Statistics Sources

ISSN 0585-198X

Statistics Sources

48th Edition

A Subject Guide to Data on Industrial, Business, Social, Educational, Financial, and Other Topics for the United States and Internationally

Volume 1
A-D

Statistics Sources, 48th Edition

Content Developer: Wolf Williams

Editorial Support Services: James A. Edwards

Composition and Electronic Prepress: Charlie Montney

Manufacturing: Rita Wimberley

Gale, part of Cengage Group
27555 Executive Dr., Ste. 350
Farmington Hills, MI 48331-3551

ISBN-13: 978-1-53-587512-7 (set)
ISBN-13: 978-1-53-587513-4 (Vol. 1)
ISBN-13: 978-1-53-587514-1 (Vol. 2)
ISBN-13: 978-1-53-587515-8 (Vol. 3)
ISBN-13: 978-1-53-587516-5 (Vol. 4)

ISSN 0585-198X

This title is also available online as part of Gale Directory Library.
ISBN-13: 978-1-53-587444-1

Printed in the USA
1 2 3 4 5 27 26 25 24 23

Table of Contents

The forty-eighth edition of *Statistics Sources* contains important statistical information that is compiled, cataloged, and indexed for efficient and authoritative research. The work continues to be an easy-to-use, alphabetically-arranged dictionary and guide to current sources of factual qualitative information on more than 29,000 specific subjects, incorporating approximately 105,000 citations and over 1,700 sources of statistical information for more than 190 countries, dependencies and areas of special sovereignty, disputed territories, and natural features of the world. *Statistics Sources* readily leads users to the widest possible range of print and non-print, published and unpublished, and electronic and other forms of U.S. and international statistical sources for economic, business, financial, industrial, cultural, social, educational, and other topics.

Preparation of This Edition

This edition of *Statistics Sources* fully and thoroughly updates, revises, and extends the scope and content of the previous edition. Complete revisions incorporate a wider range of current data sources from the *Selected Bibliography of Key Statistical Sources* and *Federal Statistical Telephone Contacts* sections, through the mainbody, as well as the appendixes.

During the preparation of the edition, as in earlier editions, the editors thoroughly analyzed and indexed hundreds of U.S. information sources, several years of Statistical Abstract of the United States, numerous basic statistical publications from many organizations, and special statistical issues of professional, technical and trade journals. Additional sources of international statistics are cited in this edition–particularly for Asian, Southeast Asian, and Middle Eastern countries–increasing the range of access points within a user's reference shelves.

Arrangement and Content

The familiar and convenient arrangement of the basic work continues as a straight alphabetic list of subjects. Sources of statistical information are arranged alphabetically by issuing organization within each subject category. In addition to both print and machine-readable sources, a considerable number of organizations, government agencies, trade and professional groups, and international bodies are cited because they are important sources of statistical data, even if they do not ordinarily publish all of the statistics they compile. In such instances, specific inquiries may be addressed to the organization mentioned. As in earlier editions, the street address of the publisher of any work cited has been provided wherever possible, followed by the telephone number of the source, as well as email and web site information, where available.

Interfiled within the subject categories are geographic headings for states and individual countries. Listings for state data center agencies that make census information and data available to the public are included within the citations of sources for each state. These listings appear under the heading State Data Center Agencies, which immediately follows the citation for Primary Statistics Sources under each state subheading.

Individual citations for each country are sub-arranged by an alphabetic list of specific subjects, enabling the user to pin-point sources of statistics on subjects such as agriculture, education, energy, imports, population and consumer prices. Two types of key statistical sources are cited in listings for countries (as applicable and available) and precede the alphabetical listing of specific subjects for the country. The first citation is the *National Statistical Office*, if the country has such an office. This is followed by a reference to the major printed sources for the country, termed the *Primary Statistics Sources*. These sources should be consulted by users seeking more in-depth data, particularly for technical and commercial activities in countries other than the U.S. and Canada.

Introductory Materials Pinpoint Key Sources and Individuals

The *Selected Bibliography of Key Statistical Sources* and *Federal Statistical Telephone Contacts* sections precede the main section. The *Selected Bibliography* provides an annotated guide to a selected group of major, general statistical compendia and related works, and includes dictionaries of terms, almanacs, census publications, periodical sources, and guides to machine-readable and online data sources. Both governmental and non-governmental sources are cited. A source's availability in machine-readable form or as an online database is noted wherever possible. The *Telephone Contacts* section provides the names and telephone numbers of individuals and agencies within the U.S. federal government with expertise in identifying the most current sources of statistical data.

Appendixes Identify Published and Nonpublished Sources

The two appendixes identify the sources of information used to compile this directory. The *Source Publications Appendix* provides an alphabetic listing of the specific publication titles of every source mentioned in *Statistics Sources*, along with the issuing or publishing bodies, their addresses and phone numbers. The *Sources of Nonpublished Statistical Data Appendix* identifies the agencies, institutions, and other organizations which are cited as sources of nonpublished statistical information in this edition.

Selected Bibliography of Key Statistical Sources

This section describes a selected group of major, general statistical compendia and related works in the English language. Both governmental and non-governmental sources are included. For ease of reference, these sources are presented according to the categories listed below.

ENCYCLOPEDIAS, DICTIONARIES OF TERMS, AND OTHER GENERAL SOURCES

Arthur S. Banks, Thomas C. Muller, William R. Overstreet, eds. *Political Handbook of the World 2022-2023.* Thousand Oaks, CA, USA, CQ Press, an Imprint of Sage Publications, ((800) 818-7243, https://us.sagepub.com/en-us/nam/cqpress, 2021.

Published since 1928, the *Political Handbook of the World* provides timely, thorough, and accurate political information with more in-depth coverage of current political controversies and political parties than any other reference guide. The updated 2022-2023 Edition continues this legacy as the most authoritative source for finding complete facts and analysis on each country's governmental and political makeup. Political science and international relations scholars have revised this edition and made understanding complex foreign affairs and political situations easy and accessible. With more than 200 entries on countries and territories throughout the world, housed in one place, these volumes are renowned for their extensive coverage of all major and minor political parties and groups in each political system. They also provide names of key ambassadors and international memberships of each country, plus detailed profiles of more than 30 intergovernmental organizations and United Nations agencies.

ALMANACS

Canadian Almanac and Directory 2023. Amenia, NY, USA, Grey House Publishing, ((800) 562-2139), https://www.greyhouse.com, 2022.

The *Canadian Almanac and Directory* is the most complete source of Canadian information available - cultural, professional and financial institutions, legislative, governmental, judicial and educational organizations. Canada's authoritative sourcebook for 176 years, the Canadian Almanac & Directory includes over 50,000 entries covering hundreds of topics, making this the number one reference for collected facts and figures about Canada.

Whitaker's 2021. Oxford, GRB, Rebellion Publishing, 1868-. (Annual). https://rebellionpublishing.com, 2021.

First published in 1868, *Whitaker's 2021* contains a comprehensive explanation of every aspect of national and local government infrastructure in the UK, astronomical and tidal data for 2021, guides to UK law, education and taxation, overviews of the water, energy and transport industries, essential calendar information, chapters on royalty and peerage, complete results for each constituency from the last UK General Election and an up-to-date list of MPs, government departments and public bodies, directory listings of trade unions and professional bodies, sports results and records, reviews of the year 2019-2020 - covering the arts, science and politics - and monthly summaries of the year's news. It is also an excellent introduction to world politics with in-depth profiles of international organisations, the European Union and every country of the world.

World Almanac and Book of Facts 2024. New York, NY, USA, World Almanac Books, ((212) 643-6816), https://www.skyhorsepublishing.com/, (Annual).

The *World Almanac and Book of Facts* is America's top-selling reference book of all time, with more than 83 million copies sold. For more than 150 years, this compendium of information has been the authoritative source for all your entertainment, reference, and learning needs. The 2024 edition of The World Almanac reviews the events of 2023 and will be your go-to source for questions on any topic in the upcoming year. Praised as a 'treasure trove of political, economic, scientific and educational statistics and information' by The Wall Street Journal, The World Almanac and Book of Facts will answer all of your trivia needs effortlessly.

U.S. STATISTICS

NON-GOVERNMENT U.S. PUBLICATIONS

Association of Religion Data Archive (ARDA), https://www.thearda.com, University Park, PA, USA, ARDA, ((814) 865-6258).

Collects quantitative data sets for the study of American religion. Most files are from surveys but all forms of quantitative data collections on religion are available as well.

Book of the States. Lexington, KY, USA, Council of State Governments, ((859) 244-8000), 1935-. (Annual) https://www.csg.org/.

The Council of State Governments continues a long tradition of 'sharing capitol ideas' with the publication of the 2021 edition of *The Book of the States.* Since 1933, CSG has served as a resource for state leaders and a catalyst for innovation and excellence in state governance. The Book of the States has been the reference tool of choice since 1935, providing relevant, accurate and timely information, answers and comparisons for all 56 states, commonwealths and territories of the United States. The 2021 volume includes in-depth tables, figures and infographics illustrating how state government operates. Staff members mined more than 500 sources to obtain the information shared in The Book of the States.

Business Rankings Annual 2023. Farmington Hills, MI, USA, Gale, ((800) 877-4253), https://www.gale.com/, 2022.

Helps librarians answer reference questions related to rankings information. Working from a bibliographic file built up over the years, Gale has culled thousands of items from periodicals, newspapers, financial services, directories, statistical annuals and other printed material. The top 10 from each of these rankings appears in this volume, grouped under standard subject headings for easy browsing. Readers can quickly locate all rankings in which a given company, person or product appears by consulting the reference's comprehensive index. In addition, a complete listing of sources used to compile Business Rankings Annual is provided in the bibliography.

CEDDS: The Complete Economic and Demographic Data Source. Washington, DC, USA, Woods and Poole Economics, Inc., ((800) 786-1915), https://www.woodsandpoole.com, 2023.

Includes data for all counties and CBSAs in the U.S. *CEDDS* contains annual historical data from 1970 (some variables begin in 1990) and annual projections to 2060 of population by age and race, employment by industry, earnings of employees by industry, GDP, personal income by source, households by income bracket and retail sales by kind of business.

cmdtyView. Chicago, IL, USA, Barchart, ((312) 283-2387), https://www.barchart.com/cmdty, 1939-..

Since 1934, CRB has been trusted by commodity traders worldwide to provide them with reliable data products, publications, fundamental data services, and rich historical data on commodities. All of this content will now be made available via cmdtyView and its innovative line of products across Data, Indexes, Trading, and Solutions. Barchart is a leading provider of market data and services to the global financial, media, and commodity industries. Our diversified client base trusts Barchart's innovative Solutions across data, software, and technology to power their operation from front to back office, while our Media brands enable financial and commodity professionals to make decisions through web content, news, and publications.

Scott Morgan, Kathleen O'Leary Morgan, eds. *State Rankings 2020: A Statistical View of America.* Thousand Oaks, CA, USA, CQ Press, an Imprint of Sage Publications, ((800) 818-7243, https://us.sagepub.com/en-us/nam/cqpress, 2020.

State Rankings features comprehensive state statistics across key measures in education, health, crime, transportation, taxes, government finance, and so much more. The editors compile useful statistics that otherwise take an enormous amount of time to research, making it a favorite resource on reference shelves throughout the United States and around the world. Overall state rankings are provided as well as a complete list of all sources used to compile the tables. The rankings have been updated using specific methodology explained in the introduction with the most current available data at publication. Explanatory notes on the source and data are also included to provide context to each statistical table.

Deirdre A. Gaquin and Mary Meghan Ryan, eds. *County and City Extra 2023.* Lanham, MD, USA, Bernan Press, ((800) 865-3457), https://rowman.com/. (Annual).

This trusted reference compiles information from many sources to provide all the key demographic and economic data for every state, county, metropolitan area, congressional district, and for all cities in the United States with a 2010 population of 25,000 or more. In one volume, you can conveniently find data from 1990 to 2022 in easy-to-read tables. The annual updating of *County and City Extra* for 31 years ensures its stature as a reliable and authoritative source for information.

Deirdre A. Gaquin and Mary Meghan Ryan, eds. 7th ed. *Places, Towns, and Townships 2021.* Lanham, MD, USA, Bernan Press, ((800) 865-3457), https://rowman.com, 2021.

An excellent resource for anyone in need of data for all of the nation's cities, towns, townships, villages, and census-designated places in one convenient source. It compiles essential information about places in the United States and the people who live in them including population, housing, income, education, employment, crime.

David Garoogian, ed. *America's Top-Rated Cities: A Statistical Handbook, 2023.* Amenia, NY, USA, Grey House Publishing, ((800) 562-2139), https://www.greyhouse.com/, 2023.

Provides current, comprehensive statistical information and other essential data in one easy-to-use source on the top 100 cities that have been cited as the best for business and living in the United States. It is designed for a wide range of readers: private individuals considering relocating a residence or business; professionals considering expanding their business or changing careers; government agencies; general and market researchers; real estate consultants; human resource personnel; urban planners and investors. This outstanding source of information will be widely useful in any reference collection.

AHA Hospital Statistics. Chicago, IL, USA, American Hospital Association, ((800) 424-4301), https://www.aha.org, 1971-. (Annual).

AHA Hospital Statistics is a comprehensive resource for analysis and comparison of health care industry trends in U.S. community hospitals. With more than 75 years of hospital data, this extensive and reliable health care statistical resource includes five-year trends in utilization, personnel, revenues and expenses across local, regional and national markets. You will also find useful community health indicators such as beds per population and expenses per capita by state. Summary level statistical information is presented in easy-to-read tables making Hospital Statistics a valuable resource for getting a snap-shot of the hospital market. The data are based on the AHA Annual Survey of Hospitals which has been conducted by the American Hospital Association since 1946.

Mary Meghan Ryan. *Handbook of U.S. Labor Statistics 2023: Employment, Earnings, Prices, Productivity, and Other Labor Data.* 26th ed. Lanham, MD, USA, Bernan Press, ((800) 865-3457), https://rowman.com/, (Annual).

Recognized as an authoritative resource on the U.S. labor force. It continues and enhances the Bureau of Labor Statistics's (BLS) discontinued publication, Labor Statistics. It allows the user to understand recent developments as well as to compare today's economy with that of the past. This publication includes several tables throughout the book examining the extensive effect that coronavirus (COVID-19) had on the labor market since 2020. A chapter titled "The Impact of Coronavirus (COVID-19) on the Labor Force" includes new information on hazard pay, safety measures businesses enforced during the pandemic, vaccine incentives, and compressed work schedules. In addition, there are several other tables within the book exploring its impact on employment, telework, and consumer expenditures. This edition also includes a completely updated chapter on prices and the most current employment projections through 2030.

Market Share Reporter. 33rd ed. Farmington Hills, MI, USA, Gale, ((800) 877-4253), https://www.gale.com/, 2023.

This is a compilation of market share reports from periodical literature and is a unique resource for competitive analysis, diversification planning, marketing research, and other forms of economic and policy analysis. *Market Share Reporter* includes more than 3,600 new entries, which are arranged under both SIC and NAICS codes, corporate, brand, product, service, and commodity market shares, coverage of private- and public-sector activities, and comprehensive indexes, including products, companies, brands, places, sources, NAICS, ISIC, Harmonized and SIC codes.

MSA Profile: Metropolitan Area Projections to 2060. Washington, DC, USA, Woods and Poole Economics, Inc., ((800) 786-1915), https://www.woodsandpoole.com, 2022.

MSA Profile has population projections and economic projections for all Core Based Statistical Areas (MSAs, CSAs, Micropolitan Statistical Areas, and Metropolitan Divisions) in the U.S. The spreadsheet files by download contain annual historical data from 1970 (some variables begin in 1990) and annual projections to 2060 of population by age and race, employment by industry, earnings of employees by industry, GDP, personal income by source, households by income bracket and retail sales by kind of business. The *MSA Profile* is also available in a printed volume: the 900-page printed volume has more than 500,000 statistics for selected years for the U.S., states, regions, and MSAs only. The data tables, and a PDF file of the entire printed volume, are available by download. The *MSA Profile* on CD-ROM is still available.

State Profile. Washington, DC, USA, Woods and Poole Economics, Inc., ((800) 786-1915), https://www.woodsandpoole.com.

Contains historical data for all counties and Metropolitan Areas in a particular state. State Profiles contain historical data from 1970 (some variables begin in 1990) and projections to 2060 of population by age and race, employment by industry, earnings of employees by industry, personal income by source, households by income bracket and retail sales by kind of business. The data and projections are for every county, MSA, and DMA in a particular state (some volumes contain more than one state).

Susan Ockert, ed. *Business Statistics of the United States: Patterns of Economic Change 2022,* 27th ed., Lanham, MD, USA, Bernan Press, ((800) 865-3457), https://rowman.com/, 2022.

Business Statistics of the United States is a comprehensive and practical collection of data from as early as 1913 that reflects the nation's economic performance. It provides several years of annual, quarterly, and monthly data in industrial and demographic detail including key indicators such as: gross domestic product, personal income, spending, saving, employment, unemployment, the capital stock, and more. *Business Statistics of the United States* is the best place to find historical perspectives on the U.S. economy. Of equal importance to the data are the introductory highlights, extensive notes, and figures for each chapter that help users to understand the data, use them appropriately, and, if desired, seek additional information from the source agencies. This edition will continue to explore the dramatic impact that COVID-19 is having on U.S. and world economies. It provides a rich and deep picture of the American economy and contains approximately 3,500 time series in all. The data are predominately from federal government sources including: Board of Governors of the Federal Reserve System; Bureau of Economic Analysis; Bureau of Labor Statistics; Census Bureau; Employment and Training Administration; Energy Information Administration; Federal Housing Finance Agency; and the U.S. Department of the Treasury.

Hannah Anderson Krog, ed. *State Profiles 2023: The Population and Economy of Each U.S. State.* Lanham, MD, USA, Bernan Press, ((800) 865-3457), https://rowman.com/, 2023.

This volume provides a wealth of current, authoritative, and comprehensive data on key demographic and economic indicators for each U.S. state and the District of Columbia. Each state is covered by a compact standardized chapter that allows for easy comparisons and timely analysis between the states. A ten-page profile for each U.S. state plus the District of Columbia provides reliable, up-to-date information on a wide range of topics, including: population, labor force, income and poverty, government finances, crime, education, health insurance coverage, voting, marital status, migration, and more.

Encyclopedia of Business Information Sources, 38th Edition. Farmington Hills, MI, USA, Gale, ((800) 877-4253) https://www.gale.com, 2021.

Includes more than 21,000 citations, dealing with more than 1,100 business, financial, and industrial topics. The subjects cover a variety of business-related concerns, such as Business Functions - Accounting; Administration; Personnel Management; Computer-Related Subjects - Computer Graphics; Computer Software Industry; Local Area Networks; Foreign Trade - International Marketing; Latin American Markets; North American Free Trade Agreement (NAFTA); Information Industry Topics--Electronic Publishing; Internet; and Multimedia.

PUBLICATIONS OF THE U.S. BUREAU OF THE CENSUS

The U.S. Bureau of the Census is a prolific publisher of statistical data in print and online formats. The data are, for the most part, based on the following periodic censuses:

Census of Housing
Census of Population
Census of Agriculture
Economic Census
Census of Construction Industries
Census of Governments
Census of Manufactures
Census of Mineral Industries
Census of Retail Trade
Census of Service Industries
Census of Transportation
Census of Wholesale Trade

Many current and historical Bureau of the Census publications are available in PDF and HTML versions online, or in microfiche from Congressional Information Service, 4520 East-West Highway, Bethesda, MD, 20814, USA, ((800) 521-0600). Available are all Decennial Censuses from 1790 to 2010, as well as Non-Decennial Census Publications.

The Census Bureau offers a web data stop that provides access to product descriptions and a wide cross section of information ranging from agriculture to industry to population. All Census Bureau publications released by the Government Printing Office since January 1996, as well as selected reports printed before January 1996, are presented in the Electronic Subscription Service section of the

Census website. The Census Bureau's website can be found at https://www.census.gov.

For more information on Census Bureau products and programs, contact U.S. Census Bureau, 4600 Silver Hill Road, Washington, DC, 20233, USA, https://www.census.gov, (800) 923-8282.

Descriptions of the Bureau's best known publication, the *Statistical Abstract of the United States*, and of other important Bureau publications follow.

Annual Survey of Manufacturers. Washington, DC, USA, U.S. Bureau of the Census, https://www.census.gov, ((800) 923-8282), 1949-. (Annual).

Provides data on manufacturing activity for industry groups; important individual industries; and for geographic divisions, states, large standard metropolitan district areas, and large industrial counties. Items include value added by manufacture; value of shipments; cost of materials, fuels, electric energy consumed, employment, man-hours, payrolls, and capital expenditures. Available in CD-ROM.

County Business Patterns. Washington, DC, USA, U.S. Bureau of the Census, https://www.census.gov, ((800) 923-8282), 1946-. (Annual).

Data are presented on employment, number and employment size of reporting units, and taxable payrolls by industry groups for private nonfarm activities. Annual edition includes a separate paper bound report for each state, District of Columbia, and Puerto Rico and Outlying Areas.

Digest of Education Statistics. Washington, DC, USA, National Center for Education Statistics (NCES), ((202) 403-5551), https://nces.ed.gov, 1962-. (Annual).

Provides an abstract of statistical information covering the entire field of American education from prekindergarten through graduate school. Listed are figures pertaining to such topics as schools, enrollments, teachers, graduates, attainment, and expenditures. A companion volume published annually, *Projections of Education Statistics*, shows trends for the past 10 years and projects data for the next 10 years. A related publication, *The Condition of Education*, provides an overview of trends and current issues.

Economic Indicators. Washington, DC, USA, U.S. President's Council of Economic Advisers, ((202) 456-4779), https://www.whitehouse.gov/cea, 1948-. (Monthly).

Available from April 1995 forward, this monthly compilation is prepared for the Joint Economic Committee by the Council of Economic Advisors and provides economic information on gross domestic product, income, employment, production, business activity, prices, money, credit, security markets, Federal finance, and international statistics.

Economic Report of the President. Washington, DC, USA, U.S. President's Council of Economic Advisers, ((202) 456-4779), https://www.whitehouse.gov/cea, 1947-. (Annual).

This publication is an annual report written by the Chair of the Council of Economic Advisers. An important vehicle for presenting the Administration's domestic and international economic policies, it provides an overview of the nation's economic progress with text and extensive data appendices.

Guide to Foreign Trade Statistics. Washington, DC, USA, U.S. Bureau of the Census, https://www.census.gov, ((800) 923-8282), periodic.

This is a guide to the published and unpublished sources of foreign trade statistics prepared by the Bureau of the Census; it describes the content and arrangement of the data and tells where the statistics can be found. It lists the titles of the published reports and illustrates the tables included in them. Unpublished tabulations are also listed and the statistics in these are illustrated. The book also describes the coverage of the import and export statistics program, and discusses the methodology of the data, such as the procedure for estimating low-valued shipments. Special services available from the Census Bureau for those wishing to obtain additional statistics are also described.

Historical Statistics of the United States, Colonial Times to 1970. Washington, DC, USA, U.S. Bureau of the Census, https://www.census.gov, ((800) 923-8282), 1976.

This periodically-revised supplement to the *Statistical Abstract of the United States* includes more than 12,500 statistical time series, largely annual, on American social and economic development covering the period 1610 to 1970. Definitions of terms and descriptive text are provided, as well as source notes guiding the reader to original published sources for further reference and additional data. Indexed by subject. Also available on CD-ROM.

International Database (IDB). Washington, DC, USA, U.S. Bureau of the Census, https://www.census.gov, ((800) 923-8282).

A computerized data bank containing statistical tables of demographic and socio-economic data for over 200 countries and areas of the world. The IDB was created in the Census Bureau's International Programs Center in response to the information requirements of IPC staff to meet the needs of organizations that sponsor IPC's research efforts. The IDB provides quick access to specialized information, with emphasis on demographic measures, for individual countries or selected groups of countries. Access IDB on the web at https://www.census.gov/data-tools/demo/idb/

Quarterly Financial Report for U.S. Manufacturing, Mining, Wholesale Trade, and Selected Service Industries. Washington, DC, USA, U.S. Bureau of the Census, https://www.census.gov, ((800) 923-8282), 1947-. (Quarterly).

The purpose of this publication is to present aggregate statistics on the financial results and position of United States corporations classified by both industry and asset size. Data are presented in financial statement and balance sheet form. Also available on diskette and online.

PUBLICATIONS AND OTHER MATERIALS FROM U.S. GOVERNMENT AGENCIES AND DEPARTMENTS

Note: Approximately 200 Federal statistical publications are available on microfiche from: Congressional Information Service, 4520 East-West Highway, Bethesda, MD, 20814, USA, (800) 638-8380.

Amber Waves. Washington, DC, USA, Department of Agriculture, Economic Research Service, ((202) 694-5000). https://www.ers.usda.gov (Quarterly).

Contains data and analysis on U.S. food, farming, resources, and rural America.

Agricultural Statistics. Washington, DC, USA, U.S. Department of Agriculture, National Agricultural Statistics Service, ((800) 727-9540), https://www.nass.usda.gov/, 1936-. (Annual).

Brings together the more important series of statistics compiled in this department and others whose work concerns agriculture. Prior to 1936, statistical data appeared in the Statistical Section of the *Yearbook of Agriculture.*

Monthly Energy Review. Washington, DC, USA, U.S. Energy Information Administration, ((202) 586-8800), https://www.eia.gov 1974-. .

A publication of recent energy statistics. This publication includes total energy production, consumption, stocks, and trade; energy prices; overviews of petroleum, natural gas, coal, electricity, nuclear energy, renewable energy, and carbon dioxide emissions; and data unit conversion values.

Economic News Releases. Washington, DC, USA, U.S. Bureau of Labor Statistics, ((202) 691-5200), https://www.bls.gov.

Economic News Releases are available at the Bureau of Labor Statistics Website, which is updated daily. Releases include the Consumer Price Index, Producer Price Index, Employment Situation, Productivity and Costs, and many more.

Budget of the United States Government. Washington, DC, USA, Office of Management and Budget, ((202) 395-3080), https://www.whitehouse.gov/omb, 1923-. (Annual).

Comprehensive details, contained in summary tables, on receipts, expenditures, etc. of the federal government. Accompanying the Budget Message is a detailed account by departments and agencies of proposed budget items, giving previous year's actual figures, present year's estimated, and coming year's proposed amounts. Available online from 1996.

Current Employment Statistics. Washington, DC, USA, U.S. Bureau of Labor Statistics, ((202) 691-6555), https://www.bls.gov.

The Current Employment Statistics (CES) program produces detailed industry estimates of nonfarm employment, hours, and earnings of workers on payrolls. CES National Estimates produces data for the nation, and 'CES State and Metro Area' produces estimates for all 50 States, the District of Columbia, Puerto Rico, the Virgin Islands, and about 450 metropolitan areas and divisions. Each month, CES surveys approximately 122,000 businesses and government agencies, representing approximately 666,000 individual worksites.

Farm Income and Wealth Statistics. Washington, DC, USA, U.S. Department of Agriculture, Economic Research Service, ((202) 694-5000), https://www.ers.usda.gov, 1945-. (Annual).

These are the latest data concerning USDA's forecasts and estimates of farm income, including net value added, net cash income, cash receipts, government payments, farm production expenses, and the balance sheet.

Federal Reserve Bulletin. Washington, DC, USA, Board of Governors of the Federal Reserve System, ((202) 452-3000), https://www.federalreserve.gov, 1915-. (Quarterly).

Articles on economic topics and news about the Federal Reserve System are included along with both national and international financial and business statistics.

Foreign Agricultural Trade of the United States (FATUS). Washington, DC, USA, U.S. Department of Agriculture, Economic Research Service, ((202) 694-5000), https://www.ers.usda.gov, 1962-. (Updated periodically).

Contains tables showing value and quantity of agricultural commodities imported and exported, with annual supplements on trade by commodities and trade by countries.

Foreign Direct Investment in the United States. Washington, DC, USA, U.S. Department of Commerce, Bureau of Economic Analysis, ((301) 278-9004), https://www.bea.gov, 1980-. (Annual).

Includes financial and operating data, and direct investment positions and balance of payment data for U.S. businesses which are owned 10 percent or more by a foreign entity.

Health, United States. Atlanta, GA, USA, U.S. National Center for Health Statistics, Centers for Disease Control and Prevention, ((800) 232-4636), https://www.cdc.gov/nchs, 1976-. (Annual).

The Health, United States program provides a wide array of trends in health statistics to policymakers, public health professionals, and the public. As part of the program's legislative mandate, Health, United States is charged with presenting a comprehensive set of health topics, and examining trends in health status and determinants, healthcare utilization, healthcare resources, and health expenditures and payers. Health, United States provides a detailed look at these topics within specific demographic and socioeconomic groups, including age, sex, race and ethnicity, disability status, education, poverty level, and geographic area.

Monthly Energy Review. Washington, DC, USA, U.S. Energy Information Administration, ((202) 586-8800), https://www.eia.gov, 1975-. (Monthly).

Current data for production, consumption, stocks, imports, exports, and prices for the major energy commodities in the U.S. Annual data is published in the *Annual Energy Outlook.*

Monthly Labor Review. Washington, DC, USA, U.S. Bureau of Labor Statistics, ((202) 691-5200), https://www.bls.gov, 1915-. (Monthly).

Established in 1915, *Monthly Labor Review* is the principal journal of fact, analysis, and research from the Bureau of Labor Statistics, an agency within the U.S. Department of Labor. Each month, economists, statisticians, and experts from the Bureau join with private sector professionals and State and local government specialists to provide a wealth of research in a wide variety of fields - the labor force, the economy, employment, inflation, productivity, occupational injuries and illnesses, wages, prices, and many more.

National Transportation Statistics. Washington, DC, USA, U.S. Department of Transportation, ((202) 366-4000), https://www.transportation.gov/, 1969-. (Annual).

National Transportation Statistics presents statistics on the U.S. transportation system, including its physical components, safety record, economic performance, the human and natural environment, and national security. This is a large online document comprising more than 260 data tables plus data source and accuracy statements, glossary and a list of acronyms and initialisms.

Science and Engineering Indicators. Arlington, VA, USA, National Science Board, National Science Foundation, ((703) 292-5111), https://www.nsf.gov, 1972-. (Biennial).

Data are presented on international research and development, resources for research and development, resources for basic research, industrial research and development and innovation, science and engineering personnel, and public attitudes toward science and technology. A combination of text, tables, and graphs is used.

Social Security Bulletin. Washington, DC, USA, Social Security Administration, ((800) 772-1213), https://www.ssa.gov, 1938-. (Monthly).

Provides current data on social security program operations. Also contains data on recipients and payments under public assistance programs; unemployment insurance; and railroad, civil service, and veterans programs. An annual statistical supplement is also published.

Personal Income and Outlays. Washington, DC, USA, U.S. Bureau of Economic Analysis, ((301) 278-9004), https://www.bea.gov, (Quarterly and annual updates).

Quarterly and annual estimates of state and local area personal income, including news releases and interactive tables.

Statistics of Income (SOI) Bulletin. Washington, DC, USA, U.S. Internal Revenue Service, ((800) 829-1040), https://www.irs.gov, 1916-. (Quarterly).

Gives summary tabulations on financial information obtained from the various tax returns. Individual reports have been issued for each type of return beginning with data from 1954. For 1953 and prior years, the information was released in two parts: Part 1 for individuals, and Part 2 for Corporations, with special studies for selected years included in Part 1.

Survey of Current Business. Washington, DC, USA, U.S. Bureau of Economic Analysis, ((301) 278-9004), https://www.bea.gov, 1921-. (Monthly).

The major reporting publication for business statistics, including indexes for income payments, industrial production, commodity prices, statistics on construction and real estate, domestic trade, employment conditions and wages, finance, foreign trade, transportation and communication, products by kind, etc. Some reports on the business situation and conditions in specific industries are included.

Treasury Bulletin. Washington, DC, USA, U.S. Department of the Treasury, ((202) 622-2000), https://www.fiscal.treasury.gov, 1939-. (Monthly).

The Treasury Bulletin contains a mix of narrative, tables, and charts related to: treasury issues, federal financial operations, international statistics, financial commitments of the U.S. government.

Uniform Crime Reports. Washington, DC, USA, Federal Bureau of Investigation, ((202) 324-3000), https://www.fbi.gov, 1930-. (Annual).

Data for this publication are received by the FBI from over 18,000 law enforcement agencies that participate in the Uniform Crime Reporting Program. Information is provided for eight offenses: murder and nonnegligent manslaughter, aggravated assault, forcible rape, robbery, burglary, larceny-theft, motor vehicle theft, and arson. National, state, county, metropolitan area, and selected city data are provided. Not indexed.

GUIDES TO MACHINE-READABLE U.S. GOVERNMENT DATA SOURCES

In addition to the print sources described below, statistics users may want to contact the National Technical Information Service (NTIS) in Alexandria, VA, USA, (703) 605-6000, https://www.ntis.gov/federal-data-products.xhtml. The strategic focus for NTIS is to expand access to data resources, with an emphasis on data concerning the nation's economy, population, and environment. NTIS serves government agencies by providing solution services to readily available data products. Partnering with companies (Joint Venture Partners) that are industry leaders in data discovery, usability, accessibility, interoperability, analytics, security, and privacy, ensures NTIS achieving the core data mission to become a center of excellence in data science.

National Archive of Criminal Justice Data (NACJD). Washington, DC, USA, Sponsored by the Bureau of Justice Statistics, U.S. Department of Justice and operated by the Inter-University Consortium for Political and Social Research, ((800) 999-0960), https://www.icpsr.umich.edu/NACJD.

The *National Archive of Criminal Justice Data (NACJD)* preserves and distributes computerized crime and justice data from Federal agencies, state agencies, and investigator initiated research projects to users for secondary statistical analysis.

INTERNATIONAL SOURCES

GENERAL INTERNATIONAL PUBLICATIONS

Africa South of the Sahara 2024. New York, NY, USA, Routledge, ((800) 634-7064), https://www.routledge.com, 2023.

The definitive one-volume guide to all sub-Saharan African countries, providing invaluable economic, political, statistical and directory data. Thoroughly revised and updated analytical articles written by experts on the region and covering both continent-wide and sub-regional issues.

Annual Statistical Bulletin 2023. Vienna, AUS, Organization of the Petroleum Exporting Countries (OPEC), https://www.opec.org, 1966-. (Annual).

The ASB provides key statistical data on oil and natural gas activities in each of OPEC's Member Countries: Algeria, Angola, Congo, Equatorial Guinea, Gabon, the Islamic Republic of Iran, Iraq, Kuwait, Libya, Nigeria, Saudi Arabia, the United Arab Emirates and Venezuela. It also provides valuable data related to non-OPEC oil producing countries while presenting data on exports, imports, production, refineries and shipping.

Central and South-Eastern Europe 2023. New York, NY, USA, Routledge, ((800) 634-7064), https://www.routledge.com, 2022.

A comprehensive survey of the countries and territories of this region, incorporating the latest economic and political developments. Offers detailed analyses by the world's foremost authorities; an accurate and impartial view of the region and individual chapters on each country containing in-depth articles on geography, history and economy, as well as economic and demographic statistics and contact details of key individuals. A comprehensive survey of the countries and territories of this region, incorporating the latest economic and sociopolitical developments.

Consumer Lifestyles in China. Chicago, IL, USA, Euromonitor International, ((312) 922-1115), https://www.euromonitor.com, 2023.

In addition to covering important core topics like household disposable income, consumer expenditure, savings and credit and housing and home ownership, this report also contains hard-to-find statistics on more specific consumer-related topics like eating and drinking habits, shopping habits, preferred types of stores and retail venues, clothing and fashion trends and descriptions of how consumers spend their leisure and recreation time. A consumer segmentation section in the report breaks down the China's consumers by specific age groups, ranging from babies and infants to pensioners; highlighting the factors that influence purchasing decisions and the products in greatest demand for each segment.

Countries of the World and Their Leaders Yearbook 2021. Farmington Hills, MI, USA, Gale, ((800) 877-4253), https://www.gale.com/, 2020.

A compilation of U.S. Department of State reports on contemporary political and economic conditions, government personnel and policies, political parties, religions, history, education, press, radio and TV, climate, and other characteristics of selected countries of the world; together with travel alerts, passport and visa information, world health information for travelers, and customs and duty tips for returning residents.

Country Report New York, NY, USA, Economist Intelligence Unit, ((212) 698-9717), https://www.eiu.com. (Annual).

Detailed insight into political and economic analysis as well as forecasts for 190 countries. The EIU's flagship report examines and explains the important political and economic trends for a country.

CountryData. New York, NY, USA, Economist Intelligence Unit, ((212) 698-9717), https://www.eiu.com. (Quarterly).

This complete country-by-country data set contains over 300 key economic indicators for a country, with data ranging from 1980 to 2050 and covering 204 countries. It provides immediate access to headline economic indicators and forecasts vital to economic, financial, and budget models. It also provides hard-edged analysis of a country's economic health and prospects.

The Developing Economies. Tokyo, JPN, Institute of Developing Economies (IDE), https://www.ide.go.jp/English. (Quarterly).

An international and interdisciplinary forum for studies on social sciences relating to the developing countries. Provides an opportunity for discussions and exchanges across a wide spectrum of scholarly opinions to promote empirical and comparative studies on the problems confronted by developing countries.

Eastern Europe, Russia and Central Asia 2024. New York, NY, USA, Routledge, ((800) 634-7064), https://www.routledge.com, 2023.

Offers detailed analyses by the world's foremost authorities; an accurate and impartial view of the region; and individual chapters on each country containing in-depth articles on geography, history and economy, as well as economic and demographic statistics and contact details of key individuals.

Insider Intelligence. New York, NY, USA, ((800) 405-0844), https://www.emarketer.com.

Research focuses on global advertising and marketing, ecommerce and retail, financial services, health, technology and more.

The Europa World Year Book 2023. New York, NY, USA, Routledge, ((800) 634-7064), https://www.routledge.com, 2023.

This reference work on the political and economic life of countries throughout the world includes a statistical survey for each country. Topics covered include: area and population, agriculture, forestry, mining industry, finance, external trade, tourism, transport, communications media, and education.

EU Transport in Figures - Statistical Pocketbook 2022. Washington, DC, USA, European Commission, https://transport.ec.europa.eu/index_en, 2022.

The European Union (EU) has released the latest issue of its annual overview of transport statistics for the EU and its member states. The report covers all modes of transportation and provides general statistics, as well as measurements on the performance of freight and passenger transport and a summary of infrastructure assets. The full report is available, as well as individual reports on general data, energy, and transport.

Far East and Australasia 2023. New York, NY, USA, Routledge, ((800) 634-7064), https://www.routledge.com, 2022.

This comprehensive survey of the countries of East and South-East Asia, Australia and New Zealand, along with 22 Pacific islands, fully revised to reflect current economic and political developments, is an essential resource for the Asia-Pacific region.

Global Financial Development Database. Washington, DC, USA, The World Bank Group, ((202) 473-1000), https://www.worldbank.org, 2022.

This is an extensive dataset of financial system characteristics for 214 economies. It contains annual data, starting from 1960. It has been last updated in September 2022 and contains data through 2021 for 108 indicators, capturing various aspects of financial institutions and markets. The final print volume of this title was published in 2022.

Government Finance Statistics (GFS) Database. Washington, DC, USA, International Monetary Fund, ((202) 623-7000), https://www.imf.org.

This database contains fiscal data for all reporting countries in the framework of the Government Finance Statistics Manual 2014. It includes detailed data on revenues, expenditures, transactions in financial assets and liabilities, and balance sheet data and includes data for the general government sector and its subsectors (e.g., central government, local government, state government and social security funds). This site also includes preset presentations of GFS data by country and by indicators, as well as provides the option to download data with customized queries.

International Financial Statistics (IFS) Database. Washington, DC, USA, International Monetary Fund, ((202) 623-7000), https://www.imf.org.

The IFS database covers about 200 countries and areas, with some aggregates calculated for selected regions, plus some world totals. Topics covered include balance of payments, commodity prices, exchange rates, fund position, government finance, industrial production, interest rates, international investment position, international liquidity, international transactions, labor statistics, money and banking, national accounts, population, prices, and real effective exchange rates. Data are available starting in 1948 for many IMF member countries.

The Middle East and North Africa 2023. New York, NY, USA, Routledge, ((800) 634-7064), https://www.routledge.com, 2022. 1948-. (Annual).

Covers the Middle East and North Africa from Algeria to Yemen. An extensive statistical survey of economic and social indicators, which include area and population, health and welfare, agriculture, forestry, fishing, mining, industry, finance, trade, transport, tourism, communications media and education. Includes all major international organizations active in the Middle East and North Africa; research institutes specializing in the region; and select bibliographies of books and periodicals.

Renewables 2022. Paris, FRA, International Energy Agency, https://www.iea.org, 2022.

Renewables 2022 is the IEA's primary analysis on the sector, based on current policies and market developments. It forecasts the deployment of renewable energy technologies in electricity, transport and heat to 2027 while also exploring key challenges to the industry and identifying barriers to faster growth.

South America, Central America, and the Caribbean 2023. New York, NY, USA, Routledge, ((800) 634-7064), https://www.routledge.com, 2022.

Published annually, this 31st edition brings together a unique combination of the latest data on, and detailed analysis of, a vast region. Scrupulously updated by Europa's experienced editors, the volume also includes contributions from regional specialists.

Statesman's Yearbook 2024. New York, NY, USA, Palgrave Macmillan, ((800) 777-4643), https://www.palgrave.com. 1864-. (Annual).

This classic reference work presents a political, economic and social account of every country of the world together with facts and analysis. The 2024 edition includes revised and updated biographical profiles of all current leaders, extensive updates to national economic overviews, accurate historical introductions, comprehensive coverage of major international organizations and think tanks, and every country ranked for the ease of doing business.

Western Europe 2024. New York, NY, USA, Routledge, ((800) 634-7064), https://www.routledge.com, 2023.

The definitive survey of the countries and territories of Western Europe, comprising expert analysis and commentary, up-to-date economic and socio-political data and extensive directory information. An extensive statistical survey of economic and demographic indicators, including area and population, health and welfare, agriculture, forestry, fishing, mining, industry, finance, trade, transport, tourism, communications media and education.

World Agricultural Supply and Demand Estimates. Washington, DC, USA, U.S. Department of Agriculture, Economic Research Service, ((202) 694-5000), https://www.ers.usda.gov. (Monthly).

The World Agricultural Outlook Board (WAOB) serves as USDA's focal point for economic intelligence and the commodity outlook for U.S. and world agriculture. The Board coordinates, reviews, and approves the monthly World Agricultural Supply and Demand Estimates (WASDE) report as well as long-term Agricultural Baseline Projections. It is also the focal point for analyzing weather-related impacts on agriculture through the Office of the Chief Meteorologist. In addition, the Board is responsible for coordinating the World Agricultural Outlook Forum, USDA's oldest and largest gathering.

World Development Indicators. Washington, DC, USA, The World Bank Group, ((202) 473-1000), https://www.worldbank.org.

A compilation of relevant, high-quality, and internationally comparable statistics about global development and the fight against poverty. The database contains 1,400 time series indicators for 217 economies and more than 40 country groups, with data for many indicators going back more than 50 years.

World Development Report 2023: Migrants, Refugees, and Societies. Washington, DC, USA, The World Bank Group, ((202) 473-1000), https://www.worldbank.org, 1978-. (Annual).

The 2023 report proposes an integrated framework to maximize the development impacts of cross-border movements on both destination and origin countries and on migrants and refugees themselves. The framework it offers, drawn from labor economics and international law, rests on a "match and motive" matrix that focuses on two factors: how closely migrants' skills and attributes match the needs of destination countries and what motives underlie their movements. This approach enables policy makers to distinguish between different types of movements and to design migration policies for each. International cooperation will be critical to the effective management of migration.

World Energy Outlook 2022. Paris, FRA, International Energy Agency, https://www.iea.org, 2022.

The annual World Energy Outlook (WEO) is an authoritative source of energy market analysis and projections, providing critical analytical insights into trends in energy demand and supply and what they mean for energy security, environmental protection and economic development. The WEO projections are used by the public and private sector as a framework on which they can base their policy-making, planning and investment decisions and to identify what needs to be done to arrive at a supportable and sustainable energy future.

The World Factbook. Washington, DC, USA, Central Intelligence Agency, ((703) 482-0623), https://www.cia.gov/the-world-factbook, 1972-. (Annual).

Provides basic intelligence on the history, people, government, economy, energy, geography, environment, communications, transportation, military, terrorism, and transnational issues for 266 world entities.

Compendium of Tourism Statistics. Madrid, SPA, World Tourism Organization (WTO), https://www.unwto.org, 19-. (Annual).

Presents data on a variety of travel topics including: international tourist arrivals; international tourism receipts and expenditures; international fare payments and receipts. Tabular data on domestic tourism is presented for major countries.

PUBLICATIONS OF THE ORGANISATION FOR ECONOMIC COOPERATION AND DEVELOPMENT (OECD)

OECD was established in 1961 and now has 38 member countries. Countries of the OECD are Australia, Austria, Belgium, Canada, Chile, Colombia, Costa Rica, Czech Republic, Denmark, Estonia, Finland, France, Germany, Greece, Hungary, Iceland, Ireland, Israel, Italy, Japan, South Korea, Latvia, Lithuania, Luxembourg, Mexico, Netherlands, New Zealand, Norway, Poland, Portugal, Slovakia, Slovenia, Spain, Sweden, Switzerland, Turkey, United Kingdom, and the United States. It is a prolific publisher of statistics as well as research and policy studies. (202) 785-6323. Visit OECD on the web at https://www.oecd.org. A selection of some of the more important OECD statistical resources follows.

OECD Agriculture Statistics Databases. Paris, FRA, Organisation for Economic Cooperation and Development, ((202) 785-6323), https://www.oecd.org.

The OECD databases on agriculture constitute a unique collection of agricultural statistics and provide a framework for quantifying and analyzing the agricultural economy. This includes forecasts regarding the evolution of the main agricultural markets and commodities, detailed estimates of policy support, as well as indicators of environmental performance of agriculture. Data concern both OECD countries and non-member economies.

Coal Information. Paris, FRA, Organisation for Economic Cooperation and Development, ((202) 785-6323) in the U.S., https://www.oecd.org, 2019.

Coal Information brings together in one volume essential statistics on coal. It therefore provides a strong foundation for policy and market analysis. Part I of the publication provides a review of the world coal market, while Part II provides a statistical overview of developments, which covers world coal production and coal reserves, coal demand by type (hard, steam, coking), hard coal trade and hard coal prices. Part III provides, in tabular and graphic form, a more detailed and comprehensive statistical picture of historical and current coal developments in the 30 OECD member countries, by region and individually. Part IV provides for selected non-OECD countries summary statistics on hard coal supply and end-use statistics for about 40 countries and regions worldwide.

Education at a Glance 2022: OECD Indicators. Paris, FRA, Organisation for Economic Cooperation and Development, ((202) 785-6323), https://www.oecd.org, 2008-. (Annual).

Education at a Glance is the authoritative source for information on the state of education around the world. It provides data on the structure, finances and performance of education systems across OECD countries and a number of partner economies. More than 100 charts and tables in this publication - as well as links to much more available on the educational database - provides key information on the output of educational institutions; the impact of learning across countries; access, participation and progression in education; the financial resources invested in education; and teachers, the learning environment and the organisation of schools. The 2022 edition focuses on tertiary education, looking at the rise of tertiary attainment and the associated benefits for individuals and for societies. It also considers the costs of tertiary education and how spending on education is divided across levels of government and between the state and individuals. A specific chapter is dedicated to the COVID crisis and the shift from crisis management to recovery. Two new indicators on professional development for teachers and school heads and on the profile of academic staff complement this year's edition.

Foreign Direct Investment (FDI) Statistics. Paris, FRA, Organisation for Economic Cooperation and Development, ((202) 785-6323), https://www.oecd.org, (Annual).

Foreign Direct Investment (FDI) flows record the value of cross-border transactions related to direct investment during a given period of time, usually a quarter or a year. Financial flows consist of equity transactions, reinvestment of earnings, and intercompany debt transactions. FDI flows are measured in USD and as a share of GDP. FDI creates stable and long-lasting links between economies. FDI is an important channel for the transfer of technology between countries, promotes international trade through access to foreign markets, and can be an important vehicle for economic development.

International Trade by Commodity Statistics. Paris, FRA, Organisation for Economic Cooperation, ((202) 785-6323), https://www.oecd.org. (Annual).

This reliable source of yearly data covers a wide range of statistics on international trade of OECD countries and provides detailed data in value by commodity and by partner country. Country tables are published in the order in which data become available. The sixth volume includes the OECD country groupings, OECD Total and EU28 Extra. For each country, this publication shows detailed tables relating to the Harmonised System HS 2012 classification, Sections and Divisions (one- and two- digit). Each table presents imports and exports of a given commodity with more than seventy partner countries or country groupings for the most recent five-year period available.

Labour Force Statistics 2022. Paris, FRA, Organisation for Economic Cooperation and Development, (202) 785-6323), https://www.oecd.org, 1961-. (Annual).

This annual edition of Labour Force Statistics provides detailed statistics on population, labour force, employment and unemployment, broken down by sex, as well as unemployment duration, employment status, employment by sector of activity and part-time employment. It also contains participation and unemployment rates by sex and detailed age groups as well as comparative tables for the main components of the labour force. Data are available for each OECD member country and for OECD-Total, Euro area and European Union. The time series presented in the publication cover 10 years for most countries. It also provides information on the sources and definitions used by member countries in the compilation of those statistics.

Main Economic Indicators (MEI). Paris, FRA, Organisation for Economic Cooperation and Development, https://www.oecd.org, ((202) 785-6323), 1965-. (Monthly).

The monthly *Main Economic Indicators* presents comparative statistics that provide an overview of recent international economic developments for OECD countries, the euro zone and a number of non-member economies. The indicators cover national accounts, business surveys and consumer opinions, leading indicators, retail sales, production, construction, prices, employment, unemployment, wages, finance, foreign trade and balance of payments.

National Accounts of OECD Countries, Volume 2022. Paris, FRA, Organisation for Economic Cooperation and Development, https://www.oecd.org, ((202) 785-6323), 1966-. (Annual).

This annual publication consists of two issues, the first covering main aggregates and the second detailed tables. The National Accounts of OECD Countries, Main Aggregates covers expenditure-based GDP, output-based GDP, income-based GDP, disposable income, saving and net lending, population and employment. It includes also comparative tables based on purchasing power parities and exchange rates. Data are shown for all OECD countries and the Euro area. Country tables are expressed in national currency. The National Accounts of OECD Countries, Detailed Tables includes, in addition to main aggregates, final consumption expenditure of households by purpose, simplified accounts for three main sectors: general government, corporations and households. Data are shown for all OECD countries and the Euro area. Country tables are expressed in national currency.

OECD Economic Outlook. Paris, FRA, Organisation for Economic Cooperation and Development, ((202) 785-6323), https://www.oecd.org, 1970-. (Biannual).

Analysis of the major economic trends and prospects for the next two years. Prepared by the OECD Economics Department, the Outlook puts forward a consistent set of projections for output, employment, government spending, prices and current balances based on a review of each member country and of the induced effect on each of them on international developments. Coverage is provided for all OECD member countries as well as for selected non-member countries. Each issue includes a general assessment, and a chapter summarizing developments and providing projections for each individual country. An extensive statistical annex with a wide variety of variables is available on-line.

OECD Economic Surveys. Paris, FRA, Organisation for Economic Cooperation and Development, ((202) 785-6323), https://www.oecd.org, 1953-. (Annual).

OECD Economic Surveys are periodic reviews of member and non-member economies. Reviews of member and some non-member economies are on a two-year cycle; other selected non-member economies are also reviewed from time to time. Each Economic Survey provides a comprehensive analysis of economic developments, with chapters covering key economic challenges and policy recommendations addressing these challenges.

OECD Health Statistics 2023 Database. Paris, FRA, Organisation for Economic Cooperation and Development, ((202) 785-6323), https://www.oecd.org, 2023.

The database offers the most comprehensive source of comparable statistics on health and health systems across OECD countries. It is an essential tool to carry out comparative analyses and draw lessons from international comparisons of diverse health systems.

OECD Main Science and Technology Indicators. Paris, FRA, Organisation for Economic Cooperation and Development, ((202) 785-6323), https://www.oecd.org, 1984-. (Biannual).

This biannual publication provides a set of indicators that reflect the level and structure of the efforts undertaken by OECD Member countries and selected non-member economies in the field of science and technology from 1981 onwards. These data include final or provisional results as well as forecasts established by government authorities.

Oil Information Database. Paris, FRA, Organisation for Economic Cooperation and Development, ((202) 785-6323), https://www.oecd.org, 1976-. (Annual).

This resource includes detailed and comprehensive annual data of oil supply, demand, trade, production and consumption by end-user for each OECD country individually and for the OECD regions. Trade data are reported extensively by origin and destination. Data are available for some 20 oil products and are provided in thousand metric tons; including conversion factors. This database also contains some major series for world-wide historical demand and supply.

Revenue Statistics 2022. Paris, FRA, Organisation for Economic Cooperation and Development, ((202) 785-6323), https://www.oecd.org, 1965-. (Annual).

Data on government sector receipts, and on taxes in particular, are basic inputs to most structural economic descriptions and economic analyses and are increasingly used in international comparisons. This annual publication gives a conceptual framework to define which government receipts should be regarded as taxes. It presents a unique set of detailed and internationally comparable tax data in a common format for all OECD countries from 1965 onwards.

PUBLICATIONS OF THE UNITED NATIONS AND AFFILIATED ORGANIZATIONS

The United Nations publishes scores of yearbooks, specialized studies, bulletins, and other compilations of interest to statistics users. The annual *United Nations Publications* catalogue provides a comprehensive guide to U.N. publications in print. Microfiche users should consult *United Nations Documentation in Microfiche. Index to Proceedings* is an annual bibliographic guide to the proceedings and documentation of the major organs. The Indexes are prepared by the Dag Hammarskjold Library and are produced at the end of the session/year.

The United Nations makes advanced multidisciplinary databases available for researchers working on a specific topic. They can be accessed by browsing its list of electronic resources by subject, such as development, disarmament, economy and finance, international law, international relations, peace and security, and social affairs.

Some U.N. databases are also available online from commercial vendors, for example as noted in the individual citations below. In addition several publications are available online from United Nations Publications at https://unog.primo.exlibrisgroup.com.

The following section covers many of the more important U.N. statistical publications.

African Statistical Yearbook 2021. New York, NY, USA, United Nations, Economic Commission for Africa, ((800) 253-9646), https://www.uneca.org/. 2022. (Annual).

The Yearbook series is a result of joint efforts by major African regional organizations to set up a joint data collection mechanism of socio-economic data on African countries as well as the development of a common harmonized database. The joint African Statistical Yearbook is meant to break with the practices of the past where each regional/sub-regional organization was publishing statistical data on African countries of the continent in an inefficient way, leading to duplication of efforts, inefficient use of scarce resources, increased burden on countries and sending different signals to users involved in tracking development efforts on the continent. It is expected that the joint collection and sharing of data between regional institutions will promote wider use of country data, reduce costs and significantly improve the quality of the data and lead to better monitoring of development initiatives on the continent.

UNAIDS Global AIDS Update 2023. Geneva, SWI, UNAIDS, https://www.unaids.org. 2023.

This report shows that there is a clear path that ends AIDS. This path will also help prepare for and tackle future pandemics and advance progress towards achieving the Sustainable Development Goals. The report contains data and case studies which highlight that ending AIDS is a political and financial choice, and that the countries and leaders who are already following the path are achieving extraordinary results.

Demographic Yearbook. New York, NY, USA, United Nations, Department of Economic and Social Affairs, (800) 253-9646), https://www.un.org/en/desa/, 1948-. (Annual).

The *Demographic Yearbook* provides official national population statistics for over 230 countries and areas of the world. Published annually since 1948, the *Demographic Yearbook* meets the needs of demographers, economists, public-health workers, sociologists, and other specialists. It presents general tables giving a world summary of basic demographic statistics and includes tables on the size, distribution, and trends of population, fertility, mortality, marriage and divorce, international migration and population census data. The information is provided in English and French.

Economic and Social Survey of Asia and the Pacific 2023. Bangkok, CHN, Economic and Social Commission for Asia and the Pacific (ESCAP), ((800) 253-9646), https://www.unescap.org/, 2023.

The Survey for 2023 examines how new perspectives on fiscal and public debt analyses and policies can help countries in Asia and the Pacific to effectively pursue not only the Sustainable Development Goals by 2030 but also improve their long-term sustainable development prospects.

Economic Report on Africa 2021: Addressing Poverty and Vulnerability in Africa during the COVID-19 Pandemic. New York, NY, USA, United Nations, Economic Commission for Africa, ((800) 253-9646), 2022, https://www.uneca.org, (Annual).

The *Economic Report on Africa* is an annual series that reviews the continent's economic performance and near-term prospects. Statistical data providing details for overall trade, trade between nations, regional trade and specific product information are presented.

Human Development Index (HDI). New York, NY, USA, United Nations Development Programme (UNDP), ((800) 253-9646), https://hdr.undp.org/en/, 2020.

With a comprehensive statistical annex, the data gives an overview of the state of development across the world, looking at long-term trends in human development indicators across multiple dimensions and for every nation, the HDI highlights the considerable progress, but also the persistent deprivations and disparities. The HDI was created to emphasize that people and their capabilities should be the ultimate criteria for assessing the development of a country, not economic growth alone.

International Trade Statistics Yearbook (ITSY). New York, NY, USA, United Nations, Department of Economic and Social Affairs, United Nations Publications, (212) 963-9851), https://unstats.un.org/home/, 1950-. (Annual).

This publication is aimed at both specialist trade data users and common audience at large. Volume I - Trade by Country - provides a condensed and integrated analytical view of the international merchandise trade, and trade in services up to the year 2021 by means of brief descriptive text, concise data tables and charts. The information presented provides insights into the latest trends of trade in goods and services of around 175 countries (and areas) in the world. Volume II - Trade by Product - provides an overview of the latest trends of trade in goods and services showing international trade for 258 individual commodities (3-digit SITC groups) and 11 main Extended Balance of Payments Services (EBOPS) categories.

Monthly Bulletin of Statistics. New York, NY, USA, United Nations, ((800) 253-9646), https://unstats.un.org, 1947-. (Monthly).

Current economic and social statistics for more than 200 countries and territories of the world. Many of these special tables are also reproduced in the *United Nations Statistical Yearbook.* Also available online.

National Accounts Statistics. New York, NY, USA, United Nations, Department of Economic and Social Affairs, (800) 253-9646), https://www.un.org/en/desa/, 1957-. (Annual).

This publication presents, in the form of analytical tables, a summary of the principal national accounting aggregates based on official detailed national accounts data for more than 200 countries and areas of the world. Where official data is not available estimates are provided by the Statistics Division of the United Nations. The analysis covers the level of total and per capita gross domestic product, economic structures, economic development and price development.

Population and Vital Statistics Report. New York, NY, USA, United Nations, Department of Economic and Social Affairs, ((800) 253-9646), https://www.un.org/en/desa/, (Annual).

The Population and Vital Statistics Report presents most recent data on population size (total, male and female) from the latest available census of the population, national official population estimates and the number and rate (births, deaths and infant deaths) for the latest available year within the past 15 years. It also presents United Nations estimates of the mid-year population of the world, and its major areas and regions.

The State of Food and Agriculture (SOFA). Rome, ITA, United Nations Food and Agriculture Organization, Information Division, FAO, ((202) 653-2400), https://www.fao.org, (Annual).

SOFA 2022 looks into the drivers of agricultural automation, including the more recent digital technologies. Based on 27 case studies, the report analyses the business case for adoption of digital automation technologies in different agricultural production systems across the world. It identifies several barriers preventing inclusive adoption of these technologies, particularly by small-scale producers. Key barriers are low digital literacy and lack of an enabling infrastructure, such as connectivity and access to electricity, in addition to financial constraints. Based on the analysis, the publication suggests policies to ensure that disadvantaged groups in developing regions can benefit from agricultural automation and that automation contributes to sustainable and resilient agrifood systems.

The State of the World's Children. New York, NY, USA, United Nations International Children's Emergency Fund (UNICEF), ((212) 326-7000), https://www.unicef.org, (Annual).

Each year, UNICEF's flagship publication, *The State of the World's Children,* closely examines a key issue affecting children. The State of the World's Children website includes digital versions of report components such as supporting data, statistics and stories in addition to online only features.

Statistical Yearbook. New York, NY, USA, United Nations, Department of Economic and Social Affairs, ((800) 253-9646), https://www.un.org/en/desa/, 1949-. (Annual).

The *Statistical Yearbook* is a comprehensive compendium of vital internationally comparable data for the analysis of socio-economic developments at the world, regional and national levels. The Yearbook provides data on the world economy, its structure, major trends and current performance, as well as on issues such as population and social statistics, economic activity and international economic relations. The information is available in English and French.

Statistical Yearbook for Latin America and the Caribbean 2021. New York, NY, USA, United Nations, Economic Commission for Latin America and the Caribbean, ((800) 253-9646), https://www.cepal.org/, 1975-. (Annual).

Provides statistical series for the overall region as well as subregions in the area. In addition, statistical series are presented for each country covering population, national accounts, agriculture, industry, transport, external trade, prices, balance of payments, and social statistics.

UNCTAD Handbook of Statistics 2022. New York, NY, USA, United Nations Conference on Trade and Development (UNCTAD), ((800) 253-9646), https://www.unctad.org, 1984-. (Annual).

The *UNCTAD Handbook of Statistics* provides a comprehensive collection of statistical data relevant to the analysis of world trade, investment and development. Since the 2017 edition, the Handbook of Statistics has been overhauled entirely to make it shorter and easier to read, and features a wealth of maps, charts, and infographics.

World Cities Report 2022: Envisaging the Future of Cities. New York, NY, USA, United Nations Human Settlements Programme (HABITAT), ((800) 253-9646), https://www.unhabitat.org, 2020.

This edition of World Cities Report seeks to provide greater clarity and insights into the future of cities based on existing trends, challenges and opportunities, as well as disruptive conditions, including the valuable lessons from the COVID-19 pandemic, and suggest ways that cities can be better prepared to address a wide range of shocks and transition to sustainable urban futures. The Report proposes a state of informed preparedness that provides us with the opportunity to anticipate change, correct the course of action and become more knowledgeable of the different scenarios or possibilities that the future of cities offers.

World Intellectual Property Indicators 2022. Geneva, SWI, World Intellectual Property Organization (WIPO), https://www.wipo.int, 2022.

This authoritative report provides an annual overview of activity in the areas of patents, utility models, trademarks, industrial designs, microorganisms, plant variety protection, geographical indications and the creative economy. It draws on statistics from around 150 national and regional IP offices and WIPO, as well as survey data and industry sources.

World Health Statistics 2023. Geneva, SWI, World Health Organization, https://www.who.int. (Telephone Number in U.S. (202) 974-3000), (Annual).

The World Health Statistics report is the World Health Organization's (WHO) annual compilation of the most recent available data on health and health-related indicators for its 194 Member States. The 2023 edition reviews more than 50 health-related indicators from the Sustainable Development Goals (SDGs) and WHO's Thirteenth General Programme of Work (GPW 13).

World Statistics Pocketbook 2022. New York, NY, USA, United Nations, ((800) 253-9646), https://unstats.un.org/unsd/publications/pocketbook/, 2022.

This volume is an annual compilation of key economic, social and environmental indicators, presented in one-page profiles and selected from the wealth of international statistical information compiled regularly by the Statistics Division and the Population Division of the United Nations, the statistical services of the United Nations specialized agencies and other international organizations and institutions.

Yearbook of Fishery and Aquaculture Statistics. United Nations Food and Agriculture Organization, FAO, (202) 653-2400, https://www.fao.org, 2021.

The FAO Fisheries and Aquaculture Department provides advice and objective information to Members to help promote responsible aquaculture and fisheries. To fulfil this role, the Department compiles, analyses and disseminates fishery data, structured within data collections. Global time series have been maintained over more than 60 years. To meet diverse user needs, data from each statistical collection are available through various formats, tools and information products.

WEBSITES

This listing of websites consists of national statistical offices and related government and non-government organizations, international statistical organizations, and United States government agencies which produce statistical information for the public. Entries are arranged alphabetically by country and organization name and include web addresses. Sites listed are for the English version where available.

NATIONAL STATISTICAL OFFICES AND RELATED ORGANIZATIONS

AFGHANISTAN

National Statistic and Information Authority (NISA)
http://nsia.gov.af

ALBANIA

Institute of Statistics (INSTAT)
https://www.instat.gov.al/en/

ALGERIA

National Office of Statistics (Office National des Statistiques)
https://www.ons.dz/

AMERICAN SAMOA

Statistics Division, Department of Commerce
https://www.doc.as.gov/

ANDORRA

Departament d'Estadistica, Edifici Administratiu de Govern
https://www.estadistica.ad/

ANGOLA

Instituto Nacional de Estatistica (INE) (National Institute of Statistics)
http://www.ine-ao.com/

ANGUILLA

Anguilla Statistics Department
http://www.gov.ai/statistics/

ARGENTINA

National Institute of Statistics and Censuses (Instituto Nacional de Estadistica y Censos (INDEC))
https://www.indec.gob.ar/

ARMENIA

Statistical Committee of the Republic of Armenia
https://www.armstat.am

ARUBA

Central Bureau of Statistics (CBS)
https://www.cbs.aw

AUSTRALIA

Australian Bureau of Statistics (ABS)
https://www.abs.gov.au/

OTHER STATISTICAL ORGANIZATIONS:

Australian Institute of Health and Welfare
https://www.aihw.gov.au

AUSTRIA

Statistik Osterreich (Statistics Austria)
https://www.statistik.at/

AZERBAIJAN

State Statistical Committee of the Republic of Azerbaijan
https://www.stat.gov.az/

BAHAMAS, THE

Bahamas National Statistical Institute
https://stats.gov.bs/

BAHRAIN

Bahrain Information and eGovernment
https://www.data.gov.bh/

BANGLADESH

Bangladesh Bureau of Statistics (BBS)
http://www.bbs.gov.bd/

BARBADOS

Barbados Statistical Service
https://www.gov.bb/Departments/statistical-services/

BELARUS

National Statistical Committee of the Republic of Belarus
https://belstat.gov.by/en/

BELGIUM

Statistics Belgium (Statbel)
https://statbel.fgov.be/

BELIZE

Statistical Institute of Belize
https://sib.org.bz/

BENIN

Institut National de la Statistique et de la Demographie (INSTAD)
https://instad.bj/

BERMUDA

Bermuda Government Department of Statistics
https://www.gov.bm/department/statistics

BHUTAN

National Statistics Bureau
https://www.nsb.gov.bt

BOLIVIA

Instituto Nacional de Estadistica (INE)
https://www.ine.gob.bo/

BOSNIA AND HERZEGOVINA

Agency for Statistics of Bosnia and Herzegovina
https://bhas.gov.ba/

BOTSWANA

Statistics Botswana
https://www.statsbots.org.bw/

BRAZIL

Brazilian Statistical and Geographic Institute (IBGE)
https://www.ibge.gov.br

BRUNEI

Department of Economic Planning and Statistics
https://deps.mofe.gov.bn/

BULGARIA

National Statistical Institute (NSI)
https://www.nsi.bg/en/

CAMBODIA

Cambodia Ministry of Planning, National Institute of Statistics (NIS)
https://www.nis.gov.kh/

CAMEROON

National Institute of Statistics of Cameroon
https://ins-cameroun.cm/en/

CANADA

Statistics Canada
https://www.statcan.gc.ca

PROVINCIAL STATISTICAL OFFICES:

Alberta
https://www.alberta.ca/office-statistics-information.aspx/

British Columbia
https://www2.gov.bc.ca/gov/content/data/statistics

Manitoba
https://vitalstats.gov.mb.ca/

New Brunswick
https://www2.snb.ca/

Newfoundland and Labrador
https://www.stats.gov.nl.ca/Statistics/

Northwest Territories
https://www.statsnwt.ca/

Nova Scotia
https://beta.novascotia.ca/programs-and-services/vital-statistics/

Nunavut
https://www.gov.nu.ca/

Ontario
https://www.ontario.ca/

Prince Edward Island
https://www.princeedwardisland.ca/

Quebec
https://www.etatcivil.gouv.qc.ca

Saskatchewan
https://www.ehealthsask.ca/vitalstats/

Yukon
https://yukon.ca/

OTHER STATISTICAL ORGANIZATIONS:

Statistical Society of Canada
https://ssc.ca/en/

Innovation, Science and Economic Development Canada
https://www.ic.gc.ca

CAPE VERDE

Instituto Nacional de Estatistica (INE)
https://ine.cv/

CAYMAN ISLANDS

Economics and Statistics Office
https://www.eso.ky

CENTRAL AFRICAN REPUBLIC

Institut Centrafricain des Statitistique et des Etudes Economiques et Sociales (ICASEES)
https://icasees.org

CHAD

Institut National de la Statistique, des Etudes Economiques et Demographiques
https://www.inseed.td

CHILE

Instituto Nacional de Estadisticas (INE)
https://www.ine.cl

CHINA

National Bureau of Statistics of China (NBS)
http://www.stats.gov.cn/english/

COLOMBIA

Departamento Administrativo Nacional de Estadisticas (DANE)
https://www.dane.gov.co

CONGO, REPUBLIC OF THE

Centre National de la Statistique et des Etudes Economiques (CNSEE)
https://www.cnsee.org

COOK ISLANDS

Cook Islands Statistics Office (CISO)
https://www.mfem.gov.ck/oldsite/index.php/statistics

COSTA RICA

Instituto Nacional de Estadistica y Censos (INEC)
https://inec.cr/

COTE d'IVOIRE

Institut National de la Statistique
https://www.ins.ci/n

CROATIA

Croatian Bureau of Statistics
https://www.dzs.hr/en

CUBA

La Oficina Nacional de Estadistica e Informacion
http://www.onei.gob.cu/

CYPRUS

Statistical Service of the Republic of Cyprus (CYSTAT), Ministry of Finance
https://www.cystat.gov.cy/en

CZECH REPUBLIC

Czech Statistical Office (CSU)
https://www.czso.cz

DENMARK

Statistics Denmark (Danmarks Statistik)
https://www.dst.dk/en

DJIBOUTI

Ministere de l'Economie, des Finances, Charge de l'Industrie
http://www.ministere-finances.dj/

DOMINICAN REPUBLIC

Oficina Nacional de Estadistica (ONE)
https://www.one.gob.do

EAST TIMOR

National Institute of Statistics Timor-Leste (INETL)
https://inetl-ip.gov.tl/

ECUADOR

Instituto Nacional de Estadistica y Censos (INEC)
https://www.ecuadorencifras.gob.ec

EGYPT

Central Agency for Public Mobilization and Statistics (CAPMAS)
https://www.capmas.gov.eg/

EL SALVADOR

Direccion General de Estadisticas y Censos (DIGESTYC)
http://www.digestyc.gob.sv

EQUATORIAL GUINEA

Direccion General de Estadistica y Cuentas Nacionales de Equatorial Guinea (DGECNSTATGE)
https://www.dgecnstat-ge.org

ESTONIA

Statistics Estonia
https://www.stat.ee/en

FIJI

Fiji Bureau of Statistics
https://www.statsfiji.gov.fj

FINLAND

Statistics Finland
https://www.stat.fi/index_en.html

OTHER STATISTICAL ORGANIZATIONS:

Bank of Finland
https://www.suomenpankki.fi/en

Geological Survey of Finland
https://www.gtk.fi/en/

Ministry of Education and Culture
https://okm.fi/en/frontpage

Finnish Institute for Health and Welfare
https://thl.fi/en/web/thlfi-en

FRANCE

National Institute of Statistics and Economic Studies (Institut National de la Statistique et des Etudes Economiques (INSEE))
https://www.insee.fr/

OTHER STATISTICAL ORGANIZATIONS:

Banque de France
https://www.banque-france.fr/en

Institut National de la Statistique et des Etudes Economiques (INSEE), Service Regional de la Martinique
https://www.insee.fr/fr/information/2017718/

French Ministry for the Economy and Finance
https://www.economie.gouv.fr

FRENCH POLYNESIA

Institut de la Statistique de la Polynesie Francaise
https://www.ispf.pf

GABON

Direction Generale des Statistiques (DGS)
https://stat-gabon.ga/

GEORGIA

National Statistics Office of Georgia
https://www.geostat.ge/en

GERMANY

Federal Statistical Office of Germany
https://www.destatis.de/

OTHER STATISTICAL ORGANIZATIONS:

German Economic Institute (IW)
https://www.iwkoeln.de/en/

Information und Technik Nordrhein-Westfalen
https://www.it.nrw/

GIBRALTAR

Statistics Office
https://www.gibraltar.gov.gi/statistics

GREECE

Hellenic Statistical Authority (ELSTAT)
https://www.statistics.gr/en/home

GREENLAND

Statistics Greenland
https://stat.gl/

GUAM

Bureau of Statistics and Plans
https://bsp.guam.gov/

GUERNSEY

States of Guernsey Data and Analysis Service
https://www.gov.gg/data

GUINEA

Institute National de la Statistique
https://www.stat-guinee.org

GUINEA-BISSAU

Instituto Nacional de Estatistica
https://www.stat-guinebissau.com/

GUYANA

Bureau of Statistics
https://statisticsguyana.gov.gy/

HONDURAS

Instituto Nacional de Estadistica (INE)
https://www.ine.gob.hn/

HONG KONG

Census and Statistics Department (CSD)
https://www.censtatd.gov.hk

HUNGARY

Hungarian Central Statistical Office (HCSO)
https://www.ksh.hu

INDIA

Ministry of Statistics and Programme Implementation
https://www.mospi.gov.in

OTHER STATISTICAL ORGANIZATIONS:

Office of the Registrar General and Census Commissioner
https://censusindia.gov.in

INDONESIA

Statistics Indonesia (Badan Pusat Statistik (BPS))
https://www.bps.go.id

IRELAND

Central Statistics Office (CSO)
https://www.cso.ie

ISRAEL

Central Bureau of Statistics (CBS) Israel
https://www.cbs.gov.il/en

Ministry of Finance
http://mof.gov.il/

ITALY

Istat - National Institute of Statistics (Instituto Nazionale di Statistica)
https://www.istat.it/en/

JAMAICA

Statistical Institute of Jamaica (STATIN)
https://statinja.gov.jm

JAPAN

Statistics Japan
https://www.stat.go.jp/

OTHER STATISTICAL ORGANIZATIONS:

Japan External Trade Organization (JETRO)
https://www.jetro.go.jp/en/

Ministry of Foreign Affairs of Japan
https://www.mofa.go.jp/

Ministry of Finance Japan
https://www.mof.go.jp/english

JORDAN

Department of Statistics (DOS)
http://dosweb.dos.gov.jo/ar/

KAZAKHSTAN

Agency for Strategic Planning and Reforms of the Republic of Kazakhstan, Bureau of National Statistics
https://stat.gov.kz/

KENYA

Kenya National Bureau of Statistics (KNBS)
https://www.knbs.or.ke/

KIRIBATI

Ministry of Finance and Economic Development, Kiribati National Statistics Office
https://nso.gov.ki/

KOREA, SOUTH

Statistics Korea
https://kostat.go.kr

KUWAIT

Kuwait Central Statistical Bureau
https://www.csb.gov.kw/Default_EN

KYRGYZSTAN

National Statistical Committee (NSC) of the Kyrgyz Republic
http://www.stat.kg/

LAOS

Lao Statistics Bureau
https://www.lsb.gov.la/en

LEBANON

Central Administration of Statistics (CAS)
http://www.cas.gov.lb/

LESOTHO

Lesotho Bureau of Statistics
https://www.bos.gov.ls

LIBYA

Bureau of Statistics and Census Libya
https://www.bsc.ly/

LIECHTENSTEIN

Amt fur Statistik
https://www.llv.li/de/landesverwaltung/amt-fuer-statistik

LITHUANIA

Statistics Lithuania
https://www.stat.gov.lt/en/

LUXEMBOURG

National Institute of Statistics and Economic Studies (STATEC), Grand-Duchy of Luxembourg
https://statistiques.public.lu/en/

MACAU

Statistics and Census Service of Macao
https://www.dsec.gov.mo/en-US

MACEDONIA, THE REPUBLIC OF

State Statistical Office of the Republic of Macedonia
https://www.stat.gov.mk

MADAGASCAR

Institut National de la Statistique (INSTAT)
https://www.instat.mg/

MALAWI

National Statistical Office of Malawi
http://www.nsomalawi.mw

MALAYSIA

Department of Statistics Malaysia
https://www.dosm.gov.my/v1

MALDIVES

Ministry of National Planning, Housing and Infrastructure, Bureau of Statistics
https://statisticsmaldives.gov.mv/

MALTA

National Statistics Office (NSO)
https://nso.gov.mt/

MAN, ISLE OF

Isle of Man Government Treasury
https://www.gov.im/treasury/

MARSHALL ISLANDS

Economic Policy, Planning and Statistics Office (EPPSO)
https://www.rmieppso.org/

MAURITANIA

Office National de la Statistique et de l'Analyse Demographique et Economique (ANSADE) Mauritania
https://ansade.mr

MAURITIUS

Statistics Mauritius
https://statsmauritius.govmu.org

MEXICO

Instituto Nacional de Estadistica y Geografia (INEGI)
https://www.inegi.org.mx/

MICRONESIA, FEDERATED STATES OF

Federated States of Micronesia Statistics Division (FSM Statistics)
https://www.fsmstatistics.fm/

MOLDOVA

National Bureau of Statistics of the Republic of Moldova
https://statistica.gov.md

MONACO

Monaco Statistics
https://www.monacostatistics.mc/

MONGOLIA

National Statistics Office of Mongolia
https://en.nso.mn/home/

MONTSERRAT

Government of Montserrat, Ministry of Finance and Economic Management, Statistics Department
https://statistics.gov.ms/

MOROCCO

Haut-Commissariat au Plan
https://www.hcp.ma

MOZAMBIQUE

Instituto Nacional de Estatistica (INE)
https://www.ine.gov.mz

NAMIBIA

Namibia Statistics Agency
https://nsa.org.na/

NAURU

Ministry of Finance, Bureau of Statistics
https://nauru.prism.spc.int/

NEPAL

Nepal Central Bureau of Statistics
https://cbs.gov.np/

NETHERLANDS

Statistics Netherlands (CBS)
https://www.cbs.nl/en-gb/

NEW CALEDONIA

Institute de la Statistique et des Etudes Economiques (ISEE)
https://www.isee.nc

NEW ZEALAND

Statistics New Zealand (Stats NZ)
https://www.stats.govt.nz

NIGER

Institut National de la Statistique (INS)
https://www.stat-niger.org

NIGERIA

National Bureau of Statistics (NBS)
https://www.nigerianstat.gov.ng/

NIUE

Statistics Niue
https://niuestatistics.nu/

NORTHERN MARIANA ISLANDS

Department of Commerce, Central Statistics Division (CSD)
https://ver1.cnmicommerce.com/divisions/central-statistics/

NORWAY

Statistics Norway
https://www.ssb.no/en/

OMAN

National Centre for Statistics and Information
https://www.ncsi.gov.om/

PAKISTAN

Pakistan Bureau of Statistics
https://www.pbs.gov.pk/

PALAU

Bureau of Budget and Planning, Office of Planning and Statistics (OPS)
https://www.palaugov.pw/budgetandplanning/

PANAMA

Instituto Nacional de Estadistica y Censo
https://www.inec.gob.pa/

PAPUA NEW GUINEA

National Statistical Office (NSO)
https://www.nso.gov.pg/

PARAGUAY

Instituto Nacional de Estadistica (INE)
https://www.ine.gov.py

PERU

Instituto Nacional de Estadistica e Informatica (INEI)
https://www.gob.pe/inei/

PHILIPPINES

Philippine Statistics Authority (PSA)
https://psa.gov.ph/

POLAND

Statistics Poland
https://stat.gov.pl/en/

PORTUGAL

Statistics Portugal
https://www.ine.pt

PUERTO RICO

Departamento de Educacion
https://de.pr.gov/

Instituto de Estadisticas de Puerto Rico
https://estadisticas.pr/

QATAR

Qatar Planning and Statistics Authority (PSA)
https://www.psa.gov.qa/en/

ROMANIA

National Institute of Statistics (NIS) Romania
https://www.insse.ro/cms/en

RUSSIA

Federal State Statistics Service (FSSS)
https://eng.rosstat.gov.ru/

RWANDA

National Institute of Statistics of Rwanda
https://www.statistics.gov.rw/

SAINT HELENA

Statistics Office, Government of Saint Helena
https://www.sainthelena.gov.sh/st-helena/statistics/

SAINT LUCIA

Central Statistical Office of Saint Lucia
https://www.stats.gov.lc

SAMOA

Samoa Bureau of Statistics (SBS)
https://www.sbs.gov.ws/

SAO TOME AND PRINCIPE

Instituto Nacional de Estatistica (INE)
https://ine.st/

SAUDI ARABIA

General Authority for Statistics (GASTAT)
https://www.stats.gov.sa/en

SENEGAL

Agence Nationale de la Statistique et de la Demographie (ANSD), Ministere de l'Economie et des Finances
https://www.ansd.sn/

SERBIA AND MONTENEGRO

Statistical Office of the Republic of Serbia
https://www.stat.gov.rs/en-US/

SEYCHELLES

National Bureau of Statistics
https://www.nbs.gov.sc/

SIERRA LEONE

Statistics Sierra Leone (Stats SL)
http://www.statistics.sl/

SINGAPORE

Department of Statistics Singapore
https://www.singstat.gov.sg

SLOVENIA

Statistical Office of the Republic of Slovenia
https://www.stat.si/

SOLOMON ISLANDS

Solomon Islands National Statistics Office (SINSO)
https://www.statistics.gov.sb/

SOUTH AFRICA

Statistics South Africa
https://www.statssa.gov.za

SPAIN

Instituto Nacional de Estadistica (INE)
https://www.ine.es/en

SRI LANKA

Department of Census and Statistics
http://www.statistics.gov.lk/

SUDAN

Central Bureau of Statistics (CBS)
http://www.cbs.gov.sd

SURINAME

General Bureau of Statistics in Suriname
https://statistics-suriname.org/en/

SWAZILAND

Ministry of Economic Planning and Development, Central Statistical Office
https://www.gov.sz/index.php/ministries-departments/ministry-of-economic-planning/

SWEDEN

Statistics Sweden
https://www.scb.se/

SWITZERLAND

Swiss Federal Statistical Office
https://www.bfs.admin.ch/bfs/en/home.html

SYRIA

Central Bureau of Statistics
https://www.cbssyr.org/

TAIWAN

Ministry of Economic Affairs
https://mnscdn.moea.gov.tw/MNS/english/

Ministry of Education
https://english.moe.gov.tw

TANZANIA

Tanzania National Bureau of Statistics (NBS)
https://www.nbs.go.tz/

THAILAND

National Statistical Office (NSO)
http://web.nso.go.th/sites/2014en

OTHER STATISTICAL ORGANIZATIONS:

Bank of Thailand (BOT)
https://www.bot.or.th/en/home.html/

TOGO

Institut National de la Statistique et des Etudes Economiques et Demographiques (INSEED)
https://inseed.tg/

TONGA

Tonga Statistics Department
https://tongastats.gov.to/

TRINIDAD AND TOBAGO

Central Statistical Office (CSO)
https://cso.gov.tt/

TUNISIA

National Institute of Statistics, Tunisia (Statistiques Tunisie)
https://www.ins.tn/

TURKEY

Turkish Statistical Institute
https://www.tuik.gov.tr/

TUVALU

Central Statistics Division of Tuvalu
https://stats.gov.tv/

UGANDA

Uganda Bureau of Statistics (UBOS)
https://www.ubos.org/

UNITED ARAB EMIRATES

Federal Competitiveness and Statistics Authority
https://uaecabinet.ae/en/the-federal-competitiveness-and-statistics-centre/

UNITED KINGDOM

Office for National Statistics (ONS)
https://www.ons.gov.uk

OTHER STATISTICAL ORGANIZATIONS:

Confederation of British Industry (CBI)
https://www.cbi.org.uk/

Bank of England, Statistics Division
https://www.bankofengland.co.uk/statistics/

His Majesty's Treasury
https://www.gov.uk/government/organisations/hm-treasury/

GOV.UK
https://www.gov.uk/

URUGUAY

Instituto Nacional de Estadistica
https://www.ine.gub.uy/

UZBEKISTAN

Statistics Agency Under the President of the Republic of Uzbekistan
https://stat.uz/en/

VANUATU

Vanuatu National Statistics Office (VNSO)
https://vnso.gov.vu/

VENEZUELA

Instituto Nacional de Estadistica (INE)
http://www.ine.gov.ve/

VIETNAM

General Statistics Office (GSO) of Vietnam
https://www.gso.gov.vn/en/

VIRGIN ISLANDS

University of the Virgin Islands Eastern Caribbean Center
https://www.uvi.edu/research/eastern-caribbean-center/

Virgin Islands Economic Development Authority
https://www.usvieda.org/

ZAMBIA

Zambia Statistics Agency (ZAMSTATS)
https://www.zamstats.gov.zm/

ZIMBABWE

Zimbabwe National Statistics Agency (ZIMSTAT)
https://www.zimstat.co.zw/

UNITED STATES GOVERNMENT AGENCIES

DEPARTMENT OF AGRICULTURE

Department of Agriculture (Home Page)
https://www.usda.gov

Economics, Statistics and Market Information System
https://usda.library.cornell.edu/

Economic Research Service
https://www.ers.usda.gov

National Agricultural Library
https://www.nal.usda.gov

National Agricultural Statistics Service
https://www.nass.usda.gov

DEPARTMENT OF COMMERCE

Department of Commerce (Home Page)
https://www.commerce.gov/

Bureau of Economic Analysis
https://www.bea.gov/

Bureau of the Census
https://www.census.gov

International Trade Administration
https://www.trade.gov/

National Marine Fisheries Service (NOAA Fisheries)
https://www.fisheries.noaa.gov/

National Oceanic and Atmospheric Administration
https://www.noaa.gov

NOAA National Centers for Environmental Information
https://www.ncei.noaa.gov

NOAA National Weather Service
https://www.weather.gov/

Patent and Trademark Office
https://www.uspto.gov

DEPARTMENT OF DEFENSE

Department of Defense (Home Page)
https://www.defense.gov/

DEPARTMENT OF EDUCATION

National Center for Education Statistics
https://nces.ed.gov

DEPARTMENT OF ENERGY

Department of Energy (Home Page)
https://www.energy.gov

Energy Information Administration
https://www.eia.gov

Federal Energy Regulatory Commission
https://www.ferc.gov

DEPARTMENT OF HEALTH AND HUMAN SERVICES

Department of Health and Human Services (Home Page)
https://www.hhs.gov

Centers for Disease Control and Prevention
https://www.cdc.gov

National Cancer Institute
https://www.cancer.gov/

National Center for Health Statistics
https://www.cdc.gov/nchs/

National Institutes of Health
https://www.nih.gov

DEPARTMENT OF HOMELAND SECURITY

Department of Homeland Security (Home Page)
https://www.dhs.gov

National Counterterrorism Center
https://www.dni.gov/index.php/nctc-home/

U.S. Coast Guard
https://www.uscg.mil

U.S. Customs and Border Protection
https://www.cbp.gov

DEPARTMENT OF HOUSING AND URBAN DEVELOPMENT

Department of Housing and Urban Development (Home Page)
https://www.hud.gov

DEPARTMENT OF JUSTICE

Department of Justice (Home Page)
https://www.justice.gov/

Bureau of Justice Statistics
https://bjs.ojp.gov/

Civil Rights Division
https://www.justice.gov/crt/

Drug Enforcement Administration
https://www.dea.gov

Federal Bureau of Investigation
https://www.fbi.gov

U.S. Citizenship and Immigration Services
https://www.uscis.gov/

National Criminal Justice Reference Service
https://www.ojp.gov/ncjrs

National Institute of Justice
https://nij.ojp.gov/

Office of Juvenile Justice and Delinquency Prevention
https://ojjdp.ojp.gov/

DEPARTMENT OF LABOR

Office of Labor-Management Standards
https://www.dol.gov/agencies/olms/

Bureau of Labor Statistics
https://www.bls.gov

Occupational Safety and Health Administration
https://www.osha.gov

DEPARTMENT OF THE INTERIOR

Department of the Interior (Home Page)
https://www.doi.gov

Bureau of Reclamation
https://www.usbr.gov

U.S. Geological Survey
https://www.usgs.gov

U.S. Geological Survey, National Minerals Information Center
https://www.usgs.gov/centers/national-minerals-information-center/

DEPARTMENT OF THE TREASURY

Department of the Treasury (Home Page)
https://home.treasury.gov

Alcohol and Tobacco Tax and Trade Bureau
https://www.ttb.gov

Internal Revenue Service
https://www.irs.gov/

Office of the Comptroller of the Currency (OCC)
https://www.ots.treas.gov

DEPARTMENT OF TRANSPORTATION

Department of Transportation (Home Page)
https://www.transportation.gov/

Bureau of Transportation Statistics
https://www.bts.gov/

Federal Aviation Administration
https://www.faa.gov

Federal Highway Administration
https://highways.dot.gov/

Federal Railroad Administration
https://railroads.dot.gov/

Federal Transit Administration
https://www.transit.dot.gov/

Maritime Administration
https://www.maritime.dot.gov/

National Highway Traffic Safety Administration
https://www.nhtsa.gov/

DEPARTMENT OF VETERANS AFFAIRS

Department of Veterans Affairs (Home Page)
https://www.va.gov

OTHER U.S. GOVERNMENT DEPARTMENTS AND AGENCIES

Federal Geographic Data Committee
https://www.fgdc.gov

Foreign Agriculture Service
https://www.fas.usda.gov

Library of Congress
https://www.loc.gov

National Archives and Records Administration
https://www.archives.gov

National Endowment for the Humanities
https://www.neh.gov/

National Institute of Standards and Technology
https://www.nist.gov

National Science Foundation
https://www.nsf.gov

National Science Foundation - National Center for Science and Engineering Statistics
https://ncses.nsf.gov/

Social Security Administration
https://www.ssa.gov

INTERNATIONAL STATISTICAL ORGANIZATIONS

EUROSTAT (Statistical Office of the European Communities)
https://ec.europa.eu/eurostat/

International Atomic Energy Agency (IAEA)
https://www.iaea.org

International Civil Aviation Organization (ICAO)
https://www.icao.int

International Fund for Agricultural Development (IFAD)
https://www.ifad.org

International Labour Organization (ILO)
https://www.ilo.org

International Maritime Organization (IMO)
https://www.imo.org

International Monetary Fund (IMF)
https://www.imf.org

International Monetary Fund (IMF) Dissemination Standards Bulletin Board (DSBB)
https://dsbb.imf.org/

International Statistical Institute (ISI)
https://isi-web.org/

International Telecommunication Union (ITU)
https://www.itu.int

Organization for Economic Co-operation and Development (OECD)
https://www.oecd.org

Oxford Economics
https://www.oxfordeconomics.com/

United Nations
https://www.un.org

United Nations Children's Fund (UNICEF)
https://www.unicef.org

United Nations Conference on Trade and Development (UNCTAD)
https://unctad.org

United Nations Industrial Development Organization (UNIDO)
https://www.unido.org

Universal Postal Union (UPU)
https://www.upu.int

UN Development Programme
https://www.undp.org

UN Economic Commission for Europe (UNECE)
https://unece.org

UN Economic Commission for Latin America and the Caribbean (ECLAC)
https://www.cepal.org/en

UN Economic Commission for Africa (ECA)
https://www.uneca.org

UN Economic and Social Commission for Asia and the Pacific (ESCAP)
https://www.unescap.org

UN Economic and Social Commission for Western Asia (ESCWA)
https://www.unescwa.org/

UN Educational, Scientific and Cultural Organization (UNESCO)
https://en.unesco.org/

UN Food and Agriculture Organization (FAO)
https://www.fao.org

UN Population Fund (UNFPA)
https://www.unfpa.org

UN Statistics Division
https://unstats.un.org/

World Bank
https://www.worldbank.org

World Food Programme (WFP)
https://www.wfp.org

World Health Organization (WHO)
https://www.who.int

World Intellectual Property Organization (WIPO)
https://www.wipo.int

World Meteorological Organization (WMO)
https://public.wmo.int/

World Tourism Organization
https://world-tourism.org

World Trade Organization (WTO)
https://www.wto.org

Federal Statistical Telephone Contacts

The federal government is the most important collector, disseminator, and repository of statistical information available, covering virtually every subject in today's society. Its highly-informed cadre of subject specialists is of great potential assistance to information-seekers. In a time when those seekers are becoming more inclined to go beyond traditional published sources in their search for the most current data, federal government specialists represent a unique, but often untapped, source of information.

An inventory of the federal government's statistical information sources is listed below. First arranged under broader subject categories, the inventory is then broken down further to name precise government units or individual specialists who can be called upon for help in a specific topic area. The specialists are experienced at answering questions, and do not charge for their time or assistance. When they cannot provide the specific data sought, the specialists can often make referrals to other expert contacts with the most current statistical information available.

AGRICULTURE

The National Agricultural Statistics Service collects data on crops, livestock, poultry, dairy, chemical use, prices, and labor. Its 45 field offices can provide information about agricultural production, stocks, prices and other data on an individual county and/or state basis. The agricultural experts are listed below. For a current listing see https://www.nass.usda.gov/Contact_Us/Ask_a_Specialist/index.php Also phone the Agricultural Statistics Hotline at (800) 727-9540.

AGRICULTURAL CHEMICAL USE
Doug Farmer
(202) 690-3229
doug.farmer@usda.gov

AGROFORESTRY
Thomas Laidley
(202) 221-9280
thomas.laidley@usda.gov

ALCOHOL COPRODUCTS
David Colwell
(202) 720-8800
david.colwell@usda.gov

ALMONDS
Deonne Holiday
(202) 720-4288
deonne.mccray@usda.gov

ALPACAS
Scott Hollis
(202) 690-2424
scott.holllis@usda.gov

AMERICAN INDIANS
Thomas Laidley
(202) 221-9280
thomas.laidley@usda.gov

APPLES
Chris Singh
(202) 720-4285
chris.singh@usda.gov

APRICOTS
Robert Little
(202) 720-3250
robert.little@usda.gov

AQUACULTURE TOTALS
Liana Cuffman
(202) 720-8784
liana.cuffman@usda.gov

ARTICHOKES
Krishna Rizal
(202) 720-5412
krishna.rizal@usda.gov

ASPARAGUS
Deonne Holiday
(202) 720-4288
deonne.mccray@usda.gov

AVOCADOS
Chris Wallace
(202) 720-4215
chris.wallace@usda.gov

BARLEY
Michelle Harder
(202) 690-8533
michelle.harder@usda.gov

BEANS, DRY EDIBLE
Robert Little
(202) 720-3250
robert.little@usda.gov

BEANS, SNAP
Robert Little
(202) 720-3250
robert.little@usda.gov

BEES
Seth Riggins
(202) 690-4870
seth.riggins@usda.gov

BISON
Ryan Cowen
(202) 720-3040
ryan.cowen@usda.gov

BISON SLAUGHTER
Sherry Bertramsen
(202) 690-8632
sherry.bertramsen@usda.gov

BLUEBERRIES
Chris Singh
(202) 720-4285
chris.singh@usda.gov

BROCCOLI
Chris Wallace
(202) 720-4215
chris.wallace@usda.gov

BROILERS
Takiyah Walker
(202) 720-6147
takiyah.walker@usda.gov

BUTTER
Donnie Fike
(202) 690-3347
donnie.fike@usda.gov

BUTTERMILK
Donnie Fike
(202) 690-3347
donnie.fike@usda.gov

CABBAGE
Chris Wallace
(202) 720-4215
chris.wallace@usda.gov

CANOLA
Travis Thorson
(202) 720-7369
travis.thorson@usda.gov

CANTALOUPES
Antonio Torres
(202) 720-2157
antonio.torres@usda.gov

CARROTS
Deonne Holiday
(202) 720-4288
deonne.mccray@usda.gov

CATFISH
Liana Cuffman
(202) 720-8784
liana.cuffman@usda.gov

CATTLE
Ryan Cowen
(202) 720-3040
ryan.cowen@usda.gov

CATTLE ON FEED
Ryan Cowen
(202) 720-3040
ryan.cowen@usda.gov

CATTLE SLAUGHTER
Sherry Bertramsen
(202) 690-8632
sherry.bertramsen@usda.gov

CAULIFLOWER
Krishna Rizal
(202) 720-5412
krishna.rizal@usda.gov

CELERY
Krishna Rizal
(202) 720-5412
krishna.rizal@usda.gov

CENSUS FACT SHEETS
Thomas Laidley
(202) 221-9280
thomas.laidley@usda.gov

CENSUS OF AGRICULTURE
NASS Statistician
(800) 727-9540
nass@usda.gov

CENSUS OF AQUACULTURE
Liana Cuffman
(202) 720-8784
liana.cuffman@usda.gov

CENSUS OF HORTICULTURE
Jamila Sani
(202) 690-3226
jamila.sani@usda.gov

CENSUS OF PR
Irvin Yeager
(202) 720-7492
irvin.yeager@usda.gov

CHEESE
Donnie Fike
(202) 690-3347
donnie.fike@usda.gov

CHEESE AMERICAN
Donnie Fike
(202) 690-3347
donnie.fike@usda.gov

CHEMICAL USE
Doug Farmer
(202) 690-3229
doug.farmer@usda.gov

CHERRIES, SWEET
Antonio Torres
(202) 720-2157
antonio.torres@usda.gov

CHERRIES TART
Antonio Torres
(202) 720-2157
antonio.torres@usda.gov

CHICKENS
Autumn Stone
(202) 690-3676
autumn.stone@usda.gov

COFFEE
Deonne Holiday
(202) 720-4288
deonne.mccray@usda.gov

COLD STORAGE
Shulonda Shaw
(202) 720-3240
shulonda.shaw@usda.gov

COMMODITY TOTALS
Bruce Boess
(202) 720-4447
bruce.boess@usda.gov

CORN
Greg Lemmons
(202) 720-9526
greg.lemmons@usda.gov

COST OF INPUTS
Ralph Mondesir
(202) 221-9280
ralph.mondesir@usda.gov

COTTON
Rebecca Sommer
(202) 720-5944
rebecca.sommer@usda.gov

COTTON PIMA
Rebecca Sommer
(202) 720-5944
rebecca.sommer@usda.gov

COTTON UPLAND
Rebecca Sommer
(202) 720-5944
rebecca.sommer@usda.gov

CRANBERRIES
Deonne Holiday
(202) 720-4288
deonne.mccray@usda.gov

CREAM
Donnie Fike
(202) 690-3347
donnie.fike@usda.gov

CROP PROGRESS
Irwin Anolik
(202) 720-7621
irwin.anolik@usda.gov

CUCUMBERS
Chris Singh
(202) 720-4285
chris.singh@usda.gov

DAIRY PRODUCTS
Donnie Fike
(202) 690-3347
donnie.fike@usda.gov

DAIRY PRODUCTS FROZEN
Donnie Fike
(202) 690-3347
donnie.fike@usda.gov

DATES
Chris Wallace
(202) 720-4215
chris.wallace@usda.gov

DEER
Donnie Fike
(202) 690-3347
donnie.fike@usda.gov

EGG PRODUCTS
Derron Martin
(202) 690-3237
derron.martin@usda.gov

EGGS
Autumn Stone
(202) 690-3676
autumn.stone@usda.gov

ELK
Donnie Fike
(202) 690-3347
donnie.fike@usda.gov

EQUINE SLAUGHTER
Sherry Bertramsen
(202) 690-8632
sherry.bertramsen@usda.gov

FARM DEMOGRAPHICS
Ginger Harris
(502) 582-5257
virginia.harris@usda.gov

FARM OPERATIONS
Michael Mathison
(202) 720-3243
michael.mathison@usda.gov

FARM PRODUCTION EXPENDITURES
Zoe Johnson
(202) 720-5446
zoe.johnson@usda.gov

FARMERS MARKET
Jeffrey Kissel
(202) 720-5777
jeff.kissel@usda.gov

FEED PRICE RATIOS
Max Reason
(202) 720-8844
max.reason@usda.gov

FIELD CROP TOTALS
Travis Thorson
(202) 720-7369
travis.thorson@usda.gov

FLAXSEED
Greg Lemmons
(202) 720-9526
greg.lemmons@usda.gov

FLORICULTURE TOTALS
Chris Wallace
(202) 720-4215
chris.wallace@usda.gov

FLOUR
David Colwell
(202) 720-8800
david.colwell@usda.gov

FOOD FISH
Liana Cuffman
(202) 720-8784
liana.cuffman@usda.gov

FORAGE
Michelle Harder
(202) 690-8533
michelle.harder@usda.gov

FOREST
Ralph Mondesir
(202) 221-9280
ralph.mondesir@usda.gov

GARLIC
Krishna Rizal
(202) 720-5412
krishna.rizal@usda.gov

GOATS
Scott Hollis
(202) 690-2424
scott.holllis@usda.gov

GOATS SLAUGHTER
Sherry Bertramsen
(515) 284-3240
sherry.bertramsen@usda.gov

GRAIN STORAGE CAPACITY
Greg Lemmons
(202) 720-9526
greg.lemmons@usda.gov

GRAPEFRUIT
Krishna Rizal
(202) 720-5412
krishna.rizal@usda.gov

GRAPES
Chris Wallace
(202) 720-4215
chris.wallace@usda.gov

GRAZING FEES PRIVATE
Michael Mathison
(202) 720-3243
michael.mathison@usda.gov

HATCHERY
Derron Martin
(202) 690-3237
derron.martin@usda.gov

HAY ALFALFA (DRY)
Michelle Harder
(202) 690-8533
michelle.harder@usda.gov

HAY ALL (DRY)
Michelle Harder
(202) 690-8533
michelle.harder@usda.gov

HAY OTHER (DRY)
Michelle Harder
(202) 690-8533
michelle.harder@usda.gov

HAZELNUTS
Chris Singh
(202) 720-4285
chris.singh@usda.gov
HEMP
Joshua Bates
(202) 690-3234
joshua.bates@usda.gov

HOGS
Anthony Fischer
(202) 720-3106
anthony.fischer@usda.gov

HOGS SLAUGHTER
Sherry Bertramsen
(202) 690-8632
sherry.bertramsen@usda.gov

HONEY
Seth Riggins
(202) 690-4870
seth.riggins@usda.gov

HONEYDEW MELONS
Antonio Torres
(202) 720-2157
antonio.torres@usda.gov

HOPS
Chris Wallace
(202) 720-4215
chris.wallace@usda.gov

ICE CREAM
Donnie Fike
(202) 690-3347
donnie.fike@usda.gov

INPUT COSTS IN PRODUCTION
Max Reason
(202) 720-8844
max.reason@usda.gov

IRRIGATION AND WATER MANAGEMENT
William Cumberland
(202) 690-1348
william.cumberland@usda.gov

IRRIGATION ORGANIZATIONS
William Cumberland
(202) 690-1348
william.cumberland@usda.gov

KIWIFRUIT
Krishna Rizal
(202) 720-5412
krishna.rizal@usda.gov

LABOR
Theresa Varner
(202) 690-3231
theresa.varner@usda.gov

LAMB & MUTTON
Sherry Bertramsen
(202) 690-8632
sherry.bertramsen@usda.gov

LAMBS
Scott Hollis
(202) 690-2424
scott.holllis@usda.gov

LAND IN FARMS
Michael Mathison
(202) 720-3243
michael.mathison@usda.gov

LEMONS
Krishna Rizal
(202) 720-5412
krishna.rizal@usda.gov

LENTILS
Antonio Torres
(202) 720-2157
antonio.torres@usda.gov

LETTUCE
Robert Little
(202) 720-3250
robert.little@usda.gov

LLAMAS
Scott Hollis
(202) 690-2424
scott.holllis@usda.gov

LOCAL FOODS
Irvin Yeager
(202) 720-7492
irvin.yeager@usda.gov

MACADAMIAS
Robert Little
(202) 720-3250
robert.little@usda.gov

MANDARINS
Krishna Rizal
(202) 720-5412
krishna.rizal@usda.gov

MANUFACTURED DAIRY
Donnie Fike
(202) 690-3347
donnie.fike@usda.gov

MANUFACTURED DAIRY OTHER
Donnie Fike
(202) 690-3347
donnie.fike@usda.gov

MAPLE SYRUP
Robert Little
(202) 720-3250
robert.little@usda.gov

MELLORINE MIX
Donnie Fike
(202) 690-3347
donnie.fike@usda.gov

MILK
Kim Dapra
(512) 501-3266
kim.dapra@usda.gov

MILLET
Greg Lemmons
(202) 720-9526
greg.lemmons@usda.gov

MILLFEED
David Colwell
(202) 720-8800
david.colwell@usda.gov

MINK
Liana Cuffman
(202) 720-8784
liana.cuffman@usda.gov

MINT
Krishna Rizal
(202) 720-5412
krishna.rizal@usda.gov

MOHAIR
Scott Hollis
(202) 690-2424
scott.holllis@usda.gov

MUSHROOMS
Krishna Rizal
(202) 720-5412
krishna.rizal@usda.gov

MUSTARD
Travis Thorson
(202) 720-7369
travis.thorson@usda.gov

NECTARINES
Robert Little
(202) 720-3250
robert.little@usda.gov

NONCITRUS FRUIT & TREE NUTS TOTALS
Krishna Rizal
(202) 720-5412
krishna.rizal@usda.gov

NONCITRUS TOTALS
Krishna Rizal
(202) 720-5412
krishna.rizal@usda.gov

OATS
Joshua Bates
(202) 690-3234
joshua.bates@usda.gov

OLIVES
Krishna Rizal
(202) 720-5412
krishna.rizal@usda.gov

ONIONS
Deonne Holiday
(202) 720-4288
deonne.mccray@usda.gov

ORANGES
Krishna Rizal
(202) 720-5412
krishna.rizal@usda.gov

ORGANICS
Ginger Harris
(502) 582-5257
virginia.harris@usda.gov

OUTLYING AREAS
Irvin Yeager
(202) 720-7492
irvin.yeager@usda.gov

PAPAYAS
Antonio Torres
(202) 720-2157
antonio.torres@usda.gov

PEACHES
Antonio Torres
(202) 720-2157
antonio.torres@usda.gov

PEANUTS
Lihan Wei
(202) 720-7688
jlihan.wei@usda.gov

PEARS
Robert Little
(202) 720-3250
robert.little@usda.gov

PEAS, DRY EDIBLE
Antonio Torres
(202) 720-2157
antonio.torres@usda.gov

PEAS, GREEN
Antonio Torres
(202) 720-2157
antonio.torres@usda.gov

PECANS
Chris Wallace
(202) 720-4215
chris.wallace@usda.gov

PEPPERS, CHILE
Chris Wallace
(202) 720-4215
chris.wallace@usda.gov

PEPPERS, BELL
Chris Wallace
(202) 720-4215
chris.wallace@usda.gov

PISTACHIOS
Deonne Holiday
(202) 720-4288
deonne.mccray@usda.gov

PLUMS
Deonne Holiday
(202) 720-4288
deonne.mccray@usda.gov

POTATOES
Chris Singh
(202) 720-4285
chris.singh@usda.gov

POULTRY
Holly Brenize
(202) 720-0585
holly.brenize@usda.gov

POULTRY SLAUGHTER
Holly Brenize
(202) 720-0585
holly.brenize@usda.gov

PRICES PAID BY FARMERS
Max Reason
(202) 720-8844
max.reason@usda.gov

PRICES RECEIVED
Ralph Mondesir
(202) 221-9280
ralph.mondesir@usda.gov
Tom Laidley
(202) 221-9280
tom.laidley@usda.gov

PRUNES
Deonne Holiday
(202) 720-4288
deonne.mccray@usda.gov

PUMPKINS
Chris Singh
(202) 720-4285
chris.singh@usda.gov

RAPESEED
Travis Thorson
(202) 720-7369
travis.thorson@usda.gov

RASPBERRIES
Chris Singh
(202) 720-4285
chris.singh@usda.gov

RENT
Michael Mathison
(202) 720-3243
michael.mathison@usda.gov

RICE
Lihan Wei
(202) 720-7688
jlihan.wei@usda.gov

RYE
James Johanson
james.johanson@usda.gov
(202) 690-8533

SAFFLOWER
Travis Thorson
(202) 720-7369
travis.thorson@usda.gov

SHEEP
Scott Hollis
(202) 690-2424
scott.holllis@usda.gov

SLAUGHTER (PLANTS)
Sherry Bertramsen
(202) 690-8632
sherry.bertramsen@usda.gov

SOIL
James Johanson
(202) 690-8533
james.johanson@usda.gov

SORGHUM
Rebecca Sommer

(202) 720-5944
rebecca.sommer@usda.gov

SOYBEANS
Joshua Bates
(202) 690-3234
joshua.bates@usda.gov

SPEARMINT OIL
Krishna Rizal
(202) 720-5412
krishna.rizal@usda.gov

SPINACH
Robert Little
(202) 720-3250
robert.little@usda.gov

SQUASH
Chris Singh
(202) 720-4285
chris.singh@usda.gov

STRAWBERRIES
Chris Singh
(202) 720-4285
chris.singh@usda.gov

SUGARBEETS
Chris Singh
(202) 720-4285
chris.singh@usda.gov

SUGARCANE
Chris Singh
(202) 720-4285
chris.singh@usda.gov

SUNFLOWER
Travis Thorson
(202) 720-7369
travis.thorson@usda.gov

SWEET CORN
Deonne Holiday
(202) 720-4288
deonne.mccray@usda.gov

SWEET POTATOES
Chris Singh
(202) 720-4285
chris.singh@usda.gov

TANGERINES
Krishna Rizal
(202) 720-5412
krishna.rizal@usda.gov

TOBACCO
Deonne Holiday
(202) 720-4288
deonne.mccray@usda.gov

TOMATOES
Robert Little
(202) 720-3250
robert.little@usda.gov

TROUT
Liana Cuffman
(202) 720-8784
liana.cuffman@usda.gov

TURKEYS
Fatema Haque
(202) 720-3244
fatema.haque@usda.gov

VEGETABLE CHEMICAL USE
Doug Farmer
(202) 690-3229
doug.farmer@usda.gov

VEGETABLE TOTALS
Krishna Rizal
(202) 720-5412
krishna.rizal@usda.gov

WAGE RATES
Theresa Varner
(202) 690-3231
theresa.varner@usda.gov

WALNUTS
Antonio Torres
(202) 720-2157
antonio.torres@usda.gov

WATER ICES
Donnie Fike
(202) 690-3347
donnie.fike@usda.gov

WATERMELON
Antonio Torres
(202) 720-2157
antonio.torres@usda.gov

WHEAT
James Johanson
james.johanson@usda.gov
(202) 690-8533

WHEAT DURUM
James Johanson
james.johanson@usda.gov
(202) 690-8533

WHEAT OTHER SPRING
James Johanson
james.johanson@usda.gov
(202) 690-8533

WHEAT WINTER
James Johanson
james.johanson@usda.gov
(202) 690-8533

WHEY
Donnie Fike
(202) 690-3347
donnie.fike@usda.gov

WOOL
Scott Hollis
(202) 690-2424
scott.holllis@usda.gov

YOGURT
Donnie Fike
(202) 690-3347
donnie.fike@usda.gov

STATE STATISTICAL OFFICES

The following people can provide information about agricultural production, stocks, prices and other data for individual States and, in many cases, for counties in those States. For an updated list, go to the website https://www.nass.usda.gov/Statistics_by_State/.

ALABAMA - Montgomery
Vacant
(800) 253-4419
Fax: (334) 279-3590
nassrfosor@nass.usda.gov

ALASKA - Palmer
Dennis Koong
(800) 435-5883
Fax: (855) 270-2721
nassrfonwr@nass.usda.gov

ARIZONA - Phoenix
Dave DeWalt
(800) 392-3202
Fax: (866) 314-4029
nassrfomtr@nass.usda.gov

ARKANSAS - Little Rock
Eugene Young
(501) 228-9926
(800) 327-2970
Fax: (855) 270-2705
nassrfodlr@nass.usda.gov

CALIFORNIA - Sacramento
Gary R. Keough
(916) 738-6600
(800) 851-1127
Fax: (855) 270-2722
nassrfopcr@nass.usda.gov

COLORADO - Lakewood
Bill Meyer
(720) 787-3150
Fax: (866) 314-4029
nassrfomtr@nass.usda.gov

CONNECTICUT - See NEW ENGLAND

DELAWARE - Dover
Shareefah Williams
(301) 347-8179
Fax: (855) 270-2719
nassrfoner@nass.usda.gov

FLORIDA - Orlando
Mark Hudson
(407) 648-6013
Fax: (855) 271-9801
nassrfosor@nass.usda.gov

GEORGIA - Athens
Anthony Prillaman
(706) 713-5400
(800) 253-4419
Fax: (855) 271-9801
nassrfosor@nass.usda.gov

HAWAII - Honolulu
Shawn Clark
(808) 522-8080
Fax: (844) 332-7146
nassrfopcr@nass.usda.gov

IDAHO - Boise
Ben Johnson
(208) 334-1507
(800) 691-9987
Fax: (208) 334-1114
nassrfonwr@nass.usda.gov

ILLINOIS - Springfield
Mark Schleusener
(217) 524-9606
Fax: (855) 270-2717
nassfohlr@nass.usda.gov

INDIANA - Lafayette
Vacant
(765) 494-8371
Fax: (765) 494-4315
nassrfoglr@nass.usda.gov

IOWA - Des Moines
Greg Thessen
(515) 776-3400
Fax: (855) 271-9802
nassrfoumr@nass.usda.gov

KANSAS - Manhattan
Doug Bounds
(800) 582-6443
Fax: (855) 270-2720
nassrfonpr@nass.usda.gov

KENTUCKY - Louisville
David Knopf
(800) 928-5277
Fax: (855) 270-2708
nassrfoemr@nass.usda.gov

LOUISIANA - Baton Rouge
Kathy Broussard
(800) 256-4485
Fax: (888) 922-0744
nassrfodlr@nass.usda.gov

MAINE
Pam Hird
(202) 615-9845
Fax: (855) 270-2719
nassrfoner@nass.usda.gov

MARYLAND - Annapolis
Shareefah Williams
(301) 347-8179
Fax: (855) 270-2719
nassrfoner@nass.usda.gov

MASSACHUSETTS - See NEW ENGLAND

MICHIGAN - Lansing
Marlo Johnson
(800) 453-7501
Fax: (855) 270-2709
nassrfoglr@nass.usda.gov

MINNESOTA - St. Paul
Dan Lofthus
(651) 728-3113
Fax: (855) 271-9802
nassrfoumr@nass.usda.gov

MISSISSIPPI - Jackson
Esmerelda Dickson
(601) 359-1259
(800) 535-9609
nassrfodlr@nass.usda.gov

MISSOURI - Columbia
Brad Summa
(314) 595-9594
(800) 551-1014
Fax: (855) 270-2717
nassrfohlr@nass.usda.gov

MONTANA - Helena
Eric Sommer
(800) 392-3202
Fax: (888) 314-4029
nassrfomtr@nass.usda.gov

NEBRASKA - Lincoln
Nicholas Streff
(402) 437-5541
(800) 582-6443
Fax: (855) 270-2720
nassrfonpr@nass.usda.gov

NEVADA - Reno
Gary R. Keough
(916) 738-6601
nassrfopcr@nass.usda.gov

NEW ENGLAND - Concord, NH
Pam Hird
(202) 615-9845
Fax: (855) 270-2719
nassrfoner@nass.usda.gov

NEW HAMPSHIRE - See NEW ENGLAND

NEW JERSEY - Trenton
Bruce Eklund
(503) 308-0404
Fax: (609) 633-9231
nassrfoner@nass.usda.gov

NEW MEXICO - Las Cruces
Bill Meyer
(800) 392-3202
Fax: (866) 314-4029
nassrfomtr@nass.usda.gov

NEW YORK - Albany
Donnie Fike
(518) 457-5570
Fax: (855) 270-2719
nassrfoner@nass.usda.gov

NORTH CAROLINA - Raleigh
Dee Webb
(919) 707-3333
Fax: (919) 856-4139
nassrfoemr@nass.usda.gov

NORTH DAKOTA - Fargo
Darin Jantzi
(800) 582-6443
Fax: (855) 270-2720
nassrfonpr@nass.usda.gov

OHIO - Reynoldsburg
Cheryl Turner
(614) 728-2100
Fax: (855) 270-2709
nassrfoglr@nass.usda.gov

OKLAHOMA - Oklahoma City
Troy Marshall
(405) 415-8850
Fax: (405) 528-2296
nassrfospr@nass.usda.gov

OREGON - Portland
Dave Losh
(503) 326-2131
(800) 338-2157
Fax: (503) 326-2549
nassrfonwr@nass.usda.gov

PENNSYLVANIA - Harrisburg
King Whetstone
(717) 787-3904
Fax: (855) 270-2719
nassrfoner@nass.usda.gov

RHODE ISLAND - See NEW ENGLAND

SOUTH CAROLINA - Columbia
Jacqueline Moore
(803) 734-2506
(800) 424-9406
Fax: (855) 271-9801
nassrfosor@nass.usda.gov

SOUTH DAKOTA - Sioux Falls
Erik Gerlach
(800) 582-6443
Fax: (855) 270-2720
nassrfonpr@nass.usda.gov

TENNESSEE - Nashville
Debra K. Kenerson
(615) 781-5300
(800) 626-0987
Fax: (615) 781-5303
nassrfoemr@nass.usda.gov

TEXAS - Austin
Wilbert Hundl, Jr.
(512) 501-3200
Fax: (855) 270-2725
nassrfospr@nass.usda.gov

UTAH - Salt Lake City
John Hilton
(800) 392-3202
Fax: (801) 314-4029
nassrfomtr@nass.usda.gov

VERMONT - See NEW ENGLAND

VIRGINIA - Richmond
Herman Ellison
(502) 907-3250
(800) 928-5277
Fax: (855) 270-2708
nassrfoemr@nass.usda.gov

WASHINGTON - Olympia
Dennis Koong
(360) 890-3300
(800) 435-5883
Fax: (855) 270-2721
nassrfonwr@nass.usda.gov

WEST VIRGINIA - Charleston
Charmaine Wilson
(304) 357-5123
(800) 535-7088
Fax: (855) 270-2708
nassrfoemr@nass.usda.gov

WISCONSIN - Madison
Greg Bussler
(608) 287-4775
Fax: (855) 271-9802
nassrfoumr@nass.usda.gov

WYOMING - Cheyenne
Bill Meyer
(800) 392-3202
Fax: (866) 314-4029
nassrfomtr@nass.usda.gov

BANKING AND FINANCIAL DATA

The Federal Reserve Board's Division of Research and Statistics is responsible for developing and presenting economic and financial data and analysis for the use of the Board, the Federal Open Market Committee, and other Federal Reserve System officials. This information serves as background for the formulation and conduct of monetary, regulatory, and supervisory policies. In addition, the division fosters a broader understanding of issues relating to economic policy by providing leadership in economic and statistical research and by supplying data and analyses for public release.

Capital Markets
Andrew Y. Chen
Economist, Capital Markets Section
(202) 973-6941
andrew.y.chen@frb.gov
Dalida Kadyrzhanova
Principal Economist, Capital Markets Section
202-452-3053
dalida.kadyrzhanova@frb.gov
Francisco Palomino
Senior Economist, Capital Markets Section
(202) 452-5220
francisco.palomino@frb.gov
Nitish R. Sinha
Senior Economist, Capital Markets Section
(202) 973-6916
nitish.r.sinha@frb.gov
Michael Smolyansky
Economist, Capital Markets Section
(202) 721-4577
Michael.smolyansky@frb.gov
Tugkan Tuzun
Senior Economist, Capital Markets Section
(202)736-5646
tugkan.tuzun@frb.gov
Jie Yang
Senior Economist, Capital Markets Section
(202) 736-1939
jie.yang@frb.gov

Consumer Finance
John C. Driscoll
Economist, Consumer Finance Section
john.c.driscoll@frb.gov
Gregory Elliehausen
Principal Economist, Consumer Finance Section
(202) 452-2326
gregory.elliehausen@frb.gov
Felicia F. Ionescu
Principal Economist, Consumer Finance Section
(202) 452-2504
felicia.ionescu@frb.gov
Geng Li
Chief, Consumer Finance Section
(202) 452-2995
geng.li@frb.gov
Alvaro Mezza
Economist, Consumer Finance Section
(202) 452-3392
alvaro.a.mezza@frb.gov

Current Macroeconomic Conditions
Edward P. Herbst
Chief, Current Macroeconomic Conditions Section
(202) 452-3369
edward.p.herbst@frb.gov
Hie Joo Ahn
Principal Economist, Current Macroeconomic Conditions Section
(202) 728-5875
hiejoo.ahn@frb.gov
Travis J. Berge
Senior Economist, Current Macroeconomic Conditions Section
(202) 452-7843
travis.j.berge@frb.gov
Andrea Stella
Senior Economist, Current Macroeconomic Conditions Section
(202) 452-2793
andrea.stella@frb.gov

Financial Structure
Cecilia R. Caglio
Group Manager, Financial Structure Section
(202) 452-3084
cecilia.r.caglio@frb.gov
Tim E. Dore
Economist, Financial Structure Section
(202) 452-2887
tim.dore@frb.gov
Jennifer L. Dlugosz
Principal Economist, Financial Studies Section
(202) 452-2638
jennifer.l.dlugosz@frb.gov
Jacob P. Gramlich
Chief, Financial Structure Section
(202) 721-4585
jacob.gramlich@frb.gov
Serafin J. Grundl
Economist, Financial Studies Section
(202) 452-2910
serafin.j.grundl@frb.gov
Marcelo Rezende
Principal Economist, Financial Studies Section
(202) 452-3264
marcelo.rezende@frb.gov
Gloria Sheu
Group Manager, Financial Structure Section
(202) 202-912-4612
gloria.sheu@frb.gov

Fiscal Analysis
David B. Cashin

Senior Economist, Fiscal Analysis Section
(202) 452-3991
david.b.cashin@frb.gov
Lisa J. Dettling
Principal Economist, Fiscal Analysis Section
lisa.j.dettling@frb.gov
William B. Peterman
Principal Economist, Fiscal Analysis Section
(202) 452-3703
william.b.peterman@frb.gov
Nick Turner
Senior Economist, Fiscal Analysis Section
(202) 452-2098
nick.turner@frb.gov

Flow of Funds
Michael M. Batty
Economist, Flow of Funds Section
mike.batty@frb.gov
Christine L. Dobridge
Principal Economist, Flow of Funds Section
christine.l.dobridge@frb.gov
Tim E. Dore
Principal Economist, Flow of Funds Section
(202) 452-2887
tim.dore@frb.gov
Traci L. Mach
Principal Economist, Flow of Funds Section
(202) 452-3906
traci.l.mach@frb.gov
Eric R. Nielsen
Economist, Flow of Funds Section
(202) 872-7591
eric.r.nielsen@frb.gov
Maria G. Perozek
Group Manager, Flow of Funds Section
maria.g.perozek@frb.gov
Ana-Maria K. Tenekedjieva
Economist, Flow of Funds Section
ana-maria.k.tenekedjieva@frb.gov
Youngsuk Yook
Senior Economist, Flow of Funds Section
(202) 457-6324
youngsuk.yook@frb.gov

Household and Business Spending
Eirik E. Brandsaas
Economist, Household and Business Spending Section
eirik.e.brandsaas@frb.gov
Han Chen
Senior Economist, Household and Business Spending Section
(202) 452-2465
han.chen@frb.gov
David Cho
Senior Economist, Household and Business Spending Section
(202) 785-6023
david.cho@frb.gov
Laura J. Feiveson
Deputy Assistant Secretary, Household and Business Spending Section
(202) 452-2758
laura.j.feiveson@frb.gov
William L. Gamber
Economist, Household and Business Spending Section
(202) 452-3606
will.gamber@frb.gov
Andrew D. Paciorek
Senior Economist, Household and Business Spending Section
(202) 974-7069
andrew.d.paciorek@frb.gov
Eugenio Pinto
Senior Economist, Household and Business Spending Section
(202) 452-3370
eugenio.p.pinto@frb.gov

Industrial Output
Kimberly N. Bayard
Economist, Industrial Output Section
(202) 452-2570
kimberly.n.bayard@frb.gov
David M. Byrne
Principal Economist, Industrial Output Section
(202) 452-3587
david.m.byrne@frb.gov
Leland D. Crane
Economist, Industrial Output Section
(202) 475-7649
leland.d.crane@frb.gov
Ryan A. Decker
Economist, Industrial Output Section
(202) 452-2478
ryan.a.decker@frb.gov
Christopher J. Kurz
Principal Economist, Industrial Output Section
(202) 452-3086
christopher.j.kurz@frb.gov
Scott W. Ohlmacher
Senior Economist, Industrial Output Section
(202) 993-3101
scott.w.ohlmacher@frb.gov
Gisela Rua
Senior Economist, Industrial Output Section
(202) 736-5664
gisela.rua@frb.gov
Paul E. Soto
Senior Economist, Industrial Output Section
(202) 912-4685
paul.e.soto@frb.gov
Maria D. Tito
Economist, Industrial Output Section
(202) 530-6236
maria.d.tito@frb.gov

Labor Markets
Hie Joo Ahn
Economist, Labor Markets Section
(202) 728-5875
hiejoo.ahn@frb.gov
Tomaz Cajner
Senior Economist, Labor Markets Section
tomaz.cajner@frb.gov
Charles A. Fleischman
Chief, Labor Markets Section
charles.a.fleischman@frb.gov
Joshua K. Montes
Senior Economist, Labor Markets Section
joshua.k.montes@frb.gov
Christopher J. Nekarda
Senior Economist, Labor Markets Section
christopher.j.nekarda@frb.gov
David D. Ratner
Senior Economist, Labor Markets Section
david.d.ratner@frb.gov
Christopher L. Smith
Principal Economist, Labor Markets Section
christopher.l.smith@frb.gov
Ivan Vidangos
Principal Economist, Labor Markets Section
ivan.vidangos@frb.gov

Macroeconomic and Quantitative Studies
Isabel Cairo
Economist, Macroeconomic and Quantitative Studies Section
isabel.cairo@frb.gov
Joonkyu Choi
Economist, Macroeconomic and Quantitative Studies Section
joonkyuchoi@frb.gov
Hess T. Chung
Principal Economist, Macroeconomic and Quantitative Studies Section
(202) 452-3992
hess.t.chung@frb.gov
Francesco Ferrante
Economist, Macroeconomic and Quantitative Studies Section
francesco.ferrante@frb.gov
Cristina Fuentes-Albero
Economist, Macroeconomic and Quantitative Studies Section
(202) 973-6971
cristina.fuentes-albero@frb.gov
Manuel P. Gonzalez-Astudillo
Senior Economist, Macroeconomic and Quantitative Studies Section
(202) 452-2468
manuel.p.gonzalez-astudillo@frb.gov
Jean-Philippe Laforte
Senior Economist, Macroeconomic and Quantitative Studies Section
jean-philippe.laforte@frb.gov
Antoine Lepetit
Economist, Macroeconomic and Quantitative Studies Section
AntoineLepetit@frb.gov
David S. Miller
Economist, Macroeconomic and Quantitative Studies Section
(202) 785-6015
david.s.miller@frb.gov
Camilo Morales-Jimenez
Economist, Macroeconomic and Quantitative Studies Section
(202) 452-2837
camilo.moralesjimenez@frb.gov
Matthias O. Paustian
Chief, Macroeconomic and Quantitative Studies Section
(202) 736-5543
matthias.o.paustian@frb.gov
Damjan Pfajfar
Senior Economist, Macroeconomic and Quantitative Studies Section
(202) 452-2813
damjan.pfajfar@frb.gov
Michael Siemer
Economist, Macroeconomic and Quantitative Studies Section
(202) 912-7860
michael.siemer@frb.gov
Jae W. Sim
Principal Economist, Macroeconomic and Quantitative Studies Section
(202) 452-2670
jae.w.sim@frb.gov
Diego Vilan
Economist, Macroeconomic and Quantitative Studies Section
(202) 452-2681
diego.vilan@frb.gov

Microeconomic Surveys
Neil Bhutta
Principal Economist, Microeconomic Surveys Section
neil.bhutta@frb.gov
Jesse Bricker
Economist, Microeconomic Surveys Section
(202) 263-4827
jesse.bricker@frb.gov
Lisa J. Dettling
Economist, Microeconomic Surveys Section
(202) 973-6956
lisa.j.dettling@frb.gov
Alice M. Henriques
Economist, Microeconomic Surveys Section
(202) 425-3080
alice.m.henriques@frb.gov
Joanne W. Hsu
Senior Economist, Microeconomic Surveys Section
(202) 973-7391
joanne.w.hsu@frb.gov
Kevin B. Moore
Chief, Microeconomic Surveys Section
(202) 452-3887
kevin.b.moore@frb.gov

Prices and Wages
Chad T. Fulton
Economist, Prices and Wages Section
(202) 452-6454
chad.t.fulton@frb.gov
Kirstin Hubrich
Chief, Prices and Wages Section
(202) 452-6604
kirstin.hubrich@frb.gov
Matteo Luciani
Senior Economist, Prices and Wages Section
(202) 452-3123
matteoluciani@frb.gov
Ekaterina Peneva
Economist, Prices and Wages Section
(202) 736-1916
ekaterina.v.peneva@frb.gov
Brad E. Strum
Economist, Prices and Wages Section
(202) 452-5244
brad.e.strum@frb.gov
Daniel Villar Vallenas
Economist, Prices and Wages Section
daniel.villar@frb.gov

Program Direction
Daniel M. Covitz
Deputy Director, Program Direction Section

(202) 452-5267
daniel.m.covitz@frb.gov
Burcu Duygan-Bump
Assistant Director, Program Direction Section
(202) 452-4663
burcu.duygan-bump@frb.gov
Eric M. Engen
Senior Associate Director, Program Direction Section
(202) 452-3715
eric.m.engen@frb.gov
Eric C. Engstrom
Adviser, Program Direction Section
(202) 452-3044
eric.c.engstrom@frb.gov
Glenn R. Follette
Assistant Director, Program Direction Section
(202) 452-2940
glenn.r.follette@frb.gov
Joshua Gallin
Deputy Associate Director, Program Direction Section
(202) 452-2788
joshua.h.gallin@frb.gov
Diana Hancock
Senior Associate Director, Program Direction Section
(202) 452-3019
diana.hancock@frb.gov
Erik A. Heitfield
Assistant Director, Program Direction Section
(202) 452-2613
erik.a.heitfield@frb.gov
Elizabeth K. Kiser
Deputy Associate Director, Program Direction Section
(202) 452-2584
elizabeth.k.kiser@frb.gov
David E. Lebow
Senior Associate Director, Program Direction Section
(202) 452-3057
david.e.lebow@frb.gov
Patrick E. McCabe
Adviser, Program Direction Section
(202) 452-3483
patrick.e.mccabe@frb.gov
Michael G. Palumbo
Senior Associate Director, Program Direction Section
michael.g.palumbo@frb.gov
Wayne Passmore
Senior Adviser, Program Direction Section
wayne.passmore@frb.gov
Karen M. Pence
Adviser, Program Direction Section
(202) 452-2342
karen.pence@frb.gov
John M. Roberts
Assistant Director, Program Direction Section
(202) 452-2946
john.m.roberts@frb.gov
Jeremy Rudd
Senior Adviser, Program Direction Section
(202) 452-3780
jeremy.b.rudd@frb.gov
Steven A. Sharpe
Assistant Director, Program Direction Section
steve.a.sharpe@frb.gov
Shane M. Sherlund
Assistant Director, Program Direction Section
(202) 452-3589
shane.m.sherlund@frb.gov
Paul A. Smith
Assistant Director, Program Direction Section
paul.a.smith@frb.gov
John J. Stevens
Deputy Associate Director, Program Direction Section
(202) 452-2206
john.j.stevens@frb.gov
Stacey Tevlin
Associate Director, Program Direction Section
stacey.tevlin@frb.gov
William L. Wascher
Deputy Director, Program Direction Section
(202) 452-2812
william.l.wascher@frb.gov

Real Estate Finance
Elliot Anenberg
Senior Economist, Real Estate Finance Section
(202) 452-2581
elliot.anenberg@frb.gov
Raven Malloy
Chief, Real Estate Finance Section
raven.s.molloy@frb.gov
Daniel R. Ringo
Economist, Real Estate Finance Section
(202) 452-2935
daniel.r.ringo@frb.gov

Risk Analysis
Erfan Danesh
Economist, Risk Analysis Section
erfan.danesh@frb.gov
Michael B. Gordy
Principal Economist, Risk Analysis Section
(202) 452-3705
michael.gordy@frb.gov
Xin Huang
Economist, Risk Analysis Section
(202) 530-6211
xin.huang@frb.gov
Yesol Huh
Economist, Risk Analysis Section
(202) 973-6943
yesol.huh@frb.gov
Yang-Ho Park
Senior Economist, Risk Analysis Section
(202) 452-3177
yang-ho.park@frb.gov
Valery Polkovnichenko
Economist, Risk Analysis Section
valery.polkovnichenko@frb.gov
Pawel J. Szerszen
Principal Economist, Risk Analysis Section
pawel.j.szerszen@frb.gov
Clara Vega
Chief, Risk Analysis Section
(202) 452-2379
clara.vega@frb.gov

Short-Term Funding Markets
Lei Li
Senior Economist, Short-Term Funding Markets Section
(202) 475-6616
yi.li@frb.gov
Yi Li
Economist, Short-Term Funding Markets Section
(202) 721-4576
yi.li@frb.gov
Xing (Alex) Zhou
Senior Economist, Short-Term Funding Markets Section
(202) 452-2596
xing.zhou@frb.gov
Francesca Zucchi
Economist, Short-Term Funding Markets Section
(202) 245-4212
francesca.zucchi@frb.gov

Systemic Financial Institutions and Markets
Celso Brunetti
Chief, Systemic Financial Institutions and Markets Section
(202) 452-3134
celso.brunetti@frb.gov
Nathan Foley-Fisher
Economist, Systemic Financial Institutions and Markets Section
(202) 452-2350
nathan.c.foley-fisher@frb.gov
Stefan Gissler
Economist, Systemic Financial Institutions and Markets Section
(202) 452-2693
stefan.gissler@frb.gov
Borghan N. Narajabad
Senior Economist, Systemic Financial Institutions and Markets Section
(202) 728-5817
borghan.narajabad@frb.gov
Carlos Ramirez
Economist, Systemic Financial Institutions and Markets Section
(202) 452-3169
carlos.ramirez@frb.gov
Doriana Ruffino
Economist, Systemic Financial Institutions and Markets Section
(202) 452-5235
doriana.ruffino@frb.gov
Stephane Verani
Senior Economist, Systemic Financial Institutions and Markets Section
(202) 912-7972
stephane.h.verani@frb.gov

CENSUS DATA

These specialists can tell precisely what statistical data is available in their subject areas. The information is arranged by program and subject area. To contact any of the specialists by mail, use their name, division and address: U.S. Census Bureau, Washington, D.C. 20233.

AMERICAN FACTFINDER

American FactFinder
Staff (MSO)
(301) 763-4636
factfinder@census.gov

CENSUS 2020

2020 Census
Staff (C2PO)
(301) 763-3977

Aging Population, U.S.
Staff (POP)
(301) 763-2378

American Community Survey
Staff (CLMSO)
(301) 763-4636

American FactFinder
Staff (CLMSO)
(301) 763-4636

Annexations/Boundary Changes
Staff (GEO)
(301) 763-1099

Apportionment
Staff (POP)
(301) 763-9291

Census History
Staff (DIR)
(301) 763-1167

Census in Schools
Staff (CLMSO)
(301) 763-6676

Citizenship
Staff (POP)
(301) 763-2411

Commuting, Means of Transportation and Place of Work
Staff (HHES)
(301) 763-2454

Confidentiality and Privacy
Staff (POL)
(301) 763-7310

Count Review
Staff (POP)
(301) 763-2390

Data Dissemination
Staff (CLMSO)
(301) 763-4636

Disability
Staff (DID)
(301) 763-2422

Employment/Unemployment (General Information)
Staff (DID)
(301) 763-2422

Foreign-born
Staff (POP)
(301) 763-2411

Geographic Entities
Staff (GEO)

(301) 763-1099

Grandparents as Caregivers
Staff (HHES)
(301) 763-2416

Group Quarters Population
Staff (POP)
(301) 763-2378

Health Insurance Statistics
Staff (DID)
(301) 763-2422

Hispanic Origin/Ethnicity/Ancestry
Staff (POP)
(301) 763-2403

Homeless
Staff (POP)
(301) 763-2378

Housing (General Information)
Staff (HHES)
(301) 763-3237

Immigration/Emigration
Staff (DID)
(301) 763-2422

Income
Staff (HHES)
(301) 763-3243

Island Areas (Puerto Rico, U.S. Virgin Islands, Pacific Islands)
Staff (DMD)
(301) 763-8443

Labor Force Status/Work Experience (General)
Staff (CLMSO)
(301) 763-4636

Living Arrangements
Staff (HHES)
(301) 763-2416

Marital Status
Staff (HHES)
(301) 763-2416

Metropolitan and Micropolitan Statistical Areas Standards
Staff (POP)
(301) 763-2419

Migration
Staff (HHES)
(301) 763-2454

News Media Inquiries
Staff (PIO)
(301) 763-3030

Occupation/Industry
Staff (HHES)
(301) 763-3239

Partnership and Data Services
Staff (FLD)
(301) 763-7879

Place of Birth/Native Born
Staff (HHES)
(301) 763-2454

Population (General Information)
Staff (DID)
(301) 763-2422

Poverty
Staff (DID)
(301) 763-2422

Public Use Microdata Files (PUMS)
Staff (POP)
(301) 763-2429

Race
Staff (POP)
(301) 763-2402

Redistricting
Staff (DIR)
(301) 763-4039

Residence Rules
Staff (POP)
(301) 763-9291

Small Area Income and Poverty Estimates
Staff (DID)
(301) 763-3193

Special Censuses
Staff (FLD)
(301) 763-1429

Special Population
Staff (POP)
(301) 763-2378

Special Tabulations
Staff (POP)
(301) 763-2429

TIGER/Line files
Staff (GEO)
(301) 763-1128

Undercount
Staff (DSSD)
(301) 763-4206

Undercount - Demographic Analysis
Staff (POP)
(301) 763-2110

Unmarried Partners
Staff (HHES)
(301) 763-2416

Urban/Rural
Staff (GEO)
(301) 763-3056

U.S. Citizens Abroad
Staff (CLMSO)
(301) 763-4636

Veteran Status
Staff (DID)
(301) 763-2422

Voting Districts
Staff (GEO)
(301) 763-1099

Women
Staff (POP)
(301) 763-2378

ZIP Codes
Staff (DID)
(301) 763-2422

CENSUS ADVISORY COMMITTEES OFFICE

National Advisory Committee

Race and Ethnic Advisory Committees
Tom Loo, Coordinator
(301) 763-2070
Fax: (301) 763-5236
tom.loo@census.gov

Census Scientific Advisory Committee
Sara Rosario-Nieves, Coordinator
(301) 763-2941
Fax: (301) 457-8608
sara.a.rosario.nieves@census.gov

CENSUS INFORMATION CENTERS

The Census Information Centers (CICs) are national, regional, and local nonprofit organizations in partnership with the Census Bureau to make census data available to underserved communities. The CICs provide access to and understanding of the value and uses of census data to communities and neighborhoods across the country.

Alaska
First Alaskans Institute
Liz Medicine Cow, Director
606 E St., Ste. 200
Anchorage, AK, USA, 99501
(907) 677-1702
Fax: (907) 677-1780
lizmedicinecrow@firstalaskans.org
qunmigu@firstalaskans.org https://firstalaskans.org/census-information-center/overview/

Arizona
The Navajo Nation
Mr. Jonathan Nez, President
PO Box 1904
Window Rock, AZ, USA, 86515
(928) 871-7181
(928) 871-7182
Fax: (928) 871-7189
nnez@nndcd.org https://www.nndcd.org

California
Asian Americans Advancing Justice - Los Angeles
Mr. Stewart Kwoh, President & Executive Director
1145 Wilshire Blvd., 2nd Fl.
Los Angeles, CA, USA, 90017
(213) 977-7500
Fax: (213) 977-7595
jlim@advancingjustice-la.org https://advancingjustice-la.org/
Asian and Pacific Islander American Health Forum
Mrs. Kathy Ko Chin, President & CEO
One Kaiser Plz., Ste. 600
Oakland, CA, USA, 94612
(415) 954-9988
Fax: (415) 954-9999
communitypartners@apiahf.org https://www.apiahf.org/
ASIAN, Inc.
Mr. Lamar Heystek, President
1167 Mission Street, 4th Fl.
San Francisco, CA, USA, 94103
(415) 928-5910
Fax: (415) 921-0182
lheystek@asianinc.org https://www.asianinc.org/census
Asian Pacific American Community Development Data Center
Dr. David K. Yoo, Director
University of California, Los Angeles (UCLA)
3230 Campbell Hall, 405 Hilgard Avenue, Box 951546
Los Angeles, CA, USA, 90095-1546
(310) 206-7738
Fax: (310) 206-9844
melanyd@ucla.edu http://www.aasc.ucla.edu/cic
California Indian Manpower Consortium
Ms. Lorenda T. Sanchez, Director
738 N Market Blvd.
Sacramento, CA, USA, 95834-1206
(916) 920-0285
Fax: (916) 641-6338
lorendas@cimcinc.com
teresaw@cimcinc.com http://www.cimcinc.org
Chinese American Voters Education Committee
Mr. David Lee, Executive Director
4444 Geary Blvd. Ste. 300
San Francisco, CA, USA, 94118
(415) 408-8833
(415) 397-8133
Fax: (415) 397-6617
delee@peralta.edu
Korean American Coalition-Census Information Center
Ms. Eunice Song, Executive Director
3727 W 6th St., Ste. 305
Los Angeles, CA, USA, 90020
(213) 365-5999
Fax: (213) 380-7990
eunice@kacla.org
ireh@kacla.org
estherj@kacla.org https://www.kacla.org/
Oakland Citizen's Committee for Urban Renewal (OCCUR)
Mrs. Sondra Alexander, Director
1330 Broadway, Ste. 1030
Oakland, CA, USA, 94612
(510) 839-2440
Fax: (510) 268-9065
denise@occurnow.org https://occurnow.org/
Special Service for Groups Census Data & Geographic Information Services
Mr. Herbert K. Hatanaka, Executive Director
905 E 8th St.
Los Angeles, CA, USA, 90021
(213) 553-1800
Fax: (213) 553-1822
jdamon@ssg.org https://www.ssg.org/
William C. Velasquez Institute
Mr. Antonio Gonzalez, President
2914 N Main St.

Los Angeles, CA, USA, 90031
(323) 332-6160
Fax: (323) 222-2011
pgonzales@wcvi.org https://www.wcvi.org/

District of Columbia

Arab American Institute Foundation
Maya Berry, President
1600 K St. NW, Ste. 601
Washington, DC, USA, 20006
(202) 429-9210
Fax: (202) 429-9214
nadia@aaiusa.org https://www.aaiusa.org/census

Children's Defense Fund, Inc.
Mrs. Marian Wright Edelman, Director
25 E St. NW, 6th Fl.
Washington, DC, USA, 20001
(202) 662-3585
Fax: (202) 662-3550
asowa@childrensdefense.org https://www.childrensdefense.org

The Leadership Conference on Civil and Human Rights
Mr. Wade Henderson, President & CEO
1629 K Street NW, 10th Fl.
Washington, DC, USA, 20006
(202) 466-3311
Fax: (202) 466-3435
yu@civilrights.org
nerurkar@civilrights.org https://www.civilrights.org/census

National Association for the Advancement of Colored People (NAACP)
Mr. Cornell William Brooks, President & CEO
Mr. Hilary Shelton, Director, Washington DC Bureau
1156 15th St. NW, Ste. 915
Washington, DC, USA, 20005
(202) 463-2940
hoshelton@naacpnet.org https://www.naacp.org

National Congress of American Indians
Mr. Kevin Allis, CEO
1516 P St. NW
Washington, DC, USA, 20005
(202) 466-7767
Fax: (202) 466-7797
gevans-lomayesva@ncai.org
yroubideaux@ncai.org https://www.ncai.org

Unidos US (formerly NCLR)
Ms. Janet Murguia, President & CEO
Raul Yzaguirre Bldg.
1126 16th St. NW, Ste. 600
Washington, DC, USA, 20036
(202) 776-1789
Fax: (202) 776-1792
pfoxen@unidosus.org
eruskin@unidosus.org https://www.unidosus.org

National Urban League Policy Institute
Mr. Marc Morial, President & CEO
1101 Connecticut Ave. NW, Ste. 810
Washington, DC, USA, 20036
(212) 558-5350
Fax: (844) 547-1600
jrichardson@nul.org

Florida

Florida A&M University Census Information Center
Dr. David Jackson, President
Center for Deliberative Democracy, Civic Engagement & Census Information Center
411 Tucker Hall
Tallahassee, FL, USA, 32307-4800
(850) 599-3447
Fax: (850) 412-7542
gary.paul@famu.edu https://www.famu.edu/index.cfm?CensusInformationCenter

Metropolitan Center of Florida International University
Dr. Howard Frank
1101 Brickell Ave., Ste S-200
Miami, FL, USA, 33131
(305) 779-7872
Fax: (305) 779-7880
milcheva@fiu.edu https://metropolitan.fiu.edu

Georgia

Spelman College Census Information Center
Dr. Celeste Lee, Professor
350 Spelman Ln., Campus Box 245
Atlanta, GA, USA, 30314
(404) 270-5629
Fax: (404) 270-5632
clee@spelman.edu https://www.spelman.edu/academics/majors-and-programs/sociology/census-information-center

Hawaii

Office of Hawaiian Affairs
Ms. Lisa M. Watkins-Victorino, Research Director
Ka Pou Kihi Kane
506 N. Nimitz Hwy., Ste. 200
Honolulu, HI, USA, 96817
(808) 594-0280
lisaw@oha.org
hollyy@oha.org https://www.oha.org

Illinois

Latin American Chamber of Commerce
Mr. D. Lorenzo Padron, Chairman & CEO
3512 W Fullerton Ave.
Chicago, IL, USA, 60647
(773) 252-5211
Fax: (773) 252-7065
d.lorenzopadron@laccusa.com
mpalaguachi@laccusa.com https://laccusa.com/

United States Hispanic Leadership Institute
Dr. Juan Andrade Jr., President
431 S Dearborn St., Ste. 1203
Chicago, IL, USA, 60605
(312) 427-8683
Fax: (312) 427-5183
tdeavours@ushli.org https://www.ushli.org

Louisiana

Dillard University
Dr. Robert A. Collins, CIC Contact
Department of Urban Studies and Public Policy
2601 Gentilly Blvd.
New Orleans, LA, USA, 70122
(504) 816-4701
Fax: (504) 816-4702
rcollins@dillard.edu https://www.dillard.edu

Louisiana State University in Shreveport, Center for Business and Economic Research
Mrs. Nancy Albers Miller, CIC Contact
College of Business, Education and Human Development
One University Place
Shreveport, LA, USA, 71115-2399
(318) 797-5146
Douglas.white@lsus.edu https://www.lsus.edu/offices-and-services/center-for-business-and-economic-research/census-information-center

Maryland

Maryland Population Research Center, University of Maryland
Michael S. Rendall, Director
2105 Morrill Hall
College Park, MD, USA, 20742
(301) 405-6403
wfennie@umd.edu https://www.popcenter.umd.edu

Goodwill Industries International, Incorporated
Mr. Jim Gibbons, President & CEO
15810 Indianola Dr.
Rockville, MD, USA, 20855
(310) 530-6500
Fax: (301) 530-1516
matthew.vile@goodwill.org
david.porton@goodwill.org https://www.goodwill.org

Michigan

Julian Samora Research Institute - Michigan State University, Interi-University Program for Latino Research (IUPLR)
Ruben Martinez, Ph.D., Director
219 S Harrison Rd. Rm. 93
E Lansing, MI, USA, 48824
(517) 432-1317
Fax: (517) 432-2221
ruben.martinez@ssu.msu.edu
kayitsin@msu.edu
torresma@uic.edu https://www.jsri.msu.edu

Piast Institute
Mrs. Virginia Skrzyniarz, Executive Vice President
11633 Jos. Campau
Hamtramck, MI, USA, 48212
(313) 733-4535
Fax: (313) 733-4527
skrzyniarz@piastinstitute.org https://www.piastinstitute.org

Mississippi

Jackson State University-Mississippi Urban Research Center
Dr. Sam Mozee Jr., Director
350 W Woodrow Wilson Ave., Ste. 2200-B
Jackson, MS, USA, 39213
(601) 979-4204
Fax: (601) 979-4075
sheryl.l.bacon@jsums.edu https://www.jsums.edu/murc/divisions/research

New York

Asian American Federation
Mrs. Jo-Ann Yoo, Executive Director
120 Wall St., 9th Fl.
New York, NY , USA, 10005
(212) 344-5878
Fax: (212) 344-5878
howard.shih@aafederation.org https://www.aafederation.org/cic

Medgar Evers College, DuBois Bunche Center for Public Policy
Mr. Wallace Ford, Chair
City University of New York, Department of Public Administration
1650 Bedford Ave. 2015-S
Brooklyn , NY, USA, 11225
(718) 270-5111
Fax: (718) 270-5181
jflat@mec.cuny.edu https://www.mec.cuny.edu/

North Dakota

Sitting Bull College Census Information Center
Dr. Koreen Ressler, Director
1341 92nd St.
Ft. Yates, ND, USA, 58538
(701) 854-8073
Fax: (701) 854-3403 https://sittingbull.edu/sitting-bull-college/students/library

Oklahoma

Community Service Council of Greater Tulsa
Ms. Pam Ballard, CEO
Main Square Towers, 16 E 16th St., Ste. 202
Tulsa , OK, USA, 74119
(918) 585-5551
Fax: (918) 585-3285
mpoulter@csctulsa.org
jfigart@csctulsa.org https://csctulsa.org/census-center-of-eastern-ok

Puerto Rico

Interdisciplinary Research Institute at the University of Puerto Rico in Cayey
Mrs. Vionex M. Marti, Director
205 Ave. Antonio R. Barcelo
Cayey, PR, USA, 00736
(787) 738-2161
Fax: (787) 263-1625
jose.caraballo8@upr.edu https://www.upr.edu/iii-cayey/centro-informacion-censal/

South Dakota

Northeast Council of Governments
Mr. Eric Senger, Executive Director
2201 6th Avenue SE, Ste. 2
Aberdeen, SD, USA, 57402-1985
(605) 626-2595
Fax: (605) 626-2975
eric@necog.org
jennifer@necog.org https://necog.org/census

Tennessee

Meharry CIC
Dr. William Washington, Director
Division of Public Health Practice/MSPH Program
School of Graduate Studies and Research (SOGSR)
1005 Dr. D.B. Todd Jr. Blvd.
Clay Simpson Bldg., Rm 206
Nashville , TN, USA, 37208
(615) 327-6069
Fax: (615) 327-6289 https://www.mmc.edu

Neighborhood 2 Neighbor
Mr. Jim Hawk, Executive Director
PO Box 100941
Nashville, TN, USA, 37224

(615) 782-8212
Fax: (615) 782-8213
jim@n2n.solutions https://www.n2n.solutions/
Vanderbilt University
Mr. Frank Lester, CIC Contact
Peabody Library
419 21st Avenue South
Nashville, TN , USA, 37023
(615) 343-7542
Fax: (615) 343-8796
frank.lester@vanderbilt.edu https://www.vanderbilt.edu

Texas
Capital Area Council of Governments
Ms. Betty Voights, Executive Director
6800 Burleson Rd., Building 310, Ste. 165
Austin, TX, USA, 78744
(512) 916-6183
Fax: (512) 916-6001
ahoekzema@capcog.org https://www.capcog.org
SER-Jobs for Progress National
Mr. Ignacio Salazar, President & CEO
100 E Royal Ln., Ste. 130
Irving, TX, USA, 75039
(469) 549-3600
Fax: (469) 549-3684
rsanta@ser-national.org https://www.ser-national.org
University of Texas Rio Grande Valley
Ms. Jessica Salina, Executive Director
1201 W University Dr.
Edinburg, TX , USA, 78539-2999
(956) 665-3361
Fax: (956) 576-1697
smullapudi@utrgv.edu https://www.utrgv.edu

Virginia
Norfolk State University Center for Applied Research and Public Policy
Dr. Rudolph Wilson, Chairman
Library Information Services
Lyman Beecher Brooks Library
Norfolk, VA, USA, 23504
(757) 823-9581
Fax: (757) 823-9413
rwilson@nsu.edu
kgaines-ra@nsu.edu https://www.nsu.edu

Washington
National Asian Pacific Center on Aging (NAPCA)
Mr. Joon Bang, Director
Legislative Policy & Analysis
1511 3rd Avenue, Ste. 914
Seattle, WA, USA, 98101-1626
(206) 838-8169
Fax: (206) 624-1023
joon@napca.org https://napca.org/

CENTER FOR ECONOMIC STUDIES

Census Research Data Centers (RDCs) have been established in partnership with academic and similar institutions to permit qualified researchers to have restricted access to confidential economic and demographic data collected by the Census Bureau in its surveys and censuses to carry out research of importance to the Census Bureau. There are currently 31 open Federal Statistical Research Data Center (RDC) locations. The RDCs partner with over 50 research organizations including universities, non-profit research institutions, and government agencies. For information on how to submit a proposal, please consult the RDC website (https://www.census.gov/about/adrm/fsrdc/locations.html). And then contact the RDC Administrator nearest to your location.

Atlanta Census RDC
Melissa Ruby Banzhaf
melissa.r.banzhaf@census.gov
(404) 498-7538 https://acrdc.gsu.edu

Boston Census RDC
Shital Sharma
shital.sharma@census.gov https://www.nber.org/brdc

California Census RDC, Berkeley
Angela Andrus
angela.andrus@census.gov
(510) 643-2262 https://www.ccrdc.ucla.edu

California Census RDC, Irvine
Kamal Sarah Bookwala
kamal.s.bookwala@census.gov https://www.ccrdc.ucla.edu

California Census RDC, Stanford
Rachel Hill
ced.fsrdc.info@census.gov https://www.ccrdc.ucla.edu

California Census RDC, UCLA
Frank Limehouse
ced.fsrdc.info@census.gov https://www.ccrdc.ucla.edu

California Census RDC, USC
Jose J. Alcocer
jose.j.alcocer@census.gov https://www.ccrdc.ucla.edu

Central Plains RDC
Seth Kingery
seth.j.kingery@census.gov
(402) 472-0362 https://rdc.unl.edu/

Chicago Census RDC
Shahin Davoudpour
shahin.davoudpour@census.gov

Dallas-Fort Worth Census RDC
Samuel Bondurant
samuel.r.bondurant@census.gov
(214) 922-6074

Federal Reserve Board RDC
Emily Wisniewski
(202) 452-6422
emily.m.wisniewski@census.gov

Florida Census RDC
John Hood
(301) 763-5003
john.hood@census.gov

Georgetown RDC
Jelena Leathard
jelena.leathard@census.gov
(202) 687-9369 https://mccourt.georgetown.edu/massive-data-institute

Kansas City Census RDC
Shawn Ratcliffe
shawn.ratcliff@census.gov
(816) 490-7981 https://www.kauffman.org/microsites/kcfsrdc

Kentucky Census RDC
Carlos Lopes
carlos.j.lopes@census.gov
(859) 323-7075 https://krdc.uky.edu/

Maryland Census RDC
Rachel Hill
rachelle.hill@census.gov https://marylandrdc.umd.edu/

Michigan Census RDC
J. Clint Carter
jack.carter@census.gov
(734) 615-2535 https://community.isr.umich.edu/public/mcrdc

Minnesota Census RDC
J. Clint Carter
jack.carter@census.gov
(734) 615-2535 https://mnrdc.umn.edu/

Missouri Census RDC
Kenneth Zahringer, Administrator
kenneth.a.zahringer@census.gov
(573) 884-9122 https://mcdc.missouri.edu/

New York Census RDC, Baruch
Shirley Liu
shirley.h.liu@census.gov
(646) 660-6788 https://www.ciser.cornell.edu/nyrdc

New York Census RDC, Cornell
Nichole Szembrot
nichole.e.szembrot@census.gov
(607) 255-8603 https://ciser.cornell.edu/nycrdc/home.shtml

Northwest Census RDC
Carlos Becerra
carlos.becerra@census.gov https://depts.washington.edu/nwfsrdc/

Penn State RDC
Emily Greenman
emily.k.greenman@census.gov
(301) 763-9236 https://psurdc.psy.edu

Philadelphia RDC
Joe Ballegeer
(215) 574-7280
joseph.n.ballegeer@census.gov https://web.sas.upenn.edu/pfsrdc/

Rocky Mountain RDC
Frank Limehouse
frank.limehouse@census.gov https://www.colorado.edu/rocky-mountain-research-data-center

Texas Census RDC
Karin Johnson
karin.johnson@census.gov
(979) 845-5618 https://txrdc.tamu.edu/

Texas - UT Austin
Ri Wade
riannan.wade@census.gov
(512) 232-4839

Triangle Census RDC, Duke
Bert Grider
william.b.grider@census.gov
(919) 660-6893 https://trdc.ssri.duke.edu

University of Illinois Urbana-Champaign
Lanwri Yang
lanwei.j.yang@census.gov

Wasatch Front Research Data Center (WFRDC)
Bryce Hannibal
bryce.hannibal@census.gov

Wisconsin Census RDC,
Robert Osley-Thomas
robert.r.thomas@census.gov
(608) 262-7347 https://rdc.wisc.edu

Yale Census RDC,
Stephanie Bailey
stephanie.m.bailey@census.gov
(203) 432-2962 https://ciser.cornell.edu/nycrdc

CENSUS 2020

2020 Census
Tasha Boone (C2PO)
(301) 763-3977

Aging Population, U.S.
Staff (POP)
(301) 763-2378

American Community Survey
Staff (CLMSO)
(301) 763-4636

American FactFinder
Staff (CLMSO)
(301) 763-4636

Annexations/Boundary Changes
Laura Waggoner (GEO)
(301) 763-9079

Apportionment
David Sheppard (POP)
(301) 763-9291

Census History

Census in Schools
Staff (POP)
(301) 763-6676

Citizenship
Staff (POP)
(301) 763-2411

Commuting, Means of Transportation and Place of Work
Brian McKenzie
(301) 763-6532
Peter Mateyka (HHES)
(301) 763-2356

Confidentiality and Privacy
Christa Jones (POL)
(301) 763-7310

Count Review
Edwin Byerly (POP)
(301) 763-2390

Data Dissemination
Staff (CLMSO)
(301) 763-4636

Disability
Staff (DID)
(301) 763-2422

Employment/Unemployment (General Information)
Staff (DID)
(301) 763-2422

Foreign-born
Staff (POP)
(301) 763-2411

Geographic Entities
Staff (GEO)
(301) 763-1099

Grandparents as Caregivers
Staff (HHES)
(301) 763-6062

Group Quarters Population
Staff (POP)
(301) 763-2378

Health Insurance Statistics
Staff (DID)
(301) 763-2422

Hispanic Origin/Ethnicity/Ancestry
Staff (POP)
(301) 763-2403

Homeless
Staff (POP)
(301) 763-2378

Housing (General Information)
Staff (HHES)
(301) 763-3237

Immigration/Emigration
Staff (DID)
(301) 763-2422

Income
Staff (HHES)
(301) 763-3243

Island Areas (Puerto Rico, U.S. Virgin Islands, Pacific Islands)
Idabelle Hovland (DMD)
(301) 763-8443

Labor Force Status/Work Experience (General)
Staff (CLMSO)
(301) 763-4636

Living Arrangements
Staff (HHES)
(301) 763-2416

Maps
Customer Services (CLMSO)
(301) 763-4636

Marital Status
Staff (HHES)
(301) 763-2416

Metropolitan and Micropolitan Statistical Areas Standards
Staff (POP)
(301) 763-2419

Migration
Staff (HHES)
(301) 763-2454

News Media Inquiries
Staff (PIO)
(301) 763-3030

Occupation/Industry
Staff (HHES)
(301) 763-3239

Partnership and Data Services
Staff (FLD)
(301) 763-7879

Place of Birth/Native Born
Staff (HHES)
(301) 763-2454

Population (General Information)
Staff (DID)
(301) 763-2422

Poverty
Staff (DID)
(301) 763-2422

Public Use Microdata Files (PUMS)
Staff (POP)
(301) 763-2429

Race
Staff (POP)
(301) 763-2402

Redistricting
Staff (DIR)
(301) 763-4039

Residence Rules
Staff (POP)
(301) 763-2381

Small Area Income and Poverty Estimates
Staff (DID)
(301) 763-2422

Special Censuses
Staff (FLD)
(301) 763-1429

Special Population
Staff (POP)
(301) 763-2378

Special Tabulations
Staff (POP)
(301) 763-2429

TIGER/Line files
Staff (GEO)
(301) 763-1128

Undercount
Staff (DSSD)
(301) 763-4206

Demographic Analysis
Staff (POP)
(301) 763-6133

Unmarried Partners
Staff (HHES)
(301) 763-2416

Urban/Rural
Staff (GEO)
(301) 763-3056

U.S. Citizens Abroad
Staff (CLMSO)
(301) 763-4636

Veteran Status
Staff (DID)
(301) 763-2422

Voting Districts
Staff (GEO)
(301) 763-1099

Women
Staff (POP)
(301) 763-2378

ZIP Codes
Staff (DID)
(301) 763-2422

CONSTRUCTION

Building Permits
Staff (MCD)
(301) 763-5160

Economic Census
Staff (MCD)
(301) 763-4680

Housing Starts and Completions
Staff (MCD)
(301) 763-5160

Manufactured Housing
Staff (MCD)
(301) 763-1605

Residential Characteristics, Price Index and Sales
Staff (MCD)
(301) 763-5160

Value of Construction Put in Place
Staff (MCD)
(301) 763-1605

DEMOGRAPHIC PROGRAMS, HOUSING AND POPULATION

Africa, Asia, Latin America, North America and Oceania
Staff (POP)
(301) 763-1358

Aging Population (Domestic)
Staff (POP)
(301) 763-2378

Aging Population (International)
Staff (POP)
(301) 763-1371

American Community Survey
Staff (CLMSO)
(301) 763-4636

American Housing Survey - Data
Staff (HHES)
(301) 763-3235

American Housing Survey - Methodology
LaTerri Bynum (DSD)
(301) 763-3858

Apportionment
David Sheppard (POP)
(301) 763-2381

Apportionment and Redistricting
Cathy McCully (DIR)
(301) 763-4039

Assets and Liabilities
Staff (DID)
(301) 763-2422
(866) 758-1060

Census - Housing
Staff (HHES)
(301) 763-3237

Census - Population
Staff (DID)
(301) 763-2422

ECONOMIC INDICATORS

Advance Monthly Sales for Retail and Food Services (MARTS)
(800) 772-7852 https://bhs.econ.census.gov/bhs/rtfs/contactus.html

Manufacturers' Shipments, Inventories and Orders https://www.census.gov/manufacturing/m3/index.html

Construction Spending https://www.census.gov/construction/c30/c30index.html

Housing Vacancies and Homeownership https://www.census.gov/housing/hvs/index.html

Manufacturers' Shipments, Inventories, and Orders (M3) https://bhs.econ.census.gov/bhs/m3/contactus.html

Manufacturing and Trade Inventories and Sales https://www.census.gov/mtis/index.html

Monthly Wholesale Trade: Sales and Inventories https://www.census.gov/wholesale/index.html

New Residential Construction https://www.census.gov/construction/nrc/index.html

New Residential Sales https://www.census.gov/construction/nrs/index.html

Quarterly Financial Report - Manufacturing, Mining and Trade https://bhs.econ.census.gov/bhs/qfr/contactus.html

Quarterly Financial Report - Retail Trade https://bhs.econ.census.gov/bhs/qfr/contactus.html

U.S. International Trade in Goods and Services https://www.census.gov/foreign-trade/index.html

GEOGRAPHIC CONCEPTS

1990 and 2000 Census Maps
Staff (CLMSO)
(301) 763-4636

Alaska Native Village Statistical Areas
Vince Osier (GEO)
Joshua Coutts (GEO)
(301) 763-3056

American Indian and Alaska Native Areas
Colleen Joyce (GEO)
Barbara Saville (GEO)
(301) 763-1099

American Indian statistical areas
Joshua Coutts (GEO)
Vince Osier (GEO)
(301) 763-3056

American National Standards Institute (ANSI) Codes
Joe Marinucci (GEO)
(301) 763-3056

Annexations/Boundary Changes
Laura Waggoner (GEO)
(301) 763-1099

Area Measurement - Land
Staff (GEO)
(301) 763-1099

Area Measurement - Water
Staff (GEO)
(301) 763-1100

Census Blocks
Matt Jennings (GEO)
Vince Osier (GEO)
(301) 763-3056

Census County Divisions
Eric Joe (GEO)
Vince Osier (GEO)
(301) 763-3056

Census Designated Places
Vince Osier (GEO)
Eric Joe (GEO)
(301) 763-3056

Census Geographic Concepts
Staff (GEO)
(301) 763-3056

Census Tracts
Vince Osier (GEO)
Eric Joe (GEO)
(301) 763-3056

Centers of Population
Staff (GEO)
(301) 763-1128

Combined Statistical Areas
Paul Mackun (POP)
(301) 763-2419

Congressional and State Legislative Districts - Address Allocations
Staff (GEO)
(301) 763-1050

Congressional and State Legislative Districts - Boundaries
John Byle (GEO)
(301) 763-1099

Core Based Statistical Areas
Paul Mackun (POP)
(301) 763-2419

Federal Geographic Data Committee and Geographic Standards
Randy Fusaro (GEO)
(301) 763-1056

Federal Information Processing System (FIPS) Codes
Mike Fournier (GEO)
Noelle Joll (GEO)
(301) 763-3056

Geographic Names
Mike Fournier (GEO)
Noelle Joll (GEO)
(301) 763-3056

Geographic Products and Services (including TIGER)
Staff (GEO)
(301) 763-1128

Governmental Unit Boundaries
Laura Waggoner (GEO)
(301) 763-1099

Internal Points
Staff (GEO)
(301) 763-1128

Island Areas
Vince Osier (GEO)
Matt Jennings (GEO)
(301) 763-3056

LandView
Staff (GEO)
(301) 763-1128

Local Update of Census Addresses
John McKay (GEO)
(301) 763-8630

Master Address File
Shawn Hanks (GEO)
(301) 763-1106

Metropolitan and Micropolitan Statistical Areas
Paul Mackun (POP)
(301) 763-2419

Native Hawaiian Areas
Barbara Saville (GEO)
(301) 763-1099

Place Concepts - General
Vince Osier (GEO)
Joe Marinucci (GEO)
(301) 763-3056

Place Concepts - Economic Census Places
Noelle Joll (GEO)
April Avnayim (GEO)
(301) 763-3056

Place Concepts - Census Designated Places
Vince Osier (GEO)
Eric Joe (GEO)
(301) 763-3056

Population Circles (Radii)
Staff (GEO)
(301) 763-1128

Postal Geography
Jeremy Hilts (GEO)
(301) 763-1106

Public Use Microdata Areas (PUMAs)
Bonny Berkner (GEO)
April Avnayim (GEO)
(301) 763-3056

School District
Pat Ream (GEO)
Ian Millet (GEO)
(301) 763-1099

Spatial Data Quality and Geographic Standards
Fred Malkus (GEO)
(301) 763-9102

Statistical Geographic Area Concepts
Staff (GEO)
(301) 763-3056

Thematic Mapping and Boundary Files
Staff (GEO)
(301) 763-1101

TIGER System
Staff (GEO)
(301) 763-1100

TIGER Update Partnerships - Tribal
Staff (GEO)
(301) 763-1099

TIGER Update Partnerships - Local, County, Regional Governments
Staff (GEO)
(301) 763-8630

TIGER Update Partnerships - National and State
Staff (GEO)
(301) 763-3056

Traffic Analysis Zones
April Avnayim (GEO)
Jeff Ocker (GEO)
(301) 763-3056

Urban/Rural Concepts
Chris Henrie (GEO)
Kevin Hawley (GEO)
(301) 763-3056

Urbanized Areas
Chris Henrie (GEO)
Kevin Hawley (GEO)
(301) 763-3056

Voting Districts
John Byle (GEO)
(301) 763-1099

ZIP Code Tabulation Areas (ZCTAs)
Matt Jennings (GEO)
Joshua Coutts (GEO)
(301) 763-3056

ZIP Codes - Demographic Data
Staff (CLMSO)
(301) 763-4636

ZIP Codes - Economic Data
Doug Miller (EPCD)
(301) 763-6751

ZIP Codes - Geography
Kevin Hawley (GEO)
Joshua Coutts (GEO)
(301) 763-3056

MANUFACTURING AND MINING

Annual Survey of Manufactures
(800) 233-6136 https://www.census.gov/programs-surveys/asm.html

Company Concentration

Exports From Manufacturing Establishments
Brian Appert (MCD)
(301) 763-5190

Financial Statistics (Quarterly Financial Report)
(800) 272-4250 https://bhs.econ.census.gov/bhs/qfr/contactus.html

Monthly Shipments, Inventories and Orders
Chris Savage (MCD)
(301) 763-4832

Plant Capacity Utilization
(800) 201-4647 https://www.census.gov/programs-surveys/qpc.html

Pollution Abatement Costs and Expenditures Survey
(301) 763-1907

RETAIL TRADE

Monthly Retail Trade Survey https://bhs.econ.census.gov/bhs/mrts/contactus.html

Quarterly Financial Report
(800) 272-4250 https://bhs.econ.census.gov/bhs/qfr/contactus.html

TRANSPORTATION

Commodity Flow Survey
John Fowler (SSSD)
(301) 763-2108

Economic Census
Amy Houtz (SSSD)
(301) 763-2786

Trucking and Warehousing
Jeffrey Barnett (SSSD)
(301) 763-2766

WHOLESALE TRADE

Monthly Wholesale Trade Survey https://bhs.econ.census.gov/bhs/mwts/index.html

Quarterly Financial Report https://bhs.econ.census.gov/bhs/qfr/contactus.html

CHILDREN

Listed below is contact information for staff from federal agencies who have expertise with National data sets in the following areas: Population and Family Characteristics; Economic Security; Health; Behavior and Social Environment; Education. For more information visit https://www.childstats.gov or contact a staff member directly.

FAMILY AND SOCIAL ENVIRONMENT

Adoptions (NCHS)
Jo Jones
drv4@cdc.gov

Adoptions (CENSUS)
Rose Kreider
rose.kreider@census.gov

Child Care (NCES)
Chris Chapman
chris.chapman@ed.gov

Child Maltreatment (ACF)
Susan Jekielek
susan.jekielek@acf.hhs.gov

Childhood Living Arrangements (CENSUS)
Rose Kreider
rose.kreider@census.gov

Childlessness (CENSUS)
Jane Dye
jane.l.dye@census.gov

English Speaking Ability
Hyon B. Shin
hyon.b.shin@census.gov

Family Structure (NCHS)
Debbie Blackwell
dblackwell@cdc.gov

Fertility and Family Statistics (CENSUS)
Jane Dye
jane.l.dye@census.gov

Fertility and Family Statistics (NICHD)
Rosalind King
rosalind.king@nih.gov

Fertility and Family Statistics (NCHS)
Stephanie Ventura
sjv1@cdc.gov

Immigrant Children (CENSUS)
Rose Kreider
rose.kreider@census.gov

Marriage/Cohabitation (NCHS)
Anjani Chandra
ayc3@cdc.gov

Marriage/Cohabitation (CENSUS)
Rose Kreider
rose.kreider@census.gov

Marriage/Cohabitation (CENSUS)
Tavia Simmons
tavia.simmons@census.gov

Migration (NICHD)
Rebecca Clark
rclark@mail.nih.gov

Mothers Race/Ethnic Composition (NCHS)
Stephanie Ventura
sjv1@cdc.gov

Nonmarital Childbearing (NCHS)
Stephanie Ventura
sjv1@cdc.gov

ECONOMIC CIRCUMSTANCES

Child Nutrition (FNS)
Jay Hirschman
jay.hirschman@ers.usda.gov

Health Insurance Statistics (NCHS)
Robin Cohen
rzc6@cdc.gov

Maternity Leave (CENSUS)
Lynda Laughlin
lynda.l.laughlin@census.gov

Parental Employment (BLS)
Stephanie Denton
denton.stephanie@bls.gov

Poverty and Health (NCHS)
John Pleis
jpleis@cdc.gov

Poverty, WIC Program (ARS)
Mary Hama
mhama@rbhnrc.usda.gov

HEALTH CARE

Childhood Immunizations (CDC)
James Singleton
xzs8@cdc.gov

Dental caries (cavities) (NCHS)
Bruce Dye
bdye@cdc.gov

Dental visits (NCHS)
Bruce Dye
bdye@cdc.gov

Health Insurance Statistics (NCHS)
Robin Cohen
rzc6@cdc.gov

PHYSICAL ENVIRONMENT AND SAFETY

Adolescent Injury (NCHS)
Margaret Warner
mwarner@cdc.gov

Adolescent Mortality (NCHS)
Margaret Warner
mwarner@cdc.gov

Air Quality (EPA)
Rhonda Thompson
thompson.rhonda@epa.gov

Child Injury (NCHS)
Margaret Warner
mwarner@cdc.gov

Child Mortality (NCHS)
Donna Hoyert
dhoyert@cdc.gov

Drinking Water Quality (EPA)
Jade Lee-Freeman
lee-freeman.jade@cdc.gov

Environmental Tobacco Smoke (NCHS)
Debra Brody
dbrody@cdc.gov

Housing Problems (OPDR)
Kathy Nelson
kathryn.p.nelson@hud.gov

Housing Problems (OPDR)
Barry Steffen
barry_steffen@hud.gov

Lead in the Blood of Children (NCHS)
Debra Brody
dbrody@cdc.gov

Violence (OJJDP)
Janet Chiancone
chiancoj@ojp.usdoj.gov

Violence (NIJ)
Carrie Mulford
carrie.mulford@usdoj.gov

Violence (BLS)
Jennifer Truman
jennifer.truman@usdoj.gov

BEHAVIOR

Alcohol Use (NIDA)
Jessica Cotto
cottoj@nida.nih.gov

Illicit Drug Use (NIDA)
Jessica Cotto
cottoj@nida.nih.gov

Sexual Activity (ACF)
Susan Jekielek
susan.jekielek@acf.hhs.gov

Smoking (NIDA)
Jessica Cotto
cottoj@nida.nih.gov

Violence (OJJDP)
Janet Chiancone
chiancoj@ojp.usdoj.gov

Violence (NIJ)
Carrie Mulford
carrie.mulford@usdoj.gov

Violence (BLS)
Jennifer Truman
jennifer.truman@usdoj.gov

EDUCATION

Achievement (NCES)
Arnold Goldstein
arnold.goldstein@ed.gov

Attainment (NCES)
Tom Snyder
tom.snyder@ed.gov

College Enrollment (NCES)
Tom Snyder
tom.snyder@ed.gov

Coursetaking/Transcripts, Secondary (NCES)
Tom Snyder
tom.snyder@ed.gov

Disabled Students (NCES)
Tom Snyder
tom.snyder@ed.gov

Dropouts (NCES)
Chris Chapman
chris.chapman@ed.gov

Education and Health (NCHS)
Debbie Blackwell
dblackwell@cdc.gov

High School Completion (NCES)
Chris Chapman
chris.chapman@ed.gov

Related Behavior and Characteristics (NCES)
Tom Snyder
tom.snyder@ed.gov

School Crime (NCES)
Kathryn Chandler
kathryn.chandler@ed.gov

School Crime (NCES)
Tom Snyder
tom.snyder@ed.gov

Vocational Education (NCES)
Lisa Hudson
lisa.hudson@ed.gov

Youth Indicators (NCES)
Tom Snyder
tom.snyder@ed.gov

HEALTH

Asthma (NCHS)
Lara Akinbami
lakinbami@cdc.gov

Birth Certificate Data (NCHS)
Joyce Martin
jmartin@cdc.gov

Birth Certificate Data (NCHS)
Stephanie Ventura
sjv1@cdc.gov

Children's Health (NCHS)
Susan Lukacs
srl2@cdc.gov

Contraception (NCHS)
Joyce Abma
jabma@cdc.gov

Disability (NIH)
Louis Quatrano
lq2n@nih.gov

Family Planning Services (NCHS)
Gladys Martinez
gmartinez@cdc.gov

Fetal Mortality (NCHS)
Joyce Martin
jmartin@cdc.gov

Growth and Nutrition (NCHS)
Cynthia Ogden
cao9@cdc.gov

Health Care Access (NCHS)
Robin Cohen
rzc6@cdc.gov

Healthy People 2010/2020 (NCHS)
Richard Klein
rjk6@cdc.gov

Infant and Child Health (NCHS)
Susan Lukacs
srl2@cdc.gov

Life Tables (NCHS)
Robert Anderson
rca7@cdc.gov

Linked Birth/Infant Death Records (NCHS)
Marian Mac Dorman
mfm1@cdc.gov

Linked Birth/Infant Death Records (NCHS)
T.J. Matthews
tjm4@cdc.gov

Low Birthweight Infants (NCHS)
Amy Branum
zvl5@cdc.gov

Mental Health (Depression) (SAMHSA)
Beth Han
beth.han@samhsa.gov

Overweight (NCHS)
Cynthia Ogden
cao9@cdc.gov

Perinatal Outcome/Maternal Nutrition and Weight Gain (NCHS)
Joyce Martin
jmartin@cdc.gov

Pregnancy & Health (NCHS)
Anjani Chandra
ayc3@cdc.gov

Pregnancy/Family Planning Services/Contraception (NICHD)
Susan Newcomer
newcomes@hd01.nichd.nih

Prenatal Care & Delivery Payment (NCHS)
Anjani Chandra
ayc3@cdc.gov

Preterm Births (NCHS)
Joyce Martin
jmartin@cdc.gov

Sexual Activity (NCHS)
Joyce Abma
jabma@cdc.gov

Sexual Activity (ACF)
Susan Jekielek
susan.jekielek@acf.hhs.gov

Sexual Activity and Fertility (NCHS)
Anjani Chandra
ayc3@cdc.gov

Teen Pregnancy (NCHS)
Stephanie Ventura
sjv1@cdc.gov

Teen Sex/Teen Pregnancy (NCHS)
Joyce Abma
jabma@cdc.gov

CRIME

The National Criminal Justice Reference Service (NCJRS) of the U.S. Justice Department's Office of Justice Programs operates a valuable fact finding service and can be a highly useful source of data on crime statistics and juvenile justice statistics in the United States. Reference assistance is available at https://www.ncjrs.gov, or by calling (800) 851-3420.

STATISTICAL ANALYSIS CENTERS

Statistical Analysis Centers (SACs) are state agencies that collect, analyze, and disseminate justice data. They contribute to effective state policies through statistical services, research, evaluation, and policy analysis. For more information about SAC activities and publications, visit https://www.jrsa.org or one of the state offices listed below.

ALABAMA
Mike Trotter
Operations Chief
Alabama Law Enforcement Agency
301 S Ripley St.
PO Box 304115
Montgomery, AL, USA, 36104
(334) 676-7700
mike.trotter@alea.gov https://www.alea.gov/sbi/criminal-justice-services https://crime.alabama.gov

ALASKA
Troy Payne, Ph.D.
Director
Alaska Justice Statistical Analysis Center
University of Alaska Anchorage Justice Center
3211 Providence Dr., LIB 213
Anchorage, AK, USA, 99508
(907) 786-1816
Fax: (907) 786-7777
tpayne@uaa.alaska.edu https://www.uaa.alaska.edu/academics/college-of-health/departments/justice-center/alaska-justice-information-center/

ARIZONA
Ana Daniels
Senior Analyst and Interim Director
Arizona Criminal Justice Commission
1110 W Washington, Ste. 230
Phoenix, AZ, USA, 85007
(602) 364-1191
Fax: (602) 364-1175
adaniels@azcjc.gov https://www.azcjc.gov/Programs/Statistical-Analysis-Center/Statistics-Overview

ARKANSAS
Ralph Ward
Manager, UCR, NIBRS, N-DEx, SAC
Arkansas Crime Information Center
322 S Main St., Ste. 615
Little Rock, AR, USA, 72201
(501) 682-2222
Fax: (501) 683-0272
ralph.war@acic.arkansas.gov https://www.dps.arkansas.gov/crime-info-support/arkansas-crime-information-center/

CALIFORNIA
Alyson Lunetta
Manager, Investigative Services Program
Criminal Justice Statistics Center
California Department of Justice
4949 Broadway
Sacramento, CA, USA, 95820
(916) 227-3282
Fax: (916) 227-0427
alyson.lunetta@doj.ca.gov https://oag.ca.gov/crime

COLORADO
Jack Reed
Research Director
Office of Research and Statistics
Division of Criminal Justice
700 Kipling St., Ste. 1000
Denver, CO, USA, 80215
(303) 239-4442
Fax: (303) 239-4491
jack.reed@cdps.state.co.us https://www.colorado.gov/dcj-ors

CONNECTICUT
Kevin Neary
Policy Development Coordinator
Criminal Justice Policy and Planning
Office of Policy and Management
450 Capitol Ave.
Hartford, CT, USA, 06106-1379
(860) 418-6350
Fax: (860) 418-6496
kevin.f.neary@ct.gov https://portal.ct.gov/OPM/CJ-About/CJ-SAC/SAC-Sites/SAC-Homepage

DELAWARE
Philisa Weidlein-Crist
Director
Delaware Statistical Analysis Center
Criminal Justice Council
410 Federal St., Ste. 6
Dover, DE, USA, 19901
(302) 739-4846
Fax: (302) 739-4630
philisa.weidlein-crist@delaware.gov https://cjc.delaware.gov/sac/

DISTRICT OF COLUMBIA
Kristy Love
Interim Executive Director
Criminal Justice Coordinating Council
441 4th St. NW, Rm. 727N
Washington, DC, USA, 20001-2714
(202) 442-8504
Fax: (202) 724-3691
kristy.love@dc.gov https://cjcc.dc.gov/page/statistical-analysis-center

FLORIDA
Phillip Suber
Statistical Analysis Center
Florida Department of Law Enforcement
2331 Phillips Rd.
Tallahassee, FL, USA, 32302
(850) 410-7140
phillipsuber@fdle.state.fl.us https://www.fdle.state.fl.us/FSAC/FSAC-Home

GEORGIA
Stefanie Lopez-Howard
Planning and Evaluation Program Coordinator
Georgia Criminal Justice Coordinating Council
104 Marietta St. NW, Ste. 440
Atlanta, GA, USA, 30303-2743
(404) 657-1960
Fax: (404) 657-1957
stefanie.lopez-howard@cjcc.ga.gov https://cjcc.georgia.gov/about-sac

HAWAII
Paul Perrone
Chief of Research and Statistics
Crime Prevention and Justice Assistance Division
Hawaii Department of the Attorney General
235 S Beretania St., Ste. 401
Honolulu, HI, USA, 96813
(808) 586-1420
Fax: (808) 586-1373
paul.a.perrone@hawaii.gov https://hawaii.gov/ag/cpja

IDAHO
Thomas Strauss
Director
Idaho Statistical Analysis Center
Planning, Grants, and Research Department
Idaho State Police
700 S Stratford Dr.
Meridian, ID, USA, 83642-6202
(208) 884-7074
Fax: (208) 884-7094
thomas.strauss@isp.idaho.gov https://isp.idaho.gov/pgr/sac/

ILLINOIS
Timothy Lavery
Manager, Center for Justice Research and Evaluation
Illinois Criminal Justice Information Authority
300 W Adams St., 7th Fl.
Chicago, IL, USA, 60606-5107
(312) 793-8550
Fax: (312) 793-8422
timothy.lavery@illinois.gov https://www.icjia.org/public/sac/index.cfm

INDIANA
Christine Reynolds
Director
Research Division
Indiana Criminal Justice Institute
101 W Washington St., Ste. 1170 East Tower

Indianapolis, IN, USA, 46204
(317) 232-1259
Fax: (317) 232-4979
chrreynolds@cji.in.gov https://www.in.gov/cji

IOWA
Mindi TenNapel, Ph.D.
SAC Director
Division of Criminal and Juvenile Justice Planning
Iowa Department of Human Rights
Lucas State Office Building
321 E 12th St., 2nd Fl.
Des Moines, IA, USA, 50319
(515) 725-2884
Fax: (515) 242-6119
mindi.tennapel@iowa.gov https://humanrights.iowa.gov/cjjp

KANSAS
John Grube
Executive Director
Kansas Sentencing Commission
700 SW Jackson St., Ste. 501
Topeka, KS, USA, 66603
(785) 296-0923
Fax: (785) 296-0927
john.grube@ks.gov https://www.accesskansas.org/ksc/

KENTUCKY
Elzie Burgher
Executive Director
Kentucky Statistical Analysis Center
Justice and Public Safety Cabinet
125 Holmes St.
Frankfort, KY, USA, 40601
(502) 564-3251
Fax: (502) 564-5244
elzie.burgher@ky.gov https://justice.ky.gov/cjsac/Pages/default.aspx

LOUISIANA
Fredia Dunn
Section Manager - Policy Planning
Louisiana Commission on Law Enforcement
602 North 5th St.
PO Box 3133
Baton Rouge, LA, USA, 70821
(225) 342-1867
Fax: (225) 342-1846
fredia.dunn@lcle.la.gov http://lcle.la.gov/programs/SAC.asp

MAINE
George Shaler
Research Associate
Maine Statistical Analysis Center
Muskie School of Public Service
University of Southern Maine
PO Box 9300
Portland, ME, USA, 04104-9300
(207) 228-8344
Fax: (207) 228-8340
gshaler@usm.maine.edu https://muskie.usm.maine.edu/justiceresearch/

MARYLAND
Nathan Kemper
Chief, Research and Analysis
Maryland Statistical Analysis Center
Governor's Office of Crime Control and Prevention
300 E Joppa Rd., Ste. 3016
Baltimore, MD, USA, 21286-3016
(410) 697-9344
nathan.kemper@maryland.gov https://goccp.maryland.gov/crime-statistics/

MASSACHUSETTS
Lisa Lundquist
Director
Patricia Bergin
SAC Contact
Office of Grants and Research
Executive Office of Public Safety and Security
10 Park Plz., Ste. 3720
Boston, MA, USA, 02116
(617) 535-0087
Fax: (617) 725-0260
lisa.lundquist@state.ma.us
patricia.bergin@state.ma.us https://www.mass.gov/orgs/office-of-grants-and-research

MICHIGAN
Scott Wolfe, Ph.D.
Director and Associate Professor
Michigan Justice Statistics Center
Michigan State University School of Criminal Justice
560 Baker Hall
East Lansing, MI, USA, 48824
(517) 355-6649
Fax: (517) 432-1787
wolfesc1@msu.edu https://cj.msu.edu/community/mich-stat.html

MINNESOTA
Tricia Hummel
Assistant Director
Minnesota Office of Justice Programs
445 Minnesota St., Ste. 2300
St. Paul, MN, USA, 55101
(651) 201-7320
Fax: (651) 284-3317
tricia.hummel@state.mn.us https://dps.mn.gov/divisions/ojp/statistical-analysis-center/Pages/default.aspx

MISSISSIPPI
Charles Scheer, Ph.D.
Director
Mississippi Statistical Analysis Center
University of Southern Mississippi
PO Box 5127
Hattiesburg, MS, USA, 39406
(601) 266-4516
Fax: (601) 266-4391
charles.scheer@usm.edu https://www.usm.edu/criminal-justice/mississippi-statistical-analysis-center

MISSOURI
Michael Mroczkowski
Research Analyst
Statistical Analysis Center
Missouri State Highway Patrol
1510 E Elm St.
PO Box 568
Jefferson City, MO, USA, 65102
(573) 526-7107
Fax: (573) 526-6383
michael.mroczkowski@mshp.dps.mo.gov https://www.mshp.dps.missouri.gov/MSHPWeb/SAC/index_960grid.html

MONTANA
Kathy Wilkins
Data Unit Manager
Montana Board of Crime Control
5 S Last Chance Gulch
PO Box 201408
Helena, MT, USA, 59620
(406) 444-3615
Fax: (406) 444-4722
kwilkins@mt.gov https://mbcc.mt.gov/Data/Data.asp

NEBRASKA
Drew Bigham
Director
Statistical Analysis Center
Nebraska Crime Commission
301 Centennial Mall South
PO Box 94946
Lincoln, NE, USA, 68509
(402) 471-3992
Fax: (402) 471-2837
drew.bigham@nebraska.gov https://ncc.nebraska.gov/

NEVADA
William H. Sousa, Ph.D.
Director
Center for Analysis of Crime Statistics
Department of Criminal Justice
University of Nevada Las Vegas
4505 Maryland Pkwy.
Box 5009
Las Vegas, NV, USA, 89154-5009
(702) 895-0247
Fax: (702) 895-0252
sousaw@unlv.nevada.edu https://www.unlv.edu/ccjp

NEW HAMPSHIRE
Lisa Lamphere
SAC Contact
New Hampshire Office of the Attorney General
33 Capitol St.
Concord, NH, USA, 03301
(603) 271-8090
Fax: (603) 271-2110
lisa.j.lamphere@doj.nh.gov https://www.doj.nh.gov/

NEW JERSEY
Kristin Golden, Ph.D.
Manager, Research and Evaluation
Department of Law and Public Safety
25 Market St., CN-085
Trenton, NJ, USA, 08625
(609) 376-2539
kristin.golden@njoag.gov https://www.state.nj.us/lps/

NEW MEXICO
Kristine Denman
Senior Research Scientist
Institute for Social Research
University of New Mexico
MSC 02-1625
1915 Las Lomas Rd. NE
Albuquerque, NM, USA, 87131
(505) 277-6247
Fax: (505) 277-4215
kdenman@unm.edu https://nmsac.unm.edu

NEW YORK
Leigh Bates
Director
Office of Justice Research and Performance
NYS Division of Criminal Justice Services
4 Tower Place
Albany, NY, USA, 12203-3764
(518) 457-7301
Fax: (518) 485-0988
leigh.bates@dcjs.ny.gov https://www.criminaljustice.ny.gov/

NORTH CAROLINA
Michelle Beck
Director, Statistical Analysis Center
North Carolina Governor's Crime Commission
1201 Front St.
Raleigh, NC, USA, 27609
(919) 733-9144
Fax: (919) 733-4625
michelle.beck@ncdps.gov https://www.ncdps.gov/

NORTH DAKOTA
Colleen Weltz
NIBRS/UCR Program Manager
North Dakota Bureau of Criminal Investigation
PO Box 1054
Bismarck, ND, USA, 58502
(701) 328-5527
Fax: (701) 328-5510
cweltz@nd.gov https://attorneygeneral.nd.gov/

OHIO
Lisa Shoaf, Ph.D.
Director
Ohio Statistical Analysis Center
Ohio Office of Criminal Justice Services
1970 W Broad St.
Columbus, OH, USA, 43223
(614) 466-5997
Fax: (614) 466-0308
lshoaf@dps.state.oh.us https://www.ocjs.ohio.gov/policy_research.stm

OKLAHOMA
Kara Miller
Director
Oklahoma Statistical Analysis Center
Administration
Oklahoma State Bureau of Investigation
6600 N Harvey
Oklahoma City, OK, USA, 73116-7912
(405) 879-5272
Fax: (405) 879-2301
kara.miller@osbi.ok.gov https://osbi.ok.gov/statistical-analysis-center

OREGON
Kelly Officer
SAC Director
Oregon Criminal Justice Commission

885 Summer St. NE
Salem, OR, USA, 97301
(503) 378-6224
Fax: (503) 378-4861
kelly.j.officer@cjc.oregon.gov https://www.oregon.gov/CJC/Pages/index.aspx

PENNSYLVANIA
Kirsten Kenyon
Director
Office of Research, Evaluation, and Strategic Policy Development
Pennsylvania Commission on Crime and Delinquency
PO Box 1167
Harrisburg, PA, USA, 17108-1167
(717) 265-8505
Fax: (717) 705-4566
kkenyon@pa.gov https://www.pacrimestats.info/About.aspx

RHODE ISLAND
Michael J. Hogan
Administrative Manager
Rhode Island Department of Public Safety
One Capitol Hill, 2nd Fl.
Providence, RI, USA, 02908-5816
(401) 222-4493
Fax: (401) 222-1294
michael.hogan@ripsga.gov

SOUTH CAROLINA
Ross Hartfield
SAC Director
Office of Justice Programs
South Carolina Department of Public Safety
PO Box 1993
Blythewood, SC, USA, 29016
(803) 896-8702
Fax: (803) 896-8714
rosshartfield@scdps.gov https://scdps.sc.gov/ohsjp/stats/sac

SOUTH DAKOTA
Vacant
DCI Director
Criminal Statistical Analysis Center
South Dakota Division of Criminal Investigation
1302 E Highway 14, Ste. 5
Pierre, SD, USA, 57501-8505
(605) 773-3331
Fax: (605) 773-4629
david.natvig@state.sd.us
sdnibrs@state.sd.us https://atg.sd.gov/OurOffice/Departments/DCI/SAC

TENNESSEE
Yeselin Pendleton
CJIS Support Center Supervisor, TIBRS and N-DEx
Tennessee Bureau of Investigation
901 R.S. Gass Blvd.
Nashville, TN, USA, 37216-2639
(615) 744-4136
Fax: (615) 744-4555
yeselin.pendleton@tn.gov https://www.tn.gov/tbi/divisions/cjis-division.html

UTAH
Benjamin Peterson, Ph.D.
SAC Director
Utah Commission on Criminal and Juvenile Justice
Senate Bldg., Ste 330
PO Box 142330
Salt Lake City, UT, USA, 84114
(801) 538-1143
Fax: (801) 538-1024
benpeterson@utah.gov https://justice.utah.gov/

VERMONT
Monica Weeber
Executive Director
Crime Research Group, Inc.
PO Box 1433
Montpelier, VT, USA, 05601
(802) 310-2576
monicaw@crgvt.org https://www.crgvt.org/

VIRGINIA
Baron Blakley
Research Analyst
Criminal Justice Research Center
Virginia Department of Criminal Justice Services
1100 Bank St.
Richmond, VA, USA, 23219
(804) 786-3057
Fax: (804) 225-3853
baron.blakley@dcjs.virginia.gov https://www.dcjs.virginia.gov/research-center

Virgin Islands
Keisha Culpepper-Smith
SAC Contact
Law Enforcement Planning Commission
8000 Nisky Center, Ste. 700/701
St. Thomas, VI, USA, 00802-5803
(340) 774-6400
Fax: (340) 776-3317
keisha.culpepper-smith@lepc.vi.gov

WASHINGTON
Vasiliki Georgoulas-Sherry, Ph.D.
SAC Director
Washington State Statistical Analysis Center
Washington Office of Financial Management
PO Box 43113
Olympia, WA, USA, 98504-3113
(360) 890-5729
Fax: (360) 725-5174
vasiliki.georgoulas-sherry@ofm.wa.gov https://sac.ofm.wa.gov/

WEST VIRGINIA
Catie Clark, Ph.D.
Director
Office of Research and Strategic Planning
Division of Administrative Services
Justice and Community Services
1124 Smith St., Ste. 3100
Charleston, WV, USA, 25301-1323
(304) 558-8814
Fax: (304) 558-0391
catie.l.clark@wv.gov https://djcs.wv.gov/ORSP/SAC/Pages/default.aspx

WISCONSIN
Ashley Billig
SAC Contact
Bureau of Justice Information and Analysis
Wisconsin Justice Information Center
Wisconsin Department of Justice
17 W Main St.
Madison, WI, USA, 53703
(608) 266-2659
Fax: (608) 267-1338
billigak@doj.state.wi.us https://www.doj.state.wi.us/dles/bjia/bureau-justice-information-and-analysis

WYOMING
Brian Harnisch, MBA
Executive Director
Wyoming Survey and Analysis Center
University of Wyoming, Dept. 3925
1000 E. University Ave.
Laramie WY, USA, 82071-2000
(307) 766-6103
Fax: (307) 760-2759
harnisch@uwyo.edu https://wysac.uwyo.edu/wysac/

DRUGS

The Drug Enforcement Administration of the U.S. Justice Department is a source of data on facts, figures and trends of the illicit use of drugs. The information includes statistics on drug-related deaths and hospital admission due to drug abuse.

Telephone inquiries can be made to the Drug Enforcement Administration (202) 307-1000. Website: https://www.dea.gov.

ECONOMICS

A list of the experts within the Bureau of Economic Analysis follows: Website: https://www.bea.gov.

NATIONAL ECONOMIC ACCOUNTS

Associate Director for National Economic Accounts
David B. Wasshausen
(301) 278-9752

Acting Chief, Expenditure and Income Division
David B. Wasshausen
(301) 278-9752

Deputy Chief, Expenditure and Income Division
Pamela A. Kelly
(301) 278-9781

Chief, Industry Economics Division
Thomas F. Howells
(301) 278-9586

Deputy Chief, Industry Economics Division
Edward T. Morgan
(301) 278-9541

Auto Output
Everette P. Johnson
(301) 278-9725

Capital Consumption Allowances
Marlyn Rodriguez
(301) 278-9702

Capital Expenditures: By Industry
Michael T. Cusick
(301) 278-9764

Capital Expenditures: By Type
Michael Armah
(301) 278-9721

Capital Stocks: Government
William A. Jolliff
(301) 278-9668

Capital Stocks: Private Nonresidential
Michael T. Cusick
(301) 278-9764

Capital Stocks: Private Residential
Michael T. Cusick
(301) 278-9764

Computer Price Index
Michael Armah
(301) 278-9721

Construction
Gregory J. Prunchak
(301) 278-9233

Consumption, goods (personal)
William H. Nicolls IV
(301) 278-9544

Consumption, services (personal)
Harvey L. Davis
(301) 278-9719

Corporate Profits and Taxes
Kate L.S. Pinard
(301) 278-9635

Depreciation
Michael T. Cusick
(301) 278-9764

Disposable Personal Income
Marissa J. Crawford
(301) 278-9729

Dividends
Kate L.S. Pinard
(301) 278-9635

Employee Benefit Plans
Brian J. Smith
(301) 278-9625

Employee Compensation
Brian J. Smith
(301) 278-9625

Equipment and Software
Gregory J. Prunchak
(301) 278-9233

Farm Output, Product, and Income
Marcelo F. Yoon
(301) 278-9106

Fixed Assets Accounts
Michael T. Cusick
(301) 278-9764

Fixed Investment: By Type
Michael Armah
(301) 278-9721

Fixed Investment: Entertainment, Literary, and Artistic Originals
Gregory J. Prunchak
(301) 278-9233

Fixed Investment: Equipment
Jennifer Bennett
(301) 278-9769

Fixed Investment: Research and Development
Gregory J. Prunchak
(301) 278-9233

Fixed Investment: Software
Gregory J. Prunchak
(301) 278-9233

Fixed Investment: Structures
Gregory J. Prunchak
(301) 278-9233

Government
Mark S. Ludwick
(301) 278-9090

Government: Capital Stocks
William A. Jolliff
(301) 278-9668

Government: Compensation
Brendan I. Brankin
(301) 278-9736

Government: Contributions for Government Social Insurance: Federal
Stan J. Bellotti
(301) 278-9779

Government: Functions: Federal
Andrea L. Cook
(301) 278-9777

Government: Functions: State & Local
Steven J. Andrews
(301) 278-9770

Government: Output, Consumption Expenditures, and Gross Investment
Peter G. Beall
(301) 278-9771

Government: Receipts and Expenditures
Andrea L. Cook
(301) 278-9777

Government: Social Benefit Payments
Aida Kurti
(301) 278-9075

Government: Taxes: Federal
Mary L. Roy
(301) 278-9664

Government: Taxes: State & Local
Christopher M. Bravo
(301) 278-9735

Gross Domestic Product (Gross National Product): Current Estimates
Lisa S. Mataloni
(301) 278-9083

Gross Domestic Product (Gross National Product): Gross Domestic Product by Industry
Thomas F. Howells
(301) 278-9586

Interest Income and Payments
Brian J. Smith
(301) 278-9625

Inventories
David T. Hill
(301) 278-9046

Inventory/Sales Ratios
David T. Hill
(301) 278-9046

Investment, Fixed: By Type
Michael Armah
(301) 278-9721

Investment, Fixed: Entertainment, Literary, and Artistic Originals
Gregory J. Prunchak
(301) 278-9233

Investment, Fixed: Equipment
Jennifer Bennett
(301) 278-9769

Investment, Fixed: Research and Development
Gregory J. Prunchak
(301) 278-9233

Investment, Fixed: Software
Gregory J. Prunchak
(301) 278-9233

Investment, Fixed: Structures
Gregory J. Prunchak
(301) 278-9233

Investment, Inventories
David T. Hill
(301) 278-9046

Investment, Inventories: Inventories
David T. Hill
(301) 278-9046

Investment, Inventories: Inventory/Sales Ratios
David T. Hill
(301) 278-9046

Motor Vehicle Output
Everette P. Johnson
(301) 278-9725

National Income
Jennifer Lee
(301) 278-9107

Net Exports
Rebecca E. Pocase
(301) 278-9082

Output Measures (Chain-type)
Robert J. Kornfeld
(301) 278-9285

Personal Consumption Expenditures, Goods
William H. Nicolls IV
(301) 278-9544

Personal Consumption Expenditures, Goods: Motor Vehicles
Everette P. Johnson
(301) 278-9725

Personal Consumption Expenditures, Goods: Other Goods
William H. Nicolls IV
(301) 278-9544

Personal Consumption Expenditures, Prices
Kyle J. Brown
(301) 278-9688

Personal Consumption Expenditures, Services
Harvey L. Davis
(301) 278-9719

Personal Income
Marissa J. Crawford
(301) 278-9729

Price Measures (Chain-type)
Robert J. Kornfeld
(301) 278-9285

Proprietors Income, Nonfarm
Howard I. Krakower
(301) 278-9717

Rental Income
Brian J. Smith
(301) 278-9625

Residential Construction
Gregory J. Prunchak
(301) 278-9233

Saving
Marissa J. Crawford
(301) 278-9729

Structures
Gregory J. Prunchak
(301) 278-9233

Taxes
Mary L. Roy
(301) 278-9664

Truck Output
Michael F. Woehrman
(301) 278-9231

United Nations and OECD System of National Accounts
Karin E. Moses
(301) 278-9620

Wages and Salaries
Brian J. Smith
(301) 278-9625

INTERNATIONAL ECONOMIC ACCOUNTS

Associate Director for International Economics
Paul Farello
(301) 278-9660

Chief, Balance of Payments Division
Patricia Abaroa
(301) 278-9591

Chief, Direct Investment Division
Jessica Hanson
(301) 278-9591

Direct Investment and Multinational Enterprises (MNEs): Activities of MNEs
Kristen Brew
(301) 278-9152

Direct Investment and Multinational Enterprises (MNEs): Direct Investment Positions and Transactions
Ricardo Limes
(301) 278-9659

Direct Investment and Multinational Enterprises (MNEs): Establishment (Linked) Data
Thomas W. Anderson
(301) 278-9117

Direct Investment and Multinational Enterprises (MNEs): Services Supplied Through Affiliates
Alexis N. Grimm
(301) 278-9696

Financial Account Transactions: Direct Investment
Ricardo Limes
(301) 278-9659

Financial Account Transactions: Financial Derivative and Reserve Asset Transactions
Douglas Weinberg
(301) 278-9590

Financial Account Transactions: Other Investment Transactions
Douglas Weinberg
(301) 278-9590

Financial Account Transactions: Portfolio Investment Transactions
Elena L. Nguyen
(301) 278-9555

Financial Account Transactions: Portfolio Investment Transactions
Tait Militana
(301) 278-9556

International Investment Position Accounts
Elena L. Nguyen
(301) 278-9555

International Investment Position Accounts: Direct Investment
Ricardo Limes
(301) 278-9659

International Investment Position Accounts: Financial Derivative and Reserve Asset Positions
Douglas Weinberg
(301) 278-9590

International Investment Position Accounts: Other Investment Positions
Douglas Weinberg
(301) 278-9590

International Investment Position Accounts: Portfolio Investment Positions
Elena L. Nguyen
(301) 278-9555

International Investment Position Accounts: Reserve Asset Positions
Tait Militana
(301) 278-9556

International Trade in Goods
Kevin Barefoot
(301) 278-9118

International Trade in Services
Molly E. Garber
(301) 278-9580

International Trade in Services: Charges for the Use of Intellectual Property
Jeffrey R. Bogen
(301) 278-9592

International Trade in Services: Financial Services
Ed Dozier
(301) 278-9559

International Trade in Services: Foreign Military Sales and other Government Transactions
Jeffrey R. Bogen
(301) 278-9592

International Trade in Services: Insurance Services
Ami Adjoh-Baliki
(301) 278-9583

International Trade in Services: Other Business Services
Jeffrey R. Bogen
(301) 278-9592

International Trade in Services: Transport
Ed Dozier
(301) 278-9559

International Trade in Services: Travel
Edward F. Dozier
(301) 278-9559

Primary Income
Elena L. Nguyen
(301) 278-9555

Secondary Income (Current Transfers): Private Remittances and Other Transfers
Theodore Peck
(301) 278-9584

Secondary Income (Current Transfers): U.S. Government Grants and Other Transfers
Edward F. Dozier
(301) 278-9559

Surveys, Foreign Direct Investment in the United States (FDIUS): Annual (BE-15) and Benchmark (BE-12)
Kirsten Brew
(301) 278-9152

Surveys, Foreign Direct Investment in the United States (FDIUS): Annual (BE-15) and Benchmark (BE-12)
Survey Staff
(301) 278-9247

Surveys, Foreign Direct Investment in the United States (FDIUS): New FDIUS (BE-13)
Amanda Budny
(301) 278-9154

Surveys, Foreign Direct Investment in the United States (FDIUS): New FDIUS (BE-13)
Survey Staff
(301) 278-9419

Surveys, Foreign Direct Investment in the United States (FDIUS): Quarterly (BE-605)
Jeannette Scott
(301) 278-9614

Surveys, Foreign Direct Investment in the United States (FDIUS): Quarterly (BE-605)
Survey Staff
(301) 278-9422

Surveys, International Services
Christopher J. Stein
(301) 278-9189

Surveys, International Services : Financial Services (BE-185/180)
Kiesha Brown
(301) 278-9122

Surveys, International Services : Insurance Services (BE-45/140)
Andre Garber
(301) 278-9288

Surveys, International Services : Other Selected Services & Intellectual Property (BE-125/120)
Steven J. Muno
(301) 278-9132

Surveys, International Services : Transport Services (BE-9/29/30/37)
Brian Goddard
(301) 278-9559

Surveys, U.S. Direct Investment Abroad (USDIA): Annual (BE-11) and Benchmark (BE-10)
Mark D. Goddard
(301) 278-9162

Surveys, U.S. Direct Investment Abroad (USDIA): Annual (BE-11) and Benchmark (BE-10)
Survey Staff
(301) 278-9418

Surveys, U.S. Direct Investment Abroad (USDIA): Quarterly (BE-577)
Leila Morrison
(301) 278-9178

Surveys, U.S. Direct Investment Abroad (USDIA): Quarterly (BE-577)
Survey Staff
(301) 278-9261

REGIONAL ECONOMIC ACCOUNTS

Acting Associate Director for Regional Economics
Mauricio Ortiz
(301) 278-9269

Chief, Regional Income Division
Marcelo Yoon
(301) 278-9106

Chief, Regional Product Division
Christian Awuku-Budu
(301) 278-9235

Gross Domestic Product by County
Sharon D. Panek
(301) 278-9228

Gross Domestic Product by Metropolitan Area
Sharon D. Panek
(301) 278-9228

Gross Domestic Product by State
Cliff Woodruff
(301) 278-9234

Gross Domestic Product by State: Banking and Services Industries
Sharon D. Panek
(301) 278-9228

Gross Domestic Product by State: Compensation of Employees
John E. Broda
(301) 278-9225

Gross Domestic Product by State: Government
Zheng Wang
(301) 278-9670

Gross Domestic Product by State: Manufacturing Industries
Todd P. Siebeneck
(301) 278-9705

Gross Domestic Product by State: Methodology Questions: Goods Industries
Cliff H. Woodruff
(301) 278-9234

Gross Domestic Product by State: Methodology Questions: Services Industries
Sharon D. Panek
(301) 278-9228

Gross Domestic Product by State: Mining
Lam Cao
(301) 278-9232

Gross Domestic Product by State: Real Estate
Sharon D. Panek
(301) 278-9228

Gross Domestic Product by State: Taxes on Production and Imports
John E. Broda
(301) 278-9225

Personal Consumption Expenditures by State
Steven Zemanek
(301) 278-9578

Personal Income and Employment
Staff
(301) 278-9321

Personal Income and Employment: Disposable Personal Income
Mauricio Ortiz
(301) 278-9269

Personal Income and Employment: Dividends, Interest, and Rental Income
Brian Maisano
(301) 278-9652

Personal Income and Employment: Farm Proprietors Income and Employment
Marcello Yoon
(301) 278-9106

Personal Income and Employment: Methodology
Mauricio Ortiz
(301) 278-9269

Personal Income and Employment: Nonfarm Proprietors Income and Employment
Brian Maisano
(301) 278-9652

Personal Income and Employment: Personal Current Transfer Receipts
Alexander Adams
(301) 278-9279

Personal Income and Employment: Residence Adjustment
Matthew A. VonKerczek
(301) 278-9250

Personal Income and Employment: State and Local Defined Benefit Pensions
Ross Stepp
(301) 278-9316

Personal Income and Employment: State Quarterly Personal Income
Matthew A. VonKerczek
(301) 278-9250

Personal Income and Employment: Supplements to Wages and Salaries
Marcelo F. Yoon
(301) 278-9106

Personal Income and Employment: Wage and Salary Income and Employment
Marcelo F. Yoon
(301) 278-9106

Regional Price Parities
Eric B. Figueroa
(301) 278-9328

RIMS II, Regional Multipliers
Staff
(301) 278-9313

Satellite Accounts: Arts and Cultural Production
Sharon Panek
(301) 278-9228

Satellite Accounts: Outdoor Recreation
Dirk van Duym
(301) 278-9560

INDUSTRY ACCOUNTS

Associate Director for National Economic Accounts
Erich H. Strassner
(301) 278-9612

Chief, Expenditure and Income Division
David B. Wasshausen
(301) 278-9752

Chief, Industry Economics Division
Thomas F. Howells
(301) 278-9586

Deputy Chief, Expenditure and Income Division
Pamela A. Kelly
(301) 278-9781

Deputy Chief, Industry Economics Division
Edward T. Morgan
(301) 278-9541

Goods
William A. Jolliff
(301) 278-9668

Goods: Agriculture, forestry, fishing, and hunting
Patricia A. Washington
(301) 278-9114

Goods: Construction
Gregory J. Prunchak
(301) 278-9233

Goods: Manufacturing (durable goods)
Jennifer Bennett
(301) 278-9769

Goods: Manufacturing (durable goods): Computer and electronic products
Jennifer Bennett
(301) 278-9769

Goods: Manufacturing (durable goods): Electrical equipment, appliances, and components
Jennifer Bennett
(301) 278-9769

Goods: Manufacturing (durable goods): Fabricated metal products
Jennifer Bennett
(301) 278-9769

Goods: Manufacturing (durable goods): Furniture and related products
Jennifer Bennett
(301) 278-9769

Goods: Manufacturing (durable goods): Machinery
Jennifer Bennett
(301) 278-9769

Goods: Manufacturing (durable goods): Miscellaneous manufacturing
Jennifer Bennett
(301) 278-9769

Goods: Manufacturing (durable goods): Motor vehicles, bodies and trailers, and parts
Patricia A. Washington
(301) 278-9114

Goods: Manufacturing (durable goods): Nonmetallic mineral products
Jennifer Bennett
(301) 278-9769

Goods: Manufacturing (durable goods): Other transportation equipment
Patricia A. Washington
(301) 278-9114

Goods: Manufacturing (durable goods): Primary metals
Jennifer Bennett
(301) 278-9769

Goods: Manufacturing (durable goods): Wood products
Jennifer Bennett
(301) 278-9769

Goods: Manufacturing (nondurable goods)
Justin M. Harper
(301) 278-9464

Goods: Manufacturing (nondurable goods): Apparel and leather and allied products
Justin M. Harper
(301) 278-9464

Goods: Manufacturing (nondurable goods): Chemical products
Justin M. Harper
(301) 278-9464

Goods: Manufacturing (nondurable goods): Food and beverage and tobacco products
Patricia A. Washington
(301) 278-9114

Goods: Manufacturing (nondurable goods): Paper products
Justin M. Harper
(301) 278-9464

Goods: Manufacturing (nondurable goods): Petroleum and coal products
Justin M. Harper
(301) 278-9464

Goods: Manufacturing (nondurable goods): Plastics and rubber products
Justin M. Harper
(301) 278-9464

Goods: Manufacturing (nondurable goods): Printing and related support activities
Justin M. Harper
(301) 278-9464

Goods: Manufacturing (nondurable goods): Textile mills and textile product mills
Justin M. Harper
(301) 278-9464

Goods: Mining
Justin M. Harper
(301) 278-9464

Government: General Government
Mark S. Ludwick
(301) 278-9090

Government: Government Enterprises
Dan W. Jackson
(301) 278-9722

Information, financial services, real estate, and rental and leasing: Financial services, real estate, and rental and leasing
Jennifer Lee
(301) 278-9107

Information, financial services, real estate, and rental and leasing: Financial services, real estate, and rental and leasing: Federal Reserve banks, credit intermediation, and related activities
Jennifer Lee
(301) 278-9107

Information, financial services, real estate, and rental and leasing: Financial services, real estate, and rental and leasing: Funds, trusts, and other financial vehicles
Jennifer Lee
(301) 278-9107

Information, financial services, real estate, and rental and leasing: Financial services, real estate, and rental and leasing: Insurance carriers and related activities
Jennifer Lee
(301) 278-9107

Information, financial services, real estate, and rental and leasing: Financial services, real estate, and rental and leasing: Real estate and rental and leasing
Brian J. Smith
(301) 278-9625

Information, financial services, real estate, and rental and leasing: Financial services, real estate, and rental and leasing: Securities, commodity contracts, and investments
Jennifer Lee
(301) 278-9107

Information, financial services, real estate, and rental and leasing: Information
Brian M. Lindberg
(301) 278-9329

Personal and administrative services and government: Arts, entertainment, accommodation, food, educational services, and government: Accommodation and food services
Harvey L. Davis
(301) 278-9719

Personal and administrative services and government: Arts, entertainment, accommodation, food, educational services, and government: Arts, entertainment, and recreation
Harvey L. Davis
(301) 278-9719

Personal and administrative services and government: Arts, entertainment, accommodation, food, educational services, and government: Educational services
Paul V. Kern
(301) 278-9596

Personal and administrative services and government: Health care, administrative, and other services
Paul V. Kern
(301) 278-9596

Personal and administrative services and government: Health care, administrative, and other services: Administrative and waste management services
Paul V. Kern
(301) 278-9596

Personal and administrative services and government: Health care, administrative, and other services: Health care and social assistance
Paul V. Kern
(301) 278-9596

Personal and administrative services and government: Health care, administrative, and other services: Management of companies and enterprises
Jennifer Lee
(301) 278-9107

Personal and administrative services and government: Health care, administrative, and other services: Other services
Paul V. Kern
(301) 278-9596

Professional and distributive services
Edward T. Morgan
(301) 278-9541

Professional and distributive services: Professional, scientific, and technical services
Nikki Y. Dubria
(301) 278-9298

Professional and distributive services: Retail trade and utilities
Ricky L. Stewart
(301) 278-9113

Professional and distributive services: Retail trade and utilities: Retail trade
Ricky L. Stewart
(301) 278-9113

Professional and distributive services: Retail trade and utilities: Utilities
Harvey L. Davis
(301) 278-9719

Professional and distributive services: Wholesale trade, transportation, and warehousing
William H. Nicolls IV
(301) 278-9544

Professional and distributive services: Wholesale trade, transportation, and warehousing: Transportation and warehousing
William H. Nicolls IV
(301) 278-9544

Professional and distributive services: Wholesale trade, transportation, and warehousing: Wholesale trade
William H. Nicolls IV
(301) 278-9544

Satellite Accounts
Paul V. Kern
(301) 278-9596

Satellite Accounts: Arts and cultural production satellite account
Paul V. Kern
(301) 278-9596

Satellite Accounts: Industry-level production account
Jon D. Samuels
(301) 278-9020

Satellite Accounts: Outdoor recreation satellite account
Kyle J. Brown
(301) 278-9688

Satellite Accounts: Travel and tourism satellite account
Sarah B. Osborne
(301) 278-9459

Special Topics
Thomas F. Howells
(301) 278-9586

Special Topics: Chain-type indexes and contributions
Robert J. Kornfeld

(301) 278-9285

Special Topics: Direct and total requirements
Gabriel W. Medeiros
(301) 278-9109

Special Topics: International trade and inventories
Rebecca E. Pocase
(301) 278-9082

Special Topics: KLEMS tables
Matthew E. Calby
(301) 278-9787

Special Topics: Make and use tables
Matthew E. Calby
(301) 278-9787

Special Topics: Seasonal adjustment
Jason W. Chute
(301) 278-9677

Special Topics: Value added components
Jennifer Lee
(301) 278-9107

EDUCATION

The National Center for Education Statistics (NCES) is the primary federal entity for collecting and analyzing data related to education in the U.S. and other nations. NCES is located within the U.S. Department of Education and the Institute of Education Sciences. NCES fulfills a Congressional mandate to collect, collate, analyze, and report complete statistics on the condition of American education; conduct and publish reports; and review and report on education activities internationally.

For more information, call the NCES at (202) 502-7300, or via the web at https://nces.ed.gov.

ENERGY

The National Energy Information Center of the U.S. Department of Energy provides statistical and analytical energy data, information, and referral assistance to the government and private sectors, academia, and the general public. For questions of a general nature about energy data call (202) 586-8800. Website: https://www.eia.gov/about/contact/. For specific topics, call information contacts listed below:

COAL
Main Fax: (202) 287-1944

Annual Distribution
infocoal@eia.gov

Annual Production
infocoal@eia.gov

Coal Reserves
infocoal@eia.gov

Coal Transportation (Rates, Trends, Analysis)
infocoal@eia.gov

Coke Plants
infocoal@eia.gov

Manufacturing Plants and Commercial and Institutional Users: Consumption, Receipts, Prices, Stocks
infocoal@eia.gov

Monthly Data: Production, Imports, Exports, Consumption, Stocks
infocoal@eia.gov

Quarterly Data: Production, Imports, Exports, Consumption, Stocks
infocoal@eia.gov

Weekly Production
infocoal@eia.gov

COAL FORECAST

International Consumption/Production
Bonnie West
(202) 586-2415
bonnie.west@eia.gov

International Trade
David Fritsch
(202) 287-6538
david.fritsch@eia.gov

Long-Term Projections (Coal Distribution/End-use Prices/Exports/Imports)
David Fritsch
(202) 287-6538
david.fritsch@eia.gov

Long-Term Projections (Coal Production, Exports and Imports)
Bonnie West
(202) 586-2415
bonnie.west@eia.gov

Short-Term Projections (Coal Markets)
Bonnie West
(202) 586-2415
bonnie.west@eia.gov

Short-Term Projections (Coal Production, Exports and Imports)
Bonnie West
(202) 586-2415
bonnie.west@eia.gov

ECONOMIC/FINANCIAL ANALYSIS
Main Fax: (202) 586-9753

Foreign Investment
Bruce Bawks
(202) 586-6579
bruce.bawks@eia.gov

Oil and Gas Exploration, Development, and Production Financial Analysis
Bruce Bawks
(202) 586-6579
bruce.bawks@eia.gov

Refining and Marketing Financial Analysis
Bruce Bawks
(202) 586-6579
bruce.bawks@eia.gov

ELECTRIC POWER
Main Fax: (202) 586-9753

Advanced Metering / Net Metering
Anodyne Linstrom
Marc Harnish

Capacity
Suparna Ray

Demand-Side Management
Patricia Hutchins

Distribution system reliability contact
Anodyne Linstrom

Electricity Imports/Exports
Tosha Beckford

Emissions
Jonathan DeVilbiss

Fuel Receipts, Cost, and Quality
Eric Harrison

Generation, Consumption, and Stocks
Chris Cassar
Brady Tyra

Sales, Revenue, Customers, and Price
Marc Harnish
Alex Gorski

Wholesale Data
Lolita Jamison

ENVIRONMENTAL EXPERTS
Main Fax: (202) 586-3045

Biodiesel/Ethanol
Steven Hanson
(202) 287-5826
steven.hanson@eia.gov

Carbon Dioxide - U.S. History and Projections (STEO and AEO)
emissions@eia.gov

Carbon Dioxide - International Projections (IEO)
emissions@eia.gov

Electric Power Emissions
Jonathan DeVilbiss
(202) 586-2992
jonathan.devilbiss@eia.gov

Electric Power Sector Pollutant Emissions - Modeling and Projections
Thad Huetteman
(202) 586-7238
thaddeus.huetteman@eia.gov

International Carbon Dioxide Emissions - Current Data
Tejasvi Raghuveer
(202) 586-8926
tejasvi.raghuveer@eia.gov

MTBE, Oxygenated Gasoline, and Reformulated Gasoline
Mason Hamilton
(202) 586-7105
mason.hamilton@eia.gov

Thermoelectric Cooling Water
Jonathan DeVilbiss
(202) 586-2992
jonathan.devilbiss@eia.gov

Tier 3 Gasoline and Ultra Low Sulfur Diesel
James Preciado
(202) 586-8769
james.preciado@eia.gov

Voluntary Reporting of Greenhouse Gas Emissions (discontinued)
Paul McArdle
(202) 586-4445
paul.mcardle@eia.gov

FORECASTING & ANALYSIS

Short-Term (STEO) Analysis and Forecasting Experts
Timothy Hess
(202) 586-4212
timothy.hess@eia.gov

Petroleum and Natural Gas Markets Review
Jeffrey Barron
(202) 586-5840
jeffrey.barron@eia.gov

Global Oil Markets
Lejla Villar
(202) 586-1398
lejla.villar@eia.gov

Crude Oil and Petroleum Product Prices
Sean Hill
(202) 586-4247
sean.hill@eia.gov

Futures Markets and Energy Price Uncertainty
James Preciado
(202) 586-8769
james.preciado@eia.gov

U.S. Crude Oil/Natural Gas Production
Naser Ameen
(202) 287-6448
naser.ameen@eia.gov

U.S. Petroleum Demand/Stocks/Trade
Matt French
(202) 586-3714
matthew.french@eia.gov

U.S. Hydrocarbon Gas Liquids
Joshua Eiermann
(202) 586-7713
joshua.eiermann@eia.gov

U.S. Refining
Kevin Hack
(202) 586-9999
kevin.hack@eia.gov

U.S. Ethanol and Biodiesel
Sean Hill
(202) 586-4247
sean.hill@eia.gov

U.S. Natural Gas
Corrina Ricker
(202) 586-0547
corrina.ricker@eia.gov

U.S. Coal
Bonnie West
(202) 586-2415
bonnie.west@eia.gov

U.S. Electricity

Tyler Hodge
(202) 586-0442
tyler.hodge@eia.gov

U.S. Renewables, Emissions
Perry Lindstrom
(202) 586-0934
perry.lindstrom@eia.gov

U.S. Nuclear Energy
Lindsay Aramayo
(202) 586-9999
lindsay.aramayo@eia.gov

Macroeconomic Projections
Russ Tarver
(202) 586-3991
russell.tarver@eia.gov

LONG-TERM (AEO) ANALYSIS AND FORECASTING
Main Fax: (202) 586-3045

Annual Energy Outlook

General Questions/Executive Summary
annualenergyoutlook@eia.gov

Carbon Dioxide Emissions
emissions@eia.gov

Coal Supply and Prices
David Fritsch
(202) 287-6538
david.fritsch@eia.gov

Commercial Demand
Kevin Jarzomski
(202) 586-3208
kevin.jarzomski@eia.gov

Economic Activity
Russell Tarver
(202) 586-3991
russell.tarver@eia.gov

Electricity Generation, Capacity, Emissions
Laura Martin
(202) 586-1494
laura.martin@eia.gov

Electricity Prices
Lori Aniti
(202) 586-2867
lori.aniti@eia.gov

Ethanol and Biodiesel
Estella Shi
(202) 586-4787
estella.shi@eia.gov

Industrial Demand
Nicholas Skarzynski
(202) 586-4821
nicholas.skarzynski@eia.gov

International Oil Demand
Peter Colletti
(202) 586-2223
peter.colletti@eia.gov

International Oil Production
Troy Cook
(202) 586-4493
troy.cook@eia.gov

National Gas Markets
Mary Lewis
(202) 586-8676
mary.lewis@eia.gov

Nuclear Energy
Michael Scott
(202) 586-0253
michael.scott@eia.gov

Oil and Natural Gas Production
Albert Painter
(202) 287-6463
albert.painter@eia.gov

Oil Refining and Markets
Peter Colletti
(202) 586-2223
peter.colletti@eia.gov

Renewable Energy
Chris Namovicz
(202) 586-7120
christopher.namovicz@eia.gov

Residential Demand
Kevin Jarzomski
(202) 586-3208
kevin.jarzomski@eia.gov

Transportation Demand
Michael Dwyer
(202) 586-8406
michael.dwyer@eia.gov

World Oil Prices
Sean Hill
(202) 586-4247
sean.hill@eia.gov

INTERNATIONAL (IEO) ANALYSIS AND FORECASTING EXPERTS
Main Fax: (202) 586-3045
internationalenergyoutlook@eia.gov

Buildings sector
Courtney Sourmehi
(202) 586-0022
courtney.sourmehi@eia.gov

Carbon Dioxide Emissions
emissions@eia.gov

Coal
David Fritsch
(202) 287-6538
david.fritsch@eia.gov

District Heat
Courtney Sourmehi
(202) 586-0022
courtney.sourmehi@eia.gov

Economic Activity
Elizabeth Sendich
(202) 586-7145
elizabeth.sendich@eia.gov

Electricity
Kenneth Dubin
(202) 586-0477
kenneth.dubin@eia.gov

Energy-Related CO2 Emissions
emissions@eia.gov

Industrial sector
Matthew Skelton
(202) 287-5660
matthew.skelton@eia.gov

International Energy Outlook
Linda Doman
(202) 586-1041
linda.doman@eia.gov

Natural Gas
David Manowitz
(202) 586-2815
david.manowitz@eia.gov

Nuclear Power
Slade Johnson
(202) 586-3945
slade.johnson@eia.gov

Petroleum and Other Liquid Fuels
Troy Cook
(202) 586-4493
troy.cook@eia.gov

Renewable Energy
Michelle Bowman
(202) 586-0526
michelle.bowman@eia.gov

Transportation Sector
Michael Dwyer
(202) 586-8406
michael.dwyer@eia.gov

RENEWABLE ENERGY/ALTERNATE FUELS DATA EXPERTS
Main Fax: (202) 586-3045

Alternative-Fueled Vehicle Suppliers and Users
Cynthia Sirk
inforenewablesdata@eia.gov

Biodiesel Production
Chris Buckner
inforenewablesdata@eia.gov

Biofuels Resources
Steven Hanson
inforenewablesdata@eia.gov

Biomass for Electricity Generation (Land Fill Gas and Waste)
Chris Cassar
inforenewablesdata@eia.gov

Densified Biomass (Such as wood pellets)
Connor Murphy
inforenewablesdata@eia.gov

Geothermal for Electricity Generation
Chris Cassar
inforenewablesdata@eia.gov

Geothermal Heat Pump
Kevin Jarzomski
inforenewablesdata@eia.gov

Hydroelectric
Chris Cassar
inforenewablesdata@eia.gov

Solar: Utility Scale Photovoltaic and Thermal
Suparna Ray
inforenewablesdata@eia.gov

Solar Distributed Generation (e.g., residential rooftop solar)
David Darling
inforenewablesdata@eia.gov

Solar Photovoltaic Manufacturing and Shipment
Lolita Jamison
inforenewablesdata@eia.gov

Wind (Onshore and Offshore)
Tosha Richardson
inforenewablesdata@eia.gov

Wind Distributed Generation
April Lee
inforenewablesdata@eia.gov

RENEWABLE ANALYSIS AND FORECASTING EXPERTS

Alternative-Fueled Vehicle
Nicolas Chase
(202) 586-1879
nicolas.chase@eia.gov
John Maples
(202) 586-1757
john.maples@eia.gov

Biofuels Resources
Steven Hanson
(202) 287-5826
steven.hanson@eia.gov

Biomass: Land Fill Gas
Fred Mayes
(202) 586-7209
fred.mayes@eia.gov

Biomass: Municipal Solid Waste
Fred Mayes
(202) 586-7209
fred.mayes@eia.gov

Biomass Resource Supply
Manussawee Sukunta
(202) 586-0279
manussawee.sukunta.mayes@eia.gov

Electricity Levelized Costs and Avoided Costs
Manussawee Sukunta
(202) 586-0279
manussawee.sukunta.mayes@eia.gov

Geothermal (Conventional)
Richard Bowers
(202) 586-8586
richard.bowers@eia.gov

Geothermal Heat Pumps
Kevin Jarzomski
(202) 586-3208
kevin.jarzomski@eia.gov

Hydroelectric (Conventional)
Michelle Bowman
(202) 586-1508
michelle.bowman@eia.gov
Fred Mayes
(202) 586-7209
fred.mayes@eia.gov

Hydrokinetics (Wave, Tidal, Thermal)
Fred Mayes
(202) 586-7209
fred.mayes@eia.gov
Chris Namovicz
(202) 586-7120
chris.namovicz@eia.gov

International Renewable Trends
Michelle Bowman
(202) 586-0526
michelle.bowman@eia.gov

Renewable RPS, Tax Incentives, Feed-in-Tariffs, etc.
Manussawee Sukunta
(202) 586-0279
manussawee.sukunta@eia.gov
Richard Bowers
(202) 586-8586
richard.bowers@eia.gov

Renewable resources assessment
Manussawee Sukunta
(202) 586-0279
manussawee.sukunta@eia.gov

Solar: Commercial Buildings PV
Meera Fickling
(202) 586-0765
meera.fickling@eia.gov

Solar Distributed Generation
Kevin Jarzomski
(202) 586-3208
kevin.jarzomski@eia.gov

Solar: Utility Scale Photovoltaic
Manussawee Sukunta
(202) 586-0279
manussawee.sukunta@eia.gov

Solar Distributed Generation
Manussawee Sukunta
(202) 586-0279
manussawee.sukunta@eia.gov
Kevin Jarzomski
(202) 586-3208
kevin.jarzomski@eia.gov

Solar Distributed Generation
Manussawee Sukunta
(202) 586-0279
manussawee.sukunta@eia.gov
Kevin Jarzomski
(202) 586-3208
kevin.jarzomski@eia.gov

Solar Thermal Power (Concentrating Solar Power)
Manussawee Sukunta
(202) 586-0279
manussawee.sukunta@eia.gov
Chris Namovicz
(202) 586-7120
chris.namovicz@eia.gov

Wind Distributed Generation
Erin Boedecker
(202) 586-4791
erin.boedecker@eia.gov

Wind Offshore
Richard Bowers
(202) 586-8586
richard.bowers@eia.gov

Wind Onshore
Richard Bowers
(202) 586-8586
richard.bowers@eia.gov

FOREIGN COUNTRIES STATISTICS OR INTERNATIONAL STATISTICS ON SPECIFIC COUNTRIES

The Census Bureau's International Programs Data Base (IPC) maintains the International Data Base (IDB). The IDB is a computerized source of demographic and socioeconomic statistics for countries and areas of the world with a population of more than 5,000. The IDB provides quick access to specialized information, with emphasis on demographic measures, for individual countries or selected groups of countries of the world. For more information about the IDB, visit https://www.census.gov/programs-surveys/international-programs/about/idb.html.

HEALTH

The National Center for Health Statistics (NCHS) of the U.S. Department of Health and Human Services (HHS) collects and disseminates data on every aspect of health and health care in the United States. To identify specific agency programs which provide inquiry assistance, visit https://www.cdc.gov/nchs.

HOUSING

The U.S. Department of Housing and Urban Development (HUD) is the principal federal agency responsible for programs concerned with the Nation's housing needs, fair housing opportunities, and improvement and development of the Nation's communities. Inquiries on housing statistics can be made to (202) 708-1112. Website: https://www.hud.gov.

INTERNATIONAL TRADE

The U.S. Department of Commerce (DOC), International Trade Administration (ITA) will provide a statistical expert from a specific country desk by contacting them toll free at (800) USA-TRADE. The website is: https://legacy.trade.gov/mas/ian/.

LABOR

EMPLOYMENT AND UNEMPLOYMENT STATISTICS

The following experts are drawn from the Department of Labor Statistics. Website: https://www.bls.gov/help/hlpcont.htm.

EMPLOYMENT PROJECTIONS

Occupational Outlook

Occupational information, general
Staff
(202) 691-5700
ep-info@bls.gov

Education and training categories and statistics
Teri Morisi
(202) 691-6501
morisi.teri@bls.gov

Career Outlook
Kathleen Green
(202) 691-5717
green.kathleen@bls.gov

Occupational separations
Michael Wolf
(202) 691-5714
wolf.michael@bls.gov

Industry Employment Projections

Aggregate economy
Kevin Dubina
(202) 691-6482
dubina.kevin@bls.gov

Final Demand
Jared Teeter
(202) 691-5688
teeter.jared@bls.gov

Industry output and employment
Andrea Gensler
(202) 691-6334
gensler.andrea@bls.gov

Industry input-output system
Richard Graham
(202) 691-5692
graham.richard@bls.gov

Labor force
Mitra Toossi
(202) 691-5721
toossi.mitra@bls.gov

INTERNATIONAL LABOR COMPARISONS

Staff
(202) 691-5654
ilchelp@bls.gov

Productivity and Unit Labor Costs
Aaron Cobet
(202) 691-5018

Labor Force, Employment, and Unemployment
Rich Esposito
(202) 691-6071

Consumer Prices
Mubarka Haq
(202) 691-5772

MULTIFACTOR PRODUCTIVITY

Multifactor Productivity for Major Sectors (Annual Measures), General Information and Help
Staff
(202) 691-5606

Multifactor Productivity for Major Sectors (Annual Measures), Analysis and methodology
Steve Rosenthal
(202) 691-5609
rosenthal.steve@bls.gov

Multifactor Productivity for Major Sectors (Annual Measures), Data
Ryan Forshay
(202) 691-5617
forshay.ryan@bls.gov
Randy Kinoshita
(202) 691-5610
kinoshita.randal@bls.gov

Multifactor Productivity for Manufacturing and 3-digit NAICS Industries (KLEMS Annual Measure)
Steve Rosenthal
(202) 691-5609
rosenthal.steve@bls.gov
Randy Kinoshita
(202) 691-5610
kinoshita.randal@bls.gov

Multifactor Productivity for 4-digit NAICS Manufacturing Industries, Air Transportation, and Line-Haul Railrod Transportation
Lisa Usher
(202) 691-5641
usher.lisa@bls.gov
Victor Torres
(202) 691-5626
torres.victor@bls.gov
Chris Kask
(202) 691-5647
kask.chris@bls.gov

Capital Measurement for Major Sector and 3-digit NAICS Industries
Steve Rosenthal
(202) 691-5609
rosenthal.steve@bls.gov
Ryan Forshay
(202) 691-5617
forshay.ryan@bls.gov
Randy Kinoshita
(202) 691-5610
kinoshita.randal@bls.gov

Labor Composition, Analysis and Methodology
Cindy Zoghi
(202) 691-5680
zoghi.cindy@bls.gov

Labor Composition, Data
Ryan Forshay
(202) 691-5617
forshay.ryan@bls.gov

Hours at Work Ratio
Shawn Sprague

(202) 691-5612
sprague.shawn@bls.gov

Research and Development, Analysis and Methodology
Leo Sveikauskas
(202) 691-5677
sveikauskas.leo@bls.gov

Research and Development, Data
Bhavani Khandrika
(202) 691-5620
khandrika.bhavani@bls.gov

LABOR PRODUCTIVITY AND COSTS

MAJOR SECTOR PRODUCTIVITY AND COST DATA (QUARTERLY AND ANNUAL)

Methodology
John Glaser
(202) 691-5607
glaser.john@bls.gov
Shawn Sprague
(202) 691-5612
sprague.shawn@bls.gov

INDUSTRY PRODUCTIVITY AND COST DATA (ANNUAL)

Methodology
Michael Brill
(202) 691-5657
Jenny Rudd
(202) 691-5816
Victor Torres
(202) 691-5626
torres.victor@bls.gov

PRODUCER PRICE INDEXES

For industry specific contacts, see the website: https://www.bls.gov/ppi/ppicon.htm
(202) 691-7705

MEDICARE AND MEDICAID

Data on Medicare and Medicaid, as well as hospitals, nursing homes, doctors, and recipients, are amassed and made available from the Department of Health and Human Services (HHS), Centers for Medicare and Medicaid Services (CMS). Inquiries can be made to (877) 267-2323.

MINES AND MINERALS

The following experts are drawn from U.S. Geological Survey (USGS). Website: https://minerals.usgs.gov.

MINERALS COMMODITY SPECIALISTS

Minerals Information commodity specialists collect and analyze information on production, trade, and consumption of minerals from raw material through refining to finished products. Mineral commodity specialists can answer questions on these aspects of a mineral commodity. https://www.usgs.gov/centers/nmic/commodity-statistics-and-information

Abrasives, Manufactured
Donald Olson
(703) 648-7721
dolson@usgs.gov

Aggregates
Jason Christopher Willett
(703) 648-6473
jwillett@usgs.gov

Alumina
Adam Merrill
(703) 648-7715
amerrill@usgs.gov

Aluminum
Adam Merrill
(703) 648-7715
amerrill@usgs.gov

Aluminum Oxide, Fused
Donald Olson
(703) 648-7721
dolson@usgs.gov

Antimony
Kateryna Klochko
(703) 648-4977
kklochko@usgs.gov

Arsenic
Michael W. George
(703) 648-4962
mgeorge@usgs.gov

Asbestos
Daniel M. Flanagan
(703) 648-7726
dflanagan@usgs.gov

Barite
Michele E. McRae
(703) 648-7743
mmcrae@usgs.gov

Bauxite
Adam Merrill
(703) 648-7715
amerrill@usgs.gov

Bentonite (Clay minerals)
Kristi Simmons
kjsimmons@usgs.gov

Beryllium
Brian W. Jaskula
(703) 648-4908
bjaskula@usgs.gov

Bismuth
Adam Merrill
(703) 648-7715
amerrill@usgs.gov

Boron
Amanda Brioche
(703) 648-7747
abrioche@usgs.gov

Bromine
Emily K. Schnebele
(703) 648-4945
eschnebele@usgs.gov

Cadmium
Robert M. Callaghan
(703) 648-7709
rcallaghan@usgs.gov

Calcium Carbonate (Crushed Stone, Lime)
Jason Christopher Willett
(703) 648-6473
jwillett@usgs.gov

Cement
Ashley Hatfield
(703) 648-7751
ahatfield@usgs.gov

Cesium
Christopher Candice Tuck
(703) 648-4912
ctuck@usgs.gov

Chromium
Ruth Schulte
(703) 648-4963
rschulte@usgs.gov

Coal Combustion Products
Robert D. Crangle
(703) 648-6410
rcrangle@usgs.gov

Cobalt
Kim B. Shedd
(703) 648-4974
kshedd@usgs.gov

Columbium (Niobium)
Chad Friedline
cfriedline@usgs.gov

Copper
Daniel M. Flanagan
(703) 648-7726
dflanagan@usgs.gov

Corundum (Manufactured Abrasives)
Donald Olson
(703) 648-7721
dolson@usgs.gov

Crushed Stone
Jason Christopher Willett
(703) 648-6473
jwillett@usgs.gov

Diamond, Industrial
Donald W. Olson
(703) 648-7721
dolson@usgs.gov

Diatomite
Robert D. Crangle
(703) 648-6410
rcrangle@usgs.gov

Dimension Stone
Jason Williams
(703) 648-7749
jrwilliams@usgs.gov

Explosives
Lori E. Apodaca
(703) 648-7724
lapodaca@usgs.gov

Feldspar
James (JJ) Barry
jbarry@usgs.gov

Ferroalloys
Ruth F. Schulte
(703) 648-4963
rschulte@usgs.gov

Fluorspar
Michele E. McRae
(703) 648-7743
mmcrae@usgs.gov

Fuller's Earth (Clay Minerals)
Kristi Simmons
kjsimmons@usgs.gov

Gallium
Brian W. Jaskula
(703) 648-4908
bjaskula@usgs.gov

Garnet, Industrial
Donald Olson
(703) 648-7721
dolson@usgs.gov

Gemstones
Donald W. Olson
(703) 648-7721
dolson@usgs.gov

Germanium
Amy Tolcin
(703) 648-4940
atolcin@usgs.gov

Gold
Kristine Sheaffer
(703) 648-4954
ksheaffer@usgs.gov

Graphite
Andrew A. Stewart
(703) 648-7723
astewart@usgs.gov

Gypsum
Robert D. Crangle
(703) 648-6410
rcrangle@usgs.gov

Hafnium
Joseph Gambogi
(703) 648-7718
jgambogi@usgs.gov

Helium
Robert C Goodin
(703) 648-7710
rgoodin@usgs.gov

Ilmenite (Titanium Mineral Concentrates)
Joseph Gambogi
(703) 648-7718
jgambogi@usgs.gov

Indium
Amy Tolcin
(703) 648-4940
atolcin@usgs.gov

Iodine
Emily K. Schnebele
(703) 648-4945
eschnebele@usgs.gov

Iridium (Platinum-Group Metals)
Ruth F. Schulte
(703) 648-4963
rschulte@usgs.gov

Iron Ore
Candice Tuck
(703) 648-4912
ctuck@usgs.gov

Iron and Steel Scrap
Candice Tuck
(703) 648-4912
ctuck@usgs.gov

Iron and Steel Slag
Candice Tuck
(703) 648-4912
ctuck@usgs.gov

Iron Oxide Pigments
Ji-Eun (JJ) Kim
ji-eunkim@usgs.gov

Kaolin (Clay Minerals)
Kristi Simmons
kjsimmons@usgs.gov

Kyanite and Related Minerals
Ashley Hatfield
(703) 648-7751
ahatfield@usgs.gov

Lead
Kateryna Klochko
(703) 648-4977
kklochko@usgs.gov

Lime
Lori Apodaca
(703) 648-7724
lapodaca@usgs.gov

Lithium
Brian W. Jaskula
(703) 648-4908
bjaskula@usgs.gov

Magnesium
Lee Bray
(703) 648-4979
lbray@usgs.gov

Magnesium Compounds
Adam Merrill
(703) 648-7715
amerrill@usgs.gov

Manganese
Ji-Eun (JJ) Kim
ji-eunkim@usgs.gov

Mercury
Kristine Sheaffer
(703) 648-4954
ksheaffer@usgs.gov

Mica
Stephen Jasinski
(703) 648-7711
sjasinsk@usgs.gov

Molybdenum
Desiree E. Polyak
(703) 648-4909
dpolyak@usgs.gov

Mullite, Synthetic (Kyanite)
Ashley Hatfield
(703) 648-7751
ahatfield@usgs.gov

Nepheline Syenite (Feldspar)
James (JJ) Barry
jbarry@usgs.gov

Nickel
Michele E. McRae
(703) 648-7743
mmcrae@usgs.gov

Niobium
Chad Friedline
cfriedline@usgs.gov

Nitrogen
Lori E. Apodaca
(703) 648-7724
lapodaca@usgs.gov

Osmium (Platinum-Group Metals)
Ruth F. Schulte
(703) 648-4963
rschulte@usgs.gov

Palladium (Platinum-Group Metals)
Ruth F. Schulte
(703) 648-4963
rschulte@usgs.gov

Peat
Amanda Brioche
(703) 648-7747
abrioche@usgs.gov

Perlite
Kristi Simmons
kjsimmons@usgs.gov

Phosphate Rock
Stephen Jasinski
(703) 648-7711
sjasinsk@usgs.gov

Platinum-Group Metals
Ruth F. Schulte
(703) 648-4963
rschulte@usgs.gov

Potash
Stephen Jasinski
(703) 648-7711
sjasinsk@usgs.gov

Pumice and Pumicite
Robert Crangle
(703) 648-6410
rcrangle@usgs.gov

Pyrophyllite (Talc)
Amanda Brioche
(703) 648-7747
abrioche@usgs.gov

Quartz Crystal (Silica)
Robert C Goodin
(703) 648-7710
rgoodin@usgs.gov

Rare Earths
Daniel J. Cordier
dcordier@usgs.gov

Recycling
Elizabeth Sangine
(703) 648-7720
escottsangine@usgs.gov

Rhenium
Desiree E. Polyak
(703) 648-4909
dpolyak@usgs.gov

Rhodium (Platinum-Group Metals)
Ruth F. Schulte
(703) 648-4963
rschulte@usgs.gov

Rubidium (Cesium)
Candice Tuck
(703) 648-4912
ctuck@usgs.gov

Ruthenium (Platinum-Group Metals)
Ruth F. Schulte
(703) 648-4963
rschulte@usgs.gov

Rutile (Titanium Mineral Concentrates)
Joseph Gambogi
(703) 648-7718
jgambogi@usgs.gov

Salt
Wallace Bolen
(703) 648-7727
wbolen@usgs.gov

Sand and Gravel, Construction
Jason Christopher Willett
(703) 648-6473
jwillett@usgs.gov

Sand and Gravel, Industrial (Silica)
Robert C Goodin
(703) 648-7710
rgoodin@usgs.gov

Scandium (Rare Earths)
Daniel J. Cordier
dcordier@usgs.gov

Selenium
Daniel M Flanagan
(703) 648-7726
dflanagan@usgs.gov

Shell (Gemstones)
Donald W. Olson
(703) 648-7721
dolson@usgs.gov

Silica
Robert C Goodin
(703) 648-7710
rgoodin@usgs.gov

Silicon
Emily Schnebele
(703) 648-4945
eschnebele@usgs.gov

Silicon Carbide (Manufactured Abrasives)
Donald Olson
(703) 648-7721
dolson@usgs.gov

Silver
Anne Hartingh
ahartingh@usgs.gov

Soda Ash
Wallace P. Bolen
(703) 648-7727
wbolen@usgs.gov

Sodium Sulfate
Wallace P. Bolen
(703) 648-7727
wbolen@usgs.gov

Steel
Candice Tuck
(703) 648-4912
ctuck@usgs.gov

Stone, Crushed
Jason Christopher Willett
(703) 648-6473
jwillett@usgs.gov

Stone, Dimension
Jason Williams
(703) 648-7740
jrwilliams@usgs.gov

Strontium
Ashley Hatfield
(703) 648-7751
ahatfield@usgs.gov

Sulfur
Lori Apodaca
(703) 648-7724
lapodaca@usgs.gov

Talc
Amanda Brioche
(703) 648-7747
abrioche@usgs.gov

Tantalum
Chad Friedline
cfriedline@usgs.gov

Tellurium
Daniel M Flanagan
(703) 648-7726
dflanagan@usgs.gov

Thallium
Robert M Callaghan
(703) 648-7709
rcallaghan@usgs.gov

Thorium
Daniel J. Cordier

dcordier@usgs.gov

Tin
Chad Friedline
cfriedline@usgs.gov

Titanium
Joseph Gambogi
(703) 648-7718
jgambogi@usgs.gov

Titanium Dioxide
Joseph Gambogi
(703) 648-7718
jgambogi@usgs.gov

Titanium Mineral Concentrates
Joseph Gambogi
(703) 648-7718
jgambogi@usgs.gov

Traprock (Crushed Stone)
Jason Christopher Willett
(703) 648-6473
jwillett@usgs.gov

Tripoli (Silica)
Robert C Goodin
(703) 648-7710
rgoodin@usgs.gov

Tungsten
Kim Shedd
(703) 648-4974
kshedd@usgs.gov

Vanadium
Desiree E. Polyak
(703) 648-4909
dpolyak@usgs.gov

Vermiculite
Kristi Simmons
kjsimmons@usgs.gov

Wollastonite
Elizabeth Sangine
(703) 648-7720
escottsangine@usgs.gov

Yttrium (Rare Earths)
Daniel J. Cordier
dcordier@usgs.gov

Zeolites
Jason Williams
(703) 648-7740
jrwilliams@usgs.gov

Zinc
Amy Tolcin
(703) 648-4940
atolcin@usgs.gov

Zirconium
Joseph Gambogi
(703) 648-7718
jgambogi@usgs.gov

COUNTRY SPECIALISTS

Minerals information country specialists at the U.S. Geological Survey collect and analyze information on the mineral industries of more than 170 nations throughout the world. The specialists are available to answer minerals-related questions concerning individual countries. https://www.usgs.gov/centers/nmic/country-specialists

Afghanistan
Keita Decarlo
(703) 648-7716
Fax: (703) 648-7737
kdecarlo@usgs.gov

Albania
Kristian Macias
(703) 648-4902
Fax: (703) 648-7737
kmacias@usgs.gov

Algeria
Mowafa Taib
(703) 648-4986
Fax: (703) 648-7737
mtaib@usgs.gov

Angola
Meralis Plaza-Toledo
(703) 648-7759
Fax: (703) 648-7737
mplaza-toledo@usgs.gov

Antarctica
Steven D. Textoris
(703) 648-4976
Fax: (703) 648-7737
stextoris@usgs.gov

Argentina
Jesse J. Inestroza
(703) 648-7779
Fax: (703) 648-7737
jinestroza@usgs.gov

Armenia
Elena Safirova
(703) 648-7731
Fax: (703) 648-7737
esafirova@usgs.gov

Aruba
Yadira Soto-Viruet
(703) 648-4957
Fax: (703) 648-7737
ysoto-viruet@usgs.gov

Australia
Loyd Trimmer
(703) 648-4983
Fax: (703) 648-7737
ltrimmer@usgs.gov

Austria
Elena Safirova
(703) 648-7731
Fax: (703) 648-7737
esafirova@usgs.gov

Azerbaijan
Elena Safirova
(703) 648-7731
Fax: (703) 648-7737
esafirova@usgs.gov

Bahamas, The
Yadira Soto-Viruet
(703) 648-4957
Fax: (703) 648-7737
ysoto-viruet@usgs.gov

Bahrain
Imam Salehihikouei
(703) 648-7744
Fax: (703) 648-7737
isalehihikouei@usgs.gov

Bangladesh
Keita Decarlo
(703) 648-7716
Fax: (703) 648-7737
kdecarlo@usgs.gov

Barbados
Yadira Soto-Viruet
(703) 648-4957
Fax: (703) 648-7737
ysoto-viruet@usgs.gov

Belarus
Elena Safirova
(703) 648-7731
Fax: (703) 648-7737
esafirova@usgs.gov

Belgium
Elizabeth Neustaedter
(703) 648-7732
Fax: (703) 648-7737
eneustaedter@usgs.gov

Belize
Jesse J. Inestroza
(703) 648-7779
Fax: (703) 648-7737
jinestroza@usgs.gov

Benin
Meralis Plaza-Toledo
(703) 648-7759
Fax: (703) 648-7737
mplaza-toledo@usgs.gov

Bhutan
Keita Decarlo
(703) 648-7716
Fax: (703) 648-7737
kdecarlo@usgs.gov

Bolivia
Yolanda Fong-Sam
(703) 648-7756
Fax: (703) 648-7737
yfong-sam@usgs.gov

Bosnia and Herzegovina
Karine Renaud
(703) 648-7748
Fax: (703) 648-7737
krenaud@usgs.gov

Botswana
Thomas R. Yager
(703) 648-7739
Fax: (703) 648-7737
tyager@usgs.gov

Brazil
Yolanda Fong-Sam
(703) 648-7756
Fax: (703) 648-7737
yfong-sam@usgs.gov

Brunei
Kathleen Gans
(703) 648-4905
Fax: (703) 648-7737
kgans@usgs.gov

Bulgaria
Karine Renaud
(703) 648-7748
Fax: (703) 648-7737
krenaud@usgs.gov

Burkina Faso
Alberto A. Perez
(703) 648-7749
Fax: (703) 648-7737
aperez@usgs.gov

Burma (Myanmar)
Kathleen Gans
(703) 648-4905
Fax: (703) 648-7737
kgans@usgs.gov

Burundi
Thomas R. Yager
(703) 648-7739
Fax: (703) 648-7737
tyager@usgs.gov

Cabo Verde (formerly Cape Verde)
Meralis Plaza-Toledo
(703) 648-7759
Fax: (703) 648-7737
mplaza-toledo@usgs.gov

Cambodia
Kathleen Gans
(703) 648-4905
Fax: (703) 648-7737
kgans@usgs.gov

Cameroon
Jaewon Chung
(703) 648-4793
Fax: (703) 648-7737
jchung@usgs.gov

Canada
Jesse J. Inestroza
(703) 648-7779
Fax: (703) 648-7737
jinestroza@usgs.gov

Central African Republic
Ji Won Moon
(703) 648-7791
Fax: (703) 648-7737
jmoon@usgs.gov

Chad
Meralis Plaza-Toledo
(703) 648-7759
Fax: (703) 648-7737
mplaza-toledo@usgs.gov

Chile
Yadira Soto-Viruet
(703) 648-4957
Fax: (703) 648-7737

ysoto-viruet@usgs

China
Ji Won Moon
(703) 648-7791
Fax: (703) 648-7737
jmoon@usgs.gov

Christmas Island
Omayra Bermudez-Lugo
(703) 648-4946
Fax: (703) 648-7737
obermude@usgs.gov

Colombia
Jesse J. Inestroza
(703) 648-7779
Fax: (703) 648-7737
jinestroza@usgs.gov

Comoros
Ji Won Moon
(703) 648-7791
Fax: (703) 648-7737
jmoon@usgs.gov

Congo (Brazzaville)
Ji Won Moon
(703) 648-7791
Fax: (703) 648-7737
jmoon@usgs.gov

Congo (Kinshasa)
Thomas R. Yager
(703) 648-7739
Fax: (703) 648-7737
tyager@usgs.gov

Costa Rica
Jesse J. Inestroza
(703) 648-7779
Fax: (703) 648-7737
jinestroza@usgs.gov

COTE d'IVOIRE
Alberto A. Perez
(703) 648-7749
Fax: (703) 648-7737
aperez@usgs.gov

Croatia
Kathleen Trafton
(703) 648-4903
Fax: (703) 648-7737
ktrafton@usgs.gov

Cuba
Yadira Soto-Viruet
(703) 648-4957
Fax: (703) 648-7737
ysoto-viruet@usgs.gov

Cyprus
Kristian Macias
(703) 648-4902
Fax: (703) 648-7737
kmacias@usgs.gov

Czechia (Czech Republic)
Elizabeth Neustaedter
(703) 648-7732
Fax: (703) 648-7737
eneustaedter@usgs.gov

Denmark
Joanna Goclawska
(703) 648-7973
Fax: (703) 648-7737
jgoclawska@usgs.gov

Djibouti
Thomas R.Yager
(703) 648-7739
Fax: (703) 648-7737
tyager@usgs.gov

Dominican Republic
Yadira Soto-Viruet
(703) 648-4957
Fax: (703) 648-7737
ysoto-viruet@usgs.gov

Ecuador
Jesse J. Inestroza
(703) 648-7779
Fax: (703) 648-7737
jinestroza@usgs.gov

Egypt
Mowafa Taib
(703) 648-4986
Fax: (703) 648-7737
mtaib@usgs.gov

El Salvador
Jesse J. Inestroza
(703) 648-7779
Fax: (703) 648-7737
jinestroza@usgs.gov

Equatorial Guinea
Meralis Plaza-Toledo
(703) 648-7759
Fax: (703) 648-7737
mplaza-toledo@usgs.gov

Eritrea
Thomas R. Yager
(703) 648-7739
Fax: (703) 648-7737
tyager@usgs.gov

Estonia
Joanna Goclawska
(703) 648-7973
Fax: (703) 648-7737
jgoclawska@usgs.gov

Eswatnini (Swaziland)
Ji Won Moon
(703) 648-7791
Fax: (703) 648-7737
jmoon@usgs.gov

Ethiopia
Meralis Plaza-Toledo
(703) 648-7759
Fax: (703) 648-7737
mplaza-toledo@usgs.gov

Faroe Islands
Joanna Goclawska
(703) 648-7973
Fax: (703) 648-7737
jgoclawska@usgs.gov

Fiji
Loyd Trimmer
(703) 648-4983
Fax: (703) 648-7737
ltrimmer@usgs.gov

Finland
Joanna Goclawska
(703) 648-7973
Fax: (703) 648-7737
jgoclawska@usgs.gov

France
Kathleen Trafton
(703) 648-4903
Fax: (703) 648-7737
ktrafton@usgs.gov

French Guiana
Yolanda Fong-Sam
(703) 648-7756
Fax: (703) 648-7737
yfong-sam@usgs.gov

Gabon
Alberto A. Perez
(703) 648-7749
Fax: (703) 648-7737
aperez@usgs.gov

Gambia, The
Meralis Plaza-Toledo
(703) 648-7759
Fax: (703) 648-7737
mplaza-toledo@usgs.gov

Georgia
Elena Safirova
(703) 648-7731
Fax: (703) 648-7737
esafirova@usgs.gov

Germany
Karine Renaud
(703) 648-7748
Fax: (703) 648-7737
krenaud@usgs.gov

Ghana
Meralis Plaza-Toledo
(703) 648-7759
Fax: (703) 648-7737
mplaza-toledo@usgs.gov

Greece
Kristian Macias
(703) 648-4902
Fax: (703) 648-7737
kmacias@usgs.gov

Greenland (See Denmark)

Guatemala
Jesse J. Inestroza
(703) 648-7779
Fax: (703) 648-7737
jinestroza@usgs.gov

Guinea
Alberto A. Perez
(703) 648-7749
Fax: (703) 648-7737
aperez@usgs.gov

Guinea-Bissau
Meralis Plaza-Toledo
(703) 648-7759
Fax: (703) 648-7737
mplaza-toledo@usgs.gov

Guyana
Yolanda Fong-Sam
(703) 648-7756
Fax: (703) 648-7737
yfong-sam@usgs.gov

Haiti
Yadira Soto-Viruet
(703) 648-4957
Fax: (703) 648-7737
ysoto-viruet@usgs.gov

Honduras
Jesse J. Inestroza
(703) 648-7779
Fax: (703) 648-7737
jinestroza@usgs.gov

Hungary
Elizabeth Neustaedter
(703) 648-7732
Fax: (703) 648-7737
eneustaedter@usgs.gov

Iceland
Joanna Goclawska
(703) 648-7973
Fax: (703) 648-7737
jgoclawska@usgs.gov

India
Keita Decarlo
(703) 648-7716
Fax: (703) 648-7737
kdecarlo@usgs.gov

Indonesia
Jaewon Chung
(703) 648-4793
Fax: (703) 648-7737
jchung@usgs.gov

Iran
Imam Salehihikouei
(703) 648-7744
Fax: (703) 648-7737
isalehihikouei@usgs.gov

Iraq
Imam Salehihikouei
(703) 648-7744
Fax: (703) 648-7737
isalehihikouei@usgs.gov

Ireland
Joanna Goclawska
(703) 648-7973
Fax: (703) 648-7737
jgoclawska@usgs.gov

Israel
Imam Salehihikouei
(703) 648-7744
Fax: (703) 648-7737
isalehihikouei@usgs.gov

Italy
Loyd Trimmer
(703) 648-4983
Fax: (703) 648-7737
ltrimmer@usgs.gov

Jamaica
Yadira Soto-Viruet
(703) 648-4957
Fax: (703) 648-7737
ysoto-viruet@usgs.gov

Japan
Keita Decarlo
(703) 648-7716
Fax: (703) 648-7737
kdecarlo@usgs.gov

Jordan
Mowafa Taib
(703) 648-4986
Fax: (703) 648-7737
mtaib@usgs.gov

Kazakhstan
Elena Safirova
(703) 648-7731
Fax: (703) 648-7737
esafirova@usgs.gov

Kenya
Thomas R. Yager
(703) 648-7739
Fax: (703) 648-7737
tyager@usgs.gov

Korea, North
Jaewon Chung
(703) 648-4793
Fax: (703) 648-7737
jchung@usgs.gov

Korea, Republic of
Jaewon Chung
(703) 648-4793
Fax: (703) 648-7737
jchung@usgs.gov

Kosovo
Kristian Macias
(703) 648-4902
Fax: (703) 648-7737
kmacias@usgs.gov

Kuwait
Imam Salehihikouei
(703) 648-7744
Fax: (703) 648-7737
isalehihikouei@usgs.gov

Kyrgyzstan
Karine Renaud
(703) 648-7748
Fax: (703) 648-7737
krenaud@usgs.gov

Laos
Kathleen Gans
(703) 648-4905
Fax: (703) 648-7737
kgans@usgs.gov

Latvia
Joanna Goclawska
(703) 648-7973
Fax: (703) 648-7737
jgoclawska@usgs.gov

Lebanon
Mowafa Taib
(703) 648-4986
Fax: (703) 648-7737
mtaib@usgs.gov

Lesotho
Ji Won Moon
(703) 648-7791
Fax: (703) 648-7737
jmoon@usgs.gov

Liberia
Meralis Plaza-Toledo
(703) 648-7759
Fax: (703) 648-7737
mplaza-toledo@usgs.gov

Libya
Mowafa Taib
(703) 648-4986
Fax: (703) 648-7737
mtaib@usgs.gov

Lithuania
Joanna Goclawska
(703) 648-7973
Fax: (703) 648-7737
jgoclawska@usgs.gov

Luxembourg
Keita Decarlo
(703) 648-7716
Fax: (703) 648-7737
kdecarlo@usgs.gov

Macedonia (See North Macedonia)

Madagascar
Thomas R. Yager
(703) 648-7739
Fax: (703) 648-7737
tyager@usgs.gov

Malawi
Thomas R. Yager
(703) 648-7739
Fax: (703) 648-7737
tyager@usgs.gov

Malaysia
Jaewon Chung
(703) 648-4793
Fax: (703) 648-7737
jchung@usgs.gov

Mali
Alberto A. Perez
(703) 648-7749
Fax: (703) 648-7737
aperez@usgs.gov

Malta
Kristian Macias
(703) 648-4902
Fax: (703) 648-7737
kmacias@usgs.gov

Mauritania
Mowafa Taib
(703) 648-4986
Fax: (703) 648-7737
mtaib@usgs.gov

Mauritius
Ji Won Moon
(703) 648-7791
Fax: (703) 648-7737
jmoon@usgs.gov

Mexico
Alberto A. Perez
(703) 648-7749
Fax: (703) 648-7737
aperez@usgs.gov

Moldova
Elena Safirova
(703) 648-7731
Fax: (703) 648-7737
esafirova@usgs.gov

Mongolia
Jaewon Chung
(703) 648-4793
Fax: (703) 648-7737
jchung@usgs.gov

Montenegro
Kristian Macias
(703) 648-4902
Fax: (703) 648-7737
kmacias@usgs.gov

Morocco & Western Sahara
Mowafa Taib
(703) 648-4986
Fax: (703) 648-7737
mtaib@usgs.gov

Mozambique
Meralis Plaza-Toledo
(703) 648-7759
Fax: (703) 648-7737
mplaza-toledo@usgs.gov

Namibia
Philip Szczesniak
(703) 648-7728
Fax: (703) 648-7737
pszczesniak@usgs.gov

Nauru
Loyd Trimmer
(703) 648-4983
Fax: (703) 648-7737
ltrimmer@usgs.gov

Nepal
Keita Decarlo
(703) 648-7716
Fax: (703) 648-7737
kdecarlo@usgs.gov

Netherlands
Elizabeth Neustaedter
(703) 648-7732
Fax: (703) 648-7737
eneustaedter@usgs.gov

New Caledonia
Loyd Trimmer
(703) 648-4983
Fax: (703) 648-7737
ltrimmer@usgs.gov

New Zealand
Loyd Trimmer
(703) 648-4983
Fax: (703) 648-7737
ltrimmer@usgs.gov

Nicaragua
Jesse J. Inestroza
(703) 648-7779
Fax: (703) 648-7737
jinestroza@usgs.gov

Niger
Alberto A. Perez
(703) 648-7749
Fax: (703) 648-7737
aperez@usgs.gov

Nigeria
Thomas R. Yager
(703) 648-7739
Fax: (703) 648-7737
tyager@usgs.gov

North Macedonia
Kathleen Trafton
(703) 648-4903
Fax: (703) 648-7737
ktrafton@usgs.gov

Norway
Joanna Goclawska
(703) 648-7973
Fax: (703) 648-7737
jgoclawska@usgs.gov

Oman
Imam Salehihikouei
(703) 648-7744
Fax: (703) 648-7737
isalehihikouei@usgs.gov

Pakistan
Kathleen Gans
(703) 648-4905
Fax: (703) 648-7737
kgans@usgs.gov

Panama
Jesse J. Inestroza
(703) 648-7779
Fax: (703) 648-7737
jinestroza@usgs.gov

Papua New Guinea
Loyd Trimmer
(703) 648-4983
Fax: (703) 648-7737
ltrimmer@usgs.gov

Paraguay
Yadira Soto-Viruet
(703) 648-4957
Fax: (703) 648-7737
ysoto-viruet@usgs.gov

Peru
Yadira Soto-Viruet
(703) 648-4957
Fax: (703) 648-7737
ysoto-viruet@usgs.gov

Philippines
Ji Won Moon
(703) 648-7791
Fax: (703) 648-7737
jmoon@usgs.gov

Poland
Joanna Goclawska
(703) 648-7973
Fax: (703) 648-7737
jgoclawska@usgs.gov

Portugal
Kristian Macias
(703) 648-4902
Fax: (703) 648-7737
kmacias@usgs.gov

Qatar
Imam Salehihikouei
(703) 648-7744
Fax: (703) 648-7737
isalehihikouei@usgs.gov

Reunion
Ji Won Moon
(703) 648-7791
Fax: (703) 648-7737
jmoon@usgs.gov

Romania
Keita Decarlo
(703) 648-7716
Fax: (703) 648-7737
kdecarlo@usgs.gov

Russia
Elena Safirova
(703) 648-7731
Fax: (703) 648-7737
esafirova@usgs.gov

Rwanda
Thomas R. Yager
(703) 648-7739
Fax: (703) 648-7737
tyager@usgs.gov

Sao Tome and Principe
Meralis Plaza-Toledo
(703) 648-7759
Fax: (703) 648-7737
mplaza-toledo@usgs.gov

Saudi Arabia
Mowafa Taib
(703) 648-4986
Fax: (703) 648-7737
mtaib@usgs.gov

Senegal
Alberto A. Perez
(703) 648-7749
Fax: (703) 648-7737
aperez@usgs.gov

Serbia
Karine Renaud
(703) 648-7748
Fax: (703) 648-7737
krenaud@usgs.gov

Seychelles
Ji Won Moon
(703) 648-7791
Fax: (703) 648-7737
jmoon@usgs.gov

Sierra Leone
Alberto A. Perez
(703) 648-7749
Fax: (703) 648-7737
aperez@usgs.gov

Singapore
Kathleen Gans
(703) 648-4905
Fax: (703) 648-7737
kgans@usgs.gov

Slovakia
Elizabeth Neustaedter
(703) 648-7732
Fax: (703) 648-7737
eneustaedter@usgs.gov

Slovenia
Elizabeth Neustaedter
(703) 648-7732
Fax: (703) 648-7737
eneustaedter@usgs.gov

Solomon Islands
Jaewon Chung
(703) 648-4793
Fax: (703) 648-7737
jchung@usgs.gov

Somalia
Loyd Trimmer
(703) 648-4983
Fax: (703) 648-7737
ltrimmer@usgs.gov

South Africa
Thomas R. Yager
(703) 648-7739
Fax: (703) 648-7737
tyager@usgs.gov

South Sudan
Alberto A. Perez
(703) 648-7749
Fax: (703) 648-7737
aperez@usgs.gov

Spain
Kristian Macias
(703) 648-4902
Fax: (703) 648-7737
kmacias@usgs.gov

Sri Lanka
Keita Decarlo
(703) 648-7716
Fax: (703) 648-7737
kdecarlo@usgs.gov

Sudan
Mowafa Taib
(703) 648-4986
Fax: (703) 648-7737
mtaib@usgs.gov

Suriname
Yolanda Fong-Sam
(703) 648-7756
Fax: (703) 648-7737
yfong-sam@usgs.gov

Swaziland (See Eswatini)

Sweden
Joanna Goclawska
(703) 648-7973
Fax: (703) 648-7737
jgoclawska@usgs.gov

Switzerland
Kathleen Trafton
(703) 648-4903
Fax: (703) 648-7737
ktrafton@usgs.gov

Syria
Mowafa Taib
(703) 648-4986
Fax: (703) 648-7737
mtaib@usgs.gov

Taiwan
Jaewon Chung
(703) 648-4793
Fax: (703) 648-7737
jchung@usgs.gov

Tajikistan
Karine Renaud
(703) 648-7748
Fax: (703) 648-7737
krenaud@usgs.gov

Tanzania
Thomas R. Yager
(703) 648-7739
Fax: (703) 648-7737
tyager@usgs.gov

Thailand
Kathleen Gans
(703) 648-4905
Fax: (703) 648-7737
kgans@usgs.gov

Timor-Leste
Loyd Trimmer
(703) 648-4983
Fax: (703) 648-7737
ltrimmer@usgs.gov

Togo
Alberto A. Perez
(703) 648-7749
Fax: (703) 648-7737
aperez@usgs.gov

Trinidad and Tobago
Yadira Soto-Viruet
(703) 648-4957
Fax: (703) 648-7737
ysoto-viruet@usgs.gov

Tunisia
Mowafa Taib
(703) 648-4986
Fax: (703) 648-7737
mtaib@usgs.gov

Turkey
Loyd Trimmer
(703) 648-4983
Fax: (703) 648-7737
ltrimmer@usgs.gov

Turkmenistan
Karine Renaud
(703) 648-7748
Fax: (703) 648-7737
krenaud@usgs.gov

Uganda
Thomas R. Yager
(703) 648-7739
Fax: (703) 648-7737
tyager@usgs.gov

Ukraine
Elena Safirova
(703) 648-7731
Fax: (703) 648-7737
esafirova@usgs.gov

United Arab Emirates
Imam Salehihikouei
(703) 648-7744
Fax: (703) 648-7737
isalehihikouei@usgs.gov

United Kingdom
Kathleen Trafton
(703) 648-4903
Fax: (703) 648-7737
ktrafton@usgs.gov

Uruguay
Yadira Soto-Viruet
(703) 648-4957
Fax: (703) 648-7737
ysoto-viruet@usgs.gov

Uzbekistan
Elena Safirova
(703) 648-7731
Fax: (703) 648-7737
esafirova@usgs.gov

Venezuela
Yolanda Fong-Sam
(703) 648-7756
Fax: (703) 648-7737
yfong-sam@usgs.gov

Vietnam
Ji Won Moon
(703) 648-7791
Fax: (703) 648-7737
jmoon@usgs.gov

Western Sahara
Mowafa Taib
(703) 648-4986
Fax: (703) 648-7737
mtaib@usgs.gov

Yemen
Mowafa Taib
(703) 648-4986
Fax: (703) 648-7737
mtaib@usgs.gov

Zaire (See Congo Kinshasa)

Zambia
Philip Szczesniak
(703) 648-7728
Fax: (703) 648-7737
pszczesniak@usgs.gov

Zimbabwe
Philip Szczesniak
(703) 648-7728
Fax: (703) 648-7737
pszczesniak@usgs.gov

Other Countries
Steven D. Textoris
(703) 648-4976
Fax: (703) 648-7737
stextoris@usgs.gov

RURAL DEVELOPMENT

The U.S. Department of Agriculture's Rural Development office administers rural business, cooperative, housing, utilities and community development programs. Its financial programs support such essential public facilities and services as water and sewer systems, housing, health clinics, emergency service facilities and electric and telephone service. The office promotes economic development by supporting loans to businesses through banks and community-managed lending pools. Valuable statistical data is collected in this process. For more information please visit https://www.rd.usda.gov/ or telephone (800) 414-1226.

SOCIAL SECURITY

The Social Security Administration (SSA) collects a great deal of data on the composition of the population in relation to demographic information such as age and income levels, and the years of population ncentration. The statistics deal with historic, current and projected trends. The main office can direct callers to staff specialists who are knowledgeable on specific subjects; the general information number is (800) 772-1213. Website: https://www.ssa.gov.

TRANSPORTATION

The U.S. Department of Transportation (DOT) establishes the nation's overall transportation policy. There are twelve separate administrations within the DOT whose main offices can direct callers to specialists who are knowledgeable on specific subjects. The website is: https://www.transportation.gov.

Office of the Secretary of Transportation (OST)
(202) 366-4000 https://www.transportation.gov/office-of-secretary

Federal Aviation Administration (FAA)
(202) 267-3883 https://www.faa.gov/

Federal Highway Administration (FHWA)
(202) 366-0660 https://highways.dot.gov/

Federal Motor Carrier Safety Administration (FMCSA)
(202) 366-9999 https://www.fmcsa.dot.gov/

Federal Railroad Administration (FRA)
(202) 493-6024 https://railroads.dot.gov/

Federal Transit Administration (FTA)
(202) 366-4043 https://www.transit.dot.gov/

Maritime Administration (MARAD)
(202) 366-5807 https://www.maritime.dot.gov/

National Highway Traffic Safety Administration (NHTSA)
(202) 366-9550 https://www.nhtsa.gov/

Office of the Inspector General (OIG)
(202) 366-8751 https://www.oig.dot.gov/

Pipeline and Hazardous Materials Administration (PHMSA)
(202) 366-4831 https://www.phmsa.dot.gov/

Saint Lawrence Seaway Development Corporation (SLSDC)
(202) 366-0091 https://www.seaway.dot.gov/

Surface Transportation Board (STB)
(202) 245-0245 https://prod.stb.gov/

ABORTION

FiveThirtyEight, 47 W 66th St., 2nd Fl., New York, NY, 10023, USA, contact@fivethirtyeight.com, https://fivethirtyeight.com/; Where Americans Stand on Abortion, in 5 Charts.

Guttmacher Institute, 125 Maiden Ln., 7th Fl., New York, NY, 10038, USA, (212) 248-1111, (800) 355-0244, (212) 248-1951, info@guttmacher.org, https://www.guttmacher.org/; Abortion Incidence and Unintended Pregnancy Among Adolescents in Zimbabwe; Anti-Abortion Judge Attempts to Ban Mifepristone Nationwide, Ignoring Science and More than Two Decades of the Drug's Safe Use in the United States; Data Center; Even Before Roe Was Overturned, Nearly One in 10 People Obtaining an Abortion Traveled Across State Lines for Care; Induced Abortion in the United States; Inequity in US Abortion Rights and Access: The End of Roe Is Deepening Existing Divides; State Facts About Abortion; State Policy Trends at Midyear 2022: With Roe About to Be Overturned, Some States Double Down on Abortion Restrictions; Unintended Pregnancy and Abortion by Income, Region, and the Legal Status of Abortion: Estimates from a Comprehensive Model for 1990-2019; Unintended Pregnancy and Abortion Worldwide; and Unintended Pregnancy in the United States.

Marist College Institute for Public Opinion, 3399 North Rd., Poughkeepsie, NY, 12601, USA, (845) 575-5050, https://maristpoll.marist.edu; Abortion Rights, May 2022.

National Organization for Women (NOW), 1100 H St. NW, Ste. 300, Washington, DC, 20005, USA, (202) 628-8669, (202) 331-9002 (TTY), https://now.org/; unpublished data.

Pew Research Center, Religion & Public Life, 1615 L St. NW, Ste. 800, Washington, DC, 20036, USA, (202) 419-4300, (202) 857-8562, https://www.pewforum.org/; What the Data Says About Abortion in the U.S..

PollingReport.com, USA, https://www.pollingreport.com/; Issues Facing the Nation.

Public Health Agency of Canada, 130 Colonnade Rd., Ottawa, ON, K1A 0K9, CAN, (844) 280-5020 (Dial from U.S.), https://www.phac-aspc.gc.ca/; Perinatal Health Indicators (PHI).

Public Religion Research Institute (PRRI), 1023 15th St. NW, 9th Fl., Washington, DC, 20005, USA, (202) 238-9424, info@prri.org, https://www.prri.org/; Competing Visions of America: An Evolving Identity or a Culture Under Attack? Findings from the 2021 American Values Survey.

United Nations UN Women, 405 E 42nd St., New York, NY, 10017-3599, USA, (646) 781-4400, (646) 781-4444, https://www.unwomen.org; Progress on the Sustainable Development Goals: The Gender Snapshot 2021.

ABORTION-LAW AND LEGISLATION

The Henry J. Kaiser Family Foundation (KFF), 185 Berry St., Ste. 2000, San Francisco, CA, 94107, USA, (650) 854-9400, (650) 854-4800, https://www.kff.org; Abortion in the United States.

Marist College Institute for Public Opinion, 3399 North Rd., Poughkeepsie, NY, 12601, USA, (845) 575-5050, https://maristpoll.marist.edu; Abortion Rights, May 2022.

Public Religion Research Institute (PRRI), 1023 15th St. NW, 9th Fl., Washington, DC, 20005, USA, (202) 238-9424, info@prri.org, https://www.prri.org/; Abortion Attitudes in a Post-Roe World: Findings From the 50-State 2022 American Values Atlas.

Union of Concerned Scientists (UCS), 2 Brattle Sq., Cambridge, MA, 02138-3780, USA, (617) 547-5552, (617) 864-9405, https://www.ucsusa.org/; Science Shows US Supreme Court Abortion, Guns, Environment Rulings Will Have Devastating Consequences.

ABORTION-POLITICAL ASPECTS

The Henry J. Kaiser Family Foundation (KFF), 185 Berry St., Ste. 2000, San Francisco, CA, 94107, USA, (650) 854-9400, (650) 854-4800, https://www.kff.org; Abortion in the United States.

Public Religion Research Institute (PRRI), 1023 15th St. NW, 9th Fl., Washington, DC, 20005, USA, (202) 238-9424, info@prri.org, https://www.prri.org/; Abortion Attitudes in a Post-Roe World: Findings From the 50-State 2022 American Values Atlas.

ABORTION APPLICANTS

The Urban Institute, 500 L'Enfant Plaza SW, Washington, DC, 20024, USA, (202) 833-7200, https://www.urban.org/; Research Shows Access to Legal Abortion Improves Women's Lives.

ABORTION SERVICES

The Henry J. Kaiser Family Foundation (KFF), 185 Berry St., Ste. 2000, San Francisco, CA, 94107, USA, (650) 854-9400, (650) 854-4800, https://www.kff.org; Abortion in the United States.

Union of Concerned Scientists (UCS), 2 Brattle Sq., Cambridge, MA, 02138-3780, USA, (617) 547-5552, (617) 864-9405, https://www.ucsusa.org/; Science Shows US Supreme Court Abortion, Guns, Environment Rulings Will Have Devastating Consequences.

The Urban Institute, 500 L'Enfant Plaza SW, Washington, DC, 20024, USA, (202) 833-7200, https://www.urban.org/; Research Shows Access to Legal Abortion Improves Women's Lives.

ABRASIVES

U.S. Department of the Interior (DOI), U.S. Geological Survey (USGS), National Minerals Information Center (NMIC), 12201 Sunrise Valley Dr., Reston, VA, 20192, USA, (703) 648-4920, (703) 648-7971, (703) 648-4995, sfortier@usgs.gov, https://www.usgs.gov/centers/nmic; Mineral Industry Surveys (MIS).

ABRASIVES-STONE

U.S. Department of the Interior (DOI), U.S. Geological Survey (USGS), National Minerals Information Center (NMIC), 12201 Sunrise Valley Dr., Reston, VA, 20192, USA, (703) 648-4920, (703) 648-7971, (703) 648-4995, sfortier@usgs.gov, https://www.usgs.gov/centers/nmic; Mineral Commodity Summaries 2022.

ABSENTEE VOTING

American Civil Liberties Union (ACLU), 125 Broad St. , 18th Fl., New York, NY, 10004, USA, (212) 549-2500, https://www.aclu.org/; Racial Justice Demands That Every Vote Is Counted: Discounting Mail-In Ballots Will Disenfranchise Communities of Color and Distort Election Outcomes in Key Counties in Michigan, Wisconsin, Pennsylvania, and Georgia.

ABUSED CHILDREN

National Indian Child Welfare Association (NICWA), 5100 SW Macadam Ave., Ste. 300, Portland, OR, 97239, USA, (503) 222-4044, info@nicwa.org, https://www.nicwa.org/; unpublished data.

The Stimson Center, 1211 Connecticut Ave. NW, 8th Fl., Washington, DC, 20036, USA, (202) 223-5956, (202) 238-9604, communications@stimson.org, https://www.stimson.org/; 2022 Human Rights Reports: Insights Into Global Child Soldier Recruitment and Use.

ABUSED MEN

U.S. Department of Defense (DOD), Sexual Assault Prevention and Response Office (SAPRO), 1400 Defense Pentagon, Washington, DC, 20301, USA, (571) 372-2657, whs.mc-alex.wso.mbx.sapro@mail.mil, https://www.sapr.mil/; Annual Report on Sexual Assault in the Military, Fiscal Year 2022.

ABUSED WOMEN

The European Institute for Crime Prevention and Control, Affiliated with the United Nations (HEUNI), Vilhonkatu 4 B 19, Helsinki, FI-00101, FIN, heuni@om.fi, https://heuni.fi/; Unseen Victims: Why Refugee Women Victims of Gender-Based Violence Do Not Receive Assistance in the EU.

ACADEMIC FREEDOM

Foundation for Individual Rights and Expression (FIRE), 510 Walnut St., Ste. 1250, Philadelphia, PA, 19106, USA, (215) 717-3473, fire@thefire.org, https://www.thefire.org/; The Academic Mind in 2022: What Faculty Think About Free Expression and Academic Freedom on Campus; 2023 College Free Speech Rankings; Scholars Under Fire: Attempts to Sanction Scholars from 2000 to 2022; and Spotlight on Speech Codes 2023.

ACCIDENTS

Association of American Railroads (AAR), 425 3rd St. SW, Washington, DC, 20024, USA, (202) 639-2100, https://www.aar.org; Analysis of Class I Railroads 2021 and Railroad Facts 2022.

European Commission, Directorate-General for Health and Food Safety, Brussels, B-1049, BEL, https://ec.europa.eu/info/departments/health-and-food-safety_en ; zzunpublished data.

Google Public Data Directory, USA, https://www.google.com/publicdata/directory; Google Public Data Directory.

Insurance Institute for Highway Safety/Highway Loss Data Institute (IIHS/HLDI), 4121 Wilson Blvd., 6th Fl., Arlington, VA, 22203, USA, (703) 247-1500, (434) 985 4600, cmatthew@iihs.org, https://www.iihs.org/; Highway Safety Topics.

National Highway Traffic Safety Administration (NHTSA), National Center for Statistics and Analysis (NCSA), 1200 New Jersey Ave. SE, West Bldg., Washington, DC, 20590, USA, (800) 934-8517, (202) 366-2746, ncsarequests@dot.gov, https://www.nhtsa.gov/research-data/national-center-statistics-and-analysis-ncsa; Analysis of Real-World Crashes Where Involved Vehicles Were Equipped With Adaptive Equipment; Occupant Restraint Use in 2021: Results From the NOPUS Controlled Intersection Study; Traffic Safety Facts; Traffic Safety Facts, 2011-2020 Data - School-Transportation-Related Crashes; Traffic Safety Facts, 2019 Data - Motorcycles; Traffic Safety Facts, 2019 Data - Rural/Urban Comparison of Traffic Fatalities; Traffic Safety Facts, 2020 Data - Alcohol-Impaired Driving; Traffic Safety Facts, 2020 Data - Bicyclists and Other Cyclists; Traffic Safety Facts, 2020 Data - Children; Traffic Safety Facts, 2020 Data - Occupant Protection in Passenger Vehicles; Traffic Safety Facts, 2020 Data - Pedestrians; and Traffic Safety Facts, 2020 Data - Young Drivers.

National Safety Council (NSC), 1121 Spring Lake Dr., Itasca, IL, 60143-3201, USA, (630) 285-1121, (800) 621-7615, customerservice@nsc.org, https://www.nsc.org/; National Safety Council Injury Facts.

Small Arms Survey, Maison de la Paix, Chemin Eugene-Rigot 2E, Geneva, CH-1202, SWI, sas@smallarmssurvey.org, https://www.smallarmssurvey.org/; Unplanned Explosions at Munitions Sites (UEMS).

U.S. Department of Health and Human Services, Centers for Disease Control and Prevention (CDC), National Center for Health Statistics (NCHS), 3311 Toledo Rd., Hyattsville, MD, 20782-2064, USA, (800) 232-4636, (301) 458-4000, https://www.cdc.gov/nchs; FastStats - Statistics by Topic.

U.S. Department of Labor (DOL), Occupational Safety and Health Administration (OSHA), 200 Constitution Ave. NW, Rm. N3626, Washington, DC, 20210, USA, (800) 321-6742, https://www.osha.gov; Fatality Inspection Data: Work-Related Fatalities for Cases Inspected by Federal or State OSHA and Severe Injury Reports.

U.S. Department of Transportation (DOT), Office of the Assistant Secretary for Research and Technology (OST-R), Bureau of Transportation Statistics (BTS), 1200 New Jersey Ave. SE, Washington, DC, 20590, USA, (800) 853-1351, (202) 366-3282, https://www.bts.gov; TranStats.

ACCIDENTS-AGE OF DRIVER

National Highway Traffic Safety Administration (NHTSA), National Center for Statistics and Analysis (NCSA), 1200 New Jersey Ave. SE, West Bldg., Washington, DC, 20590, USA, (800) 934-8517, (202) 366-2746, ncsarequests@dot.gov, https://www.nhtsa.gov/research-data/national-center-statistics-and-analysis-ncsa; Traffic Safety Facts and Traffic Safety Facts, 2020 Data - Young Drivers.

National Safety Council (NSC), 1121 Spring Lake Dr., Itasca, IL, 60143-3201, USA, (630) 285-1121, (800) 621-7615, customerservice@nsc.org, https://www.nsc.org/; National Safety Council Injury Facts.

ACCIDENTS-AIRCRAFT

International Civil Aviation Organization (ICAO), 999 Robert-Bourassa Blvd., Montreal, QC, H3C 5H7, CAN, (514) 954-8219 (Dial from U.S.), (514) 954-6077 (Fax from U.S.), icaohq@icao.int, https://www.icao.int; ICAO Regional Reports.

National Aeronautics and Space Administration (NASA), NASA Headquarters, 300 E St. SW, Ste. 5R30, Washington, DC, 20546, USA, (202) 358-0001, (202) 358-4338, https://www.nasa.gov; Aviation Safety Reporting System (ASRS).

National Transportation Safety Board (NTSB), 490 L'Enfant Plz. SW, Washington, DC, 20594, USA, (202) 314-6000, https://www.ntsb.gov; Statistical Reviews.

U.S. Department of Transportation (DOT), Federal Aviation Administration (FAA), 800 Independence Ave. SW, Washington, DC, 20591, USA, (866) 835-5322, https://www.faa.gov/; Accident and Incident Data and Runway Safety Statistics.

U.S. Department of Transportation (DOT), Office of the Assistant Secretary for Research and Technology (OST-R), Bureau of Transportation Statistics (BTS), 1200 New Jersey Ave. SE, Washington, DC, 20590, USA, (800) 853-1351, (202) 366-3282, https://www.bts.gov; Airlines, Airports, and Aviation and TranStats.

ACCIDENTS-ALCOHOL INVOLVEMENT

The Lancet, 230 Park Ave., New York, NY, 10169, USA, (212) 633-3800, editorial@lancet.com, https://www.thelancet.com/; Alcohol Use and Burden for 195 Countries and Territories, 1990-2016: A Systematic Analysis for the Global Burden of Disease Study 2016.

National Highway Traffic Safety Administration (NHTSA), National Center for Statistics and Analysis (NCSA), 1200 New Jersey Ave. SE, West Bldg., Washington, DC, 20590, USA, (800) 934-8517, (202) 366-2746, ncsarequests@dot.gov, https://www.nhtsa.gov/research-data/national-center-statistics-and-analysis-ncsa; Traffic Safety Facts and Traffic Safety Facts, 2020 Data - Alcohol-Impaired Driving.

Trust for America's Health (TFAH), 1730 M St. NW, Ste. 900, Washington, DC, 20036, USA, (202) 223-9870, (202) 223-9871, info@tfah.org, https://www.tfah.org/; Pain in the Nation Series Update: Alcohol, Drug and Suicide Deaths at Record Highs.

ACCIDENTS-COSTS

National Highway Traffic Safety Administration (NHTSA), National Center for Statistics and Analysis (NCSA), 1200 New Jersey Ave. SE, West Bldg., Washington, DC, 20590, USA, (800) 934-8517, (202) 366-2746, ncsarequests@dot.gov, https://www.nhtsa.gov/research-data/national-center-statistics-and-analysis-ncsa; Traffic Safety Facts.

National Safety Council (NSC), 1121 Spring Lake Dr., Itasca, IL, 60143-3201, USA, (630) 285-1121, (800) 621-7615, customerservice@nsc.org, https://www.nsc.org/; National Safety Council Injury Facts.

ACCIDENTS-DEATHS AND DEATH RATES

AFL-CIO, 815 16th St. NW, Washington, DC, 20006, USA, (202) 637-5000, https://aflcio.org; Death on the Job: The Toll of Neglect 2022.

Association of American Railroads (AAR), 425 3rd St. SW, Washington, DC, 20024, USA, (202) 639-2100, https://www.aar.org; Analysis of Class I Railroads 2021 and Railroad Facts 2022.

Bernan Press, 15250 NBN Way, Bldg. C, Blue Ridge Summit, PA, 17214, USA, (301) 459-2255, (800) 865-3457, (800) 865-3450, customercare@bernan.com, https://rowman.com/Page/Bernan; Vital Statistics of the United States 2022: Births, Life Expectancy, Deaths, and Selected Health Data.

Governors Highway Safety Association (GHSA), 660 N Capitol St. NW, Ste. 220, Washington, DC, 20001-1642, USA, (202) 789-0942, headquarters@ghsa.org, https://www.ghsa.org/; An Analysis of Traffic Fatalities by Race and Ethnicity.

Insurance Institute for Highway Safety/Highway Loss Data Institute (IIHS/HLDI), 4121 Wilson Blvd., 6th Fl., Arlington, VA, 22203, USA, (703) 247-1500, (434) 985 4600, cmatthew@iihs.org, https://www.iihs.org/; Fatality Facts 2021: Yearly Snapshot.

Kids and Cars, Kansas City, MO, 64114, USA, (913) 732-2792, (913) 205-6973, amber@kidsandcars.org, https://www.kidsandcars.org/.

The Lancet, 230 Park Ave., New York, NY, 10169, USA, (212) 633-3800, editorial@lancet.com, https://www.thelancet.com/; Alcohol Use and Burden for 195 Countries and Territories, 1990-2016: A Systematic Analysis for the Global Burden of Disease Study 2016.

National Highway Traffic Safety Administration (NHTSA), National Center for Statistics and Analysis (NCSA), 1200 New Jersey Ave. SE, West Bldg., Washington, DC, 20590, USA, (800) 934-8517, (202) 366-2746, ncsarequests@dot.gov, https://www.nhtsa.gov/research-data/national-center-statistics-and-analysis-ncsa; Analysis of Real-World Crashes Where Involved Vehicles Were Equipped With Adaptive Equipment; Early Estimates of Motor Vehicle Traffic Fatalities and Fatality Rate by Sub-Categories in 2021; Occupant Restraint Use in 2021: Results From the NOPUS Controlled Intersection Study; Traffic Safety Facts; Traffic Safety Facts, 2011-2020 Data - School-Transportation-Related Crashes; Traffic Safety Facts, 2019 Data - Motorcycles; Traffic Safety Facts, 2019 Data - Rural/Urban Comparison of Traffic Fatalities; Traffic Safety Facts, 2020 Data - Alcohol-Impaired Driving; Traffic Safety Facts, 2020 Data - Bicyclists and Other Cyclists; Traffic Safety Facts, 2020 Data - Children; Traffic Safety Facts, 2020 Data - Large Trucks; Traffic Safety Facts, 2020 Data - Older Population; Traffic Safety Facts, 2020 Data - Pedestrians; Traffic Safety Facts, 2020 Data - Young Drivers; and Update to Special Reports on Traffic Safety During the COVID-19 Public Health Emergency.

National Safety Council (NSC), 1121 Spring Lake Dr., Itasca, IL, 60143-3201, USA, (630) 285-1121, (800) 621-7615, customerservice@nsc.org, https://www.nsc.org/; Motor Vehicles; National Safety Council Injury Facts; and Odds of Dying Chart.

RAND Corporation, PO Box 2138, 1776 Main St., Santa Monica, CA, 90407-2138, USA, (310) 451-7002, (412) 802-4981, order@rand.org, https://www.rand.org/; Gun Policy Expert-Opinion Tool and Gun Policy in America.

U.S. Department of Health and Human Services, Centers for Disease Control and Prevention (CDC), National Center for Health Statistics (NCHS), 3311 Toledo Rd., Hyattsville, MD, 20782-2064, USA, (800) 232-4636, (301) 458-4000, https://www.cdc.gov/nchs; National Vital Statistics Reports (NVSR) and Vital Statistics Online Data Portal.

U.S. Department of Labor (DOL), Mine Safety and Health Administration (MSHA), 201 12th St. S, Ste. 401, Arlington, VA, 22202-5450, USA, (202) 693-9400, askmsha@dol.gov, https://www.msha.gov; MSHA Fatality Reports.

U.S. Department of Transportation (DOT), Office of the Secretary of Transportation, 1200 New Jersey Ave. SE, Washington, DC, 20590, USA, (202) 366-4200, https://www.transportation.gov/tags/office-secretary; Our Nation's Roadway Safety Crisis.

World Health Organization (WHO), Ave. Appia 20, Geneva, CH-1211, SWI, (202) 974-3000 (Telephone in U.S.), publications@who.int, https://www.who.int/; Road Traffic Injuries.

ACCIDENTS-DEATHS AND DEATH RATES-INFANTS

Bernan Press, 15250 NBN Way, Bldg. C, Blue Ridge Summit, PA, 17214, USA, (301) 459-2255, (800) 865-3457, (800) 865-3450, customercare@bernan.com, https://rowman.com/Page/Bernan; Vital Statistics of the United States 2022: Births, Life Expectancy, Deaths, and Selected Health Data.

U.S. Department of Health and Human Services, Centers for Disease Control and Prevention (CDC), National Center for Health Statistics (NCHS), 3311 Toledo Rd., Hyattsville, MD, 20782-2064, USA, (800) 232-4636, (301) 458-4000, https://www.cdc.gov/nchs; National Vital Statistics Reports (NVSR) and Vital Statistics Online Data Portal.

ACCIDENTS-FIRES

Bureau of Alcohol, Tobacco, Firearms and Explosives (ATF), United States Bomb Data Center (USBDC), 3750 Corporal Rd., Huntsville, AL, 35898,

USA, (800) 461-8841, usbdc@atf.gov, https://www.atf.gov/explosives/us-bomb-data-center; 2019 Juvenile Offender (Fire) Incident Report.

California Department of Forestry and Fire Protection (CAL FIRE), 1416 9th St., PO Box 944246, Sacramento, CA, 94244-2460, USA, (916) 653-5123, https://www.fire.ca.gov/; CAL Fire Incidents Overview and CAL FIRE Stats and Events.

European Commission, Joint Research Centre, EU Science Hub, Brussels, B-1049, BEL, ies-contact@jrc.ec.europa.eu, https://ec.europa.eu/jrc/en; European Forest Fire Information System (EFFIS).

National Fire Protection Association (NFPA), 1 Batterymarch Park, Quincy, MA, 02169-7471, USA, (617) 770-3000, (800) 344-3555, (508) 895-8301, https://www.nfpa.org/; Firefighter Fatalities in the United States 2021 and NFPA Journal.

United Nations Environment Programme (UNEP), 900 17th St. NW, Ste. 506, Washington, DC, 20006, USA, (202) 974-1300, publications@unep.org, https://www.unep.org/; Spreading like Wildfire: The Rising Threat of Extraordinary Landscape Fires.

ACCIDENTS-INDUSTRIAL

AFL-CIO, 815 16th St. NW, Washington, DC, 20006, USA, (202) 637-5000, https://aflcio.org; Death on the Job: The Toll of Neglect 2022.

Centre for Research on the Epidemiology of Disasters (CRED), Universite Catholique de Louvain School of Public Health, Clos Chapelle-aux-Champs, Bte B1.30.15, Brussels, B-1200, BEL, contact@cred.be, https://www.cred.be/; Technological Disasters: Trends & Transport Accidents.

Marshfield Clinic Research Institute (MCRI), National Children's Center for Rural and Agricultural Health and Safety (NCCRAHS), 1000 N Oak Ave., Marshfield, WI, 54449-5790, USA, (800) 662-6900, (715) 389-4999, nccrahs@mcrf.mfldclin.edu, https://www.marshfieldresearch.org/nccrahs; Childhood Agricultural Injuries: 2022 Fact Sheet.

National Safety Council (NSC), 1121 Spring Lake Dr., Itasca, IL, 60143-3201, USA, (630) 285-1121, (800) 621-7615, customerservice@nsc.org, https://www.nsc.org/; National Safety Council Injury Facts.

Statistics Poland, Aleja Niepodleglosci 208, Warsaw, 00-925, POL, kancelariaogolnagus@stat.gov.pl, https://stat.gov.pl/en/; Accidents at Work in 2021, Preliminary Data.

U.S. Department of Agriculture (USDA), National Agricultural Statistics Service (USDA-NASS), 1400 Independence Ave. SW, Washington, DC, 20250, USA, (800) 727-9540, nass@nass.usda.gov, https://www.nass.usda.gov; Adult Agricultural Related Injuries.

U.S. Department of Labor (DOL), Bureau of Labor Statistics (BLS), Postal Square Bldg., 2 Massachusetts Ave. NE, Washington, DC, 20212-0001, USA, (202) 691-5200, (202) 691-7890, blsdata_staff@bls.gov, https://www.bls.gov; Injuries, Illnesses, and Fatalities (IIF).

U.S. Department of Labor (DOL), Mine Safety and Health Administration (MSHA), 201 12th St. S, Ste. 401, Arlington, VA, 22202-5450, USA, (202) 693-9400, askmsha@dol.gov, https://www.msha.gov; MSHA Fatality Reports.

ACCIDENTS-INJURIES

Advocates for Highway and Auto Safety, 750 1st St. NE, Ste. 1130, Washington, DC, 20002, USA, (202) 408-1711, (202) 408-1699, advocates@saferoads.org, https://saferoads.org/; 2022 Roadmap of State Highway Safety Laws and 2023 Roadmap to Safety.

Bureau of Alcohol, Tobacco, Firearms and Explosives (ATF), United States Bomb Data Center (USBDC), 3750 Corporal Rd., Huntsville, AL, 35898 , USA, (800) 461-8841, usbdc@atf.gov, https://www.atf.gov/explosives/us-bomb-data-center; 2021 Explosives Incident Report and 2019 Juvenile Offender (Fire) Incident Report.

Canadian Institute for Health Information (CIHI), 495 Richmond Rd., Ste. 600, Ottawa, ON, K2A 4H6, CAN, (613) 241-7860 (Dial from U.S.), (613) 241-5543 (Dial from U.S.), (613) 241-8120 (Fax from U.S.), communications@cihi.ca, https://www.cihi.ca; National Trauma Registry (NTR) Metadata.

Kids and Cars, Kansas City, MO, 64114, USA, (913) 732-2792, (913) 205-6973, amber@kidsandcars.org, https://www.kidsandcars.org/.

The Lancet, 230 Park Ave., New York, NY, 10169, USA, (212) 633-3800, editorial@lancet.com, https://www.thelancet.com/; Alcohol Use and Burden for 195 Countries and Territories, 1990-2016: A Systematic Analysis for the Global Burden of Disease Study 2016.

Marshfield Clinic Research Institute (MCRI), National Children's Center for Rural and Agricultural Health and Safety (NCCRAHS), 1000 N Oak Ave., Marshfield, WI, 54449-5790, USA, (800) 662-6900, (715) 389-4999, nccrahs@mcrf.mfldclin.edu, https://www.marshfieldresearch.org/nccrahs; Childhood Agricultural Injuries: 2022 Fact Sheet.

National Highway Traffic Safety Administration (NHTSA), National Center for Statistics and Analysis (NCSA), 1200 New Jersey Ave. SE, West Bldg., Washington, DC, 20590, USA, (800) 934-8517, (202) 366-2746, ncsarequests@dot.gov, https://www.nhtsa.gov/research-data/national-center-statistics-and-analysis-ncsa; Analysis of Real-World Crashes Where Involved Vehicles Were Equipped With Adaptive Equipment; Occupant Restraint Use in 2021: Results From the NOPUS Controlled Intersection Study; Traffic Safety Facts; Traffic Safety Facts, 2019 Data - Motorcycles; Traffic Safety Facts, 2020 Data - Alcohol-Impaired Driving; Traffic Safety Facts, 2020 Data - Bicyclists and Other Cyclists; Traffic Safety Facts, 2020 Data - Children; Traffic Safety Facts, 2020 Data - Large Trucks; Traffic Safety Facts, 2020 Data - Older Population; Traffic Safety Facts, 2020 Data - Pedestrians; and Traffic Safety Facts, 2020 Data - Young Drivers.

National Safety Council (NSC), 1121 Spring Lake Dr., Itasca, IL, 60143-3201, USA, (630) 285-1121, (800) 621-7615, customerservice@nsc.org, https://www.nsc.org/; Motor Vehicles and National Safety Council Injury Facts.

Public Health Agency of Canada, 130 Colonnade Rd., Ottawa, ON, K1A 0K9, CAN, (844) 280-5020 (Dial from U.S.), https://www.phac-aspc.gc.ca/; CHIRPP Injury Reports.

RAND Corporation, PO Box 2138, 1776 Main St., Santa Monica, CA, 90407-2138, USA, (310) 451-7002, (412) 802-4981, order@rand.org, https://www.rand.org/; Gun Policy Expert-Opinion Tool and Gun Policy in America.

U.S. Department of Agriculture (USDA), National Agricultural Statistics Service (USDA-NASS), 1400 Independence Ave. SW, Washington, DC, 20250, USA, (800) 727-9540, nass@nass.usda.gov, https://www.nass.usda.gov; Adult Agricultural Related Injuries.

U.S. Department of Health and Human Services, Centers for Disease Control and Prevention (CDC), 1600 Clifton Rd., Atlanta, GA, 30329-4027, USA, (800) 232-4636, (888) 232-6348 (TTY), cdcinfo@cdc.gov, https://www.cdc.gov; WISQARS (Web-Based Injury Statistics Query and Reporting System).

U.S. Department of Labor (DOL), Bureau of Labor Statistics (BLS), Postal Square Bldg., 2 Massachusetts Ave. NE, Washington, DC, 20212-0001, USA, (202) 691-5200, (202) 691-7890, blsdata_staff@bls.gov, https://www.bls.gov; Injuries, Illnesses, and Fatalities (IIF).

U.S. Department of Transportation (DOT), Office of the Secretary of Transportation, 1200 New Jersey Ave. SE, Washington, DC, 20590, USA, (202) 366-4200, https://www.transportation.gov/tags/office-secretary; Our Nation's Roadway Safety Crisis.

University of Virginia School of Engineering and Applied Science, Center for Applied Biomechanics (CAB), 4040 Lewis and Clark Dr., Charlottesville, VA, 22911, USA, (434) 297-8001, https://engineering.virginia.edu/research/centers-institutes/center-applied-biomechanics/research; unpublished data.

World Health Organization (WHO), Ave. Appia 20, Geneva, CH-1211, SWI, (202) 974-3000 (Telephone in U.S.), publications@who.int, https://www.who.int/; Road Traffic Injuries.

ACCIDENTS-MOTOR VEHICLES

AAA Foundation for Traffic Safety (FTS), 607 14th St. NW, Ste. 201, Washington, DC, 20005, USA, (202) 638-5944, (202) 638-5943, info@aaafoundation.org, https://www.aaafoundation.org/; Cannabis Use Among Drivers in Fatal Crashes in Washington State Before and After Legalization; 2021 Traffic Safety Culture Index; and Use of Potentially Impairing Medications in Relation to Driving, United States, 2021.

Bernan Press, 15250 NBN Way, Bldg. C, Blue Ridge Summit, PA, 17214, USA, (301) 459-2255, (800) 865-3457, (800) 865-3450, customercare@bernan.com, https://rowman.com/Page/Bernan; Vital Statistics of the United States 2022: Births, Life Expectancy, Deaths, and Selected Health Data.

Centre for Research on the Epidemiology of Disasters (CRED), Universite Catholique de Louvain School of Public Health, Clos Chapelle-aux-Champs, Bte B1.30.15, Brussels, B-1200, BEL, contact@cred.be, https://www.cred.be/; Technological Disasters: Trends & Transport Accidents.

Governors Highway Safety Association (GHSA), 660 N Capitol St. NW, Ste. 220, Washington, DC, 20001-1642, USA, (202) 789-0942, headquarters@ghsa.org, https://www.ghsa.org/; An Analysis of Traffic Fatalities by Race and Ethnicity; High-Risk Impaired Drivers: Combating a Critical Threat; Motorcyclists' Attitudes on Using High-Visibility Gear to Improve Conspicuity; and Pedestrian Traffic Fatalities by State: 2022 Preliminary Data.

Insurance Institute for Highway Safety/Highway Loss Data Institute (IIHS/HLDI), 4121 Wilson Blvd., 6th Fl., Arlington, VA, 22203, USA, (703) 247-1500, (434) 985 4600, cmatthew@iihs.org, https://www.iihs.org/; Fatality Facts 2021: Yearly Snapshot and Highway Safety Topics.

Kids and Cars, Kansas City, MO, 64114, USA, (913) 732-2792, (913) 205-6973, amber@kidsandcars.org, https://www.kidsandcars.org/.

National Academies of Sciences, Engineering, and Medicine (The National Academies), Transportation Research Board (TRB), 500 5th St. NW, Washington, DC, 20001, USA, (202) 334-2934, (202) 334-2000, mytrb@nas.edu, https://www.nationalacademies.org/trb/transportation-research-board; TRID: The TRIS and ITRD Database.

National Highway Traffic Safety Administration (NHTSA), National Center for Statistics and Analysis (NCSA), 1200 New Jersey Ave. SE, West Bldg., Washington, DC, 20590, USA, (800) 934-8517, (202) 366-2746, ncsarequests@dot.gov, https://www.nhtsa.gov/research-data/national-center-statistics-and-analysis-ncsa; Analysis of Real-World Crashes Where Involved Vehicles Were Equipped With Adaptive Equipment; Early Estimates of Motor Vehicle Traffic Fatalities and Fatality Rate by Sub-Categories in 2021; Fatality Analysis Reporting System (FARS) National Statistics; Occupant Restraint Use in 2021: Results From the NOPUS Controlled Intersection Study; Traffic Safety Facts; Traffic Safety Facts, 2011-2020 Data - School-Transportation-Related Crashes; Traffic Safety Facts, 2019 Data - Motorcycles; Traffic Safety Facts, 2019 Data - Rural/Urban Comparison of Traffic Fatalities; Traffic Safety Facts, 2020 Data - Alcohol-Impaired Driving; Traffic Safety Facts, 2020 Data - Bicyclists and Other Cyclists; Traffic Safety Facts, 2020 Data - Children; Traffic Safety Facts, 2020 Data - Large Trucks; Traffic Safety Facts, 2020 Data - Occupant Protection in Passenger Vehicles; Traffic Safety Facts, 2020 Data - Older Population; Traffic Safety Facts, 2020 Data - Pedestrians; Traffic Safety Facts, 2020 Data - Speeding; and Traffic Safety Facts, 2020 Data - Young Drivers.

National Safety Council (NSC), 1121 Spring Lake Dr., Itasca, IL, 60143-3201, USA, (630) 285-1121, (800) 621-7615, customerservice@nsc.org, https://www.nsc.org/; Motor Vehicles and National Safety Council Injury Facts.

Transport Research Laboratory (TRL), Crowthorne House, Nine Mile Ride, Wokingham, Berkshire, RG40 3GA, GBR, enquiries@trl.co.uk, https://trl.co.uk/; In-Depth Investigation of E-Scooter Performance.

U.S. Department of Health and Human Services, Centers for Disease Control and Prevention (CDC), National Center for Health Statistics (NCHS), 3311 Toledo Rd., Hyattsville, MD, 20782-2064, USA, (800) 232-4636, (301) 458-4000, https://www.cdc.gov/nchs; National Vital Statistics Reports (NVSR) and Vital Statistics Online Data Portal.

U.S. Department of Transportation (DOT), Federal Highway Administration (FHA), 1200 New Jersey Ave. SE, Washington, DC, 20590, USA, (202) 366-4000, https://highways.dot.gov/; Highway Statistics 2020.

U.S. Department of Transportation (DOT), Federal Motor Carrier Safety Administration (FMCSA), 1200 New Jersey Ave. SE, Washington, DC, 20590, USA, (800) 832-5660, https://www.fmcsa.dot.gov/; Large Truck and Bus Crash Facts 2019 and 2021 Pocket Guide to Large Truck and Bus Statistics.

U.S. Department of Transportation (DOT), Office of the Assistant Secretary for Research and Technology (OST-R), Bureau of Transportation Statistics (BTS), 1200 New Jersey Ave. SE, Washington, DC, 20590, USA, (800) 853-1351, (202) 366-3282, https://www.bts.gov; TranStats.

U.S. Department of Transportation (DOT), Office of the Secretary of Transportation, 1200 New Jersey Ave. SE, Washington, DC, 20590, USA, (202) 366-4200, https://www.transportation.gov/tags/office-secretary; Our Nation's Roadway Safety Crisis.

University of Virginia School of Engineering and Applied Science, Center for Applied Biomechanics (CAB), 4040 Lewis and Clark Dr., Charlottesville, VA, 22911, USA, (434) 297-8001, https://engineering.virginia.edu/research/centers-institutes/center-applied-biomechanics/research; unpublished data.

World Health Organization (WHO), Ave. Appia 20, Geneva, CH-1211, SWI, (202) 974-3000 (Telephone in U.S.), publications@who.int, https://www.who.int/; Road Traffic Injuries.

ACCIDENTS-MOTORCYCLE

Governors Highway Safety Association (GHSA), 660 N Capitol St. NW, Ste. 220, Washington, DC, 20001-1642, USA, (202) 789-0942, headquarters@ghsa.org, https://www.ghsa.org/; Motorcyclists' Attitudes on Using High-Visibility Gear to Improve Conspicuity.

National Highway Traffic Safety Administration (NHTSA), National Center for Statistics and Analysis (NCSA), 1200 New Jersey Ave. SE, West Bldg., Washington, DC, 20590, USA, (800) 934-8517, (202) 366-2746, ncsarequests@dot.gov, https://www.nhtsa.gov/research-data/national-center-statistics-and-analysis-ncsa; Traffic Safety Facts, 2019 Data - Motorcycles.

National Safety Council (NSC), 1121 Spring Lake Dr., Itasca, IL, 60143-3201, USA, (630) 285-1121, (800) 621-7615, customerservice@nsc.org, https://www.nsc.org/; National Safety Council Injury Facts.

ACCIDENTS-POLICE OFFICERS ASSAULTED, KILLED

National Policing Institute, 2550 S Clark St., Ste. 1130, Arlington, VA, 22202, USA, (202) 833-1460, (202) 659-9149, info@policinginstitute.org, https://www.policefoundation.org; National Survey on Officer Safety Training: Findings and Implications.

U.S. Department of Justice (DOJ), Federal Bureau of Investigation (FBI), 935 Pennsylvania Ave. NW, Washington, DC, 20535-0001, USA, (202) 324-3000, https://www.fbi.gov/; Law Enforcement Officers Killed and Assaulted (LEOKA) 2020.

ACCIDENTS-RAILROAD

Association of American Railroads (AAR), 425 3rd St. SW, Washington, DC, 20024, USA, (202) 639-2100, https://www.aar.org; Analysis of Class I Railroads 2021 and Railroad Facts 2022.

U.S. Department of Transportation (DOT), Federal Railroad Administration (FRA), 1200 New Jersey Ave. SE, Washington, DC, 20590, USA, (202) 366-4000, (202) 493-6014, (202) 493-6481, frapa@dot.gov, https://railroads.dot.gov/; FRA Office of Safety Analysis Website.

ACCIDENTS-TRANSPORTATION

Centre for Research on the Epidemiology of Disasters (CRED), Universite Catholique de Louvain School of Public Health, Clos Chapelle-aux-Champs, Bte B1.30.15, Brussels, B-1200, BEL, contact@cred.be, https://www.cred.be/; Technological Disasters: Trends & Transport Accidents.

Governors Highway Safety Association (GHSA), 660 N Capitol St. NW, Ste. 220, Washington, DC, 20001-1642, USA, (202) 789-0942, headquarters@ghsa.org, https://www.ghsa.org/; High-Risk Impaired Drivers: Combating a Critical Threat; Motorcyclists' Attitudes on Using High-Visibility Gear to Improve Conspicuity; and Pedestrian Traffic Fatalities by State: 2022 Preliminary Data.

U.S. Department of Transportation (DOT), Office of the Assistant Secretary for Research and Technology (OST-R), Bureau of Transportation Statistics (BTS), 1200 New Jersey Ave. SE, Washington, DC, 20590, USA, (800) 853-1351, (202) 366-3282, https://www.bts.gov; TranStats.

World Health Organization (WHO), Ave. Appia 20, Geneva, CH-1211, SWI, (202) 974-3000 (Telephone in U.S.), publications@who.int, https://www.who.int/; Road Traffic Injuries.

ACCIDENTS-WORK FATALITIES

AFL-CIO, 815 16th St. NW, Washington, DC, 20006, USA, (202) 637-5000, https://aflcio.org; Death on the Job: The Toll of Neglect 2022.

National Fire Protection Association (NFPA), 1 Batterymarch Park, Quincy, MA, 02169-7471, USA, (617) 770-3000, (800) 344-3555, (508) 895-8301, https://www.nfpa.org/; Firefighter Fatalities in the United States 2021.

U.S. Department of Labor (DOL), Bureau of Labor Statistics (BLS), Postal Square Bldg., 2 Massachusetts Ave. NE, Washington, DC, 20212-0001, USA, (202) 691-5200, (202) 691-7890, blsdata_staff@bls.gov, https://www.bls.gov; Injuries, Illnesses, and Fatalities (IIF) and Monthly Labor Review.

U.S. Department of Labor (DOL), Occupational Safety and Health Administration (OSHA), 200 Constitution Ave. NW, Rm. N3626, Washington, DC, 20210, USA, (800) 321-6742, https://www.osha.gov; Fatality Inspection Data: Work-Related Fatalities for Cases Inspected by Federal or State OSHA and Severe Injury Reports.

ACCIDENTS-WORK TIME LOST

National Safety Council (NSC), 1121 Spring Lake Dr., Itasca, IL, 60143-3201, USA, (630) 285-1121, (800) 621-7615, customerservice@nsc.org, https://www.nsc.org/; National Safety Council Injury Facts.

U.S. Department of Labor (DOL), Occupational Safety and Health Administration (OSHA), 200 Constitution Ave. NW, Rm. N3626, Washington, DC, 20210, USA, (800) 321-6742, https://www.osha.gov; Severe Injury Reports.

ACCOUNTANTS AND AUDITORS

U.S. Department of Labor (DOL), Bureau of Labor Statistics (BLS), Postal Square Bldg., 2 Massachusetts Ave. NE, Washington, DC, 20212-0001, USA, (202) 691-5200, (202) 691-7890, blsdata_staff@bls.gov, https://www.bls.gov; Monthly Labor Review.

ACCOUNTING, TAX PREPARATION, BOOKKEEPING, AND PAYROLL SERVICES

U.S. Census Bureau, 4600 Silver Hill Rd., Washington, DC, 20233, USA, (301) 763-4636, (800) 923-8282, https://www.census.gov; County Business Patterns (CBP) 2020.

ACCOUNTING, TAX PREPARATION, BOOKKEEPING, AND PAYROLL SERVICES-EARNINGS

U.S. Census Bureau, 4600 Silver Hill Rd., Washington, DC, 20233, USA, (301) 763-4636, (800) 923-8282, https://www.census.gov; County Business Patterns (CBP) 2020.

ACCOUNTING, TAX PREPARATION, BOOKKEEPING, AND PAYROLL SERVICES-EMPLOYEES

U.S. Census Bureau, 4600 Silver Hill Rd., Washington, DC, 20233, USA, (301) 763-4636, (800) 923-8282, https://www.census.gov; County Business Patterns (CBP) 2020.

ACCOUNTING, TAX PREPARATION, BOOKKEEPING, AND PAYROLL SERVICES-FINANCES

Internal Revenue Service (IRS), Statistics of Income Division (SOI), 1111 Constitution Ave. NW, K-Room 4100-123, Washington, DC, 20224-0002, USA, (202) 874-0410, (202) 874-0964, sis@irs.gov, https://www.irs.gov/uac/soi-tax-stats-statistics-of-income; Statistics of Income Bulletin.

ACCOUNTING, TAX PREPARATION, BOOKKEEPING, AND PAYROLL SERVICES-RECEIPTS

Internal Revenue Service (IRS), Statistics of Income Division (SOI), 1111 Constitution Ave. NW, K-Room 4100-123, Washington, DC, 20224-0002, USA, (202) 874-0410, (202) 874-0964, sis@irs.gov, https://www.irs.gov/uac/soi-tax-stats-statistics-of-income; Statistics of Income Bulletin.

U.S. Census Bureau, 4600 Silver Hill Rd., Washington, DC, 20233, USA, (301) 763-4636, (800) 923-8282, https://www.census.gov; County Business Patterns (CBP) 2020.

ACT ASSESSMENT

ACT, PO Box 168, Iowa City, IA, 52243-0168, USA, (319) 337-1270, https://www.act.org; Benefits of Pre-ACT: What Does the Evidence Say? and Examining the Relationship Between School Climate and ACT Composite Scores.

ACTIVITY LIMITATION CAUSED BY CHRONIC CONDITIONS

U.S. Department of Health and Human Services, Centers for Disease Control and Prevention (CDC), 1600 Clifton Rd., Atlanta, GA, 30329-4027, USA, (800) 232-4636, (888) 232-6348 (TTY), cdcinfo@cdc.gov, https://www.cdc.gov; Health-Related Quality of Life (HRQOL).

U.S. Department of Health and Human Services, Centers for Disease Control and Prevention (CDC), National Center for Health Statistics (NCHS), 3311 Toledo Rd., Hyattsville, MD, 20782-2064, USA, (800) 232-4636, (301) 458-4000, https://www.cdc.gov/nchs; Health, United States, 2020-2021.

ACTORS

U.S. Department of Labor (DOL), Bureau of Labor Statistics (BLS), Postal Square Bldg., 2 Massachusetts Ave. NE, Washington, DC, 20212-0001, USA, (202) 691-5200, (202) 691-7890, blsdata_staff@bls.gov, https://www.bls.gov; Monthly Labor Review.

University of Southern California (USC), Annenberg School for Communication and Journalism, Annenberg Inclusion Initiative, 3630 Watt Way, Ste. 402, Los Angeles, CA, 90089, USA, (213) 740-6180, (213) 740-3772, aii@usc.edu, https://annenberg.usc.edu/research/aii; Inequality Across 1,600 Popular Films: Examining Gender, Race/Ethnicity & Age of Leads/Co Leads From 2007 to 2022.

ADAPTATION (BIOLOGY)

Global Center on Adaptation (GCA), Antoine Platekade 1006, Rotterdam, 3072 ME, NLD, info@gca.org, https://gca.org/; Adapt Now: A Global Call for Leadership on Climate Resilience.

ADDICTS

Partnership to End Addiction, 711 3rd Ave., 5th Fl., Ste. 500, New York, NY, 10017, USA, (212) 841-5200, contact@toendaddiction.org, https://drugfree.org/; unpublished data.

ADDITIVE MANUFACTURING

IDTechEx, One Boston Place, Ste. 2600, Boston, MA, 02108, USA, (617) 577-7890, (617) 577-7810, research@idtechex.com, https://www.idtechex.com/; 3D Printing and Additive Manufacturing 2022-2032: Technology and Market Outlook.

ADOPTION

Australian Institute of Health and Welfare (AIHW), GPO Box 570, Canberra, ACT, 2601, AUS, info@aihw.gov.au, https://www.aihw.gov.au/; Adoptions Australia 2021-2022.

Child Trends, 7315 Wisconsin Ave., Ste. 1200W, Bethesda, MD, 20814, USA, (240) 223-9200, https://www.childtrends.org/; Undercounting Hispanics in the 2020 Census Will Result in a Loss in Federal Funding to Many States for Child and Family Assistance Programs.

National Council For Adoption (NCFA), 431 N Lee St., Alexandria, VA, 22314-2561, USA, (703) 299-6633, (703) 299-6004, ncfa@adoptioncouncil.org, https://adoptioncouncil.org/; Adoption Advocate.

U.S. Department of Health and Human Services (HHS), Administration for Children and Families (ACF), Children's Bureau, 330 C St. SW, Washington, DC, 20201, USA, https://www.acf.hhs.gov/cb; The Adoption and Foster Care Analysis and Reporting System (AFCARS); Child Welfare Outcomes: Report to Congress Executive Summary; State-by-State Adoption and Foster Care Statistics; and Trends in Foster Care and Adoption.

U.S. Department of Health and Human Services (HHS), Administration for Children and Families (ACF), Children's Bureau, Child Welfare Information Gateway, 330 C St. SW, Washington, DC, 20201, USA, (800) 394-3366, info@childwelfare.gov, https://www.childwelfare.gov/; Adoption Statistics.

U.S. Department of State (DOS), Bureau of Consular Affairs, Office of Children's Issues, 2201 C. St. NW, SA-17, 9th Fl., Washington, DC, 20522-1709, USA, (888) 407-4747, (202) 501-4444, adoption@state.gov, https://travel.state.gov/content/travel/en/Intercountry-Adoption.html; Annual Report on Intercountry Adoption, Fiscal Year 2021 and Country Information.

ADULT EDUCATION

U.S. Department of Education (ED), Institute of Education Sciences (IES), National Center for Education Statistics (NCES), Potomac Center Plaza, 550 12th St. SW, Washington, DC, 20202, USA, (202) 403-5551, https://nces.ed.gov/; The National Household Education Surveys Program (NHES) Data.

Utah State Board of Education, PO Box 144200, Salt Lake City, UT, 84114-4200, USA, (801) 538-7500, ryan.bartlett@schools.utah.gov, https://www.schools.utah.gov/; Career and Technical Education (CTE) At a Glance 2021-2022 and Utah Schools Data and Statistics.

ADVERTISING

Interactive Advertising Bureau (IAB), 116 E 27th St., 6th Fl., New York, NY, 10016, USA, (212) 380-4700, https://www.iab.com/; U.S. Podcast Advertising Revenue Study and 2022 Video Ad Spend & 2023 Outlook: Defining the Next Generation.

Violence Policy Center (VPC), 1025 Connecticut Ave. NW, Ste. 1210, Washington, DC, 20036, USA, (202) 822-8200, https://vpc.org/; How the Firearms Industry Markets Guns to Asian Americans.

ADVERTISING-RADIO

Radio Advertising Bureau (RAB), 400 E Las Colinas Blvd., No. 350, Irving, TX, 75039, USA, (800) 232-3131, (972) 753-6700, memberresponse@rab.com, http://www.rab.com; Why Radio Radio Facts.

ADVERTISING AGENCIES

DoubleVerify, 28 Crosby St., 6th Fl., New York, NY, 10003, USA, info@doubleverify.com, https://doubleverify.com; 2023 Global Insights Report.

Television Bureau of Advertising (TVB), 120 Wall St., 15th Fl., New York, NY, 10005-3908, USA, (212) 486-1111, https://www.tvb.org; Competitive Media.

ADVERTISING AGENCIES-EARNINGS

U.S. Census Bureau, 4600 Silver Hill Rd., Washington, DC, 20233, USA, (301) 763-4636, (800) 923-8282, https://www.census.gov; County Business Patterns (CBP) 2020.

U.S. Census Bureau, Center for Economic Studies (CES), 4600 Silver Hill Rd., Washington, DC, 20233, USA, (301) 763-6460, (301) 763-5935, ces.contacts@census.gov, https://www.census.gov/programs-surveys/ces.html; Professional, Scientific and Technical Services, 2017 Economic Census.

U.S. Department of Labor (DOL), Bureau of Labor Statistics (BLS), Postal Square Bldg., 2 Massachusetts Ave. NE, Washington, DC, 20212-0001, USA, (202) 691-5200, (202) 691-7890, blsdata_staff@bls.gov, https://www.bls.gov; Current Employment Statistics (CES).

ADVERTISING AGENCIES-EMPLOYEES

U.S. Census Bureau, 4600 Silver Hill Rd., Washington, DC, 20233, USA, (301) 763-4636, (800) 923-8282, https://www.census.gov; County Business Patterns (CBP) 2020.

U.S. Census Bureau, Center for Economic Studies (CES), 4600 Silver Hill Rd., Washington, DC, 20233, USA, (301) 763-6460, (301) 763-5935, ces.contacts@census.gov, https://www.census.gov/programs-surveys/ces.html; Professional, Scientific and Technical Services, 2017 Economic Census.

U.S. Department of Labor (DOL), Bureau of Labor Statistics (BLS), Postal Square Bldg., 2 Massachusetts Ave. NE, Washington, DC, 20212-0001, USA, (202) 691-5200, (202) 691-7890, blsdata_staff@bls.gov, https://www.bls.gov; Current Employment Statistics (CES).

ADVERTISING AGENCIES-ESTABLISHMENTS

Nielsen, 675 6th Ave., New York, NY, 10011, USA, (800) 864-1224, https://www.nielsen.com; 2022 Global Annual Marketing Report and Nielsen Total Audience Report: August 2020 Special Edition on Work-From-Home.

U.S. Census Bureau, 4600 Silver Hill Rd., Washington, DC, 20233, USA, (301) 763-4636, (800) 923-8282, https://www.census.gov; County Business Patterns (CBP) 2020.

ADVERTISING AGENCIES-RECEIPTS

Interactive Advertising Bureau (IAB), 116 E 27th St., 6th Fl., New York, NY, 10016, USA, (212) 380-4700, https://www.iab.com/; 2022 Video Ad Spend & 2023 Outlook: Defining the Next Generation.

AEROBIC EXERCISES

National Sporting Goods Association (NSGA), 3041 Woodcreek Dr., Ste. 210, Downers Grove, IL, 60515, USA, (847) 296-6742, (847) 391-9827, info@nsga.org, https://www.nsga.org; Sports Participation in the United States 2022 and Sports Participation: Historical Sports Participation 2022.

The NPD Group, 900 W Shore Rd., Port Washington, NY, 11050, USA, (516) 625-0700, contactnpd@npd.com, https://www.npd.com; Sports.

AERONAUTICS, CIVIL

See AERONAUTICS, COMMERCIAL

AERONAUTICS, COMMERCIAL

Cirium, 230 Park Ave., 7th Fl., New York, NY, 10169, USA, (646) 746-6851, https://www.cirium.com/; The Impact of COVID-19 on Aviation and Taking to the Skies 2021: An Analysis of Startup Airlines in North America with Sample Profiles of the Newest Airlines.

IDTechEx, One Boston Place, Ste. 2600, Boston, MA, 02108, USA, (617) 577-7890, (617) 577-7810, research@idtechex.com, https://www.idtechex.com/; Electric Vehicles: Land, Sea & Air 2022-2042.

Janes, USA, (703) 574-7580, (888) 977-1519, customer.care@janes.com, https://www.janes.com; Jane's All the World's Aircraft: In Service 2021-2022.

U.S. Census Bureau, 4600 Silver Hill Rd., Washington, DC, 20233, USA, (301) 763-4636, (800) 923-8282, https://www.census.gov; County Business Patterns (CBP) 2020.

U.S. Census Bureau, Center for Economic Studies (CES), 4600 Silver Hill Rd., Washington, DC, 20233, USA, (301) 763-6460, (301) 763-5935, ces.contacts@census.gov, https://www.census.gov/programs-surveys/ces.html; Transportation and Warehousing, 2017 Economic Census.

U.S. Department of Transportation (DOT), Office of the Assistant Secretary for Research and Technology (OST-R), Bureau of Transportation Statistics (BTS), 1200 New Jersey Ave. SE, Washington, DC, 20590, USA, (800) 853-1351, (202) 366-3282, https://www.bts.gov; Airlines, Airports, and Aviation.

AERONAUTICS, COMMERCIAL-ACCIDENTS

International Civil Aviation Organization (ICAO), 999 Robert-Bourassa Blvd., Montreal, QC, H3C 5H7, CAN, (514) 954-8219 (Dial from U.S.), (514) 954-6077 (Fax from U.S.), icaohq@icao.int, https://www.icao.int; ICAO Regional Reports.

National Aeronautics and Space Administration (NASA), NASA Headquarters, 300 E St. SW, Ste. 5R30, Washington, DC, 20546, USA, (202) 358-0001, (202) 358-4338, https://www.nasa.gov; Aviation Safety Reporting System (ASRS).

National Transportation Safety Board (NTSB), 490 L'Enfant Plz. SW, Washington, DC, 20594, USA, (202) 314-6000, https://www.ntsb.gov; Statistical Reviews.

U.S. Department of Transportation (DOT), Federal Aviation Administration (FAA), 800 Independence Ave. SW, Washington, DC, 20591, USA, (866) 835-5322, https://www.faa.gov/; Aviation Safety Information Analysis and Sharing (ASIAS) System and Preliminary Accident and Incident Notices.

U.S. Department of Transportation (DOT), Office of the Assistant Secretary for Research and Technology (OST-R), Bureau of Transportation Statistics (BTS), 1200 New Jersey Ave. SE, Washington, DC, 20590, USA, (800) 853-1351, (202) 366-3282, https://www.bts.gov; Airlines, Airports, and Aviation and TranStats.

AERONAUTICS, COMMERCIAL-AIRLINE MARKETS

Airlines for America (A4A), 1275 Pennsylvania Ave. NW, Ste. 1300, Washington, DC, 20004, USA, (202) 626-4000, mediarelations@airlines.org, https://www.airlines.org; A4A Passenger Airline Cost Index (PACI).

S&P Global, 55 Water St., New York, NY, 10041, USA, (212) 438-2000, market.intelligence@spglobal.com, https://www.spglobal.com/; Update: Aerospace and Defense North America.

AERONAUTICS, COMMERCIAL-AIRPORT SUMMARY

FlightAware, 11 Greenway Plaza, Ste. 2900, Houston, TX, 77046, USA, (713) 877-9010, contact@flightaware.com, https://flightaware.com/; FlightAware Firehose.

Regional Airline Association (RAA), 1201 15th St. NW, Ste. 430, Washington, DC, 20005, USA, (202) 367-1170, raa@raa.org, https://www.raa.org; The Year of Community: 2021 Annual Report.

U.S. Department of Transportation (DOT), Office of Aviation Consumer Protection, 1200 New Jersey Ave. SE, Washington, DC, 20590, USA, (202) 366-2220, https://www.transportation.gov/airconsumer; Air Travel Consumer Report.

U.S. Department of Transportation (DOT), Office of the Assistant Secretary for Research and Technology (OST-R), Bureau of Transportation Statistics (BTS), 1200 New Jersey Ave. SE, Washington, DC, 20590, USA, (800) 853-1351, (202) 366-3282, https://www.bts.gov; Airlines, Airports, and Aviation.

AERONAUTICS, COMMERCIAL-AIRPORT SUMMARY-FLIGHT ON-TIME PERFORMANCE

FlightStats by Cirium, 522 SW 5th Ave., Portland, OR, 97204, USA, (503) 274-0938, https://www.flightstats.com; 2022 On-Time Performance Review.

U.S. Department of Transportation (DOT), Office of Aviation Consumer Protection, 1200 New Jersey Ave. SE, Washington, DC, 20590, USA, (202) 366-2220, https://www.transportation.gov/airconsumer; Air Travel Consumer Report.

U.S. Department of Transportation (DOT), Office of the Assistant Secretary for Research and Technology (OST-R), Bureau of Transportation Statistics (BTS), 1200 New Jersey Ave. SE, Washington, DC, 20590, USA, (800) 853-1351, (202) 366-3282, https://www.bts.gov; Airline On-Time Statistics and Delay Causes and Airlines, Airports, and Aviation.

AERONAUTICS, COMMERCIAL-CIVIL AVIATION

U.S. Department of Transportation (DOT), Office of Aviation Consumer Protection, 1200 New Jersey Ave. SE, Washington, DC, 20590, USA, (202) 366-2220, https://www.transportation.gov/airconsumer; Air Travel Consumer Report.

U.S. Department of Transportation (DOT), Office of the Assistant Secretary for Research and Technology (OST-R), Bureau of Transportation Statistics (BTS), 1200 New Jersey Ave. SE, Washington, DC, 20590, USA, (800) 853-1351, (202) 366-3282, https://www.bts.gov; TranStats.

AERONAUTICS, COMMERCIAL-COST INDEXES

Airlines for America (A4A), 1275 Pennsylvania Ave. NW, Ste. 1300, Washington, DC, 20004, USA, (202) 626-4000, mediarelations@airlines.org, https://www.airlines.org; A4A Passenger Airline Cost Index (PACI) and Economic Impact of Commercial Aviation.

AMSTAT, 44 Apple St., Ste. 5, Tinton Falls, NJ, 07724, USA, (732) 530-6400, (877) 426-7828, (732) 530-6360, service@amstatcorp.com, https://www.amstatcorp.com/; AMSTAT Premier and AMSTAT StatPak.

AERONAUTICS, COMMERCIAL-EARNINGS

S&P Global, 55 Water St., New York, NY, 10041, USA, (212) 438-2000, market.intelligence@spglobal.com, https://www.spglobal.com/; Update: Aerospace and Defense North America.

U.S. Census Bureau, 4600 Silver Hill Rd., Washington, DC, 20233, USA, (301) 763-4636, (800) 923-8282, https://www.census.gov; County Business Patterns (CBP) 2020.

U.S. Census Bureau, Center for Economic Studies (CES), 4600 Silver Hill Rd., Washington, DC, 20233, USA, (301) 763-6460, (301) 763-5935, ces.contacts@census.gov, https://www.census.gov/programs-surveys/ces.html; Transportation and Warehousing, 2017 Economic Census.

U.S. Department of Labor (DOL), Bureau of Labor Statistics (BLS), Postal Square Bldg., 2 Massachusetts Ave. NE, Washington, DC, 20212-0001, USA, (202) 691-5200, (202) 691-7890, blsdata_staff@bls.gov, https://www.bls.gov; Current Employment Statistics (CES).

AERONAUTICS, COMMERCIAL-EMPLOYEES

Airlines for America (A4A), 1275 Pennsylvania Ave. NW, Ste. 1300, Washington, DC, 20004, USA, (202) 626-4000, mediarelations@airlines.org, https://www.airlines.org; A4A Passenger Airline Cost Index (PACI).

U.S. Census Bureau, 4600 Silver Hill Rd., Washington, DC, 20233, USA, (301) 763-4636, (800) 923-8282, https://www.census.gov; County Business Patterns (CBP) 2020.

U.S. Census Bureau, Center for Economic Studies (CES), 4600 Silver Hill Rd., Washington, DC, 20233, USA, (301) 763-6460, (301) 763-5935, ces.contacts@census.gov, https://www.census.gov/programs-surveys/ces.html; Transportation and Warehousing, 2017 Economic Census.

U.S. Department of Labor (DOL), Bureau of Labor Statistics (BLS), Postal Square Bldg., 2 Massachusetts Ave. NE, Washington, DC, 20212-0001, USA, (202) 691-5200, (202) 691-7890, blsdata_staff@bls.gov, https://www.bls.gov; Current Employment Statistics (CES).

U.S. Department of Transportation (DOT), Federal Aviation Administration (FAA), 800 Independence Ave. SW, Washington, DC, 20591, USA, (866) 835-5322, https://www.faa.gov/; Airmen Knowledge Test Statistics.

U.S. Department of Transportation (DOT), Office of the Assistant Secretary for Research and Technology (OST-R), Bureau of Transportation Statistics (BTS), 1200 New Jersey Ave. SE, Washington, DC, 20590, USA, (800) 853-1351, (202) 366-3282, https://www.bts.gov; Airlines, Airports, and Aviation.

AERONAUTICS, COMMERCIAL-FEDERAL OUTLAYS

U.S. Office of Management and Budget (OMB), 725 17th St. NW, Washington, DC, 20503, USA, (202) 395-3080, https://www.whitehouse.gov/omb/; Budget of the United States Government, Fiscal Year 2023 and Historical Tables.

AERONAUTICS, COMMERCIAL-FINANCES

Airlines for America (A4A), 1275 Pennsylvania Ave. NW, Ste. 1300, Washington, DC, 20004, USA, (202) 626-4000, mediarelations@airlines.org, https://www.airlines.org; A4A Passenger Airline Cost Index (PACI) and Economic Impact of Commercial Aviation.

AMSTAT, 44 Apple St., Ste. 5, Tinton Falls, NJ, 07724, USA, (732) 530-6400, (877) 426-7828, (732) 530-6360, service@amstatcorp.com, https://www.amstatcorp.com/; AMSTAT Premier and AMSTAT StatPak.

S&P Global, 55 Water St., New York, NY, 10041, USA, (212) 438-2000, market.intelligence@spglobal.com, https://www.spglobal.com/; Update: Aerospace and Defense North America.

U.S. Department of Transportation (DOT), Office of the Assistant Secretary for Research and Technology (OST-R), Bureau of Transportation Statistics (BTS), 1200 New Jersey Ave. SE, Washington, DC, 20590, USA, (800) 853-1351, (202) 366-3282, https://www.bts.gov; Airlines, Airports, and Aviation.

AERONAUTICS, COMMERCIAL-FREIGHT

Airlines for America (A4A), 1275 Pennsylvania Ave. NW, Ste. 1300, Washington, DC, 20004, USA, (202) 626-4000, mediarelations@airlines.org, https://www.airlines.org; A4A Passenger Airline Cost Index (PACI) and Economic Impact of Commercial Aviation.

AERONAUTICS, COMMERCIAL-INDUSTRIAL SAFETY

National Transportation Safety Board (NTSB), 490 L'Enfant Plz. SW, Washington, DC, 20594, USA, (202) 314-6000, https://www.ntsb.gov; Accident Data and Statistical Reviews.

U.S. Department of Labor (DOL), Bureau of Labor Statistics (BLS), Postal Square Bldg., 2 Massachusetts Ave. NE, Washington, DC, 20212-0001, USA, (202) 691-5200, (202) 691-7890, blsdata_staff@bls.gov, https://www.bls.gov; Injuries, Illnesses, and Fatalities (IIF).

AERONAUTICS, COMMERCIAL-PASSENGER SCREENING

U.S. Department of Transportation (DOT), Office of the Assistant Secretary for Research and Technology (OST-R), Bureau of Transportation Statistics (BTS), 1200 New Jersey Ave. SE, Washington, DC, 20590, USA, (800) 853-1351, (202) 366-3282, https://www.bts.gov; TranStats.

AERONAUTICS, COMMERCIAL-PASSENGER TRAFFIC

U.S. Department of Transportation (DOT), Federal Aviation Administration (FAA), 800 Independence Ave. SW, Washington, DC, 20591, USA, (866) 835-5322, https://www.faa.gov/; Passengers & Cargo: Unruly Passengers.

AERONAUTICS, COMMERCIAL-PRICE INDEXES

U.S. Department of Labor (DOL), Bureau of Labor Statistics (BLS), Postal Square Bldg., 2 Massachusetts Ave. NE, Washington, DC, 20212-0001, USA, (202) 691-5200, (202) 691-7890, blsdata_staff@bls.gov, https://www.bls.gov; Consumer Price Index (CPI) Databases.

AERONAUTICS, COMMERCIAL-PRODUCTIVITY

U.S. Department of Labor (DOL), Bureau of Labor Statistics (BLS), Postal Square Bldg., 2 Massachusetts Ave. NE, Washington, DC, 20212-0001, USA, (202) 691-5200, (202) 691-7890, blsdata_staff@bls.gov, https://www.bls.gov; Productivity.

AERONAUTICS, COMMERCIAL-PROFITS

Airlines for America (A4A), 1275 Pennsylvania Ave. NW, Ste. 1300, Washington, DC, 20004, USA, (202) 626-4000, mediarelations@airlines.org, https://www.airlines.org; A4A Passenger Airline Cost Index (PACI).

AERONAUTICS, COMMERCIAL-SAFETY MEASURES

U.S. Department of Transportation (DOT), Federal Aviation Administration (FAA), 800 Independence Ave. SW, Washington, DC, 20591, USA, (866) 835-5322, https://www.faa.gov/; Passengers & Cargo: Unruly Passengers.

AERONAUTICS, COMMERCIAL-TRAFFIC CARRIED

Airlines for America (A4A), 1275 Pennsylvania Ave. NW, Ste. 1300, Washington, DC, 20004, USA, (202) 626-4000, mediarelations@airlines.org, https://www.airlines.org; A4A Passenger Airline Cost Index (PACI).

Regional Airline Association (RAA), 1201 15th St. NW, Ste. 430, Washington, DC, 20005, USA, (202) 367-1170, raa@raa.org, https://www.raa.org; The Year of Community: 2021 Annual Report.

AEROSPACE INDUSTRY

Aerospace Industries Association (AIA), 1000 Wilson Blvd., Ste. 1700, Arlington, VA, 22209-3928, USA, (703) 358-1000, aia@aia-aerospace.org, https://www.aia-aerospace.org/; 2021 Facts & Figures.

Euromonitor International, Inc., 1 N Dearborn St., Ste. 1700, Chicago, IL, 60602, USA, (312) 922-

1115, (312) 922-1157, info-usa@euromonitor.com, https://www.euromonitor.com/; Strategic Analysis of the World's Largest Companies.

European Cockpit Association (ECA), Rue du Commerce 20-22, Brussels, B-1000, BEL, eca@eurocockpit.be, https://www.eurocockpit.be/; COVID-19: Thousands of Aircrew Redundant.

OpenSecrets, 1300 L St. NW , Ste. 200, Washington, DC, 20005, USA, (202) 857-0044, (202) 857-7809, info@crp.org, https://www.opensecrets.org/; Blue Origin and SpaceX Lobby for Dominance and Government Contracts in Billionaire Space Race.

AEROSPACE INDUSTRY-EMPLOYEES

Aerospace Industries Association (AIA), 1000 Wilson Blvd., Ste. 1700, Arlington, VA, 22209-3928, USA, (703) 358-1000, aia@aia-aerospace.org, https://www.aia-aerospace.org/; 2022 Aerospace & Defense Workforce Study.

U.S. Department of Labor (DOL), Bureau of Labor Statistics (BLS), Postal Square Bldg., 2 Massachusetts Ave. NE, Washington, DC, 20212-0001, USA, (202) 691-5200, (202) 691-7890, blsdata_staff@bls.gov, https://www.bls.gov; Industry-Occupation Matrix Data, By Occupation.

U.S. Department of Transportation (DOT), Office of the Assistant Secretary for Research and Technology (OST-R), Bureau of Transportation Statistics (BTS), 1200 New Jersey Ave. SE, Washington, DC, 20590, USA, (800) 853-1351, (202) 366-3282, https://www.bts.gov; TranStats.

AEROSPACE INDUSTRY-INTERNATIONAL TRADE

U.S. Department of Transportation (DOT), Federal Aviation Administration (FAA), 800 Independence Ave. SW, Washington, DC, 20591, USA, (866) 835-5322, https://www.faa.gov/; FAA Aerospace Forecasts.

AEROSPACE INDUSTRY-SALES

AMSTAT, 44 Apple St., Ste. 5, Tinton Falls, NJ, 07724, USA, (732) 530-6400, (877) 426-7828, (732) 530-6360, service@amstatcorp.com, https://www.amstatcorp.com/; AMSTAT Premier and AMSTAT StatPak.

S&P Global, 55 Water St., New York, NY, 10041, USA, (212) 438-2000, market.intelligence@spglobal.com, https://www.spglobal.com/; Update: Aerospace and Defense North America.

AEROSPACE INDUSTRY-SHIPMENTS

Aerospace Industries Association (AIA), 1000 Wilson Blvd., Ste. 1700, Arlington, VA, 22209-3928, USA, (703) 358-1000, aia@aia-aerospace.org, https://www.aia-aerospace.org/; 2022 Aerospace & Defense Workforce Study.

U.S. Department of Transportation (DOT), Federal Aviation Administration (FAA), 800 Independence Ave. SW, Washington, DC, 20591, USA, (866) 835-5322, https://www.faa.gov/; FAA Aerospace Forecasts.

AFFIRMATIVE ACTION PROGRAMS

The Gallup Organization, 901 F St. NW, Washington, DC, 20004, USA, (202) 715-3030, (800) 204-1192, (202) 715-3045, https://www.gallup.com; Americans' Support for Affirmative Action Programs Rises.

Inside Higher Ed, 1150 Connecticut Ave. NW, Ste. 400, Washington, DC, 20036, USA, (202) 659-9208, (202) 659-9381, info@insidehighered.com, https://www.insidehighered.com/; Survey of College and University Admissions Directors, 2022.

University of California Los Angeles (UCLA), The Civil Rights Project, 8370 Math Sciences, PO Box 951521, Los Angeles, CA, 90095-1521, USA, crp@ucla.edu, https://www.civilrightsproject.ucla.edu/; The Walls Around Opportunity: The Failure of Colorblind Policy for Higher Education.

AFFORDABLE CARE ACT

The Brookings Institution, 1775 Massachusetts Ave. NW, Washington, DC, 20036, USA, (202) 797-6000, communications@brookings.edu, https://www.brookings.edu/; All Medicaid Expansions Are Not Created Equal: The Geography and Targeting of the Affordable Care Act.

The Henry J. Kaiser Family Foundation (KFF), 185 Berry St., Ste. 2000, San Francisco, CA, 94107, USA, (650) 854-9400, (650) 854-4800, https://www.kff.org; How ACA Marketplace Premiums are Changing by County in 2023 and Status of State Medicaid Expansion Decisions: Interactive Map.

Issue Lab by Candid, 32 Old Slip, 24th Fl., New York, NY, 10003, USA, (800) 424-9836, https://www.issuelab.org/; Issue Lab Special Collection: Affordable Care Act.

AFGHAN WAR, 2001-

Brown University, Watson Institute of International and Public Affairs, Costs of War Project, 111 Thayer St., Box 1970, Providence, RI, 02912-1970, USA, (401) 863-2809, costsofwar@brown.edu, https://watson.brown.edu/; Costs of War.

Institute for the Study of War (ISW), 1400 16th St. NW, Ste. 515, Washington, DC, 20036, USA, (202) 293-5550, https://www.understandingwar.org/; Regional Actors Eye Threats and Opportunities in Taliban Takeover.

U.S. Department of Defense (DOD), 1400 Defense Pentagon, Washington, DC, 20301-1400, USA, (703) 571-3343, https://www.defense.gov; Enhancing Security and Stability in Afghanistan.

AFGHANISTAN-NATIONAL STATISTICAL OFFICE

National Statistic and Information Authority (NSIA), PO Box 1254, Kabul, AFG, info@nsia.gov.af, https://nsia.gov.af; National Data Reports (Afghanistan).

AFGHANISTAN-AGRICULTURE

Asian Development Bank (ADB), 6 ADB Ave., Mandaluyong City, 1550, PHL, information@adb.org, https://www.adb.org/; Key Indicators for Asia and the Pacific 2022.

The Economist Group: Economist Intelligence Unit (EIU), 900 3rd Ave., 16th Fl., New York, NY, 10022, USA, (212) 541-0500, americas@eiu.com, https://www.eiu.com; Afghanistan Country Report.

Euromonitor International, Inc., 1 N Dearborn St., Ste. 1700, Chicago, IL, 60602, USA, (312) 922-1115, (312) 922-1157, info-usa@euromonitor.com, https://www.euromonitor.com/; Geographies.

Organisation of Islamic Cooperation (OIC), Statistical, Economic and Social Research and Training Centre for Islamic Countries (SESRIC), Kudus Cad. No. 9, Diplomatik Site, Ankara, 06450, TUR, statistics@sesric.org, https://www.sesric.org/; OIC Statistics (OICStat) Database and OIC-Countries in Figures (OIC-CIF).

Palgrave Macmillan, 1 New York Plaza, Ste. 4500, New York, NY, 10004-1562, USA, (800) 777-4643, orders@palgrave.com, https://www.palgrave.com/us; The Statesman's Yearbook, 2023.

Routledge - Taylor & Francis Group, 6000 Broken Sound Pkwy. NW, Ste. 300, Boca Raton, FL, 33487, USA, (800) 634-1420, (800) 634-7064, orders@taylorandfrancis.com, https://www.routledge.com/; The Europa World Year Book 2022.

United Nations Economic and Social Commission for Asia and the Pacific (ESCAP), United Nations Building, Rajadamnern Nok Ave., Bangkok, 10200, THA, https://www.unescap.org/; Asia-Pacific Development Journal and SDG Gateway Data Explorer.

United Nations Food and Agricultural Organization (FAO), 2121 K St., Ste. 800B, Washington, DC, 20037, USA, (202) 653-2400 (Dial from U.S.), (202) 653-5760 (Fax from U.S.), fao-hq@fao.org, https://www.fao.org; AQUASTAT and The State of Food and Agriculture (SOFA) 2022.

United Nations Statistics Division (UNSD), United Nations Plz., New York, NY, 10017, USA, (800) 253-9646, (212) 963-9851, statistics@un.org, https://unstats.un.org; Statistical Yearbook of the United Nations 2021.

AFGHANISTAN-AIRLINES

International Civil Aviation Organization (ICAO), 999 Robert-Bourassa Blvd., Montreal, QC, H3C 5H7, CAN, (514) 954-8219 (Dial from U.S.), (514) 954-6077 (Fax from U.S.), icaohq@icao.int, https://www.icao.int; ICAO Regional Reports.

Palgrave Macmillan, 1 New York Plaza, Ste. 4500, New York, NY, 10004-1562, USA, (800) 777-4643, orders@palgrave.com, https://www.palgrave.com/us; The Statesman's Yearbook, 2023.

Routledge - Taylor & Francis Group, 6000 Broken Sound Pkwy. NW, Ste. 300, Boca Raton, FL, 33487, USA, (800) 634-1420, (800) 634-7064, orders@taylorandfrancis.com, https://www.routledge.com/; The Europa World Year Book 2022.

AFGHANISTAN-ALUMINUM PRODUCTION

See AFGHANISTAN-MINERAL INDUSTRIES

AFGHANISTAN-ARMED FORCES

Central Intelligence Agency (CIA), Office of Public Affairs, Washington, DC, 20505, USA, (703) 482-0623, https://www.cia.gov; The World Factbook.

Institute for the Study of War (ISW), 1400 16th St. NW, Ste. 515, Washington, DC, 20036, USA, (202) 293-5550, https://www.understandingwar.org/; Regional Actors Eye Threats and Opportunities in Taliban Takeover.

International Institute for Strategic Studies (IISS) - Americas, 2121 K St. NW, Ste. 600, Washington, DC, 20037, USA, (202) 659-1490, (202) 659-1499, https://www.iiss.org/; Armed Conflict Survey 2021 and The Military Balance 2022.

Palgrave Macmillan, 1 New York Plaza, Ste. 4500, New York, NY, 10004-1562, USA, (800) 777-4643, orders@palgrave.com, https://www.palgrave.com/us; The Statesman's Yearbook, 2023.

Stockholm International Peace Research Institute (SIPRI), Signalistgatan 9, Stockholm, SE 169 72, SWE, https://www.sipri.org/; SIPRI Arms Transfers Database and SIPRI Military Expenditure Database.

AFGHANISTAN-BALANCE OF PAYMENTS

International Monetary Fund (IMF), 700 19th St. NW, Washington, DC, 20431, USA, (202) 623-7000, (202) 623-4661, publications@imf.org, https://www.imf.org; International Financial Statistics (IFS).

Routledge - Taylor & Francis Group, 6000 Broken Sound Pkwy. NW, Ste. 300, Boca Raton, FL, 33487, USA, (800) 634-1420, (800) 634-7064, orders@taylorandfrancis.com, https://www.routledge.com/; The Europa World Year Book 2022.

SAGE Publications, 2455 Teller Rd., Thousand Oaks, CA, 91320, USA, (800) 818-7243, (800) 583-2665, journals@sagepub.com, https://www.sagepub.com; Journal of South Asian Development and South Asia Economic Journal.

United Nations Conference on Trade and Development (UNCTAD), Palais des Nations, Geneva, 1211, SWI, (212) 963-6896, unctadinfo@unctad.org, https://unctad.org; Handbook of Statistics 2021.

AFGHANISTAN-BANKS AND BANKING

Asian Development Bank (ADB), 6 ADB Ave., Mandaluyong City, 1550, PHL, information@adb.org, https://www.adb.org/; Key Indicators for Asia and the Pacific 2022.

Euromonitor International, Inc., 1 N Dearborn St., Ste. 1700, Chicago, IL, 60602, USA, (312) 922-1115, (312) 922-1157, info-usa@euromonitor.com, https://www.euromonitor.com/; Geographies.

International Monetary Fund (IMF), 700 19th St. NW, Washington, DC, 20431, USA, (202) 623-7000, (202) 623-4661, publications@imf.org, https://www.imf.org; International Financial Statistics (IFS).

Routledge - Taylor & Francis Group, 6000 Broken Sound Pkwy. NW, Ste. 300, Boca Raton, FL, 33487,

USA, (800) 634-1420, (800) 634-7064, orders@taylorandfrancis.com, https://www.routledge.com/; The Europa World Year Book 2022.

SAGE Publications, 2455 Teller Rd., Thousand Oaks, CA, 91320, USA, (800) 818-7243, (800) 583-2665, journals@sagepub.com, https://www.sagepub.com; Journal of South Asian Development and South Asia Economic Journal.

AFGHANISTAN-BARLEY PRODUCTION

See AFGHANISTAN-CROPS

AFGHANISTAN-BROADCASTING

Central Intelligence Agency (CIA), Office of Public Affairs, Washington, DC, 20505, USA, (703) 482-0623, https://www.cia.gov; The World Factbook.

Euromonitor International, Inc., 1 N Dearborn St., Ste. 1700, Chicago, IL, 60602, USA, (312) 922-1115, (312) 922-1157, info-usa@euromonitor.com, https://www.euromonitor.com/; Geographies.

Palgrave Macmillan, 1 New York Plaza, Ste. 4500, New York, NY, 10004-1562, USA, (800) 777-4643, orders@palgrave.com, https://www.palgrave.com/us; The Statesman's Yearbook, 2023.

UNESCO Institute for Statistics, C.P 250 Succursale H, Montreal, QC, H3G 2K8, CAN, (514) 343-6880 (Dial from U.S.), (514) 343-5740 (Fax from U.S.), uis.publications@unesco.org, http://uis.unesco.org/; UIS.Stat.

WRTH Publications Limited, PO Box 290, Oxford, OX2 7FT, GBR, sales@wrth.com, https://www.wrth.com; World Radio TV Handbook 2023.

AFGHANISTAN-BUDGET

Central Intelligence Agency (CIA), Office of Public Affairs, Washington, DC, 20505, USA, (703) 482-0623, https://www.cia.gov; The World Factbook.

AFGHANISTAN-BUSINESS

SAGE Publications, 2455 Teller Rd., Thousand Oaks, CA, 91320, USA, (800) 818-7243, (800) 583-2665, journals@sagepub.com, https://www.sagepub.com; Journal of South Asian Development and South Asia Economic Journal.

United Nations Economic and Social Commission for Asia and the Pacific (ESCAP), United Nations Building, Rajadamnern Nok Ave., Bangkok, 10200, THA, https://www.unescap.org/; SDG Gateway Data Explorer.

AFGHANISTAN-CLIMATE

Palgrave Macmillan, 1 New York Plaza, Ste. 4500, New York, NY, 10004-1562, USA, (800) 777-4643, orders@palgrave.com, https://www.palgrave.com/us; The Statesman's Yearbook, 2023.

AFGHANISTAN-COAL PRODUCTION

See AFGHANISTAN-MINERAL INDUSTRIES

AFGHANISTAN-COMMERCE

Palgrave Macmillan, 1 New York Plaza, Ste. 4500, New York, NY, 10004-1562, USA, (800) 777-4643, orders@palgrave.com, https://www.palgrave.com/us; The Statesman's Yearbook, 2023.

SAGE Publications, 2455 Teller Rd., Thousand Oaks, CA, 91320, USA, (800) 818-7243, (800) 583-2665, journals@sagepub.com, https://www.sagepub.com; Journal of South Asian Development and South Asia Economic Journal.

UK Data Service, University of Essex, Wivenhoe Park, Colchester, Essex, CO4 3SQ, GBR, https://ukdataservice.ac.uk/; International Aggregate Data.

AFGHANISTAN-COMMODITY EXCHANGES

Barchart, 209 W Jackson Blvd., 2nd Fl., Chicago, IL, 60606, USA, (877) 247-4394, commodities@barchart.com, https://www.barchart.com/cmdty; The cmdty Yearbook 2023; cmdtyStats: Commodity Statistics and Fundamental Data; cmdtyView: Commodity Index; and Commodity Data and Prices.

International Monetary Fund (IMF), 700 19th St. NW, Washington, DC, 20431, USA, (202) 623-7000, (202) 623-4661, publications@imf.org, https://www.imf.org; IMF Primary Commodity Prices.

AFGHANISTAN-CONSUMER PRICE INDEXES

Asian Development Bank (ADB), 6 ADB Ave., Mandaluyong City, 1550, PHL, information@adb.org, https://www.adb.org/; Key Indicators for Asia and the Pacific 2022.

Routledge - Taylor & Francis Group, 6000 Broken Sound Pkwy. NW, Ste. 300, Boca Raton, FL, 33487, USA, (800) 634-1420, (800) 634-7064, orders@taylorandfrancis.com, https://www.routledge.com/; The Europa World Year Book 2022.

SAGE Publications, 2455 Teller Rd., Thousand Oaks, CA, 91320, USA, (800) 818-7243, (800) 583-2665, journals@sagepub.com, https://www.sagepub.com; Journal of South Asian Development and South Asia Economic Journal.

AFGHANISTAN-COPPER INDUSTRY AND TRADE

See AFGHANISTAN-MINERAL INDUSTRIES

AFGHANISTAN-CORN INDUSTRY

See AFGHANISTAN-CROPS

AFGHANISTAN-COTTON

See AFGHANISTAN-CROPS

AFGHANISTAN-CRIME

United Nations Office on Drugs and Crime (UNODC), Vienna International Ctre., PO Box 500, Vienna, A-1400, AUT, unodc@unodc.org, https://www.unodc.org/; Afghanistan Opium Survey 2020: Cultivation and Production.

AFGHANISTAN-CROPS

International Monetary Fund (IMF), 700 19th St. NW, Washington, DC, 20431, USA, (202) 623-7000, (202) 623-4661, publications@imf.org, https://www.imf.org; International Financial Statistics (IFS).

Palgrave Macmillan, 1 New York Plaza, Ste. 4500, New York, NY, 10004-1562, USA, (800) 777-4643, orders@palgrave.com, https://www.palgrave.com/us; The Statesman's Yearbook, 2023.

United Nations Food and Agricultural Organization (FAO), 2121 K St., Ste. 800B, Washington, DC, 20037, USA, (202) 653-2400 (Dial from U.S.), (202) 653-5760 (Fax from U.S.), fao-hq@fao.org, https://www.fao.org; The State of Food and Agriculture (SOFA) 2022.

United Nations Statistics Division (UNSD), United Nations Plz., New York, NY, 10017, USA, (800) 253-9646, (212) 963-9851, statistics@un.org, https://unstats.un.org; Statistical Yearbook of the United Nations 2021.

AFGHANISTAN-DAIRY PROCESSING

United Nations Food and Agricultural Organization (FAO), 2121 K St., Ste. 800B, Washington, DC, 20037, USA, (202) 653-2400 (Dial from U.S.), (202) 653-5760 (Fax from U.S.), fao-hq@fao.org, https://www.fao.org; The State of Food and Agriculture (SOFA) 2022.

AFGHANISTAN-DEBTS, EXTERNAL

Asian Development Bank (ADB), 6 ADB Ave., Mandaluyong City, 1550, PHL, information@adb.org, https://www.adb.org/; Key Indicators for Asia and the Pacific 2022.

Palgrave Macmillan, 1 New York Plaza, Ste. 4500, New York, NY, 10004-1562, USA, (800) 777-4643, orders@palgrave.com, https://www.palgrave.com/us; The Statesman's Yearbook, 2023.

SAGE Publications, 2455 Teller Rd., Thousand Oaks, CA, 91320, USA, (800) 818-7243, (800) 583-2665, journals@sagepub.com, https://www.sagepub.com; Journal of South Asian Development and South Asia Economic Journal.

The World Bank, 1818 H St. NW, Washington, DC, 20433, USA, (202) 473-1000, (202) 477-6391, eds03@worldbank.org, https://www.worldbank.org/; Global Financial Development Report 2019-2020: Bank Regulation and Supervision a Decade after the Global Financial Crisis.

AFGHANISTAN-DEFENSE EXPENDITURES

See AFGHANISTAN-ARMED FORCES

AFGHANISTAN-DIAMONDS

See AFGHANISTAN-MINERAL INDUSTRIES

AFGHANISTAN-ECONOMIC ASSISTANCE

United Nations Statistics Division (UNSD), United Nations Plz., New York, NY, 10017, USA, (800) 253-9646, (212) 963-9851, statistics@un.org, https://unstats.un.org; Statistical Yearbook of the United Nations 2021.

AFGHANISTAN-ECONOMIC CONDITIONS

Asian Development Bank (ADB), 6 ADB Ave., Mandaluyong City, 1550, PHL, information@adb.org, https://www.adb.org/; Key Indicators for Asia and the Pacific 2022.

Bernan Press, 15250 NBN Way, Bldg. C, Blue Ridge Summit, PA, 17214, USA, (301) 459-2255, (800) 865-3457, (800) 865-3450, customercare@bernan.com, https://rowman.com/Page/Bernan; World Economic Outlook, April 2022.

Center for Economic and Policy Research (CEPR), 1611 Connecticut Ave. NW, Ste. 400, Washington, DC, 20009, USA, (202) 293-5380, (202) 588-1356, info@cepr.net, https://cepr.net/; The Human Consequences of Economic Sanctions.

Central Intelligence Agency (CIA), Office of Public Affairs, Washington, DC, 20505, USA, (703) 482-0623, https://www.cia.gov; The World Factbook.

The Economist Group: Economist Intelligence Unit (EIU), 900 3rd Ave., 16th Fl., New York, NY, 10022, USA, (212) 541-0500, americas@eiu.com, https://www.eiu.com; Afghanistan Country Report.

Euromonitor International, Inc., 1 N Dearborn St., Ste. 1700, Chicago, IL, 60602, USA, (312) 922-1115, (312) 922-1157, info-usa@euromonitor.com, https://www.euromonitor.com/; Geographies.

International Monetary Fund (IMF), 700 19th St. NW, Washington, DC, 20431, USA, (202) 623-7000, (202) 623-4661, publications@imf.org, https://www.imf.org; IMF Data and World Economic Outlook.

Organisation of Islamic Cooperation (OIC), Statistical, Economic and Social Research and Training Centre for Islamic Countries (SESRIC), Kudus Cad. No. 9, Diplomatik Site, Ankara, 06450, TUR, statistics@sesric.org, https://www.sesric.org/; OIC Economic Outlook 2021; OIC Statistics (OICStat) Database; and OIC-Countries in Figures (OIC-CIF).

Palgrave Macmillan, 1 New York Plaza, Ste. 4500, New York, NY, 10004-1562, USA, (800) 777-4643, orders@palgrave.com, https://www.palgrave.com/us; The Statesman's Yearbook, 2023.

Routledge - Taylor & Francis Group, 6000 Broken Sound Pkwy. NW, Ste. 300, Boca Raton, FL, 33487, USA, (800) 634-1420, (800) 634-7064, orders@taylorandfrancis.com, https://www.routledge.com/; The Europa World Year Book 2022.

SAGE Publications, 2455 Teller Rd., Thousand Oaks, CA, 91320, USA, (800) 818-7243, (800) 583-2665, journals@sagepub.com, https://www.sagepub.com; Journal of South Asian Development and South Asia Economic Journal.

United Nations Statistics Division (UNSD), United Nations Plz., New York, NY, 10017, USA, (800) 253-9646, (212) 963-9851, statistics@un.org, https://unstats.un.org; World Statistics Pocketbook 2021.

The World Bank, 1818 H St. NW, Washington, DC, 20433, USA, (202) 473-1000, (202) 477-6391, eds03@worldbank.org, https://www.worldbank.org/; Global Economic Monitor (GEM); Global Economic Prospects, June 2022; and The Global Findex Database 2021.

AFGHANISTAN-EDUCATION

Euromonitor International, Inc., 1 N Dearborn St., Ste. 1700, Chicago, IL, 60602, USA, (312) 922-1115, (312) 922-1157, info-usa@euromonitor.com, https://www.euromonitor.com/; Geographies.

Infoplease, c/o Sandbox Networks, Inc., 1 Lincoln St., 24th Fl., Boston, MA, 02111, USA, https://www.infoplease.com; Countries of the World.

Organisation of Islamic Cooperation (OIC), Statistical, Economic and Social Research and Training Centre for Islamic Countries (SESRIC), Kudus Cad. No. 9, Diplomatik Site, Ankara, 06450, TUR, statistics@sesric.org, https://www.sesric.org/; OIC Statistics (OICStat) Database.

Palgrave Macmillan, 1 New York Plaza, Ste. 4500, New York, NY, 10004-1562, USA, (800) 777-4643, orders@palgrave.com, https://www.palgrave.com/us; The Statesman's Yearbook, 2023.

Routledge - Taylor & Francis Group, 6000 Broken Sound Pkwy. NW, Ste. 300, Boca Raton, FL, 33487, USA, (800) 634-1420, (800) 634-7064, orders@taylorandfrancis.com, https://www.routledge.com/; The Europa World Year Book 2022.

UNESCO Institute for Statistics, C.P 250 Succursale H, Montreal, QC, H3G 2K8, CAN, (514) 343-6880 (Dial from U.S.), (514) 343-5740 (Fax from U.S.), uis.publications@unesco.org, http://uis.unesco.org/; Literacy and UIS.Stat.

United Nations Economic and Social Commission for Asia and the Pacific (ESCAP), United Nations Building, Rajadamnern Nok Ave., Bangkok, 10200, THA, https://www.unescap.org/; Asia-Pacific Development Journal and SDG Gateway Data Explorer.

United Nations Statistics Division (UNSD), United Nations Plz., New York, NY, 10017, USA, (800) 253-9646, (212) 963-9851, statistics@un.org, https://unstats.un.org; Millennium Development Goal Indicators.

AFGHANISTAN-ELECTRICITY

United Nations Statistics Division (UNSD), United Nations Plz., New York, NY, 10017, USA, (800) 253-9646, (212) 963-9851, statistics@un.org, https://unstats.un.org; Statistical Yearbook of the United Nations 2021.

AFGHANISTAN-EMPLOYMENT

International Labour Organization (ILO), 4 Rte. des Morillons, Geneva, CH-1211, SWI, ilo@ilo.org, https://www.ilo.org; NORMLEX Information System on International Labour Standards.

SAGE Publications, 2455 Teller Rd., Thousand Oaks, CA, 91320, USA, (800) 818-7243, (800) 583-2665, journals@sagepub.com, https://www.sagepub.com; Journal of South Asian Development and South Asia Economic Journal.

UK Data Service, University of Essex, Wivenhoe Park, Colchester, Essex, CO4 3SQ, GBR, https://ukdataservice.ac.uk/; International Aggregate Data.

United Nations Economic and Social Commission for Asia and the Pacific (ESCAP), United Nations Building, Rajadamnern Nok Ave., Bangkok, 10200, THA, https://www.unescap.org/; Asia-Pacific Development Journal.

AFGHANISTAN-ENERGY INDUSTRIES

Enerdata, 47 avenue Alsace Lorraine, Grenoble, 38027, FRA, (332) 216-4534, research@enerdata.net, https://www.enerdata.net; World Refinery Database.

AFGHANISTAN-ENVIRONMENTAL CONDITIONS

DSI Data Service & Information, Xantener Strasse 51a, Rheinberg, D-47495, GER, dsi@dsidata.com, https://www.dsidata.com/; Global Environmental Database.

The Economist Group: Economist Intelligence Unit (EIU), 900 3rd Ave., 16th Fl., New York, NY, 10022, USA, (212) 541-0500, americas@eiu.com, https://www.eiu.com; Afghanistan Country Report.

Organisation of Islamic Cooperation (OIC), Statistical, Economic and Social Research and Training Centre for Islamic Countries (SESRIC), Kudus Cad. No. 9, Diplomatik Site, Ankara, 06450, TUR, statistics@sesric.org, https://www.sesric.org/; OIC Statistics (OICStat) Database and OIC-Countries in Figures (OIC-CIF).

United Nations Statistics Division (UNSD), United Nations Plz., New York, NY, 10017, USA, (800) 253-9646, (212) 963-9851, statistics@un.org, https://unstats.un.org; World Statistics Pocketbook 2021.

AFGHANISTAN-EXPORTS

Asian Development Bank (ADB), 6 ADB Ave., Mandaluyong City, 1550, PHL, information@adb.org, https://www.adb.org/; Key Indicators for Asia and the Pacific 2022.

Central Intelligence Agency (CIA), Office of Public Affairs, Washington, DC, 20505, USA, (703) 482-0623, https://www.cia.gov; The World Factbook.

The Economist Group: Economist Intelligence Unit (EIU), 900 3rd Ave., 16th Fl., New York, NY, 10022, USA, (212) 541-0500, americas@eiu.com, https://www.eiu.com; Afghanistan Country Report.

International Monetary Fund (IMF), 700 19th St. NW, Washington, DC, 20431, USA, (202) 623-7000, (202) 623-4661, publications@imf.org, https://www.imf.org; Direction of Trade Statistics (DOTS) and International Financial Statistics (IFS).

Organisation of Islamic Cooperation (OIC), Statistical, Economic and Social Research and Training Centre for Islamic Countries (SESRIC), Kudus Cad. No. 9, Diplomatik Site, Ankara, 06450, TUR, statistics@sesric.org, https://www.sesric.org/; OIC Statistics (OICStat) Database.

S&P Global, IHS Markit, 15 Inverness Way E, Englewood, CO, 80112, USA, (800) 447-2273, (800) 854-7179, https://ihsmarkit.com; Global Trade Atlas (GTA).

United Nations Conference on Trade and Development (UNCTAD), Palais des Nations, Geneva, 1211, SWI, (212) 963-6896, unctadinfo@unctad.org, https://unctad.org; Handbook of Statistics 2021.

AFGHANISTAN-FEMALE WORKING POPULATION

See AFGHANISTAN-EMPLOYMENT

AFGHANISTAN-FERTILIZER INDUSTRY

United Nations Food and Agricultural Organization (FAO), 2121 K St., Ste. 800B, Washington, DC, 20037, USA, (202) 653-2400 (Dial from U.S.), (202) 653-5760 (Fax from U.S.), fao-hq@fao.org, https://www.fao.org; The State of Food and Agriculture (SOFA) 2022.

AFGHANISTAN-FETAL MORTALITY

See AFGHANISTAN-MORTALITY

AFGHANISTAN-FINANCE

International Monetary Fund (IMF), 700 19th St. NW, Washington, DC, 20431, USA, (202) 623-7000, (202) 623-4661, publications@imf.org, https://www.imf.org; International Financial Statistics (IFS).

SAGE Publications, 2455 Teller Rd., Thousand Oaks, CA, 91320, USA, (800) 818-7243, (800) 583-2665, journals@sagepub.com, https://www.sagepub.com; Journal of South Asian Development and South Asia Economic Journal.

Stockholm International Peace Research Institute (SIPRI), Signalistgatan 9, Stockholm, SE 169 72, SWE, https://www.sipri.org/; SIPRI Arms Transfers Database and SIPRI Military Expenditure Database.

United Nations Economic and Social Commission for Asia and the Pacific (ESCAP), United Nations Building, Rajadamnern Nok Ave., Bangkok, 10200, THA, https://www.unescap.org/; Asia-Pacific Development Journal and SDG Gateway Data Explorer.

United Nations Statistics Division (UNSD), United Nations Plz., New York, NY, 10017, USA, (800) 253-9646, (212) 963-9851, statistics@un.org, https://unstats.un.org; Statistical Yearbook of the United Nations 2021.

AFGHANISTAN-FINANCE, PUBLIC

Asian Development Bank (ADB), 6 ADB Ave., Mandaluyong City, 1550, PHL, information@adb.org, https://www.adb.org/; Key Indicators for Asia and the Pacific 2022.

Bernan Press, 15250 NBN Way, Bldg. C, Blue Ridge Summit, PA, 17214, USA, (301) 459-2255, (800) 865-3457, (800) 865-3450, customercare@bernan.com, https://rowman.com/Page/Bernan; National Accounts Statistics: Analysis of Main Aggregates 2020.

The Economist Group: Economist Intelligence Unit (EIU), 900 3rd Ave., 16th Fl., New York, NY, 10022, USA, (212) 541-0500, americas@eiu.com, https://www.eiu.com; Afghanistan Country Report.

International Monetary Fund (IMF), 700 19th St. NW, Washington, DC, 20431, USA, (202) 623-7000, (202) 623-4661, publications@imf.org, https://www.imf.org; International Financial Statistics (IFS) and Regional Economic Outlook.

Palgrave Macmillan, 1 New York Plaza, Ste. 4500, New York, NY, 10004-1562, USA, (800) 777-4643, orders@palgrave.com, https://www.palgrave.com/us; The Statesman's Yearbook, 2023.

Routledge - Taylor & Francis Group, 6000 Broken Sound Pkwy. NW, Ste. 300, Boca Raton, FL, 33487, USA, (800) 634-1420, (800) 634-7064, orders@taylorandfrancis.com, https://www.routledge.com/; The Europa World Year Book 2022.

United Nations Economic and Social Commission for Asia and the Pacific (ESCAP), United Nations Building, Rajadamnern Nok Ave., Bangkok, 10200, THA, https://www.unescap.org/; SDG Gateway Data Explorer.

United Nations Statistics Division (UNSD), United Nations Plz., New York, NY, 10017, USA, (800) 253-9646, (212) 963-9851, statistics@un.org, https://unstats.un.org; National Accounts Main Aggregates Database and National Accounts Statistics: Main Aggregates and Detailed Tables.

AFGHANISTAN-FISHERIES

Routledge - Taylor & Francis Group, 6000 Broken Sound Pkwy. NW, Ste. 300, Boca Raton, FL, 33487, USA, (800) 634-1420, (800) 634-7064, orders@taylorandfrancis.com, https://www.routledge.com/; The Europa World Year Book 2022.

United Nations Food and Agricultural Organization (FAO), 2121 K St., Ste. 800B, Washington, DC, 20037, USA, (202) 653-2400 (Dial from U.S.), (202) 653-5760 (Fax from U.S.), fao-hq@fao.org, https://www.fao.org; FAO Yearbook of Fishery and Aquaculture Statistics 2019; Fishery Statistical Collections Global Capture Production; FishStatJ; and The State of Food and Agriculture (SOFA) 2022.

United Nations Statistics Division (UNSD), United Nations Plz., New York, NY, 10017, USA, (800) 253-9646, (212) 963-9851, statistics@un.org, https://unstats.un.org; Statistical Yearbook of the United Nations 2021.

AFGHANISTAN-FOOD

United Nations Economic and Social Commission for Asia and the Pacific (ESCAP), United Nations Building, Rajadamnern Nok Ave., Bangkok, 10200, THA, https://www.unescap.org/; SDG Gateway Data Explorer.

United Nations Food and Agricultural Organization (FAO), 2121 K St., Ste. 800B, Washington, DC, 20037, USA, (202) 653-2400 (Dial from U.S.), (202) 653-5760 (Fax from U.S.), fao-hq@fao.org, https://www.fao.org; The State of Food and Agriculture (SOFA) 2022.

AFGHANISTAN-FOREIGN EXCHANGE RATES

Asian Development Bank (ADB), 6 ADB Ave., Mandaluyong City, 1550, PHL, information@adb.org, https://www.adb.org/; Key Indicators for Asia and the Pacific 2022.

International Monetary Fund (IMF), 700 19th St. NW, Washington, DC, 20431, USA, (202) 623-7000, (202) 623-4661, publications@imf.org, https://www.imf.org; International Financial Statistics (IFS).

AFGHANISTAN-FORESTS AND FORESTRY

Palgrave Macmillan, 1 New York Plaza, Ste. 4500, New York, NY, 10004-1562, USA, (800) 777-4643, orders@palgrave.com, https://www.palgrave.com/us; The Statesman's Yearbook, 2023.

Routledge - Taylor & Francis Group, 6000 Broken Sound Pkwy. NW, Ste. 300, Boca Raton, FL, 33487, USA, (800) 634-1420, (800) 634-7064, orders@taylorandfrancis.com, https://www.routledge.com/; The Europa World Year Book 2022.

UNESCO Institute for Statistics, C.P 250 Succursale H, Montreal, QC, H3G 2K8, CAN, (514) 343-6880 (Dial from U.S.), (514) 343-5740 (Fax from U.S.), uis.publications@unesco.org, http://uis.unesco.org/; UIS.Stat.

United Nations Food and Agricultural Organization (FAO), 2121 K St., Ste. 800B, Washington, DC, 20037, USA, (202) 653-2400 (Dial from U.S.), (202) 653-5760 (Fax from U.S.), fao-hq@fao.org, https://www.fao.org; FAO Yearbook of Forest Products 2019 and The State of Food and Agriculture (SOFA) 2022.

United Nations Statistics Division (UNSD), United Nations Plz., New York, NY, 10017, USA, (800) 253-9646, (212) 963-9851, statistics@un.org, https://unstats.un.org; Statistical Yearbook of the United Nations 2021.

AFGHANISTAN-FRUIT PRODUCTION

See AFGHANISTAN-CROPS

AFGHANISTAN-GAS PRODUCTION

See AFGHANISTAN-MINERAL INDUSTRIES

AFGHANISTAN-GOLD PRODUCTION

See AFGHANISTAN-MINERAL INDUSTRIES

AFGHANISTAN-GROSS DOMESTIC PRODUCT

Asian Development Bank (ADB), 6 ADB Ave., Mandaluyong City, 1550, PHL, information@adb.org, https://www.adb.org/; Key Indicators for Asia and the Pacific 2022.

The Economist Group: Economist Intelligence Unit (EIU), 900 3rd Ave., 16th Fl., New York, NY, 10022, USA, (212) 541-0500, americas@eiu.com, https://www.eiu.com; Afghanistan Country Report.

United Nations Statistics Division (UNSD), United Nations Plz., New York, NY, 10017, USA, (800) 253-9646, (212) 963-9851, statistics@un.org, https://unstats.un.org; Statistical Yearbook of the United Nations 2021.

AFGHANISTAN-GROSS NATIONAL PRODUCT

Asian Development Bank (ADB), 6 ADB Ave., Mandaluyong City, 1550, PHL, information@adb.org, https://www.adb.org/; Key Indicators for Asia and the Pacific 2022.

Palgrave Macmillan, 1 New York Plaza, Ste. 4500, New York, NY, 10004-1562, USA, (800) 777-4643, orders@palgrave.com, https://www.palgrave.com/us; The Statesman's Yearbook, 2023.

United Nations Statistics Division (UNSD), United Nations Plz., New York, NY, 10017, USA, (800) 253-9646, (212) 963-9851, statistics@un.org, https://unstats.un.org; Statistical Yearbook of the United Nations 2021.

AFGHANISTAN-HIDES AND SKINS INDUSTRY

International Monetary Fund (IMF), 700 19th St. NW, Washington, DC, 20431, USA, (202) 623-7000, (202) 623-4661, publications@imf.org, https://www.imf.org; International Financial Statistics (IFS).

AFGHANISTAN-HOUSING

Euromonitor International, Inc., 1 N Dearborn St., Ste. 1700, Chicago, IL, 60602, USA, (312) 922-1115, (312) 922-1157, info-usa@euromonitor.com, https://www.euromonitor.com/; Geographies.

AFGHANISTAN-ILLITERATE PERSONS

UNESCO Institute for Statistics, C.P 250 Succursale H, Montreal, QC, H3G 2K8, CAN, (514) 343-6880 (Dial from U.S.), (514) 343-5740 (Fax from U.S.), uis.publications@unesco.org, http://uis.unesco.org/; UIS.Stat.

United Nations Economic and Social Commission for Asia and the Pacific (ESCAP), United Nations Building, Rajadamnern Nok Ave., Bangkok, 10200, THA, https://www.unescap.org/; Asia-Pacific Development Journal.

AFGHANISTAN-IMPORTS

Asian Development Bank (ADB), 6 ADB Ave., Mandaluyong City, 1550, PHL, information@adb.org, https://www.adb.org/; Key Indicators for Asia and the Pacific 2022.

Central Intelligence Agency (CIA), Office of Public Affairs, Washington, DC, 20505, USA, (703) 482-0623, https://www.cia.gov; The World Factbook.

The Economist Group: Economist Intelligence Unit (EIU), 900 3rd Ave., 16th Fl., New York, NY, 10022, USA, (212) 541-0500, americas@eiu.com, https://www.eiu.com; Afghanistan Country Report.

International Monetary Fund (IMF), 700 19th St. NW, Washington, DC, 20431, USA, (202) 623-7000, (202) 623-4661, publications@imf.org, https://www.imf.org; Direction of Trade Statistics (DOTS) and International Financial Statistics (IFS).

S&P Global, IHS Markit, 15 Inverness Way E, Englewood, CO, 80112, USA, (800) 447-2273, (800) 854-7179, https://ihsmarkit.com; Global Trade Atlas (GTA).

United Nations Conference on Trade and Development (UNCTAD), Palais des Nations, Geneva, 1211, SWI, (212) 963-6896, unctadinfo@unctad.org, https://unctad.org; Handbook of Statistics 2021.

AFGHANISTAN-INDUSTRIES

Central Intelligence Agency (CIA), Office of Public Affairs, Washington, DC, 20505, USA, (703) 482-0623, https://www.cia.gov; The World Factbook.

The Economist Group: Economist Intelligence Unit (EIU), 900 3rd Ave., 16th Fl., New York, NY, 10022, USA, (212) 541-0500, americas@eiu.com, https://www.eiu.com; Afghanistan Country Report.

Euromonitor International, Inc., 1 N Dearborn St., Ste. 1700, Chicago, IL, 60602, USA, (312) 922-1115, (312) 922-1157, info-usa@euromonitor.com, https://www.euromonitor.com/; Geographies.

International Labour Organization (ILO), 4 Rte. des Morillons, Geneva, CH-1211, SWI, ilo@ilo.org, https://www.ilo.org; NORMLEX Information System on International Labour Standards.

Palgrave Macmillan, 1 New York Plaza, Ste. 4500, New York, NY, 10004-1562, USA, (800) 777-4643, orders@palgrave.com, https://www.palgrave.com/us; The Statesman's Yearbook, 2023.

Routledge - Taylor & Francis Group, 6000 Broken Sound Pkwy. NW, Ste. 300, Boca Raton, FL, 33487, USA, (800) 634-1420, (800) 634-7064, orders@taylorandfrancis.com, https://www.routledge.com/; The Europa World Year Book 2022.

SAGE Publications, 2455 Teller Rd., Thousand Oaks, CA, 91320, USA, (800) 818-7243, (800) 583-2665, journals@sagepub.com, https://www.sagepub.com; Journal of South Asian Development and South Asia Economic Journal.

United Nations Economic and Social Commission for Asia and the Pacific (ESCAP), United Nations Building, Rajadamnern Nok Ave., Bangkok, 10200, THA, https://www.unescap.org/; Asia-Pacific Development Journal and SDG Gateway Data Explorer.

United Nations Industrial Development Organization (UNIDO), 1 United Nations Plz., Rm. DC1-1118, New York, NY, 10017, USA, (212) 963-6890, (212) 963 6885, (212) 963-7904, office.newyork@unido.org, https://www.unido.org/; Industrial Statistics Databases and International Yearbook of Industrial Statistics 2021.

AFGHANISTAN-INFANT AND MATERNAL MORTALITY

See AFGHANISTAN-MORTALITY

AFGHANISTAN-INTERNATIONAL FINANCE

Asian Development Bank (ADB), 6 ADB Ave., Mandaluyong City, 1550, PHL, information@adb.org, https://www.adb.org/; Key Indicators for Asia and the Pacific 2022.

SAGE Publications, 2455 Teller Rd., Thousand Oaks, CA, 91320, USA, (800) 818-7243, (800) 583-2665, journals@sagepub.com, https://www.sagepub.com; Journal of South Asian Development and South Asia Economic Journal.

AFGHANISTAN-INTERNATIONAL TRADE

Asian Development Bank (ADB), 6 ADB Ave., Mandaluyong City, 1550, PHL, information@adb.org, https://www.adb.org/; Key Indicators for Asia and the Pacific 2022.

The Economist Group: Economist Intelligence Unit (EIU), 900 3rd Ave., 16th Fl., New York, NY, 10022, USA, (212) 541-0500, americas@eiu.com, https://www.eiu.com; Afghanistan Country Report.

Euromonitor International, Inc., 1 N Dearborn St., Ste. 1700, Chicago, IL, 60602, USA, (312) 922-1115, (312) 922-1157, info-usa@euromonitor.com, https://www.euromonitor.com/; Geographies.

Palgrave Macmillan, 1 New York Plaza, Ste. 4500, New York, NY, 10004-1562, USA, (800) 777-4643, orders@palgrave.com, https://www.palgrave.com/us; The Statesman's Yearbook, 2023.

Routledge - Taylor & Francis Group, 6000 Broken Sound Pkwy. NW, Ste. 300, Boca Raton, FL, 33487, USA, (800) 634-1420, (800) 634-7064, orders@taylorandfrancis.com, https://www.routledge.com/; The Europa World Year Book 2022.

United Nations Conference on Trade and Development (UNCTAD), Palais des Nations, Geneva, 1211, SWI, (212) 963-6896, unctadinfo@unctad.org, https://unctad.org; Trade and Development Report 2021.

United Nations Economic and Social Commission for Asia and the Pacific (ESCAP), United Nations Building, Rajadamnern Nok Ave., Bangkok, 10200, THA, https://www.unescap.org/; Asia-Pacific Development Journal and SDG Gateway Data Explorer.

United Nations Food and Agricultural Organization (FAO), 2121 K St., Ste. 800B, Washington, DC, 20037, USA, (202) 653-2400 (Dial from U.S.), (202) 653-5760 (Fax from U.S.), fao-hq@fao.org, https://www.fao.org; The State of Food and Agriculture (SOFA) 2022.

United Nations Statistics Division (UNSD), United Nations Plz., New York, NY, 10017, USA, (800) 253-9646, (212) 963-9851, statistics@un.org, https://unstats.un.org; International Trade Statistics Yearbook 2020 and Statistical Yearbook of the United Nations 2021.

World Trade Organization (WTO), Ctre. William Rappard, Rue de Lausanne 154, Case postale, Geneva, CH-1211, SWI, enquiries@wto.org, https://www.wto.org; World Trade Statistical Review 2022.

AFGHANISTAN-INTERNET USERS

International Telecommunication Union (ITU), Place des Nations, Geneva, CH-1211, SWI, itumail@itu.

int, https://www.itu.int; Global Connectivity Report 2022; World Telecommunication/ICT Indicators Database 2021; and Yearbook of Statistics 2019.

AFGHANISTAN-INVESTMENTS

International Monetary Fund (IMF), 700 19th St. NW, Washington, DC, 20431, USA, (202) 623-7000, (202) 623-4661, publications@imf.org, https://www.imf.org; International Financial Statistics (IFS).

AFGHANISTAN-LABOR

Central Intelligence Agency (CIA), Office of Public Affairs, Washington, DC, 20505, USA, (703) 482-0623, https://www.cia.gov; The World Factbook.

Euromonitor International, Inc., 1 N Dearborn St., Ste. 1700, Chicago, IL, 60602, USA, (312) 922-1115, (312) 922-1157, info-usa@euromonitor.com, https://www.euromonitor.com/; Geographies.

International Labour Organization (ILO), 4 Rte. des Morillons, Geneva, CH-1211, SWI, ilo@ilo.org, https://www.ilo.org; NORMLEX Information System on International Labour Standards.

Organisation of Islamic Cooperation (OIC), Statistical, Economic and Social Research and Training Centre for Islamic Countries (SESRIC), Kudus Cad. No. 9, Diplomatik Site, Ankara, 06450, TUR, statistics@sesric.org, https://www.sesric.org/; OIC Statistics (OICStat) Database.

Palgrave Macmillan, 1 New York Plaza, Ste. 4500, New York, NY, 10004-1562, USA, (800) 777-4643, orders@palgrave.com, https://www.palgrave.com/us; The Statesman's Yearbook, 2023.

United Nations Food and Agricultural Organization (FAO), 2121 K St., Ste. 800B, Washington, DC, 20037, USA, (202) 653-2400 (Dial from U.S.), (202) 653-5760 (Fax from U.S.), fao-hq@fao.org, https://www.fao.org; The State of Food and Agriculture (SOFA) 2022.

AFGHANISTAN-LAND USE

United Nations Statistics Division (UNSD), United Nations Plz., New York, NY, 10017, USA, (800) 253-9646, (212) 963-9851, statistics@un.org, https://unstats.un.org; Millennium Development Goal Indicators.

AFGHANISTAN-LIFE EXPECTANCY

United Nations Department of Economic and Social Affairs (DESA), Population Division, 2 United Nations Plz., Rm. DC2-1950, New York, NY, 10017, USA, (212) 963-3209, (212) 963-2147, population@un.org, https://www.un.org/development/desa/pd/; World Population Ageing 2020 Highlights.

United Nations Economic and Social Commission for Asia and the Pacific (ESCAP), United Nations Building, Rajadamnern Nok Ave., Bangkok, 10200, THA, https://www.unescap.org/; Asia-Pacific Development Journal.

United Nations Statistics Division (UNSD), United Nations Plz., New York, NY, 10017, USA, (800) 253-9646, (212) 963-9851, statistics@un.org, https://unstats.un.org; Millennium Development Goal Indicators.

AFGHANISTAN-LITERACY

Euromonitor International, Inc., 1 N Dearborn St., Ste. 1700, Chicago, IL, 60602, USA, (312) 922-1115, (312) 922-1157, info-usa@euromonitor.com, https://www.euromonitor.com/; Geographies.

UNESCO Institute for Statistics, C.P 250 Succursale H, Montreal, QC, H3G 2K8, CAN, (514) 343-6880 (Dial from U.S.), (514) 343-5740 (Fax from U.S.), uis.publications@unesco.org, http://uis.unesco.org/; Literacy.

AFGHANISTAN-LIVESTOCK

Palgrave Macmillan, 1 New York Plaza, Ste. 4500, New York, NY, 10004-1562, USA, (800) 777-4643, orders@palgrave.com, https://www.palgrave.com/us; The Statesman's Yearbook, 2023.

Routledge - Taylor & Francis Group, 6000 Broken Sound Pkwy. NW, Ste. 300, Boca Raton, FL, 33487, USA, (800) 634-1420, (800) 634-7064, orders@taylorandfrancis.com, https://www.routledge.com/; The Europa World Year Book 2022.

United Nations Food and Agricultural Organization (FAO), 2121 K St., Ste. 800B, Washington, DC, 20037, USA, (202) 653-2400 (Dial from U.S.), (202) 653-5760 (Fax from U.S.), fao-hq@fao.org, https://www.fao.org; The State of Food and Agriculture (SOFA) 2022.

United Nations Statistics Division (UNSD), United Nations Plz., New York, NY, 10017, USA, (800) 253-9646, (212) 963-9851, statistics@un.org, https://unstats.un.org; Statistical Yearbook of the United Nations 2021.

AFGHANISTAN-MANPOWER

United Nations Economic and Social Commission for Asia and the Pacific (ESCAP), United Nations Building, Rajadamnern Nok Ave., Bangkok, 10200, THA, https://www.unescap.org/; SDG Gateway Data Explorer.

AFGHANISTAN-MANUFACTURES

Asian Development Bank (ADB), 6 ADB Ave., Mandaluyong City, 1550, PHL, information@adb.org, https://www.adb.org/; Key Indicators for Asia and the Pacific 2022.

AFGHANISTAN-MINERAL INDUSTRIES

Asian Development Bank (ADB), 6 ADB Ave., Mandaluyong City, 1550, PHL, information@adb.org, https://www.adb.org/; Key Indicators for Asia and the Pacific 2022.

International Monetary Fund (IMF), 700 19th St. NW, Washington, DC, 20431, USA, (202) 623-7000, (202) 623-4661, publications@imf.org, https://www.imf.org; International Financial Statistics (IFS).

Palgrave Macmillan, 1 New York Plaza, Ste. 4500, New York, NY, 10004-1562, USA, (800) 777-4643, orders@palgrave.com, https://www.palgrave.com/us; The Statesman's Yearbook, 2023.

Routledge - Taylor & Francis Group, 6000 Broken Sound Pkwy. NW, Ste. 300, Boca Raton, FL, 33487, USA, (800) 634-1420, (800) 634-7064, orders@taylorandfrancis.com, https://www.routledge.com/; The Europa World Year Book 2022.

United Nations Conference on Trade and Development (UNCTAD), Palais des Nations, Geneva, 1211, SWI, (212) 963-6896, unctadinfo@unctad.org, https://unctad.org; Trade and Development Report 2021.

United Nations Statistics Division (UNSD), United Nations Plz., New York, NY, 10017, USA, (800) 253-9646, (212) 963-9851, statistics@un.org, https://unstats.un.org; Statistical Yearbook of the United Nations 2021.

AFGHANISTAN-MONEY SUPPLY

The Economist Group: Economist Intelligence Unit (EIU), 900 3rd Ave., 16th Fl., New York, NY, 10022, USA, (212) 541-0500, americas@eiu.com, https://www.eiu.com; Afghanistan Country Report.

International Monetary Fund (IMF), 700 19th St. NW, Washington, DC, 20431, USA, (202) 623-7000, (202) 623-4661, publications@imf.org, https://www.imf.org; International Financial Statistics (IFS).

Routledge - Taylor & Francis Group, 6000 Broken Sound Pkwy. NW, Ste. 300, Boca Raton, FL, 33487, USA, (800) 634-1420, (800) 634-7064, orders@taylorandfrancis.com, https://www.routledge.com/; The Europa World Year Book 2022.

United Nations Statistics Division (UNSD), United Nations Plz., New York, NY, 10017, USA, (800) 253-9646, (212) 963-9851, statistics@un.org, https://unstats.un.org; Statistical Yearbook of the United Nations 2021.

AFGHANISTAN-MORTALITY

UNICEF, 3 United Nations Plz., New York, NY, 10017, USA, (212) 303-7984, (917) 244-2215, https://www.unicef.org; The State of the World's Children 2023.

United Nations Economic and Social Commission for Asia and the Pacific (ESCAP), United Nations Building, Rajadamnern Nok Ave., Bangkok, 10200, THA, https://www.unescap.org/; Asia-Pacific Development Journal.

United Nations Statistics Division (UNSD), United Nations Plz., New York, NY, 10017, USA, (800) 253-9646, (212) 963-9851, statistics@un.org, https://unstats.un.org; Millennium Development Goal Indicators and World Statistics Pocketbook 2021.

World Health Organization (WHO), Ave. Appia 20, Geneva, CH-1211, SWI, (202) 974-3000 (Telephone in U.S.), publications@who.int, https://www.who.int/; Global Health Observatory (GHO).

AFGHANISTAN-MOTOR VEHICLES

International Road Federation (IRF), Madison Place, 500 Montgomery St., 5th Fl., Alexandria, VA, 22314, USA, (703) 535-1001, (703) 535-1007, info@irf.global, https://www.irf.global/; World Road Statistics (WRS).

AFGHANISTAN-NATURAL GAS PRODUCTION

See AFGHANISTAN-MINERAL INDUSTRIES

AFGHANISTAN-NUTRITION

Asian Development Bank (ADB), 6 ADB Ave., Mandaluyong City, 1550, PHL, information@adb.org, https://www.adb.org/; Key Indicators for Asia and the Pacific 2022.

United Nations Food and Agricultural Organization (FAO), 2121 K St., Ste. 800B, Washington, DC, 20037, USA, (202) 653-2400 (Dial from U.S.), (202) 653-5760 (Fax from U.S.), fao-hq@fao.org, https://www.fao.org; The State of Food and Agriculture (SOFA) 2022.

United Nations Statistics Division (UNSD), United Nations Plz., New York, NY, 10017, USA, (800) 253-9646, (212) 963-9851, statistics@un.org, https://unstats.un.org; Millennium Development Goal Indicators.

AFGHANISTAN-PAPER

See AFGHANISTAN-FORESTS AND FORESTRY

AFGHANISTAN-PEANUT PRODUCTION

See AFGHANISTAN-CROPS

AFGHANISTAN-PESTICIDES

United Nations Food and Agricultural Organization (FAO), 2121 K St., Ste. 800B, Washington, DC, 20037, USA, (202) 653-2400 (Dial from U.S.), (202) 653-5760 (Fax from U.S.), fao-hq@fao.org, https://www.fao.org; The State of Food and Agriculture (SOFA) 2022.

AFGHANISTAN-PETROLEUM INDUSTRY AND TRADE

Asian Development Bank (ADB), 6 ADB Ave., Mandaluyong City, 1550, PHL, information@adb.org, https://www.adb.org/; Key Indicators for Asia and the Pacific 2022.

AFGHANISTAN-POLITICAL SCIENCE

Institute for the Study of War (ISW), 1400 16th St. NW, Ste. 515, Washington, DC, 20036, USA, (202) 293-5550, https://www.understandingwar.org/; Regional Actors Eye Threats and Opportunities in Taliban Takeover.

AFGHANISTAN-POPULATION

Asian Development Bank (ADB), 6 ADB Ave., Mandaluyong City, 1550, PHL, information@adb.org, https://www.adb.org/; Key Indicators for Asia and the Pacific 2022.

Center for Economic and Policy Research (CEPR), 1611 Connecticut Ave. NW, Ste. 400, Washington, DC, 20009, USA, (202) 293-5380, (202) 588-1356, info@cepr.net, https://cepr.net/; The Human Consequences of Economic Sanctions.

Central Intelligence Agency (CIA), Office of Public Affairs, Washington, DC, 20505, USA, (703) 482-0623, https://www.cia.gov; The World Factbook.

The Economist Group: Economist Intelligence Unit (EIU), 900 3rd Ave., 16th Fl., New York, NY, 10022, USA, (212) 541-0500, americas@eiu.com, https://www.eiu.com; Afghanistan Country Report.

Infoplease, c/o Sandbox Networks, Inc., 1 Lincoln St., 24th Fl., Boston, MA, 02111, USA, https://www.infoplease.com; Countries of the World.

International Labour Organization (ILO), 4 Rte. des Morillons, Geneva, CH-1211, SWI, ilo@ilo.org, https://www.ilo.org; NORMLEX Information System on International Labour Standards.

Palgrave Macmillan, 1 New York Plaza, Ste. 4500, New York, NY, 10004-1562, USA, (800) 777-4643, orders@palgrave.com, https://www.palgrave.com/us; The Statesman's Yearbook, 2023.

Routledge - Taylor & Francis Group, 6000 Broken Sound Pkwy. NW, Ste. 300, Boca Raton, FL, 33487, USA, (800) 634-1420, (800) 634-7064, orders@taylorandfrancis.com, https://www.routledge.com/; The Europa World Year Book 2022.

UK Data Service, University of Essex, Wivenhoe Park, Colchester, Essex, CO4 3SQ, GBR, https://ukdataservice.ac.uk/; International Aggregate Data.

United Nations Department of Economic and Social Affairs (DESA), Population Division, 2 United Nations Plz., Rm. DC2-1950, New York, NY, 10017, USA, (212) 963-3209, (212) 963-2147, population@un.org, https://www.un.org/development/desa/pd/; Revision of World Urbanization Prospects and World Population Ageing 2020 Highlights.

United Nations Economic and Social Commission for Asia and the Pacific (ESCAP), United Nations Building, Rajadamnern Nok Ave., Bangkok, 10200, THA, https://www.unescap.org/; Asia-Pacific Development Journal and SDG Gateway Data Explorer.

United Nations Statistics Division (UNSD), United Nations Plz., New York, NY, 10017, USA, (800) 253-9646, (212) 963-9851, statistics@un.org, https://unstats.un.org; Statistical Yearbook of the United Nations 2021 and World Statistics Pocketbook 2021.

The World Bank, 1818 H St. NW, Washington, DC, 20433, USA, (202) 473-1000, (202) 477-6391, eds03@worldbank.org, https://www.worldbank.org/; The Global Findex Database 2021.

AFGHANISTAN-POPULATION DENSITY

Central Intelligence Agency (CIA), Office of Public Affairs, Washington, DC, 20505, USA, (703) 482-0623, https://www.cia.gov; The World Factbook.

Palgrave Macmillan, 1 New York Plaza, Ste. 4500, New York, NY, 10004-1562, USA, (800) 777-4643, orders@palgrave.com, https://www.palgrave.com/us; The Statesman's Yearbook, 2023.

Routledge - Taylor & Francis Group, 6000 Broken Sound Pkwy. NW, Ste. 300, Boca Raton, FL, 33487, USA, (800) 634-1420, (800) 634-7064, orders@taylorandfrancis.com, https://www.routledge.com/; The Europa World Year Book 2022.

AFGHANISTAN-POWER RESOURCES

Euromonitor International, Inc., 1 N Dearborn St., Ste. 1700, Chicago, IL, 60602, USA, (312) 922-1115, (312) 922-1157, info-usa@euromonitor.com, https://www.euromonitor.com/; Geographies.

Palgrave Macmillan, 1 New York Plaza, Ste. 4500, New York, NY, 10004-1562, USA, (800) 777-4643, orders@palgrave.com, https://www.palgrave.com/us; The Statesman's Yearbook, 2023.

United Nations Economic and Social Commission for Asia and the Pacific (ESCAP), United Nations Building, Rajadamnern Nok Ave., Bangkok, 10200, THA, https://www.unescap.org/; Asia-Pacific Development Journal.

United Nations Food and Agricultural Organization (FAO), 2121 K St., Ste. 800B, Washington, DC, 20037, USA, (202) 653-2400 (Dial from U.S.), (202) 653-5760 (Fax from U.S.), fao-hq@fao.org, https://www.fao.org; The State of Food and Agriculture (SOFA) 2022.

United Nations Statistics Division (UNSD), United Nations Plz., New York, NY, 10017, USA, (800) 253-9646, (212) 963-9851, statistics@un.org, https://unstats.un.org; Energy Statistics Yearbook 2019; Statistical Yearbook of the United Nations 2021; and World Statistics Pocketbook 2021.

AFGHANISTAN-PRICES

Asian Development Bank (ADB), 6 ADB Ave., Mandaluyong City, 1550, PHL, information@adb.org, https://www.adb.org/; Key Indicators for Asia and the Pacific 2022.

Euromonitor International, Inc., 1 N Dearborn St., Ste. 1700, Chicago, IL, 60602, USA, (312) 922-1115, (312) 922-1157, info-usa@euromonitor.com, https://www.euromonitor.com/; Geographies.

AFGHANISTAN-PUBLIC HEALTH

Euromonitor International, Inc., 1 N Dearborn St., Ste. 1700, Chicago, IL, 60602, USA, (312) 922-1115, (312) 922-1157, info-usa@euromonitor.com, https://www.euromonitor.com/; Geographies.

Organisation of Islamic Cooperation (OIC), Statistical, Economic and Social Research and Training Centre for Islamic Countries (SESRIC), Kudus Cad. No. 9, Diplomatik Site, Ankara, 06450, TUR, statistics@sesric.org, https://www.sesric.org/; OIC Statistics (OICStat) Database.

Palgrave Macmillan, 1 New York Plaza, Ste. 4500, New York, NY, 10004-1562, USA, (800) 777-4643, orders@palgrave.com, https://www.palgrave.com/us; The Statesman's Yearbook, 2023.

U.S. Census Bureau, 4600 Silver Hill Rd., Washington, DC, 20233, USA, (301) 763-4636, (800) 923-8282, https://www.census.gov; HIV/AIDS Surveillance Data Base.

UNICEF, 3 United Nations Plz., New York, NY, 10017, USA, (212) 303-7984, (917) 244-2215, https://www.unicef.org; The State of the World's Children 2023.

United Nations Department of Economic and Social Affairs (DESA), Population Division, 2 United Nations Plz., Rm. DC2-1950, New York, NY, 10017, USA, (212) 963-3209, (212) 963-2147, population@un.org, https://www.un.org/development/desa/pd/; World Fertility Data 2019.

United Nations Economic and Social Commission for Asia and the Pacific (ESCAP), United Nations Building, Rajadamnern Nok Ave., Bangkok, 10200, THA, https://www.unescap.org/; Asia-Pacific Development Journal.

United Nations Statistics Division (UNSD), United Nations Plz., New York, NY, 10017, USA, (800) 253-9646, (212) 963-9851, statistics@un.org, https://unstats.un.org; Millennium Development Goal Indicators and Statistical Yearbook of the United Nations 2021.

World Health Organization (WHO), Ave. Appia 20, Geneva, CH-1211, SWI, (202) 974-3000 (Telephone in U.S.), publications@who.int, https://www.who.int/; Global Health Observatory (GHO) and Health Statistics and Information Systems.

AFGHANISTAN-PUBLISHERS AND PUBLISHING

UNESCO Institute for Statistics, C.P 250 Succursale H, Montreal, QC, H3G 2K8, CAN, (514) 343-6880 (Dial from U.S.), (514) 343-5740 (Fax from U.S.), uis.publications@unesco.org, http://uis.unesco.org/; UIS.Stat.

AFGHANISTAN-RAILROADS

Janes, USA, (703) 574-7580, (888) 977-1519, customer.care@janes.com, https://www.janes.com; Janes World Railways 2021-2022.

AFGHANISTAN-RELIGION

Central Intelligence Agency (CIA), Office of Public Affairs, Washington, DC, 20505, USA, (703) 482-0623, https://www.cia.gov; The World Factbook.

Palgrave Macmillan, 1 New York Plaza, Ste. 4500, New York, NY, 10004-1562, USA, (800) 777-4643, orders@palgrave.com, https://www.palgrave.com/us; The Statesman's Yearbook, 2023.

AFGHANISTAN-RETAIL TRADE

Euromonitor International, Inc., 1 N Dearborn St., Ste. 1700, Chicago, IL, 60602, USA, (312) 922-1115, (312) 922-1157, info-usa@euromonitor.com, https://www.euromonitor.com/; Geographies.

AFGHANISTAN-RICE PRODUCTION

See AFGHANISTAN-CROPS

AFGHANISTAN-ROADS

International Road Federation (IRF), Madison Place, 500 Montgomery St., 5th Fl., Alexandria, VA, 22314, USA, (703) 535-1001, (703) 535-1007, info@irf.global, https://www.irf.global/; World Road Statistics (WRS).

AFGHANISTAN-RUBBER INDUSTRY AND TRADE

International Rubber Study Group (IRSG), 51 Changi Business Park Central 2, Unit No. 6, 486066, SGP, https://www.rubberstudy.org; Monthly Rubber Bulletin (MRB); Rubber Industry Report; Rubber Statistical Bulletin; and World Rubber Industry Report (WRIO).

AFGHANISTAN-RUG AND CARPET INDUSTRY

International Monetary Fund (IMF), 700 19th St. NW, Washington, DC, 20431, USA, (202) 623-7000, (202) 623-4661, publications@imf.org, https://www.imf.org; International Financial Statistics (IFS).

AFGHANISTAN-STEEL PRODUCTION

See AFGHANISTAN-MINERAL INDUSTRIES

AFGHANISTAN-SUGAR PRODUCTION

See AFGHANISTAN-CROPS

AFGHANISTAN-TAXATION

International Road Federation (IRF), Madison Place, 500 Montgomery St., 5th Fl., Alexandria, VA, 22314, USA, (703) 535-1001, (703) 535-1007, info@irf.global, https://www.irf.global/; World Road Statistics (WRS).

AFGHANISTAN-TEA PRODUCTION

See AFGHANISTAN-CROPS

AFGHANISTAN-TEXTILE INDUSTRY

International Monetary Fund (IMF), 700 19th St. NW, Washington, DC, 20431, USA, (202) 623-7000, (202) 623-4661, publications@imf.org, https://www.imf.org; International Financial Statistics (IFS).

Palgrave Macmillan, 1 New York Plaza, Ste. 4500, New York, NY, 10004-1562, USA, (800) 777-4643, orders@palgrave.com, https://www.palgrave.com/us; The Statesman's Yearbook, 2023.

United Nations Statistics Division (UNSD), United Nations Plz., New York, NY, 10017, USA, (800) 253-9646, (212) 963-9851, statistics@un.org, https://unstats.un.org; Statistical Yearbook of the United Nations 2021.

AFGHANISTAN-TOURISM

Euromonitor International, Inc., 1 N Dearborn St., Ste. 1700, Chicago, IL, 60602, USA, (312) 922-1115, (312) 922-1157, info-usa@euromonitor.com, https://www.euromonitor.com/; Geographies.

Organisation of Islamic Cooperation (OIC), Statistical, Economic and Social Research and Training Centre for Islamic Countries (SESRIC), Kudus Cad. No. 9, Diplomatik Site, Ankara, 06450, TUR, statistics@sesric.org, https://www.sesric.org/; International Tourism in the OIC Countries: Prospects and Challenges, 2020 and OIC Statistics (OICStat) Database.

Routledge - Taylor & Francis Group, 6000 Broken Sound Pkwy. NW, Ste. 300, Boca Raton, FL, 33487, USA, (800) 634-1420, (800) 634-7064, orders@taylorandfrancis.com, https://www.routledge.com/; The Europa World Year Book 2022.

United Nations Statistics Division (UNSD), United Nations Plz., New York, NY, 10017, USA, (800) 253-9646, (212) 963-9851, statistics@un.org, https://unstats.un.org; Statistical Yearbook of the United Nations 2021.

AFGHANISTAN-TRADE

See AFGHANISTAN-INTERNATIONAL TRADE

AFGHANISTAN-TRANSPORTATION

Central Intelligence Agency (CIA), Office of Public Affairs, Washington, DC, 20505, USA, (703) 482-0623, https://www.cia.gov; The World Factbook.

Euromonitor International, Inc., 1 N Dearborn St., Ste. 1700, Chicago, IL, 60602, USA, (312) 922-1115, (312) 922-1157, info-usa@euromonitor.com, https://www.euromonitor.com/; Geographies.

Organisation of Islamic Cooperation (OIC), Statistical, Economic and Social Research and Training Centre for Islamic Countries (SESRIC), Kudus Cad. No. 9, Diplomatik Site, Ankara, 06450, TUR, statistics@sesric.org, https://www.sesric.org/; OIC Statistics (OICStat) Database.

Palgrave Macmillan, 1 New York Plaza, Ste. 4500, New York, NY, 10004-1562, USA, (800) 777-4643, orders@palgrave.com, https://www.palgrave.com/us; The Statesman's Yearbook, 2023.

Routledge - Taylor & Francis Group, 6000 Broken Sound Pkwy. NW, Ste. 300, Boca Raton, FL, 33487, USA, (800) 634-1420, (800) 634-7064, orders@taylorandfrancis.com, https://www.routledge.com/; The Europa World Year Book 2022.

United Nations Economic and Social Commission for Asia and the Pacific (ESCAP), United Nations Building, Rajadamnern Nok Ave., Bangkok, 10200, THA, https://www.unescap.org/; SDG Gateway Data Explorer.

AFGHANISTAN-UNEMPLOYMENT

International Labour Organization (ILO), 4 Rte. des Morillons, Geneva, CH-1211, SWI, ilo@ilo.org, https://www.ilo.org; NORMLEX Information System on International Labour Standards.

AFGHANISTAN-VITAL STATISTICS

Palgrave Macmillan, 1 New York Plaza, Ste. 4500, New York, NY, 10004-1562, USA, (800) 777-4643, orders@palgrave.com, https://www.palgrave.com/us; The Statesman's Yearbook, 2023.

U.S. Census Bureau, 4600 Silver Hill Rd., Washington, DC, 20233, USA, (301) 763-4636, (800) 923-8282, https://www.census.gov; HIV/AIDS Surveillance Data Base.

United Nations Department of Economic and Social Affairs (DESA), Population Division, 2 United Nations Plz., Rm. DC2-1950, New York, NY, 10017, USA, (212) 963-3209, (212) 963-2147, population@un.org, https://www.un.org/development/desa/pd/; World Contraceptive Use 2021: Estimates and Projections of Family Planning Indicators and World Marriage Data 2019.

United Nations Economic and Social Commission for Asia and the Pacific (ESCAP), United Nations Building, Rajadamnern Nok Ave., Bangkok, 10200, THA, https://www.unescap.org/; Asia-Pacific Development Journal.

United Nations Statistics Division (UNSD), United Nations Plz., New York, NY, 10017, USA, (800) 253-9646, (212) 963-9851, statistics@un.org, https://unstats.un.org; United Nations Demographic Yearbook 2020.

AFGHANISTAN-WAGES

International Labour Organization (ILO), 4 Rte. des Morillons, Geneva, CH-1211, SWI, ilo@ilo.org, https://www.ilo.org; NORMLEX Information System on International Labour Standards.

United Nations Economic and Social Commission for Asia and the Pacific (ESCAP), United Nations Building, Rajadamnern Nok Ave., Bangkok, 10200, THA, https://www.unescap.org/; SDG Gateway Data Explorer.

United Nations Statistics Division (UNSD), United Nations Plz., New York, NY, 10017, USA, (800) 253-9646, (212) 963-9851, statistics@un.org, https://unstats.un.org; Statistical Yearbook of the United Nations 2021.

AFGHANISTAN-WEATHER

See AFGHANISTAN-CLIMATE

AFGHANISTAN-WHEAT PRODUCTION

See AFGHANISTAN-CROPS

AFGHANISTAN-WOOL PRODUCTION

See AFGHANISTAN-TEXTILE INDUSTRY

AFRICA

See also Individual countries

African Development Bank Group (AfDB), Avenue Joseph Anoma, 01 BP 1387, Abidjan, 01, COT, https://www.afdb.org; Compendium of Statistics on Bank Group Operations 2019.

African Gender Institute (AGI), University of Cape Town, Private Bag, Rondebosch, 7701, SAF, afs@uct.ac.za, http://www.agi.uct.ac.za/; Feminist Africa Journal.

African Women's Development and Communication Network (FEMNET), 12 Masaba Rd., Lowerhill, PO Box 54562, Nairobi, 00200, KEN, admin@femnet.or.ke, https://femnet.org; Qualitative Study on the Impact of COVID-19 on Sexual and Reproductive Health and Rights (SRHR) of Women & Girls in Africa.

AFRISTAT, PO Box E 1600, Bamako, MLI, afristat@afristat.org, https://www.afristat.org; La lettre d'AFRISTAT.

French Institute of International Relations (Institut francais des relations internationales (IFRI)), 27 rue de la Procession, Paris, 75015, FRA, accueil@ifri.org, https://www.ifri.org/en; Land Governance in the Outskirts of African Cities: Socio-Economic Challenges of Growing Peri-Urban Land Markets.

Global Facility for Disaster Reduction and Recovery (GFDRR), 1818 H St. NW, Washington, DC, 20433, USA, (202) 473-1000, gfdrr@worldbank.org, https://www.gfdrr.org/; Turning Flood Risk Into Economic Opportunity in Dar es Salaam, Tanzania.

Global Integrity, 1110 Vermont Ave. NW, Ste. 500, Washington, DC, 20005, USA, (202) 449-4100, info@globalintegrity.org, https://www.globalintegrity.org/; Africa Integrity Indicators.

Imperial College London, South Kensington Campus, London, SW7 2AZ, GBR, https://www.imperial.ac.uk/; The Effect of Climate Change on Yellow Fever Disease Burden in Africa.

International Institute for Democracy and Electoral Assistance (International IDEA), Stromsborg, Stockholm, SE 103 34, SWE, https://www.idea.int/; The Integrity of Political Finance Systems in Africa: Tackling Political Corruption.

International Institute for Environment and Development (IIED), 235 High Holborn, London, WC1V 7DN, GBR, inforequest@iied.org, https://www.iied.org; Environment & Urbanization.

Kantar, 3 World Trade Center, 35th Fl., New York, NY, 10007, USA, (866) 471-1399, https://www.kantar.com/; Evaluating an African Reality TV Show to Promote Agriculture.

National Safety Council (NSC), 1121 Spring Lake Dr., Itasca, IL, 60143-3201, USA, (630) 285-1121, (800) 621-7615, customerservice@nsc.org, https://www.nsc.org/; National Safety Council Injury Facts.

U.S. Census Bureau, 4600 Silver Hill Rd., Washington, DC, 20233, USA, (301) 763-4636, (800) 923-8282, https://www.census.gov; Africa Aging: 2020.

UNICEF, 3 United Nations Plz., New York, NY, 10017, USA, (212) 303-7984, (917) 244-2215, https://www.unicef.org; Adolescent Girls in West and Central Africa: Data Brief and Female Genital Mutilation (FGM).

United Nations Economic Commission for Africa (UNECA), PO Box 3001, Addis Ababa, ETH, ecainfo@uneca.org, https://www.uneca.org/; African Governance Report VI and Economic Report on Africa 2021.

United Nations Economic Commission for Africa (UNECA), African Centre for Statistics (ACS), PO Box 3001, Addis Ababa, ETH, https://www.uneca.org/data-and-statistics; ECAstats Database.

United Nations Environment Programme (UNEP), 900 17th St. NW, Ste. 506, Washington, DC, 20006, USA, (202) 974-1300, publications@unep.org, https://www.unep.org/; Africa Water Atlas.

University of Washington, Institute for Health Metrics and Evaluation (IHME), Population Health Building/Hans Rosling Center, UW Campus Box 351615, 3980 15th Ave. NE, Seattle, WA, 98195, USA, (206) 897-2800, (206) 897-2899, engage@healthdata.org, https://www.healthdata.org; Mapping Male Circumcision for HIV Prevention Efforts in Sub-Saharan Africa.

World Wildlife Fund (WWF), 1250 24th St. NW, Washington, DC, 20037-1193, USA, (202) 495-4800, (202) 495-4211, https://wwf.panda.org/; Food Loss and Waste in Farming: Insights from South African Farmers.

AGE OF POPULATION

See POPULATION

AGGRESSIVENESS

Committee to Protect Journalists (CPJ), PO Box 2675, New York, NY, 10108, USA, (212) 465-1004, (212) 214-0640, info@cpj.org, https://cpj.org; Database of Attacks on the Press: 1992-2023; Journalists Killed Since 1992; Record Number of Journalists Jailed Worldwide; and Ten Most Censored Countries.

Institute on Violence, Abuse and Trauma (IVAT), 10065 Old Grove Rd. , Ste. 101, San Diego, CA, 92131, USA, (858) 527-1860, (858) 527-1743, https://www.ivatcenters.org/; Journal of Aggression, Maltreatment, and Trauma (JAMT) and Journal of Family Trauma, Child Custody, and Child Development (JFT).

International Women's Media Foundation (IWMF), 1625 K St. NW, Ste. 1275, Washington, DC, 20006, USA, (202) 496-1992, info@iwmf.org, https://www.iwmf.org/; The Missing Perspectives of Women in COVID-19 News.

National Coalition of Anti-Violence Programs (NCAVP), 116 Nassau St., 3rd Fl., New York, NY, 10038, USA, (212) 714-1184, ecruz@avp.org, https://avp.org/ncavp/; Pride and Pain: A Snapshot of Anti-LGBTQ Hate and Violence During Pride Season 2019 and Supporting LGBTQ Survivors of Violence During the COVID-19 Pandemic.

National Sexual Violence Resource Center (NSVRC), Governor's Plaza N, Bldg. 2, 2101 N Front St., Harrisburg, PA, 17110, USA, (877) 739-3895, (717) 909-0715 (TTY), (717) 909-0714, https://www.nsvrc.org/resources@nsvrc.org, https://www.nsvrc.org/; National Sexual Violence Resource Center Library Catalog.

Pew Research Center, Internet & Technology, 1615 L St. NW, Ste. 800, Washington, DC, 20036, USA, (202) 419-4300, (202) 857-8562, https://www.pewresearch.org/topic/internet-technology/; The State of Online Harassment.

Rape, Abuse & Incest National Network (RAINN), 635 Pennsylvania Ave. SE, Ste. B, Washington, DC, 20003, USA, (202) 544-1034, (800) 656-4673 , info@rainn.org, https://www.rainn.org/; Statistics.

University of Michigan Institute for Social Research, Inter-University Consortium for Political and Social Science Research (ICPSR), National Archive of Criminal Justice Data (NACJD), PO Box 1248, Ann

Arbor, MI, 48106-1248, USA, (734) 615-8400, nacjd@icpsr.umich.edu, https://www.icpsr.umich.edu/web/pages/NACJD/; Violence Against Women (VAW) Resource Guide.

VTVCare, PO Box 230024, Centreville, VA, 20120, USA, (703) 627-0932, info@vtvcare.org, https://www.vtvcare.org/vtv-family-outreach-foundation/; unpublished data.

Workplace Bullying Institute (WBI), USA, https://workplacebullying.org/; 2021 WBI U.S. Workplace Bullying Survey.

AGING

Bernan Press, 15250 NBN Way, Bldg. C, Blue Ridge Summit, PA, 17214, USA, (301) 459-2255, (800) 865-3457, (800) 865-3450, customercare@bernan.com, https://rowman.com/Page/Bernan; Aging in America 2020.

National Alliance for Caregiving (NAC), 1730 Rhode Island Ave. NW, Ste. 812, Washington, DC, 20036, USA, (202) 918-1013, (202) 918-1014, info@caregiving.org, https://www.caregiving.org/; Caregiving in the U.S. 2020.

National Bureau of Economic Research (NBER), 1050 Massachusetts Ave., Cambridge, MA, 02138, USA, (617) 868-3900, info@nber.org, https://www.nber.org/; Bulletin on Health.

Population Reference Bureau (PRB), 1875 Connecticut Ave. NW, Ste. 520, Washington, DC, 20009, USA, (800) 877-9881, (202) 483-1100, communications@prb.org, https://www.prb.org/; 2021 World Population Data Sheet.

U.S. Census Bureau, 4600 Silver Hill Rd., Washington, DC, 20233, USA, (301) 763-4636, (800) 923-8282, https://www.census.gov; Africa Aging: 2020.

University of California San Francisco (UCSF), Institute for Health & Aging (IHA), Wayne and Gladys Valley Center for Vision, 490 Illinois St., 12th Fl., Box 0646, San Francisco, CA, 94158, USA, (415) 502-5200, https://nursing.ucsf.edu/academics/departments/institute-health-aging; unpublished data.

University of Michigan Institute for Social Research, Inter-University Consortium for Political and Social Science Research (ICPSR), National Archive of Computerized Data on Aging (NACDA), PO Box 1248, Ann Arbor, MI, 48106-1248, USA, (734) 615-9520, (734) 615-9516, (734) 647-8700, jmcnally@umich.edu, https://www.icpsr.umich.edu/web/pages/NACDA/index.html; National Archive of Computerized Data on Aging (NACDA).

University of Vienna Department of Demography, Wittgenstein Centre for Demography and Global Human Capital, Dr. Ignaz Seipel-Platz 2, Vienna, A-1010, AUT, heike.barakat@univie.ac.at, https://www.wittgensteincentre.org/en/; Population Aging, Migration, and Productivity in Europe.

AGNOSTICISM

Trinity College, Institute for the Study of Secularism in Society and Culture (ISSSC), 300 Summit St., Hartford, CT, 06106, USA, (860) 297-2000, isssc@trincoll.edu, https://www.trincoll.edu/; unpublished data.

AGRICULTURAL LABORERS

Johns Hopkins Center for a Livable Future, 111 Market Pl., Ste. 840, Baltimore, MD, 21202, USA, (410) 223-1811, (410) 223-1829, clf@jhsph.edu, https://clf.jhsph.edu; Essential and in Crisis: A Review of the Public Health Threats Facing Farmworkers in the US.

Kantar, 3 World Trade Center, 35th Fl., New York, NY, 10007, USA, (866) 471-1399, https://www.kantar.com/; Evaluating an African Reality TV Show to Promote Agriculture.

Marshfield Clinic Research Institute (MCRI), National Children's Center for Rural and Agricultural Health and Safety (NCCRAHS), 1000 N Oak Ave., Marshfield, WI, 54449-5790, USA, (800) 662-6900, (715) 389-4999, nccrahs@mcrf.mfldclin.edu, https://www.marshfieldresearch.org/nccrahs; Childhood Agricultural Injuries: 2022 Fact Sheet.

U.S. Census Bureau, 4600 Silver Hill Rd., Washington, DC, 20233, USA, (301) 763-4636, (800) 923-8282, https://www.census.gov; County Business Patterns (CBP) 2020 and Statistics of U.S. Businesses (SUSB).

U.S. Department of Agriculture (USDA), National Agricultural Statistics Service (USDA-NASS), 1400 Independence Ave. SW, Washington, DC, 20250, USA, (800) 727-9540, nass@nass.usda.gov, https://www.nass.usda.gov; Adult Agricultural Related Injuries and Farm Labor.

U.S. Department of Labor (DOL), Bureau of Labor Statistics (BLS), Postal Square Bldg., 2 Massachusetts Ave. NE, Washington, DC, 20212-0001, USA, (202) 691-5200, (202) 691-7890, blsdata_staff@bls.gov, https://www.bls.gov; Monthly Labor Review.

Union of Concerned Scientists (UCS), 2 Brattle Sq., Cambridge, MA, 02138-3780, USA, (617) 547-5552, (617) 864-9405, https://www.ucsusa.org/; Too Hot to Work: Assessing the Threats Climate Change Poses to Outdoor Workers.

AGRICULTURAL LOANS

See FARM MORTGAGE LOANS

AGRICULTURAL PRODUCTS

See FARMS

AGRICULTURAL SCIENCES-DEGREES CONFERRED

National Science Foundation, National Center for Science and Engineering Statistics (NCSES), 2415 Eisenhower Ave., Ste. W14200, Arlington, VA, 22314, USA, (703) 292-8780, (703) 292-9092, info@nsf.gov, https://www.nsf.gov/statistics/; Survey of Doctorate Recipients and Survey of Earned Doctorates.

U.S. Department of Education (ED), Institute of Education Sciences (IES), National Center for Education Statistics (NCES), Potomac Center Plaza, 550 12th St. SW, Washington, DC, 20202, USA, (202) 403-5551, https://nces.ed.gov/; Digest of Education Statistics, 2020.

AGRICULTURE

See also FARMS

Bernan Press, 15250 NBN Way, Bldg. C, Blue Ridge Summit, PA, 17214, USA, (301) 459-2255, (800) 865-3457, (800) 865-3450, customercare@bernan.com, https://rowman.com/Page/Bernan; Pesticide Residues in Food 2021 - Joint FAO/WHO Meeting on Pesticide Residues.

CIRAD Agricultural Research for Development, 42, Rue Scheffer, Paris, 75116, FRA, https://www.cirad.fr/en; Agritrop: The CIRAD Information Database.

Department of Statistics of Jordan, PO Box 2015, Amman, 11181, JOR, stat@dos.gov.jo, https://dosweb.dos.gov.jo/; Agricultural Statistics 2019.

The Economist Group: Economist Intelligence Unit (EIU), 900 3rd Ave., 16th Fl., New York, NY, 10022, USA, (212) 541-0500, americas@eiu.com, https://www.eiu.com; United States Country Report.

Environmental Working Group (EWG), 1250 U St. NW, Ste. 1000, Washington, DC, 20005, USA, (202) 667-6982, https://www.ewg.org/; EWG's Quick Tips for Reducing Your Diet's Climate Footprint.

Euromonitor International, Inc., 1 N Dearborn St., Ste. 1700, Chicago, IL, 60602, USA, (312) 922-1115, (312) 922-1157, info-usa@euromonitor.com, https://www.euromonitor.com/; Strategic Analysis of the World's Largest Companies.

Food & Water Watch, 1616 P St. NW, Washington, DC, 20036, USA, (202) 683-2500, (855) 340-8083, (202) 683-2501, info@fwwatch.org, https://www.foodandwaterwatch.org; Well-Fed: A Roadmap to a Sustainable Food System That Works For All.

International Food Information Council Foundation (IFIC), 1100 Connecticut Ave. NW, Ste. 430, Washington, DC, 20036, USA, (202) 296-6540, info@foodinsight.org, https://foodinsight.org/; Food Insight.

Public Policy Institute of California (PPIC), 500 Washington St., Ste. 600, San Francisco, CA, 94111, USA, (415) 291-4400, (916) 440-1120, (415) 291-4401, https://www.ppic.org/; Droughts in California.

Public Policy Institute of California (PPIC) Water Policy Center, 500 Washington St., Ste. 600, San Francisco, CA, 94111, USA, (415) 291-4433, (415) 291-4400, (415) 291-4401, https://www.ppic.org/water/; Policy Brief: Drought and California's Agriculture.

Rapid Intelligence, Sydney, NSW, 2001, AUS, https://www.rapint.com/; NationMaster.com.

SAGE Publications, 2455 Teller Rd., Thousand Oaks, CA, 91320, USA, (800) 818-7243, (800) 583-2665, journals@sagepub.com, https://www.sagepub.com; Data Planet.

U.S. Department of Agriculture (USDA), Agricultural Marketing Service (AMS), National Organic Program (NOP), 1400 Independence Ave. SW, Rm. 2642-S, Stop 0268, Washington, DC, 20250-0268, USA, (202) 720-3252, jennifer.tucker@usda.gov, https://www.ams.usda.gov/organic; Organic Integrity Database.

U.S. Department of Agriculture (USDA), Economic Research Service (ERS), 1400 Independence Ave. SW, Mail Stop 1800, Washington, DC, 20250-0002, USA, (202) 720-2791, https://www.ers.usda.gov/; Agricultural Baseline Database; Countries and Regions: Brazil; Countries and Regions: China; Countries and Regions: European Union; Countries and Regions: India; Countries and Regions: Japan and South Korea; Countries and Regions: The United States-Mexico-Canada Agreement (USMCA), Canada and Mexico; Feed Grains Database; and Feed Outlook: June 2022.

U.S. Department of Agriculture (USDA), Foreign Agricultural Service (FAS), 1400 Independence Ave. SW, Mail Stop 1001, Washington, DC, 20250, USA, (202) 720-3935, https://www.fas.usda.gov/; World Agricultural Production.

U.S. Department of Agriculture (USDA), National Agricultural Statistics Service (USDA-NASS), 1400 Independence Ave. SW, Washington, DC, 20250, USA, (800) 727-9540, nass@nass.usda.gov, https://www.nass.usda.gov; Agricultural Statistics; Cold Storage; and Quick Stats.

United Nations Food and Agricultural Organization (FAO), 2121 K St., Ste. 800B, Washington, DC, 20037, USA, (202) 653-2400 (Dial from U.S.), (202) 653-5760 (Fax from U.S.), fao-hq@fao.org, https://www.fao.org; CountrySTAT; FAO Country Profiles; FAO Statistical Pocketbook 2021; and FAOSTAT Database.

University of Georgia, Center for Agribusiness and Economic Development, 203 Lumpkin House , Athens, GA, 30602-7509, USA, (706) 542-9809, spkane@uga.edu, https://caed.uga.edu/; 2023 Ag Snapshot and 2022 Georgia Ag Forecast.

World Resources Institute (WRI), 10 G St. NE, Ste. 800, Washington, DC, 20002, USA, (202) 729-7600, (202) 280-1314, https://www.wri.org/; World Resources Report (WRR): Creating a Sustainable Food Future.

AGRICULTURE-ACCIDENTS

Marshfield Clinic Research Institute (MCRI), National Children's Center for Rural and Agricultural Health and Safety (NCCRAHS), 1000 N Oak Ave., Marshfield, WI, 54449-5790, USA, (800) 662-6900, (715) 389-4999, nccrahs@mcrf.mfldclin.edu, https://www.marshfieldresearch.org/nccrahs; Childhood Agricultural Injuries: 2022 Fact Sheet.

National Safety Council (NSC), 1121 Spring Lake Dr., Itasca, IL, 60143-3201, USA, (630) 285-1121, (800) 621-7615, customerservice@nsc.org, https://www.nsc.org/; National Safety Council Injury Facts.

U.S. Department of Agriculture (USDA), National Agricultural Statistics Service (USDA-NASS), 1400 Independence Ave. SW, Washington, DC, 20250, USA, (800) 727-9540, nass@nass.usda.gov, https://www.nass.usda.gov; Adult Agricultural Related Injuries.

U.S. Department of Labor (DOL), Bureau of Labor Statistics (BLS), Postal Square Bldg., 2 Massachusetts Ave. NE, Washington, DC, 20212-0001, USA, (202) 691-5200, (202) 691-7890, blsdata_staff@bls.gov, https://www.bls.gov; Injuries, Illnesses, and Fatalities (IIF) and Monthly Labor Review.

Union of Concerned Scientists (UCS), 2 Brattle Sq., Cambridge, MA, 02138-3780, USA, (617) 547-5552, (617) 864-9405, https://www.ucsusa.org/; Too Hot to Work: Assessing the Threats Climate Change Poses to Outdoor Workers.

AGRICULTURE-ENERGY CONSUMPTION

Natural Resources Defence Council (NRDC), 40 W 20th St., 11th Fl., New York, NY, 10011, USA, (212) 727-2700, (202) 289-6868, nrdcinfo@nrdc.org, https://www.nrdc.org; 2023 Farm Bill Can Help Address Climate Crisis.

AGRICULTURE-ENVIRONMENTAL ASPECTS

Food & Water Watch, 1616 P St. NW, Washington, DC, 20036, USA, (202) 683-2500, (855) 340-8083, (202) 683-2501, info@fwwatch.org, https://www.foodandwaterwatch.org; Well-Fed: A Roadmap to a Sustainable Food System That Works For All.

International Fund for Agricultural Development (IFAD), Via Paolo di Dono, 44, Rome, 00142, ITA, ifad@ifad.org, https://www.ifad.org/; Climate Change and Food System Activities - A Review of Emission Trends, Climate Impacts and the Effects of Dietary Change.

Natural Resources Defence Council (NRDC), 40 W 20th St., 11th Fl., New York, NY, 10011, USA, (212) 727-2700, (202) 289-6868, nrdcinfo@nrdc.org, https://www.nrdc.org; 2023 Farm Bill Can Help Address Climate Crisis.

Organic Trade Association (OTA), 444 N Capitol St. NW, Ste. 445A, Washington, DC, 20001, USA, (202) 403-8520, https://ota.com/; U.S. Organic Trade Data and Trends: 2016 to 2020.

Project Drawdown, 3450 Sacramento St., No. 506, San Francisco, CA, 94118, USA, https://drawdown.org; Farming Our Way Out of the Climate Crisis.

U.S. Department of the Interior (DOI), U.S. Geological Survey (USGS), National Water-Quality Assessment (NAWQA) Project, 12201 Sunrise Valley Dr., Reston, VA, 20192, USA, (888) 392-8545, (770) 283-9728, msdalton@usgs.gov, https://water.usgs.gov/nawqa/; Is There an Urban Pesticide Signature? Urban Streams in Five U.S. Regions Share Common Dissolved-Phase Pesticides But Differ in Predicted Aquatic Toxicity.

Union of Concerned Scientists (UCS), 2 Brattle Sq., Cambridge, MA, 02138-3780, USA, (617) 547-5552, (617) 864-9405, https://www.ucsusa.org/; Too Hot to Work: Assessing the Threats Climate Change Poses to Outdoor Workers.

AGRICULTURE-FEDERAL AID TO STATE AND LOCAL GOVERNMENTS

U.S. Department of Agriculture (USDA), Rural Development, PO Box 66889, St. Louis, MO, 63166, USA, (800) 414-1226, (800) 438-1832 (TTY), https://www.rd.usda.gov; Rural Development Fact Sheets.

U.S. Office of Management and Budget (OMB), 725 17th St. NW, Washington, DC, 20503, USA, (202) 395-3080, https://www.whitehouse.gov/omb/; Budget of the United States Government, Fiscal Year 2023 and Historical Tables.

AGRICULTURE-FINANCE

Internal Revenue Service (IRS), Statistics of Income Division (SOI), 1111 Constitution Ave. NW, K-Room 4100-123, Washington, DC, 20224-0002, USA, (202) 874-0410, (202) 874-0964, sis@irs.gov, https://www.irs.gov/uac/soi-tax-stats-statistics-of-income; Statistics of Income Bulletin.

Sustainable Food Trust, 38 Richmond St., Totterdown, Bristol, BS3 4TQ, GBR, info@sustainablefoodtrust.org, https://sustainablefoodtrust.org/; The Case for Local Food: Building Better Local Food Systems to Benefit Society and Nature.

U.S. Census Bureau, 4600 Silver Hill Rd., Washington, DC, 20233, USA, (301) 763-4636, (800) 923-8282, https://www.census.gov; Annual Capital Expenditures Survey (ACES) 2020 and Statistics of U.S. Businesses (SUSB).

U.S. Department of Agriculture (USDA), Rural Development, PO Box 66889, St. Louis, MO, 63166, USA, (800) 414-1226, (800) 438-1832 (TTY), https://www.rd.usda.gov; Rural Development Fact Sheets.

U.S. Department of Commerce (DOC), Bureau of Economic Analysis (BEA), 4600 Silver Hill Rd., Washington, DC, 20233, USA, (301) 278-9004, customerservice@bea.gov, https://www.bea.gov; National Income and Product Accounts (NIPA): 2022 Update and Survey of Current Business (SCB).

AGRICULTURE-INTERNATIONAL TRADE

CIRAD Agricultural Research for Development, 42, Rue Scheffer, Paris, 75116, FRA, https://www.cirad.fr/en; Agritrop: The CIRAD Information Database.

Malaysian Palm Oil Board (MPOB), 3516 International Court NW, Washington, DC, 20008, USA, (202) 572-9719, (202) 572-9768, (202) 572-9783, mpobtas@gmail.com, https://www.mpob.gov.my/; Journal of Oil Palm Research; Malaysian Oil Palm Statistics 2021; Oil Palm Industry Economic Journal; Overview of the Malaysian Oil Palm Industry 2021; and Palm Oil Engineering Bulletin.

Organic Trade Association (OTA), 444 N Capitol St. NW, Ste. 445A, Washington, DC, 20001, USA, (202) 403-8520, https://ota.com/; U.S. Organic Trade Data and Trends: 2016 to 2020.

U.S. Department of Agriculture (USDA), Economic Research Service (ERS), 1400 Independence Ave. SW, Mail Stop 1800, Washington, DC, 20250-0002, USA, (202) 720-2791, https://www.ers.usda.gov/; Foreign Agricultural Trade of the United States (FATUS); Outlook for U.S. Agricultural Trade: May 2022; and USDA Agricultural Projections to 2031.

U.S. Department of Agriculture (USDA), Foreign Agricultural Service (FAS), 1400 Independence Ave. SW, Mail Stop 1001, Washington, DC, 20250, USA, (202) 720-3935, https://www.fas.usda.gov/; Export Sales Query System; Global Agricultural Trade System (GATS); and World Agricultural Production.

U.S. Department of Agriculture (USDA), National Agricultural Statistics Service (USDA-NASS), 1400 Independence Ave. SW, Washington, DC, 20250, USA, (800) 727-9540, nass@nass.usda.gov, https://www.nass.usda.gov; Agricultural Statistics.

AGRICULTURE-VALUE ADDED

U.S. Department of Agriculture (USDA), Economic Research Service (ERS), 1400 Independence Ave. SW, Mail Stop 1800, Washington, DC, 20250-0002, USA, (202) 720-2791, https://www.ers.usda.gov/; U.S. and State Farm Income and Wealth Statistics.

AGRICULTURE AND ENERGY

Project Drawdown, 3450 Sacramento St., No. 506, San Francisco, CA, 94118, USA, https://drawdown.org; Farming Our Way Out of the Climate Crisis.

U.S. Department of Agriculture (USDA), Rural Development, PO Box 66889, St. Louis, MO, 63166, USA, (800) 414-1226, (800) 438-1832 (TTY), https://www.rd.usda.gov; Rural Development Fact Sheets.

AID TO FAMILIES WITH DEPENDENT CHILDREN

See TEMPORARY ASSISTANCE FOR NEEDY FAMILIES PROGRAM

AIDS (DISEASE)

Bernan Press, 15250 NBN Way, Bldg. C, Blue Ridge Summit, PA, 17214, USA, (301) 459-2255, (800) 865-3457, (800) 865-3450, customercare@bernan.com, https://rowman.com/Page/Bernan; Vital Statistics of the United States 2022: Births, Life Expectancy, Deaths, and Selected Health Data.

Bulletin of the Atomic Scientists, PO Box 15461, Chicago, IL, 60615-5146, USA, (773) 834-3779, admin@thebulletin.org, https://thebulletin.org/; An Illustrated History of the World's Deadliest Epidemics, from Ancient Rome to Covid-19.

Directorate of Health, Iceland, Katrinartuni 2, Reykjavik, 105, ICE, mottaka@landlaeknir.is, https://island.is/en/o/directorate-of-health; HIV by Sex, Age, Citizenship, Transmission Category, and Country of Infection 2000-2021.

Gay Men's Health Crisis (GMHC), 307 W 38th St, New York, NY, 10018-9502, USA, (212) 367-1000, info@gmhc.org, https://www.gmhc.org/; unpublished data.

SIECUS: Sex Ed for Social Change, 1012 14th St. NW, Ste. 305, Washington, DC, 20005, USA, (202) 265-2405, info@siecus.org, https://siecus.org/; The SIECUS State Profiles.

U.S. Census Bureau, 4600 Silver Hill Rd., Washington, DC, 20233, USA, (301) 763-4636, (800) 923-8282, https://www.census.gov; HIV/AIDS Surveillance Data Base.

U.S. Department of Health and Human Services, Centers for Disease Control and Prevention (CDC), 1600 Clifton Rd., Atlanta, GA, 30329-4027, USA, (800) 232-4636, (888) 232-6348 (TTY), cdcinfo@cdc.gov, https://www.cdc.gov; CDC Wonder Databases; HIV Surveillance Reports; Morbidity and Mortality Weekly Report (MMWR); and National Notifiable Diseases Surveillance System (NNDSS).

U.S. Department of Health and Human Services, Centers for Disease Control and Prevention (CDC), National Center for Health Statistics (NCHS), 3311 Toledo Rd., Hyattsville, MD, 20782-2064, USA, (800) 232-4636, (301) 458-4000, https://www.cdc.gov/nchs; FastStats - Statistics by Topic; Health, United States, 2020-2021; National Vital Statistics Reports (NVSR); and Vital Statistics Online Data Portal.

U.S. Department of Health and Human Services, Centers for Disease Control and Prevention (CDC), National Center for HIV, Viral Hepatitis, STD, and TB Prevention (NCHHSTP), 1600 Clifton Rd., Atlanta, GA, 30329-4027, USA, (800) 232-4636, (888) 232-6348 (TTY), https://www.cdc.gov/nchhstp/; NCHHSTP AtlasPlus.

UNAIDS, 20, Avenue Appia, Geneva, CH-1211, SWI, unaids@unaids.org, https://www.unaids.org; 2020 AIDS Progress Reports Submitted by Countries; AIDSinfo Database; Key Populations Atlas; and UNAIDS Global AIDS Update 2022 - In Danger.

United Nations Statistics Division (UNSD), United Nations Plz., New York, NY, 10017, USA, (800) 253-9646, (212) 963-9851, statistics@un.org, https://unstats.un.org; Millennium Development Goal Indicators.

World Health Organization (WHO), Ave. Appia 20, Geneva, CH-1211, SWI, (202) 974-3000 (Telephone in U.S.), publications@who.int, https://www.who.int/; Global Health Observatory (GHO) and HIV/AIDS Surveillance in Europe 2022.

AIR CONDITIONING

U.S. Census Bureau, 4600 Silver Hill Rd., Washington, DC, 20233, USA, (301) 763-4636, (800) 923-8282, https://www.census.gov; American Community Survey (ACS) 2020 and American Housing Survey (AHS) 2019.

AIR PILOTS

Regional Airline Association (RAA), 1201 15th St. NW, Ste. 430, Washington, DC, 20005, USA, (202) 367-1170, raa@raa.org, https://www.raa.org; Pilot Supply & Air Service Update, May 2019.

AIR POLLUTION

AirNow, c/o U.S. Environmental Protection Agency (EPA), Office of Air Quality Planning and Standards (OAQPS), Information Transfer Group, Mail Code C404-07, Research Triangle Park, NC, 27711, USA, (919) 541-0242, https://www.airnow.gov/; Air Quality Index (AQI).

American Lung Association, 55 W Wacker Dr., Ste. 1150, Chicago, IL, 60601, USA, (800) 586-4872, info@lung.org, https://www.lung.org/; State of the Air.

Berkeley Earth, admin@berkeleyearth.org, https://berkeleyearth.org; Air Quality Country List.

California Air Resources Board (CARB), PO Box 2815 , Sacramento, CA, 95812, USA, (800) 242-4450, helpline@arb.ca.gov, https://ww2.arb.ca.gov/; iADAM: Air Quality Data Statistics.

Climate Central, One Palmer Square, Ste. 402, Princeton, NJ, 08542, USA, (609) 924-3800, (877) 425-4724, https://www.climatecentral.org/; Climate Change Is Threatening Air Quality Across the Country.

Global Change Data Lab, Our World in Data, GBR, info@ourworldindata.org, https://ourworldindata.org; Outdoor Air Pollution.

Harvard T.H. Chan School of Public Health, 677 Huntington Ave., Boston, MA, 02115, USA, (617) 495-1000, https://www.hsph.harvard.edu/; Air Pollution and COVID-19 Mortality in the United States: Strengths and Limitations of an Ecological Regression Analysis.

Health Effects Institute (HEI), 75 Federal St., Ste. 1400, Boston, MA, 02110-1817, USA, (617) 488-2300, (617) 488-2335, https://www.healtheffects.org/; Systematic Review and Meta-analysis of Selected Health Effects of Long-Term Exposure to Traffic-Related Air Pollution.

IQAir, 14351 Firestone Blvd., La Mirada, CA, 90638, USA, (877) 304-7247, https://www.iqair.com/us/; Air Quality in the World and 2022 World Air Quality Report.

New York University School of Law, Institute for Policy Integrity, 139 MacDougal St., Wilf Hall, 3rd Fl., New York, NY, 10012, USA, (212) 992-8932, (212) 995-4592, https://policyintegrity.org/; No Turning Back: An Analysis of EPA's Authority to Withdraw California's Preemption Waiver Under Section 209 of the Clean Air Act.

ProPublica, 155 Avenue of the Americas, 13th Fl., New York, NY, 10013, USA, (212) 514-5250, (212) 785-2634, hello@propublica.org, https://www.propublica.org/; Hazardous Air Pollutant Exposure as a Contributing Factor to COVID-19 Mortality in the United States.

World Health Organization (WHO), Ave. Appia 20, Geneva, CH-1211, SWI, (202) 974-3000 (Telephone in U.S.), publications@who.int, https://www.who.int/; Global Health Observatory (GHO) Data.

AIR POLLUTION-EMISSIONS

Carbon Tracker Initiative (CTI), 40 Bermondsey St., 2nd Fl., London, SE1 3UD, GBR, hello@carbontracker.org, https://www.carbontracker.org/; Closing the Gap to a Paris-Compliant EU-ETS.

Climate Change Committee (CCC), 151 Buckingham Palace Rd., London, SW1W 9SZ, GBR, https://www.theccc.org.uk/; Independent Assessment of UK Climate Risk and 2021 Progress Report to Parliament.

The Energy and Resources Institute (TERI), Lodhi Rd., Darbari Seth Block, IHC Complex, New Delhi, 110003, IND, mailbox@teri.res.in, https://www.teriin.org/; Air Pollution Causing Heart Diseases.

Environment and Climate Change Canada, Fontaine Bldg., 200 Sacre-Coeur Blvd., 12th Fl., Gatineau, QC, K1A 0H3, CAN, (819) 938-3838 (Dial from U.S.), enviroinfo@ec.gc.ca, https://www.canada.ca/en/environment-climate-change.html; Air Pollutant Emissions.

Environmental Defense Fund (EDF), 1875 Connecticut Ave. NW, Ste. 600, Washington, DC, 20009, USA, (202) 572-3298, (202) 387-3500, (202) 234-6049, https://www.edf.org; Making the Invisible Visible: Shining a Light on Warehouse Truck Air Pollution.

European Commission, Joint Research Centre, EU Science Hub, Brussels, B-1049, BEL, ies-contact@jrc.ec.europa.eu, https://ec.europa.eu/jrc/en; Emissions Database for Global Atmospheric Research (EDGAR).

Harvard T.H. Chan School of Public Health, Center for Climate, Health, and the Global Environment (Harvard C-CHANGE), 401 Park Dr., 4th Fl. W, Ste. 415, Boston, MA, 02215, USA, (617) 384-8350, cchange@hsph.harvard.edu, https://www.hsph.harvard.edu/c-change/; Carbon Standards Re-Examined: An Analysis of Potential Emissions Outcomes for the Affordable Clean Energy Rule and the Clean Power Plan.

INRIX, 10210 NE Points Dr., No. 400, Kirkland, WA, 98033, USA, (425) 284-3800, https://inrix.com; Signal Optimization and Climate Outcomes.

International Council on Clean Transportation (ICCT), 1500 K St. NW, Ste. 650, Washington, DC, 20005, USA, (202) 798-3986, https://theicct.org; Reassessment of Excess NOx from Diesel Cars in Europe Following the Court Justice of the European Union Rulings.

International Energy Agency (IEA), 9 Rue de la Federation, Paris, 75739, FRA, info@iea.org, https://www.iea.org/; CO2 Emissions in 2022 and Global Energy Review 2021.

New York University School of Law, Institute for Policy Integrity, 139 MacDougal St., Wilf Hall, 3rd Fl., New York, NY, 10012, USA, (212) 992-8932, (212) 995-4592, https://policyintegrity.org/; Analyzing EPA's Vehicle-Emissions Decisions: Why Withdrawing the 2022-2025 Standards Is Economically Flawed.

NewClimate Institute, Waidmarkt 11a, Cologne, D-50676, GER, info@newclimate.org, https://newclimate.org/; Exploring the Impact of the COVID-19 Pandemic on Global Emission Projections and Net Zero Stocktake 2022.

Oko-Institut e.V. (Institute for Applied Ecology), PO Box 17 71, Freiburg, D-79017, GER, info@oeko.de, https://www.oeko.de; E-Fuels Versus DACCS and Enough? The Role of Sufficiency in European Energy and Climate Plans.

Organization for Economic Cooperation and Development (OECD), 2001 L St. NW, Ste. 650, Washington, DC, 20036-4922, USA, (202) 785-6323, (800) 456-6323, (202) 785-0350, washington.contact@oecd.org, https://www.oecd.org/; Environment Statistics.

The Real Urban Emissions Initiative (TRUE), 60 Trafalgar Square, London, WC2N 5DS, GBR, info@trueinitiative.org, https://www.trueinitiative.org/; Air Quality and Health Impacts of Diesel Truck Emissions in New York City and Policy Implications.

Silent Spring Institute, 320 Nevada St., Ste. 302, Newton, MA, 02460, USA, (617) 332-4288, (617) 332-4284, info@silentspring.org, https://silentspring.org/; Identifying Toxic Consumer Products: A Novel Data Set Reveals Air Emissions of Potent Carcinogens, Reproductive Toxicants, and Developmental Toxicants.

Statistics Norway, PO Box 2633 St. Hanshaugen, Oslo, NO-0131, NOR, ssb@ssb.no, https://www.ssb.no/en/; Emissions from Norwegian Economic Activity.

U.S. Department of Energy (DOE), 1000 Independence Ave. SW, Washington, DC, 20585, USA, (202) 586-5000, (202) 586-4403, the.secretary@hq.doe.gov, https://www.energy.gov/; Greenhouse Gas Emissions from Electric and Plug-In Hybrid Vehicles.

U.S. Environmental Protection Agency (EPA), 1200 Pennsylvania Ave. NW, Washington, DC, 20460, USA, (202) 564-4700, https://www.epa.gov/; Air Data: Air Quality Data Collected at Outdoor Monitors Across the US; Clearinghouse for Inventories and Emissions Factors (CHIEF); Emissions and Generation Resource Integrated Database (eGRID); EnviroMapper for Envirofacts; Release Chemical Report; and Toxics Release Inventory (TRI) Program.

United Nations Environment Programme (UNEP), 900 17th St. NW, Ste. 506, Washington, DC, 20006, USA, (202) 974-1300, publications@unep.org, https://www.unep.org/; Emissions Gap Report 2022.

University of California Davis, Policy Institute for Energy, Environment, and the Economy, 1 Shields Ave., Davis, CA, 95616, USA, (530) 752-1011, contact@flightaware.com, https://flightaware.com/; Modeling Expected Air Quality Impacts of Oregon's Proposed Expanded Clean Fuels Program.

AIR POLLUTION-GREENHOUSE GASES

Environmental Defense Fund (EDF), 1875 Connecticut Ave. NW, Ste. 600, Washington, DC, 20009, USA, (202) 572-3298, (202) 387-3500, (202) 234-6049, https://www.edf.org; Solutions Newsletter.

European Commission, Joint Research Centre, EU Science Hub, Brussels, B-1049, BEL, ies-contact@jrc.ec.europa.eu, https://ec.europa.eu/jrc/en; Emissions Database for Global Atmospheric Research (EDGAR).

INRIX, 10210 NE Points Dr., No. 400, Kirkland, WA, 98033, USA, (425) 284-3800, https://inrix.com; Signal Optimization and Climate Outcomes.

Intergovernmental Panel on Climate Change (IPCC), C/O World Meteorological Organization, 7 bis Avenue de la Paix, C.P. 2300, Geneva, CH-1211, SWI, ipcc-sec@wmo.int, https://www.ipcc.ch/; AR6 Synthesis Report: Climate Change 2023; Climate Change 2022: Mitigation of Climate Change; and Climate Change and Land.

Statistics Norway, PO Box 2633 St. Hanshaugen, Oslo, NO-0131, NOR, ssb@ssb.no, https://www.ssb.no/en/; Emissions from Norwegian Economic Activity.

U.S. Department of Energy (DOE), 1000 Independence Ave. SW, Washington, DC, 20585, USA, (202) 586-5000, (202) 586-4403, the.secretary@hq.doe.gov, https://www.energy.gov/; Greenhouse Gas Emissions from Electric and Plug-In Hybrid Vehicles.

U.S. Department of Energy (DOE), Office of Energy Efficiency and Renewable Energy (EERE), Alternative Fuels Data Center (AFDC), Mail Stop EE-1, Washington, DC, 20585, USA, (202) 586-5000, https://www.afdc.energy.gov/; Clean Cities.

U.S. Environmental Protection Agency (EPA), 1200 Pennsylvania Ave. NW, Washington, DC, 20460, USA, (202) 564-4700, https://www.epa.gov/; 2021 Automotive Trends Report.

World Meteorological Organization (WMO), 7bis, ave. de la Paix, PO Box 2300, Geneva, CH-1211, SWI, wmo@wmo.int, https://public.wmo.int/en; WMO Greenhouse Gas Bulletin.

AIR POLLUTION-INDUSTRY

Environmental Business International, Inc. (EBI), 4452 Park Blvd., Ste. 306, San Diego, CA, 92116, USA, (619) 295-7685, info@ebionline.org, https://ebionline.org/; Climate Change Adaptation & Resilience Markets; Climate Change Business Journal (CCBJ); Environmental Business Journal (EBJ); Environmental Testing and Analytical Services; The Global Environmental Market; and U.S. Environmental Industry Overview.

Silent Spring Institute, 320 Nevada St., Ste. 302, Newton, MA, 02460, USA, (617) 332-4288, (617) 332-4284, info@silentspring.org, https://silentspring.org/; Identifying Toxic Consumer Products: A Novel Data Set Reveals Air Emissions of Potent Carcinogens, Reproductive Toxicants, and Developmental Toxicants.

AIR QUALITY

AirNow, c/o U.S. Environmental Protection Agency (EPA), Office of Air Quality Planning and Standards (OAQPS), Information Transfer Group, Mail Code C404-07, Research Triangle Park, NC, 27711, USA, (919) 541-0242, https://www.airnow.gov/; Air Quality Index (AQI).

Berkeley Earth, admin@berkeleyearth.org, https://berkeleyearth.org; Air Quality Country List.

Climate Central, One Palmer Square, Ste. 402, Princeton, NJ, 08542, USA, (609) 924-3800, (877)

425-4724, https://www.climatecentral.org/; Climate Change Is Threatening Air Quality Across the Country; Extreme Heat: When Outdoor Sports Become Risky; and Seniors at Risk: Heat and Climate Change.

International Council on Clean Transportation (ICCT), 1500 K St. NW, Ste. 650, Washington, DC, 20005, USA, (202) 798-3986, https://theicct.org; Reassessment of Excess NOx from Diesel Cars in Europe Following the Court Justice of the European Union Rulings.

IQAir, 14351 Firestone Blvd., La Mirada, CA, 90638, USA, (877) 304-7247, https://www.iqair.com/us/; Air Quality in the World and 2022 World Air Quality Report.

The Real Urban Emissions Initiative (TRUE), 60 Trafalgar Square, London, WC2N 5DS, GBR, info@trueinitiative.org, https://www.trueinitiative.org/; Air Quality and Health Impacts of Diesel Truck Emissions in New York City and Policy Implications.

Silent Spring Institute, 320 Nevada St., Ste. 302, Newton, MA, 02460, USA, (617) 332-4288, (617) 332-4284, info@silentspring.org, https://silentspring.org/; Influence of Living in the Same Home on Biomonitored Levels of Consumer Product Chemicals.

University of California Davis, Policy Institute for Energy, Environment, and the Economy, 1 Shields Ave., Davis, CA, 95616, USA, (530) 752-1011, contact@flightaware.com, https://flightaware.com/; Modeling Expected Air Quality Impacts of Oregon's Proposed Expanded Clean Fuels Program.

University of Washington, Institute for Health Metrics and Evaluation (IHME), Population Health Building/Hans Rosling Center, UW Campus Box 351615, 3980 15th Ave. NE, Seattle, WA, 98195, USA, (206) 897-2800, (206) 897-2899, engage@healthdata.org, https://www.healthdata.org; Air Quality and Health in Cities.

AIR QUALITY MANAGEMENT

California Air Resources Board (CARB), PO Box 2815 , Sacramento, CA, 95812, USA, (800) 242-4450, helpline@arb.ca.gov, https://ww2.arb.ca.gov/; iADAM: Air Quality Data Statistics.

Environment and Climate Change Canada, Fontaine Bldg., 200 Sacre-Coeur Blvd., 12th Fl., Gatineau, QC, K1A 0H3, CAN, (819) 938-3838 (Dial from U.S.), enviroinfo@ec.gc.ca, https://www.canada.ca/en/environment-climate-change.html; Air Pollutant Emissions.

Environmental Business International, Inc. (EBI), 4452 Park Blvd., Ste. 306, San Diego, CA, 92116, USA, (619) 295-7685, info@ebionline.org, https://ebionline.org/; Climate Change Adaptation & Resilience Markets; Climate Change Business Journal (CCBJ); Environmental Business Journal (EBJ); Environmental Testing and Analytical Services; The Global Environmental Market; and U.S. Environmental Industry Overview.

AIR TRAFFIC CAPACITY

FlightAware, 11 Greenway Plaza, Ste. 2900, Houston, TX, 77046, USA, (713) 877-9010, contact@flightaware.com, https://flightaware.com/; FlightAware Firehose.

AIR TRAVEL

European Cockpit Association (ECA), Rue du Commerce 20-22, Brussels, B-1000, BEL, eca@eurocockpit.be, https://www.eurocockpit.be/; COVID-19: Thousands of Aircrew Redundant.

European Commission, Eurostat, Luxembourg, 2920, LUX, https://ec.europa.eu/eurostat/; Air Transport Statistics.

U.S. Department of Transportation (DOT), Federal Aviation Administration (FAA), 800 Independence Ave. SW, Washington, DC, 20591, USA, (866) 835-5322, https://www.faa.gov/; Accident and Incident Data; Airmen Knowledge Test Statistics; and Runway Safety Statistics.

AIRCRAFT ACCIDENTS

National Transportation Safety Board (NTSB), 490 L'Enfant Plz. SW, Washington, DC, 20594, USA, (202) 314-6000, https://www.ntsb.gov; Accident Data and Statistical Reviews.

U.S. Department of Transportation (DOT), Federal Aviation Administration (FAA), 800 Independence Ave. SW, Washington, DC, 20591, USA, (866) 835-5322, https://www.faa.gov/; Accident and Incident Data; Preliminary Accident and Incident Notices; and Runway Safety Statistics.

AIRCRAFT AND PARTS INDUSTRY

AMSTAT, 44 Apple St., Ste. 5, Tinton Falls, NJ, 07724, USA, (732) 530-6400, (877) 426-7828, (732) 530-6360, service@amstatcorp.com, https://www.amstatcorp.com/; AMSTAT Premier and AMSTAT StatPak.

AIRCRAFT AND PARTS INDUSTRY-MANUFACTURING-EARNINGS

U.S. Census Bureau, Center for Economic Studies (CES), 4600 Silver Hill Rd., Washington, DC, 20233, USA, (301) 763-6460, (301) 763-5935, ces.contacts@census.gov, https://www.census.gov/programs-surveys/ces.html; Transportation and Warehousing, 2017 Economic Census.

AIRCRAFT MANUFACTURING

See AEROSPACE INDUSTRY

AIRLINES

Cirium, 230 Park Ave., 7th Fl., New York, NY, 10169, USA, (646) 746-6851, https://www.cirium.com/; The Impact of COVID-19 on Aviation and Taking to the Skies 2021: An Analysis of Startup Airlines in North America with Sample Profiles of the Newest Airlines.

AIRMAIL SERVICE

U.S. Postal Service (USPS), 475 L'Enfant Plz. SW, Washington, DC, 20260, USA, (800) 275-8777, (877) 889-2457 (TTY), https://www.usps.com/; Quarterly Statistics Report (QSR).

AIRPLANES

AMSTAT, 44 Apple St., Ste. 5, Tinton Falls, NJ, 07724, USA, (732) 530-6400, (877) 426-7828, (732) 530-6360, service@amstatcorp.com, https://www.amstatcorp.com/; AMSTAT Premier and AMSTAT StatPak.

FlightAware, 11 Greenway Plaza, Ste. 2900, Houston, TX, 77046, USA, (713) 877-9010, contact@flightaware.com, https://flightaware.com/; FlightAware Firehose.

Janes, USA, (703) 574-7580, (888) 977-1519, customer.care@janes.com, https://www.janes.com; Jane's All the World's Aircraft: In Service 2021-2022.

National Aeronautics and Space Administration (NASA), NASA Headquarters, 300 E St. SW, Ste. 5R30, Washington, DC, 20546, USA, (202) 358-0001, (202) 358-4338, https://www.nasa.gov; Aviation Safety Reporting System (ASRS).

S&P Global, 55 Water St., New York, NY, 10041, USA, (212) 438-2000, market.intelligence@spglobal.com, https://www.spglobal.com/; Update: Aerospace and Defense North America.

U.S. Census Bureau, International Trade Program, 4600 Silver Hill Rd., Washington, DC, 20233, USA, (800) 549-0595, eid.international.trade.data@census.gov, https://www.census.gov/foreign-trade; International Trade Data.

AIRPORT SECURITY PERSONNEL

U.S. Department of Homeland Security (DHS), Transportation Security Administration (TSA), 2707 Martin Luther King Jr. Ave. SE, Washington, DC, 20528, USA, (866) 289-9673, (202) 282-8000, https://www.tsa.gov; TSA Checkpoint Travel Numbers for 2022, 2021, 2020 and 2019.

AIRPORTS

European Commission, Eurostat, Luxembourg, 2920, LUX, https://ec.europa.eu/eurostat/; Air Transport Statistics.

FlightStats by Cirium, 522 SW 5th Ave., Portland, OR, 97204, USA, (503) 274-0938, https://www.flightstats.com; 2022 On-Time Performance Review.

Regional Airline Association (RAA), 1201 15th St. NW, Ste. 430, Washington, DC, 20005, USA, (202) 367-1170, raa@raa.org, https://www.raa.org; Pilot Supply & Air Service Update, May 2019.

U.S. Department of Transportation (DOT), Federal Aviation Administration (FAA), 800 Independence Ave. SW, Washington, DC, 20591, USA, (866) 835-5322, https://www.faa.gov/; Accident and Incident Data and Runway Safety Statistics.

U.S. Department of Transportation (DOT), Office of the Assistant Secretary for Research and Technology (OST-R), Bureau of Transportation Statistics (BTS), 1200 New Jersey Ave. SE, Washington, DC, 20590, USA, (800) 853-1351, (202) 366-3282, https://www.bts.gov; TranStats.

AIRPORTS-FEDERAL AID TO STATE AND LOCAL GOVERNMENTS

U.S. Office of Management and Budget (OMB), 725 17th St. NW, Washington, DC, 20503, USA, (202) 395-3080, https://www.whitehouse.gov/omb/; Budget of the United States Government, Fiscal Year 2023 and Historical Tables.

AIRPORTS-TRAFFIC

FlightAware, 11 Greenway Plaza, Ste. 2900, Houston, TX, 77046, USA, (713) 877-9010, contact@flightaware.com, https://flightaware.com/; FlightAware Firehose.

FlightStats by Cirium, 522 SW 5th Ave., Portland, OR, 97204, USA, (503) 274-0938, https://www.flightstats.com; 2022 On-Time Performance Review.

Regional Airline Association (RAA), 1201 15th St. NW, Ste. 430, Washington, DC, 20005, USA, (202) 367-1170, raa@raa.org, https://www.raa.org; The Year of Community: 2021 Annual Report.

U.S. Department of Homeland Security (DHS), Transportation Security Administration (TSA), 2707 Martin Luther King Jr. Ave. SE, Washington, DC, 20528, USA, (866) 289-9673, (202) 282-8000, https://www.tsa.gov; TSA Checkpoint Travel Numbers for 2022, 2021, 2020 and 2019.

U.S. Department of Transportation (DOT), Federal Aviation Administration (FAA), 800 Independence Ave. SW, Washington, DC, 20591, USA, (866) 835-5322, https://www.faa.gov/; Runway Safety Statistics.

U.S. Department of Transportation (DOT), Office of Aviation Consumer Protection, 1200 New Jersey Ave. SE, Washington, DC, 20590, USA, (202) 366-2220, https://www.transportation.gov/airconsumer; Air Travel Consumer Report.

U.S. Department of Transportation (DOT), Office of the Assistant Secretary for Research and Technology (OST-R), Bureau of Transportation Statistics (BTS), 1200 New Jersey Ave. SE, Washington, DC, 20590, USA, (800) 853-1351, (202) 366-3282, https://www.bts.gov; Airline On-Time Statistics and Delay Causes.

AIRPORTS-TRAFFIC-RANKINGS AND RATINGS

U.S. Department of Transportation (DOT), Office of the Assistant Secretary for Research and Technology (OST-R), Bureau of Transportation Statistics (BTS), 1200 New Jersey Ave. SE, Washington, DC, 20590, USA, (800) 853-1351, (202) 366-3282, https://www.bts.gov; Airline On-Time Statistics and Delay Causes.

AIRPORTS OR AIRFIELDS-AIRPORT AND AIRWAY TRUST FUND

U.S. Office of Management and Budget (OMB), 725 17th St. NW, Washington, DC, 20503, USA, (202)

395-3080, https://www.whitehouse.gov/omb/; Budget of the United States Government, Fiscal Year 2023.

ALABAMA

See also-STATE DATA (FOR INDIVIDUAL STATES)

ALABAMA-STATE DATA CENTERS

Alabama Department of Economic and Community Affairs (ADECA), PO Box 5690, Montgomery, AL, 36103-5690, USA, (334) 242-5100, (334) 242-5099, contact@adeca.alabama.gov, https://adeca.alabama.gov; State Data Reports (AL).

University of Alabama, Culverhouse College of Business, Center for Business and Economic Research (CBER), PO Box 870221, Tuscaloosa, AL, 35487-0221, USA, (205) 348-6191, (205) 348-2951, uacber@cba.ua.edu, uacber@culverhouse.ua.edu; State Data Reports (AL).

ALABAMA-PRIMARY STATISTICS SOURCES

Alabama State Department of Education, 50 N Ripley St., PO Box 302101, Montgomery, AL, 36104, USA, (334) 694-4900, comm@alsde.edu, https://www.alabamaachieves.org/; Alabama Education Report Card and Education Report Card: Supporting Data.

Appalachian Regional Commission (ARC), 1666 Connecticut Ave. NW, Ste. 700, Washington, DC, 20009, USA, (202) 884-7700, info@arc.gov, https://www.arc.gov/; Socioeconomic Data Profile by County and Strengthening Economic Resilience in Appalachia.

SAGE Publications, 2455 Teller Rd., Thousand Oaks, CA, 91320, USA, (800) 818-7243, (800) 583-2665, journals@sagepub.com, https://www.sagepub.com; Data Planet.

University of Alabama, Culverhouse College of Business, Center for Business and Economic Research (CBER), PO Box 870221, Tuscaloosa, AL, 35487-0221, USA, (205) 348-6191, (205) 348-2951, uacber@cba.ua.edu, uacber@culverhouse.ua.edu; Alabama Business; 2023 Alabama Economic Outlook; and Alabama Population Estimates and Projections.

ALASKA

See also-STATE DATA (FOR INDIVIDUAL STATES)

Alaska Department of Commerce, Community and Economic Development (DCCED), Division of Community and Regional Affairs (DCRA), 550 W 7th Ave., Ste. 1650, Anchorage, AK, 99501-3510, USA, (907) 269-4501, (907) 269-4563, dcra.admin@alaska.gov, https://www.commerce.alaska.gov/web/dcra; Alaska Fuel Price Report: Current Community Conditions.

State of Alaska Department of Labor and Workforce Development, Research and Analysis Section, PO Box 111149, Juneau, AK, 99811, USA, (907) 465-5970, (907) 465-2437, liz.brooks@alaska.gov, https://live.laborstats.alaska.gov/cen/; Alaska Economic Trends.

U.S. Department of Housing and Urban Development (HUD), Office of Policy Development and Research (PD&R), PO Box 23268, Washington, DC, 20026-3268, USA, (800) 245-2691, (800) 927-7589 (TDD), (202) 708-9981, helpdesk@huduser.gov, https://www.huduser.gov; Assessment of American Indian, Alaska Native, and Native Hawaiian Housing Needs.

University of Alaska Anchorage Justice Center, 3211 Providence Dr., PSB Ste. 234, Anchorage, AK, 99508, USA, (907) 786-1810, (907) 786-7777, uaa_justicecenter@alaska.edu, https://www.uaa.alaska.edu/academics/college-of-health/departments/justice-center/; Adverse Childhood Experiences, Intimate Partner Violence, and Sexual Violence Among Persons Who May Be Alaska Mental Health Trust Beneficiaries: Findings from the Alaska Victimization Survey and Alaska Victimization Survey.

ALASKA-STATE DATA CENTERS

Alaska Department of Commerce, Community and Economic Development (DCCED), Division of Community and Regional Affairs (DCRA), 550 W 7th Ave., Ste. 1650, Anchorage, AK, 99501-3510, USA, (907) 269-4501, (907) 269-4563, dcra.admin@alaska.gov, https://www.commerce.alaska.gov/web/dcra; State Data Reports (AK).

Alaska State Library, PO Box 110571, Juneau, AK, 99811-0571, USA, (907) 465-4837, (907) 465-2151, asl@alaska.gov, https://library.alaska.gov; State Data Reports (AK).

State of Alaska Department of Labor and Workforce Development, Research and Analysis Section, PO Box 111149, Juneau, AK, 99811, USA, (907) 465-5970, (907) 465-2437, liz.brooks@alaska.gov, https://live.laborstats.alaska.gov/cen/; State Data Reports (AK).

University of Alaska Anchorage, Institute of Social and Economic Research (ISER), 3211 Providence Dr., Anchorage, AK, 99508, USA, (907) 786-7710, (907) 786-7739, uaa_iser@uaa.alaska.edu, https://iseralaska.org/; State Data Reports (AK).

ALASKA-PRIMARY STATISTICS SOURCES

SAGE Publications, 2455 Teller Rd., Thousand Oaks, CA, 91320, USA, (800) 818-7243, (800) 583-2665, journals@sagepub.com, https://www.sagepub.com; Data Planet.

State of Alaska Department of Education and Early Development, PO Box 110500, Juneau, AK, 99811-0500, USA, (907) 465-2800, (800) 770-8973 (TTY), (907) 465-2441, eed.webmaster@alaska.gov, https://education.alaska.gov/; Data Center.

ALBANIA-NATIONAL STATISTICAL OFFICE

Institute of Statistics (INSTAT), St. Vllazen Huta, Bldg. 35, Tirane, 1017, ALB, info@instat.gov.al, http://www.instat.gov.al; National Data Reports (Albania).

ALBANIA-PRIMARY STATISTICS SOURCES

Institute of Statistics (INSTAT), St. Vllazen Huta, Bldg. 35, Tirane, 1017, ALB, info@instat.gov.al, http://www.instat.gov.al; Albania in Figures, 2020.

ALBANIA-AGRICULTURE

The Economist Group: Economist Intelligence Unit (EIU), 900 3rd Ave., 16th Fl., New York, NY, 10022, USA, (212) 541-0500, americas@eiu.com, https://www.eiu.com; Albania Country Report.

Euromonitor International, Inc., 1 N Dearborn St., Ste. 1700, Chicago, IL, 60602, USA, (312) 922-1115, (312) 922-1157, info-usa@euromonitor.com, https://www.euromonitor.com/; Geographies.

Organisation of Islamic Cooperation (OIC), Statistical, Economic and Social Research and Training Centre for Islamic Countries (SESRIC), Kudus Cad. No. 9, Diplomatik Site, Ankara, 06450, TUR, statistics@sesric.org, https://www.sesric.org/; OIC Statistics (OICStat) Database and OIC-Countries in Figures (OIC-CIF).

Palgrave Macmillan, 1 New York Plaza, Ste. 4500, New York, NY, 10004-1562, USA, (800) 777-4643, orders@palgrave.com, https://www.palgrave.com/us; The Statesman's Yearbook, 2023.

Routledge - Taylor & Francis Group, 6000 Broken Sound Pkwy. NW, Ste. 300, Boca Raton, FL, 33487, USA, (800) 634-1420, (800) 634-7064, orders@taylorandfrancis.com, https://www.routledge.com/; The Europa World Year Book 2022.

United Nations Food and Agricultural Organization (FAO), 2121 K St., Ste. 800B, Washington, DC, 20037, USA, (202) 653-2400 (Dial from U.S.), (202) 653-5760 (Fax from U.S.), fao-hq@fao.org, https://www.fao.org; AQUASTAT and The State of Food and Agriculture (SOFA) 2022.

United Nations Statistics Division (UNSD), United Nations Plz., New York, NY, 10017, USA, (800) 253-9646, (212) 963-9851, statistics@un.org, https://unstats.un.org; Statistical Yearbook of the United Nations 2021.

The World Bank, 1818 H St. NW, Washington, DC, 20433, USA, (202) 473-1000, (202) 477-6391, eds03@worldbank.org, https://www.worldbank.org/; Albania (report).

ALBANIA-AIRLINES

Palgrave Macmillan, 1 New York Plaza, Ste. 4500, New York, NY, 10004-1562, USA, (800) 777-4643, orders@palgrave.com, https://www.palgrave.com/us; The Statesman's Yearbook, 2023.

ALBANIA-ALUMINUM PRODUCTION

See ALBANIA-MINERAL INDUSTRIES

ALBANIA-ARMED FORCES

Central Intelligence Agency (CIA), Office of Public Affairs, Washington, DC, 20505, USA, (703) 482-0623, https://www.cia.gov; The World Factbook.

International Institute for Strategic Studies (IISS) - Americas, 2121 K St. NW, Ste. 600, Washington, DC, 20037, USA, (202) 659-1490, (202) 659-1499, https://www.iiss.org/; The Military Balance 2022.

Palgrave Macmillan, 1 New York Plaza, Ste. 4500, New York, NY, 10004-1562, USA, (800) 777-4643, orders@palgrave.com, https://www.palgrave.com/us; The Statesman's Yearbook, 2023.

Stockholm International Peace Research Institute (SIPRI), Signalistgatan 9, Stockholm, SE 169 72, SWE, https://www.sipri.org/; SIPRI Arms Transfers Database and SIPRI Military Expenditure Database.

ALBANIA-BALANCE OF PAYMENTS

United Nations Conference on Trade and Development (UNCTAD), Palais des Nations, Geneva, 1211, SWI, (212) 963-6896, unctadinfo@unctad.org, https://unctad.org; Handbook of Statistics 2021.

The World Bank, 1818 H St. NW, Washington, DC, 20433, USA, (202) 473-1000, (202) 477-6391, eds03@worldbank.org, https://www.worldbank.org/; Albania (report) and World Development Report 2022: Finance for an Equitable Recovery.

ALBANIA-BANKS AND BANKING

Euromonitor International, Inc., 1 N Dearborn St., Ste. 1700, Chicago, IL, 60602, USA, (312) 922-1115, (312) 922-1157, info-usa@euromonitor.com, https://www.euromonitor.com/; Geographies.

ALBANIA-BARLEY PRODUCTION

See ALBANIA-CROPS

ALBANIA-BROADCASTING

Central Intelligence Agency (CIA), Office of Public Affairs, Washington, DC, 20505, USA, (703) 482-0623, https://www.cia.gov; The World Factbook.

Euromonitor International, Inc., 1 N Dearborn St., Ste. 1700, Chicago, IL, 60602, USA, (312) 922-1115, (312) 922-1157, info-usa@euromonitor.com, https://www.euromonitor.com/; Geographies.

Palgrave Macmillan, 1 New York Plaza, Ste. 4500, New York, NY, 10004-1562, USA, (800) 777-4643,

orders@palgrave.com, https://www.palgrave.com/us; The Statesman's Yearbook, 2023.

WRTH Publications Limited, PO Box 290, Oxford, OX2 7FT, GBR, sales@wrth.com, https://www.wrth.com; World Radio TV Handbook 2023.

ALBANIA-BUDGET

Central Intelligence Agency (CIA), Office of Public Affairs, Washington, DC, 20505, USA, (703) 482-0623, https://www.cia.gov; The World Factbook.

ALBANIA-BUSINESS

Institute of Statistics (INSTAT), St. Vllazen Huta, Bldg. 35, Tirane, 1017, ALB, info@instat.gov.al, http://www.instat.gov.al; International Trade in Goods and Enterprises, 2016-2020.

ALBANIA-CLIMATE

Palgrave Macmillan, 1 New York Plaza, Ste. 4500, New York, NY, 10004-1562, USA, (800) 777-4643, orders@palgrave.com, https://www.palgrave.com/us; The Statesman's Yearbook, 2023.

ALBANIA-COAL PRODUCTION

See ALBANIA-MINERAL INDUSTRIES

ALBANIA-COFFEE

See ALBANIA-CROPS

ALBANIA-COMMERCE

Palgrave Macmillan, 1 New York Plaza, Ste. 4500, New York, NY, 10004-1562, USA, (800) 777-4643, orders@palgrave.com, https://www.palgrave.com/us; The Statesman's Yearbook, 2023.

UK Data Service, University of Essex, Wivenhoe Park, Colchester, Essex, CO4 3SQ, GBR, https://ukdataservice.ac.uk/; International Aggregate Data.

ALBANIA-COMMODITY EXCHANGES

Barchart, 209 W Jackson Blvd., 2nd Fl., Chicago, IL, 60606, USA, (877) 247-4394, commodities@barchart.com, https://www.barchart.com/cmdty; The cmdty Yearbook 2023; cmdtyStats: Commodity Statistics and Fundamental Data; cmdtyView: Commodity Index; and Commodity Data and Prices.

International Monetary Fund (IMF), 700 19th St. NW, Washington, DC, 20431, USA, (202) 623-7000, (202) 623-4661, publications@imf.org, https://www.imf.org; IMF Primary Commodity Prices.

ALBANIA-CONSTRUCTION INDUSTRY

Palgrave Macmillan, 1 New York Plaza, Ste. 4500, New York, NY, 10004-1562, USA, (800) 777-4643, orders@palgrave.com, https://www.palgrave.com/us; The Statesman's Yearbook, 2023.

ALBANIA-CONSUMER PRICE INDEXES

The World Bank, 1818 H St. NW, Washington, DC, 20433, USA, (202) 473-1000, (202) 477-6391, eds03@worldbank.org, https://www.worldbank.org/; Albania (report).

ALBANIA-COPPER INDUSTRY AND TRADE

See ALBANIA-MINERAL INDUSTRIES

ALBANIA-CORN INDUSTRY

See ALBANIA-CROPS

ALBANIA-COTTON

See ALBANIA-CROPS

ALBANIA-CROPS

Palgrave Macmillan, 1 New York Plaza, Ste. 4500, New York, NY, 10004-1562, USA, (800) 777-4643, orders@palgrave.com, https://www.palgrave.com/us; The Statesman's Yearbook, 2023.

United Nations Food and Agricultural Organization (FAO), 2121 K St., Ste. 800B, Washington, DC, 20037, USA, (202) 653-2400 (Dial from U.S.), (202) 653-5760 (Fax from U.S.), fao-hq@fao.org, https://www.fao.org; The State of Food and Agriculture (SOFA) 2022.

United Nations Statistics Division (UNSD), United Nations Plz., New York, NY, 10017, USA, (800) 253-9646, (212) 963-9851, statistics@un.org, https://unstats.un.org; Statistical Yearbook of the United Nations 2021.

ALBANIA-DAIRY PROCESSING

Palgrave Macmillan, 1 New York Plaza, Ste. 4500, New York, NY, 10004-1562, USA, (800) 777-4643, orders@palgrave.com, https://www.palgrave.com/us; The Statesman's Yearbook, 2023.

United Nations Food and Agricultural Organization (FAO), 2121 K St., Ste. 800B, Washington, DC, 20037, USA, (202) 653-2400 (Dial from U.S.), (202) 653-5760 (Fax from U.S.), fao-hq@fao.org, https://www.fao.org; The State of Food and Agriculture (SOFA) 2022.

ALBANIA-DEBTS, EXTERNAL

Palgrave Macmillan, 1 New York Plaza, Ste. 4500, New York, NY, 10004-1562, USA, (800) 777-4643, orders@palgrave.com, https://www.palgrave.com/us; The Statesman's Yearbook, 2023.

The World Bank, 1818 H St. NW, Washington, DC, 20433, USA, (202) 473-1000, (202) 477-6391, eds03@worldbank.org, https://www.worldbank.org/; Global Financial Development Report 2019-2020: Bank Regulation and Supervision a Decade after the Global Financial Crisis and World Development Report 2022: Finance for an Equitable Recovery.

ALBANIA-DEFENSE EXPENDITURES

See ALBANIA-ARMED FORCES

ALBANIA-DIAMONDS

See ALBANIA-MINERAL INDUSTRIES

ALBANIA-ECONOMIC CONDITIONS

Bernan Press, 15250 NBN Way, Bldg. C, Blue Ridge Summit, PA, 17214, USA, (301) 459-2255, (800) 865-3457, (800) 865-3450, customercare@bernan.com, https://rowman.com/Page/Bernan; World Economic Outlook, April 2022.

Central Intelligence Agency (CIA), Office of Public Affairs, Washington, DC, 20505, USA, (703) 482-0623, https://www.cia.gov; The World Factbook.

The Economist Group: Economist Intelligence Unit (EIU), 900 3rd Ave., 16th Fl., New York, NY, 10022, USA, (212) 541-0500, americas@eiu.com, https://www.eiu.com; Albania Country Report.

Euromonitor International, Inc., 1 N Dearborn St., Ste. 1700, Chicago, IL, 60602, USA, (312) 922-1115, (312) 922-1157, info-usa@euromonitor.com, https://www.euromonitor.com/; Geographies.

Institute of Statistics (INSTAT), St. Vllazen Huta, Bldg. 35, Tirane, 1017, ALB, info@instat.gov.al, http://www.instat.gov.al; International Trade in Goods and Enterprises, 2016-2020.

International Monetary Fund (IMF), 700 19th St. NW, Washington, DC, 20431, USA, (202) 623-7000, (202) 623-4661, publications@imf.org, https://www.imf.org; IMF Data and World Economic Outlook.

Organisation of Islamic Cooperation (OIC), Statistical, Economic and Social Research and Training Centre for Islamic Countries (SESRIC), Kudus Cad. No. 9, Diplomatik Site, Ankara, 06450, TUR, statistics@sesric.org, https://www.sesric.org/; OIC Economic Outlook 2021; OIC Statistics (OICStat) Database; and OIC-Countries in Figures (OIC-CIF).

Palgrave Macmillan, 1 New York Plaza, Ste. 4500, New York, NY, 10004-1562, USA, (800) 777-4643, orders@palgrave.com, https://www.palgrave.com/us; The Statesman's Yearbook, 2023.

Routledge - Taylor & Francis Group, 6000 Broken Sound Pkwy. NW, Ste. 300, Boca Raton, FL, 33487, USA, (800) 634-1420, (800) 634-7064, orders@taylorandfrancis.com, https://www.routledge.com/; The Europa World Year Book 2022.

United Nations Statistics Division (UNSD), United Nations Plz., New York, NY, 10017, USA, (800) 253-9646, (212) 963-9851, statistics@un.org, https://unstats.un.org; World Statistics Pocketbook 2021.

The World Bank, 1818 H St. NW, Washington, DC, 20433, USA, (202) 473-1000, (202) 477-6391, eds03@worldbank.org, https://www.worldbank.org/; Albania (report); Global Economic Monitor (GEM); Global Economic Prospects, June 2022; The Global Findex Database 2021; and World Development Report 2022: Finance for an Equitable Recovery.

ALBANIA-EDUCATION

Euromonitor International, Inc., 1 N Dearborn St., Ste. 1700, Chicago, IL, 60602, USA, (312) 922-1115, (312) 922-1157, info-usa@euromonitor.com, https://www.euromonitor.com/; Geographies.

Infoplease, c/o Sandbox Networks, Inc., 1 Lincoln St., 24th Fl., Boston, MA, 02111, USA, https://www.infoplease.com; Countries of the World.

Organisation of Islamic Cooperation (OIC), Statistical, Economic and Social Research and Training Centre for Islamic Countries (SESRIC), Kudus Cad. No. 9, Diplomatik Site, Ankara, 06450, TUR, statistics@sesric.org, https://www.sesric.org/; OIC Statistics (OICStat) Database.

Palgrave Macmillan, 1 New York Plaza, Ste. 4500, New York, NY, 10004-1562, USA, (800) 777-4643, orders@palgrave.com, https://www.palgrave.com/us; The Statesman's Yearbook, 2023.

Routledge - Taylor & Francis Group, 6000 Broken Sound Pkwy. NW, Ste. 300, Boca Raton, FL, 33487, USA, (800) 634-1420, (800) 634-7064, orders@taylorandfrancis.com, https://www.routledge.com/; The Europa World Year Book 2022.

UNESCO Institute for Statistics, C.P 250 Succursale H, Montreal, QC, H3G 2K8, CAN, (514) 343-6880 (Dial from U.S.), (514) 343-5740 (Fax from U.S.), uis.publications@unesco.org, http://uis.unesco.org/; Literacy and UIS.Stat.

United Nations Statistics Division (UNSD), United Nations Plz., New York, NY, 10017, USA, (800) 253-9646, (212) 963-9851, statistics@un.org, https://unstats.un.org; Millennium Development Goal Indicators.

The World Bank, 1818 H St. NW, Washington, DC, 20433, USA, (202) 473-1000, (202) 477-6391, eds03@worldbank.org, https://www.worldbank.org/; Albania (report) and World Development Report 2022: Finance for an Equitable Recovery.

ALBANIA-ELECTRICITY

International Energy Agency (IEA), 9 Rue de la Federation, Paris, 75739, FRA, info@iea.org, https://www.iea.org/; World Energy Outlook 2021.

S&P Global Commodity Insights, One World Trade Center, New York, NY, 10007, USA, (800) 752-8878, support@platts.com, https://www.spglobal.com/commodityinsights/en; Platts European Power Alert.

U.S. Energy Information Administration (EIA), 1000 Independence Ave. SW, Washington, DC, 20585, USA, (202) 586-8800, infoctr@eia.gov, https://www.eia.gov; International Energy Outlook 2021.

United Nations Statistics Division (UNSD), United Nations Plz., New York, NY, 10017, USA, (800) 253-9646, (212) 963-9851, statistics@un.org, https://unstats.un.org; Statistical Yearbook of the United Nations 2021.

ALBANIA-EMPLOYMENT

UK Data Service, University of Essex, Wivenhoe Park, Colchester, Essex, CO4 3SQ, GBR, https://ukdataservice.ac.uk/; International Aggregate Data.

The World Bank, 1818 H St. NW, Washington, DC, 20433, USA, (202) 473-1000, (202) 477-6391, eds03@worldbank.org, https://www.worldbank.org/; Albania (report).

ALBANIA-ENVIRONMENTAL CONDITIONS

DSI Data Service & Information, Xantener Strasse 51a, Rheinberg, D-47495, GER, dsi@dsidata.com, https://www.dsidata.com/; Global Environmental Database.

The Economist Group: Economist Intelligence Unit (EIU), 900 3rd Ave., 16th Fl., New York, NY, 10022, USA, (212) 541-0500, americas@eiu.com, https://www.eiu.com; Albania Country Report.

European Commission, Eurostat, Luxembourg, 2920, LUX, https://ec.europa.eu/eurostat/; Environment Statistics Introduced.

Organisation of Islamic Cooperation (OIC), Statistical, Economic and Social Research and Training Centre for Islamic Countries (SESRIC), Kudus Cad. No. 9, Diplomatik Site, Ankara, 06450, TUR, statistics@sesric.org, https://www.sesric.org/; OIC Statistics (OICStat) Database and OIC-Countries in Figures (OIC-CIF).

United Nations Statistics Division (UNSD), United Nations Plz., New York, NY, 10017, USA, (800) 253-9646, (212) 963-9851, statistics@un.org, https://unstats.un.org; World Statistics Pocketbook 2021.

ALBANIA-EXPORTS

Central Intelligence Agency (CIA), Office of Public Affairs, Washington, DC, 20505, USA, (703) 482-0623, https://www.cia.gov; The World Factbook.

The Economist Group: Economist Intelligence Unit (EIU), 900 3rd Ave., 16th Fl., New York, NY, 10022, USA, (212) 541-0500, americas@eiu.com, https://www.eiu.com; Albania Country Report.

International Monetary Fund (IMF), 700 19th St. NW, Washington, DC, 20431, USA, (202) 623-7000, (202) 623-4661, publications@imf.org, https://www.imf.org; Direction of Trade Statistics (DOTS).

Organisation of Islamic Cooperation (OIC), Statistical, Economic and Social Research and Training Centre for Islamic Countries (SESRIC), Kudus Cad. No. 9, Diplomatik Site, Ankara, 06450, TUR, statistics@sesric.org, https://www.sesric.org/; OIC Statistics (OICStat) Database.

S&P Global, IHS Markit, 15 Inverness Way E, Englewood, CO, 80112, USA, (800) 447-2273, (800) 854-7179, https://ihsmarkit.com; Global Trade Atlas (GTA).

United Nations Conference on Trade and Development (UNCTAD), Palais des Nations, Geneva, 1211, SWI, (212) 963-6896, unctadinfo@unctad.org, https://unctad.org; Handbook of Statistics 2021.

The World Bank, 1818 H St. NW, Washington, DC, 20433, USA, (202) 473-1000, (202) 477-6391, eds03@worldbank.org, https://www.worldbank.org/; World Development Report 2022: Finance for an Equitable Recovery.

ALBANIA-FERTILIZER INDUSTRY

United Nations Food and Agricultural Organization (FAO), 2121 K St., Ste. 800B, Washington, DC, 20037, USA, (202) 653-2400 (Dial from U.S.), (202) 653-5760 (Fax from U.S.), fao-hq@fao.org, https://www.fao.org; The State of Food and Agriculture (SOFA) 2022.

ALBANIA-FETAL MORTALITY

See ALBANIA-MORTALITY

ALBANIA-FINANCE

Stockholm International Peace Research Institute (SIPRI), Signalistgatan 9, Stockholm, SE 169 72, SWE, https://www.sipri.org/; SIPRI Arms Transfers Database and SIPRI Military Expenditure Database.

United Nations Statistics Division (UNSD), United Nations Plz., New York, NY, 10017, USA, (800) 253-9646, (212) 963-9851, statistics@un.org, https://unstats.un.org; Statistical Yearbook of the United Nations 2021.

The World Bank, 1818 H St. NW, Washington, DC, 20433, USA, (202) 473-1000, (202) 477-6391, eds03@worldbank.org, https://www.worldbank.org/; Albania (report).

ALBANIA-FINANCE, PUBLIC

Bernan Press, 15250 NBN Way, Bldg. C, Blue Ridge Summit, PA, 17214, USA, (301) 459-2255, (800) 865-3457, (800) 865-3450, customercare@bernan.com, https://rowman.com/Page/Bernan; National Accounts Statistics: Analysis of Main Aggregates 2020.

The Economist Group: Economist Intelligence Unit (EIU), 900 3rd Ave., 16th Fl., New York, NY, 10022, USA, (212) 541-0500, americas@eiu.com, https://www.eiu.com; Albania Country Report.

International Monetary Fund (IMF), 700 19th St. NW, Washington, DC, 20431, USA, (202) 623-7000, (202) 623-4661, publications@imf.org, https://www.imf.org; International Financial Statistics (IFS) and Regional Economic Outlook.

Palgrave Macmillan, 1 New York Plaza, Ste. 4500, New York, NY, 10004-1562, USA, (800) 777-4643, orders@palgrave.com, https://www.palgrave.com/us; The Statesman's Yearbook, 2023.

Routledge - Taylor & Francis Group, 6000 Broken Sound Pkwy. NW, Ste. 300, Boca Raton, FL, 33487, USA, (800) 634-1420, (800) 634-7064, orders@taylorandfrancis.com, https://www.routledge.com/; The Europa World Year Book 2022.

United Nations Statistics Division (UNSD), United Nations Plz., New York, NY, 10017, USA, (800) 253-9646, (212) 963-9851, statistics@un.org, https://unstats.un.org; National Accounts Main Aggregates Database and National Accounts Statistics: Main Aggregates and Detailed Tables.

The World Bank, 1818 H St. NW, Washington, DC, 20433, USA, (202) 473-1000, (202) 477-6391, eds03@worldbank.org, https://www.worldbank.org/; Albania (report).

ALBANIA-FISHERIES

Palgrave Macmillan, 1 New York Plaza, Ste. 4500, New York, NY, 10004-1562, USA, (800) 777-4643, orders@palgrave.com, https://www.palgrave.com/us; The Statesman's Yearbook, 2023.

Routledge - Taylor & Francis Group, 6000 Broken Sound Pkwy. NW, Ste. 300, Boca Raton, FL, 33487, USA, (800) 634-1420, (800) 634-7064, orders@taylorandfrancis.com, https://www.routledge.com/; The Europa World Year Book 2022.

United Nations Food and Agricultural Organization (FAO), 2121 K St., Ste. 800B, Washington, DC, 20037, USA, (202) 653-2400 (Dial from U.S.), (202) 653-5760 (Fax from U.S.), fao-hq@fao.org, https://www.fao.org; FAO Yearbook of Fishery and Aquaculture Statistics 2019; Fishery Statistical Collections Global Capture Production; FishStatJ; and The State of Food and Agriculture (SOFA) 2022.

United Nations Statistics Division (UNSD), United Nations Plz., New York, NY, 10017, USA, (800) 253-9646, (212) 963-9851, statistics@un.org, https://unstats.un.org; Statistical Yearbook of the United Nations 2021.

The World Bank, 1818 H St. NW, Washington, DC, 20433, USA, (202) 473-1000, (202) 477-6391, eds03@worldbank.org, https://www.worldbank.org/; Albania (report).

ALBANIA-FOOD

United Nations Food and Agricultural Organization (FAO), 2121 K St., Ste. 800B, Washington, DC, 20037, USA, (202) 653-2400 (Dial from U.S.), (202) 653-5760 (Fax from U.S.), fao-hq@fao.org, https://www.fao.org; The State of Food and Agriculture (SOFA) 2022.

ALBANIA-FORESTS AND FORESTRY

Palgrave Macmillan, 1 New York Plaza, Ste. 4500, New York, NY, 10004-1562, USA, (800) 777-4643, orders@palgrave.com, https://www.palgrave.com/us; The Statesman's Yearbook, 2023.

Routledge - Taylor & Francis Group, 6000 Broken Sound Pkwy. NW, Ste. 300, Boca Raton, FL, 33487, USA, (800) 634-1420, (800) 634-7064, orders@taylorandfrancis.com, https://www.routledge.com/; The Europa World Year Book 2022.

UNESCO Institute for Statistics, C.P 250 Succursale H, Montreal, QC, H3G 2K8, CAN, (514) 343-6880 (Dial from U.S.), (514) 343-5740 (Fax from U.S.), uis.publications@unesco.org, http://uis.unesco.org/; UIS.Stat.

United Nations Food and Agricultural Organization (FAO), 2121 K St., Ste. 800B, Washington, DC, 20037, USA, (202) 653-2400 (Dial from U.S.), (202) 653-5760 (Fax from U.S.), fao-hq@fao.org, https://www.fao.org; FAO Yearbook of Forest Products 2019 and The State of Food and Agriculture (SOFA) 2022.

United Nations Statistics Division (UNSD), United Nations Plz., New York, NY, 10017, USA, (800) 253-9646, (212) 963-9851, statistics@un.org, https://unstats.un.org; Statistical Yearbook of the United Nations 2021.

The World Bank, 1818 H St. NW, Washington, DC, 20433, USA, (202) 473-1000, (202) 477-6391, eds03@worldbank.org, https://www.worldbank.org/; Albania (report) and World Development Report 2022: Finance for an Equitable Recovery.

ALBANIA-GAS PRODUCTION

See ALBANIA-MINERAL INDUSTRIES

ALBANIA-GEOGRAPHIC INFORMATION SYSTEMS

The World Bank, 1818 H St. NW, Washington, DC, 20433, USA, (202) 473-1000, (202) 477-6391, eds03@worldbank.org, https://www.worldbank.org/; Albania (report).

ALBANIA-GOLD PRODUCTION

See ALBANIA-MINERAL INDUSTRIES

ALBANIA-GROSS DOMESTIC PRODUCT

The Economist Group: Economist Intelligence Unit (EIU), 900 3rd Ave., 16th Fl., New York, NY, 10022, USA, (212) 541-0500, americas@eiu.com, https://www.eiu.com; Albania Country Report.

The World Bank, 1818 H St. NW, Washington, DC, 20433, USA, (202) 473-1000, (202) 477-6391, eds03@worldbank.org, https://www.worldbank.org/; World Development Report 2022: Finance for an Equitable Recovery.

ALBANIA-GROSS NATIONAL PRODUCT

Palgrave Macmillan, 1 New York Plaza, Ste. 4500, New York, NY, 10004-1562, USA, (800) 777-4643, orders@palgrave.com, https://www.palgrave.com/us; The Statesman's Yearbook, 2023.

United Nations Statistics Division (UNSD), United Nations Plz., New York, NY, 10017, USA, (800) 253-9646, (212) 963-9851, statistics@un.org, https://unstats.un.org; Statistical Yearbook of the United Nations 2021.

The World Bank, 1818 H St. NW, Washington, DC, 20433, USA, (202) 473-1000, (202) 477-6391, eds03@worldbank.org, https://www.worldbank.org/; World Development Report 2022: Finance for an Equitable Recovery.

ALBANIA-HOUSING

Euromonitor International, Inc., 1 N Dearborn St., Ste. 1700, Chicago, IL, 60602, USA, (312) 922-1115, (312) 922-1157, info-usa@euromonitor.com, https://www.euromonitor.com/; Geographies.

ALBANIA-ILLITERATE PERSONS

UNESCO Institute for Statistics, C.P 250 Succursale H, Montreal, QC, H3G 2K8, CAN, (514) 343-6880 (Dial from U.S.), (514) 343-5740 (Fax from U.S.), uis.publications@unesco.org, http://uis.unesco.org/; UIS.Stat.

ALBANIA-IMPORTS

Central Intelligence Agency (CIA), Office of Public Affairs, Washington, DC, 20505, USA, (703) 482-0623, https://www.cia.gov; The World Factbook.

The Economist Group: Economist Intelligence Unit (EIU), 900 3rd Ave., 16th Fl., New York, NY, 10022, USA, (212) 541-0500, americas@eiu.com, https://www.eiu.com; Albania Country Report.

International Monetary Fund (IMF), 700 19th St. NW, Washington, DC, 20431, USA, (202) 623-7000, (202) 623-4661, publications@imf.org, https://www.imf.org; Direction of Trade Statistics (DOTS).

S&P Global, IHS Markit, 15 Inverness Way E, Englewood, CO, 80112, USA, (800) 447-2273, (800) 854-7179, https://ihsmarkit.com; Global Trade Atlas (GTA).

United Nations Conference on Trade and Development (UNCTAD), Palais des Nations, Geneva, 1211, SWI, (212) 963-6896, unctadinfo@unctad.org, https://unctad.org; Handbook of Statistics 2021.

The World Bank, 1818 H St. NW, Washington, DC, 20433, USA, (202) 473-1000, (202) 477-6391, eds03@worldbank.org, https://www.worldbank.org/; World Development Report 2022: Finance for an Equitable Recovery.

ALBANIA-INDUSTRIES

Central Intelligence Agency (CIA), Office of Public Affairs, Washington, DC, 20505, USA, (703) 482-0623, https://www.cia.gov; The World Factbook.

The Economist Group: Economist Intelligence Unit (EIU), 900 3rd Ave., 16th Fl., New York, NY, 10022, USA, (212) 541-0500, americas@eiu.com, https://www.eiu.com; Albania Country Report.

Euromonitor International, Inc., 1 N Dearborn St., Ste. 1700, Chicago, IL, 60602, USA, (312) 922-1115, (312) 922-1157, info-usa@euromonitor.com, https://www.euromonitor.com/; Geographies.

Palgrave Macmillan, 1 New York Plaza, Ste. 4500, New York, NY, 10004-1562, USA, (800) 777-4643, orders@palgrave.com, https://www.palgrave.com/us; The Statesman's Yearbook, 2023.

Routledge - Taylor & Francis Group, 6000 Broken Sound Pkwy. NW, Ste. 300, Boca Raton, FL, 33487, USA, (800) 634-1420, (800) 634-7064, orders@taylorandfrancis.com, https://www.routledge.com/; The Europa World Year Book 2022.

United Nations Industrial Development Organization (UNIDO), 1 United Nations Plz., Rm. DC1-1118, New York, NY, 10017, USA, (212) 963-6890, (212) 963 6885, (212) 963-7904, office.newyork@unido.org, https://www.unido.org/; Industrial Statistics Databases and International Yearbook of Industrial Statistics 2021.

The World Bank, 1818 H St. NW, Washington, DC, 20433, USA, (202) 473-1000, (202) 477-6391, eds03@worldbank.org, https://www.worldbank.org/; Albania (report).

ALBANIA-INFANT AND MATERNAL MORTALITY

See ALBANIA-MORTALITY

ALBANIA-INTERNATIONAL TRADE

The Economist Group: Economist Intelligence Unit (EIU), 900 3rd Ave., 16th Fl., New York, NY, 10022, USA, (212) 541-0500, americas@eiu.com, https://www.eiu.com; Albania Country Report.

Euromonitor International, Inc., 1 N Dearborn St., Ste. 1700, Chicago, IL, 60602, USA, (312) 922-1115, (312) 922-1157, info-usa@euromonitor.com, https://www.euromonitor.com/; Geographies.

Institute of Statistics (INSTAT), St. Vllazen Huta, Bldg. 35, Tirane, 1017, ALB, info@instat.gov.al, http://www.instat.gov.al; International Trade in Goods and Enterprises, 2016-2020.

Palgrave Macmillan, 1 New York Plaza, Ste. 4500, New York, NY, 10004-1562, USA, (800) 777-4643, orders@palgrave.com, https://www.palgrave.com/us; The Statesman's Yearbook, 2023.

Routledge - Taylor & Francis Group, 6000 Broken Sound Pkwy. NW, Ste. 300, Boca Raton, FL, 33487, USA, (800) 634-1420, (800) 634-7064, orders@taylorandfrancis.com, https://www.routledge.com/; The Europa World Year Book 2022.

United Nations Conference on Trade and Development (UNCTAD), Palais des Nations, Geneva, 1211, SWI, (212) 963-6896, unctadinfo@unctad.org, https://unctad.org; Trade and Development Report 2021.

United Nations Food and Agricultural Organization (FAO), 2121 K St., Ste. 800B, Washington, DC, 20037, USA, (202) 653-2400 (Dial from U.S.), (202) 653-5760 (Fax from U.S.), fao-hq@fao.org, https://www.fao.org; The State of Food and Agriculture (SOFA) 2022.

United Nations Statistics Division (UNSD), United Nations Plz., New York, NY, 10017, USA, (800) 253-9646, (212) 963-9851, statistics@un.org, https://unstats.un.org; Statistical Yearbook of the United Nations 2021.

The World Bank, 1818 H St. NW, Washington, DC, 20433, USA, (202) 473-1000, (202) 477-6391, eds03@worldbank.org, https://www.worldbank.org/; Albania (report) and World Development Report 2022: Finance for an Equitable Recovery.

World Trade Organization (WTO), Ctre. William Rappard, Rue de Lausanne 154, Case postale, Geneva, CH-1211, SWI, enquiries@wto.org, https://www.wto.org; World Trade Statistical Review 2022.

ALBANIA-INTERNET USERS

International Telecommunication Union (ITU), Place des Nations, Geneva, CH-1211, SWI, itumail@itu.int, https://www.itu.int; Global Connectivity Report 2022; World Telecommunication/ICT Indicators Database 2021; and Yearbook of Statistics 2019.

The World Bank, 1818 H St. NW, Washington, DC, 20433, USA, (202) 473-1000, (202) 477-6391, eds03@worldbank.org, https://www.worldbank.org/; Albania (report).

ALBANIA-LABOR

Central Intelligence Agency (CIA), Office of Public Affairs, Washington, DC, 20505, USA, (703) 482-0623, https://www.cia.gov; The World Factbook.

Euromonitor International, Inc., 1 N Dearborn St., Ste. 1700, Chicago, IL, 60602, USA, (312) 922-1115, (312) 922-1157, info-usa@euromonitor.com, https://www.euromonitor.com/; Geographies.

Organisation of Islamic Cooperation (OIC), Statistical, Economic and Social Research and Training Centre for Islamic Countries (SESRIC), Kudus Cad. No. 9, Diplomatik Site, Ankara, 06450, TUR, statistics@sesric.org, https://www.sesric.org/; OIC Statistics (OICStat) Database.

Palgrave Macmillan, 1 New York Plaza, Ste. 4500, New York, NY, 10004-1562, USA, (800) 777-4643, orders@palgrave.com, https://www.palgrave.com/us; The Statesman's Yearbook, 2023.

United Nations Food and Agricultural Organization (FAO), 2121 K St., Ste. 800B, Washington, DC, 20037, USA, (202) 653-2400 (Dial from U.S.), (202) 653-5760 (Fax from U.S.), fao-hq@fao.org, https://www.fao.org; The State of Food and Agriculture (SOFA) 2022.

The World Bank, 1818 H St. NW, Washington, DC, 20433, USA, (202) 473-1000, (202) 477-6391, eds03@worldbank.org, https://www.worldbank.org/; World Development Report 2022: Finance for an Equitable Recovery.

ALBANIA-LAND USE

United Nations Statistics Division (UNSD), United Nations Plz., New York, NY, 10017, USA, (800) 253-9646, (212) 963-9851, statistics@un.org, https://unstats.un.org; Millennium Development Goal Indicators.

The World Bank, 1818 H St. NW, Washington, DC, 20433, USA, (202) 473-1000, (202) 477-6391, eds03@worldbank.org, https://www.worldbank.org/; World Development Report 2022: Finance for an Equitable Recovery.

ALBANIA-LIFE EXPECTANCY

United Nations Department of Economic and Social Affairs (DESA), Population Division, 2 United Nations Plz., Rm. DC2-1950, New York, NY, 10017, USA, (212) 963-3209, (212) 963-2147, population@un.org, https://www.un.org/development/desa/pd/; World Population Ageing 2020 Highlights.

United Nations Statistics Division (UNSD), United Nations Plz., New York, NY, 10017, USA, (800) 253-9646, (212) 963-9851, statistics@un.org, https://unstats.un.org; Millennium Development Goal Indicators.

ALBANIA-LITERACY

Euromonitor International, Inc., 1 N Dearborn St., Ste. 1700, Chicago, IL, 60602, USA, (312) 922-1115, (312) 922-1157, info-usa@euromonitor.com, https://www.euromonitor.com/; Geographies.

UNESCO Institute for Statistics, C.P 250 Succursale H, Montreal, QC, H3G 2K8, CAN, (514) 343-6880 (Dial from U.S.), (514) 343-5740 (Fax from U.S.), uis.publications@unesco.org, http://uis.unesco.org/; Literacy.

ALBANIA-LIVESTOCK

Palgrave Macmillan, 1 New York Plaza, Ste. 4500, New York, NY, 10004-1562, USA, (800) 777-4643, orders@palgrave.com, https://www.palgrave.com/us; The Statesman's Yearbook, 2023.

Routledge - Taylor & Francis Group, 6000 Broken Sound Pkwy. NW, Ste. 300, Boca Raton, FL, 33487, USA, (800) 634-1420, (800) 634-7064, orders@taylorandfrancis.com, https://www.routledge.com/; The Europa World Year Book 2022.

United Nations Food and Agricultural Organization (FAO), 2121 K St., Ste. 800B, Washington, DC, 20037, USA, (202) 653-2400 (Dial from U.S.), (202) 653-5760 (Fax from U.S.), fao-hq@fao.org, https://www.fao.org; The State of Food and Agriculture (SOFA) 2022.

United Nations Statistics Division (UNSD), United Nations Plz., New York, NY, 10017, USA, (800) 253-9646, (212) 963-9851, statistics@un.org, https://unstats.un.org; Statistical Yearbook of the United Nations 2021.

ALBANIA-MARRIAGE

Routledge - Taylor & Francis Group, 6000 Broken Sound Pkwy. NW, Ste. 300, Boca Raton, FL, 33487, USA, (800) 634-1420, (800) 634-7064, orders@taylorandfrancis.com, https://www.routledge.com/; The Europa World Year Book 2022.

United Nations Statistics Division (UNSD), United Nations Plz., New York, NY, 10017, USA, (800) 253-9646, (212) 963-9851, statistics@un.org, https://unstats.un.org; Statistical Yearbook of the United Nations 2021.

ALBANIA-MINERAL INDUSTRIES

Barchart, 209 W Jackson Blvd., 2nd Fl., Chicago, IL, 60606, USA, (877) 247-4394, commodities@barchart.com, https://www.barchart.com/cmdty; The cmdty Yearbook 2023; cmdtyStats: Commodity Statistics and Fundamental Data; cmdtyView: Commodity Index; and Commodity Data and Prices.

International Energy Agency (IEA), 9 Rue de la Federation, Paris, 75739, FRA, info@iea.org, https://www.iea.org/; World Energy Outlook 2021.

Palgrave Macmillan, 1 New York Plaza, Ste. 4500, New York, NY, 10004-1562, USA, (800) 777-4643, orders@palgrave.com, https://www.palgrave.com/us; The Statesman's Yearbook, 2023.

Routledge - Taylor & Francis Group, 6000 Broken Sound Pkwy. NW, Ste. 300, Boca Raton, FL, 33487, USA, (800) 634-1420, (800) 634-7064, orders@taylorandfrancis.com, https://www.routledge.com/; The Europa World Year Book 2022.

United Nations Conference on Trade and Development (UNCTAD), Palais des Nations, Geneva, 1211, SWI, (212) 963-6896, unctadinfo@unctad.org, https://unctad.org; Trade and Development Report 2021.

United Nations Statistics Division (UNSD), United Nations Plz., New York, NY, 10017, USA, (800) 253-9646, (212) 963-9851, statistics@un.org, https://unstats.un.org; Statistical Yearbook of the United Nations 2021.

ALBANIA-MONEY SUPPLY

The Economist Group: Economist Intelligence Unit (EIU), 900 3rd Ave., 16th Fl., New York, NY, 10022, USA, (212) 541-0500, americas@eiu.com, https://www.eiu.com; Albania Country Report.

The World Bank, 1818 H St. NW, Washington, DC, 20433, USA, (202) 473-1000, (202) 477-6391, eds03@worldbank.org, https://www.worldbank.org/; Albania (report).

ALBANIA-MORTALITY

UNICEF, 3 United Nations Plz., New York, NY, 10017, USA, (212) 303-7984, (917) 244-2215, https://www.unicef.org; The State of the World's Children 2023.

United Nations Statistics Division (UNSD), United Nations Plz., New York, NY, 10017, USA, (800) 253-9646, (212) 963-9851, statistics@un.org, https://unstats.un.org; Millennium Development Goal Indicators; Statistical Yearbook of the United Nations 2021; and World Statistics Pocketbook 2021.

World Health Organization (WHO), Ave. Appia 20, Geneva, CH-1211, SWI, (202) 974-3000 (Telephone in U.S.), publications@who.int, https://www.who.int/; Global Health Observatory (GHO).

ALBANIA-MOTION PICTURES

Palgrave Macmillan, 1 New York Plaza, Ste. 4500, New York, NY, 10004-1562, USA, (800) 777-4643, orders@palgrave.com, https://www.palgrave.com/us; The Statesman's Yearbook, 2023.

ALBANIA-NATURAL GAS PRODUCTION

See ALBANIA-MINERAL INDUSTRIES

ALBANIA-NICKEL AND NICKEL ORE

See ALBANIA-MINERAL INDUSTRIES

ALBANIA-NUTRITION

United Nations Food and Agricultural Organization (FAO), 2121 K St., Ste. 800B, Washington, DC, 20037, USA, (202) 653-2400 (Dial from U.S.), (202) 653-5760 (Fax from U.S.), fao-hq@fao.org, https://www.fao.org; The State of Food and Agriculture (SOFA) 2022.

United Nations Statistics Division (UNSD), United Nations Plz., New York, NY, 10017, USA, (800) 253-9646, (212) 963-9851, statistics@un.org, https://unstats.un.org; Millennium Development Goal Indicators.

ALBANIA-PEANUT PRODUCTION

See ALBANIA-CROPS

ALBANIA-PESTICIDES

United Nations Food and Agricultural Organization (FAO), 2121 K St., Ste. 800B, Washington, DC, 20037, USA, (202) 653-2400 (Dial from U.S.), (202) 653-5760 (Fax from U.S.), fao-hq@fao.org, https://www.fao.org; The State of Food and Agriculture (SOFA) 2022.

ALBANIA-PETROLEUM INDUSTRY AND TRADE

International Energy Agency (IEA), 9 Rue de la Federation, Paris, 75739, FRA, info@iea.org, https://www.iea.org/; World Energy Outlook 2021.

Palgrave Macmillan, 1 New York Plaza, Ste. 4500, New York, NY, 10004-1562, USA, (800) 777-4643, orders@palgrave.com, https://www.palgrave.com/us; The Statesman's Yearbook, 2023.

U.S. Energy Information Administration (EIA), 1000 Independence Ave. SW, Washington, DC, 20585, USA, (202) 586-8800, infoctr@eia.gov, https://www.eia.gov; International Energy Outlook 2021.

United Nations Food and Agricultural Organization (FAO), 2121 K St., Ste. 800B, Washington, DC, 20037, USA, (202) 653-2400 (Dial from U.S.), (202) 653-5760 (Fax from U.S.), fao-hq@fao.org, https://www.fao.org; The State of Food and Agriculture (SOFA) 2022.

United Nations Statistics Division (UNSD), United Nations Plz., New York, NY, 10017, USA, (800) 253-9646, (212) 963-9851, statistics@un.org, https://unstats.un.org; Statistical Yearbook of the United Nations 2021.

ALBANIA-POPULATION

Central Intelligence Agency (CIA), Office of Public Affairs, Washington, DC, 20505, USA, (703) 482-0623, https://www.cia.gov; The World Factbook.

The Economist Group: Economist Intelligence Unit (EIU), 900 3rd Ave., 16th Fl., New York, NY, 10022, USA, (212) 541-0500, americas@eiu.com, https://www.eiu.com; Albania Country Report.

Infoplease, c/o Sandbox Networks, Inc., 1 Lincoln St., 24th Fl., Boston, MA, 02111, USA, https://www.infoplease.com; Countries of the World.

Palgrave Macmillan, 1 New York Plaza, Ste. 4500, New York, NY, 10004-1562, USA, (800) 777-4643, orders@palgrave.com, https://www.palgrave.com/us; The Statesman's Yearbook, 2023.

Routledge - Taylor & Francis Group, 6000 Broken Sound Pkwy. NW, Ste. 300, Boca Raton, FL, 33487, USA, (800) 634-1420, (800) 634-7064, orders@taylorandfrancis.com, https://www.routledge.com/; The Europa World Year Book 2022.

UK Data Service, University of Essex, Wivenhoe Park, Colchester, Essex, CO4 3SQ, GBR, https://ukdataservice.ac.uk/; International Aggregate Data.

United Nations Department of Economic and Social Affairs (DESA), Population Division, 2 United Nations Plz., Rm. DC2-1950, New York, NY, 10017, USA, (212) 963-3209, (212) 963-2147, population@un.org, https://www.un.org/development/desa/pd/; Revision of World Urbanization Prospects and World Population Ageing 2020 Highlights.

United Nations Development Programme (UNDP), One United Nations Plz., New York, NY, 10017, USA, (212) 906-5000, (212) 906-5001, https://www.undp.org; Human Development Report 2021-2022.

United Nations Statistics Division (UNSD), United Nations Plz., New York, NY, 10017, USA, (800) 253-9646, (212) 963-9851, statistics@un.org, https://unstats.un.org; Statistical Yearbook of the United Nations 2021.

The World Bank, 1818 H St. NW, Washington, DC, 20433, USA, (202) 473-1000, (202) 477-6391, eds03@worldbank.org, https://www.worldbank.org/; Albania (report); The Global Findex Database 2021; and World Development Report 2022: Finance for an Equitable Recovery.

ALBANIA-POPULATION DENSITY

Central Intelligence Agency (CIA), Office of Public Affairs, Washington, DC, 20505, USA, (703) 482-0623, https://www.cia.gov; The World Factbook.

Palgrave Macmillan, 1 New York Plaza, Ste. 4500, New York, NY, 10004-1562, USA, (800) 777-4643, orders@palgrave.com, https://www.palgrave.com/us; The Statesman's Yearbook, 2023.

Routledge - Taylor & Francis Group, 6000 Broken Sound Pkwy. NW, Ste. 300, Boca Raton, FL, 33487, USA, (800) 634-1420, (800) 634-7064, orders@taylorandfrancis.com, https://www.routledge.com/; The Europa World Year Book 2022.

The World Bank, 1818 H St. NW, Washington, DC, 20433, USA, (202) 473-1000, (202) 477-6391, eds03@worldbank.org, https://www.worldbank.org/; Albania (report) and World Development Report 2022: Finance for an Equitable Recovery.

ALBANIA-POSTAL SERVICE

Palgrave Macmillan, 1 New York Plaza, Ste. 4500, New York, NY, 10004-1562, USA, (800) 777-4643, orders@palgrave.com, https://www.palgrave.com/us; The Statesman's Yearbook, 2023.

ALBANIA-POULTRY

See ALBANIA-LIVESTOCK

ALBANIA-POWER RESOURCES

Euromonitor International, Inc., 1 N Dearborn St., Ste. 1700, Chicago, IL, 60602, USA, (312) 922-1115, (312) 922-1157, info-usa@euromonitor.com, https://www.euromonitor.com/; Geographies.

International Energy Agency (IEA), 9 Rue de la Federation, Paris, 75739, FRA, info@iea.org, https://www.iea.org/; World Energy Outlook 2021.

Palgrave Macmillan, 1 New York Plaza, Ste. 4500, New York, NY, 10004-1562, USA, (800) 777-4643, orders@palgrave.com, https://www.palgrave.com/us; The Statesman's Yearbook, 2023.

S&P Global Commodity Insights, One World Trade Center, New York, NY, 10007, USA, (800) 752-8878, support@platts.com, https://www.spglobal.com/commodityinsights/en; Platts European Power Daily.

U.S. Energy Information Administration (EIA), 1000 Independence Ave. SW, Washington, DC, 20585, USA, (202) 586-8800, infoctr@eia.gov, https://www.eia.gov; International Energy Outlook 2021.

United Nations Food and Agricultural Organization (FAO), 2121 K St., Ste. 800B, Washington, DC, 20037, USA, (202) 653-2400 (Dial from U.S.), (202) 653-5760 (Fax from U.S.), fao-hq@fao.org, https://www.fao.org; The State of Food and Agriculture (SOFA) 2022.

United Nations Statistics Division (UNSD), United Nations Plz., New York, NY, 10017, USA, (800) 253-9646, (212) 963-9851, statistics@un.org, https://unstats.un.org; Energy Statistics Yearbook 2019; Statistical Yearbook of the United Nations 2021; and World Statistics Pocketbook 2021.

The World Bank, 1818 H St. NW, Washington, DC, 20433, USA, (202) 473-1000, (202) 477-6391, eds03@worldbank.org, https://www.worldbank.org/; World Development Report 2022: Finance for an Equitable Recovery.

ALBANIA-PRICES

Euromonitor International, Inc., 1 N Dearborn St., Ste. 1700, Chicago, IL, 60602, USA, (312) 922-1115, (312) 922-1157, info-usa@euromonitor.com, https://www.euromonitor.com/; Geographies.

The World Bank, 1818 H St. NW, Washington, DC, 20433, USA, (202) 473-1000, (202) 477-6391, eds03@worldbank.org, https://www.worldbank.org/; Albania (report).

ALBANIA-PUBLIC HEALTH

Organisation of Islamic Cooperation (OIC), Statistical, Economic and Social Research and Training Centre for Islamic Countries (SESRIC), Kudus Cad. No. 9, Diplomatik Site, Ankara, 06450, TUR, statistics@sesric.org, https://www.sesric.org/; OIC Statistics (OICStat) Database.

Palgrave Macmillan, 1 New York Plaza, Ste. 4500, New York, NY, 10004-1562, USA, (800) 777-4643, orders@palgrave.com, https://www.palgrave.com/us; The Statesman's Yearbook, 2023.

U.S. Census Bureau, 4600 Silver Hill Rd., Washington, DC, 20233, USA, (301) 763-4636, (800) 923-8282, https://www.census.gov; HIV/AIDS Surveillance Data Base.

UNICEF, 3 United Nations Plz., New York, NY, 10017, USA, (212) 303-7984, (917) 244-2215, https://www.unicef.org; The State of the World's Children 2023.

United Nations Department of Economic and Social Affairs (DESA), Population Division, 2 United Nations Plz., Rm. DC2-1950, New York, NY, 10017, USA, (212) 963-3209, (212) 963-2147, population@un.org, https://www.un.org/development/desa/pd/; World Fertility Data 2019.

United Nations Development Programme (UNDP), One United Nations Plz., New York, NY, 10017,

USA, (212) 906-5000, (212) 906-5001, https://www.undp.org; Human Development Report 2021-2022.

United Nations Statistics Division (UNSD), United Nations Plz., New York, NY, 10017, USA, (800) 253-9646, (212) 963-9851, statistics@un.org, https://unstats.un.org; Millennium Development Goal Indicators and Statistical Yearbook of the United Nations 2021.

The World Bank, 1818 H St. NW, Washington, DC, 20433, USA, (202) 473-1000, (202) 477-6391, eds03@worldbank.org, https://www.worldbank.org/; Albania (report).

World Health Organization (WHO), Ave. Appia 20, Geneva, CH-1211, SWI, (202) 974-3000 (Telephone in U.S.), publications@who.int, https://www.who.int/; Global Health Observatory (GHO).

ALBANIA-PUBLISHERS AND PUBLISHING

Palgrave Macmillan, 1 New York Plaza, Ste. 4500, New York, NY, 10004-1562, USA, (800) 777-4643, orders@palgrave.com, https://www.palgrave.com/us; The Statesman's Yearbook, 2023.

Routledge - Taylor & Francis Group, 6000 Broken Sound Pkwy. NW, Ste. 300, Boca Raton, FL, 33487, USA, (800) 634-1420, (800) 634-7064, orders@taylorandfrancis.com, https://www.routledge.com/; The Europa World Year Book 2022.

ALBANIA-RAILROADS

Janes, USA, (703) 574-7580, (888) 977-1519, customer.care@janes.com, https://www.janes.com; Janes World Railways 2021-2022.

Palgrave Macmillan, 1 New York Plaza, Ste. 4500, New York, NY, 10004-1562, USA, (800) 777-4643, orders@palgrave.com, https://www.palgrave.com/us; The Statesman's Yearbook, 2023.

Routledge - Taylor & Francis Group, 6000 Broken Sound Pkwy. NW, Ste. 300, Boca Raton, FL, 33487, USA, (800) 634-1420, (800) 634-7064, orders@taylorandfrancis.com, https://www.routledge.com/; The Europa World Year Book 2022.

ALBANIA-RELIGION

Central Intelligence Agency (CIA), Office of Public Affairs, Washington, DC, 20505, USA, (703) 482-0623, https://www.cia.gov; The World Factbook.

Palgrave Macmillan, 1 New York Plaza, Ste. 4500, New York, NY, 10004-1562, USA, (800) 777-4643, orders@palgrave.com, https://www.palgrave.com/us; The Statesman's Yearbook, 2023.

ALBANIA-RETAIL TRADE

Euromonitor International, Inc., 1 N Dearborn St., Ste. 1700, Chicago, IL, 60602, USA, (312) 922-1115, (312) 922-1157, info-usa@euromonitor.com, https://www.euromonitor.com/; Geographies.

ALBANIA-RICE PRODUCTION

See ALBANIA-CROPS

ALBANIA-RUBBER INDUSTRY AND TRADE

International Rubber Study Group (IRSG), 51 Changi Business Park Central 2, Unit No. 6, 486066, SGP, https://www.rubberstudy.org; Monthly Rubber Bulletin (MRB); Rubber Industry Report; Rubber Statistical Bulletin; and World Rubber Industry Report (WRIO).

ALBANIA-SHIPPING

Routledge - Taylor & Francis Group, 6000 Broken Sound Pkwy. NW, Ste. 300, Boca Raton, FL, 33487, USA, (800) 634-1420, (800) 634-7064, orders@taylorandfrancis.com, https://www.routledge.com/; The Europa World Year Book 2022.

United Nations Statistics Division (UNSD), United Nations Plz., New York, NY, 10017, USA, (800) 253-9646, (212) 963-9851, statistics@un.org, https://unstats.un.org; Statistical Yearbook of the United Nations 2021.

ALBANIA-STEEL PRODUCTION

See ALBANIA-MINERAL INDUSTRIES

ALBANIA-SUGAR PRODUCTION

See ALBANIA-CROPS

ALBANIA-TELEPHONE

Central Intelligence Agency (CIA), Office of Public Affairs, Washington, DC, 20505, USA, (703) 482-0623, https://www.cia.gov; The World Factbook.

Palgrave Macmillan, 1 New York Plaza, Ste. 4500, New York, NY, 10004-1562, USA, (800) 777-4643, orders@palgrave.com, https://www.palgrave.com/us; The Statesman's Yearbook, 2023.

United Nations Statistics Division (UNSD), United Nations Plz., New York, NY, 10017, USA, (800) 253-9646, (212) 963-9851, statistics@un.org, https://unstats.un.org; World Statistics Pocketbook 2021.

ALBANIA-TEXTILE INDUSTRY

Palgrave Macmillan, 1 New York Plaza, Ste. 4500, New York, NY, 10004-1562, USA, (800) 777-4643, orders@palgrave.com, https://www.palgrave.com/us; The Statesman's Yearbook, 2023.

ALBANIA-TOBACCO INDUSTRY

United Nations Statistics Division (UNSD), United Nations Plz., New York, NY, 10017, USA, (800) 253-9646, (212) 963-9851, statistics@un.org, https://unstats.un.org; Statistical Yearbook of the United Nations 2021.

ALBANIA-TOURISM

Euromonitor International, Inc., 1 N Dearborn St., Ste. 1700, Chicago, IL, 60602, USA, (312) 922-1115, (312) 922-1157, info-usa@euromonitor.com, https://www.euromonitor.com/; Geographies.

Organisation of Islamic Cooperation (OIC), Statistical, Economic and Social Research and Training Centre for Islamic Countries (SESRIC), Kudus Cad. No. 9, Diplomatik Site, Ankara, 06450, TUR, statistics@sesric.org, https://www.sesric.org/; International Tourism in the OIC Countries: Prospects and Challenges, 2020 and OIC Statistics (OICStat) Database.

Palgrave Macmillan, 1 New York Plaza, Ste. 4500, New York, NY, 10004-1562, USA, (800) 777-4643, orders@palgrave.com, https://www.palgrave.com/us; The Statesman's Yearbook, 2023.

The World Bank, 1818 H St. NW, Washington, DC, 20433, USA, (202) 473-1000, (202) 477-6391, eds03@worldbank.org, https://www.worldbank.org/; Albania (report).

ALBANIA-TRADE

See ALBANIA-INTERNATIONAL TRADE

ALBANIA-TRANSPORTATION

Central Intelligence Agency (CIA), Office of Public Affairs, Washington, DC, 20505, USA, (703) 482-0623, https://www.cia.gov; The World Factbook.

Euromonitor International, Inc., 1 N Dearborn St., Ste. 1700, Chicago, IL, 60602, USA, (312) 922-1115, (312) 922-1157, info-usa@euromonitor.com, https://www.euromonitor.com/; Geographies.

Organisation of Islamic Cooperation (OIC), Statistical, Economic and Social Research and Training Centre for Islamic Countries (SESRIC), Kudus Cad. No. 9, Diplomatik Site, Ankara, 06450, TUR, statistics@sesric.org, https://www.sesric.org/; OIC Statistics (OICStat) Database.

Palgrave Macmillan, 1 New York Plaza, Ste. 4500, New York, NY, 10004-1562, USA, (800) 777-4643, orders@palgrave.com, https://www.palgrave.com/us; The Statesman's Yearbook, 2023.

Routledge - Taylor & Francis Group, 6000 Broken Sound Pkwy. NW, Ste. 300, Boca Raton, FL, 33487, USA, (800) 634-1420, (800) 634-7064, orders@taylorandfrancis.com, https://www.routledge.com/; The Europa World Year Book 2022.

The World Bank, 1818 H St. NW, Washington, DC, 20433, USA, (202) 473-1000, (202) 477-6391, eds03@worldbank.org, https://www.worldbank.org/; Albania (report).

ALBANIA-UNEMPLOYMENT

Palgrave Macmillan, 1 New York Plaza, Ste. 4500, New York, NY, 10004-1562, USA, (800) 777-4643, orders@palgrave.com, https://www.palgrave.com/us; The Statesman's Yearbook, 2023.

ALBANIA-VITAL STATISTICS

Palgrave Macmillan, 1 New York Plaza, Ste. 4500, New York, NY, 10004-1562, USA, (800) 777-4643, orders@palgrave.com, https://www.palgrave.com/us; The Statesman's Yearbook, 2023.

U.S. Census Bureau, 4600 Silver Hill Rd., Washington, DC, 20233, USA, (301) 763-4636, (800) 923-8282, https://www.census.gov; HIV/AIDS Surveillance Data Base.

United Nations Department of Economic and Social Affairs (DESA), Population Division, 2 United Nations Plz., Rm. DC2-1950, New York, NY, 10017, USA, (212) 963-3209, (212) 963-2147, population@un.org, https://www.un.org/development/desa/pd/; World Contraceptive Use 2021: Estimates and Projections of Family Planning Indicators and World Marriage Data 2019.

United Nations Statistics Division (UNSD), United Nations Plz., New York, NY, 10017, USA, (800) 253-9646, (212) 963-9851, statistics@un.org, https://unstats.un.org; Statistical Yearbook of the United Nations 2021 and United Nations Demographic Yearbook 2020.

ALBANIA-WAGES

The World Bank, 1818 H St. NW, Washington, DC, 20433, USA, (202) 473-1000, (202) 477-6391, eds03@worldbank.org, https://www.worldbank.org/; Albania (report).

ALBANIA-WEATHER

See ALBANIA-CLIMATE

ALBANIA-WHEAT PRODUCTION

See ALBANIA-CROPS

ALBANIA-WOOL PRODUCTION

See ALBANIA-TEXTILE INDUSTRY

ALBERTA

Government of Alberta, PO Box 1333, Edmonton, AB, T5J 2N2, CAN, (780) 427-2711 (Dial from U.S.), https://www.alberta.ca; Alberta Business and Economy.

ALCOHOL AND DRUG ABUSE

American Psychological Association (APA), 750 First St. NE, Washington, DC, 20002-4242, USA, (800) 374-2721, (202) 336-5500, https://www.apa.org/; One Year On: Unhealthy Weight Gains, Increased Drinking Reported by Americans Coping with Pandemic Stress.

Australian Institute of Family Studies, Child Family Community Australia (CFCA), 40 City Rd., Level 4, Southbank, VIC, 3006, AUS, enquiries@aifs.gov.au, https://aifs.gov.au/research_programs/child-family-community-australia; Alcohol-Related Harm in Families and Alcohol Consumption During COVID-19.

Police Executive Research Forum (PERF), 1120 Connecticut Ave. NW, Ste. 930, Washington, DC, 20036, USA, (202) 466-7820, https://www.policeforum.org; Policing on the Front Lines of the Opioid Crisis.

Recovery Research Institute (RRI), 151 Merrimac St., 6th Fl., Boston, MA, 02114, USA, https://www.recoveryanswers.org/; Sexual Minorities and Women Veterans Die Younger than Straight Veterans Due to Alcohol Use.

Trust for America's Health (TFAH), 1730 M St. NW, Ste. 900, Washington, DC, 20036, USA, (202) 223-9870, (202) 223-9871, info@tfah.org, https://www.tfah.org/; Pain in the Nation Series Update: Alcohol, Drug and Suicide Deaths at Record Highs.

U.S. Department of Health and Human Services (HHS), National Institutes of Health (NIH), National Institute on Alcohol Abuse and Alcoholism (NIAAA), 9000 Rockville Pike, Bethesda, MD, 20892, USA, (888) 696-4222, (301) 443-3860, askniaaa@nih.gov, https://www.niaaa.nih.gov/; Alcohol Use Disorder and Co-Occurring Mental Health Conditions and Alcohol's Negative Emotional Side: The Role of Stress Neurobiology in Alcohol Use Disorder.

World Health Organization (WHO), Ave. Appia 20, Geneva, CH-1211, SWI, (202) 974-3000 (Telephone in U.S.), publications@who.int, https://www.who.int/; Alcohol.

ALCOHOLIC BEVERAGES

See also LIQUORS AND BEVERAGES

British Beer & Pub Association (BBPA), 61 Queen St., Ground Fl., London, EC4R 1EB, GBR, contact@beerandpub.com, https://beerandpub.com/; 2021 Statistical Handbook.

Kirin Holdings Company, Limited, Nakano Central Park South, 10-2, Nakano 4-chome, Nakano-ku, Tokyo, 164-0001, JPN, https://www.kirinholdings.com/en/; Kirin CSV Report 2021.

The Lancet, 230 Park Ave., New York, NY, 10169, USA, (212) 633-3800, editorial@lancet.com, https://www.thelancet.com/; Alcohol Use and Burden for 195 Countries and Territories, 1990-2016: A Systematic Analysis for the Global Burden of Disease Study 2016.

World Health Organization (WHO), Ave. Appia 20, Geneva, CH-1211, SWI, (202) 974-3000 (Telephone in U.S.), publications@who.int, https://www.who.int/; Alcohol.

ALCOHOLIC BEVERAGES-CONSUMER EXPENDITURES

EnsembleIQ, 8550 W Bryn Mawr Ave., Ste. 200, Chicago, IL, 60631, USA, (877) 687-7321, https://ensembleiq.com/; 2021 Consumer Expenditures Report.

U.S. Department of Agriculture (USDA), Economic Research Service (ERS), 1400 Independence Ave. SW, Mail Stop 1800, Washington, DC, 20250-0002, USA, (202) 720-2791, https://www.ers.usda.gov/; Food Price Outlook.

U.S. Department of Labor (DOL), Bureau of Labor Statistics (BLS), Postal Square Bldg., 2 Massachusetts Ave. NE, Washington, DC, 20212-0001, USA, (202) 691-5200, (202) 691-7890, blsdata_staff@bls.gov, https://www.bls.gov; Consumer Expenditure Survey (CE).

ALCOHOLIC BEVERAGES-CONSUMPTION

American Psychological Association (APA), 750 First St. NE, Washington, DC, 20002-4242, USA, (800) 374-2721, (202) 336-5500, https://www.apa.org/; One Year On: Unhealthy Weight Gains, Increased Drinking Reported by Americans Coping with Pandemic Stress.

Health Canada, Address Locator 1801B, Ottawa, ON, K1A 0K9, CAN, (613) 957-2991 (Dial from U.S.), (613) 941-5366 (Fax from U.S.), hcinfo.infosc@canada.ca, https://www.hc-sc.gc.ca/; Canadian Alcohol and Drugs Survey (CADS): Summary of Results for 2019.

The Lancet, 230 Park Ave., New York, NY, 10169, USA, (212) 633-3800, editorial@lancet.com, https://www.thelancet.com/; Alcohol Use and Burden for 195 Countries and Territories, 1990-2016: A Systematic Analysis for the Global Burden of Disease Study 2016.

Substance Abuse and Mental Health Services Administration (SAMHSA), 5600 Fishers Ln., Rockville, MD, 20857, USA, (877) 726-4727, (800) 487-4889 (TTY), samhsainfo@samhsa.hhs.gov, https://www.samhsa.gov/; 2019-2020 National Survey on Drug Use and Health (NSDUH).

U.S. Department of Agriculture (USDA), Economic Research Service (ERS), 1400 Independence Ave. SW, Mail Stop 1800, Washington, DC, 20250-0002, USA, (202) 720-2791, https://www.ers.usda.gov/; Food Price Outlook.

U.S. Department of Health and Human Services (HHS), National Institutes of Health (NIH), National Institute on Alcohol Abuse and Alcoholism (NIAAA), 9000 Rockville Pike, Bethesda, MD, 20892, USA, (888) 696-4222, (301) 443-3860, askniaaa@nih.gov, https://www.niaaa.nih.gov/; Alcohol and the Hispanic Community; Alcohol Facts and Statistics; Alcohol Policy Information System (APIS); Alcohol's Unique Effects on Cognition in Women: A 2020 (Re)view to Envision Future Research and Treatment; Apparent Per Capita Alcohol Consumption: National, State, and Regional Trends, 1977-2021; Surveillance Reports; and Underage Drinking.

U.S. Department of Health and Human Services, Centers for Disease Control and Prevention (CDC), 1600 Clifton Rd., Atlanta, GA, 30329-4027, USA, (800) 232-4636, (888) 232-6348 (TTY), cdcinfo@cdc.gov, https://www.cdc.gov; Behavioral Risk Factor Surveillance System (BRFSS) Data.

U.S. Department of Health and Human Services, Centers for Disease Control and Prevention (CDC), National Center for Health Statistics (NCHS), 3311 Toledo Rd., Hyattsville, MD, 20782-2064, USA, (800) 232-4636, (301) 458-4000, https://www.cdc.gov/nchs; FastStats - Statistics by Topic.

ALCOHOLIC BEVERAGES-CONSUMPTION-BINGE USE

Substance Abuse and Mental Health Services Administration (SAMHSA), 5600 Fishers Ln., Rockville, MD, 20857, USA, (877) 726-4727, (800) 487-4889 (TTY), samhsainfo@samhsa.hhs.gov, https://www.samhsa.gov/; 2019-2020 National Survey on Drug Use and Health (NSDUH).

U.S. Department of Health and Human Services (HHS), National Institutes of Health (NIH), National Institute on Alcohol Abuse and Alcoholism (NIAAA), 9000 Rockville Pike, Bethesda, MD, 20892, USA, (888) 696-4222, (301) 443-3860, askniaaa@nih.gov, https://www.niaaa.nih.gov/; Alcohol Use Disorder and Co-Occurring Mental Health Conditions.

ALCOHOLIC BEVERAGES-INTERNATIONAL TRADE

U.S. Census Bureau, International Trade Program, 4600 Silver Hill Rd., Washington, DC, 20233, USA, (800) 549-0595, eid.international.trade.data@census.gov, https://www.census.gov/foreign-trade; International Trade Data.

ALCOHOLIC BEVERAGES-PRICE INDEXES

U.S. Department of Labor (DOL), Bureau of Labor Statistics (BLS), Postal Square Bldg., 2 Massachusetts Ave. NE, Washington, DC, 20212-0001, USA, (202) 691-5200, (202) 691-7890, blsdata_staff@bls.gov, https://www.bls.gov; Consumer Price Index (CPI) Databases.

ALCOHOLIC BEVERAGES-SALES

Beer Institute, 440 First St. NW, Ste. 350, Washington, DC, 20001, USA, (202) 737-2337, (800) 379-2739, (202) 737-7004, info@beerinstitute.org, https://www.beerinstitute.org/; Brewers Almanac.

U.S. Census Bureau, Center for Economic Studies (CES), 4600 Silver Hill Rd., Washington, DC, 20233, USA, (301) 763-6460, (301) 763-5935, ces.contacts@census.gov, https://www.census.gov/programs-surveys/ces.html; Retail Trade, 2017 Economic Census and Wholesale Trade, 2017 Economic Census.

U.S. Department of Commerce (DOC), International Trade Administration (ITA), 1401 Constitution Ave. NW, Washington, DC, 20230, USA, (800) 872-8723, https://www.trade.gov/; TradeStats Express (TSE).

ALCOHOLISM

Health Canada, Address Locator 1801B, Ottawa, ON, K1A 0K9, CAN, (613) 957-2991 (Dial from U.S.), (613) 941-5366 (Fax from U.S.), hcinfo.infosc@canada.ca, https://www.hc-sc.gc.ca/; Canadian Alcohol and Drugs Survey (CADS): Summary of Results for 2019.

Recovery Research Institute (RRI), 151 Merrimac St., 6th Fl., Boston, MA, 02114, USA, https://www.recoveryanswers.org/; Sexual Minorities and Women Veterans Die Younger than Straight Veterans Due to Alcohol Use.

Trust for America's Health (TFAH), 1730 M St. NW, Ste. 900, Washington, DC, 20036, USA, (202) 223-9870, (202) 223-9871, info@tfah.org, https://www.tfah.org/; Pain in the Nation Series Update: Alcohol, Drug and Suicide Deaths at Record Highs.

U.S. Department of Health and Human Services (HHS), National Institutes of Health (NIH), National Institute on Alcohol Abuse and Alcoholism (NIAAA), 9000 Rockville Pike, Bethesda, MD, 20892, USA, (888) 696-4222, (301) 443-3860, askniaaa@nih.gov, https://www.niaaa.nih.gov/; Alcohol and the Hispanic Community; Alcohol Facts and Statistics; Alcohol Policy Information System (APIS); Alcohol Use Disorder and Co-Occurring Mental Health Conditions; Alcohol's Negative Emotional Side: The Role of Stress Neurobiology in Alcohol Use Disorder; Alcohol's Unique Effects on Cognition in Women: A 2020 (Re)view to Envision Future Research and Treatment; Apparent Per Capita Alcohol Consumption: National, State, and Regional Trends, 1977-2021; Surveillance Reports; and Underage Drinking.

World Health Organization (WHO), Ave. Appia 20, Geneva, CH-1211, SWI, (202) 974-3000 (Telephone in U.S.), publications@who.int, https://www.who.int/; Alcohol.

ALCOHOLISM-TREATMENT

Council on Criminal Justice (CCJ), National Commission on COVID-19 and Criminal Justice, 700 Pennsylvania Ave. SE, Washington, DC, 20020, USA, info@counciloncj.org, https://counciloncj.org/covid-19/; Impact Report: COVID-19 and SUD Treatment.

Substance Abuse and Mental Health Services Administration (SAMHSA), 5600 Fishers Ln., Rockville, MD, 20857, USA, (877) 726-4727, (800) 487-4889 (TTY), samhsainfo@samhsa.hhs.gov, https://www.samhsa.gov/; 2020 National Survey of Substance Abuse Treatment Services (N-SSATS).

U.S. Department of Health and Human Services, Centers for Disease Control and Prevention (CDC), National Center for Health Statistics (NCHS), 3311 Toledo Rd., Hyattsville, MD, 20782-2064, USA, (800) 232-4636, (301) 458-4000, https://www.cdc.gov/nchs; Health, United States, 2020-2021.

ALEUT POPULATION

See AMERICAN INDIAN, ESKIMO, ALEUT POPULATION

ALFALFA-ORGANIC ACREAGE

U.S. Department of Agriculture (USDA), Economic Research Service (ERS), 1400 Independence Ave. SW, Mail Stop 1800, Washington, DC, 20250-0002, USA, (202) 720-2791, https://www.ers.usda.gov/; Organic Market Summary and Trends.

ALGERIA-NATIONAL STATISTICAL OFFICE

National Office of Statistics, Algeria, 8/10 Rue des moussebilines, Algiers, ALG, stat@ons.dz, https://www.ons.dz/; National Data Reports (Algeria).

ALGERIA-AGRICULTURE

African Development Bank Group (AfDB), Avenue Joseph Anoma, 01 BP 1387, Abidjan, 01, COT, https://www.afdb.org; African Economic Outlook 2021 and Compendium of Statistics on Bank Group Operations 2019.

The Economist Group: Economist Intelligence Unit (EIU), 900 3rd Ave., 16th Fl., New York, NY, 10022, USA, (212) 541-0500, americas@eiu.com, https://www.eiu.com; Algeria Country Report.

Euromonitor International, Inc., 1 N Dearborn St., Ste. 1700, Chicago, IL, 60602, USA, (312) 922-1115, (312) 922-1157, info-usa@euromonitor.com, https://www.euromonitor.com/; Geographies.

Organisation of Islamic Cooperation (OIC), Statistical, Economic and Social Research and Training Centre for Islamic Countries (SESRIC), Kudus Cad. No. 9, Diplomatik Site, Ankara, 06450, TUR, statistics@sesric.org, https://www.sesric.org/; OIC Statistics (OICStat) Database and OIC-Countries in Figures (OIC-CIF).

Palgrave Macmillan, 1 New York Plaza, Ste. 4500, New York, NY, 10004-1562, USA, (800) 777-4643, orders@palgrave.com, https://www.palgrave.com/us; The Statesman's Yearbook, 2023.

Routledge - Taylor & Francis Group, 6000 Broken Sound Pkwy. NW, Ste. 300, Boca Raton, FL, 33487, USA, (800) 634-1420, (800) 634-7064, orders@taylorandfrancis.com, https://www.routledge.com/; The Europa World Year Book 2022.

United Nations Economic Commission for Africa (UNECA), PO Box 3001, Addis Ababa, ETH, ecainfo@uneca.org, https://www.uneca.org/; African Statistical Yearbook 2020 and Economic Report on Africa 2021.

United Nations Food and Agricultural Organization (FAO), 2121 K St., Ste. 800B, Washington, DC, 20037, USA, (202) 653-2400 (Dial from U.S.), (202) 653-5760 (Fax from U.S.), fao-hq@fao.org, https://www.fao.org; AQUASTAT and The State of Food and Agriculture (SOFA) 2022.

United Nations Statistics Division (UNSD), United Nations Plz., New York, NY, 10017, USA, (800) 253-9646, (212) 963-9851, statistics@un.org, https://unstats.un.org; Statistical Yearbook of the United Nations 2021.

The World Bank, 1818 H St. NW, Washington, DC, 20433, USA, (202) 473-1000, (202) 477-6391, eds03@worldbank.org, https://www.worldbank.org/; Algeria (report) and World Development Indicators (WDI) 2022.

ALGERIA-AIRLINES

International Civil Aviation Organization (ICAO), 999 Robert-Bourassa Blvd., Montreal, QC, H3C 5H7, CAN, (514) 954-8219 (Dial from U.S.), (514) 954-6077 (Fax from U.S.), icaohq@icao.int, https://www.icao.int; ICAO Regional Reports.

Palgrave Macmillan, 1 New York Plaza, Ste. 4500, New York, NY, 10004-1562, USA, (800) 777-4643, orders@palgrave.com, https://www.palgrave.com/us; The Statesman's Yearbook, 2023.

Routledge - Taylor & Francis Group, 6000 Broken Sound Pkwy. NW, Ste. 300, Boca Raton, FL, 33487, USA, (800) 634-1420, (800) 634-7064, orders@taylorandfrancis.com, https://www.routledge.com/; The Europa World Year Book 2022.

United Nations Economic Commission for Africa (UNECA), PO Box 3001, Addis Ababa, ETH, ecainfo@uneca.org, https://www.uneca.org/; African Statistical Yearbook 2020.

ALGERIA-ALUMINUM PRODUCTION

See ALGERIA-MINERAL INDUSTRIES

ALGERIA-ARMED FORCES

Central Intelligence Agency (CIA), Office of Public Affairs, Washington, DC, 20505, USA, (703) 482-0623, https://www.cia.gov; The World Factbook.

International Institute for Strategic Studies (IISS) - Americas, 2121 K St. NW, Ste. 600, Washington, DC, 20037, USA, (202) 659-1490, (202) 659-1499, https://www.iiss.org/; The Military Balance 2022.

Palgrave Macmillan, 1 New York Plaza, Ste. 4500, New York, NY, 10004-1562, USA, (800) 777-4643, orders@palgrave.com, https://www.palgrave.com/us; The Statesman's Yearbook, 2023.

Stockholm International Peace Research Institute (SIPRI), Signalistgatan 9, Stockholm, SE 169 72, SWE, https://www.sipri.org/; SIPRI Arms Transfers Database and SIPRI Military Expenditure Database.

ALGERIA-ARTICHOKE PRODUCTION

See ALGERIA-CROPS

ALGERIA-BALANCE OF PAYMENTS

African Development Bank Group (AfDB), Avenue Joseph Anoma, 01 BP 1387, Abidjan, 01, COT, https://www.afdb.org; The AfDB Statistics Pocketbook 2019.

International Monetary Fund (IMF), 700 19th St. NW, Washington, DC, 20431, USA, (202) 623-7000, (202) 623-4661, publications@imf.org, https://www.imf.org; Balance of Payments Statistics: Annual Report 2021.

Routledge - Taylor & Francis Group, 6000 Broken Sound Pkwy. NW, Ste. 300, Boca Raton, FL, 33487, USA, (800) 634-1420, (800) 634-7064, orders@taylorandfrancis.com, https://www.routledge.com/; The Europa World Year Book 2022.

United Nations Conference on Trade and Development (UNCTAD), Palais des Nations, Geneva, 1211, SWI, (212) 963-6896, unctadinfo@unctad.org, https://unctad.org; Handbook of Statistics 2021.

United Nations Economic Commission for Africa (UNECA), PO Box 3001, Addis Ababa, ETH, ecainfo@uneca.org, https://www.uneca.org/; African Statistical Yearbook 2020.

The World Bank, 1818 H St. NW, Washington, DC, 20433, USA, (202) 473-1000, (202) 477-6391, eds03@worldbank.org, https://www.worldbank.org/; Algeria (report); World Development Indicators (WDI) 2022; and World Development Report 2022: Finance for an Equitable Recovery.

ALGERIA-BANKS AND BANKING

Euromonitor International, Inc., 1 N Dearborn St., Ste. 1700, Chicago, IL, 60602, USA, (312) 922-1115, (312) 922-1157, info-usa@euromonitor.com, https://www.euromonitor.com/; Geographies.

International Monetary Fund (IMF), 700 19th St. NW, Washington, DC, 20431, USA, (202) 623-7000, (202) 623-4661, publications@imf.org, https://www.imf.org; International Financial Statistics (IFS).

Routledge - Taylor & Francis Group, 6000 Broken Sound Pkwy. NW, Ste. 300, Boca Raton, FL, 33487, USA, (800) 634-1420, (800) 634-7064, orders@taylorandfrancis.com, https://www.routledge.com/; The Europa World Year Book 2022.

United Nations Economic Commission for Africa (UNECA), PO Box 3001, Addis Ababa, ETH, ecainfo@uneca.org, https://www.uneca.org/; African Statistical Yearbook 2020.

ALGERIA-BARLEY PRODUCTION

See ALGERIA-CROPS

ALGERIA-BROADCASTING

Central Intelligence Agency (CIA), Office of Public Affairs, Washington, DC, 20505, USA, (703) 482-0623, https://www.cia.gov; The World Factbook.

Euromonitor International, Inc., 1 N Dearborn St., Ste. 1700, Chicago, IL, 60602, USA, (312) 922-1115, (312) 922-1157, info-usa@euromonitor.com, https://www.euromonitor.com/; Geographies.

Palgrave Macmillan, 1 New York Plaza, Ste. 4500, New York, NY, 10004-1562, USA, (800) 777-4643, orders@palgrave.com, https://www.palgrave.com/us; The Statesman's Yearbook, 2023.

WRTH Publications Limited, PO Box 290, Oxford, OX2 7FT, GBR, sales@wrth.com, https://www.wrth.com; World Radio TV Handbook 2023.

ALGERIA-BUDGET

Central Intelligence Agency (CIA), Office of Public Affairs, Washington, DC, 20505, USA, (703) 482-0623, https://www.cia.gov; The World Factbook.

ALGERIA-BUSINESS

Global Entrepreneurship Monitor (GEM), Babson College, 231 Forest St., Babson Park, MA, 02457, USA, (781) 235-1200, info@gemconsortium.org, https://www.gemconsortium.org/; GEM 2022-2023 Global Report.

ALGERIA-CLIMATE

International Institute for Environment and Development (IIED), 235 High Holborn, London, WC1V 7DN, GBR, inforequest@iied.org, https://www.iied.org; Environment & Urbanization.

Palgrave Macmillan, 1 New York Plaza, Ste. 4500, New York, NY, 10004-1562, USA, (800) 777-4643, orders@palgrave.com, https://www.palgrave.com/us; The Statesman's Yearbook, 2023.

ALGERIA-COAL PRODUCTION

See ALGERIA-MINERAL INDUSTRIES

ALGERIA-COFFEE

See ALGERIA-CROPS

ALGERIA-COMMERCE

Palgrave Macmillan, 1 New York Plaza, Ste. 4500, New York, NY, 10004-1562, USA, (800) 777-4643, orders@palgrave.com, https://www.palgrave.com/us; The Statesman's Yearbook, 2023.

UK Data Service, University of Essex, Wivenhoe Park, Colchester, Essex, CO4 3SQ, GBR, https://ukdataservice.ac.uk/; International Aggregate Data.

ALGERIA-COMMODITY EXCHANGES

Barchart, 209 W Jackson Blvd., 2nd Fl., Chicago, IL, 60606, USA, (877) 247-4394, commodities@barchart.com, https://www.barchart.com/cmdty; The cmdty Yearbook 2023; cmdtyStats: Commodity Statistics and Fundamental Data; cmdtyView: Commodity Index; and Commodity Data and Prices.

International Monetary Fund (IMF), 700 19th St. NW, Washington, DC, 20431, USA, (202) 623-7000, (202) 623-4661, publications@imf.org, https://www.imf.org; IMF Primary Commodity Prices.

ALGERIA-CONSTRUCTION INDUSTRY

Palgrave Macmillan, 1 New York Plaza, Ste. 4500, New York, NY, 10004-1562, USA, (800) 777-4643, orders@palgrave.com, https://www.palgrave.com/us; The Statesman's Yearbook, 2023.

United Nations Economic Commission for Africa (UNECA), PO Box 3001, Addis Ababa, ETH, ecainfo@uneca.org, https://www.uneca.org/; African Statistical Yearbook 2020.

United Nations Statistics Division (UNSD), United Nations Plz., New York, NY, 10017, USA, (800) 253-9646, (212) 963-9851, statistics@un.org, https://unstats.un.org; Statistical Yearbook of the United Nations 2021.

ALGERIA-CONSUMER PRICE INDEXES

Routledge - Taylor & Francis Group, 6000 Broken Sound Pkwy. NW, Ste. 300, Boca Raton, FL, 33487, USA, (800) 634-1420, (800) 634-7064, orders@taylorandfrancis.com, https://www.routledge.com/; The Europa World Year Book 2022.

United Nations Economic Commission for Africa (UNECA), PO Box 3001, Addis Ababa, ETH, ecainfo@uneca.org, https://www.uneca.org/; African Statistical Yearbook 2020.

The World Bank, 1818 H St. NW, Washington, DC, 20433, USA, (202) 473-1000, (202) 477-6391, eds03@worldbank.org, https://www.worldbank.org/; Algeria (report).

ALGERIA-CONSUMPTION (ECONOMICS)

African Development Bank Group (AfDB), Avenue Joseph Anoma, 01 BP 1387, Abidjan, 01, COT, https://www.afdb.org; The AfDB Statistics Pocketbook 2019.

ALGERIA-COPPER INDUSTRY AND TRADE

See ALGERIA-MINERAL INDUSTRIES

ALGERIA-CORN INDUSTRY

See ALGERIA-CROPS

ALGERIA-COTTON

See ALGERIA-CROPS

ALGERIA-CROPS

Palgrave Macmillan, 1 New York Plaza, Ste. 4500, New York, NY, 10004-1562, USA, (800) 777-4643, orders@palgrave.com, https://www.palgrave.com/us; The Statesman's Yearbook, 2023.

United Nations Economic Commission for Africa (UNECA), PO Box 3001, Addis Ababa, ETH, ecainfo@uneca.org, https://www.uneca.org/; African Statistical Yearbook 2020.

United Nations Food and Agricultural Organization (FAO), 2121 K St., Ste. 800B, Washington, DC, 20037, USA, (202) 653-2400 (Dial from U.S.), (202) 653-5760 (Fax from U.S.), fao-hq@fao.org, https://www.fao.org; The State of Food and Agriculture (SOFA) 2022.

United Nations Statistics Division (UNSD), United Nations Plz., New York, NY, 10017, USA, (800) 253-9646, (212) 963-9851, statistics@un.org, https://unstats.un.org; Statistical Yearbook of the United Nations 2021.

ALGERIA-DAIRY PROCESSING

Palgrave Macmillan, 1 New York Plaza, Ste. 4500, New York, NY, 10004-1562, USA, (800) 777-4643, orders@palgrave.com, https://www.palgrave.com/us; The Statesman's Yearbook, 2023.

United Nations Food and Agricultural Organization (FAO), 2121 K St., Ste. 800B, Washington, DC, 20037, USA, (202) 653-2400 (Dial from U.S.), (202) 653-5760 (Fax from U.S.), fao-hq@fao.org, https://www.fao.org; The State of Food and Agriculture (SOFA) 2022.

ALGERIA-DEBTS, EXTERNAL

African Development Bank Group (AfDB), Avenue Joseph Anoma, 01 BP 1387, Abidjan, 01, COT, https://www.afdb.org; The AfDB Statistics Pocketbook 2019; African Economic Outlook 2021; and Compendium of Statistics on Bank Group Operations 2019.

Palgrave Macmillan, 1 New York Plaza, Ste. 4500, New York, NY, 10004-1562, USA, (800) 777-4643, orders@palgrave.com, https://www.palgrave.com/us; The Statesman's Yearbook, 2023.

United Nations Economic Commission for Africa (UNECA), PO Box 3001, Addis Ababa, ETH, ecainfo@uneca.org, https://www.uneca.org/; Economic Report on Africa 2021.

The World Bank, 1818 H St. NW, Washington, DC, 20433, USA, (202) 473-1000, (202) 477-6391, eds03@worldbank.org, https://www.worldbank.org/; Global Financial Development Report 2019-2020: Bank Regulation and Supervision a Decade after the Global Financial Crisis and World Development Indicators (WDI) 2022.

ALGERIA-DEFENSE EXPENDITURES

See ALGERIA-ARMED FORCES

ALGERIA-DIAMONDS

See ALGERIA-MINERAL INDUSTRIES

ALGERIA-ECONOMIC ASSISTANCE

United Nations Statistics Division (UNSD), United Nations Plz., New York, NY, 10017, USA, (800) 253-9646, (212) 963-9851, statistics@un.org, https://unstats.un.org; Statistical Yearbook of the United Nations 2021.

ALGERIA-ECONOMIC CONDITIONS

African Development Bank Group (AfDB), Avenue Joseph Anoma, 01 BP 1387, Abidjan, 01, COT, https://www.afdb.org; The AfDB Statistics Pocketbook 2019; Africa Economic Brief - COVID-19 Pandemic Potential Risks for Trade and Trade Finance in Africa; African Economic Outlook 2021; The African Statistical Journal; Compendium of Statistics on Bank Group Operations 2019; and Gender, Poverty and Environmental Indicators on African Countries 2019.

Bernan Press, 15250 NBN Way, Bldg. C, Blue Ridge Summit, PA, 17214, USA, (301) 459-2255, (800) 865-3457, (800) 865-3450, customercare@bernan.com, https://rowman.com/Page/Bernan; World Economic Outlook, April 2022.

Central Intelligence Agency (CIA), Office of Public Affairs, Washington, DC, 20505, USA, (703) 482-0623, https://www.cia.gov; The World Factbook.

The Economist Group: Economist Intelligence Unit (EIU), 900 3rd Ave., 16th Fl., New York, NY, 10022, USA, (212) 541-0500, americas@eiu.com, https://www.eiu.com; Algeria Country Report.

Euromonitor International, Inc., 1 N Dearborn St., Ste. 1700, Chicago, IL, 60602, USA, (312) 922-1115, (312) 922-1157, info-usa@euromonitor.com, https://www.euromonitor.com/; Geographies and Market Research on the Consumer Finance Industry.

Global Entrepreneurship Monitor (GEM), Babson College, 231 Forest St., Babson Park, MA, 02457, USA, (781) 235-1200, info@gemconsortium.org, https://www.gemconsortium.org/; GEM 2022-2023 Global Report.

International Monetary Fund (IMF), 700 19th St. NW, Washington, DC, 20431, USA, (202) 623-7000, (202) 623-4661, publications@imf.org, https://www.imf.org; IMF Data and World Economic Outlook.

Organisation of Islamic Cooperation (OIC), Statistical, Economic and Social Research and Training Centre for Islamic Countries (SESRIC), Kudus Cad. No. 9, Diplomatik Site, Ankara, 06450, TUR, statistics@sesric.org, https://www.sesric.org/; OIC Economic Outlook 2021; OIC Statistics (OICStat) Database; and OIC-Countries in Figures (OIC-CIF).

Palgrave Macmillan, 1 New York Plaza, Ste. 4500, New York, NY, 10004-1562, USA, (800) 777-4643, orders@palgrave.com, https://www.palgrave.com/us; The Statesman's Yearbook, 2023.

Routledge - Taylor & Francis Group, 6000 Broken Sound Pkwy. NW, Ste. 300, Boca Raton, FL, 33487, USA, (800) 634-1420, (800) 634-7064, orders@taylorandfrancis.com, https://www.routledge.com/; The Europa World Year Book 2022.

United Nations Economic Commission for Africa (UNECA), PO Box 3001, Addis Ababa, ETH, ecainfo@uneca.org, https://www.uneca.org/; Economic Report on Africa 2021.

United Nations Statistics Division (UNSD), United Nations Plz., New York, NY, 10017, USA, (800) 253-9646, (212) 963-9851, statistics@un.org, https://unstats.un.org; World Statistics Pocketbook 2021.

The World Bank, 1818 H St. NW, Washington, DC, 20433, USA, (202) 473-1000, (202) 477-6391, eds03@worldbank.org, https://www.worldbank.org/; Algeria (report); Global Economic Monitor (GEM); Global Economic Prospects, June 2022; The Global Findex Database 2021; and World Development Report 2022: Finance for an Equitable Recovery.

ALGERIA-EDUCATION

African Development Bank Group (AfDB), Avenue Joseph Anoma, 01 BP 1387, Abidjan, 01, COT, https://www.afdb.org; The AfDB Statistics Pocketbook 2019.

Euromonitor International, Inc., 1 N Dearborn St., Ste. 1700, Chicago, IL, 60602, USA, (312) 922-1115, (312) 922-1157, info-usa@euromonitor.com, https://www.euromonitor.com/; Geographies.

Infoplease, c/o Sandbox Networks, Inc., 1 Lincoln St., 24th Fl., Boston, MA, 02111, USA, https://www.infoplease.com; Countries of the World.

Organisation of Islamic Cooperation (OIC), Statistical, Economic and Social Research and Training Centre for Islamic Countries (SESRIC), Kudus Cad. No. 9, Diplomatik Site, Ankara, 06450, TUR, statistics@sesric.org, https://www.sesric.org/; OIC Statistics (OICStat) Database.

Palgrave Macmillan, 1 New York Plaza, Ste. 4500, New York, NY, 10004-1562, USA, (800) 777-4643, orders@palgrave.com, https://www.palgrave.com/us; The Statesman's Yearbook, 2023.

Routledge - Taylor & Francis Group, 6000 Broken Sound Pkwy. NW, Ste. 300, Boca Raton, FL, 33487, USA, (800) 634-1420, (800) 634-7064, orders@taylorandfrancis.com, https://www.routledge.com/; The Europa World Year Book 2022.

UNESCO Institute for Statistics, C.P 250 Succursale H, Montreal, QC, H3G 2K8, CAN, (514) 343-6880 (Dial from U.S.), (514) 343-5740 (Fax from U.S.), uis.publications@unesco.org, http://uis.unesco.org/; Literacy and UIS.Stat.

United Nations Economic Commission for Africa (UNECA), PO Box 3001, Addis Ababa, ETH, ecainfo@uneca.org, https://www.uneca.org/; African Statistical Yearbook 2020.

United Nations Statistics Division (UNSD), United Nations Plz., New York, NY, 10017, USA, (800) 253-9646, (212) 963-9851, statistics@un.org, https://unstats.un.org; Millennium Development Goal Indicators.

The World Bank, 1818 H St. NW, Washington, DC, 20433, USA, (202) 473-1000, (202) 477-6391, eds03@worldbank.org, https://www.worldbank.org/; Algeria (report); World Development Indicators (WDI) 2022; and World Development Report 2022: Finance for an Equitable Recovery.

ALGERIA-ELECTRICITY

International Energy Agency (IEA), 9 Rue de la Federation, Paris, 75739, FRA, info@iea.org, https://www.iea.org/; World Energy Outlook 2021.

U.S. Energy Information Administration (EIA), 1000 Independence Ave. SW, Washington, DC, 20585, USA, (202) 586-8800, infoctr@eia.gov, https://www.eia.gov; International Energy Outlook 2021.

United Nations Statistics Division (UNSD), United Nations Plz., New York, NY, 10017, USA, (800) 253-9646, (212) 963-9851, statistics@un.org, https://unstats.un.org; Statistical Yearbook of the United Nations 2021.

ALGERIA-EMPLOYMENT

International Labour Organization (ILO), 4 Rte. des Morillons, Geneva, CH-1211, SWI, ilo@ilo.org, https://www.ilo.org; NORMLEX Information System on International Labour Standards.

UK Data Service, University of Essex, Wivenhoe Park, Colchester, Essex, CO4 3SQ, GBR, https://ukdataservice.ac.uk/; International Aggregate Data.

United Nations Economic Commission for Africa (UNECA), PO Box 3001, Addis Ababa, ETH, ecainfo@uneca.org, https://www.uneca.org/; African Statistical Yearbook 2020.

The World Bank, 1818 H St. NW, Washington, DC, 20433, USA, (202) 473-1000, (202) 477-6391, eds03@worldbank.org, https://www.worldbank.org/; Algeria (report).

ALGERIA-ENVIRONMENTAL CONDITIONS

DSI Data Service & Information, Xantener Strasse 51a, Rheinberg, D-47495, GER, dsi@dsidata.com, https://www.dsidata.com/; Global Environmental Database.

The Economist Group: Economist Intelligence Unit (EIU), 900 3rd Ave., 16th Fl., New York, NY, 10022, USA, (212) 541-0500, americas@eiu.com, https://www.eiu.com; Algeria Country Report.

International Institute for Environment and Development (IIED), 235 High Holborn, London, WC1V 7DN, GBR, inforequest@iied.org, https://www.iied.org; Environment & Urbanization.

Organisation of Islamic Cooperation (OIC), Statistical, Economic and Social Research and Training

Centre for Islamic Countries (SESRIC), Kudus Cad. No. 9, Diplomatik Site, Ankara, 06450, TUR, statistics@sesric.org, https://www.sesric.org/; OIC Statistics (OICStat) Database and OIC-Countries in Figures (OIC-CIF).

United Nations Statistics Division (UNSD), United Nations Plz., New York, NY, 10017, USA, (800) 253-9646, (212) 963-9851, statistics@un.org, https://unstats.un.org; World Statistics Pocketbook 2021.

ALGERIA-EXPORTS

African Development Bank Group (AfDB), Avenue Joseph Anoma, 01 BP 1387, Abidjan, 01, COT, https://www.afdb.org; African Economic Outlook 2021.

Central Intelligence Agency (CIA), Office of Public Affairs, Washington, DC, 20505, USA, (703) 482-0623, https://www.cia.gov; The World Factbook.

The Economist Group: Economist Intelligence Unit (EIU), 900 3rd Ave., 16th Fl., New York, NY, 10022, USA, (212) 541-0500, americas@eiu.com, https://www.eiu.com; Algeria Country Report.

International Monetary Fund (IMF), 700 19th St. NW, Washington, DC, 20431, USA, (202) 623-7000, (202) 623-4661, publications@imf.org, https://www.imf.org; Direction of Trade Statistics (DOTS).

Organisation of Islamic Cooperation (OIC), Statistical, Economic and Social Research and Training Centre for Islamic Countries (SESRIC), Kudus Cad. No. 9, Diplomatik Site, Ankara, 06450, TUR, statistics@sesric.org, https://www.sesric.org/; OIC Statistics (OICStat) Database.

Organization of Petroleum Exporting Countries (OPEC), Helferstorferstrasse 17, Vienna, A-1010, AUT, https://www.opec.org/; OPEC Annual Statistical Bulletin 2021.

S&P Global, IHS Markit, 15 Inverness Way E, Englewood, CO, 80112, USA, (800) 447-2273, (800) 854-7179, https://ihsmarkit.com; Global Trade Atlas (GTA).

United Nations Conference on Trade and Development (UNCTAD), Palais des Nations, Geneva, 1211, SWI, (212) 963-6896, unctadinfo@unctad.org, https://unctad.org; Handbook of Statistics 2021.

The World Bank, 1818 H St. NW, Washington, DC, 20433, USA, (202) 473-1000, (202) 477-6391, eds03@worldbank.org, https://www.worldbank.org/; World Development Report 2022: Finance for an Equitable Recovery.

ALGERIA-FEMALE WORKING POPULATION

See ALGERIA-EMPLOYMENT

ALGERIA-FERTILIZER INDUSTRY

United Nations Food and Agricultural Organization (FAO), 2121 K St., Ste. 800B, Washington, DC, 20037, USA, (202) 653-2400 (Dial from U.S.), (202) 653-5760 (Fax from U.S.), fao-hq@fao.org, https://www.fao.org; The State of Food and Agriculture (SOFA) 2022.

ALGERIA-FETAL MORTALITY

See ALGERIA-MORTALITY

ALGERIA-FINANCE

Stockholm International Peace Research Institute (SIPRI), Signalistgatan 9, Stockholm, SE 169 72, SWE, https://www.sipri.org/; SIPRI Arms Transfers Database and SIPRI Military Expenditure Database.

United Nations Economic Commission for Africa (UNECA), PO Box 3001, Addis Ababa, ETH, ecainfo@uneca.org, https://www.uneca.org/; African Statistical Yearbook 2020.

The World Bank, 1818 H St. NW, Washington, DC, 20433, USA, (202) 473-1000, (202) 477-6391, eds03@worldbank.org, https://www.worldbank.org/; Algeria (report).

ALGERIA-FINANCE, PUBLIC

African Development Bank Group (AfDB), Avenue Joseph Anoma, 01 BP 1387, Abidjan, 01, COT, https://www.afdb.org; The AfDB Statistics Pocketbook 2019.

Bernan Press, 15250 NBN Way, Bldg. C, Blue Ridge Summit, PA, 17214, USA, (301) 459-2255, (800) 865-3457, (800) 865-3450, customercare@bernan.com, https://rowman.com/Page/Bernan; National Accounts Statistics: Analysis of Main Aggregates 2020.

The Economist Group: Economist Intelligence Unit (EIU), 900 3rd Ave., 16th Fl., New York, NY, 10022, USA, (212) 541-0500, americas@eiu.com, https://www.eiu.com; Algeria Country Report.

International Monetary Fund (IMF), 700 19th St. NW, Washington, DC, 20431, USA, (202) 623-7000, (202) 623-4661, publications@imf.org, https://www.imf.org; International Financial Statistics (IFS) and Regional Economic Outlook.

Palgrave Macmillan, 1 New York Plaza, Ste. 4500, New York, NY, 10004-1562, USA, (800) 777-4643, orders@palgrave.com, https://www.palgrave.com/us; The Statesman's Yearbook, 2023.

Routledge - Taylor & Francis Group, 6000 Broken Sound Pkwy. NW, Ste. 300, Boca Raton, FL, 33487, USA, (800) 634-1420, (800) 634-7064, orders@taylorandfrancis.com, https://www.routledge.com/; The Europa World Year Book 2022.

United Nations Economic Commission for Africa (UNECA), PO Box 3001, Addis Ababa, ETH, ecainfo@uneca.org, https://www.uneca.org/; African Statistical Yearbook 2020.

United Nations Statistics Division (UNSD), United Nations Plz., New York, NY, 10017, USA, (800) 253-9646, (212) 963-9851, statistics@un.org, https://unstats.un.org; National Accounts Main Aggregates Database and National Accounts Statistics: Main Aggregates and Detailed Tables.

The World Bank, 1818 H St. NW, Washington, DC, 20433, USA, (202) 473-1000, (202) 477-6391, eds03@worldbank.org, https://www.worldbank.org/; Algeria (report).

ALGERIA-FISHERIES

Palgrave Macmillan, 1 New York Plaza, Ste. 4500, New York, NY, 10004-1562, USA, (800) 777-4643, orders@palgrave.com, https://www.palgrave.com/us; The Statesman's Yearbook, 2023.

Routledge - Taylor & Francis Group, 6000 Broken Sound Pkwy. NW, Ste. 300, Boca Raton, FL, 33487, USA, (800) 634-1420, (800) 634-7064, orders@taylorandfrancis.com, https://www.routledge.com/; The Europa World Year Book 2022.

United Nations Economic Commission for Africa (UNECA), PO Box 3001, Addis Ababa, ETH, ecainfo@uneca.org, https://www.uneca.org/; African Statistical Yearbook 2020.

United Nations Food and Agricultural Organization (FAO), 2121 K St., Ste. 800B, Washington, DC, 20037, USA, (202) 653-2400 (Dial from U.S.), (202) 653-5760 (Fax from U.S.), fao-hq@fao.org, https://www.fao.org; FAO Yearbook of Fishery and Aquaculture Statistics 2019; Fishery Statistical Collections Global Capture Production; FishStatJ; and The State of Food and Agriculture (SOFA) 2022.

United Nations Statistics Division (UNSD), United Nations Plz., New York, NY, 10017, USA, (800) 253-9646, (212) 963-9851, statistics@un.org, https://unstats.un.org; Statistical Yearbook of the United Nations 2021.

The World Bank, 1818 H St. NW, Washington, DC, 20433, USA, (202) 473-1000, (202) 477-6391, eds03@worldbank.org, https://www.worldbank.org/; Algeria (report).

ALGERIA-FOOD

African Development Bank Group (AfDB), Avenue Joseph Anoma, 01 BP 1387, Abidjan, 01, COT, https://www.afdb.org; The AfDB Statistics Pocketbook 2019.

United Nations Food and Agricultural Organization (FAO), 2121 K St., Ste. 800B, Washington, DC, 20037, USA, (202) 653-2400 (Dial from U.S.), (202) 653-5760 (Fax from U.S.), fao-hq@fao.org, https://www.fao.org; The State of Food and Agriculture (SOFA) 2022.

ALGERIA-FOREIGN EXCHANGE RATES

African Development Bank Group (AfDB), Avenue Joseph Anoma, 01 BP 1387, Abidjan, 01, COT, https://www.afdb.org; The AfDB Statistics Pocketbook 2019 and African Economic Outlook 2021.

Organization of Petroleum Exporting Countries (OPEC), Helferstorferstrasse 17, Vienna, A-1010, AUT, https://www.opec.org/; OPEC Annual Statistical Bulletin 2021.

ALGERIA-FORESTS AND FORESTRY

Palgrave Macmillan, 1 New York Plaza, Ste. 4500, New York, NY, 10004-1562, USA, (800) 777-4643, orders@palgrave.com, https://www.palgrave.com/us; The Statesman's Yearbook, 2023.

Routledge - Taylor & Francis Group, 6000 Broken Sound Pkwy. NW, Ste. 300, Boca Raton, FL, 33487, USA, (800) 634-1420, (800) 634-7064, orders@taylorandfrancis.com, https://www.routledge.com/; The Europa World Year Book 2022.

UNESCO Institute for Statistics, C.P 250 Succursale H, Montreal, QC, H3G 2K8, CAN, (514) 343-6880 (Dial from U.S.), (514) 343-5740 (Fax from U.S.), uis.publications@unesco.org, http://uis.unesco.org/; UIS.Stat.

United Nations Economic Commission for Africa (UNECA), PO Box 3001, Addis Ababa, ETH, ecainfo@uneca.org, https://www.uneca.org/; African Statistical Yearbook 2020.

United Nations Food and Agricultural Organization (FAO), 2121 K St., Ste. 800B, Washington, DC, 20037, USA, (202) 653-2400 (Dial from U.S.), (202) 653-5760 (Fax from U.S.), fao-hq@fao.org, https://www.fao.org; FAO Yearbook of Forest Products 2019 and The State of Food and Agriculture (SOFA) 2022.

United Nations Statistics Division (UNSD), United Nations Plz., New York, NY, 10017, USA, (800) 253-9646, (212) 963-9851, statistics@un.org, https://unstats.un.org; Statistical Yearbook of the United Nations 2021.

The World Bank, 1818 H St. NW, Washington, DC, 20433, USA, (202) 473-1000, (202) 477-6391, eds03@worldbank.org, https://www.worldbank.org/; Algeria (report) and World Development Report 2022: Finance for an Equitable Recovery.

ALGERIA-GAS PRODUCTION

See ALGERIA-MINERAL INDUSTRIES

ALGERIA-GEOGRAPHIC INFORMATION SYSTEMS

The World Bank, 1818 H St. NW, Washington, DC, 20433, USA, (202) 473-1000, (202) 477-6391, eds03@worldbank.org, https://www.worldbank.org/; Algeria (report).

ALGERIA-GOLD PRODUCTION

See ALGERIA-MINERAL INDUSTRIES

ALGERIA-GROSS DOMESTIC PRODUCT

African Development Bank Group (AfDB), Avenue Joseph Anoma, 01 BP 1387, Abidjan, 01, COT, https://www.afdb.org; The AfDB Statistics Pocketbook 2019.

The Economist Group: Economist Intelligence Unit (EIU), 900 3rd Ave., 16th Fl., New York, NY, 10022, USA, (212) 541-0500, americas@eiu.com, https://www.eiu.com; Algeria Country Report.

Routledge - Taylor & Francis Group, 6000 Broken Sound Pkwy. NW, Ste. 300, Boca Raton, FL, 33487, USA, (800) 634-1420, (800) 634-7064, orders@taylorandfrancis.com, https://www.routledge.com/; The Europa World Year Book 2022.

United Nations Economic Commission for Africa (UNECA), PO Box 3001, Addis Ababa, ETH, ecainfo@uneca.org, https://www.uneca.org/; African Statistical Yearbook 2020.

United Nations Statistics Division (UNSD), United Nations Plz., New York, NY, 10017, USA, (800) 253-9646, (212) 963-9851, statistics@un.org, https://unstats.un.org; Statistical Yearbook of the United Nations 2021.

The World Bank, 1818 H St. NW, Washington, DC, 20433, USA, (202) 473-1000, (202) 477-6391, eds03@worldbank.org, https://www.worldbank.org/; World Development Indicators (WDI) 2022 and World Development Report 2022: Finance for an Equitable Recovery.

ALGERIA-GROSS NATIONAL PRODUCT

Organization of Petroleum Exporting Countries (OPEC), Helferstorferstrasse 17, Vienna, A-1010, AUT, https://www.opec.org/; OPEC Annual Statistical Bulletin 2021.

Palgrave Macmillan, 1 New York Plaza, Ste. 4500, New York, NY, 10004-1562, USA, (800) 777-4643, orders@palgrave.com, https://www.palgrave.com/us; The Statesman's Yearbook, 2023.

Routledge - Taylor & Francis Group, 6000 Broken Sound Pkwy. NW, Ste. 300, Boca Raton, FL, 33487, USA, (800) 634-1420, (800) 634-7064, orders@taylorandfrancis.com, https://www.routledge.com/; The Europa World Year Book 2022.

The World Bank, 1818 H St. NW, Washington, DC, 20433, USA, (202) 473-1000, (202) 477-6391, eds03@worldbank.org, https://www.worldbank.org/; World Development Indicators (WDI) 2022 and World Development Report 2022: Finance for an Equitable Recovery.

ALGERIA-HEALTH

See ALGERIA-PUBLIC HEALTH

ALGERIA-HOUSING

Euromonitor International, Inc., 1 N Dearborn St., Ste. 1700, Chicago, IL, 60602, USA, (312) 922-1115, (312) 922-1157, info-usa@euromonitor.com, https://www.euromonitor.com/; Geographies.

ALGERIA-ILLITERATE PERSONS

UNESCO Institute for Statistics, C.P 250 Succursale H, Montreal, QC, H3G 2K8, CAN, (514) 343-6880 (Dial from U.S.), (514) 343-5740 (Fax from U.S.), uis.publications@unesco.org, http://uis.unesco.org/; UIS.Stat.

ALGERIA-IMPORTS

African Development Bank Group (AfDB), Avenue Joseph Anoma, 01 BP 1387, Abidjan, 01, COT, https://www.afdb.org; African Economic Outlook 2021.

Central Intelligence Agency (CIA), Office of Public Affairs, Washington, DC, 20505, USA, (703) 482-0623, https://www.cia.gov; The World Factbook.

The Economist Group: Economist Intelligence Unit (EIU), 900 3rd Ave., 16th Fl., New York, NY, 10022, USA, (212) 541-0500, americas@eiu.com, https://www.eiu.com; Algeria Country Report.

International Monetary Fund (IMF), 700 19th St. NW, Washington, DC, 20431, USA, (202) 623-7000, (202) 623-4661, publications@imf.org, https://www.imf.org; Direction of Trade Statistics (DOTS).

S&P Global, IHS Markit, 15 Inverness Way E, Englewood, CO, 80112, USA, (800) 447-2273, (800) 854-7179, https://ihsmarkit.com; Global Trade Atlas (GTA).

United Nations Conference on Trade and Development (UNCTAD), Palais des Nations, Geneva, 1211, SWI, (212) 963-6896, unctadinfo@unctad.org, https://unctad.org; Handbook of Statistics 2021.

United Nations Statistics Division (UNSD), United Nations Plz., New York, NY, 10017, USA, (800) 253-9646, (212) 963-9851, statistics@un.org, https://unstats.un.org; Statistical Yearbook of the United Nations 2021.

The World Bank, 1818 H St. NW, Washington, DC, 20433, USA, (202) 473-1000, (202) 477-6391, eds03@worldbank.org, https://www.worldbank.org/; World Development Report 2022: Finance for an Equitable Recovery.

ALGERIA-INDUSTRIAL PRODUCTIVITY

International Lead and Zinc Study Group (ILZSG), Rua Almirante Barroso 38, 5th Fl., Lisbon, 1000-013, PRT, sales@ilzsg.org, https://www.ilzsg.org; Interactive Statistical Database.

ALGERIA-INDUSTRIAL PROPERTY

World Intellectual Property Organization (WIPO), 34, chemin des Colombettes, Geneva, CH-1211, SWI, https://www.wipo.int; Madrid Yearly Review 2022: International Registrations of Marks.

ALGERIA-INDUSTRIES

Central Intelligence Agency (CIA), Office of Public Affairs, Washington, DC, 20505, USA, (703) 482-0623, https://www.cia.gov; The World Factbook.

The Economist Group: Economist Intelligence Unit (EIU), 900 3rd Ave., 16th Fl., New York, NY, 10022, USA, (212) 541-0500, americas@eiu.com, https://www.eiu.com; Algeria Country Report.

Euromonitor International, Inc., 1 N Dearborn St., Ste. 1700, Chicago, IL, 60602, USA, (312) 922-1115, (312) 922-1157, info-usa@euromonitor.com, https://www.euromonitor.com/; Geographies.

International Labour Organization (ILO), 4 Rte. des Morillons, Geneva, CH-1211, SWI, ilo@ilo.org, https://www.ilo.org; NORMLEX Information System on International Labour Standards.

Palgrave Macmillan, 1 New York Plaza, Ste. 4500, New York, NY, 10004-1562, USA, (800) 777-4643, orders@palgrave.com, https://www.palgrave.com/us; The Statesman's Yearbook, 2023.

Routledge - Taylor & Francis Group, 6000 Broken Sound Pkwy. NW, Ste. 300, Boca Raton, FL, 33487, USA, (800) 634-1420, (800) 634-7064, orders@taylorandfrancis.com, https://www.routledge.com/; The Europa World Year Book 2022.

United Nations Economic and Social Commission for Western Asia (ESCWA), Riad el-Solh Sq., PO Box 11-8575, Beirut, LBN, escwa-ciu@un.org, https://www.unescwa.org; Bulletin of Industrial Statistics for Arab Countries.

United Nations Economic Commission for Africa (UNECA), PO Box 3001, Addis Ababa, ETH, ecainfo@uneca.org, https://www.uneca.org/; African Statistical Yearbook 2020.

United Nations Industrial Development Organization (UNIDO), 1 United Nations Plz., Rm. DC1-1118, New York, NY, 10017, USA, (212) 963-6890, (212) 963 6885, (212) 963-7904, office.newyork@unido.org, https://www.unido.org/; Industrial Statistics Databases and International Yearbook of Industrial Statistics 2021.

The World Bank, 1818 H St. NW, Washington, DC, 20433, USA, (202) 473-1000, (202) 477-6391, eds03@worldbank.org, https://www.worldbank.org/; Algeria (report) and World Development Indicators (WDI) 2022.

World Intellectual Property Organization (WIPO), 34, chemin des Colombettes, Geneva, CH-1211, SWI, https://www.wipo.int; Madrid Yearly Review 2022: International Registrations of Marks.

ALGERIA-INFANT AND MATERNAL MORTALITY

See ALGERIA-MORTALITY

ALGERIA-INTERNATIONAL TRADE

African Development Bank Group (AfDB), Avenue Joseph Anoma, 01 BP 1387, Abidjan, 01, COT, https://www.afdb.org; The AfDB Statistics Pocketbook 2019 and African Economic Outlook 2021.

The Economist Group: Economist Intelligence Unit (EIU), 900 3rd Ave., 16th Fl., New York, NY, 10022, USA, (212) 541-0500, americas@eiu.com, https://www.eiu.com; Algeria Country Report.

Euromonitor International, Inc., 1 N Dearborn St., Ste. 1700, Chicago, IL, 60602, USA, (312) 922-1115, (312) 922-1157, info-usa@euromonitor.com, https://www.euromonitor.com/; Geographies.

Palgrave Macmillan, 1 New York Plaza, Ste. 4500, New York, NY, 10004-1562, USA, (800) 777-4643, orders@palgrave.com, https://www.palgrave.com/us; The Statesman's Yearbook, 2023.

Routledge - Taylor & Francis Group, 6000 Broken Sound Pkwy. NW, Ste. 300, Boca Raton, FL, 33487, USA, (800) 634-1420, (800) 634-7064, orders@taylorandfrancis.com, https://www.routledge.com/; The Europa World Year Book 2022.

United Nations Conference on Trade and Development (UNCTAD), Palais des Nations, Geneva, 1211, SWI, (212) 963-6896, unctadinfo@unctad.org, https://unctad.org; Trade and Development Report 2021.

United Nations Economic Commission for Africa (UNECA), PO Box 3001, Addis Ababa, ETH, ecainfo@uneca.org, https://www.uneca.org/; African Statistical Yearbook 2020.

United Nations Food and Agricultural Organization (FAO), 2121 K St., Ste. 800B, Washington, DC, 20037, USA, (202) 653-2400 (Dial from U.S.), (202) 653-5760 (Fax from U.S.), fao-hq@fao.org, https://www.fao.org; The State of Food and Agriculture (SOFA) 2022.

United Nations Statistics Division (UNSD), United Nations Plz., New York, NY, 10017, USA, (800) 253-9646, (212) 963-9851, statistics@un.org, https://unstats.un.org; International Trade Statistics Yearbook 2020 and Statistical Yearbook of the United Nations 2021.

The World Bank, 1818 H St. NW, Washington, DC, 20433, USA, (202) 473-1000, (202) 477-6391, eds03@worldbank.org, https://www.worldbank.org/; Algeria (report); World Development Indicators (WDI) 2022; and World Development Report 2022: Finance for an Equitable Recovery.

World Trade Organization (WTO), Ctre. William Rappard, Rue de Lausanne 154, Case postale, Geneva, CH-1211, SWI, enquiries@wto.org, https://www.wto.org; World Trade Statistical Review 2022.

ALGERIA-INTERNET USERS

International Telecommunication Union (ITU), Place des Nations, Geneva, CH-1211, SWI, itumail@itu.int, https://www.itu.int; Global Connectivity Report 2022; World Telecommunication/ICT Indicators Database 2021; and Yearbook of Statistics 2019.

The World Bank, 1818 H St. NW, Washington, DC, 20433, USA, (202) 473-1000, (202) 477-6391, eds03@worldbank.org, https://www.worldbank.org/; Algeria (report).

ALGERIA-INVESTMENTS

International Monetary Fund (IMF), 700 19th St. NW, Washington, DC, 20431, USA, (202) 623-7000, (202) 623-4661, publications@imf.org, https://www.imf.org; International Financial Statistics (IFS).

ALGERIA-LABOR

African Development Bank Group (AfDB), Avenue Joseph Anoma, 01 BP 1387, Abidjan, 01, COT, https://www.afdb.org; The AfDB Statistics Pocketbook 2019.

Central Intelligence Agency (CIA), Office of Public Affairs, Washington, DC, 20505, USA, (703) 482-0623, https://www.cia.gov; The World Factbook.

Euromonitor International, Inc., 1 N Dearborn St., Ste. 1700, Chicago, IL, 60602, USA, (312) 922-1115, (312) 922-1157, info-usa@euromonitor.com, https://www.euromonitor.com/; Geographies.

International Labour Organization (ILO), 4 Rte. des Morillons, Geneva, CH-1211, SWI, ilo@ilo.org, https://www.ilo.org; NORMLEX Information System on International Labour Standards.

Organisation of Islamic Cooperation (OIC), Statistical, Economic and Social Research and Training

Centre for Islamic Countries (SESRIC), Kudus Cad. No. 9, Diplomatik Site, Ankara, 06450, TUR, statistics@sesric.org, https://www.sesric.org/; OIC Statistics (OICStat) Database.

Palgrave Macmillan, 1 New York Plaza, Ste. 4500, New York, NY, 10004-1562, USA, (800) 777-4643, orders@palgrave.com, https://www.palgrave.com/us; The Statesman's Yearbook, 2023.

United Nations Food and Agricultural Organization (FAO), 2121 K St., Ste. 800B, Washington, DC, 20037, USA, (202) 653-2400 (Dial from U.S.), (202) 653-5760 (Fax from U.S.), fao-hq@fao.org, https://www.fao.org; The State of Food and Agriculture (SOFA) 2022.

The World Bank, 1818 H St. NW, Washington, DC, 20433, USA, (202) 473-1000, (202) 477-6391, eds03@worldbank.org, https://www.worldbank.org/; World Development Indicators (WDI) 2022 and World Development Report 2022: Finance for an Equitable Recovery.

ALGERIA-LAND USE

United Nations Statistics Division (UNSD), United Nations Plz., New York, NY, 10017, USA, (800) 253-9646, (212) 963-9851, statistics@un.org, https://unstats.un.org; Millennium Development Goal Indicators.

The World Bank, 1818 H St. NW, Washington, DC, 20433, USA, (202) 473-1000, (202) 477-6391, eds03@worldbank.org, https://www.worldbank.org/; World Development Report 2022: Finance for an Equitable Recovery.

ALGERIA-LIBRARIES

UNESCO Institute for Statistics, C.P 250 Succursale H, Montreal, QC, H3G 2K8, CAN, (514) 343-6880 (Dial from U.S.), (514) 343-5740 (Fax from U.S.), uis.publications@unesco.org, http://uis.unesco.org/; UIS.Stat.

ALGERIA-LIFE EXPECTANCY

African Development Bank Group (AfDB), Avenue Joseph Anoma, 01 BP 1387, Abidjan, 01, COT, https://www.afdb.org; The AfDB Statistics Pocketbook 2019.

United Nations Department of Economic and Social Affairs (DESA), Population Division, 2 United Nations Plz., Rm. DC2-1950, New York, NY, 10017, USA, (212) 963-3209, (212) 963-2147, population@un.org, https://www.un.org/development/desa/pd/; World Population Ageing 2020 Highlights.

United Nations Statistics Division (UNSD), United Nations Plz., New York, NY, 10017, USA, (800) 253-9646, (212) 963-9851, statistics@un.org, https://unstats.un.org; Millennium Development Goal Indicators.

ALGERIA-LITERACY

Euromonitor International, Inc., 1 N Dearborn St., Ste. 1700, Chicago, IL, 60602, USA, (312) 922-1115, (312) 922-1157, info-usa@euromonitor.com, https://www.euromonitor.com/; Geographies.

UNESCO Institute for Statistics, C.P 250 Succursale H, Montreal, QC, H3G 2K8, CAN, (514) 343-6880 (Dial from U.S.), (514) 343-5740 (Fax from U.S.), uis.publications@unesco.org, http://uis.unesco.org/; Literacy.

ALGERIA-LIVESTOCK

Palgrave Macmillan, 1 New York Plaza, Ste. 4500, New York, NY, 10004-1562, USA, (800) 777-4643, orders@palgrave.com, https://www.palgrave.com/us; The Statesman's Yearbook, 2023.

Routledge - Taylor & Francis Group, 6000 Broken Sound Pkwy. NW, Ste. 300, Boca Raton, FL, 33487, USA, (800) 634-1420, (800) 634-7064, orders@taylorandfrancis.com, https://www.routledge.com/; The Europa World Year Book 2022.

United Nations Economic Commission for Africa (UNECA), PO Box 3001, Addis Ababa, ETH, ecainfo@uneca.org, https://www.uneca.org/; African Statistical Yearbook 2020.

United Nations Food and Agricultural Organization (FAO), 2121 K St., Ste. 800B, Washington, DC, 20037, USA, (202) 653-2400 (Dial from U.S.), (202) 653-5760 (Fax from U.S.), fao-hq@fao.org, https://www.fao.org; The State of Food and Agriculture (SOFA) 2022.

United Nations Statistics Division (UNSD), United Nations Plz., New York, NY, 10017, USA, (800) 253-9646, (212) 963-9851, statistics@un.org, https://unstats.un.org; Statistical Yearbook of the United Nations 2021.

ALGERIA-MARRIAGE

United Nations Statistics Division (UNSD), United Nations Plz., New York, NY, 10017, USA, (800) 253-9646, (212) 963-9851, statistics@un.org, https://unstats.un.org; Statistical Yearbook of the United Nations 2021.

ALGERIA-MERCURY PRODUCTION

See ALGERIA-MINERAL INDUSTRIES

ALGERIA-MINERAL INDUSTRIES

Barchart, 209 W Jackson Blvd., 2nd Fl., Chicago, IL, 60606, USA, (877) 247-4394, commodities@barchart.com, https://www.barchart.com/cmdty; The cmdty Yearbook 2023; cmdtyStats: Commodity Statistics and Fundamental Data; cmdtyView: Commodity Index; and Commodity Data and Prices.

International Energy Agency (IEA), 9 Rue de la Federation, Paris, 75739, FRA, info@iea.org, https://www.iea.org/; World Energy Outlook 2021.

International Lead and Zinc Study Group (ILZSG), Rua Almirante Barroso 38, 5th Fl., Lisbon, 1000-013, PRT, sales@ilzsg.org, https://www.ilzsg.org; Interactive Statistical Database.

International Monetary Fund (IMF), 700 19th St. NW, Washington, DC, 20431, USA, (202) 623-7000, (202) 623-4661, publications@imf.org, https://www.imf.org; International Financial Statistics (IFS).

Organization of Petroleum Exporting Countries (OPEC), Helferstorferstrasse 17, Vienna, A-1010, AUT, https://www.opec.org/; OPEC Annual Statistical Bulletin 2021.

Palgrave Macmillan, 1 New York Plaza, Ste. 4500, New York, NY, 10004-1562, USA, (800) 777-4643, orders@palgrave.com, https://www.palgrave.com/us; The Statesman's Yearbook, 2023.

Routledge - Taylor & Francis Group, 6000 Broken Sound Pkwy. NW, Ste. 300, Boca Raton, FL, 33487, USA, (800) 634-1420, (800) 634-7064, orders@taylorandfrancis.com, https://www.routledge.com/; The Europa World Year Book 2022.

United Nations Conference on Trade and Development (UNCTAD), Palais des Nations, Geneva, 1211, SWI, (212) 963-6896, unctadinfo@unctad.org, https://unctad.org; Trade and Development Report 2021.

United Nations Economic Commission for Africa (UNECA), PO Box 3001, Addis Ababa, ETH, ecainfo@uneca.org, https://www.uneca.org/; African Statistical Yearbook 2020.

United Nations Statistics Division (UNSD), United Nations Plz., New York, NY, 10017, USA, (800) 253-9646, (212) 963-9851, statistics@un.org, https://unstats.un.org; Statistical Yearbook of the United Nations 2021.

The World Bank, 1818 H St. NW, Washington, DC, 20433, USA, (202) 473-1000, (202) 477-6391, eds03@worldbank.org, https://www.worldbank.org/; World Development Indicators (WDI) 2022.

ALGERIA-MONEY SUPPLY

The Economist Group: Economist Intelligence Unit (EIU), 900 3rd Ave., 16th Fl., New York, NY, 10022, USA, (212) 541-0500, americas@eiu.com, https://www.eiu.com; Algeria Country Report.

Routledge - Taylor & Francis Group, 6000 Broken Sound Pkwy. NW, Ste. 300, Boca Raton, FL, 33487, USA, (800) 634-1420, (800) 634-7064, orders@taylorandfrancis.com, https://www.routledge.com/; The Europa World Year Book 2022.

United Nations Statistics Division (UNSD), United Nations Plz., New York, NY, 10017, USA, (800) 253-9646, (212) 963-9851, statistics@un.org, https://unstats.un.org; Statistical Yearbook of the United Nations 2021.

The World Bank, 1818 H St. NW, Washington, DC, 20433, USA, (202) 473-1000, (202) 477-6391, eds03@worldbank.org, https://www.worldbank.org/; Algeria (report).

ALGERIA-MORTALITY

UNICEF, 3 United Nations Plz., New York, NY, 10017, USA, (212) 303-7984, (917) 244-2215, https://www.unicef.org; The State of the World's Children 2023.

United Nations Statistics Division (UNSD), United Nations Plz., New York, NY, 10017, USA, (800) 253-9646, (212) 963-9851, statistics@un.org, https://unstats.un.org; Millennium Development Goal Indicators; Statistical Yearbook of the United Nations 2021; and World Statistics Pocketbook 2021.

The World Bank, 1818 H St. NW, Washington, DC, 20433, USA, (202) 473-1000, (202) 477-6391, eds03@worldbank.org, https://www.worldbank.org/; World Development Indicators (WDI) 2022.

World Health Organization (WHO), Ave. Appia 20, Geneva, CH-1211, SWI, (202) 974-3000 (Telephone in U.S.), publications@who.int, https://www.who.int/; Global Health Observatory (GHO).

ALGERIA-MOTION PICTURES

Palgrave Macmillan, 1 New York Plaza, Ste. 4500, New York, NY, 10004-1562, USA, (800) 777-4643, orders@palgrave.com, https://www.palgrave.com/us; The Statesman's Yearbook, 2023.

ALGERIA-MOTOR VEHICLES

International Road Federation (IRF), Madison Place, 500 Montgomery St., 5th Fl., Alexandria, VA, 22314, USA, (703) 535-1001, (703) 535-1007, info@irf.global, https://www.irf.global/; World Road Statistics (WRS).

ALGERIA-NATURAL GAS PRODUCTION

See ALGERIA-MINERAL INDUSTRIES

ALGERIA-NUTRITION

United Nations Food and Agricultural Organization (FAO), 2121 K St., Ste. 800B, Washington, DC, 20037, USA, (202) 653-2400 (Dial from U.S.), (202) 653-5760 (Fax from U.S.), fao-hq@fao.org, https://www.fao.org; The State of Food and Agriculture (SOFA) 2022.

United Nations Statistics Division (UNSD), United Nations Plz., New York, NY, 10017, USA, (800) 253-9646, (212) 963-9851, statistics@un.org, https://unstats.un.org; Millennium Development Goal Indicators.

ALGERIA-ORANGES PRODUCTION

See ALGERIA-CROPS

ALGERIA-PAPER

See ALGERIA-FORESTS AND FORESTRY

ALGERIA-PEANUT PRODUCTION

See ALGERIA-CROPS

ALGERIA-PESTICIDES

United Nations Food and Agricultural Organization (FAO), 2121 K St., Ste. 800B, Washington, DC, 20037, USA, (202) 653-2400 (Dial from U.S.), (202) 653-5760 (Fax from U.S.), fao-hq@fao.org, https://www.fao.org; The State of Food and Agriculture (SOFA) 2022.

ALGERIA-PETROLEUM INDUSTRY AND TRADE

International Energy Agency (IEA), 9 Rue de la Federation, Paris, 75739, FRA, info@iea.org, https://www.iea.org/; World Energy Outlook 2021.

International Monetary Fund (IMF), 700 19th St. NW, Washington, DC, 20431, USA, (202) 623-7000, (202) 623-4661, publications@imf.org, https://www.imf.org; International Financial Statistics (IFS).

Organization of Petroleum Exporting Countries (OPEC), Helferstorferstrasse 17, Vienna, A-1010, AUT, https://www.opec.org/; OPEC Annual Statistical Bulletin 2021.

Palgrave Macmillan, 1 New York Plaza, Ste. 4500, New York, NY, 10004-1562, USA, (800) 777-4643, orders@palgrave.com, https://www.palgrave.com/us; The Statesman's Yearbook, 2023.

U.S. Energy Information Administration (EIA), 1000 Independence Ave. SW, Washington, DC, 20585, USA, (202) 586-8800, infoctr@eia.gov, https://www.eia.gov; International Energy Outlook 2021.

United Nations Food and Agricultural Organization (FAO), 2121 K St., Ste. 800B, Washington, DC, 20037, USA, (202) 653-2400 (Dial from U.S.), (202) 653-5760 (Fax from U.S.), fao-hq@fao.org, https://www.fao.org; The State of Food and Agriculture (SOFA) 2022.

United Nations Statistics Division (UNSD), United Nations Plz., New York, NY, 10017, USA, (800) 253-9646, (212) 963-9851, statistics@un.org, https://unstats.un.org; Statistical Yearbook of the United Nations 2021.

ALGERIA-PHOSPHATES PRODUCTION

See ALGERIA-MINERAL INDUSTRIES

ALGERIA-PIPELINES

Organization of Petroleum Exporting Countries (OPEC), Helferstorferstrasse 17, Vienna, A-1010, AUT, https://www.opec.org/; OPEC Annual Statistical Bulletin 2021.

ALGERIA-POPULATION

African Development Bank Group (AfDB), Avenue Joseph Anoma, 01 BP 1387, Abidjan, 01, COT, https://www.afdb.org; The AfDB Statistics Pocketbook 2019; Africa Economic Brief - COVID-19 Pandemic Potential Risks for Trade and Trade Finance in Africa; The African Statistical Journal; and Gender, Poverty and Environmental Indicators on African Countries 2019.

Central Intelligence Agency (CIA), Office of Public Affairs, Washington, DC, 20505, USA, (703) 482-0623, https://www.cia.gov; The World Factbook.

The Economist Group: Economist Intelligence Unit (EIU), 900 3rd Ave., 16th Fl., New York, NY, 10022, USA, (212) 541-0500, americas@eiu.com, https://www.eiu.com; Algeria Country Report.

European Commission, Eurostat, Luxembourg, 2920, LUX, https://ec.europa.eu/eurostat/; EU in the World 2020.

Infoplease, c/o Sandbox Networks, Inc., 1 Lincoln St., 24th Fl., Boston, MA, 02111, USA, https://www.infoplease.com; Countries of the World.

International Labour Organization (ILO), 4 Rte. des Morillons, Geneva, CH-1211, SWI, ilo@ilo.org, https://www.ilo.org; NORMLEX Information System on International Labour Standards.

Palgrave Macmillan, 1 New York Plaza, Ste. 4500, New York, NY, 10004-1562, USA, (800) 777-4643, orders@palgrave.com, https://www.palgrave.com/us; The Statesman's Yearbook, 2023.

Routledge - Taylor & Francis Group, 6000 Broken Sound Pkwy. NW, Ste. 300, Boca Raton, FL, 33487, USA, (800) 634-1420, (800) 634-7064, orders@taylorandfrancis.com, https://www.routledge.com/; The Europa World Year Book 2022.

UK Data Service, University of Essex, Wivenhoe Park, Colchester, Essex, CO4 3SQ, GBR, https://ukdataservice.ac.uk/; International Aggregate Data.

United Nations Department of Economic and Social Affairs (DESA), Population Division, 2 United Nations Plz., Rm. DC2-1950, New York, NY, 10017, USA, (212) 963-3209, (212) 963-2147, population@un.org, https://www.un.org/development/desa/pd/; Revision of World Urbanization Prospects and World Population Ageing 2020 Highlights.

United Nations Development Programme (UNDP), One United Nations Plz., New York, NY, 10017, USA, (212) 906-5000, (212) 906-5001, https://www.undp.org; Human Development Report 2021-2022.

United Nations Statistics Division (UNSD), United Nations Plz., New York, NY, 10017, USA, (800) 253-9646, (212) 963-9851, statistics@un.org, https://unstats.un.org; Statistical Yearbook of the United Nations 2021 and World Statistics Pocketbook 2021.

The World Bank, 1818 H St. NW, Washington, DC, 20433, USA, (202) 473-1000, (202) 477-6391, eds03@worldbank.org, https://www.worldbank.org/; Algeria (report); The Global Findex Database 2021; and World Development Report 2022: Finance for an Equitable Recovery.

ALGERIA-POPULATION DENSITY

African Development Bank Group (AfDB), Avenue Joseph Anoma, 01 BP 1387, Abidjan, 01, COT, https://www.afdb.org; The AfDB Statistics Pocketbook 2019.

Central Intelligence Agency (CIA), Office of Public Affairs, Washington, DC, 20505, USA, (703) 482-0623, https://www.cia.gov; The World Factbook.

Palgrave Macmillan, 1 New York Plaza, Ste. 4500, New York, NY, 10004-1562, USA, (800) 777-4643, orders@palgrave.com, https://www.palgrave.com/us; The Statesman's Yearbook, 2023.

Routledge - Taylor & Francis Group, 6000 Broken Sound Pkwy. NW, Ste. 300, Boca Raton, FL, 33487, USA, (800) 634-1420, (800) 634-7064, orders@taylorandfrancis.com, https://www.routledge.com/; The Europa World Year Book 2022.

The World Bank, 1818 H St. NW, Washington, DC, 20433, USA, (202) 473-1000, (202) 477-6391, eds03@worldbank.org, https://www.worldbank.org/; Algeria (report) and World Development Report 2022: Finance for an Equitable Recovery.

ALGERIA-POULTRY

See ALGERIA-LIVESTOCK

ALGERIA-POWER RESOURCES

Euromonitor International, Inc., 1 N Dearborn St., Ste. 1700, Chicago, IL, 60602, USA, (312) 922-1115, (312) 922-1157, info-usa@euromonitor.com, https://www.euromonitor.com/; Geographies.

International Energy Agency (IEA), 9 Rue de la Federation, Paris, 75739, FRA, info@iea.org, https://www.iea.org/; World Energy Outlook 2021.

Palgrave Macmillan, 1 New York Plaza, Ste. 4500, New York, NY, 10004-1562, USA, (800) 777-4643, orders@palgrave.com, https://www.palgrave.com/us; The Statesman's Yearbook, 2023.

U.S. Energy Information Administration (EIA), 1000 Independence Ave. SW, Washington, DC, 20585, USA, (202) 586-8800, infoctr@eia.gov, https://www.eia.gov; International Energy Outlook 2021.

United Nations Economic Commission for Africa (UNECA), PO Box 3001, Addis Ababa, ETH, ecainfo@uneca.org, https://www.uneca.org/; African Statistical Yearbook 2020.

United Nations Food and Agricultural Organization (FAO), 2121 K St., Ste. 800B, Washington, DC, 20037, USA, (202) 653-2400 (Dial from U.S.), (202) 653-5760 (Fax from U.S.), fao-hq@fao.org, https://www.fao.org; The State of Food and Agriculture (SOFA) 2022.

United Nations Statistics Division (UNSD), United Nations Plz., New York, NY, 10017, USA, (800) 253-9646, (212) 963-9851, statistics@un.org, https://unstats.un.org; Energy Statistics Yearbook 2019; Statistical Yearbook of the United Nations 2021; and World Statistics Pocketbook 2021.

The World Bank, 1818 H St. NW, Washington, DC, 20433, USA, (202) 473-1000, (202) 477-6391, eds03@worldbank.org, https://www.worldbank.org/; World Development Report 2022: Finance for an Equitable Recovery.

ALGERIA-PRICES

Euromonitor International, Inc., 1 N Dearborn St., Ste. 1700, Chicago, IL, 60602, USA, (312) 922-1115, (312) 922-1157, info-usa@euromonitor.com, https://www.euromonitor.com/; Geographies.

International Monetary Fund (IMF), 700 19th St. NW, Washington, DC, 20431, USA, (202) 623-7000, (202) 623-4661, publications@imf.org, https://www.imf.org; International Financial Statistics (IFS).

United Nations Economic Commission for Africa (UNECA), PO Box 3001, Addis Ababa, ETH, ecainfo@uneca.org, https://www.uneca.org/; African Statistical Yearbook 2020.

The World Bank, 1818 H St. NW, Washington, DC, 20433, USA, (202) 473-1000, (202) 477-6391, eds03@worldbank.org, https://www.worldbank.org/; Algeria (report).

ALGERIA-PUBLIC HEALTH

African Development Bank Group (AfDB), Avenue Joseph Anoma, 01 BP 1387, Abidjan, 01, COT, https://www.afdb.org; The AfDB Statistics Pocketbook 2019.

Euromonitor International, Inc., 1 N Dearborn St., Ste. 1700, Chicago, IL, 60602, USA, (312) 922-1115, (312) 922-1157, info-usa@euromonitor.com, https://www.euromonitor.com/; Geographies and Market Research on the Health and Wellness Industry.

Organisation of Islamic Cooperation (OIC), Statistical, Economic and Social Research and Training Centre for Islamic Countries (SESRIC), Kudus Cad. No. 9, Diplomatik Site, Ankara, 06450, TUR, statistics@sesric.org, https://www.sesric.org/; OIC Statistics (OICStat) Database.

Palgrave Macmillan, 1 New York Plaza, Ste. 4500, New York, NY, 10004-1562, USA, (800) 777-4643, orders@palgrave.com, https://www.palgrave.com/us; The Statesman's Yearbook, 2023.

U.S. Census Bureau, 4600 Silver Hill Rd., Washington, DC, 20233, USA, (301) 763-4636, (800) 923-8282, https://www.census.gov; HIV/AIDS Surveillance Data Base.

UNICEF, 3 United Nations Plz., New York, NY, 10017, USA, (212) 303-7984, (917) 244-2215, https://www.unicef.org; The State of the World's Children 2023.

United Nations Department of Economic and Social Affairs (DESA), Population Division, 2 United Nations Plz., Rm. DC2-1950, New York, NY, 10017, USA, (212) 963-3209, (212) 963-2147, population@un.org, https://www.un.org/development/desa/pd/; World Fertility Data 2019.

United Nations Development Programme (UNDP), One United Nations Plz., New York, NY, 10017, USA, (212) 906-5000, (212) 906-5001, https://www.undp.org; Human Development Report 2021-2022.

United Nations Economic Commission for Africa (UNECA), PO Box 3001, Addis Ababa, ETH, ecainfo@uneca.org, https://www.uneca.org/; African Statistical Yearbook 2020.

United Nations Statistics Division (UNSD), United Nations Plz., New York, NY, 10017, USA, (800) 253-9646, (212) 963-9851, statistics@un.org, https://unstats.un.org; Millennium Development Goal Indicators and Statistical Yearbook of the United Nations 2021.

The World Bank, 1818 H St. NW, Washington, DC, 20433, USA, (202) 473-1000, (202) 477-6391, eds03@worldbank.org, https://www.worldbank.org/; Algeria (report).

World Health Organization (WHO), Ave. Appia 20, Geneva, CH-1211, SWI, (202) 974-3000 (Telephone in U.S.), publications@who.int, https://www.who.int/; Global Health Observatory (GHO) and Health Statistics and Information Systems.

ALGERIA-RAILROADS

Janes, USA, (703) 574-7580, (888) 977-1519, customer.care@janes.com, https://www.janes.com; Janes World Railways 2021-2022.

Palgrave Macmillan, 1 New York Plaza, Ste. 4500, New York, NY, 10004-1562, USA, (800) 777-4643, orders@palgrave.com, https://www.palgrave.com/us; The Statesman's Yearbook, 2023.

Routledge - Taylor & Francis Group, 6000 Broken Sound Pkwy. NW, Ste. 300, Boca Raton, FL, 33487, USA, (800) 634-1420, (800) 634-7064, orders@taylorandfrancis.com, https://www.routledge.com/; The Europa World Year Book 2022.

United Nations Economic Commission for Africa (UNECA), PO Box 3001, Addis Ababa, ETH, ecainfo@uneca.org, https://www.uneca.org/; African Statistical Yearbook 2020.

United Nations Statistics Division (UNSD), United Nations Plz., New York, NY, 10017, USA, (800) 253-9646, (212) 963-9851, statistics@un.org, https://unstats.un.org; Statistical Yearbook of the United Nations 2021.

ALGERIA-RELIGION

Central Intelligence Agency (CIA), Office of Public Affairs, Washington, DC, 20505, USA, (703) 482-0623, https://www.cia.gov; The World Factbook.

Palgrave Macmillan, 1 New York Plaza, Ste. 4500, New York, NY, 10004-1562, USA, (800) 777-4643, orders@palgrave.com, https://www.palgrave.com/us; The Statesman's Yearbook, 2023.

ALGERIA-RETAIL TRADE

Euromonitor International, Inc., 1 N Dearborn St., Ste. 1700, Chicago, IL, 60602, USA, (312) 922-1115, (312) 922-1157, info-usa@euromonitor.com, https://www.euromonitor.com/; Geographies and Market Research on the Retailing Industry.

ALGERIA-RICE PRODUCTION

See ALGERIA-CROPS

ALGERIA-ROADS

International Road Federation (IRF), Madison Place, 500 Montgomery St., 5th Fl., Alexandria, VA, 22314, USA, (703) 535-1001, (703) 535-1007, info@irf.global, https://www.irf.global/; World Road Statistics (WRS).

United Nations Economic Commission for Africa (UNECA), PO Box 3001, Addis Ababa, ETH, ecainfo@uneca.org, https://www.uneca.org/; African Statistical Yearbook 2020.

ALGERIA-RUBBER INDUSTRY AND TRADE

International Rubber Study Group (IRSG), 51 Changi Business Park Central 2, Unit No. 6, 486066, SGP, https://www.rubberstudy.org; Monthly Rubber Bulletin (MRB); Rubber Industry Report; Rubber Statistical Bulletin; and World Rubber Industry Report (WRIO).

ALGERIA-SHIPPING

Organization of Petroleum Exporting Countries (OPEC), Helferstorferstrasse 17, Vienna, A-1010, AUT, https://www.opec.org/; OPEC Annual Statistical Bulletin 2021.

Routledge - Taylor & Francis Group, 6000 Broken Sound Pkwy. NW, Ste. 300, Boca Raton, FL, 33487, USA, (800) 634-1420, (800) 634-7064, orders@taylorandfrancis.com, https://www.routledge.com/; The Europa World Year Book 2022.

United Nations Economic Commission for Africa (UNECA), PO Box 3001, Addis Ababa, ETH, ecainfo@uneca.org, https://www.uneca.org/; African Statistical Yearbook 2020.

United Nations Statistics Division (UNSD), United Nations Plz., New York, NY, 10017, USA, (800) 253-9646, (212) 963-9851, statistics@un.org, https://unstats.un.org; Statistical Yearbook of the United Nations 2021.

ALGERIA-STEEL PRODUCTION

See ALGERIA-MINERAL INDUSTRIES

ALGERIA-SUGAR PRODUCTION

See ALGERIA-CROPS

ALGERIA-SULPHUR PRODUCTION

See ALGERIA-MINERAL INDUSTRIES

ALGERIA-TAXATION

International Road Federation (IRF), Madison Place, 500 Montgomery St., 5th Fl., Alexandria, VA, 22314, USA, (703) 535-1001, (703) 535-1007, info@irf.global, https://www.irf.global/; World Road Statistics (WRS).

The World Bank, 1818 H St. NW, Washington, DC, 20433, USA, (202) 473-1000, (202) 477-6391, eds03@worldbank.org, https://www.worldbank.org/; World Development Indicators (WDI) 2022.

ALGERIA-TEA PRODUCTION

See ALGERIA-CROPS

ALGERIA-TELEPHONE

Central Intelligence Agency (CIA), Office of Public Affairs, Washington, DC, 20505, USA, (703) 482-0623, https://www.cia.gov; The World Factbook.

Palgrave Macmillan, 1 New York Plaza, Ste. 4500, New York, NY, 10004-1562, USA, (800) 777-4643, orders@palgrave.com, https://www.palgrave.com/us; The Statesman's Yearbook, 2023.

Routledge - Taylor & Francis Group, 6000 Broken Sound Pkwy. NW, Ste. 300, Boca Raton, FL, 33487, USA, (800) 634-1420, (800) 634-7064, orders@taylorandfrancis.com, https://www.routledge.com/; The Europa World Year Book 2022.

United Nations Statistics Division (UNSD), United Nations Plz., New York, NY, 10017, USA, (800) 253-9646, (212) 963-9851, statistics@un.org, https://unstats.un.org; World Statistics Pocketbook 2021.

ALGERIA-TEXTILE INDUSTRY

United Nations Statistics Division (UNSD), United Nations Plz., New York, NY, 10017, USA, (800) 253-9646, (212) 963-9851, statistics@un.org, https://unstats.un.org; Statistical Yearbook of the United Nations 2021.

ALGERIA-TOBACCO INDUSTRY

United Nations Statistics Division (UNSD), United Nations Plz., New York, NY, 10017, USA, (800) 253-9646, (212) 963-9851, statistics@un.org, https://unstats.un.org; Statistical Yearbook of the United Nations 2021.

ALGERIA-TOURISM

Euromonitor International, Inc., 1 N Dearborn St., Ste. 1700, Chicago, IL, 60602, USA, (312) 922-1115, (312) 922-1157, info-usa@euromonitor.com, https://www.euromonitor.com/; Geographies.

Organisation of Islamic Cooperation (OIC), Statistical, Economic and Social Research and Training Centre for Islamic Countries (SESRIC), Kudus Cad. No. 9, Diplomatik Site, Ankara, 06450, TUR, statistics@sesric.org, https://www.sesric.org/; International Tourism in the OIC Countries: Prospects and Challenges, 2020 and OIC Statistics (OICStat) Database.

Palgrave Macmillan, 1 New York Plaza, Ste. 4500, New York, NY, 10004-1562, USA, (800) 777-4643, orders@palgrave.com, https://www.palgrave.com/us; The Statesman's Yearbook, 2023.

Routledge - Taylor & Francis Group, 6000 Broken Sound Pkwy. NW, Ste. 300, Boca Raton, FL, 33487, USA, (800) 634-1420, (800) 634-7064, orders@taylorandfrancis.com, https://www.routledge.com/; The Europa World Year Book 2022.

United Nations Economic Commission for Africa (UNECA), PO Box 3001, Addis Ababa, ETH, ecainfo@uneca.org, https://www.uneca.org/; African Statistical Yearbook 2020.

The World Bank, 1818 H St. NW, Washington, DC, 20433, USA, (202) 473-1000, (202) 477-6391, eds03@worldbank.org, https://www.worldbank.org/; Algeria (report).

ALGERIA-TRADE

See ALGERIA-INTERNATIONAL TRADE

ALGERIA-TRANSPORTATION

Central Intelligence Agency (CIA), Office of Public Affairs, Washington, DC, 20505, USA, (703) 482-0623, https://www.cia.gov; The World Factbook.

Euromonitor International, Inc., 1 N Dearborn St., Ste. 1700, Chicago, IL, 60602, USA, (312) 922-1115, (312) 922-1157, info-usa@euromonitor.com, https://www.euromonitor.com/; Geographies.

Organisation of Islamic Cooperation (OIC), Statistical, Economic and Social Research and Training Centre for Islamic Countries (SESRIC), Kudus Cad. No. 9, Diplomatik Site, Ankara, 06450, TUR, statistics@sesric.org, https://www.sesric.org/; OIC Statistics (OICStat) Database.

Palgrave Macmillan, 1 New York Plaza, Ste. 4500, New York, NY, 10004-1562, USA, (800) 777-4643, orders@palgrave.com, https://www.palgrave.com/us; The Statesman's Yearbook, 2023.

Routledge - Taylor & Francis Group, 6000 Broken Sound Pkwy. NW, Ste. 300, Boca Raton, FL, 33487, USA, (800) 634-1420, (800) 634-7064, orders@taylorandfrancis.com, https://www.routledge.com/; The Europa World Year Book 2022.

United Nations Economic Commission for Africa (UNECA), PO Box 3001, Addis Ababa, ETH, ecainfo@uneca.org, https://www.uneca.org/; African Statistical Yearbook 2020.

The World Bank, 1818 H St. NW, Washington, DC, 20433, USA, (202) 473-1000, (202) 477-6391, eds03@worldbank.org, https://www.worldbank.org/; Algeria (report).

ALGERIA-UNEMPLOYMENT

International Labour Organization (ILO), 4 Rte. des Morillons, Geneva, CH-1211, SWI, ilo@ilo.org, https://www.ilo.org; NORMLEX Information System on International Labour Standards.

ALGERIA-URANIUM PRODUCTION AND CONSUMPTION

See ALGERIA-MINERAL INDUSTRIES

ALGERIA-VITAL STATISTICS

Palgrave Macmillan, 1 New York Plaza, Ste. 4500, New York, NY, 10004-1562, USA, (800) 777-4643, orders@palgrave.com, https://www.palgrave.com/us; The Statesman's Yearbook, 2023.

U.S. Census Bureau, 4600 Silver Hill Rd., Washington, DC, 20233, USA, (301) 763-4636, (800) 923-8282, https://www.census.gov; HIV/AIDS Surveillance Data Base.

United Nations Department of Economic and Social Affairs (DESA), Population Division, 2 United Nations Plz., Rm. DC2-1950, New York, NY, 10017, USA, (212) 963-3209, (212) 963-2147, population@un.org, https://www.un.org/development/desa/pd/; World Contraceptive Use 2021: Estimates and Projections of Family Planning Indicators and World Marriage Data 2019.

United Nations Statistics Division (UNSD), United Nations Plz., New York, NY, 10017, USA, (800) 253-9646, (212) 963-9851, statistics@un.org, https://unstats.un.org; Statistical Yearbook of the United Nations 2021 and United Nations Demographic Yearbook 2020.

The World Bank, 1818 H St. NW, Washington, DC, 20433, USA, (202) 473-1000, (202) 477-6391, eds03@worldbank.org, https://www.worldbank.org/; World Development Indicators (WDI) 2022.

ALGERIA-WAGES

International Labour Organization (ILO), 4 Rte. des Morillons, Geneva, CH-1211, SWI, ilo@ilo.org,

https://www.ilo.org; NORMLEX Information System on International Labour Standards.

United Nations Statistics Division (UNSD), United Nations Plz., New York, NY, 10017, USA, (800) 253-9646, (212) 963-9851, statistics@un.org, https://unstats.un.org; Statistical Yearbook of the United Nations 2021.

The World Bank, 1818 H St. NW, Washington, DC, 20433, USA, (202) 473-1000, (202) 477-6391, eds03@worldbank.org, https://www.worldbank.org/; Algeria (report).

ALGERIA-WEATHER

See ALGERIA-CLIMATE

ALGERIA-WHEAT PRODUCTION

See ALGERIA-CROPS

ALGERIA-WOOD AND WOOD PULP

See ALGERIA-FORESTS AND FORESTRY

ALGERIA-WOOL PRODUCTION

See ALGERIA-TEXTILE INDUSTRY

ALGERIA-ZINC AND ZINC ORE

See ALGERIA-MINERAL INDUSTRIES

ALGORITHMS

Center for Countering Digital Hate (CCDH), Langley House, Park Rd. , East Finchley, London, N2 8EY, GBR, info@counterhate.com, https://www.counterhate.com; Malgorithm: How Instagram's Algorithm Publishes Misinformation and Hate to Millions During a Pandemic.

ALLERGIES

Food Allergy Research & Education (FARE), 7901 Jones Branch Dr., Ste. 240, McLean, VA, 22102, USA, (800) 929-4040, (703) 691-3179, (703) 691-2713, https://www.foodallergy.org/; Food Allergy Facts and Statistics for the U.S..

U.S. Department of Health and Human Services (HHS), National Institutes of Health (NIH), National Institute of Allergy and Infectious Diseases (NIAID), Office of Communications and Government Relations, 5601 Fishers Ln., MSC 9806, Bethesda, MD, 20892-9806, USA, (866) 284-4107, (301) 496-5717, (301) 402-3573, ocpostoffice@niaid.nih.gov, https://www.niaid.nih.gov; Diseases & Conditions.

U.S. Department of Health and Human Services, Centers for Disease Control and Prevention (CDC), National Center for Health Statistics (NCHS), 3311 Toledo Rd., Hyattsville, MD, 20782-2064, USA, (800) 232-4636, (301) 458-4000, https://www.cdc.gov/nchs; FastStats - Statistics by Topic.

ALMONDS

U.S. Department of Agriculture (USDA), National Agricultural Statistics Service (USDA-NASS), 1400 Independence Ave. SW, Washington, DC, 20250, USA, (800) 727-9540, nass@nass.usda.gov, https://www.nass.usda.gov; Quick Stats.

ALTERNATIVE EDUCATION

Gap Year Association (GYA), PO Box 17427, Portland, OR, 97217, USA, (503) 206-7336, info@gapyearassociation.org, https://gapyearassociation.org/; Annual State of the Field Survey 2020-2021 and National Alumni Survey 2020 Report.

ALTERNATIVE LIFESTYLES

Numerator, 24 E Washington St., Ste. 1200, Chicago, IL, 60602, USA, (312) 585-3927, https://www.numerator.com; The Real Deal with Fake Meat: Understanding the Plant-Based Meat Alternative Buyer.

University of Michigan, Institute for Social Research, Population Studies Center, 426 Thompson St., 2nd Fl., Ann Arbor, MI, 48106-1248, USA, (734) 764-8354, (734) 615-9538, psc-director@umich.edu, https://www.psc.isr.umich.edu; How Do I Learn More About this?: Utilization and Trust of Psychedelic Information Sources Among People Naturalistically Using Psychedelics.

ALTERNATIVE MEDICINE

Global Lyme Alliance (GLA), 1290 E Main St., 3rd Fl., Stamford, CT, 06902, USA, (203) 969-1333, info@gla.org, https://globallymealliance.org/; Botanical Medicines Cryptolepsis Sanguinolenta, Artemisia Annua, Scutellaria Baicalensis, Polygonum Cuspidatum, and Alchornea Cordifolia Demonstrate Inhibitory Activity against Babesia Duncani.

ALUMINUM-CONSUMPTION

U.S. Department of the Interior (DOI), U.S. Geological Survey (USGS), National Minerals Information Center (NMIC), 12201 Sunrise Valley Dr., Reston, VA, 20192, USA, (703) 648-4920, (703) 648-7971, (703) 648-4995, sfortier@usgs.gov, https://www.usgs.gov/centers/nmic; Mineral Commodity Summaries 2022.

World Bureau of Metal Statistics (WBMS), 31 Star St., Ware, Hertfordshire, SG12 9BA, GBR, https://www.refinitiv.com/en/trading-solutions/world-bureau-metal-statistics; Long Term Production/Consumption Series - Aluminium.

ALUMINUM-EMPLOYMENT

U.S. Department of Labor (DOL), Bureau of Labor Statistics (BLS), Postal Square Bldg., 2 Massachusetts Ave. NE, Washington, DC, 20212-0001, USA, (202) 691-5200, (202) 691-7890, blsdata_staff@bls.gov, https://www.bls.gov; Industry-Occupation Matrix Data, By Occupation.

U.S. Department of the Interior (DOI), U.S. Geological Survey (USGS), National Minerals Information Center (NMIC), 12201 Sunrise Valley Dr., Reston, VA, 20192, USA, (703) 648-4920, (703) 648-7971, (703) 648-4995, sfortier@usgs.gov, https://www.usgs.gov/centers/nmic; Mineral Commodity Summaries 2022.

ALUMINUM-INTERNATIONAL TRADE

U.S. Census Bureau, International Trade Program, 4600 Silver Hill Rd., Washington, DC, 20233, USA, (800) 549-0595, eid.international.trade.data@census.gov, https://www.census.gov/foreign-trade; International Trade Data.

U.S. Department of the Interior (DOI), U.S. Geological Survey (USGS), National Minerals Information Center (NMIC), 12201 Sunrise Valley Dr., Reston, VA, 20192, USA, (703) 648-4920, (703) 648-7971, (703) 648-4995, sfortier@usgs.gov, https://www.usgs.gov/centers/nmic; Mineral Commodity Summaries 2022.

World Bureau of Metal Statistics (WBMS), 31 Star St., Ware, Hertfordshire, SG12 9BA, GBR, https://www.refinitiv.com/en/trading-solutions/world-bureau-metal-statistics; Long Term Production/Consumption Series - Aluminium.

ALUMINUM-PRICES

U.S. Department of Labor (DOL), Bureau of Labor Statistics (BLS), Postal Square Bldg., 2 Massachusetts Ave. NE, Washington, DC, 20212-0001, USA, (202) 691-5200, (202) 691-7890, blsdata_staff@bls.gov, https://www.bls.gov; Industry Data (Producer Price Index - PPI).

U.S. Department of the Interior (DOI), U.S. Geological Survey (USGS), National Minerals Information Center (NMIC), 12201 Sunrise Valley Dr., Reston, VA, 20192, USA, (703) 648-4920, (703) 648-7971, (703) 648-4995, sfortier@usgs.gov, https://www.usgs.gov/centers/nmic; Metal Industry Indicators (MII) and Mineral Commodity Summaries 2022.

ALUMINUM-PRODUCTION

Aluminum Association, 1400 Crystal Dr., Ste. 430, Arlington, VA, 22202, USA, (703) 358-2960, https://www.aluminum.org; Aluminum Association Statistics Portal; Aluminum Situation; and The Environmental Footprint of Semi-Fabricated Aluminum Products in North America Life Cycle Assessment.

U.S. Department of the Interior (DOI), U.S. Geological Survey (USGS), National Minerals Information Center (NMIC), 12201 Sunrise Valley Dr., Reston, VA, 20192, USA, (703) 648-4920, (703) 648-7971, (703) 648-4995, sfortier@usgs.gov, https://www.usgs.gov/centers/nmic; Mineral Industry Surveys (MIS).

ALUMINUM-RECYCLING

Aluminum Association, 1400 Crystal Dr., Ste. 430, Arlington, VA, 22202, USA, (703) 358-2960, https://www.aluminum.org; The Environmental Footprint of Semi-Fabricated Aluminum Products in North America Life Cycle Assessment.

U.S. Department of the Interior (DOI), U.S. Geological Survey (USGS), National Minerals Information Center (NMIC), 12201 Sunrise Valley Dr., Reston, VA, 20192, USA, (703) 648-4920, (703) 648-7971, (703) 648-4995, sfortier@usgs.gov, https://www.usgs.gov/centers/nmic; Mineral Industry Surveys (MIS).

U.S. Environmental Protection Agency (EPA), 1200 Pennsylvania Ave. NW, Washington, DC, 20460, USA, (202) 564-4700, https://www.epa.gov/; Advancing Sustainable Materials Management: Facts and Figures.

ALUMINUM-WORLD PRODUCTION

U.S. Department of the Interior (DOI), U.S. Geological Survey (USGS), National Minerals Information Center (NMIC), 12201 Sunrise Valley Dr., Reston, VA, 20192, USA, (703) 648-4920, (703) 648-7971, (703) 648-4995, sfortier@usgs.gov, https://www.usgs.gov/centers/nmic; Mineral Commodity Summaries 2022.

World Bureau of Metal Statistics (WBMS), 31 Star St., Ware, Hertfordshire, SG12 9BA, GBR, https://www.refinitiv.com/en/trading-solutions/world-bureau-metal-statistics; Long Term Production/Consumption Series - Aluminium.

ALZHEIMER'S DISEASE

AlzForum Foundation Inc., 7 Water St., Boston, MA, 02109, USA, contact@alzforum.org, https://www.alzforum.org; AlzForum.

Alzheimer's Association, 225 N Michigan Ave., 17th Fl., Chicago, IL, 60601, USA, (312) 335-8700, (800) 272-3900, (866) 699-1246, info@alz.org, https://www.alz.org/; Alzheimer's & Dementia: The Journal of the Alzheimer's Association and 2022 Alzheimer's Disease Facts and Figures.

Alzheimer's Disease International (ADI), 15 Blue Lion Pl., London, SE1 4PU, GBR, info@alzint.org, https://www.alzint.org; Global Perspective Newsletter; World Alzheimer Report 2020: Design, Dignity, Dementia: Dementia-Related Design and the Built Environment; World Alzheimer Report 2021: Journey to a Diagnosis of Dementia; and World Alzheimer Report 2022: Life After Diagnosis: Navigating Treatment, Care and Support.

Alzheimer's Foundation of America (AFA), 322 8th Ave., 16th Fl., New York, NY, 10001, USA, (866) 232-8484, (646) 638-1542, (646) 638-1546, info@alzfdn.org, https://alzfdn.org; unpublished data.

Boston University Alzheimer's Disease Center (ADC), 72 East Concord St., B-7800, Boston, MA, 02118, USA, (857) 364-2140, (888) 458-2823, (617) 358-6544, https://www.bu.edu/alzresearch/; unpublished data.

Dementia Singapore, 20 Bendemeer Rd. , No. 01-02, BS Bendemeer Centre, 339914, SGP, https://dementia.org.sg/; Voice of Dementia 2023.

National Alliance for Caregiving (NAC), 1730 Rhode Island Ave. NW, Ste. 812, Washington, DC, 20036, USA, (202) 918-1013, (202) 918-1014, info@caregiving.org, https://www.caregiving.org/; Caregiving in the U.S. 2020.

Rush Alzheimer's Disease Center (RADC), 1620 W Harrison St., Chicago, IL, 60612, USA, (312) 942-

0050, (312) 942-7100, https://www.rushu.rush.edu/research/departmental-research/rush-alzheimers-disease-center; RADC Research Resource Sharing Hub and Rush Memory Clinic Data Repository.

SAGE Publications, 2455 Teller Rd., Thousand Oaks, CA, 91320, USA, (800) 818-7243, (800) 583-2665, journals@sagepub.com, https://www.sagepub.com; American Journal of Alzheimer's Disease and Other Dementias.

Springer Nature, BMC, 1 New York Plaza, Ste. 4600, New York, NY, 10004-1562, USA, info@biomedcentral.com, https://www.biomedcentral.com/; Alzheimer's Research & Therapy.

U.S. Department of Health and Human Services (HHS), National Institutes of Health (NIH), National Institute on Aging (NIA), Alzheimer's Disease Education and Referral (ADEAR) Center, PO Box 8057, Gaithersburg, MD, 20898, USA, (800) 438-4380, adear@nia.nih.gov, https://www.nia.nih.gov/health/alzheimers; alzheimers.gov.

U.S. Department of Health and Human Services, Centers for Disease Control and Prevention (CDC), National Center for Health Statistics (NCHS), 3311 Toledo Rd., Hyattsville, MD, 20782-2064, USA, (800) 232-4636, (301) 458-4000, https://www.cdc.gov/nchs; FastStats - Statistics by Topic.

World Health Organization (WHO), Ave. Appia 20, Geneva, CH-1211, SWI, (202) 974-3000 (Telephone in U.S.), publications@who.int, https://www.who.int/; Noncommunicable Diseases Progress Monitor 2022.

AMBULATORY MEDICAL CARE

U.S. Department of Health and Human Services, Centers for Disease Control and Prevention (CDC), National Center for Health Statistics (NCHS), 3311 Toledo Rd., Hyattsville, MD, 20782-2064, USA, (800) 232-4636, (301) 458-4000, https://www.cdc.gov/nchs; FastStats - Statistics by Topic.

AMBULATORY MEDICAL CARE-EMPLOYERS

U.S. Census Bureau, 4600 Silver Hill Rd., Washington, DC, 20233, USA, (301) 763-4636, (800) 923-8282, https://www.census.gov; Economic Census, Nonemployer Statistics (NES) 2019.

AMBULATORY MEDICAL CARE-ESTABLISHMENTS

U.S. Census Bureau, 4600 Silver Hill Rd., Washington, DC, 20233, USA, (301) 763-4636, (800) 923-8282, https://www.census.gov; Economic Census, Nonemployer Statistics (NES) 2019.

AMBULATORY MEDICAL CARE-FINANCES

Internal Revenue Service (IRS), Statistics of Income Division (SOI), 1111 Constitution Ave. NW, K-Room 4100-123, Washington, DC, 20224-0002, USA, (202) 874-0410, (202) 874-0964, sis@irs.gov, https://www.irs.gov/uac/soi-tax-stats-statistics-of-income; Statistics of Income Bulletin.

AMBULATORY MEDICAL CARE-SALES-RECEIPTS

Internal Revenue Service (IRS), Statistics of Income Division (SOI), 1111 Constitution Ave. NW, K-Room 4100-123, Washington, DC, 20224-0002, USA, (202) 874-0410, (202) 874-0964, sis@irs.gov, https://www.irs.gov/uac/soi-tax-stats-statistics-of-income; Statistics of Income Bulletin.

AMERICAN INDIAN, ESKIMO, ALEUT POPULATION

U.S. Department of Health and Human Services (HHS), Indian Health Service (IHS), 5600 Fishers Ln., Mailstop 09E70, Rockville, MD, 20857, USA, (301) 443-1180, https://www.ihs.gov; Indian Health Service Fact Sheets.

U.S. Department of Housing and Urban Development (HUD), Office of Policy Development and Research (PD&R), PO Box 23268, Washington, DC, 20026-3268, USA, (800) 245-2691, (800) 927-7589 (TDD), (202) 708-9981, helpdesk@huduser.gov, https://www.huduser.gov; Assessment of American Indian, Alaska Native, and Native Hawaiian Housing Needs.

U.S. Department of the Interior (DOI), Office of Natural Resources Revenue (ONRR), 1849 C Street NW, Mail Stop 5134, Washington, DC, 20240, USA, (202) 513-0600, https://www.onrr.gov/; Natural Resources Revenue Data.

AMERICAN INDIAN, ESKIMO, ALEUT POPULATION-BUSINESS OWNERS

U.S. Census Bureau, 4600 Silver Hill Rd., Washington, DC, 20233, USA, (301) 763-4636, (800) 923-8282, https://www.census.gov; Survey of Business Owners (SBO).

AMERICAN INDIAN, ESKIMO, ALEUT POPULATION-CANCER

U.S. Department of Health and Human Services (HHS), National Institutes of Health (NIH), National Cancer Institute (NCI), 9609 Medical Center Dr., Bethesda, MD, 20850, USA, (800) 422-6237, nciinfo@nih.gov, https://www.cancer.gov; Annual Report to the Nation on the Status of Cancer and Surveillance, Epidemiology, and End Results (SEER) Incidence Data, 1975-2020.

AMERICAN INDIAN, ESKIMO, ALEUT POPULATION-CHILDREN UNDER EIGHTEEN YEARS OLD

Federal Interagency Forum on Child and Family Statistics (The Forum), USA, childstats@ed.gov, https://www.childstats.gov; America's Children: Key National Indicators of Well-Being, 2021.

National Indian Child Welfare Association (NICWA), 5100 SW Macadam Ave., Ste. 300, Portland, OR, 97239, USA, (503) 222-4044, info@nicwa.org, https://www.nicwa.org/; unpublished data.

U.S. Department of the Interior (DOI), Office of the Secretary, 1849 C St. NW, Washington, DC, 20240, USA, (202) 208-3100, https://www.doi.gov/office-of-the-secretary; Federal Indian Boarding School Initiative Investigative Report.

AMERICAN INDIAN, ESKIMO, ALEUT POPULATION-CHILDREN UNDER EIGHTEEN YEARS OLD-POVERTY

American Civil Liberties Union (ACLU), 125 Broad St. , 18th Fl., New York, NY, 10004, USA, (212) 549-2500, https://www.aclu.org/; 'If I Wasn't Poor, I Wouldn't Be Unfit': The Family Separation Crisis in the US Child Welfare System.

Bank Street Graduate School of Education, National Center for Children in Poverty (NCCP), 475 Riverside Dr., Ste. 1400, New York, NY, 10115, USA, info@nccp.org, https://www.nccp.org/; 50-State Demographics Data Generator.

Montana Office of Public Instruction, PO Box 202501, Helena, MT, 59620-2501, USA, (406) 444-3680, (406) 444-3693, https://opi.mt.gov/; Culture and Schools: American Indian Stakeholder Perspectives on the American Indian Student Achievement Gap.

AMERICAN INDIAN, ESKIMO, ALEUT POPULATION-CITIES

U.S. Census Bureau, 4600 Silver Hill Rd., Washington, DC, 20233, USA, (301) 763-4636, (800) 923-8282, https://www.census.gov; Explore Census Data; National Population by Characteristics: 2020-2022; and United States QuickFacts.

AMERICAN INDIAN, ESKIMO, ALEUT POPULATION-COLLEGE ENROLLMENT

U.S. Department of Education (ED), Institute of Education Sciences (IES), National Center for Education Statistics (NCES), Potomac Center Plaza, 550 12th St. SW, Washington, DC, 20202, USA, (202) 403-5551, https://nces.ed.gov/; Digest of Education Statistics, 2020.

AMERICAN INDIAN, ESKIMO, ALEUT POPULATION-CONSUMER EXPENDITURES

EnsembleIQ, 8550 W Bryn Mawr Ave., Ste. 200, Chicago, IL, 60631, USA, (877) 687-7321, https://ensembleiq.com/; 2021 Consumer Expenditures Report.

University of Georgia, Terry College of Business, Selig Center for Economic Growth, E201 Ivester Hall, 650 S Lumpkin St., Athens, GA, 30602, USA, (706) 425-9782, jhumphre@uga.edu, https://www.terry.uga.edu/about/selig//; The Multicultural Economy 2021.

AMERICAN INDIAN, ESKIMO, ALEUT POPULATION-CRIMES AGAINST

U.S. Department of Justice (DOJ), Office on Violence Against Women (OVW), 145 N St. NE, Ste. 10W.121, Washington, DC, 20530, USA, (202) 307-6026, (202) 307-2277 (TTY), (202) 305-2589, ovw.info@usdoj.gov, https://www.justice.gov/ovw; Office on Violence Against Women 2021 Tribal Consultation Report.

U.S. Department of the Interior (DOI), Office of the Secretary, 1849 C St. NW, Washington, DC, 20240, USA, (202) 208-3100, https://www.doi.gov/office-of-the-secretary; Federal Indian Boarding School Initiative Investigative Report.

AMERICAN INDIAN, ESKIMO, ALEUT POPULATION-CRIMINAL STATISTICS

U.S. Department of Justice (DOJ), Bureau of Justice Statistics (BJS), 810 7th St. NW, Washington, DC, 20531, USA, (202) 307-0765, askbjs@usdoj.gov, https://www.bjs.gov/; Annual Survey of Jails, 2019 and Jails in Indian Country, 2019-2020 and the Impact of COVID-19 on the Tribal Jail Population.

U.S. Department of Justice (DOJ), Federal Bureau of Investigation (FBI), 935 Pennsylvania Ave. NW, Washington, DC, 20535-0001, USA, (202) 324-3000, https://www.fbi.gov/; Crime in the United States 2019.

AMERICAN INDIAN, ESKIMO, ALEUT POPULATION-DEATHS AND DEATH RATES

The COVID Tracking Project at The Atlantic, support@covidtracking.com, https://covidtracking.com; The COVID Racial Data Tracker.

Governors Highway Safety Association (GHSA), 660 N Capitol St. NW, Ste. 220, Washington, DC, 20001-1642, USA, (202) 789-0942, headquarters@ghsa.org, https://www.ghsa.org/; An Analysis of Traffic Fatalities by Race and Ethnicity.

Massachusetts Institute of Technology (MIT), Living Wage Calculator, 77 Massachusetts Ave., Cambridge, MA, 02139, USA, (617) 324-6565, (617) 253-1000, amyglas@mit.edu, https://livingwage.mit.edu; Nothing New Under the Sun: Covid-19 Brings to Light Persistent Issues in the Navajo Nation.

U.S. Department of Health and Human Services (HHS), Indian Health Service (IHS), 5600 Fishers Ln., Mailstop 09E70, Rockville, MD, 20857, USA, (301) 443-1180, https://www.ihs.gov; Indian Health Service Fact Sheets.

U.S. Department of Health and Human Services, Centers for Disease Control and Prevention (CDC), 1600 Clifton Rd., Atlanta, GA, 30329-4027, USA, (800) 232-4636, (888) 232-6348 (TTY), cdcinfo@cdc.gov, https://www.cdc.gov; Provisional COVID-19 Deaths: Distribution of Deaths by Race and Hispanic Origin.

U.S. Department of the Interior (DOI), Office of the Secretary, 1849 C St. NW, Washington, DC, 20240, USA, (202) 208-3100, https://www.doi.gov/office-of-the-secretary; Federal Indian Boarding School Initiative Investigative Report.

AMERICAN INDIAN, ESKIMO, ALEUT POPULATION-DEGREES CONFERRED

U.S. Department of Education (ED), Institute of Education Sciences (IES), National Center for

Education Statistics (NCES), Potomac Center Plaza, 550 12th St. SW, Washington, DC, 20202, USA, (202) 403-5551, https://nces.ed.gov/; Digest of Education Statistics, 2020.

AMERICAN INDIAN, ESKIMO, ALEUT POPULATION-EDUCATIONAL ATTAINMENT

Alliance for Excellent Education (All4Ed), 1425 K St. NW, Ste. 700, Washington, DC, 20005, USA, (202) 828-0828, (202) 828-0821, https://all4ed.org; Ready for What? How Multiple Graduation Pathways Do - and Do Not - Signal Readiness for College and Careers.

Montana Office of Public Instruction, PO Box 202501, Helena, MT, 59620-2501, USA, (406) 444-3680, (406) 444-3693, https://opi.mt.gov/; Culture and Schools: American Indian Stakeholder Perspectives on the American Indian Student Achievement Gap.

U.S. Department of Education (ED), Institute of Education Sciences (IES), National Center for Education Statistics (NCES), Potomac Center Plaza, 550 12th St. SW, Washington, DC, 20202, USA, (202) 403-5551, https://nces.ed.gov/; National Indian Education Study (NIES).

University of California Los Angeles (UCLA), The Civil Rights Project, 8370 Math Sciences, PO Box 951521, Los Angeles, CA, 90095-1521, USA, crp@ucla.edu, https://www.civilrightsproject.ucla.edu/; The Walls Around Opportunity: The Failure of Colorblind Policy for Higher Education.

AMERICAN INDIAN, ESKIMO, ALEUT POPULATION-FOOD STAMP PARTICIPANTS

U.S. Department of Agriculture (USDA), Food and Nutrition Service (FNS), Braddock Metro Center II, 1320 Braddock Pl., Alexandria, VA, 22314, USA, (703) 305-2062, https://www.fns.usda.gov/; Characteristics of SNAP Households: FY 2019.

AMERICAN INDIAN, ESKIMO, ALEUT POPULATION-HEALTH CARE VISITS TO PROFESSIONALS

U.S. Department of Health and Human Services (HHS), Indian Health Service (IHS), 5600 Fishers Ln., Mailstop 09E70, Rockville, MD, 20857, USA, (301) 443-1180, https://www.ihs.gov; Indian Health Service Fact Sheets.

U.S. Department of Health and Human Services, Centers for Disease Control and Prevention (CDC), 1600 Clifton Rd., Atlanta, GA, 30329-4027, USA, (800) 232-4636, (888) 232-6348 (TTY), cdcinfo@cdc.gov, https://www.cdc.gov; Emergency Department Visits for COVID-19 by Race and Ethnicity - 13 States, October - December 2020 and Trends in Racial and Ethnic Disparities in COVID-19 Hospitalizations, by Region - United States, March - December 2020.

U.S. Department of Health and Human Services, Centers for Disease Control and Prevention (CDC), National Center for Health Statistics (NCHS), 3311 Toledo Rd., Hyattsville, MD, 20782-2064, USA, (800) 232-4636, (301) 458-4000, https://www.cdc.gov/nchs; Health, United States, 2020-2021.

AMERICAN INDIAN, ESKIMO, ALEUT POPULATION-HEALTH INSURANCE COVERAGE

U.S. Department of Health and Human Services (HHS), Indian Health Service (IHS), 5600 Fishers Ln., Mailstop 09E70, Rockville, MD, 20857, USA, (301) 443-1180, https://www.ihs.gov; Indian Health Service Fact Sheets.

U.S. Department of Health and Human Services, Centers for Disease Control and Prevention (CDC), National Center for Health Statistics (NCHS), 3311 Toledo Rd., Hyattsville, MD, 20782-2064, USA, (800) 232-4636, (301) 458-4000, https://www.cdc.gov/nchs; FastStats - Statistics by Topic.

AMERICAN INDIAN, ESKIMO, ALEUT POPULATION-HOSPITAL UTILIZATION

U.S. Department of Health and Human Services (HHS), Indian Health Service (IHS), 5600 Fishers Ln., Mailstop 09E70, Rockville, MD, 20857, USA, (301) 443-1180, https://www.ihs.gov; Indian Health Service Fact Sheets.

U.S. Department of Health and Human Services, Centers for Disease Control and Prevention (CDC), 1600 Clifton Rd., Atlanta, GA, 30329-4027, USA, (800) 232-4636, (888) 232-6348 (TTY), cdcinfo@cdc.gov, https://www.cdc.gov; Emergency Department Visits for COVID-19 by Race and Ethnicity - 13 States, October - December 2020 and Trends in Racial and Ethnic Disparities in COVID-19 Hospitalizations, by Region - United States, March - December 2020.

AMERICAN INDIAN, ESKIMO, ALEUT POPULATION-HOUSEHOLDS

U.S. Department of Housing and Urban Development (HUD), Office of Policy Development and Research (PD&R), PO Box 23268, Washington, DC, 20026-3268, USA, (800) 245-2691, (800) 927-7589 (TDD), (202) 708-9981, helpdesk@huduser.gov, https://www.huduser.gov; Assessment of American Indian, Alaska Native, and Native Hawaiian Housing Needs.

AMERICAN INDIAN, ESKIMO, ALEUT POPULATION-IMMUNIZATION OF CHILDREN

U.S. Department of Health and Human Services (HHS), Indian Health Service (IHS), 5600 Fishers Ln., Mailstop 09E70, Rockville, MD, 20857, USA, (301) 443-1180, https://www.ihs.gov; Indian Health Service Fact Sheets.

U.S. Department of Health and Human Services, Centers for Disease Control and Prevention (CDC), 1600 Clifton Rd., Atlanta, GA, 30329-4027, USA, (800) 232-4636, (888) 232-6348 (TTY), cdcinfo@cdc.gov, https://www.cdc.gov; Morbidity and Mortality Weekly Report (MMWR) and VaxView: Vaccination Coverage in the U.S..

U.S. Department of Health and Human Services, Centers for Disease Control and Prevention (CDC), National Center for Health Statistics (NCHS), 3311 Toledo Rd., Hyattsville, MD, 20782-2064, USA, (800) 232-4636, (301) 458-4000, https://www.cdc.gov/nchs; National Immunization Surveys (NIS).

AMERICAN INDIAN, ESKIMO, ALEUT POPULATION-INCOME

University of Georgia, Terry College of Business, Selig Center for Economic Growth, E201 Ivester Hall, 650 S Lumpkin St., Athens, GA, 30602, USA, (706) 425-9782, jhumphre@uga.edu, https://www.terry.uga.edu/about/selig//; The Multicultural Economy 2021.

AMERICAN INDIAN, ESKIMO, ALEUT POPULATION-MEDICAL CARE

Massachusetts Institute of Technology (MIT), Living Wage Calculator, 77 Massachusetts Ave., Cambridge, MA, 02139, USA, (617) 324-6565, (617) 253-1000, amyglas@mit.edu, https://livingwage.mit.edu; Nothing New Under the Sun: Covid-19 Brings to Light Persistent Issues in the Navajo Nation.

U.S. Department of Health and Human Services (HHS), Indian Health Service (IHS), 5600 Fishers Ln., Mailstop 09E70, Rockville, MD, 20857, USA, (301) 443-1180, https://www.ihs.gov; Indian Health Service Fact Sheets.

U.S. Department of Health and Human Services, Centers for Disease Control and Prevention (CDC), 1600 Clifton Rd., Atlanta, GA, 30329-4027, USA, (800) 232-4636, (888) 232-6348 (TTY), cdcinfo@cdc.gov, https://www.cdc.gov; Emergency Department Visits for COVID-19 by Race and Ethnicity - 13 States, October - December 2020 and Trends in Racial and Ethnic Disparities in COVID-19 Hospitalizations, by Region - United States, March - December 2020.

U.S. Department of Health and Human Services, Centers for Disease Control and Prevention (CDC), National Center for Health Statistics (NCHS), 3311 Toledo Rd., Hyattsville, MD, 20782-2064, USA, (800) 232-4636, (301) 458-4000, https://www.cdc.gov/nchs; FastStats - Statistics by Topic.

AMERICAN INDIAN, ESKIMO, ALEUT POPULATION-POVERTY

Massachusetts Institute of Technology (MIT), Living Wage Calculator, 77 Massachusetts Ave., Cambridge, MA, 02139, USA, (617) 324-6565, (617) 253-1000, amyglas@mit.edu, https://livingwage.mit.edu; Nothing New Under the Sun: Covid-19 Brings to Light Persistent Issues in the Navajo Nation.

National Indian Child Welfare Association (NICWA), 5100 SW Macadam Ave., Ste. 300, Portland, OR, 97239, USA, (503) 222-4044, info@nicwa.org, https://www.nicwa.org/; unpublished data.

AMERICAN INDIAN, ESKIMO, ALEUT POPULATION-SCHOOLS AND EDUCATION

Montana Office of Public Instruction, PO Box 202501, Helena, MT, 59620-2501, USA, (406) 444-3680, (406) 444-3693, https://opi.mt.gov/; Culture and Schools: American Indian Stakeholder Perspectives on the American Indian Student Achievement Gap.

U.S. Department of the Interior (DOI), Office of the Secretary, 1849 C St. NW, Washington, DC, 20240, USA, (202) 208-3100, https://www.doi.gov/office-of-the-secretary; Federal Indian Boarding School Initiative Investigative Report.

AMERICAN SAMOA-NATIONAL STATISTICAL OFFICE

American Samoa Government, Department of Commerce, A.P. Lutali Executive Office Bldg., 2nd Fl., Pago Pago, 96799, ASM, (684) 633-5155 (Dial from U.S.), (684) 699-9411 (Dial from U.S.), (684) 633-4195 (Fax from U.S.), info@doc.as, https://www.doc.as.gov/; Regional Data Reports (American Samoa).

AMERICAN SAMOA-PRIMARY STATISTICS SOURCES

American Samoa Government, Department of Commerce, A.P. Lutali Executive Office Bldg., 2nd Fl., Pago Pago, 96799, ASM, (684) 633-5155 (Dial from U.S.), (684) 699-9411 (Dial from U.S.), (684) 633-4195 (Fax from U.S.), info@doc.as, https://www.doc.as.gov/; Statistical Yearbook of American Samoa 2020.

AMERICAN SAMOA-AGRICULTURE

Euromonitor International, Inc., 1 N Dearborn St., Ste. 1700, Chicago, IL, 60602, USA, (312) 922-1115, (312) 922-1157, info-usa@euromonitor.com, https://www.euromonitor.com/; Geographies.

Palgrave Macmillan, 1 New York Plaza, Ste. 4500, New York, NY, 10004-1562, USA, (800) 777-4643, orders@palgrave.com, https://www.palgrave.com/us; The Statesman's Yearbook, 2023.

Routledge - Taylor & Francis Group, 6000 Broken Sound Pkwy. NW, Ste. 300, Boca Raton, FL, 33487, USA, (800) 634-1420, (800) 634-7064, orders@taylorandfrancis.com, https://www.routledge.com/; The Europa World Year Book 2022.

United Nations Food and Agricultural Organization (FAO), 2121 K St., Ste. 800B, Washington, DC, 20037, USA, (202) 653-2400 (Dial from U.S.), (202) 653-5760 (Fax from U.S.), fao-hq@fao.org, https://www.fao.org; AQUASTAT and The State of Food and Agriculture (SOFA) 2022.

United Nations Statistics Division (UNSD), United Nations Plz., New York, NY, 10017, USA, (800) 253-9646, (212) 963-9851, statistics@un.org, https://unstats.un.org; Statistical Yearbook of the United Nations 2021.

AMERICAN SAMOA-AIRLINES

Palgrave Macmillan, 1 New York Plaza, Ste. 4500, New York, NY, 10004-1562, USA, (800) 777-4643, orders@palgrave.com, https://www.palgrave.com/us; The Statesman's Yearbook, 2023.

Routledge - Taylor & Francis Group, 6000 Broken Sound Pkwy. NW, Ste. 300, Boca Raton, FL, 33487, USA, (800) 634-1420, (800) 634-7064, orders@taylorandfrancis.com, https://www.routledge.com/; The Europa World Year Book 2022.

AMERICAN SAMOA-ARMED FORCES

Central Intelligence Agency (CIA), Office of Public Affairs, Washington, DC, 20505, USA, (703) 482-0623, https://www.cia.gov; The World Factbook.

Stockholm International Peace Research Institute (SIPRI), Signalistgatan 9, Stockholm, SE 169 72, SWE, https://www.sipri.org/; SIPRI Arms Transfers Database and SIPRI Military Expenditure Database.

AMERICAN SAMOA-BANKS AND BANKING

Euromonitor International, Inc., 1 N Dearborn St., Ste. 1700, Chicago, IL, 60602, USA, (312) 922-1115, (312) 922-1157, info-usa@euromonitor.com, https://www.euromonitor.com/; Geographies.

AMERICAN SAMOA-BROADCASTING

Central Intelligence Agency (CIA), Office of Public Affairs, Washington, DC, 20505, USA, (703) 482-0623, https://www.cia.gov; The World Factbook.

Euromonitor International, Inc., 1 N Dearborn St., Ste. 1700, Chicago, IL, 60602, USA, (312) 922-1115, (312) 922-1157, info-usa@euromonitor.com, https://www.euromonitor.com/; Geographies.

Palgrave Macmillan, 1 New York Plaza, Ste. 4500, New York, NY, 10004-1562, USA, (800) 777-4643, orders@palgrave.com, https://www.palgrave.com/us; The Statesman's Yearbook, 2023.

WRTH Publications Limited, PO Box 290, Oxford, OX2 7FT, GBR, sales@wrth.com, https://www.wrth.com; World Radio TV Handbook 2023.

AMERICAN SAMOA-BUDGET

Central Intelligence Agency (CIA), Office of Public Affairs, Washington, DC, 20505, USA, (703) 482-0623, https://www.cia.gov; The World Factbook.

AMERICAN SAMOA-CLIMATE

Palgrave Macmillan, 1 New York Plaza, Ste. 4500, New York, NY, 10004-1562, USA, (800) 777-4643, orders@palgrave.com, https://www.palgrave.com/us; The Statesman's Yearbook, 2023.

AMERICAN SAMOA-COMMERCE

Palgrave Macmillan, 1 New York Plaza, Ste. 4500, New York, NY, 10004-1562, USA, (800) 777-4643, orders@palgrave.com, https://www.palgrave.com/us; The Statesman's Yearbook, 2023.

UK Data Service, University of Essex, Wivenhoe Park, Colchester, Essex, CO4 3SQ, GBR, https://ukdataservice.ac.uk/; International Aggregate Data.

AMERICAN SAMOA-COMMODITY EXCHANGES

Barchart, 209 W Jackson Blvd., 2nd Fl., Chicago, IL, 60606, USA, (877) 247-4394, commodities@barchart.com, https://www.barchart.com/cmdty; The cmdty Yearbook 2023; cmdtyStats: Commodity Statistics and Fundamental Data; cmdtyView: Commodity Index; and Commodity Data and Prices.

International Monetary Fund (IMF), 700 19th St. NW, Washington, DC, 20431, USA, (202) 623-7000, (202) 623-4661, publications@imf.org, https://www.imf.org; IMF Primary Commodity Prices.

AMERICAN SAMOA-CONSTRUCTION INDUSTRY

United Nations Statistics Division (UNSD), United Nations Plz., New York, NY, 10017, USA, (800) 253-9646, (212) 963-9851, statistics@un.org, https://unstats.un.org; Statistical Yearbook of the United Nations 2021.

AMERICAN SAMOA-CONSUMER PRICE INDEXES

International Labour Organization (ILO), 4 Rte. des Morillons, Geneva, CH-1211, SWI, ilo@ilo.org, https://www.ilo.org; NORMLEX Information System on International Labour Standards.

Routledge - Taylor & Francis Group, 6000 Broken Sound Pkwy. NW, Ste. 300, Boca Raton, FL, 33487, USA, (800) 634-1420, (800) 634-7064, orders@taylorandfrancis.com, https://www.routledge.com/; The Europa World Year Book 2022.

AMERICAN SAMOA-CORN INDUSTRY

See AMERICAN SAMOA-CROPS

AMERICAN SAMOA-CROPS

Palgrave Macmillan, 1 New York Plaza, Ste. 4500, New York, NY, 10004-1562, USA, (800) 777-4643, orders@palgrave.com, https://www.palgrave.com/us; The Statesman's Yearbook, 2023.

United Nations Food and Agricultural Organization (FAO), 2121 K St., Ste. 800B, Washington, DC, 20037, USA, (202) 653-2400 (Dial from U.S.), (202) 653-5760 (Fax from U.S.), fao-hq@fao.org, https://www.fao.org; The State of Food and Agriculture (SOFA) 2022.

AMERICAN SAMOA-DAIRY PROCESSING

Palgrave Macmillan, 1 New York Plaza, Ste. 4500, New York, NY, 10004-1562, USA, (800) 777-4643, orders@palgrave.com, https://www.palgrave.com/us; The Statesman's Yearbook, 2023.

United Nations Food and Agricultural Organization (FAO), 2121 K St., Ste. 800B, Washington, DC, 20037, USA, (202) 653-2400 (Dial from U.S.), (202) 653-5760 (Fax from U.S.), fao-hq@fao.org, https://www.fao.org; The State of Food and Agriculture (SOFA) 2022.

AMERICAN SAMOA-DEBTS, EXTERNAL

The World Bank, 1818 H St. NW, Washington, DC, 20433, USA, (202) 473-1000, (202) 477-6391, eds03@worldbank.org, https://www.worldbank.org/; Global Financial Development Report 2019-2020: Bank Regulation and Supervision a Decade after the Global Financial Crisis.

AMERICAN SAMOA-ECONOMIC CONDITIONS

Bernan Press, 15250 NBN Way, Bldg. C, Blue Ridge Summit, PA, 17214, USA, (301) 459-2255, (800) 865-3457, (800) 865-3450, customercare@bernan.com, https://rowman.com/Page/Bernan; World Economic Outlook, April 2022.

Central Intelligence Agency (CIA), Office of Public Affairs, Washington, DC, 20505, USA, (703) 482-0623, https://www.cia.gov; The World Factbook.

Euromonitor International, Inc., 1 N Dearborn St., Ste. 1700, Chicago, IL, 60602, USA, (312) 922-1115, (312) 922-1157, info-usa@euromonitor.com, https://www.euromonitor.com/; Geographies.

International Monetary Fund (IMF), 700 19th St. NW, Washington, DC, 20431, USA, (202) 623-7000, (202) 623-4661, publications@imf.org, https://www.imf.org; IMF Data and World Economic Outlook.

Palgrave Macmillan, 1 New York Plaza, Ste. 4500, New York, NY, 10004-1562, USA, (800) 777-4643, orders@palgrave.com, https://www.palgrave.com/us; The Statesman's Yearbook, 2023.

Routledge - Taylor & Francis Group, 6000 Broken Sound Pkwy. NW, Ste. 300, Boca Raton, FL, 33487, USA, (800) 634-1420, (800) 634-7064, orders@taylorandfrancis.com, https://www.routledge.com/; The Europa World Year Book 2022.

Secretariat of the Pacific Community (SPC), Statistics for Development Division (SDD), 95 Promenade Roger Laroque, Anse Vata , BP D5, Noumea, 98848, NCL, spc@spc.int, https://sdd.spc.int/; The Economic and Social Impact of the COVID-19 Pandemic on the Pacific Island Economies and Statistics for Development Division Data.

U.S. Census Bureau, 4600 Silver Hill Rd., Washington, DC, 20233, USA, (301) 763-4636, (800) 923-8282, https://www.census.gov; Economic Census of Island Areas.

United Nations Statistics Division (UNSD), United Nations Plz., New York, NY, 10017, USA, (800) 253-9646, (212) 963-9851, statistics@un.org, https://unstats.un.org; World Statistics Pocketbook 2021.

The World Bank, 1818 H St. NW, Washington, DC, 20433, USA, (202) 473-1000, (202) 477-6391, eds03@worldbank.org, https://www.worldbank.org/; Global Economic Monitor (GEM); Global Economic Prospects, June 2022; and The Global Findex Database 2021.

AMERICAN SAMOA-EDUCATION

Euromonitor International, Inc., 1 N Dearborn St., Ste. 1700, Chicago, IL, 60602, USA, (312) 922-1115, (312) 922-1157, info-usa@euromonitor.com, https://www.euromonitor.com/; Geographies.

Infoplease, c/o Sandbox Networks, Inc., 1 Lincoln St., 24th Fl., Boston, MA, 02111, USA, https://www.infoplease.com; Countries of the World.

Palgrave Macmillan, 1 New York Plaza, Ste. 4500, New York, NY, 10004-1562, USA, (800) 777-4643, orders@palgrave.com, https://www.palgrave.com/us; The Statesman's Yearbook, 2023.

Routledge - Taylor & Francis Group, 6000 Broken Sound Pkwy. NW, Ste. 300, Boca Raton, FL, 33487, USA, (800) 634-1420, (800) 634-7064, orders@taylorandfrancis.com, https://www.routledge.com/; The Europa World Year Book 2022.

UNESCO Institute for Statistics, C.P 250 Succursale H, Montreal, QC, H3G 2K8, CAN, (514) 343-6880 (Dial from U.S.), (514) 343-5740 (Fax from U.S.), uis.publications@unesco.org, http://uis.unesco.org/; Literacy and UIS.Stat.

United Nations Statistics Division (UNSD), United Nations Plz., New York, NY, 10017, USA, (800) 253-9646, (212) 963-9851, statistics@un.org, https://unstats.un.org; Millennium Development Goal Indicators.

AMERICAN SAMOA-ELECTRICITY

United Nations Statistics Division (UNSD), United Nations Plz., New York, NY, 10017, USA, (800) 253-9646, (212) 963-9851, statistics@un.org, https://unstats.un.org; Statistical Yearbook of the United Nations 2021.

AMERICAN SAMOA-EMPLOYMENT

International Labour Organization (ILO), 4 Rte. des Morillons, Geneva, CH-1211, SWI, ilo@ilo.org, https://www.ilo.org; NORMLEX Information System on International Labour Standards.

UK Data Service, University of Essex, Wivenhoe Park, Colchester, Essex, CO4 3SQ, GBR, https://ukdataservice.ac.uk/; International Aggregate Data.

AMERICAN SAMOA-ENVIRONMENTAL CONDITIONS

DSI Data Service & Information, Xantener Strasse 51a, Rheinberg, D-47495, GER, dsi@dsidata.com, https://www.dsidata.com/; Global Environmental Database.

United Nations Statistics Division (UNSD), United Nations Plz., New York, NY, 10017, USA, (800) 253-9646, (212) 963-9851, statistics@un.org, https://unstats.un.org; World Statistics Pocketbook 2021.

AMERICAN SAMOA-EXPORTS

Central Intelligence Agency (CIA), Office of Public Affairs, Washington, DC, 20505, USA, (703) 482-0623, https://www.cia.gov; The World Factbook.

AMERICAN SAMOA-FERTILIZER INDUSTRY

United Nations Food and Agricultural Organization (FAO), 2121 K St., Ste. 800B, Washington, DC, 20037, USA, (202) 653-2400 (Dial from U.S.), (202) 653-5760 (Fax from U.S.), fao-hq@fao.org, https://www.fao.org; The State of Food and Agriculture (SOFA) 2022.

AMERICAN SAMOA-FETAL MORTALITY

See AMERICAN SAMOA-MORTALITY

AMERICAN SAMOA-FINANCE, PUBLIC

Bernan Press, 15250 NBN Way, Bldg. C, Blue Ridge Summit, PA, 17214, USA, (301) 459-2255, (800) 865-3457, (800) 865-3450, customercare@bernan.com, https://rowman.com/Page/Bernan; National Accounts Statistics: Analysis of Main Aggregates 2020.

International Monetary Fund (IMF), 700 19th St. NW, Washington, DC, 20431, USA, (202) 623-7000, (202) 623-4661, publications@imf.org, https://www.imf.org; International Financial Statistics (IFS) and Regional Economic Outlook.

Routledge - Taylor & Francis Group, 6000 Broken Sound Pkwy. NW, Ste. 300, Boca Raton, FL, 33487, USA, (800) 634-1420, (800) 634-7064, orders@taylorandfrancis.com, https://www.routledge.com/; The Europa World Year Book 2022.

United Nations Statistics Division (UNSD), United Nations Plz., New York, NY, 10017, USA, (800) 253-9646, (212) 963-9851, statistics@un.org, https://unstats.un.org; National Accounts Main Aggregates Database and National Accounts Statistics: Main Aggregates and Detailed Tables.

AMERICAN SAMOA-FISHERIES

Palgrave Macmillan, 1 New York Plaza, Ste. 4500, New York, NY, 10004-1562, USA, (800) 777-4643, orders@palgrave.com, https://www.palgrave.com/us; The Statesman's Yearbook, 2023.

Routledge - Taylor & Francis Group, 6000 Broken Sound Pkwy. NW, Ste. 300, Boca Raton, FL, 33487, USA, (800) 634-1420, (800) 634-7064, orders@taylorandfrancis.com, https://www.routledge.com/; The Europa World Year Book 2022.

United Nations Food and Agricultural Organization (FAO), 2121 K St., Ste. 800B, Washington, DC, 20037, USA, (202) 653-2400 (Dial from U.S.), (202) 653-5760 (Fax from U.S.), fao-hq@fao.org, https://www.fao.org; FAO Yearbook of Fishery and Aquaculture Statistics 2019; Fishery Statistical Collections Global Capture Production; FishStatJ; and The State of Food and Agriculture (SOFA) 2022.

AMERICAN SAMOA-FOOD

United Nations Food and Agricultural Organization (FAO), 2121 K St., Ste. 800B, Washington, DC, 20037, USA, (202) 653-2400 (Dial from U.S.), (202) 653-5760 (Fax from U.S.), fao-hq@fao.org, https://www.fao.org; The State of Food and Agriculture (SOFA) 2022.

AMERICAN SAMOA-FORESTS AND FORESTRY

UNESCO Institute for Statistics, C.P 250 Succursale H, Montreal, QC, H3G 2K8, CAN, (514) 343-6880 (Dial from U.S.), (514) 343-5740 (Fax from U.S.), uis.publications@unesco.org, http://uis.unesco.org/; UIS.Stat.

United Nations Food and Agricultural Organization (FAO), 2121 K St., Ste. 800B, Washington, DC, 20037, USA, (202) 653-2400 (Dial from U.S.), (202) 653-5760 (Fax from U.S.), fao-hq@fao.org, https://www.fao.org; The State of Food and Agriculture (SOFA) 2022.

United Nations Statistics Division (UNSD), United Nations Plz., New York, NY, 10017, USA, (800) 253-9646, (212) 963-9851, statistics@un.org, https://unstats.un.org; Statistical Yearbook of the United Nations 2021.

AMERICAN SAMOA-HOUSING

Euromonitor International, Inc., 1 N Dearborn St., Ste. 1700, Chicago, IL, 60602, USA, (312) 922-1115, (312) 922-1157, info-usa@euromonitor.com, https://www.euromonitor.com/; Geographies.

AMERICAN SAMOA-IMPORTS

Central Intelligence Agency (CIA), Office of Public Affairs, Washington, DC, 20505, USA, (703) 482-0623, https://www.cia.gov; The World Factbook.

AMERICAN SAMOA-INDUSTRIES

Central Intelligence Agency (CIA), Office of Public Affairs, Washington, DC, 20505, USA, (703) 482-0623, https://www.cia.gov; The World Factbook.

Euromonitor International, Inc., 1 N Dearborn St., Ste. 1700, Chicago, IL, 60602, USA, (312) 922-1115, (312) 922-1157, info-usa@euromonitor.com, https://www.euromonitor.com/; Geographies.

International Labour Organization (ILO), 4 Rte. des Morillons, Geneva, CH-1211, SWI, ilo@ilo.org, https://www.ilo.org; NORMLEX Information System on International Labour Standards.

Palgrave Macmillan, 1 New York Plaza, Ste. 4500, New York, NY, 10004-1562, USA, (800) 777-4643, orders@palgrave.com, https://www.palgrave.com/us; The Statesman's Yearbook, 2023.

Routledge - Taylor & Francis Group, 6000 Broken Sound Pkwy. NW, Ste. 300, Boca Raton, FL, 33487, USA, (800) 634-1420, (800) 634-7064, orders@taylorandfrancis.com, https://www.routledge.com/; The Europa World Year Book 2022.

United Nations Industrial Development Organization (UNIDO), 1 United Nations Plz., Rm. DC1-1118, New York, NY, 10017, USA, (212) 963-6890, (212) 963 6885, (212) 963-7904, office.newyork@unido.org, https://www.unido.org/; Industrial Statistics Databases and International Yearbook of Industrial Statistics 2021.

AMERICAN SAMOA-INFANT AND MATERNAL MORTALITY

See AMERICAN SAMOA-MORTALITY

AMERICAN SAMOA-INTERNATIONAL TRADE

Euromonitor International, Inc., 1 N Dearborn St., Ste. 1700, Chicago, IL, 60602, USA, (312) 922-1115, (312) 922-1157, info-usa@euromonitor.com, https://www.euromonitor.com/; Geographies.

Palgrave Macmillan, 1 New York Plaza, Ste. 4500, New York, NY, 10004-1562, USA, (800) 777-4643, orders@palgrave.com, https://www.palgrave.com/us; The Statesman's Yearbook, 2023.

Routledge - Taylor & Francis Group, 6000 Broken Sound Pkwy. NW, Ste. 300, Boca Raton, FL, 33487, USA, (800) 634-1420, (800) 634-7064, orders@taylorandfrancis.com, https://www.routledge.com/; The Europa World Year Book 2022.

United Nations Conference on Trade and Development (UNCTAD), Palais des Nations, Geneva, 1211, SWI, (212) 963-6896, unctadinfo@unctad.org, https://unctad.org; Trade and Development Report 2021.

United Nations Food and Agricultural Organization (FAO), 2121 K St., Ste. 800B, Washington, DC, 20037, USA, (202) 653-2400 (Dial from U.S.), (202) 653-5760 (Fax from U.S.), fao-hq@fao.org, https://www.fao.org; The State of Food and Agriculture (SOFA) 2022.

United Nations Statistics Division (UNSD), United Nations Plz., New York, NY, 10017, USA, (800) 253-9646, (212) 963-9851, statistics@un.org, https://unstats.un.org; Statistical Yearbook of the United Nations 2021.

World Trade Organization (WTO), Ctre. William Rappard, Rue de Lausanne 154, Case postale, Geneva, CH-1211, SWI, enquiries@wto.org, https://www.wto.org; World Trade Statistical Review 2022.

AMERICAN SAMOA-INTERNET USERS

International Telecommunication Union (ITU), Place des Nations, Geneva, CH-1211, SWI, itumail@itu.int, https://www.itu.int; Global Connectivity Report 2022; World Telecommunication/ICT Indicators Database 2021; and Yearbook of Statistics 2019.

AMERICAN SAMOA-LABOR

Central Intelligence Agency (CIA), Office of Public Affairs, Washington, DC, 20505, USA, (703) 482-0623, https://www.cia.gov; The World Factbook.

Euromonitor International, Inc., 1 N Dearborn St., Ste. 1700, Chicago, IL, 60602, USA, (312) 922-1115, (312) 922-1157, info-usa@euromonitor.com, https://www.euromonitor.com/; Geographies.

International Labour Organization (ILO), 4 Rte. des Morillons, Geneva, CH-1211, SWI, ilo@ilo.org, https://www.ilo.org; NORMLEX Information System on International Labour Standards.

Palgrave Macmillan, 1 New York Plaza, Ste. 4500, New York, NY, 10004-1562, USA, (800) 777-4643, orders@palgrave.com, https://www.palgrave.com/us; The Statesman's Yearbook, 2023.

United Nations Food and Agricultural Organization (FAO), 2121 K St., Ste. 800B, Washington, DC, 20037, USA, (202) 653-2400 (Dial from U.S.), (202) 653-5760 (Fax from U.S.), fao-hq@fao.org, https://www.fao.org; The State of Food and Agriculture (SOFA) 2022.

AMERICAN SAMOA-LAND USE

United Nations Statistics Division (UNSD), United Nations Plz., New York, NY, 10017, USA, (800) 253-9646, (212) 963-9851, statistics@un.org, https://unstats.un.org; Millennium Development Goal Indicators.

AMERICAN SAMOA-LIBRARIES

UNESCO Institute for Statistics, C.P 250 Succursale H, Montreal, QC, H3G 2K8, CAN, (514) 343-6880 (Dial from U.S.), (514) 343-5740 (Fax from U.S.), uis.publications@unesco.org, http://uis.unesco.org/; UIS.Stat.

AMERICAN SAMOA-LIFE EXPECTANCY

United Nations Department of Economic and Social Affairs (DESA), Population Division, 2 United Nations Plz., Rm. DC2-1950, New York, NY, 10017, USA, (212) 963-3209, (212) 963-2147, population@un.org, https://www.un.org/development/desa/pd/; World Population Ageing 2020 Highlights.

United Nations Statistics Division (UNSD), United Nations Plz., New York, NY, 10017, USA, (800) 253-9646, (212) 963-9851, statistics@un.org, https://unstats.un.org; Millennium Development Goal Indicators.

AMERICAN SAMOA-LITERACY

Euromonitor International, Inc., 1 N Dearborn St., Ste. 1700, Chicago, IL, 60602, USA, (312) 922-1115, (312) 922-1157, info-usa@euromonitor.com, https://www.euromonitor.com/; Geographies.

UNESCO Institute for Statistics, C.P 250 Succursale H, Montreal, QC, H3G 2K8, CAN, (514) 343-6880 (Dial from U.S.), (514) 343-5740 (Fax from U.S.), uis.publications@unesco.org, http://uis.unesco.org/; Literacy.

AMERICAN SAMOA-LIVESTOCK

Palgrave Macmillan, 1 New York Plaza, Ste. 4500, New York, NY, 10004-1562, USA, (800) 777-4643, orders@palgrave.com, https://www.palgrave.com/us; The Statesman's Yearbook, 2023.

Routledge - Taylor & Francis Group, 6000 Broken Sound Pkwy. NW, Ste. 300, Boca Raton, FL, 33487, USA, (800) 634-1420, (800) 634-7064, orders@taylorandfrancis.com, https://www.routledge.com/; The Europa World Year Book 2022.

United Nations Food and Agricultural Organization (FAO), 2121 K St., Ste. 800B, Washington, DC, 20037, USA, (202) 653-2400 (Dial from U.S.), (202) 653-5760 (Fax from U.S.), fao-hq@fao.org, https://www.fao.org; The State of Food and Agriculture (SOFA) 2022.

AMERICAN SAMOA-MARRIAGE

Routledge - Taylor & Francis Group, 6000 Broken Sound Pkwy. NW, Ste. 300, Boca Raton, FL, 33487, USA, (800) 634-1420, (800) 634-7064, orders@taylorandfrancis.com, https://www.routledge.com/; The Europa World Year Book 2022.

United Nations Statistics Division (UNSD), United Nations Plz., New York, NY, 10017, USA, (800) 253-9646, (212) 963-9851, statistics@un.org, https://unstats.un.org; Statistical Yearbook of the United Nations 2021.

AMERICAN SAMOA-MINERAL INDUSTRIES

Routledge - Taylor & Francis Group, 6000 Broken Sound Pkwy. NW, Ste. 300, Boca Raton, FL, 33487,

USA, (800) 634-1420, (800) 634-7064, orders@taylorandfrancis.com, https://www.routledge.com/; The Europa World Year Book 2022.

United Nations Conference on Trade and Development (UNCTAD), Palais des Nations, Geneva, 1211, SWI, (212) 963-6896, unctadinfo@unctad.org, https://unctad.org; Trade and Development Report 2021.

AMERICAN SAMOA-MORTALITY

United Nations Statistics Division (UNSD), United Nations Plz., New York, NY, 10017, USA, (800) 253-9646, (212) 963-9851, statistics@un.org, https://unstats.un.org; Millennium Development Goal Indicators; Statistical Yearbook of the United Nations 2021; and World Statistics Pocketbook 2021.

World Health Organization (WHO), Ave. Appia 20, Geneva, CH-1211, SWI, (202) 974-3000 (Telephone in U.S.), publications@who.int, https://www.who.int/; Global Health Observatory (GHO).

AMERICAN SAMOA-NUTRITION

United Nations Food and Agricultural Organization (FAO), 2121 K St., Ste. 800B, Washington, DC, 20037, USA, (202) 653-2400 (Dial from U.S.), (202) 653-5760 (Fax from U.S.), fao-hq@fao.org, https://www.fao.org; The State of Food and Agriculture (SOFA) 2022.

United Nations Statistics Division (UNSD), United Nations Plz., New York, NY, 10017, USA, (800) 253-9646, (212) 963-9851, statistics@un.org, https://unstats.un.org; Millennium Development Goal Indicators.

AMERICAN SAMOA-PESTICIDES

United Nations Food and Agricultural Organization (FAO), 2121 K St., Ste. 800B, Washington, DC, 20037, USA, (202) 653-2400 (Dial from U.S.), (202) 653-5760 (Fax from U.S.), fao-hq@fao.org, https://www.fao.org; The State of Food and Agriculture (SOFA) 2022.

AMERICAN SAMOA-PETROLEUM INDUSTRY AND TRADE

United Nations Food and Agricultural Organization (FAO), 2121 K St., Ste. 800B, Washington, DC, 20037, USA, (202) 653-2400 (Dial from U.S.), (202) 653-5760 (Fax from U.S.), fao-hq@fao.org, https://www.fao.org; The State of Food and Agriculture (SOFA) 2022.

AMERICAN SAMOA-POPULATION

Central Intelligence Agency (CIA), Office of Public Affairs, Washington, DC, 20505, USA, (703) 482-0623, https://www.cia.gov; The World Factbook.

Infoplease, c/o Sandbox Networks, Inc., 1 Lincoln St., 24th Fl., Boston, MA, 02111, USA, https://www.infoplease.com; Countries of the World.

International Labour Organization (ILO), 4 Rte. des Morillons, Geneva, CH-1211, SWI, ilo@ilo.org, https://www.ilo.org; NORMLEX Information System on International Labour Standards.

Palgrave Macmillan, 1 New York Plaza, Ste. 4500, New York, NY, 10004-1562, USA, (800) 777-4643, orders@palgrave.com, https://www.palgrave.com/us; The Statesman's Yearbook, 2023.

Routledge - Taylor & Francis Group, 6000 Broken Sound Pkwy. NW, Ste. 300, Boca Raton, FL, 33487, USA, (800) 634-1420, (800) 634-7064, orders@taylorandfrancis.com, https://www.routledge.com/; The Europa World Year Book 2022.

UK Data Service, University of Essex, Wivenhoe Park, Colchester, Essex, CO4 3SQ, GBR, https://ukdataservice.ac.uk/; International Aggregate Data.

United Nations Department of Economic and Social Affairs (DESA), Population Division, 2 United Nations Plz., Rm. DC2-1950, New York, NY, 10017, USA, (212) 963-3209, (212) 963-2147, population@un.org, https://www.un.org/development/desa/pd/; Revision of World Urbanization Prospects and World Population Ageing 2020 Highlights.

United Nations Statistics Division (UNSD), United Nations Plz., New York, NY, 10017, USA, (800) 253-9646, (212) 963-9851, statistics@un.org, https://unstats.un.org; Statistical Yearbook of the United Nations 2021 and World Statistics Pocketbook 2021.

The World Bank, 1818 H St. NW, Washington, DC, 20433, USA, (202) 473-1000, (202) 477-6391, eds03@worldbank.org, https://www.worldbank.org/; The Global Findex Database 2021.

AMERICAN SAMOA-POPULATION DENSITY

Central Intelligence Agency (CIA), Office of Public Affairs, Washington, DC, 20505, USA, (703) 482-0623, https://www.cia.gov; The World Factbook.

Palgrave Macmillan, 1 New York Plaza, Ste. 4500, New York, NY, 10004-1562, USA, (800) 777-4643, orders@palgrave.com, https://www.palgrave.com/us; The Statesman's Yearbook, 2023.

Routledge - Taylor & Francis Group, 6000 Broken Sound Pkwy. NW, Ste. 300, Boca Raton, FL, 33487, USA, (800) 634-1420, (800) 634-7064, orders@taylorandfrancis.com, https://www.routledge.com/; The Europa World Year Book 2022.

AMERICAN SAMOA-POWER RESOURCES

Euromonitor International, Inc., 1 N Dearborn St., Ste. 1700, Chicago, IL, 60602, USA, (312) 922-1115, (312) 922-1157, info-usa@euromonitor.com, https://www.euromonitor.com/; Geographies.

Palgrave Macmillan, 1 New York Plaza, Ste. 4500, New York, NY, 10004-1562, USA, (800) 777-4643, orders@palgrave.com, https://www.palgrave.com/us; The Statesman's Yearbook, 2023.

United Nations Food and Agricultural Organization (FAO), 2121 K St., Ste. 800B, Washington, DC, 20037, USA, (202) 653-2400 (Dial from U.S.), (202) 653-5760 (Fax from U.S.), fao-hq@fao.org, https://www.fao.org; The State of Food and Agriculture (SOFA) 2022.

United Nations Statistics Division (UNSD), United Nations Plz., New York, NY, 10017, USA, (800) 253-9646, (212) 963-9851, statistics@un.org, https://unstats.un.org; Energy Statistics Yearbook 2019; Statistical Yearbook of the United Nations 2021; and World Statistics Pocketbook 2021.

AMERICAN SAMOA-PRICES

Euromonitor International, Inc., 1 N Dearborn St., Ste. 1700, Chicago, IL, 60602, USA, (312) 922-1115, (312) 922-1157, info-usa@euromonitor.com, https://www.euromonitor.com/; Geographies.

AMERICAN SAMOA-PUBLIC HEALTH

Euromonitor International, Inc., 1 N Dearborn St., Ste. 1700, Chicago, IL, 60602, USA, (312) 922-1115, (312) 922-1157, info-usa@euromonitor.com, https://www.euromonitor.com/; Geographies.

U.S. Census Bureau, 4600 Silver Hill Rd., Washington, DC, 20233, USA, (301) 763-4636, (800) 923-8282, https://www.census.gov; HIV/AIDS Surveillance Data Base.

United Nations Department of Economic and Social Affairs (DESA), Population Division, 2 United Nations Plz., Rm. DC2-1950, New York, NY, 10017, USA, (212) 963-3209, (212) 963-2147, population@un.org, https://www.un.org/development/desa/pd/; World Fertility Data 2019.

United Nations Statistics Division (UNSD), United Nations Plz., New York, NY, 10017, USA, (800) 253-9646, (212) 963-9851, statistics@un.org, https://unstats.un.org; Millennium Development Goal Indicators and Statistical Yearbook of the United Nations 2021.

World Health Organization (WHO), Ave. Appia 20, Geneva, CH-1211, SWI, (202) 974-3000 (Telephone in U.S.), publications@who.int, https://www.who.int/; Global Health Observatory (GHO) and Health Statistics and Information Systems.

AMERICAN SAMOA-PUBLISHERS AND PUBLISHING

UNESCO Institute for Statistics, C.P 250 Succursale H, Montreal, QC, H3G 2K8, CAN, (514) 343-6880 (Dial from U.S.), (514) 343-5740 (Fax from U.S.), uis.publications@unesco.org, http://uis.unesco.org/; UIS.Stat.

AMERICAN SAMOA-RELIGION

Central Intelligence Agency (CIA), Office of Public Affairs, Washington, DC, 20505, USA, (703) 482-0623, https://www.cia.gov; The World Factbook.

Palgrave Macmillan, 1 New York Plaza, Ste. 4500, New York, NY, 10004-1562, USA, (800) 777-4643, orders@palgrave.com, https://www.palgrave.com/us; The Statesman's Yearbook, 2023.

AMERICAN SAMOA-RETAIL TRADE

Euromonitor International, Inc., 1 N Dearborn St., Ste. 1700, Chicago, IL, 60602, USA, (312) 922-1115, (312) 922-1157, info-usa@euromonitor.com, https://www.euromonitor.com/; Geographies.

AMERICAN SAMOA-SHIPPING

Routledge - Taylor & Francis Group, 6000 Broken Sound Pkwy. NW, Ste. 300, Boca Raton, FL, 33487, USA, (800) 634-1420, (800) 634-7064, orders@taylorandfrancis.com, https://www.routledge.com/; The Europa World Year Book 2022.

United Nations Statistics Division (UNSD), United Nations Plz., New York, NY, 10017, USA, (800) 253-9646, (212) 963-9851, statistics@un.org, https://unstats.un.org; Statistical Yearbook of the United Nations 2021.

AMERICAN SAMOA-TELEPHONE

Routledge - Taylor & Francis Group, 6000 Broken Sound Pkwy. NW, Ste. 300, Boca Raton, FL, 33487, USA, (800) 634-1420, (800) 634-7064, orders@taylorandfrancis.com, https://www.routledge.com/; The Europa World Year Book 2022.

United Nations Statistics Division (UNSD), United Nations Plz., New York, NY, 10017, USA, (800) 253-9646, (212) 963-9851, statistics@un.org, https://unstats.un.org; World Statistics Pocketbook 2021.

AMERICAN SAMOA-TOURISM

Euromonitor International, Inc., 1 N Dearborn St., Ste. 1700, Chicago, IL, 60602, USA, (312) 922-1115, (312) 922-1157, info-usa@euromonitor.com, https://www.euromonitor.com/; Geographies.

Routledge - Taylor & Francis Group, 6000 Broken Sound Pkwy. NW, Ste. 300, Boca Raton, FL, 33487, USA, (800) 634-1420, (800) 634-7064, orders@taylorandfrancis.com, https://www.routledge.com/; The Europa World Year Book 2022.

United Nations World Tourism Organization (UNWTO), Calle Poeta Joan Maragall 42, Madrid, 28020, SPA, info@unwto.org, https://www.unwto.org/; Yearbook of Tourism Statistics, 2021 Edition.

AMERICAN SAMOA-TRADE

See AMERICAN SAMOA-INTERNATIONAL TRADE

AMERICAN SAMOA-TRANSPORTATION

Central Intelligence Agency (CIA), Office of Public Affairs, Washington, DC, 20505, USA, (703) 482-0623, https://www.cia.gov; The World Factbook.

Euromonitor International, Inc., 1 N Dearborn St., Ste. 1700, Chicago, IL, 60602, USA, (312) 922-1115, (312) 922-1157, info-usa@euromonitor.com, https://www.euromonitor.com/; Geographies.

Palgrave Macmillan, 1 New York Plaza, Ste. 4500, New York, NY, 10004-1562, USA, (800) 777-4643, orders@palgrave.com, https://www.palgrave.com/us; The Statesman's Yearbook, 2023.

Routledge - Taylor & Francis Group, 6000 Broken Sound Pkwy. NW, Ste. 300, Boca Raton, FL, 33487, USA, (800) 634-1420, (800) 634-7064,

orders@taylorandfrancis.com, https://www.routledge.com/; The Europa World Year Book 2022.

AMERICAN SAMOA-UNEMPLOYMENT

International Labour Organization (ILO), 4 Rte. des Morillons, Geneva, CH-1211, SWI, ilo@ilo.org, https://www.ilo.org; NORMLEX Information System on International Labour Standards.

Palgrave Macmillan, 1 New York Plaza, Ste. 4500, New York, NY, 10004-1562, USA, (800) 777-4643, orders@palgrave.com, https://www.palgrave.com/us; The Statesman's Yearbook, 2023.

United Nations Statistics Division (UNSD), United Nations Plz., New York, NY, 10017, USA, (800) 253-9646, (212) 963-9851, statistics@un.org, https://unstats.un.org; Statistical Yearbook of the United Nations 2021.

AMERICAN SAMOA-VITAL STATISTICS

U.S. Census Bureau, 4600 Silver Hill Rd., Washington, DC, 20233, USA, (301) 763-4636, (800) 923-8282, https://www.census.gov; HIV/AIDS Surveillance Data Base.

United Nations Department of Economic and Social Affairs (DESA), Population Division, 2 United Nations Plz., Rm. DC2-1950, New York, NY, 10017, USA, (212) 963-3209, (212) 963-2147, population@un.org, https://www.un.org/development/desa/pd/; World Contraceptive Use 2021: Estimates and Projections of Family Planning Indicators and World Marriage Data 2019.

United Nations Statistics Division (UNSD), United Nations Plz., New York, NY, 10017, USA, (800) 253-9646, (212) 963-9851, statistics@un.org, https://unstats.un.org; Statistical Yearbook of the United Nations 2021 and United Nations Demographic Yearbook 2020.

AMERICAN SAMOA-WAGES

International Labour Organization (ILO), 4 Rte. des Morillons, Geneva, CH-1211, SWI, ilo@ilo.org, https://www.ilo.org; NORMLEX Information System on International Labour Standards.

AMERICAN SIGN LANGUAGE

Modern Language Association (MLA) Academic Program Services (MAPS), 85 Broad St., Ste. 500, New York, NY, 10004-2434, USA, (646) 576-5000, jutell@mla.org, https://www.maps.mla.org; ADFL Bulletin.

AMERICAN STOCK EXCHANGE

U.S. Securities and Exchange Commission (SEC), 100 F St. NE, Washington, DC, 20549, USA, (202) 551-6551, (202) 551-4119, https://www.sec.gov; 2021 Agency Financial Report.

AMERICAN STOCK EXCHANGE-COMPOSITE INDEX

Global Financial Data, Inc., 29122 Rancho Viejo Rd., Ste. 215, San Juan Capistrano, CA, 92675, USA, (949) 542-4200, sales@globalfinancialdata.com, https://globalfinancialdata.com/; Macroversal Database.

AMTRAK

Association of American Railroads (AAR), 425 3rd St. SW, Washington, DC, 20024, USA, (202) 639-2100, https://www.aar.org; Analysis of Class I Railroads 2021 and Railroad Facts 2022.

AMUSEMENT PARKS

National Safety Council (NSC), 1121 Spring Lake Dr., Itasca, IL, 60143-3201, USA, (630) 285-1121, (800) 621-7615, customerservice@nsc.org, https://www.nsc.org/; International Association of Amusement Parks and Attractions (IAAPA) Ride Safety Report - North America - 2019.

U.S. Census Bureau, Center for Economic Studies (CES), 4600 Silver Hill Rd., Washington, DC, 20233, USA, (301) 763-6460, (301) 763-5935, ces.contacts@census.gov, https://www.census.gov/programs-surveys/ces.html; Arts, Entertainment and Recreation, 2017 Economic Census.

AMUSEMENT, GAMBLING, AND RECREATION INDUSTRY

U.S. Census Bureau, 4600 Silver Hill Rd., Washington, DC, 20233, USA, (301) 763-4636, (800) 923-8282, https://www.census.gov; County Business Patterns (CBP) 2020.

AMUSEMENT, GAMBLING, AND RECREATION INDUSTRY-EARNINGS

U.S. Census Bureau, 4600 Silver Hill Rd., Washington, DC, 20233, USA, (301) 763-4636, (800) 923-8282, https://www.census.gov; County Business Patterns (CBP) 2020.

AMUSEMENT, GAMBLING, AND RECREATION INDUSTRY-EMPLOYEES

U.S. Census Bureau, 4600 Silver Hill Rd., Washington, DC, 20233, USA, (301) 763-4636, (800) 923-8282, https://www.census.gov; County Business Patterns (CBP) 2020.

AMUSEMENT, GAMBLING, AND RECREATION INDUSTRY-NONEMPLOYER ESTABLISHMENTS

U.S. Census Bureau, 4600 Silver Hill Rd., Washington, DC, 20233, USA, (301) 763-4636, (800) 923-8282, https://www.census.gov; Economic Census, Nonemployer Statistics (NES) 2019.

AMUSEMENT, GAMBLING, AND RECREATION INDUSTRY-RECEIPTS AND REVENUE

U.S. Census Bureau, 4600 Silver Hill Rd., Washington, DC, 20233, USA, (301) 763-4636, (800) 923-8282, https://www.census.gov; County Business Patterns (CBP) 2020.

ANALGESICS

KFF Health News, 1330 G St. NW, Washington, DC, 20005, USA, (202) 347-5270, https://khn.org/; $50 Billion in Opioid Settlement Cash Is on the Way. We're Tracking How It's Spent..

Substance Abuse and Mental Health Services Administration (SAMHSA), 5600 Fishers Ln., Rockville, MD, 20857, USA, (877) 726-4727, (800) 487-4889 (TTY), samhsainfo@samhsa.hhs.gov, https://www.samhsa.gov/; 2019-2020 National Survey on Drug Use and Health (NSDUH).

ANCESTRY

U.S. Census Bureau, 4600 Silver Hill Rd., Washington, DC, 20233, USA, (301) 763-4636, (800) 923-8282, https://www.census.gov; Explore Census Data and United States QuickFacts.

ANCHOVIES

National Oceanic and Atmospheric Administration (NOAA), National Marine Fisheries Service (NOAA Fisheries), 1315 East-West Hwy., 14th Fl., Silver Spring, MD, 20910, USA, (301) 427-8000, https://www.fisheries.noaa.gov/; Fisheries of the United States, 2020.

ANDORRA-NATIONAL STATISTICAL OFFICE

Govern d'Andorra, Departament d'Estadistica, Edifici Administratiu de Govern, Carrer de les Boigues, 2, 3a planta, Escaldes Engordany, AD700, AND, estadistica@govern.ad, https://www.estadistica.ad; National Data Reports (Andorra).

ANDORRA-AGRICULTURE

Palgrave Macmillan, 1 New York Plaza, Ste. 4500, New York, NY, 10004-1562, USA, (800) 777-4643, orders@palgrave.com, https://www.palgrave.com/us; The Statesman's Yearbook, 2023.

Routledge - Taylor & Francis Group, 6000 Broken Sound Pkwy. NW, Ste. 300, Boca Raton, FL, 33487, USA, (800) 634-1420, (800) 634-7064, orders@taylorandfrancis.com, https://www.routledge.com/; The Europa World Year Book 2022.

United Nations Food and Agricultural Organization (FAO), 2121 K St., Ste. 800B, Washington, DC, 20037, USA, (202) 653-2400 (Dial from U.S.), (202) 653-5760 (Fax from U.S.), fao-hq@fao.org, https://www.fao.org; AQUASTAT and The State of Food and Agriculture (SOFA) 2022.

ANDORRA-AIRLINES

Palgrave Macmillan, 1 New York Plaza, Ste. 4500, New York, NY, 10004-1562, USA, (800) 777-4643, orders@palgrave.com, https://www.palgrave.com/us; The Statesman's Yearbook, 2023.

ANDORRA-ARMED FORCES

Central Intelligence Agency (CIA), Office of Public Affairs, Washington, DC, 20505, USA, (703) 482-0623, https://www.cia.gov; The World Factbook.

Stockholm International Peace Research Institute (SIPRI), Signalistgatan 9, Stockholm, SE 169 72, SWE, https://www.sipri.org/; SIPRI Arms Transfers Database and SIPRI Military Expenditure Database.

ANDORRA-BROADCASTING

Central Intelligence Agency (CIA), Office of Public Affairs, Washington, DC, 20505, USA, (703) 482-0623, https://www.cia.gov; The World Factbook.

Palgrave Macmillan, 1 New York Plaza, Ste. 4500, New York, NY, 10004-1562, USA, (800) 777-4643, orders@palgrave.com, https://www.palgrave.com/us; The Statesman's Yearbook, 2023.

WRTH Publications Limited, PO Box 290, Oxford, OX2 7FT, GBR, sales@wrth.com, https://www.wrth.com; World Radio TV Handbook 2023.

ANDORRA-BUDGET

Central Intelligence Agency (CIA), Office of Public Affairs, Washington, DC, 20505, USA, (703) 482-0623, https://www.cia.gov; The World Factbook.

ANDORRA-CLIMATE

Palgrave Macmillan, 1 New York Plaza, Ste. 4500, New York, NY, 10004-1562, USA, (800) 777-4643, orders@palgrave.com, https://www.palgrave.com/us; The Statesman's Yearbook, 2023.

ANDORRA-COMMERCE

Palgrave Macmillan, 1 New York Plaza, Ste. 4500, New York, NY, 10004-1562, USA, (800) 777-4643, orders@palgrave.com, https://www.palgrave.com/us; The Statesman's Yearbook, 2023.

UK Data Service, University of Essex, Wivenhoe Park, Colchester, Essex, CO4 3SQ, GBR, https://ukdataservice.ac.uk/; International Aggregate Data.

ANDORRA-CORN INDUSTRY

See ANDORRA-CROPS

ANDORRA-CROPS

Palgrave Macmillan, 1 New York Plaza, Ste. 4500, New York, NY, 10004-1562, USA, (800) 777-4643, orders@palgrave.com, https://www.palgrave.com/us; The Statesman's Yearbook, 2023.

United Nations Food and Agricultural Organization (FAO), 2121 K St., Ste. 800B, Washington, DC, 20037, USA, (202) 653-2400 (Dial from U.S.), (202) 653-5760 (Fax from U.S.), fao-hq@fao.org, https://www.fao.org; The State of Food and Agriculture (SOFA) 2022.

ANDORRA-ECONOMIC CONDITIONS

Bernan Press, 15250 NBN Way, Bldg. C, Blue Ridge Summit, PA, 17214, USA, (301) 459-2255, (800) 865-3457, (800) 865-3450, customercare@bernan.com, https://rowman.com/Page/Bernan; World Economic Outlook, April 2022.

Central Intelligence Agency (CIA), Office of Public Affairs, Washington, DC, 20505, USA, (703) 482-0623, https://www.cia.gov; The World Factbook.

Palgrave Macmillan, 1 New York Plaza, Ste. 4500, New York, NY, 10004-1562, USA, (800) 777-4643, orders@palgrave.com, https://www.palgrave.com/us; The Statesman's Yearbook, 2023.

Routledge - Taylor & Francis Group, 6000 Broken Sound Pkwy. NW, Ste. 300, Boca Raton, FL, 33487, USA, (800) 634-1420, (800) 634-7064, orders@taylorandfrancis.com, https://www.routledge.com/; The Europa World Year Book 2022.

United Nations Economic Commission for Europe (UNECE), Palais des Nations, Geneva, CH-1211, SWI, unece_info@un.org, https://unece.org/; UN-ECE Countries in Figures 2019.

United Nations Statistics Division (UNSD), United Nations Plz., New York, NY, 10017, USA, (800) 253-9646, (212) 963-9851, statistics@un.org, https://unstats.un.org; World Statistics Pocketbook 2021.

The World Bank, 1818 H St. NW, Washington, DC, 20433, USA, (202) 473-1000, (202) 477-6391, eds03@worldbank.org, https://www.worldbank.org/; The Global Findex Database 2021.

ANDORRA-EDUCATION

Palgrave Macmillan, 1 New York Plaza, Ste. 4500, New York, NY, 10004-1562, USA, (800) 777-4643, orders@palgrave.com, https://www.palgrave.com/us; The Statesman's Yearbook, 2023.

Routledge - Taylor & Francis Group, 6000 Broken Sound Pkwy. NW, Ste. 300, Boca Raton, FL, 33487, USA, (800) 634-1420, (800) 634-7064, orders@taylorandfrancis.com, https://www.routledge.com/; The Europa World Year Book 2022.

ANDORRA-EGG TRADE

United Nations Food and Agricultural Organization (FAO), 2121 K St., Ste. 800B, Washington, DC, 20037, USA, (202) 653-2400 (Dial from U.S.), (202) 653-5760 (Fax from U.S.), fao-hq@fao.org, https://www.fao.org; The State of Food and Agriculture (SOFA) 2022.

ANDORRA-EMPLOYMENT

UK Data Service, University of Essex, Wivenhoe Park, Colchester, Essex, CO4 3SQ, GBR, https://ukdataservice.ac.uk/; International Aggregate Data.

ANDORRA-ENVIRONMENTAL CONDITIONS

European Commission, Eurostat, Luxembourg, 2920, LUX, https://ec.europa.eu/eurostat/; Environment Statistics Introduced.

United Nations Statistics Division (UNSD), United Nations Plz., New York, NY, 10017, USA, (800) 253-9646, (212) 963-9851, statistics@un.org, https://unstats.un.org; World Statistics Pocketbook 2021.

ANDORRA-EXPORTS

Central Intelligence Agency (CIA), Office of Public Affairs, Washington, DC, 20505, USA, (703) 482-0623, https://www.cia.gov; The World Factbook.

ANDORRA-FERTILIZER INDUSTRY

United Nations Food and Agricultural Organization (FAO), 2121 K St., Ste. 800B, Washington, DC, 20037, USA, (202) 653-2400 (Dial from U.S.), (202) 653-5760 (Fax from U.S.), fao-hq@fao.org, https://www.fao.org; The State of Food and Agriculture (SOFA) 2022.

ANDORRA-FETAL MORTALITY

See ANDORRA-MORTALITY

ANDORRA-FINANCE, PUBLIC

Palgrave Macmillan, 1 New York Plaza, Ste. 4500, New York, NY, 10004-1562, USA, (800) 777-4643, orders@palgrave.com, https://www.palgrave.com/us; The Statesman's Yearbook, 2023.

Routledge - Taylor & Francis Group, 6000 Broken Sound Pkwy. NW, Ste. 300, Boca Raton, FL, 33487, USA, (800) 634-1420, (800) 634-7064, orders@taylorandfrancis.com, https://www.routledge.com/; The Europa World Year Book 2022.

United Nations Statistics Division (UNSD), United Nations Plz., New York, NY, 10017, USA, (800) 253-9646, (212) 963-9851, statistics@un.org, https://unstats.un.org; National Accounts Main Aggregates Database and National Accounts Statistics: Main Aggregates and Detailed Tables.

ANDORRA-FISHERIES

United Nations Food and Agricultural Organization (FAO), 2121 K St., Ste. 800B, Washington, DC, 20037, USA, (202) 653-2400 (Dial from U.S.), (202) 653-5760 (Fax from U.S.), fao-hq@fao.org, https://www.fao.org; FAO Yearbook of Fishery and Aquaculture Statistics 2019; Fishery Statistical Collections Global Capture Production; FishStatJ; and The State of Food and Agriculture (SOFA) 2022.

ANDORRA-FOOD

United Nations Food and Agricultural Organization (FAO), 2121 K St., Ste. 800B, Washington, DC, 20037, USA, (202) 653-2400 (Dial from U.S.), (202) 653-5760 (Fax from U.S.), fao-hq@fao.org, https://www.fao.org; The State of Food and Agriculture (SOFA) 2022.

ANDORRA-FORESTS AND FORESTRY

Palgrave Macmillan, 1 New York Plaza, Ste. 4500, New York, NY, 10004-1562, USA, (800) 777-4643, orders@palgrave.com, https://www.palgrave.com/us; The Statesman's Yearbook, 2023.

UNESCO Institute for Statistics, C.P 250 Succursale H, Montreal, QC, H3G 2K8, CAN, (514) 343-6880 (Dial from U.S.), (514) 343-5740 (Fax from U.S.), uis.publications@unesco.org, http://uis.unesco.org/; UIS.Stat.

United Nations Food and Agricultural Organization (FAO), 2121 K St., Ste. 800B, Washington, DC, 20037, USA, (202) 653-2400 (Dial from U.S.), (202) 653-5760 (Fax from U.S.), fao-hq@fao.org, https://www.fao.org; The State of Food and Agriculture (SOFA) 2022.

ANDORRA-IMPORTS

Central Intelligence Agency (CIA), Office of Public Affairs, Washington, DC, 20505, USA, (703) 482-0623, https://www.cia.gov; The World Factbook.

ANDORRA-INDUSTRIES

Central Intelligence Agency (CIA), Office of Public Affairs, Washington, DC, 20505, USA, (703) 482-0623, https://www.cia.gov; The World Factbook.

Palgrave Macmillan, 1 New York Plaza, Ste. 4500, New York, NY, 10004-1562, USA, (800) 777-4643, orders@palgrave.com, https://www.palgrave.com/us; The Statesman's Yearbook, 2023.

ANDORRA-INFANT AND MATERNAL MORTALITY

See ANDORRA-MORTALITY

ANDORRA-INTERNATIONAL TRADE

Banque de France, 31 rue Croix des Petits-Champs, Paris, 75049, FRA, infos@banque-france.fr, https://www.banque-france.fr/en; Key Figures France and Abroad.

Palgrave Macmillan, 1 New York Plaza, Ste. 4500, New York, NY, 10004-1562, USA, (800) 777-4643, orders@palgrave.com, https://www.palgrave.com/us; The Statesman's Yearbook, 2023.

Routledge - Taylor & Francis Group, 6000 Broken Sound Pkwy. NW, Ste. 300, Boca Raton, FL, 33487, USA, (800) 634-1420, (800) 634-7064, orders@taylorandfrancis.com, https://www.routledge.com/; The Europa World Year Book 2022.

United Nations Conference on Trade and Development (UNCTAD), Palais des Nations, Geneva, 1211, SWI, (212) 963-6896, unctadinfo@unctad.org, https://unctad.org; Trade and Development Report 2021.

United Nations Food and Agricultural Organization (FAO), 2121 K St., Ste. 800B, Washington, DC, 20037, USA, (202) 653-2400 (Dial from U.S.), (202) 653-5760 (Fax from U.S.), fao-hq@fao.org, https://www.fao.org; The State of Food and Agriculture (SOFA) 2022.

World Trade Organization (WTO), Ctre. William Rappard, Rue de Lausanne 154, Case postale, Geneva, CH-1211, SWI, enquiries@wto.org, https://www.wto.org; World Trade Statistical Review 2022.

ANDORRA-LABOR

Central Intelligence Agency (CIA), Office of Public Affairs, Washington, DC, 20505, USA, (703) 482-0623, https://www.cia.gov; The World Factbook.

Palgrave Macmillan, 1 New York Plaza, Ste. 4500, New York, NY, 10004-1562, USA, (800) 777-4643, orders@palgrave.com, https://www.palgrave.com/us; The Statesman's Yearbook, 2023.

United Nations Economic Commission for Europe (UNECE), Palais des Nations, Geneva, CH-1211, SWI, unece_info@un.org, https://unece.org/; UN-ECE Countries in Figures 2019.

United Nations Food and Agricultural Organization (FAO), 2121 K St., Ste. 800B, Washington, DC, 20037, USA, (202) 653-2400 (Dial from U.S.), (202) 653-5760 (Fax from U.S.), fao-hq@fao.org, https://www.fao.org; The State of Food and Agriculture (SOFA) 2022.

ANDORRA-LIFE EXPECTANCY

United Nations Department of Economic and Social Affairs (DESA), Population Division, 2 United Nations Plz., Rm. DC2-1950, New York, NY, 10017, USA, (212) 963-3209, (212) 963-2147, population@un.org, https://www.un.org/development/desa/pd/; World Population Ageing 2020 Highlights.

United Nations Economic Commission for Europe (UNECE), Palais des Nations, Geneva, CH-1211, SWI, unece_info@un.org, https://unece.org/; UN-ECE Countries in Figures 2019.

ANDORRA-LIVESTOCK

Routledge - Taylor & Francis Group, 6000 Broken Sound Pkwy. NW, Ste. 300, Boca Raton, FL, 33487, USA, (800) 634-1420, (800) 634-7064, orders@taylorandfrancis.com, https://www.routledge.com/; The Europa World Year Book 2022.

United Nations Food and Agricultural Organization (FAO), 2121 K St., Ste. 800B, Washington, DC, 20037, USA, (202) 653-2400 (Dial from U.S.), (202) 653-5760 (Fax from U.S.), fao-hq@fao.org, https://www.fao.org; The State of Food and Agriculture (SOFA) 2022.

ANDORRA-MARRIAGE

Routledge - Taylor & Francis Group, 6000 Broken Sound Pkwy. NW, Ste. 300, Boca Raton, FL, 33487, USA, (800) 634-1420, (800) 634-7064, orders@taylorandfrancis.com, https://www.routledge.com/; The Europa World Year Book 2022.

ANDORRA-MINERAL INDUSTRIES

United Nations Conference on Trade and Development (UNCTAD), Palais des Nations, Geneva, 1211, SWI, (212) 963-6896, unctadinfo@unctad.org, https://unctad.org; Trade and Development Report 2021.

ANDORRA-MORTALITY

United Nations Statistics Division (UNSD), United Nations Plz., New York, NY, 10017, USA, (800) 253-9646, (212) 963-9851, statistics@un.org, https://unstats.un.org; World Statistics Pocketbook 2021.

ANDORRA-NUTRITION

United Nations Food and Agricultural Organization (FAO), 2121 K St., Ste. 800B, Washington, DC,

20037, USA, (202) 653-2400 (Dial from U.S.), (202) 653-5760 (Fax from U.S.), fao-hq@fao.org, https://www.fao.org; The State of Food and Agriculture (SOFA) 2022.

ANDORRA-PESTICIDES

United Nations Food and Agricultural Organization (FAO), 2121 K St., Ste. 800B, Washington, DC, 20037, USA, (202) 653-2400 (Dial from U.S.), (202) 653-5760 (Fax from U.S.), fao-hq@fao.org, https://www.fao.org; The State of Food and Agriculture (SOFA) 2022.

ANDORRA-PETROLEUM INDUSTRY AND TRADE

United Nations Food and Agricultural Organization (FAO), 2121 K St., Ste. 800B, Washington, DC, 20037, USA, (202) 653-2400 (Dial from U.S.), (202) 653-5760 (Fax from U.S.), fao-hq@fao.org, https://www.fao.org; The State of Food and Agriculture (SOFA) 2022.

ANDORRA-POPULATION

Central Intelligence Agency (CIA), Office of Public Affairs, Washington, DC, 20505, USA, (703) 482-0623, https://www.cia.gov; The World Factbook.

Palgrave Macmillan, 1 New York Plaza, Ste. 4500, New York, NY, 10004-1562, USA, (800) 777-4643, orders@palgrave.com, https://www.palgrave.com/us; The Statesman's Yearbook, 2023.

Routledge - Taylor & Francis Group, 6000 Broken Sound Pkwy. NW, Ste. 300, Boca Raton, FL, 33487, USA, (800) 634-1420, (800) 634-7064, orders@taylorandfrancis.com, https://www.routledge.com/; The Europa World Year Book 2022.

UK Data Service, University of Essex, Wivenhoe Park, Colchester, Essex, CO4 3SQ, GBR, https://ukdataservice.ac.uk/; International Aggregate Data.

United Nations Department of Economic and Social Affairs (DESA), Population Division, 2 United Nations Plz., Rm. DC2-1950, New York, NY, 10017, USA, (212) 963-3209, (212) 963-2147, population@un.org, https://www.un.org/development/desa/pd/; Revision of World Urbanization Prospects and World Population Ageing 2020 Highlights.

United Nations Statistics Division (UNSD), United Nations Plz., New York, NY, 10017, USA, (800) 253-9646, (212) 963-9851, statistics@un.org, https://unstats.un.org; Statistical Yearbook of the United Nations 2021 and World Statistics Pocketbook 2021.

The World Bank, 1818 H St. NW, Washington, DC, 20433, USA, (202) 473-1000, (202) 477-6391, eds03@worldbank.org, https://www.worldbank.org/; The Global Findex Database 2021.

ANDORRA-POPULATION DENSITY

Central Intelligence Agency (CIA), Office of Public Affairs, Washington, DC, 20505, USA, (703) 482-0623, https://www.cia.gov; The World Factbook.

Palgrave Macmillan, 1 New York Plaza, Ste. 4500, New York, NY, 10004-1562, USA, (800) 777-4643, orders@palgrave.com, https://www.palgrave.com/us; The Statesman's Yearbook, 2023.

Routledge - Taylor & Francis Group, 6000 Broken Sound Pkwy. NW, Ste. 300, Boca Raton, FL, 33487, USA, (800) 634-1420, (800) 634-7064, orders@taylorandfrancis.com, https://www.routledge.com/; The Europa World Year Book 2022.

ANDORRA-POWER RESOURCES

Palgrave Macmillan, 1 New York Plaza, Ste. 4500, New York, NY, 10004-1562, USA, (800) 777-4643, orders@palgrave.com, https://www.palgrave.com/us; The Statesman's Yearbook, 2023.

United Nations Food and Agricultural Organization (FAO), 2121 K St., Ste. 800B, Washington, DC, 20037, USA, (202) 653-2400 (Dial from U.S.), (202) 653-5760 (Fax from U.S.), fao-hq@fao.org, https://www.fao.org; The State of Food and Agriculture (SOFA) 2022.

United Nations Statistics Division (UNSD), United Nations Plz., New York, NY, 10017, USA, (800) 253-9646, (212) 963-9851, statistics@un.org, https://unstats.un.org; World Statistics Pocketbook 2021.

ANDORRA-PUBLIC HEALTH

Palgrave Macmillan, 1 New York Plaza, Ste. 4500, New York, NY, 10004-1562, USA, (800) 777-4643, orders@palgrave.com, https://www.palgrave.com/us; The Statesman's Yearbook, 2023.

U.S. Census Bureau, 4600 Silver Hill Rd., Washington, DC, 20233, USA, (301) 763-4636, (800) 923-8282, https://www.census.gov; HIV/AIDS Surveillance Data Base.

United Nations Department of Economic and Social Affairs (DESA), Population Division, 2 United Nations Plz., Rm. DC2-1950, New York, NY, 10017, USA, (212) 963-3209, (212) 963-2147, population@un.org, https://www.un.org/development/desa/pd/; World Fertility Data 2019.

ANDORRA-RELIGION

Central Intelligence Agency (CIA), Office of Public Affairs, Washington, DC, 20505, USA, (703) 482-0623, https://www.cia.gov; The World Factbook.

Palgrave Macmillan, 1 New York Plaza, Ste. 4500, New York, NY, 10004-1562, USA, (800) 777-4643, orders@palgrave.com, https://www.palgrave.com/us; The Statesman's Yearbook, 2023.

ANDORRA-TELEPHONE

Palgrave Macmillan, 1 New York Plaza, Ste. 4500, New York, NY, 10004-1562, USA, (800) 777-4643, orders@palgrave.com, https://www.palgrave.com/us; The Statesman's Yearbook, 2023.

Routledge - Taylor & Francis Group, 6000 Broken Sound Pkwy. NW, Ste. 300, Boca Raton, FL, 33487, USA, (800) 634-1420, (800) 634-7064, orders@taylorandfrancis.com, https://www.routledge.com/; The Europa World Year Book 2022.

United Nations Statistics Division (UNSD), United Nations Plz., New York, NY, 10017, USA, (800) 253-9646, (212) 963-9851, statistics@un.org, https://unstats.un.org; World Statistics Pocketbook 2021.

ANDORRA-THEATER

UNESCO Institute for Statistics, C.P 250 Succursale H, Montreal, QC, H3G 2K8, CAN, (514) 343-6880 (Dial from U.S.), (514) 343-5740 (Fax from U.S.), uis.publications@unesco.org, http://uis.unesco.org/; UIS.Stat.

ANDORRA-TOURISM

Palgrave Macmillan, 1 New York Plaza, Ste. 4500, New York, NY, 10004-1562, USA, (800) 777-4643, orders@palgrave.com, https://www.palgrave.com/us; The Statesman's Yearbook, 2023.

Routledge - Taylor & Francis Group, 6000 Broken Sound Pkwy. NW, Ste. 300, Boca Raton, FL, 33487, USA, (800) 634-1420, (800) 634-7064, orders@taylorandfrancis.com, https://www.routledge.com/; The Europa World Year Book 2022.

ANDORRA-TRADE

See ANDORRA-INTERNATIONAL TRADE

ANDORRA-TRANSPORTATION

Central Intelligence Agency (CIA), Office of Public Affairs, Washington, DC, 20505, USA, (703) 482-0623, https://www.cia.gov; The World Factbook.

Palgrave Macmillan, 1 New York Plaza, Ste. 4500, New York, NY, 10004-1562, USA, (800) 777-4643, orders@palgrave.com, https://www.palgrave.com/us; The Statesman's Yearbook, 2023.

Routledge - Taylor & Francis Group, 6000 Broken Sound Pkwy. NW, Ste. 300, Boca Raton, FL, 33487, USA, (800) 634-1420, (800) 634-7064, orders@taylorandfrancis.com, https://www.routledge.com/; The Europa World Year Book 2022.

United Nations Economic Commission for Europe (UNECE), Palais des Nations, Geneva, CH-1211, SWI, unece_info@un.org, https://unece.org/; UNECE Countries in Figures 2019.

ANDORRA-VITAL STATISTICS

Palgrave Macmillan, 1 New York Plaza, Ste. 4500, New York, NY, 10004-1562, USA, (800) 777-4643, orders@palgrave.com, https://www.palgrave.com/us; The Statesman's Yearbook, 2023.

U.S. Census Bureau, 4600 Silver Hill Rd., Washington, DC, 20233, USA, (301) 763-4636, (800) 923-8282, https://www.census.gov; HIV/AIDS Surveillance Data Base.

United Nations Department of Economic and Social Affairs (DESA), Population Division, 2 United Nations Plz., Rm. DC2-1950, New York, NY, 10017, USA, (212) 963-3209, (212) 963-2147, population@un.org, https://www.un.org/development/desa/pd/; World Contraceptive Use 2021: Estimates and Projections of Family Planning Indicators and World Marriage Data 2019.

United Nations Statistics Division (UNSD), United Nations Plz., New York, NY, 10017, USA, (800) 253-9646, (212) 963-9851, statistics@un.org, https://unstats.un.org; Statistical Yearbook of the United Nations 2021 and United Nations Demographic Yearbook 2020.

ANEMIA

U.S. Department of Health and Human Services, Centers for Disease Control and Prevention (CDC), National Center for Health Statistics (NCHS), 3311 Toledo Rd., Hyattsville, MD, 20782-2064, USA, (800) 232-4636, (301) 458-4000, https://www.cdc.gov/nchs; FastStats - Statistics by Topic.

ANEMIA-DEATHS

U.S. Department of Health and Human Services, Centers for Disease Control and Prevention (CDC), National Center for Health Statistics (NCHS), 3311 Toledo Rd., Hyattsville, MD, 20782-2064, USA, (800) 232-4636, (301) 458-4000, https://www.cdc.gov/nchs; Vital Statistics Online Data Portal.

ANGOLA-NATIONAL STATISTICAL OFFICE

Instituto Nacional de Estatistica, Angola, Rua Ho-Chi-Min, Luanda, CP 1215, ANG, luisa.dasilva@ine.gov.ao, http://www.ine-ao.com/; National Data Reports (Angola).

ANGOLA-AGRICULTURE

African Development Bank Group (AfDB), Avenue Joseph Anoma, 01 BP 1387, Abidjan, 01, COT, https://www.afdb.org; African Economic Outlook 2021 and Compendium of Statistics on Bank Group Operations 2019.

The Economist Group: Economist Intelligence Unit (EIU), 900 3rd Ave., 16th Fl., New York, NY, 10022, USA, (212) 541-0500, americas@eiu.com, https://www.eiu.com; Angola Country Report.

Euromonitor International, Inc., 1 N Dearborn St., Ste. 1700, Chicago, IL, 60602, USA, (312) 922-1115, (312) 922-1157, info-usa@euromonitor.com, https://www.euromonitor.com/; Geographies.

Palgrave Macmillan, 1 New York Plaza, Ste. 4500, New York, NY, 10004-1562, USA, (800) 777-4643, orders@palgrave.com, https://www.palgrave.com/us; The Statesman's Yearbook, 2023.

Routledge - Taylor & Francis Group, 6000 Broken Sound Pkwy. NW, Ste. 300, Boca Raton, FL, 33487, USA, (800) 634-1420, (800) 634-7064, orders@taylorandfrancis.com, https://www.routledge.com/; The Europa World Year Book 2022.

United Nations Economic Commission for Africa (UNECA), PO Box 3001, Addis Ababa, ETH, ecainfo@uneca.org, https://www.uneca.org/; African Statistical Yearbook 2020 and Economic Report on Africa 2021.

United Nations Food and Agricultural Organization (FAO), 2121 K St., Ste. 800B, Washington, DC,

20037, USA, (202) 653-2400 (Dial from U.S.), (202) 653-5760 (Fax from U.S.), fao-hq@fao.org, https://www.fao.org; AQUASTAT and The State of Food and Agriculture (SOFA) 2022.

United Nations Statistics Division (UNSD), United Nations Plz., New York, NY, 10017, USA, (800) 253-9646, (212) 963-9851, statistics@un.org, https://unstats.un.org; Statistical Yearbook of the United Nations 2021.

The World Bank, 1818 H St. NW, Washington, DC, 20433, USA, (202) 473-1000, (202) 477-6391, eds03@worldbank.org, https://www.worldbank.org/; Angola (report).

ANGOLA-AIRLINES

Palgrave Macmillan, 1 New York Plaza, Ste. 4500, New York, NY, 10004-1562, USA, (800) 777-4643, orders@palgrave.com, https://www.palgrave.com/us; The Statesman's Yearbook, 2023.

Routledge - Taylor & Francis Group, 6000 Broken Sound Pkwy. NW, Ste. 300, Boca Raton, FL, 33487, USA, (800) 634-1420, (800) 634-7064, orders@taylorandfrancis.com, https://www.routledge.com/; The Europa World Year Book 2022.

United Nations Economic Commission for Africa (UNECA), PO Box 3001, Addis Ababa, ETH, ecainfo@uneca.org, https://www.uneca.org/; African Statistical Yearbook 2020.

ANGOLA-ALUMINUM PRODUCTION

See ANGOLA-MINERAL INDUSTRIES

ANGOLA-ANIMAL FEEDING

United Nations Statistics Division (UNSD), United Nations Plz., New York, NY, 10017, USA, (800) 253-9646, (212) 963-9851, statistics@un.org, https://unstats.un.org; Statistical Yearbook of the United Nations 2021.

ANGOLA-ARMED FORCES

Central Intelligence Agency (CIA), Office of Public Affairs, Washington, DC, 20505, USA, (703) 482-0623, https://www.cia.gov; The World Factbook.

International Institute for Strategic Studies (IISS) - Americas, 2121 K St. NW, Ste. 600, Washington, DC, 20037, USA, (202) 659-1490, (202) 659-1499, https://www.iiss.org/; The Military Balance 2022.

Palgrave Macmillan, 1 New York Plaza, Ste. 4500, New York, NY, 10004-1562, USA, (800) 777-4643, orders@palgrave.com, https://www.palgrave.com/us; The Statesman's Yearbook, 2023.

Stockholm International Peace Research Institute (SIPRI), Signalistgatan 9, Stockholm, SE 169 72, SWE, https://www.sipri.org/; SIPRI Arms Transfers Database and SIPRI Military Expenditure Database.

ANGOLA-BALANCE OF PAYMENTS

African Development Bank Group (AfDB), Avenue Joseph Anoma, 01 BP 1387, Abidjan, 01, COT, https://www.afdb.org; The AfDB Statistics Pocketbook 2019.

Routledge - Taylor & Francis Group, 6000 Broken Sound Pkwy. NW, Ste. 300, Boca Raton, FL, 33487, USA, (800) 634-1420, (800) 634-7064, orders@taylorandfrancis.com, https://www.routledge.com/; The Europa World Year Book 2022.

The World Bank, 1818 H St. NW, Washington, DC, 20433, USA, (202) 473-1000, (202) 477-6391, eds03@worldbank.org, https://www.worldbank.org/; Angola (report).

ANGOLA-BANKS AND BANKING

Euromonitor International, Inc., 1 N Dearborn St., Ste. 1700, Chicago, IL, 60602, USA, (312) 922-1115, (312) 922-1157, info-usa@euromonitor.com, https://www.euromonitor.com/; Geographies.

ANGOLA-BARLEY PRODUCTION

See ANGOLA-CROPS

ANGOLA-BROADCASTING

Central Intelligence Agency (CIA), Office of Public Affairs, Washington, DC, 20505, USA, (703) 482-0623, https://www.cia.gov; The World Factbook.

Euromonitor International, Inc., 1 N Dearborn St., Ste. 1700, Chicago, IL, 60602, USA, (312) 922-1115, (312) 922-1157, info-usa@euromonitor.com, https://www.euromonitor.com/; Geographies.

Palgrave Macmillan, 1 New York Plaza, Ste. 4500, New York, NY, 10004-1562, USA, (800) 777-4643, orders@palgrave.com, https://www.palgrave.com/us; The Statesman's Yearbook, 2023.

WRTH Publications Limited, PO Box 290, Oxford, OX2 7FT, GBR, sales@wrth.com, https://www.wrth.com; World Radio TV Handbook 2023.

ANGOLA-BUDGET

Central Intelligence Agency (CIA), Office of Public Affairs, Washington, DC, 20505, USA, (703) 482-0623, https://www.cia.gov; The World Factbook.

ANGOLA-BUSINESS

Global Entrepreneurship Monitor (GEM), Babson College, 231 Forest St., Babson Park, MA, 02457, USA, (781) 235-1200, info@gemconsortium.org, https://www.gemconsortium.org/; Angola Economy Profile.

ANGOLA-CLIMATE

International Institute for Environment and Development (IIED), 235 High Holborn, London, WC1V 7DN, GBR, inforequest@iied.org, https://www.iied.org; Environment & Urbanization.

Palgrave Macmillan, 1 New York Plaza, Ste. 4500, New York, NY, 10004-1562, USA, (800) 777-4643, orders@palgrave.com, https://www.palgrave.com/us; The Statesman's Yearbook, 2023.

ANGOLA-COAL PRODUCTION

See ANGOLA-MINERAL INDUSTRIES

ANGOLA-COCOA PRODUCTION

See ANGOLA-CROPS

ANGOLA-COFFEE

See ANGOLA-CROPS

ANGOLA-COMMERCE

Palgrave Macmillan, 1 New York Plaza, Ste. 4500, New York, NY, 10004-1562, USA, (800) 777-4643, orders@palgrave.com, https://www.palgrave.com/us; The Statesman's Yearbook, 2023.

UK Data Service, University of Essex, Wivenhoe Park, Colchester, Essex, CO4 3SQ, GBR, https://ukdataservice.ac.uk/; International Aggregate Data.

ANGOLA-COMMODITY EXCHANGES

Barchart, 209 W Jackson Blvd., 2nd Fl., Chicago, IL, 60606, USA, (877) 247-4394, commodities@barchart.com, https://www.barchart.com/cmdty; The cmdty Yearbook 2023; cmdtyStats: Commodity Statistics and Fundamental Data; cmdtyView: Commodity Index; and Commodity Data and Prices.

International Monetary Fund (IMF), 700 19th St. NW, Washington, DC, 20431, USA, (202) 623-7000, (202) 623-4661, publications@imf.org, https://www.imf.org; IMF Primary Commodity Prices.

ANGOLA-CONSTRUCTION INDUSTRY

United Nations Economic Commission for Africa (UNECA), PO Box 3001, Addis Ababa, ETH, ecainfo@uneca.org, https://www.uneca.org/; African Statistical Yearbook 2020.

United Nations Statistics Division (UNSD), United Nations Plz., New York, NY, 10017, USA, (800) 253-9646, (212) 963-9851, statistics@un.org, https://unstats.un.org; Statistical Yearbook of the United Nations 2021.

ANGOLA-CONSUMER PRICE INDEXES

The World Bank, 1818 H St. NW, Washington, DC, 20433, USA, (202) 473-1000, (202) 477-6391, eds03@worldbank.org, https://www.worldbank.org/; Angola (report).

ANGOLA-CONSUMPTION (ECONOMICS)

African Development Bank Group (AfDB), Avenue Joseph Anoma, 01 BP 1387, Abidjan, 01, COT, https://www.afdb.org; The AfDB Statistics Pocketbook 2019.

ANGOLA-COPPER INDUSTRY AND TRADE

See ANGOLA-MINERAL INDUSTRIES

ANGOLA-CORN INDUSTRY

See ANGOLA-CROPS

ANGOLA-COTTON

See ANGOLA-CROPS

ANGOLA-CROPS

Palgrave Macmillan, 1 New York Plaza, Ste. 4500, New York, NY, 10004-1562, USA, (800) 777-4643, orders@palgrave.com, https://www.palgrave.com/us; The Statesman's Yearbook, 2023.

United Nations Economic Commission for Africa (UNECA), PO Box 3001, Addis Ababa, ETH, ecainfo@uneca.org, https://www.uneca.org/; African Statistical Yearbook 2020.

United Nations Food and Agricultural Organization (FAO), 2121 K St., Ste. 800B, Washington, DC, 20037, USA, (202) 653-2400 (Dial from U.S.), (202) 653-5760 (Fax from U.S.), fao-hq@fao.org, https://www.fao.org; The State of Food and Agriculture (SOFA) 2022.

United Nations Statistics Division (UNSD), United Nations Plz., New York, NY, 10017, USA, (800) 253-9646, (212) 963-9851, statistics@un.org, https://unstats.un.org; Statistical Yearbook of the United Nations 2021.

ANGOLA-DAIRY PROCESSING

Palgrave Macmillan, 1 New York Plaza, Ste. 4500, New York, NY, 10004-1562, USA, (800) 777-4643, orders@palgrave.com, https://www.palgrave.com/us; The Statesman's Yearbook, 2023.

United Nations Food and Agricultural Organization (FAO), 2121 K St., Ste. 800B, Washington, DC, 20037, USA, (202) 653-2400 (Dial from U.S.), (202) 653-5760 (Fax from U.S.), fao-hq@fao.org, https://www.fao.org; The State of Food and Agriculture (SOFA) 2022.

ANGOLA-DEBTS, EXTERNAL

African Development Bank Group (AfDB), Avenue Joseph Anoma, 01 BP 1387, Abidjan, 01, COT, https://www.afdb.org; The AfDB Statistics Pocketbook 2019; African Economic Outlook 2021; and Compendium of Statistics on Bank Group Operations 2019.

Palgrave Macmillan, 1 New York Plaza, Ste. 4500, New York, NY, 10004-1562, USA, (800) 777-4643, orders@palgrave.com, https://www.palgrave.com/us; The Statesman's Yearbook, 2023.

United Nations Economic Commission for Africa (UNECA), PO Box 3001, Addis Ababa, ETH, ecainfo@uneca.org, https://www.uneca.org/; Economic Report on Africa 2021.

The World Bank, 1818 H St. NW, Washington, DC, 20433, USA, (202) 473-1000, (202) 477-6391, eds03@worldbank.org, https://www.worldbank.org/; Global Financial Development Report 2019-2020: Bank Regulation and Supervision a Decade after the Global Financial Crisis.

ANGOLA-DEFENSE EXPENDITURES

See ANGOLA-ARMED FORCES

ANGOLA-DIAMONDS

See ANGOLA-MINERAL INDUSTRIES

ANGOLA-ECONOMIC ASSISTANCE

United Nations Statistics Division (UNSD), United Nations Plz., New York, NY, 10017, USA, (800) 253-9646, (212) 963-9851, statistics@un.org, https://unstats.un.org; Statistical Yearbook of the United Nations 2021.

ANGOLA-ECONOMIC CONDITIONS

African Development Bank Group (AfDB), Avenue Joseph Anoma, 01 BP 1387, Abidjan, 01, COT, https://www.afdb.org; The AfDB Statistics Pocketbook 2019; Africa Economic Brief - COVID-19 Pandemic Potential Risks for Trade and Trade Finance in Africa; African Economic Outlook 2021; The African Statistical Journal; Compendium of Statistics on Bank Group Operations 2019; and Gender, Poverty and Environmental Indicators on African Countries 2019.

Bernan Press, 15250 NBN Way, Bldg. C, Blue Ridge Summit, PA, 17214, USA, (301) 459-2255, (800) 865-3457, (800) 865-3450, customercare@bernan.com, https://rowman.com/Page/Bernan; World Economic Outlook, April 2022.

Central Intelligence Agency (CIA), Office of Public Affairs, Washington, DC, 20505, USA, (703) 482-0623, https://www.cia.gov; The World Factbook.

The Economist Group: Economist Intelligence Unit (EIU), 900 3rd Ave., 16th Fl., New York, NY, 10022, USA, (212) 541-0500, americas@eiu.com, https://www.eiu.com; Angola Country Report.

Euromonitor International, Inc., 1 N Dearborn St., Ste. 1700, Chicago, IL, 60602, USA, (312) 922-1115, (312) 922-1157, info-usa@euromonitor.com, https://www.euromonitor.com/; Geographies.

Global Entrepreneurship Monitor (GEM), Babson College, 231 Forest St., Babson Park, MA, 02457, USA, (781) 235-1200, info@gemconsortium.org, https://www.gemconsortium.org/; Angola Economy Profile.

International Monetary Fund (IMF), 700 19th St. NW, Washington, DC, 20431, USA, (202) 623-7000, (202) 623-4661, publications@imf.org, https://www.imf.org; IMF Data and World Economic Outlook.

Palgrave Macmillan, 1 New York Plaza, Ste. 4500, New York, NY, 10004-1562, USA, (800) 777-4643, orders@palgrave.com, https://www.palgrave.com/us; The Statesman's Yearbook, 2023.

Routledge - Taylor & Francis Group, 6000 Broken Sound Pkwy. NW, Ste. 300, Boca Raton, FL, 33487, USA, (800) 634-1420, (800) 634-7064, orders@taylorandfrancis.com, https://www.routledge.com/; The Europa World Year Book 2022.

United Nations Economic Commission for Africa (UNECA), PO Box 3001, Addis Ababa, ETH, ecainfo@uneca.org, https://www.uneca.org/; Economic Report on Africa 2021.

United Nations Statistics Division (UNSD), United Nations Plz., New York, NY, 10017, USA, (800) 253-9646, (212) 963-9851, statistics@un.org, https://unstats.un.org; World Statistics Pocketbook 2021.

The World Bank, 1818 H St. NW, Washington, DC, 20433, USA, (202) 473-1000, (202) 477-6391, eds03@worldbank.org, https://www.worldbank.org/; Angola (report); Global Economic Monitor (GEM); Global Economic Prospects, June 2022; and The Global Findex Database 2021.

ANGOLA-EDUCATION

African Development Bank Group (AfDB), Avenue Joseph Anoma, 01 BP 1387, Abidjan, 01, COT, https://www.afdb.org; The AfDB Statistics Pocketbook 2019.

Euromonitor International, Inc., 1 N Dearborn St., Ste. 1700, Chicago, IL, 60602, USA, (312) 922-1115, (312) 922-1157, info-usa@euromonitor.com, https://www.euromonitor.com/; Geographies.

Infoplease, c/o Sandbox Networks, Inc., 1 Lincoln St., 24th Fl., Boston, MA, 02111, USA, https://www.infoplease.com; Countries of the World.

Palgrave Macmillan, 1 New York Plaza, Ste. 4500, New York, NY, 10004-1562, USA, (800) 777-4643, orders@palgrave.com, https://www.palgrave.com/us; The Statesman's Yearbook, 2023.

Routledge - Taylor & Francis Group, 6000 Broken Sound Pkwy. NW, Ste. 300, Boca Raton, FL, 33487, USA, (800) 634-1420, (800) 634-7064, orders@taylorandfrancis.com, https://www.routledge.com/; The Europa World Year Book 2022.

UNESCO Institute for Statistics, C.P 250 Succursale H, Montreal, QC, H3G 2K8, CAN, (514) 343-6880 (Dial from U.S.), (514) 343-5740 (Fax from U.S.), uis.publications@unesco.org, http://uis.unesco.org/; Literacy and UIS.Stat.

United Nations Economic Commission for Africa (UNECA), PO Box 3001, Addis Ababa, ETH, ecainfo@uneca.org, https://www.uneca.org/; African Statistical Yearbook 2020.

United Nations Statistics Division (UNSD), United Nations Plz., New York, NY, 10017, USA, (800) 253-9646, (212) 963-9851, statistics@un.org, https://unstats.un.org; Millennium Development Goal Indicators.

The World Bank, 1818 H St. NW, Washington, DC, 20433, USA, (202) 473-1000, (202) 477-6391, eds03@worldbank.org, https://www.worldbank.org/; Angola (report).

ANGOLA-ELECTRICITY

International Energy Agency (IEA), 9 Rue de la Federation, Paris, 75739, FRA, info@iea.org, https://www.iea.org/; World Energy Outlook 2021.

U.S. Energy Information Administration (EIA), 1000 Independence Ave. SW, Washington, DC, 20585, USA, (202) 586-8800, infoctr@eia.gov, https://www.eia.gov; International Energy Outlook 2021.

United Nations Statistics Division (UNSD), United Nations Plz., New York, NY, 10017, USA, (800) 253-9646, (212) 963-9851, statistics@un.org, https://unstats.un.org; Statistical Yearbook of the United Nations 2021.

ANGOLA-EMPLOYMENT

UK Data Service, University of Essex, Wivenhoe Park, Colchester, Essex, CO4 3SQ, GBR, https://ukdataservice.ac.uk/; International Aggregate Data.

United Nations Economic Commission for Africa (UNECA), PO Box 3001, Addis Ababa, ETH, ecainfo@uneca.org, https://www.uneca.org/; African Statistical Yearbook 2020.

United Nations Statistics Division (UNSD), United Nations Plz., New York, NY, 10017, USA, (800) 253-9646, (212) 963-9851, statistics@un.org, https://unstats.un.org; Statistical Yearbook of the United Nations 2021.

The World Bank, 1818 H St. NW, Washington, DC, 20433, USA, (202) 473-1000, (202) 477-6391, eds03@worldbank.org, https://www.worldbank.org/; Angola (report).

ANGOLA-ENVIRONMENTAL CONDITIONS

DSI Data Service & Information, Xantener Strasse 51a, Rheinberg, D-47495, GER, dsi@dsidata.com, https://www.dsidata.com/; Global Environmental Database.

The Economist Group: Economist Intelligence Unit (EIU), 900 3rd Ave., 16th Fl., New York, NY, 10022, USA, (212) 541-0500, americas@eiu.com, https://www.eiu.com; Angola Country Report.

International Institute for Environment and Development (IIED), 235 High Holborn, London, WC1V 7DN, GBR, inforequest@iied.org, https://www.iied.org; Environment & Urbanization.

United Nations Statistics Division (UNSD), United Nations Plz., New York, NY, 10017, USA, (800) 253-9646, (212) 963-9851, statistics@un.org, https://unstats.un.org; World Statistics Pocketbook 2021.

ANGOLA-EXPORTS

African Development Bank Group (AfDB), Avenue Joseph Anoma, 01 BP 1387, Abidjan, 01, COT, https://www.afdb.org; African Economic Outlook 2021.

Central Intelligence Agency (CIA), Office of Public Affairs, Washington, DC, 20505, USA, (703) 482-0623, https://www.cia.gov; The World Factbook.

The Economist Group: Economist Intelligence Unit (EIU), 900 3rd Ave., 16th Fl., New York, NY, 10022, USA, (212) 541-0500, americas@eiu.com, https://www.eiu.com; Angola Country Report.

International Monetary Fund (IMF), 700 19th St. NW, Washington, DC, 20431, USA, (202) 623-7000, (202) 623-4661, publications@imf.org, https://www.imf.org; Direction of Trade Statistics (DOTS).

Organization of Petroleum Exporting Countries (OPEC), Helferstorferstrasse 17, Vienna, A-1010, AUT, https://www.opec.org/; OPEC Annual Statistical Bulletin 2021.

S&P Global, IHS Markit, 15 Inverness Way E, Englewood, CO, 80112, USA, (800) 447-2273, (800) 854-7179, https://ihsmarkit.com; Global Trade Atlas (GTA).

ANGOLA-FEMALE WORKING POPULATION

See ANGOLA-EMPLOYMENT

ANGOLA-FERTILIZER INDUSTRY

United Nations Food and Agricultural Organization (FAO), 2121 K St., Ste. 800B, Washington, DC, 20037, USA, (202) 653-2400 (Dial from U.S.), (202) 653-5760 (Fax from U.S.), fao-hq@fao.org, https://www.fao.org; The State of Food and Agriculture (SOFA) 2022.

ANGOLA-FETAL MORTALITY

See ANGOLA-MORTALITY

ANGOLA-FINANCE

Stockholm International Peace Research Institute (SIPRI), Signalistgatan 9, Stockholm, SE 169 72, SWE, https://www.sipri.org/; SIPRI Arms Transfers Database and SIPRI Military Expenditure Database.

United Nations Economic Commission for Africa (UNECA), PO Box 3001, Addis Ababa, ETH, ecainfo@uneca.org, https://www.uneca.org/; African Statistical Yearbook 2020.

The World Bank, 1818 H St. NW, Washington, DC, 20433, USA, (202) 473-1000, (202) 477-6391, eds03@worldbank.org, https://www.worldbank.org/; Angola (report).

ANGOLA-FINANCE, PUBLIC

African Development Bank Group (AfDB), Avenue Joseph Anoma, 01 BP 1387, Abidjan, 01, COT, https://www.afdb.org; The AfDB Statistics Pocketbook 2019.

Bernan Press, 15250 NBN Way, Bldg. C, Blue Ridge Summit, PA, 17214, USA, (301) 459-2255, (800) 865-3457, (800) 865-3450, customercare@bernan.com, https://rowman.com/Page/Bernan; National Accounts Statistics: Analysis of Main Aggregates 2020.

The Economist Group: Economist Intelligence Unit (EIU), 900 3rd Ave., 16th Fl., New York, NY, 10022, USA, (212) 541-0500, americas@eiu.com, https://www.eiu.com; Angola Country Report.

International Monetary Fund (IMF), 700 19th St. NW, Washington, DC, 20431, USA, (202) 623-7000, (202) 623-4661, publications@imf.org, https://www.imf.org; International Financial Statistics (IFS) and Regional Economic Outlook.

Palgrave Macmillan, 1 New York Plaza, Ste. 4500, New York, NY, 10004-1562, USA, (800) 777-4643, orders@palgrave.com, https://www.palgrave.com/us; The Statesman's Yearbook, 2023.

Routledge - Taylor & Francis Group, 6000 Broken Sound Pkwy. NW, Ste. 300, Boca Raton, FL, 33487,

USA, (800) 634-1420, (800) 634-7064, orders@taylorandfrancis.com, https://www.routledge.com/; The Europa World Year Book 2022.

United Nations Statistics Division (UNSD), United Nations Plz., New York, NY, 10017, USA, (800) 253-9646, (212) 963-9851, statistics@un.org, https://unstats.un.org; National Accounts Main Aggregates Database and National Accounts Statistics: Main Aggregates and Detailed Tables.

The World Bank, 1818 H St. NW, Washington, DC, 20433, USA, (202) 473-1000, (202) 477-6391, eds03@worldbank.org, https://www.worldbank.org/; Angola (report).

ANGOLA-FISHERIES

Palgrave Macmillan, 1 New York Plaza, Ste. 4500, New York, NY, 10004-1562, USA, (800) 777-4643, orders@palgrave.com, https://www.palgrave.com/us; The Statesman's Yearbook, 2023.

Routledge - Taylor & Francis Group, 6000 Broken Sound Pkwy. NW, Ste. 300, Boca Raton, FL, 33487, USA, (800) 634-1420, (800) 634-7064, orders@taylorandfrancis.com, https://www.routledge.com/; The Europa World Year Book 2022.

United Nations Economic Commission for Africa (UNECA), PO Box 3001, Addis Ababa, ETH, ecainfo@uneca.org, https://www.uneca.org/; African Statistical Yearbook 2020.

United Nations Food and Agricultural Organization (FAO), 2121 K St., Ste. 800B, Washington, DC, 20037, USA, (202) 653-2400 (Dial from U.S.), (202) 653-5760 (Fax from U.S.), fao-hq@fao.org, https://www.fao.org; FAO Yearbook of Fishery and Aquaculture Statistics 2019; Fishery Statistical Collections Global Capture Production; FishStatJ; and The State of Food and Agriculture (SOFA) 2022.

United Nations Statistics Division (UNSD), United Nations Plz., New York, NY, 10017, USA, (800) 253-9646, (212) 963-9851, statistics@un.org, https://unstats.un.org; Statistical Yearbook of the United Nations 2021.

The World Bank, 1818 H St. NW, Washington, DC, 20433, USA, (202) 473-1000, (202) 477-6391, eds03@worldbank.org, https://www.worldbank.org/; Angola (report).

ANGOLA-FOOD

African Development Bank Group (AfDB), Avenue Joseph Anoma, 01 BP 1387, Abidjan, 01, COT, https://www.afdb.org; The AfDB Statistics Pocketbook 2019.

United Nations Food and Agricultural Organization (FAO), 2121 K St., Ste. 800B, Washington, DC, 20037, USA, (202) 653-2400 (Dial from U.S.), (202) 653-5760 (Fax from U.S.), fao-hq@fao.org, https://www.fao.org; The State of Food and Agriculture (SOFA) 2022.

ANGOLA-FOREIGN EXCHANGE RATES

African Development Bank Group (AfDB), Avenue Joseph Anoma, 01 BP 1387, Abidjan, 01, COT, https://www.afdb.org; The AfDB Statistics Pocketbook 2019 and African Economic Outlook 2021.

Organization of Petroleum Exporting Countries (OPEC), Helferstorferstrasse 17, Vienna, A-1010, AUT, https://www.opec.org/; OPEC Annual Statistical Bulletin 2021.

ANGOLA-FORESTS AND FORESTRY

Palgrave Macmillan, 1 New York Plaza, Ste. 4500, New York, NY, 10004-1562, USA, (800) 777-4643, orders@palgrave.com, https://www.palgrave.com/us; The Statesman's Yearbook, 2023.

Routledge - Taylor & Francis Group, 6000 Broken Sound Pkwy. NW, Ste. 300, Boca Raton, FL, 33487, USA, (800) 634-1420, (800) 634-7064, orders@taylorandfrancis.com, https://www.routledge.com/; The Europa World Year Book 2022.

UNESCO Institute for Statistics, C.P 250 Succursale H, Montreal, QC, H3G 2K8, CAN, (514) 343-6880 (Dial from U.S.), (514) 343-5740 (Fax from U.S.), uis.publications@unesco.org, http://uis.unesco.org/; UIS.Stat.

United Nations Economic Commission for Africa (UNECA), PO Box 3001, Addis Ababa, ETH, ecainfo@uneca.org, https://www.uneca.org/; African Statistical Yearbook 2020.

United Nations Food and Agricultural Organization (FAO), 2121 K St., Ste. 800B, Washington, DC, 20037, USA, (202) 653-2400 (Dial from U.S.), (202) 653-5760 (Fax from U.S.), fao-hq@fao.org, https://www.fao.org; FAO Yearbook of Forest Products 2019 and The State of Food and Agriculture (SOFA) 2022.

United Nations Statistics Division (UNSD), United Nations Plz., New York, NY, 10017, USA, (800) 253-9646, (212) 963-9851, statistics@un.org, https://unstats.un.org; Statistical Yearbook of the United Nations 2021.

The World Bank, 1818 H St. NW, Washington, DC, 20433, USA, (202) 473-1000, (202) 477-6391, eds03@worldbank.org, https://www.worldbank.org/; Angola (report).

ANGOLA-GAS PRODUCTION

See ANGOLA-MINERAL INDUSTRIES

ANGOLA-GEOGRAPHIC INFORMATION SYSTEMS

The World Bank, 1818 H St. NW, Washington, DC, 20433, USA, (202) 473-1000, (202) 477-6391, eds03@worldbank.org, https://www.worldbank.org/; Angola (report).

ANGOLA-GOLD PRODUCTION

See ANGOLA-MINERAL INDUSTRIES

ANGOLA-GROSS DOMESTIC PRODUCT

African Development Bank Group (AfDB), Avenue Joseph Anoma, 01 BP 1387, Abidjan, 01, COT, https://www.afdb.org; The AfDB Statistics Pocketbook 2019.

The Economist Group: Economist Intelligence Unit (EIU), 900 3rd Ave., 16th Fl., New York, NY, 10022, USA, (212) 541-0500, americas@eiu.com, https://www.eiu.com; Angola Country Report.

Routledge - Taylor & Francis Group, 6000 Broken Sound Pkwy. NW, Ste. 300, Boca Raton, FL, 33487, USA, (800) 634-1420, (800) 634-7064, orders@taylorandfrancis.com, https://www.routledge.com/; The Europa World Year Book 2022.

United Nations Economic Commission for Africa (UNECA), PO Box 3001, Addis Ababa, ETH, ecainfo@uneca.org, https://www.uneca.org/; African Statistical Yearbook 2020.

United Nations Statistics Division (UNSD), United Nations Plz., New York, NY, 10017, USA, (800) 253-9646, (212) 963-9851, statistics@un.org, https://unstats.un.org; Statistical Yearbook of the United Nations 2021.

ANGOLA-GROSS NATIONAL PRODUCT

Organization of Petroleum Exporting Countries (OPEC), Helferstorferstrasse 17, Vienna, A-1010, AUT, https://www.opec.org/; OPEC Annual Statistical Bulletin 2021.

Palgrave Macmillan, 1 New York Plaza, Ste. 4500, New York, NY, 10004-1562, USA, (800) 777-4643, orders@palgrave.com, https://www.palgrave.com/us; The Statesman's Yearbook, 2023.

Routledge - Taylor & Francis Group, 6000 Broken Sound Pkwy. NW, Ste. 300, Boca Raton, FL, 33487, USA, (800) 634-1420, (800) 634-7064, orders@taylorandfrancis.com, https://www.routledge.com/; The Europa World Year Book 2022.

ANGOLA-HOUSING

Euromonitor International, Inc., 1 N Dearborn St., Ste. 1700, Chicago, IL, 60602, USA, (312) 922-1115, (312) 922-1157, info-usa@euromonitor.com, https://www.euromonitor.com/; Geographies.

ANGOLA-ILLITERATE PERSONS

UNESCO Institute for Statistics, C.P 250 Succursale H, Montreal, QC, H3G 2K8, CAN, (514) 343-6880 (Dial from U.S.), (514) 343-5740 (Fax from U.S.), uis.publications@unesco.org, http://uis.unesco.org/; UIS.Stat.

ANGOLA-IMPORTS

African Development Bank Group (AfDB), Avenue Joseph Anoma, 01 BP 1387, Abidjan, 01, COT, https://www.afdb.org; African Economic Outlook 2021.

Central Intelligence Agency (CIA), Office of Public Affairs, Washington, DC, 20505, USA, (703) 482-0623, https://www.cia.gov; The World Factbook.

The Economist Group: Economist Intelligence Unit (EIU), 900 3rd Ave., 16th Fl., New York, NY, 10022, USA, (212) 541-0500, americas@eiu.com, https://www.eiu.com; Angola Country Report.

International Monetary Fund (IMF), 700 19th St. NW, Washington, DC, 20431, USA, (202) 623-7000, (202) 623-4661, publications@imf.org, https://www.imf.org; Direction of Trade Statistics (DOTS).

S&P Global, IHS Markit, 15 Inverness Way E, Englewood, CO, 80112, USA, (800) 447-2273, (800) 854-7179, https://ihsmarkit.com; Global Trade Atlas (GTA).

ANGOLA-INDUSTRIAL METALS PRODUCTION

See ANGOLA-MINERAL INDUSTRIES

ANGOLA-INDUSTRIES

Central Intelligence Agency (CIA), Office of Public Affairs, Washington, DC, 20505, USA, (703) 482-0623, https://www.cia.gov; The World Factbook.

The Economist Group: Economist Intelligence Unit (EIU), 900 3rd Ave., 16th Fl., New York, NY, 10022, USA, (212) 541-0500, americas@eiu.com, https://www.eiu.com; Angola Country Report.

Euromonitor International, Inc., 1 N Dearborn St., Ste. 1700, Chicago, IL, 60602, USA, (312) 922-1115, (312) 922-1157, info-usa@euromonitor.com, https://www.euromonitor.com/; Geographies.

Palgrave Macmillan, 1 New York Plaza, Ste. 4500, New York, NY, 10004-1562, USA, (800) 777-4643, orders@palgrave.com, https://www.palgrave.com/us; The Statesman's Yearbook, 2023.

Routledge - Taylor & Francis Group, 6000 Broken Sound Pkwy. NW, Ste. 300, Boca Raton, FL, 33487, USA, (800) 634-1420, (800) 634-7064, orders@taylorandfrancis.com, https://www.routledge.com/; The Europa World Year Book 2022.

United Nations Economic Commission for Africa (UNECA), PO Box 3001, Addis Ababa, ETH, ecainfo@uneca.org, https://www.uneca.org/; African Statistical Yearbook 2020.

United Nations Industrial Development Organization (UNIDO), 1 United Nations Plz., Rm. DC1-1118, New York, NY, 10017, USA, (212) 963-6890, (212) 963 6885, (212) 963-7904, office.newyork@unido.org, https://www.unido.org/; Industrial Statistics Databases and International Yearbook of Industrial Statistics 2021.

The World Bank, 1818 H St. NW, Washington, DC, 20433, USA, (202) 473-1000, (202) 477-6391, eds03@worldbank.org, https://www.worldbank.org/; Angola (report).

ANGOLA-INFANT AND MATERNAL MORTALITY

See ANGOLA-MORTALITY

ANGOLA-INTERNATIONAL TRADE

African Development Bank Group (AfDB), Avenue Joseph Anoma, 01 BP 1387, Abidjan, 01, COT, https://www.afdb.org; The AfDB Statistics Pocketbook 2019 and African Economic Outlook 2021.

The Economist Group: Economist Intelligence Unit (EIU), 900 3rd Ave., 16th Fl., New York, NY, 10022, USA, (212) 541-0500, americas@eiu.com, https://www.eiu.com; Angola Country Report.

Euromonitor International, Inc., 1 N Dearborn St., Ste. 1700, Chicago, IL, 60602, USA, (312) 922-1115, (312) 922-1157, info-usa@euromonitor.com, https://www.euromonitor.com/; Geographies.

Palgrave Macmillan, 1 New York Plaza, Ste. 4500, New York, NY, 10004-1562, USA, (800) 777-4643, orders@palgrave.com, https://www.palgrave.com/us; The Statesman's Yearbook, 2023.

Routledge - Taylor & Francis Group, 6000 Broken Sound Pkwy. NW, Ste. 300, Boca Raton, FL, 33487, USA, (800) 634-1420, (800) 634-7064, orders@taylorandfrancis.com, https://www.routledge.com/; The Europa World Year Book 2022.

United Nations Conference on Trade and Development (UNCTAD), Palais des Nations, Geneva, 1211, SWI, (212) 963-6896, unctadinfo@unctad.org, https://unctad.org; Trade and Development Report 2021.

United Nations Economic Commission for Africa (UNECA), PO Box 3001, Addis Ababa, ETH, ecainfo@uneca.org, https://www.uneca.org/; African Statistical Yearbook 2020.

United Nations Food and Agricultural Organization (FAO), 2121 K St., Ste. 800B, Washington, DC, 20037, USA, (202) 653-2400 (Dial from U.S.), (202) 653-5760 (Fax from U.S.), fao-hq@fao.org, https://www.fao.org; The State of Food and Agriculture (SOFA) 2022.

United Nations Statistics Division (UNSD), United Nations Plz., New York, NY, 10017, USA, (800) 253-9646, (212) 963-9851, statistics@un.org, https://unstats.un.org; International Trade Statistics Yearbook 2020 and Statistical Yearbook of the United Nations 2021.

The World Bank, 1818 H St. NW, Washington, DC, 20433, USA, (202) 473-1000, (202) 477-6391, eds03@worldbank.org, https://www.worldbank.org/; Angola (report).

World Trade Organization (WTO), Ctre. William Rappard, Rue de Lausanne 154, Case postale, Geneva, CH-1211, SWI, enquiries@wto.org, https://www.wto.org; World Trade Statistical Review 2022.

ANGOLA-INTERNET USERS

International Telecommunication Union (ITU), Place des Nations, Geneva, CH-1211, SWI, itumail@itu.int, https://www.itu.int; Global Connectivity Report 2022; World Telecommunication/ICT Indicators Database 2021; and Yearbook of Statistics 2019.

The World Bank, 1818 H St. NW, Washington, DC, 20433, USA, (202) 473-1000, (202) 477-6391, eds03@worldbank.org, https://www.worldbank.org/; Angola (report).

ANGOLA-LABOR

African Development Bank Group (AfDB), Avenue Joseph Anoma, 01 BP 1387, Abidjan, 01, COT, https://www.afdb.org; The AfDB Statistics Pocketbook 2019.

Central Intelligence Agency (CIA), Office of Public Affairs, Washington, DC, 20505, USA, (703) 482-0623, https://www.cia.gov; The World Factbook.

Euromonitor International, Inc., 1 N Dearborn St., Ste. 1700, Chicago, IL, 60602, USA, (312) 922-1115, (312) 922-1157, info-usa@euromonitor.com, https://www.euromonitor.com/; Geographies.

Palgrave Macmillan, 1 New York Plaza, Ste. 4500, New York, NY, 10004-1562, USA, (800) 777-4643, orders@palgrave.com, https://www.palgrave.com/us; The Statesman's Yearbook, 2023.

United Nations Food and Agricultural Organization (FAO), 2121 K St., Ste. 800B, Washington, DC, 20037, USA, (202) 653-2400 (Dial from U.S.), (202) 653-5760 (Fax from U.S.), fao-hq@fao.org, https://www.fao.org; The State of Food and Agriculture (SOFA) 2022.

ANGOLA-LAND USE

United Nations Statistics Division (UNSD), United Nations Plz., New York, NY, 10017, USA, (800) 253-9646, (212) 963-9851, statistics@un.org, https://unstats.un.org; Millennium Development Goal Indicators.

ANGOLA-LIFE EXPECTANCY

African Development Bank Group (AfDB), Avenue Joseph Anoma, 01 BP 1387, Abidjan, 01, COT, https://www.afdb.org; The AfDB Statistics Pocketbook 2019.

United Nations Department of Economic and Social Affairs (DESA), Population Division, 2 United Nations Plz., Rm. DC2-1950, New York, NY, 10017, USA, (212) 963-3209, (212) 963-2147, population@un.org, https://www.un.org/development/desa/pd/; World Population Ageing 2020 Highlights.

United Nations Statistics Division (UNSD), United Nations Plz., New York, NY, 10017, USA, (800) 253-9646, (212) 963-9851, statistics@un.org, https://unstats.un.org; Millennium Development Goal Indicators.

ANGOLA-LITERACY

Euromonitor International, Inc., 1 N Dearborn St., Ste. 1700, Chicago, IL, 60602, USA, (312) 922-1115, (312) 922-1157, info-usa@euromonitor.com, https://www.euromonitor.com/; Geographies.

Palgrave Macmillan, 1 New York Plaza, Ste. 4500, New York, NY, 10004-1562, USA, (800) 777-4643, orders@palgrave.com, https://www.palgrave.com/us; The Statesman's Yearbook, 2023.

Routledge - Taylor & Francis Group, 6000 Broken Sound Pkwy. NW, Ste. 300, Boca Raton, FL, 33487, USA, (800) 634-1420, (800) 634-7064, orders@taylorandfrancis.com, https://www.routledge.com/; The Europa World Year Book 2022.

UNESCO Institute for Statistics, C.P 250 Succursale H, Montreal, QC, H3G 2K8, CAN, (514) 343-6880 (Dial from U.S.), (514) 343-5740 (Fax from U.S.), uis.publications@unesco.org, http://uis.unesco.org/; Literacy.

United Nations Economic Commission for Africa (UNECA), PO Box 3001, Addis Ababa, ETH, ecainfo@uneca.org, https://www.uneca.org/; African Statistical Yearbook 2020.

United Nations Food and Agricultural Organization (FAO), 2121 K St., Ste. 800B, Washington, DC, 20037, USA, (202) 653-2400 (Dial from U.S.), (202) 653-5760 (Fax from U.S.), fao-hq@fao.org, https://www.fao.org; The State of Food and Agriculture (SOFA) 2022.

United Nations Statistics Division (UNSD), United Nations Plz., New York, NY, 10017, USA, (800) 253-9646, (212) 963-9851, statistics@un.org, https://unstats.un.org; Statistical Yearbook of the United Nations 2021.

ANGOLA-MARRIAGE

United Nations Statistics Division (UNSD), United Nations Plz., New York, NY, 10017, USA, (800) 253-9646, (212) 963-9851, statistics@un.org, https://unstats.un.org; Statistical Yearbook of the United Nations 2021.

ANGOLA-MINERAL INDUSTRIES

International Energy Agency (IEA), 9 Rue de la Federation, Paris, 75739, FRA, info@iea.org, https://www.iea.org/; World Energy Outlook 2021.

Palgrave Macmillan, 1 New York Plaza, Ste. 4500, New York, NY, 10004-1562, USA, (800) 777-4643, orders@palgrave.com, https://www.palgrave.com/us; The Statesman's Yearbook, 2023.

Routledge - Taylor & Francis Group, 6000 Broken Sound Pkwy. NW, Ste. 300, Boca Raton, FL, 33487, USA, (800) 634-1420, (800) 634-7064, orders@taylorandfrancis.com, https://www.routledge.com/; The Europa World Year Book 2022.

United Nations Conference on Trade and Development (UNCTAD), Palais des Nations, Geneva, 1211, SWI, (212) 963-6896, unctadinfo@unctad.org, https://unctad.org; Trade and Development Report 2021.

United Nations Economic Commission for Africa (UNECA), PO Box 3001, Addis Ababa, ETH, ecainfo@uneca.org, https://www.uneca.org/; African Statistical Yearbook 2020.

United Nations Statistics Division (UNSD), United Nations Plz., New York, NY, 10017, USA, (800) 253-9646, (212) 963-9851, statistics@un.org, https://unstats.un.org; Statistical Yearbook of the United Nations 2021.

ANGOLA-MONEY SUPPLY

The Economist Group: Economist Intelligence Unit (EIU), 900 3rd Ave., 16th Fl., New York, NY, 10022, USA, (212) 541-0500, americas@eiu.com, https://www.eiu.com; Angola Country Report.

The World Bank, 1818 H St. NW, Washington, DC, 20433, USA, (202) 473-1000, (202) 477-6391, eds03@worldbank.org, https://www.worldbank.org/; Angola (report).

ANGOLA-MORTALITY

UNICEF, 3 United Nations Plz., New York, NY, 10017, USA, (212) 303-7984, (917) 244-2215, https://www.unicef.org; The State of the World's Children 2023.

United Nations Statistics Division (UNSD), United Nations Plz., New York, NY, 10017, USA, (800) 253-9646, (212) 963-9851, statistics@un.org, https://unstats.un.org; Millennium Development Goal Indicators; Statistical Yearbook of the United Nations 2021; and World Statistics Pocketbook 2021.

World Health Organization (WHO), Ave. Appia 20, Geneva, CH-1211, SWI, (202) 974-3000 (Telephone in U.S.), publications@who.int, https://www.who.int/; Global Health Observatory (GHO).

ANGOLA-MOTION PICTURES

Palgrave Macmillan, 1 New York Plaza, Ste. 4500, New York, NY, 10004-1562, USA, (800) 777-4643, orders@palgrave.com, https://www.palgrave.com/us; The Statesman's Yearbook, 2023.

ANGOLA-MOTOR VEHICLES

International Road Federation (IRF), Madison Place, 500 Montgomery St., 5th Fl., Alexandria, VA, 22314, USA, (703) 535-1001, (703) 535-1007, info@irf.global, https://www.irf.global/; World Road Statistics (WRS).

ANGOLA-NATURAL GAS PRODUCTION

See ANGOLA-MINERAL INDUSTRIES

ANGOLA-NUTRITION

United Nations Food and Agricultural Organization (FAO), 2121 K St., Ste. 800B, Washington, DC, 20037, USA, (202) 653-2400 (Dial from U.S.), (202) 653-5760 (Fax from U.S.), fao-hq@fao.org, https://www.fao.org; The State of Food and Agriculture (SOFA) 2022.

United Nations Statistics Division (UNSD), United Nations Plz., New York, NY, 10017, USA, (800) 253-9646, (212) 963-9851, statistics@un.org, https://unstats.un.org; Millennium Development Goal Indicators.

ANGOLA-PAPER

See ANGOLA-FORESTS AND FORESTRY

ANGOLA-PEANUT PRODUCTION

See ANGOLA-CROPS

ANGOLA-PESTICIDES

United Nations Food and Agricultural Organization (FAO), 2121 K St., Ste. 800B, Washington, DC, 20037, USA, (202) 653-2400 (Dial from U.S.), (202) 653-5760 (Fax from U.S.), fao-hq@fao.org, https://www.fao.org; The State of Food and Agriculture (SOFA) 2022.

ANGOLA-PETROLEUM INDUSTRY AND TRADE

International Energy Agency (IEA), 9 Rue de la Federation, Paris, 75739, FRA, info@iea.org, https://www.iea.org/; World Energy Outlook 2021.

Organization of Petroleum Exporting Countries (OPEC), Helferstorferstrasse 17, Vienna, A-1010, AUT, https://www.opec.org/; OPEC Annual Statistical Bulletin 2021.

Palgrave Macmillan, 1 New York Plaza, Ste. 4500, New York, NY, 10004-1562, USA, (800) 777-4643, orders@palgrave.com, https://www.palgrave.com/us; The Statesman's Yearbook, 2023.

United Nations Food and Agricultural Organization (FAO), 2121 K St., Ste. 800B, Washington, DC, 20037, USA, (202) 653-2400 (Dial from U.S.), (202) 653-5760 (Fax from U.S.), fao-hq@fao.org, https://www.fao.org; The State of Food and Agriculture (SOFA) 2022.

United Nations Statistics Division (UNSD), United Nations Plz., New York, NY, 10017, USA, (800) 253-9646, (212) 963-9851, statistics@un.org, https://unstats.un.org; Statistical Yearbook of the United Nations 2021.

ANGOLA-PIPELINES

Organization of Petroleum Exporting Countries (OPEC), Helferstorferstrasse 17, Vienna, A-1010, AUT, https://www.opec.org/; OPEC Annual Statistical Bulletin 2021.

ANGOLA-POPULATION

African Development Bank Group (AfDB), Avenue Joseph Anoma, 01 BP 1387, Abidjan, 01, COT, https://www.afdb.org; The AfDB Statistics Pocketbook 2019; Africa Economic Brief - COVID-19 Pandemic Potential Risks for Trade and Trade Finance in Africa; The African Statistical Journal; and Gender, Poverty and Environmental Indicators on African Countries 2019.

Central Intelligence Agency (CIA), Office of Public Affairs, Washington, DC, 20505, USA, (703) 482-0623, https://www.cia.gov; The World Factbook.

The Economist Group: Economist Intelligence Unit (EIU), 900 3rd Ave., 16th Fl., New York, NY, 10022, USA, (212) 541-0500, americas@eiu.com, https://www.eiu.com; Angola Country Report.

European Commission, Eurostat, Luxembourg, 2920, LUX, https://ec.europa.eu/eurostat/; EU in the World 2020.

Infoplease, c/o Sandbox Networks, Inc., 1 Lincoln St., 24th Fl., Boston, MA, 02111, USA, https://www.infoplease.com; Countries of the World.

Palgrave Macmillan, 1 New York Plaza, Ste. 4500, New York, NY, 10004-1562, USA, (800) 777-4643, orders@palgrave.com, https://www.palgrave.com/us; The Statesman's Yearbook, 2023.

Routledge - Taylor & Francis Group, 6000 Broken Sound Pkwy. NW, Ste. 300, Boca Raton, FL, 33487, USA, (800) 634-1420, (800) 634-7064, orders@taylorandfrancis.com, https://www.routledge.com/; The Europa World Year Book 2022.

UK Data Service, University of Essex, Wivenhoe Park, Colchester, Essex, CO4 3SQ, GBR, https://ukdataservice.ac.uk/; International Aggregate Data.

United Nations Department of Economic and Social Affairs (DESA), Population Division, 2 United Nations Plz., Rm. DC2-1950, New York, NY, 10017, USA, (212) 963-3209, (212) 963-2147, population@un.org, https://www.un.org/development/desa/pd/; Revision of World Urbanization Prospects and World Population Ageing 2020 Highlights.

United Nations Development Programme (UNDP), One United Nations Plz., New York, NY, 10017, USA, (212) 906-5000, (212) 906-5001, https://www.undp.org; Human Development Report 2021-2022.

United Nations Statistics Division (UNSD), United Nations Plz., New York, NY, 10017, USA, (800) 253-9646, (212) 963-9851, statistics@un.org, https://unstats.un.org; Statistical Yearbook of the United Nations 2021 and World Statistics Pocketbook 2021.

The World Bank, 1818 H St. NW, Washington, DC, 20433, USA, (202) 473-1000, (202) 477-6391, eds03@worldbank.org, https://www.worldbank.org/; Angola (report) and The Global Findex Database 2021.

ANGOLA-POPULATION DENSITY

African Development Bank Group (AfDB), Avenue Joseph Anoma, 01 BP 1387, Abidjan, 01, COT, https://www.afdb.org; The AfDB Statistics Pocketbook 2019.

Central Intelligence Agency (CIA), Office of Public Affairs, Washington, DC, 20505, USA, (703) 482-0623, https://www.cia.gov; The World Factbook.

Palgrave Macmillan, 1 New York Plaza, Ste. 4500, New York, NY, 10004-1562, USA, (800) 777-4643, orders@palgrave.com, https://www.palgrave.com/us; The Statesman's Yearbook, 2023.

Routledge - Taylor & Francis Group, 6000 Broken Sound Pkwy. NW, Ste. 300, Boca Raton, FL, 33487, USA, (800) 634-1420, (800) 634-7064, orders@taylorandfrancis.com, https://www.routledge.com/; The Europa World Year Book 2022.

The World Bank, 1818 H St. NW, Washington, DC, 20433, USA, (202) 473-1000, (202) 477-6391, eds03@worldbank.org, https://www.worldbank.org/; Angola (report).

ANGOLA-POULTRY

See ANGOLA-LIVESTOCK

ANGOLA-POWER RESOURCES

Euromonitor International, Inc., 1 N Dearborn St., Ste. 1700, Chicago, IL, 60602, USA, (312) 922-1115, (312) 922-1157, info-usa@euromonitor.com, https://www.euromonitor.com/; Geographies.

International Energy Agency (IEA), 9 Rue de la Federation, Paris, 75739, FRA, info@iea.org, https://www.iea.org/; World Energy Outlook 2021.

Palgrave Macmillan, 1 New York Plaza, Ste. 4500, New York, NY, 10004-1562, USA, (800) 777-4643, orders@palgrave.com, https://www.palgrave.com/us; The Statesman's Yearbook, 2023.

U.S. Energy Information Administration (EIA), 1000 Independence Ave. SW, Washington, DC, 20585, USA, (202) 586-8800, infoctr@eia.gov, https://www.eia.gov; International Energy Outlook 2021.

United Nations Economic Commission for Africa (UNECA), PO Box 3001, Addis Ababa, ETH, ecainfo@uneca.org, https://www.uneca.org/; African Statistical Yearbook 2020.

United Nations Food and Agricultural Organization (FAO), 2121 K St., Ste. 800B, Washington, DC, 20037, USA, (202) 653-2400 (Dial from U.S.), (202) 653-5760 (Fax from U.S.), fao-hq@fao.org, https://www.fao.org; The State of Food and Agriculture (SOFA) 2022.

United Nations Statistics Division (UNSD), United Nations Plz., New York, NY, 10017, USA, (800) 253-9646, (212) 963-9851, statistics@un.org, https://unstats.un.org; Energy Statistics Yearbook 2019; Statistical Yearbook of the United Nations 2021; and World Statistics Pocketbook 2021.

ANGOLA-PRICES

Euromonitor International, Inc., 1 N Dearborn St., Ste. 1700, Chicago, IL, 60602, USA, (312) 922-1115, (312) 922-1157, info-usa@euromonitor.com, https://www.euromonitor.com/; Geographies.

The World Bank, 1818 H St. NW, Washington, DC, 20433, USA, (202) 473-1000, (202) 477-6391, eds03@worldbank.org, https://www.worldbank.org/; Angola (report).

ANGOLA-PUBLIC HEALTH

African Development Bank Group (AfDB), Avenue Joseph Anoma, 01 BP 1387, Abidjan, 01, COT, https://www.afdb.org; The AfDB Statistics Pocketbook 2019.

Euromonitor International, Inc., 1 N Dearborn St., Ste. 1700, Chicago, IL, 60602, USA, (312) 922-1115, (312) 922-1157, info-usa@euromonitor.com, https://www.euromonitor.com/; Geographies.

Palgrave Macmillan, 1 New York Plaza, Ste. 4500, New York, NY, 10004-1562, USA, (800) 777-4643, orders@palgrave.com, https://www.palgrave.com/us; The Statesman's Yearbook, 2023.

U.S. Census Bureau, 4600 Silver Hill Rd., Washington, DC, 20233, USA, (301) 763-4636, (800) 923-8282, https://www.census.gov; HIV/AIDS Surveillance Data Base.

UNICEF, 3 United Nations Plz., New York, NY, 10017, USA, (212) 303-7984, (917) 244-2215, https://www.unicef.org; The State of the World's Children 2023.

United Nations Department of Economic and Social Affairs (DESA), Population Division, 2 United Nations Plz., Rm. DC2-1950, New York, NY, 10017, USA, (212) 963-3209, (212) 963-2147, population@un.org, https://www.un.org/development/desa/pd/; World Fertility Data 2019.

United Nations Development Programme (UNDP), One United Nations Plz., New York, NY, 10017, USA, (212) 906-5000, (212) 906-5001, https://www.undp.org; Human Development Report 2021-2022.

United Nations Economic Commission for Africa (UNECA), PO Box 3001, Addis Ababa, ETH, ecainfo@uneca.org, https://www.uneca.org/; African Statistical Yearbook 2020.

United Nations Statistics Division (UNSD), United Nations Plz., New York, NY, 10017, USA, (800) 253-9646, (212) 963-9851, statistics@un.org, https://unstats.un.org; Millennium Development Goal Indicators and Statistical Yearbook of the United Nations 2021.

The World Bank, 1818 H St. NW, Washington, DC, 20433, USA, (202) 473-1000, (202) 477-6391, eds03@worldbank.org, https://www.worldbank.org/; Angola (report).

World Health Organization (WHO), Ave. Appia 20, Geneva, CH-1211, SWI, (202) 974-3000 (Telephone in U.S.), publications@who.int, https://www.who.int/; Global Health Observatory (GHO).

ANGOLA-PUBLISHERS AND PUBLISHING

Routledge - Taylor & Francis Group, 6000 Broken Sound Pkwy. NW, Ste. 300, Boca Raton, FL, 33487, USA, (800) 634-1420, (800) 634-7064, orders@taylorandfrancis.com, https://www.routledge.com/; The Europa World Year Book 2022.

UNESCO Institute for Statistics, C.P 250 Succursale H, Montreal, QC, H3G 2K8, CAN, (514) 343-6880 (Dial from U.S.), (514) 343-5740 (Fax from U.S.), uis.publications@unesco.org, http://uis.unesco.org/; UIS.Stat.

ANGOLA-RAILROADS

Janes, USA, (703) 574-7580, (888) 977-1519, customer.care@janes.com, https://www.janes.com; Janes World Railways 2021-2022.

Palgrave Macmillan, 1 New York Plaza, Ste. 4500, New York, NY, 10004-1562, USA, (800) 777-4643, orders@palgrave.com, https://www.palgrave.com/us; The Statesman's Yearbook, 2023.

United Nations Economic Commission for Africa (UNECA), PO Box 3001, Addis Ababa, ETH, ecainfo@uneca.org, https://www.uneca.org/; African Statistical Yearbook 2020.

United Nations Statistics Division (UNSD), United Nations Plz., New York, NY, 10017, USA, (800) 253-9646, (212) 963-9851, statistics@un.org, https://unstats.un.org; Statistical Yearbook of the United Nations 2021.

ANGOLA-RELIGION

Central Intelligence Agency (CIA), Office of Public Affairs, Washington, DC, 20505, USA, (703) 482-0623, https://www.cia.gov; The World Factbook.

Palgrave Macmillan, 1 New York Plaza, Ste. 4500, New York, NY, 10004-1562, USA, (800) 777-4643, orders@palgrave.com, https://www.palgrave.com/us; The Statesman's Yearbook, 2023.

ANGOLA-RETAIL TRADE

Euromonitor International, Inc., 1 N Dearborn St., Ste. 1700, Chicago, IL, 60602, USA, (312) 922-

1115, (312) 922-1157, info-usa@euromonitor.com, https://www.euromonitor.com/; Geographies.

ANGOLA-RICE PRODUCTION

See ANGOLA-CROPS

ANGOLA-ROADS

International Road Federation (IRF), Madison Place, 500 Montgomery St., 5th Fl., Alexandria, VA, 22314, USA, (703) 535-1001, (703) 535-1007, info@irf.global, https://www.irf.global/; World Road Statistics (WRS).

United Nations Economic Commission for Africa (UNECA), PO Box 3001, Addis Ababa, ETH, ecainfo@uneca.org, https://www.uneca.org/; African Statistical Yearbook 2020.

ANGOLA-RUBBER INDUSTRY AND TRADE

International Rubber Study Group (IRSG), 51 Changi Business Park Central 2, Unit No. 6, 486066, SGP, https://www.rubberstudy.org; Monthly Rubber Bulletin (MRB); Rubber Industry Report; Rubber Statistical Bulletin; and World Rubber Industry Report (WRIO).

ANGOLA-SHIPPING

Organization of Petroleum Exporting Countries (OPEC), Helferstorferstrasse 17, Vienna, A-1010, AUT, https://www.opec.org/; OPEC Annual Statistical Bulletin 2021.

Routledge - Taylor & Francis Group, 6000 Broken Sound Pkwy. NW, Ste. 300, Boca Raton, FL, 33487, USA, (800) 634-1420, (800) 634-7064, orders@taylorandfrancis.com, https://www.routledge.com/; The Europa World Year Book 2022.

S&P Global, IHS Markit, 15 Inverness Way E, Englewood, CO, 80112, USA, (800) 447-2273, (800) 854-7179, https://ihsmarkit.com; IHS Maritime World Shipbuilding Statistics; Journal of Commerce; Lloyd's Register of Ships 2021-2022; and Maritime Portal Desktop.

United Nations Economic Commission for Africa (UNECA), PO Box 3001, Addis Ababa, ETH, ecainfo@uneca.org, https://www.uneca.org/; African Statistical Yearbook 2020.

United Nations Statistics Division (UNSD), United Nations Plz., New York, NY, 10017, USA, (800) 253-9646, (212) 963-9851, statistics@un.org, https://unstats.un.org; Statistical Yearbook of the United Nations 2021.

ANGOLA-STEEL PRODUCTION

See ANGOLA-MINERAL INDUSTRIES

ANGOLA-SUGAR PRODUCTION

See ANGOLA-CROPS

ANGOLA-TAXATION

International Road Federation (IRF), Madison Place, 500 Montgomery St., 5th Fl., Alexandria, VA, 22314, USA, (703) 535-1001, (703) 535-1007, info@irf.global, https://www.irf.global/; World Road Statistics (WRS).

ANGOLA-TELEPHONE

Palgrave Macmillan, 1 New York Plaza, Ste. 4500, New York, NY, 10004-1562, USA, (800) 777-4643, orders@palgrave.com, https://www.palgrave.com/us; The Statesman's Yearbook, 2023.

United Nations Statistics Division (UNSD), United Nations Plz., New York, NY, 10017, USA, (800) 253-9646, (212) 963-9851, statistics@un.org, https://unstats.un.org; World Statistics Pocketbook 2021.

ANGOLA-TEXTILE INDUSTRY

Palgrave Macmillan, 1 New York Plaza, Ste. 4500, New York, NY, 10004-1562, USA, (800) 777-4643, orders@palgrave.com, https://www.palgrave.com/us; The Statesman's Yearbook, 2023.

United Nations Statistics Division (UNSD), United Nations Plz., New York, NY, 10017, USA, (800) 253-9646, (212) 963-9851, statistics@un.org, https://unstats.un.org; Statistical Yearbook of the United Nations 2021.

ANGOLA-TOBACCO INDUSTRY

United Nations Statistics Division (UNSD), United Nations Plz., New York, NY, 10017, USA, (800) 253-9646, (212) 963-9851, statistics@un.org, https://unstats.un.org; Statistical Yearbook of the United Nations 2021.

ANGOLA-TOURISM

Euromonitor International, Inc., 1 N Dearborn St., Ste. 1700, Chicago, IL, 60602, USA, (312) 922-1115, (312) 922-1157, info-usa@euromonitor.com, https://www.euromonitor.com/; Geographies.

United Nations Economic Commission for Africa (UNECA), PO Box 3001, Addis Ababa, ETH, ecainfo@uneca.org, https://www.uneca.org/; African Statistical Yearbook 2020.

The World Bank, 1818 H St. NW, Washington, DC, 20433, USA, (202) 473-1000, (202) 477-6391, eds03@worldbank.org, https://www.worldbank.org/; Angola (report).

ANGOLA-TRADE

See ANGOLA-INTERNATIONAL TRADE

ANGOLA-TRANSPORTATION

Central Intelligence Agency (CIA), Office of Public Affairs, Washington, DC, 20505, USA, (703) 482-0623, https://www.cia.gov; The World Factbook.

Euromonitor International, Inc., 1 N Dearborn St., Ste. 1700, Chicago, IL, 60602, USA, (312) 922-1115, (312) 922-1157, info-usa@euromonitor.com, https://www.euromonitor.com/; Geographies.

Palgrave Macmillan, 1 New York Plaza, Ste. 4500, New York, NY, 10004-1562, USA, (800) 777-4643, orders@palgrave.com, https://www.palgrave.com/us; The Statesman's Yearbook, 2023.

Routledge - Taylor & Francis Group, 6000 Broken Sound Pkwy. NW, Ste. 300, Boca Raton, FL, 33487, USA, (800) 634-1420, (800) 634-7064, orders@taylorandfrancis.com, https://www.routledge.com/; The Europa World Year Book 2022.

United Nations Economic Commission for Africa (UNECA), PO Box 3001, Addis Ababa, ETH, ecainfo@uneca.org, https://www.uneca.org/; African Statistical Yearbook 2020.

The World Bank, 1818 H St. NW, Washington, DC, 20433, USA, (202) 473-1000, (202) 477-6391, eds03@worldbank.org, https://www.worldbank.org/; Angola (report).

ANGOLA-VITAL STATISTICS

Palgrave Macmillan, 1 New York Plaza, Ste. 4500, New York, NY, 10004-1562, USA, (800) 777-4643, orders@palgrave.com, https://www.palgrave.com/us; The Statesman's Yearbook, 2023.

U.S. Census Bureau, 4600 Silver Hill Rd., Washington, DC, 20233, USA, (301) 763-4636, (800) 923-8282, https://www.census.gov; HIV/AIDS Surveillance Data Base.

United Nations Department of Economic and Social Affairs (DESA), Population Division, 2 United Nations Plz., Rm. DC2-1950, New York, NY, 10017, USA, (212) 963-3209, (212) 963-2147, population@un.org, https://www.un.org/development/desa/pd/; World Contraceptive Use 2021: Estimates and Projections of Family Planning Indicators and World Marriage Data 2019.

United Nations Statistics Division (UNSD), United Nations Plz., New York, NY, 10017, USA, (800) 253-9646, (212) 963-9851, statistics@un.org, https://unstats.un.org; Statistical Yearbook of the United Nations 2021 and United Nations Demographic Yearbook 2020.

ANGOLA-WAGES

The World Bank, 1818 H St. NW, Washington, DC, 20433, USA, (202) 473-1000, (202) 477-6391, eds03@worldbank.org, https://www.worldbank.org/; Angola (report).

ANGOLA-WEATHER

See ANGOLA-CLIMATE

ANGOLA-WHEAT PRODUCTION

See ANGOLA-CROPS

ANGOLA-WOOD AND WOOD PULP

See ANGOLA-FORESTS AND FORESTRY

ANGOLA-WOOL PRODUCTION

See ANGOLA-TEXTILE INDUSTRY

ANGUILLA-NATIONAL STATISTICAL OFFICE

Anguilla Statistics Department, Old Court House Bldg., PO Box 60, The Valley, AIA, (264) 497-5731 (Dial from U.S.), (264) 497-3986 (Fax from U.S.), statistics@gov.ai, http://www.gov.ai/statistics; National Data Reports (Anguilla).

ANGUILLA-AGRICULTURE

Euromonitor International, Inc., 1 N Dearborn St., Ste. 1700, Chicago, IL, 60602, USA, (312) 922-1115, (312) 922-1157, info-usa@euromonitor.com, https://www.euromonitor.com/; Geographies.

Palgrave Macmillan, 1 New York Plaza, Ste. 4500, New York, NY, 10004-1562, USA, (800) 777-4643, orders@palgrave.com, https://www.palgrave.com/us; The Statesman's Yearbook, 2023.

Routledge - Taylor & Francis Group, 6000 Broken Sound Pkwy. NW, Ste. 300, Boca Raton, FL, 33487, USA, (800) 634-1420, (800) 634-7064, orders@taylorandfrancis.com, https://www.routledge.com/; The Europa World Year Book 2022.

United Nations Food and Agricultural Organization (FAO), 2121 K St., Ste. 800B, Washington, DC, 20037, USA, (202) 653-2400 (Dial from U.S.), (202) 653-5760 (Fax from U.S.), fao-hq@fao.org, https://www.fao.org; AQUASTAT.

ANGUILLA-AIRLINES

Palgrave Macmillan, 1 New York Plaza, Ste. 4500, New York, NY, 10004-1562, USA, (800) 777-4643, orders@palgrave.com, https://www.palgrave.com/us; The Statesman's Yearbook, 2023.

ANGUILLA-ARMED FORCES

Central Intelligence Agency (CIA), Office of Public Affairs, Washington, DC, 20505, USA, (703) 482-0623, https://www.cia.gov; The World Factbook.

Stockholm International Peace Research Institute (SIPRI), Signalistgatan 9, Stockholm, SE 169 72, SWE, https://www.sipri.org/; SIPRI Arms Transfers Database and SIPRI Military Expenditure Database.

ANGUILLA-BALANCE OF PAYMENTS

Routledge - Taylor & Francis Group, 6000 Broken Sound Pkwy. NW, Ste. 300, Boca Raton, FL, 33487, USA, (800) 634-1420, (800) 634-7064, orders@taylorandfrancis.com, https://www.routledge.com/; The Europa World Year Book 2022.

ANGUILLA-BANKS AND BANKING

Euromonitor International, Inc., 1 N Dearborn St., Ste. 1700, Chicago, IL, 60602, USA, (312) 922-1115, (312) 922-1157, info-usa@euromonitor.com, https://www.euromonitor.com/; Geographies.

ANGUILLA-BROADCASTING

Central Intelligence Agency (CIA), Office of Public Affairs, Washington, DC, 20505, USA, (703) 482-0623, https://www.cia.gov; The World Factbook.

Euromonitor International, Inc., 1 N Dearborn St., Ste. 1700, Chicago, IL, 60602, USA, (312) 922-1115, (312) 922-1157, info-usa@euromonitor.com, https://www.euromonitor.com/; Geographies.

WRTH Publications Limited, PO Box 290, Oxford, OX2 7FT, GBR, sales@wrth.com, https://www.wrth.com; World Radio TV Handbook 2023.

ANGUILLA-BUDGET

Central Intelligence Agency (CIA), Office of Public Affairs, Washington, DC, 20505, USA, (703) 482-0623, https://www.cia.gov; The World Factbook.

ANGUILLA-CLIMATE

Palgrave Macmillan, 1 New York Plaza, Ste. 4500, New York, NY, 10004-1562, USA, (800) 777-4643, orders@palgrave.com, https://www.palgrave.com/us; The Statesman's Yearbook, 2023.

ANGUILLA-COMMERCE

Palgrave Macmillan, 1 New York Plaza, Ste. 4500, New York, NY, 10004-1562, USA, (800) 777-4643, orders@palgrave.com, https://www.palgrave.com/us; The Statesman's Yearbook, 2023.

UK Data Service, University of Essex, Wivenhoe Park, Colchester, Essex, CO4 3SQ, GBR, https://ukdataservice.ac.uk/; International Aggregate Data.

ANGUILLA-CONSUMER PRICE INDEXES

Routledge - Taylor & Francis Group, 6000 Broken Sound Pkwy. NW, Ste. 300, Boca Raton, FL, 33487, USA, (800) 634-1420, (800) 634-7064, orders@taylorandfrancis.com, https://www.routledge.com/; The Europa World Year Book 2022.

ANGUILLA-DAIRY PROCESSING

Palgrave Macmillan, 1 New York Plaza, Ste. 4500, New York, NY, 10004-1562, USA, (800) 777-4643, orders@palgrave.com, https://www.palgrave.com/us; The Statesman's Yearbook, 2023.

ANGUILLA-ECONOMIC CONDITIONS

Bernan Press, 15250 NBN Way, Bldg. C, Blue Ridge Summit, PA, 17214, USA, (301) 459-2255, (800) 865-3457, (800) 865-3450, customercare@bernan.com, https://rowman.com/Page/Bernan; World Economic Outlook, April 2022.

Central Intelligence Agency (CIA), Office of Public Affairs, Washington, DC, 20505, USA, (703) 482-0623, https://www.cia.gov; The World Factbook.

Euromonitor International, Inc., 1 N Dearborn St., Ste. 1700, Chicago, IL, 60602, USA, (312) 922-1115, (312) 922-1157, info-usa@euromonitor.com, https://www.euromonitor.com/; Geographies.

International Monetary Fund (IMF), 700 19th St. NW, Washington, DC, 20431, USA, (202) 623-7000, (202) 623-4661, publications@imf.org, https://www.imf.org; IMF Data and World Economic Outlook.

Palgrave Macmillan, 1 New York Plaza, Ste. 4500, New York, NY, 10004-1562, USA, (800) 777-4643, orders@palgrave.com, https://www.palgrave.com/us; The Statesman's Yearbook, 2023.

United Nations Economic Commission for Latin America and the Caribbean (ECLAC), Casilla 179-D, Santiago, 7630412, CHL, (202) 596-3713, prensa@cepal.org, https://www.cepal.org/en; CEPALSTAT.

The World Bank, 1818 H St. NW, Washington, DC, 20433, USA, (202) 473-1000, (202) 477-6391, eds03@worldbank.org, https://www.worldbank.org/; Global Economic Monitor (GEM) and Global Economic Prospects, June 2022.

ANGUILLA-EDUCATION

Euromonitor International, Inc., 1 N Dearborn St., Ste. 1700, Chicago, IL, 60602, USA, (312) 922-1115, (312) 922-1157, info-usa@euromonitor.com, https://www.euromonitor.com/; Geographies.

Infoplease, c/o Sandbox Networks, Inc., 1 Lincoln St., 24th Fl., Boston, MA, 02111, USA, https://www.infoplease.com; Countries of the World.

Palgrave Macmillan, 1 New York Plaza, Ste. 4500, New York, NY, 10004-1562, USA, (800) 777-4643, orders@palgrave.com, https://www.palgrave.com/us; The Statesman's Yearbook, 2023.

Routledge - Taylor & Francis Group, 6000 Broken Sound Pkwy. NW, Ste. 300, Boca Raton, FL, 33487, USA, (800) 634-1420, (800) 634-7064, orders@taylorandfrancis.com, https://www.routledge.com/; The Europa World Year Book 2022.

UNESCO Institute for Statistics, C.P 250 Succursale H, Montreal, QC, H3G 2K8, CAN, (514) 343-6880 (Dial from U.S.), (514) 343-5740 (Fax from U.S.), uis.publications@unesco.org, http://uis.unesco.org/; Literacy.

United Nations Statistics Division (UNSD), United Nations Plz., New York, NY, 10017, USA, (800) 253-9646, (212) 963-9851, statistics@un.org, https://unstats.un.org; Millennium Development Goal Indicators.

ANGUILLA-EMPLOYMENT

UK Data Service, University of Essex, Wivenhoe Park, Colchester, Essex, CO4 3SQ, GBR, https://ukdataservice.ac.uk/; International Aggregate Data.

ANGUILLA-EXPORTS

Central Intelligence Agency (CIA), Office of Public Affairs, Washington, DC, 20505, USA, (703) 482-0623, https://www.cia.gov; The World Factbook.

ANGUILLA-FINANCE, PUBLIC

Bernan Press, 15250 NBN Way, Bldg. C, Blue Ridge Summit, PA, 17214, USA, (301) 459-2255, (800) 865-3457, (800) 865-3450, customercare@bernan.com, https://rowman.com/Page/Bernan; National Accounts Statistics: Analysis of Main Aggregates 2020.

International Monetary Fund (IMF), 700 19th St. NW, Washington, DC, 20431, USA, (202) 623-7000, (202) 623-4661, publications@imf.org, https://www.imf.org; Regional Economic Outlook.

Routledge - Taylor & Francis Group, 6000 Broken Sound Pkwy. NW, Ste. 300, Boca Raton, FL, 33487, USA, (800) 634-1420, (800) 634-7064, orders@taylorandfrancis.com, https://www.routledge.com/; The Europa World Year Book 2022.

United Nations Statistics Division (UNSD), United Nations Plz., New York, NY, 10017, USA, (800) 253-9646, (212) 963-9851, statistics@un.org, https://unstats.un.org; National Accounts Main Aggregates Database and National Accounts Statistics: Main Aggregates and Detailed Tables.

ANGUILLA-FISHERIES

Palgrave Macmillan, 1 New York Plaza, Ste. 4500, New York, NY, 10004-1562, USA, (800) 777-4643, orders@palgrave.com, https://www.palgrave.com/us; The Statesman's Yearbook, 2023.

Routledge - Taylor & Francis Group, 6000 Broken Sound Pkwy. NW, Ste. 300, Boca Raton, FL, 33487, USA, (800) 634-1420, (800) 634-7064, orders@taylorandfrancis.com, https://www.routledge.com/; The Europa World Year Book 2022.

ANGUILLA-GROSS DOMESTIC PRODUCT

Routledge - Taylor & Francis Group, 6000 Broken Sound Pkwy. NW, Ste. 300, Boca Raton, FL, 33487, USA, (800) 634-1420, (800) 634-7064, orders@taylorandfrancis.com, https://www.routledge.com/; The Europa World Year Book 2022.

ANGUILLA-HOUSING

Euromonitor International, Inc., 1 N Dearborn St., Ste. 1700, Chicago, IL, 60602, USA, (312) 922-1115, (312) 922-1157, info-usa@euromonitor.com, https://www.euromonitor.com/; Geographies.

ANGUILLA-IMPORTS

Central Intelligence Agency (CIA), Office of Public Affairs, Washington, DC, 20505, USA, (703) 482-0623, https://www.cia.gov; The World Factbook.

ANGUILLA-INDUSTRIES

Central Intelligence Agency (CIA), Office of Public Affairs, Washington, DC, 20505, USA, (703) 482-0623, https://www.cia.gov; The World Factbook.

Euromonitor International, Inc., 1 N Dearborn St., Ste. 1700, Chicago, IL, 60602, USA, (312) 922-1115, (312) 922-1157, info-usa@euromonitor.com, https://www.euromonitor.com/; Geographies.

Palgrave Macmillan, 1 New York Plaza, Ste. 4500, New York, NY, 10004-1562, USA, (800) 777-4643, orders@palgrave.com, https://www.palgrave.com/us; The Statesman's Yearbook, 2023.

United Nations Industrial Development Organization (UNIDO), 1 United Nations Plz., Rm. DC1-1118, New York, NY, 10017, USA, (212) 963-6890, (212) 963 6885, (212) 963-7904, office.newyork@unido.org, https://www.unido.org/; Industrial Statistics Databases and International Yearbook of Industrial Statistics 2021.

ANGUILLA-INTERNATIONAL TRADE

Euromonitor International, Inc., 1 N Dearborn St., Ste. 1700, Chicago, IL, 60602, USA, (312) 922-1115, (312) 922-1157, info-usa@euromonitor.com, https://www.euromonitor.com/; Geographies.

World Trade Organization (WTO), Ctre. William Rappard, Rue de Lausanne 154, Case postale, Geneva, CH-1211, SWI, enquiries@wto.org, https://www.wto.org; World Trade Statistical Review 2022.

ANGUILLA-INTERNET USERS

International Telecommunication Union (ITU), Place des Nations, Geneva, CH-1211, SWI, itumail@itu.int, https://www.itu.int; Global Connectivity Report 2022; World Telecommunication/ICT Indicators Database 2021; and Yearbook of Statistics 2019.

ANGUILLA-LABOR

Central Intelligence Agency (CIA), Office of Public Affairs, Washington, DC, 20505, USA, (703) 482-0623, https://www.cia.gov; The World Factbook.

Euromonitor International, Inc., 1 N Dearborn St., Ste. 1700, Chicago, IL, 60602, USA, (312) 922-1115, (312) 922-1157, info-usa@euromonitor.com, https://www.euromonitor.com/; Geographies.

ANGUILLA-LAND USE

United Nations Statistics Division (UNSD), United Nations Plz., New York, NY, 10017, USA, (800) 253-9646, (212) 963-9851, statistics@un.org, https://unstats.un.org; Millennium Development Goal Indicators.

ANGUILLA-LIFE EXPECTANCY

United Nations Department of Economic and Social Affairs (DESA), Population Division, 2 United Nations Plz., Rm. DC2-1950, New York, NY, 10017, USA, (212) 963-3209, (212) 963-2147, population@un.org, https://www.un.org/development/desa/pd/; World Population Ageing 2020 Highlights.

United Nations Statistics Division (UNSD), United Nations Plz., New York, NY, 10017, USA, (800) 253-9646, (212) 963-9851, statistics@un.org, https://unstats.un.org; Millennium Development Goal Indicators.

ANGUILLA-LITERACY

Euromonitor International, Inc., 1 N Dearborn St., Ste. 1700, Chicago, IL, 60602, USA, (312) 922-1115, (312) 922-1157, info-usa@euromonitor.com, https://www.euromonitor.com/; Geographies.

UNESCO Institute for Statistics, C.P 250 Succursale H, Montreal, QC, H3G 2K8, CAN, (514) 343-6880 (Dial from U.S.), (514) 343-5740 (Fax from U.S.), uis.publications@unesco.org, http://uis.unesco.org/; Literacy.

ANGUILLA-LIVESTOCK

Palgrave Macmillan, 1 New York Plaza, Ste. 4500, New York, NY, 10004-1562, USA, (800) 777-4643,

orders@palgrave.com, https://www.palgrave.com/us; The Statesman's Yearbook, 2023.

Routledge - Taylor & Francis Group, 6000 Broken Sound Pkwy. NW, Ste. 300, Boca Raton, FL, 33487, USA, (800) 634-1420, (800) 634-7064, orders@taylorandfrancis.com, https://www.routledge.com/; The Europa World Year Book 2022.

ANGUILLA-MARRIAGE

Routledge - Taylor & Francis Group, 6000 Broken Sound Pkwy. NW, Ste. 300, Boca Raton, FL, 33487, USA, (800) 634-1420, (800) 634-7064, orders@taylorandfrancis.com, https://www.routledge.com/; The Europa World Year Book 2022.

ANGUILLA-MINERAL INDUSTRIES

Routledge - Taylor & Francis Group, 6000 Broken Sound Pkwy. NW, Ste. 300, Boca Raton, FL, 33487, USA, (800) 634-1420, (800) 634-7064, orders@taylorandfrancis.com, https://www.routledge.com/; The Europa World Year Book 2022.

ANGUILLA-MORTALITY

United Nations Statistics Division (UNSD), United Nations Plz., New York, NY, 10017, USA, (800) 253-9646, (212) 963-9851, statistics@un.org, https://unstats.un.org; Millennium Development Goal Indicators.

World Health Organization (WHO), Ave. Appia 20, Geneva, CH-1211, SWI, (202) 974-3000 (Telephone in U.S.), publications@who.int, https://www.who.int/; Global Health Observatory (GHO).

ANGUILLA-POPULATION

Caribbean Public Health Agency (CARPHA), Federation Park, 16-18 Jamaica Blvd., Port of Spain, TTO, (868) 622-4261 (Dial from U.S.), (868) 299-0820 (Dial from U.S.), postmaster@carpha.org, https://carpha.org/; unpublished data.

Central Intelligence Agency (CIA), Office of Public Affairs, Washington, DC, 20505, USA, (703) 482-0623, https://www.cia.gov; The World Factbook.

Infoplease, c/o Sandbox Networks, Inc., 1 Lincoln St., 24th Fl., Boston, MA, 02111, USA, https://www.infoplease.com; Countries of the World.

Palgrave Macmillan, 1 New York Plaza, Ste. 4500, New York, NY, 10004-1562, USA, (800) 777-4643, orders@palgrave.com, https://www.palgrave.com/us; The Statesman's Yearbook, 2023.

Routledge - Taylor & Francis Group, 6000 Broken Sound Pkwy. NW, Ste. 300, Boca Raton, FL, 33487, USA, (800) 634-1420, (800) 634-7064, orders@taylorandfrancis.com, https://www.routledge.com/; The Europa World Year Book 2022.

UK Data Service, University of Essex, Wivenhoe Park, Colchester, Essex, CO4 3SQ, GBR, https://ukdataservice.ac.uk/; International Aggregate Data.

United Nations Department of Economic and Social Affairs (DESA), Population Division, 2 United Nations Plz., Rm. DC2-1950, New York, NY, 10017, USA, (212) 963-3209, (212) 963-2147, population@un.org, https://www.un.org/development/desa/pd/; Revision of World Urbanization Prospects and World Population Ageing 2020 Highlights.

United Nations Economic Commission for Latin America and the Caribbean (ECLAC), Casilla 179-D, Santiago, 7630412, CHL, (202) 596-3713, prensa@cepal.org, https://www.cepal.org/en; CEPALSTAT.

ANGUILLA-POPULATION DENSITY

Central Intelligence Agency (CIA), Office of Public Affairs, Washington, DC, 20505, USA, (703) 482-0623, https://www.cia.gov; The World Factbook.

Palgrave Macmillan, 1 New York Plaza, Ste. 4500, New York, NY, 10004-1562, USA, (800) 777-4643, orders@palgrave.com, https://www.palgrave.com/us; The Statesman's Yearbook, 2023.

Routledge - Taylor & Francis Group, 6000 Broken Sound Pkwy. NW, Ste. 300, Boca Raton, FL, 33487, USA, (800) 634-1420, (800) 634-7064, orders@taylorandfrancis.com, https://www.routledge.com/; The Europa World Year Book 2022.

ANGUILLA-POWER RESOURCES

Euromonitor International, Inc., 1 N Dearborn St., Ste. 1700, Chicago, IL, 60602, USA, (312) 922-1115, (312) 922-1157, info-usa@euromonitor.com, https://www.euromonitor.com/; Geographies.

ANGUILLA-PRICES

Euromonitor International, Inc., 1 N Dearborn St., Ste. 1700, Chicago, IL, 60602, USA, (312) 922-1115, (312) 922-1157, info-usa@euromonitor.com, https://www.euromonitor.com/; Geographies.

ANGUILLA-PUBLIC HEALTH

Euromonitor International, Inc., 1 N Dearborn St., Ste. 1700, Chicago, IL, 60602, USA, (312) 922-1115, (312) 922-1157, info-usa@euromonitor.com, https://www.euromonitor.com/; Geographies.

Palgrave Macmillan, 1 New York Plaza, Ste. 4500, New York, NY, 10004-1562, USA, (800) 777-4643, orders@palgrave.com, https://www.palgrave.com/us; The Statesman's Yearbook, 2023.

U.S. Census Bureau, 4600 Silver Hill Rd., Washington, DC, 20233, USA, (301) 763-4636, (800) 923-8282, https://www.census.gov; HIV/AIDS Surveillance Data Base.

United Nations Department of Economic and Social Affairs (DESA), Population Division, 2 United Nations Plz., Rm. DC2-1950, New York, NY, 10017, USA, (212) 963-3209, (212) 963-2147, population@un.org, https://www.un.org/development/desa/pd/; World Fertility Data 2019.

United Nations Statistics Division (UNSD), United Nations Plz., New York, NY, 10017, USA, (800) 253-9646, (212) 963-9851, statistics@un.org, https://unstats.un.org; Millennium Development Goal Indicators.

World Health Organization (WHO), Ave. Appia 20, Geneva, CH-1211, SWI, (202) 974-3000 (Telephone in U.S.), publications@who.int, https://www.who.int/; Global Health Observatory (GHO).

ANGUILLA-RELIGION

Central Intelligence Agency (CIA), Office of Public Affairs, Washington, DC, 20505, USA, (703) 482-0623, https://www.cia.gov; The World Factbook.

Palgrave Macmillan, 1 New York Plaza, Ste. 4500, New York, NY, 10004-1562, USA, (800) 777-4643, orders@palgrave.com, https://www.palgrave.com/us; The Statesman's Yearbook, 2023.

ANGUILLA-RETAIL TRADE

Euromonitor International, Inc., 1 N Dearborn St., Ste. 1700, Chicago, IL, 60602, USA, (312) 922-1115, (312) 922-1157, info-usa@euromonitor.com, https://www.euromonitor.com/; Geographies.

ANGUILLA-TELEPHONE

Palgrave Macmillan, 1 New York Plaza, Ste. 4500, New York, NY, 10004-1562, USA, (800) 777-4643, orders@palgrave.com, https://www.palgrave.com/us; The Statesman's Yearbook, 2023.

Routledge - Taylor & Francis Group, 6000 Broken Sound Pkwy. NW, Ste. 300, Boca Raton, FL, 33487, USA, (800) 634-1420, (800) 634-7064, orders@taylorandfrancis.com, https://www.routledge.com/; The Europa World Year Book 2022.

ANGUILLA-TOURISM

Euromonitor International, Inc., 1 N Dearborn St., Ste. 1700, Chicago, IL, 60602, USA, (312) 922-1115, (312) 922-1157, info-usa@euromonitor.com, https://www.euromonitor.com/; Geographies.

Palgrave Macmillan, 1 New York Plaza, Ste. 4500, New York, NY, 10004-1562, USA, (800) 777-4643, orders@palgrave.com, https://www.palgrave.com/us; The Statesman's Yearbook, 2023.

Routledge - Taylor & Francis Group, 6000 Broken Sound Pkwy. NW, Ste. 300, Boca Raton, FL, 33487, USA, (800) 634-1420, (800) 634-7064, orders@taylorandfrancis.com, https://www.routledge.com/; The Europa World Year Book 2022.

United Nations World Tourism Organization (UNWTO), Calle Poeta Joan Maragall 42, Madrid, 28020, SPA, info@unwto.org, https://www.unwto.org/; Yearbook of Tourism Statistics, 2021 Edition.

ANGUILLA-TRANSPORTATION

Central Intelligence Agency (CIA), Office of Public Affairs, Washington, DC, 20505, USA, (703) 482-0623, https://www.cia.gov; The World Factbook.

Euromonitor International, Inc., 1 N Dearborn St., Ste. 1700, Chicago, IL, 60602, USA, (312) 922-1115, (312) 922-1157, info-usa@euromonitor.com, https://www.euromonitor.com/; Geographies.

Palgrave Macmillan, 1 New York Plaza, Ste. 4500, New York, NY, 10004-1562, USA, (800) 777-4643, orders@palgrave.com, https://www.palgrave.com/us; The Statesman's Yearbook, 2023.

Routledge - Taylor & Francis Group, 6000 Broken Sound Pkwy. NW, Ste. 300, Boca Raton, FL, 33487, USA, (800) 634-1420, (800) 634-7064, orders@taylorandfrancis.com, https://www.routledge.com/; The Europa World Year Book 2022.

ANIMAL OILS AND FATS

See OILS-ANIMAL

ANIMAL WELFARE

Food & Water Watch, 1616 P St. NW, Washington, DC, 20036, USA, (202) 683-2500, (855) 340-8083, (202) 683-2501, info@fwwatch.org, https://www.foodandwaterwatch.org; Factory Farm Pollution Threatens the Great Lakes and Well-Fed: A Roadmap to a Sustainable Food System That Works For All.

Global Change Data Lab, Our World in Data, GBR, info@ourworldindata.org, https://ourworldindata.org; The Largest Mammals Have Always Been at the Greatest Risk of Extinction - This Is Still the Case Today.

Global Penguin Society (GPS), 209 Mississippi St., San Francisco, CA, 94107, USA, (415) 202-6380 , info@globalpenguinsociety.org, https://www.globalpenguinsociety.org/; Learn About Penguins.

Lake Research Partners (LRP), 1101 17th St. NW, Ste. 301, Washington, DC, 20036, USA, (202) 776-9066, (202) 776-9074, info@lakeresearch.com, https://www.lakeresearch.com/; unpublished data.

Natural Resources Defence Council (NRDC), 40 W 20th St., 11th Fl., New York, NY, 10011, USA, (212) 727-2700, (202) 289-6868, nrdcinfo@nrdc.org, https://www.nrdc.org; Unintentional Partner: How the United States Helps the Illegal Shark Fin Market.

TRAFFIC, David Attenborough Bldg., Pembroke St., Cambridge, CB2 3QZ, GBR, traffic@traffic.org, https://www.traffic.org/; TRAFFIC Bulletin and TRAFFIC Bulletin: Seizures and Prosecutions 1997-2019.

World Organisation for Animal Health (WOAH), 12, rue de Prony, Paris, 75017, FRA, woah@woah.org, https://www.woah.org/; Scientific and Technical Review 2023; WOAH Bulletin; and World Animal Health Information System (WAHIS).

ANIMALS

American Veterinary Medical Association (AVMA), 1931 N Meacham Rd., Ste. 100, Schaumburg, IL, 60173-4360, USA, (800) 248-2862, (847) 925-1329, https://www.avma.org; 2022 Economic State of the Profession.

ConsumerLab, 333 Mamaroneck Ave., White Plains, NY, 10605, USA, (914) 722-9149, info@consumerlab.com, https://www.consumerlab.com; Probiotic Supplements Review (Including Pet Probiotics).

Department for Environment, Food and Rural Affairs (Defra), Seacole Bldg., 2 Marsham St., London,

SW1P 4DF, GBR, defra.helpline@defra.gov.uk, https://www.gov.uk/defra; Farming Statistics 2021, UK Wheat and Barley Production First Estimate.

Environmental Working Group (EWG), 1250 U St. NW, Ste. 1000, Washington, DC, 20005, USA, (202) 667-6982, https://www.ewg.org/; EWG's Quick Tips for Reducing Your Diet's Climate Footprint.

Food & Water Watch, 1616 P St. NW, Washington, DC, 20036, USA, (202) 683-2500, (855) 340-8083, (202) 683-2501, info@fwwatch.org, https://www.foodandwaterwatch.org; Factory Farm Pollution Threatens the Great Lakes and Well-Fed: A Roadmap to a Sustainable Food System That Works For All.

Global Penguin Society (GPS), 209 Mississippi St., San Francisco, CA, 94107, USA, (415) 202-6380 , info@globalpenguinsociety.org, https://www.globalpenguinsociety.org/; Learn About Penguins.

National Audubon Society, 225 Varick St., New York, NY, 10014, USA, (212) 979-3196, (844) 428-3826, customerservice@audubon.org, https://www.audubon.org/; Annual Summaries of the Christmas Bird Count, 1901-Present.

U.S. Department of the Interior (DOI), Fish & Wildlife Service (FWS), 1849 C St. NW, Washington, DC, 20240, USA, (800) 344-9453, https://www.fws.gov; Species.

United Kingdom National Wildlife Crime Unit (NWCU), GBR, https://www.nwcu.police.uk/; U.K. Wildlife Crime 2020 and Wildlife Crime in Scotland: 2021 Annual Report.

World Organisation for Animal Health (WOAH), 12, rue de Prony, Paris, 75017, FRA, woah@woah.org, https://www.woah.org/; Scientific and Technical Review 2023; WOAH Bulletin; and World Animal Health Information System (WAHIS).

World Wildlife Fund (WWF), 1250 24th St. NW, Washington, DC, 20037-1193, USA, (202) 495-4800, (202) 495-4211, https://wwf.panda.org/; Living Planet Report 2022.

Zoological Society of London (ZSL), Outer Circle, Regent's Park, London, NW1 4RY, GBR, generalenquiries@zsl.org, https://www.zsl.org/; Animal Conservation; International Zoo Yearbook; and Journal of Zoology.

ANIMALS-EFFECT OF GLOBAL WARMING ON

Global Center on Adaptation (GCA), Antoine Platekade 1006, Rotterdam, 3072 ME, NLD, info@gca.org, https://gca.org/; Adapt Now: A Global Call for Leadership on Climate Resilience.

United Nations Intergovernmental Science-Policy Platform on Biodiversity and Ecosystem Services (IPBES), Platz der Vereinten Nationen 1, 10th Fl., Bonn, D-53113, GER, secretariat@ipbes.net, https://www.ipbes.net/; Global Assessment Report on Biodiversity and Ecosystem Services.

ANIMALS-HABITATIONS

Center for Biological Diversity, PO Box 710, Tucson, AZ, 85702-0710, USA, (520) 623-5252, (866) 357-3349, (520) 623-9797, center@biologicaldiversity.org, https://www.biologicaldiversity.org/; Endangered Earth Online.

United Nations Intergovernmental Science-Policy Platform on Biodiversity and Ecosystem Services (IPBES), Platz der Vereinten Nationen 1, 10th Fl., Bonn, D-53113, GER, secretariat@ipbes.net, https://www.ipbes.net/; Global Assessment Report on Biodiversity and Ecosystem Services.

Xerces Society for Invertebrate Conservation, 628 NE Broadway, Ste. 200, Portland, OR, 97232, USA, (855) 232-6639, (503) 233-6794, info@xerces.org, https://xerces.org/; Drifting Toward Disaster: How Dicamba Herbicides are Harming Cultivated and Wild Landscapes.

ANIMALS-HABITS AND BEHAVIOR

Center for Whale Research, PO Box 1577, Friday Harbor, WA, 98250, USA, info@whaleresearch.com, https://www.whaleresearch.com; Inbreeding in an Endangered Killer Whale Population.

United Nations Intergovernmental Science-Policy Platform on Biodiversity and Ecosystem Services (IPBES), Platz der Vereinten Nationen 1, 10th Fl., Bonn, D-53113, GER, secretariat@ipbes.net, https://www.ipbes.net/; Global Assessment Report on Biodiversity and Ecosystem Services.

The Whale Sanctuary Project, 4100 Kanab Canyon Rd., Kanab, UT, 84741, USA, info@whalesanctuaryproject.org, https://whalesanctuaryproject.org; unpublished data.

ANIMALS OF THE BIOMES

Global Change Data Lab, Our World in Data, GBR, info@ourworldindata.org, https://ourworldindata.org; The Largest Mammals Have Always Been at the Greatest Risk of Extinction - This Is Still the Case Today.

International Union for Conservation of Nature (IUCN), Rue Mauverney 28, Gland, CH-1196, SWI, membership@iucn.org, https://www.iucn.org/; IUCN Red List of Threatened Species.

U.S. Department of the Interior (DOI), Fish & Wildlife Service (FWS), 1849 C St. NW, Washington, DC, 20240, USA, (800) 344-9453, https://www.fws.gov; Species.

ANIMALS OF THE FOREST

Global Change Data Lab, Our World in Data, GBR, info@ourworldindata.org, https://ourworldindata.org; The Largest Mammals Have Always Been at the Greatest Risk of Extinction - This Is Still the Case Today.

International Union for Conservation of Nature (IUCN), Rue Mauverney 28, Gland, CH-1196, SWI, membership@iucn.org, https://www.iucn.org/; IUCN Red List of Threatened Species.

U.S. Department of the Interior (DOI), Fish & Wildlife Service (FWS), 1849 C St. NW, Washington, DC, 20240, USA, (800) 344-9453, https://www.fws.gov; Species.

ANIMALS OF THE OCEANS

Center for Whale Research, PO Box 1577, Friday Harbor, WA, 98250, USA, info@whaleresearch.com, https://www.whaleresearch.com; Inbreeding in an Endangered Killer Whale Population.

Global Change Data Lab, Our World in Data, GBR, info@ourworldindata.org, https://ourworldindata.org; The Largest Mammals Have Always Been at the Greatest Risk of Extinction - This Is Still the Case Today.

Global Penguin Society (GPS), 209 Mississippi St., San Francisco, CA, 94107, USA, (415) 202-6380 , info@globalpenguinsociety.org, https://www.globalpenguinsociety.org/; Learn About Penguins.

International Union for Conservation of Nature (IUCN), Rue Mauverney 28, Gland, CH-1196, SWI, membership@iucn.org, https://www.iucn.org/; IUCN Red List of Threatened Species.

Natural Resources Defence Council (NRDC), 40 W 20th St., 11th Fl., New York, NY, 10011, USA, (212) 727-2700, (202) 289-6868, nrdcinfo@nrdc.org, https://www.nrdc.org; Unintentional Partner: How the United States Helps the Illegal Shark Fin Market.

U.S. Department of the Interior (DOI), Fish & Wildlife Service (FWS), 1849 C St. NW, Washington, DC, 20240, USA, (800) 344-9453, https://www.fws.gov; Species.

The Whale Sanctuary Project, 4100 Kanab Canyon Rd., Kanab, UT, 84741, USA, info@whalesanctuaryproject.org, https://whalesanctuaryproject.org; unpublished data.

ANIMALS, DOMESTIC-INVENTORY AND PRODUCTION

Department for Environment, Food and Rural Affairs (Defra), Seacole Bldg., 2 Marsham St., London, SW1P 4DF, GBR, defra.helpline@defra.gov.uk, https://www.gov.uk/defra; Farming Statistics 2021, UK Wheat and Barley Production First Estimate.

Public Health Agency of Canada, 130 Colonnade Rd., Ottawa, ON, K1A 0K9, CAN, (844) 280-5020 (Dial from U.S.), https://www.phac-aspc.gc.ca/; Canadian Integrated Program for Antimicrobial Resistance Surveillance (CIPARS).

U.S. Department of Agriculture (USDA), Foreign Agricultural Service (FAS), 1400 Independence Ave. SW, Mail Stop 1001, Washington, DC, 20250, USA, (202) 720-3935, https://www.fas.usda.gov/; Livestock and Poultry: World Markets and Trade.

U.S. Department of Agriculture (USDA), National Agricultural Statistics Service (USDA-NASS), 1400 Independence Ave. SW, Washington, DC, 20250, USA, (800) 727-9540, nass@nass.usda.gov, https://www.nass.usda.gov; Agricultural Statistics; Hogs and Pigs; and Meat Animals Production, Disposition, and Income Annual Summary.

ANNUITIES

See PENSIONS AND RETIREMENT BENEFITS

ANTI-INFECTIVE AGENTS

U.S. Department of Health and Human Services, Centers for Disease Control and Prevention (CDC), 1600 Clifton Rd., Atlanta, GA, 30329-4027, USA, (800) 232-4636, (888) 232-6348 (TTY), cdcinfo@cdc.gov, https://www.cdc.gov; COVID-19: U.S. Impact on Antimicrobial Resistance.

ANTI-JEWISH PROPAGANDA

Anti-Defamation League (ADL), 605 3rd Ave., New York, NY, 10158-3650, USA, (212) 885-7700, adlmedia@adl.org, https://www.adl.org; U.S. White Supremacist Propaganda Remained at Historic Levels in 2021, With 27 Percent Rise in Antisemitic Messaging.

Institute for Strategic Dialogue (ISD), PO Box 75769, London, SW1P 9ER, GBR, info@isdglobal.org, https://www.isdglobal.org/; Islamogram: Salafism and Alt-Right Online Subcultures.

ANTI-VACCINATION MOVEMENT

Center for Countering Digital Hate (CCDH), Langley House, Park Rd. , East Finchley, London, N2 8EY, GBR, info@counterhate.com, https://www.counterhate.com; The Disinformation Dozen: Why Platforms Must Act on Twelve Leading Online Anti-Vaxxers and Malgorithm: How Instagram's Algorithm Publishes Misinformation and Hate to Millions During a Pandemic.

ANTIBACTERIAL AGENTS

Biotechnology Innovation Organization (BIO), 1201 New York NW, Ste. 1300, Washington, DC, 20005, USA, (202) 962-9200, info@bio.org, https://www.bio.org/; The State of Innovation in Antibacterial Therapeutics.

ANTIBIOTICS

Review on Antimicrobial Resistance, Gibbs Bldg., 215 Euston Rd., London, NW1 2BE, GBR, info@amr-review.org, https://amr-review.org/; unpublished data.

U.S. Department of Health and Human Services, Centers for Disease Control and Prevention (CDC), 1600 Clifton Rd., Atlanta, GA, 30329-4027, USA, (800) 232-4636, (888) 232-6348 (TTY), cdcinfo@cdc.gov, https://www.cdc.gov; COVID-19: U.S. Impact on Antimicrobial Resistance.

ANTIBIOTICS IN AGRICULTURE

Johns Hopkins Center for a Livable Future, 111 Market Pl., Ste. 840, Baltimore, MD, 21202, USA, (410) 223-1811, (410) 223-1829, clf@jhsph.edu, https://clf.jhsph.edu; Contamination of Retail Meat Samples with Multidrug-Resistant Organisms in Relation to Organic and Conventional Production and Processing: A Cross-Sectional Analysis of Data from the United States National Antimicrobial Resistance Monitoring System.

ANTIBIOTICS IN ANIMAL NUTRITION

Johns Hopkins Center for a Livable Future, 111 Market Pl., Ste. 840, Baltimore, MD, 21202, USA, (410) 223-1811, (410) 223-1829, clf@jhsph.edu, https://clf.jhsph.edu; Contamination of Retail Meat Samples with Multidrug-Resistant Organisms in Relation to Organic and Conventional Production and Processing: A Cross-Sectional Analysis of Data from the United States National Antimicrobial Resistance Monitoring System.

ANTIGUA AND BARBUDA-NATIONAL STATISTICAL OFFICE

Antigua and Barbuda Ministry of Finance and Corporate Governance, Statistics Division, ACT Bldg., Market and Church Sts., 1st Fl., St. John's, ATG, (268) 462-4775 (Dial from U.S.), (268) 562-7492 (Dial from U.S.), (268) 562-2542 (Fax from U.S.), info.stats@ab.gov.ag, https://statistics.gov.ag; National Data Reports (Antigua and Barbuda).

ANTIGUA AND BARBUDA-AGRICULTURE

Euromonitor International, Inc., 1 N Dearborn St., Ste. 1700, Chicago, IL, 60602, USA, (312) 922-1115, (312) 922-1157, info-usa@euromonitor.com, https://www.euromonitor.com/; Geographies.

Palgrave Macmillan, 1 New York Plaza, Ste. 4500, New York, NY, 10004-1562, USA, (800) 777-4643, orders@palgrave.com, https://www.palgrave.com/us; The Statesman's Yearbook, 2023.

Routledge - Taylor & Francis Group, 6000 Broken Sound Pkwy. NW, Ste. 300, Boca Raton, FL, 33487, USA, (800) 634-1420, (800) 634-7064, orders@taylorandfrancis.com, https://www.routledge.com/; The Europa World Year Book 2022.

United Nations Food and Agricultural Organization (FAO), 2121 K St., Ste. 800B, Washington, DC, 20037, USA, (202) 653-2400 (Dial from U.S.), (202) 653-5760 (Fax from U.S.), fao-hq@fao.org, https://www.fao.org; AQUASTAT and The State of Food and Agriculture (SOFA) 2022.

United Nations Statistics Division (UNSD), United Nations Plz., New York, NY, 10017, USA, (800) 253-9646, (212) 963-9851, statistics@un.org, https://unstats.un.org; Statistical Yearbook of the United Nations 2021.

The World Bank, 1818 H St. NW, Washington, DC, 20433, USA, (202) 473-1000, (202) 477-6391, eds03@worldbank.org, https://www.worldbank.org/; World Development Indicators (WDI) 2022.

ANTIGUA AND BARBUDA-AIRLINES

International Civil Aviation Organization (ICAO), 999 Robert-Bourassa Blvd., Montreal, QC, H3C 5H7, CAN, (514) 954-8219 (Dial from U.S.), (514) 954-6077 (Fax from U.S.), icaohq@icao.int, https://www.icao.int; ICAO Regional Reports.

Palgrave Macmillan, 1 New York Plaza, Ste. 4500, New York, NY, 10004-1562, USA, (800) 777-4643, orders@palgrave.com, https://www.palgrave.com/us; The Statesman's Yearbook, 2023.

Routledge - Taylor & Francis Group, 6000 Broken Sound Pkwy. NW, Ste. 300, Boca Raton, FL, 33487, USA, (800) 634-1420, (800) 634-7064, orders@taylorandfrancis.com, https://www.routledge.com/; The Europa World Year Book 2022.

ANTIGUA AND BARBUDA-ARMED FORCES

Central Intelligence Agency (CIA), Office of Public Affairs, Washington, DC, 20505, USA, (703) 482-0623, https://www.cia.gov; The World Factbook.

Palgrave Macmillan, 1 New York Plaza, Ste. 4500, New York, NY, 10004-1562, USA, (800) 777-4643, orders@palgrave.com, https://www.palgrave.com/us; The Statesman's Yearbook, 2023.

Stockholm International Peace Research Institute (SIPRI), Signalistgatan 9, Stockholm, SE 169 72, SWE, https://www.sipri.org/; SIPRI Arms Transfers Database and SIPRI Military Expenditure Database.

ANTIGUA AND BARBUDA-BALANCE OF PAYMENTS

International Monetary Fund (IMF), 700 19th St. NW, Washington, DC, 20431, USA, (202) 623-7000, (202) 623-4661, publications@imf.org, https://www.imf.org; Balance of Payments Statistics: Annual Report 2021.

Routledge - Taylor & Francis Group, 6000 Broken Sound Pkwy. NW, Ste. 300, Boca Raton, FL, 33487, USA, (800) 634-1420, (800) 634-7064, orders@taylorandfrancis.com, https://www.routledge.com/; The Europa World Year Book 2022.

United Nations Economic Commission for Latin America and the Caribbean (ECLAC), Casilla 179-D, Santiago, 7630412, CHL, (202) 596-3713, prensa@cepal.org, https://www.cepal.org/en; Economic Survey of Latin America and the Caribbean 2021: Labour Dynamics and Employment Policies for Sustainable and Inclusive Recovery Beyond the COVID-19 Crisis.

The World Bank, 1818 H St. NW, Washington, DC, 20433, USA, (202) 473-1000, (202) 477-6391, eds03@worldbank.org, https://www.worldbank.org/; World Development Indicators (WDI) 2022.

ANTIGUA AND BARBUDA-BANKS AND BANKING

Euromonitor International, Inc., 1 N Dearborn St., Ste. 1700, Chicago, IL, 60602, USA, (312) 922-1115, (312) 922-1157, info-usa@euromonitor.com, https://www.euromonitor.com/; Geographies.

Routledge - Taylor & Francis Group, 6000 Broken Sound Pkwy. NW, Ste. 300, Boca Raton, FL, 33487, USA, (800) 634-1420, (800) 634-7064, orders@taylorandfrancis.com, https://www.routledge.com/; The Europa World Year Book 2022.

ANTIGUA AND BARBUDA-BROADCASTING

Central Intelligence Agency (CIA), Office of Public Affairs, Washington, DC, 20505, USA, (703) 482-0623, https://www.cia.gov; The World Factbook.

Euromonitor International, Inc., 1 N Dearborn St., Ste. 1700, Chicago, IL, 60602, USA, (312) 922-1115, (312) 922-1157, info-usa@euromonitor.com, https://www.euromonitor.com/; Geographies.

Palgrave Macmillan, 1 New York Plaza, Ste. 4500, New York, NY, 10004-1562, USA, (800) 777-4643, orders@palgrave.com, https://www.palgrave.com/us; The Statesman's Yearbook, 2023.

WRTH Publications Limited, PO Box 290, Oxford, OX2 7FT, GBR, sales@wrth.com, https://www.wrth.com; World Radio TV Handbook 2023.

ANTIGUA AND BARBUDA-BUDGET

Central Intelligence Agency (CIA), Office of Public Affairs, Washington, DC, 20505, USA, (703) 482-0623, https://www.cia.gov; The World Factbook.

ANTIGUA AND BARBUDA-CLIMATE

Palgrave Macmillan, 1 New York Plaza, Ste. 4500, New York, NY, 10004-1562, USA, (800) 777-4643, orders@palgrave.com, https://www.palgrave.com/us; The Statesman's Yearbook, 2023.

ANTIGUA AND BARBUDA-COMMERCE

Palgrave Macmillan, 1 New York Plaza, Ste. 4500, New York, NY, 10004-1562, USA, (800) 777-4643, orders@palgrave.com, https://www.palgrave.com/us; The Statesman's Yearbook, 2023.

UK Data Service, University of Essex, Wivenhoe Park, Colchester, Essex, CO4 3SQ, GBR, https://ukdataservice.ac.uk/; International Aggregate Data.

ANTIGUA AND BARBUDA-CORN INDUSTRY

See ANTIGUA AND BARBUDA-CROPS

ANTIGUA AND BARBUDA-CROPS

Palgrave Macmillan, 1 New York Plaza, Ste. 4500, New York, NY, 10004-1562, USA, (800) 777-4643, orders@palgrave.com, https://www.palgrave.com/us; The Statesman's Yearbook, 2023.

United Nations Food and Agricultural Organization (FAO), 2121 K St., Ste. 800B, Washington, DC, 20037, USA, (202) 653-2400 (Dial from U.S.), (202) 653-5760 (Fax from U.S.), fao-hq@fao.org, https://www.fao.org; The State of Food and Agriculture (SOFA) 2022.

United Nations Statistics Division (UNSD), United Nations Plz., New York, NY, 10017, USA, (800) 253-9646, (212) 963-9851, statistics@un.org, https://unstats.un.org; Statistical Yearbook of the United Nations 2021.

ANTIGUA AND BARBUDA-DAIRY PROCESSING

Palgrave Macmillan, 1 New York Plaza, Ste. 4500, New York, NY, 10004-1562, USA, (800) 777-4643, orders@palgrave.com, https://www.palgrave.com/us; The Statesman's Yearbook, 2023.

United Nations Food and Agricultural Organization (FAO), 2121 K St., Ste. 800B, Washington, DC, 20037, USA, (202) 653-2400 (Dial from U.S.), (202) 653-5760 (Fax from U.S.), fao-hq@fao.org, https://www.fao.org; The State of Food and Agriculture (SOFA) 2022.

ANTIGUA AND BARBUDA-DEBTS, EXTERNAL

United Nations Economic Commission for Latin America and the Caribbean (ECLAC), Casilla 179-D, Santiago, 7630412, CHL, (202) 596-3713, prensa@cepal.org, https://www.cepal.org/en; Economic Survey of Latin America and the Caribbean 2021: Labour Dynamics and Employment Policies for Sustainable and Inclusive Recovery Beyond the COVID-19 Crisis.

The World Bank, 1818 H St. NW, Washington, DC, 20433, USA, (202) 473-1000, (202) 477-6391, eds03@worldbank.org, https://www.worldbank.org/; World Development Indicators (WDI) 2022.

ANTIGUA AND BARBUDA-ECONOMIC CONDITIONS

Bernan Press, 15250 NBN Way, Bldg. C, Blue Ridge Summit, PA, 17214, USA, (301) 459-2255, (800) 865-3457, (800) 865-3450, customercare@bernan.com, https://rowman.com/Page/Bernan; World Economic Outlook, April 2022.

Central Intelligence Agency (CIA), Office of Public Affairs, Washington, DC, 20505, USA, (703) 482-0623, https://www.cia.gov; The World Factbook.

Euromonitor International, Inc., 1 N Dearborn St., Ste. 1700, Chicago, IL, 60602, USA, (312) 922-1115, (312) 922-1157, info-usa@euromonitor.com, https://www.euromonitor.com/; Geographies.

Palgrave Macmillan, 1 New York Plaza, Ste. 4500, New York, NY, 10004-1562, USA, (800) 777-4643, orders@palgrave.com, https://www.palgrave.com/us; The Statesman's Yearbook, 2023.

Routledge - Taylor & Francis Group, 6000 Broken Sound Pkwy. NW, Ste. 300, Boca Raton, FL, 33487, USA, (800) 634-1420, (800) 634-7064, orders@taylorandfrancis.com, https://www.routledge.com/; The Europa World Year Book 2022.

UNESCO Institute for Statistics, C.P 250 Succursale H, Montreal, QC, H3G 2K8, CAN, (514) 343-6880 (Dial from U.S.), (514) 343-5740 (Fax from U.S.), uis.publications@unesco.org, http://uis.unesco.org/; UIS.Stat.

United Nations Economic Commission for Latin America and the Caribbean (ECLAC), Casilla 179-D, Santiago, 7630412, CHL, (202) 596-3713, prensa@cepal.org, https://www.cepal.org/en; Economic Survey of Latin America and the Caribbean 2021: Labour Dynamics and Employment Policies for Sustainable and Inclusive Recovery Beyond the COVID-19 Crisis and Foreign Direct Investment in Latin America and the Caribbean 2022.

United Nations Statistics Division (UNSD), United Nations Plz., New York, NY, 10017, USA, (800) 253-9646, (212) 963-9851, statistics@un.org, https://unstats.un.org; World Statistics Pocketbook 2021.

The World Bank, 1818 H St. NW, Washington, DC, 20433, USA, (202) 473-1000, (202) 477-6391, eds03@worldbank.org, https://www.worldbank.org/; Caribbean (report); The Global Findex Database 2021; and World Development Indicators (WDI) 2022.

ANTIGUA AND BARBUDA-EDUCATION

The World Bank, 1818 H St. NW, Washington, DC, 20433, USA, (202) 473-1000, (202) 477-6391, eds03@worldbank.org, https://www.worldbank.org/; Caribbean (report).

ANTIGUA AND BARBUDA-ELECTRICITY

United Nations Statistics Division (UNSD), United Nations Plz., New York, NY, 10017, USA, (800) 253-9646, (212) 963-9851, statistics@un.org, https://unstats.un.org; Statistical Yearbook of the United Nations 2021.

ANTIGUA AND BARBUDA-EMPLOYMENT

International Labour Organization (ILO), 4 Rte. des Morillons, Geneva, CH-1211, SWI, ilo@ilo.org, https://www.ilo.org; NORMLEX Information System on International Labour Standards.

UK Data Service, University of Essex, Wivenhoe Park, Colchester, Essex, CO4 3SQ, GBR, https://ukdataservice.ac.uk/; International Aggregate Data.

ANTIGUA AND BARBUDA-ENVIRONMENTAL CONDITIONS

United Nations Statistics Division (UNSD), United Nations Plz., New York, NY, 10017, USA, (800) 253-9646, (212) 963-9851, statistics@un.org, https://unstats.un.org; World Statistics Pocketbook 2021.

The World Bank, 1818 H St. NW, Washington, DC, 20433, USA, (202) 473-1000, (202) 477-6391, eds03@worldbank.org, https://www.worldbank.org/; Caribbean (report).

ANTIGUA AND BARBUDA-EXPORTS

Central Intelligence Agency (CIA), Office of Public Affairs, Washington, DC, 20505, USA, (703) 482-0623, https://www.cia.gov; The World Factbook.

ANTIGUA AND BARBUDA-FERTILIZER INDUSTRY

United Nations Food and Agricultural Organization (FAO), 2121 K St., Ste. 800B, Washington, DC, 20037, USA, (202) 653-2400 (Dial from U.S.), (202) 653-5760 (Fax from U.S.), fao-hq@fao.org, https://www.fao.org; The State of Food and Agriculture (SOFA) 2022.

ANTIGUA AND BARBUDA-FETAL MORTALITY

See ANTIGUA AND BARBUDA-MORTALITY

ANTIGUA AND BARBUDA-FINANCE

Stockholm International Peace Research Institute (SIPRI), Signalistgatan 9, Stockholm, SE 169 72, SWE, https://www.sipri.org/; SIPRI Arms Transfers Database and SIPRI Military Expenditure Database.

The World Bank, 1818 H St. NW, Washington, DC, 20433, USA, (202) 473-1000, (202) 477-6391, eds03@worldbank.org, https://www.worldbank.org/; Caribbean (report).

ANTIGUA AND BARBUDA-FINANCE, PUBLIC

International Monetary Fund (IMF), 700 19th St. NW, Washington, DC, 20431, USA, (202) 623-7000, (202) 623-4661, publications@imf.org, https://www.imf.org; International Financial Statistics (IFS).

Palgrave Macmillan, 1 New York Plaza, Ste. 4500, New York, NY, 10004-1562, USA, (800) 777-4643, orders@palgrave.com, https://www.palgrave.com/us; The Statesman's Yearbook, 2023.

Routledge - Taylor & Francis Group, 6000 Broken Sound Pkwy. NW, Ste. 300, Boca Raton, FL, 33487, USA, (800) 634-1420, (800) 634-7064, orders@taylorandfrancis.com, https://www.routledge.com/; The Europa World Year Book 2022.

United Nations Statistics Division (UNSD), United Nations Plz., New York, NY, 10017, USA, (800) 253-9646, (212) 963-9851, statistics@un.org, https://unstats.un.org; National Accounts Main Aggregates Database and National Accounts Statistics: Main Aggregates and Detailed Tables.

ANTIGUA AND BARBUDA-FISHERIES

Routledge - Taylor & Francis Group, 6000 Broken Sound Pkwy. NW, Ste. 300, Boca Raton, FL, 33487, USA, (800) 634-1420, (800) 634-7064, orders@taylorandfrancis.com, https://www.routledge.com/; The Europa World Year Book 2022.

United Nations Food and Agricultural Organization (FAO), 2121 K St., Ste. 800B, Washington, DC, 20037, USA, (202) 653-2400 (Dial from U.S.), (202) 653-5760 (Fax from U.S.), fao-hq@fao.org, https://www.fao.org; FAO Yearbook of Fishery and Aquaculture Statistics 2019; Fishery Statistical Collections Global Capture Production; FishStatJ; and The State of Food and Agriculture (SOFA) 2022.

ANTIGUA AND BARBUDA-FOOD

United Nations Food and Agricultural Organization (FAO), 2121 K St., Ste. 800B, Washington, DC, 20037, USA, (202) 653-2400 (Dial from U.S.), (202) 653-5760 (Fax from U.S.), fao-hq@fao.org, https://www.fao.org; The State of Food and Agriculture (SOFA) 2022.

ANTIGUA AND BARBUDA-FORESTS AND FORESTRY

UNESCO Institute for Statistics, C.P 250 Succursale H, Montreal, QC, H3G 2K8, CAN, (514) 343-6880 (Dial from U.S.), (514) 343-5740 (Fax from U.S.), uis.publications@unesco.org, http://uis.unesco.org/; UIS.Stat.

United Nations Food and Agricultural Organization (FAO), 2121 K St., Ste. 800B, Washington, DC, 20037, USA, (202) 653-2400 (Dial from U.S.), (202) 653-5760 (Fax from U.S.), fao-hq@fao.org, https://www.fao.org; The State of Food and Agriculture (SOFA) 2022.

United Nations Statistics Division (UNSD), United Nations Plz., New York, NY, 10017, USA, (800) 253-9646, (212) 963-9851, statistics@un.org, https://unstats.un.org; Statistical Yearbook of the United Nations 2021.

ANTIGUA AND BARBUDA-GOLD INDUSTRY

The World Bank, 1818 H St. NW, Washington, DC, 20433, USA, (202) 473-1000, (202) 477-6391, eds03@worldbank.org, https://www.worldbank.org/; World Development Indicators (WDI) 2022.

ANTIGUA AND BARBUDA-GROSS DOMESTIC PRODUCT

Routledge - Taylor & Francis Group, 6000 Broken Sound Pkwy. NW, Ste. 300, Boca Raton, FL, 33487, USA, (800) 634-1420, (800) 634-7064, orders@taylorandfrancis.com, https://www.routledge.com/; The Europa World Year Book 2022.

United Nations Statistics Division (UNSD), United Nations Plz., New York, NY, 10017, USA, (800) 253-9646, (212) 963-9851, statistics@un.org, https://unstats.un.org; Statistical Yearbook of the United Nations 2021.

The World Bank, 1818 H St. NW, Washington, DC, 20433, USA, (202) 473-1000, (202) 477-6391, eds03@worldbank.org, https://www.worldbank.org/; World Development Indicators (WDI) 2022.

ANTIGUA AND BARBUDA-GROSS NATIONAL PRODUCT

Palgrave Macmillan, 1 New York Plaza, Ste. 4500, New York, NY, 10004-1562, USA, (800) 777-4643, orders@palgrave.com, https://www.palgrave.com/us; The Statesman's Yearbook, 2023.

The World Bank, 1818 H St. NW, Washington, DC, 20433, USA, (202) 473-1000, (202) 477-6391, eds03@worldbank.org, https://www.worldbank.org/; World Development Indicators (WDI) 2022.

ANTIGUA AND BARBUDA-HOUSING

Euromonitor International, Inc., 1 N Dearborn St., Ste. 1700, Chicago, IL, 60602, USA, (312) 922-1115, (312) 922-1157, info-usa@euromonitor.com, https://www.euromonitor.com/; Geographies.

ANTIGUA AND BARBUDA-ILLITERATE PERSONS

UNESCO Institute for Statistics, C.P 250 Succursale H, Montreal, QC, H3G 2K8, CAN, (514) 343-6880 (Dial from U.S.), (514) 343-5740 (Fax from U.S.), uis.publications@unesco.org, http://uis.unesco.org/; UIS.Stat.

ANTIGUA AND BARBUDA-IMPORTS

Central Intelligence Agency (CIA), Office of Public Affairs, Washington, DC, 20505, USA, (703) 482-0623, https://www.cia.gov; The World Factbook.

ANTIGUA AND BARBUDA-INDUSTRIES

Central Intelligence Agency (CIA), Office of Public Affairs, Washington, DC, 20505, USA, (703) 482-0623, https://www.cia.gov; The World Factbook.

International Labour Organization (ILO), 4 Rte. des Morillons, Geneva, CH-1211, SWI, ilo@ilo.org, https://www.ilo.org; NORMLEX Information System on International Labour Standards.

Palgrave Macmillan, 1 New York Plaza, Ste. 4500, New York, NY, 10004-1562, USA, (800) 777-4643, orders@palgrave.com, https://www.palgrave.com/us; The Statesman's Yearbook, 2023.

Routledge - Taylor & Francis Group, 6000 Broken Sound Pkwy. NW, Ste. 300, Boca Raton, FL, 33487, USA, (800) 634-1420, (800) 634-7064, orders@taylorandfrancis.com, https://www.routledge.com/; The Europa World Year Book 2022.

United Nations Economic Commission for Latin America and the Caribbean (ECLAC), Casilla 179-D, Santiago, 7630412, CHL, (202) 596-3713, prensa@cepal.org, https://www.cepal.org/en; Economic Survey of Latin America and the Caribbean 2021: Labour Dynamics and Employment Policies for Sustainable and Inclusive Recovery Beyond the COVID-19 Crisis.

The World Bank, 1818 H St. NW, Washington, DC, 20433, USA, (202) 473-1000, (202) 477-6391, eds03@worldbank.org, https://www.worldbank.org/; World Development Indicators (WDI) 2022.

ANTIGUA AND BARBUDA-INFANT AND MATERNAL MORTALITY

See ANTIGUA AND BARBUDA-MORTALITY

ANTIGUA AND BARBUDA-INFLATION (FINANCE)

United Nations Economic Commission for Latin America and the Caribbean (ECLAC), Casilla 179-D, Santiago, 7630412, CHL, (202) 596-3713, prensa@cepal.org, https://www.cepal.org/en; Economic Survey of Latin America and the Caribbean 2021: Labour Dynamics and Employment Policies for Sustainable and Inclusive Recovery Beyond the COVID-19 Crisis.

ANTIGUA AND BARBUDA-INTERNATIONAL TRADE

Euromonitor International, Inc., 1 N Dearborn St., Ste. 1700, Chicago, IL, 60602, USA, (312) 922-1115, (312) 922-1157, info-usa@euromonitor.com, https://www.euromonitor.com/; Geographies.

Palgrave Macmillan, 1 New York Plaza, Ste. 4500, New York, NY, 10004-1562, USA, (800) 777-4643, orders@palgrave.com, https://www.palgrave.com/us; The Statesman's Yearbook, 2023.

Routledge - Taylor & Francis Group, 6000 Broken Sound Pkwy. NW, Ste. 300, Boca Raton, FL, 33487, USA, (800) 634-1420, (800) 634-7064, orders@taylorandfrancis.com, https://www.routledge.com/; The Europa World Year Book 2022.

United Nations Conference on Trade and Development (UNCTAD), Palais des Nations, Geneva, 1211, SWI, (212) 963-6896, unctadinfo@unctad.org, https://unctad.org; Trade and Development Report 2021.

United Nations Economic Commission for Latin America and the Caribbean (ECLAC), Casilla 179-D, Santiago, 7630412, CHL, (202) 596-3713, prensa@cepal.org, https://www.cepal.org/en; Economic Survey of Latin America and the Caribbean 2021: Labour Dynamics and Employment Policies for Sustainable and Inclusive Recovery Beyond the COVID-19 Crisis.

United Nations Food and Agricultural Organization (FAO), 2121 K St., Ste. 800B, Washington, DC, 20037, USA, (202) 653-2400 (Dial from U.S.), (202) 653-5760 (Fax from U.S.), fao-hq@fao.org, https://www.fao.org; The State of Food and Agriculture (SOFA) 2022.

United Nations Statistics Division (UNSD), United Nations Plz., New York, NY, 10017, USA, (800) 253-9646, (212) 963-9851, statistics@un.org, https://unstats.un.org; International Trade Statistics Yearbook 2020.

The World Bank, 1818 H St. NW, Washington, DC, 20433, USA, (202) 473-1000, (202) 477-6391, eds03@worldbank.org, https://www.worldbank.org/; World Development Indicators (WDI) 2022.

World Trade Organization (WTO), Ctre. William Rappard, Rue de Lausanne 154, Case postale, Geneva, CH-1211, SWI, enquiries@wto.org, https://www.wto.org; World Trade Statistical Review 2022.

ANTIGUA AND BARBUDA-LABOR

Central Intelligence Agency (CIA), Office of Public Affairs, Washington, DC, 20505, USA, (703) 482-0623, https://www.cia.gov; The World Factbook.

Euromonitor International, Inc., 1 N Dearborn St., Ste. 1700, Chicago, IL, 60602, USA, (312) 922-1115, (312) 922-1157, info-usa@euromonitor.com, https://www.euromonitor.com/; Geographies.

International Labour Organization (ILO), 4 Rte. des Morillons, Geneva, CH-1211, SWI, ilo@ilo.org, https://www.ilo.org; NORMLEX Information System on International Labour Standards.

Palgrave Macmillan, 1 New York Plaza, Ste. 4500, New York, NY, 10004-1562, USA, (800) 777-4643, orders@palgrave.com, https://www.palgrave.com/us; The Statesman's Yearbook, 2023.

United Nations Food and Agricultural Organization (FAO), 2121 K St., Ste. 800B, Washington, DC, 20037, USA, (202) 653-2400 (Dial from U.S.), (202) 653-5760 (Fax from U.S.), fao-hq@fao.org, https://www.fao.org; The State of Food and Agriculture (SOFA) 2022.

The World Bank, 1818 H St. NW, Washington, DC, 20433, USA, (202) 473-1000, (202) 477-6391, eds03@worldbank.org, https://www.worldbank.org/; World Development Indicators (WDI) 2022.

ANTIGUA AND BARBUDA-LIFE EXPECTANCY

United Nations Department of Economic and Social Affairs (DESA), Population Division, 2 United Nations Plz., Rm. DC2-1950, New York, NY, 10017, USA, (212) 963-3209, (212) 963-2147, population@un.org, https://www.un.org/development/desa/pd/; World Population Ageing 2020 Highlights.

The World Bank, 1818 H St. NW, Washington, DC, 20433, USA, (202) 473-1000, (202) 477-6391, eds03@worldbank.org, https://www.worldbank.org/; Caribbean (report).

ANTIGUA AND BARBUDA-LITERACY

Euromonitor International, Inc., 1 N Dearborn St., Ste. 1700, Chicago, IL, 60602, USA, (312) 922-1115, (312) 922-1157, info-usa@euromonitor.com, https://www.euromonitor.com/; Geographies.

ANTIGUA AND BARBUDA-LIVESTOCK

Palgrave Macmillan, 1 New York Plaza, Ste. 4500, New York, NY, 10004-1562, USA, (800) 777-4643, orders@palgrave.com, https://www.palgrave.com/us; The Statesman's Yearbook, 2023.

Routledge - Taylor & Francis Group, 6000 Broken Sound Pkwy. NW, Ste. 300, Boca Raton, FL, 33487, USA, (800) 634-1420, (800) 634-7064, orders@taylorandfrancis.com, https://www.routledge.com/; The Europa World Year Book 2022.

United Nations Food and Agricultural Organization (FAO), 2121 K St., Ste. 800B, Washington, DC, 20037, USA, (202) 653-2400 (Dial from U.S.), (202) 653-5760 (Fax from U.S.), fao-hq@fao.org, https://www.fao.org; The State of Food and Agriculture (SOFA) 2022.

United Nations Statistics Division (UNSD), United Nations Plz., New York, NY, 10017, USA, (800) 253-9646, (212) 963-9851, statistics@un.org, https://unstats.un.org; Statistical Yearbook of the United Nations 2021.

ANTIGUA AND BARBUDA-MARRIAGE

Routledge - Taylor & Francis Group, 6000 Broken Sound Pkwy. NW, Ste. 300, Boca Raton, FL, 33487, USA, (800) 634-1420, (800) 634-7064, orders@taylorandfrancis.com, https://www.routledge.com/; The Europa World Year Book 2022.

United Nations Statistics Division (UNSD), United Nations Plz., New York, NY, 10017, USA, (800) 253-9646, (212) 963-9851, statistics@un.org, https://unstats.un.org; Statistical Yearbook of the United Nations 2021.

ANTIGUA AND BARBUDA-MINERAL INDUSTRIES

United Nations Conference on Trade and Development (UNCTAD), Palais des Nations, Geneva, 1211, SWI, (212) 963-6896, unctadinfo@unctad.org, https://unctad.org; Trade and Development Report 2021.

ANTIGUA AND BARBUDA-MONEY SUPPLY

Routledge - Taylor & Francis Group, 6000 Broken Sound Pkwy. NW, Ste. 300, Boca Raton, FL, 33487, USA, (800) 634-1420, (800) 634-7064, orders@taylorandfrancis.com, https://www.routledge.com/; The Europa World Year Book 2022.

ANTIGUA AND BARBUDA-MORTALITY

United Nations Statistics Division (UNSD), United Nations Plz., New York, NY, 10017, USA, (800) 253-9646, (212) 963-9851, statistics@un.org, https://unstats.un.org; Statistical Yearbook of the United Nations 2021 and World Statistics Pocketbook 2021.

The World Bank, 1818 H St. NW, Washington, DC, 20433, USA, (202) 473-1000, (202) 477-6391, eds03@worldbank.org, https://www.worldbank.org/; World Development Indicators (WDI) 2022.

ANTIGUA AND BARBUDA-NUTRITION

United Nations Food and Agricultural Organization (FAO), 2121 K St., Ste. 800B, Washington, DC, 20037, USA, (202) 653-2400 (Dial from U.S.), (202) 653-5760 (Fax from U.S.), fao-hq@fao.org, https://www.fao.org; The State of Food and Agriculture (SOFA) 2022.

ANTIGUA AND BARBUDA-PESTICIDES

United Nations Food and Agricultural Organization (FAO), 2121 K St., Ste. 800B, Washington, DC, 20037, USA, (202) 653-2400 (Dial from U.S.), (202) 653-5760 (Fax from U.S.), fao-hq@fao.org, https://www.fao.org; The State of Food and Agriculture (SOFA) 2022.

ANTIGUA AND BARBUDA-PETROLEUM INDUSTRY AND TRADE

United Nations Food and Agricultural Organization (FAO), 2121 K St., Ste. 800B, Washington, DC, 20037, USA, (202) 653-2400 (Dial from U.S.), (202) 653-5760 (Fax from U.S.), fao-hq@fao.org, https://www.fao.org; The State of Food and Agriculture (SOFA) 2022.

United Nations Statistics Division (UNSD), United Nations Plz., New York, NY, 10017, USA, (800) 253-9646, (212) 963-9851, statistics@un.org, https://unstats.un.org; Statistical Yearbook of the United Nations 2021.

ANTIGUA AND BARBUDA-POPULATION

Caribbean Public Health Agency (CARPHA), Federation Park, 16-18 Jamaica Blvd., Port of Spain, TTO, (868) 622-4261 (Dial from U.S.), (868) 299-0820 (Dial from U.S.), postmaster@carpha.org, https://carpha.org/; unpublished data.

Central Intelligence Agency (CIA), Office of Public Affairs, Washington, DC, 20505, USA, (703) 482-0623, https://www.cia.gov; The World Factbook.

European Commission, Eurostat, Luxembourg, 2920, LUX, https://ec.europa.eu/eurostat/; EU in the World 2020.

International Labour Organization (ILO), 4 Rte. des Morillons, Geneva, CH-1211, SWI, ilo@ilo.org, https://www.ilo.org; NORMLEX Information System on International Labour Standards.

Palgrave Macmillan, 1 New York Plaza, Ste. 4500, New York, NY, 10004-1562, USA, (800) 777-4643, orders@palgrave.com, https://www.palgrave.com/us; The Statesman's Yearbook, 2023.

Routledge - Taylor & Francis Group, 6000 Broken Sound Pkwy. NW, Ste. 300, Boca Raton, FL, 33487, USA, (800) 634-1420, (800) 634-7064, orders@taylorandfrancis.com, https://www.routledge.com/; The Europa World Year Book 2022.

UK Data Service, University of Essex, Wivenhoe Park, Colchester, Essex, CO4 3SQ, GBR, https://ukdataservice.ac.uk/; International Aggregate Data.

United Nations Department of Economic and Social Affairs (DESA), Population Division, 2 United Nations Plz., Rm. DC2-1950, New York, NY, 10017, USA, (212) 963-3209, (212) 963-2147, population@un.org, https://www.un.org/development/desa/pd/; Revision of World Urbanization Prospects and World Population Ageing 2020 Highlights.

United Nations Development Programme (UNDP), One United Nations Plz., New York, NY, 10017, USA, (212) 906-5000, (212) 906-5001, https://www.undp.org; Human Development Report 2021-2022.

United Nations Statistics Division (UNSD), United Nations Plz., New York, NY, 10017, USA, (800) 253-9646, (212) 963-9851, statistics@un.org, https://unstats.un.org; Statistical Yearbook of the United Nations 2021 and World Statistics Pocketbook 2021.

The World Bank, 1818 H St. NW, Washington, DC, 20433, USA, (202) 473-1000, (202) 477-6391, eds03@worldbank.org, https://www.worldbank.org/; Caribbean (report) and The Global Findex Database 2021.

ANTIGUA AND BARBUDA-POPULATION DENSITY

Central Intelligence Agency (CIA), Office of Public Affairs, Washington, DC, 20505, USA, (703) 482-0623, https://www.cia.gov; The World Factbook.

Palgrave Macmillan, 1 New York Plaza, Ste. 4500, New York, NY, 10004-1562, USA, (800) 777-4643, orders@palgrave.com, https://www.palgrave.com/us; The Statesman's Yearbook, 2023.

Routledge - Taylor & Francis Group, 6000 Broken Sound Pkwy. NW, Ste. 300, Boca Raton, FL, 33487, USA, (800) 634-1420, (800) 634-7064, orders@taylorandfrancis.com, https://www.routledge.com/; The Europa World Year Book 2022.

ANTIGUA AND BARBUDA-POWER RESOURCES

Euromonitor International, Inc., 1 N Dearborn St., Ste. 1700, Chicago, IL, 60602, USA, (312) 922-1115, (312) 922-1157, info-usa@euromonitor.com, https://www.euromonitor.com/; Geographies.

United Nations Food and Agricultural Organization (FAO), 2121 K St., Ste. 800B, Washington, DC, 20037, USA, (202) 653-2400 (Dial from U.S.), (202) 653-5760 (Fax from U.S.), fao-hq@fao.org, https://www.fao.org; The State of Food and Agriculture (SOFA) 2022.

United Nations Statistics Division (UNSD), United Nations Plz., New York, NY, 10017, USA, (800) 253-9646, (212) 963-9851, statistics@un.org, https://unstats.un.org; Energy Statistics Yearbook 2019; Statistical Yearbook of the United Nations 2021; and World Statistics Pocketbook 2021.

ANTIGUA AND BARBUDA-PRICES

Euromonitor International, Inc., 1 N Dearborn St., Ste. 1700, Chicago, IL, 60602, USA, (312) 922-1115, (312) 922-1157, info-usa@euromonitor.com, https://www.euromonitor.com/; Geographies.

United Nations Economic Commission for Latin America and the Caribbean (ECLAC), Casilla 179-D, Santiago, 7630412, CHL, (202) 596-3713, prensa@cepal.org, https://www.cepal.org/en; Economic Survey of Latin America and the Caribbean 2021: Labour Dynamics and Employment Policies for Sustainable and Inclusive Recovery Beyond the COVID-19 Crisis.

ANTIGUA AND BARBUDA-PUBLIC HEALTH

Euromonitor International, Inc., 1 N Dearborn St., Ste. 1700, Chicago, IL, 60602, USA, (312) 922-1115, (312) 922-1157, info-usa@euromonitor.com, https://www.euromonitor.com/; Geographies.

Palgrave Macmillan, 1 New York Plaza, Ste. 4500, New York, NY, 10004-1562, USA, (800) 777-4643, orders@palgrave.com, https://www.palgrave.com/us; The Statesman's Yearbook, 2023.

U.S. Census Bureau, 4600 Silver Hill Rd., Washington, DC, 20233, USA, (301) 763-4636, (800) 923-8282, https://www.census.gov; HIV/AIDS Surveillance Data Base.

United Nations Department of Economic and Social Affairs (DESA), Population Division, 2 United Nations Plz., Rm. DC2-1950, New York, NY, 10017, USA, (212) 963-3209, (212) 963-2147, population@un.org, https://www.un.org/development/desa/pd/; World Fertility Data 2019.

United Nations Development Programme (UNDP), One United Nations Plz., New York, NY, 10017, USA, (212) 906-5000, (212) 906-5001, https://www.undp.org; Human Development Report 2021-2022.

United Nations Statistics Division (UNSD), United Nations Plz., New York, NY, 10017, USA, (800) 253-9646, (212) 963-9851, statistics@un.org, https://unstats.un.org; Statistical Yearbook of the United Nations 2021.

The World Bank, 1818 H St. NW, Washington, DC, 20433, USA, (202) 473-1000, (202) 477-6391, eds03@worldbank.org, https://www.worldbank.org/; Caribbean (report).

World Health Organization (WHO), Ave. Appia 20, Geneva, CH-1211, SWI, (202) 974-3000 (Telephone in U.S.), publications@who.int, https://www.who.int/; Health Statistics and Information Systems.

ANTIGUA AND BARBUDA-RELIGION

Central Intelligence Agency (CIA), Office of Public Affairs, Washington, DC, 20505, USA, (703) 482-0623, https://www.cia.gov; The World Factbook.

Palgrave Macmillan, 1 New York Plaza, Ste. 4500, New York, NY, 10004-1562, USA, (800) 777-4643, orders@palgrave.com, https://www.palgrave.com/us; The Statesman's Yearbook, 2023.

ANTIGUA AND BARBUDA-RETAIL TRADE

Euromonitor International, Inc., 1 N Dearborn St., Ste. 1700, Chicago, IL, 60602, USA, (312) 922-1115, (312) 922-1157, info-usa@euromonitor.com, https://www.euromonitor.com/; Geographies.

ANTIGUA AND BARBUDA-SHIPPING

Routledge - Taylor & Francis Group, 6000 Broken Sound Pkwy. NW, Ste. 300, Boca Raton, FL, 33487, USA, (800) 634-1420, (800) 634-7064, orders@taylorandfrancis.com, https://www.routledge.com/; The Europa World Year Book 2022.

United Nations Statistics Division (UNSD), United Nations Plz., New York, NY, 10017, USA, (800) 253-9646, (212) 963-9851, statistics@un.org, https://unstats.un.org; Statistical Yearbook of the United Nations 2021.

ANTIGUA AND BARBUDA-SUGAR PRODUCTION

See ANTIGUA AND BARBUDA-CROPS

ANTIGUA AND BARBUDA-TAXATION

The World Bank, 1818 H St. NW, Washington, DC, 20433, USA, (202) 473-1000, (202) 477-6391, eds03@worldbank.org, https://www.worldbank.org/; World Development Indicators (WDI) 2022.

ANTIGUA AND BARBUDA-TELEPHONE

Palgrave Macmillan, 1 New York Plaza, Ste. 4500, New York, NY, 10004-1562, USA, (800) 777-4643, orders@palgrave.com, https://www.palgrave.com/us; The Statesman's Yearbook, 2023.

Routledge - Taylor & Francis Group, 6000 Broken Sound Pkwy. NW, Ste. 300, Boca Raton, FL, 33487, USA, (800) 634-1420, (800) 634-7064, orders@taylorandfrancis.com, https://www.routledge.com/; The Europa World Year Book 2022.

United Nations Statistics Division (UNSD), United Nations Plz., New York, NY, 10017, USA, (800) 253-9646, (212) 963-9851, statistics@un.org, https://unstats.un.org; World Statistics Pocketbook 2021.

ANTIGUA AND BARBUDA-TEXTILE INDUSTRY

Palgrave Macmillan, 1 New York Plaza, Ste. 4500, New York, NY, 10004-1562, USA, (800) 777-4643, orders@palgrave.com, https://www.palgrave.com/us; The Statesman's Yearbook, 2023.

ANTIGUA AND BARBUDA-TOURISM

Euromonitor International, Inc., 1 N Dearborn St., Ste. 1700, Chicago, IL, 60602, USA, (312) 922-1115, (312) 922-1157, info-usa@euromonitor.com, https://www.euromonitor.com/; Geographies.

Palgrave Macmillan, 1 New York Plaza, Ste. 4500, New York, NY, 10004-1562, USA, (800) 777-4643, orders@palgrave.com, https://www.palgrave.com/us; The Statesman's Yearbook, 2023.

Routledge - Taylor & Francis Group, 6000 Broken Sound Pkwy. NW, Ste. 300, Boca Raton, FL, 33487, USA, (800) 634-1420, (800) 634-7064, orders@taylorandfrancis.com, https://www.routledge.com/; The Europa World Year Book 2022.

United Nations World Tourism Organization (UNWTO), Calle Poeta Joan Maragall 42, Madrid, 28020, SPA, info@unwto.org, https://www.unwto.org/; Yearbook of Tourism Statistics, 2021 Edition.

ANTIGUA AND BARBUDA-TRADE

See ANTIGUA AND BARBUDA-INTERNATIONAL TRADE

ANTIGUA AND BARBUDA-TRANSPORTATION

Central Intelligence Agency (CIA), Office of Public Affairs, Washington, DC, 20505, USA, (703) 482-0623, https://www.cia.gov; The World Factbook.

Euromonitor International, Inc., 1 N Dearborn St., Ste. 1700, Chicago, IL, 60602, USA, (312) 922-1115, (312) 922-1157, info-usa@euromonitor.com, https://www.euromonitor.com/; Geographies.

Palgrave Macmillan, 1 New York Plaza, Ste. 4500, New York, NY, 10004-1562, USA, (800) 777-4643, orders@palgrave.com, https://www.palgrave.com/us; The Statesman's Yearbook, 2023.

Routledge - Taylor & Francis Group, 6000 Broken Sound Pkwy. NW, Ste. 300, Boca Raton, FL, 33487, USA, (800) 634-1420, (800) 634-7064, orders@taylorandfrancis.com, https://www.routledge.com/; The Europa World Year Book 2022.

ANTIGUA AND BARBUDA-UNEMPLOYMENT

International Labour Organization (ILO), 4 Rte. des Morillons, Geneva, CH-1211, SWI, ilo@ilo.org, https://www.ilo.org; NORMLEX Information System on International Labour Standards.

Palgrave Macmillan, 1 New York Plaza, Ste. 4500, New York, NY, 10004-1562, USA, (800) 777-4643, orders@palgrave.com, https://www.palgrave.com/us; The Statesman's Yearbook, 2023.

United Nations Statistics Division (UNSD), United Nations Plz., New York, NY, 10017, USA, (800) 253-9646, (212) 963-9851, statistics@un.org, https://unstats.un.org; Statistical Yearbook of the United Nations 2021.

ANTIGUA AND BARBUDA-VITAL STATISTICS

Palgrave Macmillan, 1 New York Plaza, Ste. 4500, New York, NY, 10004-1562, USA, (800) 777-4643, orders@palgrave.com, https://www.palgrave.com/us; The Statesman's Yearbook, 2023.

U.S. Census Bureau, 4600 Silver Hill Rd., Washington, DC, 20233, USA, (301) 763-4636, (800) 923-8282, https://www.census.gov; HIV/AIDS Surveillance Data Base.

United Nations Department of Economic and Social Affairs (DESA), Population Division, 2 United Nations Plz., Rm. DC2-1950, New York, NY, 10017, USA, (212) 963-3209, (212) 963-2147, population@un.org, https://www.un.org/development/desa/pd/; World Contraceptive Use 2021: Estimates and Projections of Family Planning Indicators and World Marriage Data 2019.

United Nations Statistics Division (UNSD), United Nations Plz., New York, NY, 10017, USA, (800) 253-9646, (212) 963-9851, statistics@un.org, https://unstats.un.org; Statistical Yearbook of the United Nations 2021 and United Nations Demographic Yearbook 2020.

ANTIGUA AND BARBUDA-WAGES

International Labour Organization (ILO), 4 Rte. des Morillons, Geneva, CH-1211, SWI, ilo@ilo.org, https://www.ilo.org; NORMLEX Information System on International Labour Standards.

ANTIMONY

U.S. Department of the Interior (DOI), U.S. Geological Survey (USGS), National Minerals Information Center (NMIC), 12201 Sunrise Valley Dr., Reston, VA, 20192, USA, (703) 648-4920, (703) 648-7971, (703) 648-4995, sfortier@usgs.gov, https://www.usgs.gov/centers/nmic; Mineral Commodity Summaries 2022 and Mineral Industry Surveys (MIS).

ANTINUCLEAR MOVEMENT

Federation of American Scientists (FAS), 1112 16th St. NW, Ste. 600, Washington, DC, 20036, USA, (202) 546-3300, (202) 675-1010, fas@fas.org, https://fas.org/; Siloed Thinking: A Closer Look at the Ground-Based Strategic Deterrent.

ANTISEMITISM

American Jewish Committee (AJC), 165 E 56th St., New York, NY, 10022, USA, (212) 891-1443, (212) 751-4000, newyork@ajc.org, https://www.ajc.org; Numbers Do Lie: Experts Say Extent of White Supremacist Terrorism Is Worse than Data Depicts.

Anti-Defamation League (ADL), 605 3rd Ave., New York, NY, 10158-3650, USA, (212) 885-7700, adlmedia@adl.org, https://www.adl.org; ADL H.E.A.T. Map: Hate, Extremism, Antisemitism and Terrorism; ADL Hate Crime Map; Audit of Antisemitic Incidents 2022; Murder and Extremism in the United States in 2021; and U.S. White Supremacist Propaganda Remained at Historic Levels in 2021, With 27 Percent Rise in Antisemitic Messaging.

California State University San Bernardino, Center for the Study of Hate and Extremism, 5500 University Pkwy., San Bernardino, CA, 92407, USA, (909) 537-7503, (909) 537-7711, blevin8@aol.com, https://csbs.csusb.edu/hate-and-extremism-center; Report to the Nation: Factbook on Hate and Extremism in the U.S. and Internationally; Report to the Nation: Illustrated Almanac; Report to the Nation: Visual Almanac 2020 Preview, with the Latest FBI/DHS Data; and Special Status Report: Hate Crime in the U.S. 1992-2016.

Center for Countering Digital Hate (CCDH), Langley House, Park Rd. , East Finchley, London, N2 8EY, GBR, info@counterhate.com, https://www.counterhate.com; Malgorithm: How Instagram's Algorithm Publishes Misinformation and Hate to Millions During a Pandemic.

Institute for Strategic Dialogue (ISD), PO Box 75769, London, SW1P 9ER, GBR, info@isdglobal.org, https://www.isdglobal.org/; Islamogram: Salafism and Alt-Right Online Subcultures.

The Leadership Conference Education Fund (The Education Fund), 1620 L St. NW, Ste. 1100, Washington, DC, 20036, USA, (202) 466-3311, https://civilrights.org/edfund/#; Cause for Concern 2024: The State of Hate.

Network Contagion Research Institute (NCRI), https://networkcontagion.us/; #Twittertakeover: How the Musk Acquisition Became a Launchpad for Gen-Z Neo-Nazis, Ye, and Widespread Antisemitism.

U.S. Department of Justice (DOJ), Federal Bureau of Investigation (FBI), 935 Pennsylvania Ave. NW, Washington, DC, 20535-0001, USA, (202) 324-3000, https://www.fbi.gov/; Hate Crime in the United States Incident Analysis.

University of Maryland, National Consortium for the Study of Terrorism and Responses to Terrorism (START), PO Box 266, 5245 Greenbelt Rd., College Park, MD, 20740, USA, (301) 405-6600, (301) 314-1980, infostart@start.umd.edu, https://www.start.umd.edu; Characteristics and Targets of Mass Casualty Hate Crime Offenders.

ANTIVIRAL AGENTS

Biotechnology Innovation Organization (BIO), 1201 New York NW, Ste. 1300, Washington, DC, 20005, USA, (202) 962-9200, info@bio.org, https://www.bio.org/; BIO COVID-19 Therapeutic Development Tracker.

ANXIETY

American Institute of Stress, 220 Adams Dr., Ste 280, Weatherford, TX, 76086, USA, (682) 239-6823, info@stress.org, https://www.stress.org; Stress Research: 2022 Stress Statistics.

The Gallup Organization, 901 F St. NW, Washington, DC, 20004, USA, (202) 715-3030, (800) 204-1192, (202) 715-3045, https://www.gallup.com; 2020 Sets Records for Negative Emotions.

The Henry J. Kaiser Family Foundation (KFF), 185 Berry St., Ste. 2000, San Francisco, CA, 94107, USA, (650) 854-9400, (650) 854-4800, https://www.kff.org; The Implications of COVID-19 for Mental Health and Substance Use.

U.S. Department of Health and Human Services, Centers for Disease Control and Prevention (CDC), 1600 Clifton Rd., Atlanta, GA, 30329-4027, USA, (800) 232-4636, (888) 232-6348 (TTY), cdcinfo@cdc.gov, https://www.cdc.gov; Symptoms of Anxiety or Depressive Disorder and Use of Mental Health Care Among Adults During the COVID-19 Pandemic - United States, August 2020 - February 2021.

U.S. Department of Health and Human Services, Centers for Disease Control and Prevention (CDC), National Center for Health Statistics (NCHS), 3311 Toledo Rd., Hyattsville, MD, 20782-2064, USA, (800) 232-4636, (301) 458-4000, https://www.cdc.gov/nchs; Household Pulse Survey: Anxiety and Depression.

ANXIETY DISORDERS

The Henry J. Kaiser Family Foundation (KFF), 185 Berry St., Ste. 2000, San Francisco, CA, 94107, USA, (650) 854-9400, (650) 854-4800, https://www.kff.org; The Implications of COVID-19 for Mental Health and Substance Use.

U.S. Department of Health and Human Services (HHS), National Institutes of Health (NIH), National Institute of Mental Health (NIMH), 6001 Executive Blvd., Room 6200, MSC 9663, Bethesda, MD, 20892-9663, USA, (866) 615-6464, (301) 443-8431 (TTY), (301) 443-4279, nimhinfo@nih.gov, https://www.nimh.nih.gov/; Mental Health Statistics.

U.S. Department of Health and Human Services, Centers for Disease Control and Prevention (CDC), 1600 Clifton Rd., Atlanta, GA, 30329-4027, USA, (800) 232-4636, (888) 232-6348 (TTY), cdcinfo@cdc.gov, https://www.cdc.gov; Symptoms of Anxiety or Depressive Disorder and Use of Mental Health Care Among Adults During the COVID-19 Pandemic - United States, August 2020 - February 2021.

Yale School of Medicine, Yale Child Study Center, 230 S Frontage Rd., New Haven, CT, 06520, USA, (844) 362-9272, https://medicine.yale.edu/childstudy; unpublished data.

APARTMENTS

Apartment List, USA, https://www.apartmentlist.com; National Rent Report; Rent Growth & Inflation Explainer; and Renter Stigma: Social and Economic Pressure in the Housing Market.

National Association of Realtors (NAR), 430 N Michigan Ave., Chicago, IL, 60611-4087, USA, (800) 874-6500, (202) 383-1000, https://www.nar.realtor; Monthly Housing Affordability Index.

APIARIES

Bee Informed Partnership (BIP), 4112 Plant Sciences Bldg., College Park, MD, 20742, USA, (443) 296-2470, https://beeinformed.org/; Loss & Management Survey and 2021-2022 Weighted Average Winter All Colony Loss.

APPALACHIAN REGION

Appalachian Regional Commission (ARC), 1666 Connecticut Ave. NW, Ste. 700, Washington, DC, 20009, USA, (202) 884-7700, info@arc.gov, https://www.arc.gov/; Socioeconomic Data Profile by County and Strengthening Economic Resilience in Appalachia.

APPAREL GOODS-ADVERTISING

The NPD Group, 900 W Shore Rd., Port Washington, NY, 11050, USA, (516) 625-0700, contactnpd@npd.com, https://www.npd.com; Fashion Accessories.

APPAREL GOODS-CONSUMER EXPENDITURES

The NPD Group, 900 W Shore Rd., Port Washington, NY, 11050, USA, (516) 625-0700, contactnpd@npd.com, https://www.npd.com; Fashion Accessories.

U.S. Department of Labor (DOL), Bureau of Labor Statistics (BLS), Postal Square Bldg., 2 Massachusetts Ave. NE, Washington, DC, 20212-0001, USA, (202) 691-5200, (202) 691-7890, blsdata_staff@bls.gov, https://www.bls.gov; Consumer Expenditure Survey (CE).

APPAREL GOODS-INTERNATIONAL TRADE

The NPD Group, 900 W Shore Rd., Port Washington, NY, 11050, USA, (516) 625-0700, contactnpd@npd.com, https://www.npd.com; Fashion Accessories.

U.S. Census Bureau, International Trade Program, 4600 Silver Hill Rd., Washington, DC, 20233, USA, (800) 549-0595, eid.international.trade.data@census.gov, https://www.census.gov/foreign-trade; International Trade Data.

APPAREL GOODS-PRICES

The NPD Group, 900 W Shore Rd., Port Washington, NY, 11050, USA, (516) 625-0700, contactnpd@npd.com, https://www.npd.com; Fashion Accessories.

U.S. Department of Commerce (DOC), Bureau of Economic Analysis (BEA), 4600 Silver Hill Rd., Washington, DC, 20233, USA, (301) 278-9004, customerservice@bea.gov, https://www.bea.gov; National Income and Product Accounts (NIPA): 2022 Update and Survey of Current Business (SCB).

U.S. Department of Labor (DOL), Bureau of Labor Statistics (BLS), Postal Square Bldg., 2 Massachusetts Ave. NE, Washington, DC, 20212-0001, USA, (202) 691-5200, (202) 691-7890, blsdata_staff@bls.gov, https://www.bls.gov; All Urban Consumers (Chained CPI) (Consumer Price Index - CPI); All Urban Consumers (Current Series) (Consumer Price Index - CPI); Consumer Price Indexe (CPI) Publications; and Urban Wage Earners and Clerical Workers (Current Series) (Consumer Price Index - CPI).

APPAREL MANUFACTURING-EARNINGS

The NPD Group, 900 W Shore Rd., Port Washington, NY, 11050, USA, (516) 625-0700, contactnpd@npd.com, https://www.npd.com; Fashion Accessories.

U.S. Census Bureau, 4600 Silver Hill Rd., Washington, DC, 20233, USA, (301) 763-4636, (800) 923-8282, https://www.census.gov; County Business Patterns (CBP) 2020.

U.S. Department of Labor (DOL), Bureau of Labor Statistics (BLS), Postal Square Bldg., 2 Massachusetts Ave. NE, Washington, DC, 20212-0001, USA, (202) 691-5200, (202) 691-7890, blsdata_staff@bls.gov, https://www.bls.gov; Current Employment Statistics (CES).

APPAREL MANUFACTURING-EMPLOYEES

U.S. Census Bureau, 4600 Silver Hill Rd., Washington, DC, 20233, USA, (301) 763-4636, (800) 923-8282, https://www.census.gov; County Business Patterns (CBP) 2020.

U.S. Department of Commerce (DOC), Bureau of Economic Analysis (BEA), 4600 Silver Hill Rd., Washington, DC, 20233, USA, (301) 278-9004, customerservice@bea.gov, https://www.bea.gov; Survey of Current Business (SCB).

U.S. Department of Labor (DOL), Bureau of Labor Statistics (BLS), Postal Square Bldg., 2 Massachusetts Ave. NE, Washington, DC, 20212-0001, USA, (202) 691-5200, (202) 691-7890, blsdata_staff@bls.gov, https://www.bls.gov; Current Employment Statistics (CES) and Industry-Occupation Matrix Data, By Occupation.

APPAREL MANUFACTURING-ESTABLISHMENTS

U.S. Census Bureau, 4600 Silver Hill Rd., Washington, DC, 20233, USA, (301) 763-4636, (800) 923-8282, https://www.census.gov; County Business Patterns (CBP) 2020.

APPAREL MANUFACTURING-GROSS DOMESTIC PRODUCT

The NPD Group, 900 W Shore Rd., Port Washington, NY, 11050, USA, (516) 625-0700, contactnpd@npd.com, https://www.npd.com; Fashion Accessories.

U.S. Department of Commerce (DOC), Bureau of Economic Analysis (BEA), 4600 Silver Hill Rd., Washington, DC, 20233, USA, (301) 278-9004, customerservice@bea.gov, https://www.bea.gov; National Income and Product Accounts (NIPA): 2022 Update and Survey of Current Business (SCB).

APPAREL MANUFACTURING-INDUSTRIAL SAFETY

U.S. Department of Labor (DOL), Bureau of Labor Statistics (BLS), Postal Square Bldg., 2 Massachusetts Ave. NE, Washington, DC, 20212-0001, USA, (202) 691-5200, (202) 691-7890, blsdata_staff@bls.gov, https://www.bls.gov; Injuries, Illnesses, and Fatalities (IIF).

APPAREL MANUFACTURING-INTERNATIONAL TRADE

The NPD Group, 900 W Shore Rd., Port Washington, NY, 11050, USA, (516) 625-0700, contactnpd@npd.com, https://www.npd.com; Fashion Accessories.

U.S. Census Bureau, International Trade Program, 4600 Silver Hill Rd., Washington, DC, 20233, USA, (800) 549-0595, eid.international.trade.data@census.gov, https://www.census.gov/foreign-trade; International Trade Data.

APPAREL MANUFACTURING-PRODUCTIVITY

The NPD Group, 900 W Shore Rd., Port Washington, NY, 11050, USA, (516) 625-0700, contactnpd@npd.com, https://www.npd.com; Fashion Accessories.

U.S. Department of Labor (DOL), Bureau of Labor Statistics (BLS), Postal Square Bldg., 2 Massachusetts Ave. NE, Washington, DC, 20212-0001, USA, (202) 691-5200, (202) 691-7890, blsdata_staff@bls.gov, https://www.bls.gov; Productivity.

APPAREL MANUFACTURING-TOXIC CHEMICAL RELEASES

U.S. Environmental Protection Agency (EPA), 1200 Pennsylvania Ave. NW, Washington, DC, 20460, USA, (202) 564-4700, https://www.epa.gov/; Toxics Release Inventory (TRI) Program.

APPLES

U.S. Department of Agriculture (USDA), Economic Research Service (ERS), 1400 Independence Ave. SW, Mail Stop 1800, Washington, DC, 20250-0002, USA, (202) 720-2791, https://www.ers.usda.gov/; Food Price Outlook.

U.S. Department of Agriculture (USDA), National Agricultural Statistics Service (USDA-NASS), 1400 Independence Ave. SW, Washington, DC, 20250, USA, (800) 727-9540, nass@nass.usda.gov, https://www.nass.usda.gov; Quick Stats.

U.S. Department of Labor (DOL), Bureau of Labor Statistics (BLS), Postal Square Bldg., 2 Massachusetts Ave. NE, Washington, DC, 20212-0001, USA, (202) 691-5200, (202) 691-7890, blsdata_staff@bls.gov, https://www.bls.gov; Consumer Price Index (CPI) Databases.

APRICOTS

U.S. Department of Agriculture (USDA), National Agricultural Statistics Service (USDA-NASS), 1400 Independence Ave. SW, Washington, DC, 20250, USA, (800) 727-9540, nass@nass.usda.gov, https://www.nass.usda.gov; Quick Stats.

AQUACULTURE

U.S. Department of Agriculture (USDA), National Agricultural Statistics Service (USDA-NASS), 1400 Independence Ave. SW, Washington, DC, 20250, USA, (800) 727-9540, nass@nass.usda.gov, https://www.nass.usda.gov; Catfish Processing; Catfish Production; and Trout Production.

ARAB COUNTRIES

Organisation of Islamic Cooperation (OIC), Statistical, Economic and Social Research and Training Centre for Islamic Countries (SESRIC), Kudus Cad. No. 9, Diplomatik Site, Ankara, 06450, TUR, statistics@sesric.org, https://www.sesric.org/; OIC Statistics (OICStat) Database and OIC-Countries in Figures (OIC-CIF).

United Nations Economic and Social Commission for Western Asia (ESCWA), Riad el-Solh Sq., PO Box 11-8575, Beirut, LBN, escwa-ciu@un.org, https://www.unescwa.org; ESCWA Annual Report 2019.

ARCHERY

National Sporting Goods Association (NSGA), 3041 Woodcreek Dr., Ste. 210, Downers Grove, IL, 60515, USA, (847) 296-6742, (847) 391-9827, info@nsga.org, https://www.nsga.org; Sports Participation in the United States 2022 and Sports Participation: Historical Sports Participation 2022.

ARCHITECTURAL DESIGN

Alzheimer's Disease International (ADI), 15 Blue Lion Pl., London, SE1 4PU, GBR, info@alzint.org, https://www.alzint.org; World Alzheimer Report 2020: Design, Dignity, Dementia: Dementia-Related Design and the Built Environment.

ARCHITECTURAL SERVICES

See ENGINEERING AND ARCHITECTURAL SERVICES

ARCHIVAL RESOURCES

U.S. National Archives and Records Administration, 8601 Adelphi Rd., College Park, MD, 20740-6001, USA, (866) 272-6272, (301) 837-0483, https://www.archives.gov; Access to Archival Databases (AAD).

AREA OF-FOREIGN COUNTRIES

U.S. Census Bureau, 4600 Silver Hill Rd., Washington, DC, 20233, USA, (301) 763-4636, (800) 923-8282, https://www.census.gov; International Database: World Population Estimates and Projections.

AREA OF-FOREST LAND

U.S. Department of Agriculture (USDA), U.S. Forest Service, 1400 Independence Ave. SW, Washington, DC, 20250-0003, USA, (800) 832-1355, https://www.fs.usda.gov; Land Areas of the National Forest System 2021.

United Nations Food and Agricultural Organization (FAO), 2121 K St., Ste. 800B, Washington, DC, 20037, USA, (202) 653-2400 (Dial from U.S.), (202) 653-5760 (Fax from U.S.), fao-hq@fao.org, https://www.fao.org; FAO Soils Portal: Legacy Soil Maps and Soils Databases.

AREA OF-PARKS

National Association of State Park Directors (NASPD), PO Box 24114, Winston-Salem, NC, 27114-4114, USA, info@stateparks.org, https://www.stateparks.org/; unpublished data.

U.S. Department of the Interior (DOI), National Park Service (NPS), 1849 C St. NW, Washington, DC, 20240, USA, (202) 208-6843, https://www.nps.gov/; Park Science Magazine.

AREA OF-UNITED STATES

U.S. Census Bureau, 4600 Silver Hill Rd., Washington, DC, 20233, USA, (301) 763-4636, (800) 923-8282, https://www.census.gov; International Database: World Population Estimates and Projections.

AREA OF-UNITED STATES-WATER

University of Nebraska-Lincoln, National Drought Mitigation Center, 3310 Holdrege St., PO Box 830988, Lincoln, NE, 68583-0988, USA, (402) 472-6707, (402) 472-2946, https://droughtmonitor.unl.edu/; U.S. Drought Monitor.

AREA OF-WORLD

U.S. Census Bureau, 4600 Silver Hill Rd., Washington, DC, 20233, USA, (301) 763-4636, (800) 923-8282, https://www.census.gov; International Database: World Population Estimates and Projections.

ARGENTINA-NATIONAL STATISTICAL OFFICE

Instituto Nacional de Estadistica y Censos de Argentina, Av. Presidente Julio A. Roca 609, PB C1067ABB, Buenos Aires, ARG, https://www.indec.gob.ar/; National Data Reports (Argentina).

ARGENTINA-AGRICULTURE

The Economist Group: Economist Intelligence Unit (EIU), 900 3rd Ave., 16th Fl., New York, NY, 10022, USA, (212) 541-0500, americas@eiu.com, https://www.eiu.com; Argentina Country Report.

Euromonitor International, Inc., 1 N Dearborn St., Ste. 1700, Chicago, IL, 60602, USA, (312) 922-1115, (312) 922-1157, info-usa@euromonitor.com, https://www.euromonitor.com/; Geographies.

Inter-American Development Bank (IDB), 1300 New York Ave. NW, Washington, DC, 20577, USA, (202) 623-1000, (202) 623-3096, https://www.iadb.org/en; Latin Macro Watch (LMW).

Palgrave Macmillan, 1 New York Plaza, Ste. 4500, New York, NY, 10004-1562, USA, (800) 777-4643, orders@palgrave.com, https://www.palgrave.com/us; The Statesman's Yearbook, 2023.

Routledge - Taylor & Francis Group, 6000 Broken Sound Pkwy. NW, Ste. 300, Boca Raton, FL, 33487, USA, (800) 634-1420, (800) 634-7064, orders@taylorandfrancis.com, https://www.routledge.com/; The Europa World Year Book 2022.

United Nations Food and Agricultural Organization (FAO), 2121 K St., Ste. 800B, Washington, DC, 20037, USA, (202) 653-2400 (Dial from U.S.), (202) 653-5760 (Fax from U.S.), fao-hq@fao.org, https://www.fao.org; AQUASTAT and The State of Food and Agriculture (SOFA) 2022.

United Nations Statistics Division (UNSD), United Nations Plz., New York, NY, 10017, USA, (800) 253-9646, (212) 963-9851, statistics@un.org, https://unstats.un.org; Statistical Yearbook of the United Nations 2021.

University of California Los Angeles (UCLA), Latin American Institute (LAI), 10343 Bunche Hall, 315 Portola Plaza, Los Angeles, CA, 90095-1447, USA, (310) 825-4571, lai@international.ucla.edu, https://www.international.ucla.edu/lai; unpublished data.

The World Bank, 1818 H St. NW, Washington, DC, 20433, USA, (202) 473-1000, (202) 477-6391, eds03@worldbank.org, https://www.worldbank.org/; Argentina (report) and World Development Indicators (WDI) 2022.

ARGENTINA-AIRLINES

International Civil Aviation Organization (ICAO), 999 Robert-Bourassa Blvd., Montreal, QC, H3C 5H7, CAN, (514) 954-8219 (Dial from U.S.), (514) 954-6077 (Fax from U.S.), icaohq@icao.int, https://www.icao.int; ICAO Regional Reports.

Palgrave Macmillan, 1 New York Plaza, Ste. 4500, New York, NY, 10004-1562, USA, (800) 777-4643, orders@palgrave.com, https://www.palgrave.com/us; The Statesman's Yearbook, 2023.

Routledge - Taylor & Francis Group, 6000 Broken Sound Pkwy. NW, Ste. 300, Boca Raton, FL, 33487, USA, (800) 634-1420, (800) 634-7064, orders@taylorandfrancis.com, https://www.routledge.com/; The Europa World Year Book 2022.

ARGENTINA-ALUMINUM PRODUCTION

See ARGENTINA-MINERAL INDUSTRIES

ARGENTINA-ARMED FORCES

Central Intelligence Agency (CIA), Office of Public Affairs, Washington, DC, 20505, USA, (703) 482-0623, https://www.cia.gov; The World Factbook.

International Institute for Strategic Studies (IISS) - Americas, 2121 K St. NW, Ste. 600, Washington, DC, 20037, USA, (202) 659-1490, (202) 659-1499, https://www.iiss.org/; The Military Balance 2022.

Palgrave Macmillan, 1 New York Plaza, Ste. 4500, New York, NY, 10004-1562, USA, (800) 777-4643, orders@palgrave.com, https://www.palgrave.com/us; The Statesman's Yearbook, 2023.

Stockholm International Peace Research Institute (SIPRI), Signalistgatan 9, Stockholm, SE 169 72, SWE, https://www.sipri.org/; SIPRI Arms Transfers Database and SIPRI Military Expenditure Database.

ARGENTINA-ARTICHOKE PRODUCTION

See ARGENTINA-CROPS

ARGENTINA-BALANCE OF PAYMENTS

Inter-American Development Bank (IDB), 1300 New York Ave. NW, Washington, DC, 20577, USA, (202) 623-1000, (202) 623-3096, https://www.iadb.org/en; Latin Macro Watch (LMW).

International Monetary Fund (IMF), 700 19th St. NW, Washington, DC, 20431, USA, (202) 623-7000, (202) 623-4661, publications@imf.org, https://www.imf.org; Balance of Payments Statistics: Annual Report 2021 and International Financial Statistics (IFS).

Routledge - Taylor & Francis Group, 6000 Broken Sound Pkwy. NW, Ste. 300, Boca Raton, FL, 33487, USA, (800) 634-1420, (800) 634-7064, orders@taylorandfrancis.com, https://www.routledge.com/; The Europa World Year Book 2022.

United Nations Conference on Trade and Development (UNCTAD), Palais des Nations, Geneva, 1211, SWI, (212) 963-6896, unctadinfo@unctad.org, https://unctad.org; Handbook of Statistics 2021.

United Nations Economic Commission for Latin America and the Caribbean (ECLAC), Casilla 179-D, Santiago, 7630412, CHL, (202) 596-3713, prensa@cepal.org, https://www.cepal.org/en; Economic Survey of Latin America and the Caribbean 2021: Labour Dynamics and Employment Policies for Sustainable and Inclusive Recovery Beyond the COVID-19 Crisis.

The World Bank, 1818 H St. NW, Washington, DC, 20433, USA, (202) 473-1000, (202) 477-6391, eds03@worldbank.org, https://www.worldbank.org/; Argentina (report); World Development Indicators (WDI) 2022; and World Development Report 2022: Finance for an Equitable Recovery.

ARGENTINA-BANKS AND BANKING

Euromonitor International, Inc., 1 N Dearborn St., Ste. 1700, Chicago, IL, 60602, USA, (312) 922-1115, (312) 922-1157, info-usa@euromonitor.com, https://www.euromonitor.com/; Geographies.

Inter-American Development Bank (IDB), 1300 New York Ave. NW, Washington, DC, 20577, USA, (202) 623-1000, (202) 623-3096, https://www.iadb.org/en; Latin Macro Watch (LMW).

International Monetary Fund (IMF), 700 19th St. NW, Washington, DC, 20431, USA, (202) 623-7000, (202) 623-4661, publications@imf.org, https://www.imf.org; International Financial Statistics (IFS).

Routledge - Taylor & Francis Group, 6000 Broken Sound Pkwy. NW, Ste. 300, Boca Raton, FL, 33487, USA, (800) 634-1420, (800) 634-7064, orders@taylorandfrancis.com, https://www.routledge.com/; The Europa World Year Book 2022.

ARGENTINA-BARLEY PRODUCTION

See ARGENTINA-CROPS

ARGENTINA-BONDS

Inter-American Development Bank (IDB), 1300 New York Ave. NW, Washington, DC, 20577, USA, (202) 623-1000, (202) 623-3096, https://www.iadb.org/en; Latin Macro Watch (LMW).

ARGENTINA-BROADCASTING

Central Intelligence Agency (CIA), Office of Public Affairs, Washington, DC, 20505, USA, (703) 482-0623, https://www.cia.gov; The World Factbook.

Euromonitor International, Inc., 1 N Dearborn St., Ste. 1700, Chicago, IL, 60602, USA, (312) 922-1115, (312) 922-1157, info-usa@euromonitor.com, https://www.euromonitor.com/; Geographies.

Palgrave Macmillan, 1 New York Plaza, Ste. 4500, New York, NY, 10004-1562, USA, (800) 777-4643, orders@palgrave.com, https://www.palgrave.com/us; The Statesman's Yearbook, 2023.

WRTH Publications Limited, PO Box 290, Oxford, OX2 7FT, GBR, sales@wrth.com, https://www.wrth.com; World Radio TV Handbook 2023.

ARGENTINA-BUDGET

Central Intelligence Agency (CIA), Office of Public Affairs, Washington, DC, 20505, USA, (703) 482-0623, https://www.cia.gov; The World Factbook.

ARGENTINA-BUSINESS

Global Entrepreneurship Monitor (GEM), Babson College, 231 Forest St., Babson Park, MA, 02457, USA, (781) 235-1200, info@gemconsortium.org, https://www.gemconsortium.org/; Argentina Economy Profile and GEM 2022-2023 Global Report.

Inter-American Development Bank (IDB), 1300 New York Ave. NW, Washington, DC, 20577, USA, (202) 623-1000, (202) 623-3096, https://www.iadb.org/en; Latin Macro Watch (LMW).

ARGENTINA-CAPITAL INVESTMENTS

Inter-American Development Bank (IDB), 1300 New York Ave. NW, Washington, DC, 20577, USA, (202) 623-1000, (202) 623-3096, https://www.iadb.org/en; Latin Macro Watch (LMW).

ARGENTINA-CLIMATE

Palgrave Macmillan, 1 New York Plaza, Ste. 4500, New York, NY, 10004-1562, USA, (800) 777-4643, orders@palgrave.com, https://www.palgrave.com/us; The Statesman's Yearbook, 2023.

University of California Los Angeles (UCLA), Latin American Institute (LAI), 10343 Bunche Hall, 315 Portola Plaza, Los Angeles, CA, 90095-1447, USA, (310) 825-4571, lai@international.ucla.edu, https://www.international.ucla.edu/lai; unpublished data.

ARGENTINA-COAL PRODUCTION

See ARGENTINA-MINERAL INDUSTRIES

ARGENTINA-COFFEE

See ARGENTINA-CROPS

ARGENTINA-COMMERCE

Palgrave Macmillan, 1 New York Plaza, Ste. 4500, New York, NY, 10004-1562, USA, (800) 777-4643, orders@palgrave.com, https://www.palgrave.com/us; The Statesman's Yearbook, 2023.

UK Data Service, University of Essex, Wivenhoe Park, Colchester, Essex, CO4 3SQ, GBR, https://ukdataservice.ac.uk/; International Aggregate Data.

ARGENTINA-COMMODITY EXCHANGES

Barchart, 209 W Jackson Blvd., 2nd Fl., Chicago, IL, 60606, USA, (877) 247-4394, commodities@barchart.com, https://www.barchart.com/cmdty; The cmdty Yearbook 2023; cmdtyStats: Commodity Statistics and Fundamental Data; cmdtyView: Commodity Index; and Commodity Data and Prices.

International Monetary Fund (IMF), 700 19th St. NW, Washington, DC, 20431, USA, (202) 623-7000, (202) 623-4661, publications@imf.org, https://www.imf.org; IMF Primary Commodity Prices.

ARGENTINA-CONSTRUCTION INDUSTRY

Copenhagen Centre on Energy Efficiency, Marmorvej 51, Copenhagen, DK-2100, DEN, c2e2@dtu.dk, https://c2e2.unepdtu.org/; Assessment of Skills and Knowledge Gap in Energy Efficiency within the Building Sector in Argentina.

Inter-American Development Bank (IDB), 1300 New York Ave. NW, Washington, DC, 20577, USA, (202) 623-1000, (202) 623-3096, https://www.iadb.org/en; Latin Macro Watch (LMW).

United Nations Statistics Division (UNSD), United Nations Plz., New York, NY, 10017, USA, (800) 253-9646, (212) 963-9851, statistics@un.org, https://unstats.un.org; Statistical Yearbook of the United Nations 2021.

ARGENTINA-CONSUMER PRICE INDEXES

Routledge - Taylor & Francis Group, 6000 Broken Sound Pkwy. NW, Ste. 300, Boca Raton, FL, 33487, USA, (800) 634-1420, (800) 634-7064, orders@taylorandfrancis.com, https://www.routledge.com/; The Europa World Year Book 2022.

The World Bank, 1818 H St. NW, Washington, DC, 20433, USA, (202) 473-1000, (202) 477-6391, eds03@worldbank.org, https://www.worldbank.org/; Argentina (report).

ARGENTINA-CONSUMPTION (ECONOMICS)

Inter-American Development Bank (IDB), 1300 New York Ave. NW, Washington, DC, 20577, USA, (202) 623-1000, (202) 623-3096, https://www.iadb.org/en; Latin Macro Watch (LMW).

ARGENTINA-COPPER INDUSTRY AND TRADE

See ARGENTINA-MINERAL INDUSTRIES

ARGENTINA-CORN INDUSTRY

See ARGENTINA-CROPS

ARGENTINA-COTTON

See ARGENTINA-CROPS

ARGENTINA-CROPS

International Monetary Fund (IMF), 700 19th St. NW, Washington, DC, 20431, USA, (202) 623-7000, (202) 623-4661, publications@imf.org, https://www.imf.org; International Financial Statistics (IFS).

Palgrave Macmillan, 1 New York Plaza, Ste. 4500, New York, NY, 10004-1562, USA, (800) 777-4643, orders@palgrave.com, https://www.palgrave.com/us; The Statesman's Yearbook, 2023.

United Nations Food and Agricultural Organization (FAO), 2121 K St., Ste. 800B, Washington, DC, 20037, USA, (202) 653-2400 (Dial from U.S.), (202) 653-5760 (Fax from U.S.), fao-hq@fao.org, https://www.fao.org; The State of Food and Agriculture (SOFA) 2022.

United Nations Statistics Division (UNSD), United Nations Plz., New York, NY, 10017, USA, (800) 253-9646, (212) 963-9851, statistics@un.org, https://unstats.un.org; Statistical Yearbook of the United Nations 2021.

ARGENTINA-CUSTOMS ADMINISTRATION

Inter-American Development Bank (IDB), 1300 New York Ave. NW, Washington, DC, 20577, USA, (202) 623-1000, (202) 623-3096, https://www.iadb.org/en; Latin Macro Watch (LMW).

ARGENTINA-DAIRY PROCESSING

Palgrave Macmillan, 1 New York Plaza, Ste. 4500, New York, NY, 10004-1562, USA, (800) 777-4643, orders@palgrave.com, https://www.palgrave.com/us; The Statesman's Yearbook, 2023.

United Nations Food and Agricultural Organization (FAO), 2121 K St., Ste. 800B, Washington, DC, 20037, USA, (202) 653-2400 (Dial from U.S.), (202) 653-5760 (Fax from U.S.), fao-hq@fao.org, https://www.fao.org; The State of Food and Agriculture (SOFA) 2022.

ARGENTINA-DEBTS, EXTERNAL

Inter-American Development Bank (IDB), 1300 New York Ave. NW, Washington, DC, 20577, USA, (202) 623-1000, (202) 623-3096, https://www.iadb.org/en; Latin Macro Watch (LMW).

Palgrave Macmillan, 1 New York Plaza, Ste. 4500, New York, NY, 10004-1562, USA, (800) 777-4643, orders@palgrave.com, https://www.palgrave.com/us; The Statesman's Yearbook, 2023.

United Nations Economic Commission for Latin America and the Caribbean (ECLAC), Casilla 179-D, Santiago, 7630412, CHL, (202) 596-3713, prensa@cepal.org, https://www.cepal.org/en; Economic Survey of Latin America and the Caribbean 2021: Labour Dynamics and Employment Policies for Sustainable and Inclusive Recovery Beyond the COVID-19 Crisis.

The World Bank, 1818 H St. NW, Washington, DC, 20433, USA, (202) 473-1000, (202) 477-6391,

eds03@worldbank.org, https://www.worldbank.org/; Global Financial Development Report 2019-2020: Bank Regulation and Supervision a Decade after the Global Financial Crisis; World Development Indicators (WDI) 2022; and World Development Report 2022: Finance for an Equitable Recovery.

ARGENTINA-DEFENSE EXPENDITURES

See ARGENTINA-ARMED FORCES

ARGENTINA-DIAMONDS

See ARGENTINA-MINERAL INDUSTRIES

ARGENTINA-DISPOSABLE INCOME

Inter-American Development Bank (IDB), 1300 New York Ave. NW, Washington, DC, 20577, USA, (202) 623-1000, (202) 623-3096, https://www.iadb.org/en; Latin Macro Watch (LMW).

ARGENTINA-ECONOMIC ASSISTANCE

Inter-American Development Bank (IDB), 1300 New York Ave. NW, Washington, DC, 20577, USA, (202) 623-1000, (202) 623-3096, https://www.iadb.org/en; Latin Macro Watch (LMW).

United Nations Statistics Division (UNSD), United Nations Plz., New York, NY, 10017, USA, (800) 253-9646, (212) 963-9851, statistics@un.org, https://unstats.un.org; Statistical Yearbook of the United Nations 2021.

ARGENTINA-ECONOMIC CONDITIONS

Bernan Press, 15250 NBN Way, Bldg. C, Blue Ridge Summit, PA, 17214, USA, (301) 459-2255, (800) 865-3457, (800) 865-3450, customercare@bernan.com, https://rowman.com/Page/Bernan; World Economic Outlook, April 2022.

Central Intelligence Agency (CIA), Office of Public Affairs, Washington, DC, 20505, USA, (703) 482-0623, https://www.cia.gov; The World Factbook.

The Economist Group: Economist Intelligence Unit (EIU), 900 3rd Ave., 16th Fl., New York, NY, 10022, USA, (212) 541-0500, americas@eiu.com, https://www.eiu.com; Argentina Country Report.

Euromonitor International, Inc., 1 N Dearborn St., Ste. 1700, Chicago, IL, 60602, USA, (312) 922-1115, (312) 922-1157, info-usa@euromonitor.com, https://www.euromonitor.com/; Geographies and Market Research on the Consumer Finance Industry.

Federal Statistical Office Germany, Gustav-Stresemann-Ring 11, Wiesbaden, D-65189, GER, https://www.destatis.de; Basic Indicators: Argentina.

Global Entrepreneurship Monitor (GEM), Babson College, 231 Forest St., Babson Park, MA, 02457, USA, (781) 235-1200, info@gemconsortium.org, https://www.gemconsortium.org/; Argentina Economy Profile and GEM 2022-2023 Global Report.

Inter-American Development Bank (IDB), 1300 New York Ave. NW, Washington, DC, 20577, USA, (202) 623-1000, (202) 623-3096, https://www.iadb.org/en; Latin Macro Watch (LMW).

International Monetary Fund (IMF), 700 19th St. NW, Washington, DC, 20431, USA, (202) 623-7000, (202) 623-4661, publications@imf.org, https://www.imf.org; IMF Data and World Economic Outlook.

Palgrave Macmillan, 1 New York Plaza, Ste. 4500, New York, NY, 10004-1562, USA, (800) 777-4643, orders@palgrave.com, https://www.palgrave.com/us; The Statesman's Yearbook, 2023.

Routledge - Taylor & Francis Group, 6000 Broken Sound Pkwy. NW, Ste. 300, Boca Raton, FL, 33487, USA, (800) 634-1420, (800) 634-7064, orders@taylorandfrancis.com, https://www.routledge.com/; The Europa World Year Book 2022.

United Nations Economic Commission for Latin America and the Caribbean (ECLAC), Casilla 179-D, Santiago, 7630412, CHL, (202) 596-3713, prensa@cepal.org, https://www.cepal.org/en; CEPALSTAT; Economic Survey of Latin America and the Caribbean 2021: Labour Dynamics and Employment Policies for Sustainable and Inclusive Recovery Beyond the COVID-19 Crisis; Foreign Direct Investment in Latin America and the Caribbean 2022; and Social Panorama of Latin America and the Caribbean 2022: Transforming Education as a Basis for Sustainable Development.

United Nations Statistics Division (UNSD), United Nations Plz., New York, NY, 10017, USA, (800) 253-9646, (212) 963-9851, statistics@un.org, https://unstats.un.org; World Statistics Pocketbook 2021.

University of California Los Angeles (UCLA), Latin American Institute (LAI), 10343 Bunche Hall, 315 Portola Plaza, Los Angeles, CA, 90095-1447, USA, (310) 825-4571, lai@international.ucla.edu, https://www.international.ucla.edu/lai; unpublished data.

The World Bank, 1818 H St. NW, Washington, DC, 20433, USA, (202) 473-1000, (202) 477-6391, eds03@worldbank.org, https://www.worldbank.org/; Argentina (report); Global Economic Monitor (GEM); Global Economic Prospects, June 2022; The Global Findex Database 2021; and World Development Report 2022: Finance for an Equitable Recovery.

ARGENTINA-EDUCATION

Euromonitor International, Inc., 1 N Dearborn St., Ste. 1700, Chicago, IL, 60602, USA, (312) 922-1115, (312) 922-1157, info-usa@euromonitor.com, https://www.euromonitor.com/; Geographies.

Infoplease, c/o Sandbox Networks, Inc., 1 Lincoln St., 24th Fl., Boston, MA, 02111, USA, https://www.infoplease.com; Countries of the World.

Palgrave Macmillan, 1 New York Plaza, Ste. 4500, New York, NY, 10004-1562, USA, (800) 777-4643, orders@palgrave.com, https://www.palgrave.com/us; The Statesman's Yearbook, 2023.

Routledge - Taylor & Francis Group, 6000 Broken Sound Pkwy. NW, Ste. 300, Boca Raton, FL, 33487, USA, (800) 634-1420, (800) 634-7064, orders@taylorandfrancis.com, https://www.routledge.com/; The Europa World Year Book 2022.

UNESCO Institute for Statistics, C.P 250 Succursale H, Montreal, QC, H3G 2K8, CAN, (514) 343-6880 (Dial from U.S.), (514) 343-5740 (Fax from U.S.), uis.publications@unesco.org, http://uis.unesco.org/; Literacy and UIS.Stat.

United Nations Statistics Division (UNSD), United Nations Plz., New York, NY, 10017, USA, (800) 253-9646, (212) 963-9851, statistics@un.org, https://unstats.un.org; Millennium Development Goal Indicators.

The World Bank, 1818 H St. NW, Washington, DC, 20433, USA, (202) 473-1000, (202) 477-6391, eds03@worldbank.org, https://www.worldbank.org/; Argentina (report); World Development Indicators (WDI) 2022; and World Development Report 2022: Finance for an Equitable Recovery.

ARGENTINA-ELECTRICITY

Copenhagen Centre on Energy Efficiency, Marmorvej 51, Copenhagen, DK-2100, DEN, c2e2@dtu.dk, https://c2e2.unepdtu.org/; Assessment of Skills and Knowledge Gap in Energy Efficiency within the Building Sector in Argentina.

Inter-American Development Bank (IDB), 1300 New York Ave. NW, Washington, DC, 20577, USA, (202) 623-1000, (202) 623-3096, https://www.iadb.org/en; Latin Macro Watch (LMW).

International Energy Agency (IEA), 9 Rue de la Federation, Paris, 75739, FRA, info@iea.org, https://www.iea.org/; World Energy Outlook 2021.

U.S. Energy Information Administration (EIA), 1000 Independence Ave. SW, Washington, DC, 20585, USA, (202) 586-8800, infoctr@eia.gov, https://www.eia.gov; International Energy Outlook 2021.

United Nations Statistics Division (UNSD), United Nations Plz., New York, NY, 10017, USA, (800) 253-9646, (212) 963-9851, statistics@un.org, https://unstats.un.org; Statistical Yearbook of the United Nations 2021.

ARGENTINA-EMIGRATION AND IMMIGRATION

University of California Los Angeles (UCLA), Latin American Institute (LAI), 10343 Bunche Hall, 315 Portola Plaza, Los Angeles, CA, 90095-1447, USA, (310) 825-4571, lai@international.ucla.edu, https://www.international.ucla.edu/lai; unpublished data.

ARGENTINA-EMPLOYMENT

International Labour Organization (ILO), 4 Rte. des Morillons, Geneva, CH-1211, SWI, ilo@ilo.org, https://www.ilo.org; NORMLEX Information System on International Labour Standards.

UK Data Service, University of Essex, Wivenhoe Park, Colchester, Essex, CO4 3SQ, GBR, https://ukdataservice.ac.uk/; International Aggregate Data.

The World Bank, 1818 H St. NW, Washington, DC, 20433, USA, (202) 473-1000, (202) 477-6391, eds03@worldbank.org, https://www.worldbank.org/; Argentina (report).

ARGENTINA-ENERGY INDUSTRIES

Copenhagen Centre on Energy Efficiency, Marmorvej 51, Copenhagen, DK-2100, DEN, c2e2@dtu.dk, https://c2e2.unepdtu.org/; Assessment of Skills and Knowledge Gap in Energy Efficiency within the Building Sector in Argentina.

ARGENTINA-ENVIRONMENTAL CONDITIONS

DSI Data Service & Information, Xantener Strasse 51a, Rheinberg, D-47495, GER, dsi@dsidata.com, https://www.dsidata.com/; Global Environmental Database.

The Economist Group: Economist Intelligence Unit (EIU), 900 3rd Ave., 16th Fl., New York, NY, 10022, USA, (212) 541-0500, americas@eiu.com, https://www.eiu.com; Argentina Country Report.

Federal Statistical Office Germany, Gustav-Stresemann-Ring 11, Wiesbaden, D-65189, GER, https://www.destatis.de; Basic Indicators: Argentina.

United Nations Economic Commission for Latin America and the Caribbean (ECLAC), Casilla 179-D, Santiago, 7630412, CHL, (202) 596-3713, prensa@cepal.org, https://www.cepal.org/en; CEPALSTAT.

United Nations Statistics Division (UNSD), United Nations Plz., New York, NY, 10017, USA, (800) 253-9646, (212) 963-9851, statistics@un.org, https://unstats.un.org; World Statistics Pocketbook 2021.

ARGENTINA-EXCISE TAX

United Nations Statistics Division (UNSD), United Nations Plz., New York, NY, 10017, USA, (800) 253-9646, (212) 963-9851, statistics@un.org, https://unstats.un.org; World Statistics Pocketbook 2021.

ARGENTINA-EXPENDITURES, PUBLIC

Inter-American Development Bank (IDB), 1300 New York Ave. NW, Washington, DC, 20577, USA, (202) 623-1000, (202) 623-3096, https://www.iadb.org/en; Latin Macro Watch (LMW).

ARGENTINA-EXPORTS

Central Intelligence Agency (CIA), Office of Public Affairs, Washington, DC, 20505, USA, (703) 482-0623, https://www.cia.gov; The World Factbook.

The Economist Group: Economist Intelligence Unit (EIU), 900 3rd Ave., 16th Fl., New York, NY, 10022, USA, (212) 541-0500, americas@eiu.com, https://www.eiu.com; Argentina Country Report.

Inter-American Development Bank (IDB), 1300 New York Ave. NW, Washington, DC, 20577, USA, (202) 623-1000, (202) 623-3096, https://www.iadb.org/en; Latin Macro Watch (LMW).

International Monetary Fund (IMF), 700 19th St. NW, Washington, DC, 20431, USA, (202) 623-7000, (202) 623-4661, publications@imf.org, https://www.imf.org; Direction of Trade Statistics (DOTS) and International Financial Statistics (IFS).

S&P Global, IHS Markit, 15 Inverness Way E, Englewood, CO, 80112, USA, (800) 447-2273, (800) 854-7179, https://ihsmarkit.com; Global Trade Atlas (GTA).

United Nations Conference on Trade and Development (UNCTAD), Palais des Nations, Geneva, 1211, SWI, (212) 963-6896, unctadinfo@unctad.org, https://unctad.org; Handbook of Statistics 2021.

United Nations Statistics Division (UNSD), United Nations Plz., New York, NY, 10017, USA, (800) 253-9646, (212) 963-9851, statistics@un.org, https://unstats.un.org; United Nations Commodity Trade Statistics Database (UN Comtrade).

The World Bank, 1818 H St. NW, Washington, DC, 20433, USA, (202) 473-1000, (202) 477-6391, eds03@worldbank.org, https://www.worldbank.org/; World Development Report 2022: Finance for an Equitable Recovery.

ARGENTINA-FEMALE WORKING POPULATION

See ARGENTINA-EMPLOYMENT

ARGENTINA-FERTILIZER INDUSTRY

United Nations Food and Agricultural Organization (FAO), 2121 K St., Ste. 800B, Washington, DC, 20037, USA, (202) 653-2400 (Dial from U.S.), (202) 653-5760 (Fax from U.S.), fao-hq@fao.org, https://www.fao.org; The State of Food and Agriculture (SOFA) 2022.

ARGENTINA-FETAL MORTALITY

See ARGENTINA-MORTALITY

ARGENTINA-FINANCE

Inter-American Development Bank (IDB), 1300 New York Ave. NW, Washington, DC, 20577, USA, (202) 623-1000, (202) 623-3096, https://www.iadb.org/en; Latin Macro Watch (LMW).

International Monetary Fund (IMF), 700 19th St. NW, Washington, DC, 20431, USA, (202) 623-7000, (202) 623-4661, publications@imf.org, https://www.imf.org; International Financial Statistics (IFS).

Stockholm International Peace Research Institute (SIPRI), Signalistgatan 9, Stockholm, SE 169 72, SWE, https://www.sipri.org/; SIPRI Arms Transfers Database and SIPRI Military Expenditure Database.

The World Bank, 1818 H St. NW, Washington, DC, 20433, USA, (202) 473-1000, (202) 477-6391, eds03@worldbank.org, https://www.worldbank.org/; Argentina (report).

ARGENTINA-FINANCE, PUBLIC

Bernan Press, 15250 NBN Way, Bldg. C, Blue Ridge Summit, PA, 17214, USA, (301) 459-2255, (800) 865-3457, (800) 865-3450, customercare@bernan.com, https://rowman.com/Page/Bernan; National Accounts Statistics: Analysis of Main Aggregates 2020.

The Economist Group: Economist Intelligence Unit (EIU), 900 3rd Ave., 16th Fl., New York, NY, 10022, USA, (212) 541-0500, americas@eiu.com, https://www.eiu.com; Argentina Country Report.

Inter-American Development Bank (IDB), 1300 New York Ave. NW, Washington, DC, 20577, USA, (202) 623-1000, (202) 623-3096, https://www.iadb.org/en; Latin Macro Watch (LMW).

International Monetary Fund (IMF), 700 19th St. NW, Washington, DC, 20431, USA, (202) 623-7000, (202) 623-4661, publications@imf.org, https://www.imf.org; International Financial Statistics (IFS) and Regional Economic Outlook.

Palgrave Macmillan, 1 New York Plaza, Ste. 4500, New York, NY, 10004-1562, USA, (800) 777-4643, orders@palgrave.com, https://www.palgrave.com/us; The Statesman's Yearbook, 2023.

Routledge - Taylor & Francis Group, 6000 Broken Sound Pkwy. NW, Ste. 300, Boca Raton, FL, 33487, USA, (800) 634-1420, (800) 634-7064, orders@taylorandfrancis.com, https://www.routledge.com/; The Europa World Year Book 2022.

United Nations Statistics Division (UNSD), United Nations Plz., New York, NY, 10017, USA, (800) 253-9646, (212) 963-9851, statistics@un.org, https://unstats.un.org; National Accounts Main Aggregates Database and National Accounts Statistics: Main Aggregates and Detailed Tables.

The World Bank, 1818 H St. NW, Washington, DC, 20433, USA, (202) 473-1000, (202) 477-6391, eds03@worldbank.org, https://www.worldbank.org/; Argentina (report).

ARGENTINA-FISHERIES

Inter-American Development Bank (IDB), 1300 New York Ave. NW, Washington, DC, 20577, USA, (202) 623-1000, (202) 623-3096, https://www.iadb.org/en; Latin Macro Watch (LMW).

Palgrave Macmillan, 1 New York Plaza, Ste. 4500, New York, NY, 10004-1562, USA, (800) 777-4643, orders@palgrave.com, https://www.palgrave.com/us; The Statesman's Yearbook, 2023.

Routledge - Taylor & Francis Group, 6000 Broken Sound Pkwy. NW, Ste. 300, Boca Raton, FL, 33487, USA, (800) 634-1420, (800) 634-7064, orders@taylorandfrancis.com, https://www.routledge.com/; The Europa World Year Book 2022.

United Nations Food and Agricultural Organization (FAO), 2121 K St., Ste. 800B, Washington, DC, 20037, USA, (202) 653-2400 (Dial from U.S.), (202) 653-5760 (Fax from U.S.), fao-hq@fao.org, https://www.fao.org; FAO Yearbook of Fishery and Aquaculture Statistics 2019; Fishery Statistical Collections Global Capture Production; FishStatJ; and The State of Food and Agriculture (SOFA) 2022.

United Nations Statistics Division (UNSD), United Nations Plz., New York, NY, 10017, USA, (800) 253-9646, (212) 963-9851, statistics@un.org, https://unstats.un.org; Statistical Yearbook of the United Nations 2021.

The World Bank, 1818 H St. NW, Washington, DC, 20433, USA, (202) 473-1000, (202) 477-6391, eds03@worldbank.org, https://www.worldbank.org/; Argentina (report).

ARGENTINA-FOOD

Euromonitor International, Inc., 1 N Dearborn St., Ste. 1700, Chicago, IL, 60602, USA, (312) 922-1115, (312) 922-1157, info-usa@euromonitor.com, https://www.euromonitor.com/; Market Research on the Retailing Industry.

United Nations Food and Agricultural Organization (FAO), 2121 K St., Ste. 800B, Washington, DC, 20037, USA, (202) 653-2400 (Dial from U.S.), (202) 653-5760 (Fax from U.S.), fao-hq@fao.org, https://www.fao.org; The State of Food and Agriculture (SOFA) 2022.

United Nations Statistics Division (UNSD), United Nations Plz., New York, NY, 10017, USA, (800) 253-9646, (212) 963-9851, statistics@un.org, https://unstats.un.org; United Nations Commodity Trade Statistics Database (UN Comtrade).

ARGENTINA-FOREIGN EXCHANGE RATES

Inter-American Development Bank (IDB), 1300 New York Ave. NW, Washington, DC, 20577, USA, (202) 623-1000, (202) 623-3096, https://www.iadb.org/en; Latin Macro Watch (LMW).

International Monetary Fund (IMF), 700 19th St. NW, Washington, DC, 20431, USA, (202) 623-7000, (202) 623-4661, publications@imf.org, https://www.imf.org; International Financial Statistics (IFS).

ARGENTINA-FORESTS AND FORESTRY

Inter-American Development Bank (IDB), 1300 New York Ave. NW, Washington, DC, 20577, USA, (202) 623-1000, (202) 623-3096, https://www.iadb.org/en; Latin Macro Watch (LMW).

Palgrave Macmillan, 1 New York Plaza, Ste. 4500, New York, NY, 10004-1562, USA, (800) 777-4643, orders@palgrave.com, https://www.palgrave.com/us; The Statesman's Yearbook, 2023.

Routledge - Taylor & Francis Group, 6000 Broken Sound Pkwy. NW, Ste. 300, Boca Raton, FL, 33487, USA, (800) 634-1420, (800) 634-7064, orders@taylorandfrancis.com, https://www.routledge.com/; The Europa World Year Book 2022.

UNESCO Institute for Statistics, C.P 250 Succursale H, Montreal, QC, H3G 2K8, CAN, (514) 343-6880 (Dial from U.S.), (514) 343-5740 (Fax from U.S.), uis.publications@unesco.org, http://uis.unesco.org/; UIS.Stat.

United Nations Food and Agricultural Organization (FAO), 2121 K St., Ste. 800B, Washington, DC, 20037, USA, (202) 653-2400 (Dial from U.S.), (202) 653-5760 (Fax from U.S.), fao-hq@fao.org, https://www.fao.org; FAO Yearbook of Forest Products 2019 and The State of Food and Agriculture (SOFA) 2022.

United Nations Statistics Division (UNSD), United Nations Plz., New York, NY, 10017, USA, (800) 253-9646, (212) 963-9851, statistics@un.org, https://unstats.un.org; Statistical Yearbook of the United Nations 2021.

The World Bank, 1818 H St. NW, Washington, DC, 20433, USA, (202) 473-1000, (202) 477-6391, eds03@worldbank.org, https://www.worldbank.org/; Argentina (report) and World Development Report 2022: Finance for an Equitable Recovery.

ARGENTINA-GAS PRODUCTION

See ARGENTINA-MINERAL INDUSTRIES

ARGENTINA-GEOGRAPHIC INFORMATION SYSTEMS

The World Bank, 1818 H St. NW, Washington, DC, 20433, USA, (202) 473-1000, (202) 477-6391, eds03@worldbank.org, https://www.worldbank.org/; Argentina (report).

ARGENTINA-GOLD INDUSTRY

The World Bank, 1818 H St. NW, Washington, DC, 20433, USA, (202) 473-1000, (202) 477-6391, eds03@worldbank.org, https://www.worldbank.org/; World Development Indicators (WDI) 2022.

ARGENTINA-GOLD PRODUCTION

See ARGENTINA-MINERAL INDUSTRIES

ARGENTINA-GROSS DOMESTIC PRODUCT

The Economist Group: Economist Intelligence Unit (EIU), 900 3rd Ave., 16th Fl., New York, NY, 10022, USA, (212) 541-0500, americas@eiu.com, https://www.eiu.com; Argentina Country Report.

Inter-American Development Bank (IDB), 1300 New York Ave. NW, Washington, DC, 20577, USA, (202) 623-1000, (202) 623-3096, https://www.iadb.org/en; Latin Macro Watch (LMW).

International Monetary Fund (IMF), 700 19th St. NW, Washington, DC, 20431, USA, (202) 623-7000, (202) 623-4661, publications@imf.org, https://www.imf.org; International Financial Statistics (IFS).

Routledge - Taylor & Francis Group, 6000 Broken Sound Pkwy. NW, Ste. 300, Boca Raton, FL, 33487, USA, (800) 634-1420, (800) 634-7064, orders@taylorandfrancis.com, https://www.routledge.com/; The Europa World Year Book 2022.

United Nations Statistics Division (UNSD), United Nations Plz., New York, NY, 10017, USA, (800) 253-9646, (212) 963-9851, statistics@un.org, https://unstats.un.org; Statistical Yearbook of the United Nations 2021.

The World Bank, 1818 H St. NW, Washington, DC, 20433, USA, (202) 473-1000, (202) 477-6391, eds03@worldbank.org, https://www.worldbank.org/; World Development Indicators (WDI) 2022 and World Development Report 2022: Finance for an Equitable Recovery.

ARGENTINA-GROSS NATIONAL PRODUCT

Inter-American Development Bank (IDB), 1300 New York Ave. NW, Washington, DC, 20577, USA, (202)

623-1000, (202) 623-3096, https://www.iadb.org/en; Latin Macro Watch (LMW).

Palgrave Macmillan, 1 New York Plaza, Ste. 4500, New York, NY, 10004-1562, USA, (800) 777-4643, orders@palgrave.com, https://www.palgrave.com/us; The Statesman's Yearbook, 2023.

United Nations Statistics Division (UNSD), United Nations Plz., New York, NY, 10017, USA, (800) 253-9646, (212) 963-9851, statistics@un.org, https://unstats.un.org; Statistical Yearbook of the United Nations 2021.

The World Bank, 1818 H St. NW, Washington, DC, 20433, USA, (202) 473-1000, (202) 477-6391, eds03@worldbank.org, https://www.worldbank.org/; World Development Indicators (WDI) 2022 and World Development Report 2022: Finance for an Equitable Recovery.

ARGENTINA-HIDES AND SKINS INDUSTRY

International Monetary Fund (IMF), 700 19th St. NW, Washington, DC, 20431, USA, (202) 623-7000, (202) 623-4661, publications@imf.org, https://www.imf.org; International Financial Statistics (IFS).

ARGENTINA-HOUSING

Euromonitor International, Inc., 1 N Dearborn St., Ste. 1700, Chicago, IL, 60602, USA, (312) 922-1115, (312) 922-1157, info-usa@euromonitor.com, https://www.euromonitor.com/; Geographies.

ARGENTINA-ILLITERATE PERSONS

UNESCO Institute for Statistics, C.P 250 Succursale H, Montreal, QC, H3G 2K8, CAN, (514) 343-6880 (Dial from U.S.), (514) 343-5740 (Fax from U.S.), uis.publications@unesco.org, http://uis.unesco.org/; UIS.Stat.

ARGENTINA-IMPORTS

Central Intelligence Agency (CIA), Office of Public Affairs, Washington, DC, 20505, USA, (703) 482-0623, https://www.cia.gov; The World Factbook.

The Economist Group: Economist Intelligence Unit (EIU), 900 3rd Ave., 16th Fl., New York, NY, 10022, USA, (212) 541-0500, americas@eiu.com, https://www.eiu.com; Argentina Country Report.

Inter-American Development Bank (IDB), 1300 New York Ave. NW, Washington, DC, 20577, USA, (202) 623-1000, (202) 623-3096, https://www.iadb.org/en; Latin Macro Watch (LMW).

International Monetary Fund (IMF), 700 19th St. NW, Washington, DC, 20431, USA, (202) 623-7000, (202) 623-4661, publications@imf.org, https://www.imf.org; Direction of Trade Statistics (DOTS) and International Financial Statistics (IFS).

S&P Global, IHS Markit, 15 Inverness Way E, Englewood, CO, 80112, USA, (800) 447-2273, (800) 854-7179, https://ihsmarkit.com; Global Trade Atlas (GTA).

United Nations Conference on Trade and Development (UNCTAD), Palais des Nations, Geneva, 1211, SWI, (212) 963-6896, unctadinfo@unctad.org, https://unctad.org; Handbook of Statistics 2021.

United Nations Statistics Division (UNSD), United Nations Plz., New York, NY, 10017, USA, (800) 253-9646, (212) 963-9851, statistics@un.org, https://unstats.un.org; United Nations Commodity Trade Statistics Database (UN Comtrade).

The World Bank, 1818 H St. NW, Washington, DC, 20433, USA, (202) 473-1000, (202) 477-6391, eds03@worldbank.org, https://www.worldbank.org/; World Development Report 2022: Finance for an Equitable Recovery.

ARGENTINA-INDUSTRIAL METALS PRODUCTION

See ARGENTINA-MINERAL INDUSTRIES

ARGENTINA-INDUSTRIES

Central Intelligence Agency (CIA), Office of Public Affairs, Washington, DC, 20505, USA, (703) 482-0623, https://www.cia.gov; The World Factbook.

The Economist Group: Economist Intelligence Unit (EIU), 900 3rd Ave., 16th Fl., New York, NY, 10022, USA, (212) 541-0500, americas@eiu.com, https://www.eiu.com; Argentina Country Report.

Euromonitor International, Inc., 1 N Dearborn St., Ste. 1700, Chicago, IL, 60602, USA, (312) 922-1115, (312) 922-1157, info-usa@euromonitor.com, https://www.euromonitor.com/; Geographies.

International Labour Organization (ILO), 4 Rte. des Morillons, Geneva, CH-1211, SWI, ilo@ilo.org, https://www.ilo.org; NORMLEX Information System on International Labour Standards.

Palgrave Macmillan, 1 New York Plaza, Ste. 4500, New York, NY, 10004-1562, USA, (800) 777-4643, orders@palgrave.com, https://www.palgrave.com/us; The Statesman's Yearbook, 2023.

Routledge - Taylor & Francis Group, 6000 Broken Sound Pkwy. NW, Ste. 300, Boca Raton, FL, 33487, USA, (800) 634-1420, (800) 634-7064, orders@taylorandfrancis.com, https://www.routledge.com/; The Europa World Year Book 2022.

United Nations Economic Commission for Latin America and the Caribbean (ECLAC), Casilla 179-D, Santiago, 7630412, CHL, (202) 596-3713, prensa@cepal.org, https://www.cepal.org/en; Economic Survey of Latin America and the Caribbean 2021: Labour Dynamics and Employment Policies for Sustainable and Inclusive Recovery Beyond the COVID-19 Crisis.

United Nations Industrial Development Organization (UNIDO), 1 United Nations Plz., Rm. DC1-1118, New York, NY, 10017, USA, (212) 963-6890, (212) 963 6885, (212) 963-7904, office.newyork@unido.org, https://www.unido.org/; Industrial Statistics Databases and International Yearbook of Industrial Statistics 2021.

University of California Los Angeles (UCLA), Latin American Institute (LAI), 10343 Bunche Hall, 315 Portola Plaza, Los Angeles, CA, 90095-1447, USA, (310) 825-4571, lai@international.ucla.edu, https://www.international.ucla.edu/lai; unpublished data.

The World Bank, 1818 H St. NW, Washington, DC, 20433, USA, (202) 473-1000, (202) 477-6391, eds03@worldbank.org, https://www.worldbank.org/; Argentina (report) and World Development Indicators (WDI) 2022.

ARGENTINA-INFANT AND MATERNAL MORTALITY

See ARGENTINA-MORTALITY

ARGENTINA-INFLATION (FINANCE)

United Nations Economic Commission for Latin America and the Caribbean (ECLAC), Casilla 179-D, Santiago, 7630412, CHL, (202) 596-3713, prensa@cepal.org, https://www.cepal.org/en; Economic Survey of Latin America and the Caribbean 2021: Labour Dynamics and Employment Policies for Sustainable and Inclusive Recovery Beyond the COVID-19 Crisis.

ARGENTINA-INTEREST RATES

Inter-American Development Bank (IDB), 1300 New York Ave. NW, Washington, DC, 20577, USA, (202) 623-1000, (202) 623-3096, https://www.iadb.org/en; Latin Macro Watch (LMW).

ARGENTINA-INTERNAL REVENUE

Inter-American Development Bank (IDB), 1300 New York Ave. NW, Washington, DC, 20577, USA, (202) 623-1000, (202) 623-3096, https://www.iadb.org/en; Latin Macro Watch (LMW).

ARGENTINA-INTERNATIONAL FINANCE

Inter-American Development Bank (IDB), 1300 New York Ave. NW, Washington, DC, 20577, USA, (202) 623-1000, (202) 623-3096, https://www.iadb.org/en; Latin Macro Watch (LMW).

ARGENTINA-INTERNATIONAL LIQUIDITY

Inter-American Development Bank (IDB), 1300 New York Ave. NW, Washington, DC, 20577, USA, (202) 623-1000, (202) 623-3096, https://www.iadb.org/en; Latin Macro Watch (LMW).

ARGENTINA-INTERNATIONAL TRADE

The Economist Group: Economist Intelligence Unit (EIU), 900 3rd Ave., 16th Fl., New York, NY, 10022, USA, (212) 541-0500, americas@eiu.com, https://www.eiu.com; Argentina Country Report.

Euromonitor International, Inc., 1 N Dearborn St., Ste. 1700, Chicago, IL, 60602, USA, (312) 922-1115, (312) 922-1157, info-usa@euromonitor.com, https://www.euromonitor.com/; Geographies.

Inter-American Development Bank (IDB), 1300 New York Ave. NW, Washington, DC, 20577, USA, (202) 623-1000, (202) 623-3096, https://www.iadb.org/en; Latin Macro Watch (LMW).

Palgrave Macmillan, 1 New York Plaza, Ste. 4500, New York, NY, 10004-1562, USA, (800) 777-4643, orders@palgrave.com, https://www.palgrave.com/us; The Statesman's Yearbook, 2023.

Routledge - Taylor & Francis Group, 6000 Broken Sound Pkwy. NW, Ste. 300, Boca Raton, FL, 33487, USA, (800) 634-1420, (800) 634-7064, orders@taylorandfrancis.com, https://www.routledge.com/; The Europa World Year Book 2022.

United Nations Conference on Trade and Development (UNCTAD), Palais des Nations, Geneva, 1211, SWI, (212) 963-6896, unctadinfo@unctad.org, https://unctad.org; Trade and Development Report 2021.

United Nations Economic Commission for Latin America and the Caribbean (ECLAC), Casilla 179-D, Santiago, 7630412, CHL, (202) 596-3713, prensa@cepal.org, https://www.cepal.org/en; Economic Survey of Latin America and the Caribbean 2021: Labour Dynamics and Employment Policies for Sustainable and Inclusive Recovery Beyond the COVID-19 Crisis.

United Nations Food and Agricultural Organization (FAO), 2121 K St., Ste. 800B, Washington, DC, 20037, USA, (202) 653-2400 (Dial from U.S.), (202) 653-5760 (Fax from U.S.), fao-hq@fao.org, https://www.fao.org; The State of Food and Agriculture (SOFA) 2022.

United Nations Statistics Division (UNSD), United Nations Plz., New York, NY, 10017, USA, (800) 253-9646, (212) 963-9851, statistics@un.org, https://unstats.un.org; International Trade Statistics Yearbook 2020 and Statistical Yearbook of the United Nations 2021.

The World Bank, 1818 H St. NW, Washington, DC, 20433, USA, (202) 473-1000, (202) 477-6391, eds03@worldbank.org, https://www.worldbank.org/; Argentina (report); World Development Indicators (WDI) 2022; and World Development Report 2022: Finance for an Equitable Recovery.

World Trade Organization (WTO), Ctre. William Rappard, Rue de Lausanne 154, Case postale, Geneva, CH-1211, SWI, enquiries@wto.org, https://www.wto.org; World Trade Statistical Review 2022.

ARGENTINA-INTERNET USERS

International Telecommunication Union (ITU), Place des Nations, Geneva, CH-1211, SWI, itumail@itu.int, https://www.itu.int; Global Connectivity Report 2022; World Telecommunication/ICT Indicators Database 2021; and Yearbook of Statistics 2019.

The World Bank, 1818 H St. NW, Washington, DC, 20433, USA, (202) 473-1000, (202) 477-6391, eds03@worldbank.org, https://www.worldbank.org/; Argentina (report).

ARGENTINA-INVESTMENTS

Inter-American Development Bank (IDB), 1300 New York Ave. NW, Washington, DC, 20577, USA, (202) 623-1000, (202) 623-3096, https://www.iadb.org/en; Latin Macro Watch (LMW).

International Monetary Fund (IMF), 700 19th St. NW, Washington, DC, 20431, USA, (202) 623-7000, (202) 623-4661, publications@imf.org, https://www.imf.org; International Financial Statistics (IFS).

ARGENTINA-IRRIGATION

Inter-American Development Bank (IDB), 1300 New York Ave. NW, Washington, DC, 20577, USA, (202) 623-1000, (202) 623-3096, https://www.iadb.org/en; Latin Macro Watch (LMW).

ARGENTINA-LABOR

Central Intelligence Agency (CIA), Office of Public Affairs, Washington, DC, 20505, USA, (703) 482-0623, https://www.cia.gov; The World Factbook.

Euromonitor International, Inc., 1 N Dearborn St., Ste. 1700, Chicago, IL, 60602, USA, (312) 922-1115, (312) 922-1157, info-usa@euromonitor.com, https://www.euromonitor.com/; Geographies.

Federal Statistical Office Germany, Gustav-Stresemann-Ring 11, Wiesbaden, D-65189, GER, https://www.destatis.de; Basic Indicators: Argentina.

International Labour Organization (ILO), 4 Rte. des Morillons, Geneva, CH-1211, SWI, ilo@ilo.org, https://www.ilo.org; NORMLEX Information System on International Labour Standards.

Palgrave Macmillan, 1 New York Plaza, Ste. 4500, New York, NY, 10004-1562, USA, (800) 777-4643, orders@palgrave.com, https://www.palgrave.com/us; The Statesman's Yearbook, 2023.

United Nations Food and Agricultural Organization (FAO), 2121 K St., Ste. 800B, Washington, DC, 20037, USA, (202) 653-2400 (Dial from U.S.), (202) 653-5760 (Fax from U.S.), fao-hq@fao.org, https://www.fao.org; The State of Food and Agriculture (SOFA) 2022.

The World Bank, 1818 H St. NW, Washington, DC, 20433, USA, (202) 473-1000, (202) 477-6391, eds03@worldbank.org, https://www.worldbank.org/; World Development Indicators (WDI) 2022 and World Development Report 2022: Finance for an Equitable Recovery.

ARGENTINA-LAND USE

Inter-American Development Bank (IDB), 1300 New York Ave. NW, Washington, DC, 20577, USA, (202) 623-1000, (202) 623-3096, https://www.iadb.org/en; Latin Macro Watch (LMW).

United Nations Statistics Division (UNSD), United Nations Plz., New York, NY, 10017, USA, (800) 253-9646, (212) 963-9851, statistics@un.org, https://unstats.un.org; Millennium Development Goal Indicators.

The World Bank, 1818 H St. NW, Washington, DC, 20433, USA, (202) 473-1000, (202) 477-6391, eds03@worldbank.org, https://www.worldbank.org/; World Development Report 2022: Finance for an Equitable Recovery.

ARGENTINA-LEATHER INDUSTRY AND TRADE

United Nations Statistics Division (UNSD), United Nations Plz., New York, NY, 10017, USA, (800) 253-9646, (212) 963-9851, statistics@un.org, https://unstats.un.org; United Nations Commodity Trade Statistics Database (UN Comtrade).

ARGENTINA-LIBRARIES

UNESCO Institute for Statistics, C.P 250 Succursale H, Montreal, QC, H3G 2K8, CAN, (514) 343-6880 (Dial from U.S.), (514) 343-5740 (Fax from U.S.), uis.publications@unesco.org, http://uis.unesco.org/; UIS.Stat.

ARGENTINA-LIFE EXPECTANCY

United Nations Department of Economic and Social Affairs (DESA), Population Division, 2 United Nations Plz., Rm. DC2-1950, New York, NY, 10017, USA, (212) 963-3209, (212) 963-2147, population@un.org, https://www.un.org/development/desa/pd/; World Population Ageing 2020 Highlights.

United Nations Statistics Division (UNSD), United Nations Plz., New York, NY, 10017, USA, (800) 253-9646, (212) 963-9851, statistics@un.org, https://unstats.un.org; Millennium Development Goal Indicators.

ARGENTINA-LITERACY

Euromonitor International, Inc., 1 N Dearborn St., Ste. 1700, Chicago, IL, 60602, USA, (312) 922-1115, (312) 922-1157, info-usa@euromonitor.com, https://www.euromonitor.com/; Geographies.

UNESCO Institute for Statistics, C.P 250 Succursale H, Montreal, QC, H3G 2K8, CAN, (514) 343-6880 (Dial from U.S.), (514) 343-5740 (Fax from U.S.), uis.publications@unesco.org, http://uis.unesco.org/; Literacy.

ARGENTINA-LIVESTOCK

Palgrave Macmillan, 1 New York Plaza, Ste. 4500, New York, NY, 10004-1562, USA, (800) 777-4643, orders@palgrave.com, https://www.palgrave.com/us; The Statesman's Yearbook, 2023.

Routledge - Taylor & Francis Group, 6000 Broken Sound Pkwy. NW, Ste. 300, Boca Raton, FL, 33487, USA, (800) 634-1420, (800) 634-7064, orders@taylorandfrancis.com, https://www.routledge.com/; The Europa World Year Book 2022.

United Nations Food and Agricultural Organization (FAO), 2121 K St., Ste. 800B, Washington, DC, 20037, USA, (202) 653-2400 (Dial from U.S.), (202) 653-5760 (Fax from U.S.), fao-hq@fao.org, https://www.fao.org; The State of Food and Agriculture (SOFA) 2022.

United Nations Statistics Division (UNSD), United Nations Plz., New York, NY, 10017, USA, (800) 253-9646, (212) 963-9851, statistics@un.org, https://unstats.un.org; Statistical Yearbook of the United Nations 2021.

ARGENTINA-MANUFACTURES

Inter-American Development Bank (IDB), 1300 New York Ave. NW, Washington, DC, 20577, USA, (202) 623-1000, (202) 623-3096, https://www.iadb.org/en; Latin Macro Watch (LMW).

International Monetary Fund (IMF), 700 19th St. NW, Washington, DC, 20431, USA, (202) 623-7000, (202) 623-4661, publications@imf.org, https://www.imf.org; International Financial Statistics (IFS).

ARGENTINA-MARRIAGE

United Nations Statistics Division (UNSD), United Nations Plz., New York, NY, 10017, USA, (800) 253-9646, (212) 963-9851, statistics@un.org, https://unstats.un.org; Statistical Yearbook of the United Nations 2021.

ARGENTINA-MEAT INDUSTRY AND TRADE

International Monetary Fund (IMF), 700 19th St. NW, Washington, DC, 20431, USA, (202) 623-7000, (202) 623-4661, publications@imf.org, https://www.imf.org; International Financial Statistics (IFS).

ARGENTINA-METAL PRODUCTS

United Nations Statistics Division (UNSD), United Nations Plz., New York, NY, 10017, USA, (800) 253-9646, (212) 963-9851, statistics@un.org, https://unstats.un.org; United Nations Commodity Trade Statistics Database (UN Comtrade).

ARGENTINA-MINERAL INDUSTRIES

Barchart, 209 W Jackson Blvd., 2nd Fl., Chicago, IL, 60606, USA, (877) 247-4394, commodities@barchart.com, https://www.barchart.com/cmdty; The cmdty Yearbook 2023; cmdtyStats: Commodity Statistics and Fundamental Data; cmdtyView: Commodity Index; and Commodity Data and Prices.

Inter-American Development Bank (IDB), 1300 New York Ave. NW, Washington, DC, 20577, USA, (202) 623-1000, (202) 623-3096, https://www.iadb.org/en; Latin Macro Watch (LMW).

International Energy Agency (IEA), 9 Rue de la Federation, Paris, 75739, FRA, info@iea.org, https://www.iea.org/; World Energy Outlook 2021.

International Lead and Zinc Study Group (ILZSG), Rua Almirante Barroso 38, 5th Fl., Lisbon, 1000-013, PRT, sales@ilzsg.org, https://www.ilzsg.org; Interactive Statistical Database.

Palgrave Macmillan, 1 New York Plaza, Ste. 4500, New York, NY, 10004-1562, USA, (800) 777-4643, orders@palgrave.com, https://www.palgrave.com/us; The Statesman's Yearbook, 2023.

Routledge - Taylor & Francis Group, 6000 Broken Sound Pkwy. NW, Ste. 300, Boca Raton, FL, 33487, USA, (800) 634-1420, (800) 634-7064, orders@taylorandfrancis.com, https://www.routledge.com/; The Europa World Year Book 2022.

United Nations Conference on Trade and Development (UNCTAD), Palais des Nations, Geneva, 1211, SWI, (212) 963-6896, unctadinfo@unctad.org, https://unctad.org; Trade and Development Report 2021.

United Nations Statistics Division (UNSD), United Nations Plz., New York, NY, 10017, USA, (800) 253-9646, (212) 963-9851, statistics@un.org, https://unstats.un.org; Statistical Yearbook of the United Nations 2021.

ARGENTINA-MOLASSES PRODUCTION

See ARGENTINA-CROPS

ARGENTINA-MONEY SUPPLY

The Economist Group: Economist Intelligence Unit (EIU), 900 3rd Ave., 16th Fl., New York, NY, 10022, USA, (212) 541-0500, americas@eiu.com, https://www.eiu.com; Argentina Country Report.

Inter-American Development Bank (IDB), 1300 New York Ave. NW, Washington, DC, 20577, USA, (202) 623-1000, (202) 623-3096, https://www.iadb.org/en; Latin Macro Watch (LMW).

International Monetary Fund (IMF), 700 19th St. NW, Washington, DC, 20431, USA, (202) 623-7000, (202) 623-4661, publications@imf.org, https://www.imf.org; International Financial Statistics (IFS).

Routledge - Taylor & Francis Group, 6000 Broken Sound Pkwy. NW, Ste. 300, Boca Raton, FL, 33487, USA, (800) 634-1420, (800) 634-7064, orders@taylorandfrancis.com, https://www.routledge.com/; The Europa World Year Book 2022.

United Nations Statistics Division (UNSD), United Nations Plz., New York, NY, 10017, USA, (800) 253-9646, (212) 963-9851, statistics@un.org, https://unstats.un.org; Statistical Yearbook of the United Nations 2021.

The World Bank, 1818 H St. NW, Washington, DC, 20433, USA, (202) 473-1000, (202) 477-6391, eds03@worldbank.org, https://www.worldbank.org/; Argentina (report).

ARGENTINA-MORTALITY

UNICEF, 3 United Nations Plz., New York, NY, 10017, USA, (212) 303-7984, (917) 244-2215, https://www.unicef.org; The State of the World's Children 2023.

United Nations Statistics Division (UNSD), United Nations Plz., New York, NY, 10017, USA, (800) 253-9646, (212) 963-9851, statistics@un.org, https://unstats.un.org; Millennium Development Goal Indicators; Statistical Yearbook of the United Nations 2021; and World Statistics Pocketbook 2021.

The World Bank, 1818 H St. NW, Washington, DC, 20433, USA, (202) 473-1000, (202) 477-6391, eds03@worldbank.org, https://www.worldbank.org/; World Development Indicators (WDI) 2022.

World Health Organization (WHO), Ave. Appia 20, Geneva, CH-1211, SWI, (202) 974-3000 (Telephone in U.S.), publications@who.int, https://www.who.int/; Global Health Observatory (GHO).

ARGENTINA-MOTION PICTURES

Palgrave Macmillan, 1 New York Plaza, Ste. 4500, New York, NY, 10004-1562, USA, (800) 777-4643, orders@palgrave.com, https://www.palgrave.com/us; The Statesman's Yearbook, 2023.

ARGENTINA-MOTOR VEHICLES

International Road Federation (IRF), Madison Place, 500 Montgomery St., 5th Fl., Alexandria, VA, 22314,

USA, (703) 535-1001, (703) 535-1007, info@irf.global, https://www.irf.global/; World Road Statistics (WRS).

ARGENTINA-NATURAL GAS PRODUCTION

See ARGENTINA-MINERAL INDUSTRIES

ARGENTINA-NUTRITION

United Nations Food and Agricultural Organization (FAO), 2121 K St., Ste. 800B, Washington, DC, 20037, USA, (202) 653-2400 (Dial from U.S.), (202) 653-5760 (Fax from U.S.), fao-hq@fao.org, https://www.fao.org; The State of Food and Agriculture (SOFA) 2022.

United Nations Statistics Division (UNSD), United Nations Plz., New York, NY, 10017, USA, (800) 253-9646, (212) 963-9851, statistics@un.org, https://unstats.un.org; Millennium Development Goal Indicators.

ARGENTINA-ORANGES PRODUCTION

See ARGENTINA-CROPS

ARGENTINA-PAPER

See ARGENTINA-FORESTS AND FORESTRY

ARGENTINA-PEANUT PRODUCTION

See ARGENTINA-CROPS

ARGENTINA-PESTICIDES

United Nations Food and Agricultural Organization (FAO), 2121 K St., Ste. 800B, Washington, DC, 20037, USA, (202) 653-2400 (Dial from U.S.), (202) 653-5760 (Fax from U.S.), fao-hq@fao.org, https://www.fao.org; The State of Food and Agriculture (SOFA) 2022.

ARGENTINA-PETROLEUM INDUSTRY AND TRADE

Inter-American Development Bank (IDB), 1300 New York Ave. NW, Washington, DC, 20577, USA, (202) 623-1000, (202) 623-3096, https://www.iadb.org/en; Latin Macro Watch (LMW).

International Energy Agency (IEA), 9 Rue de la Federation, Paris, 75739, FRA, info@iea.org, https://www.iea.org/; World Energy Outlook 2021.

International Monetary Fund (IMF), 700 19th St. NW, Washington, DC, 20431, USA, (202) 623-7000, (202) 623-4661, publications@imf.org, https://www.imf.org; International Financial Statistics (IFS).

Palgrave Macmillan, 1 New York Plaza, Ste. 4500, New York, NY, 10004-1562, USA, (800) 777-4643, orders@palgrave.com, https://www.palgrave.com/us; The Statesman's Yearbook, 2023.

U.S. Energy Information Administration (EIA), 1000 Independence Ave. SW, Washington, DC, 20585, USA, (202) 586-8800, infoctr@eia.gov, https://www.eia.gov; International Energy Outlook 2021.

United Nations Food and Agricultural Organization (FAO), 2121 K St., Ste. 800B, Washington, DC, 20037, USA, (202) 653-2400 (Dial from U.S.), (202) 653-5760 (Fax from U.S.), fao-hq@fao.org, https://www.fao.org; The State of Food and Agriculture (SOFA) 2022.

United Nations Statistics Division (UNSD), United Nations Plz., New York, NY, 10017, USA, (800) 253-9646, (212) 963-9851, statistics@un.org, https://unstats.un.org; Statistical Yearbook of the United Nations 2021.

ARGENTINA-PLASTICS INDUSTRY AND TRADE

United Nations Statistics Division (UNSD), United Nations Plz., New York, NY, 10017, USA, (800) 253-9646, (212) 963-9851, statistics@un.org, https://unstats.un.org; Statistical Yearbook of the United Nations 2021.

ARGENTINA-POPULATION

Central Intelligence Agency (CIA), Office of Public Affairs, Washington, DC, 20505, USA, (703) 482-0623, https://www.cia.gov; The World Factbook.

The Economist Group: Economist Intelligence Unit (EIU), 900 3rd Ave., 16th Fl., New York, NY, 10022, USA, (212) 541-0500, americas@eiu.com, https://www.eiu.com; Argentina Country Report.

Federal Statistical Office Germany, Gustav-Stresemann-Ring 11, Wiesbaden, D-65189, GER, https://www.destatis.de; Basic Indicators: Argentina.

Infoplease, c/o Sandbox Networks, Inc., 1 Lincoln St., 24th Fl., Boston, MA, 02111, USA, https://www.infoplease.com; Countries of the World.

Inter-American Development Bank (IDB), 1300 New York Ave. NW, Washington, DC, 20577, USA, (202) 623-1000, (202) 623-3096, https://www.iadb.org/en; Latin Macro Watch (LMW).

International Labour Organization (ILO), 4 Rte. des Morillons, Geneva, CH-1211, SWI, ilo@ilo.org, https://www.ilo.org; NORMLEX Information System on International Labour Standards.

Palgrave Macmillan, 1 New York Plaza, Ste. 4500, New York, NY, 10004-1562, USA, (800) 777-4643, orders@palgrave.com, https://www.palgrave.com/us; The Statesman's Yearbook, 2023.

Routledge - Taylor & Francis Group, 6000 Broken Sound Pkwy. NW, Ste. 300, Boca Raton, FL, 33487, USA, (800) 634-1420, (800) 634-7064, orders@taylorandfrancis.com, https://www.routledge.com/; The Europa World Year Book 2022.

UK Data Service, University of Essex, Wivenhoe Park, Colchester, Essex, CO4 3SQ, GBR, https://ukdataservice.ac.uk/; International Aggregate Data.

United Nations Department of Economic and Social Affairs (DESA), Population Division, 2 United Nations Plz., Rm. DC2-1950, New York, NY, 10017, USA, (212) 963-3209, (212) 963-2147, population@un.org, https://www.un.org/development/desa/pd/; Revision of World Urbanization Prospects and World Population Ageing 2020 Highlights.

United Nations Development Programme (UNDP), One United Nations Plz., New York, NY, 10017, USA, (212) 906-5000, (212) 906-5001, https://www.undp.org; Human Development Report 2021-2022.

United Nations Economic Commission for Latin America and the Caribbean (ECLAC), Casilla 179-D, Santiago, 7630412, CHL, (202) 596-3713, prensa@cepal.org, https://www.cepal.org/en; CEPALSTAT and Social Panorama of Latin America and the Caribbean 2022: Transforming Education as a Basis for Sustainable Development.

United Nations Statistics Division (UNSD), United Nations Plz., New York, NY, 10017, USA, (800) 253-9646, (212) 963-9851, statistics@un.org, https://unstats.un.org; Statistical Yearbook of the United Nations 2021 and World Statistics Pocketbook 2021.

University of California Los Angeles (UCLA), Latin American Institute (LAI), 10343 Bunche Hall, 315 Portola Plaza, Los Angeles, CA, 90095-1447, USA, (310) 825-4571, lai@international.ucla.edu, https://www.international.ucla.edu/lai; unpublished data.

The World Bank, 1818 H St. NW, Washington, DC, 20433, USA, (202) 473-1000, (202) 477-6391, eds03@worldbank.org, https://www.worldbank.org/; Argentina (report); The Global Findex Database 2021; and World Development Report 2022: Finance for an Equitable Recovery.

ARGENTINA-POPULATION DENSITY

Central Intelligence Agency (CIA), Office of Public Affairs, Washington, DC, 20505, USA, (703) 482-0623, https://www.cia.gov; The World Factbook.

Inter-American Development Bank (IDB), 1300 New York Ave. NW, Washington, DC, 20577, USA, (202) 623-1000, (202) 623-3096, https://www.iadb.org/en; Latin Macro Watch (LMW).

Palgrave Macmillan, 1 New York Plaza, Ste. 4500, New York, NY, 10004-1562, USA, (800) 777-4643, orders@palgrave.com, https://www.palgrave.com/us; The Statesman's Yearbook, 2023.

Routledge - Taylor & Francis Group, 6000 Broken Sound Pkwy. NW, Ste. 300, Boca Raton, FL, 33487, USA, (800) 634-1420, (800) 634-7064, orders@taylorandfrancis.com, https://www.routledge.com/; The Europa World Year Book 2022.

The World Bank, 1818 H St. NW, Washington, DC, 20433, USA, (202) 473-1000, (202) 477-6391, eds03@worldbank.org, https://www.worldbank.org/; Argentina (report) and World Development Report 2022: Finance for an Equitable Recovery.

ARGENTINA-POWER RESOURCES

Euromonitor International, Inc., 1 N Dearborn St., Ste. 1700, Chicago, IL, 60602, USA, (312) 922-1115, (312) 922-1157, info-usa@euromonitor.com, https://www.euromonitor.com/; Geographies.

International Energy Agency (IEA), 9 Rue de la Federation, Paris, 75739, FRA, info@iea.org, https://www.iea.org/; World Energy Outlook 2021.

Palgrave Macmillan, 1 New York Plaza, Ste. 4500, New York, NY, 10004-1562, USA, (800) 777-4643, orders@palgrave.com, https://www.palgrave.com/us; The Statesman's Yearbook, 2023.

U.S. Energy Information Administration (EIA), 1000 Independence Ave. SW, Washington, DC, 20585, USA, (202) 586-8800, infoctr@eia.gov, https://www.eia.gov; International Energy Outlook 2021.

United Nations Food and Agricultural Organization (FAO), 2121 K St., Ste. 800B, Washington, DC, 20037, USA, (202) 653-2400 (Dial from U.S.), (202) 653-5760 (Fax from U.S.), fao-hq@fao.org, https://www.fao.org; The State of Food and Agriculture (SOFA) 2022.

United Nations Statistics Division (UNSD), United Nations Plz., New York, NY, 10017, USA, (800) 253-9646, (212) 963-9851, statistics@un.org, https://unstats.un.org; Energy Statistics Yearbook 2019; Statistical Yearbook of the United Nations 2021; and World Statistics Pocketbook 2021.

The World Bank, 1818 H St. NW, Washington, DC, 20433, USA, (202) 473-1000, (202) 477-6391, eds03@worldbank.org, https://www.worldbank.org/; World Development Report 2022: Finance for an Equitable Recovery.

ARGENTINA-PRICES

Euromonitor International, Inc., 1 N Dearborn St., Ste. 1700, Chicago, IL, 60602, USA, (312) 922-1115, (312) 922-1157, info-usa@euromonitor.com, https://www.euromonitor.com/; Geographies.

International Monetary Fund (IMF), 700 19th St. NW, Washington, DC, 20431, USA, (202) 623-7000, (202) 623-4661, publications@imf.org, https://www.imf.org; International Financial Statistics (IFS).

The World Bank, 1818 H St. NW, Washington, DC, 20433, USA, (202) 473-1000, (202) 477-6391, eds03@worldbank.org, https://www.worldbank.org/; Argentina (report).

ARGENTINA-PUBLIC HEALTH

Euromonitor International, Inc., 1 N Dearborn St., Ste. 1700, Chicago, IL, 60602, USA, (312) 922-1115, (312) 922-1157, info-usa@euromonitor.com, https://www.euromonitor.com/; Geographies and Market Research on the Health and Wellness Industry.

Palgrave Macmillan, 1 New York Plaza, Ste. 4500, New York, NY, 10004-1562, USA, (800) 777-4643, orders@palgrave.com, https://www.palgrave.com/us; The Statesman's Yearbook, 2023.

U.S. Census Bureau, 4600 Silver Hill Rd., Washington, DC, 20233, USA, (301) 763-4636, (800) 923-8282, https://www.census.gov; HIV/AIDS Surveillance Data Base.

UNICEF, 3 United Nations Plz., New York, NY, 10017, USA, (212) 303-7984, (917) 244-2215, https://www.unicef.org; The State of the World's Children 2023.

United Nations Department of Economic and Social Affairs (DESA), Population Division, 2 United Nations Plz., Rm. DC2-1950, New York, NY, 10017, USA, (212) 963-3209, (212) 963-2147, population@un.org, https://www.un.org/development/desa/pd/; World Fertility Data 2019.

United Nations Development Programme (UNDP), One United Nations Plz., New York, NY, 10017, USA, (212) 906-5000, (212) 906-5001, https://www.undp.org; Human Development Report 2021-2022.

United Nations Statistics Division (UNSD), United Nations Plz., New York, NY, 10017, USA, (800) 253-9646, (212) 963-9851, statistics@un.org, https://unstats.un.org; Millennium Development Goal Indicators and Statistical Yearbook of the United Nations 2021.

University of California Los Angeles (UCLA), Latin American Institute (LAI), 10343 Bunche Hall, 315 Portola Plaza, Los Angeles, CA, 90095-1447, USA, (310) 825-4571, lai@international.ucla.edu, https://www.international.ucla.edu/lai; unpublished data.

The World Bank, 1818 H St. NW, Washington, DC, 20433, USA, (202) 473-1000, (202) 477-6391, eds03@worldbank.org, https://www.worldbank.org/; Argentina (report).

World Health Organization (WHO), Ave. Appia 20, Geneva, CH-1211, SWI, (202) 974-3000 (Telephone in U.S.), publications@who.int, https://www.who.int/; Global Health Observatory (GHO) and Health Statistics and Information Systems.

ARGENTINA-PUBLISHERS AND PUBLISHING

Palgrave Macmillan, 1 New York Plaza, Ste. 4500, New York, NY, 10004-1562, USA, (800) 777-4643, orders@palgrave.com, https://www.palgrave.com/us; The Statesman's Yearbook, 2023.

Routledge - Taylor & Francis Group, 6000 Broken Sound Pkwy. NW, Ste. 300, Boca Raton, FL, 33487, USA, (800) 634-1420, (800) 634-7064, orders@taylorandfrancis.com, https://www.routledge.com/; The Europa World Year Book 2022.

UNESCO Institute for Statistics, C.P 250 Succursale H, Montreal, QC, H3G 2K8, CAN, (514) 343-6880 (Dial from U.S.), (514) 343-5740 (Fax from U.S.), uis.publications@unesco.org, http://uis.unesco.org/; UIS.Stat.

ARGENTINA-RAILROADS

Janes, USA, (703) 574-7580, (888) 977-1519, customer.care@janes.com, https://www.janes.com; Janes World Railways 2021-2022.

Palgrave Macmillan, 1 New York Plaza, Ste. 4500, New York, NY, 10004-1562, USA, (800) 777-4643, orders@palgrave.com, https://www.palgrave.com/us; The Statesman's Yearbook, 2023.

Routledge - Taylor & Francis Group, 6000 Broken Sound Pkwy. NW, Ste. 300, Boca Raton, FL, 33487, USA, (800) 634-1420, (800) 634-7064, orders@taylorandfrancis.com, https://www.routledge.com/; The Europa World Year Book 2022.

United Nations Statistics Division (UNSD), United Nations Plz., New York, NY, 10017, USA, (800) 253-9646, (212) 963-9851, statistics@un.org, https://unstats.un.org; Statistical Yearbook of the United Nations 2021.

ARGENTINA-RELIGION

Central Intelligence Agency (CIA), Office of Public Affairs, Washington, DC, 20505, USA, (703) 482-0623, https://www.cia.gov; The World Factbook.

Palgrave Macmillan, 1 New York Plaza, Ste. 4500, New York, NY, 10004-1562, USA, (800) 777-4643, orders@palgrave.com, https://www.palgrave.com/us; The Statesman's Yearbook, 2023.

ARGENTINA-RETAIL TRADE

Euromonitor International, Inc., 1 N Dearborn St., Ste. 1700, Chicago, IL, 60602, USA, (312) 922-1115, (312) 922-1157, info-usa@euromonitor.com, https://www.euromonitor.com/; Geographies and Market Research on the Retailing Industry.

Inter-American Development Bank (IDB), 1300 New York Ave. NW, Washington, DC, 20577, USA, (202) 623-1000, (202) 623-3096, https://www.iadb.org/en; Latin Macro Watch (LMW).

ARGENTINA-RICE PRODUCTION

See ARGENTINA-CROPS

ARGENTINA-ROADS

International Road Federation (IRF), Madison Place, 500 Montgomery St., 5th Fl., Alexandria, VA, 22314, USA, (703) 535-1001, (703) 535-1007, info@irf.global, https://www.irf.global/; World Road Statistics (WRS).

ARGENTINA-RUBBER INDUSTRY AND TRADE

International Rubber Study Group (IRSG), 51 Changi Business Park Central 2, Unit No. 6, 486066, SGP, https://www.rubberstudy.org; Monthly Rubber Bulletin (MRB); Rubber Industry Report; Rubber Statistical Bulletin; and World Rubber Industry Report (WRIO).

United Nations Statistics Division (UNSD), United Nations Plz., New York, NY, 10017, USA, (800) 253-9646, (212) 963-9851, statistics@un.org, https://unstats.un.org; Statistical Yearbook of the United Nations 2021.

ARGENTINA-RYE PRODUCTION

See ARGENTINA-CROPS

ARGENTINA-SHIPPING

Inter-American Development Bank (IDB), 1300 New York Ave. NW, Washington, DC, 20577, USA, (202) 623-1000, (202) 623-3096, https://www.iadb.org/en; Latin Macro Watch (LMW).

Routledge - Taylor & Francis Group, 6000 Broken Sound Pkwy. NW, Ste. 300, Boca Raton, FL, 33487, USA, (800) 634-1420, (800) 634-7064, orders@taylorandfrancis.com, https://www.routledge.com/; The Europa World Year Book 2022.

S&P Global, IHS Markit, 15 Inverness Way E, Englewood, CO, 80112, USA, (800) 447-2273, (800) 854-7179, https://ihsmarkit.com; IHS Maritime World Shipbuilding Statistics; Journal of Commerce; Lloyd's Register of Ships 2021-2022; and Maritime Portal Desktop.

United Nations Statistics Division (UNSD), United Nations Plz., New York, NY, 10017, USA, (800) 253-9646, (212) 963-9851, statistics@un.org, https://unstats.un.org; Statistical Yearbook of the United Nations 2021.

ARGENTINA-SOYBEAN PRODUCTION

See ARGENTINA-CROPS

ARGENTINA-STEEL PRODUCTION

See ARGENTINA-MINERAL INDUSTRIES

ARGENTINA-SUGAR PRODUCTION

See ARGENTINA-CROPS

ARGENTINA-SULPHUR PRODUCTION

See ARGENTINA-MINERAL INDUSTRIES

ARGENTINA-TAXATION

Inter-American Development Bank (IDB), 1300 New York Ave. NW, Washington, DC, 20577, USA, (202) 623-1000, (202) 623-3096, https://www.iadb.org/en; Latin Macro Watch (LMW).

The World Bank, 1818 H St. NW, Washington, DC, 20433, USA, (202) 473-1000, (202) 477-6391, eds03@worldbank.org, https://www.worldbank.org/; World Development Indicators (WDI) 2022.

ARGENTINA-TEA PRODUCTION

See ARGENTINA-CROPS

ARGENTINA-TELEPHONE

Palgrave Macmillan, 1 New York Plaza, Ste. 4500, New York, NY, 10004-1562, USA, (800) 777-4643, orders@palgrave.com, https://www.palgrave.com/us; The Statesman's Yearbook, 2023.

Routledge - Taylor & Francis Group, 6000 Broken Sound Pkwy. NW, Ste. 300, Boca Raton, FL, 33487, USA, (800) 634-1420, (800) 634-7064, orders@taylorandfrancis.com, https://www.routledge.com/; The Europa World Year Book 2022.

United Nations Statistics Division (UNSD), United Nations Plz., New York, NY, 10017, USA, (800) 253-9646, (212) 963-9851, statistics@un.org, https://unstats.un.org; World Statistics Pocketbook 2021.

ARGENTINA-TELEVISION-RECEIVERS AND RECEPTION

Euromonitor International, Inc., 1 N Dearborn St., Ste. 1700, Chicago, IL, 60602, USA, (312) 922-1115, (312) 922-1157, info-usa@euromonitor.com, https://www.euromonitor.com/; Market Research on the Retailing Industry.

International Monetary Fund (IMF), 700 19th St. NW, Washington, DC, 20431, USA, (202) 623-7000, (202) 623-4661, publications@imf.org, https://www.imf.org; International Financial Statistics (IFS).

Palgrave Macmillan, 1 New York Plaza, Ste. 4500, New York, NY, 10004-1562, USA, (800) 777-4643, orders@palgrave.com, https://www.palgrave.com/us; The Statesman's Yearbook, 2023.

ARGENTINA-TEXTILE INDUSTRY

United Nations Statistics Division (UNSD), United Nations Plz., New York, NY, 10017, USA, (800) 253-9646, (212) 963-9851, statistics@un.org, https://unstats.un.org; Statistical Yearbook of the United Nations 2021.

ARGENTINA-TOBACCO INDUSTRY

United Nations Statistics Division (UNSD), United Nations Plz., New York, NY, 10017, USA, (800) 253-9646, (212) 963-9851, statistics@un.org, https://unstats.un.org; Statistical Yearbook of the United Nations 2021.

ARGENTINA-TOURISM

Euromonitor International, Inc., 1 N Dearborn St., Ste. 1700, Chicago, IL, 60602, USA, (312) 922-1115, (312) 922-1157, info-usa@euromonitor.com, https://www.euromonitor.com/; Geographies.

Palgrave Macmillan, 1 New York Plaza, Ste. 4500, New York, NY, 10004-1562, USA, (800) 777-4643, orders@palgrave.com, https://www.palgrave.com/us; The Statesman's Yearbook, 2023.

Routledge - Taylor & Francis Group, 6000 Broken Sound Pkwy. NW, Ste. 300, Boca Raton, FL, 33487, USA, (800) 634-1420, (800) 634-7064, orders@taylorandfrancis.com, https://www.routledge.com/; The Europa World Year Book 2022.

United Nations Statistics Division (UNSD), United Nations Plz., New York, NY, 10017, USA, (800) 253-9646, (212) 963-9851, statistics@un.org, https://unstats.un.org; Statistical Yearbook of the United Nations 2021.

United Nations World Tourism Organization (UNWTO), Calle Poeta Joan Maragall 42, Madrid, 28020, SPA, info@unwto.org, https://www.unwto.org/; Yearbook of Tourism Statistics, 2021 Edition.

The World Bank, 1818 H St. NW, Washington, DC, 20433, USA, (202) 473-1000, (202) 477-6391, eds03@worldbank.org, https://www.worldbank.org/; Argentina (report).

ARGENTINA-TRADE

See ARGENTINA-INTERNATIONAL TRADE

ARGENTINA-TRANSPORTATION

Central Intelligence Agency (CIA), Office of Public Affairs, Washington, DC, 20505, USA, (703) 482-0623, https://www.cia.gov; The World Factbook.

Euromonitor International, Inc., 1 N Dearborn St., Ste. 1700, Chicago, IL, 60602, USA, (312) 922-1115, (312) 922-1157, info-usa@euromonitor.com, https://www.euromonitor.com/; Geographies.

Inter-American Development Bank (IDB), 1300 New York Ave. NW, Washington, DC, 20577, USA, (202) 623-1000, (202) 623-3096, https://www.iadb.org/en; Latin Macro Watch (LMW).

Palgrave Macmillan, 1 New York Plaza, Ste. 4500, New York, NY, 10004-1562, USA, (800) 777-4643, orders@palgrave.com, https://www.palgrave.com/us; The Statesman's Yearbook, 2023.

Routledge - Taylor & Francis Group, 6000 Broken Sound Pkwy. NW, Ste. 300, Boca Raton, FL, 33487, USA, (800) 634-1420, (800) 634-7064, orders@taylorandfrancis.com, https://www.routledge.com/; The Europa World Year Book 2022.

The World Bank, 1818 H St. NW, Washington, DC, 20433, USA, (202) 473-1000, (202) 477-6391, eds03@worldbank.org, https://www.worldbank.org/; Argentina (report).

ARGENTINA-UNEMPLOYMENT

International Labour Organization (ILO), 4 Rte. des Morillons, Geneva, CH-1211, SWI, ilo@ilo.org, https://www.ilo.org; NORMLEX Information System on International Labour Standards.

United Nations Statistics Division (UNSD), United Nations Plz., New York, NY, 10017, USA, (800) 253-9646, (212) 963-9851, statistics@un.org, https://unstats.un.org; Statistical Yearbook of the United Nations 2021.

ARGENTINA-URANIUM PRODUCTION AND CONSUMPTION

See ARGENTINA-MINERAL INDUSTRIES

ARGENTINA-VITAL STATISTICS

Palgrave Macmillan, 1 New York Plaza, Ste. 4500, New York, NY, 10004-1562, USA, (800) 777-4643, orders@palgrave.com, https://www.palgrave.com/us; The Statesman's Yearbook, 2023.

U.S. Census Bureau, 4600 Silver Hill Rd., Washington, DC, 20233, USA, (301) 763-4636, (800) 923-8282, https://www.census.gov; HIV/AIDS Surveillance Data Base.

United Nations Department of Economic and Social Affairs (DESA), Population Division, 2 United Nations Plz., Rm. DC2-1950, New York, NY, 10017, USA, (212) 963-3209, (212) 963-2147, population@un.org, https://www.un.org/development/desa/pd/; World Contraceptive Use 2021: Estimates and Projections of Family Planning Indicators and World Marriage Data 2019.

United Nations Statistics Division (UNSD), United Nations Plz., New York, NY, 10017, USA, (800) 253-9646, (212) 963-9851, statistics@un.org, https://unstats.un.org; Statistical Yearbook of the United Nations 2021 and United Nations Demographic Yearbook 2020.

The World Bank, 1818 H St. NW, Washington, DC, 20433, USA, (202) 473-1000, (202) 477-6391, eds03@worldbank.org, https://www.worldbank.org/; World Development Indicators (WDI) 2022.

ARGENTINA-WAGES

International Labour Organization (ILO), 4 Rte. des Morillons, Geneva, CH-1211, SWI, ilo@ilo.org, https://www.ilo.org; NORMLEX Information System on International Labour Standards.

United Nations Statistics Division (UNSD), United Nations Plz., New York, NY, 10017, USA, (800) 253-9646, (212) 963-9851, statistics@un.org, https://unstats.un.org; Statistical Yearbook of the United Nations 2021.

The World Bank, 1818 H St. NW, Washington, DC, 20433, USA, (202) 473-1000, (202) 477-6391, eds03@worldbank.org, https://www.worldbank.org/; Argentina (report).

ARGENTINA-WEATHER

See ARGENTINA-CLIMATE

ARGENTINA-WHEAT PRODUCTION

See ARGENTINA-CROPS

ARGENTINA-WHOLESALE PRICE INDEXES

Inter-American Development Bank (IDB), 1300 New York Ave. NW, Washington, DC, 20577, USA, (202) 623-1000, (202) 623-3096, https://www.iadb.org/en; Latin Macro Watch (LMW).

International Monetary Fund (IMF), 700 19th St. NW, Washington, DC, 20431, USA, (202) 623-7000, (202) 623-4661, publications@imf.org, https://www.imf.org; International Financial Statistics (IFS).

ARGENTINA-WHOLESALE TRADE

Inter-American Development Bank (IDB), 1300 New York Ave. NW, Washington, DC, 20577, USA, (202) 623-1000, (202) 623-3096, https://www.iadb.org/en; Latin Macro Watch (LMW).

United Nations Statistics Division (UNSD), United Nations Plz., New York, NY, 10017, USA, (800) 253-9646, (212) 963-9851, statistics@un.org, https://unstats.un.org; Statistical Yearbook of the United Nations 2021.

ARGENTINA-WOOD AND WOOD PULP

See ARGENTINA-FORESTS AND FORESTRY

ARGENTINA-WOOL PRODUCTION

See ARGENTINA-TEXTILE INDUSTRY

ARGENTINA-ZINC AND ZINC ORE

See ARGENTINA-MINERAL INDUSTRIES

ARGENTINA-ZOOS

UNESCO Institute for Statistics, C.P 250 Succursale H, Montreal, QC, H3G 2K8, CAN, (514) 343-6880 (Dial from U.S.), (514) 343-5740 (Fax from U.S.), uis.publications@unesco.org, http://uis.unesco.org/; UIS.Stat.

ARIZONA

See also-STATE DATA (FOR INDIVIDUAL STATES)

ARIZONA-STATE DATA CENTERS

Arizona Commerce Authority, Arizona State Data Center, 100 N 7th Ave., Ste. 400, Phoenix, AZ, 85007, USA, (602) 771-1155, (602) 845-1200, https://www.azcommerce.com/oeo/population/arizona-state-data-center-sdc/; State Data Reports (AZ).

Arizona State Library, Archives and Public Records, 1901 W Madison St., Phoenix, AZ, 85009, USA, (602) 926-3720, (602) 256-7982, abourgeois@azlibrary.gov, https://azlibrary.gov/; State Data Reports (AZ).

Arizona State University, W. P. Carey School of Business, L. William Seidman Research Institute, 660 S Mill Ave., Ste. 300, Tempe, AZ, 85281, USA, (480) 965-5362, (480) 965-5458, seidman@asu.edu, https://seidmaninstitute.com/; State Data Reports (AZ).

Northern Arizona University, W. A. Franke College of Business, PO Box 15066, Flagstaff, AZ, 86011-5066, USA, (928) 523-3657, (928) 523-7331, fcb@nau.edu, https://nau.edu/franke-college-business/; State Data Reports (AZ).

University of Arizona, Eller College of Management, Economic and Business Research Center, McClelland Hall 103, PO Box 210108, Tucson, AZ, 85721-0108, USA, (520) 621-2155, (520) 621-2150, ebrpublications@email.arizona.edu, https://eller.arizona.edu/departments-research/centers-labs/economic-business-research; State Data Reports (AZ).

ARIZONA-PRIMARY STATISTICS SOURCES

Arizona Department of Education, 1535 W Jefferson St., Phoenix, AZ, 85007, USA, (602) 542-5393, (800) 352-4558, adeinbox@azed.gov, https://www.azed.gov/; Arizona School Report Cards.

SAGE Publications, 2455 Teller Rd., Thousand Oaks, CA, 91320, USA, (800) 818-7243, (800) 583-2665, journals@sagepub.com, https://www.sagepub.com; Data Planet.

University of Arizona, Eller College of Management, Economic and Business Research Center, McClelland Hall 103, PO Box 210108, Tucson, AZ, 85721-0108, USA, (520) 621-2155, (520) 621-2150, ebrpublications@email.arizona.edu, https://eller.arizona.edu/departments-research/centers-labs/economic-business-research; Arizona's Economy.

ARKANSAS

See also-STATE DATA (FOR INDIVIDUAL STATES)

Arkansas Division of Workforce Services, PO Box 2981, Little Rock, AR, 72203, USA, (501) 682-2121, (501) 682-8845, adws.info@arkansas.gov, https://www.dws.arkansas.gov/; unpublished data.

U.S. Department of Health and Human Services, Centers for Disease Control and Prevention (CDC), 1600 Clifton Rd., Atlanta, GA, 30329-4027, USA, (800) 232-4636, (888) 232-6348 (TTY), cdcinfo@cdc.gov, https://www.cdc.gov; SARS-CoV-2 Incidence in K-12 School Districts with Mask-Required Versus Mask-Optional Policies: Arkansas, August-October 2021.

ARKANSAS-STATE DATA CENTERS

Arkansas State Library, 900 W Capitol, Ste. 100, Little Rock, AR, 72201, USA, (501) 682-2053, (501) 682-1529, aslib-ref@ade.arkansas.gov, https://www.library.arkansas.gov/; State Data Reports (AR).

University of Arkansas at Little Rock, Arkansas Economic Development Institute (AEDI), 2801 S University Ave., Little Rock, AR, 72204-1099, USA, (501) 916-3519, grow@youraedi.com, https://youraedi.com/; State Data Reports (AR).

ARKANSAS-PRIMARY STATISTICS SOURCES

SAGE Publications, 2455 Teller Rd., Thousand Oaks, CA, 91320, USA, (800) 818-7243, (800) 583-2665, journals@sagepub.com, https://www.sagepub.com; Data Planet.

ARMED FORCES

The Stimson Center, 1211 Connecticut Ave. NW, 8th Fl., Washington, DC, 20036, USA, (202) 223-5956, (202) 238-9604, communications@stimson.org, https://www.stimson.org/; 25 Years of Security Cooperation Beneath the Nuclear Shadow: Shifting U.S. Arms Transfers to India and Pakistan.

U.S. Army War College, Public Affairs Office, 122 Forbes Ave., Carlisle, PA, 17013-5234, USA, usarmy.carlisle.awc.mbx.atwc-cpa@mail.mil, https://www.armywarcollege.edu/; Implications of Climate Change for the U.S. Army.

U.S. Department of Defense (DOD), Sexual Assault Prevention and Response Office (SAPRO), 1400 Defense Pentagon, Washington, DC, 20301, USA, (571) 372-2657, whs.mc-alex.wso.mbx.sapro@mail.mil, https://www.sapr.mil/; Annual Report on Sexual Assault in the Military, Fiscal Year 2022.

United States Merchant Marine Academy (USMMA), 300 Steamboat Rd., Kings Point, NY, 11024, USA, (516) 726-5800, (516) 726-6048, https://www.usmma.edu/; Final Signed 2018-2019 Sexual Harassment Report.

ARMED FORCES-FOREIGN COUNTRIES

Central Intelligence Agency (CIA), Office of Public Affairs, Washington, DC, 20505, USA, (703) 482-0623, https://www.cia.gov; The World Factbook.

International Institute for Strategic Studies (IISS) - Americas, 2121 K St. NW, Ste. 600, Washington, DC, 20037, USA, (202) 659-1490, (202) 659-1499, https://www.iiss.org/; Armed Conflict Survey 2021.

Oryx, NLD, oryxspioenkop@gmail.com, https://www.oryxspioenkop.com/; Attack on Europe: Documenting Russian Equipment Losses During the 2022 Russian Invasion of Ukraine.

ARMED FORCES-PERSONNEL

See SOLDIERS

ARMENIA-NATIONAL STATISTICAL OFFICE

Statistical Committee of the Republic of Armenia, Republic Ave., Government Bldg. 3, Yerevan, 0010, AMA, info@armstat.am, https://www.armstat.am/en/; National Data Reports (Armenia).

ARMENIA-PRIMARY STATISTICS SOURCES

Interstate Statistical Committee of the Commonwealth of Independent States, USA, cisstat@cisstat.org, http://www.cisstat.com/eng; Population and Social Indicators of the CIS and Other Countries of the World 2016-2019.

Statistical Committee of the Republic of Armenia, Republic Ave., Government Bldg. 3, Yerevan, 0010, AMA, info@armstat.am, https://www.armstat.am/en/; Statistical Yearbook of Armenia, 2023.

ARMENIA-AGRICULTURE

The Economist Group: Economist Intelligence Unit (EIU), 900 3rd Ave., 16th Fl., New York, NY, 10022, USA, (212) 541-0500, americas@eiu.com, https://www.eiu.com; Armenia Country Report.

Euromonitor International, Inc., 1 N Dearborn St., Ste. 1700, Chicago, IL, 60602, USA, (312) 922-1115, (312) 922-1157, info-usa@euromonitor.com, https://www.euromonitor.com/; Geographies.

Palgrave Macmillan, 1 New York Plaza, Ste. 4500, New York, NY, 10004-1562, USA, (800) 777-4643, orders@palgrave.com, https://www.palgrave.com/us; The Statesman's Yearbook, 2023.

Routledge - Taylor & Francis Group, 6000 Broken Sound Pkwy. NW, Ste. 300, Boca Raton, FL, 33487, USA, (800) 634-1420, (800) 634-7064, orders@taylorandfrancis.com, https://www.routledge.com/; The Europa World Year Book 2022.

United Nations Food and Agricultural Organization (FAO), 2121 K St., Ste. 800B, Washington, DC, 20037, USA, (202) 653-2400 (Dial from U.S.), (202) 653-5760 (Fax from U.S.), fao-hq@fao.org, https://www.fao.org; AQUASTAT and The State of Food and Agriculture (SOFA) 2022.

United Nations Statistics Division (UNSD), United Nations Plz., New York, NY, 10017, USA, (800) 253-9646, (212) 963-9851, statistics@un.org, https://unstats.un.org; Statistical Yearbook of the United Nations 2021.

The World Bank, 1818 H St. NW, Washington, DC, 20433, USA, (202) 473-1000, (202) 477-6391, eds03@worldbank.org, https://www.worldbank.org/; Armenia (report) and World Development Indicators (WDI) 2022.

ARMENIA-AIRLINES

International Civil Aviation Organization (ICAO), 999 Robert-Bourassa Blvd., Montreal, QC, H3C 5H7, CAN, (514) 954-8219 (Dial from U.S.), (514) 954-6077 (Fax from U.S.), icaohq@icao.int, https://www.icao.int; ICAO Regional Reports.

Palgrave Macmillan, 1 New York Plaza, Ste. 4500, New York, NY, 10004-1562, USA, (800) 777-4643, orders@palgrave.com, https://www.palgrave.com/us; The Statesman's Yearbook, 2023.

ARMENIA-ARMED FORCES

Central Intelligence Agency (CIA), Office of Public Affairs, Washington, DC, 20505, USA, (703) 482-0623, https://www.cia.gov; The World Factbook.

International Institute for Strategic Studies (IISS) - Americas, 2121 K St. NW, Ste. 600, Washington, DC, 20037, USA, (202) 659-1490, (202) 659-1499, https://www.iiss.org/; Armed Conflict Survey 2021 and The Military Balance 2022.

Palgrave Macmillan, 1 New York Plaza, Ste. 4500, New York, NY, 10004-1562, USA, (800) 777-4643, orders@palgrave.com, https://www.palgrave.com/us; The Statesman's Yearbook, 2023.

Stockholm International Peace Research Institute (SIPRI), Signalistgatan 9, Stockholm, SE 169 72, SWE, https://www.sipri.org/; SIPRI Arms Transfers Database and SIPRI Military Expenditure Database.

ARMENIA-BALANCE OF PAYMENTS

Routledge - Taylor & Francis Group, 6000 Broken Sound Pkwy. NW, Ste. 300, Boca Raton, FL, 33487, USA, (800) 634-1420, (800) 634-7064, orders@taylorandfrancis.com, https://www.routledge.com/; The Europa World Year Book 2022.

United Nations Conference on Trade and Development (UNCTAD), Palais des Nations, Geneva, 1211, SWI, (212) 963-6896, unctadinfo@unctad.org, https://unctad.org; Handbook of Statistics 2021.

The World Bank, 1818 H St. NW, Washington, DC, 20433, USA, (202) 473-1000, (202) 477-6391, eds03@worldbank.org, https://www.worldbank.org/; Armenia (report); World Development Indicators (WDI) 2022; and World Development Report 2022: Finance for an Equitable Recovery.

ARMENIA-BANKS AND BANKING

Euromonitor International, Inc., 1 N Dearborn St., Ste. 1700, Chicago, IL, 60602, USA, (312) 922-1115, (312) 922-1157, info-usa@euromonitor.com, https://www.euromonitor.com/; Geographies.

ARMENIA-BROADCASTING

Central Intelligence Agency (CIA), Office of Public Affairs, Washington, DC, 20505, USA, (703) 482-0623, https://www.cia.gov; The World Factbook.

Euromonitor International, Inc., 1 N Dearborn St., Ste. 1700, Chicago, IL, 60602, USA, (312) 922-1115, (312) 922-1157, info-usa@euromonitor.com, https://www.euromonitor.com/; Geographies.

Palgrave Macmillan, 1 New York Plaza, Ste. 4500, New York, NY, 10004-1562, USA, (800) 777-4643, orders@palgrave.com, https://www.palgrave.com/us; The Statesman's Yearbook, 2023.

UNESCO Institute for Statistics, C.P 250 Succursale H, Montreal, QC, H3G 2K8, CAN, (514) 343-6880 (Dial from U.S.), (514) 343-5740 (Fax from U.S.), uis.publications@unesco.org, http://uis.unesco.org/; UIS.Stat.

ARMENIA-BUDGET

Central Intelligence Agency (CIA), Office of Public Affairs, Washington, DC, 20505, USA, (703) 482-0623, https://www.cia.gov; The World Factbook.

ARMENIA-BUSINESS

United Nations Statistics Division (UNSD), United Nations Plz., New York, NY, 10017, USA, (800) 253-9646, (212) 963-9851, statistics@un.org, https://unstats.un.org; Statistical Yearbook of the United Nations 2021.

ARMENIA-COAL PRODUCTION

See ARMENIA-MINERAL INDUSTRIES

ARMENIA-COMMERCE

Palgrave Macmillan, 1 New York Plaza, Ste. 4500, New York, NY, 10004-1562, USA, (800) 777-4643, orders@palgrave.com, https://www.palgrave.com/us; The Statesman's Yearbook, 2023.

UK Data Service, University of Essex, Wivenhoe Park, Colchester, Essex, CO4 3SQ, GBR, https://ukdataservice.ac.uk/; International Aggregate Data.

ARMENIA-CONSTRUCTION INDUSTRY

United Nations Statistics Division (UNSD), United Nations Plz., New York, NY, 10017, USA, (800) 253-9646, (212) 963-9851, statistics@un.org, https://unstats.un.org; Statistical Yearbook of the United Nations 2021.

ARMENIA-CONSUMER PRICE INDEXES

The World Bank, 1818 H St. NW, Washington, DC, 20433, USA, (202) 473-1000, (202) 477-6391, eds03@worldbank.org, https://www.worldbank.org/; Armenia (report).

ARMENIA-COTTON

See ARMENIA-CROPS

ARMENIA-CROPS

Palgrave Macmillan, 1 New York Plaza, Ste. 4500, New York, NY, 10004-1562, USA, (800) 777-4643, orders@palgrave.com, https://www.palgrave.com/us; The Statesman's Yearbook, 2023.

United Nations Food and Agricultural Organization (FAO), 2121 K St., Ste. 800B, Washington, DC, 20037, USA, (202) 653-2400 (Dial from U.S.), (202) 653-5760 (Fax from U.S.), fao-hq@fao.org, https://www.fao.org; The State of Food and Agriculture (SOFA) 2022.

United Nations Statistics Division (UNSD), United Nations Plz., New York, NY, 10017, USA, (800) 253-9646, (212) 963-9851, statistics@un.org, https://unstats.un.org; Statistical Yearbook of the United Nations 2021.

ARMENIA-DAIRY PROCESSING

Palgrave Macmillan, 1 New York Plaza, Ste. 4500, New York, NY, 10004-1562, USA, (800) 777-4643, orders@palgrave.com, https://www.palgrave.com/us; The Statesman's Yearbook, 2023.

United Nations Food and Agricultural Organization (FAO), 2121 K St., Ste. 800B, Washington, DC, 20037, USA, (202) 653-2400 (Dial from U.S.), (202) 653-5760 (Fax from U.S.), fao-hq@fao.org, https://www.fao.org; The State of Food and Agriculture (SOFA) 2022.

ARMENIA-DEBTS, EXTERNAL

The World Bank, 1818 H St. NW, Washington, DC, 20433, USA, (202) 473-1000, (202) 477-6391, eds03@worldbank.org, https://www.worldbank.org/; Global Financial Development Report 2019-2020: Bank Regulation and Supervision a Decade after the Global Financial Crisis; World Development Indicators (WDI) 2022; and World Development Report 2022: Finance for an Equitable Recovery.

ARMENIA-ECONOMIC CONDITIONS

Bernan Press, 15250 NBN Way, Bldg. C, Blue Ridge Summit, PA, 17214, USA, (301) 459-2255, (800) 865-3457, (800) 865-3450, customercare@bernan.com, https://rowman.com/Page/Bernan; World Economic Outlook, April 2022.

Central Intelligence Agency (CIA), Office of Public Affairs, Washington, DC, 20505, USA, (703) 482-0623, https://www.cia.gov; The World Factbook.

The Economist Group: Economist Intelligence Unit (EIU), 900 3rd Ave., 16th Fl., New York, NY, 10022, USA, (212) 541-0500, americas@eiu.com, https://www.eiu.com; Armenia Country Report.

Euromonitor International, Inc., 1 N Dearborn St., Ste. 1700, Chicago, IL, 60602, USA, (312) 922-1115, (312) 922-1157, info-usa@euromonitor.com, https://www.euromonitor.com/; Geographies.

International Monetary Fund (IMF), 700 19th St. NW, Washington, DC, 20431, USA, (202) 623-7000, (202) 623-4661, publications@imf.org, https://www.imf.org; IMF Data and World Economic Outlook.

Palgrave Macmillan, 1 New York Plaza, Ste. 4500, New York, NY, 10004-1562, USA, (800) 777-4643, orders@palgrave.com, https://www.palgrave.com/us; The Statesman's Yearbook, 2023.

Routledge - Taylor & Francis Group, 6000 Broken Sound Pkwy. NW, Ste. 300, Boca Raton, FL, 33487, USA, (800) 634-1420, (800) 634-7064,

orders@taylorandfrancis.com, https://www.routledge.com/; The Europa World Year Book 2022.

United Nations Economic and Social Commission for Western Asia (ESCWA), Riad el-Solh Sq., PO Box 11-8575, Beirut, LBN, escwa-ciu@un.org, https://www.unescwa.org; ESCWA Annual Report 2019; ESCWA Data Portal for the Arab Region; and Survey of Economic and Social Developments in the Arab Region 2020-2021.

United Nations Statistics Division (UNSD), United Nations Plz., New York, NY, 10017, USA, (800) 253-9646, (212) 963-9851, statistics@un.org, https://unstats.un.org; World Statistics Pocketbook 2021.

The World Bank, 1818 H St. NW, Washington, DC, 20433, USA, (202) 473-1000, (202) 477-6391, eds03@worldbank.org, https://www.worldbank.org/; Armenia (report); Global Economic Monitor (GEM); Global Economic Prospects, June 2022; The Global Findex Database 2021; and World Development Report 2022: Finance for an Equitable Recovery.

ARMENIA-EDUCATION

Euromonitor International, Inc., 1 N Dearborn St., Ste. 1700, Chicago, IL, 60602, USA, (312) 922-1115, (312) 922-1157, info-usa@euromonitor.com, https://www.euromonitor.com/; Geographies.

Infoplease, c/o Sandbox Networks, Inc., 1 Lincoln St., 24th Fl., Boston, MA, 02111, USA, https://www.infoplease.com; Countries of the World.

Palgrave Macmillan, 1 New York Plaza, Ste. 4500, New York, NY, 10004-1562, USA, (800) 777-4643, orders@palgrave.com, https://www.palgrave.com/us; The Statesman's Yearbook, 2023.

Routledge - Taylor & Francis Group, 6000 Broken Sound Pkwy. NW, Ste. 300, Boca Raton, FL, 33487, USA, (800) 634-1420, (800) 634-7064, orders@taylorandfrancis.com, https://www.routledge.com/; The Europa World Year Book 2022.

UNESCO Institute for Statistics, C.P 250 Succursale H, Montreal, QC, H3G 2K8, CAN, (514) 343-6880 (Dial from U.S.), (514) 343-5740 (Fax from U.S.), uis.publications@unesco.org, http://uis.unesco.org/; Literacy and UIS.Stat.

United Nations Statistics Division (UNSD), United Nations Plz., New York, NY, 10017, USA, (800) 253-9646, (212) 963-9851, statistics@un.org, https://unstats.un.org; Millennium Development Goal Indicators.

The World Bank, 1818 H St. NW, Washington, DC, 20433, USA, (202) 473-1000, (202) 477-6391, eds03@worldbank.org, https://www.worldbank.org/; Armenia (report) and World Development Report 2022: Finance for an Equitable Recovery.

ARMENIA-ELECTRICITY

U.S. Energy Information Administration (EIA), 1000 Independence Ave. SW, Washington, DC, 20585, USA, (202) 586-8800, infoctr@eia.gov, https://www.eia.gov; International Energy Outlook 2021.

United Nations Statistics Division (UNSD), United Nations Plz., New York, NY, 10017, USA, (800) 253-9646, (212) 963-9851, statistics@un.org, https://unstats.un.org; Energy Statistics Yearbook 2019 and Statistical Yearbook of the United Nations 2021.

ARMENIA-EMPLOYMENT

UK Data Service, University of Essex, Wivenhoe Park, Colchester, Essex, CO4 3SQ, GBR, https://ukdataservice.ac.uk/; International Aggregate Data.

United Nations Statistics Division (UNSD), United Nations Plz., New York, NY, 10017, USA, (800) 253-9646, (212) 963-9851, statistics@un.org, https://unstats.un.org; Statistical Yearbook of the United Nations 2021.

The World Bank, 1818 H St. NW, Washington, DC, 20433, USA, (202) 473-1000, (202) 477-6391, eds03@worldbank.org, https://www.worldbank.org/; Armenia (report).

ARMENIA-ENVIRONMENTAL CONDITIONS

DSI Data Service & Information, Xantener Strasse 51a, Rheinberg, D-47495, GER, dsi@dsidata.com, https://www.dsidata.com/; Global Environmental Database.

The Economist Group: Economist Intelligence Unit (EIU), 900 3rd Ave., 16th Fl., New York, NY, 10022, USA, (212) 541-0500, americas@eiu.com, https://www.eiu.com; Armenia Country Report.

United Nations Statistics Division (UNSD), United Nations Plz., New York, NY, 10017, USA, (800) 253-9646, (212) 963-9851, statistics@un.org, https://unstats.un.org; Statistical Yearbook of the United Nations 2021 and World Statistics Pocketbook 2021.

ARMENIA-EXPORTS

Central Intelligence Agency (CIA), Office of Public Affairs, Washington, DC, 20505, USA, (703) 482-0623, https://www.cia.gov; The World Factbook.

The Economist Group: Economist Intelligence Unit (EIU), 900 3rd Ave., 16th Fl., New York, NY, 10022, USA, (212) 541-0500, americas@eiu.com, https://www.eiu.com; Armenia Country Report.

International Monetary Fund (IMF), 700 19th St. NW, Washington, DC, 20431, USA, (202) 623-7000, (202) 623-4661, publications@imf.org, https://www.imf.org; Direction of Trade Statistics (DOTS).

S&P Global, IHS Markit, 15 Inverness Way E, Englewood, CO, 80112, USA, (800) 447-2273, (800) 854-7179, https://ihsmarkit.com; Global Trade Atlas (GTA).

United Nations Conference on Trade and Development (UNCTAD), Palais des Nations, Geneva, 1211, SWI, (212) 963-6896, unctadinfo@unctad.org, https://unctad.org; Handbook of Statistics 2021.

United Nations Statistics Division (UNSD), United Nations Plz., New York, NY, 10017, USA, (800) 253-9646, (212) 963-9851, statistics@un.org, https://unstats.un.org; International Trade Statistics Yearbook 2020.

The World Bank, 1818 H St. NW, Washington, DC, 20433, USA, (202) 473-1000, (202) 477-6391, eds03@worldbank.org, https://www.worldbank.org/; World Development Report 2022: Finance for an Equitable Recovery.

ARMENIA-FINANCE

Stockholm International Peace Research Institute (SIPRI), Signalistgatan 9, Stockholm, SE 169 72, SWE, https://www.sipri.org/; SIPRI Arms Transfers Database and SIPRI Military Expenditure Database.

United Nations Statistics Division (UNSD), United Nations Plz., New York, NY, 10017, USA, (800) 253-9646, (212) 963-9851, statistics@un.org, https://unstats.un.org; Statistical Yearbook of the United Nations 2021.

The World Bank, 1818 H St. NW, Washington, DC, 20433, USA, (202) 473-1000, (202) 477-6391, eds03@worldbank.org, https://www.worldbank.org/; Armenia (report).

ARMENIA-FINANCE, PUBLIC

Bernan Press, 15250 NBN Way, Bldg. C, Blue Ridge Summit, PA, 17214, USA, (301) 459-2255, (800) 865-3457, (800) 865-3450, customercare@bernan.com, https://rowman.com/Page/Bernan; National Accounts Statistics: Analysis of Main Aggregates 2020.

The Economist Group: Economist Intelligence Unit (EIU), 900 3rd Ave., 16th Fl., New York, NY, 10022, USA, (212) 541-0500, americas@eiu.com, https://www.eiu.com; Armenia Country Report.

International Monetary Fund (IMF), 700 19th St. NW, Washington, DC, 20431, USA, (202) 623-7000, (202) 623-4661, publications@imf.org, https://www.imf.org; Regional Economic Outlook.

Palgrave Macmillan, 1 New York Plaza, Ste. 4500, New York, NY, 10004-1562, USA, (800) 777-4643, orders@palgrave.com, https://www.palgrave.com/us; The Statesman's Yearbook, 2023.

Routledge - Taylor & Francis Group, 6000 Broken Sound Pkwy. NW, Ste. 300, Boca Raton, FL, 33487, USA, (800) 634-1420, (800) 634-7064, orders@taylorandfrancis.com, https://www.routledge.com/; The Europa World Year Book 2022.

United Nations Statistics Division (UNSD), United Nations Plz., New York, NY, 10017, USA, (800) 253-9646, (212) 963-9851, statistics@un.org, https://unstats.un.org; National Accounts Main Aggregates Database and National Accounts Statistics: Main Aggregates and Detailed Tables.

The World Bank, 1818 H St. NW, Washington, DC, 20433, USA, (202) 473-1000, (202) 477-6391, eds03@worldbank.org, https://www.worldbank.org/; Armenia (report).

ARMENIA-FISHERIES

United Nations Food and Agricultural Organization (FAO), 2121 K St., Ste. 800B, Washington, DC, 20037, USA, (202) 653-2400 (Dial from U.S.), (202) 653-5760 (Fax from U.S.), fao-hq@fao.org, https://www.fao.org; FAO Yearbook of Fishery and Aquaculture Statistics 2019; Fishery Statistical Collections Global Capture Production; FishStatJ; and The State of Food and Agriculture (SOFA) 2022.

United Nations Statistics Division (UNSD), United Nations Plz., New York, NY, 10017, USA, (800) 253-9646, (212) 963-9851, statistics@un.org, https://unstats.un.org; Statistical Yearbook of the United Nations 2021.

The World Bank, 1818 H St. NW, Washington, DC, 20433, USA, (202) 473-1000, (202) 477-6391, eds03@worldbank.org, https://www.worldbank.org/; Armenia (report).

ARMENIA-FOOD

United Nations Food and Agricultural Organization (FAO), 2121 K St., Ste. 800B, Washington, DC, 20037, USA, (202) 653-2400 (Dial from U.S.), (202) 653-5760 (Fax from U.S.), fao-hq@fao.org, https://www.fao.org; The State of Food and Agriculture (SOFA) 2022.

ARMENIA-FORESTS AND FORESTRY

United Nations Food and Agricultural Organization (FAO), 2121 K St., Ste. 800B, Washington, DC, 20037, USA, (202) 653-2400 (Dial from U.S.), (202) 653-5760 (Fax from U.S.), fao-hq@fao.org, https://www.fao.org; FAO Yearbook of Forest Products 2019 and The State of Food and Agriculture (SOFA) 2022.

United Nations Statistics Division (UNSD), United Nations Plz., New York, NY, 10017, USA, (800) 253-9646, (212) 963-9851, statistics@un.org, https://unstats.un.org; Statistical Yearbook of the United Nations 2021.

The World Bank, 1818 H St. NW, Washington, DC, 20433, USA, (202) 473-1000, (202) 477-6391, eds03@worldbank.org, https://www.worldbank.org/; Armenia (report) and World Development Report 2022: Finance for an Equitable Recovery.

ARMENIA-GROSS DOMESTIC PRODUCT

The Economist Group: Economist Intelligence Unit (EIU), 900 3rd Ave., 16th Fl., New York, NY, 10022, USA, (212) 541-0500, americas@eiu.com, https://www.eiu.com; Armenia Country Report.

United Nations Statistics Division (UNSD), United Nations Plz., New York, NY, 10017, USA, (800) 253-9646, (212) 963-9851, statistics@un.org, https://unstats.un.org; Statistical Yearbook of the United Nations 2021.

The World Bank, 1818 H St. NW, Washington, DC, 20433, USA, (202) 473-1000, (202) 477-6391, eds03@worldbank.org, https://www.worldbank.org/; World Development Indicators (WDI) 2022 and World Development Report 2022: Finance for an Equitable Recovery.

ARMENIA-GROSS NATIONAL PRODUCT

Palgrave Macmillan, 1 New York Plaza, Ste. 4500, New York, NY, 10004-1562, USA, (800) 777-4643,

orders@palgrave.com, https://www.palgrave.com/us; The Statesman's Yearbook, 2023.

United Nations Statistics Division (UNSD), United Nations Plz., New York, NY, 10017, USA, (800) 253-9646, (212) 963-9851, statistics@un.org, https://unstats.un.org; Statistical Yearbook of the United Nations 2021.

The World Bank, 1818 H St. NW, Washington, DC, 20433, USA, (202) 473-1000, (202) 477-6391, eds03@worldbank.org, https://www.worldbank.org/; World Development Indicators (WDI) 2022 and World Development Report 2022: Finance for an Equitable Recovery.

ARMENIA-HOUSING

Euromonitor International, Inc., 1 N Dearborn St., Ste. 1700, Chicago, IL, 60602, USA, (312) 922-1115, (312) 922-1157, info-usa@euromonitor.com, https://www.euromonitor.com/; Geographies.

ARMENIA-ILLITERATE PERSONS

Central Intelligence Agency (CIA), Office of Public Affairs, Washington, DC, 20505, USA, (703) 482-0623, https://www.cia.gov; The World Factbook.

UNESCO Institute for Statistics, C.P 250 Succursale H, Montreal, QC, H3G 2K8, CAN, (514) 343-6880 (Dial from U.S.), (514) 343-5740 (Fax from U.S.), uis.publications@unesco.org, http://uis.unesco.org/; UIS.Stat.

ARMENIA-IMPORTS

Central Intelligence Agency (CIA), Office of Public Affairs, Washington, DC, 20505, USA, (703) 482-0623, https://www.cia.gov; The World Factbook.

The Economist Group: Economist Intelligence Unit (EIU), 900 3rd Ave., 16th Fl., New York, NY, 10022, USA, (212) 541-0500, americas@eiu.com, https://www.eiu.com; Armenia Country Report.

International Monetary Fund (IMF), 700 19th St. NW, Washington, DC, 20431, USA, (202) 623-7000, (202) 623-4661, publications@imf.org, https://www.imf.org; Direction of Trade Statistics (DOTS).

S&P Global, IHS Markit, 15 Inverness Way E, Englewood, CO, 80112, USA, (800) 447-2273, (800) 854-7179, https://ihsmarkit.com; Global Trade Atlas (GTA).

United Nations Conference on Trade and Development (UNCTAD), Palais des Nations, Geneva, 1211, SWI, (212) 963-6896, unctadinfo@unctad.org, https://unctad.org; Handbook of Statistics 2021.

United Nations Statistics Division (UNSD), United Nations Plz., New York, NY, 10017, USA, (800) 253-9646, (212) 963-9851, statistics@un.org, https://unstats.un.org; International Trade Statistics Yearbook 2020.

The World Bank, 1818 H St. NW, Washington, DC, 20433, USA, (202) 473-1000, (202) 477-6391, eds03@worldbank.org, https://www.worldbank.org/; World Development Report 2022: Finance for an Equitable Recovery.

ARMENIA-INDUSTRIES

The Economist Group: Economist Intelligence Unit (EIU), 900 3rd Ave., 16th Fl., New York, NY, 10022, USA, (212) 541-0500, americas@eiu.com, https://www.eiu.com; Armenia Country Report.

Euromonitor International, Inc., 1 N Dearborn St., Ste. 1700, Chicago, IL, 60602, USA, (312) 922-1115, (312) 922-1157, info-usa@euromonitor.com, https://www.euromonitor.com/; Geographies.

Routledge - Taylor & Francis Group, 6000 Broken Sound Pkwy. NW, Ste. 300, Boca Raton, FL, 33487, USA, (800) 634-1420, (800) 634-7064, orders@taylorandfrancis.com, https://www.routledge.com/; The Europa World Year Book 2022.

United Nations Industrial Development Organization (UNIDO), 1 United Nations Plz., Rm. DC1-1118, New York, NY, 10017, USA, (212) 963-6890, (212) 963 6885, (212) 963-7904, office.newyork@unido.org, https://www.unido.org/; Industrial Statistics Databases and International Yearbook of Industrial Statistics 2021.

The World Bank, 1818 H St. NW, Washington, DC, 20433, USA, (202) 473-1000, (202) 477-6391, eds03@worldbank.org, https://www.worldbank.org/; Armenia (report) and World Development Indicators (WDI) 2022.

ARMENIA-INFANT AND MATERNAL MORTALITY

See ARMENIA-MORTALITY

ARMENIA-INTERNATIONAL TRADE

The Economist Group: Economist Intelligence Unit (EIU), 900 3rd Ave., 16th Fl., New York, NY, 10022, USA, (212) 541-0500, americas@eiu.com, https://www.eiu.com; Armenia Country Report.

Euromonitor International, Inc., 1 N Dearborn St., Ste. 1700, Chicago, IL, 60602, USA, (312) 922-1115, (312) 922-1157, info-usa@euromonitor.com, https://www.euromonitor.com/; Geographies.

International Monetary Fund (IMF), 700 19th St. NW, Washington, DC, 20431, USA, (202) 623-7000, (202) 623-4661, publications@imf.org, https://www.imf.org; Direction of Trade Statistics (DOTS).

S&P Global, IHS Markit, 15 Inverness Way E, Englewood, CO, 80112, USA, (800) 447-2273, (800) 854-7179, https://ihsmarkit.com; Global Trade Atlas (GTA).

United Nations Statistics Division (UNSD), United Nations Plz., New York, NY, 10017, USA, (800) 253-9646, (212) 963-9851, statistics@un.org, https://unstats.un.org; International Trade Statistics Yearbook 2020 and Statistical Yearbook of the United Nations 2021.

The World Bank, 1818 H St. NW, Washington, DC, 20433, USA, (202) 473-1000, (202) 477-6391, eds03@worldbank.org, https://www.worldbank.org/; Armenia (report); World Development Indicators (WDI) 2022; and World Development Report 2022: Finance for an Equitable Recovery.

World Trade Organization (WTO), Ctre. William Rappard, Rue de Lausanne 154, Case postale, Geneva, CH-1211, SWI, enquiries@wto.org, https://www.wto.org; World Trade Statistical Review 2022.

ARMENIA-INTERNET USERS

International Telecommunication Union (ITU), Place des Nations, Geneva, CH-1211, SWI, itumail@itu.int, https://www.itu.int; Global Connectivity Report 2022; World Telecommunication/ICT Indicators Database 2021; and Yearbook of Statistics 2019.

The World Bank, 1818 H St. NW, Washington, DC, 20433, USA, (202) 473-1000, (202) 477-6391, eds03@worldbank.org, https://www.worldbank.org/; Armenia (report).

ARMENIA-LABOR

Central Intelligence Agency (CIA), Office of Public Affairs, Washington, DC, 20505, USA, (703) 482-0623, https://www.cia.gov; The World Factbook.

Euromonitor International, Inc., 1 N Dearborn St., Ste. 1700, Chicago, IL, 60602, USA, (312) 922-1115, (312) 922-1157, info-usa@euromonitor.com, https://www.euromonitor.com/; Geographies.

Palgrave Macmillan, 1 New York Plaza, Ste. 4500, New York, NY, 10004-1562, USA, (800) 777-4643, orders@palgrave.com, https://www.palgrave.com/us; The Statesman's Yearbook, 2023.

United Nations Statistics Division (UNSD), United Nations Plz., New York, NY, 10017, USA, (800) 253-9646, (212) 963-9851, statistics@un.org, https://unstats.un.org; Statistical Yearbook of the United Nations 2021.

The World Bank, 1818 H St. NW, Washington, DC, 20433, USA, (202) 473-1000, (202) 477-6391, eds03@worldbank.org, https://www.worldbank.org/; World Development Indicators (WDI) 2022 and World Development Report 2022: Finance for an Equitable Recovery.

ARMENIA-LAND USE

United Nations Statistics Division (UNSD), United Nations Plz., New York, NY, 10017, USA, (800) 253-9646, (212) 963-9851, statistics@un.org, https://unstats.un.org; Millennium Development Goal Indicators.

The World Bank, 1818 H St. NW, Washington, DC, 20433, USA, (202) 473-1000, (202) 477-6391, eds03@worldbank.org, https://www.worldbank.org/; World Development Report 2022: Finance for an Equitable Recovery.

ARMENIA-LIBRARIES

UNESCO Institute for Statistics, C.P 250 Succursale H, Montreal, QC, H3G 2K8, CAN, (514) 343-6880 (Dial from U.S.), (514) 343-5740 (Fax from U.S.), uis.publications@unesco.org, http://uis.unesco.org/; UIS.Stat.

ARMENIA-LIFE EXPECTANCY

United Nations Department of Economic and Social Affairs (DESA), Population Division, 2 United Nations Plz., Rm. DC2-1950, New York, NY, 10017, USA, (212) 963-3209, (212) 963-2147, population@un.org, https://www.un.org/development/desa/pd/; World Population Ageing 2020 Highlights.

United Nations Statistics Division (UNSD), United Nations Plz., New York, NY, 10017, USA, (800) 253-9646, (212) 963-9851, statistics@un.org, https://unstats.un.org; Millennium Development Goal Indicators.

The World Bank, 1818 H St. NW, Washington, DC, 20433, USA, (202) 473-1000, (202) 477-6391, eds03@worldbank.org, https://www.worldbank.org/; World Development Indicators (WDI) 2022.

ARMENIA-LITERACY

Euromonitor International, Inc., 1 N Dearborn St., Ste. 1700, Chicago, IL, 60602, USA, (312) 922-1115, (312) 922-1157, info-usa@euromonitor.com, https://www.euromonitor.com/; Geographies.

UNESCO Institute for Statistics, C.P 250 Succursale H, Montreal, QC, H3G 2K8, CAN, (514) 343-6880 (Dial from U.S.), (514) 343-5740 (Fax from U.S.), uis.publications@unesco.org, http://uis.unesco.org/; Literacy.

ARMENIA-LIVESTOCK

Palgrave Macmillan, 1 New York Plaza, Ste. 4500, New York, NY, 10004-1562, USA, (800) 777-4643, orders@palgrave.com, https://www.palgrave.com/us; The Statesman's Yearbook, 2023.

Routledge - Taylor & Francis Group, 6000 Broken Sound Pkwy. NW, Ste. 300, Boca Raton, FL, 33487, USA, (800) 634-1420, (800) 634-7064, orders@taylorandfrancis.com, https://www.routledge.com/; The Europa World Year Book 2022.

United Nations Food and Agricultural Organization (FAO), 2121 K St., Ste. 800B, Washington, DC, 20037, USA, (202) 653-2400 (Dial from U.S.), (202) 653-5760 (Fax from U.S.), fao-hq@fao.org, https://www.fao.org; The State of Food and Agriculture (SOFA) 2022.

United Nations Statistics Division (UNSD), United Nations Plz., New York, NY, 10017, USA, (800) 253-9646, (212) 963-9851, statistics@un.org, https://unstats.un.org; Statistical Yearbook of the United Nations 2021.

ARMENIA-MARRIAGE

Routledge - Taylor & Francis Group, 6000 Broken Sound Pkwy. NW, Ste. 300, Boca Raton, FL, 33487, USA, (800) 634-1420, (800) 634-7064, orders@taylorandfrancis.com, https://www.routledge.com/; The Europa World Year Book 2022.

United Nations Statistics Division (UNSD), United Nations Plz., New York, NY, 10017, USA, (800) 253-9646, (212) 963-9851, statistics@un.org, https://unstats.un.org; Statistical Yearbook of the United Nations 2021.

ARMENIA-MINERAL INDUSTRIES

Palgrave Macmillan, 1 New York Plaza, Ste. 4500, New York, NY, 10004-1562, USA, (800) 777-4643,

orders@palgrave.com, https://www.palgrave.com/us; The Statesman's Yearbook, 2023.

United Nations Statistics Division (UNSD), United Nations Plz., New York, NY, 10017, USA, (800) 253-9646, (212) 963-9851, statistics@un.org, https://unstats.un.org; Energy Statistics Yearbook 2019 and Statistical Yearbook of the United Nations 2021.

The World Bank, 1818 H St. NW, Washington, DC, 20433, USA, (202) 473-1000, (202) 477-6391, eds03@worldbank.org, https://www.worldbank.org/; Armenia (report).

ARMENIA-MONEY SUPPLY

The Economist Group: Economist Intelligence Unit (EIU), 900 3rd Ave., 16th Fl., New York, NY, 10022, USA, (212) 541-0500, americas@eiu.com, https://www.eiu.com; Armenia Country Report.

The World Bank, 1818 H St. NW, Washington, DC, 20433, USA, (202) 473-1000, (202) 477-6391, eds03@worldbank.org, https://www.worldbank.org/; Armenia (report).

ARMENIA-MONUMENTS AND HISTORIC SITES

UNESCO Institute for Statistics, C.P 250 Succursale H, Montreal, QC, H3G 2K8, CAN, (514) 343-6880 (Dial from U.S.), (514) 343-5740 (Fax from U.S.), uis.publications@unesco.org, http://uis.unesco.org/; UIS.Stat.

ARMENIA-MORTALITY

United Nations Statistics Division (UNSD), United Nations Plz., New York, NY, 10017, USA, (800) 253-9646, (212) 963-9851, statistics@un.org, https://unstats.un.org; Millennium Development Goal Indicators; Statistical Yearbook of the United Nations 2021; and World Statistics Pocketbook 2021.

The World Bank, 1818 H St. NW, Washington, DC, 20433, USA, (202) 473-1000, (202) 477-6391, eds03@worldbank.org, https://www.worldbank.org/; World Development Indicators (WDI) 2022.

World Health Organization (WHO), Ave. Appia 20, Geneva, CH-1211, SWI, (202) 974-3000 (Telephone in U.S.), publications@who.int, https://www.who.int/; Global Health Observatory (GHO).

ARMENIA-PETROLEUM INDUSTRY AND TRADE

U.S. Energy Information Administration (EIA), 1000 Independence Ave. SW, Washington, DC, 20585, USA, (202) 586-8800, infoctr@eia.gov, https://www.eia.gov; International Energy Outlook 2021.

United Nations Food and Agricultural Organization (FAO), 2121 K St., Ste. 800B, Washington, DC, 20037, USA, (202) 653-2400 (Dial from U.S.), (202) 653-5760 (Fax from U.S.), fao-hq@fao.org, https://www.fao.org; The State of Food and Agriculture (SOFA) 2022.

United Nations Statistics Division (UNSD), United Nations Plz., New York, NY, 10017, USA, (800) 253-9646, (212) 963-9851, statistics@un.org, https://unstats.un.org; Energy Statistics Yearbook 2019 and Statistical Yearbook of the United Nations 2021.

ARMENIA-POPULATION

Central Intelligence Agency (CIA), Office of Public Affairs, Washington, DC, 20505, USA, (703) 482-0623, https://www.cia.gov; The World Factbook.

The Economist Group: Economist Intelligence Unit (EIU), 900 3rd Ave., 16th Fl., New York, NY, 10022, USA, (212) 541-0500, americas@eiu.com, https://www.eiu.com; Armenia Country Report.

Infoplease, c/o Sandbox Networks, Inc., 1 Lincoln St., 24th Fl., Boston, MA, 02111, USA, https://www.infoplease.com; Countries of the World.

Palgrave Macmillan, 1 New York Plaza, Ste. 4500, New York, NY, 10004-1562, USA, (800) 777-4643, orders@palgrave.com, https://www.palgrave.com/us; The Statesman's Yearbook, 2023.

Routledge - Taylor & Francis Group, 6000 Broken Sound Pkwy. NW, Ste. 300, Boca Raton, FL, 33487, USA, (800) 634-1420, (800) 634-7064, orders@taylorandfrancis.com, https://www.routledge.com/; The Europa World Year Book 2022.

UK Data Service, University of Essex, Wivenhoe Park, Colchester, Essex, CO4 3SQ, GBR, https://ukdataservice.ac.uk/; International Aggregate Data.

UNESCO Institute for Statistics, C.P 250 Succursale H, Montreal, QC, H3G 2K8, CAN, (514) 343-6880 (Dial from U.S.), (514) 343-5740 (Fax from U.S.), uis.publications@unesco.org, http://uis.unesco.org/; UIS.Stat.

United Nations Department of Economic and Social Affairs (DESA), Population Division, 2 United Nations Plz., Rm. DC2-1950, New York, NY, 10017, USA, (212) 963-3209, (212) 963-2147, population@un.org, https://www.un.org/development/desa/pd/; Revision of World Urbanization Prospects and World Population Ageing 2020 Highlights.

United Nations Development Programme (UNDP), One United Nations Plz., New York, NY, 10017, USA, (212) 906-5000, (212) 906-5001, https://www.undp.org; Human Development Report 2021-2022.

United Nations Statistics Division (UNSD), United Nations Plz., New York, NY, 10017, USA, (800) 253-9646, (212) 963-9851, statistics@un.org, https://unstats.un.org; Statistical Yearbook of the United Nations 2021 and World Statistics Pocketbook 2021.

The World Bank, 1818 H St. NW, Washington, DC, 20433, USA, (202) 473-1000, (202) 477-6391, eds03@worldbank.org, https://www.worldbank.org/; Armenia (report); The Global Findex Database 2021; World Development Indicators (WDI) 2022; and World Development Report 2022: Finance for an Equitable Recovery.

ARMENIA-POPULATION DENSITY

Central Intelligence Agency (CIA), Office of Public Affairs, Washington, DC, 20505, USA, (703) 482-0623, https://www.cia.gov; The World Factbook.

Palgrave Macmillan, 1 New York Plaza, Ste. 4500, New York, NY, 10004-1562, USA, (800) 777-4643, orders@palgrave.com, https://www.palgrave.com/us; The Statesman's Yearbook, 2023.

Routledge - Taylor & Francis Group, 6000 Broken Sound Pkwy. NW, Ste. 300, Boca Raton, FL, 33487, USA, (800) 634-1420, (800) 634-7064, orders@taylorandfrancis.com, https://www.routledge.com/; The Europa World Year Book 2022.

UNESCO Institute for Statistics, C.P 250 Succursale H, Montreal, QC, H3G 2K8, CAN, (514) 343-6880 (Dial from U.S.), (514) 343-5740 (Fax from U.S.), uis.publications@unesco.org, http://uis.unesco.org/; UIS.Stat.

The World Bank, 1818 H St. NW, Washington, DC, 20433, USA, (202) 473-1000, (202) 477-6391, eds03@worldbank.org, https://www.worldbank.org/; Armenia (report) and World Development Report 2022: Finance for an Equitable Recovery.

ARMENIA-POULTRY

See ARMENIA-LIVESTOCK

ARMENIA-POWER RESOURCES

Euromonitor International, Inc., 1 N Dearborn St., Ste. 1700, Chicago, IL, 60602, USA, (312) 922-1115, (312) 922-1157, info-usa@euromonitor.com, https://www.euromonitor.com/; Geographies.

Palgrave Macmillan, 1 New York Plaza, Ste. 4500, New York, NY, 10004-1562, USA, (800) 777-4643, orders@palgrave.com, https://www.palgrave.com/us; The Statesman's Yearbook, 2023.

U.S. Energy Information Administration (EIA), 1000 Independence Ave. SW, Washington, DC, 20585, USA, (202) 586-8800, infoctr@eia.gov, https://www.eia.gov; International Energy Outlook 2021.

United Nations Statistics Division (UNSD), United Nations Plz., New York, NY, 10017, USA, (800) 253-9646, (212) 963-9851, statistics@un.org, https://unstats.un.org; Energy Statistics Yearbook 2019; Statistical Yearbook of the United Nations 2021; and World Statistics Pocketbook 2021.

The World Bank, 1818 H St. NW, Washington, DC, 20433, USA, (202) 473-1000, (202) 477-6391, eds03@worldbank.org, https://www.worldbank.org/; World Development Report 2022: Finance for an Equitable Recovery.

ARMENIA-PRICES

Euromonitor International, Inc., 1 N Dearborn St., Ste. 1700, Chicago, IL, 60602, USA, (312) 922-1115, (312) 922-1157, info-usa@euromonitor.com, https://www.euromonitor.com/; Geographies.

The World Bank, 1818 H St. NW, Washington, DC, 20433, USA, (202) 473-1000, (202) 477-6391, eds03@worldbank.org, https://www.worldbank.org/; Armenia (report).

ARMENIA-PUBLIC HEALTH

Euromonitor International, Inc., 1 N Dearborn St., Ste. 1700, Chicago, IL, 60602, USA, (312) 922-1115, (312) 922-1157, info-usa@euromonitor.com, https://www.euromonitor.com/; Geographies.

Palgrave Macmillan, 1 New York Plaza, Ste. 4500, New York, NY, 10004-1562, USA, (800) 777-4643, orders@palgrave.com, https://www.palgrave.com/us; The Statesman's Yearbook, 2023.

U.S. Census Bureau, 4600 Silver Hill Rd., Washington, DC, 20233, USA, (301) 763-4636, (800) 923-8282, https://www.census.gov; HIV/AIDS Surveillance Data Base.

United Nations Department of Economic and Social Affairs (DESA), Population Division, 2 United Nations Plz., Rm. DC2-1950, New York, NY, 10017, USA, (212) 963-3209, (212) 963-2147, population@un.org, https://www.un.org/development/desa/pd/; World Fertility Data 2019.

United Nations Development Programme (UNDP), One United Nations Plz., New York, NY, 10017, USA, (212) 906-5000, (212) 906-5001, https://www.undp.org; Human Development Report 2021-2022.

United Nations Statistics Division (UNSD), United Nations Plz., New York, NY, 10017, USA, (800) 253-9646, (212) 963-9851, statistics@un.org, https://unstats.un.org; Millennium Development Goal Indicators and Statistical Yearbook of the United Nations 2021.

The World Bank, 1818 H St. NW, Washington, DC, 20433, USA, (202) 473-1000, (202) 477-6391, eds03@worldbank.org, https://www.worldbank.org/; Armenia (report).

World Health Organization (WHO), Ave. Appia 20, Geneva, CH-1211, SWI, (202) 974-3000 (Telephone in U.S.), publications@who.int, https://www.who.int/; Global Health Observatory (GHO) and Health Statistics and Information Systems.

ARMENIA-PUBLISHERS AND PUBLISHING

UNESCO Institute for Statistics, C.P 250 Succursale H, Montreal, QC, H3G 2K8, CAN, (514) 343-6880 (Dial from U.S.), (514) 343-5740 (Fax from U.S.), uis.publications@unesco.org, http://uis.unesco.org/; UIS.Stat.

ARMENIA-RAILROADS

Palgrave Macmillan, 1 New York Plaza, Ste. 4500, New York, NY, 10004-1562, USA, (800) 777-4643, orders@palgrave.com, https://www.palgrave.com/us; The Statesman's Yearbook, 2023.

United Nations Statistics Division (UNSD), United Nations Plz., New York, NY, 10017, USA, (800) 253-9646, (212) 963-9851, statistics@un.org, https://unstats.un.org; Statistical Yearbook of the United Nations 2021.

ARMENIA-RELIGION

Central Intelligence Agency (CIA), Office of Public Affairs, Washington, DC, 20505, USA, (703) 482-0623, https://www.cia.gov; The World Factbook.

Palgrave Macmillan, 1 New York Plaza, Ste. 4500, New York, NY, 10004-1562, USA, (800) 777-4643, orders@palgrave.com, https://www.palgrave.com/us; The Statesman's Yearbook, 2023.

ARMENIA-RETAIL TRADE

Euromonitor International, Inc., 1 N Dearborn St., Ste. 1700, Chicago, IL, 60602, USA, (312) 922-1115, (312) 922-1157, info-usa@euromonitor.com, https://www.euromonitor.com/; Geographies.

United Nations Statistics Division (UNSD), United Nations Plz., New York, NY, 10017, USA, (800) 253-9646, (212) 963-9851, statistics@un.org, https://unstats.un.org; Statistical Yearbook of the United Nations 2021.

ARMENIA-RUBBER INDUSTRY AND TRADE

International Rubber Study Group (IRSG), 51 Changi Business Park Central 2, Unit No. 6, 486066, SGP, https://www.rubberstudy.org; Monthly Rubber Bulletin (MRB); Rubber Industry Report; Rubber Statistical Bulletin; and World Rubber Industry Report (WRIO).

United Nations Statistics Division (UNSD), United Nations Plz., New York, NY, 10017, USA, (800) 253-9646, (212) 963-9851, statistics@un.org, https://unstats.un.org; Statistical Yearbook of the United Nations 2021.

ARMENIA-SHIPPING

United Nations Statistics Division (UNSD), United Nations Plz., New York, NY, 10017, USA, (800) 253-9646, (212) 963-9851, statistics@un.org, https://unstats.un.org; Statistical Yearbook of the United Nations 2021.

ARMENIA-STEEL PRODUCTION

See ARMENIA-MINERAL INDUSTRIES

ARMENIA-TELEPHONE

United Nations Statistics Division (UNSD), United Nations Plz., New York, NY, 10017, USA, (800) 253-9646, (212) 963-9851, statistics@un.org, https://unstats.un.org; World Statistics Pocketbook 2021.

ARMENIA-TEXTILE INDUSTRY

Palgrave Macmillan, 1 New York Plaza, Ste. 4500, New York, NY, 10004-1562, USA, (800) 777-4643, orders@palgrave.com, https://www.palgrave.com/us; The Statesman's Yearbook, 2023.

United Nations Statistics Division (UNSD), United Nations Plz., New York, NY, 10017, USA, (800) 253-9646, (212) 963-9851, statistics@un.org, https://unstats.un.org; Statistical Yearbook of the United Nations 2021.

ARMENIA-THEATER

UNESCO Institute for Statistics, C.P 250 Succursale H, Montreal, QC, H3G 2K8, CAN, (514) 343-6880 (Dial from U.S.), (514) 343-5740 (Fax from U.S.), uis.publications@unesco.org, http://uis.unesco.org/; UIS.Stat.

ARMENIA-TOBACCO INDUSTRY

United Nations Statistics Division (UNSD), United Nations Plz., New York, NY, 10017, USA, (800) 253-9646, (212) 963-9851, statistics@un.org, https://unstats.un.org; Statistical Yearbook of the United Nations 2021.

ARMENIA-TOURISM

Euromonitor International, Inc., 1 N Dearborn St., Ste. 1700, Chicago, IL, 60602, USA, (312) 922-1115, (312) 922-1157, info-usa@euromonitor.com, https://www.euromonitor.com/; Geographies.

United Nations Statistics Division (UNSD), United Nations Plz., New York, NY, 10017, USA, (800) 253-9646, (212) 963-9851, statistics@un.org, https://unstats.un.org; Statistical Yearbook of the United Nations 2021.

The World Bank, 1818 H St. NW, Washington, DC, 20433, USA, (202) 473-1000, (202) 477-6391, eds03@worldbank.org, https://www.worldbank.org/; Armenia (report).

ARMENIA-TRANSPORTATION

Central Intelligence Agency (CIA), Office of Public Affairs, Washington, DC, 20505, USA, (703) 482-0623, https://www.cia.gov; The World Factbook.

Euromonitor International, Inc., 1 N Dearborn St., Ste. 1700, Chicago, IL, 60602, USA, (312) 922-1115, (312) 922-1157, info-usa@euromonitor.com, https://www.euromonitor.com/; Geographies.

Palgrave Macmillan, 1 New York Plaza, Ste. 4500, New York, NY, 10004-1562, USA, (800) 777-4643, orders@palgrave.com, https://www.palgrave.com/us; The Statesman's Yearbook, 2023.

The World Bank, 1818 H St. NW, Washington, DC, 20433, USA, (202) 473-1000, (202) 477-6391, eds03@worldbank.org, https://www.worldbank.org/; Armenia (report).

ARMENIA-UNEMPLOYMENT

Palgrave Macmillan, 1 New York Plaza, Ste. 4500, New York, NY, 10004-1562, USA, (800) 777-4643, orders@palgrave.com, https://www.palgrave.com/us; The Statesman's Yearbook, 2023.

United Nations Statistics Division (UNSD), United Nations Plz., New York, NY, 10017, USA, (800) 253-9646, (212) 963-9851, statistics@un.org, https://unstats.un.org; Statistical Yearbook of the United Nations 2021.

The World Bank, 1818 H St. NW, Washington, DC, 20433, USA, (202) 473-1000, (202) 477-6391, eds03@worldbank.org, https://www.worldbank.org/; Armenia (report).

ARMENIA-VITAL STATISTICS

Palgrave Macmillan, 1 New York Plaza, Ste. 4500, New York, NY, 10004-1562, USA, (800) 777-4643, orders@palgrave.com, https://www.palgrave.com/us; The Statesman's Yearbook, 2023.

U.S. Census Bureau, 4600 Silver Hill Rd., Washington, DC, 20233, USA, (301) 763-4636, (800) 923-8282, https://www.census.gov; HIV/AIDS Surveillance Data Base.

United Nations Department of Economic and Social Affairs (DESA), Population Division, 2 United Nations Plz., Rm. DC2-1950, New York, NY, 10017, USA, (212) 963-3209, (212) 963-2147, population@un.org, https://www.un.org/development/desa/pd/; World Contraceptive Use 2021: Estimates and Projections of Family Planning Indicators and World Marriage Data 2019.

United Nations Economic and Social Commission for Western Asia (ESCWA), Riad el-Solh Sq., PO Box 11-8575, Beirut, LBN, escwa-ciu@un.org, https://www.unescwa.org; ESCWA Annual Report 2019; ESCWA Data Portal for the Arab Region; and Survey of Economic and Social Developments in the Arab Region 2020-2021.

United Nations Statistics Division (UNSD), United Nations Plz., New York, NY, 10017, USA, (800) 253-9646, (212) 963-9851, statistics@un.org, https://unstats.un.org; Statistical Yearbook of the United Nations 2021.

ARMENIA-WAGES

United Nations Statistics Division (UNSD), United Nations Plz., New York, NY, 10017, USA, (800) 253-9646, (212) 963-9851, statistics@un.org, https://unstats.un.org; Statistical Yearbook of the United Nations 2021.

The World Bank, 1818 H St. NW, Washington, DC, 20433, USA, (202) 473-1000, (202) 477-6391, eds03@worldbank.org, https://www.worldbank.org/; Armenia (report).

ARMENIA-WHOLESALE TRADE

United Nations Statistics Division (UNSD), United Nations Plz., New York, NY, 10017, USA, (800) 253-9646, (212) 963-9851, statistics@un.org, https://unstats.un.org; Statistical Yearbook of the United Nations 2021.

ARMENIA-WOOL PRODUCTION

See ARMENIA-TEXTILE INDUSTRY

ARMS RACE

Federation of American Scientists (FAS), 1112 16th St. NW, Ste. 600, Washington, DC, 20036, USA, (202) 546-3300, (202) 675-1010, fas@fas.org, https://fas.org/; Siloed Thinking: A Closer Look at the Ground-Based Strategic Deterrent.

ARMS TRANSFERS

The Stimson Center, 1211 Connecticut Ave. NW, 8th Fl., Washington, DC, 20036, USA, (202) 223-5956, (202) 238-9604, communications@stimson.org, https://www.stimson.org/; 25 Years of Security Cooperation Beneath the Nuclear Shadow: Shifting U.S. Arms Transfers to India and Pakistan.

Stockholm International Peace Research Institute (SIPRI), Signalistgatan 9, Stockholm, SE 169 72, SWE, https://www.sipri.org/; SIPRI Arms Transfers Database.

ARRESTS

See also LAW ENFORCEMENT

Center for Policing Equity (CPE), 8605 Santa Monica Blvd., PMB 54596, West Hollywood, CA, 90069-4109, USA, (347) 948-9953, https://policingequity.org/; National Justice Database (NJD).

National Center for Juvenile Justice (NCJJ), 3700 S Water St., Ste. 200, Pittsburgh, PA, 15203, USA, (412) 227-6950, (412) 227-6955, ncjj@ncjfcj.org, https://www.ncjj.org/; Criminological Highlights: Children and Youth and Trends and Characteristics of Delinquency Cases Handled in Juvenile Court, 2019.

U.S. Department of Homeland Security (DHS), 2707 Martin Luther King Jr. Ave. SE, Washington, DC, 20528-0525, USA, (202) 282-8000, https://www.dhs.gov; Department of Homeland Security Border Security Metrics Report: 2021.

U.S. Department of Homeland Security (DHS), Office of Immigration Statistics (OIS), 2707 Martin Luther King Jr. Ave. SE, Washington, DC, 20528-0525, USA, (202) 282-8000, immigrationstatistics@hq.dhs.gov, https://www.dhs.gov/office-immigration-statistics; Fiscal Year 2021 Enforcement Lifecycle Report and Immigration Enforcement Actions: 2020.

U.S. Department of Homeland Security (DHS), U.S. Customs and Border Protection (CBP), 1300 Pennsylvania Ave. NW, Washington, DC, 20229, USA, (877) 227-5511, (202) 325-8000, https://www.cbp.gov; CBP Public Data Portal and Southwest Land Border Encounters (By Component).

U.S. Department of Justice (DOJ), Federal Bureau of Investigation (FBI), 935 Pennsylvania Ave. NW, Washington, DC, 20535-0001, USA, (202) 324-3000, https://www.fbi.gov/; Crime in the United States 2019.

U.S. Department of Justice (DOJ), National Institute of Justice (NIJ), 810 7th St. NW, Washington, DC, 20531, USA, (202) 307-2942, (800) 851-3420, https://www.nij.gov/; 2021 Annual Report to Congress.

ARSENIC

U.S. Department of the Interior (DOI), U.S. Geological Survey (USGS), National Minerals Information Center (NMIC), 12201 Sunrise Valley Dr., Reston, VA, 20192, USA, (703) 648-4920, (703) 648-7971, (703) 648-4995, sfortier@usgs.gov, https://www.usgs.gov/centers/nmic; Mineral Commodity Summaries 2022.

ARSON

Bureau of Alcohol, Tobacco, Firearms and Explosives (ATF), United States Bomb Data Center (USBDC), 3750 Corporal Rd., Huntsville, AL, 35898, USA, (800) 461-8841, usbdc@atf.gov, https://www.atf.gov/explosives/us-bomb-data-center; 2020 Arson Incident Report and 2019 House of Worship Incidents in the United States.

ART

Art Basel, 176-180 Grand St., Ste. 601, New York, NY, 10013, USA, https://www.artbasel.com; The Art Market 2022.

International Criminal Police Organization (INTERPOL), General Secretariat, 200 quai Charles de Gaulle, Lyon, 69006, FRA, https://www.interpol.int; Stolen Works of Art Database.

National Endowment for the Arts (NEA), 400 7th St. SW, Washington, DC, 20506-0001, USA, (202) 682-5400, https://www.arts.gov; Arts Data Profile Series.

ARTERIOSCLEROSIS-DEATHS

Bernan Press, 15250 NBN Way, Bldg. C, Blue Ridge Summit, PA, 17214, USA, (301) 459-2255, (800) 865-3457, (800) 865-3450, customercare@bernan.com, https://rowman.com/Page/Bernan; Vital Statistics of the United States 2022: Births, Life Expectancy, Deaths, and Selected Health Data.

U.S. Department of Health and Human Services, Centers for Disease Control and Prevention (CDC), National Center for Health Statistics (NCHS), 3311 Toledo Rd., Hyattsville, MD, 20782-2064, USA, (800) 232-4636, (301) 458-4000, https://www.cdc.gov/nchs; National Vital Statistics Reports (NVSR) and Vital Statistics Online Data Portal.

ARTHRITIS

U.S. Department of Health and Human Services, Centers for Disease Control and Prevention (CDC), 1600 Clifton Rd., Atlanta, GA, 30329-4027, USA, (800) 232-4636, (888) 232-6348 (TTY), cdcinfo@cdc.gov, https://www.cdc.gov; Behavioral Risk Factor Surveillance System (BRFSS) Data.

U.S. Department of Health and Human Services, Centers for Disease Control and Prevention (CDC), National Center for Chronic Disease Prevention and Health Promotion (NCCDPHP), 1600 Clifton Rd., Atlanta, GA, 30329, USA, (800) 232-4636, (888) 232-6348 (TTY), https://www.cdc.gov/chronicdisease/; Leading Indicators for Chronic Diseases and Risk Factors Open Data Portal.

U.S. Department of Health and Human Services, Centers for Disease Control and Prevention (CDC), National Center for Health Statistics (NCHS), 3311 Toledo Rd., Hyattsville, MD, 20782-2064, USA, (800) 232-4636, (301) 458-4000, https://www.cdc.gov/nchs; FastStats - Statistics by Topic.

ARTICHOKES

U.S. Department of Agriculture (USDA), National Agricultural Statistics Service (USDA-NASS), 1400 Independence Ave. SW, Washington, DC, 20250, USA, (800) 727-9540, nass@nass.usda.gov, https://www.nass.usda.gov; Quick Stats.

ARTIFICIAL INTELLIGENCE

Network Contagion Research Institute (NCRI), https://networkcontagion.us/; Exploiting Tragedy: The Rise of Computer-Generative Enabled Hoaxes and Malicious Information in the Wake of Mass Shootings.

ARTIFICIAL INTELLIGENCE-SOCIAL ASPECTS

Microsoft Research, 14820 NE 36th St., Bldg. 99, Redmond, WA, 98052, USA, https://research.microsoft.com; Assessing Human-AI Interaction Early through Factorial Surveys: A Study on the Guidelines for Human-AI Interaction.

ARTIFICIAL INTELLIGENCE AND SOCIETY

Microsoft Research, 14820 NE 36th St., Bldg. 99, Redmond, WA, 98052, USA, https://research.microsoft.com; Assessing Human-AI Interaction Early through Factorial Surveys: A Study on the Guidelines for Human-AI Interaction.

Pew Research Center, Internet & Technology, 1615 L St. NW, Ste. 800, Washington, DC, 20036, USA, (202) 419-4300, (202) 857-8562, https://www.pewresearch.org/topic/internet-technology/; AI in Hiring and Evaluating Workers: What Americans Think.

ARTISTS

Art Basel, 176-180 Grand St., Ste. 601, New York, NY, 10013, USA, https://www.artbasel.com; The Art Market 2022.

National Endowment for the Arts (NEA), 400 7th St. SW, Washington, DC, 20506-0001, USA, (202) 682-5400, https://www.arts.gov; Arts Data Profile Series.

United Nations Conference on Trade and Development (UNCTAD), Palais des Nations, Geneva, 1211, SWI, (212) 963-6896, unctadinfo@unctad.org, https://unctad.org; UNCTADstat Database.

ARTS AND HUMANITIES

Art Basel, 176-180 Grand St., Ste. 601, New York, NY, 10013, USA, https://www.artbasel.com; The Art Market 2022.

The Broadway League, 729 7th Ave., 5th Fl., New York, NY, 10019, USA, (212) 764-1122, (212) 944-2136, league@broadway.org, https://www.broadwayleague.com/; Broadway's Economic Contribution to New York City 2018-2019 Season.

National Endowment for the Arts (NEA), 400 7th St. SW, Washington, DC, 20506-0001, USA, (202) 682-5400, https://www.arts.gov; Arts Data Profile Series.

United Nations Conference on Trade and Development (UNCTAD), Palais des Nations, Geneva, 1211, SWI, (212) 963-6896, unctadinfo@unctad.org, https://unctad.org; UNCTADstat Database.

The Wallace Foundation, 140 Broadway, 49th Fl., New York, NY, 10005, USA, (212) 251-9700, (212) 679-6990, https://www.wallacefoundation.org; Knowledge Center.

ARTS AND HUMANITIES-ARTS EDUCATION IN SCHOOLS

See ARTS EDUCATION

ARTS AND HUMANITIES-ATTENDANCE

The Broadway League, 729 7th Ave., 5th Fl., New York, NY, 10019, USA, (212) 764-1122, (212) 944-2136, league@broadway.org, https://www.broadwayleague.com/; Broadway Season Statistics; The Demographics of the Broadway Audience 2018-2019; and Statistics - Touring Broadway.

The National Opera Center America (OPERA America), 330 7th Ave., New York, NY, 10001, USA, (212) 796-8620, (212) 796-8621, info@operaamerica.org, https://www.operaamerica.org/; 2021 Annual Field Report.

SMU DataArts, 461 N 3rd St., 4th Fl., Philadelphia, PA, 19123, USA, (215) 383-0700, (215) 383-0750, info@culturaldata.org, https://culturaldata.org/; Cultural Data Profile (CDP).

Theatre Communications Group (TCG), 520 8h Ave., 24th Fl., New York, NY, 10018-4156, USA, (212) 609-5900, (212) 609-5901, info@tcg.org, https://circle.tcg.org/; Centerpieces.

ARTS AND HUMANITIES-CHARITABLE CONTRIBUTIONS

Independent Sector, 1602 L St. NW, Ste. 900, Washington, DC, 20036, USA, (202) 467-6100, (202) 467-6101, info@independentsector.org, https://independentsector.org/; Health of the U.S. Nonprofit Sector Quarterly Review.

ARTS AND HUMANITIES-FEDERAL AID

National Assembly of State Arts Agencies (NASAA), 1200 18th St. NW, Ste. 1100, Washington, DC, 20036, USA, (202) 347-6352, (202) 296-0567 (TDD), (202) 737-0526, nasaa@nasaa-arts.org, https://nasaa-arts.org/; State Arts Agency Legislative Appropriations Preview, Fiscal Year 2021.

National Endowment for the Arts (NEA), 400 7th St. SW, Washington, DC, 20506-0001, USA, (202) 682-5400, https://www.arts.gov; 2022 Annual Performance Report.

National Endowment for the Humanities (NEH), 400 7th St. SW, Washington, DC, 20506, USA, (202) 606-8400, questions@neh.gov, https://www.neh.gov; Humanities.

ARTS AND HUMANITIES-GRANTS, FOUNDATIONS

SMU DataArts, 461 N 3rd St., 4th Fl., Philadelphia, PA, 19123, USA, (215) 383-0700, (215) 383-0750, info@culturaldata.org, https://culturaldata.org/; Cultural Data Profile (CDP).

ARTS AND HUMANITIES-PARTICIPATION

American Academy of Arts & Sciences, 136 Irving St., Cambridge, MA, 02138, USA, (617) 576-5000, https://www.amacad.org/; Humanities Indicators.

National Endowment for the Humanities (NEH), 400 7th St. SW, Washington, DC, 20506, USA, (202) 606-8400, questions@neh.gov, https://www.neh.gov; Humanities.

Poetry Foundation, 61 W Superior St., Chicago, IL, 60654, USA, (312) 787-7070, info@poetryfoundation.org, https://www.poetryfoundation.org/; unpublished data.

SMU DataArts, 461 N 3rd St., 4th Fl., Philadelphia, PA, 19123, USA, (215) 383-0700, (215) 383-0750, info@culturaldata.org, https://culturaldata.org/; Cultural Data Profile (CDP).

University of Chicago, Center for the Study of Race, Politics and Culture, Black Youth Project, 5733 S University Ave., Chicago, IL, 60637, USA, info@blackyouthproject.com, https://www.blackyouthproject.com/; GenForward Survey 2022.

ARTS AND HUMANITIES-PHILANTHROPY

The Chronicle of Philanthropy, 1255 23rd St. NW, 7th Fl., Washington, DC, 20037, USA, (202) 466-1200, philanthropy@pubservice.com, https://www.philanthropy.com/; America's Favorite Charities 2021; The Chronicle of Philanthropy; and Data & Research.

Giving Institute, 7918 Jones Branch Dr., No. 300, McLean, VA, 22102, USA, (312) 981-6794, (312) 265-2908, info@givinginstitute.org, https://www.givinginstitute.org/; Giving USA 2021: The Annual Report on Philanthropy for the Year 2020.

ARTS EDUCATION

National Assembly of State Arts Agencies (NASAA), 1200 18th St. NW, Ste. 1100, Washington, DC, 20036, USA, (202) 347-6352, (202) 296-0567 (TDD), (202) 737-0526, nasaa@nasaa-arts.org, https://nasaa-arts.org/; State Arts Agency Revenues Report, Fiscal Year 2022.

ARTS, ENTERTAINMENT AND RECREATION

National Assembly of State Arts Agencies (NASAA), 1200 18th St. NW, Ste. 1100, Washington, DC, 20036, USA, (202) 347-6352, (202) 296-0567 (TDD), (202) 737-0526, nasaa@nasaa-arts.org, https://nasaa-arts.org/; State Arts Agency Revenues Report, Fiscal Year 2022.

National Endowment for the Arts (NEA), 400 7th St. SW, Washington, DC, 20506-0001, USA, (202) 682-5400, https://www.arts.gov; Arts Data Profile Series.

PricewaterhouseCoopers (PwC) Strategy&, 90 Park Ave., Ste. 400, New York, NY, 10016, USA, (212) 697-1900, (212) 551-6732, https://www.strategyand.pwc.com/gx/en/; Global Entertainment & Media Outlook 2022-2026.

U.S. Census Bureau, Center for Economic Studies (CES), 4600 Silver Hill Rd., Washington, DC, 20233, USA, (301) 763-6460, (301) 763-5935, ces.contacts@census.gov, https://www.census.gov/programs-surveys/ces.html; 2017 Economic Census Data.

U.S. Department of Labor (DOL), Bureau of Labor Statistics (BLS), Postal Square Bldg., 2 Massachusetts Ave. NE, Washington, DC, 20212-0001, USA, (202) 691-5200, (202) 691-7890, blsdata_staff@bls.gov, https://www.bls.gov; Industries at a Glance.

ARTS, ENTERTAINMENT AND RECREATION-CAPITAL

U.S. Census Bureau, 4600 Silver Hill Rd., Washington, DC, 20233, USA, (301) 763-4636, (800) 923-8282, https://www.census.gov; Annual Capital Expenditures Survey (ACES) 2020.

U.S. Census Bureau, Center for Economic Studies (CES), 4600 Silver Hill Rd., Washington, DC, 20233, USA, (301) 763-6460, (301) 763-5935, ces.contacts@census.gov, https://www.census.gov/programs-surveys/ces.html; Arts, Entertainment and Recreation, 2017 Economic Census.

ARTS, ENTERTAINMENT AND RECREATION-EARNINGS

Forbes, Inc., 499 Washington Blvd., Jersey City, NJ, 07310, USA, (800) 295-0893, https://www.forbes.com; The Highest-Paid Entertainers 2022.

U.S. Census Bureau, 4600 Silver Hill Rd., Washington, DC, 20233, USA, (301) 763-4636, (800) 923-8282, https://www.census.gov; Economic Census, Nonemployer Statistics (NES) 2019.

U.S. Census Bureau, Center for Economic Studies (CES), 4600 Silver Hill Rd., Washington, DC, 20233, USA, (301) 763-6460, (301) 763-5935, ces.contacts@census.gov, https://www.census.gov/programs-surveys/ces.html; Arts, Entertainment and Recreation, 2017 Economic Census and Geographic Area, 2017 Economic Census.

ARTS, ENTERTAINMENT AND RECREATION-EMPLOYEES

Institute for Supply Management (ISM), 309 W Elliot Rd. , Ste. 113, Tempe, AZ, 85284-1556, USA, (480) 752-6276, (480) 752-7890, membersvcs@ismworld.org, https://www.ismworld.org/; 2022 Salary Survey.

U.S. Department of Labor (DOL), Bureau of Labor Statistics (BLS), Postal Square Bldg., 2 Massachusetts Ave. NE, Washington, DC, 20212-0001, USA, (202) 691-5200, (202) 691-7890, blsdata_staff@bls.gov, https://www.bls.gov; Industry-Occupation Matrix Data, By Occupation.

ARTS, ENTERTAINMENT AND RECREATION-FINANCES

U.S. Census Bureau, 4600 Silver Hill Rd., Washington, DC, 20233, USA, (301) 763-4636, (800) 923-8282, https://www.census.gov; County Business Patterns (CBP) 2020 and Survey of Income and Program Participation (SIPP) 2020.

U.S. Census Bureau, Center for Economic Studies (CES), 4600 Silver Hill Rd., Washington, DC, 20233, USA, (301) 763-6460, (301) 763-5935, ces.contacts@census.gov, https://www.census.gov/programs-surveys/ces.html; Arts, Entertainment and Recreation, 2017 Economic Census.

ARTS, ENTERTAINMENT AND RECREATION-INDUSTRIAL SAFETY

U.S. Department of Labor (DOL), Bureau of Labor Statistics (BLS), Postal Square Bldg., 2 Massachusetts Ave. NE, Washington, DC, 20212-0001, USA, (202) 691-5200, (202) 691-7890, blsdata_staff@bls.gov, https://www.bls.gov; Injuries, Illnesses, and Fatalities (IIF).

ARTS, ENTERTAINMENT AND RECREATION-REVENUE, RECEIPTS

Internal Revenue Service (IRS), Statistics of Income Division (SOI), 1111 Constitution Ave. NW, K-Room 4100-123, Washington, DC, 20224-0002, USA, (202) 874-0410, (202) 874-0964, sis@irs.gov, https://www.irs.gov/uac/soi-tax-stats-statistics-of-income; Statistics of Income Bulletin.

National Association of Theatre Owners (NATO), 1705 N St. NW, Washington, DC, 20036, USA, (202) 962-0054, (818) 506-1778, nato@natodc.com, https://www.natoonline.org/; Exhibition Data and Statistics.

U.S. Census Bureau, Center for Economic Studies (CES), 4600 Silver Hill Rd., Washington, DC, 20233, USA, (301) 763-6460, (301) 763-5935, ces.contacts@census.gov, https://www.census.gov/programs-surveys/ces.html; Arts, Entertainment and Recreation, 2017 Economic Census.

ARUBA-NATIONAL STATISTICAL OFFICE

Central Bureau of Statistics of Aruba, L.G. Smith Blvd. 160, Sun Plaza Bldg., 3rd Fl., Oranjestad, ARU, (297) 524-7433 (Dial from U.S.), (297) 583-8057 (Fax from U.S.), cbs@setarnet.aw, https://cbs.aw/wp/; National Data Reports (Aruba).

ARUBA-AGRICULTURE

The Economist Group: Economist Intelligence Unit (EIU), 900 3rd Ave., 16th Fl., New York, NY, 10022, USA, (212) 541-0500, americas@eiu.com, https://www.eiu.com; Aruba Country Report.

Euromonitor International, Inc., 1 N Dearborn St., Ste. 1700, Chicago, IL, 60602, USA, (312) 922-1115, (312) 922-1157, info-usa@euromonitor.com, https://www.euromonitor.com/; Geographies.

United Nations Food and Agricultural Organization (FAO), 2121 K St., Ste. 800B, Washington, DC, 20037, USA, (202) 653-2400 (Dial from U.S.), (202) 653-5760 (Fax from U.S.), fao-hq@fao.org, https://www.fao.org; AQUASTAT.

ARUBA-AIRLINES

Palgrave Macmillan, 1 New York Plaza, Ste. 4500, New York, NY, 10004-1562, USA, (800) 777-4643, orders@palgrave.com, https://www.palgrave.com/us; The Statesman's Yearbook, 2023.

ARUBA-ARMED FORCES

Central Intelligence Agency (CIA), Office of Public Affairs, Washington, DC, 20505, USA, (703) 482-0623, https://www.cia.gov; The World Factbook.

Stockholm International Peace Research Institute (SIPRI), Signalistgatan 9, Stockholm, SE 169 72, SWE, https://www.sipri.org/; SIPRI Arms Transfers Database and SIPRI Military Expenditure Database.

ARUBA-BALANCE OF PAYMENTS

Routledge - Taylor & Francis Group, 6000 Broken Sound Pkwy. NW, Ste. 300, Boca Raton, FL, 33487, USA, (800) 634-1420, (800) 634-7064, orders@taylorandfrancis.com, https://www.routledge.com/; The Europa World Year Book 2022.

ARUBA-BANKS AND BANKING

Euromonitor International, Inc., 1 N Dearborn St., Ste. 1700, Chicago, IL, 60602, USA, (312) 922-1115, (312) 922-1157, info-usa@euromonitor.com, https://www.euromonitor.com/; Geographies.

Routledge - Taylor & Francis Group, 6000 Broken Sound Pkwy. NW, Ste. 300, Boca Raton, FL, 33487, USA, (800) 634-1420, (800) 634-7064, orders@taylorandfrancis.com, https://www.routledge.com/; The Europa World Year Book 2022.

ARUBA-BROADCASTING

Central Intelligence Agency (CIA), Office of Public Affairs, Washington, DC, 20505, USA, (703) 482-0623, https://www.cia.gov; The World Factbook.

Euromonitor International, Inc., 1 N Dearborn St., Ste. 1700, Chicago, IL, 60602, USA, (312) 922-1115, (312) 922-1157, info-usa@euromonitor.com, https://www.euromonitor.com/; Geographies.

Palgrave Macmillan, 1 New York Plaza, Ste. 4500, New York, NY, 10004-1562, USA, (800) 777-4643, orders@palgrave.com, https://www.palgrave.com/us; The Statesman's Yearbook, 2023.

WRTH Publications Limited, PO Box 290, Oxford, OX2 7FT, GBR, sales@wrth.com, https://www.wrth.com; World Radio TV Handbook 2023.

ARUBA-BUDGET

Central Intelligence Agency (CIA), Office of Public Affairs, Washington, DC, 20505, USA, (703) 482-0623, https://www.cia.gov; The World Factbook.

ARUBA-CLIMATE

Palgrave Macmillan, 1 New York Plaza, Ste. 4500, New York, NY, 10004-1562, USA, (800) 777-4643, orders@palgrave.com, https://www.palgrave.com/us; The Statesman's Yearbook, 2023.

ARUBA-COMMERCE

Palgrave Macmillan, 1 New York Plaza, Ste. 4500, New York, NY, 10004-1562, USA, (800) 777-4643, orders@palgrave.com, https://www.palgrave.com/us; The Statesman's Yearbook, 2023.

UK Data Service, University of Essex, Wivenhoe Park, Colchester, Essex, CO4 3SQ, GBR, https://ukdataservice.ac.uk/; International Aggregate Data.

ARUBA-CONSUMER PRICE INDEXES

Routledge - Taylor & Francis Group, 6000 Broken Sound Pkwy. NW, Ste. 300, Boca Raton, FL, 33487, USA, (800) 634-1420, (800) 634-7064, orders@taylorandfrancis.com, https://www.routledge.com/; The Europa World Year Book 2022.

ARUBA-ECONOMIC CONDITIONS

Bernan Press, 15250 NBN Way, Bldg. C, Blue Ridge Summit, PA, 17214, USA, (301) 459-2255, (800) 865-3457, (800) 865-3450, customercare@bernan.com, https://rowman.com/Page/Bernan; World Economic Outlook, April 2022.

Central Intelligence Agency (CIA), Office of Public Affairs, Washington, DC, 20505, USA, (703) 482-0623, https://www.cia.gov; The World Factbook.

The Economist Group: Economist Intelligence Unit (EIU), 900 3rd Ave., 16th Fl., New York, NY, 10022, USA, (212) 541-0500, americas@eiu.com, https://www.eiu.com; Aruba Country Report.

International Monetary Fund (IMF), 700 19th St. NW, Washington, DC, 20431, USA, (202) 623-7000, (202) 623-4661, publications@imf.org, https://www.imf.org; IMF Data and World Economic Outlook.

United Nations Economic Commission for Latin America and the Caribbean (ECLAC), Casilla 179-D, Santiago, 7630412, CHL, (202) 596-3713, prensa@cepal.org, https://www.cepal.org/en; CEPALSTAT.

United Nations Statistics Division (UNSD), United Nations Plz., New York, NY, 10017, USA, (800) 253-9646, (212) 963-9851, statistics@un.org, https://unstats.un.org; World Statistics Pocketbook 2021.

The World Bank, 1818 H St. NW, Washington, DC, 20433, USA, (202) 473-1000, (202) 477-6391, eds03@worldbank.org, https://www.worldbank.org/; Global Economic Monitor (GEM); Global Economic Prospects, June 2022; and The Global Findex Database 2021.

ARUBA-EDUCATION

Euromonitor International, Inc., 1 N Dearborn St., Ste. 1700, Chicago, IL, 60602, USA, (312) 922-1115, (312) 922-1157, info-usa@euromonitor.com, https://www.euromonitor.com/; Geographies.

Infoplease, c/o Sandbox Networks, Inc., 1 Lincoln St., 24th Fl., Boston, MA, 02111, USA, https://www.infoplease.com; Countries of the World.

Palgrave Macmillan, 1 New York Plaza, Ste. 4500, New York, NY, 10004-1562, USA, (800) 777-4643, orders@palgrave.com, https://www.palgrave.com/us; The Statesman's Yearbook, 2023.

Routledge - Taylor & Francis Group, 6000 Broken Sound Pkwy. NW, Ste. 300, Boca Raton, FL, 33487, USA, (800) 634-1420, (800) 634-7064, orders@taylorandfrancis.com, https://www.routledge.com/; The Europa World Year Book 2022.

UNESCO Institute for Statistics, C.P 250 Succursale H, Montreal, QC, H3G 2K8, CAN, (514) 343-6880 (Dial from U.S.), (514) 343-5740 (Fax from U.S.), uis.publications@unesco.org, http://uis.unesco.org/; Literacy.

United Nations Statistics Division (UNSD), United Nations Plz., New York, NY, 10017, USA, (800) 253-9646, (212) 963-9851, statistics@un.org, https://unstats.un.org; Millennium Development Goal Indicators.

ARUBA-EMPLOYMENT

UK Data Service, University of Essex, Wivenhoe Park, Colchester, Essex, CO4 3SQ, GBR, https://ukdataservice.ac.uk/; International Aggregate Data.

ARUBA-ENVIRONMENTAL CONDITIONS

DSI Data Service & Information, Xantener Strasse 51a, Rheinberg, D-47495, GER, dsi@dsidata.com, https://www.dsidata.com/; Global Environmental Database.

The Economist Group: Economist Intelligence Unit (EIU), 900 3rd Ave., 16th Fl., New York, NY, 10022, USA, (212) 541-0500, americas@eiu.com, https://www.eiu.com; Aruba Country Report.

United Nations Economic Commission for Latin America and the Caribbean (ECLAC), Casilla 179-D, Santiago, 7630412, CHL, (202) 596-3713, prensa@cepal.org, https://www.cepal.org/en; CEPALSTAT.

United Nations Statistics Division (UNSD), United Nations Plz., New York, NY, 10017, USA, (800) 253-9646, (212) 963-9851, statistics@un.org, https://unstats.un.org; World Statistics Pocketbook 2021.

ARUBA-EXPORTS

Central Intelligence Agency (CIA), Office of Public Affairs, Washington, DC, 20505, USA, (703) 482-0623, https://www.cia.gov; The World Factbook.

The Economist Group: Economist Intelligence Unit (EIU), 900 3rd Ave., 16th Fl., New York, NY, 10022, USA, (212) 541-0500, americas@eiu.com, https://www.eiu.com; Aruba Country Report.

ARUBA-FINANCE, PUBLIC

Bernan Press, 15250 NBN Way, Bldg. C, Blue Ridge Summit, PA, 17214, USA, (301) 459-2255, (800) 865-3457, (800) 865-3450, customercare@bernan.com, https://rowman.com/Page/Bernan; National Accounts Statistics: Analysis of Main Aggregates 2020.

The Economist Group: Economist Intelligence Unit (EIU), 900 3rd Ave., 16th Fl., New York, NY, 10022, USA, (212) 541-0500, americas@eiu.com, https://www.eiu.com; Aruba Country Report.

International Monetary Fund (IMF), 700 19th St. NW, Washington, DC, 20431, USA, (202) 623-7000, (202) 623-4661, publications@imf.org, https://www.imf.org; Regional Economic Outlook.

Palgrave Macmillan, 1 New York Plaza, Ste. 4500, New York, NY, 10004-1562, USA, (800) 777-4643, orders@palgrave.com, https://www.palgrave.com/us; The Statesman's Yearbook, 2023.

Routledge - Taylor & Francis Group, 6000 Broken Sound Pkwy. NW, Ste. 300, Boca Raton, FL, 33487, USA, (800) 634-1420, (800) 634-7064, orders@taylorandfrancis.com, https://www.routledge.com/; The Europa World Year Book 2022.

United Nations Statistics Division (UNSD), United Nations Plz., New York, NY, 10017, USA, (800) 253-9646, (212) 963-9851, statistics@un.org, https://unstats.un.org; National Accounts Main Aggregates Database and National Accounts Statistics: Main Aggregates and Detailed Tables.

ARUBA-FISHERIES

Routledge - Taylor & Francis Group, 6000 Broken Sound Pkwy. NW, Ste. 300, Boca Raton, FL, 33487, USA, (800) 634-1420, (800) 634-7064, orders@taylorandfrancis.com, https://www.routledge.com/; The Europa World Year Book 2022.

ARUBA-GROSS DOMESTIC PRODUCT

The Economist Group: Economist Intelligence Unit (EIU), 900 3rd Ave., 16th Fl., New York, NY, 10022, USA, (212) 541-0500, americas@eiu.com, https://www.eiu.com; Aruba Country Report.

Routledge - Taylor & Francis Group, 6000 Broken Sound Pkwy. NW, Ste. 300, Boca Raton, FL, 33487, USA, (800) 634-1420, (800) 634-7064, orders@taylorandfrancis.com, https://www.routledge.com/; The Europa World Year Book 2022.

ARUBA-HOUSING

Euromonitor International, Inc., 1 N Dearborn St., Ste. 1700, Chicago, IL, 60602, USA, (312) 922-1115, (312) 922-1157, info-usa@euromonitor.com, https://www.euromonitor.com/; Geographies.

ARUBA-ILLITERATE PERSONS

Central Intelligence Agency (CIA), Office of Public Affairs, Washington, DC, 20505, USA, (703) 482-0623, https://www.cia.gov; The World Factbook.

ARUBA-IMPORTS

Central Intelligence Agency (CIA), Office of Public Affairs, Washington, DC, 20505, USA, (703) 482-0623, https://www.cia.gov; The World Factbook.

The Economist Group: Economist Intelligence Unit (EIU), 900 3rd Ave., 16th Fl., New York, NY, 10022, USA, (212) 541-0500, americas@eiu.com, https://www.eiu.com; Aruba Country Report.

ARUBA-INDUSTRIES

Central Intelligence Agency (CIA), Office of Public Affairs, Washington, DC, 20505, USA, (703) 482-0623, https://www.cia.gov; The World Factbook.

The Economist Group: Economist Intelligence Unit (EIU), 900 3rd Ave., 16th Fl., New York, NY, 10022, USA, (212) 541-0500, americas@eiu.com, https://www.eiu.com; Aruba Country Report.

Euromonitor International, Inc., 1 N Dearborn St., Ste. 1700, Chicago, IL, 60602, USA, (312) 922-1115, (312) 922-1157, info-usa@euromonitor.com, https://www.euromonitor.com/; Geographies.

Routledge - Taylor & Francis Group, 6000 Broken Sound Pkwy. NW, Ste. 300, Boca Raton, FL, 33487, USA, (800) 634-1420, (800) 634-7064, orders@taylorandfrancis.com, https://www.routledge.com/; The Europa World Year Book 2022.

United Nations Industrial Development Organization (UNIDO), 1 United Nations Plz., Rm. DC1-1118, New York, NY, 10017, USA, (212) 963-6890, (212) 963 6885, (212) 963-7904, office.newyork@unido.org, https://www.unido.org/; Industrial Statistics Databases and International Yearbook of Industrial Statistics 2021.

ARUBA-INTERNATIONAL TRADE

The Economist Group: Economist Intelligence Unit (EIU), 900 3rd Ave., 16th Fl., New York, NY, 10022, USA, (212) 541-0500, americas@eiu.com, https://www.eiu.com; Aruba Country Report.

Euromonitor International, Inc., 1 N Dearborn St., Ste. 1700, Chicago, IL, 60602, USA, (312) 922-1115, (312) 922-1157, info-usa@euromonitor.com, https://www.euromonitor.com/; Geographies.

Palgrave Macmillan, 1 New York Plaza, Ste. 4500, New York, NY, 10004-1562, USA, (800) 777-4643, orders@palgrave.com, https://www.palgrave.com/us; The Statesman's Yearbook, 2023.

Routledge - Taylor & Francis Group, 6000 Broken Sound Pkwy. NW, Ste. 300, Boca Raton, FL, 33487, USA, (800) 634-1420, (800) 634-7064, orders@taylorandfrancis.com, https://www.routledge.com/; The Europa World Year Book 2022.

World Trade Organization (WTO), Ctre. William Rappard, Rue de Lausanne 154, Case postale, Geneva, CH-1211, SWI, enquiries@wto.org, https://www.wto.org; World Trade Statistical Review 2022.

ARUBA-INTERNET USERS

International Telecommunication Union (ITU), Place des Nations, Geneva, CH-1211, SWI, itumail@itu.int, https://www.itu.int; Global Connectivity Report 2022; World Telecommunication/ICT Indicators Database 2021; and Yearbook of Statistics 2019.

ARUBA-LABOR

Central Intelligence Agency (CIA), Office of Public Affairs, Washington, DC, 20505, USA, (703) 482-0623, https://www.cia.gov; The World Factbook.

Euromonitor International, Inc., 1 N Dearborn St., Ste. 1700, Chicago, IL, 60602, USA, (312) 922-1115, (312) 922-1157, info-usa@euromonitor.com, https://www.euromonitor.com/; Geographies.

ARUBA-LAND USE

United Nations Statistics Division (UNSD), United Nations Plz., New York, NY, 10017, USA, (800) 253-9646, (212) 963-9851, statistics@un.org, https://unstats.un.org; Millennium Development Goal Indicators.

ARUBA-LIFE EXPECTANCY

United Nations Department of Economic and Social Affairs (DESA), Population Division, 2 United Nations Plz., Rm. DC2-1950, New York, NY, 10017, USA, (212) 963-3209, (212) 963-2147, population@un.org, https://www.un.org/development/desa/pd/; World Population Ageing 2020 Highlights.

United Nations Statistics Division (UNSD), United Nations Plz., New York, NY, 10017, USA, (800) 253-9646, (212) 963-9851, statistics@un.org, https://unstats.un.org; Millennium Development Goal Indicators.

ARUBA-LITERACY

Euromonitor International, Inc., 1 N Dearborn St., Ste. 1700, Chicago, IL, 60602, USA, (312) 922-1115, (312) 922-1157, info-usa@euromonitor.com, https://www.euromonitor.com/; Geographies.

UNESCO Institute for Statistics, C.P 250 Succursale H, Montreal, QC, H3G 2K8, CAN, (514) 343-6880 (Dial from U.S.), (514) 343-5740 (Fax from U.S.), uis.publications@unesco.org, http://uis.unesco.org/; Literacy.

ARUBA-MINERAL INDUSTRIES

Palgrave Macmillan, 1 New York Plaza, Ste. 4500, New York, NY, 10004-1562, USA, (800) 777-4643, orders@palgrave.com, https://www.palgrave.com/us; The Statesman's Yearbook, 2023.

ARUBA-MONEY SUPPLY

The Economist Group: Economist Intelligence Unit (EIU), 900 3rd Ave., 16th Fl., New York, NY, 10022, USA, (212) 541-0500, americas@eiu.com, https://www.eiu.com; Aruba Country Report.

Routledge - Taylor & Francis Group, 6000 Broken Sound Pkwy. NW, Ste. 300, Boca Raton, FL, 33487, USA, (800) 634-1420, (800) 634-7064, orders@taylorandfrancis.com, https://www.routledge.com/; The Europa World Year Book 2022.

ARUBA-MORTALITY

United Nations Statistics Division (UNSD), United Nations Plz., New York, NY, 10017, USA, (800) 253-9646, (212) 963-9851, statistics@un.org, https://unstats.un.org; Millennium Development Goal Indicators and World Statistics Pocketbook 2021.

World Health Organization (WHO), Ave. Appia 20, Geneva, CH-1211, SWI, (202) 974-3000 (Telephone in U.S.), publications@who.int, https://www.who.int/; Global Health Observatory (GHO).

ARUBA-POPULATION

Caribbean Public Health Agency (CARPHA), Federation Park, 16-18 Jamaica Blvd., Port of Spain, TTO, (868) 622-4261 (Dial from U.S.), (868) 299-0820 (Dial from U.S.), postmaster@carpha.org, https://carpha.org/; unpublished data.

Central Intelligence Agency (CIA), Office of Public Affairs, Washington, DC, 20505, USA, (703) 482-0623, https://www.cia.gov; The World Factbook.

The Economist Group: Economist Intelligence Unit (EIU), 900 3rd Ave., 16th Fl., New York, NY, 10022, USA, (212) 541-0500, americas@eiu.com, https://www.eiu.com; Aruba Country Report.

European Commission, Eurostat, Luxembourg, 2920, LUX, https://ec.europa.eu/eurostat/; EU in the World 2020.

Infoplease, c/o Sandbox Networks, Inc., 1 Lincoln St., 24th Fl., Boston, MA, 02111, USA, https://www.infoplease.com; Countries of the World.

Palgrave Macmillan, 1 New York Plaza, Ste. 4500, New York, NY, 10004-1562, USA, (800) 777-4643, orders@palgrave.com, https://www.palgrave.com/us; The Statesman's Yearbook, 2023.

Routledge - Taylor & Francis Group, 6000 Broken Sound Pkwy. NW, Ste. 300, Boca Raton, FL, 33487, USA, (800) 634-1420, (800) 634-7064, orders@taylorandfrancis.com, https://www.routledge.com/; The Europa World Year Book 2022.

UK Data Service, University of Essex, Wivenhoe Park, Colchester, Essex, CO4 3SQ, GBR, https://ukdataservice.ac.uk/; International Aggregate Data.

United Nations Department of Economic and Social Affairs (DESA), Population Division, 2 United Nations Plz., Rm. DC2-1950, New York, NY, 10017, USA, (212) 963-3209, (212) 963-2147, population@un.org, https://www.un.org/development/desa/pd/; Revision of World Urbanization Prospects and World Population Ageing 2020 Highlights.

United Nations Economic Commission for Latin America and the Caribbean (ECLAC), Casilla 179-D, Santiago, 7630412, CHL, (202) 596-3713, prensa@cepal.org, https://www.cepal.org/en; CEPALSTAT.

United Nations Statistics Division (UNSD), United Nations Plz., New York, NY, 10017, USA, (800) 253-9646, (212) 963-9851, statistics@un.org, https://unstats.un.org; World Statistics Pocketbook 2021.

The World Bank, 1818 H St. NW, Washington, DC, 20433, USA, (202) 473-1000, (202) 477-6391, eds03@worldbank.org, https://www.worldbank.org/; The Global Findex Database 2021.

ARUBA-POPULATION DENSITY

Central Intelligence Agency (CIA), Office of Public Affairs, Washington, DC, 20505, USA, (703) 482-0623, https://www.cia.gov; The World Factbook.

Palgrave Macmillan, 1 New York Plaza, Ste. 4500, New York, NY, 10004-1562, USA, (800) 777-4643, orders@palgrave.com, https://www.palgrave.com/us; The Statesman's Yearbook, 2023.

Routledge - Taylor & Francis Group, 6000 Broken Sound Pkwy. NW, Ste. 300, Boca Raton, FL, 33487, USA, (800) 634-1420, (800) 634-7064, orders@taylorandfrancis.com, https://www.routledge.com/; The Europa World Year Book 2022.

ARUBA-POWER RESOURCES

Euromonitor International, Inc., 1 N Dearborn St., Ste. 1700, Chicago, IL, 60602, USA, (312) 922-1115, (312) 922-1157, info-usa@euromonitor.com, https://www.euromonitor.com/; Geographies.

Palgrave Macmillan, 1 New York Plaza, Ste. 4500, New York, NY, 10004-1562, USA, (800) 777-4643, orders@palgrave.com, https://www.palgrave.com/us; The Statesman's Yearbook, 2023.

United Nations Statistics Division (UNSD), United Nations Plz., New York, NY, 10017, USA, (800) 253-9646, (212) 963-9851, statistics@un.org, https://unstats.un.org; World Statistics Pocketbook 2021.

ARUBA-PRICES

Euromonitor International, Inc., 1 N Dearborn St., Ste. 1700, Chicago, IL, 60602, USA, (312) 922-1115, (312) 922-1157, info-usa@euromonitor.com, https://www.euromonitor.com/; Geographies.

ARUBA-PUBLIC HEALTH

Euromonitor International, Inc., 1 N Dearborn St., Ste. 1700, Chicago, IL, 60602, USA, (312) 922-1115, (312) 922-1157, info-usa@euromonitor.com, https://www.euromonitor.com/; Geographies.

Palgrave Macmillan, 1 New York Plaza, Ste. 4500, New York, NY, 10004-1562, USA, (800) 777-4643, orders@palgrave.com, https://www.palgrave.com/us; The Statesman's Yearbook, 2023.

U.S. Census Bureau, 4600 Silver Hill Rd., Washington, DC, 20233, USA, (301) 763-4636, (800) 923-8282, https://www.census.gov; HIV/AIDS Surveillance Data Base.

United Nations Department of Economic and Social Affairs (DESA), Population Division, 2 United Nations Plz., Rm. DC2-1950, New York, NY, 10017, USA, (212) 963-3209, (212) 963-2147, population@un.org, https://www.un.org/development/desa/pd/; World Fertility Data 2019.

United Nations Statistics Division (UNSD), United Nations Plz., New York, NY, 10017, USA, (800) 253-9646, (212) 963-9851, statistics@un.org, https://unstats.un.org; Millennium Development Goal Indicators.

World Health Organization (WHO), Ave. Appia 20, Geneva, CH-1211, SWI, (202) 974-3000 (Telephone in U.S.), publications@who.int, https://www.who.int/; Global Health Observatory (GHO).

ARUBA-RELIGION

Central Intelligence Agency (CIA), Office of Public Affairs, Washington, DC, 20505, USA, (703) 482-0623, https://www.cia.gov; The World Factbook.

Palgrave Macmillan, 1 New York Plaza, Ste. 4500, New York, NY, 10004-1562, USA, (800) 777-4643, orders@palgrave.com, https://www.palgrave.com/us; The Statesman's Yearbook, 2023.

ARUBA-RETAIL TRADE

Euromonitor International, Inc., 1 N Dearborn St., Ste. 1700, Chicago, IL, 60602, USA, (312) 922-1115, (312) 922-1157, info-usa@euromonitor.com, https://www.euromonitor.com/; Geographies.

ARUBA-TOURISM

Euromonitor International, Inc., 1 N Dearborn St., Ste. 1700, Chicago, IL, 60602, USA, (312) 922-1115, (312) 922-1157, info-usa@euromonitor.com, https://www.euromonitor.com/; Geographies.

Palgrave Macmillan, 1 New York Plaza, Ste. 4500, New York, NY, 10004-1562, USA, (800) 777-4643, orders@palgrave.com, https://www.palgrave.com/us; The Statesman's Yearbook, 2023.

Routledge - Taylor & Francis Group, 6000 Broken Sound Pkwy. NW, Ste. 300, Boca Raton, FL, 33487, USA, (800) 634-1420, (800) 634-7064, orders@taylorandfrancis.com, https://www.routledge.com/; The Europa World Year Book 2022.

United Nations World Tourism Organization (UNWTO), Calle Poeta Joan Maragall 42, Madrid, 28020, SPA, info@unwto.org, https://www.unwto.org/; Yearbook of Tourism Statistics, 2021 Edition.

ARUBA-TRANSPORTATION

Central Intelligence Agency (CIA), Office of Public Affairs, Washington, DC, 20505, USA, (703) 482-0623, https://www.cia.gov; The World Factbook.

Euromonitor International, Inc., 1 N Dearborn St., Ste. 1700, Chicago, IL, 60602, USA, (312) 922-1115, (312) 922-1157, info-usa@euromonitor.com, https://www.euromonitor.com/; Geographies.

Palgrave Macmillan, 1 New York Plaza, Ste. 4500, New York, NY, 10004-1562, USA, (800) 777-4643, orders@palgrave.com, https://www.palgrave.com/us; The Statesman's Yearbook, 2023.

Routledge - Taylor & Francis Group, 6000 Broken Sound Pkwy. NW, Ste. 300, Boca Raton, FL, 33487, USA, (800) 634-1420, (800) 634-7064, orders@taylorandfrancis.com, https://www.routledge.com/; The Europa World Year Book 2022.

ASBESTOS

Environmental Business International, Inc. (EBI), 4452 Park Blvd., Ste. 306, San Diego, CA, 92116, USA, (619) 295-7685, info@ebionline.org, https://ebionline.org/; Environmental Business Journal (EBJ); Environmental Testing and Analytical Services; and The Global Environmental Market.

U.S. Department of the Interior (DOI), U.S. Geological Survey (USGS), 12201 Sunrise Valley Dr., Reston, VA, 20192, USA, (888) 392-8545, https://www.usgs.gov/; Asbestos Statistics and Information.

U.S. Department of the Interior (DOI), U.S. Geological Survey (USGS), National Minerals Information Center (NMIC), 12201 Sunrise Valley Dr., Reston, VA, 20192, USA, (703) 648-4920, (703) 648-7971, (703) 648-4995, sfortier@usgs.gov, https://www.usgs.gov/centers/nmic; Mineral Commodity Summaries 2022.

ASEXUAL PEOPLE

GLAAD, USA, rferraro@glaad.org, https://www.glaad.org/; Accelerating Acceptance 2021; Social Media Safety Index (SMSI); and Where We Are on TV Report 2021-2022.

ASIA

See also Individual countries

Asia Pacific Economic Cooperation (APEC), 35 Heng Mui Keng Terrace, 119616, SGP, info@apec.org, https://www.apec.org/; APEC at a Glance, 2021; APEC Regional Trends Analysis - What Goes Around Comes Around: Pivoting to a Circular Economy; Uncertainty Tests APEC's Resilience amid COVID-19; and APEC Senior Officials' Report on Economic and Technical Cooperation, 2021.

Asian Development Bank (ADB), 6 ADB Ave., Mandaluyong City, 1550, PHL, information@adb.org, https://www.adb.org/; Statistical Database System (SDBS).

Association of Southeast Asian Nations (ASEAN), 70A Jl. Sisingamangaraja, Jakarta, 12110, IDN, statistics@asean.org, https://asean.org/; ASEAN Key Figures 2022; ASEAN Statistical Highlights 2022; ASEAN Statistical Yearbook 2021; and ASEANStatsDataPortal.

The East-West Center, 1601 East-West Rd., Honolulu, HI, 96848-1601, USA, (808) 944-7111, (808) 944-7212, ewccontact@eastwestcenter.org, https://www.eastwestcenter.org/; Asia Pacific Bulletin (APB).

European Commission, Eurostat, Luxembourg, 2920, LUX, https://ec.europa.eu/eurostat/; EU in the World 2020.

Global Facility for Disaster Reduction and Recovery (GFDRR), 1818 H St. NW, Washington, DC, 20433, USA, (202) 473-1000, gfdrr@worldbank.org, https://www.gfdrr.org/; Overlooked : Examining the Impact of Disasters and Climate Shocks on Poverty in the Europe and Central Asia Region.

Government of Japan, Cabinet Office, 1-6-1 Nagatacho, Chiyoda-ku, Tokyo, 100-8914, JPN, https://www.cao.go.jp/; Economy Watchers Survey; Indexes of Business Conditions; and Monthly Economic Report.

Institute for the Study of War (ISW), 1400 16th St. NW, Ste. 515, Washington, DC, 20036, USA, (202) 293-5550, https://www.understandingwar.org/; Regional Actors Eye Threats and Opportunities in Taliban Takeover and Russia in Review.

Institute of Southeast Asian Studies (ISEAS)/Yusof Ishak Institute, 30, Heng Mui Keng Terrace, Pasir Panjang, 119614, SGP, https://www.iseas.edu.sg; Contemporary Southeast Asia (CSEA); ISEAS Perspective; SOJOURN: Journal of Social Issues in Southeast Asia; and Trends in Southeast Asia.

International Institute for Democracy and Electoral Assistance (International IDEA), Stromsborg, Stockholm, SE 103 34, SWE, https://www.idea.int/; The Integrity of Political Finance Systems in Asia: Tackling Political Corruption.

International Institute for Environment and Development (IIED), 235 High Holborn, London, WC1V 7DN, GBR, inforequest@iied.org, https://www.iied.org; Environment & Urbanization.

Japan Center for Economic Research (JCER), Nikkei Inc. Bldg. 11F, 1-3-7 Otemachi, Chiyoda-ku, Tokyo, 100-8066, JPN, https://www.jcer.or.jp/en; East Asia Risk and Japan-China Relations.

Japan Ministry of Economy, Trade and Industry (METI), 1-3-1 Kasumigaseki, Chiyoda-ku, Tokyo, 100-8901, JPN, https://www.meti.go.jp/english/; Indices of All Industry Activity, 2020; Yearbook of Current Production Statistics, 2020; and Yearbook of the Current Survey of Commerce, 2021.

Nikkei Inc., 1-3-7 Ohtemachi Chiyoda-ku, Tokyo, 100-8066, JPN, https://www.nikkei.co.jp/nikkeiinfo/en/; Nikkei Asia.

S&P Global Commodity Insights, One World Trade Center, New York, NY, 10007, USA, (800) 752-8878, support@platts.com, https://www.spglobal.com/commodityinsights/en; Platts Asia Pacific / Arab Gulf Marketscan (APAG Marketscan).

Singapore Tourism Board (STB), 589 5th Ave., Ste. 710, New York, NY, 10017, USA, (212) 302-4861, (212) 302-4801, americas@stb.gov.sg, https://www.stb.gov.sg/; Quarterly Tourism Performance Report.

U.S. Department of Labor (DOL), Bureau of Labor Statistics (BLS), Postal Square Bldg., 2 Massachusetts Ave. NE, Washington, DC, 20212-0001, USA, (202) 691-5200, (202) 691-7890, blsdata_staff@bls.gov, https://www.bls.gov; Import/Export Price Indexes (International Price Program - IPP).

United Nations Economic and Social Commission for Asia and the Pacific (ESCAP), United Nations Building, Rajadamnern Nok Ave., Bangkok, 10200, THA, https://www.unescap.org/; Asia-Pacific SDG Gateway.

United Nations Economic and Social Commission for Western Asia (ESCWA), Riad el-Solh Sq., PO Box 11-8575, Beirut, LBN, escwa-ciu@un.org, https://www.unescwa.org; ESCWA Annual Report 2019 and Survey of Economic and Social Developments in the Arab Region 2020-2021.

United Nations Human Settlements Programme (UN-HABITAT), PO Box 30030, Nairobi, 00100, KEN, unhabitat-info@un.org, https://unhabitat.org/; The Future of Asian & Pacific Cities 2019.

United Nations Office on Drugs and Crime (UNODC), Vienna International Ctre., PO Box 500, Vienna, A-1400, AUT, unodc@unodc.org, https://www.unodc.org/; Myanmar Opium Survey 2022 - Cultivation, Production and Implications.

United Nations Statistics Division (UNSD), United Nations Plz., New York, NY, 10017, USA, (800) 253-9646, (212) 963-9851, statistics@un.org, https://unstats.un.org; National Accounts Main Aggregates Database.

US-ASEAN Business Council, Inc., 1101 17th St. NW, Ste. 411, Washington, DC, 20036, USA, (202) 289-1911, mail@usasean.org, https://www.usasean.org/; ASEAN Matters for America, America Matters for ASEAN.

World Health Organization (WHO), Ave. Appia 20, Geneva, CH-1211, SWI, (202) 974-3000 (Telephone in U.S.), publications@who.int, https://www.who.int/; WHO South-East Asia Journal of Public Health.

ASIAN AND PACIFIC ISLANDER POPULATION

Asian Development Bank (ADB), 6 ADB Ave., Mandaluyong City, 1550, PHL, information@adb.org, https://www.adb.org/; ADB's Support for the Sustainable Development Goals: Enabling the 2030 Agenda for Sustainable Development through Strategy 2030.

Bernan Press, 15250 NBN Way, Bldg. C, Blue Ridge Summit, PA, 17214, USA, (301) 459-2255, (800) 865-3457, (800) 865-3450, customercare@bernan.com, https://rowman.com/Page/Bernan; Vital Statistics of the United States 2022: Births, Life Expectancy, Deaths, and Selected Health Data.

European Commission, Eurostat, Luxembourg, 2920, LUX, https://ec.europa.eu/eurostat/; EU in the World 2020.

Institute for Strategic Dialogue (ISD), Strong Cities Network (SCN), PO Box 75769, London, SW1P 9ER, GBR, https://strongcitiesnetwork.org; Online Russian-Language Hate and Discrimination Against Central Asian Migrants: Challenges and Ways Forward.

National Science Foundation, National Center for Science and Engineering Statistics (NCSES), 2415 Eisenhower Ave., Ste. W14200, Arlington, VA, 22314, USA, (703) 292-8780, (703) 292-9092, info@nsf.gov, https://www.nsf.gov/statistics/; Survey of Doctorate Recipients and Survey of Earned Doctorates.

Pew Research Center, 1615 L St. NW, Ste. 800, Washington, DC, 20036, USA, (202) 419-4300, (202) 857-8562, info@pewresearch.org, https://www.pewresearch.org/; Many Black and Asian Americans Say They Have Experienced Discrimination Amid the COVID-19 Outbreak.

U.S. Census Bureau, 4600 Silver Hill Rd., Washington, DC, 20233, USA, (301) 763-4636, (800) 923-8282, https://www.census.gov; Asian-American and Pacific Islander Heritage Month: May 2023; Explore Census Data; and United States QuickFacts.

U.S. Department of Health and Human Services, Centers for Disease Control and Prevention (CDC), National Center for Health Statistics (NCHS), 3311 Toledo Rd., Hyattsville, MD, 20782-2064, USA, (800) 232-4636, (301) 458-4000, https://www.cdc.gov/nchs; National Vital Statistics Reports (NVSR) and Vital Statistics Online Data Portal.

United Nations Economic and Social Commission for Western Asia (ESCWA), Riad el-Solh Sq., PO Box 11-8575, Beirut, LBN, escwa-ciu@un.org, https://www.unescwa.org; ESCWA Data Portal for the Arab Region.

Violence Policy Center (VPC), 1025 Connecticut Ave. NW, Ste. 1210, Washington, DC, 20036, USA, (202) 822-8200, https://vpc.org/; How the Firearms Industry Markets Guns to Asian Americans.

ASIAN AND PACIFIC ISLANDER POPULATION-BUSINESS OWNERS

U.S. Census Bureau, 4600 Silver Hill Rd., Washington, DC, 20233, USA, (301) 763-4636, (800) 923-8282, https://www.census.gov; Survey of Business Owners (SBO).

ASIAN AND PACIFIC ISLANDER POPULATION-CHILDBIRTH

Bernan Press, 15250 NBN Way, Bldg. C, Blue Ridge Summit, PA, 17214, USA, (301) 459-2255, (800) 865-3457, (800) 865-3450, customercare@bernan.com, https://rowman.com/Page/Bernan; Vital Statistics of the United States 2022: Births, Life Expectancy, Deaths, and Selected Health Data.

Guttmacher Institute, 125 Maiden Ln., 7th Fl., New York, NY, 10038, USA, (212) 248-1111, (800) 355-0244, (212) 248-1951, info@guttmacher.org, https://www.guttmacher.org/; Adolescent Sexual and Reproductive Health in the United States.

U.S. Department of Health and Human Services, Centers for Disease Control and Prevention (CDC), National Center for Health Statistics (NCHS), 3311 Toledo Rd., Hyattsville, MD, 20782-2064, USA, (800) 232-4636, (301) 458-4000, https://www.cdc.gov/nchs; National Vital Statistics Reports (NVSR) and Vital Statistics Online Data Portal.

ASIAN AND PACIFIC ISLANDER POPULATION-CHILDREN UNDER EIGHTEEN YEARS OLD-POVERTY

Bank Street Graduate School of Education, National Center for Children in Poverty (NCCP), 475 Riverside Dr., Ste. 1400, New York, NY, 10115, USA, info@nccp.org, https://www.nccp.org/; 50-State Demographics Data Generator.

ASIAN AND PACIFIC ISLANDER POPULATION-CITIES

U.S. Census Bureau, 4600 Silver Hill Rd., Washington, DC, 20233, USA, (301) 763-4636, (800) 923-8282, https://www.census.gov; Explore Census Data and United States QuickFacts.

ASIAN AND PACIFIC ISLANDER POPULATION-COLLEGE ENROLLMENT

U.S. Department of Education (ED), Institute of Education Sciences (IES), National Center for Education Statistics (NCES), Potomac Center Plaza, 550 12th St. SW, Washington, DC, 20202, USA, (202) 403-5551, https://nces.ed.gov/; Digest of Education Statistics, 2020.

ASIAN AND PACIFIC ISLANDER POPULATION-COMPUTER USE

U.S. Census Bureau, 4600 Silver Hill Rd., Washington, DC, 20233, USA, (301) 763-4636, (800) 923-8282, https://www.census.gov; Asian-American and Pacific Islander Heritage Month: May 2023.

ASIAN AND PACIFIC ISLANDER POPULATION-CONGRESS, MEMBERS OF

Joint Center for Political and Economic Studies, 633 Pennsylvania Ave. NW, Washington, DC, 20004, USA, (202) 789-3500, info@jointcenter.org, https://jointcenter.org/; Racial Diversity Among Top House Staff and Racial Diversity Among Top Staff in Senate Personal Offices.

U.S. Government Publishing Office (GPO),, 732 N Capitol St. NW, Washington, DC, 20401-0001, USA, (202) 512-1800, (866) 512-1800, (202) 512-2104, contactcenter@gpo.gov, https://www.gpo.gov/; Congressional Directory.

ASIAN AND PACIFIC ISLANDER POPULATION-CONSUMER EXPENDITURES

EnsembleIQ, 8550 W Bryn Mawr Ave., Ste. 200, Chicago, IL, 60631, USA, (877) 687-7321, https://ensembleiq.com/; 2021 Consumer Expenditures Report.

NielsenIQ (NIQ), 200 W Jackson Blvd., Chicago, IL, 60606, USA, https://nielseniq.com; Multicultural Consumers Are Set to Drive Beauty Growth Amid Continued Category Shifts in 2021.

University of Georgia, Terry College of Business, Selig Center for Economic Growth, E201 Ivester Hall, 650 S Lumpkin St., Athens, GA, 30602, USA, (706) 425-9782, jhumphre@uga.edu, https://www.terry.uga.edu/about/selig//; The Multicultural Economy 2021.

ASIAN AND PACIFIC ISLANDER POPULATION-CRIMES AGAINST

California State University San Bernardino, Center for the Study of Hate and Extremism, 5500 University Pkwy., San Bernardino, CA, 92407, USA, (909) 537-7503, (909) 537-7711, blevin8@aol.com, https://csbs.csusb.edu/hate-and-extremism-center; Report to the Nation: Anti-Asian Prejudice & Hate Crime.

National Asian Pacific American Women's Forum (NAPAWF), PO Box 13255, Chicago, IL, 60613, USA, info@napawf.org, https://www.napawf.org/; The State of Safety for Asian American, Native Hawaiian, and Pacific Islander Women.

Stop AAPI Hate, C/O Chinese for Affirmative Action, 17 Walter U. Lum Place, San Francisco, CA, 94108, USA, (415) 274-6750, (415) 397-8770, community@stopaapihate.org, https://stopaapihate.org; The Rising Tide of Violence and Discrimination Against Asian American and Pacific Islander Women and Girls; Stop AAPI Hate Mental Health Report; Stop AAPI Hate National Report; and Two Years and Thousands of Voices: What Community-Generated Data Tells Us About Anti-AAPI Hate.

ASIAN AND PACIFIC ISLANDER POPULATION-CRIMINAL STATISTICS

U.S. Department of Justice (DOJ), Bureau of Justice Statistics (BJS), 810 7th St. NW, Washington, DC, 20531, USA, (202) 307-0765, askbjs@usdoj.gov, https://www.bjs.gov/; Annual Survey of Jails, 2019.

U.S. Department of Justice (DOJ), Federal Bureau of Investigation (FBI), 935 Pennsylvania Ave. NW, Washington, DC, 20535-0001, USA, (202) 324-3000, https://www.fbi.gov/; Crime in the United States 2019.

United Nations Office on Drugs and Crime (UNODC), Vienna International Ctre., PO Box 500, Vienna, A-1400, AUT, unodc@unodc.org, https://www.unodc.org/; Myanmar Opium Survey 2022 - Cultivation, Production and Implications.

ASIAN AND PACIFIC ISLANDER POPULATION-DEATHS AND DEATH RATES

Governors Highway Safety Association (GHSA), 660 N Capitol St. NW, Ste. 220, Washington, DC, 20001-

1642, USA, (202) 789-0942, headquarters@ghsa.org, https://www.ghsa.org/; An Analysis of Traffic Fatalities by Race and Ethnicity.

National Asian Pacific American Women's Forum (NAPAWF), PO Box 13255, Chicago, IL, 60613, USA, info@napawf.org, https://www.napawf.org/; The State of Safety for Asian American, Native Hawaiian, and Pacific Islander Women.

U.S. Department of Health and Human Services, Centers for Disease Control and Prevention (CDC), 1600 Clifton Rd., Atlanta, GA, 30329-4027, USA, (800) 232-4636, (888) 232-6348 (TTY), cdcinfo@cdc.gov, https://www.cdc.gov; Provisional COVID-19 Deaths: Distribution of Deaths by Race and Hispanic Origin.

World Health Organization (WHO), Ave. Appia 20, Geneva, CH-1211, SWI, (202) 974-3000 (Telephone in U.S.), publications@who.int, https://www.who.int/; Western Pacific Surveillance and Response Journal.

ASIAN AND PACIFIC ISLANDER POPULATION-EDUCATIONAL ATTAINMENT

U.S. Census Bureau, 4600 Silver Hill Rd., Washington, DC, 20233, USA, (301) 763-4636, (800) 923-8282, https://www.census.gov; Asian-American and Pacific Islander Heritage Month: May 2023.

ASIAN AND PACIFIC ISLANDER POPULATION-ELECTIONS-VOTER REGISTRATION AND TURNOUT

Tufts University, Tisch College of Civic Life, Center for Information and Research on Civic Learning and Engagement (CIRCLE), Barnum Hall, Medford, MA, 02155, USA, (617) 627-2593, circle@tufts.edu, https://circle.tufts.edu/; Driven by Key Issues, Asian Youth Increased Their Political Participation.

ASIAN AND PACIFIC ISLANDER POPULATION-FAMILIES

Stop AAPI Hate, C/O Chinese for Affirmative Action, 17 Walter U. Lum Place, San Francisco, CA, 94108, USA, (415) 274-6750, (415) 397-8770, community@stopaapihate.org, https://stopaapihate.org; Two Years and Thousands of Voices: What Community-Generated Data Tells Us About Anti-AAPI Hate.

U.S. Census Bureau, 4600 Silver Hill Rd., Washington, DC, 20233, USA, (301) 763-4636, (800) 923-8282, https://www.census.gov; Asian-American and Pacific Islander Heritage Month: May 2023.

ASIAN AND PACIFIC ISLANDER POPULATION-FOOD STAMP PARTICIPANTS

U.S. Department of Agriculture (USDA), Food and Nutrition Service (FNS), Braddock Metro Center II, 1320 Braddock Pl., Alexandria, VA, 22314, USA, (703) 305-2062, https://www.fns.usda.gov/; Characteristics of SNAP Households: FY 2019.

ASIAN AND PACIFIC ISLANDER POPULATION-FOREIGN BORN POPULATION

Migration Policy Institute (MPI), 1275 K St. NW, Ste. 800, Washington, DC, 20005, USA, (202) 266-1940, (202) 266-1900, info@migrationpolicy.org, https://www.migrationpolicy.org/; Frequently Requested Statistics on Immigrants and Immigration in the United States; Maps of Immigrants in the United States; State Immigration Data Profiles; and U.S. Immigration Policy under Trump: Deep Changes and Lasting Impacts.

U.S. Census Bureau, 4600 Silver Hill Rd., Washington, DC, 20233, USA, (301) 763-4636, (800) 923-8282, https://www.census.gov; Asian-American and Pacific Islander Heritage Month: May 2023.

ASIAN AND PACIFIC ISLANDER POPULATION-HEALTH INSURANCE COVERAGE

U.S. Department of Health and Human Services, Centers for Disease Control and Prevention (CDC), National Center for Health Statistics (NCHS), 3311 Toledo Rd., Hyattsville, MD, 20782-2064, USA, (800) 232-4636, (301) 458-4000, https://www.cdc.gov/nchs; FastStats - Statistics by Topic and Household Pulse Survey: Health Insurance Coverage.

World Health Organization (WHO), Ave. Appia 20, Geneva, CH-1211, SWI, (202) 974-3000 (Telephone in U.S.), publications@who.int, https://www.who.int/; Western Pacific Surveillance and Response Journal.

ASIAN AND PACIFIC ISLANDER POPULATION-HOSPITAL UTILIZATION

World Health Organization (WHO), Ave. Appia 20, Geneva, CH-1211, SWI, (202) 974-3000 (Telephone in U.S.), publications@who.int, https://www.who.int/; Western Pacific Surveillance and Response Journal.

ASIAN AND PACIFIC ISLANDER POPULATION-HOUSING TENURE

U.S. Census Bureau, 4600 Silver Hill Rd., Washington, DC, 20233, USA, (301) 763-4636, (800) 923-8282, https://www.census.gov; Asian-American and Pacific Islander Heritage Month: May 2023.

ASIAN AND PACIFIC ISLANDER POPULATION-IMMUNIZATION OF CHILDREN

U.S. Department of Health and Human Services, Centers for Disease Control and Prevention (CDC), 1600 Clifton Rd., Atlanta, GA, 30329-4027, USA, (800) 232-4636, (888) 232-6348 (TTY), cdcinfo@cdc.gov, https://www.cdc.gov; Morbidity and Mortality Weekly Report (MMWR) and VaxView: Vaccination Coverage in the U.S..

U.S. Department of Health and Human Services, Centers for Disease Control and Prevention (CDC), National Center for Health Statistics (NCHS), 3311 Toledo Rd., Hyattsville, MD, 20782-2064, USA, (800) 232-4636, (301) 458-4000, https://www.cdc.gov/nchs; National Immunization Surveys (NIS).

World Health Organization (WHO), Ave. Appia 20, Geneva, CH-1211, SWI, (202) 974-3000 (Telephone in U.S.), publications@who.int, https://www.who.int/; Western Pacific Surveillance and Response Journal.

ASIAN AND PACIFIC ISLANDER POPULATION-INCOME

Pew Research Center, 1615 L St. NW, Ste. 800, Washington, DC, 20036, USA, (202) 419-4300, (202) 857-8562, info@pewresearch.org, https://www.pewresearch.org/; Key Findings on the Rise in Income Inequality within America's Racial and Ethnic Groups.

U.S. Census Bureau, 4600 Silver Hill Rd., Washington, DC, 20233, USA, (301) 763-4636, (800) 923-8282, https://www.census.gov; Asian-American and Pacific Islander Heritage Month: May 2023.

University of Georgia, Terry College of Business, Selig Center for Economic Growth, E201 Ivester Hall, 650 S Lumpkin St., Athens, GA, 30602, USA, (706) 425-9782, jhumphre@uga.edu, https://www.terry.uga.edu/about/selig//; The Multicultural Economy 2021.

ASIAN AND PACIFIC ISLANDER POPULATION-LIVING ARRANGEMENTS

U.S. Census Bureau, 4600 Silver Hill Rd., Washington, DC, 20233, USA, (301) 763-4636, (800) 923-8282, https://www.census.gov; Families and Living Arrangements.

ASIAN AND PACIFIC ISLANDER POPULATION-MEDICAL CARE

U.S. Department of Health and Human Services, Centers for Disease Control and Prevention (CDC), National Center for Health Statistics (NCHS), 3311 Toledo Rd., Hyattsville, MD, 20782-2064, USA, (800) 232-4636, (301) 458-4000, https://www.cdc.gov/nchs; FastStats - Statistics by Topic and Health, United States, 2020-2021.

World Health Organization (WHO), Ave. Appia 20, Geneva, CH-1211, SWI, (202) 974-3000 (Telephone in U.S.), publications@who.int, https://www.who.int/; Western Pacific Surveillance and Response Journal.

ASIAN AND PACIFIC ISLANDER POPULATION-OVERWEIGHT

University of California Los Angeles (UCLA), Center for Health Policy Research (CHPR), 10960 Wilshire Blvd., Ste. 1550, Campus Mail Code 714346, Los Angeles, CA, 90024, USA, (310) 794-0909, (310) 794-2686, healthpolicy@ucla.edu, https://healthpolicy.ucla.edu; Racial/Ethnic Variations in Weight Management Among Patients with Overweight and Obesity Status Who Are Served by Health Centres (Clinical Obesity).

ASIAN AND PACIFIC ISLANDER POPULATION-POVERTY

U.S. Census Bureau, 4600 Silver Hill Rd., Washington, DC, 20233, USA, (301) 763-4636, (800) 923-8282, https://www.census.gov; Asian-American and Pacific Islander Heritage Month: May 2023.

ASIAN AND PACIFIC ISLANDER POPULATION-PRISONERS

Council on Criminal Justice (CCJ), 700 Pennsylvania Ave. SE, Washington, DC, 20003, USA, info@counciloncj.org, https://counciloncj.org; Justice System Disparities: Black-White National Imprisonment Trends, 2000 to 2020.

U.S. Department of Justice (DOJ), Bureau of Justice Statistics (BJS), 810 7th St. NW, Washington, DC, 20531, USA, (202) 307-0765, askbjs@usdoj.gov, https://www.bjs.gov/; Data Collection: National Corrections Reporting Program (NCRP) and Probation and Parole in the United States, 2020.

ASIAN AND PACIFIC ISLANDER POPULATION-SCHOOL ENROLLMENT

U.S. Census Bureau, 4600 Silver Hill Rd., Washington, DC, 20233, USA, (301) 763-4636, (800) 923-8282, https://www.census.gov; Asian-American and Pacific Islander Heritage Month: May 2023 and School Enrollment in the United States: 2020.

ASIAN AND PACIFIC ISLANDER POPULATION-VOTER REGISTRATION AND TURNOUT

Tufts University, Tisch College of Civic Life, Center for Information and Research on Civic Learning and Engagement (CIRCLE), Barnum Hall, Medford, MA, 02155, USA, (617) 627-2593, circle@tufts.edu, https://circle.tufts.edu/; Driven by Key Issues, Asian Youth Increased Their Political Participation.

ASPARAGUS

U.S. Department of Agriculture (USDA), Economic Research Service (ERS), 1400 Independence Ave. SW, Mail Stop 1800, Washington, DC, 20250-0002, USA, (202) 720-2791, https://www.ers.usda.gov/; Food Price Outlook.

U.S. Department of Agriculture (USDA), National Agricultural Statistics Service (USDA-NASS), 1400 Independence Ave. SW, Washington, DC, 20250, USA, (800) 727-9540, nass@nass.usda.gov, https://www.nass.usda.gov; Vegetables Annual Summary.

ASPHALT

U.S. Department of Labor (DOL), Bureau of Labor Statistics (BLS), Postal Square Bldg., 2 Massachusetts Ave. NE, Washington, DC, 20212-0001, USA, (202) 691-5200, (202) 691-7890, blsdata_staff@bls.gov, https://www.bls.gov; Producer Price Indexes (PPI).

U.S. Department of the Interior (DOI), U.S. Geological Survey (USGS), National Minerals Information Center (NMIC), 12201 Sunrise Valley Dr., Reston, VA, 20192, USA, (703) 648-4920, (703) 648-7971, (703) 648-4995, sfortier@usgs.gov, https://www.usgs.gov/centers/nmic; Mineral Commodity Summaries 2022 and Minerals Yearbook.

ASPHYXIA

Council on Criminal Justice (CCJ), Task Force on Policing, 700 Pennsylvania Ave. SE, Washington,

DC, 20020, USA, info@counciloncj.org, https://counciloncj.org/tfp/; Policy Assessment: Chokeholds and Other Neck Restraints.

ASSAULT

See CRIME-ASSAULT

ASSET-BACKED FINANCING

Board of Governors of the Federal Reserve System, Constitution Ave. NW, Washington, DC, 20551, USA, (202) 452-3000, (202) 263-4869 (TDD), https://www.federalreserve.gov; Financial Accounts of the United States 2023.

ASSETS-PERSONAL

See HOUSEHOLDS OR FAMILIES-NET WORTH

ASTHMA

Bernan Press, 15250 NBN Way, Bldg. C, Blue Ridge Summit, PA, 17214, USA, (301) 459-2255, (800) 865-3457, (800) 865-3450, customercare@bernan.com, https://rowman.com/Page/Bernan; Vital Statistics of the United States 2022: Births, Life Expectancy, Deaths, and Selected Health Data.

U.S. Department of Health and Human Services, Centers for Disease Control and Prevention (CDC), 1600 Clifton Rd., Atlanta, GA, 30329-4027, USA, (800) 232-4636, (888) 232-6348 (TTY), cdcinfo@cdc.gov, https://www.cdc.gov; Behavioral Risk Factor Surveillance System (BRFSS) Data.

U.S. Department of Health and Human Services, Centers for Disease Control and Prevention (CDC), National Center for Health Statistics (NCHS), 3311 Toledo Rd., Hyattsville, MD, 20782-2064, USA, (800) 232-4636, (301) 458-4000, https://www.cdc.gov/nchs; FastStats - Statistics by Topic; National Vital Statistics Reports (NVSR); and Vital Statistics Online Data Portal.

ASTRONOMY

American Meteor Society (AMS), USA, https://www.amsmeteors.org; Meteor Trails.

National Aeronautics and Space Administration (NASA), NASA Headquarters, 300 E St. SW, Ste. 5R30, Washington, DC, 20546, USA, (202) 358-0001, (202) 358-4338, https://www.nasa.gov; Discovery Statistics.

ASYLUM-RIGHT OF

LGBT Freedom and Asylum Network (LGBT-FAN), USA, info@lgbt-fan.org, https://www.lgbt-fan.org; unpublished data.

U.S. Department of Justice (DOJ), Executive Office for Immigration Review (EOIR), 5107 Leesburg Pike, 18th Fl., Falls Church, VA, 22041, USA, (703) 305-0289, (703) 605-0365, pao.eoir@usdoj.gov, https://www.justice.gov/eoir/; Asylum Statistics by Nationality.

United Nations High Commissioner for Refugees (UNHCR), Case Postale 2500, Geneva, 1211, SWI, (202) 296-5191, https://www.unhcr.org/; Refugee Population Statistics Database.

University of California San Diego, U.S. Immigration Policy Center (USIPC), 9500 Gilman Dr., La Jolla, CA, 92093, USA, (858) 534-2230, usipc@ucsd.edu, https://usipc.ucsd.edu/; COVID-19 and the Remaking of U.S. Immigration Policy? Empirically Evaluating the Myth of Immigration and Disease; Public Preferences for Admitting Migrants Displaced by Climate Change; Seeking Asylum: Part 1; and Seeking Asylum: Part 2.

ATHEROSCLEROSIS-DEATHS

Bernan Press, 15250 NBN Way, Bldg. C, Blue Ridge Summit, PA, 17214, USA, (301) 459-2255, (800) 865-3457, (800) 865-3450, customercare@bernan.com, https://rowman.com/Page/Bernan; Vital Statistics of the United States 2022: Births, Life Expectancy, Deaths, and Selected Health Data.

U.S. Department of Health and Human Services, Centers for Disease Control and Prevention (CDC), National Center for Health Statistics (NCHS), 3311 Toledo Rd., Hyattsville, MD, 20782-2064, USA, (800) 232-4636, (301) 458-4000, https://www.cdc.gov/nchs; National Vital Statistics Reports (NVSR) and Vital Statistics Online Data Portal.

ATHLETES

Elias Sports Bureau, Inc., 500 5th Ave., New York, NY, 10110, USA, (212) 869-1530, https://www.esb.com; Elias Book of Baseball Records 2022.

National Hockey League Players' Association (NHLPA), 10 Bay St., Ste. 1200, Toronto, ON, M5J 2R8 , CAN, https://www.nhlpa.com/; Player Profiles.

Stats Perform, 203 N LaSalle St., Ste. 2350, Chicago, IL, 60601, USA, (866) 221-1426, https://www.statsperform.com/; unpublished data.

Stats Perform/Opta, The Point, 37 N Wharf Rd., London, W2 1AF, GBR, https://www.statsperform.com/opta/; Opta Sports Data.

U.S. Department of Labor (DOL), Bureau of Labor Statistics (BLS), Postal Square Bldg., 2 Massachusetts Ave. NE, Washington, DC, 20212-0001, USA, (202) 691-5200, (202) 691-7890, blsdata_staff@bls.gov, https://www.bls.gov; Monthly Labor Review.

The Washington Post, 1301 K St. NW, Washington, DC, 20071, USA, (800) 477-4679, https://www.washingtonpost.com/; Most Americans Oppose Trans Athletes in Female Sports, Poll Finds.

ATHLETIC ASSOCIATIONS

Stats Perform, 203 N LaSalle St., Ste. 2350, Chicago, IL, 60601, USA, (866) 221-1426, https://www.statsperform.com/; unpublished data.

Stats Perform/Opta, The Point, 37 N Wharf Rd., London, W2 1AF, GBR, https://www.statsperform.com/opta/; Opta Sports Data.

ATHLETIC GOODS

See SPORTING AND ATHLETIC GOODS

ATTENTION DEFICIT HYPERACTIVITY DISORDERS

U.S. Department of Health and Human Services (HHS), National Institutes of Health (NIH), National Institute of Mental Health (NIMH), 6001 Executive Blvd., Room 6200, MSC 9663, Bethesda, MD, 20892-9663, USA, (866) 615-6464, (301) 443-8431 (TTY), (301) 443-4279, nimhinfo@nih.gov, https://www.nimh.nih.gov/; Mental Health Statistics.

U.S. Department of Health and Human Services, Centers for Disease Control and Prevention (CDC), National Center for Health Statistics (NCHS), 3311 Toledo Rd., Hyattsville, MD, 20782-2064, USA, (800) 232-4636, (301) 458-4000, https://www.cdc.gov/nchs; FastStats - Statistics by Topic.

AUDIO EQUIPMENT INDUSTRY

U.S. Census Bureau, Center for Economic Studies (CES), 4600 Silver Hill Rd., Washington, DC, 20233, USA, (301) 763-6460, (301) 763-5935, ces.contacts@census.gov, https://www.census.gov/programs-surveys/ces.html; Retail Trade, 2017 Economic Census and Wholesale Trade, 2017 Economic Census.

U.S. Department of Commerce (DOC), International Trade Administration (ITA), 1401 Constitution Ave. NW, Washington, DC, 20230, USA, (800) 872-8723, https://www.trade.gov/; TradeStats Express (TSE).

AUDITING

See ACCOUNTING, TAX PREPARATION, BOOKKEEPING, AND PAYROLL SERVICES

AUGMENTED REALITY

IDTechEx, One Boston Place, Ste. 2600, Boston, MA, 02108, USA, (617) 577-7890, (617) 577-7810, research@idtechex.com, https://www.idtechex.com/; Optics and Displays in AR, VR, and MR 2020-2030: Technologies, Players and Markets.

AUSTRALIA-NATIONAL STATISTICAL OFFICE

Australian Bureau of Statistics (ABS), Locked Bag 10, Belconnen, ACT, 2616, AUS, client.services@abs.gov.au, https://www.abs.gov.au/; National Data Reports (Australia).

AUSTRALIA-PRIMARY STATISTICS SOURCES

Australian Bureau of Statistics (ABS), Locked Bag 10, Belconnen, ACT, 2616, AUS, client.services@abs.gov.au, https://www.abs.gov.au/; Regional Population by Age and Sex.

AUSTRALIA-DATABASES

Reserve Bank of Australia (RBA), GPO Box 3947, Sydney, NSW, 2001, AUS, rbainfo@rba.gov.au, https://www.rba.gov.au/; Reserve Bank of Australia Bulletin.

AUSTRALIA-AGRICULTURE

Australian Bureau of Statistics (ABS), Locked Bag 10, Belconnen, ACT, 2616, AUS, client.services@abs.gov.au, https://www.abs.gov.au/; Regional Population by Age and Sex.

Australian Government Department of Agriculture, Water and the Environment, GPO Box 858, Canberra, ACT, 2601, AUS, https://www.agriculture.gov.au/; Australian Agricultural Trade and the COVID-19 Pandemic and Red Meat Export Statistics 2022.

The Economist Group: Economist Intelligence Unit (EIU), 900 3rd Ave., 16th Fl., New York, NY, 10022, USA, (212) 541-0500, americas@eiu.com, https://www.eiu.com; Australia Country Report.

Euromonitor International, Inc., 1 N Dearborn St., Ste. 1700, Chicago, IL, 60602, USA, (312) 922-1115, (312) 922-1157, info-usa@euromonitor.com, https://www.euromonitor.com/; Geographies.

Organization for Economic Cooperation and Development (OECD), 2001 L St. NW, Ste. 650, Washington, DC, 20036-4922, USA, (202) 785-6323, (800) 456-6323, (202) 785-0350, washington.contact@oecd.org, https://www.oecd.org/; Economic Survey of Australia 2021; OECD-FAO Agricultural Outlook 2022-2031; and STAN (STructural ANalysis) Database.

Palgrave Macmillan, 1 New York Plaza, Ste. 4500, New York, NY, 10004-1562, USA, (800) 777-4643, orders@palgrave.com, https://www.palgrave.com/us; The Statesman's Yearbook, 2023.

Routledge - Taylor & Francis Group, 6000 Broken Sound Pkwy. NW, Ste. 300, Boca Raton, FL, 33487, USA, (800) 634-1420, (800) 634-7064, orders@taylorandfrancis.com, https://www.routledge.com/; The Europa World Year Book 2022.

United Nations Economic and Social Commission for Asia and the Pacific (ESCAP), United Nations Building, Rajadamnern Nok Ave., Bangkok, 10200, THA, https://www.unescap.org/; Asia-Pacific Development Journal and SDG Gateway Data Explorer.

United Nations Food and Agricultural Organization (FAO), 2121 K St., Ste. 800B, Washington, DC, 20037, USA, (202) 653-2400 (Dial from U.S.), (202) 653-5760 (Fax from U.S.), fao-hq@fao.org, https://www.fao.org; AQUASTAT and The State of Food and Agriculture (SOFA) 2022.

United Nations Statistics Division (UNSD), United Nations Plz., New York, NY, 10017, USA, (800) 253-9646, (212) 963-9851, statistics@un.org, https://unstats.un.org; Statistical Yearbook of the United Nations 2021.

The World Bank, 1818 H St. NW, Washington, DC, 20433, USA, (202) 473-1000, (202) 477-6391, eds03@worldbank.org, https://www.worldbank.org/; World Development Indicators (WDI) 2022.

AUSTRALIA-AIRLINES

International Civil Aviation Organization (ICAO), 999 Robert-Bourassa Blvd., Montreal, QC, H3C 5H7,

CAN, (514) 954-8219 (Dial from U.S.), (514) 954-6077 (Fax from U.S.), icaohq@icao.int, https://www.icao.int; ICAO Regional Reports.

Organization for Economic Cooperation and Development (OECD), 2001 L St. NW, Ste. 650, Washington, DC, 20036-4922, USA, (202) 785-6323, (800) 456-6323, (202) 785-0350, washington.contact@oecd.org, https://www.oecd.org/; OECD Tourism Trends and Policies 2022.

Palgrave Macmillan, 1 New York Plaza, Ste. 4500, New York, NY, 10004-1562, USA, (800) 777-4643, orders@palgrave.com, https://www.palgrave.com/us; The Statesman's Yearbook, 2023.

Routledge - Taylor & Francis Group, 6000 Broken Sound Pkwy. NW, Ste. 300, Boca Raton, FL, 33487, USA, (800) 634-1420, (800) 634-7064, orders@taylorandfrancis.com, https://www.routledge.com/; The Europa World Year Book 2022.

AUSTRALIA-ALUMINUM PRODUCTION

See AUSTRALIA-MINERAL INDUSTRIES

AUSTRALIA-ANIMAL FEEDING

United Nations Statistics Division (UNSD), United Nations Plz., New York, NY, 10017, USA, (800) 253-9646, (212) 963-9851, statistics@un.org, https://unstats.un.org; Statistical Yearbook of the United Nations 2021.

AUSTRALIA-ARMED FORCES

Australian Bureau of Statistics (ABS), Locked Bag 10, Belconnen, ACT, 2616, AUS, client.services@abs.gov.au, https://www.abs.gov.au/; Regional Population by Age and Sex.

Central Intelligence Agency (CIA), Office of Public Affairs, Washington, DC, 20505, USA, (703) 482-0623, https://www.cia.gov; The World Factbook.

International Institute for Strategic Studies (IISS) - Americas, 2121 K St. NW, Ste. 600, Washington, DC, 20037, USA, (202) 659-1490, (202) 659-1499, https://www.iiss.org/; The Military Balance 2022.

Palgrave Macmillan, 1 New York Plaza, Ste. 4500, New York, NY, 10004-1562, USA, (800) 777-4643, orders@palgrave.com, https://www.palgrave.com/us; The Statesman's Yearbook, 2023.

Stockholm International Peace Research Institute (SIPRI), Signalistgatan 9, Stockholm, SE 169 72, SWE, https://www.sipri.org/; SIPRI Arms Transfers Database and SIPRI Military Expenditure Database.

AUSTRALIA-AUTOMOBILE INDUSTRY AND TRADE

Australian Bureau of Statistics (ABS), Locked Bag 10, Belconnen, ACT, 2616, AUS, client.services@abs.gov.au, https://www.abs.gov.au/; Regional Population by Age and Sex.

AUSTRALIA-BALANCE OF PAYMENTS

Australian Bureau of Statistics (ABS), Locked Bag 10, Belconnen, ACT, 2616, AUS, client.services@abs.gov.au, https://www.abs.gov.au/; Key Economic Indicators and Regional Population by Age and Sex.

International Monetary Fund (IMF), 700 19th St. NW, Washington, DC, 20431, USA, (202) 623-7000, (202) 623-4661, publications@imf.org, https://www.imf.org; Balance of Payments Statistics: Annual Report 2021 and International Financial Statistics (IFS).

Organization for Economic Cooperation and Development (OECD), 2001 L St. NW, Ste. 650, Washington, DC, 20036-4922, USA, (202) 785-6323, (800) 456-6323, (202) 785-0350, washington.contact@oecd.org, https://www.oecd.org/; Economic Survey of Australia 2021; Geographical Distribution of Financial Flows to Developing Countries 2023; OECD Digital Economy Outlook 2020; and OECD Main Economic Indicators (MEI).

Routledge - Taylor & Francis Group, 6000 Broken Sound Pkwy. NW, Ste. 300, Boca Raton, FL, 33487, USA, (800) 634-1420, (800) 634-7064, orders@taylorandfrancis.com, https://www.routledge.com/; The Europa World Year Book 2022.

United Nations Conference on Trade and Development (UNCTAD), Palais des Nations, Geneva, 1211, SWI, (212) 963-6896, unctadinfo@unctad.org, https://unctad.org; Handbook of Statistics 2021.

The World Bank, 1818 H St. NW, Washington, DC, 20433, USA, (202) 473-1000, (202) 477-6391, eds03@worldbank.org, https://www.worldbank.org/; World Development Indicators (WDI) 2022 and World Development Report 2022: Finance for an Equitable Recovery.

AUSTRALIA-BANKS AND BANKING

Euromonitor International, Inc., 1 N Dearborn St., Ste. 1700, Chicago, IL, 60602, USA, (312) 922-1115, (312) 922-1157, info-usa@euromonitor.com, https://www.euromonitor.com/; Geographies.

International Monetary Fund (IMF), 700 19th St. NW, Washington, DC, 20431, USA, (202) 623-7000, (202) 623-4661, publications@imf.org, https://www.imf.org; International Financial Statistics (IFS).

Organization for Economic Cooperation and Development (OECD), 2001 L St. NW, Ste. 650, Washington, DC, 20036-4922, USA, (202) 785-6323, (800) 456-6323, (202) 785-0350, washington.contact@oecd.org, https://www.oecd.org/; Economic Survey of Australia 2021; OECD Business and Finance Outlook 2021; and OECD Digital Economy Outlook 2020.

Reserve Bank of Australia (RBA), GPO Box 3947, Sydney, NSW, 2001, AUS, rbainfo@rba.gov.au, https://www.rba.gov.au/; Financial Stability Review; Reserve Bank of Australia Annual Report 2021; and Statement on Monetary Policy.

Routledge - Taylor & Francis Group, 6000 Broken Sound Pkwy. NW, Ste. 300, Boca Raton, FL, 33487, USA, (800) 634-1420, (800) 634-7064, orders@taylorandfrancis.com, https://www.routledge.com/; The Europa World Year Book 2022.

AUSTRALIA-BARLEY PRODUCTION

See AUSTRALIA-CROPS

AUSTRALIA-BONDS

Organization for Economic Cooperation and Development (OECD), 2001 L St. NW, Ste. 650, Washington, DC, 20036-4922, USA, (202) 785-6323, (800) 456-6323, (202) 785-0350, washington.contact@oecd.org, https://www.oecd.org/; OECD Business and Finance Outlook 2021.

United Nations Statistics Division (UNSD), United Nations Plz., New York, NY, 10017, USA, (800) 253-9646, (212) 963-9851, statistics@un.org, https://unstats.un.org; Statistical Yearbook of the United Nations 2021.

AUSTRALIA-BROADCASTING

Central Intelligence Agency (CIA), Office of Public Affairs, Washington, DC, 20505, USA, (703) 482-0623, https://www.cia.gov; The World Factbook.

Euromonitor International, Inc., 1 N Dearborn St., Ste. 1700, Chicago, IL, 60602, USA, (312) 922-1115, (312) 922-1157, info-usa@euromonitor.com, https://www.euromonitor.com/; Geographies.

Palgrave Macmillan, 1 New York Plaza, Ste. 4500, New York, NY, 10004-1562, USA, (800) 777-4643, orders@palgrave.com, https://www.palgrave.com/us; The Statesman's Yearbook, 2023.

UNESCO Institute for Statistics, C.P 250 Succursale H, Montreal, QC, H3G 2K8, CAN, (514) 343-6880 (Dial from U.S.), (514) 343-5740 (Fax from U.S.), uis.publications@unesco.org, http://uis.unesco.org/; UIS.Stat.

WRTH Publications Limited, PO Box 290, Oxford, OX2 7FT, GBR, sales@wrth.com, https://www.wrth.com; World Radio TV Handbook 2023.

AUSTRALIA-BUDGET

Central Intelligence Agency (CIA), Office of Public Affairs, Washington, DC, 20505, USA, (703) 482-0623, https://www.cia.gov; The World Factbook.

AUSTRALIA-BUSINESS

Australian Bureau of Statistics (ABS), Locked Bag 10, Belconnen, ACT, 2616, AUS, client.services@abs.gov.au, https://www.abs.gov.au/; Regional Population by Age and Sex.

Organization for Economic Cooperation and Development (OECD), 2001 L St. NW, Ste. 650, Washington, DC, 20036-4922, USA, (202) 785-6323, (800) 456-6323, (202) 785-0350, washington.contact@oecd.org, https://www.oecd.org/; OECD Main Economic Indicators (MEI).

United Nations Economic and Social Commission for Asia and the Pacific (ESCAP), United Nations Building, Rajadamnern Nok Ave., Bangkok, 10200, THA, https://www.unescap.org/; SDG Gateway Data Explorer.

AUSTRALIA-CAPITAL INVESTMENTS

Organization for Economic Cooperation and Development (OECD), 2001 L St. NW, Ste. 650, Washington, DC, 20036-4922, USA, (202) 785-6323, (800) 456-6323, (202) 785-0350, washington.contact@oecd.org, https://www.oecd.org/; OECD Business and Finance Outlook 2021.

AUSTRALIA-CHILDBIRTH-STATISTICS

Australian Bureau of Statistics (ABS), Locked Bag 10, Belconnen, ACT, 2616, AUS, client.services@abs.gov.au, https://www.abs.gov.au/; Regional Population by Age and Sex.

United Nations Economic and Social Commission for Asia and the Pacific (ESCAP), United Nations Building, Rajadamnern Nok Ave., Bangkok, 10200, THA, https://www.unescap.org/; Asia-Pacific Development Journal.

The World Bank, 1818 H St. NW, Washington, DC, 20433, USA, (202) 473-1000, (202) 477-6391, eds03@worldbank.org, https://www.worldbank.org/; World Development Indicators (WDI) 2022.

AUSTRALIA-CLIMATE

Palgrave Macmillan, 1 New York Plaza, Ste. 4500, New York, NY, 10004-1562, USA, (800) 777-4643, orders@palgrave.com, https://www.palgrave.com/us; The Statesman's Yearbook, 2023.

World Weather Attribution (WWA), wwamedia@imperial.ac.uk, https://www.worldweatherattribution.org; Attribution of the Australian Bushfire Risk to Anthropogenic Climate Change.

AUSTRALIA-COAL PRODUCTION

See AUSTRALIA-MINERAL INDUSTRIES

AUSTRALIA-COFFEE

See AUSTRALIA-CROPS

AUSTRALIA-COMMERCE

Palgrave Macmillan, 1 New York Plaza, Ste. 4500, New York, NY, 10004-1562, USA, (800) 777-4643, orders@palgrave.com, https://www.palgrave.com/us; The Statesman's Yearbook, 2023.

UK Data Service, University of Essex, Wivenhoe Park, Colchester, Essex, CO4 3SQ, GBR, https://ukdataservice.ac.uk/; International Aggregate Data.

AUSTRALIA-COMMODITY EXCHANGES

Barchart, 209 W Jackson Blvd., 2nd Fl., Chicago, IL, 60606, USA, (877) 247-4394, commodities@barchart.com, https://www.barchart.com/cmdty; The cmdty Yearbook 2023; cmdtyStats: Commodity Statistics and Fundamental Data; cmdtyView: Commodity Index; and Commodity Data and Prices.

International Monetary Fund (IMF), 700 19th St. NW, Washington, DC, 20431, USA, (202) 623-7000, (202) 623-4661, publications@imf.org, https://www.imf.org; IMF Primary Commodity Prices.

Organization for Economic Cooperation and Development (OECD), 2001 L St. NW, Ste. 650, Washington, DC, 20036-4922, USA, (202) 785-6323, (800)

456-6323, (202) 785-0350, washington. contact@oecd.org, https://www.oecd.org/; OECD Main Economic Indicators (MEI).

United Nations Statistics Division (UNSD), United Nations Plz., New York, NY, 10017, USA, (800) 253-9646, (212) 963-9851, statistics@un.org, https://unstats.un.org; Statistical Yearbook of the United Nations 2021.

World Bureau of Metal Statistics (WBMS), 31 Star St., Ware, Hertfordshire, SG12 9BA, GBR, https://www.refinitiv.com/en/trading-solutions/world-bureau-metal-statistics; Annual Stainless Steel Statistics; Long Term Production/Consumption Series - All Metals; World Flow Charts; and World Metal Statistics.

AUSTRALIA-CONSTRUCTION INDUSTRY

Australian Bureau of Statistics (ABS), Locked Bag 10, Belconnen, ACT, 2616, AUS, client.services@abs.gov.au, https://www.abs.gov.au/; Regional Population by Age and Sex.

Australian Institute of Health and Welfare (AIHW), GPO Box 570, Canberra, ACT, 2601, AUS, info@aihw.gov.au, https://www.aihw.gov.au/; National Social Housing Survey 2021.

Organization for Economic Cooperation and Development (OECD), 2001 L St. NW, Ste. 650, Washington, DC, 20036-4922, USA, (202) 785-6323, (800) 456-6323, (202) 785-0350, washington.contact@oecd.org, https://www.oecd.org/; Economic Survey of Australia 2021; OECD Main Economic Indicators (MEI); and STAN (STructural ANalysis) Database.

Palgrave Macmillan, 1 New York Plaza, Ste. 4500, New York, NY, 10004-1562, USA, (800) 777-4643, orders@palgrave.com, https://www.palgrave.com/us; The Statesman's Yearbook, 2023.

United Nations Statistics Division (UNSD), United Nations Plz., New York, NY, 10017, USA, (800) 253-9646, (212) 963-9851, statistics@un.org, https://unstats.un.org; Statistical Yearbook of the United Nations 2021.

AUSTRALIA-CONSUMER PRICE INDEXES

Australian Bureau of Statistics (ABS), Locked Bag 10, Belconnen, ACT, 2616, AUS, client.services@abs.gov.au, https://www.abs.gov.au/; Regional Population by Age and Sex.

Organization for Economic Cooperation and Development (OECD), 2001 L St. NW, Ste. 650, Washington, DC, 20036-4922, USA, (202) 785-6323, (800) 456-6323, (202) 785-0350, washington.contact@oecd.org, https://www.oecd.org/; OECD Digital Economy Outlook 2020.

Routledge - Taylor & Francis Group, 6000 Broken Sound Pkwy. NW, Ste. 300, Boca Raton, FL, 33487, USA, (800) 634-1420, (800) 634-7064, orders@taylorandfrancis.com, https://www.routledge.com/; The Europa World Year Book 2022.

AUSTRALIA-CONSUMPTION (ECONOMICS)

International Monetary Fund (IMF), 700 19th St. NW, Washington, DC, 20431, USA, (202) 623-7000, (202) 623-4661, publications@imf.org, https://www.imf.org; International Financial Statistics (IFS).

Organization for Economic Cooperation and Development (OECD), 2001 L St. NW, Ste. 650, Washington, DC, 20036-4922, USA, (202) 785-6323, (800) 456-6323, (202) 785-0350, washington.contact@oecd.org, https://www.oecd.org/; OECD-FAO Agricultural Outlook 2022-2031 and Revenue Statistics 2022.

TAPPI - Technical Association of the Pulp and Paper Industry, 15 Technology Pkwy. S, Ste. 115, Peachtree Corners, GA, 30092, USA, (770) 446-1400, (800) 332-8686, (770) 446-6947, memberconnection@tappi.org, https://www.tappi.org/; TAPPI Journal.

World Steel Association (Worldsteel), Avenue de Tervueren 270, Brussels, B-1150, BEL, steel@worldsteel.org, https://www.worldsteel.org; Steel Statistical Yearbook 2021.

AUSTRALIA-COPPER INDUSTRY AND TRADE

See AUSTRALIA-MINERAL INDUSTRIES

AUSTRALIA-CORN INDUSTRY

See AUSTRALIA-CROPS

AUSTRALIA-COST AND STANDARD OF LIVING

United Nations Economic and Social Commission for Asia and the Pacific (ESCAP), United Nations Building, Rajadamnern Nok Ave., Bangkok, 10200, THA, https://www.unescap.org/; SDG Gateway Data Explorer.

AUSTRALIA-COTTON

See AUSTRALIA-CROPS

AUSTRALIA-CRIME

Australia's National Research Organisation for Women's Safety Limited (ANROWS), Queen Victoria Bldg., PO Box Q389, New South Wales, NSW, 1230, AUS, enquiries@anrows.org.au, https://www.anrows.org.au/; It Depends on What the Definition of Domestic Violence Is: How Young Australians Conceptualise Domestic Violence and Abuse.

Australian Institute of Criminology (AIC), GPO Box 1936, Canberra, ACT, 2601, AUS, front.desk@aic.gov.au, https://www.aic.gov.au/; Deaths in Custody in Australia 2021-2022; Drug Use Monitoring in Australia: Drug Use Among Police Detainees, 2021; and Estimating the Costs of Serious and Organised Crime in Australia, 2020-2021.

AUSTRALIA-CROPS

International Monetary Fund (IMF), 700 19th St. NW, Washington, DC, 20431, USA, (202) 623-7000, (202) 623-4661, publications@imf.org, https://www.imf.org; International Financial Statistics (IFS).

Organization for Economic Cooperation and Development (OECD), 2001 L St. NW, Ste. 650, Washington, DC, 20036-4922, USA, (202) 785-6323, (800) 456-6323, (202) 785-0350, washington.contact@oecd.org, https://www.oecd.org/; OECD-FAO Agricultural Outlook 2022-2031.

Palgrave Macmillan, 1 New York Plaza, Ste. 4500, New York, NY, 10004-1562, USA, (800) 777-4643, orders@palgrave.com, https://www.palgrave.com/us; The Statesman's Yearbook, 2023.

United Nations Food and Agricultural Organization (FAO), 2121 K St., Ste. 800B, Washington, DC, 20037, USA, (202) 653-2400 (Dial from U.S.), (202) 653-5760 (Fax from U.S.), fao-hq@fao.org, https://www.fao.org; The State of Food and Agriculture (SOFA) 2022.

United Nations Statistics Division (UNSD), United Nations Plz., New York, NY, 10017, USA, (800) 253-9646, (212) 963-9851, statistics@un.org, https://unstats.un.org; Statistical Yearbook of the United Nations 2021.

AUSTRALIA-CULTURE

Australian Bureau of Statistics (ABS), Locked Bag 10, Belconnen, ACT, 2616, AUS, client.services@abs.gov.au, https://www.abs.gov.au/; Regional Population by Age and Sex.

AUSTRALIA-DAIRY PROCESSING

Organization for Economic Cooperation and Development (OECD), 2001 L St. NW, Ste. 650, Washington, DC, 20036-4922, USA, (202) 785-6323, (800) 456-6323, (202) 785-0350, washington.contact@oecd.org, https://www.oecd.org/; OECD-FAO Agricultural Outlook 2022-2031.

Palgrave Macmillan, 1 New York Plaza, Ste. 4500, New York, NY, 10004-1562, USA, (800) 777-4643, orders@palgrave.com, https://www.palgrave.com/us; The Statesman's Yearbook, 2023.

United Nations Food and Agricultural Organization (FAO), 2121 K St., Ste. 800B, Washington, DC, 20037, USA, (202) 653-2400 (Dial from U.S.), (202) 653-5760 (Fax from U.S.), fao-hq@fao.org, https://www.fao.org; The State of Food and Agriculture (SOFA) 2022.

AUSTRALIA-DEBTS, EXTERNAL

Organization for Economic Cooperation and Development (OECD), 2001 L St. NW, Ste. 650, Washington, DC, 20036-4922, USA, (202) 785-6323, (800) 456-6323, (202) 785-0350, washington.contact@oecd.org, https://www.oecd.org/; Geographical Distribution of Financial Flows to Developing Countries 2023; OECD Business and Finance Outlook 2021; and OECD Digital Economy Outlook 2020.

Palgrave Macmillan, 1 New York Plaza, Ste. 4500, New York, NY, 10004-1562, USA, (800) 777-4643, orders@palgrave.com, https://www.palgrave.com/us; The Statesman's Yearbook, 2023.

The World Bank, 1818 H St. NW, Washington, DC, 20433, USA, (202) 473-1000, (202) 477-6391, eds03@worldbank.org, https://www.worldbank.org/; Global Financial Development Report 2019-2020: Bank Regulation and Supervision a Decade after the Global Financial Crisis; World Development Indicators (WDI) 2022; and World Development Report 2022: Finance for an Equitable Recovery.

AUSTRALIA-DEFENSE EXPENDITURES

See AUSTRALIA-ARMED FORCES

AUSTRALIA-DIAMONDS

See AUSTRALIA-MINERAL INDUSTRIES

AUSTRALIA-DISPOSABLE INCOME

Australian Bureau of Statistics (ABS), Locked Bag 10, Belconnen, ACT, 2616, AUS, client.services@abs.gov.au, https://www.abs.gov.au/; Regional Population by Age and Sex.

AUSTRALIA-ECONOMIC ASSISTANCE

Organization for Economic Cooperation and Development (OECD), 2001 L St. NW, Ste. 650, Washington, DC, 20036-4922, USA, (202) 785-6323, (800) 456-6323, (202) 785-0350, washington.contact@oecd.org, https://www.oecd.org/; Geographical Distribution of Financial Flows to Developing Countries 2023.

United Nations Statistics Division (UNSD), United Nations Plz., New York, NY, 10017, USA, (800) 253-9646, (212) 963-9851, statistics@un.org, https://unstats.un.org; Statistical Yearbook of the United Nations 2021.

AUSTRALIA-ECONOMIC CONDITIONS

Australian Bureau of Statistics (ABS), Locked Bag 10, Belconnen, ACT, 2616, AUS, client.services@abs.gov.au, https://www.abs.gov.au/; Aboriginal and Torres Strait Islander Peoples.

Australian Government Department of Agriculture, Water and the Environment, GPO Box 858, Canberra, ACT, 2601, AUS, https://www.agriculture.gov.au/; Australian Agricultural Trade and the COVID-19 Pandemic.

Bernan Press, 15250 NBN Way, Bldg. C, Blue Ridge Summit, PA, 17214, USA, (301) 459-2255, (800) 865-3457, (800) 865-3450, customercare@bernan.com, https://rowman.com/Page/Bernan; World Economic Outlook, April 2022.

Central Intelligence Agency (CIA), Office of Public Affairs, Washington, DC, 20505, USA, (703) 482-0623, https://www.cia.gov; The World Factbook.

The Economist Group: Economist Intelligence Unit (EIU), 900 3rd Ave., 16th Fl., New York, NY, 10022, USA, (212) 541-0500, americas@eiu.com, https://www.eiu.com; Australia Country Report.

Euromonitor International, Inc., 1 N Dearborn St., Ste. 1700, Chicago, IL, 60602, USA, (312) 922-1115, (312) 922-1157, info-usa@euromonitor.com, https://www.euromonitor.com/; Geographies and Market Research on the Consumer Finance Industry.

Federal Statistical Office Germany, Gustav-Stresemann-Ring 11, Wiesbaden, D-65189, GER, https://www.destatis.de; Basic Indicators: Australia.

International Monetary Fund (IMF), 700 19th St. NW, Washington, DC, 20431, USA, (202) 623-7000, (202) 623-4661, publications@imf.org, https://www.imf.org; IMF Data and World Economic Outlook.

Organization for Economic Cooperation and Development (OECD), 2001 L St. NW, Ste. 650, Washington, DC, 20036-4922, USA, (202) 785-6323, (800) 456-6323, (202) 785-0350, washington.contact@oecd.org, https://www.oecd.org/; Economic Survey of Australia 2021; Geographical Distribution of Financial Flows to Developing Countries 2023; OECD Composite Leading Indicator (CLI); OECD Digital Economy Outlook 2020; OECD Employment Outlook 2022: Building Back More Inclusive Labour Markets; OECD Labour Force Statistics 2022; and OECD Main Economic Indicators (MEI).

Palgrave Macmillan, 1 New York Plaza, Ste. 4500, New York, NY, 10004-1562, USA, (800) 777-4643, orders@palgrave.com, https://www.palgrave.com/us; The Statesman's Yearbook, 2023.

Reserve Bank of Australia (RBA), GPO Box 3947, Sydney, NSW, 2001, AUS, rbainfo@rba.gov.au, https://www.rba.gov.au/; Financial Stability Review; Reserve Bank of Australia Research Discussion Papers; and Statement on Monetary Policy.

Routledge - Taylor & Francis Group, 6000 Broken Sound Pkwy. NW, Ste. 300, Boca Raton, FL, 33487, USA, (800) 634-1420, (800) 634-7064, orders@taylorandfrancis.com, https://www.routledge.com/; The Europa World Year Book 2022.

United Nations Statistics Division (UNSD), United Nations Plz., New York, NY, 10017, USA, (800) 253-9646, (212) 963-9851, statistics@un.org, https://unstats.un.org; World Statistics Pocketbook 2021.

The World Bank, 1818 H St. NW, Washington, DC, 20433, USA, (202) 473-1000, (202) 477-6391, eds03@worldbank.org, https://www.worldbank.org/; Global Economic Monitor (GEM); Global Economic Prospects, June 2022; The Global Findex Database 2021; and World Development Report 2022: Finance for an Equitable Recovery.

AUSTRALIA-EDUCATION

Australian Bureau of Statistics (ABS), Locked Bag 10, Belconnen, ACT, 2616, AUS, client.services@abs.gov.au, https://www.abs.gov.au/; Regional Population by Age and Sex.

Euromonitor International, Inc., 1 N Dearborn St., Ste. 1700, Chicago, IL, 60602, USA, (312) 922-1115, (312) 922-1157, info-usa@euromonitor.com, https://www.euromonitor.com/; Geographies.

Infoplease, c/o Sandbox Networks, Inc., 1 Lincoln St., 24th Fl., Boston, MA, 02111, USA, https://www.infoplease.com; Countries of the World.

Organization for Economic Cooperation and Development (OECD), 2001 L St. NW, Ste. 650, Washington, DC, 20036-4922, USA, (202) 785-6323, (800) 456-6323, (202) 785-0350, washington.contact@oecd.org, https://www.oecd.org/; Education at a Glance 2022: OECD Indicators.

Palgrave Macmillan, 1 New York Plaza, Ste. 4500, New York, NY, 10004-1562, USA, (800) 777-4643, orders@palgrave.com, https://www.palgrave.com/us; The Statesman's Yearbook, 2023.

Routledge - Taylor & Francis Group, 6000 Broken Sound Pkwy. NW, Ste. 300, Boca Raton, FL, 33487, USA, (800) 634-1420, (800) 634-7064, orders@taylorandfrancis.com, https://www.routledge.com/; The Europa World Year Book 2022.

UNESCO Institute for Statistics, C.P 250 Succursale H, Montreal, QC, H3G 2K8, CAN, (514) 343-6880 (Dial from U.S.), (514) 343-5740 (Fax from U.S.), uis.publications@unesco.org, http://uis.unesco.org/; Literacy and UIS.Stat.

United Nations Economic and Social Commission for Asia and the Pacific (ESCAP), United Nations Building, Rajadamnern Nok Ave., Bangkok, 10200, THA, https://www.unescap.org/; Asia-Pacific Development Journal and SDG Gateway Data Explorer.

United Nations Statistics Division (UNSD), United Nations Plz., New York, NY, 10017, USA, (800) 253-9646, (212) 963-9851, statistics@un.org, https://unstats.un.org; Millennium Development Goal Indicators.

The World Bank, 1818 H St. NW, Washington, DC, 20433, USA, (202) 473-1000, (202) 477-6391, eds03@worldbank.org, https://www.worldbank.org/; World Development Indicators (WDI) 2022 and World Development Report 2022: Finance for an Equitable Recovery.

AUSTRALIA-ELECTRICITY

International Energy Agency (IEA), 9 Rue de la Federation, Paris, 75739, FRA, info@iea.org, https://www.iea.org/; Coal 2021: Analysis and Forecast to 2024 and World Energy Outlook 2021.

Organization for Economic Cooperation and Development (OECD), 2001 L St. NW, Ste. 650, Washington, DC, 20036-4922, USA, (202) 785-6323, (800) 456-6323, (202) 785-0350, washington.contact@oecd.org, https://www.oecd.org/; Energy Prices and Taxes for OECD Countries 2020 and STAN (STructural ANalysis) Database.

S&P Global Commodity Insights, One World Trade Center, New York, NY, 10007, USA, (800) 752-8878, support@platts.com, https://www.spglobal.com/commodityinsights/en; Platts Asia Pacific / Arab Gulf Marketscan (APAG Marketscan).

U.S. Energy Information Administration (EIA), 1000 Independence Ave. SW, Washington, DC, 20585, USA, (202) 586-8800, infoctr@eia.gov, https://www.eia.gov; International Energy Outlook 2021.

United Nations Statistics Division (UNSD), United Nations Plz., New York, NY, 10017, USA, (800) 253-9646, (212) 963-9851, statistics@un.org, https://unstats.un.org; Statistical Yearbook of the United Nations 2021.

AUSTRALIA-EMPLOYMENT

Australian Bureau of Statistics (ABS), Locked Bag 10, Belconnen, ACT, 2616, AUS, client.services@abs.gov.au, https://www.abs.gov.au/; Aboriginal and Torres Strait Islander Peoples.

International Labour Organization (ILO), 4 Rte. des Morillons, Geneva, CH-1211, SWI, ilo@ilo.org, https://www.ilo.org; NORMLEX Information System on International Labour Standards.

Organization for Economic Cooperation and Development (OECD), 2001 L St. NW, Ste. 650, Washington, DC, 20036-4922, USA, (202) 785-6323, (800) 456-6323, (202) 785-0350, washington.contact@oecd.org, https://www.oecd.org/; Economic Survey of Australia 2021; OECD Composite Leading Indicator (CLI); OECD Digital Economy Outlook 2020; OECD Employment Outlook 2022: Building Back More Inclusive Labour Markets; and OECD Labour Force Statistics 2022.

UK Data Service, University of Essex, Wivenhoe Park, Colchester, Essex, CO4 3SQ, GBR, https://ukdataservice.ac.uk/; International Aggregate Data.

United Nations Economic and Social Commission for Asia and the Pacific (ESCAP), United Nations Building, Rajadamnern Nok Ave., Bangkok, 10200, THA, https://www.unescap.org/; Asia-Pacific Development Journal.

United Nations Statistics Division (UNSD), United Nations Plz., New York, NY, 10017, USA, (800) 253-9646, (212) 963-9851, statistics@un.org, https://unstats.un.org; Statistical Yearbook of the United Nations 2021.

AUSTRALIA-ENERGY INDUSTRIES

Enerdata, 47 avenue Alsace Lorraine, Grenoble, 38027, FRA, (332) 216-4534, research@enerdata.net, https://www.enerdata.net; World Refinery Database.

International Energy Agency (IEA), 9 Rue de la Federation, Paris, 75739, FRA, info@iea.org, https://www.iea.org/; Renewables Information and World Energy Statistics and Balances.

S&P Global Commodity Insights, One World Trade Center, New York, NY, 10007, USA, (800) 752-8878, support@platts.com, https://www.spglobal.com/commodityinsights/en; Platts Asia Pacific / Arab Gulf Marketscan (APAG Marketscan).

United Nations Statistics Division (UNSD), United Nations Plz., New York, NY, 10017, USA, (800) 253-9646, (212) 963-9851, statistics@un.org, https://unstats.un.org; Statistical Yearbook of the United Nations 2021.

AUSTRALIA-ENVIRONMENTAL CONDITIONS

DSI Data Service & Information, Xantener Strasse 51a, Rheinberg, D-47495, GER, dsi@dsidata.com, https://www.dsidata.com/; Global Environmental Database.

The Economist Group: Economist Intelligence Unit (EIU), 900 3rd Ave., 16th Fl., New York, NY, 10022, USA, (212) 541-0500, americas@eiu.com, https://www.eiu.com; Australia Country Report.

Federal Statistical Office Germany, Gustav-Stresemann-Ring 11, Wiesbaden, D-65189, GER, https://www.destatis.de; Basic Indicators: Australia.

Organization for Economic Cooperation and Development (OECD), 2001 L St. NW, Ste. 650, Washington, DC, 20036-4922, USA, (202) 785-6323, (800) 456-6323, (202) 785-0350, washington.contact@oecd.org, https://www.oecd.org/; Environment Statistics.

United Nations Statistics Division (UNSD), United Nations Plz., New York, NY, 10017, USA, (800) 253-9646, (212) 963-9851, statistics@un.org, https://unstats.un.org; World Statistics Pocketbook 2021.

AUSTRALIA-EXPENDITURES, PUBLIC

Australian Institute of Health and Welfare (AIHW), GPO Box 570, Canberra, ACT, 2601, AUS, info@aihw.gov.au, https://www.aihw.gov.au/; Health Expenditure Australia 2020-2021.

Organization for Economic Cooperation and Development (OECD), 2001 L St. NW, Ste. 650, Washington, DC, 20036-4922, USA, (202) 785-6323, (800) 456-6323, (202) 785-0350, washington.contact@oecd.org, https://www.oecd.org/; Revenue Statistics 2022.

AUSTRALIA-EXPORTS

Australian Government Department of Agriculture, Water and the Environment, GPO Box 858, Canberra, ACT, 2601, AUS, https://www.agriculture.gov.au/; Red Meat Export Statistics 2022.

BC Stats, Stn Prov Govt, PO Box 9410, Victoria, BC, V8W 9V1, CAN, (250) 387-6121 (Dial from U.S.), bc.stats@gov.bc.ca, https://www2.gov.bc.ca/gov/content/data/about-data-management/bc-stats; Country Trade Profile - Australia.

Central Intelligence Agency (CIA), Office of Public Affairs, Washington, DC, 20505, USA, (703) 482-0623, https://www.cia.gov; The World Factbook.

The Economist Group: Economist Intelligence Unit (EIU), 900 3rd Ave., 16th Fl., New York, NY, 10022, USA, (212) 541-0500, americas@eiu.com, https://www.eiu.com; Australia Country Report.

International Monetary Fund (IMF), 700 19th St. NW, Washington, DC, 20431, USA, (202) 623-7000, (202) 623-4661, publications@imf.org, https://www.imf.org; Direction of Trade Statistics (DOTS) and International Financial Statistics (IFS).

Organization for Economic Cooperation and Development (OECD), 2001 L St. NW, Ste. 650, Washington, DC, 20036-4922, USA, (202) 785-6323, (800) 456-6323, (202) 785-0350, washington.contact@oecd.org, https://www.oecd.org/; Economic Survey of Australia 2021; Geographical Distribution of Financial Flows to Developing Countries 2023; OECD Digital Economy Outlook 2020; OECD Review of Fisheries 2022; OECD-FAO Agricultural Outlook 2022-2031; and STAN (STructural ANalysis) Database.

S&P Global, IHS Markit, 15 Inverness Way E, Englewood, CO, 80112, USA, (800) 447-2273, (800) 854-7179, https://ihsmarkit.com; Global Trade Atlas (GTA).

TAPPI - Technical Association of the Pulp and Paper Industry, 15 Technology Pkwy. S, Ste. 115, Peachtree Corners, GA, 30092, USA, (770) 446-1400, (800) 332-8686, (770) 446-6947, memberconnection@tappi.org, https://www.tappi.org/; TAPPI Journal.

United Nations Conference on Trade and Development (UNCTAD), Palais des Nations, Geneva, 1211, SWI, (212) 963-6896, unctadinfo@unctad.org, https://unctad.org; Handbook of Statistics 2021.

The World Bank, 1818 H St. NW, Washington, DC, 20433, USA, (202) 473-1000, (202) 477-6391, eds03@worldbank.org, https://www.worldbank.org/; World Development Report 2022: Finance for an Equitable Recovery.

World Steel Association (Worldsteel), Avenue de Tervueren 270, Brussels, B-1150, BEL, steel@worldsteel.org, https://www.worldsteel.org; Steel Statistical Yearbook 2021.

AUSTRALIA-FEMALE WORKING POPULATION

See AUSTRALIA-EMPLOYMENT

AUSTRALIA-FERTILIZER INDUSTRY

Organization for Economic Cooperation and Development (OECD), 2001 L St. NW, Ste. 650, Washington, DC, 20036-4922, USA, (202) 785-6323, (800) 456-6323, (202) 785-0350, washington.contact@oecd.org, https://www.oecd.org/; OECD-FAO Agricultural Outlook 2022-2031.

United Nations Food and Agricultural Organization (FAO), 2121 K St., Ste. 800B, Washington, DC, 20037, USA, (202) 653-2400 (Dial from U.S.), (202) 653-5760 (Fax from U.S.), fao-hq@fao.org, https://www.fao.org; The State of Food and Agriculture (SOFA) 2022.

AUSTRALIA-FETAL MORTALITY

See AUSTRALIA-MORTALITY

AUSTRALIA-FINANCE

Australian Bureau of Statistics (ABS), Locked Bag 10, Belconnen, ACT, 2616, AUS, client.services@abs.gov.au, https://www.abs.gov.au/; Regional Population by Age and Sex.

International Monetary Fund (IMF), 700 19th St. NW, Washington, DC, 20431, USA, (202) 623-7000, (202) 623-4661, publications@imf.org, https://www.imf.org; International Financial Statistics (IFS).

Organization for Economic Cooperation and Development (OECD), 2001 L St. NW, Ste. 650, Washington, DC, 20036-4922, USA, (202) 785-6323, (800) 456-6323, (202) 785-0350, washington.contact@oecd.org, https://www.oecd.org/; OECD Digital Economy Outlook 2020.

Reserve Bank of Australia (RBA), GPO Box 3947, Sydney, NSW, 2001, AUS, rbainfo@rba.gov.au, https://www.rba.gov.au/; Financial Stability Review and Reserve Bank of Australia Research Discussion Papers.

Stockholm International Peace Research Institute (SIPRI), Signalistgatan 9, Stockholm, SE 169 72, SWE, https://www.sipri.org/; SIPRI Arms Transfers Database and SIPRI Military Expenditure Database.

United Nations Economic and Social Commission for Asia and the Pacific (ESCAP), United Nations Building, Rajadamnern Nok Ave., Bangkok, 10200, THA, https://www.unescap.org/; Asia-Pacific Development Journal and SDG Gateway Data Explorer.

AUSTRALIA-FINANCE, PUBLIC

Bernan Press, 15250 NBN Way, Bldg. C, Blue Ridge Summit, PA, 17214, USA, (301) 459-2255, (800) 865-3457, (800) 865-3450, customercare@bernan.com, https://rowman.com/Page/Bernan; National Accounts Statistics: Analysis of Main Aggregates 2020.

The Economist Group: Economist Intelligence Unit (EIU), 900 3rd Ave., 16th Fl., New York, NY, 10022, USA, (212) 541-0500, americas@eiu.com, https://www.eiu.com; Australia Country Report.

International Monetary Fund (IMF), 700 19th St. NW, Washington, DC, 20431, USA, (202) 623-7000, (202) 623-4661, publications@imf.org, https://www.imf.org; International Financial Statistics (IFS) and Regional Economic Outlook.

Organization for Economic Cooperation and Development (OECD), 2001 L St. NW, Ste. 650, Washington, DC, 20036-4922, USA, (202) 785-6323, (800) 456-6323, (202) 785-0350, washington.contact@oecd.org, https://www.oecd.org/; Geographical Distribution of Financial Flows to Developing Countries 2023; OECD Business and Finance Outlook 2021; OECD Digital Economy Outlook 2020; OECD Main Economic Indicators (MEI); and Revenue Statistics 2022.

Palgrave Macmillan, 1 New York Plaza, Ste. 4500, New York, NY, 10004-1562, USA, (800) 777-4643, orders@palgrave.com, https://www.palgrave.com/us; The Statesman's Yearbook, 2023.

Reserve Bank of Australia (RBA), GPO Box 3947, Sydney, NSW, 2001, AUS, rbainfo@rba.gov.au, https://www.rba.gov.au/; Financial Stability Review.

Routledge - Taylor & Francis Group, 6000 Broken Sound Pkwy. NW, Ste. 300, Boca Raton, FL, 33487, USA, (800) 634-1420, (800) 634-7064, orders@taylorandfrancis.com, https://www.routledge.com/; The Europa World Year Book 2022.

United Nations Economic and Social Commission for Asia and the Pacific (ESCAP), United Nations Building, Rajadamnern Nok Ave., Bangkok, 10200, THA, https://www.unescap.org/; SDG Gateway Data Explorer.

United Nations Statistics Division (UNSD), United Nations Plz., New York, NY, 10017, USA, (800) 253-9646, (212) 963-9851, statistics@un.org, https://unstats.un.org; National Accounts Main Aggregates Database and National Accounts Statistics: Main Aggregates and Detailed Tables.

AUSTRALIA-FISHERIES

Australian Bureau of Statistics (ABS), Locked Bag 10, Belconnen, ACT, 2616, AUS, client.services@abs.gov.au, https://www.abs.gov.au/; Regional Population by Age and Sex.

Organization for Economic Cooperation and Development (OECD), 2001 L St. NW, Ste. 650, Washington, DC, 20036-4922, USA, (202) 785-6323, (800) 456-6323, (202) 785-0350, washington.contact@oecd.org, https://www.oecd.org/; OECD Review of Fisheries 2022 and STAN (STructural ANalysis) Database.

Palgrave Macmillan, 1 New York Plaza, Ste. 4500, New York, NY, 10004-1562, USA, (800) 777-4643, orders@palgrave.com, https://www.palgrave.com/us; The Statesman's Yearbook, 2023.

Routledge - Taylor & Francis Group, 6000 Broken Sound Pkwy. NW, Ste. 300, Boca Raton, FL, 33487, USA, (800) 634-1420, (800) 634-7064, orders@taylorandfrancis.com, https://www.routledge.com/; The Europa World Year Book 2022.

United Nations Food and Agricultural Organization (FAO), 2121 K St., Ste. 800B, Washington, DC, 20037, USA, (202) 653-2400 (Dial from U.S.), (202) 653-5760 (Fax from U.S.), fao-hq@fao.org, https://www.fao.org; The State of Food and Agriculture (SOFA) 2022.

United Nations Statistics Division (UNSD), United Nations Plz., New York, NY, 10017, USA, (800) 253-9646, (212) 963-9851, statistics@un.org, https://unstats.un.org; Statistical Yearbook of the United Nations 2021.

AUSTRALIA-FOOD

Australian Government Department of Agriculture, Water and the Environment, GPO Box 858, Canberra, ACT, 2601, AUS, https://www.agriculture.gov.au/; Red Meat Export Statistics 2022.

Euromonitor International, Inc., 1 N Dearborn St., Ste. 1700, Chicago, IL, 60602, USA, (312) 922-1115, (312) 922-1157, info-usa@euromonitor.com, https://www.euromonitor.com/; Market Research on the Retailing Industry.

United Nations Economic and Social Commission for Asia and the Pacific (ESCAP), United Nations Building, Rajadamnern Nok Ave., Bangkok, 10200, THA, https://www.unescap.org/; SDG Gateway Data Explorer.

United Nations Food and Agricultural Organization (FAO), 2121 K St., Ste. 800B, Washington, DC, 20037, USA, (202) 653-2400 (Dial from U.S.), (202) 653-5760 (Fax from U.S.), fao-hq@fao.org, https://www.fao.org; The State of Food and Agriculture (SOFA) 2022.

AUSTRALIA-FOREIGN EXCHANGE RATES

International Monetary Fund (IMF), 700 19th St. NW, Washington, DC, 20431, USA, (202) 623-7000, (202) 623-4661, publications@imf.org, https://www.imf.org; International Financial Statistics (IFS).

Organization for Economic Cooperation and Development (OECD), 2001 L St. NW, Ste. 650, Washington, DC, 20036-4922, USA, (202) 785-6323, (800) 456-6323, (202) 785-0350, washington.contact@oecd.org, https://www.oecd.org/; OECD Business and Finance Outlook 2021; OECD Digital Economy Outlook 2020; OECD Tourism Trends and Policies 2022; and Revenue Statistics 2022.

AUSTRALIA-FORESTS AND FORESTRY

Australian Bureau of Statistics (ABS), Locked Bag 10, Belconnen, ACT, 2616, AUS, client.services@abs.gov.au, https://www.abs.gov.au/; Regional Population by Age and Sex.

Organization for Economic Cooperation and Development (OECD), 2001 L St. NW, Ste. 650, Washington, DC, 20036-4922, USA, (202) 785-6323, (800) 456-6323, (202) 785-0350, washington.contact@oecd.org, https://www.oecd.org/; STAN (STructural ANalysis) Database.

Palgrave Macmillan, 1 New York Plaza, Ste. 4500, New York, NY, 10004-1562, USA, (800) 777-4643, orders@palgrave.com, https://www.palgrave.com/us; The Statesman's Yearbook, 2023.

Routledge - Taylor & Francis Group, 6000 Broken Sound Pkwy. NW, Ste. 300, Boca Raton, FL, 33487, USA, (800) 634-1420, (800) 634-7064, orders@taylorandfrancis.com, https://www.routledge.com/; The Europa World Year Book 2022.

TAPPI - Technical Association of the Pulp and Paper Industry, 15 Technology Pkwy. S, Ste. 115, Peachtree Corners, GA, 30092, USA, (770) 446-1400, (800) 332-8686, (770) 446-6947, memberconnection@tappi.org, https://www.tappi.org/; TAPPI Journal.

UNESCO Institute for Statistics, C.P 250 Succursale H, Montreal, QC, H3G 2K8, CAN, (514) 343-6880 (Dial from U.S.), (514) 343-5740 (Fax from U.S.), uis.publications@unesco.org, http://uis.unesco.org/; UIS.Stat.

United Nations Food and Agricultural Organization (FAO), 2121 K St., Ste. 800B, Washington, DC, 20037, USA, (202) 653-2400 (Dial from U.S.), (202) 653-5760 (Fax from U.S.), fao-hq@fao.org, https://www.fao.org; FAO Yearbook of Forest Products 2019 and The State of Food and Agriculture (SOFA) 2022.

United Nations Statistics Division (UNSD), United Nations Plz., New York, NY, 10017, USA, (800) 253-9646, (212) 963-9851, statistics@un.org, https://unstats.un.org; Statistical Yearbook of the United Nations 2021.

The World Bank, 1818 H St. NW, Washington, DC, 20433, USA, (202) 473-1000, (202) 477-6391, eds03@worldbank.org, https://www.worldbank.org/; World Development Report 2022: Finance for an Equitable Recovery.

AUSTRALIA-FRUIT PRODUCTION

See AUSTRALIA-CROPS

AUSTRALIA-GAS PRODUCTION

See AUSTRALIA-MINERAL INDUSTRIES

AUSTRALIA-GOLD PRODUCTION

See AUSTRALIA-MINERAL INDUSTRIES

AUSTRALIA-GRANTS-IN-AID

Organization for Economic Cooperation and Development (OECD), 2001 L St. NW, Ste. 650, Washington, DC, 20036-4922, USA, (202) 785-6323, (800) 456-6323, (202) 785-0350, washington.contact@oecd.org, https://www.oecd.org/; Geographical Distribution of Financial Flows to Developing Countries 2023.

AUSTRALIA-GROSS DOMESTIC PRODUCT

Australian Bureau of Statistics (ABS), Locked Bag 10, Belconnen, ACT, 2616, AUS, client.services@abs.gov.au, https://www.abs.gov.au/; Regional Population by Age and Sex.

The Economist Group: Economist Intelligence Unit (EIU), 900 3rd Ave., 16th Fl., New York, NY, 10022, USA, (212) 541-0500, americas@eiu.com, https://www.eiu.com; Australia Country Report.

International Monetary Fund (IMF), 700 19th St. NW, Washington, DC, 20431, USA, (202) 623-7000, (202) 623-4661, publications@imf.org, https://www.imf.org; International Financial Statistics (IFS).

Organization for Economic Cooperation and Development (OECD), 2001 L St. NW, Ste. 650, Washington, DC, 20036-4922, USA, (202) 785-6323, (800) 456-6323, (202) 785-0350, washington.contact@oecd.org, https://www.oecd.org/; Geographical Distribution of Financial Flows to Developing Countries 2023; OECD Digital Economy Outlook 2020; and Revenue Statistics 2022.

Routledge - Taylor & Francis Group, 6000 Broken Sound Pkwy. NW, Ste. 300, Boca Raton, FL, 33487, USA, (800) 634-1420, (800) 634-7064, orders@taylorandfrancis.com, https://www.routledge.com/; The Europa World Year Book 2022.

United Nations Statistics Division (UNSD), United Nations Plz., New York, NY, 10017, USA, (800) 253-9646, (212) 963-9851, statistics@un.org, https://unstats.un.org; Statistical Yearbook of the United Nations 2021.

The World Bank, 1818 H St. NW, Washington, DC, 20433, USA, (202) 473-1000, (202) 477-6391, eds03@worldbank.org, https://www.worldbank.org/; World Development Indicators (WDI) 2022 and World Development Report 2022: Finance for an Equitable Recovery.

AUSTRALIA-GROSS NATIONAL PRODUCT

Organization for Economic Cooperation and Development (OECD), 2001 L St. NW, Ste. 650, Washington, DC, 20036-4922, USA, (202) 785-6323, (800) 456-6323, (202) 785-0350, washington.contact@oecd.org, https://www.oecd.org/; Geographical Distribution of Financial Flows to Developing Countries 2023; OECD Composite Leading Indicator (CLI); OECD Digital Economy Outlook 2020; and OECD Main Economic Indicators (MEI).

Palgrave Macmillan, 1 New York Plaza, Ste. 4500, New York, NY, 10004-1562, USA, (800) 777-4643, orders@palgrave.com, https://www.palgrave.com/us; The Statesman's Yearbook, 2023.

Routledge - Taylor & Francis Group, 6000 Broken Sound Pkwy. NW, Ste. 300, Boca Raton, FL, 33487, USA, (800) 634-1420, (800) 634-7064, orders@taylorandfrancis.com, https://www.routledge.com/; The Europa World Year Book 2022.

United Nations Statistics Division (UNSD), United Nations Plz., New York, NY, 10017, USA, (800) 253-9646, (212) 963-9851, statistics@un.org, https://unstats.un.org; Statistical Yearbook of the United Nations 2021.

The World Bank, 1818 H St. NW, Washington, DC, 20433, USA, (202) 473-1000, (202) 477-6391, eds03@worldbank.org, https://www.worldbank.org/; World Development Indicators (WDI) 2022 and World Development Report 2022: Finance for an Equitable Recovery.

AUSTRALIA-HOUSING

Australian Bureau of Statistics (ABS), Locked Bag 10, Belconnen, ACT, 2616, AUS, client.services@abs.gov.au, https://www.abs.gov.au/; Regional Population by Age and Sex.

Australian Institute of Health and Welfare (AIHW), GPO Box 570, Canberra, ACT, 2601, AUS, info@aihw.gov.au, https://www.aihw.gov.au/; National Social Housing Survey 2021.

Euromonitor International, Inc., 1 N Dearborn St., Ste. 1700, Chicago, IL, 60602, USA, (312) 922-1115, (312) 922-1157, info-usa@euromonitor.com, https://www.euromonitor.com/; Geographies.

AUSTRALIA-HOUSING-FINANCE

Organization for Economic Cooperation and Development (OECD), 2001 L St. NW, Ste. 650, Washington, DC, 20036-4922, USA, (202) 785-6323, (800) 456-6323, (202) 785-0350, washington.contact@oecd.org, https://www.oecd.org/; OECD Main Economic Indicators (MEI).

AUSTRALIA-HOUSING CONSTRUCTION

See AUSTRALIA-CONSTRUCTION INDUSTRY

AUSTRALIA-ILLITERATE PERSONS

United Nations Economic and Social Commission for Asia and the Pacific (ESCAP), United Nations Building, Rajadamnern Nok Ave., Bangkok, 10200, THA, https://www.unescap.org/; Asia-Pacific Development Journal.

AUSTRALIA-IMPORTS

BC Stats, Stn Prov Govt, PO Box 9410, Victoria, BC, V8W 9V1, CAN, (250) 387-6121 (Dial from U.S.), bc.stats@gov.bc.ca, https://www2.gov.bc.ca/gov/content/data/about-data-management/bc-stats; Country Trade Profile - Australia.

Central Intelligence Agency (CIA), Office of Public Affairs, Washington, DC, 20505, USA, (703) 482-0623, https://www.cia.gov; The World Factbook.

The Economist Group: Economist Intelligence Unit (EIU), 900 3rd Ave., 16th Fl., New York, NY, 10022, USA, (212) 541-0500, americas@eiu.com, https://www.eiu.com; Australia Country Report.

International Monetary Fund (IMF), 700 19th St. NW, Washington, DC, 20431, USA, (202) 623-7000, (202) 623-4661, publications@imf.org, https://www.imf.org; Direction of Trade Statistics (DOTS).

Organization for Economic Cooperation and Development (OECD), 2001 L St. NW, Ste. 650, Washington, DC, 20036-4922, USA, (202) 785-6323, (800) 456-6323, (202) 785-0350, washington.contact@oecd.org, https://www.oecd.org/; Economic Survey of Australia 2021; OECD Digital Economy Outlook 2020; OECD Review of Fisheries 2022; OECD-FAO Agricultural Outlook 2022-2031; and STAN (STructural ANalysis) Database.

S&P Global, IHS Markit, 15 Inverness Way E, Englewood, CO, 80112, USA, (800) 447-2273, (800) 854-7179, https://ihsmarkit.com; Global Trade Atlas (GTA).

TAPPI - Technical Association of the Pulp and Paper Industry, 15 Technology Pkwy. S, Ste. 115, Peachtree Corners, GA, 30092, USA, (770) 446-1400, (800) 332-8686, (770) 446-6947, memberconnection@tappi.org, https://www.tappi.org/; TAPPI Journal.

United Nations Conference on Trade and Development (UNCTAD), Palais des Nations, Geneva, 1211, SWI, (212) 963-6896, unctadinfo@unctad.org, https://unctad.org; Handbook of Statistics 2021.

The World Bank, 1818 H St. NW, Washington, DC, 20433, USA, (202) 473-1000, (202) 477-6391, eds03@worldbank.org, https://www.worldbank.org/; World Development Report 2022: Finance for an Equitable Recovery.

World Steel Association (Worldsteel), Avenue de Tervueren 270, Brussels, B-1150, BEL, steel@worldsteel.org, https://www.worldsteel.org; Steel Statistical Yearbook 2021.

AUSTRALIA-INDUSTRIAL METALS PRODUCTION

See AUSTRALIA-MINERAL INDUSTRIES

AUSTRALIA-INDUSTRIAL PRODUCTIVITY

International Lead and Zinc Study Group (ILZSG), Rua Almirante Barroso 38, 5th Fl., Lisbon, 1000-013, PRT, sales@ilzsg.org, https://www.ilzsg.org; Interactive Statistical Database.

Organization for Economic Cooperation and Development (OECD), 2001 L St. NW, Ste. 650, Washington, DC, 20036-4922, USA, (202) 785-6323, (800) 456-6323, (202) 785-0350, washington.contact@oecd.org, https://www.oecd.org/; OECD Digital Economy Outlook 2020; OECD-FAO Agricultural Outlook 2022-2031; and STAN (STructural ANalysis) Database.

TAPPI - Technical Association of the Pulp and Paper Industry, 15 Technology Pkwy. S, Ste. 115, Peachtree Corners, GA, 30092, USA, (770) 446-1400, (800) 332-8686, (770) 446-6947, memberconnection@tappi.org, https://www.tappi.org/; TAPPI Journal.

World Steel Association (Worldsteel), Avenue de Tervueren 270, Brussels, B-1150, BEL, steel@worldsteel.org, https://www.worldsteel.org; Steel Statistical Yearbook 2021.

AUSTRALIA-INDUSTRIAL PROPERTY

World Intellectual Property Organization (WIPO), 34, chemin des Colombettes, Geneva, CH-1211, SWI, https://www.wipo.int; Madrid Yearly Review 2022: International Registrations of Marks.

AUSTRALIA-INDUSTRIES

Central Intelligence Agency (CIA), Office of Public Affairs, Washington, DC, 20505, USA, (703) 482-0623, https://www.cia.gov; The World Factbook.

The Economist Group: Economist Intelligence Unit (EIU), 900 3rd Ave., 16th Fl., New York, NY, 10022, USA, (212) 541-0500, americas@eiu.com, https://www.eiu.com; Australia Country Report.

Euromonitor International, Inc., 1 N Dearborn St., Ste. 1700, Chicago, IL, 60602, USA, (312) 922-1115, (312) 922-1157, info-usa@euromonitor.com, https://www.euromonitor.com/; Geographies.

International Labour Organization (ILO), 4 Rte. des Morillons, Geneva, CH-1211, SWI, ilo@ilo.org, https://www.ilo.org; NORMLEX Information System on International Labour Standards.

Organization for Economic Cooperation and Development (OECD), 2001 L St. NW, Ste. 650, Washington, DC, 20036-4922, USA, (202) 785-6323, (800) 456-6323, (202) 785-0350, washington.contact@oecd.org, https://www.oecd.org/; Environment Statistics; OECD Digital Economy Outlook 2020; OECD Main Economic Indicators (MEI); and STAN (STructural ANalysis) Database.

Palgrave Macmillan, 1 New York Plaza, Ste. 4500, New York, NY, 10004-1562, USA, (800) 777-4643, orders@palgrave.com, https://www.palgrave.com/us; The Statesman's Yearbook, 2023.

Routledge - Taylor & Francis Group, 6000 Broken Sound Pkwy. NW, Ste. 300, Boca Raton, FL, 33487, USA, (800) 634-1420, (800) 634-7064, orders@taylorandfrancis.com, https://www.routledge.com/; The Europa World Year Book 2022.

Tourism Research Australia (AUSTRADE), Embassy of Australia, 1145 17th St., Ste. GP410, Washington, DC, 20036, USA, (202) 454-9744, (202) 454-9760, https://www.tra.gov.au/; International Visitor Survey (IVS) Results March 2022.

United Nations Economic and Social Commission for Asia and the Pacific (ESCAP), United Nations Building, Rajadamnern Nok Ave., Bangkok, 10200, THA, https://www.unescap.org/; Asia-Pacific Development Journal and SDG Gateway Data Explorer.

United Nations Industrial Development Organization (UNIDO), 1 United Nations Plz., Rm. DC1-1118, New York, NY, 10017, USA, (212) 963-6890, (212) 963 6885, (212) 963-7904, office.newyork@unido.

org, https://www.unido.org/; Industrial Statistics Databases and International Yearbook of Industrial Statistics 2021.

The World Bank, 1818 H St. NW, Washington, DC, 20433, USA, (202) 473-1000, (202) 477-6391, eds03@worldbank.org, https://www.worldbank.org/; World Development Indicators (WDI) 2022.

World Intellectual Property Organization (WIPO), 34, chemin des Colombettes, Geneva, CH-1211, SWI, https://www.wipo.int; Madrid Yearly Review 2022: International Registrations of Marks.

AUSTRALIA-INFANT AND MATERNAL MORTALITY

See AUSTRALIA-MORTALITY

AUSTRALIA-INTEREST RATES

Organization for Economic Cooperation and Development (OECD), 2001 L St. NW, Ste. 650, Washington, DC, 20036-4922, USA, (202) 785-6323, (800) 456-6323, (202) 785-0350, washington.contact@oecd.org, https://www.oecd.org/; OECD Business and Finance Outlook 2021; OECD Digital Economy Outlook 2020; and OECD Main Economic Indicators (MEI).

AUSTRALIA-INTERNAL REVENUE

Organization for Economic Cooperation and Development (OECD), 2001 L St. NW, Ste. 650, Washington, DC, 20036-4922, USA, (202) 785-6323, (800) 456-6323, (202) 785-0350, washington.contact@oecd.org, https://www.oecd.org/; Revenue Statistics 2022.

AUSTRALIA-INTERNATIONAL FINANCE

Organization for Economic Cooperation and Development (OECD), 2001 L St. NW, Ste. 650, Washington, DC, 20036-4922, USA, (202) 785-6323, (800) 456-6323, (202) 785-0350, washington.contact@oecd.org, https://www.oecd.org/; OECD Business and Finance Outlook 2021 and OECD Digital Economy Outlook 2020.

World Bank Group: International Finance Corporation (IFC), 2121 Pennsylvania Ave. NW, Washington, DC, 20433, USA, (202) 473-1000, (202) 473-7711, (202) 974-4384, https://www.ifc.org; Annual Report 2021: Meeting the Moment.

AUSTRALIA-INTERNATIONAL LIQUIDITY

Organization for Economic Cooperation and Development (OECD), 2001 L St. NW, Ste. 650, Washington, DC, 20036-4922, USA, (202) 785-6323, (800) 456-6323, (202) 785-0350, washington.contact@oecd.org, https://www.oecd.org/; OECD Business and Finance Outlook 2021.

AUSTRALIA-INTERNATIONAL TRADE

Asia Pacific Economic Cooperation (APEC), 35 Heng Mui Keng Terrace, 119616, SGP, info@apec.org, https://www.apec.org/; APEC Regional Trends Analysis - What Goes Around Comes Around: Pivoting to a Circular Economy; Uncertainty Tests APEC's Resilience amid COVID-19.

Australian Bureau of Statistics (ABS), Locked Bag 10, Belconnen, ACT, 2616, AUS, client.services@abs.gov.au, https://www.abs.gov.au/; Key Economic Indicators.

Australian Government Department of Agriculture, Water and the Environment, GPO Box 858, Canberra, ACT, 2601, AUS, https://www.agriculture.gov.au/; Australian Agricultural Trade and the COVID-19 Pandemic.

The Economist Group: Economist Intelligence Unit (EIU), 900 3rd Ave., 16th Fl., New York, NY, 10022, USA, (212) 541-0500, americas@eiu.com, https://www.eiu.com; Australia Country Report.

Euromonitor International, Inc., 1 N Dearborn St., Ste. 1700, Chicago, IL, 60602, USA, (312) 922-1115, (312) 922-1157, info-usa@euromonitor.com, https://www.euromonitor.com/; Geographies.

Organization for Economic Cooperation and Development (OECD), 2001 L St. NW, Ste. 650, Washington, DC, 20036-4922, USA, (202) 785-6323, (800) 456-6323, (202) 785-0350, washington.contact@oecd.org, https://www.oecd.org/; Economic Survey of Australia 2021; OECD Digital Economy Outlook 2020; OECD Main Economic Indicators (MEI); and OECD-FAO Agricultural Outlook 2022-2031.

Palgrave Macmillan, 1 New York Plaza, Ste. 4500, New York, NY, 10004-1562, USA, (800) 777-4643, orders@palgrave.com, https://www.palgrave.com/us; The Statesman's Yearbook, 2023.

Routledge - Taylor & Francis Group, 6000 Broken Sound Pkwy. NW, Ste. 300, Boca Raton, FL, 33487, USA, (800) 634-1420, (800) 634-7064, orders@taylorandfrancis.com, https://www.routledge.com/; The Europa World Year Book 2022.

United Nations Conference on Trade and Development (UNCTAD), Palais des Nations, Geneva, 1211, SWI, (212) 963-6896, unctadinfo@unctad.org, https://unctad.org; Trade and Development Report 2021.

United Nations Economic and Social Commission for Asia and the Pacific (ESCAP), United Nations Building, Rajadamnern Nok Ave., Bangkok, 10200, THA, https://www.unescap.org/; Asia-Pacific Development Journal and SDG Gateway Data Explorer.

United Nations Food and Agricultural Organization (FAO), 2121 K St., Ste. 800B, Washington, DC, 20037, USA, (202) 653-2400 (Dial from U.S.), (202) 653-5760 (Fax from U.S.), fao-hq@fao.org, https://www.fao.org; The State of Food and Agriculture (SOFA) 2022.

United Nations Statistics Division (UNSD), United Nations Plz., New York, NY, 10017, USA, (800) 253-9646, (212) 963-9851, statistics@un.org, https://unstats.un.org; International Trade Statistics Yearbook 2020; Statistical Yearbook of the United Nations 2021; and United Nations Commodity Trade Statistics Database (UN Comtrade).

The World Bank, 1818 H St. NW, Washington, DC, 20433, USA, (202) 473-1000, (202) 477-6391, eds03@worldbank.org, https://www.worldbank.org/; World Development Indicators (WDI) 2022 and World Development Report 2022: Finance for an Equitable Recovery.

World Steel Association (Worldsteel), Avenue de Tervueren 270, Brussels, B-1150, BEL, steel@worldsteel.org, https://www.worldsteel.org; Steel Statistical Yearbook 2021.

World Trade Organization (WTO), Ctre. William Rappard, Rue de Lausanne 154, Case postale, Geneva, CH-1211, SWI, enquiries@wto.org, https://www.wto.org; World Trade Statistical Review 2022.

AUSTRALIA-INTERNET USERS

International Telecommunication Union (ITU), Place des Nations, Geneva, CH-1211, SWI, itumail@itu.int, https://www.itu.int; Global Connectivity Report 2022; World Telecommunication/ICT Indicators Database 2021; and Yearbook of Statistics 2019.

AUSTRALIA-INVESTMENTS

Australian Bureau of Statistics (ABS), Locked Bag 10, Belconnen, ACT, 2616, AUS, client.services@abs.gov.au, https://www.abs.gov.au/; Key Economic Indicators.

International Monetary Fund (IMF), 700 19th St. NW, Washington, DC, 20431, USA, (202) 623-7000, (202) 623-4661, publications@imf.org, https://www.imf.org; International Financial Statistics (IFS).

Organization for Economic Cooperation and Development (OECD), 2001 L St. NW, Ste. 650, Washington, DC, 20036-4922, USA, (202) 785-6323, (800) 456-6323, (202) 785-0350, washington.contact@oecd.org, https://www.oecd.org/; OECD Business and Finance Outlook 2021; OECD Digital Economy Outlook 2020; and STAN (STructural ANalysis) Database.

AUSTRALIA-LABOR

Australian Bureau of Statistics (ABS), Locked Bag 10, Belconnen, ACT, 2616, AUS, client.services@abs.gov.au, https://www.abs.gov.au/; Regional Population by Age and Sex.

Central Intelligence Agency (CIA), Office of Public Affairs, Washington, DC, 20505, USA, (703) 482-0623, https://www.cia.gov; The World Factbook.

Euromonitor International, Inc., 1 N Dearborn St., Ste. 1700, Chicago, IL, 60602, USA, (312) 922-1115, (312) 922-1157, info-usa@euromonitor.com, https://www.euromonitor.com/; Geographies.

Federal Statistical Office Germany, Gustav-Stresemann-Ring 11, Wiesbaden, D-65189, GER, https://www.destatis.de; Basic Indicators: Australia.

International Labour Organization (ILO), 4 Rte. des Morillons, Geneva, CH-1211, SWI, ilo@ilo.org, https://www.ilo.org; NORMLEX Information System on International Labour Standards.

Organization for Economic Cooperation and Development (OECD), 2001 L St. NW, Ste. 650, Washington, DC, 20036-4922, USA, (202) 785-6323, (800) 456-6323, (202) 785-0350, washington.contact@oecd.org, https://www.oecd.org/; Economic Survey of Australia 2021; OECD Digital Economy Outlook 2020; OECD Employment Outlook 2022: Building Back More Inclusive Labour Markets; and OECD Main Economic Indicators (MEI).

Palgrave Macmillan, 1 New York Plaza, Ste. 4500, New York, NY, 10004-1562, USA, (800) 777-4643, orders@palgrave.com, https://www.palgrave.com/us; The Statesman's Yearbook, 2023.

United Nations Food and Agricultural Organization (FAO), 2121 K St., Ste. 800B, Washington, DC, 20037, USA, (202) 653-2400 (Dial from U.S.), (202) 653-5760 (Fax from U.S.), fao-hq@fao.org, https://www.fao.org; The State of Food and Agriculture (SOFA) 2022.

The World Bank, 1818 H St. NW, Washington, DC, 20433, USA, (202) 473-1000, (202) 477-6391, eds03@worldbank.org, https://www.worldbank.org/; World Development Indicators (WDI) 2022 and World Development Report 2022: Finance for an Equitable Recovery.

AUSTRALIA-LAND USE

United Nations Statistics Division (UNSD), United Nations Plz., New York, NY, 10017, USA, (800) 253-9646, (212) 963-9851, statistics@un.org, https://unstats.un.org; Millennium Development Goal Indicators.

The World Bank, 1818 H St. NW, Washington, DC, 20433, USA, (202) 473-1000, (202) 477-6391, eds03@worldbank.org, https://www.worldbank.org/; World Development Report 2022: Finance for an Equitable Recovery.

AUSTRALIA-LIBRARIES

UNESCO Institute for Statistics, C.P 250 Succursale H, Montreal, QC, H3G 2K8, CAN, (514) 343-6880 (Dial from U.S.), (514) 343-5740 (Fax from U.S.), uis.publications@unesco.org, http://uis.unesco.org/; UIS.Stat.

AUSTRALIA-LIFE EXPECTANCY

Central Intelligence Agency (CIA), Office of Public Affairs, Washington, DC, 20505, USA, (703) 482-0623, https://www.cia.gov; The World Factbook.

United Nations Department of Economic and Social Affairs (DESA), Population Division, 2 United Nations Plz., Rm. DC2-1950, New York, NY, 10017, USA, (212) 963-3209, (212) 963-2147, population@un.org, https://www.un.org/development/desa/pd/; World Population Ageing 2020 Highlights.

United Nations Economic and Social Commission for Asia and the Pacific (ESCAP), United Nations Building, Rajadamnern Nok Ave., Bangkok, 10200, THA, https://www.unescap.org/; Asia-Pacific Development Journal.

United Nations Statistics Division (UNSD), United Nations Plz., New York, NY, 10017, USA, (800) 253-9646, (212) 963-9851, statistics@un.org, https://unstats.un.org; Millennium Development Goal Indicators.

AUSTRALIA-LITERACY

Euromonitor International, Inc., 1 N Dearborn St., Ste. 1700, Chicago, IL, 60602, USA, (312) 922-1115, (312) 922-1157, info-usa@euromonitor.com, https://www.euromonitor.com/; Geographies.

UNESCO Institute for Statistics, C.P 250 Succursale H, Montreal, QC, H3G 2K8, CAN, (514) 343-6880 (Dial from U.S.), (514) 343-5740 (Fax from U.S.), uis.publications@unesco.org, http://uis.unesco.org/; Literacy.

AUSTRALIA-LIVESTOCK

Australian Government Department of Agriculture, Water and the Environment, GPO Box 858, Canberra, ACT, 2601, AUS, https://www.agriculture.gov.au/; Red Meat Export Statistics 2022.

Organization for Economic Cooperation and Development (OECD), 2001 L St. NW, Ste. 650, Washington, DC, 20036-4922, USA, (202) 785-6323, (800) 456-6323, (202) 785-0350, washington.contact@oecd.org, https://www.oecd.org/; OECD-FAO Agricultural Outlook 2022-2031.

Palgrave Macmillan, 1 New York Plaza, Ste. 4500, New York, NY, 10004-1562, USA, (800) 777-4643, orders@palgrave.com, https://www.palgrave.com/us; The Statesman's Yearbook, 2023.

Routledge - Taylor & Francis Group, 6000 Broken Sound Pkwy. NW, Ste. 300, Boca Raton, FL, 33487, USA, (800) 634-1420, (800) 634-7064, orders@taylorandfrancis.com, https://www.routledge.com/; The Europa World Year Book 2022.

United Nations Food and Agricultural Organization (FAO), 2121 K St., Ste. 800B, Washington, DC, 20037, USA, (202) 653-2400 (Dial from U.S.), (202) 653-5760 (Fax from U.S.), fao-hq@fao.org, https://www.fao.org; The State of Food and Agriculture (SOFA) 2022.

United Nations Statistics Division (UNSD), United Nations Plz., New York, NY, 10017, USA, (800) 253-9646, (212) 963-9851, statistics@un.org, https://unstats.un.org; Statistical Yearbook of the United Nations 2021.

AUSTRALIA-MAGNESIUM PRODUCTION AND CONSUMPTION

See AUSTRALIA-MINERAL INDUSTRIES

AUSTRALIA-MANPOWER

United Nations Economic and Social Commission for Asia and the Pacific (ESCAP), United Nations Building, Rajadamnern Nok Ave., Bangkok, 10200, THA, https://www.unescap.org/; SDG Gateway Data Explorer.

AUSTRALIA-MANUFACTURES

Australian Bureau of Statistics (ABS), Locked Bag 10, Belconnen, ACT, 2616, AUS, client.services@abs.gov.au, https://www.abs.gov.au/; Regional Population by Age and Sex.

International Monetary Fund (IMF), 700 19th St. NW, Washington, DC, 20431, USA, (202) 623-7000, (202) 623-4661, publications@imf.org, https://www.imf.org; International Financial Statistics (IFS).

Organization for Economic Cooperation and Development (OECD), 2001 L St. NW, Ste. 650, Washington, DC, 20036-4922, USA, (202) 785-6323, (800) 456-6323, (202) 785-0350, washington.contact@oecd.org, https://www.oecd.org/; Economic Survey of Australia 2021.

AUSTRALIA-MARRIAGE

Routledge - Taylor & Francis Group, 6000 Broken Sound Pkwy. NW, Ste. 300, Boca Raton, FL, 33487, USA, (800) ,634-1420, (800) 634-7064, orders@taylorandfrancis.com, https://www.routledge.com/; The Europa World Year Book 2022.

United Nations Statistics Division (UNSD), United Nations Plz., New York, NY, 10017, USA, (800) 253-9646, (212) 963-9851, statistics@un.org, https://unstats.un.org; Statistical Yearbook of the United Nations 2021.

AUSTRALIA-MEAT INDUSTRY AND TRADE

International Monetary Fund (IMF), 700 19th St. NW, Washington, DC, 20431, USA, (202) 623-7000, (202) 623-4661, publications@imf.org, https://www.imf.org; International Financial Statistics (IFS).

AUSTRALIA-MEDICAL CARE, COST OF

Australian Institute of Health and Welfare (AIHW), GPO Box 570, Canberra, ACT, 2601, AUS, info@aihw.gov.au, https://www.aihw.gov.au/; Australia's Health 2022; Disability Support Services: Services Provided Under the National Disability Agreement 2018-2019; and Health Expenditure Australia 2020-2021.

AUSTRALIA-MERCURY PRODUCTION

See AUSTRALIA-MINERAL INDUSTRIES

AUSTRALIA-METAL PRODUCTS

United Nations Statistics Division (UNSD), United Nations Plz., New York, NY, 10017, USA, (800) 253-9646, (212) 963-9851, statistics@un.org, https://unstats.un.org; United Nations Commodity Trade Statistics Database (UN Comtrade).

AUSTRALIA-MINERAL INDUSTRIES

Australian Bureau of Statistics (ABS), Locked Bag 10, Belconnen, ACT, 2616, AUS, client.services@abs.gov.au, https://www.abs.gov.au/; Regional Population by Age and Sex.

Barchart, 209 W Jackson Blvd., 2nd Fl., Chicago, IL, 60606, USA, (877) 247-4394, commodities@barchart.com, https://www.barchart.com/cmdty; The cmdty Yearbook 2023; cmdtyStats: Commodity Statistics and Fundamental Data; cmdtyView: Commodity Index; and Commodity Data and Prices.

International Energy Agency (IEA), 9 Rue de la Federation, Paris, 75739, FRA, info@iea.org, https://www.iea.org/; Coal 2021: Analysis and Forecast to 2024; World Energy Outlook 2021; and World Energy Statistics and Balances.

International Lead and Zinc Study Group (ILZSG), Rua Almirante Barroso 38, 5th Fl., Lisbon, 1000-013, PRT, sales@ilzsg.org, https://www.ilzsg.org; Interactive Statistical Database.

International Monetary Fund (IMF), 700 19th St. NW, Washington, DC, 20431, USA, (202) 623-7000, (202) 623-4661, publications@imf.org, https://www.imf.org; International Financial Statistics (IFS).

Organization for Economic Cooperation and Development (OECD), 2001 L St. NW, Ste. 650, Washington, DC, 20036-4922, USA, (202) 785-6323, (800) 456-6323, (202) 785-0350, washington.contact@oecd.org, https://www.oecd.org/; Economic Survey of Australia 2021; Energy Prices and Taxes for OECD Countries 2020; and STAN (STructural ANalysis) Database.

Palgrave Macmillan, 1 New York Plaza, Ste. 4500, New York, NY, 10004-1562, USA, (800) 777-4643, orders@palgrave.com, https://www.palgrave.com/us; The Statesman's Yearbook, 2023.

Routledge - Taylor & Francis Group, 6000 Broken Sound Pkwy. NW, Ste. 300, Boca Raton, FL, 33487, USA, (800) 634-1420, (800) 634-7064, orders@taylorandfrancis.com, https://www.routledge.com/; The Europa World Year Book 2022.

United Nations Conference on Trade and Development (UNCTAD), Palais des Nations, Geneva, 1211, SWI, (212) 963-6896, unctadinfo@unctad.org, https://unctad.org; Trade and Development Report 2021.

United Nations Statistics Division (UNSD), United Nations Plz., New York, NY, 10017, USA, (800) 253-9646, (212) 963-9851, statistics@un.org, https://unstats.un.org; Statistical Yearbook of the United Nations 2021.

The World Bank, 1818 H St. NW, Washington, DC, 20433, USA, (202) 473-1000, (202) 477-6391, eds03@worldbank.org, https://www.worldbank.org/; World Development Indicators (WDI) 2022.

World Bureau of Metal Statistics (WBMS), 31 Star St., Ware, Hertfordshire, SG12 9BA, GBR, https://www.refinitiv.com/en/trading-solutions/world-bureau-metal-statistics; Annual Stainless Steel Statistics; Long Term Production/Consumption Series - All Metals; World Flow Charts; and World Metal Statistics.

World Steel Association (Worldsteel), Avenue de Tervueren 270, Brussels, B-1150, BEL, steel@worldsteel.org, https://www.worldsteel.org; Steel Statistical Yearbook 2021.

AUSTRALIA-MOLASSES PRODUCTION

See AUSTRALIA-CROPS

AUSTRALIA-MONEY

European Central Bank (ECB), Frankfurt am Main, D-60640, GER, info@ecb.europa.eu, https://www.ecb.europa.eu; Economic Bulletin; Monetary Developments in the Euro Area; and Research Bulletin.

Organization for Economic Cooperation and Development (OECD), 2001 L St. NW, Ste. 650, Washington, DC, 20036-4922, USA, (202) 785-6323, (800) 456-6323, (202) 785-0350, washington.contact@oecd.org, https://www.oecd.org/; Economic Survey of Australia 2021.

AUSTRALIA-MONEY SUPPLY

The Economist Group: Economist Intelligence Unit (EIU), 900 3rd Ave., 16th Fl., New York, NY, 10022, USA, (212) 541-0500, americas@eiu.com, https://www.eiu.com; Australia Country Report.

International Monetary Fund (IMF), 700 19th St. NW, Washington, DC, 20431, USA, (202) 623-7000, (202) 623-4661, publications@imf.org, https://www.imf.org; International Financial Statistics (IFS).

Routledge - Taylor & Francis Group, 6000 Broken Sound Pkwy. NW, Ste. 300, Boca Raton, FL, 33487, USA, (800) 634-1420, (800) 634-7064, orders@taylorandfrancis.com, https://www.routledge.com/; The Europa World Year Book 2022.

United Nations Statistics Division (UNSD), United Nations Plz., New York, NY, 10017, USA, (800) 253-9646, (212) 963-9851, statistics@un.org, https://unstats.un.org; Statistical Yearbook of the United Nations 2021.

AUSTRALIA-MORTALITY

UNICEF, 3 United Nations Plz., New York, NY, 10017, USA, (212) 303-7984, (917) 244-2215, https://www.unicef.org; The State of the World's Children 2023.

United Nations Economic and Social Commission for Asia and the Pacific (ESCAP), United Nations Building, Rajadamnern Nok Ave., Bangkok, 10200, THA, https://www.unescap.org/; Asia-Pacific Development Journal.

United Nations Statistics Division (UNSD), United Nations Plz., New York, NY, 10017, USA, (800) 253-9646, (212) 963-9851, statistics@un.org, https://unstats.un.org; Millennium Development Goal Indicators; Statistical Yearbook of the United Nations 2021; and World Statistics Pocketbook 2021.

The World Bank, 1818 H St. NW, Washington, DC, 20433, USA, (202) 473-1000, (202) 477-6391, eds03@worldbank.org, https://www.worldbank.org/; World Development Indicators (WDI) 2022.

World Health Organization (WHO), Ave. Appia 20, Geneva, CH-1211, SWI, (202) 974-3000 (Telephone in U.S.), publications@who.int, https://www.who.int/; Global Health Observatory (GHO).

AUSTRALIA-MOTION PICTURES

Palgrave Macmillan, 1 New York Plaza, Ste. 4500, New York, NY, 10004-1562, USA, (800) 777-4643, orders@palgrave.com, https://www.palgrave.com/us; The Statesman's Yearbook, 2023.

AUSTRALIA-MOTOR VEHICLES

International Road Federation (IRF), Madison Place, 500 Montgomery St., 5th Fl., Alexandria, VA, 22314,

USA, (703) 535-1001, (703) 535-1007, info@irf.global, https://www.irf.global/; World Road Statistics (WRS).

AUSTRALIA-NATURAL GAS PRODUCTION

See AUSTRALIA-MINERAL INDUSTRIES

AUSTRALIA-NICKEL AND NICKEL ORE

See AUSTRALIA-MINERAL INDUSTRIES

AUSTRALIA-NUTRITION

United Nations Food and Agricultural Organization (FAO), 2121 K St., Ste. 800B, Washington, DC, 20037, USA, (202) 653-2400 (Dial from U.S.), (202) 653-5760 (Fax from U.S.), fao-hq@fao.org, https://www.fao.org; The State of Food and Agriculture (SOFA) 2022.

United Nations Statistics Division (UNSD), United Nations Plz., New York, NY, 10017, USA, (800) 253-9646, (212) 963-9851, statistics@un.org, https://unstats.un.org; Millennium Development Goal Indicators.

AUSTRALIA-ORANGES PRODUCTION

See AUSTRALIA-CROPS

AUSTRALIA-PAPER

See AUSTRALIA-FORESTS AND FORESTRY

AUSTRALIA-PEANUT PRODUCTION

See AUSTRALIA-CROPS

AUSTRALIA-PESTICIDES

United Nations Food and Agricultural Organization (FAO), 2121 K St., Ste. 800B, Washington, DC, 20037, USA, (202) 653-2400 (Dial from U.S.), (202) 653-5760 (Fax from U.S.), fao-hq@fao.org, https://www.fao.org; The State of Food and Agriculture (SOFA) 2022.

AUSTRALIA-PETROLEUM INDUSTRY AND TRADE

International Energy Agency (IEA), 9 Rue de la Federation, Paris, 75739, FRA, info@iea.org, https://www.iea.org/; World Energy Outlook 2021 and World Energy Statistics and Balances.

Organization for Economic Cooperation and Development (OECD), 2001 L St. NW, Ste. 650, Washington, DC, 20036-4922, USA, (202) 785-6323, (800) 456-6323, (202) 785-0350, washington.contact@oecd.org, https://www.oecd.org/; Energy Prices and Taxes for OECD Countries 2020.

Palgrave Macmillan, 1 New York Plaza, Ste. 4500, New York, NY, 10004-1562, USA, (800) 777-4643, orders@palgrave.com, https://www.palgrave.com/us; The Statesman's Yearbook, 2023.

U.S. Energy Information Administration (EIA), 1000 Independence Ave. SW, Washington, DC, 20585, USA, (202) 586-8800, infoctr@eia.gov, https://www.eia.gov; International Energy Outlook 2021.

United Nations Food and Agricultural Organization (FAO), 2121 K St., Ste. 800B, Washington, DC, 20037, USA, (202) 653-2400 (Dial from U.S.), (202) 653-5760 (Fax from U.S.), fao-hq@fao.org, https://www.fao.org; The State of Food and Agriculture (SOFA) 2022.

United Nations Statistics Division (UNSD), United Nations Plz., New York, NY, 10017, USA, (800) 253-9646, (212) 963-9851, statistics@un.org, https://unstats.un.org; Statistical Yearbook of the United Nations 2021.

AUSTRALIA-PHOSPHATES PRODUCTION

See AUSTRALIA-MINERAL INDUSTRIES

AUSTRALIA-PLASTICS INDUSTRY AND TRADE

United Nations Statistics Division (UNSD), United Nations Plz., New York, NY, 10017, USA, (800) 253-9646, (212) 963-9851, statistics@un.org, https://unstats.un.org; Statistical Yearbook of the United Nations 2021.

AUSTRALIA-PLATINUM PRODUCTION

See AUSTRALIA-MINERAL INDUSTRIES

AUSTRALIA-POPULATION

Australian Bureau of Statistics (ABS), Locked Bag 10, Belconnen, ACT, 2616, AUS, client.services@abs.gov.au, https://www.abs.gov.au/; Aboriginal and Torres Strait Islander Peoples and Regional Population by Age and Sex.

Australian Government Department of Social Services, 71 Athllon Dr., Canberra, ACT, 2900, AUS, https://www.dss.gov.au/; Growing Up in Australia: The Longitudinal Study of Australian Children Annual Statistical Report.

Australian Institute of Family Studies, Child Family Community Australia (CFCA), 40 City Rd., Level 4, Southbank, VIC, 3006, AUS, enquiries@aifs.gov.au, https://aifs.gov.au/research_programs/child-family-community-australia; Alcohol-Related Harm in Families and Alcohol Consumption During COVID-19 and Child Wellbeing During the COVID Pandemic: Parental Concerns.

Australian Institute of Health and Welfare (AIHW), GPO Box 570, Canberra, ACT, 2601, AUS, info@aihw.gov.au, https://www.aihw.gov.au/; Adoptions Australia 2021-2022; Australia's Welfare 2021; Child Protection Australia 2020-2021; Disability Support Services: Services Provided Under the National Disability Agreement 2018-2019; Health Expenditure Australia 2020-2021; Heart, Stroke and Vascular Disease: Australian Facts; Incidence of Insulin-Treated Diabetes in Australia; and National Social Housing Survey 2021.

Central Intelligence Agency (CIA), Office of Public Affairs, Washington, DC, 20505, USA, (703) 482-0623, https://www.cia.gov; The World Factbook.

The Economist Group: Economist Intelligence Unit (EIU), 900 3rd Ave., 16th Fl., New York, NY, 10022, USA, (212) 541-0500, americas@eiu.com, https://www.eiu.com; Australia Country Report.

Federal Statistical Office Germany, Gustav-Stresemann-Ring 11, Wiesbaden, D-65189, GER, https://www.destatis.de; Basic Indicators: Australia.

Infoplease, c/o Sandbox Networks, Inc., 1 Lincoln St., 24th Fl., Boston, MA, 02111, USA, https://www.infoplease.com; Countries of the World.

International Labour Organization (ILO), 4 Rte. des Morillons, Geneva, CH-1211, SWI, ilo@ilo.org, https://www.ilo.org; NORMLEX Information System on International Labour Standards.

Organization for Economic Cooperation and Development (OECD), 2001 L St. NW, Ste. 650, Washington, DC, 20036-4922, USA, (202) 785-6323, (800) 456-6323, (202) 785-0350, washington.contact@oecd.org, https://www.oecd.org/; OECD Labour Force Statistics 2022.

Palgrave Macmillan, 1 New York Plaza, Ste. 4500, New York, NY, 10004-1562, USA, (800) 777-4643, orders@palgrave.com, https://www.palgrave.com/us; The Statesman's Yearbook, 2023.

Routledge - Taylor & Francis Group, 6000 Broken Sound Pkwy. NW, Ste. 300, Boca Raton, FL, 33487, USA, (800) 634-1420, (800) 634-7064, orders@taylorandfrancis.com, https://www.routledge.com/; The Europa World Year Book 2022.

UK Data Service, University of Essex, Wivenhoe Park, Colchester, Essex, CO4 3SQ, GBR, https://ukdataservice.ac.uk/; International Aggregate Data.

United Nations Department of Economic and Social Affairs (DESA), Population Division, 2 United Nations Plz., Rm. DC2-1950, New York, NY, 10017, USA, (212) 963-3209, (212) 963-2147, population@un.org, https://www.un.org/development/desa/pd/; Revision of World Urbanization Prospects and World Population Ageing 2020 Highlights.

United Nations Development Programme (UNDP), One United Nations Plz., New York, NY, 10017, USA, (212) 906-5000, (212) 906-5001, https://www.undp.org; Human Development Report 2021-2022.

United Nations Economic and Social Commission for Asia and the Pacific (ESCAP), United Nations Building, Rajadamnern Nok Ave., Bangkok, 10200, THA, https://www.unescap.org/; Asia-Pacific Development Journal and SDG Gateway Data Explorer.

United Nations Statistics Division (UNSD), United Nations Plz., New York, NY, 10017, USA, (800) 253-9646, (212) 963-9851, statistics@un.org, https://unstats.un.org; Statistical Yearbook of the United Nations 2021 and World Statistics Pocketbook 2021.

University of Sydney, Sydney School of Public Health, GunPolicy.org, Edward Ford Bldg. , Sydney, NSW, 2006, AUS, ssph.education-support@sydney.edu.au, https://www.gunpolicy.org/; Mass Gun Killings in Australia, 1971-2022.

The World Bank, 1818 H St. NW, Washington, DC, 20433, USA, (202) 473-1000, (202) 477-6391, eds03@worldbank.org, https://www.worldbank.org/; The Global Findex Database 2021 and World Development Report 2022: Finance for an Equitable Recovery.

AUSTRALIA-POPULATION DENSITY

Central Intelligence Agency (CIA), Office of Public Affairs, Washington, DC, 20505, USA, (703) 482-0623, https://www.cia.gov; The World Factbook.

Palgrave Macmillan, 1 New York Plaza, Ste. 4500, New York, NY, 10004-1562, USA, (800) 777-4643, orders@palgrave.com, https://www.palgrave.com/us; The Statesman's Yearbook, 2023.

Routledge - Taylor & Francis Group, 6000 Broken Sound Pkwy. NW, Ste. 300, Boca Raton, FL, 33487, USA, (800) 634-1420, (800) 634-7064, orders@taylorandfrancis.com, https://www.routledge.com/; The Europa World Year Book 2022.

The World Bank, 1818 H St. NW, Washington, DC, 20433, USA, (202) 473-1000, (202) 477-6391, eds03@worldbank.org, https://www.worldbank.org/; World Development Report 2022: Finance for an Equitable Recovery.

AUSTRALIA-POSTAL SERVICE

Palgrave Macmillan, 1 New York Plaza, Ste. 4500, New York, NY, 10004-1562, USA, (800) 777-4643, orders@palgrave.com, https://www.palgrave.com/us; The Statesman's Yearbook, 2023.

AUSTRALIA-POULTRY

See AUSTRALIA-LIVESTOCK

AUSTRALIA-POWER RESOURCES

Australian Bureau of Statistics (ABS), Locked Bag 10, Belconnen, ACT, 2616, AUS, client.services@abs.gov.au, https://www.abs.gov.au/; Regional Population by Age and Sex.

Euromonitor International, Inc., 1 N Dearborn St., Ste. 1700, Chicago, IL, 60602, USA, (312) 922-1115, (312) 922-1157, info-usa@euromonitor.com, https://www.euromonitor.com/; Geographies.

International Energy Agency (IEA), 9 Rue de la Federation, Paris, 75739, FRA, info@iea.org, https://www.iea.org/; Coal 2021: Analysis and Forecast to 2024 and World Energy Outlook 2021.

Organization for Economic Cooperation and Development (OECD), 2001 L St. NW, Ste. 650, Washington, DC, 20036-4922, USA, (202) 785-6323, (800) 456-6323, (202) 785-0350, washington.contact@oecd.org, https://www.oecd.org/; Energy Prices and Taxes for OECD Countries 2020 and Environment Statistics.

Palgrave Macmillan, 1 New York Plaza, Ste. 4500, New York, NY, 10004-1562, USA, (800) 777-4643, orders@palgrave.com, https://www.palgrave.com/us; The Statesman's Yearbook, 2023.

S&P Global Commodity Insights, One World Trade Center, New York, NY, 10007, USA, (800) 752-8878, support@platts.com, https://www.spglobal.com/commodityinsights/en; Platts Asia Pacific / Arab Gulf Marketscan (APAG Marketscan).

U.S. Energy Information Administration (EIA), 1000 Independence Ave. SW, Washington, DC, 20585, USA, (202) 586-8800, infoctr@eia.gov, https://www.eia.gov; International Energy Outlook 2021.

United Nations Economic and Social Commission for Asia and the Pacific (ESCAP), United Nations Building, Rajadamnern Nok Ave., Bangkok, 10200, THA, https://www.unescap.org/; Asia-Pacific Development Journal.

United Nations Statistics Division (UNSD), United Nations Plz., New York, NY, 10017, USA, (800) 253-9646, (212) 963-9851, statistics@un.org, https://unstats.un.org; Energy Statistics Yearbook 2019; Statistical Yearbook of the United Nations 2021; and World Statistics Pocketbook 2021.

The World Bank, 1818 H St. NW, Washington, DC, 20433, USA, (202) 473-1000, (202) 477-6391, eds03@worldbank.org, https://www.worldbank.org/; World Development Report 2022: Finance for an Equitable Recovery.

AUSTRALIA-PRICES

Euromonitor International, Inc., 1 N Dearborn St., Ste. 1700, Chicago, IL, 60602, USA, (312) 922-1115, (312) 922-1157, info-usa@euromonitor.com, https://www.euromonitor.com/; Geographies.

International Monetary Fund (IMF), 700 19th St. NW, Washington, DC, 20431, USA, (202) 623-7000, (202) 623-4661, publications@imf.org, https://www.imf.org; International Financial Statistics (IFS).

Organization for Economic Cooperation and Development (OECD), 2001 L St. NW, Ste. 650, Washington, DC, 20036-4922, USA, (202) 785-6323, (800) 456-6323, (202) 785-0350, washington.contact@oecd.org, https://www.oecd.org/; OECD Digital Economy Outlook 2020 and OECD Main Economic Indicators (MEI).

TAPPI - Technical Association of the Pulp and Paper Industry, 15 Technology Pkwy. S, Ste. 115, Peachtree Corners, GA, 30092, USA, (770) 446-1400, (800) 332-8686, (770) 446-6947, memberconnection@tappi.org, https://www.tappi.org/; TAPPI Journal.

World Bureau of Metal Statistics (WBMS), 31 Star St., Ware, Hertfordshire, SG12 9BA, GBR, https://www.refinitiv.com/en/trading-solutions/world-bureau-metal-statistics; Long Term Production/Consumption Series - All Metals; World Flow Charts; and World Metal Statistics.

AUSTRALIA-PUBLIC HEALTH

Australia's National Research Organisation for Women's Safety Limited (ANROWS), Queen Victoria Bldg., PO Box Q389, New South Wales, NSW, 1230, AUS, enquiries@anrows.org.au, https://www.anrows.org.au/; It Depends on What the Definition of Domestic Violence Is: How Young Australians Conceptualise Domestic Violence and Abuse.

Australian Bureau of Statistics (ABS), Locked Bag 10, Belconnen, ACT, 2616, AUS, client.services@abs.gov.au, https://www.abs.gov.au/; Regional Population by Age and Sex.

Australian Government Department of Agriculture, Water and the Environment, GPO Box 858, Canberra, ACT, 2601, AUS, https://www.agriculture.gov.au/; Australian Agricultural Trade and the COVID-19 Pandemic.

Australian Government Department of Health and Aged Care, GPO Box 9848, Canberra, ACT, 2601, AUS, enquiries@health.gov.au, https://www.health.gov.au/; Australian Statistics on Medicines; Medicare Data, Statistics and Reporting; and Pharmaceutical Benefits Scheme Expenditure and Prescriptions 1 July 2021 to 30 June 2022.

Australian Government Department of Social Services, 71 Athllon Dr., Canberra, ACT, 2900, AUS, https://www.dss.gov.au/; Growing Up in Australia: The Longitudinal Study of Australian Children Annual Statistical Report.

Australian Institute of Family Studies, Child Family Community Australia (CFCA), 40 City Rd., Level 4, Southbank, VIC, 3006, AUS, enquiries@aifs.gov.au, https://aifs.gov.au/research_programs/child-family-community-australia; Alcohol-Related Harm in Families and Alcohol Consumption During COVID-19 and Child Wellbeing During the COVID Pandemic: Parental Concerns.

Australian Institute of Health and Welfare (AIHW), GPO Box 570, Canberra, ACT, 2601, AUS, info@aihw.gov.au, https://www.aihw.gov.au/; Australia's Health 2022; Child Protection Australia 2020-2021; Health Expenditure Australia 2020-2021; Heart, Stroke and Vascular Disease: Australian Facts; and Incidence of Insulin-Treated Diabetes in Australia.

Euromonitor International, Inc., 1 N Dearborn St., Ste. 1700, Chicago, IL, 60602, USA, (312) 922-1115, (312) 922-1157, info-usa@euromonitor.com, https://www.euromonitor.com/; Geographies and Market Research on the Health and Wellness Industry.

Organization for Economic Cooperation and Development (OECD), 2001 L St. NW, Ste. 650, Washington, DC, 20036-4922, USA, (202) 785-6323, (800) 456-6323, (202) 785-0350, washington.contact@oecd.org, https://www.oecd.org/; Health at a Glance 2021.

Palgrave Macmillan, 1 New York Plaza, Ste. 4500, New York, NY, 10004-1562, USA, (800) 777-4643, orders@palgrave.com, https://www.palgrave.com/us; The Statesman's Yearbook, 2023.

U.S. Census Bureau, 4600 Silver Hill Rd., Washington, DC, 20233, USA, (301) 763-4636, (800) 923-8282, https://www.census.gov; HIV/AIDS Surveillance Data Base.

UNICEF, 3 United Nations Plz., New York, NY, 10017, USA, (212) 303-7984, (917) 244-2215, https://www.unicef.org; The State of the World's Children 2023.

United Nations Department of Economic and Social Affairs (DESA), Population Division, 2 United Nations Plz., Rm. DC2-1950, New York, NY, 10017, USA, (212) 963-3209, (212) 963-2147, population@un.org, https://www.un.org/development/desa/pd/; World Fertility Data 2019.

United Nations Development Programme (UNDP), One United Nations Plz., New York, NY, 10017, USA, (212) 906-5000, (212) 906-5001, https://www.undp.org; Human Development Report 2021-2022.

United Nations Economic and Social Commission for Asia and the Pacific (ESCAP), United Nations Building, Rajadamnern Nok Ave., Bangkok, 10200, THA, https://www.unescap.org/; Asia-Pacific Development Journal.

United Nations Statistics Division (UNSD), United Nations Plz., New York, NY, 10017, USA, (800) 253-9646, (212) 963-9851, statistics@un.org, https://unstats.un.org; Millennium Development Goal Indicators and Statistical Yearbook of the United Nations 2021.

University of Sydney, Sydney School of Public Health, GunPolicy.org, Edward Ford Bldg. , Sydney, NSW, 2006, AUS, ssph.education-support@sydney.edu.au, https://www.gunpolicy.org/; From Policy Inertia to World Leader: Australia's 'Perfect Storm' of Gun Control and Mass Gun Killings in Australia, 1971-2022.

World Health Organization (WHO), Ave. Appia 20, Geneva, CH-1211, SWI, (202) 974-3000 (Telephone in U.S.), publications@who.int, https://www.who.int/; Global Health Observatory (GHO) and Health Statistics and Information Systems.

AUSTRALIA-PUBLISHERS AND PUBLISHING

Palgrave Macmillan, 1 New York Plaza, Ste. 4500, New York, NY, 10004-1562, USA, (800) 777-4643, orders@palgrave.com, https://www.palgrave.com/us; The Statesman's Yearbook, 2023.

Routledge - Taylor & Francis Group, 6000 Broken Sound Pkwy. NW, Ste. 300, Boca Raton, FL, 33487, USA, (800) 634-1420, (800) 634-7064, orders@taylorandfrancis.com, https://www.routledge.com/; The Europa World Year Book 2022.

UNESCO Institute for Statistics, C.P 250 Succursale H, Montreal, QC, H3G 2K8, CAN, (514) 343-6880 (Dial from U.S.), (514) 343-5740 (Fax from U.S.), uis.publications@unesco.org, http://uis.unesco.org/; UIS.Stat.

AUSTRALIA-RAILROADS

Janes, USA, (703) 574-7580, (888) 977-1519, customer.care@janes.com, https://www.janes.com; Janes World Railways 2021-2022.

Palgrave Macmillan, 1 New York Plaza, Ste. 4500, New York, NY, 10004-1562, USA, (800) 777-4643, orders@palgrave.com, https://www.palgrave.com/us; The Statesman's Yearbook, 2023.

Routledge - Taylor & Francis Group, 6000 Broken Sound Pkwy. NW, Ste. 300, Boca Raton, FL, 33487, USA, (800) 634-1420, (800) 634-7064, orders@taylorandfrancis.com, https://www.routledge.com/; The Europa World Year Book 2022.

United Nations Statistics Division (UNSD), United Nations Plz., New York, NY, 10017, USA, (800) 253-9646, (212) 963-9851, statistics@un.org, https://unstats.un.org; Statistical Yearbook of the United Nations 2021.

AUSTRALIA-RECREATION

Australian Bureau of Statistics (ABS), Locked Bag 10, Belconnen, ACT, 2616, AUS, client.services@abs.gov.au, https://www.abs.gov.au/; Regional Population by Age and Sex.

AUSTRALIA-RELIGION

Central Intelligence Agency (CIA), Office of Public Affairs, Washington, DC, 20505, USA, (703) 482-0623, https://www.cia.gov; The World Factbook.

Palgrave Macmillan, 1 New York Plaza, Ste. 4500, New York, NY, 10004-1562, USA, (800) 777-4643, orders@palgrave.com, https://www.palgrave.com/us; The Statesman's Yearbook, 2023.

AUSTRALIA-RETAIL TRADE

Australian Bureau of Statistics (ABS), Locked Bag 10, Belconnen, ACT, 2616, AUS, client.services@abs.gov.au, https://www.abs.gov.au/; Regional Population by Age and Sex.

Euromonitor International, Inc., 1 N Dearborn St., Ste. 1700, Chicago, IL, 60602, USA, (312) 922-1115, (312) 922-1157, info-usa@euromonitor.com, https://www.euromonitor.com/; Geographies and Market Research on the Retailing Industry.

United Nations Statistics Division (UNSD), United Nations Plz., New York, NY, 10017, USA, (800) 253-9646, (212) 963-9851, statistics@un.org, https://unstats.un.org; Statistical Yearbook of the United Nations 2021.

AUSTRALIA-RICE PRODUCTION

See AUSTRALIA-CROPS

AUSTRALIA-ROADS

International Road Federation (IRF), Madison Place, 500 Montgomery St., 5th Fl., Alexandria, VA, 22314, USA, (703) 535-1001, (703) 535-1007, info@irf.global, https://www.irf.global/; World Road Statistics (WRS).

AUSTRALIA-RUBBER INDUSTRY AND TRADE

International Rubber Study Group (IRSG), 51 Changi Business Park Central 2, Unit No. 6, 486066, SGP, https://www.rubberstudy.org; Monthly Rubber Bulletin (MRB); Rubber Industry Report; Rubber Statistical Bulletin; and World Rubber Industry Report (WRIO).

United Nations Statistics Division (UNSD), United Nations Plz., New York, NY, 10017, USA, (800) 253-9646, (212) 963-9851, statistics@un.org, https://unstats.un.org; Statistical Yearbook of the United Nations 2021.

AUSTRALIA-SHIPPING

Routledge - Taylor & Francis Group, 6000 Broken Sound Pkwy. NW, Ste. 300, Boca Raton, FL, 33487,

USA, (800) 634-1420, (800) 634-7064, orders@taylorandfrancis.com, https://www.routledge.com/; The Europa World Year Book 2022.

S&P Global, IHS Markit, 15 Inverness Way E, Englewood, CO, 80112, USA, (800) 447-2273, (800) 854-7179, https://ihsmarkit.com; IHS Maritime World Shipbuilding Statistics; Journal of Commerce; Lloyd's Register of Ships 2021-2022; and Maritime Portal Desktop.

United Nations Statistics Division (UNSD), United Nations Plz., New York, NY, 10017, USA, (800) 253-9646, (212) 963-9851, statistics@un.org, https://unstats.un.org; Statistical Yearbook of the United Nations 2021.

AUSTRALIA-SOYBEAN PRODUCTION

See AUSTRALIA-CROPS

AUSTRALIA-STEEL PRODUCTION

See AUSTRALIA-MINERAL INDUSTRIES

AUSTRALIA-SUGAR PRODUCTION

See AUSTRALIA-CROPS

AUSTRALIA-SULPHUR PRODUCTION

See AUSTRALIA-MINERAL INDUSTRIES

AUSTRALIA-TAXATION

International Road Federation (IRF), Madison Place, 500 Montgomery St., 5th Fl., Alexandria, VA, 22314, USA, (703) 535-1001, (703) 535-1007, info@irf.global, https://www.irf.global/; World Road Statistics (WRS).

Organization for Economic Cooperation and Development (OECD), 2001 L St. NW, Ste. 650, Washington, DC, 20036-4922, USA, (202) 785-6323, (800) 456-6323, (202) 785-0350, washington.contact@oecd.org, https://www.oecd.org/; Revenue Statistics 2022.

Palgrave Macmillan, 1 New York Plaza, Ste. 4500, New York, NY, 10004-1562, USA, (800) 777-4643, orders@palgrave.com, https://www.palgrave.com/us; The Statesman's Yearbook, 2023.

The World Bank, 1818 H St. NW, Washington, DC, 20433, USA, (202) 473-1000, (202) 477-6391, eds03@worldbank.org, https://www.worldbank.org/; World Development Indicators (WDI) 2022.

AUSTRALIA-TEA PRODUCTION

See AUSTRALIA-CROPS

AUSTRALIA-TEXTILE INDUSTRY

Euromonitor International, Inc., 1 N Dearborn St., Ste. 1700, Chicago, IL, 60602, USA, (312) 922-1115, (312) 922-1157, info-usa@euromonitor.com, https://www.euromonitor.com/; Market Research on the Retailing Industry.

International Monetary Fund (IMF), 700 19th St. NW, Washington, DC, 20431, USA, (202) 623-7000, (202) 623-4661, publications@imf.org, https://www.imf.org; International Financial Statistics (IFS).

Organization for Economic Cooperation and Development (OECD), 2001 L St. NW, Ste. 650, Washington, DC, 20036-4922, USA, (202) 785-6323, (800) 456-6323, (202) 785-0350, washington.contact@oecd.org, https://www.oecd.org/; OECD-FAO Agricultural Outlook 2022-2031 and STAN (STructural ANalysis) Database.

Palgrave Macmillan, 1 New York Plaza, Ste. 4500, New York, NY, 10004-1562, USA, (800) 777-4643, orders@palgrave.com, https://www.palgrave.com/us; The Statesman's Yearbook, 2023.

United Nations Statistics Division (UNSD), United Nations Plz., New York, NY, 10017, USA, (800) 253-9646, (212) 963-9851, statistics@un.org, https://unstats.un.org; Statistical Yearbook of the United Nations 2021 and United Nations Commodity Trade Statistics Database (UN Comtrade).

AUSTRALIA-TOBACCO INDUSTRY

Organization for Economic Cooperation and Development (OECD), 2001 L St. NW, Ste. 650, Washington, DC, 20036-4922, USA, (202) 785-6323, (800) 456-6323, (202) 785-0350, washington.contact@oecd.org, https://www.oecd.org/; STAN (STructural ANalysis) Database.

United Nations Statistics Division (UNSD), United Nations Plz., New York, NY, 10017, USA, (800) 253-9646, (212) 963-9851, statistics@un.org, https://unstats.un.org; Statistical Yearbook of the United Nations 2021.

AUSTRALIA-TOURISM

Euromonitor International, Inc., 1 N Dearborn St., Ste. 1700, Chicago, IL, 60602, USA, (312) 922-1115, (312) 922-1157, info-usa@euromonitor.com, https://www.euromonitor.com/; Geographies.

Organization for Economic Cooperation and Development (OECD), 2001 L St. NW, Ste. 650, Washington, DC, 20036-4922, USA, (202) 785-6323, (800) 456-6323, (202) 785-0350, washington.contact@oecd.org, https://www.oecd.org/; OECD Tourism Trends and Policies 2022.

Palgrave Macmillan, 1 New York Plaza, Ste. 4500, New York, NY, 10004-1562, USA, (800) 777-4643, orders@palgrave.com, https://www.palgrave.com/us; The Statesman's Yearbook, 2023.

Routledge - Taylor & Francis Group, 6000 Broken Sound Pkwy. NW, Ste. 300, Boca Raton, FL, 33487, USA, (800) 634-1420, (800) 634-7064, orders@taylorandfrancis.com, https://www.routledge.com/; The Europa World Year Book 2022.

Tourism Research Australia (AUSTRADE), Embassy of Australia, 1145 17th St., Ste. GP410, Washington, DC, 20036, USA, (202) 454-9744, (202) 454-9760, https://www.tra.gov.au/; International Visitor Survey (IVS) Results March 2022.

United Nations Statistics Division (UNSD), United Nations Plz., New York, NY, 10017, USA, (800) 253-9646, (212) 963-9851, statistics@un.org, https://unstats.un.org; Statistical Yearbook of the United Nations 2021.

United Nations World Tourism Organization (UNWTO), Calle Poeta Joan Maragall 42, Madrid, 28020, SPA, info@unwto.org, https://www.unwto.org/; Yearbook of Tourism Statistics, 2021 Edition.

AUSTRALIA-TRADE

See AUSTRALIA-INTERNATIONAL TRADE

AUSTRALIA-TRANSPORTATION

Australian Bureau of Statistics (ABS), Locked Bag 10, Belconnen, ACT, 2616, AUS, client.services@abs.gov.au, https://www.abs.gov.au/; Regional Population by Age and Sex.

Central Intelligence Agency (CIA), Office of Public Affairs, Washington, DC, 20505, USA, (703) 482-0623, https://www.cia.gov; The World Factbook.

Euromonitor International, Inc., 1 N Dearborn St., Ste. 1700, Chicago, IL, 60602, USA, (312) 922-1115, (312) 922-1157, info-usa@euromonitor.com, https://www.euromonitor.com/; Geographies.

Palgrave Macmillan, 1 New York Plaza, Ste. 4500, New York, NY, 10004-1562, USA, (800) 777-4643, orders@palgrave.com, https://www.palgrave.com/us; The Statesman's Yearbook, 2023.

Routledge - Taylor & Francis Group, 6000 Broken Sound Pkwy. NW, Ste. 300, Boca Raton, FL, 33487, USA, (800) 634-1420, (800) 634-7064, orders@taylorandfrancis.com, https://www.routledge.com/; The Europa World Year Book 2022.

United Nations Economic and Social Commission for Asia and the Pacific (ESCAP), United Nations Building, Rajadamnern Nok Ave., Bangkok, 10200, THA, https://www.unescap.org/; SDG Gateway Data Explorer.

AUSTRALIA-TRAVEL COSTS

Australian Bureau of Statistics (ABS), Locked Bag 10, Belconnen, ACT, 2616, AUS, client.services@abs.gov.au, https://www.abs.gov.au/; Regional Population by Age and Sex.

Tourism Research Australia (AUSTRADE), Embassy of Australia, 1145 17th St., Ste. GP410, Washington, DC, 20036, USA, (202) 454-9744, (202) 454-9760, https://www.tra.gov.au/; International Visitor Survey (IVS) Results March 2022.

AUSTRALIA-UNEMPLOYMENT

Australian Bureau of Statistics (ABS), Locked Bag 10, Belconnen, ACT, 2616, AUS, client.services@abs.gov.au, https://www.abs.gov.au/; Regional Population by Age and Sex.

International Labour Organization (ILO), 4 Rte. des Morillons, Geneva, CH-1211, SWI, ilo@ilo.org, https://www.ilo.org; NORMLEX Information System on International Labour Standards.

Organization for Economic Cooperation and Development (OECD), 2001 L St. NW, Ste. 650, Washington, DC, 20036-4922, USA, (202) 785-6323, (800) 456-6323, (202) 785-0350, washington.contact@oecd.org, https://www.oecd.org/; Economic Survey of Australia 2021; OECD Composite Leading Indicator (CLI); OECD Employment Outlook 2022: Building Back More Inclusive Labour Markets; and OECD Labour Force Statistics 2022.

Palgrave Macmillan, 1 New York Plaza, Ste. 4500, New York, NY, 10004-1562, USA, (800) 777-4643, orders@palgrave.com, https://www.palgrave.com/us; The Statesman's Yearbook, 2023.

United Nations Statistics Division (UNSD), United Nations Plz., New York, NY, 10017, USA, (800) 253-9646, (212) 963-9851, statistics@un.org, https://unstats.un.org; Statistical Yearbook of the United Nations 2021.

AUSTRALIA-URANIUM PRODUCTION AND CONSUMPTION

See AUSTRALIA-MINERAL INDUSTRIES

AUSTRALIA-VITAL STATISTICS

Australian Bureau of Statistics (ABS), Locked Bag 10, Belconnen, ACT, 2616, AUS, client.services@abs.gov.au, https://www.abs.gov.au/; Regional Population by Age and Sex.

Australian Institute of Health and Welfare (AIHW), GPO Box 570, Canberra, ACT, 2601, AUS, info@aihw.gov.au, https://www.aihw.gov.au/; Adoptions Australia 2021-2022 and Disability Support Services: Services Provided Under the National Disability Agreement 2018-2019.

Palgrave Macmillan, 1 New York Plaza, Ste. 4500, New York, NY, 10004-1562, USA, (800) 777-4643, orders@palgrave.com, https://www.palgrave.com/us; The Statesman's Yearbook, 2023.

U.S. Census Bureau, 4600 Silver Hill Rd., Washington, DC, 20233, USA, (301) 763-4636, (800) 923-8282, https://www.census.gov; HIV/AIDS Surveillance Data Base.

United Nations Department of Economic and Social Affairs (DESA), Population Division, 2 United Nations Plz., Rm. DC2-1950, New York, NY, 10017, USA, (212) 963-3209, (212) 963-2147, population@un.org, https://www.un.org/development/desa/pd/; World Contraceptive Use 2021: Estimates and Projections of Family Planning Indicators and World Marriage Data 2019.

United Nations Economic and Social Commission for Asia and the Pacific (ESCAP), United Nations Building, Rajadamnern Nok Ave., Bangkok, 10200, THA, https://www.unescap.org/; Asia-Pacific Development Journal.

United Nations Statistics Division (UNSD), United Nations Plz., New York, NY, 10017, USA, (800) 253-9646, (212) 963-9851, statistics@un.org, https://unstats.un.org; Statistical Yearbook of the United Nations 2021 and United Nations Demographic Yearbook 2020.

University of Sydney, Sydney School of Public Health, GunPolicy.org, Edward Ford Bldg. , Sydney, NSW, 2006, AUS, ssph.education-support@sydney.edu.au, https://www.gunpolicy.org/; Mass Gun Killings in Australia, 1971-2022.

The World Bank, 1818 H St. NW, Washington, DC, 20433, USA, (202) 473-1000, (202) 477-6391,

eds03@worldbank.org, https://www.worldbank.org/; World Development Indicators (WDI) 2022.

AUSTRALIA-WAGES

Australian Bureau of Statistics (ABS), Locked Bag 10, Belconnen, ACT, 2616, AUS, client.services@abs.gov.au, https://www.abs.gov.au/; Regional Population by Age and Sex.

International Labour Organization (ILO), 4 Rte. des Morillons, Geneva, CH-1211, SWI, ilo@ilo.org, https://www.ilo.org; NORMLEX Information System on International Labour Standards.

Organization for Economic Cooperation and Development (OECD), 2001 L St. NW, Ste. 650, Washington, DC, 20036-4922, USA, (202) 785-6323, (800) 456-6323, (202) 785-0350, washington.contact@oecd.org, https://www.oecd.org/; OECD Digital Economy Outlook 2020; OECD Main Economic Indicators (MEI); and STAN (STructural ANalysis) Database.

United Nations Statistics Division (UNSD), United Nations Plz., New York, NY, 10017, USA, (800) 253-9646, (212) 963-9851, statistics@un.org, https://unstats.un.org; Statistical Yearbook of the United Nations 2021.

AUSTRALIA-WEATHER

See AUSTRALIA-CLIMATE

AUSTRALIA-WHALES

See AUSTRALIA-FISHERIES

AUSTRALIA-WHEAT PRODUCTION

See AUSTRALIA-CROPS

AUSTRALIA-WHOLESALE PRICE INDEXES

International Monetary Fund (IMF), 700 19th St. NW, Washington, DC, 20431, USA, (202) 623-7000, (202) 623-4661, publications@imf.org, https://www.imf.org; International Financial Statistics (IFS).

AUSTRALIA-WHOLESALE TRADE

United Nations Statistics Division (UNSD), United Nations Plz., New York, NY, 10017, USA, (800) 253-9646, (212) 963-9851, statistics@un.org, https://unstats.un.org; Statistical Yearbook of the United Nations 2021.

AUSTRALIA-WOOD AND WOOD PULP

See AUSTRALIA-FORESTS AND FORESTRY

AUSTRALIA-WOOD PRODUCTS

Organization for Economic Cooperation and Development (OECD), 2001 L St. NW, Ste. 650, Washington, DC, 20036-4922, USA, (202) 785-6323, (800) 456-6323, (202) 785-0350, washington.contact@oecd.org, https://www.oecd.org/; STAN (STructural ANalysis) Database.

United Nations Statistics Division (UNSD), United Nations Plz., New York, NY, 10017, USA, (800) 253-9646, (212) 963-9851, statistics@un.org, https://unstats.un.org; United Nations Commodity Trade Statistics Database (UN Comtrade).

AUSTRALIA-WOOL PRODUCTION

See AUSTRALIA-TEXTILE INDUSTRY

AUSTRALIA-ZINC AND ZINC ORE

See AUSTRALIA-MINERAL INDUSTRIES

AUSTRIA-NATIONAL STATISTICAL OFFICE

Statistics Austria, Guglgasse 13, Vienna, A-1110, AUT, info@statistik.gv.at, https://www.statistik.at; National Data Reports (Austria).

AUSTRIA-PRIMARY STATISTICS SOURCES

European Commission, Eurostat, Luxembourg, 2920, LUX, https://ec.europa.eu/eurostat/; Key Figures on Enlargement Countries, 2019.

Statistics Austria, Guglgasse 13, Vienna, A-1110, AUT, info@statistik.gv.at, https://www.statistik.at; Statistical Yearbook of Austria, 2023.

AUSTRIA-DATABASES

Austrian Institute of Economic Research (WIFO), Arsenal, Objekt 20, Vienna, A-1030, AUT, office@wifo.ac.at, https://www.wifo.ac.at/en; WIFO Economic Data Service.

Statistics Austria, Guglgasse 13, Vienna, A-1110, AUT, info@statistik.gv.at, https://www.statistik.at; STATcube - Statistical Database.

AUSTRIA-AGRICULTURE

The Economist Group: Economist Intelligence Unit (EIU), 900 3rd Ave., 16th Fl., New York, NY, 10022, USA, (212) 541-0500, americas@eiu.com, https://www.eiu.com; Austria Country Report.

Euromonitor International, Inc., 1 N Dearborn St., Ste. 1700, Chicago, IL, 60602, USA, (312) 922-1115, (312) 922-1157, info-usa@euromonitor.com, https://www.euromonitor.com/; Geographies.

European Commission, Rue de la Loi, 170, Brussels, B-1040, BEL, https://ec.europa.eu; Common Agricultural Policy (CAPF) Context Indicators, 2019 Update.

European Commission, Eurostat, Luxembourg, 2920, LUX, https://ec.europa.eu/eurostat/; Farmers and the Agricultural Labour Force - Statistics.

Organization for Economic Cooperation and Development (OECD), 2001 L St. NW, Ste. 650, Washington, DC, 20036-4922, USA, (202) 785-6323, (800) 456-6323, (202) 785-0350, washington.contact@oecd.org, https://www.oecd.org/; Economic Survey of Austria 2021; OECD-FAO Agricultural Outlook 2022-2031; and STAN (STructural ANalysis) Database.

Palgrave Macmillan, 1 New York Plaza, Ste. 4500, New York, NY, 10004-1562, USA, (800) 777-4643, orders@palgrave.com, https://www.palgrave.com/us; The Statesman's Yearbook, 2023.

Routledge - Taylor & Francis Group, 6000 Broken Sound Pkwy. NW, Ste. 300, Boca Raton, FL, 33487, USA, (800) 634-1420, (800) 634-7064, orders@taylorandfrancis.com, https://www.routledge.com/; The Europa World Year Book 2022.

United Nations Food and Agricultural Organization (FAO), 2121 K St., Ste. 800B, Washington, DC, 20037, USA, (202) 653-2400 (Dial from U.S.), (202) 653-5760 (Fax from U.S.), fao-hq@fao.org, https://www.fao.org; AQUASTAT and The State of Food and Agriculture (SOFA) 2022.

United Nations Statistics Division (UNSD), United Nations Plz., New York, NY, 10017, USA, (800) 253-9646, (212) 963-9851, statistics@un.org, https://unstats.un.org; Statistical Yearbook of the United Nations 2021.

The World Bank, 1818 H St. NW, Washington, DC, 20433, USA, (202) 473-1000, (202) 477-6391, eds03@worldbank.org, https://www.worldbank.org/; Austria (report) and World Development Indicators (WDI) 2022.

AUSTRIA-AIRLINES

European Commission, Eurostat, Luxembourg, 2920, LUX, https://ec.europa.eu/eurostat/; Air Transport Statistics.

International Civil Aviation Organization (ICAO), 999 Robert-Bourassa Blvd., Montreal, QC, H3C 5H7, CAN, (514) 954-8219 (Dial from U.S.), (514) 954-6077 (Fax from U.S.), icaohq@icao.int, https://www.icao.int; ICAO Regional Reports.

Organization for Economic Cooperation and Development (OECD), 2001 L St. NW, Ste. 650, Washington, DC, 20036-4922, USA, (202) 785-6323, (800) 456-6323, (202) 785-0350, washington.contact@oecd.org, https://www.oecd.org/; OECD Tourism Trends and Policies 2022.

Palgrave Macmillan, 1 New York Plaza, Ste. 4500, New York, NY, 10004-1562, USA, (800) 777-4643, orders@palgrave.com, https://www.palgrave.com/us; The Statesman's Yearbook, 2023.

Routledge - Taylor & Francis Group, 6000 Broken Sound Pkwy. NW, Ste. 300, Boca Raton, FL, 33487, USA, (800) 634-1420, (800) 634-7064, orders@taylorandfrancis.com, https://www.routledge.com/; The Europa World Year Book 2022.

AUSTRIA-ALUMINUM PRODUCTION

See AUSTRIA-MINERAL INDUSTRIES

AUSTRIA-ARMED FORCES

Central Intelligence Agency (CIA), Office of Public Affairs, Washington, DC, 20505, USA, (703) 482-0623, https://www.cia.gov; The World Factbook.

International Institute for Strategic Studies (IISS) - Americas, 2121 K St. NW, Ste. 600, Washington, DC, 20037, USA, (202) 659-1490, (202) 659-1499, https://www.iiss.org/; The Military Balance 2022.

Palgrave Macmillan, 1 New York Plaza, Ste. 4500, New York, NY, 10004-1562, USA, (800) 777-4643, orders@palgrave.com, https://www.palgrave.com/us; The Statesman's Yearbook, 2023.

Stockholm International Peace Research Institute (SIPRI), Signalistgatan 9, Stockholm, SE 169 72, SWE, https://www.sipri.org/; SIPRI Arms Transfers Database and SIPRI Military Expenditure Database.

AUSTRIA-BALANCE OF PAYMENTS

International Monetary Fund (IMF), 700 19th St. NW, Washington, DC, 20431, USA, (202) 623-7000, (202) 623-4661, publications@imf.org, https://www.imf.org; Balance of Payments Statistics: Annual Report 2021 and International Financial Statistics (IFS).

Organization for Economic Cooperation and Development (OECD), 2001 L St. NW, Ste. 650, Washington, DC, 20036-4922, USA, (202) 785-6323, (800) 456-6323, (202) 785-0350, washington.contact@oecd.org, https://www.oecd.org/; Economic Survey of Austria 2021; Geographical Distribution of Financial Flows to Developing Countries 2023; OECD Digital Economy Outlook 2020; and OECD Main Economic Indicators (MEI).

Routledge - Taylor & Francis Group, 6000 Broken Sound Pkwy. NW, Ste. 300, Boca Raton, FL, 33487, USA, (800) 634-1420, (800) 634-7064, orders@taylorandfrancis.com, https://www.routledge.com/; The Europa World Year Book 2022.

United Nations Conference on Trade and Development (UNCTAD), Palais des Nations, Geneva, 1211, SWI, (212) 963-6896, unctadinfo@unctad.org, https://unctad.org; Handbook of Statistics 2021.

The World Bank, 1818 H St. NW, Washington, DC, 20433, USA, (202) 473-1000, (202) 477-6391, eds03@worldbank.org, https://www.worldbank.org/; Austria (report); World Development Indicators (WDI) 2022; and World Development Report 2022: Finance for an Equitable Recovery.

AUSTRIA-BANKS AND BANKING

Euromonitor International, Inc., 1 N Dearborn St., Ste. 1700, Chicago, IL, 60602, USA, (312) 922-1115, (312) 922-1157, info-usa@euromonitor.com, https://www.euromonitor.com/; Geographies.

International Monetary Fund (IMF), 700 19th St. NW, Washington, DC, 20431, USA, (202) 623-7000, (202) 623-4661, publications@imf.org, https://www.imf.org; International Financial Statistics (IFS).

Organization for Economic Cooperation and Development (OECD), 2001 L St. NW, Ste. 650, Washington, DC, 20036-4922, USA, (202) 785-6323, (800) 456-6323, (202) 785-0350, washington.contact@oecd.org, https://www.oecd.org/; Economic Survey of Austria 2021; OECD Business and Finance Outlook 2021; OECD Digital Economy Outlook 2020; and OECD Main Economic Indicators (MEI).

Routledge - Taylor & Francis Group, 6000 Broken Sound Pkwy. NW, Ste. 300, Boca Raton, FL, 33487, USA, (800) 634-1420, (800) 634-7064, orders@taylorandfrancis.com, https://www.routledge.com/; The Europa World Year Book 2022.

United Nations Statistics Division (UNSD), United Nations Plz., New York, NY, 10017, USA, (800) 253-9646, (212) 963-9851, statistics@un.org, https://unstats.un.org; Statistical Yearbook of the United Nations 2021.

AUSTRIA-BARLEY PRODUCTION

See AUSTRIA-CROPS

AUSTRIA-BONDS

Organization for Economic Cooperation and Development (OECD), 2001 L St. NW, Ste. 650, Washington, DC, 20036-4922, USA, (202) 785-6323, (800) 456-6323, (202) 785-0350, washington.contact@oecd.org, https://www.oecd.org/; OECD Business and Finance Outlook 2021.

United Nations Statistics Division (UNSD), United Nations Plz., New York, NY, 10017, USA, (800) 253-9646, (212) 963-9851, statistics@un.org, https://unstats.un.org; Statistical Yearbook of the United Nations 2021.

AUSTRIA-BROADCASTING

Central Intelligence Agency (CIA), Office of Public Affairs, Washington, DC, 20505, USA, (703) 482-0623, https://www.cia.gov; The World Factbook.

Euromonitor International, Inc., 1 N Dearborn St., Ste. 1700, Chicago, IL, 60602, USA, (312) 922-1115, (312) 922-1157, info-usa@euromonitor.com, https://www.euromonitor.com/; Geographies.

Palgrave Macmillan, 1 New York Plaza, Ste. 4500, New York, NY, 10004-1562, USA, (800) 777-4643, orders@palgrave.com, https://www.palgrave.com/us; The Statesman's Yearbook, 2023.

UNESCO Institute for Statistics, C.P 250 Succursale H, Montreal, QC, H3G 2K8, CAN, (514) 343-6880 (Dial from U.S.), (514) 343-5740 (Fax from U.S.), uis.publications@unesco.org, http://uis.unesco.org/; UIS.Stat.

WRTH Publications Limited, PO Box 290, Oxford, OX2 7FT, GBR, sales@wrth.com, https://www.wrth.com; World Radio TV Handbook 2023.

AUSTRIA-BUDGET

Central Intelligence Agency (CIA), Office of Public Affairs, Washington, DC, 20505, USA, (703) 482-0623, https://www.cia.gov; The World Factbook.

European Commission, Eurostat, Luxembourg, 2920, LUX, https://ec.europa.eu/eurostat/; Share of Government Budget Appropriations or Outlays on Research and Development.

AUSTRIA-BUSINESS

Global Entrepreneurship Monitor (GEM), Babson College, 231 Forest St., Babson Park, MA, 02457, USA, (781) 235-1200, info@gemconsortium.org, https://www.gemconsortium.org/; Austria Economy Profile.

Organization for Economic Cooperation and Development (OECD), 2001 L St. NW, Ste. 650, Washington, DC, 20036-4922, USA, (202) 785-6323, (800) 456-6323, (202) 785-0350, washington.contact@oecd.org, https://www.oecd.org/; OECD Main Economic Indicators (MEI).

AUSTRIA-CAPITAL INVESTMENTS

Organization for Economic Cooperation and Development (OECD), 2001 L St. NW, Ste. 650, Washington, DC, 20036-4922, USA, (202) 785-6323, (800) 456-6323, (202) 785-0350, washington.contact@oecd.org, https://www.oecd.org/; OECD Business and Finance Outlook 2021.

AUSTRIA-CHILDBIRTH-STATISTICS

The World Bank, 1818 H St. NW, Washington, DC, 20433, USA, (202) 473-1000, (202) 477-6391, eds03@worldbank.org, https://www.worldbank.org/; World Development Indicators (WDI) 2022.

AUSTRIA-CLIMATE

Palgrave Macmillan, 1 New York Plaza, Ste. 4500, New York, NY, 10004-1562, USA, (800) 777-4643, orders@palgrave.com, https://www.palgrave.com/us; The Statesman's Yearbook, 2023.

AUSTRIA-COAL PRODUCTION

See AUSTRIA-MINERAL INDUSTRIES

AUSTRIA-COFFEE

See AUSTRIA-CROPS

AUSTRIA-COMMERCE

Palgrave Macmillan, 1 New York Plaza, Ste. 4500, New York, NY, 10004-1562, USA, (800) 777-4643, orders@palgrave.com, https://www.palgrave.com/us; The Statesman's Yearbook, 2023.

UK Data Service, University of Essex, Wivenhoe Park, Colchester, Essex, CO4 3SQ, GBR, https://ukdataservice.ac.uk/; International Aggregate Data.

AUSTRIA-COMMODITY EXCHANGES

Barchart, 209 W Jackson Blvd., 2nd Fl., Chicago, IL, 60606, USA, (877) 247-4394, commodities@barchart.com, https://www.barchart.com/cmdty; The cmdty Yearbook 2023; cmdtyStats: Commodity Statistics and Fundamental Data; cmdtyView: Commodity Index; and Commodity Data and Prices.

International Monetary Fund (IMF), 700 19th St. NW, Washington, DC, 20431, USA, (202) 623-7000, (202) 623-4661, publications@imf.org, https://www.imf.org; IMF Primary Commodity Prices.

United Nations Statistics Division (UNSD), United Nations Plz., New York, NY, 10017, USA, (800) 253-9646, (212) 963-9851, statistics@un.org, https://unstats.un.org; Statistical Yearbook of the United Nations 2021.

World Bureau of Metal Statistics (WBMS), 31 Star St., Ware, Hertfordshire, SG12 9BA, GBR, https://www.refinitiv.com/en/trading-solutions/world-bureau-metal-statistics; Annual Stainless Steel Statistics; Long Term Production/Consumption Series - All Metals; World Flow Charts; and World Metal Statistics.

AUSTRIA-CONSTRUCTION INDUSTRY

Organization for Economic Cooperation and Development (OECD), 2001 L St. NW, Ste. 650, Washington, DC, 20036-4922, USA, (202) 785-6323, (800) 456-6323, (202) 785-0350, washington.contact@oecd.org, https://www.oecd.org/; Economic Survey of Austria 2021; OECD Main Economic Indicators (MEI); and STAN (STructural ANalysis) Database.

Palgrave Macmillan, 1 New York Plaza, Ste. 4500, New York, NY, 10004-1562, USA, (800) 777-4643, orders@palgrave.com, https://www.palgrave.com/us; The Statesman's Yearbook, 2023.

United Nations Statistics Division (UNSD), United Nations Plz., New York, NY, 10017, USA, (800) 253-9646, (212) 963-9851, statistics@un.org, https://unstats.un.org; Statistical Yearbook of the United Nations 2021.

AUSTRIA-CONSUMER PRICE INDEXES

Organization for Economic Cooperation and Development (OECD), 2001 L St. NW, Ste. 650, Washington, DC, 20036-4922, USA, (202) 785-6323, (800) 456-6323, (202) 785-0350, washington.contact@oecd.org, https://www.oecd.org/; OECD Digital Economy Outlook 2020.

Routledge - Taylor & Francis Group, 6000 Broken Sound Pkwy. NW, Ste. 300, Boca Raton, FL, 33487, USA, (800) 634-1420, (800) 634-7064, orders@taylorandfrancis.com, https://www.routledge.com/; The Europa World Year Book 2022.

The World Bank, 1818 H St. NW, Washington, DC, 20433, USA, (202) 473-1000, (202) 477-6391, eds03@worldbank.org, https://www.worldbank.org/; Austria (report).

AUSTRIA-CONSUMPTION (ECONOMICS)

International Monetary Fund (IMF), 700 19th St. NW, Washington, DC, 20431, USA, (202) 623-7000, (202) 623-4661, publications@imf.org, https://www.imf.org; International Financial Statistics (IFS).

Organization for Economic Cooperation and Development (OECD), 2001 L St. NW, Ste. 650, Washington, DC, 20036-4922, USA, (202) 785-6323, (800) 456-6323, (202) 785-0350, washington.contact@oecd.org, https://www.oecd.org/; OECD-FAO Agricultural Outlook 2022-2031 and Revenue Statistics 2022.

TAPPI - Technical Association of the Pulp and Paper Industry, 15 Technology Pkwy. S, Ste. 115, Peachtree Corners, GA, 30092, USA, (770) 446-1400, (800) 332-8686, (770) 446-6947, memberconnection@tappi.org, https://www.tappi.org/; TAPPI Journal.

World Steel Association (Worldsteel), Avenue de Tervueren 270, Brussels, B-1150, BEL, steel@worldsteel.org, https://www.worldsteel.org; Steel Statistical Yearbook 2021.

AUSTRIA-COPPER INDUSTRY AND TRADE

See AUSTRIA-MINERAL INDUSTRIES

AUSTRIA-CORN INDUSTRY

See AUSTRIA-CROPS

AUSTRIA-COTTON

See AUSTRIA-CROPS

AUSTRIA-CRIME

European Commission, Eurostat, Luxembourg, 2920, LUX, https://ec.europa.eu/eurostat/; Crime and Criminal Justice Database and Crime Statistics.

AUSTRIA-CROPS

Organization for Economic Cooperation and Development (OECD), 2001 L St. NW, Ste. 650, Washington, DC, 20036-4922, USA, (202) 785-6323, (800) 456-6323, (202) 785-0350, washington.contact@oecd.org, https://www.oecd.org/; OECD-FAO Agricultural Outlook 2022-2031.

Palgrave Macmillan, 1 New York Plaza, Ste. 4500, New York, NY, 10004-1562, USA, (800) 777-4643, orders@palgrave.com, https://www.palgrave.com/us; The Statesman's Yearbook, 2023.

United Nations Food and Agricultural Organization (FAO), 2121 K St., Ste. 800B, Washington, DC, 20037, USA, (202) 653-2400 (Dial from U.S.), (202) 653-5760 (Fax from U.S.), fao-hq@fao.org, https://www.fao.org; The State of Food and Agriculture (SOFA) 2022.

United Nations Statistics Division (UNSD), United Nations Plz., New York, NY, 10017, USA, (800) 253-9646, (212) 963-9851, statistics@un.org, https://unstats.un.org; Statistical Yearbook of the United Nations 2021.

AUSTRIA-DAIRY PROCESSING

Organization for Economic Cooperation and Development (OECD), 2001 L St. NW, Ste. 650, Washington, DC, 20036-4922, USA, (202) 785-6323, (800) 456-6323, (202) 785-0350, washington.contact@oecd.org, https://www.oecd.org/; OECD-FAO Agricultural Outlook 2022-2031.

Palgrave Macmillan, 1 New York Plaza, Ste. 4500, New York, NY, 10004-1562, USA, (800) 777-4643, orders@palgrave.com, https://www.palgrave.com/us; The Statesman's Yearbook, 2023.

United Nations Food and Agricultural Organization (FAO), 2121 K St., Ste. 800B, Washington, DC,

20037, USA, (202) 653-2400 (Dial from U.S.), (202) 653-5760 (Fax from U.S.), fao-hq@fao.org, https://www.fao.org; The State of Food and Agriculture (SOFA) 2022.

AUSTRIA-DEBTS, EXTERNAL

Organization for Economic Cooperation and Development (OECD), 2001 L St. NW, Ste. 650, Washington, DC, 20036-4922, USA, (202) 785-6323, (800) 456-6323, (202) 785-0350, washington.contact@oecd.org, https://www.oecd.org/; Geographical Distribution of Financial Flows to Developing Countries 2023; OECD Business and Finance Outlook 2021; and OECD Digital Economy Outlook 2020.

Palgrave Macmillan, 1 New York Plaza, Ste. 4500, New York, NY, 10004-1562, USA, (800) 777-4643, orders@palgrave.com, https://www.palgrave.com/us; The Statesman's Yearbook, 2023.

The World Bank, 1818 H St. NW, Washington, DC, 20433, USA, (202) 473-1000, (202) 477-6391, eds03@worldbank.org, https://www.worldbank.org/; Global Financial Development Report 2019-2020: Bank Regulation and Supervision a Decade after the Global Financial Crisis; World Development Indicators (WDI) 2022; and World Development Report 2022: Finance for an Equitable Recovery.

AUSTRIA-DEFENSE EXPENDITURES

See AUSTRIA-ARMED FORCES

AUSTRIA-DIAMONDS

See AUSTRIA-MINERAL INDUSTRIES

AUSTRIA-ECONOMIC ASSISTANCE

Organization for Economic Cooperation and Development (OECD), 2001 L St. NW, Ste. 650, Washington, DC, 20036-4922, USA, (202) 785-6323, (800) 456-6323, (202) 785-0350, washington.contact@oecd.org, https://www.oecd.org/; Geographical Distribution of Financial Flows to Developing Countries 2023.

United Nations Statistics Division (UNSD), United Nations Plz., New York, NY, 10017, USA, (800) 253-9646, (212) 963-9851, statistics@un.org, https://unstats.un.org; Statistical Yearbook of the United Nations 2021.

AUSTRIA-ECONOMIC CONDITIONS

Austrian Institute of Economic Research (WIFO), Arsenal, Objekt 20, Vienna, A-1030, AUT, office@wifo.ac.at, https://www.wifo.ac.at/en; WIFO Economic Data Service.

Banque de France, 31 rue Croix des Petits-Champs, Paris, 75049, FRA, infos@banque-france.fr, https://www.banque-france.fr/en; Webstat: Access to Statistical Series of Banque de France.

Bernan Press, 15250 NBN Way, Bldg. C, Blue Ridge Summit, PA, 17214, USA, (301) 459-2255, (800) 865-3457, (800) 865-3450, customercare@bernan.com, https://rowman.com/Page/Bernan; World Economic Outlook, April 2022.

Central Intelligence Agency (CIA), Office of Public Affairs, Washington, DC, 20505, USA, (703) 482-0623, https://www.cia.gov; The World Factbook.

The Economist Group: Economist Intelligence Unit (EIU), 900 3rd Ave., 16th Fl., New York, NY, 10022, USA, (212) 541-0500, americas@eiu.com, https://www.eiu.com; Austria Country Report.

Euromonitor International, Inc., 1 N Dearborn St., Ste. 1700, Chicago, IL, 60602, USA, (312) 922-1115, (312) 922-1157, info-usa@euromonitor.com, https://www.euromonitor.com/; Geographies and Market Research on the Consumer Finance Industry.

European Commission, Rue de la Loi, 170, Brussels, B-1040, BEL, https://ec.europa.eu; Common Agricultural Policy (CAPF) Context Indicators, 2019 Update.

Global Entrepreneurship Monitor (GEM), Babson College, 231 Forest St., Babson Park, MA, 02457, USA, (781) 235-1200, info@gemconsortium.org, https://www.gemconsortium.org/; Austria Economy Profile.

International Monetary Fund (IMF), 700 19th St. NW, Washington, DC, 20431, USA, (202) 623-7000, (202) 623-4661, publications@imf.org, https://www.imf.org; IMF Data and World Economic Outlook.

Organization for Economic Cooperation and Development (OECD), 2001 L St. NW, Ste. 650, Washington, DC, 20036-4922, USA, (202) 785-6323, (800) 456-6323, (202) 785-0350, washington.contact@oecd.org, https://www.oecd.org/; Economic Survey of Austria 2021; Geographical Distribution of Financial Flows to Developing Countries 2023; OECD Composite Leading Indicator (CLI); OECD Digital Economy Outlook 2020; OECD Employment Outlook 2022: Building Back More Inclusive Labour Markets; OECD Labour Force Statistics 2022; and OECD Main Economic Indicators (MEI).

Palgrave Macmillan, 1 New York Plaza, Ste. 4500, New York, NY, 10004-1562, USA, (800) 777-4643, orders@palgrave.com, https://www.palgrave.com/us; The Statesman's Yearbook, 2023.

Routledge - Taylor & Francis Group, 6000 Broken Sound Pkwy. NW, Ste. 300, Boca Raton, FL, 33487, USA, (800) 634-1420, (800) 634-7064, orders@taylorandfrancis.com, https://www.routledge.com/; The Europa World Year Book 2022.

United Nations Economic Commission for Europe (UNECE), Palais des Nations, Geneva, CH-1211, SWI, unece_info@un.org, https://unece.org/; UNECE Countries in Figures 2019.

United Nations Statistics Division (UNSD), United Nations Plz., New York, NY, 10017, USA, (800) 253-9646, (212) 963-9851, statistics@un.org, https://unstats.un.org; World Statistics Pocketbook 2021.

The World Bank, 1818 H St. NW, Washington, DC, 20433, USA, (202) 473-1000, (202) 477-6391, eds03@worldbank.org, https://www.worldbank.org/; Austria (report); Global Economic Monitor (GEM); Global Economic Prospects, June 2022; The Global Findex Database 2021; and World Development Report 2022: Finance for an Equitable Recovery.

AUSTRIA-EDUCATION

Euromonitor International, Inc., 1 N Dearborn St., Ste. 1700, Chicago, IL, 60602, USA, (312) 922-1115, (312) 922-1157, info-usa@euromonitor.com, https://www.euromonitor.com/; Geographies.

European Commission, Rue de la Loi, 170, Brussels, B-1040, BEL, https://ec.europa.eu; Common Agricultural Policy (CAPF) Context Indicators, 2019 Update.

Infoplease, c/o Sandbox Networks, Inc., 1 Lincoln St., 24th Fl., Boston, MA, 02111, USA, https://www.infoplease.com; Countries of the World.

Organization for Economic Cooperation and Development (OECD), 2001 L St. NW, Ste. 650, Washington, DC, 20036-4922, USA, (202) 785-6323, (800) 456-6323, (202) 785-0350, washington.contact@oecd.org, https://www.oecd.org/; Education at a Glance 2022: OECD Indicators.

Palgrave Macmillan, 1 New York Plaza, Ste. 4500, New York, NY, 10004-1562, USA, (800) 777-4643, orders@palgrave.com, https://www.palgrave.com/us; The Statesman's Yearbook, 2023.

Routledge - Taylor & Francis Group, 6000 Broken Sound Pkwy. NW, Ste. 300, Boca Raton, FL, 33487, USA, (800) 634-1420, (800) 634-7064, orders@taylorandfrancis.com, https://www.routledge.com/; The Europa World Year Book 2022.

UNESCO Institute for Statistics, C.P 250 Succursale H, Montreal, QC, H3G 2K8, CAN, (514) 343-6880 (Dial from U.S.), (514) 343-5740 (Fax from U.S.), uis.publications@unesco.org, http://uis.unesco.org/; Literacy and UIS.Stat.

United Nations Statistics Division (UNSD), United Nations Plz., New York, NY, 10017, USA, (800) 253-9646, (212) 963-9851, statistics@un.org, https://unstats.un.org; Millennium Development Goal Indicators.

The World Bank, 1818 H St. NW, Washington, DC, 20433, USA, (202) 473-1000, (202) 477-6391, eds03@worldbank.org, https://www.worldbank.org/; Austria (report); World Development Indicators (WDI) 2022; and World Development Report 2022: Finance for an Equitable Recovery.

AUSTRIA-ELECTRICITY

European Commission, Eurostat, Luxembourg, 2920, LUX, https://ec.europa.eu/eurostat/; Final Energy Consumption in Transport by Type of Fuel.

International Energy Agency (IEA), 9 Rue de la Federation, Paris, 75739, FRA, info@iea.org, https://www.iea.org/; Coal 2021: Analysis and Forecast to 2024 and World Energy Outlook 2021.

Organization for Economic Cooperation and Development (OECD), 2001 L St. NW, Ste. 650, Washington, DC, 20036-4922, USA, (202) 785-6323, (800) 456-6323, (202) 785-0350, washington.contact@oecd.org, https://www.oecd.org/; Energy Prices and Taxes for OECD Countries 2020 and STAN (STructural ANalysis) Database.

S&P Global Commodity Insights, One World Trade Center, New York, NY, 10007, USA, (800) 752-8878, support@platts.com, https://www.spglobal.com/commodityinsights/en; Platts European Power Alert and Platts Power in Europe.

U.S. Energy Information Administration (EIA), 1000 Independence Ave. SW, Washington, DC, 20585, USA, (202) 586-8800, infoctr@eia.gov, https://www.eia.gov; International Energy Outlook 2021.

United Nations Statistics Division (UNSD), United Nations Plz., New York, NY, 10017, USA, (800) 253-9646, (212) 963-9851, statistics@un.org, https://unstats.un.org; Statistical Yearbook of the United Nations 2021.

AUSTRIA-EMPLOYMENT

International Labour Organization (ILO), 4 Rte. des Morillons, Geneva, CH-1211, SWI, ilo@ilo.org, https://www.ilo.org; NORMLEX Information System on International Labour Standards.

Organization for Economic Cooperation and Development (OECD), 2001 L St. NW, Ste. 650, Washington, DC, 20036-4922, USA, (202) 785-6323, (800) 456-6323, (202) 785-0350, washington.contact@oecd.org, https://www.oecd.org/; Economic Survey of Austria 2021; OECD Composite Leading Indicator (CLI); OECD Digital Economy Outlook 2020; OECD Employment Outlook 2022: Building Back More Inclusive Labour Markets; and OECD Labour Force Statistics 2022.

UK Data Service, University of Essex, Wivenhoe Park, Colchester, Essex, CO4 3SQ, GBR, https://ukdataservice.ac.uk/; International Aggregate Data.

United Nations Statistics Division (UNSD), United Nations Plz., New York, NY, 10017, USA, (800) 253-9646, (212) 963-9851, statistics@un.org, https://unstats.un.org; Statistical Yearbook of the United Nations 2021.

The World Bank, 1818 H St. NW, Washington, DC, 20433, USA, (202) 473-1000, (202) 477-6391, eds03@worldbank.org, https://www.worldbank.org/; Austria (report).

AUSTRIA-ENERGY INDUSTRIES

European Commission, Eurostat, Luxembourg, 2920, LUX, https://ec.europa.eu/eurostat/; Final Energy Consumption in Transport by Type of Fuel.

European Institute for Energy Research (EIFER), Emmy-Noether-Strasse 11, Ground Fl., Karlsruhe, D-76131, GER, contact@eifer.org, https://www.eifer.kit.edu/; unpublished data.

International Energy Agency (IEA), 9 Rue de la Federation, Paris, 75739, FRA, info@iea.org, https://www.iea.org/; World Energy Statistics and Balances.

S&P Global Commodity Insights, One World Trade Center, New York, NY, 10007, USA, (800) 752-8878, support@platts.com, https://www.spglobal.com/commodityinsights/en; Platts Power in Europe.

AUSTRIA-ENVIRONMENTAL CONDITIONS

DSI Data Service & Information, Xantener Strasse 51a, Rheinberg, D-47495, GER, dsi@dsidata.com, https://www.dsidata.com/; Global Environmental Database.

The Economist Group: Economist Intelligence Unit (EIU), 900 3rd Ave., 16th Fl., New York, NY, 10022, USA, (212) 541-0500, americas@eiu.com, https://www.eiu.com; Austria Country Report.

European Commission, Rue de la Loi, 170, Brussels, B-1040, BEL, https://ec.europa.eu; Common Agricultural Policy (CAPF) Context Indicators, 2019 Update.

United Nations Statistics Division (UNSD), United Nations Plz., New York, NY, 10017, USA, (800) 253-9646, (212) 963-9851, statistics@un.org, https://unstats.un.org; World Statistics Pocketbook 2021.

AUSTRIA-EXPENDITURES, PUBLIC

Organization for Economic Cooperation and Development (OECD), 2001 L St. NW, Ste. 650, Washington, DC, 20036-4922, USA, (202) 785-6323, (800) 456-6323, (202) 785-0350, washington.contact@oecd.org, https://www.oecd.org/; Revenue Statistics 2022.

AUSTRIA-EXPORTS

Central Intelligence Agency (CIA), Office of Public Affairs, Washington, DC, 20505, USA, (703) 482-0623, https://www.cia.gov; The World Factbook.

The Economist Group: Economist Intelligence Unit (EIU), 900 3rd Ave., 16th Fl., New York, NY, 10022, USA, (212) 541-0500, americas@eiu.com, https://www.eiu.com; Austria Country Report.

International Monetary Fund (IMF), 700 19th St. NW, Washington, DC, 20431, USA, (202) 623-7000, (202) 623-4661, publications@imf.org, https://www.imf.org; Direction of Trade Statistics (DOTS) and International Financial Statistics (IFS).

Organization for Economic Cooperation and Development (OECD), 2001 L St. NW, Ste. 650, Washington, DC, 20036-4922, USA, (202) 785-6323, (800) 456-6323, (202) 785-0350, washington.contact@oecd.org, https://www.oecd.org/; Economic Survey of Austria 2021; Geographical Distribution of Financial Flows to Developing Countries 2023; OECD Digital Economy Outlook 2020; OECD-FAO Agricultural Outlook 2022-2031; and STAN (STructural ANalysis) Database.

S&P Global, IHS Markit, 15 Inverness Way E, Englewood, CO, 80112, USA, (800) 447-2273, (800) 854-7179, https://ihsmarkit.com; Global Trade Atlas (GTA).

TAPPI - Technical Association of the Pulp and Paper Industry, 15 Technology Pkwy. S, Ste. 115, Peachtree Corners, GA, 30092, USA, (770) 446-1400, (800) 332-8686, (770) 446-6947, memberconnection@tappi.org, https://www.tappi.org/; TAPPI Journal.

United Nations Conference on Trade and Development (UNCTAD), Palais des Nations, Geneva, 1211, SWI, (212) 963-6896, unctadinfo@unctad.org, https://unctad.org; Handbook of Statistics 2021.

The World Bank, 1818 H St. NW, Washington, DC, 20433, USA, (202) 473-1000, (202) 477-6391, eds03@worldbank.org, https://www.worldbank.org/; World Development Report 2022: Finance for an Equitable Recovery.

World Steel Association (Worldsteel), Avenue de Tervueren 270, Brussels, B-1150, BEL, steel@worldsteel.org, https://www.worldsteel.org; Steel Statistical Yearbook 2021.

AUSTRIA-FERTILIZER INDUSTRY

Organization for Economic Cooperation and Development (OECD), 2001 L St. NW, Ste. 650, Washington, DC, 20036-4922, USA, (202) 785-6323, (800) 456-6323, (202) 785-0350, washington.contact@oecd.org, https://www.oecd.org/; OECD-FAO Agricultural Outlook 2022-2031.

United Nations Food and Agricultural Organization (FAO), 2121 K St., Ste. 800B, Washington, DC, 20037, USA, (202) 653-2400 (Dial from U.S.), (202) 653-5760 (Fax from U.S.), fao-hq@fao.org, https://www.fao.org; The State of Food and Agriculture (SOFA) 2022.

AUSTRIA-FETAL MORTALITY

See AUSTRIA-MORTALITY

AUSTRIA-FINANCE

International Monetary Fund (IMF), 700 19th St. NW, Washington, DC, 20431, USA, (202) 623-7000, (202) 623-4661, publications@imf.org, https://www.imf.org; International Financial Statistics (IFS).

Organization for Economic Cooperation and Development (OECD), 2001 L St. NW, Ste. 650, Washington, DC, 20036-4922, USA, (202) 785-6323, (800) 456-6323, (202) 785-0350, washington.contact@oecd.org, https://www.oecd.org/; OECD Digital Economy Outlook 2020.

Stockholm International Peace Research Institute (SIPRI), Signalistgatan 9, Stockholm, SE 169 72, SWE, https://www.sipri.org/; SIPRI Arms Transfers Database and SIPRI Military Expenditure Database.

The World Bank, 1818 H St. NW, Washington, DC, 20433, USA, (202) 473-1000, (202) 477-6391, eds03@worldbank.org, https://www.worldbank.org/; Austria (report).

AUSTRIA-FINANCE, PUBLIC

Banque de France, 31 rue Croix des Petits-Champs, Paris, 75049, FRA, infos@banque-france.fr, https://www.banque-france.fr/en; Webstat: Access to Statistical Series of Banque de France.

Bernan Press, 15250 NBN Way, Bldg. C, Blue Ridge Summit, PA, 17214, USA, (301) 459-2255, (800) 865-3457, (800) 865-3450, customercare@bernan.com, https://rowman.com/Page/Bernan; National Accounts Statistics: Analysis of Main Aggregates 2020.

The Economist Group: Economist Intelligence Unit (EIU), 900 3rd Ave., 16th Fl., New York, NY, 10022, USA, (212) 541-0500, americas@eiu.com, https://www.eiu.com; Austria Country Report.

International Monetary Fund (IMF), 700 19th St. NW, Washington, DC, 20431, USA, (202) 623-7000, (202) 623-4661, publications@imf.org, https://www.imf.org; International Financial Statistics (IFS) and Regional Economic Outlook.

Organization for Economic Cooperation and Development (OECD), 2001 L St. NW, Ste. 650, Washington, DC, 20036-4922, USA, (202) 785-6323, (800) 456-6323, (202) 785-0350, washington.contact@oecd.org, https://www.oecd.org/; Geographical Distribution of Financial Flows to Developing Countries 2023; OECD Business and Finance Outlook 2021; OECD Digital Economy Outlook 2020; and Revenue Statistics 2022.

Palgrave Macmillan, 1 New York Plaza, Ste. 4500, New York, NY, 10004-1562, USA, (800) 777-4643, orders@palgrave.com, https://www.palgrave.com/us; The Statesman's Yearbook, 2023.

Routledge - Taylor & Francis Group, 6000 Broken Sound Pkwy. NW, Ste. 300, Boca Raton, FL, 33487, USA, (800) 634-1420, (800) 634-7064, orders@taylorandfrancis.com, https://www.routledge.com/; The Europa World Year Book 2022.

United Nations Statistics Division (UNSD), United Nations Plz., New York, NY, 10017, USA, (800) 253-9646, (212) 963-9851, statistics@un.org, https://unstats.un.org; National Accounts Main Aggregates Database and National Accounts Statistics: Main Aggregates and Detailed Tables.

The World Bank, 1818 H St. NW, Washington, DC, 20433, USA, (202) 473-1000, (202) 477-6391, eds03@worldbank.org, https://www.worldbank.org/; Austria (report).

AUSTRIA-FISHERIES

Organization for Economic Cooperation and Development (OECD), 2001 L St. NW, Ste. 650, Washington, DC, 20036-4922, USA, (202) 785-6323, (800) 456-6323, (202) 785-0350, washington.contact@oecd.org, https://www.oecd.org/; STAN (STructural ANalysis) Database.

Palgrave Macmillan, 1 New York Plaza, Ste. 4500, New York, NY, 10004-1562, USA, (800) 777-4643, orders@palgrave.com, https://www.palgrave.com/us; The Statesman's Yearbook, 2023.

Routledge - Taylor & Francis Group, 6000 Broken Sound Pkwy. NW, Ste. 300, Boca Raton, FL, 33487, USA, (800) 634-1420, (800) 634-7064, orders@taylorandfrancis.com, https://www.routledge.com/; The Europa World Year Book 2022.

United Nations Food and Agricultural Organization (FAO), 2121 K St., Ste. 800B, Washington, DC, 20037, USA, (202) 653-2400 (Dial from U.S.), (202) 653-5760 (Fax from U.S.), fao-hq@fao.org, https://www.fao.org; FAO Yearbook of Fishery and Aquaculture Statistics 2019; Fishery Statistical Collections Global Capture Production; FishStatJ; and The State of Food and Agriculture (SOFA) 2022.

United Nations Statistics Division (UNSD), United Nations Plz., New York, NY, 10017, USA, (800) 253-9646, (212) 963-9851, statistics@un.org, https://unstats.un.org; Statistical Yearbook of the United Nations 2021.

The World Bank, 1818 H St. NW, Washington, DC, 20433, USA, (202) 473-1000, (202) 477-6391, eds03@worldbank.org, https://www.worldbank.org/; Austria (report).

AUSTRIA-FOOD

Euromonitor International, Inc., 1 N Dearborn St., Ste. 1700, Chicago, IL, 60602, USA, (312) 922-1115, (312) 922-1157, info-usa@euromonitor.com, https://www.euromonitor.com/; Market Research on the Retailing Industry.

United Nations Food and Agricultural Organization (FAO), 2121 K St., Ste. 800B, Washington, DC, 20037, USA, (202) 653-2400 (Dial from U.S.), (202) 653-5760 (Fax from U.S.), fao-hq@fao.org, https://www.fao.org; The State of Food and Agriculture (SOFA) 2022.

AUSTRIA-FOREIGN EXCHANGE RATES

International Monetary Fund (IMF), 700 19th St. NW, Washington, DC, 20431, USA, (202) 623-7000, (202) 623-4661, publications@imf.org, https://www.imf.org; International Financial Statistics (IFS).

Organization for Economic Cooperation and Development (OECD), 2001 L St. NW, Ste. 650, Washington, DC, 20036-4922, USA, (202) 785-6323, (800) 456-6323, (202) 785-0350, washington.contact@oecd.org, https://www.oecd.org/; OECD Business and Finance Outlook 2021; OECD Digital Economy Outlook 2020; OECD Tourism Trends and Policies 2022; and Revenue Statistics 2022.

AUSTRIA-FORESTS AND FORESTRY

Organization for Economic Cooperation and Development (OECD), 2001 L St. NW, Ste. 650, Washington, DC, 20036-4922, USA, (202) 785-6323, (800) 456-6323, (202) 785-0350, washington.contact@oecd.org, https://www.oecd.org/; STAN (STructural ANalysis) Database.

Palgrave Macmillan, 1 New York Plaza, Ste. 4500, New York, NY, 10004-1562, USA, (800) 777-4643, orders@palgrave.com, https://www.palgrave.com/us; The Statesman's Yearbook, 2023.

Routledge - Taylor & Francis Group, 6000 Broken Sound Pkwy. NW, Ste. 300, Boca Raton, FL, 33487, USA, (800) 634-1420, (800) 634-7064, orders@taylorandfrancis.com, https://www.routledge.com/; The Europa World Year Book 2022.

TAPPI - Technical Association of the Pulp and Paper Industry, 15 Technology Pkwy. S, Ste. 115, Peachtree Corners, GA, 30092, USA, (770) 446-1400, (800) 332-8686, (770) 446-6947, memberconnection@tappi.org, https://www.tappi.org/; TAPPI Journal.

UNESCO Institute for Statistics, C.P 250 Succursale H, Montreal, QC, H3G 2K8, CAN, (514) 343-6880 (Dial from U.S.), (514) 343-5740 (Fax from U.S.), uis.publications@unesco.org, http://uis.unesco.org/; UIS.Stat.

United Nations Food and Agricultural Organization (FAO), 2121 K St., Ste. 800B, Washington, DC, 20037, USA, (202) 653-2400 (Dial from U.S.), (202) 653-5760 (Fax from U.S.), fao-hq@fao.org, https://www.fao.org; FAO Yearbook of Forest Products 2019 and The State of Food and Agriculture (SOFA) 2022.

United Nations Statistics Division (UNSD), United Nations Plz., New York, NY, 10017, USA, (800) 253-9646, (212) 963-9851, statistics@un.org, https://unstats.un.org; Statistical Yearbook of the United Nations 2021.

The World Bank, 1818 H St. NW, Washington, DC, 20433, USA, (202) 473-1000, (202) 477-6391, eds03@worldbank.org, https://www.worldbank.org/; Austria (report) and World Development Report 2022: Finance for an Equitable Recovery.

AUSTRIA-FRUIT PRODUCTION

See AUSTRIA-CROPS

AUSTRIA-GAS PRODUCTION

See AUSTRIA-MINERAL INDUSTRIES

AUSTRIA-GEOGRAPHIC INFORMATION SYSTEMS

The World Bank, 1818 H St. NW, Washington, DC, 20433, USA, (202) 473-1000, (202) 477-6391, eds03@worldbank.org, https://www.worldbank.org/; Austria (report).

AUSTRIA-GOLD INDUSTRY

The World Bank, 1818 H St. NW, Washington, DC, 20433, USA, (202) 473-1000, (202) 477-6391, eds03@worldbank.org, https://www.worldbank.org/; World Development Indicators (WDI) 2022.

AUSTRIA-GOLD PRODUCTION

See AUSTRIA-MINERAL INDUSTRIES

AUSTRIA-GRANTS-IN-AID

Organization for Economic Cooperation and Development (OECD), 2001 L St. NW, Ste. 650, Washington, DC, 20036-4922, USA, (202) 785-6323, (800) 456-6323, (202) 785-0350, washington.contact@oecd.org, https://www.oecd.org/; Geographical Distribution of Financial Flows to Developing Countries 2023.

AUSTRIA-GROSS DOMESTIC PRODUCT

The Economist Group: Economist Intelligence Unit (EIU), 900 3rd Ave., 16th Fl., New York, NY, 10022, USA, (212) 541-0500, americas@eiu.com, https://www.eiu.com; Austria Country Report.

International Monetary Fund (IMF), 700 19th St. NW, Washington, DC, 20431, USA, (202) 623-7000, (202) 623-4661, publications@imf.org, https://www.imf.org; International Financial Statistics (IFS).

Organization for Economic Cooperation and Development (OECD), 2001 L St. NW, Ste. 650, Washington, DC, 20036-4922, USA, (202) 785-6323, (800) 456-6323, (202) 785-0350, washington.contact@oecd.org, https://www.oecd.org/; Geographical Distribution of Financial Flows to Developing Countries 2023; OECD Digital Economy Outlook 2020; and Revenue Statistics 2022.

Routledge - Taylor & Francis Group, 6000 Broken Sound Pkwy. NW, Ste. 300, Boca Raton, FL, 33487, USA, (800) 634-1420, (800) 634-7064, orders@taylorandfrancis.com, https://www.routledge.com/; The Europa World Year Book 2022.

United Nations Statistics Division (UNSD), United Nations Plz., New York, NY, 10017, USA, (800) 253-9646, (212) 963-9851, statistics@un.org, https://unstats.un.org; Statistical Yearbook of the United Nations 2021.

The World Bank, 1818 H St. NW, Washington, DC, 20433, USA, (202) 473-1000, (202) 477-6391, eds03@worldbank.org, https://www.worldbank.org/; World Development Indicators (WDI) 2022 and World Development Report 2022: Finance for an Equitable Recovery.

AUSTRIA-GROSS NATIONAL PRODUCT

Organization for Economic Cooperation and Development (OECD), 2001 L St. NW, Ste. 650, Washington, DC, 20036-4922, USA, (202) 785-6323, (800) 456-6323, (202) 785-0350, washington.contact@oecd.org, https://www.oecd.org/; Geographical Distribution of Financial Flows to Developing Countries 2023; OECD Composite Leading Indicator (CLI); and OECD Digital Economy Outlook 2020.

Palgrave Macmillan, 1 New York Plaza, Ste. 4500, New York, NY, 10004-1562, USA, (800) 777-4643, orders@palgrave.com, https://www.palgrave.com/us; The Statesman's Yearbook, 2023.

Routledge - Taylor & Francis Group, 6000 Broken Sound Pkwy. NW, Ste. 300, Boca Raton, FL, 33487, USA, (800) 634-1420, (800) 634-7064, orders@taylorandfrancis.com, https://www.routledge.com/; The Europa World Year Book 2022.

United Nations Economic Commission for Africa (UNECA), PO Box 3001, Addis Ababa, ETH, ecainfo@uneca.org, https://www.uneca.org/; African Statistical Yearbook 2020.

United Nations Statistics Division (UNSD), United Nations Plz., New York, NY, 10017, USA, (800) 253-9646, (212) 963-9851, statistics@un.org, https://unstats.un.org; Statistical Yearbook of the United Nations 2021.

The World Bank, 1818 H St. NW, Washington, DC, 20433, USA, (202) 473-1000, (202) 477-6391, eds03@worldbank.org, https://www.worldbank.org/; World Development Indicators (WDI) 2022 and World Development Report 2022: Finance for an Equitable Recovery.

AUSTRIA-HOUSING

Euromonitor International, Inc., 1 N Dearborn St., Ste. 1700, Chicago, IL, 60602, USA, (312) 922-1115, (312) 922-1157, info-usa@euromonitor.com, https://www.euromonitor.com/; Geographies.

AUSTRIA-HOUSING-FINANCE

Organization for Economic Cooperation and Development (OECD), 2001 L St. NW, Ste. 650, Washington, DC, 20036-4922, USA, (202) 785-6323, (800) 456-6323, (202) 785-0350, washington.contact@oecd.org, https://www.oecd.org/; OECD Main Economic Indicators (MEI).

AUSTRIA-HOUSING CONSTRUCTION

See AUSTRIA-CONSTRUCTION INDUSTRY

AUSTRIA-IMPORTS

Central Intelligence Agency (CIA), Office of Public Affairs, Washington, DC, 20505, USA, (703) 482-0623, https://www.cia.gov; The World Factbook.

The Economist Group: Economist Intelligence Unit (EIU), 900 3rd Ave., 16th Fl., New York, NY, 10022, USA, (212) 541-0500, americas@eiu.com, https://www.eiu.com; Austria Country Report.

Euromonitor International, Inc., 1 N Dearborn St., Ste. 1700, Chicago, IL, 60602, USA, (312) 922-1115, (312) 922-1157, info-usa@euromonitor.com, https://www.euromonitor.com/; Geographies.

International Monetary Fund (IMF), 700 19th St. NW, Washington, DC, 20431, USA, (202) 623-7000, (202) 623-4661, publications@imf.org, https://www.imf.org; Direction of Trade Statistics (DOTS) and International Financial Statistics (IFS).

Organization for Economic Cooperation and Development (OECD), 2001 L St. NW, Ste. 650, Washington, DC, 20036-4922, USA, (202) 785-6323, (800) 456-6323, (202) 785-0350, washington.contact@oecd.org, https://www.oecd.org/; Economic Survey of Austria 2021; OECD Digital Economy Outlook 2020; OECD-FAO Agricultural Outlook 2022-2031; and STAN (STructural ANalysis) Database.

S&P Global, IHS Markit, 15 Inverness Way E, Englewood, CO, 80112, USA, (800) 447-2273, (800) 854-7179, https://ihsmarkit.com; Global Trade Atlas (GTA).

TAPPI - Technical Association of the Pulp and Paper Industry, 15 Technology Pkwy. S, Ste. 115, Peachtree Corners, GA, 30092, USA, (770) 446-1400, (800) 332-8686, (770) 446-6947, memberconnection@tappi.org, https://www.tappi.org/; TAPPI Journal.

United Nations Conference on Trade and Development (UNCTAD), Palais des Nations, Geneva, 1211, SWI, (212) 963-6896, unctadinfo@unctad.org, https://unctad.org; Handbook of Statistics 2021.

The World Bank, 1818 H St. NW, Washington, DC, 20433, USA, (202) 473-1000, (202) 477-6391, eds03@worldbank.org, https://www.worldbank.org/; World Development Report 2022: Finance for an Equitable Recovery.

World Steel Association (Worldsteel), Avenue de Tervueren 270, Brussels, B-1150, BEL, steel@worldsteel.org, https://www.worldsteel.org; Steel Statistical Yearbook 2021.

AUSTRIA-INDUSTRIAL METALS PRODUCTION

See AUSTRIA-MINERAL INDUSTRIES

AUSTRIA-INDUSTRIAL PRODUCTIVITY

International Lead and Zinc Study Group (ILZSG), Rua Almirante Barroso 38, 5th Fl., Lisbon, 1000-013, PRT, sales@ilzsg.org, https://www.ilzsg.org; Interactive Statistical Database.

Organization for Economic Cooperation and Development (OECD), 2001 L St. NW, Ste. 650, Washington, DC, 20036-4922, USA, (202) 785-6323, (800) 456-6323, (202) 785-0350, washington.contact@oecd.org, https://www.oecd.org/; OECD Digital Economy Outlook 2020; OECD-FAO Agricultural Outlook 2022-2031; and STAN (STructural ANalysis) Database.

TAPPI - Technical Association of the Pulp and Paper Industry, 15 Technology Pkwy. S, Ste. 115, Peachtree Corners, GA, 30092, USA, (770) 446-1400, (800) 332-8686, (770) 446-6947, memberconnection@tappi.org, https://www.tappi.org/; TAPPI Journal.

World Steel Association (Worldsteel), Avenue de Tervueren 270, Brussels, B-1150, BEL, steel@worldsteel.org, https://www.worldsteel.org; Steel Statistical Yearbook 2021.

AUSTRIA-INDUSTRIAL PROPERTY

International Energy Agency (IEA), 9 Rue de la Federation, Paris, 75739, FRA, info@iea.org, https://www.iea.org/; World Energy Outlook 2021.

AUSTRIA-INDUSTRIES

Central Intelligence Agency (CIA), Office of Public Affairs, Washington, DC, 20505, USA, (703) 482-0623, https://www.cia.gov; The World Factbook.

The Economist Group: Economist Intelligence Unit (EIU), 900 3rd Ave., 16th Fl., New York, NY, 10022, USA, (212) 541-0500, americas@eiu.com, https://www.eiu.com; Austria Country Report.

International Energy Agency (IEA), 9 Rue de la Federation, Paris, 75739, FRA, info@iea.org, https://www.iea.org/; World Energy Outlook 2021.

International Labour Organization (ILO), 4 Rte. des Morillons, Geneva, CH-1211, SWI, ilo@ilo.org, https://www.ilo.org; NORMLEX Information System on International Labour Standards.

Palgrave Macmillan, 1 New York Plaza, Ste. 4500, New York, NY, 10004-1562, USA, (800) 777-4643, orders@palgrave.com, https://www.palgrave.com/us; The Statesman's Yearbook, 2023.

Routledge - Taylor & Francis Group, 6000 Broken Sound Pkwy. NW, Ste. 300, Boca Raton, FL, 33487, USA, (800) 634-1420, (800) 634-7064, orders@taylorandfrancis.com, https://www.routledge.com/; The Europa World Year Book 2022.

United Nations Industrial Development Organization (UNIDO), 1 United Nations Plz., Rm. DC1-1118, New York, NY, 10017, USA, (212) 963-6890, (212)

963 6885, (212) 963-7904, office.newyork@unido.org, https://www.unido.org/; Industrial Statistics Databases and International Yearbook of Industrial Statistics 2021.

The World Bank, 1818 H St. NW, Washington, DC, 20433, USA, (202) 473-1000, (202) 477-6391, eds03@worldbank.org, https://www.worldbank.org/; Austria (report) and World Development Indicators (WDI) 2022.

AUSTRIA-INFANT AND MATERNAL MORTALITY

See AUSTRIA-MORTALITY

AUSTRIA-INTEREST RATES

Organization for Economic Cooperation and Development (OECD), 2001 L St. NW, Ste. 650, Washington, DC, 20036-4922, USA, (202) 785-6323, (800) 456-6323, (202) 785-0350, washington.contact@oecd.org, https://www.oecd.org/; OECD Business and Finance Outlook 2021 and OECD Digital Economy Outlook 2020.

AUSTRIA-INTERNAL REVENUE

Organization for Economic Cooperation and Development (OECD), 2001 L St. NW, Ste. 650, Washington, DC, 20036-4922, USA, (202) 785-6323, (800) 456-6323, (202) 785-0350, washington.contact@oecd.org, https://www.oecd.org/; Revenue Statistics 2022.

AUSTRIA-INTERNATIONAL FINANCE

Organization for Economic Cooperation and Development (OECD), 2001 L St. NW, Ste. 650, Washington, DC, 20036-4922, USA, (202) 785-6323, (800) 456-6323, (202) 785-0350, washington.contact@oecd.org, https://www.oecd.org/; OECD Business and Finance Outlook 2021; OECD Digital Economy Outlook 2020; and OECD Main Economic Indicators (MEI).

AUSTRIA-INTERNATIONAL LIQUIDITY

Organization for Economic Cooperation and Development (OECD), 2001 L St. NW, Ste. 650, Washington, DC, 20036-4922, USA, (202) 785-6323, (800) 456-6323, (202) 785-0350, washington.contact@oecd.org, https://www.oecd.org/; OECD Business and Finance Outlook 2021.

AUSTRIA-INTERNATIONAL TRADE

Banque de France, 31 rue Croix des Petits-Champs, Paris, 75049, FRA, infos@banque-france.fr, https://www.banque-france.fr/en; Key Figures France and Abroad.

The Economist Group: Economist Intelligence Unit (EIU), 900 3rd Ave., 16th Fl., New York, NY, 10022, USA, (212) 541-0500, americas@eiu.com, https://www.eiu.com; Austria Country Report.

Euromonitor International, Inc., 1 N Dearborn St., Ste. 1700, Chicago, IL, 60602, USA, (312) 922-1115, (312) 922-1157, info-usa@euromonitor.com, https://www.euromonitor.com/; Geographies.

European Commission, Eurostat, Luxembourg, 2920, LUX, https://ec.europa.eu/eurostat/; Extra-EU Trade in Goods.

Organization for Economic Cooperation and Development (OECD), 2001 L St. NW, Ste. 650, Washington, DC, 20036-4922, USA, (202) 785-6323, (800) 456-6323, (202) 785-0350, washington.contact@oecd.org, https://www.oecd.org/; Economic Survey of Austria 2021; OECD Digital Economy Outlook 2020; OECD Main Economic Indicators (MEI); and OECD-FAO Agricultural Outlook 2022-2031.

Palgrave Macmillan, 1 New York Plaza, Ste. 4500, New York, NY, 10004-1562, USA, (800) 777-4643, orders@palgrave.com, https://www.palgrave.com/us; The Statesman's Yearbook, 2023.

Routledge - Taylor & Francis Group, 6000 Broken Sound Pkwy. NW, Ste. 300, Boca Raton, FL, 33487, USA, (800) 634-1420, (800) 634-7064, orders@taylorandfrancis.com, https://www.routledge.com/; The Europa World Year Book 2022.

United Nations Conference on Trade and Development (UNCTAD), Palais des Nations, Geneva, 1211, SWI, (212) 963-6896, unctadinfo@unctad.org, https://unctad.org; Trade and Development Report 2021.

United Nations Food and Agricultural Organization (FAO), 2121 K St., Ste. 800B, Washington, DC, 20037, USA, (202) 653-2400 (Dial from U.S.), (202) 653-5760 (Fax from U.S.), fao-hq@fao.org, https://www.fao.org; The State of Food and Agriculture (SOFA) 2022.

United Nations Statistics Division (UNSD), United Nations Plz., New York, NY, 10017, USA, (800) 253-9646, (212) 963-9851, statistics@un.org, https://unstats.un.org; International Trade Statistics Yearbook 2020 and Statistical Yearbook of the United Nations 2021.

The World Bank, 1818 H St. NW, Washington, DC, 20433, USA, (202) 473-1000, (202) 477-6391, eds03@worldbank.org, https://www.worldbank.org/; Austria (report); World Development Indicators (WDI) 2022; and World Development Report 2022: Finance for an Equitable Recovery.

World Steel Association (Worldsteel), Avenue de Tervueren 270, Brussels, B-1150, BEL, steel@worldsteel.org, https://www.worldsteel.org; Steel Statistical Yearbook 2021.

World Trade Organization (WTO), Ctre. William Rappard, Rue de Lausanne 154, Case postale, Geneva, CH-1211, SWI, enquiries@wto.org, https://www.wto.org; World Trade Statistical Review 2022.

AUSTRIA-INTERNET USERS

International Telecommunication Union (ITU), Place des Nations, Geneva, CH-1211, SWI, itumail@itu.int, https://www.itu.int; Global Connectivity Report 2022; World Telecommunication/ICT Indicators Database 2021; and Yearbook of Statistics 2019.

AUSTRIA-INVESTMENTS

International Monetary Fund (IMF), 700 19th St. NW, Washington, DC, 20431, USA, (202) 623-7000, (202) 623-4661, publications@imf.org, https://www.imf.org; International Financial Statistics (IFS).

Organization for Economic Cooperation and Development (OECD), 2001 L St. NW, Ste. 650, Washington, DC, 20036-4922, USA, (202) 785-6323, (800) 456-6323, (202) 785-0350, washington.contact@oecd.org, https://www.oecd.org/; OECD Business and Finance Outlook 2021; OECD Digital Economy Outlook 2020; and STAN (STructural ANalysis) Database.

AUSTRIA-LABOR

Central Intelligence Agency (CIA), Office of Public Affairs, Washington, DC, 20505, USA, (703) 482-0623, https://www.cia.gov; The World Factbook.

Euromonitor International, Inc., 1 N Dearborn St., Ste. 1700, Chicago, IL, 60602, USA, (312) 922-1115, (312) 922-1157, info-usa@euromonitor.com, https://www.euromonitor.com/; Geographies.

International Labour Organization (ILO), 4 Rte. des Morillons, Geneva, CH-1211, SWI, ilo@ilo.org, https://www.ilo.org; NORMLEX Information System on International Labour Standards.

Organization for Economic Cooperation and Development (OECD), 2001 L St. NW, Ste. 650, Washington, DC, 20036-4922, USA, (202) 785-6323, (800) 456-6323, (202) 785-0350, washington.contact@oecd.org, https://www.oecd.org/; Economic Survey of Austria 2021; OECD Digital Economy Outlook 2020; OECD Employment Outlook 2022: Building Back More Inclusive Labour Markets; and OECD Main Economic Indicators (MEI).

Palgrave Macmillan, 1 New York Plaza, Ste. 4500, New York, NY, 10004-1562, USA, (800) 777-4643, orders@palgrave.com, https://www.palgrave.com/us; The Statesman's Yearbook, 2023.

United Nations Economic Commission for Europe (UNECE), Palais des Nations, Geneva, CH-1211, SWI, unece_info@un.org, https://unece.org/; UNECE Countries in Figures 2019.

United Nations Food and Agricultural Organization (FAO), 2121 K St., Ste. 800B, Washington, DC, 20037, USA, (202) 653-2400 (Dial from U.S.), (202) 653-5760 (Fax from U.S.), fao-hq@fao.org, https://www.fao.org; The State of Food and Agriculture (SOFA) 2022.

The World Bank, 1818 H St. NW, Washington, DC, 20433, USA, (202) 473-1000, (202) 477-6391, eds03@worldbank.org, https://www.worldbank.org/; World Development Indicators (WDI) 2022 and World Development Report 2022: Finance for an Equitable Recovery.

AUSTRIA-LAND USE

United Nations Statistics Division (UNSD), United Nations Plz., New York, NY, 10017, USA, (800) 253-9646, (212) 963-9851, statistics@un.org, https://unstats.un.org; Millennium Development Goal Indicators.

The World Bank, 1818 H St. NW, Washington, DC, 20433, USA, (202) 473-1000, (202) 477-6391, eds03@worldbank.org, https://www.worldbank.org/; World Development Report 2022: Finance for an Equitable Recovery.

AUSTRIA-LIBRARIES

UNESCO Institute for Statistics, C.P 250 Succursale H, Montreal, QC, H3G 2K8, CAN, (514) 343-6880 (Dial from U.S.), (514) 343-5740 (Fax from U.S.), uis.publications@unesco.org, http://uis.unesco.org/; UIS.Stat.

AUSTRIA-LIFE EXPECTANCY

Central Intelligence Agency (CIA), Office of Public Affairs, Washington, DC, 20505, USA, (703) 482-0623, https://www.cia.gov; The World Factbook.

United Nations Department of Economic and Social Affairs (DESA), Population Division, 2 United Nations Plz., Rm. DC2-1950, New York, NY, 10017, USA, (212) 963-3209, (212) 963-2147, population@un.org, https://www.un.org/development/desa/pd/; World Population Ageing 2020 Highlights.

United Nations Economic Commission for Europe (UNECE), Palais des Nations, Geneva, CH-1211, SWI, unece_info@un.org, https://unece.org/; UNECE Countries in Figures 2019.

United Nations Statistics Division (UNSD), United Nations Plz., New York, NY, 10017, USA, (800) 253-9646, (212) 963-9851, statistics@un.org, https://unstats.un.org; Millennium Development Goal Indicators.

AUSTRIA-LITERACY

Euromonitor International, Inc., 1 N Dearborn St., Ste. 1700, Chicago, IL, 60602, USA, (312) 922-1115, (312) 922-1157, info-usa@euromonitor.com, https://www.euromonitor.com/; Geographies.

UNESCO Institute for Statistics, C.P 250 Succursale H, Montreal, QC, H3G 2K8, CAN, (514) 343-6880 (Dial from U.S.), (514) 343-5740 (Fax from U.S.), uis.publications@unesco.org, http://uis.unesco.org/; Literacy.

AUSTRIA-LIVESTOCK

Organization for Economic Cooperation and Development (OECD), 2001 L St. NW, Ste. 650, Washington, DC, 20036-4922, USA, (202) 785-6323, (800) 456-6323, (202) 785-0350, washington.contact@oecd.org, https://www.oecd.org/; OECD-FAO Agricultural Outlook 2022-2031.

Palgrave Macmillan, 1 New York Plaza, Ste. 4500, New York, NY, 10004-1562, USA, (800) 777-4643, orders@palgrave.com, https://www.palgrave.com/us; The Statesman's Yearbook, 2023.

Routledge - Taylor & Francis Group, 6000 Broken Sound Pkwy. NW, Ste. 300, Boca Raton, FL, 33487, USA, (800) 634-1420, (800) 634-7064, orders@taylorandfrancis.com, https://www.routledge.com/; The Europa World Year Book 2022.

United Nations Food and Agricultural Organization (FAO), 2121 K St., Ste. 800B, Washington, DC, 20037, USA, (202) 653-2400 (Dial from U.S.), (202) 653-5760 (Fax from U.S.), fao-hq@fao.org, https://www.fao.org; The State of Food and Agriculture (SOFA) 2022.

United Nations Statistics Division (UNSD), United Nations Plz., New York, NY, 10017, USA, (800) 253-9646, (212) 963-9851, statistics@un.org, https://unstats.un.org; Statistical Yearbook of the United Nations 2021.

AUSTRIA-MAGNESIUM PRODUCTION AND CONSUMPTION

See AUSTRIA-MINERAL INDUSTRIES

AUSTRIA-MANUFACTURES

Organization for Economic Cooperation and Development (OECD), 2001 L St. NW, Ste. 650, Washington, DC, 20036-4922, USA, (202) 785-6323, (800) 456-6323, (202) 785-0350, washington.contact@oecd.org, https://www.oecd.org/; Economic Survey of Austria 2021; OECD Main Economic Indicators (MEI); and STAN (STructural ANalysis) Database.

AUSTRIA-MARRIAGE

Routledge - Taylor & Francis Group, 6000 Broken Sound Pkwy. NW, Ste. 300, Boca Raton, FL, 33487, USA, (800) 634-1420, (800) 634-7064, orders@taylorandfrancis.com, https://www.routledge.com/; The Europa World Year Book 2022.

United Nations Statistics Division (UNSD), United Nations Plz., New York, NY, 10017, USA, (800) 253-9646, (212) 963-9851, statistics@un.org, https://unstats.un.org; Statistical Yearbook of the United Nations 2021.

AUSTRIA-MERCURY PRODUCTION

See AUSTRIA-MINERAL INDUSTRIES

AUSTRIA-MINERAL INDUSTRIES

Barchart, 209 W Jackson Blvd., 2nd Fl., Chicago, IL, 60606, USA, (877) 247-4394, commodities@barchart.com, https://www.barchart.com/cmdty; The cmdty Yearbook 2023; cmdtyStats: Commodity Statistics and Fundamental Data; cmdtyView: Commodity Index; and Commodity Data and Prices.

European Commission, Eurostat, Luxembourg, 2920, LUX, https://ec.europa.eu/eurostat/; Final Energy Consumption in Transport by Type of Fuel.

International Energy Agency (IEA), 9 Rue de la Federation, Paris, 75739, FRA, info@iea.org, https://www.iea.org/; Coal 2021: Analysis and Forecast to 2024; World Energy Outlook 2021; and World Energy Statistics and Balances.

International Lead and Zinc Study Group (ILZSG), Rua Almirante Barroso 38, 5th Fl., Lisbon, 1000-013, PRT, sales@ilzsg.org, https://www.ilzsg.org; Interactive Statistical Database.

Organization for Economic Cooperation and Development (OECD), 2001 L St. NW, Ste. 650, Washington, DC, 20036-4922, USA, (202) 785-6323, (800) 456-6323, (202) 785-0350, washington.contact@oecd.org, https://www.oecd.org/; Economic Survey of Austria 2021; Energy Prices and Taxes for OECD Countries 2020; OECD Employment Outlook 2022: Building Back More Inclusive Labour Markets; OECD Main Economic Indicators (MEI); and STAN (STructural ANalysis) Database.

Palgrave Macmillan, 1 New York Plaza, Ste. 4500, New York, NY, 10004-1562, USA, (800) 777-4643, orders@palgrave.com, https://www.palgrave.com/us; The Statesman's Yearbook, 2023.

Routledge - Taylor & Francis Group, 6000 Broken Sound Pkwy. NW, Ste. 300, Boca Raton, FL, 33487, USA, (800) 634-1420, (800) 634-7064, orders@taylorandfrancis.com, https://www.routledge.com/; The Europa World Year Book 2022.

S&P Global Commodity Insights, One World Trade Center, New York, NY, 10007, USA, (800) 752-8878, support@platts.com, https://www.spglobal.com/commodityinsights/en; Platts Power in Europe.

United Nations Conference on Trade and Development (UNCTAD), Palais des Nations, Geneva, 1211, SWI, (212) 963-6896, unctadinfo@unctad.org, https://unctad.org; Trade and Development Report 2021.

United Nations Statistics Division (UNSD), United Nations Plz., New York, NY, 10017, USA, (800) 253-9646, (212) 963-9851, statistics@un.org, https://unstats.un.org; Statistical Yearbook of the United Nations 2021.

The World Bank, 1818 H St. NW, Washington, DC, 20433, USA, (202) 473-1000, (202) 477-6391, eds03@worldbank.org, https://www.worldbank.org/; Austria (report).

World Bureau of Metal Statistics (WBMS), 31 Star St., Ware, Hertfordshire, SG12 9BA, GBR, https://www.refinitiv.com/en/trading-solutions/world-bureau-metal-statistics; Annual Stainless Steel Statistics; Long Term Production/Consumption Series - All Metals; World Flow Charts; and World Metal Statistics.

World Steel Association (Worldsteel), Avenue de Tervueren 270, Brussels, B-1150, BEL, steel@worldsteel.org, https://www.worldsteel.org; Steel Statistical Yearbook 2021.

AUSTRIA-MONEY

European Central Bank (ECB), Frankfurt am Main, D-60640, GER, info@ecb.europa.eu, https://www.ecb.europa.eu; Economic Bulletin; Monetary Developments in the Euro Area; and Research Bulletin.

Organization for Economic Cooperation and Development (OECD), 2001 L St. NW, Ste. 650, Washington, DC, 20036-4922, USA, (202) 785-6323, (800) 456-6323, (202) 785-0350, washington.contact@oecd.org, https://www.oecd.org/; Economic Survey of Austria 2021.

AUSTRIA-MONEY SUPPLY

The Economist Group: Economist Intelligence Unit (EIU), 900 3rd Ave., 16th Fl., New York, NY, 10022, USA, (212) 541-0500, americas@eiu.com, https://www.eiu.com; Austria Country Report.

International Monetary Fund (IMF), 700 19th St. NW, Washington, DC, 20431, USA, (202) 623-7000, (202) 623-4661, publications@imf.org, https://www.imf.org; International Financial Statistics (IFS).

Routledge - Taylor & Francis Group, 6000 Broken Sound Pkwy. NW, Ste. 300, Boca Raton, FL, 33487, USA, (800) 634-1420, (800) 634-7064, orders@taylorandfrancis.com, https://www.routledge.com/; The Europa World Year Book 2022.

United Nations Statistics Division (UNSD), United Nations Plz., New York, NY, 10017, USA, (800) 253-9646, (212) 963-9851, statistics@un.org, https://unstats.un.org; Statistical Yearbook of the United Nations 2021.

The World Bank, 1818 H St. NW, Washington, DC, 20433, USA, (202) 473-1000, (202) 477-6391, eds03@worldbank.org, https://www.worldbank.org/; Austria (report).

AUSTRIA-MORTALITY

UNICEF, 3 United Nations Plz., New York, NY, 10017, USA, (212) 303-7984, (917) 244-2215, https://www.unicef.org; The State of the World's Children 2023.

United Nations Statistics Division (UNSD), United Nations Plz., New York, NY, 10017, USA, (800) 253-9646, (212) 963-9851, statistics@un.org, https://unstats.un.org; Millennium Development Goal Indicators; Statistical Yearbook of the United Nations 2021; and World Statistics Pocketbook 2021.

The World Bank, 1818 H St. NW, Washington, DC, 20433, USA, (202) 473-1000, (202) 477-6391, eds03@worldbank.org, https://www.worldbank.org/; World Development Indicators (WDI) 2022.

World Health Organization (WHO), Ave. Appia 20, Geneva, CH-1211, SWI, (202) 974-3000 (Telephone in U.S.), publications@who.int, https://www.who.int/; Global Health Observatory (GHO).

AUSTRIA-MOTION PICTURES

Palgrave Macmillan, 1 New York Plaza, Ste. 4500, New York, NY, 10004-1562, USA, (800) 777-4643, orders@palgrave.com, https://www.palgrave.com/us; The Statesman's Yearbook, 2023.

AUSTRIA-MOTOR VEHICLES

International Labour Organization (ILO), 4 Rte. des Morillons, Geneva, CH-1211, SWI, ilo@ilo.org, https://www.ilo.org; NORMLEX Information System on International Labour Standards.

AUSTRIA-NATURAL GAS PRODUCTION

See AUSTRIA-MINERAL INDUSTRIES

AUSTRIA-NICKEL AND NICKEL ORE

See AUSTRIA-MINERAL INDUSTRIES

AUSTRIA-NUTRITION

United Nations Food and Agricultural Organization (FAO), 2121 K St., Ste. 800B, Washington, DC, 20037, USA, (202) 653-2400 (Dial from U.S.), (202) 653-5760 (Fax from U.S.), fao-hq@fao.org, https://www.fao.org; The State of Food and Agriculture (SOFA) 2022.

United Nations Statistics Division (UNSD), United Nations Plz., New York, NY, 10017, USA, (800) 253-9646, (212) 963-9851, statistics@un.org, https://unstats.un.org; Millennium Development Goal Indicators.

AUSTRIA-PAPER

See AUSTRIA-FORESTS AND FORESTRY

AUSTRIA-PEANUT PRODUCTION

See AUSTRIA-CROPS

AUSTRIA-PESTICIDES

United Nations Food and Agricultural Organization (FAO), 2121 K St., Ste. 800B, Washington, DC, 20037, USA, (202) 653-2400 (Dial from U.S.), (202) 653-5760 (Fax from U.S.), fao-hq@fao.org, https://www.fao.org; The State of Food and Agriculture (SOFA) 2022.

AUSTRIA-PETROLEUM INDUSTRY AND TRADE

International Energy Agency (IEA), 9 Rue de la Federation, Paris, 75739, FRA, info@iea.org, https://www.iea.org/; World Energy Outlook 2021 and World Energy Statistics and Balances.

Organization for Economic Cooperation and Development (OECD), 2001 L St. NW, Ste. 650, Washington, DC, 20036-4922, USA, (202) 785-6323, (800) 456-6323, (202) 785-0350, washington.contact@oecd.org, https://www.oecd.org/; Energy Prices and Taxes for OECD Countries 2020.

Palgrave Macmillan, 1 New York Plaza, Ste. 4500, New York, NY, 10004-1562, USA, (800) 777-4643, orders@palgrave.com, https://www.palgrave.com/us; The Statesman's Yearbook, 2023.

U.S. Energy Information Administration (EIA), 1000 Independence Ave. SW, Washington, DC, 20585, USA, (202) 586-8800, infoctr@eia.gov, https://www.eia.gov; International Energy Outlook 2021.

United Nations Food and Agricultural Organization (FAO), 2121 K St., Ste. 800B, Washington, DC, 20037, USA, (202) 653-2400 (Dial from U.S.), (202) 653-5760 (Fax from U.S.), fao-hq@fao.org, https://www.fao.org; The State of Food and Agriculture (SOFA) 2022.

United Nations Statistics Division (UNSD), United Nations Plz., New York, NY, 10017, USA, (800) 253-9646, (212) 963-9851, statistics@un.org, https://unstats.un.org; Statistical Yearbook of the United Nations 2021.

AUSTRIA-PHOSPHATES PRODUCTION

See AUSTRIA-MINERAL INDUSTRIES

AUSTRIA-PLASTICS INDUSTRY AND TRADE

United Nations Statistics Division (UNSD), United Nations Plz., New York, NY, 10017, USA, (800) 253-9646, (212) 963-9851, statistics@un.org, https://unstats.un.org; Statistical Yearbook of the United Nations 2021.

AUSTRIA-PLATINUM PRODUCTION

See AUSTRIA-MINERAL INDUSTRIES

AUSTRIA-POPULATION

Austrian Academy of Sciences, Vienna Institute of Demography (VID), Vordere Zollamtsstrasse 3, Vienna, A-1030, AUT, vid@oeaw.ac.at, https://www.oeaw.ac.at/vid/; European Demographic Data Sheet 2022 and Vienna Yearbook of Population Research 2022.

Banque de France, 31 rue Croix des Petits-Champs, Paris, 75049, FRA, infos@banque-france.fr, https://www.banque-france.fr/en; Webstat: Access to Statistical Series of Banque de France.

Central Intelligence Agency (CIA), Office of Public Affairs, Washington, DC, 20505, USA, (703) 482-0623, https://www.cia.gov; The World Factbook.

The Economist Group: Economist Intelligence Unit (EIU), 900 3rd Ave., 16th Fl., New York, NY, 10022, USA, (212) 541-0500, americas@eiu.com, https://www.eiu.com; Austria Country Report.

Infoplease, c/o Sandbox Networks, Inc., 1 Lincoln St., 24th Fl., Boston, MA, 02111, USA, https://www.infoplease.com; Countries of the World.

International Labour Organization (ILO), 4 Rte. des Morillons, Geneva, CH-1211, SWI, ilo@ilo.org, https://www.ilo.org; NORMLEX Information System on International Labour Standards.

Organization for Economic Cooperation and Development (OECD), 2001 L St. NW, Ste. 650, Washington, DC, 20036-4922, USA, (202) 785-6323, (800) 456-6323, (202) 785-0350, washington.contact@oecd.org, https://www.oecd.org/; OECD Labour Force Statistics 2022.

Palgrave Macmillan, 1 New York Plaza, Ste. 4500, New York, NY, 10004-1562, USA, (800) 777-4643, orders@palgrave.com, https://www.palgrave.com/us; The Statesman's Yearbook, 2023.

Routledge - Taylor & Francis Group, 6000 Broken Sound Pkwy. NW, Ste. 300, Boca Raton, FL, 33487, USA, (800) 634-1420, (800) 634-7064, orders@taylorandfrancis.com, https://www.routledge.com/; The Europa World Year Book 2022.

UK Data Service, University of Essex, Wivenhoe Park, Colchester, Essex, CO4 3SQ, GBR, https://ukdataservice.ac.uk/; International Aggregate Data.

United Nations Department of Economic and Social Affairs (DESA), Population Division, 2 United Nations Plz., Rm. DC2-1950, New York, NY, 10017, USA, (212) 963-3209, (212) 963-2147, population@un.org, https://www.un.org/development/desa/pd/; Revision of World Urbanization Prospects and World Population Ageing 2020 Highlights.

United Nations Development Programme (UNDP), One United Nations Plz., New York, NY, 10017, USA, (212) 906-5000, (212) 906-5001, https://www.undp.org; Human Development Report 2021-2022.

United Nations Statistics Division (UNSD), United Nations Plz., New York, NY, 10017, USA, (800) 253-9646, (212) 963-9851, statistics@un.org, https://unstats.un.org; Statistical Yearbook of the United Nations 2021 and World Statistics Pocketbook 2021.

The World Bank, 1818 H St. NW, Washington, DC, 20433, USA, (202) 473-1000, (202) 477-6391, eds03@worldbank.org, https://www.worldbank.org/; Austria (report); The Global Findex Database 2021; and World Development Report 2022: Finance for an Equitable Recovery.

AUSTRIA-POPULATION DENSITY

Central Intelligence Agency (CIA), Office of Public Affairs, Washington, DC, 20505, USA, (703) 482-0623, https://www.cia.gov; The World Factbook.

Palgrave Macmillan, 1 New York Plaza, Ste. 4500, New York, NY, 10004-1562, USA, (800) 777-4643, orders@palgrave.com, https://www.palgrave.com/us; The Statesman's Yearbook, 2023.

Routledge - Taylor & Francis Group, 6000 Broken Sound Pkwy. NW, Ste. 300, Boca Raton, FL, 33487, USA, (800) 634-1420, (800) 634-7064, orders@taylorandfrancis.com, https://www.routledge.com/; The Europa World Year Book 2022.

The World Bank, 1818 H St. NW, Washington, DC, 20433, USA, (202) 473-1000, (202) 477-6391, eds03@worldbank.org, https://www.worldbank.org/; Austria (report) and World Development Report 2022: Finance for an Equitable Recovery.

AUSTRIA-POSTAL SERVICE

Palgrave Macmillan, 1 New York Plaza, Ste. 4500, New York, NY, 10004-1562, USA, (800) 777-4643, orders@palgrave.com, https://www.palgrave.com/us; The Statesman's Yearbook, 2023.

AUSTRIA-POULTRY

See AUSTRIA-LIVESTOCK

AUSTRIA-POWER RESOURCES

Euromonitor International, Inc., 1 N Dearborn St., Ste. 1700, Chicago, IL, 60602, USA, (312) 922-1115, (312) 922-1157, info-usa@euromonitor.com, https://www.euromonitor.com/; Geographies.

International Energy Agency (IEA), 9 Rue de la Federation, Paris, 75739, FRA, info@iea.org, https://www.iea.org/; Coal 2021: Analysis and Forecast to 2024 and World Energy Outlook 2021.

Organization for Economic Cooperation and Development (OECD), 2001 L St. NW, Ste. 650, Washington, DC, 20036-4922, USA, (202) 785-6323, (800) 456-6323, (202) 785-0350, washington.contact@oecd.org, https://www.oecd.org/; Energy Prices and Taxes for OECD Countries 2020 and Environment Statistics.

Palgrave Macmillan, 1 New York Plaza, Ste. 4500, New York, NY, 10004-1562, USA, (800) 777-4643, orders@palgrave.com, https://www.palgrave.com/us; The Statesman's Yearbook, 2023.

S&P Global Commodity Insights, One World Trade Center, New York, NY, 10007, USA, (800) 752-8878, support@platts.com, https://www.spglobal.com/commodityinsights/en; Platts European Power Daily.

U.S. Energy Information Administration (EIA), 1000 Independence Ave. SW, Washington, DC, 20585, USA, (202) 586-8800, infoctr@eia.gov, https://www.eia.gov; International Energy Outlook 2021.

United Nations Food and Agricultural Organization (FAO), 2121 K St., Ste. 800B, Washington, DC, 20037, USA, (202) 653-2400 (Dial from U.S.), (202) 653-5760 (Fax from U.S.), fao-hq@fao.org, https://www.fao.org; The State of Food and Agriculture (SOFA) 2022.

United Nations Statistics Division (UNSD), United Nations Plz., New York, NY, 10017, USA, (800) 253-9646, (212) 963-9851, statistics@un.org, https://unstats.un.org; Energy Statistics Yearbook 2019 and World Statistics Pocketbook 2021.

The World Bank, 1818 H St. NW, Washington, DC, 20433, USA, (202) 473-1000, (202) 477-6391, eds03@worldbank.org, https://www.worldbank.org/; World Development Report 2022: Finance for an Equitable Recovery.

AUSTRIA-PRICES

Euromonitor International, Inc., 1 N Dearborn St., Ste. 1700, Chicago, IL, 60602, USA, (312) 922-1115, (312) 922-1157, info-usa@euromonitor.com, https://www.euromonitor.com/; Geographies.

International Monetary Fund (IMF), 700 19th St. NW, Washington, DC, 20431, USA, (202) 623-7000, (202) 623-4661, publications@imf.org, https://www.imf.org; International Financial Statistics (IFS).

Organization for Economic Cooperation and Development (OECD), 2001 L St. NW, Ste. 650, Washington, DC, 20036-4922, USA, (202) 785-6323, (800) 456-6323, (202) 785-0350, washington.contact@oecd.org, https://www.oecd.org/; OECD Digital Economy Outlook 2020 and OECD Main Economic Indicators (MEI).

TAPPI - Technical Association of the Pulp and Paper Industry, 15 Technology Pkwy. S, Ste. 115, Peachtree Corners, GA, 30092, USA, (770) 446-1400, (800) 332-8686, (770) 446-6947, memberconnection@tappi.org, https://www.tappi.org/; TAPPI Journal.

The World Bank, 1818 H St. NW, Washington, DC, 20433, USA, (202) 473-1000, (202) 477-6391, eds03@worldbank.org, https://www.worldbank.org/; Austria (report).

World Bureau of Metal Statistics (WBMS), 31 Star St., Ware, Hertfordshire, SG12 9BA, GBR, https://www.refinitiv.com/en/trading-solutions/world-bureau-metal-statistics; Long Term Production/Consumption Series - All Metals; World Flow Charts; and World Metal Statistics.

AUSTRIA-PUBLIC HEALTH

Euromonitor International, Inc., 1 N Dearborn St., Ste. 1700, Chicago, IL, 60602, USA, (312) 922-1115, (312) 922-1157, info-usa@euromonitor.com, https://www.euromonitor.com/; Geographies and Market Research on the Health and Wellness Industry.

European Commission, Directorate-General for Health and Food Safety, Brussels, B-1049, BEL, https://ec.europa.eu/info/departments/health-and-food-safety_en ; zzunpublished data.

Organization for Economic Cooperation and Development (OECD), 2001 L St. NW, Ste. 650, Washington, DC, 20036-4922, USA, (202) 785-6323, (800) 456-6323, (202) 785-0350, washington.contact@oecd.org, https://www.oecd.org/; Health at a Glance 2021.

Palgrave Macmillan, 1 New York Plaza, Ste. 4500, New York, NY, 10004-1562, USA, (800) 777-4643, orders@palgrave.com, https://www.palgrave.com/us; The Statesman's Yearbook, 2023.

U.S. Census Bureau, 4600 Silver Hill Rd., Washington, DC, 20233, USA, (301) 763-4636, (800) 923-8282, https://www.census.gov; HIV/AIDS Surveillance Data Base.

UNICEF, 3 United Nations Plz., New York, NY, 10017, USA, (212) 303-7984, (917) 244-2215, https://www.unicef.org; The State of the World's Children 2023.

United Nations Department of Economic and Social Affairs (DESA), Population Division, 2 United Nations Plz., Rm. DC2-1950, New York, NY, 10017, USA, (212) 963-3209, (212) 963-2147, population@un.org, https://www.un.org/development/desa/pd/; World Fertility Data 2019.

United Nations Development Programme (UNDP), One United Nations Plz., New York, NY, 10017, USA, (212) 906-5000, (212) 906-5001, https://www.undp.org; Human Development Report 2021-2022.

United Nations Statistics Division (UNSD), United Nations Plz., New York, NY, 10017, USA, (800) 253-9646, (212) 963-9851, statistics@un.org, https://unstats.un.org; Millennium Development Goal Indicators and Statistical Yearbook of the United Nations 2021.

The World Bank, 1818 H St. NW, Washington, DC, 20433, USA, (202) 473-1000, (202) 477-6391, eds03@worldbank.org, https://www.worldbank.org/; Austria (report).

World Health Organization (WHO), Ave. Appia 20, Geneva, CH-1211, SWI, (202) 974-3000 (Telephone in U.S.), publications@who.int, https://www.who.int/; Global Health Observatory (GHO) and Health Statistics and Information Systems.

AUSTRIA-PUBLISHERS AND PUBLISHING

Routledge - Taylor & Francis Group, 6000 Broken Sound Pkwy. NW, Ste. 300, Boca Raton, FL, 33487, USA, (800) 634-1420, (800) 634-7064,

orders@taylorandfrancis.com, https://www.routledge.com/; The Europa World Year Book 2022.

UNESCO Institute for Statistics, C.P 250 Succursale H, Montreal, QC, H3G 2K8, CAN, (514) 343-6880 (Dial from U.S.), (514) 343-5740 (Fax from U.S.), uis.publications@unesco.org, http://uis.unesco.org/; UIS.Stat.

AUSTRIA-RAILROADS

Janes, USA, (703) 574-7580, (888) 977-1519, customer.care@janes.com, https://www.janes.com; Janes World Railways 2021-2022.

Palgrave Macmillan, 1 New York Plaza, Ste. 4500, New York, NY, 10004-1562, USA, (800) 777-4643, orders@palgrave.com, https://www.palgrave.com/us; The Statesman's Yearbook, 2023.

Routledge - Taylor & Francis Group, 6000 Broken Sound Pkwy. NW, Ste. 300, Boca Raton, FL, 33487, USA, (800) 634-1420, (800) 634-7064, orders@taylorandfrancis.com, https://www.routledge.com/; The Europa World Year Book 2022.

United Nations Statistics Division (UNSD), United Nations Plz., New York, NY, 10017, USA, (800) 253-9646, (212) 963-9851, statistics@un.org, https://unstats.un.org; Statistical Yearbook of the United Nations 2021.

AUSTRIA-RELIGION

Central Intelligence Agency (CIA), Office of Public Affairs, Washington, DC, 20505, USA, (703) 482-0623, https://www.cia.gov; The World Factbook.

Palgrave Macmillan, 1 New York Plaza, Ste. 4500, New York, NY, 10004-1562, USA, (800) 777-4643, orders@palgrave.com, https://www.palgrave.com/us; The Statesman's Yearbook, 2023.

AUSTRIA-RETAIL TRADE

Banque de France, 31 rue Croix des Petits-Champs, Paris, 75049, FRA, infos@banque-france.fr, https://www.banque-france.fr/en; Key Figures France and Abroad.

Euromonitor International, Inc., 1 N Dearborn St., Ste. 1700, Chicago, IL, 60602, USA, (312) 922-1115, (312) 922-1157, info-usa@euromonitor.com, https://www.euromonitor.com/; Geographies and Market Research on the Retailing Industry.

United Nations Statistics Division (UNSD), United Nations Plz., New York, NY, 10017, USA, (800) 253-9646, (212) 963-9851, statistics@un.org, https://unstats.un.org; Statistical Yearbook of the United Nations 2021.

AUSTRIA-RICE PRODUCTION

See AUSTRIA-CROPS

AUSTRIA-ROADS

International Road Federation (IRF), Madison Place, 500 Montgomery St., 5th Fl., Alexandria, VA, 22314, USA, (703) 535-1001, (703) 535-1007, info@irf.global, https://www.irf.global/; World Road Statistics (WRS).

AUSTRIA-RUBBER INDUSTRY AND TRADE

International Rubber Study Group (IRSG), 51 Changi Business Park Central 2, Unit No. 6, 486066, SGP, https://www.rubberstudy.org; Monthly Rubber Bulletin (MRB); Rubber Industry Report; Rubber Statistical Bulletin; and World Rubber Industry Report (WRIO).

AUSTRIA-RYE PRODUCTION

See AUSTRIA-CROPS

AUSTRIA-SHIPPING

Routledge - Taylor & Francis Group, 6000 Broken Sound Pkwy. NW, Ste. 300, Boca Raton, FL, 33487, USA, (800) 634-1420, (800) 634-7064, orders@taylorandfrancis.com, https://www.routledge.com/; The Europa World Year Book 2022.

AUSTRIA-STEEL PRODUCTION

See AUSTRIA-MINERAL INDUSTRIES

AUSTRIA-SUGAR PRODUCTION

See AUSTRIA-CROPS

AUSTRIA-SULPHUR PRODUCTION

See AUSTRIA-MINERAL INDUSTRIES

AUSTRIA-TAXATION

International Labour Organization (ILO), 4 Rte. des Morillons, Geneva, CH-1211, SWI, ilo@ilo.org, https://www.ilo.org; NORMLEX Information System on International Labour Standards.

Organization for Economic Cooperation and Development (OECD), 2001 L St. NW, Ste. 650, Washington, DC, 20036-4922, USA, (202) 785-6323, (800) 456-6323, (202) 785-0350, washington.contact@oecd.org, https://www.oecd.org/; Revenue Statistics 2022.

The World Bank, 1818 H St. NW, Washington, DC, 20433, USA, (202) 473-1000, (202) 477-6391, eds03@worldbank.org, https://www.worldbank.org/; World Development Indicators (WDI) 2022.

AUSTRIA-TELEPHONE

Palgrave Macmillan, 1 New York Plaza, Ste. 4500, New York, NY, 10004-1562, USA, (800) 777-4643, orders@palgrave.com, https://www.palgrave.com/us; The Statesman's Yearbook, 2023.

Routledge - Taylor & Francis Group, 6000 Broken Sound Pkwy. NW, Ste. 300, Boca Raton, FL, 33487, USA, (800) 634-1420, (800) 634-7064, orders@taylorandfrancis.com, https://www.routledge.com/; The Europa World Year Book 2022.

United Nations Statistics Division (UNSD), United Nations Plz., New York, NY, 10017, USA, (800) 253-9646, (212) 963-9851, statistics@un.org, https://unstats.un.org; World Statistics Pocketbook 2021.

AUSTRIA-TEXTILE INDUSTRY

Euromonitor International, Inc., 1 N Dearborn St., Ste. 1700, Chicago, IL, 60602, USA, (312) 922-1115, (312) 922-1157, info-usa@euromonitor.com, https://www.euromonitor.com/; Market Research on the Retailing Industry.

Organization for Economic Cooperation and Development (OECD), 2001 L St. NW, Ste. 650, Washington, DC, 20036-4922, USA, (202) 785-6323, (800) 456-6323, (202) 785-0350, washington.contact@oecd.org, https://www.oecd.org/; OECD-FAO Agricultural Outlook 2022-2031 and STAN (STructural ANalysis) Database.

Palgrave Macmillan, 1 New York Plaza, Ste. 4500, New York, NY, 10004-1562, USA, (800) 777-4643, orders@palgrave.com, https://www.palgrave.com/us; The Statesman's Yearbook, 2023.

United Nations Statistics Division (UNSD), United Nations Plz., New York, NY, 10017, USA, (800) 253-9646, (212) 963-9851, statistics@un.org, https://unstats.un.org; Statistical Yearbook of the United Nations 2021.

AUSTRIA-TOBACCO INDUSTRY

Organization for Economic Cooperation and Development (OECD), 2001 L St. NW, Ste. 650, Washington, DC, 20036-4922, USA, (202) 785-6323, (800) 456-6323, (202) 785-0350, washington.contact@oecd.org, https://www.oecd.org/; STAN (STructural ANalysis) Database.

United Nations Statistics Division (UNSD), United Nations Plz., New York, NY, 10017, USA, (800) 253-9646, (212) 963-9851, statistics@un.org, https://unstats.un.org; Statistical Yearbook of the United Nations 2021.

AUSTRIA-TOURISM

Euromonitor International, Inc., 1 N Dearborn St., Ste. 1700, Chicago, IL, 60602, USA, (312) 922-1115, (312) 922-1157, info-usa@euromonitor.com, https://www.euromonitor.com/; Geographies.

European Commission, Rue de la Loi, 170, Brussels, B-1040, BEL, https://ec.europa.eu; Common Agricultural Policy (CAPF) Context Indicators, 2019 Update.

European Commission, Eurostat, Luxembourg, 2920, LUX, https://ec.europa.eu/eurostat/; European Union Tourism Database.

Organization for Economic Cooperation and Development (OECD), 2001 L St. NW, Ste. 650, Washington, DC, 20036-4922, USA, (202) 785-6323, (800) 456-6323, (202) 785-0350, washington.contact@oecd.org, https://www.oecd.org/; OECD Tourism Trends and Policies 2022.

Palgrave Macmillan, 1 New York Plaza, Ste. 4500, New York, NY, 10004-1562, USA, (800) 777-4643, orders@palgrave.com, https://www.palgrave.com/us; The Statesman's Yearbook, 2023.

Routledge - Taylor & Francis Group, 6000 Broken Sound Pkwy. NW, Ste. 300, Boca Raton, FL, 33487, USA, (800) 634-1420, (800) 634-7064, orders@taylorandfrancis.com, https://www.routledge.com/; The Europa World Year Book 2022.

United Nations Statistics Division (UNSD), United Nations Plz., New York, NY, 10017, USA, (800) 253-9646, (212) 963-9851, statistics@un.org, https://unstats.un.org; Statistical Yearbook of the United Nations 2021.

United Nations World Tourism Organization (UNWTO), Calle Poeta Joan Maragall 42, Madrid, 28020, SPA, info@unwto.org, https://www.unwto.org/; Yearbook of Tourism Statistics, 2021 Edition.

The World Bank, 1818 H St. NW, Washington, DC, 20433, USA, (202) 473-1000, (202) 477-6391, eds03@worldbank.org, https://www.worldbank.org/; Austria (report).

AUSTRIA-TRADE

See AUSTRIA-INTERNATIONAL TRADE

AUSTRIA-TRANSPORTATION

Central Intelligence Agency (CIA), Office of Public Affairs, Washington, DC, 20505, USA, (703) 482-0623, https://www.cia.gov; The World Factbook.

European Commission, Eurostat, Luxembourg, 2920, LUX, https://ec.europa.eu/eurostat/; Air Transport Statistics.

Palgrave Macmillan, 1 New York Plaza, Ste. 4500, New York, NY, 10004-1562, USA, (800) 777-4643, orders@palgrave.com, https://www.palgrave.com/us; The Statesman's Yearbook, 2023.

Routledge - Taylor & Francis Group, 6000 Broken Sound Pkwy. NW, Ste. 300, Boca Raton, FL, 33487, USA, (800) 634-1420, (800) 634-7064, orders@taylorandfrancis.com, https://www.routledge.com/; The Europa World Year Book 2022.

United Nations Economic Commission for Europe (UNECE), Palais des Nations, Geneva, CH-1211, SWI, unece_info@un.org, https://unece.org/; UN-ECE Countries in Figures 2019.

The World Bank, 1818 H St. NW, Washington, DC, 20433, USA, (202) 473-1000, (202) 477-6391, eds03@worldbank.org, https://www.worldbank.org/; Austria (report).

AUSTRIA-UNEMPLOYMENT

International Labour Organization (ILO), 4 Rte. des Morillons, Geneva, CH-1211, SWI, ilo@ilo.org, https://www.ilo.org; NORMLEX Information System on International Labour Standards.

Organization for Economic Cooperation and Development (OECD), 2001 L St. NW, Ste. 650, Washington, DC, 20036-4922, USA, (202) 785-6323, (800) 456-6323, (202) 785-0350, washington.contact@oecd.org, https://www.oecd.org/; Economic Survey of Austria 2021; OECD Composite Leading Indicator (CLI); OECD Employment Outlook 2022: Building Back More Inclusive Labour Markets; and OECD Labour Force Statistics 2022.

Palgrave Macmillan, 1 New York Plaza, Ste. 4500, New York, NY, 10004-1562, USA, (800) 777-4643, orders@palgrave.com, https://www.palgrave.com/us; The Statesman's Yearbook, 2023.

United Nations Statistics Division (UNSD), United Nations Plz., New York, NY, 10017, USA, (800) 253-9646, (212) 963-9851, statistics@un.org, https://unstats.un.org; Statistical Yearbook of the United Nations 2021.

AUSTRIA-URANIUM PRODUCTION AND CONSUMPTION

See AUSTRIA-MINERAL INDUSTRIES

AUSTRIA-VITAL STATISTICS

Palgrave Macmillan, 1 New York Plaza, Ste. 4500, New York, NY, 10004-1562, USA, (800) 777-4643, orders@palgrave.com, https://www.palgrave.com/us; The Statesman's Yearbook, 2023.

U.S. Census Bureau, 4600 Silver Hill Rd., Washington, DC, 20233, USA, (301) 763-4636, (800) 923-8282, https://www.census.gov; HIV/AIDS Surveillance Data Base.

United Nations Department of Economic and Social Affairs (DESA), Population Division, 2 United Nations Plz., Rm. DC2-1950, New York, NY, 10017, USA, (212) 963-3209, (212) 963-2147, population@un.org, https://www.un.org/development/desa/pd/; World Contraceptive Use 2021: Estimates and Projections of Family Planning Indicators and World Marriage Data 2019.

United Nations Statistics Division (UNSD), United Nations Plz., New York, NY, 10017, USA, (800) 253-9646, (212) 963-9851, statistics@un.org, https://unstats.un.org; Statistical Yearbook of the United Nations 2021.

AUSTRIA-WAGES

International Labour Organization (ILO), 4 Rte. des Morillons, Geneva, CH-1211, SWI, ilo@ilo.org, https://www.ilo.org; NORMLEX Information System on International Labour Standards.

Organization for Economic Cooperation and Development (OECD), 2001 L St. NW, Ste. 650, Washington, DC, 20036-4922, USA, (202) 785-6323, (800) 456-6323, (202) 785-0350, washington.contact@oecd.org, https://www.oecd.org/; OECD Digital Economy Outlook 2020; OECD Main Economic Indicators (MEI); and STAN (STructural ANalysis) Database.

United Nations Statistics Division (UNSD), United Nations Plz., New York, NY, 10017, USA, (800) 253-9646, (212) 963-9851, statistics@un.org, https://unstats.un.org; Statistical Yearbook of the United Nations 2021.

The World Bank, 1818 H St. NW, Washington, DC, 20433, USA, (202) 473-1000, (202) 477-6391, eds03@worldbank.org, https://www.worldbank.org/; Austria (report).

AUSTRIA-WEATHER

See AUSTRIA-CLIMATE

AUSTRIA-WHEAT PRODUCTION

See AUSTRIA-CROPS

AUSTRIA-WHOLESALE PRICE INDEXES

International Monetary Fund (IMF), 700 19th St. NW, Washington, DC, 20431, USA, (202) 623-7000, (202) 623-4661, publications@imf.org, https://www.imf.org; International Financial Statistics (IFS).

AUSTRIA-WHOLESALE TRADE

United Nations Statistics Division (UNSD), United Nations Plz., New York, NY, 10017, USA, (800) 253-9646, (212) 963-9851, statistics@un.org, https://unstats.un.org; Statistical Yearbook of the United Nations 2021.

AUSTRIA-WOOD AND WOOD PULP

See AUSTRIA-FORESTS AND FORESTRY

AUSTRIA-WOOD PRODUCTS

Organization for Economic Cooperation and Development (OECD), 2001 L St. NW, Ste. 650, Washington, DC, 20036-4922, USA, (202) 785-6323, (800) 456-6323, (202) 785-0350, washington.contact@oecd.org, https://www.oecd.org/; STAN (STructural ANalysis) Database.

AUSTRIA-WOOL PRODUCTION

See AUSTRIA-TEXTILE INDUSTRY

AUSTRIA-ZINC AND ZINC ORE

See AUSTRIA-MINERAL INDUSTRIES

AUSTRIA-ZOOS

UNESCO Institute for Statistics, C.P 250 Succursale H, Montreal, QC, H3G 2K8, CAN, (514) 343-6880 (Dial from U.S.), (514) 343-5740 (Fax from U.S.), uis.publications@unesco.org, http://uis.unesco.org/; UIS.Stat.

AUTHORITARIANISM

Civis Analytics, 200 W Monroe St., 22nd Fl., Chicago, IL, 60606, USA, https://www.civisanalytics.com/; BLM and Policing Survey Identifies Broad Support for Common-Sense Reform.

Democracy Fund Voter Study Group, 1200 17th St. NW, Ste. 300, Washington, DC, 20036, USA, (202) 420-7900, https://www.voterstudygroup.org/; Democracy Maybe: Attitudes on Authoritarianism in America.

Freedom House, 1850 M St. NW, 11th Fl., Washington, DC, 20036, USA, (202) 296-5101, info@freedomhouse.org, https://freedomhouse.org; Freedom in the World 2022: The Global Expansion of Authoritarian Rule.

AUTHORS

U.S. Department of Labor (DOL), Bureau of Labor Statistics (BLS), Postal Square Bldg., 2 Massachusetts Ave. NE, Washington, DC, 20212-0001, USA, (202) 691-5200, (202) 691-7890, blsdata_staff@bls.gov, https://www.bls.gov; Monthly Labor Review.

AUTISM

A.J. Drexel Autism Institute, 3020 Market St., Ste. 560, Philadelphia, PA, 19104-3734, USA, (215) 571-3401, (215) 571-3187, autisminstitute@drexel.edu, https://drexel.edu/autisminstitute/; National Autism Indicators Report: Family Perspectives on Services and Supports; National Autism Indicators Report: Health and Health Care; National Autism Indicators Report: High School Students on the Autism Spectrum; and National Autism Indicators Report: Mental Health.

U.S. Department of Health and Human Services (HHS), National Institutes of Health (NIH), National Institute of Mental Health (NIMH), 6001 Executive Blvd., Room 6200, MSC 9663, Bethesda, MD, 20892-9663, USA, (866) 615-6464, (301) 443-8431 (TTY), (301) 443-4279, nimhinfo@nih.gov, https://www.nimh.nih.gov/; Mental Health Statistics.

AUTISM SPECTRUM DISORDERS

A.J. Drexel Autism Institute, 3020 Market St., Ste. 560, Philadelphia, PA, 19104-3734, USA, (215) 571-3401, (215) 571-3187, autisminstitute@drexel.edu, https://drexel.edu/autisminstitute/; National Autism Indicators Report: Family Perspectives on Services and Supports; National Autism Indicators Report: Health and Health Care; National Autism Indicators Report: High School Students on the Autism Spectrum; and National Autism Indicators Report: Mental Health.

Yale School of Medicine, Yale Child Study Center, 230 S Frontage Rd., New Haven, CT, 06520, USA, (844) 362-9272, https://medicine.yale.edu/childstudy; unpublished data.

AUTOMOBILE DEALERS-EARNINGS

The NPD Group, 900 W Shore Rd., Port Washington, NY, 11050, USA, (516) 625-0700, contactnpd@npd.com, https://www.npd.com; Automotive.

U.S. Census Bureau, 4600 Silver Hill Rd., Washington, DC, 20233, USA, (301) 763-4636, (800) 923-8282, https://www.census.gov; County Business Patterns (CBP) 2020.

U.S. Census Bureau, Center for Economic Studies (CES), 4600 Silver Hill Rd., Washington, DC, 20233, USA, (301) 763-6460, (301) 763-5935, ces.contacts@census.gov, https://www.census.gov/programs-surveys/ces.html; Retail Trade, 2017 Economic Census and Wholesale Trade, 2017 Economic Census.

U.S. Department of Commerce (DOC), International Trade Administration (ITA), 1401 Constitution Ave. NW, Washington, DC, 20230, USA, (800) 872-8723, https://www.trade.gov/; TradeStats Express (TSE).

AUTOMOBILE DEALERS-EMPLOYEES

U.S. Census Bureau, 4600 Silver Hill Rd., Washington, DC, 20233, USA, (301) 763-4636, (800) 923-8282, https://www.census.gov; County Business Patterns (CBP) 2020.

U.S. Census Bureau, Center for Economic Studies (CES), 4600 Silver Hill Rd., Washington, DC, 20233, USA, (301) 763-6460, (301) 763-5935, ces.contacts@census.gov, https://www.census.gov/programs-surveys/ces.html; Retail Trade, 2017 Economic Census and Wholesale Trade, 2017 Economic Census.

AUTOMOBILE DEALERS-ESTABLISHMENTS

U.S. Census Bureau, 4600 Silver Hill Rd., Washington, DC, 20233, USA, (301) 763-4636, (800) 923-8282, https://www.census.gov; County Business Patterns (CBP) 2020.

U.S. Census Bureau, Center for Economic Studies (CES), 4600 Silver Hill Rd., Washington, DC, 20233, USA, (301) 763-6460, (301) 763-5935, ces.contacts@census.gov, https://www.census.gov/programs-surveys/ces.html; Retail Trade, 2017 Economic Census and Wholesale Trade, 2017 Economic Census.

U.S. Department of Commerce (DOC), International Trade Administration (ITA), 1401 Constitution Ave. NW, Washington, DC, 20230, USA, (800) 872-8723, https://www.trade.gov/; TradeStats Express (TSE).

AUTOMOBILE DEALERS-INVENTORIES

U.S. Census Bureau, Center for Economic Studies (CES), 4600 Silver Hill Rd., Washington, DC, 20233, USA, (301) 763-6460, (301) 763-5935, ces.contacts@census.gov, https://www.census.gov/programs-surveys/ces.html; Retail Trade, 2017 Economic Census and Wholesale Trade, 2017 Economic Census.

U.S. Department of Commerce (DOC), International Trade Administration (ITA), 1401 Constitution Ave. NW, Washington, DC, 20230, USA, (800) 872-8723, https://www.trade.gov/; TradeStats Express (TSE).

AUTOMOBILE DEALERS-PRODUCTION

The NPD Group, 900 W Shore Rd., Port Washington, NY, 11050, USA, (516) 625-0700, contactnpd@npd.com, https://www.npd.com; Automotive.

U.S. Department of Labor (DOL), Bureau of Labor Statistics (BLS), Postal Square Bldg., 2 Massachusetts Ave. NE, Washington, DC, 20212-0001, USA, (202) 691-5200, (202) 691-7890, blsdata_staff@bls.gov, https://www.bls.gov; Productivity.

AUTOMOBILE DEALERS-SALES

Alliance for Automotive Innovation, 1050 K St., Ste. 650, Washington, DC, 20001, USA, (202) 326-5500, (916) 447-7315, info@autosinnovate.org, https://www.autosinnovate.org; Electric Vehicle Sales Dashboard and Reading the Meter: State of the Industry Report.

The NPD Group, 900 W Shore Rd., Port Washington, NY, 11050, USA, (516) 625-0700, contactnpd@npd.com, https://www.npd.com; Automotive.

U.S. Census Bureau, Center for Economic Studies (CES), 4600 Silver Hill Rd., Washington, DC, 20233, USA, (301) 763-6460, (301) 763-5935, ces.contacts@census.gov, https://www.census.gov/programs-surveys/ces.html; Retail Trade, 2017 Economic Census and Wholesale Trade, 2017 Economic Census.

U.S. Department of Commerce (DOC), International Trade Administration (ITA), 1401 Constitution Ave. NW, Washington, DC, 20230, USA, (800) 872-8723, https://www.trade.gov/; TradeStats Express (TSE).

AUTOMOBILE REPAIR SHOPS-EMPLOYEES

U.S. Department of Labor (DOL), Bureau of Labor Statistics (BLS), Postal Square Bldg., 2 Massachusetts Ave. NE, Washington, DC, 20212-0001, USA, (202) 691-5200, (202) 691-7890, blsdata_staff@bls.gov, https://www.bls.gov; Industry-Occupation Matrix Data, By Occupation.

AUTOMOBILE REPAIR SHOPS-ESTABLISHMENTS

U.S. Census Bureau, 4600 Silver Hill Rd., Washington, DC, 20233, USA, (301) 763-4636, (800) 923-8282, https://www.census.gov; County Business Patterns (CBP) 2020 and Economic Census, Nonemployer Statistics (NES) 2019.

AUTOMOBILE REPAIR SHOPS-PRODUCTIVITY

U.S. Department of Labor (DOL), Bureau of Labor Statistics (BLS), Postal Square Bldg., 2 Massachusetts Ave. NE, Washington, DC, 20212-0001, USA, (202) 691-5200, (202) 691-7890, blsdata_staff@bls.gov, https://www.bls.gov; Productivity.

AUTOMOBILE REPAIR SHOPS-RECEIPTS

U.S. Census Bureau, 4600 Silver Hill Rd., Washington, DC, 20233, USA, (301) 763-4636, (800) 923-8282, https://www.census.gov; Economic Census, Nonemployer Statistics (NES) 2019.

AUTOMOBILES

See also MOTOR VEHICLES

The NPD Group, 900 W Shore Rd., Port Washington, NY, 11050, USA, (516) 625-0700, contactnpd@npd.com, https://www.npd.com; Automotive.

Transport Research Laboratory (TRL), Crowthorne House, Nine Mile Ride, Wokingham, Berkshire, RG40 3GA, GBR, enquiries@trl.co.uk, https://trl.co.uk/; Skid Resistance Benchmark Surveys 2021.

U.S. Department of Energy (DOE), Office of Energy Efficiency and Renewable Energy (EERE), Alternative Fuels Data Center (AFDC), Mail Stop EE-1, Washington, DC, 20585, USA, (202) 586-5000, https://www.afdc.energy.gov/; Clean Cities; Fuels & Infrastructure; and Regulated Fleets.

U.S. Environmental Protection Agency (EPA), 1200 Pennsylvania Ave. NW, Washington, DC, 20460, USA, (202) 564-4700, https://www.epa.gov/; 2021 Automotive Trends Report.

WardsAuto, 3000 Town Ctr., Ste. 2750, Southfield, MI, 48075, USA, (248) 799-2642, (248) 799-2622, (248) 357-9747, wards@wardsauto.com, https://www.wardsauto.com/; Ward's InfoBank and Ward's World Motor Vehicle Data 2020.

AUTOMOBILES-ENVIRONMENTAL ASPECTS

BloombergNEF, New York, NY, 10022, USA, (212) 617-4050, https://about.bnef.com; Electric Vehicle Outlook 2022.

New York University School of Law, Institute for Policy Integrity, 139 MacDougal St., Wilf Hall, 3rd Fl., New York, NY, 10012, USA, (212) 992-8932, (212) 995-4592, https://policyintegrity.org/; Analyzing EPA's Vehicle-Emissions Decisions: Why Withdrawing the 2022-2025 Standards Is Economically Flawed.

RAC Motoring Services, RAC House, Brockhurst Crescent, Walsall, WS5 4AW, GBR, https://www.rac.co.uk; More Drivers than Ever Plan to 'Go Electric' When They Next Change Their Cars and RAC Report on Motoring 2022.

Society of Motor Manufacturers and Traders (SMMT), 71 Great Peter St., London, SW1P 2BN, GBR, https://www.smmt.co.uk; 2022 Automotive Sustainability Report.

AUTOMOBILES-EXPENDITURE PER NEW CAR

U.S. Department of Commerce (DOC), Bureau of Economic Analysis (BEA), 4600 Silver Hill Rd., Washington, DC, 20233, USA, (301) 278-9004, customerservice@bea.gov, https://www.bea.gov; Survey of Current Business (SCB).

AUTOMOBILES-FOREIGN COUNTRIES

Bain & Company, 131 Dartmouth St., Boston, MA, 02116, USA, (617) 572-2000, (617) 572-2427, https://www.bain.com/; The Coronavirus Demand Challenge Awaiting China's Auto Industry.

International Energy Agency (IEA), 9 Rue de la Federation, Paris, 75739, FRA, info@iea.org, https://www.iea.org/; Global EV Data Explorer and Global EV Outlook 2023.

Japan Automobile Manufacturers Association (JAMA), Jidosha Kaikan (NBF Tower), 16th Fl., 1-30, Shiba Daimon 1-chome, Minato-ku, Tokyo, 105-0012, JPN, https://www.jama.or.jp/english/; The Motor Industry of Japan 2022 and Motor Vehicle Statistics of Japan 2020.

Oko-Institut e.V. (Institute for Applied Ecology), PO Box 17 71, Freiburg, D-79017, GER, info@oeko.de, https://www.oeko.de; E-Fuels Versus DACCS.

RAC Motoring Services, RAC House, Brockhurst Crescent, Walsall, WS5 4AW, GBR, https://www.rac.co.uk; More Drivers than Ever Plan to 'Go Electric' When They Next Change Their Cars and RAC Report on Motoring 2022.

Society of Motor Manufacturers and Traders (SMMT), 71 Great Peter St., London, SW1P 2BN, GBR, https://www.smmt.co.uk; 2022 Automotive Sustainability Report.

U.S. Department of Transportation (DOT), Federal Highway Administration (FHA), 1200 New Jersey Ave. SE, Washington, DC, 20590, USA, (202) 366-4000, https://highways.dot.gov/; Highway Statistics 2020.

AUTOMOBILES-IMPORTS

U.S. Department of Commerce (DOC), Bureau of Economic Analysis (BEA), 4600 Silver Hill Rd., Washington, DC, 20233, USA, (301) 278-9004, customerservice@bea.gov, https://www.bea.gov; Survey of Current Business (SCB).

WardsAuto, 3000 Town Ctr., Ste. 2750, Southfield, MI, 48075, USA, (248) 799-2642, (248) 799-2622, (248) 357-9747, wards@wardsauto.com, https://www.wardsauto.com/; Ward's Motor Vehicle Facts & Figures 2019.

AUTOMOBILES-INSURANCE

National Association of Insurance Commissioners (NAIC), 1100 Walnut St., Ste. 1500, Kansas City, MO, 64106-2197, USA, (816) 842-3600, (202) 471-3990, (816) 783-8175, help@naic.org, https://www.naic.org/; Insurance Department Resources Report.

U.S. Department of Transportation (DOT), Office of the Assistant Secretary for Research and Technology (OST-R), Bureau of Transportation Statistics (BTS), 1200 New Jersey Ave. SE, Washington, DC, 20590, USA, (800) 853-1351, (202) 366-3282, https://www.bts.gov; TranStats.

ValuePenguin, 600 3rd Ave. , 8th Fl., New York, NY, 10016, USA, media@valuepenguin.com, https://www.valuepenguin.com; State of Auto Insurance in 2023.

AUTOMOBILES-INTERNATIONAL TRADE

Alliance for Automotive Innovation, 1050 K St., Ste. 650, Washington, DC, 20001, USA, (202) 326-5500, (916) 447-7315, info@autosinnovate.org, https://www.autosinnovate.org; Economic Insights: See Auto Industry Impacts at the National, State, and Congressional District Levels.

WardsAuto, 3000 Town Ctr., Ste. 2750, Southfield, MI, 48075, USA, (248) 799-2642, (248) 799-2622, (248) 357-9747, wards@wardsauto.com, https://www.wardsauto.com/; Ward's InfoBank; Ward's Motor Vehicle Facts & Figures 2019; and Ward's World Motor Vehicle Data 2020.

AUTOMOBILES-LOANS

Board of Governors of the Federal Reserve System, Constitution Ave. NW, Washington, DC, 20551, USA, (202) 452-3000, (202) 263-4869 (TDD), https://www.federalreserve.gov; Federal Reserve Bulletin.

AUTOMOBILES-PRICE INDEXES

The NPD Group, 900 W Shore Rd., Port Washington, NY, 11050, USA, (516) 625-0700, contactnpd@npd.com, https://www.npd.com; Automotive.

U.S. Department of Labor (DOL), Bureau of Labor Statistics (BLS), Postal Square Bldg., 2 Massachusetts Ave. NE, Washington, DC, 20212-0001, USA, (202) 691-5200, (202) 691-7890, blsdata_staff@bls.gov, https://www.bls.gov; Consumer Price Index (CPI) Databases and Industry Data (Producer Price Index - PPI).

AUTOMOBILES-PRODUCTION

Alliance for Automotive Innovation, 1050 K St., Ste. 650, Washington, DC, 20001, USA, (202) 326-5500, (916) 447-7315, info@autosinnovate.org, https://www.autosinnovate.org; Economic Insights: See Auto Industry Impacts at the National, State, and Congressional District Levels and Reading the Meter: State of the Industry Report.

BloombergNEF, New York, NY, 10022, USA, (212) 617-4050, https://about.bnef.com; Lithium-ion Battery Pack Prices Rise for First Time to an Average of $151/kWh.

Consumer Technology Association (CTA), 1919 S Eads St., Arlington, VA, 22202, USA, (703) 907-7600, (866) 858-1555, (703) 907-7675, cta@cta.tech, https://www.cta.tech; Mobility and Auto Technology in the COVID-19 Era.

IDTechEx, One Boston Place, Ste. 2600, Boston, MA, 02108, USA, (617) 577-7890, (617) 577-7810, research@idtechex.com, https://www.idtechex.com/; Electric Vehicles: Land, Sea & Air 2022-2042.

International Energy Agency (IEA), 9 Rue de la Federation, Paris, 75739, FRA, info@iea.org, https://www.iea.org/; Global EV Data Explorer and Global EV Outlook 2023.

The NPD Group, 900 W Shore Rd., Port Washington, NY, 11050, USA, (516) 625-0700, contactnpd@npd.com, https://www.npd.com; Automotive.

Society of Motor Manufacturers and Traders (SMMT), 71 Great Peter St., London, SW1P 2BN, GBR, https://www.smmt.co.uk; 2022 Automotive Sustainability Report.

U.S. Department of Commerce (DOC), Bureau of Economic Analysis (BEA), 4600 Silver Hill Rd., Washington, DC, 20233, USA, (301) 278-9004, customerservice@bea.gov, https://www.bea.gov; Survey of Current Business (SCB).

WardsAuto, 3000 Town Ctr., Ste. 2750, Southfield, MI, 48075, USA, (248) 799-2642, (248) 799-2622, (248) 357-9747, wards@wardsauto.com, https://www.wardsauto.com/; Ward's Automotive Yearbook 2022; Ward's InfoBank; Ward's Motor Vehicle Facts & Figures 2019; and Ward's World Motor Vehicle Data 2020.

AUTOMOBILES-SALES

Alliance for Automotive Innovation, 1050 K St., Ste. 650, Washington, DC, 20001, USA, (202) 326-5500, (916) 447-7315, info@autosinnovate.org, https://www.autosinnovate.org; Economic Insights: See

Auto Industry Impacts at the National, State, and Congressional District Levels; Electric Vehicle Sales Dashboard; and Reading the Meter: State of the Industry Report.

Bain & Company, 131 Dartmouth St., Boston, MA, 02116, USA, (617) 572-2000, (617) 572-2427, https://www.bain.com/; The Coronavirus Demand Challenge Awaiting China's Auto Industry.

Board of Governors of the Federal Reserve System, Constitution Ave. NW, Washington, DC, 20551, USA, (202) 452-3000, (202) 263-4869 (TDD), https://www.federalreserve.gov; Annual Report of the FED, 2021.

EV-volumes.com, Strandgatan 28, Trollhattan, SE 461 30, SWE, info@ev-volumes.com, https://www.ev-volumes.com; EV Data Center; EV-volumes.com: The Electric Vehicle World Sales Database; and Global EV Sales for 2022.

IDTechEx, One Boston Place, Ste. 2600, Boston, MA, 02108, USA, (617) 577-7890, (617) 577-7810, research@idtechex.com, https://www.idtechex.com/; Electric Vehicles: Land, Sea & Air 2022-2042.

Manheim, 6325 Peachtree Dunwoody Rd. NE, Atlanta, GA, 30328, USA, (866) 626-4346, info@manheim.com, https://www.manheim.com; Manheim Market Report (MMR) and Manheim Used Vehicle Value Index.

The NPD Group, 900 W Shore Rd., Port Washington, NY, 11050, USA, (516) 625-0700, contactnpd@npd.com, https://www.npd.com; Automotive.

RAC Motoring Services, RAC House, Brockhurst Crescent, Walsall, WS5 4AW, GBR, https://www.rac.co.uk; RAC Report on Motoring 2022.

U.S. Department of Commerce (DOC), Bureau of Economic Analysis (BEA), 4600 Silver Hill Rd., Washington, DC, 20233, USA, (301) 278-9004, customerservice@bea.gov, https://www.bea.gov; Survey of Current Business (SCB).

U.S. Department of Energy (DOE), Office of Energy Efficiency and Renewable Energy (EERE), Alternative Fuels Data Center (AFDC), Mail Stop EE-1, Washington, DC, 20585, USA, (202) 586-5000, https://www.afdc.energy.gov/; Average Fuel Economy by Major Vehicle Category.

WardsAuto, 3000 Town Ctr., Ste. 2750, Southfield, MI, 48075, USA, (248) 799-2642, (248) 799-2622, (248) 357-9747, wards@wardsauto.com, https://www.wardsauto.com/; Ward's Automotive Yearbook 2022; Ward's Motor Vehicle Facts & Figures 2019; and Ward's World Motor Vehicle Data 2020.

Worldometer, https://www.worldometers.info/; Worldometers.info.

AVALANCHES

Colorado Avalanche Information Center (CAIC), 1313 Sherman St., Rm. 423, Denver, CO, 80203, USA, (303) 499-9650, help@caic.com, https://www.avalanche.state.co.us; US Avalanche Accidents 2022.

AVALANCHES-ACCIDENTS

Colorado Avalanche Information Center (CAIC), 1313 Sherman St., Rm. 423, Denver, CO, 80203, USA, (303) 499-9650, help@caic.com, https://www.avalanche.state.co.us; US Avalanche Accidents 2022.

AVOCADOS

U.S. Department of Agriculture (USDA), National Agricultural Statistics Service (USDA-NASS), 1400 Independence Ave. SW, Washington, DC, 20250, USA, (800) 727-9540, nass@nass.usda.gov, https://www.nass.usda.gov; Quick Stats.

AZERBAIJAN-NATIONAL STATISTICAL OFFICE

State Statistical Committee of the Republic of Azerbaijan, Inshaatchilar Ave. 81, Baku, AZ 1136, AJN, sc@azstat.org, https://www.stat.gov.az/; National Data Reports (Azerbaijan).

AZERBAIJAN-PRIMARY STATISTICS SOURCES

Interstate Statistical Committee of the Commonwealth of Independent States, USA, cisstat@cisstat.org, http://www.cisstat.com/eng; Population and Social Indicators of the CIS and Other Countries of the World 2016-2019.

State Statistical Committee of the Republic of Azerbaijan, Inshaatchilar Ave. 81, Baku, AZ 1136, AJN, sc@azstat.org, https://www.stat.gov.az/; Azerbaijan in Figures, 2023; Education, Science and Culture in Azerbaijan, 2023; and Statistical Indicators of Azerbaijan, 2023.

AZERBAIJAN-AGRICULTURE

The Economist Group: Economist Intelligence Unit (EIU), 900 3rd Ave., 16th Fl., New York, NY, 10022, USA, (212) 541-0500, americas@eiu.com, https://www.eiu.com; Azerbaijan Country Report.

Euromonitor International, Inc., 1 N Dearborn St., Ste. 1700, Chicago, IL, 60602, USA, (312) 922-1115, (312) 922-1157, info-usa@euromonitor.com, https://www.euromonitor.com/; Geographies.

Organisation of Islamic Cooperation (OIC), Statistical, Economic and Social Research and Training Centre for Islamic Countries (SESRIC), Kudus Cad. No. 9, Diplomatik Site, Ankara, 06450, TUR, statistics@sesric.org, https://www.sesric.org/; OIC Statistics (OICStat) Database and OIC-Countries in Figures (OIC-CIF).

Palgrave Macmillan, 1 New York Plaza, Ste. 4500, New York, NY, 10004-1562, USA, (800) 777-4643, orders@palgrave.com, https://www.palgrave.com/us; The Statesman's Yearbook, 2023.

Routledge - Taylor & Francis Group, 6000 Broken Sound Pkwy. NW, Ste. 300, Boca Raton, FL, 33487, USA, (800) 634-1420, (800) 634-7064, orders@taylorandfrancis.com, https://www.routledge.com/; The Europa World Year Book 2022.

United Nations Food and Agricultural Organization (FAO), 2121 K St., Ste. 800B, Washington, DC, 20037, USA, (202) 653-2400 (Dial from U.S.), (202) 653-5760 (Fax from U.S.), fao-hq@fao.org, https://www.fao.org; AQUASTAT and The State of Food and Agriculture (SOFA) 2022.

United Nations Statistics Division (UNSD), United Nations Plz., New York, NY, 10017, USA, (800) 253-9646, (212) 963-9851, statistics@un.org, https://unstats.un.org; Statistical Yearbook of the United Nations 2021.

The World Bank, 1818 H St. NW, Washington, DC, 20433, USA, (202) 473-1000, (202) 477-6391, eds03@worldbank.org, https://www.worldbank.org/; Azerbaijan (report) and World Development Indicators (WDI) 2022.

AZERBAIJAN-AIRLINES

International Civil Aviation Organization (ICAO), 999 Robert-Bourassa Blvd., Montreal, QC, H3C 5H7, CAN, (514) 954-8219 (Dial from U.S.), (514) 954-6077 (Fax from U.S.), icaohq@icao.int, https://www.icao.int; ICAO Regional Reports.

Palgrave Macmillan, 1 New York Plaza, Ste. 4500, New York, NY, 10004-1562, USA, (800) 777-4643, orders@palgrave.com, https://www.palgrave.com/us; The Statesman's Yearbook, 2023.

AZERBAIJAN-ARMED FORCES

Central Intelligence Agency (CIA), Office of Public Affairs, Washington, DC, 20505, USA, (703) 482-0623, https://www.cia.gov; The World Factbook.

International Institute for Strategic Studies (IISS) - Americas, 2121 K St. NW, Ste. 600, Washington, DC, 20037, USA, (202) 659-1490, (202) 659-1499, https://www.iiss.org/; Armed Conflict Survey 2021 and The Military Balance 2022.

Palgrave Macmillan, 1 New York Plaza, Ste. 4500, New York, NY, 10004-1562, USA, (800) 777-4643, orders@palgrave.com, https://www.palgrave.com/us; The Statesman's Yearbook, 2023.

Stockholm International Peace Research Institute (SIPRI), Signalistgatan 9, Stockholm, SE 169 72, SWE, https://www.sipri.org/; SIPRI Arms Transfers Database and SIPRI Military Expenditure Database.

AZERBAIJAN-BALANCE OF PAYMENTS

The World Bank, 1818 H St. NW, Washington, DC, 20433, USA, (202) 473-1000, (202) 477-6391, eds03@worldbank.org, https://www.worldbank.org/; Azerbaijan (report); World Development Indicators (WDI) 2022; and World Development Report 2022: Finance for an Equitable Recovery.

AZERBAIJAN-BANKS AND BANKING

Euromonitor International, Inc., 1 N Dearborn St., Ste. 1700, Chicago, IL, 60602, USA, (312) 922-1115, (312) 922-1157, info-usa@euromonitor.com, https://www.euromonitor.com/; Geographies.

AZERBAIJAN-BROADCASTING

Central Intelligence Agency (CIA), Office of Public Affairs, Washington, DC, 20505, USA, (703) 482-0623, https://www.cia.gov; The World Factbook.

Euromonitor International, Inc., 1 N Dearborn St., Ste. 1700, Chicago, IL, 60602, USA, (312) 922-1115, (312) 922-1157, info-usa@euromonitor.com, https://www.euromonitor.com/; Geographies.

Palgrave Macmillan, 1 New York Plaza, Ste. 4500, New York, NY, 10004-1562, USA, (800) 777-4643, orders@palgrave.com, https://www.palgrave.com/us; The Statesman's Yearbook, 2023.

UNESCO Institute for Statistics, C.P 250 Succursale H, Montreal, QC, H3G 2K8, CAN, (514) 343-6880 (Dial from U.S.), (514) 343-5740 (Fax from U.S.), uis.publications@unesco.org, http://uis.unesco.org/; UIS.Stat.

AZERBAIJAN-BUDGET

Central Intelligence Agency (CIA), Office of Public Affairs, Washington, DC, 20505, USA, (703) 482-0623, https://www.cia.gov; The World Factbook.

AZERBAIJAN-BUSINESS

United Nations Statistics Division (UNSD), United Nations Plz., New York, NY, 10017, USA, (800) 253-9646, (212) 963-9851, statistics@un.org, https://unstats.un.org; Statistical Yearbook of the United Nations 2021.

AZERBAIJAN-COAL PRODUCTION

See AZERBAIJAN-MINERAL INDUSTRIES

AZERBAIJAN-COMMERCE

Palgrave Macmillan, 1 New York Plaza, Ste. 4500, New York, NY, 10004-1562, USA, (800) 777-4643, orders@palgrave.com, https://www.palgrave.com/us; The Statesman's Yearbook, 2023.

UK Data Service, University of Essex, Wivenhoe Park, Colchester, Essex, CO4 3SQ, GBR, https://ukdataservice.ac.uk/; International Aggregate Data.

AZERBAIJAN-CONSTRUCTION INDUSTRY

United Nations Statistics Division (UNSD), United Nations Plz., New York, NY, 10017, USA, (800) 253-9646, (212) 963-9851, statistics@un.org, https://unstats.un.org; Statistical Yearbook of the United Nations 2021.

AZERBAIJAN-CONSUMER GOODS

The World Bank, 1818 H St. NW, Washington, DC, 20433, USA, (202) 473-1000, (202) 477-6391, eds03@worldbank.org, https://www.worldbank.org/; World Development Report 2022: Finance for an Equitable Recovery.

AZERBAIJAN-CONSUMER PRICE INDEXES

The World Bank, 1818 H St. NW, Washington, DC, 20433, USA, (202) 473-1000, (202) 477-6391, eds03@worldbank.org, https://www.worldbank.org/; Azerbaijan (report).

AZERBAIJAN-COTTON

See AZERBAIJAN-CROPS

AZERBAIJAN-CROPS

Palgrave Macmillan, 1 New York Plaza, Ste. 4500, New York, NY, 10004-1562, USA, (800) 777-4643, orders@palgrave.com, https://www.palgrave.com/us; The Statesman's Yearbook, 2023.

United Nations Food and Agricultural Organization (FAO), 2121 K St., Ste. 800B, Washington, DC, 20037, USA, (202) 653-2400 (Dial from U.S.), (202) 653-5760 (Fax from U.S.), fao-hq@fao.org, https://www.fao.org; The State of Food and Agriculture (SOFA) 2022.

United Nations Statistics Division (UNSD), United Nations Plz., New York, NY, 10017, USA, (800) 253-9646, (212) 963-9851, statistics@un.org, https://unstats.un.org; Statistical Yearbook of the United Nations 2021.

AZERBAIJAN-DAIRY PROCESSING

Palgrave Macmillan, 1 New York Plaza, Ste. 4500, New York, NY, 10004-1562, USA, (800) 777-4643, orders@palgrave.com, https://www.palgrave.com/us; The Statesman's Yearbook, 2023.

United Nations Food and Agricultural Organization (FAO), 2121 K St., Ste. 800B, Washington, DC, 20037, USA, (202) 653-2400 (Dial from U.S.), (202) 653-5760 (Fax from U.S.), fao-hq@fao.org, https://www.fao.org; The State of Food and Agriculture (SOFA) 2022.

AZERBAIJAN-DEBTS, EXTERNAL

The World Bank, 1818 H St. NW, Washington, DC, 20433, USA, (202) 473-1000, (202) 477-6391, eds03@worldbank.org, https://www.worldbank.org/; Global Financial Development Report 2019-2020: Bank Regulation and Supervision a Decade after the Global Financial Crisis; World Development Indicators (WDI) 2022; and World Development Report 2022: Finance for an Equitable Recovery.

AZERBAIJAN-ECONOMIC CONDITIONS

Bernan Press, 15250 NBN Way, Bldg. C, Blue Ridge Summit, PA, 17214, USA, (301) 459-2255, (800) 865-3457, (800) 865-3450, customercare@bernan.com, https://rowman.com/Page/Bernan; World Economic Outlook, April 2022.

Central Intelligence Agency (CIA), Office of Public Affairs, Washington, DC, 20505, USA, (703) 482-0623, https://www.cia.gov; The World Factbook.

The Economist Group: Economist Intelligence Unit (EIU), 900 3rd Ave., 16th Fl., New York, NY, 10022, USA, (212) 541-0500, americas@eiu.com, https://www.eiu.com; Azerbaijan Country Report.

Euromonitor International, Inc., 1 N Dearborn St., Ste. 1700, Chicago, IL, 60602, USA, (312) 922-1115, (312) 922-1157, info-usa@euromonitor.com, https://www.euromonitor.com/; Geographies and Market Research on the Consumer Finance Industry.

International Monetary Fund (IMF), 700 19th St. NW, Washington, DC, 20431, USA, (202) 623-7000, (202) 623-4661, publications@imf.org, https://www.imf.org; IMF Data and World Economic Outlook.

Organisation of Islamic Cooperation (OIC), Statistical, Economic and Social Research and Training Centre for Islamic Countries (SESRIC), Kudus Cad. No. 9, Diplomatik Site, Ankara, 06450, TUR, statistics@sesric.org, https://www.sesric.org/; OIC Economic Outlook 2021; OIC Statistics (OICStat) Database; and OIC-Countries in Figures (OIC-CIF).

Palgrave Macmillan, 1 New York Plaza, Ste. 4500, New York, NY, 10004-1562, USA, (800) 777-4643, orders@palgrave.com, https://www.palgrave.com/us; The Statesman's Yearbook, 2023.

Routledge - Taylor & Francis Group, 6000 Broken Sound Pkwy. NW, Ste. 300, Boca Raton, FL, 33487, USA, (800) 634-1420, (800) 634-7064, orders@taylorandfrancis.com, https://www.routledge.com/; The Europa World Year Book 2022.

State Statistical Committee of the Republic of Azerbaijan, Inshaatchilar Ave. 81, Baku, AZ 1136, AJN, sc@azstat.org, https://www.stat.gov.az/; Foreign Trade of Azerbaijan, 2023.

United Nations Economic and Social Commission for Western Asia (ESCWA), Riad el-Solh Sq., PO Box 11-8575, Beirut, LBN, escwa-ciu@un.org, https://www.unescwa.org; ESCWA Annual Report 2019; ESCWA Data Portal for the Arab Region; and Survey of Economic and Social Developments in the Arab Region 2020-2021.

United Nations Statistics Division (UNSD), United Nations Plz., New York, NY, 10017, USA, (800) 253-9646, (212) 963-9851, statistics@un.org, https://unstats.un.org; World Statistics Pocketbook 2021.

The World Bank, 1818 H St. NW, Washington, DC, 20433, USA, (202) 473-1000, (202) 477-6391, eds03@worldbank.org, https://www.worldbank.org/; Azerbaijan (report); Global Economic Monitor (GEM); Global Economic Prospects, June 2022; The Global Findex Database 2021; and World Development Report 2022: Finance for an Equitable Recovery.

AZERBAIJAN-EDUCATION

Euromonitor International, Inc., 1 N Dearborn St., Ste. 1700, Chicago, IL, 60602, USA, (312) 922-1115, (312) 922-1157, info-usa@euromonitor.com, https://www.euromonitor.com/; Geographies.

Infoplease, c/o Sandbox Networks, Inc., 1 Lincoln St., 24th Fl., Boston, MA, 02111, USA, https://www.infoplease.com; Countries of the World.

Organisation of Islamic Cooperation (OIC), Statistical, Economic and Social Research and Training Centre for Islamic Countries (SESRIC), Kudus Cad. No. 9, Diplomatik Site, Ankara, 06450, TUR, statistics@sesric.org, https://www.sesric.org/; OIC Statistics (OICStat) Database.

Palgrave Macmillan, 1 New York Plaza, Ste. 4500, New York, NY, 10004-1562, USA, (800) 777-4643, orders@palgrave.com, https://www.palgrave.com/us; The Statesman's Yearbook, 2023.

Routledge - Taylor & Francis Group, 6000 Broken Sound Pkwy. NW, Ste. 300, Boca Raton, FL, 33487, USA, (800) 634-1420, (800) 634-7064, orders@taylorandfrancis.com, https://www.routledge.com/; The Europa World Year Book 2022.

State Statistical Committee of the Republic of Azerbaijan, Inshaatchilar Ave. 81, Baku, AZ 1136, AJN, sc@azstat.org, https://www.stat.gov.az/; Education, Science and Culture in Azerbaijan, 2023.

UNESCO Institute for Statistics, C.P 250 Succursale H, Montreal, QC, H3G 2K8, CAN, (514) 343-6880 (Dial from U.S.), (514) 343-5740 (Fax from U.S.), uis.publications@unesco.org, http://uis.unesco.org/; Literacy and UIS.Stat.

United Nations Statistics Division (UNSD), United Nations Plz., New York, NY, 10017, USA, (800) 253-9646, (212) 963-9851, statistics@un.org, https://unstats.un.org; Millennium Development Goal Indicators.

The World Bank, 1818 H St. NW, Washington, DC, 20433, USA, (202) 473-1000, (202) 477-6391, eds03@worldbank.org, https://www.worldbank.org/; Azerbaijan (report) and World Development Report 2022: Finance for an Equitable Recovery.

AZERBAIJAN-ELECTRICITY

U.S. Energy Information Administration (EIA), 1000 Independence Ave. SW, Washington, DC, 20585, USA, (202) 586-8800, infoctr@eia.gov, https://www.eia.gov; International Energy Outlook 2021.

United Nations Statistics Division (UNSD), United Nations Plz., New York, NY, 10017, USA, (800) 253-9646, (212) 963-9851, statistics@un.org, https://unstats.un.org; Energy Statistics Yearbook 2019 and Statistical Yearbook of the United Nations 2021.

AZERBAIJAN-EMPLOYMENT

UK Data Service, University of Essex, Wivenhoe Park, Colchester, Essex, CO4 3SQ, GBR, https://ukdataservice.ac.uk/; International Aggregate Data.

United Nations Statistics Division (UNSD), United Nations Plz., New York, NY, 10017, USA, (800) 253-9646, (212) 963-9851, statistics@un.org, https://unstats.un.org; Statistical Yearbook of the United Nations 2021.

The World Bank, 1818 H St. NW, Washington, DC, 20433, USA, (202) 473-1000, (202) 477-6391, eds03@worldbank.org, https://www.worldbank.org/; Azerbaijan (report).

AZERBAIJAN-ENVIRONMENTAL CONDITIONS

DSI Data Service & Information, Xantener Strasse 51a, Rheinberg, D-47495, GER, dsi@dsidata.com, https://www.dsidata.com/; Global Environmental Database.

The Economist Group: Economist Intelligence Unit (EIU), 900 3rd Ave., 16th Fl., New York, NY, 10022, USA, (212) 541-0500, americas@eiu.com, https://www.eiu.com; Azerbaijan Country Report.

Organisation of Islamic Cooperation (OIC), Statistical, Economic and Social Research and Training Centre for Islamic Countries (SESRIC), Kudus Cad. No. 9, Diplomatik Site, Ankara, 06450, TUR, statistics@sesric.org, https://www.sesric.org/; OIC Statistics (OICStat) Database and OIC-Countries in Figures (OIC-CIF).

United Nations Statistics Division (UNSD), United Nations Plz., New York, NY, 10017, USA, (800) 253-9646, (212) 963-9851, statistics@un.org, https://unstats.un.org; Statistical Yearbook of the United Nations 2021 and World Statistics Pocketbook 2021.

AZERBAIJAN-EXPORTS

Central Intelligence Agency (CIA), Office of Public Affairs, Washington, DC, 20505, USA, (703) 482-0623, https://www.cia.gov; The World Factbook.

The Economist Group: Economist Intelligence Unit (EIU), 900 3rd Ave., 16th Fl., New York, NY, 10022, USA, (212) 541-0500, americas@eiu.com, https://www.eiu.com; Azerbaijan Country Report.

International Monetary Fund (IMF), 700 19th St. NW, Washington, DC, 20431, USA, (202) 623-7000, (202) 623-4661, publications@imf.org, https://www.imf.org; Direction of Trade Statistics (DOTS).

Organisation of Islamic Cooperation (OIC), Statistical, Economic and Social Research and Training Centre for Islamic Countries (SESRIC), Kudus Cad. No. 9, Diplomatik Site, Ankara, 06450, TUR, statistics@sesric.org, https://www.sesric.org/; OIC Statistics (OICStat) Database.

S&P Global, IHS Markit, 15 Inverness Way E, Englewood, CO, 80112, USA, (800) 447-2273, (800) 854-7179, https://ihsmarkit.com; Global Trade Atlas (GTA).

State Statistical Committee of the Republic of Azerbaijan, Inshaatchilar Ave. 81, Baku, AZ 1136, AJN, sc@azstat.org, https://www.stat.gov.az/; Foreign Trade of Azerbaijan, 2023.

United Nations Statistics Division (UNSD), United Nations Plz., New York, NY, 10017, USA, (800) 253-9646, (212) 963-9851, statistics@un.org, https://unstats.un.org; International Trade Statistics Yearbook 2020.

The World Bank, 1818 H St. NW, Washington, DC, 20433, USA, (202) 473-1000, (202) 477-6391, eds03@worldbank.org, https://www.worldbank.org/; World Development Report 2022: Finance for an Equitable Recovery.

AZERBAIJAN-FERTILITY, HUMAN

Central Intelligence Agency (CIA), Office of Public Affairs, Washington, DC, 20505, USA, (703) 482-0623, https://www.cia.gov; The World Factbook.

AZERBAIJAN-FETAL MORTALITY

See AZERBAIJAN-MORTALITY

AZERBAIJAN-FINANCE

Stockholm International Peace Research Institute (SIPRI), Signalistgatan 9, Stockholm, SE 169 72,

SWE, https://www.sipri.org/; SIPRI Arms Transfers Database and SIPRI Military Expenditure Database.

United Nations Statistics Division (UNSD), United Nations Plz., New York, NY, 10017, USA, (800) 253-9646, (212) 963-9851, statistics@un.org, https://unstats.un.org; Statistical Yearbook of the United Nations 2021.

The World Bank, 1818 H St. NW, Washington, DC, 20433, USA, (202) 473-1000, (202) 477-6391, eds03@worldbank.org, https://www.worldbank.org/; Azerbaijan (report).

AZERBAIJAN-FINANCE, PUBLIC

Bernan Press, 15250 NBN Way, Bldg. C, Blue Ridge Summit, PA, 17214, USA, (301) 459-2255, (800) 865-3457, (800) 865-3450, customercare@bernan.com, https://rowman.com/Page/Bernan; National Accounts Statistics: Analysis of Main Aggregates 2020.

The Economist Group: Economist Intelligence Unit (EIU), 900 3rd Ave., 16th Fl., New York, NY, 10022, USA, (212) 541-0500, americas@eiu.com, https://www.eiu.com; Azerbaijan Country Report.

International Monetary Fund (IMF), 700 19th St. NW, Washington, DC, 20431, USA, (202) 623-7000, (202) 623-4661, publications@imf.org, https://www.imf.org; Regional Economic Outlook.

Palgrave Macmillan, 1 New York Plaza, Ste. 4500, New York, NY, 10004-1562, USA, (800) 777-4643, orders@palgrave.com, https://www.palgrave.com/us; The Statesman's Yearbook, 2023.

Routledge - Taylor & Francis Group, 6000 Broken Sound Pkwy. NW, Ste. 300, Boca Raton, FL, 33487, USA, (800) 634-1420, (800) 634-7064, orders@taylorandfrancis.com, https://www.routledge.com/; The Europa World Year Book 2022.

United Nations Statistics Division (UNSD), United Nations Plz., New York, NY, 10017, USA, (800) 253-9646, (212) 963-9851, statistics@un.org, https://unstats.un.org; National Accounts Main Aggregates Database and National Accounts Statistics: Main Aggregates and Detailed Tables.

The World Bank, 1818 H St. NW, Washington, DC, 20433, USA, (202) 473-1000, (202) 477-6391, eds03@worldbank.org, https://www.worldbank.org/; Azerbaijan (report).

AZERBAIJAN-FISHERIES

Palgrave Macmillan, 1 New York Plaza, Ste. 4500, New York, NY, 10004-1562, USA, (800) 777-4643, orders@palgrave.com, https://www.palgrave.com/us; The Statesman's Yearbook, 2023.

United Nations Food and Agricultural Organization (FAO), 2121 K St., Ste. 800B, Washington, DC, 20037, USA, (202) 653-2400 (Dial from U.S.), (202) 653-5760 (Fax from U.S.), fao-hq@fao.org, https://www.fao.org; FAO Yearbook of Fishery and Aquaculture Statistics 2019; Fishery Statistical Collections Global Capture Production; FishStatJ; and The State of Food and Agriculture (SOFA) 2022.

United Nations Statistics Division (UNSD), United Nations Plz., New York, NY, 10017, USA, (800) 253-9646, (212) 963-9851, statistics@un.org, https://unstats.un.org; Statistical Yearbook of the United Nations 2021.

The World Bank, 1818 H St. NW, Washington, DC, 20433, USA, (202) 473-1000, (202) 477-6391, eds03@worldbank.org, https://www.worldbank.org/; Azerbaijan (report).

AZERBAIJAN-FOOD

United Nations Food and Agricultural Organization (FAO), 2121 K St., Ste. 800B, Washington, DC, 20037, USA, (202) 653-2400 (Dial from U.S.), (202) 653-5760 (Fax from U.S.), fao-hq@fao.org, https://www.fao.org; The State of Food and Agriculture (SOFA) 2022.

AZERBAIJAN-FORESTS AND FORESTRY

Palgrave Macmillan, 1 New York Plaza, Ste. 4500, New York, NY, 10004-1562, USA, (800) 777-4643, orders@palgrave.com, https://www.palgrave.com/us; The Statesman's Yearbook, 2023.

UNESCO Institute for Statistics, C.P 250 Succursale H, Montreal, QC, H3G 2K8, CAN, (514) 343-6880 (Dial from U.S.), (514) 343-5740 (Fax from U.S.), uis.publications@unesco.org, http://uis.unesco.org/; UIS.Stat.

United Nations Food and Agricultural Organization (FAO), 2121 K St., Ste. 800B, Washington, DC, 20037, USA, (202) 653-2400 (Dial from U.S.), (202) 653-5760 (Fax from U.S.), fao-hq@fao.org, https://www.fao.org; FAO Yearbook of Forest Products 2019 and The State of Food and Agriculture (SOFA) 2022.

United Nations Statistics Division (UNSD), United Nations Plz., New York, NY, 10017, USA, (800) 253-9646, (212) 963-9851, statistics@un.org, https://unstats.un.org; Statistical Yearbook of the United Nations 2021.

The World Bank, 1818 H St. NW, Washington, DC, 20433, USA, (202) 473-1000, (202) 477-6391, eds03@worldbank.org, https://www.worldbank.org/; Azerbaijan (report) and World Development Report 2022: Finance for an Equitable Recovery.

AZERBAIJAN-GROSS DOMESTIC PRODUCT

The Economist Group: Economist Intelligence Unit (EIU), 900 3rd Ave., 16th Fl., New York, NY, 10022, USA, (212) 541-0500, americas@eiu.com, https://www.eiu.com; Azerbaijan Country Report.

United Nations Statistics Division (UNSD), United Nations Plz., New York, NY, 10017, USA, (800) 253-9646, (212) 963-9851, statistics@un.org, https://unstats.un.org; Statistical Yearbook of the United Nations 2021.

The World Bank, 1818 H St. NW, Washington, DC, 20433, USA, (202) 473-1000, (202) 477-6391, eds03@worldbank.org, https://www.worldbank.org/; World Development Indicators (WDI) 2022 and World Development Report 2022: Finance for an Equitable Recovery.

AZERBAIJAN-GROSS NATIONAL PRODUCT

Palgrave Macmillan, 1 New York Plaza, Ste. 4500, New York, NY, 10004-1562, USA, (800) 777-4643, orders@palgrave.com, https://www.palgrave.com/us; The Statesman's Yearbook, 2023.

United Nations Statistics Division (UNSD), United Nations Plz., New York, NY, 10017, USA, (800) 253-9646, (212) 963-9851, statistics@un.org, https://unstats.un.org; Statistical Yearbook of the United Nations 2021.

The World Bank, 1818 H St. NW, Washington, DC, 20433, USA, (202) 473-1000, (202) 477-6391, eds03@worldbank.org, https://www.worldbank.org/; World Development Indicators (WDI) 2022 and World Development Report 2022: Finance for an Equitable Recovery.

AZERBAIJAN-HOUSING

Euromonitor International, Inc., 1 N Dearborn St., Ste. 1700, Chicago, IL, 60602, USA, (312) 922-1115, (312) 922-1157, info-usa@euromonitor.com, https://www.euromonitor.com/; Geographies.

United Nations Statistics Division (UNSD), United Nations Plz., New York, NY, 10017, USA, (800) 253-9646, (212) 963-9851, statistics@un.org, https://unstats.un.org; Statistical Yearbook of the United Nations 2021.

AZERBAIJAN-ILLITERATE PERSONS

UNESCO Institute for Statistics, C.P 250 Succursale H, Montreal, QC, H3G 2K8, CAN, (514) 343-6880 (Dial from U.S.), (514) 343-5740 (Fax from U.S.), uis.publications@unesco.org, http://uis.unesco.org/; UIS.Stat.

AZERBAIJAN-IMPORTS

Central Intelligence Agency (CIA), Office of Public Affairs, Washington, DC, 20505, USA, (703) 482-0623, https://www.cia.gov; The World Factbook.

The Economist Group: Economist Intelligence Unit (EIU), 900 3rd Ave., 16th Fl., New York, NY, 10022, USA, (212) 541-0500, americas@eiu.com, https://www.eiu.com; Azerbaijan Country Report.

International Monetary Fund (IMF), 700 19th St. NW, Washington, DC, 20431, USA, (202) 623-7000, (202) 623-4661, publications@imf.org, https://www.imf.org; Direction of Trade Statistics (DOTS).

S&P Global, IHS Markit, 15 Inverness Way E, Englewood, CO, 80112, USA, (800) 447-2273, (800) 854-7179, https://ihsmarkit.com; Global Trade Atlas (GTA).

State Statistical Committee of the Republic of Azerbaijan, Inshaatchilar Ave. 81, Baku, AZ 1136, AJN, sc@azstat.org, https://www.stat.gov.az/; Foreign Trade of Azerbaijan, 2023.

United Nations Statistics Division (UNSD), United Nations Plz., New York, NY, 10017, USA, (800) 253-9646, (212) 963-9851, statistics@un.org, https://unstats.un.org; International Trade Statistics Yearbook 2020.

The World Bank, 1818 H St. NW, Washington, DC, 20433, USA, (202) 473-1000, (202) 477-6391, eds03@worldbank.org, https://www.worldbank.org/; World Development Report 2022: Finance for an Equitable Recovery.

AZERBAIJAN-INDUSTRIES

Central Intelligence Agency (CIA), Office of Public Affairs, Washington, DC, 20505, USA, (703) 482-0623, https://www.cia.gov; The World Factbook.

The Economist Group: Economist Intelligence Unit (EIU), 900 3rd Ave., 16th Fl., New York, NY, 10022, USA, (212) 541-0500, americas@eiu.com, https://www.eiu.com; Azerbaijan Country Report.

Euromonitor International, Inc., 1 N Dearborn St., Ste. 1700, Chicago, IL, 60602, USA, (312) 922-1115, (312) 922-1157, info-usa@euromonitor.com, https://www.euromonitor.com/; Geographies.

Palgrave Macmillan, 1 New York Plaza, Ste. 4500, New York, NY, 10004-1562, USA, (800) 777-4643, orders@palgrave.com, https://www.palgrave.com/us; The Statesman's Yearbook, 2023.

Routledge - Taylor & Francis Group, 6000 Broken Sound Pkwy. NW, Ste. 300, Boca Raton, FL, 33487, USA, (800) 634-1420, (800) 634-7064, orders@taylorandfrancis.com, https://www.routledge.com/; The Europa World Year Book 2022.

United Nations Industrial Development Organization (UNIDO), 1 United Nations Plz., Rm. DC1-1118, New York, NY, 10017, USA, (212) 963-6890, (212) 963 6885, (212) 963-7904, office.newyork@unido.org, https://www.unido.org/; Industrial Statistics Databases and International Yearbook of Industrial Statistics 2021.

The World Bank, 1818 H St. NW, Washington, DC, 20433, USA, (202) 473-1000, (202) 477-6391, eds03@worldbank.org, https://www.worldbank.org/; Azerbaijan (report) and World Development Indicators (WDI) 2022.

AZERBAIJAN-INFANT AND MATERNAL MORTALITY

See AZERBAIJAN-MORTALITY

AZERBAIJAN-INTERNATIONAL TRADE

The Economist Group: Economist Intelligence Unit (EIU), 900 3rd Ave., 16th Fl., New York, NY, 10022, USA, (212) 541-0500, americas@eiu.com, https://www.eiu.com; Azerbaijan Country Report.

Euromonitor International, Inc., 1 N Dearborn St., Ste. 1700, Chicago, IL, 60602, USA, (312) 922-1115, (312) 922-1157, info-usa@euromonitor.com, https://www.euromonitor.com/; Geographies.

International Monetary Fund (IMF), 700 19th St. NW, Washington, DC, 20431, USA, (202) 623-7000, (202) 623-4661, publications@imf.org, https://www.imf.org; Direction of Trade Statistics (DOTS).

Palgrave Macmillan, 1 New York Plaza, Ste. 4500, New York, NY, 10004-1562, USA, (800) 777-4643, orders@palgrave.com, https://www.palgrave.com/us; The Statesman's Yearbook, 2023.

Routledge - Taylor & Francis Group, 6000 Broken Sound Pkwy. NW, Ste. 300, Boca Raton, FL, 33487, USA, (800) 634-1420, (800) 634-7064, orders@taylorandfrancis.com, https://www.routledge.com/; The Europa World Year Book 2022.

S&P Global, IHS Markit, 15 Inverness Way E, Englewood, CO, 80112, USA, (800) 447-2273, (800) 854-7179, https://ihsmarkit.com; Global Trade Atlas (GTA).

State Statistical Committee of the Republic of Azerbaijan, Inshaatchilar Ave. 81, Baku, AZ 1136, AJN, sc@azstat.org, https://www.stat.gov.az/; Foreign Trade of Azerbaijan, 2023.

United Nations Statistics Division (UNSD), United Nations Plz., New York, NY, 10017, USA, (800) 253-9646, (212) 963-9851, statistics@un.org, https://unstats.un.org; International Trade Statistics Yearbook 2020 and Statistical Yearbook of the United Nations 2021.

The World Bank, 1818 H St. NW, Washington, DC, 20433, USA, (202) 473-1000, (202) 477-6391, eds03@worldbank.org, https://www.worldbank.org/; Azerbaijan (report); World Development Indicators (WDI) 2022; and World Development Report 2022: Finance for an Equitable Recovery.

World Trade Organization (WTO), Ctre. William Rappard, Rue de Lausanne 154, Case postale, Geneva, CH-1211, SWI, enquiries@wto.org, https://www.wto.org; World Trade Statistical Review 2022.

AZERBAIJAN-INTERNET USERS

International Telecommunication Union (ITU), Place des Nations, Geneva, CH-1211, SWI, itumail@itu.int, https://www.itu.int; Global Connectivity Report 2022; World Telecommunication/ICT Indicators Database 2021; and Yearbook of Statistics 2019.

The World Bank, 1818 H St. NW, Washington, DC, 20433, USA, (202) 473-1000, (202) 477-6391, eds03@worldbank.org, https://www.worldbank.org/; Azerbaijan (report).

AZERBAIJAN-LABOR

Central Intelligence Agency (CIA), Office of Public Affairs, Washington, DC, 20505, USA, (703) 482-0623, https://www.cia.gov; The World Factbook.

Euromonitor International, Inc., 1 N Dearborn St., Ste. 1700, Chicago, IL, 60602, USA, (312) 922-1115, (312) 922-1157, info-usa@euromonitor.com, https://www.euromonitor.com/; Geographies.

Organisation of Islamic Cooperation (OIC), Statistical, Economic and Social Research and Training Centre for Islamic Countries (SESRIC), Kudus Cad. No. 9, Diplomatik Site, Ankara, 06450, TUR, statistics@sesric.org, https://www.sesric.org/; OIC Statistics (OICStat) Database.

Palgrave Macmillan, 1 New York Plaza, Ste. 4500, New York, NY, 10004-1562, USA, (800) 777-4643, orders@palgrave.com, https://www.palgrave.com/us; The Statesman's Yearbook, 2023.

United Nations Statistics Division (UNSD), United Nations Plz., New York, NY, 10017, USA, (800) 253-9646, (212) 963-9851, statistics@un.org, https://unstats.un.org; Statistical Yearbook of the United Nations 2021.

The World Bank, 1818 H St. NW, Washington, DC, 20433, USA, (202) 473-1000, (202) 477-6391, eds03@worldbank.org, https://www.worldbank.org/; World Development Indicators (WDI) 2022 and World Development Report 2022: Finance for an Equitable Recovery.

AZERBAIJAN-LAND USE

United Nations Statistics Division (UNSD), United Nations Plz., New York, NY, 10017, USA, (800) 253-9646, (212) 963-9851, statistics@un.org, https://unstats.un.org; Millennium Development Goal Indicators.

The World Bank, 1818 H St. NW, Washington, DC, 20433, USA, (202) 473-1000, (202) 477-6391, eds03@worldbank.org, https://www.worldbank.org/; World Development Report 2022: Finance for an Equitable Recovery.

AZERBAIJAN-LIBRARIES

UNESCO Institute for Statistics, C.P 250 Succursale H, Montreal, QC, H3G 2K8, CAN, (514) 343-6880 (Dial from U.S.), (514) 343-5740 (Fax from U.S.), uis.publications@unesco.org, http://uis.unesco.org/; UIS.Stat.

United Nations Statistics Division (UNSD), United Nations Plz., New York, NY, 10017, USA, (800) 253-9646, (212) 963-9851, statistics@un.org, https://unstats.un.org; Statistical Yearbook of the United Nations 2021.

AZERBAIJAN-LIFE EXPECTANCY

Central Intelligence Agency (CIA), Office of Public Affairs, Washington, DC, 20505, USA, (703) 482-0623, https://www.cia.gov; The World Factbook.

United Nations Department of Economic and Social Affairs (DESA), Population Division, 2 United Nations Plz., Rm. DC2-1950, New York, NY, 10017, USA, (212) 963-3209, (212) 963-2147, population@un.org, https://www.un.org/development/desa/pd/; World Population Ageing 2020 Highlights.

United Nations Statistics Division (UNSD), United Nations Plz., New York, NY, 10017, USA, (800) 253-9646, (212) 963-9851, statistics@un.org, https://unstats.un.org; Millennium Development Goal Indicators.

The World Bank, 1818 H St. NW, Washington, DC, 20433, USA, (202) 473-1000, (202) 477-6391, eds03@worldbank.org, https://www.worldbank.org/; World Development Indicators (WDI) 2022.

AZERBAIJAN-LITERACY

Euromonitor International, Inc., 1 N Dearborn St., Ste. 1700, Chicago, IL, 60602, USA, (312) 922-1115, (312) 922-1157, info-usa@euromonitor.com, https://www.euromonitor.com/; Geographies.

UNESCO Institute for Statistics, C.P 250 Succursale H, Montreal, QC, H3G 2K8, CAN, (514) 343-6880 (Dial from U.S.), (514) 343-5740 (Fax from U.S.), uis.publications@unesco.org, http://uis.unesco.org/; Literacy.

AZERBAIJAN-LIVESTOCK

Palgrave Macmillan, 1 New York Plaza, Ste. 4500, New York, NY, 10004-1562, USA, (800) 777-4643, orders@palgrave.com, https://www.palgrave.com/us; The Statesman's Yearbook, 2023.

Routledge - Taylor & Francis Group, 6000 Broken Sound Pkwy. NW, Ste. 300, Boca Raton, FL, 33487, USA, (800) 634-1420, (800) 634-7064, orders@taylorandfrancis.com, https://www.routledge.com/; The Europa World Year Book 2022.

United Nations Food and Agricultural Organization (FAO), 2121 K St., Ste. 800B, Washington, DC, 20037, USA, (202) 653-2400 (Dial from U.S.), (202) 653-5760 (Fax from U.S.), fao-hq@fao.org, https://www.fao.org; The State of Food and Agriculture (SOFA) 2022.

United Nations Statistics Division (UNSD), United Nations Plz., New York, NY, 10017, USA, (800) 253-9646, (212) 963-9851, statistics@un.org, https://unstats.un.org; Statistical Yearbook of the United Nations 2021.

AZERBAIJAN-MARRIAGE

Routledge - Taylor & Francis Group, 6000 Broken Sound Pkwy. NW, Ste. 300, Boca Raton, FL, 33487, USA, (800) 634-1420, (800) 634-7064, orders@taylorandfrancis.com, https://www.routledge.com/; The Europa World Year Book 2022.

United Nations Statistics Division (UNSD), United Nations Plz., New York, NY, 10017, USA, (800) 253-9646, (212) 963-9851, statistics@un.org, https://unstats.un.org; Statistical Yearbook of the United Nations 2021.

AZERBAIJAN-MINERAL INDUSTRIES

Palgrave Macmillan, 1 New York Plaza, Ste. 4500, New York, NY, 10004-1562, USA, (800) 777-4643, orders@palgrave.com, https://www.palgrave.com/us; The Statesman's Yearbook, 2023.

Routledge - Taylor & Francis Group, 6000 Broken Sound Pkwy. NW, Ste. 300, Boca Raton, FL, 33487, USA, (800) 634-1420, (800) 634-7064, orders@taylorandfrancis.com, https://www.routledge.com/; The Europa World Year Book 2022.

United Nations Statistics Division (UNSD), United Nations Plz., New York, NY, 10017, USA, (800) 253-9646, (212) 963-9851, statistics@un.org, https://unstats.un.org; Energy Statistics Yearbook 2019 and Statistical Yearbook of the United Nations 2021.

The World Bank, 1818 H St. NW, Washington, DC, 20433, USA, (202) 473-1000, (202) 477-6391, eds03@worldbank.org, https://www.worldbank.org/; Azerbaijan (report).

AZERBAIJAN-MONEY SUPPLY

The Economist Group: Economist Intelligence Unit (EIU), 900 3rd Ave., 16th Fl., New York, NY, 10022, USA, (212) 541-0500, americas@eiu.com, https://www.eiu.com; Azerbaijan Country Report.

Routledge - Taylor & Francis Group, 6000 Broken Sound Pkwy. NW, Ste. 300, Boca Raton, FL, 33487, USA, (800) 634-1420, (800) 634-7064, orders@taylorandfrancis.com, https://www.routledge.com/; The Europa World Year Book 2022.

The World Bank, 1818 H St. NW, Washington, DC, 20433, USA, (202) 473-1000, (202) 477-6391, eds03@worldbank.org, https://www.worldbank.org/; Azerbaijan (report).

AZERBAIJAN-MONUMENTS AND HISTORIC SITES

UNESCO Institute for Statistics, C.P 250 Succursale H, Montreal, QC, H3G 2K8, CAN, (514) 343-6880 (Dial from U.S.), (514) 343-5740 (Fax from U.S.), uis.publications@unesco.org, http://uis.unesco.org/; UIS.Stat.

AZERBAIJAN-MORTALITY

UNICEF, 3 United Nations Plz., New York, NY, 10017, USA, (212) 303-7984, (917) 244-2215, https://www.unicef.org; The State of the World's Children 2023.

United Nations Statistics Division (UNSD), United Nations Plz., New York, NY, 10017, USA, (800) 253-9646, (212) 963-9851, statistics@un.org, https://unstats.un.org; Millennium Development Goal Indicators; Statistical Yearbook of the United Nations 2021; and World Statistics Pocketbook 2021.

The World Bank, 1818 H St. NW, Washington, DC, 20433, USA, (202) 473-1000, (202) 477-6391, eds03@worldbank.org, https://www.worldbank.org/; World Development Indicators (WDI) 2022.

World Health Organization (WHO), Ave. Appia 20, Geneva, CH-1211, SWI, (202) 974-3000 (Telephone in U.S.), publications@who.int, https://www.who.int/; Global Health Observatory (GHO).

AZERBAIJAN-PETROLEUM INDUSTRY AND TRADE

Palgrave Macmillan, 1 New York Plaza, Ste. 4500, New York, NY, 10004-1562, USA, (800) 777-4643, orders@palgrave.com, https://www.palgrave.com/us; The Statesman's Yearbook, 2023.

U.S. Energy Information Administration (EIA), 1000 Independence Ave. SW, Washington, DC, 20585, USA, (202) 586-8800, infoctr@eia.gov, https://www.eia.gov; International Energy Outlook 2021.

United Nations Food and Agricultural Organization (FAO), 2121 K St., Ste. 800B, Washington, DC, 20037, USA, (202) 653-2400 (Dial from U.S.), (202) 653-5760 (Fax from U.S.), fao-hq@fao.org, https://www.fao.org; The State of Food and Agriculture (SOFA) 2022.

United Nations Statistics Division (UNSD), United Nations Plz., New York, NY, 10017, USA, (800) 253-9646, (212) 963-9851, statistics@un.org, https://unstats.un.org; Energy Statistics Yearbook 2019 and Statistical Yearbook of the United Nations 2021.

AZERBAIJAN-POPULATION

Central Intelligence Agency (CIA), Office of Public Affairs, Washington, DC, 20505, USA, (703) 482-0623, https://www.cia.gov; The World Factbook.

The Economist Group: Economist Intelligence Unit (EIU), 900 3rd Ave., 16th Fl., New York, NY, 10022, USA, (212) 541-0500, americas@eiu.com, https://www.eiu.com; Azerbaijan Country Report.

Infoplease, c/o Sandbox Networks, Inc., 1 Lincoln St., 24th Fl., Boston, MA, 02111, USA, https://www.infoplease.com; Countries of the World.

Palgrave Macmillan, 1 New York Plaza, Ste. 4500, New York, NY, 10004-1562, USA, (800) 777-4643, orders@palgrave.com, https://www.palgrave.com/us; The Statesman's Yearbook, 2023.

Routledge - Taylor & Francis Group, 6000 Broken Sound Pkwy. NW, Ste. 300, Boca Raton, FL, 33487, USA, (800) 634-1420, (800) 634-7064, orders@taylorandfrancis.com, https://www.routledge.com/; The Europa World Year Book 2022.

State Statistical Committee of the Republic of Azerbaijan, Inshaatchilar Ave. 81, Baku, AZ 1136, AJN, sc@azstat.org, https://www.stat.gov.az/; Children in Azerbaijan, 2023 and Women and Men in Azerbaijan, 2023.

UK Data Service, University of Essex, Wivenhoe Park, Colchester, Essex, CO4 3SQ, GBR, https://ukdataservice.ac.uk/; International Aggregate Data.

UNESCO Institute for Statistics, C.P 250 Succursale H, Montreal, QC, H3G 2K8, CAN, (514) 343-6880 (Dial from U.S.), (514) 343-5740 (Fax from U.S.), uis.publications@unesco.org, http://uis.unesco.org/; UIS.Stat.

United Nations Department of Economic and Social Affairs (DESA), Population Division, 2 United Nations Plz., Rm. DC2-1950, New York, NY, 10017, USA, (212) 963-3209, (212) 963-2147, population@un.org, https://www.un.org/development/desa/pd/; Revision of World Urbanization Prospects and World Population Ageing 2020 Highlights.

United Nations Development Programme (UNDP), One United Nations Plz., New York, NY, 10017, USA, (212) 906-5000, (212) 906-5001, https://www.undp.org; Human Development Report 2021-2022.

United Nations Statistics Division (UNSD), United Nations Plz., New York, NY, 10017, USA, (800) 253-9646, (212) 963-9851, statistics@un.org, https://unstats.un.org; Statistical Yearbook of the United Nations 2021 and World Statistics Pocketbook 2021.

The World Bank, 1818 H St. NW, Washington, DC, 20433, USA, (202) 473-1000, (202) 477-6391, eds03@worldbank.org, https://www.worldbank.org/; Azerbaijan (report); The Global Findex Database 2021; World Development Indicators (WDI) 2022; and World Development Report 2022: Finance for an Equitable Recovery.

AZERBAIJAN-POPULATION DENSITY

Central Intelligence Agency (CIA), Office of Public Affairs, Washington, DC, 20505, USA, (703) 482-0623, https://www.cia.gov; The World Factbook.

Palgrave Macmillan, 1 New York Plaza, Ste. 4500, New York, NY, 10004-1562, USA, (800) 777-4643, orders@palgrave.com, https://www.palgrave.com/us; The Statesman's Yearbook, 2023.

Routledge - Taylor & Francis Group, 6000 Broken Sound Pkwy. NW, Ste. 300, Boca Raton, FL, 33487, USA, (800) 634-1420, (800) 634-7064, orders@taylorandfrancis.com, https://www.routledge.com/; The Europa World Year Book 2022.

UNESCO Institute for Statistics, C.P 250 Succursale H, Montreal, QC, H3G 2K8, CAN, (514) 343-6880 (Dial from U.S.), (514) 343-5740 (Fax from U.S.), uis.publications@unesco.org, http://uis.unesco.org/; UIS.Stat.

The World Bank, 1818 H St. NW, Washington, DC, 20433, USA, (202) 473-1000, (202) 477-6391, eds03@worldbank.org, https://www.worldbank.org/; Azerbaijan (report) and World Development Report 2022: Finance for an Equitable Recovery.

AZERBAIJAN-POULTRY

See AZERBAIJAN-LIVESTOCK

AZERBAIJAN-POWER RESOURCES

Euromonitor International, Inc., 1 N Dearborn St., Ste. 1700, Chicago, IL, 60602, USA, (312) 922-1115, (312) 922-1157, info-usa@euromonitor.com, https://www.euromonitor.com/; Geographies.

Palgrave Macmillan, 1 New York Plaza, Ste. 4500, New York, NY, 10004-1562, USA, (800) 777-4643, orders@palgrave.com, https://www.palgrave.com/us; The Statesman's Yearbook, 2023.

U.S. Energy Information Administration (EIA), 1000 Independence Ave. SW, Washington, DC, 20585, USA, (202) 586-8800, infoctr@eia.gov, https://www.eia.gov; International Energy Outlook 2021.

United Nations Statistics Division (UNSD), United Nations Plz., New York, NY, 10017, USA, (800) 253-9646, (212) 963-9851, statistics@un.org, https://unstats.un.org; Energy Statistics Yearbook 2019; Statistical Yearbook of the United Nations 2021; and World Statistics Pocketbook 2021.

The World Bank, 1818 H St. NW, Washington, DC, 20433, USA, (202) 473-1000, (202) 477-6391, eds03@worldbank.org, https://www.worldbank.org/; World Development Report 2022: Finance for an Equitable Recovery.

AZERBAIJAN-PRICES

Euromonitor International, Inc., 1 N Dearborn St., Ste. 1700, Chicago, IL, 60602, USA, (312) 922-1115, (312) 922-1157, info-usa@euromonitor.com, https://www.euromonitor.com/; Geographies.

The World Bank, 1818 H St. NW, Washington, DC, 20433, USA, (202) 473-1000, (202) 477-6391, eds03@worldbank.org, https://www.worldbank.org/; Azerbaijan (report).

AZERBAIJAN-PUBLIC HEALTH

Euromonitor International, Inc., 1 N Dearborn St., Ste. 1700, Chicago, IL, 60602, USA, (312) 922-1115, (312) 922-1157, info-usa@euromonitor.com, https://www.euromonitor.com/; Geographies and Market Research on the Health and Wellness Industry.

Organisation of Islamic Cooperation (OIC), Statistical, Economic and Social Research and Training Centre for Islamic Countries (SESRIC), Kudus Cad. No. 9, Diplomatik Site, Ankara, 06450, TUR, statistics@sesric.org, https://www.sesric.org/; OIC Statistics (OICStat) Database.

Palgrave Macmillan, 1 New York Plaza, Ste. 4500, New York, NY, 10004-1562, USA, (800) 777-4643, orders@palgrave.com, https://www.palgrave.com/us; The Statesman's Yearbook, 2023.

U.S. Census Bureau, 4600 Silver Hill Rd., Washington, DC, 20233, USA, (301) 763-4636, (800) 923-8282, https://www.census.gov; HIV/AIDS Surveillance Data Base.

UNICEF, 3 United Nations Plz., New York, NY, 10017, USA, (212) 303-7984, (917) 244-2215, https://www.unicef.org; The State of the World's Children 2023.

United Nations Department of Economic and Social Affairs (DESA), Population Division, 2 United Nations Plz., Rm. DC2-1950, New York, NY, 10017, USA, (212) 963-3209, (212) 963-2147, population@un.org, https://www.un.org/development/desa/pd/; World Fertility Data 2019.

United Nations Development Programme (UNDP), One United Nations Plz., New York, NY, 10017, USA, (212) 906-5000, (212) 906-5001, https://www.undp.org; Human Development Report 2021-2022.

United Nations Statistics Division (UNSD), United Nations Plz., New York, NY, 10017, USA, (800) 253-9646, (212) 963-9851, statistics@un.org, https://unstats.un.org; Millennium Development Goal Indicators and Statistical Yearbook of the United Nations 2021.

The World Bank, 1818 H St. NW, Washington, DC, 20433, USA, (202) 473-1000, (202) 477-6391, eds03@worldbank.org, https://www.worldbank.org/; Azerbaijan (report).

World Health Organization (WHO), Ave. Appia 20, Geneva, CH-1211, SWI, (202) 974-3000 (Telephone in U.S.), publications@who.int, https://www.who.int/; Global Health Observatory (GHO) and Health Statistics and Information Systems.

AZERBAIJAN-PUBLISHERS AND PUBLISHING

UNESCO Institute for Statistics, C.P 250 Succursale H, Montreal, QC, H3G 2K8, CAN, (514) 343-6880 (Dial from U.S.), (514) 343-5740 (Fax from U.S.), uis.publications@unesco.org, http://uis.unesco.org/; UIS.Stat.

AZERBAIJAN-RAILROADS

Palgrave Macmillan, 1 New York Plaza, Ste. 4500, New York, NY, 10004-1562, USA, (800) 777-4643, orders@palgrave.com, https://www.palgrave.com/us; The Statesman's Yearbook, 2023.

United Nations Statistics Division (UNSD), United Nations Plz., New York, NY, 10017, USA, (800) 253-9646, (212) 963-9851, statistics@un.org, https://unstats.un.org; Statistical Yearbook of the United Nations 2021.

AZERBAIJAN-RELIGION

Central Intelligence Agency (CIA), Office of Public Affairs, Washington, DC, 20505, USA, (703) 482-0623, https://www.cia.gov; The World Factbook.

Palgrave Macmillan, 1 New York Plaza, Ste. 4500, New York, NY, 10004-1562, USA, (800) 777-4643, orders@palgrave.com, https://www.palgrave.com/us; The Statesman's Yearbook, 2023.

AZERBAIJAN-RETAIL TRADE

Euromonitor International, Inc., 1 N Dearborn St., Ste. 1700, Chicago, IL, 60602, USA, (312) 922-1115, (312) 922-1157, info-usa@euromonitor.com, https://www.euromonitor.com/; Geographies.

United Nations Statistics Division (UNSD), United Nations Plz., New York, NY, 10017, USA, (800) 253-9646, (212) 963-9851, statistics@un.org, https://unstats.un.org; Statistical Yearbook of the United Nations 2021.

AZERBAIJAN-ROADS

United Nations Statistics Division (UNSD), United Nations Plz., New York, NY, 10017, USA, (800) 253-9646, (212) 963-9851, statistics@un.org, https://unstats.un.org; Statistical Yearbook of the United Nations 2021.

AZERBAIJAN-RUBBER INDUSTRY AND TRADE

International Rubber Study Group (IRSG), 51 Changi Business Park Central 2, Unit No. 6, 486066, SGP, https://www.rubberstudy.org; Monthly Rubber Bulletin (MRB); Rubber Industry Report; Rubber Statistical Bulletin; and World Rubber Industry Report (WRIO).

United Nations Statistics Division (UNSD), United Nations Plz., New York, NY, 10017, USA, (800) 253-9646, (212) 963-9851, statistics@un.org, https://unstats.un.org; Statistical Yearbook of the United Nations 2021.

AZERBAIJAN-SHIPPING

United Nations Statistics Division (UNSD), United Nations Plz., New York, NY, 10017, USA, (800) 253-9646, (212) 963-9851, statistics@un.org, https://unstats.un.org; Statistical Yearbook of the United Nations 2021.

AZERBAIJAN-STEEL PRODUCTION

See AZERBAIJAN-MINERAL INDUSTRIES

AZERBAIJAN-TELEPHONE

United Nations Statistics Division (UNSD), United Nations Plz., New York, NY, 10017, USA, (800) 253-

9646, (212) 963-9851, statistics@un.org, https://unstats.un.org; World Statistics Pocketbook 2021.

AZERBAIJAN-TEXTILE INDUSTRY

Palgrave Macmillan, 1 New York Plaza, Ste. 4500, New York, NY, 10004-1562, USA, (800) 777-4643, orders@palgrave.com, https://www.palgrave.com/us; The Statesman's Yearbook, 2023.

United Nations Statistics Division (UNSD), United Nations Plz., New York, NY, 10017, USA, (800) 253-9646, (212) 963-9851, statistics@un.org, https://unstats.un.org; Statistical Yearbook of the United Nations 2021.

AZERBAIJAN-THEATER

UNESCO Institute for Statistics, C.P 250 Succursale H, Montreal, QC, H3G 2K8, CAN, (514) 343-6880 (Dial from U.S.), (514) 343-5740 (Fax from U.S.), uis.publications@unesco.org, http://uis.unesco.org/; UIS.Stat.

AZERBAIJAN-TOBACCO INDUSTRY

United Nations Statistics Division (UNSD), United Nations Plz., New York, NY, 10017, USA, (800) 253-9646, (212) 963-9851, statistics@un.org, https://unstats.un.org; Statistical Yearbook of the United Nations 2021.

AZERBAIJAN-TOURISM

Euromonitor International, Inc., 1 N Dearborn St., Ste. 1700, Chicago, IL, 60602, USA, (312) 922-1115, (312) 922-1157, info-usa@euromonitor.com, https://www.euromonitor.com/; Geographies.

Organisation of Islamic Cooperation (OIC), Statistical, Economic and Social Research and Training Centre for Islamic Countries (SESRIC), Kudus Cad. No. 9, Diplomatik Site, Ankara, 06450, TUR, statistics@sesric.org, https://www.sesric.org/; International Tourism in the OIC Countries: Prospects and Challenges, 2020 and OIC Statistics (OICStat) Database.

United Nations Statistics Division (UNSD), United Nations Plz., New York, NY, 10017, USA, (800) 253-9646, (212) 963-9851, statistics@un.org, https://unstats.un.org; Statistical Yearbook of the United Nations 2021.

The World Bank, 1818 H St. NW, Washington, DC, 20433, USA, (202) 473-1000, (202) 477-6391, eds03@worldbank.org, https://www.worldbank.org/; Azerbaijan (report).

AZERBAIJAN-TRANSPORTATION

Central Intelligence Agency (CIA), Office of Public Affairs, Washington, DC, 20505, USA, (703) 482-0623, https://www.cia.gov; The World Factbook.

Euromonitor International, Inc., 1 N Dearborn St., Ste. 1700, Chicago, IL, 60602, USA, (312) 922-1115, (312) 922-1157, info-usa@euromonitor.com, https://www.euromonitor.com/; Geographies.

Organisation of Islamic Cooperation (OIC), Statistical, Economic and Social Research and Training Centre for Islamic Countries (SESRIC), Kudus Cad. No. 9, Diplomatik Site, Ankara, 06450, TUR, statistics@sesric.org, https://www.sesric.org/; OIC Statistics (OICStat) Database.

Palgrave Macmillan, 1 New York Plaza, Ste. 4500, New York, NY, 10004-1562, USA, (800) 777-4643, orders@palgrave.com, https://www.palgrave.com/us; The Statesman's Yearbook, 2023.

The World Bank, 1818 H St. NW, Washington, DC, 20433, USA, (202) 473-1000, (202) 477-6391, eds03@worldbank.org, https://www.worldbank.org/; Azerbaijan (report).

AZERBAIJAN-UNEMPLOYMENT

Palgrave Macmillan, 1 New York Plaza, Ste. 4500, New York, NY, 10004-1562, USA, (800) 777-4643, orders@palgrave.com, https://www.palgrave.com/us; The Statesman's Yearbook, 2023.

United Nations Statistics Division (UNSD), United Nations Plz., New York, NY, 10017, USA, (800) 253-9646, (212) 963-9851, statistics@un.org, https://unstats.un.org; Statistical Yearbook of the United Nations 2021.

The World Bank, 1818 H St. NW, Washington, DC, 20433, USA, (202) 473-1000, (202) 477-6391, eds03@worldbank.org, https://www.worldbank.org/; Azerbaijan (report).

AZERBAIJAN-VITAL STATISTICS

Palgrave Macmillan, 1 New York Plaza, Ste. 4500, New York, NY, 10004-1562, USA, (800) 777-4643, orders@palgrave.com, https://www.palgrave.com/us; The Statesman's Yearbook, 2023.

State Statistical Committee of the Republic of Azerbaijan, Inshaatchilar Ave. 81, Baku, AZ 1136, AJN, sc@azstat.org, https://www.stat.gov.az/; Azerbaijan in Figures, 2023; Children in Azerbaijan, 2023; and Women and Men in Azerbaijan, 2023.

U.S. Census Bureau, 4600 Silver Hill Rd., Washington, DC, 20233, USA, (301) 763-4636, (800) 923-8282, https://www.census.gov; HIV/AIDS Surveillance Data Base.

United Nations Department of Economic and Social Affairs (DESA), Population Division, 2 United Nations Plz., Rm. DC2-1950, New York, NY, 10017, USA, (212) 963-3209, (212) 963-2147, population@un.org, https://www.un.org/development/desa/pd/; World Contraceptive Use 2021: Estimates and Projections of Family Planning Indicators and World Marriage Data 2019.

United Nations Economic and Social Commission for Western Asia (ESCWA), Riad el-Solh Sq., PO Box 11-8575, Beirut, LBN, escwa-ciu@un.org, https://www.unescwa.org; ESCWA Annual Report 2019; ESCWA Data Portal for the Arab Region; and Survey of Economic and Social Developments in the Arab Region 2020-2021.

United Nations Statistics Division (UNSD), United Nations Plz., New York, NY, 10017, USA, (800) 253-9646, (212) 963-9851, statistics@un.org, https://unstats.un.org; Statistical Yearbook of the United Nations 2021.

AZERBAIJAN-WAGES

United Nations Statistics Division (UNSD), United Nations Plz., New York, NY, 10017, USA, (800) 253-9646, (212) 963-9851, statistics@un.org, https://unstats.un.org; Statistical Yearbook of the United Nations 2021.

The World Bank, 1818 H St. NW, Washington, DC, 20433, USA, (202) 473-1000, (202) 477-6391, eds03@worldbank.org, https://www.worldbank.org/; Azerbaijan (report).

AZERBAIJAN-WHOLESALE TRADE

United Nations Statistics Division (UNSD), United Nations Plz., New York, NY, 10017, USA, (800) 253-9646, (212) 963-9851, statistics@un.org, https://unstats.un.org; Statistical Yearbook of the United Nations 2021.

BABY BOOM GENERATION

The Gallup Organization, 901 F St. NW, Washington, DC, 20004, USA, (202) 715-3030, (800) 204-1192, (202) 715-3045, https://www.gallup.com; LGBT Identification in U.S. Ticks Up to 7.1%.

Yale Project on Climate Change Communication (YPCCC), Yale School of the Environment, 195 Prospect St., New Haven, CT, 06511, USA, (203) 432-5055, climatechange@yale.edu, https://climatecommunication.yale.edu/; Global Warming's Six Americas Across Age, Race/Ethnicity, and Gender.

BACKPACKING

National Sporting Goods Association (NSGA), 3041 Woodcreek Dr., Ste. 210, Downers Grove, IL, 60515, USA, (847) 296-6742, (847) 391-9827, info@nsga.org, https://www.nsga.org; Sports Participation in the United States 2022.

BACON

U.S. Department of Labor (DOL), Bureau of Labor Statistics (BLS), Postal Square Bldg., 2 Massachusetts Ave. NE, Washington, DC, 20212-0001, USA, (202) 691-5200, (202) 691-7890, blsdata_staff@bls.gov, https://www.bls.gov; Consumer Price Index (CPI) Databases.

BADMINTON

National Sporting Goods Association (NSGA), 3041 Woodcreek Dr., Ste. 210, Downers Grove, IL, 60515, USA, (847) 296-6742, (847) 391-9827, info@nsga.org, https://www.nsga.org; Sports Participation in the United States 2022.

BAHAMAS, THE-NATIONAL STATISTICAL OFFICE

Bahamas National Statistical Institute, Bellagio Plaza, Palmdale, PO Box N 3904, Nassau, BHS, (242) 604-4000 (Dial from U.S.), (242) 604-4090 (Fax from U.S.), statsnp@bahamas.gov.bs, https://stats.gov.bs; National Data Reports (Bahamas).

BAHAMAS, THE-AGRICULTURE

The Economist Group: Economist Intelligence Unit (EIU), 900 3rd Ave., 16th Fl., New York, NY, 10022, USA, (212) 541-0500, americas@eiu.com, https://www.eiu.com; Bahamas Country Report.

Euromonitor International, Inc., 1 N Dearborn St., Ste. 1700, Chicago, IL, 60602, USA, (312) 922-1115, (312) 922-1157, info-usa@euromonitor.com, https://www.euromonitor.com/; Geographies.

Inter-American Development Bank (IDB), 1300 New York Ave. NW, Washington, DC, 20577, USA, (202) 623-1000, (202) 623-3096, https://www.iadb.org/en; Latin Macro Watch (LMW).

Palgrave Macmillan, 1 New York Plaza, Ste. 4500, New York, NY, 10004-1562, USA, (800) 777-4643, orders@palgrave.com, https://www.palgrave.com/us; The Statesman's Yearbook, 2023.

Routledge - Taylor & Francis Group, 6000 Broken Sound Pkwy. NW, Ste. 300, Boca Raton, FL, 33487, USA, (800) 634-1420, (800) 634-7064, orders@taylorandfrancis.com, https://www.routledge.com/; The Europa World Year Book 2022.

United Nations Food and Agricultural Organization (FAO), 2121 K St., Ste. 800B, Washington, DC, 20037, USA, (202) 653-2400 (Dial from U.S.), (202) 653-5760 (Fax from U.S.), fao-hq@fao.org, https://www.fao.org; AQUASTAT and The State of Food and Agriculture (SOFA) 2022.

United Nations Statistics Division (UNSD), United Nations Plz., New York, NY, 10017, USA, (800) 253-9646, (212) 963-9851, statistics@un.org, https://unstats.un.org; Statistical Yearbook of the United Nations 2021.

The World Bank, 1818 H St. NW, Washington, DC, 20433, USA, (202) 473-1000, (202) 477-6391, eds03@worldbank.org, https://www.worldbank.org/; World Development Indicators (WDI) 2022.

BAHAMAS, THE-AIRLINES

Palgrave Macmillan, 1 New York Plaza, Ste. 4500, New York, NY, 10004-1562, USA, (800) 777-4643, orders@palgrave.com, https://www.palgrave.com/us; The Statesman's Yearbook, 2023.

Routledge - Taylor & Francis Group, 6000 Broken Sound Pkwy. NW, Ste. 300, Boca Raton, FL, 33487, USA, (800) 634-1420, (800) 634-7064, orders@taylorandfrancis.com, https://www.routledge.com/; The Europa World Year Book 2022.

BAHAMAS, THE-ALUMINUM PRODUCTION

See BAHAMAS, THE-MINERAL INDUSTRIES

BAHAMAS, THE-ARMED FORCES

Central Intelligence Agency (CIA), Office of Public Affairs, Washington, DC, 20505, USA, (703) 482-0623, https://www.cia.gov; The World Factbook.

International Institute for Strategic Studies (IISS) - Americas, 2121 K St. NW, Ste. 600, Washington, DC, 20037, USA, (202) 659-1490, (202) 659-1499, https://www.iiss.org/; The Military Balance 2022.

Palgrave Macmillan, 1 New York Plaza, Ste. 4500, New York, NY, 10004-1562, USA, (800) 777-4643, orders@palgrave.com, https://www.palgrave.com/us; The Statesman's Yearbook, 2023.

Stockholm International Peace Research Institute (SIPRI), Signalistgatan 9, Stockholm, SE 169 72, SWE, https://www.sipri.org/; SIPRI Arms Transfers Database and SIPRI Military Expenditure Database.

BAHAMAS, THE-BALANCE OF PAYMENTS

Inter-American Development Bank (IDB), 1300 New York Ave. NW, Washington, DC, 20577, USA, (202) 623-1000, (202) 623-3096, https://www.iadb.org/en; Latin Macro Watch (LMW).

International Monetary Fund (IMF), 700 19th St. NW, Washington, DC, 20431, USA, (202) 623-7000, (202) 623-4661, publications@imf.org, https://www.imf.org; Balance of Payments Statistics: Annual Report 2021.

Routledge - Taylor & Francis Group, 6000 Broken Sound Pkwy. NW, Ste. 300, Boca Raton, FL, 33487, USA, (800) 634-1420, (800) 634-7064, orders@taylorandfrancis.com, https://www.routledge.com/; The Europa World Year Book 2022.

United Nations Conference on Trade and Development (UNCTAD), Palais des Nations, Geneva, 1211, SWI, (212) 963-6896, unctadinfo@unctad.org, https://unctad.org; Handbook of Statistics 2021.

United Nations Economic Commission for Latin America and the Caribbean (ECLAC), Casilla 179-D, Santiago, 7630412, CHL, (202) 596-3713, prensa@cepal.org, https://www.cepal.org/en; Economic Survey of Latin America and the Caribbean 2021: Labour Dynamics and Employment Policies for Sustainable and Inclusive Recovery Beyond the COVID-19 Crisis.

The World Bank, 1818 H St. NW, Washington, DC, 20433, USA, (202) 473-1000, (202) 477-6391, eds03@worldbank.org, https://www.worldbank.org/; World Development Indicators (WDI) 2022.

BAHAMAS, THE-BANKS AND BANKING

Euromonitor International, Inc., 1 N Dearborn St., Ste. 1700, Chicago, IL, 60602, USA, (312) 922-1115, (312) 922-1157, info-usa@euromonitor.com, https://www.euromonitor.com/; Geographies.

Inter-American Development Bank (IDB), 1300 New York Ave. NW, Washington, DC, 20577, USA, (202) 623-1000, (202) 623-3096, https://www.iadb.org/en; Latin Macro Watch (LMW).

International Monetary Fund (IMF), 700 19th St. NW, Washington, DC, 20431, USA, (202) 623-7000, (202) 623-4661, publications@imf.org, https://www.imf.org; International Financial Statistics (IFS).

Routledge - Taylor & Francis Group, 6000 Broken Sound Pkwy. NW, Ste. 300, Boca Raton, FL, 33487, USA, (800) 634-1420, (800) 634-7064, orders@taylorandfrancis.com, https://www.routledge.com/; The Europa World Year Book 2022.

BAHAMAS, THE-BARLEY PRODUCTION

See BAHAMAS, THE-CROPS

BAHAMAS, THE-BONDS

Inter-American Development Bank (IDB), 1300 New York Ave. NW, Washington, DC, 20577, USA, (202) 623-1000, (202) 623-3096, https://www.iadb.org/en; Latin Macro Watch (LMW).

The World Bank, 1818 H St. NW, Washington, DC, 20433, USA, (202) 473-1000, (202) 477-6391, eds03@worldbank.org, https://www.worldbank.org/; World Development Indicators (WDI) 2022.

BAHAMAS, THE-BROADCASTING

Central Intelligence Agency (CIA), Office of Public Affairs, Washington, DC, 20505, USA, (703) 482-0623, https://www.cia.gov; The World Factbook.

Euromonitor International, Inc., 1 N Dearborn St., Ste. 1700, Chicago, IL, 60602, USA, (312) 922-1115, (312) 922-1157, info-usa@euromonitor.com, https://www.euromonitor.com/; Geographies.

Palgrave Macmillan, 1 New York Plaza, Ste. 4500, New York, NY, 10004-1562, USA, (800) 777-4643, orders@palgrave.com, https://www.palgrave.com/us; The Statesman's Yearbook, 2023.

WRTH Publications Limited, PO Box 290, Oxford, OX2 7FT, GBR, sales@wrth.com, https://www.wrth.com; World Radio TV Handbook 2023.

BAHAMAS, THE-BUDGET

Central Intelligence Agency (CIA), Office of Public Affairs, Washington, DC, 20505, USA, (703) 482-0623, https://www.cia.gov; The World Factbook.

BAHAMAS, THE-BUSINESS

Inter-American Development Bank (IDB), 1300 New York Ave. NW, Washington, DC, 20577, USA, (202) 623-1000, (202) 623-3096, https://www.iadb.org/en; Latin Macro Watch (LMW).

BAHAMAS, THE-CAPITAL INVESTMENTS

Inter-American Development Bank (IDB), 1300 New York Ave. NW, Washington, DC, 20577, USA, (202) 623-1000, (202) 623-3096, https://www.iadb.org/en; Latin Macro Watch (LMW).

BAHAMAS, THE-CHILDBIRTH-STATISTICS

The World Bank, 1818 H St. NW, Washington, DC, 20433, USA, (202) 473-1000, (202) 477-6391, eds03@worldbank.org, https://www.worldbank.org/; World Development Indicators (WDI) 2022.

BAHAMAS, THE-CLIMATE

Palgrave Macmillan, 1 New York Plaza, Ste. 4500, New York, NY, 10004-1562, USA, (800) 777-4643, orders@palgrave.com, https://www.palgrave.com/us; The Statesman's Yearbook, 2023.

BAHAMAS, THE-COAL PRODUCTION

See BAHAMAS, THE-MINERAL INDUSTRIES

BAHAMAS, THE-COFFEE

See BAHAMAS, THE-CROPS

BAHAMAS, THE-COMMERCE

Palgrave Macmillan, 1 New York Plaza, Ste. 4500, New York, NY, 10004-1562, USA, (800) 777-4643, orders@palgrave.com, https://www.palgrave.com/us; The Statesman's Yearbook, 2023.

UK Data Service, University of Essex, Wivenhoe Park, Colchester, Essex, CO4 3SQ, GBR, https://ukdataservice.ac.uk/; International Aggregate Data.

BAHAMAS, THE-COMMODITY EXCHANGES

Barchart, 209 W Jackson Blvd., 2nd Fl., Chicago, IL, 60606, USA, (877) 247-4394, commodities@barchart.com, https://www.barchart.com/cmdty; The cmdty Yearbook 2023; cmdtyStats: Commodity Statistics and Fundamental Data; cmdtyView: Commodity Index; and Commodity Data and Prices.

International Monetary Fund (IMF), 700 19th St. NW, Washington, DC, 20431, USA, (202) 623-7000, (202) 623-4661, publications@imf.org, https://www.imf.org; IMF Primary Commodity Prices.

BAHAMAS, THE-CONSTRUCTION INDUSTRY

Bahamas National Statistical Institute, Bellagio Plaza, Palmdale, PO Box N 3904, Nassau, BHS, (242) 604-4000 (Dial from U.S.), (242) 604-4090 (Fax from U.S.), statsnp@bahamas.gov.bs, https://stats.gov.bs; Building Construction Statistics Report.

Inter-American Development Bank (IDB), 1300 New York Ave. NW, Washington, DC, 20577, USA, (202) 623-1000, (202) 623-3096, https://www.iadb.org/en; Latin Macro Watch (LMW).

United Nations Statistics Division (UNSD), United Nations Plz., New York, NY, 10017, USA, (800) 253-9646, (212) 963-9851, statistics@un.org, https://unstats.un.org; Statistical Yearbook of the United Nations 2021.

BAHAMAS, THE-CONSUMER PRICE INDEXES

Routledge - Taylor & Francis Group, 6000 Broken Sound Pkwy. NW, Ste. 300, Boca Raton, FL, 33487, USA, (800) 634-1420, (800) 634-7064, orders@taylorandfrancis.com, https://www.routledge.com/; The Europa World Year Book 2022.

BAHAMAS, THE-CONSUMPTION (ECONOMICS)

Inter-American Development Bank (IDB), 1300 New York Ave. NW, Washington, DC, 20577, USA, (202) 623-1000, (202) 623-3096, https://www.iadb.org/en; Latin Macro Watch (LMW).

BAHAMAS, THE-COPPER INDUSTRY AND TRADE

See BAHAMAS, THE-MINERAL INDUSTRIES

BAHAMAS, THE-CORN INDUSTRY

See BAHAMAS, THE-CROPS

BAHAMAS, THE-COTTON

See BAHAMAS, THE-CROPS

BAHAMAS, THE-CROPS

Palgrave Macmillan, 1 New York Plaza, Ste. 4500, New York, NY, 10004-1562, USA, (800) 777-4643, orders@palgrave.com, https://www.palgrave.com/us; The Statesman's Yearbook, 2023.

United Nations Food and Agricultural Organization (FAO), 2121 K St., Ste. 800B, Washington, DC, 20037, USA, (202) 653-2400 (Dial from U.S.), (202) 653-5760 (Fax from U.S.), fao-hq@fao.org, https://www.fao.org; The State of Food and Agriculture (SOFA) 2022.

BAHAMAS, THE-CUSTOMS ADMINISTRATION

Inter-American Development Bank (IDB), 1300 New York Ave. NW, Washington, DC, 20577, USA, (202) 623-1000, (202) 623-3096, https://www.iadb.org/en; Latin Macro Watch (LMW).

BAHAMAS, THE-DAIRY PROCESSING

Palgrave Macmillan, 1 New York Plaza, Ste. 4500, New York, NY, 10004-1562, USA, (800) 777-4643, orders@palgrave.com, https://www.palgrave.com/us; The Statesman's Yearbook, 2023.

United Nations Food and Agricultural Organization (FAO), 2121 K St., Ste. 800B, Washington, DC, 20037, USA, (202) 653-2400 (Dial from U.S.), (202) 653-5760 (Fax from U.S.), fao-hq@fao.org, https://www.fao.org; The State of Food and Agriculture (SOFA) 2022.

BAHAMAS, THE-DEBTS, EXTERNAL

Inter-American Development Bank (IDB), 1300 New York Ave. NW, Washington, DC, 20577, USA, (202) 623-1000, (202) 623-3096, https://www.iadb.org/en; Latin Macro Watch (LMW).

Palgrave Macmillan, 1 New York Plaza, Ste. 4500, New York, NY, 10004-1562, USA, (800) 777-4643, orders@palgrave.com, https://www.palgrave.com/us; The Statesman's Yearbook, 2023.

United Nations Economic Commission for Latin America and the Caribbean (ECLAC), Casilla 179-D, Santiago, 7630412, CHL, (202) 596-3713, prensa@cepal.org, https://www.cepal.org/en; Economic Survey of Latin America and the Caribbean 2021: Labour Dynamics and Employment Policies for Sustainable and Inclusive Recovery Beyond the COVID-19 Crisis.

The World Bank, 1818 H St. NW, Washington, DC, 20433, USA, (202) 473-1000, (202) 477-6391, eds03@worldbank.org, https://www.worldbank.org/; Global Financial Development Report 2019-2020: Bank Regulation and Supervision a Decade after the Global Financial Crisis and World Development Indicators (WDI) 2022.

BAHAMAS, THE-DEFENSE EXPENDITURES

See BAHAMAS, THE-ARMED FORCES

BAHAMAS, THE-DIAMONDS

See BAHAMAS, THE-MINERAL INDUSTRIES

BAHAMAS, THE-DISPOSABLE INCOME

Inter-American Development Bank (IDB), 1300 New York Ave. NW, Washington, DC, 20577, USA, (202) 623-1000, (202) 623-3096, https://www.iadb.org/en; Latin Macro Watch (LMW).

BAHAMAS, THE-ECONOMIC ASSISTANCE

Inter-American Development Bank (IDB), 1300 New York Ave. NW, Washington, DC, 20577, USA, (202) 623-1000, (202) 623-3096, https://www.iadb.org/en; Latin Macro Watch (LMW).

United Nations Statistics Division (UNSD), United Nations Plz., New York, NY, 10017, USA, (800) 253-9646, (212) 963-9851, statistics@un.org, https://unstats.un.org; Statistical Yearbook of the United Nations 2021.

BAHAMAS, THE-ECONOMIC CONDITIONS

Bahamas National Statistical Institute, Bellagio Plaza, Palmdale, PO Box N 3904, Nassau, BHS, (242) 604-4000 (Dial from U.S.), (242) 604-4090 (Fax from U.S.), statsnp@bahamas.gov.bs, https://stats.gov.bs; Building Construction Statistics Report; Foreign Trade Statistics Quarterly Report; and Labour Market December 2019.

Bernan Press, 15250 NBN Way, Bldg. C, Blue Ridge Summit, PA, 17214, USA, (301) 459-2255, (800) 865-3457, (800) 865-3450, customercare@bernan.com, https://rowman.com/Page/Bernan; World Economic Outlook, April 2022.

Central Intelligence Agency (CIA), Office of Public Affairs, Washington, DC, 20505, USA, (703) 482-0623, https://www.cia.gov; The World Factbook.

The Economist Group: Economist Intelligence Unit (EIU), 900 3rd Ave., 16th Fl., New York, NY, 10022, USA, (212) 541-0500, americas@eiu.com, https://www.eiu.com; Bahamas Country Report.

Euromonitor International, Inc., 1 N Dearborn St., Ste. 1700, Chicago, IL, 60602, USA, (312) 922-1115, (312) 922-1157, info-usa@euromonitor.com, https://www.euromonitor.com/; Geographies.

Inter-American Development Bank (IDB), 1300 New York Ave. NW, Washington, DC, 20577, USA, (202) 623-1000, (202) 623-3096, https://www.iadb.org/en; Latin Macro Watch (LMW).

International Monetary Fund (IMF), 700 19th St. NW, Washington, DC, 20431, USA, (202) 623-7000, (202) 623-4661, publications@imf.org, https://www.imf.org; IMF Data and World Economic Outlook.

Palgrave Macmillan, 1 New York Plaza, Ste. 4500, New York, NY, 10004-1562, USA, (800) 777-4643, orders@palgrave.com, https://www.palgrave.com/us; The Statesman's Yearbook, 2023.

Routledge - Taylor & Francis Group, 6000 Broken Sound Pkwy. NW, Ste. 300, Boca Raton, FL, 33487, USA, (800) 634-1420, (800) 634-7064, orders@taylorandfrancis.com, https://www.routledge.com/; The Europa World Year Book 2022.

United Nations Economic Commission for Latin America and the Caribbean (ECLAC), Casilla 179-D,

Santiago, 7630412, CHL, (202) 596-3713, prensa@cepal.org, https://www.cepal.org/en; Economic Survey of Latin America and the Caribbean 2021: Labour Dynamics and Employment Policies for Sustainable and Inclusive Recovery Beyond the COVID-19 Crisis and Foreign Direct Investment in Latin America and the Caribbean 2022.

United Nations Statistics Division (UNSD), United Nations Plz., New York, NY, 10017, USA, (800) 253-9646, (212) 963-9851, statistics@un.org, https://unstats.un.org; World Statistics Pocketbook 2021.

The World Bank, 1818 H St. NW, Washington, DC, 20433, USA, (202) 473-1000, (202) 477-6391, eds03@worldbank.org, https://www.worldbank.org/; Global Economic Monitor (GEM); Global Economic Prospects, June 2022; and The Global Findex Database 2021.

BAHAMAS, THE-EDUCATION

Euromonitor International, Inc., 1 N Dearborn St., Ste. 1700, Chicago, IL, 60602, USA, (312) 922-1115, (312) 922-1157, info-usa@euromonitor.com, https://www.euromonitor.com/; Geographies.

Infoplease, c/o Sandbox Networks, Inc., 1 Lincoln St., 24th Fl., Boston, MA, 02111, USA, https://www.infoplease.com; Countries of the World.

Palgrave Macmillan, 1 New York Plaza, Ste. 4500, New York, NY, 10004-1562, USA, (800) 777-4643, orders@palgrave.com, https://www.palgrave.com/us; The Statesman's Yearbook, 2023.

Routledge - Taylor & Francis Group, 6000 Broken Sound Pkwy. NW, Ste. 300, Boca Raton, FL, 33487, USA, (800) 634-1420, (800) 634-7064, orders@taylorandfrancis.com, https://www.routledge.com/; The Europa World Year Book 2022.

UNESCO Institute for Statistics, C.P 250 Succursale H, Montreal, QC, H3G 2K8, CAN, (514) 343-6880 (Dial from U.S.), (514) 343-5740 (Fax from U.S.), uis.publications@unesco.org, http://uis.unesco.org/; Literacy and UIS.Stat.

United Nations Statistics Division (UNSD), United Nations Plz., New York, NY, 10017, USA, (800) 253-9646, (212) 963-9851, statistics@un.org, https://unstats.un.org; Millennium Development Goal Indicators.

The World Bank, 1818 H St. NW, Washington, DC, 20433, USA, (202) 473-1000, (202) 477-6391, eds03@worldbank.org, https://www.worldbank.org/; World Development Indicators (WDI) 2022.

BAHAMAS, THE-ELECTRICITY

Inter-American Development Bank (IDB), 1300 New York Ave. NW, Washington, DC, 20577, USA, (202) 623-1000, (202) 623-3096, https://www.iadb.org/en; Latin Macro Watch (LMW).

United Nations Statistics Division (UNSD), United Nations Plz., New York, NY, 10017, USA, (800) 253-9646, (212) 963-9851, statistics@un.org, https://unstats.un.org; Statistical Yearbook of the United Nations 2021.

BAHAMAS, THE-EMPLOYMENT

International Labour Organization (ILO), 4 Rte. des Morillons, Geneva, CH-1211, SWI, ilo@ilo.org, https://www.ilo.org; NORMLEX Information System on International Labour Standards.

UK Data Service, University of Essex, Wivenhoe Park, Colchester, Essex, CO4 3SQ, GBR, https://ukdataservice.ac.uk/; International Aggregate Data.

BAHAMAS, THE-ENVIRONMENTAL CONDITIONS

DSI Data Service & Information, Xantener Strasse 51a, Rheinberg, D-47495, GER, dsi@dsidata.com, https://www.dsidata.com/; Global Environmental Database.

The Economist Group: Economist Intelligence Unit (EIU), 900 3rd Ave., 16th Fl., New York, NY, 10022, USA, (212) 541-0500, americas@eiu.com, https://www.eiu.com; Bahamas Country Report.

United Nations Statistics Division (UNSD), United Nations Plz., New York, NY, 10017, USA, (800) 253-9646, (212) 963-9851, statistics@un.org, https://unstats.un.org; World Statistics Pocketbook 2021.

BAHAMAS, THE-EXCISE TAX

International Monetary Fund (IMF), 700 19th St. NW, Washington, DC, 20431, USA, (202) 623-7000, (202) 623-4661, publications@imf.org, https://www.imf.org; International Financial Statistics (IFS).

BAHAMAS, THE-EXPENDITURES, PUBLIC

Inter-American Development Bank (IDB), 1300 New York Ave. NW, Washington, DC, 20577, USA, (202) 623-1000, (202) 623-3096, https://www.iadb.org/en; Latin Macro Watch (LMW).

BAHAMAS, THE-EXPORTS

Central Intelligence Agency (CIA), Office of Public Affairs, Washington, DC, 20505, USA, (703) 482-0623, https://www.cia.gov; The World Factbook.

The Economist Group: Economist Intelligence Unit (EIU), 900 3rd Ave., 16th Fl., New York, NY, 10022, USA, (212) 541-0500, americas@eiu.com, https://www.eiu.com; Bahamas Country Report.

Inter-American Development Bank (IDB), 1300 New York Ave. NW, Washington, DC, 20577, USA, (202) 623-1000, (202) 623-3096, https://www.iadb.org/en; Latin Macro Watch (LMW).

International Monetary Fund (IMF), 700 19th St. NW, Washington, DC, 20431, USA, (202) 623-7000, (202) 623-4661, publications@imf.org, https://www.imf.org; Direction of Trade Statistics (DOTS) and International Financial Statistics (IFS).

S&P Global, IHS Markit, 15 Inverness Way E, Englewood, CO, 80112, USA, (800) 447-2273, (800) 854-7179, https://ihsmarkit.com; Global Trade Atlas (GTA).

United Nations Conference on Trade and Development (UNCTAD), Palais des Nations, Geneva, 1211, SWI, (212) 963-6896, unctadinfo@unctad.org, https://unctad.org; Handbook of Statistics 2021.

BAHAMAS, THE-FERTILIZER INDUSTRY

United Nations Food and Agricultural Organization (FAO), 2121 K St., Ste. 800B, Washington, DC, 20037, USA, (202) 653-2400 (Dial from U.S.), (202) 653-5760 (Fax from U.S.), fao-hq@fao.org, https://www.fao.org; The State of Food and Agriculture (SOFA) 2022.

BAHAMAS, THE-FETAL MORTALITY

See BAHAMAS, THE-MORTALITY

BAHAMAS, THE-FINANCE

Inter-American Development Bank (IDB), 1300 New York Ave. NW, Washington, DC, 20577, USA, (202) 623-1000, (202) 623-3096, https://www.iadb.org/en; Latin Macro Watch (LMW).

Stockholm International Peace Research Institute (SIPRI), Signalistgatan 9, Stockholm, SE 169 72, SWE, https://www.sipri.org/; SIPRI Arms Transfers Database and SIPRI Military Expenditure Database.

BAHAMAS, THE-FINANCE, PUBLIC

Bernan Press, 15250 NBN Way, Bldg. C, Blue Ridge Summit, PA, 17214, USA, (301) 459-2255, (800) 865-3457, (800) 865-3450, customercare@bernan.com, https://rowman.com/Page/Bernan; National Accounts Statistics: Analysis of Main Aggregates 2020.

The Economist Group: Economist Intelligence Unit (EIU), 900 3rd Ave., 16th Fl., New York, NY, 10022, USA, (212) 541-0500, americas@eiu.com, https://www.eiu.com; Bahamas Country Report.

Inter-American Development Bank (IDB), 1300 New York Ave. NW, Washington, DC, 20577, USA, (202) 623-1000, (202) 623-3096, https://www.iadb.org/en; Latin Macro Watch (LMW).

International Monetary Fund (IMF), 700 19th St. NW, Washington, DC, 20431, USA, (202) 623-7000, (202) 623-4661, publications@imf.org, https://www.imf.org; Regional Economic Outlook.

Palgrave Macmillan, 1 New York Plaza, Ste. 4500, New York, NY, 10004-1562, USA, (800) 777-4643, orders@palgrave.com, https://www.palgrave.com/us; The Statesman's Yearbook, 2023.

Routledge - Taylor & Francis Group, 6000 Broken Sound Pkwy. NW, Ste. 300, Boca Raton, FL, 33487, USA, (800) 634-1420, (800) 634-7064, orders@taylorandfrancis.com, https://www.routledge.com/; The Europa World Year Book 2022.

United Nations Statistics Division (UNSD), United Nations Plz., New York, NY, 10017, USA, (800) 253-9646, (212) 963-9851, statistics@un.org, https://unstats.un.org; National Accounts Main Aggregates Database and National Accounts Statistics: Main Aggregates and Detailed Tables.

BAHAMAS, THE-FISHERIES

Inter-American Development Bank (IDB), 1300 New York Ave. NW, Washington, DC, 20577, USA, (202) 623-1000, (202) 623-3096, https://www.iadb.org/en; Latin Macro Watch (LMW).

Palgrave Macmillan, 1 New York Plaza, Ste. 4500, New York, NY, 10004-1562, USA, (800) 777-4643, orders@palgrave.com, https://www.palgrave.com/us; The Statesman's Yearbook, 2023.

Routledge - Taylor & Francis Group, 6000 Broken Sound Pkwy. NW, Ste. 300, Boca Raton, FL, 33487, USA, (800) 634-1420, (800) 634-7064, orders@taylorandfrancis.com, https://www.routledge.com/; The Europa World Year Book 2022.

United Nations Food and Agricultural Organization (FAO), 2121 K St., Ste. 800B, Washington, DC, 20037, USA, (202) 653-2400 (Dial from U.S.), (202) 653-5760 (Fax from U.S.), fao-hq@fao.org, https://www.fao.org; FAO Yearbook of Fishery and Aquaculture Statistics 2019; Fishery Statistical Collections Global Capture Production; FishStatJ; and The State of Food and Agriculture (SOFA) 2022.

United Nations Statistics Division (UNSD), United Nations Plz., New York, NY, 10017, USA, (800) 253-9646, (212) 963-9851, statistics@un.org, https://unstats.un.org; Statistical Yearbook of the United Nations 2021.

BAHAMAS, THE-FOOD

United Nations Food and Agricultural Organization (FAO), 2121 K St., Ste. 800B, Washington, DC, 20037, USA, (202) 653-2400 (Dial from U.S.), (202) 653-5760 (Fax from U.S.), fao-hq@fao.org, https://www.fao.org; The State of Food and Agriculture (SOFA) 2022.

BAHAMAS, THE-FOREIGN EXCHANGE RATES

Inter-American Development Bank (IDB), 1300 New York Ave. NW, Washington, DC, 20577, USA, (202) 623-1000, (202) 623-3096, https://www.iadb.org/en; Latin Macro Watch (LMW).

International Monetary Fund (IMF), 700 19th St. NW, Washington, DC, 20431, USA, (202) 623-7000, (202) 623-4661, publications@imf.org, https://www.imf.org; International Financial Statistics (IFS).

BAHAMAS, THE-FORESTS AND FORESTRY

Inter-American Development Bank (IDB), 1300 New York Ave. NW, Washington, DC, 20577, USA, (202) 623-1000, (202) 623-3096, https://www.iadb.org/en; Latin Macro Watch (LMW).

Routledge - Taylor & Francis Group, 6000 Broken Sound Pkwy. NW, Ste. 300, Boca Raton, FL, 33487, USA, (800) 634-1420, (800) 634-7064, orders@taylorandfrancis.com, https://www.routledge.com/; The Europa World Year Book 2022.

UNESCO Institute for Statistics, C.P 250 Succursale H, Montreal, QC, H3G 2K8, CAN, (514) 343-6880 (Dial from U.S.), (514) 343-5740 (Fax from U.S.), uis.publications@unesco.org, http://uis.unesco.org/; UIS.Stat.

United Nations Food and Agricultural Organization (FAO), 2121 K St., Ste. 800B, Washington, DC, 20037, USA, (202) 653-2400 (Dial from U.S.), (202) 653-5760 (Fax from U.S.), fao-hq@fao.org, https://www.fao.org; FAO Yearbook of Forest Products 2019 and The State of Food and Agriculture (SOFA) 2022.

United Nations Statistics Division (UNSD), United Nations Plz., New York, NY, 10017, USA, (800) 253-9646, (212) 963-9851, statistics@un.org, https://unstats.un.org; Statistical Yearbook of the United Nations 2021.

BAHAMAS, THE-GAS PRODUCTION

See BAHAMAS, THE-MINERAL INDUSTRIES

BAHAMAS, THE-GOLD INDUSTRY

The World Bank, 1818 H St. NW, Washington, DC, 20433, USA, (202) 473-1000, (202) 477-6391, eds03@worldbank.org, https://www.worldbank.org/; World Development Indicators (WDI) 2022.

BAHAMAS, THE-GOLD PRODUCTION

See BAHAMAS, THE-MINERAL INDUSTRIES

BAHAMAS, THE-GROSS DOMESTIC PRODUCT

The Economist Group: Economist Intelligence Unit (EIU), 900 3rd Ave., 16th Fl., New York, NY, 10022, USA, (212) 541-0500, americas@eiu.com, https://www.eiu.com; Bahamas Country Report.

Inter-American Development Bank (IDB), 1300 New York Ave. NW, Washington, DC, 20577, USA, (202) 623-1000, (202) 623-3096, https://www.iadb.org/en; Latin Macro Watch (LMW).

Routledge - Taylor & Francis Group, 6000 Broken Sound Pkwy. NW, Ste. 300, Boca Raton, FL, 33487, USA, (800) 634-1420, (800) 634-7064, orders@taylorandfrancis.com, https://www.routledge.com/; The Europa World Year Book 2022.

The World Bank, 1818 H St. NW, Washington, DC, 20433, USA, (202) 473-1000, (202) 477-6391, eds03@worldbank.org, https://www.worldbank.org/; World Development Indicators (WDI) 2022.

BAHAMAS, THE-GROSS NATIONAL PRODUCT

Inter-American Development Bank (IDB), 1300 New York Ave. NW, Washington, DC, 20577, USA, (202) 623-1000, (202) 623-3096, https://www.iadb.org/en; Latin Macro Watch (LMW).

Palgrave Macmillan, 1 New York Plaza, Ste. 4500, New York, NY, 10004-1562, USA, (800) 777-4643, orders@palgrave.com, https://www.palgrave.com/us; The Statesman's Yearbook, 2023.

The World Bank, 1818 H St. NW, Washington, DC, 20433, USA, (202) 473-1000, (202) 477-6391, eds03@worldbank.org, https://www.worldbank.org/; World Development Indicators (WDI) 2022.

BAHAMAS, THE-HOUSING

Euromonitor International, Inc., 1 N Dearborn St., Ste. 1700, Chicago, IL, 60602, USA, (312) 922-1115, (312) 922-1157, info-usa@euromonitor.com, https://www.euromonitor.com/; Geographies.

BAHAMAS, THE-ILLITERATE PERSONS

UNESCO Institute for Statistics, C.P 250 Succursale H, Montreal, QC, H3G 2K8, CAN, (514) 343-6880 (Dial from U.S.), (514) 343-5740 (Fax from U.S.), uis.publications@unesco.org, http://uis.unesco.org/; UIS.Stat.

BAHAMAS, THE-IMPORTS

Central Intelligence Agency (CIA), Office of Public Affairs, Washington, DC, 20505, USA, (703) 482-0623, https://www.cia.gov; The World Factbook.

The Economist Group: Economist Intelligence Unit (EIU), 900 3rd Ave., 16th Fl., New York, NY, 10022, USA, (212) 541-0500, americas@eiu.com, https://www.eiu.com; Bahamas Country Report.

Inter-American Development Bank (IDB), 1300 New York Ave. NW, Washington, DC, 20577, USA, (202) 623-1000, (202) 623-3096, https://www.iadb.org/en; Latin Macro Watch (LMW).

International Monetary Fund (IMF), 700 19th St. NW, Washington, DC, 20431, USA, (202) 623-7000, (202) 623-4661, publications@imf.org, https://www.imf.org; Direction of Trade Statistics (DOTS) and International Financial Statistics (IFS).

S&P Global, IHS Markit, 15 Inverness Way E, Englewood, CO, 80112, USA, (800) 447-2273, (800) 854-7179, https://ihsmarkit.com; Global Trade Atlas (GTA).

United Nations Conference on Trade and Development (UNCTAD), Palais des Nations, Geneva, 1211, SWI, (212) 963-6896, unctadinfo@unctad.org, https://unctad.org; Handbook of Statistics 2021.

BAHAMAS, THE-INDUSTRIES

Central Intelligence Agency (CIA), Office of Public Affairs, Washington, DC, 20505, USA, (703) 482-0623, https://www.cia.gov; The World Factbook.

The Economist Group: Economist Intelligence Unit (EIU), 900 3rd Ave., 16th Fl., New York, NY, 10022, USA, (212) 541-0500, americas@eiu.com, https://www.eiu.com; Bahamas Country Report.

Euromonitor International, Inc., 1 N Dearborn St., Ste. 1700, Chicago, IL, 60602, USA, (312) 922-1115, (312) 922-1157, info-usa@euromonitor.com, https://www.euromonitor.com/; Geographies.

International Labour Organization (ILO), 4 Rte. des Morillons, Geneva, CH-1211, SWI, ilo@ilo.org, https://www.ilo.org; NORMLEX Information System on International Labour Standards.

Palgrave Macmillan, 1 New York Plaza, Ste. 4500, New York, NY, 10004-1562, USA, (800) 777-4643, orders@palgrave.com, https://www.palgrave.com/us; The Statesman's Yearbook, 2023.

Routledge - Taylor & Francis Group, 6000 Broken Sound Pkwy. NW, Ste. 300, Boca Raton, FL, 33487, USA, (800) 634-1420, (800) 634-7064, orders@taylorandfrancis.com, https://www.routledge.com/; The Europa World Year Book 2022.

United Nations Economic Commission for Latin America and the Caribbean (ECLAC), Casilla 179-D, Santiago, 7630412, CHL, (202) 596-3713, prensa@cepal.org, https://www.cepal.org/en; Economic Survey of Latin America and the Caribbean 2021: Labour Dynamics and Employment Policies for Sustainable and Inclusive Recovery Beyond the COVID-19 Crisis.

United Nations Industrial Development Organization (UNIDO), 1 United Nations Plz., Rm. DC1-1118, New York, NY, 10017, USA, (212) 963-6890, (212) 963 6885, (212) 963-7904, office.newyork@unido.org, https://www.unido.org/; Industrial Statistics Databases and International Yearbook of Industrial Statistics 2021.

The World Bank, 1818 H St. NW, Washington, DC, 20433, USA, (202) 473-1000, (202) 477-6391, eds03@worldbank.org, https://www.worldbank.org/; World Development Indicators (WDI) 2022.

BAHAMAS, THE-INFANT AND MATERNAL MORTALITY

See BAHAMAS, THE-MORTALITY

BAHAMAS, THE-INFLATION (FINANCE)

United Nations Economic Commission for Latin America and the Caribbean (ECLAC), Casilla 179-D, Santiago, 7630412, CHL, (202) 596-3713, prensa@cepal.org, https://www.cepal.org/en; Economic Survey of Latin America and the Caribbean 2021: Labour Dynamics and Employment Policies for Sustainable and Inclusive Recovery Beyond the COVID-19 Crisis.

BAHAMAS, THE-INTEREST RATES

Inter-American Development Bank (IDB), 1300 New York Ave. NW, Washington, DC, 20577, USA, (202) 623-1000, (202) 623-3096, https://www.iadb.org/en; Latin Macro Watch (LMW).

United Nations Statistics Division (UNSD), United Nations Plz., New York, NY, 10017, USA, (800) 253-9646, (212) 963-9851, statistics@un.org, https://unstats.un.org; Statistical Yearbook of the United Nations 2021.

BAHAMAS, THE-INTERNAL REVENUE

Inter-American Development Bank (IDB), 1300 New York Ave. NW, Washington, DC, 20577, USA, (202) 623-1000, (202) 623-3096, https://www.iadb.org/en; Latin Macro Watch (LMW).

BAHAMAS, THE-INTERNATIONAL FINANCE

Inter-American Development Bank (IDB), 1300 New York Ave. NW, Washington, DC, 20577, USA, (202) 623-1000, (202) 623-3096, https://www.iadb.org/en; Latin Macro Watch (LMW).

BAHAMAS, THE-INTERNATIONAL LIQUIDITY

Inter-American Development Bank (IDB), 1300 New York Ave. NW, Washington, DC, 20577, USA, (202) 623-1000, (202) 623-3096, https://www.iadb.org/en; Latin Macro Watch (LMW).

BAHAMAS, THE-INTERNATIONAL TRADE

Bahamas National Statistical Institute, Bellagio Plaza, Palmdale, PO Box N 3904, Nassau, BHS, (242) 604-4000 (Dial from U.S.), (242) 604-4090 (Fax from U.S.), statsnp@bahamas.gov.bs, https://stats.gov.bs; Foreign Trade Statistics Quarterly Report.

The Economist Group: Economist Intelligence Unit (EIU), 900 3rd Ave., 16th Fl., New York, NY, 10022, USA, (212) 541-0500, americas@eiu.com, https://www.eiu.com; Bahamas Country Report.

Euromonitor International, Inc., 1 N Dearborn St., Ste. 1700, Chicago, IL, 60602, USA, (312) 922-1115, (312) 922-1157, info-usa@euromonitor.com, https://www.euromonitor.com/; Geographies.

Inter-American Development Bank (IDB), 1300 New York Ave. NW, Washington, DC, 20577, USA, (202) 623-1000, (202) 623-3096, https://www.iadb.org/en; Latin Macro Watch (LMW).

Palgrave Macmillan, 1 New York Plaza, Ste. 4500, New York, NY, 10004-1562, USA, (800) 777-4643, orders@palgrave.com, https://www.palgrave.com/us; The Statesman's Yearbook, 2023.

Routledge - Taylor & Francis Group, 6000 Broken Sound Pkwy. NW, Ste. 300, Boca Raton, FL, 33487, USA, (800) 634-1420, (800) 634-7064, orders@taylorandfrancis.com, https://www.routledge.com/; The Europa World Year Book 2022.

United Nations Conference on Trade and Development (UNCTAD), Palais des Nations, Geneva, 1211, SWI, (212) 963-6896, unctadinfo@unctad.org, https://unctad.org; Trade and Development Report 2021.

United Nations Economic Commission for Latin America and the Caribbean (ECLAC), Casilla 179-D, Santiago, 7630412, CHL, (202) 596-3713, prensa@cepal.org, https://www.cepal.org/en; Economic Survey of Latin America and the Caribbean 2021: Labour Dynamics and Employment Policies for Sustainable and Inclusive Recovery Beyond the COVID-19 Crisis.

United Nations Food and Agricultural Organization (FAO), 2121 K St., Ste. 800B, Washington, DC, 20037, USA, (202) 653-2400 (Dial from U.S.), (202) 653-5760 (Fax from U.S.), fao-hq@fao.org, https://www.fao.org; The State of Food and Agriculture (SOFA) 2022.

United Nations Statistics Division (UNSD), United Nations Plz., New York, NY, 10017, USA, (800) 253-9646, (212) 963-9851, statistics@un.org, https://unstats.un.org; International Trade Statistics Yearbook 2020 and Statistical Yearbook of the United Nations 2021.

The World Bank, 1818 H St. NW, Washington, DC, 20433, USA, (202) 473-1000, (202) 477-6391,

eds03@worldbank.org, https://www.worldbank.org/; World Development Indicators (WDI) 2022.

World Trade Organization (WTO), Ctre. William Rappard, Rue de Lausanne 154, Case postale, Geneva, CH-1211, SWI, enquiries@wto.org, https://www.wto.org; World Trade Statistical Review 2022.

BAHAMAS, THE-INTERNET USERS

International Telecommunication Union (ITU), Place des Nations, Geneva, CH-1211, SWI, itumail@itu.int, https://www.itu.int; Global Connectivity Report 2022; World Telecommunication/ICT Indicators Database 2021; and Yearbook of Statistics 2019.

BAHAMAS, THE-INVESTMENTS

Inter-American Development Bank (IDB), 1300 New York Ave. NW, Washington, DC, 20577, USA, (202) 623-1000, (202) 623-3096, https://www.iadb.org/en; Latin Macro Watch (LMW).

BAHAMAS, THE-IRRIGATION

Inter-American Development Bank (IDB), 1300 New York Ave. NW, Washington, DC, 20577, USA, (202) 623-1000, (202) 623-3096, https://www.iadb.org/en; Latin Macro Watch (LMW).

BAHAMAS, THE-LABOR

Bahamas National Statistical Institute, Bellagio Plaza, Palmdale, PO Box N 3904, Nassau, BHS, (242) 604-4000 (Dial from U.S.), (242) 604-4090 (Fax from U.S.), statsnp@bahamas.gov.bs, https://stats.gov.bs; Labour Market December 2019.

Central Intelligence Agency (CIA), Office of Public Affairs, Washington, DC, 20505, USA, (703) 482-0623, https://www.cia.gov; The World Factbook.

Euromonitor International, Inc., 1 N Dearborn St., Ste. 1700, Chicago, IL, 60602, USA, (312) 922-1115, (312) 922-1157, info-usa@euromonitor.com, https://www.euromonitor.com/; Geographies.

International Labour Organization (ILO), 4 Rte. des Morillons, Geneva, CH-1211, SWI, ilo@ilo.org, https://www.ilo.org; NORMLEX Information System on International Labour Standards.

Palgrave Macmillan, 1 New York Plaza, Ste. 4500, New York, NY, 10004-1562, USA, (800) 777-4643, orders@palgrave.com, https://www.palgrave.com/us; The Statesman's Yearbook, 2023.

United Nations Food and Agricultural Organization (FAO), 2121 K St., Ste. 800B, Washington, DC, 20037, USA, (202) 653-2400 (Dial from U.S.), (202) 653-5760 (Fax from U.S.), fao-hq@fao.org, https://www.fao.org; The State of Food and Agriculture (SOFA) 2022.

The World Bank, 1818 H St. NW, Washington, DC, 20433, USA, (202) 473-1000, (202) 477-6391, eds03@worldbank.org, https://www.worldbank.org/; World Development Indicators (WDI) 2022.

BAHAMAS, THE-LAND USE

Inter-American Development Bank (IDB), 1300 New York Ave. NW, Washington, DC, 20577, USA, (202) 623-1000, (202) 623-3096, https://www.iadb.org/en; Latin Macro Watch (LMW).

United Nations Statistics Division (UNSD), United Nations Plz., New York, NY, 10017, USA, (800) 253-9646, (212) 963-9851, statistics@un.org, https://unstats.un.org; Millennium Development Goal Indicators.

BAHAMAS, THE-LIBRARIES

UNESCO Institute for Statistics, C.P 250 Succursale H, Montreal, QC, H3G 2K8, CAN, (514) 343-6880 (Dial from U.S.), (514) 343-5740 (Fax from U.S.), uis.publications@unesco.org, http://uis.unesco.org/; UIS.Stat.

BAHAMAS, THE-LIFE EXPECTANCY

United Nations Department of Economic and Social Affairs (DESA), Population Division, 2 United Nations Plz., Rm. DC2-1950, New York, NY, 10017, USA, (212) 963-3209, (212) 963-2147, population@un.org, https://www.un.org/development/desa/pd/; World Population Ageing 2020 Highlights.

United Nations Statistics Division (UNSD), United Nations Plz., New York, NY, 10017, USA, (800) 253-9646, (212) 963-9851, statistics@un.org, https://unstats.un.org; Millennium Development Goal Indicators.

BAHAMAS, THE-LITERACY

Euromonitor International, Inc., 1 N Dearborn St., Ste. 1700, Chicago, IL, 60602, USA, (312) 922-1115, (312) 922-1157, info-usa@euromonitor.com, https://www.euromonitor.com/; Geographies.

UNESCO Institute for Statistics, C.P 250 Succursale H, Montreal, QC, H3G 2K8, CAN, (514) 343-6880 (Dial from U.S.), (514) 343-5740 (Fax from U.S.), uis.publications@unesco.org, http://uis.unesco.org/; Literacy.

BAHAMAS, THE-LIVESTOCK

Palgrave Macmillan, 1 New York Plaza, Ste. 4500, New York, NY, 10004-1562, USA, (800) 777-4643, orders@palgrave.com, https://www.palgrave.com/us; The Statesman's Yearbook, 2023.

Routledge - Taylor & Francis Group, 6000 Broken Sound Pkwy. NW, Ste. 300, Boca Raton, FL, 33487, USA, (800) 634-1420, (800) 634-7064, orders@taylorandfrancis.com, https://www.routledge.com/; The Europa World Year Book 2022.

United Nations Food and Agricultural Organization (FAO), 2121 K St., Ste. 800B, Washington, DC, 20037, USA, (202) 653-2400 (Dial from U.S.), (202) 653-5760 (Fax from U.S.), fao-hq@fao.org, https://www.fao.org; The State of Food and Agriculture (SOFA) 2022.

United Nations Statistics Division (UNSD), United Nations Plz., New York, NY, 10017, USA, (800) 253-9646, (212) 963-9851, statistics@un.org, https://unstats.un.org; Statistical Yearbook of the United Nations 2021.

BAHAMAS, THE-MANUFACTURES

Inter-American Development Bank (IDB), 1300 New York Ave. NW, Washington, DC, 20577, USA, (202) 623-1000, (202) 623-3096, https://www.iadb.org/en; Latin Macro Watch (LMW).

BAHAMAS, THE-MARRIAGE

Routledge - Taylor & Francis Group, 6000 Broken Sound Pkwy. NW, Ste. 300, Boca Raton, FL, 33487, USA, (800) 634-1420, (800) 634-7064, orders@taylorandfrancis.com, https://www.routledge.com/; The Europa World Year Book 2022.

United Nations Statistics Division (UNSD), United Nations Plz., New York, NY, 10017, USA, (800) 253-9646, (212) 963-9851, statistics@un.org, https://unstats.un.org; Statistical Yearbook of the United Nations 2021.

BAHAMAS, THE-MINERAL INDUSTRIES

Inter-American Development Bank (IDB), 1300 New York Ave. NW, Washington, DC, 20577, USA, (202) 623-1000, (202) 623-3096, https://www.iadb.org/en; Latin Macro Watch (LMW).

Palgrave Macmillan, 1 New York Plaza, Ste. 4500, New York, NY, 10004-1562, USA, (800) 777-4643, orders@palgrave.com, https://www.palgrave.com/us; The Statesman's Yearbook, 2023.

Routledge - Taylor & Francis Group, 6000 Broken Sound Pkwy. NW, Ste. 300, Boca Raton, FL, 33487, USA, (800) 634-1420, (800) 634-7064, orders@taylorandfrancis.com, https://www.routledge.com/; The Europa World Year Book 2022.

United Nations Conference on Trade and Development (UNCTAD), Palais des Nations, Geneva, 1211, SWI, (212) 963-6896, unctadinfo@unctad.org, https://unctad.org; Trade and Development Report 2021.

United Nations Statistics Division (UNSD), United Nations Plz., New York, NY, 10017, USA, (800) 253-9646, (212) 963-9851, statistics@un.org, https://unstats.un.org; Statistical Yearbook of the United Nations 2021.

BAHAMAS, THE-MONEY SUPPLY

The Economist Group: Economist Intelligence Unit (EIU), 900 3rd Ave., 16th Fl., New York, NY, 10022, USA, (212) 541-0500, americas@eiu.com, https://www.eiu.com; Bahamas Country Report.

Inter-American Development Bank (IDB), 1300 New York Ave. NW, Washington, DC, 20577, USA, (202) 623-1000, (202) 623-3096, https://www.iadb.org/en; Latin Macro Watch (LMW).

International Monetary Fund (IMF), 700 19th St. NW, Washington, DC, 20431, USA, (202) 623-7000, (202) 623-4661, publications@imf.org, https://www.imf.org; International Financial Statistics (IFS).

Routledge - Taylor & Francis Group, 6000 Broken Sound Pkwy. NW, Ste. 300, Boca Raton, FL, 33487, USA, (800) 634-1420, (800) 634-7064, orders@taylorandfrancis.com, https://www.routledge.com/; The Europa World Year Book 2022.

United Nations Statistics Division (UNSD), United Nations Plz., New York, NY, 10017, USA, (800) 253-9646, (212) 963-9851, statistics@un.org, https://unstats.un.org; Statistical Yearbook of the United Nations 2021.

BAHAMAS, THE-MORTALITY

United Nations Statistics Division (UNSD), United Nations Plz., New York, NY, 10017, USA, (800) 253-9646, (212) 963-9851, statistics@un.org, https://unstats.un.org; Millennium Development Goal Indicators; Statistical Yearbook of the United Nations 2021; and World Statistics Pocketbook 2021.

The World Bank, 1818 H St. NW, Washington, DC, 20433, USA, (202) 473-1000, (202) 477-6391, eds03@worldbank.org, https://www.worldbank.org/; World Development Indicators (WDI) 2022.

World Health Organization (WHO), Ave. Appia 20, Geneva, CH-1211, SWI, (202) 974-3000 (Telephone in U.S.), publications@who.int, https://www.who.int/; Global Health Observatory (GHO).

BAHAMAS, THE-MOTION PICTURES

Palgrave Macmillan, 1 New York Plaza, Ste. 4500, New York, NY, 10004-1562, USA, (800) 777-4643, orders@palgrave.com, https://www.palgrave.com/us; The Statesman's Yearbook, 2023.

BAHAMAS, THE-NATURAL GAS PRODUCTION

See BAHAMAS, THE-MINERAL INDUSTRIES

BAHAMAS, THE-NUTRITION

United Nations Food and Agricultural Organization (FAO), 2121 K St., Ste. 800B, Washington, DC, 20037, USA, (202) 653-2400 (Dial from U.S.), (202) 653-5760 (Fax from U.S.), fao-hq@fao.org, https://www.fao.org; The State of Food and Agriculture (SOFA) 2022.

United Nations Statistics Division (UNSD), United Nations Plz., New York, NY, 10017, USA, (800) 253-9646, (212) 963-9851, statistics@un.org, https://unstats.un.org; Millennium Development Goal Indicators.

BAHAMAS, THE-PAPER

See BAHAMAS, THE-FORESTS AND FORESTRY

BAHAMAS, THE-PEANUT PRODUCTION

See BAHAMAS, THE-CROPS

BAHAMAS, THE-PESTICIDES

United Nations Food and Agricultural Organization (FAO), 2121 K St., Ste. 800B, Washington, DC, 20037, USA, (202) 653-2400 (Dial from U.S.), (202) 653-5760 (Fax from U.S.), fao-hq@fao.org, https://www.fao.org; The State of Food and Agriculture (SOFA) 2022.

BAHAMAS, THE-PETROLEUM INDUSTRY AND TRADE

Inter-American Development Bank (IDB), 1300 New York Ave. NW, Washington, DC, 20577, USA, (202) 623-1000, (202) 623-3096, https://www.iadb.org/en; Latin Macro Watch (LMW).

United Nations Food and Agricultural Organization (FAO), 2121 K St., Ste. 800B, Washington, DC, 20037, USA, (202) 653-2400 (Dial from U.S.), (202) 653-5760 (Fax from U.S.), fao-hq@fao.org, https://www.fao.org; The State of Food and Agriculture (SOFA) 2022.

United Nations Statistics Division (UNSD), United Nations Plz., New York, NY, 10017, USA, (800) 253-9646, (212) 963-9851, statistics@un.org, https://unstats.un.org; Statistical Yearbook of the United Nations 2021.

BAHAMAS, THE-POPULATION

Caribbean Public Health Agency (CARPHA), Federation Park, 16-18 Jamaica Blvd., Port of Spain, TTO, (868) 622-4261 (Dial from U.S.), (868) 299-0820 (Dial from U.S.), postmaster@carpha.org, https://carpha.org/; unpublished data.

Central Intelligence Agency (CIA), Office of Public Affairs, Washington, DC, 20505, USA, (703) 482-0623, https://www.cia.gov; The World Factbook.

The Economist Group: Economist Intelligence Unit (EIU), 900 3rd Ave., 16th Fl., New York, NY, 10022, USA, (212) 541-0500, americas@eiu.com, https://www.eiu.com; Bahamas Country Report.

European Commission, Eurostat, Luxembourg, 2920, LUX, https://ec.europa.eu/eurostat/; EU in the World 2020.

Infoplease, c/o Sandbox Networks, Inc., 1 Lincoln St., 24th Fl., Boston, MA, 02111, USA, https://www.infoplease.com; Countries of the World.

Inter-American Development Bank (IDB), 1300 New York Ave. NW, Washington, DC, 20577, USA, (202) 623-1000, (202) 623-3096, https://www.iadb.org/en; Latin Macro Watch (LMW).

International Labour Organization (ILO), 4 Rte. des Morillons, Geneva, CH-1211, SWI, ilo@ilo.org, https://www.ilo.org; NORMLEX Information System on International Labour Standards.

Palgrave Macmillan, 1 New York Plaza, Ste. 4500, New York, NY, 10004-1562, USA, (800) 777-4643, orders@palgrave.com, https://www.palgrave.com/us; The Statesman's Yearbook, 2023.

Routledge - Taylor & Francis Group, 6000 Broken Sound Pkwy. NW, Ste. 300, Boca Raton, FL, 33487, USA, (800) 634-1420, (800) 634-7064, orders@taylorandfrancis.com, https://www.routledge.com/; The Europa World Year Book 2022.

UK Data Service, University of Essex, Wivenhoe Park, Colchester, Essex, CO4 3SQ, GBR, https://ukdataservice.ac.uk/; International Aggregate Data.

UNESCO Institute for Statistics, C.P 250 Succursale H, Montreal, QC, H3G 2K8, CAN, (514) 343-6880 (Dial from U.S.), (514) 343-5740 (Fax from U.S.), uis.publications@unesco.org, http://uis.unesco.org/; UIS.Stat.

United Nations Department of Economic and Social Affairs (DESA), Population Division, 2 United Nations Plz., Rm. DC2-1950, New York, NY, 10017, USA, (212) 963-3209, (212) 963-2147, population@un.org, https://www.un.org/development/desa/pd/; Revision of World Urbanization Prospects and World Population Ageing 2020 Highlights.

United Nations Development Programme (UNDP), One United Nations Plz., New York, NY, 10017, USA, (212) 906-5000, (212) 906-5001, https://www.undp.org; Human Development Report 2021-2022.

United Nations Statistics Division (UNSD), United Nations Plz., New York, NY, 10017, USA, (800) 253-9646, (212) 963-9851, statistics@un.org, https://unstats.un.org; Statistical Yearbook of the United Nations 2021 and World Statistics Pocketbook 2021.

The World Bank, 1818 H St. NW, Washington, DC, 20433, USA, (202) 473-1000, (202) 477-6391, eds03@worldbank.org, https://www.worldbank.org/; The Global Findex Database 2021.

BAHAMAS, THE-POPULATION DENSITY

Central Intelligence Agency (CIA), Office of Public Affairs, Washington, DC, 20505, USA, (703) 482-0623, https://www.cia.gov; The World Factbook.

Inter-American Development Bank (IDB), 1300 New York Ave. NW, Washington, DC, 20577, USA, (202) 623-1000, (202) 623-3096, https://www.iadb.org/en; Latin Macro Watch (LMW).

Palgrave Macmillan, 1 New York Plaza, Ste. 4500, New York, NY, 10004-1562, USA, (800) 777-4643, orders@palgrave.com, https://www.palgrave.com/us; The Statesman's Yearbook, 2023.

Routledge - Taylor & Francis Group, 6000 Broken Sound Pkwy. NW, Ste. 300, Boca Raton, FL, 33487, USA, (800) 634-1420, (800) 634-7064, orders@taylorandfrancis.com, https://www.routledge.com/; The Europa World Year Book 2022.

BAHAMAS, THE-POSTAL SERVICE

Palgrave Macmillan, 1 New York Plaza, Ste. 4500, New York, NY, 10004-1562, USA, (800) 777-4643, orders@palgrave.com, https://www.palgrave.com/us; The Statesman's Yearbook, 2023.

BAHAMAS, THE-POWER RESOURCES

Euromonitor International, Inc., 1 N Dearborn St., Ste. 1700, Chicago, IL, 60602, USA, (312) 922-1115, (312) 922-1157, info-usa@euromonitor.com, https://www.euromonitor.com/; Geographies.

Palgrave Macmillan, 1 New York Plaza, Ste. 4500, New York, NY, 10004-1562, USA, (800) 777-4643, orders@palgrave.com, https://www.palgrave.com/us; The Statesman's Yearbook, 2023.

United Nations Food and Agricultural Organization (FAO), 2121 K St., Ste. 800B, Washington, DC, 20037, USA, (202) 653-2400 (Dial from U.S.), (202) 653-5760 (Fax from U.S.), fao-hq@fao.org, https://www.fao.org; The State of Food and Agriculture (SOFA) 2022.

United Nations Statistics Division (UNSD), United Nations Plz., New York, NY, 10017, USA, (800) 253-9646, (212) 963-9851, statistics@un.org, https://unstats.un.org; Energy Statistics Yearbook 2019; Statistical Yearbook of the United Nations 2021; and World Statistics Pocketbook 2021.

BAHAMAS, THE-PRICES

Bahamas National Statistical Institute, Bellagio Plaza, Palmdale, PO Box N 3904, Nassau, BHS, (242) 604-4000 (Dial from U.S.), (242) 604-4090 (Fax from U.S.), statsnp@bahamas.gov.bs, https://stats.gov.bs; All Bahamas Consumer Price Index.

Euromonitor International, Inc., 1 N Dearborn St., Ste. 1700, Chicago, IL, 60602, USA, (312) 922-1115, (312) 922-1157, info-usa@euromonitor.com, https://www.euromonitor.com/; Geographies.

International Monetary Fund (IMF), 700 19th St. NW, Washington, DC, 20431, USA, (202) 623-7000, (202) 623-4661, publications@imf.org, https://www.imf.org; International Financial Statistics (IFS).

United Nations Economic Commission for Latin America and the Caribbean (ECLAC), Casilla 179-D, Santiago, 7630412, CHL, (202) 596-3713, prensa@cepal.org, https://www.cepal.org/en; Economic Survey of Latin America and the Caribbean 2021: Labour Dynamics and Employment Policies for Sustainable and Inclusive Recovery Beyond the COVID-19 Crisis.

BAHAMAS, THE-PUBLIC HEALTH

Euromonitor International, Inc., 1 N Dearborn St., Ste. 1700, Chicago, IL, 60602, USA, (312) 922-1115, (312) 922-1157, info-usa@euromonitor.com, https://www.euromonitor.com/; Geographies.

Palgrave Macmillan, 1 New York Plaza, Ste. 4500, New York, NY, 10004-1562, USA, (800) 777-4643, orders@palgrave.com, https://www.palgrave.com/us; The Statesman's Yearbook, 2023.

U.S. Census Bureau, 4600 Silver Hill Rd., Washington, DC, 20233, USA, (301) 763-4636, (800) 923-8282, https://www.census.gov; HIV/AIDS Surveillance Data Base.

United Nations Department of Economic and Social Affairs (DESA), Population Division, 2 United Nations Plz., Rm. DC2-1950, New York, NY, 10017, USA, (212) 963-3209, (212) 963-2147, population@un.org, https://www.un.org/development/desa/pd/; World Fertility Data 2019.

United Nations Development Programme (UNDP), One United Nations Plz., New York, NY, 10017, USA, (212) 906-5000, (212) 906-5001, https://www.undp.org; Human Development Report 2021-2022.

United Nations Statistics Division (UNSD), United Nations Plz., New York, NY, 10017, USA, (800) 253-9646, (212) 963-9851, statistics@un.org, https://unstats.un.org; Millennium Development Goal Indicators and Statistical Yearbook of the United Nations 2021.

World Health Organization (WHO), Ave. Appia 20, Geneva, CH-1211, SWI, (202) 974-3000 (Telephone in U.S.), publications@who.int, https://www.who.int/; Global Health Observatory (GHO) and Health Statistics and Information Systems.

BAHAMAS, THE-RELIGION

Central Intelligence Agency (CIA), Office of Public Affairs, Washington, DC, 20505, USA, (703) 482-0623, https://www.cia.gov; The World Factbook.

Palgrave Macmillan, 1 New York Plaza, Ste. 4500, New York, NY, 10004-1562, USA, (800) 777-4643, orders@palgrave.com, https://www.palgrave.com/us; The Statesman's Yearbook, 2023.

BAHAMAS, THE-RETAIL TRADE

Euromonitor International, Inc., 1 N Dearborn St., Ste. 1700, Chicago, IL, 60602, USA, (312) 922-1115, (312) 922-1157, info-usa@euromonitor.com, https://www.euromonitor.com/; Geographies.

Inter-American Development Bank (IDB), 1300 New York Ave. NW, Washington, DC, 20577, USA, (202) 623-1000, (202) 623-3096, https://www.iadb.org/en; Latin Macro Watch (LMW).

BAHAMAS, THE-RICE PRODUCTION

See BAHAMAS, THE-CROPS

BAHAMAS, THE-RUBBER INDUSTRY AND TRADE

International Rubber Study Group (IRSG), 51 Changi Business Park Central 2, Unit No. 6, 486066, SGP, https://www.rubberstudy.org; Monthly Rubber Bulletin (MRB); Rubber Industry Report; Rubber Statistical Bulletin; and World Rubber Industry Report (WRIO).

BAHAMAS, THE-SHIPPING

Routledge - Taylor & Francis Group, 6000 Broken Sound Pkwy. NW, Ste. 300, Boca Raton, FL, 33487, USA, (800) 634-1420, (800) 634-7064, orders@taylorandfrancis.com, https://www.routledge.com/; The Europa World Year Book 2022.

S&P Global, IHS Markit, 15 Inverness Way E, Englewood, CO, 80112, USA, (800) 447-2273, (800) 854-7179, https://ihsmarkit.com; IHS Maritime World Shipbuilding Statistics; Journal of Commerce; Lloyd's Register of Ships 2021-2022; and Maritime Portal Desktop.

United Nations Statistics Division (UNSD), United Nations Plz., New York, NY, 10017, USA, (800) 253-9646, (212) 963-9851, statistics@un.org, https://unstats.un.org; Statistical Yearbook of the United Nations 2021.

BAHAMAS, THE-STEEL PRODUCTION

See BAHAMAS, THE-MINERAL INDUSTRIES

BAHAMAS, THE-SUGAR PRODUCTION

See BAHAMAS, THE-CROPS

BAHAMAS, THE-TAXATION

Inter-American Development Bank (IDB), 1300 New York Ave. NW, Washington, DC, 20577, USA, (202) 623-1000, (202) 623-3096, https://www.iadb.org/en; Latin Macro Watch (LMW).

The World Bank, 1818 H St. NW, Washington, DC, 20433, USA, (202) 473-1000, (202) 477-6391, eds03@worldbank.org, https://www.worldbank.org/; World Development Indicators (WDI) 2022.

BAHAMAS, THE-TELEPHONE

Palgrave Macmillan, 1 New York Plaza, Ste. 4500, New York, NY, 10004-1562, USA, (800) 777-4643, orders@palgrave.com, https://www.palgrave.com/us; The Statesman's Yearbook, 2023.

Routledge - Taylor & Francis Group, 6000 Broken Sound Pkwy. NW, Ste. 300, Boca Raton, FL, 33487, USA, (800) 634-1420, (800) 634-7064, orders@taylorandfrancis.com, https://www.routledge.com/; The Europa World Year Book 2022.

United Nations Statistics Division (UNSD), United Nations Plz., New York, NY, 10017, USA, (800) 253-9646, (212) 963-9851, statistics@un.org, https://unstats.un.org; World Statistics Pocketbook 2021.

BAHAMAS, THE-TEXTILE INDUSTRY

Palgrave Macmillan, 1 New York Plaza, Ste. 4500, New York, NY, 10004-1562, USA, (800) 777-4643, orders@palgrave.com, https://www.palgrave.com/us; The Statesman's Yearbook, 2023.

BAHAMAS, THE-TOURISM

Euromonitor International, Inc., 1 N Dearborn St., Ste. 1700, Chicago, IL, 60602, USA, (312) 922-1115, (312) 922-1157, info-usa@euromonitor.com, https://www.euromonitor.com/; Geographies.

Palgrave Macmillan, 1 New York Plaza, Ste. 4500, New York, NY, 10004-1562, USA, (800) 777-4643, orders@palgrave.com, https://www.palgrave.com/us; The Statesman's Yearbook, 2023.

Routledge - Taylor & Francis Group, 6000 Broken Sound Pkwy. NW, Ste. 300, Boca Raton, FL, 33487, USA, (800) 634-1420, (800) 634-7064, orders@taylorandfrancis.com, https://www.routledge.com/; The Europa World Year Book 2022.

United Nations Statistics Division (UNSD), United Nations Plz., New York, NY, 10017, USA, (800) 253-9646, (212) 963-9851, statistics@un.org, https://unstats.un.org; Statistical Yearbook of the United Nations 2021.

United Nations World Tourism Organization (UNWTO), Calle Poeta Joan Maragall 42, Madrid, 28020, SPA, info@unwto.org, https://www.unwto.org/; Yearbook of Tourism Statistics, 2021 Edition.

BAHAMAS, THE-TRADE

See BAHAMAS, THE-INTERNATIONAL TRADE

BAHAMAS, THE-TRANSPORTATION

Central Intelligence Agency (CIA), Office of Public Affairs, Washington, DC, 20505, USA, (703) 482-0623, https://www.cia.gov; The World Factbook.

Euromonitor International, Inc., 1 N Dearborn St., Ste. 1700, Chicago, IL, 60602, USA, (312) 922-1115, (312) 922-1157, info-usa@euromonitor.com, https://www.euromonitor.com/; Geographies.

Inter-American Development Bank (IDB), 1300 New York Ave. NW, Washington, DC, 20577, USA, (202) 623-1000, (202) 623-3096, https://www.iadb.org/en; Latin Macro Watch (LMW).

Palgrave Macmillan, 1 New York Plaza, Ste. 4500, New York, NY, 10004-1562, USA, (800) 777-4643, orders@palgrave.com, https://www.palgrave.com/us; The Statesman's Yearbook, 2023.

Routledge - Taylor & Francis Group, 6000 Broken Sound Pkwy. NW, Ste. 300, Boca Raton, FL, 33487, USA, (800) 634-1420, (800) 634-7064, orders@taylorandfrancis.com, https://www.routledge.com/; The Europa World Year Book 2022.

BAHAMAS, THE-UNEMPLOYMENT

International Labour Organization (ILO), 4 Rte. des Morillons, Geneva, CH-1211, SWI, ilo@ilo.org, https://www.ilo.org; NORMLEX Information System on International Labour Standards.

BAHAMAS, THE-VITAL STATISTICS

Palgrave Macmillan, 1 New York Plaza, Ste. 4500, New York, NY, 10004-1562, USA, (800) 777-4643, orders@palgrave.com, https://www.palgrave.com/us; The Statesman's Yearbook, 2023.

U.S. Census Bureau, 4600 Silver Hill Rd., Washington, DC, 20233, USA, (301) 763-4636, (800) 923-8282, https://www.census.gov; HIV/AIDS Surveillance Data Base.

United Nations Department of Economic and Social Affairs (DESA), Population Division, 2 United Nations Plz., Rm. DC2-1950, New York, NY, 10017, USA, (212) 963-3209, (212) 963-2147, population@un.org, https://www.un.org/development/desa/pd/; World Contraceptive Use 2021: Estimates and Projections of Family Planning Indicators and World Marriage Data 2019.

United Nations Statistics Division (UNSD), United Nations Plz., New York, NY, 10017, USA, (800) 253-9646, (212) 963-9851, statistics@un.org, https://unstats.un.org; Statistical Yearbook of the United Nations 2021.

BAHAMAS, THE-WAGES

Bahamas National Statistical Institute, Bellagio Plaza, Palmdale, PO Box N 3904, Nassau, BHS, (242) 604-4000 (Dial from U.S.), (242) 604-4090 (Fax from U.S.), statsnp@bahamas.gov.bs, https://stats.gov.bs; Labour Market December 2019.

International Labour Organization (ILO), 4 Rte. des Morillons, Geneva, CH-1211, SWI, ilo@ilo.org, https://www.ilo.org; NORMLEX Information System on International Labour Standards.

BAHAMAS, THE-WEATHER

See BAHAMAS, THE-CLIMATE

BAHAMAS, THE-WHALES

See BAHAMAS, THE-FISHERIES

BAHAMAS, THE-WHEAT PRODUCTION

See BAHAMAS, THE-CROPS

BAHAMAS, THE-WHOLESALE PRICE INDEXES

Inter-American Development Bank (IDB), 1300 New York Ave. NW, Washington, DC, 20577, USA, (202) 623-1000, (202) 623-3096, https://www.iadb.org/en; Latin Macro Watch (LMW).

BAHAMAS, THE-WHOLESALE TRADE

Inter-American Development Bank (IDB), 1300 New York Ave. NW, Washington, DC, 20577, USA, (202) 623-1000, (202) 623-3096, https://www.iadb.org/en; Latin Macro Watch (LMW).

BAHAMAS, THE-WOOL PRODUCTION

See BAHAMAS, THE-TEXTILE INDUSTRY

BAHRAIN-NATIONAL STATISTICAL OFFICE

Bahrain Information & eGovernment Authority, PO Box 33305, Isa Town, 17878000, BHR, statistics@iga.gov.bh, https://www.data.gov.bh/; National Data Reports (Bahrain).

BAHRAIN-AGRICULTURE

The Economist Group: Economist Intelligence Unit (EIU), 900 3rd Ave., 16th Fl., New York, NY, 10022, USA, (212) 541-0500, americas@eiu.com, https://www.eiu.com; Bahrain Country Report.

Euromonitor International, Inc., 1 N Dearborn St., Ste. 1700, Chicago, IL, 60602, USA, (312) 922-1115, (312) 922-1157, info-usa@euromonitor.com, https://www.euromonitor.com/; Geographies.

Organisation of Islamic Cooperation (OIC), Statistical, Economic and Social Research and Training Centre for Islamic Countries (SESRIC), Kudus Cad. No. 9, Diplomatik Site, Ankara, 06450, TUR, statistics@sesric.org, https://www.sesric.org/; OIC Statistics (OICStat) Database and OIC-Countries in Figures (OIC-CIF).

Palgrave Macmillan, 1 New York Plaza, Ste. 4500, New York, NY, 10004-1562, USA, (800) 777-4643, orders@palgrave.com, https://www.palgrave.com/us; The Statesman's Yearbook, 2023.

Routledge - Taylor & Francis Group, 6000 Broken Sound Pkwy. NW, Ste. 300, Boca Raton, FL, 33487, USA, (800) 634-1420, (800) 634-7064, orders@taylorandfrancis.com, https://www.routledge.com/; The Europa World Year Book 2022.

United Nations Economic and Social Commission for Western Asia (ESCWA), Riad el-Solh Sq., PO Box 11-8575, Beirut, LBN, escwa-ciu@un.org, https://www.unescwa.org; ESCWA Annual Report 2019.

United Nations Food and Agricultural Organization (FAO), 2121 K St., Ste. 800B, Washington, DC, 20037, USA, (202) 653-2400 (Dial from U.S.), (202) 653-5760 (Fax from U.S.), fao-hq@fao.org, https://www.fao.org; AQUASTAT and The State of Food and Agriculture (SOFA) 2022.

The World Bank, 1818 H St. NW, Washington, DC, 20433, USA, (202) 473-1000, (202) 477-6391, eds03@worldbank.org, https://www.worldbank.org/; Gulf Cooperation Council (report) and World Development Indicators (WDI) 2022.

BAHRAIN-AIRLINES

Palgrave Macmillan, 1 New York Plaza, Ste. 4500, New York, NY, 10004-1562, USA, (800) 777-4643, orders@palgrave.com, https://www.palgrave.com/us; The Statesman's Yearbook, 2023.

Routledge - Taylor & Francis Group, 6000 Broken Sound Pkwy. NW, Ste. 300, Boca Raton, FL, 33487, USA, (800) 634-1420, (800) 634-7064, orders@taylorandfrancis.com, https://www.routledge.com/; The Europa World Year Book 2022.

BAHRAIN-ALUMINUM PRODUCTION

See BAHRAIN-MINERAL INDUSTRIES

BAHRAIN-ARMED FORCES

Central Intelligence Agency (CIA), Office of Public Affairs, Washington, DC, 20505, USA, (703) 482-0623, https://www.cia.gov; The World Factbook.

International Institute for Strategic Studies (IISS) - Americas, 2121 K St. NW, Ste. 600, Washington, DC, 20037, USA, (202) 659-1490, (202) 659-1499, https://www.iiss.org/; The Military Balance 2022.

Palgrave Macmillan, 1 New York Plaza, Ste. 4500, New York, NY, 10004-1562, USA, (800) 777-4643, orders@palgrave.com, https://www.palgrave.com/us; The Statesman's Yearbook, 2023.

Stockholm International Peace Research Institute (SIPRI), Signalistgatan 9, Stockholm, SE 169 72, SWE, https://www.sipri.org/; SIPRI Arms Transfers Database and SIPRI Military Expenditure Database.

BAHRAIN-BALANCE OF PAYMENTS

International Monetary Fund (IMF), 700 19th St. NW, Washington, DC, 20431, USA, (202) 623-7000, (202) 623-4661, publications@imf.org, https://www.imf.org; Balance of Payments Statistics: Annual Report 2021.

Routledge - Taylor & Francis Group, 6000 Broken Sound Pkwy. NW, Ste. 300, Boca Raton, FL, 33487, USA, (800) 634-1420, (800) 634-7064, orders@taylorandfrancis.com, https://www.routledge.com/; The Europa World Year Book 2022.

United Nations Conference on Trade and Development (UNCTAD), Palais des Nations, Geneva, 1211,

SWI, (212) 963-6896, unctadinfo@unctad.org, https://unctad.org; Handbook of Statistics 2021.

The World Bank, 1818 H St. NW, Washington, DC, 20433, USA, (202) 473-1000, (202) 477-6391, eds03@worldbank.org, https://www.worldbank.org/; Gulf Cooperation Council (report) and World Development Indicators (WDI) 2022.

BAHRAIN-BANKS AND BANKING

Euromonitor International, Inc., 1 N Dearborn St., Ste. 1700, Chicago, IL, 60602, USA, (312) 922-1115, (312) 922-1157, info-usa@euromonitor.com, https://www.euromonitor.com/; Geographies.

International Monetary Fund (IMF), 700 19th St. NW, Washington, DC, 20431, USA, (202) 623-7000, (202) 623-4661, publications@imf.org, https://www.imf.org; International Financial Statistics (IFS).

Routledge - Taylor & Francis Group, 6000 Broken Sound Pkwy. NW, Ste. 300, Boca Raton, FL, 33487, USA, (800) 634-1420, (800) 634-7064, orders@taylorandfrancis.com, https://www.routledge.com/; The Europa World Year Book 2022.

United Nations Economic and Social Commission for Western Asia (ESCWA), Riad el-Solh Sq., PO Box 11-8575, Beirut, LBN, escwa-ciu@un.org, https://www.unescwa.org; ESCWA Annual Report 2019.

BAHRAIN-BARLEY PRODUCTION

See BAHRAIN-CROPS

BAHRAIN-BROADCASTING

Central Intelligence Agency (CIA), Office of Public Affairs, Washington, DC, 20505, USA, (703) 482-0623, https://www.cia.gov; The World Factbook.

Euromonitor International, Inc., 1 N Dearborn St., Ste. 1700, Chicago, IL, 60602, USA, (312) 922-1115, (312) 922-1157, info-usa@euromonitor.com, https://www.euromonitor.com/; Geographies.

Palgrave Macmillan, 1 New York Plaza, Ste. 4500, New York, NY, 10004-1562, USA, (800) 777-4643, orders@palgrave.com, https://www.palgrave.com/us; The Statesman's Yearbook, 2023.

UNESCO Institute for Statistics, C.P 250 Succursale H, Montreal, QC, H3G 2K8, CAN, (514) 343-6880 (Dial from U.S.), (514) 343-5740 (Fax from U.S.), uis.publications@unesco.org, http://uis.unesco.org/; UIS.Stat.

WRTH Publications Limited, PO Box 290, Oxford, OX2 7FT, GBR, sales@wrth.com, https://www.wrth.com; World Radio TV Handbook 2023.

BAHRAIN-BUDGET

Central Intelligence Agency (CIA), Office of Public Affairs, Washington, DC, 20505, USA, (703) 482-0623, https://www.cia.gov; The World Factbook.

BAHRAIN-CHILDBIRTH-STATISTICS

The World Bank, 1818 H St. NW, Washington, DC, 20433, USA, (202) 473-1000, (202) 477-6391, eds03@worldbank.org, https://www.worldbank.org/; World Development Indicators (WDI) 2022.

BAHRAIN-CLIMATE

Palgrave Macmillan, 1 New York Plaza, Ste. 4500, New York, NY, 10004-1562, USA, (800) 777-4643, orders@palgrave.com, https://www.palgrave.com/us; The Statesman's Yearbook, 2023.

BAHRAIN-COAL PRODUCTION

See BAHRAIN-MINERAL INDUSTRIES

BAHRAIN-COFFEE

See BAHRAIN-CROPS

BAHRAIN-COMMERCE

Palgrave Macmillan, 1 New York Plaza, Ste. 4500, New York, NY, 10004-1562, USA, (800) 777-4643, orders@palgrave.com, https://www.palgrave.com/us; The Statesman's Yearbook, 2023.

UK Data Service, University of Essex, Wivenhoe Park, Colchester, Essex, CO4 3SQ, GBR, https://ukdataservice.ac.uk/; International Aggregate Data.

BAHRAIN-COMMODITY EXCHANGES

Barchart, 209 W Jackson Blvd., 2nd Fl., Chicago, IL, 60606, USA, (877) 247-4394, commodities@barchart.com, https://www.barchart.com/cmdty; The cmdty Yearbook 2023; cmdtyStats: Commodity Statistics and Fundamental Data; cmdtyView: Commodity Index; and Commodity Data and Prices.

International Monetary Fund (IMF), 700 19th St. NW, Washington, DC, 20431, USA, (202) 623-7000, (202) 623-4661, publications@imf.org, https://www.imf.org; IMF Primary Commodity Prices.

BAHRAIN-CONSTRUCTION INDUSTRY

Palgrave Macmillan, 1 New York Plaza, Ste. 4500, New York, NY, 10004-1562, USA, (800) 777-4643, orders@palgrave.com, https://www.palgrave.com/us; The Statesman's Yearbook, 2023.

BAHRAIN-CONSUMER PRICE INDEXES

Routledge - Taylor & Francis Group, 6000 Broken Sound Pkwy. NW, Ste. 300, Boca Raton, FL, 33487, USA, (800) 634-1420, (800) 634-7064, orders@taylorandfrancis.com, https://www.routledge.com/; The Europa World Year Book 2022.

The World Bank, 1818 H St. NW, Washington, DC, 20433, USA, (202) 473-1000, (202) 477-6391, eds03@worldbank.org, https://www.worldbank.org/; Gulf Cooperation Council (report).

BAHRAIN-COPPER INDUSTRY AND TRADE

See BAHRAIN-MINERAL INDUSTRIES

BAHRAIN-CORN INDUSTRY

See BAHRAIN-CROPS

BAHRAIN-COTTON

See BAHRAIN-CROPS

BAHRAIN-CROPS

Palgrave Macmillan, 1 New York Plaza, Ste. 4500, New York, NY, 10004-1562, USA, (800) 777-4643, orders@palgrave.com, https://www.palgrave.com/us; The Statesman's Yearbook, 2023.

United Nations Food and Agricultural Organization (FAO), 2121 K St., Ste. 800B, Washington, DC, 20037, USA, (202) 653-2400 (Dial from U.S.), (202) 653-5760 (Fax from U.S.), fao-hq@fao.org, https://www.fao.org; The State of Food and Agriculture (SOFA) 2022.

BAHRAIN-DAIRY PROCESSING

United Nations Food and Agricultural Organization (FAO), 2121 K St., Ste. 800B, Washington, DC, 20037, USA, (202) 653-2400 (Dial from U.S.), (202) 653-5760 (Fax from U.S.), fao-hq@fao.org, https://www.fao.org; The State of Food and Agriculture (SOFA) 2022.

BAHRAIN-DEBTS, EXTERNAL

Palgrave Macmillan, 1 New York Plaza, Ste. 4500, New York, NY, 10004-1562, USA, (800) 777-4643, orders@palgrave.com, https://www.palgrave.com/us; The Statesman's Yearbook, 2023.

The World Bank, 1818 H St. NW, Washington, DC, 20433, USA, (202) 473-1000, (202) 477-6391, eds03@worldbank.org, https://www.worldbank.org/; Global Financial Development Report 2019-2020: Bank Regulation and Supervision a Decade after the Global Financial Crisis and World Development Indicators (WDI) 2022.

BAHRAIN-DEFENSE EXPENDITURES

See BAHRAIN-ARMED FORCES

BAHRAIN-DIAMONDS

See BAHRAIN-MINERAL INDUSTRIES

BAHRAIN-ECONOMIC ASSISTANCE

United Nations Statistics Division (UNSD), United Nations Plz., New York, NY, 10017, USA, (800) 253-9646, (212) 963-9851, statistics@un.org, https://unstats.un.org; Statistical Yearbook of the United Nations 2021.

BAHRAIN-ECONOMIC CONDITIONS

Bernan Press, 15250 NBN Way, Bldg. C, Blue Ridge Summit, PA, 17214, USA, (301) 459-2255, (800) 865-3457, (800) 865-3450, customercare@bernan.com, https://rowman.com/Page/Bernan; World Economic Outlook, April 2022.

Central Intelligence Agency (CIA), Office of Public Affairs, Washington, DC, 20505, USA, (703) 482-0623, https://www.cia.gov; The World Factbook.

The Economist Group: Economist Intelligence Unit (EIU), 900 3rd Ave., 16th Fl., New York, NY, 10022, USA, (212) 541-0500, americas@eiu.com, https://www.eiu.com; Bahrain Country Report.

Euromonitor International, Inc., 1 N Dearborn St., Ste. 1700, Chicago, IL, 60602, USA, (312) 922-1115, (312) 922-1157, info-usa@euromonitor.com, https://www.euromonitor.com/; Geographies.

International Monetary Fund (IMF), 700 19th St. NW, Washington, DC, 20431, USA, (202) 623-7000, (202) 623-4661, publications@imf.org, https://www.imf.org; IMF Data and World Economic Outlook.

Organisation of Islamic Cooperation (OIC), Statistical, Economic and Social Research and Training Centre for Islamic Countries (SESRIC), Kudus Cad. No. 9, Diplomatik Site, Ankara, 06450, TUR, statistics@sesric.org, https://www.sesric.org/; OIC Economic Outlook 2021; OIC Statistics (OICStat) Database; and OIC-Countries in Figures (OIC-CIF).

Palgrave Macmillan, 1 New York Plaza, Ste. 4500, New York, NY, 10004-1562, USA, (800) 777-4643, orders@palgrave.com, https://www.palgrave.com/us; The Statesman's Yearbook, 2023.

Routledge - Taylor & Francis Group, 6000 Broken Sound Pkwy. NW, Ste. 300, Boca Raton, FL, 33487, USA, (800) 634-1420, (800) 634-7064, orders@taylorandfrancis.com, https://www.routledge.com/; The Europa World Year Book 2022.

United Nations Economic and Social Commission for Western Asia (ESCWA), Riad el-Solh Sq., PO Box 11-8575, Beirut, LBN, escwa-ciu@un.org, https://www.unescwa.org; ESCWA Annual Report 2019; ESCWA Data Portal for the Arab Region; and Survey of Economic and Social Developments in the Arab Region 2020-2021.

United Nations Statistics Division (UNSD), United Nations Plz., New York, NY, 10017, USA, (800) 253-9646, (212) 963-9851, statistics@un.org, https://unstats.un.org; World Statistics Pocketbook 2021.

The World Bank, 1818 H St. NW, Washington, DC, 20433, USA, (202) 473-1000, (202) 477-6391, eds03@worldbank.org, https://www.worldbank.org/; Global Economic Monitor (GEM); Global Economic Prospects, June 2022; The Global Findex Database 2021; and Gulf Cooperation Council (report).

BAHRAIN-EDUCATION

Euromonitor International, Inc., 1 N Dearborn St., Ste. 1700, Chicago, IL, 60602, USA, (312) 922-1115, (312) 922-1157, info-usa@euromonitor.com, https://www.euromonitor.com/; Geographies.

Infoplease, c/o Sandbox Networks, Inc., 1 Lincoln St., 24th Fl., Boston, MA, 02111, USA, https://www.infoplease.com; Countries of the World.

Organisation of Islamic Cooperation (OIC), Statistical, Economic and Social Research and Training Centre for Islamic Countries (SESRIC), Kudus Cad. No. 9, Diplomatik Site, Ankara, 06450, TUR, statistics@sesric.org, https://www.sesric.org/; OIC Statistics (OICStat) Database.

Palgrave Macmillan, 1 New York Plaza, Ste. 4500, New York, NY, 10004-1562, USA, (800) 777-4643,

orders@palgrave.com, https://www.palgrave.com/us; The Statesman's Yearbook, 2023.

Routledge - Taylor & Francis Group, 6000 Broken Sound Pkwy. NW, Ste. 300, Boca Raton, FL, 33487, USA, (800) 634-1420, (800) 634-7064, orders@taylorandfrancis.com, https://www.routledge.com/; The Europa World Year Book 2022.

UNESCO Institute for Statistics, C.P 250 Succursale H, Montreal, QC, H3G 2K8, CAN, (514) 343-6880 (Dial from U.S.), (514) 343-5740 (Fax from U.S.), uis.publications@unesco.org, http://uis.unesco.org/; Literacy and UIS.Stat.

United Nations Economic and Social Commission for Western Asia (ESCWA), Riad el-Solh Sq., PO Box 11-8575, Beirut, LBN, escwa-ciu@un.org, https://www.unescwa.org; ESCWA Annual Report 2019.

United Nations Statistics Division (UNSD), United Nations Plz., New York, NY, 10017, USA, (800) 253-9646, (212) 963-9851, statistics@un.org, https://unstats.un.org; Millennium Development Goal Indicators.

The World Bank, 1818 H St. NW, Washington, DC, 20433, USA, (202) 473-1000, (202) 477-6391, eds03@worldbank.org, https://www.worldbank.org/; Gulf Cooperation Council (report) and World Development Indicators (WDI) 2022.

BAHRAIN-ELECTRICITY

International Energy Agency (IEA), 9 Rue de la Federation, Paris, 75739, FRA, info@iea.org, https://www.iea.org/; World Energy Outlook 2021.

U.S. Energy Information Administration (EIA), 1000 Independence Ave. SW, Washington, DC, 20585, USA, (202) 586-8800, infoctr@eia.gov, https://www.eia.gov; International Energy Outlook 2021.

United Nations Statistics Division (UNSD), United Nations Plz., New York, NY, 10017, USA, (800) 253-9646, (212) 963-9851, statistics@un.org, https://unstats.un.org; Statistical Yearbook of the United Nations 2021.

BAHRAIN-EMPLOYMENT

International Labour Organization (ILO), 4 Rte. des Morillons, Geneva, CH-1211, SWI, ilo@ilo.org, https://www.ilo.org; NORMLEX Information System on International Labour Standards.

UK Data Service, University of Essex, Wivenhoe Park, Colchester, Essex, CO4 3SQ, GBR, https://ukdataservice.ac.uk/; International Aggregate Data.

United Nations Economic and Social Commission for Western Asia (ESCWA), Riad el-Solh Sq., PO Box 11-8575, Beirut, LBN, escwa-ciu@un.org, https://www.unescwa.org; ESCWA Annual Report 2019.

The World Bank, 1818 H St. NW, Washington, DC, 20433, USA, (202) 473-1000, (202) 477-6391, eds03@worldbank.org, https://www.worldbank.org/; Gulf Cooperation Council (report).

BAHRAIN-ENVIRONMENTAL CONDITIONS

DSI Data Service & Information, Xantener Strasse 51a, Rheinberg, D-47495, GER, dsi@dsidata.com, https://www.dsidata.com/; Global Environmental Database.

The Economist Group: Economist Intelligence Unit (EIU), 900 3rd Ave., 16th Fl., New York, NY, 10022, USA, (212) 541-0500, americas@eiu.com, https://www.eiu.com; Bahrain Country Report.

Organisation of Islamic Cooperation (OIC), Statistical, Economic and Social Research and Training Centre for Islamic Countries (SESRIC), Kudus Cad. No. 9, Diplomatik Site, Ankara, 06450, TUR, statistics@sesric.org, https://www.sesric.org/; OIC Statistics (OICStat) Database and OIC-Countries in Figures (OIC-CIF).

United Nations Statistics Division (UNSD), United Nations Plz., New York, NY, 10017, USA, (800) 253-9646, (212) 963-9851, statistics@un.org, https://unstats.un.org; World Statistics Pocketbook 2021.

BAHRAIN-EXPORTS

Central Intelligence Agency (CIA), Office of Public Affairs, Washington, DC, 20505, USA, (703) 482-0623, https://www.cia.gov; The World Factbook.

The Economist Group: Economist Intelligence Unit (EIU), 900 3rd Ave., 16th Fl., New York, NY, 10022, USA, (212) 541-0500, americas@eiu.com, https://www.eiu.com; Bahrain Country Report.

International Monetary Fund (IMF), 700 19th St. NW, Washington, DC, 20431, USA, (202) 623-7000, (202) 623-4661, publications@imf.org, https://www.imf.org; Direction of Trade Statistics (DOTS) and International Financial Statistics (IFS).

Organisation of Islamic Cooperation (OIC), Statistical, Economic and Social Research and Training Centre for Islamic Countries (SESRIC), Kudus Cad. No. 9, Diplomatik Site, Ankara, 06450, TUR, statistics@sesric.org, https://www.sesric.org/; OIC Statistics (OICStat) Database.

S&P Global, IHS Markit, 15 Inverness Way E, Englewood, CO, 80112, USA, (800) 447-2273, (800) 854-7179, https://ihsmarkit.com; Global Trade Atlas (GTA).

United Nations Conference on Trade and Development (UNCTAD), Palais des Nations, Geneva, 1211, SWI, (212) 963-6896, unctadinfo@unctad.org, https://unctad.org; Handbook of Statistics 2021.

United Nations Economic and Social Commission for Western Asia (ESCWA), Riad el-Solh Sq., PO Box 11-8575, Beirut, LBN, escwa-ciu@un.org, https://www.unescwa.org; ESCWA Annual Report 2019.

BAHRAIN-FEMALE WORKING POPULATION

See BAHRAIN-EMPLOYMENT

BAHRAIN-FERTILIZER INDUSTRY

United Nations Food and Agricultural Organization (FAO), 2121 K St., Ste. 800B, Washington, DC, 20037, USA, (202) 653-2400 (Dial from U.S.), (202) 653-5760 (Fax from U.S.), fao-hq@fao.org, https://www.fao.org; The State of Food and Agriculture (SOFA) 2022.

BAHRAIN-FETAL MORTALITY

See BAHRAIN-MORTALITY

BAHRAIN-FINANCE

Stockholm International Peace Research Institute (SIPRI), Signalistgatan 9, Stockholm, SE 169 72, SWE, https://www.sipri.org/; SIPRI Arms Transfers Database and SIPRI Military Expenditure Database.

United Nations Economic and Social Commission for Western Asia (ESCWA), Riad el-Solh Sq., PO Box 11-8575, Beirut, LBN, escwa-ciu@un.org, https://www.unescwa.org; ESCWA Annual Report 2019.

United Nations Statistics Division (UNSD), United Nations Plz., New York, NY, 10017, USA, (800) 253-9646, (212) 963-9851, statistics@un.org, https://unstats.un.org; Statistical Yearbook of the United Nations 2021.

The World Bank, 1818 H St. NW, Washington, DC, 20433, USA, (202) 473-1000, (202) 477-6391, eds03@worldbank.org, https://www.worldbank.org/; Gulf Cooperation Council (report).

BAHRAIN-FINANCE, PUBLIC

Bernan Press, 15250 NBN Way, Bldg. C, Blue Ridge Summit, PA, 17214, USA, (301) 459-2255, (800) 865-3457, (800) 865-3450, customercare@bernan.com, https://rowman.com/Page/Bernan; National Accounts Statistics: Analysis of Main Aggregates 2020.

The Economist Group: Economist Intelligence Unit (EIU), 900 3rd Ave., 16th Fl., New York, NY, 10022, USA, (212) 541-0500, americas@eiu.com, https://www.eiu.com; Bahrain Country Report.

International Monetary Fund (IMF), 700 19th St. NW, Washington, DC, 20431, USA, (202) 623-7000, (202) 623-4661, publications@imf.org, https://www.imf.org; Regional Economic Outlook.

Palgrave Macmillan, 1 New York Plaza, Ste. 4500, New York, NY, 10004-1562, USA, (800) 777-4643, orders@palgrave.com, https://www.palgrave.com/us; The Statesman's Yearbook, 2023.

Routledge - Taylor & Francis Group, 6000 Broken Sound Pkwy. NW, Ste. 300, Boca Raton, FL, 33487, USA, (800) 634-1420, (800) 634-7064, orders@taylorandfrancis.com, https://www.routledge.com/; The Europa World Year Book 2022.

United Nations Economic and Social Commission for Western Asia (ESCWA), Riad el-Solh Sq., PO Box 11-8575, Beirut, LBN, escwa-ciu@un.org, https://www.unescwa.org; ESCWA Annual Report 2019.

United Nations Statistics Division (UNSD), United Nations Plz., New York, NY, 10017, USA, (800) 253-9646, (212) 963-9851, statistics@un.org, https://unstats.un.org; National Accounts Main Aggregates Database and National Accounts Statistics: Main Aggregates and Detailed Tables.

The World Bank, 1818 H St. NW, Washington, DC, 20433, USA, (202) 473-1000, (202) 477-6391, eds03@worldbank.org, https://www.worldbank.org/; Gulf Cooperation Council (report).

BAHRAIN-FISHERIES

Palgrave Macmillan, 1 New York Plaza, Ste. 4500, New York, NY, 10004-1562, USA, (800) 777-4643, orders@palgrave.com, https://www.palgrave.com/us; The Statesman's Yearbook, 2023.

Routledge - Taylor & Francis Group, 6000 Broken Sound Pkwy. NW, Ste. 300, Boca Raton, FL, 33487, USA, (800) 634-1420, (800) 634-7064, orders@taylorandfrancis.com, https://www.routledge.com/; The Europa World Year Book 2022.

United Nations Economic and Social Commission for Western Asia (ESCWA), Riad el-Solh Sq., PO Box 11-8575, Beirut, LBN, escwa-ciu@un.org, https://www.unescwa.org; ESCWA Annual Report 2019.

United Nations Food and Agricultural Organization (FAO), 2121 K St., Ste. 800B, Washington, DC, 20037, USA, (202) 653-2400 (Dial from U.S.), (202) 653-5760 (Fax from U.S.), fao-hq@fao.org, https://www.fao.org; FAO Yearbook of Fishery and Aquaculture Statistics 2019; Fishery Statistical Collections Global Capture Production; FishStatJ; and The State of Food and Agriculture (SOFA) 2022.

United Nations Statistics Division (UNSD), United Nations Plz., New York, NY, 10017, USA, (800) 253-9646, (212) 963-9851, statistics@un.org, https://unstats.un.org; Statistical Yearbook of the United Nations 2021.

The World Bank, 1818 H St. NW, Washington, DC, 20433, USA, (202) 473-1000, (202) 477-6391, eds03@worldbank.org, https://www.worldbank.org/; Gulf Cooperation Council (report).

BAHRAIN-FOOD

United Nations Food and Agricultural Organization (FAO), 2121 K St., Ste. 800B, Washington, DC, 20037, USA, (202) 653-2400 (Dial from U.S.), (202) 653-5760 (Fax from U.S.), fao-hq@fao.org, https://www.fao.org; The State of Food and Agriculture (SOFA) 2022.

BAHRAIN-FOREIGN EXCHANGE RATES

International Monetary Fund (IMF), 700 19th St. NW, Washington, DC, 20431, USA, (202) 623-7000, (202) 623-4661, publications@imf.org, https://www.imf.org; International Financial Statistics (IFS).

BAHRAIN-FORESTS AND FORESTRY

UNESCO Institute for Statistics, C.P 250 Succursale H, Montreal, QC, H3G 2K8, CAN, (514) 343-6880 (Dial from U.S.), (514) 343-5740 (Fax from U.S.), uis.publications@unesco.org, http://uis.unesco.org/; UIS.Stat.

United Nations Food and Agricultural Organization (FAO), 2121 K St., Ste. 800B, Washington, DC,

20037, USA, (202) 653-2400 (Dial from U.S.), (202) 653-5760 (Fax from U.S.), fao-hq@fao.org, https://www.fao.org; FAO Yearbook of Forest Products 2019 and The State of Food and Agriculture (SOFA) 2022.

United Nations Statistics Division (UNSD), United Nations Plz., New York, NY, 10017, USA, (800) 253-9646, (212) 963-9851, statistics@un.org, https://unstats.un.org; Statistical Yearbook of the United Nations 2021.

The World Bank, 1818 H St. NW, Washington, DC, 20433, USA, (202) 473-1000, (202) 477-6391, eds03@worldbank.org, https://www.worldbank.org/; Gulf Cooperation Council (report).

BAHRAIN-GAS PRODUCTION

See BAHRAIN-MINERAL INDUSTRIES

BAHRAIN-GEOGRAPHIC INFORMATION SYSTEMS

The World Bank, 1818 H St. NW, Washington, DC, 20433, USA, (202) 473-1000, (202) 477-6391, eds03@worldbank.org, https://www.worldbank.org/; Gulf Cooperation Council (report).

BAHRAIN-GOLD INDUSTRY

The World Bank, 1818 H St. NW, Washington, DC, 20433, USA, (202) 473-1000, (202) 477-6391, eds03@worldbank.org, https://www.worldbank.org/; World Development Indicators (WDI) 2022.

BAHRAIN-GOLD PRODUCTION

See BAHRAIN-MINERAL INDUSTRIES

BAHRAIN-GROSS DOMESTIC PRODUCT

The Economist Group: Economist Intelligence Unit (EIU), 900 3rd Ave., 16th Fl., New York, NY, 10022, USA, (212) 541-0500, americas@eiu.com, https://www.eiu.com; Bahrain Country Report.

Routledge - Taylor & Francis Group, 6000 Broken Sound Pkwy. NW, Ste. 300, Boca Raton, FL, 33487, USA, (800) 634-1420, (800) 634-7064, orders@taylorandfrancis.com, https://www.routledge.com/; The Europa World Year Book 2022.

United Nations Economic and Social Commission for Western Asia (ESCWA), Riad el-Solh Sq., PO Box 11-8575, Beirut, LBN, escwa-ciu@un.org, https://www.unescwa.org; ESCWA Annual Report 2019.

United Nations Statistics Division (UNSD), United Nations Plz., New York, NY, 10017, USA, (800) 253-9646, (212) 963-9851, statistics@un.org, https://unstats.un.org; Statistical Yearbook of the United Nations 2021.

The World Bank, 1818 H St. NW, Washington, DC, 20433, USA, (202) 473-1000, (202) 477-6391, eds03@worldbank.org, https://www.worldbank.org/; World Development Indicators (WDI) 2022.

BAHRAIN-GROSS NATIONAL PRODUCT

Palgrave Macmillan, 1 New York Plaza, Ste. 4500, New York, NY, 10004-1562, USA, (800) 777-4643, orders@palgrave.com, https://www.palgrave.com/us; The Statesman's Yearbook, 2023.

The World Bank, 1818 H St. NW, Washington, DC, 20433, USA, (202) 473-1000, (202) 477-6391, eds03@worldbank.org, https://www.worldbank.org/; World Development Indicators (WDI) 2022.

BAHRAIN-HOUSING

Euromonitor International, Inc., 1 N Dearborn St., Ste. 1700, Chicago, IL, 60602, USA, (312) 922-1115, (312) 922-1157, info-usa@euromonitor.com, https://www.euromonitor.com/; Geographies.

United Nations Statistics Division (UNSD), United Nations Plz., New York, NY, 10017, USA, (800) 253-9646, (212) 963-9851, statistics@un.org, https://unstats.un.org; Statistical Yearbook of the United Nations 2021.

BAHRAIN-ILLITERATE PERSONS

Central Intelligence Agency (CIA), Office of Public Affairs, Washington, DC, 20505, USA, (703) 482-0623, https://www.cia.gov; The World Factbook.

UNESCO Institute for Statistics, C.P 250 Succursale H, Montreal, QC, H3G 2K8, CAN, (514) 343-6880 (Dial from U.S.), (514) 343-5740 (Fax from U.S.), uis.publications@unesco.org, http://uis.unesco.org/; UIS.Stat.

BAHRAIN-IMPORTS

Central Intelligence Agency (CIA), Office of Public Affairs, Washington, DC, 20505, USA, (703) 482-0623, https://www.cia.gov; The World Factbook.

The Economist Group: Economist Intelligence Unit (EIU), 900 3rd Ave., 16th Fl., New York, NY, 10022, USA, (212) 541-0500, americas@eiu.com, https://www.eiu.com; Bahrain Country Report.

International Monetary Fund (IMF), 700 19th St. NW, Washington, DC, 20431, USA, (202) 623-7000, (202) 623-4661, publications@imf.org, https://www.imf.org; Direction of Trade Statistics (DOTS) and International Financial Statistics (IFS).

S&P Global, IHS Markit, 15 Inverness Way E, Englewood, CO, 80112, USA, (800) 447-2273, (800) 854-7179, https://ihsmarkit.com; Global Trade Atlas (GTA).

United Nations Conference on Trade and Development (UNCTAD), Palais des Nations, Geneva, 1211, SWI, (212) 963-6896, unctadinfo@unctad.org, https://unctad.org; Handbook of Statistics 2021.

United Nations Economic and Social Commission for Western Asia (ESCWA), Riad el-Solh Sq., PO Box 11-8575, Beirut, LBN, escwa-ciu@un.org, https://www.unescwa.org; ESCWA Annual Report 2019.

BAHRAIN-INDUSTRIAL PROPERTY

United Nations World Tourism Organization (UNWTO), Calle Poeta Joan Maragall 42, Madrid, 28020, SPA, info@unwto.org, https://www.unwto.org/; Yearbook of Tourism Statistics, 2021 Edition.

World Intellectual Property Organization (WIPO), 34, chemin des Colombettes, Geneva, CH-1211, SWI, https://www.wipo.int; Madrid Yearly Review 2022: International Registrations of Marks.

BAHRAIN-INDUSTRIES

Central Intelligence Agency (CIA), Office of Public Affairs, Washington, DC, 20505, USA, (703) 482-0623, https://www.cia.gov; The World Factbook.

The Economist Group: Economist Intelligence Unit (EIU), 900 3rd Ave., 16th Fl., New York, NY, 10022, USA, (212) 541-0500, americas@eiu.com, https://www.eiu.com; Bahrain Country Report.

Euromonitor International, Inc., 1 N Dearborn St., Ste. 1700, Chicago, IL, 60602, USA, (312) 922-1115, (312) 922-1157, info-usa@euromonitor.com, https://www.euromonitor.com/; Geographies.

International Labour Organization (ILO), 4 Rte. des Morillons, Geneva, CH-1211, SWI, ilo@ilo.org, https://www.ilo.org; NORMLEX Information System on International Labour Standards.

Palgrave Macmillan, 1 New York Plaza, Ste. 4500, New York, NY, 10004-1562, USA, (800) 777-4643, orders@palgrave.com, https://www.palgrave.com/us; The Statesman's Yearbook, 2023.

Routledge - Taylor & Francis Group, 6000 Broken Sound Pkwy. NW, Ste. 300, Boca Raton, FL, 33487, USA, (800) 634-1420, (800) 634-7064, orders@taylorandfrancis.com, https://www.routledge.com/; The Europa World Year Book 2022.

United Nations Economic and Social Commission for Western Asia (ESCWA), Riad el-Solh Sq., PO Box 11-8575, Beirut, LBN, escwa-ciu@un.org, https://www.unescwa.org; Bulletin of Industrial Statistics for Arab Countries.

United Nations Industrial Development Organization (UNIDO), 1 United Nations Plz., Rm. DC1-1118, New York, NY, 10017, USA, (212) 963-6890, (212) 963 6885, (212) 963-7904, office.newyork@unido.org, https://www.unido.org/; Industrial Statistics Databases and International Yearbook of Industrial Statistics 2021.

The World Bank, 1818 H St. NW, Washington, DC, 20433, USA, (202) 473-1000, (202) 477-6391, eds03@worldbank.org, https://www.worldbank.org/; Gulf Cooperation Council (report) and World Development Indicators (WDI) 2022.

World Intellectual Property Organization (WIPO), 34, chemin des Colombettes, Geneva, CH-1211, SWI, https://www.wipo.int; Madrid Yearly Review 2022: International Registrations of Marks.

BAHRAIN-INFANT AND MATERNAL MORTALITY

See BAHRAIN-MORTALITY

BAHRAIN-INTERNATIONAL TRADE

The Economist Group: Economist Intelligence Unit (EIU), 900 3rd Ave., 16th Fl., New York, NY, 10022, USA, (212) 541-0500, americas@eiu.com, https://www.eiu.com; Bahrain Country Report.

Euromonitor International, Inc., 1 N Dearborn St., Ste. 1700, Chicago, IL, 60602, USA, (312) 922-1115, (312) 922-1157, info-usa@euromonitor.com, https://www.euromonitor.com/; Geographies.

Palgrave Macmillan, 1 New York Plaza, Ste. 4500, New York, NY, 10004-1562, USA, (800) 777-4643, orders@palgrave.com, https://www.palgrave.com/us; The Statesman's Yearbook, 2023.

Routledge - Taylor & Francis Group, 6000 Broken Sound Pkwy. NW, Ste. 300, Boca Raton, FL, 33487, USA, (800) 634-1420, (800) 634-7064, orders@taylorandfrancis.com, https://www.routledge.com/; The Europa World Year Book 2022.

United Nations Conference on Trade and Development (UNCTAD), Palais des Nations, Geneva, 1211, SWI, (212) 963-6896, unctadinfo@unctad.org, https://unctad.org; Trade and Development Report 2021.

United Nations Economic and Social Commission for Western Asia (ESCWA), Riad el-Solh Sq., PO Box 11-8575, Beirut, LBN, escwa-ciu@un.org, https://www.unescwa.org; ESCWA Annual Report 2019.

United Nations Food and Agricultural Organization (FAO), 2121 K St., Ste. 800B, Washington, DC, 20037, USA, (202) 653-2400 (Dial from U.S.), (202) 653-5760 (Fax from U.S.), fao-hq@fao.org, https://www.fao.org; The State of Food and Agriculture (SOFA) 2022.

United Nations Statistics Division (UNSD), United Nations Plz., New York, NY, 10017, USA, (800) 253-9646, (212) 963-9851, statistics@un.org, https://unstats.un.org; International Trade Statistics Yearbook 2020 and Statistical Yearbook of the United Nations 2021.

The World Bank, 1818 H St. NW, Washington, DC, 20433, USA, (202) 473-1000, (202) 477-6391, eds03@worldbank.org, https://www.worldbank.org/; Gulf Cooperation Council (report) and World Development Indicators (WDI) 2022.

World Trade Organization (WTO), Ctre. William Rappard, Rue de Lausanne 154, Case postale, Geneva, CH-1211, SWI, enquiries@wto.org, https://www.wto.org; World Trade Statistical Review 2022.

BAHRAIN-INTERNET USERS

International Telecommunication Union (ITU), Place des Nations, Geneva, CH-1211, SWI, itumail@itu.int, https://www.itu.int; Global Connectivity Report 2022; World Telecommunication/ICT Indicators Database 2021; and Yearbook of Statistics 2019.

The World Bank, 1818 H St. NW, Washington, DC, 20433, USA, (202) 473-1000, (202) 477-6391, eds03@worldbank.org, https://www.worldbank.org/; Gulf Cooperation Council (report).

BAHRAIN-LABOR

Central Intelligence Agency (CIA), Office of Public Affairs, Washington, DC, 20505, USA, (703) 482-0623, https://www.cia.gov; The World Factbook.

Euromonitor International, Inc., 1 N Dearborn St., Ste. 1700, Chicago, IL, 60602, USA, (312) 922-1115, (312) 922-1157, info-usa@euromonitor.com, https://www.euromonitor.com/; Geographies.

International Labour Organization (ILO), 4 Rte. des Morillons, Geneva, CH-1211, SWI, ilo@ilo.org, https://www.ilo.org; NORMLEX Information System on International Labour Standards.

Organisation of Islamic Cooperation (OIC), Statistical, Economic and Social Research and Training Centre for Islamic Countries (SESRIC), Kudus Cad. No. 9, Diplomatik Site, Ankara, 06450, TUR, statistics@sesric.org, https://www.sesric.org/; OIC Statistics (OICStat) Database.

Palgrave Macmillan, 1 New York Plaza, Ste. 4500, New York, NY, 10004-1562, USA, (800) 777-4643, orders@palgrave.com, https://www.palgrave.com/us; The Statesman's Yearbook, 2023.

United Nations Economic and Social Commission for Western Asia (ESCWA), Riad el-Solh Sq., PO Box 11-8575, Beirut, LBN, escwa-ciu@un.org, https://www.unescwa.org; ESCWA Annual Report 2019.

United Nations Food and Agricultural Organization (FAO), 2121 K St., Ste. 800B, Washington, DC, 20037, USA, (202) 653-2400 (Dial from U.S.), (202) 653-5760 (Fax from U.S.), fao-hq@fao.org, https://www.fao.org; The State of Food and Agriculture (SOFA) 2022.

The World Bank, 1818 H St. NW, Washington, DC, 20433, USA, (202) 473-1000, (202) 477-6391, eds03@worldbank.org, https://www.worldbank.org/; World Development Indicators (WDI) 2022.

BAHRAIN-LAND USE

United Nations Economic and Social Commission for Western Asia (ESCWA), Riad el-Solh Sq., PO Box 11-8575, Beirut, LBN, escwa-ciu@un.org, https://www.unescwa.org; ESCWA Annual Report 2019.

United Nations Statistics Division (UNSD), United Nations Plz., New York, NY, 10017, USA, (800) 253-9646, (212) 963-9851, statistics@un.org, https://unstats.un.org; Millennium Development Goal Indicators.

BAHRAIN-LIBRARIES

UNESCO Institute for Statistics, C.P 250 Succursale H, Montreal, QC, H3G 2K8, CAN, (514) 343-6880 (Dial from U.S.), (514) 343-5740 (Fax from U.S.), uis.publications@unesco.org, http://uis.unesco.org/; UIS.Stat.

BAHRAIN-LIFE EXPECTANCY

United Nations Department of Economic and Social Affairs (DESA), Population Division, 2 United Nations Plz., Rm. DC2-1950, New York, NY, 10017, USA, (212) 963-3209, (212) 963-2147, population@un.org, https://www.un.org/development/desa/pd/; World Population Ageing 2020 Highlights.

United Nations Statistics Division (UNSD), United Nations Plz., New York, NY, 10017, USA, (800) 253-9646, (212) 963-9851, statistics@un.org, https://unstats.un.org; Millennium Development Goal Indicators.

BAHRAIN-LITERACY

Euromonitor International, Inc., 1 N Dearborn St., Ste. 1700, Chicago, IL, 60602, USA, (312) 922-1115, (312) 922-1157, info-usa@euromonitor.com, https://www.euromonitor.com/; Geographies.

UNESCO Institute for Statistics, C.P 250 Succursale H, Montreal, QC, H3G 2K8, CAN, (514) 343-6880 (Dial from U.S.), (514) 343-5740 (Fax from U.S.), uis.publications@unesco.org, http://uis.unesco.org/; Literacy.

BAHRAIN-LIVESTOCK

Palgrave Macmillan, 1 New York Plaza, Ste. 4500, New York, NY, 10004-1562, USA, (800) 777-4643, orders@palgrave.com, https://www.palgrave.com/us; The Statesman's Yearbook, 2023.

Routledge - Taylor & Francis Group, 6000 Broken Sound Pkwy. NW, Ste. 300, Boca Raton, FL, 33487, USA, (800) 634-1420, (800) 634-7064, orders@taylorandfrancis.com, https://www.routledge.com/; The Europa World Year Book 2022.

United Nations Food and Agricultural Organization (FAO), 2121 K St., Ste. 800B, Washington, DC, 20037, USA, (202) 653-2400 (Dial from U.S.), (202) 653-5760 (Fax from U.S.), fao-hq@fao.org, https://www.fao.org; The State of Food and Agriculture (SOFA) 2022.

United Nations Statistics Division (UNSD), United Nations Plz., New York, NY, 10017, USA, (800) 253-9646, (212) 963-9851, statistics@un.org, https://unstats.un.org; Statistical Yearbook of the United Nations 2021.

BAHRAIN-MARRIAGE

Routledge - Taylor & Francis Group, 6000 Broken Sound Pkwy. NW, Ste. 300, Boca Raton, FL, 33487, USA, (800) 634-1420, (800) 634-7064, orders@taylorandfrancis.com, https://www.routledge.com/; The Europa World Year Book 2022.

BAHRAIN-MINERAL INDUSTRIES

International Energy Agency (IEA), 9 Rue de la Federation, Paris, 75739, FRA, info@iea.org, https://www.iea.org/; World Energy Outlook 2021.

International Monetary Fund (IMF), 700 19th St. NW, Washington, DC, 20431, USA, (202) 623-7000, (202) 623-4661, publications@imf.org, https://www.imf.org; International Financial Statistics (IFS).

Palgrave Macmillan, 1 New York Plaza, Ste. 4500, New York, NY, 10004-1562, USA, (800) 777-4643, orders@palgrave.com, https://www.palgrave.com/us; The Statesman's Yearbook, 2023.

Routledge - Taylor & Francis Group, 6000 Broken Sound Pkwy. NW, Ste. 300, Boca Raton, FL, 33487, USA, (800) 634-1420, (800) 634-7064, orders@taylorandfrancis.com, https://www.routledge.com/; The Europa World Year Book 2022.

United Nations Conference on Trade and Development (UNCTAD), Palais des Nations, Geneva, 1211, SWI, (212) 963-6896, unctadinfo@unctad.org, https://unctad.org; Trade and Development Report 2021.

United Nations Economic and Social Commission for Western Asia (ESCWA), Riad el-Solh Sq., PO Box 11-8575, Beirut, LBN, escwa-ciu@un.org, https://www.unescwa.org; ESCWA Annual Report 2019.

United Nations Statistics Division (UNSD), United Nations Plz., New York, NY, 10017, USA, (800) 253-9646, (212) 963-9851, statistics@un.org, https://unstats.un.org; Statistical Yearbook of the United Nations 2021.

BAHRAIN-MONEY SUPPLY

The Economist Group: Economist Intelligence Unit (EIU), 900 3rd Ave., 16th Fl., New York, NY, 10022, USA, (212) 541-0500, americas@eiu.com, https://www.eiu.com; Bahrain Country Report.

International Monetary Fund (IMF), 700 19th St. NW, Washington, DC, 20431, USA, (202) 623-7000, (202) 623-4661, publications@imf.org, https://www.imf.org; International Financial Statistics (IFS).

Routledge - Taylor & Francis Group, 6000 Broken Sound Pkwy. NW, Ste. 300, Boca Raton, FL, 33487, USA, (800) 634-1420, (800) 634-7064, orders@taylorandfrancis.com, https://www.routledge.com/; The Europa World Year Book 2022.

United Nations Economic and Social Commission for Western Asia (ESCWA), Riad el-Solh Sq., PO Box 11-8575, Beirut, LBN, escwa-ciu@un.org, https://www.unescwa.org; ESCWA Annual Report 2019.

United Nations Statistics Division (UNSD), United Nations Plz., New York, NY, 10017, USA, (800) 253-9646, (212) 963-9851, statistics@un.org, https://unstats.un.org; Statistical Yearbook of the United Nations 2021.

The World Bank, 1818 H St. NW, Washington, DC, 20433, USA, (202) 473-1000, (202) 477-6391, eds03@worldbank.org, https://www.worldbank.org/; Gulf Cooperation Council (report).

BAHRAIN-MORTALITY

United Nations Statistics Division (UNSD), United Nations Plz., New York, NY, 10017, USA, (800) 253-9646, (212) 963-9851, statistics@un.org, https://unstats.un.org; Millennium Development Goal Indicators and World Statistics Pocketbook 2021.

World Health Organization (WHO), Ave. Appia 20, Geneva, CH-1211, SWI, (202) 974-3000 (Telephone in U.S.), publications@who.int, https://www.who.int/; Global Health Observatory (GHO).

BAHRAIN-MOTION PICTURES

Palgrave Macmillan, 1 New York Plaza, Ste. 4500, New York, NY, 10004-1562, USA, (800) 777-4643, orders@palgrave.com, https://www.palgrave.com/us; The Statesman's Yearbook, 2023.

BAHRAIN-NATURAL GAS PRODUCTION

See BAHRAIN-MINERAL INDUSTRIES

BAHRAIN-NUTRITION

United Nations Food and Agricultural Organization (FAO), 2121 K St., Ste. 800B, Washington, DC, 20037, USA, (202) 653-2400 (Dial from U.S.), (202) 653-5760 (Fax from U.S.), fao-hq@fao.org, https://www.fao.org; The State of Food and Agriculture (SOFA) 2022.

United Nations Statistics Division (UNSD), United Nations Plz., New York, NY, 10017, USA, (800) 253-9646, (212) 963-9851, statistics@un.org, https://unstats.un.org; Millennium Development Goal Indicators.

BAHRAIN-PAPER

See BAHRAIN-FORESTS AND FORESTRY

BAHRAIN-PEANUT PRODUCTION

See BAHRAIN-CROPS

BAHRAIN-PESTICIDES

United Nations Food and Agricultural Organization (FAO), 2121 K St., Ste. 800B, Washington, DC, 20037, USA, (202) 653-2400 (Dial from U.S.), (202) 653-5760 (Fax from U.S.), fao-hq@fao.org, https://www.fao.org; The State of Food and Agriculture (SOFA) 2022.

BAHRAIN-PETROLEUM INDUSTRY AND TRADE

International Energy Agency (IEA), 9 Rue de la Federation, Paris, 75739, FRA, info@iea.org, https://www.iea.org/; World Energy Outlook 2021.

International Monetary Fund (IMF), 700 19th St. NW, Washington, DC, 20431, USA, (202) 623-7000, (202) 623-4661, publications@imf.org, https://www.imf.org; International Financial Statistics (IFS).

Palgrave Macmillan, 1 New York Plaza, Ste. 4500, New York, NY, 10004-1562, USA, (800) 777-4643, orders@palgrave.com, https://www.palgrave.com/us; The Statesman's Yearbook, 2023.

U.S. Energy Information Administration (EIA), 1000 Independence Ave. SW, Washington, DC, 20585, USA, (202) 586-8800, infoctr@eia.gov, https://www.eia.gov; International Energy Outlook 2021.

United Nations Food and Agricultural Organization (FAO), 2121 K St., Ste. 800B, Washington, DC, 20037, USA, (202) 653-2400 (Dial from U.S.), (202) 653-5760 (Fax from U.S.), fao-hq@fao.org, https://www.fao.org; The State of Food and Agriculture (SOFA) 2022.

United Nations Statistics Division (UNSD), United Nations Plz., New York, NY, 10017, USA, (800) 253-9646, (212) 963-9851, statistics@un.org, https://unstats.un.org; Statistical Yearbook of the United Nations 2021.

BAHRAIN-POPULATION

Central Intelligence Agency (CIA), Office of Public Affairs, Washington, DC, 20505, USA, (703) 482-0623, https://www.cia.gov; The World Factbook.

The Economist Group: Economist Intelligence Unit (EIU), 900 3rd Ave., 16th Fl., New York, NY, 10022, USA, (212) 541-0500, americas@eiu.com, https://www.eiu.com; Bahrain Country Report.

Infoplease, c/o Sandbox Networks, Inc., 1 Lincoln St., 24th Fl., Boston, MA, 02111, USA, https://www.infoplease.com; Countries of the World.

International Labour Organization (ILO), 4 Rte. des Morillons, Geneva, CH-1211, SWI, ilo@ilo.org, https://www.ilo.org; NORMLEX Information System on International Labour Standards.

Palgrave Macmillan, 1 New York Plaza, Ste. 4500, New York, NY, 10004-1562, USA, (800) 777-4643, orders@palgrave.com, https://www.palgrave.com/us; The Statesman's Yearbook, 2023.

Routledge - Taylor & Francis Group, 6000 Broken Sound Pkwy. NW, Ste. 300, Boca Raton, FL, 33487, USA, (800) 634-1420, (800) 634-7064, orders@taylorandfrancis.com, https://www.routledge.com/; The Europa World Year Book 2022.

UK Data Service, University of Essex, Wivenhoe Park, Colchester, Essex, CO4 3SQ, GBR, https://ukdataservice.ac.uk/; International Aggregate Data.

United Nations Department of Economic and Social Affairs (DESA), Population Division, 2 United Nations Plz., Rm. DC2-1950, New York, NY, 10017, USA, (212) 963-3209, (212) 963-2147, population@un.org, https://www.un.org/development/desa/pd/; Revision of World Urbanization Prospects and World Population Ageing 2020 Highlights.

United Nations Development Programme (UNDP), One United Nations Plz., New York, NY, 10017, USA, (212) 906-5000, (212) 906-5001, https://www.undp.org; Human Development Report 2021-2022.

United Nations Economic and Social Commission for Western Asia (ESCWA), Riad el-Solh Sq., PO Box 11-8575, Beirut, LBN, escwa-ciu@un.org, https://www.unescwa.org; ESCWA Annual Report 2019.

United Nations Statistics Division (UNSD), United Nations Plz., New York, NY, 10017, USA, (800) 253-9646, (212) 963-9851, statistics@un.org, https://unstats.un.org; Statistical Yearbook of the United Nations 2021 and World Statistics Pocketbook 2021.

The World Bank, 1818 H St. NW, Washington, DC, 20433, USA, (202) 473-1000, (202) 477-6391, eds03@worldbank.org, https://www.worldbank.org/; The Global Findex Database 2021 and Gulf Cooperation Council (report).

BAHRAIN-POPULATION DENSITY

Central Intelligence Agency (CIA), Office of Public Affairs, Washington, DC, 20505, USA, (703) 482-0623, https://www.cia.gov; The World Factbook.

Palgrave Macmillan, 1 New York Plaza, Ste. 4500, New York, NY, 10004-1562, USA, (800) 777-4643, orders@palgrave.com, https://www.palgrave.com/us; The Statesman's Yearbook, 2023.

Routledge - Taylor & Francis Group, 6000 Broken Sound Pkwy. NW, Ste. 300, Boca Raton, FL, 33487, USA, (800) 634-1420, (800) 634-7064, orders@taylorandfrancis.com, https://www.routledge.com/; The Europa World Year Book 2022.

United Nations Economic and Social Commission for Western Asia (ESCWA), Riad el-Solh Sq., PO Box 11-8575, Beirut, LBN, escwa-ciu@un.org, https://www.unescwa.org; ESCWA Annual Report 2019.

The World Bank, 1818 H St. NW, Washington, DC, 20433, USA, (202) 473-1000, (202) 477-6391, eds03@worldbank.org, https://www.worldbank.org/; Gulf Cooperation Council (report).

BAHRAIN-POWER RESOURCES

Euromonitor International, Inc., 1 N Dearborn St., Ste. 1700, Chicago, IL, 60602, USA, (312) 922-1115, (312) 922-1157, info-usa@euromonitor.com, https://www.euromonitor.com/; Geographies.

International Energy Agency (IEA), 9 Rue de la Federation, Paris, 75739, FRA, info@iea.org, https://www.iea.org/; World Energy Outlook 2021.

Palgrave Macmillan, 1 New York Plaza, Ste. 4500, New York, NY, 10004-1562, USA, (800) 777-4643, orders@palgrave.com, https://www.palgrave.com/us; The Statesman's Yearbook, 2023.

U.S. Energy Information Administration (EIA), 1000 Independence Ave. SW, Washington, DC, 20585, USA, (202) 586-8800, infoctr@eia.gov, https://www.eia.gov; International Energy Outlook 2021.

United Nations Economic and Social Commission for Western Asia (ESCWA), Riad el-Solh Sq., PO Box 11-8575, Beirut, LBN, escwa-ciu@un.org, https://www.unescwa.org; ESCWA Annual Report 2019.

United Nations Food and Agricultural Organization (FAO), 2121 K St., Ste. 800B, Washington, DC, 20037, USA, (202) 653-2400 (Dial from U.S.), (202) 653-5760 (Fax from U.S.), fao-hq@fao.org, https://www.fao.org; The State of Food and Agriculture (SOFA) 2022.

United Nations Statistics Division (UNSD), United Nations Plz., New York, NY, 10017, USA, (800) 253-9646, (212) 963-9851, statistics@un.org, https://unstats.un.org; Energy Statistics Yearbook 2019; Statistical Yearbook of the United Nations 2021; and World Statistics Pocketbook 2021.

BAHRAIN-PRICES

Euromonitor International, Inc., 1 N Dearborn St., Ste. 1700, Chicago, IL, 60602, USA, (312) 922-1115, (312) 922-1157, info-usa@euromonitor.com, https://www.euromonitor.com/; Geographies.

International Monetary Fund (IMF), 700 19th St. NW, Washington, DC, 20431, USA, (202) 623-7000, (202) 623-4661, publications@imf.org, https://www.imf.org; International Financial Statistics (IFS).

The World Bank, 1818 H St. NW, Washington, DC, 20433, USA, (202) 473-1000, (202) 477-6391, eds03@worldbank.org, https://www.worldbank.org/; Gulf Cooperation Council (report).

BAHRAIN-PUBLIC HEALTH

Euromonitor International, Inc., 1 N Dearborn St., Ste. 1700, Chicago, IL, 60602, USA, (312) 922-1115, (312) 922-1157, info-usa@euromonitor.com, https://www.euromonitor.com/; Geographies.

Organisation of Islamic Cooperation (OIC), Statistical, Economic and Social Research and Training Centre for Islamic Countries (SESRIC), Kudus Cad. No. 9, Diplomatik Site, Ankara, 06450, TUR, statistics@sesric.org, https://www.sesric.org/; OIC Statistics (OICStat) Database.

Palgrave Macmillan, 1 New York Plaza, Ste. 4500, New York, NY, 10004-1562, USA, (800) 777-4643, orders@palgrave.com, https://www.palgrave.com/us; The Statesman's Yearbook, 2023.

U.S. Census Bureau, 4600 Silver Hill Rd., Washington, DC, 20233, USA, (301) 763-4636, (800) 923-8282, https://www.census.gov; HIV/AIDS Surveillance Data Base.

United Nations Department of Economic and Social Affairs (DESA), Population Division, 2 United Nations Plz., Rm. DC2-1950, New York, NY, 10017, USA, (212) 963-3209, (212) 963-2147, population@un.org, https://www.un.org/development/desa/pd/; World Fertility Data 2019.

United Nations Development Programme (UNDP), One United Nations Plz., New York, NY, 10017, USA, (212) 906-5000, (212) 906-5001, https://www.undp.org; Human Development Report 2021-2022.

United Nations Economic and Social Commission for Western Asia (ESCWA), Riad el-Solh Sq., PO Box 11-8575, Beirut, LBN, escwa-ciu@un.org, https://www.unescwa.org; ESCWA Annual Report 2019.

United Nations Statistics Division (UNSD), United Nations Plz., New York, NY, 10017, USA, (800) 253-9646, (212) 963-9851, statistics@un.org, https://unstats.un.org; Millennium Development Goal Indicators and Statistical Yearbook of the United Nations 2021.

The World Bank, 1818 H St. NW, Washington, DC, 20433, USA, (202) 473-1000, (202) 477-6391, eds03@worldbank.org, https://www.worldbank.org/; Gulf Cooperation Council (report).

World Health Organization (WHO), Ave. Appia 20, Geneva, CH-1211, SWI, (202) 974-3000 (Telephone in U.S.), publications@who.int, https://www.who.int/; Global Health Observatory (GHO) and Health Statistics and Information Systems.

BAHRAIN-PUBLISHERS AND PUBLISHING

Routledge - Taylor & Francis Group, 6000 Broken Sound Pkwy. NW, Ste. 300, Boca Raton, FL, 33487, USA, (800) 634-1420, (800) 634-7064, orders@taylorandfrancis.com, https://www.routledge.com/; The Europa World Year Book 2022.

BAHRAIN-RAILROADS

Routledge - Taylor & Francis Group, 6000 Broken Sound Pkwy. NW, Ste. 300, Boca Raton, FL, 33487, USA, (800) 634-1420, (800) 634-7064, orders@taylorandfrancis.com, https://www.routledge.com/; The Europa World Year Book 2022.

BAHRAIN-RELIGION

Central Intelligence Agency (CIA), Office of Public Affairs, Washington, DC, 20505, USA, (703) 482-0623, https://www.cia.gov; The World Factbook.

BAHRAIN-RETAIL TRADE

Euromonitor International, Inc., 1 N Dearborn St., Ste. 1700, Chicago, IL, 60602, USA, (312) 922-1115, (312) 922-1157, info-usa@euromonitor.com, https://www.euromonitor.com/; Geographies.

BAHRAIN-RICE PRODUCTION

See BAHRAIN-CROPS

BAHRAIN-RUBBER INDUSTRY AND TRADE

International Rubber Study Group (IRSG), 51 Changi Business Park Central 2, Unit No. 6, 486066, SGP, https://www.rubberstudy.org; Monthly Rubber Bulletin (MRB); Rubber Industry Report; Rubber Statistical Bulletin; and World Rubber Industry Report (WRIO).

BAHRAIN-SHIPPING

Routledge - Taylor & Francis Group, 6000 Broken Sound Pkwy. NW, Ste. 300, Boca Raton, FL, 33487, USA, (800) 634-1420, (800) 634-7064, orders@taylorandfrancis.com, https://www.routledge.com/; The Europa World Year Book 2022.

United Nations Statistics Division (UNSD), United Nations Plz., New York, NY, 10017, USA, (800) 253-9646, (212) 963-9851, statistics@un.org, https://unstats.un.org; Statistical Yearbook of the United Nations 2021.

BAHRAIN-STEEL PRODUCTION

See BAHRAIN-MINERAL INDUSTRIES

BAHRAIN-SUGAR PRODUCTION

See BAHRAIN-CROPS

BAHRAIN-TAXATION

The World Bank, 1818 H St. NW, Washington, DC, 20433, USA, (202) 473-1000, (202) 477-6391, eds03@worldbank.org, https://www.worldbank.org/; World Development Indicators (WDI) 2022.

BAHRAIN-TELEPHONE

Palgrave Macmillan, 1 New York Plaza, Ste. 4500, New York, NY, 10004-1562, USA, (800) 777-4643, orders@palgrave.com, https://www.palgrave.com/us; The Statesman's Yearbook, 2023.

Routledge - Taylor & Francis Group, 6000 Broken Sound Pkwy. NW, Ste. 300, Boca Raton, FL, 33487, USA, (800) 634-1420, (800) 634-7064, orders@taylorandfrancis.com, https://www.routledge.com/; The Europa World Year Book 2022.

United Nations Statistics Division (UNSD), United Nations Plz., New York, NY, 10017, USA, (800) 253-9646, (212) 963-9851, statistics@un.org, https://unstats.un.org; World Statistics Pocketbook 2021.

BAHRAIN-TELEVISION BROADCASTING

UNESCO Institute for Statistics, C.P 250 Succursale H, Montreal, QC, H3G 2K8, CAN, (514) 343-6880 (Dial from U.S.), (514) 343-5740 (Fax from U.S.), uis.publications@unesco.org, http://uis.unesco.org/; UIS.Stat.

BAHRAIN-TEXTILE INDUSTRY

Palgrave Macmillan, 1 New York Plaza, Ste. 4500, New York, NY, 10004-1562, USA, (800) 777-4643, orders@palgrave.com, https://www.palgrave.com/us; The Statesman's Yearbook, 2023.

BAHRAIN-TOURISM

Euromonitor International, Inc., 1 N Dearborn St., Ste. 1700, Chicago, IL, 60602, USA, (312) 922-1115, (312) 922-1157, info-usa@euromonitor.com, https://www.euromonitor.com/; Geographies.

Organisation of Islamic Cooperation (OIC), Statistical, Economic and Social Research and Training Centre for Islamic Countries (SESRIC), Kudus Cad. No. 9, Diplomatik Site, Ankara, 06450, TUR, statistics@sesric.org, https://www.sesric.org/; International Tourism in the OIC Countries: Prospects and Challenges, 2020 and OIC Statistics (OICStat) Database.

Palgrave Macmillan, 1 New York Plaza, Ste. 4500, New York, NY, 10004-1562, USA, (800) 777-4643, orders@palgrave.com, https://www.palgrave.com/us; The Statesman's Yearbook, 2023.

Routledge - Taylor & Francis Group, 6000 Broken Sound Pkwy. NW, Ste. 300, Boca Raton, FL, 33487, USA, (800) 634-1420, (800) 634-7064, orders@taylorandfrancis.com, https://www.routledge.com/; The Europa World Year Book 2022.

United Nations Economic and Social Commission for Western Asia (ESCWA), Riad el-Solh Sq., PO Box 11-8575, Beirut, LBN, escwa-ciu@un.org, https://www.unescwa.org; ESCWA Annual Report 2019.

The World Bank, 1818 H St. NW, Washington, DC, 20433, USA, (202) 473-1000, (202) 477-6391, eds03@worldbank.org, https://www.worldbank.org/; Gulf Cooperation Council (report).

BAHRAIN-TRADE

See BAHRAIN-INTERNATIONAL TRADE

BAHRAIN-TRANSPORTATION

Central Intelligence Agency (CIA), Office of Public Affairs, Washington, DC, 20505, USA, (703) 482-0623, https://www.cia.gov; The World Factbook.

Euromonitor International, Inc., 1 N Dearborn St., Ste. 1700, Chicago, IL, 60602, USA, (312) 922-1115, (312) 922-1157, info-usa@euromonitor.com, https://www.euromonitor.com/; Geographies.

Organisation of Islamic Cooperation (OIC), Statistical, Economic and Social Research and Training Centre for Islamic Countries (SESRIC), Kudus Cad. No. 9, Diplomatik Site, Ankara, 06450, TUR, statistics@sesric.org, https://www.sesric.org/; OIC Statistics (OICStat) Database.

Palgrave Macmillan, 1 New York Plaza, Ste. 4500, New York, NY, 10004-1562, USA, (800) 777-4643, orders@palgrave.com, https://www.palgrave.com/us; The Statesman's Yearbook, 2023.

Routledge - Taylor & Francis Group, 6000 Broken Sound Pkwy. NW, Ste. 300, Boca Raton, FL, 33487, USA, (800) 634-1420, (800) 634-7064, orders@taylorandfrancis.com, https://www.routledge.com/; The Europa World Year Book 2022.

United Nations Economic and Social Commission for Western Asia (ESCWA), Riad el-Solh Sq., PO Box 11-8575, Beirut, LBN, escwa-ciu@un.org, https://www.unescwa.org; ESCWA Annual Report 2019.

The World Bank, 1818 H St. NW, Washington, DC, 20433, USA, (202) 473-1000, (202) 477-6391, eds03@worldbank.org, https://www.worldbank.org/; Gulf Cooperation Council (report).

BAHRAIN-UNEMPLOYMENT

International Labour Organization (ILO), 4 Rte. des Morillons, Geneva, CH-1211, SWI, ilo@ilo.org, https://www.ilo.org; NORMLEX Information System on International Labour Standards.

Palgrave Macmillan, 1 New York Plaza, Ste. 4500, New York, NY, 10004-1562, USA, (800) 777-4643, orders@palgrave.com, https://www.palgrave.com/us; The Statesman's Yearbook, 2023.

BAHRAIN-VITAL STATISTICS

Palgrave Macmillan, 1 New York Plaza, Ste. 4500, New York, NY, 10004-1562, USA, (800) 777-4643, orders@palgrave.com, https://www.palgrave.com/us; The Statesman's Yearbook, 2023.

U.S. Census Bureau, 4600 Silver Hill Rd., Washington, DC, 20233, USA, (301) 763-4636, (800) 923-8282, https://www.census.gov; HIV/AIDS Surveillance Data Base.

United Nations Department of Economic and Social Affairs (DESA), Population Division, 2 United Nations Plz., Rm. DC2-1950, New York, NY, 10017, USA, (212) 963-3209, (212) 963-2147, population@un.org, https://www.un.org/development/desa/pd/; World Contraceptive Use 2021: Estimates and Projections of Family Planning Indicators and World Marriage Data 2019.

United Nations Economic and Social Commission for Western Asia (ESCWA), Riad el-Solh Sq., PO Box 11-8575, Beirut, LBN, escwa-ciu@un.org, https://www.unescwa.org; ESCWA Annual Report 2019; ESCWA Data Portal for the Arab Region; and Survey of Economic and Social Developments in the Arab Region 2020-2021.

BAHRAIN-WAGES

International Labour Organization (ILO), 4 Rte. des Morillons, Geneva, CH-1211, SWI, ilo@ilo.org, https://www.ilo.org; NORMLEX Information System on International Labour Standards.

The World Bank, 1818 H St. NW, Washington, DC, 20433, USA, (202) 473-1000, (202) 477-6391, eds03@worldbank.org, https://www.worldbank.org/; Gulf Cooperation Council (report).

BAHRAIN-WEATHER

See BAHRAIN-CLIMATE

BAHRAIN-WHEAT PRODUCTION

See BAHRAIN-CROPS

BAHRAIN-WOOL PRODUCTION

See BAHRAIN-TEXTILE INDUSTRY

BAKERY PRODUCTS

U.S. Department of Labor (DOL), Bureau of Labor Statistics (BLS), Postal Square Bldg., 2 Massachusetts Ave. NE, Washington, DC, 20212-0001, USA, (202) 691-5200, (202) 691-7890, blsdata_staff@bls.gov, https://www.bls.gov; Consumer Price Index (CPI) Databases.

BALANCE OF PAYMENTS

Google Public Data Directory, USA, https://www.google.com/publicdata/directory; Google Public Data Directory.

BALLET

National Endowment for the Arts (NEA), 400 7th St. SW, Washington, DC, 20506-0001, USA, (202) 682-5400, https://www.arts.gov; 2022 Annual Performance Report.

BANANAS

U.S. Department of Agriculture (USDA), Economic Research Service (ERS), 1400 Independence Ave. SW, Mail Stop 1800, Washington, DC, 20250-0002, USA, (202) 720-2791, https://www.ers.usda.gov/; Food Price Outlook; Foreign Agricultural Trade of the United States (FATUS); and Outlook for U.S. Agricultural Trade: May 2022.

U.S. Department of Agriculture (USDA), National Agricultural Statistics Service (USDA-NASS), 1400 Independence Ave. SW, Washington, DC, 20250, USA, (800) 727-9540, nass@nass.usda.gov, https://www.nass.usda.gov; Quick Stats.

U.S. Department of Labor (DOL), Bureau of Labor Statistics (BLS), Postal Square Bldg., 2 Massachusetts Ave. NE, Washington, DC, 20212-0001, USA, (202) 691-5200, (202) 691-7890, blsdata_staff@bls.gov, https://www.bls.gov; Consumer Price Index (CPI) Databases.

BANGLADESH-NATIONAL STATISTICAL OFFICE

Bangladesh Bureau of Statistics (BBS), Director General, Parishankhyan Bhaban E-27/A, Agargaon, Dhaka, 1207, BGD, dg@bbs.gov.bd, http://www.bbs.gov.bd; National Data Reports (Bangladesh).

BANGLADESH-AGRICULTURE

Asian Development Bank (ADB), 6 ADB Ave., Mandaluyong City, 1550, PHL, information@adb.org, https://www.adb.org/; Key Indicators for Asia and the Pacific 2022.

The Economist Group: Economist Intelligence Unit (EIU), 900 3rd Ave., 16th Fl., New York, NY, 10022, USA, (212) 541-0500, americas@eiu.com, https://www.eiu.com; Bangladesh Country Report.

Euromonitor International, Inc., 1 N Dearborn St., Ste. 1700, Chicago, IL, 60602, USA, (312) 922-1115, (312) 922-1157, info-usa@euromonitor.com, https://www.euromonitor.com/; Geographies.

Organisation of Islamic Cooperation (OIC), Statistical, Economic and Social Research and Training Centre for Islamic Countries (SESRIC), Kudus Cad. No. 9, Diplomatik Site, Ankara, 06450, TUR, statistics@sesric.org, https://www.sesric.org/; OIC Statistics (OICStat) Database and OIC-Countries in Figures (OIC-CIF).

Palgrave Macmillan, 1 New York Plaza, Ste. 4500, New York, NY, 10004-1562, USA, (800) 777-4643, orders@palgrave.com, https://www.palgrave.com/us; The Statesman's Yearbook, 2023.

Routledge - Taylor & Francis Group, 6000 Broken Sound Pkwy. NW, Ste. 300, Boca Raton, FL, 33487, USA, (800) 634-1420, (800) 634-7064, orders@taylorandfrancis.com, https://www.routledge.com/; The Europa World Year Book 2022.

United Nations Economic and Social Commission for Asia and the Pacific (ESCAP), United Nations Building, Rajadamnern Nok Ave., Bangkok, 10200, THA, https://www.unescap.org/; Asia-Pacific Development Journal and SDG Gateway Data Explorer.

United Nations Food and Agricultural Organization (FAO), 2121 K St., Ste. 800B, Washington, DC, 20037, USA, (202) 653-2400 (Dial from U.S.), (202) 653-5760 (Fax from U.S.), fao-hq@fao.org, https://www.fao.org; AQUASTAT and The State of Food and Agriculture (SOFA) 2022.

United Nations Statistics Division (UNSD), United Nations Plz., New York, NY, 10017, USA, (800) 253-9646, (212) 963-9851, statistics@un.org, https://unstats.un.org; Statistical Yearbook of the United Nations 2021.

The World Bank, 1818 H St. NW, Washington, DC, 20433, USA, (202) 473-1000, (202) 477-6391, eds03@worldbank.org, https://www.worldbank.org/; Bangladesh (report) and World Development Indicators (WDI) 2022.

BANGLADESH-AIRLINES

International Civil Aviation Organization (ICAO), 999 Robert-Bourassa Blvd., Montreal, QC, H3C 5H7,

CAN, (514) 954-8219 (Dial from U.S.), (514) 954-6077 (Fax from U.S.), icaohq@icao.int, https://www.icao.int; ICAO Regional Reports.

Palgrave Macmillan, 1 New York Plaza, Ste. 4500, New York, NY, 10004-1562, USA, (800) 777-4643, orders@palgrave.com, https://www.palgrave.com/us; The Statesman's Yearbook, 2023.

BANGLADESH-ALUMINUM PRODUCTION

See BANGLADESH-MINERAL INDUSTRIES

BANGLADESH-ARMED FORCES

Central Intelligence Agency (CIA), Office of Public Affairs, Washington, DC, 20505, USA, (703) 482-0623, https://www.cia.gov; The World Factbook.

International Institute for Strategic Studies (IISS) - Americas, 2121 K St. NW, Ste. 600, Washington, DC, 20037, USA, (202) 659-1490, (202) 659-1499, https://www.iiss.org/; The Military Balance 2022.

Palgrave Macmillan, 1 New York Plaza, Ste. 4500, New York, NY, 10004-1562, USA, (800) 777-4643, orders@palgrave.com, https://www.palgrave.com/us; The Statesman's Yearbook, 2023.

Stockholm International Peace Research Institute (SIPRI), Signalistgatan 9, Stockholm, SE 169 72, SWE, https://www.sipri.org/; SIPRI Arms Transfers Database and SIPRI Military Expenditure Database.

BANGLADESH-BALANCE OF PAYMENTS

Routledge - Taylor & Francis Group, 6000 Broken Sound Pkwy. NW, Ste. 300, Boca Raton, FL, 33487, USA, (800) 634-1420, (800) 634-7064, orders@taylorandfrancis.com, https://www.routledge.com/; The Europa World Year Book 2022.

SAGE Publications, 2455 Teller Rd., Thousand Oaks, CA, 91320, USA, (800) 818-7243, (800) 583-2665, journals@sagepub.com, https://www.sagepub.com; Journal of South Asian Development and South Asia Economic Journal.

United Nations Conference on Trade and Development (UNCTAD), Palais des Nations, Geneva, 1211, SWI, (212) 963-6896, unctadinfo@unctad.org, https://unctad.org; Handbook of Statistics 2021.

The World Bank, 1818 H St. NW, Washington, DC, 20433, USA, (202) 473-1000, (202) 477-6391, eds03@worldbank.org, https://www.worldbank.org/; Bangladesh (report); World Development Indicators (WDI) 2022; and World Development Report 2022: Finance for an Equitable Recovery.

BANGLADESH-BANKS AND BANKING

Asian Development Bank (ADB), 6 ADB Ave., Mandaluyong City, 1550, PHL, information@adb.org, https://www.adb.org/; Key Indicators for Asia and the Pacific 2022.

Euromonitor International, Inc., 1 N Dearborn St., Ste. 1700, Chicago, IL, 60602, USA, (312) 922-1115, (312) 922-1157, info-usa@euromonitor.com, https://www.euromonitor.com/; Geographies.

International Monetary Fund (IMF), 700 19th St. NW, Washington, DC, 20431, USA, (202) 623-7000, (202) 623-4661, publications@imf.org, https://www.imf.org; International Financial Statistics (IFS).

Routledge - Taylor & Francis Group, 6000 Broken Sound Pkwy. NW, Ste. 300, Boca Raton, FL, 33487, USA, (800) 634-1420, (800) 634-7064, orders@taylorandfrancis.com, https://www.routledge.com/; The Europa World Year Book 2022.

SAGE Publications, 2455 Teller Rd., Thousand Oaks, CA, 91320, USA, (800) 818-7243, (800) 583-2665, journals@sagepub.com, https://www.sagepub.com; Journal of South Asian Development and South Asia Economic Journal.

BANGLADESH-BARLEY PRODUCTION

See BANGLADESH-CROPS

BANGLADESH-BROADCASTING

Central Intelligence Agency (CIA), Office of Public Affairs, Washington, DC, 20505, USA, (703) 482-0623, https://www.cia.gov; The World Factbook.

Euromonitor International, Inc., 1 N Dearborn St., Ste. 1700, Chicago, IL, 60602, USA, (312) 922-1115, (312) 922-1157, info-usa@euromonitor.com, https://www.euromonitor.com/; Geographies.

Palgrave Macmillan, 1 New York Plaza, Ste. 4500, New York, NY, 10004-1562, USA, (800) 777-4643, orders@palgrave.com, https://www.palgrave.com/us; The Statesman's Yearbook, 2023.

UNESCO Institute for Statistics, C.P 250 Succursale H, Montreal, QC, H3G 2K8, CAN, (514) 343-6880 (Dial from U.S.), (514) 343-5740 (Fax from U.S.), uis.publications@unesco.org, http://uis.unesco.org/; UIS.Stat.

WRTH Publications Limited, PO Box 290, Oxford, OX2 7FT, GBR, sales@wrth.com, https://www.wrth.com; World Radio TV Handbook 2023.

BANGLADESH-BUDGET

Central Intelligence Agency (CIA), Office of Public Affairs, Washington, DC, 20505, USA, (703) 482-0623, https://www.cia.gov; The World Factbook.

BANGLADESH-BUSINESS

SAGE Publications, 2455 Teller Rd., Thousand Oaks, CA, 91320, USA, (800) 818-7243, (800) 583-2665, journals@sagepub.com, https://www.sagepub.com; Journal of South Asian Development and South Asia Economic Journal.

United Nations Economic and Social Commission for Asia and the Pacific (ESCAP), United Nations Building, Rajadamnern Nok Ave., Bangkok, 10200, THA, https://www.unescap.org/; SDG Gateway Data Explorer.

BANGLADESH-CHILDBIRTH-STATISTICS

United Nations Economic and Social Commission for Asia and the Pacific (ESCAP), United Nations Building, Rajadamnern Nok Ave., Bangkok, 10200, THA, https://www.unescap.org/; Asia-Pacific Development Journal.

The World Bank, 1818 H St. NW, Washington, DC, 20433, USA, (202) 473-1000, (202) 477-6391, eds03@worldbank.org, https://www.worldbank.org/; World Development Indicators (WDI) 2022.

BANGLADESH-CLIMATE

International Institute for Environment and Development (IIED), 235 High Holborn, London, WC1V 7DN, GBR, inforequest@iied.org, https://www.iied.org; Environment & Urbanization.

Palgrave Macmillan, 1 New York Plaza, Ste. 4500, New York, NY, 10004-1562, USA, (800) 777-4643, orders@palgrave.com, https://www.palgrave.com/us; The Statesman's Yearbook, 2023.

BANGLADESH-COAL PRODUCTION

See BANGLADESH-MINERAL INDUSTRIES

BANGLADESH-COFFEE

See BANGLADESH-CROPS

BANGLADESH-COMMERCE

Palgrave Macmillan, 1 New York Plaza, Ste. 4500, New York, NY, 10004-1562, USA, (800) 777-4643, orders@palgrave.com, https://www.palgrave.com/us; The Statesman's Yearbook, 2023.

SAGE Publications, 2455 Teller Rd., Thousand Oaks, CA, 91320, USA, (800) 818-7243, (800) 583-2665, journals@sagepub.com, https://www.sagepub.com; Journal of South Asian Development and South Asia Economic Journal.

UK Data Service, University of Essex, Wivenhoe Park, Colchester, Essex, CO4 3SQ, GBR, https://ukdataservice.ac.uk/; International Aggregate Data.

BANGLADESH-COMMODITY EXCHANGES

Barchart, 209 W Jackson Blvd., 2nd Fl., Chicago, IL, 60606, USA, (877) 247-4394, commodities@barchart.com, https://www.barchart.com/cmdty; The cmdty Yearbook 2023; cmdtyStats: Commodity Statistics and Fundamental Data; cmdtyView: Commodity Index; and Commodity Data and Prices.

International Monetary Fund (IMF), 700 19th St. NW, Washington, DC, 20431, USA, (202) 623-7000, (202) 623-4661, publications@imf.org, https://www.imf.org; IMF Primary Commodity Prices.

BANGLADESH-CONSTRUCTION INDUSTRY

United Nations Statistics Division (UNSD), United Nations Plz., New York, NY, 10017, USA, (800) 253-9646, (212) 963-9851, statistics@un.org, https://unstats.un.org; Statistical Yearbook of the United Nations 2021.

BANGLADESH-CONSUMER PRICE INDEXES

Asian Development Bank (ADB), 6 ADB Ave., Mandaluyong City, 1550, PHL, information@adb.org, https://www.adb.org/; Key Indicators for Asia and the Pacific 2022.

Routledge - Taylor & Francis Group, 6000 Broken Sound Pkwy. NW, Ste. 300, Boca Raton, FL, 33487, USA, (800) 634-1420, (800) 634-7064, orders@taylorandfrancis.com, https://www.routledge.com/; The Europa World Year Book 2022.

SAGE Publications, 2455 Teller Rd., Thousand Oaks, CA, 91320, USA, (800) 818-7243, (800) 583-2665, journals@sagepub.com, https://www.sagepub.com; Journal of South Asian Development and South Asia Economic Journal.

The World Bank, 1818 H St. NW, Washington, DC, 20433, USA, (202) 473-1000, (202) 477-6391, eds03@worldbank.org, https://www.worldbank.org/; Bangladesh (report).

BANGLADESH-COPPER INDUSTRY AND TRADE

See BANGLADESH-MINERAL INDUSTRIES

BANGLADESH-CORN INDUSTRY

See BANGLADESH-CROPS

BANGLADESH-COTTON

See BANGLADESH-CROPS

BANGLADESH-CROPS

International Monetary Fund (IMF), 700 19th St. NW, Washington, DC, 20431, USA, (202) 623-7000, (202) 623-4661, publications@imf.org, https://www.imf.org; International Financial Statistics (IFS).

Palgrave Macmillan, 1 New York Plaza, Ste. 4500, New York, NY, 10004-1562, USA, (800) 777-4643, orders@palgrave.com, https://www.palgrave.com/us; The Statesman's Yearbook, 2023.

United Nations Food and Agricultural Organization (FAO), 2121 K St., Ste. 800B, Washington, DC, 20037, USA, (202) 653-2400 (Dial from U.S.), (202) 653-5760 (Fax from U.S.), fao-hq@fao.org, https://www.fao.org; The State of Food and Agriculture (SOFA) 2022.

United Nations Statistics Division (UNSD), United Nations Plz., New York, NY, 10017, USA, (800) 253-9646, (212) 963-9851, statistics@un.org, https://unstats.un.org; Statistical Yearbook of the United Nations 2021.

BANGLADESH-DAIRY PROCESSING

Palgrave Macmillan, 1 New York Plaza, Ste. 4500, New York, NY, 10004-1562, USA, (800) 777-4643, orders@palgrave.com, https://www.palgrave.com/us; The Statesman's Yearbook, 2023.

United Nations Food and Agricultural Organization (FAO), 2121 K St., Ste. 800B, Washington, DC, 20037, USA, (202) 653-2400 (Dial from U.S.), (202) 653-5760 (Fax from U.S.), fao-hq@fao.org, https://www.fao.org; The State of Food and Agriculture (SOFA) 2022.

BANGLADESH-DEBTS, EXTERNAL

Asian Development Bank (ADB), 6 ADB Ave., Mandaluyong City, 1550, PHL, information@adb.org, https://www.adb.org/; Key Indicators for Asia and the Pacific 2022.

Palgrave Macmillan, 1 New York Plaza, Ste. 4500, New York, NY, 10004-1562, USA, (800) 777-4643, orders@palgrave.com, https://www.palgrave.com/us; The Statesman's Yearbook, 2023.

SAGE Publications, 2455 Teller Rd., Thousand Oaks, CA, 91320, USA, (800) 818-7243, (800) 583-2665, journals@sagepub.com, https://www.sagepub.com; Journal of South Asian Development and South Asia Economic Journal.

The World Bank, 1818 H St. NW, Washington, DC, 20433, USA, (202) 473-1000, (202) 477-6391, eds03@worldbank.org, https://www.worldbank.org/; Global Financial Development Report 2019-2020: Bank Regulation and Supervision a Decade after the Global Financial Crisis; World Development Indicators (WDI) 2022; and World Development Report 2022: Finance for an Equitable Recovery.

BANGLADESH-DEFENSE EXPENDITURES

See BANGLADESH-ARMED FORCES

BANGLADESH-DIAMONDS

See BANGLADESH-MINERAL INDUSTRIES

BANGLADESH-ECONOMIC ASSISTANCE

United Nations Statistics Division (UNSD), United Nations Plz., New York, NY, 10017, USA, (800) 253-9646, (212) 963-9851, statistics@un.org, https://unstats.un.org; Statistical Yearbook of the United Nations 2021.

BANGLADESH-ECONOMIC CONDITIONS

Asian Development Bank (ADB), 6 ADB Ave., Mandaluyong City, 1550, PHL, information@adb.org, https://www.adb.org/; Key Indicators for Asia and the Pacific 2022.

Bernan Press, 15250 NBN Way, Bldg. C, Blue Ridge Summit, PA, 17214, USA, (301) 459-2255, (800) 865-3457, (800) 865-3450, customercare@bernan.com, https://rowman.com/Page/Bernan; World Economic Outlook, April 2022.

Central Intelligence Agency (CIA), Office of Public Affairs, Washington, DC, 20505, USA, (703) 482-0623, https://www.cia.gov; The World Factbook.

The Economist Group: Economist Intelligence Unit (EIU), 900 3rd Ave., 16th Fl., New York, NY, 10022, USA, (212) 541-0500, americas@eiu.com, https://www.eiu.com; Bangladesh Country Report.

Euromonitor International, Inc., 1 N Dearborn St., Ste. 1700, Chicago, IL, 60602, USA, (312) 922-1115, (312) 922-1157, info-usa@euromonitor.com, https://www.euromonitor.com/; Geographies.

International Monetary Fund (IMF), 700 19th St. NW, Washington, DC, 20431, USA, (202) 623-7000, (202) 623-4661, publications@imf.org, https://www.imf.org; IMF Data and World Economic Outlook.

Organisation of Islamic Cooperation (OIC), Statistical, Economic and Social Research and Training Centre for Islamic Countries (SESRIC), Kudus Cad. No. 9, Diplomatik Site, Ankara, 06450, TUR, statistics@sesric.org, https://www.sesric.org/; OIC Economic Outlook 2021; OIC Statistics (OICStat) Database; and OIC-Countries in Figures (OIC-CIF).

Palgrave Macmillan, 1 New York Plaza, Ste. 4500, New York, NY, 10004-1562, USA, (800) 777-4643, orders@palgrave.com, https://www.palgrave.com/us; The Statesman's Yearbook, 2023.

Routledge - Taylor & Francis Group, 6000 Broken Sound Pkwy. NW, Ste. 300, Boca Raton, FL, 33487, USA, (800) 634-1420, (800) 634-7064, orders@taylorandfrancis.com, https://www.routledge.com/; The Europa World Year Book 2022.

SAGE Publications, 2455 Teller Rd., Thousand Oaks, CA, 91320, USA, (800) 818-7243, (800) 583-2665, journals@sagepub.com, https://www.sagepub.com; Journal of South Asian Development and South Asia Economic Journal.

United Nations Statistics Division (UNSD), United Nations Plz., New York, NY, 10017, USA, (800) 253-9646, (212) 963-9851, statistics@un.org, https://unstats.un.org; World Statistics Pocketbook 2021.

The World Bank, 1818 H St. NW, Washington, DC, 20433, USA, (202) 473-1000, (202) 477-6391, eds03@worldbank.org, https://www.worldbank.org/; Bangladesh (report); Global Economic Monitor (GEM); Global Economic Prospects, June 2022; The Global Findex Database 2021; and World Development Report 2022: Finance for an Equitable Recovery.

BANGLADESH-EDUCATION

Euromonitor International, Inc., 1 N Dearborn St., Ste. 1700, Chicago, IL, 60602, USA, (312) 922-1115, (312) 922-1157, info-usa@euromonitor.com, https://www.euromonitor.com/; Geographies.

Infoplease, c/o Sandbox Networks, Inc., 1 Lincoln St., 24th Fl., Boston, MA, 02111, USA, https://www.infoplease.com; Countries of the World.

Organisation of Islamic Cooperation (OIC), Statistical, Economic and Social Research and Training Centre for Islamic Countries (SESRIC), Kudus Cad. No. 9, Diplomatik Site, Ankara, 06450, TUR, statistics@sesric.org, https://www.sesric.org/; OIC Statistics (OICStat) Database.

Palgrave Macmillan, 1 New York Plaza, Ste. 4500, New York, NY, 10004-1562, USA, (800) 777-4643, orders@palgrave.com, https://www.palgrave.com/us; The Statesman's Yearbook, 2023.

Routledge - Taylor & Francis Group, 6000 Broken Sound Pkwy. NW, Ste. 300, Boca Raton, FL, 33487, USA, (800) 634-1420, (800) 634-7064, orders@taylorandfrancis.com, https://www.routledge.com/; The Europa World Year Book 2022.

UNESCO Institute for Statistics, C.P 250 Succursale H, Montreal, QC, H3G 2K8, CAN, (514) 343-6880 (Dial from U.S.), (514) 343-5740 (Fax from U.S.), uis.publications@unesco.org, http://uis.unesco.org/; Literacy and UIS.Stat.

United Nations Economic and Social Commission for Asia and the Pacific (ESCAP), United Nations Building, Rajadamnern Nok Ave., Bangkok, 10200, THA, https://www.unescap.org/; Asia-Pacific Development Journal and SDG Gateway Data Explorer.

United Nations Statistics Division (UNSD), United Nations Plz., New York, NY, 10017, USA, (800) 253-9646, (212) 963-9851, statistics@un.org, https://unstats.un.org; Millennium Development Goal Indicators.

The World Bank, 1818 H St. NW, Washington, DC, 20433, USA, (202) 473-1000, (202) 477-6391, eds03@worldbank.org, https://www.worldbank.org/; Bangladesh (report); World Development Indicators (WDI) 2022; and World Development Report 2022: Finance for an Equitable Recovery.

BANGLADESH-ELECTRICITY

International Energy Agency (IEA), 9 Rue de la Federation, Paris, 75739, FRA, info@iea.org, https://www.iea.org/; World Energy Outlook 2021.

U.S. Energy Information Administration (EIA), 1000 Independence Ave. SW, Washington, DC, 20585, USA, (202) 586-8800, infoctr@eia.gov, https://www.eia.gov; International Energy Outlook 2021.

BANGLADESH-EMPLOYMENT

International Labour Organization (ILO), 4 Rte. des Morillons, Geneva, CH-1211, SWI, ilo@ilo.org, https://www.ilo.org; NORMLEX Information System on International Labour Standards.

SAGE Publications, 2455 Teller Rd., Thousand Oaks, CA, 91320, USA, (800) 818-7243, (800) 583-2665, journals@sagepub.com, https://www.sagepub.com; Journal of South Asian Development and South Asia Economic Journal.

UK Data Service, University of Essex, Wivenhoe Park, Colchester, Essex, CO4 3SQ, GBR, https://ukdataservice.ac.uk/; International Aggregate Data.

United Nations Economic and Social Commission for Asia and the Pacific (ESCAP), United Nations Building, Rajadamnern Nok Ave., Bangkok, 10200, THA, https://www.unescap.org/; Asia-Pacific Development Journal.

United Nations Statistics Division (UNSD), United Nations Plz., New York, NY, 10017, USA, (800) 253-9646, (212) 963-9851, statistics@un.org, https://unstats.un.org; Statistical Yearbook of the United Nations 2021.

The World Bank, 1818 H St. NW, Washington, DC, 20433, USA, (202) 473-1000, (202) 477-6391, eds03@worldbank.org, https://www.worldbank.org/; Bangladesh (report).

BANGLADESH-ENERGY INDUSTRIES

Enerdata, 47 avenue Alsace Lorraine, Grenoble, 38027, FRA, (332) 216-4534, research@enerdata.net, https://www.enerdata.net; World Refinery Database.

BANGLADESH-ENVIRONMENTAL CONDITIONS

DSI Data Service & Information, Xantener Strasse 51a, Rheinberg, D-47495, GER, dsi@dsidata.com, https://www.dsidata.com/; Global Environmental Database.

The Economist Group: Economist Intelligence Unit (EIU), 900 3rd Ave., 16th Fl., New York, NY, 10022, USA, (212) 541-0500, americas@eiu.com, https://www.eiu.com; Bangladesh Country Report.

International Institute for Environment and Development (IIED), 235 High Holborn, London, WC1V 7DN, GBR, inforequest@iied.org, https://www.iied.org; Environment & Urbanization.

Organisation of Islamic Cooperation (OIC), Statistical, Economic and Social Research and Training Centre for Islamic Countries (SESRIC), Kudus Cad. No. 9, Diplomatik Site, Ankara, 06450, TUR, statistics@sesric.org, https://www.sesric.org/; OIC Statistics (OICStat) Database and OIC-Countries in Figures (OIC-CIF).

United Nations Statistics Division (UNSD), United Nations Plz., New York, NY, 10017, USA, (800) 253-9646, (212) 963-9851, statistics@un.org, https://unstats.un.org; World Statistics Pocketbook 2021.

BANGLADESH-EXPORTS

Asian Development Bank (ADB), 6 ADB Ave., Mandaluyong City, 1550, PHL, information@adb.org, https://www.adb.org/; Key Indicators for Asia and the Pacific 2022.

Central Intelligence Agency (CIA), Office of Public Affairs, Washington, DC, 20505, USA, (703) 482-0623, https://www.cia.gov; The World Factbook.

The Economist Group: Economist Intelligence Unit (EIU), 900 3rd Ave., 16th Fl., New York, NY, 10022, USA, (212) 541-0500, americas@eiu.com, https://www.eiu.com; Bangladesh Country Report.

International Monetary Fund (IMF), 700 19th St. NW, Washington, DC, 20431, USA, (202) 623-7000, (202) 623-4661, publications@imf.org, https://www.imf.org; Direction of Trade Statistics (DOTS) and International Financial Statistics (IFS).

Organisation of Islamic Cooperation (OIC), Statistical, Economic and Social Research and Training Centre for Islamic Countries (SESRIC), Kudus Cad. No. 9, Diplomatik Site, Ankara, 06450, TUR, statistics@sesric.org, https://www.sesric.org/; OIC Statistics (OICStat) Database.

S&P Global, IHS Markit, 15 Inverness Way E, Englewood, CO, 80112, USA, (800) 447-2273, (800) 854-7179, https://ihsmarkit.com; Global Trade Atlas (GTA).

United Nations Conference on Trade and Development (UNCTAD), Palais des Nations, Geneva, 1211, SWI, (212) 963-6896, unctadinfo@unctad.org, https://unctad.org; Handbook of Statistics 2021.

The World Bank, 1818 H St. NW, Washington, DC, 20433, USA, (202) 473-1000, (202) 477-6391, eds03@worldbank.org, https://www.worldbank.org/; World Development Report 2022: Finance for an Equitable Recovery.

BANGLADESH-FEMALE WORKING POPULATION

See BANGLADESH-EMPLOYMENT

BANGLADESH-FERTILITY, HUMAN

Central Intelligence Agency (CIA), Office of Public Affairs, Washington, DC, 20505, USA, (703) 482-0623, https://www.cia.gov; The World Factbook.

BANGLADESH-FERTILIZER INDUSTRY

United Nations Food and Agricultural Organization (FAO), 2121 K St., Ste. 800B, Washington, DC, 20037, USA, (202) 653-2400 (Dial from U.S.), (202) 653-5760 (Fax from U.S.), fao-hq@fao.org, https://www.fao.org; The State of Food and Agriculture (SOFA) 2022.

BANGLADESH-FETAL MORTALITY

See BANGLADESH-MORTALITY

BANGLADESH-FINANCE

SAGE Publications, 2455 Teller Rd., Thousand Oaks, CA, 91320, USA, (800) 818-7243, (800) 583-2665, journals@sagepub.com, https://www.sagepub.com; Journal of South Asian Development and South Asia Economic Journal.

Stockholm International Peace Research Institute (SIPRI), Signalistgatan 9, Stockholm, SE 169 72, SWE, https://www.sipri.org/; SIPRI Arms Transfers Database and SIPRI Military Expenditure Database.

United Nations Economic and Social Commission for Asia and the Pacific (ESCAP), United Nations Building, Rajadamnern Nok Ave., Bangkok, 10200, THA, https://www.unescap.org/; Asia-Pacific Development Journal and SDG Gateway Data Explorer.

United Nations Statistics Division (UNSD), United Nations Plz., New York, NY, 10017, USA, (800) 253-9646, (212) 963-9851, statistics@un.org, https://unstats.un.org; Statistical Yearbook of the United Nations 2021.

The World Bank, 1818 H St. NW, Washington, DC, 20433, USA, (202) 473-1000, (202) 477-6391, eds03@worldbank.org, https://www.worldbank.org/; Bangladesh (report).

BANGLADESH-FINANCE, PUBLIC

Asian Development Bank (ADB), 6 ADB Ave., Mandaluyong City, 1550, PHL, information@adb.org, https://www.adb.org/; Key Indicators for Asia and the Pacific 2022.

Bernan Press, 15250 NBN Way, Bldg. C, Blue Ridge Summit, PA, 17214, USA, (301) 459-2255, (800) 865-3457, (800) 865-3450, customercare@bernan.com, https://rowman.com/Page/Bernan; National Accounts Statistics: Analysis of Main Aggregates 2020.

The Economist Group: Economist Intelligence Unit (EIU), 900 3rd Ave., 16th Fl., New York, NY, 10022, USA, (212) 541-0500, americas@eiu.com, https://www.eiu.com; Bangladesh Country Report.

International Monetary Fund (IMF), 700 19th St. NW, Washington, DC, 20431, USA, (202) 623-7000, (202) 623-4661, publications@imf.org, https://www.imf.org; International Financial Statistics (IFS) and Regional Economic Outlook.

Routledge - Taylor & Francis Group, 6000 Broken Sound Pkwy. NW, Ste. 300, Boca Raton, FL, 33487, USA, (800) 634-1420, (800) 634-7064, orders@taylorandfrancis.com, https://www.routledge.com/; The Europa World Year Book 2022.

United Nations Economic and Social Commission for Asia and the Pacific (ESCAP), United Nations Building, Rajadamnern Nok Ave., Bangkok, 10200, THA, https://www.unescap.org/; SDG Gateway Data Explorer.

United Nations Statistics Division (UNSD), United Nations Plz., New York, NY, 10017, USA, (800) 253-9646, (212) 963-9851, statistics@un.org, https://unstats.un.org; National Accounts Main Aggregates Database and National Accounts Statistics: Main Aggregates and Detailed Tables.

The World Bank, 1818 H St. NW, Washington, DC, 20433, USA, (202) 473-1000, (202) 477-6391, eds03@worldbank.org, https://www.worldbank.org/; Bangladesh (report).

BANGLADESH-FISHERIES

Palgrave Macmillan, 1 New York Plaza, Ste. 4500, New York, NY, 10004-1562, USA, (800) 777-4643, orders@palgrave.com, https://www.palgrave.com/us; The Statesman's Yearbook, 2023.

Routledge - Taylor & Francis Group, 6000 Broken Sound Pkwy. NW, Ste. 300, Boca Raton, FL, 33487, USA, (800) 634-1420, (800) 634-7064, orders@taylorandfrancis.com, https://www.routledge.com/; The Europa World Year Book 2022.

United Nations Food and Agricultural Organization (FAO), 2121 K St., Ste. 800B, Washington, DC, 20037, USA, (202) 653-2400 (Dial from U.S.), (202) 653-5760 (Fax from U.S.), fao-hq@fao.org, https://www.fao.org; FAO Yearbook of Fishery and Aquaculture Statistics 2019; Fishery Statistical Collections Global Capture Production; FishStatJ; and The State of Food and Agriculture (SOFA) 2022.

United Nations Statistics Division (UNSD), United Nations Plz., New York, NY, 10017, USA, (800) 253-9646, (212) 963-9851, statistics@un.org, https://unstats.un.org; Statistical Yearbook of the United Nations 2021.

The World Bank, 1818 H St. NW, Washington, DC, 20433, USA, (202) 473-1000, (202) 477-6391, eds03@worldbank.org, https://www.worldbank.org/; Bangladesh (report).

BANGLADESH-FOOD

United Nations Economic and Social Commission for Asia and the Pacific (ESCAP), United Nations Building, Rajadamnern Nok Ave., Bangkok, 10200, THA, https://www.unescap.org/; SDG Gateway Data Explorer.

United Nations Food and Agricultural Organization (FAO), 2121 K St., Ste. 800B, Washington, DC, 20037, USA, (202) 653-2400 (Dial from U.S.), (202) 653-5760 (Fax from U.S.), fao-hq@fao.org, https://www.fao.org; The State of Food and Agriculture (SOFA) 2022.

BANGLADESH-FOREIGN EXCHANGE RATES

Asian Development Bank (ADB), 6 ADB Ave., Mandaluyong City, 1550, PHL, information@adb.org, https://www.adb.org/; Key Indicators for Asia and the Pacific 2022.

International Monetary Fund (IMF), 700 19th St. NW, Washington, DC, 20431, USA, (202) 623-7000, (202) 623-4661, publications@imf.org, https://www.imf.org; International Financial Statistics (IFS).

BANGLADESH-FORESTS AND FORESTRY

Palgrave Macmillan, 1 New York Plaza, Ste. 4500, New York, NY, 10004-1562, USA, (800) 777-4643, orders@palgrave.com, https://www.palgrave.com/us; The Statesman's Yearbook, 2023.

Routledge - Taylor & Francis Group, 6000 Broken Sound Pkwy. NW, Ste. 300, Boca Raton, FL, 33487, USA, (800) 634-1420, (800) 634-7064, orders@taylorandfrancis.com, https://www.routledge.com/; The Europa World Year Book 2022.

UNESCO Institute for Statistics, C.P 250 Succursale H, Montreal, QC, H3G 2K8, CAN, (514) 343-6880 (Dial from U.S.), (514) 343-5740 (Fax from U.S.), uis.publications@unesco.org, http://uis.unesco.org/; UIS.Stat.

United Nations Food and Agricultural Organization (FAO), 2121 K St., Ste. 800B, Washington, DC, 20037, USA, (202) 653-2400 (Dial from U.S.), (202) 653-5760 (Fax from U.S.), fao-hq@fao.org, https://www.fao.org; FAO Yearbook of Forest Products 2019 and The State of Food and Agriculture (SOFA) 2022.

United Nations Statistics Division (UNSD), United Nations Plz., New York, NY, 10017, USA, (800) 253-9646, (212) 963-9851, statistics@un.org, https://unstats.un.org; Statistical Yearbook of the United Nations 2021.

The World Bank, 1818 H St. NW, Washington, DC, 20433, USA, (202) 473-1000, (202) 477-6391, eds03@worldbank.org, https://www.worldbank.org/; Bangladesh (report) and World Development Report 2022: Finance for an Equitable Recovery.

BANGLADESH-GAS PRODUCTION

See BANGLADESH-MINERAL INDUSTRIES

BANGLADESH-GEOGRAPHIC INFORMATION SYSTEMS

The World Bank, 1818 H St. NW, Washington, DC, 20433, USA, (202) 473-1000, (202) 477-6391, eds03@worldbank.org, https://www.worldbank.org/; Bangladesh (report).

BANGLADESH-GOLD INDUSTRY

The World Bank, 1818 H St. NW, Washington, DC, 20433, USA, (202) 473-1000, (202) 477-6391, eds03@worldbank.org, https://www.worldbank.org/; World Development Indicators (WDI) 2022.

BANGLADESH-GOLD PRODUCTION

See BANGLADESH-MINERAL INDUSTRIES

BANGLADESH-GROSS DOMESTIC PRODUCT

Asian Development Bank (ADB), 6 ADB Ave., Mandaluyong City, 1550, PHL, information@adb.org, https://www.adb.org/; Key Indicators for Asia and the Pacific 2022.

The Economist Group: Economist Intelligence Unit (EIU), 900 3rd Ave., 16th Fl., New York, NY, 10022, USA, (212) 541-0500, americas@eiu.com, https://www.eiu.com; Bangladesh Country Report.

Routledge - Taylor & Francis Group, 6000 Broken Sound Pkwy. NW, Ste. 300, Boca Raton, FL, 33487, USA, (800) 634-1420, (800) 634-7064, orders@taylorandfrancis.com, https://www.routledge.com/; The Europa World Year Book 2022.

United Nations Statistics Division (UNSD), United Nations Plz., New York, NY, 10017, USA, (800) 253-9646, (212) 963-9851, statistics@un.org, https://unstats.un.org; Statistical Yearbook of the United Nations 2021.

The World Bank, 1818 H St. NW, Washington, DC, 20433, USA, (202) 473-1000, (202) 477-6391, eds03@worldbank.org, https://www.worldbank.org/; World Development Indicators (WDI) 2022 and World Development Report 2022: Finance for an Equitable Recovery.

BANGLADESH-GROSS NATIONAL PRODUCT

Asian Development Bank (ADB), 6 ADB Ave., Mandaluyong City, 1550, PHL, information@adb.org, https://www.adb.org/; Key Indicators for Asia and the Pacific 2022.

Palgrave Macmillan, 1 New York Plaza, Ste. 4500, New York, NY, 10004-1562, USA, (800) 777-4643, orders@palgrave.com, https://www.palgrave.com/us; The Statesman's Yearbook, 2023.

United Nations Statistics Division (UNSD), United Nations Plz., New York, NY, 10017, USA, (800) 253-9646, (212) 963-9851, statistics@un.org, https://unstats.un.org; Statistical Yearbook of the United Nations 2021.

The World Bank, 1818 H St. NW, Washington, DC, 20433, USA, (202) 473-1000, (202) 477-6391, eds03@worldbank.org, https://www.worldbank.org/; World Development Indicators (WDI) 2022 and World Development Report 2022: Finance for an Equitable Recovery.

BANGLADESH-HEMP FIBRE PRODUCTION

See BANGLADESH-TEXTILE INDUSTRY

BANGLADESH-HOUSING

Euromonitor International, Inc., 1 N Dearborn St., Ste. 1700, Chicago, IL, 60602, USA, (312) 922-1115, (312) 922-1157, info-usa@euromonitor.com, https://www.euromonitor.com/; Geographies.

BANGLADESH-ILLITERATE PERSONS

Central Intelligence Agency (CIA), Office of Public Affairs, Washington, DC, 20505, USA, (703) 482-0623, https://www.cia.gov; The World Factbook.

UNESCO Institute for Statistics, C.P 250 Succursale H, Montreal, QC, H3G 2K8, CAN, (514) 343-6880 (Dial from U.S.), (514) 343-5740 (Fax from U.S.), uis.publications@unesco.org, http://uis.unesco.org/; UIS.Stat.

United Nations Economic and Social Commission for Asia and the Pacific (ESCAP), United Nations Building, Rajadamnern Nok Ave., Bangkok, 10200, THA, https://www.unescap.org/; Asia-Pacific Development Journal.

BANGLADESH-IMPORTS

Asian Development Bank (ADB), 6 ADB Ave., Mandaluyong City, 1550, PHL, information@adb.org, https://www.adb.org/; Key Indicators for Asia and the Pacific 2022.

Central Intelligence Agency (CIA), Office of Public Affairs, Washington, DC, 20505, USA, (703) 482-0623, https://www.cia.gov; The World Factbook.

The Economist Group: Economist Intelligence Unit (EIU), 900 3rd Ave., 16th Fl., New York, NY, 10022, USA, (212) 541-0500, americas@eiu.com, https://www.eiu.com; Bangladesh Country Report.

International Monetary Fund (IMF), 700 19th St. NW, Washington, DC, 20431, USA, (202) 623-7000, (202) 623-4661, publications@imf.org, https://www.imf.org; Direction of Trade Statistics (DOTS) and International Financial Statistics (IFS).

S&P Global, IHS Markit, 15 Inverness Way E, Englewood, CO, 80112, USA, (800) 447-2273, (800) 854-7179, https://ihsmarkit.com; Global Trade Atlas (GTA).

United Nations Conference on Trade and Development (UNCTAD), Palais des Nations, Geneva, 1211, SWI, (212) 963-6896, unctadinfo@unctad.org, https://unctad.org; Handbook of Statistics 2021.

The World Bank, 1818 H St. NW, Washington, DC, 20433, USA, (202) 473-1000, (202) 477-6391, eds03@worldbank.org, https://www.worldbank.org/; World Development Report 2022: Finance for an Equitable Recovery.

BANGLADESH-INDUSTRIES

Central Intelligence Agency (CIA), Office of Public Affairs, Washington, DC, 20505, USA, (703) 482-0623, https://www.cia.gov; The World Factbook.

The Economist Group: Economist Intelligence Unit (EIU), 900 3rd Ave., 16th Fl., New York, NY, 10022, USA, (212) 541-0500, americas@eiu.com, https://www.eiu.com; Bangladesh Country Report.

Euromonitor International, Inc., 1 N Dearborn St., Ste. 1700, Chicago, IL, 60602, USA, (312) 922-1115, (312) 922-1157, info-usa@euromonitor.com, https://www.euromonitor.com/; Geographies.

International Labour Organization (ILO), 4 Rte. des Morillons, Geneva, CH-1211, SWI, ilo@ilo.org, https://www.ilo.org; NORMLEX Information System on International Labour Standards.

Palgrave Macmillan, 1 New York Plaza, Ste. 4500, New York, NY, 10004-1562, USA, (800) 777-4643, orders@palgrave.com, https://www.palgrave.com/us; The Statesman's Yearbook, 2023.

Routledge - Taylor & Francis Group, 6000 Broken Sound Pkwy. NW, Ste. 300, Boca Raton, FL, 33487, USA, (800) 634-1420, (800) 634-7064, orders@taylorandfrancis.com, https://www.routledge.com/; The Europa World Year Book 2022.

SAGE Publications, 2455 Teller Rd., Thousand Oaks, CA, 91320, USA, (800) 818-7243, (800) 583-2665, journals@sagepub.com, https://www.sagepub.com; Journal of South Asian Development and South Asia Economic Journal.

United Nations Economic and Social Commission for Asia and the Pacific (ESCAP), United Nations Building, Rajadamnern Nok Ave., Bangkok, 10200, THA, https://www.unescap.org/; Asia-Pacific Development Journal and SDG Gateway Data Explorer.

United Nations Industrial Development Organization (UNIDO), 1 United Nations Plz., Rm. DC1-1118, New York, NY, 10017, USA, (212) 963-6890, (212) 963 6885, (212) 963-7904, office.newyork@unido.org, https://www.unido.org/; Industrial Statistics Databases and International Yearbook of Industrial Statistics 2021.

The World Bank, 1818 H St. NW, Washington, DC, 20433, USA, (202) 473-1000, (202) 477-6391, eds03@worldbank.org, https://www.worldbank.org/; Bangladesh (report) and World Development Indicators (WDI) 2022.

BANGLADESH-INFANT AND MATERNAL MORTALITY

See BANGLADESH-MORTALITY

BANGLADESH-INTERNATIONAL FINANCE

Asian Development Bank (ADB), 6 ADB Ave., Mandaluyong City, 1550, PHL, information@adb.org, https://www.adb.org/; Key Indicators for Asia and the Pacific 2022.

SAGE Publications, 2455 Teller Rd., Thousand Oaks, CA, 91320, USA, (800) 818-7243, (800) 583-2665, journals@sagepub.com, https://www.sagepub.com; Journal of South Asian Development and South Asia Economic Journal.

BANGLADESH-INTERNATIONAL TRADE

Asian Development Bank (ADB), 6 ADB Ave., Mandaluyong City, 1550, PHL, information@adb.org, https://www.adb.org/; Key Indicators for Asia and the Pacific 2022.

The Economist Group: Economist Intelligence Unit (EIU), 900 3rd Ave., 16th Fl., New York, NY, 10022, USA, (212) 541-0500, americas@eiu.com, https://www.eiu.com; Bangladesh Country Report.

Euromonitor International, Inc., 1 N Dearborn St., Ste. 1700, Chicago, IL, 60602, USA, (312) 922-1115, (312) 922-1157, info-usa@euromonitor.com, https://www.euromonitor.com/; Geographies.

Palgrave Macmillan, 1 New York Plaza, Ste. 4500, New York, NY, 10004-1562, USA, (800) 777-4643, orders@palgrave.com, https://www.palgrave.com/us; The Statesman's Yearbook, 2023.

Routledge - Taylor & Francis Group, 6000 Broken Sound Pkwy. NW, Ste. 300, Boca Raton, FL, 33487, USA, (800) 634-1420, (800) 634-7064, orders@taylorandfrancis.com, https://www.routledge.com/; The Europa World Year Book 2022.

United Nations Conference on Trade and Development (UNCTAD), Palais des Nations, Geneva, 1211, SWI, (212) 963-6896, unctadinfo@unctad.org, https://unctad.org; Trade and Development Report 2021.

United Nations Economic and Social Commission for Asia and the Pacific (ESCAP), United Nations Building, Rajadamnern Nok Ave., Bangkok, 10200, THA, https://www.unescap.org/; Asia-Pacific Development Journal and SDG Gateway Data Explorer.

United Nations Food and Agricultural Organization (FAO), 2121 K St., Ste. 800B, Washington, DC, 20037, USA, (202) 653-2400 (Dial from U.S.), (202) 653-5760 (Fax from U.S.), fao-hq@fao.org, https://www.fao.org; The State of Food and Agriculture (SOFA) 2022.

United Nations Statistics Division (UNSD), United Nations Plz., New York, NY, 10017, USA, (800) 253-9646, (212) 963-9851, statistics@un.org, https://unstats.un.org; International Trade Statistics Yearbook 2020 and Statistical Yearbook of the United Nations 2021.

The World Bank, 1818 H St. NW, Washington, DC, 20433, USA, (202) 473-1000, (202) 477-6391, eds03@worldbank.org, https://www.worldbank.org/; Bangladesh (report); World Development Indicators (WDI) 2022; and World Development Report 2022: Finance for an Equitable Recovery.

World Trade Organization (WTO), Ctre. William Rappard, Rue de Lausanne 154, Case postale, Geneva, CH-1211, SWI, enquiries@wto.org, https://www.wto.org; World Trade Statistical Review 2022.

BANGLADESH-INTERNET USERS

International Telecommunication Union (ITU), Place des Nations, Geneva, CH-1211, SWI, itumail@itu.int, https://www.itu.int; Global Connectivity Report 2022; World Telecommunication/ICT Indicators Database 2021; and Yearbook of Statistics 2019.

The World Bank, 1818 H St. NW, Washington, DC, 20433, USA, (202) 473-1000, (202) 477-6391, eds03@worldbank.org, https://www.worldbank.org/; Bangladesh (report).

BANGLADESH-LABOR

Central Intelligence Agency (CIA), Office of Public Affairs, Washington, DC, 20505, USA, (703) 482-0623, https://www.cia.gov; The World Factbook.

Euromonitor International, Inc., 1 N Dearborn St., Ste. 1700, Chicago, IL, 60602, USA, (312) 922-1115, (312) 922-1157, info-usa@euromonitor.com, https://www.euromonitor.com/; Geographies.

International Labour Organization (ILO), 4 Rte. des Morillons, Geneva, CH-1211, SWI, ilo@ilo.org, https://www.ilo.org; NORMLEX Information System on International Labour Standards.

Organisation of Islamic Cooperation (OIC), Statistical, Economic and Social Research and Training Centre for Islamic Countries (SESRIC), Kudus Cad. No. 9, Diplomatik Site, Ankara, 06450, TUR, statistics@sesric.org, https://www.sesric.org/; OIC Statistics (OICStat) Database.

Palgrave Macmillan, 1 New York Plaza, Ste. 4500, New York, NY, 10004-1562, USA, (800) 777-4643, orders@palgrave.com, https://www.palgrave.com/us; The Statesman's Yearbook, 2023.

United Nations Food and Agricultural Organization (FAO), 2121 K St., Ste. 800B, Washington, DC, 20037, USA, (202) 653-2400 (Dial from U.S.), (202) 653-5760 (Fax from U.S.), fao-hq@fao.org, https://www.fao.org; The State of Food and Agriculture (SOFA) 2022.

The World Bank, 1818 H St. NW, Washington, DC, 20433, USA, (202) 473-1000, (202) 477-6391, eds03@worldbank.org, https://www.worldbank.org/; World Development Indicators (WDI) 2022 and World Development Report 2022: Finance for an Equitable Recovery.

BANGLADESH-LAND USE

United Nations Statistics Division (UNSD), United Nations Plz., New York, NY, 10017, USA, (800) 253-9646, (212) 963-9851, statistics@un.org, https://unstats.un.org; Millennium Development Goal Indicators.

The World Bank, 1818 H St. NW, Washington, DC, 20433, USA, (202) 473-1000, (202) 477-6391, eds03@worldbank.org, https://www.worldbank.org/; World Development Report 2022: Finance for an Equitable Recovery.

BANGLADESH-LIFE EXPECTANCY

Central Intelligence Agency (CIA), Office of Public Affairs, Washington, DC, 20505, USA, (703) 482-0623, https://www.cia.gov; The World Factbook.

United Nations Department of Economic and Social Affairs (DESA), Population Division, 2 United Nations Plz., Rm. DC2-1950, New York, NY, 10017, USA, (212) 963-3209, (212) 963-2147, population@un.org, https://www.un.org/development/desa/pd/; World Population Ageing 2020 Highlights.

United Nations Economic and Social Commission for Asia and the Pacific (ESCAP), United Nations Building, Rajadamnern Nok Ave., Bangkok, 10200, THA, https://www.unescap.org/; Asia-Pacific Development Journal.

United Nations Statistics Division (UNSD), United Nations Plz., New York, NY, 10017, USA, (800) 253-9646, (212) 963-9851, statistics@un.org, https://unstats.un.org; Millennium Development Goal Indicators.

BANGLADESH-LITERACY

Euromonitor International, Inc., 1 N Dearborn St., Ste. 1700, Chicago, IL, 60602, USA, (312) 922-1115, (312) 922-1157, info-usa@euromonitor.com, https://www.euromonitor.com/; Geographies.

UNESCO Institute for Statistics, C.P 250 Succursale H, Montreal, QC, H3G 2K8, CAN, (514) 343-6880 (Dial from U.S.), (514) 343-5740 (Fax from U.S.), uis.publications@unesco.org, http://uis.unesco.org/; Literacy.

BANGLADESH-LIVESTOCK

Palgrave Macmillan, 1 New York Plaza, Ste. 4500, New York, NY, 10004-1562, USA, (800) 777-4643, orders@palgrave.com, https://www.palgrave.com/us; The Statesman's Yearbook, 2023.

Routledge - Taylor & Francis Group, 6000 Broken Sound Pkwy. NW, Ste. 300, Boca Raton, FL, 33487, USA, (800) 634-1420, (800) 634-7064, orders@taylorandfrancis.com, https://www.routledge.com/; The Europa World Year Book 2022.

United Nations Food and Agricultural Organization (FAO), 2121 K St., Ste. 800B, Washington, DC, 20037, USA, (202) 653-2400 (Dial from U.S.), (202) 653-5760 (Fax from U.S.), fao-hq@fao.org, https://www.fao.org; The State of Food and Agriculture (SOFA) 2022.

United Nations Statistics Division (UNSD), United Nations Plz., New York, NY, 10017, USA, (800) 253-9646, (212) 963-9851, statistics@un.org, https://unstats.un.org; Statistical Yearbook of the United Nations 2021.

BANGLADESH-MANPOWER

United Nations Economic and Social Commission for Asia and the Pacific (ESCAP), United Nations Building, Rajadamnern Nok Ave., Bangkok, 10200, THA, https://www.unescap.org/; SDG Gateway Data Explorer.

BANGLADESH-MANUFACTURES

Asian Development Bank (ADB), 6 ADB Ave., Mandaluyong City, 1550, PHL, information@adb.org, https://www.adb.org/; Key Indicators for Asia and the Pacific 2022.

BANGLADESH-MINERAL INDUSTRIES

Asian Development Bank (ADB), 6 ADB Ave., Mandaluyong City, 1550, PHL, information@adb.org, https://www.adb.org/; Key Indicators for Asia and the Pacific 2022.

International Energy Agency (IEA), 9 Rue de la Federation, Paris, 75739, FRA, info@iea.org, https://www.iea.org/; World Energy Outlook 2021.

Palgrave Macmillan, 1 New York Plaza, Ste. 4500, New York, NY, 10004-1562, USA, (800) 777-4643, orders@palgrave.com, https://www.palgrave.com/us; The Statesman's Yearbook, 2023.

Routledge - Taylor & Francis Group, 6000 Broken Sound Pkwy. NW, Ste. 300, Boca Raton, FL, 33487, USA, (800) 634-1420, (800) 634-7064, orders@taylorandfrancis.com, https://www.routledge.com/; The Europa World Year Book 2022.

United Nations Conference on Trade and Development (UNCTAD), Palais des Nations, Geneva, 1211, SWI, (212) 963-6896, unctadinfo@unctad.org, https://unctad.org; Trade and Development Report 2021.

United Nations Statistics Division (UNSD), United Nations Plz., New York, NY, 10017, USA, (800) 253-9646, (212) 963-9851, statistics@un.org, https://unstats.un.org; Statistical Yearbook of the United Nations 2021.

BANGLADESH-MONEY SUPPLY

The Economist Group: Economist Intelligence Unit (EIU), 900 3rd Ave., 16th Fl., New York, NY, 10022, USA, (212) 541-0500, americas@eiu.com, https://www.eiu.com; Bangladesh Country Report.

International Monetary Fund (IMF), 700 19th St. NW, Washington, DC, 20431, USA, (202) 623-7000, (202) 623-4661, publications@imf.org, https://www.imf.org; International Financial Statistics (IFS).

Routledge - Taylor & Francis Group, 6000 Broken Sound Pkwy. NW, Ste. 300, Boca Raton, FL, 33487, USA, (800) 634-1420, (800) 634-7064, orders@taylorandfrancis.com, https://www.routledge.com/; The Europa World Year Book 2022.

United Nations Statistics Division (UNSD), United Nations Plz., New York, NY, 10017, USA, (800) 253-9646, (212) 963-9851, statistics@un.org, https://unstats.un.org; Statistical Yearbook of the United Nations 2021.

The World Bank, 1818 H St. NW, Washington, DC, 20433, USA, (202) 473-1000, (202) 477-6391, eds03@worldbank.org, https://www.worldbank.org/; Bangladesh (report).

BANGLADESH-MORTALITY

UNICEF, 3 United Nations Plz., New York, NY, 10017, USA, (212) 303-7984, (917) 244-2215, https://www.unicef.org; The State of the World's Children 2023.

United Nations Economic and Social Commission for Asia and the Pacific (ESCAP), United Nations Building, Rajadamnern Nok Ave., Bangkok, 10200, THA, https://www.unescap.org/; Asia-Pacific Development Journal.

United Nations Statistics Division (UNSD), United Nations Plz., New York, NY, 10017, USA, (800) 253-9646, (212) 963-9851, statistics@un.org, https://unstats.un.org; Millennium Development Goal Indicators; Statistical Yearbook of the United Nations 2021; and World Statistics Pocketbook 2021.

The World Bank, 1818 H St. NW, Washington, DC, 20433, USA, (202) 473-1000, (202) 477-6391, eds03@worldbank.org, https://www.worldbank.org/; World Development Indicators (WDI) 2022.

World Health Organization (WHO), Ave. Appia 20, Geneva, CH-1211, SWI, (202) 974-3000 (Telephone in U.S.), publications@who.int, https://www.who.int/; Global Health Observatory (GHO).

BANGLADESH-MOTION PICTURES

Palgrave Macmillan, 1 New York Plaza, Ste. 4500, New York, NY, 10004-1562, USA, (800) 777-4643, orders@palgrave.com, https://www.palgrave.com/us; The Statesman's Yearbook, 2023.

BANGLADESH-NATURAL GAS PRODUCTION

See BANGLADESH-MINERAL INDUSTRIES

BANGLADESH-NUTRITION

Asian Development Bank (ADB), 6 ADB Ave., Mandaluyong City, 1550, PHL, information@adb.org, https://www.adb.org/; Key Indicators for Asia and the Pacific 2022.

United Nations Food and Agricultural Organization (FAO), 2121 K St., Ste. 800B, Washington, DC, 20037, USA, (202) 653-2400 (Dial from U.S.), (202) 653-5760 (Fax from U.S.), fao-hq@fao.org, https://www.fao.org; The State of Food and Agriculture (SOFA) 2022.

United Nations Statistics Division (UNSD), United Nations Plz., New York, NY, 10017, USA, (800) 253-9646, (212) 963-9851, statistics@un.org, https://unstats.un.org; Millennium Development Goal Indicators.

BANGLADESH-PAPER

See BANGLADESH-FORESTS AND FORESTRY

BANGLADESH-PEANUT PRODUCTION

See BANGLADESH-CROPS

BANGLADESH-PESTICIDES

United Nations Food and Agricultural Organization (FAO), 2121 K St., Ste. 800B, Washington, DC, 20037, USA, (202) 653-2400 (Dial from U.S.), (202) 653-5760 (Fax from U.S.), fao-hq@fao.org, https://www.fao.org; The State of Food and Agriculture (SOFA) 2022.

BANGLADESH-PETROLEUM INDUSTRY AND TRADE

Asian Development Bank (ADB), 6 ADB Ave., Mandaluyong City, 1550, PHL, information@adb.org, https://www.adb.org/; Key Indicators for Asia and the Pacific 2022.

International Energy Agency (IEA), 9 Rue de la Federation, Paris, 75739, FRA, info@iea.org, https://www.iea.org/; World Energy Outlook 2021.

Palgrave Macmillan, 1 New York Plaza, Ste. 4500, New York, NY, 10004-1562, USA, (800) 777-4643, orders@palgrave.com, https://www.palgrave.com/us; The Statesman's Yearbook, 2023.

U.S. Energy Information Administration (EIA), 1000 Independence Ave. SW, Washington, DC, 20585, USA, (202) 586-8800, infoctr@eia.gov, https://www.eia.gov; International Energy Outlook 2021.

United Nations Food and Agricultural Organization (FAO), 2121 K St., Ste. 800B, Washington, DC, 20037, USA, (202) 653-2400 (Dial from U.S.), (202) 653-5760 (Fax from U.S.), fao-hq@fao.org, https://www.fao.org; The State of Food and Agriculture (SOFA) 2022.

United Nations Statistics Division (UNSD), United Nations Plz., New York, NY, 10017, USA, (800) 253-9646, (212) 963-9851, statistics@un.org, https://unstats.un.org; Statistical Yearbook of the United Nations 2021.

BANGLADESH-POPULATION

Asian Development Bank (ADB), 6 ADB Ave., Mandaluyong City, 1550, PHL, information@adb.org, https://www.adb.org/; Key Indicators for Asia and the Pacific 2022.

Central Intelligence Agency (CIA), Office of Public Affairs, Washington, DC, 20505, USA, (703) 482-0623, https://www.cia.gov; The World Factbook.

The Economist Group: Economist Intelligence Unit (EIU), 900 3rd Ave., 16th Fl., New York, NY, 10022, USA, (212) 541-0500, americas@eiu.com, https://www.eiu.com; Bangladesh Country Report.

Infoplease, c/o Sandbox Networks, Inc., 1 Lincoln St., 24th Fl., Boston, MA, 02111, USA, https://www.infoplease.com; Countries of the World.

International Labour Organization (ILO), 4 Rte. des Morillons, Geneva, CH-1211, SWI, ilo@ilo.org, https://www.ilo.org; NORMLEX Information System on International Labour Standards.

Palgrave Macmillan, 1 New York Plaza, Ste. 4500, New York, NY, 10004-1562, USA, (800) 777-4643, orders@palgrave.com, https://www.palgrave.com/us; The Statesman's Yearbook, 2023.

Routledge - Taylor & Francis Group, 6000 Broken Sound Pkwy. NW, Ste. 300, Boca Raton, FL, 33487, USA, (800) 634-1420, (800) 634-7064, orders@taylorandfrancis.com, https://www.routledge.com/; The Europa World Year Book 2022.

UK Data Service, University of Essex, Wivenhoe Park, Colchester, Essex, CO4 3SQ, GBR, https://ukdataservice.ac.uk/; International Aggregate Data.

United Nations Department of Economic and Social Affairs (DESA), Population Division, 2 United Nations Plz., Rm. DC2-1950, New York, NY, 10017, USA, (212) 963-3209, (212) 963-2147, population@un.org, https://www.un.org/

development/desa/pd/; Revision of World Urbanization Prospects and World Population Ageing 2020 Highlights.

United Nations Development Programme (UNDP), One United Nations Plz., New York, NY, 10017, USA, (212) 906-5000, (212) 906-5001, https://www.undp.org; Human Development Report 2021-2022.

United Nations Economic and Social Commission for Asia and the Pacific (ESCAP), United Nations Building, Rajadamnern Nok Ave., Bangkok, 10200, THA, https://www.unescap.org/; Asia-Pacific Development Journal.

United Nations Statistics Division (UNSD), United Nations Plz., New York, NY, 10017, USA, (800) 253-9646, (212) 963-9851, statistics@un.org, https://unstats.un.org; Statistical Yearbook of the United Nations 2021 and World Statistics Pocketbook 2021.

The World Bank, 1818 H St. NW, Washington, DC, 20433, USA, (202) 473-1000, (202) 477-6391, eds03@worldbank.org, https://www.worldbank.org/; Bangladesh (report); The Global Findex Database 2021; and World Development Report 2022: Finance for an Equitable Recovery.

BANGLADESH-POPULATION DENSITY

Central Intelligence Agency (CIA), Office of Public Affairs, Washington, DC, 20505, USA, (703) 482-0623, https://www.cia.gov; The World Factbook.

Palgrave Macmillan, 1 New York Plaza, Ste. 4500, New York, NY, 10004-1562, USA, (800) 777-4643, orders@palgrave.com, https://www.palgrave.com/us; The Statesman's Yearbook, 2023.

Routledge - Taylor & Francis Group, 6000 Broken Sound Pkwy. NW, Ste. 300, Boca Raton, FL, 33487, USA, (800) 634-1420, (800) 634-7064, orders@taylorandfrancis.com, https://www.routledge.com/; The Europa World Year Book 2022.

The World Bank, 1818 H St. NW, Washington, DC, 20433, USA, (202) 473-1000, (202) 477-6391, eds03@worldbank.org, https://www.worldbank.org/; Bangladesh (report) and World Development Report 2022: Finance for an Equitable Recovery.

BANGLADESH-POSTAL SERVICE

Palgrave Macmillan, 1 New York Plaza, Ste. 4500, New York, NY, 10004-1562, USA, (800) 777-4643, orders@palgrave.com, https://www.palgrave.com/us; The Statesman's Yearbook, 2023.

BANGLADESH-POWER RESOURCES

Euromonitor International, Inc., 1 N Dearborn St., Ste. 1700, Chicago, IL, 60602, USA, (312) 922-1115, (312) 922-1157, info-usa@euromonitor.com, https://www.euromonitor.com/; Geographies.

International Energy Agency (IEA), 9 Rue de la Federation, Paris, 75739, FRA, info@iea.org, https://www.iea.org/; World Energy Outlook 2021.

Palgrave Macmillan, 1 New York Plaza, Ste. 4500, New York, NY, 10004-1562, USA, (800) 777-4643, orders@palgrave.com, https://www.palgrave.com/us; The Statesman's Yearbook, 2023.

U.S. Energy Information Administration (EIA), 1000 Independence Ave. SW, Washington, DC, 20585, USA, (202) 586-8800, infoctr@eia.gov, https://www.eia.gov; International Energy Outlook 2021.

United Nations Economic and Social Commission for Asia and the Pacific (ESCAP), United Nations Building, Rajadamnern Nok Ave., Bangkok, 10200, THA, https://www.unescap.org/; Asia-Pacific Development Journal and SDG Gateway Data Explorer.

United Nations Food and Agricultural Organization (FAO), 2121 K St., Ste. 800B, Washington, DC, 20037, USA, (202) 653-2400 (Dial from U.S.), (202) 653-5760 (Fax from U.S.), fao-hq@fao.org, https://www.fao.org; The State of Food and Agriculture (SOFA) 2022.

United Nations Statistics Division (UNSD), United Nations Plz., New York, NY, 10017, USA, (800) 253-9646, (212) 963-9851, statistics@un.org, https://unstats.un.org; Statistical Yearbook of the United Nations 2021 and World Statistics Pocketbook 2021.

The World Bank, 1818 H St. NW, Washington, DC, 20433, USA, (202) 473-1000, (202) 477-6391, eds03@worldbank.org, https://www.worldbank.org/; World Development Report 2022: Finance for an Equitable Recovery.

BANGLADESH-PRICES

Asian Development Bank (ADB), 6 ADB Ave., Mandaluyong City, 1550, PHL, information@adb.org, https://www.adb.org/; Key Indicators for Asia and the Pacific 2022.

Euromonitor International, Inc., 1 N Dearborn St., Ste. 1700, Chicago, IL, 60602, USA, (312) 922-1115, (312) 922-1157, info-usa@euromonitor.com, https://www.euromonitor.com/; Geographies.

International Monetary Fund (IMF), 700 19th St. NW, Washington, DC, 20431, USA, (202) 623-7000, (202) 623-4661, publications@imf.org, https://www.imf.org; International Financial Statistics (IFS).

The World Bank, 1818 H St. NW, Washington, DC, 20433, USA, (202) 473-1000, (202) 477-6391, eds03@worldbank.org, https://www.worldbank.org/; Bangladesh (report).

BANGLADESH-PUBLIC HEALTH

Euromonitor International, Inc., 1 N Dearborn St., Ste. 1700, Chicago, IL, 60602, USA, (312) 922-1115, (312) 922-1157, info-usa@euromonitor.com, https://www.euromonitor.com/; Geographies.

Organisation of Islamic Cooperation (OIC), Statistical, Economic and Social Research and Training Centre for Islamic Countries (SESRIC), Kudus Cad. No. 9, Diplomatik Site, Ankara, 06450, TUR, statistics@sesric.org, https://www.sesric.org/; OIC Statistics (OICStat) Database.

Palgrave Macmillan, 1 New York Plaza, Ste. 4500, New York, NY, 10004-1562, USA, (800) 777-4643, orders@palgrave.com, https://www.palgrave.com/us; The Statesman's Yearbook, 2023.

U.S. Census Bureau, 4600 Silver Hill Rd., Washington, DC, 20233, USA, (301) 763-4636, (800) 923-8282, https://www.census.gov; HIV/AIDS Surveillance Data Base.

UNICEF, 3 United Nations Plz., New York, NY, 10017, USA, (212) 303-7984, (917) 244-2215, https://www.unicef.org; The State of the World's Children 2023.

United Nations Department of Economic and Social Affairs (DESA), Population Division, 2 United Nations Plz., Rm. DC2-1950, New York, NY, 10017, USA, (212) 963-3209, (212) 963-2147, population@un.org, https://www.un.org/development/desa/pd/; World Fertility Data 2019.

United Nations Development Programme (UNDP), One United Nations Plz., New York, NY, 10017, USA, (212) 906-5000, (212) 906-5001, https://www.undp.org; Human Development Report 2021-2022.

United Nations Economic and Social Commission for Asia and the Pacific (ESCAP), United Nations Building, Rajadamnern Nok Ave., Bangkok, 10200, THA, https://www.unescap.org/; Asia-Pacific Development Journal.

United Nations Statistics Division (UNSD), United Nations Plz., New York, NY, 10017, USA, (800) 253-9646, (212) 963-9851, statistics@un.org, https://unstats.un.org; Millennium Development Goal Indicators and Statistical Yearbook of the United Nations 2021.

The World Bank, 1818 H St. NW, Washington, DC, 20433, USA, (202) 473-1000, (202) 477-6391, eds03@worldbank.org, https://www.worldbank.org/; Bangladesh (report).

World Health Organization (WHO), Ave. Appia 20, Geneva, CH-1211, SWI, (202) 974-3000 (Telephone in U.S.), publications@who.int, https://www.who.int/; Global Health Observatory (GHO) and Health Statistics and Information Systems.

BANGLADESH-PUBLISHERS AND PUBLISHING

Palgrave Macmillan, 1 New York Plaza, Ste. 4500, New York, NY, 10004-1562, USA, (800) 777-4643, orders@palgrave.com, https://www.palgrave.com/us; The Statesman's Yearbook, 2023.

Routledge - Taylor & Francis Group, 6000 Broken Sound Pkwy. NW, Ste. 300, Boca Raton, FL, 33487, USA, (800) 634-1420, (800) 634-7064, orders@taylorandfrancis.com, https://www.routledge.com/; The Europa World Year Book 2022.

BANGLADESH-RAILROADS

Janes, USA, (703) 574-7580, (888) 977-1519, customer.care@janes.com, https://www.janes.com; Janes World Railways 2021-2022.

Palgrave Macmillan, 1 New York Plaza, Ste. 4500, New York, NY, 10004-1562, USA, (800) 777-4643, orders@palgrave.com, https://www.palgrave.com/us; The Statesman's Yearbook, 2023.

Routledge - Taylor & Francis Group, 6000 Broken Sound Pkwy. NW, Ste. 300, Boca Raton, FL, 33487, USA, (800) 634-1420, (800) 634-7064, orders@taylorandfrancis.com, https://www.routledge.com/; The Europa World Year Book 2022.

United Nations Statistics Division (UNSD), United Nations Plz., New York, NY, 10017, USA, (800) 253-9646, (212) 963-9851, statistics@un.org, https://unstats.un.org; Statistical Yearbook of the United Nations 2021.

BANGLADESH-RELIGION

Central Intelligence Agency (CIA), Office of Public Affairs, Washington, DC, 20505, USA, (703) 482-0623, https://www.cia.gov; The World Factbook.

Palgrave Macmillan, 1 New York Plaza, Ste. 4500, New York, NY, 10004-1562, USA, (800) 777-4643, orders@palgrave.com, https://www.palgrave.com/us; The Statesman's Yearbook, 2023.

BANGLADESH-RETAIL TRADE

Euromonitor International, Inc., 1 N Dearborn St., Ste. 1700, Chicago, IL, 60602, USA, (312) 922-1115, (312) 922-1157, info-usa@euromonitor.com, https://www.euromonitor.com/; Geographies.

BANGLADESH-RICE PRODUCTION

See BANGLADESH-CROPS

BANGLADESH-RUBBER INDUSTRY AND TRADE

International Rubber Study Group (IRSG), 51 Changi Business Park Central 2, Unit No. 6, 486066, SGP, https://www.rubberstudy.org; Monthly Rubber Bulletin (MRB); Rubber Industry Report; Rubber Statistical Bulletin; and World Rubber Industry Report (WRIO).

BANGLADESH-SHIPPING

Routledge - Taylor & Francis Group, 6000 Broken Sound Pkwy. NW, Ste. 300, Boca Raton, FL, 33487, USA, (800) 634-1420, (800) 634-7064, orders@taylorandfrancis.com, https://www.routledge.com/; The Europa World Year Book 2022.

S&P Global, IHS Markit, 15 Inverness Way E, Englewood, CO, 80112, USA, (800) 447-2273, (800) 854-7179, https://ihsmarkit.com; IHS Maritime World Shipbuilding Statistics; Journal of Commerce; Lloyd's Register of Ships 2021-2022; and Maritime Portal Desktop.

United Nations Statistics Division (UNSD), United Nations Plz., New York, NY, 10017, USA, (800) 253-9646, (212) 963-9851, statistics@un.org, https://unstats.un.org; Statistical Yearbook of the United Nations 2021.

BANGLADESH-STEEL PRODUCTION

See BANGLADESH-MINERAL INDUSTRIES

BANGLADESH-SUGAR PRODUCTION

See BANGLADESH-CROPS

BANGLADESH-SULPHUR PRODUCTION

See BANGLADESH-MINERAL INDUSTRIES

BANGLADESH-TAXATION

The World Bank, 1818 H St. NW, Washington, DC, 20433, USA, (202) 473-1000, (202) 477-6391, eds03@worldbank.org, https://www.worldbank.org/; World Development Indicators (WDI) 2022.

BANGLADESH-TEA PRODUCTION

See BANGLADESH-CROPS

BANGLADESH-TELEPHONE

Palgrave Macmillan, 1 New York Plaza, Ste. 4500, New York, NY, 10004-1562, USA, (800) 777-4643, orders@palgrave.com, https://www.palgrave.com/us; The Statesman's Yearbook, 2023.

Routledge - Taylor & Francis Group, 6000 Broken Sound Pkwy. NW, Ste. 300, Boca Raton, FL, 33487, USA, (800) 634-1420, (800) 634-7064, orders@taylorandfrancis.com, https://www.routledge.com/; The Europa World Year Book 2022.

United Nations Statistics Division (UNSD), United Nations Plz., New York, NY, 10017, USA, (800) 253-9646, (212) 963-9851, statistics@un.org, https://unstats.un.org; World Statistics Pocketbook 2021.

BANGLADESH-TEXTILE INDUSTRY

Palgrave Macmillan, 1 New York Plaza, Ste. 4500, New York, NY, 10004-1562, USA, (800) 777-4643, orders@palgrave.com, https://www.palgrave.com/us; The Statesman's Yearbook, 2023.

United Nations Statistics Division (UNSD), United Nations Plz., New York, NY, 10017, USA, (800) 253-9646, (212) 963-9851, statistics@un.org, https://unstats.un.org; Statistical Yearbook of the United Nations 2021.

BANGLADESH-TOBACCO INDUSTRY

United Nations Statistics Division (UNSD), United Nations Plz., New York, NY, 10017, USA, (800) 253-9646, (212) 963-9851, statistics@un.org, https://unstats.un.org; Statistical Yearbook of the United Nations 2021.

BANGLADESH-TOURISM

Euromonitor International, Inc., 1 N Dearborn St., Ste. 1700, Chicago, IL, 60602, USA, (312) 922-1115, (312) 922-1157, info-usa@euromonitor.com, https://www.euromonitor.com/; Geographies.

Organisation of Islamic Cooperation (OIC), Statistical, Economic and Social Research and Training Centre for Islamic Countries (SESRIC), Kudus Cad. No. 9, Diplomatik Site, Ankara, 06450, TUR, statistics@sesric.org, https://www.sesric.org/; International Tourism in the OIC Countries: Prospects and Challenges, 2020 and OIC Statistics (OICStat) Database.

Palgrave Macmillan, 1 New York Plaza, Ste. 4500, New York, NY, 10004-1562, USA, (800) 777-4643, orders@palgrave.com, https://www.palgrave.com/us; The Statesman's Yearbook, 2023.

Routledge - Taylor & Francis Group, 6000 Broken Sound Pkwy. NW, Ste. 300, Boca Raton, FL, 33487, USA, (800) 634-1420, (800) 634-7064, orders@taylorandfrancis.com, https://www.routledge.com/; The Europa World Year Book 2022.

United Nations Statistics Division (UNSD), United Nations Plz., New York, NY, 10017, USA, (800) 253-9646, (212) 963-9851, statistics@un.org, https://unstats.un.org; Statistical Yearbook of the United Nations 2021.

United Nations World Tourism Organization (UNWTO), Calle Poeta Joan Maragall 42, Madrid, 28020, SPA, info@unwto.org, https://www.unwto.org/; Yearbook of Tourism Statistics, 2021 Edition.

The World Bank, 1818 H St. NW, Washington, DC, 20433, USA, (202) 473-1000, (202) 477-6391, eds03@worldbank.org, https://www.worldbank.org/; Bangladesh (report).

BANGLADESH-TRADE

See BANGLADESH-INTERNATIONAL TRADE

BANGLADESH-TRANSPORTATION

Central Intelligence Agency (CIA), Office of Public Affairs, Washington, DC, 20505, USA, (703) 482-0623, https://www.cia.gov; The World Factbook.

Euromonitor International, Inc., 1 N Dearborn St., Ste. 1700, Chicago, IL, 60602, USA, (312) 922-1115, (312) 922-1157, info-usa@euromonitor.com, https://www.euromonitor.com/; Geographies.

Organisation of Islamic Cooperation (OIC), Statistical, Economic and Social Research and Training Centre for Islamic Countries (SESRIC), Kudus Cad. No. 9, Diplomatik Site, Ankara, 06450, TUR, statistics@sesric.org, https://www.sesric.org/; OIC Statistics (OICStat) Database.

Palgrave Macmillan, 1 New York Plaza, Ste. 4500, New York, NY, 10004-1562, USA, (800) 777-4643, orders@palgrave.com, https://www.palgrave.com/us; The Statesman's Yearbook, 2023.

Routledge - Taylor & Francis Group, 6000 Broken Sound Pkwy. NW, Ste. 300, Boca Raton, FL, 33487, USA, (800) 634-1420, (800) 634-7064, orders@taylorandfrancis.com, https://www.routledge.com/; The Europa World Year Book 2022.

United Nations Economic and Social Commission for Asia and the Pacific (ESCAP), United Nations Building, Rajadamnern Nok Ave., Bangkok, 10200, THA, https://www.unescap.org/; SDG Gateway Data Explorer.

The World Bank, 1818 H St. NW, Washington, DC, 20433, USA, (202) 473-1000, (202) 477-6391, eds03@worldbank.org, https://www.worldbank.org/; Bangladesh (report).

BANGLADESH-UNEMPLOYMENT

International Labour Organization (ILO), 4 Rte. des Morillons, Geneva, CH-1211, SWI, ilo@ilo.org, https://www.ilo.org; NORMLEX Information System on International Labour Standards.

Palgrave Macmillan, 1 New York Plaza, Ste. 4500, New York, NY, 10004-1562, USA, (800) 777-4643, orders@palgrave.com, https://www.palgrave.com/us; The Statesman's Yearbook, 2023.

BANGLADESH-VITAL STATISTICS

Palgrave Macmillan, 1 New York Plaza, Ste. 4500, New York, NY, 10004-1562, USA, (800) 777-4643, orders@palgrave.com, https://www.palgrave.com/us; The Statesman's Yearbook, 2023.

U.S. Census Bureau, 4600 Silver Hill Rd., Washington, DC, 20233, USA, (301) 763-4636, (800) 923-8282, https://www.census.gov; HIV/AIDS Surveillance Data Base.

United Nations Department of Economic and Social Affairs (DESA), Population Division, 2 United Nations Plz., Rm. DC2-1950, New York, NY, 10017, USA, (212) 963-3209, (212) 963-2147, population@un.org, https://www.un.org/development/desa/pd/; World Contraceptive Use 2021: Estimates and Projections of Family Planning Indicators and World Marriage Data 2019.

United Nations Statistics Division (UNSD), United Nations Plz., New York, NY, 10017, USA, (800) 253-9646, (212) 963-9851, statistics@un.org, https://unstats.un.org; Statistical Yearbook of the United Nations 2021.

BANGLADESH-WAGES

International Labour Organization (ILO), 4 Rte. des Morillons, Geneva, CH-1211, SWI, ilo@ilo.org, https://www.ilo.org; NORMLEX Information System on International Labour Standards.

United Nations Economic and Social Commission for Asia and the Pacific (ESCAP), United Nations Building, Rajadamnern Nok Ave., Bangkok, 10200, THA, https://www.unescap.org/; SDG Gateway Data Explorer.

United Nations Statistics Division (UNSD), United Nations Plz., New York, NY, 10017, USA, (800) 253-9646, (212) 963-9851, statistics@un.org, https://unstats.un.org; Statistical Yearbook of the United Nations 2021.

The World Bank, 1818 H St. NW, Washington, DC, 20433, USA, (202) 473-1000, (202) 477-6391, eds03@worldbank.org, https://www.worldbank.org/; Bangladesh (report).

BANGLADESH-WEATHER

See BANGLADESH-CLIMATE

BANGLADESH-WHEAT PRODUCTION

See BANGLADESH-CROPS

BANGLADESH-WOOL PRODUCTION

See BANGLADESH-TEXTILE INDUSTRY

BANKRUPTCY

Administrative Office of the United States Courts, One Columbus Cir. NE, Washington, DC, 20544, USA, (202) 502-2600, https://www.uscourts.gov; Bankruptcy Abuse Prevention and Consumer Protection Act Report 2021; Bankruptcy Filings Statistics; Civil Justice Reform Act Report 2022; Judicial Business of the U.S. Courts, 2022; and Statistical Tables for the Federal Judiciary 2022.

Dun & Bradstreet (D&B) Corporation, 5335 Gate Parkway, Jacksonville, FL, 32256, USA, (904) 648-6350, (800) 526-9018, https://www.dnb.com/; 2020 Global Bankruptcy Report.

BANKS, COMMERCIAL

Bank for International Settlements (BIS), Postfach, Basel, CH-4002, SWI, email@bis.org, https://www.bis.org/; BIS Statistics Explorer.

Bank of England, Statistics Division, Threadneedle St., London, EC2R 8AH, GBR, enquiries@bankofengland.co.uk, https://www.bankofengland.co.uk/statistics; BIS Statistics Explorer.

European Central Bank (ECB), Frankfurt am Main, D-60640, GER, info@ecb.europa.eu, https://www.ecb.europa.eu; Monetary Financial Institutions (MFI) Interest Rate Statistics.

Federal Deposit Insurance Corporation (FDIC), 550 17th St. NW, Washington, DC, 20429-9990, USA, (877) 275-3342, (800) 925-4618 (TTY), publicinfo@fdic.gov, https://www.fdic.gov; Annual Report of the FDIC, 2021; BankFind Suite; FDIC State Profiles; Quarterly Banking Profile (QBP); Statistics at a Glance; and Statistics on Depository Institutions (SDI).

The Federal Reserve Bank of Richmond, PO Box 27622, Richmond, VA, 23261, USA, (804) 697-8000, (410) 576-3300, https://www.richmondfed.org/; Economic Quarterly.

Rainforest Action Network (RAN), 425 Bush St., Ste. 300, San Francisco, CA, 94108, USA, (415) 398-4404, (415) 398-2732, answers@ran.org, https://www.ran.org/; Fracking Fiasco: The Banks that Fueled the U.S. Shale Bust.

U.S. Census Bureau, 4600 Silver Hill Rd., Washington, DC, 20233, USA, (301) 763-4636, (800) 923-8282, https://www.census.gov; County Business Patterns (CBP) 2020.

U.S. Census Bureau, Center for Economic Studies (CES), 4600 Silver Hill Rd., Washington, DC, 20233, USA, (301) 763-6460, (301) 763-5935, ces.contacts@census.gov, https://www.census.gov/programs-surveys/ces.html; Management of Companies and Enterprises, 2017 Economic Census.

U.S. Department of Justice (DOJ), Federal Bureau of Investigation (FBI), 935 Pennsylvania Ave. NW, Washington, DC, 20535-0001, USA, (202) 324-3000, https://www.fbi.gov/; Bank Crime Statistics 2020.

UK Finance, 1 Angel Court, 5th Fl., London, EC2R 7HJ, GBR, membership@ukfinance.org.uk, https://www.ukfinance.org.uk/; UK Payment Markets 2021.

BANKS, COMMERCIAL-CHECKING ACCOUNTS

Board of Governors of the Federal Reserve System, Constitution Ave. NW, Washington, DC, 20551,

USA, (202) 452-3000, (202) 263-4869 (TDD), https://www.federalreserve.gov; Federal Reserve Bulletin.

ValuePenguin, 600 3rd Ave. , 8th Fl., New York, NY, 10016, USA, media@valuepenguin.com, https://www.valuepenguin.com; Average U.S. Checking Account Balance 2022: A Demographic Breakdown.

BANKS, COMMERCIAL-CONSUMER CREDIT FINANCE RATES

Board of Governors of the Federal Reserve System, Constitution Ave. NW, Washington, DC, 20551, USA, (202) 452-3000, (202) 263-4869 (TDD), https://www.federalreserve.gov; Federal Reserve Bulletin.

BANKS, COMMERCIAL-CREDIT CARDS

Federal Deposit Insurance Corporation (FDIC), 550 17th St. NW, Washington, DC, 20429-9990, USA, (877) 275-3342, (800) 925-4618 (TTY), publicinfo@fdic.gov, https://www.fdic.gov; Annual Report of the FDIC, 2021; FDIC State Profiles; and Quarterly Banking Profile (QBP).

Federal Financial Institutions Examination Council (FFIEC), 3501 Fairfax Dr., L. William Seidman Center, Mail Stop: B-7081a, Arlington, VA, 22226-3550 , USA, (703) 516-5590, https://www.ffiec.gov/; Uniform Bank Performance Report (UBPR).

The Nilson Report, PO Box 50539, Santa Barbara, CA, 93150, USA, (805) 684-8800, (805) 684-8825, info@nilsonreport.com, https://www.nilsonreport.com; The Nilson Report and The World's Top Card Issuers and Merchant Acquirers.

BANKS, COMMERCIAL-DEBIT CARDS

The Nilson Report, PO Box 50539, Santa Barbara, CA, 93150, USA, (805) 684-8800, (805) 684-8825, info@nilsonreport.com, https://www.nilsonreport.com; The Nilson Report and The World's Top Card Issuers and Merchant Acquirers.

BANKS, COMMERCIAL-DELINQUENCY RATES, REPOSSESSIONS, LOANS

Federal Financial Institutions Examination Council (FFIEC), 3501 Fairfax Dr., L. William Seidman Center, Mail Stop: B-7081a, Arlington, VA, 22226-3550 , USA, (703) 516-5590, https://www.ffiec.gov/; Uniform Bank Performance Report (UBPR).

BANKS, COMMERCIAL-DEPOSITS

Federal Deposit Insurance Corporation (FDIC), 550 17th St. NW, Washington, DC, 20429-9990, USA, (877) 275-3342, (800) 925-4618 (TTY), publicinfo@fdic.gov, https://www.fdic.gov; Annual Report of the FDIC, 2021; FDIC State Profiles; and Quarterly Banking Profile (QBP).

BANKS, COMMERCIAL-EARNINGS

U.S. Census Bureau, 4600 Silver Hill Rd., Washington, DC, 20233, USA, (301) 763-4636, (800) 923-8282, https://www.census.gov; County Business Patterns (CBP) 2020.

U.S. Department of Labor (DOL), Bureau of Labor Statistics (BLS), Postal Square Bldg., 2 Massachusetts Ave. NE, Washington, DC, 20212-0001, USA, (202) 691-5200, (202) 691-7890, blsdata_staff@bls.gov, https://www.bls.gov; Current Employment Statistics (CES).

BANKS, COMMERCIAL-EMPLOYEES

U.S. Census Bureau, 4600 Silver Hill Rd., Washington, DC, 20233, USA, (301) 763-4636, (800) 923-8282, https://www.census.gov; County Business Patterns (CBP) 2020.

U.S. Department of Labor (DOL), Bureau of Labor Statistics (BLS), Postal Square Bldg., 2 Massachusetts Ave. NE, Washington, DC, 20212-0001, USA, (202) 691-5200, (202) 691-7890, blsdata_staff@bls.gov, https://www.bls.gov; Current Employment Statistics (CES).

BANKS, COMMERCIAL-FEDERAL RESERVE BANKS

Board of Governors of the Federal Reserve System, Constitution Ave. NW, Washington, DC, 20551, USA, (202) 452-3000, (202) 263-4869 (TDD), https://www.federalreserve.gov; Annual Report of the FED, 2021.

Federal Deposit Insurance Corporation (FDIC), 550 17th St. NW, Washington, DC, 20429-9990, USA, (877) 275-3342, (800) 925-4618 (TTY), publicinfo@fdic.gov, https://www.fdic.gov; FDIC State Profiles.

BANKS, COMMERCIAL-FINANCES

Board of Governors of the Federal Reserve System, Constitution Ave. NW, Washington, DC, 20551, USA, (202) 452-3000, (202) 263-4869 (TDD), https://www.federalreserve.gov; Financial Accounts of the United States 2023.

Federal Deposit Insurance Corporation (FDIC), 550 17th St. NW, Washington, DC, 20429-9990, USA, (877) 275-3342, (800) 925-4618 (TTY), publicinfo@fdic.gov, https://www.fdic.gov; Annual Report of the FDIC, 2021; FDIC State Profiles; and Quarterly Banking Profile (QBP).

Federal Financial Institutions Examination Council (FFIEC), 3501 Fairfax Dr., L. William Seidman Center, Mail Stop: B-7081a, Arlington, VA, 22226-3550 , USA, (703) 516-5590, https://www.ffiec.gov/; Annual Report of the FFIEC 2021 and Reports of Condition and Income (Call Reports).

Financial Industry Regulatory Authority (FINRA), 1735 K St. NW, Washington, DC, 20006, USA, (301) 590-6500, https://www.finra.org; Margin Statistics.

Rainforest Action Network (RAN), 425 Bush St., Ste. 300, San Francisco, CA, 94108, USA, (415) 398-4404, (415) 398-2732, answers@ran.org, https://www.ran.org/; Banking on Climate Chaos: Fossil Fuel Finance Report, 2021.

Reserve Bank of Australia (RBA), GPO Box 3947, Sydney, NSW, 2001, AUS, rbainfo@rba.gov.au, https://www.rba.gov.au/; Reserve Bank of Australia Annual Report 2021 and Statement on Monetary Policy.

BANKS, COMMERCIAL-FLOW OF FUNDS

Board of Governors of the Federal Reserve System, Constitution Ave. NW, Washington, DC, 20551, USA, (202) 452-3000, (202) 263-4869 (TDD), https://www.federalreserve.gov; Financial Accounts of the United States 2023.

BANKS, COMMERCIAL-FOREIGN BANKING OFFICES IN THE UNITED STATES

Board of Governors of the Federal Reserve System, Constitution Ave. NW, Washington, DC, 20551, USA, (202) 452-3000, (202) 263-4869 (TDD), https://www.federalreserve.gov; Structure and Share Data for U.S. Banking Offices of Foreign Entities 2022.

BANKS, COMMERCIAL-GROSS DOMESTIC PRODUCT

U.S. Department of Commerce (DOC), Bureau of Economic Analysis (BEA), 4600 Silver Hill Rd., Washington, DC, 20233, USA, (301) 278-9004, customerservice@bea.gov, https://www.bea.gov; Survey of Current Business (SCB).

BANKS, COMMERCIAL-HOME EQUITY LOANS

Board of Governors of the Federal Reserve System, Constitution Ave. NW, Washington, DC, 20551, USA, (202) 452-3000, (202) 263-4869 (TDD), https://www.federalreserve.gov; Federal Reserve Bulletin.

Federal Deposit Insurance Corporation (FDIC), 550 17th St. NW, Washington, DC, 20429-9990, USA, (877) 275-3342, (800) 925-4618 (TTY), publicinfo@fdic.gov, https://www.fdic.gov; Annual Report of the FDIC, 2021; FDIC State Profiles; and Quarterly Banking Profile (QBP).

BANKS, COMMERCIAL-INDIVIDUAL RETIREMENT ACCOUNTS-401K PLANS

Investment Company Institute (ICI), 1401 H St. NW, Ste. 1200, Washington, DC, 20005, USA, (202) 326-5800, doug.richardson@ici.org, https://www.ici.org/; Quarterly 529 Plan Program Statistics and Quarterly Retirement Market Data.

BANKS, COMMERCIAL-INDUSTRIAL SAFETY

U.S. Department of Labor (DOL), Bureau of Labor Statistics (BLS), Postal Square Bldg., 2 Massachusetts Ave. NE, Washington, DC, 20212-0001, USA, (202) 691-5200, (202) 691-7890, blsdata_staff@bls.gov, https://www.bls.gov; Injuries, Illnesses, and Fatalities (IIF).

BANKS, COMMERCIAL-INSURED BANKS

Federal Deposit Insurance Corporation (FDIC), 550 17th St. NW, Washington, DC, 20429-9990, USA, (877) 275-3342, (800) 925-4618 (TTY), publicinfo@fdic.gov, https://www.fdic.gov; FDIC State Profiles.

BANKS, COMMERCIAL-PRODUCTIVITY

U.S. Department of Labor (DOL), Bureau of Labor Statistics (BLS), Postal Square Bldg., 2 Massachusetts Ave. NE, Washington, DC, 20212-0001, USA, (202) 691-5200, (202) 691-7890, blsdata_staff@bls.gov, https://www.bls.gov; Productivity.

BANKS, COMMERCIAL-PROFITS

Federal Deposit Insurance Corporation (FDIC), 550 17th St. NW, Washington, DC, 20429-9990, USA, (877) 275-3342, (800) 925-4618 (TTY), publicinfo@fdic.gov, https://www.fdic.gov; Annual Report of the FDIC, 2021; FDIC State Profiles; and Quarterly Banking Profile (QBP).

BANKS, COMMERCIAL-ROBBERY

U.S. Department of Justice (DOJ), Federal Bureau of Investigation (FBI), 935 Pennsylvania Ave. NW, Washington, DC, 20535-0001, USA, (202) 324-3000, https://www.fbi.gov/; Crime in the United States 2019.

BANKS, COMMERCIAL-STOCK AND BOND PRICES AND YIELDS

Global Financial Data, Inc., 29122 Rancho Viejo Rd., Ste. 215, San Juan Capistrano, CA, 92675, USA, (949) 542-4200, sales@globalfinancialdata.com, https://globalfinancialdata.com/; GFD Finaeon: U.S. Equities Database.

BARBADOS-NATIONAL STATISTICAL OFFICE

Barbados Statistical Service (BSS), Baobab Tower Bldg., 5th Fl., Warrens, BRB, (246) 535-2600 (Dial from U.S.), (246) 535-2601 (Dial from U.S.), (246) 421-8294 (Fax from U.S.), barstats@caribsurf.com, https://www.gov.bb/Departments/statistical-services; National Data Reports (Barbados).

BARBADOS-AGRICULTURE

The Economist Group: Economist Intelligence Unit (EIU), 900 3rd Ave., 16th Fl., New York, NY, 10022, USA, (212) 541-0500, americas@eiu.com, https://www.eiu.com; Barbados Country Report.

Euromonitor International, Inc., 1 N Dearborn St., Ste. 1700, Chicago, IL, 60602, USA, (312) 922-1115, (312) 922-1157, info-usa@euromonitor.com, https://www.euromonitor.com/; Geographies.

Inter-American Development Bank (IDB), 1300 New York Ave. NW, Washington, DC, 20577, USA, (202) 623-1000, (202) 623-3096, https://www.iadb.org/en; Latin Macro Watch (LMW).

Palgrave Macmillan, 1 New York Plaza, Ste. 4500, New York, NY, 10004-1562, USA, (800) 777-4643, orders@palgrave.com, https://www.palgrave.com/us; The Statesman's Yearbook, 2023.

Routledge - Taylor & Francis Group, 6000 Broken Sound Pkwy. NW, Ste. 300, Boca Raton, FL, 33487, USA, (800) 634-1420, (800) 634-7064,

orders@taylorandfrancis.com, https://www.routledge.com/; The Europa World Year Book 2022.

United Nations Food and Agricultural Organization (FAO), 2121 K St., Ste. 800B, Washington, DC, 20037, USA, (202) 653-2400 (Dial from U.S.), (202) 653-5760 (Fax from U.S.), fao-hq@fao.org, https://www.fao.org; AQUASTAT and The State of Food and Agriculture (SOFA) 2022.

United Nations Statistics Division (UNSD), United Nations Plz., New York, NY, 10017, USA, (800) 253-9646, (212) 963-9851, statistics@un.org, https://unstats.un.org; Statistical Yearbook of the United Nations 2021.

The World Bank, 1818 H St. NW, Washington, DC, 20433, USA, (202) 473-1000, (202) 477-6391, eds03@worldbank.org, https://www.worldbank.org/; World Development Indicators (WDI) 2022.

BARBADOS-AIRLINES

International Civil Aviation Organization (ICAO), 999 Robert-Bourassa Blvd., Montreal, QC, H3C 5H7, CAN, (514) 954-8219 (Dial from U.S.), (514) 954-6077 (Fax from U.S.), icaohq@icao.int, https://www.icao.int; ICAO Regional Reports.

Palgrave Macmillan, 1 New York Plaza, Ste. 4500, New York, NY, 10004-1562, USA, (800) 777-4643, orders@palgrave.com, https://www.palgrave.com/us; The Statesman's Yearbook, 2023.

Routledge - Taylor & Francis Group, 6000 Broken Sound Pkwy. NW, Ste. 300, Boca Raton, FL, 33487, USA, (800) 634-1420, (800) 634-7064, orders@taylorandfrancis.com, https://www.routledge.com/; The Europa World Year Book 2022.

BARBADOS-ALUMINUM PRODUCTION

See BARBADOS-MINERAL INDUSTRIES

BARBADOS-ARMED FORCES

Central Intelligence Agency (CIA), Office of Public Affairs, Washington, DC, 20505, USA, (703) 482-0623, https://www.cia.gov; The World Factbook.

Stockholm International Peace Research Institute (SIPRI), Signalistgatan 9, Stockholm, SE 169 72, SWE, https://www.sipri.org/; SIPRI Arms Transfers Database and SIPRI Military Expenditure Database.

BARBADOS-BALANCE OF PAYMENTS

Inter-American Development Bank (IDB), 1300 New York Ave. NW, Washington, DC, 20577, USA, (202) 623-1000, (202) 623-3096, https://www.iadb.org/en; Latin Macro Watch (LMW).

International Monetary Fund (IMF), 700 19th St. NW, Washington, DC, 20431, USA, (202) 623-7000, (202) 623-4661, publications@imf.org, https://www.imf.org; Balance of Payments Statistics: Annual Report 2021.

Routledge - Taylor & Francis Group, 6000 Broken Sound Pkwy. NW, Ste. 300, Boca Raton, FL, 33487, USA, (800) 634-1420, (800) 634-7064, orders@taylorandfrancis.com, https://www.routledge.com/; The Europa World Year Book 2022.

United Nations Conference on Trade and Development (UNCTAD), Palais des Nations, Geneva, 1211, SWI, (212) 963-6896, unctadinfo@unctad.org, https://unctad.org; Handbook of Statistics 2021.

United Nations Economic Commission for Latin America and the Caribbean (ECLAC), Casilla 179-D, Santiago, 7630412, CHL, (202) 596-3713, prensa@cepal.org, https://www.cepal.org/en; Economic Survey of Latin America and the Caribbean 2021: Labour Dynamics and Employment Policies for Sustainable and Inclusive Recovery Beyond the COVID-19 Crisis.

The World Bank, 1818 H St. NW, Washington, DC, 20433, USA, (202) 473-1000, (202) 477-6391, eds03@worldbank.org, https://www.worldbank.org/; World Development Indicators (WDI) 2022.

BARBADOS-BANKS AND BANKING

Euromonitor International, Inc., 1 N Dearborn St., Ste. 1700, Chicago, IL, 60602, USA, (312) 922-1115, (312) 922-1157, info-usa@euromonitor.com, https://www.euromonitor.com/; Geographies.

Inter-American Development Bank (IDB), 1300 New York Ave. NW, Washington, DC, 20577, USA, (202) 623-1000, (202) 623-3096, https://www.iadb.org/en; Latin Macro Watch (LMW).

International Monetary Fund (IMF), 700 19th St. NW, Washington, DC, 20431, USA, (202) 623-7000, (202) 623-4661, publications@imf.org, https://www.imf.org; International Financial Statistics (IFS).

Routledge - Taylor & Francis Group, 6000 Broken Sound Pkwy. NW, Ste. 300, Boca Raton, FL, 33487, USA, (800) 634-1420, (800) 634-7064, orders@taylorandfrancis.com, https://www.routledge.com/; The Europa World Year Book 2022.

BARBADOS-BARLEY PRODUCTION

See BARBADOS-CROPS

BARBADOS-BONDS

Inter-American Development Bank (IDB), 1300 New York Ave. NW, Washington, DC, 20577, USA, (202) 623-1000, (202) 623-3096, https://www.iadb.org/en; Latin Macro Watch (LMW).

BARBADOS-BROADCASTING

Central Intelligence Agency (CIA), Office of Public Affairs, Washington, DC, 20505, USA, (703) 482-0623, https://www.cia.gov; The World Factbook.

Euromonitor International, Inc., 1 N Dearborn St., Ste. 1700, Chicago, IL, 60602, USA, (312) 922-1115, (312) 922-1157, info-usa@euromonitor.com, https://www.euromonitor.com/; Geographies.

Palgrave Macmillan, 1 New York Plaza, Ste. 4500, New York, NY, 10004-1562, USA, (800) 777-4643, orders@palgrave.com, https://www.palgrave.com/us; The Statesman's Yearbook, 2023.

UNESCO Institute for Statistics, C.P 250 Succursale H, Montreal, QC, H3G 2K8, CAN, (514) 343-6880 (Dial from U.S.), (514) 343-5740 (Fax from U.S.), uis.publications@unesco.org, http://uis.unesco.org/; UIS.Stat.

WRTH Publications Limited, PO Box 290, Oxford, OX2 7FT, GBR, sales@wrth.com, https://www.wrth.com; World Radio TV Handbook 2023.

BARBADOS-BUDGET

Central Intelligence Agency (CIA), Office of Public Affairs, Washington, DC, 20505, USA, (703) 482-0623, https://www.cia.gov; The World Factbook.

BARBADOS-BUSINESS

Global Entrepreneurship Monitor (GEM), Babson College, 231 Forest St., Babson Park, MA, 02457, USA, (781) 235-1200, info@gemconsortium.org, https://www.gemconsortium.org/; Barbados Economy Profile.

Inter-American Development Bank (IDB), 1300 New York Ave. NW, Washington, DC, 20577, USA, (202) 623-1000, (202) 623-3096, https://www.iadb.org/en; Latin Macro Watch (LMW).

BARBADOS-CAPITAL INVESTMENTS

Inter-American Development Bank (IDB), 1300 New York Ave. NW, Washington, DC, 20577, USA, (202) 623-1000, (202) 623-3096, https://www.iadb.org/en; Latin Macro Watch (LMW).

BARBADOS-CHILDBIRTH-STATISTICS

The World Bank, 1818 H St. NW, Washington, DC, 20433, USA, (202) 473-1000, (202) 477-6391, eds03@worldbank.org, https://www.worldbank.org/; World Development Indicators (WDI) 2022.

BARBADOS-CLIMATE

Palgrave Macmillan, 1 New York Plaza, Ste. 4500, New York, NY, 10004-1562, USA, (800) 777-4643, orders@palgrave.com, https://www.palgrave.com/us; The Statesman's Yearbook, 2023.

BARBADOS-COAL PRODUCTION

See BARBADOS-MINERAL INDUSTRIES

BARBADOS-COFFEE

See BARBADOS-CROPS

BARBADOS-COMMERCE

Palgrave Macmillan, 1 New York Plaza, Ste. 4500, New York, NY, 10004-1562, USA, (800) 777-4643, orders@palgrave.com, https://www.palgrave.com/us; The Statesman's Yearbook, 2023.

UK Data Service, University of Essex, Wivenhoe Park, Colchester, Essex, CO4 3SQ, GBR, https://ukdataservice.ac.uk/; International Aggregate Data.

BARBADOS-COMMODITY EXCHANGES

Barchart, 209 W Jackson Blvd., 2nd Fl., Chicago, IL, 60606, USA, (877) 247-4394, commodities@barchart.com, https://www.barchart.com/cmdty; The cmdty Yearbook 2023; cmdtyStats: Commodity Statistics and Fundamental Data; cmdtyView: Commodity Index; and Commodity Data and Prices.

International Monetary Fund (IMF), 700 19th St. NW, Washington, DC, 20431, USA, (202) 623-7000, (202) 623-4661, publications@imf.org, https://www.imf.org; IMF Primary Commodity Prices.

BARBADOS-CONSTRUCTION INDUSTRY

Inter-American Development Bank (IDB), 1300 New York Ave. NW, Washington, DC, 20577, USA, (202) 623-1000, (202) 623-3096, https://www.iadb.org/en; Latin Macro Watch (LMW).

United Nations Statistics Division (UNSD), United Nations Plz., New York, NY, 10017, USA, (800) 253-9646, (212) 963-9851, statistics@un.org, https://unstats.un.org; Statistical Yearbook of the United Nations 2021.

BARBADOS-CONSUMER PRICE INDEXES

Routledge - Taylor & Francis Group, 6000 Broken Sound Pkwy. NW, Ste. 300, Boca Raton, FL, 33487, USA, (800) 634-1420, (800) 634-7064, orders@taylorandfrancis.com, https://www.routledge.com/; The Europa World Year Book 2022.

BARBADOS-CONSUMPTION (ECONOMICS)

Inter-American Development Bank (IDB), 1300 New York Ave. NW, Washington, DC, 20577, USA, (202) 623-1000, (202) 623-3096, https://www.iadb.org/en; Latin Macro Watch (LMW).

BARBADOS-COPPER INDUSTRY AND TRADE

See BARBADOS-MINERAL INDUSTRIES

BARBADOS-CORN INDUSTRY

See BARBADOS-CROPS

BARBADOS-COTTON

See BARBADOS-CROPS

BARBADOS-CROPS

International Monetary Fund (IMF), 700 19th St. NW, Washington, DC, 20431, USA, (202) 623-7000, (202) 623-4661, publications@imf.org, https://www.imf.org; International Financial Statistics (IFS).

Palgrave Macmillan, 1 New York Plaza, Ste. 4500, New York, NY, 10004-1562, USA, (800) 777-4643, orders@palgrave.com, https://www.palgrave.com/us; The Statesman's Yearbook, 2023.

United Nations Food and Agricultural Organization (FAO), 2121 K St., Ste. 800B, Washington, DC, 20037, USA, (202) 653-2400 (Dial from U.S.), (202) 653-5760 (Fax from U.S.), fao-hq@fao.org, https://www.fao.org; The State of Food and Agriculture (SOFA) 2022.

BARBADOS-CUSTOMS ADMINISTRATION

Inter-American Development Bank (IDB), 1300 New York Ave. NW, Washington, DC, 20577, USA, (202) 623-1000, (202) 623-3096, https://www.iadb.org/en; Latin Macro Watch (LMW).

BARBADOS-DAIRY PROCESSING

Palgrave Macmillan, 1 New York Plaza, Ste. 4500, New York, NY, 10004-1562, USA, (800) 777-4643, orders@palgrave.com, https://www.palgrave.com/us; The Statesman's Yearbook, 2023.

United Nations Food and Agricultural Organization (FAO), 2121 K St., Ste. 800B, Washington, DC, 20037, USA, (202) 653-2400 (Dial from U.S.), (202) 653-5760 (Fax from U.S.), fao-hq@fao.org, https://www.fao.org; The State of Food and Agriculture (SOFA) 2022.

BARBADOS-DEBTS, EXTERNAL

Inter-American Development Bank (IDB), 1300 New York Ave. NW, Washington, DC, 20577, USA, (202) 623-1000, (202) 623-3096, https://www.iadb.org/en; Latin Macro Watch (LMW).

Palgrave Macmillan, 1 New York Plaza, Ste. 4500, New York, NY, 10004-1562, USA, (800) 777-4643, orders@palgrave.com, https://www.palgrave.com/us; The Statesman's Yearbook, 2023.

United Nations Economic Commission for Latin America and the Caribbean (ECLAC), Casilla 179-D, Santiago, 7630412, CHL, (202) 596-3713, prensa@cepal.org, https://www.cepal.org/en; Economic Survey of Latin America and the Caribbean 2021: Labour Dynamics and Employment Policies for Sustainable and Inclusive Recovery Beyond the COVID-19 Crisis.

The World Bank, 1818 H St. NW, Washington, DC, 20433, USA, (202) 473-1000, (202) 477-6391, eds03@worldbank.org, https://www.worldbank.org/; Global Financial Development Report 2019-2020: Bank Regulation and Supervision a Decade after the Global Financial Crisis and World Development Indicators (WDI) 2022.

BARBADOS-DEFENSE EXPENDITURES

See BARBADOS-ARMED FORCES

BARBADOS-DIAMONDS

See BARBADOS-MINERAL INDUSTRIES

BARBADOS-DISPOSABLE INCOME

Inter-American Development Bank (IDB), 1300 New York Ave. NW, Washington, DC, 20577, USA, (202) 623-1000, (202) 623-3096, https://www.iadb.org/en; Latin Macro Watch (LMW).

BARBADOS-ECONOMIC ASSISTANCE

Inter-American Development Bank (IDB), 1300 New York Ave. NW, Washington, DC, 20577, USA, (202) 623-1000, (202) 623-3096, https://www.iadb.org/en; Latin Macro Watch (LMW).

United Nations Statistics Division (UNSD), United Nations Plz., New York, NY, 10017, USA, (800) 253-9646, (212) 963-9851, statistics@un.org, https://unstats.un.org; Statistical Yearbook of the United Nations 2021.

BARBADOS-ECONOMIC CONDITIONS

Bernan Press, 15250 NBN Way, Bldg. C, Blue Ridge Summit, PA, 17214, USA, (301) 459-2255, (800) 865-3457, (800) 865-3450, customercare@bernan.com, https://rowman.com/Page/Bernan; World Economic Outlook, April 2022.

Central Intelligence Agency (CIA), Office of Public Affairs, Washington, DC, 20505, USA, (703) 482-0623, https://www.cia.gov; The World Factbook.

The Economist Group: Economist Intelligence Unit (EIU), 900 3rd Ave., 16th Fl., New York, NY, 10022, USA, (212) 541-0500, americas@eiu.com, https://www.eiu.com; Barbados Country Report.

Euromonitor International, Inc., 1 N Dearborn St., Ste. 1700, Chicago, IL, 60602, USA, (312) 922-1115, (312) 922-1157, info-usa@euromonitor.com, https://www.euromonitor.com/; Geographies.

Global Entrepreneurship Monitor (GEM), Babson College, 231 Forest St., Babson Park, MA, 02457, USA, (781) 235-1200, info@gemconsortium.org, https://www.gemconsortium.org/; Barbados Economy Profile.

Inter-American Development Bank (IDB), 1300 New York Ave. NW, Washington, DC, 20577, USA, (202) 623-1000, (202) 623-3096, https://www.iadb.org/en; Latin Macro Watch (LMW).

International Monetary Fund (IMF), 700 19th St. NW, Washington, DC, 20431, USA, (202) 623-7000, (202) 623-4661, publications@imf.org, https://www.imf.org; IMF Data and World Economic Outlook.

Palgrave Macmillan, 1 New York Plaza, Ste. 4500, New York, NY, 10004-1562, USA, (800) 777-4643, orders@palgrave.com, https://www.palgrave.com/us; The Statesman's Yearbook, 2023.

Routledge - Taylor & Francis Group, 6000 Broken Sound Pkwy. NW, Ste. 300, Boca Raton, FL, 33487, USA, (800) 634-1420, (800) 634-7064, orders@taylorandfrancis.com, https://www.routledge.com/; The Europa World Year Book 2022.

United Nations Economic Commission for Latin America and the Caribbean (ECLAC), Casilla 179-D, Santiago, 7630412, CHL, (202) 596-3713, prensa@cepal.org, https://www.cepal.org/en; CEPALSTAT; Economic Survey of Latin America and the Caribbean 2021: Labour Dynamics and Employment Policies for Sustainable and Inclusive Recovery Beyond the COVID-19 Crisis; and Foreign Direct Investment in Latin America and the Caribbean 2022.

United Nations Statistics Division (UNSD), United Nations Plz., New York, NY, 10017, USA, (800) 253-9646, (212) 963-9851, statistics@un.org, https://unstats.un.org; World Statistics Pocketbook 2021.

The World Bank, 1818 H St. NW, Washington, DC, 20433, USA, (202) 473-1000, (202) 477-6391, eds03@worldbank.org, https://www.worldbank.org/; Caribbean (report); Global Economic Monitor (GEM); Global Economic Prospects, June 2022; and The Global Findex Database 2021.

BARBADOS-EDUCATION

Euromonitor International, Inc., 1 N Dearborn St., Ste. 1700, Chicago, IL, 60602, USA, (312) 922-1115, (312) 922-1157, info-usa@euromonitor.com, https://www.euromonitor.com/; Geographies.

Infoplease, c/o Sandbox Networks, Inc., 1 Lincoln St., 24th Fl., Boston, MA, 02111, USA, https://www.infoplease.com; Countries of the World.

Palgrave Macmillan, 1 New York Plaza, Ste. 4500, New York, NY, 10004-1562, USA, (800) 777-4643, orders@palgrave.com, https://www.palgrave.com/us; The Statesman's Yearbook, 2023.

Routledge - Taylor & Francis Group, 6000 Broken Sound Pkwy. NW, Ste. 300, Boca Raton, FL, 33487, USA, (800) 634-1420, (800) 634-7064, orders@taylorandfrancis.com, https://www.routledge.com/; The Europa World Year Book 2022.

UNESCO Institute for Statistics, C.P 250 Succursale H, Montreal, QC, H3G 2K8, CAN, (514) 343-6880 (Dial from U.S.), (514) 343-5740 (Fax from U.S.), uis.publications@unesco.org, http://uis.unesco.org/; Literacy and UIS.Stat.

United Nations Statistics Division (UNSD), United Nations Plz., New York, NY, 10017, USA, (800) 253-9646, (212) 963-9851, statistics@un.org, https://unstats.un.org; Millennium Development Goal Indicators.

The World Bank, 1818 H St. NW, Washington, DC, 20433, USA, (202) 473-1000, (202) 477-6391, eds03@worldbank.org, https://www.worldbank.org/; World Development Indicators (WDI) 2022.

BARBADOS-ELECTRICITY

Inter-American Development Bank (IDB), 1300 New York Ave. NW, Washington, DC, 20577, USA, (202) 623-1000, (202) 623-3096, https://www.iadb.org/en; Latin Macro Watch (LMW).

International Energy Agency (IEA), 9 Rue de la Federation, Paris, 75739, FRA, info@iea.org, https://www.iea.org/; World Energy Outlook 2021.

United Nations Statistics Division (UNSD), United Nations Plz., New York, NY, 10017, USA, (800) 253-9646, (212) 963-9851, statistics@un.org, https://unstats.un.org; Statistical Yearbook of the United Nations 2021.

BARBADOS-EMPLOYMENT

International Labour Organization (ILO), 4 Rte. des Morillons, Geneva, CH-1211, SWI, ilo@ilo.org, https://www.ilo.org; NORMLEX Information System on International Labour Standards.

UK Data Service, University of Essex, Wivenhoe Park, Colchester, Essex, CO4 3SQ, GBR, https://ukdataservice.ac.uk/; International Aggregate Data.

United Nations Statistics Division (UNSD), United Nations Plz., New York, NY, 10017, USA, (800) 253-9646, (212) 963-9851, statistics@un.org, https://unstats.un.org; Statistical Yearbook of the United Nations 2021.

BARBADOS-ENERGY INDUSTRIES

Enerdata, 47 avenue Alsace Lorraine, Grenoble, 38027, FRA, (332) 216-4534, research@enerdata.net, https://www.enerdata.net; World Refinery Database.

United Nations Statistics Division (UNSD), United Nations Plz., New York, NY, 10017, USA, (800) 253-9646, (212) 963-9851, statistics@un.org, https://unstats.un.org; Statistical Yearbook of the United Nations 2021.

BARBADOS-ENVIRONMENTAL CONDITIONS

DSI Data Service & Information, Xantener Strasse 51a, Rheinberg, D-47495, GER, dsi@dsidata.com, https://www.dsidata.com/; Global Environmental Database.

The Economist Group: Economist Intelligence Unit (EIU), 900 3rd Ave., 16th Fl., New York, NY, 10022, USA, (212) 541-0500, americas@eiu.com, https://www.eiu.com; Barbados Country Report.

United Nations Economic Commission for Latin America and the Caribbean (ECLAC), Casilla 179-D, Santiago, 7630412, CHL, (202) 596-3713, prensa@cepal.org, https://www.cepal.org/en; CEPALSTAT.

United Nations Statistics Division (UNSD), United Nations Plz., New York, NY, 10017, USA, (800) 253-9646, (212) 963-9851, statistics@un.org, https://unstats.un.org; World Statistics Pocketbook 2021.

BARBADOS-EXPENDITURES, PUBLIC

Inter-American Development Bank (IDB), 1300 New York Ave. NW, Washington, DC, 20577, USA, (202) 623-1000, (202) 623-3096, https://www.iadb.org/en; Latin Macro Watch (LMW).

BARBADOS-EXPORTS

Central Intelligence Agency (CIA), Office of Public Affairs, Washington, DC, 20505, USA, (703) 482-0623, https://www.cia.gov; The World Factbook.

The Economist Group: Economist Intelligence Unit (EIU), 900 3rd Ave., 16th Fl., New York, NY, 10022, USA, (212) 541-0500, americas@eiu.com, https://www.eiu.com; Barbados Country Report.

Inter-American Development Bank (IDB), 1300 New York Ave. NW, Washington, DC, 20577, USA, (202) 623-1000, (202) 623-3096, https://www.iadb.org/en; Latin Macro Watch (LMW).

International Monetary Fund (IMF), 700 19th St. NW, Washington, DC, 20431, USA, (202) 623-7000, (202) 623-4661, publications@imf.org, https://www.imf.org; Direction of Trade Statistics (DOTS) and International Financial Statistics (IFS).

S&P Global, IHS Markit, 15 Inverness Way E, Englewood, CO, 80112, USA, (800) 447-2273, (800) 854-7179, https://ihsmarkit.com; Global Trade Atlas (GTA).

United Nations Conference on Trade and Development (UNCTAD), Palais des Nations, Geneva, 1211, SWI, (212) 963-6896, unctadinfo@unctad.org, https://unctad.org; Handbook of Statistics 2021.

BARBADOS-FERTILITY, HUMAN

Central Intelligence Agency (CIA), Office of Public Affairs, Washington, DC, 20505, USA, (703) 482-0623, https://www.cia.gov; The World Factbook.

BARBADOS-FERTILIZER INDUSTRY

United Nations Food and Agricultural Organization (FAO), 2121 K St., Ste. 800B, Washington, DC, 20037, USA, (202) 653-2400 (Dial from U.S.), (202) 653-5760 (Fax from U.S.), fao-hq@fao.org, https://www.fao.org; The State of Food and Agriculture (SOFA) 2022.

The World Bank, 1818 H St. NW, Washington, DC, 20433, USA, (202) 473-1000, (202) 477-6391, eds03@worldbank.org, https://www.worldbank.org/; World Development Indicators (WDI) 2022.

BARBADOS-FETAL MORTALITY

See BARBADOS-MORTALITY

BARBADOS-FINANCE

Inter-American Development Bank (IDB), 1300 New York Ave. NW, Washington, DC, 20577, USA, (202) 623-1000, (202) 623-3096, https://www.iadb.org/en; Latin Macro Watch (LMW).

Stockholm International Peace Research Institute (SIPRI), Signalistgatan 9, Stockholm, SE 169 72, SWE, https://www.sipri.org/; SIPRI Arms Transfers Database and SIPRI Military Expenditure Database.

United Nations Statistics Division (UNSD), United Nations Plz., New York, NY, 10017, USA, (800) 253-9646, (212) 963-9851, statistics@un.org, https://unstats.un.org; Statistical Yearbook of the United Nations 2021.

BARBADOS-FINANCE, PUBLIC

Bernan Press, 15250 NBN Way, Bldg. C, Blue Ridge Summit, PA, 17214, USA, (301) 459-2255, (800) 865-3457, (800) 865-3450, customercare@bernan.com, https://rowman.com/Page/Bernan; National Accounts Statistics: Analysis of Main Aggregates 2020.

The Economist Group: Economist Intelligence Unit (EIU), 900 3rd Ave., 16th Fl., New York, NY, 10022, USA, (212) 541-0500, americas@eiu.com, https://www.eiu.com; Barbados Country Report.

Inter-American Development Bank (IDB), 1300 New York Ave. NW, Washington, DC, 20577, USA, (202) 623-1000, (202) 623-3096, https://www.iadb.org/en; Latin Macro Watch (LMW).

International Monetary Fund (IMF), 700 19th St. NW, Washington, DC, 20431, USA, (202) 623-7000, (202) 623-4661, publications@imf.org, https://www.imf.org; International Financial Statistics (IFS) and Regional Economic Outlook.

Palgrave Macmillan, 1 New York Plaza, Ste. 4500, New York, NY, 10004-1562, USA, (800) 777-4643, orders@palgrave.com, https://www.palgrave.com/us; The Statesman's Yearbook, 2023.

Routledge - Taylor & Francis Group, 6000 Broken Sound Pkwy. NW, Ste. 300, Boca Raton, FL, 33487, USA, (800) 634-1420, (800) 634-7064, orders@taylorandfrancis.com, https://www.routledge.com/; The Europa World Year Book 2022.

United Nations Statistics Division (UNSD), United Nations Plz., New York, NY, 10017, USA, (800) 253-9646, (212) 963-9851, statistics@un.org, https://unstats.un.org; National Accounts Main Aggregates Database and National Accounts Statistics: Main Aggregates and Detailed Tables.

BARBADOS-FISHERIES

Inter-American Development Bank (IDB), 1300 New York Ave. NW, Washington, DC, 20577, USA, (202) 623-1000, (202) 623-3096, https://www.iadb.org/en; Latin Macro Watch (LMW).

Palgrave Macmillan, 1 New York Plaza, Ste. 4500, New York, NY, 10004-1562, USA, (800) 777-4643, orders@palgrave.com, https://www.palgrave.com/us; The Statesman's Yearbook, 2023.

United Nations Food and Agricultural Organization (FAO), 2121 K St., Ste. 800B, Washington, DC, 20037, USA, (202) 653-2400 (Dial from U.S.), (202) 653-5760 (Fax from U.S.), fao-hq@fao.org, https://www.fao.org; FAO Yearbook of Fishery and Aquaculture Statistics 2019; Fishery Statistical Collections Global Capture Production; FishStatJ; and The State of Food and Agriculture (SOFA) 2022.

United Nations Statistics Division (UNSD), United Nations Plz., New York, NY, 10017, USA, (800) 253-9646, (212) 963-9851, statistics@un.org, https://unstats.un.org; Statistical Yearbook of the United Nations 2021.

BARBADOS-FOOD

United Nations Food and Agricultural Organization (FAO), 2121 K St., Ste. 800B, Washington, DC, 20037, USA, (202) 653-2400 (Dial from U.S.), (202) 653-5760 (Fax from U.S.), fao-hq@fao.org, https://www.fao.org; The State of Food and Agriculture (SOFA) 2022.

BARBADOS-FOREIGN EXCHANGE RATES

Inter-American Development Bank (IDB), 1300 New York Ave. NW, Washington, DC, 20577, USA, (202) 623-1000, (202) 623-3096, https://www.iadb.org/en; Latin Macro Watch (LMW).

International Monetary Fund (IMF), 700 19th St. NW, Washington, DC, 20431, USA, (202) 623-7000, (202) 623-4661, publications@imf.org, https://www.imf.org; International Financial Statistics (IFS).

BARBADOS-FORESTS AND FORESTRY

Inter-American Development Bank (IDB), 1300 New York Ave. NW, Washington, DC, 20577, USA, (202) 623-1000, (202) 623-3096, https://www.iadb.org/en; Latin Macro Watch (LMW).

UNESCO Institute for Statistics, C.P 250 Succursale H, Montreal, QC, H3G 2K8, CAN, (514) 343-6880 (Dial from U.S.), (514) 343-5740 (Fax from U.S.), uis.publications@unesco.org, http://uis.unesco.org/; UIS.Stat.

United Nations Food and Agricultural Organization (FAO), 2121 K St., Ste. 800B, Washington, DC, 20037, USA, (202) 653-2400 (Dial from U.S.), (202) 653-5760 (Fax from U.S.), fao-hq@fao.org, https://www.fao.org; FAO Yearbook of Forest Products 2019 and The State of Food and Agriculture (SOFA) 2022.

United Nations Statistics Division (UNSD), United Nations Plz., New York, NY, 10017, USA, (800) 253-9646, (212) 963-9851, statistics@un.org, https://unstats.un.org; Statistical Yearbook of the United Nations 2021.

BARBADOS-GAS PRODUCTION

See BARBADOS-MINERAL INDUSTRIES

BARBADOS-GOLD INDUSTRY

The World Bank, 1818 H St. NW, Washington, DC, 20433, USA, (202) 473-1000, (202) 477-6391, eds03@worldbank.org, https://www.worldbank.org/; World Development Indicators (WDI) 2022.

BARBADOS-GOLD PRODUCTION

See BARBADOS-MINERAL INDUSTRIES

BARBADOS-GROSS DOMESTIC PRODUCT

The Economist Group: Economist Intelligence Unit (EIU), 900 3rd Ave., 16th Fl., New York, NY, 10022, USA, (212) 541-0500, americas@eiu.com, https://www.eiu.com; Barbados Country Report.

Inter-American Development Bank (IDB), 1300 New York Ave. NW, Washington, DC, 20577, USA, (202) 623-1000, (202) 623-3096, https://www.iadb.org/en; Latin Macro Watch (LMW).

Routledge - Taylor & Francis Group, 6000 Broken Sound Pkwy. NW, Ste. 300, Boca Raton, FL, 33487, USA, (800) 634-1420, (800) 634-7064, orders@taylorandfrancis.com, https://www.routledge.com/; The Europa World Year Book 2022.

United Nations Statistics Division (UNSD), United Nations Plz., New York, NY, 10017, USA, (800) 253-9646, (212) 963-9851, statistics@un.org, https://unstats.un.org; Statistical Yearbook of the United Nations 2021.

The World Bank, 1818 H St. NW, Washington, DC, 20433, USA, (202) 473-1000, (202) 477-6391, eds03@worldbank.org, https://www.worldbank.org/; World Development Indicators (WDI) 2022.

BARBADOS-GROSS NATIONAL PRODUCT

Inter-American Development Bank (IDB), 1300 New York Ave. NW, Washington, DC, 20577, USA, (202) 623-1000, (202) 623-3096, https://www.iadb.org/en; Latin Macro Watch (LMW).

Palgrave Macmillan, 1 New York Plaza, Ste. 4500, New York, NY, 10004-1562, USA, (800) 777-4643, orders@palgrave.com, https://www.palgrave.com/us; The Statesman's Yearbook, 2023.

United Nations Statistics Division (UNSD), United Nations Plz., New York, NY, 10017, USA, (800) 253-9646, (212) 963-9851, statistics@un.org, https://unstats.un.org; Statistical Yearbook of the United Nations 2021.

The World Bank, 1818 H St. NW, Washington, DC, 20433, USA, (202) 473-1000, (202) 477-6391, eds03@worldbank.org, https://www.worldbank.org/; World Development Indicators (WDI) 2022.

BARBADOS-HOUSING

Euromonitor International, Inc., 1 N Dearborn St., Ste. 1700, Chicago, IL, 60602, USA, (312) 922-1115, (312) 922-1157, info-usa@euromonitor.com, https://www.euromonitor.com/; Geographies.

BARBADOS-ILLITERATE PERSONS

UNESCO Institute for Statistics, C.P 250 Succursale H, Montreal, QC, H3G 2K8, CAN, (514) 343-6880 (Dial from U.S.), (514) 343-5740 (Fax from U.S.), uis.publications@unesco.org, http://uis.unesco.org/; UIS.Stat.

BARBADOS-IMPORTS

Central Intelligence Agency (CIA), Office of Public Affairs, Washington, DC, 20505, USA, (703) 482-0623, https://www.cia.gov; The World Factbook.

The Economist Group: Economist Intelligence Unit (EIU), 900 3rd Ave., 16th Fl., New York, NY, 10022, USA, (212) 541-0500, americas@eiu.com, https://www.eiu.com; Barbados Country Report.

Inter-American Development Bank (IDB), 1300 New York Ave. NW, Washington, DC, 20577, USA, (202) 623-1000, (202) 623-3096, https://www.iadb.org/en; Latin Macro Watch (LMW).

International Monetary Fund (IMF), 700 19th St. NW, Washington, DC, 20431, USA, (202) 623-7000, (202) 623-4661, publications@imf.org, https://www.imf.org; Direction of Trade Statistics (DOTS) and International Financial Statistics (IFS).

S&P Global, IHS Markit, 15 Inverness Way E, Englewood, CO, 80112, USA, (800) 447-2273, (800) 854-7179, https://ihsmarkit.com; Global Trade Atlas (GTA).

United Nations Conference on Trade and Development (UNCTAD), Palais des Nations, Geneva, 1211, SWI, (212) 963-6896, unctadinfo@unctad.org, https://unctad.org; Handbook of Statistics 2021.

BARBADOS-INDUSTRIES

Central Intelligence Agency (CIA), Office of Public Affairs, Washington, DC, 20505, USA, (703) 482-0623, https://www.cia.gov; The World Factbook.

The Economist Group: Economist Intelligence Unit (EIU), 900 3rd Ave., 16th Fl., New York, NY, 10022, USA, (212) 541-0500, americas@eiu.com, https://www.eiu.com; Barbados Country Report.

Euromonitor International, Inc., 1 N Dearborn St., Ste. 1700, Chicago, IL, 60602, USA, (312) 922-1115, (312) 922-1157, info-usa@euromonitor.com, https://www.euromonitor.com/; Geographies.

International Labour Organization (ILO), 4 Rte. des Morillons, Geneva, CH-1211, SWI, ilo@ilo.org, https://www.ilo.org; NORMLEX Information System on International Labour Standards.

Palgrave Macmillan, 1 New York Plaza, Ste. 4500, New York, NY, 10004-1562, USA, (800) 777-4643, orders@palgrave.com, https://www.palgrave.com/us; The Statesman's Yearbook, 2023.

Routledge - Taylor & Francis Group, 6000 Broken Sound Pkwy. NW, Ste. 300, Boca Raton, FL, 33487, USA, (800) 634-1420, (800) 634-7064, orders@taylorandfrancis.com, https://www.routledge.com/; The Europa World Year Book 2022.

United Nations Economic Commission for Latin America and the Caribbean (ECLAC), Casilla 179-D, Santiago, 7630412, CHL, (202) 596-3713, prensa@cepal.org, https://www.cepal.org/en; Economic Survey of Latin America and the Caribbean 2021: Labour Dynamics and Employment Policies for Sustainable and Inclusive Recovery Beyond the COVID-19 Crisis.

United Nations Industrial Development Organization (UNIDO), 1 United Nations Plz., Rm. DC1-1118, New York, NY, 10017, USA, (212) 963-6890, (212) 963 6885, (212) 963-7904, office.newyork@unido.org, https://www.unido.org/; Industrial Statistics Databases and International Yearbook of Industrial Statistics 2021.

The World Bank, 1818 H St. NW, Washington, DC, 20433, USA, (202) 473-1000, (202) 477-6391, eds03@worldbank.org, https://www.worldbank.org/; World Development Indicators (WDI) 2022.

BARBADOS-INFANT AND MATERNAL MORTALITY

See BARBADOS-MORTALITY

BARBADOS-INFLATION (FINANCE)

United Nations Economic Commission for Latin America and the Caribbean (ECLAC), Casilla 179-D, Santiago, 7630412, CHL, (202) 596-3713, prensa@cepal.org, https://www.cepal.org/en; Economic Survey of Latin America and the Caribbean 2021: Labour Dynamics and Employment Policies for Sustainable and Inclusive Recovery Beyond the COVID-19 Crisis.

BARBADOS-INTEREST RATES

Inter-American Development Bank (IDB), 1300 New York Ave. NW, Washington, DC, 20577, USA, (202) 623-1000, (202) 623-3096, https://www.iadb.org/en; Latin Macro Watch (LMW).

United Nations Statistics Division (UNSD), United Nations Plz., New York, NY, 10017, USA, (800) 253-9646, (212) 963-9851, statistics@un.org, https://unstats.un.org; Statistical Yearbook of the United Nations 2021.

BARBADOS-INTERNAL REVENUE

Inter-American Development Bank (IDB), 1300 New York Ave. NW, Washington, DC, 20577, USA, (202) 623-1000, (202) 623-3096, https://www.iadb.org/en; Latin Macro Watch (LMW).

BARBADOS-INTERNATIONAL FINANCE

Inter-American Development Bank (IDB), 1300 New York Ave. NW, Washington, DC, 20577, USA, (202) 623-1000, (202) 623-3096, https://www.iadb.org/en; Latin Macro Watch (LMW).

BARBADOS-INTERNATIONAL LIQUIDITY

Inter-American Development Bank (IDB), 1300 New York Ave. NW, Washington, DC, 20577, USA, (202) 623-1000, (202) 623-3096, https://www.iadb.org/en; Latin Macro Watch (LMW).

BARBADOS-INTERNATIONAL TRADE

The Economist Group: Economist Intelligence Unit (EIU), 900 3rd Ave., 16th Fl., New York, NY, 10022, USA, (212) 541-0500, americas@eiu.com, https://www.eiu.com; Barbados Country Report.

Euromonitor International, Inc., 1 N Dearborn St., Ste. 1700, Chicago, IL, 60602, USA, (312) 922-1115, (312) 922-1157, info-usa@euromonitor.com, https://www.euromonitor.com/; Geographies.

Inter-American Development Bank (IDB), 1300 New York Ave. NW, Washington, DC, 20577, USA, (202) 623-1000, (202) 623-3096, https://www.iadb.org/en; Latin Macro Watch (LMW).

Palgrave Macmillan, 1 New York Plaza, Ste. 4500, New York, NY, 10004-1562, USA, (800) 777-4643, orders@palgrave.com, https://www.palgrave.com/us; The Statesman's Yearbook, 2023.

Routledge - Taylor & Francis Group, 6000 Broken Sound Pkwy. NW, Ste. 300, Boca Raton, FL, 33487, USA, (800) 634-1420, (800) 634-7064, orders@taylorandfrancis.com, https://www.routledge.com/; The Europa World Year Book 2022.

United Nations Conference on Trade and Development (UNCTAD), Palais des Nations, Geneva, 1211, SWI, (212) 963-6896, unctadinfo@unctad.org, https://unctad.org; Trade and Development Report 2021.

United Nations Economic Commission for Latin America and the Caribbean (ECLAC), Casilla 179-D, Santiago, 7630412, CHL, (202) 596-3713, prensa@cepal.org, https://www.cepal.org/en; Economic Survey of Latin America and the Caribbean 2021: Labour Dynamics and Employment Policies for Sustainable and Inclusive Recovery Beyond the COVID-19 Crisis.

United Nations Food and Agricultural Organization (FAO), 2121 K St., Ste. 800B, Washington, DC, 20037, USA, (202) 653-2400 (Dial from U.S.), (202) 653-5760 (Fax from U.S.), fao-hq@fao.org, https://www.fao.org; The State of Food and Agriculture (SOFA) 2022.

United Nations Statistics Division (UNSD), United Nations Plz., New York, NY, 10017, USA, (800) 253-9646, (212) 963-9851, statistics@un.org, https://unstats.un.org; International Trade Statistics Yearbook 2020 and Statistical Yearbook of the United Nations 2021.

The World Bank, 1818 H St. NW, Washington, DC, 20433, USA, (202) 473-1000, (202) 477-6391, eds03@worldbank.org, https://www.worldbank.org/; World Development Indicators (WDI) 2022.

World Trade Organization (WTO), Ctre. William Rappard, Rue de Lausanne 154, Case postale, Geneva, CH-1211, SWI, enquiries@wto.org, https://www.wto.org; World Trade Statistical Review 2022.

BARBADOS-INTERNET USERS

International Telecommunication Union (ITU), Place des Nations, Geneva, CH-1211, SWI, itumail@itu.int, https://www.itu.int; Global Connectivity Report 2022; World Telecommunication/ICT Indicators Database 2021; and Yearbook of Statistics 2019.

BARBADOS-INVESTMENTS

Inter-American Development Bank (IDB), 1300 New York Ave. NW, Washington, DC, 20577, USA, (202) 623-1000, (202) 623-3096, https://www.iadb.org/en; Latin Macro Watch (LMW).

BARBADOS-IRRIGATION

Inter-American Development Bank (IDB), 1300 New York Ave. NW, Washington, DC, 20577, USA, (202) 623-1000, (202) 623-3096, https://www.iadb.org/en; Latin Macro Watch (LMW).

BARBADOS-LABOR

Central Intelligence Agency (CIA), Office of Public Affairs, Washington, DC, 20505, USA, (703) 482-0623, https://www.cia.gov; The World Factbook.

Euromonitor International, Inc., 1 N Dearborn St., Ste. 1700, Chicago, IL, 60602, USA, (312) 922-1115, (312) 922-1157, info-usa@euromonitor.com, https://www.euromonitor.com/; Geographies.

International Labour Organization (ILO), 4 Rte. des Morillons, Geneva, CH-1211, SWI, ilo@ilo.org, https://www.ilo.org; NORMLEX Information System on International Labour Standards.

Palgrave Macmillan, 1 New York Plaza, Ste. 4500, New York, NY, 10004-1562, USA, (800) 777-4643, orders@palgrave.com, https://www.palgrave.com/us; The Statesman's Yearbook, 2023.

United Nations Food and Agricultural Organization (FAO), 2121 K St., Ste. 800B, Washington, DC, 20037, USA, (202) 653-2400 (Dial from U.S.), (202) 653-5760 (Fax from U.S.), fao-hq@fao.org, https://www.fao.org; The State of Food and Agriculture (SOFA) 2022.

The World Bank, 1818 H St. NW, Washington, DC, 20433, USA, (202) 473-1000, (202) 477-6391, eds03@worldbank.org, https://www.worldbank.org/; World Development Indicators (WDI) 2022.

BARBADOS-LAND USE

Inter-American Development Bank (IDB), 1300 New York Ave. NW, Washington, DC, 20577, USA, (202) 623-1000, (202) 623-3096, https://www.iadb.org/en; Latin Macro Watch (LMW).

United Nations Statistics Division (UNSD), United Nations Plz., New York, NY, 10017, USA, (800) 253-9646, (212) 963-9851, statistics@un.org, https://unstats.un.org; Millennium Development Goal Indicators.

BARBADOS-LIBRARIES

UNESCO Institute for Statistics, C.P 250 Succursale H, Montreal, QC, H3G 2K8, CAN, (514) 343-6880 (Dial from U.S.), (514) 343-5740 (Fax from U.S.), uis.publications@unesco.org, http://uis.unesco.org/; UIS.Stat.

BARBADOS-LIFE EXPECTANCY

Central Intelligence Agency (CIA), Office of Public Affairs, Washington, DC, 20505, USA, (703) 482-0623, https://www.cia.gov; The World Factbook.

United Nations Department of Economic and Social Affairs (DESA), Population Division, 2 United Nations Plz., Rm. DC2-1950, New York, NY, 10017, USA, (212) 963-3209, (212) 963-2147, population@un.org, https://www.un.org/development/desa/pd/; World Population Ageing 2020 Highlights.

United Nations Statistics Division (UNSD), United Nations Plz., New York, NY, 10017, USA, (800) 253-9646, (212) 963-9851, statistics@un.org, https://unstats.un.org; Millennium Development Goal Indicators.

BARBADOS-LITERACY

Euromonitor International, Inc., 1 N Dearborn St., Ste. 1700, Chicago, IL, 60602, USA, (312) 922-1115, (312) 922-1157, info-usa@euromonitor.com, https://www.euromonitor.com/; Geographies.

UNESCO Institute for Statistics, C.P 250 Succursale H, Montreal, QC, H3G 2K8, CAN, (514) 343-6880 (Dial from U.S.), (514) 343-5740 (Fax from U.S.), uis.publications@unesco.org, http://uis.unesco.org/; Literacy.

BARBADOS-LIVESTOCK

Palgrave Macmillan, 1 New York Plaza, Ste. 4500, New York, NY, 10004-1562, USA, (800) 777-4643, orders@palgrave.com, https://www.palgrave.com/us; The Statesman's Yearbook, 2023.

Routledge - Taylor & Francis Group, 6000 Broken Sound Pkwy. NW, Ste. 300, Boca Raton, FL, 33487, USA, (800) 634-1420, (800) 634-7064, orders@taylorandfrancis.com, https://www.routledge.com/; The Europa World Year Book 2022.

United Nations Food and Agricultural Organization (FAO), 2121 K St., Ste. 800B, Washington, DC,

20037, USA, (202) 653-2400 (Dial from U.S.), (202) 653-5760 (Fax from U.S.), fao-hq@fao.org, https://www.fao.org; The State of Food and Agriculture (SOFA) 2022.

United Nations Statistics Division (UNSD), United Nations Plz., New York, NY, 10017, USA, (800) 253-9646, (212) 963-9851, statistics@un.org, https://unstats.un.org; Statistical Yearbook of the United Nations 2021.

BARBADOS-MANUFACTURES

Inter-American Development Bank (IDB), 1300 New York Ave. NW, Washington, DC, 20577, USA, (202) 623-1000, (202) 623-3096, https://www.iadb.org/en; Latin Macro Watch (LMW).

BARBADOS-MARRIAGE

Routledge - Taylor & Francis Group, 6000 Broken Sound Pkwy. NW, Ste. 300, Boca Raton, FL, 33487, USA, (800) 634-1420, (800) 634-7064, orders@taylorandfrancis.com, https://www.routledge.com/; The Europa World Year Book 2022.

United Nations Statistics Division (UNSD), United Nations Plz., New York, NY, 10017, USA, (800) 253-9646, (212) 963-9851, statistics@un.org, https://unstats.un.org; Statistical Yearbook of the United Nations 2021.

BARBADOS-MINERAL INDUSTRIES

Inter-American Development Bank (IDB), 1300 New York Ave. NW, Washington, DC, 20577, USA, (202) 623-1000, (202) 623-3096, https://www.iadb.org/en; Latin Macro Watch (LMW).

International Energy Agency (IEA), 9 Rue de la Federation, Paris, 75739, FRA, info@iea.org, https://www.iea.org/; World Energy Outlook 2021.

Routledge - Taylor & Francis Group, 6000 Broken Sound Pkwy. NW, Ste. 300, Boca Raton, FL, 33487, USA, (800) 634-1420, (800) 634-7064, orders@taylorandfrancis.com, https://www.routledge.com/; The Europa World Year Book 2022.

United Nations Conference on Trade and Development (UNCTAD), Palais des Nations, Geneva, 1211, SWI, (212) 963-6896, unctadinfo@unctad.org, https://unctad.org; Trade and Development Report 2021.

United Nations Statistics Division (UNSD), United Nations Plz., New York, NY, 10017, USA, (800) 253-9646, (212) 963-9851, statistics@un.org, https://unstats.un.org; Statistical Yearbook of the United Nations 2021.

BARBADOS-MONEY SUPPLY

The Economist Group: Economist Intelligence Unit (EIU), 900 3rd Ave., 16th Fl., New York, NY, 10022, USA, (212) 541-0500, americas@eiu.com, https://www.eiu.com; Barbados Country Report.

Inter-American Development Bank (IDB), 1300 New York Ave. NW, Washington, DC, 20577, USA, (202) 623-1000, (202) 623-3096, https://www.iadb.org/en; Latin Macro Watch (LMW).

International Monetary Fund (IMF), 700 19th St. NW, Washington, DC, 20431, USA, (202) 623-7000, (202) 623-4661, publications@imf.org, https://www.imf.org; International Financial Statistics (IFS).

Routledge - Taylor & Francis Group, 6000 Broken Sound Pkwy. NW, Ste. 300, Boca Raton, FL, 33487, USA, (800) 634-1420, (800) 634-7064, orders@taylorandfrancis.com, https://www.routledge.com/; The Europa World Year Book 2022.

United Nations Statistics Division (UNSD), United Nations Plz., New York, NY, 10017, USA, (800) 253-9646, (212) 963-9851, statistics@un.org, https://unstats.un.org; Statistical Yearbook of the United Nations 2021.

BARBADOS-MORTALITY

United Nations Statistics Division (UNSD), United Nations Plz., New York, NY, 10017, USA, (800) 253-9646, (212) 963-9851, statistics@un.org, https://unstats.un.org; Millennium Development Goal Indicators; Statistical Yearbook of the United Nations 2021; and World Statistics Pocketbook 2021.

The World Bank, 1818 H St. NW, Washington, DC, 20433, USA, (202) 473-1000, (202) 477-6391, eds03@worldbank.org, https://www.worldbank.org/; World Development Indicators (WDI) 2022.

World Health Organization (WHO), Ave. Appia 20, Geneva, CH-1211, SWI, (202) 974-3000 (Telephone in U.S.), publications@who.int, https://www.who.int/; Global Health Observatory (GHO).

BARBADOS-MOTION PICTURES

Palgrave Macmillan, 1 New York Plaza, Ste. 4500, New York, NY, 10004-1562, USA, (800) 777-4643, orders@palgrave.com, https://www.palgrave.com/us; The Statesman's Yearbook, 2023.

BARBADOS-NATURAL GAS PRODUCTION

See BARBADOS-MINERAL INDUSTRIES

BARBADOS-NUTRITION

United Nations Food and Agricultural Organization (FAO), 2121 K St., Ste. 800B, Washington, DC, 20037, USA, (202) 653-2400 (Dial from U.S.), (202) 653-5760 (Fax from U.S.), fao-hq@fao.org, https://www.fao.org; The State of Food and Agriculture (SOFA) 2022.

United Nations Statistics Division (UNSD), United Nations Plz., New York, NY, 10017, USA, (800) 253-9646, (212) 963-9851, statistics@un.org, https://unstats.un.org; Millennium Development Goal Indicators.

BARBADOS-PAPER

See BARBADOS-FORESTS AND FORESTRY

BARBADOS-PEANUT PRODUCTION

See BARBADOS-CROPS

BARBADOS-PESTICIDES

United Nations Food and Agricultural Organization (FAO), 2121 K St., Ste. 800B, Washington, DC, 20037, USA, (202) 653-2400 (Dial from U.S.), (202) 653-5760 (Fax from U.S.), fao-hq@fao.org, https://www.fao.org; The State of Food and Agriculture (SOFA) 2022.

BARBADOS-PETROLEUM INDUSTRY AND TRADE

Inter-American Development Bank (IDB), 1300 New York Ave. NW, Washington, DC, 20577, USA, (202) 623-1000, (202) 623-3096, https://www.iadb.org/en; Latin Macro Watch (LMW).

International Energy Agency (IEA), 9 Rue de la Federation, Paris, 75739, FRA, info@iea.org, https://www.iea.org/; World Energy Outlook 2021.

Palgrave Macmillan, 1 New York Plaza, Ste. 4500, New York, NY, 10004-1562, USA, (800) 777-4643, orders@palgrave.com, https://www.palgrave.com/us; The Statesman's Yearbook, 2023.

United Nations Food and Agricultural Organization (FAO), 2121 K St., Ste. 800B, Washington, DC, 20037, USA, (202) 653-2400 (Dial from U.S.), (202) 653-5760 (Fax from U.S.), fao-hq@fao.org, https://www.fao.org; The State of Food and Agriculture (SOFA) 2022.

United Nations Statistics Division (UNSD), United Nations Plz., New York, NY, 10017, USA, (800) 253-9646, (212) 963-9851, statistics@un.org, https://unstats.un.org; Statistical Yearbook of the United Nations 2021.

BARBADOS-POPULATION

Caribbean Public Health Agency (CARPHA), Federation Park, 16-18 Jamaica Blvd., Port of Spain, TTO, (868) 622-4261 (Dial from U.S.), (868) 299-0820 (Dial from U.S.), postmaster@carpha.org, https://carpha.org/; unpublished data.

Central Intelligence Agency (CIA), Office of Public Affairs, Washington, DC, 20505, USA, (703) 482-0623, https://www.cia.gov; The World Factbook.

The Economist Group: Economist Intelligence Unit (EIU), 900 3rd Ave., 16th Fl., New York, NY, 10022, USA, (212) 541-0500, americas@eiu.com, https://www.eiu.com; Barbados Country Report.

European Commission, Eurostat, Luxembourg, 2920, LUX, https://ec.europa.eu/eurostat/; EU in the World 2020.

Infoplease, c/o Sandbox Networks, Inc., 1 Lincoln St., 24th Fl., Boston, MA, 02111, USA, https://www.infoplease.com; Countries of the World.

Inter-American Development Bank (IDB), 1300 New York Ave. NW, Washington, DC, 20577, USA, (202) 623-1000, (202) 623-3096, https://www.iadb.org/en; Latin Macro Watch (LMW).

International Labour Organization (ILO), 4 Rte. des Morillons, Geneva, CH-1211, SWI, ilo@ilo.org, https://www.ilo.org; NORMLEX Information System on International Labour Standards.

Palgrave Macmillan, 1 New York Plaza, Ste. 4500, New York, NY, 10004-1562, USA, (800) 777-4643, orders@palgrave.com, https://www.palgrave.com/us; The Statesman's Yearbook, 2023.

Routledge - Taylor & Francis Group, 6000 Broken Sound Pkwy. NW, Ste. 300, Boca Raton, FL, 33487, USA, (800) 634-1420, (800) 634-7064, orders@taylorandfrancis.com, https://www.routledge.com/; The Europa World Year Book 2022.

UK Data Service, University of Essex, Wivenhoe Park, Colchester, Essex, CO4 3SQ, GBR, https://ukdataservice.ac.uk/; International Aggregate Data.

United Nations Department of Economic and Social Affairs (DESA), Population Division, 2 United Nations Plz., Rm. DC2-1950, New York, NY, 10017, USA, (212) 963-3209, (212) 963-2147, population@un.org, https://www.un.org/development/desa/pd/; Revision of World Urbanization Prospects and World Population Ageing 2020 Highlights.

United Nations Development Programme (UNDP), One United Nations Plz., New York, NY, 10017, USA, (212) 906-5000, (212) 906-5001, https://www.undp.org; Human Development Report 2021-2022.

United Nations Economic Commission for Latin America and the Caribbean (ECLAC), Casilla 179-D, Santiago, 7630412, CHL, (202) 596-3713, prensa@cepal.org, https://www.cepal.org/en; CEPALSTAT.

United Nations Statistics Division (UNSD), United Nations Plz., New York, NY, 10017, USA, (800) 253-9646, (212) 963-9851, statistics@un.org, https://unstats.un.org; Statistical Yearbook of the United Nations 2021 and World Statistics Pocketbook 2021.

The World Bank, 1818 H St. NW, Washington, DC, 20433, USA, (202) 473-1000, (202) 477-6391, eds03@worldbank.org, https://www.worldbank.org/; Caribbean (report) and The Global Findex Database 2021.

BARBADOS-POPULATION DENSITY

Central Intelligence Agency (CIA), Office of Public Affairs, Washington, DC, 20505, USA, (703) 482-0623, https://www.cia.gov; The World Factbook.

Inter-American Development Bank (IDB), 1300 New York Ave. NW, Washington, DC, 20577, USA, (202) 623-1000, (202) 623-3096, https://www.iadb.org/en; Latin Macro Watch (LMW).

Palgrave Macmillan, 1 New York Plaza, Ste. 4500, New York, NY, 10004-1562, USA, (800) 777-4643, orders@palgrave.com, https://www.palgrave.com/us; The Statesman's Yearbook, 2023.

Routledge - Taylor & Francis Group, 6000 Broken Sound Pkwy. NW, Ste. 300, Boca Raton, FL, 33487, USA, (800) 634-1420, (800) 634-7064, orders@taylorandfrancis.com, https://www.routledge.com/; The Europa World Year Book 2022.

BARBADOS-POSTAL SERVICE

Palgrave Macmillan, 1 New York Plaza, Ste. 4500, New York, NY, 10004-1562, USA, (800) 777-4643, orders@palgrave.com, https://www.palgrave.com/us; The Statesman's Yearbook, 2023.

BARBADOS-POWER RESOURCES

Euromonitor International, Inc., 1 N Dearborn St., Ste. 1700, Chicago, IL, 60602, USA, (312) 922-1115, (312) 922-1157, info-usa@euromonitor.com, https://www.euromonitor.com/; Geographies.

International Energy Agency (IEA), 9 Rue de la Federation, Paris, 75739, FRA, info@iea.org, https://www.iea.org/; World Energy Outlook 2021.

Palgrave Macmillan, 1 New York Plaza, Ste. 4500, New York, NY, 10004-1562, USA, (800) 777-4643, orders@palgrave.com, https://www.palgrave.com/us; The Statesman's Yearbook, 2023.

United Nations Food and Agricultural Organization (FAO), 2121 K St., Ste. 800B, Washington, DC, 20037, USA, (202) 653-2400 (Dial from U.S.), (202) 653-5760 (Fax from U.S.), fao-hq@fao.org, https://www.fao.org; The State of Food and Agriculture (SOFA) 2022.

United Nations Statistics Division (UNSD), United Nations Plz., New York, NY, 10017, USA, (800) 253-9646, (212) 963-9851, statistics@un.org, https://unstats.un.org; Energy Statistics Yearbook 2019; Statistical Yearbook of the United Nations 2021; and World Statistics Pocketbook 2021.

BARBADOS-PRICES

Euromonitor International, Inc., 1 N Dearborn St., Ste. 1700, Chicago, IL, 60602, USA, (312) 922-1115, (312) 922-1157, info-usa@euromonitor.com, https://www.euromonitor.com/; Geographies.

International Monetary Fund (IMF), 700 19th St. NW, Washington, DC, 20431, USA, (202) 623-7000, (202) 623-4661, publications@imf.org, https://www.imf.org; International Financial Statistics (IFS).

BARBADOS-PUBLIC HEALTH

Euromonitor International, Inc., 1 N Dearborn St., Ste. 1700, Chicago, IL, 60602, USA, (312) 922-1115, (312) 922-1157, info-usa@euromonitor.com, https://www.euromonitor.com/; Geographies.

Palgrave Macmillan, 1 New York Plaza, Ste. 4500, New York, NY, 10004-1562, USA, (800) 777-4643, orders@palgrave.com, https://www.palgrave.com/us; The Statesman's Yearbook, 2023.

U.S. Census Bureau, 4600 Silver Hill Rd., Washington, DC, 20233, USA, (301) 763-4636, (800) 923-8282, https://www.census.gov; HIV/AIDS Surveillance Data Base.

United Nations Department of Economic and Social Affairs (DESA), Population Division, 2 United Nations Plz., Rm. DC2-1950, New York, NY, 10017, USA, (212) 963-3209, (212) 963-2147, population@un.org, https://www.un.org/development/desa/pd/; World Fertility Data 2019.

United Nations Development Programme (UNDP), One United Nations Plz., New York, NY, 10017, USA, (212) 906-5000, (212) 906-5001, https://www.undp.org; Human Development Report 2021-2022.

United Nations Statistics Division (UNSD), United Nations Plz., New York, NY, 10017, USA, (800) 253-9646, (212) 963-9851, statistics@un.org, https://unstats.un.org; Millennium Development Goal Indicators and Statistical Yearbook of the United Nations 2021.

World Health Organization (WHO), Ave. Appia 20, Geneva, CH-1211, SWI, (202) 974-3000 (Telephone in U.S.), publications@who.int, https://www.who.int/; Global Health Observatory (GHO) and Health Statistics and Information Systems.

BARBADOS-PUBLISHERS AND PUBLISHING

Routledge - Taylor & Francis Group, 6000 Broken Sound Pkwy. NW, Ste. 300, Boca Raton, FL, 33487, USA, (800) 634-1420, (800) 634-7064, orders@taylorandfrancis.com, https://www.routledge.com/; The Europa World Year Book 2022.

UNESCO Institute for Statistics, C.P 250 Succursale H, Montreal, QC, H3G 2K8, CAN, (514) 343-6880 (Dial from U.S.), (514) 343-5740 (Fax from U.S.), uis.publications@unesco.org, http://uis.unesco.org/; UIS.Stat.

BARBADOS-RELIGION

Central Intelligence Agency (CIA), Office of Public Affairs, Washington, DC, 20505, USA, (703) 482-0623, https://www.cia.gov; The World Factbook.

Palgrave Macmillan, 1 New York Plaza, Ste. 4500, New York, NY, 10004-1562, USA, (800) 777-4643, orders@palgrave.com, https://www.palgrave.com/us; The Statesman's Yearbook, 2023.

BARBADOS-RETAIL TRADE

Euromonitor International, Inc., 1 N Dearborn St., Ste. 1700, Chicago, IL, 60602, USA, (312) 922-1115, (312) 922-1157, info-usa@euromonitor.com, https://www.euromonitor.com/; Geographies.

Inter-American Development Bank (IDB), 1300 New York Ave. NW, Washington, DC, 20577, USA, (202) 623-1000, (202) 623-3096, https://www.iadb.org/en; Latin Macro Watch (LMW).

BARBADOS-RICE PRODUCTION

See BARBADOS-CROPS

BARBADOS-RUBBER INDUSTRY AND TRADE

International Rubber Study Group (IRSG), 51 Changi Business Park Central 2, Unit No. 6, 486066, SGP, https://www.rubberstudy.org; Monthly Rubber Bulletin (MRB); Rubber Industry Report; Rubber Statistical Bulletin; and World Rubber Industry Report (WRIO).

BARBADOS-SHIPPING

Routledge - Taylor & Francis Group, 6000 Broken Sound Pkwy. NW, Ste. 300, Boca Raton, FL, 33487, USA, (800) 634-1420, (800) 634-7064, orders@taylorandfrancis.com, https://www.routledge.com/; The Europa World Year Book 2022.

United Nations Statistics Division (UNSD), United Nations Plz., New York, NY, 10017, USA, (800) 253-9646, (212) 963-9851, statistics@un.org, https://unstats.un.org; Statistical Yearbook of the United Nations 2021.

BARBADOS-STEEL PRODUCTION

See BARBADOS-MINERAL INDUSTRIES

BARBADOS-SUGAR PRODUCTION

See BARBADOS-CROPS

BARBADOS-TAXATION

Inter-American Development Bank (IDB), 1300 New York Ave. NW, Washington, DC, 20577, USA, (202) 623-1000, (202) 623-3096, https://www.iadb.org/en; Latin Macro Watch (LMW).

The World Bank, 1818 H St. NW, Washington, DC, 20433, USA, (202) 473-1000, (202) 477-6391, eds03@worldbank.org, https://www.worldbank.org/; World Development Indicators (WDI) 2022.

BARBADOS-TELEPHONE

Palgrave Macmillan, 1 New York Plaza, Ste. 4500, New York, NY, 10004-1562, USA, (800) 777-4643, orders@palgrave.com, https://www.palgrave.com/us; The Statesman's Yearbook, 2023.

Routledge - Taylor & Francis Group, 6000 Broken Sound Pkwy. NW, Ste. 300, Boca Raton, FL, 33487, USA, (800) 634-1420, (800) 634-7064, orders@taylorandfrancis.com, https://www.routledge.com/; The Europa World Year Book 2022.

United Nations Statistics Division (UNSD), United Nations Plz., New York, NY, 10017, USA, (800) 253-9646, (212) 963-9851, statistics@un.org, https://unstats.un.org; World Statistics Pocketbook 2021.

BARBADOS-TEXTILE INDUSTRY

Palgrave Macmillan, 1 New York Plaza, Ste. 4500, New York, NY, 10004-1562, USA, (800) 777-4643, orders@palgrave.com, https://www.palgrave.com/us; The Statesman's Yearbook, 2023.

BARBADOS-THEATER

UNESCO Institute for Statistics, C.P 250 Succursale H, Montreal, QC, H3G 2K8, CAN, (514) 343-6880 (Dial from U.S.), (514) 343-5740 (Fax from U.S.), uis.publications@unesco.org, http://uis.unesco.org/; UIS.Stat.

BARBADOS-TOBACCO INDUSTRY

United Nations Statistics Division (UNSD), United Nations Plz., New York, NY, 10017, USA, (800) 253-9646, (212) 963-9851, statistics@un.org, https://unstats.un.org; Statistical Yearbook of the United Nations 2021.

BARBADOS-TOURISM

Euromonitor International, Inc., 1 N Dearborn St., Ste. 1700, Chicago, IL, 60602, USA, (312) 922-1115, (312) 922-1157, info-usa@euromonitor.com, https://www.euromonitor.com/; Geographies.

Palgrave Macmillan, 1 New York Plaza, Ste. 4500, New York, NY, 10004-1562, USA, (800) 777-4643, orders@palgrave.com, https://www.palgrave.com/us; The Statesman's Yearbook, 2023.

Routledge - Taylor & Francis Group, 6000 Broken Sound Pkwy. NW, Ste. 300, Boca Raton, FL, 33487, USA, (800) 634-1420, (800) 634-7064, orders@taylorandfrancis.com, https://www.routledge.com/; The Europa World Year Book 2022.

United Nations Statistics Division (UNSD), United Nations Plz., New York, NY, 10017, USA, (800) 253-9646, (212) 963-9851, statistics@un.org, https://unstats.un.org; Statistical Yearbook of the United Nations 2021.

United Nations World Tourism Organization (UNWTO), Calle Poeta Joan Maragall 42, Madrid, 28020, SPA, info@unwto.org, https://www.unwto.org/; Yearbook of Tourism Statistics, 2021 Edition.

BARBADOS-TRADE

See BARBADOS-INTERNATIONAL TRADE

BARBADOS-TRANSPORTATION

Central Intelligence Agency (CIA), Office of Public Affairs, Washington, DC, 20505, USA, (703) 482-0623, https://www.cia.gov; The World Factbook.

Euromonitor International, Inc., 1 N Dearborn St., Ste. 1700, Chicago, IL, 60602, USA, (312) 922-1115, (312) 922-1157, info-usa@euromonitor.com, https://www.euromonitor.com/; Geographies.

Inter-American Development Bank (IDB), 1300 New York Ave. NW, Washington, DC, 20577, USA, (202) 623-1000, (202) 623-3096, https://www.iadb.org/en; Latin Macro Watch (LMW).

Palgrave Macmillan, 1 New York Plaza, Ste. 4500, New York, NY, 10004-1562, USA, (800) 777-4643, orders@palgrave.com, https://www.palgrave.com/us; The Statesman's Yearbook, 2023.

Routledge - Taylor & Francis Group, 6000 Broken Sound Pkwy. NW, Ste. 300, Boca Raton, FL, 33487, USA, (800) 634-1420, (800) 634-7064, orders@taylorandfrancis.com, https://www.routledge.com/; The Europa World Year Book 2022.

BARBADOS-UNEMPLOYMENT

International Labour Organization (ILO), 4 Rte. des Morillons, Geneva, CH-1211, SWI, ilo@ilo.org, https://www.ilo.org; NORMLEX Information System on International Labour Standards.

United Nations Statistics Division (UNSD), United Nations Plz., New York, NY, 10017, USA, (800) 253-9646, (212) 963-9851, statistics@un.org, https://unstats.un.org; Statistical Yearbook of the United Nations 2021.

BARBADOS-VITAL STATISTICS

Palgrave Macmillan, 1 New York Plaza, Ste. 4500, New York, NY, 10004-1562, USA, (800) 777-4643, orders@palgrave.com, https://www.palgrave.com/us; The Statesman's Yearbook, 2023.

U.S. Census Bureau, 4600 Silver Hill Rd., Washington, DC, 20233, USA, (301) 763-4636, (800) 923-8282, https://www.census.gov; HIV/AIDS Surveillance Data Base.

United Nations Department of Economic and Social Affairs (DESA), Population Division, 2 United Nations Plz., Rm. DC2-1950, New York, NY, 10017, USA, (212) 963-3209, (212) 963-2147, population@un.org, https://www.un.org/development/desa/pd/; World Contraceptive Use 2021: Estimates and Projections of Family Planning Indicators and World Marriage Data 2019.

United Nations Statistics Division (UNSD), United Nations Plz., New York, NY, 10017, USA, (800) 253-9646, (212) 963-9851, statistics@un.org, https://unstats.un.org; Statistical Yearbook of the United Nations 2021.

BARBADOS-WAGES

International Labour Organization (ILO), 4 Rte. des Morillons, Geneva, CH-1211, SWI, ilo@ilo.org, https://www.ilo.org; NORMLEX Information System on International Labour Standards.

United Nations Statistics Division (UNSD), United Nations Plz., New York, NY, 10017, USA, (800) 253-9646, (212) 963-9851, statistics@un.org, https://unstats.un.org; Statistical Yearbook of the United Nations 2021.

BARBADOS-WEATHER

See BARBADOS-CLIMATE

BARBADOS-WHEAT PRODUCTION

See BARBADOS-CROPS

BARBADOS-WHOLESALE PRICE INDEXES

Inter-American Development Bank (IDB), 1300 New York Ave. NW, Washington, DC, 20577, USA, (202) 623-1000, (202) 623-3096, https://www.iadb.org/en; Latin Macro Watch (LMW).

BARBADOS-WHOLESALE TRADE

Inter-American Development Bank (IDB), 1300 New York Ave. NW, Washington, DC, 20577, USA, (202) 623-1000, (202) 623-3096, https://www.iadb.org/en; Latin Macro Watch (LMW).

BARBADOS-WOOL PRODUCTION

See BARBADOS-TEXTILE INDUSTRY

BARBECUING

MRI Simmons, 200 Liberty St., 4th Fl., New York, NY, 10281, USA, (866) 256-4468, info.ms@mrisimmons.com, https://www.mrisimmons.com/; MRI-Simmons USA.

BARBERSHOPS

U.S. Census Bureau, Center for Economic Studies (CES), 4600 Silver Hill Rd., Washington, DC, 20233, USA, (301) 763-6460, (301) 763-5935, ces.contacts@census.gov, https://www.census.gov/programs-surveys/ces.html; Other Services (except Public Administration), 2017 Economic Census.

U.S. Department of Labor (DOL), Bureau of Labor Statistics (BLS), Postal Square Bldg., 2 Massachusetts Ave. NE, Washington, DC, 20212-0001, USA, (202) 691-5200, (202) 691-7890, blsdata_staff@bls.gov, https://www.bls.gov; Productivity.

BARITE

U.S. Department of the Interior (DOI), U.S. Geological Survey (USGS), National Minerals Information Center (NMIC), 12201 Sunrise Valley Dr., Reston, VA, 20192, USA, (703) 648-4920, (703) 648-7971, (703) 648-4995, sfortier@usgs.gov, https://www.usgs.gov/centers/nmic; Mineral Commodity Summaries 2022.

BARIUM

U.S. Department of the Interior (DOI), U.S. Geological Survey (USGS), National Minerals Information Center (NMIC), 12201 Sunrise Valley Dr., Reston, VA, 20192, USA, (703) 648-4920, (703) 648-7971, (703) 648-4995, sfortier@usgs.gov, https://www.usgs.gov/centers/nmic; Mineral Commodity Summaries 2022.

BARLEY

U.S. Department of Agriculture (USDA), Economic Research Service (ERS), 1400 Independence Ave. SW, Mail Stop 1800, Washington, DC, 20250-0002, USA, (202) 720-2791, https://www.ers.usda.gov/; Organic Market Summary and Trends and U.S. and State Farm Income and Wealth Statistics.

U.S. Department of Agriculture (USDA), National Agricultural Statistics Service (USDA-NASS), 1400 Independence Ave. SW, Washington, DC, 20250, USA, (800) 727-9540, nass@nass.usda.gov, https://www.nass.usda.gov; Crop Progress; Grain Stocks; and Quick Stats.

BARS

See RESTAURANTS

BASEBALL

The Baseball Archive, 48 Cedarwood Rd., Rochester, NY, 14617, USA, http://www.seanlahman.com/baseball-archive/; The Lahman Baseball Database.

Elias Sports Bureau, Inc., 500 5th Ave., New York, NY, 10110, USA, (212) 869-1530, https://www.esb.com; Elias Book of Baseball Records 2022.

Major League Baseball (MLB), 1271 Avenue of the Americas, New York, NY, 10020, USA, (866) 244-2291, (315) 203-6761, customerservice@website.mlb.com, https://www.mlb.com/; unpublished data.

MRI Simmons, 200 Liberty St., 4th Fl., New York, NY, 10281, USA, (866) 256-4468, info.ms@mrisimmons.com, https://www.mrisimmons.com/; MRI-Simmons USA.

National Collegiate Athletic Association (NCAA), PO Box 6222, Indianapolis, IN, 46206-6222, USA, (317) 917-6222, (317) 917-6888, https://www.ncaa.org/; NCAA Sports Sponsorship and Participation Rates Report: 1956-1957 through 2020-2021.

National Federation of State High School Associations (NFHS), PO Box 690, Indianapolis, IN, 46206, USA, (317) 972-6900, https://www.nfhs.org/; High School Athletics Participation Survey, 2021-2022.

National Sporting Goods Association (NSGA), 3041 Woodcreek Dr., Ste. 210, Downers Grove, IL, 60515, USA, (847) 296-6742, (847) 391-9827, info@nsga.org, https://www.nsga.org; Sports Participation in the United States 2022 and Sports Participation: Historical Sports Participation 2022.

The NPD Group, 900 W Shore Rd., Port Washington, NY, 11050, USA, (516) 625-0700, contactnpd@npd.com, https://www.npd.com; Sports.

Sports Reference LLC, 6757 Greene St., Ste. 315, Philadelphia, PA, 19119, USA, (888) 512-8907, https://www.sports-reference.com/; Baseball-Reference.com.

Stats Perform, 203 N LaSalle St., Ste. 2350, Chicago, IL, 60601, USA, (866) 221-1426, https://www.statsperform.com/; unpublished data.

BASIC INCOME

Basic Income Earth Network (BIEN), 286 Ivydale Rd., London, SE15 3DF, GBR, bien@basicincome.org, https://basicincome.org/; Basic Income Studies.

BASKETBALL

MRI Simmons, 200 Liberty St., 4th Fl., New York, NY, 10281, USA, (866) 256-4468, info.ms@mrisimmons.com, https://www.mrisimmons.com/; MRI-Simmons USA.

National Basketball Association (NBA), 645 5th Ave., 18th Fl., New York, NY, 10022, USA, (212) 407-8000, https://www.nba.com/; unpublished data.

National Collegiate Athletic Association (NCAA), PO Box 6222, Indianapolis, IN, 46206-6222, USA, (317) 917-6222, (317) 917-6888, https://www.ncaa.org/; NCAA Sports Sponsorship and Participation Rates Report: 1956-1957 through 2020-2021.

National Federation of State High School Associations (NFHS), PO Box 690, Indianapolis, IN, 46206, USA, (317) 972-6900, https://www.nfhs.org/; High School Athletics Participation Survey, 2021-2022.

National Sporting Goods Association (NSGA), 3041 Woodcreek Dr., Ste. 210, Downers Grove, IL, 60515, USA, (847) 296-6742, (847) 391-9827, info@nsga.org, https://www.nsga.org; Sports Participation in the United States 2022 and Sports Participation: Historical Sports Participation 2022.

The NPD Group, 900 W Shore Rd., Port Washington, NY, 11050, USA, (516) 625-0700, contactnpd@npd.com, https://www.npd.com; Sports.

Sports Reference LLC, 6757 Greene St., Ste. 315, Philadelphia, PA, 19119, USA, (888) 512-8907, https://www.sports-reference.com/; Basketball-Reference.com.

Stats Perform, 203 N LaSalle St., Ste. 2350, Chicago, IL, 60601, USA, (866) 221-1426, https://www.statsperform.com/; unpublished data.

BAUXITE

U.S. Department of the Interior (DOI), U.S. Geological Survey (USGS), National Minerals Information Center (NMIC), 12201 Sunrise Valley Dr., Reston, VA, 20192, USA, (703) 648-4920, (703) 648-7971, (703) 648-4995, sfortier@usgs.gov, https://www.usgs.gov/centers/nmic; Mineral Commodity Summaries 2022; Mineral Industry Surveys (MIS); and Minerals Yearbook.

BAUXITE-CONSUMPTION

U.S. Department of the Interior (DOI), U.S. Geological Survey (USGS), National Minerals Information Center (NMIC), 12201 Sunrise Valley Dr., Reston, VA, 20192, USA, (703) 648-4920, (703) 648-7971, (703) 648-4995, sfortier@usgs.gov, https://www.usgs.gov/centers/nmic; Mineral Commodity Summaries 2022.

BAUXITE-EMPLOYMENT

U.S. Department of the Interior (DOI), U.S. Geological Survey (USGS), National Minerals Information Center (NMIC), 12201 Sunrise Valley Dr., Reston, VA, 20192, USA, (703) 648-4920, (703) 648-7971, (703) 648-4995, sfortier@usgs.gov, https://www.usgs.gov/centers/nmic; Mineral Commodity Summaries 2022.

BAUXITE-INTERNATIONAL TRADE

U.S. Department of the Interior (DOI), U.S. Geological Survey (USGS), National Minerals Information Center (NMIC), 12201 Sunrise Valley Dr., Reston, VA, 20192, USA, (703) 648-4920, (703) 648-7971, (703) 648-4995, sfortier@usgs.gov, https://www.usgs.gov/centers/nmic; Mineral Commodity Summaries 2022.

BAUXITE-PRICES

U.S. Department of the Interior (DOI), U.S. Geological Survey (USGS), National Minerals Information Center (NMIC), 12201 Sunrise Valley Dr., Reston, VA, 20192, USA, (703) 648-4920, (703) 648-7971, (703) 648-4995, sfortier@usgs.gov, https://www.usgs.gov/centers/nmic; Mineral Commodity Summaries 2022.

BAUXITE-PRODUCTION

U.S. Department of the Interior (DOI), U.S. Geological Survey (USGS), National Minerals Information Center (NMIC), 12201 Sunrise Valley Dr., Reston, VA, 20192, USA, (703) 648-4920, (703) 648-7971, (703) 648-4995, sfortier@usgs.gov, https://www.usgs.gov/centers/nmic; Mineral Commodity Summaries 2022 and Minerals Yearbook.

BAUXITE-WORLD PRODUCTION

U.S. Department of the Interior (DOI), U.S. Geological Survey (USGS), National Minerals Information Center (NMIC), 12201 Sunrise Valley Dr., Reston, VA, 20192, USA, (703) 648-4920, (703) 648-7971, (703) 648-4995, sfortier@usgs.gov, https://www.

usgs.gov/centers/nmic; Mineral Commodity Summaries 2022 and Minerals Yearbook.

BEANS

U.S. Department of Agriculture (USDA), National Agricultural Statistics Service (USDA-NASS), 1400 Independence Ave. SW, Washington, DC, 20250, USA, (800) 727-9540, nass@nass.usda.gov, https://www.nass.usda.gov; Agricultural Prices; Quick Stats; and Vegetables Annual Summary.

BEAUTY SHOPS

The NPD Group, 900 W Shore Rd., Port Washington, NY, 11050, USA, (516) 625-0700, contactnpd@npd.com, https://www.npd.com; Beauty.

U.S. Census Bureau, Center for Economic Studies (CES), 4600 Silver Hill Rd., Washington, DC, 20233, USA, (301) 763-6460, (301) 763-5935, ces.contacts@census.gov, https://www.census.gov/programs-surveys/ces.html; Other Services (except Public Administration), 2017 Economic Census.

U.S. Department of Labor (DOL), Bureau of Labor Statistics (BLS), Postal Square Bldg., 2 Massachusetts Ave. NE, Washington, DC, 20212-0001, USA, (202) 691-5200, (202) 691-7890, blsdata_staff@bls.gov, https://www.bls.gov; Productivity.

BEAUTY SHOPS-PRICE INDEXES

The NPD Group, 900 W Shore Rd., Port Washington, NY, 11050, USA, (516) 625-0700, contactnpd@npd.com, https://www.npd.com; Beauty.

U.S. Department of Labor (DOL), Bureau of Labor Statistics (BLS), Postal Square Bldg., 2 Massachusetts Ave. NE, Washington, DC, 20212-0001, USA, (202) 691-5200, (202) 691-7890, blsdata_staff@bls.gov, https://www.bls.gov; Consumer Price Index (CPI) Databases.

BEAUTY, PERSONAL

NielsenIQ (NIQ), 200 W Jackson Blvd., Chicago, IL, 60606, USA, https://nielseniq.com; Multicultural Consumers Are Set to Drive Beauty Growth Amid Continued Category Shifts in 2021.

BEE CULTURE

Bee Informed Partnership (BIP), 4112 Plant Sciences Bldg., College Park, MD, 20742, USA, (443) 296-2470, https://beeinformed.org/; Loss & Management Survey and 2021-2022 Weighted Average Winter All Colony Loss.

BEEF

See also MEAT INDUSTRY AND TRADE

EnsembleIQ, 8550 W Bryn Mawr Ave., Ste. 200, Chicago, IL, 60631, USA, (877) 687-7321, https://ensembleiq.com/; Progressive Grocer's Retail Meat Review, 2020.

Public Health Agency of Canada, 130 Colonnade Rd., Ottawa, ON, K1A 0K9, CAN, (844) 280-5020 (Dial from U.S.), https://www.phac-aspc.gc.ca/; Canadian Integrated Program for Antimicrobial Resistance Surveillance (CIPARS).

U.S. Department of Agriculture (USDA), National Agricultural Statistics Service (USDA-NASS), 1400 Independence Ave. SW, Washington, DC, 20250, USA, (800) 727-9540, nass@nass.usda.gov, https://www.nass.usda.gov; Cold Storage.

BEEF-CONSUMER EXPENDITURES

EnsembleIQ, 8550 W Bryn Mawr Ave., Ste. 200, Chicago, IL, 60631, USA, (877) 687-7321, https://ensembleiq.com/; 2021 Consumer Expenditures Report.

U.S. Department of Labor (DOL), Bureau of Labor Statistics (BLS), Postal Square Bldg., 2 Massachusetts Ave. NE, Washington, DC, 20212-0001, USA, (202) 691-5200, (202) 691-7890, blsdata_staff@bls.gov, https://www.bls.gov; Consumer Expenditure Survey (CE).

BEEF-CONSUMPTION

U.S. Department of Agriculture (USDA), Economic Research Service (ERS), 1400 Independence Ave. SW, Mail Stop 1800, Washington, DC, 20250-0002, USA, (202) 720-2791, https://www.ers.usda.gov/; Food Price Outlook.

U.S. Department of Agriculture (USDA), Foreign Agricultural Service (FAS), 1400 Independence Ave. SW, Mail Stop 1001, Washington, DC, 20250, USA, (202) 720-3935, https://www.fas.usda.gov/; Livestock and Poultry: World Markets and Trade.

BEEF-CONSUMPTION-FOREIGN COUNTRIES

U.S. Department of Agriculture (USDA), Foreign Agricultural Service (FAS), 1400 Independence Ave. SW, Mail Stop 1001, Washington, DC, 20250, USA, (202) 720-3935, https://www.fas.usda.gov/; Livestock and Poultry: World Markets and Trade.

BEEF-INTERNATIONAL TRADE

U.S. Department of Agriculture (USDA), Economic Research Service (ERS), 1400 Independence Ave. SW, Mail Stop 1800, Washington, DC, 20250-0002, USA, (202) 720-2791, https://www.ers.usda.gov/; Food Price Outlook; Foreign Agricultural Trade of the United States (FATUS); and Outlook for U.S. Agricultural Trade: May 2022.

BEEF-PRICE INDEXES

U.S. Department of Labor (DOL), Bureau of Labor Statistics (BLS), Postal Square Bldg., 2 Massachusetts Ave. NE, Washington, DC, 20212-0001, USA, (202) 691-5200, (202) 691-7890, blsdata_staff@bls.gov, https://www.bls.gov; Consumer Price Index (CPI) Databases.

BEEF-PRICES

U.S. Department of Labor (DOL), Bureau of Labor Statistics (BLS), Postal Square Bldg., 2 Massachusetts Ave. NE, Washington, DC, 20212-0001, USA, (202) 691-5200, (202) 691-7890, blsdata_staff@bls.gov, https://www.bls.gov; Consumer Price Index (CPI) Databases.

BEEF-PRODUCTION

U.S. Department of Agriculture (USDA), National Agricultural Statistics Service (USDA-NASS), 1400 Independence Ave. SW, Washington, DC, 20250, USA, (800) 727-9540, nass@nass.usda.gov, https://www.nass.usda.gov; Cold Storage and Livestock Slaughter.

BEEF-SUPPLY

U.S. Department of Agriculture (USDA), Economic Research Service (ERS), 1400 Independence Ave. SW, Mail Stop 1800, Washington, DC, 20250-0002, USA, (202) 720-2791, https://www.ers.usda.gov/; Food Price Outlook.

BEEHIVES

Bee Informed Partnership (BIP), 4112 Plant Sciences Bldg., College Park, MD, 20742, USA, (443) 296-2470, https://beeinformed.org/; Loss & Management Survey and 2021-2022 Weighted Average Winter All Colony Loss.

BEER

See BEVERAGES-CONSUMPTION

BEER, WINE, AND LIQUOR STORES-EARNINGS

U.S. Census Bureau, 4600 Silver Hill Rd., Washington, DC, 20233, USA, (301) 763-4636, (800) 923-8282, https://www.census.gov; County Business Patterns (CBP) 2020.

U.S. Census Bureau, Center for Economic Studies (CES), 4600 Silver Hill Rd., Washington, DC, 20233, USA, (301) 763-6460, (301) 763-5935, ces.contacts@census.gov, https://www.census.gov/programs-surveys/ces.html; Retail Trade, 2017 Economic Census and Wholesale Trade, 2017 Economic Census.

U.S. Department of Commerce (DOC), International Trade Administration (ITA), 1401 Constitution Ave. NW, Washington, DC, 20230, USA, (800) 872-8723, https://www.trade.gov/; TradeStats Express (TSE).

BEER, WINE, AND LIQUOR STORES-EMPLOYEES

U.S. Census Bureau, 4600 Silver Hill Rd., Washington, DC, 20233, USA, (301) 763-4636, (800) 923-8282, https://www.census.gov; County Business Patterns (CBP) 2020.

U.S. Census Bureau, Center for Economic Studies (CES), 4600 Silver Hill Rd., Washington, DC, 20233, USA, (301) 763-6460, (301) 763-5935, ces.contacts@census.gov, https://www.census.gov/programs-surveys/ces.html; Retail Trade, 2017 Economic Census and Wholesale Trade, 2017 Economic Census.

U.S. Department of Labor (DOL), Bureau of Labor Statistics (BLS), Postal Square Bldg., 2 Massachusetts Ave. NE, Washington, DC, 20212-0001, USA, (202) 691-5200, (202) 691-7890, blsdata_staff@bls.gov, https://www.bls.gov; Industry-Occupation Matrix Data, By Occupation.

BEER, WINE, AND LIQUOR STORES-ESTABLISHMENTS

Beer Institute, 440 First St. NW, Ste. 350, Washington, DC, 20001, USA, (202) 737-2337, (800) 379-2739, (202) 737-7004, info@beerinstitute.org, https://www.beerinstitute.org/; Industry Insights.

British Beer & Pub Association (BBPA), 61 Queen St., Ground Fl., London, EC4R 1EB, GBR, contact@beerandpub.com, https://beerandpub.com/; 2021 Statistical Handbook.

U.S. Census Bureau, 4600 Silver Hill Rd., Washington, DC, 20233, USA, (301) 763-4636, (800) 923-8282, https://www.census.gov; County Business Patterns (CBP) 2020 and Economic Census, Nonemployer Statistics (NES) 2019.

U.S. Census Bureau, Center for Economic Studies (CES), 4600 Silver Hill Rd., Washington, DC, 20233, USA, (301) 763-6460, (301) 763-5935, ces.contacts@census.gov, https://www.census.gov/programs-surveys/ces.html; Retail Trade, 2017 Economic Census and Wholesale Trade, 2017 Economic Census.

U.S. Department of Commerce (DOC), International Trade Administration (ITA), 1401 Constitution Ave. NW, Washington, DC, 20230, USA, (800) 872-8723, https://www.trade.gov/; TradeStats Express (TSE).

BEER, WINE, AND LIQUOR STORES-NONEMPLOYERS

U.S. Census Bureau, 4600 Silver Hill Rd., Washington, DC, 20233, USA, (301) 763-4636, (800) 923-8282, https://www.census.gov; County Business Patterns (CBP) 2020 and Economic Census, Nonemployer Statistics (NES) 2019.

U.S. Census Bureau, Center for Economic Studies (CES), 4600 Silver Hill Rd., Washington, DC, 20233, USA, (301) 763-6460, (301) 763-5935, ces.contacts@census.gov, https://www.census.gov/programs-surveys/ces.html; Retail Trade, 2017 Economic Census and Wholesale Trade, 2017 Economic Census.

U.S. Department of Commerce (DOC), International Trade Administration (ITA), 1401 Constitution Ave. NW, Washington, DC, 20230, USA, (800) 872-8723, https://www.trade.gov/; TradeStats Express (TSE).

BEER, WINE, AND LIQUOR STORES-PRODUCTIVITY

U.S. Department of Labor (DOL), Bureau of Labor Statistics (BLS), Postal Square Bldg., 2 Massachusetts Ave. NE, Washington, DC, 20212-0001, USA, (202) 691-5200, (202) 691-7890, blsdata_staff@bls.gov, https://www.bls.gov; Productivity.

BEER, WINE, AND LIQUOR STORES-SALES

Beer Institute, 440 First St. NW, Ste. 350, Washington, DC, 20001, USA, (202) 737-2337, (800) 379-2739, (202) 737-7004, info@beerinstitute.org, https://www.beerinstitute.org/; Brewers Almanac and Industry Insights.

U.S. Census Bureau, 4600 Silver Hill Rd., Washington, DC, 20233, USA, (301) 763-4636, (800) 923-8282, https://www.census.gov; Economic Census, Nonemployer Statistics (NES) 2019.

U.S. Census Bureau, Center for Economic Studies (CES), 4600 Silver Hill Rd., Washington, DC, 20233, USA, (301) 763-6460, (301) 763-5935, ces.contacts@census.gov, https://www.census.gov/programs-surveys/ces.html; Retail Trade, 2017 Economic Census and Wholesale Trade, 2017 Economic Census.

U.S. Department of Commerce (DOC), International Trade Administration (ITA), 1401 Constitution Ave. NW, Washington, DC, 20230, USA, (800) 872-8723, https://www.trade.gov/; TradeStats Express (TSE).

BEES

Bee Informed Partnership (BIP), 4112 Plant Sciences Bldg., College Park, MD, 20742, USA, (443) 296-2470, https://beeinformed.org/; Loss & Management Survey and 2021-2022 Weighted Average Winter All Colony Loss.

Xerces Society for Invertebrate Conservation, 628 NE Broadway, Ste. 200, Portland, OR, 97232, USA, (855) 232-6639, (503) 233-6794, info@xerces.org, https://xerces.org/; Drifting Toward Disaster: How Dicamba Herbicides are Harming Cultivated and Wild Landscapes.

BELARUS-NATIONAL STATISTICAL OFFICE

National Statistical Committee of the Republic of Belarus, 12 Partizansky Ave., Minsk, 220070, BLR, belstat@beltstat.gov.by, https://belstat.gov.by/en/; National Data Reports (Belarus).

BELARUS-PRIMARY STATISTICS SOURCES

Interstate Statistical Committee of the Commonwealth of Independent States, USA, cisstat@cisstat.org, http://www.cisstat.com/eng; Population and Social Indicators of the CIS and Other Countries of the World 2016-2019.

National Statistical Committee of the Republic of Belarus, 12 Partizansky Ave., Minsk, 220070, BLR, belstat@beltstat.gov.by, https://belstat.gov.by/en/; Belarus in Figures, 2023 and Statistical Yearbook of the Republic of Belarus, 2022.

BELARUS-AGRICULTURE

The Economist Group: Economist Intelligence Unit (EIU), 900 3rd Ave., 16th Fl., New York, NY, 10022, USA, (212) 541-0500, americas@eiu.com, https://www.eiu.com; Belarus Country Report.

Euromonitor International, Inc., 1 N Dearborn St., Ste. 1700, Chicago, IL, 60602, USA, (312) 922-1115, (312) 922-1157, info-usa@euromonitor.com, https://www.euromonitor.com/; Geographies.

Palgrave Macmillan, 1 New York Plaza, Ste. 4500, New York, NY, 10004-1562, USA, (800) 777-4643, orders@palgrave.com, https://www.palgrave.com/us; The Statesman's Yearbook, 2023.

Routledge - Taylor & Francis Group, 6000 Broken Sound Pkwy. NW, Ste. 300, Boca Raton, FL, 33487, USA, (800) 634-1420, (800) 634-7064, orders@taylorandfrancis.com, https://www.routledge.com/; The Europa World Year Book 2022.

United Nations Food and Agricultural Organization (FAO), 2121 K St., Ste. 800B, Washington, DC, 20037, USA, (202) 653-2400 (Dial from U.S.), (202) 653-5760 (Fax from U.S.), fao-hq@fao.org, https://www.fao.org; AQUASTAT and The State of Food and Agriculture (SOFA) 2022.

United Nations Statistics Division (UNSD), United Nations Plz., New York, NY, 10017, USA, (800) 253-9646, (212) 963-9851, statistics@un.org, https://unstats.un.org; Statistical Yearbook of the United Nations 2021.

The World Bank, 1818 H St. NW, Washington, DC, 20433, USA, (202) 473-1000, (202) 477-6391, eds03@worldbank.org, https://www.worldbank.org/; Belarus (report) and World Development Indicators (WDI) 2022.

BELARUS-AIRLINES

International Civil Aviation Organization (ICAO), 999 Robert-Bourassa Blvd., Montreal, QC, H3C 5H7, CAN, (514) 954-8219 (Dial from U.S.), (514) 954-6077 (Fax from U.S.), icaohq@icao.int, https://www.icao.int; ICAO Regional Reports.

BELARUS-ARMED FORCES

Central Intelligence Agency (CIA), Office of Public Affairs, Washington, DC, 20505, USA, (703) 482-0623, https://www.cia.gov; The World Factbook.

International Institute for Strategic Studies (IISS) - Americas, 2121 K St. NW, Ste. 600, Washington, DC, 20037, USA, (202) 659-1490, (202) 659-1499, https://www.iiss.org/; The Military Balance 2022.

Palgrave Macmillan, 1 New York Plaza, Ste. 4500, New York, NY, 10004-1562, USA, (800) 777-4643, orders@palgrave.com, https://www.palgrave.com/us; The Statesman's Yearbook, 2023.

Stockholm International Peace Research Institute (SIPRI), Signalistgatan 9, Stockholm, SE 169 72, SWE, https://www.sipri.org/; SIPRI Arms Transfers Database and SIPRI Military Expenditure Database.

BELARUS-BALANCE OF PAYMENTS

The World Bank, 1818 H St. NW, Washington, DC, 20433, USA, (202) 473-1000, (202) 477-6391, eds03@worldbank.org, https://www.worldbank.org/; Belarus (report); World Development Indicators (WDI) 2022; and World Development Report 2022: Finance for an Equitable Recovery.

BELARUS-BANKS AND BANKING

Euromonitor International, Inc., 1 N Dearborn St., Ste. 1700, Chicago, IL, 60602, USA, (312) 922-1115, (312) 922-1157, info-usa@euromonitor.com, https://www.euromonitor.com/; Geographies.

BELARUS-BROADCASTING

Central Intelligence Agency (CIA), Office of Public Affairs, Washington, DC, 20505, USA, (703) 482-0623, https://www.cia.gov; The World Factbook.

Euromonitor International, Inc., 1 N Dearborn St., Ste. 1700, Chicago, IL, 60602, USA, (312) 922-1115, (312) 922-1157, info-usa@euromonitor.com, https://www.euromonitor.com/; Geographies.

Palgrave Macmillan, 1 New York Plaza, Ste. 4500, New York, NY, 10004-1562, USA, (800) 777-4643, orders@palgrave.com, https://www.palgrave.com/us; The Statesman's Yearbook, 2023.

UNESCO Institute for Statistics, C.P 250 Succursale H, Montreal, QC, H3G 2K8, CAN, (514) 343-6880 (Dial from U.S.), (514) 343-5740 (Fax from U.S.), uis.publications@unesco.org, http://uis.unesco.org/; UIS.Stat.

BELARUS-BUDGET

Central Intelligence Agency (CIA), Office of Public Affairs, Washington, DC, 20505, USA, (703) 482-0623, https://www.cia.gov; The World Factbook.

BELARUS-BUSINESS

United Nations Statistics Division (UNSD), United Nations Plz., New York, NY, 10017, USA, (800) 253-9646, (212) 963-9851, statistics@un.org, https://unstats.un.org; Statistical Yearbook of the United Nations 2021.

BELARUS-COAL PRODUCTION

See BELARUS-MINERAL INDUSTRIES

BELARUS-COMMERCE

Palgrave Macmillan, 1 New York Plaza, Ste. 4500, New York, NY, 10004-1562, USA, (800) 777-4643, orders@palgrave.com, https://www.palgrave.com/us; The Statesman's Yearbook, 2023.

UK Data Service, University of Essex, Wivenhoe Park, Colchester, Essex, CO4 3SQ, GBR, https://ukdataservice.ac.uk/; International Aggregate Data.

BELARUS-CONSTRUCTION INDUSTRY

United Nations Statistics Division (UNSD), United Nations Plz., New York, NY, 10017, USA, (800) 253-9646, (212) 963-9851, statistics@un.org, https://unstats.un.org; Statistical Yearbook of the United Nations 2021.

BELARUS-CONSUMER PRICE INDEXES

Routledge - Taylor & Francis Group, 6000 Broken Sound Pkwy. NW, Ste. 300, Boca Raton, FL, 33487, USA, (800) 634-1420, (800) 634-7064, orders@taylorandfrancis.com, https://www.routledge.com/; The Europa World Year Book 2022.

The World Bank, 1818 H St. NW, Washington, DC, 20433, USA, (202) 473-1000, (202) 477-6391, eds03@worldbank.org, https://www.worldbank.org/; Belarus (report).

BELARUS-COTTON

See BELARUS-CROPS

BELARUS-CROPS

Palgrave Macmillan, 1 New York Plaza, Ste. 4500, New York, NY, 10004-1562, USA, (800) 777-4643, orders@palgrave.com, https://www.palgrave.com/us; The Statesman's Yearbook, 2023.

United Nations Food and Agricultural Organization (FAO), 2121 K St., Ste. 800B, Washington, DC, 20037, USA, (202) 653-2400 (Dial from U.S.), (202) 653-5760 (Fax from U.S.), fao-hq@fao.org, https://www.fao.org; The State of Food and Agriculture (SOFA) 2022.

United Nations Statistics Division (UNSD), United Nations Plz., New York, NY, 10017, USA, (800) 253-9646, (212) 963-9851, statistics@un.org, https://unstats.un.org; Statistical Yearbook of the United Nations 2021.

BELARUS-DAIRY PROCESSING

Palgrave Macmillan, 1 New York Plaza, Ste. 4500, New York, NY, 10004-1562, USA, (800) 777-4643, orders@palgrave.com, https://www.palgrave.com/us; The Statesman's Yearbook, 2023.

United Nations Food and Agricultural Organization (FAO), 2121 K St., Ste. 800B, Washington, DC, 20037, USA, (202) 653-2400 (Dial from U.S.), (202) 653-5760 (Fax from U.S.), fao-hq@fao.org, https://www.fao.org; The State of Food and Agriculture (SOFA) 2022.

BELARUS-DEBTS, EXTERNAL

The World Bank, 1818 H St. NW, Washington, DC, 20433, USA, (202) 473-1000, (202) 477-6391, eds03@worldbank.org, https://www.worldbank.org/; Global Financial Development Report 2019-2020: Bank Regulation and Supervision a Decade after the Global Financial Crisis; World Development Indicators (WDI) 2022; and World Development Report 2022: Finance for an Equitable Recovery.

BELARUS-ECONOMIC CONDITIONS

Bernan Press, 15250 NBN Way, Bldg. C, Blue Ridge Summit, PA, 17214, USA, (301) 459-2255, (800) 865-3457, (800) 865-3450, customercare@bernan.com, https://rowman.com/Page/Bernan; World Economic Outlook, April 2022.

Central Intelligence Agency (CIA), Office of Public Affairs, Washington, DC, 20505, USA, (703) 482-0623, https://www.cia.gov; The World Factbook.

The Economist Group: Economist Intelligence Unit (EIU), 900 3rd Ave., 16th Fl., New York, NY, 10022, USA, (212) 541-0500, americas@eiu.com, https://www.eiu.com; Belarus Country Report.

Euromonitor International, Inc., 1 N Dearborn St., Ste. 1700, Chicago, IL, 60602, USA, (312) 922-1115, (312) 922-1157, info-usa@euromonitor.com, https://www.euromonitor.com/; Geographies and Market Research on the Consumer Finance Industry.

International Monetary Fund (IMF), 700 19th St. NW, Washington, DC, 20431, USA, (202) 623-7000, (202) 623-4661, publications@imf.org, https://www.imf.org; IMF Data and World Economic Outlook.

National Statistical Committee of the Republic of Belarus, 12 Partizansky Ave., Minsk, 220070, BLR, belstat@beltstat.gov.by, https://belstat.gov.by/en/; National Accounts of the Republic of Belarus, 2023 and Social Conditions and Living Standards of the Population in the Republic of Belarus, 2021.

Palgrave Macmillan, 1 New York Plaza, Ste. 4500, New York, NY, 10004-1562, USA, (800) 777-4643, orders@palgrave.com, https://www.palgrave.com/us; The Statesman's Yearbook, 2023.

Routledge - Taylor & Francis Group, 6000 Broken Sound Pkwy. NW, Ste. 300, Boca Raton, FL, 33487, USA, (800) 634-1420, (800) 634-7064, orders@taylorandfrancis.com, https://www.routledge.com/; The Europa World Year Book 2022.

United Nations Economic Commission for Europe (UNECE), Palais des Nations, Geneva, CH-1211, SWI, unece_info@un.org, https://unece.org/; UN-ECE Countries in Figures 2019.

United Nations Statistics Division (UNSD), United Nations Plz., New York, NY, 10017, USA, (800) 253-9646, (212) 963-9851, statistics@un.org, https://unstats.un.org; World Statistics Pocketbook 2021.

The World Bank, 1818 H St. NW, Washington, DC, 20433, USA, (202) 473-1000, (202) 477-6391, eds03@worldbank.org, https://www.worldbank.org/; Belarus (report); Global Economic Monitor (GEM); Global Economic Prospects, June 2022; The Global Findex Database 2021; and World Development Report 2022: Finance for an Equitable Recovery.

BELARUS-EDUCATION

Euromonitor International, Inc., 1 N Dearborn St., Ste. 1700, Chicago, IL, 60602, USA, (312) 922-1115, (312) 922-1157, info-usa@euromonitor.com, https://www.euromonitor.com/; Geographies.

Infoplease, c/o Sandbox Networks, Inc., 1 Lincoln St., 24th Fl., Boston, MA, 02111, USA, https://www.infoplease.com; Countries of the World.

Palgrave Macmillan, 1 New York Plaza, Ste. 4500, New York, NY, 10004-1562, USA, (800) 777-4643, orders@palgrave.com, https://www.palgrave.com/us; The Statesman's Yearbook, 2023.

Routledge - Taylor & Francis Group, 6000 Broken Sound Pkwy. NW, Ste. 300, Boca Raton, FL, 33487, USA, (800) 634-1420, (800) 634-7064, orders@taylorandfrancis.com, https://www.routledge.com/; The Europa World Year Book 2022.

UNESCO Institute for Statistics, C.P 250 Succursale H, Montreal, QC, H3G 2K8, CAN, (514) 343-6880 (Dial from U.S.), (514) 343-5740 (Fax from U.S.), uis.publications@unesco.org, http://uis.unesco.org/; Literacy and UIS.Stat.

United Nations Statistics Division (UNSD), United Nations Plz., New York, NY, 10017, USA, (800) 253-9646, (212) 963-9851, statistics@un.org, https://unstats.un.org; Millennium Development Goal Indicators.

The World Bank, 1818 H St. NW, Washington, DC, 20433, USA, (202) 473-1000, (202) 477-6391, eds03@worldbank.org, https://www.worldbank.org/; Belarus (report) and World Development Report 2022: Finance for an Equitable Recovery.

BELARUS-ELECTRICITY

S&P Global Commodity Insights, One World Trade Center, New York, NY, 10007, USA, (800) 752-8878, support@platts.com, https://www.spglobal.com/commodityinsights/en; Platts European Power Alert.

U.S. Energy Information Administration (EIA), 1000 Independence Ave. SW, Washington, DC, 20585, USA, (202) 586-8800, infoctr@eia.gov, https://www.eia.gov; International Energy Outlook 2021.

United Nations Statistics Division (UNSD), United Nations Plz., New York, NY, 10017, USA, (800) 253-9646, (212) 963-9851, statistics@un.org, https://unstats.un.org; Energy Statistics Yearbook 2019 and Statistical Yearbook of the United Nations 2021.

BELARUS-EMPLOYMENT

International Labour Organization (ILO), 4 Rte. des Morillons, Geneva, CH-1211, SWI, ilo@ilo.org, https://www.ilo.org; NORMLEX Information System on International Labour Standards.

UK Data Service, University of Essex, Wivenhoe Park, Colchester, Essex, CO4 3SQ, GBR, https://ukdataservice.ac.uk/; International Aggregate Data.

United Nations Statistics Division (UNSD), United Nations Plz., New York, NY, 10017, USA, (800) 253-9646, (212) 963-9851, statistics@un.org, https://unstats.un.org; Statistical Yearbook of the United Nations 2021.

The World Bank, 1818 H St. NW, Washington, DC, 20433, USA, (202) 473-1000, (202) 477-6391, eds03@worldbank.org, https://www.worldbank.org/; Belarus (report).

BELARUS-ENVIRONMENTAL CONDITIONS

DSI Data Service & Information, Xantener Strasse 51a, Rheinberg, D-47495, GER, dsi@dsidata.com, https://www.dsidata.com/; Global Environmental Database.

The Economist Group: Economist Intelligence Unit (EIU), 900 3rd Ave., 16th Fl., New York, NY, 10022, USA, (212) 541-0500, americas@eiu.com, https://www.eiu.com; Belarus Country Report.

European Commission, Eurostat, Luxembourg, 2920, LUX, https://ec.europa.eu/eurostat/; Environment Statistics Introduced.

National Statistical Committee of the Republic of Belarus, 12 Partizansky Ave., Minsk, 220070, BLR, belstat@beltstat.gov.by, https://belstat.gov.by/en/; Environmental Protection in the Republic of Belarus, 2022.

United Nations Statistics Division (UNSD), United Nations Plz., New York, NY, 10017, USA, (800) 253-9646, (212) 963-9851, statistics@un.org, https://unstats.un.org; Statistical Yearbook of the United Nations 2021 and World Statistics Pocketbook 2021.

BELARUS-EXPORTS

Central Intelligence Agency (CIA), Office of Public Affairs, Washington, DC, 20505, USA, (703) 482-0623, https://www.cia.gov; The World Factbook.

The Economist Group: Economist Intelligence Unit (EIU), 900 3rd Ave., 16th Fl., New York, NY, 10022, USA, (212) 541-0500, americas@eiu.com, https://www.eiu.com; Belarus Country Report.

International Monetary Fund (IMF), 700 19th St. NW, Washington, DC, 20431, USA, (202) 623-7000, (202) 623-4661, publications@imf.org, https://www.imf.org; Direction of Trade Statistics (DOTS).

National Statistical Committee of the Republic of Belarus, 12 Partizansky Ave., Minsk, 220070, BLR, belstat@beltstat.gov.by, https://belstat.gov.by/en/; Foreign Trade of the Republic of Belarus, 2022.

S&P Global, IHS Markit, 15 Inverness Way E, Englewood, CO, 80112, USA, (800) 447-2273, (800) 854-7179, https://ihsmarkit.com; Global Trade Atlas (GTA).

United Nations Statistics Division (UNSD), United Nations Plz., New York, NY, 10017, USA, (800) 253-9646, (212) 963-9851, statistics@un.org, https://unstats.un.org; International Trade Statistics Yearbook 2020.

The World Bank, 1818 H St. NW, Washington, DC, 20433, USA, (202) 473-1000, (202) 477-6391, eds03@worldbank.org, https://www.worldbank.org/; World Development Report 2022: Finance for an Equitable Recovery.

BELARUS-FERTILITY, HUMAN

Central Intelligence Agency (CIA), Office of Public Affairs, Washington, DC, 20505, USA, (703) 482-0623, https://www.cia.gov; The World Factbook.

BELARUS-FETAL MORTALITY

See BELARUS-MORTALITY

BELARUS-FINANCE

National Statistical Committee of the Republic of Belarus, 12 Partizansky Ave., Minsk, 220070, BLR, belstat@beltstat.gov.by, https://belstat.gov.by/en/; National Accounts of the Republic of Belarus, 2023.

Stockholm International Peace Research Institute (SIPRI), Signalistgatan 9, Stockholm, SE 169 72, SWE, https://www.sipri.org/; SIPRI Arms Transfers Database and SIPRI Military Expenditure Database.

United Nations Statistics Division (UNSD), United Nations Plz., New York, NY, 10017, USA, (800) 253-9646, (212) 963-9851, statistics@un.org, https://unstats.un.org; Statistical Yearbook of the United Nations 2021.

The World Bank, 1818 H St. NW, Washington, DC, 20433, USA, (202) 473-1000, (202) 477-6391, eds03@worldbank.org, https://www.worldbank.org/; Belarus (report).

BELARUS-FINANCE, PUBLIC

Bernan Press, 15250 NBN Way, Bldg. C, Blue Ridge Summit, PA, 17214, USA, (301) 459-2255, (800) 865-3457, (800) 865-3450, customercare@bernan.com, https://rowman.com/Page/Bernan; National Accounts Statistics: Analysis of Main Aggregates 2020.

The Economist Group: Economist Intelligence Unit (EIU), 900 3rd Ave., 16th Fl., New York, NY, 10022, USA, (212) 541-0500, americas@eiu.com, https://www.eiu.com; Belarus Country Report.

International Monetary Fund (IMF), 700 19th St. NW, Washington, DC, 20431, USA, (202) 623-7000, (202) 623-4661, publications@imf.org, https://www.imf.org; Regional Economic Outlook.

Palgrave Macmillan, 1 New York Plaza, Ste. 4500, New York, NY, 10004-1562, USA, (800) 777-4643, orders@palgrave.com, https://www.palgrave.com/us; The Statesman's Yearbook, 2023.

Routledge - Taylor & Francis Group, 6000 Broken Sound Pkwy. NW, Ste. 300, Boca Raton, FL, 33487, USA, (800) 634-1420, (800) 634-7064, orders@taylorandfrancis.com, https://www.routledge.com/; The Europa World Year Book 2022.

United Nations Statistics Division (UNSD), United Nations Plz., New York, NY, 10017, USA, (800) 253-9646, (212) 963-9851, statistics@un.org, https://unstats.un.org; National Accounts Main Aggregates Database and National Accounts Statistics: Main Aggregates and Detailed Tables.

The World Bank, 1818 H St. NW, Washington, DC, 20433, USA, (202) 473-1000, (202) 477-6391, eds03@worldbank.org, https://www.worldbank.org/; Belarus (report).

BELARUS-FISHERIES

United Nations Food and Agricultural Organization (FAO), 2121 K St., Ste. 800B, Washington, DC, 20037, USA, (202) 653-2400 (Dial from U.S.), (202) 653-5760 (Fax from U.S.), fao-hq@fao.org, https://www.fao.org; FAO Yearbook of Fishery and Aquaculture Statistics 2019; Fishery Statistical Collections Global Capture Production; FishStatJ; and The State of Food and Agriculture (SOFA) 2022.

United Nations Statistics Division (UNSD), United Nations Plz., New York, NY, 10017, USA, (800) 253-9646, (212) 963-9851, statistics@un.org, https://unstats.un.org; Statistical Yearbook of the United Nations 2021.

The World Bank, 1818 H St. NW, Washington, DC, 20433, USA, (202) 473-1000, (202) 477-6391, eds03@worldbank.org, https://www.worldbank.org/; Belarus (report).

BELARUS-FLOUR PRODUCTION

See BELARUS-CROPS

BELARUS-FOOD

United Nations Food and Agricultural Organization (FAO), 2121 K St., Ste. 800B, Washington, DC, 20037, USA, (202) 653-2400 (Dial from U.S.), (202) 653-5760 (Fax from U.S.), fao-hq@fao.org, https://www.fao.org; The State of Food and Agriculture (SOFA) 2022.

BELARUS-FORESTS AND FORESTRY

National Statistical Committee of the Republic of Belarus, 12 Partizansky Ave., Minsk, 220070, BLR, belstat@beltstat.gov.by, https://belstat.gov.by/en/; Environmental Protection in the Republic of Belarus, 2022.

Palgrave Macmillan, 1 New York Plaza, Ste. 4500, New York, NY, 10004-1562, USA, (800) 777-4643, orders@palgrave.com, https://www.palgrave.com/us; The Statesman's Yearbook, 2023.

UNESCO Institute for Statistics, C.P 250 Succursale H, Montreal, QC, H3G 2K8, CAN, (514) 343-6880 (Dial from U.S.), (514) 343-5740 (Fax from U.S.), uis.publications@unesco.org, http://uis.unesco.org/; UIS.Stat.

United Nations Food and Agricultural Organization (FAO), 2121 K St., Ste. 800B, Washington, DC, 20037, USA, (202) 653-2400 (Dial from U.S.), (202) 653-5760 (Fax from U.S.), fao-hq@fao.org, https://www.fao.org; FAO Yearbook of Forest Products 2019 and The State of Food and Agriculture (SOFA) 2022.

United Nations Statistics Division (UNSD), United Nations Plz., New York, NY, 10017, USA, (800) 253-9646, (212) 963-9851, statistics@un.org, https://unstats.un.org; Statistical Yearbook of the United Nations 2021.

The World Bank, 1818 H St. NW, Washington, DC, 20433, USA, (202) 473-1000, (202) 477-6391, eds03@worldbank.org, https://www.worldbank.org/; Belarus (report) and World Development Report 2022: Finance for an Equitable Recovery.

BELARUS-GAS PRODUCTION

See BELARUS-MINERAL INDUSTRIES

BELARUS-GROSS DOMESTIC PRODUCT

The Economist Group: Economist Intelligence Unit (EIU), 900 3rd Ave., 16th Fl., New York, NY, 10022, USA, (212) 541-0500, americas@eiu.com, https://www.eiu.com; Belarus Country Report.

United Nations Statistics Division (UNSD), United Nations Plz., New York, NY, 10017, USA, (800) 253-9646, (212) 963-9851, statistics@un.org, https://unstats.un.org; Statistical Yearbook of the United Nations 2021.

The World Bank, 1818 H St. NW, Washington, DC, 20433, USA, (202) 473-1000, (202) 477-6391, eds03@worldbank.org, https://www.worldbank.org/; World Development Indicators (WDI) 2022 and World Development Report 2022: Finance for an Equitable Recovery.

BELARUS-GROSS NATIONAL PRODUCT

Palgrave Macmillan, 1 New York Plaza, Ste. 4500, New York, NY, 10004-1562, USA, (800) 777-4643, orders@palgrave.com, https://www.palgrave.com/us; The Statesman's Yearbook, 2023.

United Nations Statistics Division (UNSD), United Nations Plz., New York, NY, 10017, USA, (800) 253-9646, (212) 963-9851, statistics@un.org, https://unstats.un.org; Statistical Yearbook of the United Nations 2021.

The World Bank, 1818 H St. NW, Washington, DC, 20433, USA, (202) 473-1000, (202) 477-6391, eds03@worldbank.org, https://www.worldbank.org/; World Development Indicators (WDI) 2022 and World Development Report 2022: Finance for an Equitable Recovery.

BELARUS-HOUSING

Euromonitor International, Inc., 1 N Dearborn St., Ste. 1700, Chicago, IL, 60602, USA, (312) 922-1115, (312) 922-1157, info-usa@euromonitor.com, https://www.euromonitor.com/; Geographies.

BELARUS-ILLITERATE PERSONS

UNESCO Institute for Statistics, C.P 250 Succursale H, Montreal, QC, H3G 2K8, CAN, (514) 343-6880 (Dial from U.S.), (514) 343-5740 (Fax from U.S.), uis.publications@unesco.org, http://uis.unesco.org/; UIS.Stat.

BELARUS-IMPORTS

Central Intelligence Agency (CIA), Office of Public Affairs, Washington, DC, 20505, USA, (703) 482-0623, https://www.cia.gov; The World Factbook.

The Economist Group: Economist Intelligence Unit (EIU), 900 3rd Ave., 16th Fl., New York, NY, 10022, USA, (212) 541-0500, americas@eiu.com, https://www.eiu.com; Belarus Country Report.

International Monetary Fund (IMF), 700 19th St. NW, Washington, DC, 20431, USA, (202) 623-7000, (202) 623-4661, publications@imf.org, https://www.imf.org; Direction of Trade Statistics (DOTS).

S&P Global, IHS Markit, 15 Inverness Way E, Englewood, CO, 80112, USA, (800) 447-2273, (800) 854-7179, https://ihsmarkit.com; Global Trade Atlas (GTA).

United Nations Statistics Division (UNSD), United Nations Plz., New York, NY, 10017, USA, (800) 253-9646, (212) 963-9851, statistics@un.org, https://unstats.un.org; International Trade Statistics Yearbook 2020.

The World Bank, 1818 H St. NW, Washington, DC, 20433, USA, (202) 473-1000, (202) 477-6391, eds03@worldbank.org, https://www.worldbank.org/; World Development Report 2022: Finance for an Equitable Recovery.

BELARUS-INDUSTRIES

Central Intelligence Agency (CIA), Office of Public Affairs, Washington, DC, 20505, USA, (703) 482-0623, https://www.cia.gov; The World Factbook.

The Economist Group: Economist Intelligence Unit (EIU), 900 3rd Ave., 16th Fl., New York, NY, 10022, USA, (212) 541-0500, americas@eiu.com, https://www.eiu.com; Belarus Country Report.

Euromonitor International, Inc., 1 N Dearborn St., Ste. 1700, Chicago, IL, 60602, USA, (312) 922-1115, (312) 922-1157, info-usa@euromonitor.com, https://www.euromonitor.com/; Geographies.

International Labour Organization (ILO), 4 Rte. des Morillons, Geneva, CH-1211, SWI, ilo@ilo.org, https://www.ilo.org; NORMLEX Information System on International Labour Standards.

Palgrave Macmillan, 1 New York Plaza, Ste. 4500, New York, NY, 10004-1562, USA, (800) 777-4643, orders@palgrave.com, https://www.palgrave.com/us; The Statesman's Yearbook, 2023.

Routledge - Taylor & Francis Group, 6000 Broken Sound Pkwy. NW, Ste. 300, Boca Raton, FL, 33487, USA, (800) 634-1420, (800) 634-7064, orders@taylorandfrancis.com, https://www.routledge.com/; The Europa World Year Book 2022.

United Nations Industrial Development Organization (UNIDO), 1 United Nations Plz., Rm. DC1-1118, New York, NY, 10017, USA, (212) 963-6890, (212) 963 6885, (212) 963-7904, office.newyork@unido.org, https://www.unido.org/; Industrial Statistics Databases and International Yearbook of Industrial Statistics 2021.

The World Bank, 1818 H St. NW, Washington, DC, 20433, USA, (202) 473-1000, (202) 477-6391, eds03@worldbank.org, https://www.worldbank.org/; Belarus (report) and World Development Indicators (WDI) 2022.

BELARUS-INFANT AND MATERNAL MORTALITY

See BELARUS-MORTALITY

BELARUS-INTERNATIONAL TRADE

Banque de France, 31 rue Croix des Petits-Champs, Paris, 75049, FRA, infos@banque-france.fr, https://www.banque-france.fr/en; Key Figures France and Abroad.

The Economist Group: Economist Intelligence Unit (EIU), 900 3rd Ave., 16th Fl., New York, NY, 10022, USA, (212) 541-0500, americas@eiu.com, https://www.eiu.com; Belarus Country Report.

Euromonitor International, Inc., 1 N Dearborn St., Ste. 1700, Chicago, IL, 60602, USA, (312) 922-1115, (312) 922-1157, info-usa@euromonitor.com, https://www.euromonitor.com/; Geographies.

International Monetary Fund (IMF), 700 19th St. NW, Washington, DC, 20431, USA, (202) 623-7000, (202) 623-4661, publications@imf.org, https://www.imf.org; Direction of Trade Statistics (DOTS).

National Statistical Committee of the Republic of Belarus, 12 Partizansky Ave., Minsk, 220070, BLR, belstat@beltstat.gov.by, https://belstat.gov.by/en/; Foreign Trade of the Republic of Belarus, 2022.

S&P Global, IHS Markit, 15 Inverness Way E, Englewood, CO, 80112, USA, (800) 447-2273, (800) 854-7179, https://ihsmarkit.com; Global Trade Atlas (GTA).

United Nations Statistics Division (UNSD), United Nations Plz., New York, NY, 10017, USA, (800) 253-9646, (212) 963-9851, statistics@un.org, https://unstats.un.org; International Trade Statistics Yearbook 2020 and Statistical Yearbook of the United Nations 2021.

The World Bank, 1818 H St. NW, Washington, DC, 20433, USA, (202) 473-1000, (202) 477-6391, eds03@worldbank.org, https://www.worldbank.org/; Belarus (report); World Development Indicators (WDI) 2022; and World Development Report 2022: Finance for an Equitable Recovery.

World Trade Organization (WTO), Ctre. William Rappard, Rue de Lausanne 154, Case postale, Geneva, CH-1211, SWI, enquiries@wto.org, https://www.wto.org; World Trade Statistical Review 2022.

BELARUS-INTERNET USERS

International Telecommunication Union (ITU), Place des Nations, Geneva, CH-1211, SWI, itumail@itu.int, https://www.itu.int; Global Connectivity Report 2022; World Telecommunication/ICT Indicators Database 2021; and Yearbook of Statistics 2019.

The World Bank, 1818 H St. NW, Washington, DC, 20433, USA, (202) 473-1000, (202) 477-6391, eds03@worldbank.org, https://www.worldbank.org/; Belarus (report).

BELARUS-LABOR

Central Intelligence Agency (CIA), Office of Public Affairs, Washington, DC, 20505, USA, (703) 482-0623, https://www.cia.gov; The World Factbook.

Euromonitor International, Inc., 1 N Dearborn St., Ste. 1700, Chicago, IL, 60602, USA, (312) 922-1115, (312) 922-1157, info-usa@euromonitor.com, https://www.euromonitor.com/; Geographies.

International Labour Organization (ILO), 4 Rte. des Morillons, Geneva, CH-1211, SWI, ilo@ilo.org, https://www.ilo.org; NORMLEX Information System on International Labour Standards.

Palgrave Macmillan, 1 New York Plaza, Ste. 4500, New York, NY, 10004-1562, USA, (800) 777-4643, orders@palgrave.com, https://www.palgrave.com/us; The Statesman's Yearbook, 2023.

United Nations Economic Commission for Europe (UNECE), Palais des Nations, Geneva, CH-1211, SWI, unece_info@un.org, https://unece.org/; UNECE Countries in Figures 2019.

United Nations Statistics Division (UNSD), United Nations Plz., New York, NY, 10017, USA, (800) 253-9646, (212) 963-9851, statistics@un.org, https://unstats.un.org; Statistical Yearbook of the United Nations 2021.

The World Bank, 1818 H St. NW, Washington, DC, 20433, USA, (202) 473-1000, (202) 477-6391,

eds03@worldbank.org, https://www.worldbank.org/; World Development Indicators (WDI) 2022 and World Development Report 2022: Finance for an Equitable Recovery.

BELARUS-LAND USE

United Nations Statistics Division (UNSD), United Nations Plz., New York, NY, 10017, USA, (800) 253-9646, (212) 963-9851, statistics@un.org, https://unstats.un.org; Millennium Development Goal Indicators.

The World Bank, 1818 H St. NW, Washington, DC, 20433, USA, (202) 473-1000, (202) 477-6391, eds03@worldbank.org, https://www.worldbank.org/; World Development Report 2022: Finance for an Equitable Recovery.

BELARUS-LIBRARIES

UNESCO Institute for Statistics, C.P 250 Succursale H, Montreal, QC, H3G 2K8, CAN, (514) 343-6880 (Dial from U.S.), (514) 343-5740 (Fax from U.S.), uis.publications@unesco.org, http://uis.unesco.org/; UIS.Stat.

BELARUS-LIFE EXPECTANCY

Central Intelligence Agency (CIA), Office of Public Affairs, Washington, DC, 20505, USA, (703) 482-0623, https://www.cia.gov; The World Factbook.

United Nations Department of Economic and Social Affairs (DESA), Population Division, 2 United Nations Plz., Rm. DC2-1950, New York, NY, 10017, USA, (212) 963-3209, (212) 963-2147, population@un.org, https://www.un.org/development/desa/pd/; World Population Ageing 2020 Highlights.

United Nations Economic Commission for Europe (UNECE), Palais des Nations, Geneva, CH-1211, SWI, unece_info@un.org, https://unece.org/; UNECE Countries in Figures 2019.

United Nations Statistics Division (UNSD), United Nations Plz., New York, NY, 10017, USA, (800) 253-9646, (212) 963-9851, statistics@un.org, https://unstats.un.org; Millennium Development Goal Indicators.

The World Bank, 1818 H St. NW, Washington, DC, 20433, USA, (202) 473-1000, (202) 477-6391, eds03@worldbank.org, https://www.worldbank.org/; World Development Indicators (WDI) 2022.

BELARUS-LITERACY

Euromonitor International, Inc., 1 N Dearborn St., Ste. 1700, Chicago, IL, 60602, USA, (312) 922-1115, (312) 922-1157, info-usa@euromonitor.com, https://www.euromonitor.com/; Geographies.

UNESCO Institute for Statistics, C.P 250 Succursale H, Montreal, QC, H3G 2K8, CAN, (514) 343-6880 (Dial from U.S.), (514) 343-5740 (Fax from U.S.), uis.publications@unesco.org, http://uis.unesco.org/; Literacy.

BELARUS-LIVESTOCK

Palgrave Macmillan, 1 New York Plaza, Ste. 4500, New York, NY, 10004-1562, USA, (800) 777-4643, orders@palgrave.com, https://www.palgrave.com/us; The Statesman's Yearbook, 2023.

Routledge - Taylor & Francis Group, 6000 Broken Sound Pkwy. NW, Ste. 300, Boca Raton, FL, 33487, USA, (800) 634-1420, (800) 634-7064, orders@taylorandfrancis.com, https://www.routledge.com/; The Europa World Year Book 2022.

United Nations Food and Agricultural Organization (FAO), 2121 K St., Ste. 800B, Washington, DC, 20037, USA, (202) 653-2400 (Dial from U.S.), (202) 653-5760 (Fax from U.S.), fao-hq@fao.org, https://www.fao.org; The State of Food and Agriculture (SOFA) 2022.

BELARUS-MARRIAGE

Routledge - Taylor & Francis Group, 6000 Broken Sound Pkwy. NW, Ste. 300, Boca Raton, FL, 33487, USA, (800) 634-1420, (800) 634-7064, orders@taylorandfrancis.com, https://www.routledge.com/; The Europa World Year Book 2022.

United Nations Statistics Division (UNSD), United Nations Plz., New York, NY, 10017, USA, (800) 253-9646, (212) 963-9851, statistics@un.org, https://unstats.un.org; Statistical Yearbook of the United Nations 2021.

BELARUS-MINERAL INDUSTRIES

Palgrave Macmillan, 1 New York Plaza, Ste. 4500, New York, NY, 10004-1562, USA, (800) 777-4643, orders@palgrave.com, https://www.palgrave.com/us; The Statesman's Yearbook, 2023.

Routledge - Taylor & Francis Group, 6000 Broken Sound Pkwy. NW, Ste. 300, Boca Raton, FL, 33487, USA, (800) 634-1420, (800) 634-7064, orders@taylorandfrancis.com, https://www.routledge.com/; The Europa World Year Book 2022.

United Nations Statistics Division (UNSD), United Nations Plz., New York, NY, 10017, USA, (800) 253-9646, (212) 963-9851, statistics@un.org, https://unstats.un.org; Energy Statistics Yearbook 2019 and Statistical Yearbook of the United Nations 2021.

The World Bank, 1818 H St. NW, Washington, DC, 20433, USA, (202) 473-1000, (202) 477-6391, eds03@worldbank.org, https://www.worldbank.org/; Belarus (report).

BELARUS-MONEY SUPPLY

The Economist Group: Economist Intelligence Unit (EIU), 900 3rd Ave., 16th Fl., New York, NY, 10022, USA, (212) 541-0500, americas@eiu.com, https://www.eiu.com; Belarus Country Report.

Routledge - Taylor & Francis Group, 6000 Broken Sound Pkwy. NW, Ste. 300, Boca Raton, FL, 33487, USA, (800) 634-1420, (800) 634-7064, orders@taylorandfrancis.com, https://www.routledge.com/; The Europa World Year Book 2022.

The World Bank, 1818 H St. NW, Washington, DC, 20433, USA, (202) 473-1000, (202) 477-6391, eds03@worldbank.org, https://www.worldbank.org/; Belarus (report).

BELARUS-MORTALITY

UNICEF, 3 United Nations Plz., New York, NY, 10017, USA, (212) 303-7984, (917) 244-2215, https://www.unicef.org; The State of the World's Children 2023.

United Nations Statistics Division (UNSD), United Nations Plz., New York, NY, 10017, USA, (800) 253-9646, (212) 963-9851, statistics@un.org, https://unstats.un.org; Millennium Development Goal Indicators; Statistical Yearbook of the United Nations 2021; and World Statistics Pocketbook 2021.

The World Bank, 1818 H St. NW, Washington, DC, 20433, USA, (202) 473-1000, (202) 477-6391, eds03@worldbank.org, https://www.worldbank.org/; World Development Indicators (WDI) 2022.

World Health Organization (WHO), Ave. Appia 20, Geneva, CH-1211, SWI, (202) 974-3000 (Telephone in U.S.), publications@who.int, https://www.who.int/; Global Health Observatory (GHO).

BELARUS-MOTION PICTURES

Palgrave Macmillan, 1 New York Plaza, Ste. 4500, New York, NY, 10004-1562, USA, (800) 777-4643, orders@palgrave.com, https://www.palgrave.com/us; The Statesman's Yearbook, 2023.

BELARUS-NATURAL GAS PRODUCTION

See BELARUS-MINERAL INDUSTRIES

BELARUS-PAPER

See BELARUS-FORESTS AND FORESTRY

BELARUS-PETROLEUM INDUSTRY AND TRADE

Palgrave Macmillan, 1 New York Plaza, Ste. 4500, New York, NY, 10004-1562, USA, (800) 777-4643, orders@palgrave.com, https://www.palgrave.com/us; The Statesman's Yearbook, 2023.

U.S. Energy Information Administration (EIA), 1000 Independence Ave. SW, Washington, DC, 20585, USA, (202) 586-8800, infoctr@eia.gov, https://www.eia.gov; International Energy Outlook 2021.

United Nations Food and Agricultural Organization (FAO), 2121 K St., Ste. 800B, Washington, DC, 20037, USA, (202) 653-2400 (Dial from U.S.), (202) 653-5760 (Fax from U.S.), fao-hq@fao.org, https://www.fao.org; The State of Food and Agriculture (SOFA) 2022.

United Nations Statistics Division (UNSD), United Nations Plz., New York, NY, 10017, USA, (800) 253-9646, (212) 963-9851, statistics@un.org, https://unstats.un.org; Energy Statistics Yearbook 2019 and Statistical Yearbook of the United Nations 2021.

BELARUS-POPULATION

Central Intelligence Agency (CIA), Office of Public Affairs, Washington, DC, 20505, USA, (703) 482-0623, https://www.cia.gov; The World Factbook.

The Economist Group: Economist Intelligence Unit (EIU), 900 3rd Ave., 16th Fl., New York, NY, 10022, USA, (212) 541-0500, americas@eiu.com, https://www.eiu.com; Belarus Country Report.

Infoplease, c/o Sandbox Networks, Inc., 1 Lincoln St., 24th Fl., Boston, MA, 02111, USA, https://www.infoplease.com; Countries of the World.

International Labour Organization (ILO), 4 Rte. des Morillons, Geneva, CH-1211, SWI, ilo@ilo.org, https://www.ilo.org; NORMLEX Information System on International Labour Standards.

National Statistical Committee of the Republic of Belarus, 12 Partizansky Ave., Minsk, 220070, BLR, belstat@beltstat.gov.by, https://belstat.gov.by/en/; Social Conditions and Living Standards of the Population in the Republic of Belarus, 2021.

Palgrave Macmillan, 1 New York Plaza, Ste. 4500, New York, NY, 10004-1562, USA, (800) 777-4643, orders@palgrave.com, https://www.palgrave.com/us; The Statesman's Yearbook, 2023.

Routledge - Taylor & Francis Group, 6000 Broken Sound Pkwy. NW, Ste. 300, Boca Raton, FL, 33487, USA, (800) 634-1420, (800) 634-7064, orders@taylorandfrancis.com, https://www.routledge.com/; The Europa World Year Book 2022.

UK Data Service, University of Essex, Wivenhoe Park, Colchester, Essex, CO4 3SQ, GBR, https://ukdataservice.ac.uk/; International Aggregate Data.

United Nations Department of Economic and Social Affairs (DESA), Population Division, 2 United Nations Plz., Rm. DC2-1950, New York, NY, 10017, USA, (212) 963-3209, (212) 963-2147, population@un.org, https://www.un.org/development/desa/pd/; Revision of World Urbanization Prospects and World Population Ageing 2020 Highlights.

United Nations Development Programme (UNDP), One United Nations Plz., New York, NY, 10017, USA, (212) 906-5000, (212) 906-5001, https://www.undp.org; Human Development Report 2021-2022.

United Nations Statistics Division (UNSD), United Nations Plz., New York, NY, 10017, USA, (800) 253-9646, (212) 963-9851, statistics@un.org, https://unstats.un.org; Statistical Yearbook of the United Nations 2021 and World Statistics Pocketbook 2021.

The World Bank, 1818 H St. NW, Washington, DC, 20433, USA, (202) 473-1000, (202) 477-6391, eds03@worldbank.org, https://www.worldbank.org/; Belarus (report); The Global Findex Database 2021; World Development Indicators (WDI) 2022; and World Development Report 2022: Finance for an Equitable Recovery.

BELARUS-POPULATION DENSITY

Central Intelligence Agency (CIA), Office of Public Affairs, Washington, DC, 20505, USA, (703) 482-0623, https://www.cia.gov; The World Factbook.

Palgrave Macmillan, 1 New York Plaza, Ste. 4500, New York, NY, 10004-1562, USA, (800) 777-4643,

orders@palgrave.com, https://www.palgrave.com/us; The Statesman's Yearbook, 2023.

Routledge - Taylor & Francis Group, 6000 Broken Sound Pkwy. NW, Ste. 300, Boca Raton, FL, 33487, USA, (800) 634-1420, (800) 634-7064, orders@taylorandfrancis.com, https://www.routledge.com/; The Europa World Year Book 2022.

UNESCO Institute for Statistics, C.P 250 Succursale H, Montreal, QC, H3G 2K8, CAN, (514) 343-6880 (Dial from U.S.), (514) 343-5740 (Fax from U.S.), uis.publications@unesco.org, http://uis.unesco.org/; UIS.Stat.

The World Bank, 1818 H St. NW, Washington, DC, 20433, USA, (202) 473-1000, (202) 477-6391, eds03@worldbank.org, https://www.worldbank.org/; Belarus (report) and World Development Report 2022: Finance for an Equitable Recovery.

BELARUS-POULTRY

See BELARUS-LIVESTOCK

BELARUS-POWER RESOURCES

Euromonitor International, Inc., 1 N Dearborn St., Ste. 1700, Chicago, IL, 60602, USA, (312) 922-1115, (312) 922-1157, info-usa@euromonitor.com, https://www.euromonitor.com/; Geographies.

Palgrave Macmillan, 1 New York Plaza, Ste. 4500, New York, NY, 10004-1562, USA, (800) 777-4643, orders@palgrave.com, https://www.palgrave.com/us; The Statesman's Yearbook, 2023.

S&P Global Commodity Insights, One World Trade Center, New York, NY, 10007, USA, (800) 752-8878, support@platts.com, https://www.spglobal.com/commodityinsights/en; Platts European Power Daily.

U.S. Energy Information Administration (EIA), 1000 Independence Ave. SW, Washington, DC, 20585, USA, (202) 586-8800, infoctr@eia.gov, https://www.eia.gov; International Energy Outlook 2021.

United Nations Statistics Division (UNSD), United Nations Plz., New York, NY, 10017, USA, (800) 253-9646, (212) 963-9851, statistics@un.org, https://unstats.un.org; Energy Statistics Yearbook 2019; Statistical Yearbook of the United Nations 2021; and World Statistics Pocketbook 2021.

The World Bank, 1818 H St. NW, Washington, DC, 20433, USA, (202) 473-1000, (202) 477-6391, eds03@worldbank.org, https://www.worldbank.org/; World Development Report 2022: Finance for an Equitable Recovery.

BELARUS-PRICES

Euromonitor International, Inc., 1 N Dearborn St., Ste. 1700, Chicago, IL, 60602, USA, (312) 922-1115, (312) 922-1157, info-usa@euromonitor.com, https://www.euromonitor.com/; Geographies.

The World Bank, 1818 H St. NW, Washington, DC, 20433, USA, (202) 473-1000, (202) 477-6391, eds03@worldbank.org, https://www.worldbank.org/; Belarus (report).

BELARUS-PUBLIC HEALTH

Euromonitor International, Inc., 1 N Dearborn St., Ste. 1700, Chicago, IL, 60602, USA, (312) 922-1115, (312) 922-1157, info-usa@euromonitor.com, https://www.euromonitor.com/; Geographies and Market Research on the Health and Wellness Industry.

Palgrave Macmillan, 1 New York Plaza, Ste. 4500, New York, NY, 10004-1562, USA, (800) 777-4643, orders@palgrave.com, https://www.palgrave.com/us; The Statesman's Yearbook, 2023.

U.S. Census Bureau, 4600 Silver Hill Rd., Washington, DC, 20233, USA, (301) 763-4636, (800) 923-8282, https://www.census.gov; HIV/AIDS Surveillance Data Base.

UNICEF, 3 United Nations Plz., New York, NY, 10017, USA, (212) 303-7984, (917) 244-2215, https://www.unicef.org; The State of the World's Children 2023.

United Nations Department of Economic and Social Affairs (DESA), Population Division, 2 United Nations Plz., Rm. DC2-1950, New York, NY, 10017, USA, (212) 963-3209, (212) 963-2147, population@un.org, https://www.un.org/development/desa/pd/; World Fertility Data 2019.

United Nations Development Programme (UNDP), One United Nations Plz., New York, NY, 10017, USA, (212) 906-5000, (212) 906-5001, https://www.undp.org; Human Development Report 2021-2022.

United Nations Statistics Division (UNSD), United Nations Plz., New York, NY, 10017, USA, (800) 253-9646, (212) 963-9851, statistics@un.org, https://unstats.un.org; Millennium Development Goal Indicators and Statistical Yearbook of the United Nations 2021.

The World Bank, 1818 H St. NW, Washington, DC, 20433, USA, (202) 473-1000, (202) 477-6391, eds03@worldbank.org, https://www.worldbank.org/; Belarus (report).

World Health Organization (WHO), Ave. Appia 20, Geneva, CH-1211, SWI, (202) 974-3000 (Telephone in U.S.), publications@who.int, https://www.who.int/; Global Health Observatory (GHO) and Health Statistics and Information Systems.

BELARUS-PUBLISHERS AND PUBLISHING

Routledge - Taylor & Francis Group, 6000 Broken Sound Pkwy. NW, Ste. 300, Boca Raton, FL, 33487, USA, (800) 634-1420, (800) 634-7064, orders@taylorandfrancis.com, https://www.routledge.com/; The Europa World Year Book 2022.

UNESCO Institute for Statistics, C.P 250 Succursale H, Montreal, QC, H3G 2K8, CAN, (514) 343-6880 (Dial from U.S.), (514) 343-5740 (Fax from U.S.), uis.publications@unesco.org, http://uis.unesco.org/; UIS.Stat.

BELARUS-RAILROADS

Palgrave Macmillan, 1 New York Plaza, Ste. 4500, New York, NY, 10004-1562, USA, (800) 777-4643, orders@palgrave.com, https://www.palgrave.com/us; The Statesman's Yearbook, 2023.

Routledge - Taylor & Francis Group, 6000 Broken Sound Pkwy. NW, Ste. 300, Boca Raton, FL, 33487, USA, (800) 634-1420, (800) 634-7064, orders@taylorandfrancis.com, https://www.routledge.com/; The Europa World Year Book 2022.

United Nations Statistics Division (UNSD), United Nations Plz., New York, NY, 10017, USA, (800) 253-9646, (212) 963-9851, statistics@un.org, https://unstats.un.org; Statistical Yearbook of the United Nations 2021.

BELARUS-RELIGION

Central Intelligence Agency (CIA), Office of Public Affairs, Washington, DC, 20505, USA, (703) 482-0623, https://www.cia.gov; The World Factbook.

Palgrave Macmillan, 1 New York Plaza, Ste. 4500, New York, NY, 10004-1562, USA, (800) 777-4643, orders@palgrave.com, https://www.palgrave.com/us; The Statesman's Yearbook, 2023.

BELARUS-RETAIL TRADE

Banque de France, 31 rue Croix des Petits-Champs, Paris, 75049, FRA, infos@banque-france.fr, https://www.banque-france.fr/en; Key Figures France and Abroad.

Euromonitor International, Inc., 1 N Dearborn St., Ste. 1700, Chicago, IL, 60602, USA, (312) 922-1115, (312) 922-1157, info-usa@euromonitor.com, https://www.euromonitor.com/; Geographies.

United Nations Statistics Division (UNSD), United Nations Plz., New York, NY, 10017, USA, (800) 253-9646, (212) 963-9851, statistics@un.org, https://unstats.un.org; Statistical Yearbook of the United Nations 2021.

BELARUS-RUBBER INDUSTRY AND TRADE

International Rubber Study Group (IRSG), 51 Changi Business Park Central 2, Unit No. 6, 486066, SGP, https://www.rubberstudy.org; Monthly Rubber Bulletin (MRB); Rubber Industry Report; Rubber Statistical Bulletin; and World Rubber Industry Report (WRIO).

United Nations Statistics Division (UNSD), United Nations Plz., New York, NY, 10017, USA, (800) 253-9646, (212) 963-9851, statistics@un.org, https://unstats.un.org; Statistical Yearbook of the United Nations 2021.

BELARUS-SHIPPING

United Nations Statistics Division (UNSD), United Nations Plz., New York, NY, 10017, USA, (800) 253-9646, (212) 963-9851, statistics@un.org, https://unstats.un.org; Statistical Yearbook of the United Nations 2021.

BELARUS-STEEL PRODUCTION

See BELARUS-MINERAL INDUSTRIES

BELARUS-SUGAR PRODUCTION

See BELARUS-CROPS

BELARUS-SULPHUR PRODUCTION

See BELARUS-MINERAL INDUSTRIES

BELARUS-TELEPHONE

United Nations Statistics Division (UNSD), United Nations Plz., New York, NY, 10017, USA, (800) 253-9646, (212) 963-9851, statistics@un.org, https://unstats.un.org; World Statistics Pocketbook 2021.

BELARUS-TEXTILE INDUSTRY

United Nations Statistics Division (UNSD), United Nations Plz., New York, NY, 10017, USA, (800) 253-9646, (212) 963-9851, statistics@un.org, https://unstats.un.org; Statistical Yearbook of the United Nations 2021.

BELARUS-THEATER

UNESCO Institute for Statistics, C.P 250 Succursale H, Montreal, QC, H3G 2K8, CAN, (514) 343-6880 (Dial from U.S.), (514) 343-5740 (Fax from U.S.), uis.publications@unesco.org, http://uis.unesco.org/; UIS.Stat.

BELARUS-TOBACCO INDUSTRY

United Nations Statistics Division (UNSD), United Nations Plz., New York, NY, 10017, USA, (800) 253-9646, (212) 963-9851, statistics@un.org, https://unstats.un.org; Statistical Yearbook of the United Nations 2021.

BELARUS-TOURISM

Euromonitor International, Inc., 1 N Dearborn St., Ste. 1700, Chicago, IL, 60602, USA, (312) 922-1115, (312) 922-1157, info-usa@euromonitor.com, https://www.euromonitor.com/; Geographies.

United Nations Statistics Division (UNSD), United Nations Plz., New York, NY, 10017, USA, (800) 253-9646, (212) 963-9851, statistics@un.org, https://unstats.un.org; Statistical Yearbook of the United Nations 2021.

The World Bank, 1818 H St. NW, Washington, DC, 20433, USA, (202) 473-1000, (202) 477-6391, eds03@worldbank.org, https://www.worldbank.org/; Belarus (report).

BELARUS-TRANSPORTATION

Central Intelligence Agency (CIA), Office of Public Affairs, Washington, DC, 20505, USA, (703) 482-0623, https://www.cia.gov; The World Factbook.

Euromonitor International, Inc., 1 N Dearborn St., Ste. 1700, Chicago, IL, 60602, USA, (312) 922-1115, (312) 922-1157, info-usa@euromonitor.com, https://www.euromonitor.com/; Geographies.

Palgrave Macmillan, 1 New York Plaza, Ste. 4500, New York, NY, 10004-1562, USA, (800) 777-4643, orders@palgrave.com, https://www.palgrave.com/us; The Statesman's Yearbook, 2023.

Routledge - Taylor & Francis Group, 6000 Broken Sound Pkwy. NW, Ste. 300, Boca Raton, FL, 33487, USA, (800) 634-1420, (800) 634-7064, orders@taylorandfrancis.com, https://www.routledge.com/; The Europa World Year Book 2022.

United Nations Economic Commission for Europe (UNECE), Palais des Nations, Geneva, CH-1211, SWI, unece_info@un.org, https://unece.org/; UNECE Countries in Figures 2019.

The World Bank, 1818 H St. NW, Washington, DC, 20433, USA, (202) 473-1000, (202) 477-6391, eds03@worldbank.org, https://www.worldbank.org/; Belarus (report).

BELARUS-UNEMPLOYMENT

International Labour Organization (ILO), 4 Rte. des Morillons, Geneva, CH-1211, SWI, ilo@ilo.org, https://www.ilo.org; NORMLEX Information System on International Labour Standards.

Palgrave Macmillan, 1 New York Plaza, Ste. 4500, New York, NY, 10004-1562, USA, (800) 777-4643, orders@palgrave.com, https://www.palgrave.com/us; The Statesman's Yearbook, 2023.

United Nations Statistics Division (UNSD), United Nations Plz., New York, NY, 10017, USA, (800) 253-9646, (212) 963-9851, statistics@un.org, https://unstats.un.org; Statistical Yearbook of the United Nations 2021.

The World Bank, 1818 H St. NW, Washington, DC, 20433, USA, (202) 473-1000, (202) 477-6391, eds03@worldbank.org, https://www.worldbank.org/; Belarus (report).

BELARUS-VITAL STATISTICS

National Statistical Committee of the Republic of Belarus, 12 Partizansky Ave., Minsk, 220070, BLR, belstat@beltstat.gov.by, https://belstat.gov.by/en/; Belarus in Figures, 2023; Social Conditions and Living Standards of the Population in the Republic of Belarus, 2021; and Statistical Yearbook of the Republic of Belarus, 2022.

Palgrave Macmillan, 1 New York Plaza, Ste. 4500, New York, NY, 10004-1562, USA, (800) 777-4643, orders@palgrave.com, https://www.palgrave.com/us; The Statesman's Yearbook, 2023.

U.S. Census Bureau, 4600 Silver Hill Rd., Washington, DC, 20233, USA, (301) 763-4636, (800) 923-8282, https://www.census.gov; HIV/AIDS Surveillance Data Base.

United Nations Department of Economic and Social Affairs (DESA), Population Division, 2 United Nations Plz., Rm. DC2-1950, New York, NY, 10017, USA, (212) 963-3209, (212) 963-2147, population@un.org, https://www.un.org/development/desa/pd/; World Contraceptive Use 2021: Estimates and Projections of Family Planning Indicators and World Marriage Data 2019.

United Nations Statistics Division (UNSD), United Nations Plz., New York, NY, 10017, USA, (800) 253-9646, (212) 963-9851, statistics@un.org, https://unstats.un.org; Statistical Yearbook of the United Nations 2021.

BELARUS-WAGES

International Labour Organization (ILO), 4 Rte. des Morillons, Geneva, CH-1211, SWI, ilo@ilo.org, https://www.ilo.org; NORMLEX Information System on International Labour Standards.

United Nations Statistics Division (UNSD), United Nations Plz., New York, NY, 10017, USA, (800) 253-9646, (212) 963-9851, statistics@un.org, https://unstats.un.org; Statistical Yearbook of the United Nations 2021.

The World Bank, 1818 H St. NW, Washington, DC, 20433, USA, (202) 473-1000, (202) 477-6391, eds03@worldbank.org, https://www.worldbank.org/; Belarus (report).

BELARUS-WHEAT PRODUCTION

See BELARUS-CROPS

BELARUS-WHOLESALE TRADE

United Nations Statistics Division (UNSD), United Nations Plz., New York, NY, 10017, USA, (800) 253-9646, (212) 963-9851, statistics@un.org, https://unstats.un.org; Statistical Yearbook of the United Nations 2021.

BELARUS-WOOL PRODUCTION

See BELARUS-TEXTILE INDUSTRY

BELGIUM-NATIONAL STATISTICAL OFFICE

Statistics Belgium (Statbel), Boulevard du Roi Albert II, 16 , North Gate, Brussels, B-1000, BEL, statbel@economie.fgov.be, https://statbel.fgov.be/en; National Data Reports (Belgium).

BELGIUM-PRIMARY STATISTICS SOURCES

European Commission, Eurostat, Luxembourg, 2920, LUX, https://ec.europa.eu/eurostat/; Key Figures on Enlargement Countries, 2019.

BELGIUM-AGRICULTURAL MACHINERY

European Commission, Rue de la Loi, 170, Brussels, B-1040, BEL, https://ec.europa.eu; EU Energy in Figures: Statistical Pocketbook 2021.

BELGIUM-AGRICULTURE

The Economist Group: Economist Intelligence Unit (EIU), 900 3rd Ave., 16th Fl., New York, NY, 10022, USA, (212) 541-0500, americas@eiu.com, https://www.eiu.com; Belgium Country Report.

Euromonitor International, Inc., 1 N Dearborn St., Ste. 1700, Chicago, IL, 60602, USA, (312) 922-1115, (312) 922-1157, info-usa@euromonitor.com, https://www.euromonitor.com/; Geographies.

European Commission, Rue de la Loi, 170, Brussels, B-1040, BEL, https://ec.europa.eu; Common Agricultural Policy (CAPF) Context Indicators, 2019 Update.

European Commission, Eurostat, Luxembourg, 2920, LUX, https://ec.europa.eu/eurostat/; Eurostat Regional Yearbook 2021 and Farmers and the Agricultural Labour Force - Statistics.

Organization for Economic Cooperation and Development (OECD), 2001 L St. NW, Ste. 650, Washington, DC, 20036-4922, USA, (202) 785-6323, (800) 456-6323, (202) 785-0350, washington.contact@oecd.org, https://www.oecd.org/; Economic Survey of Belgium 2022; OECD-FAO Agricultural Outlook 2022-2031; and STAN (STructural ANalysis) Database.

Palgrave Macmillan, 1 New York Plaza, Ste. 4500, New York, NY, 10004-1562, USA, (800) 777-4643, orders@palgrave.com, https://www.palgrave.com/us; The Statesman's Yearbook, 2023.

Routledge - Taylor & Francis Group, 6000 Broken Sound Pkwy. NW, Ste. 300, Boca Raton, FL, 33487, USA, (800) 634-1420, (800) 634-7064, orders@taylorandfrancis.com, https://www.routledge.com/; The Europa World Year Book 2022.

United Nations Food and Agricultural Organization (FAO), 2121 K St., Ste. 800B, Washington, DC, 20037, USA, (202) 653-2400 (Dial from U.S.), (202) 653-5760 (Fax from U.S.), fao-hq@fao.org, https://www.fao.org; AQUASTAT and The State of Food and Agriculture (SOFA) 2022.

United Nations Statistics Division (UNSD), United Nations Plz., New York, NY, 10017, USA, (800) 253-9646, (212) 963-9851, statistics@un.org, https://unstats.un.org; Statistical Yearbook of the United Nations 2021.

The World Bank, 1818 H St. NW, Washington, DC, 20433, USA, (202) 473-1000, (202) 477-6391, eds03@worldbank.org, https://www.worldbank.org/; Belgium (report) and World Development Indicators (WDI) 2022.

BELGIUM-AIRLINES

European Commission, Rue de la Loi, 170, Brussels, B-1040, BEL, https://ec.europa.eu; EU Energy in Figures: Statistical Pocketbook 2021.

European Commission, Eurostat, Luxembourg, 2920, LUX, https://ec.europa.eu/eurostat/; Air Transport Statistics.

International Civil Aviation Organization (ICAO), 999 Robert-Bourassa Blvd., Montreal, QC, H3C 5H7, CAN, (514) 954-8219 (Dial from U.S.), (514) 954-6077 (Fax from U.S.), icaohq@icao.int, https://www.icao.int; ICAO Regional Reports.

Organization for Economic Cooperation and Development (OECD), 2001 L St. NW, Ste. 650, Washington, DC, 20036-4922, USA, (202) 785-6323, (800) 456-6323, (202) 785-0350, washington.contact@oecd.org, https://www.oecd.org/; OECD Tourism Trends and Policies 2022.

Palgrave Macmillan, 1 New York Plaza, Ste. 4500, New York, NY, 10004-1562, USA, (800) 777-4643, orders@palgrave.com, https://www.palgrave.com/us; The Statesman's Yearbook, 2023.

Routledge - Taylor & Francis Group, 6000 Broken Sound Pkwy. NW, Ste. 300, Boca Raton, FL, 33487, USA, (800) 634-1420, (800) 634-7064, orders@taylorandfrancis.com, https://www.routledge.com/; The Europa World Year Book 2022.

BELGIUM-ALUMINUM PRODUCTION

See BELGIUM-MINERAL INDUSTRIES

BELGIUM-ANIMAL FEEDING

United Nations Statistics Division (UNSD), United Nations Plz., New York, NY, 10017, USA, (800) 253-9646, (212) 963-9851, statistics@un.org, https://unstats.un.org; Statistical Yearbook of the United Nations 2021.

BELGIUM-ARMED FORCES

Central Intelligence Agency (CIA), Office of Public Affairs, Washington, DC, 20505, USA, (703) 482-0623, https://www.cia.gov; The World Factbook.

International Institute for Strategic Studies (IISS) - Americas, 2121 K St. NW, Ste. 600, Washington, DC, 20037, USA, (202) 659-1490, (202) 659-1499, https://www.iiss.org/; The Military Balance 2022.

Palgrave Macmillan, 1 New York Plaza, Ste. 4500, New York, NY, 10004-1562, USA, (800) 777-4643, orders@palgrave.com, https://www.palgrave.com/us; The Statesman's Yearbook, 2023.

Stockholm International Peace Research Institute (SIPRI), Signalistgatan 9, Stockholm, SE 169 72, SWE, https://www.sipri.org/; SIPRI Arms Transfers Database and SIPRI Military Expenditure Database.

BELGIUM-BALANCE OF PAYMENTS

European Commission, Eurostat, Luxembourg, 2920, LUX, https://ec.europa.eu/eurostat/; Eurostat Regional Yearbook 2021.

International Monetary Fund (IMF), 700 19th St. NW, Washington, DC, 20431, USA, (202) 623-7000, (202) 623-4661, publications@imf.org, https://www.imf.org; Balance of Payments Statistics: Annual Report 2021 and International Financial Statistics (IFS).

Organization for Economic Cooperation and Development (OECD), 2001 L St. NW, Ste. 650, Washington, DC, 20036-4922, USA, (202) 785-6323, (800) 456-6323, (202) 785-0350, washington.contact@oecd.org, https://www.oecd.org/; Economic Survey of Belgium 2022; Geographical Distribution of Financial Flows to Developing Countries 2023; and OECD Digital Economy Outlook 2020.

Routledge - Taylor & Francis Group, 6000 Broken Sound Pkwy. NW, Ste. 300, Boca Raton, FL, 33487, USA, (800) 634-1420, (800) 634-7064, orders@taylorandfrancis.com, https://www.routledge.com/; The Europa World Year Book 2022.

United Nations Conference on Trade and Development (UNCTAD), Palais des Nations, Geneva, 1211,

SWI, (212) 963-6896, unctadinfo@unctad.org, https://unctad.org; Handbook of Statistics 2021.

United Nations Statistics Division (UNSD), United Nations Plz., New York, NY, 10017, USA, (800) 253-9646, (212) 963-9851, statistics@un.org, https://unstats.un.org; Energy Statistics Yearbook 2019.

The World Bank, 1818 H St. NW, Washington, DC, 20433, USA, (202) 473-1000, (202) 477-6391, eds03@worldbank.org, https://www.worldbank.org/; Belgium (report); World Development Indicators (WDI) 2022; and World Development Report 2022: Finance for an Equitable Recovery.

BELGIUM-BANANAS

See BELGIUM-CROPS

BELGIUM-BANKS AND BANKING

Euromonitor International, Inc., 1 N Dearborn St., Ste. 1700, Chicago, IL, 60602, USA, (312) 922-1115, (312) 922-1157, info-usa@euromonitor.com, https://www.euromonitor.com/; Geographies.

European Commission, Eurostat, Luxembourg, 2920, LUX, https://ec.europa.eu/eurostat/; Eurostat Regional Yearbook 2021.

International Monetary Fund (IMF), 700 19th St. NW, Washington, DC, 20431, USA, (202) 623-7000, (202) 623-4661, publications@imf.org, https://www.imf.org; International Financial Statistics (IFS).

Organization for Economic Cooperation and Development (OECD), 2001 L St. NW, Ste. 650, Washington, DC, 20036-4922, USA, (202) 785-6323, (800) 456-6323, (202) 785-0350, washington.contact@oecd.org, https://www.oecd.org/; Economic Survey of Belgium 2022; OECD Business and Finance Outlook 2021; and OECD Digital Economy Outlook 2020.

Routledge - Taylor & Francis Group, 6000 Broken Sound Pkwy. NW, Ste. 300, Boca Raton, FL, 33487, USA, (800) 634-1420, (800) 634-7064, orders@taylorandfrancis.com, https://www.routledge.com/; The Europa World Year Book 2022.

United Nations Statistics Division (UNSD), United Nations Plz., New York, NY, 10017, USA, (800) 253-9646, (212) 963-9851, statistics@un.org, https://unstats.un.org; Statistical Yearbook of the United Nations 2021.

BELGIUM-BARLEY PRODUCTION

See BELGIUM-CROPS

BELGIUM-BONDS

Organization for Economic Cooperation and Development (OECD), 2001 L St. NW, Ste. 650, Washington, DC, 20036-4922, USA, (202) 785-6323, (800) 456-6323, (202) 785-0350, washington.contact@oecd.org, https://www.oecd.org/; OECD Business and Finance Outlook 2021.

United Nations Statistics Division (UNSD), United Nations Plz., New York, NY, 10017, USA, (800) 253-9646, (212) 963-9851, statistics@un.org, https://unstats.un.org; Statistical Yearbook of the United Nations 2021.

BELGIUM-BROADCASTING

Central Intelligence Agency (CIA), Office of Public Affairs, Washington, DC, 20505, USA, (703) 482-0623, https://www.cia.gov; The World Factbook.

Euromonitor International, Inc., 1 N Dearborn St., Ste. 1700, Chicago, IL, 60602, USA, (312) 922-1115, (312) 922-1157, info-usa@euromonitor.com, https://www.euromonitor.com/; Geographies.

Palgrave Macmillan, 1 New York Plaza, Ste. 4500, New York, NY, 10004-1562, USA, (800) 777-4643, orders@palgrave.com, https://www.palgrave.com/us; The Statesman's Yearbook, 2023.

UNESCO Institute for Statistics, C.P 250 Succursale H, Montreal, QC, H3G 2K8, CAN, (514) 343-6880 (Dial from U.S.), (514) 343-5740 (Fax from U.S.), uis.publications@unesco.org, http://uis.unesco.org/; UIS.Stat.

WRTH Publications Limited, PO Box 290, Oxford, OX2 7FT, GBR, sales@wrth.com, https://www.wrth.com; World Radio TV Handbook 2023.

BELGIUM-BUDGET

Central Intelligence Agency (CIA), Office of Public Affairs, Washington, DC, 20505, USA, (703) 482-0623, https://www.cia.gov; The World Factbook.

European Commission, Eurostat, Luxembourg, 2920, LUX, https://ec.europa.eu/eurostat/; Share of Government Budget Appropriations or Outlays on Research and Development.

BELGIUM-BUSINESS

European Commission, Eurostat, Luxembourg, 2920, LUX, https://ec.europa.eu/eurostat/; Eurostat Regional Yearbook 2021.

Global Entrepreneurship Monitor (GEM), Babson College, 231 Forest St., Babson Park, MA, 02457, USA, (781) 235-1200, info@gemconsortium.org, https://www.gemconsortium.org/; GEM 2022-2023 Global Report.

Organization for Economic Cooperation and Development (OECD), 2001 L St. NW, Ste. 650, Washington, DC, 20036-4922, USA, (202) 785-6323, (800) 456-6323, (202) 785-0350, washington.contact@oecd.org, https://www.oecd.org/; OECD Main Economic Indicators (MEI).

BELGIUM-CAPITAL INVESTMENTS

Organization for Economic Cooperation and Development (OECD), 2001 L St. NW, Ste. 650, Washington, DC, 20036-4922, USA, (202) 785-6323, (800) 456-6323, (202) 785-0350, washington.contact@oecd.org, https://www.oecd.org/; OECD Business and Finance Outlook 2021.

BELGIUM-CHILDBIRTH-STATISTICS

European Commission, Eurostat, Luxembourg, 2920, LUX, https://ec.europa.eu/eurostat/; Eurostat Regional Yearbook 2021.

The World Bank, 1818 H St. NW, Washington, DC, 20433, USA, (202) 473-1000, (202) 477-6391, eds03@worldbank.org, https://www.worldbank.org/; World Development Indicators (WDI) 2022.

BELGIUM-CLIMATE

Palgrave Macmillan, 1 New York Plaza, Ste. 4500, New York, NY, 10004-1562, USA, (800) 777-4643, orders@palgrave.com, https://www.palgrave.com/us; The Statesman's Yearbook, 2023.

BELGIUM-COAL PRODUCTION

See BELGIUM-MINERAL INDUSTRIES

BELGIUM-COCOA PRODUCTION

See BELGIUM-CROPS

BELGIUM-COFFEE

See BELGIUM-CROPS

BELGIUM-COMMERCE

Palgrave Macmillan, 1 New York Plaza, Ste. 4500, New York, NY, 10004-1562, USA, (800) 777-4643, orders@palgrave.com, https://www.palgrave.com/us; The Statesman's Yearbook, 2023.

UK Data Service, University of Essex, Wivenhoe Park, Colchester, Essex, CO4 3SQ, GBR, https://ukdataservice.ac.uk/; International Aggregate Data.

BELGIUM-COMMODITY EXCHANGES

Barchart, 209 W Jackson Blvd., 2nd Fl., Chicago, IL, 60606, USA, (877) 247-4394, commodities@barchart.com, https://www.barchart.com/cmdty; The cmdty Yearbook 2023; cmdtyStats: Commodity Statistics and Fundamental Data; cmdtyView: Commodity Index; and Commodity Data and Prices.

International Lead and Zinc Study Group (ILZSG), Rua Almirante Barroso 38, 5th Fl., Lisbon, 1000-013, PRT, sales@ilzsg.org, https://www.ilzsg.org; Interactive Statistical Database.

International Monetary Fund (IMF), 700 19th St. NW, Washington, DC, 20431, USA, (202) 623-7000, (202) 623-4661, publications@imf.org, https://www.imf.org; IMF Primary Commodity Prices.

United Nations Statistics Division (UNSD), United Nations Plz., New York, NY, 10017, USA, (800) 253-9646, (212) 963-9851, statistics@un.org, https://unstats.un.org; Statistical Yearbook of the United Nations 2021.

World Bureau of Metal Statistics (WBMS), 31 Star St., Ware, Hertfordshire, SG12 9BA, GBR, https://www.refinitiv.com/en/trading-solutions/world-bureau-metal-statistics; Annual Stainless Steel Statistics; Long Term Production/Consumption Series - All Metals; World Flow Charts; and World Metal Statistics.

BELGIUM-CONSTRUCTION INDUSTRY

Organization for Economic Cooperation and Development (OECD), 2001 L St. NW, Ste. 650, Washington, DC, 20036-4922, USA, (202) 785-6323, (800) 456-6323, (202) 785-0350, washington.contact@oecd.org, https://www.oecd.org/; Economic Survey of Belgium 2022.

Palgrave Macmillan, 1 New York Plaza, Ste. 4500, New York, NY, 10004-1562, USA, (800) 777-4643, orders@palgrave.com, https://www.palgrave.com/us; The Statesman's Yearbook, 2023.

United Nations Statistics Division (UNSD), United Nations Plz., New York, NY, 10017, USA, (800) 253-9646, (212) 963-9851, statistics@un.org, https://unstats.un.org; Statistical Yearbook of the United Nations 2021.

BELGIUM-CONSUMER PRICE INDEXES

European Commission, Eurostat, Luxembourg, 2920, LUX, https://ec.europa.eu/eurostat/; Eurostat Regional Yearbook 2021.

Organization for Economic Cooperation and Development (OECD), 2001 L St. NW, Ste. 650, Washington, DC, 20036-4922, USA, (202) 785-6323, (800) 456-6323, (202) 785-0350, washington.contact@oecd.org, https://www.oecd.org/; OECD Digital Economy Outlook 2020.

Routledge - Taylor & Francis Group, 6000 Broken Sound Pkwy. NW, Ste. 300, Boca Raton, FL, 33487, USA, (800) 634-1420, (800) 634-7064, orders@taylorandfrancis.com, https://www.routledge.com/; The Europa World Year Book 2022.

The World Bank, 1818 H St. NW, Washington, DC, 20433, USA, (202) 473-1000, (202) 477-6391, eds03@worldbank.org, https://www.worldbank.org/; Belgium (report).

BELGIUM-CONSUMPTION (ECONOMICS)

European Commission, Eurostat, Luxembourg, 2920, LUX, https://ec.europa.eu/eurostat/; Eurostat Regional Yearbook 2021.

Organization for Economic Cooperation and Development (OECD), 2001 L St. NW, Ste. 650, Washington, DC, 20036-4922, USA, (202) 785-6323, (800) 456-6323, (202) 785-0350, washington.contact@oecd.org, https://www.oecd.org/; OECD-FAO Agricultural Outlook 2022-2031 and Revenue Statistics 2022.

TAPPI - Technical Association of the Pulp and Paper Industry, 15 Technology Pkwy. S, Ste. 115, Peachtree Corners, GA, 30092, USA, (770) 446-1400, (800) 332-8686, (770) 446-6947, memberconnection@tappi.org, https://www.tappi.org/; TAPPI Journal.

World Steel Association (Worldsteel), Avenue de Tervueren 270, Brussels, B-1150, BEL, steel@worldsteel.org, https://www.worldsteel.org; Steel Statistical Yearbook 2021.

BELGIUM-COPPER INDUSTRY AND TRADE

See BELGIUM-MINERAL INDUSTRIES

BELGIUM-CORN INDUSTRY

See BELGIUM-CROPS

BELGIUM-COST AND STANDARD OF LIVING

European Commission, Eurostat, Luxembourg, 2920, LUX, https://ec.europa.eu/eurostat/; Eurostat Regional Yearbook 2021.

BELGIUM-COTTON

See BELGIUM-CROPS

BELGIUM-CRIME

European Commission, Eurostat, Luxembourg, 2920, LUX, https://ec.europa.eu/eurostat/; Crime and Criminal Justice Database and Crime Statistics.

BELGIUM-CROPS

European Commission, Eurostat, Luxembourg, 2920, LUX, https://ec.europa.eu/eurostat/; Eurostat Regional Yearbook 2021.

Organization for Economic Cooperation and Development (OECD), 2001 L St. NW, Ste. 650, Washington, DC, 20036-4922, USA, (202) 785-6323, (800) 456-6323, (202) 785-0350, washington.contact@oecd.org, https://www.oecd.org/; OECD-FAO Agricultural Outlook 2022-2031.

Palgrave Macmillan, 1 New York Plaza, Ste. 4500, New York, NY, 10004-1562, USA, (800) 777-4643, orders@palgrave.com, https://www.palgrave.com/us; The Statesman's Yearbook, 2023.

United Nations Food and Agricultural Organization (FAO), 2121 K St., Ste. 800B, Washington, DC, 20037, USA, (202) 653-2400 (Dial from U.S.), (202) 653-5760 (Fax from U.S.), fao-hq@fao.org, https://www.fao.org; The State of Food and Agriculture (SOFA) 2022.

United Nations Statistics Division (UNSD), United Nations Plz., New York, NY, 10017, USA, (800) 253-9646, (212) 963-9851, statistics@un.org, https://unstats.un.org; Statistical Yearbook of the United Nations 2021.

BELGIUM-CUSTOMS ADMINISTRATION

European Commission, Eurostat, Luxembourg, 2920, LUX, https://ec.europa.eu/eurostat/; Eurostat Regional Yearbook 2021.

BELGIUM-DAIRY PROCESSING

Organization for Economic Cooperation and Development (OECD), 2001 L St. NW, Ste. 650, Washington, DC, 20036-4922, USA, (202) 785-6323, (800) 456-6323, (202) 785-0350, washington.contact@oecd.org, https://www.oecd.org/; OECD-FAO Agricultural Outlook 2022-2031.

Palgrave Macmillan, 1 New York Plaza, Ste. 4500, New York, NY, 10004-1562, USA, (800) 777-4643, orders@palgrave.com, https://www.palgrave.com/us; The Statesman's Yearbook, 2023.

United Nations Food and Agricultural Organization (FAO), 2121 K St., Ste. 800B, Washington, DC, 20037, USA, (202) 653-2400 (Dial from U.S.), (202) 653-5760 (Fax from U.S.), fao-hq@fao.org, https://www.fao.org; The State of Food and Agriculture (SOFA) 2022.

BELGIUM-DEBTS, EXTERNAL

Organization for Economic Cooperation and Development (OECD), 2001 L St. NW, Ste. 650, Washington, DC, 20036-4922, USA, (202) 785-6323, (800) 456-6323, (202) 785-0350, washington.contact@oecd.org, https://www.oecd.org/; Geographical Distribution of Financial Flows to Developing Countries 2023; OECD Business and Finance Outlook 2021; and OECD Digital Economy Outlook 2020.

Palgrave Macmillan, 1 New York Plaza, Ste. 4500, New York, NY, 10004-1562, USA, (800) 777-4643, orders@palgrave.com, https://www.palgrave.com/us; The Statesman's Yearbook, 2023.

The World Bank, 1818 H St. NW, Washington, DC, 20433, USA, (202) 473-1000, (202) 477-6391, eds03@worldbank.org, https://www.worldbank.org/; Global Financial Development Report 2019-2020: Bank Regulation and Supervision a Decade after the Global Financial Crisis; World Development Indicators (WDI) 2022; and World Development Report 2022: Finance for an Equitable Recovery.

BELGIUM-DEFENSE EXPENDITURES

See BELGIUM-ARMED FORCES

BELGIUM-DIAMONDS

See BELGIUM-MINERAL INDUSTRIES

BELGIUM-ECONOMIC ASSISTANCE

Organization for Economic Cooperation and Development (OECD), 2001 L St. NW, Ste. 650, Washington, DC, 20036-4922, USA, (202) 785-6323, (800) 456-6323, (202) 785-0350, washington.contact@oecd.org, https://www.oecd.org/; Geographical Distribution of Financial Flows to Developing Countries 2023.

United Nations Statistics Division (UNSD), United Nations Plz., New York, NY, 10017, USA, (800) 253-9646, (212) 963-9851, statistics@un.org, https://unstats.un.org; Statistical Yearbook of the United Nations 2021.

BELGIUM-ECONOMIC CONDITIONS

Banque de France, 31 rue Croix des Petits-Champs, Paris, 75049, FRA, infos@banque-france.fr, https://www.banque-france.fr/en; Webstat: Access to Statistical Series of Banque de France.

Bernan Press, 15250 NBN Way, Bldg. C, Blue Ridge Summit, PA, 17214, USA, (301) 459-2255, (800) 865-3457, (800) 865-3450, customercare@bernan.com, https://rowman.com/Page/Bernan; World Economic Outlook, April 2022.

Central Intelligence Agency (CIA), Office of Public Affairs, Washington, DC, 20505, USA, (703) 482-0623, https://www.cia.gov; The World Factbook.

The Economist Group: Economist Intelligence Unit (EIU), 900 3rd Ave., 16th Fl., New York, NY, 10022, USA, (212) 541-0500, americas@eiu.com, https://www.eiu.com; Belgium Country Report.

Euromonitor International, Inc., 1 N Dearborn St., Ste. 1700, Chicago, IL, 60602, USA, (312) 922-1115, (312) 922-1157, info-usa@euromonitor.com, https://www.euromonitor.com/; Geographies and Market Research on the Consumer Finance Industry.

European Commission, Rue de la Loi, 170, Brussels, B-1040, BEL, https://ec.europa.eu; Common Agricultural Policy (CAPF) Context Indicators, 2019 Update.

European Commission, Eurostat, Luxembourg, 2920, LUX, https://ec.europa.eu/eurostat/; Eurostat Regional Yearbook 2021.

Global Entrepreneurship Monitor (GEM), Babson College, 231 Forest St., Babson Park, MA, 02457, USA, (781) 235-1200, info@gemconsortium.org, https://www.gemconsortium.org/; GEM 2022-2023 Global Report.

International Monetary Fund (IMF), 700 19th St. NW, Washington, DC, 20431, USA, (202) 623-7000, (202) 623-4661, publications@imf.org, https://www.imf.org; IMF Data and World Economic Outlook.

Organization for Economic Cooperation and Development (OECD), 2001 L St. NW, Ste. 650, Washington, DC, 20036-4922, USA, (202) 785-6323, (800) 456-6323, (202) 785-0350, washington.contact@oecd.org, https://www.oecd.org/; Economic Survey of Belgium 2022; Geographical Distribution of Financial Flows to Developing Countries 2023; OECD Composite Leading Indicator (CLI); OECD Digital Economy Outlook 2020; OECD Employment Outlook 2022: Building Back More Inclusive Labour Markets; and OECD Labour Force Statistics 2022.

Palgrave Macmillan, 1 New York Plaza, Ste. 4500, New York, NY, 10004-1562, USA, (800) 777-4643, orders@palgrave.com, https://www.palgrave.com/us; The Statesman's Yearbook, 2023.

Routledge - Taylor & Francis Group, 6000 Broken Sound Pkwy. NW, Ste. 300, Boca Raton, FL, 33487, USA, (800) 634-1420, (800) 634-7064, orders@taylorandfrancis.com, https://www.routledge.com/; The Europa World Year Book 2022.

United Nations Economic Commission for Europe (UNECE), Palais des Nations, Geneva, CH-1211, SWI, unece_info@un.org, https://unece.org/; UNECE Countries in Figures 2019.

United Nations Statistics Division (UNSD), United Nations Plz., New York, NY, 10017, USA, (800) 253-9646, (212) 963-9851, statistics@un.org, https://unstats.un.org; Energy Statistics Yearbook 2019 and World Statistics Pocketbook 2021.

The World Bank, 1818 H St. NW, Washington, DC, 20433, USA, (202) 473-1000, (202) 477-6391, eds03@worldbank.org, https://www.worldbank.org/; Belgium (report); Global Economic Monitor (GEM); Global Economic Prospects, June 2022; The Global Findex Database 2021; and World Development Report 2022: Finance for an Equitable Recovery.

BELGIUM-EDUCATION

Euromonitor International, Inc., 1 N Dearborn St., Ste. 1700, Chicago, IL, 60602, USA, (312) 922-1115, (312) 922-1157, info-usa@euromonitor.com, https://www.euromonitor.com/; Geographies.

European Commission, Rue de la Loi, 170, Brussels, B-1040, BEL, https://ec.europa.eu; Common Agricultural Policy (CAPF) Context Indicators, 2019 Update.

European Commission, Eurostat, Luxembourg, 2920, LUX, https://ec.europa.eu/eurostat/; Eurostat Regional Yearbook 2021.

Infoplease, c/o Sandbox Networks, Inc., 1 Lincoln St., 24th Fl., Boston, MA, 02111, USA, https://www.infoplease.com; Countries of the World.

Organization for Economic Cooperation and Development (OECD), 2001 L St. NW, Ste. 650, Washington, DC, 20036-4922, USA, (202) 785-6323, (800) 456-6323, (202) 785-0350, washington.contact@oecd.org, https://www.oecd.org/; Education at a Glance 2022: OECD Indicators.

Palgrave Macmillan, 1 New York Plaza, Ste. 4500, New York, NY, 10004-1562, USA, (800) 777-4643, orders@palgrave.com, https://www.palgrave.com/us; The Statesman's Yearbook, 2023.

Routledge - Taylor & Francis Group, 6000 Broken Sound Pkwy. NW, Ste. 300, Boca Raton, FL, 33487, USA, (800) 634-1420, (800) 634-7064, orders@taylorandfrancis.com, https://www.routledge.com/; The Europa World Year Book 2022.

UNESCO Institute for Statistics, C.P 250 Succursale H, Montreal, QC, H3G 2K8, CAN, (514) 343-6880 (Dial from U.S.), (514) 343-5740 (Fax from U.S.), uis.publications@unesco.org, http://uis.unesco.org/; Literacy and UIS.Stat.

United Nations Statistics Division (UNSD), United Nations Plz., New York, NY, 10017, USA, (800) 253-9646, (212) 963-9851, statistics@un.org, https://unstats.un.org; Millennium Development Goal Indicators.

The World Bank, 1818 H St. NW, Washington, DC, 20433, USA, (202) 473-1000, (202) 477-6391, eds03@worldbank.org, https://www.worldbank.org/; Belgium (report); World Development Indicators (WDI) 2022; and World Development Report 2022: Finance for an Equitable Recovery.

BELGIUM-ELECTRICITY

European Commission, Eurostat, Luxembourg, 2920, LUX, https://ec.europa.eu/eurostat/; Eurostat Regional Yearbook 2021 and Final Energy Consumption in Transport by Type of Fuel.

International Energy Agency (IEA), 9 Rue de la Federation, Paris, 75739, FRA, info@iea.org, https://www.iea.org/; Coal 2021: Analysis and Forecast to 2024.

Organization for Economic Cooperation and Development (OECD), 2001 L St. NW, Ste. 650, Washington, DC, 20036-4922, USA, (202) 785-6323, (800) 456-6323, (202) 785-0350, washington.contact@oecd.org, https://www.oecd.org/; Energy

Prices and Taxes for OECD Countries 2020 and STAN (STructural ANalysis) Database.

S&P Global Commodity Insights, One World Trade Center, New York, NY, 10007, USA, (800) 752-8878, support@platts.com, https://www.spglobal.com/commodityinsights/en; Platts European Power Alert and Platts Power in Europe.

U.S. Energy Information Administration (EIA), 1000 Independence Ave. SW, Washington, DC, 20585, USA, (202) 586-8800, infoctr@eia.gov, https://www.eia.gov; International Energy Outlook 2021.

United Nations Statistics Division (UNSD), United Nations Plz., New York, NY, 10017, USA, (800) 253-9646, (212) 963-9851, statistics@un.org, https://unstats.un.org; Energy Statistics Yearbook 2019 and Statistical Yearbook of the United Nations 2021.

BELGIUM-EMPLOYMENT

European Commission, Eurostat, Luxembourg, 2920, LUX, https://ec.europa.eu/eurostat/; Eurostat Regional Yearbook 2021.

International Energy Agency (IEA), 9 Rue de la Federation, Paris, 75739, FRA, info@iea.org, https://www.iea.org/; Coal 2021: Analysis and Forecast to 2024.

International Labour Organization (ILO), 4 Rte. des Morillons, Geneva, CH-1211, SWI, ilo@ilo.org, https://www.ilo.org; NORMLEX Information System on International Labour Standards.

Organization for Economic Cooperation and Development (OECD), 2001 L St. NW, Ste. 650, Washington, DC, 20036-4922, USA, (202) 785-6323, (800) 456-6323, (202) 785-0350, washington.contact@oecd.org, https://www.oecd.org/; Economic Survey of Belgium 2022; OECD Composite Leading Indicator (CLI); OECD Digital Economy Outlook 2020; OECD Employment Outlook 2022: Building Back More Inclusive Labour Markets; and OECD Labour Force Statistics 2022.

UK Data Service, University of Essex, Wivenhoe Park, Colchester, Essex, CO4 3SQ, GBR, https://ukdataservice.ac.uk/; International Aggregate Data.

United Nations Statistics Division (UNSD), United Nations Plz., New York, NY, 10017, USA, (800) 253-9646, (212) 963-9851, statistics@un.org, https://unstats.un.org; Statistical Yearbook of the United Nations 2021.

The World Bank, 1818 H St. NW, Washington, DC, 20433, USA, (202) 473-1000, (202) 477-6391, eds03@worldbank.org, https://www.worldbank.org/; Belgium (report).

BELGIUM-ENERGY INDUSTRIES

Enerdata, 47 avenue Alsace Lorraine, Grenoble, 38027, FRA, (332) 216-4534, research@enerdata.net, https://www.enerdata.net; World Refinery Database.

European Commission, Rue de la Loi, 170, Brussels, B-1040, BEL, https://ec.europa.eu; EU Energy in Figures: Statistical Pocketbook 2021.

European Commission, Eurostat, Luxembourg, 2920, LUX, https://ec.europa.eu/eurostat/; Eurostat Regional Yearbook 2021 and Final Energy Consumption in Transport by Type of Fuel.

European Institute for Energy Research (EIFER), Emmy-Noether-Strasse 11, Ground Fl., Karlsruhe, D-76131, GER, contact@eifer.org, https://www.eifer.kit.edu/; unpublished data.

International Energy Agency (IEA), 9 Rue de la Federation, Paris, 75739, FRA, info@iea.org, https://www.iea.org/; Renewables Information and World Energy Statistics and Balances.

S&P Global Commodity Insights, One World Trade Center, New York, NY, 10007, USA, (800) 752-8878, support@platts.com, https://www.spglobal.com/commodityinsights/en; Platts European Power Daily and Platts Power in Europe.

United Nations Statistics Division (UNSD), United Nations Plz., New York, NY, 10017, USA, (800) 253-9646, (212) 963-9851, statistics@un.org, https://unstats.un.org; Statistical Yearbook of the United Nations 2021.

BELGIUM-ENVIRONMENTAL CONDITIONS

DSI Data Service & Information, Xantener Strasse 51a, Rheinberg, D-47495, GER, dsi@dsidata.com, https://www.dsidata.com/; Global Environmental Database.

The Economist Group: Economist Intelligence Unit (EIU), 900 3rd Ave., 16th Fl., New York, NY, 10022, USA, (212) 541-0500, americas@eiu.com, https://www.eiu.com; Belgium Country Report.

European Commission, Rue de la Loi, 170, Brussels, B-1040, BEL, https://ec.europa.eu; Common Agricultural Policy (CAPF) Context Indicators, 2019 Update.

European Commission, Eurostat, Luxembourg, 2920, LUX, https://ec.europa.eu/eurostat/; Environment Statistics Introduced.

Organization for Economic Cooperation and Development (OECD), 2001 L St. NW, Ste. 650, Washington, DC, 20036-4922, USA, (202) 785-6323, (800) 456-6323, (202) 785-0350, washington.contact@oecd.org, https://www.oecd.org/; Environment Statistics.

United Nations Statistics Division (UNSD), United Nations Plz., New York, NY, 10017, USA, (800) 253-9646, (212) 963-9851, statistics@un.org, https://unstats.un.org; World Statistics Pocketbook 2021.

BELGIUM-EXPENDITURES, PUBLIC

European Commission, Eurostat, Luxembourg, 2920, LUX, https://ec.europa.eu/eurostat/; Eurostat Regional Yearbook 2021.

Organization for Economic Cooperation and Development (OECD), 2001 L St. NW, Ste. 650, Washington, DC, 20036-4922, USA, (202) 785-6323, (800) 456-6323, (202) 785-0350, washington.contact@oecd.org, https://www.oecd.org/; Revenue Statistics 2022.

BELGIUM-EXPORTS

Central Intelligence Agency (CIA), Office of Public Affairs, Washington, DC, 20505, USA, (703) 482-0623, https://www.cia.gov; The World Factbook.

The Economist Group: Economist Intelligence Unit (EIU), 900 3rd Ave., 16th Fl., New York, NY, 10022, USA, (212) 541-0500, americas@eiu.com, https://www.eiu.com; Belgium Country Report.

European Commission, Eurostat, Luxembourg, 2920, LUX, https://ec.europa.eu/eurostat/; Eurostat Regional Yearbook 2021.

International Monetary Fund (IMF), 700 19th St. NW, Washington, DC, 20431, USA, (202) 623-7000, (202) 623-4661, publications@imf.org, https://www.imf.org; Direction of Trade Statistics (DOTS) and International Financial Statistics (IFS).

Organization for Economic Cooperation and Development (OECD), 2001 L St. NW, Ste. 650, Washington, DC, 20036-4922, USA, (202) 785-6323, (800) 456-6323, (202) 785-0350, washington.contact@oecd.org, https://www.oecd.org/; Economic Survey of Belgium 2022; Geographical Distribution of Financial Flows to Developing Countries 2023; OECD Digital Economy Outlook 2020; OECD Review of Fisheries 2022; OECD-FAO Agricultural Outlook 2022-2031; and STAN (STructural ANalysis) Database.

S&P Global, IHS Markit, 15 Inverness Way E, Englewood, CO, 80112, USA, (800) 447-2273, (800) 854-7179, https://ihsmarkit.com; Global Trade Atlas (GTA).

TAPPI - Technical Association of the Pulp and Paper Industry, 15 Technology Pkwy. S, Ste. 115, Peachtree Corners, GA, 30092, USA, (770) 446-1400, (800) 332-8686, (770) 446-6947, memberconnection@tappi.org, https://www.tappi.org/; TAPPI Journal.

United Nations Conference on Trade and Development (UNCTAD), Palais des Nations, Geneva, 1211, SWI, (212) 963-6896, unctadinfo@unctad.org, https://unctad.org; Handbook of Statistics 2021.

United Nations Statistics Division (UNSD), United Nations Plz., New York, NY, 10017, USA, (800) 253-9646, (212) 963-9851, statistics@un.org, https://unstats.un.org; Energy Statistics Yearbook 2019.

The World Bank, 1818 H St. NW, Washington, DC, 20433, USA, (202) 473-1000, (202) 477-6391, eds03@worldbank.org, https://www.worldbank.org/; World Development Report 2022: Finance for an Equitable Recovery.

World Steel Association (Worldsteel), Avenue de Tervueren 270, Brussels, B-1150, BEL, steel@worldsteel.org, https://www.worldsteel.org; Steel Statistical Yearbook 2021.

BELGIUM-FEMALE WORKING POPULATION

See BELGIUM-EMPLOYMENT

BELGIUM-FERTILITY, HUMAN

Central Intelligence Agency (CIA), Office of Public Affairs, Washington, DC, 20505, USA, (703) 482-0623, https://www.cia.gov; The World Factbook.

BELGIUM-FERTILIZER INDUSTRY

Organization for Economic Cooperation and Development (OECD), 2001 L St. NW, Ste. 650, Washington, DC, 20036-4922, USA, (202) 785-6323, (800) 456-6323, (202) 785-0350, washington.contact@oecd.org, https://www.oecd.org/; OECD-FAO Agricultural Outlook 2022-2031.

United Nations Food and Agricultural Organization (FAO), 2121 K St., Ste. 800B, Washington, DC, 20037, USA, (202) 653-2400 (Dial from U.S.), (202) 653-5760 (Fax from U.S.), fao-hq@fao.org, https://www.fao.org; The State of Food and Agriculture (SOFA) 2022.

BELGIUM-FETAL MORTALITY

See BELGIUM-MORTALITY

BELGIUM-FINANCE

European Commission, Eurostat, Luxembourg, 2920, LUX, https://ec.europa.eu/eurostat/; Eurostat Regional Yearbook 2021.

International Monetary Fund (IMF), 700 19th St. NW, Washington, DC, 20431, USA, (202) 623-7000, (202) 623-4661, publications@imf.org, https://www.imf.org; International Financial Statistics (IFS).

Organization for Economic Cooperation and Development (OECD), 2001 L St. NW, Ste. 650, Washington, DC, 20036-4922, USA, (202) 785-6323, (800) 456-6323, (202) 785-0350, washington.contact@oecd.org, https://www.oecd.org/; OECD Digital Economy Outlook 2020.

Stockholm International Peace Research Institute (SIPRI), Signalistgatan 9, Stockholm, SE 169 72, SWE, https://www.sipri.org/; SIPRI Arms Transfers Database and SIPRI Military Expenditure Database.

United Nations Statistics Division (UNSD), United Nations Plz., New York, NY, 10017, USA, (800) 253-9646, (212) 963-9851, statistics@un.org, https://unstats.un.org; Statistical Yearbook of the United Nations 2021.

The World Bank, 1818 H St. NW, Washington, DC, 20433, USA, (202) 473-1000, (202) 477-6391, eds03@worldbank.org, https://www.worldbank.org/; Belgium (report).

BELGIUM-FINANCE, PUBLIC

Banque de France, 31 rue Croix des Petits-Champs, Paris, 75049, FRA, infos@banque-france.fr, https://www.banque-france.fr/en; Webstat: Access to Statistical Series of Banque de France.

Bernan Press, 15250 NBN Way, Bldg. C, Blue Ridge Summit, PA, 17214, USA, (301) 459-2255, (800) 865-3457, (800) 865-3450, customercare@bernan.com, https://rowman.com/Page/Bernan; National Accounts Statistics: Analysis of Main Aggregates 2020.

The Economist Group: Economist Intelligence Unit (EIU), 900 3rd Ave., 16th Fl., New York, NY, 10022, USA, (212) 541-0500, americas@eiu.com, https://www.eiu.com; Belgium Country Report.

European Commission, Eurostat, Luxembourg, 2920, LUX, https://ec.europa.eu/eurostat/; Eurostat Regional Yearbook 2021.

International Monetary Fund (IMF), 700 19th St. NW, Washington, DC, 20431, USA, (202) 623-7000, (202) 623-4661, publications@imf.org, https://www.imf.org; International Financial Statistics (IFS) and Regional Economic Outlook.

Organization for Economic Cooperation and Development (OECD), 2001 L St. NW, Ste. 650, Washington, DC, 20036-4922, USA, (202) 785-6323, (800) 456-6323, (202) 785-0350, washington.contact@oecd.org, https://www.oecd.org/; Geographical Distribution of Financial Flows to Developing Countries 2023; OECD Business and Finance Outlook 2021; OECD Digital Economy Outlook 2020; and Revenue Statistics 2022.

Palgrave Macmillan, 1 New York Plaza, Ste. 4500, New York, NY, 10004-1562, USA, (800) 777-4643, orders@palgrave.com, https://www.palgrave.com/us; The Statesman's Yearbook, 2023.

Routledge - Taylor & Francis Group, 6000 Broken Sound Pkwy. NW, Ste. 300, Boca Raton, FL, 33487, USA, (800) 634-1420, (800) 634-7064, orders@taylorandfrancis.com, https://www.routledge.com/; The Europa World Year Book 2022.

United Nations Statistics Division (UNSD), United Nations Plz., New York, NY, 10017, USA, (800) 253-9646, (212) 963-9851, statistics@un.org, https://unstats.un.org; National Accounts Main Aggregates Database and National Accounts Statistics: Main Aggregates and Detailed Tables.

The World Bank, 1818 H St. NW, Washington, DC, 20433, USA, (202) 473-1000, (202) 477-6391, eds03@worldbank.org, https://www.worldbank.org/; Belgium (report).

BELGIUM-FISHERIES

European Commission, Eurostat, Luxembourg, 2920, LUX, https://ec.europa.eu/eurostat/; Eurostat Regional Yearbook 2021.

Organization for Economic Cooperation and Development (OECD), 2001 L St. NW, Ste. 650, Washington, DC, 20036-4922, USA, (202) 785-6323, (800) 456-6323, (202) 785-0350, washington.contact@oecd.org, https://www.oecd.org/; OECD Review of Fisheries 2022 and STAN (STructural ANalysis) Database.

Palgrave Macmillan, 1 New York Plaza, Ste. 4500, New York, NY, 10004-1562, USA, (800) 777-4643, orders@palgrave.com, https://www.palgrave.com/us; The Statesman's Yearbook, 2023.

Routledge - Taylor & Francis Group, 6000 Broken Sound Pkwy. NW, Ste. 300, Boca Raton, FL, 33487, USA, (800) 634-1420, (800) 634-7064, orders@taylorandfrancis.com, https://www.routledge.com/; The Europa World Year Book 2022.

United Nations Food and Agricultural Organization (FAO), 2121 K St., Ste. 800B, Washington, DC, 20037, USA, (202) 653-2400 (Dial from U.S.), (202) 653-5760 (Fax from U.S.), fao-hq@fao.org, https://www.fao.org; FAO Yearbook of Fishery and Aquaculture Statistics 2019; Fishery Statistical Collections Global Capture Production; FishStatJ; and The State of Food and Agriculture (SOFA) 2022.

United Nations Statistics Division (UNSD), United Nations Plz., New York, NY, 10017, USA, (800) 253-9646, (212) 963-9851, statistics@un.org, https://unstats.un.org; Statistical Yearbook of the United Nations 2021.

The World Bank, 1818 H St. NW, Washington, DC, 20433, USA, (202) 473-1000, (202) 477-6391, eds03@worldbank.org, https://www.worldbank.org/; Belgium (report).

BELGIUM-FOOD

Euromonitor International, Inc., 1 N Dearborn St., Ste. 1700, Chicago, IL, 60602, USA, (312) 922-1115, (312) 922-1157, info-usa@euromonitor.com, https://www.euromonitor.com/; Geographies.

European Commission, Eurostat, Luxembourg, 2920, LUX, https://ec.europa.eu/eurostat/; Eurostat Regional Yearbook 2021.

United Nations Food and Agricultural Organization (FAO), 2121 K St., Ste. 800B, Washington, DC, 20037, USA, (202) 653-2400 (Dial from U.S.), (202) 653-5760 (Fax from U.S.), fao-hq@fao.org, https://www.fao.org; The State of Food and Agriculture (SOFA) 2022.

BELGIUM-FOREIGN EXCHANGE RATES

European Commission, Eurostat, Luxembourg, 2920, LUX, https://ec.europa.eu/eurostat/; Eurostat Regional Yearbook 2021.

International Monetary Fund (IMF), 700 19th St. NW, Washington, DC, 20431, USA, (202) 623-7000, (202) 623-4661, publications@imf.org, https://www.imf.org; International Financial Statistics (IFS).

Organization for Economic Cooperation and Development (OECD), 2001 L St. NW, Ste. 650, Washington, DC, 20036-4922, USA, (202) 785-6323, (800) 456-6323, (202) 785-0350, washington.contact@oecd.org, https://www.oecd.org/; OECD Business and Finance Outlook 2021; OECD Digital Economy Outlook 2020; OECD Tourism Trends and Policies 2022; and Revenue Statistics 2022.

BELGIUM-FORESTS AND FORESTRY

European Commission, Eurostat, Luxembourg, 2920, LUX, https://ec.europa.eu/eurostat/; Eurostat Regional Yearbook 2021.

Organization for Economic Cooperation and Development (OECD), 2001 L St. NW, Ste. 650, Washington, DC, 20036-4922, USA, (202) 785-6323, (800) 456-6323, (202) 785-0350, washington.contact@oecd.org, https://www.oecd.org/; STAN (STructural ANalysis) Database.

Palgrave Macmillan, 1 New York Plaza, Ste. 4500, New York, NY, 10004-1562, USA, (800) 777-4643, orders@palgrave.com, https://www.palgrave.com/us; The Statesman's Yearbook, 2023.

TAPPI - Technical Association of the Pulp and Paper Industry, 15 Technology Pkwy. S, Ste. 115, Peachtree Corners, GA, 30092, USA, (770) 446-1400, (800) 332-8686, (770) 446-6947, memberconnection@tappi.org, https://www.tappi.org/; TAPPI Journal.

UNESCO Institute for Statistics, C.P 250 Succursale H, Montreal, QC, H3G 2K8, CAN, (514) 343-6880 (Dial from U.S.), (514) 343-5740 (Fax from U.S.), uis.publications@unesco.org, http://uis.unesco.org/; UIS.Stat.

United Nations Food and Agricultural Organization (FAO), 2121 K St., Ste. 800B, Washington, DC, 20037, USA, (202) 653-2400 (Dial from U.S.), (202) 653-5760 (Fax from U.S.), fao-hq@fao.org, https://www.fao.org; FAO Yearbook of Forest Products 2019 and The State of Food and Agriculture (SOFA) 2022.

The World Bank, 1818 H St. NW, Washington, DC, 20433, USA, (202) 473-1000, (202) 477-6391, eds03@worldbank.org, https://www.worldbank.org/; Belgium (report) and World Development Report 2022: Finance for an Equitable Recovery.

BELGIUM-FRUIT PRODUCTION

See BELGIUM-CROPS

BELGIUM-GAS PRODUCTION

See BELGIUM-MINERAL INDUSTRIES

BELGIUM-GEOGRAPHIC INFORMATION SYSTEMS

The World Bank, 1818 H St. NW, Washington, DC, 20433, USA, (202) 473-1000, (202) 477-6391, eds03@worldbank.org, https://www.worldbank.org/; Belgium (report).

BELGIUM-GOLD INDUSTRY

The World Bank, 1818 H St. NW, Washington, DC, 20433, USA, (202) 473-1000, (202) 477-6391, eds03@worldbank.org, https://www.worldbank.org/; World Development Indicators (WDI) 2022.

BELGIUM-GOLD PRODUCTION

See BELGIUM-MINERAL INDUSTRIES

BELGIUM-GRANTS-IN-AID

Organization for Economic Cooperation and Development (OECD), 2001 L St. NW, Ste. 650, Washington, DC, 20036-4922, USA, (202) 785-6323, (800) 456-6323, (202) 785-0350, washington.contact@oecd.org, https://www.oecd.org/; Geographical Distribution of Financial Flows to Developing Countries 2023.

BELGIUM-GROSS DOMESTIC PRODUCT

The Economist Group: Economist Intelligence Unit (EIU), 900 3rd Ave., 16th Fl., New York, NY, 10022, USA, (212) 541-0500, americas@eiu.com, https://www.eiu.com; Belgium Country Report.

European Commission, Eurostat, Luxembourg, 2920, LUX, https://ec.europa.eu/eurostat/; Eurostat Regional Yearbook 2021.

Organization for Economic Cooperation and Development (OECD), 2001 L St. NW, Ste. 650, Washington, DC, 20036-4922, USA, (202) 785-6323, (800) 456-6323, (202) 785-0350, washington.contact@oecd.org, https://www.oecd.org/; Geographical Distribution of Financial Flows to Developing Countries 2023; OECD Digital Economy Outlook 2020; and Revenue Statistics 2022.

Routledge - Taylor & Francis Group, 6000 Broken Sound Pkwy. NW, Ste. 300, Boca Raton, FL, 33487, USA, (800) 634-1420, (800) 634-7064, orders@taylorandfrancis.com, https://www.routledge.com/; The Europa World Year Book 2022.

United Nations Statistics Division (UNSD), United Nations Plz., New York, NY, 10017, USA, (800) 253-9646, (212) 963-9851, statistics@un.org, https://unstats.un.org; Statistical Yearbook of the United Nations 2021.

The World Bank, 1818 H St. NW, Washington, DC, 20433, USA, (202) 473-1000, (202) 477-6391, eds03@worldbank.org, https://www.worldbank.org/; World Development Indicators (WDI) 2022 and World Development Report 2022: Finance for an Equitable Recovery.

BELGIUM-GROSS NATIONAL PRODUCT

European Commission, Eurostat, Luxembourg, 2920, LUX, https://ec.europa.eu/eurostat/; Eurostat Regional Yearbook 2021.

Organization for Economic Cooperation and Development (OECD), 2001 L St. NW, Ste. 650, Washington, DC, 20036-4922, USA, (202) 785-6323, (800) 456-6323, (202) 785-0350, washington.contact@oecd.org, https://www.oecd.org/; Geographical Distribution of Financial Flows to Developing Countries 2023; OECD Composite Leading Indicator (CLI); and OECD Digital Economy Outlook 2020.

Palgrave Macmillan, 1 New York Plaza, Ste. 4500, New York, NY, 10004-1562, USA, (800) 777-4643, orders@palgrave.com, https://www.palgrave.com/us; The Statesman's Yearbook, 2023.

United Nations Statistics Division (UNSD), United Nations Plz., New York, NY, 10017, USA, (800) 253-9646, (212) 963-9851, statistics@un.org, https://unstats.un.org; Statistical Yearbook of the United Nations 2021.

The World Bank, 1818 H St. NW, Washington, DC, 20433, USA, (202) 473-1000, (202) 477-6391, eds03@worldbank.org, https://www.worldbank.org/; World Development Indicators (WDI) 2022 and World Development Report 2022: Finance for an Equitable Recovery.

BELGIUM-HAY PRODUCTION

See BELGIUM-CROPS

BELGIUM-HAZELNUT PRODUCTION

See BELGIUM-CROPS

BELGIUM-HEALTH

See BELGIUM-PUBLIC HEALTH

BELGIUM-HEMP FIBRE PRODUCTION

See BELGIUM-TEXTILE INDUSTRY

BELGIUM-HOUSING

Euromonitor International, Inc., 1 N Dearborn St., Ste. 1700, Chicago, IL, 60602, USA, (312) 922-1115, (312) 922-1157, info-usa@euromonitor.com, https://www.euromonitor.com/; Geographies.

European Commission, Eurostat, Luxembourg, 2920, LUX, https://ec.europa.eu/eurostat/; Eurostat Regional Yearbook 2021.

BELGIUM-HOUSING-FINANCE

Organization for Economic Cooperation and Development (OECD), 2001 L St. NW, Ste. 650, Washington, DC, 20036-4922, USA, (202) 785-6323, (800) 456-6323, (202) 785-0350, washington.contact@oecd.org, https://www.oecd.org/; OECD Main Economic Indicators (MEI).

BELGIUM-HOUSING CONSTRUCTION

See BELGIUM-CONSTRUCTION INDUSTRY

BELGIUM-ILLITERATE PERSONS

UNESCO Institute for Statistics, C.P 250 Succursale H, Montreal, QC, H3G 2K8, CAN, (514) 343-6880 (Dial from U.S.), (514) 343-5740 (Fax from U.S.), uis.publications@unesco.org, http://uis.unesco.org/; UIS.Stat.

BELGIUM-IMPORTS

Central Intelligence Agency (CIA), Office of Public Affairs, Washington, DC, 20505, USA, (703) 482-0623, https://www.cia.gov; The World Factbook.

The Economist Group: Economist Intelligence Unit (EIU), 900 3rd Ave., 16th Fl., New York, NY, 10022, USA, (212) 541-0500, americas@eiu.com, https://www.eiu.com; Belgium Country Report.

European Commission, Eurostat, Luxembourg, 2920, LUX, https://ec.europa.eu/eurostat/; Eurostat Regional Yearbook 2021.

International Monetary Fund (IMF), 700 19th St. NW, Washington, DC, 20431, USA, (202) 623-7000, (202) 623-4661, publications@imf.org, https://www.imf.org; Direction of Trade Statistics (DOTS).

Organization for Economic Cooperation and Development (OECD), 2001 L St. NW, Ste. 650, Washington, DC, 20036-4922, USA, (202) 785-6323, (800) 456-6323, (202) 785-0350, washington.contact@oecd.org, https://www.oecd.org/; OECD Digital Economy Outlook 2020; OECD Review of Fisheries 2022; OECD-FAO Agricultural Outlook 2022-2031; and STAN (STructural ANalysis) Database.

S&P Global, IHS Markit, 15 Inverness Way E, Englewood, CO, 80112, USA, (800) 447-2273, (800) 854-7179, https://ihsmarkit.com; Global Trade Atlas (GTA).

TAPPI - Technical Association of the Pulp and Paper Industry, 15 Technology Pkwy. S, Ste. 115, Peachtree Corners, GA, 30092, USA, (770) 446-1400, (800) 332-8686, (770) 446-6947, memberconnection@tappi.org, https://www.tappi.org/; TAPPI Journal.

United Nations Conference on Trade and Development (UNCTAD), Palais des Nations, Geneva, 1211, SWI, (212) 963-6896, unctadinfo@unctad.org, https://unctad.org; Handbook of Statistics 2021.

United Nations Statistics Division (UNSD), United Nations Plz., New York, NY, 10017, USA, (800) 253-9646, (212) 963-9851, statistics@un.org, https://unstats.un.org; Energy Statistics Yearbook 2019.

The World Bank, 1818 H St. NW, Washington, DC, 20433, USA, (202) 473-1000, (202) 477-6391, eds03@worldbank.org, https://www.worldbank.org/; World Development Report 2022: Finance for an Equitable Recovery.

World Steel Association (Worldsteel), Avenue de Tervueren 270, Brussels, B-1150, BEL, steel@worldsteel.org, https://www.worldsteel.org; Steel Statistical Yearbook 2021.

BELGIUM-INDUSTRIAL METALS PRODUCTION

See BELGIUM-MINERAL INDUSTRIES

BELGIUM-INDUSTRIAL PRODUCTIVITY

European Commission, Eurostat, Luxembourg, 2920, LUX, https://ec.europa.eu/eurostat/; Eurostat Regional Yearbook 2021.

Organization for Economic Cooperation and Development (OECD), 2001 L St. NW, Ste. 650, Washington, DC, 20036-4922, USA, (202) 785-6323, (800) 456-6323, (202) 785-0350, washington.contact@oecd.org, https://www.oecd.org/; OECD Digital Economy Outlook 2020; OECD-FAO Agricultural Outlook 2022-2031; and STAN (STructural ANalysis) Database.

TAPPI - Technical Association of the Pulp and Paper Industry, 15 Technology Pkwy. S, Ste. 115, Peachtree Corners, GA, 30092, USA, (770) 446-1400, (800) 332-8686, (770) 446-6947, memberconnection@tappi.org, https://www.tappi.org/; TAPPI Journal.

World Steel Association (Worldsteel), Avenue de Tervueren 270, Brussels, B-1150, BEL, steel@worldsteel.org, https://www.worldsteel.org; Steel Statistical Yearbook 2021.

BELGIUM-INDUSTRIES

Central Intelligence Agency (CIA), Office of Public Affairs, Washington, DC, 20505, USA, (703) 482-0623, https://www.cia.gov; The World Factbook.

The Economist Group: Economist Intelligence Unit (EIU), 900 3rd Ave., 16th Fl., New York, NY, 10022, USA, (212) 541-0500, americas@eiu.com, https://www.eiu.com; Belgium Country Report.

Euromonitor International, Inc., 1 N Dearborn St., Ste. 1700, Chicago, IL, 60602, USA, (312) 922-1115, (312) 922-1157, info-usa@euromonitor.com, https://www.euromonitor.com/; Geographies.

European Commission, Eurostat, Luxembourg, 2920, LUX, https://ec.europa.eu/eurostat/; Eurostat Regional Yearbook 2021.

International Labour Organization (ILO), 4 Rte. des Morillons, Geneva, CH-1211, SWI, ilo@ilo.org, https://www.ilo.org; NORMLEX Information System on International Labour Standards.

Organization for Economic Cooperation and Development (OECD), 2001 L St. NW, Ste. 650, Washington, DC, 20036-4922, USA, (202) 785-6323, (800) 456-6323, (202) 785-0350, washington.contact@oecd.org, https://www.oecd.org/; Environment Statistics; OECD Digital Economy Outlook 2020; OECD Main Economic Indicators (MEI); and STAN (STructural ANalysis) Database.

Palgrave Macmillan, 1 New York Plaza, Ste. 4500, New York, NY, 10004-1562, USA, (800) 777-4643, orders@palgrave.com, https://www.palgrave.com/us; The Statesman's Yearbook, 2023.

Routledge - Taylor & Francis Group, 6000 Broken Sound Pkwy. NW, Ste. 300, Boca Raton, FL, 33487, USA, (800) 634-1420, (800) 634-7064, orders@taylorandfrancis.com, https://www.routledge.com/; The Europa World Year Book 2022.

United Nations Industrial Development Organization (UNIDO), 1 United Nations Plz., Rm. DC1-1118, New York, NY, 10017, USA, (212) 963-6890, (212) 963 6885, (212) 963-7904, office.newyork@unido.org, https://www.unido.org/; Industrial Statistics Databases and International Yearbook of Industrial Statistics 2021.

The World Bank, 1818 H St. NW, Washington, DC, 20433, USA, (202) 473-1000, (202) 477-6391, eds03@worldbank.org, https://www.worldbank.org/; Belgium (report) and World Development Indicators (WDI) 2022.

BELGIUM-INFANT AND MATERNAL MORTALITY

See BELGIUM-MORTALITY

BELGIUM-INTEREST RATES

Organization for Economic Cooperation and Development (OECD), 2001 L St. NW, Ste. 650, Washington, DC, 20036-4922, USA, (202) 785-6323, (800) 456-6323, (202) 785-0350, washington.contact@oecd.org, https://www.oecd.org/; OECD Business and Finance Outlook 2021; OECD Digital Economy Outlook 2020; and OECD Main Economic Indicators (MEI).

United Nations Statistics Division (UNSD), United Nations Plz., New York, NY, 10017, USA, (800) 253-9646, (212) 963-9851, statistics@un.org, https://unstats.un.org; Statistical Yearbook of the United Nations 2021.

BELGIUM-INTERNAL REVENUE

Organization for Economic Cooperation and Development (OECD), 2001 L St. NW, Ste. 650, Washington, DC, 20036-4922, USA, (202) 785-6323, (800) 456-6323, (202) 785-0350, washington.contact@oecd.org, https://www.oecd.org/; Revenue Statistics 2022.

BELGIUM-INTERNATIONAL FINANCE

European Commission, Eurostat, Luxembourg, 2920, LUX, https://ec.europa.eu/eurostat/; Eurostat Regional Yearbook 2021.

Inter-American Development Bank (IDB), 1300 New York Ave. NW, Washington, DC, 20577, USA, (202) 623-1000, (202) 623-3096, https://www.iadb.org/en; Latin Macro Watch (LMW).

Organization for Economic Cooperation and Development (OECD), 2001 L St. NW, Ste. 650, Washington, DC, 20036-4922, USA, (202) 785-6323, (800) 456-6323, (202) 785-0350, washington.contact@oecd.org, https://www.oecd.org/; OECD Business and Finance Outlook 2021; OECD Digital Economy Outlook 2020; and OECD Main Economic Indicators (MEI).

World Bank Group: International Finance Corporation (IFC), 2121 Pennsylvania Ave. NW, Washington, DC, 20433, USA, (202) 473-1000, (202) 473-7711, (202) 974-4384, https://www.ifc.org; Annual Report 2021: Meeting the Moment.

BELGIUM-INTERNATIONAL LIQUIDITY

Organization for Economic Cooperation and Development (OECD), 2001 L St. NW, Ste. 650, Washington, DC, 20036-4922, USA, (202) 785-6323, (800) 456-6323, (202) 785-0350, washington.contact@oecd.org, https://www.oecd.org/; OECD Business and Finance Outlook 2021.

BELGIUM-INTERNATIONAL TRADE

Banque de France, 31 rue Croix des Petits-Champs, Paris, 75049, FRA, infos@banque-france.fr, https://www.banque-france.fr/en; Key Figures France and Abroad.

The Economist Group: Economist Intelligence Unit (EIU), 900 3rd Ave., 16th Fl., New York, NY, 10022, USA, (212) 541-0500, americas@eiu.com, https://www.eiu.com; Belgium Country Report.

Euromonitor International, Inc., 1 N Dearborn St., Ste. 1700, Chicago, IL, 60602, USA, (312) 922-1115, (312) 922-1157, info-usa@euromonitor.com, https://www.euromonitor.com/; Geographies.

European Commission, Eurostat, Luxembourg, 2920, LUX, https://ec.europa.eu/eurostat/; Eurostat Regional Yearbook 2021 and Extra-EU Trade in Goods.

Organization for Economic Cooperation and Development (OECD), 2001 L St. NW, Ste. 650, Washington, DC, 20036-4922, USA, (202) 785-6323, (800) 456-6323, (202) 785-0350, washington.contact@oecd.org, https://www.oecd.org/; Economic Survey of Belgium 2022; OECD Digital Economy Outlook 2020; OECD Main Economic Indicators (MEI); and OECD-FAO Agricultural Outlook 2022-2031.

Palgrave Macmillan, 1 New York Plaza, Ste. 4500, New York, NY, 10004-1562, USA, (800) 777-4643, orders@palgrave.com, https://www.palgrave.com/us; The Statesman's Yearbook, 2023.

Routledge - Taylor & Francis Group, 6000 Broken Sound Pkwy. NW, Ste. 300, Boca Raton, FL, 33487, USA, (800) 634-1420, (800) 634-7064, orders@taylorandfrancis.com, https://www.routledge.com/; The Europa World Year Book 2022.

United Nations Conference on Trade and Development (UNCTAD), Palais des Nations, Geneva, 1211, SWI, (212) 963-6896, unctadinfo@unctad.org, https://unctad.org; Trade and Development Report 2021.

United Nations Food and Agricultural Organization (FAO), 2121 K St., Ste. 800B, Washington, DC, 20037, USA, (202) 653-2400 (Dial from U.S.), (202) 653-5760 (Fax from U.S.), fao-hq@fao.org, https://www.fao.org; The State of Food and Agriculture (SOFA) 2022.

United Nations Statistics Division (UNSD), United Nations Plz., New York, NY, 10017, USA, (800) 253-9646, (212) 963-9851, statistics@un.org, https://unstats.un.org; International Trade Statistics Yearbook 2020 and Statistical Yearbook of the United Nations 2021.

The World Bank, 1818 H St. NW, Washington, DC, 20433, USA, (202) 473-1000, (202) 477-6391, eds03@worldbank.org, https://www.worldbank.org/; Belgium (report); World Development Indicators (WDI) 2022; and World Development Report 2022: Finance for an Equitable Recovery.

World Bureau of Metal Statistics (WBMS), 31 Star St., Ware, Hertfordshire, SG12 9BA, GBR, https://www.refinitiv.com/en/trading-solutions/world-bureau-metal-statistics; Long Term Production/Consumption Series - All Metals; World Flow Charts; and World Metal Statistics.

World Steel Association (Worldsteel), Avenue de Tervueren 270, Brussels, B-1150, BEL, steel@worldsteel.org, https://www.worldsteel.org; Steel Statistical Yearbook 2021.

World Trade Organization (WTO), Ctre. William Rappard, Rue de Lausanne 154, Case postale, Geneva, CH-1211, SWI, enquiries@wto.org, https://www.wto.org; World Trade Statistical Review 2022.

BELGIUM-INTERNET USERS

International Telecommunication Union (ITU), Place des Nations, Geneva, CH-1211, SWI, itumail@itu.int, https://www.itu.int; Global Connectivity Report 2022; World Telecommunication/ICT Indicators Database 2021; and Yearbook of Statistics 2019.

The World Bank, 1818 H St. NW, Washington, DC, 20433, USA, (202) 473-1000, (202) 477-6391, eds03@worldbank.org, https://www.worldbank.org/; Belgium (report).

BELGIUM-INVESTMENTS

International Monetary Fund (IMF), 700 19th St. NW, Washington, DC, 20431, USA, (202) 623-7000, (202) 623-4661, publications@imf.org, https://www.imf.org; International Financial Statistics (IFS).

Organization for Economic Cooperation and Development (OECD), 2001 L St. NW, Ste. 650, Washington, DC, 20036-4922, USA, (202) 785-6323, (800) 456-6323, (202) 785-0350, washington.contact@oecd.org, https://www.oecd.org/; OECD Business and Finance Outlook 2021; OECD Digital Economy Outlook 2020; and STAN (STructural ANalysis) Database.

BELGIUM-LABOR

Central Intelligence Agency (CIA), Office of Public Affairs, Washington, DC, 20505, USA, (703) 482-0623, https://www.cia.gov; The World Factbook.

Euromonitor International, Inc., 1 N Dearborn St., Ste. 1700, Chicago, IL, 60602, USA, (312) 922-1115, (312) 922-1157, info-usa@euromonitor.com, https://www.euromonitor.com/; Geographies.

European Commission, Eurostat, Luxembourg, 2920, LUX, https://ec.europa.eu/eurostat/; Eurostat Regional Yearbook 2021.

International Labour Organization (ILO), 4 Rte. des Morillons, Geneva, CH-1211, SWI, ilo@ilo.org, https://www.ilo.org; NORMLEX Information System on International Labour Standards.

Organization for Economic Cooperation and Development (OECD), 2001 L St. NW, Ste. 650, Washington, DC, 20036-4922, USA, (202) 785-6323, (800) 456-6323, (202) 785-0350, washington.contact@oecd.org, https://www.oecd.org/; Economic Survey of Belgium 2022; OECD Digital Economy Outlook 2020; OECD Employment Outlook 2022: Building Back More Inclusive Labour Markets; and OECD Main Economic Indicators (MEI).

Palgrave Macmillan, 1 New York Plaza, Ste. 4500, New York, NY, 10004-1562, USA, (800) 777-4643, orders@palgrave.com, https://www.palgrave.com/us; The Statesman's Yearbook, 2023.

United Nations Economic Commission for Europe (UNECE), Palais des Nations, Geneva, CH-1211, SWI, unece_info@un.org, https://unece.org/; UNECE Countries in Figures 2019.

United Nations Food and Agricultural Organization (FAO), 2121 K St., Ste. 800B, Washington, DC, 20037, USA, (202) 653-2400 (Dial from U.S.), (202) 653-5760 (Fax from U.S.), fao-hq@fao.org, https://www.fao.org; The State of Food and Agriculture (SOFA) 2022.

The World Bank, 1818 H St. NW, Washington, DC, 20433, USA, (202) 473-1000, (202) 477-6391, eds03@worldbank.org, https://www.worldbank.org/; World Development Indicators (WDI) 2022 and World Development Report 2022: Finance for an Equitable Recovery.

BELGIUM-LAND USE

European Commission, Eurostat, Luxembourg, 2920, LUX, https://ec.europa.eu/eurostat/; Eurostat Regional Yearbook 2021.

United Nations Statistics Division (UNSD), United Nations Plz., New York, NY, 10017, USA, (800) 253-9646, (212) 963-9851, statistics@un.org, https://unstats.un.org; Millennium Development Goal Indicators.

The World Bank, 1818 H St. NW, Washington, DC, 20433, USA, (202) 473-1000, (202) 477-6391, eds03@worldbank.org, https://www.worldbank.org/; World Development Report 2022: Finance for an Equitable Recovery.

BELGIUM-LIBRARIES

UNESCO Institute for Statistics, C.P 250 Succursale H, Montreal, QC, H3G 2K8, CAN, (514) 343-6880 (Dial from U.S.), (514) 343-5740 (Fax from U.S.), uis.publications@unesco.org, http://uis.unesco.org/; UIS.Stat.

BELGIUM-LIFE EXPECTANCY

Central Intelligence Agency (CIA), Office of Public Affairs, Washington, DC, 20505, USA, (703) 482-0623, https://www.cia.gov; The World Factbook.

United Nations Department of Economic and Social Affairs (DESA), Population Division, 2 United Nations Plz., Rm. DC2-1950, New York, NY, 10017, USA, (212) 963-3209, (212) 963-2147, population@un.org, https://www.un.org/development/desa/pd/; World Population Ageing 2020 Highlights.

United Nations Economic Commission for Europe (UNECE), Palais des Nations, Geneva, CH-1211, SWI, unece_info@un.org, https://unece.org/; UNECE Countries in Figures 2019.

United Nations Statistics Division (UNSD), United Nations Plz., New York, NY, 10017, USA, (800) 253-9646, (212) 963-9851, statistics@un.org, https://unstats.un.org; Millennium Development Goal Indicators.

BELGIUM-LITERACY

Euromonitor International, Inc., 1 N Dearborn St., Ste. 1700, Chicago, IL, 60602, USA, (312) 922-1115, (312) 922-1157, info-usa@euromonitor.com, https://www.euromonitor.com/; Geographies.

UNESCO Institute for Statistics, C.P 250 Succursale H, Montreal, QC, H3G 2K8, CAN, (514) 343-6880 (Dial from U.S.), (514) 343-5740 (Fax from U.S.), uis.publications@unesco.org, http://uis.unesco.org/; Literacy.

BELGIUM-LIVESTOCK

European Commission, Eurostat, Luxembourg, 2920, LUX, https://ec.europa.eu/eurostat/; Eurostat Regional Yearbook 2021.

Organization for Economic Cooperation and Development (OECD), 2001 L St. NW, Ste. 650, Washington, DC, 20036-4922, USA, (202) 785-6323, (800) 456-6323, (202) 785-0350, washington.contact@oecd.org, https://www.oecd.org/; OECD-FAO Agricultural Outlook 2022-2031.

Palgrave Macmillan, 1 New York Plaza, Ste. 4500, New York, NY, 10004-1562, USA, (800) 777-4643, orders@palgrave.com, https://www.palgrave.com/us; The Statesman's Yearbook, 2023.

Routledge - Taylor & Francis Group, 6000 Broken Sound Pkwy. NW, Ste. 300, Boca Raton, FL, 33487, USA, (800) 634-1420, (800) 634-7064, orders@taylorandfrancis.com, https://www.routledge.com/; The Europa World Year Book 2022.

United Nations Food and Agricultural Organization (FAO), 2121 K St., Ste. 800B, Washington, DC, 20037, USA, (202) 653-2400 (Dial from U.S.), (202) 653-5760 (Fax from U.S.), fao-hq@fao.org, https://www.fao.org; The State of Food and Agriculture (SOFA) 2022.

United Nations Statistics Division (UNSD), United Nations Plz., New York, NY, 10017, USA, (800) 253-9646, (212) 963-9851, statistics@un.org, https://unstats.un.org; Statistical Yearbook of the United Nations 2021.

BELGIUM-MAGNESIUM PRODUCTION AND CONSUMPTION

See BELGIUM-MINERAL INDUSTRIES

BELGIUM-MANUFACTURES

European Commission, Eurostat, Luxembourg, 2920, LUX, https://ec.europa.eu/eurostat/; Eurostat Regional Yearbook 2021.

Organization for Economic Cooperation and Development (OECD), 2001 L St. NW, Ste. 650, Washington, DC, 20036-4922, USA, (202) 785-6323, (800) 456-6323, (202) 785-0350, washington.contact@oecd.org, https://www.oecd.org/; Economic Survey of Belgium 2022 and STAN (STructural ANalysis) Database.

BELGIUM-MARRIAGE

European Commission, Eurostat, Luxembourg, 2920, LUX, https://ec.europa.eu/eurostat/; Eurostat Regional Yearbook 2021.

Routledge - Taylor & Francis Group, 6000 Broken Sound Pkwy. NW, Ste. 300, Boca Raton, FL, 33487, USA, (800) 634-1420, (800) 634-7064, orders@taylorandfrancis.com, https://www.routledge.com/; The Europa World Year Book 2022.

United Nations Statistics Division (UNSD), United Nations Plz., New York, NY, 10017, USA, (800) 253-9646, (212) 963-9851, statistics@un.org, https://unstats.un.org; Statistical Yearbook of the United Nations 2021.

BELGIUM-MERCURY PRODUCTION

See BELGIUM-MINERAL INDUSTRIES

BELGIUM-METAL PRODUCTS

European Commission, Eurostat, Luxembourg, 2920, LUX, https://ec.europa.eu/eurostat/; Eurostat Regional Yearbook 2021.

BELGIUM-MINERAL INDUSTRIES

Barchart, 209 W Jackson Blvd., 2nd Fl., Chicago, IL, 60606, USA, (877) 247-4394, commodities@barchart.com, https://www.barchart.com/cmdty; The cmdty Yearbook 2023; cmdtyStats:

Commodity Statistics and Fundamental Data; cmdtyView: Commodity Index; and Commodity Data and Prices.

European Commission, Eurostat, Luxembourg, 2920, LUX, https://ec.europa.eu/eurostat/; Eurostat Regional Yearbook 2021 and Final Energy Consumption in Transport by Type of Fuel.

International Energy Agency (IEA), 9 Rue de la Federation, Paris, 75739, FRA, info@iea.org, https://www.iea.org/; Coal 2021: Analysis and Forecast to 2024 and World Energy Statistics and Balances.

International Lead and Zinc Study Group (ILZSG), Rua Almirante Barroso 38, 5th Fl., Lisbon, 1000-013, PRT, sales@ilzsg.org, https://www.ilzsg.org; Interactive Statistical Database.

Organization for Economic Cooperation and Development (OECD), 2001 L St. NW, Ste. 650, Washington, DC, 20036-4922, USA, (202) 785-6323, (800) 456-6323, (202) 785-0350, washington.contact@oecd.org, https://www.oecd.org/; Economic Survey of Belgium 2022; Energy Prices and Taxes for OECD Countries 2020; OECD Main Economic Indicators (MEI); and STAN (STructural ANalysis) Database.

Palgrave Macmillan, 1 New York Plaza, Ste. 4500, New York, NY, 10004-1562, USA, (800) 777-4643, orders@palgrave.com, https://www.palgrave.com/us; The Statesman's Yearbook, 2023.

Routledge - Taylor & Francis Group, 6000 Broken Sound Pkwy. NW, Ste. 300, Boca Raton, FL, 33487, USA, (800) 634-1420, (800) 634-7064, orders@taylorandfrancis.com, https://www.routledge.com/; The Europa World Year Book 2022.

S&P Global Commodity Insights, One World Trade Center, New York, NY, 10007, USA, (800) 752-8878, support@platts.com, https://www.spglobal.com/commodityinsights/en; Platts Power in Europe.

United Nations Conference on Trade and Development (UNCTAD), Palais des Nations, Geneva, 1211, SWI, (212) 963-6896, unctadinfo@unctad.org, https://unctad.org; Trade and Development Report 2021.

United Nations Statistics Division (UNSD), United Nations Plz., New York, NY, 10017, USA, (800) 253-9646, (212) 963-9851, statistics@un.org, https://unstats.un.org; Energy Statistics Yearbook 2019 and Statistical Yearbook of the United Nations 2021.

World Bureau of Metal Statistics (WBMS), 31 Star St., Ware, Hertfordshire, SG12 9BA, GBR, https://www.refinitiv.com/en/trading-solutions/world-bureau-metal-statistics; Annual Stainless Steel Statistics; Long Term Production/Consumption Series - All Metals; World Flow Charts; and World Metal Statistics.

World Steel Association (Worldsteel), Avenue de Tervueren 270, Brussels, B-1150, BEL, steel@worldsteel.org, https://www.worldsteel.org; Steel Statistical Yearbook 2021.

BELGIUM-MONEY

European Central Bank (ECB), Frankfurt am Main, D-60640, GER, info@ecb.europa.eu, https://www.ecb.europa.eu; Economic Bulletin; Monetary Developments in the Euro Area; and Research Bulletin.

Organization for Economic Cooperation and Development (OECD), 2001 L St. NW, Ste. 650, Washington, DC, 20036-4922, USA, (202) 785-6323, (800) 456-6323, (202) 785-0350, washington.contact@oecd.org, https://www.oecd.org/; Economic Survey of Belgium 2022.

BELGIUM-MONEY SUPPLY

The Economist Group: Economist Intelligence Unit (EIU), 900 3rd Ave., 16th Fl., New York, NY, 10022, USA, (212) 541-0500, americas@eiu.com, https://www.eiu.com; Belgium Country Report.

International Monetary Fund (IMF), 700 19th St. NW, Washington, DC, 20431, USA, (202) 623-7000, (202) 623-4661, publications@imf.org, https://www.imf.org; International Financial Statistics (IFS).

Routledge - Taylor & Francis Group, 6000 Broken Sound Pkwy. NW, Ste. 300, Boca Raton, FL, 33487, USA, (800) 634-1420, (800) 634-7064, orders@taylorandfrancis.com, https://www.routledge.com/; The Europa World Year Book 2022.

United Nations Statistics Division (UNSD), United Nations Plz., New York, NY, 10017, USA, (800) 253-9646, (212) 963-9851, statistics@un.org, https://unstats.un.org; Statistical Yearbook of the United Nations 2021.

The World Bank, 1818 H St. NW, Washington, DC, 20433, USA, (202) 473-1000, (202) 477-6391, eds03@worldbank.org, https://www.worldbank.org/; Belgium (report).

BELGIUM-MORTALITY

European Commission, Eurostat, Luxembourg, 2920, LUX, https://ec.europa.eu/eurostat/; Eurostat Regional Yearbook 2021.

United Nations Statistics Division (UNSD), United Nations Plz., New York, NY, 10017, USA, (800) 253-9646, (212) 963-9851, statistics@un.org, https://unstats.un.org; Millennium Development Goal Indicators; Statistical Yearbook of the United Nations 2021; and World Statistics Pocketbook 2021.

World Health Organization (WHO), Ave. Appia 20, Geneva, CH-1211, SWI, (202) 974-3000 (Telephone in U.S.), publications@who.int, https://www.who.int/; Global Health Observatory (GHO).

BELGIUM-MOTION PICTURES

Palgrave Macmillan, 1 New York Plaza, Ste. 4500, New York, NY, 10004-1562, USA, (800) 777-4643, orders@palgrave.com, https://www.palgrave.com/us; The Statesman's Yearbook, 2023.

BELGIUM-MOTOR VEHICLES

European Commission, Rue de la Loi, 170, Brussels, B-1040, BEL, https://ec.europa.eu; EU Energy in Figures: Statistical Pocketbook 2021.

International Road Federation (IRF), Madison Place, 500 Montgomery St., 5th Fl., Alexandria, VA, 22314, USA, (703) 535-1001, (703) 535-1007, info@irf.global, https://www.irf.global/; World Road Statistics (WRS).

BELGIUM-NATURAL GAS PRODUCTION

See BELGIUM-MINERAL INDUSTRIES

BELGIUM-NICKEL AND NICKEL ORE

See BELGIUM-MINERAL INDUSTRIES

BELGIUM-NUTRITION

United Nations Food and Agricultural Organization (FAO), 2121 K St., Ste. 800B, Washington, DC, 20037, USA, (202) 653-2400 (Dial from U.S.), (202) 653-5760 (Fax from U.S.), fao-hq@fao.org, https://www.fao.org; The State of Food and Agriculture (SOFA) 2022.

United Nations Statistics Division (UNSD), United Nations Plz., New York, NY, 10017, USA, (800) 253-9646, (212) 963-9851, statistics@un.org, https://unstats.un.org; Millennium Development Goal Indicators.

BELGIUM-PAPER

See BELGIUM-FORESTS AND FORESTRY

BELGIUM-PEANUT PRODUCTION

See BELGIUM-CROPS

BELGIUM-PEPPER PRODUCTION

See BELGIUM-CROPS

BELGIUM-PESTICIDES

United Nations Food and Agricultural Organization (FAO), 2121 K St., Ste. 800B, Washington, DC, 20037, USA, (202) 653-2400 (Dial from U.S.), (202) 653-5760 (Fax from U.S.), fao-hq@fao.org, https://www.fao.org; The State of Food and Agriculture (SOFA) 2022.

BELGIUM-PETROLEUM INDUSTRY AND TRADE

International Energy Agency (IEA), 9 Rue de la Federation, Paris, 75739, FRA, info@iea.org, https://www.iea.org/; World Energy Statistics and Balances.

Organization for Economic Cooperation and Development (OECD), 2001 L St. NW, Ste. 650, Washington, DC, 20036-4922, USA, (202) 785-6323, (800) 456-6323, (202) 785-0350, washington.contact@oecd.org, https://www.oecd.org/; Energy Prices and Taxes for OECD Countries 2020.

Palgrave Macmillan, 1 New York Plaza, Ste. 4500, New York, NY, 10004-1562, USA, (800) 777-4643, orders@palgrave.com, https://www.palgrave.com/us; The Statesman's Yearbook, 2023.

U.S. Energy Information Administration (EIA), 1000 Independence Ave. SW, Washington, DC, 20585, USA, (202) 586-8800, infoctr@eia.gov, https://www.eia.gov; International Energy Outlook 2021.

United Nations Food and Agricultural Organization (FAO), 2121 K St., Ste. 800B, Washington, DC, 20037, USA, (202) 653-2400 (Dial from U.S.), (202) 653-5760 (Fax from U.S.), fao-hq@fao.org, https://www.fao.org; The State of Food and Agriculture (SOFA) 2022.

United Nations Statistics Division (UNSD), United Nations Plz., New York, NY, 10017, USA, (800) 253-9646, (212) 963-9851, statistics@un.org, https://unstats.un.org; Energy Statistics Yearbook 2019 and Statistical Yearbook of the United Nations 2021.

BELGIUM-PHOSPHATES PRODUCTION

See BELGIUM-MINERAL INDUSTRIES

BELGIUM-PIPELINES

European Commission, Rue de la Loi, 170, Brussels, B-1040, BEL, https://ec.europa.eu; EU Energy in Figures: Statistical Pocketbook 2021.

BELGIUM-PLASTICS INDUSTRY AND TRADE

European Commission, Eurostat, Luxembourg, 2920, LUX, https://ec.europa.eu/eurostat/; Eurostat Regional Yearbook 2021.

United Nations Statistics Division (UNSD), United Nations Plz., New York, NY, 10017, USA, (800) 253-9646, (212) 963-9851, statistics@un.org, https://unstats.un.org; Statistical Yearbook of the United Nations 2021.

BELGIUM-PLATINUM PRODUCTION

See BELGIUM-MINERAL INDUSTRIES

BELGIUM-POPULATION

Banque de France, 31 rue Croix des Petits-Champs, Paris, 75049, FRA, infos@banque-france.fr, https://www.banque-france.fr/en; Webstat: Access to Statistical Series of Banque de France.

Central Intelligence Agency (CIA), Office of Public Affairs, Washington, DC, 20505, USA, (703) 482-0623, https://www.cia.gov; The World Factbook.

The Economist Group: Economist Intelligence Unit (EIU), 900 3rd Ave., 16th Fl., New York, NY, 10022, USA, (212) 541-0500, americas@eiu.com, https://www.eiu.com; Belgium Country Report.

European Commission, Eurostat, Luxembourg, 2920, LUX, https://ec.europa.eu/eurostat/; Eurostat Regional Yearbook 2021.

Infoplease, c/o Sandbox Networks, Inc., 1 Lincoln St., 24th Fl., Boston, MA, 02111, USA, https://www.infoplease.com; Countries of the World.

International Labour Organization (ILO), 4 Rte. des Morillons, Geneva, CH-1211, SWI, ilo@ilo.org, https://www.ilo.org; NORMLEX Information System on International Labour Standards.

Organization for Economic Cooperation and Development (OECD), 2001 L St. NW, Ste. 650, Washington, DC, 20036-4922, USA, (202) 785-6323, (800) 456-6323, (202) 785-0350, washington.

contact@oecd.org, https://www.oecd.org/; OECD Labour Force Statistics 2022.

Palgrave Macmillan, 1 New York Plaza, Ste. 4500, New York, NY, 10004-1562, USA, (800) 777-4643, orders@palgrave.com, https://www.palgrave.com/us; The Statesman's Yearbook, 2023.

Routledge - Taylor & Francis Group, 6000 Broken Sound Pkwy. NW, Ste. 300, Boca Raton, FL, 33487, USA, (800) 634-1420, (800) 634-7064, orders@taylorandfrancis.com, https://www.routledge.com/; The Europa World Year Book 2022.

UK Data Service, University of Essex, Wivenhoe Park, Colchester, Essex, CO4 3SQ, GBR, https://ukdataservice.ac.uk/; International Aggregate Data.

UNESCO Institute for Statistics, C.P 250 Succursale H, Montreal, QC, H3G 2K8, CAN, (514) 343-6880 (Dial from U.S.), (514) 343-5740 (Fax from U.S.), uis.publications@unesco.org, http://uis.unesco.org/; UIS.Stat.

United Nations Department of Economic and Social Affairs (DESA), Population Division, 2 United Nations Plz., Rm. DC2-1950, New York, NY, 10017, USA, (212) 963-3209, (212) 963-2147, population@un.org, https://www.un.org/development/desa/pd/; Revision of World Urbanization Prospects and World Population Ageing 2020 Highlights.

United Nations Development Programme (UNDP), One United Nations Plz., New York, NY, 10017, USA, (212) 906-5000, (212) 906-5001, https://www.undp.org; Human Development Report 2021-2022.

United Nations Statistics Division (UNSD), United Nations Plz., New York, NY, 10017, USA, (800) 253-9646, (212) 963-9851, statistics@un.org, https://unstats.un.org; Statistical Yearbook of the United Nations 2021 and World Statistics Pocketbook 2021.

The World Bank, 1818 H St. NW, Washington, DC, 20433, USA, (202) 473-1000, (202) 477-6391, eds03@worldbank.org, https://www.worldbank.org/; Belgium (report); The Global Findex Database 2021; and World Development Report 2022: Finance for an Equitable Recovery.

BELGIUM-POPULATION DENSITY

Central Intelligence Agency (CIA), Office of Public Affairs, Washington, DC, 20505, USA, (703) 482-0623, https://www.cia.gov; The World Factbook.

European Commission, Eurostat, Luxembourg, 2920, LUX, https://ec.europa.eu/eurostat/; Eurostat Regional Yearbook 2021.

Palgrave Macmillan, 1 New York Plaza, Ste. 4500, New York, NY, 10004-1562, USA, (800) 777-4643, orders@palgrave.com, https://www.palgrave.com/us; The Statesman's Yearbook, 2023.

Routledge - Taylor & Francis Group, 6000 Broken Sound Pkwy. NW, Ste. 300, Boca Raton, FL, 33487, USA, (800) 634-1420, (800) 634-7064, orders@taylorandfrancis.com, https://www.routledge.com/; The Europa World Year Book 2022.

The World Bank, 1818 H St. NW, Washington, DC, 20433, USA, (202) 473-1000, (202) 477-6391, eds03@worldbank.org, https://www.worldbank.org/; Belgium (report) and World Development Report 2022: Finance for an Equitable Recovery.

BELGIUM-POSTAL SERVICE

European Commission, Rue de la Loi, 170, Brussels, B-1040, BEL, https://ec.europa.eu; EU Energy in Figures: Statistical Pocketbook 2021.

Palgrave Macmillan, 1 New York Plaza, Ste. 4500, New York, NY, 10004-1562, USA, (800) 777-4643, orders@palgrave.com, https://www.palgrave.com/us; The Statesman's Yearbook, 2023.

BELGIUM-POULTRY

See BELGIUM-LIVESTOCK

BELGIUM-POWER RESOURCES

Euromonitor International, Inc., 1 N Dearborn St., Ste. 1700, Chicago, IL, 60602, USA, (312) 922-1115, (312) 922-1157, info-usa@euromonitor.com, https://www.euromonitor.com/; Geographies.

European Commission, Rue de la Loi, 170, Brussels, B-1040, BEL, https://ec.europa.eu; EU Energy in Figures: Statistical Pocketbook 2021.

European Commission, Eurostat, Luxembourg, 2920, LUX, https://ec.europa.eu/eurostat/; Eurostat Regional Yearbook 2021.

International Energy Agency (IEA), 9 Rue de la Federation, Paris, 75739, FRA, info@iea.org, https://www.iea.org/; Coal 2021: Analysis and Forecast to 2024.

Organization for Economic Cooperation and Development (OECD), 2001 L St. NW, Ste. 650, Washington, DC, 20036-4922, USA, (202) 785-6323, (800) 456-6323, (202) 785-0350, washington.contact@oecd.org, https://www.oecd.org/; Energy Prices and Taxes for OECD Countries 2020 and Environment Statistics.

Palgrave Macmillan, 1 New York Plaza, Ste. 4500, New York, NY, 10004-1562, USA, (800) 777-4643, orders@palgrave.com, https://www.palgrave.com/us; The Statesman's Yearbook, 2023.

S&P Global Commodity Insights, One World Trade Center, New York, NY, 10007, USA, (800) 752-8878, support@platts.com, https://www.spglobal.com/commodityinsights/en; Platts European Power Daily.

U.S. Energy Information Administration (EIA), 1000 Independence Ave. SW, Washington, DC, 20585, USA, (202) 586-8800, infoctr@eia.gov, https://www.eia.gov; International Energy Outlook 2021.

United Nations Food and Agricultural Organization (FAO), 2121 K St., Ste. 800B, Washington, DC, 20037, USA, (202) 653-2400 (Dial from U.S.), (202) 653-5760 (Fax from U.S.), fao-hq@fao.org, https://www.fao.org; The State of Food and Agriculture (SOFA) 2022.

United Nations Statistics Division (UNSD), United Nations Plz., New York, NY, 10017, USA, (800) 253-9646, (212) 963-9851, statistics@un.org, https://unstats.un.org; Energy Statistics Yearbook 2019; Statistical Yearbook of the United Nations 2021; and World Statistics Pocketbook 2021.

The World Bank, 1818 H St. NW, Washington, DC, 20433, USA, (202) 473-1000, (202) 477-6391, eds03@worldbank.org, https://www.worldbank.org/; World Development Report 2022: Finance for an Equitable Recovery.

BELGIUM-PRICES

Euromonitor International, Inc., 1 N Dearborn St., Ste. 1700, Chicago, IL, 60602, USA, (312) 922-1115, (312) 922-1157, info-usa@euromonitor.com, https://www.euromonitor.com/; Geographies.

European Commission, Eurostat, Luxembourg, 2920, LUX, https://ec.europa.eu/eurostat/; Eurostat Regional Yearbook 2021.

Organization for Economic Cooperation and Development (OECD), 2001 L St. NW, Ste. 650, Washington, DC, 20036-4922, USA, (202) 785-6323, (800) 456-6323, (202) 785-0350, washington.contact@oecd.org, https://www.oecd.org/; OECD Digital Economy Outlook 2020 and OECD Main Economic Indicators (MEI).

TAPPI - Technical Association of the Pulp and Paper Industry, 15 Technology Pkwy. S, Ste. 115, Peachtree Corners, GA, 30092, USA, (770) 446-1400, (800) 332-8686, (770) 446-6947, memberconnection@tappi.org, https://www.tappi.org/; TAPPI Journal.

The World Bank, 1818 H St. NW, Washington, DC, 20433, USA, (202) 473-1000, (202) 477-6391, eds03@worldbank.org, https://www.worldbank.org/; Belgium (report).

World Bureau of Metal Statistics (WBMS), 31 Star St., Ware, Hertfordshire, SG12 9BA, GBR, https://www.refinitiv.com/en/trading-solutions/world-bureau-metal-statistics; Long Term Production/Consumption Series - All Metals; World Flow Charts; and World Metal Statistics.

BELGIUM-PUBLIC HEALTH

Euromonitor International, Inc., 1 N Dearborn St., Ste. 1700, Chicago, IL, 60602, USA, (312) 922-1115, (312) 922-1157, info-usa@euromonitor.com, https://www.euromonitor.com/; Geographies and Market Research on the Health and Wellness Industry.

European Centre for Disease Prevention and Control (ECDC), Stockholm, SE 171 83, SWE, ecdc.info@ecdc.europa.eu, https://ecdc.europa.eu; Eurosurveillance.

European Commission, Eurostat, Luxembourg, 2920, LUX, https://ec.europa.eu/eurostat/; Eurostat Regional Yearbook 2021.

Organization for Economic Cooperation and Development (OECD), 2001 L St. NW, Ste. 650, Washington, DC, 20036-4922, USA, (202) 785-6323, (800) 456-6323, (202) 785-0350, washington.contact@oecd.org, https://www.oecd.org/; Health at a Glance 2021.

Palgrave Macmillan, 1 New York Plaza, Ste. 4500, New York, NY, 10004-1562, USA, (800) 777-4643, orders@palgrave.com, https://www.palgrave.com/us; The Statesman's Yearbook, 2023.

U.S. Census Bureau, 4600 Silver Hill Rd., Washington, DC, 20233, USA, (301) 763-4636, (800) 923-8282, https://www.census.gov; HIV/AIDS Surveillance Data Base.

UNICEF, 3 United Nations Plz., New York, NY, 10017, USA, (212) 303-7984, (917) 244-2215, https://www.unicef.org; The State of the World's Children 2023.

United Nations Department of Economic and Social Affairs (DESA), Population Division, 2 United Nations Plz., Rm. DC2-1950, New York, NY, 10017, USA, (212) 963-3209, (212) 963-2147, population@un.org, https://www.un.org/development/desa/pd/; World Fertility Data 2019.

United Nations Development Programme (UNDP), One United Nations Plz., New York, NY, 10017, USA, (212) 906-5000, (212) 906-5001, https://www.undp.org; Human Development Report 2021-2022.

United Nations Statistics Division (UNSD), United Nations Plz., New York, NY, 10017, USA, (800) 253-9646, (212) 963-9851, statistics@un.org, https://unstats.un.org; Millennium Development Goal Indicators and Statistical Yearbook of the United Nations 2021.

The World Bank, 1818 H St. NW, Washington, DC, 20433, USA, (202) 473-1000, (202) 477-6391, eds03@worldbank.org, https://www.worldbank.org/; Belgium (report).

World Health Organization (WHO), Ave. Appia 20, Geneva, CH-1211, SWI, (202) 974-3000 (Telephone in U.S.), publications@who.int, https://www.who.int/; Global Health Observatory (GHO) and Health Statistics and Information Systems.

BELGIUM-PUBLISHERS AND PUBLISHING

Routledge - Taylor & Francis Group, 6000 Broken Sound Pkwy. NW, Ste. 300, Boca Raton, FL, 33487, USA, (800) 634-1420, (800) 634-7064, orders@taylorandfrancis.com, https://www.routledge.com/; The Europa World Year Book 2022.

UNESCO Institute for Statistics, C.P 250 Succursale H, Montreal, QC, H3G 2K8, CAN, (514) 343-6880 (Dial from U.S.), (514) 343-5740 (Fax from U.S.), uis.publications@unesco.org, http://uis.unesco.org/; UIS.Stat.

BELGIUM-RAILROADS

European Commission, Rue de la Loi, 170, Brussels, B-1040, BEL, https://ec.europa.eu; EU Energy in Figures: Statistical Pocketbook 2021.

Janes, USA, (703) 574-7580, (888) 977-1519, customer.care@janes.com, https://www.janes.com; Janes World Railways 2021-2022.

Palgrave Macmillan, 1 New York Plaza, Ste. 4500, New York, NY, 10004-1562, USA, (800) 777-4643,

orders@palgrave.com, https://www.palgrave.com/us; The Statesman's Yearbook, 2023.

Routledge - Taylor & Francis Group, 6000 Broken Sound Pkwy. NW, Ste. 300, Boca Raton, FL, 33487, USA, (800) 634-1420, (800) 634-7064, orders@taylorandfrancis.com, https://www.routledge.com/; The Europa World Year Book 2022.

United Nations Statistics Division (UNSD), United Nations Plz., New York, NY, 10017, USA, (800) 253-9646, (212) 963-9851, statistics@un.org, https://unstats.un.org; Statistical Yearbook of the United Nations 2021.

BELGIUM-RELIGION

Central Intelligence Agency (CIA), Office of Public Affairs, Washington, DC, 20505, USA, (703) 482-0623, https://www.cia.gov; The World Factbook.

Palgrave Macmillan, 1 New York Plaza, Ste. 4500, New York, NY, 10004-1562, USA, (800) 777-4643, orders@palgrave.com, https://www.palgrave.com/us; The Statesman's Yearbook, 2023.

BELGIUM-RETAIL TRADE

Banque de France, 31 rue Croix des Petits-Champs, Paris, 75049, FRA, infos@banque-france.fr, https://www.banque-france.fr/en; Key Figures France and Abroad.

Euromonitor International, Inc., 1 N Dearborn St., Ste. 1700, Chicago, IL, 60602, USA, (312) 922-1115, (312) 922-1157, info-usa@euromonitor.com, https://www.euromonitor.com/; Geographies and Market Research on the Retailing Industry.

United Nations Statistics Division (UNSD), United Nations Plz., New York, NY, 10017, USA, (800) 253-9646, (212) 963-9851, statistics@un.org, https://unstats.un.org; Statistical Yearbook of the United Nations 2021.

BELGIUM-RICE PRODUCTION

See BELGIUM-CROPS

BELGIUM-ROADS

European Commission, Rue de la Loi, 170, Brussels, B-1040, BEL, https://ec.europa.eu; EU Energy in Figures: Statistical Pocketbook 2021.

International Road Federation (IRF), Madison Place, 500 Montgomery St., 5th Fl., Alexandria, VA, 22314, USA, (703) 535-1001, (703) 535-1007, info@irf.global, https://www.irf.global/; World Road Statistics (WRS).

BELGIUM-RUBBER INDUSTRY AND TRADE

International Rubber Study Group (IRSG), 51 Changi Business Park Central 2, Unit No. 6, 486066, SGP, https://www.rubberstudy.org; Monthly Rubber Bulletin (MRB); Rubber Industry Report; Rubber Statistical Bulletin; and World Rubber Industry Report (WRIO).

United Nations Statistics Division (UNSD), United Nations Plz., New York, NY, 10017, USA, (800) 253-9646, (212) 963-9851, statistics@un.org, https://unstats.un.org; Statistical Yearbook of the United Nations 2021.

BELGIUM-RYE PRODUCTION

See BELGIUM-CROPS

BELGIUM-SAVING AND INVESTMENT

Organization for Economic Cooperation and Development (OECD), 2001 L St. NW, Ste. 650, Washington, DC, 20036-4922, USA, (202) 785-6323, (800) 456-6323, (202) 785-0350, washington.contact@oecd.org, https://www.oecd.org/; OECD Digital Economy Outlook 2020.

BELGIUM-SAVINGS ACCOUNT DEPOSITS

See BELGIUM-BANKS AND BANKING

BELGIUM-SHIPPING

European Commission, Rue de la Loi, 170, Brussels, B-1040, BEL, https://ec.europa.eu; EU Energy in Figures: Statistical Pocketbook 2021.

Routledge - Taylor & Francis Group, 6000 Broken Sound Pkwy. NW, Ste. 300, Boca Raton, FL, 33487, USA, (800) 634-1420, (800) 634-7064, orders@taylorandfrancis.com, https://www.routledge.com/; The Europa World Year Book 2022.

S&P Global, IHS Markit, 15 Inverness Way E, Englewood, CO, 80112, USA, (800) 447-2273, (800) 854-7179, https://ihsmarkit.com; IHS Maritime World Shipbuilding Statistics; Journal of Commerce; Lloyd's Register of Ships 2021-2022; and Maritime Portal Desktop.

United Nations Statistics Division (UNSD), United Nations Plz., New York, NY, 10017, USA, (800) 253-9646, (212) 963-9851, statistics@un.org, https://unstats.un.org; Statistical Yearbook of the United Nations 2021.

BELGIUM-SOYBEAN PRODUCTION

See BELGIUM-CROPS

BELGIUM-STEEL PRODUCTION

See BELGIUM-MINERAL INDUSTRIES

BELGIUM-STRAW PRODUCTION

See BELGIUM-CROPS

BELGIUM-SUGAR PRODUCTION

See BELGIUM-CROPS

BELGIUM-SULPHUR PRODUCTION

See BELGIUM-MINERAL INDUSTRIES

BELGIUM-SUNFLOWER PRODUCTION

See BELGIUM-CROPS

BELGIUM-TAXATION

European Commission, Eurostat, Luxembourg, 2920, LUX, https://ec.europa.eu/eurostat/; Eurostat Regional Yearbook 2021 and Taxation Trends in the European Union.

International Road Federation (IRF), Madison Place, 500 Montgomery St., 5th Fl., Alexandria, VA, 22314, USA, (703) 535-1001, (703) 535-1007, info@irf.global, https://www.irf.global/; World Road Statistics (WRS).

Organization for Economic Cooperation and Development (OECD), 2001 L St. NW, Ste. 650, Washington, DC, 20036-4922, USA, (202) 785-6323, (800) 456-6323, (202) 785-0350, washington.contact@oecd.org, https://www.oecd.org/; Revenue Statistics 2022.

The World Bank, 1818 H St. NW, Washington, DC, 20433, USA, (202) 473-1000, (202) 477-6391, eds03@worldbank.org, https://www.worldbank.org/; World Development Indicators (WDI) 2022.

BELGIUM-TEA PRODUCTION

See BELGIUM-CROPS

BELGIUM-TELEPHONE

European Commission, Rue de la Loi, 170, Brussels, B-1040, BEL, https://ec.europa.eu; EU Energy in Figures: Statistical Pocketbook 2021.

Palgrave Macmillan, 1 New York Plaza, Ste. 4500, New York, NY, 10004-1562, USA, (800) 777-4643, orders@palgrave.com, https://www.palgrave.com/us; The Statesman's Yearbook, 2023.

BELGIUM-TEXTILE INDUSTRY

Euromonitor International, Inc., 1 N Dearborn St., Ste. 1700, Chicago, IL, 60602, USA, (312) 922-1115, (312) 922-1157, info-usa@euromonitor.com, https://www.euromonitor.com/; Market Research on the Retailing Industry.

European Commission, Eurostat, Luxembourg, 2920, LUX, https://ec.europa.eu/eurostat/; Eurostat Regional Yearbook 2021.

Organization for Economic Cooperation and Development (OECD), 2001 L St. NW, Ste. 650, Washington, DC, 20036-4922, USA, (202) 785-6323, (800) 456-6323, (202) 785-0350, washington.contact@oecd.org, https://www.oecd.org/; STAN (STructural ANalysis) Database.

Palgrave Macmillan, 1 New York Plaza, Ste. 4500, New York, NY, 10004-1562, USA, (800) 777-4643, orders@palgrave.com, https://www.palgrave.com/us; The Statesman's Yearbook, 2023.

United Nations Food and Agricultural Organization (FAO), 2121 K St., Ste. 800B, Washington, DC, 20037, USA, (202) 653-2400 (Dial from U.S.), (202) 653-5760 (Fax from U.S.), fao-hq@fao.org, https://www.fao.org; The State of Food and Agriculture (SOFA) 2022.

United Nations Statistics Division (UNSD), United Nations Plz., New York, NY, 10017, USA, (800) 253-9646, (212) 963-9851, statistics@un.org, https://unstats.un.org; Statistical Yearbook of the United Nations 2021.

BELGIUM-TIMBER

See BELGIUM-FORESTS AND FORESTRY

BELGIUM-TOBACCO INDUSTRY

European Commission, Eurostat, Luxembourg, 2920, LUX, https://ec.europa.eu/eurostat/; Eurostat Regional Yearbook 2021.

Organization for Economic Cooperation and Development (OECD), 2001 L St. NW, Ste. 650, Washington, DC, 20036-4922, USA, (202) 785-6323, (800) 456-6323, (202) 785-0350, washington.contact@oecd.org, https://www.oecd.org/; STAN (STructural ANalysis) Database.

United Nations Statistics Division (UNSD), United Nations Plz., New York, NY, 10017, USA, (800) 253-9646, (212) 963-9851, statistics@un.org, https://unstats.un.org; Statistical Yearbook of the United Nations 2021.

BELGIUM-TOURISM

Euromonitor International, Inc., 1 N Dearborn St., Ste. 1700, Chicago, IL, 60602, USA, (312) 922-1115, (312) 922-1157, info-usa@euromonitor.com, https://www.euromonitor.com/; Geographies.

European Commission, Rue de la Loi, 170, Brussels, B-1040, BEL, https://ec.europa.eu; Common Agricultural Policy (CAPF) Context Indicators, 2019 Update and EU Energy in Figures: Statistical Pocketbook 2021.

European Commission, Eurostat, Luxembourg, 2920, LUX, https://ec.europa.eu/eurostat/; European Union Tourism Database.

Organization for Economic Cooperation and Development (OECD), 2001 L St. NW, Ste. 650, Washington, DC, 20036-4922, USA, (202) 785-6323, (800) 456-6323, (202) 785-0350, washington.contact@oecd.org, https://www.oecd.org/; OECD Tourism Trends and Policies 2022.

Palgrave Macmillan, 1 New York Plaza, Ste. 4500, New York, NY, 10004-1562, USA, (800) 777-4643, orders@palgrave.com, https://www.palgrave.com/us; The Statesman's Yearbook, 2023.

Routledge - Taylor & Francis Group, 6000 Broken Sound Pkwy. NW, Ste. 300, Boca Raton, FL, 33487, USA, (800) 634-1420, (800) 634-7064, orders@taylorandfrancis.com, https://www.routledge.com/; The Europa World Year Book 2022.

United Nations Statistics Division (UNSD), United Nations Plz., New York, NY, 10017, USA, (800) 253-9646, (212) 963-9851, statistics@un.org, https://unstats.un.org; Statistical Yearbook of the United Nations 2021.

United Nations World Tourism Organization (UNWTO), Calle Poeta Joan Maragall 42, Madrid, 28020, SPA, info@unwto.org, https://www.unwto.org/; Yearbook of Tourism Statistics, 2021 Edition.

The World Bank, 1818 H St. NW, Washington, DC, 20433, USA, (202) 473-1000, (202) 477-6391, eds03@worldbank.org, https://www.worldbank.org/; Belgium (report).

BELGIUM-TRADE

See BELGIUM-INTERNATIONAL TRADE

BELGIUM-TRANSPORTATION

Central Intelligence Agency (CIA), Office of Public Affairs, Washington, DC, 20505, USA, (703) 482-0623, https://www.cia.gov; The World Factbook.

Euromonitor International, Inc., 1 N Dearborn St., Ste. 1700, Chicago, IL, 60602, USA, (312) 922-1115, (312) 922-1157, info-usa@euromonitor.com, https://www.euromonitor.com/; Geographies.

European Commission, Rue de la Loi, 170, Brussels, B-1040, BEL, https://ec.europa.eu; EU Energy in Figures: Statistical Pocketbook 2021.

European Commission, Eurostat, Luxembourg, 2920, LUX, https://ec.europa.eu/eurostat/; Air Transport Statistics and Eurostat Regional Yearbook 2021.

Palgrave Macmillan, 1 New York Plaza, Ste. 4500, New York, NY, 10004-1562, USA, (800) 777-4643, orders@palgrave.com, https://www.palgrave.com/us; The Statesman's Yearbook, 2023.

Routledge - Taylor & Francis Group, 6000 Broken Sound Pkwy. NW, Ste. 300, Boca Raton, FL, 33487, USA, (800) 634-1420, (800) 634-7064, orders@taylorandfrancis.com, https://www.routledge.com/; The Europa World Year Book 2022.

United Nations Economic Commission for Europe (UNECE), Palais des Nations, Geneva, CH-1211, SWI, unece_info@un.org, https://unece.org/; UNECE Countries in Figures 2019.

United Nations Statistics Division (UNSD), United Nations Plz., New York, NY, 10017, USA, (800) 253-9646, (212) 963-9851, statistics@un.org, https://unstats.un.org; Energy Statistics Yearbook 2019.

The World Bank, 1818 H St. NW, Washington, DC, 20433, USA, (202) 473-1000, (202) 477-6391, eds03@worldbank.org, https://www.worldbank.org/; Belgium (report).

BELGIUM-UNEMPLOYMENT

European Commission, Eurostat, Luxembourg, 2920, LUX, https://ec.europa.eu/eurostat/; Eurostat Regional Yearbook 2021.

International Labour Organization (ILO), 4 Rte. des Morillons, Geneva, CH-1211, SWI, ilo@ilo.org, https://www.ilo.org; NORMLEX Information System on International Labour Standards.

Organization for Economic Cooperation and Development (OECD), 2001 L St. NW, Ste. 650, Washington, DC, 20036-4922, USA, (202) 785-6323, (800) 456-6323, (202) 785-0350, washington.contact@oecd.org, https://www.oecd.org/; Economic Survey of Belgium 2022; OECD Composite Leading Indicator (CLI); OECD Employment Outlook 2022: Building Back More Inclusive Labour Markets; and OECD Labour Force Statistics 2022.

Palgrave Macmillan, 1 New York Plaza, Ste. 4500, New York, NY, 10004-1562, USA, (800) 777-4643, orders@palgrave.com, https://www.palgrave.com/us; The Statesman's Yearbook, 2023.

United Nations Statistics Division (UNSD), United Nations Plz., New York, NY, 10017, USA, (800) 253-9646, (212) 963-9851, statistics@un.org, https://unstats.un.org; Statistical Yearbook of the United Nations 2021.

BELGIUM-URANIUM PRODUCTION AND CONSUMPTION

See BELGIUM-MINERAL INDUSTRIES

BELGIUM-VITAL STATISTICS

European Commission, Eurostat, Luxembourg, 2920, LUX, https://ec.europa.eu/eurostat/; Eurostat Regional Yearbook 2021.

Palgrave Macmillan, 1 New York Plaza, Ste. 4500, New York, NY, 10004-1562, USA, (800) 777-4643, orders@palgrave.com, https://www.palgrave.com/us; The Statesman's Yearbook, 2023.

Royal Statistical Society of Belgium (RSSB), Boulevard du Roi Albert II, 16, Brussels, B-1000, BEL, https://www.rssb.be/; unpublished data.

U.S. Census Bureau, 4600 Silver Hill Rd., Washington, DC, 20233, USA, (301) 763-4636, (800) 923-8282, https://www.census.gov; HIV/AIDS Surveillance Data Base.

United Nations Department of Economic and Social Affairs (DESA), Population Division, 2 United Nations Plz., Rm. DC2-1950, New York, NY, 10017, USA, (212) 963-3209, (212) 963-2147, population@un.org, https://www.un.org/development/desa/pd/; World Contraceptive Use 2021: Estimates and Projections of Family Planning Indicators and World Marriage Data 2019.

United Nations Statistics Division (UNSD), United Nations Plz., New York, NY, 10017, USA, (800) 253-9646, (212) 963-9851, statistics@un.org, https://unstats.un.org; Statistical Yearbook of the United Nations 2021.

BELGIUM-WAGES

European Commission, Eurostat, Luxembourg, 2920, LUX, https://ec.europa.eu/eurostat/; Eurostat Regional Yearbook 2021.

International Labour Organization (ILO), 4 Rte. des Morillons, Geneva, CH-1211, SWI, ilo@ilo.org, https://www.ilo.org; NORMLEX Information System on International Labour Standards.

Organization for Economic Cooperation and Development (OECD), 2001 L St. NW, Ste. 650, Washington, DC, 20036-4922, USA, (202) 785-6323, (800) 456-6323, (202) 785-0350, washington.contact@oecd.org, https://www.oecd.org/; OECD Digital Economy Outlook 2020; OECD Main Economic Indicators (MEI); and STAN (STructural ANalysis) Database.

United Nations Statistics Division (UNSD), United Nations Plz., New York, NY, 10017, USA, (800) 253-9646, (212) 963-9851, statistics@un.org, https://unstats.un.org; Statistical Yearbook of the United Nations 2021.

The World Bank, 1818 H St. NW, Washington, DC, 20433, USA, (202) 473-1000, (202) 477-6391, eds03@worldbank.org, https://www.worldbank.org/; Belgium (report).

BELGIUM-WEATHER

See BELGIUM-CLIMATE

BELGIUM-WHEAT PRODUCTION

See BELGIUM-CROPS

BELGIUM-WHOLESALE PRICE INDEXES

International Monetary Fund (IMF), 700 19th St. NW, Washington, DC, 20431, USA, (202) 623-7000, (202) 623-4661, publications@imf.org, https://www.imf.org; International Financial Statistics (IFS).

BELGIUM-WHOLESALE TRADE

European Commission, Eurostat, Luxembourg, 2920, LUX, https://ec.europa.eu/eurostat/; Eurostat Regional Yearbook 2021.

United Nations Statistics Division (UNSD), United Nations Plz., New York, NY, 10017, USA, (800) 253-9646, (212) 963-9851, statistics@un.org, https://unstats.un.org; Statistical Yearbook of the United Nations 2021.

BELGIUM-WOOD AND WOOD PULP

See BELGIUM-FORESTS AND FORESTRY

BELGIUM-WOOD PRODUCTS

Organization for Economic Cooperation and Development (OECD), 2001 L St. NW, Ste. 650, Washington, DC, 20036-4922, USA, (202) 785-6323, (800) 456-6323, (202) 785-0350, washington.contact@oecd.org, https://www.oecd.org/; Economic Survey of Belgium 2022 and STAN (STructural ANalysis) Database.

BELGIUM-WOOL PRODUCTION

See BELGIUM-TEXTILE INDUSTRY

BELGIUM-ZINC AND ZINC ORE

See BELGIUM-MINERAL INDUSTRIES

BELGIUM-ZOOS

UNESCO Institute for Statistics, C.P 250 Succursale H, Montreal, QC, H3G 2K8, CAN, (514) 343-6880 (Dial from U.S.), (514) 343-5740 (Fax from U.S.), uis.publications@unesco.org, http://uis.unesco.org/; UIS.Stat.

BELIZE-NATIONAL STATISTICAL OFFICE

Statistical Institute of Belize, 1902 Constitution Dr., Belmopan, BLZ, https://sib.org.bz/; National Data Reports (Belize).

BELIZE-AGRICULTURE

The Economist Group: Economist Intelligence Unit (EIU), 900 3rd Ave., 16th Fl., New York, NY, 10022, USA, (212) 541-0500, americas@eiu.com, https://www.eiu.com; Belize Country Report.

Euromonitor International, Inc., 1 N Dearborn St., Ste. 1700, Chicago, IL, 60602, USA, (312) 922-1115, (312) 922-1157, info-usa@euromonitor.com, https://www.euromonitor.com/; Geographies.

Palgrave Macmillan, 1 New York Plaza, Ste. 4500, New York, NY, 10004-1562, USA, (800) 777-4643, orders@palgrave.com, https://www.palgrave.com/us; The Statesman's Yearbook, 2023.

Routledge - Taylor & Francis Group, 6000 Broken Sound Pkwy. NW, Ste. 300, Boca Raton, FL, 33487, USA, (800) 634-1420, (800) 634-7064, orders@taylorandfrancis.com, https://www.routledge.com/; The Europa World Year Book 2022.

United Nations Food and Agricultural Organization (FAO), 2121 K St., Ste. 800B, Washington, DC, 20037, USA, (202) 653-2400 (Dial from U.S.), (202) 653-5760 (Fax from U.S.), fao-hq@fao.org, https://www.fao.org; AQUASTAT and The State of Food and Agriculture (SOFA) 2022.

United Nations Statistics Division (UNSD), United Nations Plz., New York, NY, 10017, USA, (800) 253-9646, (212) 963-9851, statistics@un.org, https://unstats.un.org; Statistical Yearbook of the United Nations 2021.

The World Bank, 1818 H St. NW, Washington, DC, 20433, USA, (202) 473-1000, (202) 477-6391, eds03@worldbank.org, https://www.worldbank.org/; World Development Indicators (WDI) 2022.

BELIZE-AIRLINES

Palgrave Macmillan, 1 New York Plaza, Ste. 4500, New York, NY, 10004-1562, USA, (800) 777-4643, orders@palgrave.com, https://www.palgrave.com/us; The Statesman's Yearbook, 2023.

Routledge - Taylor & Francis Group, 6000 Broken Sound Pkwy. NW, Ste. 300, Boca Raton, FL, 33487, USA, (800) 634-1420, (800) 634-7064, orders@taylorandfrancis.com, https://www.routledge.com/; The Europa World Year Book 2022.

BELIZE-ARMED FORCES

Central Intelligence Agency (CIA), Office of Public Affairs, Washington, DC, 20505, USA, (703) 482-0623, https://www.cia.gov; The World Factbook.

International Institute for Strategic Studies (IISS) - Americas, 2121 K St. NW, Ste. 600, Washington, DC, 20037, USA, (202) 659-1490, (202) 659-1499, https://www.iiss.org/; The Military Balance 2022.

Palgrave Macmillan, 1 New York Plaza, Ste. 4500, New York, NY, 10004-1562, USA, (800) 777-4643, orders@palgrave.com, https://www.palgrave.com/us; The Statesman's Yearbook, 2023.

Stockholm International Peace Research Institute (SIPRI), Signalistgatan 9, Stockholm, SE 169 72,

SWE, https://www.sipri.org/; SIPRI Arms Transfers Database and SIPRI Military Expenditure Database.

BELIZE-BALANCE OF PAYMENTS

Routledge - Taylor & Francis Group, 6000 Broken Sound Pkwy. NW, Ste. 300, Boca Raton, FL, 33487, USA, (800) 634-1420, (800) 634-7064, orders@taylorandfrancis.com, https://www.routledge.com/; The Europa World Year Book 2022.

United Nations Conference on Trade and Development (UNCTAD), Palais des Nations, Geneva, 1211, SWI, (212) 963-6896, unctadinfo@unctad.org, https://unctad.org; Handbook of Statistics 2021.

United Nations Economic Commission for Latin America and the Caribbean (ECLAC), Casilla 179-D, Santiago, 7630412, CHL, (202) 596-3713, prensa@cepal.org, https://www.cepal.org/en; Economic Survey of Latin America and the Caribbean 2021: Labour Dynamics and Employment Policies for Sustainable and Inclusive Recovery Beyond the COVID-19 Crisis.

The World Bank, 1818 H St. NW, Washington, DC, 20433, USA, (202) 473-1000, (202) 477-6391, eds03@worldbank.org, https://www.worldbank.org/; World Development Indicators (WDI) 2022.

BELIZE-BANKS AND BANKING

Euromonitor International, Inc., 1 N Dearborn St., Ste. 1700, Chicago, IL, 60602, USA, (312) 922-1115, (312) 922-1157, info-usa@euromonitor.com, https://www.euromonitor.com/; Geographies.

Routledge - Taylor & Francis Group, 6000 Broken Sound Pkwy. NW, Ste. 300, Boca Raton, FL, 33487, USA, (800) 634-1420, (800) 634-7064, orders@taylorandfrancis.com, https://www.routledge.com/; The Europa World Year Book 2022.

BELIZE-BROADCASTING

Central Intelligence Agency (CIA), Office of Public Affairs, Washington, DC, 20505, USA, (703) 482-0623, https://www.cia.gov; The World Factbook.

Euromonitor International, Inc., 1 N Dearborn St., Ste. 1700, Chicago, IL, 60602, USA, (312) 922-1115, (312) 922-1157, info-usa@euromonitor.com, https://www.euromonitor.com/; Geographies.

Palgrave Macmillan, 1 New York Plaza, Ste. 4500, New York, NY, 10004-1562, USA, (800) 777-4643, orders@palgrave.com, https://www.palgrave.com/us; The Statesman's Yearbook, 2023.

WRTH Publications Limited, PO Box 290, Oxford, OX2 7FT, GBR, sales@wrth.com, https://www.wrth.com; World Radio TV Handbook 2023.

BELIZE-BUDGET

Central Intelligence Agency (CIA), Office of Public Affairs, Washington, DC, 20505, USA, (703) 482-0623, https://www.cia.gov; The World Factbook.

BELIZE-CHILDBIRTH-STATISTICS

The World Bank, 1818 H St. NW, Washington, DC, 20433, USA, (202) 473-1000, (202) 477-6391, eds03@worldbank.org, https://www.worldbank.org/; World Development Indicators (WDI) 2022.

BELIZE-CLIMATE

Palgrave Macmillan, 1 New York Plaza, Ste. 4500, New York, NY, 10004-1562, USA, (800) 777-4643, orders@palgrave.com, https://www.palgrave.com/us; The Statesman's Yearbook, 2023.

BELIZE-COMMERCE

Palgrave Macmillan, 1 New York Plaza, Ste. 4500, New York, NY, 10004-1562, USA, (800) 777-4643, orders@palgrave.com, https://www.palgrave.com/us; The Statesman's Yearbook, 2023.

UK Data Service, University of Essex, Wivenhoe Park, Colchester, Essex, CO4 3SQ, GBR, https://ukdataservice.ac.uk/; International Aggregate Data.

BELIZE-COMMODITY EXCHANGES

Barchart, 209 W Jackson Blvd., 2nd Fl., Chicago, IL, 60606, USA, (877) 247-4394, commodities@barchart.com, https://www.barchart.com/cmdty; The cmdty Yearbook 2023; cmdtyStats: Commodity Statistics and Fundamental Data; cmdtyView: Commodity Index; and Commodity Data and Prices.

International Monetary Fund (IMF), 700 19th St. NW, Washington, DC, 20431, USA, (202) 623-7000, (202) 623-4661, publications@imf.org, https://www.imf.org; IMF Primary Commodity Prices.

BELIZE-CONSTRUCTION INDUSTRY

United Nations Statistics Division (UNSD), United Nations Plz., New York, NY, 10017, USA, (800) 253-9646, (212) 963-9851, statistics@un.org, https://unstats.un.org; Statistical Yearbook of the United Nations 2021.

BELIZE-CONSUMER PRICE INDEXES

Euromonitor International, Inc., 1 N Dearborn St., Ste. 1700, Chicago, IL, 60602, USA, (312) 922-1115, (312) 922-1157, info-usa@euromonitor.com, https://www.euromonitor.com/; Geographies.

Routledge - Taylor & Francis Group, 6000 Broken Sound Pkwy. NW, Ste. 300, Boca Raton, FL, 33487, USA, (800) 634-1420, (800) 634-7064, orders@taylorandfrancis.com, https://www.routledge.com/; The Europa World Year Book 2022.

BELIZE-CORN INDUSTRY

See BELIZE-CROPS

BELIZE-CROPS

Palgrave Macmillan, 1 New York Plaza, Ste. 4500, New York, NY, 10004-1562, USA, (800) 777-4643, orders@palgrave.com, https://www.palgrave.com/us; The Statesman's Yearbook, 2023.

United Nations Food and Agricultural Organization (FAO), 2121 K St., Ste. 800B, Washington, DC, 20037, USA, (202) 653-2400 (Dial from U.S.), (202) 653-5760 (Fax from U.S.), fao-hq@fao.org, https://www.fao.org; The State of Food and Agriculture (SOFA) 2022.

United Nations Statistics Division (UNSD), United Nations Plz., New York, NY, 10017, USA, (800) 253-9646, (212) 963-9851, statistics@un.org, https://unstats.un.org; Statistical Yearbook of the United Nations 2021.

BELIZE-DAIRY PROCESSING

Palgrave Macmillan, 1 New York Plaza, Ste. 4500, New York, NY, 10004-1562, USA, (800) 777-4643, orders@palgrave.com, https://www.palgrave.com/us; The Statesman's Yearbook, 2023.

United Nations Food and Agricultural Organization (FAO), 2121 K St., Ste. 800B, Washington, DC, 20037, USA, (202) 653-2400 (Dial from U.S.), (202) 653-5760 (Fax from U.S.), fao-hq@fao.org, https://www.fao.org; The State of Food and Agriculture (SOFA) 2022.

BELIZE-DEBTS, EXTERNAL

Palgrave Macmillan, 1 New York Plaza, Ste. 4500, New York, NY, 10004-1562, USA, (800) 777-4643, orders@palgrave.com, https://www.palgrave.com/us; The Statesman's Yearbook, 2023.

United Nations Economic Commission for Latin America and the Caribbean (ECLAC), Casilla 179-D, Santiago, 7630412, CHL, (202) 596-3713, prensa@cepal.org, https://www.cepal.org/en; Economic Survey of Latin America and the Caribbean 2021: Labour Dynamics and Employment Policies for Sustainable and Inclusive Recovery Beyond the COVID-19 Crisis.

The World Bank, 1818 H St. NW, Washington, DC, 20433, USA, (202) 473-1000, (202) 477-6391, eds03@worldbank.org, https://www.worldbank.org/; Global Financial Development Report 2019-2020: Bank Regulation and Supervision a Decade after the Global Financial Crisis and World Development Indicators (WDI) 2022.

BELIZE-ECONOMIC ASSISTANCE

United Nations Statistics Division (UNSD), United Nations Plz., New York, NY, 10017, USA, (800) 253-9646, (212) 963-9851, statistics@un.org, https://unstats.un.org; Statistical Yearbook of the United Nations 2021.

BELIZE-ECONOMIC CONDITIONS

Bernan Press, 15250 NBN Way, Bldg. C, Blue Ridge Summit, PA, 17214, USA, (301) 459-2255, (800) 865-3457, (800) 865-3450, customercare@bernan.com, https://rowman.com/Page/Bernan; World Economic Outlook, April 2022.

Central Intelligence Agency (CIA), Office of Public Affairs, Washington, DC, 20505, USA, (703) 482-0623, https://www.cia.gov; The World Factbook.

The Economist Group: Economist Intelligence Unit (EIU), 900 3rd Ave., 16th Fl., New York, NY, 10022, USA, (212) 541-0500, americas@eiu.com, https://www.eiu.com; Belize Country Report.

Euromonitor International, Inc., 1 N Dearborn St., Ste. 1700, Chicago, IL, 60602, USA, (312) 922-1115, (312) 922-1157, info-usa@euromonitor.com, https://www.euromonitor.com/; Geographies.

International Monetary Fund (IMF), 700 19th St. NW, Washington, DC, 20431, USA, (202) 623-7000, (202) 623-4661, publications@imf.org, https://www.imf.org; IMF Data and World Economic Outlook.

Palgrave Macmillan, 1 New York Plaza, Ste. 4500, New York, NY, 10004-1562, USA, (800) 777-4643, orders@palgrave.com, https://www.palgrave.com/us; The Statesman's Yearbook, 2023.

Routledge - Taylor & Francis Group, 6000 Broken Sound Pkwy. NW, Ste. 300, Boca Raton, FL, 33487, USA, (800) 634-1420, (800) 634-7064, orders@taylorandfrancis.com, https://www.routledge.com/; The Europa World Year Book 2022.

United Nations Economic Commission for Latin America and the Caribbean (ECLAC), Casilla 179-D, Santiago, 7630412, CHL, (202) 596-3713, prensa@cepal.org, https://www.cepal.org/en; Economic Survey of Latin America and the Caribbean 2021: Labour Dynamics and Employment Policies for Sustainable and Inclusive Recovery Beyond the COVID-19 Crisis and Foreign Direct Investment in Latin America and the Caribbean 2022.

United Nations Statistics Division (UNSD), United Nations Plz., New York, NY, 10017, USA, (800) 253-9646, (212) 963-9851, statistics@un.org, https://unstats.un.org; World Statistics Pocketbook 2021.

The World Bank, 1818 H St. NW, Washington, DC, 20433, USA, (202) 473-1000, (202) 477-6391, eds03@worldbank.org, https://www.worldbank.org/; Caribbean (report); Global Economic Monitor (GEM); Global Economic Prospects, June 2022; and The Global Findex Database 2021.

BELIZE-EDUCATION

Euromonitor International, Inc., 1 N Dearborn St., Ste. 1700, Chicago, IL, 60602, USA, (312) 922-1115, (312) 922-1157, info-usa@euromonitor.com, https://www.euromonitor.com/; Geographies.

Infoplease, c/o Sandbox Networks, Inc., 1 Lincoln St., 24th Fl., Boston, MA, 02111, USA, https://www.infoplease.com; Countries of the World.

Organization for Economic Cooperation and Development (OECD), 2001 L St. NW, Ste. 650, Washington, DC, 20036-4922, USA, (202) 785-6323, (800) 456-6323, (202) 785-0350, washington.contact@oecd.org, https://www.oecd.org/; Education at a Glance 2022: OECD Indicators.

Palgrave Macmillan, 1 New York Plaza, Ste. 4500, New York, NY, 10004-1562, USA, (800) 777-4643, orders@palgrave.com, https://www.palgrave.com/us; The Statesman's Yearbook, 2023.

Routledge - Taylor & Francis Group, 6000 Broken Sound Pkwy. NW, Ste. 300, Boca Raton, FL, 33487, USA, (800) 634-1420, (800) 634-7064, orders@taylorandfrancis.com, https://www.routledge.com/; The Europa World Year Book 2022.

UNESCO Institute for Statistics, C.P 250 Succursale H, Montreal, QC, H3G 2K8, CAN, (514) 343-6880 (Dial from U.S.), (514) 343-5740 (Fax from U.S.), uis.publications@unesco.org, http://uis.unesco.org/; Literacy and UIS.Stat.

United Nations Statistics Division (UNSD), United Nations Plz., New York, NY, 10017, USA, (800) 253-9646, (212) 963-9851, statistics@un.org, https://unstats.un.org; Millennium Development Goal Indicators.

The World Bank, 1818 H St. NW, Washington, DC, 20433, USA, (202) 473-1000, (202) 477-6391, eds03@worldbank.org, https://www.worldbank.org/; Caribbean (report) and World Development Indicators (WDI) 2022.

BELIZE-ELECTRICITY

United Nations Statistics Division (UNSD), United Nations Plz., New York, NY, 10017, USA, (800) 253-9646, (212) 963-9851, statistics@un.org, https://unstats.un.org; Statistical Yearbook of the United Nations 2021.

BELIZE-EMPLOYMENT

UK Data Service, University of Essex, Wivenhoe Park, Colchester, Essex, CO4 3SQ, GBR, https://ukdataservice.ac.uk/; International Aggregate Data.

United Nations Statistics Division (UNSD), United Nations Plz., New York, NY, 10017, USA, (800) 253-9646, (212) 963-9851, statistics@un.org, https://unstats.un.org; Statistical Yearbook of the United Nations 2021.

BELIZE-ENVIRONMENTAL CONDITIONS

DSI Data Service & Information, Xantener Strasse 51a, Rheinberg, D-47495, GER, dsi@dsidata.com, https://www.dsidata.com/; Global Environmental Database.

The Economist Group: Economist Intelligence Unit (EIU), 900 3rd Ave., 16th Fl., New York, NY, 10022, USA, (212) 541-0500, americas@eiu.com, https://www.eiu.com; Belize Country Report.

United Nations Statistics Division (UNSD), United Nations Plz., New York, NY, 10017, USA, (800) 253-9646, (212) 963-9851, statistics@un.org, https://unstats.un.org; World Statistics Pocketbook 2021.

The World Bank, 1818 H St. NW, Washington, DC, 20433, USA, (202) 473-1000, (202) 477-6391, eds03@worldbank.org, https://www.worldbank.org/; Caribbean (report).

BELIZE-EXPORTS

Central Intelligence Agency (CIA), Office of Public Affairs, Washington, DC, 20505, USA, (703) 482-0623, https://www.cia.gov; The World Factbook.

The Economist Group: Economist Intelligence Unit (EIU), 900 3rd Ave., 16th Fl., New York, NY, 10022, USA, (212) 541-0500, americas@eiu.com, https://www.eiu.com; Belize Country Report.

United Nations Conference on Trade and Development (UNCTAD), Palais des Nations, Geneva, 1211, SWI, (212) 963-6896, unctadinfo@unctad.org, https://unctad.org; Handbook of Statistics 2021.

BELIZE-FERTILITY, HUMAN

Central Intelligence Agency (CIA), Office of Public Affairs, Washington, DC, 20505, USA, (703) 482-0623, https://www.cia.gov; The World Factbook.

BELIZE-FERTILIZER INDUSTRY

United Nations Food and Agricultural Organization (FAO), 2121 K St., Ste. 800B, Washington, DC, 20037, USA, (202) 653-2400 (Dial from U.S.), (202) 653-5760 (Fax from U.S.), fao-hq@fao.org, https://www.fao.org; The State of Food and Agriculture (SOFA) 2022.

BELIZE-FETAL MORTALITY

See BELIZE-MORTALITY

BELIZE-FINANCE

Stockholm International Peace Research Institute (SIPRI), Signalistgatan 9, Stockholm, SE 169 72, SWE, https://www.sipri.org/; SIPRI Arms Transfers Database and SIPRI Military Expenditure Database.

United Nations Statistics Division (UNSD), United Nations Plz., New York, NY, 10017, USA, (800) 253-9646, (212) 963-9851, statistics@un.org, https://unstats.un.org; Statistical Yearbook of the United Nations 2021.

The World Bank, 1818 H St. NW, Washington, DC, 20433, USA, (202) 473-1000, (202) 477-6391, eds03@worldbank.org, https://www.worldbank.org/; Caribbean (report).

BELIZE-FINANCE, PUBLIC

Bernan Press, 15250 NBN Way, Bldg. C, Blue Ridge Summit, PA, 17214, USA, (301) 459-2255, (800) 865-3457, (800) 865-3450, customercare@bernan.com, https://rowman.com/Page/Bernan; National Accounts Statistics: Analysis of Main Aggregates 2020.

The Economist Group: Economist Intelligence Unit (EIU), 900 3rd Ave., 16th Fl., New York, NY, 10022, USA, (212) 541-0500, americas@eiu.com, https://www.eiu.com; Belize Country Report.

International Monetary Fund (IMF), 700 19th St. NW, Washington, DC, 20431, USA, (202) 623-7000, (202) 623-4661, publications@imf.org, https://www.imf.org; Regional Economic Outlook.

Palgrave Macmillan, 1 New York Plaza, Ste. 4500, New York, NY, 10004-1562, USA, (800) 777-4643, orders@palgrave.com, https://www.palgrave.com/us; The Statesman's Yearbook, 2023.

Routledge - Taylor & Francis Group, 6000 Broken Sound Pkwy. NW, Ste. 300, Boca Raton, FL, 33487, USA, (800) 634-1420, (800) 634-7064, orders@taylorandfrancis.com, https://www.routledge.com/; The Europa World Year Book 2022.

United Nations Statistics Division (UNSD), United Nations Plz., New York, NY, 10017, USA, (800) 253-9646, (212) 963-9851, statistics@un.org, https://unstats.un.org; National Accounts Main Aggregates Database and National Accounts Statistics: Main Aggregates and Detailed Tables.

BELIZE-FISHERIES

Routledge - Taylor & Francis Group, 6000 Broken Sound Pkwy. NW, Ste. 300, Boca Raton, FL, 33487, USA, (800) 634-1420, (800) 634-7064, orders@taylorandfrancis.com, https://www.routledge.com/; The Europa World Year Book 2022.

United Nations Food and Agricultural Organization (FAO), 2121 K St., Ste. 800B, Washington, DC, 20037, USA, (202) 653-2400 (Dial from U.S.), (202) 653-5760 (Fax from U.S.), fao-hq@fao.org, https://www.fao.org; FAO Yearbook of Fishery and Aquaculture Statistics 2019; Fishery Statistical Collections Global Capture Production; FishStatJ; and The State of Food and Agriculture (SOFA) 2022.

United Nations Statistics Division (UNSD), United Nations Plz., New York, NY, 10017, USA, (800) 253-9646, (212) 963-9851, statistics@un.org, https://unstats.un.org; Statistical Yearbook of the United Nations 2021.

BELIZE-FOOD

United Nations Food and Agricultural Organization (FAO), 2121 K St., Ste. 800B, Washington, DC, 20037, USA, (202) 653-2400 (Dial from U.S.), (202) 653-5760 (Fax from U.S.), fao-hq@fao.org, https://www.fao.org; The State of Food and Agriculture (SOFA) 2022.

BELIZE-FORESTS AND FORESTRY

Palgrave Macmillan, 1 New York Plaza, Ste. 4500, New York, NY, 10004-1562, USA, (800) 777-4643, orders@palgrave.com, https://www.palgrave.com/us; The Statesman's Yearbook, 2023.

Routledge - Taylor & Francis Group, 6000 Broken Sound Pkwy. NW, Ste. 300, Boca Raton, FL, 33487, USA, (800) 634-1420, (800) 634-7064, orders@taylorandfrancis.com, https://www.routledge.com/; The Europa World Year Book 2022.

UNESCO Institute for Statistics, C.P 250 Succursale H, Montreal, QC, H3G 2K8, CAN, (514) 343-6880 (Dial from U.S.), (514) 343-5740 (Fax from U.S.), uis.publications@unesco.org, http://uis.unesco.org/; UIS.Stat.

United Nations Food and Agricultural Organization (FAO), 2121 K St., Ste. 800B, Washington, DC, 20037, USA, (202) 653-2400 (Dial from U.S.), (202) 653-5760 (Fax from U.S.), fao-hq@fao.org, https://www.fao.org; FAO Yearbook of Forest Products 2019 and The State of Food and Agriculture (SOFA) 2022.

United Nations Statistics Division (UNSD), United Nations Plz., New York, NY, 10017, USA, (800) 253-9646, (212) 963-9851, statistics@un.org, https://unstats.un.org; Statistical Yearbook of the United Nations 2021.

BELIZE-GOLD INDUSTRY

The World Bank, 1818 H St. NW, Washington, DC, 20433, USA, (202) 473-1000, (202) 477-6391, eds03@worldbank.org, https://www.worldbank.org/; World Development Indicators (WDI) 2022.

BELIZE-GROSS DOMESTIC PRODUCT

The Economist Group: Economist Intelligence Unit (EIU), 900 3rd Ave., 16th Fl., New York, NY, 10022, USA, (212) 541-0500, americas@eiu.com, https://www.eiu.com; Belize Country Report.

Routledge - Taylor & Francis Group, 6000 Broken Sound Pkwy. NW, Ste. 300, Boca Raton, FL, 33487, USA, (800) 634-1420, (800) 634-7064, orders@taylorandfrancis.com, https://www.routledge.com/; The Europa World Year Book 2022.

United Nations Statistics Division (UNSD), United Nations Plz., New York, NY, 10017, USA, (800) 253-9646, (212) 963-9851, statistics@un.org, https://unstats.un.org; Statistical Yearbook of the United Nations 2021.

The World Bank, 1818 H St. NW, Washington, DC, 20433, USA, (202) 473-1000, (202) 477-6391, eds03@worldbank.org, https://www.worldbank.org/; World Development Indicators (WDI) 2022.

BELIZE-GROSS NATIONAL PRODUCT

Palgrave Macmillan, 1 New York Plaza, Ste. 4500, New York, NY, 10004-1562, USA, (800) 777-4643, orders@palgrave.com, https://www.palgrave.com/us; The Statesman's Yearbook, 2023.

United Nations Statistics Division (UNSD), United Nations Plz., New York, NY, 10017, USA, (800) 253-9646, (212) 963-9851, statistics@un.org, https://unstats.un.org; Statistical Yearbook of the United Nations 2021.

The World Bank, 1818 H St. NW, Washington, DC, 20433, USA, (202) 473-1000, (202) 477-6391, eds03@worldbank.org, https://www.worldbank.org/; World Development Indicators (WDI) 2022.

BELIZE-HOUSING

Euromonitor International, Inc., 1 N Dearborn St., Ste. 1700, Chicago, IL, 60602, USA, (312) 922-1115, (312) 922-1157, info-usa@euromonitor.com, https://www.euromonitor.com/; Geographies.

BELIZE-ILLITERATE PERSONS

UNESCO Institute for Statistics, C.P 250 Succursale H, Montreal, QC, H3G 2K8, CAN, (514) 343-6880 (Dial from U.S.), (514) 343-5740 (Fax from U.S.), uis.publications@unesco.org, http://uis.unesco.org/; UIS.Stat.

BELIZE-IMPORTS

Central Intelligence Agency (CIA), Office of Public Affairs, Washington, DC, 20505, USA, (703) 482-0623, https://www.cia.gov; The World Factbook.

The Economist Group: Economist Intelligence Unit (EIU), 900 3rd Ave., 16th Fl., New York, NY, 10022, USA, (212) 541-0500, americas@eiu.com, https://www.eiu.com; Belize Country Report.

International Monetary Fund (IMF), 700 19th St. NW, Washington, DC, 20431, USA, (202) 623-7000, (202) 623-4661, publications@imf.org, https://www.imf.org; Direction of Trade Statistics (DOTS).

S&P Global, IHS Markit, 15 Inverness Way E, Englewood, CO, 80112, USA, (800) 447-2273, (800) 854-7179, https://ihsmarkit.com; Global Trade Atlas (GTA).

United Nations Conference on Trade and Development (UNCTAD), Palais des Nations, Geneva, 1211, SWI, (212) 963-6896, unctadinfo@unctad.org, https://unctad.org; Handbook of Statistics 2021.

BELIZE-INDUSTRIES

Central Intelligence Agency (CIA), Office of Public Affairs, Washington, DC, 20505, USA, (703) 482-0623, https://www.cia.gov; The World Factbook.

The Economist Group: Economist Intelligence Unit (EIU), 900 3rd Ave., 16th Fl., New York, NY, 10022, USA, (212) 541-0500, americas@eiu.com, https://www.eiu.com; Belize Country Report.

Euromonitor International, Inc., 1 N Dearborn St., Ste. 1700, Chicago, IL, 60602, USA, (312) 922-1115, (312) 922-1157, info-usa@euromonitor.com, https://www.euromonitor.com/; Geographies.

Palgrave Macmillan, 1 New York Plaza, Ste. 4500, New York, NY, 10004-1562, USA, (800) 777-4643, orders@palgrave.com, https://www.palgrave.com/us; The Statesman's Yearbook, 2023.

Routledge - Taylor & Francis Group, 6000 Broken Sound Pkwy. NW, Ste. 300, Boca Raton, FL, 33487, USA, (800) 634-1420, (800) 634-7064, orders@taylorandfrancis.com, https://www.routledge.com/; The Europa World Year Book 2022.

United Nations Economic Commission for Latin America and the Caribbean (ECLAC), Casilla 179-D, Santiago, 7630412, CHL, (202) 596-3713, prensa@cepal.org, https://www.cepal.org/en; Economic Survey of Latin America and the Caribbean 2021: Labour Dynamics and Employment Policies for Sustainable and Inclusive Recovery Beyond the COVID-19 Crisis.

United Nations Industrial Development Organization (UNIDO), 1 United Nations Plz., Rm. DC1-1118, New York, NY, 10017, USA, (212) 963-6890, (212) 963 6885, (212) 963-7904, office.newyork@unido.org, https://www.unido.org/; Industrial Statistics Databases and International Yearbook of Industrial Statistics 2021.

The World Bank, 1818 H St. NW, Washington, DC, 20433, USA, (202) 473-1000, (202) 477-6391, eds03@worldbank.org, https://www.worldbank.org/; World Development Indicators (WDI) 2022.

BELIZE-INFANT AND MATERNAL MORTALITY

See BELIZE-MORTALITY

BELIZE-INFLATION (FINANCE)

United Nations Economic Commission for Latin America and the Caribbean (ECLAC), Casilla 179-D, Santiago, 7630412, CHL, (202) 596-3713, prensa@cepal.org, https://www.cepal.org/en; Economic Survey of Latin America and the Caribbean 2021: Labour Dynamics and Employment Policies for Sustainable and Inclusive Recovery Beyond the COVID-19 Crisis.

BELIZE-INTERNATIONAL TRADE

The Economist Group: Economist Intelligence Unit (EIU), 900 3rd Ave., 16th Fl., New York, NY, 10022, USA, (212) 541-0500, americas@eiu.com, https://www.eiu.com; Belize Country Report.

Euromonitor International, Inc., 1 N Dearborn St., Ste. 1700, Chicago, IL, 60602, USA, (312) 922-1115, (312) 922-1157, info-usa@euromonitor.com, https://www.euromonitor.com/; Geographies.

Palgrave Macmillan, 1 New York Plaza, Ste. 4500, New York, NY, 10004-1562, USA, (800) 777-4643, orders@palgrave.com, https://www.palgrave.com/us; The Statesman's Yearbook, 2023.

Routledge - Taylor & Francis Group, 6000 Broken Sound Pkwy. NW, Ste. 300, Boca Raton, FL, 33487, USA, (800) 634-1420, (800) 634-7064, orders@taylorandfrancis.com, https://www.routledge.com/; The Europa World Year Book 2022.

United Nations Conference on Trade and Development (UNCTAD), Palais des Nations, Geneva, 1211, SWI, (212) 963-6896, unctadinfo@unctad.org, https://unctad.org; Trade and Development Report 2021.

United Nations Economic Commission for Latin America and the Caribbean (ECLAC), Casilla 179-D, Santiago, 7630412, CHL, (202) 596-3713, prensa@cepal.org, https://www.cepal.org/en; Economic Survey of Latin America and the Caribbean 2021: Labour Dynamics and Employment Policies for Sustainable and Inclusive Recovery Beyond the COVID-19 Crisis.

United Nations Food and Agricultural Organization (FAO), 2121 K St., Ste. 800B, Washington, DC, 20037, USA, (202) 653-2400 (Dial from U.S.), (202) 653-5760 (Fax from U.S.), fao-hq@fao.org, https://www.fao.org; The State of Food and Agriculture (SOFA) 2022.

United Nations Statistics Division (UNSD), United Nations Plz., New York, NY, 10017, USA, (800) 253-9646, (212) 963-9851, statistics@un.org, https://unstats.un.org; International Trade Statistics Yearbook 2020 and Statistical Yearbook of the United Nations 2021.

The World Bank, 1818 H St. NW, Washington, DC, 20433, USA, (202) 473-1000, (202) 477-6391, eds03@worldbank.org, https://www.worldbank.org/; World Development Indicators (WDI) 2022.

World Trade Organization (WTO), Ctre. William Rappard, Rue de Lausanne 154, Case postale, Geneva, CH-1211, SWI, enquiries@wto.org, https://www.wto.org; World Trade Statistical Review 2022.

BELIZE-INTERNET USERS

International Telecommunication Union (ITU), Place des Nations, Geneva, CH-1211, SWI, itumail@itu.int, https://www.itu.int; Global Connectivity Report 2022; World Telecommunication/ICT Indicators Database 2021; and Yearbook of Statistics 2019.

BELIZE-LABOR

Central Intelligence Agency (CIA), Office of Public Affairs, Washington, DC, 20505, USA, (703) 482-0623, https://www.cia.gov; The World Factbook.

Euromonitor International, Inc., 1 N Dearborn St., Ste. 1700, Chicago, IL, 60602, USA, (312) 922-1115, (312) 922-1157, info-usa@euromonitor.com, https://www.euromonitor.com/; Geographies.

Palgrave Macmillan, 1 New York Plaza, Ste. 4500, New York, NY, 10004-1562, USA, (800) 777-4643, orders@palgrave.com, https://www.palgrave.com/us; The Statesman's Yearbook, 2023.

United Nations Food and Agricultural Organization (FAO), 2121 K St., Ste. 800B, Washington, DC, 20037, USA, (202) 653-2400 (Dial from U.S.), (202) 653-5760 (Fax from U.S.), fao-hq@fao.org, https://www.fao.org; The State of Food and Agriculture (SOFA) 2022.

The World Bank, 1818 H St. NW, Washington, DC, 20433, USA, (202) 473-1000, (202) 477-6391, eds03@worldbank.org, https://www.worldbank.org/; World Development Indicators (WDI) 2022.

BELIZE-LAND USE

United Nations Statistics Division (UNSD), United Nations Plz., New York, NY, 10017, USA, (800) 253-9646, (212) 963-9851, statistics@un.org, https://unstats.un.org; Millennium Development Goal Indicators.

BELIZE-LIBRARIES

UNESCO Institute for Statistics, C.P 250 Succursale H, Montreal, QC, H3G 2K8, CAN, (514) 343-6880 (Dial from U.S.), (514) 343-5740 (Fax from U.S.), uis.publications@unesco.org, http://uis.unesco.org/; UIS.Stat.

BELIZE-LIFE EXPECTANCY

Central Intelligence Agency (CIA), Office of Public Affairs, Washington, DC, 20505, USA, (703) 482-0623, https://www.cia.gov; The World Factbook.

United Nations Department of Economic and Social Affairs (DESA), Population Division, 2 United Nations Plz., Rm. DC2-1950, New York, NY, 10017, USA, (212) 963-3209, (212) 963-2147, population@un.org, https://www.un.org/development/desa/pd/; World Population Ageing 2020 Highlights.

United Nations Statistics Division (UNSD), United Nations Plz., New York, NY, 10017, USA, (800) 253-9646, (212) 963-9851, statistics@un.org, https://unstats.un.org; Millennium Development Goal Indicators.

The World Bank, 1818 H St. NW, Washington, DC, 20433, USA, (202) 473-1000, (202) 477-6391, eds03@worldbank.org, https://www.worldbank.org/; Caribbean (report).

BELIZE-LITERACY

Euromonitor International, Inc., 1 N Dearborn St., Ste. 1700, Chicago, IL, 60602, USA, (312) 922-1115, (312) 922-1157, info-usa@euromonitor.com, https://www.euromonitor.com/; Geographies.

UNESCO Institute for Statistics, C.P 250 Succursale H, Montreal, QC, H3G 2K8, CAN, (514) 343-6880 (Dial from U.S.), (514) 343-5740 (Fax from U.S.), uis.publications@unesco.org, http://uis.unesco.org/; Literacy.

BELIZE-LIVESTOCK

Palgrave Macmillan, 1 New York Plaza, Ste. 4500, New York, NY, 10004-1562, USA, (800) 777-4643, orders@palgrave.com, https://www.palgrave.com/us; The Statesman's Yearbook, 2023.

Routledge - Taylor & Francis Group, 6000 Broken Sound Pkwy. NW, Ste. 300, Boca Raton, FL, 33487, USA, (800) 634-1420, (800) 634-7064, orders@taylorandfrancis.com, https://www.routledge.com/; The Europa World Year Book 2022.

United Nations Food and Agricultural Organization (FAO), 2121 K St., Ste. 800B, Washington, DC, 20037, USA, (202) 653-2400 (Dial from U.S.), (202) 653-5760 (Fax from U.S.), fao-hq@fao.org, https://www.fao.org; The State of Food and Agriculture (SOFA) 2022.

United Nations Statistics Division (UNSD), United Nations Plz., New York, NY, 10017, USA, (800) 253-9646, (212) 963-9851, statistics@un.org, https://unstats.un.org; Statistical Yearbook of the United Nations 2021.

BELIZE-MARRIAGE

Routledge - Taylor & Francis Group, 6000 Broken Sound Pkwy. NW, Ste. 300, Boca Raton, FL, 33487, USA, (800) 634-1420, (800) 634-7064, orders@taylorandfrancis.com, https://www.routledge.com/; The Europa World Year Book 2022.

United Nations Statistics Division (UNSD), United Nations Plz., New York, NY, 10017, USA, (800) 253-9646, (212) 963-9851, statistics@un.org, https://unstats.un.org; Statistical Yearbook of the United Nations 2021.

BELIZE-MINERAL INDUSTRIES

Palgrave Macmillan, 1 New York Plaza, Ste. 4500, New York, NY, 10004-1562, USA, (800) 777-4643, orders@palgrave.com, https://www.palgrave.com/us; The Statesman's Yearbook, 2023.

United Nations Conference on Trade and Development (UNCTAD), Palais des Nations, Geneva, 1211, SWI, (212) 963-6896, unctadinfo@unctad.org, https://unctad.org; Trade and Development Report 2021.

BELIZE-MONEY SUPPLY

The Economist Group: Economist Intelligence Unit (EIU), 900 3rd Ave., 16th Fl., New York, NY, 10022, USA, (212) 541-0500, americas@eiu.com, https://www.eiu.com; Belize Country Report.

Routledge - Taylor & Francis Group, 6000 Broken Sound Pkwy. NW, Ste. 300, Boca Raton, FL, 33487, USA, (800) 634-1420, (800) 634-7064, orders@taylorandfrancis.com, https://www.routledge.com/; The Europa World Year Book 2022.

BELIZE-MONUMENTS AND HISTORIC SITES

UNESCO Institute for Statistics, C.P 250 Succursale H, Montreal, QC, H3G 2K8, CAN, (514) 343-

6880 (Dial from U.S.), (514) 343-5740 (Fax from U.S.), uis.publications@unesco.org, http://uis.unesco.org/; UIS.Stat.

BELIZE-MORTALITY

United Nations Statistics Division (UNSD), United Nations Plz., New York, NY, 10017, USA, (800) 253-9646, (212) 963-9851, statistics@un.org, https://unstats.un.org; Millennium Development Goal Indicators; Statistical Yearbook of the United Nations 2021; and World Statistics Pocketbook 2021.

World Health Organization (WHO), Ave. Appia 20, Geneva, CH-1211, SWI, (202) 974-3000 (Telephone in U.S.), publications@who.int, https://www.who.int/; Global Health Observatory (GHO).

BELIZE-MOTION PICTURES

Palgrave Macmillan, 1 New York Plaza, Ste. 4500, New York, NY, 10004-1562, USA, (800) 777-4643, orders@palgrave.com, https://www.palgrave.com/us; The Statesman's Yearbook, 2023.

BELIZE-NUTRITION

United Nations Food and Agricultural Organization (FAO), 2121 K St., Ste. 800B, Washington, DC, 20037, USA, (202) 653-2400 (Dial from U.S.), (202) 653-5760 (Fax from U.S.), fao-hq@fao.org, https://www.fao.org; The State of Food and Agriculture (SOFA) 2022.

United Nations Statistics Division (UNSD), United Nations Plz., New York, NY, 10017, USA, (800) 253-9646, (212) 963-9851, statistics@un.org, https://unstats.un.org; Millennium Development Goal Indicators.

BELIZE-PAPER

See BELIZE-FORESTS AND FORESTRY

BELIZE-PESTICIDES

United Nations Food and Agricultural Organization (FAO), 2121 K St., Ste. 800B, Washington, DC, 20037, USA, (202) 653-2400 (Dial from U.S.), (202) 653-5760 (Fax from U.S.), fao-hq@fao.org, https://www.fao.org; The State of Food and Agriculture (SOFA) 2022.

BELIZE-PETROLEUM INDUSTRY AND TRADE

United Nations Food and Agricultural Organization (FAO), 2121 K St., Ste. 800B, Washington, DC, 20037, USA, (202) 653-2400 (Dial from U.S.), (202) 653-5760 (Fax from U.S.), fao-hq@fao.org, https://www.fao.org; The State of Food and Agriculture (SOFA) 2022.

BELIZE-POPULATION

Caribbean Public Health Agency (CARPHA), Federation Park, 16-18 Jamaica Blvd., Port of Spain, TTO, (868) 622-4261 (Dial from U.S.), (868) 299-0820 (Dial from U.S.), postmaster@carpha.org, https://carpha.org/; unpublished data.

Central Intelligence Agency (CIA), Office of Public Affairs, Washington, DC, 20505, USA, (703) 482-0623, https://www.cia.gov; The World Factbook.

The Economist Group: Economist Intelligence Unit (EIU), 900 3rd Ave., 16th Fl., New York, NY, 10022, USA, (212) 541-0500, americas@eiu.com, https://www.eiu.com; Belize Country Report.

Infoplease, c/o Sandbox Networks, Inc., 1 Lincoln St., 24th Fl., Boston, MA, 02111, USA, https://www.infoplease.com; Countries of the World.

Palgrave Macmillan, 1 New York Plaza, Ste. 4500, New York, NY, 10004-1562, USA, (800) 777-4643, orders@palgrave.com, https://www.palgrave.com/us; The Statesman's Yearbook, 2023.

Routledge - Taylor & Francis Group, 6000 Broken Sound Pkwy. NW, Ste. 300, Boca Raton, FL, 33487, USA, (800) 634-1420, (800) 634-7064, orders@taylorandfrancis.com, https://www.routledge.com/; The Europa World Year Book 2022.

UK Data Service, University of Essex, Wivenhoe Park, Colchester, Essex, CO4 3SQ, GBR, https://ukdataservice.ac.uk/; International Aggregate Data.

UNESCO Institute for Statistics, C.P 250 Succursale H, Montreal, QC, H3G 2K8, CAN, (514) 343-6880 (Dial from U.S.), (514) 343-5740 (Fax from U.S.), uis.publications@unesco.org, http://uis.unesco.org/; UIS.Stat.

United Nations Department of Economic and Social Affairs (DESA), Population Division, 2 United Nations Plz., Rm. DC2-1950, New York, NY, 10017, USA, (212) 963-3209, (212) 963-2147, population@un.org, https://www.un.org/development/desa/pd/; Revision of World Urbanization Prospects and World Population Ageing 2020 Highlights.

United Nations Development Programme (UNDP), One United Nations Plz., New York, NY, 10017, USA, (212) 906-5000, (212) 906-5001, https://www.undp.org; Human Development Report 2021-2022.

United Nations Statistics Division (UNSD), United Nations Plz., New York, NY, 10017, USA, (800) 253-9646, (212) 963-9851, statistics@un.org, https://unstats.un.org; Statistical Yearbook of the United Nations 2021 and World Statistics Pocketbook 2021.

The World Bank, 1818 H St. NW, Washington, DC, 20433, USA, (202) 473-1000, (202) 477-6391, eds03@worldbank.org, https://www.worldbank.org/; Caribbean (report) and World Development Report 2022: Finance for an Equitable Recovery.

BELIZE-POPULATION DENSITY

Central Intelligence Agency (CIA), Office of Public Affairs, Washington, DC, 20505, USA, (703) 482-0623, https://www.cia.gov; The World Factbook.

Palgrave Macmillan, 1 New York Plaza, Ste. 4500, New York, NY, 10004-1562, USA, (800) 777-4643, orders@palgrave.com, https://www.palgrave.com/us; The Statesman's Yearbook, 2023.

Routledge - Taylor & Francis Group, 6000 Broken Sound Pkwy. NW, Ste. 300, Boca Raton, FL, 33487, USA, (800) 634-1420, (800) 634-7064, orders@taylorandfrancis.com, https://www.routledge.com/; The Europa World Year Book 2022.

BELIZE-POSTAL SERVICE

Palgrave Macmillan, 1 New York Plaza, Ste. 4500, New York, NY, 10004-1562, USA, (800) 777-4643, orders@palgrave.com, https://www.palgrave.com/us; The Statesman's Yearbook, 2023.

BELIZE-POWER RESOURCES

Euromonitor International, Inc., 1 N Dearborn St., Ste. 1700, Chicago, IL, 60602, USA, (312) 922-1115, (312) 922-1157, info-usa@euromonitor.com, https://www.euromonitor.com/; Geographies.

Palgrave Macmillan, 1 New York Plaza, Ste. 4500, New York, NY, 10004-1562, USA, (800) 777-4643, orders@palgrave.com, https://www.palgrave.com/us; The Statesman's Yearbook, 2023.

United Nations Food and Agricultural Organization (FAO), 2121 K St., Ste. 800B, Washington, DC, 20037, USA, (202) 653-2400 (Dial from U.S.), (202) 653-5760 (Fax from U.S.), fao-hq@fao.org, https://www.fao.org; The State of Food and Agriculture (SOFA) 2022.

United Nations Statistics Division (UNSD), United Nations Plz., New York, NY, 10017, USA, (800) 253-9646, (212) 963-9851, statistics@un.org, https://unstats.un.org; Energy Statistics Yearbook 2019; Statistical Yearbook of the United Nations 2021; and World Statistics Pocketbook 2021.

BELIZE-PRICES

United Nations Economic Commission for Latin America and the Caribbean (ECLAC), Casilla 179-D, Santiago, 7630412, CHL, (202) 596-3713, prensa@cepal.org, https://www.cepal.org/en; Economic Survey of Latin America and the Caribbean 2021: Labour Dynamics and Employment Policies for Sustainable and Inclusive Recovery Beyond the COVID-19 Crisis.

BELIZE-PUBLIC HEALTH

Euromonitor International, Inc., 1 N Dearborn St., Ste. 1700, Chicago, IL, 60602, USA, (312) 922-1115, (312) 922-1157, info-usa@euromonitor.com, https://www.euromonitor.com/; Geographies.

Palgrave Macmillan, 1 New York Plaza, Ste. 4500, New York, NY, 10004-1562, USA, (800) 777-4643, orders@palgrave.com, https://www.palgrave.com/us; The Statesman's Yearbook, 2023.

U.S. Census Bureau, 4600 Silver Hill Rd., Washington, DC, 20233, USA, (301) 763-4636, (800) 923-8282, https://www.census.gov; HIV/AIDS Surveillance Data Base.

United Nations Department of Economic and Social Affairs (DESA), Population Division, 2 United Nations Plz., Rm. DC2-1950, New York, NY, 10017, USA, (212) 963-3209, (212) 963-2147, population@un.org, https://www.un.org/development/desa/pd/; World Fertility Data 2019.

United Nations Development Programme (UNDP), One United Nations Plz., New York, NY, 10017, USA, (212) 906-5000, (212) 906-5001, https://www.undp.org; Human Development Report 2021-2022.

United Nations Statistics Division (UNSD), United Nations Plz., New York, NY, 10017, USA, (800) 253-9646, (212) 963-9851, statistics@un.org, https://unstats.un.org; Millennium Development Goal Indicators and Statistical Yearbook of the United Nations 2021.

The World Bank, 1818 H St. NW, Washington, DC, 20433, USA, (202) 473-1000, (202) 477-6391, eds03@worldbank.org, https://www.worldbank.org/; Caribbean (report).

World Health Organization (WHO), Ave. Appia 20, Geneva, CH-1211, SWI, (202) 974-3000 (Telephone in U.S.), publications@who.int, https://www.who.int/; Global Health Observatory (GHO) and Health Statistics and Information Systems.

BELIZE-RELIGION

Central Intelligence Agency (CIA), Office of Public Affairs, Washington, DC, 20505, USA, (703) 482-0623, https://www.cia.gov; The World Factbook.

Palgrave Macmillan, 1 New York Plaza, Ste. 4500, New York, NY, 10004-1562, USA, (800) 777-4643, orders@palgrave.com, https://www.palgrave.com/us; The Statesman's Yearbook, 2023.

BELIZE-RETAIL TRADE

Euromonitor International, Inc., 1 N Dearborn St., Ste. 1700, Chicago, IL, 60602, USA, (312) 922-1115, (312) 922-1157, info-usa@euromonitor.com, https://www.euromonitor.com/; Geographies.

BELIZE-RICE PRODUCTION

See BELIZE-CROPS

BELIZE-SHIPPING

Routledge - Taylor & Francis Group, 6000 Broken Sound Pkwy. NW, Ste. 300, Boca Raton, FL, 33487, USA, (800) 634-1420, (800) 634-7064, orders@taylorandfrancis.com, https://www.routledge.com/; The Europa World Year Book 2022.

United Nations Statistics Division (UNSD), United Nations Plz., New York, NY, 10017, USA, (800) 253-9646, (212) 963-9851, statistics@un.org, https://unstats.un.org; Statistical Yearbook of the United Nations 2021.

BELIZE-SUGAR PRODUCTION

See BELIZE-CROPS

BELIZE-TAXATION

The World Bank, 1818 H St. NW, Washington, DC, 20433, USA, (202) 473-1000, (202) 477-6391, eds03@worldbank.org, https://www.worldbank.org/; World Development Indicators (WDI) 2022.

BELIZE-TELEPHONE

Central Intelligence Agency (CIA), Office of Public Affairs, Washington, DC, 20505, USA, (703) 482-0623, https://www.cia.gov; The World Factbook.

Palgrave Macmillan, 1 New York Plaza, Ste. 4500, New York, NY, 10004-1562, USA, (800) 777-4643, orders@palgrave.com, https://www.palgrave.com/us; The Statesman's Yearbook, 2023.

Routledge - Taylor & Francis Group, 6000 Broken Sound Pkwy. NW, Ste. 300, Boca Raton, FL, 33487, USA, (800) 634-1420, (800) 634-7064, orders@taylorandfrancis.com, https://www.routledge.com/; The Europa World Year Book 2022.

United Nations Statistics Division (UNSD), United Nations Plz., New York, NY, 10017, USA, (800) 253-9646, (212) 963-9851, statistics@un.org, https://unstats.un.org; World Statistics Pocketbook 2021.

BELIZE-TOBACCO INDUSTRY

United Nations Statistics Division (UNSD), United Nations Plz., New York, NY, 10017, USA, (800) 253-9646, (212) 963-9851, statistics@un.org, https://unstats.un.org; Statistical Yearbook of the United Nations 2021.

BELIZE-TOURISM

Euromonitor International, Inc., 1 N Dearborn St., Ste. 1700, Chicago, IL, 60602, USA, (312) 922-1115, (312) 922-1157, info-usa@euromonitor.com, https://www.euromonitor.com/; Geographies.

International Institute for Strategic Studies (IISS) - Americas, 2121 K St. NW, Ste. 600, Washington, DC, 20037, USA, (202) 659-1490, (202) 659-1499, https://www.iiss.org/; The Military Balance 2022.

Palgrave Macmillan, 1 New York Plaza, Ste. 4500, New York, NY, 10004-1562, USA, (800) 777-4643, orders@palgrave.com, https://www.palgrave.com/us; The Statesman's Yearbook, 2023.

Routledge - Taylor & Francis Group, 6000 Broken Sound Pkwy. NW, Ste. 300, Boca Raton, FL, 33487, USA, (800) 634-1420, (800) 634-7064, orders@taylorandfrancis.com, https://www.routledge.com/; The Europa World Year Book 2022.

United Nations World Tourism Organization (UNWTO), Calle Poeta Joan Maragall 42, Madrid, 28020, SPA, info@unwto.org, https://www.unwto.org/; Yearbook of Tourism Statistics, 2021 Edition.

BELIZE-TRADE

See BELIZE-INTERNATIONAL TRADE

BELIZE-TRANSPORTATION

Central Intelligence Agency (CIA), Office of Public Affairs, Washington, DC, 20505, USA, (703) 482-0623, https://www.cia.gov; The World Factbook.

Euromonitor International, Inc., 1 N Dearborn St., Ste. 1700, Chicago, IL, 60602, USA, (312) 922-1115, (312) 922-1157, info-usa@euromonitor.com, https://www.euromonitor.com/; Geographies.

Palgrave Macmillan, 1 New York Plaza, Ste. 4500, New York, NY, 10004-1562, USA, (800) 777-4643, orders@palgrave.com, https://www.palgrave.com/us; The Statesman's Yearbook, 2023.

Routledge - Taylor & Francis Group, 6000 Broken Sound Pkwy. NW, Ste. 300, Boca Raton, FL, 33487, USA, (800) 634-1420, (800) 634-7064, orders@taylorandfrancis.com, https://www.routledge.com/; The Europa World Year Book 2022.

BELIZE-VITAL STATISTICS

Palgrave Macmillan, 1 New York Plaza, Ste. 4500, New York, NY, 10004-1562, USA, (800) 777-4643, orders@palgrave.com, https://www.palgrave.com/us; The Statesman's Yearbook, 2023.

U.S. Census Bureau, 4600 Silver Hill Rd., Washington, DC, 20233, USA, (301) 763-4636, (800) 923-8282, https://www.census.gov; HIV/AIDS Surveillance Data Base.

United Nations Department of Economic and Social Affairs (DESA), Population Division, 2 United Nations Plz., Rm. DC2-1950, New York, NY, 10017, USA, (212) 963-3209, (212) 963-2147, population@un.org, https://www.un.org/development/desa/pd/; World Contraceptive Use 2021: Estimates and Projections of Family Planning Indicators and World Marriage Data 2019.

United Nations Statistics Division (UNSD), United Nations Plz., New York, NY, 10017, USA, (800) 253-9646, (212) 963-9851, statistics@un.org, https://unstats.un.org; Statistical Yearbook of the United Nations 2021.

BENIN-NATIONAL STATISTICAL OFFICE

L'Institut National de la Statistique et de la Démographie (INSTAD), Route de l'aeroport, 01 BP 323, Cotonou, BEN, instad@instad.bj, https://instad.bj/; National Data Reports (Benin).

BENIN-AGRICULTURE

African Development Bank Group (AfDB), Avenue Joseph Anoma, 01 BP 1387, Abidjan, 01, COT, https://www.afdb.org; African Economic Outlook 2021 and Compendium of Statistics on Bank Group Operations 2019.

The Economist Group: Economist Intelligence Unit (EIU), 900 3rd Ave., 16th Fl., New York, NY, 10022, USA, (212) 541-0500, americas@eiu.com, https://www.eiu.com; Benin Country Report.

Euromonitor International, Inc., 1 N Dearborn St., Ste. 1700, Chicago, IL, 60602, USA, (312) 922-1115, (312) 922-1157, info-usa@euromonitor.com, https://www.euromonitor.com/; Geographies.

Organisation of Islamic Cooperation (OIC), Statistical, Economic and Social Research and Training Centre for Islamic Countries (SESRIC), Kudus Cad. No. 9, Diplomatik Site, Ankara, 06450, TUR, statistics@sesric.org, https://www.sesric.org/; OIC Statistics (OICStat) Database and OIC-Countries in Figures (OIC-CIF).

Palgrave Macmillan, 1 New York Plaza, Ste. 4500, New York, NY, 10004-1562, USA, (800) 777-4643, orders@palgrave.com, https://www.palgrave.com/us; The Statesman's Yearbook, 2023.

Routledge - Taylor & Francis Group, 6000 Broken Sound Pkwy. NW, Ste. 300, Boca Raton, FL, 33487, USA, (800) 634-1420, (800) 634-7064, orders@taylorandfrancis.com, https://www.routledge.com/; The Europa World Year Book 2022.

United Nations Economic Commission for Africa (UNECA), PO Box 3001, Addis Ababa, ETH, ecainfo@uneca.org, https://www.uneca.org/; African Statistical Yearbook 2020 and Economic Report on Africa 2021.

United Nations Food and Agricultural Organization (FAO), 2121 K St., Ste. 800B, Washington, DC, 20037, USA, (202) 653-2400 (Dial from U.S.), (202) 653-5760 (Fax from U.S.), fao-hq@fao.org, https://www.fao.org; AQUASTAT and The State of Food and Agriculture (SOFA) 2022.

United Nations Statistics Division (UNSD), United Nations Plz., New York, NY, 10017, USA, (800) 253-9646, (212) 963-9851, statistics@un.org, https://unstats.un.org; Statistical Yearbook of the United Nations 2021.

The World Bank, 1818 H St. NW, Washington, DC, 20433, USA, (202) 473-1000, (202) 477-6391, eds03@worldbank.org, https://www.worldbank.org/; Benin (report) and World Development Indicators (WDI) 2022.

BENIN-AIRLINES

Palgrave Macmillan, 1 New York Plaza, Ste. 4500, New York, NY, 10004-1562, USA, (800) 777-4643, orders@palgrave.com, https://www.palgrave.com/us; The Statesman's Yearbook, 2023.

Routledge - Taylor & Francis Group, 6000 Broken Sound Pkwy. NW, Ste. 300, Boca Raton, FL, 33487, USA, (800) 634-1420, (800) 634-7064, orders@taylorandfrancis.com, https://www.routledge.com/; The Europa World Year Book 2022.

United Nations Economic Commission for Africa (UNECA), PO Box 3001, Addis Ababa, ETH, ecainfo@uneca.org, https://www.uneca.org/; African Statistical Yearbook 2020.

BENIN-ALUMINUM PRODUCTION

See BENIN-MINERAL INDUSTRIES

BENIN-ARMED FORCES

Central Intelligence Agency (CIA), Office of Public Affairs, Washington, DC, 20505, USA, (703) 482-0623, https://www.cia.gov; The World Factbook.

International Institute for Strategic Studies (IISS) - Americas, 2121 K St. NW, Ste. 600, Washington, DC, 20037, USA, (202) 659-1490, (202) 659-1499, https://www.iiss.org/; The Military Balance 2022.

Palgrave Macmillan, 1 New York Plaza, Ste. 4500, New York, NY, 10004-1562, USA, (800) 777-4643, orders@palgrave.com, https://www.palgrave.com/us; The Statesman's Yearbook, 2023.

Stockholm International Peace Research Institute (SIPRI), Signalistgatan 9, Stockholm, SE 169 72, SWE, https://www.sipri.org/; SIPRI Arms Transfers Database and SIPRI Military Expenditure Database.

BENIN-BALANCE OF PAYMENTS

African Development Bank Group (AfDB), Avenue Joseph Anoma, 01 BP 1387, Abidjan, 01, COT, https://www.afdb.org; The AfDB Statistics Pocketbook 2019.

International Monetary Fund (IMF), 700 19th St. NW, Washington, DC, 20431, USA, (202) 623-7000, (202) 623-4661, publications@imf.org, https://www.imf.org; Balance of Payments Statistics: Annual Report 2021.

Routledge - Taylor & Francis Group, 6000 Broken Sound Pkwy. NW, Ste. 300, Boca Raton, FL, 33487, USA, (800) 634-1420, (800) 634-7064, orders@taylorandfrancis.com, https://www.routledge.com/; The Europa World Year Book 2022.

United Nations Conference on Trade and Development (UNCTAD), Palais des Nations, Geneva, 1211, SWI, (212) 963-6896, unctadinfo@unctad.org, https://unctad.org; Handbook of Statistics 2021.

United Nations Economic Commission for Africa (UNECA), PO Box 3001, Addis Ababa, ETH, ecainfo@uneca.org, https://www.uneca.org/; African Statistical Yearbook 2020.

The World Bank, 1818 H St. NW, Washington, DC, 20433, USA, (202) 473-1000, (202) 477-6391, eds03@worldbank.org, https://www.worldbank.org/; Benin (report); World Development Indicators (WDI) 2022; and World Development Report 2022: Finance for an Equitable Recovery.

BENIN-BANKS AND BANKING

Euromonitor International, Inc., 1 N Dearborn St., Ste. 1700, Chicago, IL, 60602, USA, (312) 922-1115, (312) 922-1157, info-usa@euromonitor.com, https://www.euromonitor.com/; Geographies.

International Monetary Fund (IMF), 700 19th St. NW, Washington, DC, 20431, USA, (202) 623-7000, (202) 623-4661, publications@imf.org, https://www.imf.org; International Financial Statistics (IFS).

Routledge - Taylor & Francis Group, 6000 Broken Sound Pkwy. NW, Ste. 300, Boca Raton, FL, 33487, USA, (800) 634-1420, (800) 634-7064, orders@taylorandfrancis.com, https://www.routledge.com/; The Europa World Year Book 2022.

United Nations Statistics Division (UNSD), United Nations Plz., New York, NY, 10017, USA, (800) 253-9646, (212) 963-9851, statistics@un.org, https://unstats.un.org; Statistical Yearbook of the United Nations 2021.

BENIN-BARLEY PRODUCTION

See BENIN-CROPS

BENIN-BROADCASTING

Central Intelligence Agency (CIA), Office of Public Affairs, Washington, DC, 20505, USA, (703) 482-0623, https://www.cia.gov; The World Factbook.

Euromonitor International, Inc., 1 N Dearborn St., Ste. 1700, Chicago, IL, 60602, USA, (312) 922-1115, (312) 922-1157, info-usa@euromonitor.com, https://www.euromonitor.com/; Geographies.

WRTH Publications Limited, PO Box 290, Oxford, OX2 7FT, GBR, sales@wrth.com, https://www.wrth.com; World Radio TV Handbook 2023.

BENIN-BUDGET

Central Intelligence Agency (CIA), Office of Public Affairs, Washington, DC, 20505, USA, (703) 482-0623, https://www.cia.gov; The World Factbook.

BENIN-CHILDBIRTH-STATISTICS

The World Bank, 1818 H St. NW, Washington, DC, 20433, USA, (202) 473-1000, (202) 477-6391, eds03@worldbank.org, https://www.worldbank.org/; World Development Indicators (WDI) 2022.

BENIN-CLIMATE

International Institute for Environment and Development (IIED), 235 High Holborn, London, WC1V 7DN, GBR, inforequest@iied.org, https://www.iied.org; Environment & Urbanization.

Palgrave Macmillan, 1 New York Plaza, Ste. 4500, New York, NY, 10004-1562, USA, (800) 777-4643, orders@palgrave.com, https://www.palgrave.com/us; The Statesman's Yearbook, 2023.

BENIN-COAL PRODUCTION

See BENIN-MINERAL INDUSTRIES

BENIN-COFFEE

See BENIN-CROPS

BENIN-COMMERCE

Palgrave Macmillan, 1 New York Plaza, Ste. 4500, New York, NY, 10004-1562, USA, (800) 777-4643, orders@palgrave.com, https://www.palgrave.com/us; The Statesman's Yearbook, 2023.

UK Data Service, University of Essex, Wivenhoe Park, Colchester, Essex, CO4 3SQ, GBR, https://ukdataservice.ac.uk/; International Aggregate Data.

BENIN-COMMODITY EXCHANGES

Barchart, 209 W Jackson Blvd., 2nd Fl., Chicago, IL, 60606, USA, (877) 247-4394, commodities@barchart.com, https://www.barchart.com/cmdty; The cmdty Yearbook 2023; cmdtyStats: Commodity Statistics and Fundamental Data; cmdtyView: Commodity Index; and Commodity Data and Prices.

International Monetary Fund (IMF), 700 19th St. NW, Washington, DC, 20431, USA, (202) 623-7000, (202) 623-4661, publications@imf.org, https://www.imf.org; IMF Primary Commodity Prices.

BENIN-CONSTRUCTION INDUSTRY

United Nations Economic Commission for Africa (UNECA), PO Box 3001, Addis Ababa, ETH, ecainfo@uneca.org, https://www.uneca.org/; African Statistical Yearbook 2020.

BENIN-CONSUMER PRICE INDEXES

Euromonitor International, Inc., 1 N Dearborn St., Ste. 1700, Chicago, IL, 60602, USA, (312) 922-1115, (312) 922-1157, info-usa@euromonitor.com, https://www.euromonitor.com/; Geographies.

The World Bank, 1818 H St. NW, Washington, DC, 20433, USA, (202) 473-1000, (202) 477-6391, eds03@worldbank.org, https://www.worldbank.org/; Benin (report).

BENIN-CONSUMPTION (ECONOMICS)

African Development Bank Group (AfDB), Avenue Joseph Anoma, 01 BP 1387, Abidjan, 01, COT, https://www.afdb.org; The AfDB Statistics Pocketbook 2019.

BENIN-COPPER INDUSTRY AND TRADE

See BENIN-MINERAL INDUSTRIES

BENIN-CORN INDUSTRY

See BENIN-CROPS

BENIN-COTTON

See BENIN-CROPS

BENIN-CROPS

Palgrave Macmillan, 1 New York Plaza, Ste. 4500, New York, NY, 10004-1562, USA, (800) 777-4643, orders@palgrave.com, https://www.palgrave.com/us; The Statesman's Yearbook, 2023.

United Nations Economic Commission for Africa (UNECA), PO Box 3001, Addis Ababa, ETH, ecainfo@uneca.org, https://www.uneca.org/; African Statistical Yearbook 2020.

United Nations Food and Agricultural Organization (FAO), 2121 K St., Ste. 800B, Washington, DC, 20037, USA, (202) 653-2400 (Dial from U.S.), (202) 653-5760 (Fax from U.S.), fao-hq@fao.org, https://www.fao.org; The State of Food and Agriculture (SOFA) 2022.

United Nations Statistics Division (UNSD), United Nations Plz., New York, NY, 10017, USA, (800) 253-9646, (212) 963-9851, statistics@un.org, https://unstats.un.org; Statistical Yearbook of the United Nations 2021.

BENIN-DAIRY PROCESSING

Palgrave Macmillan, 1 New York Plaza, Ste. 4500, New York, NY, 10004-1562, USA, (800) 777-4643, orders@palgrave.com, https://www.palgrave.com/us; The Statesman's Yearbook, 2023.

United Nations Food and Agricultural Organization (FAO), 2121 K St., Ste. 800B, Washington, DC, 20037, USA, (202) 653-2400 (Dial from U.S.), (202) 653-5760 (Fax from U.S.), fao-hq@fao.org, https://www.fao.org; The State of Food and Agriculture (SOFA) 2022.

BENIN-DEBTS, EXTERNAL

African Development Bank Group (AfDB), Avenue Joseph Anoma, 01 BP 1387, Abidjan, 01, COT, https://www.afdb.org; The AfDB Statistics Pocketbook 2019; African Economic Outlook 2021; and Compendium of Statistics on Bank Group Operations 2019.

Palgrave Macmillan, 1 New York Plaza, Ste. 4500, New York, NY, 10004-1562, USA, (800) 777-4643, orders@palgrave.com, https://www.palgrave.com/us; The Statesman's Yearbook, 2023.

United Nations Economic Commission for Africa (UNECA), PO Box 3001, Addis Ababa, ETH, ecainfo@uneca.org, https://www.uneca.org/; Economic Report on Africa 2021.

The World Bank, 1818 H St. NW, Washington, DC, 20433, USA, (202) 473-1000, (202) 477-6391, eds03@worldbank.org, https://www.worldbank.org/; Global Financial Development Report 2019-2020: Bank Regulation and Supervision a Decade after the Global Financial Crisis; World Development Indicators (WDI) 2022; and World Development Report 2022: Finance for an Equitable Recovery.

BENIN-DEFENSE EXPENDITURES

See BENIN-ARMED FORCES

BENIN-DIAMONDS

See BENIN-MINERAL INDUSTRIES

BENIN-ECONOMIC ASSISTANCE

United Nations Statistics Division (UNSD), United Nations Plz., New York, NY, 10017, USA, (800) 253-9646, (212) 963-9851, statistics@un.org, https://unstats.un.org; Statistical Yearbook of the United Nations 2021.

BENIN-ECONOMIC CONDITIONS

African Development Bank Group (AfDB), Avenue Joseph Anoma, 01 BP 1387, Abidjan, 01, COT, https://www.afdb.org; The AfDB Statistics Pocketbook 2019; Africa Economic Brief - COVID-19 Pandemic Potential Risks for Trade and Trade Finance in Africa; African Economic Outlook 2021; The African Statistical Journal; Compendium of Statistics on Bank Group Operations 2019; and Gender, Poverty and Environmental Indicators on African Countries 2019.

Bernan Press, 15250 NBN Way, Bldg. C, Blue Ridge Summit, PA, 17214, USA, (301) 459-2255, (800) 865-3457, (800) 865-3450, customercare@bernan.com, https://rowman.com/Page/Bernan; World Economic Outlook, April 2022.

Central Intelligence Agency (CIA), Office of Public Affairs, Washington, DC, 20505, USA, (703) 482-0623, https://www.cia.gov; The World Factbook.

The Economist Group: Economist Intelligence Unit (EIU), 900 3rd Ave., 16th Fl., New York, NY, 10022, USA, (212) 541-0500, americas@eiu.com, https://www.eiu.com; Benin Country Report.

Euromonitor International, Inc., 1 N Dearborn St., Ste. 1700, Chicago, IL, 60602, USA, (312) 922-1115, (312) 922-1157, info-usa@euromonitor.com, https://www.euromonitor.com/; Geographies.

International Monetary Fund (IMF), 700 19th St. NW, Washington, DC, 20431, USA, (202) 623-7000, (202) 623-4661, publications@imf.org, https://www.imf.org; IMF Data and World Economic Outlook.

Organisation of Islamic Cooperation (OIC), Statistical, Economic and Social Research and Training Centre for Islamic Countries (SESRIC), Kudus Cad. No. 9, Diplomatik Site, Ankara, 06450, TUR, statistics@sesric.org, https://www.sesric.org/; OIC Economic Outlook 2021; OIC Statistics (OICStat) Database; and OIC-Countries in Figures (OIC-CIF).

Palgrave Macmillan, 1 New York Plaza, Ste. 4500, New York, NY, 10004-1562, USA, (800) 777-4643, orders@palgrave.com, https://www.palgrave.com/us; The Statesman's Yearbook, 2023.

Routledge - Taylor & Francis Group, 6000 Broken Sound Pkwy. NW, Ste. 300, Boca Raton, FL, 33487, USA, (800) 634-1420, (800) 634-7064, orders@taylorandfrancis.com, https://www.routledge.com/; The Europa World Year Book 2022.

United Nations Economic Commission for Africa (UNECA), PO Box 3001, Addis Ababa, ETH, ecainfo@uneca.org, https://www.uneca.org/; Economic Report on Africa 2021.

United Nations Statistics Division (UNSD), United Nations Plz., New York, NY, 10017, USA, (800) 253-9646, (212) 963-9851, statistics@un.org, https://unstats.un.org; World Statistics Pocketbook 2021.

The World Bank, 1818 H St. NW, Washington, DC, 20433, USA, (202) 473-1000, (202) 477-6391, eds03@worldbank.org, https://www.worldbank.org/; Benin (report); Global Economic Monitor (GEM); Global Economic Prospects, June 2022; The Global Findex Database 2021; and World Development Report 2022: Finance for an Equitable Recovery.

BENIN-EDUCATION

African Development Bank Group (AfDB), Avenue Joseph Anoma, 01 BP 1387, Abidjan, 01, COT, https://www.afdb.org; The AfDB Statistics Pocketbook 2019.

Euromonitor International, Inc., 1 N Dearborn St., Ste. 1700, Chicago, IL, 60602, USA, (312) 922-1115, (312) 922-1157, info-usa@euromonitor.com, https://www.euromonitor.com/; Geographies.

Infoplease, c/o Sandbox Networks, Inc., 1 Lincoln St., 24th Fl., Boston, MA, 02111, USA, https://www.infoplease.com; Countries of the World.

Organisation of Islamic Cooperation (OIC), Statistical, Economic and Social Research and Training Centre for Islamic Countries (SESRIC), Kudus Cad. No. 9, Diplomatik Site, Ankara, 06450, TUR, statistics@sesric.org, https://www.sesric.org/; OIC Statistics (OICStat) Database.

Palgrave Macmillan, 1 New York Plaza, Ste. 4500, New York, NY, 10004-1562, USA, (800) 777-4643, orders@palgrave.com, https://www.palgrave.com/us; The Statesman's Yearbook, 2023.

Routledge - Taylor & Francis Group, 6000 Broken Sound Pkwy. NW, Ste. 300, Boca Raton, FL, 33487, USA, (800) 634-1420, (800) 634-7064, orders@taylorandfrancis.com, https://www.routledge.com/; The Europa World Year Book 2022.

UNESCO Institute for Statistics, C.P 250 Succursale H, Montreal, QC, H3G 2K8, CAN, (514) 343-6880 (Dial from U.S.), (514) 343-5740 (Fax from U.S.), uis.publications@unesco.org, http://uis.unesco.org/; Literacy and UIS.Stat.

United Nations Economic Commission for Africa (UNECA), PO Box 3001, Addis Ababa, ETH, ecainfo@uneca.org, https://www.uneca.org/; African Statistical Yearbook 2020.

United Nations Statistics Division (UNSD), United Nations Plz., New York, NY, 10017, USA, (800) 253-9646, (212) 963-9851, statistics@un.org, https://unstats.un.org; Millennium Development Goal Indicators.

The World Bank, 1818 H St. NW, Washington, DC, 20433, USA, (202) 473-1000, (202) 477-6391, eds03@worldbank.org, https://www.worldbank.org/; Benin (report); World Development Indicators (WDI) 2022; and World Development Report 2022: Finance for an Equitable Recovery.

BENIN-ELECTRICITY

International Energy Agency (IEA), 9 Rue de la Federation, Paris, 75739, FRA, info@iea.org, https://www.iea.org/; World Energy Outlook 2021.

United Nations Statistics Division (UNSD), United Nations Plz., New York, NY, 10017, USA, (800) 253-9646, (212) 963-9851, statistics@un.org, https://unstats.un.org; Statistical Yearbook of the United Nations 2021.

BENIN-EMPLOYMENT

International Labour Organization (ILO), 4 Rte. des Morillons, Geneva, CH-1211, SWI, ilo@ilo.org, https://www.ilo.org; NORMLEX Information System on International Labour Standards.

UK Data Service, University of Essex, Wivenhoe Park, Colchester, Essex, CO4 3SQ, GBR, https://ukdataservice.ac.uk/; International Aggregate Data.

United Nations Economic Commission for Africa (UNECA), PO Box 3001, Addis Ababa, ETH, ecainfo@uneca.org, https://www.uneca.org/; African Statistical Yearbook 2020.

The World Bank, 1818 H St. NW, Washington, DC, 20433, USA, (202) 473-1000, (202) 477-6391, eds03@worldbank.org, https://www.worldbank.org/; Benin (report).

BENIN-ENVIRONMENTAL CONDITIONS

DSI Data Service & Information, Xantener Strasse 51a, Rheinberg, D-47495, GER, dsi@dsidata.com, https://www.dsidata.com/; Global Environmental Database.

The Economist Group: Economist Intelligence Unit (EIU), 900 3rd Ave., 16th Fl., New York, NY, 10022, USA, (212) 541-0500, americas@eiu.com, https://www.eiu.com; Benin Country Report.

International Institute for Environment and Development (IIED), 235 High Holborn, London, WC1V 7DN, GBR, inforequest@iied.org, https://www.iied.org; Environment & Urbanization.

Organisation of Islamic Cooperation (OIC), Statistical, Economic and Social Research and Training Centre for Islamic Countries (SESRIC), Kudus Cad. No. 9, Diplomatik Site, Ankara, 06450, TUR, statistics@sesric.org, https://www.sesric.org/; OIC Statistics (OICStat) Database and OIC-Countries in Figures (OIC-CIF).

United Nations Statistics Division (UNSD), United Nations Plz., New York, NY, 10017, USA, (800) 253-9646, (212) 963-9851, statistics@un.org, https://unstats.un.org; World Statistics Pocketbook 2021.

BENIN-EXPORTS

African Development Bank Group (AfDB), Avenue Joseph Anoma, 01 BP 1387, Abidjan, 01, COT, https://www.afdb.org; African Economic Outlook 2021.

Central Intelligence Agency (CIA), Office of Public Affairs, Washington, DC, 20505, USA, (703) 482-0623, https://www.cia.gov; The World Factbook.

The Economist Group: Economist Intelligence Unit (EIU), 900 3rd Ave., 16th Fl., New York, NY, 10022, USA, (212) 541-0500, americas@eiu.com, https://www.eiu.com; Benin Country Report.

International Monetary Fund (IMF), 700 19th St. NW, Washington, DC, 20431, USA, (202) 623-7000, (202) 623-4661, publications@imf.org, https://www.imf.org; Direction of Trade Statistics (DOTS).

Organisation of Islamic Cooperation (OIC), Statistical, Economic and Social Research and Training Centre for Islamic Countries (SESRIC), Kudus Cad. No. 9, Diplomatik Site, Ankara, 06450, TUR, statistics@sesric.org, https://www.sesric.org/; OIC Statistics (OICStat) Database.

S&P Global, IHS Markit, 15 Inverness Way E, Englewood, CO, 80112, USA, (800) 447-2273, (800) 854-7179, https://ihsmarkit.com; Global Trade Atlas (GTA).

United Nations Conference on Trade and Development (UNCTAD), Palais des Nations, Geneva, 1211, SWI, (212) 963-6896, unctadinfo@unctad.org, https://unctad.org; Handbook of Statistics 2021.

The World Bank, 1818 H St. NW, Washington, DC, 20433, USA, (202) 473-1000, (202) 477-6391, eds03@worldbank.org, https://www.worldbank.org/; World Development Report 2022: Finance for an Equitable Recovery.

BENIN-FEMALE WORKING POPULATION

See BENIN-EMPLOYMENT

BENIN-FERTILITY, HUMAN

Central Intelligence Agency (CIA), Office of Public Affairs, Washington, DC, 20505, USA, (703) 482-0623, https://www.cia.gov; The World Factbook.

BENIN-FERTILIZER INDUSTRY

United Nations Food and Agricultural Organization (FAO), 2121 K St., Ste. 800B, Washington, DC, 20037, USA, (202) 653-2400 (Dial from U.S.), (202) 653-5760 (Fax from U.S.), fao-hq@fao.org, https://www.fao.org; The State of Food and Agriculture (SOFA) 2022.

BENIN-FINANCE

Stockholm International Peace Research Institute (SIPRI), Signalistgatan 9, Stockholm, SE 169 72, SWE, https://www.sipri.org/; SIPRI Arms Transfers Database and SIPRI Military Expenditure Database.

United Nations Economic Commission for Africa (UNECA), PO Box 3001, Addis Ababa, ETH, ecainfo@uneca.org, https://www.uneca.org/; African Statistical Yearbook 2020.

United Nations Statistics Division (UNSD), United Nations Plz., New York, NY, 10017, USA, (800) 253-9646, (212) 963-9851, statistics@un.org, https://unstats.un.org; Statistical Yearbook of the United Nations 2021.

The World Bank, 1818 H St. NW, Washington, DC, 20433, USA, (202) 473-1000, (202) 477-6391, eds03@worldbank.org, https://www.worldbank.org/; Benin (report).

BENIN-FINANCE, PUBLIC

African Development Bank Group (AfDB), Avenue Joseph Anoma, 01 BP 1387, Abidjan, 01, COT, https://www.afdb.org; The AfDB Statistics Pocketbook 2019.

Bernan Press, 15250 NBN Way, Bldg. C, Blue Ridge Summit, PA, 17214, USA, (301) 459-2255, (800) 865-3457, (800) 865-3450, customercare@bernan.com, https://rowman.com/Page/Bernan; National Accounts Statistics: Analysis of Main Aggregates 2020.

The Economist Group: Economist Intelligence Unit (EIU), 900 3rd Ave., 16th Fl., New York, NY, 10022, USA, (212) 541-0500, americas@eiu.com, https://www.eiu.com; Benin Country Report.

International Monetary Fund (IMF), 700 19th St. NW, Washington, DC, 20431, USA, (202) 623-7000, (202) 623-4661, publications@imf.org, https://www.imf.org; Regional Economic Outlook.

Palgrave Macmillan, 1 New York Plaza, Ste. 4500, New York, NY, 10004-1562, USA, (800) 777-4643, orders@palgrave.com, https://www.palgrave.com/us; The Statesman's Yearbook, 2023.

Routledge - Taylor & Francis Group, 6000 Broken Sound Pkwy. NW, Ste. 300, Boca Raton, FL, 33487, USA, (800) 634-1420, (800) 634-7064, orders@taylorandfrancis.com, https://www.routledge.com/; The Europa World Year Book 2022.

United Nations Economic Commission for Africa (UNECA), PO Box 3001, Addis Ababa, ETH, ecainfo@uneca.org, https://www.uneca.org/; African Statistical Yearbook 2020.

United Nations Statistics Division (UNSD), United Nations Plz., New York, NY, 10017, USA, (800) 253-9646, (212) 963-9851, statistics@un.org, https://unstats.un.org; National Accounts Main Aggregates Database and National Accounts Statistics: Main Aggregates and Detailed Tables.

The World Bank, 1818 H St. NW, Washington, DC, 20433, USA, (202) 473-1000, (202) 477-6391, eds03@worldbank.org, https://www.worldbank.org/; Benin (report).

BENIN-FISHERIES

Palgrave Macmillan, 1 New York Plaza, Ste. 4500, New York, NY, 10004-1562, USA, (800) 777-4643, orders@palgrave.com, https://www.palgrave.com/us; The Statesman's Yearbook, 2023.

Routledge - Taylor & Francis Group, 6000 Broken Sound Pkwy. NW, Ste. 300, Boca Raton, FL, 33487, USA, (800) 634-1420, (800) 634-7064, orders@taylorandfrancis.com, https://www.routledge.com/; The Europa World Year Book 2022.

United Nations Economic Commission for Africa (UNECA), PO Box 3001, Addis Ababa, ETH, ecainfo@uneca.org, https://www.uneca.org/; African Statistical Yearbook 2020.

United Nations Food and Agricultural Organization (FAO), 2121 K St., Ste. 800B, Washington, DC, 20037, USA, (202) 653-2400 (Dial from U.S.), (202) 653-5760 (Fax from U.S.), fao-hq@fao.org, https://www.fao.org; FAO Yearbook of Fishery and Aquaculture Statistics 2019; Fishery Statistical Collections Global Capture Production; FishStatJ; and The State of Food and Agriculture (SOFA) 2022.

United Nations Statistics Division (UNSD), United Nations Plz., New York, NY, 10017, USA, (800) 253-9646, (212) 963-9851, statistics@un.org, https://unstats.un.org; Statistical Yearbook of the United Nations 2021.

The World Bank, 1818 H St. NW, Washington, DC, 20433, USA, (202) 473-1000, (202) 477-6391, eds03@worldbank.org, https://www.worldbank.org/; Benin (report).

BENIN-FOOD

African Development Bank Group (AfDB), Avenue Joseph Anoma, 01 BP 1387, Abidjan, 01, COT, https://www.afdb.org; The AfDB Statistics Pocketbook 2019.

United Nations Food and Agricultural Organization (FAO), 2121 K St., Ste. 800B, Washington, DC, 20037, USA, (202) 653-2400 (Dial from U.S.), (202) 653-5760 (Fax from U.S.), fao-hq@fao.org, https://www.fao.org; The State of Food and Agriculture (SOFA) 2022.

BENIN-FOREIGN EXCHANGE RATES

African Development Bank Group (AfDB), Avenue Joseph Anoma, 01 BP 1387, Abidjan, 01, COT, https://www.afdb.org; The AfDB Statistics Pocketbook 2019 and African Economic Outlook 2021.

BENIN-FORESTS AND FORESTRY

Palgrave Macmillan, 1 New York Plaza, Ste. 4500, New York, NY, 10004-1562, USA, (800) 777-4643,

orders@palgrave.com, https://www.palgrave.com/us; The Statesman's Yearbook, 2023.

Routledge - Taylor & Francis Group, 6000 Broken Sound Pkwy. NW, Ste. 300, Boca Raton, FL, 33487, USA, (800) 634-1420, (800) 634-7064, orders@taylorandfrancis.com, https://www.routledge.com/; The Europa World Year Book 2022.

UNESCO Institute for Statistics, C.P 250 Succursale H, Montreal, QC, H3G 2K8, CAN, (514) 343-6880 (Dial from U.S.), (514) 343-5740 (Fax from U.S.), uis.publications@unesco.org, http://uis.unesco.org/; UIS.Stat.

United Nations Economic Commission for Africa (UNECA), PO Box 3001, Addis Ababa, ETH, ecainfo@uneca.org, https://www.uneca.org/; African Statistical Yearbook 2020.

United Nations Food and Agricultural Organization (FAO), 2121 K St., Ste. 800B, Washington, DC, 20037, USA, (202) 653-2400 (Dial from U.S.), (202) 653-5760 (Fax from U.S.), fao-hq@fao.org, https://www.fao.org; FAO Yearbook of Forest Products 2019 and The State of Food and Agriculture (SOFA) 2022.

United Nations Statistics Division (UNSD), United Nations Plz., New York, NY, 10017, USA, (800) 253-9646, (212) 963-9851, statistics@un.org, https://unstats.un.org; Statistical Yearbook of the United Nations 2021.

The World Bank, 1818 H St. NW, Washington, DC, 20433, USA, (202) 473-1000, (202) 477-6391, eds03@worldbank.org, https://www.worldbank.org/; Benin (report) and World Development Report 2022: Finance for an Equitable Recovery.

BENIN-GAS PRODUCTION

See BENIN-MINERAL INDUSTRIES

BENIN-GEOGRAPHIC INFORMATION SYSTEMS

The World Bank, 1818 H St. NW, Washington, DC, 20433, USA, (202) 473-1000, (202) 477-6391, eds03@worldbank.org, https://www.worldbank.org/; Benin (report).

BENIN-GOLD INDUSTRY

The World Bank, 1818 H St. NW, Washington, DC, 20433, USA, (202) 473-1000, (202) 477-6391, eds03@worldbank.org, https://www.worldbank.org/; World Development Indicators (WDI) 2022.

BENIN-GOLD PRODUCTION

See BENIN-MINERAL INDUSTRIES

BENIN-GROSS DOMESTIC PRODUCT

African Development Bank Group (AfDB), Avenue Joseph Anoma, 01 BP 1387, Abidjan, 01, COT, https://www.afdb.org; The AfDB Statistics Pocketbook 2019.

The Economist Group: Economist Intelligence Unit (EIU), 900 3rd Ave., 16th Fl., New York, NY, 10022, USA, (212) 541-0500, americas@eiu.com, https://www.eiu.com; Benin Country Report.

Routledge - Taylor & Francis Group, 6000 Broken Sound Pkwy. NW, Ste. 300, Boca Raton, FL, 33487, USA, (800) 634-1420, (800) 634-7064, orders@taylorandfrancis.com, https://www.routledge.com/; The Europa World Year Book 2022.

United Nations Economic Commission for Africa (UNECA), PO Box 3001, Addis Ababa, ETH, ecainfo@uneca.org, https://www.uneca.org/; African Statistical Yearbook 2020.

United Nations Statistics Division (UNSD), United Nations Plz., New York, NY, 10017, USA, (800) 253-9646, (212) 963-9851, statistics@un.org, https://unstats.un.org; Statistical Yearbook of the United Nations 2021.

The World Bank, 1818 H St. NW, Washington, DC, 20433, USA, (202) 473-1000, (202) 477-6391, eds03@worldbank.org, https://www.worldbank.org/; World Development Indicators (WDI) 2022 and World Development Report 2022: Finance for an Equitable Recovery.

BENIN-GROSS NATIONAL PRODUCT

Palgrave Macmillan, 1 New York Plaza, Ste. 4500, New York, NY, 10004-1562, USA, (800) 777-4643, orders@palgrave.com, https://www.palgrave.com/us; The Statesman's Yearbook, 2023.

Routledge - Taylor & Francis Group, 6000 Broken Sound Pkwy. NW, Ste. 300, Boca Raton, FL, 33487, USA, (800) 634-1420, (800) 634-7064, orders@taylorandfrancis.com, https://www.routledge.com/; The Europa World Year Book 2022.

United Nations Statistics Division (UNSD), United Nations Plz., New York, NY, 10017, USA, (800) 253-9646, (212) 963-9851, statistics@un.org, https://unstats.un.org; Statistical Yearbook of the United Nations 2021.

The World Bank, 1818 H St. NW, Washington, DC, 20433, USA, (202) 473-1000, (202) 477-6391, eds03@worldbank.org, https://www.worldbank.org/; World Development Indicators (WDI) 2022 and World Development Report 2022: Finance for an Equitable Recovery.

BENIN-ILLITERATE PERSONS

UNESCO Institute for Statistics, C.P 250 Succursale H, Montreal, QC, H3G 2K8, CAN, (514) 343-6880 (Dial from U.S.), (514) 343-5740 (Fax from U.S.), uis.publications@unesco.org, http://uis.unesco.org/; UIS.Stat.

BENIN-IMPORTS

African Development Bank Group (AfDB), Avenue Joseph Anoma, 01 BP 1387, Abidjan, 01, COT, https://www.afdb.org; African Economic Outlook 2021.

Central Intelligence Agency (CIA), Office of Public Affairs, Washington, DC, 20505, USA, (703) 482-0623, https://www.cia.gov; The World Factbook.

The Economist Group: Economist Intelligence Unit (EIU), 900 3rd Ave., 16th Fl., New York, NY, 10022, USA, (212) 541-0500, americas@eiu.com, https://www.eiu.com; Benin Country Report.

International Monetary Fund (IMF), 700 19th St. NW, Washington, DC, 20431, USA, (202) 623-7000, (202) 623-4661, publications@imf.org, https://www.imf.org; Direction of Trade Statistics (DOTS).

S&P Global, IHS Markit, 15 Inverness Way E, Englewood, CO, 80112, USA, (800) 447-2273, (800) 854-7179, https://ihsmarkit.com; Global Trade Atlas (GTA).

United Nations Conference on Trade and Development (UNCTAD), Palais des Nations, Geneva, 1211, SWI, (212) 963-6896, unctadinfo@unctad.org, https://unctad.org; Handbook of Statistics 2021.

The World Bank, 1818 H St. NW, Washington, DC, 20433, USA, (202) 473-1000, (202) 477-6391, eds03@worldbank.org, https://www.worldbank.org/; World Development Report 2022: Finance for an Equitable Recovery.

BENIN-INDUSTRIES

Central Intelligence Agency (CIA), Office of Public Affairs, Washington, DC, 20505, USA, (703) 482-0623, https://www.cia.gov; The World Factbook.

The Economist Group: Economist Intelligence Unit (EIU), 900 3rd Ave., 16th Fl., New York, NY, 10022, USA, (212) 541-0500, americas@eiu.com, https://www.eiu.com; Benin Country Report.

Euromonitor International, Inc., 1 N Dearborn St., Ste. 1700, Chicago, IL, 60602, USA, (312) 922-1115, (312) 922-1157, info-usa@euromonitor.com, https://www.euromonitor.com/; Geographies.

International Labour Organization (ILO), 4 Rte. des Morillons, Geneva, CH-1211, SWI, ilo@ilo.org, https://www.ilo.org; NORMLEX Information System on International Labour Standards.

Palgrave Macmillan, 1 New York Plaza, Ste. 4500, New York, NY, 10004-1562, USA, (800) 777-4643, orders@palgrave.com, https://www.palgrave.com/us; The Statesman's Yearbook, 2023.

Routledge - Taylor & Francis Group, 6000 Broken Sound Pkwy. NW, Ste. 300, Boca Raton, FL, 33487, USA, (800) 634-1420, (800) 634-7064, orders@taylorandfrancis.com, https://www.routledge.com/; The Europa World Year Book 2022.

United Nations Economic Commission for Africa (UNECA), PO Box 3001, Addis Ababa, ETH, ecainfo@uneca.org, https://www.uneca.org/; African Statistical Yearbook 2020.

United Nations Industrial Development Organization (UNIDO), 1 United Nations Plz., Rm. DC1-1118, New York, NY, 10017, USA, (212) 963-6890, (212) 963 6885, (212) 963-7904, office.newyork@unido.org, https://www.unido.org/; Industrial Statistics Databases and International Yearbook of Industrial Statistics 2021.

The World Bank, 1818 H St. NW, Washington, DC, 20433, USA, (202) 473-1000, (202) 477-6391, eds03@worldbank.org, https://www.worldbank.org/; Benin (report) and World Development Indicators (WDI) 2022.

BENIN-INFANT AND MATERNAL MORTALITY

See BENIN-MORTALITY

BENIN-INTERNATIONAL TRADE

African Development Bank Group (AfDB), Avenue Joseph Anoma, 01 BP 1387, Abidjan, 01, COT, https://www.afdb.org; The AfDB Statistics Pocketbook 2019 and African Economic Outlook 2021.

The Economist Group: Economist Intelligence Unit (EIU), 900 3rd Ave., 16th Fl., New York, NY, 10022, USA, (212) 541-0500, americas@eiu.com, https://www.eiu.com; Benin Country Report.

Euromonitor International, Inc., 1 N Dearborn St., Ste. 1700, Chicago, IL, 60602, USA, (312) 922-1115, (312) 922-1157, info-usa@euromonitor.com, https://www.euromonitor.com/; Geographies.

Palgrave Macmillan, 1 New York Plaza, Ste. 4500, New York, NY, 10004-1562, USA, (800) 777-4643, orders@palgrave.com, https://www.palgrave.com/us; The Statesman's Yearbook, 2023.

Routledge - Taylor & Francis Group, 6000 Broken Sound Pkwy. NW, Ste. 300, Boca Raton, FL, 33487, USA, (800) 634-1420, (800) 634-7064, orders@taylorandfrancis.com, https://www.routledge.com/; The Europa World Year Book 2022.

United Nations Conference on Trade and Development (UNCTAD), Palais des Nations, Geneva, 1211, SWI, (212) 963-6896, unctadinfo@unctad.org, https://unctad.org; Trade and Development Report 2021.

United Nations Economic Commission for Africa (UNECA), PO Box 3001, Addis Ababa, ETH, ecainfo@uneca.org, https://www.uneca.org/; African Statistical Yearbook 2020.

United Nations Food and Agricultural Organization (FAO), 2121 K St., Ste. 800B, Washington, DC, 20037, USA, (202) 653-2400 (Dial from U.S.), (202) 653-5760 (Fax from U.S.), fao-hq@fao.org, https://www.fao.org; The State of Food and Agriculture (SOFA) 2022.

United Nations Statistics Division (UNSD), United Nations Plz., New York, NY, 10017, USA, (800) 253-9646, (212) 963-9851, statistics@un.org, https://unstats.un.org; International Trade Statistics Yearbook 2020 and Statistical Yearbook of the United Nations 2021.

The World Bank, 1818 H St. NW, Washington, DC, 20433, USA, (202) 473-1000, (202) 477-6391, eds03@worldbank.org, https://www.worldbank.org/; Benin (report); World Development Indicators (WDI) 2022; and World Development Report 2022: Finance for an Equitable Recovery.

World Trade Organization (WTO), Ctre. William Rappard, Rue de Lausanne 154, Case postale, Geneva, CH-1211, SWI, enquiries@wto.org, https://www.wto.org; World Trade Statistical Review 2022.

BENIN-INTERNET USERS

International Telecommunication Union (ITU), Place des Nations, Geneva, CH-1211, SWI, itumail@itu.

int, https://www.itu.int; Global Connectivity Report 2022; World Telecommunication/ICT Indicators Database 2021; and Yearbook of Statistics 2019.

The World Bank, 1818 H St. NW, Washington, DC, 20433, USA, (202) 473-1000, (202) 477-6391, eds03@worldbank.org, https://www.worldbank.org/; Benin (report).

BENIN-LABOR

African Development Bank Group (AfDB), Avenue Joseph Anoma, 01 BP 1387, Abidjan, 01, COT, https://www.afdb.org; The AfDB Statistics Pocketbook 2019.

Central Intelligence Agency (CIA), Office of Public Affairs, Washington, DC, 20505, USA, (703) 482-0623, https://www.cia.gov; The World Factbook.

Euromonitor International, Inc., 1 N Dearborn St., Ste. 1700, Chicago, IL, 60602, USA, (312) 922-1115, (312) 922-1157, info-usa@euromonitor.com, https://www.euromonitor.com/; Geographies.

International Labour Organization (ILO), 4 Rte. des Morillons, Geneva, CH-1211, SWI, ilo@ilo.org, https://www.ilo.org; NORMLEX Information System on International Labour Standards.

Organisation of Islamic Cooperation (OIC), Statistical, Economic and Social Research and Training Centre for Islamic Countries (SESRIC), Kudus Cad. No. 9, Diplomatik Site, Ankara, 06450, TUR, statistics@sesric.org, https://www.sesric.org/; OIC Statistics (OICStat) Database.

Palgrave Macmillan, 1 New York Plaza, Ste. 4500, New York, NY, 10004-1562, USA, (800) 777-4643, orders@palgrave.com, https://www.palgrave.com/us; The Statesman's Yearbook, 2023.

United Nations Food and Agricultural Organization (FAO), 2121 K St., Ste. 800B, Washington, DC, 20037, USA, (202) 653-2400 (Dial from U.S.), (202) 653-5760 (Fax from U.S.), fao-hq@fao.org, https://www.fao.org; The State of Food and Agriculture (SOFA) 2022.

The World Bank, 1818 H St. NW, Washington, DC, 20433, USA, (202) 473-1000, (202) 477-6391, eds03@worldbank.org, https://www.worldbank.org/; World Development Indicators (WDI) 2022 and World Development Report 2022: Finance for an Equitable Recovery.

BENIN-LAND USE

United Nations Statistics Division (UNSD), United Nations Plz., New York, NY, 10017, USA, (800) 253-9646, (212) 963-9851, statistics@un.org, https://unstats.un.org; Millennium Development Goal Indicators.

The World Bank, 1818 H St. NW, Washington, DC, 20433, USA, (202) 473-1000, (202) 477-6391, eds03@worldbank.org, https://www.worldbank.org/; World Development Report 2022: Finance for an Equitable Recovery.

BENIN-LIBRARIES

UNESCO Institute for Statistics, C.P 250 Succursale H, Montreal, QC, H3G 2K8, CAN, (514) 343-6880 (Dial from U.S.), (514) 343-5740 (Fax from U.S.), uis.publications@unesco.org, http://uis.unesco.org/; UIS.Stat.

BENIN-LIFE EXPECTANCY

African Development Bank Group (AfDB), Avenue Joseph Anoma, 01 BP 1387, Abidjan, 01, COT, https://www.afdb.org; The AfDB Statistics Pocketbook 2019.

Central Intelligence Agency (CIA), Office of Public Affairs, Washington, DC, 20505, USA, (703) 482-0623, https://www.cia.gov; The World Factbook.

United Nations Department of Economic and Social Affairs (DESA), Population Division, 2 United Nations Plz., Rm. DC2-1950, New York, NY, 10017, USA, (212) 963-3209, (212) 963-2147, population@un.org, https://www.un.org/development/desa/pd/; World Population Ageing 2020 Highlights.

United Nations Statistics Division (UNSD), United Nations Plz., New York, NY, 10017, USA, (800) 253-9646, (212) 963-9851, statistics@un.org, https://unstats.un.org; Millennium Development Goal Indicators.

BENIN-LITERACY

Euromonitor International, Inc., 1 N Dearborn St., Ste. 1700, Chicago, IL, 60602, USA, (312) 922-1115, (312) 922-1157, info-usa@euromonitor.com, https://www.euromonitor.com/; Geographies.

UNESCO Institute for Statistics, C.P 250 Succursale H, Montreal, QC, H3G 2K8, CAN, (514) 343-6880 (Dial from U.S.), (514) 343-5740 (Fax from U.S.), uis.publications@unesco.org, http://uis.unesco.org/; Literacy.

BENIN-LIVESTOCK

Palgrave Macmillan, 1 New York Plaza, Ste. 4500, New York, NY, 10004-1562, USA, (800) 777-4643, orders@palgrave.com, https://www.palgrave.com/us; The Statesman's Yearbook, 2023.

Routledge - Taylor & Francis Group, 6000 Broken Sound Pkwy. NW, Ste. 300, Boca Raton, FL, 33487, USA, (800) 634-1420, (800) 634-7064, orders@taylorandfrancis.com, https://www.routledge.com/; The Europa World Year Book 2022.

United Nations Economic Commission for Africa (UNECA), PO Box 3001, Addis Ababa, ETH, ecainfo@uneca.org, https://www.uneca.org/; African Statistical Yearbook 2020.

United Nations Food and Agricultural Organization (FAO), 2121 K St., Ste. 800B, Washington, DC, 20037, USA, (202) 653-2400 (Dial from U.S.), (202) 653-5760 (Fax from U.S.), fao-hq@fao.org, https://www.fao.org; The State of Food and Agriculture (SOFA) 2022.

United Nations Statistics Division (UNSD), United Nations Plz., New York, NY, 10017, USA, (800) 253-9646, (212) 963-9851, statistics@un.org, https://unstats.un.org; Statistical Yearbook of the United Nations 2021.

BENIN-MINERAL INDUSTRIES

International Energy Agency (IEA), 9 Rue de la Federation, Paris, 75739, FRA, info@iea.org, https://www.iea.org/; World Energy Outlook 2021.

Routledge - Taylor & Francis Group, 6000 Broken Sound Pkwy. NW, Ste. 300, Boca Raton, FL, 33487, USA, (800) 634-1420, (800) 634-7064, orders@taylorandfrancis.com, https://www.routledge.com/; The Europa World Year Book 2022.

United Nations Conference on Trade and Development (UNCTAD), Palais des Nations, Geneva, 1211, SWI, (212) 963-6896, unctadinfo@unctad.org, https://unctad.org; Trade and Development Report 2021.

United Nations Economic Commission for Africa (UNECA), PO Box 3001, Addis Ababa, ETH, ecainfo@uneca.org, https://www.uneca.org/; African Statistical Yearbook 2020.

United Nations Statistics Division (UNSD), United Nations Plz., New York, NY, 10017, USA, (800) 253-9646, (212) 963-9851, statistics@un.org, https://unstats.un.org; Statistical Yearbook of the United Nations 2021.

BENIN-MONEY SUPPLY

The Economist Group: Economist Intelligence Unit (EIU), 900 3rd Ave., 16th Fl., New York, NY, 10022, USA, (212) 541-0500, americas@eiu.com, https://www.eiu.com; Benin Country Report.

Routledge - Taylor & Francis Group, 6000 Broken Sound Pkwy. NW, Ste. 300, Boca Raton, FL, 33487, USA, (800) 634-1420, (800) 634-7064, orders@taylorandfrancis.com, https://www.routledge.com/; The Europa World Year Book 2022.

United Nations Statistics Division (UNSD), United Nations Plz., New York, NY, 10017, USA, (800) 253-9646, (212) 963-9851, statistics@un.org, https://unstats.un.org; Statistical Yearbook of the United Nations 2021.

The World Bank, 1818 H St. NW, Washington, DC, 20433, USA, (202) 473-1000, (202) 477-6391, eds03@worldbank.org, https://www.worldbank.org/; Benin (report).

BENIN-MORTALITY

United Nations Statistics Division (UNSD), United Nations Plz., New York, NY, 10017, USA, (800) 253-9646, (212) 963-9851, statistics@un.org, https://unstats.un.org; Millennium Development Goal Indicators; Statistical Yearbook of the United Nations 2021; and World Statistics Pocketbook 2021.

The World Bank, 1818 H St. NW, Washington, DC, 20433, USA, (202) 473-1000, (202) 477-6391, eds03@worldbank.org, https://www.worldbank.org/; World Development Indicators (WDI) 2022.

World Health Organization (WHO), Ave. Appia 20, Geneva, CH-1211, SWI, (202) 974-3000 (Telephone in U.S.), publications@who.int, https://www.who.int/; Global Health Observatory (GHO).

BENIN-MOTOR VEHICLES

International Road Federation (IRF), Madison Place, 500 Montgomery St., 5th Fl., Alexandria, VA, 22314, USA, (703) 535-1001, (703) 535-1007, info@irf.global, https://www.irf.global/; World Road Statistics (WRS).

BENIN-NATURAL GAS PRODUCTION

See BENIN-MINERAL INDUSTRIES

BENIN-NUTRITION

United Nations Food and Agricultural Organization (FAO), 2121 K St., Ste. 800B, Washington, DC, 20037, USA, (202) 653-2400 (Dial from U.S.), (202) 653-5760 (Fax from U.S.), fao-hq@fao.org, https://www.fao.org; The State of Food and Agriculture (SOFA) 2022.

United Nations Statistics Division (UNSD), United Nations Plz., New York, NY, 10017, USA, (800) 253-9646, (212) 963-9851, statistics@un.org, https://unstats.un.org; Millennium Development Goal Indicators.

BENIN-PAPER

See BENIN-FORESTS AND FORESTRY

BENIN-PEANUT PRODUCTION

See BENIN-CROPS

BENIN-PESTICIDES

United Nations Food and Agricultural Organization (FAO), 2121 K St., Ste. 800B, Washington, DC, 20037, USA, (202) 653-2400 (Dial from U.S.), (202) 653-5760 (Fax from U.S.), fao-hq@fao.org, https://www.fao.org; The State of Food and Agriculture (SOFA) 2022.

BENIN-PETROLEUM INDUSTRY AND TRADE

International Energy Agency (IEA), 9 Rue de la Federation, Paris, 75739, FRA, info@iea.org, https://www.iea.org/; World Energy Outlook 2021.

Palgrave Macmillan, 1 New York Plaza, Ste. 4500, New York, NY, 10004-1562, USA, (800) 777-4643, orders@palgrave.com, https://www.palgrave.com/us; The Statesman's Yearbook, 2023.

United Nations Food and Agricultural Organization (FAO), 2121 K St., Ste. 800B, Washington, DC, 20037, USA, (202) 653-2400 (Dial from U.S.), (202) 653-5760 (Fax from U.S.), fao-hq@fao.org, https://www.fao.org; The State of Food and Agriculture (SOFA) 2022.

BENIN-POPULATION

African Development Bank Group (AfDB), Avenue Joseph Anoma, 01 BP 1387, Abidjan, 01, COT, https://www.afdb.org; The AfDB Statistics Pocketbook 2019; Africa Economic Brief - COVID-19 Pandemic Potential Risks for Trade and Trade Finance in Africa; The African Statistical Journal;

and Gender, Poverty and Environmental Indicators on African Countries 2019.

Central Intelligence Agency (CIA), Office of Public Affairs, Washington, DC, 20505, USA, (703) 482-0623, https://www.cia.gov; The World Factbook.

The Economist Group: Economist Intelligence Unit (EIU), 900 3rd Ave., 16th Fl., New York, NY, 10022, USA, (212) 541-0500, americas@eiu.com, https://www.eiu.com; Benin Country Report.

European Commission, Eurostat, Luxembourg, 2920, LUX, https://ec.europa.eu/eurostat/; EU in the World 2020.

Infoplease, c/o Sandbox Networks, Inc., 1 Lincoln St., 24th Fl., Boston, MA, 02111, USA, https://www.infoplease.com; Countries of the World.

International Labour Organization (ILO), 4 Rte. des Morillons, Geneva, CH-1211, SWI, ilo@ilo.org, https://www.ilo.org; NORMLEX Information System on International Labour Standards.

Palgrave Macmillan, 1 New York Plaza, Ste. 4500, New York, NY, 10004-1562, USA, (800) 777-4643, orders@palgrave.com, https://www.palgrave.com/us; The Statesman's Yearbook, 2023.

Routledge - Taylor & Francis Group, 6000 Broken Sound Pkwy. NW, Ste. 300, Boca Raton, FL, 33487, USA, (800) 634-1420, (800) 634-7064, orders@taylorandfrancis.com, https://www.routledge.com/; The Europa World Year Book 2022.

UK Data Service, University of Essex, Wivenhoe Park, Colchester, Essex, CO4 3SQ, GBR, https://ukdataservice.ac.uk/; International Aggregate Data.

UNESCO Institute for Statistics, C.P 250 Succursale H, Montreal, QC, H3G 2K8, CAN, (514) 343-6880 (Dial from U.S.), (514) 343-5740 (Fax from U.S.), uis.publications@unesco.org, http://uis.unesco.org/; UIS.Stat.

United Nations Department of Economic and Social Affairs (DESA), Population Division, 2 United Nations Plz., Rm. DC2-1950, New York, NY, 10017, USA, (212) 963-3209, (212) 963-2147, population@un.org, https://www.un.org/development/desa/pd/; Revision of World Urbanization Prospects and World Population Ageing 2020 Highlights.

United Nations Development Programme (UNDP), One United Nations Plz., New York, NY, 10017, USA, (212) 906-5000, (212) 906-5001, https://www.undp.org; Human Development Report 2021-2022.

United Nations Statistics Division (UNSD), United Nations Plz., New York, NY, 10017, USA, (800) 253-9646, (212) 963-9851, statistics@un.org, https://unstats.un.org; Statistical Yearbook of the United Nations 2021 and World Statistics Pocketbook 2021.

The World Bank, 1818 H St. NW, Washington, DC, 20433, USA, (202) 473-1000, (202) 477-6391, eds03@worldbank.org, https://www.worldbank.org/; Benin (report); The Global Findex Database 2021; and World Development Report 2022: Finance for an Equitable Recovery.

BENIN-POPULATION DENSITY

African Development Bank Group (AfDB), Avenue Joseph Anoma, 01 BP 1387, Abidjan, 01, COT, https://www.afdb.org; The AfDB Statistics Pocketbook 2019.

Central Intelligence Agency (CIA), Office of Public Affairs, Washington, DC, 20505, USA, (703) 482-0623, https://www.cia.gov; The World Factbook.

Palgrave Macmillan, 1 New York Plaza, Ste. 4500, New York, NY, 10004-1562, USA, (800) 777-4643, orders@palgrave.com, https://www.palgrave.com/us; The Statesman's Yearbook, 2023.

Routledge - Taylor & Francis Group, 6000 Broken Sound Pkwy. NW, Ste. 300, Boca Raton, FL, 33487, USA, (800) 634-1420, (800) 634-7064, orders@taylorandfrancis.com, https://www.routledge.com/; The Europa World Year Book 2022.

UNESCO Institute for Statistics, C.P 250 Succursale H, Montreal, QC, H3G 2K8, CAN, (514) 343-6880 (Dial from U.S.), (514) 343-5740 (Fax from U.S.), uis.publications@unesco.org, http://uis.unesco.org/; UIS.Stat.

The World Bank, 1818 H St. NW, Washington, DC, 20433, USA, (202) 473-1000, (202) 477-6391, eds03@worldbank.org, https://www.worldbank.org/; Benin (report) and World Development Report 2022: Finance for an Equitable Recovery.

BENIN-POWER RESOURCES

Euromonitor International, Inc., 1 N Dearborn St., Ste. 1700, Chicago, IL, 60602, USA, (312) 922-1115, (312) 922-1157, info-usa@euromonitor.com, https://www.euromonitor.com/; Geographies.

International Energy Agency (IEA), 9 Rue de la Federation, Paris, 75739, FRA, info@iea.org, https://www.iea.org/; World Energy Outlook 2021.

Palgrave Macmillan, 1 New York Plaza, Ste. 4500, New York, NY, 10004-1562, USA, (800) 777-4643, orders@palgrave.com, https://www.palgrave.com/us; The Statesman's Yearbook, 2023.

United Nations Economic Commission for Africa (UNECA), PO Box 3001, Addis Ababa, ETH, ecainfo@uneca.org, https://www.uneca.org/; African Statistical Yearbook 2020.

United Nations Food and Agricultural Organization (FAO), 2121 K St., Ste. 800B, Washington, DC, 20037, USA, (202) 653-2400 (Dial from U.S.), (202) 653-5760 (Fax from U.S.), fao-hq@fao.org, https://www.fao.org; The State of Food and Agriculture (SOFA) 2022.

United Nations Statistics Division (UNSD), United Nations Plz., New York, NY, 10017, USA, (800) 253-9646, (212) 963-9851, statistics@un.org, https://unstats.un.org; World Statistics Pocketbook 2021.

The World Bank, 1818 H St. NW, Washington, DC, 20433, USA, (202) 473-1000, (202) 477-6391, eds03@worldbank.org, https://www.worldbank.org/; World Development Report 2022: Finance for an Equitable Recovery.

BENIN-PRICES

Euromonitor International, Inc., 1 N Dearborn St., Ste. 1700, Chicago, IL, 60602, USA, (312) 922-1115, (312) 922-1157, info-usa@euromonitor.com, https://www.euromonitor.com/; Geographies.

The World Bank, 1818 H St. NW, Washington, DC, 20433, USA, (202) 473-1000, (202) 477-6391, eds03@worldbank.org, https://www.worldbank.org/; Benin (report).

BENIN-PUBLIC HEALTH

African Development Bank Group (AfDB), Avenue Joseph Anoma, 01 BP 1387, Abidjan, 01, COT, https://www.afdb.org; The AfDB Statistics Pocketbook 2019.

Euromonitor International, Inc., 1 N Dearborn St., Ste. 1700, Chicago, IL, 60602, USA, (312) 922-1115, (312) 922-1157, info-usa@euromonitor.com, https://www.euromonitor.com/; Geographies.

Organisation of Islamic Cooperation (OIC), Statistical, Economic and Social Research and Training Centre for Islamic Countries (SESRIC), Kudus Cad. No. 9, Diplomatik Site, Ankara, 06450, TUR, statistics@sesric.org, https://www.sesric.org/; OIC Statistics (OICStat) Database.

Palgrave Macmillan, 1 New York Plaza, Ste. 4500, New York, NY, 10004-1562, USA, (800) 777-4643, orders@palgrave.com, https://www.palgrave.com/us; The Statesman's Yearbook, 2023.

U.S. Census Bureau, 4600 Silver Hill Rd., Washington, DC, 20233, USA, (301) 763-4636, (800) 923-8282, https://www.census.gov; HIV/AIDS Surveillance Data Base.

United Nations Department of Economic and Social Affairs (DESA), Population Division, 2 United Nations Plz., Rm. DC2-1950, New York, NY, 10017, USA, (212) 963-3209, (212) 963-2147, population@un.org, https://www.un.org/development/desa/pd/; World Fertility Data 2019.

United Nations Development Programme (UNDP), One United Nations Plz., New York, NY, 10017, USA, (212) 906-5000, (212) 906-5001, https://www.undp.org; Human Development Report 2021-2022.

United Nations Economic Commission for Africa (UNECA), PO Box 3001, Addis Ababa, ETH, ecainfo@uneca.org, https://www.uneca.org/; African Statistical Yearbook 2020.

United Nations Statistics Division (UNSD), United Nations Plz., New York, NY, 10017, USA, (800) 253-9646, (212) 963-9851, statistics@un.org, https://unstats.un.org; Millennium Development Goal Indicators and Statistical Yearbook of the United Nations 2021.

The World Bank, 1818 H St. NW, Washington, DC, 20433, USA, (202) 473-1000, (202) 477-6391, eds03@worldbank.org, https://www.worldbank.org/; Benin (report).

World Health Organization (WHO), Ave. Appia 20, Geneva, CH-1211, SWI, (202) 974-3000 (Telephone in U.S.), publications@who.int, https://www.who.int/; Global Health Observatory (GHO) and Health Statistics and Information Systems.

BENIN-PUBLISHERS AND PUBLISHING

UNESCO Institute for Statistics, C.P 250 Succursale H, Montreal, QC, H3G 2K8, CAN, (514) 343-6880 (Dial from U.S.), (514) 343-5740 (Fax from U.S.), uis.publications@unesco.org, http://uis.unesco.org/; UIS.Stat.

BENIN-RAILROADS

Janes, USA, (703) 574-7580, (888) 977-1519, customer.care@janes.com, https://www.janes.com; Janes World Railways 2021-2022.

Palgrave Macmillan, 1 New York Plaza, Ste. 4500, New York, NY, 10004-1562, USA, (800) 777-4643, orders@palgrave.com, https://www.palgrave.com/us; The Statesman's Yearbook, 2023.

Routledge - Taylor & Francis Group, 6000 Broken Sound Pkwy. NW, Ste. 300, Boca Raton, FL, 33487, USA, (800) 634-1420, (800) 634-7064, orders@taylorandfrancis.com, https://www.routledge.com/; The Europa World Year Book 2022.

United Nations Economic Commission for Africa (UNECA), PO Box 3001, Addis Ababa, ETH, ecainfo@uneca.org, https://www.uneca.org/; African Statistical Yearbook 2020.

United Nations Statistics Division (UNSD), United Nations Plz., New York, NY, 10017, USA, (800) 253-9646, (212) 963-9851, statistics@un.org, https://unstats.un.org; Statistical Yearbook of the United Nations 2021.

BENIN-RELIGION

Central Intelligence Agency (CIA), Office of Public Affairs, Washington, DC, 20505, USA, (703) 482-0623, https://www.cia.gov; The World Factbook.

Palgrave Macmillan, 1 New York Plaza, Ste. 4500, New York, NY, 10004-1562, USA, (800) 777-4643, orders@palgrave.com, https://www.palgrave.com/us; The Statesman's Yearbook, 2023.

BENIN-RETAIL TRADE

Euromonitor International, Inc., 1 N Dearborn St., Ste. 1700, Chicago, IL, 60602, USA, (312) 922-1115, (312) 922-1157, info-usa@euromonitor.com, https://www.euromonitor.com/; Geographies.

BENIN-RICE PRODUCTION

See BENIN-CROPS

BENIN-ROADS

International Road Federation (IRF), Madison Place, 500 Montgomery St., 5th Fl., Alexandria, VA, 22314, USA, (703) 535-1001, (703) 535-1007, info@irf.global, https://www.irf.global/; World Road Statistics (WRS).

United Nations Economic Commission for Africa (UNECA), PO Box 3001, Addis Ababa, ETH, ecainfo@uneca.org, https://www.uneca.org/; African Statistical Yearbook 2020.

BENIN-RUBBER INDUSTRY AND TRADE

International Rubber Study Group (IRSG), 51 Changi Business Park Central 2, Unit No. 6, 486066, SGP, https://www.rubberstudy.org; Monthly Rubber Bulletin (MRB); Rubber Industry Report; Rubber Statistical Bulletin; and World Rubber Industry Report (WRIO).

BENIN-SAVING AND INVESTMENT

International Monetary Fund (IMF), 700 19th St. NW, Washington, DC, 20431, USA, (202) 623-7000, (202) 623-4661, publications@imf.org, https://www.imf.org; International Financial Statistics (IFS).

BENIN-SHIPPING

Routledge - Taylor & Francis Group, 6000 Broken Sound Pkwy. NW, Ste. 300, Boca Raton, FL, 33487, USA, (800) 634-1420, (800) 634-7064, orders@taylorandfrancis.com, https://www.routledge.com/; The Europa World Year Book 2022.

United Nations Economic Commission for Africa (UNECA), PO Box 3001, Addis Ababa, ETH, ecainfo@uneca.org, https://www.uneca.org/; African Statistical Yearbook 2020.

United Nations Statistics Division (UNSD), United Nations Plz., New York, NY, 10017, USA, (800) 253-9646, (212) 963-9851, statistics@un.org, https://unstats.un.org; Statistical Yearbook of the United Nations 2021.

BENIN-STEEL PRODUCTION

See BENIN-MINERAL INDUSTRIES

BENIN-SUGAR PRODUCTION

See BENIN-CROPS

BENIN-TAXATION

International Road Federation (IRF), Madison Place, 500 Montgomery St., 5th Fl., Alexandria, VA, 22314, USA, (703) 535-1001, (703) 535-1007, info@irf.global, https://www.irf.global/; World Road Statistics (WRS).

The World Bank, 1818 H St. NW, Washington, DC, 20433, USA, (202) 473-1000, (202) 477-6391, eds03@worldbank.org, https://www.worldbank.org/; World Development Indicators (WDI) 2022.

BENIN-TELEPHONE

Palgrave Macmillan, 1 New York Plaza, Ste. 4500, New York, NY, 10004-1562, USA, (800) 777-4643, orders@palgrave.com, https://www.palgrave.com/us; The Statesman's Yearbook, 2023.

Routledge - Taylor & Francis Group, 6000 Broken Sound Pkwy. NW, Ste. 300, Boca Raton, FL, 33487, USA, (800) 634-1420, (800) 634-7064, orders@taylorandfrancis.com, https://www.routledge.com/; The Europa World Year Book 2022.

United Nations Statistics Division (UNSD), United Nations Plz., New York, NY, 10017, USA, (800) 253-9646, (212) 963-9851, statistics@un.org, https://unstats.un.org; World Statistics Pocketbook 2021.

BENIN-TOBACCO INDUSTRY

United Nations Statistics Division (UNSD), United Nations Plz., New York, NY, 10017, USA, (800) 253-9646, (212) 963-9851, statistics@un.org, https://unstats.un.org; Statistical Yearbook of the United Nations 2021.

BENIN-TOURISM

Euromonitor International, Inc., 1 N Dearborn St., Ste. 1700, Chicago, IL, 60602, USA, (312) 922-1115, (312) 922-1157, info-usa@euromonitor.com, https://www.euromonitor.com/; Geographies.

Organisation of Islamic Cooperation (OIC), Statistical, Economic and Social Research and Training Centre for Islamic Countries (SESRIC), Kudus Cad. No. 9, Diplomatik Site, Ankara, 06450, TUR, statistics@sesric.org, https://www.sesric.org/; International Tourism in the OIC Countries: Prospects and Challenges, 2020 and OIC Statistics (OICStat) Database.

Routledge - Taylor & Francis Group, 6000 Broken Sound Pkwy. NW, Ste. 300, Boca Raton, FL, 33487, USA, (800) 634-1420, (800) 634-7064, orders@taylorandfrancis.com, https://www.routledge.com/; The Europa World Year Book 2022.

United Nations Economic Commission for Africa (UNECA), PO Box 3001, Addis Ababa, ETH, ecainfo@uneca.org, https://www.uneca.org/; African Statistical Yearbook 2020.

United Nations Statistics Division (UNSD), United Nations Plz., New York, NY, 10017, USA, (800) 253-9646, (212) 963-9851, statistics@un.org, https://unstats.un.org; Statistical Yearbook of the United Nations 2021.

The World Bank, 1818 H St. NW, Washington, DC, 20433, USA, (202) 473-1000, (202) 477-6391, eds03@worldbank.org, https://www.worldbank.org/; Benin (report).

BENIN-TRADE

See BENIN-INTERNATIONAL TRADE

BENIN-TRANSPORTATION

Central Intelligence Agency (CIA), Office of Public Affairs, Washington, DC, 20505, USA, (703) 482-0623, https://www.cia.gov; The World Factbook.

Euromonitor International, Inc., 1 N Dearborn St., Ste. 1700, Chicago, IL, 60602, USA, (312) 922-1115, (312) 922-1157, info-usa@euromonitor.com, https://www.euromonitor.com/; Geographies.

Organisation of Islamic Cooperation (OIC), Statistical, Economic and Social Research and Training Centre for Islamic Countries (SESRIC), Kudus Cad. No. 9, Diplomatik Site, Ankara, 06450, TUR, statistics@sesric.org, https://www.sesric.org/; OIC Statistics (OICStat) Database.

Palgrave Macmillan, 1 New York Plaza, Ste. 4500, New York, NY, 10004-1562, USA, (800) 777-4643, orders@palgrave.com, https://www.palgrave.com/us; The Statesman's Yearbook, 2023.

Routledge - Taylor & Francis Group, 6000 Broken Sound Pkwy. NW, Ste. 300, Boca Raton, FL, 33487, USA, (800) 634-1420, (800) 634-7064, orders@taylorandfrancis.com, https://www.routledge.com/; The Europa World Year Book 2022.

United Nations Economic Commission for Africa (UNECA), PO Box 3001, Addis Ababa, ETH, ecainfo@uneca.org, https://www.uneca.org/; African Statistical Yearbook 2020.

The World Bank, 1818 H St. NW, Washington, DC, 20433, USA, (202) 473-1000, (202) 477-6391, eds03@worldbank.org, https://www.worldbank.org/; Benin (report).

BENIN-UNEMPLOYMENT

International Labour Organization (ILO), 4 Rte. des Morillons, Geneva, CH-1211, SWI, ilo@ilo.org, https://www.ilo.org; NORMLEX Information System on International Labour Standards.

BENIN-VITAL STATISTICS

Palgrave Macmillan, 1 New York Plaza, Ste. 4500, New York, NY, 10004-1562, USA, (800) 777-4643, orders@palgrave.com, https://www.palgrave.com/us; The Statesman's Yearbook, 2023.

U.S. Census Bureau, 4600 Silver Hill Rd., Washington, DC, 20233, USA, (301) 763-4636, (800) 923-8282, https://www.census.gov; HIV/AIDS Surveillance Data Base.

United Nations Department of Economic and Social Affairs (DESA), Population Division, 2 United Nations Plz., Rm. DC2-1950, New York, NY, 10017, USA, (212) 963-3209, (212) 963-2147, population@un.org, https://www.un.org/development/desa/pd/; World Contraceptive Use 2021: Estimates and Projections of Family Planning Indicators and World Marriage Data 2019.

United Nations Statistics Division (UNSD), United Nations Plz., New York, NY, 10017, USA, (800) 253-9646, (212) 963-9851, statistics@un.org, https://unstats.un.org; Statistical Yearbook of the United Nations 2021.

BENIN-WAGES

International Labour Organization (ILO), 4 Rte. des Morillons, Geneva, CH-1211, SWI, ilo@ilo.org, https://www.ilo.org; NORMLEX Information System on International Labour Standards.

The World Bank, 1818 H St. NW, Washington, DC, 20433, USA, (202) 473-1000, (202) 477-6391, eds03@worldbank.org, https://www.worldbank.org/; Benin (report).

BENIN-WEATHER

See BENIN-CLIMATE

BENIN-WHEAT PRODUCTION

See BENIN-CROPS

BENIN-WOOL PRODUCTION

See BENIN-TEXTILE INDUSTRY

BERMUDA-NATIONAL STATISTICAL OFFICE

Bermuda Government Department of Statistics, PO Box HM 3015, Hamilton, HM MX, BMU, (441) 297-7761 (Dial from U.S.), statistics@gov.bm, https://www.gov.bm/department/statistics; National Data Reports (Bermuda).

BERMUDA-PRIMARY STATISTICS SOURCES

Bermuda Government Department of Statistics, PO Box HM 3015, Hamilton, HM MX, BMU, (441) 297-7761 (Dial from U.S.), statistics@gov.bm, https://www.gov.bm/department/statistics; 2021 Digest of Statistics.

BERMUDA-AGRICULTURE

The Economist Group: Economist Intelligence Unit (EIU), 900 3rd Ave., 16th Fl., New York, NY, 10022, USA, (212) 541-0500, americas@eiu.com, https://www.eiu.com; Bermuda Country Report.

Euromonitor International, Inc., 1 N Dearborn St., Ste. 1700, Chicago, IL, 60602, USA, (312) 922-1115, (312) 922-1157, info-usa@euromonitor.com, https://www.euromonitor.com/; Geographies.

Palgrave Macmillan, 1 New York Plaza, Ste. 4500, New York, NY, 10004-1562, USA, (800) 777-4643, orders@palgrave.com, https://www.palgrave.com/us; The Statesman's Yearbook, 2023.

Routledge - Taylor & Francis Group, 6000 Broken Sound Pkwy. NW, Ste. 300, Boca Raton, FL, 33487, USA, (800) 634-1420, (800) 634-7064, orders@taylorandfrancis.com, https://www.routledge.com/; The Europa World Year Book 2022.

United Nations Food and Agricultural Organization (FAO), 2121 K St., Ste. 800B, Washington, DC, 20037, USA, (202) 653-2400 (Dial from U.S.), (202) 653-5760 (Fax from U.S.), fao-hq@fao.org, https://www.fao.org; AQUASTAT and The State of Food and Agriculture (SOFA) 2022.

United Nations Statistics Division (UNSD), United Nations Plz., New York, NY, 10017, USA, (800) 253-9646, (212) 963-9851, statistics@un.org, https://unstats.un.org; Statistical Yearbook of the United Nations 2021.

BERMUDA-AIRLINES

Palgrave Macmillan, 1 New York Plaza, Ste. 4500, New York, NY, 10004-1562, USA, (800) 777-4643, orders@palgrave.com, https://www.palgrave.com/us; The Statesman's Yearbook, 2023.

Routledge - Taylor & Francis Group, 6000 Broken Sound Pkwy. NW, Ste. 300, Boca Raton, FL, 33487, USA, (800) 634-1420, (800) 634-7064, orders@taylorandfrancis.com, https://www.routledge.com/; The Europa World Year Book 2022.

BERMUDA-ALUMINUM PRODUCTION

See BERMUDA-MINERAL INDUSTRIES

BERMUDA-ARMED FORCES

Central Intelligence Agency (CIA), Office of Public Affairs, Washington, DC, 20505, USA, (703) 482-0623, https://www.cia.gov; The World Factbook.

Palgrave Macmillan, 1 New York Plaza, Ste. 4500, New York, NY, 10004-1562, USA, (800) 777-4643, orders@palgrave.com, https://www.palgrave.com/us; The Statesman's Yearbook, 2023.

Stockholm International Peace Research Institute (SIPRI), Signalistgatan 9, Stockholm, SE 169 72, SWE, https://www.sipri.org/; SIPRI Arms Transfers Database and SIPRI Military Expenditure Database.

BERMUDA-BALANCE OF PAYMENTS

Routledge - Taylor & Francis Group, 6000 Broken Sound Pkwy. NW, Ste. 300, Boca Raton, FL, 33487, USA, (800) 634-1420, (800) 634-7064, orders@taylorandfrancis.com, https://www.routledge.com/; The Europa World Year Book 2022.

BERMUDA-BANKS AND BANKING

Euromonitor International, Inc., 1 N Dearborn St., Ste. 1700, Chicago, IL, 60602, USA, (312) 922-1115, (312) 922-1157, info-usa@euromonitor.com, https://www.euromonitor.com/; Geographies.

BERMUDA-BARLEY PRODUCTION

See BERMUDA-CROPS

BERMUDA-BROADCASTING

Central Intelligence Agency (CIA), Office of Public Affairs, Washington, DC, 20505, USA, (703) 482-0623, https://www.cia.gov; The World Factbook.

Euromonitor International, Inc., 1 N Dearborn St., Ste. 1700, Chicago, IL, 60602, USA, (312) 922-1115, (312) 922-1157, info-usa@euromonitor.com, https://www.euromonitor.com/; Geographies.

Palgrave Macmillan, 1 New York Plaza, Ste. 4500, New York, NY, 10004-1562, USA, (800) 777-4643, orders@palgrave.com, https://www.palgrave.com/us; The Statesman's Yearbook, 2023.

WRTH Publications Limited, PO Box 290, Oxford, OX2 7FT, GBR, sales@wrth.com, https://www.wrth.com; World Radio TV Handbook 2023.

BERMUDA-BUDGET

Central Intelligence Agency (CIA), Office of Public Affairs, Washington, DC, 20505, USA, (703) 482-0623, https://www.cia.gov; The World Factbook.

BERMUDA-CLIMATE

Palgrave Macmillan, 1 New York Plaza, Ste. 4500, New York, NY, 10004-1562, USA, (800) 777-4643, orders@palgrave.com, https://www.palgrave.com/us; The Statesman's Yearbook, 2023.

BERMUDA-COAL PRODUCTION

See BERMUDA-MINERAL INDUSTRIES

BERMUDA-COFFEE

See BERMUDA-CROPS

BERMUDA-COMMERCE

Palgrave Macmillan, 1 New York Plaza, Ste. 4500, New York, NY, 10004-1562, USA, (800) 777-4643, orders@palgrave.com, https://www.palgrave.com/us; The Statesman's Yearbook, 2023.

UK Data Service, University of Essex, Wivenhoe Park, Colchester, Essex, CO4 3SQ, GBR, https://ukdataservice.ac.uk/; International Aggregate Data.

BERMUDA-COMMODITY EXCHANGES

Barchart, 209 W Jackson Blvd., 2nd Fl., Chicago, IL, 60606, USA, (877) 247-4394, commodities@barchart.com, https://www.barchart.com/cmdty; The cmdty Yearbook 2023; cmdtyStats: Commodity Statistics and Fundamental Data; cmdtyView: Commodity Index; and Commodity Data and Prices.

International Monetary Fund (IMF), 700 19th St. NW, Washington, DC, 20431, USA, (202) 623-7000, (202) 623-4661, publications@imf.org, https://www.imf.org; IMF Primary Commodity Prices.

BERMUDA-CONSTRUCTION INDUSTRY

United Nations Statistics Division (UNSD), United Nations Plz., New York, NY, 10017, USA, (800) 253-9646, (212) 963-9851, statistics@un.org, https://unstats.un.org; Statistical Yearbook of the United Nations 2021.

BERMUDA-CONSUMER PRICE INDEXES

Routledge - Taylor & Francis Group, 6000 Broken Sound Pkwy. NW, Ste. 300, Boca Raton, FL, 33487, USA, (800) 634-1420, (800) 634-7064, orders@taylorandfrancis.com, https://www.routledge.com/; The Europa World Year Book 2022.

BERMUDA-COPPER INDUSTRY AND TRADE

See BERMUDA-MINERAL INDUSTRIES

BERMUDA-CORN INDUSTRY

See BERMUDA-CROPS

BERMUDA-COTTON

See BERMUDA-CROPS

BERMUDA-CROPS

Palgrave Macmillan, 1 New York Plaza, Ste. 4500, New York, NY, 10004-1562, USA, (800) 777-4643, orders@palgrave.com, https://www.palgrave.com/us; The Statesman's Yearbook, 2023.

United Nations Food and Agricultural Organization (FAO), 2121 K St., Ste. 800B, Washington, DC, 20037, USA, (202) 653-2400 (Dial from U.S.), (202) 653-5760 (Fax from U.S.), fao-hq@fao.org, https://www.fao.org; The State of Food and Agriculture (SOFA) 2022.

BERMUDA-DAIRY PROCESSING

United Nations Food and Agricultural Organization (FAO), 2121 K St., Ste. 800B, Washington, DC, 20037, USA, (202) 653-2400 (Dial from U.S.), (202) 653-5760 (Fax from U.S.), fao-hq@fao.org, https://www.fao.org; The State of Food and Agriculture (SOFA) 2022.

BERMUDA-DEBTS, EXTERNAL

Palgrave Macmillan, 1 New York Plaza, Ste. 4500, New York, NY, 10004-1562, USA, (800) 777-4643, orders@palgrave.com, https://www.palgrave.com/us; The Statesman's Yearbook, 2023.

The World Bank, 1818 H St. NW, Washington, DC, 20433, USA, (202) 473-1000, (202) 477-6391, eds03@worldbank.org, https://www.worldbank.org/; Global Financial Development Report 2019-2020: Bank Regulation and Supervision a Decade after the Global Financial Crisis.

BERMUDA-DIAMONDS

See BERMUDA-MINERAL INDUSTRIES

BERMUDA-ECONOMIC ASSISTANCE

United Nations Statistics Division (UNSD), United Nations Plz., New York, NY, 10017, USA, (800) 253-9646, (212) 963-9851, statistics@un.org, https://unstats.un.org; Statistical Yearbook of the United Nations 2021.

BERMUDA-ECONOMIC CONDITIONS

Bermuda Government Department of Statistics, PO Box HM 3015, Hamilton, HM MX, BMU, (441) 297-7761 (Dial from U.S.), statistics@gov.bm, https://www.gov.bm/department/statistics; Bermuda Employment Statistics and Quarterly Gross Domestic Product.

Bernan Press, 15250 NBN Way, Bldg. C, Blue Ridge Summit, PA, 17214, USA, (301) 459-2255, (800) 865-3457, (800) 865-3450, customercare@bernan.com, https://rowman.com/Page/Bernan; World Economic Outlook, April 2022.

Central Intelligence Agency (CIA), Office of Public Affairs, Washington, DC, 20505, USA, (703) 482-0623, https://www.cia.gov; The World Factbook.

The Economist Group: Economist Intelligence Unit (EIU), 900 3rd Ave., 16th Fl., New York, NY, 10022, USA, (212) 541-0500, americas@eiu.com, https://www.eiu.com; Bermuda Country Report.

Euromonitor International, Inc., 1 N Dearborn St., Ste. 1700, Chicago, IL, 60602, USA, (312) 922-1115, (312) 922-1157, info-usa@euromonitor.com, https://www.euromonitor.com/; Geographies.

International Monetary Fund (IMF), 700 19th St. NW, Washington, DC, 20431, USA, (202) 623-7000, (202) 623-4661, publications@imf.org, https://www.imf.org; IMF Data and World Economic Outlook.

Palgrave Macmillan, 1 New York Plaza, Ste. 4500, New York, NY, 10004-1562, USA, (800) 777-4643, orders@palgrave.com, https://www.palgrave.com/us; The Statesman's Yearbook, 2023.

Routledge - Taylor & Francis Group, 6000 Broken Sound Pkwy. NW, Ste. 300, Boca Raton, FL, 33487, USA, (800) 634-1420, (800) 634-7064, orders@taylorandfrancis.com, https://www.routledge.com/; The Europa World Year Book 2022.

United Nations Statistics Division (UNSD), United Nations Plz., New York, NY, 10017, USA, (800) 253-9646, (212) 963-9851, statistics@un.org, https://unstats.un.org; World Statistics Pocketbook 2021.

The World Bank, 1818 H St. NW, Washington, DC, 20433, USA, (202) 473-1000, (202) 477-6391, eds03@worldbank.org, https://www.worldbank.org/; Global Economic Monitor (GEM); Global Economic Prospects, June 2022; and The Global Findex Database 2021.

BERMUDA-EDUCATION

Euromonitor International, Inc., 1 N Dearborn St., Ste. 1700, Chicago, IL, 60602, USA, (312) 922-1115, (312) 922-1157, info-usa@euromonitor.com, https://www.euromonitor.com/; Geographies.

Infoplease, c/o Sandbox Networks, Inc., 1 Lincoln St., 24th Fl., Boston, MA, 02111, USA, https://www.infoplease.com; Countries of the World.

Palgrave Macmillan, 1 New York Plaza, Ste. 4500, New York, NY, 10004-1562, USA, (800) 777-4643, orders@palgrave.com, https://www.palgrave.com/us; The Statesman's Yearbook, 2023.

Routledge - Taylor & Francis Group, 6000 Broken Sound Pkwy. NW, Ste. 300, Boca Raton, FL, 33487, USA, (800) 634-1420, (800) 634-7064, orders@taylorandfrancis.com, https://www.routledge.com/; The Europa World Year Book 2022.

UNESCO Institute for Statistics, C.P 250 Succursale H, Montreal, QC, H3G 2K8, CAN, (514) 343-6880 (Dial from U.S.), (514) 343-5740 (Fax from U.S.), uis.publications@unesco.org, http://uis.unesco.org/; Literacy and UIS.Stat.

United Nations Statistics Division (UNSD), United Nations Plz., New York, NY, 10017, USA, (800) 253-9646, (212) 963-9851, statistics@un.org, https://unstats.un.org; Millennium Development Goal Indicators.

BERMUDA-ELECTRICITY

United Nations Statistics Division (UNSD), United Nations Plz., New York, NY, 10017, USA, (800) 253-9646, (212) 963-9851, statistics@un.org, https://unstats.un.org; Statistical Yearbook of the United Nations 2021.

BERMUDA-EMPLOYMENT

International Labour Organization (ILO), 4 Rte. des Morillons, Geneva, CH-1211, SWI, ilo@ilo.org, https://www.ilo.org; NORMLEX Information System on International Labour Standards.

UK Data Service, University of Essex, Wivenhoe Park, Colchester, Essex, CO4 3SQ, GBR, https://ukdataservice.ac.uk/; International Aggregate Data.

BERMUDA-ENVIRONMENTAL CONDITIONS

DSI Data Service & Information, Xantener Strasse 51a, Rheinberg, D-47495, GER, dsi@dsidata.com, https://www.dsidata.com/; Global Environmental Database.

The Economist Group: Economist Intelligence Unit (EIU), 900 3rd Ave., 16th Fl., New York, NY, 10022, USA, (212) 541-0500, americas@eiu.com, https://www.eiu.com; Bermuda Country Report.

United Nations Statistics Division (UNSD), United Nations Plz., New York, NY, 10017, USA, (800) 253-9646, (212) 963-9851, statistics@un.org, https://unstats.un.org; World Statistics Pocketbook 2021.

BERMUDA-EXPORTS

Central Intelligence Agency (CIA), Office of Public Affairs, Washington, DC, 20505, USA, (703) 482-0623, https://www.cia.gov; The World Factbook.

The Economist Group: Economist Intelligence Unit (EIU), 900 3rd Ave., 16th Fl., New York, NY, 10022, USA, (212) 541-0500, americas@eiu.com, https://www.eiu.com; Bermuda Country Report.

International Monetary Fund (IMF), 700 19th St. NW, Washington, DC, 20431, USA, (202) 623-7000, (202) 623-4661, publications@imf.org, https://www.imf.org; Direction of Trade Statistics (DOTS).

S&P Global, IHS Markit, 15 Inverness Way E, Englewood, CO, 80112, USA, (800) 447-2273, (800) 854-7179, https://ihsmarkit.com; Global Trade Atlas (GTA).

BERMUDA-FERTILITY, HUMAN

Central Intelligence Agency (CIA), Office of Public Affairs, Washington, DC, 20505, USA, (703) 482-0623, https://www.cia.gov; The World Factbook.

BERMUDA-FERTILIZER INDUSTRY

United Nations Food and Agricultural Organization (FAO), 2121 K St., Ste. 800B, Washington, DC, 20037, USA, (202) 653-2400 (Dial from U.S.), (202) 653-5760 (Fax from U.S.), fao-hq@fao.org, https://www.fao.org; The State of Food and Agriculture (SOFA) 2022.

BERMUDA-FETAL MORTALITY

See BERMUDA-MORTALITY

BERMUDA-FINANCE, PUBLIC

Bernan Press, 15250 NBN Way, Bldg. C, Blue Ridge Summit, PA, 17214, USA, (301) 459-2255, (800) 865-3457, (800) 865-3450, customercare@bernan.com, https://rowman.com/Page/Bernan; National Accounts Statistics: Analysis of Main Aggregates 2020.

The Economist Group: Economist Intelligence Unit (EIU), 900 3rd Ave., 16th Fl., New York, NY, 10022, USA, (212) 541-0500, americas@eiu.com, https://www.eiu.com; Bermuda Country Report.

International Monetary Fund (IMF), 700 19th St. NW, Washington, DC, 20431, USA, (202) 623-7000, (202) 623-4661, publications@imf.org, https://www.imf.org; Regional Economic Outlook.

Palgrave Macmillan, 1 New York Plaza, Ste. 4500, New York, NY, 10004-1562, USA, (800) 777-4643, orders@palgrave.com, https://www.palgrave.com/us; The Statesman's Yearbook, 2023.

Routledge - Taylor & Francis Group, 6000 Broken Sound Pkwy. NW, Ste. 300, Boca Raton, FL, 33487, USA, (800) 634-1420, (800) 634-7064, orders@taylorandfrancis.com, https://www.routledge.com/; The Europa World Year Book 2022.

United Nations Statistics Division (UNSD), United Nations Plz., New York, NY, 10017, USA, (800) 253-9646, (212) 963-9851, statistics@un.org, https://unstats.un.org; National Accounts Main Aggregates Database and National Accounts Statistics: Main Aggregates and Detailed Tables.

BERMUDA-FISHERIES

Palgrave Macmillan, 1 New York Plaza, Ste. 4500, New York, NY, 10004-1562, USA, (800) 777-4643, orders@palgrave.com, https://www.palgrave.com/us; The Statesman's Yearbook, 2023.

Routledge - Taylor & Francis Group, 6000 Broken Sound Pkwy. NW, Ste. 300, Boca Raton, FL, 33487, USA, (800) 634-1420, (800) 634-7064, orders@taylorandfrancis.com, https://www.routledge.com/; The Europa World Year Book 2022.

United Nations Food and Agricultural Organization (FAO), 2121 K St., Ste. 800B, Washington, DC, 20037, USA, (202) 653-2400 (Dial from U.S.), (202) 653-5760 (Fax from U.S.), fao-hq@fao.org, https://www.fao.org; FAO Yearbook of Fishery and Aquaculture Statistics 2019; Fishery Statistical Collections Global Capture Production; FishStatJ; and The State of Food and Agriculture (SOFA) 2022.

United Nations Statistics Division (UNSD), United Nations Plz., New York, NY, 10017, USA, (800) 253-9646, (212) 963-9851, statistics@un.org, https://unstats.un.org; Statistical Yearbook of the United Nations 2021.

BERMUDA-FOOD

United Nations Food and Agricultural Organization (FAO), 2121 K St., Ste. 800B, Washington, DC, 20037, USA, (202) 653-2400 (Dial from U.S.), (202) 653-5760 (Fax from U.S.), fao-hq@fao.org, https://www.fao.org; The State of Food and Agriculture (SOFA) 2022.

BERMUDA-FORESTS AND FORESTRY

UNESCO Institute for Statistics, C.P 250 Succursale H, Montreal, QC, H3G 2K8, CAN, (514) 343-6880 (Dial from U.S.), (514) 343-5740 (Fax from U.S.), uis.publications@unesco.org, http://uis.unesco.org/; UIS.Stat.

United Nations Food and Agricultural Organization (FAO), 2121 K St., Ste. 800B, Washington, DC, 20037, USA, (202) 653-2400 (Dial from U.S.), (202) 653-5760 (Fax from U.S.), fao-hq@fao.org, https://www.fao.org; The State of Food and Agriculture (SOFA) 2022.

BERMUDA-GAS PRODUCTION

See BERMUDA-MINERAL INDUSTRIES

BERMUDA-GOLD PRODUCTION

See BERMUDA-MINERAL INDUSTRIES

BERMUDA-GROSS DOMESTIC PRODUCT

The Economist Group: Economist Intelligence Unit (EIU), 900 3rd Ave., 16th Fl., New York, NY, 10022, USA, (212) 541-0500, americas@eiu.com, https://www.eiu.com; Bermuda Country Report.

Routledge - Taylor & Francis Group, 6000 Broken Sound Pkwy. NW, Ste. 300, Boca Raton, FL, 33487, USA, (800) 634-1420, (800) 634-7064, orders@taylorandfrancis.com, https://www.routledge.com/; The Europa World Year Book 2022.

BERMUDA-GROSS NATIONAL PRODUCT

Palgrave Macmillan, 1 New York Plaza, Ste. 4500, New York, NY, 10004-1562, USA, (800) 777-4643, orders@palgrave.com, https://www.palgrave.com/us; The Statesman's Yearbook, 2023.

BERMUDA-HOUSING

Euromonitor International, Inc., 1 N Dearborn St., Ste. 1700, Chicago, IL, 60602, USA, (312) 922-1115, (312) 922-1157, info-usa@euromonitor.com, https://www.euromonitor.com/; Geographies.

BERMUDA-ILLITERATE PERSONS

UNESCO Institute for Statistics, C.P 250 Succursale H, Montreal, QC, H3G 2K8, CAN, (514) 343-6880 (Dial from U.S.), (514) 343-5740 (Fax from U.S.), uis.publications@unesco.org, http://uis.unesco.org/; UIS.Stat.

BERMUDA-IMPORTS

Central Intelligence Agency (CIA), Office of Public Affairs, Washington, DC, 20505, USA, (703) 482-0623, https://www.cia.gov; The World Factbook.

The Economist Group: Economist Intelligence Unit (EIU), 900 3rd Ave., 16th Fl., New York, NY, 10022, USA, (212) 541-0500, americas@eiu.com, https://www.eiu.com; Bermuda Country Report.

International Monetary Fund (IMF), 700 19th St. NW, Washington, DC, 20431, USA, (202) 623-7000, (202) 623-4661, publications@imf.org, https://www.imf.org; Direction of Trade Statistics (DOTS).

S&P Global, IHS Markit, 15 Inverness Way E, Englewood, CO, 80112, USA, (800) 447-2273, (800) 854-7179, https://ihsmarkit.com; Global Trade Atlas (GTA).

BERMUDA-INDUSTRIES

Central Intelligence Agency (CIA), Office of Public Affairs, Washington, DC, 20505, USA, (703) 482-0623, https://www.cia.gov; The World Factbook.

The Economist Group: Economist Intelligence Unit (EIU), 900 3rd Ave., 16th Fl., New York, NY, 10022, USA, (212) 541-0500, americas@eiu.com, https://www.eiu.com; Bermuda Country Report.

Euromonitor International, Inc., 1 N Dearborn St., Ste. 1700, Chicago, IL, 60602, USA, (312) 922-1115, (312) 922-1157, info-usa@euromonitor.com, https://www.euromonitor.com/; Geographies.

International Labour Organization (ILO), 4 Rte. des Morillons, Geneva, CH-1211, SWI, ilo@ilo.org, https://www.ilo.org; NORMLEX Information System on International Labour Standards.

Palgrave Macmillan, 1 New York Plaza, Ste. 4500, New York, NY, 10004-1562, USA, (800) 777-4643, orders@palgrave.com, https://www.palgrave.com/us; The Statesman's Yearbook, 2023.

Routledge - Taylor & Francis Group, 6000 Broken Sound Pkwy. NW, Ste. 300, Boca Raton, FL, 33487, USA, (800) 634-1420, (800) 634-7064, orders@taylorandfrancis.com, https://www.routledge.com/; The Europa World Year Book 2022.

United Nations Industrial Development Organization (UNIDO), 1 United Nations Plz., Rm. DC1-1118, New York, NY, 10017, USA, (212) 963-6890, (212) 963 6885, (212) 963-7904, office.newyork@unido.org, https://www.unido.org/; Industrial Statistics Databases and International Yearbook of Industrial Statistics 2021.

BERMUDA-INFANT AND MATERNAL MORTALITY

See BERMUDA-MORTALITY

BERMUDA-INTERNATIONAL TRADE

The Economist Group: Economist Intelligence Unit (EIU), 900 3rd Ave., 16th Fl., New York, NY, 10022, USA, (212) 541-0500, americas@eiu.com, https://www.eiu.com; Bermuda Country Report.

Euromonitor International, Inc., 1 N Dearborn St., Ste. 1700, Chicago, IL, 60602, USA, (312) 922-1115, (312) 922-1157, info-usa@euromonitor.com, https://www.euromonitor.com/; Geographies.

Palgrave Macmillan, 1 New York Plaza, Ste. 4500, New York, NY, 10004-1562, USA, (800) 777-4643, orders@palgrave.com, https://www.palgrave.com/us; The Statesman's Yearbook, 2023.

Routledge - Taylor & Francis Group, 6000 Broken Sound Pkwy. NW, Ste. 300, Boca Raton, FL, 33487, USA, (800) 634-1420, (800) 634-7064, orders@taylorandfrancis.com, https://www.routledge.com/; The Europa World Year Book 2022.

United Nations Conference on Trade and Development (UNCTAD), Palais des Nations, Geneva, 1211, SWI, (212) 963-6896, unctadinfo@unctad.org, https://unctad.org; Trade and Development Report 2021.

United Nations Food and Agricultural Organization (FAO), 2121 K St., Ste. 800B, Washington, DC, 20037, USA, (202) 653-2400 (Dial from U.S.), (202) 653-5760 (Fax from U.S.), fao-hq@fao.org, https://www.fao.org; The State of Food and Agriculture (SOFA) 2022.

United Nations Statistics Division (UNSD), United Nations Plz., New York, NY, 10017, USA, (800) 253-

9646, (212) 963-9851, statistics@un.org, https://unstats.un.org; International Trade Statistics Yearbook 2020 and Statistical Yearbook of the United Nations 2021.

World Trade Organization (WTO), Ctre. William Rappard, Rue de Lausanne 154, Case postale, Geneva, CH-1211, SWI, enquiries@wto.org, https://www.wto.org; World Trade Statistical Review 2022.

BERMUDA-INTERNET USERS

International Telecommunication Union (ITU), Place des Nations, Geneva, CH-1211, SWI, itumail@itu.int, https://www.itu.int; Global Connectivity Report 2022; World Telecommunication/ICT Indicators Database 2021; and Yearbook of Statistics 2019.

BERMUDA-LABOR

Bermuda Government Department of Statistics, PO Box HM 3015, Hamilton, HM MX, BMU, (441) 297-7761 (Dial from U.S.), statistics@gov.bm, https://www.gov.bm/department/statistics; Bermuda Employment Statistics.

Central Intelligence Agency (CIA), Office of Public Affairs, Washington, DC, 20505, USA, (703) 482-0623, https://www.cia.gov; The World Factbook.

Euromonitor International, Inc., 1 N Dearborn St., Ste. 1700, Chicago, IL, 60602, USA, (312) 922-1115, (312) 922-1157, info-usa@euromonitor.com, https://www.euromonitor.com/; Geographies.

International Labour Organization (ILO), 4 Rte. des Morillons, Geneva, CH-1211, SWI, ilo@ilo.org, https://www.ilo.org; NORMLEX Information System on International Labour Standards.

Palgrave Macmillan, 1 New York Plaza, Ste. 4500, New York, NY, 10004-1562, USA, (800) 777-4643, orders@palgrave.com, https://www.palgrave.com/us; The Statesman's Yearbook, 2023.

United Nations Food and Agricultural Organization (FAO), 2121 K St., Ste. 800B, Washington, DC, 20037, USA, (202) 653-2400 (Dial from U.S.), (202) 653-5760 (Fax from U.S.), fao-hq@fao.org, https://www.fao.org; The State of Food and Agriculture (SOFA) 2022.

BERMUDA-LAND USE

United Nations Statistics Division (UNSD), United Nations Plz., New York, NY, 10017, USA, (800) 253-9646, (212) 963-9851, statistics@un.org, https://unstats.un.org; Millennium Development Goal Indicators.

BERMUDA-LIBRARIES

UNESCO Institute for Statistics, C.P 250 Succursale H, Montreal, QC, H3G 2K8, CAN, (514) 343-6880 (Dial from U.S.), (514) 343-5740 (Fax from U.S.), uis.publications@unesco.org, http://uis.unesco.org/; UIS.Stat.

BERMUDA-LIFE EXPECTANCY

Central Intelligence Agency (CIA), Office of Public Affairs, Washington, DC, 20505, USA, (703) 482-0623, https://www.cia.gov; The World Factbook.

United Nations Department of Economic and Social Affairs (DESA), Population Division, 2 United Nations Plz., Rm. DC2-1950, New York, NY, 10017, USA, (212) 963-3209, (212) 963-2147, population@un.org, https://www.un.org/development/desa/pd/; World Population Ageing 2020 Highlights.

United Nations Statistics Division (UNSD), United Nations Plz., New York, NY, 10017, USA, (800) 253-9646, (212) 963-9851, statistics@un.org, https://unstats.un.org; Millennium Development Goal Indicators.

BERMUDA-LITERACY

Euromonitor International, Inc., 1 N Dearborn St., Ste. 1700, Chicago, IL, 60602, USA, (312) 922-1115, (312) 922-1157, info-usa@euromonitor.com, https://www.euromonitor.com/; Geographies.

UNESCO Institute for Statistics, C.P 250 Succursale H, Montreal, QC, H3G 2K8, CAN, (514) 343-6880 (Dial from U.S.), (514) 343-5740 (Fax from U.S.), uis.publications@unesco.org, http://uis.unesco.org/; Literacy.

BERMUDA-LIVESTOCK

Routledge - Taylor & Francis Group, 6000 Broken Sound Pkwy. NW, Ste. 300, Boca Raton, FL, 33487, USA, (800) 634-1420, (800) 634-7064, orders@taylorandfrancis.com, https://www.routledge.com/; The Europa World Year Book 2022.

United Nations Food and Agricultural Organization (FAO), 2121 K St., Ste. 800B, Washington, DC, 20037, USA, (202) 653-2400 (Dial from U.S.), (202) 653-5760 (Fax from U.S.), fao-hq@fao.org, https://www.fao.org; The State of Food and Agriculture (SOFA) 2022.

United Nations Statistics Division (UNSD), United Nations Plz., New York, NY, 10017, USA, (800) 253-9646, (212) 963-9851, statistics@un.org, https://unstats.un.org; Statistical Yearbook of the United Nations 2021.

BERMUDA-MARRIAGE

Routledge - Taylor & Francis Group, 6000 Broken Sound Pkwy. NW, Ste. 300, Boca Raton, FL, 33487, USA, (800) 634-1420, (800) 634-7064, orders@taylorandfrancis.com, https://www.routledge.com/; The Europa World Year Book 2022.

United Nations Statistics Division (UNSD), United Nations Plz., New York, NY, 10017, USA, (800) 253-9646, (212) 963-9851, statistics@un.org, https://unstats.un.org; Statistical Yearbook of the United Nations 2021.

BERMUDA-MINERAL INDUSTRIES

United Nations Conference on Trade and Development (UNCTAD), Palais des Nations, Geneva, 1211, SWI, (212) 963-6896, unctadinfo@unctad.org, https://unctad.org; Trade and Development Report 2021.

BERMUDA-MONEY SUPPLY

The Economist Group: Economist Intelligence Unit (EIU), 900 3rd Ave., 16th Fl., New York, NY, 10022, USA, (212) 541-0500, americas@eiu.com, https://www.eiu.com; Bermuda Country Report.

BERMUDA-MORTALITY

United Nations Statistics Division (UNSD), United Nations Plz., New York, NY, 10017, USA, (800) 253-9646, (212) 963-9851, statistics@un.org, https://unstats.un.org; Millennium Development Goal Indicators; Statistical Yearbook of the United Nations 2021; and World Statistics Pocketbook 2021.

World Health Organization (WHO), Ave. Appia 20, Geneva, CH-1211, SWI, (202) 974-3000 (Telephone in U.S.), publications@who.int, https://www.who.int/; Global Health Observatory (GHO).

BERMUDA-NATURAL GAS PRODUCTION

See BERMUDA-MINERAL INDUSTRIES

BERMUDA-NUTRITION

United Nations Food and Agricultural Organization (FAO), 2121 K St., Ste. 800B, Washington, DC, 20037, USA, (202) 653-2400 (Dial from U.S.), (202) 653-5760 (Fax from U.S.), fao-hq@fao.org, https://www.fao.org; The State of Food and Agriculture (SOFA) 2022.

United Nations Statistics Division (UNSD), United Nations Plz., New York, NY, 10017, USA, (800) 253-9646, (212) 963-9851, statistics@un.org, https://unstats.un.org; Millennium Development Goal Indicators.

BERMUDA-PEANUT PRODUCTION

See BERMUDA-CROPS

BERMUDA-PESTICIDES

United Nations Food and Agricultural Organization (FAO), 2121 K St., Ste. 800B, Washington, DC, 20037, USA, (202) 653-2400 (Dial from U.S.), (202) 653-5760 (Fax from U.S.), fao-hq@fao.org, https://www.fao.org; The State of Food and Agriculture (SOFA) 2022.

BERMUDA-PETROLEUM INDUSTRY AND TRADE

United Nations Food and Agricultural Organization (FAO), 2121 K St., Ste. 800B, Washington, DC, 20037, USA, (202) 653-2400 (Dial from U.S.), (202) 653-5760 (Fax from U.S.), fao-hq@fao.org, https://www.fao.org; The State of Food and Agriculture (SOFA) 2022.

BERMUDA-POPULATION

Caribbean Public Health Agency (CARPHA), Federation Park, 16-18 Jamaica Blvd., Port of Spain, TTO, (868) 622-4261 (Dial from U.S.), (868) 299-0820 (Dial from U.S.), postmaster@carpha.org, https://carpha.org/; unpublished data.

Central Intelligence Agency (CIA), Office of Public Affairs, Washington, DC, 20505, USA, (703) 482-0623, https://www.cia.gov; The World Factbook.

The Economist Group: Economist Intelligence Unit (EIU), 900 3rd Ave., 16th Fl., New York, NY, 10022, USA, (212) 541-0500, americas@eiu.com, https://www.eiu.com; Bermuda Country Report.

Infoplease, c/o Sandbox Networks, Inc., 1 Lincoln St., 24th Fl., Boston, MA, 02111, USA, https://www.infoplease.com; Countries of the World.

International Labour Organization (ILO), 4 Rte. des Morillons, Geneva, CH-1211, SWI, ilo@ilo.org, https://www.ilo.org; NORMLEX Information System on International Labour Standards.

Palgrave Macmillan, 1 New York Plaza, Ste. 4500, New York, NY, 10004-1562, USA, (800) 777-4643, orders@palgrave.com, https://www.palgrave.com/us; The Statesman's Yearbook, 2023.

Routledge - Taylor & Francis Group, 6000 Broken Sound Pkwy. NW, Ste. 300, Boca Raton, FL, 33487, USA, (800) 634-1420, (800) 634-7064, orders@taylorandfrancis.com, https://www.routledge.com/; The Europa World Year Book 2022.

UK Data Service, University of Essex, Wivenhoe Park, Colchester, Essex, CO4 3SQ, GBR, https://ukdataservice.ac.uk/; International Aggregate Data.

United Nations Department of Economic and Social Affairs (DESA), Population Division, 2 United Nations Plz., Rm. DC2-1950, New York, NY, 10017, USA, (212) 963-3209, (212) 963-2147, population@un.org, https://www.un.org/development/desa/pd/; Revision of World Urbanization Prospects and World Population Ageing 2020 Highlights.

United Nations Statistics Division (UNSD), United Nations Plz., New York, NY, 10017, USA, (800) 253-9646, (212) 963-9851, statistics@un.org, https://unstats.un.org; Statistical Yearbook of the United Nations 2021 and World Statistics Pocketbook 2021.

The World Bank, 1818 H St. NW, Washington, DC, 20433, USA, (202) 473-1000, (202) 477-6391, eds03@worldbank.org, https://www.worldbank.org/; The Global Findex Database 2021.

BERMUDA-POPULATION DENSITY

Central Intelligence Agency (CIA), Office of Public Affairs, Washington, DC, 20505, USA, (703) 482-0623, https://www.cia.gov; The World Factbook.

Palgrave Macmillan, 1 New York Plaza, Ste. 4500, New York, NY, 10004-1562, USA, (800) 777-4643, orders@palgrave.com, https://www.palgrave.com/us; The Statesman's Yearbook, 2023.

Routledge - Taylor & Francis Group, 6000 Broken Sound Pkwy. NW, Ste. 300, Boca Raton, FL, 33487, USA, (800) 634-1420, (800) 634-7064, orders@taylorandfrancis.com, https://www.routledge.com/; The Europa World Year Book 2022.

BERMUDA-POSTAL SERVICE

Palgrave Macmillan, 1 New York Plaza, Ste. 4500, New York, NY, 10004-1562, USA, (800) 777-4643,

orders@palgrave.com, https://www.palgrave.com/us; The Statesman's Yearbook, 2023.

BERMUDA-POWER RESOURCES

Euromonitor International, Inc., 1 N Dearborn St., Ste. 1700, Chicago, IL, 60602, USA, (312) 922-1115, (312) 922-1157, info-usa@euromonitor.com, https://www.euromonitor.com/; Geographies.

Palgrave Macmillan, 1 New York Plaza, Ste. 4500, New York, NY, 10004-1562, USA, (800) 777-4643, orders@palgrave.com, https://www.palgrave.com/us; The Statesman's Yearbook, 2023.

United Nations Food and Agricultural Organization (FAO), 2121 K St., Ste. 800B, Washington, DC, 20037, USA, (202) 653-2400 (Dial from U.S.), (202) 653-5760 (Fax from U.S.), fao-hq@fao.org, https://www.fao.org; The State of Food and Agriculture (SOFA) 2022.

United Nations Statistics Division (UNSD), United Nations Plz., New York, NY, 10017, USA, (800) 253-9646, (212) 963-9851, statistics@un.org, https://unstats.un.org; Energy Statistics Yearbook 2019 and World Statistics Pocketbook 2021.

BERMUDA-PRICES

Euromonitor International, Inc., 1 N Dearborn St., Ste. 1700, Chicago, IL, 60602, USA, (312) 922-1115, (312) 922-1157, info-usa@euromonitor.com, https://www.euromonitor.com/; Geographies.

BERMUDA-PUBLIC HEALTH

Euromonitor International, Inc., 1 N Dearborn St., Ste. 1700, Chicago, IL, 60602, USA, (312) 922-1115, (312) 922-1157, info-usa@euromonitor.com, https://www.euromonitor.com/; Geographies.

Palgrave Macmillan, 1 New York Plaza, Ste. 4500, New York, NY, 10004-1562, USA, (800) 777-4643, orders@palgrave.com, https://www.palgrave.com/us; The Statesman's Yearbook, 2023.

U.S. Census Bureau, 4600 Silver Hill Rd., Washington, DC, 20233, USA, (301) 763-4636, (800) 923-8282, https://www.census.gov; HIV/AIDS Surveillance Data Base.

United Nations Department of Economic and Social Affairs (DESA), Population Division, 2 United Nations Plz., Rm. DC2-1950, New York, NY, 10017, USA, (212) 963-3209, (212) 963-2147, population@un.org, https://www.un.org/development/desa/pd/; World Fertility Data 2019.

United Nations Statistics Division (UNSD), United Nations Plz., New York, NY, 10017, USA, (800) 253-9646, (212) 963-9851, statistics@un.org, https://unstats.un.org; Millennium Development Goal Indicators and Statistical Yearbook of the United Nations 2021.

World Health Organization (WHO), Ave. Appia 20, Geneva, CH-1211, SWI, (202) 974-3000 (Telephone in U.S.), publications@who.int, https://www.who.int/; Global Health Observatory (GHO) and Health Statistics and Information Systems.

BERMUDA-RELIGION

Central Intelligence Agency (CIA), Office of Public Affairs, Washington, DC, 20505, USA, (703) 482-0623, https://www.cia.gov; The World Factbook.

BERMUDA-RETAIL TRADE

Euromonitor International, Inc., 1 N Dearborn St., Ste. 1700, Chicago, IL, 60602, USA, (312) 922-1115, (312) 922-1157, info-usa@euromonitor.com, https://www.euromonitor.com/; Geographies.

BERMUDA-RICE PRODUCTION

See BERMUDA-CROPS

BERMUDA-RUBBER INDUSTRY AND TRADE

International Rubber Study Group (IRSG), 51 Changi Business Park Central 2, Unit No. 6, 486066, SGP, https://www.rubberstudy.org; Monthly Rubber Bulletin (MRB); Rubber Industry Report; Rubber Statistical Bulletin; and World Rubber Industry Report (WRIO).

BERMUDA-SHIPPING

Routledge - Taylor & Francis Group, 6000 Broken Sound Pkwy. NW, Ste. 300, Boca Raton, FL, 33487, USA, (800) 634-1420, (800) 634-7064, orders@taylorandfrancis.com, https://www.routledge.com/; The Europa World Year Book 2022.

United Nations Statistics Division (UNSD), United Nations Plz., New York, NY, 10017, USA, (800) 253-9646, (212) 963-9851, statistics@un.org, https://unstats.un.org; Statistical Yearbook of the United Nations 2021.

BERMUDA-STEEL PRODUCTION

See BERMUDA-MINERAL INDUSTRIES

BERMUDA-SUGAR PRODUCTION

See BERMUDA-CROPS

BERMUDA-TAXATION

Palgrave Macmillan, 1 New York Plaza, Ste. 4500, New York, NY, 10004-1562, USA, (800) 777-4643, orders@palgrave.com, https://www.palgrave.com/us; The Statesman's Yearbook, 2023.

BERMUDA-TEXTILE INDUSTRY

Palgrave Macmillan, 1 New York Plaza, Ste. 4500, New York, NY, 10004-1562, USA, (800) 777-4643, orders@palgrave.com, https://www.palgrave.com/us; The Statesman's Yearbook, 2023.

BERMUDA-THEATER

UNESCO Institute for Statistics, C.P 250 Succursale H, Montreal, QC, H3G 2K8, CAN, (514) 343-6880 (Dial from U.S.), (514) 343-5740 (Fax from U.S.), uis.publications@unesco.org, http://uis.unesco.org/; UIS.Stat.

BERMUDA-TOURISM

Euromonitor International, Inc., 1 N Dearborn St., Ste. 1700, Chicago, IL, 60602, USA, (312) 922-1115, (312) 922-1157, info-usa@euromonitor.com, https://www.euromonitor.com/; Geographies.

Palgrave Macmillan, 1 New York Plaza, Ste. 4500, New York, NY, 10004-1562, USA, (800) 777-4643, orders@palgrave.com, https://www.palgrave.com/us; The Statesman's Yearbook, 2023.

Routledge - Taylor & Francis Group, 6000 Broken Sound Pkwy. NW, Ste. 300, Boca Raton, FL, 33487, USA, (800) 634-1420, (800) 634-7064, orders@taylorandfrancis.com, https://www.routledge.com/; The Europa World Year Book 2022.

United Nations Statistics Division (UNSD), United Nations Plz., New York, NY, 10017, USA, (800) 253-9646, (212) 963-9851, statistics@un.org, https://unstats.un.org; Statistical Yearbook of the United Nations 2021.

United Nations World Tourism Organization (UNWTO), Calle Poeta Joan Maragall 42, Madrid, 28020, SPA, info@unwto.org, https://www.unwto.org/; Yearbook of Tourism Statistics, 2021 Edition.

BERMUDA-TRADE

See BERMUDA-INTERNATIONAL TRADE

BERMUDA-TRANSPORTATION

Central Intelligence Agency (CIA), Office of Public Affairs, Washington, DC, 20505, USA, (703) 482-0623, https://www.cia.gov; The World Factbook.

Euromonitor International, Inc., 1 N Dearborn St., Ste. 1700, Chicago, IL, 60602, USA, (312) 922-1115, (312) 922-1157, info-usa@euromonitor.com, https://www.euromonitor.com/; Geographies.

Palgrave Macmillan, 1 New York Plaza, Ste. 4500, New York, NY, 10004-1562, USA, (800) 777-4643, orders@palgrave.com, https://www.palgrave.com/us; The Statesman's Yearbook, 2023.

Routledge - Taylor & Francis Group, 6000 Broken Sound Pkwy. NW, Ste. 300, Boca Raton, FL, 33487, USA, (800) 634-1420, (800) 634-7064, orders@taylorandfrancis.com, https://www.routledge.com/; The Europa World Year Book 2022.

BERMUDA-UNEMPLOYMENT

International Labour Organization (ILO), 4 Rte. des Morillons, Geneva, CH-1211, SWI, ilo@ilo.org, https://www.ilo.org; NORMLEX Information System on International Labour Standards.

BERMUDA-VITAL STATISTICS

Palgrave Macmillan, 1 New York Plaza, Ste. 4500, New York, NY, 10004-1562, USA, (800) 777-4643, orders@palgrave.com, https://www.palgrave.com/us; The Statesman's Yearbook, 2023.

U.S. Census Bureau, 4600 Silver Hill Rd., Washington, DC, 20233, USA, (301) 763-4636, (800) 923-8282, https://www.census.gov; HIV/AIDS Surveillance Data Base.

United Nations Department of Economic and Social Affairs (DESA), Population Division, 2 United Nations Plz., Rm. DC2-1950, New York, NY, 10017, USA, (212) 963-3209, (212) 963-2147, population@un.org, https://www.un.org/development/desa/pd/; World Contraceptive Use 2021: Estimates and Projections of Family Planning Indicators and World Marriage Data 2019.

United Nations Statistics Division (UNSD), United Nations Plz., New York, NY, 10017, USA, (800) 253-9646, (212) 963-9851, statistics@un.org, https://unstats.un.org; Statistical Yearbook of the United Nations 2021.

BERMUDA-WAGES

International Labour Organization (ILO), 4 Rte. des Morillons, Geneva, CH-1211, SWI, ilo@ilo.org, https://www.ilo.org; NORMLEX Information System on International Labour Standards.

BERMUDA-WEATHER

See BERMUDA-CLIMATE

BERMUDA-WHEAT PRODUCTION

See BERMUDA-CROPS

BERMUDA-WOOL PRODUCTION

See BERMUDA-TEXTILE INDUSTRY

BERRIES

U.S. Department of Agriculture (USDA), National Agricultural Statistics Service (USDA-NASS), 1400 Independence Ave. SW, Washington, DC, 20250, USA, (800) 727-9540, nass@nass.usda.gov, https://www.nass.usda.gov; Quick Stats.

BERYLLIUM

U.S. Department of the Interior (DOI), U.S. Geological Survey (USGS), National Minerals Information Center (NMIC), 12201 Sunrise Valley Dr., Reston, VA, 20192, USA, (703) 648-4920, (703) 648-7971, (703) 648-4995, sfortier@usgs.gov, https://www.usgs.gov/centers/nmic; Mineral Commodity Summaries 2022.

BEVERAGE INDUSTRY

Can Manufacturers Institute (CMI), 1730 Rhode Island Ave. NW, Ste. 1000, Washington, DC, 20036, USA, (202) 232-4677, (202) 232-5756, https://www.cancentral.com/; 1970-2020 CMI Food Can Shipments Report.

BEVERAGES

See also ALCOHOLIC BEVERAGES

The Lancet, 230 Park Ave., New York, NY, 10169, USA, (212) 633-3800, editorial@lancet.com, https://www.thelancet.com/; Alcohol Use and Burden for 195 Countries and Territories, 1990-2016: A Systematic Analysis for the Global Burden of Disease Study 2016.

BEVERAGES-CONSUMPTION

American Heart Association (AHA), 7272 Greenville Ave., Dallas, TX, 75231, USA, (800) 242-8721, (214) 570-5943, https://www.heart.org; AHA/ACC/HRS Guideline for the Management of Patients with Atrial Fibrillation.

Kirin Holdings Company, Limited, Nakano Central Park South, 10-2, Nakano 4-chome, Nakano-ku, Tokyo, 164-0001, JPN, https://www.kirinholdings.com/en/; Kirin CSV Report 2021.

National Coffee Association (NCA), 45 Broadway, Ste. 1140, New York, NY, 10006, USA, (212) 766-4007, (212) 766-5815, https://www.ncausa.org; Coffee, Consumers, & COVID-19: Road Map to Recovery and National Coffee Data Trends (NCDT) 2022.

U.S. Department of Agriculture (USDA), Economic Research Service (ERS), 1400 Independence Ave. SW, Mail Stop 1800, Washington, DC, 20250-0002, USA, (202) 720-2791, https://www.ers.usda.gov/; Food Price Outlook.

BEVERAGES-PRICE INDEXES

U.S. Department of Labor (DOL), Bureau of Labor Statistics (BLS), Postal Square Bldg., 2 Massachusetts Ave. NE, Washington, DC, 20212-0001, USA, (202) 691-5200, (202) 691-7890, blsdata_staff@bls.gov, https://www.bls.gov; Consumer Price Index (CPI) Databases and Consumer Price Indexe (CPI) Publications.

BEVERAGES-WHISKEY

U.S. Department of Labor (DOL), Bureau of Labor Statistics (BLS), Postal Square Bldg., 2 Massachusetts Ave. NE, Washington, DC, 20212-0001, USA, (202) 691-5200, (202) 691-7890, blsdata_staff@bls.gov, https://www.bls.gov; Consumer Price Index (CPI) Databases.

BEVERAGES-WINE

U.S. Department of Labor (DOL), Bureau of Labor Statistics (BLS), Postal Square Bldg., 2 Massachusetts Ave. NE, Washington, DC, 20212-0001, USA, (202) 691-5200, (202) 691-7890, blsdata_staff@bls.gov, https://www.bls.gov; Consumer Price Index (CPI) Databases.

BEVERAGES AND TOBACCO PRODUCT MANUFACTURING-EARNINGS

U.S. Department of Labor (DOL), Bureau of Labor Statistics (BLS), Postal Square Bldg., 2 Massachusetts Ave. NE, Washington, DC, 20212-0001, USA, (202) 691-5200, (202) 691-7890, blsdata_staff@bls.gov, https://www.bls.gov; Current Employment Statistics (CES).

BEVERAGES AND TOBACCO PRODUCT MANUFACTURING-EMPLOYEES

U.S. Department of Labor (DOL), Bureau of Labor Statistics (BLS), Postal Square Bldg., 2 Massachusetts Ave. NE, Washington, DC, 20212-0001, USA, (202) 691-5200, (202) 691-7890, blsdata_staff@bls.gov, https://www.bls.gov; Current Employment Statistics (CES) and Industry-Occupation Matrix Data, By Occupation.

BEVERAGES AND TOBACCO PRODUCT MANUFACTURING-PRODUCTIVITY

U.S. Department of Labor (DOL), Bureau of Labor Statistics (BLS), Postal Square Bldg., 2 Massachusetts Ave. NE, Washington, DC, 20212-0001, USA, (202) 691-5200, (202) 691-7890, blsdata_staff@bls.gov, https://www.bls.gov; Productivity.

BEVERAGES AND TOBACCO PRODUCT MANUFACTURING-SHIPMENTS

U.S. Census Bureau, 4600 Silver Hill Rd., Washington, DC, 20233, USA, (301) 763-4636, (800) 923-8282, https://www.census.gov; Manufacturers' Shipments, Inventories and Orders.

BHUTAN-NATIONAL STATISTICAL OFFICE

National Statistics Bureau of Bhutan, PO Box 338, Thimphu, BTN, nsbictinfo@gmail.com, https://www.nsb.gov.bt/; National Data Reports (Bhutan).

BHUTAN-PRIMARY STATISTICS SOURCES

National Statistics Bureau of Bhutan, PO Box 338, Thimphu, BTN, nsbictinfo@gmail.com, https://www.nsb.gov.bt/; Bhutan at a Glance 2021 and Statistical Yearbook of Bhutan 2021.

BHUTAN-AGRICULTURE

Asian Development Bank (ADB), 6 ADB Ave., Mandaluyong City, 1550, PHL, information@adb.org, https://www.adb.org/; Key Indicators for Asia and the Pacific 2022.

The Economist Group: Economist Intelligence Unit (EIU), 900 3rd Ave., 16th Fl., New York, NY, 10022, USA, (212) 541-0500, americas@eiu.com, https://www.eiu.com; Bhutan Country Report.

Euromonitor International, Inc., 1 N Dearborn St., Ste. 1700, Chicago, IL, 60602, USA, (312) 922-1115, (312) 922-1157, info-usa@euromonitor.com, https://www.euromonitor.com/; Geographies.

Palgrave Macmillan, 1 New York Plaza, Ste. 4500, New York, NY, 10004-1562, USA, (800) 777-4643, orders@palgrave.com, https://www.palgrave.com/us; The Statesman's Yearbook, 2023.

Routledge - Taylor & Francis Group, 6000 Broken Sound Pkwy. NW, Ste. 300, Boca Raton, FL, 33487, USA, (800) 634-1420, (800) 634-7064, orders@taylorandfrancis.com, https://www.routledge.com/; The Europa World Year Book 2022.

United Nations Economic and Social Commission for Asia and the Pacific (ESCAP), United Nations Building, Rajadamnern Nok Ave., Bangkok, 10200, THA, https://www.unescap.org/; Asia-Pacific Development Journal and SDG Gateway Data Explorer.

United Nations Food and Agricultural Organization (FAO), 2121 K St., Ste. 800B, Washington, DC, 20037, USA, (202) 653-2400 (Dial from U.S.), (202) 653-5760 (Fax from U.S.), fao-hq@fao.org, https://www.fao.org; AQUASTAT and The State of Food and Agriculture (SOFA) 2022.

The World Bank, 1818 H St. NW, Washington, DC, 20433, USA, (202) 473-1000, (202) 477-6391, eds03@worldbank.org, https://www.worldbank.org/; Bhutan (report) and World Development Indicators (WDI) 2022.

BHUTAN-AIRLINES

Palgrave Macmillan, 1 New York Plaza, Ste. 4500, New York, NY, 10004-1562, USA, (800) 777-4643, orders@palgrave.com, https://www.palgrave.com/us; The Statesman's Yearbook, 2023.

Routledge - Taylor & Francis Group, 6000 Broken Sound Pkwy. NW, Ste. 300, Boca Raton, FL, 33487, USA, (800) 634-1420, (800) 634-7064, orders@taylorandfrancis.com, https://www.routledge.com/; The Europa World Year Book 2022.

BHUTAN-ALUMINUM PRODUCTION

See BHUTAN-MINERAL INDUSTRIES

BHUTAN-ARMED FORCES

Central Intelligence Agency (CIA), Office of Public Affairs, Washington, DC, 20505, USA, (703) 482-0623, https://www.cia.gov; The World Factbook.

Palgrave Macmillan, 1 New York Plaza, Ste. 4500, New York, NY, 10004-1562, USA, (800) 777-4643, orders@palgrave.com, https://www.palgrave.com/us; The Statesman's Yearbook, 2023.

Stockholm International Peace Research Institute (SIPRI), Signalistgatan 9, Stockholm, SE 169 72, SWE, https://www.sipri.org/; SIPRI Arms Transfers Database and SIPRI Military Expenditure Database.

BHUTAN-BALANCE OF PAYMENTS

Routledge - Taylor & Francis Group, 6000 Broken Sound Pkwy. NW, Ste. 300, Boca Raton, FL, 33487, USA, (800) 634-1420, (800) 634-7064, orders@taylorandfrancis.com, https://www.routledge.com/; The Europa World Year Book 2022.

SAGE Publications, 2455 Teller Rd., Thousand Oaks, CA, 91320, USA, (800) 818-7243, (800) 583-2665, journals@sagepub.com, https://www.sagepub.com; Journal of South Asian Development and South Asia Economic Journal.

The World Bank, 1818 H St. NW, Washington, DC, 20433, USA, (202) 473-1000, (202) 477-6391, eds03@worldbank.org, https://www.worldbank.org/; Bhutan (report) and World Development Indicators (WDI) 2022.

BHUTAN-BANKS AND BANKING

Asian Development Bank (ADB), 6 ADB Ave., Mandaluyong City, 1550, PHL, information@adb.org, https://www.adb.org/; Key Indicators for Asia and the Pacific 2022.

Euromonitor International, Inc., 1 N Dearborn St., Ste. 1700, Chicago, IL, 60602, USA, (312) 922-1115, (312) 922-1157, info-usa@euromonitor.com, https://www.euromonitor.com/; Geographies.

Routledge - Taylor & Francis Group, 6000 Broken Sound Pkwy. NW, Ste. 300, Boca Raton, FL, 33487, USA, (800) 634-1420, (800) 634-7064, orders@taylorandfrancis.com, https://www.routledge.com/; The Europa World Year Book 2022.

SAGE Publications, 2455 Teller Rd., Thousand Oaks, CA, 91320, USA, (800) 818-7243, (800) 583-2665, journals@sagepub.com, https://www.sagepub.com; Journal of South Asian Development and South Asia Economic Journal.

BHUTAN-BARLEY PRODUCTION

See BHUTAN-CROPS

BHUTAN-BROADCASTING

Central Intelligence Agency (CIA), Office of Public Affairs, Washington, DC, 20505, USA, (703) 482-0623, https://www.cia.gov; The World Factbook.

Euromonitor International, Inc., 1 N Dearborn St., Ste. 1700, Chicago, IL, 60602, USA, (312) 922-1115, (312) 922-1157, info-usa@euromonitor.com, https://www.euromonitor.com/; Geographies.

Palgrave Macmillan, 1 New York Plaza, Ste. 4500, New York, NY, 10004-1562, USA, (800) 777-4643, orders@palgrave.com, https://www.palgrave.com/us; The Statesman's Yearbook, 2023.

WRTH Publications Limited, PO Box 290, Oxford, OX2 7FT, GBR, sales@wrth.com, https://www.wrth.com; World Radio TV Handbook 2023.

BHUTAN-BUDGET

Central Intelligence Agency (CIA), Office of Public Affairs, Washington, DC, 20505, USA, (703) 482-0623, https://www.cia.gov; The World Factbook.

BHUTAN-BUSINESS

SAGE Publications, 2455 Teller Rd., Thousand Oaks, CA, 91320, USA, (800) 818-7243, (800) 583-2665, journals@sagepub.com, https://www.sagepub.com; Journal of South Asian Development and South Asia Economic Journal.

United Nations Economic and Social Commission for Asia and the Pacific (ESCAP), United Nations Building, Rajadamnern Nok Ave., Bangkok, 10200, THA, https://www.unescap.org/; SDG Gateway Data Explorer.

BHUTAN-CHILDBIRTH-STATISTICS

United Nations Economic and Social Commission for Asia and the Pacific (ESCAP), United Nations Building, Rajadamnern Nok Ave., Bangkok, 10200, THA, https://www.unescap.org/; Asia-Pacific Development Journal.

The World Bank, 1818 H St. NW, Washington, DC, 20433, USA, (202) 473-1000, (202) 477-6391,

eds03@worldbank.org, https://www.worldbank.org/; World Development Indicators (WDI) 2022.

BHUTAN-CLIMATE

International Institute for Environment and Development (IIED), 235 High Holborn, London, WC1V 7DN, GBR, inforequest@iied.org, https://www.iied.org; Environment & Urbanization.

Palgrave Macmillan, 1 New York Plaza, Ste. 4500, New York, NY, 10004-1562, USA, (800) 777-4643, orders@palgrave.com, https://www.palgrave.com/us; The Statesman's Yearbook, 2023.

BHUTAN-COAL PRODUCTION

See BHUTAN-MINERAL INDUSTRIES

BHUTAN-COFFEE

See BHUTAN-CROPS

BHUTAN-COMMERCE

Palgrave Macmillan, 1 New York Plaza, Ste. 4500, New York, NY, 10004-1562, USA, (800) 777-4643, orders@palgrave.com, https://www.palgrave.com/us; The Statesman's Yearbook, 2023.

SAGE Publications, 2455 Teller Rd., Thousand Oaks, CA, 91320, USA, (800) 818-7243, (800) 583-2665, journals@sagepub.com, https://www.sagepub.com; Journal of South Asian Development and South Asia Economic Journal.

UK Data Service, University of Essex, Wivenhoe Park, Colchester, Essex, CO4 3SQ, GBR, https://ukdataservice.ac.uk/; International Aggregate Data.

BHUTAN-CONSUMER PRICE INDEXES

Asian Development Bank (ADB), 6 ADB Ave., Mandaluyong City, 1550, PHL, information@adb.org, https://www.adb.org/; Key Indicators for Asia and the Pacific 2022.

Routledge - Taylor & Francis Group, 6000 Broken Sound Pkwy. NW, Ste. 300, Boca Raton, FL, 33487, USA, (800) 634-1420, (800) 634-7064, orders@taylorandfrancis.com, https://www.routledge.com/; The Europa World Year Book 2022.

SAGE Publications, 2455 Teller Rd., Thousand Oaks, CA, 91320, USA, (800) 818-7243, (800) 583-2665, journals@sagepub.com, https://www.sagepub.com; Journal of South Asian Development and South Asia Economic Journal.

The World Bank, 1818 H St. NW, Washington, DC, 20433, USA, (202) 473-1000, (202) 477-6391, eds03@worldbank.org, https://www.worldbank.org/; Bhutan (report).

BHUTAN-COPPER INDUSTRY AND TRADE

See BHUTAN-MINERAL INDUSTRIES

BHUTAN-CORN INDUSTRY

See BHUTAN-CROPS

BHUTAN-COTTON

See BHUTAN-CROPS

BHUTAN-CROPS

Palgrave Macmillan, 1 New York Plaza, Ste. 4500, New York, NY, 10004-1562, USA, (800) 777-4643, orders@palgrave.com, https://www.palgrave.com/us; The Statesman's Yearbook, 2023.

United Nations Food and Agricultural Organization (FAO), 2121 K St., Ste. 800B, Washington, DC, 20037, USA, (202) 653-2400 (Dial from U.S.), (202) 653-5760 (Fax from U.S.), fao-hq@fao.org, https://www.fao.org; The State of Food and Agriculture (SOFA) 2022.

United Nations Statistics Division (UNSD), United Nations Plz., New York, NY, 10017, USA, (800) 253-9646, (212) 963-9851, statistics@un.org, https://unstats.un.org; Statistical Yearbook of the United Nations 2021.

BHUTAN-DAIRY PROCESSING

United Nations Food and Agricultural Organization (FAO), 2121 K St., Ste. 800B, Washington, DC, 20037, USA, (202) 653-2400 (Dial from U.S.), (202) 653-5760 (Fax from U.S.), fao-hq@fao.org, https://www.fao.org; The State of Food and Agriculture (SOFA) 2022.

BHUTAN-DEBTS, EXTERNAL

Asian Development Bank (ADB), 6 ADB Ave., Mandaluyong City, 1550, PHL, information@adb.org, https://www.adb.org/; Key Indicators for Asia and the Pacific 2022.

SAGE Publications, 2455 Teller Rd., Thousand Oaks, CA, 91320, USA, (800) 818-7243, (800) 583-2665, journals@sagepub.com, https://www.sagepub.com; Journal of South Asian Development and South Asia Economic Journal.

The World Bank, 1818 H St. NW, Washington, DC, 20433, USA, (202) 473-1000, (202) 477-6391, eds03@worldbank.org, https://www.worldbank.org/; World Development Indicators (WDI) 2022.

BHUTAN-DIAMONDS

See BHUTAN-MINERAL INDUSTRIES

BHUTAN-ECONOMIC ASSISTANCE

United Nations Statistics Division (UNSD), United Nations Plz., New York, NY, 10017, USA, (800) 253-9646, (212) 963-9851, statistics@un.org, https://unstats.un.org; Statistical Yearbook of the United Nations 2021.

BHUTAN-ECONOMIC CONDITIONS

Asian Development Bank (ADB), 6 ADB Ave., Mandaluyong City, 1550, PHL, information@adb.org, https://www.adb.org/; Key Indicators for Asia and the Pacific 2022.

Bernan Press, 15250 NBN Way, Bldg. C, Blue Ridge Summit, PA, 17214, USA, (301) 459-2255, (800) 865-3457, (800) 865-3450, customercare@bernan.com, https://rowman.com/Page/Bernan; World Economic Outlook, April 2022.

Central Intelligence Agency (CIA), Office of Public Affairs, Washington, DC, 20505, USA, (703) 482-0623, https://www.cia.gov; The World Factbook.

The Economist Group: Economist Intelligence Unit (EIU), 900 3rd Ave., 16th Fl., New York, NY, 10022, USA, (212) 541-0500, americas@eiu.com, https://www.eiu.com; Bhutan Country Report.

Euromonitor International, Inc., 1 N Dearborn St., Ste. 1700, Chicago, IL, 60602, USA, (312) 922-1115, (312) 922-1157, info-usa@euromonitor.com, https://www.euromonitor.com/; Geographies.

Palgrave Macmillan, 1 New York Plaza, Ste. 4500, New York, NY, 10004-1562, USA, (800) 777-4643, orders@palgrave.com, https://www.palgrave.com/us; The Statesman's Yearbook, 2023.

Routledge - Taylor & Francis Group, 6000 Broken Sound Pkwy. NW, Ste. 300, Boca Raton, FL, 33487, USA, (800) 634-1420, (800) 634-7064, orders@taylorandfrancis.com, https://www.routledge.com/; The Europa World Year Book 2022.

SAGE Publications, 2455 Teller Rd., Thousand Oaks, CA, 91320, USA, (800) 818-7243, (800) 583-2665, journals@sagepub.com, https://www.sagepub.com; Journal of South Asian Development and South Asia Economic Journal.

United Nations Statistics Division (UNSD), United Nations Plz., New York, NY, 10017, USA, (800) 253-9646, (212) 963-9851, statistics@un.org, https://unstats.un.org; World Statistics Pocketbook 2021.

The World Bank, 1818 H St. NW, Washington, DC, 20433, USA, (202) 473-1000, (202) 477-6391, eds03@worldbank.org, https://www.worldbank.org/; Bhutan (report) and The Global Findex Database 2021.

BHUTAN-EDUCATION

Euromonitor International, Inc., 1 N Dearborn St., Ste. 1700, Chicago, IL, 60602, USA, (312) 922-1115, (312) 922-1157, info-usa@euromonitor.com, https://www.euromonitor.com/; Geographies.

Palgrave Macmillan, 1 New York Plaza, Ste. 4500, New York, NY, 10004-1562, USA, (800) 777-4643, orders@palgrave.com, https://www.palgrave.com/us; The Statesman's Yearbook, 2023.

Routledge - Taylor & Francis Group, 6000 Broken Sound Pkwy. NW, Ste. 300, Boca Raton, FL, 33487, USA, (800) 634-1420, (800) 634-7064, orders@taylorandfrancis.com, https://www.routledge.com/; The Europa World Year Book 2022.

UNESCO Institute for Statistics, C.P 250 Succursale H, Montreal, QC, H3G 2K8, CAN, (514) 343-6880 (Dial from U.S.), (514) 343-5740 (Fax from U.S.), uis.publications@unesco.org, http://uis.unesco.org/; UIS.Stat.

United Nations Economic and Social Commission for Asia and the Pacific (ESCAP), United Nations Building, Rajadamnern Nok Ave., Bangkok, 10200, THA, https://www.unescap.org/; Asia-Pacific Development Journal and SDG Gateway Data Explorer.

The World Bank, 1818 H St. NW, Washington, DC, 20433, USA, (202) 473-1000, (202) 477-6391, eds03@worldbank.org, https://www.worldbank.org/; Bhutan (report) and World Development Indicators (WDI) 2022.

BHUTAN-ELECTRICITY

U.S. Energy Information Administration (EIA), 1000 Independence Ave. SW, Washington, DC, 20585, USA, (202) 586-8800, infoctr@eia.gov, https://www.eia.gov; International Energy Outlook 2021.

BHUTAN-EMPLOYMENT

SAGE Publications, 2455 Teller Rd., Thousand Oaks, CA, 91320, USA, (800) 818-7243, (800) 583-2665, journals@sagepub.com, https://www.sagepub.com; Journal of South Asian Development and South Asia Economic Journal.

UK Data Service, University of Essex, Wivenhoe Park, Colchester, Essex, CO4 3SQ, GBR, https://ukdataservice.ac.uk/; International Aggregate Data.

United Nations Economic and Social Commission for Asia and the Pacific (ESCAP), United Nations Building, Rajadamnern Nok Ave., Bangkok, 10200, THA, https://www.unescap.org/; Asia-Pacific Development Journal.

The World Bank, 1818 H St. NW, Washington, DC, 20433, USA, (202) 473-1000, (202) 477-6391, eds03@worldbank.org, https://www.worldbank.org/; Bhutan (report).

BHUTAN-ENVIRONMENTAL CONDITIONS

The Economist Group: Economist Intelligence Unit (EIU), 900 3rd Ave., 16th Fl., New York, NY, 10022, USA, (212) 541-0500, americas@eiu.com, https://www.eiu.com; Bhutan Country Report.

International Institute for Environment and Development (IIED), 235 High Holborn, London, WC1V 7DN, GBR, inforequest@iied.org, https://www.iied.org; Environment & Urbanization.

United Nations Statistics Division (UNSD), United Nations Plz., New York, NY, 10017, USA, (800) 253-9646, (212) 963-9851, statistics@un.org, https://unstats.un.org; World Statistics Pocketbook 2021.

BHUTAN-EXPORTS

Asian Development Bank (ADB), 6 ADB Ave., Mandaluyong City, 1550, PHL, information@adb.org, https://www.adb.org/; Key Indicators for Asia and the Pacific 2022.

Central Intelligence Agency (CIA), Office of Public Affairs, Washington, DC, 20505, USA, (703) 482-0623, https://www.cia.gov; The World Factbook.

The Economist Group: Economist Intelligence Unit (EIU), 900 3rd Ave., 16th Fl., New York, NY, 10022, USA, (212) 541-0500, americas@eiu.com, https://www.eiu.com; Bhutan Country Report.

BHUTAN-FEMALE WORKING POPULATION

See BHUTAN-EMPLOYMENT

BHUTAN-FERTILITY, HUMAN

Central Intelligence Agency (CIA), Office of Public Affairs, Washington, DC, 20505, USA, (703) 482-0623, https://www.cia.gov; The World Factbook.

BHUTAN-FERTILIZER INDUSTRY

United Nations Food and Agricultural Organization (FAO), 2121 K St., Ste. 800B, Washington, DC, 20037, USA, (202) 653-2400 (Dial from U.S.), (202) 653-5760 (Fax from U.S.), fao-hq@fao.org, https://www.fao.org; The State of Food and Agriculture (SOFA) 2022.

BHUTAN-FETAL MORTALITY

See BHUTAN-MORTALITY

BHUTAN-FINANCE

SAGE Publications, 2455 Teller Rd., Thousand Oaks, CA, 91320, USA, (800) 818-7243, (800) 583-2665, journals@sagepub.com, https://www.sagepub.com; Journal of South Asian Development and South Asia Economic Journal.

Stockholm International Peace Research Institute (SIPRI), Signalistgatan 9, Stockholm, SE 169 72, SWE, https://www.sipri.org/; SIPRI Arms Transfers Database and SIPRI Military Expenditure Database.

United Nations Economic and Social Commission for Asia and the Pacific (ESCAP), United Nations Building, Rajadamnern Nok Ave., Bangkok, 10200, THA, https://www.unescap.org/; Asia-Pacific Development Journal and SDG Gateway Data Explorer.

The World Bank, 1818 H St. NW, Washington, DC, 20433, USA, (202) 473-1000, (202) 477-6391, eds03@worldbank.org, https://www.worldbank.org/; Bhutan (report).

BHUTAN-FINANCE, PUBLIC

Asian Development Bank (ADB), 6 ADB Ave., Mandaluyong City, 1550, PHL, information@adb.org, https://www.adb.org/; Key Indicators for Asia and the Pacific 2022.

The Economist Group: Economist Intelligence Unit (EIU), 900 3rd Ave., 16th Fl., New York, NY, 10022, USA, (212) 541-0500, americas@eiu.com, https://www.eiu.com; Bhutan Country Report.

Palgrave Macmillan, 1 New York Plaza, Ste. 4500, New York, NY, 10004-1562, USA, (800) 777-4643, orders@palgrave.com, https://www.palgrave.com/us; The Statesman's Yearbook, 2023.

Routledge - Taylor & Francis Group, 6000 Broken Sound Pkwy. NW, Ste. 300, Boca Raton, FL, 33487, USA, (800) 634-1420, (800) 634-7064, orders@taylorandfrancis.com, https://www.routledge.com/; The Europa World Year Book 2022.

United Nations Economic and Social Commission for Asia and the Pacific (ESCAP), United Nations Building, Rajadamnern Nok Ave., Bangkok, 10200, THA, https://www.unescap.org/; SDG Gateway Data Explorer.

United Nations Statistics Division (UNSD), United Nations Plz., New York, NY, 10017, USA, (800) 253-9646, (212) 963-9851, statistics@un.org, https://unstats.un.org; National Accounts Main Aggregates Database and National Accounts Statistics: Main Aggregates and Detailed Tables.

The World Bank, 1818 H St. NW, Washington, DC, 20433, USA, (202) 473-1000, (202) 477-6391, eds03@worldbank.org, https://www.worldbank.org/; Bhutan (report).

BHUTAN-FISHERIES

Routledge - Taylor & Francis Group, 6000 Broken Sound Pkwy. NW, Ste. 300, Boca Raton, FL, 33487, USA, (800) 634-1420, (800) 634-7064, orders@taylorandfrancis.com, https://www.routledge.com/; The Europa World Year Book 2022.

United Nations Food and Agricultural Organization (FAO), 2121 K St., Ste. 800B, Washington, DC, 20037, USA, (202) 653-2400 (Dial from U.S.), (202) 653-5760 (Fax from U.S.), fao-hq@fao.org, https://www.fao.org; FAO Yearbook of Fishery and Aquaculture Statistics 2019; Fishery Statistical Collections Global Capture Production; FishStatJ; and The State of Food and Agriculture (SOFA) 2022.

United Nations Statistics Division (UNSD), United Nations Plz., New York, NY, 10017, USA, (800) 253-9646, (212) 963-9851, statistics@un.org, https://unstats.un.org; Statistical Yearbook of the United Nations 2021.

The World Bank, 1818 H St. NW, Washington, DC, 20433, USA, (202) 473-1000, (202) 477-6391, eds03@worldbank.org, https://www.worldbank.org/; Bhutan (report).

BHUTAN-FOOD

United Nations Economic and Social Commission for Asia and the Pacific (ESCAP), United Nations Building, Rajadamnern Nok Ave., Bangkok, 10200, THA, https://www.unescap.org/; SDG Gateway Data Explorer.

United Nations Food and Agricultural Organization (FAO), 2121 K St., Ste. 800B, Washington, DC, 20037, USA, (202) 653-2400 (Dial from U.S.), (202) 653-5760 (Fax from U.S.), fao-hq@fao.org, https://www.fao.org; The State of Food and Agriculture (SOFA) 2022.

BHUTAN-FOREIGN EXCHANGE RATES

Asian Development Bank (ADB), 6 ADB Ave., Mandaluyong City, 1550, PHL, information@adb.org, https://www.adb.org/; Key Indicators for Asia and the Pacific 2022.

BHUTAN-FORESTS AND FORESTRY

Palgrave Macmillan, 1 New York Plaza, Ste. 4500, New York, NY, 10004-1562, USA, (800) 777-4643, orders@palgrave.com, https://www.palgrave.com/us; The Statesman's Yearbook, 2023.

Routledge - Taylor & Francis Group, 6000 Broken Sound Pkwy. NW, Ste. 300, Boca Raton, FL, 33487, USA, (800) 634-1420, (800) 634-7064, orders@taylorandfrancis.com, https://www.routledge.com/; The Europa World Year Book 2022.

United Nations Food and Agricultural Organization (FAO), 2121 K St., Ste. 800B, Washington, DC, 20037, USA, (202) 653-2400 (Dial from U.S.), (202) 653-5760 (Fax from U.S.), fao-hq@fao.org, https://www.fao.org; The State of Food and Agriculture (SOFA) 2022.

The World Bank, 1818 H St. NW, Washington, DC, 20433, USA, (202) 473-1000, (202) 477-6391, eds03@worldbank.org, https://www.worldbank.org/; Bhutan (report).

BHUTAN-GAS PRODUCTION

See BHUTAN-MINERAL INDUSTRIES

BHUTAN-GEOGRAPHIC INFORMATION SYSTEMS

The World Bank, 1818 H St. NW, Washington, DC, 20433, USA, (202) 473-1000, (202) 477-6391, eds03@worldbank.org, https://www.worldbank.org/; Bhutan (report).

BHUTAN-GOLD INDUSTRY

The World Bank, 1818 H St. NW, Washington, DC, 20433, USA, (202) 473-1000, (202) 477-6391, eds03@worldbank.org, https://www.worldbank.org/; World Development Indicators (WDI) 2022.

BHUTAN-GOLD PRODUCTION

See BHUTAN-MINERAL INDUSTRIES

BHUTAN-GROSS DOMESTIC PRODUCT

Asian Development Bank (ADB), 6 ADB Ave., Mandaluyong City, 1550, PHL, information@adb.org, https://www.adb.org/; Key Indicators for Asia and the Pacific 2022.

The Economist Group: Economist Intelligence Unit (EIU), 900 3rd Ave., 16th Fl., New York, NY, 10022, USA, (212) 541-0500, americas@eiu.com, https://www.eiu.com; Bhutan Country Report.

Routledge - Taylor & Francis Group, 6000 Broken Sound Pkwy. NW, Ste. 300, Boca Raton, FL, 33487, USA, (800) 634-1420, (800) 634-7064, orders@taylorandfrancis.com, https://www.routledge.com/; The Europa World Year Book 2022.

United Nations Statistics Division (UNSD), United Nations Plz., New York, NY, 10017, USA, (800) 253-9646, (212) 963-9851, statistics@un.org, https://unstats.un.org; Statistical Yearbook of the United Nations 2021.

The World Bank, 1818 H St. NW, Washington, DC, 20433, USA, (202) 473-1000, (202) 477-6391, eds03@worldbank.org, https://www.worldbank.org/; World Development Indicators (WDI) 2022.

BHUTAN-GROSS NATIONAL PRODUCT

Asian Development Bank (ADB), 6 ADB Ave., Mandaluyong City, 1550, PHL, information@adb.org, https://www.adb.org/; Key Indicators for Asia and the Pacific 2022.

Palgrave Macmillan, 1 New York Plaza, Ste. 4500, New York, NY, 10004-1562, USA, (800) 777-4643, orders@palgrave.com, https://www.palgrave.com/us; The Statesman's Yearbook, 2023.

The World Bank, 1818 H St. NW, Washington, DC, 20433, USA, (202) 473-1000, (202) 477-6391, eds03@worldbank.org, https://www.worldbank.org/; World Development Indicators (WDI) 2022.

BHUTAN-HOUSING

Euromonitor International, Inc., 1 N Dearborn St., Ste. 1700, Chicago, IL, 60602, USA, (312) 922-1115, (312) 922-1157, info-usa@euromonitor.com, https://www.euromonitor.com/; Geographies.

BHUTAN-ILLITERATE PERSONS

United Nations Economic and Social Commission for Asia and the Pacific (ESCAP), United Nations Building, Rajadamnern Nok Ave., Bangkok, 10200, THA, https://www.unescap.org/; Asia-Pacific Development Journal.

BHUTAN-IMPORTS

Asian Development Bank (ADB), 6 ADB Ave., Mandaluyong City, 1550, PHL, information@adb.org, https://www.adb.org/; Key Indicators for Asia and the Pacific 2022.

Central Intelligence Agency (CIA), Office of Public Affairs, Washington, DC, 20505, USA, (703) 482-0623, https://www.cia.gov; The World Factbook.

The Economist Group: Economist Intelligence Unit (EIU), 900 3rd Ave., 16th Fl., New York, NY, 10022, USA, (212) 541-0500, americas@eiu.com, https://www.eiu.com; Bhutan Country Report.

BHUTAN-INDUSTRIES

Central Intelligence Agency (CIA), Office of Public Affairs, Washington, DC, 20505, USA, (703) 482-0623, https://www.cia.gov; The World Factbook.

The Economist Group: Economist Intelligence Unit (EIU), 900 3rd Ave., 16th Fl., New York, NY, 10022, USA, (212) 541-0500, americas@eiu.com, https://www.eiu.com; Bhutan Country Report.

Euromonitor International, Inc., 1 N Dearborn St., Ste. 1700, Chicago, IL, 60602, USA, (312) 922-1115, (312) 922-1157, info-usa@euromonitor.com, https://www.euromonitor.com/; Geographies.

Palgrave Macmillan, 1 New York Plaza, Ste. 4500, New York, NY, 10004-1562, USA, (800) 777-4643, orders@palgrave.com, https://www.palgrave.com/us; The Statesman's Yearbook, 2023.

Routledge - Taylor & Francis Group, 6000 Broken Sound Pkwy. NW, Ste. 300, Boca Raton, FL, 33487, USA, (800) 634-1420, (800) 634-7064, orders@taylorandfrancis.com, https://www.routledge.com/; The Europa World Year Book 2022.

SAGE Publications, 2455 Teller Rd., Thousand Oaks, CA, 91320, USA, (800) 818-7243, (800) 583-

2665, journals@sagepub.com, https://www.sagepub.com; Journal of South Asian Development and South Asia Economic Journal.

United Nations Economic and Social Commission for Asia and the Pacific (ESCAP), United Nations Building, Rajadamnern Nok Ave., Bangkok, 10200, THA, https://www.unescap.org/; Asia-Pacific Development Journal and SDG Gateway Data Explorer.

The World Bank, 1818 H St. NW, Washington, DC, 20433, USA, (202) 473-1000, (202) 477-6391, eds03@worldbank.org, https://www.worldbank.org/; Bhutan (report) and World Development Indicators (WDI) 2022.

BHUTAN-INFANT AND MATERNAL MORTALITY

See BHUTAN-MORTALITY

BHUTAN-INTERNATIONAL FINANCE

Asian Development Bank (ADB), 6 ADB Ave., Mandaluyong City, 1550, PHL, information@adb.org, https://www.adb.org/; Key Indicators for Asia and the Pacific 2022.

SAGE Publications, 2455 Teller Rd., Thousand Oaks, CA, 91320, USA, (800) 818-7243, (800) 583-2665, journals@sagepub.com, https://www.sagepub.com; Journal of South Asian Development and South Asia Economic Journal.

The World Bank, 1818 H St. NW, Washington, DC, 20433, USA, (202) 473-1000, (202) 477-6391, eds03@worldbank.org, https://www.worldbank.org/; Bhutan (report).

BHUTAN-INTERNATIONAL TRADE

Asian Development Bank (ADB), 6 ADB Ave., Mandaluyong City, 1550, PHL, information@adb.org, https://www.adb.org/; Key Indicators for Asia and the Pacific 2022.

The Economist Group: Economist Intelligence Unit (EIU), 900 3rd Ave., 16th Fl., New York, NY, 10022, USA, (212) 541-0500, americas@eiu.com, https://www.eiu.com; Bhutan Country Report.

Euromonitor International, Inc., 1 N Dearborn St., Ste. 1700, Chicago, IL, 60602, USA, (312) 922-1115, (312) 922-1157, info-usa@euromonitor.com, https://www.euromonitor.com/; Geographies.

Palgrave Macmillan, 1 New York Plaza, Ste. 4500, New York, NY, 10004-1562, USA, (800) 777-4643, orders@palgrave.com, https://www.palgrave.com/us; The Statesman's Yearbook, 2023.

Routledge - Taylor & Francis Group, 6000 Broken Sound Pkwy. NW, Ste. 300, Boca Raton, FL, 33487, USA, (800) 634-1420, (800) 634-7064, orders@taylorandfrancis.com, https://www.routledge.com/; The Europa World Year Book 2022.

United Nations Conference on Trade and Development (UNCTAD), Palais des Nations, Geneva, 1211, SWI, (212) 963-6896, unctadinfo@unctad.org, https://unctad.org; Trade and Development Report 2021.

United Nations Economic and Social Commission for Asia and the Pacific (ESCAP), United Nations Building, Rajadamnern Nok Ave., Bangkok, 10200, THA, https://www.unescap.org/; Asia-Pacific Development Journal and SDG Gateway Data Explorer.

United Nations Food and Agricultural Organization (FAO), 2121 K St., Ste. 800B, Washington, DC, 20037, USA, (202) 653-2400 (Dial from U.S.), (202) 653-5760 (Fax from U.S.), fao-hq@fao.org, https://www.fao.org; The State of Food and Agriculture (SOFA) 2022.

The World Bank, 1818 H St. NW, Washington, DC, 20433, USA, (202) 473-1000, (202) 477-6391, eds03@worldbank.org, https://www.worldbank.org/; Bhutan (report) and World Development Indicators (WDI) 2022.

World Trade Organization (WTO), Ctre. William Rappard, Rue de Lausanne 154, Case postale, Geneva, CH-1211, SWI, enquiries@wto.org, https://www.wto.org; World Trade Statistical Review 2022.

BHUTAN-LABOR

Central Intelligence Agency (CIA), Office of Public Affairs, Washington, DC, 20505, USA, (703) 482-0623, https://www.cia.gov; The World Factbook.

Euromonitor International, Inc., 1 N Dearborn St., Ste. 1700, Chicago, IL, 60602, USA, (312) 922-1115, (312) 922-1157, info-usa@euromonitor.com, https://www.euromonitor.com/; Geographies.

Palgrave Macmillan, 1 New York Plaza, Ste. 4500, New York, NY, 10004-1562, USA, (800) 777-4643, orders@palgrave.com, https://www.palgrave.com/us; The Statesman's Yearbook, 2023.

United Nations Food and Agricultural Organization (FAO), 2121 K St., Ste. 800B, Washington, DC, 20037, USA, (202) 653-2400 (Dial from U.S.), (202) 653-5760 (Fax from U.S.), fao-hq@fao.org, https://www.fao.org; The State of Food and Agriculture (SOFA) 2022.

The World Bank, 1818 H St. NW, Washington, DC, 20433, USA, (202) 473-1000, (202) 477-6391, eds03@worldbank.org, https://www.worldbank.org/; World Development Indicators (WDI) 2022.

BHUTAN-LIFE EXPECTANCY

Central Intelligence Agency (CIA), Office of Public Affairs, Washington, DC, 20505, USA, (703) 482-0623, https://www.cia.gov; The World Factbook.

United Nations Department of Economic and Social Affairs (DESA), Population Division, 2 United Nations Plz., Rm. DC2-1950, New York, NY, 10017, USA, (212) 963-3209, (212) 963-2147, population@un.org, https://www.un.org/development/desa/pd/; World Population Ageing 2020 Highlights.

United Nations Economic and Social Commission for Asia and the Pacific (ESCAP), United Nations Building, Rajadamnern Nok Ave., Bangkok, 10200, THA, https://www.unescap.org/; Asia-Pacific Development Journal.

BHUTAN-LITERACY

Euromonitor International, Inc., 1 N Dearborn St., Ste. 1700, Chicago, IL, 60602, USA, (312) 922-1115, (312) 922-1157, info-usa@euromonitor.com, https://www.euromonitor.com/; Geographies.

BHUTAN-LIVESTOCK

Palgrave Macmillan, 1 New York Plaza, Ste. 4500, New York, NY, 10004-1562, USA, (800) 777-4643, orders@palgrave.com, https://www.palgrave.com/us; The Statesman's Yearbook, 2023.

Routledge - Taylor & Francis Group, 6000 Broken Sound Pkwy. NW, Ste. 300, Boca Raton, FL, 33487, USA, (800) 634-1420, (800) 634-7064, orders@taylorandfrancis.com, https://www.routledge.com/; The Europa World Year Book 2022.

United Nations Food and Agricultural Organization (FAO), 2121 K St., Ste. 800B, Washington, DC, 20037, USA, (202) 653-2400 (Dial from U.S.), (202) 653-5760 (Fax from U.S.), fao-hq@fao.org, https://www.fao.org; The State of Food and Agriculture (SOFA) 2022.

United Nations Statistics Division (UNSD), United Nations Plz., New York, NY, 10017, USA, (800) 253-9646, (212) 963-9851, statistics@un.org, https://unstats.un.org; Statistical Yearbook of the United Nations 2021.

BHUTAN-MANPOWER

United Nations Economic and Social Commission for Asia and the Pacific (ESCAP), United Nations Building, Rajadamnern Nok Ave., Bangkok, 10200, THA, https://www.unescap.org/; SDG Gateway Data Explorer.

BHUTAN-MANUFACTURES

Asian Development Bank (ADB), 6 ADB Ave., Mandaluyong City, 1550, PHL, information@adb.org, https://www.adb.org/; Key Indicators for Asia and the Pacific 2022.

BHUTAN-MINERAL INDUSTRIES

Asian Development Bank (ADB), 6 ADB Ave., Mandaluyong City, 1550, PHL, information@adb.org, https://www.adb.org/; Key Indicators for Asia and the Pacific 2022.

Palgrave Macmillan, 1 New York Plaza, Ste. 4500, New York, NY, 10004-1562, USA, (800) 777-4643, orders@palgrave.com, https://www.palgrave.com/us; The Statesman's Yearbook, 2023.

Routledge - Taylor & Francis Group, 6000 Broken Sound Pkwy. NW, Ste. 300, Boca Raton, FL, 33487, USA, (800) 634-1420, (800) 634-7064, orders@taylorandfrancis.com, https://www.routledge.com/; The Europa World Year Book 2022.

United Nations Conference on Trade and Development (UNCTAD), Palais des Nations, Geneva, 1211, SWI, (212) 963-6896, unctadinfo@unctad.org, https://unctad.org; Trade and Development Report 2021.

The World Bank, 1818 H St. NW, Washington, DC, 20433, USA, (202) 473-1000, (202) 477-6391, eds03@worldbank.org, https://www.worldbank.org/; Bhutan (report).

BHUTAN-MONEY SUPPLY

The Economist Group: Economist Intelligence Unit (EIU), 900 3rd Ave., 16th Fl., New York, NY, 10022, USA, (212) 541-0500, americas@eiu.com, https://www.eiu.com; Bhutan Country Report.

Routledge - Taylor & Francis Group, 6000 Broken Sound Pkwy. NW, Ste. 300, Boca Raton, FL, 33487, USA, (800) 634-1420, (800) 634-7064, orders@taylorandfrancis.com, https://www.routledge.com/; The Europa World Year Book 2022.

The World Bank, 1818 H St. NW, Washington, DC, 20433, USA, (202) 473-1000, (202) 477-6391, eds03@worldbank.org, https://www.worldbank.org/; Bhutan (report).

BHUTAN-MORTALITY

UNICEF, 3 United Nations Plz., New York, NY, 10017, USA, (212) 303-7984, (917) 244-2215, https://www.unicef.org; The State of the World's Children 2023.

United Nations Economic and Social Commission for Asia and the Pacific (ESCAP), United Nations Building, Rajadamnern Nok Ave., Bangkok, 10200, THA, https://www.unescap.org/; Asia-Pacific Development Journal.

United Nations Statistics Division (UNSD), United Nations Plz., New York, NY, 10017, USA, (800) 253-9646, (212) 963-9851, statistics@un.org, https://unstats.un.org; Statistical Yearbook of the United Nations 2021 and World Statistics Pocketbook 2021.

BHUTAN-MOTION PICTURES

Palgrave Macmillan, 1 New York Plaza, Ste. 4500, New York, NY, 10004-1562, USA, (800) 777-4643, orders@palgrave.com, https://www.palgrave.com/us; The Statesman's Yearbook, 2023.

BHUTAN-NATURAL GAS PRODUCTION

See BHUTAN-MINERAL INDUSTRIES

BHUTAN-NUTRITION

Asian Development Bank (ADB), 6 ADB Ave., Mandaluyong City, 1550, PHL, information@adb.org, https://www.adb.org/; Key Indicators for Asia and the Pacific 2022.

United Nations Food and Agricultural Organization (FAO), 2121 K St., Ste. 800B, Washington, DC, 20037, USA, (202) 653-2400 (Dial from U.S.), (202) 653-5760 (Fax from U.S.), fao-hq@fao.org, https://www.fao.org; The State of Food and Agriculture (SOFA) 2022.

BHUTAN-PEANUT PRODUCTION

See BHUTAN-CROPS

BHUTAN-PESTICIDES

United Nations Food and Agricultural Organization (FAO), 2121 K St., Ste. 800B, Washington, DC,

20037, USA, (202) 653-2400 (Dial from U.S.), (202) 653-5760 (Fax from U.S.), fao-hq@fao.org, https://www.fao.org; The State of Food and Agriculture (SOFA) 2022.

BHUTAN-PETROLEUM INDUSTRY AND TRADE

Asian Development Bank (ADB), 6 ADB Ave., Mandaluyong City, 1550, PHL, information@adb.org, https://www.adb.org/; Key Indicators for Asia and the Pacific 2022.

U.S. Energy Information Administration (EIA), 1000 Independence Ave. SW, Washington, DC, 20585, USA, (202) 586-8800, infoctr@eia.gov, https://www.eia.gov; International Energy Outlook 2021.

United Nations Food and Agricultural Organization (FAO), 2121 K St., Ste. 800B, Washington, DC, 20037, USA, (202) 653-2400 (Dial from U.S.), (202) 653-5760 (Fax from U.S.), fao-hq@fao.org, https://www.fao.org; The State of Food and Agriculture (SOFA) 2022.

BHUTAN-POPULATION

Asian Development Bank (ADB), 6 ADB Ave., Mandaluyong City, 1550, PHL, information@adb.org, https://www.adb.org/; Key Indicators for Asia and the Pacific 2022.

Central Intelligence Agency (CIA), Office of Public Affairs, Washington, DC, 20505, USA, (703) 482-0623, https://www.cia.gov; The World Factbook.

The Economist Group: Economist Intelligence Unit (EIU), 900 3rd Ave., 16th Fl., New York, NY, 10022, USA, (212) 541-0500, americas@eiu.com, https://www.eiu.com; Bhutan Country Report.

Palgrave Macmillan, 1 New York Plaza, Ste. 4500, New York, NY, 10004-1562, USA, (800) 777-4643, orders@palgrave.com, https://www.palgrave.com/us; The Statesman's Yearbook, 2023.

Routledge - Taylor & Francis Group, 6000 Broken Sound Pkwy. NW, Ste. 300, Boca Raton, FL, 33487, USA, (800) 634-1420, (800) 634-7064, orders@taylorandfrancis.com, https://www.routledge.com/; The Europa World Year Book 2022.

UK Data Service, University of Essex, Wivenhoe Park, Colchester, Essex, CO4 3SQ, GBR, https://ukdataservice.ac.uk/; International Aggregate Data.

United Nations Department of Economic and Social Affairs (DESA), Population Division, 2 United Nations Plz., Rm. DC2-1950, New York, NY, 10017, USA, (212) 963-3209, (212) 963-2147, population@un.org, https://www.un.org/development/desa/pd/; Revision of World Urbanization Prospects and World Population Ageing 2020 Highlights.

United Nations Development Programme (UNDP), One United Nations Plz., New York, NY, 10017, USA, (212) 906-5000, (212) 906-5001, https://www.undp.org; Human Development Report 2021-2022.

United Nations Economic and Social Commission for Asia and the Pacific (ESCAP), United Nations Building, Rajadamnern Nok Ave., Bangkok, 10200, THA, https://www.unescap.org/; Asia-Pacific Development Journal and SDG Gateway Data Explorer.

United Nations Statistics Division (UNSD), United Nations Plz., New York, NY, 10017, USA, (800) 253-9646, (212) 963-9851, statistics@un.org, https://unstats.un.org; Statistical Yearbook of the United Nations 2021 and World Statistics Pocketbook 2021.

The World Bank, 1818 H St. NW, Washington, DC, 20433, USA, (202) 473-1000, (202) 477-6391, eds03@worldbank.org, https://www.worldbank.org/; Bhutan (report) and The Global Findex Database 2021.

BHUTAN-POPULATION DENSITY

Central Intelligence Agency (CIA), Office of Public Affairs, Washington, DC, 20505, USA, (703) 482-0623, https://www.cia.gov; The World Factbook.

Palgrave Macmillan, 1 New York Plaza, Ste. 4500, New York, NY, 10004-1562, USA, (800) 777-4643, orders@palgrave.com, https://www.palgrave.com/us; The Statesman's Yearbook, 2023.

Routledge - Taylor & Francis Group, 6000 Broken Sound Pkwy. NW, Ste. 300, Boca Raton, FL, 33487, USA, (800) 634-1420, (800) 634-7064, orders@taylorandfrancis.com, https://www.routledge.com/; The Europa World Year Book 2022.

The World Bank, 1818 H St. NW, Washington, DC, 20433, USA, (202) 473-1000, (202) 477-6391, eds03@worldbank.org, https://www.worldbank.org/; Bhutan (report).

BHUTAN-POSTAL SERVICE

Palgrave Macmillan, 1 New York Plaza, Ste. 4500, New York, NY, 10004-1562, USA, (800) 777-4643, orders@palgrave.com, https://www.palgrave.com/us; The Statesman's Yearbook, 2023.

BHUTAN-POWER RESOURCES

Euromonitor International, Inc., 1 N Dearborn St., Ste. 1700, Chicago, IL, 60602, USA, (312) 922-1115, (312) 922-1157, info-usa@euromonitor.com, https://www.euromonitor.com/; Geographies.

Palgrave Macmillan, 1 New York Plaza, Ste. 4500, New York, NY, 10004-1562, USA, (800) 777-4643, orders@palgrave.com, https://www.palgrave.com/us; The Statesman's Yearbook, 2023.

U.S. Energy Information Administration (EIA), 1000 Independence Ave. SW, Washington, DC, 20585, USA, (202) 586-8800, infoctr@eia.gov, https://www.eia.gov; International Energy Outlook 2021.

United Nations Economic and Social Commission for Asia and the Pacific (ESCAP), United Nations Building, Rajadamnern Nok Ave., Bangkok, 10200, THA, https://www.unescap.org/; Asia-Pacific Development Journal and SDG Gateway Data Explorer.

United Nations Food and Agricultural Organization (FAO), 2121 K St., Ste. 800B, Washington, DC, 20037, USA, (202) 653-2400 (Dial from U.S.), (202) 653-5760 (Fax from U.S.), fao-hq@fao.org, https://www.fao.org; The State of Food and Agriculture (SOFA) 2022.

United Nations Statistics Division (UNSD), United Nations Plz., New York, NY, 10017, USA, (800) 253-9646, (212) 963-9851, statistics@un.org, https://unstats.un.org; World Statistics Pocketbook 2021.

BHUTAN-PRICES

Asian Development Bank (ADB), 6 ADB Ave., Mandaluyong City, 1550, PHL, information@adb.org, https://www.adb.org/; Key Indicators for Asia and the Pacific 2022.

Euromonitor International, Inc., 1 N Dearborn St., Ste. 1700, Chicago, IL, 60602, USA, (312) 922-1115, (312) 922-1157, info-usa@euromonitor.com, https://www.euromonitor.com/; Geographies.

The World Bank, 1818 H St. NW, Washington, DC, 20433, USA, (202) 473-1000, (202) 477-6391, eds03@worldbank.org, https://www.worldbank.org/; Bhutan (report).

BHUTAN-PUBLIC HEALTH

Euromonitor International, Inc., 1 N Dearborn St., Ste. 1700, Chicago, IL, 60602, USA, (312) 922-1115, (312) 922-1157, info-usa@euromonitor.com, https://www.euromonitor.com/; Geographies.

Palgrave Macmillan, 1 New York Plaza, Ste. 4500, New York, NY, 10004-1562, USA, (800) 777-4643, orders@palgrave.com, https://www.palgrave.com/us; The Statesman's Yearbook, 2023.

U.S. Census Bureau, 4600 Silver Hill Rd., Washington, DC, 20233, USA, (301) 763-4636, (800) 923-8282, https://www.census.gov; HIV/AIDS Surveillance Data Base.

UNICEF, 3 United Nations Plz., New York, NY, 10017, USA, (212) 303-7984, (917) 244-2215, https://www.unicef.org; The State of the World's Children 2023.

United Nations Department of Economic and Social Affairs (DESA), Population Division, 2 United Nations Plz., Rm. DC2-1950, New York, NY, 10017, USA, (212) 963-3209, (212) 963-2147, population@un.org, https://www.un.org/development/desa/pd/; World Fertility Data 2019.

United Nations Development Programme (UNDP), One United Nations Plz., New York, NY, 10017, USA, (212) 906-5000, (212) 906-5001, https://www.undp.org; Human Development Report 2021-2022.

United Nations Economic and Social Commission for Asia and the Pacific (ESCAP), United Nations Building, Rajadamnern Nok Ave., Bangkok, 10200, THA, https://www.unescap.org/; Asia-Pacific Development Journal.

The World Bank, 1818 H St. NW, Washington, DC, 20433, USA, (202) 473-1000, (202) 477-6391, eds03@worldbank.org, https://www.worldbank.org/; Bhutan (report).

BHUTAN-RELIGION

Central Intelligence Agency (CIA), Office of Public Affairs, Washington, DC, 20505, USA, (703) 482-0623, https://www.cia.gov; The World Factbook.

Palgrave Macmillan, 1 New York Plaza, Ste. 4500, New York, NY, 10004-1562, USA, (800) 777-4643, orders@palgrave.com, https://www.palgrave.com/us; The Statesman's Yearbook, 2023.

BHUTAN-RETAIL TRADE

Euromonitor International, Inc., 1 N Dearborn St., Ste. 1700, Chicago, IL, 60602, USA, (312) 922-1115, (312) 922-1157, info-usa@euromonitor.com, https://www.euromonitor.com/; Geographies.

BHUTAN-RICE PRODUCTION

See BHUTAN-CROPS

BHUTAN-RUBBER INDUSTRY AND TRADE

International Rubber Study Group (IRSG), 51 Changi Business Park Central 2, Unit No. 6, 486066, SGP, https://www.rubberstudy.org; Monthly Rubber Bulletin (MRB); Rubber Industry Report; Rubber Statistical Bulletin; and World Rubber Industry Report (WRIO).

BHUTAN-STEEL PRODUCTION

See BHUTAN-MINERAL INDUSTRIES

BHUTAN-SUGAR PRODUCTION

See BHUTAN-CROPS

BHUTAN-TAXATION

The World Bank, 1818 H St. NW, Washington, DC, 20433, USA, (202) 473-1000, (202) 477-6391, eds03@worldbank.org, https://www.worldbank.org/; World Development Indicators (WDI) 2022.

BHUTAN-TOBACCO INDUSTRY

United Nations Statistics Division (UNSD), United Nations Plz., New York, NY, 10017, USA, (800) 253-9646, (212) 963-9851, statistics@un.org, https://unstats.un.org; Statistical Yearbook of the United Nations 2021.

BHUTAN-TOURISM

Euromonitor International, Inc., 1 N Dearborn St., Ste. 1700, Chicago, IL, 60602, USA, (312) 922-1115, (312) 922-1157, info-usa@euromonitor.com, https://www.euromonitor.com/; Geographies.

Palgrave Macmillan, 1 New York Plaza, Ste. 4500, New York, NY, 10004-1562, USA, (800) 777-4643, orders@palgrave.com, https://www.palgrave.com/us; The Statesman's Yearbook, 2023.

Routledge - Taylor & Francis Group, 6000 Broken Sound Pkwy. NW, Ste. 300, Boca Raton, FL, 33487, USA, (800) 634-1420, (800) 634-7064, orders@taylorandfrancis.com, https://www.routledge.com/; The Europa World Year Book 2022.

United Nations World Tourism Organization (UNWTO), Calle Poeta Joan Maragall 42, Madrid, 28020, SPA, info@unwto.org, https://www.unwto.org/; Yearbook of Tourism Statistics, 2021 Edition.

The World Bank, 1818 H St. NW, Washington, DC, 20433, USA, (202) 473-1000, (202) 477-6391, eds03@worldbank.org, https://www.worldbank.org/; Bhutan (report).

BHUTAN-TRADE

See BHUTAN-INTERNATIONAL TRADE

BHUTAN-TRANSPORTATION

Central Intelligence Agency (CIA), Office of Public Affairs, Washington, DC, 20505, USA, (703) 482-0623, https://www.cia.gov; The World Factbook.

Euromonitor International, Inc., 1 N Dearborn St., Ste. 1700, Chicago, IL, 60602, USA, (312) 922-1115, (312) 922-1157, info-usa@euromonitor.com, https://www.euromonitor.com/; Geographies.

Palgrave Macmillan, 1 New York Plaza, Ste. 4500, New York, NY, 10004-1562, USA, (800) 777-4643, orders@palgrave.com, https://www.palgrave.com/us; The Statesman's Yearbook, 2023.

Routledge - Taylor & Francis Group, 6000 Broken Sound Pkwy. NW, Ste. 300, Boca Raton, FL, 33487, USA, (800) 634-1420, (800) 634-7064, orders@taylorandfrancis.com, https://www.routledge.com/; The Europa World Year Book 2022.

United Nations Economic and Social Commission for Asia and the Pacific (ESCAP), United Nations Building, Rajadamnern Nok Ave., Bangkok, 10200, THA, https://www.unescap.org/; SDG Gateway Data Explorer.

The World Bank, 1818 H St. NW, Washington, DC, 20433, USA, (202) 473-1000, (202) 477-6391, eds03@worldbank.org, https://www.worldbank.org/; Bhutan (report).

BHUTAN-UNEMPLOYMENT

The World Bank, 1818 H St. NW, Washington, DC, 20433, USA, (202) 473-1000, (202) 477-6391, eds03@worldbank.org, https://www.worldbank.org/; Bhutan (report).

BHUTAN-VITAL STATISTICS

Palgrave Macmillan, 1 New York Plaza, Ste. 4500, New York, NY, 10004-1562, USA, (800) 777-4643, orders@palgrave.com, https://www.palgrave.com/us; The Statesman's Yearbook, 2023.

U.S. Census Bureau, 4600 Silver Hill Rd., Washington, DC, 20233, USA, (301) 763-4636, (800) 923-8282, https://www.census.gov; HIV/AIDS Surveillance Data Base.

United Nations Department of Economic and Social Affairs (DESA), Population Division, 2 United Nations Plz., Rm. DC2-1950, New York, NY, 10017, USA, (212) 963-3209, (212) 963-2147, population@un.org, https://www.un.org/development/desa/pd/; World Contraceptive Use 2021: Estimates and Projections of Family Planning Indicators and World Marriage Data 2019.

BHUTAN-WAGES

United Nations Economic and Social Commission for Asia and the Pacific (ESCAP), United Nations Building, Rajadamnern Nok Ave., Bangkok, 10200, THA, https://www.unescap.org/; SDG Gateway Data Explorer.

The World Bank, 1818 H St. NW, Washington, DC, 20433, USA, (202) 473-1000, (202) 477-6391, eds03@worldbank.org, https://www.worldbank.org/; Bhutan (report).

BHUTAN-WEATHER

See BHUTAN-CLIMATE

BHUTAN-WHEAT PRODUCTION

See BHUTAN-CROPS

BHUTAN-WOOL PRODUCTION

See BHUTAN-TEXTILE INDUSTRY

BIAS CRIMES

See HATE CRIMES

BICYCLE SHARING PROGRAMS

Mineta Transportation Institute (MTI), San Jose State University Research Foundation, 210 N 4th St., 4th Fl., San Jose, CA, 95112, USA, (408) 924-7560, (408) 924-7565, mineta-institute@sjsu.edu, https://transweb.sjsu.edu/; Examining the Effects of a Bike and E-Bike Lending Program on Commuting Behavior.

University of California Davis, Institute of Transportation Studies (ITS-Davis), 1605 Tilia St., Davis, CA, 95616, USA, (530) 752-6548, kcswayze@ucdavis.edu, https://its.ucdavis.edu; Investigating the Influence of Dockless Electric Bike-share on Travel Behavior, Attitudes, Health, and Equity.

BICYCLES

Insurance Institute for Highway Safety/Highway Loss Data Institute (IIHS/HLDI), 4121 Wilson Blvd., 6th Fl., Arlington, VA, 22203, USA, (703) 247-1500, (434) 985 4600, cmatthew@iihs.org, https://www.iihs.org/; Fatality Facts 2021: Yearly Snapshot.

Mineta Transportation Institute (MTI), San Jose State University Research Foundation, 210 N 4th St., 4th Fl., San Jose, CA, 95112, USA, (408) 924-7560, (408) 924-7565, mineta-institute@sjsu.edu, https://transweb.sjsu.edu/; Examining the Effects of a Bike and E-Bike Lending Program on Commuting Behavior.

National Highway Traffic Safety Administration (NHTSA), National Center for Statistics and Analysis (NCSA), 1200 New Jersey Ave. SE, West Bldg., Washington, DC, 20590, USA, (800) 934-8517, (202) 366-2746, ncsarequests@dot.gov, https://www.nhtsa.gov/research-data/national-center-statistics-and-analysis-ncsa; Traffic Safety Facts, 2020 Data - Bicyclists and Other Cyclists.

National Sporting Goods Association (NSGA), 3041 Woodcreek Dr., Ste. 210, Downers Grove, IL, 60515, USA, (847) 296-6742, (847) 391-9827, info@nsga.org, https://www.nsga.org; Sports Participation in the United States 2022 and Sports Participation: Historical Sports Participation 2022.

Oxford University Centre for the Environment, Centre for Research into Energy Demand Solutions (CREDS), South Parks Rd., Oxford, OX1 3QY, GBR, credsadmin@ouce.ox.ac.uk, https://www.creds.ac.uk; E-bike Carbon Savings - How Much and Where?.

PeopleForBikes, PO Box 2359, Boulder, CO, 80306, USA, (303) 449-4893, info@peopleforbikes.org, https://www.peopleforbikes.org; COVID Participation Study and Statistics Library.

Stats Perform, 203 N LaSalle St., Ste. 2350, Chicago, IL, 60601, USA, (866) 221-1426, https://www.statsperform.com/; unpublished data.

University of California Davis, Institute of Transportation Studies (ITS-Davis), 1605 Tilia St., Davis, CA, 95616, USA, (530) 752-6548, kcswayze@ucdavis.edu, https://its.ucdavis.edu; Investigating the Influence of Dockless Electric Bike-share on Travel Behavior, Attitudes, Health, and Equity.

Worldometer, https://www.worldometers.info/; Worldometers.info.

BICYCLES-THEFT

U.S. Department of Justice (DOJ), Federal Bureau of Investigation (FBI), 935 Pennsylvania Ave. NW, Washington, DC, 20535-0001, USA, (202) 324-3000, https://www.fbi.gov/; Crime in the United States 2019.

BICYCLISTS

European Cyclists' Federation (ECF), Rue de la Charite, 22, Brussels, B-1210, BEL, office@ecf.com, https://www.ecf.com; Cyclists Love Trains - An Analysis of the Bicycle Friendliness of European Railway Operators.

League of American Bicyclists, 1612 K St. NW, Ste. 1102, Washington, DC, 20006, USA, (202) 822-1333, communications@bikeleague.org, https://bikeleague.org/; Bicycling & Walking in the United States: Benchmarking Progress.

BILLIARDS

National Sporting Goods Association (NSGA), 3041 Woodcreek Dr., Ste. 210, Downers Grove, IL, 60515, USA, (847) 296-6742, (847) 391-9827, info@nsga.org, https://www.nsga.org; Sports Participation in the United States 2022 and Sports Participation: Historical Sports Participation 2022.

BILLIONAIRES

Bloomberg, 731 Lexington Ave., New York, NY, 10022, USA, (212) 318-2000, https://www.bloomberg.com/; Bloomberg Billionaires Index.

Forbes, Inc., 499 Washington Blvd., Jersey City, NJ, 07310, USA, (800) 295-0893, https://www.forbes.com; Forbes Billionaires 2022: The Richest People In The World.

BIODEGRADABLE PLASTICS

The 5 Gyres Institute, PO Box 5699, Santa Monica, CA, 90409, USA, info@5gyres.org, https://www.5gyres.org/; Plastic & Climate Change: The Hidden Costs of a Plastic Planet and Understanding Microplastic Levels, Pathways, and Transport in the San Francisco Bay Region.

BIODEGRADABLE PRODUCTS

The 5 Gyres Institute, PO Box 5699, Santa Monica, CA, 90409, USA, info@5gyres.org, https://www.5gyres.org/; Plastic & Climate Change: The Hidden Costs of a Plastic Planet and Understanding Microplastic Levels, Pathways, and Transport in the San Francisco Bay Region.

BIODIESEL FUELS

Clean Fuels Alliance America, PO Box 104898, Jefferson City, MO, 65110-4898, USA, (573) 635-3893, (800) 841-5849, info@cleanfuels.org, https://www.biodiesel.org/; Clean Fuels Bulletin.

U.S. Department of Energy (DOE), Office of Energy Efficiency and Renewable Energy (EERE), Alternative Fuels Data Center (AFDC), Mail Stop EE-1, Washington, DC, 20585, USA, (202) 586-5000, https://www.afdc.energy.gov/; Clean Cities and Fuels & Infrastructure.

BIODIVERSITY

Centro del Agua del Tropico Humedo para America Latina y el Caribe (CATHALAC) (Water Center for the Humid Tropics of Latin America and the Caribbean), Ciudad del Saber , Edificio 111, Panama, 0843-03102, PAN, (507) 317-3200, cathalac@cathalac.int, https://cathalac.int/; unpublished data.

National Audubon Society, 225 Varick St., New York, NY, 10014, USA, (212) 979-3196, (844) 428-3826, customerservice@audubon.org, https://www.audubon.org/; Annual Summaries of the Christmas Bird Count, 1901-Present.

Natural England, County Hall, Spetchley Rd., Worcester, WR5 2NP, GBR, enquiries@naturalengland.org.uk, https://www.gov.uk/government/organisations/natural-england; Access to Evidence Catalogue.

United Nations Intergovernmental Science-Policy Platform on Biodiversity and Ecosystem Services (IPBES), Platz der Vereinten Nationen 1, 10th Fl., Bonn, D-53113, GER, secretariat@ipbes.net, https://www.ipbes.net/; Global Assessment Report on Biodiversity and Ecosystem Services.

World Wildlife Fund (WWF), 1250 24th St. NW, Washington, DC, 20037-1193, USA, (202) 495-4800, (202) 495-4211, https://wwf.panda.org/; Living Planet Report 2022.

BIOLOGY

American Association for the Advancement of Science (AAAS), 1200 New York Ave. NW, Washington, DC, 20005, USA, (202) 326-6400, https://www.aaas.org; Science; Science Advances; and Science Signaling.

Elsevier, Radarweg 29, Amsterdam, 1043 NX, NLD, https://www.elsevier.com; ScienceDirect.

SAGE Publications, 2455 Teller Rd., Thousand Oaks, CA, 91320, USA, (800) 818-7243, (800) 583-2665, journals@sagepub.com, https://www.sagepub.com; Experimental Biology and Medicine.

U.S. Department of Health and Human Services (HHS), National Toxicology Program (NTP), PO Box 12233, MD K2-03, Research Triangle Park, NC, 27709, USA, (984) 287-3209, cdm@niehs.nih.gov, https://ntp.niehs.nih.gov; Chemical Effects in Biological Systems (CEBS).

U.S. Department of Health and Human Services (HHS), U.S. National Library of Medicine (NLM), National Center for Biotechnology Information (NCBI), 8600 Rockville Pike, Bethesda, MD, 20894, USA, info@ncbi.nlm.nih.gov, https://www.ncbi.nlm.nih.gov; BioProject.

World Wildlife Fund (WWF), 1250 24th St. NW, Washington, DC, 20037-1193, USA, (202) 495-4800, (202) 495-4211, https://wwf.panda.org/; Living Planet Report 2022.

Zoological Society of London (ZSL), Outer Circle, Regent's Park, London, NW1 4RY, GBR, generalenquiries@zsl.org, https://www.zsl.org/; Animal Conservation; International Zoo Yearbook; and Journal of Zoology.

BIOTECHNOLOGY

American Association for the Advancement of Science (AAAS), 1200 New York Ave. NW, Washington, DC, 20005, USA, (202) 326-6400, https://www.aaas.org; Science Robotics.

International Food Information Council Foundation (IFIC), 1100 Connecticut Ave. NW, Ste. 430, Washington, DC, 20036, USA, (202) 296-6540, info@foodinsight.org, https://foodinsight.org/; Food Insight.

U.S. Department of Health and Human Services (HHS), U.S. National Library of Medicine (NLM), National Center for Biotechnology Information (NCBI), 8600 Rockville Pike, Bethesda, MD, 20894, USA, info@ncbi.nlm.nih.gov, https://www.ncbi.nlm.nih.gov; BioProject.

BIRDS

Center for Biological Diversity, PO Box 710, Tucson, AZ, 85702-0710, USA, (520) 623-5252, (866) 357-3349, (520) 623-9797, center@biologicaldiversity.org, https://www.biologicaldiversity.org/; Endangered Earth Online.

Global Penguin Society (GPS), 209 Mississippi St., San Francisco, CA, 94107, USA, (415) 202-6380 , info@globalpenguinsociety.org, https://www.globalpenguinsociety.org/; Learn About Penguins.

Gulf Coast Ecosystem Restoration Council, 500 Poydras St., Ste. 1117, New Orleans, LA, 70130, USA, (504) 717-7235, restorecouncil@restorethegulf.gov, https://www.restorethegulf.gov/; RESTORE Council - 10 Year Commemoration Report.

National Audubon Society, 225 Varick St., New York, NY, 10014, USA, (212) 979-3196, (844) 428-3826, customerservice@audubon.org, https://www.audubon.org/; Annual Summaries of the Christmas Bird Count, 1901-Present.

BIRTH CONTROL

Guttmacher Institute, 125 Maiden Ln., 7th Fl., New York, NY, 10038, USA, (212) 248-1111, (800) 355-0244, (212) 248-1951, info@guttmacher.org, https://www.guttmacher.org/; Contraceptive Use in the United States; Data Center; and Unintended Pregnancy in the United States.

National Organization for Women (NOW), 1100 H St. NW, Ste. 300, Washington, DC, 20005, USA, (202) 628-8669, (202) 331-9002 (TTY), https://now.org/; unpublished data.

U.S. Department of Health and Human Services, Centers for Disease Control and Prevention (CDC), National Center for Health Statistics (NCHS), 3311 Toledo Rd., Hyattsville, MD, 20782-2064, USA, (800) 232-4636, (301) 458-4000, https://www.cdc.gov/nchs; FastStats - Statistics by Topic and National Survey of Family Growth (NSFG).

United Nations Department of Economic and Social Affairs (DESA), Population Division, 2 United Nations Plz., Rm. DC2-1950, New York, NY, 10017, USA, (212) 963-3209, (212) 963-2147, population@un.org, https://www.un.org/development/desa/pd/; Family Planning Indicators: Estimates and Projections of Family Planning Indicators 2022; World Contraceptive Use 2021: Estimates and Projections of Family Planning Indicators; World Family Planning 2022; and World Fertility and Family Planning 2020.

World Resources Institute (WRI), 10 G St. NE, Ste. 800, Washington, DC, 20002, USA, (202) 729-7600, (202) 280-1314, https://www.wri.org/; World Resources Report (WRR): Creating a Sustainable Food Future.

BIRTH WEIGHTS

Bernan Press, 15250 NBN Way, Bldg. C, Blue Ridge Summit, PA, 17214, USA, (301) 459-2255, (800) 865-3457, (800) 865-3450, customercare@bernan.com, https://rowman.com/Page/Bernan; Vital Statistics of the United States 2022: Births, Life Expectancy, Deaths, and Selected Health Data.

March of Dimes Perinatal Data Center (PeriStats), 1550 Crystal Dr., Ste. 1300, Arlington, VA, 22202, USA, (888) 663-4637, https://www.marchofdimes.org/peristats; PeriStats.

U.S. Department of Health and Human Services, Centers for Disease Control and Prevention (CDC), National Center for Health Statistics (NCHS), 3311 Toledo Rd., Hyattsville, MD, 20782-2064, USA, (800) 232-4636, (301) 458-4000, https://www.cdc.gov/nchs; National Vital Statistics Reports (NVSR) and Vital Statistics Online Data Portal.

BISEXUAL/LGBTQ PEOPLE-IDENTITY

The Gallup Organization, 901 F St. NW, Washington, DC, 20004, USA, (202) 715-3030, (800) 204-1192, (202) 715-3045, https://www.gallup.com; LGBT Identification in U.S. Ticks Up to 7.1%.

Human Rights Campaign (HRC), 1640 Rhode Island Ave. NW, Washington, DC, 20036-3278, USA, (202) 628-4160, (202) 216-1572 (TTY), (202) 347-5323, feedback@hrc.org, https://www.hrc.org/; A Workplace Divided: Understanding the Climate for LGBTQ Workers Nationwide.

University of California Los Angeles (UCLA) School of Law, The Williams Institute, 1060 Veteran Ave., Ste. 134, PO Box 957092, Los Angeles, CA, 90095-7092, USA, (310) 267-4382, (310) 825-7270, williamsinstitute@law.ucla.edu, https://williamsinstitute.law.ucla.edu/; Nonbinary LGBTQ Adults in the United States.

BISEXUAL/LGBTQ PEOPLE-LEGAL STATUS, LAWS, ETC.

The Henry J. Kaiser Family Foundation (KFF), 185 Berry St., Ste. 2000, San Francisco, CA, 94107, USA, (650) 854-9400, (650) 854-4800, https://www.kff.org; Majorities Support Policies Banning Discrimination Against LGBTQ Individuals' Health Care Access.

Movement Advancement Project (MAP), 1905 15th St., No. 1097, Boulder, CO, 80301-1097, USA, (303) 578-4600, info@lgbtmap.org, https://www.lgbtmap.org/; Mapping LGBTQ Equality: 2010 to 2020 and Snapshot: LGBTQ Equality by State.

Public Religion Research Institute (PRRI), 1023 15th St. NW, 9th Fl., Washington, DC, 20005, USA, (202) 238-9424, info@prri.org, https://www.prri.org/; Americans' Support for Key LGBTQ Rights Continues to Tick Upward.

BISEXUAL/LGBTQ PEOPLE

See also SEXUAL MINORITIES and LGBTQ+ PEOPLE

Community Marketing & Insights (CMI), 611 S Palm Canyon Dr., Nos. 7-244, Palm Springs, CA, 92264, USA, (415) 343-4656, info@cmi.info, https://cmi.info/; LGBTQ Consumer Products Survey 2019 Report; LGBTQ Health Survey Report 2019; and 16th Annual LGBT Community Survey.

GLAAD, USA, rferraro@glaad.org, https://www.glaad.org/; Accelerating Acceptance 2021; Social Media Safety Index (SMSI); and Where We Are on TV Report 2021-2022.

Recovery Research Institute (RRI), 151 Merrimac St., 6th Fl., Boston, MA, 02114, USA, https://www.recoveryanswers.org/; Sexual Minorities and Women Veterans Die Younger than Straight Veterans Due to Alcohol Use.

U.S. Department of Health and Human Services, Centers for Disease Control and Prevention (CDC), 1600 Clifton Rd., Atlanta, GA, 30329-4027, USA, (800) 232-4636, (888) 232-6348 (TTY), cdcinfo@cdc.gov, https://www.cdc.gov; Sexual Orientation Disparities in Risk Factors for Adverse COVID-19-Related Outcomes, by Race/Ethnicity - Behavioral Risk Factor Surveillance System, United States, 2017-2019.

University of California Los Angeles (UCLA) School of Law, The Williams Institute, 1060 Veteran Ave., Ste. 134, PO Box 957092, Los Angeles, CA, 90095-7092, USA, (310) 267-4382, (310) 825-7270, williamsinstitute@law.ucla.edu, https://williamsinstitute.law.ucla.edu/; LGBT Poverty in the United States: A Study of Differences Between Sexual Orientation and Gender Identity Groups; LGBTQ People in the US: Select Findings from the Generations and TransPop Studies; and Sexual Orientation Change Efforts, Adverse Childhood Experiences, and Suicide Ideation and Attempt Among Sexual Minority Adults: United States.

BISEXUAL/LGBTQ PEOPLE-VIOLENCE AGAINST

California State University San Bernardino, Center for the Study of Hate and Extremism, 5500 University Pkwy., San Bernardino, CA, 92407, USA, (909) 537-7503, (909) 537-7711, blevin8@aol.com, https://csbs.csusb.edu/hate-and-extremism-center; Report to the Nation: Factbook on Hate and Extremism in the U.S. and Internationally; Report to the Nation: Illustrated Almanac; Report to the Nation: Visual Almanac 2020 Preview, with the Latest FBI/DHS Data; and Special Status Report: Hate Crime in the U.S. 1992-2016.

National Coalition of Anti-Violence Programs (NCAVP), 116 Nassau St., 3rd Fl., New York, NY, 10038, USA, (212) 714-1184, ecruz@avp.org, https://avp.org/ncavp/; Pride and Pain: A Snapshot of Anti-LGBTQ Hate and Violence During Pride Season 2019 and Supporting LGBTQ Survivors of Violence During the COVID-19 Pandemic.

V-Day, 4104 24th St., No. 4515, San Francisco, CA, 94114, USA, (212) 645-8329, info@vday.org, https://www.vday.org/; unpublished data.

BISEXUAL/LGBTQ TEENAGERS

The Trevor Project, PO Box 69232, West Hollywood, CA, 90069, USA, (212) 695-8650, info@thetrevorproject.org, https://www.thetrevorproject.org/; Facts About LGBTQ Youth Suicide and 2022 National Survey on LGBTQ Youth Mental Health.

University of California Los Angeles (UCLA) School of Law, The Williams Institute, 1060 Veteran Ave., Ste. 134, PO Box 957092, Los Angeles, CA, 90095-7092, USA, (310) 267-4382, (310) 825-7270, williamsinstitute@law.ucla.edu, https://williamsinstitute.law.ucla.edu/; LGBT 'Dreamers' and Deferred Action for Childhood Arrivals (DACA).

BISEXUAL/LGBTQ YOUTH

The Trevor Project, PO Box 69232, West Hollywood, CA, 90069, USA, (212) 695-8650, info@thetrevorproject.org, https://www.thetrevorproject.org/; Facts About LGBTQ Youth Suicide and 2022 National Survey on LGBTQ Youth Mental Health.

University of California Los Angeles (UCLA) School of Law, The Williams Institute, 1060 Veteran Ave., Ste. 134, PO Box 957092, Los Angeles, CA, 90095-7092, USA, (310) 267-4382, (310) 825-7270, williamsinstitute@law.ucla.edu, https://williamsinstitute.law.ucla.edu/; LGBT 'Dreamers' and Deferred Action for Childhood Arrivals (DACA).

BISEXUALITY

Indiana University, Kinsey Institute, 150 S Woodlawn Ave., Lindley Hall 428, Bloomington, IN, 47405, USA, (812) 855-7686, (812) 855-3058, kinsey@indiana.edu, https://kinseyinstitute.org; FAQs & Sex Information.

BISMUTH

U.S. Department of the Interior (DOI), U.S. Geological Survey (USGS), National Minerals Information Center (NMIC), 12201 Sunrise Valley Dr., Reston, VA, 20192, USA, (703) 648-4920, (703) 648-7971, (703) 648-4995, sfortier@usgs.gov, https://www.usgs.gov/centers/nmic; Mineral Commodity Summaries 2022 and Mineral Industry Surveys (MIS).

BITCOIN

Greenpeace, 1300 I St. NW, Ste. 1100 E, Washington, DC, 20001, USA, (800) 722-6995, (202) 462-1177, (202) 462-4507, connect@greenpeace.us, https://www.greenpeace.org; Financial Institutions Need to Support a Code Change to Cleanup Bitcoin.

Thomson Reuters, 3 Times Square, New York, NY, 10036, USA, (646) 540-3000, general.info@thomsonreuters.com, https://thomsonreuters.com/; Cryptos on the Rise 2022.

BLACK LIVES MATTER MOVEMENT

The Brookings Institution, 1775 Massachusetts Ave. NW, Washington, DC, 20036, USA, (202) 797-6000, communications@brookings.edu, https://www.brookings.edu/; Three Million More Guns: The Spring 2020 Spike in Firearm Sales.

Civiqs, PO Box 70008, Oakland, CA, 94612, USA, (510) 394-5664, inquiries@civiqs.com, https://civiqs.com/; Poll: Do You Support or Oppose the Black Lives Matter Movement?.

Civis Analytics, 200 W Monroe St., 22nd Fl., Chicago, IL, 60606, USA, https://www.civisanalytics.com/; BLM and Policing Survey Identifies Broad Support for Common-Sense Reform.

The Henry J. Kaiser Family Foundation (KFF), 185 Berry St., Ste. 2000, San Francisco, CA, 94107, USA, (650) 854-9400, (650) 854-4800, https://www.kff.org; KFF Health Tracking Poll: Racial Disparities and Protests.

Ipsos, 360 Park Ave. S, 17th Fl., New York, NY, 10010, USA, (212) 265-3200, https://www.ipsos.com/en-us; Poll: Black Americans Wholly Support Protest Movement, But Optimism for Change Is Muted.

Major Cities Chiefs Association (MCCA), PO Box 71690, Salt Lake City, UT, 84171, USA, (801) 209-1815, patricia@majorcitieschiefs.com, https://majorcitieschiefs.com/; MCCA Report on the 2020 Protest and Civil Unrest.

Pew Research Center, 1615 L St. NW, Ste. 800, Washington, DC, 20036, USA, (202) 419-4300, (202) 857-8562, info@pewresearch.org, https://www.pewresearch.org/; Younger Adults Differ from Older Ones in Perceptions of News about COVID-19, George Floyd Protests.

Pew Research Center, Internet & Technology, 1615 L St. NW, Ste. 800, Washington, DC, 20036, USA, (202) 419-4300, (202) 857-8562, https://www.pewresearch.org/topic/internet-technology/; Activism in the Social Media Age.

BLACK LUNG BENEFIT PROGRAM

Social Security Administration (SSA), Office of Public Inquiries and Communications Support, 1100 W High Rise, 6401 Security Blvd., Baltimore, MD, 21235, USA, (800) 772-1213, (800) 325-0778 (TTY), https://www.ssa.gov; Social Security Bulletin.

BLACK POPULATION

The Gallup Organization, 901 F St. NW, Washington, DC, 20004, USA, (202) 715-3030, (800) 204-1192, (202) 715-3045, https://www.gallup.com; New Low: 35% in U.S. Satisfied With Treatment of Black People.

Pew Research Center, 1615 L St. NW, Ste. 800, Washington, DC, 20036, USA, (202) 419-4300, (202) 857-8562, info@pewresearch.org, https://www.pewresearch.org/; Black Muslims Account for a Fifth of All U.S. Muslims, and About Half Are Converts to Islam and Many Black and Asian Americans Say They Have Experienced Discrimination Amid the COVID-19 Outbreak.

Pew Research Center, Politics & Policy, 1615 L St. NW, Ste. 800, Washington, DC, 20036, USA, (202) 419-4300, (202) 857-8562, https://www.pewresearch.org/topic/politics-policy/; Ten Facts About Black Republicans.

U.S. Census Bureau, 4600 Silver Hill Rd., Washington, DC, 20233, USA, (301) 763-4636, (800) 923-8282, https://www.census.gov; Explore Census Data and United States QuickFacts.

BLACK POPULATION-ABORTION

Guttmacher Institute, 125 Maiden Ln., 7th Fl., New York, NY, 10038, USA, (212) 248-1111, (800) 355-0244, (212) 248-1951, info@guttmacher.org, https://www.guttmacher.org/; Even Before Roe Was Overturned, Nearly One in 10 People Obtaining an Abortion Traveled Across State Lines for Care.

BLACK POPULATION-ACTIVITY LIMITATION

U.S. Department of Health and Human Services, Centers for Disease Control and Prevention (CDC), National Center for Health Statistics (NCHS), 3311 Toledo Rd., Hyattsville, MD, 20782-2064, USA, (800) 232-4636, (301) 458-4000, https://www.cdc.gov/nchs; Health, United States, 2020-2021.

BLACK POPULATION-ADULT EDUCATION

U.S. Department of Education (ED), Institute of Education Sciences (IES), National Center for Education Statistics (NCES), Potomac Center Plaza, 550 12th St. SW, Washington, DC, 20202, USA, (202) 403-5551, https://nces.ed.gov/; The National Household Education Surveys Program (NHES) Data.

BLACK POPULATION-AIDS

U.S. Department of Health and Human Services, Centers for Disease Control and Prevention (CDC), 1600 Clifton Rd., Atlanta, GA, 30329-4027, USA, (800) 232-4636, (888) 232-6348 (TTY), cdcinfo@cdc.gov, https://www.cdc.gov; HIV Surveillance Reports.

BLACK POPULATION-BUSINESS OWNERS

U.S. Census Bureau, 4600 Silver Hill Rd., Washington, DC, 20233, USA, (301) 763-4636, (800) 923-8282, https://www.census.gov; Survey of Business Owners (SBO).

BLACK POPULATION-CANCER

American Cancer Society (ACS), 3380 Chastain Meadows Pkwy NW, Ste. 200, Kennesaw, GA, 30144, USA, (800) 227-2345, https://www.cancer.org; Cancer Facts & Figures 2023 and Cancer Facts & Figures for African American/Black People 2022-2024.

Bernan Press, 15250 NBN Way, Bldg. C, Blue Ridge Summit, PA, 17214, USA, (301) 459-2255, (800) 865-3457, (800) 865-3450, customercare@bernan.com, https://rowman.com/Page/Bernan; Vital Statistics of the United States 2022: Births, Life Expectancy, Deaths, and Selected Health Data.

U.S. Department of Health and Human Services (HHS), National Institutes of Health (NIH), National Cancer Institute (NCI), 9609 Medical Center Dr., Bethesda, MD, 20850, USA, (800) 422-6237, nciinfo@nih.gov, https://www.cancer.gov; Annual Report to the Nation on the Status of Cancer and Surveillance, Epidemiology, and End Results (SEER) Incidence Data, 1975-2020.

U.S. Department of Health and Human Services, Centers for Disease Control and Prevention (CDC), National Center for Health Statistics (NCHS), 3311 Toledo Rd., Hyattsville, MD, 20782-2064, USA, (800) 232-4636, (301) 458-4000, https://www.cdc.gov/nchs; National Vital Statistics Reports (NVSR) and Vital Statistics Online Data Portal.

BLACK POPULATION-CHILD CARE

U.S. Department of Education (ED), Institute of Education Sciences (IES), National Center for Education Statistics (NCES), Potomac Center Plaza, 550 12th St. SW, Washington, DC, 20202, USA, (202) 403-5551, https://nces.ed.gov/; Digest of Education Statistics, 2020.

BLACK POPULATION-CHILDBIRTH-STATISTICS

Bernan Press, 15250 NBN Way, Bldg. C, Blue Ridge Summit, PA, 17214, USA, (301) 459-2255, (800) 865-3457, (800) 865-3450, customercare@bernan.com, https://rowman.com/Page/Bernan; Vital Statistics of the United States 2022: Births, Life Expectancy, Deaths, and Selected Health Data.

Guttmacher Institute, 125 Maiden Ln., 7th Fl., New York, NY, 10038, USA, (212) 248-1111, (800) 355-0244, (212) 248-1951, info@guttmacher.org, https://www.guttmacher.org/; Adolescent Sexual and Reproductive Health in the United States.

U.S. Department of Health and Human Services, Centers for Disease Control and Prevention (CDC), National Center for Health Statistics (NCHS), 3311 Toledo Rd., Hyattsville, MD, 20782-2064, USA, (800) 232-4636, (301) 458-4000, https://www.cdc.gov/nchs; National Vital Statistics Reports (NVSR) and Vital Statistics Online Data Portal.

BLACK POPULATION-CHILDREN UNDER EIGHTEEN YEARS OLD

Federal Interagency Forum on Child and Family Statistics (The Forum), USA, childstats@ed.gov, https://www.childstats.gov; America's Children: Key National Indicators of Well-Being, 2021.

University of Chicago, Center for the Study of Race, Politics and Culture, Black Youth Project, 5733 S University Ave., Chicago, IL, 60637, USA, info@blackyouthproject.com, https://www.blackyouthproject.com/; GenForward Survey 2022.

BLACK POPULATION-CHILDREN UNDER EIGHTEEN YEARS OLD-POVERTY

Bank Street Graduate School of Education, National Center for Children in Poverty (NCCP), 475 Riverside Dr., Ste. 1400, New York, NY, 10115, USA, info@nccp.org, https://www.nccp.org/; 50-State Demographics Data Generator.

Children's Defense Fund (CDF), 840 1st St. NE, Ste. 300, Washington, DC, 20002, USA, (202) 628-8787, cdfinfo@childrensdefense.org, https://www.childrensdefense.org/; Ending Child Poverty Now and The State of America's Children 2021.

BLACK POPULATION-CIGARETTE SMOKING

U.S. Department of Health and Human Services, Centers for Disease Control and Prevention (CDC), National Center for Health Statistics (NCHS), 3311 Toledo Rd., Hyattsville, MD, 20782-2064, USA, (800) 232-4636, (301) 458-4000, https://www.cdc.gov/nchs; Health, United States, 2020-2021.

BLACK POPULATION-CITIES

U.S. Census Bureau, 4600 Silver Hill Rd., Washington, DC, 20233, USA, (301) 763-4636, (800) 923-8282, https://www.census.gov; Explore Census Data and United States QuickFacts.

BLACK POPULATION-COHABITATION EXPERIENCE

U.S. Department of Health and Human Services, Centers for Disease Control and Prevention (CDC), National Center for Health Statistics (NCHS), 3311 Toledo Rd., Hyattsville, MD, 20782-2064, USA, (800) 232-4636, (301) 458-4000, https://www.cdc.gov/nchs; National Survey of Family Growth (NSFG).

BLACK POPULATION-COMPUTER USE

U.S. Department of Education (ED), Institute of Education Sciences (IES), National Center for Education Statistics (NCES), Potomac Center Plaza, 550 12th St. SW, Washington, DC, 20202, USA, (202) 403-5551, https://nces.ed.gov/; Digest of Education Statistics, 2020.

BLACK POPULATION-CONGRESS, MEMBERS OF

U.S. Government Publishing Office (GPO),, 732 N Capitol St. NW, Washington, DC, 20401-0001, USA, (202) 512-1800, (866) 512-1800, (202) 512-2104, contactcenter@gpo.gov, https://www.gpo.gov/; Congressional Directory.

BLACK POPULATION-CONSUMER EXPENDITURES

EnsembleIQ, 8550 W Bryn Mawr Ave., Ste. 200, Chicago, IL, 60631, USA, (877) 687-7321, https://ensembleiq.com/; 2021 Consumer Expenditures Report.

NielsenIQ (NIQ), 200 W Jackson Blvd., Chicago, IL, 60606, USA, https://nielseniq.com; Multicultural Consumers Are Set to Drive Beauty Growth Amid Continued Category Shifts in 2021.

U.S. Department of Labor (DOL), Bureau of Labor Statistics (BLS), Postal Square Bldg., 2 Massachusetts Ave. NE, Washington, DC, 20212-0001, USA, (202) 691-5200, (202) 691-7890, blsdata_staff@bls.gov, https://www.bls.gov; Consumer Expenditure Survey (CE).

University of Georgia, Terry College of Business, Selig Center for Economic Growth, E201 Ivester Hall, 650 S Lumpkin St., Athens, GA, 30602, USA, (706) 425-9782, jhumphre@uga.edu, https://www.terry.uga.edu/about/selig//; The Multicultural Economy 2021.

BLACK POPULATION-CONTRACEPTIVE USE

Guttmacher Institute, 125 Maiden Ln., 7th Fl., New York, NY, 10038, USA, (212) 248-1111, (800) 355-0244, (212) 248-1951, info@guttmacher.org, https://www.guttmacher.org/; Contraceptive Use in the United States.

U.S. Department of Health and Human Services, Centers for Disease Control and Prevention (CDC), National Center for Health Statistics (NCHS), 3311 Toledo Rd., Hyattsville, MD, 20782-2064, USA, (800) 232-4636, (301) 458-4000, https://www.cdc.gov/nchs; National Survey of Family Growth (NSFG).

BLACK POPULATION-CRIMES AGAINST

Human Rights Campaign (HRC), 1640 Rhode Island Ave. NW, Washington, DC, 20036-3278, USA, (202) 628-4160, (202) 216-1572 (TTY), (202) 347-5323, feedback@hrc.org, https://www.hrc.org/; A National Epidemic: Fatal Anti-Transgender Violence in the United States in 2019.

U.S. Department of Education (ED), Institute of Education Sciences (IES), National Center for Education Statistics (NCES), Potomac Center Plaza, 550 12th St. SW, Washington, DC, 20202, USA, (202) 403-5551, https://nces.ed.gov/; Indicators of School Crime and Safety: 2021.

U.S. Department of Justice (DOJ), Bureau of Justice Statistics (BJS), 810 7th St. NW, Washington, DC, 20531, USA, (202) 307-0765, askbjs@usdoj.gov, https://www.bjs.gov/; Criminal Victimization, 2020.

BLACK POPULATION-CRIMINAL STATISTICS

The Guardian, 61 Broadway, New York, NY, 10006, USA, (844) 632-2010, (917) 900-4663, usinfo@theguardian.com, https://www.theguardian.com; 'No Progress' Since George Floyd: US Police Killing Three People a Day.

Monmouth University Polling Institute, 400 Cedar Ave., West Long Branch, NJ, 07764, USA, (732) 263-5860, polling@monmouth.edu, https://www.monmouth.edu/polling-institute/; Protestors' Anger Justified Even If Actions May Not Be: Most Say Police More Likely to Use Excessive Force on Black Individuals.

National Registry of Exonerations, USA, https://www.law.umich.edu/special/exoneration/; Race and Wrongful Convictions in the United States 2022.

Public Religion Research Institute (PRRI), 1023 15th St. NW, 9th Fl., Washington, DC, 20005, USA, (202) 238-9424, info@prri.org, https://www.prri.org/; Summer Unrest over Racial Injustice Moves the Country, But Not Republicans or White Evangelicals.

The Sentencing Project, 1705 DeSales St. NW, 8th Fl., Washington, DC, 20036, USA, (202) 628-0871, staff@sentencingproject.org, https://www.sentencingproject.org; Mass Incarceration Trends.

U.S. Department of Justice (DOJ), Bureau of Justice Statistics (BJS), 810 7th St. NW, Washington, DC, 20531, USA, (202) 307-0765, askbjs@usdoj.gov, https://www.bjs.gov/; Annual Survey of Jails, 2019 and Criminal Victimization, 2020.

U.S. Department of Justice (DOJ), Federal Bureau of Investigation (FBI), 935 Pennsylvania Ave. NW, Washington, DC, 20535-0001, USA, (202) 324-3000, https://www.fbi.gov/; Crime in the United States 2019.

BLACK POPULATION-DEATHS AND DEATH RATES

Bernan Press, 15250 NBN Way, Bldg. C, Blue Ridge Summit, PA, 17214, USA, (301) 459-2255, (800) 865-3457, (800) 865-3450, customercare@bernan.com, https://rowman.com/Page/Bernan; Vital Statistics of the United States 2022: Births, Life Expectancy, Deaths, and Selected Health Data.

Campaign Zero, USA, info@campaignzero.org, https://campaignzero.org; Mapping Police Violence.

The COVID Tracking Project at The Atlantic, support@covidtracking.com, https://covidtracking.com; The COVID Racial Data Tracker.

Governors Highway Safety Association (GHSA), 660 N Capitol St. NW, Ste. 220, Washington, DC, 20001-1642, USA, (202) 789-0942, headquarters@ghsa.org, https://www.ghsa.org/; An Analysis of Traffic Fatalities by Race and Ethnicity.

The Guardian, 61 Broadway, New York, NY, 10006, USA, (844) 632-2010, (917) 900-4663, usinfo@theguardian.com, https://www.theguardian.com; 'No Progress' Since George Floyd: US Police Killing Three People a Day.

KFF Health News, 1330 G St. NW, Washington, DC, 20005, USA, (202) 347-5270, https://khn.org/; Black and Hispanic Americans Suffer Most in Biggest US Decline in Life Expectancy Since WWII.

Public Religion Research Institute (PRRI), 1023 15th St. NW, 9th Fl., Washington, DC, 20005, USA, (202) 238-9424, info@prri.org, https://www.prri.org/; Summer Unrest over Racial Injustice Moves the Country, But Not Republicans or White Evangelicals.

U.S. Department of Health and Human Services (HHS), National Institutes of Health (NIH), Researching COVID to Enhance Recovery (RECOVER), 9000 Rockville Pike, Bethesda, MD, 20892, USA, (301) 496-4000, (301) 402-9612 (TTY), https://recovercovid.org; Racial/Ethnic Disparities in Post-Acute Sequelae of SARS-CoV-2 Infection in New York: An EHR-Based Cohort Study from the RECOVER Program.

U.S. Department of Health and Human Services, Centers for Disease Control and Prevention (CDC), 1600 Clifton Rd., Atlanta, GA, 30329-4027, USA, (800) 232-4636, (888) 232-6348 (TTY), cdcinfo@cdc.gov, https://www.cdc.gov; Provisional COVID-19 Deaths: Distribution of Deaths by Race and Hispanic Origin.

U.S. Department of Health and Human Services, Centers for Disease Control and Prevention (CDC), National Center for Health Statistics (NCHS), 3311 Toledo Rd., Hyattsville, MD, 20782-2064, USA, (800) 232-4636, (301) 458-4000, https://www.cdc.gov/nchs; National Vital Statistics Reports (NVSR) and Vital Statistics Online Data Portal.

BLACK POPULATION-EDUCATIONAL ATTAINMENT

Alliance for Excellent Education (All4Ed), 1425 K St. NW, Ste. 700, Washington, DC, 20005, USA, (202) 828-0828, (202) 828-0821, https://all4ed.org; Ready for What? How Multiple Graduation Pathways Do - and Do Not - Signal Readiness for College and Careers.

University of California Los Angeles (UCLA), The Civil Rights Project, 8370 Math Sciences, PO Box 951521, Los Angeles, CA, 90095-1521, USA, crp@ucla.edu, https://www.civilrightsproject.ucla.edu/; The Walls Around Opportunity: The Failure of Colorblind Policy for Higher Education.

BLACK POPULATION-ELECTED OFFICIALS

Joint Center for Political and Economic Studies, 633 Pennsylvania Ave. NW, Washington, DC, 20004, USA, (202) 789-3500, info@jointcenter.org, https://jointcenter.org/; Racial Diversity Among Top House Staff and Racial Diversity Among Top Staff in Senate Personal Offices.

U.S. Government Publishing Office (GPO),, 732 N Capitol St. NW, Washington, DC, 20401-0001, USA, (202) 512-1800, (866) 512-1800, (202) 512-2104, contactcenter@gpo.gov, https://www.gpo.gov/; Congressional Directory.

U.S. House of Representatives, Office of the Clerk, U.S. Capitol, Rm. H154, Washington, DC, 20515-6601, USA, (202) 225-7000, (202) 228-2125, https://clerk.house.gov/; Black Americans in Congress.

BLACK POPULATION-ELECTIONS-VOTER REGISTRATION AND TURNOUT

Poor People's Campaign, USA, https://www.poorpeoplescampaign.org/; Waking the Sleeping Giant: Poor and Low-Income Voters in the 2020 Elections.

BLACK POPULATION-EMPLOYMENT STATUS

U.S. Department of Labor (DOL), Bureau of Labor Statistics (BLS), Postal Square Bldg., 2 Massachusetts Ave. NE, Washington, DC, 20212-0001, USA, (202) 691-5200, (202) 691-7890, blsdata_staff@bls.gov, https://www.bls.gov; Labor Force Statistics from the Current Population Survey (CPS).

BLACK POPULATION-EMPLOYMENT STATUS-EDUCATIONAL ATTAINMENT

U.S. Department of Labor (DOL), Bureau of Labor Statistics (BLS), Postal Square Bldg., 2 Massachusetts Ave. NE, Washington, DC, 20212-0001, USA, (202) 691-5200, (202) 691-7890, blsdata_staff@bls.gov, https://www.bls.gov; Monthly Labor Review.

BLACK POPULATION-EMPLOYMENT STATUS-HIGH SCHOOL GRADUATES AND DROPOUTS

U.S. Department of Labor (DOL), Bureau of Labor Statistics (BLS), Postal Square Bldg., 2 Massachusetts Ave. NE, Washington, DC, 20212-0001, USA, (202) 691-5200, (202) 691-7890, blsdata_staff@bls.gov, https://www.bls.gov; Labor Force Statistics from the Current Population Survey (CPS) and Monthly Labor Review.

BLACK POPULATION-EMPLOYMENT STATUS-SCHOOL ENROLLMENT

U.S. Department of Labor (DOL), Bureau of Labor Statistics (BLS), Postal Square Bldg., 2 Massachusetts Ave. NE, Washington, DC, 20212-0001, USA, (202) 691-5200, (202) 691-7890, blsdata_staff@bls.gov, https://www.bls.gov; Labor Force Statistics from the Current Population Survey (CPS) and Monthly Labor Review.

BLACK POPULATION-EMPLOYMENT STATUS-UNEMPLOYED

U.S. Department of Labor (DOL), Bureau of Labor Statistics (BLS), Postal Square Bldg., 2 Massachusetts Ave. NE, Washington, DC, 20212-0001, USA, (202) 691-5200, (202) 691-7890, blsdata_staff@bls.gov, https://www.bls.gov; Monthly Labor Review.

BLACK POPULATION-FAMILIES-CHARACTERISTICS

Children's Defense Fund (CDF), 840 1st St. NE, Ste. 300, Washington, DC, 20002, USA, (202) 628-8787, cdfinfo@childrensdefense.org, https://www.childrensdefense.org/; Ending Child Poverty Now and The State of America's Children 2021.

BLACK POPULATION-FERTILITY RATE

U.S. Department of Health and Human Services, Centers for Disease Control and Prevention (CDC), National Center for Health Statistics (NCHS), 3311 Toledo Rd., Hyattsville, MD, 20782-2064, USA, (800) 232-4636, (301) 458-4000, https://www.cdc.gov/nchs; Vital Statistics Online Data Portal.

BLACK POPULATION-FOOD STAMP PARTICIPANTS

U.S. Department of Agriculture (USDA), Food and Nutrition Service (FNS), Braddock Metro Center II, 1320 Braddock Pl., Alexandria, VA, 22314, USA, (703) 305-2062, https://www.fns.usda.gov/; Characteristics of SNAP Households: FY 2019.

BLACK POPULATION-FOREIGN BORN POPULATION

Migration Policy Institute (MPI), 1275 K St. NW, Ste. 800, Washington, DC, 20005, USA, (202) 266-1940, (202) 266-1900, info@migrationpolicy.org, https://www.migrationpolicy.org/; Frequently Requested Statistics on Immigrants and Immigration in the United States; Maps of Immigrants in the United States; State Immigration Data Profiles; and U.S. Immigration Policy under Trump: Deep Changes and Lasting Impacts.

BLACK POPULATION-HEALTH CARE VISITS TO PROFESSIONALS

U.S. Department of Health and Human Services (HHS), National Institutes of Health (NIH), Researching COVID to Enhance Recovery (RECOVER), 9000 Rockville Pike, Bethesda, MD, 20892, USA, (301) 496-4000, (301) 402-9612 (TTY), https://recovercovid.org; Racial/Ethnic Disparities in Post-Acute Sequelae of SARS-CoV-2 Infection in New York: An EHR-Based Cohort Study from the RECOVER Program.

U.S. Department of Health and Human Services, Centers for Disease Control and Prevention (CDC), 1600 Clifton Rd., Atlanta, GA, 30329-4027, USA, (800) 232-4636, (888) 232-6348 (TTY), cdcinfo@cdc.gov, https://www.cdc.gov; Emergency Department Visits for COVID-19 by Race and Ethnicity - 13 States, October - December 2020 and Trends in Racial and Ethnic Disparities in COVID-19 Hospitalizations, by Region - United States, March - December 2020.

U.S. Department of Health and Human Services, Centers for Disease Control and Prevention (CDC), National Center for Health Statistics (NCHS), 3311 Toledo Rd., Hyattsville, MD, 20782-2064, USA, (800) 232-4636, (301) 458-4000, https://www.cdc.gov/nchs; Health, United States, 2020-2021.

BLACK POPULATION-HEALTH INSURANCE COVERAGE

U.S. Department of Health and Human Services, Centers for Disease Control and Prevention (CDC), National Center for Health Statistics (NCHS), 3311 Toledo Rd., Hyattsville, MD, 20782-2064, USA, (800) 232-4636, (301) 458-4000, https://www.cdc.gov/nchs; FastStats - Statistics by Topic and Household Pulse Survey: Health Insurance Coverage.

BLACK POPULATION-HOME HEALTH AND HOSPICE CARE

U.S. Department of Health and Human Services, Centers for Disease Control and Prevention (CDC), National Center for Health Statistics (NCHS), 3311 Toledo Rd., Hyattsville, MD, 20782-2064, USA, (800) 232-4636, (301) 458-4000, https://www.cdc.gov/nchs; Health, United States, 2020-2021.

BLACK POPULATION-HOMICIDES

Bernan Press, 15250 NBN Way, Bldg. C, Blue Ridge Summit, PA, 17214, USA, (301) 459-2255, (800) 865-3457, (800) 865-3450, customercare@bernan.com, https://rowman.com/Page/Bernan; Vital Statistics of the United States 2022: Births, Life Expectancy, Deaths, and Selected Health Data.

U.S. Department of Health and Human Services, Centers for Disease Control and Prevention (CDC), 1600 Clifton Rd., Atlanta, GA, 30329-4027, USA, (800) 232-4636, (888) 232-6348 (TTY), cdcinfo@cdc.gov, https://www.cdc.gov; Racial and Ethnic Differences in Homicides of Adult Women and the Role of Intimate Partner Violence.

U.S. Department of Health and Human Services, Centers for Disease Control and Prevention (CDC), National Center for Health Statistics (NCHS), 3311 Toledo Rd., Hyattsville, MD, 20782-2064, USA, (800) 232-4636, (301) 458-4000, https://www.cdc.gov/nchs; National Vital Statistics Reports (NVSR) and Vital Statistics Online Data Portal.

BLACK POPULATION-HOSPITAL UTILIZATION

U.S. Department of Health and Human Services, Centers for Disease Control and Prevention (CDC), 1600 Clifton Rd., Atlanta, GA, 30329-4027, USA, (800) 232-4636, (888) 232-6348 (TTY), cdcinfo@cdc.gov, https://www.cdc.gov; Emergency Department Visits for COVID-19 by Race and Ethnicity - 13 States, October - December 2020 and Trends in Racial and Ethnic Disparities in COVID-19 Hospitalizations, by Region - United States, March - December 2020.

BLACK POPULATION-HOUSING

U.S. Census Bureau, 4600 Silver Hill Rd., Washington, DC, 20233, USA, (301) 763-4636, (800) 923-8282, https://www.census.gov; American Community Survey (ACS) 2020 and American Housing Survey (AHS) 2019.

BLACK POPULATION-IMMUNIZATION OF CHILDREN

U.S. Department of Health and Human Services, Centers for Disease Control and Prevention (CDC), 1600 Clifton Rd., Atlanta, GA, 30329-4027, USA, (800) 232-4636, (888) 232-6348 (TTY), cdcinfo@cdc.gov, https://www.cdc.gov; Morbidity and Mortality Weekly Report (MMWR).

BLACK POPULATION-INCOME

Pew Research Center, 1615 L St. NW, Ste. 800, Washington, DC, 20036, USA, (202) 419-4300, (202) 857-8562, info@pewresearch.org, https://www.pewresearch.org/; Key Findings on the Rise in Income Inequality within America's Racial and Ethnic Groups.

University of Georgia, Terry College of Business, Selig Center for Economic Growth, E201 Ivester Hall, 650 S Lumpkin St., Athens, GA, 30602, USA, (706) 425-9782, jhumphre@uga.edu, https://www.terry.uga.edu/about/selig//; The Multicultural Economy 2021.

BLACK POPULATION-INFANT DEATHS

Bernan Press, 15250 NBN Way, Bldg. C, Blue Ridge Summit, PA, 17214, USA, (301) 459-2255, (800) 865-3457, (800) 865-3450, customercare@bernan.com, https://rowman.com/Page/Bernan; Vital Statistics of the United States 2022: Births, Life Expectancy, Deaths, and Selected Health Data.

U.S. Department of Health and Human Services, Centers for Disease Control and Prevention (CDC), National Center for Health Statistics (NCHS), 3311 Toledo Rd., Hyattsville, MD, 20782-2064, USA, (800) 232-4636, (301) 458-4000, https://www.cdc.gov/nchs; National Vital Statistics Reports (NVSR) and Vital Statistics Online Data Portal.

BLACK POPULATION-INTERNET ACCESS

MRI Simmons, 200 Liberty St., 4th Fl., New York, NY, 10281, USA, (866) 256-4468, info.ms@mrisimmons.com, https://www.mrisimmons.com/; MRI-Simmons USA.

BLACK POPULATION-LABOR FORCE

Center for American Progress Action Fund (CAP Action), 1333 H St. NW, 10th Fl., Washington, DC, 20005, USA, (202) 682-1611, https://www.americanprogressaction.org; Who Makes Up the Working Class? A State-by-State Look at America's Diverse Working Class.

National Organization of Black Law Enforcement Executives (NOBLE), 4609-F Pinecrest Office Park Dr., Alexandria, VA, 22312-1442, USA, (703) 658-1529, (703) 658-9479, info@noblenatl.org, https://noblenational.org/; unpublished data.

U.S. Department of Labor (DOL), Bureau of Labor Statistics (BLS), Postal Square Bldg., 2 Massachusetts Ave. NE, Washington, DC, 20212-0001, USA, (202) 691-5200, (202) 691-7890, blsdata_staff@bls.gov, https://www.bls.gov; Labor Force Statistics from the Current Population Survey (CPS) and Monthly Labor Review.

University of Southern California (USC), Annenberg School for Communication and Journalism, Annenberg Inclusion Initiative, 3630 Watt Way, Ste. 402, Los Angeles, CA, 90089, USA, (213) 740-6180, (213) 740-3772, aii@usc.edu, https://annenberg.usc.edu/research/aii; Inclusion at Film Festivals: Examining the Gender and Race/Ethnicity of Narrative Directors from 2017-2019 and Inclusion in the Director's Chair: Analysis of Director Gender & Race/Ethnicity Across 1,500 Top Films from 2007 to 2021.

BLACK POPULATION-LABOR FORCE-DISPLACED WORKERS

U.S. Department of Labor (DOL), Bureau of Labor Statistics (BLS), Postal Square Bldg., 2 Massachusetts Ave. NE, Washington, DC, 20212-0001, USA, (202) 691-5200, (202) 691-7890, blsdata_staff@bls.gov, https://www.bls.gov; Monthly Labor Review.

BLACK POPULATION-LABOR FORCE-EARNINGS

U.S. Department of Labor (DOL), Bureau of Labor Statistics (BLS), Postal Square Bldg., 2 Massachusetts Ave. NE, Washington, DC, 20212-0001, USA, (202) 691-5200, (202) 691-7890, blsdata_staff@bls.gov, https://www.bls.gov; Labor Force Statistics from the Current Population Survey (CPS) and Monthly Labor Review.

BLACK POPULATION-LABOR FORCE-EMPLOYED

U.S. Department of Labor (DOL), Bureau of Labor Statistics (BLS), Postal Square Bldg., 2 Massachusetts Ave. NE, Washington, DC, 20212-0001, USA, (202) 691-5200, (202) 691-7890, blsdata_staff@bls.gov, https://www.bls.gov; Labor Force Statistics from the Current Population Survey (CPS) and Monthly Labor Review.

BLACK POPULATION-LIFE EXPECTANCY

Bernan Press, 15250 NBN Way, Bldg. C, Blue Ridge Summit, PA, 17214, USA, (301) 459-2255, (800) 865-3457, (800) 865-3450, customercare@bernan.com, https://rowman.com/Page/Bernan; Vital Statistics of the United States 2022: Births, Life Expectancy, Deaths, and Selected Health Data.

U.S. Department of Health and Human Services, Centers for Disease Control and Prevention (CDC), National Center for Health Statistics (NCHS), 3311 Toledo Rd., Hyattsville, MD, 20782-2064, USA, (800) 232-4636, (301) 458-4000, https://www.cdc.gov/nchs; National Vital Statistics Reports (NVSR) and Vital Statistics Online Data Portal.

BLACK POPULATION-LIVING ARRANGEMENTS

U.S. Census Bureau, 4600 Silver Hill Rd., Washington, DC, 20233, USA, (301) 763-4636, (800) 923-8282, https://www.census.gov; Families and Living Arrangements.

BLACK POPULATION-MEDIA USERS

MRI Simmons, 200 Liberty St., 4th Fl., New York, NY, 10281, USA, (866) 256-4468, info.ms@mrisimmons.com, https://www.mrisimmons.com/; MRI-Simmons USA.

Pew Research Center, 1615 L St. NW, Ste. 800, Washington, DC, 20036, USA, (202) 419-4300, (202) 857-8562, info@pewresearch.org, https://www.pewresearch.org/; 7 Facts about Black Americans and the News Media.

BLACK POPULATION-MEDICAL CARE

American Cancer Society (ACS), 3380 Chastain Meadows Pkwy NW, Ste. 200, Kennesaw, GA, 30144, USA, (800) 227-2345, https://www.cancer.org; Cancer Facts & Figures for African American/Black People 2022-2024.

U.S. Department of Health and Human Services (HHS), National Institutes of Health (NIH), Researching COVID to Enhance Recovery (RECOVER), 9000 Rockville Pike, Bethesda, MD, 20892, USA, (301) 496-4000, (301) 402-9612 (TTY), https://recovercovid.org; Racial/Ethnic Disparities in Post-Acute Sequelae of SARS-CoV-2 Infection in New York: An EHR-Based Cohort Study from the RECOVER Program.

U.S. Department of Health and Human Services, Centers for Disease Control and Prevention (CDC), 1600 Clifton Rd., Atlanta, GA, 30329-4027, USA, (800) 232-4636, (888) 232-6348 (TTY), cdcinfo@cdc.gov, https://www.cdc.gov; Emergency Department Visits for COVID-19 by Race and Ethnicity - 13 States, October - December 2020 and Trends in Racial and Ethnic Disparities in COVID-19 Hospitalizations, by Region - United States, March - December 2020.

U.S. Department of Health and Human Services, Centers for Disease Control and Prevention (CDC), National Center for Health Statistics (NCHS), 3311 Toledo Rd., Hyattsville, MD, 20782-2064, USA, (800) 232-4636, (301) 458-4000, https://www.cdc.gov/nchs; FastStats - Statistics by Topic.

BLACK POPULATION-MINIMUM WAGE WORKERS

Center for American Progress Action Fund (CAP Action), 1333 H St. NW, 10th Fl., Washington, DC, 20005, USA, (202) 682-1611, https://www.americanprogressaction.org; Who Makes Up the Working Class? A State-by-State Look at America's Diverse Working Class.

U.S. Department of Labor (DOL), Bureau of Labor Statistics (BLS), Postal Square Bldg., 2 Massachusetts Ave. NE, Washington, DC, 20212-0001, USA, (202) 691-5200, (202) 691-7890, blsdata_staff@bls.gov, https://www.bls.gov; Monthly Labor Review.

BLACK POPULATION-OVERWEIGHT

University of California Los Angeles (UCLA), Center for Health Policy Research (CHPR), 10960 Wilshire Blvd., Ste. 1550, Campus Mail Code 714346, Los Angeles, CA, 90024, USA, (310) 794-0909, (310) 794-2686, healthpolicy@ucla.edu, https://healthpolicy.ucla.edu; Racial/Ethnic Variations in Weight Management Among Patients with Overweight and Obesity Status Who Are Served by Health Centres (Clinical Obesity).

BLACK POPULATION-POLICE CONTACT

American Civil Liberties Union (ACLU), 125 Broad St. , 18th Fl., New York, NY, 10004, USA, (212) 549-2500, https://www.aclu.org/; License to Abuse: How ICE's 287(g) Program Empowers Racist Sheriffs and Civil Rights Violations and The Other Epidemic: Fatal Police Shootings in the Time of COVID-19.

Blue Ribbon Panel on Transparency, Accountability, and Fairness in Law Enforcement (The Panel), San Francisco, CA, 94108, USA, info@sfblueribbonpanel.com, https://sfblueribbonpanel.com/; unpublished data.

Campaign Zero, USA, info@campaignzero.org, https://campaignzero.org; Mapping Police Violence.

Center for Policing Equity (CPE), 8605 Santa Monica Blvd., PMB 54596, West Hollywood, CA, 90069-4109, USA, (347) 948-9953, https://policingequity.org/; National Justice Database (NJD).

Chicago Police Accountability Task Force, PO Box 6289, Chicago, IL, 60606-6289, USA, comments@chicagopatf.org, https://chicagopatf.org; unpublished data.

Civis Analytics, 200 W Monroe St., 22nd Fl., Chicago, IL, 60606, USA, https://www.civisanalytics.com/; BLM and Policing Survey Identifies Broad Support for Common-Sense Reform.

The Guardian, 61 Broadway, New York, NY, 10006, USA, (844) 632-2010, (917) 900-4663, usinfo@theguardian.com, https://www.theguardian.com; 'No Progress' Since George Floyd: US Police Killing Three People a Day.

The Henry J. Kaiser Family Foundation (KFF), 185 Berry St., Ste. 2000, San Francisco, CA, 94107, USA, (650) 854-9400, (650) 854-4800, https://www.kff.org; KFF Health Tracking Poll: Racial Disparities and Protests.

Monmouth University Polling Institute, 400 Cedar Ave., West Long Branch, NJ, 07764, USA, (732) 263-5860, polling@monmouth.edu, https://www.monmouth.edu/polling-institute/; Protestors' Anger Justified Even If Actions May Not Be: Most Say Police More Likely to Use Excessive Force on Black Individuals.

Physicians for Human Rights (PHR), 256 W 38th St., 9th Fl., New York, NY, 10018, USA, (646) 564-3720, (646) 564-3750, https://phr.org/; 'Excited Delirium' and Deaths in Police Custody: The Deadly Impact of a Baseless Diagnosis.

Public Agenda, 1 Dock 72 Way, No. 6101, Brooklyn, NY, 11205-1242, USA, (212) 686-6610, info@publicagenda.org, https://www.publicagenda.org/; America's Hidden Common Ground on Race and Police Reform.

Public Religion Research Institute (PRRI), 1023 15th St. NW, 9th Fl., Washington, DC, 20005, USA, (202) 238-9424, info@prri.org, https://www.prri.org/; Summer Unrest over Racial Injustice Moves the Country, But Not Republicans or White Evangelicals.

BLACK POPULATION-POVERTY

The Urban Institute, 500 L'Enfant Plaza SW, Washington, DC, 20024, USA, (202) 833-7200, https://www.urban.org/; 2021 Poverty Projections: Assessing the Impact of Benefits and Stimulus Measures.

BLACK POPULATION-PRISONERS

Council on Criminal Justice (CCJ), 700 Pennsylvania Ave. SE, Washington, DC, 20003, USA, info@counciloncj.org, https://counciloncj.org; Justice System Disparities: Black-White National Imprisonment Trends, 2000 to 2020 and The 1994 Crime Bill: Legacy and Lessons.

Pew Research Center, 1615 L St. NW, Ste. 800, Washington, DC, 20036, USA, (202) 419-4300, (202) 857-8562, info@pewresearch.org, https://www.pewresearch.org/; Black Imprisonment Rate in the U.S. Has Fallen by a Third Since 2006.

Southern Poverty Law Center (SPLC), 400 Washington Ave., Montgomery, AL, 36104, USA, (334) 956-8200, (888) 414-7752, https://www.splcenter.org/; Cut Off From Caregivers: The Children of Incarcerated Parents in Louisiana.

U.S. Department of Justice (DOJ), Bureau of Justice Statistics (BJS), 810 7th St. NW, Washington, DC, 20531, USA, (202) 307-0765, askbjs@usdoj.gov, https://www.bjs.gov/; Annual Survey of Jails, 2019; Data Collection: National Corrections Reporting Program (NCRP); Prisoners in 2020; and Probation and Parole in the United States, 2020.

Vera Institute of Justice, 34 35th St., Ste. 4-2A, Brooklyn, NY, 11232, USA, (212) 334-1300, (212) 941-9407, contactvera@vera.org, https://www.vera.org/; The New Dynamics of Mass Incarceration and An Unjust Burden: The Disparate Treatment of Black Americans in the Criminal Justice System.

BLACK POPULATION-PROPERTY OWNERS

U.S. Census Bureau, 4600 Silver Hill Rd., Washington, DC, 20233, USA, (301) 763-4636, (800) 923-8282, https://www.census.gov; American Community Survey (ACS) 2020 and American Housing Survey (AHS) 2019.

BLACK POPULATION-SCHOOLS AND EDUCATION-ADULT EDUCATION

U.S. Department of Education (ED), Institute of Education Sciences (IES), National Center for Education Statistics (NCES), Potomac Center Plaza, 550 12th St. SW, Washington, DC, 20202, USA, (202) 403-5551, https://nces.ed.gov/; The National Household Education Surveys Program (NHES) Data.

BLACK POPULATION-SCHOOLS AND EDUCATION-ATTAINMENT

Alliance for Excellent Education (All4Ed), 1425 K St. NW, Ste. 700, Washington, DC, 20005, USA, (202) 828-0828, (202) 828-0821, https://all4ed.org; Ready for What? How Multiple Graduation Pathways Do - and Do Not - Signal Readiness for College and Careers.

BLACK POPULATION-SCHOOLS AND EDUCATION-EMPLOYED STUDENTS

U.S. Department of Labor (DOL), Bureau of Labor Statistics (BLS), Postal Square Bldg., 2 Massachusetts Ave. NE, Washington, DC, 20212-0001, USA, (202) 691-5200, (202) 691-7890, blsdata_staff@bls.gov, https://www.bls.gov; Labor Market Experience, Education, Partner Status, and Health for those Born 1980-1984.

BLACK POPULATION-SCHOOLS AND EDUCATION-ENROLLMENT

U.S. Census Bureau, 4600 Silver Hill Rd., Washington, DC, 20233, USA, (301) 763-4636, (800) 923-8282, https://www.census.gov; School Enrollment in the United States: 2020.

BLACK POPULATION-SCHOOLS AND EDUCATION-ENROLLMENT-COLLEGE ENROLLMENT

U.S. Department of Education (ED), Institute of Education Sciences (IES), National Center for Education Statistics (NCES), Potomac Center Plaza, 550 12th St. SW, Washington, DC, 20202, USA, (202) 403-5551, https://nces.ed.gov/; Digest of Education Statistics, 2020.

BLACK POPULATION-SCHOOLS AND EDUCATION-HIGH SCHOOL DROPOUTS

U.S. Department of Labor (DOL), Bureau of Labor Statistics (BLS), Postal Square Bldg., 2 Massachusetts Ave. NE, Washington, DC, 20212-0001, USA, (202) 691-5200, (202) 691-7890, blsdata_staff@bls.gov, https://www.bls.gov; Labor Force Statistics from the Current Population Survey (CPS) and Monthly Labor Review.

BLACK POPULATION-SCHOOLS AND EDUCATION-HIGH SCHOOL GRADUATES

U.S. Department of Labor (DOL), Bureau of Labor Statistics (BLS), Postal Square Bldg., 2 Massachusetts Ave. NE, Washington, DC, 20212-0001, USA, (202) 691-5200, (202) 691-7890, blsdata_staff@bls.gov, https://www.bls.gov; Labor Force Statistics from the Current Population Survey (CPS) and Monthly Labor Review.

BLACK POPULATION-SCHOOLS AND EDUCATION-HIGHER EDUCATION INSTITUTIONS-DEGREES CONFERRED

National Science Foundation, National Center for Science and Engineering Statistics (NCSES), 2415

Eisenhower Ave., Ste. W14200, Arlington, VA, 22314, USA, (703) 292-8780, (703) 292-9092, info@nsf.gov, https://www.nsf.gov/statistics/; Survey of Doctorate Recipients and Survey of Earned Doctorates.

BLACK POPULATION-SCHOOLS AND EDUCATION-HIGHER EDUCATION INSTITUTIONS-ENROLLMENT

U.S. Department of Education (ED), Institute of Education Sciences (IES), National Center for Education Statistics (NCES), Potomac Center Plaza, 550 12th St. SW, Washington, DC, 20202, USA, (202) 403-5551, https://nces.ed.gov/; Digest of Education Statistics, 2020.

BLACK POPULATION-SCHOOLS AND EDUCATION-SCHOLASTIC APTITUDE TEST

College Board, 250 Vesey St., New York, NY, 10281, USA, (212) 713-8000, (800) 323-7155, (212) 713-8143, store_help@collegeboard.org, https://www.collegeboard.com; 2022 Total Group SAT Suite of Assessments Annual Report.

BLACK POPULATION-SCHOOLS AND EDUCATION-SPORTS PARTICIPATION

U.S. Department of Health and Human Services, Centers for Disease Control and Prevention (CDC), 1600 Clifton Rd., Atlanta, GA, 30329-4027, USA, (800) 232-4636, (888) 232-6348 (TTY), cdcinfo@cdc.gov, https://www.cdc.gov; Morbidity and Mortality Weekly Report (MMWR) and Youth Risk Behavior Survey (YRBS): 2021 Results.

BLACK POPULATION-SCHOOLS AND EDUCATION-TEACHERS

U.S. Department of Labor (DOL), Bureau of Labor Statistics (BLS), Postal Square Bldg., 2 Massachusetts Ave. NE, Washington, DC, 20212-0001, USA, (202) 691-5200, (202) 691-7890, blsdata_staff@bls.gov, https://www.bls.gov; Monthly Labor Review.

BLACK POPULATION-SENIOR CITIZEN COMMUNITIES

U.S. Census Bureau, 4600 Silver Hill Rd., Washington, DC, 20233, USA, (301) 763-4636, (800) 923-8282, https://www.census.gov; American Community Survey (ACS) 2020 and American Housing Survey (AHS) 2019.

BLACK POPULATION-SINGLE MOTHERS

Bernan Press, 15250 NBN Way, Bldg. C, Blue Ridge Summit, PA, 17214, USA, (301) 459-2255, (800) 865-3457, (800) 865-3450, customercare@bernan.com, https://rowman.com/Page/Bernan; Vital Statistics of the United States 2022: Births, Life Expectancy, Deaths, and Selected Health Data.

U.S. Department of Health and Human Services, Centers for Disease Control and Prevention (CDC), National Center for Health Statistics (NCHS), 3311 Toledo Rd., Hyattsville, MD, 20782-2064, USA, (800) 232-4636, (301) 458-4000, https://www.cdc.gov/nchs; National Vital Statistics Reports (NVSR) and Vital Statistics Online Data Portal.

BLACK POPULATION-SUICIDE

American Association of Suicidology (AAS), 448 Walton Ave., No. 790, Hummelstown, PA, 17036, USA, (202) 237-2280, (202) 237-2282, info@suicidology.org, https://suicidology.org; U.S.A. Suicide: 2019 Official Final Data.

American Psychological Association (APA), 750 First St. NE, Washington, DC, 20002-4242, USA, (800) 374-2721, (202) 336-5500, https://www.apa.org/; More Than 20% of Teens Have Seriously Considered Suicide. Psychologists and Communities Can Help Tackle the Problem.

Bernan Press, 15250 NBN Way, Bldg. C, Blue Ridge Summit, PA, 17214, USA, (301) 459-2255, (800) 865-3457, (800) 865-3450, customercare@bernan.com, https://rowman.com/Page/Bernan; Vital Statistics of the United States 2022: Births, Life Expectancy, Deaths, and Selected Health Data.

The Trevor Project, PO Box 69232, West Hollywood, CA, 90069, USA, (212) 695-8650, info@thetrevorproject.org, https://www.thetrevorproject.org/; Facts About LGBTQ Youth Suicide and 2022 National Survey on LGBTQ Youth Mental Health.

U.S. Department of Health and Human Services, Centers for Disease Control and Prevention (CDC), 1600 Clifton Rd., Atlanta, GA, 30329-4027, USA, (800) 232-4636, (888) 232-6348 (TTY), cdcinfo@cdc.gov, https://www.cdc.gov; Notes from the Field: Recent Changes in Suicide Rates, by Race and Ethnicity and Age Group - United States, 2021.

U.S. Department of Health and Human Services, Centers for Disease Control and Prevention (CDC), National Center for Health Statistics (NCHS), 3311 Toledo Rd., Hyattsville, MD, 20782-2064, USA, (800) 232-4636, (301) 458-4000, https://www.cdc.gov/nchs; National Vital Statistics Reports (NVSR) and Vital Statistics Online Data Portal.

U.S. Department of Justice (DOJ), Bureau of Justice Statistics (BJS), 810 7th St. NW, Washington, DC, 20531, USA, (202) 307-0765, askbjs@usdoj.gov, https://www.bjs.gov/; Mortality in State and Federal Prisons, 2001-2019 - Statistical Tables.

BLACK POPULATION-TEENAGE MOTHERS

Bernan Press, 15250 NBN Way, Bldg. C, Blue Ridge Summit, PA, 17214, USA, (301) 459-2255, (800) 865-3457, (800) 865-3450, customercare@bernan.com, https://rowman.com/Page/Bernan; Vital Statistics of the United States 2022: Births, Life Expectancy, Deaths, and Selected Health Data.

U.S. Department of Health and Human Services, Centers for Disease Control and Prevention (CDC), National Center for Health Statistics (NCHS), 3311 Toledo Rd., Hyattsville, MD, 20782-2064, USA, (800) 232-4636, (301) 458-4000, https://www.cdc.gov/nchs; National Vital Statistics Reports (NVSR) and Vital Statistics Online Data Portal.

BLACK POPULATION-YOUNG ADULTS

University of Chicago, Center for the Study of Race, Politics and Culture, Black Youth Project, 5733 S University Ave., Chicago, IL, 60637, USA, info@blackyouthproject.com, https://www.blackyouthproject.com/; GenForward Survey 2022.

BLAST FURNACE AND BASIC STEEL PRODUCTS

See IRON AND STEEL

BLIND PERSONS

SAGE Publications, 2455 Teller Rd., Thousand Oaks, CA, 91320, USA, (800) 818-7243, (800) 583-2665, journals@sagepub.com, https://www.sagepub.com; British Journal of Visual Impairment.

Social Security Administration (SSA), Office of Public Inquiries and Communications Support, 1100 W High Rise, 6401 Security Blvd., Baltimore, MD, 21235, USA, (800) 772-1213, (800) 325-0778 (TTY), https://www.ssa.gov/; Annual Statistical Supplement, 2021 and Social Security Bulletin.

BLIND PERSONS-MEDICAID PAYMENTS AND RECIPIENTS

U.S. Department of Health and Human Services (HHS), Centers for Medicare and Medicaid Services (CMS), 7500 Security Blvd., Baltimore, MD, 21244, USA, (410) 786-3000, (877) 267-2323, https://www.cms.gov; Medicare Current Beneficiary Survey (MCBS).

BLOGS

Pew Research Center, 1615 L St. NW, Ste. 800, Washington, DC, 20036, USA, (202) 419-4300, (202) 857-8562, info@pewresearch.org, https://www.pewresearch.org/; Distinguishing Between Factual and Opinion Statements in the News and State of the News Media.

Pew Research Center, News Habits & Media, 1615 L St. NW, Ste. 800, Washington, DC, 20036, USA, (202) 419-4300, (202) 857-8562, https://www.pewresearch.org/topic/news-habits-media/; Digital News Fact Sheet.

BLOOD ALCOHOL CONCENTRATION

National Highway Traffic Safety Administration (NHTSA), National Center for Statistics and Analysis (NCSA), 1200 New Jersey Ave. SE, West Bldg., Washington, DC, 20590, USA, (800) 934-8517, (202) 366-2746, ncsarequests@dot.gov, https://www.nhtsa.gov/research-data/national-center-statistics-and-analysis-ncsa; Traffic Safety Facts and Traffic Safety Facts, 2020 Data - Alcohol-Impaired Driving.

BLUE-COLLAR WORKERS

U.S. Department of Labor (DOL), Bureau of Labor Statistics (BLS), Postal Square Bldg., 2 Massachusetts Ave. NE, Washington, DC, 20212-0001, USA, (202) 691-5200, (202) 691-7890, blsdata_staff@bls.gov, https://www.bls.gov; Employment Cost Index; Monthly Labor Review; National Compensation Survey - Employment Cost Trends; and National Compensation Survey - Wages.

BLUEFISH

National Oceanic and Atmospheric Administration (NOAA), National Marine Fisheries Service (NOAA Fisheries), 1315 East-West Hwy., 14th Fl., Silver Spring, MD, 20910, USA, (301) 427-8000, https://www.fisheries.noaa.gov/; Fisheries of the United States, 2020.

BOARD GAMES

Unites States Chess Federation (USCF), PO Box 3967, Crossville, TN, 38557-3967, USA, (931) 787-1234, https://www.uschess.org; unpublished data.

BOARDING SCHOOLS

U.S. Department of the Interior (DOI), Office of the Secretary, 1849 C St. NW, Washington, DC, 20240, USA, (202) 208-3100, https://www.doi.gov/office-of-the-secretary; Federal Indian Boarding School Initiative Investigative Report.

BOATS AND BOATING

Clean Fuels Alliance America, PO Box 104898, Jefferson City, MO, 65110-4898, USA, (573) 635-3893, (800) 841-5849, info@cleanfuels.org, https://www.biodiesel.org/; Clean Fuels Bulletin.

National Marine Manufacturers Association (NMMA), 231 S LaSalle St., Ste. 2050, Chicago, IL, 60604, USA, (312) 946-6200, (312) 946-6212, pdalal@nmma.org, https://www.nmma.org/; Economic Impact Infographics by State and U.S. Recreational Boating Statistical Abstract 2021.

National Sporting Goods Association (NSGA), 3041 Woodcreek Dr., Ste. 210, Downers Grove, IL, 60515, USA, (847) 296-6742, (847) 391-9827, info@nsga.org, https://www.nsga.org; Sports Participation in the United States 2022 and Sports Participation: Historical Sports Participation 2022.

U.S. Department of Health and Human Services (HHS), National Institutes of Health (NIH), National Institute on Alcohol Abuse and Alcoholism (NIAAA), 9000 Rockville Pike, Bethesda, MD, 20892, USA, (888) 696-4222, (301) 443-3860, askniaaa@nih.gov, https://www.niaaa.nih.gov/; Alcohol Policy Information System (APIS).

BOATS AND BOATING-ACCIDENTS

U.S. Department of Transportation (DOT), Office of the Assistant Secretary for Research and Technology (OST-R), Bureau of Transportation Statistics (BTS), 1200 New Jersey Ave. SE, Washington, DC, 20590, USA, (800) 853-1351, (202) 366-3282, https://www.bts.gov; TranStats.

BODY CAMERAS

See WEARABLE VIDEO DEVICES

BOLIVIA-NATIONAL STATISTICAL OFFICE

Instituto Nacional de Estadistica, Bolivia, Avenida Jose Carrasco 1391, La Paz, BOL, info@ine.gob.bo, https://www.ine.gob.bo/; National Data Reports (Bolivia).

BOLIVIA-PRIMARY STATISTICS SOURCES

Unidad de Analisis de Politicas Sociales y Economicas, Bolivia, Av. Mariscal Santa Cruz, Edificio Centro de Comunicaciones , Piso 18 , La Paz, BOL, udape@udape.gob.bo, http://www.udape.gob.bo/; Dossier de Estadisticas Sociales y Economicas.

BOLIVIA-AGRICULTURE

The Economist Group: Economist Intelligence Unit (EIU), 900 3rd Ave., 16th Fl., New York, NY, 10022, USA, (212) 541-0500, americas@eiu.com, https://www.eiu.com; Bolivia Country Report.

Euromonitor International, Inc., 1 N Dearborn St., Ste. 1700, Chicago, IL, 60602, USA, (312) 922-1115, (312) 922-1157, info-usa@euromonitor.com, https://www.euromonitor.com/; Geographies.

Inter-American Development Bank (IDB), 1300 New York Ave. NW, Washington, DC, 20577, USA, (202) 623-1000, (202) 623-3096, https://www.iadb.org/en; Latin Macro Watch (LMW).

Palgrave Macmillan, 1 New York Plaza, Ste. 4500, New York, NY, 10004-1562, USA, (800) 777-4643, orders@palgrave.com, https://www.palgrave.com/us; The Statesman's Yearbook, 2023.

Routledge - Taylor & Francis Group, 6000 Broken Sound Pkwy. NW, Ste. 300, Boca Raton, FL, 33487, USA, (800) 634-1420, (800) 634-7064, orders@taylorandfrancis.com, https://www.routledge.com/; The Europa World Year Book 2022.

United Nations Food and Agricultural Organization (FAO), 2121 K St., Ste. 800B, Washington, DC, 20037, USA, (202) 653-2400 (Dial from U.S.), (202) 653-5760 (Fax from U.S.), fao-hq@fao.org, https://www.fao.org; AQUASTAT and The State of Food and Agriculture (SOFA) 2022.

United Nations Statistics Division (UNSD), United Nations Plz., New York, NY, 10017, USA, (800) 253-9646, (212) 963-9851, statistics@un.org, https://unstats.un.org; Statistical Yearbook of the United Nations 2021.

The World Bank, 1818 H St. NW, Washington, DC, 20433, USA, (202) 473-1000, (202) 477-6391, eds03@worldbank.org, https://www.worldbank.org/; Bolivia (report) and World Development Indicators (WDI) 2022.

BOLIVIA-AIRLINES

International Civil Aviation Organization (ICAO), 999 Robert-Bourassa Blvd., Montreal, QC, H3C 5H7, CAN, (514) 954-8219 (Dial from U.S.), (514) 954-6077 (Fax from U.S.), icaohq@icao.int, https://www.icao.int; ICAO Regional Reports.

Palgrave Macmillan, 1 New York Plaza, Ste. 4500, New York, NY, 10004-1562, USA, (800) 777-4643, orders@palgrave.com, https://www.palgrave.com/us; The Statesman's Yearbook, 2023.

Routledge - Taylor & Francis Group, 6000 Broken Sound Pkwy. NW, Ste. 300, Boca Raton, FL, 33487, USA, (800) 634-1420, (800) 634-7064, orders@taylorandfrancis.com, https://www.routledge.com/; The Europa World Year Book 2022.

BOLIVIA-ALUMINUM PRODUCTION

See BOLIVIA-MINERAL INDUSTRIES

BOLIVIA-ARMED FORCES

Central Intelligence Agency (CIA), Office of Public Affairs, Washington, DC, 20505, USA, (703) 482-0623, https://www.cia.gov; The World Factbook.

International Institute for Strategic Studies (IISS) - Americas, 2121 K St. NW, Ste. 600, Washington, DC, 20037, USA, (202) 659-1490, (202) 659-1499, https://www.iiss.org/; The Military Balance 2022.

Palgrave Macmillan, 1 New York Plaza, Ste. 4500, New York, NY, 10004-1562, USA, (800) 777-4643, orders@palgrave.com, https://www.palgrave.com/us; The Statesman's Yearbook, 2023.

Stockholm International Peace Research Institute (SIPRI), Signalistgatan 9, Stockholm, SE 169 72, SWE, https://www.sipri.org/; SIPRI Arms Transfers Database and SIPRI Military Expenditure Database.

BOLIVIA-BALANCE OF PAYMENTS

Inter-American Development Bank (IDB), 1300 New York Ave. NW, Washington, DC, 20577, USA, (202) 623-1000, (202) 623-3096, https://www.iadb.org/en; Latin Macro Watch (LMW).

International Monetary Fund (IMF), 700 19th St. NW, Washington, DC, 20431, USA, (202) 623-7000, (202) 623-4661, publications@imf.org, https://www.imf.org; Balance of Payments Statistics: Annual Report 2021 and International Financial Statistics (IFS).

Routledge - Taylor & Francis Group, 6000 Broken Sound Pkwy. NW, Ste. 300, Boca Raton, FL, 33487, USA, (800) 634-1420, (800) 634-7064, orders@taylorandfrancis.com, https://www.routledge.com/; The Europa World Year Book 2022.

United Nations Conference on Trade and Development (UNCTAD), Palais des Nations, Geneva, 1211, SWI, (212) 963-6896, unctadinfo@unctad.org, https://unctad.org; Handbook of Statistics 2021.

United Nations Economic Commission for Latin America and the Caribbean (ECLAC), Casilla 179-D, Santiago, 7630412, CHL, (202) 596-3713, prensa@cepal.org, https://www.cepal.org/en; Economic Survey of Latin America and the Caribbean 2021: Labour Dynamics and Employment Policies for Sustainable and Inclusive Recovery Beyond the COVID-19 Crisis.

The World Bank, 1818 H St. NW, Washington, DC, 20433, USA, (202) 473-1000, (202) 477-6391, eds03@worldbank.org, https://www.worldbank.org/; Bolivia (report); World Development Indicators (WDI) 2022; and World Development Report 2022: Finance for an Equitable Recovery.

BOLIVIA-BANKS AND BANKING

Euromonitor International, Inc., 1 N Dearborn St., Ste. 1700, Chicago, IL, 60602, USA, (312) 922-1115, (312) 922-1157, info-usa@euromonitor.com, https://www.euromonitor.com/; Geographies.

Inter-American Development Bank (IDB), 1300 New York Ave. NW, Washington, DC, 20577, USA, (202) 623-1000, (202) 623-3096, https://www.iadb.org/en; Latin Macro Watch (LMW).

International Monetary Fund (IMF), 700 19th St. NW, Washington, DC, 20431, USA, (202) 623-7000, (202) 623-4661, publications@imf.org, https://www.imf.org; International Financial Statistics (IFS).

Routledge - Taylor & Francis Group, 6000 Broken Sound Pkwy. NW, Ste. 300, Boca Raton, FL, 33487, USA, (800) 634-1420, (800) 634-7064, orders@taylorandfrancis.com, https://www.routledge.com/; The Europa World Year Book 2022.

BOLIVIA-BARLEY PRODUCTION

See BOLIVIA-CROPS

BOLIVIA-BONDS

Inter-American Development Bank (IDB), 1300 New York Ave. NW, Washington, DC, 20577, USA, (202) 623-1000, (202) 623-3096, https://www.iadb.org/en; Latin Macro Watch (LMW).

BOLIVIA-BROADCASTING

Central Intelligence Agency (CIA), Office of Public Affairs, Washington, DC, 20505, USA, (703) 482-0623, https://www.cia.gov; The World Factbook.

Euromonitor International, Inc., 1 N Dearborn St., Ste. 1700, Chicago, IL, 60602, USA, (312) 922-1115, (312) 922-1157, info-usa@euromonitor.com, https://www.euromonitor.com/; Geographies.

Palgrave Macmillan, 1 New York Plaza, Ste. 4500, New York, NY, 10004-1562, USA, (800) 777-4643, orders@palgrave.com, https://www.palgrave.com/us; The Statesman's Yearbook, 2023.

WRTH Publications Limited, PO Box 290, Oxford, OX2 7FT, GBR, sales@wrth.com, https://www.wrth.com; World Radio TV Handbook 2023.

BOLIVIA-BUDGET

Central Intelligence Agency (CIA), Office of Public Affairs, Washington, DC, 20505, USA, (703) 482-0623, https://www.cia.gov; The World Factbook.

BOLIVIA-BUSINESS

Inter-American Development Bank (IDB), 1300 New York Ave. NW, Washington, DC, 20577, USA, (202) 623-1000, (202) 623-3096, https://www.iadb.org/en; Latin Macro Watch (LMW).

BOLIVIA-CAPITAL INVESTMENTS

Inter-American Development Bank (IDB), 1300 New York Ave. NW, Washington, DC, 20577, USA, (202) 623-1000, (202) 623-3096, https://www.iadb.org/en; Latin Macro Watch (LMW).

BOLIVIA-CHESTNUT PRODUCTION

See BOLIVIA-CROPS

BOLIVIA-CHILDBIRTH-STATISTICS

The World Bank, 1818 H St. NW, Washington, DC, 20433, USA, (202) 473-1000, (202) 477-6391, eds03@worldbank.org, https://www.worldbank.org/; World Development Indicators (WDI) 2022.

BOLIVIA-CLIMATE

Palgrave Macmillan, 1 New York Plaza, Ste. 4500, New York, NY, 10004-1562, USA, (800) 777-4643, orders@palgrave.com, https://www.palgrave.com/us; The Statesman's Yearbook, 2023.

BOLIVIA-COAL PRODUCTION

See BOLIVIA-MINERAL INDUSTRIES

BOLIVIA-COCOA PRODUCTION

See BOLIVIA-CROPS

BOLIVIA-COFFEE

See BOLIVIA-CROPS

BOLIVIA-COMMERCE

Palgrave Macmillan, 1 New York Plaza, Ste. 4500, New York, NY, 10004-1562, USA, (800) 777-4643, orders@palgrave.com, https://www.palgrave.com/us; The Statesman's Yearbook, 2023.

UK Data Service, University of Essex, Wivenhoe Park, Colchester, Essex, CO4 3SQ, GBR, https://ukdataservice.ac.uk/; International Aggregate Data.

BOLIVIA-COMMODITY EXCHANGES

Barchart, 209 W Jackson Blvd., 2nd Fl., Chicago, IL, 60606, USA, (877) 247-4394, commodities@barchart.com, https://www.barchart.com/cmdty; The cmdty Yearbook 2023; cmdtyStats: Commodity Statistics and Fundamental Data; cmdtyView: Commodity Index; and Commodity Data and Prices.

International Monetary Fund (IMF), 700 19th St. NW, Washington, DC, 20431, USA, (202) 623-7000, (202) 623-4661, publications@imf.org, https://www.imf.org; IMF Primary Commodity Prices.

BOLIVIA-CONSTRUCTION INDUSTRY

Inter-American Development Bank (IDB), 1300 New York Ave. NW, Washington, DC, 20577, USA, (202) 623-1000, (202) 623-3096, https://www.iadb.org/en; Latin Macro Watch (LMW).

United Nations Statistics Division (UNSD), United Nations Plz., New York, NY, 10017, USA, (800) 253-9646, (212) 963-9851, statistics@un.org, https://unstats.un.org; Statistical Yearbook of the United Nations 2021.

BOLIVIA-CONSUMER PRICE INDEXES

Routledge - Taylor & Francis Group, 6000 Broken Sound Pkwy. NW, Ste. 300, Boca Raton, FL, 33487, USA, (800) 634-1420, (800) 634-7064, orders@taylorandfrancis.com, https://www.routledge.com/; The Europa World Year Book 2022.

The World Bank, 1818 H St. NW, Washington, DC, 20433, USA, (202) 473-1000, (202) 477-6391, eds03@worldbank.org, https://www.worldbank.org/; Bolivia (report).

BOLIVIA-CONSUMPTION (ECONOMICS)

Inter-American Development Bank (IDB), 1300 New York Ave. NW, Washington, DC, 20577, USA, (202) 623-1000, (202) 623-3096, https://www.iadb.org/en; Latin Macro Watch (LMW).

BOLIVIA-COPPER INDUSTRY AND TRADE

See BOLIVIA-MINERAL INDUSTRIES

BOLIVIA-CORN INDUSTRY

See BOLIVIA-CROPS

BOLIVIA-COTTON

See BOLIVIA-CROPS

BOLIVIA-CROPS

Inter-American Development Bank (IDB), 1300 New York Ave. NW, Washington, DC, 20577, USA, (202) 623-1000, (202) 623-3096, https://www.iadb.org/en; Latin Macro Watch (LMW).

Palgrave Macmillan, 1 New York Plaza, Ste. 4500, New York, NY, 10004-1562, USA, (800) 777-4643, orders@palgrave.com, https://www.palgrave.com/us; The Statesman's Yearbook, 2023.

United Nations Food and Agricultural Organization (FAO), 2121 K St., Ste. 800B, Washington, DC, 20037, USA, (202) 653-2400 (Dial from U.S.), (202) 653-5760 (Fax from U.S.), fao-hq@fao.org, https://www.fao.org; The State of Food and Agriculture (SOFA) 2022.

United Nations Statistics Division (UNSD), United Nations Plz., New York, NY, 10017, USA, (800) 253-9646, (212) 963-9851, statistics@un.org, https://unstats.un.org; Statistical Yearbook of the United Nations 2021.

BOLIVIA-CUSTOMS ADMINISTRATION

Inter-American Development Bank (IDB), 1300 New York Ave. NW, Washington, DC, 20577, USA, (202) 623-1000, (202) 623-3096, https://www.iadb.org/en; Latin Macro Watch (LMW).

BOLIVIA-DAIRY PROCESSING

Palgrave Macmillan, 1 New York Plaza, Ste. 4500, New York, NY, 10004-1562, USA, (800) 777-4643, orders@palgrave.com, https://www.palgrave.com/us; The Statesman's Yearbook, 2023.

United Nations Food and Agricultural Organization (FAO), 2121 K St., Ste. 800B, Washington, DC, 20037, USA, (202) 653-2400 (Dial from U.S.), (202) 653-5760 (Fax from U.S.), fao-hq@fao.org, https://www.fao.org; The State of Food and Agriculture (SOFA) 2022.

BOLIVIA-DEBT

The World Bank, 1818 H St. NW, Washington, DC, 20433, USA, (202) 473-1000, (202) 477-6391, eds03@worldbank.org, https://www.worldbank.org/; Global Financial Development Report 2019-2020: Bank Regulation and Supervision a Decade after the Global Financial Crisis.

BOLIVIA-DEBTS, EXTERNAL

Inter-American Development Bank (IDB), 1300 New York Ave. NW, Washington, DC, 20577, USA, (202) 623-1000, (202) 623-3096, https://www.iadb.org/en; Latin Macro Watch (LMW).

Palgrave Macmillan, 1 New York Plaza, Ste. 4500, New York, NY, 10004-1562, USA, (800) 777-4643, orders@palgrave.com, https://www.palgrave.com/us; The Statesman's Yearbook, 2023.

United Nations Economic Commission for Latin America and the Caribbean (ECLAC), Casilla 179-D, Santiago, 7630412, CHL, (202) 596-3713, prensa@cepal.org, https://www.cepal.org/en; Economic Survey of Latin America and the Caribbean 2021: Labour Dynamics and Employment Policies for Sustainable and Inclusive Recovery Beyond the COVID-19 Crisis.

The World Bank, 1818 H St. NW, Washington, DC, 20433, USA, (202) 473-1000, (202) 477-6391, eds03@worldbank.org, https://www.worldbank.org/; Global Financial Development Report 2019-2020: Bank Regulation and Supervision a Decade after the Global Financial Crisis; World Development Indicators (WDI) 2022; and World Development Report 2022: Finance for an Equitable Recovery.

BOLIVIA-DEFENSE EXPENDITURES

See BOLIVIA-ARMED FORCES

BOLIVIA-DIAMONDS

See BOLIVIA-MINERAL INDUSTRIES

BOLIVIA-DISPOSABLE INCOME

Inter-American Development Bank (IDB), 1300 New York Ave. NW, Washington, DC, 20577, USA, (202) 623-1000, (202) 623-3096, https://www.iadb.org/en; Latin Macro Watch (LMW).

BOLIVIA-ECONOMIC ASSISTANCE

Inter-American Development Bank (IDB), 1300 New York Ave. NW, Washington, DC, 20577, USA, (202) 623-1000, (202) 623-3096, https://www.iadb.org/en; Latin Macro Watch (LMW).

United Nations Statistics Division (UNSD), United Nations Plz., New York, NY, 10017, USA, (800) 253-9646, (212) 963-9851, statistics@un.org, https://unstats.un.org; Statistical Yearbook of the United Nations 2021.

BOLIVIA-ECONOMIC CONDITIONS

Bernan Press, 15250 NBN Way, Bldg. C, Blue Ridge Summit, PA, 17214, USA, (301) 459-2255, (800) 865-3457, (800) 865-3450, customercare@bernan.com, https://rowman.com/Page/Bernan; World Economic Outlook, April 2022.

Central Intelligence Agency (CIA), Office of Public Affairs, Washington, DC, 20505, USA, (703) 482-0623, https://www.cia.gov; The World Factbook.

The Economist Group: Economist Intelligence Unit (EIU), 900 3rd Ave., 16th Fl., New York, NY, 10022, USA, (212) 541-0500, americas@eiu.com, https://www.eiu.com; Bolivia Country Report.

Euromonitor International, Inc., 1 N Dearborn St., Ste. 1700, Chicago, IL, 60602, USA, (312) 922-1115, (312) 922-1157, info-usa@euromonitor.com, https://www.euromonitor.com/; Geographies and Market Research on the Consumer Finance Industry.

Inter-American Development Bank (IDB), 1300 New York Ave. NW, Washington, DC, 20577, USA, (202) 623-1000, (202) 623-3096, https://www.iadb.org/en; Latin Macro Watch (LMW).

International Monetary Fund (IMF), 700 19th St. NW, Washington, DC, 20431, USA, (202) 623-7000, (202) 623-4661, publications@imf.org, https://www.imf.org; IMF Data and World Economic Outlook.

Palgrave Macmillan, 1 New York Plaza, Ste. 4500, New York, NY, 10004-1562, USA, (800) 777-4643, orders@palgrave.com, https://www.palgrave.com/us; The Statesman's Yearbook, 2023.

Routledge - Taylor & Francis Group, 6000 Broken Sound Pkwy. NW, Ste. 300, Boca Raton, FL, 33487, USA, (800) 634-1420, (800) 634-7064, orders@taylorandfrancis.com, https://www.routledge.com/; The Europa World Year Book 2022.

United Nations Economic Commission for Latin America and the Caribbean (ECLAC), Casilla 179-D, Santiago, 7630412, CHL, (202) 596-3713, prensa@cepal.org, https://www.cepal.org/en; CEPALSTAT; Economic Survey of Latin America and the Caribbean 2021: Labour Dynamics and Employment Policies for Sustainable and Inclusive Recovery Beyond the COVID-19 Crisis; Foreign Direct Investment in Latin America and the Caribbean 2022; and Social Panorama of Latin America and the Caribbean 2022: Transforming Education as a Basis for Sustainable Development.

United Nations Statistics Division (UNSD), United Nations Plz., New York, NY, 10017, USA, (800) 253-9646, (212) 963-9851, statistics@un.org, https://unstats.un.org; World Statistics Pocketbook 2021.

The World Bank, 1818 H St. NW, Washington, DC, 20433, USA, (202) 473-1000, (202) 477-6391, eds03@worldbank.org, https://www.worldbank.org/; Bolivia (report); Global Economic Monitor (GEM); Global Economic Prospects, June 2022; The Global Findex Database 2021; and World Development Report 2022: Finance for an Equitable Recovery.

BOLIVIA-EDUCATION

Euromonitor International, Inc., 1 N Dearborn St., Ste. 1700, Chicago, IL, 60602, USA, (312) 922-1115, (312) 922-1157, info-usa@euromonitor.com, https://www.euromonitor.com/; Geographies.

Infoplease, c/o Sandbox Networks, Inc., 1 Lincoln St., 24th Fl., Boston, MA, 02111, USA, https://www.infoplease.com; Countries of the World.

Palgrave Macmillan, 1 New York Plaza, Ste. 4500, New York, NY, 10004-1562, USA, (800) 777-4643, orders@palgrave.com, https://www.palgrave.com/us; The Statesman's Yearbook, 2023.

Routledge - Taylor & Francis Group, 6000 Broken Sound Pkwy. NW, Ste. 300, Boca Raton, FL, 33487, USA, (800) 634-1420, (800) 634-7064, orders@taylorandfrancis.com, https://www.routledge.com/; The Europa World Year Book 2022.

UNESCO Institute for Statistics, C.P 250 Succursale H, Montreal, QC, H3G 2K8, CAN, (514) 343-6880 (Dial from U.S.), (514) 343-5740 (Fax from U.S.), uis.publications@unesco.org, http://uis.unesco.org/; Literacy and UIS.Stat.

United Nations Statistics Division (UNSD), United Nations Plz., New York, NY, 10017, USA, (800) 253-9646, (212) 963-9851, statistics@un.org, https://unstats.un.org; Millennium Development Goal Indicators.

The World Bank, 1818 H St. NW, Washington, DC, 20433, USA, (202) 473-1000, (202) 477-6391, eds03@worldbank.org, https://www.worldbank.org/; Bolivia (report); World Development Indicators (WDI) 2022; and World Development Report 2022: Finance for an Equitable Recovery.

BOLIVIA-ELECTRICITY

Inter-American Development Bank (IDB), 1300 New York Ave. NW, Washington, DC, 20577, USA, (202) 623-1000, (202) 623-3096, https://www.iadb.org/en; Latin Macro Watch (LMW).

International Energy Agency (IEA), 9 Rue de la Federation, Paris, 75739, FRA, info@iea.org, https://www.iea.org/; World Energy Outlook 2021.

U.S. Energy Information Administration (EIA), 1000 Independence Ave. SW, Washington, DC, 20585, USA, (202) 586-8800, infoctr@eia.gov, https://www.eia.gov; International Energy Outlook 2021.

United Nations Statistics Division (UNSD), United Nations Plz., New York, NY, 10017, USA, (800) 253-9646, (212) 963-9851, statistics@un.org, https://unstats.un.org; Statistical Yearbook of the United Nations 2021.

BOLIVIA-EMPLOYMENT

International Labour Organization (ILO), 4 Rte. des Morillons, Geneva, CH-1211, SWI, ilo@ilo.org,

https://www.ilo.org; NORMLEX Information System on International Labour Standards.

UK Data Service, University of Essex, Wivenhoe Park, Colchester, Essex, CO4 3SQ, GBR, https://ukdataservice.ac.uk/; International Aggregate Data.

United Nations Statistics Division (UNSD), United Nations Plz., New York, NY, 10017, USA, (800) 253-9646, (212) 963-9851, statistics@un.org, https://unstats.un.org; Statistical Yearbook of the United Nations 2021.

The World Bank, 1818 H St. NW, Washington, DC, 20433, USA, (202) 473-1000, (202) 477-6391, eds03@worldbank.org, https://www.worldbank.org/; Bolivia (report).

BOLIVIA-ENERGY INDUSTRIES

Enerdata, 47 avenue Alsace Lorraine, Grenoble, 38027, FRA, (332) 216-4534, research@enerdata.net, https://www.enerdata.net; World Refinery Database.

United Nations Statistics Division (UNSD), United Nations Plz., New York, NY, 10017, USA, (800) 253-9646, (212) 963-9851, statistics@un.org, https://unstats.un.org; Statistical Yearbook of the United Nations 2021.

BOLIVIA-ENVIRONMENTAL CONDITIONS

DSI Data Service & Information, Xantener Strasse 51a, Rheinberg, D-47495, GER, dsi@dsidata.com, https://www.dsidata.com/; Global Environmental Database.

The Economist Group: Economist Intelligence Unit (EIU), 900 3rd Ave., 16th Fl., New York, NY, 10022, USA, (212) 541-0500, americas@eiu.com, https://www.eiu.com; Bolivia Country Report.

United Nations Economic Commission for Latin America and the Caribbean (ECLAC), Casilla 179-D, Santiago, 7630412, CHL, (202) 596-3713, prensa@cepal.org, https://www.cepal.org/en; CEPALSTAT.

United Nations Statistics Division (UNSD), United Nations Plz., New York, NY, 10017, USA, (800) 253-9646, (212) 963-9851, statistics@un.org, https://unstats.un.org; World Statistics Pocketbook 2021.

BOLIVIA-EXPENDITURES, PUBLIC

Inter-American Development Bank (IDB), 1300 New York Ave. NW, Washington, DC, 20577, USA, (202) 623-1000, (202) 623-3096, https://www.iadb.org/en; Latin Macro Watch (LMW).

BOLIVIA-EXPORTS

Central Intelligence Agency (CIA), Office of Public Affairs, Washington, DC, 20505, USA, (703) 482-0623, https://www.cia.gov; The World Factbook.

The Economist Group: Economist Intelligence Unit (EIU), 900 3rd Ave., 16th Fl., New York, NY, 10022, USA, (212) 541-0500, americas@eiu.com, https://www.eiu.com; Bolivia Country Report.

Inter-American Development Bank (IDB), 1300 New York Ave. NW, Washington, DC, 20577, USA, (202) 623-1000, (202) 623-3096, https://www.iadb.org/en; Latin Macro Watch (LMW).

International Monetary Fund (IMF), 700 19th St. NW, Washington, DC, 20431, USA, (202) 623-7000, (202) 623-4661, publications@imf.org, https://www.imf.org; Direction of Trade Statistics (DOTS) and International Financial Statistics (IFS).

S&P Global, IHS Markit, 15 Inverness Way E, Englewood, CO, 80112, USA, (800) 447-2273, (800) 854-7179, https://ihsmarkit.com; Global Trade Atlas (GTA).

United Nations Conference on Trade and Development (UNCTAD), Palais des Nations, Geneva, 1211, SWI, (212) 963-6896, unctadinfo@unctad.org, https://unctad.org; Handbook of Statistics 2021.

The World Bank, 1818 H St. NW, Washington, DC, 20433, USA, (202) 473-1000, (202) 477-6391, eds03@worldbank.org, https://www.worldbank.org/; World Development Report 2022: Finance for an Equitable Recovery.

BOLIVIA-FEMALE WORKING POPULATION

See BOLIVIA-EMPLOYMENT

BOLIVIA-FERTILITY, HUMAN

Central Intelligence Agency (CIA), Office of Public Affairs, Washington, DC, 20505, USA, (703) 482-0623, https://www.cia.gov; The World Factbook.

BOLIVIA-FERTILIZER INDUSTRY

United Nations Food and Agricultural Organization (FAO), 2121 K St., Ste. 800B, Washington, DC, 20037, USA, (202) 653-2400 (Dial from U.S.), (202) 653-5760 (Fax from U.S.), fao-hq@fao.org, https://www.fao.org; The State of Food and Agriculture (SOFA) 2022.

BOLIVIA-FETAL MORTALITY

See BOLIVIA-MORTALITY

BOLIVIA-FINANCE

Inter-American Development Bank (IDB), 1300 New York Ave. NW, Washington, DC, 20577, USA, (202) 623-1000, (202) 623-3096, https://www.iadb.org/en; Latin Macro Watch (LMW).

Stockholm International Peace Research Institute (SIPRI), Signalistgatan 9, Stockholm, SE 169 72, SWE, https://www.sipri.org/; SIPRI Arms Transfers Database and SIPRI Military Expenditure Database.

The World Bank, 1818 H St. NW, Washington, DC, 20433, USA, (202) 473-1000, (202) 477-6391, eds03@worldbank.org, https://www.worldbank.org/; Bolivia (report).

BOLIVIA-FINANCE, PUBLIC

Bernan Press, 15250 NBN Way, Bldg. C, Blue Ridge Summit, PA, 17214, USA, (301) 459-2255, (800) 865-3457, (800) 865-3450, customercare@bernan.com, https://rowman.com/Page/Bernan; National Accounts Statistics: Analysis of Main Aggregates 2020.

The Economist Group: Economist Intelligence Unit (EIU), 900 3rd Ave., 16th Fl., New York, NY, 10022, USA, (212) 541-0500, americas@eiu.com, https://www.eiu.com; Bolivia Country Report.

Inter-American Development Bank (IDB), 1300 New York Ave. NW, Washington, DC, 20577, USA, (202) 623-1000, (202) 623-3096, https://www.iadb.org/en; Latin Macro Watch (LMW).

International Monetary Fund (IMF), 700 19th St. NW, Washington, DC, 20431, USA, (202) 623-7000, (202) 623-4661, publications@imf.org, https://www.imf.org; International Financial Statistics (IFS) and Regional Economic Outlook.

Palgrave Macmillan, 1 New York Plaza, Ste. 4500, New York, NY, 10004-1562, USA, (800) 777-4643, orders@palgrave.com, https://www.palgrave.com/us; The Statesman's Yearbook, 2023.

Routledge - Taylor & Francis Group, 6000 Broken Sound Pkwy. NW, Ste. 300, Boca Raton, FL, 33487, USA, (800) 634-1420, (800) 634-7064, orders@taylorandfrancis.com, https://www.routledge.com/; The Europa World Year Book 2022.

United Nations Statistics Division (UNSD), United Nations Plz., New York, NY, 10017, USA, (800) 253-9646, (212) 963-9851, statistics@un.org, https://unstats.un.org; National Accounts Main Aggregates Database and National Accounts Statistics: Main Aggregates and Detailed Tables.

The World Bank, 1818 H St. NW, Washington, DC, 20433, USA, (202) 473-1000, (202) 477-6391, eds03@worldbank.org, https://www.worldbank.org/; Bolivia (report).

BOLIVIA-FISHERIES

Inter-American Development Bank (IDB), 1300 New York Ave. NW, Washington, DC, 20577, USA, (202) 623-1000, (202) 623-3096, https://www.iadb.org/en; Latin Macro Watch (LMW).

Routledge - Taylor & Francis Group, 6000 Broken Sound Pkwy. NW, Ste. 300, Boca Raton, FL, 33487, USA, (800) 634-1420, (800) 634-7064, orders@taylorandfrancis.com, https://www.routledge.com/; The Europa World Year Book 2022.

United Nations Food and Agricultural Organization (FAO), 2121 K St., Ste. 800B, Washington, DC, 20037, USA, (202) 653-2400 (Dial from U.S.), (202) 653-5760 (Fax from U.S.), fao-hq@fao.org, https://www.fao.org; FAO Yearbook of Fishery and Aquaculture Statistics 2019; Fishery Statistical Collections Global Capture Production; FishStatJ; and The State of Food and Agriculture (SOFA) 2022.

United Nations Statistics Division (UNSD), United Nations Plz., New York, NY, 10017, USA, (800) 253-9646, (212) 963-9851, statistics@un.org, https://unstats.un.org; Statistical Yearbook of the United Nations 2021.

The World Bank, 1818 H St. NW, Washington, DC, 20433, USA, (202) 473-1000, (202) 477-6391, eds03@worldbank.org, https://www.worldbank.org/; Bolivia (report).

BOLIVIA-FOOD

United Nations Food and Agricultural Organization (FAO), 2121 K St., Ste. 800B, Washington, DC, 20037, USA, (202) 653-2400 (Dial from U.S.), (202) 653-5760 (Fax from U.S.), fao-hq@fao.org, https://www.fao.org; The State of Food and Agriculture (SOFA) 2022.

BOLIVIA-FOREIGN EXCHANGE RATES

Inter-American Development Bank (IDB), 1300 New York Ave. NW, Washington, DC, 20577, USA, (202) 623-1000, (202) 623-3096, https://www.iadb.org/en; Latin Macro Watch (LMW).

International Monetary Fund (IMF), 700 19th St. NW, Washington, DC, 20431, USA, (202) 623-7000, (202) 623-4661, publications@imf.org, https://www.imf.org; International Financial Statistics (IFS).

BOLIVIA-FORESTS AND FORESTRY

Inter-American Development Bank (IDB), 1300 New York Ave. NW, Washington, DC, 20577, USA, (202) 623-1000, (202) 623-3096, https://www.iadb.org/en; Latin Macro Watch (LMW).

Palgrave Macmillan, 1 New York Plaza, Ste. 4500, New York, NY, 10004-1562, USA, (800) 777-4643, orders@palgrave.com, https://www.palgrave.com/us; The Statesman's Yearbook, 2023.

Routledge - Taylor & Francis Group, 6000 Broken Sound Pkwy. NW, Ste. 300, Boca Raton, FL, 33487, USA, (800) 634-1420, (800) 634-7064, orders@taylorandfrancis.com, https://www.routledge.com/; The Europa World Year Book 2022.

United Nations Food and Agricultural Organization (FAO), 2121 K St., Ste. 800B, Washington, DC, 20037, USA, (202) 653-2400 (Dial from U.S.), (202) 653-5760 (Fax from U.S.), fao-hq@fao.org, https://www.fao.org; FAO Yearbook of Forest Products 2019 and The State of Food and Agriculture (SOFA) 2022.

United Nations Statistics Division (UNSD), United Nations Plz., New York, NY, 10017, USA, (800) 253-9646, (212) 963-9851, statistics@un.org, https://unstats.un.org; Statistical Yearbook of the United Nations 2021.

The World Bank, 1818 H St. NW, Washington, DC, 20433, USA, (202) 473-1000, (202) 477-6391, eds03@worldbank.org, https://www.worldbank.org/; Bolivia (report) and World Development Report 2022: Finance for an Equitable Recovery.

BOLIVIA-GAS PRODUCTION

See BOLIVIA-MINERAL INDUSTRIES

BOLIVIA-GEOGRAPHIC INFORMATION SYSTEMS

The World Bank, 1818 H St. NW, Washington, DC, 20433, USA, (202) 473-1000, (202) 477-6391, eds03@worldbank.org, https://www.worldbank.org/; Bolivia (report).

BOLIVIA-GOLD INDUSTRY

The World Bank, 1818 H St. NW, Washington, DC, 20433, USA, (202) 473-1000, (202) 477-6391,

eds03@worldbank.org, https://www.worldbank.org/; World Development Indicators (WDI) 2022.

BOLIVIA-GOLD PRODUCTION

See BOLIVIA-MINERAL INDUSTRIES

BOLIVIA-GROSS DOMESTIC PRODUCT

The Economist Group: Economist Intelligence Unit (EIU), 900 3rd Ave., 16th Fl., New York, NY, 10022, USA, (212) 541-0500, americas@eiu.com, https://www.eiu.com; Bolivia Country Report.

Inter-American Development Bank (IDB), 1300 New York Ave. NW, Washington, DC, 20577, USA, (202) 623-1000, (202) 623-3096, https://www.iadb.org/en; Latin Macro Watch (LMW).

Routledge - Taylor & Francis Group, 6000 Broken Sound Pkwy. NW, Ste. 300, Boca Raton, FL, 33487, USA, (800) 634-1420, (800) 634-7064, orders@taylorandfrancis.com, https://www.routledge.com/; The Europa World Year Book 2022.

United Nations Statistics Division (UNSD), United Nations Plz., New York, NY, 10017, USA, (800) 253-9646, (212) 963-9851, statistics@un.org, https://unstats.un.org; Statistical Yearbook of the United Nations 2021.

The World Bank, 1818 H St. NW, Washington, DC, 20433, USA, (202) 473-1000, (202) 477-6391, eds03@worldbank.org, https://www.worldbank.org/; World Development Indicators (WDI) 2022 and World Development Report 2022: Finance for an Equitable Recovery.

BOLIVIA-GROSS NATIONAL PRODUCT

Inter-American Development Bank (IDB), 1300 New York Ave. NW, Washington, DC, 20577, USA, (202) 623-1000, (202) 623-3096, https://www.iadb.org/en; Latin Macro Watch (LMW).

Palgrave Macmillan, 1 New York Plaza, Ste. 4500, New York, NY, 10004-1562, USA, (800) 777-4643, orders@palgrave.com, https://www.palgrave.com/us; The Statesman's Yearbook, 2023.

United Nations Statistics Division (UNSD), United Nations Plz., New York, NY, 10017, USA, (800) 253-9646, (212) 963-9851, statistics@un.org, https://unstats.un.org; Statistical Yearbook of the United Nations 2021.

The World Bank, 1818 H St. NW, Washington, DC, 20433, USA, (202) 473-1000, (202) 477-6391, eds03@worldbank.org, https://www.worldbank.org/; World Development Indicators (WDI) 2022 and World Development Report 2022: Finance for an Equitable Recovery.

BOLIVIA-HOUSING

Euromonitor International, Inc., 1 N Dearborn St., Ste. 1700, Chicago, IL, 60602, USA, (312) 922-1115, (312) 922-1157, info-usa@euromonitor.com, https://www.euromonitor.com/; Geographies.

BOLIVIA-ILLITERATE PERSONS

UNESCO Institute for Statistics, C.P 250 Succursale H, Montreal, QC, H3G 2K8, CAN, (514) 343-6880 (Dial from U.S.), (514) 343-5740 (Fax from U.S.), uis.publications@unesco.org, http://uis.unesco.org/; UIS.Stat.

BOLIVIA-IMPORTS

Central Intelligence Agency (CIA), Office of Public Affairs, Washington, DC, 20505, USA, (703) 482-0623, https://www.cia.gov; The World Factbook.

The Economist Group: Economist Intelligence Unit (EIU), 900 3rd Ave., 16th Fl., New York, NY, 10022, USA, (212) 541-0500, americas@eiu.com, https://www.eiu.com; Bolivia Country Report.

Inter-American Development Bank (IDB), 1300 New York Ave. NW, Washington, DC, 20577, USA, (202) 623-1000, (202) 623-3096, https://www.iadb.org/en; Latin Macro Watch (LMW).

International Monetary Fund (IMF), 700 19th St. NW, Washington, DC, 20431, USA, (202) 623-7000, (202) 623-4661, publications@imf.org, https://www.imf.org; Direction of Trade Statistics (DOTS) and International Financial Statistics (IFS).

S&P Global, IHS Markit, 15 Inverness Way E, Englewood, CO, 80112, USA, (800) 447-2273, (800) 854-7179, https://ihsmarkit.com; Global Trade Atlas (GTA).

United Nations Conference on Trade and Development (UNCTAD), Palais des Nations, Geneva, 1211, SWI, (212) 963-6896, unctadinfo@unctad.org, https://unctad.org; Handbook of Statistics 2021.

The World Bank, 1818 H St. NW, Washington, DC, 20433, USA, (202) 473-1000, (202) 477-6391, eds03@worldbank.org, https://www.worldbank.org/; World Development Report 2022: Finance for an Equitable Recovery.

BOLIVIA-INDUSTRIES

Central Intelligence Agency (CIA), Office of Public Affairs, Washington, DC, 20505, USA, (703) 482-0623, https://www.cia.gov; The World Factbook.

The Economist Group: Economist Intelligence Unit (EIU), 900 3rd Ave., 16th Fl., New York, NY, 10022, USA, (212) 541-0500, americas@eiu.com, https://www.eiu.com; Bolivia Country Report.

Euromonitor International, Inc., 1 N Dearborn St., Ste. 1700, Chicago, IL, 60602, USA, (312) 922-1115, (312) 922-1157, info-usa@euromonitor.com, https://www.euromonitor.com/; Geographies.

International Labour Organization (ILO), 4 Rte. des Morillons, Geneva, CH-1211, SWI, ilo@ilo.org, https://www.ilo.org; NORMLEX Information System on International Labour Standards.

Palgrave Macmillan, 1 New York Plaza, Ste. 4500, New York, NY, 10004-1562, USA, (800) 777-4643, orders@palgrave.com, https://www.palgrave.com/us; The Statesman's Yearbook, 2023.

Routledge - Taylor & Francis Group, 6000 Broken Sound Pkwy. NW, Ste. 300, Boca Raton, FL, 33487, USA, (800) 634-1420, (800) 634-7064, orders@taylorandfrancis.com, https://www.routledge.com/; The Europa World Year Book 2022.

United Nations Economic Commission for Latin America and the Caribbean (ECLAC), Casilla 179-D, Santiago, 7630412, CHL, (202) 596-3713, prensa@cepal.org, https://www.cepal.org/en; Economic Survey of Latin America and the Caribbean 2021: Labour Dynamics and Employment Policies for Sustainable and Inclusive Recovery Beyond the COVID-19 Crisis.

United Nations Industrial Development Organization (UNIDO), 1 United Nations Plz., Rm. DC1-1118, New York, NY, 10017, USA, (212) 963-6890, (212) 963 6885, (212) 963-7904, office.newyork@unido.org, https://www.unido.org/; Industrial Statistics Databases and International Yearbook of Industrial Statistics 2021.

The World Bank, 1818 H St. NW, Washington, DC, 20433, USA, (202) 473-1000, (202) 477-6391, eds03@worldbank.org, https://www.worldbank.org/; Bolivia (report) and World Development Indicators (WDI) 2022.

BOLIVIA-INFANT AND MATERNAL MORTALITY

See BOLIVIA-MORTALITY

BOLIVIA-INFLATION (FINANCE)

United Nations Economic Commission for Latin America and the Caribbean (ECLAC), Casilla 179-D, Santiago, 7630412, CHL, (202) 596-3713, prensa@cepal.org, https://www.cepal.org/en; Economic Survey of Latin America and the Caribbean 2021: Labour Dynamics and Employment Policies for Sustainable and Inclusive Recovery Beyond the COVID-19 Crisis.

BOLIVIA-INTEREST RATES

Inter-American Development Bank (IDB), 1300 New York Ave. NW, Washington, DC, 20577, USA, (202) 623-1000, (202) 623-3096, https://www.iadb.org/en; Latin Macro Watch (LMW).

BOLIVIA-INTERNAL REVENUE

Inter-American Development Bank (IDB), 1300 New York Ave. NW, Washington, DC, 20577, USA, (202) 623-1000, (202) 623-3096, https://www.iadb.org/en; Latin Macro Watch (LMW).

BOLIVIA-INTERNATIONAL FINANCE

Inter-American Development Bank (IDB), 1300 New York Ave. NW, Washington, DC, 20577, USA, (202) 623-1000, (202) 623-3096, https://www.iadb.org/en; Latin Macro Watch (LMW).

BOLIVIA-INTERNATIONAL LIQUIDITY

Inter-American Development Bank (IDB), 1300 New York Ave. NW, Washington, DC, 20577, USA, (202) 623-1000, (202) 623-3096, https://www.iadb.org/en; Latin Macro Watch (LMW).

BOLIVIA-INTERNATIONAL TRADE

The Economist Group: Economist Intelligence Unit (EIU), 900 3rd Ave., 16th Fl., New York, NY, 10022, USA, (212) 541-0500, americas@eiu.com, https://www.eiu.com; Bolivia Country Report.

Euromonitor International, Inc., 1 N Dearborn St., Ste. 1700, Chicago, IL, 60602, USA, (312) 922-1115, (312) 922-1157, info-usa@euromonitor.com, https://www.euromonitor.com/; Geographies.

Inter-American Development Bank (IDB), 1300 New York Ave. NW, Washington, DC, 20577, USA, (202) 623-1000, (202) 623-3096, https://www.iadb.org/en; Latin Macro Watch (LMW).

Palgrave Macmillan, 1 New York Plaza, Ste. 4500, New York, NY, 10004-1562, USA, (800) 777-4643, orders@palgrave.com, https://www.palgrave.com/us; The Statesman's Yearbook, 2023.

Routledge - Taylor & Francis Group, 6000 Broken Sound Pkwy. NW, Ste. 300, Boca Raton, FL, 33487, USA, (800) 634-1420, (800) 634-7064, orders@taylorandfrancis.com, https://www.routledge.com/; The Europa World Year Book 2022.

United Nations Conference on Trade and Development (UNCTAD), Palais des Nations, Geneva, 1211, SWI, (212) 963-6896, unctadinfo@unctad.org, https://unctad.org; Trade and Development Report 2021.

United Nations Economic Commission for Latin America and the Caribbean (ECLAC), Casilla 179-D, Santiago, 7630412, CHL, (202) 596-3713, prensa@cepal.org, https://www.cepal.org/en; Economic Survey of Latin America and the Caribbean 2021: Labour Dynamics and Employment Policies for Sustainable and Inclusive Recovery Beyond the COVID-19 Crisis.

United Nations Food and Agricultural Organization (FAO), 2121 K St., Ste. 800B, Washington, DC, 20037, USA, (202) 653-2400 (Dial from U.S.), (202) 653-5760 (Fax from U.S.), fao-hq@fao.org, https://www.fao.org; The State of Food and Agriculture (SOFA) 2022.

United Nations Statistics Division (UNSD), United Nations Plz., New York, NY, 10017, USA, (800) 253-9646, (212) 963-9851, statistics@un.org, https://unstats.un.org; International Trade Statistics Yearbook 2020 and Statistical Yearbook of the United Nations 2021.

The World Bank, 1818 H St. NW, Washington, DC, 20433, USA, (202) 473-1000, (202) 477-6391, eds03@worldbank.org, https://www.worldbank.org/; Bolivia (report); World Development Indicators (WDI) 2022; and World Development Report 2022: Finance for an Equitable Recovery.

World Trade Organization (WTO), Ctre. William Rappard, Rue de Lausanne 154, Case postale, Geneva, CH-1211, SWI, enquiries@wto.org, https://www.wto.org; World Trade Statistical Review 2022.

BOLIVIA-INTERNET USERS

International Telecommunication Union (ITU), Place des Nations, Geneva, CH-1211, SWI, itumail@itu.int, https://www.itu.int; Global Connectivity Report 2022; World Telecommunication/ICT Indicators Database 2021; and Yearbook of Statistics 2019.

The World Bank, 1818 H St. NW, Washington, DC, 20433, USA, (202) 473-1000, (202) 477-6391, eds03@worldbank.org, https://www.worldbank.org/; Bolivia (report).

BOLIVIA-INVESTMENTS

Inter-American Development Bank (IDB), 1300 New York Ave. NW, Washington, DC, 20577, USA, (202) 623-1000, (202) 623-3096, https://www.iadb.org/en; Latin Macro Watch (LMW).

International Monetary Fund (IMF), 700 19th St. NW, Washington, DC, 20431, USA, (202) 623-7000, (202) 623-4661, publications@imf.org, https://www.imf.org; International Financial Statistics (IFS).

BOLIVIA-IRRIGATION

Inter-American Development Bank (IDB), 1300 New York Ave. NW, Washington, DC, 20577, USA, (202) 623-1000, (202) 623-3096, https://www.iadb.org/en; Latin Macro Watch (LMW).

BOLIVIA-LABOR

Central Intelligence Agency (CIA), Office of Public Affairs, Washington, DC, 20505, USA, (703) 482-0623, https://www.cia.gov; The World Factbook.

Euromonitor International, Inc., 1 N Dearborn St., Ste. 1700, Chicago, IL, 60602, USA, (312) 922-1115, (312) 922-1157, info-usa@euromonitor.com, https://www.euromonitor.com/; Geographies.

International Labour Organization (ILO), 4 Rte. des Morillons, Geneva, CH-1211, SWI, ilo@ilo.org, https://www.ilo.org; NORMLEX Information System on International Labour Standards.

Palgrave Macmillan, 1 New York Plaza, Ste. 4500, New York, NY, 10004-1562, USA, (800) 777-4643, orders@palgrave.com, https://www.palgrave.com/us; The Statesman's Yearbook, 2023.

United Nations Food and Agricultural Organization (FAO), 2121 K St., Ste. 800B, Washington, DC, 20037, USA, (202) 653-2400 (Dial from U.S.), (202) 653-5760 (Fax from U.S.), fao-hq@fao.org, https://www.fao.org; The State of Food and Agriculture (SOFA) 2022.

The World Bank, 1818 H St. NW, Washington, DC, 20433, USA, (202) 473-1000, (202) 477-6391, eds03@worldbank.org, https://www.worldbank.org/; World Development Indicators (WDI) 2022 and World Development Report 2022: Finance for an Equitable Recovery.

BOLIVIA-LAND USE

Inter-American Development Bank (IDB), 1300 New York Ave. NW, Washington, DC, 20577, USA, (202) 623-1000, (202) 623-3096, https://www.iadb.org/en; Latin Macro Watch (LMW).

United Nations Statistics Division (UNSD), United Nations Plz., New York, NY, 10017, USA, (800) 253-9646, (212) 963-9851, statistics@un.org, https://unstats.un.org; Millennium Development Goal Indicators.

The World Bank, 1818 H St. NW, Washington, DC, 20433, USA, (202) 473-1000, (202) 477-6391, eds03@worldbank.org, https://www.worldbank.org/; World Development Report 2022: Finance for an Equitable Recovery.

BOLIVIA-LIFE EXPECTANCY

Central Intelligence Agency (CIA), Office of Public Affairs, Washington, DC, 20505, USA, (703) 482-0623, https://www.cia.gov; The World Factbook.

United Nations Department of Economic and Social Affairs (DESA), Population Division, 2 United Nations Plz., Rm. DC2-1950, New York, NY, 10017, USA, (212) 963-3209, (212) 963-2147, population@un.org, https://www.un.org/development/desa/pd/; World Population Ageing 2020 Highlights.

United Nations Statistics Division (UNSD), United Nations Plz., New York, NY, 10017, USA, (800) 253-9646, (212) 963-9851, statistics@un.org, https://unstats.un.org; Millennium Development Goal Indicators.

BOLIVIA-LITERACY

Central Intelligence Agency (CIA), Office of Public Affairs, Washington, DC, 20505, USA, (703) 482-0623, https://www.cia.gov; The World Factbook.

Euromonitor International, Inc., 1 N Dearborn St., Ste. 1700, Chicago, IL, 60602, USA, (312) 922-1115, (312) 922-1157, info-usa@euromonitor.com, https://www.euromonitor.com/; Geographies.

UNESCO Institute for Statistics, C.P 250 Succursale H, Montreal, QC, H3G 2K8, CAN, (514) 343-6880 (Dial from U.S.), (514) 343-5740 (Fax from U.S.), uis.publications@unesco.org, http://uis.unesco.org/; Literacy.

BOLIVIA-LIVESTOCK

Palgrave Macmillan, 1 New York Plaza, Ste. 4500, New York, NY, 10004-1562, USA, (800) 777-4643, orders@palgrave.com, https://www.palgrave.com/us; The Statesman's Yearbook, 2023.

Routledge - Taylor & Francis Group, 6000 Broken Sound Pkwy. NW, Ste. 300, Boca Raton, FL, 33487, USA, (800) 634-1420, (800) 634-7064, orders@taylorandfrancis.com, https://www.routledge.com/; The Europa World Year Book 2022.

United Nations Food and Agricultural Organization (FAO), 2121 K St., Ste. 800B, Washington, DC, 20037, USA, (202) 653-2400 (Dial from U.S.), (202) 653-5760 (Fax from U.S.), fao-hq@fao.org, https://www.fao.org; The State of Food and Agriculture (SOFA) 2022.

United Nations Statistics Division (UNSD), United Nations Plz., New York, NY, 10017, USA, (800) 253-9646, (212) 963-9851, statistics@un.org, https://unstats.un.org; Statistical Yearbook of the United Nations 2021.

BOLIVIA-MANUFACTURES

Inter-American Development Bank (IDB), 1300 New York Ave. NW, Washington, DC, 20577, USA, (202) 623-1000, (202) 623-3096, https://www.iadb.org/en; Latin Macro Watch (LMW).

BOLIVIA-MARRIAGE

United Nations Statistics Division (UNSD), United Nations Plz., New York, NY, 10017, USA, (800) 253-9646, (212) 963-9851, statistics@un.org, https://unstats.un.org; Statistical Yearbook of the United Nations 2021.

BOLIVIA-MERCURY PRODUCTION

See BOLIVIA-MINERAL INDUSTRIES

BOLIVIA-MINERAL INDUSTRIES

Barchart, 209 W Jackson Blvd., 2nd Fl., Chicago, IL, 60606, USA, (877) 247-4394, commodities@barchart.com, https://www.barchart.com/cmdty; The cmdty Yearbook 2023; cmdtyStats: Commodity Statistics and Fundamental Data; cmdtyView: Commodity Index; and Commodity Data and Prices.

Inter-American Development Bank (IDB), 1300 New York Ave. NW, Washington, DC, 20577, USA, (202) 623-1000, (202) 623-3096, https://www.iadb.org/en; Latin Macro Watch (LMW).

International Energy Agency (IEA), 9 Rue de la Federation, Paris, 75739, FRA, info@iea.org, https://www.iea.org/; World Energy Outlook 2021.

International Monetary Fund (IMF), 700 19th St. NW, Washington, DC, 20431, USA, (202) 623-7000, (202) 623-4661, publications@imf.org, https://www.imf.org; International Financial Statistics (IFS).

Palgrave Macmillan, 1 New York Plaza, Ste. 4500, New York, NY, 10004-1562, USA, (800) 777-4643, orders@palgrave.com, https://www.palgrave.com/us; The Statesman's Yearbook, 2023.

Routledge - Taylor & Francis Group, 6000 Broken Sound Pkwy. NW, Ste. 300, Boca Raton, FL, 33487, USA, (800) 634-1420, (800) 634-7064, orders@taylorandfrancis.com, https://www.routledge.com/; The Europa World Year Book 2022.

United Nations Conference on Trade and Development (UNCTAD), Palais des Nations, Geneva, 1211, SWI, (212) 963-6896, unctadinfo@unctad.org, https://unctad.org; Trade and Development Report 2021.

United Nations Statistics Division (UNSD), United Nations Plz., New York, NY, 10017, USA, (800) 253-9646, (212) 963-9851, statistics@un.org, https://unstats.un.org; Statistical Yearbook of the United Nations 2021.

BOLIVIA-MONEY SUPPLY

The Economist Group: Economist Intelligence Unit (EIU), 900 3rd Ave., 16th Fl., New York, NY, 10022, USA, (212) 541-0500, americas@eiu.com, https://www.eiu.com; Bolivia Country Report.

Inter-American Development Bank (IDB), 1300 New York Ave. NW, Washington, DC, 20577, USA, (202) 623-1000, (202) 623-3096, https://www.iadb.org/en; Latin Macro Watch (LMW).

International Monetary Fund (IMF), 700 19th St. NW, Washington, DC, 20431, USA, (202) 623-7000, (202) 623-4661, publications@imf.org, https://www.imf.org; International Financial Statistics (IFS).

Routledge - Taylor & Francis Group, 6000 Broken Sound Pkwy. NW, Ste. 300, Boca Raton, FL, 33487, USA, (800) 634-1420, (800) 634-7064, orders@taylorandfrancis.com, https://www.routledge.com/; The Europa World Year Book 2022.

United Nations Statistics Division (UNSD), United Nations Plz., New York, NY, 10017, USA, (800) 253-9646, (212) 963-9851, statistics@un.org, https://unstats.un.org; Statistical Yearbook of the United Nations 2021.

The World Bank, 1818 H St. NW, Washington, DC, 20433, USA, (202) 473-1000, (202) 477-6391, eds03@worldbank.org, https://www.worldbank.org/; Bolivia (report).

BOLIVIA-MORTALITY

UNICEF, 3 United Nations Plz., New York, NY, 10017, USA, (212) 303-7984, (917) 244-2215, https://www.unicef.org; The State of the World's Children 2023.

United Nations Statistics Division (UNSD), United Nations Plz., New York, NY, 10017, USA, (800) 253-9646, (212) 963-9851, statistics@un.org, https://unstats.un.org; Millennium Development Goal Indicators; Statistical Yearbook of the United Nations 2021; and World Statistics Pocketbook 2021.

The World Bank, 1818 H St. NW, Washington, DC, 20433, USA, (202) 473-1000, (202) 477-6391, eds03@worldbank.org, https://www.worldbank.org/; World Development Indicators (WDI) 2022.

World Health Organization (WHO), Ave. Appia 20, Geneva, CH-1211, SWI, (202) 974-3000 (Telephone in U.S.), publications@who.int, https://www.who.int/; Global Health Observatory (GHO).

BOLIVIA-MOTION PICTURES

Palgrave Macmillan, 1 New York Plaza, Ste. 4500, New York, NY, 10004-1562, USA, (800) 777-4643, orders@palgrave.com, https://www.palgrave.com/us; The Statesman's Yearbook, 2023.

BOLIVIA-MOTOR VEHICLES

International Road Federation (IRF), Madison Place, 500 Montgomery St., 5th Fl., Alexandria, VA, 22314, USA, (703) 535-1001, (703) 535-1007, info@irf.global, https://www.irf.global/; World Road Statistics (WRS).

BOLIVIA-NATURAL GAS PRODUCTION

See BOLIVIA-MINERAL INDUSTRIES

BOLIVIA-NUTRITION

United Nations Food and Agricultural Organization (FAO), 2121 K St., Ste. 800B, Washington, DC, 20037, USA, (202) 653-2400 (Dial from U.S.), (202) 653-5760 (Fax from U.S.), fao-hq@fao.org, https://www.fao.org; The State of Food and Agriculture (SOFA) 2022.

United Nations Statistics Division (UNSD), United Nations Plz., New York, NY, 10017, USA, (800) 253-9646, (212) 963-9851, statistics@un.org, https://unstats.un.org; Millennium Development Goal Indicators.

BOLIVIA-PAPER

See BOLIVIA-FORESTS AND FORESTRY

BOLIVIA-PEANUT PRODUCTION

See BOLIVIA-CROPS

BOLIVIA-PESTICIDES

United Nations Food and Agricultural Organization (FAO), 2121 K St., Ste. 800B, Washington, DC, 20037, USA, (202) 653-2400 (Dial from U.S.), (202) 653-5760 (Fax from U.S.), fao-hq@fao.org, https://www.fao.org; The State of Food and Agriculture (SOFA) 2022.

BOLIVIA-PETROLEUM INDUSTRY AND TRADE

Inter-American Development Bank (IDB), 1300 New York Ave. NW, Washington, DC, 20577, USA, (202) 623-1000, (202) 623-3096, https://www.iadb.org/en; Latin Macro Watch (LMW).

International Energy Agency (IEA), 9 Rue de la Federation, Paris, 75739, FRA, info@iea.org, https://www.iea.org/; World Energy Outlook 2021.

International Monetary Fund (IMF), 700 19th St. NW, Washington, DC, 20431, USA, (202) 623-7000, (202) 623-4661, publications@imf.org, https://www.imf.org; International Financial Statistics (IFS).

Palgrave Macmillan, 1 New York Plaza, Ste. 4500, New York, NY, 10004-1562, USA, (800) 777-4643, orders@palgrave.com, https://www.palgrave.com/us; The Statesman's Yearbook, 2023.

U.S. Energy Information Administration (EIA), 1000 Independence Ave. SW, Washington, DC, 20585, USA, (202) 586-8800, infoctr@eia.gov, https://www.eia.gov; International Energy Outlook 2021.

United Nations Statistics Division (UNSD), United Nations Plz., New York, NY, 10017, USA, (800) 253-9646, (212) 963-9851, statistics@un.org, https://unstats.un.org; Statistical Yearbook of the United Nations 2021.

BOLIVIA-POPULATION

Central Intelligence Agency (CIA), Office of Public Affairs, Washington, DC, 20505, USA, (703) 482-0623, https://www.cia.gov; The World Factbook.

The Economist Group: Economist Intelligence Unit (EIU), 900 3rd Ave., 16th Fl., New York, NY, 10022, USA, (212) 541-0500, americas@eiu.com, https://www.eiu.com; Bolivia Country Report.

Infoplease, c/o Sandbox Networks, Inc., 1 Lincoln St., 24th Fl., Boston, MA, 02111, USA, https://www.infoplease.com; Countries of the World.

Inter-American Development Bank (IDB), 1300 New York Ave. NW, Washington, DC, 20577, USA, (202) 623-1000, (202) 623-3096, https://www.iadb.org/en; Latin Macro Watch (LMW).

International Labour Organization (ILO), 4 Rte. des Morillons, Geneva, CH-1211, SWI, ilo@ilo.org, https://www.ilo.org; NORMLEX Information System on International Labour Standards.

Palgrave Macmillan, 1 New York Plaza, Ste. 4500, New York, NY, 10004-1562, USA, (800) 777-4643, orders@palgrave.com, https://www.palgrave.com/us; The Statesman's Yearbook, 2023.

Routledge - Taylor & Francis Group, 6000 Broken Sound Pkwy. NW, Ste. 300, Boca Raton, FL, 33487, USA, (800) 634-1420, (800) 634-7064, orders@taylorandfrancis.com, https://www.routledge.com/; The Europa World Year Book 2022.

UK Data Service, University of Essex, Wivenhoe Park, Colchester, Essex, CO4 3SQ, GBR, https://ukdataservice.ac.uk/; International Aggregate Data.

UNESCO Institute for Statistics, C.P 250 Succursale H, Montreal, QC, H3G 2K8, CAN, (514) 343-6880 (Dial from U.S.), (514) 343-5740 (Fax from U.S.), uis.publications@unesco.org, http://uis.unesco.org/; UIS.Stat.

United Nations Department of Economic and Social Affairs (DESA), Population Division, 2 United Nations Plz., Rm. DC2-1950, New York, NY, 10017, USA, (212) 963-3209, (212) 963-2147, population@un.org, https://www.un.org/development/desa/pd/; Revision of World Urbanization Prospects and World Population Ageing 2020 Highlights.

United Nations Development Programme (UNDP), One United Nations Plz., New York, NY, 10017, USA, (212) 906-5000, (212) 906-5001, https://www.undp.org; Human Development Report 2021-2022.

United Nations Economic Commission for Latin America and the Caribbean (ECLAC), Casilla 179-D, Santiago, 7630412, CHL, (202) 596-3713, prensa@cepal.org, https://www.cepal.org/en; CEPALSTAT and Social Panorama of Latin America and the Caribbean 2022: Transforming Education as a Basis for Sustainable Development.

United Nations Statistics Division (UNSD), United Nations Plz., New York, NY, 10017, USA, (800) 253-9646, (212) 963-9851, statistics@un.org, https://unstats.un.org; Statistical Yearbook of the United Nations 2021 and World Statistics Pocketbook 2021.

The World Bank, 1818 H St. NW, Washington, DC, 20433, USA, (202) 473-1000, (202) 477-6391, eds03@worldbank.org, https://www.worldbank.org/; Bolivia (report); The Global Findex Database 2021; and World Development Report 2022: Finance for an Equitable Recovery.

BOLIVIA-POPULATION DENSITY

Central Intelligence Agency (CIA), Office of Public Affairs, Washington, DC, 20505, USA, (703) 482-0623, https://www.cia.gov; The World Factbook.

Inter-American Development Bank (IDB), 1300 New York Ave. NW, Washington, DC, 20577, USA, (202) 623-1000, (202) 623-3096, https://www.iadb.org/en; Latin Macro Watch (LMW).

Palgrave Macmillan, 1 New York Plaza, Ste. 4500, New York, NY, 10004-1562, USA, (800) 777-4643, orders@palgrave.com, https://www.palgrave.com/us; The Statesman's Yearbook, 2023.

Routledge - Taylor & Francis Group, 6000 Broken Sound Pkwy. NW, Ste. 300, Boca Raton, FL, 33487, USA, (800) 634-1420, (800) 634-7064, orders@taylorandfrancis.com, https://www.routledge.com/; The Europa World Year Book 2022.

The World Bank, 1818 H St. NW, Washington, DC, 20433, USA, (202) 473-1000, (202) 477-6391, eds03@worldbank.org, https://www.worldbank.org/; Bolivia (report) and World Development Report 2022: Finance for an Equitable Recovery.

BOLIVIA-POWER RESOURCES

Euromonitor International, Inc., 1 N Dearborn St., Ste. 1700, Chicago, IL, 60602, USA, (312) 922-1115, (312) 922-1157, info-usa@euromonitor.com, https://www.euromonitor.com/; Geographies.

International Energy Agency (IEA), 9 Rue de la Federation, Paris, 75739, FRA, info@iea.org, https://www.iea.org/; World Energy Outlook 2021.

Palgrave Macmillan, 1 New York Plaza, Ste. 4500, New York, NY, 10004-1562, USA, (800) 777-4643, orders@palgrave.com, https://www.palgrave.com/us; The Statesman's Yearbook, 2023.

U.S. Energy Information Administration (EIA), 1000 Independence Ave. SW, Washington, DC, 20585, USA, (202) 586-8800, infoctr@eia.gov, https://www.eia.gov; International Energy Outlook 2021.

United Nations Statistics Division (UNSD), United Nations Plz., New York, NY, 10017, USA, (800) 253-9646, (212) 963-9851, statistics@un.org, https://unstats.un.org; Energy Statistics Yearbook 2019 and World Statistics Pocketbook 2021.

The World Bank, 1818 H St. NW, Washington, DC, 20433, USA, (202) 473-1000, (202) 477-6391, eds03@worldbank.org, https://www.worldbank.org/; World Development Report 2022: Finance for an Equitable Recovery.

BOLIVIA-PRICES

Euromonitor International, Inc., 1 N Dearborn St., Ste. 1700, Chicago, IL, 60602, USA, (312) 922-1115, (312) 922-1157, info-usa@euromonitor.com, https://www.euromonitor.com/; Geographies.

International Monetary Fund (IMF), 700 19th St. NW, Washington, DC, 20431, USA, (202) 623-7000, (202) 623-4661, publications@imf.org, https://www.imf.org; International Financial Statistics (IFS).

The World Bank, 1818 H St. NW, Washington, DC, 20433, USA, (202) 473-1000, (202) 477-6391, eds03@worldbank.org, https://www.worldbank.org/; Bolivia (report).

BOLIVIA-PUBLIC HEALTH

Euromonitor International, Inc., 1 N Dearborn St., Ste. 1700, Chicago, IL, 60602, USA, (312) 922-1115, (312) 922-1157, info-usa@euromonitor.com, https://www.euromonitor.com/; Geographies and Market Research on the Health and Wellness Industry.

Palgrave Macmillan, 1 New York Plaza, Ste. 4500, New York, NY, 10004-1562, USA, (800) 777-4643, orders@palgrave.com, https://www.palgrave.com/us; The Statesman's Yearbook, 2023.

U.S. Census Bureau, 4600 Silver Hill Rd., Washington, DC, 20233, USA, (301) 763-4636, (800) 923-8282, https://www.census.gov; HIV/AIDS Surveillance Data Base.

UNICEF, 3 United Nations Plz., New York, NY, 10017, USA, (212) 303-7984, (917) 244-2215, https://www.unicef.org; The State of the World's Children 2023.

United Nations Department of Economic and Social Affairs (DESA), Population Division, 2 United Nations Plz., Rm. DC2-1950, New York, NY, 10017, USA, (212) 963-3209, (212) 963-2147, population@un.org, https://www.un.org/development/desa/pd/; World Fertility Data 2019.

United Nations Development Programme (UNDP), One United Nations Plz., New York, NY, 10017, USA, (212) 906-5000, (212) 906-5001, https://www.undp.org; Human Development Report 2021-2022.

United Nations Statistics Division (UNSD), United Nations Plz., New York, NY, 10017, USA, (800) 253-9646, (212) 963-9851, statistics@un.org, https://unstats.un.org; Millennium Development Goal Indicators and Statistical Yearbook of the United Nations 2021.

The World Bank, 1818 H St. NW, Washington, DC, 20433, USA, (202) 473-1000, (202) 477-6391, eds03@worldbank.org, https://www.worldbank.org/; Bolivia (report).

World Health Organization (WHO), Ave. Appia 20, Geneva, CH-1211, SWI, (202) 974-3000 (Telephone in U.S.), publications@who.int, https://www.who.int/; Global Health Observatory (GHO) and Health Statistics and Information Systems.

BOLIVIA-PUBLISHERS AND PUBLISHING

Routledge - Taylor & Francis Group, 6000 Broken Sound Pkwy. NW, Ste. 300, Boca Raton, FL, 33487, USA, (800) 634-1420, (800) 634-7064, orders@taylorandfrancis.com, https://www.routledge.com/; The Europa World Year Book 2022.

BOLIVIA-RAILROADS

Janes, USA, (703) 574-7580, (888) 977-1519, customer.care@janes.com, https://www.janes.com; Janes World Railways 2021-2022.

Palgrave Macmillan, 1 New York Plaza, Ste. 4500, New York, NY, 10004-1562, USA, (800) 777-4643, orders@palgrave.com, https://www.palgrave.com/us; The Statesman's Yearbook, 2023.

Routledge - Taylor & Francis Group, 6000 Broken Sound Pkwy. NW, Ste. 300, Boca Raton, FL, 33487,

USA, (800) 634-1420, (800) 634-7064, orders@taylorandfrancis.com, https://www.routledge.com/; The Europa World Year Book 2022.

United Nations Statistics Division (UNSD), United Nations Plz., New York, NY, 10017, USA, (800) 253-9646, (212) 963-9851, statistics@un.org, https://unstats.un.org; Statistical Yearbook of the United Nations 2021.

BOLIVIA-RELIGION

Central Intelligence Agency (CIA), Office of Public Affairs, Washington, DC, 20505, USA, (703) 482-0623, https://www.cia.gov; The World Factbook.

Palgrave Macmillan, 1 New York Plaza, Ste. 4500, New York, NY, 10004-1562, USA, (800) 777-4643, orders@palgrave.com, https://www.palgrave.com/us; The Statesman's Yearbook, 2023.

BOLIVIA-RETAIL TRADE

Euromonitor International, Inc., 1 N Dearborn St., Ste. 1700, Chicago, IL, 60602, USA, (312) 922-1115, (312) 922-1157, info-usa@euromonitor.com, https://www.euromonitor.com/; Geographies.

Inter-American Development Bank (IDB), 1300 New York Ave. NW, Washington, DC, 20577, USA, (202) 623-1000, (202) 623-3096, https://www.iadb.org/en; Latin Macro Watch (LMW).

BOLIVIA-RICE PRODUCTION

See BOLIVIA-CROPS

BOLIVIA-ROADS

International Road Federation (IRF), Madison Place, 500 Montgomery St., 5th Fl., Alexandria, VA, 22314, USA, (703) 535-1001, (703) 535-1007, info@irf.global, https://www.irf.global/; World Road Statistics (WRS).

BOLIVIA-RUBBER INDUSTRY AND TRADE

International Rubber Study Group (IRSG), 51 Changi Business Park Central 2, Unit No. 6, 486066, SGP, https://www.rubberstudy.org; Monthly Rubber Bulletin (MRB); Rubber Industry Report; Rubber Statistical Bulletin; and World Rubber Industry Report (WRIO).

BOLIVIA-SOYBEAN PRODUCTION

See BOLIVIA-CROPS

BOLIVIA-STEEL PRODUCTION

See BOLIVIA-MINERAL INDUSTRIES

BOLIVIA-SUGAR PRODUCTION

See BOLIVIA-CROPS

BOLIVIA-SULPHUR PRODUCTION

See BOLIVIA-MINERAL INDUSTRIES

BOLIVIA-TAXATION

Inter-American Development Bank (IDB), 1300 New York Ave. NW, Washington, DC, 20577, USA, (202) 623-1000, (202) 623-3096, https://www.iadb.org/en; Latin Macro Watch (LMW).

International Road Federation (IRF), Madison Place, 500 Montgomery St., 5th Fl., Alexandria, VA, 22314, USA, (703) 535-1001, (703) 535-1007, info@irf.global, https://www.irf.global/; World Road Statistics (WRS).

The World Bank, 1818 H St. NW, Washington, DC, 20433, USA, (202) 473-1000, (202) 477-6391, eds03@worldbank.org, https://www.worldbank.org/; World Development Report 2022: Finance for an Equitable Recovery.

BOLIVIA-TELEPHONE

Palgrave Macmillan, 1 New York Plaza, Ste. 4500, New York, NY, 10004-1562, USA, (800) 777-4643, orders@palgrave.com, https://www.palgrave.com/us; The Statesman's Yearbook, 2023.

Routledge - Taylor & Francis Group, 6000 Broken Sound Pkwy. NW, Ste. 300, Boca Raton, FL, 33487, USA, (800) 634-1420, (800) 634-7064, orders@taylorandfrancis.com, https://www.routledge.com/; The Europa World Year Book 2022.

United Nations Statistics Division (UNSD), United Nations Plz., New York, NY, 10017, USA, (800) 253-9646, (212) 963-9851, statistics@un.org, https://unstats.un.org; World Statistics Pocketbook 2021.

BOLIVIA-TEXTILE INDUSTRY

United Nations Statistics Division (UNSD), United Nations Plz., New York, NY, 10017, USA, (800) 253-9646, (212) 963-9851, statistics@un.org, https://unstats.un.org; Statistical Yearbook of the United Nations 2021.

BOLIVIA-TOBACCO INDUSTRY

United Nations Statistics Division (UNSD), United Nations Plz., New York, NY, 10017, USA, (800) 253-9646, (212) 963-9851, statistics@un.org, https://unstats.un.org; Statistical Yearbook of the United Nations 2021.

BOLIVIA-TOURISM

Euromonitor International, Inc., 1 N Dearborn St., Ste. 1700, Chicago, IL, 60602, USA, (312) 922-1115, (312) 922-1157, info-usa@euromonitor.com, https://www.euromonitor.com/; Geographies.

Palgrave Macmillan, 1 New York Plaza, Ste. 4500, New York, NY, 10004-1562, USA, (800) 777-4643, orders@palgrave.com, https://www.palgrave.com/us; The Statesman's Yearbook, 2023.

Routledge - Taylor & Francis Group, 6000 Broken Sound Pkwy. NW, Ste. 300, Boca Raton, FL, 33487, USA, (800) 634-1420, (800) 634-7064, orders@taylorandfrancis.com, https://www.routledge.com/; The Europa World Year Book 2022.

United Nations Statistics Division (UNSD), United Nations Plz., New York, NY, 10017, USA, (800) 253-9646, (212) 963-9851, statistics@un.org, https://unstats.un.org; Statistical Yearbook of the United Nations 2021.

United Nations World Tourism Organization (UNWTO), Calle Poeta Joan Maragall 42, Madrid, 28020, SPA, info@unwto.org, https://www.unwto.org/; Yearbook of Tourism Statistics, 2021 Edition.

The World Bank, 1818 H St. NW, Washington, DC, 20433, USA, (202) 473-1000, (202) 477-6391, eds03@worldbank.org, https://www.worldbank.org/; Bolivia (report).

BOLIVIA-TRADE

See BOLIVIA-INTERNATIONAL TRADE

BOLIVIA-TRANSPORTATION

Central Intelligence Agency (CIA), Office of Public Affairs, Washington, DC, 20505, USA, (703) 482-0623, https://www.cia.gov; The World Factbook.

Euromonitor International, Inc., 1 N Dearborn St., Ste. 1700, Chicago, IL, 60602, USA, (312) 922-1115, (312) 922-1157, info-usa@euromonitor.com, https://www.euromonitor.com/; Geographies.

Inter-American Development Bank (IDB), 1300 New York Ave. NW, Washington, DC, 20577, USA, (202) 623-1000, (202) 623-3096, https://www.iadb.org/en; Latin Macro Watch (LMW).

Palgrave Macmillan, 1 New York Plaza, Ste. 4500, New York, NY, 10004-1562, USA, (800) 777-4643, orders@palgrave.com, https://www.palgrave.com/us; The Statesman's Yearbook, 2023.

Routledge - Taylor & Francis Group, 6000 Broken Sound Pkwy. NW, Ste. 300, Boca Raton, FL, 33487, USA, (800) 634-1420, (800) 634-7064, orders@taylorandfrancis.com, https://www.routledge.com/; The Europa World Year Book 2022.

The World Bank, 1818 H St. NW, Washington, DC, 20433, USA, (202) 473-1000, (202) 477-6391, eds03@worldbank.org, https://www.worldbank.org/; Bolivia (report).

BOLIVIA-UNEMPLOYMENT

International Labour Organization (ILO), 4 Rte. des Morillons, Geneva, CH-1211, SWI, ilo@ilo.org, https://www.ilo.org; NORMLEX Information System on International Labour Standards.

United Nations Statistics Division (UNSD), United Nations Plz., New York, NY, 10017, USA, (800) 253-9646, (212) 963-9851, statistics@un.org, https://unstats.un.org; Statistical Yearbook of the United Nations 2021.

BOLIVIA-VITAL STATISTICS

Palgrave Macmillan, 1 New York Plaza, Ste. 4500, New York, NY, 10004-1562, USA, (800) 777-4643, orders@palgrave.com, https://www.palgrave.com/us; The Statesman's Yearbook, 2023.

U.S. Census Bureau, 4600 Silver Hill Rd., Washington, DC, 20233, USA, (301) 763-4636, (800) 923-8282, https://www.census.gov; HIV/AIDS Surveillance Data Base.

United Nations Department of Economic and Social Affairs (DESA), Population Division, 2 United Nations Plz., Rm. DC2-1950, New York, NY, 10017, USA, (212) 963-3209, (212) 963-2147, population@un.org, https://www.un.org/development/desa/pd/; World Contraceptive Use 2021: Estimates and Projections of Family Planning Indicators and World Marriage Data 2019.

BOLIVIA-WAGES

International Labour Organization (ILO), 4 Rte. des Morillons, Geneva, CH-1211, SWI, ilo@ilo.org, https://www.ilo.org; NORMLEX Information System on International Labour Standards.

United Nations Statistics Division (UNSD), United Nations Plz., New York, NY, 10017, USA, (800) 253-9646, (212) 963-9851, statistics@un.org, https://unstats.un.org; Statistical Yearbook of the United Nations 2021.

The World Bank, 1818 H St. NW, Washington, DC, 20433, USA, (202) 473-1000, (202) 477-6391, eds03@worldbank.org, https://www.worldbank.org/; Bolivia (report).

BOLIVIA-WEATHER

See BOLIVIA-CLIMATE

BOLIVIA-WHEAT PRODUCTION

See BOLIVIA-CROPS

BOLIVIA-WHOLESALE PRICE INDEXES

Inter-American Development Bank (IDB), 1300 New York Ave. NW, Washington, DC, 20577, USA, (202) 623-1000, (202) 623-3096, https://www.iadb.org/en; Latin Macro Watch (LMW).

BOLIVIA-WHOLESALE TRADE

Inter-American Development Bank (IDB), 1300 New York Ave. NW, Washington, DC, 20577, USA, (202) 623-1000, (202) 623-3096, https://www.iadb.org/en; Latin Macro Watch (LMW).

BOLIVIA-WOOL PRODUCTION

See BOLIVIA-TEXTILE INDUSTRY

BOLIVIA-ZINC AND ZINC ORE

See BOLIVIA-MINERAL INDUSTRIES

BOMB THREATS

Bureau of Alcohol, Tobacco, Firearms and Explosives (ATF), United States Bomb Data Center (USBDC), 3750 Corporal Rd., Huntsville, AL, 35898 , USA, (800) 461-8841, usbdc@atf.gov, https://www.atf.gov/explosives/us-bomb-data-center; 2021 Explosives Incident Report.

BOMBINGS

Bureau of Alcohol, Tobacco, Firearms and Explosives (ATF), United States Bomb Data Center (USBDC), 3750 Corporal Rd., Huntsville, AL, 35898

, USA, (800) 461-8841, usbdc@atf.gov, https://www.atf.gov/explosives/us-bomb-data-center; 2021 Explosives Incident Report.

BONDS-FOREIGN-UNITED STATES PURCHASES AND SALES OF

U.S. Department of Commerce (DOC), Bureau of Economic Analysis (BEA), 4600 Silver Hill Rd., Washington, DC, 20233, USA, (301) 278-9004, customerservice@bea.gov, https://www.bea.gov; Survey of Current Business (SCB).

U.S. Department of the Treasury (DOT), 1500 Pennsylvania Ave. NW, Washington, DC, 20220, USA, (202) 622-2000, (202) 622-6415, https://home.treasury.gov; Treasury Bulletin.

BONDS-HOLDINGS BY SECTOR

Board of Governors of the Federal Reserve System, Constitution Ave. NW, Washington, DC, 20551, USA, (202) 452-3000, (202) 263-4869 (TDD), https://www.federalreserve.gov; Financial Accounts of the United States 2023.

BONDS-LIFE INSURANCE COMPANIES

American Council of Life Insurers (ACLI), 101 Constitution Ave. NW, Ste. 700, Washington, DC, 20001-2133, USA, (202) 624-2000, contact@acli.com, https://www.acli.com; Life Insurers Fact Book 2022.

Board of Governors of the Federal Reserve System, Constitution Ave. NW, Washington, DC, 20551, USA, (202) 452-3000, (202) 263-4869 (TDD), https://www.federalreserve.gov; Financial Accounts of the United States 2023.

BONDS-NEW ISSUES

Board of Governors of the Federal Reserve System, Constitution Ave. NW, Washington, DC, 20551, USA, (202) 452-3000, (202) 263-4869 (TDD), https://www.federalreserve.gov; Federal Reserve Bulletin.

BONDS-OWNERSHIP BY EQUITY HOLDERS

Investment Company Institute (ICI), 1401 H St. NW, Ste. 1200, Washington, DC, 20005, USA, (202) 326-5800, doug.richardson@ici.org, https://www.ici.org/; Quarterly Worldwide Mutual Fund Market.

BONDS-PRICES, YIELDS, SALES, AND ISSUES

Board of Governors of the Federal Reserve System, Constitution Ave. NW, Washington, DC, 20551, USA, (202) 452-3000, (202) 263-4869 (TDD), https://www.federalreserve.gov; Federal Reserve Bulletin.

Global Financial Data, Inc., 29122 Rancho Viejo Rd., Ste. 215, San Juan Capistrano, CA, 92675, USA, (949) 542-4200, sales@globalfinancialdata.com, https://globalfinancialdata.com/; Macroversal Database.

New York Stock Exchange (NYSE), 11 Wall St., New York, NY, 10005, USA, (212) 656-3000, (800) 281-3659, https://www.nyse.com; Real-Time Data Products.

U.S. Department of the Treasury (DOT), 1500 Pennsylvania Ave. NW, Washington, DC, 20220, USA, (202) 622-2000, (202) 622-6415, https://home.treasury.gov; Treasury Bulletin.

BONDS-RATINGS

Moody's Investors Service, 7 World Trade Center at 250 Greenwich St., New York, NY, 10007, USA, (212) 553-1653, (866) 330-6397, clientservices@moodys.com, https://www.moodys.com; unpublished data.

BONDS-UNITED STATES SAVINGS

Board of Governors of the Federal Reserve System, Constitution Ave. NW, Washington, DC, 20551, USA, (202) 452-3000, (202) 263-4869 (TDD), https://www.federalreserve.gov; Federal Reserve Bulletin.

U.S. Department of the Treasury (DOT), 1500 Pennsylvania Ave. NW, Washington, DC, 20220, USA, (202) 622-2000, (202) 622-6415, https://home.treasury.gov; Treasury Bulletin.

BOOKKEEPING

See ACCOUNTING, TAX PREPARATION, BOOKKEEPING, AND PAYROLL SERVICES

BOOKS

See also INFORMATION INDUSTRY and PUBLISHING INDUSTRIES

BOOKS-PRICES

Information Today, Inc., 143 Old Marlton Pike, Medford, NJ, 08055-8750, USA, (609) 654-6266, (609) 654-4309, custserv@infotoday.com, https://www.infotoday.com/; Library and Book Trade Almanac 2021.

U.S. Department of Labor (DOL), Bureau of Labor Statistics (BLS), Postal Square Bldg., 2 Massachusetts Ave. NE, Washington, DC, 20212-0001, USA, (202) 691-5200, (202) 691-7890, blsdata_staff@bls.gov, https://www.bls.gov; Industry Data (Producer Price Index - PPI).

BOOKS-PRODUCTION

Information Today, Inc., 143 Old Marlton Pike, Medford, NJ, 08055-8750, USA, (609) 654-6266, (609) 654-4309, custserv@infotoday.com, https://www.infotoday.com/; Library and Book Trade Almanac 2021.

BOOKS-READING

American Academy of Arts & Sciences, 136 Irving St., Cambridge, MA, 02138, USA, (617) 576-5000, https://www.amacad.org/; Humanities Indicators.

BOOKS-SALES

Book Industry Study Group (BISG), 232 Madison Ave., Ste. 1400, New York, NY, 10016, USA, (646) 336-7141, info@bisg.org, https://bisg.org/; unpublished data.

U.S. Census Bureau, 4600 Silver Hill Rd., Washington, DC, 20233, USA, (301) 763-4636, (800) 923-8282, https://www.census.gov; 2019 E-Stats Report: Measuring the Electronic Economy.

U.S. Department of Commerce (DOC), Bureau of Economic Analysis (BEA), 4600 Silver Hill Rd., Washington, DC, 20233, USA, (301) 278-9004, customerservice@bea.gov, https://www.bea.gov; National Income and Product Accounts (NIPA): 2022 Update and Survey of Current Business (SCB).

BOOTS

See FOOTWEAR

BORDER PATROLS

Bipartisan Policy Center (BPC), 1225 Eye St. NW, Ste. 1000, Washington, DC, 20005, USA, (202) 204-2400, bipartisaninfo@bipartisanpolicy.org, https://bipartisanpolicy.org/; What the Border Looked Like in FY2022.

Issue Lab by Candid, 32 Old Slip, 24th Fl., New York, NY, 10003, USA, (800) 424-9836, https://www.issuelab.org/; Issue Lab Special Collection: Immigration Strategies.

Migration Policy Institute (MPI), 1275 K St. NW, Ste. 800, Washington, DC, 20005, USA, (202) 266-1940, (202) 266-1900, info@migrationpolicy.org, https://www.migrationpolicy.org/; From Control to Crisis: Changing Trends and Policies Reshaping U.S.-Mexico Border Enforcement.

U.S. Department of Homeland Security (DHS), 2707 Martin Luther King Jr. Ave. SE, Washington, DC, 20528-0525, USA, (202) 282-8000, https://www.dhs.gov; Department of Homeland Security Border Security Metrics Report: 2021 and 2020 Homeland Threat Assessment.

U.S. Department of Homeland Security (DHS), Office of Immigration Statistics (OIS), 2707 Martin Luther King Jr. Ave. SE, Washington, DC, 20528-0525, USA, (202) 282-8000, immigrationstatistics@hq.dhs.gov, https://www.dhs.gov/office-immigration-statistics; Fiscal Year 2021 Enforcement Lifecycle Report; Immigration Enforcement Actions: 2020; and Yearbook of Immigration Statistics 2020.

U.S. Department of Homeland Security (DHS), U.S. Customs and Border Protection (CBP), 1300 Pennsylvania Ave. NW, Washington, DC, 20229, USA, (877) 227-5511, (202) 325-8000, https://www.cbp.gov; CBP Public Data Portal; Intellectual Property Rights (IPR) Seizure Statistics - Fiscal Year 2020; Quarterly CBP Trade Enforcement Bulletins; Snapshot: A Summary of CBP Facts and Figures; and Southwest Land Border Encounters (By Component).

Western Washington University, Border Policy Research Institute (BPRI), 516 High St., Bellingham, WA, 98225, USA, (360) 650-3000, laurie.trautman@wwu.edu, https://bpri.wwu.edu/; Border Barometer and COVID-19 and the US-Canada Border.

BORDER SECURITY

Bipartisan Policy Center (BPC), 1225 Eye St. NW, Ste. 1000, Washington, DC, 20005, USA, (202) 204-2400, bipartisaninfo@bipartisanpolicy.org, https://bipartisanpolicy.org/; What the Border Looked Like in FY2022.

Migration Policy Institute (MPI), 1275 K St. NW, Ste. 800, Washington, DC, 20005, USA, (202) 266-1940, (202) 266-1900, info@migrationpolicy.org, https://www.migrationpolicy.org/; From Control to Crisis: Changing Trends and Policies Reshaping U.S.-Mexico Border Enforcement.

Physicians for Human Rights (PHR), 256 W 38th St., 9th Fl., New York, NY, 10018, USA, (646) 564-3720, (646) 564-3750, https://phr.org/; Neither Safety nor Health: How Title 42 Expulsions Harm Health and Violate Rights.

Quinnipiac University Poll, Mount Carmel Campus, 275 Mount Carmel Ave., Hamden, CT, 06518, USA, (203) 582-5201, (800) 462-1944, poll@qu.edu, https://poll.qu.edu; 78% of Republicans Want to See Trump Run for President in 2024, Quinnipiac University National Poll Finds; Americans Now Split on Border Wall as Opposition Softens.

U.S. Department of Health and Human Services (HHS), Office of Inspector General (OIG), 330 Independence Ave. SW, Washington, DC, 20201, USA, (877) 696-6775, public.affairs@oig.hhs.gov, https://oig.hhs.gov/; Care Provider Facilities Described Challenges Addressing Mental Health Needs of Children in HHS Custody.

U.S. Department of Homeland Security (DHS), 2707 Martin Luther King Jr. Ave. SE, Washington, DC, 20528-0525, USA, (202) 282-8000, https://www.dhs.gov; Department of Homeland Security Border Security Metrics Report: 2021 and 2020 Homeland Threat Assessment.

U.S. Department of Homeland Security (DHS), Office of Immigration Statistics (OIS), 2707 Martin Luther King Jr. Ave. SE, Washington, DC, 20528-0525, USA, (202) 282-8000, immigrationstatistics@hq.dhs.gov, https://www.dhs.gov/office-immigration-statistics; Fiscal Year 2021 Enforcement Lifecycle Report.

U.S. Department of Homeland Security (DHS), U.S. Customs and Border Protection (CBP), 1300 Pennsylvania Ave. NW, Washington, DC, 20229, USA, (877) 227-5511, (202) 325-8000, https://www.cbp.gov; CBP Public Data Portal and Southwest Land Border Encounters (By Component).

Western Washington University, Border Policy Research Institute (BPRI), 516 High St., Bellingham, WA, 98225, USA, (360) 650-3000, laurie.trautman@wwu.edu, https://bpri.wwu.edu/; Border Barometer.

BORON

U.S. Department of the Interior (DOI), U.S. Geological Survey (USGS), National Minerals Information

Center (NMIC), 12201 Sunrise Valley Dr., Reston, VA, 20192, USA, (703) 648-4920, (703) 648-7971, (703) 648-4995, sfortier@usgs.gov, https://www.usgs.gov/centers/nmic; Mineral Commodity Summaries 2022 and Minerals Yearbook.

BOSNIA AND HERZEGOVINA-NATIONAL STATISTICAL OFFICE

Agency for Statistics of Bosnia and Herzegovina, Zelenih Beretki 26, Sarajevo, 71000, HBO, info@bhas.ba, https://bhas.gov.ba/; National Data Reports (Bosnia and Herzegovina).

BOSNIA AND HERZEGOVINA-AGRICULTURE

The Economist Group: Economist Intelligence Unit (EIU), 900 3rd Ave., 16th Fl., New York, NY, 10022, USA, (212) 541-0500, americas@eiu.com, https://www.eiu.com; Bosnia & Herzegovina Country Report.

Euromonitor International, Inc., 1 N Dearborn St., Ste. 1700, Chicago, IL, 60602, USA, (312) 922-1115, (312) 922-1157, info-usa@euromonitor.com, https://www.euromonitor.com/; Geographies.

Palgrave Macmillan, 1 New York Plaza, Ste. 4500, New York, NY, 10004-1562, USA, (800) 777-4643, orders@palgrave.com, https://www.palgrave.com/us; The Statesman's Yearbook, 2023.

Routledge - Taylor & Francis Group, 6000 Broken Sound Pkwy. NW, Ste. 300, Boca Raton, FL, 33487, USA, (800) 634-1420, (800) 634-7064, orders@taylorandfrancis.com, https://www.routledge.com/; The Europa World Year Book 2022.

United Nations Food and Agricultural Organization (FAO), 2121 K St., Ste. 800B, Washington, DC, 20037, USA, (202) 653-2400 (Dial from U.S.), (202) 653-5760 (Fax from U.S.), fao-hq@fao.org, https://www.fao.org; AQUASTAT and The State of Food and Agriculture (SOFA) 2022.

United Nations Statistics Division (UNSD), United Nations Plz., New York, NY, 10017, USA, (800) 253-9646, (212) 963-9851, statistics@un.org, https://unstats.un.org; Statistical Yearbook of the United Nations 2021.

The World Bank, 1818 H St. NW, Washington, DC, 20433, USA, (202) 473-1000, (202) 477-6391, eds03@worldbank.org, https://www.worldbank.org/; Bosnia and Herzegovina (report).

BOSNIA AND HERZEGOVINA-AIRLINES

International Civil Aviation Organization (ICAO), 999 Robert-Bourassa Blvd., Montreal, QC, H3C 5H7, CAN, (514) 954-8219 (Dial from U.S.), (514) 954-6077 (Fax from U.S.), icaohq@icao.int, https://www.icao.int; ICAO Regional Reports.

BOSNIA AND HERZEGOVINA-ARMED FORCES

Central Intelligence Agency (CIA), Office of Public Affairs, Washington, DC, 20505, USA, (703) 482-0623, https://www.cia.gov; The World Factbook.

Stockholm International Peace Research Institute (SIPRI), Signalistgatan 9, Stockholm, SE 169 72, SWE, https://www.sipri.org/; SIPRI Arms Transfers Database and SIPRI Military Expenditure Database.

BOSNIA AND HERZEGOVINA-BANKS AND BANKING

Euromonitor International, Inc., 1 N Dearborn St., Ste. 1700, Chicago, IL, 60602, USA, (312) 922-1115, (312) 922-1157, info-usa@euromonitor.com, https://www.euromonitor.com/; Geographies.

BOSNIA AND HERZEGOVINA-BROADCASTING

Central Intelligence Agency (CIA), Office of Public Affairs, Washington, DC, 20505, USA, (703) 482-0623, https://www.cia.gov; The World Factbook.

Euromonitor International, Inc., 1 N Dearborn St., Ste. 1700, Chicago, IL, 60602, USA, (312) 922-1115, (312) 922-1157, info-usa@euromonitor.com, https://www.euromonitor.com/; Geographies.

UNESCO Institute for Statistics, C.P 250 Succursale H, Montreal, QC, H3G 2K8, CAN, (514) 343-6880 (Dial from U.S.), (514) 343-5740 (Fax from U.S.), uis.publications@unesco.org, http://uis.unesco.org/; UIS.Stat.

BOSNIA AND HERZEGOVINA-BUDGET

Central Intelligence Agency (CIA), Office of Public Affairs, Washington, DC, 20505, USA, (703) 482-0623, https://www.cia.gov; The World Factbook.

BOSNIA AND HERZEGOVINA-BUSINESS

Global Entrepreneurship Monitor (GEM), Babson College, 231 Forest St., Babson Park, MA, 02457, USA, (781) 235-1200, info@gemconsortium.org, https://www.gemconsortium.org/; GEM 2022-2023 Global Report.

United Nations Statistics Division (UNSD), United Nations Plz., New York, NY, 10017, USA, (800) 253-9646, (212) 963-9851, statistics@un.org, https://unstats.un.org; Statistical Yearbook of the United Nations 2021.

BOSNIA AND HERZEGOVINA-COMMERCE

Palgrave Macmillan, 1 New York Plaza, Ste. 4500, New York, NY, 10004-1562, USA, (800) 777-4643, orders@palgrave.com, https://www.palgrave.com/us; The Statesman's Yearbook, 2023.

UK Data Service, University of Essex, Wivenhoe Park, Colchester, Essex, CO4 3SQ, GBR, https://ukdataservice.ac.uk/; International Aggregate Data.

BOSNIA AND HERZEGOVINA-CONSTRUCTION INDUSTRY

United Nations Statistics Division (UNSD), United Nations Plz., New York, NY, 10017, USA, (800) 253-9646, (212) 963-9851, statistics@un.org, https://unstats.un.org; Statistical Yearbook of the United Nations 2021.

BOSNIA AND HERZEGOVINA-CONSUMER PRICE INDEXES

Euromonitor International, Inc., 1 N Dearborn St., Ste. 1700, Chicago, IL, 60602, USA, (312) 922-1115, (312) 922-1157, info-usa@euromonitor.com, https://www.euromonitor.com/; Geographies.

The World Bank, 1818 H St. NW, Washington, DC, 20433, USA, (202) 473-1000, (202) 477-6391, eds03@worldbank.org, https://www.worldbank.org/; Bosnia and Herzegovina (report).

BOSNIA AND HERZEGOVINA-CROPS

Palgrave Macmillan, 1 New York Plaza, Ste. 4500, New York, NY, 10004-1562, USA, (800) 777-4643, orders@palgrave.com, https://www.palgrave.com/us; The Statesman's Yearbook, 2023.

United Nations Food and Agricultural Organization (FAO), 2121 K St., Ste. 800B, Washington, DC, 20037, USA, (202) 653-2400 (Dial from U.S.), (202) 653-5760 (Fax from U.S.), fao-hq@fao.org, https://www.fao.org; The State of Food and Agriculture (SOFA) 2022.

United Nations Statistics Division (UNSD), United Nations Plz., New York, NY, 10017, USA, (800) 253-9646, (212) 963-9851, statistics@un.org, https://unstats.un.org; Statistical Yearbook of the United Nations 2021.

BOSNIA AND HERZEGOVINA-DAIRY PROCESSING

Palgrave Macmillan, 1 New York Plaza, Ste. 4500, New York, NY, 10004-1562, USA, (800) 777-4643, orders@palgrave.com, https://www.palgrave.com/us; The Statesman's Yearbook, 2023.

United Nations Food and Agricultural Organization (FAO), 2121 K St., Ste. 800B, Washington, DC, 20037, USA, (202) 653-2400 (Dial from U.S.), (202) 653-5760 (Fax from U.S.), fao-hq@fao.org, https://www.fao.org; The State of Food and Agriculture (SOFA) 2022.

BOSNIA AND HERZEGOVINA-ECONOMIC CONDITIONS

Bernan Press, 15250 NBN Way, Bldg. C, Blue Ridge Summit, PA, 17214, USA, (301) 459-2255, (800) 865-3457, (800) 865-3450, customercare@bernan.com, https://rowman.com/Page/Bernan; World Economic Outlook, April 2022.

Central Intelligence Agency (CIA), Office of Public Affairs, Washington, DC, 20505, USA, (703) 482-0623, https://www.cia.gov; The World Factbook.

The Economist Group: Economist Intelligence Unit (EIU), 900 3rd Ave., 16th Fl., New York, NY, 10022, USA, (212) 541-0500, americas@eiu.com, https://www.eiu.com; Bosnia & Herzegovina Country Report.

Euromonitor International, Inc., 1 N Dearborn St., Ste. 1700, Chicago, IL, 60602, USA, (312) 922-1115, (312) 922-1157, info-usa@euromonitor.com, https://www.euromonitor.com/; Geographies.

Global Entrepreneurship Monitor (GEM), Babson College, 231 Forest St., Babson Park, MA, 02457, USA, (781) 235-1200, info@gemconsortium.org, https://www.gemconsortium.org/; GEM 2022-2023 Global Report.

International Monetary Fund (IMF), 700 19th St. NW, Washington, DC, 20431, USA, (202) 623-7000, (202) 623-4661, publications@imf.org, https://www.imf.org; IMF Data and World Economic Outlook.

Palgrave Macmillan, 1 New York Plaza, Ste. 4500, New York, NY, 10004-1562, USA, (800) 777-4643, orders@palgrave.com, https://www.palgrave.com/us; The Statesman's Yearbook, 2023.

United Nations Statistics Division (UNSD), United Nations Plz., New York, NY, 10017, USA, (800) 253-9646, (212) 963-9851, statistics@un.org, https://unstats.un.org; World Statistics Pocketbook 2021.

The World Bank, 1818 H St. NW, Washington, DC, 20433, USA, (202) 473-1000, (202) 477-6391, eds03@worldbank.org, https://www.worldbank.org/; Bosnia and Herzegovina (report); Global Economic Monitor (GEM); Global Economic Prospects, June 2022; and The Global Findex Database 2021.

BOSNIA AND HERZEGOVINA-EDUCATION

Euromonitor International, Inc., 1 N Dearborn St., Ste. 1700, Chicago, IL, 60602, USA, (312) 922-1115, (312) 922-1157, info-usa@euromonitor.com, https://www.euromonitor.com/; Geographies.

Infoplease, c/o Sandbox Networks, Inc., 1 Lincoln St., 24th Fl., Boston, MA, 02111, USA, https://www.infoplease.com; Countries of the World.

Palgrave Macmillan, 1 New York Plaza, Ste. 4500, New York, NY, 10004-1562, USA, (800) 777-4643, orders@palgrave.com, https://www.palgrave.com/us; The Statesman's Yearbook, 2023.

UNESCO Institute for Statistics, C.P 250 Succursale H, Montreal, QC, H3G 2K8, CAN, (514) 343-6880 (Dial from U.S.), (514) 343-5740 (Fax from U.S.), uis.publications@unesco.org, http://uis.unesco.org/; Literacy and UIS.Stat.

United Nations Statistics Division (UNSD), United Nations Plz., New York, NY, 10017, USA, (800) 253-9646, (212) 963-9851, statistics@un.org, https://unstats.un.org; Millennium Development Goal Indicators.

The World Bank, 1818 H St. NW, Washington, DC, 20433, USA, (202) 473-1000, (202) 477-6391, eds03@worldbank.org, https://www.worldbank.org/; Bosnia and Herzegovina (report).

BOSNIA AND HERZEGOVINA-ELECTRICITY

S&P Global Commodity Insights, One World Trade Center, New York, NY, 10007, USA, (800) 752-8878, support@platts.com, https://www.spglobal.com/commodityinsights/en; Platts European Power Alert.

U.S. Energy Information Administration (EIA), 1000 Independence Ave. SW, Washington, DC, 20585, USA, (202) 586-8800, infoctr@eia.gov, https://www.eia.gov; International Energy Outlook 2021.

United Nations Statistics Division (UNSD), United Nations Plz., New York, NY, 10017, USA, (800) 253-9646, (212) 963-9851, statistics@un.org, https://unstats.un.org; Energy Statistics Yearbook 2019 and Statistical Yearbook of the United Nations 2021.

BOSNIA AND HERZEGOVINA-EMPLOYMENT

UK Data Service, University of Essex, Wivenhoe Park, Colchester, Essex, CO4 3SQ, GBR, https://ukdataservice.ac.uk/; International Aggregate Data.

United Nations Statistics Division (UNSD), United Nations Plz., New York, NY, 10017, USA, (800) 253-9646, (212) 963-9851, statistics@un.org, https://unstats.un.org; Statistical Yearbook of the United Nations 2021.

The World Bank, 1818 H St. NW, Washington, DC, 20433, USA, (202) 473-1000, (202) 477-6391, eds03@worldbank.org, https://www.worldbank.org/; Bosnia and Herzegovina (report).

BOSNIA AND HERZEGOVINA-ENVIRONMENTAL CONDITIONS

DSI Data Service & Information, Xantener Strasse 51a, Rheinberg, D-47495, GER, dsi@dsidata.com, https://www.dsidata.com/; Global Environmental Database.

The Economist Group: Economist Intelligence Unit (EIU), 900 3rd Ave., 16th Fl., New York, NY, 10022, USA, (212) 541-0500, americas@eiu.com, https://www.eiu.com; Bosnia & Herzegovina Country Report.

United Nations Statistics Division (UNSD), United Nations Plz., New York, NY, 10017, USA, (800) 253-9646, (212) 963-9851, statistics@un.org, https://unstats.un.org; Statistical Yearbook of the United Nations 2021 and World Statistics Pocketbook 2021.

BOSNIA AND HERZEGOVINA-EXPORTS

Central Intelligence Agency (CIA), Office of Public Affairs, Washington, DC, 20505, USA, (703) 482-0623, https://www.cia.gov; The World Factbook.

The Economist Group: Economist Intelligence Unit (EIU), 900 3rd Ave., 16th Fl., New York, NY, 10022, USA, (212) 541-0500, americas@eiu.com, https://www.eiu.com; Bosnia & Herzegovina Country Report.

United Nations Statistics Division (UNSD), United Nations Plz., New York, NY, 10017, USA, (800) 253-9646, (212) 963-9851, statistics@un.org, https://unstats.un.org; International Trade Statistics Yearbook 2020.

BOSNIA AND HERZEGOVINA-FERTILITY, HUMAN

Central Intelligence Agency (CIA), Office of Public Affairs, Washington, DC, 20505, USA, (703) 482-0623, https://www.cia.gov; The World Factbook.

BOSNIA AND HERZEGOVINA-FINANCE

Stockholm International Peace Research Institute (SIPRI), Signalistgatan 9, Stockholm, SE 169 72, SWE, https://www.sipri.org/; SIPRI Arms Transfers Database and SIPRI Military Expenditure Database.

United Nations Statistics Division (UNSD), United Nations Plz., New York, NY, 10017, USA, (800) 253-9646, (212) 963-9851, statistics@un.org, https://unstats.un.org; Statistical Yearbook of the United Nations 2021.

The World Bank, 1818 H St. NW, Washington, DC, 20433, USA, (202) 473-1000, (202) 477-6391, eds03@worldbank.org, https://www.worldbank.org/; Bosnia and Herzegovina (report).

BOSNIA AND HERZEGOVINA-FINANCE, PUBLIC

Bernan Press, 15250 NBN Way, Bldg. C, Blue Ridge Summit, PA, 17214, USA, (301) 459-2255, (800) 865-3457, (800) 865-3450, customercare@bernan.com, https://rowman.com/Page/Bernan; National Accounts Statistics: Analysis of Main Aggregates 2020.

The Economist Group: Economist Intelligence Unit (EIU), 900 3rd Ave., 16th Fl., New York, NY, 10022, USA, (212) 541-0500, americas@eiu.com, https://www.eiu.com; Bosnia & Herzegovina Country Report.

International Monetary Fund (IMF), 700 19th St. NW, Washington, DC, 20431, USA, (202) 623-7000, (202) 623-4661, publications@imf.org, https://www.imf.org; Regional Economic Outlook.

Routledge - Taylor & Francis Group, 6000 Broken Sound Pkwy. NW, Ste. 300, Boca Raton, FL, 33487, USA, (800) 634-1420, (800) 634-7064, orders@taylorandfrancis.com, https://www.routledge.com/; The Europa World Year Book 2022.

United Nations Statistics Division (UNSD), United Nations Plz., New York, NY, 10017, USA, (800) 253-9646, (212) 963-9851, statistics@un.org, https://unstats.un.org; National Accounts Main Aggregates Database and National Accounts Statistics: Main Aggregates and Detailed Tables.

The World Bank, 1818 H St. NW, Washington, DC, 20433, USA, (202) 473-1000, (202) 477-6391, eds03@worldbank.org, https://www.worldbank.org/; Bosnia and Herzegovina (report).

BOSNIA AND HERZEGOVINA-FISHERIES

United Nations Food and Agricultural Organization (FAO), 2121 K St., Ste. 800B, Washington, DC, 20037, USA, (202) 653-2400 (Dial from U.S.), (202) 653-5760 (Fax from U.S.), fao-hq@fao.org, https://www.fao.org; FAO Yearbook of Fishery and Aquaculture Statistics 2019; Fishery Statistical Collections Global Capture Production; FishStatJ; and The State of Food and Agriculture (SOFA) 2022.

United Nations Statistics Division (UNSD), United Nations Plz., New York, NY, 10017, USA, (800) 253-9646, (212) 963-9851, statistics@un.org, https://unstats.un.org; Statistical Yearbook of the United Nations 2021.

The World Bank, 1818 H St. NW, Washington, DC, 20433, USA, (202) 473-1000, (202) 477-6391, eds03@worldbank.org, https://www.worldbank.org/; Bosnia and Herzegovina (report).

BOSNIA AND HERZEGOVINA-FOOD

United Nations Food and Agricultural Organization (FAO), 2121 K St., Ste. 800B, Washington, DC, 20037, USA, (202) 653-2400 (Dial from U.S.), (202) 653-5760 (Fax from U.S.), fao-hq@fao.org, https://www.fao.org; The State of Food and Agriculture (SOFA) 2022.

BOSNIA AND HERZEGOVINA-FORESTS AND FORESTRY

UNESCO Institute for Statistics, C.P 250 Succursale H, Montreal, QC, H3G 2K8, CAN, (514) 343-6880 (Dial from U.S.), (514) 343-5740 (Fax from U.S.), uis.publications@unesco.org, http://uis.unesco.org/; UIS.Stat.

United Nations Food and Agricultural Organization (FAO), 2121 K St., Ste. 800B, Washington, DC, 20037, USA, (202) 653-2400 (Dial from U.S.), (202) 653-5760 (Fax from U.S.), fao-hq@fao.org, https://www.fao.org; FAO Yearbook of Forest Products 2019 and The State of Food and Agriculture (SOFA) 2022.

United Nations Statistics Division (UNSD), United Nations Plz., New York, NY, 10017, USA, (800) 253-9646, (212) 963-9851, statistics@un.org, https://unstats.un.org; Statistical Yearbook of the United Nations 2021.

The World Bank, 1818 H St. NW, Washington, DC, 20433, USA, (202) 473-1000, (202) 477-6391, eds03@worldbank.org, https://www.worldbank.org/; Bosnia and Herzegovina (report).

BOSNIA AND HERZEGOVINA-GROSS DOMESTIC PRODUCT

The Economist Group: Economist Intelligence Unit (EIU), 900 3rd Ave., 16th Fl., New York, NY, 10022, USA, (212) 541-0500, americas@eiu.com, https://www.eiu.com; Bosnia & Herzegovina Country Report.

United Nations Statistics Division (UNSD), United Nations Plz., New York, NY, 10017, USA, (800) 253-9646, (212) 963-9851, statistics@un.org, https://unstats.un.org; Statistical Yearbook of the United Nations 2021.

BOSNIA AND HERZEGOVINA-GROSS NATIONAL PRODUCT

United Nations Statistics Division (UNSD), United Nations Plz., New York, NY, 10017, USA, (800) 253-9646, (212) 963-9851, statistics@un.org, https://unstats.un.org; Statistical Yearbook of the United Nations 2021.

BOSNIA AND HERZEGOVINA-HOUSING

Euromonitor International, Inc., 1 N Dearborn St., Ste. 1700, Chicago, IL, 60602, USA, (312) 922-1115, (312) 922-1157, info-usa@euromonitor.com, https://www.euromonitor.com/; Geographies.

BOSNIA AND HERZEGOVINA-ILLITERATE PERSONS

Central Intelligence Agency (CIA), Office of Public Affairs, Washington, DC, 20505, USA, (703) 482-0623, https://www.cia.gov; The World Factbook.

UNESCO Institute for Statistics, C.P 250 Succursale H, Montreal, QC, H3G 2K8, CAN, (514) 343-6880 (Dial from U.S.), (514) 343-5740 (Fax from U.S.), uis.publications@unesco.org, http://uis.unesco.org/; UIS.Stat.

BOSNIA AND HERZEGOVINA-IMPORTS

Central Intelligence Agency (CIA), Office of Public Affairs, Washington, DC, 20505, USA, (703) 482-0623, https://www.cia.gov; The World Factbook.

The Economist Group: Economist Intelligence Unit (EIU), 900 3rd Ave., 16th Fl., New York, NY, 10022, USA, (212) 541-0500, americas@eiu.com, https://www.eiu.com; Bosnia & Herzegovina Country Report.

United Nations Statistics Division (UNSD), United Nations Plz., New York, NY, 10017, USA, (800) 253-9646, (212) 963-9851, statistics@un.org, https://unstats.un.org; International Trade Statistics Yearbook 2020.

BOSNIA AND HERZEGOVINA-INDUSTRIES

Central Intelligence Agency (CIA), Office of Public Affairs, Washington, DC, 20505, USA, (703) 482-0623, https://www.cia.gov; The World Factbook.

The Economist Group: Economist Intelligence Unit (EIU), 900 3rd Ave., 16th Fl., New York, NY, 10022, USA, (212) 541-0500, americas@eiu.com, https://www.eiu.com; Bosnia & Herzegovina Country Report.

Euromonitor International, Inc., 1 N Dearborn St., Ste. 1700, Chicago, IL, 60602, USA, (312) 922-1115, (312) 922-1157, info-usa@euromonitor.com, https://www.euromonitor.com/; Geographies.

Palgrave Macmillan, 1 New York Plaza, Ste. 4500, New York, NY, 10004-1562, USA, (800) 777-4643, orders@palgrave.com, https://www.palgrave.com/us; The Statesman's Yearbook, 2023.

Routledge - Taylor & Francis Group, 6000 Broken Sound Pkwy. NW, Ste. 300, Boca Raton, FL, 33487, USA, (800) 634-1420, (800) 634-7064, orders@taylorandfrancis.com, https://www.routledge.com/; The Europa World Year Book 2022.

United Nations Industrial Development Organization (UNIDO), 1 United Nations Plz., Rm. DC1-1118, New York, NY, 10017, USA, (212) 963-6890, (212) 963 6885, (212) 963-7904, office.newyork@unido.org, https://www.unido.org/; Industrial Statistics Databases and International Yearbook of Industrial Statistics 2021.

The World Bank, 1818 H St. NW, Washington, DC, 20433, USA, (202) 473-1000, (202) 477-6391,

eds03@worldbank.org, https://www.worldbank.org/; Bosnia and Herzegovina (report).

BOSNIA AND HERZEGOVINA-INTERNATIONAL TRADE

The Economist Group: Economist Intelligence Unit (EIU), 900 3rd Ave., 16th Fl., New York, NY, 10022, USA, (212) 541-0500, americas@eiu.com, https://www.eiu.com; Bosnia & Herzegovina Country Report.

Euromonitor International, Inc., 1 N Dearborn St., Ste. 1700, Chicago, IL, 60602, USA, (312) 922-1115, (312) 922-1157, info-usa@euromonitor.com, https://www.euromonitor.com/; Geographies.

United Nations Statistics Division (UNSD), United Nations Plz., New York, NY, 10017, USA, (800) 253-9646, (212) 963-9851, statistics@un.org, https://unstats.un.org; International Trade Statistics Yearbook 2020 and Statistical Yearbook of the United Nations 2021.

The World Bank, 1818 H St. NW, Washington, DC, 20433, USA, (202) 473-1000, (202) 477-6391, eds03@worldbank.org, https://www.worldbank.org/; Bosnia and Herzegovina (report).

World Trade Organization (WTO), Ctre. William Rappard, Rue de Lausanne 154, Case postale, Geneva, CH-1211, SWI, enquiries@wto.org, https://www.wto.org; World Trade Statistical Review 2022.

BOSNIA AND HERZEGOVINA-INTERNET USERS

International Telecommunication Union (ITU), Place des Nations, Geneva, CH-1211, SWI, itumail@itu.int, https://www.itu.int; Global Connectivity Report 2022; World Telecommunication/ICT Indicators Database 2021; and Yearbook of Statistics 2019.

The World Bank, 1818 H St. NW, Washington, DC, 20433, USA, (202) 473-1000, (202) 477-6391, eds03@worldbank.org, https://www.worldbank.org/; Bosnia and Herzegovina (report).

BOSNIA AND HERZEGOVINA-LABOR

Central Intelligence Agency (CIA), Office of Public Affairs, Washington, DC, 20505, USA, (703) 482-0623, https://www.cia.gov; The World Factbook.

Euromonitor International, Inc., 1 N Dearborn St., Ste. 1700, Chicago, IL, 60602, USA, (312) 922-1115, (312) 922-1157, info-usa@euromonitor.com, https://www.euromonitor.com/; Geographies.

Palgrave Macmillan, 1 New York Plaza, Ste. 4500, New York, NY, 10004-1562, USA, (800) 777-4643, orders@palgrave.com, https://www.palgrave.com/us; The Statesman's Yearbook, 2023.

United Nations Statistics Division (UNSD), United Nations Plz., New York, NY, 10017, USA, (800) 253-9646, (212) 963-9851, statistics@un.org, https://unstats.un.org; Statistical Yearbook of the United Nations 2021.

BOSNIA AND HERZEGOVINA-LAND USE

United Nations Statistics Division (UNSD), United Nations Plz., New York, NY, 10017, USA, (800) 253-9646, (212) 963-9851, statistics@un.org, https://unstats.un.org; Millennium Development Goal Indicators.

BOSNIA AND HERZEGOVINA-LIBRARIES

UNESCO Institute for Statistics, C.P 250 Succursale H, Montreal, QC, H3G 2K8, CAN, (514) 343-6880 (Dial from U.S.), (514) 343-5740 (Fax from U.S.), uis.publications@unesco.org, http://uis.unesco.org/; UIS.Stat.

BOSNIA AND HERZEGOVINA-LIFE EXPECTANCY

Central Intelligence Agency (CIA), Office of Public Affairs, Washington, DC, 20505, USA, (703) 482-0623, https://www.cia.gov; The World Factbook.

United Nations Department of Economic and Social Affairs (DESA), Population Division, 2 United Nations Plz., Rm. DC2-1950, New York, NY, 10017, USA, (212) 963-3209, (212) 963-2147, population@un.org, https://www.un.org/development/desa/pd/; World Population Ageing 2020 Highlights.

United Nations Statistics Division (UNSD), United Nations Plz., New York, NY, 10017, USA, (800) 253-9646, (212) 963-9851, statistics@un.org, https://unstats.un.org; Millennium Development Goal Indicators.

BOSNIA AND HERZEGOVINA-LITERACY

Euromonitor International, Inc., 1 N Dearborn St., Ste. 1700, Chicago, IL, 60602, USA, (312) 922-1115, (312) 922-1157, info-usa@euromonitor.com, https://www.euromonitor.com/; Geographies.

UNESCO Institute for Statistics, C.P 250 Succursale H, Montreal, QC, H3G 2K8, CAN, (514) 343-6880 (Dial from U.S.), (514) 343-5740 (Fax from U.S.), uis.publications@unesco.org, http://uis.unesco.org/; Literacy.

BOSNIA AND HERZEGOVINA-LIVESTOCK

Palgrave Macmillan, 1 New York Plaza, Ste. 4500, New York, NY, 10004-1562, USA, (800) 777-4643, orders@palgrave.com, https://www.palgrave.com/us; The Statesman's Yearbook, 2023.

Routledge - Taylor & Francis Group, 6000 Broken Sound Pkwy. NW, Ste. 300, Boca Raton, FL, 33487, USA, (800) 634-1420, (800) 634-7064, orders@taylorandfrancis.com, https://www.routledge.com/; The Europa World Year Book 2022.

United Nations Food and Agricultural Organization (FAO), 2121 K St., Ste. 800B, Washington, DC, 20037, USA, (202) 653-2400 (Dial from U.S.), (202) 653-5760 (Fax from U.S.), fao-hq@fao.org, https://www.fao.org; The State of Food and Agriculture (SOFA) 2022.

United Nations Statistics Division (UNSD), United Nations Plz., New York, NY, 10017, USA, (800) 253-9646, (212) 963-9851, statistics@un.org, https://unstats.un.org; Statistical Yearbook of the United Nations 2021.

BOSNIA AND HERZEGOVINA-MARRIAGE

United Nations Statistics Division (UNSD), United Nations Plz., New York, NY, 10017, USA, (800) 253-9646, (212) 963-9851, statistics@un.org, https://unstats.un.org; Statistical Yearbook of the United Nations 2021.

BOSNIA AND HERZEGOVINA-MINERAL INDUSTRIES

Routledge - Taylor & Francis Group, 6000 Broken Sound Pkwy. NW, Ste. 300, Boca Raton, FL, 33487, USA, (800) 634-1420, (800) 634-7064, orders@taylorandfrancis.com, https://www.routledge.com/; The Europa World Year Book 2022.

United Nations Statistics Division (UNSD), United Nations Plz., New York, NY, 10017, USA, (800) 253-9646, (212) 963-9851, statistics@un.org, https://unstats.un.org; Energy Statistics Yearbook 2019 and Statistical Yearbook of the United Nations 2021.

The World Bank, 1818 H St. NW, Washington, DC, 20433, USA, (202) 473-1000, (202) 477-6391, eds03@worldbank.org, https://www.worldbank.org/; Bosnia and Herzegovina (report).

BOSNIA AND HERZEGOVINA-MONEY SUPPLY

The Economist Group: Economist Intelligence Unit (EIU), 900 3rd Ave., 16th Fl., New York, NY, 10022, USA, (212) 541-0500, americas@eiu.com, https://www.eiu.com; Bosnia & Herzegovina Country Report.

The World Bank, 1818 H St. NW, Washington, DC, 20433, USA, (202) 473-1000, (202) 477-6391, eds03@worldbank.org, https://www.worldbank.org/; Bosnia and Herzegovina (report).

BOSNIA AND HERZEGOVINA-MONUMENTS AND HISTORIC SITES

UNESCO Institute for Statistics, C.P 250 Succursale H, Montreal, QC, H3G 2K8, CAN, (514) 343-6880 (Dial from U.S.), (514) 343-5740 (Fax from U.S.), uis.publications@unesco.org, http://uis.unesco.org/; UIS.Stat.

BOSNIA AND HERZEGOVINA-MORTALITY

UNICEF, 3 United Nations Plz., New York, NY, 10017, USA, (212) 303-7984, (917) 244-2215, https://www.unicef.org; The State of the World's Children 2023.

United Nations Statistics Division (UNSD), United Nations Plz., New York, NY, 10017, USA, (800) 253-9646, (212) 963-9851, statistics@un.org, https://unstats.un.org; Millennium Development Goal Indicators; Statistical Yearbook of the United Nations 2021; and World Statistics Pocketbook 2021.

World Health Organization (WHO), Ave. Appia 20, Geneva, CH-1211, SWI, (202) 974-3000 (Telephone in U.S.), publications@who.int, https://www.who.int/; Global Health Observatory (GHO).

BOSNIA AND HERZEGOVINA-PETROLEUM INDUSTRY AND TRADE

U.S. Energy Information Administration (EIA), 1000 Independence Ave. SW, Washington, DC, 20585, USA, (202) 586-8800, infoctr@eia.gov, https://www.eia.gov; International Energy Outlook 2021.

United Nations Food and Agricultural Organization (FAO), 2121 K St., Ste. 800B, Washington, DC, 20037, USA, (202) 653-2400 (Dial from U.S.), (202) 653-5760 (Fax from U.S.), fao-hq@fao.org, https://www.fao.org; The State of Food and Agriculture (SOFA) 2022.

United Nations Statistics Division (UNSD), United Nations Plz., New York, NY, 10017, USA, (800) 253-9646, (212) 963-9851, statistics@un.org, https://unstats.un.org; Energy Statistics Yearbook 2019 and Statistical Yearbook of the United Nations 2021.

BOSNIA AND HERZEGOVINA-POPULATION

Central Intelligence Agency (CIA), Office of Public Affairs, Washington, DC, 20505, USA, (703) 482-0623, https://www.cia.gov; The World Factbook.

The Economist Group: Economist Intelligence Unit (EIU), 900 3rd Ave., 16th Fl., New York, NY, 10022, USA, (212) 541-0500, americas@eiu.com, https://www.eiu.com; Bosnia & Herzegovina Country Report.

Infoplease, c/o Sandbox Networks, Inc., 1 Lincoln St., 24th Fl., Boston, MA, 02111, USA, https://www.infoplease.com; Countries of the World.

Palgrave Macmillan, 1 New York Plaza, Ste. 4500, New York, NY, 10004-1562, USA, (800) 777-4643, orders@palgrave.com, https://www.palgrave.com/us; The Statesman's Yearbook, 2023.

Routledge - Taylor & Francis Group, 6000 Broken Sound Pkwy. NW, Ste. 300, Boca Raton, FL, 33487, USA, (800) 634-1420, (800) 634-7064, orders@taylorandfrancis.com, https://www.routledge.com/; The Europa World Year Book 2022.

UK Data Service, University of Essex, Wivenhoe Park, Colchester, Essex, CO4 3SQ, GBR, https://ukdataservice.ac.uk/; International Aggregate Data.

UNESCO Institute for Statistics, C.P 250 Succursale H, Montreal, QC, H3G 2K8, CAN, (514) 343-6880 (Dial from U.S.), (514) 343-5740 (Fax from U.S.), uis.publications@unesco.org, http://uis.unesco.org/; UIS.Stat.

United Nations Department of Economic and Social Affairs (DESA), Population Division, 2 United Nations Plz., Rm. DC2-1950, New York, NY, 10017, USA, (212) 963-3209, (212) 963-2147, population@un.org, https://www.un.org/development/desa/pd/; Revision of World Urbanization Prospects and World Population Ageing 2020 Highlights.

United Nations Statistics Division (UNSD), United Nations Plz., New York, NY, 10017, USA, (800) 253-9646, (212) 963-9851, statistics@un.org, https://unstats.un.org; Statistical Yearbook of the United Nations 2021 and World Statistics Pocketbook 2021.

The World Bank, 1818 H St. NW, Washington, DC, 20433, USA, (202) 473-1000, (202) 477-6391, eds03@worldbank.org, https://www.worldbank.org/; Bosnia and Herzegovina (report) and The Global Findex Database 2021.

BOSNIA AND HERZEGOVINA-POPULATION DENSITY

Central Intelligence Agency (CIA), Office of Public Affairs, Washington, DC, 20505, USA, (703) 482-0623, https://www.cia.gov; The World Factbook.

Palgrave Macmillan, 1 New York Plaza, Ste. 4500, New York, NY, 10004-1562, USA, (800) 777-4643, orders@palgrave.com, https://www.palgrave.com/us; The Statesman's Yearbook, 2023.

Routledge - Taylor & Francis Group, 6000 Broken Sound Pkwy. NW, Ste. 300, Boca Raton, FL, 33487, USA, (800) 634-1420, (800) 634-7064, orders@taylorandfrancis.com, https://www.routledge.com/; The Europa World Year Book 2022.

UNESCO Institute for Statistics, C.P 250 Succursale H, Montreal, QC, H3G 2K8, CAN, (514) 343-6880 (Dial from U.S.), (514) 343-5740 (Fax from U.S.), uis.publications@unesco.org, http://uis.unesco.org/; UIS.Stat.

The World Bank, 1818 H St. NW, Washington, DC, 20433, USA, (202) 473-1000, (202) 477-6391, eds03@worldbank.org, https://www.worldbank.org/; Bosnia and Herzegovina (report).

BOSNIA AND HERZEGOVINA-POWER RESOURCES

Euromonitor International, Inc., 1 N Dearborn St., Ste. 1700, Chicago, IL, 60602, USA, (312) 922-1115, (312) 922-1157, info-usa@euromonitor.com, https://www.euromonitor.com/; Geographies.

S&P Global Commodity Insights, One World Trade Center, New York, NY, 10007, USA, (800) 752-8878, support@platts.com, https://www.spglobal.com/commodityinsights/en; Platts European Power Daily.

U.S. Energy Information Administration (EIA), 1000 Independence Ave. SW, Washington, DC, 20585, USA, (202) 586-8800, infoctr@eia.gov, https://www.eia.gov; International Energy Outlook 2021.

United Nations Statistics Division (UNSD), United Nations Plz., New York, NY, 10017, USA, (800) 253-9646, (212) 963-9851, statistics@un.org, https://unstats.un.org; Energy Statistics Yearbook 2019; Statistical Yearbook of the United Nations 2021; and World Statistics Pocketbook 2021.

BOSNIA AND HERZEGOVINA-PRICES

The World Bank, 1818 H St. NW, Washington, DC, 20433, USA, (202) 473-1000, (202) 477-6391, eds03@worldbank.org, https://www.worldbank.org/; Bosnia and Herzegovina (report).

BOSNIA AND HERZEGOVINA-PUBLIC HEALTH

Euromonitor International, Inc., 1 N Dearborn St., Ste. 1700, Chicago, IL, 60602, USA, (312) 922-1115, (312) 922-1157, info-usa@euromonitor.com, https://www.euromonitor.com/; Geographies.

Palgrave Macmillan, 1 New York Plaza, Ste. 4500, New York, NY, 10004-1562, USA, (800) 777-4643, orders@palgrave.com, https://www.palgrave.com/us; The Statesman's Yearbook, 2023.

U.S. Census Bureau, 4600 Silver Hill Rd., Washington, DC, 20233, USA, (301) 763-4636, (800) 923-8282, https://www.census.gov; HIV/AIDS Surveillance Data Base.

UNICEF, 3 United Nations Plz., New York, NY, 10017, USA, (212) 303-7984, (917) 244-2215, https://www.unicef.org; The State of the World's Children 2023.

United Nations Department of Economic and Social Affairs (DESA), Population Division, 2 United Nations Plz., Rm. DC2-1950, New York, NY, 10017, USA, (212) 963-3209, (212) 963-2147, population@un.org, https://www.un.org/development/desa/pd/; World Fertility Data 2019.

United Nations Statistics Division (UNSD), United Nations Plz., New York, NY, 10017, USA, (800) 253-9646, (212) 963-9851, statistics@un.org, https://unstats.un.org; Millennium Development Goal Indicators and Statistical Yearbook of the United Nations 2021.

The World Bank, 1818 H St. NW, Washington, DC, 20433, USA, (202) 473-1000, (202) 477-6391, eds03@worldbank.org, https://www.worldbank.org/; Bosnia and Herzegovina (report).

World Health Organization (WHO), Ave. Appia 20, Geneva, CH-1211, SWI, (202) 974-3000 (Telephone in U.S.), publications@who.int, https://www.who.int/; Global Health Observatory (GHO).

BOSNIA AND HERZEGOVINA-PUBLISHERS AND PUBLISHING

UNESCO Institute for Statistics, C.P 250 Succursale H, Montreal, QC, H3G 2K8, CAN, (514) 343-6880 (Dial from U.S.), (514) 343-5740 (Fax from U.S.), uis.publications@unesco.org, http://uis.unesco.org/; UIS.Stat.

BOSNIA AND HERZEGOVINA-RAILROADS

Palgrave Macmillan, 1 New York Plaza, Ste. 4500, New York, NY, 10004-1562, USA, (800) 777-4643, orders@palgrave.com, https://www.palgrave.com/us; The Statesman's Yearbook, 2023.

United Nations Statistics Division (UNSD), United Nations Plz., New York, NY, 10017, USA, (800) 253-9646, (212) 963-9851, statistics@un.org, https://unstats.un.org; Statistical Yearbook of the United Nations 2021.

BOSNIA AND HERZEGOVINA-RELIGION

Central Intelligence Agency (CIA), Office of Public Affairs, Washington, DC, 20505, USA, (703) 482-0623, https://www.cia.gov; The World Factbook.

BOSNIA AND HERZEGOVINA-RETAIL TRADE

Euromonitor International, Inc., 1 N Dearborn St., Ste. 1700, Chicago, IL, 60602, USA, (312) 922-1115, (312) 922-1157, info-usa@euromonitor.com, https://www.euromonitor.com/; Geographies.

United Nations Statistics Division (UNSD), United Nations Plz., New York, NY, 10017, USA, (800) 253-9646, (212) 963-9851, statistics@un.org, https://unstats.un.org; Statistical Yearbook of the United Nations 2021.

BOSNIA AND HERZEGOVINA-RUBBER INDUSTRY AND TRADE

International Rubber Study Group (IRSG), 51 Changi Business Park Central 2, Unit No. 6, 486066, SGP, https://www.rubberstudy.org; Monthly Rubber Bulletin (MRB); Rubber Industry Report; Rubber Statistical Bulletin; and World Rubber Industry Report (WRIO).

United Nations Statistics Division (UNSD), United Nations Plz., New York, NY, 10017, USA, (800) 253-9646, (212) 963-9851, statistics@un.org, https://unstats.un.org; Statistical Yearbook of the United Nations 2021.

BOSNIA AND HERZEGOVINA-SHIPPING

United Nations Statistics Division (UNSD), United Nations Plz., New York, NY, 10017, USA, (800) 253-9646, (212) 963-9851, statistics@un.org, https://unstats.un.org; Statistical Yearbook of the United Nations 2021.

BOSNIA AND HERZEGOVINA-TELEPHONE

United Nations Statistics Division (UNSD), United Nations Plz., New York, NY, 10017, USA, (800) 253-9646, (212) 963-9851, statistics@un.org, https://unstats.un.org; World Statistics Pocketbook 2021.

BOSNIA AND HERZEGOVINA-TEXTILE INDUSTRY

Palgrave Macmillan, 1 New York Plaza, Ste. 4500, New York, NY, 10004-1562, USA, (800) 777-4643, orders@palgrave.com, https://www.palgrave.com/us; The Statesman's Yearbook, 2023.

United Nations Statistics Division (UNSD), United Nations Plz., New York, NY, 10017, USA, (800) 253-9646, (212) 963-9851, statistics@un.org, https://unstats.un.org; Statistical Yearbook of the United Nations 2021.

BOSNIA AND HERZEGOVINA-THEATER

UNESCO Institute for Statistics, C.P 250 Succursale H, Montreal, QC, H3G 2K8, CAN, (514) 343-6880 (Dial from U.S.), (514) 343-5740 (Fax from U.S.), uis.publications@unesco.org, http://uis.unesco.org/; UIS.Stat.

BOSNIA AND HERZEGOVINA-TOBACCO INDUSTRY

United Nations Statistics Division (UNSD), United Nations Plz., New York, NY, 10017, USA, (800) 253-9646, (212) 963-9851, statistics@un.org, https://unstats.un.org; Statistical Yearbook of the United Nations 2021.

BOSNIA AND HERZEGOVINA-TOURISM

Euromonitor International, Inc., 1 N Dearborn St., Ste. 1700, Chicago, IL, 60602, USA, (312) 922-1115, (312) 922-1157, info-usa@euromonitor.com, https://www.euromonitor.com/; Geographies.

United Nations Statistics Division (UNSD), United Nations Plz., New York, NY, 10017, USA, (800) 253-9646, (212) 963-9851, statistics@un.org, https://unstats.un.org; Statistical Yearbook of the United Nations 2021.

The World Bank, 1818 H St. NW, Washington, DC, 20433, USA, (202) 473-1000, (202) 477-6391, eds03@worldbank.org, https://www.worldbank.org/; Bosnia and Herzegovina (report).

BOSNIA AND HERZEGOVINA-TRANSPORTATION

Central Intelligence Agency (CIA), Office of Public Affairs, Washington, DC, 20505, USA, (703) 482-0623, https://www.cia.gov; The World Factbook.

Euromonitor International, Inc., 1 N Dearborn St., Ste. 1700, Chicago, IL, 60602, USA, (312) 922-1115, (312) 922-1157, info-usa@euromonitor.com, https://www.euromonitor.com/; Geographies.

Palgrave Macmillan, 1 New York Plaza, Ste. 4500, New York, NY, 10004-1562, USA, (800) 777-4643, orders@palgrave.com, https://www.palgrave.com/us; The Statesman's Yearbook, 2023.

The World Bank, 1818 H St. NW, Washington, DC, 20433, USA, (202) 473-1000, (202) 477-6391, eds03@worldbank.org, https://www.worldbank.org/; Bosnia and Herzegovina (report).

BOSNIA AND HERZEGOVINA-UNEMPLOYMENT

Palgrave Macmillan, 1 New York Plaza, Ste. 4500, New York, NY, 10004-1562, USA, (800) 777-4643, orders@palgrave.com, https://www.palgrave.com/us; The Statesman's Yearbook, 2023.

United Nations Statistics Division (UNSD), United Nations Plz., New York, NY, 10017, USA, (800) 253-9646, (212) 963-9851, statistics@un.org, https://unstats.un.org; Statistical Yearbook of the United Nations 2021.

The World Bank, 1818 H St. NW, Washington, DC, 20433, USA, (202) 473-1000, (202) 477-6391, eds03@worldbank.org, https://www.worldbank.org/; Bosnia and Herzegovina (report).

BOSNIA AND HERZEGOVINA-VITAL STATISTICS

Palgrave Macmillan, 1 New York Plaza, Ste. 4500, New York, NY, 10004-1562, USA, (800) 777-4643, orders@palgrave.com, https://www.palgrave.com/us; The Statesman's Yearbook, 2023.

U.S. Census Bureau, 4600 Silver Hill Rd., Washington, DC, 20233, USA, (301) 763-4636, (800) 923-8282, https://www.census.gov; HIV/AIDS Surveillance Data Base.

United Nations Department of Economic and Social Affairs (DESA), Population Division, 2 United Nations Plz., Rm. DC2-1950, New York, NY, 10017, USA, (212) 963-3209, (212) 963-2147, population@un.org, https://www.un.org/development/desa/pd/; World Contraceptive Use 2021: Estimates and Projections of Family Planning Indicators and World Marriage Data 2019.

United Nations Statistics Division (UNSD), United Nations Plz., New York, NY, 10017, USA, (800) 253-9646, (212) 963-9851, statistics@un.org, https://unstats.un.org; Statistical Yearbook of the United Nations 2021.

BOSNIA AND HERZEGOVINA-WAGES

United Nations Statistics Division (UNSD), United Nations Plz., New York, NY, 10017, USA, (800) 253-9646, (212) 963-9851, statistics@un.org, https://unstats.un.org; Statistical Yearbook of the United Nations 2021.

The World Bank, 1818 H St. NW, Washington, DC, 20433, USA, (202) 473-1000, (202) 477-6391, eds03@worldbank.org, https://www.worldbank.org/; Bosnia and Herzegovina (report).

BOSNIA AND HERZEGOVINA-WHOLESALE TRADE

United Nations Statistics Division (UNSD), United Nations Plz., New York, NY, 10017, USA, (800) 253-9646, (212) 963-9851, statistics@un.org, https://unstats.un.org; Statistical Yearbook of the United Nations 2021.

BOTSWANA-NATIONAL STATISTICAL OFFICE

Statistics Botswana, Ministry of Finance and Development Planning, Private Bag 0024, Gaborone, BWA, info@statsbots.org.bw, https://www.statsbots.org.bw/; National Data Reports (Botswana).

BOTSWANA-PRIMARY STATISTICS SOURCES

Statistics Botswana, Ministry of Finance and Development Planning, Private Bag 0024, Gaborone, BWA, info@statsbots.org.bw, https://www.statsbots.org.bw/; Statistical Yearbook of Botswana and Vital Statistics Report 2019.

BOTSWANA-AGRICULTURE

African Development Bank Group (AfDB), Avenue Joseph Anoma, 01 BP 1387, Abidjan, 01, COT, https://www.afdb.org; African Economic Outlook 2021 and Compendium of Statistics on Bank Group Operations 2019.

The Economist Group: Economist Intelligence Unit (EIU), 900 3rd Ave., 16th Fl., New York, NY, 10022, USA, (212) 541-0500, americas@eiu.com, https://www.eiu.com; Botswana Country Report.

Euromonitor International, Inc., 1 N Dearborn St., Ste. 1700, Chicago, IL, 60602, USA, (312) 922-1115, (312) 922-1157, info-usa@euromonitor.com, https://www.euromonitor.com/; Geographies.

Palgrave Macmillan, 1 New York Plaza, Ste. 4500, New York, NY, 10004-1562, USA, (800) 777-4643, orders@palgrave.com, https://www.palgrave.com/us; The Statesman's Yearbook, 2023.

Routledge - Taylor & Francis Group, 6000 Broken Sound Pkwy. NW, Ste. 300, Boca Raton, FL, 33487, USA, (800) 634-1420, (800) 634-7064, orders@taylorandfrancis.com, https://www.routledge.com/; The Europa World Year Book 2022.

United Nations Economic Commission for Africa (UNECA), PO Box 3001, Addis Ababa, ETH, ecainfo@uneca.org, https://www.uneca.org/; African Statistical Yearbook 2020 and Economic Report on Africa 2021.

United Nations Food and Agricultural Organization (FAO), 2121 K St., Ste. 800B, Washington, DC, 20037, USA, (202) 653-2400 (Dial from U.S.), (202) 653-5760 (Fax from U.S.), fao-hq@fao.org, https://www.fao.org; AQUASTAT and The State of Food and Agriculture (SOFA) 2022.

United Nations Statistics Division (UNSD), United Nations Plz., New York, NY, 10017, USA, (800) 253-9646, (212) 963-9851, statistics@un.org, https://unstats.un.org; Statistical Yearbook of the United Nations 2021.

The World Bank, 1818 H St. NW, Washington, DC, 20433, USA, (202) 473-1000, (202) 477-6391, eds03@worldbank.org, https://www.worldbank.org/; Botswana (report) and World Development Indicators (WDI) 2022.

BOTSWANA-AIRLINES

Palgrave Macmillan, 1 New York Plaza, Ste. 4500, New York, NY, 10004-1562, USA, (800) 777-4643, orders@palgrave.com, https://www.palgrave.com/us; The Statesman's Yearbook, 2023.

Routledge - Taylor & Francis Group, 6000 Broken Sound Pkwy. NW, Ste. 300, Boca Raton, FL, 33487, USA, (800) 634-1420, (800) 634-7064, orders@taylorandfrancis.com, https://www.routledge.com/; The Europa World Year Book 2022.

United Nations Economic Commission for Africa (UNECA), PO Box 3001, Addis Ababa, ETH, ecainfo@uneca.org, https://www.uneca.org/; African Statistical Yearbook 2020.

BOTSWANA-ALUMINUM PRODUCTION

See BOTSWANA-MINERAL INDUSTRIES

BOTSWANA-ARMED FORCES

Central Intelligence Agency (CIA), Office of Public Affairs, Washington, DC, 20505, USA, (703) 482-0623, https://www.cia.gov; The World Factbook.

International Institute for Strategic Studies (IISS) - Americas, 2121 K St. NW, Ste. 600, Washington, DC, 20037, USA, (202) 659-1490, (202) 659-1499, https://www.iiss.org/; The Military Balance 2022.

Palgrave Macmillan, 1 New York Plaza, Ste. 4500, New York, NY, 10004-1562, USA, (800) 777-4643, orders@palgrave.com, https://www.palgrave.com/us; The Statesman's Yearbook, 2023.

Stockholm International Peace Research Institute (SIPRI), Signalistgatan 9, Stockholm, SE 169 72, SWE, https://www.sipri.org/; SIPRI Arms Transfers Database and SIPRI Military Expenditure Database.

BOTSWANA-BALANCE OF PAYMENTS

African Development Bank Group (AfDB), Avenue Joseph Anoma, 01 BP 1387, Abidjan, 01, COT, https://www.afdb.org; The AfDB Statistics Pocketbook 2019.

International Monetary Fund (IMF), 700 19th St. NW, Washington, DC, 20431, USA, (202) 623-7000, (202) 623-4661, publications@imf.org, https://www.imf.org; Balance of Payments Statistics: Annual Report 2021.

Routledge - Taylor & Francis Group, 6000 Broken Sound Pkwy. NW, Ste. 300, Boca Raton, FL, 33487, USA, (800) 634-1420, (800) 634-7064, orders@taylorandfrancis.com, https://www.routledge.com/; The Europa World Year Book 2022.

United Nations Conference on Trade and Development (UNCTAD), Palais des Nations, Geneva, 1211, SWI, (212) 963-6896, unctadinfo@unctad.org, https://unctad.org; Handbook of Statistics 2021.

United Nations Economic Commission for Africa (UNECA), PO Box 3001, Addis Ababa, ETH, ecainfo@uneca.org, https://www.uneca.org/; African Statistical Yearbook 2020.

The World Bank, 1818 H St. NW, Washington, DC, 20433, USA, (202) 473-1000, (202) 477-6391, eds03@worldbank.org, https://www.worldbank.org/; Botswana (report); World Development Indicators (WDI) 2022; and World Development Report 2022: Finance for an Equitable Recovery.

BOTSWANA-BANKS AND BANKING

Euromonitor International, Inc., 1 N Dearborn St., Ste. 1700, Chicago, IL, 60602, USA, (312) 922-1115, (312) 922-1157, info-usa@euromonitor.com, https://www.euromonitor.com/; Geographies.

International Monetary Fund (IMF), 700 19th St. NW, Washington, DC, 20431, USA, (202) 623-7000, (202) 623-4661, publications@imf.org, https://www.imf.org; International Financial Statistics (IFS).

Routledge - Taylor & Francis Group, 6000 Broken Sound Pkwy. NW, Ste. 300, Boca Raton, FL, 33487, USA, (800) 634-1420, (800) 634-7064, orders@taylorandfrancis.com, https://www.routledge.com/; The Europa World Year Book 2022.

United Nations Economic Commission for Africa (UNECA), PO Box 3001, Addis Ababa, ETH, ecainfo@uneca.org, https://www.uneca.org/; African Statistical Yearbook 2020.

BOTSWANA-BARLEY PRODUCTION

See BOTSWANA-CROPS

BOTSWANA-BROADCASTING

Central Intelligence Agency (CIA), Office of Public Affairs, Washington, DC, 20505, USA, (703) 482-0623, https://www.cia.gov; The World Factbook.

Euromonitor International, Inc., 1 N Dearborn St., Ste. 1700, Chicago, IL, 60602, USA, (312) 922-1115, (312) 922-1157, info-usa@euromonitor.com, https://www.euromonitor.com/; Geographies.

Palgrave Macmillan, 1 New York Plaza, Ste. 4500, New York, NY, 10004-1562, USA, (800) 777-4643, orders@palgrave.com, https://www.palgrave.com/us; The Statesman's Yearbook, 2023.

WRTH Publications Limited, PO Box 290, Oxford, OX2 7FT, GBR, sales@wrth.com, https://www.wrth.com; World Radio TV Handbook 2023.

BOTSWANA-BUDGET

Central Intelligence Agency (CIA), Office of Public Affairs, Washington, DC, 20505, USA, (703) 482-0623, https://www.cia.gov; The World Factbook.

BOTSWANA-CHILDBIRTH-STATISTICS

The World Bank, 1818 H St. NW, Washington, DC, 20433, USA, (202) 473-1000, (202) 477-6391, eds03@worldbank.org, https://www.worldbank.org/; World Development Indicators (WDI) 2022.

BOTSWANA-CLIMATE

International Institute for Environment and Development (IIED), 235 High Holborn, London, WC1V 7DN, GBR, inforequest@iied.org, https://www.iied.org; Environment & Urbanization.

Palgrave Macmillan, 1 New York Plaza, Ste. 4500, New York, NY, 10004-1562, USA, (800) 777-4643, orders@palgrave.com, https://www.palgrave.com/us; The Statesman's Yearbook, 2023.

BOTSWANA-COAL PRODUCTION

See BOTSWANA-MINERAL INDUSTRIES

BOTSWANA-COFFEE

See BOTSWANA-CROPS

BOTSWANA-COMMERCE

Palgrave Macmillan, 1 New York Plaza, Ste. 4500, New York, NY, 10004-1562, USA, (800) 777-4643, orders@palgrave.com, https://www.palgrave.com/us; The Statesman's Yearbook, 2023.

UK Data Service, University of Essex, Wivenhoe Park, Colchester, Essex, CO4 3SQ, GBR, https://ukdataservice.ac.uk/; International Aggregate Data.

BOTSWANA-COMMODITY EXCHANGES

Barchart, 209 W Jackson Blvd., 2nd Fl., Chicago, IL, 60606, USA, (877) 247-4394, commodities@barchart.com, https://www.barchart.com/cmdty; The cmdty Yearbook 2023; cmdtyStats: Commodity Statistics and Fundamental Data; cmdtyView: Commodity Index; and Commodity Data and Prices.

International Monetary Fund (IMF), 700 19th St. NW, Washington, DC, 20431, USA, (202) 623-7000, (202) 623-4661, publications@imf.org, https://www.imf.org; IMF Primary Commodity Prices.

BOTSWANA-CONSTRUCTION INDUSTRY

United Nations Economic Commission for Africa (UNECA), PO Box 3001, Addis Ababa, ETH, ecainfo@uneca.org, https://www.uneca.org/; African Statistical Yearbook 2020.

United Nations Statistics Division (UNSD), United Nations Plz., New York, NY, 10017, USA, (800) 253-9646, (212) 963-9851, statistics@un.org, https://unstats.un.org; Statistical Yearbook of the United Nations 2021.

BOTSWANA-CONSUMER PRICE INDEXES

Routledge - Taylor & Francis Group, 6000 Broken Sound Pkwy. NW, Ste. 300, Boca Raton, FL, 33487, USA, (800) 634-1420, (800) 634-7064, orders@taylorandfrancis.com, https://www.routledge.com/; The Europa World Year Book 2022.

United Nations Economic Commission for Africa (UNECA), PO Box 3001, Addis Ababa, ETH, ecainfo@uneca.org, https://www.uneca.org/; African Statistical Yearbook 2020.

The World Bank, 1818 H St. NW, Washington, DC, 20433, USA, (202) 473-1000, (202) 477-6391, eds03@worldbank.org, https://www.worldbank.org/; Botswana (report).

BOTSWANA-CONSUMPTION (ECONOMICS)

African Development Bank Group (AfDB), Avenue Joseph Anoma, 01 BP 1387, Abidjan, 01, COT, https://www.afdb.org; The AfDB Statistics Pocketbook 2019.

BOTSWANA-COPPER INDUSTRY AND TRADE

See BOTSWANA-MINERAL INDUSTRIES

BOTSWANA-CORN INDUSTRY

See BOTSWANA-CROPS

BOTSWANA-COTTON

See BOTSWANA-CROPS

BOTSWANA-CROPS

Palgrave Macmillan, 1 New York Plaza, Ste. 4500, New York, NY, 10004-1562, USA, (800) 777-4643, orders@palgrave.com, https://www.palgrave.com/us; The Statesman's Yearbook, 2023.

United Nations Economic Commission for Africa (UNECA), PO Box 3001, Addis Ababa, ETH, ecainfo@uneca.org, https://www.uneca.org/; African Statistical Yearbook 2020.

United Nations Food and Agricultural Organization (FAO), 2121 K St., Ste. 800B, Washington, DC, 20037, USA, (202) 653-2400 (Dial from U.S.), (202) 653-5760 (Fax from U.S.), fao-hq@fao.org, https://www.fao.org; The State of Food and Agriculture (SOFA) 2022.

United Nations Statistics Division (UNSD), United Nations Plz., New York, NY, 10017, USA, (800) 253-9646, (212) 963-9851, statistics@un.org, https://unstats.un.org; Statistical Yearbook of the United Nations 2021.

BOTSWANA-DAIRY PROCESSING

Palgrave Macmillan, 1 New York Plaza, Ste. 4500, New York, NY, 10004-1562, USA, (800) 777-4643, orders@palgrave.com, https://www.palgrave.com/us; The Statesman's Yearbook, 2023.

United Nations Food and Agricultural Organization (FAO), 2121 K St., Ste. 800B, Washington, DC, 20037, USA, (202) 653-2400 (Dial from U.S.), (202) 653-5760 (Fax from U.S.), fao-hq@fao.org, https://www.fao.org; The State of Food and Agriculture (SOFA) 2022.

BOTSWANA-DEBTS, EXTERNAL

African Development Bank Group (AfDB), Avenue Joseph Anoma, 01 BP 1387, Abidjan, 01, COT, https://www.afdb.org; The AfDB Statistics Pocketbook 2019; African Economic Outlook 2021; and Compendium of Statistics on Bank Group Operations 2019.

Palgrave Macmillan, 1 New York Plaza, Ste. 4500, New York, NY, 10004-1562, USA, (800) 777-4643, orders@palgrave.com, https://www.palgrave.com/us; The Statesman's Yearbook, 2023.

United Nations Economic Commission for Africa (UNECA), PO Box 3001, Addis Ababa, ETH, ecainfo@uneca.org, https://www.uneca.org/; Economic Report on Africa 2021.

The World Bank, 1818 H St. NW, Washington, DC, 20433, USA, (202) 473-1000, (202) 477-6391, eds03@worldbank.org, https://www.worldbank.org/; Global Financial Development Report 2019-2020: Bank Regulation and Supervision a Decade after the Global Financial Crisis; World Development Indicators (WDI) 2022; and World Development Report 2022: Finance for an Equitable Recovery.

BOTSWANA-DEFENSE EXPENDITURES

See BOTSWANA-ARMED FORCES

BOTSWANA-DIAMONDS

See BOTSWANA-MINERAL INDUSTRIES

BOTSWANA-ECONOMIC ASSISTANCE

United Nations Statistics Division (UNSD), United Nations Plz., New York, NY, 10017, USA, (800) 253-9646, (212) 963-9851, statistics@un.org, https://unstats.un.org; Statistical Yearbook of the United Nations 2021.

BOTSWANA-ECONOMIC CONDITIONS

African Development Bank Group (AfDB), Avenue Joseph Anoma, 01 BP 1387, Abidjan, 01, COT, https://www.afdb.org; The AfDB Statistics Pocketbook 2019; Africa Economic Brief - COVID-19 Pandemic Potential Risks for Trade and Trade Finance in Africa; African Economic Outlook 2021; The African Statistical Journal; Compendium of Statistics on Bank Group Operations 2019; and Gender, Poverty and Environmental Indicators on African Countries 2019.

Bernan Press, 15250 NBN Way, Bldg. C, Blue Ridge Summit, PA, 17214, USA, (301) 459-2255, (800) 865-3457, (800) 865-3450, customercare@bernan.com, https://rowman.com/Page/Bernan; World Economic Outlook, April 2022.

Central Intelligence Agency (CIA), Office of Public Affairs, Washington, DC, 20505, USA, (703) 482-0623, https://www.cia.gov; The World Factbook.

The Economist Group: Economist Intelligence Unit (EIU), 900 3rd Ave., 16th Fl., New York, NY, 10022, USA, (212) 541-0500, americas@eiu.com, https://www.eiu.com; Botswana Country Report.

Euromonitor International, Inc., 1 N Dearborn St., Ste. 1700, Chicago, IL, 60602, USA, (312) 922-1115, (312) 922-1157, info-usa@euromonitor.com, https://www.euromonitor.com/; Geographies.

International Monetary Fund (IMF), 700 19th St. NW, Washington, DC, 20431, USA, (202) 623-7000, (202) 623-4661, publications@imf.org, https://www.imf.org; IMF Data and World Economic Outlook.

Palgrave Macmillan, 1 New York Plaza, Ste. 4500, New York, NY, 10004-1562, USA, (800) 777-4643, orders@palgrave.com, https://www.palgrave.com/us; The Statesman's Yearbook, 2023.

Routledge - Taylor & Francis Group, 6000 Broken Sound Pkwy. NW, Ste. 300, Boca Raton, FL, 33487, USA, (800) 634-1420, (800) 634-7064, orders@taylorandfrancis.com, https://www.routledge.com/; The Europa World Year Book 2022.

Statistics Botswana, Ministry of Finance and Development Planning, Private Bag 0024, Gaborone, BWA, info@statsbots.org.bw, https://www.statsbots.org.bw/; International Merchandise Trade Statistics (IMTS) Monthly Digest.

United Nations Economic Commission for Africa (UNECA), PO Box 3001, Addis Ababa, ETH, ecainfo@uneca.org, https://www.uneca.org/; Economic Report on Africa 2021.

United Nations Statistics Division (UNSD), United Nations Plz., New York, NY, 10017, USA, (800) 253-9646, (212) 963-9851, statistics@un.org, https://unstats.un.org; World Statistics Pocketbook 2021.

The World Bank, 1818 H St. NW, Washington, DC, 20433, USA, (202) 473-1000, (202) 477-6391, eds03@worldbank.org, https://www.worldbank.org/; Botswana (report); Global Economic Monitor (GEM); Global Economic Prospects, June 2022; The Global Findex Database 2021; and World Development Report 2022: Finance for an Equitable Recovery.

BOTSWANA-EDUCATION

African Development Bank Group (AfDB), Avenue Joseph Anoma, 01 BP 1387, Abidjan, 01, COT, https://www.afdb.org; The AfDB Statistics Pocketbook 2019.

Euromonitor International, Inc., 1 N Dearborn St., Ste. 1700, Chicago, IL, 60602, USA, (312) 922-1115, (312) 922-1157, info-usa@euromonitor.com, https://www.euromonitor.com/; Geographies.

Infoplease, c/o Sandbox Networks, Inc., 1 Lincoln St., 24th Fl., Boston, MA, 02111, USA, https://www.infoplease.com; Countries of the World.

Palgrave Macmillan, 1 New York Plaza, Ste. 4500, New York, NY, 10004-1562, USA, (800) 777-4643, orders@palgrave.com, https://www.palgrave.com/us; The Statesman's Yearbook, 2023.

Routledge - Taylor & Francis Group, 6000 Broken Sound Pkwy. NW, Ste. 300, Boca Raton, FL, 33487, USA, (800) 634-1420, (800) 634-7064, orders@taylorandfrancis.com, https://www.routledge.com/; The Europa World Year Book 2022.

UNESCO Institute for Statistics, C.P 250 Succursale H, Montreal, QC, H3G 2K8, CAN, (514) 343-6880 (Dial from U.S.), (514) 343-5740 (Fax from U.S.), uis.publications@unesco.org, http://uis.unesco.org/; Literacy and UIS.Stat.

United Nations Economic Commission for Africa (UNECA), PO Box 3001, Addis Ababa, ETH, ecainfo@uneca.org, https://www.uneca.org/; African Statistical Yearbook 2020.

United Nations Statistics Division (UNSD), United Nations Plz., New York, NY, 10017, USA, (800) 253-9646, (212) 963-9851, statistics@un.org, https://unstats.un.org; Millennium Development Goal Indicators.

The World Bank, 1818 H St. NW, Washington, DC, 20433, USA, (202) 473-1000, (202) 477-6391, eds03@worldbank.org, https://www.worldbank.org/; Botswana (report); World Development Indicators (WDI) 2022; and World Development Report 2022: Finance for an Equitable Recovery.

BOTSWANA-ELECTRICITY

Central Intelligence Agency (CIA), Office of Public Affairs, Washington, DC, 20505, USA, (703) 482-0623, https://www.cia.gov; The World Factbook.

U.S. Energy Information Administration (EIA), 1000 Independence Ave. SW, Washington, DC, 20585, USA, (202) 586-8800, infoctr@eia.gov, https://www.eia.gov; International Energy Outlook 2021.

BOTSWANA-EMPLOYMENT

International Labour Organization (ILO), 4 Rte. des Morillons, Geneva, CH-1211, SWI, ilo@ilo.org, https://www.ilo.org; NORMLEX Information System on International Labour Standards.

UK Data Service, University of Essex, Wivenhoe Park, Colchester, Essex, CO4 3SQ, GBR, https://ukdataservice.ac.uk/; International Aggregate Data.

United Nations Economic Commission for Africa (UNECA), PO Box 3001, Addis Ababa, ETH, ecainfo@uneca.org, https://www.uneca.org/; African Statistical Yearbook 2020.

United Nations Statistics Division (UNSD), United Nations Plz., New York, NY, 10017, USA, (800) 253-

9646, (212) 963-9851, statistics@un.org, https://unstats.un.org; Statistical Yearbook of the United Nations 2021.

The World Bank, 1818 H St. NW, Washington, DC, 20433, USA, (202) 473-1000, (202) 477-6391, eds03@worldbank.org, https://www.worldbank.org/; Botswana (report).

BOTSWANA-ENVIRONMENTAL CONDITIONS

DSI Data Service & Information, Xantener Strasse 51a, Rheinberg, D-47495, GER, dsi@dsidata.com, https://www.dsidata.com/; Global Environmental Database.

The Economist Group: Economist Intelligence Unit (EIU), 900 3rd Ave., 16th Fl., New York, NY, 10022, USA, (212) 541-0500, americas@eiu.com, https://www.eiu.com; Botswana Country Report.

International Institute for Environment and Development (IIED), 235 High Holborn, London, WC1V 7DN, GBR, inforequest@iied.org, https://www.iied.org; Environment & Urbanization.

United Nations Statistics Division (UNSD), United Nations Plz., New York, NY, 10017, USA, (800) 253-9646, (212) 963-9851, statistics@un.org, https://unstats.un.org; World Statistics Pocketbook 2021.

BOTSWANA-EXPORTS

Central Intelligence Agency (CIA), Office of Public Affairs, Washington, DC, 20505, USA, (703) 482-0623, https://www.cia.gov; The World Factbook.

The Economist Group: Economist Intelligence Unit (EIU), 900 3rd Ave., 16th Fl., New York, NY, 10022, USA, (212) 541-0500, americas@eiu.com, https://www.eiu.com; Botswana Country Report.

International Monetary Fund (IMF), 700 19th St. NW, Washington, DC, 20431, USA, (202) 623-7000, (202) 623-4661, publications@imf.org, https://www.imf.org; Direction of Trade Statistics (DOTS).

S&P Global, IHS Markit, 15 Inverness Way E, Englewood, CO, 80112, USA, (800) 447-2273, (800) 854-7179, https://ihsmarkit.com; Global Trade Atlas (GTA).

United Nations Conference on Trade and Development (UNCTAD), Palais des Nations, Geneva, 1211, SWI, (212) 963-6896, unctadinfo@unctad.org, https://unctad.org; Handbook of Statistics 2021.

The World Bank, 1818 H St. NW, Washington, DC, 20433, USA, (202) 473-1000, (202) 477-6391, eds03@worldbank.org, https://www.worldbank.org/; World Development Report 2022: Finance for an Equitable Recovery.

BOTSWANA-FERTILITY, HUMAN

Central Intelligence Agency (CIA), Office of Public Affairs, Washington, DC, 20505, USA, (703) 482-0623, https://www.cia.gov; The World Factbook.

BOTSWANA-FERTILIZER INDUSTRY

United Nations Food and Agricultural Organization (FAO), 2121 K St., Ste. 800B, Washington, DC, 20037, USA, (202) 653-2400 (Dial from U.S.), (202) 653-5760 (Fax from U.S.), fao-hq@fao.org, https://www.fao.org; The State of Food and Agriculture (SOFA) 2022.

BOTSWANA-FETAL MORTALITY

See BOTSWANA-MORTALITY

BOTSWANA-FINANCE

Stockholm International Peace Research Institute (SIPRI), Signalistgatan 9, Stockholm, SE 169 72, SWE, https://www.sipri.org/; SIPRI Arms Transfers Database and SIPRI Military Expenditure Database.

United Nations Economic Commission for Africa (UNECA), PO Box 3001, Addis Ababa, ETH, ecainfo@uneca.org, https://www.uneca.org/; African Statistical Yearbook 2020.

United Nations Statistics Division (UNSD), United Nations Plz., New York, NY, 10017, USA, (800) 253-9646, (212) 963-9851, statistics@un.org, https://unstats.un.org; Statistical Yearbook of the United Nations 2021.

The World Bank, 1818 H St. NW, Washington, DC, 20433, USA, (202) 473-1000, (202) 477-6391, eds03@worldbank.org, https://www.worldbank.org/; Botswana (report).

BOTSWANA-FINANCE, PUBLIC

African Development Bank Group (AfDB), Avenue Joseph Anoma, 01 BP 1387, Abidjan, 01, COT, https://www.afdb.org; The AfDB Statistics Pocketbook 2019.

Bernan Press, 15250 NBN Way, Bldg. C, Blue Ridge Summit, PA, 17214, USA, (301) 459-2255, (800) 865-3457, (800) 865-3450, customercare@bernan.com, https://rowman.com/Page/Bernan; National Accounts Statistics: Analysis of Main Aggregates 2020.

The Economist Group: Economist Intelligence Unit (EIU), 900 3rd Ave., 16th Fl., New York, NY, 10022, USA, (212) 541-0500, americas@eiu.com, https://www.eiu.com; Botswana Country Report.

International Monetary Fund (IMF), 700 19th St. NW, Washington, DC, 20431, USA, (202) 623-7000, (202) 623-4661, publications@imf.org, https://www.imf.org; International Financial Statistics (IFS) and Regional Economic Outlook.

Palgrave Macmillan, 1 New York Plaza, Ste. 4500, New York, NY, 10004-1562, USA, (800) 777-4643, orders@palgrave.com, https://www.palgrave.com/us; The Statesman's Yearbook, 2023.

Routledge - Taylor & Francis Group, 6000 Broken Sound Pkwy. NW, Ste. 300, Boca Raton, FL, 33487, USA, (800) 634-1420, (800) 634-7064, orders@taylorandfrancis.com, https://www.routledge.com/; The Europa World Year Book 2022.

United Nations Economic Commission for Africa (UNECA), PO Box 3001, Addis Ababa, ETH, ecainfo@uneca.org, https://www.uneca.org/; African Statistical Yearbook 2020.

United Nations Statistics Division (UNSD), United Nations Plz., New York, NY, 10017, USA, (800) 253-9646, (212) 963-9851, statistics@un.org, https://unstats.un.org; National Accounts Main Aggregates Database and National Accounts Statistics: Main Aggregates and Detailed Tables.

The World Bank, 1818 H St. NW, Washington, DC, 20433, USA, (202) 473-1000, (202) 477-6391, eds03@worldbank.org, https://www.worldbank.org/; Botswana (report).

BOTSWANA-FISHERIES

Routledge - Taylor & Francis Group, 6000 Broken Sound Pkwy. NW, Ste. 300, Boca Raton, FL, 33487, USA, (800) 634-1420, (800) 634-7064, orders@taylorandfrancis.com, https://www.routledge.com/; The Europa World Year Book 2022.

United Nations Economic Commission for Africa (UNECA), PO Box 3001, Addis Ababa, ETH, ecainfo@uneca.org, https://www.uneca.org/; African Statistical Yearbook 2020.

United Nations Food and Agricultural Organization (FAO), 2121 K St., Ste. 800B, Washington, DC, 20037, USA, (202) 653-2400 (Dial from U.S.), (202) 653-5760 (Fax from U.S.), fao-hq@fao.org, https://www.fao.org; FAO Yearbook of Fishery and Aquaculture Statistics 2019; Fishery Statistical Collections Global Capture Production; FishStatJ; and The State of Food and Agriculture (SOFA) 2022.

United Nations Statistics Division (UNSD), United Nations Plz., New York, NY, 10017, USA, (800) 253-9646, (212) 963-9851, statistics@un.org, https://unstats.un.org; Statistical Yearbook of the United Nations 2021.

The World Bank, 1818 H St. NW, Washington, DC, 20433, USA, (202) 473-1000, (202) 477-6391, eds03@worldbank.org, https://www.worldbank.org/; Botswana (report).

BOTSWANA-FOOD

African Development Bank Group (AfDB), Avenue Joseph Anoma, 01 BP 1387, Abidjan, 01, COT, https://www.afdb.org; The AfDB Statistics Pocketbook 2019.

United Nations Food and Agricultural Organization (FAO), 2121 K St., Ste. 800B, Washington, DC, 20037, USA, (202) 653-2400 (Dial from U.S.), (202) 653-5760 (Fax from U.S.), fao-hq@fao.org, https://www.fao.org; The State of Food and Agriculture (SOFA) 2022.

BOTSWANA-FOREIGN EXCHANGE RATES

African Development Bank Group (AfDB), Avenue Joseph Anoma, 01 BP 1387, Abidjan, 01, COT, https://www.afdb.org; The AfDB Statistics Pocketbook 2019.

BOTSWANA-FORESTS AND FORESTRY

Palgrave Macmillan, 1 New York Plaza, Ste. 4500, New York, NY, 10004-1562, USA, (800) 777-4643, orders@palgrave.com, https://www.palgrave.com/us; The Statesman's Yearbook, 2023.

Routledge - Taylor & Francis Group, 6000 Broken Sound Pkwy. NW, Ste. 300, Boca Raton, FL, 33487, USA, (800) 634-1420, (800) 634-7064, orders@taylorandfrancis.com, https://www.routledge.com/; The Europa World Year Book 2022.

UNESCO Institute for Statistics, C.P 250 Succursale H, Montreal, QC, H3G 2K8, CAN, (514) 343-6880 (Dial from U.S.), (514) 343-5740 (Fax from U.S.), uis.publications@unesco.org, http://uis.unesco.org/; UIS.Stat.

United Nations Economic Commission for Africa (UNECA), PO Box 3001, Addis Ababa, ETH, ecainfo@uneca.org, https://www.uneca.org/; African Statistical Yearbook 2020.

United Nations Food and Agricultural Organization (FAO), 2121 K St., Ste. 800B, Washington, DC, 20037, USA, (202) 653-2400 (Dial from U.S.), (202) 653-5760 (Fax from U.S.), fao-hq@fao.org, https://www.fao.org; FAO Yearbook of Forest Products 2019 and The State of Food and Agriculture (SOFA) 2022.

United Nations Statistics Division (UNSD), United Nations Plz., New York, NY, 10017, USA, (800) 253-9646, (212) 963-9851, statistics@un.org, https://unstats.un.org; Statistical Yearbook of the United Nations 2021.

The World Bank, 1818 H St. NW, Washington, DC, 20433, USA, (202) 473-1000, (202) 477-6391, eds03@worldbank.org, https://www.worldbank.org/; Botswana (report) and World Development Report 2022: Finance for an Equitable Recovery.

BOTSWANA-GAS PRODUCTION

See BOTSWANA-MINERAL INDUSTRIES

BOTSWANA-GEOGRAPHIC INFORMATION SYSTEMS

The World Bank, 1818 H St. NW, Washington, DC, 20433, USA, (202) 473-1000, (202) 477-6391, eds03@worldbank.org, https://www.worldbank.org/; Botswana (report).

BOTSWANA-GOLD INDUSTRY

The World Bank, 1818 H St. NW, Washington, DC, 20433, USA, (202) 473-1000, (202) 477-6391, eds03@worldbank.org, https://www.worldbank.org/; World Development Indicators (WDI) 2022.

BOTSWANA-GOLD PRODUCTION

See BOTSWANA-MINERAL INDUSTRIES

BOTSWANA-GROSS DOMESTIC PRODUCT

African Development Bank Group (AfDB), Avenue Joseph Anoma, 01 BP 1387, Abidjan, 01, COT, https://www.afdb.org; The AfDB Statistics Pocketbook 2019.

The Economist Group: Economist Intelligence Unit (EIU), 900 3rd Ave., 16th Fl., New York, NY, 10022, USA, (212) 541-0500, americas@eiu.com, https://www.eiu.com; Botswana Country Report.

Routledge - Taylor & Francis Group, 6000 Broken Sound Pkwy. NW, Ste. 300, Boca Raton, FL, 33487, USA, (800) 634-1420, (800) 634-7064, orders@taylorandfrancis.com, https://www.routledge.com/; The Europa World Year Book 2022.

United Nations Economic Commission for Africa (UNECA), PO Box 3001, Addis Ababa, ETH, ecainfo@uneca.org, https://www.uneca.org/; African Statistical Yearbook 2020.

United Nations Statistics Division (UNSD), United Nations Plz., New York, NY, 10017, USA, (800) 253-9646, (212) 963-9851, statistics@un.org, https://unstats.un.org; Statistical Yearbook of the United Nations 2021.

The World Bank, 1818 H St. NW, Washington, DC, 20433, USA, (202) 473-1000, (202) 477-6391, eds03@worldbank.org, https://www.worldbank.org/; World Development Indicators (WDI) 2022 and World Development Report 2022: Finance for an Equitable Recovery.

BOTSWANA-GROSS NATIONAL PRODUCT

Palgrave Macmillan, 1 New York Plaza, Ste. 4500, New York, NY, 10004-1562, USA, (800) 777-4643, orders@palgrave.com, https://www.palgrave.com/us; The Statesman's Yearbook, 2023.

Routledge - Taylor & Francis Group, 6000 Broken Sound Pkwy. NW, Ste. 300, Boca Raton, FL, 33487, USA, (800) 634-1420, (800) 634-7064, orders@taylorandfrancis.com, https://www.routledge.com/; The Europa World Year Book 2022.

The World Bank, 1818 H St. NW, Washington, DC, 20433, USA, (202) 473-1000, (202) 477-6391, eds03@worldbank.org, https://www.worldbank.org/; World Development Indicators (WDI) 2022 and World Development Report 2022: Finance for an Equitable Recovery.

BOTSWANA-HOURS OF LABOR

International Labour Organization (ILO), 4 Rte. des Morillons, Geneva, CH-1211, SWI, ilo@ilo.org, https://www.ilo.org; NORMLEX Information System on International Labour Standards.

BOTSWANA-HOUSING

Euromonitor International, Inc., 1 N Dearborn St., Ste. 1700, Chicago, IL, 60602, USA, (312) 922-1115, (312) 922-1157, info-usa@euromonitor.com, https://www.euromonitor.com/; Geographies.

BOTSWANA-ILLITERATE PERSONS

UNESCO Institute for Statistics, C.P 250 Succursale H, Montreal, QC, H3G 2K8, CAN, (514) 343-6880 (Dial from U.S.), (514) 343-5740 (Fax from U.S.), uis.publications@unesco.org, http://uis.unesco.org/; UIS.Stat.

BOTSWANA-IMPORTS

Central Intelligence Agency (CIA), Office of Public Affairs, Washington, DC, 20505, USA, (703) 482-0623, https://www.cia.gov; The World Factbook.

The Economist Group: Economist Intelligence Unit (EIU), 900 3rd Ave., 16th Fl., New York, NY, 10022, USA, (212) 541-0500, americas@eiu.com, https://www.eiu.com; Botswana Country Report.

International Monetary Fund (IMF), 700 19th St. NW, Washington, DC, 20431, USA, (202) 623-7000, (202) 623-4661, publications@imf.org, https://www.imf.org; Direction of Trade Statistics (DOTS).

S&P Global, IHS Markit, 15 Inverness Way E, Englewood, CO, 80112, USA, (800) 447-2273, (800) 854-7179, https://ihsmarkit.com; Global Trade Atlas (GTA).

United Nations Conference on Trade and Development (UNCTAD), Palais des Nations, Geneva, 1211, SWI, (212) 963-6896, unctadinfo@unctad.org, https://unctad.org; Handbook of Statistics 2021.

The World Bank, 1818 H St. NW, Washington, DC, 20433, USA, (202) 473-1000, (202) 477-6391, eds03@worldbank.org, https://www.worldbank.org/; World Development Report 2022: Finance for an Equitable Recovery.

BOTSWANA-INDUSTRIAL PROPERTY

World Intellectual Property Organization (WIPO), 34, chemin des Colombettes, Geneva, CH-1211, SWI, https://www.wipo.int; Madrid Yearly Review 2022: International Registrations of Marks.

BOTSWANA-INDUSTRIES

Central Intelligence Agency (CIA), Office of Public Affairs, Washington, DC, 20505, USA, (703) 482-0623, https://www.cia.gov; The World Factbook.

The Economist Group: Economist Intelligence Unit (EIU), 900 3rd Ave., 16th Fl., New York, NY, 10022, USA, (212) 541-0500, americas@eiu.com, https://www.eiu.com; Botswana Country Report.

Euromonitor International, Inc., 1 N Dearborn St., Ste. 1700, Chicago, IL, 60602, USA, (312) 922-1115, (312) 922-1157, info-usa@euromonitor.com, https://www.euromonitor.com/; Geographies.

International Labour Organization (ILO), 4 Rte. des Morillons, Geneva, CH-1211, SWI, ilo@ilo.org, https://www.ilo.org; NORMLEX Information System on International Labour Standards.

Palgrave Macmillan, 1 New York Plaza, Ste. 4500, New York, NY, 10004-1562, USA, (800) 777-4643, orders@palgrave.com, https://www.palgrave.com/us; The Statesman's Yearbook, 2023.

Routledge - Taylor & Francis Group, 6000 Broken Sound Pkwy. NW, Ste. 300, Boca Raton, FL, 33487, USA, (800) 634-1420, (800) 634-7064, orders@taylorandfrancis.com, https://www.routledge.com/; The Europa World Year Book 2022.

United Nations Economic Commission for Africa (UNECA), PO Box 3001, Addis Ababa, ETH, ecainfo@uneca.org, https://www.uneca.org/; African Statistical Yearbook 2020.

United Nations Industrial Development Organization (UNIDO), 1 United Nations Plz., Rm. DC1-1118, New York, NY, 10017, USA, (212) 963-6890, (212) 963 6885, (212) 963-7904, office.newyork@unido.org, https://www.unido.org/; Industrial Statistics Databases and International Yearbook of Industrial Statistics 2021.

The World Bank, 1818 H St. NW, Washington, DC, 20433, USA, (202) 473-1000, (202) 477-6391, eds03@worldbank.org, https://www.worldbank.org/; Botswana (report) and World Development Indicators (WDI) 2022.

World Intellectual Property Organization (WIPO), 34, chemin des Colombettes, Geneva, CH-1211, SWI, https://www.wipo.int; Madrid Yearly Review 2022: International Registrations of Marks.

BOTSWANA-INFANT AND MATERNAL MORTALITY

See BOTSWANA-MORTALITY

BOTSWANA-INTERNATIONAL TRADE

African Development Bank Group (AfDB), Avenue Joseph Anoma, 01 BP 1387, Abidjan, 01, COT, https://www.afdb.org; The AfDB Statistics Pocketbook 2019.

The Economist Group: Economist Intelligence Unit (EIU), 900 3rd Ave., 16th Fl., New York, NY, 10022, USA, (212) 541-0500, americas@eiu.com, https://www.eiu.com; Botswana Country Report.

Euromonitor International, Inc., 1 N Dearborn St., Ste. 1700, Chicago, IL, 60602, USA, (312) 922-1115, (312) 922-1157, info-usa@euromonitor.com, https://www.euromonitor.com/; Geographies.

Routledge - Taylor & Francis Group, 6000 Broken Sound Pkwy. NW, Ste. 300, Boca Raton, FL, 33487, USA, (800) 634-1420, (800) 634-7064, orders@taylorandfrancis.com, https://www.routledge.com/; The Europa World Year Book 2022.

Statistics Botswana, Ministry of Finance and Development Planning, Private Bag 0024, Gaborone, BWA, info@statsbots.org.bw, https://www.statsbots.org.bw/; International Merchandise Trade Statistics (IMTS) Monthly Digest.

United Nations Conference on Trade and Development (UNCTAD), Palais des Nations, Geneva, 1211, SWI, (212) 963-6896, unctadinfo@unctad.org, https://unctad.org; Trade and Development Report 2021.

United Nations Economic Commission for Africa (UNECA), PO Box 3001, Addis Ababa, ETH, ecainfo@uneca.org, https://www.uneca.org/; African Statistical Yearbook 2020.

United Nations Food and Agricultural Organization (FAO), 2121 K St., Ste. 800B, Washington, DC, 20037, USA, (202) 653-2400 (Dial from U.S.), (202) 653-5760 (Fax from U.S.), fao-hq@fao.org, https://www.fao.org; The State of Food and Agriculture (SOFA) 2022.

The World Bank, 1818 H St. NW, Washington, DC, 20433, USA, (202) 473-1000, (202) 477-6391, eds03@worldbank.org, https://www.worldbank.org/; Botswana (report); World Development Indicators (WDI) 2022; and World Development Report 2022: Finance for an Equitable Recovery.

World Trade Organization (WTO), Ctre. William Rappard, Rue de Lausanne 154, Case postale, Geneva, CH-1211, SWI, enquiries@wto.org, https://www.wto.org; World Trade Statistical Review 2022.

BOTSWANA-INTERNET USERS

International Telecommunication Union (ITU), Place des Nations, Geneva, CH-1211, SWI, itumail@itu.int, https://www.itu.int; Global Connectivity Report 2022; World Telecommunication/ICT Indicators Database 2021; and Yearbook of Statistics 2019.

The World Bank, 1818 H St. NW, Washington, DC, 20433, USA, (202) 473-1000, (202) 477-6391, eds03@worldbank.org, https://www.worldbank.org/; Botswana (report).

BOTSWANA-LABOR

African Development Bank Group (AfDB), Avenue Joseph Anoma, 01 BP 1387, Abidjan, 01, COT, https://www.afdb.org; The AfDB Statistics Pocketbook 2019.

Central Intelligence Agency (CIA), Office of Public Affairs, Washington, DC, 20505, USA, (703) 482-0623, https://www.cia.gov; The World Factbook.

Euromonitor International, Inc., 1 N Dearborn St., Ste. 1700, Chicago, IL, 60602, USA, (312) 922-1115, (312) 922-1157, info-usa@euromonitor.com, https://www.euromonitor.com/; Geographies.

International Labour Organization (ILO), 4 Rte. des Morillons, Geneva, CH-1211, SWI, ilo@ilo.org, https://www.ilo.org; NORMLEX Information System on International Labour Standards.

Palgrave Macmillan, 1 New York Plaza, Ste. 4500, New York, NY, 10004-1562, USA, (800) 777-4643, orders@palgrave.com, https://www.palgrave.com/us; The Statesman's Yearbook, 2023.

United Nations Food and Agricultural Organization (FAO), 2121 K St., Ste. 800B, Washington, DC, 20037, USA, (202) 653-2400 (Dial from U.S.), (202) 653-5760 (Fax from U.S.), fao-hq@fao.org, https://www.fao.org; The State of Food and Agriculture (SOFA) 2022.

The World Bank, 1818 H St. NW, Washington, DC, 20433, USA, (202) 473-1000, (202) 477-6391, eds03@worldbank.org, https://www.worldbank.org/; World Development Indicators (WDI) 2022 and World Development Report 2022: Finance for an Equitable Recovery.

BOTSWANA-LAND USE

United Nations Statistics Division (UNSD), United Nations Plz., New York, NY, 10017, USA, (800) 253-9646, (212) 963-9851, statistics@un.org, https://unstats.un.org; Millennium Development Goal Indicators.

The World Bank, 1818 H St. NW, Washington, DC, 20433, USA, (202) 473-1000, (202) 477-6391, eds03@worldbank.org, https://www.worldbank.org/; World Development Report 2022: Finance for an Equitable Recovery.

BOTSWANA-LIFE EXPECTANCY

African Development Bank Group (AfDB), Avenue Joseph Anoma, 01 BP 1387, Abidjan, 01, COT, https://www.afdb.org; The AfDB Statistics Pocketbook 2019.

Central Intelligence Agency (CIA), Office of Public Affairs, Washington, DC, 20505, USA, (703) 482-0623, https://www.cia.gov; The World Factbook.

United Nations Department of Economic and Social Affairs (DESA), Population Division, 2 United Nations Plz., Rm. DC2-1950, New York, NY, 10017, USA, (212) 963-3209, (212) 963-2147, population@un.org, https://www.un.org/development/desa/pd/; World Population Ageing 2020 Highlights.

United Nations Statistics Division (UNSD), United Nations Plz., New York, NY, 10017, USA, (800) 253-9646, (212) 963-9851, statistics@un.org, https://unstats.un.org; Millennium Development Goal Indicators.

BOTSWANA-LITERACY

Euromonitor International, Inc., 1 N Dearborn St., Ste. 1700, Chicago, IL, 60602, USA, (312) 922-1115, (312) 922-1157, info-usa@euromonitor.com, https://www.euromonitor.com/; Geographies.

UNESCO Institute for Statistics, C.P 250 Succursale H, Montreal, QC, H3G 2K8, CAN, (514) 343-6880 (Dial from U.S.), (514) 343-5740 (Fax from U.S.), uis.publications@unesco.org, http://uis.unesco.org/; Literacy.

BOTSWANA-LIVESTOCK

Palgrave Macmillan, 1 New York Plaza, Ste. 4500, New York, NY, 10004-1562, USA, (800) 777-4643, orders@palgrave.com, https://www.palgrave.com/us; The Statesman's Yearbook, 2023.

Routledge - Taylor & Francis Group, 6000 Broken Sound Pkwy. NW, Ste. 300, Boca Raton, FL, 33487, USA, (800) 634-1420, (800) 634-7064, orders@taylorandfrancis.com, https://www.routledge.com/; The Europa World Year Book 2022.

United Nations Economic Commission for Africa (UNECA), PO Box 3001, Addis Ababa, ETH, ecainfo@uneca.org, https://www.uneca.org/; African Statistical Yearbook 2020.

United Nations Food and Agricultural Organization (FAO), 2121 K St., Ste. 800B, Washington, DC, 20037, USA, (202) 653-2400 (Dial from U.S.), (202) 653-5760 (Fax from U.S.), fao-hq@fao.org, https://www.fao.org; The State of Food and Agriculture (SOFA) 2022.

United Nations Statistics Division (UNSD), United Nations Plz., New York, NY, 10017, USA, (800) 253-9646, (212) 963-9851, statistics@un.org, https://unstats.un.org; Statistical Yearbook of the United Nations 2021.

BOTSWANA-MINERAL INDUSTRIES

International Monetary Fund (IMF), 700 19th St. NW, Washington, DC, 20431, USA, (202) 623-7000, (202) 623-4661, publications@imf.org, https://www.imf.org; International Financial Statistics (IFS).

Palgrave Macmillan, 1 New York Plaza, Ste. 4500, New York, NY, 10004-1562, USA, (800) 777-4643, orders@palgrave.com, https://www.palgrave.com/us; The Statesman's Yearbook, 2023.

Routledge - Taylor & Francis Group, 6000 Broken Sound Pkwy. NW, Ste. 300, Boca Raton, FL, 33487, USA, (800) 634-1420, (800) 634-7064, orders@taylorandfrancis.com, https://www.routledge.com/; The Europa World Year Book 2022.

United Nations Conference on Trade and Development (UNCTAD), Palais des Nations, Geneva, 1211, SWI, (212) 963-6896, unctadinfo@unctad.org, https://unctad.org; Trade and Development Report 2021.

United Nations Economic Commission for Africa (UNECA), PO Box 3001, Addis Ababa, ETH, ecainfo@uneca.org, https://www.uneca.org/; African Statistical Yearbook 2020.

United Nations Statistics Division (UNSD), United Nations Plz., New York, NY, 10017, USA, (800) 253-9646, (212) 963-9851, statistics@un.org, https://unstats.un.org; Statistical Yearbook of the United Nations 2021.

BOTSWANA-MONEY SUPPLY

The Economist Group: Economist Intelligence Unit (EIU), 900 3rd Ave., 16th Fl., New York, NY, 10022, USA, (212) 541-0500, americas@eiu.com, https://www.eiu.com; Botswana Country Report.

Routledge - Taylor & Francis Group, 6000 Broken Sound Pkwy. NW, Ste. 300, Boca Raton, FL, 33487, USA, (800) 634-1420, (800) 634-7064, orders@taylorandfrancis.com, https://www.routledge.com/; The Europa World Year Book 2022.

The World Bank, 1818 H St. NW, Washington, DC, 20433, USA, (202) 473-1000, (202) 477-6391, eds03@worldbank.org, https://www.worldbank.org/; Botswana (report).

BOTSWANA-MONUMENTS AND HISTORIC SITES

UNESCO Institute for Statistics, C.P 250 Succursale H, Montreal, QC, H3G 2K8, CAN, (514) 343-6880 (Dial from U.S.), (514) 343-5740 (Fax from U.S.), uis.publications@unesco.org, http://uis.unesco.org/; UIS.Stat.

BOTSWANA-MORTALITY

UNICEF, 3 United Nations Plz., New York, NY, 10017, USA, (212) 303-7984, (917) 244-2215, https://www.unicef.org; The State of the World's Children 2023.

United Nations Statistics Division (UNSD), United Nations Plz., New York, NY, 10017, USA, (800) 253-9646, (212) 963-9851, statistics@un.org, https://unstats.un.org; Millennium Development Goal Indicators; Statistical Yearbook of the United Nations 2021; and World Statistics Pocketbook 2021.

The World Bank, 1818 H St. NW, Washington, DC, 20433, USA, (202) 473-1000, (202) 477-6391, eds03@worldbank.org, https://www.worldbank.org/; World Development Indicators (WDI) 2022.

World Health Organization (WHO), Ave. Appia 20, Geneva, CH-1211, SWI, (202) 974-3000 (Telephone in U.S.), publications@who.int, https://www.who.int/; Global Health Observatory (GHO).

BOTSWANA-MOTOR VEHICLES

International Road Federation (IRF), Madison Place, 500 Montgomery St., 5th Fl., Alexandria, VA, 22314, USA, (703) 535-1001, (703) 535-1007, info@irf.global, https://www.irf.global/; World Road Statistics (WRS).

BOTSWANA-NATURAL GAS PRODUCTION

See BOTSWANA-MINERAL INDUSTRIES

BOTSWANA-NICKEL AND NICKEL ORE

See BOTSWANA-MINERAL INDUSTRIES

BOTSWANA-NUTRITION

United Nations Food and Agricultural Organization (FAO), 2121 K St., Ste. 800B, Washington, DC, 20037, USA, (202) 653-2400 (Dial from U.S.), (202) 653-5760 (Fax from U.S.), fao-hq@fao.org, https://www.fao.org; The State of Food and Agriculture (SOFA) 2022.

United Nations Statistics Division (UNSD), United Nations Plz., New York, NY, 10017, USA, (800) 253-9646, (212) 963-9851, statistics@un.org, https://unstats.un.org; Millennium Development Goal Indicators.

BOTSWANA-PEANUT PRODUCTION

See BOTSWANA-CROPS

BOTSWANA-PESTICIDES

United Nations Food and Agricultural Organization (FAO), 2121 K St., Ste. 800B, Washington, DC, 20037, USA, (202) 653-2400 (Dial from U.S.), (202) 653-5760 (Fax from U.S.), fao-hq@fao.org, https://www.fao.org; The State of Food and Agriculture (SOFA) 2022.

BOTSWANA-PETROLEUM INDUSTRY AND TRADE

U.S. Energy Information Administration (EIA), 1000 Independence Ave. SW, Washington, DC, 20585, USA, (202) 586-8800, infoctr@eia.gov, https://www.eia.gov; International Energy Outlook 2021.

United Nations Food and Agricultural Organization (FAO), 2121 K St., Ste. 800B, Washington, DC, 20037, USA, (202) 653-2400 (Dial from U.S.), (202) 653-5760 (Fax from U.S.), fao-hq@fao.org, https://www.fao.org; The State of Food and Agriculture (SOFA) 2022.

BOTSWANA-POPULATION

African Development Bank Group (AfDB), Avenue Joseph Anoma, 01 BP 1387, Abidjan, 01, COT, https://www.afdb.org; The AfDB Statistics Pocketbook 2019; Africa Economic Brief - COVID-19 Pandemic Potential Risks for Trade and Trade Finance in Africa; The African Statistical Journal; and Gender, Poverty and Environmental Indicators on African Countries 2019.

Central Intelligence Agency (CIA), Office of Public Affairs, Washington, DC, 20505, USA, (703) 482-0623, https://www.cia.gov; The World Factbook.

The Economist Group: Economist Intelligence Unit (EIU), 900 3rd Ave., 16th Fl., New York, NY, 10022, USA, (212) 541-0500, americas@eiu.com, https://www.eiu.com; Botswana Country Report.

European Commission, Eurostat, Luxembourg, 2920, LUX, https://ec.europa.eu/eurostat/; EU in the World 2020.

Infoplease, c/o Sandbox Networks, Inc., 1 Lincoln St., 24th Fl., Boston, MA, 02111, USA, https://www.infoplease.com; Countries of the World.

International Labour Organization (ILO), 4 Rte. des Morillons, Geneva, CH-1211, SWI, ilo@ilo.org, https://www.ilo.org; NORMLEX Information System on International Labour Standards.

Palgrave Macmillan, 1 New York Plaza, Ste. 4500, New York, NY, 10004-1562, USA, (800) 777-4643, orders@palgrave.com, https://www.palgrave.com/us; The Statesman's Yearbook, 2023.

Routledge - Taylor & Francis Group, 6000 Broken Sound Pkwy. NW, Ste. 300, Boca Raton, FL, 33487, USA, (800) 634-1420, (800) 634-7064, orders@taylorandfrancis.com, https://www.routledge.com/; The Europa World Year Book 2022.

UK Data Service, University of Essex, Wivenhoe Park, Colchester, Essex, CO4 3SQ, GBR, https://ukdataservice.ac.uk/; International Aggregate Data.

UNESCO Institute for Statistics, C.P 250 Succursale H, Montreal, QC, H3G 2K8, CAN, (514) 343-6880 (Dial from U.S.), (514) 343-5740 (Fax from U.S.), uis.publications@unesco.org, http://uis.unesco.org/; UIS.Stat.

United Nations Department of Economic and Social Affairs (DESA), Population Division, 2 United Nations Plz., Rm. DC2-1950, New York, NY, 10017, USA, (212) 963-3209, (212) 963-2147, population@un.org, https://www.un.org/development/desa/pd/; Revision of World Urbanization Prospects and World Population Ageing 2020 Highlights.

United Nations Development Programme (UNDP), One United Nations Plz., New York, NY, 10017, USA, (212) 906-5000, (212) 906-5001, https://www.undp.org; Human Development Report 2021-2022.

United Nations Statistics Division (UNSD), United Nations Plz., New York, NY, 10017, USA, (800) 253-9646, (212) 963-9851, statistics@un.org, https://unstats.un.org; Statistical Yearbook of the United Nations 2021 and World Statistics Pocketbook 2021.

The World Bank, 1818 H St. NW, Washington, DC, 20433, USA, (202) 473-1000, (202) 477-6391, eds03@worldbank.org, https://www.worldbank.org/; Botswana (report); The Global Findex Database 2021; and World Development Report 2022: Finance for an Equitable Recovery.

BOTSWANA-POPULATION DENSITY

African Development Bank Group (AfDB), Avenue Joseph Anoma, 01 BP 1387, Abidjan, 01, COT, https://www.afdb.org; The AfDB Statistics Pocketbook 2019.

Central Intelligence Agency (CIA), Office of Public Affairs, Washington, DC, 20505, USA, (703) 482-0623, https://www.cia.gov; The World Factbook.

Palgrave Macmillan, 1 New York Plaza, Ste. 4500, New York, NY, 10004-1562, USA, (800) 777-4643, orders@palgrave.com, https://www.palgrave.com/us; The Statesman's Yearbook, 2023.

Routledge - Taylor & Francis Group, 6000 Broken Sound Pkwy. NW, Ste. 300, Boca Raton, FL, 33487, USA, (800) 634-1420, (800) 634-7064, orders@taylorandfrancis.com, https://www.routledge.com/; The Europa World Year Book 2022.

The World Bank, 1818 H St. NW, Washington, DC, 20433, USA, (202) 473-1000, (202) 477-6391, eds03@worldbank.org, https://www.worldbank.org/; Botswana (report) and World Development Report 2022: Finance for an Equitable Recovery.

BOTSWANA-POSTAL SERVICE

Palgrave Macmillan, 1 New York Plaza, Ste. 4500, New York, NY, 10004-1562, USA, (800) 777-4643, orders@palgrave.com, https://www.palgrave.com/us; The Statesman's Yearbook, 2023.

BOTSWANA-POWER RESOURCES

Euromonitor International, Inc., 1 N Dearborn St., Ste. 1700, Chicago, IL, 60602, USA, (312) 922-1115, (312) 922-1157, info-usa@euromonitor.com, https://www.euromonitor.com/; Geographies.

Palgrave Macmillan, 1 New York Plaza, Ste. 4500, New York, NY, 10004-1562, USA, (800) 777-4643, orders@palgrave.com, https://www.palgrave.com/us; The Statesman's Yearbook, 2023.

U.S. Energy Information Administration (EIA), 1000 Independence Ave. SW, Washington, DC, 20585, USA, (202) 586-8800, infoctr@eia.gov, https://www.eia.gov; International Energy Outlook 2021.

United Nations Economic Commission for Africa (UNECA), PO Box 3001, Addis Ababa, ETH, ecainfo@uneca.org, https://www.uneca.org/; African Statistical Yearbook 2020.

United Nations Food and Agricultural Organization (FAO), 2121 K St., Ste. 800B, Washington, DC, 20037, USA, (202) 653-2400 (Dial from U.S.), (202) 653-5760 (Fax from U.S.), fao-hq@fao.org, https://www.fao.org; The State of Food and Agriculture (SOFA) 2022.

United Nations Statistics Division (UNSD), United Nations Plz., New York, NY, 10017, USA, (800) 253-9646, (212) 963-9851, statistics@un.org, https://unstats.un.org; Energy Statistics Yearbook 2019; Statistical Yearbook of the United Nations 2021; and World Statistics Pocketbook 2021.

The World Bank, 1818 H St. NW, Washington, DC, 20433, USA, (202) 473-1000, (202) 477-6391, eds03@worldbank.org, https://www.worldbank.org/; World Development Report 2022: Finance for an Equitable Recovery.

BOTSWANA-PRICES

Euromonitor International, Inc., 1 N Dearborn St., Ste. 1700, Chicago, IL, 60602, USA, (312) 922-1115, (312) 922-1157, info-usa@euromonitor.com, https://www.euromonitor.com/; Geographies.

International Monetary Fund (IMF), 700 19th St. NW, Washington, DC, 20431, USA, (202) 623-7000, (202) 623-4661, publications@imf.org, https://www.imf.org; International Financial Statistics (IFS).

United Nations Economic Commission for Africa (UNECA), PO Box 3001, Addis Ababa, ETH, ecainfo@uneca.org, https://www.uneca.org/; African Statistical Yearbook 2020.

The World Bank, 1818 H St. NW, Washington, DC, 20433, USA, (202) 473-1000, (202) 477-6391, eds03@worldbank.org, https://www.worldbank.org/; Botswana (report).

BOTSWANA-PUBLIC HEALTH

African Development Bank Group (AfDB), Avenue Joseph Anoma, 01 BP 1387, Abidjan, 01, COT, https://www.afdb.org; The AfDB Statistics Pocketbook 2019.

Euromonitor International, Inc., 1 N Dearborn St., Ste. 1700, Chicago, IL, 60602, USA, (312) 922-1115, (312) 922-1157, info-usa@euromonitor.com, https://www.euromonitor.com/; Geographies.

Palgrave Macmillan, 1 New York Plaza, Ste. 4500, New York, NY, 10004-1562, USA, (800) 777-4643, orders@palgrave.com, https://www.palgrave.com/us; The Statesman's Yearbook, 2023.

U.S. Census Bureau, 4600 Silver Hill Rd., Washington, DC, 20233, USA, (301) 763-4636, (800) 923-8282, https://www.census.gov; HIV/AIDS Surveillance Data Base.

UNICEF, 3 United Nations Plz., New York, NY, 10017, USA, (212) 303-7984, (917) 244-2215, https://www.unicef.org; The State of the World's Children 2023.

United Nations Department of Economic and Social Affairs (DESA), Population Division, 2 United Nations Plz., Rm. DC2-1950, New York, NY, 10017, USA, (212) 963-3209, (212) 963-2147, population@un.org, https://www.un.org/development/desa/pd/; World Fertility Data 2019.

United Nations Development Programme (UNDP), One United Nations Plz., New York, NY, 10017, USA, (212) 906-5000, (212) 906-5001, https://www.undp.org; Human Development Report 2021-2022.

United Nations Economic Commission for Africa (UNECA), PO Box 3001, Addis Ababa, ETH, ecainfo@uneca.org, https://www.uneca.org/; African Statistical Yearbook 2020.

United Nations Statistics Division (UNSD), United Nations Plz., New York, NY, 10017, USA, (800) 253-9646, (212) 963-9851, statistics@un.org, https://unstats.un.org; Millennium Development Goal Indicators and Statistical Yearbook of the United Nations 2021.

The World Bank, 1818 H St. NW, Washington, DC, 20433, USA, (202) 473-1000, (202) 477-6391, eds03@worldbank.org, https://www.worldbank.org/; Botswana (report).

World Health Organization (WHO), Ave. Appia 20, Geneva, CH-1211, SWI, (202) 974-3000 (Telephone in U.S.), publications@who.int, https://www.who.int/; Global Health Observatory (GHO).

BOTSWANA-PUBLISHERS AND PUBLISHING

Routledge - Taylor & Francis Group, 6000 Broken Sound Pkwy. NW, Ste. 300, Boca Raton, FL, 33487, USA, (800) 634-1420, (800) 634-7064, orders@taylorandfrancis.com, https://www.routledge.com/; The Europa World Year Book 2022.

UNESCO Institute for Statistics, C.P 250 Succursale H, Montreal, QC, H3G 2K8, CAN, (514) 343-6880 (Dial from U.S.), (514) 343-5740 (Fax from U.S.), uis.publications@unesco.org, http://uis.unesco.org/; UIS.Stat.

BOTSWANA-RAILROADS

Janes, USA, (703) 574-7580, (888) 977-1519, customer.care@janes.com, https://www.janes.com; Janes World Railways 2021-2022.

Palgrave Macmillan, 1 New York Plaza, Ste. 4500, New York, NY, 10004-1562, USA, (800) 777-4643, orders@palgrave.com, https://www.palgrave.com/us; The Statesman's Yearbook, 2023.

Routledge - Taylor & Francis Group, 6000 Broken Sound Pkwy. NW, Ste. 300, Boca Raton, FL, 33487, USA, (800) 634-1420, (800) 634-7064, orders@taylorandfrancis.com, https://www.routledge.com/; The Europa World Year Book 2022.

United Nations Economic Commission for Africa (UNECA), PO Box 3001, Addis Ababa, ETH, ecainfo@uneca.org, https://www.uneca.org/; African Statistical Yearbook 2020.

United Nations Statistics Division (UNSD), United Nations Plz., New York, NY, 10017, USA, (800) 253-9646, (212) 963-9851, statistics@un.org, https://unstats.un.org; Statistical Yearbook of the United Nations 2021.

BOTSWANA-RELIGION

Central Intelligence Agency (CIA), Office of Public Affairs, Washington, DC, 20505, USA, (703) 482-0623, https://www.cia.gov; The World Factbook.

Palgrave Macmillan, 1 New York Plaza, Ste. 4500, New York, NY, 10004-1562, USA, (800) 777-4643, orders@palgrave.com, https://www.palgrave.com/us; The Statesman's Yearbook, 2023.

BOTSWANA-RETAIL TRADE

Euromonitor International, Inc., 1 N Dearborn St., Ste. 1700, Chicago, IL, 60602, USA, (312) 922-1115, (312) 922-1157, info-usa@euromonitor.com, https://www.euromonitor.com/; Geographies.

BOTSWANA-RICE PRODUCTION

See BOTSWANA-CROPS

BOTSWANA-ROADS

International Road Federation (IRF), Madison Place, 500 Montgomery St., 5th Fl., Alexandria, VA, 22314, USA, (703) 535-1001, (703) 535-1007, info@irf.global, https://www.irf.global/; World Road Statistics (WRS).

United Nations Economic Commission for Africa (UNECA), PO Box 3001, Addis Ababa, ETH, ecainfo@uneca.org, https://www.uneca.org/; African Statistical Yearbook 2020.

BOTSWANA-RUBBER INDUSTRY AND TRADE

International Rubber Study Group (IRSG), 51 Changi Business Park Central 2, Unit No. 6, 486066, SGP, https://www.rubberstudy.org; Monthly Rubber Bulletin (MRB); Rubber Industry Report; Rubber Statistical Bulletin; and World Rubber Industry Report (WRIO).

BOTSWANA-SHIPPING

United Nations Economic Commission for Africa (UNECA), PO Box 3001, Addis Ababa, ETH, ecainfo@uneca.org, https://www.uneca.org/; African Statistical Yearbook 2020.

BOTSWANA-STEEL PRODUCTION

See BOTSWANA-MINERAL INDUSTRIES

BOTSWANA-SUGAR PRODUCTION

See BOTSWANA-CROPS

BOTSWANA-TAXATION

International Road Federation (IRF), Madison Place, 500 Montgomery St., 5th Fl., Alexandria, VA, 22314, USA, (703) 535-1001, (703) 535-1007, info@irf.global, https://www.irf.global/; World Road Statistics (WRS).

The World Bank, 1818 H St. NW, Washington, DC, 20433, USA, (202) 473-1000, (202) 477-6391, eds03@worldbank.org, https://www.worldbank.org/; World Development Indicators (WDI) 2022.

BOTSWANA-TELEPHONE

Palgrave Macmillan, 1 New York Plaza, Ste. 4500, New York, NY, 10004-1562, USA, (800) 777-4643, orders@palgrave.com, https://www.palgrave.com/us; The Statesman's Yearbook, 2023.

Routledge - Taylor & Francis Group, 6000 Broken Sound Pkwy. NW, Ste. 300, Boca Raton, FL, 33487, USA, (800) 634-1420, (800) 634-7064, orders@taylorandfrancis.com, https://www.routledge.com/; The Europa World Year Book 2022.

United Nations Statistics Division (UNSD), United Nations Plz., New York, NY, 10017, USA, (800) 253-9646, (212) 963-9851, statistics@un.org, https://unstats.un.org; World Statistics Pocketbook 2021.

BOTSWANA-TEXTILE INDUSTRY

Palgrave Macmillan, 1 New York Plaza, Ste. 4500, New York, NY, 10004-1562, USA, (800) 777-4643, orders@palgrave.com, https://www.palgrave.com/us; The Statesman's Yearbook, 2023.

BOTSWANA-THEATER

UNESCO Institute for Statistics, C.P 250 Succursale H, Montreal, QC, H3G 2K8, CAN, (514) 343-6880 (Dial from U.S.), (514) 343-5740 (Fax from U.S.), uis.publications@unesco.org, http://uis.unesco.org/; UIS.Stat.

BOTSWANA-TOURISM

Euromonitor International, Inc., 1 N Dearborn St., Ste. 1700, Chicago, IL, 60602, USA, (312) 922-1115, (312) 922-1157, info-usa@euromonitor.com, https://www.euromonitor.com/; Geographies.

Palgrave Macmillan, 1 New York Plaza, Ste. 4500, New York, NY, 10004-1562, USA, (800) 777-4643, orders@palgrave.com, https://www.palgrave.com/us; The Statesman's Yearbook, 2023.

Routledge - Taylor & Francis Group, 6000 Broken Sound Pkwy. NW, Ste. 300, Boca Raton, FL, 33487, USA, (800) 634-1420, (800) 634-7064, orders@taylorandfrancis.com, https://www.routledge.com/; The Europa World Year Book 2022.

United Nations Economic Commission for Africa (UNECA), PO Box 3001, Addis Ababa, ETH, ecainfo@uneca.org, https://www.uneca.org/; African Statistical Yearbook 2020.

United Nations World Tourism Organization (UNWTO), Calle Poeta Joan Maragall 42, Madrid, 28020, SPA, info@unwto.org, https://www.unwto.org/; Yearbook of Tourism Statistics, 2021 Edition.

The World Bank, 1818 H St. NW, Washington, DC, 20433, USA, (202) 473-1000, (202) 477-6391, eds03@worldbank.org, https://www.worldbank.org/; Botswana (report).

BOTSWANA-TRADE

See BOTSWANA-INTERNATIONAL TRADE

BOTSWANA-TRANSPORTATION

Central Intelligence Agency (CIA), Office of Public Affairs, Washington, DC, 20505, USA, (703) 482-0623, https://www.cia.gov; The World Factbook.

Euromonitor International, Inc., 1 N Dearborn St., Ste. 1700, Chicago, IL, 60602, USA, (312) 922-1115, (312) 922-1157, info-usa@euromonitor.com, https://www.euromonitor.com/; Geographies.

Palgrave Macmillan, 1 New York Plaza, Ste. 4500, New York, NY, 10004-1562, USA, (800) 777-4643, orders@palgrave.com, https://www.palgrave.com/us; The Statesman's Yearbook, 2023.

Routledge - Taylor & Francis Group, 6000 Broken Sound Pkwy. NW, Ste. 300, Boca Raton, FL, 33487, USA, (800) 634-1420, (800) 634-7064, orders@taylorandfrancis.com, https://www.routledge.com/; The Europa World Year Book 2022.

United Nations Economic Commission for Africa (UNECA), PO Box 3001, Addis Ababa, ETH, ecainfo@uneca.org, https://www.uneca.org/; African Statistical Yearbook 2020.

The World Bank, 1818 H St. NW, Washington, DC, 20433, USA, (202) 473-1000, (202) 477-6391, eds03@worldbank.org, https://www.worldbank.org/; Botswana (report).

BOTSWANA-UNEMPLOYMENT

International Labour Organization (ILO), 4 Rte. des Morillons, Geneva, CH-1211, SWI, ilo@ilo.org, https://www.ilo.org; NORMLEX Information System on International Labour Standards.

Palgrave Macmillan, 1 New York Plaza, Ste. 4500, New York, NY, 10004-1562, USA, (800) 777-4643, orders@palgrave.com, https://www.palgrave.com/us; The Statesman's Yearbook, 2023.

BOTSWANA-VITAL STATISTICS

Palgrave Macmillan, 1 New York Plaza, Ste. 4500, New York, NY, 10004-1562, USA, (800) 777-4643, orders@palgrave.com, https://www.palgrave.com/us; The Statesman's Yearbook, 2023.

U.S. Census Bureau, 4600 Silver Hill Rd., Washington, DC, 20233, USA, (301) 763-4636, (800) 923-8282, https://www.census.gov; HIV/AIDS Surveillance Data Base.

United Nations Department of Economic and Social Affairs (DESA), Population Division, 2 United Nations Plz., Rm. DC2-1950, New York, NY, 10017, USA, (212) 963-3209, (212) 963-2147, population@un.org, https://www.un.org/development/desa/pd/; World Contraceptive Use 2021: Estimates and Projections of Family Planning Indicators and World Marriage Data 2019.

BOTSWANA-WAGES

International Labour Organization (ILO), 4 Rte. des Morillons, Geneva, CH-1211, SWI, ilo@ilo.org, https://www.ilo.org; NORMLEX Information System on International Labour Standards.

The World Bank, 1818 H St. NW, Washington, DC, 20433, USA, (202) 473-1000, (202) 477-6391, eds03@worldbank.org, https://www.worldbank.org/; Botswana (report).

BOTSWANA-WEATHER

See BOTSWANA-CLIMATE

BOTSWANA-WHEAT PRODUCTION

See BOTSWANA-CROPS

BOTSWANA-WOOL PRODUCTION

See BOTSWANA-TEXTILE INDUSTRY

BOTULISM

U.S. Department of Health and Human Services, Centers for Disease Control and Prevention (CDC), 1600 Clifton Rd., Atlanta, GA, 30329-4027, USA, (800) 232-4636, (888) 232-6348 (TTY), cdcinfo@cdc.gov, https://www.cdc.gov; Morbidity and Mortality Weekly Report (MMWR) and National Notifiable Diseases Surveillance System (NNDSS).

BOWLING

National Sporting Goods Association (NSGA), 3041 Woodcreek Dr., Ste. 210, Downers Grove, IL, 60515, USA, (847) 296-6742, (847) 391-9827, info@nsga.org, https://www.nsga.org; Sports Participation in the United States 2022 and Sports Participation: Historical Sports Participation 2022.

United States Bowling Congress (USBC), 621 Six Flags Dr., Arlington, TX, 76011, USA, (800) 514-2695, bowlinfo@bowl.com, https://www.bowl.com; unpublished data.

BOXING

MRI Simmons, 200 Liberty St., 4th Fl., New York, NY, 10281, USA, (866) 256-4468, info.ms@mrisimmons.com, https://www.mrisimmons.com/; MRI-Simmons USA.

Stats Perform, 203 N LaSalle St., Ste. 2350, Chicago, IL, 60601, USA, (866) 221-1426, https://www.statsperform.com/; unpublished data.

BOY SCOUTS-MEMBERSHIP AND UNITS

Boy Scouts of America (BSA), PO Box 152079, Irving, TX, 75015-2079, USA, (972) 580-2000, https://www.scouting.org/; Annual Report of the Boy Scouts of America, 2019.

BRAINWASHING

Cult Education Institute (CEI), 1977 N Olden Ave., Ext. 272, Trenton, NJ, 08618, USA, (609) 396-6684, info@culteducation.com, https://www.culteducation.com; unpublished data.

University of Maryland, National Consortium for the Study of Terrorism and Responses to Terrorism (START), PO Box 266, 5245 Greenbelt Rd., College Park, MD, 20740, USA, (301) 405-6600, (301) 314-1980, infostart@start.umd.edu, https://www.start.umd.edu; Profiles of Individual Radicalization in the United States - PIRUS (Keshif).

BRAND LOYALTY

Morning Consult, 729 15th St. NW, Washington, DC, 20005, USA, (202) 506-1957, contact@morningconsult.com, https://morningconsult.com; Most Trusted Brands 2022.

BRAZIL-NATIONAL STATISTICAL OFFICE

Instituto Brasileiro de Geografia e Estatistica (IBGE), Rua General Canabarro, 706 - Maracana, Rio de Janeiro, 20271-205, BRZ, ibge@ibge.gov.br, https://www.ibge.gov.br/; National Data Reports (Brazil).

BRAZIL-AGRICULTURE

The Economist Group: Economist Intelligence Unit (EIU), 900 3rd Ave., 16th Fl., New York, NY, 10022, USA, (212) 541-0500, americas@eiu.com, https://www.eiu.com; Brazil Country Report.

Euromonitor International, Inc., 1 N Dearborn St., Ste. 1700, Chicago, IL, 60602, USA, (312) 922-1115, (312) 922-1157, info-usa@euromonitor.com, https://www.euromonitor.com/; Geographies.

Federal Statistical Office Germany, Gustav-Stresemann-Ring 11, Wiesbaden, D-65189, GER, https://www.destatis.de; Basic Indicators: Brazil.

Inter-American Development Bank (IDB), 1300 New York Ave. NW, Washington, DC, 20577, USA, (202) 623-1000, (202) 623-3096, https://www.iadb.org/en; Latin Macro Watch (LMW).

Organization for Economic Cooperation and Development (OECD), 2001 L St. NW, Ste. 650, Washington, DC, 20036-4922, USA, (202) 785-6323, (800) 456-6323, (202) 785-0350, washington.contact@oecd.org, https://www.oecd.org/; Economic Survey of Brazil 2020.

Palgrave Macmillan, 1 New York Plaza, Ste. 4500, New York, NY, 10004-1562, USA, (800) 777-4643, orders@palgrave.com, https://www.palgrave.com/us; The Statesman's Yearbook, 2023.

Routledge - Taylor & Francis Group, 6000 Broken Sound Pkwy. NW, Ste. 300, Boca Raton, FL, 33487, USA, (800) 634-1420, (800) 634-7064, orders@taylorandfrancis.com, https://www.routledge.com/; The Europa World Year Book 2022.

U.S. Department of Agriculture (USDA), Economic Research Service (ERS), 1400 Independence Ave. SW, Mail Stop 1800, Washington, DC, 20250-0002, USA, (202) 720-2791, https://www.ers.usda.gov/; Countries and Regions: Brazil.

United Nations Food and Agricultural Organization (FAO), 2121 K St., Ste. 800B, Washington, DC, 20037, USA, (202) 653-2400 (Dial from U.S.), (202) 653-5760 (Fax from U.S.), fao-hq@fao.org, https://www.fao.org; AQUASTAT and The State of Food and Agriculture (SOFA) 2022.

United Nations Statistics Division (UNSD), United Nations Plz., New York, NY, 10017, USA, (800) 253-9646, (212) 963-9851, statistics@un.org, https://unstats.un.org; Statistical Yearbook of the United Nations 2021.

The World Bank, 1818 H St. NW, Washington, DC, 20433, USA, (202) 473-1000, (202) 477-6391, eds03@worldbank.org, https://www.worldbank.org/; Brazil (report) and World Development Indicators (WDI) 2022.

BRAZIL-AIRLINES

International Civil Aviation Organization (ICAO), 999 Robert-Bourassa Blvd., Montreal, QC, H3C 5H7, CAN, (514) 954-8219 (Dial from U.S.), (514) 954-6077 (Fax from U.S.), icaohq@icao.int, https://www.icao.int; ICAO Regional Reports.

Palgrave Macmillan, 1 New York Plaza, Ste. 4500, New York, NY, 10004-1562, USA, (800) 777-4643, orders@palgrave.com, https://www.palgrave.com/us; The Statesman's Yearbook, 2023.

Routledge - Taylor & Francis Group, 6000 Broken Sound Pkwy. NW, Ste. 300, Boca Raton, FL, 33487, USA, (800) 634-1420, (800) 634-7064, orders@taylorandfrancis.com, https://www.routledge.com/; The Europa World Year Book 2022.

BRAZIL-ALUMINUM PRODUCTION

See BRAZIL-MINERAL INDUSTRIES

BRAZIL-ANIMAL FEEDING

United Nations Statistics Division (UNSD), United Nations Plz., New York, NY, 10017, USA, (800) 253-9646, (212) 963-9851, statistics@un.org, https://unstats.un.org; Statistical Yearbook of the United Nations 2021.

BRAZIL-ARMED FORCES

Central Intelligence Agency (CIA), Office of Public Affairs, Washington, DC, 20505, USA, (703) 482-0623, https://www.cia.gov; The World Factbook.

International Institute for Strategic Studies (IISS) - Americas, 2121 K St. NW, Ste. 600, Washington, DC, 20037, USA, (202) 659-1490, (202) 659-1499, https://www.iiss.org/; The Military Balance 2022.

Palgrave Macmillan, 1 New York Plaza, Ste. 4500, New York, NY, 10004-1562, USA, (800) 777-4643, orders@palgrave.com, https://www.palgrave.com/us; The Statesman's Yearbook, 2023.

Stockholm International Peace Research Institute (SIPRI), Signalistgatan 9, Stockholm, SE 169 72, SWE, https://www.sipri.org/; SIPRI Arms Transfers Database and SIPRI Military Expenditure Database.

BRAZIL-BALANCE OF PAYMENTS

Federal Statistical Office Germany, Gustav-Stresemann-Ring 11, Wiesbaden, D-65189, GER, https://www.destatis.de; Basic Indicators: Brazil.

Inter-American Development Bank (IDB), 1300 New York Ave. NW, Washington, DC, 20577, USA, (202) 623-1000, (202) 623-3096, https://www.iadb.org/en; Latin Macro Watch (LMW).

International Monetary Fund (IMF), 700 19th St. NW, Washington, DC, 20431, USA, (202) 623-7000, (202) 623-4661, publications@imf.org, https://www.imf.org; Balance of Payments Statistics: Annual Report 2021 and International Financial Statistics (IFS).

Organization for Economic Cooperation and Development (OECD), 2001 L St. NW, Ste. 650, Washington, DC, 20036-4922, USA, (202) 785-6323, (800) 456-6323, (202) 785-0350, washington.contact@oecd.org, https://www.oecd.org/; Economic Survey of Brazil 2020.

Routledge - Taylor & Francis Group, 6000 Broken Sound Pkwy. NW, Ste. 300, Boca Raton, FL, 33487, USA, (800) 634-1420, (800) 634-7064, orders@taylorandfrancis.com, https://www.routledge.com/; The Europa World Year Book 2022.

United Nations Conference on Trade and Development (UNCTAD), Palais des Nations, Geneva, 1211, SWI, (212) 963-6896, unctadinfo@unctad.org, https://unctad.org; Handbook of Statistics 2021.

United Nations Economic Commission for Latin America and the Caribbean (ECLAC), Casilla 179-D, Santiago, 7630412, CHL, (202) 596-3713, prensa@cepal.org, https://www.cepal.org/en; Economic Survey of Latin America and the Caribbean 2021: Labour Dynamics and Employment Policies for Sustainable and Inclusive Recovery Beyond the COVID-19 Crisis.

The World Bank, 1818 H St. NW, Washington, DC, 20433, USA, (202) 473-1000, (202) 477-6391, eds03@worldbank.org, https://www.worldbank.org/; Brazil (report); World Development Indicators (WDI) 2022; and World Development Report 2022: Finance for an Equitable Recovery.

BRAZIL-BANKS AND BANKING

Euromonitor International, Inc., 1 N Dearborn St., Ste. 1700, Chicago, IL, 60602, USA, (312) 922-1115, (312) 922-1157, info-usa@euromonitor.com, https://www.euromonitor.com/; Geographies.

Inter-American Development Bank (IDB), 1300 New York Ave. NW, Washington, DC, 20577, USA, (202) 623-1000, (202) 623-3096, https://www.iadb.org/en; Latin Macro Watch (LMW).

International Monetary Fund (IMF), 700 19th St. NW, Washington, DC, 20431, USA, (202) 623-7000, (202) 623-4661, publications@imf.org, https://www.imf.org; International Financial Statistics (IFS).

Organization for Economic Cooperation and Development (OECD), 2001 L St. NW, Ste. 650, Washington, DC, 20036-4922, USA, (202) 785-6323, (800) 456-6323, (202) 785-0350, washington.contact@oecd.org, https://www.oecd.org/; Economic Survey of Brazil 2020.

Routledge - Taylor & Francis Group, 6000 Broken Sound Pkwy. NW, Ste. 300, Boca Raton, FL, 33487, USA, (800) 634-1420, (800) 634-7064, orders@taylorandfrancis.com, https://www.routledge.com/; The Europa World Year Book 2022.

United Nations Statistics Division (UNSD), United Nations Plz., New York, NY, 10017, USA, (800) 253-9646, (212) 963-9851, statistics@un.org, https://unstats.un.org; Statistical Yearbook of the United Nations 2021.

BRAZIL-BARLEY PRODUCTION

See BRAZIL-CROPS

BRAZIL-BONDS

Inter-American Development Bank (IDB), 1300 New York Ave. NW, Washington, DC, 20577, USA, (202) 623-1000, (202) 623-3096, https://www.iadb.org/en; Latin Macro Watch (LMW).

BRAZIL-BROADCASTING

Central Intelligence Agency (CIA), Office of Public Affairs, Washington, DC, 20505, USA, (703) 482-0623, https://www.cia.gov; The World Factbook.

Euromonitor International, Inc., 1 N Dearborn St., Ste. 1700, Chicago, IL, 60602, USA, (312) 922-1115, (312) 922-1157, info-usa@euromonitor.com, https://www.euromonitor.com/; Geographies.

Palgrave Macmillan, 1 New York Plaza, Ste. 4500, New York, NY, 10004-1562, USA, (800) 777-4643, orders@palgrave.com, https://www.palgrave.com/us; The Statesman's Yearbook, 2023.

UNESCO Institute for Statistics, C.P 250 Succursale H, Montreal, QC, H3G 2K8, CAN, (514) 343-6880 (Dial from U.S.), (514) 343-5740 (Fax from U.S.), uis.publications@unesco.org, http://uis.unesco.org/; UIS.Stat.

WRTH Publications Limited, PO Box 290, Oxford, OX2 7FT, GBR, sales@wrth.com, https://www.wrth.com; World Radio TV Handbook 2023.

BRAZIL-BUDGET

Central Intelligence Agency (CIA), Office of Public Affairs, Washington, DC, 20505, USA, (703) 482-0623, https://www.cia.gov; The World Factbook.

BRAZIL-BUSINESS

Global Entrepreneurship Monitor (GEM), Babson College, 231 Forest St., Babson Park, MA, 02457, USA, (781) 235-1200, info@gemconsortium.org, https://www.gemconsortium.org/; Brazil Economy Profile and GEM 2022-2023 Global Report.

Inter-American Development Bank (IDB), 1300 New York Ave. NW, Washington, DC, 20577, USA, (202) 623-1000, (202) 623-3096, https://www.iadb.org/en; Latin Macro Watch (LMW).

United Nations Statistics Division (UNSD), United Nations Plz., New York, NY, 10017, USA, (800) 253-9646, (212) 963-9851, statistics@un.org, https://unstats.un.org; Statistical Yearbook of the United Nations 2021.

BRAZIL-CAPITAL INVESTMENTS

Inter-American Development Bank (IDB), 1300 New York Ave. NW, Washington, DC, 20577, USA, (202) 623-1000, (202) 623-3096, https://www.iadb.org/en; Latin Macro Watch (LMW).

BRAZIL-CHESTNUT PRODUCTION

See BRAZIL-CROPS

BRAZIL-CHILDBIRTH-STATISTICS

The World Bank, 1818 H St. NW, Washington, DC, 20433, USA, (202) 473-1000, (202) 477-6391, eds03@worldbank.org, https://www.worldbank.org/; World Development Indicators (WDI) 2022.

BRAZIL-CLIMATE

Palgrave Macmillan, 1 New York Plaza, Ste. 4500, New York, NY, 10004-1562, USA, (800) 777-4643, orders@palgrave.com, https://www.palgrave.com/us; The Statesman's Yearbook, 2023.

BRAZIL-COAL PRODUCTION

See BRAZIL-MINERAL INDUSTRIES

BRAZIL-COCOA PRODUCTION

See BRAZIL-CROPS

BRAZIL-COFFEE

See BRAZIL-CROPS

BRAZIL-COMMERCE

Palgrave Macmillan, 1 New York Plaza, Ste. 4500, New York, NY, 10004-1562, USA, (800) 777-4643, orders@palgrave.com, https://www.palgrave.com/us; The Statesman's Yearbook, 2023.

UK Data Service, University of Essex, Wivenhoe Park, Colchester, Essex, CO4 3SQ, GBR, https://ukdataservice.ac.uk/; International Aggregate Data.

BRAZIL-COMMODITY EXCHANGES

Barchart, 209 W Jackson Blvd., 2nd Fl., Chicago, IL, 60606, USA, (877) 247-4394, commodities@barchart.com, https://www.barchart.com/cmdty; The cmdty Yearbook 2023; cmdtyStats: Commodity Statistics and Fundamental Data; cmdtyView: Commodity Index; and Commodity Data and Prices.

International Monetary Fund (IMF), 700 19th St. NW, Washington, DC, 20431, USA, (202) 623-7000, (202) 623-4661, publications@imf.org, https://www.imf.org; IMF Primary Commodity Prices.

World Bureau of Metal Statistics (WBMS), 31 Star St., Ware, Hertfordshire, SG12 9BA, GBR, https://www.refinitiv.com/en/trading-solutions/world-bureau-metal-statistics; Annual Stainless Steel Statistics; Long Term Production/Consumption Series - All Metals; World Flow Charts; and World Metal Statistics.

BRAZIL-CONSTRUCTION INDUSTRY

Inter-American Development Bank (IDB), 1300 New York Ave. NW, Washington, DC, 20577, USA, (202) 623-1000, (202) 623-3096, https://www.iadb.org/en; Latin Macro Watch (LMW).

Organization for Economic Cooperation and Development (OECD), 2001 L St. NW, Ste. 650, Washington, DC, 20036-4922, USA, (202) 785-6323, (800) 456-6323, (202) 785-0350, washington.contact@oecd.org, https://www.oecd.org/; Economic Survey of Brazil 2020.

Palgrave Macmillan, 1 New York Plaza, Ste. 4500, New York, NY, 10004-1562, USA, (800) 777-4643,

orders@palgrave.com, https://www.palgrave.com/us; The Statesman's Yearbook, 2023.

United Nations Statistics Division (UNSD), United Nations Plz., New York, NY, 10017, USA, (800) 253-9646, (212) 963-9851, statistics@un.org, https://unstats.un.org; Statistical Yearbook of the United Nations 2021.

BRAZIL-CONSUMER PRICE INDEXES

Federal Statistical Office Germany, Gustav-Stresemann-Ring 11, Wiesbaden, D-65189, GER, https://www.destatis.de; Basic Indicators: Brazil.

Routledge - Taylor & Francis Group, 6000 Broken Sound Pkwy. NW, Ste. 300, Boca Raton, FL, 33487, USA, (800) 634-1420, (800) 634-7064, orders@taylorandfrancis.com, https://www.routledge.com/; The Europa World Year Book 2022.

The World Bank, 1818 H St. NW, Washington, DC, 20433, USA, (202) 473-1000, (202) 477-6391, eds03@worldbank.org, https://www.worldbank.org/; Brazil (report).

BRAZIL-CONSUMPTION (ECONOMICS)

Inter-American Development Bank (IDB), 1300 New York Ave. NW, Washington, DC, 20577, USA, (202) 623-1000, (202) 623-3096, https://www.iadb.org/en; Latin Macro Watch (LMW).

BRAZIL-COPPER INDUSTRY AND TRADE

See BRAZIL-MINERAL INDUSTRIES

BRAZIL-CORN INDUSTRY

See BRAZIL-CROPS

BRAZIL-COTTON

See BRAZIL-CROPS

BRAZIL-CROPS

Palgrave Macmillan, 1 New York Plaza, Ste. 4500, New York, NY, 10004-1562, USA, (800) 777-4643, orders@palgrave.com, https://www.palgrave.com/us; The Statesman's Yearbook, 2023.

United Nations Food and Agricultural Organization (FAO), 2121 K St., Ste. 800B, Washington, DC, 20037, USA, (202) 653-2400 (Dial from U.S.), (202) 653-5760 (Fax from U.S.), fao-hq@fao.org, https://www.fao.org; The State of Food and Agriculture (SOFA) 2022.

United Nations Statistics Division (UNSD), United Nations Plz., New York, NY, 10017, USA, (800) 253-9646, (212) 963-9851, statistics@un.org, https://unstats.un.org; Statistical Yearbook of the United Nations 2021.

BRAZIL-CUSTOMS ADMINISTRATION

Inter-American Development Bank (IDB), 1300 New York Ave. NW, Washington, DC, 20577, USA, (202) 623-1000, (202) 623-3096, https://www.iadb.org/en; Latin Macro Watch (LMW).

BRAZIL-DAIRY PROCESSING

Palgrave Macmillan, 1 New York Plaza, Ste. 4500, New York, NY, 10004-1562, USA, (800) 777-4643, orders@palgrave.com, https://www.palgrave.com/us; The Statesman's Yearbook, 2023.

United Nations Food and Agricultural Organization (FAO), 2121 K St., Ste. 800B, Washington, DC, 20037, USA, (202) 653-2400 (Dial from U.S.), (202) 653-5760 (Fax from U.S.), fao-hq@fao.org, https://www.fao.org; The State of Food and Agriculture (SOFA) 2022.

BRAZIL-DEBT

The World Bank, 1818 H St. NW, Washington, DC, 20433, USA, (202) 473-1000, (202) 477-6391, eds03@worldbank.org, https://www.worldbank.org/; Global Financial Development Report 2019-2020: Bank Regulation and Supervision a Decade after the Global Financial Crisis.

BRAZIL-DEBTS, EXTERNAL

Inter-American Development Bank (IDB), 1300 New York Ave. NW, Washington, DC, 20577, USA, (202) 623-1000, (202) 623-3096, https://www.iadb.org/en; Latin Macro Watch (LMW).

Palgrave Macmillan, 1 New York Plaza, Ste. 4500, New York, NY, 10004-1562, USA, (800) 777-4643, orders@palgrave.com, https://www.palgrave.com/us; The Statesman's Yearbook, 2023.

United Nations Economic Commission for Latin America and the Caribbean (ECLAC), Casilla 179-D, Santiago, 7630412, CHL, (202) 596-3713, prensa@cepal.org, https://www.cepal.org/en; Economic Survey of Latin America and the Caribbean 2021: Labour Dynamics and Employment Policies for Sustainable and Inclusive Recovery Beyond the COVID-19 Crisis.

The World Bank, 1818 H St. NW, Washington, DC, 20433, USA, (202) 473-1000, (202) 477-6391, eds03@worldbank.org, https://www.worldbank.org/; Global Financial Development Report 2019-2020: Bank Regulation and Supervision a Decade after the Global Financial Crisis; World Development Indicators (WDI) 2022; and World Development Report 2022: Finance for an Equitable Recovery.

BRAZIL-DEFENSE EXPENDITURES

See BRAZIL-ARMED FORCES

BRAZIL-DIAMONDS

See BRAZIL-MINERAL INDUSTRIES

BRAZIL-DISPOSABLE INCOME

Inter-American Development Bank (IDB), 1300 New York Ave. NW, Washington, DC, 20577, USA, (202) 623-1000, (202) 623-3096, https://www.iadb.org/en; Latin Macro Watch (LMW).

BRAZIL-ECONOMIC ASSISTANCE

Inter-American Development Bank (IDB), 1300 New York Ave. NW, Washington, DC, 20577, USA, (202) 623-1000, (202) 623-3096, https://www.iadb.org/en; Latin Macro Watch (LMW).

United Nations Statistics Division (UNSD), United Nations Plz., New York, NY, 10017, USA, (800) 253-9646, (212) 963-9851, statistics@un.org, https://unstats.un.org; Statistical Yearbook of the United Nations 2021.

BRAZIL-ECONOMIC CONDITIONS

Bernan Press, 15250 NBN Way, Bldg. C, Blue Ridge Summit, PA, 17214, USA, (301) 459-2255, (800) 865-3457, (800) 865-3450, customercare@bernan.com, https://rowman.com/Page/Bernan; World Economic Outlook, April 2022.

Central Intelligence Agency (CIA), Office of Public Affairs, Washington, DC, 20505, USA, (703) 482-0623, https://www.cia.gov; The World Factbook.

The Economist Group: Economist Intelligence Unit (EIU), 900 3rd Ave., 16th Fl., New York, NY, 10022, USA, (212) 541-0500, americas@eiu.com, https://www.eiu.com; Brazil Country Report.

Euromonitor International, Inc., 1 N Dearborn St., Ste. 1700, Chicago, IL, 60602, USA, (312) 922-1115, (312) 922-1157, info-usa@euromonitor.com, https://www.euromonitor.com/; Geographies and Market Research on the Consumer Finance Industry.

Federal Statistical Office Germany, Gustav-Stresemann-Ring 11, Wiesbaden, D-65189, GER, https://www.destatis.de; Basic Indicators: Brazil.

Global Entrepreneurship Monitor (GEM), Babson College, 231 Forest St., Babson Park, MA, 02457, USA, (781) 235-1200, info@gemconsortium.org, https://www.gemconsortium.org/; Brazil Economy Profile and GEM 2022-2023 Global Report.

Inter-American Development Bank (IDB), 1300 New York Ave. NW, Washington, DC, 20577, USA, (202) 623-1000, (202) 623-3096, https://www.iadb.org/en; Latin Macro Watch (LMW).

International Monetary Fund (IMF), 700 19th St. NW, Washington, DC, 20431, USA, (202) 623-7000, (202) 623-4661, publications@imf.org, https://www.imf.org; IMF Data and World Economic Outlook.

Organization for Economic Cooperation and Development (OECD), 2001 L St. NW, Ste. 650, Washington, DC, 20036-4922, USA, (202) 785-6323, (800) 456-6323, (202) 785-0350, washington.contact@oecd.org, https://www.oecd.org/; Economic Survey of Brazil 2020.

Palgrave Macmillan, 1 New York Plaza, Ste. 4500, New York, NY, 10004-1562, USA, (800) 777-4643, orders@palgrave.com, https://www.palgrave.com/us; The Statesman's Yearbook, 2023.

Routledge - Taylor & Francis Group, 6000 Broken Sound Pkwy. NW, Ste. 300, Boca Raton, FL, 33487, USA, (800) 634-1420, (800) 634-7064, orders@taylorandfrancis.com, https://www.routledge.com/; The Europa World Year Book 2022.

United Nations Economic Commission for Latin America and the Caribbean (ECLAC), Casilla 179-D, Santiago, 7630412, CHL, (202) 596-3713, prensa@cepal.org, https://www.cepal.org/en; CEPALSTAT; Economic Survey of Latin America and the Caribbean 2021: Labour Dynamics and Employment Policies for Sustainable and Inclusive Recovery Beyond the COVID-19 Crisis; Foreign Direct Investment in Latin America and the Caribbean 2022; and Social Panorama of Latin America and the Caribbean 2022: Transforming Education as a Basis for Sustainable Development.

United Nations Statistics Division (UNSD), United Nations Plz., New York, NY, 10017, USA, (800) 253-9646, (212) 963-9851, statistics@un.org, https://unstats.un.org; World Statistics Pocketbook 2021.

University of California Los Angeles (UCLA), Latin American Institute (LAI), 10343 Bunche Hall, 315 Portola Plaza, Los Angeles, CA, 90095-1447, USA, (310) 825-4571, lai@international.ucla.edu, https://www.international.ucla.edu/lai; unpublished data.

The World Bank, 1818 H St. NW, Washington, DC, 20433, USA, (202) 473-1000, (202) 477-6391, eds03@worldbank.org, https://www.worldbank.org/; Brazil (report); Global Economic Monitor (GEM); Global Economic Prospects, June 2022; The Global Findex Database 2021; and World Development Report 2022: Finance for an Equitable Recovery.

BRAZIL-EDUCATION

Euromonitor International, Inc., 1 N Dearborn St., Ste. 1700, Chicago, IL, 60602, USA, (312) 922-1115, (312) 922-1157, info-usa@euromonitor.com, https://www.euromonitor.com/; Geographies.

Federal Statistical Office Germany, Gustav-Stresemann-Ring 11, Wiesbaden, D-65189, GER, https://www.destatis.de; Basic Indicators: Brazil.

Infoplease, c/o Sandbox Networks, Inc., 1 Lincoln St., 24th Fl., Boston, MA, 02111, USA, https://www.infoplease.com; Countries of the World.

Palgrave Macmillan, 1 New York Plaza, Ste. 4500, New York, NY, 10004-1562, USA, (800) 777-4643, orders@palgrave.com, https://www.palgrave.com/us; The Statesman's Yearbook, 2023.

Routledge - Taylor & Francis Group, 6000 Broken Sound Pkwy. NW, Ste. 300, Boca Raton, FL, 33487, USA, (800) 634-1420, (800) 634-7064, orders@taylorandfrancis.com, https://www.routledge.com/; The Europa World Year Book 2022.

UNESCO Institute for Statistics, C.P 250 Succursale H, Montreal, QC, H3G 2K8, CAN, (514) 343-6880 (Dial from U.S.), (514) 343-5740 (Fax from U.S.), uis.publications@unesco.org, http://uis.unesco.org/; Literacy and UIS.Stat.

United Nations Statistics Division (UNSD), United Nations Plz., New York, NY, 10017, USA, (800) 253-9646, (212) 963-9851, statistics@un.org, https://unstats.un.org; Millennium Development Goal Indicators.

The World Bank, 1818 H St. NW, Washington, DC, 20433, USA, (202) 473-1000, (202) 477-6391, eds03@worldbank.org, https://www.worldbank.org/; Brazil (report); World Development Indicators (WDI)

2022; and World Development Report 2022: Finance for an Equitable Recovery.

BRAZIL-ELECTRICITY

Inter-American Development Bank (IDB), 1300 New York Ave. NW, Washington, DC, 20577, USA, (202) 623-1000, (202) 623-3096, https://www.iadb.org/en; Latin Macro Watch (LMW).

International Energy Agency (IEA), 9 Rue de la Federation, Paris, 75739, FRA, info@iea.org, https://www.iea.org/; World Energy Outlook 2021.

U.S. Energy Information Administration (EIA), 1000 Independence Ave. SW, Washington, DC, 20585, USA, (202) 586-8800, infoctr@eia.gov, https://www.eia.gov; International Energy Outlook 2021.

United Nations Statistics Division (UNSD), United Nations Plz., New York, NY, 10017, USA, (800) 253-9646, (212) 963-9851, statistics@un.org, https://unstats.un.org; Statistical Yearbook of the United Nations 2021.

BRAZIL-EMPLOYMENT

Federal Statistical Office Germany, Gustav-Stresemann-Ring 11, Wiesbaden, D-65189, GER, https://www.destatis.de; Basic Indicators: Brazil.

International Labour Organization (ILO), 4 Rte. des Morillons, Geneva, CH-1211, SWI, ilo@ilo.org, https://www.ilo.org; NORMLEX Information System on International Labour Standards.

Organization for Economic Cooperation and Development (OECD), 2001 L St. NW, Ste. 650, Washington, DC, 20036-4922, USA, (202) 785-6323, (800) 456-6323, (202) 785-0350, washington.contact@oecd.org, https://www.oecd.org/; Economic Survey of Brazil 2020.

UK Data Service, University of Essex, Wivenhoe Park, Colchester, Essex, CO4 3SQ, GBR, https://ukdataservice.ac.uk/; International Aggregate Data.

United Nations Statistics Division (UNSD), United Nations Plz., New York, NY, 10017, USA, (800) 253-9646, (212) 963-9851, statistics@un.org, https://unstats.un.org; Statistical Yearbook of the United Nations 2021.

The World Bank, 1818 H St. NW, Washington, DC, 20433, USA, (202) 473-1000, (202) 477-6391, eds03@worldbank.org, https://www.worldbank.org/; Brazil (report).

BRAZIL-ENVIRONMENTAL CONDITIONS

DSI Data Service & Information, Xantener Strasse 51a, Rheinberg, D-47495, GER, dsi@dsidata.com, https://www.dsidata.com/; Global Environmental Database.

The Economist Group: Economist Intelligence Unit (EIU), 900 3rd Ave., 16th Fl., New York, NY, 10022, USA, (212) 541-0500, americas@eiu.com, https://www.eiu.com; Brazil Country Report.

United Nations Economic Commission for Latin America and the Caribbean (ECLAC), Casilla 179-D, Santiago, 7630412, CHL, (202) 596-3713, prensa@cepal.org, https://www.cepal.org/en; CEPALSTAT.

United Nations Statistics Division (UNSD), United Nations Plz., New York, NY, 10017, USA, (800) 253-9646, (212) 963-9851, statistics@un.org, https://unstats.un.org; World Statistics Pocketbook 2021.

BRAZIL-EXPENDITURES, PUBLIC

Inter-American Development Bank (IDB), 1300 New York Ave. NW, Washington, DC, 20577, USA, (202) 623-1000, (202) 623-3096, https://www.iadb.org/en; Latin Macro Watch (LMW).

BRAZIL-EXPORTS

BC Stats, Stn Prov Govt, PO Box 9410, Victoria, BC, V8W 9V1, CAN, (250) 387-6121 (Dial from U.S.), bc.stats@gov.bc.ca, https://www2.gov.bc.ca/gov/content/data/about-data-management/bc-stats; Country Trade Profile - Brazil.

Central Intelligence Agency (CIA), Office of Public Affairs, Washington, DC, 20505, USA, (703) 482-0623, https://www.cia.gov; The World Factbook.

The Economist Group: Economist Intelligence Unit (EIU), 900 3rd Ave., 16th Fl., New York, NY, 10022, USA, (212) 541-0500, americas@eiu.com, https://www.eiu.com; Brazil Country Report.

Euromonitor International, Inc., 1 N Dearborn St., Ste. 1700, Chicago, IL, 60602, USA, (312) 922-1115, (312) 922-1157, info-usa@euromonitor.com, https://www.euromonitor.com/; Geographies.

Inter-American Development Bank (IDB), 1300 New York Ave. NW, Washington, DC, 20577, USA, (202) 623-1000, (202) 623-3096, https://www.iadb.org/en; Latin Macro Watch (LMW).

International Monetary Fund (IMF), 700 19th St. NW, Washington, DC, 20431, USA, (202) 623-7000, (202) 623-4661, publications@imf.org, https://www.imf.org; Direction of Trade Statistics (DOTS) and International Financial Statistics (IFS).

Organization for Economic Cooperation and Development (OECD), 2001 L St. NW, Ste. 650, Washington, DC, 20036-4922, USA, (202) 785-6323, (800) 456-6323, (202) 785-0350, washington.contact@oecd.org, https://www.oecd.org/; Economic Survey of Brazil 2020.

S&P Global, IHS Markit, 15 Inverness Way E, Englewood, CO, 80112, USA, (800) 447-2273, (800) 854-7179, https://ihsmarkit.com; Global Trade Atlas (GTA).

The World Bank, 1818 H St. NW, Washington, DC, 20433, USA, (202) 473-1000, (202) 477-6391, eds03@worldbank.org, https://www.worldbank.org/; World Development Report 2022: Finance for an Equitable Recovery.

BRAZIL-FEMALE WORKING POPULATION

See BRAZIL-EMPLOYMENT

BRAZIL-FERTILITY, HUMAN

Central Intelligence Agency (CIA), Office of Public Affairs, Washington, DC, 20505, USA, (703) 482-0623, https://www.cia.gov; The World Factbook.

BRAZIL-FERTILIZER INDUSTRY

United Nations Food and Agricultural Organization (FAO), 2121 K St., Ste. 800B, Washington, DC, 20037, USA, (202) 653-2400 (Dial from U.S.), (202) 653-5760 (Fax from U.S.), fao-hq@fao.org, https://www.fao.org; The State of Food and Agriculture (SOFA) 2022.

BRAZIL-FETAL MORTALITY

See BRAZIL-MORTALITY

BRAZIL-FINANCE

Federal Statistical Office Germany, Gustav-Stresemann-Ring 11, Wiesbaden, D-65189, GER, https://www.destatis.de; Basic Indicators: Brazil.

Inter-American Development Bank (IDB), 1300 New York Ave. NW, Washington, DC, 20577, USA, (202) 623-1000, (202) 623-3096, https://www.iadb.org/en; Latin Macro Watch (LMW).

Stockholm International Peace Research Institute (SIPRI), Signalistgatan 9, Stockholm, SE 169 72, SWE, https://www.sipri.org/; SIPRI Arms Transfers Database and SIPRI Military Expenditure Database.

United Nations Statistics Division (UNSD), United Nations Plz., New York, NY, 10017, USA, (800) 253-9646, (212) 963-9851, statistics@un.org, https://unstats.un.org; Statistical Yearbook of the United Nations 2021.

The World Bank, 1818 H St. NW, Washington, DC, 20433, USA, (202) 473-1000, (202) 477-6391, eds03@worldbank.org, https://www.worldbank.org/; Brazil (report).

BRAZIL-FINANCE, PUBLIC

Bernan Press, 15250 NBN Way, Bldg. C, Blue Ridge Summit, PA, 17214, USA, (301) 459-2255, (800) 865-3457, (800) 865-3450, customercare@bernan.com, https://rowman.com/Page/Bernan; National Accounts Statistics: Analysis of Main Aggregates 2020.

The Economist Group: Economist Intelligence Unit (EIU), 900 3rd Ave., 16th Fl., New York, NY, 10022, USA, (212) 541-0500, americas@eiu.com, https://www.eiu.com; Brazil Country Report.

Federal Statistical Office Germany, Gustav-Stresemann-Ring 11, Wiesbaden, D-65189, GER, https://www.destatis.de; Basic Indicators: Brazil.

Inter-American Development Bank (IDB), 1300 New York Ave. NW, Washington, DC, 20577, USA, (202) 623-1000, (202) 623-3096, https://www.iadb.org/en; Latin Macro Watch (LMW).

International Monetary Fund (IMF), 700 19th St. NW, Washington, DC, 20431, USA, (202) 623-7000, (202) 623-4661, publications@imf.org, https://www.imf.org; International Financial Statistics (IFS) and Regional Economic Outlook.

Palgrave Macmillan, 1 New York Plaza, Ste. 4500, New York, NY, 10004-1562, USA, (800) 777-4643, orders@palgrave.com, https://www.palgrave.com/us; The Statesman's Yearbook, 2023.

Routledge - Taylor & Francis Group, 6000 Broken Sound Pkwy. NW, Ste. 300, Boca Raton, FL, 33487, USA, (800) 634-1420, (800) 634-7064, orders@taylorandfrancis.com, https://www.routledge.com/; The Europa World Year Book 2022.

United Nations Statistics Division (UNSD), United Nations Plz., New York, NY, 10017, USA, (800) 253-9646, (212) 963-9851, statistics@un.org, https://unstats.un.org; National Accounts Main Aggregates Database and National Accounts Statistics: Main Aggregates and Detailed Tables.

The World Bank, 1818 H St. NW, Washington, DC, 20433, USA, (202) 473-1000, (202) 477-6391, eds03@worldbank.org, https://www.worldbank.org/; Brazil (report).

BRAZIL-FISHERIES

Federal Statistical Office Germany, Gustav-Stresemann-Ring 11, Wiesbaden, D-65189, GER, https://www.destatis.de; Basic Indicators: Brazil.

Inter-American Development Bank (IDB), 1300 New York Ave. NW, Washington, DC, 20577, USA, (202) 623-1000, (202) 623-3096, https://www.iadb.org/en; Latin Macro Watch (LMW).

Palgrave Macmillan, 1 New York Plaza, Ste. 4500, New York, NY, 10004-1562, USA, (800) 777-4643, orders@palgrave.com, https://www.palgrave.com/us; The Statesman's Yearbook, 2023.

Routledge - Taylor & Francis Group, 6000 Broken Sound Pkwy. NW, Ste. 300, Boca Raton, FL, 33487, USA, (800) 634-1420, (800) 634-7064, orders@taylorandfrancis.com, https://www.routledge.com/; The Europa World Year Book 2022.

United Nations Food and Agricultural Organization (FAO), 2121 K St., Ste. 800B, Washington, DC, 20037, USA, (202) 653-2400 (Dial from U.S.), (202) 653-5760 (Fax from U.S.), fao-hq@fao.org, https://www.fao.org; FAO Yearbook of Fishery and Aquaculture Statistics 2019; Fishery Statistical Collections Global Capture Production; FishStatJ; and The State of Food and Agriculture (SOFA) 2022.

United Nations Statistics Division (UNSD), United Nations Plz., New York, NY, 10017, USA, (800) 253-9646, (212) 963-9851, statistics@un.org, https://unstats.un.org; Statistical Yearbook of the United Nations 2021.

The World Bank, 1818 H St. NW, Washington, DC, 20433, USA, (202) 473-1000, (202) 477-6391, eds03@worldbank.org, https://www.worldbank.org/; Brazil (report).

BRAZIL-FOOD

Euromonitor International, Inc., 1 N Dearborn St., Ste. 1700, Chicago, IL, 60602, USA, (312) 922-1115, (312) 922-1157, info-usa@euromonitor.com, https://www.euromonitor.com/; Market Research on the Retailing Industry.

United Nations Food and Agricultural Organization (FAO), 2121 K St., Ste. 800B, Washington, DC, 20037, USA, (202) 653-2400 (Dial from U.S.), (202)

653-5760 (Fax from U.S.), fao-hq@fao.org, https://www.fao.org; The State of Food and Agriculture (SOFA) 2022.

BRAZIL-FOREIGN EXCHANGE RATES

Inter-American Development Bank (IDB), 1300 New York Ave. NW, Washington, DC, 20577, USA, (202) 623-1000, (202) 623-3096, https://www.iadb.org/en; Latin Macro Watch (LMW).

International Monetary Fund (IMF), 700 19th St. NW, Washington, DC, 20431, USA, (202) 623-7000, (202) 623-4661, publications@imf.org, https://www.imf.org; International Financial Statistics (IFS).

BRAZIL-FORESTS AND FORESTRY

Federal Statistical Office Germany, Gustav-Stresemann-Ring 11, Wiesbaden, D-65189, GER, https://www.destatis.de; Basic Indicators: Brazil.

Inter-American Development Bank (IDB), 1300 New York Ave. NW, Washington, DC, 20577, USA, (202) 623-1000, (202) 623-3096, https://www.iadb.org/en; Latin Macro Watch (LMW).

Palgrave Macmillan, 1 New York Plaza, Ste. 4500, New York, NY, 10004-1562, USA, (800) 777-4643, orders@palgrave.com, https://www.palgrave.com/us; The Statesman's Yearbook, 2023.

Routledge - Taylor & Francis Group, 6000 Broken Sound Pkwy. NW, Ste. 300, Boca Raton, FL, 33487, USA, (800) 634-1420, (800) 634-7064, orders@taylorandfrancis.com, https://www.routledge.com/; The Europa World Year Book 2022.

UNESCO Institute for Statistics, C.P 250 Succursale H, Montreal, QC, H3G 2K8, CAN, (514) 343-6880 (Dial from U.S.), (514) 343-5740 (Fax from U.S.), uis.publications@unesco.org, http://uis.unesco.org/; UIS.Stat.

United Nations Food and Agricultural Organization (FAO), 2121 K St., Ste. 800B, Washington, DC, 20037, USA, (202) 653-2400 (Dial from U.S.), (202) 653-5760 (Fax from U.S.), fao-hq@fao.org, https://www.fao.org; FAO Yearbook of Forest Products 2019 and The State of Food and Agriculture (SOFA) 2022.

The World Bank, 1818 H St. NW, Washington, DC, 20433, USA, (202) 473-1000, (202) 477-6391, eds03@worldbank.org, https://www.worldbank.org/; Brazil (report) and World Development Report 2022: Finance for an Equitable Recovery.

BRAZIL-GAS PRODUCTION

See BRAZIL-MINERAL INDUSTRIES

BRAZIL-GEOGRAPHIC INFORMATION SYSTEMS

Federal Statistical Office Germany, Gustav-Stresemann-Ring 11, Wiesbaden, D-65189, GER, https://www.destatis.de; Basic Indicators: Brazil.

The World Bank, 1818 H St. NW, Washington, DC, 20433, USA, (202) 473-1000, (202) 477-6391, eds03@worldbank.org, https://www.worldbank.org/; Brazil (report).

BRAZIL-GOLD INDUSTRY

The World Bank, 1818 H St. NW, Washington, DC, 20433, USA, (202) 473-1000, (202) 477-6391, eds03@worldbank.org, https://www.worldbank.org/; World Development Indicators (WDI) 2022.

BRAZIL-GOLD PRODUCTION

See BRAZIL-MINERAL INDUSTRIES

BRAZIL-GROSS DOMESTIC PRODUCT

The Economist Group: Economist Intelligence Unit (EIU), 900 3rd Ave., 16th Fl., New York, NY, 10022, USA, (212) 541-0500, americas@eiu.com, https://www.eiu.com; Brazil Country Report.

Inter-American Development Bank (IDB), 1300 New York Ave. NW, Washington, DC, 20577, USA, (202) 623-1000, (202) 623-3096, https://www.iadb.org/en; Latin Macro Watch (LMW).

Routledge - Taylor & Francis Group, 6000 Broken Sound Pkwy. NW, Ste. 300, Boca Raton, FL, 33487, USA, (800) 634-1420, (800) 634-7064, orders@taylorandfrancis.com, https://www.routledge.com/; The Europa World Year Book 2022.

United Nations Statistics Division (UNSD), United Nations Plz., New York, NY, 10017, USA, (800) 253-9646, (212) 963-9851, statistics@un.org, https://unstats.un.org; Statistical Yearbook of the United Nations 2021.

The World Bank, 1818 H St. NW, Washington, DC, 20433, USA, (202) 473-1000, (202) 477-6391, eds03@worldbank.org, https://www.worldbank.org/; World Development Indicators (WDI) 2022 and World Development Report 2022: Finance for an Equitable Recovery.

BRAZIL-GROSS NATIONAL PRODUCT

Inter-American Development Bank (IDB), 1300 New York Ave. NW, Washington, DC, 20577, USA, (202) 623-1000, (202) 623-3096, https://www.iadb.org/en; Latin Macro Watch (LMW).

Palgrave Macmillan, 1 New York Plaza, Ste. 4500, New York, NY, 10004-1562, USA, (800) 777-4643, orders@palgrave.com, https://www.palgrave.com/us; The Statesman's Yearbook, 2023.

Routledge - Taylor & Francis Group, 6000 Broken Sound Pkwy. NW, Ste. 300, Boca Raton, FL, 33487, USA, (800) 634-1420, (800) 634-7064, orders@taylorandfrancis.com, https://www.routledge.com/; The Europa World Year Book 2022.

United Nations Statistics Division (UNSD), United Nations Plz., New York, NY, 10017, USA, (800) 253-9646, (212) 963-9851, statistics@un.org, https://unstats.un.org; Statistical Yearbook of the United Nations 2021.

The World Bank, 1818 H St. NW, Washington, DC, 20433, USA, (202) 473-1000, (202) 477-6391, eds03@worldbank.org, https://www.worldbank.org/; World Development Indicators (WDI) 2022 and World Development Report 2022: Finance for an Equitable Recovery.

BRAZIL-HOUSING

Euromonitor International, Inc., 1 N Dearborn St., Ste. 1700, Chicago, IL, 60602, USA, (312) 922-1115, (312) 922-1157, info-usa@euromonitor.com, https://www.euromonitor.com/; Geographies.

BRAZIL-ILLITERATE PERSONS

UNESCO Institute for Statistics, C.P 250 Succursale H, Montreal, QC, H3G 2K8, CAN, (514) 343-6880 (Dial from U.S.), (514) 343-5740 (Fax from U.S.), uis.publications@unesco.org, http://uis.unesco.org/; UIS.Stat.

BRAZIL-IMPORTS

BC Stats, Stn Prov Govt, PO Box 9410, Victoria, BC, V8W 9V1, CAN, (250) 387-6121 (Dial from U.S.), bc.stats@gov.bc.ca, https://www2.gov.bc.ca/gov/content/data/about-data-management/bc-stats; Country Trade Profile - Brazil.

Central Intelligence Agency (CIA), Office of Public Affairs, Washington, DC, 20505, USA, (703) 482-0623, https://www.cia.gov; The World Factbook.

The Economist Group: Economist Intelligence Unit (EIU), 900 3rd Ave., 16th Fl., New York, NY, 10022, USA, (212) 541-0500, americas@eiu.com, https://www.eiu.com; Brazil Country Report.

Euromonitor International, Inc., 1 N Dearborn St., Ste. 1700, Chicago, IL, 60602, USA, (312) 922-1115, (312) 922-1157, info-usa@euromonitor.com, https://www.euromonitor.com/; Geographies.

Inter-American Development Bank (IDB), 1300 New York Ave. NW, Washington, DC, 20577, USA, (202) 623-1000, (202) 623-3096, https://www.iadb.org/en; Latin Macro Watch (LMW).

International Monetary Fund (IMF), 700 19th St. NW, Washington, DC, 20431, USA, (202) 623-7000, (202) 623-4661, publications@imf.org, https://www.imf.org; Direction of Trade Statistics (DOTS) and International Financial Statistics (IFS).

Organization for Economic Cooperation and Development (OECD), 2001 L St. NW, Ste. 650, Washington, DC, 20036-4922, USA, (202) 785-6323, (800) 456-6323, (202) 785-0350, washington.contact@oecd.org, https://www.oecd.org/; Economic Survey of Brazil 2020.

S&P Global, IHS Markit, 15 Inverness Way E, Englewood, CO, 80112, USA, (800) 447-2273, (800) 854-7179, https://ihsmarkit.com; Global Trade Atlas (GTA).

United Nations Conference on Trade and Development (UNCTAD), Palais des Nations, Geneva, 1211, SWI, (212) 963-6896, unctadinfo@unctad.org, https://unctad.org; Handbook of Statistics 2021.

The World Bank, 1818 H St. NW, Washington, DC, 20433, USA, (202) 473-1000, (202) 477-6391, eds03@worldbank.org, https://www.worldbank.org/; World Development Report 2022: Finance for an Equitable Recovery.

BRAZIL-INDUSTRIAL METALS PRODUCTION

See BRAZIL-MINERAL INDUSTRIES

BRAZIL-INDUSTRIAL PROPERTY

World Intellectual Property Organization (WIPO), 34, chemin des Colombettes, Geneva, CH-1211, SWI, https://www.wipo.int; Madrid Yearly Review 2022: International Registrations of Marks.

BRAZIL-INDUSTRIES

Central Intelligence Agency (CIA), Office of Public Affairs, Washington, DC, 20505, USA, (703) 482-0623, https://www.cia.gov; The World Factbook.

The Economist Group: Economist Intelligence Unit (EIU), 900 3rd Ave., 16th Fl., New York, NY, 10022, USA, (212) 541-0500, americas@eiu.com, https://www.eiu.com; Brazil Country Report.

Euromonitor International, Inc., 1 N Dearborn St., Ste. 1700, Chicago, IL, 60602, USA, (312) 922-1115, (312) 922-1157, info-usa@euromonitor.com, https://www.euromonitor.com/; Geographies.

Federal Statistical Office Germany, Gustav-Stresemann-Ring 11, Wiesbaden, D-65189, GER, https://www.destatis.de; Basic Indicators: Brazil.

International Labour Organization (ILO), 4 Rte. des Morillons, Geneva, CH-1211, SWI, ilo@ilo.org, https://www.ilo.org; NORMLEX Information System on International Labour Standards.

Palgrave Macmillan, 1 New York Plaza, Ste. 4500, New York, NY, 10004-1562, USA, (800) 777-4643, orders@palgrave.com, https://www.palgrave.com/us; The Statesman's Yearbook, 2023.

Routledge - Taylor & Francis Group, 6000 Broken Sound Pkwy. NW, Ste. 300, Boca Raton, FL, 33487, USA, (800) 634-1420, (800) 634-7064, orders@taylorandfrancis.com, https://www.routledge.com/; The Europa World Year Book 2022.

United Nations Economic Commission for Latin America and the Caribbean (ECLAC), Casilla 179-D, Santiago, 7630412, CHL, (202) 596-3713, prensa@cepal.org, https://www.cepal.org/en; Economic Survey of Latin America and the Caribbean 2021: Labour Dynamics and Employment Policies for Sustainable and Inclusive Recovery Beyond the COVID-19 Crisis.

United Nations Industrial Development Organization (UNIDO), 1 United Nations Plz., Rm. DC1-1118, New York, NY, 10017, USA, (212) 963-6890, (212) 963 6885, (212) 963-7904, office.newyork@unido.org, https://www.unido.org/; Industrial Statistics Databases and International Yearbook of Industrial Statistics 2021.

University of California Los Angeles (UCLA), Latin American Institute (LAI), 10343 Bunche Hall, 315 Portola Plaza, Los Angeles, CA, 90095-1447, USA, (310) 825-4571, lai@international.ucla.edu, https://www.international.ucla.edu/lai; unpublished data.

The World Bank, 1818 H St. NW, Washington, DC, 20433, USA, (202) 473-1000, (202) 477-6391,

eds03@worldbank.org, https://www.worldbank.org/; Brazil (report) and World Development Indicators (WDI) 2022.

World Intellectual Property Organization (WIPO), 34, chemin des Colombettes, Geneva, CH-1211, SWI, https://www.wipo.int; Madrid Yearly Review 2022: International Registrations of Marks.

BRAZIL-INFANT AND MATERNAL MORTALITY

See BRAZIL-MORTALITY

BRAZIL-INFLATION (FINANCE)

United Nations Economic Commission for Latin America and the Caribbean (ECLAC), Casilla 179-D, Santiago, 7630412, CHL, (202) 596-3713, prensa@cepal.org, https://www.cepal.org/en; Economic Survey of Latin America and the Caribbean 2021: Labour Dynamics and Employment Policies for Sustainable and Inclusive Recovery Beyond the COVID-19 Crisis.

BRAZIL-INTEREST RATES

Inter-American Development Bank (IDB), 1300 New York Ave. NW, Washington, DC, 20577, USA, (202) 623-1000, (202) 623-3096, https://www.iadb.org/en; Latin Macro Watch (LMW).

BRAZIL-INTERNAL REVENUE

Inter-American Development Bank (IDB), 1300 New York Ave. NW, Washington, DC, 20577, USA, (202) 623-1000, (202) 623-3096, https://www.iadb.org/en; Latin Macro Watch (LMW).

BRAZIL-INTERNATIONAL FINANCE

Federal Statistical Office Germany, Gustav-Stresemann-Ring 11, Wiesbaden, D-65189, GER, https://www.destatis.de; Basic Indicators: Brazil.

Inter-American Development Bank (IDB), 1300 New York Ave. NW, Washington, DC, 20577, USA, (202) 623-1000, (202) 623-3096, https://www.iadb.org/en; Latin Macro Watch (LMW).

BRAZIL-INTERNATIONAL LIQUIDITY

Inter-American Development Bank (IDB), 1300 New York Ave. NW, Washington, DC, 20577, USA, (202) 623-1000, (202) 623-3096, https://www.iadb.org/en; Latin Macro Watch (LMW).

BRAZIL-INTERNATIONAL TRADE

The Economist Group: Economist Intelligence Unit (EIU), 900 3rd Ave., 16th Fl., New York, NY, 10022, USA, (212) 541-0500, americas@eiu.com, https://www.eiu.com; Brazil Country Report.

Euromonitor International, Inc., 1 N Dearborn St., Ste. 1700, Chicago, IL, 60602, USA, (312) 922-1115, (312) 922-1157, info-usa@euromonitor.com, https://www.euromonitor.com/; Geographies.

Federal Statistical Office Germany, Gustav-Stresemann-Ring 11, Wiesbaden, D-65189, GER, https://www.destatis.de; Basic Indicators: Brazil.

Inter-American Development Bank (IDB), 1300 New York Ave. NW, Washington, DC, 20577, USA, (202) 623-1000, (202) 623-3096, https://www.iadb.org/en; Latin Macro Watch (LMW).

Organization for Economic Cooperation and Development (OECD), 2001 L St. NW, Ste. 650, Washington, DC, 20036-4922, USA, (202) 785-6323, (800) 456-6323, (202) 785-0350, washington.contact@oecd.org, https://www.oecd.org/; Economic Survey of Brazil 2020.

Palgrave Macmillan, 1 New York Plaza, Ste. 4500, New York, NY, 10004-1562, USA, (800) 777-4643, orders@palgrave.com, https://www.palgrave.com/us; The Statesman's Yearbook, 2023.

Routledge - Taylor & Francis Group, 6000 Broken Sound Pkwy. NW, Ste. 300, Boca Raton, FL, 33487, USA, (800) 634-1420, (800) 634-7064, orders@taylorandfrancis.com, https://www.routledge.com/; The Europa World Year Book 2022.

United Nations Conference on Trade and Development (UNCTAD), Palais des Nations, Geneva, 1211, SWI, (212) 963-6896, unctadinfo@unctad.org, https://unctad.org; Trade and Development Report 2021.

United Nations Economic Commission for Latin America and the Caribbean (ECLAC), Casilla 179-D, Santiago, 7630412, CHL, (202) 596-3713, prensa@cepal.org, https://www.cepal.org/en; Economic Survey of Latin America and the Caribbean 2021: Labour Dynamics and Employment Policies for Sustainable and Inclusive Recovery Beyond the COVID-19 Crisis.

United Nations Food and Agricultural Organization (FAO), 2121 K St., Ste. 800B, Washington, DC, 20037, USA, (202) 653-2400 (Dial from U.S.), (202) 653-5760 (Fax from U.S.), fao-hq@fao.org, https://www.fao.org; The State of Food and Agriculture (SOFA) 2022.

United Nations Statistics Division (UNSD), United Nations Plz., New York, NY, 10017, USA, (800) 253-9646, (212) 963-9851, statistics@un.org, https://unstats.un.org; International Trade Statistics Yearbook 2020 and Statistical Yearbook of the United Nations 2021.

The World Bank, 1818 H St. NW, Washington, DC, 20433, USA, (202) 473-1000, (202) 477-6391, eds03@worldbank.org, https://www.worldbank.org/; Brazil (report); World Development Indicators (WDI) 2022; and World Development Report 2022: Finance for an Equitable Recovery.

World Bureau of Metal Statistics (WBMS), 31 Star St., Ware, Hertfordshire, SG12 9BA, GBR, https://www.refinitiv.com/en/trading-solutions/world-bureau-metal-statistics; Annual Stainless Steel Statistics; Long Term Production/Consumption Series - All Metals; World Flow Charts; and World Metal Statistics.

World Trade Organization (WTO), Ctre. William Rappard, Rue de Lausanne 154, Case postale, Geneva, CH-1211, SWI, enquiries@wto.org, https://www.wto.org; World Trade Statistical Review 2022.

BRAZIL-INTERNET USERS

Federal Statistical Office Germany, Gustav-Stresemann-Ring 11, Wiesbaden, D-65189, GER, https://www.destatis.de; Basic Indicators: Brazil.

International Telecommunication Union (ITU), Place des Nations, Geneva, CH-1211, SWI, itumail@itu.int, https://www.itu.int; Global Connectivity Report 2022; World Telecommunication/ICT Indicators Database 2021; and Yearbook of Statistics 2019.

The World Bank, 1818 H St. NW, Washington, DC, 20433, USA, (202) 473-1000, (202) 477-6391, eds03@worldbank.org, https://www.worldbank.org/; Brazil (report).

BRAZIL-INVESTMENTS

Inter-American Development Bank (IDB), 1300 New York Ave. NW, Washington, DC, 20577, USA, (202) 623-1000, (202) 623-3096, https://www.iadb.org/en; Latin Macro Watch (LMW).

International Monetary Fund (IMF), 700 19th St. NW, Washington, DC, 20431, USA, (202) 623-7000, (202) 623-4661, publications@imf.org, https://www.imf.org; International Financial Statistics (IFS).

BRAZIL-IRRIGATION

Inter-American Development Bank (IDB), 1300 New York Ave. NW, Washington, DC, 20577, USA, (202) 623-1000, (202) 623-3096, https://www.iadb.org/en; Latin Macro Watch (LMW).

BRAZIL-LABOR

Central Intelligence Agency (CIA), Office of Public Affairs, Washington, DC, 20505, USA, (703) 482-0623, https://www.cia.gov; The World Factbook.

Euromonitor International, Inc., 1 N Dearborn St., Ste. 1700, Chicago, IL, 60602, USA, (312) 922-1115, (312) 922-1157, info-usa@euromonitor.com, https://www.euromonitor.com/; Geographies.

International Labour Organization (ILO), 4 Rte. des Morillons, Geneva, CH-1211, SWI, ilo@ilo.org, https://www.ilo.org; NORMLEX Information System on International Labour Standards.

Organization for Economic Cooperation and Development (OECD), 2001 L St. NW, Ste. 650, Washington, DC, 20036-4922, USA, (202) 785-6323, (800) 456-6323, (202) 785-0350, washington.contact@oecd.org, https://www.oecd.org/; Economic Survey of Brazil 2020.

Palgrave Macmillan, 1 New York Plaza, Ste. 4500, New York, NY, 10004-1562, USA, (800) 777-4643, orders@palgrave.com, https://www.palgrave.com/us; The Statesman's Yearbook, 2023.

United Nations Food and Agricultural Organization (FAO), 2121 K St., Ste. 800B, Washington, DC, 20037, USA, (202) 653-2400 (Dial from U.S.), (202) 653-5760 (Fax from U.S.), fao-hq@fao.org, https://www.fao.org; The State of Food and Agriculture (SOFA) 2022.

The World Bank, 1818 H St. NW, Washington, DC, 20433, USA, (202) 473-1000, (202) 477-6391, eds03@worldbank.org, https://www.worldbank.org/; World Development Indicators (WDI) 2022 and World Development Report 2022: Finance for an Equitable Recovery.

BRAZIL-LAND USE

Inter-American Development Bank (IDB), 1300 New York Ave. NW, Washington, DC, 20577, USA, (202) 623-1000, (202) 623-3096, https://www.iadb.org/en; Latin Macro Watch (LMW).

United Nations Statistics Division (UNSD), United Nations Plz., New York, NY, 10017, USA, (800) 253-9646, (212) 963-9851, statistics@un.org, https://unstats.un.org; Millennium Development Goal Indicators.

The World Bank, 1818 H St. NW, Washington, DC, 20433, USA, (202) 473-1000, (202) 477-6391, eds03@worldbank.org, https://www.worldbank.org/; World Development Report 2022: Finance for an Equitable Recovery.

BRAZIL-LIBRARIES

UNESCO Institute for Statistics, C.P 250 Succursale H, Montreal, QC, H3G 2K8, CAN, (514) 343-6880 (Dial from U.S.), (514) 343-5740 (Fax from U.S.), uis.publications@unesco.org, http://uis.unesco.org/; UIS.Stat.

BRAZIL-LIFE EXPECTANCY

Central Intelligence Agency (CIA), Office of Public Affairs, Washington, DC, 20505, USA, (703) 482-0623, https://www.cia.gov; The World Factbook.

United Nations Department of Economic and Social Affairs (DESA), Population Division, 2 United Nations Plz., Rm. DC2-1950, New York, NY, 10017, USA, (212) 963-3209, (212) 963-2147, population@un.org, https://www.un.org/development/desa/pd/; World Population Ageing 2020 Highlights.

United Nations Statistics Division (UNSD), United Nations Plz., New York, NY, 10017, USA, (800) 253-9646, (212) 963-9851, statistics@un.org, https://unstats.un.org; Millennium Development Goal Indicators.

BRAZIL-LITERACY

Euromonitor International, Inc., 1 N Dearborn St., Ste. 1700, Chicago, IL, 60602, USA, (312) 922-1115, (312) 922-1157, info-usa@euromonitor.com, https://www.euromonitor.com/; Geographies.

UNESCO Institute for Statistics, C.P 250 Succursale H, Montreal, QC, H3G 2K8, CAN, (514) 343-6880 (Dial from U.S.), (514) 343-5740 (Fax from U.S.), uis.publications@unesco.org, http://uis.unesco.org/; Literacy.

BRAZIL-LIVESTOCK

Palgrave Macmillan, 1 New York Plaza, Ste. 4500, New York, NY, 10004-1562, USA, (800) 777-4643, orders@palgrave.com, https://www.palgrave.com/us; The Statesman's Yearbook, 2023.

Routledge - Taylor & Francis Group, 6000 Broken Sound Pkwy. NW, Ste. 300, Boca Raton, FL, 33487, USA, (800) 634-1420, (800) 634-7064, orders@taylorandfrancis.com, https://www.routledge.com/; The Europa World Year Book 2022.

United Nations Food and Agricultural Organization (FAO), 2121 K St., Ste. 800B, Washington, DC, 20037, USA, (202) 653-2400 (Dial from U.S.), (202) 653-5760 (Fax from U.S.), fao-hq@fao.org, https://www.fao.org; The State of Food and Agriculture (SOFA) 2022.

United Nations Statistics Division (UNSD), United Nations Plz., New York, NY, 10017, USA, (800) 253-9646, (212) 963-9851, statistics@un.org, https://unstats.un.org; Statistical Yearbook of the United Nations 2021.

BRAZIL-MANUFACTURES

Inter-American Development Bank (IDB), 1300 New York Ave. NW, Washington, DC, 20577, USA, (202) 623-1000, (202) 623-3096, https://www.iadb.org/en; Latin Macro Watch (LMW).

Organization for Economic Cooperation and Development (OECD), 2001 L St. NW, Ste. 650, Washington, DC, 20036-4922, USA, (202) 785-6323, (800) 456-6323, (202) 785-0350, washington.contact@oecd.org, https://www.oecd.org/; Economic Survey of Brazil 2020.

BRAZIL-MINERAL INDUSTRIES

Barchart, 209 W Jackson Blvd., 2nd Fl., Chicago, IL, 60606, USA, (877) 247-4394, commodities@barchart.com, https://www.barchart.com/cmdty; The cmdty Yearbook 2023; cmdtyStats: Commodity Statistics and Fundamental Data; cmdtyView: Commodity Index; and Commodity Data and Prices.

Federal Statistical Office Germany, Gustav-Stresemann-Ring 11, Wiesbaden, D-65189, GER, https://www.destatis.de; Basic Indicators: Brazil.

Inter-American Development Bank (IDB), 1300 New York Ave. NW, Washington, DC, 20577, USA, (202) 623-1000, (202) 623-3096, https://www.iadb.org/en; Latin Macro Watch (LMW).

International Energy Agency (IEA), 9 Rue de la Federation, Paris, 75739, FRA, info@iea.org, https://www.iea.org/; World Energy Outlook 2021.

International Monetary Fund (IMF), 700 19th St. NW, Washington, DC, 20431, USA, (202) 623-7000, (202) 623-4661, publications@imf.org, https://www.imf.org; International Financial Statistics (IFS).

Organization for Economic Cooperation and Development (OECD), 2001 L St. NW, Ste. 650, Washington, DC, 20036-4922, USA, (202) 785-6323, (800) 456-6323, (202) 785-0350, washington.contact@oecd.org, https://www.oecd.org/; Economic Survey of Brazil 2020.

Palgrave Macmillan, 1 New York Plaza, Ste. 4500, New York, NY, 10004-1562, USA, (800) 777-4643, orders@palgrave.com, https://www.palgrave.com/us; The Statesman's Yearbook, 2023.

Routledge - Taylor & Francis Group, 6000 Broken Sound Pkwy. NW, Ste. 300, Boca Raton, FL, 33487, USA, (800) 634-1420, (800) 634-7064, orders@taylorandfrancis.com, https://www.routledge.com/; The Europa World Year Book 2022.

United Nations Conference on Trade and Development (UNCTAD), Palais des Nations, Geneva, 1211, SWI, (212) 963-6896, unctadinfo@unctad.org, https://unctad.org; Trade and Development Report 2021.

United Nations Statistics Division (UNSD), United Nations Plz., New York, NY, 10017, USA, (800) 253-9646, (212) 963-9851, statistics@un.org, https://unstats.un.org; Statistical Yearbook of the United Nations 2021.

World Bureau of Metal Statistics (WBMS), 31 Star St., Ware, Hertfordshire, SG12 9BA, GBR, https://www.refinitiv.com/en/trading-solutions/world-bureau-metal-statistics; Annual Stainless Steel Statistics; Long Term Production/Consumption Series - All Metals; World Flow Charts; and World Metal Statistics.

BRAZIL-MOLASSES PRODUCTION

See BRAZIL-CROPS

BRAZIL-MONEY SUPPLY

The Economist Group: Economist Intelligence Unit (EIU), 900 3rd Ave., 16th Fl., New York, NY, 10022, USA, (212) 541-0500, americas@eiu.com, https://www.eiu.com; Brazil Country Report.

Federal Statistical Office Germany, Gustav-Stresemann-Ring 11, Wiesbaden, D-65189, GER, https://www.destatis.de; Basic Indicators: Brazil.

Inter-American Development Bank (IDB), 1300 New York Ave. NW, Washington, DC, 20577, USA, (202) 623-1000, (202) 623-3096, https://www.iadb.org/en; Latin Macro Watch (LMW).

International Monetary Fund (IMF), 700 19th St. NW, Washington, DC, 20431, USA, (202) 623-7000, (202) 623-4661, publications@imf.org, https://www.imf.org; International Financial Statistics (IFS).

Organization for Economic Cooperation and Development (OECD), 2001 L St. NW, Ste. 650, Washington, DC, 20036-4922, USA, (202) 785-6323, (800) 456-6323, (202) 785-0350, washington.contact@oecd.org, https://www.oecd.org/; Economic Survey of Brazil 2020.

Routledge - Taylor & Francis Group, 6000 Broken Sound Pkwy. NW, Ste. 300, Boca Raton, FL, 33487, USA, (800) 634-1420, (800) 634-7064, orders@taylorandfrancis.com, https://www.routledge.com/; The Europa World Year Book 2022.

United Nations Statistics Division (UNSD), United Nations Plz., New York, NY, 10017, USA, (800) 253-9646, (212) 963-9851, statistics@un.org, https://unstats.un.org; Statistical Yearbook of the United Nations 2021.

The World Bank, 1818 H St. NW, Washington, DC, 20433, USA, (202) 473-1000, (202) 477-6391, eds03@worldbank.org, https://www.worldbank.org/; Brazil (report).

BRAZIL-MORTALITY

UNICEF, 3 United Nations Plz., New York, NY, 10017, USA, (212) 303-7984, (917) 244-2215, https://www.unicef.org; The State of the World's Children 2023.

United Nations Statistics Division (UNSD), United Nations Plz., New York, NY, 10017, USA, (800) 253-9646, (212) 963-9851, statistics@un.org, https://unstats.un.org; Millennium Development Goal Indicators; Statistical Yearbook of the United Nations 2021; and World Statistics Pocketbook 2021.

The World Bank, 1818 H St. NW, Washington, DC, 20433, USA, (202) 473-1000, (202) 477-6391, eds03@worldbank.org, https://www.worldbank.org/; World Development Indicators (WDI) 2022.

World Health Organization (WHO), Ave. Appia 20, Geneva, CH-1211, SWI, (202) 974-3000 (Telephone in U.S.), publications@who.int, https://www.who.int/; Global Health Observatory (GHO).

BRAZIL-MOTION PICTURES

Palgrave Macmillan, 1 New York Plaza, Ste. 4500, New York, NY, 10004-1562, USA, (800) 777-4643, orders@palgrave.com, https://www.palgrave.com/us; The Statesman's Yearbook, 2023.

BRAZIL-MOTOR VEHICLES

International Road Federation (IRF), Madison Place, 500 Montgomery St., 5th Fl., Alexandria, VA, 22314, USA, (703) 535-1001, (703) 535-1007, info@irf.global, https://www.irf.global/; World Road Statistics (WRS).

BRAZIL-NATURAL GAS PRODUCTION

See BRAZIL-MINERAL INDUSTRIES

BRAZIL-NICKEL AND NICKEL ORE

See BRAZIL-MINERAL INDUSTRIES

BRAZIL-NUTRITION

United Nations Food and Agricultural Organization (FAO), 2121 K St., Ste. 800B, Washington, DC, 20037, USA, (202) 653-2400 (Dial from U.S.), (202) 653-5760 (Fax from U.S.), fao-hq@fao.org, https://www.fao.org; The State of Food and Agriculture (SOFA) 2022.

United Nations Statistics Division (UNSD), United Nations Plz., New York, NY, 10017, USA, (800) 253-9646, (212) 963-9851, statistics@un.org, https://unstats.un.org; Millennium Development Goal Indicators.

BRAZIL-ORANGES PRODUCTION

See BRAZIL-CROPS

BRAZIL-PAPER

See BRAZIL-FORESTS AND FORESTRY

BRAZIL-PEANUT PRODUCTION

See BRAZIL-CROPS

BRAZIL-PEPPER PRODUCTION

See BRAZIL-CROPS

BRAZIL-PESTICIDES

United Nations Food and Agricultural Organization (FAO), 2121 K St., Ste. 800B, Washington, DC, 20037, USA, (202) 653-2400 (Dial from U.S.), (202) 653-5760 (Fax from U.S.), fao-hq@fao.org, https://www.fao.org; The State of Food and Agriculture (SOFA) 2022.

BRAZIL-PETROLEUM INDUSTRY AND TRADE

Inter-American Development Bank (IDB), 1300 New York Ave. NW, Washington, DC, 20577, USA, (202) 623-1000, (202) 623-3096, https://www.iadb.org/en; Latin Macro Watch (LMW).

International Energy Agency (IEA), 9 Rue de la Federation, Paris, 75739, FRA, info@iea.org, https://www.iea.org/; World Energy Outlook 2021.

Palgrave Macmillan, 1 New York Plaza, Ste. 4500, New York, NY, 10004-1562, USA, (800) 777-4643, orders@palgrave.com, https://www.palgrave.com/us; The Statesman's Yearbook, 2023.

U.S. Energy Information Administration (EIA), 1000 Independence Ave. SW, Washington, DC, 20585, USA, (202) 586-8800, infoctr@eia.gov, https://www.eia.gov; International Energy Outlook 2021.

United Nations Food and Agricultural Organization (FAO), 2121 K St., Ste. 800B, Washington, DC, 20037, USA, (202) 653-2400 (Dial from U.S.), (202) 653-5760 (Fax from U.S.), fao-hq@fao.org, https://www.fao.org; The State of Food and Agriculture (SOFA) 2022.

United Nations Statistics Division (UNSD), United Nations Plz., New York, NY, 10017, USA, (800) 253-9646, (212) 963-9851, statistics@un.org, https://unstats.un.org; Statistical Yearbook of the United Nations 2021.

BRAZIL-PHOSPHATES PRODUCTION

See BRAZIL-MINERAL INDUSTRIES

BRAZIL-PLASTICS INDUSTRY AND TRADE

United Nations Statistics Division (UNSD), United Nations Plz., New York, NY, 10017, USA, (800) 253-9646, (212) 963-9851, statistics@un.org, https://unstats.un.org; Statistical Yearbook of the United Nations 2021.

BRAZIL-POPULATION

Central Intelligence Agency (CIA), Office of Public Affairs, Washington, DC, 20505, USA, (703) 482-0623, https://www.cia.gov; The World Factbook.

The Economist Group: Economist Intelligence Unit (EIU), 900 3rd Ave., 16th Fl., New York, NY, 10022, USA, (212) 541-0500, americas@eiu.com, https://www.eiu.com; Brazil Country Report.

Federal Statistical Office Germany, Gustav-Stresemann-Ring 11, Wiesbaden, D-65189, GER, https://www.destatis.de; Basic Indicators: Brazil.

Infoplease, c/o Sandbox Networks, Inc., 1 Lincoln St., 24th Fl., Boston, MA, 02111, USA, https://www.infoplease.com; Countries of the World.

Inter-American Development Bank (IDB), 1300 New York Ave. NW, Washington, DC, 20577, USA, (202) 623-1000, (202) 623-3096, https://www.iadb.org/en; Latin Macro Watch (LMW).

International Labour Organization (ILO), 4 Rte. des Morillons, Geneva, CH-1211, SWI, ilo@ilo.org, https://www.ilo.org; NORMLEX Information System on International Labour Standards.

Palgrave Macmillan, 1 New York Plaza, Ste. 4500, New York, NY, 10004-1562, USA, (800) 777-4643, orders@palgrave.com, https://www.palgrave.com/us; The Statesman's Yearbook, 2023.

Routledge - Taylor & Francis Group, 6000 Broken Sound Pkwy. NW, Ste. 300, Boca Raton, FL, 33487, USA, (800) 634-1420, (800) 634-7064, orders@taylorandfrancis.com, https://www.routledge.com/; The Europa World Year Book 2022.

UK Data Service, University of Essex, Wivenhoe Park, Colchester, Essex, CO4 3SQ, GBR, https://ukdataservice.ac.uk/; International Aggregate Data.

UNESCO Institute for Statistics, C.P 250 Succursale H, Montreal, QC, H3G 2K8, CAN, (514) 343-6880 (Dial from U.S.), (514) 343-5740 (Fax from U.S.), uis.publications@unesco.org, http://uis.unesco.org/; UIS.Stat.

United Nations Department of Economic and Social Affairs (DESA), Population Division, 2 United Nations Plz., Rm. DC2-1950, New York, NY, 10017, USA, (212) 963-3209, (212) 963-2147, population@un.org, https://www.un.org/development/desa/pd/; Revision of World Urbanization Prospects and World Population Ageing 2020 Highlights.

United Nations Economic Commission for Latin America and the Caribbean (ECLAC), Casilla 179-D, Santiago, 7630412, CHL, (202) 596-3713, prensa@cepal.org, https://www.cepal.org/en; CEPALSTAT and Social Panorama of Latin America and the Caribbean 2022: Transforming Education as a Basis for Sustainable Development.

United Nations Statistics Division (UNSD), United Nations Plz., New York, NY, 10017, USA, (800) 253-9646, (212) 963-9851, statistics@un.org, https://unstats.un.org; Statistical Yearbook of the United Nations 2021 and World Statistics Pocketbook 2021.

University of California Los Angeles (UCLA), Latin American Institute (LAI), 10343 Bunche Hall, 315 Portola Plaza, Los Angeles, CA, 90095-1447, USA, (310) 825-4571, lai@international.ucla.edu, https://www.international.ucla.edu/lai; unpublished data.

The World Bank, 1818 H St. NW, Washington, DC, 20433, USA, (202) 473-1000, (202) 477-6391, eds03@worldbank.org, https://www.worldbank.org/; Brazil (report); The Global Findex Database 2021; and World Development Report 2022: Finance for an Equitable Recovery.

BRAZIL-POPULATION DENSITY

Central Intelligence Agency (CIA), Office of Public Affairs, Washington, DC, 20505, USA, (703) 482-0623, https://www.cia.gov; The World Factbook.

Federal Statistical Office Germany, Gustav-Stresemann-Ring 11, Wiesbaden, D-65189, GER, https://www.destatis.de; Basic Indicators: Brazil.

Inter-American Development Bank (IDB), 1300 New York Ave. NW, Washington, DC, 20577, USA, (202) 623-1000, (202) 623-3096, https://www.iadb.org/en; Latin Macro Watch (LMW).

Palgrave Macmillan, 1 New York Plaza, Ste. 4500, New York, NY, 10004-1562, USA, (800) 777-4643, orders@palgrave.com, https://www.palgrave.com/us; The Statesman's Yearbook, 2023.

Routledge - Taylor & Francis Group, 6000 Broken Sound Pkwy. NW, Ste. 300, Boca Raton, FL, 33487, USA, (800) 634-1420, (800) 634-7064, orders@taylorandfrancis.com, https://www.routledge.com/; The Europa World Year Book 2022.

The World Bank, 1818 H St. NW, Washington, DC, 20433, USA, (202) 473-1000, (202) 477-6391, eds03@worldbank.org, https://www.worldbank.org/; Brazil (report) and World Development Report 2022: Finance for an Equitable Recovery.

BRAZIL-POSTAL SERVICE

Palgrave Macmillan, 1 New York Plaza, Ste. 4500, New York, NY, 10004-1562, USA, (800) 777-4643, orders@palgrave.com, https://www.palgrave.com/us; The Statesman's Yearbook, 2023.

BRAZIL-POWER RESOURCES

Euromonitor International, Inc., 1 N Dearborn St., Ste. 1700, Chicago, IL, 60602, USA, (312) 922-1115, (312) 922-1157, info-usa@euromonitor.com, https://www.euromonitor.com/; Geographies.

International Energy Agency (IEA), 9 Rue de la Federation, Paris, 75739, FRA, info@iea.org, https://www.iea.org/; World Energy Outlook 2021.

Palgrave Macmillan, 1 New York Plaza, Ste. 4500, New York, NY, 10004-1562, USA, (800) 777-4643, orders@palgrave.com, https://www.palgrave.com/us; The Statesman's Yearbook, 2023.

U.S. Energy Information Administration (EIA), 1000 Independence Ave. SW, Washington, DC, 20585, USA, (202) 586-8800, infoctr@eia.gov, https://www.eia.gov; International Energy Outlook 2021.

United Nations Food and Agricultural Organization (FAO), 2121 K St., Ste. 800B, Washington, DC, 20037, USA, (202) 653-2400 (Dial from U.S.), (202) 653-5760 (Fax from U.S.), fao-hq@fao.org, https://www.fao.org; The State of Food and Agriculture (SOFA) 2022.

United Nations Statistics Division (UNSD), United Nations Plz., New York, NY, 10017, USA, (800) 253-9646, (212) 963-9851, statistics@un.org, https://unstats.un.org; Energy Statistics Yearbook 2019 and World Statistics Pocketbook 2021.

The World Bank, 1818 H St. NW, Washington, DC, 20433, USA, (202) 473-1000, (202) 477-6391, eds03@worldbank.org, https://www.worldbank.org/; World Development Report 2022: Finance for an Equitable Recovery.

BRAZIL-PRICES

Euromonitor International, Inc., 1 N Dearborn St., Ste. 1700, Chicago, IL, 60602, USA, (312) 922-1115, (312) 922-1157, info-usa@euromonitor.com, https://www.euromonitor.com/; Geographies.

Federal Statistical Office Germany, Gustav-Stresemann-Ring 11, Wiesbaden, D-65189, GER, https://www.destatis.de; Basic Indicators: Brazil.

International Monetary Fund (IMF), 700 19th St. NW, Washington, DC, 20431, USA, (202) 623-7000, (202) 623-4661, publications@imf.org, https://www.imf.org; International Financial Statistics (IFS).

Routledge - Taylor & Francis Group, 6000 Broken Sound Pkwy. NW, Ste. 300, Boca Raton, FL, 33487, USA, (800) 634-1420, (800) 634-7064, orders@taylorandfrancis.com, https://www.routledge.com/; The Europa World Year Book 2022.

The World Bank, 1818 H St. NW, Washington, DC, 20433, USA, (202) 473-1000, (202) 477-6391, eds03@worldbank.org, https://www.worldbank.org/; Brazil (report).

World Bureau of Metal Statistics (WBMS), 31 Star St., Ware, Hertfordshire, SG12 9BA, GBR, https://www.refinitiv.com/en/trading-solutions/world-bureau-metal-statistics; Long Term Production/Consumption Series - All Metals; World Flow Charts; and World Metal Statistics.

BRAZIL-PUBLIC HEALTH

Euromonitor International, Inc., 1 N Dearborn St., Ste. 1700, Chicago, IL, 60602, USA, (312) 922-1115, (312) 922-1157, info-usa@euromonitor.com, https://www.euromonitor.com/; Geographies and Market Research on the Health and Wellness Industry.

Federal Statistical Office Germany, Gustav-Stresemann-Ring 11, Wiesbaden, D-65189, GER, https://www.destatis.de; Basic Indicators: Brazil.

Palgrave Macmillan, 1 New York Plaza, Ste. 4500, New York, NY, 10004-1562, USA, (800) 777-4643, orders@palgrave.com, https://www.palgrave.com/us; The Statesman's Yearbook, 2023.

U.S. Census Bureau, 4600 Silver Hill Rd., Washington, DC, 20233, USA, (301) 763-4636, (800) 923-8282, https://www.census.gov; HIV/AIDS Surveillance Data Base.

UNICEF, 3 United Nations Plz., New York, NY, 10017, USA, (212) 303-7984, (917) 244-2215, https://www.unicef.org; The State of the World's Children 2023.

United Nations Department of Economic and Social Affairs (DESA), Population Division, 2 United Nations Plz., Rm. DC2-1950, New York, NY, 10017, USA, (212) 963-3209, (212) 963-2147, population@un.org, https://www.un.org/development/desa/pd/; World Fertility Data 2019.

United Nations Development Programme (UNDP), One United Nations Plz., New York, NY, 10017, USA, (212) 906-5000, (212) 906-5001, https://www.undp.org; Human Development Report 2021-2022.

United Nations Statistics Division (UNSD), United Nations Plz., New York, NY, 10017, USA, (800) 253-9646, (212) 963-9851, statistics@un.org, https://unstats.un.org; Millennium Development Goal Indicators and Statistical Yearbook of the United Nations 2021.

The World Bank, 1818 H St. NW, Washington, DC, 20433, USA, (202) 473-1000, (202) 477-6391, eds03@worldbank.org, https://www.worldbank.org/; Brazil (report).

World Health Organization (WHO), Ave. Appia 20, Geneva, CH-1211, SWI, (202) 974-3000 (Telephone in U.S.), publications@who.int, https://www.who.int/; Global Health Observatory (GHO) and Health Statistics and Information Systems.

BRAZIL-PUBLISHERS AND PUBLISHING

United Nations Statistics Division (UNSD), United Nations Plz., New York, NY, 10017, USA, (800) 253-9646, (212) 963-9851, statistics@un.org, https://unstats.un.org; Statistical Yearbook of the United Nations 2021.

BRAZIL-RAILROADS

Janes, USA, (703) 574-7580, (888) 977-1519, customer.care@janes.com, https://www.janes.com; Janes World Railways 2021-2022.

Palgrave Macmillan, 1 New York Plaza, Ste. 4500, New York, NY, 10004-1562, USA, (800) 777-4643, orders@palgrave.com, https://www.palgrave.com/us; The Statesman's Yearbook, 2023.

Routledge - Taylor & Francis Group, 6000 Broken Sound Pkwy. NW, Ste. 300, Boca Raton, FL, 33487, USA, (800) 634-1420, (800) 634-7064, orders@taylorandfrancis.com, https://www.routledge.com/; The Europa World Year Book 2022.

United Nations Statistics Division (UNSD), United Nations Plz., New York, NY, 10017, USA, (800) 253-9646, (212) 963-9851, statistics@un.org, https://unstats.un.org; Statistical Yearbook of the United Nations 2021.

BRAZIL-RELIGION

Central Intelligence Agency (CIA), Office of Public Affairs, Washington, DC, 20505, USA, (703) 482-0623, https://www.cia.gov; The World Factbook.

Palgrave Macmillan, 1 New York Plaza, Ste. 4500, New York, NY, 10004-1562, USA, (800) 777-4643, orders@palgrave.com, https://www.palgrave.com/us; The Statesman's Yearbook, 2023.

BRAZIL-RETAIL TRADE

Euromonitor International, Inc., 1 N Dearborn St., Ste. 1700, Chicago, IL, 60602, USA, (312) 922-1115, (312) 922-1157, info-usa@euromonitor.com, https://www.euromonitor.com/; Geographies and Market Research on the Retailing Industry.

Inter-American Development Bank (IDB), 1300 New York Ave. NW, Washington, DC, 20577, USA, (202)

623-1000, (202) 623-3096, https://www.iadb.org/en; Latin Macro Watch (LMW).

United Nations Statistics Division (UNSD), United Nations Plz., New York, NY, 10017, USA, (800) 253-9646, (212) 963-9851, statistics@un.org, https://unstats.un.org; Statistical Yearbook of the United Nations 2021.

BRAZIL-RICE PRODUCTION

See BRAZIL-CROPS

BRAZIL-ROADS

International Road Federation (IRF), Madison Place, 500 Montgomery St., 5th Fl., Alexandria, VA, 22314, USA, (703) 535-1001, (703) 535-1007, info@irf.global, https://www.irf.global/; World Road Statistics (WRS).

BRAZIL-RUBBER INDUSTRY AND TRADE

International Rubber Study Group (IRSG), 51 Changi Business Park Central 2, Unit No. 6, 486066, SGP, https://www.rubberstudy.org; Monthly Rubber Bulletin (MRB); Rubber Industry Report; Rubber Statistical Bulletin; and World Rubber Industry Report (WRIO).

United Nations Statistics Division (UNSD), United Nations Plz., New York, NY, 10017, USA, (800) 253-9646, (212) 963-9851, statistics@un.org, https://unstats.un.org; Statistical Yearbook of the United Nations 2021.

BRAZIL-SHIPPING

Routledge - Taylor & Francis Group, 6000 Broken Sound Pkwy. NW, Ste. 300, Boca Raton, FL, 33487, USA, (800) 634-1420, (800) 634-7064, orders@taylorandfrancis.com, https://www.routledge.com/; The Europa World Year Book 2022.

S&P Global, IHS Markit, 15 Inverness Way E, Englewood, CO, 80112, USA, (800) 447-2273, (800) 854-7179, https://ihsmarkit.com; IHS Maritime World Shipbuilding Statistics; Journal of Commerce; Lloyd's Register of Ships 2021-2022; and Maritime Portal Desktop.

United Nations Statistics Division (UNSD), United Nations Plz., New York, NY, 10017, USA, (800) 253-9646, (212) 963-9851, statistics@un.org, https://unstats.un.org; Statistical Yearbook of the United Nations 2021.

BRAZIL-SOYBEAN PRODUCTION

See BRAZIL-CROPS

BRAZIL-STEEL PRODUCTION

See BRAZIL-MINERAL INDUSTRIES

BRAZIL-SUGAR PRODUCTION

See BRAZIL-CROPS

BRAZIL-SULPHUR PRODUCTION

See BRAZIL-MINERAL INDUSTRIES

BRAZIL-TAXATION

Inter-American Development Bank (IDB), 1300 New York Ave. NW, Washington, DC, 20577, USA, (202) 623-1000, (202) 623-3096, https://www.iadb.org/en; Latin Macro Watch (LMW).

International Road Federation (IRF), Madison Place, 500 Montgomery St., 5th Fl., Alexandria, VA, 22314, USA, (703) 535-1001, (703) 535-1007, info@irf.global, https://www.irf.global/; World Road Statistics (WRS).

The World Bank, 1818 H St. NW, Washington, DC, 20433, USA, (202) 473-1000, (202) 477-6391, eds03@worldbank.org, https://www.worldbank.org/; World Development Indicators (WDI) 2022.

BRAZIL-TEA PRODUCTION

See BRAZIL-CROPS

BRAZIL-TELEPHONE

Palgrave Macmillan, 1 New York Plaza, Ste. 4500, New York, NY, 10004-1562, USA, (800) 777-4643, orders@palgrave.com, https://www.palgrave.com/us; The Statesman's Yearbook, 2023.

Routledge - Taylor & Francis Group, 6000 Broken Sound Pkwy. NW, Ste. 300, Boca Raton, FL, 33487, USA, (800) 634-1420, (800) 634-7064, orders@taylorandfrancis.com, https://www.routledge.com/; The Europa World Year Book 2022.

United Nations Statistics Division (UNSD), United Nations Plz., New York, NY, 10017, USA, (800) 253-9646, (212) 963-9851, statistics@un.org, https://unstats.un.org; World Statistics Pocketbook 2021.

BRAZIL-TEXTILE INDUSTRY

Euromonitor International, Inc., 1 N Dearborn St., Ste. 1700, Chicago, IL, 60602, USA, (312) 922-1115, (312) 922-1157, info-usa@euromonitor.com, https://www.euromonitor.com/; Geographies.

Palgrave Macmillan, 1 New York Plaza, Ste. 4500, New York, NY, 10004-1562, USA, (800) 777-4643, orders@palgrave.com, https://www.palgrave.com/us; The Statesman's Yearbook, 2023.

United Nations Statistics Division (UNSD), United Nations Plz., New York, NY, 10017, USA, (800) 253-9646, (212) 963-9851, statistics@un.org, https://unstats.un.org; Statistical Yearbook of the United Nations 2021.

BRAZIL-THEATER

UNESCO Institute for Statistics, C.P 250 Succursale H, Montreal, QC, H3G 2K8, CAN, (514) 343-6880 (Dial from U.S.), (514) 343-5740 (Fax from U.S.), uis.publications@unesco.org, http://uis.unesco.org/; UIS.Stat.

BRAZIL-TOBACCO INDUSTRY

United Nations Statistics Division (UNSD), United Nations Plz., New York, NY, 10017, USA, (800) 253-9646, (212) 963-9851, statistics@un.org, https://unstats.un.org; Statistical Yearbook of the United Nations 2021.

BRAZIL-TOURISM

Euromonitor International, Inc., 1 N Dearborn St., Ste. 1700, Chicago, IL, 60602, USA, (312) 922-1115, (312) 922-1157, info-usa@euromonitor.com, https://www.euromonitor.com/; Geographies.

Federal Statistical Office Germany, Gustav-Stresemann-Ring 11, Wiesbaden, D-65189, GER, https://www.destatis.de; Basic Indicators: Brazil.

Palgrave Macmillan, 1 New York Plaza, Ste. 4500, New York, NY, 10004-1562, USA, (800) 777-4643, orders@palgrave.com, https://www.palgrave.com/us; The Statesman's Yearbook, 2023.

Routledge - Taylor & Francis Group, 6000 Broken Sound Pkwy. NW, Ste. 300, Boca Raton, FL, 33487, USA, (800) 634-1420, (800) 634-7064, orders@taylorandfrancis.com, https://www.routledge.com/; The Europa World Year Book 2022.

United Nations Statistics Division (UNSD), United Nations Plz., New York, NY, 10017, USA, (800) 253-9646, (212) 963-9851, statistics@un.org, https://unstats.un.org; Statistical Yearbook of the United Nations 2021.

United Nations World Tourism Organization (UNWTO), Calle Poeta Joan Maragall 42, Madrid, 28020, SPA, info@unwto.org, https://www.unwto.org/; Yearbook of Tourism Statistics, 2021 Edition.

The World Bank, 1818 H St. NW, Washington, DC, 20433, USA, (202) 473-1000, (202) 477-6391, eds03@worldbank.org, https://www.worldbank.org/; Brazil (report).

BRAZIL-TRADE

See BRAZIL-INTERNATIONAL TRADE

BRAZIL-TRANSPORTATION

Central Intelligence Agency (CIA), Office of Public Affairs, Washington, DC, 20505, USA, (703) 482-0623, https://www.cia.gov; The World Factbook.

Euromonitor International, Inc., 1 N Dearborn St., Ste. 1700, Chicago, IL, 60602, USA, (312) 922-1115, (312) 922-1157, info-usa@euromonitor.com, https://www.euromonitor.com/; Geographies.

Federal Statistical Office Germany, Gustav-Stresemann-Ring 11, Wiesbaden, D-65189, GER, https://www.destatis.de; Basic Indicators: Brazil.

Inter-American Development Bank (IDB), 1300 New York Ave. NW, Washington, DC, 20577, USA, (202) 623-1000, (202) 623-3096, https://www.iadb.org/en; Latin Macro Watch (LMW).

Palgrave Macmillan, 1 New York Plaza, Ste. 4500, New York, NY, 10004-1562, USA, (800) 777-4643, orders@palgrave.com, https://www.palgrave.com/us; The Statesman's Yearbook, 2023.

Routledge - Taylor & Francis Group, 6000 Broken Sound Pkwy. NW, Ste. 300, Boca Raton, FL, 33487, USA, (800) 634-1420, (800) 634-7064, orders@taylorandfrancis.com, https://www.routledge.com/; The Europa World Year Book 2022.

The World Bank, 1818 H St. NW, Washington, DC, 20433, USA, (202) 473-1000, (202) 477-6391, eds03@worldbank.org, https://www.worldbank.org/; Brazil (report).

BRAZIL-UNEMPLOYMENT

Federal Statistical Office Germany, Gustav-Stresemann-Ring 11, Wiesbaden, D-65189, GER, https://www.destatis.de; Basic Indicators: Brazil.

International Labour Organization (ILO), 4 Rte. des Morillons, Geneva, CH-1211, SWI, ilo@ilo.org, https://www.ilo.org; NORMLEX Information System on International Labour Standards.

Organization for Economic Cooperation and Development (OECD), 2001 L St. NW, Ste. 650, Washington, DC, 20036-4922, USA, (202) 785-6323, (800) 456-6323, (202) 785-0350, washington.contact@oecd.org, https://www.oecd.org/; Economic Survey of Brazil 2020.

United Nations Statistics Division (UNSD), United Nations Plz., New York, NY, 10017, USA, (800) 253-9646, (212) 963-9851, statistics@un.org, https://unstats.un.org; Statistical Yearbook of the United Nations 2021.

BRAZIL-URANIUM PRODUCTION AND CONSUMPTION

See BRAZIL-MINERAL INDUSTRIES

BRAZIL-VITAL STATISTICS

Palgrave Macmillan, 1 New York Plaza, Ste. 4500, New York, NY, 10004-1562, USA, (800) 777-4643, orders@palgrave.com, https://www.palgrave.com/us; The Statesman's Yearbook, 2023.

U.S. Census Bureau, 4600 Silver Hill Rd., Washington, DC, 20233, USA, (301) 763-4636, (800) 923-8282, https://www.census.gov; HIV/AIDS Surveillance Data Base.

United Nations Department of Economic and Social Affairs (DESA), Population Division, 2 United Nations Plz., Rm. DC2-1950, New York, NY, 10017, USA, (212) 963-3209, (212) 963-2147, population@un.org, https://www.un.org/development/desa/pd/; World Contraceptive Use 2021: Estimates and Projections of Family Planning Indicators and World Marriage Data 2019.

United Nations Statistics Division (UNSD), United Nations Plz., New York, NY, 10017, USA, (800) 253-9646, (212) 963-9851, statistics@un.org, https://unstats.un.org; Statistical Yearbook of the United Nations 2021.

BRAZIL-WAGES

Federal Statistical Office Germany, Gustav-Stresemann-Ring 11, Wiesbaden, D-65189, GER, https://www.destatis.de; Basic Indicators: Brazil.

International Labour Organization (ILO), 4 Rte. des Morillons, Geneva, CH-1211, SWI, ilo@ilo.org, https://www.ilo.org; NORMLEX Information System on International Labour Standards.

Routledge - Taylor & Francis Group, 6000 Broken Sound Pkwy. NW, Ste. 300, Boca Raton, FL, 33487, USA, (800) 634-1420, (800) 634-7064, orders@taylorandfrancis.com, https://www.routledge.com/; The Europa World Year Book 2022.

United Nations Statistics Division (UNSD), United Nations Plz., New York, NY, 10017, USA, (800) 253-9646, (212) 963-9851, statistics@un.org, https://unstats.un.org; Statistical Yearbook of the United Nations 2021.

The World Bank, 1818 H St. NW, Washington, DC, 20433, USA, (202) 473-1000, (202) 477-6391, eds03@worldbank.org, https://www.worldbank.org/; Brazil (report).

BRAZIL-WEATHER

See BRAZIL-CLIMATE

BRAZIL-WHALES

See BRAZIL-FISHERIES

BRAZIL-WHEAT PRODUCTION

See BRAZIL-CROPS

BRAZIL-WHOLESALE PRICE INDEXES

Inter-American Development Bank (IDB), 1300 New York Ave. NW, Washington, DC, 20577, USA, (202) 623-1000, (202) 623-3096, https://www.iadb.org/en; Latin Macro Watch (LMW).

International Monetary Fund (IMF), 700 19th St. NW, Washington, DC, 20431, USA, (202) 623-7000, (202) 623-4661, publications@imf.org, https://www.imf.org; International Financial Statistics (IFS).

BRAZIL-WHOLESALE TRADE

Inter-American Development Bank (IDB), 1300 New York Ave. NW, Washington, DC, 20577, USA, (202) 623-1000, (202) 623-3096, https://www.iadb.org/en; Latin Macro Watch (LMW).

United Nations Statistics Division (UNSD), United Nations Plz., New York, NY, 10017, USA, (800) 253-9646, (212) 963-9851, statistics@un.org, https://unstats.un.org; Statistical Yearbook of the United Nations 2021.

BRAZIL-WINE AND WINE MAKING

United Nations Statistics Division (UNSD), United Nations Plz., New York, NY, 10017, USA, (800) 253-9646, (212) 963-9851, statistics@un.org, https://unstats.un.org; Statistical Yearbook of the United Nations 2021.

BRAZIL-WOOD AND WOOD PULP

See BRAZIL-FORESTS AND FORESTRY

BRAZIL-WOOL PRODUCTION

See BRAZIL-TEXTILE INDUSTRY

BRAZIL-ZINC AND ZINC ORE

See BRAZIL-MINERAL INDUSTRIES

BRAZIL-ZOOS

UNESCO Institute for Statistics, C.P 250 Succursale H, Montreal, QC, H3G 2K8, CAN, (514) 343-6880 (Dial from U.S.), (514) 343-5740 (Fax from U.S.), uis.publications@unesco.org, http://uis.unesco.org/; UIS.Stat.

BREAD

U.S. Department of Labor (DOL), Bureau of Labor Statistics (BLS), Postal Square Bldg., 2 Massachusetts Ave. NE, Washington, DC, 20212-0001, USA, (202) 691-5200, (202) 691-7890, blsdata_staff@bls.gov, https://www.bls.gov; Consumer Price Index (CPI) Databases.

BREAST-CANCER

American Cancer Society (ACS), 3380 Chastain Meadows Pkwy NW, Ste. 200, Kennesaw, GA, 30144, USA, (800) 227-2345, https://www.cancer.org; Breast Cancer Facts & Figures 2022-2024; Cancer Facts & Figures 2023; Cancer Treatment & Survivorship Facts & Figures 2022-2024; and Global Cancer Facts & Figures.

Cancer Treatment Centers of America Global, Inc. (CTCA), 5900 Broken Sound Pkwy NW, Boca Raton, FL, 33487, USA, (800) 234-7139, (844) 374-2443, https://www.cancercenter.com/; unpublished data.

The Lancet, 230 Park Ave., New York, NY, 10169, USA, (212) 633-3800, editorial@lancet.com, https://www.thelancet.com/; The Lancet Oncology.

U.S. Department of Health and Human Services (HHS), National Institutes of Health (NIH), National Cancer Institute (NCI), 9609 Medical Center Dr., Bethesda, MD, 20850, USA, (800) 422-6237, nciinfo@nih.gov, https://www.cancer.gov; Annual Report to the Nation on the Status of Cancer; Cancer Stat Facts; Surveillance, Epidemiology, and End Results (SEER) Incidence Data, 1975-2020; and U.S. Atlas of Cancer Mortality 1950-1994.

U.S. Preventive Services Task Force (USPSTF), 5600 Fishers Ln., Mail Stop 06E53A, Rockville, MD, 20857, USA, https://www.uspreventiveservicestaskforce.org/uspstf/; Annual Report to Congress on High-Priority Evidence Gaps for Clinical Preventive Services.

BREASTFEEDING

Australian Government Department of Social Services, 71 Athllon Dr., Canberra, ACT, 2900, AUS, https://www.dss.gov.au/; Growing Up in Australia: The Longitudinal Study of Australian Children Annual Statistical Report.

Public Health Agency of Canada, 130 Colonnade Rd., Ottawa, ON, K1A 0K9, CAN, (844) 280-5020 (Dial from U.S.), https://www.phac-aspc.gc.ca/; Perinatal Health Indicators (PHI).

U.S. Department of Health and Human Services, Centers for Disease Control and Prevention (CDC), 1600 Clifton Rd., Atlanta, GA, 30329-4027, USA, (800) 232-4636, (888) 232-6348 (TTY), cdcinfo@cdc.gov, https://www.cdc.gov; Breastfeeding Report Card: United States, 2022.

University of California Hastings College of the Law, Center for WorkLife Law, Project for Attorney Retention (PAR-Davis) Research Institute, 200 McAllister St., San Francisco, CA, 94102, USA, (415) 565-4640, https://worklifelaw.org/projects/women-in-the-legal-profession/; Exposed: Discrimination Against Breastfeeding Workers.

BRIDGES

National Bridge Inventory Study Foundation (NBISF), USA, https://www.nationalbridgeinventory.org/; National Bridge Inventory Database.

U.S. Department of Homeland Security (DHS), 2707 Martin Luther King Jr. Ave. SE, Washington, DC, 20528-0525, USA, (202) 282-8000, https://www.dhs.gov; Homeland Infrastructure Foundation-Level Data (HIFLD).

U.S. Department of Transportation (DOT), Federal Highway Administration (FHA), 1200 New Jersey Ave. SE, Washington, DC, 20590, USA, (202) 366-4000, https://highways.dot.gov/; Core Highway Topics.

BRITISH COLUMBIA

British Columbia Vital Statistics Agency, Stn Prov Govt, PO Box 9408, Victoria, BC, V8W 9V1, CAN, (250) 387-6121 (Dial from U.S.), (250) 952-4124 (Fax from U.S.), servicebc@gov.bc.ca, https://www2.gov.bc.ca/gov/content/family-social-supports/seniors/health-safety/health-care-programs-and-services/vital-statistics; Statistics and Reports.

BRITISH HONDURAS

See BELIZE

BRITISH INDIAN OCEAN TERRITORY-AGRICULTURE

African Development Bank Group (AfDB), Avenue Joseph Anoma, 01 BP 1387, Abidjan, 01, COT, https://www.afdb.org; African Economic Outlook 2021 and Compendium of Statistics on Bank Group Operations 2019.

United Nations Economic Commission for Africa (UNECA), PO Box 3001, Addis Ababa, ETH, ecainfo@uneca.org, https://www.uneca.org/; Economic Report on Africa 2021.

United Nations Food and Agricultural Organization (FAO), 2121 K St., Ste. 800B, Washington, DC, 20037, USA, (202) 653-2400 (Dial from U.S.), (202) 653-5760 (Fax from U.S.), fao-hq@fao.org, https://www.fao.org; AQUASTAT and The State of Food and Agriculture (SOFA) 2022.

BRITISH INDIAN OCEAN TERRITORY-ARMED FORCES

Central Intelligence Agency (CIA), Office of Public Affairs, Washington, DC, 20505, USA, (703) 482-0623, https://www.cia.gov; The World Factbook.

Stockholm International Peace Research Institute (SIPRI), Signalistgatan 9, Stockholm, SE 169 72, SWE, https://www.sipri.org/; SIPRI Arms Transfers Database and SIPRI Military Expenditure Database.

BRITISH INDIAN OCEAN TERRITORY-BROADCASTING

Central Intelligence Agency (CIA), Office of Public Affairs, Washington, DC, 20505, USA, (703) 482-0623, https://www.cia.gov; The World Factbook.

BRITISH INDIAN OCEAN TERRITORY-BUDGET

Central Intelligence Agency (CIA), Office of Public Affairs, Washington, DC, 20505, USA, (703) 482-0623, https://www.cia.gov; The World Factbook.

BRITISH INDIAN OCEAN TERRITORY-CORN INDUSTRY

See BRITISH INDIAN OCEAN TERRITORY-CROPS

BRITISH INDIAN OCEAN TERRITORY-CROPS

United Nations Food and Agricultural Organization (FAO), 2121 K St., Ste. 800B, Washington, DC, 20037, USA, (202) 653-2400 (Dial from U.S.), (202) 653-5760 (Fax from U.S.), fao-hq@fao.org, https://www.fao.org; The State of Food and Agriculture (SOFA) 2022.

BRITISH INDIAN OCEAN TERRITORY-DAIRY PROCESSING

United Nations Food and Agricultural Organization (FAO), 2121 K St., Ste. 800B, Washington, DC, 20037, USA, (202) 653-2400 (Dial from U.S.), (202) 653-5760 (Fax from U.S.), fao-hq@fao.org, https://www.fao.org; The State of Food and Agriculture (SOFA) 2022.

BRITISH INDIAN OCEAN TERRITORY-ECONOMIC CONDITIONS

African Development Bank Group (AfDB), Avenue Joseph Anoma, 01 BP 1387, Abidjan, 01, COT, https://www.afdb.org; Africa Economic Brief - COVID-19 Pandemic Potential Risks for Trade and Trade Finance in Africa; African Economic Outlook 2021; The African Statistical Journal; Compendium of Statistics on Bank Group Operations 2019; and Gender, Poverty and Environmental Indicators on African Countries 2019.

Bernan Press, 15250 NBN Way, Bldg. C, Blue Ridge Summit, PA, 17214, USA, (301) 459-2255, (800) 865-3457, (800) 865-3450, customercare@bernan.com, https://rowman.com/Page/Bernan; World Economic Outlook, April 2022.

Central Intelligence Agency (CIA), Office of Public Affairs, Washington, DC, 20505, USA, (703) 482-0623, https://www.cia.gov; The World Factbook.

United Nations Economic Commission for Africa (UNECA), PO Box 3001, Addis Ababa, ETH, ecainfo@uneca.org, https://www.uneca.org/; Economic Report on Africa 2021.

BRITISH INDIAN OCEAN TERRITORY-EXPORTS

Central Intelligence Agency (CIA), Office of Public Affairs, Washington, DC, 20505, USA, (703) 482-0623, https://www.cia.gov; The World Factbook.

BRITISH INDIAN OCEAN TERRITORY-FERTILITY, HUMAN

Central Intelligence Agency (CIA), Office of Public Affairs, Washington, DC, 20505, USA, (703) 482-0623, https://www.cia.gov; The World Factbook.

BRITISH INDIAN OCEAN TERRITORY-FERTILIZER INDUSTRY

United Nations Food and Agricultural Organization (FAO), 2121 K St., Ste. 800B, Washington, DC, 20037, USA, (202) 653-2400 (Dial from U.S.), (202) 653-5760 (Fax from U.S.), fao-hq@fao.org, https://www.fao.org; The State of Food and Agriculture (SOFA) 2022.

BRITISH INDIAN OCEAN TERRITORY-FETAL MORTALITY

See BRITISH INDIAN OCEAN TERRITORY-MORTALITY

BRITISH INDIAN OCEAN TERRITORY-FISHERIES

United Nations Food and Agricultural Organization (FAO), 2121 K St., Ste. 800B, Washington, DC, 20037, USA, (202) 653-2400 (Dial from U.S.), (202) 653-5760 (Fax from U.S.), fao-hq@fao.org, https://www.fao.org; FAO Yearbook of Fishery and Aquaculture Statistics 2019; Fishery Statistical Collections Global Capture Production; FishStatJ; and The State of Food and Agriculture (SOFA) 2022.

BRITISH INDIAN OCEAN TERRITORY-FOOD

United Nations Food and Agricultural Organization (FAO), 2121 K St., Ste. 800B, Washington, DC, 20037, USA, (202) 653-2400 (Dial from U.S.), (202) 653-5760 (Fax from U.S.), fao-hq@fao.org, https://www.fao.org; The State of Food and Agriculture (SOFA) 2022.

BRITISH INDIAN OCEAN TERRITORY-FORESTS AND FORESTRY

United Nations Food and Agricultural Organization (FAO), 2121 K St., Ste. 800B, Washington, DC, 20037, USA, (202) 653-2400 (Dial from U.S.), (202) 653-5760 (Fax from U.S.), fao-hq@fao.org, https://www.fao.org; The State of Food and Agriculture (SOFA) 2022.

BRITISH INDIAN OCEAN TERRITORY-IMPORTS

Central Intelligence Agency (CIA), Office of Public Affairs, Washington, DC, 20505, USA, (703) 482-0623, https://www.cia.gov; The World Factbook.

BRITISH INDIAN OCEAN TERRITORY-INDUSTRIES

Central Intelligence Agency (CIA), Office of Public Affairs, Washington, DC, 20505, USA, (703) 482-0623, https://www.cia.gov; The World Factbook.

BRITISH INDIAN OCEAN TERRITORY-INFANT AND MATERNAL MORTALITY

See BRITISH INDIAN OCEAN TERRITORY-MORTALITY

BRITISH INDIAN OCEAN TERRITORY-INTERNATIONAL TRADE

United Nations Food and Agricultural Organization (FAO), 2121 K St., Ste. 800B, Washington, DC, 20037, USA, (202) 653-2400 (Dial from U.S.), (202) 653-5760 (Fax from U.S.), fao-hq@fao.org, https://www.fao.org; The State of Food and Agriculture (SOFA) 2022.

World Trade Organization (WTO), Ctre. William Rappard, Rue de Lausanne 154, Case postale, Geneva, CH-1211, SWI, enquiries@wto.org, https://www.wto.org; World Trade Statistical Review 2022.

BRITISH INDIAN OCEAN TERRITORY-LABOR

Central Intelligence Agency (CIA), Office of Public Affairs, Washington, DC, 20505, USA, (703) 482-0623, https://www.cia.gov; The World Factbook.

United Nations Food and Agricultural Organization (FAO), 2121 K St., Ste. 800B, Washington, DC, 20037, USA, (202) 653-2400 (Dial from U.S.), (202) 653-5760 (Fax from U.S.), fao-hq@fao.org, https://www.fao.org; The State of Food and Agriculture (SOFA) 2022.

BRITISH INDIAN OCEAN TERRITORY-LIFE EXPECTANCY

Central Intelligence Agency (CIA), Office of Public Affairs, Washington, DC, 20505, USA, (703) 482-0623, https://www.cia.gov; The World Factbook.

United Nations Department of Economic and Social Affairs (DESA), Population Division, 2 United Nations Plz., Rm. DC2-1950, New York, NY, 10017, USA, (212) 963-3209, (212) 963-2147, population@un.org, https://www.un.org/development/desa/pd/; World Population Ageing 2020 Highlights.

BRITISH INDIAN OCEAN TERRITORY-LIVESTOCK

United Nations Food and Agricultural Organization (FAO), 2121 K St., Ste. 800B, Washington, DC, 20037, USA, (202) 653-2400 (Dial from U.S.), (202) 653-5760 (Fax from U.S.), fao-hq@fao.org, https://www.fao.org; The State of Food and Agriculture (SOFA) 2022.

BRITISH INDIAN OCEAN TERRITORY-NUTRITION

United Nations Food and Agricultural Organization (FAO), 2121 K St., Ste. 800B, Washington, DC, 20037, USA, (202) 653-2400 (Dial from U.S.), (202) 653-5760 (Fax from U.S.), fao-hq@fao.org, https://www.fao.org; The State of Food and Agriculture (SOFA) 2022.

BRITISH INDIAN OCEAN TERRITORY-PESTICIDES

United Nations Food and Agricultural Organization (FAO), 2121 K St., Ste. 800B, Washington, DC, 20037, USA, (202) 653-2400 (Dial from U.S.), (202) 653-5760 (Fax from U.S.), fao-hq@fao.org, https://www.fao.org; The State of Food and Agriculture (SOFA) 2022.

BRITISH INDIAN OCEAN TERRITORY-PETROLEUM INDUSTRY AND TRADE

United Nations Food and Agricultural Organization (FAO), 2121 K St., Ste. 800B, Washington, DC, 20037, USA, (202) 653-2400 (Dial from U.S.), (202) 653-5760 (Fax from U.S.), fao-hq@fao.org, https://www.fao.org; The State of Food and Agriculture (SOFA) 2022.

BRITISH INDIAN OCEAN TERRITORY-POPULATION

African Development Bank Group (AfDB), Avenue Joseph Anoma, 01 BP 1387, Abidjan, 01, COT, https://www.afdb.org; Africa Economic Brief - COVID-19 Pandemic Potential Risks for Trade and Trade Finance in Africa; The African Statistical Journal; and Gender, Poverty and Environmental Indicators on African Countries 2019.

Central Intelligence Agency (CIA), Office of Public Affairs, Washington, DC, 20505, USA, (703) 482-0623, https://www.cia.gov; The World Factbook.

UK Data Service, University of Essex, Wivenhoe Park, Colchester, Essex, CO4 3SQ, GBR, https://ukdataservice.ac.uk/; International Aggregate Data.

United Nations Department of Economic and Social Affairs (DESA), Population Division, 2 United Nations Plz., Rm. DC2-1950, New York, NY, 10017, USA, (212) 963-3209, (212) 963-2147, population@un.org, https://www.un.org/development/desa/pd/; Revision of World Urbanization Prospects and World Population Ageing 2020 Highlights.

United Nations Statistics Division (UNSD), United Nations Plz., New York, NY, 10017, USA, (800) 253-9646, (212) 963-9851, statistics@un.org, https://unstats.un.org; Statistical Yearbook of the United Nations 2021.

BRITISH INDIAN OCEAN TERRITORY-POPULATION DENSITY

Central Intelligence Agency (CIA), Office of Public Affairs, Washington, DC, 20505, USA, (703) 482-0623, https://www.cia.gov; The World Factbook.

BRITISH INDIAN OCEAN TERRITORY-POWER RESOURCES

United Nations Food and Agricultural Organization (FAO), 2121 K St., Ste. 800B, Washington, DC, 20037, USA, (202) 653-2400 (Dial from U.S.), (202) 653-5760 (Fax from U.S.), fao-hq@fao.org, https://www.fao.org; The State of Food and Agriculture (SOFA) 2022.

BRITISH INDIAN OCEAN TERRITORY-RELIGION

Central Intelligence Agency (CIA), Office of Public Affairs, Washington, DC, 20505, USA, (703) 482-0623, https://www.cia.gov; The World Factbook.

BRITISH INDIAN OCEAN TERRITORY-TELEPHONE

Central Intelligence Agency (CIA), Office of Public Affairs, Washington, DC, 20505, USA, (703) 482-0623, https://www.cia.gov; The World Factbook.

BRITISH INDIAN OCEAN TERRITORY-TRADE

See BRITISH INDIAN OCEAN TERRITORY-INTERNATIONAL TRADE

BRITISH INDIAN OCEAN TERRITORY-TRANSPORTATION

Central Intelligence Agency (CIA), Office of Public Affairs, Washington, DC, 20505, USA, (703) 482-0623, https://www.cia.gov; The World Factbook.

BRITISH INDIAN OCEAN TERRITORY-VITAL STATISTICS

U.S. Census Bureau, 4600 Silver Hill Rd., Washington, DC, 20233, USA, (301) 763-4636, (800) 923-8282, https://www.census.gov; HIV/AIDS Surveillance Data Base.

United Nations Department of Economic and Social Affairs (DESA), Population Division, 2 United Nations Plz., Rm. DC2-1950, New York, NY, 10017, USA, (212) 963-3209, (212) 963-2147, population@un.org, https://www.un.org/development/desa/pd/; World Contraceptive Use 2021: Estimates and Projections of Family Planning Indicators and World Marriage Data 2019.

BRITISH VIRGIN ISLANDS-AGRICULTURE

The Economist Group: Economist Intelligence Unit (EIU), 900 3rd Ave., 16th Fl., New York, NY, 10022, USA, (212) 541-0500, americas@eiu.com, https://www.eiu.com; Virgin Islands (British) Country Report.

Euromonitor International, Inc., 1 N Dearborn St., Ste. 1700, Chicago, IL, 60602, USA, (312) 922-1115, (312) 922-1157, info-usa@euromonitor.com, https://www.euromonitor.com/; Geographies.

Palgrave Macmillan, 1 New York Plaza, Ste. 4500, New York, NY, 10004-1562, USA, (800) 777-4643, orders@palgrave.com, https://www.palgrave.com/us; The Statesman's Yearbook, 2023.

Routledge - Taylor & Francis Group, 6000 Broken Sound Pkwy. NW, Ste. 300, Boca Raton, FL, 33487, USA, (800) 634-1420, (800) 634-7064,

orders@taylorandfrancis.com, https://www.routledge.com/; The Europa World Year Book 2022.

United Nations Food and Agricultural Organization (FAO), 2121 K St., Ste. 800B, Washington, DC, 20037, USA, (202) 653-2400 (Dial from U.S.), (202) 653-5760 (Fax from U.S.), fao-hq@fao.org, https://www.fao.org; AQUASTAT and The State of Food and Agriculture (SOFA) 2022.

United Nations Statistics Division (UNSD), United Nations Plz., New York, NY, 10017, USA, (800) 253-9646, (212) 963-9851, statistics@un.org, https://unstats.un.org; Statistical Yearbook of the United Nations 2021.

BRITISH VIRGIN ISLANDS-AIRLINES

International Civil Aviation Organization (ICAO), 999 Robert-Bourassa Blvd., Montreal, QC, H3C 5H7, CAN, (514) 954-8219 (Dial from U.S.), (514) 954-6077 (Fax from U.S.), icaohq@icao.int, https://www.icao.int; ICAO Regional Reports.

Palgrave Macmillan, 1 New York Plaza, Ste. 4500, New York, NY, 10004-1562, USA, (800) 777-4643, orders@palgrave.com, https://www.palgrave.com/us; The Statesman's Yearbook, 2023.

Routledge - Taylor & Francis Group, 6000 Broken Sound Pkwy. NW, Ste. 300, Boca Raton, FL, 33487, USA, (800) 634-1420, (800) 634-7064, orders@taylorandfrancis.com, https://www.routledge.com/; The Europa World Year Book 2022.

BRITISH VIRGIN ISLANDS-ARMED FORCES

Central Intelligence Agency (CIA), Office of Public Affairs, Washington, DC, 20505, USA, (703) 482-0623, https://www.cia.gov; The World Factbook.

Stockholm International Peace Research Institute (SIPRI), Signalistgatan 9, Stockholm, SE 169 72, SWE, https://www.sipri.org/; SIPRI Arms Transfers Database and SIPRI Military Expenditure Database.

BRITISH VIRGIN ISLANDS-BANKS AND BANKING

Euromonitor International, Inc., 1 N Dearborn St., Ste. 1700, Chicago, IL, 60602, USA, (312) 922-1115, (312) 922-1157, info-usa@euromonitor.com, https://www.euromonitor.com/; Geographies.

BRITISH VIRGIN ISLANDS-BROADCASTING

Central Intelligence Agency (CIA), Office of Public Affairs, Washington, DC, 20505, USA, (703) 482-0623, https://www.cia.gov; The World Factbook.

Euromonitor International, Inc., 1 N Dearborn St., Ste. 1700, Chicago, IL, 60602, USA, (312) 922-1115, (312) 922-1157, info-usa@euromonitor.com, https://www.euromonitor.com/; Geographies.

Palgrave Macmillan, 1 New York Plaza, Ste. 4500, New York, NY, 10004-1562, USA, (800) 777-4643, orders@palgrave.com, https://www.palgrave.com/us; The Statesman's Yearbook, 2023.

UNESCO Institute for Statistics, C.P 250 Succursale H, Montreal, QC, H3G 2K8, CAN, (514) 343-6880 (Dial from U.S.), (514) 343-5740 (Fax from U.S.), uis.publications@unesco.org, http://uis.unesco.org/; UIS.Stat.

WRTH Publications Limited, PO Box 290, Oxford, OX2 7FT, GBR, sales@wrth.com, https://www.wrth.com; World Radio TV Handbook 2023.

BRITISH VIRGIN ISLANDS-BUDGET

Central Intelligence Agency (CIA), Office of Public Affairs, Washington, DC, 20505, USA, (703) 482-0623, https://www.cia.gov; The World Factbook.

BRITISH VIRGIN ISLANDS-CLIMATE

Palgrave Macmillan, 1 New York Plaza, Ste. 4500, New York, NY, 10004-1562, USA, (800) 777-4643, orders@palgrave.com, https://www.palgrave.com/us; The Statesman's Yearbook, 2023.

BRITISH VIRGIN ISLANDS-COMMERCE

Palgrave Macmillan, 1 New York Plaza, Ste. 4500, New York, NY, 10004-1562, USA, (800) 777-4643, orders@palgrave.com, https://www.palgrave.com/us; The Statesman's Yearbook, 2023.

UK Data Service, University of Essex, Wivenhoe Park, Colchester, Essex, CO4 3SQ, GBR, https://ukdataservice.ac.uk/; International Aggregate Data.

BRITISH VIRGIN ISLANDS-CONSTRUCTION INDUSTRY

Palgrave Macmillan, 1 New York Plaza, Ste. 4500, New York, NY, 10004-1562, USA, (800) 777-4643, orders@palgrave.com, https://www.palgrave.com/us; The Statesman's Yearbook, 2023.

BRITISH VIRGIN ISLANDS-CONSUMER PRICE INDEXES

Routledge - Taylor & Francis Group, 6000 Broken Sound Pkwy. NW, Ste. 300, Boca Raton, FL, 33487, USA, (800) 634-1420, (800) 634-7064, orders@taylorandfrancis.com, https://www.routledge.com/; The Europa World Year Book 2022.

BRITISH VIRGIN ISLANDS-CORN INDUSTRY

See BRITISH VIRGIN ISLANDS-CROPS

BRITISH VIRGIN ISLANDS-CROPS

Palgrave Macmillan, 1 New York Plaza, Ste. 4500, New York, NY, 10004-1562, USA, (800) 777-4643, orders@palgrave.com, https://www.palgrave.com/us; The Statesman's Yearbook, 2023.

United Nations Food and Agricultural Organization (FAO), 2121 K St., Ste. 800B, Washington, DC, 20037, USA, (202) 653-2400 (Dial from U.S.), (202) 653-5760 (Fax from U.S.), fao-hq@fao.org, https://www.fao.org; The State of Food and Agriculture (SOFA) 2022.

BRITISH VIRGIN ISLANDS-DAIRY PROCESSING

United Nations Food and Agricultural Organization (FAO), 2121 K St., Ste. 800B, Washington, DC, 20037, USA, (202) 653-2400 (Dial from U.S.), (202) 653-5760 (Fax from U.S.), fao-hq@fao.org, https://www.fao.org; The State of Food and Agriculture (SOFA) 2022.

BRITISH VIRGIN ISLANDS-ECONOMIC CONDITIONS

Bernan Press, 15250 NBN Way, Bldg. C, Blue Ridge Summit, PA, 17214, USA, (301) 459-2255, (800) 865-3457, (800) 865-3450, customercare@bernan.com, https://rowman.com/Page/Bernan; World Economic Outlook, April 2022.

Central Intelligence Agency (CIA), Office of Public Affairs, Washington, DC, 20505, USA, (703) 482-0623, https://www.cia.gov; The World Factbook.

The Economist Group: Economist Intelligence Unit (EIU), 900 3rd Ave., 16th Fl., New York, NY, 10022, USA, (212) 541-0500, americas@eiu.com, https://www.eiu.com; Virgin Islands (British) Country Report.

Palgrave Macmillan, 1 New York Plaza, Ste. 4500, New York, NY, 10004-1562, USA, (800) 777-4643, orders@palgrave.com, https://www.palgrave.com/us; The Statesman's Yearbook, 2023.

Routledge - Taylor & Francis Group, 6000 Broken Sound Pkwy. NW, Ste. 300, Boca Raton, FL, 33487, USA, (800) 634-1420, (800) 634-7064, orders@taylorandfrancis.com, https://www.routledge.com/; The Europa World Year Book 2022.

United Nations Economic Commission for Latin America and the Caribbean (ECLAC), Casilla 179-D, Santiago, 7630412, CHL, (202) 596-3713, prensa@cepal.org, https://www.cepal.org/en; CEPALSTAT.

BRITISH VIRGIN ISLANDS-EDUCATION

Euromonitor International, Inc., 1 N Dearborn St., Ste. 1700, Chicago, IL, 60602, USA, (312) 922-1115, (312) 922-1157, info-usa@euromonitor.com, https://www.euromonitor.com/; Geographies.

Palgrave Macmillan, 1 New York Plaza, Ste. 4500, New York, NY, 10004-1562, USA, (800) 777-4643, orders@palgrave.com, https://www.palgrave.com/us; The Statesman's Yearbook, 2023.

Routledge - Taylor & Francis Group, 6000 Broken Sound Pkwy. NW, Ste. 300, Boca Raton, FL, 33487, USA, (800) 634-1420, (800) 634-7064, orders@taylorandfrancis.com, https://www.routledge.com/; The Europa World Year Book 2022.

UNESCO Institute for Statistics, C.P 250 Succursale H, Montreal, QC, H3G 2K8, CAN, (514) 343-6880 (Dial from U.S.), (514) 343-5740 (Fax from U.S.), uis.publications@unesco.org, http://uis.unesco.org/; UIS.Stat.

BRITISH VIRGIN ISLANDS-EMPLOYMENT

International Labour Organization (ILO), 4 Rte. des Morillons, Geneva, CH-1211, SWI, ilo@ilo.org, https://www.ilo.org; NORMLEX Information System on International Labour Standards.

UK Data Service, University of Essex, Wivenhoe Park, Colchester, Essex, CO4 3SQ, GBR, https://ukdataservice.ac.uk/; International Aggregate Data.

BRITISH VIRGIN ISLANDS-ENVIRONMENTAL CONDITIONS

The Economist Group: Economist Intelligence Unit (EIU), 900 3rd Ave., 16th Fl., New York, NY, 10022, USA, (212) 541-0500, americas@eiu.com, https://www.eiu.com; Virgin Islands (British) Country Report.

United Nations Economic Commission for Latin America and the Caribbean (ECLAC), Casilla 179-D, Santiago, 7630412, CHL, (202) 596-3713, prensa@cepal.org, https://www.cepal.org/en; CEPALSTAT.

BRITISH VIRGIN ISLANDS-EXPORTS

Central Intelligence Agency (CIA), Office of Public Affairs, Washington, DC, 20505, USA, (703) 482-0623, https://www.cia.gov; The World Factbook.

The Economist Group: Economist Intelligence Unit (EIU), 900 3rd Ave., 16th Fl., New York, NY, 10022, USA, (212) 541-0500, americas@eiu.com, https://www.eiu.com; Virgin Islands (British) Country Report.

BRITISH VIRGIN ISLANDS-FERTILITY, HUMAN

Central Intelligence Agency (CIA), Office of Public Affairs, Washington, DC, 20505, USA, (703) 482-0623, https://www.cia.gov; The World Factbook.

BRITISH VIRGIN ISLANDS-FERTILIZER INDUSTRY

United Nations Food and Agricultural Organization (FAO), 2121 K St., Ste. 800B, Washington, DC, 20037, USA, (202) 653-2400 (Dial from U.S.), (202) 653-5760 (Fax from U.S.), fao-hq@fao.org, https://www.fao.org; The State of Food and Agriculture (SOFA) 2022.

BRITISH VIRGIN ISLANDS-FETAL MORTALITY

See BRITISH VIRGIN ISLANDS-MORTALITY

BRITISH VIRGIN ISLANDS-FINANCE

Stockholm International Peace Research Institute (SIPRI), Signalistgatan 9, Stockholm, SE 169 72, SWE, https://www.sipri.org/; SIPRI Arms Transfers Database and SIPRI Military Expenditure Database.

United Nations Statistics Division (UNSD), United Nations Plz., New York, NY, 10017, USA, (800) 253-9646, (212) 963-9851, statistics@un.org, https://unstats.un.org; Statistical Yearbook of the United Nations 2021.

BRITISH VIRGIN ISLANDS-FINANCE, PUBLIC

The Economist Group: Economist Intelligence Unit (EIU), 900 3rd Ave., 16th Fl., New York, NY, 10022,

USA, (212) 541-0500, americas@eiu.com, https://www.eiu.com; Virgin Islands (British) Country Report.

Palgrave Macmillan, 1 New York Plaza, Ste. 4500, New York, NY, 10004-1562, USA, (800) 777-4643, orders@palgrave.com, https://www.palgrave.com/us; The Statesman's Yearbook, 2023.

Routledge - Taylor & Francis Group, 6000 Broken Sound Pkwy. NW, Ste. 300, Boca Raton, FL, 33487, USA, (800) 634-1420, (800) 634-7064, orders@taylorandfrancis.com, https://www.routledge.com/; The Europa World Year Book 2022.

United Nations Statistics Division (UNSD), United Nations Plz., New York, NY, 10017, USA, (800) 253-9646, (212) 963-9851, statistics@un.org, https://unstats.un.org; National Accounts Main Aggregates Database and National Accounts Statistics: Main Aggregates and Detailed Tables.

BRITISH VIRGIN ISLANDS-FISHERIES

Palgrave Macmillan, 1 New York Plaza, Ste. 4500, New York, NY, 10004-1562, USA, (800) 777-4643, orders@palgrave.com, https://www.palgrave.com/us; The Statesman's Yearbook, 2023.

Routledge - Taylor & Francis Group, 6000 Broken Sound Pkwy. NW, Ste. 300, Boca Raton, FL, 33487, USA, (800) 634-1420, (800) 634-7064, orders@taylorandfrancis.com, https://www.routledge.com/; The Europa World Year Book 2022.

United Nations Food and Agricultural Organization (FAO), 2121 K St., Ste. 800B, Washington, DC, 20037, USA, (202) 653-2400 (Dial from U.S.), (202) 653-5760 (Fax from U.S.), fao-hq@fao.org, https://www.fao.org; FAO Yearbook of Fishery and Aquaculture Statistics 2019; Fishery Statistical Collections Global Capture Production; FishStatJ; and The State of Food and Agriculture (SOFA) 2022.

BRITISH VIRGIN ISLANDS-FOOD

United Nations Food and Agricultural Organization (FAO), 2121 K St., Ste. 800B, Washington, DC, 20037, USA, (202) 653-2400 (Dial from U.S.), (202) 653-5760 (Fax from U.S.), fao-hq@fao.org, https://www.fao.org; The State of Food and Agriculture (SOFA) 2022.

BRITISH VIRGIN ISLANDS-FORESTS AND FORESTRY

United Nations Food and Agricultural Organization (FAO), 2121 K St., Ste. 800B, Washington, DC, 20037, USA, (202) 653-2400 (Dial from U.S.), (202) 653-5760 (Fax from U.S.), fao-hq@fao.org, https://www.fao.org; The State of Food and Agriculture (SOFA) 2022.

United Nations Statistics Division (UNSD), United Nations Plz., New York, NY, 10017, USA, (800) 253-9646, (212) 963-9851, statistics@un.org, https://unstats.un.org; Statistical Yearbook of the United Nations 2021.

BRITISH VIRGIN ISLANDS-GROSS DOMESTIC PRODUCT

The Economist Group: Economist Intelligence Unit (EIU), 900 3rd Ave., 16th Fl., New York, NY, 10022, USA, (212) 541-0500, americas@eiu.com, https://www.eiu.com; Virgin Islands (British) Country Report.

Routledge - Taylor & Francis Group, 6000 Broken Sound Pkwy. NW, Ste. 300, Boca Raton, FL, 33487, USA, (800) 634-1420, (800) 634-7064, orders@taylorandfrancis.com, https://www.routledge.com/; The Europa World Year Book 2022.

United Nations Statistics Division (UNSD), United Nations Plz., New York, NY, 10017, USA, (800) 253-9646, (212) 963-9851, statistics@un.org, https://unstats.un.org; Statistical Yearbook of the United Nations 2021.

BRITISH VIRGIN ISLANDS-GROSS NATIONAL PRODUCT

Palgrave Macmillan, 1 New York Plaza, Ste. 4500, New York, NY, 10004-1562, USA, (800) 777-4643, orders@palgrave.com, https://www.palgrave.com/us; The Statesman's Yearbook, 2023.

BRITISH VIRGIN ISLANDS-HOUSING

Euromonitor International, Inc., 1 N Dearborn St., Ste. 1700, Chicago, IL, 60602, USA, (312) 922-1115, (312) 922-1157, info-usa@euromonitor.com, https://www.euromonitor.com/; Geographies.

BRITISH VIRGIN ISLANDS-ILLITERATE PERSONS

UNESCO Institute for Statistics, C.P 250 Succursale H, Montreal, QC, H3G 2K8, CAN, (514) 343-6880 (Dial from U.S.), (514) 343-5740 (Fax from U.S.), uis.publications@unesco.org, http://uis.unesco.org/; UIS.Stat.

BRITISH VIRGIN ISLANDS-IMPORTS

Central Intelligence Agency (CIA), Office of Public Affairs, Washington, DC, 20505, USA, (703) 482-0623, https://www.cia.gov; The World Factbook.

The Economist Group: Economist Intelligence Unit (EIU), 900 3rd Ave., 16th Fl., New York, NY, 10022, USA, (212) 541-0500, americas@eiu.com, https://www.eiu.com; Virgin Islands (British) Country Report.

BRITISH VIRGIN ISLANDS-INDUSTRIES

Central Intelligence Agency (CIA), Office of Public Affairs, Washington, DC, 20505, USA, (703) 482-0623, https://www.cia.gov; The World Factbook.

The Economist Group: Economist Intelligence Unit (EIU), 900 3rd Ave., 16th Fl., New York, NY, 10022, USA, (212) 541-0500, americas@eiu.com, https://www.eiu.com; Virgin Islands (British) Country Report.

Euromonitor International, Inc., 1 N Dearborn St., Ste. 1700, Chicago, IL, 60602, USA, (312) 922-1115, (312) 922-1157, info-usa@euromonitor.com, https://www.euromonitor.com/; Geographies.

International Labour Organization (ILO), 4 Rte. des Morillons, Geneva, CH-1211, SWI, ilo@ilo.org, https://www.ilo.org; NORMLEX Information System on International Labour Standards.

Palgrave Macmillan, 1 New York Plaza, Ste. 4500, New York, NY, 10004-1562, USA, (800) 777-4643, orders@palgrave.com, https://www.palgrave.com/us; The Statesman's Yearbook, 2023.

Routledge - Taylor & Francis Group, 6000 Broken Sound Pkwy. NW, Ste. 300, Boca Raton, FL, 33487, USA, (800) 634-1420, (800) 634-7064, orders@taylorandfrancis.com, https://www.routledge.com/; The Europa World Year Book 2022.

BRITISH VIRGIN ISLANDS-INFANT AND MATERNAL MORTALITY

See BRITISH VIRGIN ISLANDS-MORTALITY

BRITISH VIRGIN ISLANDS-INTERNATIONAL TRADE

The Economist Group: Economist Intelligence Unit (EIU), 900 3rd Ave., 16th Fl., New York, NY, 10022, USA, (212) 541-0500, americas@eiu.com, https://www.eiu.com; Virgin Islands (British) Country Report.

Euromonitor International, Inc., 1 N Dearborn St., Ste. 1700, Chicago, IL, 60602, USA, (312) 922-1115, (312) 922-1157, info-usa@euromonitor.com, https://www.euromonitor.com/; Geographies.

Palgrave Macmillan, 1 New York Plaza, Ste. 4500, New York, NY, 10004-1562, USA, (800) 777-4643, orders@palgrave.com, https://www.palgrave.com/us; The Statesman's Yearbook, 2023.

Routledge - Taylor & Francis Group, 6000 Broken Sound Pkwy. NW, Ste. 300, Boca Raton, FL, 33487, USA, (800) 634-1420, (800) 634-7064, orders@taylorandfrancis.com, https://www.routledge.com/; The Europa World Year Book 2022.

United Nations Conference on Trade and Development (UNCTAD), Palais des Nations, Geneva, 1211, SWI, (212) 963-6896, unctadinfo@unctad.org, https://unctad.org; Trade and Development Report 2021.

United Nations Food and Agricultural Organization (FAO), 2121 K St., Ste. 800B, Washington, DC, 20037, USA, (202) 653-2400 (Dial from U.S.), (202) 653-5760 (Fax from U.S.), fao-hq@fao.org, https://www.fao.org; The State of Food and Agriculture (SOFA) 2022.

United Nations Statistics Division (UNSD), United Nations Plz., New York, NY, 10017, USA, (800) 253-9646, (212) 963-9851, statistics@un.org, https://unstats.un.org; International Trade Statistics Yearbook 2020.

World Trade Organization (WTO), Ctre. William Rappard, Rue de Lausanne 154, Case postale, Geneva, CH-1211, SWI, enquiries@wto.org, https://www.wto.org; World Trade Statistical Review 2022.

BRITISH VIRGIN ISLANDS-LABOR

Central Intelligence Agency (CIA), Office of Public Affairs, Washington, DC, 20505, USA, (703) 482-0623, https://www.cia.gov; The World Factbook.

Euromonitor International, Inc., 1 N Dearborn St., Ste. 1700, Chicago, IL, 60602, USA, (312) 922-1115, (312) 922-1157, info-usa@euromonitor.com, https://www.euromonitor.com/; Geographies.

International Labour Organization (ILO), 4 Rte. des Morillons, Geneva, CH-1211, SWI, ilo@ilo.org, https://www.ilo.org; NORMLEX Information System on International Labour Standards.

United Nations Food and Agricultural Organization (FAO), 2121 K St., Ste. 800B, Washington, DC, 20037, USA, (202) 653-2400 (Dial from U.S.), (202) 653-5760 (Fax from U.S.), fao-hq@fao.org, https://www.fao.org; The State of Food and Agriculture (SOFA) 2022.

BRITISH VIRGIN ISLANDS-LIBRARIES

UNESCO Institute for Statistics, C.P 250 Succursale H, Montreal, QC, H3G 2K8, CAN, (514) 343-6880 (Dial from U.S.), (514) 343-5740 (Fax from U.S.), uis.publications@unesco.org, http://uis.unesco.org/; UIS.Stat.

BRITISH VIRGIN ISLANDS-LIFE EXPECTANCY

Central Intelligence Agency (CIA), Office of Public Affairs, Washington, DC, 20505, USA, (703) 482-0623, https://www.cia.gov; The World Factbook.

United Nations Department of Economic and Social Affairs (DESA), Population Division, 2 United Nations Plz., Rm. DC2-1950, New York, NY, 10017, USA, (212) 963-3209, (212) 963-2147, population@un.org, https://www.un.org/development/desa/pd/; World Population Ageing 2020 Highlights.

BRITISH VIRGIN ISLANDS-LITERACY

Euromonitor International, Inc., 1 N Dearborn St., Ste. 1700, Chicago, IL, 60602, USA, (312) 922-1115, (312) 922-1157, info-usa@euromonitor.com, https://www.euromonitor.com/; Geographies.

BRITISH VIRGIN ISLANDS-LIVESTOCK

Palgrave Macmillan, 1 New York Plaza, Ste. 4500, New York, NY, 10004-1562, USA, (800) 777-4643, orders@palgrave.com, https://www.palgrave.com/us; The Statesman's Yearbook, 2023.

United Nations Food and Agricultural Organization (FAO), 2121 K St., Ste. 800B, Washington, DC, 20037, USA, (202) 653-2400 (Dial from U.S.), (202) 653-5760 (Fax from U.S.), fao-hq@fao.org, https://www.fao.org; The State of Food and Agriculture (SOFA) 2022.

United Nations Statistics Division (UNSD), United Nations Plz., New York, NY, 10017, USA, (800) 253-9646, (212) 963-9851, statistics@un.org, https://unstats.un.org; Statistical Yearbook of the United Nations 2021.

BRITISH VIRGIN ISLANDS-MARRIAGE

Routledge - Taylor & Francis Group, 6000 Broken Sound Pkwy. NW, Ste. 300, Boca Raton, FL, 33487,

USA, (800) 634-1420, (800) 634-7064, orders@taylorandfrancis.com, https://www.routledge.com/; The Europa World Year Book 2022.

United Nations Statistics Division (UNSD), United Nations Plz., New York, NY, 10017, USA, (800) 253-9646, (212) 963-9851, statistics@un.org, https://unstats.un.org; Statistical Yearbook of the United Nations 2021.

BRITISH VIRGIN ISLANDS-MINERAL INDUSTRIES

United Nations Conference on Trade and Development (UNCTAD), Palais des Nations, Geneva, 1211, SWI, (212) 963-6896, unctadinfo@unctad.org, https://unctad.org; Trade and Development Report 2021.

BRITISH VIRGIN ISLANDS-MONEY SUPPLY

The Economist Group: Economist Intelligence Unit (EIU), 900 3rd Ave., 16th Fl., New York, NY, 10022, USA, (212) 541-0500, americas@eiu.com, https://www.eiu.com; Virgin Islands (British) Country Report.

BRITISH VIRGIN ISLANDS-MORTALITY

United Nations Statistics Division (UNSD), United Nations Plz., New York, NY, 10017, USA, (800) 253-9646, (212) 963-9851, statistics@un.org, https://unstats.un.org; Statistical Yearbook of the United Nations 2021.

BRITISH VIRGIN ISLANDS-NUTRITION

United Nations Food and Agricultural Organization (FAO), 2121 K St., Ste. 800B, Washington, DC, 20037, USA, (202) 653-2400 (Dial from U.S.), (202) 653-5760 (Fax from U.S.), fao-hq@fao.org, https://www.fao.org; The State of Food and Agriculture (SOFA) 2022.

BRITISH VIRGIN ISLANDS-PESTICIDES

United Nations Food and Agricultural Organization (FAO), 2121 K St., Ste. 800B, Washington, DC, 20037, USA, (202) 653-2400 (Dial from U.S.), (202) 653-5760 (Fax from U.S.), fao-hq@fao.org, https://www.fao.org; The State of Food and Agriculture (SOFA) 2022.

BRITISH VIRGIN ISLANDS-PETROLEUM INDUSTRY AND TRADE

United Nations Food and Agricultural Organization (FAO), 2121 K St., Ste. 800B, Washington, DC, 20037, USA, (202) 653-2400 (Dial from U.S.), (202) 653-5760 (Fax from U.S.), fao-hq@fao.org, https://www.fao.org; The State of Food and Agriculture (SOFA) 2022.

BRITISH VIRGIN ISLANDS-POPULATION

Caribbean Public Health Agency (CARPHA), Federation Park, 16-18 Jamaica Blvd., Port of Spain, TTO, (868) 622-4261 (Dial from U.S.), (868) 299-0820 (Dial from U.S.), postmaster@carpha.org, https://carpha.org/; unpublished data.

Central Intelligence Agency (CIA), Office of Public Affairs, Washington, DC, 20505, USA, (703) 482-0623, https://www.cia.gov; The World Factbook.

The Economist Group: Economist Intelligence Unit (EIU), 900 3rd Ave., 16th Fl., New York, NY, 10022, USA, (212) 541-0500, americas@eiu.com, https://www.eiu.com; Virgin Islands (British) Country Report.

International Labour Organization (ILO), 4 Rte. des Morillons, Geneva, CH-1211, SWI, ilo@ilo.org, https://www.ilo.org; NORMLEX Information System on International Labour Standards.

Palgrave Macmillan, 1 New York Plaza, Ste. 4500, New York, NY, 10004-1562, USA, (800) 777-4643, orders@palgrave.com, https://www.palgrave.com/us; The Statesman's Yearbook, 2023.

Routledge - Taylor & Francis Group, 6000 Broken Sound Pkwy. NW, Ste. 300, Boca Raton, FL, 33487, USA, (800) 634-1420, (800) 634-7064, orders@taylorandfrancis.com, https://www.routledge.com/; The Europa World Year Book 2022.

UK Data Service, University of Essex, Wivenhoe Park, Colchester, Essex, CO4 3SQ, GBR, https://ukdataservice.ac.uk/; International Aggregate Data.

United Nations Department of Economic and Social Affairs (DESA), Population Division, 2 United Nations Plz., Rm. DC2-1950, New York, NY, 10017, USA, (212) 963-3209, (212) 963-2147, population@un.org, https://www.un.org/development/desa/pd/; Revision of World Urbanization Prospects and World Population Ageing 2020 Highlights.

United Nations Economic Commission for Latin America and the Caribbean (ECLAC), Casilla 179-D, Santiago, 7630412, CHL, (202) 596-3713, prensa@cepal.org, https://www.cepal.org/en; CEPALSTAT.

United Nations Statistics Division (UNSD), United Nations Plz., New York, NY, 10017, USA, (800) 253-9646, (212) 963-9851, statistics@un.org, https://unstats.un.org; Statistical Yearbook of the United Nations 2021.

BRITISH VIRGIN ISLANDS-POPULATION DENSITY

Central Intelligence Agency (CIA), Office of Public Affairs, Washington, DC, 20505, USA, (703) 482-0623, https://www.cia.gov; The World Factbook.

Palgrave Macmillan, 1 New York Plaza, Ste. 4500, New York, NY, 10004-1562, USA, (800) 777-4643, orders@palgrave.com, https://www.palgrave.com/us; The Statesman's Yearbook, 2023.

Routledge - Taylor & Francis Group, 6000 Broken Sound Pkwy. NW, Ste. 300, Boca Raton, FL, 33487, USA, (800) 634-1420, (800) 634-7064, orders@taylorandfrancis.com, https://www.routledge.com/; The Europa World Year Book 2022.

BRITISH VIRGIN ISLANDS-POWER RESOURCES

Euromonitor International, Inc., 1 N Dearborn St., Ste. 1700, Chicago, IL, 60602, USA, (312) 922-1115, (312) 922-1157, info-usa@euromonitor.com, https://www.euromonitor.com/; Geographies.

United Nations Food and Agricultural Organization (FAO), 2121 K St., Ste. 800B, Washington, DC, 20037, USA, (202) 653-2400 (Dial from U.S.), (202) 653-5760 (Fax from U.S.), fao-hq@fao.org, https://www.fao.org; The State of Food and Agriculture (SOFA) 2022.

United Nations Statistics Division (UNSD), United Nations Plz., New York, NY, 10017, USA, (800) 253-9646, (212) 963-9851, statistics@un.org, https://unstats.un.org; Energy Statistics Yearbook 2019.

BRITISH VIRGIN ISLANDS-PRICES

Euromonitor International, Inc., 1 N Dearborn St., Ste. 1700, Chicago, IL, 60602, USA, (312) 922-1115, (312) 922-1157, info-usa@euromonitor.com, https://www.euromonitor.com/; Geographies.

BRITISH VIRGIN ISLANDS-PUBLIC HEALTH

Euromonitor International, Inc., 1 N Dearborn St., Ste. 1700, Chicago, IL, 60602, USA, (312) 922-1115, (312) 922-1157, info-usa@euromonitor.com, https://www.euromonitor.com/; Geographies.

Palgrave Macmillan, 1 New York Plaza, Ste. 4500, New York, NY, 10004-1562, USA, (800) 777-4643, orders@palgrave.com, https://www.palgrave.com/us; The Statesman's Yearbook, 2023.

U.S. Census Bureau, 4600 Silver Hill Rd., Washington, DC, 20233, USA, (301) 763-4636, (800) 923-8282, https://www.census.gov; HIV/AIDS Surveillance Data Base.

United Nations Department of Economic and Social Affairs (DESA), Population Division, 2 United Nations Plz., Rm. DC2-1950, New York, NY, 10017, USA, (212) 963-3209, (212) 963-2147, population@un.org, https://www.un.org/development/desa/pd/; World Fertility Data 2019.

United Nations Statistics Division (UNSD), United Nations Plz., New York, NY, 10017, USA, (800) 253-9646, (212) 963-9851, statistics@un.org, https://unstats.un.org; Statistical Yearbook of the United Nations 2021.

World Health Organization (WHO), Ave. Appia 20, Geneva, CH-1211, SWI, (202) 974-3000 (Telephone in U.S.), publications@who.int, https://www.who.int/; Health Statistics and Information Systems.

BRITISH VIRGIN ISLANDS-RELIGION

Central Intelligence Agency (CIA), Office of Public Affairs, Washington, DC, 20505, USA, (703) 482-0623, https://www.cia.gov; The World Factbook.

Palgrave Macmillan, 1 New York Plaza, Ste. 4500, New York, NY, 10004-1562, USA, (800) 777-4643, orders@palgrave.com, https://www.palgrave.com/us; The Statesman's Yearbook, 2023.

BRITISH VIRGIN ISLANDS-RETAIL TRADE

Euromonitor International, Inc., 1 N Dearborn St., Ste. 1700, Chicago, IL, 60602, USA, (312) 922-1115, (312) 922-1157, info-usa@euromonitor.com, https://www.euromonitor.com/; Geographies.

BRITISH VIRGIN ISLANDS-SHIPPING

Routledge - Taylor & Francis Group, 6000 Broken Sound Pkwy. NW, Ste. 300, Boca Raton, FL, 33487, USA, (800) 634-1420, (800) 634-7064, orders@taylorandfrancis.com, https://www.routledge.com/; The Europa World Year Book 2022.

United Nations Statistics Division (UNSD), United Nations Plz., New York, NY, 10017, USA, (800) 253-9646, (212) 963-9851, statistics@un.org, https://unstats.un.org; Statistical Yearbook of the United Nations 2021.

BRITISH VIRGIN ISLANDS-TELEPHONE

Palgrave Macmillan, 1 New York Plaza, Ste. 4500, New York, NY, 10004-1562, USA, (800) 777-4643, orders@palgrave.com, https://www.palgrave.com/us; The Statesman's Yearbook, 2023.

Routledge - Taylor & Francis Group, 6000 Broken Sound Pkwy. NW, Ste. 300, Boca Raton, FL, 33487, USA, (800) 634-1420, (800) 634-7064, orders@taylorandfrancis.com, https://www.routledge.com/; The Europa World Year Book 2022.

BRITISH VIRGIN ISLANDS-THEATER

UNESCO Institute for Statistics, C.P 250 Succursale H, Montreal, QC, H3G 2K8, CAN, (514) 343-6880 (Dial from U.S.), (514) 343-5740 (Fax from U.S.), uis.publications@unesco.org, http://uis.unesco.org/; UIS.Stat.

BRITISH VIRGIN ISLANDS-TOURISM

Euromonitor International, Inc., 1 N Dearborn St., Ste. 1700, Chicago, IL, 60602, USA, (312) 922-1115, (312) 922-1157, info-usa@euromonitor.com, https://www.euromonitor.com/; Geographies.

Palgrave Macmillan, 1 New York Plaza, Ste. 4500, New York, NY, 10004-1562, USA, (800) 777-4643, orders@palgrave.com, https://www.palgrave.com/us; The Statesman's Yearbook, 2023.

Routledge - Taylor & Francis Group, 6000 Broken Sound Pkwy. NW, Ste. 300, Boca Raton, FL, 33487, USA, (800) 634-1420, (800) 634-7064, orders@taylorandfrancis.com, https://www.routledge.com/; The Europa World Year Book 2022.

BRITISH VIRGIN ISLANDS-TRADE

See BRITISH VIRGIN ISLANDS-INTERNATIONAL TRADE

BRITISH VIRGIN ISLANDS-TRANSPORTATION

Central Intelligence Agency (CIA), Office of Public Affairs, Washington, DC, 20505, USA, (703) 482-0623, https://www.cia.gov; The World Factbook.

Euromonitor International, Inc., 1 N Dearborn St., Ste. 1700, Chicago, IL, 60602, USA, (312) 922-

1115, (312) 922-1157, info-usa@euromonitor.com, https://www.euromonitor.com/; Geographies.

Palgrave Macmillan, 1 New York Plaza, Ste. 4500, New York, NY, 10004-1562, USA, (800) 777-4643, orders@palgrave.com, https://www.palgrave.com/us; The Statesman's Yearbook, 2023.

Routledge - Taylor & Francis Group, 6000 Broken Sound Pkwy. NW, Ste. 300, Boca Raton, FL, 33487, USA, (800) 634-1420, (800) 634-7064, orders@taylorandfrancis.com, https://www.routledge.com/; The Europa World Year Book 2022.

BRITISH VIRGIN ISLANDS-UNEMPLOYMENT

International Labour Organization (ILO), 4 Rte. des Morillons, Geneva, CH-1211, SWI, ilo@ilo.org, https://www.ilo.org; NORMLEX Information System on International Labour Standards.

BRITISH VIRGIN ISLANDS-WAGES

International Labour Organization (ILO), 4 Rte. des Morillons, Geneva, CH-1211, SWI, ilo@ilo.org, https://www.ilo.org; NORMLEX Information System on International Labour Standards.

BROADBAND COMMUNICATION SYSTEMS

EducationSuperHighway, 6 Presidio Terrace, San Francisco, CA, 94118, USA, (415) 275-1307, info@educationsuperhighway.org, https://www.educationsuperhighway.org; No Home Left Offline: Accelerating Affordable Connectivity Program Adoption.

Federal Communications Commission (FCC), International Bureau (IB), 45 L St. NE, Washington, DC, 20554, USA, (888) 225-5322, (844) 432-2275 (ASL Video Call), (866) 418-0232, https://www.fcc.gov/international; International Broadband Data Report.

Federal Communications Commission (FCC), Wireline Competition Bureau (WCB), 45 L St. NE, Washington, DC, 20554, USA, (202) 418-1500, (888) 225-5322, (202) 418-2825, https://www.fcc.gov/wireline-competition; Fourteenth Broadband Deployment Report.

National Alliance for Public Charter Schools, 800 Connecticut Ave. NW, Ste. 300, Washington, DC, 20006, USA, (202) 289-2700, (202) 289-4009, datarequest@publiccharters.org, https://www.publiccharters.org/; Closing the Digital Divide.

Pew Research Center, Internet & Technology, 1615 L St. NW, Ste. 800, Washington, DC, 20036, USA, (202) 419-4300, (202) 857-8562, https://www.pewresearch.org/topic/internet-technology/; Mobile Technology and Home Broadband 2019.

U.S. Department of Commerce (DOC), National Telecommunications and Information Administration (NTIA), Herbert C. Hoover Bldg., 1401 Constitution Ave. NW, Washington, DC, 20230, USA, (202) 482-2000, https://www.ntia.doc.gov; Data Central and National Broadband Availability Map.

United States Telecom Association (USTelecom), 601 New Jersey Ave. NW, Ste. 600, Washington, DC, 20001, USA, (202) 326-7300, https://www.ustelecom.org/; Broadband Industry Stats and USTelecom Industry Metrics and Trends 2020 Update.

BROADCASTING AND TELECOMMUNICATION INDUSTRY

Euromonitor International, Inc., 1 N Dearborn St., Ste. 1700, Chicago, IL, 60602, USA, (312) 922-1115, (312) 922-1157, info-usa@euromonitor.com, https://www.euromonitor.com/; Strategic Analysis of the World's Largest Companies.

Federal Communications Commission (FCC), Media Bureau (MB), 45 L St. NE, Washington, DC, 20554, USA, (202) 418-7200, (888) 225-5322, (866) 418-0232, mediarelations@fcc.gov, https://www.fcc.gov/media; Media Bureau Public Databases.

Federal Communications Commission (FCC), Wireless Telecommunications Bureau (WTB), 45 L St. NE, Washington, DC, 20554, USA, (202) 418-0600, (888) 225-5322, (202) 418-0787, https://www.fcc.gov/wireless-telecommunications; unpublished data.

Federal Communications Commission (FCC), Wireline Competition Bureau (WCB), 45 L St. NE, Washington, DC, 20554, USA, (202) 418-1500, (888) 225-5322, (202) 418-2825, https://www.fcc.gov/wireline-competition; Fourteenth Broadband Deployment Report.

International Telecommunication Union (ITU), Place des Nations, Geneva, CH-1211, SWI, itumail@itu.int, https://www.itu.int; Global Connectivity Report 2022; Measuring Digital Development: Facts and Figures 2021; World Telecommunication/ICT Indicators Database 2021; and Yearbook of Statistics 2019.

Ofcom, Riverside House , 2a Southwark Bridge Rd., London, SE1 9HA, GBR, https://www.ofcom.org.uk/; Communications Industry Facts and Statistics; Number of Hours Broadcast by Public Service Television Broadcasters; and Open Data.

BROADCASTING AND TELECOMMUNICATION INDUSTRY-EARNINGS

U.S. Census Bureau, 4600 Silver Hill Rd., Washington, DC, 20233, USA, (301) 763-4636, (800) 923-8282, https://www.census.gov; County Business Patterns (CBP) 2020.

BROADCASTING AND TELECOMMUNICATION INDUSTRY-EMPLOYEES

U.S. Census Bureau, 4600 Silver Hill Rd., Washington, DC, 20233, USA, (301) 763-4636, (800) 923-8282, https://www.census.gov; County Business Patterns (CBP) 2020.

BROADCASTING AND TELECOMMUNICATION INDUSTRY-ESTABLISHMENTS

U.S. Census Bureau, 4600 Silver Hill Rd., Washington, DC, 20233, USA, (301) 763-4636, (800) 923-8282, https://www.census.gov; County Business Patterns (CBP) 2020.

BROADCASTING AND TELECOMMUNICATION INDUSTRY-FINANCES

U.S. Census Bureau, 4600 Silver Hill Rd., Washington, DC, 20233, USA, (301) 763-4636, (800) 923-8282, https://www.census.gov; Service Annual Survey 2021.

BROADCASTING AND TELECOMMUNICATION INDUSTRY-RECEIPTS, REVENUE

U.S. Census Bureau, 4600 Silver Hill Rd., Washington, DC, 20233, USA, (301) 763-4636, (800) 923-8282, https://www.census.gov; Service Annual Survey 2021.

BROADCASTING AND TELECOMMUNICATION INDUSTRY-WORLD

Federal Communications Commission (FCC), International Bureau (IB), 45 L St. NE, Washington, DC, 20554, USA, (888) 225-5322, (844) 432-2275 (ASL Video Call), (866) 418-0232, https://www.fcc.gov/international; International Broadband Data Report.

International Telecommunication Union (ITU), Place des Nations, Geneva, CH-1211, SWI, itumail@itu.int, https://www.itu.int; Measuring Digital Development: Facts and Figures 2021.

BROADWAY AND OFF-BROADWAY SHOWS

The Broadway League, 729 7th Ave., 5th Fl., New York, NY, 10019, USA, (212) 764-1122, (212) 944-2136, league@broadway.org, https://www.broadwayleague.com/; Broadway Season Statistics; Broadway's Economic Contribution to New York City 2018-2019 Season; The Demographics of the Broadway Audience 2018-2019; and Statistics - Touring Broadway.

BROCCOLI

U.S. Department of Agriculture (USDA), Economic Research Service (ERS), 1400 Independence Ave. SW, Mail Stop 1800, Washington, DC, 20250-0002, USA, (202) 720-2791, https://www.ers.usda.gov/; Food Price Outlook.

U.S. Department of Agriculture (USDA), National Agricultural Statistics Service (USDA-NASS), 1400 Independence Ave. SW, Washington, DC, 20250, USA, (800) 727-9540, nass@nass.usda.gov, https://www.nass.usda.gov; Quick Stats and Vegetables Annual Summary.

BROILERS (POULTRY)

U.S. Department of Agriculture (USDA), Economic Research Service (ERS), 1400 Independence Ave. SW, Mail Stop 1800, Washington, DC, 20250-0002, USA, (202) 720-2791, https://www.ers.usda.gov/; Food Price Outlook.

U.S. Department of Agriculture (USDA), National Agricultural Statistics Service (USDA-NASS), 1400 Independence Ave. SW, Washington, DC, 20250, USA, (800) 727-9540, nass@nass.usda.gov, https://www.nass.usda.gov; Poultry Production and Value.

BROMINE

U.S. Department of the Interior (DOI), U.S. Geological Survey (USGS), National Minerals Information Center (NMIC), 12201 Sunrise Valley Dr., Reston, VA, 20192, USA, (703) 648-4920, (703) 648-7971, (703) 648-4995, sfortier@usgs.gov, https://www.usgs.gov/centers/nmic; Mineral Commodity Summaries 2022.

BRONCHITIS, EMPHYSEMA, ETC

Bernan Press, 15250 NBN Way, Bldg. C, Blue Ridge Summit, PA, 17214, USA, (301) 459-2255, (800) 865-3457, (800) 865-3450, customercare@bernan.com, https://rowman.com/Page/Bernan; Vital Statistics of the United States 2022: Births, Life Expectancy, Deaths, and Selected Health Data.

U.S. Department of Health and Human Services, Centers for Disease Control and Prevention (CDC), National Center for Health Statistics (NCHS), 3311 Toledo Rd., Hyattsville, MD, 20782-2064, USA, (800) 232-4636, (301) 458-4000, https://www.cdc.gov/nchs; FastStats - Statistics by Topic; National Vital Statistics Reports (NVSR); and Vital Statistics Online Data Portal.

BRUNEI-NATIONAL STATISTICAL OFFICE

Brunei Ministry of Finance and Economy, Department of Economic Planning and Statistics, Block 2A, Jalan Ong Sum Ping, Bandar Seri Begawan, Brunei Darussalam, BA 1311, BRN, info@jpes.gov.bn, https://deps.mofe.gov.bn; National Data Reports (Brunei).

BRUNEI-AGRICULTURE

The Economist Group: Economist Intelligence Unit (EIU), 900 3rd Ave., 16th Fl., New York, NY, 10022, USA, (212) 541-0500, americas@eiu.com, https://www.eiu.com; Brunei Country Report.

Euromonitor International, Inc., 1 N Dearborn St., Ste. 1700, Chicago, IL, 60602, USA, (312) 922-1115, (312) 922-1157, info-usa@euromonitor.com, https://www.euromonitor.com/; Geographies.

Organisation of Islamic Cooperation (OIC), Statistical, Economic and Social Research and Training Centre for Islamic Countries (SESRIC), Kudus Cad. No. 9, Diplomatik Site, Ankara, 06450, TUR, statistics@sesric.org, https://www.sesric.org/; OIC Statistics (OICStat) Database and OIC-Countries in Figures (OIC-CIF).

Palgrave Macmillan, 1 New York Plaza, Ste. 4500, New York, NY, 10004-1562, USA, (800) 777-4643, orders@palgrave.com, https://www.palgrave.com/us; The Statesman's Yearbook, 2023.

Routledge - Taylor & Francis Group, 6000 Broken Sound Pkwy. NW, Ste. 300, Boca Raton, FL, 33487, USA, (800) 634-1420, (800) 634-7064, orders@taylorandfrancis.com, https://www.routledge.com/; The Europa World Year Book 2022.

United Nations Economic and Social Commission for Asia and the Pacific (ESCAP), United Nations Building, Rajadamnern Nok Ave., Bangkok, 10200, THA, https://www.unescap.org/; Asia-Pacific Development Journal and SDG Gateway Data Explorer.

United Nations Food and Agricultural Organization (FAO), 2121 K St., Ste. 800B, Washington, DC, 20037, USA, (202) 653-2400 (Dial from U.S.), (202) 653-5760 (Fax from U.S.), fao-hq@fao.org, https://www.fao.org; AQUASTAT and The State of Food and Agriculture (SOFA) 2022.

United Nations Statistics Division (UNSD), United Nations Plz., New York, NY, 10017, USA, (800) 253-9646, (212) 963-9851, statistics@un.org, https://unstats.un.org; Statistical Yearbook of the United Nations 2021.

BRUNEI-AIRLINES

Palgrave Macmillan, 1 New York Plaza, Ste. 4500, New York, NY, 10004-1562, USA, (800) 777-4643, orders@palgrave.com, https://www.palgrave.com/us; The Statesman's Yearbook, 2023.

Routledge - Taylor & Francis Group, 6000 Broken Sound Pkwy. NW, Ste. 300, Boca Raton, FL, 33487, USA, (800) 634-1420, (800) 634-7064, orders@taylorandfrancis.com, https://www.routledge.com/; The Europa World Year Book 2022.

BRUNEI-ARMED FORCES

Central Intelligence Agency (CIA), Office of Public Affairs, Washington, DC, 20505, USA, (703) 482-0623, https://www.cia.gov; The World Factbook.

International Institute for Strategic Studies (IISS) - Americas, 2121 K St. NW, Ste. 600, Washington, DC, 20037, USA, (202) 659-1490, (202) 659-1499, https://www.iiss.org/; The Military Balance 2022.

Palgrave Macmillan, 1 New York Plaza, Ste. 4500, New York, NY, 10004-1562, USA, (800) 777-4643, orders@palgrave.com, https://www.palgrave.com/us; The Statesman's Yearbook, 2023.

Stockholm International Peace Research Institute (SIPRI), Signalistgatan 9, Stockholm, SE 169 72, SWE, https://www.sipri.org/; SIPRI Arms Transfers Database and SIPRI Military Expenditure Database.

BRUNEI-BANKS AND BANKING

Euromonitor International, Inc., 1 N Dearborn St., Ste. 1700, Chicago, IL, 60602, USA, (312) 922-1115, (312) 922-1157, info-usa@euromonitor.com, https://www.euromonitor.com/; Geographies.

BRUNEI-BROADCASTING

Central Intelligence Agency (CIA), Office of Public Affairs, Washington, DC, 20505, USA, (703) 482-0623, https://www.cia.gov; The World Factbook.

Euromonitor International, Inc., 1 N Dearborn St., Ste. 1700, Chicago, IL, 60602, USA, (312) 922-1115, (312) 922-1157, info-usa@euromonitor.com, https://www.euromonitor.com/; Geographies.

Palgrave Macmillan, 1 New York Plaza, Ste. 4500, New York, NY, 10004-1562, USA, (800) 777-4643, orders@palgrave.com, https://www.palgrave.com/us; The Statesman's Yearbook, 2023.

UNESCO Institute for Statistics, C.P 250 Succursale H, Montreal, QC, H3G 2K8, CAN, (514) 343-6880 (Dial from U.S.), (514) 343-5740 (Fax from U.S.), uis.publications@unesco.org, http://uis.unesco.org/; UIS.Stat.

WRTH Publications Limited, PO Box 290, Oxford, OX2 7FT, GBR, sales@wrth.com, https://www.wrth.com; World Radio TV Handbook 2023.

BRUNEI-BUDGET

Central Intelligence Agency (CIA), Office of Public Affairs, Washington, DC, 20505, USA, (703) 482-0623, https://www.cia.gov; The World Factbook.

BRUNEI-BUSINESS

United Nations Economic and Social Commission for Asia and the Pacific (ESCAP), United Nations Building, Rajadamnern Nok Ave., Bangkok, 10200, THA, https://www.unescap.org/; SDG Gateway Data Explorer.

BRUNEI-CHILDBIRTH-STATISTICS

United Nations Economic and Social Commission for Asia and the Pacific (ESCAP), United Nations Building, Rajadamnern Nok Ave., Bangkok, 10200, THA, https://www.unescap.org/; Asia-Pacific Development Journal.

BRUNEI-CLIMATE

Palgrave Macmillan, 1 New York Plaza, Ste. 4500, New York, NY, 10004-1562, USA, (800) 777-4643, orders@palgrave.com, https://www.palgrave.com/us; The Statesman's Yearbook, 2023.

BRUNEI-COAL PRODUCTION

See BRUNEI-MINERAL INDUSTRIES

BRUNEI-COMMERCE

Palgrave Macmillan, 1 New York Plaza, Ste. 4500, New York, NY, 10004-1562, USA, (800) 777-4643, orders@palgrave.com, https://www.palgrave.com/us; The Statesman's Yearbook, 2023.

UK Data Service, University of Essex, Wivenhoe Park, Colchester, Essex, CO4 3SQ, GBR, https://ukdataservice.ac.uk/; International Aggregate Data.

BRUNEI-COMMODITY EXCHANGES

Barchart, 209 W Jackson Blvd., 2nd Fl., Chicago, IL, 60606, USA, (877) 247-4394, commodities@barchart.com, https://www.barchart.com/cmdty; The cmdty Yearbook 2023; cmdtyStats: Commodity Statistics and Fundamental Data; cmdtyView: Commodity Index; and Commodity Data and Prices.

International Monetary Fund (IMF), 700 19th St. NW, Washington, DC, 20431, USA, (202) 623-7000, (202) 623-4661, publications@imf.org, https://www.imf.org; IMF Primary Commodity Prices.

BRUNEI-CONSUMER PRICE INDEXES

Routledge - Taylor & Francis Group, 6000 Broken Sound Pkwy. NW, Ste. 300, Boca Raton, FL, 33487, USA, (800) 634-1420, (800) 634-7064, orders@taylorandfrancis.com, https://www.routledge.com/; The Europa World Year Book 2022.

BRUNEI-CORN INDUSTRY

See BRUNEI-CROPS

BRUNEI-CROPS

Palgrave Macmillan, 1 New York Plaza, Ste. 4500, New York, NY, 10004-1562, USA, (800) 777-4643, orders@palgrave.com, https://www.palgrave.com/us; The Statesman's Yearbook, 2023.

United Nations Food and Agricultural Organization (FAO), 2121 K St., Ste. 800B, Washington, DC, 20037, USA, (202) 653-2400 (Dial from U.S.), (202) 653-5760 (Fax from U.S.), fao-hq@fao.org, https://www.fao.org; The State of Food and Agriculture (SOFA) 2022.

United Nations Statistics Division (UNSD), United Nations Plz., New York, NY, 10017, USA, (800) 253-9646, (212) 963-9851, statistics@un.org, https://unstats.un.org; Statistical Yearbook of the United Nations 2021.

BRUNEI-DAIRY PROCESSING

United Nations Food and Agricultural Organization (FAO), 2121 K St., Ste. 800B, Washington, DC, 20037, USA, (202) 653-2400 (Dial from U.S.), (202) 653-5760 (Fax from U.S.), fao-hq@fao.org, https://www.fao.org; The State of Food and Agriculture (SOFA) 2022.

BRUNEI-DEBTS, EXTERNAL

Palgrave Macmillan, 1 New York Plaza, Ste. 4500, New York, NY, 10004-1562, USA, (800) 777-4643, orders@palgrave.com, https://www.palgrave.com/us; The Statesman's Yearbook, 2023.

The World Bank, 1818 H St. NW, Washington, DC, 20433, USA, (202) 473-1000, (202) 477-6391, eds03@worldbank.org, https://www.worldbank.org/; Global Financial Development Report 2019-2020: Bank Regulation and Supervision a Decade after the Global Financial Crisis.

BRUNEI-ECONOMIC ASSISTANCE

United Nations Statistics Division (UNSD), United Nations Plz., New York, NY, 10017, USA, (800) 253-9646, (212) 963-9851, statistics@un.org, https://unstats.un.org; Statistical Yearbook of the United Nations 2021.

BRUNEI-ECONOMIC CONDITIONS

Bernan Press, 15250 NBN Way, Bldg. C, Blue Ridge Summit, PA, 17214, USA, (301) 459-2255, (800) 865-3457, (800) 865-3450, customercare@bernan.com, https://rowman.com/Page/Bernan; World Economic Outlook, April 2022.

Central Intelligence Agency (CIA), Office of Public Affairs, Washington, DC, 20505, USA, (703) 482-0623, https://www.cia.gov; The World Factbook.

The Economist Group: Economist Intelligence Unit (EIU), 900 3rd Ave., 16th Fl., New York, NY, 10022, USA, (212) 541-0500, americas@eiu.com, https://www.eiu.com; Brunei Country Report.

Euromonitor International, Inc., 1 N Dearborn St., Ste. 1700, Chicago, IL, 60602, USA, (312) 922-1115, (312) 922-1157, info-usa@euromonitor.com, https://www.euromonitor.com/; Geographies.

International Monetary Fund (IMF), 700 19th St. NW, Washington, DC, 20431, USA, (202) 623-7000, (202) 623-4661, publications@imf.org, https://www.imf.org; IMF Data and World Economic Outlook.

Organisation of Islamic Cooperation (OIC), Statistical, Economic and Social Research and Training Centre for Islamic Countries (SESRIC), Kudus Cad. No. 9, Diplomatik Site, Ankara, 06450, TUR, statistics@sesric.org, https://www.sesric.org/; OIC Economic Outlook 2021; OIC Statistics (OICStat) Database; and OIC-Countries in Figures (OIC-CIF).

Palgrave Macmillan, 1 New York Plaza, Ste. 4500, New York, NY, 10004-1562, USA, (800) 777-4643, orders@palgrave.com, https://www.palgrave.com/us; The Statesman's Yearbook, 2023.

Routledge - Taylor & Francis Group, 6000 Broken Sound Pkwy. NW, Ste. 300, Boca Raton, FL, 33487, USA, (800) 634-1420, (800) 634-7064, orders@taylorandfrancis.com, https://www.routledge.com/; The Europa World Year Book 2022.

United Nations Statistics Division (UNSD), United Nations Plz., New York, NY, 10017, USA, (800) 253-9646, (212) 963-9851, statistics@un.org, https://unstats.un.org; World Statistics Pocketbook 2021.

The World Bank, 1818 H St. NW, Washington, DC, 20433, USA, (202) 473-1000, (202) 477-6391, eds03@worldbank.org, https://www.worldbank.org/; Global Economic Monitor (GEM); Global Economic Prospects, June 2022; and The Global Findex Database 2021.

BRUNEI-EDUCATION

Euromonitor International, Inc., 1 N Dearborn St., Ste. 1700, Chicago, IL, 60602, USA, (312) 922-1115, (312) 922-1157, info-usa@euromonitor.com, https://www.euromonitor.com/; Geographies.

Infoplease, c/o Sandbox Networks, Inc., 1 Lincoln St., 24th Fl., Boston, MA, 02111, USA, https://www.infoplease.com; Countries of the World.

Organisation of Islamic Cooperation (OIC), Statistical, Economic and Social Research and Training Centre for Islamic Countries (SESRIC), Kudus Cad. No. 9, Diplomatik Site, Ankara, 06450, TUR, statistics@sesric.org, https://www.sesric.org/; OIC Statistics (OICStat) Database.

Palgrave Macmillan, 1 New York Plaza, Ste. 4500, New York, NY, 10004-1562, USA, (800) 777-4643, orders@palgrave.com, https://www.palgrave.com/us; The Statesman's Yearbook, 2023.

Routledge - Taylor & Francis Group, 6000 Broken Sound Pkwy. NW, Ste. 300, Boca Raton, FL, 33487, USA, (800) 634-1420, (800) 634-7064, orders@taylorandfrancis.com, https://www.routledge.com/; The Europa World Year Book 2022.

UNESCO Institute for Statistics, C.P 250 Succursale H, Montreal, QC, H3G 2K8, CAN, (514) 343-6880 (Dial from U.S.), (514) 343-5740 (Fax from U.S.), uis.publications@unesco.org, http://uis.unesco.org/; Literacy and UIS.Stat.

United Nations Economic and Social Commission for Asia and the Pacific (ESCAP), United Nations Building, Rajadamnern Nok Ave., Bangkok, 10200, THA, https://www.unescap.org/; Asia-Pacific Development Journal and SDG Gateway Data Explorer.

United Nations Statistics Division (UNSD), United Nations Plz., New York, NY, 10017, USA, (800) 253-9646, (212) 963-9851, statistics@un.org, https://unstats.un.org; Millennium Development Goal Indicators.

BRUNEI-ELECTRICITY

International Energy Agency (IEA), 9 Rue de la Federation, Paris, 75739, FRA, info@iea.org, https://www.iea.org/; World Energy Outlook 2021.

U.S. Energy Information Administration (EIA), 1000 Independence Ave. SW, Washington, DC, 20585, USA, (202) 586-8800, infoctr@eia.gov, https://www.eia.gov; International Energy Outlook 2021.

United Nations Statistics Division (UNSD), United Nations Plz., New York, NY, 10017, USA, (800) 253-9646, (212) 963-9851, statistics@un.org, https://unstats.un.org; Statistical Yearbook of the United Nations 2021.

BRUNEI-EMPLOYMENT

International Labour Organization (ILO), 4 Rte. des Morillons, Geneva, CH-1211, SWI, ilo@ilo.org, https://www.ilo.org; NORMLEX Information System on International Labour Standards.

UK Data Service, University of Essex, Wivenhoe Park, Colchester, Essex, CO4 3SQ, GBR, https://ukdataservice.ac.uk/; International Aggregate Data.

United Nations Economic and Social Commission for Asia and the Pacific (ESCAP), United Nations Building, Rajadamnern Nok Ave., Bangkok, 10200, THA, https://www.unescap.org/; Asia-Pacific Development Journal.

United Nations Statistics Division (UNSD), United Nations Plz., New York, NY, 10017, USA, (800) 253-9646, (212) 963-9851, statistics@un.org, https://unstats.un.org; Statistical Yearbook of the United Nations 2021.

BRUNEI-ENVIRONMENTAL CONDITIONS

DSI Data Service & Information, Xantener Strasse 51a, Rheinberg, D-47495, GER, dsi@dsidata.com, https://www.dsidata.com/; Global Environmental Database.

The Economist Group: Economist Intelligence Unit (EIU), 900 3rd Ave., 16th Fl., New York, NY, 10022, USA, (212) 541-0500, americas@eiu.com, https://www.eiu.com; Brunei Country Report.

Organisation of Islamic Cooperation (OIC), Statistical, Economic and Social Research and Training Centre for Islamic Countries (SESRIC), Kudus Cad. No. 9, Diplomatik Site, Ankara, 06450, TUR, statistics@sesric.org, https://www.sesric.org/; OIC Statistics (OICStat) Database and OIC-Countries in Figures (OIC-CIF).

United Nations Statistics Division (UNSD), United Nations Plz., New York, NY, 10017, USA, (800) 253-9646, (212) 963-9851, statistics@un.org, https://unstats.un.org; World Statistics Pocketbook 2021.

BRUNEI-EXPORTS

Central Intelligence Agency (CIA), Office of Public Affairs, Washington, DC, 20505, USA, (703) 482-0623, https://www.cia.gov; The World Factbook.

The Economist Group: Economist Intelligence Unit (EIU), 900 3rd Ave., 16th Fl., New York, NY, 10022, USA, (212) 541-0500, americas@eiu.com, https://www.eiu.com; Brunei Country Report.

International Monetary Fund (IMF), 700 19th St. NW, Washington, DC, 20431, USA, (202) 623-7000, (202) 623-4661, publications@imf.org, https://www.imf.org; Direction of Trade Statistics (DOTS).

Organisation of Islamic Cooperation (OIC), Statistical, Economic and Social Research and Training Centre for Islamic Countries (SESRIC), Kudus Cad. No. 9, Diplomatik Site, Ankara, 06450, TUR, statistics@sesric.org, https://www.sesric.org/; OIC Statistics (OICStat) Database.

S&P Global, IHS Markit, 15 Inverness Way E, Englewood, CO, 80112, USA, (800) 447-2273, (800) 854-7179, https://ihsmarkit.com; Global Trade Atlas (GTA).

United Nations Economic and Social Commission for Asia and the Pacific (ESCAP), United Nations Building, Rajadamnern Nok Ave., Bangkok, 10200, THA, https://www.unescap.org/; SDG Gateway Data Explorer.

BRUNEI-FERTILITY, HUMAN

Central Intelligence Agency (CIA), Office of Public Affairs, Washington, DC, 20505, USA, (703) 482-0623, https://www.cia.gov; The World Factbook.

BRUNEI-FERTILIZER INDUSTRY

United Nations Food and Agricultural Organization (FAO), 2121 K St., Ste. 800B, Washington, DC, 20037, USA, (202) 653-2400 (Dial from U.S.), (202) 653-5760 (Fax from U.S.), fao-hq@fao.org, https://www.fao.org; The State of Food and Agriculture (SOFA) 2022.

BRUNEI-FETAL MORTALITY

See BRUNEI-MORTALITY

BRUNEI-FINANCE

Stockholm International Peace Research Institute (SIPRI), Signalistgatan 9, Stockholm, SE 169 72, SWE, https://www.sipri.org/; SIPRI Arms Transfers Database and SIPRI Military Expenditure Database.

United Nations Economic and Social Commission for Asia and the Pacific (ESCAP), United Nations Building, Rajadamnern Nok Ave., Bangkok, 10200, THA, https://www.unescap.org/; Asia-Pacific Development Journal and SDG Gateway Data Explorer.

United Nations Statistics Division (UNSD), United Nations Plz., New York, NY, 10017, USA, (800) 253-9646, (212) 963-9851, statistics@un.org, https://unstats.un.org; Statistical Yearbook of the United Nations 2021.

BRUNEI-FINANCE, PUBLIC

Bernan Press, 15250 NBN Way, Bldg. C, Blue Ridge Summit, PA, 17214, USA, (301) 459-2255, (800) 865-3457, (800) 865-3450, customercare@bernan.com, https://rowman.com/Page/Bernan; National Accounts Statistics: Analysis of Main Aggregates 2020.

The Economist Group: Economist Intelligence Unit (EIU), 900 3rd Ave., 16th Fl., New York, NY, 10022, USA, (212) 541-0500, americas@eiu.com, https://www.eiu.com; Brunei Country Report.

International Monetary Fund (IMF), 700 19th St. NW, Washington, DC, 20431, USA, (202) 623-7000, (202) 623-4661, publications@imf.org, https://www.imf.org; Regional Economic Outlook.

Palgrave Macmillan, 1 New York Plaza, Ste. 4500, New York, NY, 10004-1562, USA, (800) 777-4643, orders@palgrave.com, https://www.palgrave.com/us; The Statesman's Yearbook, 2023.

Routledge - Taylor & Francis Group, 6000 Broken Sound Pkwy. NW, Ste. 300, Boca Raton, FL, 33487, USA, (800) 634-1420, (800) 634-7064, orders@taylorandfrancis.com, https://www.routledge.com/; The Europa World Year Book 2022.

United Nations Economic and Social Commission for Asia and the Pacific (ESCAP), United Nations Building, Rajadamnern Nok Ave., Bangkok, 10200, THA, https://www.unescap.org/; SDG Gateway Data Explorer.

United Nations Statistics Division (UNSD), United Nations Plz., New York, NY, 10017, USA, (800) 253-9646, (212) 963-9851, statistics@un.org, https://unstats.un.org; National Accounts Main Aggregates Database and National Accounts Statistics: Main Aggregates and Detailed Tables.

BRUNEI-FISHERIES

Palgrave Macmillan, 1 New York Plaza, Ste. 4500, New York, NY, 10004-1562, USA, (800) 777-4643, orders@palgrave.com, https://www.palgrave.com/us; The Statesman's Yearbook, 2023.

Routledge - Taylor & Francis Group, 6000 Broken Sound Pkwy. NW, Ste. 300, Boca Raton, FL, 33487, USA, (800) 634-1420, (800) 634-7064, orders@taylorandfrancis.com, https://www.routledge.com/; The Europa World Year Book 2022.

United Nations Food and Agricultural Organization (FAO), 2121 K St., Ste. 800B, Washington, DC, 20037, USA, (202) 653-2400 (Dial from U.S.), (202) 653-5760 (Fax from U.S.), fao-hq@fao.org, https://www.fao.org; FAO Yearbook of Fishery and Aquaculture Statistics 2019; Fishery Statistical Collections Global Capture Production; FishStatJ; and The State of Food and Agriculture (SOFA) 2022.

United Nations Statistics Division (UNSD), United Nations Plz., New York, NY, 10017, USA, (800) 253-9646, (212) 963-9851, statistics@un.org, https://unstats.un.org; Statistical Yearbook of the United Nations 2021.

BRUNEI-FOOD

United Nations Economic and Social Commission for Asia and the Pacific (ESCAP), United Nations Building, Rajadamnern Nok Ave., Bangkok, 10200, THA, https://www.unescap.org/; SDG Gateway Data Explorer.

United Nations Food and Agricultural Organization (FAO), 2121 K St., Ste. 800B, Washington, DC, 20037, USA, (202) 653-2400 (Dial from U.S.), (202) 653-5760 (Fax from U.S.), fao-hq@fao.org, https://www.fao.org; The State of Food and Agriculture (SOFA) 2022.

BRUNEI-FORESTS AND FORESTRY

Palgrave Macmillan, 1 New York Plaza, Ste. 4500, New York, NY, 10004-1562, USA, (800) 777-4643, orders@palgrave.com, https://www.palgrave.com/us; The Statesman's Yearbook, 2023.

Routledge - Taylor & Francis Group, 6000 Broken Sound Pkwy. NW, Ste. 300, Boca Raton, FL, 33487, USA, (800) 634-1420, (800) 634-7064, orders@taylorandfrancis.com, https://www.routledge.com/; The Europa World Year Book 2022.

UNESCO Institute for Statistics, C.P 250 Succursale H, Montreal, QC, H3G 2K8, CAN, (514) 343-6880 (Dial from U.S.), (514) 343-5740 (Fax from U.S.), uis.publications@unesco.org, http://uis.unesco.org/; UIS.Stat.

United Nations Food and Agricultural Organization (FAO), 2121 K St., Ste. 800B, Washington, DC, 20037, USA, (202) 653-2400 (Dial from U.S.), (202) 653-5760 (Fax from U.S.), fao-hq@fao.org, https://www.fao.org; FAO Yearbook of Forest Products 2019 and The State of Food and Agriculture (SOFA) 2022.

United Nations Statistics Division (UNSD), United Nations Plz., New York, NY, 10017, USA, (800) 253-9646, (212) 963-9851, statistics@un.org, https://unstats.un.org; Statistical Yearbook of the United Nations 2021.

BRUNEI-GAS PRODUCTION

See BRUNEI-MINERAL INDUSTRIES

BRUNEI-GROSS DOMESTIC PRODUCT

The Economist Group: Economist Intelligence Unit (EIU), 900 3rd Ave., 16th Fl., New York, NY, 10022, USA, (212) 541-0500, americas@eiu.com, https://www.eiu.com; Brunei Country Report.

Routledge - Taylor & Francis Group, 6000 Broken Sound Pkwy. NW, Ste. 300, Boca Raton, FL, 33487,

USA, (800) 634-1420, (800) 634-7064, orders@taylorandfrancis.com, https://www.routledge.com/; The Europa World Year Book 2022.

United Nations Statistics Division (UNSD), United Nations Plz., New York, NY, 10017, USA, (800) 253-9646, (212) 963-9851, statistics@un.org, https://unstats.un.org; Statistical Yearbook of the United Nations 2021.

BRUNEI-GROSS NATIONAL PRODUCT

Palgrave Macmillan, 1 New York Plaza, Ste. 4500, New York, NY, 10004-1562, USA, (800) 777-4643, orders@palgrave.com, https://www.palgrave.com/us; The Statesman's Yearbook, 2023.

BRUNEI-HOUSING

Euromonitor International, Inc., 1 N Dearborn St., Ste. 1700, Chicago, IL, 60602, USA, (312) 922-1115, (312) 922-1157, info-usa@euromonitor.com, https://www.euromonitor.com/; Geographies.

BRUNEI-ILLITERATE PERSONS

UNESCO Institute for Statistics, C.P 250 Succursale H, Montreal, QC, H3G 2K8, CAN, (514) 343-6880 (Dial from U.S.), (514) 343-5740 (Fax from U.S.), uis.publications@unesco.org, http://uis.unesco.org/; UIS.Stat.

United Nations Economic and Social Commission for Asia and the Pacific (ESCAP), United Nations Building, Rajadamnern Nok Ave., Bangkok, 10200, THA, https://www.unescap.org/; Asia-Pacific Development Journal.

BRUNEI-IMPORTS

Central Intelligence Agency (CIA), Office of Public Affairs, Washington, DC, 20505, USA, (703) 482-0623, https://www.cia.gov; The World Factbook.

The Economist Group: Economist Intelligence Unit (EIU), 900 3rd Ave., 16th Fl., New York, NY, 10022, USA, (212) 541-0500, americas@eiu.com, https://www.eiu.com; Brunei Country Report.

International Monetary Fund (IMF), 700 19th St. NW, Washington, DC, 20431, USA, (202) 623-7000, (202) 623-4661, publications@imf.org, https://www.imf.org; Direction of Trade Statistics (DOTS).

S&P Global, IHS Markit, 15 Inverness Way E, Englewood, CO, 80112, USA, (800) 447-2273, (800) 854-7179, https://ihsmarkit.com; Global Trade Atlas (GTA).

BRUNEI-INDUSTRIES

Central Intelligence Agency (CIA), Office of Public Affairs, Washington, DC, 20505, USA, (703) 482-0623, https://www.cia.gov; The World Factbook.

The Economist Group: Economist Intelligence Unit (EIU), 900 3rd Ave., 16th Fl., New York, NY, 10022, USA, (212) 541-0500, americas@eiu.com, https://www.eiu.com; Brunei Country Report.

Euromonitor International, Inc., 1 N Dearborn St., Ste. 1700, Chicago, IL, 60602, USA, (312) 922-1115, (312) 922-1157, info-usa@euromonitor.com, https://www.euromonitor.com/; Geographies.

International Labour Organization (ILO), 4 Rte. des Morillons, Geneva, CH-1211, SWI, ilo@ilo.org, https://www.ilo.org; NORMLEX Information System on International Labour Standards.

Palgrave Macmillan, 1 New York Plaza, Ste. 4500, New York, NY, 10004-1562, USA, (800) 777-4643, orders@palgrave.com, https://www.palgrave.com/us; The Statesman's Yearbook, 2023.

Routledge - Taylor & Francis Group, 6000 Broken Sound Pkwy. NW, Ste. 300, Boca Raton, FL, 33487, USA, (800) 634-1420, (800) 634-7064, orders@taylorandfrancis.com, https://www.routledge.com/; The Europa World Year Book 2022.

United Nations Economic and Social Commission for Asia and the Pacific (ESCAP), United Nations Building, Rajadamnern Nok Ave., Bangkok, 10200, THA, https://www.unescap.org/; Asia-Pacific Development Journal and SDG Gateway Data Explorer.

United Nations Industrial Development Organization (UNIDO), 1 United Nations Plz., Rm. DC1-1118, New York, NY, 10017, USA, (212) 963-6890, (212) 963 6885, (212) 963-7904, office.newyork@unido.org, https://www.unido.org/; Industrial Statistics Databases and International Yearbook of Industrial Statistics 2021.

BRUNEI-INFANT AND MATERNAL MORTALITY

See BRUNEI-MORTALITY

BRUNEI-INTERNATIONAL TRADE

Asia Pacific Economic Cooperation (APEC), 35 Heng Mui Keng Terrace, 119616, SGP, info@apec.org, https://www.apec.org/; APEC Regional Trends Analysis - What Goes Around Comes Around: Pivoting to a Circular Economy; Uncertainty Tests APEC's Resilience amid COVID-19.

The Economist Group: Economist Intelligence Unit (EIU), 900 3rd Ave., 16th Fl., New York, NY, 10022, USA, (212) 541-0500, americas@eiu.com, https://www.eiu.com; Brunei Country Report.

Euromonitor International, Inc., 1 N Dearborn St., Ste. 1700, Chicago, IL, 60602, USA, (312) 922-1115, (312) 922-1157, info-usa@euromonitor.com, https://www.euromonitor.com/; Geographies.

Palgrave Macmillan, 1 New York Plaza, Ste. 4500, New York, NY, 10004-1562, USA, (800) 777-4643, orders@palgrave.com, https://www.palgrave.com/us; The Statesman's Yearbook, 2023.

Routledge - Taylor & Francis Group, 6000 Broken Sound Pkwy. NW, Ste. 300, Boca Raton, FL, 33487, USA, (800) 634-1420, (800) 634-7064, orders@taylorandfrancis.com, https://www.routledge.com/; The Europa World Year Book 2022.

United Nations Conference on Trade and Development (UNCTAD), Palais des Nations, Geneva, 1211, SWI, (212) 963-6896, unctadinfo@unctad.org, https://unctad.org; Trade and Development Report 2021.

United Nations Economic and Social Commission for Asia and the Pacific (ESCAP), United Nations Building, Rajadamnern Nok Ave., Bangkok, 10200, THA, https://www.unescap.org/; Asia-Pacific Development Journal.

United Nations Food and Agricultural Organization (FAO), 2121 K St., Ste. 800B, Washington, DC, 20037, USA, (202) 653-2400 (Dial from U.S.), (202) 653-5760 (Fax from U.S.), fao-hq@fao.org, https://www.fao.org; The State of Food and Agriculture (SOFA) 2022.

United Nations Statistics Division (UNSD), United Nations Plz., New York, NY, 10017, USA, (800) 253-9646, (212) 963-9851, statistics@un.org, https://unstats.un.org; International Trade Statistics Yearbook 2020 and Statistical Yearbook of the United Nations 2021.

World Trade Organization (WTO), Ctre. William Rappard, Rue de Lausanne 154, Case postale, Geneva, CH-1211, SWI, enquiries@wto.org, https://www.wto.org; World Trade Statistical Review 2022.

BRUNEI-INTERNET USERS

International Telecommunication Union (ITU), Place des Nations, Geneva, CH-1211, SWI, itumail@itu.int, https://www.itu.int; Global Connectivity Report 2022; World Telecommunication/ICT Indicators Database 2021; and Yearbook of Statistics 2019.

BRUNEI-LABOR

Central Intelligence Agency (CIA), Office of Public Affairs, Washington, DC, 20505, USA, (703) 482-0623, https://www.cia.gov; The World Factbook.

Euromonitor International, Inc., 1 N Dearborn St., Ste. 1700, Chicago, IL, 60602, USA, (312) 922-1115, (312) 922-1157, info-usa@euromonitor.com, https://www.euromonitor.com/; Geographies.

International Labour Organization (ILO), 4 Rte. des Morillons, Geneva, CH-1211, SWI, ilo@ilo.org, https://www.ilo.org; NORMLEX Information System on International Labour Standards.

Organisation of Islamic Cooperation (OIC), Statistical, Economic and Social Research and Training Centre for Islamic Countries (SESRIC), Kudus Cad. No. 9, Diplomatik Site, Ankara, 06450, TUR, statistics@sesric.org, https://www.sesric.org/; OIC Statistics (OICStat) Database.

Palgrave Macmillan, 1 New York Plaza, Ste. 4500, New York, NY, 10004-1562, USA, (800) 777-4643, orders@palgrave.com, https://www.palgrave.com/us; The Statesman's Yearbook, 2023.

United Nations Food and Agricultural Organization (FAO), 2121 K St., Ste. 800B, Washington, DC, 20037, USA, (202) 653-2400 (Dial from U.S.), (202) 653-5760 (Fax from U.S.), fao-hq@fao.org, https://www.fao.org; The State of Food and Agriculture (SOFA) 2022.

BRUNEI-LAND USE

United Nations Statistics Division (UNSD), United Nations Plz., New York, NY, 10017, USA, (800) 253-9646, (212) 963-9851, statistics@un.org, https://unstats.un.org; Millennium Development Goal Indicators.

BRUNEI-LIBRARIES

UNESCO Institute for Statistics, C.P 250 Succursale H, Montreal, QC, H3G 2K8, CAN, (514) 343-6880 (Dial from U.S.), (514) 343-5740 (Fax from U.S.), uis.publications@unesco.org, http://uis.unesco.org/; UIS.Stat.

BRUNEI-LIFE EXPECTANCY

Central Intelligence Agency (CIA), Office of Public Affairs, Washington, DC, 20505, USA, (703) 482-0623, https://www.cia.gov; The World Factbook.

United Nations Department of Economic and Social Affairs (DESA), Population Division, 2 United Nations Plz., Rm. DC2-1950, New York, NY, 10017, USA, (212) 963-3209, (212) 963-2147, population@un.org, https://www.un.org/development/desa/pd/; World Population Ageing 2020 Highlights.

United Nations Economic and Social Commission for Asia and the Pacific (ESCAP), United Nations Building, Rajadamnern Nok Ave., Bangkok, 10200, THA, https://www.unescap.org/; Asia-Pacific Development Journal.

United Nations Statistics Division (UNSD), United Nations Plz., New York, NY, 10017, USA, (800) 253-9646, (212) 963-9851, statistics@un.org, https://unstats.un.org; Millennium Development Goal Indicators.

BRUNEI-LITERACY

Euromonitor International, Inc., 1 N Dearborn St., Ste. 1700, Chicago, IL, 60602, USA, (312) 922-1115, (312) 922-1157, info-usa@euromonitor.com, https://www.euromonitor.com/; Geographies.

UNESCO Institute for Statistics, C.P 250 Succursale H, Montreal, QC, H3G 2K8, CAN, (514) 343-6880 (Dial from U.S.), (514) 343-5740 (Fax from U.S.), uis.publications@unesco.org, http://uis.unesco.org/; Literacy.

BRUNEI-LIVESTOCK

Palgrave Macmillan, 1 New York Plaza, Ste. 4500, New York, NY, 10004-1562, USA, (800) 777-4643, orders@palgrave.com, https://www.palgrave.com/us; The Statesman's Yearbook, 2023.

Routledge - Taylor & Francis Group, 6000 Broken Sound Pkwy. NW, Ste. 300, Boca Raton, FL, 33487, USA, (800) 634-1420, (800) 634-7064, orders@taylorandfrancis.com, https://www.routledge.com/; The Europa World Year Book 2022.

United Nations Food and Agricultural Organization (FAO), 2121 K St., Ste. 800B, Washington, DC, 20037, USA, (202) 653-2400 (Dial from U.S.), (202) 653-5760 (Fax from U.S.), fao-hq@fao.org, https://www.fao.org; The State of Food and Agriculture (SOFA) 2022.

United Nations Statistics Division (UNSD), United Nations Plz., New York, NY, 10017, USA, (800) 253-

9646, (212) 963-9851, statistics@un.org, https://unstats.un.org; Statistical Yearbook of the United Nations 2021.

BRUNEI-MANPOWER

United Nations Economic and Social Commission for Asia and the Pacific (ESCAP), United Nations Building, Rajadamnern Nok Ave., Bangkok, 10200, THA, https://www.unescap.org/; SDG Gateway Data Explorer.

BRUNEI-MARRIAGE

Routledge - Taylor & Francis Group, 6000 Broken Sound Pkwy. NW, Ste. 300, Boca Raton, FL, 33487, USA, (800) 634-1420, (800) 634-7064, orders@taylorandfrancis.com, https://www.routledge.com/; The Europa World Year Book 2022.

United Nations Statistics Division (UNSD), United Nations Plz., New York, NY, 10017, USA, (800) 253-9646, (212) 963-9851, statistics@un.org, https://unstats.un.org; Statistical Yearbook of the United Nations 2021.

BRUNEI-MINERAL INDUSTRIES

International Energy Agency (IEA), 9 Rue de la Federation, Paris, 75739, FRA, info@iea.org, https://www.iea.org/; World Energy Outlook 2021.

Palgrave Macmillan, 1 New York Plaza, Ste. 4500, New York, NY, 10004-1562, USA, (800) 777-4643, orders@palgrave.com, https://www.palgrave.com/us; The Statesman's Yearbook, 2023.

Routledge - Taylor & Francis Group, 6000 Broken Sound Pkwy. NW, Ste. 300, Boca Raton, FL, 33487, USA, (800) 634-1420, (800) 634-7064, orders@taylorandfrancis.com, https://www.routledge.com/; The Europa World Year Book 2022.

United Nations Conference on Trade and Development (UNCTAD), Palais des Nations, Geneva, 1211, SWI, (212) 963-6896, unctadinfo@unctad.org, https://unctad.org; Trade and Development Report 2021.

United Nations Statistics Division (UNSD), United Nations Plz., New York, NY, 10017, USA, (800) 253-9646, (212) 963-9851, statistics@un.org, https://unstats.un.org; Statistical Yearbook of the United Nations 2021.

BRUNEI-MONEY SUPPLY

The Economist Group: Economist Intelligence Unit (EIU), 900 3rd Ave., 16th Fl., New York, NY, 10022, USA, (212) 541-0500, americas@eiu.com, https://www.eiu.com; Brunei Country Report.

BRUNEI-MORTALITY

United Nations Economic and Social Commission for Asia and the Pacific (ESCAP), United Nations Building, Rajadamnern Nok Ave., Bangkok, 10200, THA, https://www.unescap.org/; Asia-Pacific Development Journal.

United Nations Statistics Division (UNSD), United Nations Plz., New York, NY, 10017, USA, (800) 253-9646, (212) 963-9851, statistics@un.org, https://unstats.un.org; Millennium Development Goal Indicators; Statistical Yearbook of the United Nations 2021; and World Statistics Pocketbook 2021.

World Health Organization (WHO), Ave. Appia 20, Geneva, CH-1211, SWI, (202) 974-3000 (Telephone in U.S.), publications@who.int, https://www.who.int/; Global Health Observatory (GHO).

BRUNEI-NATURAL GAS PRODUCTION

See BRUNEI-MINERAL INDUSTRIES

BRUNEI-NUTRITION

United Nations Food and Agricultural Organization (FAO), 2121 K St., Ste. 800B, Washington, DC, 20037, USA, (202) 653-2400 (Dial from U.S.), (202) 653-5760 (Fax from U.S.), fao-hq@fao.org, https://www.fao.org; The State of Food and Agriculture (SOFA) 2022.

United Nations Statistics Division (UNSD), United Nations Plz., New York, NY, 10017, USA, (800) 253-9646, (212) 963-9851, statistics@un.org, https://unstats.un.org; Millennium Development Goal Indicators.

BRUNEI-PAPER

See BRUNEI-FORESTS AND FORESTRY

BRUNEI-PESTICIDES

United Nations Food and Agricultural Organization (FAO), 2121 K St., Ste. 800B, Washington, DC, 20037, USA, (202) 653-2400 (Dial from U.S.), (202) 653-5760 (Fax from U.S.), fao-hq@fao.org, https://www.fao.org; The State of Food and Agriculture (SOFA) 2022.

BRUNEI-PETROLEUM INDUSTRY AND TRADE

International Energy Agency (IEA), 9 Rue de la Federation, Paris, 75739, FRA, info@iea.org, https://www.iea.org/; World Energy Outlook 2021.

Palgrave Macmillan, 1 New York Plaza, Ste. 4500, New York, NY, 10004-1562, USA, (800) 777-4643, orders@palgrave.com, https://www.palgrave.com/us; The Statesman's Yearbook, 2023.

U.S. Energy Information Administration (EIA), 1000 Independence Ave. SW, Washington, DC, 20585, USA, (202) 586-8800, infoctr@eia.gov, https://www.eia.gov; International Energy Outlook 2021.

United Nations Food and Agricultural Organization (FAO), 2121 K St., Ste. 800B, Washington, DC, 20037, USA, (202) 653-2400 (Dial from U.S.), (202) 653-5760 (Fax from U.S.), fao-hq@fao.org, https://www.fao.org; The State of Food and Agriculture (SOFA) 2022.

United Nations Statistics Division (UNSD), United Nations Plz., New York, NY, 10017, USA, (800) 253-9646, (212) 963-9851, statistics@un.org, https://unstats.un.org; Statistical Yearbook of the United Nations 2021.

BRUNEI-POPULATION

Central Intelligence Agency (CIA), Office of Public Affairs, Washington, DC, 20505, USA, (703) 482-0623, https://www.cia.gov; The World Factbook.

The Economist Group: Economist Intelligence Unit (EIU), 900 3rd Ave., 16th Fl., New York, NY, 10022, USA, (212) 541-0500, americas@eiu.com, https://www.eiu.com; Brunei Country Report.

Infoplease, c/o Sandbox Networks, Inc., 1 Lincoln St., 24th Fl., Boston, MA, 02111, USA, https://www.infoplease.com; Countries of the World.

International Labour Organization (ILO), 4 Rte. des Morillons, Geneva, CH-1211, SWI, ilo@ilo.org, https://www.ilo.org; NORMLEX Information System on International Labour Standards.

Palgrave Macmillan, 1 New York Plaza, Ste. 4500, New York, NY, 10004-1562, USA, (800) 777-4643, orders@palgrave.com, https://www.palgrave.com/us; The Statesman's Yearbook, 2023.

Routledge - Taylor & Francis Group, 6000 Broken Sound Pkwy. NW, Ste. 300, Boca Raton, FL, 33487, USA, (800) 634-1420, (800) 634-7064, orders@taylorandfrancis.com, https://www.routledge.com/; The Europa World Year Book 2022.

UK Data Service, University of Essex, Wivenhoe Park, Colchester, Essex, CO4 3SQ, GBR, https://ukdataservice.ac.uk/; International Aggregate Data.

UNESCO Institute for Statistics, C.P 250 Succursale H, Montreal, QC, H3G 2K8, CAN, (514) 343-6880 (Dial from U.S.), (514) 343-5740 (Fax from U.S.), uis.publications@unesco.org, http://uis.unesco.org/; UIS.Stat.

United Nations Department of Economic and Social Affairs (DESA), Population Division, 2 United Nations Plz., Rm. DC2-1950, New York, NY, 10017, USA, (212) 963-3209, (212) 963-2147, population@un.org, https://www.un.org/development/desa/pd/; Revision of World Urbanization Prospects and World Population Ageing 2020 Highlights.

United Nations Development Programme (UNDP), One United Nations Plz., New York, NY, 10017, USA, (212) 906-5000, (212) 906-5001, https://www.undp.org; Human Development Report 2021-2022.

United Nations Economic and Social Commission for Asia and the Pacific (ESCAP), United Nations Building, Rajadamnern Nok Ave., Bangkok, 10200, THA, https://www.unescap.org/; Asia-Pacific Development Journal and SDG Gateway Data Explorer.

United Nations Statistics Division (UNSD), United Nations Plz., New York, NY, 10017, USA, (800) 253-9646, (212) 963-9851, statistics@un.org, https://unstats.un.org; Statistical Yearbook of the United Nations 2021.

The World Bank, 1818 H St. NW, Washington, DC, 20433, USA, (202) 473-1000, (202) 477-6391, eds03@worldbank.org, https://www.worldbank.org/; The Global Findex Database 2021.

BRUNEI-POPULATION DENSITY

Central Intelligence Agency (CIA), Office of Public Affairs, Washington, DC, 20505, USA, (703) 482-0623, https://www.cia.gov; The World Factbook.

Palgrave Macmillan, 1 New York Plaza, Ste. 4500, New York, NY, 10004-1562, USA, (800) 777-4643, orders@palgrave.com, https://www.palgrave.com/us; The Statesman's Yearbook, 2023.

Routledge - Taylor & Francis Group, 6000 Broken Sound Pkwy. NW, Ste. 300, Boca Raton, FL, 33487, USA, (800) 634-1420, (800) 634-7064, orders@taylorandfrancis.com, https://www.routledge.com/; The Europa World Year Book 2022.

BRUNEI-POSTAL SERVICE

Palgrave Macmillan, 1 New York Plaza, Ste. 4500, New York, NY, 10004-1562, USA, (800) 777-4643, orders@palgrave.com, https://www.palgrave.com/us; The Statesman's Yearbook, 2023.

BRUNEI-POWER RESOURCES

Euromonitor International, Inc., 1 N Dearborn St., Ste. 1700, Chicago, IL, 60602, USA, (312) 922-1115, (312) 922-1157, info-usa@euromonitor.com, https://www.euromonitor.com/; Geographies.

International Energy Agency (IEA), 9 Rue de la Federation, Paris, 75739, FRA, info@iea.org, https://www.iea.org/; World Energy Outlook 2021.

Palgrave Macmillan, 1 New York Plaza, Ste. 4500, New York, NY, 10004-1562, USA, (800) 777-4643, orders@palgrave.com, https://www.palgrave.com/us; The Statesman's Yearbook, 2023.

U.S. Energy Information Administration (EIA), 1000 Independence Ave. SW, Washington, DC, 20585, USA, (202) 586-8800, infoctr@eia.gov, https://www.eia.gov; International Energy Outlook 2021.

United Nations Economic and Social Commission for Asia and the Pacific (ESCAP), United Nations Building, Rajadamnern Nok Ave., Bangkok, 10200, THA, https://www.unescap.org/; Asia-Pacific Development Journal and SDG Gateway Data Explorer.

United Nations Food and Agricultural Organization (FAO), 2121 K St., Ste. 800B, Washington, DC, 20037, USA, (202) 653-2400 (Dial from U.S.), (202) 653-5760 (Fax from U.S.), fao-hq@fao.org, https://www.fao.org; The State of Food and Agriculture (SOFA) 2022.

United Nations Statistics Division (UNSD), United Nations Plz., New York, NY, 10017, USA, (800) 253-9646, (212) 963-9851, statistics@un.org, https://unstats.un.org; Energy Statistics Yearbook 2019 and World Statistics Pocketbook 2021.

BRUNEI-PRICES

Euromonitor International, Inc., 1 N Dearborn St., Ste. 1700, Chicago, IL, 60602, USA, (312) 922-1115, (312) 922-1157, info-usa@euromonitor.com, https://www.euromonitor.com/; Geographies.

BRUNEI-PUBLIC HEALTH

Euromonitor International, Inc., 1 N Dearborn St., Ste. 1700, Chicago, IL, 60602, USA, (312) 922-

1115, (312) 922-1157, info-usa@euromonitor.com, https://www.euromonitor.com/; Geographies.

Organisation of Islamic Cooperation (OIC), Statistical, Economic and Social Research and Training Centre for Islamic Countries (SESRIC), Kudus Cad. No. 9, Diplomatik Site, Ankara, 06450, TUR, statistics@sesric.org, https://www.sesric.org/; OIC Statistics (OICStat) Database.

Palgrave Macmillan, 1 New York Plaza, Ste. 4500, New York, NY, 10004-1562, USA, (800) 777-4643, orders@palgrave.com, https://www.palgrave.com/us; The Statesman's Yearbook, 2023.

U.S. Census Bureau, 4600 Silver Hill Rd., Washington, DC, 20233, USA, (301) 763-4636, (800) 923-8282, https://www.census.gov; HIV/AIDS Surveillance Data Base.

United Nations Department of Economic and Social Affairs (DESA), Population Division, 2 United Nations Plz., Rm. DC2-1950, New York, NY, 10017, USA, (212) 963-3209, (212) 963-2147, population@un.org, https://www.un.org/development/desa/pd/; World Fertility Data 2019.

United Nations Development Programme (UNDP), One United Nations Plz., New York, NY, 10017, USA, (212) 906-5000, (212) 906-5001, https://www.undp.org; Human Development Report 2021-2022.

United Nations Economic and Social Commission for Asia and the Pacific (ESCAP), United Nations Building, Rajadamnern Nok Ave., Bangkok, 10200, THA, https://www.unescap.org/; Asia-Pacific Development Journal.

United Nations Statistics Division (UNSD), United Nations Plz., New York, NY, 10017, USA, (800) 253-9646, (212) 963-9851, statistics@un.org, https://unstats.un.org; Millennium Development Goal Indicators and Statistical Yearbook of the United Nations 2021.

World Health Organization (WHO), Ave. Appia 20, Geneva, CH-1211, SWI, (202) 974-3000 (Telephone in U.S.), publications@who.int, https://www.who.int/; Global Health Observatory (GHO) and Health Statistics and Information Systems.

BRUNEI-PUBLISHERS AND PUBLISHING

Routledge - Taylor & Francis Group, 6000 Broken Sound Pkwy. NW, Ste. 300, Boca Raton, FL, 33487, USA, (800) 634-1420, (800) 634-7064, orders@taylorandfrancis.com, https://www.routledge.com/; The Europa World Year Book 2022.

UNESCO Institute for Statistics, C.P 250 Succursale H, Montreal, QC, H3G 2K8, CAN, (514) 343-6880 (Dial from U.S.), (514) 343-5740 (Fax from U.S.), uis.publications@unesco.org, http://uis.unesco.org/; UIS.Stat.

BRUNEI-RELIGION

Central Intelligence Agency (CIA), Office of Public Affairs, Washington, DC, 20505, USA, (703) 482-0623, https://www.cia.gov; The World Factbook.

Palgrave Macmillan, 1 New York Plaza, Ste. 4500, New York, NY, 10004-1562, USA, (800) 777-4643, orders@palgrave.com, https://www.palgrave.com/us; The Statesman's Yearbook, 2023.

BRUNEI-RETAIL TRADE

Euromonitor International, Inc., 1 N Dearborn St., Ste. 1700, Chicago, IL, 60602, USA, (312) 922-1115, (312) 922-1157, info-usa@euromonitor.com, https://www.euromonitor.com/; Geographies.

BRUNEI-RICE PRODUCTION

See BRUNEI-CROPS

BRUNEI-SHIPPING

Routledge - Taylor & Francis Group, 6000 Broken Sound Pkwy. NW, Ste. 300, Boca Raton, FL, 33487, USA, (800) 634-1420, (800) 634-7064, orders@taylorandfrancis.com, https://www.routledge.com/; The Europa World Year Book 2022.

United Nations Statistics Division (UNSD), United Nations Plz., New York, NY, 10017, USA, (800) 253-9646, (212) 963-9851, statistics@un.org, https://unstats.un.org; Statistical Yearbook of the United Nations 2021.

BRUNEI-TELEPHONE

Routledge - Taylor & Francis Group, 6000 Broken Sound Pkwy. NW, Ste. 300, Boca Raton, FL, 33487, USA, (800) 634-1420, (800) 634-7064, orders@taylorandfrancis.com, https://www.routledge.com/; The Europa World Year Book 2022.

United Nations Statistics Division (UNSD), United Nations Plz., New York, NY, 10017, USA, (800) 253-9646, (212) 963-9851, statistics@un.org, https://unstats.un.org; World Statistics Pocketbook 2021.

BRUNEI-THEATER

UNESCO Institute for Statistics, C.P 250 Succursale H, Montreal, QC, H3G 2K8, CAN, (514) 343-6880 (Dial from U.S.), (514) 343-5740 (Fax from U.S.), uis.publications@unesco.org, http://uis.unesco.org/; UIS.Stat.

BRUNEI-TOURISM

Euromonitor International, Inc., 1 N Dearborn St., Ste. 1700, Chicago, IL, 60602, USA, (312) 922-1115, (312) 922-1157, info-usa@euromonitor.com, https://www.euromonitor.com/; Geographies.

Organisation of Islamic Cooperation (OIC), Statistical, Economic and Social Research and Training Centre for Islamic Countries (SESRIC), Kudus Cad. No. 9, Diplomatik Site, Ankara, 06450, TUR, statistics@sesric.org, https://www.sesric.org/; International Tourism in the OIC Countries: Prospects and Challenges, 2020 and OIC Statistics (OICStat) Database.

Palgrave Macmillan, 1 New York Plaza, Ste. 4500, New York, NY, 10004-1562, USA, (800) 777-4643, orders@palgrave.com, https://www.palgrave.com/us; The Statesman's Yearbook, 2023.

Routledge - Taylor & Francis Group, 6000 Broken Sound Pkwy. NW, Ste. 300, Boca Raton, FL, 33487, USA, (800) 634-1420, (800) 634-7064, orders@taylorandfrancis.com, https://www.routledge.com/; The Europa World Year Book 2022.

United Nations World Tourism Organization (UNWTO), Calle Poeta Joan Maragall 42, Madrid, 28020, SPA, info@unwto.org, https://www.unwto.org/; Yearbook of Tourism Statistics, 2021 Edition.

BRUNEI-TRADE

See BRUNEI-INTERNATIONAL TRADE

BRUNEI-TRANSPORTATION

Central Intelligence Agency (CIA), Office of Public Affairs, Washington, DC, 20505, USA, (703) 482-0623, https://www.cia.gov; The World Factbook.

Euromonitor International, Inc., 1 N Dearborn St., Ste. 1700, Chicago, IL, 60602, USA, (312) 922-1115, (312) 922-1157, info-usa@euromonitor.com, https://www.euromonitor.com/; Geographies.

Organisation of Islamic Cooperation (OIC), Statistical, Economic and Social Research and Training Centre for Islamic Countries (SESRIC), Kudus Cad. No. 9, Diplomatik Site, Ankara, 06450, TUR, statistics@sesric.org, https://www.sesric.org/; OIC Statistics (OICStat) Database.

Routledge - Taylor & Francis Group, 6000 Broken Sound Pkwy. NW, Ste. 300, Boca Raton, FL, 33487, USA, (800) 634-1420, (800) 634-7064, orders@taylorandfrancis.com, https://www.routledge.com/; The Europa World Year Book 2022.

United Nations Economic and Social Commission for Asia and the Pacific (ESCAP), United Nations Building, Rajadamnern Nok Ave., Bangkok, 10200, THA, https://www.unescap.org/; SDG Gateway Data Explorer.

BRUNEI-UNEMPLOYMENT

International Labour Organization (ILO), 4 Rte. des Morillons, Geneva, CH-1211, SWI, ilo@ilo.org, https://www.ilo.org; NORMLEX Information System on International Labour Standards.

United Nations Statistics Division (UNSD), United Nations Plz., New York, NY, 10017, USA, (800) 253-9646, (212) 963-9851, statistics@un.org, https://unstats.un.org; Statistical Yearbook of the United Nations 2021.

BRUNEI-VITAL STATISTICS

Palgrave Macmillan, 1 New York Plaza, Ste. 4500, New York, NY, 10004-1562, USA, (800) 777-4643, orders@palgrave.com, https://www.palgrave.com/us; The Statesman's Yearbook, 2023.

U.S. Census Bureau, 4600 Silver Hill Rd., Washington, DC, 20233, USA, (301) 763-4636, (800) 923-8282, https://www.census.gov; HIV/AIDS Surveillance Data Base.

United Nations Department of Economic and Social Affairs (DESA), Population Division, 2 United Nations Plz., Rm. DC2-1950, New York, NY, 10017, USA, (212) 963-3209, (212) 963-2147, population@un.org, https://www.un.org/development/desa/pd/; World Contraceptive Use 2021: Estimates and Projections of Family Planning Indicators and World Marriage Data 2019.

United Nations Statistics Division (UNSD), United Nations Plz., New York, NY, 10017, USA, (800) 253-9646, (212) 963-9851, statistics@un.org, https://unstats.un.org; Statistical Yearbook of the United Nations 2021.

BRUNEI-WAGES

International Labour Organization (ILO), 4 Rte. des Morillons, Geneva, CH-1211, SWI, ilo@ilo.org, https://www.ilo.org; NORMLEX Information System on International Labour Standards.

United Nations Economic and Social Commission for Asia and the Pacific (ESCAP), United Nations Building, Rajadamnern Nok Ave., Bangkok, 10200, THA, https://www.unescap.org/; SDG Gateway Data Explorer.

United Nations Statistics Division (UNSD), United Nations Plz., New York, NY, 10017, USA, (800) 253-9646, (212) 963-9851, statistics@un.org, https://unstats.un.org; Statistical Yearbook of the United Nations 2021.

BRUNEI-ZOOS

UNESCO Institute for Statistics, C.P 250 Succursale H, Montreal, QC, H3G 2K8, CAN, (514) 343-6880 (Dial from U.S.), (514) 343-5740 (Fax from U.S.), uis.publications@unesco.org, http://uis.unesco.org/; UIS.Stat.

BUDDHIST POPULATION

See RELIGION

BUDGET, FEDERAL-OUTLAYS

Monmouth University Polling Institute, 400 Cedar Ave., West Long Branch, NJ, 07764, USA, (732) 263-5860, polling@monmouth.edu, https://www.monmouth.edu/polling-institute/; Biden Spending Plans Remain Popular.

PollingReport.com, USA, https://www.pollingreport.com/; Issues Facing the Nation.

Trust for America's Health (TFAH), 1730 M St. NW, Ste. 900, Washington, DC, 20036, USA, (202) 223-9870, (202) 223-9871, info@tfah.org, https://www.tfah.org/; The Impact of Chronic Underfunding of America's Public Health System: Trends, Risks, and Recommendations, 2022.

U.S. Department of Defense (DOD), 1400 Defense Pentagon, Washington, DC, 20301-1400, USA, (703) 571-3343, https://www.defense.gov; Agency Financial Report: Fiscal Year 2021.

U.S. Office of Management and Budget (OMB), 725 17th St. NW, Washington, DC, 20503, USA, (202) 395-3080, https://www.whitehouse.gov/omb/; Budget of the United States Government, Fiscal Year 2023 and Historical Tables.

The Urban Institute, 500 L'Enfant Plaza SW, Washington, DC, 20024, USA, (202) 833-7200, https://

www.urban.org/; Kids' Share 2022: Report on Federal Expenditures on Children through 2021 and Future Projections.

BUDGET, FEDERAL-RECEIPTS

U.S. Office of Management and Budget (OMB), 725 17th St. NW, Washington, DC, 20503, USA, (202) 395-3080, https://www.whitehouse.gov/omb/; Historical Tables.

BUDGET, FEDERAL-REVENUE LOSSES (TAX EXPENDITURES)

U.S. Office of Management and Budget (OMB), 725 17th St. NW, Washington, DC, 20503, USA, (202) 395-3080, https://www.whitehouse.gov/omb/; Budget of the United States Government, Fiscal Year 2023.

BUDGET, FEDERAL-TAX EXPENDITURES

U.S. Office of Management and Budget (OMB), 725 17th St. NW, Washington, DC, 20503, USA, (202) 395-3080, https://www.whitehouse.gov/omb/; Budget of the United States Government, Fiscal Year 2023.

BUDGET, FEDERAL-TAXES

U.S. Office of Management and Budget (OMB), 725 17th St. NW, Washington, DC, 20503, USA, (202) 395-3080, https://www.whitehouse.gov/omb/; Budget of the United States Government, Fiscal Year 2023 and Historical Tables.

BUDGET, FEDERAL-TRUST FUNDS

U.S. Office of Management and Budget (OMB), 725 17th St. NW, Washington, DC, 20503, USA, (202) 395-3080, https://www.whitehouse.gov/omb/; Analytical Perspectives: Budget of the United States Government and Budget of the United States Government, Fiscal Year 2023.

BUILDING CONTRACTORS, GENERAL-EARNINGS

U.S. Census Bureau, 4600 Silver Hill Rd., Washington, DC, 20233, USA, (301) 763-4636, (800) 923-8282, https://www.census.gov; County Business Patterns (CBP) 2020.

U.S. Census Bureau, Center for Economic Studies (CES), 4600 Silver Hill Rd., Washington, DC, 20233, USA, (301) 763-6460, (301) 763-5935, ces.contacts@census.gov, https://www.census.gov/programs-surveys/ces.html; Construction, 2017 Economic Census.

U.S. Department of Labor (DOL), Bureau of Labor Statistics (BLS), Postal Square Bldg., 2 Massachusetts Ave. NE, Washington, DC, 20212-0001, USA, (202) 691-5200, (202) 691-7890, blsdata_staff@bls.gov, https://www.bls.gov; Current Employment Statistics (CES).

BUILDING CONTRACTORS, GENERAL-EMPLOYEES

U.S. Census Bureau, 4600 Silver Hill Rd., Washington, DC, 20233, USA, (301) 763-4636, (800) 923-8282, https://www.census.gov; County Business Patterns (CBP) 2020.

U.S. Census Bureau, Center for Economic Studies (CES), 4600 Silver Hill Rd., Washington, DC, 20233, USA, (301) 763-6460, (301) 763-5935, ces.contacts@census.gov, https://www.census.gov/programs-surveys/ces.html; Construction, 2017 Economic Census.

U.S. Department of Labor (DOL), Bureau of Labor Statistics (BLS), Postal Square Bldg., 2 Massachusetts Ave. NE, Washington, DC, 20212-0001, USA, (202) 691-5200, (202) 691-7890, blsdata_staff@bls.gov, https://www.bls.gov; Current Employment Statistics (CES) and Industry-Occupation Matrix Data, By Occupation.

BUILDING CONTRACTORS, GENERAL-ESTABLISHMENTS

U.S. Census Bureau, 4600 Silver Hill Rd., Washington, DC, 20233, USA, (301) 763-4636, (800) 923-8282, https://www.census.gov; County Business Patterns (CBP) 2020.

U.S. Census Bureau, Center for Economic Studies (CES), 4600 Silver Hill Rd., Washington, DC, 20233, USA, (301) 763-6460, (301) 763-5935, ces.contacts@census.gov, https://www.census.gov/programs-surveys/ces.html; Construction, 2017 Economic Census.

BUILDING CONTRACTORS, GENERAL-INDUSTRIAL SAFETY

U.S. Department of Labor (DOL), Bureau of Labor Statistics (BLS), Postal Square Bldg., 2 Massachusetts Ave. NE, Washington, DC, 20212-0001, USA, (202) 691-5200, (202) 691-7890, blsdata_staff@bls.gov, https://www.bls.gov; Injuries, Illnesses, and Fatalities (IIF).

BUILDING CONTRACTORS, GENERAL-VALUE OF WORK

U.S. Census Bureau, Center for Economic Studies (CES), 4600 Silver Hill Rd., Washington, DC, 20233, USA, (301) 763-6460, (301) 763-5935, ces.contacts@census.gov, https://www.census.gov/programs-surveys/ces.html; Construction, 2017 Economic Census.

BUILDING MATERIALS AND GARDEN SUPPLIES, RETAIL STORES

U.S. Census Bureau, 4600 Silver Hill Rd., Washington, DC, 20233, USA, (301) 763-4636, (800) 923-8282, https://www.census.gov; County Business Patterns (CBP) 2020.

U.S. Census Bureau, Center for Economic Studies (CES), 4600 Silver Hill Rd., Washington, DC, 20233, USA, (301) 763-6460, (301) 763-5935, ces.contacts@census.gov, https://www.census.gov/programs-surveys/ces.html; Retail Trade, 2017 Economic Census and Wholesale Trade, 2017 Economic Census.

U.S. Department of Commerce (DOC), International Trade Administration (ITA), 1401 Constitution Ave. NW, Washington, DC, 20230, USA, (800) 872-8723, https://www.trade.gov/; TradeStats Express (TSE).

BUILDING MATERIALS AND GARDEN SUPPLIES, RETAIL STORES-EARNINGS

U.S. Census Bureau, 4600 Silver Hill Rd., Washington, DC, 20233, USA, (301) 763-4636, (800) 923-8282, https://www.census.gov; County Business Patterns (CBP) 2020.

U.S. Census Bureau, Center for Economic Studies (CES), 4600 Silver Hill Rd., Washington, DC, 20233, USA, (301) 763-6460, (301) 763-5935, ces.contacts@census.gov, https://www.census.gov/programs-surveys/ces.html; Retail Trade, 2017 Economic Census and Wholesale Trade, 2017 Economic Census.

U.S. Department of Commerce (DOC), International Trade Administration (ITA), 1401 Constitution Ave. NW, Washington, DC, 20230, USA, (800) 872-8723, https://www.trade.gov/; TradeStats Express (TSE).

BUILDING MATERIALS AND GARDEN SUPPLIES, RETAIL STORES-EMPLOYEES

U.S. Census Bureau, 4600 Silver Hill Rd., Washington, DC, 20233, USA, (301) 763-4636, (800) 923-8282, https://www.census.gov; County Business Patterns (CBP) 2020.

U.S. Census Bureau, Center for Economic Studies (CES), 4600 Silver Hill Rd., Washington, DC, 20233, USA, (301) 763-6460, (301) 763-5935, ces.contacts@census.gov, https://www.census.gov/programs-surveys/ces.html; Retail Trade, 2017 Economic Census and Wholesale Trade, 2017 Economic Census.

U.S. Department of Labor (DOL), Bureau of Labor Statistics (BLS), Postal Square Bldg., 2 Massachusetts Ave. NE, Washington, DC, 20212-0001, USA, (202) 691-5200, (202) 691-7890, blsdata_staff@bls.gov, https://www.bls.gov; Industry-Occupation Matrix Data, By Occupation.

BUILDING MATERIALS AND GARDEN SUPPLIES, RETAIL STORES-INVENTORIES

U.S. Census Bureau, Center for Economic Studies (CES), 4600 Silver Hill Rd., Washington, DC, 20233, USA, (301) 763-6460, (301) 763-5935, ces.contacts@census.gov, https://www.census.gov/programs-surveys/ces.html; Retail Trade, 2017 Economic Census and Wholesale Trade, 2017 Economic Census.

U.S. Department of Commerce (DOC), International Trade Administration (ITA), 1401 Constitution Ave. NW, Washington, DC, 20230, USA, (800) 872-8723, https://www.trade.gov/; TradeStats Express (TSE).

BUILDING MATERIALS AND GARDEN SUPPLIES, RETAIL STORES-NONEMPLOYERS

U.S. Census Bureau, 4600 Silver Hill Rd., Washington, DC, 20233, USA, (301) 763-4636, (800) 923-8282, https://www.census.gov; Economic Census, Nonemployer Statistics (NES) 2019.

BUILDING MATERIALS AND GARDEN SUPPLIES, RETAIL STORES-PRODUCTIVITY

U.S. Department of Labor (DOL), Bureau of Labor Statistics (BLS), Postal Square Bldg., 2 Massachusetts Ave. NE, Washington, DC, 20212-0001, USA, (202) 691-5200, (202) 691-7890, blsdata_staff@bls.gov, https://www.bls.gov; Productivity.

BUILDING MATERIALS AND GARDEN SUPPLIES, RETAIL STORES-PURCHASES

U.S. Census Bureau, Center for Economic Studies (CES), 4600 Silver Hill Rd., Washington, DC, 20233, USA, (301) 763-6460, (301) 763-5935, ces.contacts@census.gov, https://www.census.gov/programs-surveys/ces.html; Retail Trade, 2017 Economic Census and Wholesale Trade, 2017 Economic Census.

U.S. Department of Commerce (DOC), International Trade Administration (ITA), 1401 Constitution Ave. NW, Washington, DC, 20230, USA, (800) 872-8723, https://www.trade.gov/; TradeStats Express (TSE).

BUILDING MATERIALS AND GARDEN SUPPLIES, RETAIL STORES-SALES

U.S. Census Bureau, Center for Economic Studies (CES), 4600 Silver Hill Rd., Washington, DC, 20233, USA, (301) 763-6460, (301) 763-5935, ces.contacts@census.gov, https://www.census.gov/programs-surveys/ces.html; Retail Trade, 2017 Economic Census and Wholesale Trade, 2017 Economic Census.

U.S. Department of Commerce (DOC), International Trade Administration (ITA), 1401 Constitution Ave. NW, Washington, DC, 20230, USA, (800) 872-8723, https://www.trade.gov/; TradeStats Express (TSE).

BUILDING PERMITS

See CONSTRUCTION INDUSTRY-BUILDING PERMITS-VALUE

BUILDINGS

See also CONSTRUCTION INDUSTRY

Dodge Construction Network, 300 American Metro Blvd., Ste. 185, Hamilton, NJ, 08619, USA, (877) 784-9556, support@construction.com, https://www.construction.com/; Dodge MarketShare.

Federal Housing Finance Agency (FHFA), 400 7th St. SW, Washington, DC, 20019, USA, (202) 649-3800, (202) 649-1071, https://www.fhfa.gov/; House Price Index.

BUILDINGS-FEDERAL

U.S. General Services Administration (GSA), 1800 F St. NW, Washington, DC, 20405, USA, (844) 472-4111, https://www.gsa.gov/; Federal Real Property Profile (FRPP) Summary Reports.

BUILDINGS-FLOOR SPACE

U.S. General Services Administration (GSA), 1800 F St. NW, Washington, DC, 20405, USA, (844) 472-4111, https://www.gsa.gov/; Federal Real Property Profile (FRPP) Summary Reports.

BULGARIA-NATIONAL STATISTICAL OFFICE

National Statistical Insitute of Bulgaria, 2 P. Volov St., Sofia, 1038, BUL, info@nsi.bg, https://www.nsi.bg/en; National Data Reports (Bulgaria).

BULGARIA-PRIMARY STATISTICS SOURCES

European Commission, Eurostat, Luxembourg, 2920, LUX, https://ec.europa.eu/eurostat/; Key Figures on Enlargement Countries, 2019.

National Statistical Insitute of Bulgaria, 2 P. Volov St., Sofia, 1038, BUL, info@nsi.bg, https://www.nsi.bg/en; Statistical Reference Book 2021 and Statistical Yearbook of Bulgaria 2021.

BULGARIA-AGRICULTURE

The Economist Group: Economist Intelligence Unit (EIU), 900 3rd Ave., 16th Fl., New York, NY, 10022, USA, (212) 541-0500, americas@eiu.com, https://www.eiu.com; Bulgaria Country Report.

Euromonitor International, Inc., 1 N Dearborn St., Ste. 1700, Chicago, IL, 60602, USA, (312) 922-1115, (312) 922-1157, info-usa@euromonitor.com, https://www.euromonitor.com/; Geographies.

European Commission, Rue de la Loi, 170, Brussels, B-1040, BEL, https://ec.europa.eu; Common Agricultural Policy (CAPF) Context Indicators, 2019 Update.

European Commission, Eurostat, Luxembourg, 2920, LUX, https://ec.europa.eu/eurostat/; Farmers and the Agricultural Labour Force - Statistics.

Palgrave Macmillan, 1 New York Plaza, Ste. 4500, New York, NY, 10004-1562, USA, (800) 777-4643, orders@palgrave.com, https://www.palgrave.com/us; The Statesman's Yearbook, 2023.

Routledge - Taylor & Francis Group, 6000 Broken Sound Pkwy. NW, Ste. 300, Boca Raton, FL, 33487, USA, (800) 634-1420, (800) 634-7064, orders@taylorandfrancis.com, https://www.routledge.com/; The Europa World Year Book 2022.

United Nations Food and Agricultural Organization (FAO), 2121 K St., Ste. 800B, Washington, DC, 20037, USA, (202) 653-2400 (Dial from U.S.), (202) 653-5760 (Fax from U.S.), fao-hq@fao.org, https://www.fao.org; AQUASTAT and The State of Food and Agriculture (SOFA) 2022.

United Nations Statistics Division (UNSD), United Nations Plz., New York, NY, 10017, USA, (800) 253-9646, (212) 963-9851, statistics@un.org, https://unstats.un.org; Statistical Yearbook of the United Nations 2021.

The World Bank, 1818 H St. NW, Washington, DC, 20433, USA, (202) 473-1000, (202) 477-6391, eds03@worldbank.org, https://www.worldbank.org/; Bulgaria (report).

BULGARIA-AIRLINES

European Commission, Eurostat, Luxembourg, 2920, LUX, https://ec.europa.eu/eurostat/; Air Transport Statistics.

Palgrave Macmillan, 1 New York Plaza, Ste. 4500, New York, NY, 10004-1562, USA, (800) 777-4643, orders@palgrave.com, https://www.palgrave.com/us; The Statesman's Yearbook, 2023.

Routledge - Taylor & Francis Group, 6000 Broken Sound Pkwy. NW, Ste. 300, Boca Raton, FL, 33487, USA, (800) 634-1420, (800) 634-7064, orders@taylorandfrancis.com, https://www.routledge.com/; The Europa World Year Book 2022.

BULGARIA-ALUMINUM PRODUCTION

See BULGARIA-MINERAL INDUSTRIES

BULGARIA-ARMED FORCES

Central Intelligence Agency (CIA), Office of Public Affairs, Washington, DC, 20505, USA, (703) 482-0623, https://www.cia.gov; The World Factbook.

International Institute for Strategic Studies (IISS) - Americas, 2121 K St. NW, Ste. 600, Washington, DC, 20037, USA, (202) 659-1490, (202) 659-1499, https://www.iiss.org/; The Military Balance 2022.

Palgrave Macmillan, 1 New York Plaza, Ste. 4500, New York, NY, 10004-1562, USA, (800) 777-4643, orders@palgrave.com, https://www.palgrave.com/us; The Statesman's Yearbook, 2023.

Stockholm International Peace Research Institute (SIPRI), Signalistgatan 9, Stockholm, SE 169 72, SWE, https://www.sipri.org/; SIPRI Arms Transfers Database and SIPRI Military Expenditure Database.

BULGARIA-AUTOMOBILE INDUSTRY AND TRADE

National Statistical Insitute of Bulgaria, 2 P. Volov St., Sofia, 1038, BUL, info@nsi.bg, https://www.nsi.bg/en; Road Traffic Accidents in the Republic of Bulgaria 2020.

BULGARIA-BALANCE OF PAYMENTS

United Nations Conference on Trade and Development (UNCTAD), Palais des Nations, Geneva, 1211, SWI, (212) 963-6896, unctadinfo@unctad.org, https://unctad.org; Handbook of Statistics 2021.

The World Bank, 1818 H St. NW, Washington, DC, 20433, USA, (202) 473-1000, (202) 477-6391, eds03@worldbank.org, https://www.worldbank.org/; Bulgaria (report) and World Development Report 2022: Finance for an Equitable Recovery.

BULGARIA-BANKS AND BANKING

Euromonitor International, Inc., 1 N Dearborn St., Ste. 1700, Chicago, IL, 60602, USA, (312) 922-1115, (312) 922-1157, info-usa@euromonitor.com, https://www.euromonitor.com/; Geographies.

BULGARIA-BARLEY PRODUCTION

See BULGARIA-CROPS

BULGARIA-BROADCASTING

Central Intelligence Agency (CIA), Office of Public Affairs, Washington, DC, 20505, USA, (703) 482-0623, https://www.cia.gov; The World Factbook.

Euromonitor International, Inc., 1 N Dearborn St., Ste. 1700, Chicago, IL, 60602, USA, (312) 922-1115, (312) 922-1157, info-usa@euromonitor.com, https://www.euromonitor.com/; Geographies.

Palgrave Macmillan, 1 New York Plaza, Ste. 4500, New York, NY, 10004-1562, USA, (800) 777-4643, orders@palgrave.com, https://www.palgrave.com/us; The Statesman's Yearbook, 2023.

WRTH Publications Limited, PO Box 290, Oxford, OX2 7FT, GBR, sales@wrth.com, https://www.wrth.com; World Radio TV Handbook 2023.

BULGARIA-BUDGET

Central Intelligence Agency (CIA), Office of Public Affairs, Washington, DC, 20505, USA, (703) 482-0623, https://www.cia.gov; The World Factbook.

European Commission, Eurostat, Luxembourg, 2920, LUX, https://ec.europa.eu/eurostat/; Share of Government Budget Appropriations or Outlays on Research and Development.

BULGARIA-BUSINESS

United Nations Statistics Division (UNSD), United Nations Plz., New York, NY, 10017, USA, (800) 253-9646, (212) 963-9851, statistics@un.org, https://unstats.un.org; Statistical Yearbook of the United Nations 2021.

BULGARIA-CLIMATE

Palgrave Macmillan, 1 New York Plaza, Ste. 4500, New York, NY, 10004-1562, USA, (800) 777-4643, orders@palgrave.com, https://www.palgrave.com/us; The Statesman's Yearbook, 2023.

BULGARIA-COAL PRODUCTION

See BULGARIA-MINERAL INDUSTRIES

BULGARIA-COFFEE

See BULGARIA-CROPS

BULGARIA-COMMERCE

Palgrave Macmillan, 1 New York Plaza, Ste. 4500, New York, NY, 10004-1562, USA, (800) 777-4643, orders@palgrave.com, https://www.palgrave.com/us; The Statesman's Yearbook, 2023.

UK Data Service, University of Essex, Wivenhoe Park, Colchester, Essex, CO4 3SQ, GBR, https://ukdataservice.ac.uk/; International Aggregate Data.

BULGARIA-COMMODITY EXCHANGES

Barchart, 209 W Jackson Blvd., 2nd Fl., Chicago, IL, 60606, USA, (877) 247-4394, commodities@barchart.com, https://www.barchart.com/cmdty; The cmdty Yearbook 2023; cmdtyStats: Commodity Statistics and Fundamental Data; cmdtyView: Commodity Index; and Commodity Data and Prices.

International Lead and Zinc Study Group (ILZSG), Rua Almirante Barroso 38, 5th Fl., Lisbon, 1000-013, PRT, sales@ilzsg.org, https://www.ilzsg.org; Interactive Statistical Database.

International Monetary Fund (IMF), 700 19th St. NW, Washington, DC, 20431, USA, (202) 623-7000, (202) 623-4661, publications@imf.org, https://www.imf.org; IMF Primary Commodity Prices.

BULGARIA-CONSTRUCTION INDUSTRY

Palgrave Macmillan, 1 New York Plaza, Ste. 4500, New York, NY, 10004-1562, USA, (800) 777-4643, orders@palgrave.com, https://www.palgrave.com/us; The Statesman's Yearbook, 2023.

United Nations Statistics Division (UNSD), United Nations Plz., New York, NY, 10017, USA, (800) 253-9646, (212) 963-9851, statistics@un.org, https://unstats.un.org; Statistical Yearbook of the United Nations 2021.

BULGARIA-CONSUMER PRICE INDEXES

Routledge - Taylor & Francis Group, 6000 Broken Sound Pkwy. NW, Ste. 300, Boca Raton, FL, 33487, USA, (800) 634-1420, (800) 634-7064, orders@taylorandfrancis.com, https://www.routledge.com/; The Europa World Year Book 2022.

The World Bank, 1818 H St. NW, Washington, DC, 20433, USA, (202) 473-1000, (202) 477-6391, eds03@worldbank.org, https://www.worldbank.org/; Bulgaria (report).

BULGARIA-COPPER INDUSTRY AND TRADE

See BULGARIA-MINERAL INDUSTRIES

BULGARIA-CORN INDUSTRY

See BULGARIA-CROPS

BULGARIA-COTTON

See BULGARIA-CROPS

BULGARIA-CRIME

European Commission, Eurostat, Luxembourg, 2920, LUX, https://ec.europa.eu/eurostat/; Crime and Criminal Justice Database and Crime Statistics.

National Statistical Insitute of Bulgaria, 2 P. Volov St., Sofia, 1038, BUL, info@nsi.bg, https://www.nsi.bg/en; Crimes, Accused and Persons Convicted.

BULGARIA-CROPS

Palgrave Macmillan, 1 New York Plaza, Ste. 4500, New York, NY, 10004-1562, USA, (800) 777-4643, orders@palgrave.com, https://www.palgrave.com/us; The Statesman's Yearbook, 2023.

United Nations Food and Agricultural Organization (FAO), 2121 K St., Ste. 800B, Washington, DC, 20037, USA, (202) 653-2400 (Dial from U.S.), (202) 653-5760 (Fax from U.S.), fao-hq@fao.org, https://www.fao.org; The State of Food and Agriculture (SOFA) 2022.

BULGARIA-DAIRY PROCESSING

Palgrave Macmillan, 1 New York Plaza, Ste. 4500, New York, NY, 10004-1562, USA, (800) 777-4643, orders@palgrave.com, https://www.palgrave.com/us; The Statesman's Yearbook, 2023.

United Nations Food and Agricultural Organization (FAO), 2121 K St., Ste. 800B, Washington, DC, 20037, USA, (202) 653-2400 (Dial from U.S.), (202) 653-5760 (Fax from U.S.), fao-hq@fao.org, https://www.fao.org; The State of Food and Agriculture (SOFA) 2022.

BULGARIA-DEBTS, EXTERNAL

Palgrave Macmillan, 1 New York Plaza, Ste. 4500, New York, NY, 10004-1562, USA, (800) 777-4643, orders@palgrave.com, https://www.palgrave.com/us; The Statesman's Yearbook, 2023.

The World Bank, 1818 H St. NW, Washington, DC, 20433, USA, (202) 473-1000, (202) 477-6391, eds03@worldbank.org, https://www.worldbank.org/; Global Financial Development Report 2019-2020: Bank Regulation and Supervision a Decade after the Global Financial Crisis and World Development Report 2022: Finance for an Equitable Recovery.

BULGARIA-DIAMONDS

See BULGARIA-MINERAL INDUSTRIES

BULGARIA-ECONOMIC ASSISTANCE

National Statistical Insitute of Bulgaria, 2 P. Volov St., Sofia, 1038, BUL, info@nsi.bg, https://www.nsi.bg/en; Bulgaria 2021.

United Nations Statistics Division (UNSD), United Nations Plz., New York, NY, 10017, USA, (800) 253-9646, (212) 963-9851, statistics@un.org, https://unstats.un.org; Statistical Yearbook of the United Nations 2021.

BULGARIA-ECONOMIC CONDITIONS

Bernan Press, 15250 NBN Way, Bldg. C, Blue Ridge Summit, PA, 17214, USA, (301) 459-2255, (800) 865-3457, (800) 865-3450, customercare@bernan.com, https://rowman.com/Page/Bernan; World Economic Outlook, April 2022.

Central Intelligence Agency (CIA), Office of Public Affairs, Washington, DC, 20505, USA, (703) 482-0623, https://www.cia.gov; The World Factbook.

The Economist Group: Economist Intelligence Unit (EIU), 900 3rd Ave., 16th Fl., New York, NY, 10022, USA, (212) 541-0500, americas@eiu.com, https://www.eiu.com; Bulgaria Country Report.

Euromonitor International, Inc., 1 N Dearborn St., Ste. 1700, Chicago, IL, 60602, USA, (312) 922-1115, (312) 922-1157, info-usa@euromonitor.com, https://www.euromonitor.com/; Geographies and Market Research on the Consumer Finance Industry.

European Commission, Rue de la Loi, 170, Brussels, B-1040, BEL, https://ec.europa.eu; Common Agricultural Policy (CAPF) Context Indicators, 2019 Update.

International Monetary Fund (IMF), 700 19th St. NW, Washington, DC, 20431, USA, (202) 623-7000, (202) 623-4661, publications@imf.org, https://www.imf.org; IMF Data and World Economic Outlook.

Palgrave Macmillan, 1 New York Plaza, Ste. 4500, New York, NY, 10004-1562, USA, (800) 777-4643, orders@palgrave.com, https://www.palgrave.com/us; The Statesman's Yearbook, 2023.

Routledge - Taylor & Francis Group, 6000 Broken Sound Pkwy. NW, Ste. 300, Boca Raton, FL, 33487, USA, (800) 634-1420, (800) 634-7064, orders@taylorandfrancis.com, https://www.routledge.com/; The Europa World Year Book 2022.

United Nations Statistics Division (UNSD), United Nations Plz., New York, NY, 10017, USA, (800) 253-9646, (212) 963-9851, statistics@un.org, https://unstats.un.org; World Statistics Pocketbook 2021.

The World Bank, 1818 H St. NW, Washington, DC, 20433, USA, (202) 473-1000, (202) 477-6391, eds03@worldbank.org, https://www.worldbank.org/; Bulgaria (report); Global Economic Monitor (GEM); Global Economic Prospects, June 2022; The Global Findex Database 2021; and World Development Report 2022: Finance for an Equitable Recovery.

BULGARIA-EDUCATION

Euromonitor International, Inc., 1 N Dearborn St., Ste. 1700, Chicago, IL, 60602, USA, (312) 922-1115, (312) 922-1157, info-usa@euromonitor.com, https://www.euromonitor.com/; Geographies.

European Commission, Rue de la Loi, 170, Brussels, B-1040, BEL, https://ec.europa.eu; Common Agricultural Policy (CAPF) Context Indicators, 2019 Update.

Infoplease, c/o Sandbox Networks, Inc., 1 Lincoln St., 24th Fl., Boston, MA, 02111, USA, https://www.infoplease.com; Countries of the World.

National Statistical Insitute of Bulgaria, 2 P. Volov St., Sofia, 1038, BUL, info@nsi.bg, https://www.nsi.bg/en; Education and Lifelong Learning.

Palgrave Macmillan, 1 New York Plaza, Ste. 4500, New York, NY, 10004-1562, USA, (800) 777-4643, orders@palgrave.com, https://www.palgrave.com/us; The Statesman's Yearbook, 2023.

Routledge - Taylor & Francis Group, 6000 Broken Sound Pkwy. NW, Ste. 300, Boca Raton, FL, 33487, USA, (800) 634-1420, (800) 634-7064, orders@taylorandfrancis.com, https://www.routledge.com/; The Europa World Year Book 2022.

UNESCO Institute for Statistics, C.P 250 Succursale H, Montreal, QC, H3G 2K8, CAN, (514) 343-6880 (Dial from U.S.), (514) 343-5740 (Fax from U.S.), uis.publications@unesco.org, http://uis.unesco.org/; Literacy and UIS.Stat.

United Nations Statistics Division (UNSD), United Nations Plz., New York, NY, 10017, USA, (800) 253-9646, (212) 963-9851, statistics@un.org, https://unstats.un.org; Millennium Development Goal Indicators.

The World Bank, 1818 H St. NW, Washington, DC, 20433, USA, (202) 473-1000, (202) 477-6391, eds03@worldbank.org, https://www.worldbank.org/; Bulgaria (report) and World Development Report 2022: Finance for an Equitable Recovery.

BULGARIA-ELECTRICITY

European Commission, Eurostat, Luxembourg, 2920, LUX, https://ec.europa.eu/eurostat/; Final Energy Consumption in Transport by Type of Fuel.

International Energy Agency (IEA), 9 Rue de la Federation, Paris, 75739, FRA, info@iea.org, https://www.iea.org/; World Energy Outlook 2021.

S&P Global Commodity Insights, One World Trade Center, New York, NY, 10007, USA, (800) 752-8878, support@platts.com, https://www.spglobal.com/commodityinsights/en; Platts European Power Alert and Platts Power in Europe.

U.S. Energy Information Administration (EIA), 1000 Independence Ave. SW, Washington, DC, 20585, USA, (202) 586-8800, infoctr@eia.gov, https://www.eia.gov; International Energy Outlook 2021.

United Nations Statistics Division (UNSD), United Nations Plz., New York, NY, 10017, USA, (800) 253-9646, (212) 963-9851, statistics@un.org, https://unstats.un.org; Statistical Yearbook of the United Nations 2021.

BULGARIA-EMPLOYMENT

International Labour Organization (ILO), 4 Rte. des Morillons, Geneva, CH-1211, SWI, ilo@ilo.org, https://www.ilo.org; NORMLEX Information System on International Labour Standards.

UK Data Service, University of Essex, Wivenhoe Park, Colchester, Essex, CO4 3SQ, GBR, https://ukdataservice.ac.uk/; International Aggregate Data.

United Nations Statistics Division (UNSD), United Nations Plz., New York, NY, 10017, USA, (800) 253-9646, (212) 963-9851, statistics@un.org, https://unstats.un.org; Statistical Yearbook of the United Nations 2021.

The World Bank, 1818 H St. NW, Washington, DC, 20433, USA, (202) 473-1000, (202) 477-6391, eds03@worldbank.org, https://www.worldbank.org/; Bulgaria (report).

BULGARIA-ENERGY INDUSTRIES

Enerdata, 47 avenue Alsace Lorraine, Grenoble, 38027, FRA, (332) 216-4534, research@enerdata.net, https://www.enerdata.net; World Refinery Database.

European Commission, Eurostat, Luxembourg, 2920, LUX, https://ec.europa.eu/eurostat/; Final Energy Consumption in Transport by Type of Fuel.

S&P Global Commodity Insights, One World Trade Center, New York, NY, 10007, USA, (800) 752-8878, support@platts.com, https://www.spglobal.com/commodityinsights/en; Platts European Power Daily and Platts Power in Europe.

United Nations Statistics Division (UNSD), United Nations Plz., New York, NY, 10017, USA, (800) 253-9646, (212) 963-9851, statistics@un.org, https://unstats.un.org; Statistical Yearbook of the United Nations 2021.

BULGARIA-ENVIRONMENTAL CONDITIONS

DSI Data Service & Information, Xantener Strasse 51a, Rheinberg, D-47495, GER, dsi@dsidata.com, https://www.dsidata.com/; Global Environmental Database.

The Economist Group: Economist Intelligence Unit (EIU), 900 3rd Ave., 16th Fl., New York, NY, 10022, USA, (212) 541-0500, americas@eiu.com, https://www.eiu.com; Bulgaria Country Report.

European Commission, Rue de la Loi, 170, Brussels, B-1040, BEL, https://ec.europa.eu; Common Agricultural Policy (CAPF) Context Indicators, 2019 Update.

European Commission, Eurostat, Luxembourg, 2920, LUX, https://ec.europa.eu/eurostat/; Environment Statistics Introduced.

United Nations Statistics Division (UNSD), United Nations Plz., New York, NY, 10017, USA, (800) 253-9646, (212) 963-9851, statistics@un.org, https://unstats.un.org; World Statistics Pocketbook 2021.

BULGARIA-EXPORTS

Central Intelligence Agency (CIA), Office of Public Affairs, Washington, DC, 20505, USA, (703) 482-0623, https://www.cia.gov; The World Factbook.

The Economist Group: Economist Intelligence Unit (EIU), 900 3rd Ave., 16th Fl., New York, NY, 10022, USA, (212) 541-0500, americas@eiu.com, https://www.eiu.com; Bulgaria Country Report.

International Monetary Fund (IMF), 700 19th St. NW, Washington, DC, 20431, USA, (202) 623-7000, (202) 623-4661, publications@imf.org, https://www.imf.org; Direction of Trade Statistics (DOTS).

S&P Global, IHS Markit, 15 Inverness Way E, Englewood, CO, 80112, USA, (800) 447-2273, (800) 854-7179, https://ihsmarkit.com; Global Trade Atlas (GTA).

United Nations Conference on Trade and Development (UNCTAD), Palais des Nations, Geneva, 1211, SWI, (212) 963-6896, unctadinfo@unctad.org, https://unctad.org; Handbook of Statistics 2021.

The World Bank, 1818 H St. NW, Washington, DC, 20433, USA, (202) 473-1000, (202) 477-6391, eds03@worldbank.org, https://www.worldbank.org/; World Development Report 2022: Finance for an Equitable Recovery.

BULGARIA-FERTILITY, HUMAN

Central Intelligence Agency (CIA), Office of Public Affairs, Washington, DC, 20505, USA, (703) 482-0623, https://www.cia.gov; The World Factbook.

BULGARIA-FERTILIZER INDUSTRY

United Nations Food and Agricultural Organization (FAO), 2121 K St., Ste. 800B, Washington, DC,

20037, USA, (202) 653-2400 (Dial from U.S.), (202) 653-5760 (Fax from U.S.), fao-hq@fao.org, https://www.fao.org; The State of Food and Agriculture (SOFA) 2022.

BULGARIA-FETAL MORTALITY

See BULGARIA-MORTALITY

BULGARIA-FINANCE

Stockholm International Peace Research Institute (SIPRI), Signalistgatan 9, Stockholm, SE 169 72, SWE, https://www.sipri.org/; SIPRI Arms Transfers Database and SIPRI Military Expenditure Database.

United Nations Statistics Division (UNSD), United Nations Plz., New York, NY, 10017, USA, (800) 253-9646, (212) 963-9851, statistics@un.org, https://unstats.un.org; Statistical Yearbook of the United Nations 2021.

The World Bank, 1818 H St. NW, Washington, DC, 20433, USA, (202) 473-1000, (202) 477-6391, eds03@worldbank.org, https://www.worldbank.org/; Bulgaria (report).

BULGARIA-FINANCE, PUBLIC

Bernan Press, 15250 NBN Way, Bldg. C, Blue Ridge Summit, PA, 17214, USA, (301) 459-2255, (800) 865-3457, (800) 865-3450, customercare@bernan.com, https://rowman.com/Page/Bernan; National Accounts Statistics: Analysis of Main Aggregates 2020.

The Economist Group: Economist Intelligence Unit (EIU), 900 3rd Ave., 16th Fl., New York, NY, 10022, USA, (212) 541-0500, americas@eiu.com, https://www.eiu.com; Bulgaria Country Report.

International Monetary Fund (IMF), 700 19th St. NW, Washington, DC, 20431, USA, (202) 623-7000, (202) 623-4661, publications@imf.org, https://www.imf.org; International Financial Statistics (IFS) and Regional Economic Outlook.

Palgrave Macmillan, 1 New York Plaza, Ste. 4500, New York, NY, 10004-1562, USA, (800) 777-4643, orders@palgrave.com, https://www.palgrave.com/us; The Statesman's Yearbook, 2023.

Routledge - Taylor & Francis Group, 6000 Broken Sound Pkwy. NW, Ste. 300, Boca Raton, FL, 33487, USA, (800) 634-1420, (800) 634-7064, orders@taylorandfrancis.com, https://www.routledge.com/; The Europa World Year Book 2022.

United Nations Statistics Division (UNSD), United Nations Plz., New York, NY, 10017, USA, (800) 253-9646, (212) 963-9851, statistics@un.org, https://unstats.un.org; National Accounts Main Aggregates Database and National Accounts Statistics: Main Aggregates and Detailed Tables.

The World Bank, 1818 H St. NW, Washington, DC, 20433, USA, (202) 473-1000, (202) 477-6391, eds03@worldbank.org, https://www.worldbank.org/; Bulgaria (report).

BULGARIA-FISHERIES

Routledge - Taylor & Francis Group, 6000 Broken Sound Pkwy. NW, Ste. 300, Boca Raton, FL, 33487, USA, (800) 634-1420, (800) 634-7064, orders@taylorandfrancis.com, https://www.routledge.com/; The Europa World Year Book 2022.

United Nations Food and Agricultural Organization (FAO), 2121 K St., Ste. 800B, Washington, DC, 20037, USA, (202) 653-2400 (Dial from U.S.), (202) 653-5760 (Fax from U.S.), fao-hq@fao.org, https://www.fao.org; FAO Yearbook of Fishery and Aquaculture Statistics 2019; Fishery Statistical Collections Global Capture Production; FishStatJ; and The State of Food and Agriculture (SOFA) 2022.

United Nations Statistics Division (UNSD), United Nations Plz., New York, NY, 10017, USA, (800) 253-9646, (212) 963-9851, statistics@un.org, https://unstats.un.org; Statistical Yearbook of the United Nations 2021.

The World Bank, 1818 H St. NW, Washington, DC, 20433, USA, (202) 473-1000, (202) 477-6391, eds03@worldbank.org, https://www.worldbank.org/; Bulgaria (report).

BULGARIA-FOOD

Euromonitor International, Inc., 1 N Dearborn St., Ste. 1700, Chicago, IL, 60602, USA, (312) 922-1115, (312) 922-1157, info-usa@euromonitor.com, https://www.euromonitor.com/; Market Research on the Retailing Industry.

United Nations Food and Agricultural Organization (FAO), 2121 K St., Ste. 800B, Washington, DC, 20037, USA, (202) 653-2400 (Dial from U.S.), (202) 653-5760 (Fax from U.S.), fao-hq@fao.org, https://www.fao.org; The State of Food and Agriculture (SOFA) 2022.

BULGARIA-FORESTS AND FORESTRY

Palgrave Macmillan, 1 New York Plaza, Ste. 4500, New York, NY, 10004-1562, USA, (800) 777-4643, orders@palgrave.com, https://www.palgrave.com/us; The Statesman's Yearbook, 2023.

Routledge - Taylor & Francis Group, 6000 Broken Sound Pkwy. NW, Ste. 300, Boca Raton, FL, 33487, USA, (800) 634-1420, (800) 634-7064, orders@taylorandfrancis.com, https://www.routledge.com/; The Europa World Year Book 2022.

UNESCO Institute for Statistics, C.P 250 Succursale H, Montreal, QC, H3G 2K8, CAN, (514) 343-6880 (Dial from U.S.), (514) 343-5740 (Fax from U.S.), uis.publications@unesco.org, http://uis.unesco.org/; UIS.Stat.

United Nations Food and Agricultural Organization (FAO), 2121 K St., Ste. 800B, Washington, DC, 20037, USA, (202) 653-2400 (Dial from U.S.), (202) 653-5760 (Fax from U.S.), fao-hq@fao.org, https://www.fao.org; FAO Yearbook of Forest Products 2019 and The State of Food and Agriculture (SOFA) 2022.

United Nations Statistics Division (UNSD), United Nations Plz., New York, NY, 10017, USA, (800) 253-9646, (212) 963-9851, statistics@un.org, https://unstats.un.org; Statistical Yearbook of the United Nations 2021.

The World Bank, 1818 H St. NW, Washington, DC, 20433, USA, (202) 473-1000, (202) 477-6391, eds03@worldbank.org, https://www.worldbank.org/; Bulgaria (report) and World Development Report 2022: Finance for an Equitable Recovery.

BULGARIA-GAS PRODUCTION

See BULGARIA-MINERAL INDUSTRIES

BULGARIA-GEOGRAPHIC INFORMATION SYSTEMS

The World Bank, 1818 H St. NW, Washington, DC, 20433, USA, (202) 473-1000, (202) 477-6391, eds03@worldbank.org, https://www.worldbank.org/; Bulgaria (report).

BULGARIA-GOLD PRODUCTION

See BULGARIA-MINERAL INDUSTRIES

BULGARIA-GROSS DOMESTIC PRODUCT

The Economist Group: Economist Intelligence Unit (EIU), 900 3rd Ave., 16th Fl., New York, NY, 10022, USA, (212) 541-0500, americas@eiu.com, https://www.eiu.com; Bulgaria Country Report.

United Nations Statistics Division (UNSD), United Nations Plz., New York, NY, 10017, USA, (800) 253-9646, (212) 963-9851, statistics@un.org, https://unstats.un.org; Statistical Yearbook of the United Nations 2021.

The World Bank, 1818 H St. NW, Washington, DC, 20433, USA, (202) 473-1000, (202) 477-6391, eds03@worldbank.org, https://www.worldbank.org/; World Development Report 2022: Finance for an Equitable Recovery.

BULGARIA-GROSS NATIONAL PRODUCT

Palgrave Macmillan, 1 New York Plaza, Ste. 4500, New York, NY, 10004-1562, USA, (800) 777-4643, orders@palgrave.com, https://www.palgrave.com/us; The Statesman's Yearbook, 2023.

United Nations Statistics Division (UNSD), United Nations Plz., New York, NY, 10017, USA, (800) 253-9646, (212) 963-9851, statistics@un.org, https://unstats.un.org; Statistical Yearbook of the United Nations 2021.

The World Bank, 1818 H St. NW, Washington, DC, 20433, USA, (202) 473-1000, (202) 477-6391, eds03@worldbank.org, https://www.worldbank.org/; World Development Report 2022: Finance for an Equitable Recovery.

BULGARIA-HAZELNUT PRODUCTION

See BULGARIA-CROPS

BULGARIA-HEMP FIBRE PRODUCTION

See BULGARIA-TEXTILE INDUSTRY

BULGARIA-HOUSING

Euromonitor International, Inc., 1 N Dearborn St., Ste. 1700, Chicago, IL, 60602, USA, (312) 922-1115, (312) 922-1157, info-usa@euromonitor.com, https://www.euromonitor.com/; Geographies.

BULGARIA-ILLITERATE PERSONS

UNESCO Institute for Statistics, C.P 250 Succursale H, Montreal, QC, H3G 2K8, CAN, (514) 343-6880 (Dial from U.S.), (514) 343-5740 (Fax from U.S.), uis.publications@unesco.org, http://uis.unesco.org/; UIS.Stat.

BULGARIA-IMPORTS

Central Intelligence Agency (CIA), Office of Public Affairs, Washington, DC, 20505, USA, (703) 482-0623, https://www.cia.gov; The World Factbook.

The Economist Group: Economist Intelligence Unit (EIU), 900 3rd Ave., 16th Fl., New York, NY, 10022, USA, (212) 541-0500, americas@eiu.com, https://www.eiu.com; Bulgaria Country Report.

International Monetary Fund (IMF), 700 19th St. NW, Washington, DC, 20431, USA, (202) 623-7000, (202) 623-4661, publications@imf.org, https://www.imf.org; Direction of Trade Statistics (DOTS).

S&P Global, IHS Markit, 15 Inverness Way E, Englewood, CO, 80112, USA, (800) 447-2273, (800) 854-7179, https://ihsmarkit.com; Global Trade Atlas (GTA).

United Nations Conference on Trade and Development (UNCTAD), Palais des Nations, Geneva, 1211, SWI, (212) 963-6896, unctadinfo@unctad.org, https://unctad.org; Handbook of Statistics 2021.

The World Bank, 1818 H St. NW, Washington, DC, 20433, USA, (202) 473-1000, (202) 477-6391, eds03@worldbank.org, https://www.worldbank.org/; World Development Report 2022: Finance for an Equitable Recovery.

BULGARIA-INDUSTRIAL METALS PRODUCTION

See BULGARIA-MINERAL INDUSTRIES

BULGARIA-INDUSTRIAL PRODUCTIVITY

International Lead and Zinc Study Group (ILZSG), Rua Almirante Barroso 38, 5th Fl., Lisbon, 1000-013, PRT, sales@ilzsg.org, https://www.ilzsg.org; Interactive Statistical Database.

BULGARIA-INDUSTRIAL PROPERTY

World Intellectual Property Organization (WIPO), 34, chemin des Colombettes, Geneva, CH-1211, SWI, https://www.wipo.int; Madrid Yearly Review 2022: International Registrations of Marks.

BULGARIA-INDUSTRIES

Central Intelligence Agency (CIA), Office of Public Affairs, Washington, DC, 20505, USA, (703) 482-0623, https://www.cia.gov; The World Factbook.

The Economist Group: Economist Intelligence Unit (EIU), 900 3rd Ave., 16th Fl., New York, NY, 10022, USA, (212) 541-0500, americas@eiu.com, https://www.eiu.com; Bulgaria Country Report.

Euromonitor International, Inc., 1 N Dearborn St., Ste. 1700, Chicago, IL, 60602, USA, (312) 922-1115, (312) 922-1157, info-usa@euromonitor.com, https://www.euromonitor.com/; Geographies.

International Labour Organization (ILO), 4 Rte. des Morillons, Geneva, CH-1211, SWI, ilo@ilo.org, https://www.ilo.org; NORMLEX Information System on International Labour Standards.

National Statistical Insitute of Bulgaria, 2 P. Volov St., Sofia, 1038, BUL, info@nsi.bg, https://www.nsi.bg/en; Expenditure on Tourist Trips of Persons 15 Years and Over.

Palgrave Macmillan, 1 New York Plaza, Ste. 4500, New York, NY, 10004-1562, USA, (800) 777-4643, orders@palgrave.com, https://www.palgrave.com/us; The Statesman's Yearbook, 2023.

Routledge - Taylor & Francis Group, 6000 Broken Sound Pkwy. NW, Ste. 300, Boca Raton, FL, 33487, USA, (800) 634-1420, (800) 634-7064, orders@taylorandfrancis.com, https://www.routledge.com/; The Europa World Year Book 2022.

United Nations Food and Agricultural Organization (FAO), 2121 K St., Ste. 800B, Washington, DC, 20037, USA, (202) 653-2400 (Dial from U.S.), (202) 653-5760 (Fax from U.S.), fao-hq@fao.org, https://www.fao.org; The State of Food and Agriculture (SOFA) 2022.

United Nations Industrial Development Organization (UNIDO), 1 United Nations Plz., Rm. DC1-1118, New York, NY, 10017, USA, (212) 963-6890, (212) 963 6885, (212) 963-7904, office.newyork@unido.org, https://www.unido.org/; Industrial Statistics Databases and International Yearbook of Industrial Statistics 2021.

The World Bank, 1818 H St. NW, Washington, DC, 20433, USA, (202) 473-1000, (202) 477-6391, eds03@worldbank.org, https://www.worldbank.org/; Bulgaria (report).

World Intellectual Property Organization (WIPO), 34, chemin des Colombettes, Geneva, CH-1211, SWI, https://www.wipo.int; Madrid Yearly Review 2022: International Registrations of Marks.

BULGARIA-INFANT AND MATERNAL MORTALITY

See BULGARIA-MORTALITY

BULGARIA-INTERNATIONAL TRADE

The Economist Group: Economist Intelligence Unit (EIU), 900 3rd Ave., 16th Fl., New York, NY, 10022, USA, (212) 541-0500, americas@eiu.com, https://www.eiu.com; Bulgaria Country Report.

Euromonitor International, Inc., 1 N Dearborn St., Ste. 1700, Chicago, IL, 60602, USA, (312) 922-1115, (312) 922-1157, info-usa@euromonitor.com, https://www.euromonitor.com/; Geographies.

European Commission, Eurostat, Luxembourg, 2920, LUX, https://ec.europa.eu/eurostat/; Extra-EU Trade in Goods.

Palgrave Macmillan, 1 New York Plaza, Ste. 4500, New York, NY, 10004-1562, USA, (800) 777-4643, orders@palgrave.com, https://www.palgrave.com/us; The Statesman's Yearbook, 2023.

Routledge - Taylor & Francis Group, 6000 Broken Sound Pkwy. NW, Ste. 300, Boca Raton, FL, 33487, USA, (800) 634-1420, (800) 634-7064, orders@taylorandfrancis.com, https://www.routledge.com/; The Europa World Year Book 2022.

United Nations Conference on Trade and Development (UNCTAD), Palais des Nations, Geneva, 1211, SWI, (212) 963-6896, unctadinfo@unctad.org, https://unctad.org; Trade and Development Report 2021.

United Nations Food and Agricultural Organization (FAO), 2121 K St., Ste. 800B, Washington, DC, 20037, USA, (202) 653-2400 (Dial from U.S.), (202) 653-5760 (Fax from U.S.), fao-hq@fao.org, https://www.fao.org; The State of Food and Agriculture (SOFA) 2022.

United Nations Statistics Division (UNSD), United Nations Plz., New York, NY, 10017, USA, (800) 253-9646, (212) 963-9851, statistics@un.org, https://unstats.un.org; International Trade Statistics Yearbook 2020 and Statistical Yearbook of the United Nations 2021.

The World Bank, 1818 H St. NW, Washington, DC, 20433, USA, (202) 473-1000, (202) 477-6391, eds03@worldbank.org, https://www.worldbank.org/; Bulgaria (report) and World Development Report 2022: Finance for an Equitable Recovery.

World Trade Organization (WTO), Ctre. William Rappard, Rue de Lausanne 154, Case postale, Geneva, CH-1211, SWI, enquiries@wto.org, https://www.wto.org; World Trade Statistical Review 2022.

BULGARIA-INTERNET USERS

International Telecommunication Union (ITU), Place des Nations, Geneva, CH-1211, SWI, itumail@itu.int, https://www.itu.int; Global Connectivity Report 2022; World Telecommunication/ICT Indicators Database 2021; and Yearbook of Statistics 2019.

The World Bank, 1818 H St. NW, Washington, DC, 20433, USA, (202) 473-1000, (202) 477-6391, eds03@worldbank.org, https://www.worldbank.org/; Bulgaria (report).

BULGARIA-LABOR

Central Intelligence Agency (CIA), Office of Public Affairs, Washington, DC, 20505, USA, (703) 482-0623, https://www.cia.gov; The World Factbook.

Euromonitor International, Inc., 1 N Dearborn St., Ste. 1700, Chicago, IL, 60602, USA, (312) 922-1115, (312) 922-1157, info-usa@euromonitor.com, https://www.euromonitor.com/; Geographies.

International Labour Organization (ILO), 4 Rte. des Morillons, Geneva, CH-1211, SWI, ilo@ilo.org, https://www.ilo.org; NORMLEX Information System on International Labour Standards.

Palgrave Macmillan, 1 New York Plaza, Ste. 4500, New York, NY, 10004-1562, USA, (800) 777-4643, orders@palgrave.com, https://www.palgrave.com/us; The Statesman's Yearbook, 2023.

United Nations Food and Agricultural Organization (FAO), 2121 K St., Ste. 800B, Washington, DC, 20037, USA, (202) 653-2400 (Dial from U.S.), (202) 653-5760 (Fax from U.S.), fao-hq@fao.org, https://www.fao.org; The State of Food and Agriculture (SOFA) 2022.

The World Bank, 1818 H St. NW, Washington, DC, 20433, USA, (202) 473-1000, (202) 477-6391, eds03@worldbank.org, https://www.worldbank.org/; World Development Report 2022: Finance for an Equitable Recovery.

BULGARIA-LAND USE

United Nations Statistics Division (UNSD), United Nations Plz., New York, NY, 10017, USA, (800) 253-9646, (212) 963-9851, statistics@un.org, https://unstats.un.org; Millennium Development Goal Indicators.

The World Bank, 1818 H St. NW, Washington, DC, 20433, USA, (202) 473-1000, (202) 477-6391, eds03@worldbank.org, https://www.worldbank.org/; World Development Report 2022: Finance for an Equitable Recovery.

BULGARIA-LIBRARIES

UNESCO Institute for Statistics, C.P 250 Succursale H, Montreal, QC, H3G 2K8, CAN, (514) 343-6880 (Dial from U.S.), (514) 343-5740 (Fax from U.S.), uis.publications@unesco.org, http://uis.unesco.org/; UIS.Stat.

BULGARIA-LIFE EXPECTANCY

Central Intelligence Agency (CIA), Office of Public Affairs, Washington, DC, 20505, USA, (703) 482-0623, https://www.cia.gov; The World Factbook.

United Nations Department of Economic and Social Affairs (DESA), Population Division, 2 United Nations Plz., Rm. DC2-1950, New York, NY, 10017, USA, (212) 963-3209, (212) 963-2147, population@un.org, https://www.un.org/development/desa/pd/; World Population Ageing 2020 Highlights.

United Nations Statistics Division (UNSD), United Nations Plz., New York, NY, 10017, USA, (800) 253-9646, (212) 963-9851, statistics@un.org, https://unstats.un.org; Millennium Development Goal Indicators.

BULGARIA-LITERACY

Euromonitor International, Inc., 1 N Dearborn St., Ste. 1700, Chicago, IL, 60602, USA, (312) 922-1115, (312) 922-1157, info-usa@euromonitor.com, https://www.euromonitor.com/; Geographies.

UNESCO Institute for Statistics, C.P 250 Succursale H, Montreal, QC, H3G 2K8, CAN, (514) 343-6880 (Dial from U.S.), (514) 343-5740 (Fax from U.S.), uis.publications@unesco.org, http://uis.unesco.org/; Literacy.

BULGARIA-LIVESTOCK

Palgrave Macmillan, 1 New York Plaza, Ste. 4500, New York, NY, 10004-1562, USA, (800) 777-4643, orders@palgrave.com, https://www.palgrave.com/us; The Statesman's Yearbook, 2023.

Routledge - Taylor & Francis Group, 6000 Broken Sound Pkwy. NW, Ste. 300, Boca Raton, FL, 33487, USA, (800) 634-1420, (800) 634-7064, orders@taylorandfrancis.com, https://www.routledge.com/; The Europa World Year Book 2022.

United Nations Food and Agricultural Organization (FAO), 2121 K St., Ste. 800B, Washington, DC, 20037, USA, (202) 653-2400 (Dial from U.S.), (202) 653-5760 (Fax from U.S.), fao-hq@fao.org, https://www.fao.org; The State of Food and Agriculture (SOFA) 2022.

United Nations Statistics Division (UNSD), United Nations Plz., New York, NY, 10017, USA, (800) 253-9646, (212) 963-9851, statistics@un.org, https://unstats.un.org; Statistical Yearbook of the United Nations 2021.

BULGARIA-MARRIAGE

Routledge - Taylor & Francis Group, 6000 Broken Sound Pkwy. NW, Ste. 300, Boca Raton, FL, 33487, USA, (800) 634-1420, (800) 634-7064, orders@taylorandfrancis.com, https://www.routledge.com/; The Europa World Year Book 2022.

United Nations Statistics Division (UNSD), United Nations Plz., New York, NY, 10017, USA, (800) 253-9646, (212) 963-9851, statistics@un.org, https://unstats.un.org; Statistical Yearbook of the United Nations 2021.

BULGARIA-MINERAL INDUSTRIES

Barchart, 209 W Jackson Blvd., 2nd Fl., Chicago, IL, 60606, USA, (877) 247-4394, commodities@barchart.com, https://www.barchart.com/cmdty; The cmdty Yearbook 2023; cmdtyStats: Commodity Statistics and Fundamental Data; cmdtyView: Commodity Index; and Commodity Data and Prices.

European Commission, Eurostat, Luxembourg, 2920, LUX, https://ec.europa.eu/eurostat/; Final Energy Consumption in Transport by Type of Fuel.

International Energy Agency (IEA), 9 Rue de la Federation, Paris, 75739, FRA, info@iea.org, https://www.iea.org/; World Energy Outlook 2021.

International Lead and Zinc Study Group (ILZSG), Rua Almirante Barroso 38, 5th Fl., Lisbon, 1000-013, PRT, sales@ilzsg.org, https://www.ilzsg.org; Interactive Statistical Database.

Palgrave Macmillan, 1 New York Plaza, Ste. 4500, New York, NY, 10004-1562, USA, (800) 777-4643, orders@palgrave.com, https://www.palgrave.com/us; The Statesman's Yearbook, 2023.

Routledge - Taylor & Francis Group, 6000 Broken Sound Pkwy. NW, Ste. 300, Boca Raton, FL, 33487, USA, (800) 634-1420, (800) 634-7064, orders@taylorandfrancis.com, https://www.routledge.com/; The Europa World Year Book 2022.

S&P Global Commodity Insights, One World Trade Center, New York, NY, 10007, USA, (800) 752-8878, support@platts.com, https://www.spglobal.com/commodityinsights/en; Platts Power in Europe.

United Nations Conference on Trade and Development (UNCTAD), Palais des Nations, Geneva, 1211, SWI, (212) 963-6896, unctadinfo@unctad.org, https://unctad.org; Trade and Development Report 2021.

United Nations Statistics Division (UNSD), United Nations Plz., New York, NY, 10017, USA, (800) 253-9646, (212) 963-9851, statistics@un.org, https://unstats.un.org; Statistical Yearbook of the United Nations 2021.

BULGARIA-MONEY SUPPLY

The Economist Group: Economist Intelligence Unit (EIU), 900 3rd Ave., 16th Fl., New York, NY, 10022, USA, (212) 541-0500, americas@eiu.com, https://www.eiu.com; Bulgaria Country Report.

The World Bank, 1818 H St. NW, Washington, DC, 20433, USA, (202) 473-1000, (202) 477-6391, eds03@worldbank.org, https://www.worldbank.org/; Bulgaria (report).

BULGARIA-MORTALITY

UNICEF, 3 United Nations Plz., New York, NY, 10017, USA, (212) 303-7984, (917) 244-2215, https://www.unicef.org; The State of the World's Children 2023.

United Nations Statistics Division (UNSD), United Nations Plz., New York, NY, 10017, USA, (800) 253-9646, (212) 963-9851, statistics@un.org, https://unstats.un.org; Millennium Development Goal Indicators; Statistical Yearbook of the United Nations 2021; and World Statistics Pocketbook 2021.

World Health Organization (WHO), Ave. Appia 20, Geneva, CH-1211, SWI, (202) 974-3000 (Telephone in U.S.), publications@who.int, https://www.who.int/; Global Health Observatory (GHO).

BULGARIA-MOTION PICTURES

Palgrave Macmillan, 1 New York Plaza, Ste. 4500, New York, NY, 10004-1562, USA, (800) 777-4643, orders@palgrave.com, https://www.palgrave.com/us; The Statesman's Yearbook, 2023.

BULGARIA-MOTOR VEHICLES

International Road Federation (IRF), Madison Place, 500 Montgomery St., 5th Fl., Alexandria, VA, 22314, USA, (703) 535-1001, (703) 535-1007, info@irf.global, https://www.irf.global/; World Road Statistics (WRS).

BULGARIA-NATURAL GAS PRODUCTION

See BULGARIA-MINERAL INDUSTRIES

BULGARIA-NUTRITION

United Nations Food and Agricultural Organization (FAO), 2121 K St., Ste. 800B, Washington, DC, 20037, USA, (202) 653-2400 (Dial from U.S.), (202) 653-5760 (Fax from U.S.), fao-hq@fao.org, https://www.fao.org; The State of Food and Agriculture (SOFA) 2022.

United Nations Statistics Division (UNSD), United Nations Plz., New York, NY, 10017, USA, (800) 253-9646, (212) 963-9851, statistics@un.org, https://unstats.un.org; Millennium Development Goal Indicators.

BULGARIA-PAPER

See BULGARIA-FORESTS AND FORESTRY

BULGARIA-PEANUT PRODUCTION

See BULGARIA-CROPS

BULGARIA-PESTICIDES

United Nations Food and Agricultural Organization (FAO), 2121 K St., Ste. 800B, Washington, DC, 20037, USA, (202) 653-2400 (Dial from U.S.), (202) 653-5760 (Fax from U.S.), fao-hq@fao.org, https://www.fao.org; The State of Food and Agriculture (SOFA) 2022.

BULGARIA-PETROLEUM INDUSTRY AND TRADE

International Energy Agency (IEA), 9 Rue de la Federation, Paris, 75739, FRA, info@iea.org, https://www.iea.org/; World Energy Outlook 2021.

Palgrave Macmillan, 1 New York Plaza, Ste. 4500, New York, NY, 10004-1562, USA, (800) 777-4643, orders@palgrave.com, https://www.palgrave.com/us; The Statesman's Yearbook, 2023.

U.S. Energy Information Administration (EIA), 1000 Independence Ave. SW, Washington, DC, 20585, USA, (202) 586-8800, infoctr@eia.gov, https://www.eia.gov; International Energy Outlook 2021.

United Nations Food and Agricultural Organization (FAO), 2121 K St., Ste. 800B, Washington, DC, 20037, USA, (202) 653-2400 (Dial from U.S.), (202) 653-5760 (Fax from U.S.), fao-hq@fao.org, https://www.fao.org; The State of Food and Agriculture (SOFA) 2022.

United Nations Statistics Division (UNSD), United Nations Plz., New York, NY, 10017, USA, (800) 253-9646, (212) 963-9851, statistics@un.org, https://unstats.un.org; Statistical Yearbook of the United Nations 2021.

BULGARIA-PLASTICS INDUSTRY AND TRADE

United Nations Statistics Division (UNSD), United Nations Plz., New York, NY, 10017, USA, (800) 253-9646, (212) 963-9851, statistics@un.org, https://unstats.un.org; Statistical Yearbook of the United Nations 2021.

BULGARIA-POPULATION

Central Intelligence Agency (CIA), Office of Public Affairs, Washington, DC, 20505, USA, (703) 482-0623, https://www.cia.gov; The World Factbook.

The Economist Group: Economist Intelligence Unit (EIU), 900 3rd Ave., 16th Fl., New York, NY, 10022, USA, (212) 541-0500, americas@eiu.com, https://www.eiu.com; Bulgaria Country Report.

Infoplease, c/o Sandbox Networks, Inc., 1 Lincoln St., 24th Fl., Boston, MA, 02111, USA, https://www.infoplease.com; Countries of the World.

International Labour Organization (ILO), 4 Rte. des Morillons, Geneva, CH-1211, SWI, ilo@ilo.org, https://www.ilo.org; NORMLEX Information System on International Labour Standards.

National Statistical Insitute of Bulgaria, 2 P. Volov St., Sofia, 1038, BUL, info@nsi.bg, https://www.nsi.bg/en; Bulgaria 2021.

Palgrave Macmillan, 1 New York Plaza, Ste. 4500, New York, NY, 10004-1562, USA, (800) 777-4643, orders@palgrave.com, https://www.palgrave.com/us; The Statesman's Yearbook, 2023.

Routledge - Taylor & Francis Group, 6000 Broken Sound Pkwy. NW, Ste. 300, Boca Raton, FL, 33487, USA, (800) 634-1420, (800) 634-7064, orders@taylorandfrancis.com, https://www.routledge.com/; The Europa World Year Book 2022.

UK Data Service, University of Essex, Wivenhoe Park, Colchester, Essex, CO4 3SQ, GBR, https://ukdataservice.ac.uk/; International Aggregate Data.

UNESCO Institute for Statistics, C.P 250 Succursale H, Montreal, QC, H3G 2K8, CAN, (514) 343-6880 (Dial from U.S.), (514) 343-5740 (Fax from U.S.), uis.publications@unesco.org, http://uis.unesco.org/; UIS.Stat.

United Nations Department of Economic and Social Affairs (DESA), Population Division, 2 United Nations Plz., Rm. DC2-1950, New York, NY, 10017, USA, (212) 963-3209, (212) 963-2147, population@un.org, https://www.un.org/development/desa/pd/; Revision of World Urbanization Prospects and World Population Ageing 2020 Highlights.

United Nations Development Programme (UNDP), One United Nations Plz., New York, NY, 10017, USA, (212) 906-5000, (212) 906-5001, https://www.undp.org; Human Development Report 2021-2022.

United Nations Statistics Division (UNSD), United Nations Plz., New York, NY, 10017, USA, (800) 253-9646, (212) 963-9851, statistics@un.org, https://unstats.un.org; Statistical Yearbook of the United Nations 2021 and World Statistics Pocketbook 2021.

The World Bank, 1818 H St. NW, Washington, DC, 20433, USA, (202) 473-1000, (202) 477-6391, eds03@worldbank.org, https://www.worldbank.org/; Bulgaria (report); The Global Findex Database 2021; and World Development Report 2022: Finance for an Equitable Recovery.

BULGARIA-POPULATION DENSITY

Central Intelligence Agency (CIA), Office of Public Affairs, Washington, DC, 20505, USA, (703) 482-0623, https://www.cia.gov; The World Factbook.

Palgrave Macmillan, 1 New York Plaza, Ste. 4500, New York, NY, 10004-1562, USA, (800) 777-4643, orders@palgrave.com, https://www.palgrave.com/us; The Statesman's Yearbook, 2023.

Routledge - Taylor & Francis Group, 6000 Broken Sound Pkwy. NW, Ste. 300, Boca Raton, FL, 33487, USA, (800) 634-1420, (800) 634-7064, orders@taylorandfrancis.com, https://www.routledge.com/; The Europa World Year Book 2022.

The World Bank, 1818 H St. NW, Washington, DC, 20433, USA, (202) 473-1000, (202) 477-6391, eds03@worldbank.org, https://www.worldbank.org/; Bulgaria (report) and World Development Report 2022: Finance for an Equitable Recovery.

BULGARIA-POSTAL SERVICE

Palgrave Macmillan, 1 New York Plaza, Ste. 4500, New York, NY, 10004-1562, USA, (800) 777-4643, orders@palgrave.com, https://www.palgrave.com/us; The Statesman's Yearbook, 2023.

BULGARIA-POULTRY

See BULGARIA-LIVESTOCK

BULGARIA-POWER RESOURCES

Euromonitor International, Inc., 1 N Dearborn St., Ste. 1700, Chicago, IL, 60602, USA, (312) 922-1115, (312) 922-1157, info-usa@euromonitor.com, https://www.euromonitor.com/; Geographies.

International Energy Agency (IEA), 9 Rue de la Federation, Paris, 75739, FRA, info@iea.org, https://www.iea.org/; World Energy Outlook 2021.

Palgrave Macmillan, 1 New York Plaza, Ste. 4500, New York, NY, 10004-1562, USA, (800) 777-4643, orders@palgrave.com, https://www.palgrave.com/us; The Statesman's Yearbook, 2023.

S&P Global Commodity Insights, One World Trade Center, New York, NY, 10007, USA, (800) 752-8878, support@platts.com, https://www.spglobal.com/commodityinsights/en; Platts European Power Daily.

U.S. Energy Information Administration (EIA), 1000 Independence Ave. SW, Washington, DC, 20585, USA, (202) 586-8800, infoctr@eia.gov, https://www.eia.gov; International Energy Outlook 2021.

United Nations Food and Agricultural Organization (FAO), 2121 K St., Ste. 800B, Washington, DC, 20037, USA, (202) 653-2400 (Dial from U.S.), (202) 653-5760 (Fax from U.S.), fao-hq@fao.org, https://www.fao.org; The State of Food and Agriculture (SOFA) 2022.

United Nations Statistics Division (UNSD), United Nations Plz., New York, NY, 10017, USA, (800) 253-9646, (212) 963-9851, statistics@un.org, https://unstats.un.org; Energy Statistics Yearbook 2019; Statistical Yearbook of the United Nations 2021; and World Statistics Pocketbook 2021.

The World Bank, 1818 H St. NW, Washington, DC, 20433, USA, (202) 473-1000, (202) 477-6391, eds03@worldbank.org, https://www.worldbank.org/; World Development Report 2022: Finance for an Equitable Recovery.

BULGARIA-PRICES

Euromonitor International, Inc., 1 N Dearborn St., Ste. 1700, Chicago, IL, 60602, USA, (312) 922-1115, (312) 922-1157, info-usa@euromonitor.com, https://www.euromonitor.com/; Geographies.

The World Bank, 1818 H St. NW, Washington, DC, 20433, USA, (202) 473-1000, (202) 477-6391, eds03@worldbank.org, https://www.worldbank.org/; Bulgaria (report).

BULGARIA-PUBLIC HEALTH

Euromonitor International, Inc., 1 N Dearborn St., Ste. 1700, Chicago, IL, 60602, USA, (312) 922-1115, (312) 922-1157, info-usa@euromonitor.com, https://www.euromonitor.com/; Geographies and Market Research on the Health and Wellness Industry.

European Commission, Directorate-General for Health and Food Safety, Brussels, B-1049, BEL, https://ec.europa.eu/info/departments/health-and-food-safety_en ; zzunpublished data.

National Statistical Insitute of Bulgaria, 2 P. Volov St., Sofia, 1038, BUL, info@nsi.bg, https://www.nsi.bg/en; Road Traffic Accidents in the Republic of Bulgaria 2020.

Palgrave Macmillan, 1 New York Plaza, Ste. 4500, New York, NY, 10004-1562, USA, (800) 777-4643, orders@palgrave.com, https://www.palgrave.com/us; The Statesman's Yearbook, 2023.

U.S. Census Bureau, 4600 Silver Hill Rd., Washington, DC, 20233, USA, (301) 763-4636, (800) 923-8282, https://www.census.gov; HIV/AIDS Surveillance Data Base.

UNICEF, 3 United Nations Plz., New York, NY, 10017, USA, (212) 303-7984, (917) 244-2215, https://www.unicef.org; The State of the World's Children 2023.

United Nations Department of Economic and Social Affairs (DESA), Population Division, 2 United Nations Plz., Rm. DC2-1950, New York, NY, 10017, USA, (212) 963-3209, (212) 963-2147, population@un.org, https://www.un.org/development/desa/pd/; World Fertility Data 2019.

United Nations Development Programme (UNDP), One United Nations Plz., New York, NY, 10017, USA, (212) 906-5000, (212) 906-5001, https://www.undp.org; Human Development Report 2021-2022.

United Nations Statistics Division (UNSD), United Nations Plz., New York, NY, 10017, USA, (800) 253-9646, (212) 963-9851, statistics@un.org, https://unstats.un.org; Millennium Development Goal Indicators and Statistical Yearbook of the United Nations 2021.

The World Bank, 1818 H St. NW, Washington, DC, 20433, USA, (202) 473-1000, (202) 477-6391, eds03@worldbank.org, https://www.worldbank.org/; Bulgaria (report).

World Health Organization (WHO), Ave. Appia 20, Geneva, CH-1211, SWI, (202) 974-3000 (Telephone in U.S.), publications@who.int, https://www.who.int/; Global Health Observatory (GHO) and Health Statistics and Information Systems.

BULGARIA-PUBLISHERS AND PUBLISHING

Palgrave Macmillan, 1 New York Plaza, Ste. 4500, New York, NY, 10004-1562, USA, (800) 777-4643, orders@palgrave.com, https://www.palgrave.com/us; The Statesman's Yearbook, 2023.

Routledge - Taylor & Francis Group, 6000 Broken Sound Pkwy. NW, Ste. 300, Boca Raton, FL, 33487, USA, (800) 634-1420, (800) 634-7064, orders@taylorandfrancis.com, https://www.routledge.com/; The Europa World Year Book 2022.

UNESCO Institute for Statistics, C.P 250 Succursale H, Montreal, QC, H3G 2K8, CAN, (514) 343-6880 (Dial from U.S.), (514) 343-5740 (Fax from U.S.), uis.publications@unesco.org, http://uis.unesco.org/; UIS.Stat.

BULGARIA-RAILROADS

Janes, USA, (703) 574-7580, (888) 977-1519, customer.care@janes.com, https://www.janes.com; Janes World Railways 2021-2022.

Palgrave Macmillan, 1 New York Plaza, Ste. 4500, New York, NY, 10004-1562, USA, (800) 777-4643, orders@palgrave.com, https://www.palgrave.com/us; The Statesman's Yearbook, 2023.

Routledge - Taylor & Francis Group, 6000 Broken Sound Pkwy. NW, Ste. 300, Boca Raton, FL, 33487, USA, (800) 634-1420, (800) 634-7064, orders@taylorandfrancis.com, https://www.routledge.com/; The Europa World Year Book 2022.

United Nations Statistics Division (UNSD), United Nations Plz., New York, NY, 10017, USA, (800) 253-9646, (212) 963-9851, statistics@un.org, https://unstats.un.org; Statistical Yearbook of the United Nations 2021.

BULGARIA-RELIGION

Central Intelligence Agency (CIA), Office of Public Affairs, Washington, DC, 20505, USA, (703) 482-0623, https://www.cia.gov; The World Factbook.

Palgrave Macmillan, 1 New York Plaza, Ste. 4500, New York, NY, 10004-1562, USA, (800) 777-4643, orders@palgrave.com, https://www.palgrave.com/us; The Statesman's Yearbook, 2023.

BULGARIA-RETAIL TRADE

Euromonitor International, Inc., 1 N Dearborn St., Ste. 1700, Chicago, IL, 60602, USA, (312) 922-1115, (312) 922-1157, info-usa@euromonitor.com, https://www.euromonitor.com/; Geographies and Market Research on the Retailing Industry.

United Nations Statistics Division (UNSD), United Nations Plz., New York, NY, 10017, USA, (800) 253-9646, (212) 963-9851, statistics@un.org, https://unstats.un.org; Statistical Yearbook of the United Nations 2021.

BULGARIA-RICE PRODUCTION

See BULGARIA-CROPS

BULGARIA-ROADS

International Road Federation (IRF), Madison Place, 500 Montgomery St., 5th Fl., Alexandria, VA, 22314, USA, (703) 535-1001, (703) 535-1007, info@irf.global, https://www.irf.global/; World Road Statistics (WRS).

National Statistical Insitute of Bulgaria, 2 P. Volov St., Sofia, 1038, BUL, info@nsi.bg, https://www.nsi.bg/en; Road Traffic Accidents in the Republic of Bulgaria 2020.

BULGARIA-RUBBER INDUSTRY AND TRADE

International Rubber Study Group (IRSG), 51 Changi Business Park Central 2, Unit No. 6, 486066, SGP, https://www.rubberstudy.org; Monthly Rubber Bulletin (MRB); Rubber Industry Report; Rubber Statistical Bulletin; and World Rubber Industry Report (WRIO).

United Nations Statistics Division (UNSD), United Nations Plz., New York, NY, 10017, USA, (800) 253-9646, (212) 963-9851, statistics@un.org, https://unstats.un.org; Statistical Yearbook of the United Nations 2021.

BULGARIA-SHIPPING

Routledge - Taylor & Francis Group, 6000 Broken Sound Pkwy. NW, Ste. 300, Boca Raton, FL, 33487, USA, (800) 634-1420, (800) 634-7064, orders@taylorandfrancis.com, https://www.routledge.com/; The Europa World Year Book 2022.

S&P Global, IHS Markit, 15 Inverness Way E, Englewood, CO, 80112, USA, (800) 447-2273, (800) 854-7179, https://ihsmarkit.com; IHS Maritime World Shipbuilding Statistics; Journal of Commerce; Lloyd's Register of Ships 2021-2022; and Maritime Portal Desktop.

United Nations Statistics Division (UNSD), United Nations Plz., New York, NY, 10017, USA, (800) 253-9646, (212) 963-9851, statistics@un.org, https://unstats.un.org; Statistical Yearbook of the United Nations 2021.

BULGARIA-SOYBEAN PRODUCTION

See BULGARIA-CROPS

BULGARIA-STEEL PRODUCTION

See BULGARIA-MINERAL INDUSTRIES

BULGARIA-SUGAR PRODUCTION

See BULGARIA-CROPS

BULGARIA-SULPHUR PRODUCTION

See BULGARIA-MINERAL INDUSTRIES

BULGARIA-TAXATION

International Road Federation (IRF), Madison Place, 500 Montgomery St., 5th Fl., Alexandria, VA, 22314, USA, (703) 535-1001, (703) 535-1007, info@irf.global, https://www.irf.global/; World Road Statistics (WRS).

Palgrave Macmillan, 1 New York Plaza, Ste. 4500, New York, NY, 10004-1562, USA, (800) 777-4643, orders@palgrave.com, https://www.palgrave.com/us; The Statesman's Yearbook, 2023.

BULGARIA-TELEPHONE

Palgrave Macmillan, 1 New York Plaza, Ste. 4500, New York, NY, 10004-1562, USA, (800) 777-4643, orders@palgrave.com, https://www.palgrave.com/us; The Statesman's Yearbook, 2023.

Routledge - Taylor & Francis Group, 6000 Broken Sound Pkwy. NW, Ste. 300, Boca Raton, FL, 33487, USA, (800) 634-1420, (800) 634-7064, orders@taylorandfrancis.com, https://www.routledge.com/; The Europa World Year Book 2022.

United Nations Statistics Division (UNSD), United Nations Plz., New York, NY, 10017, USA, (800) 253-9646, (212) 963-9851, statistics@un.org, https://unstats.un.org; World Statistics Pocketbook 2021.

BULGARIA-THEATER

UNESCO Institute for Statistics, C.P 250 Succursale H, Montreal, QC, H3G 2K8, CAN, (514) 343-6880 (Dial from U.S.), (514) 343-5740 (Fax from U.S.), uis.publications@unesco.org, http://uis.unesco.org/; UIS.Stat.

BULGARIA-TOBACCO INDUSTRY

United Nations Statistics Division (UNSD), United Nations Plz., New York, NY, 10017, USA, (800) 253-9646, (212) 963-9851, statistics@un.org, https://unstats.un.org; Statistical Yearbook of the United Nations 2021.

BULGARIA-TOURISM

Euromonitor International, Inc., 1 N Dearborn St., Ste. 1700, Chicago, IL, 60602, USA, (312) 922-1115, (312) 922-1157, info-usa@euromonitor.com, https://www.euromonitor.com/; Geographies.

European Commission, Rue de la Loi, 170, Brussels, B-1040, BEL, https://ec.europa.eu; Common Agricultural Policy (CAPF) Context Indicators, 2019 Update.

National Statistical Insitute of Bulgaria, 2 P. Volov St., Sofia, 1038, BUL, info@nsi.bg, https://www.nsi.bg/en; Expenditure on Tourist Trips of Persons 15 Years and Over.

Palgrave Macmillan, 1 New York Plaza, Ste. 4500, New York, NY, 10004-1562, USA, (800) 777-4643, orders@palgrave.com, https://www.palgrave.com/us; The Statesman's Yearbook, 2023.

Routledge - Taylor & Francis Group, 6000 Broken Sound Pkwy. NW, Ste. 300, Boca Raton, FL, 33487, USA, (800) 634-1420, (800) 634-7064, orders@taylorandfrancis.com, https://www.routledge.com/; The Europa World Year Book 2022.

United Nations Statistics Division (UNSD), United Nations Plz., New York, NY, 10017, USA, (800) 253-9646, (212) 963-9851, statistics@un.org, https://unstats.un.org; Statistical Yearbook of the United Nations 2021.

United Nations World Tourism Organization (UNWTO), Calle Poeta Joan Maragall 42, Madrid, 28020, SPA, info@unwto.org, https://www.unwto.org/; Yearbook of Tourism Statistics, 2021 Edition.

The World Bank, 1818 H St. NW, Washington, DC, 20433, USA, (202) 473-1000, (202) 477-6391, eds03@worldbank.org, https://www.worldbank.org/; Bulgaria (report).

BULGARIA-TRADE

See BULGARIA-INTERNATIONAL TRADE

BULGARIA-TRANSPORTATION

Central Intelligence Agency (CIA), Office of Public Affairs, Washington, DC, 20505, USA, (703) 482-0623, https://www.cia.gov; The World Factbook.

Euromonitor International, Inc., 1 N Dearborn St., Ste. 1700, Chicago, IL, 60602, USA, (312) 922-1115, (312) 922-1157, info-usa@euromonitor.com, https://www.euromonitor.com/; Geographies.

European Commission, Eurostat, Luxembourg, 2920, LUX, https://ec.europa.eu/eurostat/; Air Transport Statistics.

Palgrave Macmillan, 1 New York Plaza, Ste. 4500, New York, NY, 10004-1562, USA, (800) 777-4643, orders@palgrave.com, https://www.palgrave.com/us; The Statesman's Yearbook, 2023.

Routledge - Taylor & Francis Group, 6000 Broken Sound Pkwy. NW, Ste. 300, Boca Raton, FL, 33487, USA, (800) 634-1420, (800) 634-7064, orders@taylorandfrancis.com, https://www.routledge.com/; The Europa World Year Book 2022.

The World Bank, 1818 H St. NW, Washington, DC, 20433, USA, (202) 473-1000, (202) 477-6391, eds03@worldbank.org, https://www.worldbank.org/; Bulgaria (report).

BULGARIA-UNEMPLOYMENT

International Labour Organization (ILO), 4 Rte. des Morillons, Geneva, CH-1211, SWI, ilo@ilo.org, https://www.ilo.org; NORMLEX Information System on International Labour Standards.

Palgrave Macmillan, 1 New York Plaza, Ste. 4500, New York, NY, 10004-1562, USA, (800) 777-4643, orders@palgrave.com, https://www.palgrave.com/us; The Statesman's Yearbook, 2023.

BULGARIA-VITAL STATISTICS

Palgrave Macmillan, 1 New York Plaza, Ste. 4500, New York, NY, 10004-1562, USA, (800) 777-4643, orders@palgrave.com, https://www.palgrave.com/us; The Statesman's Yearbook, 2023.

U.S. Census Bureau, 4600 Silver Hill Rd., Washington, DC, 20233, USA, (301) 763-4636, (800) 923-8282, https://www.census.gov; HIV/AIDS Surveillance Data Base.

United Nations Department of Economic and Social Affairs (DESA), Population Division, 2 United Nations Plz., Rm. DC2-1950, New York, NY, 10017, USA, (212) 963-3209, (212) 963-2147, population@un.org, https://www.un.org/development/desa/pd/; World Contraceptive Use 2021: Estimates and Projections of Family Planning Indicators and World Marriage Data 2019.

United Nations Statistics Division (UNSD), United Nations Plz., New York, NY, 10017, USA, (800) 253-9646, (212) 963-9851, statistics@un.org, https://unstats.un.org; Statistical Yearbook of the United Nations 2021.

BULGARIA-WAGES

International Labour Organization (ILO), 4 Rte. des Morillons, Geneva, CH-1211, SWI, ilo@ilo.org, https://www.ilo.org; NORMLEX Information System on International Labour Standards.

United Nations Statistics Division (UNSD), United Nations Plz., New York, NY, 10017, USA, (800) 253-9646, (212) 963-9851, statistics@un.org, https://unstats.un.org; Statistical Yearbook of the United Nations 2021.

The World Bank, 1818 H St. NW, Washington, DC, 20433, USA, (202) 473-1000, (202) 477-6391, eds03@worldbank.org, https://www.worldbank.org/; Bulgaria (report).

BULGARIA-WEATHER

See BULGARIA-CLIMATE

BULGARIA-WHEAT PRODUCTION

See BULGARIA-CROPS

BULGARIA-WOOD AND WOOD PULP

See BULGARIA-FORESTS AND FORESTRY

BULGARIA-WOOL PRODUCTION

See BULGARIA-TEXTILE INDUSTRY

BULGARIA-ZINC AND ZINC ORE

See BULGARIA-MINERAL INDUSTRIES

BULLYING

Cyberbullying Research Center, USA, hinduja@cyberbullying.org, https://cyberbullying.org; Bullying, Cyberbullying, and Sexting by State; 2021 Cyberbullying Data; Summary of Our Cyberbullying Research (2007-2021); and Tween Cyberbullying in 2020.

U.S. Department of Education (ED), Institute of Education Sciences (IES), National Center for Education Statistics (NCES), Potomac Center Plaza, 550 12th St. SW, Washington, DC, 20202, USA, (202) 403-5551, https://nces.ed.gov/; Students' Perceptions of Bullying.

Youth Pride, Inc. (YPI), 743 Westminster St., Providence, RI, 02903, USA, (401) 421-5626, (401) 274-1990, info@youthprideri.org, https://www.youthprideri.org/; unpublished data.

BULLYING IN SCHOOLS

Council on American-Islamic Relations (CAIR), 453 New Jersey Ave. SE, Washington, DC, 20003, USA, (202) 488-8787, (202) 488-0833, info@cair.com, https://www.islamophobia.org/; Islamophobia in the Mainstream.

BULLYING IN THE WORKPLACE

Workplace Bullying Institute (WBI), USA, https://workplacebullying.org/; 2021 WBI U.S. Workplace Bullying Survey.

BUPRENORPHINE

Recovery Research Institute (RRI), 151 Merrimac St., 6th Fl., Boston, MA, 02114, USA, https://www.recoveryanswers.org/; Can Buprenorphine-Equipped Ambulances Help Link Overdose Survivors to Addiction Treatment?.

BURGLARY

U.S. Department of Justice (DOJ), Bureau of Justice Statistics (BJS), 810 7th St. NW, Washington, DC, 20531, USA, (202) 307-0765, askbjs@usdoj.gov, https://www.bjs.gov/; Criminal Victimization, 2020.

U.S. Department of Justice (DOJ), Federal Bureau of Investigation (FBI), 935 Pennsylvania Ave. NW, Washington, DC, 20535-0001, USA, (202) 324-3000, https://www.fbi.gov/; Crime in the United States 2019.

BURIAL

Green Burial Council (GBC), 2720 Cold Springs Rd., Placerville, CA, 95667, USA, (888) 966-3330, info@greenburialcouncil.org, https://www.greenburialcouncil.org; Disposition Statistics.

BURKINA FASO-NATIONAL STATISTICAL OFFICE

Institut National de la Statistique et de la Demographie de Burkina Faso (INSD), BP 374, Ouaga 2000, Ouagadougou, 01, BFA, insd@insd.bf, https://www.insd.bf/; National Data Reports (Burkina Faso).

BURKINA FASO-AGRICULTURE

African Development Bank Group (AfDB), Avenue Joseph Anoma, 01 BP 1387, Abidjan, 01, COT, https://www.afdb.org; African Economic Outlook 2021 and Compendium of Statistics on Bank Group Operations 2019.

The Economist Group: Economist Intelligence Unit (EIU), 900 3rd Ave., 16th Fl., New York, NY, 10022, USA, (212) 541-0500, americas@eiu.com, https://www.eiu.com; Burkina Faso Country Report.

Euromonitor International, Inc., 1 N Dearborn St., Ste. 1700, Chicago, IL, 60602, USA, (312) 922-1115, (312) 922-1157, info-usa@euromonitor.com, https://www.euromonitor.com/; Geographies.

Organisation of Islamic Cooperation (OIC), Statistical, Economic and Social Research and Training Centre for Islamic Countries (SESRIC), Kudus Cad. No. 9, Diplomatik Site, Ankara, 06450, TUR, statistics@sesric.org, https://www.sesric.org/; OIC Statistics (OICStat) Database and OIC-Countries in Figures (OIC-CIF).

Palgrave Macmillan, 1 New York Plaza, Ste. 4500, New York, NY, 10004-1562, USA, (800) 777-4643, orders@palgrave.com, https://www.palgrave.com/us; The Statesman's Yearbook, 2023.

Routledge - Taylor & Francis Group, 6000 Broken Sound Pkwy. NW, Ste. 300, Boca Raton, FL, 33487, USA, (800) 634-1420, (800) 634-7064, orders@taylorandfrancis.com, https://www.routledge.com/; The Europa World Year Book 2022.

United Nations Economic Commission for Africa (UNECA), PO Box 3001, Addis Ababa, ETH, ecainfo@uneca.org, https://www.uneca.org/; African Statistical Yearbook 2020 and Economic Report on Africa 2021.

United Nations Food and Agricultural Organization (FAO), 2121 K St., Ste. 800B, Washington, DC, 20037, USA, (202) 653-2400 (Dial from U.S.), (202) 653-5760 (Fax from U.S.), fao-hq@fao.org, https://www.fao.org; AQUASTAT and The State of Food and Agriculture (SOFA) 2022.

United Nations Statistics Division (UNSD), United Nations Plz., New York, NY, 10017, USA, (800) 253-9646, (212) 963-9851, statistics@un.org, https://unstats.un.org; Statistical Yearbook of the United Nations 2021.

The World Bank, 1818 H St. NW, Washington, DC, 20433, USA, (202) 473-1000, (202) 477-6391, eds03@worldbank.org, https://www.worldbank.org/; Burkina Faso (report) and World Development Indicators (WDI) 2022.

BURKINA FASO-AIRLINES

Palgrave Macmillan, 1 New York Plaza, Ste. 4500, New York, NY, 10004-1562, USA, (800) 777-4643, orders@palgrave.com, https://www.palgrave.com/us; The Statesman's Yearbook, 2023.

Routledge - Taylor & Francis Group, 6000 Broken Sound Pkwy. NW, Ste. 300, Boca Raton, FL, 33487, USA, (800) 634-1420, (800) 634-7064, orders@taylorandfrancis.com, https://www.routledge.com/; The Europa World Year Book 2022.

United Nations Economic Commission for Africa (UNECA), PO Box 3001, Addis Ababa, ETH, ecainfo@uneca.org, https://www.uneca.org/; African Statistical Yearbook 2020.

BURKINA FASO-ARMED FORCES

Central Intelligence Agency (CIA), Office of Public Affairs, Washington, DC, 20505, USA, (703) 482-0623, https://www.cia.gov; The World Factbook.

International Institute for Strategic Studies (IISS) - Americas, 2121 K St. NW, Ste. 600, Washington, DC, 20037, USA, (202) 659-1490, (202) 659-1499, https://www.iiss.org/; The Military Balance 2022.

Palgrave Macmillan, 1 New York Plaza, Ste. 4500, New York, NY, 10004-1562, USA, (800) 777-4643, orders@palgrave.com, https://www.palgrave.com/us; The Statesman's Yearbook, 2023.

Stockholm International Peace Research Institute (SIPRI), Signalistgatan 9, Stockholm, SE 169 72, SWE, https://www.sipri.org/; SIPRI Arms Transfers Database and SIPRI Military Expenditure Database.

BURKINA FASO-BALANCE OF PAYMENTS

African Development Bank Group (AfDB), Avenue Joseph Anoma, 01 BP 1387, Abidjan, 01, COT, https://www.afdb.org; The AfDB Statistics Pocketbook 2019.

International Monetary Fund (IMF), 700 19th St. NW, Washington, DC, 20431, USA, (202) 623-7000, (202) 623-4661, publications@imf.org, https://www.imf.org; Balance of Payments Statistics: Annual Report 2021.

Routledge - Taylor & Francis Group, 6000 Broken Sound Pkwy. NW, Ste. 300, Boca Raton, FL, 33487, USA, (800) 634-1420, (800) 634-7064, orders@taylorandfrancis.com, https://www.routledge.com/; The Europa World Year Book 2022.

United Nations Conference on Trade and Development (UNCTAD), Palais des Nations, Geneva, 1211, SWI, (212) 963-6896, unctadinfo@unctad.org, https://unctad.org; Handbook of Statistics 2021.

United Nations Economic Commission for Africa (UNECA), PO Box 3001, Addis Ababa, ETH, ecainfo@uneca.org, https://www.uneca.org/; African Statistical Yearbook 2020.

The World Bank, 1818 H St. NW, Washington, DC, 20433, USA, (202) 473-1000, (202) 477-6391, eds03@worldbank.org, https://www.worldbank.org/; Burkina Faso (report); World Development Indicators (WDI) 2022; and World Development Report 2022: Finance for an Equitable Recovery.

BURKINA FASO-BANKS AND BANKING

Euromonitor International, Inc., 1 N Dearborn St., Ste. 1700, Chicago, IL, 60602, USA, (312) 922-1115, (312) 922-1157, info-usa@euromonitor.com, https://www.euromonitor.com/; Geographies.

International Monetary Fund (IMF), 700 19th St. NW, Washington, DC, 20431, USA, (202) 623-7000, (202) 623-4661, publications@imf.org, https://www.imf.org; International Financial Statistics (IFS).

Routledge - Taylor & Francis Group, 6000 Broken Sound Pkwy. NW, Ste. 300, Boca Raton, FL, 33487, USA, (800) 634-1420, (800) 634-7064, orders@taylorandfrancis.com, https://www.routledge.com/; The Europa World Year Book 2022.

United Nations Economic Commission for Africa (UNECA), PO Box 3001, Addis Ababa, ETH, ecainfo@uneca.org, https://www.uneca.org/; African Statistical Yearbook 2020.

United Nations Statistics Division (UNSD), United Nations Plz., New York, NY, 10017, USA, (800) 253-9646, (212) 963-9851, statistics@un.org, https://unstats.un.org; Statistical Yearbook of the United Nations 2021.

BURKINA FASO-BROADCASTING

Central Intelligence Agency (CIA), Office of Public Affairs, Washington, DC, 20505, USA, (703) 482-0623, https://www.cia.gov; The World Factbook.

Euromonitor International, Inc., 1 N Dearborn St., Ste. 1700, Chicago, IL, 60602, USA, (312) 922-1115, (312) 922-1157, info-usa@euromonitor.com, https://www.euromonitor.com/; Geographies.

Palgrave Macmillan, 1 New York Plaza, Ste. 4500, New York, NY, 10004-1562, USA, (800) 777-4643, orders@palgrave.com, https://www.palgrave.com/us; The Statesman's Yearbook, 2023.

UNESCO Institute for Statistics, C.P 250 Succursale H, Montreal, QC, H3G 2K8, CAN, (514) 343-6880 (Dial from U.S.), (514) 343-5740 (Fax from U.S.), uis.publications@unesco.org, http://uis.unesco.org/; UIS.Stat.

WRTH Publications Limited, PO Box 290, Oxford, OX2 7FT, GBR, sales@wrth.com, https://www.wrth.com; World Radio TV Handbook 2023.

BURKINA FASO-BUDGET

Central Intelligence Agency (CIA), Office of Public Affairs, Washington, DC, 20505, USA, (703) 482-0623, https://www.cia.gov; The World Factbook.

BURKINA FASO-CHILDBIRTH-STATISTICS

The World Bank, 1818 H St. NW, Washington, DC, 20433, USA, (202) 473-1000, (202) 477-6391, eds03@worldbank.org, https://www.worldbank.org/; World Development Indicators (WDI) 2022.

BURKINA FASO-CLIMATE

International Institute for Environment and Development (IIED), 235 High Holborn, London, WC1V 7DN, GBR, inforequest@iied.org, https://www.iied.org; Environment & Urbanization.

Palgrave Macmillan, 1 New York Plaza, Ste. 4500, New York, NY, 10004-1562, USA, (800) 777-4643, orders@palgrave.com, https://www.palgrave.com/us; The Statesman's Yearbook, 2023.

BURKINA FASO-COAL PRODUCTION

See BURKINA FASO-MINERAL INDUSTRIES

BURKINA FASO-COMMERCE

Palgrave Macmillan, 1 New York Plaza, Ste. 4500, New York, NY, 10004-1562, USA, (800) 777-4643, orders@palgrave.com, https://www.palgrave.com/us; The Statesman's Yearbook, 2023.

UK Data Service, University of Essex, Wivenhoe Park, Colchester, Essex, CO4 3SQ, GBR, https://ukdataservice.ac.uk/; International Aggregate Data.

BURKINA FASO-COMMODITY EXCHANGES

Barchart, 209 W Jackson Blvd., 2nd Fl., Chicago, IL, 60606, USA, (877) 247-4394, commodities@barchart.com, https://www.barchart.com/cmdty; The cmdty Yearbook 2023; cmdtyStats: Commodity Statistics and Fundamental Data; cmdtyView: Commodity Index; and Commodity Data and Prices.

International Monetary Fund (IMF), 700 19th St. NW, Washington, DC, 20431, USA, (202) 623-7000, (202) 623-4661, publications@imf.org, https://www.imf.org; IMF Primary Commodity Prices.

BURKINA FASO-CONSTRUCTION INDUSTRY

United Nations Economic Commission for Africa (UNECA), PO Box 3001, Addis Ababa, ETH, ecainfo@uneca.org, https://www.uneca.org/; African Statistical Yearbook 2020.

BURKINA FASO-CONSUMER PRICE INDEXES

Routledge - Taylor & Francis Group, 6000 Broken Sound Pkwy. NW, Ste. 300, Boca Raton, FL, 33487, USA, (800) 634-1420, (800) 634-7064, orders@taylorandfrancis.com, https://www.routledge.com/; The Europa World Year Book 2022.

United Nations Economic Commission for Africa (UNECA), PO Box 3001, Addis Ababa, ETH, ecainfo@uneca.org, https://www.uneca.org/; African Statistical Yearbook 2020.

The World Bank, 1818 H St. NW, Washington, DC, 20433, USA, (202) 473-1000, (202) 477-6391, eds03@worldbank.org, https://www.worldbank.org/; Burkina Faso (report).

BURKINA FASO-CONSUMPTION (ECONOMICS)

African Development Bank Group (AfDB), Avenue Joseph Anoma, 01 BP 1387, Abidjan, 01, COT, https://www.afdb.org; The AfDB Statistics Pocketbook 2019.

BURKINA FASO-CORN INDUSTRY

See BURKINA FASO-CROPS

BURKINA FASO-COTTON

See BURKINA FASO-CROPS

BURKINA FASO-CROPS

International Monetary Fund (IMF), 700 19th St. NW, Washington, DC, 20431, USA, (202) 623-7000, (202) 623-4661, publications@imf.org, https://www.imf.org; International Financial Statistics (IFS).

Palgrave Macmillan, 1 New York Plaza, Ste. 4500, New York, NY, 10004-1562, USA, (800) 777-4643, orders@palgrave.com, https://www.palgrave.com/us; The Statesman's Yearbook, 2023.

United Nations Economic Commission for Africa (UNECA), PO Box 3001, Addis Ababa, ETH, ecainfo@uneca.org, https://www.uneca.org/; African Statistical Yearbook 2020.

United Nations Food and Agricultural Organization (FAO), 2121 K St., Ste. 800B, Washington, DC, 20037, USA, (202) 653-2400 (Dial from U.S.), (202) 653-5760 (Fax from U.S.), fao-hq@fao.org, https://www.fao.org; The State of Food and Agriculture (SOFA) 2022.

United Nations Statistics Division (UNSD), United Nations Plz., New York, NY, 10017, USA, (800) 253-9646, (212) 963-9851, statistics@un.org, https://unstats.un.org; Statistical Yearbook of the United Nations 2021.

BURKINA FASO-DAIRY PROCESSING

Palgrave Macmillan, 1 New York Plaza, Ste. 4500, New York, NY, 10004-1562, USA, (800) 777-4643, orders@palgrave.com, https://www.palgrave.com/us; The Statesman's Yearbook, 2023.

United Nations Food and Agricultural Organization (FAO), 2121 K St., Ste. 800B, Washington, DC, 20037, USA, (202) 653-2400 (Dial from U.S.), (202) 653-5760 (Fax from U.S.), fao-hq@fao.org, https://www.fao.org; The State of Food and Agriculture (SOFA) 2022.

BURKINA FASO-DEBTS, EXTERNAL

African Development Bank Group (AfDB), Avenue Joseph Anoma, 01 BP 1387, Abidjan, 01, COT, https://www.afdb.org; The AfDB Statistics Pocketbook 2019; African Economic Outlook 2021; and Compendium of Statistics on Bank Group Operations 2019.

Palgrave Macmillan, 1 New York Plaza, Ste. 4500, New York, NY, 10004-1562, USA, (800) 777-4643, orders@palgrave.com, https://www.palgrave.com/us; The Statesman's Yearbook, 2023.

United Nations Economic Commission for Africa (UNECA), PO Box 3001, Addis Ababa, ETH, ecainfo@uneca.org, https://www.uneca.org/; Economic Report on Africa 2021.

The World Bank, 1818 H St. NW, Washington, DC, 20433, USA, (202) 473-1000, (202) 477-6391, eds03@worldbank.org, https://www.worldbank.org/; Global Financial Development Report 2019-2020: Bank Regulation and Supervision a Decade after the Global Financial Crisis; World Development Indicators (WDI) 2022; and World Development Report 2022: Finance for an Equitable Recovery.

BURKINA FASO-DEFENSE EXPENDITURES

See BURKINA FASO-ARMED FORCES

BURKINA FASO-ECONOMIC ASSISTANCE

United Nations Statistics Division (UNSD), United Nations Plz., New York, NY, 10017, USA, (800) 253-9646, (212) 963-9851, statistics@un.org, https://unstats.un.org; Statistical Yearbook of the United Nations 2021.

BURKINA FASO-ECONOMIC CONDITIONS

African Development Bank Group (AfDB), Avenue Joseph Anoma, 01 BP 1387, Abidjan, 01, COT, https://www.afdb.org; The AfDB Statistics Pocketbook 2019; Africa Economic Brief - COVID-19 Pandemic Potential Risks for Trade and Trade Finance in Africa; African Economic Outlook 2021; The African Statistical Journal; Compendium of Statistics on Bank Group Operations 2019; and Gender, Poverty and Environmental Indicators on African Countries 2019.

Bernan Press, 15250 NBN Way, Bldg. C, Blue Ridge Summit, PA, 17214, USA, (301) 459-2255, (800) 865-3457, (800) 865-3450, customercare@bernan.com, https://rowman.com/Page/Bernan; World Economic Outlook, April 2022.

Central Intelligence Agency (CIA), Office of Public Affairs, Washington, DC, 20505, USA, (703) 482-0623, https://www.cia.gov; The World Factbook.

The Economist Group: Economist Intelligence Unit (EIU), 900 3rd Ave., 16th Fl., New York, NY, 10022, USA, (212) 541-0500, americas@eiu.com, https://www.eiu.com; Burkina Faso Country Report.

Euromonitor International, Inc., 1 N Dearborn St., Ste. 1700, Chicago, IL, 60602, USA, (312) 922-1115, (312) 922-1157, info-usa@euromonitor.com, https://www.euromonitor.com/; Geographies.

International Monetary Fund (IMF), 700 19th St. NW, Washington, DC, 20431, USA, (202) 623-7000, (202) 623-4661, publications@imf.org, https://www.imf.org; IMF Data and World Economic Outlook.

Organisation of Islamic Cooperation (OIC), Statistical, Economic and Social Research and Training Centre for Islamic Countries (SESRIC), Kudus Cad. No. 9, Diplomatik Site, Ankara, 06450, TUR, statistics@sesric.org, https://www.sesric.org/; OIC Economic Outlook 2021; OIC Statistics (OICStat) Database; and OIC-Countries in Figures (OIC-CIF).

Palgrave Macmillan, 1 New York Plaza, Ste. 4500, New York, NY, 10004-1562, USA, (800) 777-4643, orders@palgrave.com, https://www.palgrave.com/us; The Statesman's Yearbook, 2023.

Routledge - Taylor & Francis Group, 6000 Broken Sound Pkwy. NW, Ste. 300, Boca Raton, FL, 33487, USA, (800) 634-1420, (800) 634-7064, orders@taylorandfrancis.com, https://www.routledge.com/; The Europa World Year Book 2022.

United Nations Economic Commission for Africa (UNECA), PO Box 3001, Addis Ababa, ETH, ecainfo@uneca.org, https://www.uneca.org/; Economic Report on Africa 2021.

United Nations Statistics Division (UNSD), United Nations Plz., New York, NY, 10017, USA, (800) 253-9646, (212) 963-9851, statistics@un.org, https://unstats.un.org; World Statistics Pocketbook 2021.

The World Bank, 1818 H St. NW, Washington, DC, 20433, USA, (202) 473-1000, (202) 477-6391, eds03@worldbank.org, https://www.worldbank.org/; Burkina Faso (report); Global Economic Monitor (GEM); Global Economic Prospects, June 2022; The Global Findex Database 2021; and World Development Report 2022: Finance for an Equitable Recovery.

BURKINA FASO-EDUCATION

African Development Bank Group (AfDB), Avenue Joseph Anoma, 01 BP 1387, Abidjan, 01, COT, https://www.afdb.org; The AfDB Statistics Pocketbook 2019.

Euromonitor International, Inc., 1 N Dearborn St., Ste. 1700, Chicago, IL, 60602, USA, (312) 922-1115, (312) 922-1157, info-usa@euromonitor.com, https://www.euromonitor.com/; Geographies.

Infoplease, c/o Sandbox Networks, Inc., 1 Lincoln St., 24th Fl., Boston, MA, 02111, USA, https://www.infoplease.com; Countries of the World.

Organisation of Islamic Cooperation (OIC), Statistical, Economic and Social Research and Training Centre for Islamic Countries (SESRIC), Kudus Cad. No. 9, Diplomatik Site, Ankara, 06450, TUR, statistics@sesric.org, https://www.sesric.org/; OIC Statistics (OICStat) Database.

Palgrave Macmillan, 1 New York Plaza, Ste. 4500, New York, NY, 10004-1562, USA, (800) 777-4643, orders@palgrave.com, https://www.palgrave.com/us; The Statesman's Yearbook, 2023.

Routledge - Taylor & Francis Group, 6000 Broken Sound Pkwy. NW, Ste. 300, Boca Raton, FL, 33487, USA, (800) 634-1420, (800) 634-7064, orders@taylorandfrancis.com, https://www.routledge.com/; The Europa World Year Book 2022.

UNESCO Institute for Statistics, C.P 250 Succursale H, Montreal, QC, H3G 2K8, CAN, (514) 343-6880 (Dial from U.S.), (514) 343-5740 (Fax from U.S.), uis.publications@unesco.org, http://uis.unesco.org/; Literacy and UIS.Stat.

United Nations Economic Commission for Africa (UNECA), PO Box 3001, Addis Ababa, ETH, ecainfo@uneca.org, https://www.uneca.org/; African Statistical Yearbook 2020.

United Nations Statistics Division (UNSD), United Nations Plz., New York, NY, 10017, USA, (800) 253-9646, (212) 963-9851, statistics@un.org, https://unstats.un.org; Millennium Development Goal Indicators.

The World Bank, 1818 H St. NW, Washington, DC, 20433, USA, (202) 473-1000, (202) 477-6391, eds03@worldbank.org, https://www.worldbank.org/; Burkina Faso (report); World Development Indicators (WDI) 2022; and World Development Report 2022: Finance for an Equitable Recovery.

BURKINA FASO-ELECTRICITY

United Nations Statistics Division (UNSD), United Nations Plz., New York, NY, 10017, USA, (800) 253-9646, (212) 963-9851, statistics@un.org, https://unstats.un.org; Statistical Yearbook of the United Nations 2021.

BURKINA FASO-EMPLOYMENT

International Labour Organization (ILO), 4 Rte. des Morillons, Geneva, CH-1211, SWI, ilo@ilo.org, https://www.ilo.org; NORMLEX Information System on International Labour Standards.

UK Data Service, University of Essex, Wivenhoe Park, Colchester, Essex, CO4 3SQ, GBR, https://ukdataservice.ac.uk/; International Aggregate Data.

United Nations Economic Commission for Africa (UNECA), PO Box 3001, Addis Ababa, ETH, ecainfo@uneca.org, https://www.uneca.org/; African Statistical Yearbook 2020.

United Nations Statistics Division (UNSD), United Nations Plz., New York, NY, 10017, USA, (800) 253-9646, (212) 963-9851, statistics@un.org, https://unstats.un.org; Statistical Yearbook of the United Nations 2021.

The World Bank, 1818 H St. NW, Washington, DC, 20433, USA, (202) 473-1000, (202) 477-6391, eds03@worldbank.org, https://www.worldbank.org/; Burkina Faso (report).

BURKINA FASO-ENVIRONMENTAL CONDITIONS

DSI Data Service & Information, Xantener Strasse 51a, Rheinberg, D-47495, GER, dsi@dsidata.com, https://www.dsidata.com/; Global Environmental Database.

The Economist Group: Economist Intelligence Unit (EIU), 900 3rd Ave., 16th Fl., New York, NY, 10022, USA, (212) 541-0500, americas@eiu.com, https://www.eiu.com; Burkina Faso Country Report.

International Institute for Environment and Development (IIED), 235 High Holborn, London, WC1V 7DN, GBR, inforequest@iied.org, https://www.iied.org; Environment & Urbanization.

Organisation of Islamic Cooperation (OIC), Statistical, Economic and Social Research and Training Centre for Islamic Countries (SESRIC), Kudus Cad. No. 9, Diplomatik Site, Ankara, 06450, TUR, statistics@sesric.org, https://www.sesric.org/; OIC Statistics (OICStat) Database and OIC-Countries in Figures (OIC-CIF).

United Nations Statistics Division (UNSD), United Nations Plz., New York, NY, 10017, USA, (800) 253-9646, (212) 963-9851, statistics@un.org, https://unstats.un.org; World Statistics Pocketbook 2021.

BURKINA FASO-EXPORTS

African Development Bank Group (AfDB), Avenue Joseph Anoma, 01 BP 1387, Abidjan, 01, COT, https://www.afdb.org; African Economic Outlook 2021.

Central Intelligence Agency (CIA), Office of Public Affairs, Washington, DC, 20505, USA, (703) 482-0623, https://www.cia.gov; The World Factbook.

The Economist Group: Economist Intelligence Unit (EIU), 900 3rd Ave., 16th Fl., New York, NY, 10022, USA, (212) 541-0500, americas@eiu.com, https://www.eiu.com; Burkina Faso Country Report.

International Monetary Fund (IMF), 700 19th St. NW, Washington, DC, 20431, USA, (202) 623-7000, (202) 623-4661, publications@imf.org, https://www.imf.org; Direction of Trade Statistics (DOTS).

Organisation of Islamic Cooperation (OIC), Statistical, Economic and Social Research and Training Centre for Islamic Countries (SESRIC), Kudus Cad. No. 9, Diplomatik Site, Ankara, 06450, TUR, statistics@sesric.org, https://www.sesric.org/; OIC Statistics (OICStat) Database.

S&P Global, IHS Markit, 15 Inverness Way E, Englewood, CO, 80112, USA, (800) 447-2273, (800) 854-7179, https://ihsmarkit.com; Global Trade Atlas (GTA).

United Nations Conference on Trade and Development (UNCTAD), Palais des Nations, Geneva, 1211, SWI, (212) 963-6896, unctadinfo@unctad.org, https://unctad.org; Handbook of Statistics 2021.

The World Bank, 1818 H St. NW, Washington, DC, 20433, USA, (202) 473-1000, (202) 477-6391, eds03@worldbank.org, https://www.worldbank.org/; World Development Report 2022: Finance for an Equitable Recovery.

BURKINA FASO-FEMALE WORKING POPULATION

See BURKINA FASO-EMPLOYMENT

BURKINA FASO-FERTILITY, HUMAN

Central Intelligence Agency (CIA), Office of Public Affairs, Washington, DC, 20505, USA, (703) 482-0623, https://www.cia.gov; The World Factbook.

BURKINA FASO-FERTILIZER INDUSTRY

United Nations Food and Agricultural Organization (FAO), 2121 K St., Ste. 800B, Washington, DC, 20037, USA, (202) 653-2400 (Dial from U.S.), (202) 653-5760 (Fax from U.S.), fao-hq@fao.org, https://www.fao.org; The State of Food and Agriculture (SOFA) 2022.

BURKINA FASO-FINANCE

Stockholm International Peace Research Institute (SIPRI), Signalistgatan 9, Stockholm, SE 169 72, SWE, https://www.sipri.org/; SIPRI Arms Transfers Database and SIPRI Military Expenditure Database.

United Nations Economic Commission for Africa (UNECA), PO Box 3001, Addis Ababa, ETH, ecainfo@uneca.org, https://www.uneca.org/; African Statistical Yearbook 2020.

United Nations Statistics Division (UNSD), United Nations Plz., New York, NY, 10017, USA, (800) 253-9646, (212) 963-9851, statistics@un.org, https://unstats.un.org; Statistical Yearbook of the United Nations 2021.

The World Bank, 1818 H St. NW, Washington, DC, 20433, USA, (202) 473-1000, (202) 477-6391, eds03@worldbank.org, https://www.worldbank.org/; Burkina Faso (report).

BURKINA FASO-FINANCE, PUBLIC

African Development Bank Group (AfDB), Avenue Joseph Anoma, 01 BP 1387, Abidjan, 01, COT, https://www.afdb.org; The AfDB Statistics Pocketbook 2019.

Bernan Press, 15250 NBN Way, Bldg. C, Blue Ridge Summit, PA, 17214, USA, (301) 459-2255, (800) 865-3457, (800) 865-3450, customercare@bernan.com, https://rowman.com/Page/Bernan; National Accounts Statistics: Analysis of Main Aggregates 2020.

The Economist Group: Economist Intelligence Unit (EIU), 900 3rd Ave., 16th Fl., New York, NY, 10022, USA, (212) 541-0500, americas@eiu.com, https://www.eiu.com; Burkina Faso Country Report.

International Monetary Fund (IMF), 700 19th St. NW, Washington, DC, 20431, USA, (202) 623-7000, (202) 623-4661, publications@imf.org, https://www.imf.org; Regional Economic Outlook.

Palgrave Macmillan, 1 New York Plaza, Ste. 4500, New York, NY, 10004-1562, USA, (800) 777-4643, orders@palgrave.com, https://www.palgrave.com/us; The Statesman's Yearbook, 2023.

Routledge - Taylor & Francis Group, 6000 Broken Sound Pkwy. NW, Ste. 300, Boca Raton, FL, 33487, USA, (800) 634-1420, (800) 634-7064, orders@taylorandfrancis.com, https://www.routledge.com/; The Europa World Year Book 2022.

United Nations Economic Commission for Africa (UNECA), PO Box 3001, Addis Ababa, ETH, ecainfo@uneca.org, https://www.uneca.org/; African Statistical Yearbook 2020.

United Nations Statistics Division (UNSD), United Nations Plz., New York, NY, 10017, USA, (800) 253-9646, (212) 963-9851, statistics@un.org, https://unstats.un.org; National Accounts Main Aggregates Database and National Accounts Statistics: Main Aggregates and Detailed Tables.

The World Bank, 1818 H St. NW, Washington, DC, 20433, USA, (202) 473-1000, (202) 477-6391, eds03@worldbank.org, https://www.worldbank.org/; Burkina Faso (report).

BURKINA FASO-FISHERIES

Palgrave Macmillan, 1 New York Plaza, Ste. 4500, New York, NY, 10004-1562, USA, (800) 777-4643, orders@palgrave.com, https://www.palgrave.com/us; The Statesman's Yearbook, 2023.

Routledge - Taylor & Francis Group, 6000 Broken Sound Pkwy. NW, Ste. 300, Boca Raton, FL, 33487, USA, (800) 634-1420, (800) 634-7064, orders@taylorandfrancis.com, https://www.routledge.com/; The Europa World Year Book 2022.

United Nations Economic Commission for Africa (UNECA), PO Box 3001, Addis Ababa, ETH, ecainfo@uneca.org, https://www.uneca.org/; African Statistical Yearbook 2020.

United Nations Food and Agricultural Organization (FAO), 2121 K St., Ste. 800B, Washington, DC, 20037, USA, (202) 653-2400 (Dial from U.S.), (202) 653-5760 (Fax from U.S.), fao-hq@fao.org, https://www.fao.org; FAO Yearbook of Fishery and Aquaculture Statistics 2019; Fishery Statistical Collections Global Capture Production; FishStatJ; and The State of Food and Agriculture (SOFA) 2022.

United Nations Statistics Division (UNSD), United Nations Plz., New York, NY, 10017, USA, (800) 253-9646, (212) 963-9851, statistics@un.org, https://unstats.un.org; Statistical Yearbook of the United Nations 2021.

The World Bank, 1818 H St. NW, Washington, DC, 20433, USA, (202) 473-1000, (202) 477-6391, eds03@worldbank.org, https://www.worldbank.org/; Burkina Faso (report).

BURKINA FASO-FOOD

African Development Bank Group (AfDB), Avenue Joseph Anoma, 01 BP 1387, Abidjan, 01, COT, https://www.afdb.org; The AfDB Statistics Pocketbook 2019.

United Nations Food and Agricultural Organization (FAO), 2121 K St., Ste. 800B, Washington, DC, 20037, USA, (202) 653-2400 (Dial from U.S.), (202) 653-5760 (Fax from U.S.), fao-hq@fao.org, https://www.fao.org; The State of Food and Agriculture (SOFA) 2022.

BURKINA FASO-FOREIGN EXCHANGE RATES

African Development Bank Group (AfDB), Avenue Joseph Anoma, 01 BP 1387, Abidjan, 01, COT, https://www.afdb.org; The AfDB Statistics Pocketbook 2019 and African Economic Outlook 2021.

International Monetary Fund (IMF), 700 19th St. NW, Washington, DC, 20431, USA, (202) 623-7000, (202) 623-4661, publications@imf.org, https://www.imf.org; International Financial Statistics (IFS).

BURKINA FASO-FORESTS AND FORESTRY

Palgrave Macmillan, 1 New York Plaza, Ste. 4500, New York, NY, 10004-1562, USA, (800) 777-4643, orders@palgrave.com, https://www.palgrave.com/us; The Statesman's Yearbook, 2023.

Routledge - Taylor & Francis Group, 6000 Broken Sound Pkwy. NW, Ste. 300, Boca Raton, FL, 33487, USA, (800) 634-1420, (800) 634-7064, orders@taylorandfrancis.com, https://www.routledge.com/; The Europa World Year Book 2022.

United Nations Economic Commission for Africa (UNECA), PO Box 3001, Addis Ababa, ETH, ecainfo@uneca.org, https://www.uneca.org/; African Statistical Yearbook 2020.

United Nations Food and Agricultural Organization (FAO), 2121 K St., Ste. 800B, Washington, DC, 20037, USA, (202) 653-2400 (Dial from U.S.), (202) 653-5760 (Fax from U.S.), fao-hq@fao.org, https://www.fao.org; FAO Yearbook of Forest Products 2019 and The State of Food and Agriculture (SOFA) 2022.

The World Bank, 1818 H St. NW, Washington, DC, 20433, USA, (202) 473-1000, (202) 477-6391, eds03@worldbank.org, https://www.worldbank.org/; Burkina Faso (report) and World Development Report 2022: Finance for an Equitable Recovery.

BURKINA FASO-GEOGRAPHIC INFORMATION SYSTEMS

The World Bank, 1818 H St. NW, Washington, DC, 20433, USA, (202) 473-1000, (202) 477-6391, eds03@worldbank.org, https://www.worldbank.org/; Burkina Faso (report).

BURKINA FASO-GOLD INDUSTRY

The World Bank, 1818 H St. NW, Washington, DC, 20433, USA, (202) 473-1000, (202) 477-6391, eds03@worldbank.org, https://www.worldbank.org/; World Development Indicators (WDI) 2022.

BURKINA FASO-GROSS DOMESTIC PRODUCT

African Development Bank Group (AfDB), Avenue Joseph Anoma, 01 BP 1387, Abidjan, 01, COT, https://www.afdb.org; The AfDB Statistics Pocketbook 2019.

The Economist Group: Economist Intelligence Unit (EIU), 900 3rd Ave., 16th Fl., New York, NY, 10022, USA, (212) 541-0500, americas@eiu.com, https://www.eiu.com; Burkina Faso Country Report.

Routledge - Taylor & Francis Group, 6000 Broken Sound Pkwy. NW, Ste. 300, Boca Raton, FL, 33487, USA, (800) 634-1420, (800) 634-7064, orders@taylorandfrancis.com, https://www.routledge.com/; The Europa World Year Book 2022.

United Nations Economic Commission for Africa (UNECA), PO Box 3001, Addis Ababa, ETH, ecainfo@uneca.org, https://www.uneca.org/; African Statistical Yearbook 2020.

United Nations Statistics Division (UNSD), United Nations Plz., New York, NY, 10017, USA, (800) 253-9646, (212) 963-9851, statistics@un.org, https://unstats.un.org; Statistical Yearbook of the United Nations 2021.

The World Bank, 1818 H St. NW, Washington, DC, 20433, USA, (202) 473-1000, (202) 477-6391, eds03@worldbank.org, https://www.worldbank.org/; World Development Indicators (WDI) 2022 and World Development Report 2022: Finance for an Equitable Recovery.

BURKINA FASO-GROSS NATIONAL PRODUCT

Palgrave Macmillan, 1 New York Plaza, Ste. 4500, New York, NY, 10004-1562, USA, (800) 777-4643, orders@palgrave.com, https://www.palgrave.com/us; The Statesman's Yearbook, 2023.

Routledge - Taylor & Francis Group, 6000 Broken Sound Pkwy. NW, Ste. 300, Boca Raton, FL, 33487, USA, (800) 634-1420, (800) 634-7064, orders@taylorandfrancis.com, https://www.routledge.com/; The Europa World Year Book 2022.

The World Bank, 1818 H St. NW, Washington, DC, 20433, USA, (202) 473-1000, (202) 477-6391, eds03@worldbank.org, https://www.worldbank.org/; World Development Indicators (WDI) 2022 and World Development Report 2022: Finance for an Equitable Recovery.

BURKINA FASO-HOUSING

Euromonitor International, Inc., 1 N Dearborn St., Ste. 1700, Chicago, IL, 60602, USA, (312) 922-1115, (312) 922-1157, info-usa@euromonitor.com, https://www.euromonitor.com/; Geographies.

BURKINA FASO-ILLITERATE PERSONS

UNESCO Institute for Statistics, C.P 250 Succursale H, Montreal, QC, H3G 2K8, CAN, (514) 343-6880 (Dial from U.S.), (514) 343-5740 (Fax from U.S.), uis.publications@unesco.org, http://uis.unesco.org/; UIS.Stat.

BURKINA FASO-IMPORTS

African Development Bank Group (AfDB), Avenue Joseph Anoma, 01 BP 1387, Abidjan, 01, COT, https://www.afdb.org; African Economic Outlook 2021.

Central Intelligence Agency (CIA), Office of Public Affairs, Washington, DC, 20505, USA, (703) 482-0623, https://www.cia.gov; The World Factbook.

The Economist Group: Economist Intelligence Unit (EIU), 900 3rd Ave., 16th Fl., New York, NY, 10022, USA, (212) 541-0500, americas@eiu.com, https://www.eiu.com; Burkina Faso Country Report.

International Monetary Fund (IMF), 700 19th St. NW, Washington, DC, 20431, USA, (202) 623-7000, (202) 623-4661, publications@imf.org, https://www.imf.org; Direction of Trade Statistics (DOTS).

S&P Global, IHS Markit, 15 Inverness Way E, Englewood, CO, 80112, USA, (800) 447-2273, (800) 854-7179, https://ihsmarkit.com; Global Trade Atlas (GTA).

United Nations Conference on Trade and Development (UNCTAD), Palais des Nations, Geneva, 1211, SWI, (212) 963-6896, unctadinfo@unctad.org, https://unctad.org; Handbook of Statistics 2021.

The World Bank, 1818 H St. NW, Washington, DC, 20433, USA, (202) 473-1000, (202) 477-6391, eds03@worldbank.org, https://www.worldbank.org/; World Development Report 2022: Finance for an Equitable Recovery.

BURKINA FASO-INDUSTRIES

Central Intelligence Agency (CIA), Office of Public Affairs, Washington, DC, 20505, USA, (703) 482-0623, https://www.cia.gov; The World Factbook.

The Economist Group: Economist Intelligence Unit (EIU), 900 3rd Ave., 16th Fl., New York, NY, 10022, USA, (212) 541-0500, americas@eiu.com, https://www.eiu.com; Burkina Faso Country Report.

Euromonitor International, Inc., 1 N Dearborn St., Ste. 1700, Chicago, IL, 60602, USA, (312) 922-1115, (312) 922-1157, info-usa@euromonitor.com, https://www.euromonitor.com/; Geographies.

International Labour Organization (ILO), 4 Rte. des Morillons, Geneva, CH-1211, SWI, ilo@ilo.org, https://www.ilo.org; NORMLEX Information System on International Labour Standards.

Palgrave Macmillan, 1 New York Plaza, Ste. 4500, New York, NY, 10004-1562, USA, (800) 777-4643, orders@palgrave.com, https://www.palgrave.com/us; The Statesman's Yearbook, 2023.

Routledge - Taylor & Francis Group, 6000 Broken Sound Pkwy. NW, Ste. 300, Boca Raton, FL, 33487, USA, (800) 634-1420, (800) 634-7064, orders@taylorandfrancis.com, https://www.routledge.com/; The Europa World Year Book 2022.

United Nations Economic Commission for Africa (UNECA), PO Box 3001, Addis Ababa, ETH, ecainfo@uneca.org, https://www.uneca.org/; African Statistical Yearbook 2020.

United Nations Industrial Development Organization (UNIDO), 1 United Nations Plz., Rm. DC1-1118, New York, NY, 10017, USA, (212) 963-6890, (212) 963 6885, (212) 963-7904, office.newyork@unido.org, https://www.unido.org/; Industrial Statistics Databases and International Yearbook of Industrial Statistics 2021.

The World Bank, 1818 H St. NW, Washington, DC, 20433, USA, (202) 473-1000, (202) 477-6391,

eds03@worldbank.org, https://www.worldbank.org/; Burkina Faso (report) and World Development Indicators (WDI) 2022.

BURKINA FASO-INFANT AND MATERNAL MORTALITY

See BURKINA FASO-MORTALITY

BURKINA FASO-INTERNATIONAL TRADE

African Development Bank Group (AfDB), Avenue Joseph Anoma, 01 BP 1387, Abidjan, 01, COT, https://www.afdb.org; The AfDB Statistics Pocketbook 2019 and African Economic Outlook 2021.

The Economist Group: Economist Intelligence Unit (EIU), 900 3rd Ave., 16th Fl., New York, NY, 10022, USA, (212) 541-0500, americas@eiu.com, https://www.eiu.com; Burkina Faso Country Report.

Euromonitor International, Inc., 1 N Dearborn St., Ste. 1700, Chicago, IL, 60602, USA, (312) 922-1115, (312) 922-1157, info-usa@euromonitor.com, https://www.euromonitor.com/; Geographies.

Palgrave Macmillan, 1 New York Plaza, Ste. 4500, New York, NY, 10004-1562, USA, (800) 777-4643, orders@palgrave.com, https://www.palgrave.com/us; The Statesman's Yearbook, 2023.

Routledge - Taylor & Francis Group, 6000 Broken Sound Pkwy. NW, Ste. 300, Boca Raton, FL, 33487, USA, (800) 634-1420, (800) 634-7064, orders@taylorandfrancis.com, https://www.routledge.com/; The Europa World Year Book 2022.

United Nations Conference on Trade and Development (UNCTAD), Palais des Nations, Geneva, 1211, SWI, (212) 963-6896, unctadinfo@unctad.org, https://unctad.org; Trade and Development Report 2021.

United Nations Economic Commission for Africa (UNECA), PO Box 3001, Addis Ababa, ETH, ecainfo@uneca.org, https://www.uneca.org/; African Statistical Yearbook 2020.

United Nations Food and Agricultural Organization (FAO), 2121 K St., Ste. 800B, Washington, DC, 20037, USA, (202) 653-2400 (Dial from U.S.), (202) 653-5760 (Fax from U.S.), fao-hq@fao.org, https://www.fao.org; The State of Food and Agriculture (SOFA) 2022.

United Nations Statistics Division (UNSD), United Nations Plz., New York, NY, 10017, USA, (800) 253-9646, (212) 963-9851, statistics@un.org, https://unstats.un.org; International Trade Statistics Yearbook 2020 and Statistical Yearbook of the United Nations 2021.

The World Bank, 1818 H St. NW, Washington, DC, 20433, USA, (202) 473-1000, (202) 477-6391, eds03@worldbank.org, https://www.worldbank.org/; Burkina Faso (report); World Development Indicators (WDI) 2022; and World Development Report 2022: Finance for an Equitable Recovery.

World Trade Organization (WTO), Ctre. William Rappard, Rue de Lausanne 154, Case postale, Geneva, CH-1211, SWI, enquiries@wto.org, https://www.wto.org; World Trade Statistical Review 2022.

BURKINA FASO-INTERNET USERS

International Telecommunication Union (ITU), Place des Nations, Geneva, CH-1211, SWI, itumail@itu.int, https://www.itu.int; Global Connectivity Report 2022; World Telecommunication/ICT Indicators Database 2021; and Yearbook of Statistics 2019.

The World Bank, 1818 H St. NW, Washington, DC, 20433, USA, (202) 473-1000, (202) 477-6391, eds03@worldbank.org, https://www.worldbank.org/; Burkina Faso (report).

BURKINA FASO-LABOR

African Development Bank Group (AfDB), Avenue Joseph Anoma, 01 BP 1387, Abidjan, 01, COT, https://www.afdb.org; The AfDB Statistics Pocketbook 2019.

Central Intelligence Agency (CIA), Office of Public Affairs, Washington, DC, 20505, USA, (703) 482-0623, https://www.cia.gov; The World Factbook.

Euromonitor International, Inc., 1 N Dearborn St., Ste. 1700, Chicago, IL, 60602, USA, (312) 922-1115, (312) 922-1157, info-usa@euromonitor.com, https://www.euromonitor.com/; Geographies.

International Labour Organization (ILO), 4 Rte. des Morillons, Geneva, CH-1211, SWI, ilo@ilo.org, https://www.ilo.org; NORMLEX Information System on International Labour Standards.

Organisation of Islamic Cooperation (OIC), Statistical, Economic and Social Research and Training Centre for Islamic Countries (SESRIC), Kudus Cad. No. 9, Diplomatik Site, Ankara, 06450, TUR, statistics@sesric.org, https://www.sesric.org/; OIC Statistics (OICStat) Database.

Palgrave Macmillan, 1 New York Plaza, Ste. 4500, New York, NY, 10004-1562, USA, (800) 777-4643, orders@palgrave.com, https://www.palgrave.com/us; The Statesman's Yearbook, 2023.

United Nations Food and Agricultural Organization (FAO), 2121 K St., Ste. 800B, Washington, DC, 20037, USA, (202) 653-2400 (Dial from U.S.), (202) 653-5760 (Fax from U.S.), fao-hq@fao.org, https://www.fao.org; The State of Food and Agriculture (SOFA) 2022.

The World Bank, 1818 H St. NW, Washington, DC, 20433, USA, (202) 473-1000, (202) 477-6391, eds03@worldbank.org, https://www.worldbank.org/; World Development Indicators (WDI) 2022 and World Development Report 2022: Finance for an Equitable Recovery.

BURKINA FASO-LAND USE

United Nations Statistics Division (UNSD), United Nations Plz., New York, NY, 10017, USA, (800) 253-9646, (212) 963-9851, statistics@un.org, https://unstats.un.org; Millennium Development Goal Indicators.

The World Bank, 1818 H St. NW, Washington, DC, 20433, USA, (202) 473-1000, (202) 477-6391, eds03@worldbank.org, https://www.worldbank.org/; World Development Report 2022: Finance for an Equitable Recovery.

BURKINA FASO-LIBRARIES

UNESCO Institute for Statistics, C.P 250 Succursale H, Montreal, QC, H3G 2K8, CAN, (514) 343-6880 (Dial from U.S.), (514) 343-5740 (Fax from U.S.), uis.publications@unesco.org, http://uis.unesco.org/; UIS.Stat.

BURKINA FASO-LIFE EXPECTANCY

African Development Bank Group (AfDB), Avenue Joseph Anoma, 01 BP 1387, Abidjan, 01, COT, https://www.afdb.org; The AfDB Statistics Pocketbook 2019.

Central Intelligence Agency (CIA), Office of Public Affairs, Washington, DC, 20505, USA, (703) 482-0623, https://www.cia.gov; The World Factbook.

United Nations Department of Economic and Social Affairs (DESA), Population Division, 2 United Nations Plz., Rm. DC2-1950, New York, NY, 10017, USA, (212) 963-3209, (212) 963-2147, population@un.org, https://www.un.org/development/desa/pd/; World Population Ageing 2020 Highlights.

United Nations Statistics Division (UNSD), United Nations Plz., New York, NY, 10017, USA, (800) 253-9646, (212) 963-9851, statistics@un.org, https://unstats.un.org; Millennium Development Goal Indicators.

BURKINA FASO-LITERACY

Euromonitor International, Inc., 1 N Dearborn St., Ste. 1700, Chicago, IL, 60602, USA, (312) 922-1115, (312) 922-1157, info-usa@euromonitor.com, https://www.euromonitor.com/; Geographies.

UNESCO Institute for Statistics, C.P 250 Succursale H, Montreal, QC, H3G 2K8, CAN, (514) 343-6880 (Dial from U.S.), (514) 343-5740 (Fax from U.S.), uis.publications@unesco.org, http://uis.unesco.org/; Literacy.

BURKINA FASO-LIVESTOCK

Palgrave Macmillan, 1 New York Plaza, Ste. 4500, New York, NY, 10004-1562, USA, (800) 777-4643, orders@palgrave.com, https://www.palgrave.com/us; The Statesman's Yearbook, 2023.

Routledge - Taylor & Francis Group, 6000 Broken Sound Pkwy. NW, Ste. 300, Boca Raton, FL, 33487, USA, (800) 634-1420, (800) 634-7064, orders@taylorandfrancis.com, https://www.routledge.com/; The Europa World Year Book 2022.

United Nations Economic Commission for Africa (UNECA), PO Box 3001, Addis Ababa, ETH, ecainfo@uneca.org, https://www.uneca.org/; African Statistical Yearbook 2020.

United Nations Food and Agricultural Organization (FAO), 2121 K St., Ste. 800B, Washington, DC, 20037, USA, (202) 653-2400 (Dial from U.S.), (202) 653-5760 (Fax from U.S.), fao-hq@fao.org, https://www.fao.org; The State of Food and Agriculture (SOFA) 2022.

United Nations Statistics Division (UNSD), United Nations Plz., New York, NY, 10017, USA, (800) 253-9646, (212) 963-9851, statistics@un.org, https://unstats.un.org; Statistical Yearbook of the United Nations 2021.

BURKINA FASO-MINERAL INDUSTRIES

Palgrave Macmillan, 1 New York Plaza, Ste. 4500, New York, NY, 10004-1562, USA, (800) 777-4643, orders@palgrave.com, https://www.palgrave.com/us; The Statesman's Yearbook, 2023.

United Nations Conference on Trade and Development (UNCTAD), Palais des Nations, Geneva, 1211, SWI, (212) 963-6896, unctadinfo@unctad.org, https://unctad.org; Trade and Development Report 2021.

United Nations Economic Commission for Africa (UNECA), PO Box 3001, Addis Ababa, ETH, ecainfo@uneca.org, https://www.uneca.org/; African Statistical Yearbook 2020.

BURKINA FASO-MONEY SUPPLY

The Economist Group: Economist Intelligence Unit (EIU), 900 3rd Ave., 16th Fl., New York, NY, 10022, USA, (212) 541-0500, americas@eiu.com, https://www.eiu.com; Burkina Faso Country Report.

Routledge - Taylor & Francis Group, 6000 Broken Sound Pkwy. NW, Ste. 300, Boca Raton, FL, 33487, USA, (800) 634-1420, (800) 634-7064, orders@taylorandfrancis.com, https://www.routledge.com/; The Europa World Year Book 2022.

United Nations Statistics Division (UNSD), United Nations Plz., New York, NY, 10017, USA, (800) 253-9646, (212) 963-9851, statistics@un.org, https://unstats.un.org; Statistical Yearbook of the United Nations 2021.

The World Bank, 1818 H St. NW, Washington, DC, 20433, USA, (202) 473-1000, (202) 477-6391, eds03@worldbank.org, https://www.worldbank.org/; Burkina Faso (report).

BURKINA FASO-MORTALITY

UNICEF, 3 United Nations Plz., New York, NY, 10017, USA, (212) 303-7984, (917) 244-2215, https://www.unicef.org; The State of the World's Children 2023.

United Nations Statistics Division (UNSD), United Nations Plz., New York, NY, 10017, USA, (800) 253-9646, (212) 963-9851, statistics@un.org, https://unstats.un.org; Millennium Development Goal Indicators; Statistical Yearbook of the United Nations 2021; and World Statistics Pocketbook 2021.

The World Bank, 1818 H St. NW, Washington, DC, 20433, USA, (202) 473-1000, (202) 477-6391, eds03@worldbank.org, https://www.worldbank.org/; World Development Indicators (WDI) 2022.

World Health Organization (WHO), Ave. Appia 20, Geneva, CH-1211, SWI, (202) 974-3000 (Telephone in U.S.), publications@who.int, https://www.who.int/; Global Health Observatory (GHO).

BURKINA FASO-MOTION PICTURES

Palgrave Macmillan, 1 New York Plaza, Ste. 4500, New York, NY, 10004-1562, USA, (800) 777-4643, orders@palgrave.com, https://www.palgrave.com/us; The Statesman's Yearbook, 2023.

BURKINA FASO-MOTOR VEHICLES

International Road Federation (IRF), Madison Place, 500 Montgomery St., 5th Fl., Alexandria, VA, 22314, USA, (703) 535-1001, (703) 535-1007, info@irf.global, https://www.irf.global/; World Road Statistics (WRS).

BURKINA FASO-NUTRITION

United Nations Food and Agricultural Organization (FAO), 2121 K St., Ste. 800B, Washington, DC, 20037, USA, (202) 653-2400 (Dial from U.S.), (202) 653-5760 (Fax from U.S.), fao-hq@fao.org, https://www.fao.org; The State of Food and Agriculture (SOFA) 2022.

United Nations Statistics Division (UNSD), United Nations Plz., New York, NY, 10017, USA, (800) 253-9646, (212) 963-9851, statistics@un.org, https://unstats.un.org; Millennium Development Goal Indicators.

BURKINA FASO-PESTICIDES

United Nations Food and Agricultural Organization (FAO), 2121 K St., Ste. 800B, Washington, DC, 20037, USA, (202) 653-2400 (Dial from U.S.), (202) 653-5760 (Fax from U.S.), fao-hq@fao.org, https://www.fao.org; The State of Food and Agriculture (SOFA) 2022.

BURKINA FASO-PETROLEUM INDUSTRY AND TRADE

United Nations Food and Agricultural Organization (FAO), 2121 K St., Ste. 800B, Washington, DC, 20037, USA, (202) 653-2400 (Dial from U.S.), (202) 653-5760 (Fax from U.S.), fao-hq@fao.org, https://www.fao.org; The State of Food and Agriculture (SOFA) 2022.

BURKINA FASO-POPULATION

African Development Bank Group (AfDB), Avenue Joseph Anoma, 01 BP 1387, Abidjan, 01, COT, https://www.afdb.org; The AfDB Statistics Pocketbook 2019; Africa Economic Brief - COVID-19 Pandemic Potential Risks for Trade and Trade Finance in Africa; The African Statistical Journal; and Gender, Poverty and Environmental Indicators on African Countries 2019.

Central Intelligence Agency (CIA), Office of Public Affairs, Washington, DC, 20505, USA, (703) 482-0623, https://www.cia.gov; The World Factbook.

The Economist Group: Economist Intelligence Unit (EIU), 900 3rd Ave., 16th Fl., New York, NY, 10022, USA, (212) 541-0500, americas@eiu.com, https://www.eiu.com; Burkina Faso Country Report.

European Commission, Eurostat, Luxembourg, 2920, LUX, https://ec.europa.eu/eurostat/; EU in the World 2020.

Infoplease, c/o Sandbox Networks, Inc., 1 Lincoln St., 24th Fl., Boston, MA, 02111, USA, https://www.infoplease.com; Countries of the World.

International Labour Organization (ILO), 4 Rte. des Morillons, Geneva, CH-1211, SWI, ilo@ilo.org, https://www.ilo.org; NORMLEX Information System on International Labour Standards.

Palgrave Macmillan, 1 New York Plaza, Ste. 4500, New York, NY, 10004-1562, USA, (800) 777-4643, orders@palgrave.com, https://www.palgrave.com/us; The Statesman's Yearbook, 2023.

Routledge - Taylor & Francis Group, 6000 Broken Sound Pkwy. NW, Ste. 300, Boca Raton, FL, 33487, USA, (800) 634-1420, (800) 634-7064, orders@taylorandfrancis.com, https://www.routledge.com/; The Europa World Year Book 2022.

UK Data Service, University of Essex, Wivenhoe Park, Colchester, Essex, CO4 3SQ, GBR, https://ukdataservice.ac.uk/; International Aggregate Data.

UNESCO Institute for Statistics, C.P 250 Succursale H, Montreal, QC, H3G 2K8, CAN, (514) 343-6880 (Dial from U.S.), (514) 343-5740 (Fax from U.S.), uis.publications@unesco.org, http://uis.unesco.org/; UIS.Stat.

United Nations Department of Economic and Social Affairs (DESA), Population Division, 2 United Nations Plz., Rm. DC2-1950, New York, NY, 10017, USA, (212) 963-3209, (212) 963-2147, population@un.org, https://www.un.org/development/desa/pd/; Revision of World Urbanization Prospects and World Population Ageing 2020 Highlights.

United Nations Development Programme (UNDP), One United Nations Plz., New York, NY, 10017, USA, (212) 906-5000, (212) 906-5001, https://www.undp.org; Human Development Report 2021-2022.

United Nations Statistics Division (UNSD), United Nations Plz., New York, NY, 10017, USA, (800) 253-9646, (212) 963-9851, statistics@un.org, https://unstats.un.org; Statistical Yearbook of the United Nations 2021 and World Statistics Pocketbook 2021.

The World Bank, 1818 H St. NW, Washington, DC, 20433, USA, (202) 473-1000, (202) 477-6391, eds03@worldbank.org, https://www.worldbank.org/; Burkina Faso (report); The Global Findex Database 2021; and World Development Report 2022: Finance for an Equitable Recovery.

BURKINA FASO-POPULATION DENSITY

African Development Bank Group (AfDB), Avenue Joseph Anoma, 01 BP 1387, Abidjan, 01, COT, https://www.afdb.org; The AfDB Statistics Pocketbook 2019.

Central Intelligence Agency (CIA), Office of Public Affairs, Washington, DC, 20505, USA, (703) 482-0623, https://www.cia.gov; The World Factbook.

Palgrave Macmillan, 1 New York Plaza, Ste. 4500, New York, NY, 10004-1562, USA, (800) 777-4643, orders@palgrave.com, https://www.palgrave.com/us; The Statesman's Yearbook, 2023.

Routledge - Taylor & Francis Group, 6000 Broken Sound Pkwy. NW, Ste. 300, Boca Raton, FL, 33487, USA, (800) 634-1420, (800) 634-7064, orders@taylorandfrancis.com, https://www.routledge.com/; The Europa World Year Book 2022.

UNESCO Institute for Statistics, C.P 250 Succursale H, Montreal, QC, H3G 2K8, CAN, (514) 343-6880 (Dial from U.S.), (514) 343-5740 (Fax from U.S.), uis.publications@unesco.org, http://uis.unesco.org/; UIS.Stat.

The World Bank, 1818 H St. NW, Washington, DC, 20433, USA, (202) 473-1000, (202) 477-6391, eds03@worldbank.org, https://www.worldbank.org/; Burkina Faso (report) and World Development Report 2022: Finance for an Equitable Recovery.

BURKINA FASO-POSTAL SERVICE

Palgrave Macmillan, 1 New York Plaza, Ste. 4500, New York, NY, 10004-1562, USA, (800) 777-4643, orders@palgrave.com, https://www.palgrave.com/us; The Statesman's Yearbook, 2023.

BURKINA FASO-POWER RESOURCES

Euromonitor International, Inc., 1 N Dearborn St., Ste. 1700, Chicago, IL, 60602, USA, (312) 922-1115, (312) 922-1157, info-usa@euromonitor.com, https://www.euromonitor.com/; Geographies.

Palgrave Macmillan, 1 New York Plaza, Ste. 4500, New York, NY, 10004-1562, USA, (800) 777-4643, orders@palgrave.com, https://www.palgrave.com/us; The Statesman's Yearbook, 2023.

United Nations Economic Commission for Africa (UNECA), PO Box 3001, Addis Ababa, ETH, ecainfo@uneca.org, https://www.uneca.org/; African Statistical Yearbook 2020.

United Nations Food and Agricultural Organization (FAO), 2121 K St., Ste. 800B, Washington, DC, 20037, USA, (202) 653-2400 (Dial from U.S.), (202) 653-5760 (Fax from U.S.), fao-hq@fao.org, https://www.fao.org; The State of Food and Agriculture (SOFA) 2022.

United Nations Statistics Division (UNSD), United Nations Plz., New York, NY, 10017, USA, (800) 253-9646, (212) 963-9851, statistics@un.org, https://unstats.un.org; Energy Statistics Yearbook 2019; Statistical Yearbook of the United Nations 2021; and World Statistics Pocketbook 2021.

The World Bank, 1818 H St. NW, Washington, DC, 20433, USA, (202) 473-1000, (202) 477-6391, eds03@worldbank.org, https://www.worldbank.org/; World Development Report 2022: Finance for an Equitable Recovery.

BURKINA FASO-PRICES

Euromonitor International, Inc., 1 N Dearborn St., Ste. 1700, Chicago, IL, 60602, USA, (312) 922-1115, (312) 922-1157, info-usa@euromonitor.com, https://www.euromonitor.com/; Geographies.

International Monetary Fund (IMF), 700 19th St. NW, Washington, DC, 20431, USA, (202) 623-7000, (202) 623-4661, publications@imf.org, https://www.imf.org; International Financial Statistics (IFS).

United Nations Economic Commission for Africa (UNECA), PO Box 3001, Addis Ababa, ETH, ecainfo@uneca.org, https://www.uneca.org/; African Statistical Yearbook 2020.

The World Bank, 1818 H St. NW, Washington, DC, 20433, USA, (202) 473-1000, (202) 477-6391, eds03@worldbank.org, https://www.worldbank.org/; Burkina Faso (report).

BURKINA FASO-PUBLIC HEALTH

African Development Bank Group (AfDB), Avenue Joseph Anoma, 01 BP 1387, Abidjan, 01, COT, https://www.afdb.org; The AfDB Statistics Pocketbook 2019.

Euromonitor International, Inc., 1 N Dearborn St., Ste. 1700, Chicago, IL, 60602, USA, (312) 922-1115, (312) 922-1157, info-usa@euromonitor.com, https://www.euromonitor.com/; Geographies.

Organisation of Islamic Cooperation (OIC), Statistical, Economic and Social Research and Training Centre for Islamic Countries (SESRIC), Kudus Cad. No. 9, Diplomatik Site, Ankara, 06450, TUR, statistics@sesric.org, https://www.sesric.org/; OIC Statistics (OICStat) Database.

Palgrave Macmillan, 1 New York Plaza, Ste. 4500, New York, NY, 10004-1562, USA, (800) 777-4643, orders@palgrave.com, https://www.palgrave.com/us; The Statesman's Yearbook, 2023.

U.S. Census Bureau, 4600 Silver Hill Rd., Washington, DC, 20233, USA, (301) 763-4636, (800) 923-8282, https://www.census.gov; HIV/AIDS Surveillance Data Base.

UNICEF, 3 United Nations Plz., New York, NY, 10017, USA, (212) 303-7984, (917) 244-2215, https://www.unicef.org; The State of the World's Children 2023.

United Nations Department of Economic and Social Affairs (DESA), Population Division, 2 United Nations Plz., Rm. DC2-1950, New York, NY, 10017, USA, (212) 963-3209, (212) 963-2147, population@un.org, https://www.un.org/development/desa/pd/; World Fertility Data 2019.

United Nations Development Programme (UNDP), One United Nations Plz., New York, NY, 10017, USA, (212) 906-5000, (212) 906-5001, https://www.undp.org; Human Development Report 2021-2022.

United Nations Economic Commission for Africa (UNECA), PO Box 3001, Addis Ababa, ETH, ecainfo@uneca.org, https://www.uneca.org/; African Statistical Yearbook 2020.

United Nations Statistics Division (UNSD), United Nations Plz., New York, NY, 10017, USA, (800) 253-9646, (212) 963-9851, statistics@un.org, https://unstats.un.org; Millennium Development Goal Indicators and Statistical Yearbook of the United Nations 2021.

The World Bank, 1818 H St. NW, Washington, DC, 20433, USA, (202) 473-1000, (202) 477-6391, eds03@worldbank.org, https://www.worldbank.org/; Burkina Faso (report).

World Health Organization (WHO), Ave. Appia 20, Geneva, CH-1211, SWI, (202) 974-3000 (Telephone in U.S.), publications@who.int, https://www.who.int/; Global Health Observatory (GHO) and Health Statistics and Information Systems.

BURKINA FASO-PUBLISHERS AND PUBLISHING

Routledge - Taylor & Francis Group, 6000 Broken Sound Pkwy. NW, Ste. 300, Boca Raton, FL, 33487, USA, (800) 634-1420, (800) 634-7064, orders@taylorandfrancis.com, https://www.routledge.com/; The Europa World Year Book 2022.

BURKINA FASO-RAILROADS

Janes, USA, (703) 574-7580, (888) 977-1519, customer.care@janes.com, https://www.janes.com; Janes World Railways 2021-2022.

Palgrave Macmillan, 1 New York Plaza, Ste. 4500, New York, NY, 10004-1562, USA, (800) 777-4643, orders@palgrave.com, https://www.palgrave.com/us; The Statesman's Yearbook, 2023.

Routledge - Taylor & Francis Group, 6000 Broken Sound Pkwy. NW, Ste. 300, Boca Raton, FL, 33487, USA, (800) 634-1420, (800) 634-7064, orders@taylorandfrancis.com, https://www.routledge.com/; The Europa World Year Book 2022.

United Nations Economic Commission for Africa (UNECA), PO Box 3001, Addis Ababa, ETH, ecainfo@uneca.org, https://www.uneca.org/; African Statistical Yearbook 2020.

United Nations Statistics Division (UNSD), United Nations Plz., New York, NY, 10017, USA, (800) 253-9646, (212) 963-9851, statistics@un.org, https://unstats.un.org; Statistical Yearbook of the United Nations 2021.

BURKINA FASO-RELIGION

Central Intelligence Agency (CIA), Office of Public Affairs, Washington, DC, 20505, USA, (703) 482-0623, https://www.cia.gov; The World Factbook.

BURKINA FASO-RETAIL TRADE

Euromonitor International, Inc., 1 N Dearborn St., Ste. 1700, Chicago, IL, 60602, USA, (312) 922-1115, (312) 922-1157, info-usa@euromonitor.com, https://www.euromonitor.com/; Geographies.

BURKINA FASO-RICE PRODUCTION

See BURKINA FASO-CROPS

BURKINA FASO-ROADS

International Road Federation (IRF), Madison Place, 500 Montgomery St., 5th Fl., Alexandria, VA, 22314, USA, (703) 535-1001, (703) 535-1007, info@irf.global, https://www.irf.global/; World Road Statistics (WRS).

United Nations Economic Commission for Africa (UNECA), PO Box 3001, Addis Ababa, ETH, ecainfo@uneca.org, https://www.uneca.org/; African Statistical Yearbook 2020.

BURKINA FASO-SAVING AND INVESTMENT

International Monetary Fund (IMF), 700 19th St. NW, Washington, DC, 20431, USA, (202) 623-7000, (202) 623-4661, publications@imf.org, https://www.imf.org; International Financial Statistics (IFS).

BURKINA FASO-SHIPPING

United Nations Economic Commission for Africa (UNECA), PO Box 3001, Addis Ababa, ETH, ecainfo@uneca.org, https://www.uneca.org/; African Statistical Yearbook 2020.

BURKINA FASO-SUGAR PRODUCTION

See BURKINA FASO-CROPS

BURKINA FASO-TAXATION

International Road Federation (IRF), Madison Place, 500 Montgomery St., 5th Fl., Alexandria, VA, 22314, USA, (703) 535-1001, (703) 535-1007, info@irf.global, https://www.irf.global/; World Road Statistics (WRS).

The World Bank, 1818 H St. NW, Washington, DC, 20433, USA, (202) 473-1000, (202) 477-6391, eds03@worldbank.org, https://www.worldbank.org/; World Development Indicators (WDI) 2022.

BURKINA FASO-TELEPHONE

Routledge - Taylor & Francis Group, 6000 Broken Sound Pkwy. NW, Ste. 300, Boca Raton, FL, 33487, USA, (800) 634-1420, (800) 634-7064, orders@taylorandfrancis.com, https://www.routledge.com/; The Europa World Year Book 2022.

United Nations Statistics Division (UNSD), United Nations Plz., New York, NY, 10017, USA, (800) 253-9646, (212) 963-9851, statistics@un.org, https://unstats.un.org; World Statistics Pocketbook 2021.

BURKINA FASO-TEXTILE INDUSTRY

Palgrave Macmillan, 1 New York Plaza, Ste. 4500, New York, NY, 10004-1562, USA, (800) 777-4643, orders@palgrave.com, https://www.palgrave.com/us; The Statesman's Yearbook, 2023.

United Nations Food and Agricultural Organization (FAO), 2121 K St., Ste. 800B, Washington, DC, 20037, USA, (202) 653-2400 (Dial from U.S.), (202) 653-5760 (Fax from U.S.), fao-hq@fao.org, https://www.fao.org; The State of Food and Agriculture (SOFA) 2022.

United Nations Statistics Division (UNSD), United Nations Plz., New York, NY, 10017, USA, (800) 253-9646, (212) 963-9851, statistics@un.org, https://unstats.un.org; Statistical Yearbook of the United Nations 2021.

BURKINA FASO-TOBACCO INDUSTRY

United Nations Statistics Division (UNSD), United Nations Plz., New York, NY, 10017, USA, (800) 253-9646, (212) 963-9851, statistics@un.org, https://unstats.un.org; Statistical Yearbook of the United Nations 2021.

BURKINA FASO-TOURISM

Euromonitor International, Inc., 1 N Dearborn St., Ste. 1700, Chicago, IL, 60602, USA, (312) 922-1115, (312) 922-1157, info-usa@euromonitor.com, https://www.euromonitor.com/; Geographies.

Organisation of Islamic Cooperation (OIC), Statistical, Economic and Social Research and Training Centre for Islamic Countries (SESRIC), Kudus Cad. No. 9, Diplomatik Site, Ankara, 06450, TUR, statistics@sesric.org, https://www.sesric.org/; International Tourism in the OIC Countries: Prospects and Challenges, 2020 and OIC Statistics (OICStat) Database.

Palgrave Macmillan, 1 New York Plaza, Ste. 4500, New York, NY, 10004-1562, USA, (800) 777-4643, orders@palgrave.com, https://www.palgrave.com/us; The Statesman's Yearbook, 2023.

Routledge - Taylor & Francis Group, 6000 Broken Sound Pkwy. NW, Ste. 300, Boca Raton, FL, 33487, USA, (800) 634-1420, (800) 634-7064, orders@taylorandfrancis.com, https://www.routledge.com/; The Europa World Year Book 2022.

United Nations Economic Commission for Africa (UNECA), PO Box 3001, Addis Ababa, ETH, ecainfo@uneca.org, https://www.uneca.org/; African Statistical Yearbook 2020.

United Nations Statistics Division (UNSD), United Nations Plz., New York, NY, 10017, USA, (800) 253-9646, (212) 963-9851, statistics@un.org, https://unstats.un.org; Statistical Yearbook of the United Nations 2021.

United Nations World Tourism Organization (UNWTO), Calle Poeta Joan Maragall 42, Madrid, 28020, SPA, info@unwto.org, https://www.unwto.org/; Yearbook of Tourism Statistics, 2021 Edition.

The World Bank, 1818 H St. NW, Washington, DC, 20433, USA, (202) 473-1000, (202) 477-6391, eds03@worldbank.org, https://www.worldbank.org/; Burkina Faso (report).

BURKINA FASO-TRADE

See BURKINA FASO-INTERNATIONAL TRADE

BURKINA FASO-TRANSPORTATION

Euromonitor International, Inc., 1 N Dearborn St., Ste. 1700, Chicago, IL, 60602, USA, (312) 922-1115, (312) 922-1157, info-usa@euromonitor.com, https://www.euromonitor.com/; Geographies.

Organisation of Islamic Cooperation (OIC), Statistical, Economic and Social Research and Training Centre for Islamic Countries (SESRIC), Kudus Cad. No. 9, Diplomatik Site, Ankara, 06450, TUR, statistics@sesric.org, https://www.sesric.org/; OIC Statistics (OICStat) Database.

Palgrave Macmillan, 1 New York Plaza, Ste. 4500, New York, NY, 10004-1562, USA, (800) 777-4643, orders@palgrave.com, https://www.palgrave.com/us; The Statesman's Yearbook, 2023.

Routledge - Taylor & Francis Group, 6000 Broken Sound Pkwy. NW, Ste. 300, Boca Raton, FL, 33487, USA, (800) 634-1420, (800) 634-7064, orders@taylorandfrancis.com, https://www.routledge.com/; The Europa World Year Book 2022.

United Nations Economic Commission for Africa (UNECA), PO Box 3001, Addis Ababa, ETH, ecainfo@uneca.org, https://www.uneca.org/; African Statistical Yearbook 2020.

The World Bank, 1818 H St. NW, Washington, DC, 20433, USA, (202) 473-1000, (202) 477-6391, eds03@worldbank.org, https://www.worldbank.org/; Burkina Faso (report).

BURKINA FASO-UNEMPLOYMENT

International Labour Organization (ILO), 4 Rte. des Morillons, Geneva, CH-1211, SWI, ilo@ilo.org, https://www.ilo.org; NORMLEX Information System on International Labour Standards.

United Nations Statistics Division (UNSD), United Nations Plz., New York, NY, 10017, USA, (800) 253-9646, (212) 963-9851, statistics@un.org, https://unstats.un.org; Statistical Yearbook of the United Nations 2021.

BURKINA FASO-VITAL STATISTICS

Palgrave Macmillan, 1 New York Plaza, Ste. 4500, New York, NY, 10004-1562, USA, (800) 777-4643, orders@palgrave.com, https://www.palgrave.com/us; The Statesman's Yearbook, 2023.

U.S. Census Bureau, 4600 Silver Hill Rd., Washington, DC, 20233, USA, (301) 763-4636, (800) 923-8282, https://www.census.gov; HIV/AIDS Surveillance Data Base.

United Nations Department of Economic and Social Affairs (DESA), Population Division, 2 United Nations Plz., Rm. DC2-1950, New York, NY, 10017, USA, (212) 963-3209, (212) 963-2147, population@un.org, https://www.un.org/development/desa/pd/; World Contraceptive Use 2021: Estimates and Projections of Family Planning Indicators and World Marriage Data 2019.

BURKINA FASO-WAGES

International Labour Organization (ILO), 4 Rte. des Morillons, Geneva, CH-1211, SWI, ilo@ilo.org, https://www.ilo.org; NORMLEX Information System on International Labour Standards.

United Nations Statistics Division (UNSD), United Nations Plz., New York, NY, 10017, USA, (800) 253-9646, (212) 963-9851, statistics@un.org, https://unstats.un.org; Statistical Yearbook of the United Nations 2021.

The World Bank, 1818 H St. NW, Washington, DC, 20433, USA, (202) 473-1000, (202) 477-6391, eds03@worldbank.org, https://www.worldbank.org/; Burkina Faso (report).

BURMA-NATIONAL STATISTICAL OFFICE

Central Statistical Organization of Myanmar, Ministry of Planning, Finance and Industry, Office 32, Nay

Pyi Taw, MYA, dgcso32.mopf@gmail.com, https://www.csostat.gov.mm/; National Data Reports (Burma).

BURMA-AGRICULTURE

Asian Development Bank (ADB), 6 ADB Ave., Mandaluyong City, 1550, PHL, information@adb.org, https://www.adb.org/; Key Indicators for Asia and the Pacific 2022.

The Economist Group: Economist Intelligence Unit (EIU), 900 3rd Ave., 16th Fl., New York, NY, 10022, USA, (212) 541-0500, americas@eiu.com, https://www.eiu.com; Myanmar (Burma) Country Report.

Euromonitor International, Inc., 1 N Dearborn St., Ste. 1700, Chicago, IL, 60602, USA, (312) 922-1115, (312) 922-1157, info-usa@euromonitor.com, https://www.euromonitor.com/; Geographies.

Palgrave Macmillan, 1 New York Plaza, Ste. 4500, New York, NY, 10004-1562, USA, (800) 777-4643, orders@palgrave.com, https://www.palgrave.com/us; The Statesman's Yearbook, 2023.

Routledge - Taylor & Francis Group, 6000 Broken Sound Pkwy. NW, Ste. 300, Boca Raton, FL, 33487, USA, (800) 634-1420, (800) 634-7064, orders@taylorandfrancis.com, https://www.routledge.com/; The Europa World Year Book 2022.

United Nations Economic and Social Commission for Asia and the Pacific (ESCAP), United Nations Building, Rajadamnern Nok Ave., Bangkok, 10200, THA, https://www.unescap.org/; Asia-Pacific Development Journal.

United Nations Food and Agricultural Organization (FAO), 2121 K St., Ste. 800B, Washington, DC, 20037, USA, (202) 653-2400 (Dial from U.S.), (202) 653-5760 (Fax from U.S.), fao-hq@fao.org, https://www.fao.org; AQUASTAT and The State of Food and Agriculture (SOFA) 2022.

United Nations Statistics Division (UNSD), United Nations Plz., New York, NY, 10017, USA, (800) 253-9646, (212) 963-9851, statistics@un.org, https://unstats.un.org; Statistical Yearbook of the United Nations 2021.

The World Bank, 1818 H St. NW, Washington, DC, 20433, USA, (202) 473-1000, (202) 477-6391, eds03@worldbank.org, https://www.worldbank.org/; Myanmar (report).

BURMA-AIRLINES

International Civil Aviation Organization (ICAO), 999 Robert-Bourassa Blvd., Montreal, QC, H3C 5H7, CAN, (514) 954-8219 (Dial from U.S.), (514) 954-6077 (Fax from U.S.), icaohq@icao.int, https://www.icao.int; ICAO Regional Reports.

Palgrave Macmillan, 1 New York Plaza, Ste. 4500, New York, NY, 10004-1562, USA, (800) 777-4643, orders@palgrave.com, https://www.palgrave.com/us; The Statesman's Yearbook, 2023.

Routledge - Taylor & Francis Group, 6000 Broken Sound Pkwy. NW, Ste. 300, Boca Raton, FL, 33487, USA, (800) 634-1420, (800) 634-7064, orders@taylorandfrancis.com, https://www.routledge.com/; The Europa World Year Book 2022.

BURMA-ALUMINUM PRODUCTION

See BURMA-MINERAL INDUSTRIES

BURMA-ARMED FORCES

Central Intelligence Agency (CIA), Office of Public Affairs, Washington, DC, 20505, USA, (703) 482-0623, https://www.cia.gov; The World Factbook.

International Institute for Strategic Studies (IISS) - Americas, 2121 K St. NW, Ste. 600, Washington, DC, 20037, USA, (202) 659-1490, (202) 659-1499, https://www.iiss.org/; Armed Conflict Survey 2021 and The Military Balance 2022.

Palgrave Macmillan, 1 New York Plaza, Ste. 4500, New York, NY, 10004-1562, USA, (800) 777-4643, orders@palgrave.com, https://www.palgrave.com/us; The Statesman's Yearbook, 2023.

Stockholm International Peace Research Institute (SIPRI), Signalistgatan 9, Stockholm, SE 169 72, SWE, https://www.sipri.org/; SIPRI Arms Transfers Database and SIPRI Military Expenditure Database.

BURMA-BALANCE OF PAYMENTS

International Monetary Fund (IMF), 700 19th St. NW, Washington, DC, 20431, USA, (202) 623-7000, (202) 623-4661, publications@imf.org, https://www.imf.org; International Financial Statistics (IFS).

Routledge - Taylor & Francis Group, 6000 Broken Sound Pkwy. NW, Ste. 300, Boca Raton, FL, 33487, USA, (800) 634-1420, (800) 634-7064, orders@taylorandfrancis.com, https://www.routledge.com/; The Europa World Year Book 2022.

United Nations Conference on Trade and Development (UNCTAD), Palais des Nations, Geneva, 1211, SWI, (212) 963-6896, unctadinfo@unctad.org, https://unctad.org; Handbook of Statistics 2021.

The World Bank, 1818 H St. NW, Washington, DC, 20433, USA, (202) 473-1000, (202) 477-6391, eds03@worldbank.org, https://www.worldbank.org/; Myanmar (report) and World Development Report 2022: Finance for an Equitable Recovery.

BURMA-BANKS AND BANKING

Asian Development Bank (ADB), 6 ADB Ave., Mandaluyong City, 1550, PHL, information@adb.org, https://www.adb.org/; Key Indicators for Asia and the Pacific 2022.

Euromonitor International, Inc., 1 N Dearborn St., Ste. 1700, Chicago, IL, 60602, USA, (312) 922-1115, (312) 922-1157, info-usa@euromonitor.com, https://www.euromonitor.com/; Geographies.

International Monetary Fund (IMF), 700 19th St. NW, Washington, DC, 20431, USA, (202) 623-7000, (202) 623-4661, publications@imf.org, https://www.imf.org; International Financial Statistics (IFS).

Routledge - Taylor & Francis Group, 6000 Broken Sound Pkwy. NW, Ste. 300, Boca Raton, FL, 33487, USA, (800) 634-1420, (800) 634-7064, orders@taylorandfrancis.com, https://www.routledge.com/; The Europa World Year Book 2022.

BURMA-BARLEY PRODUCTION

See BURMA-CROPS

BURMA-BROADCASTING

Central Intelligence Agency (CIA), Office of Public Affairs, Washington, DC, 20505, USA, (703) 482-0623, https://www.cia.gov; The World Factbook.

Euromonitor International, Inc., 1 N Dearborn St., Ste. 1700, Chicago, IL, 60602, USA, (312) 922-1115, (312) 922-1157, info-usa@euromonitor.com, https://www.euromonitor.com/; Geographies.

Palgrave Macmillan, 1 New York Plaza, Ste. 4500, New York, NY, 10004-1562, USA, (800) 777-4643, orders@palgrave.com, https://www.palgrave.com/us; The Statesman's Yearbook, 2023.

WRTH Publications Limited, PO Box 290, Oxford, OX2 7FT, GBR, sales@wrth.com, https://www.wrth.com; World Radio TV Handbook 2023.

BURMA-BUDGET

Central Intelligence Agency (CIA), Office of Public Affairs, Washington, DC, 20505, USA, (703) 482-0623, https://www.cia.gov; The World Factbook.

BURMA-BUSINESS

United Nations Economic and Social Commission for Asia and the Pacific (ESCAP), United Nations Building, Rajadamnern Nok Ave., Bangkok, 10200, THA, https://www.unescap.org/; SDG Gateway Data Explorer.

BURMA-CHILDBIRTH-STATISTICS

United Nations Economic and Social Commission for Asia and the Pacific (ESCAP), United Nations Building, Rajadamnern Nok Ave., Bangkok, 10200, THA, https://www.unescap.org/; Asia-Pacific Development Journal.

BURMA-CLIMATE

International Institute for Environment and Development (IIED), 235 High Holborn, London, WC1V 7DN, GBR, inforequest@iied.org, https://www.iied.org; Environment & Urbanization.

Palgrave Macmillan, 1 New York Plaza, Ste. 4500, New York, NY, 10004-1562, USA, (800) 777-4643, orders@palgrave.com, https://www.palgrave.com/us; The Statesman's Yearbook, 2023.

BURMA-COAL PRODUCTION

See BURMA-MINERAL INDUSTRIES

BURMA-COFFEE

See BURMA-CROPS

BURMA-COMMERCE

Palgrave Macmillan, 1 New York Plaza, Ste. 4500, New York, NY, 10004-1562, USA, (800) 777-4643, orders@palgrave.com, https://www.palgrave.com/us; The Statesman's Yearbook, 2023.

UK Data Service, University of Essex, Wivenhoe Park, Colchester, Essex, CO4 3SQ, GBR, https://ukdataservice.ac.uk/; International Aggregate Data.

BURMA-COMMODITY EXCHANGES

Barchart, 209 W Jackson Blvd., 2nd Fl., Chicago, IL, 60606, USA, (877) 247-4394, commodities@barchart.com, https://www.barchart.com/cmdty; The cmdty Yearbook 2023; cmdtyStats: Commodity Statistics and Fundamental Data; cmdtyView: Commodity Index; and Commodity Data and Prices.

International Monetary Fund (IMF), 700 19th St. NW, Washington, DC, 20431, USA, (202) 623-7000, (202) 623-4661, publications@imf.org, https://www.imf.org; IMF Primary Commodity Prices.

BURMA-CONSTRUCTION INDUSTRY

United Nations Statistics Division (UNSD), United Nations Plz., New York, NY, 10017, USA, (800) 253-9646, (212) 963-9851, statistics@un.org, https://unstats.un.org; Statistical Yearbook of the United Nations 2021.

BURMA-CONSUMER PRICE INDEXES

Asian Development Bank (ADB), 6 ADB Ave., Mandaluyong City, 1550, PHL, information@adb.org, https://www.adb.org/; Key Indicators for Asia and the Pacific 2022.

Routledge - Taylor & Francis Group, 6000 Broken Sound Pkwy. NW, Ste. 300, Boca Raton, FL, 33487, USA, (800) 634-1420, (800) 634-7064, orders@taylorandfrancis.com, https://www.routledge.com/; The Europa World Year Book 2022.

The World Bank, 1818 H St. NW, Washington, DC, 20433, USA, (202) 473-1000, (202) 477-6391, eds03@worldbank.org, https://www.worldbank.org/; Myanmar (report).

BURMA-COPPER INDUSTRY AND TRADE

See BURMA-MINERAL INDUSTRIES

BURMA-CORN INDUSTRY

See BURMA-CROPS

BURMA-COST AND STANDARD OF LIVING

Asian Development Bank (ADB), 6 ADB Ave., Mandaluyong City, 1550, PHL, information@adb.org, https://www.adb.org/; Key Indicators for Asia and the Pacific 2022.

International Labour Organization (ILO), 4 Rte. des Morillons, Geneva, CH-1211, SWI, ilo@ilo.org, https://www.ilo.org; NORMLEX Information System on International Labour Standards.

International Monetary Fund (IMF), 700 19th St. NW, Washington, DC, 20431, USA, (202) 623-7000, (202) 623-4661, publications@imf.org, https://www.imf.org; International Financial Statistics (IFS).

United Nations Food and Agricultural Organization (FAO), 2121 K St., Ste. 800B, Washington, DC, 20037, USA, (202) 653-2400 (Dial from U.S.), (202) 653-5760 (Fax from U.S.), fao-hq@fao.org, https://www.fao.org; The State of Food and Agriculture (SOFA) 2022.

The World Bank, 1818 H St. NW, Washington, DC, 20433, USA, (202) 473-1000, (202) 477-6391, eds03@worldbank.org, https://www.worldbank.org/; Myanmar (report).

BURMA-COTTON

See BURMA-CROPS

BURMA-CRIME

United Nations Office on Drugs and Crime (UNODC), Vienna International Ctre., PO Box 500, Vienna, A-1400, AUT, unodc@unodc.org, https://www.unodc.org/; Myanmar Opium Survey 2022 - Cultivation, Production and Implications.

BURMA-CROPS

International Monetary Fund (IMF), 700 19th St. NW, Washington, DC, 20431, USA, (202) 623-7000, (202) 623-4661, publications@imf.org, https://www.imf.org; International Financial Statistics (IFS).

Palgrave Macmillan, 1 New York Plaza, Ste. 4500, New York, NY, 10004-1562, USA, (800) 777-4643, orders@palgrave.com, https://www.palgrave.com/us; The Statesman's Yearbook, 2023.

United Nations Food and Agricultural Organization (FAO), 2121 K St., Ste. 800B, Washington, DC, 20037, USA, (202) 653-2400 (Dial from U.S.), (202) 653-5760 (Fax from U.S.), fao-hq@fao.org, https://www.fao.org; The State of Food and Agriculture (SOFA) 2022.

United Nations Statistics Division (UNSD), United Nations Plz., New York, NY, 10017, USA, (800) 253-9646, (212) 963-9851, statistics@un.org, https://unstats.un.org; Statistical Yearbook of the United Nations 2021.

BURMA-DAIRY PROCESSING

Palgrave Macmillan, 1 New York Plaza, Ste. 4500, New York, NY, 10004-1562, USA, (800) 777-4643, orders@palgrave.com, https://www.palgrave.com/us; The Statesman's Yearbook, 2023.

United Nations Food and Agricultural Organization (FAO), 2121 K St., Ste. 800B, Washington, DC, 20037, USA, (202) 653-2400 (Dial from U.S.), (202) 653-5760 (Fax from U.S.), fao-hq@fao.org, https://www.fao.org; The State of Food and Agriculture (SOFA) 2022.

BURMA-DEBTS, EXTERNAL

Asian Development Bank (ADB), 6 ADB Ave., Mandaluyong City, 1550, PHL, information@adb.org, https://www.adb.org/; Key Indicators for Asia and the Pacific 2022.

Palgrave Macmillan, 1 New York Plaza, Ste. 4500, New York, NY, 10004-1562, USA, (800) 777-4643, orders@palgrave.com, https://www.palgrave.com/us; The Statesman's Yearbook, 2023.

The World Bank, 1818 H St. NW, Washington, DC, 20433, USA, (202) 473-1000, (202) 477-6391, eds03@worldbank.org, https://www.worldbank.org/; Global Financial Development Report 2019-2020: Bank Regulation and Supervision a Decade after the Global Financial Crisis and World Development Report 2022: Finance for an Equitable Recovery.

BURMA-DEFENSE EXPENDITURES

See BURMA-ARMED FORCES

BURMA-DIAMONDS

See BURMA-MINERAL INDUSTRIES

BURMA-ECONOMIC ASSISTANCE

United Nations Statistics Division (UNSD), United Nations Plz., New York, NY, 10017, USA, (800) 253-9646, (212) 963-9851, statistics@un.org, https://unstats.un.org; Statistical Yearbook of the United Nations 2021.

BURMA-ECONOMIC CONDITIONS

Asian Development Bank (ADB), 6 ADB Ave., Mandaluyong City, 1550, PHL, information@adb.org, https://www.adb.org/; Key Indicators for Asia and the Pacific 2022.

Bernan Press, 15250 NBN Way, Bldg. C, Blue Ridge Summit, PA, 17214, USA, (301) 459-2255, (800) 865-3457, (800) 865-3450, customercare@bernan.com, https://rowman.com/Page/Bernan; World Economic Outlook, April 2022.

Central Intelligence Agency (CIA), Office of Public Affairs, Washington, DC, 20505, USA, (703) 482-0623, https://www.cia.gov; The World Factbook.

The Economist Group: Economist Intelligence Unit (EIU), 900 3rd Ave., 16th Fl., New York, NY, 10022, USA, (212) 541-0500, americas@eiu.com, https://www.eiu.com; Myanmar (Burma) Country Report.

Euromonitor International, Inc., 1 N Dearborn St., Ste. 1700, Chicago, IL, 60602, USA, (312) 922-1115, (312) 922-1157, info-usa@euromonitor.com, https://www.euromonitor.com/; Geographies.

International Monetary Fund (IMF), 700 19th St. NW, Washington, DC, 20431, USA, (202) 623-7000, (202) 623-4661, publications@imf.org, https://www.imf.org; IMF Data and World Economic Outlook.

Palgrave Macmillan, 1 New York Plaza, Ste. 4500, New York, NY, 10004-1562, USA, (800) 777-4643, orders@palgrave.com, https://www.palgrave.com/us; The Statesman's Yearbook, 2023.

Routledge - Taylor & Francis Group, 6000 Broken Sound Pkwy. NW, Ste. 300, Boca Raton, FL, 33487, USA, (800) 634-1420, (800) 634-7064, orders@taylorandfrancis.com, https://www.routledge.com/; The Europa World Year Book 2022.

United Nations Statistics Division (UNSD), United Nations Plz., New York, NY, 10017, USA, (800) 253-9646, (212) 963-9851, statistics@un.org, https://unstats.un.org; World Statistics Pocketbook 2021.

The World Bank, 1818 H St. NW, Washington, DC, 20433, USA, (202) 473-1000, (202) 477-6391, eds03@worldbank.org, https://www.worldbank.org/; Global Economic Monitor (GEM); Global Economic Prospects, June 2022; The Global Findex Database 2021; Myanmar (report); and World Development Report 2022: Finance for an Equitable Recovery.

BURMA-EDUCATION

Infoplease, c/o Sandbox Networks, Inc., 1 Lincoln St., 24th Fl., Boston, MA, 02111, USA, https://www.infoplease.com; Countries of the World.

Palgrave Macmillan, 1 New York Plaza, Ste. 4500, New York, NY, 10004-1562, USA, (800) 777-4643, orders@palgrave.com, https://www.palgrave.com/us; The Statesman's Yearbook, 2023.

Routledge - Taylor & Francis Group, 6000 Broken Sound Pkwy. NW, Ste. 300, Boca Raton, FL, 33487, USA, (800) 634-1420, (800) 634-7064, orders@taylorandfrancis.com, https://www.routledge.com/; The Europa World Year Book 2022.

UNESCO Institute for Statistics, C.P 250 Succursale H, Montreal, QC, H3G 2K8, CAN, (514) 343-6880 (Dial from U.S.), (514) 343-5740 (Fax from U.S.), uis.publications@unesco.org, http://uis.unesco.org/; Literacy and UIS.Stat.

United Nations Economic and Social Commission for Asia and the Pacific (ESCAP), United Nations Building, Rajadamnern Nok Ave., Bangkok, 10200, THA, https://www.unescap.org/; Asia-Pacific Development Journal and SDG Gateway Data Explorer.

United Nations Statistics Division (UNSD), United Nations Plz., New York, NY, 10017, USA, (800) 253-9646, (212) 963-9851, statistics@un.org, https://unstats.un.org; Millennium Development Goal Indicators.

The World Bank, 1818 H St. NW, Washington, DC, 20433, USA, (202) 473-1000, (202) 477-6391, eds03@worldbank.org, https://www.worldbank.org/; Myanmar (report) and World Development Report 2022: Finance for an Equitable Recovery.

BURMA-ELECTRICITY

Central Intelligence Agency (CIA), Office of Public Affairs, Washington, DC, 20505, USA, (703) 482-0623, https://www.cia.gov; The World Factbook.

International Energy Agency (IEA), 9 Rue de la Federation, Paris, 75739, FRA, info@iea.org, https://www.iea.org/; World Energy Outlook 2021.

U.S. Energy Information Administration (EIA), 1000 Independence Ave. SW, Washington, DC, 20585, USA, (202) 586-8800, infoctr@eia.gov, https://www.eia.gov; International Energy Outlook 2021.

United Nations Statistics Division (UNSD), United Nations Plz., New York, NY, 10017, USA, (800) 253-9646, (212) 963-9851, statistics@un.org, https://unstats.un.org; Statistical Yearbook of the United Nations 2021.

BURMA-EMPLOYMENT

International Labour Organization (ILO), 4 Rte. des Morillons, Geneva, CH-1211, SWI, ilo@ilo.org, https://www.ilo.org; NORMLEX Information System on International Labour Standards.

UK Data Service, University of Essex, Wivenhoe Park, Colchester, Essex, CO4 3SQ, GBR, https://ukdataservice.ac.uk/; International Aggregate Data.

United Nations Economic and Social Commission for Asia and the Pacific (ESCAP), United Nations Building, Rajadamnern Nok Ave., Bangkok, 10200, THA, https://www.unescap.org/; Asia-Pacific Development Journal.

United Nations Statistics Division (UNSD), United Nations Plz., New York, NY, 10017, USA, (800) 253-9646, (212) 963-9851, statistics@un.org, https://unstats.un.org; Statistical Yearbook of the United Nations 2021.

The World Bank, 1818 H St. NW, Washington, DC, 20433, USA, (202) 473-1000, (202) 477-6391, eds03@worldbank.org, https://www.worldbank.org/; Myanmar (report).

BURMA-ENERGY INDUSTRIES

Enerdata, 47 avenue Alsace Lorraine, Grenoble, 38027, FRA, (332) 216-4534, research@enerdata.net, https://www.enerdata.net; World Refinery Database.

Euromonitor International, Inc., 1 N Dearborn St., Ste. 1700, Chicago, IL, 60602, USA, (312) 922-1115, (312) 922-1157, info-usa@euromonitor.com, https://www.euromonitor.com/; Geographies.

International Energy Agency (IEA), 9 Rue de la Federation, Paris, 75739, FRA, info@iea.org, https://www.iea.org/; World Energy Outlook 2021.

Palgrave Macmillan, 1 New York Plaza, Ste. 4500, New York, NY, 10004-1562, USA, (800) 777-4643, orders@palgrave.com, https://www.palgrave.com/us; The Statesman's Yearbook, 2023.

U.S. Energy Information Administration (EIA), 1000 Independence Ave. SW, Washington, DC, 20585, USA, (202) 586-8800, infoctr@eia.gov, https://www.eia.gov; International Energy Outlook 2021.

United Nations Economic and Social Commission for Asia and the Pacific (ESCAP), United Nations Building, Rajadamnern Nok Ave., Bangkok, 10200, THA, https://www.unescap.org/; Asia-Pacific Development Journal and SDG Gateway Data Explorer.

United Nations Statistics Division (UNSD), United Nations Plz., New York, NY, 10017, USA, (800) 253-9646, (212) 963-9851, statistics@un.org, https://unstats.un.org; Energy Statistics Yearbook 2019; Statistical Yearbook of the United Nations 2021; and World Statistics Pocketbook 2021.

The World Bank, 1818 H St. NW, Washington, DC, 20433, USA, (202) 473-1000, (202) 477-6391, eds03@worldbank.org, https://www.worldbank.org/; World Development Report 2022: Finance for an Equitable Recovery.

BURMA-ENVIRONMENTAL CONDITIONS

DSI Data Service & Information, Xantener Strasse 51a, Rheinberg, D-47495, GER, dsi@dsidata.com, https://www.dsidata.com/; Global Environmental Database.

The Economist Group: Economist Intelligence Unit (EIU), 900 3rd Ave., 16th Fl., New York, NY, 10022, USA, (212) 541-0500, americas@eiu.com, https://www.eiu.com; Myanmar (Burma) Country Report.

International Institute for Environment and Development (IIED), 235 High Holborn, London, WC1V 7DN, GBR, inforequest@iied.org, https://www.iied.org; Environment & Urbanization.

United Nations Statistics Division (UNSD), United Nations Plz., New York, NY, 10017, USA, (800) 253-9646, (212) 963-9851, statistics@un.org, https://unstats.un.org; World Statistics Pocketbook 2021.

BURMA-EXPORTS

Asian Development Bank (ADB), 6 ADB Ave., Mandaluyong City, 1550, PHL, information@adb.org, https://www.adb.org/; Key Indicators for Asia and the Pacific 2022.

Central Intelligence Agency (CIA), Office of Public Affairs, Washington, DC, 20505, USA, (703) 482-0623, https://www.cia.gov; The World Factbook.

The Economist Group: Economist Intelligence Unit (EIU), 900 3rd Ave., 16th Fl., New York, NY, 10022, USA, (212) 541-0500, americas@eiu.com, https://www.eiu.com; Myanmar (Burma) Country Report.

International Monetary Fund (IMF), 700 19th St. NW, Washington, DC, 20431, USA, (202) 623-7000, (202) 623-4661, publications@imf.org, https://www.imf.org; Direction of Trade Statistics (DOTS) and International Financial Statistics (IFS).

S&P Global, IHS Markit, 15 Inverness Way E, Englewood, CO, 80112, USA, (800) 447-2273, (800) 854-7179, https://ihsmarkit.com; Global Trade Atlas (GTA).

United Nations Conference on Trade and Development (UNCTAD), Palais des Nations, Geneva, 1211, SWI, (212) 963-6896, unctadinfo@unctad.org, https://unctad.org; Handbook of Statistics 2021.

The World Bank, 1818 H St. NW, Washington, DC, 20433, USA, (202) 473-1000, (202) 477-6391, eds03@worldbank.org, https://www.worldbank.org/; World Development Report 2022: Finance for an Equitable Recovery.

BURMA-FEMALE WORKING POPULATION

See BURMA-EMPLOYMENT

BURMA-FERTILITY, HUMAN

Central Intelligence Agency (CIA), Office of Public Affairs, Washington, DC, 20505, USA, (703) 482-0623, https://www.cia.gov; The World Factbook.

BURMA-FERTILIZER INDUSTRY

United Nations Food and Agricultural Organization (FAO), 2121 K St., Ste. 800B, Washington, DC, 20037, USA, (202) 653-2400 (Dial from U.S.), (202) 653-5760 (Fax from U.S.), fao-hq@fao.org, https://www.fao.org; The State of Food and Agriculture (SOFA) 2022.

BURMA-FETAL MORTALITY

See BURMA-MORTALITY

BURMA-FINANCE

The Economist Group: Economist Intelligence Unit (EIU), 900 3rd Ave., 16th Fl., New York, NY, 10022, USA, (212) 541-0500, americas@eiu.com, https://www.eiu.com; Myanmar (Burma) Country Report.

International Monetary Fund (IMF), 700 19th St. NW, Washington, DC, 20431, USA, (202) 623-7000, (202) 623-4661, publications@imf.org, https://www.imf.org; International Financial Statistics (IFS).

Palgrave Macmillan, 1 New York Plaza, Ste. 4500, New York, NY, 10004-1562, USA, (800) 777-4643, orders@palgrave.com, https://www.palgrave.com/us; The Statesman's Yearbook, 2023.

Stockholm International Peace Research Institute (SIPRI), Signalistgatan 9, Stockholm, SE 169 72, SWE, https://www.sipri.org/; SIPRI Arms Transfers Database and SIPRI Military Expenditure Database.

United Nations Economic and Social Commission for Asia and the Pacific (ESCAP), United Nations Building, Rajadamnern Nok Ave., Bangkok, 10200, THA, https://www.unescap.org/; Asia-Pacific Development Journal and SDG Gateway Data Explorer.

United Nations Statistics Division (UNSD), United Nations Plz., New York, NY, 10017, USA, (800) 253-9646, (212) 963-9851, statistics@un.org, https://unstats.un.org; Statistical Yearbook of the United Nations 2021.

The World Bank, 1818 H St. NW, Washington, DC, 20433, USA, (202) 473-1000, (202) 477-6391, eds03@worldbank.org, https://www.worldbank.org/; Myanmar (report).

BURMA-FISHERIES

Palgrave Macmillan, 1 New York Plaza, Ste. 4500, New York, NY, 10004-1562, USA, (800) 777-4643, orders@palgrave.com, https://www.palgrave.com/us; The Statesman's Yearbook, 2023.

Routledge - Taylor & Francis Group, 6000 Broken Sound Pkwy. NW, Ste. 300, Boca Raton, FL, 33487, USA, (800) 634-1420, (800) 634-7064, orders@taylorandfrancis.com, https://www.routledge.com/; The Europa World Year Book 2022.

United Nations Food and Agricultural Organization (FAO), 2121 K St., Ste. 800B, Washington, DC, 20037, USA, (202) 653-2400 (Dial from U.S.), (202) 653-5760 (Fax from U.S.), fao-hq@fao.org, https://www.fao.org; FAO Yearbook of Fishery and Aquaculture Statistics 2019; Fishery Statistical Collections Global Capture Production; FishStatJ; and The State of Food and Agriculture (SOFA) 2022.

United Nations Statistics Division (UNSD), United Nations Plz., New York, NY, 10017, USA, (800) 253-9646, (212) 963-9851, statistics@un.org, https://unstats.un.org; Statistical Yearbook of the United Nations 2021.

The World Bank, 1818 H St. NW, Washington, DC, 20433, USA, (202) 473-1000, (202) 477-6391, eds03@worldbank.org, https://www.worldbank.org/; Myanmar (report).

BURMA-FOOD

United Nations Economic and Social Commission for Asia and the Pacific (ESCAP), United Nations Building, Rajadamnern Nok Ave., Bangkok, 10200, THA, https://www.unescap.org/; SDG Gateway Data Explorer.

United Nations Food and Agricultural Organization (FAO), 2121 K St., Ste. 800B, Washington, DC, 20037, USA, (202) 653-2400 (Dial from U.S.), (202) 653-5760 (Fax from U.S.), fao-hq@fao.org, https://www.fao.org; The State of Food and Agriculture (SOFA) 2022.

BURMA-FOREIGN EXCHANGE RATES

Asian Development Bank (ADB), 6 ADB Ave., Mandaluyong City, 1550, PHL, information@adb.org, https://www.adb.org/; Key Indicators for Asia and the Pacific 2022.

International Monetary Fund (IMF), 700 19th St. NW, Washington, DC, 20431, USA, (202) 623-7000, (202) 623-4661, publications@imf.org, https://www.imf.org; International Financial Statistics (IFS).

BURMA-FORESTS AND FORESTRY

Palgrave Macmillan, 1 New York Plaza, Ste. 4500, New York, NY, 10004-1562, USA, (800) 777-4643, orders@palgrave.com, https://www.palgrave.com/us; The Statesman's Yearbook, 2023.

Routledge - Taylor & Francis Group, 6000 Broken Sound Pkwy. NW, Ste. 300, Boca Raton, FL, 33487, USA, (800) 634-1420, (800) 634-7064, orders@taylorandfrancis.com, https://www.routledge.com/; The Europa World Year Book 2022.

UNESCO Institute for Statistics, C.P 250 Succursale H, Montreal, QC, H3G 2K8, CAN, (514) 343-6880 (Dial from U.S.), (514) 343-5740 (Fax from U.S.), uis.publications@unesco.org, http://uis.unesco.org/; UIS.Stat.

United Nations Food and Agricultural Organization (FAO), 2121 K St., Ste. 800B, Washington, DC, 20037, USA, (202) 653-2400 (Dial from U.S.), (202) 653-5760 (Fax from U.S.), fao-hq@fao.org, https://www.fao.org; FAO Yearbook of Forest Products 2019 and The State of Food and Agriculture (SOFA) 2022.

United Nations Statistics Division (UNSD), United Nations Plz., New York, NY, 10017, USA, (800) 253-9646, (212) 963-9851, statistics@un.org, https://unstats.un.org; Statistical Yearbook of the United Nations 2021.

The World Bank, 1818 H St. NW, Washington, DC, 20433, USA, (202) 473-1000, (202) 477-6391, eds03@worldbank.org, https://www.worldbank.org/; Myanmar (report) and World Development Report 2022: Finance for an Equitable Recovery.

BURMA-GAS PRODUCTION

See BURMA-MINERAL INDUSTRIES

BURMA-GEOGRAPHIC INFORMATION SYSTEMS

The World Bank, 1818 H St. NW, Washington, DC, 20433, USA, (202) 473-1000, (202) 477-6391, eds03@worldbank.org, https://www.worldbank.org/; Myanmar (report).

BURMA-GOLD PRODUCTION

See BURMA-MINERAL INDUSTRIES

BURMA-GRAIN TRADE

United Nations Food and Agricultural Organization (FAO), 2121 K St., Ste. 800B, Washington, DC, 20037, USA, (202) 653-2400 (Dial from U.S.), (202) 653-5760 (Fax from U.S.), fao-hq@fao.org, https://www.fao.org; The State of Food and Agriculture (SOFA) 2022.

BURMA-GROSS DOMESTIC PRODUCT

Asian Development Bank (ADB), 6 ADB Ave., Mandaluyong City, 1550, PHL, information@adb.org, https://www.adb.org/; Key Indicators for Asia and the Pacific 2022.

The Economist Group: Economist Intelligence Unit (EIU), 900 3rd Ave., 16th Fl., New York, NY, 10022, USA, (212) 541-0500, americas@eiu.com, https://www.eiu.com; Myanmar (Burma) Country Report.

Routledge - Taylor & Francis Group, 6000 Broken Sound Pkwy. NW, Ste. 300, Boca Raton, FL, 33487, USA, (800) 634-1420, (800) 634-7064, orders@taylorandfrancis.com, https://www.routledge.com/; The Europa World Year Book 2022.

United Nations Statistics Division (UNSD), United Nations Plz., New York, NY, 10017, USA, (800) 253-9646, (212) 963-9851, statistics@un.org, https://unstats.un.org; Statistical Yearbook of the United Nations 2021.

The World Bank, 1818 H St. NW, Washington, DC, 20433, USA, (202) 473-1000, (202) 477-6391, eds03@worldbank.org, https://www.worldbank.org/; World Development Report 2022: Finance for an Equitable Recovery.

BURMA-GROSS NATIONAL PRODUCT

Asian Development Bank (ADB), 6 ADB Ave., Mandaluyong City, 1550, PHL, information@adb.org, https://www.adb.org/; Key Indicators for Asia and the Pacific 2022.

United Nations Statistics Division (UNSD), United Nations Plz., New York, NY, 10017, USA, (800) 253-9646, (212) 963-9851, statistics@un.org, https://unstats.un.org; Statistical Yearbook of the United Nations 2021.

The World Bank, 1818 H St. NW, Washington, DC, 20433, USA, (202) 473-1000, (202) 477-6391,

eds03@worldbank.org, https://www.worldbank.org/; World Development Report 2022: Finance for an Equitable Recovery.

BURMA-HOUSING

Euromonitor International, Inc., 1 N Dearborn St., Ste. 1700, Chicago, IL, 60602, USA, (312) 922-1115, (312) 922-1157, info-usa@euromonitor.com, https://www.euromonitor.com/; Geographies.

BURMA-ILLITERATE PERSONS

UNESCO Institute for Statistics, C.P 250 Succursale H, Montreal, QC, H3G 2K8, CAN, (514) 343-6880 (Dial from U.S.), (514) 343-5740 (Fax from U.S.), uis.publications@unesco.org, http://uis.unesco.org/; UIS.Stat.

United Nations Economic and Social Commission for Asia and the Pacific (ESCAP), United Nations Building, Rajadamnern Nok Ave., Bangkok, 10200, THA, https://www.unescap.org/; Asia-Pacific Development Journal.

BURMA-IMPORTS

Asian Development Bank (ADB), 6 ADB Ave., Mandaluyong City, 1550, PHL, information@adb.org, https://www.adb.org/; Key Indicators for Asia and the Pacific 2022.

Central Intelligence Agency (CIA), Office of Public Affairs, Washington, DC, 20505, USA, (703) 482-0623, https://www.cia.gov; The World Factbook.

The Economist Group: Economist Intelligence Unit (EIU), 900 3rd Ave., 16th Fl., New York, NY, 10022, USA, (212) 541-0500, americas@eiu.com, https://www.eiu.com; Myanmar (Burma) Country Report.

International Monetary Fund (IMF), 700 19th St. NW, Washington, DC, 20431, USA, (202) 623-7000, (202) 623-4661, publications@imf.org, https://www.imf.org; Direction of Trade Statistics (DOTS) and International Financial Statistics (IFS).

S&P Global, IHS Markit, 15 Inverness Way E, Englewood, CO, 80112, USA, (800) 447-2273, (800) 854-7179, https://ihsmarkit.com; Global Trade Atlas (GTA).

United Nations Conference on Trade and Development (UNCTAD), Palais des Nations, Geneva, 1211, SWI, (212) 963-6896, unctadinfo@unctad.org, https://unctad.org; Handbook of Statistics 2021.

The World Bank, 1818 H St. NW, Washington, DC, 20433, USA, (202) 473-1000, (202) 477-6391, eds03@worldbank.org, https://www.worldbank.org/; World Development Report 2022: Finance for an Equitable Recovery.

BURMA-INDUSTRIAL METALS PRODUCTION

See BURMA-MINERAL INDUSTRIES

BURMA-INDUSTRIES

Central Intelligence Agency (CIA), Office of Public Affairs, Washington, DC, 20505, USA, (703) 482-0623, https://www.cia.gov; The World Factbook.

The Economist Group: Economist Intelligence Unit (EIU), 900 3rd Ave., 16th Fl., New York, NY, 10022, USA, (212) 541-0500, americas@eiu.com, https://www.eiu.com; Myanmar (Burma) Country Report.

Euromonitor International, Inc., 1 N Dearborn St., Ste. 1700, Chicago, IL, 60602, USA, (312) 922-1115, (312) 922-1157, info-usa@euromonitor.com, https://www.euromonitor.com/; Geographies.

International Labour Organization (ILO), 4 Rte. des Morillons, Geneva, CH-1211, SWI, ilo@ilo.org, https://www.ilo.org; NORMLEX Information System on International Labour Standards.

Routledge - Taylor & Francis Group, 6000 Broken Sound Pkwy. NW, Ste. 300, Boca Raton, FL, 33487, USA, (800) 634-1420, (800) 634-7064, orders@taylorandfrancis.com, https://www.routledge.com/; The Europa World Year Book 2022.

United Nations Economic and Social Commission for Asia and the Pacific (ESCAP), United Nations Building, Rajadamnern Nok Ave., Bangkok, 10200, THA, https://www.unescap.org/; Asia-Pacific Development Journal and SDG Gateway Data Explorer.

United Nations Industrial Development Organization (UNIDO), 1 United Nations Plz., Rm. DC1-1118, New York, NY, 10017, USA, (212) 963-6890, (212) 963 6885, (212) 963-7904, office.newyork@unido.org, https://www.unido.org/; Industrial Statistics Databases and International Yearbook of Industrial Statistics 2021.

The World Bank, 1818 H St. NW, Washington, DC, 20433, USA, (202) 473-1000, (202) 477-6391, eds03@worldbank.org, https://www.worldbank.org/; Myanmar (report).

BURMA-INFANT AND MATERNAL MORTALITY

See BURMA-MORTALITY

BURMA-INTERNATIONAL FINANCE

Asian Development Bank (ADB), 6 ADB Ave., Mandaluyong City, 1550, PHL, information@adb.org, https://www.adb.org/; Key Indicators for Asia and the Pacific 2022.

BURMA-INTERNATIONAL TRADE

Asian Development Bank (ADB), 6 ADB Ave., Mandaluyong City, 1550, PHL, information@adb.org, https://www.adb.org/; Key Indicators for Asia and the Pacific 2022.

The Economist Group: Economist Intelligence Unit (EIU), 900 3rd Ave., 16th Fl., New York, NY, 10022, USA, (212) 541-0500, americas@eiu.com, https://www.eiu.com; Myanmar (Burma) Country Report.

Euromonitor International, Inc., 1 N Dearborn St., Ste. 1700, Chicago, IL, 60602, USA, (312) 922-1115, (312) 922-1157, info-usa@euromonitor.com, https://www.euromonitor.com/; Geographies.

Palgrave Macmillan, 1 New York Plaza, Ste. 4500, New York, NY, 10004-1562, USA, (800) 777-4643, orders@palgrave.com, https://www.palgrave.com/us; The Statesman's Yearbook, 2023.

Routledge - Taylor & Francis Group, 6000 Broken Sound Pkwy. NW, Ste. 300, Boca Raton, FL, 33487, USA, (800) 634-1420, (800) 634-7064, orders@taylorandfrancis.com, https://www.routledge.com/; The Europa World Year Book 2022.

United Nations Conference on Trade and Development (UNCTAD), Palais des Nations, Geneva, 1211, SWI, (212) 963-6896, unctadinfo@unctad.org, https://unctad.org; Trade and Development Report 2021.

United Nations Economic and Social Commission for Asia and the Pacific (ESCAP), United Nations Building, Rajadamnern Nok Ave., Bangkok, 10200, THA, https://www.unescap.org/; Asia-Pacific Development Journal and SDG Gateway Data Explorer.

United Nations Food and Agricultural Organization (FAO), 2121 K St., Ste. 800B, Washington, DC, 20037, USA, (202) 653-2400 (Dial from U.S.), (202) 653-5760 (Fax from U.S.), fao-hq@fao.org, https://www.fao.org; The State of Food and Agriculture (SOFA) 2022.

United Nations Statistics Division (UNSD), United Nations Plz., New York, NY, 10017, USA, (800) 253-9646, (212) 963-9851, statistics@un.org, https://unstats.un.org; International Trade Statistics Yearbook 2020 and Statistical Yearbook of the United Nations 2021.

The World Bank, 1818 H St. NW, Washington, DC, 20433, USA, (202) 473-1000, (202) 477-6391, eds03@worldbank.org, https://www.worldbank.org/; Myanmar (report) and World Development Report 2022: Finance for an Equitable Recovery.

World Trade Organization (WTO), Ctre. William Rappard, Rue de Lausanne 154, Case postale, Geneva, CH-1211, SWI, enquiries@wto.org, https://www.wto.org; World Trade Statistical Review 2022.

BURMA-INTERNET USERS

International Telecommunication Union (ITU), Place des Nations, Geneva, CH-1211, SWI, itumail@itu.int, https://www.itu.int; Global Connectivity Report 2022; World Telecommunication/ICT Indicators Database 2021; and Yearbook of Statistics 2019.

BURMA-INVESTMENTS

International Monetary Fund (IMF), 700 19th St. NW, Washington, DC, 20431, USA, (202) 623-7000, (202) 623-4661, publications@imf.org, https://www.imf.org; International Financial Statistics (IFS).

BURMA-LABOR

Central Intelligence Agency (CIA), Office of Public Affairs, Washington, DC, 20505, USA, (703) 482-0623, https://www.cia.gov; The World Factbook.

Euromonitor International, Inc., 1 N Dearborn St., Ste. 1700, Chicago, IL, 60602, USA, (312) 922-1115, (312) 922-1157, info-usa@euromonitor.com, https://www.euromonitor.com/; Geographies.

International Labour Organization (ILO), 4 Rte. des Morillons, Geneva, CH-1211, SWI, ilo@ilo.org, https://www.ilo.org; NORMLEX Information System on International Labour Standards.

Palgrave Macmillan, 1 New York Plaza, Ste. 4500, New York, NY, 10004-1562, USA, (800) 777-4643, orders@palgrave.com, https://www.palgrave.com/us; The Statesman's Yearbook, 2023.

United Nations Food and Agricultural Organization (FAO), 2121 K St., Ste. 800B, Washington, DC, 20037, USA, (202) 653-2400 (Dial from U.S.), (202) 653-5760 (Fax from U.S.), fao-hq@fao.org, https://www.fao.org; The State of Food and Agriculture (SOFA) 2022.

The World Bank, 1818 H St. NW, Washington, DC, 20433, USA, (202) 473-1000, (202) 477-6391, eds03@worldbank.org, https://www.worldbank.org/; World Development Report 2022: Finance for an Equitable Recovery.

BURMA-LAND USE

United Nations Statistics Division (UNSD), United Nations Plz., New York, NY, 10017, USA, (800) 253-9646, (212) 963-9851, statistics@un.org, https://unstats.un.org; Millennium Development Goal Indicators.

The World Bank, 1818 H St. NW, Washington, DC, 20433, USA, (202) 473-1000, (202) 477-6391, eds03@worldbank.org, https://www.worldbank.org/; World Development Report 2022: Finance for an Equitable Recovery.

BURMA-LIFE EXPECTANCY

Central Intelligence Agency (CIA), Office of Public Affairs, Washington, DC, 20505, USA, (703) 482-0623, https://www.cia.gov; The World Factbook.

United Nations Department of Economic and Social Affairs (DESA), Population Division, 2 United Nations Plz., Rm. DC2-1950, New York, NY, 10017, USA, (212) 963-3209, (212) 963-2147, population@un.org, https://www.un.org/development/desa/pd/; World Population Ageing 2020 Highlights.

United Nations Economic and Social Commission for Asia and the Pacific (ESCAP), United Nations Building, Rajadamnern Nok Ave., Bangkok, 10200, THA, https://www.unescap.org/; Asia-Pacific Development Journal.

United Nations Statistics Division (UNSD), United Nations Plz., New York, NY, 10017, USA, (800) 253-9646, (212) 963-9851, statistics@un.org, https://unstats.un.org; Millennium Development Goal Indicators.

BURMA-LITERACY

Euromonitor International, Inc., 1 N Dearborn St., Ste. 1700, Chicago, IL, 60602, USA, (312) 922-1115, (312) 922-1157, info-usa@euromonitor.com, https://www.euromonitor.com/; Geographies.

UNESCO Institute for Statistics, C.P 250 Succursale H, Montreal, QC, H3G 2K8, CAN, (514) 343-6880 (Dial from U.S.), (514) 343-5740 (Fax from U.S.), uis.publications@unesco.org, http://uis.unesco.org/; Literacy.

BURMA-LIVESTOCK

Routledge - Taylor & Francis Group, 6000 Broken Sound Pkwy. NW, Ste. 300, Boca Raton, FL, 33487, USA, (800) 634-1420, (800) 634-7064, orders@taylorandfrancis.com, https://www.routledge.com/; The Europa World Year Book 2022.

United Nations Food and Agricultural Organization (FAO), 2121 K St., Ste. 800B, Washington, DC, 20037, USA, (202) 653-2400 (Dial from U.S.), (202) 653-5760 (Fax from U.S.), fao-hq@fao.org, https://www.fao.org; The State of Food and Agriculture (SOFA) 2022.

United Nations Statistics Division (UNSD), United Nations Plz., New York, NY, 10017, USA, (800) 253-9646, (212) 963-9851, statistics@un.org, https://unstats.un.org; Statistical Yearbook of the United Nations 2021.

BURMA-MANPOWER

United Nations Economic and Social Commission for Asia and the Pacific (ESCAP), United Nations Building, Rajadamnern Nok Ave., Bangkok, 10200, THA, https://www.unescap.org/; SDG Gateway Data Explorer.

BURMA-MANUFACTURES

Asian Development Bank (ADB), 6 ADB Ave., Mandaluyong City, 1550, PHL, information@adb.org, https://www.adb.org/; Key Indicators for Asia and the Pacific 2022.

BURMA-MEDICAL CARE

United Nations Statistics Division (UNSD), United Nations Plz., New York, NY, 10017, USA, (800) 253-9646, (212) 963-9851, statistics@un.org, https://unstats.un.org; Statistical Yearbook of the United Nations 2021.

The World Bank, 1818 H St. NW, Washington, DC, 20433, USA, (202) 473-1000, (202) 477-6391, eds03@worldbank.org, https://www.worldbank.org/; Myanmar (report).

BURMA-MINERAL INDUSTRIES

Asian Development Bank (ADB), 6 ADB Ave., Mandaluyong City, 1550, PHL, information@adb.org, https://www.adb.org/; Key Indicators for Asia and the Pacific 2022.

International Energy Agency (IEA), 9 Rue de la Federation, Paris, 75739, FRA, info@iea.org, https://www.iea.org/; World Energy Outlook 2021.

Palgrave Macmillan, 1 New York Plaza, Ste. 4500, New York, NY, 10004-1562, USA, (800) 777-4643, orders@palgrave.com, https://www.palgrave.com/us; The Statesman's Yearbook, 2023.

Routledge - Taylor & Francis Group, 6000 Broken Sound Pkwy. NW, Ste. 300, Boca Raton, FL, 33487, USA, (800) 634-1420, (800) 634-7064, orders@taylorandfrancis.com, https://www.routledge.com/; The Europa World Year Book 2022.

United Nations Conference on Trade and Development (UNCTAD), Palais des Nations, Geneva, 1211, SWI, (212) 963-6896, unctadinfo@unctad.org, https://unctad.org; Trade and Development Report 2021.

United Nations Statistics Division (UNSD), United Nations Plz., New York, NY, 10017, USA, (800) 253-9646, (212) 963-9851, statistics@un.org, https://unstats.un.org; Statistical Yearbook of the United Nations 2021.

BURMA-MONEY SUPPLY

The Economist Group: Economist Intelligence Unit (EIU), 900 3rd Ave., 16th Fl., New York, NY, 10022, USA, (212) 541-0500, americas@eiu.com, https://www.eiu.com; Myanmar (Burma) Country Report.

International Monetary Fund (IMF), 700 19th St. NW, Washington, DC, 20431, USA, (202) 623-7000, (202) 623-4661, publications@imf.org, https://www.imf.org; International Financial Statistics (IFS).

Routledge - Taylor & Francis Group, 6000 Broken Sound Pkwy. NW, Ste. 300, Boca Raton, FL, 33487, USA, (800) 634-1420, (800) 634-7064, orders@taylorandfrancis.com, https://www.routledge.com/; The Europa World Year Book 2022.

United Nations Statistics Division (UNSD), United Nations Plz., New York, NY, 10017, USA, (800) 253-9646, (212) 963-9851, statistics@un.org, https://unstats.un.org; Statistical Yearbook of the United Nations 2021.

The World Bank, 1818 H St. NW, Washington, DC, 20433, USA, (202) 473-1000, (202) 477-6391, eds03@worldbank.org, https://www.worldbank.org/; Myanmar (report).

BURMA-MORTALITY

UNICEF, 3 United Nations Plz., New York, NY, 10017, USA, (212) 303-7984, (917) 244-2215, https://www.unicef.org; The State of the World's Children 2023.

United Nations Economic and Social Commission for Asia and the Pacific (ESCAP), United Nations Building, Rajadamnern Nok Ave., Bangkok, 10200, THA, https://www.unescap.org/; Asia-Pacific Development Journal.

United Nations Statistics Division (UNSD), United Nations Plz., New York, NY, 10017, USA, (800) 253-9646, (212) 963-9851, statistics@un.org, https://unstats.un.org; Millennium Development Goal Indicators; Statistical Yearbook of the United Nations 2021; and World Statistics Pocketbook 2021.

World Health Organization (WHO), Ave. Appia 20, Geneva, CH-1211, SWI, (202) 974-3000 (Telephone in U.S.), publications@who.int, https://www.who.int/; Global Health Observatory (GHO).

BURMA-MOTOR VEHICLES

International Road Federation (IRF), Madison Place, 500 Montgomery St., 5th Fl., Alexandria, VA, 22314, USA, (703) 535-1001, (703) 535-1007, info@irf.global, https://www.irf.global/; World Road Statistics (WRS).

BURMA-NATURAL GAS PRODUCTION

See BURMA-MINERAL INDUSTRIES

BURMA-NICKEL AND NICKEL ORE

See BURMA-MINERAL INDUSTRIES

BURMA-NUTRITION

Asian Development Bank (ADB), 6 ADB Ave., Mandaluyong City, 1550, PHL, information@adb.org, https://www.adb.org/; Key Indicators for Asia and the Pacific 2022.

Kantar, 3 World Trade Center, 35th Fl., New York, NY, 10007, USA, (866) 471-1399, https://www.kantar.com/; Improving Child Nutrition in Myanmar.

United Nations Food and Agricultural Organization (FAO), 2121 K St., Ste. 800B, Washington, DC, 20037, USA, (202) 653-2400 (Dial from U.S.), (202) 653-5760 (Fax from U.S.), fao-hq@fao.org, https://www.fao.org; The State of Food and Agriculture (SOFA) 2022.

United Nations Statistics Division (UNSD), United Nations Plz., New York, NY, 10017, USA, (800) 253-9646, (212) 963-9851, statistics@un.org, https://unstats.un.org; Millennium Development Goal Indicators.

BURMA-OIL INDUSTRY

International Monetary Fund (IMF), 700 19th St. NW, Washington, DC, 20431, USA, (202) 623-7000, (202) 623-4661, publications@imf.org, https://www.imf.org; International Financial Statistics (IFS).

BURMA-PAPER

See BURMA-FORESTS AND FORESTRY

BURMA-PEANUT PRODUCTION

See BURMA-CROPS

BURMA-PESTICIDES

United Nations Food and Agricultural Organization (FAO), 2121 K St., Ste. 800B, Washington, DC, 20037, USA, (202) 653-2400 (Dial from U.S.), (202) 653-5760 (Fax from U.S.), fao-hq@fao.org, https://www.fao.org; The State of Food and Agriculture (SOFA) 2022.

BURMA-PETROLEUM INDUSTRY AND TRADE

Asian Development Bank (ADB), 6 ADB Ave., Mandaluyong City, 1550, PHL, information@adb.org, https://www.adb.org/; Key Indicators for Asia and the Pacific 2022.

International Energy Agency (IEA), 9 Rue de la Federation, Paris, 75739, FRA, info@iea.org, https://www.iea.org/; World Energy Outlook 2021.

Palgrave Macmillan, 1 New York Plaza, Ste. 4500, New York, NY, 10004-1562, USA, (800) 777-4643, orders@palgrave.com, https://www.palgrave.com/us; The Statesman's Yearbook, 2023.

U.S. Energy Information Administration (EIA), 1000 Independence Ave. SW, Washington, DC, 20585, USA, (202) 586-8800, infoctr@eia.gov, https://www.eia.gov; International Energy Outlook 2021.

United Nations Food and Agricultural Organization (FAO), 2121 K St., Ste. 800B, Washington, DC, 20037, USA, (202) 653-2400 (Dial from U.S.), (202) 653-5760 (Fax from U.S.), fao-hq@fao.org, https://www.fao.org; The State of Food and Agriculture (SOFA) 2022.

United Nations Statistics Division (UNSD), United Nations Plz., New York, NY, 10017, USA, (800) 253-9646, (212) 963-9851, statistics@un.org, https://unstats.un.org; Statistical Yearbook of the United Nations 2021.

BURMA-POPULATION

Asian Development Bank (ADB), 6 ADB Ave., Mandaluyong City, 1550, PHL, information@adb.org, https://www.adb.org/; Key Indicators for Asia and the Pacific 2022.

Central Intelligence Agency (CIA), Office of Public Affairs, Washington, DC, 20505, USA, (703) 482-0623, https://www.cia.gov; The World Factbook.

The Economist Group: Economist Intelligence Unit (EIU), 900 3rd Ave., 16th Fl., New York, NY, 10022, USA, (212) 541-0500, americas@eiu.com, https://www.eiu.com; Myanmar (Burma) Country Report.

Infoplease, c/o Sandbox Networks, Inc., 1 Lincoln St., 24th Fl., Boston, MA, 02111, USA, https://www.infoplease.com; Countries of the World.

International Labour Organization (ILO), 4 Rte. des Morillons, Geneva, CH-1211, SWI, ilo@ilo.org, https://www.ilo.org; NORMLEX Information System on International Labour Standards.

Kantar, 3 World Trade Center, 35th Fl., New York, NY, 10007, USA, (866) 471-1399, https://www.kantar.com/; Improving Child Nutrition in Myanmar.

Palgrave Macmillan, 1 New York Plaza, Ste. 4500, New York, NY, 10004-1562, USA, (800) 777-4643, orders@palgrave.com, https://www.palgrave.com/us; The Statesman's Yearbook, 2023.

Routledge - Taylor & Francis Group, 6000 Broken Sound Pkwy. NW, Ste. 300, Boca Raton, FL, 33487, USA, (800) 634-1420, (800) 634-7064, orders@taylorandfrancis.com, https://www.routledge.com/; The Europa World Year Book 2022.

UK Data Service, University of Essex, Wivenhoe Park, Colchester, Essex, CO4 3SQ, GBR, https://ukdataservice.ac.uk/; International Aggregate Data.

UNESCO Institute for Statistics, C.P 250 Succursale H, Montreal, QC, H3G 2K8, CAN, (514) 343-6880 (Dial from U.S.), (514) 343-5740 (Fax from U.S.), uis.publications@unesco.org, http://uis.unesco.org/; UIS.Stat.

United Nations Department of Economic and Social Affairs (DESA), Population Division, 2 United Nations Plz., Rm. DC2-1950, New York, NY, 10017, USA, (212) 963-3209, (212) 963-2147, population@un.org, https://www.un.org/development/desa/pd/; Revision of World Urbanization Prospects and World Population Ageing 2020 Highlights.

United Nations Development Programme (UNDP), One United Nations Plz., New York, NY, 10017, USA, (212) 906-5000, (212) 906-5001, https://www.undp.org; Human Development Report 2021-2022.

United Nations Economic and Social Commission for Asia and the Pacific (ESCAP), United Nations Building, Rajadamnern Nok Ave., Bangkok, 10200, THA, https://www.unescap.org/; Asia-Pacific Development Journal and SDG Gateway Data Explorer.

United Nations Statistics Division (UNSD), United Nations Plz., New York, NY, 10017, USA, (800) 253-9646, (212) 963-9851, statistics@un.org, https://unstats.un.org; Statistical Yearbook of the United Nations 2021 and World Statistics Pocketbook 2021.

The World Bank, 1818 H St. NW, Washington, DC, 20433, USA, (202) 473-1000, (202) 477-6391, eds03@worldbank.org, https://www.worldbank.org/; The Global Findex Database 2021; Myanmar (report); and World Development Report 2022: Finance for an Equitable Recovery.

BURMA-POPULATION DENSITY

Central Intelligence Agency (CIA), Office of Public Affairs, Washington, DC, 20505, USA, (703) 482-0623, https://www.cia.gov; The World Factbook.

Palgrave Macmillan, 1 New York Plaza, Ste. 4500, New York, NY, 10004-1562, USA, (800) 777-4643, orders@palgrave.com, https://www.palgrave.com/us; The Statesman's Yearbook, 2023.

Routledge - Taylor & Francis Group, 6000 Broken Sound Pkwy. NW, Ste. 300, Boca Raton, FL, 33487, USA, (800) 634-1420, (800) 634-7064, orders@taylorandfrancis.com, https://www.routledge.com/; The Europa World Year Book 2022.

The World Bank, 1818 H St. NW, Washington, DC, 20433, USA, (202) 473-1000, (202) 477-6391, eds03@worldbank.org, https://www.worldbank.org/; Myanmar (report) and World Development Report 2022: Finance for an Equitable Recovery.

BURMA-POSTAL SERVICE

Palgrave Macmillan, 1 New York Plaza, Ste. 4500, New York, NY, 10004-1562, USA, (800) 777-4643, orders@palgrave.com, https://www.palgrave.com/us; The Statesman's Yearbook, 2023.

BURMA-PRICES

Euromonitor International, Inc., 1 N Dearborn St., Ste. 1700, Chicago, IL, 60602, USA, (312) 922-1115, (312) 922-1157, info-usa@euromonitor.com, https://www.euromonitor.com/; Geographies.

International Monetary Fund (IMF), 700 19th St. NW, Washington, DC, 20431, USA, (202) 623-7000, (202) 623-4661, publications@imf.org, https://www.imf.org; International Financial Statistics (IFS).

The World Bank, 1818 H St. NW, Washington, DC, 20433, USA, (202) 473-1000, (202) 477-6391, eds03@worldbank.org, https://www.worldbank.org/; Myanmar (report).

BURMA-PUBLIC HEALTH

Euromonitor International, Inc., 1 N Dearborn St., Ste. 1700, Chicago, IL, 60602, USA, (312) 922-1115, (312) 922-1157, info-usa@euromonitor.com, https://www.euromonitor.com/; Geographies.

Palgrave Macmillan, 1 New York Plaza, Ste. 4500, New York, NY, 10004-1562, USA, (800) 777-4643, orders@palgrave.com, https://www.palgrave.com/us; The Statesman's Yearbook, 2023.

U.S. Census Bureau, 4600 Silver Hill Rd., Washington, DC, 20233, USA, (301) 763-4636, (800) 923-8282, https://www.census.gov; HIV/AIDS Surveillance Data Base.

UNICEF, 3 United Nations Plz., New York, NY, 10017, USA, (212) 303-7984, (917) 244-2215, https://www.unicef.org; The State of the World's Children 2023.

United Nations Department of Economic and Social Affairs (DESA), Population Division, 2 United Nations Plz., Rm. DC2-1950, New York, NY, 10017, USA, (212) 963-3209, (212) 963-2147, population@un.org, https://www.un.org/development/desa/pd/; World Fertility Data 2019.

United Nations Development Programme (UNDP), One United Nations Plz., New York, NY, 10017, USA, (212) 906-5000, (212) 906-5001, https://www.undp.org; Human Development Report 2021-2022.

United Nations Economic and Social Commission for Asia and the Pacific (ESCAP), United Nations Building, Rajadamnern Nok Ave., Bangkok, 10200, THA, https://www.unescap.org/; Asia-Pacific Development Journal.

United Nations Statistics Division (UNSD), United Nations Plz., New York, NY, 10017, USA, (800) 253-9646, (212) 963-9851, statistics@un.org, https://unstats.un.org; Millennium Development Goal Indicators and Statistical Yearbook of the United Nations 2021.

The World Bank, 1818 H St. NW, Washington, DC, 20433, USA, (202) 473-1000, (202) 477-6391, eds03@worldbank.org, https://www.worldbank.org/; Myanmar (report).

World Health Organization (WHO), Ave. Appia 20, Geneva, CH-1211, SWI, (202) 974-3000 (Telephone in U.S.), publications@who.int, https://www.who.int/; Global Health Observatory (GHO) and Health Statistics and Information Systems.

BURMA-RAILROADS

Palgrave Macmillan, 1 New York Plaza, Ste. 4500, New York, NY, 10004-1562, USA, (800) 777-4643, orders@palgrave.com, https://www.palgrave.com/us; The Statesman's Yearbook, 2023.

Routledge - Taylor & Francis Group, 6000 Broken Sound Pkwy. NW, Ste. 300, Boca Raton, FL, 33487, USA, (800) 634-1420, (800) 634-7064, orders@taylorandfrancis.com, https://www.routledge.com/; The Europa World Year Book 2022.

United Nations Statistics Division (UNSD), United Nations Plz., New York, NY, 10017, USA, (800) 253-9646, (212) 963-9851, statistics@un.org, https://unstats.un.org; Statistical Yearbook of the United Nations 2021.

BURMA-RELIGION

Central Intelligence Agency (CIA), Office of Public Affairs, Washington, DC, 20505, USA, (703) 482-0623, https://www.cia.gov; The World Factbook.

Palgrave Macmillan, 1 New York Plaza, Ste. 4500, New York, NY, 10004-1562, USA, (800) 777-4643, orders@palgrave.com, https://www.palgrave.com/us; The Statesman's Yearbook, 2023.

BURMA-RETAIL TRADE

Euromonitor International, Inc., 1 N Dearborn St., Ste. 1700, Chicago, IL, 60602, USA, (312) 922-1115, (312) 922-1157, info-usa@euromonitor.com, https://www.euromonitor.com/; Geographies.

BURMA-RICE PRODUCTION

See BURMA-CROPS

BURMA-ROADS

International Road Federation (IRF), Madison Place, 500 Montgomery St., 5th Fl., Alexandria, VA, 22314, USA, (703) 535-1001, (703) 535-1007, info@irf.global, https://www.irf.global/; World Road Statistics (WRS).

BURMA-RUBBER INDUSTRY AND TRADE

International Rubber Study Group (IRSG), 51 Changi Business Park Central 2, Unit No. 6, 486066, SGP, https://www.rubberstudy.org; Monthly Rubber Bulletin (MRB); Rubber Statistical Bulletin; and World Rubber Industry Report (WRIO).

United Nations Statistics Division (UNSD), United Nations Plz., New York, NY, 10017, USA, (800) 253-9646, (212) 963-9851, statistics@un.org, https://unstats.un.org; Statistical Yearbook of the United Nations 2021.

BURMA-SHIPPING

Routledge - Taylor & Francis Group, 6000 Broken Sound Pkwy. NW, Ste. 300, Boca Raton, FL, 33487, USA, (800) 634-1420, (800) 634-7064, orders@taylorandfrancis.com, https://www.routledge.com/; The Europa World Year Book 2022.

S&P Global, IHS Markit, 15 Inverness Way E, Englewood, CO, 80112, USA, (800) 447-2273, (800) 854-7179, https://ihsmarkit.com; IHS Maritime World Shipbuilding Statistics; Journal of Commerce; Lloyd's Register of Ships 2021-2022; and Maritime Portal Desktop.

United Nations Statistics Division (UNSD), United Nations Plz., New York, NY, 10017, USA, (800) 253-9646, (212) 963-9851, statistics@un.org, https://unstats.un.org; Statistical Yearbook of the United Nations 2021.

BURMA-SOYBEAN PRODUCTION

See BURMA-CROPS

BURMA-STEEL PRODUCTION

See BURMA-MINERAL INDUSTRIES

BURMA-SUGAR PRODUCTION

See BURMA-CROPS

BURMA-TAXATION

International Road Federation (IRF), Madison Place, 500 Montgomery St., 5th Fl., Alexandria, VA, 22314, USA, (703) 535-1001, (703) 535-1007, info@irf.global, https://www.irf.global/; World Road Statistics (WRS).

BURMA-TEAK

International Monetary Fund (IMF), 700 19th St. NW, Washington, DC, 20431, USA, (202) 623-7000, (202) 623-4661, publications@imf.org, https://www.imf.org; International Financial Statistics (IFS).

BURMA-TELEPHONE

Palgrave Macmillan, 1 New York Plaza, Ste. 4500, New York, NY, 10004-1562, USA, (800) 777-4643, orders@palgrave.com, https://www.palgrave.com/us; The Statesman's Yearbook, 2023.

Routledge - Taylor & Francis Group, 6000 Broken Sound Pkwy. NW, Ste. 300, Boca Raton, FL, 33487, USA, (800) 634-1420, (800) 634-7064, orders@taylorandfrancis.com, https://www.routledge.com/; The Europa World Year Book 2022.

United Nations Statistics Division (UNSD), United Nations Plz., New York, NY, 10017, USA, (800) 253-9646, (212) 963-9851, statistics@un.org, https://unstats.un.org; World Statistics Pocketbook 2021.

BURMA-TEXTILE INDUSTRY

United Nations Statistics Division (UNSD), United Nations Plz., New York, NY, 10017, USA, (800) 253-9646, (212) 963-9851, statistics@un.org, https://unstats.un.org; Statistical Yearbook of the United Nations 2021.

BURMA-TOBACCO INDUSTRY

United Nations Statistics Division (UNSD), United Nations Plz., New York, NY, 10017, USA, (800) 253-9646, (212) 963-9851, statistics@un.org, https://unstats.un.org; Statistical Yearbook of the United Nations 2021.

BURMA-TOURISM

Euromonitor International, Inc., 1 N Dearborn St., Ste. 1700, Chicago, IL, 60602, USA, (312) 922-1115, (312) 922-1157, info-usa@euromonitor.com, https://www.euromonitor.com/; Geographies.

Palgrave Macmillan, 1 New York Plaza, Ste. 4500, New York, NY, 10004-1562, USA, (800) 777-4643, orders@palgrave.com, https://www.palgrave.com/us; The Statesman's Yearbook, 2023.

Routledge - Taylor & Francis Group, 6000 Broken Sound Pkwy. NW, Ste. 300, Boca Raton, FL, 33487,

USA, (800) 634-1420, (800) 634-7064, orders@taylorandfrancis.com, https://www.routledge.com/; The Europa World Year Book 2022.

The World Bank, 1818 H St. NW, Washington, DC, 20433, USA, (202) 473-1000, (202) 477-6391, eds03@worldbank.org, https://www.worldbank.org/; Myanmar (report).

BURMA-TRADE

See BURMA-INTERNATIONAL TRADE

BURMA-TRANSPORTATION

Central Intelligence Agency (CIA), Office of Public Affairs, Washington, DC, 20505, USA, (703) 482-0623, https://www.cia.gov; The World Factbook.

Euromonitor International, Inc., 1 N Dearborn St., Ste. 1700, Chicago, IL, 60602, USA, (312) 922-1115, (312) 922-1157, info-usa@euromonitor.com, https://www.euromonitor.com/; Geographies.

Palgrave Macmillan, 1 New York Plaza, Ste. 4500, New York, NY, 10004-1562, USA, (800) 777-4643, orders@palgrave.com, https://www.palgrave.com/us; The Statesman's Yearbook, 2023.

Routledge - Taylor & Francis Group, 6000 Broken Sound Pkwy. NW, Ste. 300, Boca Raton, FL, 33487, USA, (800) 634-1420, (800) 634-7064, orders@taylorandfrancis.com, https://www.routledge.com/; The Europa World Year Book 2022.

United Nations Economic and Social Commission for Asia and the Pacific (ESCAP), United Nations Building, Rajadamnern Nok Ave., Bangkok, 10200, THA, https://www.unescap.org/; SDG Gateway Data Explorer.

The World Bank, 1818 H St. NW, Washington, DC, 20433, USA, (202) 473-1000, (202) 477-6391, eds03@worldbank.org, https://www.worldbank.org/; Myanmar (report).

BURMA-TUNGSTEN

United Nations Statistics Division (UNSD), United Nations Plz., New York, NY, 10017, USA, (800) 253-9646, (212) 963-9851, statistics@un.org, https://unstats.un.org; Statistical Yearbook of the United Nations 2021.

BURMA-UNEMPLOYMENT

International Labour Organization (ILO), 4 Rte. des Morillons, Geneva, CH-1211, SWI, ilo@ilo.org, https://www.ilo.org; NORMLEX Information System on International Labour Standards.

United Nations Statistics Division (UNSD), United Nations Plz., New York, NY, 10017, USA, (800) 253-9646, (212) 963-9851, statistics@un.org, https://unstats.un.org; Statistical Yearbook of the United Nations 2021.

BURMA-VITAL STATISTICS

Palgrave Macmillan, 1 New York Plaza, Ste. 4500, New York, NY, 10004-1562, USA, (800) 777-4643, orders@palgrave.com, https://www.palgrave.com/us; The Statesman's Yearbook, 2023.

U.S. Census Bureau, 4600 Silver Hill Rd., Washington, DC, 20233, USA, (301) 763-4636, (800) 923-8282, https://www.census.gov; HIV/AIDS Surveillance Data Base.

United Nations Department of Economic and Social Affairs (DESA), Population Division, 2 United Nations Plz., Rm. DC2-1950, New York, NY, 10017, USA, (212) 963-3209, (212) 963-2147, population@un.org, https://www.un.org/development/desa/pd/; World Contraceptive Use 2021: Estimates and Projections of Family Planning Indicators and World Marriage Data 2019.

United Nations Statistics Division (UNSD), United Nations Plz., New York, NY, 10017, USA, (800) 253-9646, (212) 963-9851, statistics@un.org, https://unstats.un.org; Statistical Yearbook of the United Nations 2021.

BURMA-WAGES

International Labour Organization (ILO), 4 Rte. des Morillons, Geneva, CH-1211, SWI, ilo@ilo.org, https://www.ilo.org; NORMLEX Information System on International Labour Standards.

United Nations Economic and Social Commission for Asia and the Pacific (ESCAP), United Nations Building, Rajadamnern Nok Ave., Bangkok, 10200, THA, https://www.unescap.org/; SDG Gateway Data Explorer.

The World Bank, 1818 H St. NW, Washington, DC, 20433, USA, (202) 473-1000, (202) 477-6391, eds03@worldbank.org, https://www.worldbank.org/; Myanmar (report).

BURMA-WEATHER

See BURMA-CLIMATE

BURMA-WHEAT PRODUCTION

See BURMA-CROPS

BURN OUT (PSYCHOLOGY)

American Academy of Pediatrics (AAP), 345 Park Blvd., Itasca, IL, 60143, USA, (800) 433-9016, (847) 434-8000, mcc@aap.org, https://www.aap.org; Longitudinal Analyses of Pediatrician Burnout.

BURUNDI-PRIMARY STATISTICS SOURCES

Institut de Statistiques et d'Etudes Economiques du Burundi (ISTEEBU), BP 1156, Bujumbura, BDI, https://www.isteebu.bi/; Annuaires Statistiques du Burundi 2020.

BURUNDI-AGRICULTURE

The Economist Group: Economist Intelligence Unit (EIU), 900 3rd Ave., 16th Fl., New York, NY, 10022, USA, (212) 541-0500, americas@eiu.com, https://www.eiu.com; Burundi Country Report.

Euromonitor International, Inc., 1 N Dearborn St., Ste. 1700, Chicago, IL, 60602, USA, (312) 922-1115, (312) 922-1157, info-usa@euromonitor.com, https://www.euromonitor.com/; Geographies.

Palgrave Macmillan, 1 New York Plaza, Ste. 4500, New York, NY, 10004-1562, USA, (800) 777-4643, orders@palgrave.com, https://www.palgrave.com/us; The Statesman's Yearbook, 2023.

Routledge - Taylor & Francis Group, 6000 Broken Sound Pkwy. NW, Ste. 300, Boca Raton, FL, 33487, USA, (800) 634-1420, (800) 634-7064, orders@taylorandfrancis.com, https://www.routledge.com/; The Europa World Year Book 2022.

United Nations Economic Commission for Africa (UNECA), PO Box 3001, Addis Ababa, ETH, ecainfo@uneca.org, https://www.uneca.org/; African Statistical Yearbook 2020.

United Nations Food and Agricultural Organization (FAO), 2121 K St., Ste. 800B, Washington, DC, 20037, USA, (202) 653-2400 (Dial from U.S.), (202) 653-5760 (Fax from U.S.), fao-hq@fao.org, https://www.fao.org; AQUASTAT and The State of Food and Agriculture (SOFA) 2022.

United Nations Statistics Division (UNSD), United Nations Plz., New York, NY, 10017, USA, (800) 253-9646, (212) 963-9851, statistics@un.org, https://unstats.un.org; Statistical Yearbook of the United Nations 2021.

The World Bank, 1818 H St. NW, Washington, DC, 20433, USA, (202) 473-1000, (202) 477-6391, eds03@worldbank.org, https://www.worldbank.org/; Burundi (report).

BURUNDI-AIRLINES

Palgrave Macmillan, 1 New York Plaza, Ste. 4500, New York, NY, 10004-1562, USA, (800) 777-4643, orders@palgrave.com, https://www.palgrave.com/us; The Statesman's Yearbook, 2023.

Routledge - Taylor & Francis Group, 6000 Broken Sound Pkwy. NW, Ste. 300, Boca Raton, FL, 33487, USA, (800) 634-1420, (800) 634-7064, orders@taylorandfrancis.com, https://www.routledge.com/; The Europa World Year Book 2022.

United Nations Economic Commission for Africa (UNECA), PO Box 3001, Addis Ababa, ETH, ecainfo@uneca.org, https://www.uneca.org/; African Statistical Yearbook 2020.

BURUNDI-ARMED FORCES

Central Intelligence Agency (CIA), Office of Public Affairs, Washington, DC, 20505, USA, (703) 482-0623, https://www.cia.gov; The World Factbook.

International Institute for Strategic Studies (IISS) - Americas, 2121 K St. NW, Ste. 600, Washington, DC, 20037, USA, (202) 659-1490, (202) 659-1499, https://www.iiss.org/; Armed Conflict Survey 2021 and The Military Balance 2022.

Palgrave Macmillan, 1 New York Plaza, Ste. 4500, New York, NY, 10004-1562, USA, (800) 777-4643, orders@palgrave.com, https://www.palgrave.com/us; The Statesman's Yearbook, 2023.

Stockholm International Peace Research Institute (SIPRI), Signalistgatan 9, Stockholm, SE 169 72, SWE, https://www.sipri.org/; SIPRI Arms Transfers Database and SIPRI Military Expenditure Database.

BURUNDI-BALANCE OF PAYMENTS

African Development Bank Group (AfDB), Avenue Joseph Anoma, 01 BP 1387, Abidjan, 01, COT, https://www.afdb.org; The AfDB Statistics Pocketbook 2019.

Routledge - Taylor & Francis Group, 6000 Broken Sound Pkwy. NW, Ste. 300, Boca Raton, FL, 33487, USA, (800) 634-1420, (800) 634-7064, orders@taylorandfrancis.com, https://www.routledge.com/; The Europa World Year Book 2022.

United Nations Conference on Trade and Development (UNCTAD), Palais des Nations, Geneva, 1211, SWI, (212) 963-6896, unctadinfo@unctad.org, https://unctad.org; Handbook of Statistics 2021.

United Nations Economic Commission for Africa (UNECA), PO Box 3001, Addis Ababa, ETH, ecainfo@uneca.org, https://www.uneca.org/; African Statistical Yearbook 2020.

The World Bank, 1818 H St. NW, Washington, DC, 20433, USA, (202) 473-1000, (202) 477-6391, eds03@worldbank.org, https://www.worldbank.org/; Burundi (report) and World Development Report 2022: Finance for an Equitable Recovery.

BURUNDI-BANKS AND BANKING

Euromonitor International, Inc., 1 N Dearborn St., Ste. 1700, Chicago, IL, 60602, USA, (312) 922-1115, (312) 922-1157, info-usa@euromonitor.com, https://www.euromonitor.com/; Geographies.

International Monetary Fund (IMF), 700 19th St. NW, Washington, DC, 20431, USA, (202) 623-7000, (202) 623-4661, publications@imf.org, https://www.imf.org; International Financial Statistics (IFS).

Routledge - Taylor & Francis Group, 6000 Broken Sound Pkwy. NW, Ste. 300, Boca Raton, FL, 33487, USA, (800) 634-1420, (800) 634-7064, orders@taylorandfrancis.com, https://www.routledge.com/; The Europa World Year Book 2022.

BURUNDI-BROADCASTING

Central Intelligence Agency (CIA), Office of Public Affairs, Washington, DC, 20505, USA, (703) 482-0623, https://www.cia.gov; The World Factbook.

Euromonitor International, Inc., 1 N Dearborn St., Ste. 1700, Chicago, IL, 60602, USA, (312) 922-1115, (312) 922-1157, info-usa@euromonitor.com, https://www.euromonitor.com/; Geographies.

Palgrave Macmillan, 1 New York Plaza, Ste. 4500, New York, NY, 10004-1562, USA, (800) 777-4643, orders@palgrave.com, https://www.palgrave.com/us; The Statesman's Yearbook, 2023.

WRTH Publications Limited, PO Box 290, Oxford, OX2 7FT, GBR, sales@wrth.com, https://www.wrth.com; World Radio TV Handbook 2023.

BURUNDI-BUDGET

Central Intelligence Agency (CIA), Office of Public Affairs, Washington, DC, 20505, USA, (703) 482-0623, https://www.cia.gov; The World Factbook.

BURUNDI-CLIMATE

International Institute for Environment and Development (IIED), 235 High Holborn, London, WC1V 7DN, GBR, inforequest@iied.org, https://www.iied.org; Environment & Urbanization.

Palgrave Macmillan, 1 New York Plaza, Ste. 4500, New York, NY, 10004-1562, USA, (800) 777-4643, orders@palgrave.com, https://www.palgrave.com/us; The Statesman's Yearbook, 2023.

BURUNDI-COAL PRODUCTION

See BURUNDI-MINERAL INDUSTRIES

BURUNDI-COFFEE

See BURUNDI-CROPS

BURUNDI-COMMERCE

Palgrave Macmillan, 1 New York Plaza, Ste. 4500, New York, NY, 10004-1562, USA, (800) 777-4643, orders@palgrave.com, https://www.palgrave.com/us; The Statesman's Yearbook, 2023.

UK Data Service, University of Essex, Wivenhoe Park, Colchester, Essex, CO4 3SQ, GBR, https://ukdataservice.ac.uk/; International Aggregate Data.

BURUNDI-COMMODITY EXCHANGES

Barchart, 209 W Jackson Blvd., 2nd Fl., Chicago, IL, 60606, USA, (877) 247-4394, commodities@barchart.com, https://www.barchart.com/cmdty; The cmdty Yearbook 2023; cmdtyStats: Commodity Statistics and Fundamental Data; cmdtyView: Commodity Index; and Commodity Data and Prices.

International Monetary Fund (IMF), 700 19th St. NW, Washington, DC, 20431, USA, (202) 623-7000, (202) 623-4661, publications@imf.org, https://www.imf.org; IMF Primary Commodity Prices.

BURUNDI-CONSTRUCTION INDUSTRY

United Nations Economic Commission for Africa (UNECA), PO Box 3001, Addis Ababa, ETH, ecainfo@uneca.org, https://www.uneca.org/; African Statistical Yearbook 2020.

BURUNDI-CONSUMER PRICE INDEXES

Routledge - Taylor & Francis Group, 6000 Broken Sound Pkwy. NW, Ste. 300, Boca Raton, FL, 33487, USA, (800) 634-1420, (800) 634-7064, orders@taylorandfrancis.com, https://www.routledge.com/; The Europa World Year Book 2022.

United Nations Economic Commission for Africa (UNECA), PO Box 3001, Addis Ababa, ETH, ecainfo@uneca.org, https://www.uneca.org/; African Statistical Yearbook 2020.

The World Bank, 1818 H St. NW, Washington, DC, 20433, USA, (202) 473-1000, (202) 477-6391, eds03@worldbank.org, https://www.worldbank.org/; Burundi (report).

BURUNDI-CONSUMPTION (ECONOMICS)

African Development Bank Group (AfDB), Avenue Joseph Anoma, 01 BP 1387, Abidjan, 01, COT, https://www.afdb.org; The AfDB Statistics Pocketbook 2019.

BURUNDI-CORN INDUSTRY

United Nations Food and Agricultural Organization (FAO), 2121 K St., Ste. 800B, Washington, DC, 20037, USA, (202) 653-2400 (Dial from U.S.), (202) 653-5760 (Fax from U.S.), fao-hq@fao.org, https://www.fao.org; The State of Food and Agriculture (SOFA) 2022.

United Nations Statistics Division (UNSD), United Nations Plz., New York, NY, 10017, USA, (800) 253-9646, (212) 963-9851, statistics@un.org, https://unstats.un.org; Statistical Yearbook of the United Nations 2021.

BURUNDI-COTTON

See BURUNDI-CROPS

BURUNDI-CROPS

International Monetary Fund (IMF), 700 19th St. NW, Washington, DC, 20431, USA, (202) 623-7000, (202) 623-4661, publications@imf.org, https://www.imf.org; International Financial Statistics (IFS).

Palgrave Macmillan, 1 New York Plaza, Ste. 4500, New York, NY, 10004-1562, USA, (800) 777-4643, orders@palgrave.com, https://www.palgrave.com/us; The Statesman's Yearbook, 2023.

United Nations Economic Commission for Africa (UNECA), PO Box 3001, Addis Ababa, ETH, ecainfo@uneca.org, https://www.uneca.org/; African Statistical Yearbook 2020.

United Nations Food and Agricultural Organization (FAO), 2121 K St., Ste. 800B, Washington, DC, 20037, USA, (202) 653-2400 (Dial from U.S.), (202) 653-5760 (Fax from U.S.), fao-hq@fao.org, https://www.fao.org; The State of Food and Agriculture (SOFA) 2022.

United Nations Statistics Division (UNSD), United Nations Plz., New York, NY, 10017, USA, (800) 253-9646, (212) 963-9851, statistics@un.org, https://unstats.un.org; Statistical Yearbook of the United Nations 2021.

BURUNDI-DAIRY PROCESSING

Palgrave Macmillan, 1 New York Plaza, Ste. 4500, New York, NY, 10004-1562, USA, (800) 777-4643, orders@palgrave.com, https://www.palgrave.com/us; The Statesman's Yearbook, 2023.

United Nations Food and Agricultural Organization (FAO), 2121 K St., Ste. 800B, Washington, DC, 20037, USA, (202) 653-2400 (Dial from U.S.), (202) 653-5760 (Fax from U.S.), fao-hq@fao.org, https://www.fao.org; The State of Food and Agriculture (SOFA) 2022.

BURUNDI-DEBTS, EXTERNAL

African Development Bank Group (AfDB), Avenue Joseph Anoma, 01 BP 1387, Abidjan, 01, COT, https://www.afdb.org; The AfDB Statistics Pocketbook 2019.

Palgrave Macmillan, 1 New York Plaza, Ste. 4500, New York, NY, 10004-1562, USA, (800) 777-4643, orders@palgrave.com, https://www.palgrave.com/us; The Statesman's Yearbook, 2023.

The World Bank, 1818 H St. NW, Washington, DC, 20433, USA, (202) 473-1000, (202) 477-6391, eds03@worldbank.org, https://www.worldbank.org/; Global Financial Development Report 2019-2020: Bank Regulation and Supervision a Decade after the Global Financial Crisis and World Development Report 2022: Finance for an Equitable Recovery.

BURUNDI-DEFENSE EXPENDITURES

See BURUNDI-ARMED FORCES

BURUNDI-ECONOMIC ASSISTANCE

United Nations Statistics Division (UNSD), United Nations Plz., New York, NY, 10017, USA, (800) 253-9646, (212) 963-9851, statistics@un.org, https://unstats.un.org; Statistical Yearbook of the United Nations 2021.

BURUNDI-ECONOMIC CONDITIONS

African Development Bank Group (AfDB), Avenue Joseph Anoma, 01 BP 1387, Abidjan, 01, COT, https://www.afdb.org; The AfDB Statistics Pocketbook 2019 and African Economic Outlook 2021.

Bernan Press, 15250 NBN Way, Bldg. C, Blue Ridge Summit, PA, 17214, USA, (301) 459-2255, (800) 865-3457, (800) 865-3450, customercare@bernan.com, https://rowman.com/Page/Bernan; World Economic Outlook, April 2022.

Central Intelligence Agency (CIA), Office of Public Affairs, Washington, DC, 20505, USA, (703) 482-0623, https://www.cia.gov; The World Factbook.

The Economist Group: Economist Intelligence Unit (EIU), 900 3rd Ave., 16th Fl., New York, NY, 10022, USA, (212) 541-0500, americas@eiu.com, https://www.eiu.com; Burundi Country Report.

Euromonitor International, Inc., 1 N Dearborn St., Ste. 1700, Chicago, IL, 60602, USA, (312) 922-1115, (312) 922-1157, info-usa@euromonitor.com, https://www.euromonitor.com/; Geographies.

International Monetary Fund (IMF), 700 19th St. NW, Washington, DC, 20431, USA, (202) 623-7000, (202) 623-4661, publications@imf.org, https://www.imf.org; IMF Data and World Economic Outlook.

Palgrave Macmillan, 1 New York Plaza, Ste. 4500, New York, NY, 10004-1562, USA, (800) 777-4643, orders@palgrave.com, https://www.palgrave.com/us; The Statesman's Yearbook, 2023.

Routledge - Taylor & Francis Group, 6000 Broken Sound Pkwy. NW, Ste. 300, Boca Raton, FL, 33487, USA, (800) 634-1420, (800) 634-7064, orders@taylorandfrancis.com, https://www.routledge.com/; The Europa World Year Book 2022.

United Nations Statistics Division (UNSD), United Nations Plz., New York, NY, 10017, USA, (800) 253-9646, (212) 963-9851, statistics@un.org, https://unstats.un.org; World Statistics Pocketbook 2021.

The World Bank, 1818 H St. NW, Washington, DC, 20433, USA, (202) 473-1000, (202) 477-6391, eds03@worldbank.org, https://www.worldbank.org/; Burundi (report); Global Economic Monitor (GEM); Global Economic Prospects, June 2022; The Global Findex Database 2021; and World Development Report 2022: Finance for an Equitable Recovery.

BURUNDI-EDUCATION

African Development Bank Group (AfDB), Avenue Joseph Anoma, 01 BP 1387, Abidjan, 01, COT, https://www.afdb.org; The AfDB Statistics Pocketbook 2019.

Euromonitor International, Inc., 1 N Dearborn St., Ste. 1700, Chicago, IL, 60602, USA, (312) 922-1115, (312) 922-1157, info-usa@euromonitor.com, https://www.euromonitor.com/; Geographies.

Infoplease, c/o Sandbox Networks, Inc., 1 Lincoln St., 24th Fl., Boston, MA, 02111, USA, https://www.infoplease.com; Countries of the World.

Palgrave Macmillan, 1 New York Plaza, Ste. 4500, New York, NY, 10004-1562, USA, (800) 777-4643, orders@palgrave.com, https://www.palgrave.com/us; The Statesman's Yearbook, 2023.

Routledge - Taylor & Francis Group, 6000 Broken Sound Pkwy. NW, Ste. 300, Boca Raton, FL, 33487, USA, (800) 634-1420, (800) 634-7064, orders@taylorandfrancis.com, https://www.routledge.com/; The Europa World Year Book 2022.

UNESCO Institute for Statistics, C.P 250 Succursale H, Montreal, QC, H3G 2K8, CAN, (514) 343-6880 (Dial from U.S.), (514) 343-5740 (Fax from U.S.), uis.publications@unesco.org, http://uis.unesco.org/; Literacy and UIS.Stat.

United Nations Economic Commission for Africa (UNECA), PO Box 3001, Addis Ababa, ETH, ecainfo@uneca.org, https://www.uneca.org/; African Statistical Yearbook 2020.

United Nations Statistics Division (UNSD), United Nations Plz., New York, NY, 10017, USA, (800) 253-9646, (212) 963-9851, statistics@un.org, https://unstats.un.org; Millennium Development Goal Indicators.

The World Bank, 1818 H St. NW, Washington, DC, 20433, USA, (202) 473-1000, (202) 477-6391, eds03@worldbank.org, https://www.worldbank.org/; Burundi (report) and World Development Report 2022: Finance for an Equitable Recovery.

BURUNDI-EMPLOYMENT

International Labour Organization (ILO), 4 Rte. des Morillons, Geneva, CH-1211, SWI, ilo@ilo.org, https://www.ilo.org; NORMLEX Information System on International Labour Standards.

UK Data Service, University of Essex, Wivenhoe Park, Colchester, Essex, CO4 3SQ, GBR, https://ukdataservice.ac.uk/; International Aggregate Data.

United Nations Economic Commission for Africa (UNECA), PO Box 3001, Addis Ababa, ETH,

ecainfo@uneca.org, https://www.uneca.org/; African Statistical Yearbook 2020.

United Nations Statistics Division (UNSD), United Nations Plz., New York, NY, 10017, USA, (800) 253-9646, (212) 963-9851, statistics@un.org, https://unstats.un.org; Statistical Yearbook of the United Nations 2021.

The World Bank, 1818 H St. NW, Washington, DC, 20433, USA, (202) 473-1000, (202) 477-6391, eds03@worldbank.org, https://www.worldbank.org/; Burundi (report).

BURUNDI-ENVIRONMENTAL CONDITIONS

DSI Data Service & Information, Xantener Strasse 51a, Rheinberg, D-47495, GER, dsi@dsidata.com, https://www.dsidata.com/; Global Environmental Database.

The Economist Group: Economist Intelligence Unit (EIU), 900 3rd Ave., 16th Fl., New York, NY, 10022, USA, (212) 541-0500, americas@eiu.com, https://www.eiu.com; Burundi Country Report.

International Institute for Environment and Development (IIED), 235 High Holborn, London, WC1V 7DN, GBR, inforequest@iied.org, https://www.iied.org; Environment & Urbanization.

United Nations Statistics Division (UNSD), United Nations Plz., New York, NY, 10017, USA, (800) 253-9646, (212) 963-9851, statistics@un.org, https://unstats.un.org; World Statistics Pocketbook 2021.

BURUNDI-EXPORTS

African Development Bank Group (AfDB), Avenue Joseph Anoma, 01 BP 1387, Abidjan, 01, COT, https://www.afdb.org; African Economic Outlook 2021.

Central Intelligence Agency (CIA), Office of Public Affairs, Washington, DC, 20505, USA, (703) 482-0623, https://www.cia.gov; The World Factbook.

The Economist Group: Economist Intelligence Unit (EIU), 900 3rd Ave., 16th Fl., New York, NY, 10022, USA, (212) 541-0500, americas@eiu.com, https://www.eiu.com; Burundi Country Report.

International Monetary Fund (IMF), 700 19th St. NW, Washington, DC, 20431, USA, (202) 623-7000, (202) 623-4661, publications@imf.org, https://www.imf.org; Direction of Trade Statistics (DOTS).

S&P Global, IHS Markit, 15 Inverness Way E, Englewood, CO, 80112, USA, (800) 447-2273, (800) 854-7179, https://ihsmarkit.com; Global Trade Atlas (GTA).

United Nations Conference on Trade and Development (UNCTAD), Palais des Nations, Geneva, 1211, SWI, (212) 963-6896, unctadinfo@unctad.org, https://unctad.org; Handbook of Statistics 2021.

The World Bank, 1818 H St. NW, Washington, DC, 20433, USA, (202) 473-1000, (202) 477-6391, eds03@worldbank.org, https://www.worldbank.org/; World Development Report 2022: Finance for an Equitable Recovery.

BURUNDI-FEMALE WORKING POPULATION

See BURUNDI-EMPLOYMENT

BURUNDI-FERTILITY, HUMAN

Central Intelligence Agency (CIA), Office of Public Affairs, Washington, DC, 20505, USA, (703) 482-0623, https://www.cia.gov; The World Factbook.

BURUNDI-FERTILIZER INDUSTRY

United Nations Food and Agricultural Organization (FAO), 2121 K St., Ste. 800B, Washington, DC, 20037, USA, (202) 653-2400 (Dial from U.S.), (202) 653-5760 (Fax from U.S.), fao-hq@fao.org, https://www.fao.org; The State of Food and Agriculture (SOFA) 2022.

BURUNDI-FETAL MORTALITY

See BURUNDI-MORTALITY

BURUNDI-FINANCE

Stockholm International Peace Research Institute (SIPRI), Signalistgatan 9, Stockholm, SE 169 72, SWE, https://www.sipri.org/; SIPRI Arms Transfers Database and SIPRI Military Expenditure Database.

United Nations Economic Commission for Africa (UNECA), PO Box 3001, Addis Ababa, ETH, ecainfo@uneca.org, https://www.uneca.org/; African Statistical Yearbook 2020.

United Nations Statistics Division (UNSD), United Nations Plz., New York, NY, 10017, USA, (800) 253-9646, (212) 963-9851, statistics@un.org, https://unstats.un.org; Statistical Yearbook of the United Nations 2021.

The World Bank, 1818 H St. NW, Washington, DC, 20433, USA, (202) 473-1000, (202) 477-6391, eds03@worldbank.org, https://www.worldbank.org/; Burundi (report).

BURUNDI-FINANCE, PUBLIC

African Development Bank Group (AfDB), Avenue Joseph Anoma, 01 BP 1387, Abidjan, 01, COT, https://www.afdb.org; The AfDB Statistics Pocketbook 2019.

Bernan Press, 15250 NBN Way, Bldg. C, Blue Ridge Summit, PA, 17214, USA, (301) 459-2255, (800) 865-3457, (800) 865-3450, customercare@bernan.com, https://rowman.com/Page/Bernan; National Accounts Statistics: Analysis of Main Aggregates 2020.

The Economist Group: Economist Intelligence Unit (EIU), 900 3rd Ave., 16th Fl., New York, NY, 10022, USA, (212) 541-0500, americas@eiu.com, https://www.eiu.com; Burundi Country Report.

International Monetary Fund (IMF), 700 19th St. NW, Washington, DC, 20431, USA, (202) 623-7000, (202) 623-4661, publications@imf.org, https://www.imf.org; Regional Economic Outlook.

Palgrave Macmillan, 1 New York Plaza, Ste. 4500, New York, NY, 10004-1562, USA, (800) 777-4643, orders@palgrave.com, https://www.palgrave.com/us; The Statesman's Yearbook, 2023.

Routledge - Taylor & Francis Group, 6000 Broken Sound Pkwy. NW, Ste. 300, Boca Raton, FL, 33487, USA, (800) 634-1420, (800) 634-7064, orders@taylorandfrancis.com, https://www.routledge.com/; The Europa World Year Book 2022.

United Nations Economic Commission for Africa (UNECA), PO Box 3001, Addis Ababa, ETH, ecainfo@uneca.org, https://www.uneca.org/; African Statistical Yearbook 2020.

United Nations Statistics Division (UNSD), United Nations Plz., New York, NY, 10017, USA, (800) 253-9646, (212) 963-9851, statistics@un.org, https://unstats.un.org; National Accounts Main Aggregates Database and National Accounts Statistics: Main Aggregates and Detailed Tables.

The World Bank, 1818 H St. NW, Washington, DC, 20433, USA, (202) 473-1000, (202) 477-6391, eds03@worldbank.org, https://www.worldbank.org/; Burundi (report).

BURUNDI-FISHERIES

Palgrave Macmillan, 1 New York Plaza, Ste. 4500, New York, NY, 10004-1562, USA, (800) 777-4643, orders@palgrave.com, https://www.palgrave.com/us; The Statesman's Yearbook, 2023.

Routledge - Taylor & Francis Group, 6000 Broken Sound Pkwy. NW, Ste. 300, Boca Raton, FL, 33487, USA, (800) 634-1420, (800) 634-7064, orders@taylorandfrancis.com, https://www.routledge.com/; The Europa World Year Book 2022.

United Nations Economic Commission for Africa (UNECA), PO Box 3001, Addis Ababa, ETH, ecainfo@uneca.org, https://www.uneca.org/; African Statistical Yearbook 2020.

United Nations Food and Agricultural Organization (FAO), 2121 K St., Ste. 800B, Washington, DC, 20037, USA, (202) 653-2400 (Dial from U.S.), (202) 653-5760 (Fax from U.S.), fao-hq@fao.org, https://www.fao.org; FAO Yearbook of Fishery and Aquaculture Statistics 2019; Fishery Statistical Collections Global Capture Production; FishStatJ; and The State of Food and Agriculture (SOFA) 2022.

United Nations Statistics Division (UNSD), United Nations Plz., New York, NY, 10017, USA, (800) 253-9646, (212) 963-9851, statistics@un.org, https://unstats.un.org; Statistical Yearbook of the United Nations 2021.

The World Bank, 1818 H St. NW, Washington, DC, 20433, USA, (202) 473-1000, (202) 477-6391, eds03@worldbank.org, https://www.worldbank.org/; Burundi (report).

BURUNDI-FOOD

African Development Bank Group (AfDB), Avenue Joseph Anoma, 01 BP 1387, Abidjan, 01, COT, https://www.afdb.org; The AfDB Statistics Pocketbook 2019.

United Nations Food and Agricultural Organization (FAO), 2121 K St., Ste. 800B, Washington, DC, 20037, USA, (202) 653-2400 (Dial from U.S.), (202) 653-5760 (Fax from U.S.), fao-hq@fao.org, https://www.fao.org; The State of Food and Agriculture (SOFA) 2022.

BURUNDI-FOREIGN EXCHANGE RATES

African Development Bank Group (AfDB), Avenue Joseph Anoma, 01 BP 1387, Abidjan, 01, COT, https://www.afdb.org; The AfDB Statistics Pocketbook 2019 and African Economic Outlook 2021.

BURUNDI-FORESTS AND FORESTRY

Palgrave Macmillan, 1 New York Plaza, Ste. 4500, New York, NY, 10004-1562, USA, (800) 777-4643, orders@palgrave.com, https://www.palgrave.com/us; The Statesman's Yearbook, 2023.

Routledge - Taylor & Francis Group, 6000 Broken Sound Pkwy. NW, Ste. 300, Boca Raton, FL, 33487, USA, (800) 634-1420, (800) 634-7064, orders@taylorandfrancis.com, https://www.routledge.com/; The Europa World Year Book 2022.

UNESCO Institute for Statistics, C.P 250 Succursale H, Montreal, QC, H3G 2K8, CAN, (514) 343-6880 (Dial from U.S.), (514) 343-5740 (Fax from U.S.), uis.publications@unesco.org, http://uis.unesco.org/; UIS.Stat.

United Nations Economic Commission for Africa (UNECA), PO Box 3001, Addis Ababa, ETH, ecainfo@uneca.org, https://www.uneca.org/; African Statistical Yearbook 2020.

United Nations Food and Agricultural Organization (FAO), 2121 K St., Ste. 800B, Washington, DC, 20037, USA, (202) 653-2400 (Dial from U.S.), (202) 653-5760 (Fax from U.S.), fao-hq@fao.org, https://www.fao.org; FAO Yearbook of Forest Products 2019 and The State of Food and Agriculture (SOFA) 2022.

United Nations Statistics Division (UNSD), United Nations Plz., New York, NY, 10017, USA, (800) 253-9646, (212) 963-9851, statistics@un.org, https://unstats.un.org; Statistical Yearbook of the United Nations 2021.

The World Bank, 1818 H St. NW, Washington, DC, 20433, USA, (202) 473-1000, (202) 477-6391, eds03@worldbank.org, https://www.worldbank.org/; Burundi (report) and World Development Report 2022: Finance for an Equitable Recovery.

BURUNDI-GEOGRAPHIC INFORMATION SYSTEMS

The World Bank, 1818 H St. NW, Washington, DC, 20433, USA, (202) 473-1000, (202) 477-6391, eds03@worldbank.org, https://www.worldbank.org/; Burundi (report).

BURUNDI-GROSS DOMESTIC PRODUCT

African Development Bank Group (AfDB), Avenue Joseph Anoma, 01 BP 1387, Abidjan, 01, COT, https://www.afdb.org; The AfDB Statistics Pocketbook 2019.

The Economist Group: Economist Intelligence Unit (EIU), 900 3rd Ave., 16th Fl., New York, NY, 10022,

USA, (212) 541-0500, americas@eiu.com, https://www.eiu.com; Burundi Country Report.

Palgrave Macmillan, 1 New York Plaza, Ste. 4500, New York, NY, 10004-1562, USA, (800) 777-4643, orders@palgrave.com, https://www.palgrave.com/us; The Statesman's Yearbook, 2023.

Routledge - Taylor & Francis Group, 6000 Broken Sound Pkwy. NW, Ste. 300, Boca Raton, FL, 33487, USA, (800) 634-1420, (800) 634-7064, orders@taylorandfrancis.com, https://www.routledge.com/; The Europa World Year Book 2022.

United Nations Economic Commission for Africa (UNECA), PO Box 3001, Addis Ababa, ETH, ecainfo@uneca.org, https://www.uneca.org/; African Statistical Yearbook 2020.

United Nations Statistics Division (UNSD), United Nations Plz., New York, NY, 10017, USA, (800) 253-9646, (212) 963-9851, statistics@un.org, https://unstats.un.org; Statistical Yearbook of the United Nations 2021.

The World Bank, 1818 H St. NW, Washington, DC, 20433, USA, (202) 473-1000, (202) 477-6391, eds03@worldbank.org, https://www.worldbank.org/; World Development Report 2022: Finance for an Equitable Recovery.

BURUNDI-GROSS NATIONAL PRODUCT

The World Bank, 1818 H St. NW, Washington, DC, 20433, USA, (202) 473-1000, (202) 477-6391, eds03@worldbank.org, https://www.worldbank.org/; World Development Report 2022: Finance for an Equitable Recovery.

BURUNDI-HOUSING

Euromonitor International, Inc., 1 N Dearborn St., Ste. 1700, Chicago, IL, 60602, USA, (312) 922-1115, (312) 922-1157, info-usa@euromonitor.com, https://www.euromonitor.com/; Geographies.

BURUNDI-ILLITERATE PERSONS

UNESCO Institute for Statistics, C.P 250 Succursale H, Montreal, QC, H3G 2K8, CAN, (514) 343-6880 (Dial from U.S.), (514) 343-5740 (Fax from U.S.), uis.publications@unesco.org, http://uis.unesco.org/; UIS.Stat.

BURUNDI-IMPORTS

African Development Bank Group (AfDB), Avenue Joseph Anoma, 01 BP 1387, Abidjan, 01, COT, https://www.afdb.org; African Economic Outlook 2021.

Central Intelligence Agency (CIA), Office of Public Affairs, Washington, DC, 20505, USA, (703) 482-0623, https://www.cia.gov; The World Factbook.

The Economist Group: Economist Intelligence Unit (EIU), 900 3rd Ave., 16th Fl., New York, NY, 10022, USA, (212) 541-0500, americas@eiu.com, https://www.eiu.com; Burundi Country Report.

International Monetary Fund (IMF), 700 19th St. NW, Washington, DC, 20431, USA, (202) 623-7000, (202) 623-4661, publications@imf.org, https://www.imf.org; Direction of Trade Statistics (DOTS).

S&P Global, IHS Markit, 15 Inverness Way E, Englewood, CO, 80112, USA, (800) 447-2273, (800) 854-7179, https://ihsmarkit.com; Global Trade Atlas (GTA).

United Nations Conference on Trade and Development (UNCTAD), Palais des Nations, Geneva, 1211, SWI, (212) 963-6896, unctadinfo@unctad.org, https://unctad.org; Handbook of Statistics 2021.

The World Bank, 1818 H St. NW, Washington, DC, 20433, USA, (202) 473-1000, (202) 477-6391, eds03@worldbank.org, https://www.worldbank.org/; World Development Report 2022: Finance for an Equitable Recovery.

BURUNDI-INDUSTRIES

Central Intelligence Agency (CIA), Office of Public Affairs, Washington, DC, 20505, USA, (703) 482-0623, https://www.cia.gov; The World Factbook.

The Economist Group: Economist Intelligence Unit (EIU), 900 3rd Ave., 16th Fl., New York, NY, 10022, USA, (212) 541-0500, americas@eiu.com, https://www.eiu.com; Burundi Country Report.

Euromonitor International, Inc., 1 N Dearborn St., Ste. 1700, Chicago, IL, 60602, USA, (312) 922-1115, (312) 922-1157, info-usa@euromonitor.com, https://www.euromonitor.com/; Geographies.

International Labour Organization (ILO), 4 Rte. des Morillons, Geneva, CH-1211, SWI, ilo@ilo.org, https://www.ilo.org; NORMLEX Information System on International Labour Standards.

Palgrave Macmillan, 1 New York Plaza, Ste. 4500, New York, NY, 10004-1562, USA, (800) 777-4643, orders@palgrave.com, https://www.palgrave.com/us; The Statesman's Yearbook, 2023.

Routledge - Taylor & Francis Group, 6000 Broken Sound Pkwy. NW, Ste. 300, Boca Raton, FL, 33487, USA, (800) 634-1420, (800) 634-7064, orders@taylorandfrancis.com, https://www.routledge.com/; The Europa World Year Book 2022.

United Nations Economic Commission for Africa (UNECA), PO Box 3001, Addis Ababa, ETH, ecainfo@uneca.org, https://www.uneca.org/; African Statistical Yearbook 2020.

United Nations Industrial Development Organization (UNIDO), 1 United Nations Plz., Rm. DC1-1118, New York, NY, 10017, USA, (212) 963-6890, (212) 963 6885, (212) 963-7904, office.newyork@unido.org, https://www.unido.org/; Industrial Statistics Databases and International Yearbook of Industrial Statistics 2021.

The World Bank, 1818 H St. NW, Washington, DC, 20433, USA, (202) 473-1000, (202) 477-6391, eds03@worldbank.org, https://www.worldbank.org/; Burundi (report).

World Intellectual Property Organization (WIPO), 34, chemin des Colombettes, Geneva, CH-1211, SWI, https://www.wipo.int; Madrid Yearly Review 2022: International Registrations of Marks.

BURUNDI-INFANT AND MATERNAL MORTALITY

See BURUNDI-MORTALITY

BURUNDI-INTERNATIONAL TRADE

African Development Bank Group (AfDB), Avenue Joseph Anoma, 01 BP 1387, Abidjan, 01, COT, https://www.afdb.org; The AfDB Statistics Pocketbook 2019 and African Economic Outlook 2021.

The Economist Group: Economist Intelligence Unit (EIU), 900 3rd Ave., 16th Fl., New York, NY, 10022, USA, (212) 541-0500, americas@eiu.com, https://www.eiu.com; Burundi Country Report.

Euromonitor International, Inc., 1 N Dearborn St., Ste. 1700, Chicago, IL, 60602, USA, (312) 922-1115, (312) 922-1157, info-usa@euromonitor.com, https://www.euromonitor.com/; Geographies.

Palgrave Macmillan, 1 New York Plaza, Ste. 4500, New York, NY, 10004-1562, USA, (800) 777-4643, orders@palgrave.com, https://www.palgrave.com/us; The Statesman's Yearbook, 2023.

Routledge - Taylor & Francis Group, 6000 Broken Sound Pkwy. NW, Ste. 300, Boca Raton, FL, 33487, USA, (800) 634-1420, (800) 634-7064, orders@taylorandfrancis.com, https://www.routledge.com/; The Europa World Year Book 2022.

United Nations Conference on Trade and Development (UNCTAD), Palais des Nations, Geneva, 1211, SWI, (212) 963-6896, unctadinfo@unctad.org, https://unctad.org; Trade and Development Report 2021.

United Nations Economic Commission for Africa (UNECA), PO Box 3001, Addis Ababa, ETH, ecainfo@uneca.org, https://www.uneca.org/; African Statistical Yearbook 2020.

United Nations Food and Agricultural Organization (FAO), 2121 K St., Ste. 800B, Washington, DC, 20037, USA, (202) 653-2400 (Dial from U.S.), (202) 653-5760 (Fax from U.S.), fao-hq@fao.org, https://www.fao.org; The State of Food and Agriculture (SOFA) 2022.

United Nations Statistics Division (UNSD), United Nations Plz., New York, NY, 10017, USA, (800) 253-9646, (212) 963-9851, statistics@un.org, https://unstats.un.org; International Trade Statistics Yearbook 2020 and Statistical Yearbook of the United Nations 2021.

The World Bank, 1818 H St. NW, Washington, DC, 20433, USA, (202) 473-1000, (202) 477-6391, eds03@worldbank.org, https://www.worldbank.org/; Burundi (report) and World Development Report 2022: Finance for an Equitable Recovery.

World Trade Organization (WTO), Ctre. William Rappard, Rue de Lausanne 154, Case postale, Geneva, CH-1211, SWI, enquiries@wto.org, https://www.wto.org; World Trade Statistical Review 2022.

BURUNDI-INTERNET USERS

International Telecommunication Union (ITU), Place des Nations, Geneva, CH-1211, SWI, itumail@itu.int, https://www.itu.int; Global Connectivity Report 2022; World Telecommunication/ICT Indicators Database 2021; and Yearbook of Statistics 2019.

The World Bank, 1818 H St. NW, Washington, DC, 20433, USA, (202) 473-1000, (202) 477-6391, eds03@worldbank.org, https://www.worldbank.org/; Burundi (report).

BURUNDI-LABOR

African Development Bank Group (AfDB), Avenue Joseph Anoma, 01 BP 1387, Abidjan, 01, COT, https://www.afdb.org; The AfDB Statistics Pocketbook 2019.

Central Intelligence Agency (CIA), Office of Public Affairs, Washington, DC, 20505, USA, (703) 482-0623, https://www.cia.gov; The World Factbook.

Euromonitor International, Inc., 1 N Dearborn St., Ste. 1700, Chicago, IL, 60602, USA, (312) 922-1115, (312) 922-1157, info-usa@euromonitor.com, https://www.euromonitor.com/; Geographies.

International Labour Organization (ILO), 4 Rte. des Morillons, Geneva, CH-1211, SWI, ilo@ilo.org, https://www.ilo.org; NORMLEX Information System on International Labour Standards.

Palgrave Macmillan, 1 New York Plaza, Ste. 4500, New York, NY, 10004-1562, USA, (800) 777-4643, orders@palgrave.com, https://www.palgrave.com/us; The Statesman's Yearbook, 2023.

United Nations Food and Agricultural Organization (FAO), 2121 K St., Ste. 800B, Washington, DC, 20037, USA, (202) 653-2400 (Dial from U.S.), (202) 653-5760 (Fax from U.S.), fao-hq@fao.org, https://www.fao.org; The State of Food and Agriculture (SOFA) 2022.

The World Bank, 1818 H St. NW, Washington, DC, 20433, USA, (202) 473-1000, (202) 477-6391, eds03@worldbank.org, https://www.worldbank.org/; World Development Report 2022: Finance for an Equitable Recovery.

BURUNDI-LAND USE

United Nations Statistics Division (UNSD), United Nations Plz., New York, NY, 10017, USA, (800) 253-9646, (212) 963-9851, statistics@un.org, https://unstats.un.org; Millennium Development Goal Indicators.

The World Bank, 1818 H St. NW, Washington, DC, 20433, USA, (202) 473-1000, (202) 477-6391, eds03@worldbank.org, https://www.worldbank.org/; World Development Report 2022: Finance for an Equitable Recovery.

BURUNDI-LIBRARIES

UNESCO Institute for Statistics, C.P 250 Succursale H, Montreal, QC, H3G 2K8, CAN, (514) 343-6880 (Dial from U.S.), (514) 343-5740 (Fax from U.S.), uis.publications@unesco.org, http://uis.unesco.org/; UIS.Stat.

BURUNDI-LIFE EXPECTANCY

African Development Bank Group (AfDB), Avenue Joseph Anoma, 01 BP 1387, Abidjan, 01, COT, https://www.afdb.org; The AfDB Statistics Pocketbook 2019.

Central Intelligence Agency (CIA), Office of Public Affairs, Washington, DC, 20505, USA, (703) 482-0623, https://www.cia.gov; The World Factbook.

United Nations Department of Economic and Social Affairs (DESA), Population Division, 2 United Nations Plz., Rm. DC2-1950, New York, NY, 10017, USA, (212) 963-3209, (212) 963-2147, population@un.org, https://www.un.org/development/desa/pd/; World Population Ageing 2020 Highlights.

United Nations Statistics Division (UNSD), United Nations Plz., New York, NY, 10017, USA, (800) 253-9646, (212) 963-9851, statistics@un.org, https://unstats.un.org; Millennium Development Goal Indicators.

BURUNDI-LITERACY

Euromonitor International, Inc., 1 N Dearborn St., Ste. 1700, Chicago, IL, 60602, USA, (312) 922-1115, (312) 922-1157, info-usa@euromonitor.com, https://www.euromonitor.com/; Geographies.

UNESCO Institute for Statistics, C.P 250 Succursale H, Montreal, QC, H3G 2K8, CAN, (514) 343-6880 (Dial from U.S.), (514) 343-5740 (Fax from U.S.), uis.publications@unesco.org, http://uis.unesco.org/; Literacy.

BURUNDI-LIVESTOCK

Routledge - Taylor & Francis Group, 6000 Broken Sound Pkwy. NW, Ste. 300, Boca Raton, FL, 33487, USA, (800) 634-1420, (800) 634-7064, orders@taylorandfrancis.com, https://www.routledge.com/; The Europa World Year Book 2022.

United Nations Economic Commission for Africa (UNECA), PO Box 3001, Addis Ababa, ETH, ecainfo@uneca.org, https://www.uneca.org/; African Statistical Yearbook 2020.

United Nations Food and Agricultural Organization (FAO), 2121 K St., Ste. 800B, Washington, DC, 20037, USA, (202) 653-2400 (Dial from U.S.), (202) 653-5760 (Fax from U.S.), fao-hq@fao.org, https://www.fao.org; The State of Food and Agriculture (SOFA) 2022.

United Nations Statistics Division (UNSD), United Nations Plz., New York, NY, 10017, USA, (800) 253-9646, (212) 963-9851, statistics@un.org, https://unstats.un.org; Statistical Yearbook of the United Nations 2021.

BURUNDI-MINERAL INDUSTRIES

Palgrave Macmillan, 1 New York Plaza, Ste. 4500, New York, NY, 10004-1562, USA, (800) 777-4643, orders@palgrave.com, https://www.palgrave.com/us; The Statesman's Yearbook, 2023.

Routledge - Taylor & Francis Group, 6000 Broken Sound Pkwy. NW, Ste. 300, Boca Raton, FL, 33487, USA, (800) 634-1420, (800) 634-7064, orders@taylorandfrancis.com, https://www.routledge.com/; The Europa World Year Book 2022.

United Nations Conference on Trade and Development (UNCTAD), Palais des Nations, Geneva, 1211, SWI, (212) 963-6896, unctadinfo@unctad.org, https://unctad.org; Trade and Development Report 2021.

United Nations Economic Commission for Africa (UNECA), PO Box 3001, Addis Ababa, ETH, ecainfo@uneca.org, https://www.uneca.org/; African Statistical Yearbook 2020.

BURUNDI-MONEY SUPPLY

The Economist Group: Economist Intelligence Unit (EIU), 900 3rd Ave., 16th Fl., New York, NY, 10022, USA, (212) 541-0500, americas@eiu.com, https://www.eiu.com; Burundi Country Report.

Routledge - Taylor & Francis Group, 6000 Broken Sound Pkwy. NW, Ste. 300, Boca Raton, FL, 33487, USA, (800) 634-1420, (800) 634-7064, orders@taylorandfrancis.com, https://www.routledge.com/; The Europa World Year Book 2022.

United Nations Statistics Division (UNSD), United Nations Plz., New York, NY, 10017, USA, (800) 253-9646, (212) 963-9851, statistics@un.org, https://unstats.un.org; Statistical Yearbook of the United Nations 2021.

The World Bank, 1818 H St. NW, Washington, DC, 20433, USA, (202) 473-1000, (202) 477-6391, eds03@worldbank.org, https://www.worldbank.org/; Burundi (report).

BURUNDI-MORTALITY

UNICEF, 3 United Nations Plz., New York, NY, 10017, USA, (212) 303-7984, (917) 244-2215, https://www.unicef.org; The State of the World's Children 2023.

United Nations Statistics Division (UNSD), United Nations Plz., New York, NY, 10017, USA, (800) 253-9646, (212) 963-9851, statistics@un.org, https://unstats.un.org; Millennium Development Goal Indicators; Statistical Yearbook of the United Nations 2021; and World Statistics Pocketbook 2021.

World Health Organization (WHO), Ave. Appia 20, Geneva, CH-1211, SWI, (202) 974-3000 (Telephone in U.S.), publications@who.int, https://www.who.int/; Global Health Observatory (GHO).

BURUNDI-MOTION PICTURES

Palgrave Macmillan, 1 New York Plaza, Ste. 4500, New York, NY, 10004-1562, USA, (800) 777-4643, orders@palgrave.com, https://www.palgrave.com/us; The Statesman's Yearbook, 2023.

BURUNDI-NUTRITION

United Nations Food and Agricultural Organization (FAO), 2121 K St., Ste. 800B, Washington, DC, 20037, USA, (202) 653-2400 (Dial from U.S.), (202) 653-5760 (Fax from U.S.), fao-hq@fao.org, https://www.fao.org; The State of Food and Agriculture (SOFA) 2022.

United Nations Statistics Division (UNSD), United Nations Plz., New York, NY, 10017, USA, (800) 253-9646, (212) 963-9851, statistics@un.org, https://unstats.un.org; Millennium Development Goal Indicators.

BURUNDI-PESTICIDES

United Nations Food and Agricultural Organization (FAO), 2121 K St., Ste. 800B, Washington, DC, 20037, USA, (202) 653-2400 (Dial from U.S.), (202) 653-5760 (Fax from U.S.), fao-hq@fao.org, https://www.fao.org; The State of Food and Agriculture (SOFA) 2022.

BURUNDI-PETROLEUM INDUSTRY AND TRADE

United Nations Food and Agricultural Organization (FAO), 2121 K St., Ste. 800B, Washington, DC, 20037, USA, (202) 653-2400 (Dial from U.S.), (202) 653-5760 (Fax from U.S.), fao-hq@fao.org, https://www.fao.org; The State of Food and Agriculture (SOFA) 2022.

BURUNDI-POPULATION

African Development Bank Group (AfDB), Avenue Joseph Anoma, 01 BP 1387, Abidjan, 01, COT, https://www.afdb.org; The AfDB Statistics Pocketbook 2019.

Central Intelligence Agency (CIA), Office of Public Affairs, Washington, DC, 20505, USA, (703) 482-0623, https://www.cia.gov; The World Factbook.

The Economist Group: Economist Intelligence Unit (EIU), 900 3rd Ave., 16th Fl., New York, NY, 10022, USA, (212) 541-0500, americas@eiu.com, https://www.eiu.com; Burundi Country Report.

European Commission, Eurostat, Luxembourg, 2920, LUX, https://ec.europa.eu/eurostat/; EU in the World 2020.

Infoplease, c/o Sandbox Networks, Inc., 1 Lincoln St., 24th Fl., Boston, MA, 02111, USA, https://www.infoplease.com; Countries of the World.

International Labour Organization (ILO), 4 Rte. des Morillons, Geneva, CH-1211, SWI, ilo@ilo.org, https://www.ilo.org; NORMLEX Information System on International Labour Standards.

Palgrave Macmillan, 1 New York Plaza, Ste. 4500, New York, NY, 10004-1562, USA, (800) 777-4643, orders@palgrave.com, https://www.palgrave.com/us; The Statesman's Yearbook, 2023.

Routledge - Taylor & Francis Group, 6000 Broken Sound Pkwy. NW, Ste. 300, Boca Raton, FL, 33487, USA, (800) 634-1420, (800) 634-7064, orders@taylorandfrancis.com, https://www.routledge.com/; The Europa World Year Book 2022.

UK Data Service, University of Essex, Wivenhoe Park, Colchester, Essex, CO4 3SQ, GBR, https://ukdataservice.ac.uk/; International Aggregate Data.

United Nations Department of Economic and Social Affairs (DESA), Population Division, 2 United Nations Plz., Rm. DC2-1950, New York, NY, 10017, USA, (212) 963-3209, (212) 963-2147, population@un.org, https://www.un.org/development/desa/pd/; Revision of World Urbanization Prospects and World Population Ageing 2020 Highlights.

United Nations Development Programme (UNDP), One United Nations Plz., New York, NY, 10017, USA, (212) 906-5000, (212) 906-5001, https://www.undp.org; Human Development Report 2021-2022.

United Nations Statistics Division (UNSD), United Nations Plz., New York, NY, 10017, USA, (800) 253-9646, (212) 963-9851, statistics@un.org, https://unstats.un.org; Statistical Yearbook of the United Nations 2021 and World Statistics Pocketbook 2021.

The World Bank, 1818 H St. NW, Washington, DC, 20433, USA, (202) 473-1000, (202) 477-6391, eds03@worldbank.org, https://www.worldbank.org/; Burundi (report); The Global Findex Database 2021; and World Development Report 2022: Finance for an Equitable Recovery.

BURUNDI-POPULATION DENSITY

African Development Bank Group (AfDB), Avenue Joseph Anoma, 01 BP 1387, Abidjan, 01, COT, https://www.afdb.org; The AfDB Statistics Pocketbook 2019.

Central Intelligence Agency (CIA), Office of Public Affairs, Washington, DC, 20505, USA, (703) 482-0623, https://www.cia.gov; The World Factbook.

Palgrave Macmillan, 1 New York Plaza, Ste. 4500, New York, NY, 10004-1562, USA, (800) 777-4643, orders@palgrave.com, https://www.palgrave.com/us; The Statesman's Yearbook, 2023.

Routledge - Taylor & Francis Group, 6000 Broken Sound Pkwy. NW, Ste. 300, Boca Raton, FL, 33487, USA, (800) 634-1420, (800) 634-7064, orders@taylorandfrancis.com, https://www.routledge.com/; The Europa World Year Book 2022.

The World Bank, 1818 H St. NW, Washington, DC, 20433, USA, (202) 473-1000, (202) 477-6391, eds03@worldbank.org, https://www.worldbank.org/; Burundi (report) and World Development Report 2022: Finance for an Equitable Recovery.

BURUNDI-POSTAL SERVICE

Palgrave Macmillan, 1 New York Plaza, Ste. 4500, New York, NY, 10004-1562, USA, (800) 777-4643, orders@palgrave.com, https://www.palgrave.com/us; The Statesman's Yearbook, 2023.

BURUNDI-POWER RESOURCES

Palgrave Macmillan, 1 New York Plaza, Ste. 4500, New York, NY, 10004-1562, USA, (800) 777-4643, orders@palgrave.com, https://www.palgrave.com/us; The Statesman's Yearbook, 2023.

United Nations Economic Commission for Africa (UNECA), PO Box 3001, Addis Ababa, ETH, ecainfo@uneca.org, https://www.uneca.org/; African Statistical Yearbook 2020.

United Nations Food and Agricultural Organization (FAO), 2121 K St., Ste. 800B, Washington, DC, 20037, USA, (202) 653-2400 (Dial from U.S.), (202)

653-5760 (Fax from U.S.), fao-hq@fao.org, https://www.fao.org; The State of Food and Agriculture (SOFA) 2022.

United Nations Statistics Division (UNSD), United Nations Plz., New York, NY, 10017, USA, (800) 253-9646, (212) 963-9851, statistics@un.org, https://unstats.un.org; Energy Statistics Yearbook 2019; Statistical Yearbook of the United Nations 2021; and World Statistics Pocketbook 2021.

The World Bank, 1818 H St. NW, Washington, DC, 20433, USA, (202) 473-1000, (202) 477-6391, eds03@worldbank.org, https://www.worldbank.org/; World Development Report 2022: Finance for an Equitable Recovery.

BURUNDI-PRICES

Euromonitor International, Inc., 1 N Dearborn St., Ste. 1700, Chicago, IL, 60602, USA, (312) 922-1115, (312) 922-1157, info-usa@euromonitor.com, https://www.euromonitor.com/; Geographies.

International Monetary Fund (IMF), 700 19th St. NW, Washington, DC, 20431, USA, (202) 623-7000, (202) 623-4661, publications@imf.org, https://www.imf.org; International Financial Statistics (IFS).

United Nations Economic Commission for Africa (UNECA), PO Box 3001, Addis Ababa, ETH, ecainfo@uneca.org, https://www.uneca.org/; African Statistical Yearbook 2020.

The World Bank, 1818 H St. NW, Washington, DC, 20433, USA, (202) 473-1000, (202) 477-6391, eds03@worldbank.org, https://www.worldbank.org/; Burundi (report).

BURUNDI-PUBLIC HEALTH

African Development Bank Group (AfDB), Avenue Joseph Anoma, 01 BP 1387, Abidjan, 01, COT, https://www.afdb.org; The AfDB Statistics Pocketbook 2019.

Euromonitor International, Inc., 1 N Dearborn St., Ste. 1700, Chicago, IL, 60602, USA, (312) 922-1115, (312) 922-1157, info-usa@euromonitor.com, https://www.euromonitor.com/; Geographies.

Palgrave Macmillan, 1 New York Plaza, Ste. 4500, New York, NY, 10004-1562, USA, (800) 777-4643, orders@palgrave.com, https://www.palgrave.com/us; The Statesman's Yearbook, 2023.

U.S. Census Bureau, 4600 Silver Hill Rd., Washington, DC, 20233, USA, (301) 763-4636, (800) 923-8282, https://www.census.gov; HIV/AIDS Surveillance Data Base.

UNICEF, 3 United Nations Plz., New York, NY, 10017, USA, (212) 303-7984, (917) 244-2215, https://www.unicef.org; The State of the World's Children 2023.

United Nations Department of Economic and Social Affairs (DESA), Population Division, 2 United Nations Plz., Rm. DC2-1950, New York, NY, 10017, USA, (212) 963-3209, (212) 963-2147, population@un.org, https://www.un.org/development/desa/pd/; World Fertility Data 2019.

United Nations Development Programme (UNDP), One United Nations Plz., New York, NY, 10017, USA, (212) 906-5000, (212) 906-5001, https://www.undp.org; Human Development Report 2021-2022.

United Nations Economic Commission for Africa (UNECA), PO Box 3001, Addis Ababa, ETH, ecainfo@uneca.org, https://www.uneca.org/; African Statistical Yearbook 2020.

United Nations Statistics Division (UNSD), United Nations Plz., New York, NY, 10017, USA, (800) 253-9646, (212) 963-9851, statistics@un.org, https://unstats.un.org; Millennium Development Goal Indicators and Statistical Yearbook of the United Nations 2021.

The World Bank, 1818 H St. NW, Washington, DC, 20433, USA, (202) 473-1000, (202) 477-6391, eds03@worldbank.org, https://www.worldbank.org/; Burundi (report).

World Health Organization (WHO), Ave. Appia 20, Geneva, CH-1211, SWI, (202) 974-3000 (Telephone in U.S.), publications@who.int, https://www.who.int/; Global Health Observatory (GHO).

BURUNDI-RAILROADS

United Nations Economic Commission for Africa (UNECA), PO Box 3001, Addis Ababa, ETH, ecainfo@uneca.org, https://www.uneca.org/; African Statistical Yearbook 2020.

BURUNDI-RELIGION

Central Intelligence Agency (CIA), Office of Public Affairs, Washington, DC, 20505, USA, (703) 482-0623, https://www.cia.gov; The World Factbook.

Palgrave Macmillan, 1 New York Plaza, Ste. 4500, New York, NY, 10004-1562, USA, (800) 777-4643, orders@palgrave.com, https://www.palgrave.com/us; The Statesman's Yearbook, 2023.

BURUNDI-RETAIL TRADE

Euromonitor International, Inc., 1 N Dearborn St., Ste. 1700, Chicago, IL, 60602, USA, (312) 922-1115, (312) 922-1157, info-usa@euromonitor.com, https://www.euromonitor.com/; Geographies.

BURUNDI-RICE PRODUCTION

See BURUNDI-CROPS

BURUNDI-ROADS

United Nations Economic Commission for Africa (UNECA), PO Box 3001, Addis Ababa, ETH, ecainfo@uneca.org, https://www.uneca.org/; African Statistical Yearbook 2020.

BURUNDI-SHIPPING

United Nations Economic Commission for Africa (UNECA), PO Box 3001, Addis Ababa, ETH, ecainfo@uneca.org, https://www.uneca.org/; African Statistical Yearbook 2020.

BURUNDI-TEA PRODUCTION

See BURUNDI-CROPS

BURUNDI-TELEPHONE

Palgrave Macmillan, 1 New York Plaza, Ste. 4500, New York, NY, 10004-1562, USA, (800) 777-4643, orders@palgrave.com, https://www.palgrave.com/us; The Statesman's Yearbook, 2023.

Routledge - Taylor & Francis Group, 6000 Broken Sound Pkwy. NW, Ste. 300, Boca Raton, FL, 33487, USA, (800) 634-1420, (800) 634-7064, orders@taylorandfrancis.com, https://www.routledge.com/; The Europa World Year Book 2022.

United Nations Statistics Division (UNSD), United Nations Plz., New York, NY, 10017, USA, (800) 253-9646, (212) 963-9851, statistics@un.org, https://unstats.un.org; World Statistics Pocketbook 2021.

BURUNDI-TEXTILE INDUSTRY

Palgrave Macmillan, 1 New York Plaza, Ste. 4500, New York, NY, 10004-1562, USA, (800) 777-4643, orders@palgrave.com, https://www.palgrave.com/us; The Statesman's Yearbook, 2023.

BURUNDI-THEATER

UNESCO Institute for Statistics, C.P 250 Succursale H, Montreal, QC, H3G 2K8, CAN, (514) 343-6880 (Dial from U.S.), (514) 343-5740 (Fax from U.S.), uis.publications@unesco.org, http://uis.unesco.org/; UIS.Stat.

BURUNDI-TOBACCO INDUSTRY

United Nations Statistics Division (UNSD), United Nations Plz., New York, NY, 10017, USA, (800) 253-9646, (212) 963-9851, statistics@un.org, https://unstats.un.org; Statistical Yearbook of the United Nations 2021.

BURUNDI-TOURISM

Euromonitor International, Inc., 1 N Dearborn St., Ste. 1700, Chicago, IL, 60602, USA, (312) 922-1115, (312) 922-1157, info-usa@euromonitor.com, https://www.euromonitor.com/; Geographies.

Palgrave Macmillan, 1 New York Plaza, Ste. 4500, New York, NY, 10004-1562, USA, (800) 777-4643, orders@palgrave.com, https://www.palgrave.com/us; The Statesman's Yearbook, 2023.

Routledge - Taylor & Francis Group, 6000 Broken Sound Pkwy. NW, Ste. 300, Boca Raton, FL, 33487, USA, (800) 634-1420, (800) 634-7064, orders@taylorandfrancis.com, https://www.routledge.com/; The Europa World Year Book 2022.

United Nations Economic Commission for Africa (UNECA), PO Box 3001, Addis Ababa, ETH, ecainfo@uneca.org, https://www.uneca.org/; African Statistical Yearbook 2020.

United Nations Statistics Division (UNSD), United Nations Plz., New York, NY, 10017, USA, (800) 253-9646, (212) 963-9851, statistics@un.org, https://unstats.un.org; Statistical Yearbook of the United Nations 2021.

United Nations World Tourism Organization (UN-WTO), Calle Poeta Joan Maragall 42, Madrid, 28020, SPA, info@unwto.org, https://www.unwto.org/; Yearbook of Tourism Statistics, 2021 Edition.

The World Bank, 1818 H St. NW, Washington, DC, 20433, USA, (202) 473-1000, (202) 477-6391, eds03@worldbank.org, https://www.worldbank.org/; Burundi (report).

BURUNDI-TRADE

See BURUNDI-INTERNATIONAL TRADE

BURUNDI-TRANSPORTATION

Central Intelligence Agency (CIA), Office of Public Affairs, Washington, DC, 20505, USA, (703) 482-0623, https://www.cia.gov; The World Factbook.

Euromonitor International, Inc., 1 N Dearborn St., Ste. 1700, Chicago, IL, 60602, USA, (312) 922-1115, (312) 922-1157, info-usa@euromonitor.com, https://www.euromonitor.com/; Geographies.

Palgrave Macmillan, 1 New York Plaza, Ste. 4500, New York, NY, 10004-1562, USA, (800) 777-4643, orders@palgrave.com, https://www.palgrave.com/us; The Statesman's Yearbook, 2023.

Routledge - Taylor & Francis Group, 6000 Broken Sound Pkwy. NW, Ste. 300, Boca Raton, FL, 33487, USA, (800) 634-1420, (800) 634-7064, orders@taylorandfrancis.com, https://www.routledge.com/; The Europa World Year Book 2022.

United Nations Economic Commission for Africa (UNECA), PO Box 3001, Addis Ababa, ETH, ecainfo@uneca.org, https://www.uneca.org/; African Statistical Yearbook 2020.

The World Bank, 1818 H St. NW, Washington, DC, 20433, USA, (202) 473-1000, (202) 477-6391, eds03@worldbank.org, https://www.worldbank.org/; Burundi (report).

BURUNDI-UNEMPLOYMENT

International Labour Organization (ILO), 4 Rte. des Morillons, Geneva, CH-1211, SWI, ilo@ilo.org, https://www.ilo.org; NORMLEX Information System on International Labour Standards.

BURUNDI-VITAL STATISTICS

U.S. Census Bureau, 4600 Silver Hill Rd., Washington, DC, 20233, USA, (301) 763-4636, (800) 923-8282, https://www.census.gov; HIV/AIDS Surveillance Data Base.

United Nations Department of Economic and Social Affairs (DESA), Population Division, 2 United Nations Plz., Rm. DC2-1950, New York, NY, 10017, USA, (212) 963-3209, (212) 963-2147, population@un.org, https://www.un.org/development/desa/pd/; World Contraceptive Use 2021: Estimates and Projections of Family Planning Indicators and World Marriage Data 2019.

United Nations Statistics Division (UNSD), United Nations Plz., New York, NY, 10017, USA, (800) 253-9646, (212) 963-9851, statistics@un.org, https://unstats.un.org; Statistical Yearbook of the United Nations 2021.

BURUNDI-WAGES

International Labour Organization (ILO), 4 Rte. des Morillons, Geneva, CH-1211, SWI, ilo@ilo.org, https://www.ilo.org; NORMLEX Information System on International Labour Standards.

United Nations Statistics Division (UNSD), United Nations Plz., New York, NY, 10017, USA, (800) 253-9646, (212) 963-9851, statistics@un.org, https://unstats.un.org; Statistical Yearbook of the United Nations 2021.

The World Bank, 1818 H St. NW, Washington, DC, 20433, USA, (202) 473-1000, (202) 477-6391, eds03@worldbank.org, https://www.worldbank.org/; Burundi (report).

BURUNDI-WHEAT PRODUCTION

See BURUNDI-CROPS

BUS TRAVEL-FINANCES

American Bus Association (ABA), 111 K St. NE, 9th Fl., Washington, DC, 20002, USA, (202) 842-1645, (800) 283-2877, (202) 842-0850, abainfo@buses.org, https://www.buses.org; Motorcoach Census: A Study of the Size and Activity of the Motorcoach Industry in the United States and Canada in 2020.

BUS TRAVEL-FOREIGN COUNTRIES

U.S. Department of Transportation (DOT), Federal Highway Administration (FHA), 1200 New Jersey Ave. SE, Washington, DC, 20590, USA, (202) 366-4000, https://highways.dot.gov/; Highway Statistics 2020.

BUS TRAVEL-PASSENGER TRAFFIC

American Bus Association (ABA), 111 K St. NE, 9th Fl., Washington, DC, 20002, USA, (202) 842-1645, (800) 283-2877, (202) 842-0850, abainfo@buses.org, https://www.buses.org; Motorcoach Census: A Study of the Size and Activity of the Motorcoach Industry in the United States and Canada in 2020.

BUS TRAVEL

See also PASSENGER TRANSIT INDUSTRY

American Public Transportation Association (APTA), 1300 I St. NW, Ste. 1200 E, Washington, DC, 20005, USA, (202) 496-4800, (202) 496-4324, https://www.apta.com; Public Transportation Fact Book, 2022.

National Highway Traffic Safety Administration (NHTSA), National Center for Statistics and Analysis (NCSA), 1200 New Jersey Ave. SE, West Bldg., Washington, DC, 20590, USA, (800) 934-8517, (202) 366-2746, ncsarequests@dot.gov, https://www.nhtsa.gov/research-data/national-center-statistics-and-analysis-ncsa; Traffic Safety Facts, 2011-2020 Data - School-Transportation-Related Crashes.

U.S. Department of Transportation (DOT), Federal Motor Carrier Safety Administration (FMCSA), 1200 New Jersey Ave. SE, Washington, DC, 20590, USA, (800) 832-5660, https://www.fmcsa.dot.gov/; Motor Carrier Safety Progress Report.

U.S. Department of Transportation (DOT), Office of the Assistant Secretary for Research and Technology (OST-R), Bureau of Transportation Statistics (BTS), 1200 New Jersey Ave. SE, Washington, DC, 20590, USA, (800) 853-1351, (202) 366-3282, https://www.bts.gov; TranStats.

BUSINESS ENTERPRISES

American Customer Satisfaction Index (ACSI), 3916 Ranchero Dr., Ann Arbor, MI, 48108, USA, (734) 913-0788, (734) 913-0790, info@theacsi.org, https://www.theacsi.org; Benchmarks by Company and Benchmarks by Industry.

Banque de France, 31 rue Croix des Petits-Champs, Paris, 75049, FRA, infos@banque-france.fr, https://www.banque-france.fr/en; Key Figures France and Abroad.

Bernan Press, 15250 NBN Way, Bldg. C, Blue Ridge Summit, PA, 17214, USA, (301) 459-2255, (800) 865-3457, (800) 865-3450, customercare@bernan.com, https://rowman.com/Page/Bernan; Patterns of Economic Change by State and Area 2022: Income, Employment, and Gross Domestic Product.

Cirium, 230 Park Ave., 7th Fl., New York, NY, 10169, USA, (646) 746-6851, https://www.cirium.com/; Taking to the Skies 2021: An Analysis of Startup Airlines in North America with Sample Profiles of the Newest Airlines.

The Economist Group, 900 3rd Ave., 16th Fl., New York, NY, 10022, USA, (212) 541-0500, (202) 429-0890, customerhelp@economist.com, https://www.economistgroup.com; The Economist.

Environmental Business International, Inc. (EBI), 4452 Park Blvd., Ste. 306, San Diego, CA, 92116, USA, (619) 295-7685, info@ebionline.org, https://ebionline.org/; Climate Change Adaptation & Resilience Markets; Climate Change Business Journal (CCBJ); Environmental Business Journal (EBJ); Environmental Testing and Analytical Services; The Global Environmental Market; and U.S. Environmental Industry Overview.

Euromonitor International, Inc., 1 N Dearborn St., Ste. 1700, Chicago, IL, 60602, USA, (312) 922-1115, (312) 922-1157, info-usa@euromonitor.com, https://www.euromonitor.com/; Strategic Analysis of the World's Largest Companies.

Ewing Marion Kauffman Foundation, 4801 Rockhill Rd., Kansas City, MO, 64110, USA, (816) 932-1000, https://www.kauffman.org/; Community-Engaged Entrepreneurship Research: Methodologies to Advance Equity and Inclusion; COVID-19 and Entrepreneurial Firms: Seeding an Inclusive and Equitable Recovery; Kauffman Indicators of Entrepreneurship; State of Entrepreneurship Address 2019; and Who is the Entrepreneur? New Entrepreneurs in the United States, 1996-2021.

The Federal Reserve Bank of Richmond, PO Box 27622, Richmond, VA, 23261, USA, (804) 697-8000, (410) 576-3300, https://www.richmondfed.org/; Economic Quarterly.

Forbes, Inc., 499 Washington Blvd., Jersey City, NJ, 07310, USA, (800) 295-0893, https://www.forbes.com; America's Best Small Companies 2022.

Glassdoor, 100 Shoreline Hwy., Mill Valley, CA, 94941, USA, (415) 339-9105, (415) 944-6888, pr@glassdoor.com, https://www.glassdoor.com; Best Places to Work 2023 and Workplace Trends 2023.

Institute for Supply Management (ISM), 309 W Elliot Rd. , Ste. 113, Tempe, AZ, 85284-1556, USA, (480) 752-6276, (480) 752-7890, membersvcs@ismworld.org, https://www.ismworld.org/; Inside Supply Management Magazine and Report on Business.

MIT Sloan School of Management, 100 Main St., Cambridge, MA, 02142, USA, (617) 253-1000, https://mitsloan.mit.edu/; MIT Sloan Management Review and MIT Technology Review.

Plunkett Research, Ltd., PO Drawer 541737, Houston, TX, 77254-1737, USA, (713) 932-0000, (713) 961-3282, (713) 932-7080, customersupport@plunkettresearch.com, https://www.plunkettresearch.com; Industry Almanacs.

Public Religion Research Institute (PRRI), 1023 15th St. NW, 9th Fl., Washington, DC, 20005, USA, (202) 238-9424, info@prri.org, https://www.prri.org/; Increasing Support for Religiously Based Service Refusals.

Refinitiv, 22 Thomson Pl., Boston, MA, 02210, USA, (857) 365-1200, https://www.refinitiv.com; Thomson ONE Wealth.

SAGE Publications, 2455 Teller Rd., Thousand Oaks, CA, 91320, USA, (800) 818-7243, (800) 583-2665, journals@sagepub.com, https://www.sagepub.com; European Journal of Industrial Relations; Family Business Review; Global Business Review; and Journal of Sports Economics.

Tax Foundation, 1325 G St. NW, Ste. 950, Washington, DC, 20005, USA, (202) 464-6200, https://taxfoundation.org/; U.S. Businesses Pay or Remit 93 Percent of All Taxes Collected in America.

U.S. Census Bureau, 4600 Silver Hill Rd., Washington, DC, 20233, USA, (301) 763-4636, (800) 923-8282, https://www.census.gov; County Business Patterns (CBP) 2020 and Economic Census, Nonemployer Statistics (NES) 2019.

U.S. Census Bureau, Center for Economic Studies (CES), 4600 Silver Hill Rd., Washington, DC, 20233, USA, (301) 763-6460, (301) 763-5935, ces.contacts@census.gov, https://www.census.gov/programs-surveys/ces.html; Geographic Area, 2017 Economic Census.

U.S. Department of Commerce (DOC), 1401 Constitution Ave. NW, Washington, DC, 20230, USA, (202) 482-2000, https://www.commerce.gov/; Commerce 2022-2026 Strategic Plan Progress Summary and Intellectual Property.

U.S. Department of Commerce (DOC), National Technical Information Service (NTIS), 5301 Shawnee Rd., Alexandria, VA, 22312, USA, (202) 482-2000, (703) 605-6880, info@ntis.gov, https://www.ntis.gov/; NTIS Bibliographic Database.

University of Pennsylvania, The Wharton School, 3733 Spruce St., Philadelphia, PA, 19104, USA, (215) 898-2575, https://www.wharton.upenn.edu/; Knowledge at Wharton.

BUSINESS ENTERPRISES-AMERICAN INDIAN AND ALAKSA NATIVE OWNED BUSINESS

U.S. Census Bureau, 4600 Silver Hill Rd., Washington, DC, 20233, USA, (301) 763-4636, (800) 923-8282, https://www.census.gov; Survey of Business Owners (SBO).

BUSINESS ENTERPRISES-BANKRUPTCIES FILED

Administrative Office of the United States Courts, One Columbus Cir. NE, Washington, DC, 20544, USA, (202) 502-2600, https://www.uscourts.gov; Statistical Tables for the Federal Judiciary 2022.

BUSINESS ENTERPRISES-BLACK-OWNED BUSINESS

U.S. Census Bureau, 4600 Silver Hill Rd., Washington, DC, 20233, USA, (301) 763-4636, (800) 923-8282, https://www.census.gov; Survey of Business Owners (SBO).

BUSINESS ENTERPRISES-CAPITAL, FIXED BY INDUSTRY

U.S. Department of Commerce (DOC), Bureau of Economic Analysis (BEA), 4600 Silver Hill Rd., Washington, DC, 20233, USA, (301) 278-9004, customerservice@bea.gov, https://www.bea.gov; Survey of Current Business (SCB).

BUSINESS ENTERPRISES-CORPORATIONS-PHILANTHROPY

The Chronicle of Philanthropy, 1255 23rd St. NW, 7th Fl., Washington, DC, 20037, USA, (202) 466-1200, philanthropy@pubservice.com, https://www.philanthropy.com/; America's Favorite Charities 2021; The Chronicle of Philanthropy; and Data & Research.

Giving Institute, 7918 Jones Branch Dr., No. 300, McLean, VA, 22102, USA, (312) 981-6794, (312) 265-2908, info@givinginstitute.org, https://www.givinginstitute.org/; Giving USA 2021: The Annual Report on Philanthropy for the Year 2020.

Independent Sector, 1602 L St. NW, Ste. 900, Washington, DC, 20036, USA, (202) 467-6100, (202) 467-6101, info@independentsector.org, https://independentsector.org/; Health of the U.S. Nonprofit Sector Quarterly Review.

BUSINESS ENTERPRISES-CORPORATIONS-PROFITS AND SALES

Internal Revenue Service (IRS), Statistics of Income Division (SOI), 1111 Constitution Ave. NW, K-Room 4100-123, Washington, DC, 20224-0002, USA, (202) 874-0410, (202) 874-0964, sis@irs.gov, https://www.irs.gov/uac/soi-tax-stats-statistics-of-income; Statistics of Income Bulletin.

S&P Global, S&P Global Market Intelligence, 55 Water St., New York, NY, 10041, USA, (877) 863-1306, market.intelligence@spglobal.com, https://www.spglobal.com/marketintelligence/en/; S&P Global Market Intelligence.

BUSINESS ENTERPRISES-CORPORATIONS, PARTNERSHIPS, AND PROPRIETORSHIPS

Internal Revenue Service (IRS), Statistics of Income Division (SOI), 1111 Constitution Ave. NW, K-Room 4100-123, Washington, DC, 20224-0002, USA, (202) 874-0410, (202) 874-0964, sis@irs.gov, https://www.irs.gov/uac/soi-tax-stats-statistics-of-income; SOI Tax Stats - Historical Data Tables and Statistics of Income Bulletin.

BUSINESS ENTERPRISES-ECONOMIC INDICATORS

American Economic Association (AEA), 2403 Sidney St., Ste. 260, Pittsburgh, PA, 15203, USA, (412) 432-2300, (412) 431-3014, https://www.aeaweb.org/; American Economic Review (AER).

Boston Consulting Group (BCG), 200 Pier 4 Blvd., Boston, MA, 02210, USA, (617) 973-1200, https://www.bcg.com/; The Business Impact of COVID-19.

The Brookings Institution, 1775 Massachusetts Ave. NW, Washington, DC, 20036, USA, (202) 797-6000, communications@brookings.edu, https://www.brookings.edu/; Advancing Inclusion Through Clean Energy Jobs.

Chief Executive Group, 9 W Broad St., Ste. 430, Stamford, CT, 06902, USA, (203) 930-2700, (203) 930-2701, contact@chiefexecutive.net, https://chiefexecutive.net/; CEO and Senior Executive Compensation Report for Private Companies 2021-2022.

The Conference Board, 845 3rd Ave., New York, NY, 10022-6660, USA, (212) 759-0900, (212) 339-0345, customer.service@conferenceboard.org, https://www.conference-board.org; Global Leading Indicators.

Customer Growth Partners (CGP), 13 Evarts Ln., Ste. 100, Madison, CT, 06443, USA, https://www.customergrowthpartners.com; Retail Growth Vectors and Retail Read Report.

Dun & Bradstreet (D&B) Corporation, 5335 Gate Parkway, Jacksonville, FL, 32256, USA, (904) 648-6350, (800) 526-9018, https://www.dnb.com/; 2020 Global Bankruptcy Report and UK Quarterly Industry Report.

Eno Center for Transportation, 1629 K St. NW, Ste. 200, Washington, DC, 20006, USA, (202) 879-4700, publicaffairs@enotrans.org, https://www.enotrans.org/; Centennial Anthology: A Collection of Essays and Ideas.

The Federal Reserve Bank of Richmond, PO Box 27622, Richmond, VA, 23261, USA, (804) 697-8000, (410) 576-3300, https://www.richmondfed.org/; Carolinas Survey of Business Activity and Maryland Survey of Business Activity.

Harris Interactive, 85 Uxbridge Rd., 11th Fl., Ealing, W5 5TH, GBR, https://harris-interactive.co.uk/; The Grocer: Ethical Trading.

Interactive Advertising Bureau (IAB), 116 E 27th St., 6th Fl., New York, NY, 10016, USA, (212) 380-4700, https://www.iab.com/; U.S. Podcast Advertising Revenue Study.

Kantar Worldpanel, 6 More London Place, London, SE1 2QY, GBR, https://www.kantarworldpanel.com; Grocery Market Share.

MSCI, 7 World Trade Center, 250 Greenwich St., New York, NY, 10007, USA, (888) 588-4567, https://www.msci.com/; 2021 Annual Market Classification Review.

Organization for Economic Cooperation and Development (OECD), 2001 L St. NW, Ste. 650, Washington, DC, 20036-4922, USA, (202) 785-6323, (800) 456-6323, (202) 785-0350, washington.contact@oecd.org, https://www.oecd.org/; The Future of Corporate Governance in Capital Markets Following the COVID-19 Crisis.

PeoplePerHour, London, GBR, https://www.peopleperhour.com/; Start-up Cities: The World's Best 25 Cities to Start a Business.

PricewaterhouseCoopers (PwC), 300 Madison Ave., New York, NY, 10017, USA, (646) 471-3000, (646) 471-4000, https://www.pwc.com/; unpublished data.

PricewaterhouseCoopers (PwC) Strategy&, 90 Park Ave., Ste. 400, New York, NY, 10016, USA, (212) 697-1900, (212) 551-6732, https://www.strategyand.pwc.com/gx/en/; 2019 Chief Digital Officer Study and Global Entertainment & Media Outlook 2022-2026.

ProPublica, 155 Avenue of the Americas, 13th Fl., New York, NY, 10013, USA, (212) 514-5250, (212) 785-2634, hello@propublica.org, https://www.propublica.org/; Nonprofit Explorer.

Refinitiv, 22 Thomson Pl., Boston, MA, 02210, USA, (857) 365-1200, https://www.refinitiv.com; Thomson ONE Wealth.

S&P Global, S&P Global Market Intelligence, 55 Water St., New York, NY, 10041, USA, (877) 863-1306, market.intelligence@spglobal.com, https://www.spglobal.com/marketintelligence/en/; S&P Global Market Intelligence.

Southern Mississippi Planning and Development District (SMPDD), 10441 Corporate Dr., Ste. 1, Gulfport, MS, 39503, USA, (228) 868-2311, (800) 444-8014, info@smpdd.com, http://smpdd.com/; unpublished data.

StatCounter, Guinness Enterprise Centre, Taylor's Ln., Dublin, 8, IRL, https://statcounter.com/; StatCounter.

Statista, 3 World Trade Center, 175 Greenwich St., 36th Fl., New York, NY, 10007, USA, (212) 433-2270, support@statista.com, https://www.statista.com; Statista: The Statistics Portal.

U.S. Census Bureau, Center for Economic Studies (CES), 4600 Silver Hill Rd., Washington, DC, 20233, USA, (301) 763-6460, (301) 763-5935, ces.contacts@census.gov, https://www.census.gov/programs-surveys/ces.html; Finance and Insurance, 2017 Economic Census and Management of Companies and Enterprises, 2017 Economic Census.

U.S. Department of Commerce (DOC), 1401 Constitution Ave. NW, Washington, DC, 20230, USA, (202) 482-2000, https://www.commerce.gov/; Digital Trade in North America.

U.S. Department of Commerce (DOC), International Trade Administration (ITA), 1401 Constitution Ave. NW, Washington, DC, 20230, USA, (800) 872-8723, https://www.trade.gov/; ITA Exporter Database (EDB).

U.S. Securities and Exchange Commission (SEC), 100 F St. NE, Washington, DC, 20549, USA, (202) 551-6551, (202) 551-4119, https://www.sec.gov; Electronic Data Gathering, Analysis, and Retrieval (EDGAR) System.

University of Arizona, Eller College of Management, Economic and Business Research Center, McClelland Hall 103, PO Box 210108, Tucson, AZ, 85721-0108, USA, (520) 621-2155, (520) 621-2150, ebrpublications@email.arizona.edu, https://eller.arizona.edu/departments-research/centers-labs/economic-business-research; Forecasting Project Economic Forecast Databases.

The World Bank, 1818 H St. NW, Washington, DC, 20433, USA, (202) 473-1000, (202) 477-6391, eds03@worldbank.org, https://www.worldbank.org/; Doing Business 2019: Training for Reform and Doing Business 2020: Comparing Business Regulation in 190 Economies.

BUSINESS ENTERPRISES-EMPLOYEES

Chief Executive Group, 9 W Broad St., Ste. 430, Stamford, CT, 06902, USA, (203) 930-2700, (203) 930-2701, contact@chiefexecutive.net, https://chiefexecutive.net/; CEO and Senior Executive Compensation Report for Private Companies 2021-2022.

The Minority Corporate Counsel Association (MCCA), 1111 Pennsylvania Ave. NW, Washington, DC, 20004, USA, (202) 739-5901, https://www.mcca.com/; 2020 Inclusion Index Survey Report.

Nestpick Global Services, GmbH, Neue Schonhauser Strasse 3-5, Berlin, D-10178, GER, info@nestpick.com, https://www.nestpick.com; Best Cities for Startup Employees.

PricewaterhouseCoopers (PwC) Strategy&, 90 Park Ave., Ste. 400, New York, NY, 10016, USA, (212) 697-1900, (212) 551-6732, https://www.strategyand.pwc.com/gx/en/; 2019 Chief Digital Officer Study.

U.S. Census Bureau, 4600 Silver Hill Rd., Washington, DC, 20233, USA, (301) 763-4636, (800) 923-8282, https://www.census.gov; County Business Patterns (CBP) 2020 and Statistics of U.S. Businesses (SUSB).

U.S. Department of Labor (DOL), Bureau of Labor Statistics (BLS), Postal Square Bldg., 2 Massachusetts Ave. NE, Washington, DC, 20212-0001, USA, (202) 691-5200, (202) 691-7890, blsdata_staff@bls.gov, https://www.bls.gov; Employer Costs for Employee Compensation.

BUSINESS ENTERPRISES-ENVIRONMENTAL ASPECTS

NielsenIQ (NIQ), 200 W Jackson Blvd., Chicago, IL, 60606, USA, https://nielseniq.com; The CPG Sustainability Report.

BUSINESS ENTERPRISES-EXPENDITURES

U.S. Census Bureau, 4600 Silver Hill Rd., Washington, DC, 20233, USA, (301) 763-4636, (800) 923-8282, https://www.census.gov; Annual Capital Expenditures Survey (ACES) 2020 and Statistics of U.S. Businesses (SUSB).

U.S. Department of Commerce (DOC), International Trade Administration (ITA), 1401 Constitution Ave. NW, Washington, DC, 20230, USA, (800) 872-8723, https://www.trade.gov/; ITA Exporter Database (EDB).

U.S. Department of Labor (DOL), Bureau of Labor Statistics (BLS), Postal Square Bldg., 2 Massachusetts Ave. NE, Washington, DC, 20212-0001, USA, (202) 691-5200, (202) 691-7890, blsdata_staff@bls.gov, https://www.bls.gov; Employer Costs for Employee Compensation.

BUSINESS ENTERPRISES-EXPENDITURES-RESEARCH AND DEVELOPMENT

National Science Foundation, National Center for Science and Engineering Statistics (NCSES), 2415 Eisenhower Ave., Ste. W14200, Arlington, VA, 22314, USA, (703) 292-8780, (703) 292-9092, info@nsf.gov, https://www.nsf.gov/statistics/; Business Enterprise Research and Development Survey (BERD) and National Patterns of R & D Resources.

BUSINESS ENTERPRISES-FAMILY-OWNED BUSINESSES

SAGE Publications, 2455 Teller Rd., Thousand Oaks, CA, 91320, USA, (800) 818-7243, (800) 583-2665, journals@sagepub.com, https://www.sagepub.com; Family Business Review.

BUSINESS ENTERPRISES-FINANCES

Board of Governors of the Federal Reserve System, Constitution Ave. NW, Washington, DC, 20551, USA, (202) 452-3000, (202) 263-4869 (TDD), https://www.federalreserve.gov; Financial Accounts of the United States 2023.

CDP, 60 Great Tower St., 4th Fl., London, EC3R 5AZ, GBR, https://www.cdp.net; The TIme to Green Finance.

Dun & Bradstreet (D&B) Corporation, 5335 Gate Parkway, Jacksonville, FL, 32256, USA, (904) 648-6350, (800) 526-9018, https://www.dnb.com/; 2020 Global Bankruptcy Report.

Interactive Advertising Bureau (IAB), 116 E 27th St., 6th Fl., New York, NY, 10016, USA, (212) 380-4700, https://www.iab.com/; U.S. Podcast Advertising Revenue Study.

Internal Revenue Service (IRS), Statistics of Income Division (SOI), 1111 Constitution Ave. NW, K-Room 4100-123, Washington, DC, 20224-0002, USA, (202) 874-0410, (202) 874-0964, sis@irs.gov, https://www.irs.gov/uac/soi-tax-stats-statistics-of-income; Statistics of Income Bulletin.

Mississippi Development Authority, PO Box 849, Jackson, MS, 39205-0849 , USA, (601) 359-3449, (800) 360-3323, https://mississippi.org/; unpublished data.

PeoplePerHour, London, GBR, https://www.peopleperhour.com/; Start-up Cities: The World's Best 25 Cities to Start a Business.

ProPublica, 155 Avenue of the Americas, 13th Fl., New York, NY, 10013, USA, (212) 514-5250, (212) 785-2634, hello@propublica.org, https://www.propublica.org/; Nonprofit Explorer.

S&P Global, S&P Global Market Intelligence, 55 Water St., New York, NY, 10041, USA, (877) 863-1306, market.intelligence@spglobal.com, https://www.spglobal.com/marketintelligence/en/; S&P Global Market Intelligence.

Southern Mississippi Planning and Development District (SMPDD), 10441 Corporate Dr., Ste. 1, Gulfport, MS, 39503, USA, (228) 868-2311, (800) 444-8014, info@smpdd.com, http://smpdd.com/; unpublished data.

Statista, 3 World Trade Center, 175 Greenwich St., 36th Fl., New York, NY, 10007, USA, (212) 433-2270, support@statista.com, https://www.statista.com; Statista: The Statistics Portal.

U.S. Census Bureau, 4600 Silver Hill Rd., Washington, DC, 20233, USA, (301) 763-4636, (800) 923-8282, https://www.census.gov; Annual Capital Expenditures Survey (ACES) 2020; Quarterly Financial Report for Manufacturing, Mining, Trade, and Selected Service Industries; and Statistics of U.S. Businesses (SUSB).

U.S. Census Bureau, Center for Economic Studies (CES), 4600 Silver Hill Rd., Washington, DC, 20233, USA, (301) 763-6460, (301) 763-5935, ces.contacts@census.gov, https://www.census.gov/programs-surveys/ces.html; Finance and Insurance, 2017 Economic Census.

U.S. Department of Commerce (DOC), 1401 Constitution Ave. NW, Washington, DC, 20230, USA, (202) 482-2000, https://www.commerce.gov/; Digital Trade in North America.

U.S. Department of Commerce (DOC), Bureau of Economic Analysis (BEA), 4600 Silver Hill Rd., Washington, DC, 20233, USA, (301) 278-9004, customerservice@bea.gov, https://www.bea.gov; National Income and Product Accounts (NIPA): 2022 Update and Survey of Current Business (SCB).

U.S. Department of Labor (DOL), Bureau of Labor Statistics (BLS), Postal Square Bldg., 2 Massachusetts Ave. NE, Washington, DC, 20212-0001, USA, (202) 691-5200, (202) 691-7890, blsdata_staff@bls.gov, https://www.bls.gov; Employer Costs for Employee Compensation.

U.S. Securities and Exchange Commission (SEC), 100 F St. NE, Washington, DC, 20549, USA, (202) 551-6551, (202) 551-4119, https://www.sec.gov; Electronic Data Gathering, Analysis, and Retrieval (EDGAR) System.

ValuePenguin, 600 3rd Ave. , 8th Fl., New York, NY, 10016, USA, media@valuepenguin.com, https://www.valuepenguin.com; State of Auto Insurance in 2023.

The World Bank, 1818 H St. NW, Washington, DC, 20433, USA, (202) 473-1000, (202) 477-6391, eds03@worldbank.org, https://www.worldbank.org/; Doing Business 2019: Training for Reform and Doing Business 2020: Comparing Business Regulation in 190 Economies.

World Intellectual Property Organization (WIPO), 34, chemin des Colombettes, Geneva, CH-1211, SWI, https://www.wipo.int; IP Facts and Figures 2022.

BUSINESS ENTERPRISES-FLOW OF FUNDS

Board of Governors of the Federal Reserve System, Constitution Ave. NW, Washington, DC, 20551, USA, (202) 452-3000, (202) 263-4869 (TDD), https://www.federalreserve.gov; Financial Accounts of the United States 2023.

U.S. Census Bureau, 4600 Silver Hill Rd., Washington, DC, 20233, USA, (301) 763-4636, (800) 923-8282, https://www.census.gov; Annual Capital Expenditures Survey (ACES) 2020 and Statistics of U.S. Businesses (SUSB).

BUSINESS ENTERPRISES-FOREIGN INVESTMENT IN THE UNITED STATES

U.S. Department of Commerce (DOC), Bureau of Economic Analysis (BEA), 4600 Silver Hill Rd., Washington, DC, 20233, USA, (301) 278-9004, customerservice@bea.gov, https://www.bea.gov; Foreign Direct Investment in the United States (FDIUS) and Survey of Current Business (SCB).

BUSINESS ENTERPRISES-HISPANIC-OWNED BUSINESSES

U.S. Census Bureau, 4600 Silver Hill Rd., Washington, DC, 20233, USA, (301) 763-4636, (800) 923-8282, https://www.census.gov; Survey of Business Owners (SBO).

BUSINESS ENTERPRISES-LEADING INDICATORS

The Conference Board, 845 3rd Ave., New York, NY, 10022-6660, USA, (212) 759-0900, (212) 339-0345, customer.service@conferenceboard.org, https://www.conference-board.org; Global Leading Indicators.

Gartner, Inc., 56 Top Gallant Rd., Stamford, CT, 06902, USA, (203) 964-0096, https://www.gartner.com; IDEAS Competitive Profiles.

Organization for Economic Cooperation and Development (OECD), 2001 L St. NW, Ste. 650, Washington, DC, 20036-4922, USA, (202) 785-6323, (800) 456-6323, (202) 785-0350, washington.contact@oecd.org, https://www.oecd.org/; The Future of Corporate Governance in Capital Markets Following the COVID-19 Crisis.

S&P Global, S&P Global Market Intelligence, 55 Water St., New York, NY, 10041, USA, (877) 863-1306, market.intelligence@spglobal.com, https://www.spglobal.com/marketintelligence/en/; S&P Global Market Intelligence.

U.S. Department of Commerce (DOC), 1401 Constitution Ave. NW, Washington, DC, 20230, USA, (202) 482-2000, https://www.commerce.gov/; Digital Trade in North America.

BUSINESS ENTERPRISES-LOANS TO MINORITY-OPERATED SMALL BUSINESSES

U.S. Small Business Administration (SBA), 409 3rd St. SW, Washington, DC, 20416, USA, (800) 827-5722, answerdesk@sba.gov, https://www.sba.gov; Small Business Administration (SBA) Loan Program Performance.

U.S. Small Business Administration (SBA), Office of Advocacy, 409 3rd St. SW, Washington, DC, 20416, USA, (202) 205-6533, advocacy@sba.gov, https://advocacy.sba.gov; 2021 Small Business Profiles for the States, the District of Columbia, and the U.S..

BUSINESS ENTERPRISES-MERGERS AND ACQUISITIONS

Refinitiv, 22 Thomson Pl., Boston, MA, 02210, USA, (857) 365-1200, https://www.refinitiv.com; Thomson ONE Wealth.

BUSINESS ENTERPRISES-MINORITY-OWNED BUSINESSES

U.S. Census Bureau, 4600 Silver Hill Rd., Washington, DC, 20233, USA, (301) 763-4636, (800) 923-8282, https://www.census.gov; United States QuickFacts.

BUSINESS ENTERPRISES-MULTINATIONAL COMPANIES

U.S. Department of Commerce (DOC), Bureau of Economic Analysis (BEA), 4600 Silver Hill Rd., Washington, DC, 20233, USA, (301) 278-9004, customerservice@bea.gov, https://www.bea.gov; Survey of Current Business (SCB).

BUSINESS ENTERPRISES-PATENTS

U.S. Department of Commerce (DOC), 1401 Constitution Ave. NW, Washington, DC, 20230, USA, (202) 482-2000, https://www.commerce.gov/; Intellectual Property.

U.S. Patent and Trademark Office (USPTO), Madison Bldg., 600 Dulany St., Alexandria, VA, 22314, USA, (571) 272-1000, (800) 786-9199, https://www.uspto.gov; Calendar Year Patent Statistics for 2020; Patent Trial and Appeal Board (PTAB) Performance Benchmarks for Dispositions, Pendency, Inventory, and Other Tracking Measures; Patents Data, at a Glance; and Performance and Accountability Report (PAR) Fiscal Year 2021.

BUSINESS ENTERPRISES-PAYROLL

Chief Executive Group, 9 W Broad St., Ste. 430, Stamford, CT, 06902, USA, (203) 930-2700, (203) 930-2701, contact@chiefexecutive.net, https://chiefexecutive.net/; CEO and Senior Executive Compensation Report for Private Companies 2021-2022.

U.S. Census Bureau, 4600 Silver Hill Rd., Washington, DC, 20233, USA, (301) 763-4636, (800) 923-8282, https://www.census.gov; County Business Patterns (CBP) 2020 and Statistics of U.S. Businesses (SUSB).

BUSINESS ENTERPRISES-PROFITS

The Federal Reserve Bank of Richmond, PO Box 27622, Richmond, VA, 23261, USA, (804) 697-8000, (410) 576-3300, https://www.richmondfed.org/; Fifth District Survey of Manufacturing Activity.

U.S. Census Bureau, 4600 Silver Hill Rd., Washington, DC, 20233, USA, (301) 763-4636, (800) 923-8282, https://www.census.gov; Quarterly Financial Report for Manufacturing, Mining, Trade, and Selected Service Industries.

U.S. Department of Commerce (DOC), Bureau of Economic Analysis (BEA), 4600 Silver Hill Rd., Washington, DC, 20233, USA, (301) 278-9004, customerservice@bea.gov, https://www.bea.gov; National Income and Product Accounts (NIPA): 2022 Update.

BUSINESS ENTERPRISES-SALES, SHIPMENTS AND RECEIPTS

CDP, 60 Great Tower St., 4th Fl., London, EC3R 5AZ, GBR, https://www.cdp.net; Engaging the Chain: Driving Speed and Scale.

Institute for Supply Management (ISM), 309 W Elliot Rd. , Ste. 113, Tempe, AZ, 85284-1556, USA, (480) 752-6276, (480) 752-7890, membersvcs@ismworld.org, https://www.ismworld.org/; Inside Supply Management Magazine and Report on Business.

S&P Global, S&P Global Market Intelligence, 55 Water St., New York, NY, 10041, USA, (877) 863-1306, market.intelligence@spglobal.com, https://www.spglobal.com/marketintelligence/en/; S&P Global Market Intelligence.

U.S. Census Bureau, 4600 Silver Hill Rd., Washington, DC, 20233, USA, (301) 763-4636, (800) 923-8282, https://www.census.gov; Quarterly Financial Report for Manufacturing, Mining, Trade, and Selected Service Industries and United States QuickFacts.

U.S. Department of Commerce (DOC), International Trade Administration (ITA), 1401 Constitution Ave. NW, Washington, DC, 20230, USA, (800) 872-8723, https://www.trade.gov/; ITA Exporter Database (EDB).

BUSINESS ENTERPRISES-SMALL BUSINESS

Forbes, Inc., 499 Washington Blvd., Jersey City, NJ, 07310, USA, (800) 295-0893, https://www.forbes.com; America's Best Small Companies 2022.

Gaebler Ventures/Resources for Entrepreneurs, 1153 S Plymouth Ct., Unit B, Chicago, IL, 60605, USA, https://www.gaebler.com/; Number of Small Businesses by State.

Global Entrepreneurship Monitor (GEM), Babson College, 231 Forest St., Babson Park, MA, 02457, USA, (781) 235-1200, info@gemconsortium.org, https://www.gemconsortium.org/; Angola Economy Profile; Argentina Economy Profile; Austria Economy Profile; Barbados Economy Profile; Brazil Economy Profile; Canada Economy Profile; Chile Economy Profile; Colombia Economy Profile; Costa Rica Economy Profile; Ecuador Economy Profile; Egypt Economy Profile; Estonia Economy Profile; Finland Economy Profile; France Economy Profile; GEM 2022-2023 Global Report; GEM Women's Entrepreneurship 2021-2022 Report; Germany Economy Profile; Greece Economy Profile; Hungary Economy Profile; India Economy Profile; Indonesia Economy Profile; Iran Economy Profile; Ireland Economy Profile; Israel Economy Profile; Italy Economy Profile; Jamaica Economy Profile; Latvia Economy Profile; Libya Economy Profile; Lithuania Economy Profile; Luxembourg Economy Profile; Mexico Economy Profile; Netherlands Economy Profile; Norway Economy Profile; Panama Economy Profile; Philippines Economy Profile; Poland Economy Profile; Portugal Economy Profile; Puerto Rico Economy Profile; Romania Economy Profile; Singapore Economy Profile; Slovakia Economy Profile; Slovenia Economy Profile; South Africa Economy Profile; South Korea Economy Profile; Spain Economy Profile; Suriname Economic Profile; Sweden Economy Profile; Switzerland Economy Profile; Thailand Economy Profile; Trinidad and Tobago Economy Profile; Tunisia Economy Profile; Uganda Economy Profile; United Kingdom Economy Profile; United States Economy Profile; and 2021-2022 United States Report.

PeoplePerHour, London, GBR, https://www.peopleperhour.com/; Start-up Cities: The World's Best 25 Cities to Start a Business.

Statista, 3 World Trade Center, 175 Greenwich St., 36th Fl., New York, NY, 10007, USA, (212) 433-2270, support@statista.com, https://www.statista.com; Statista: The Statistics Portal.

Sustainable Food Trust, 38 Richmond St., Totterdown, Bristol, BS3 4TQ, GBR, info@sustainablefoodtrust.org, https://sustainablefoodtrust.org/; The Case for Local Food: Building Better Local Food Systems to Benefit Society and Nature.

U.S. Small Business Administration (SBA), 409 3rd St. SW, Washington, DC, 20416, USA, (800) 827-5722, answerdesk@sba.gov, https://www.sba.gov; Small Business Administration (SBA) Loan Program Performance and Small Business Economic Bulletin.

U.S. Small Business Administration (SBA), Office of Advocacy, 409 3rd St. SW, Washington, DC, 20416, USA, (202) 205-6533, advocacy@sba.gov, https://advocacy.sba.gov; 2021 Small Business Profiles for the States, the District of Columbia, and the U.S..

BUSINESS ENTERPRISES-VENTURE CAPITAL

PEI Media, 130 W 42nd St., New York, NY, 10036, USA, (212) 633-1073, https://www.thisispei.com/; Venture Capital Journal (VCJ).

U.S. Census Bureau, 4600 Silver Hill Rd., Washington, DC, 20233, USA, (301) 763-4636, (800) 923-8282, https://www.census.gov; Annual Capital Expenditures Survey (ACES) 2020.

BUSINESS ENTERPRISES-WOMEN-OWNED BUSINESSES

Global Entrepreneurship Monitor (GEM), Babson College, 231 Forest St., Babson Park, MA, 02457, USA, (781) 235-1200, info@gemconsortium.org, https://www.gemconsortium.org/; GEM Women's Entrepreneurship 2021-2022 Report.

U.S. Census Bureau, 4600 Silver Hill Rd., Washington, DC, 20233, USA, (301) 763-4636, (800) 923-8282, https://www.census.gov; Survey of Business Owners (SBO) and United States QuickFacts.

BUSINESS LOGISTICS

CDP, 60 Great Tower St., 4th Fl., London, EC3R 5AZ, GBR, https://www.cdp.net; Engaging the Chain: Driving Speed and Scale.

BUSINESS MANAGEMENT

CDP, 60 Great Tower St., 4th Fl., London, EC3R 5AZ, GBR, https://www.cdp.net; Engaging the Chain: Driving Speed and Scale.

Euromonitor International, Inc., 1 N Dearborn St., Ste. 1700, Chicago, IL, 60602, USA, (312) 922-1115, (312) 922-1157, info-usa@euromonitor.com, https://www.euromonitor.com/; Strategic Analysis of the World's Largest Companies.

Higher Education Statistics Agency (HESA), 95 Promenade, Cheltenham, GL50 1HZ, GBR, official.statistics@hesa.ac.uk, https://www.hesa.ac.uk/; Estates Management Record for Higher Education Providers 2021-2022.

MIT Sloan School of Management, 100 Main St., Cambridge, MA, 02142, USA, (617) 253-1000, https://mitsloan.mit.edu/; MIT Sloan Management Review and MIT Technology Review.

U.S. Census Bureau, Center for Economic Studies (CES), 4600 Silver Hill Rd., Washington, DC, 20233, USA, (301) 763-6460, (301) 763-5935, ces.contacts@census.gov, https://www.census.gov/programs-surveys/ces.html; Management of Companies and Enterprises, 2017 Economic Census.

The World Bank, 1818 H St. NW, Washington, DC, 20433, USA, (202) 473-1000, (202) 477-6391, eds03@worldbank.org, https://www.worldbank.org/; Doing Business 2020: Comparing Business Regulation in 190 Economies.

BUSINESS MANAGEMENT-DEGREES CONFERRED

U.S. Department of Education (ED), Institute of Education Sciences (IES), National Center for Education Statistics (NCES), Potomac Center Plaza, 550 12th St. SW, Washington, DC, 20202, USA, (202) 403-5551, https://nces.ed.gov/; Digest of Education Statistics, 2020.

BUSINESS MANAGEMENT-DEGREES CONFERRED-SALARY OFFERS

National Association of Colleges and Employers (NACE), 1 E Broad St., Ste 130-1005, Bethlehem, PA, 18018, USA, (610) 868-1421, customerservice@naceweb.org, https://www.naceweb.org/; Salary Survey.

BUSINESS SERVICES-CAPITAL

U.S. Department of Commerce (DOC), Bureau of Economic Analysis (BEA), 4600 Silver Hill Rd., Washington, DC, 20233, USA, (301) 278-9004, customerservice@bea.gov, https://www.bea.gov; Survey of Current Business (SCB).

BUSINESS SERVICES-EARNINGS

U.S. Department of Labor (DOL), Bureau of Labor Statistics (BLS), Postal Square Bldg., 2 Massachusetts Ave. NE, Washington, DC, 20212-0001, USA, (202) 691-5200, (202) 691-7890, blsdata_staff@bls.gov, https://www.bls.gov; Current Employment Statistics (CES).

BUSINESS SERVICES-EMPLOYEES

U.S. Department of Labor (DOL), Bureau of Labor Statistics (BLS), Postal Square Bldg., 2 Massachusetts Ave. NE, Washington, DC, 20212-0001, USA, (202) 691-5200, (202) 691-7890, blsdata_staff@bls.gov, https://www.bls.gov; Current Employment Statistics (CES) and Monthly Labor Review.

BUSINESS SERVICES-GROSS DOMESTIC PRODUCT

U.S. Department of Commerce (DOC), Bureau of Economic Analysis (BEA), 4600 Silver Hill Rd., Washington, DC, 20233, USA, (301) 278-9004, customerservice@bea.gov, https://www.bea.gov; Survey of Current Business (SCB).

BUSINESS SERVICES-INDUSTRIAL SAFETY

U.S. Department of Labor (DOL), Bureau of Labor Statistics (BLS), Postal Square Bldg., 2 Massachusetts Ave. NE, Washington, DC, 20212-0001, USA, (202) 691-5200, (202) 691-7890, blsdata_staff@bls.gov, https://www.bls.gov; Injuries, Illnesses, and Fatalities (IIF).

BUSINESS SERVICES-MERGERS AND ACQUISITIONS

Refinitiv, 22 Thomson Pl., Boston, MA, 02210, USA, (857) 365-1200, https://www.refinitiv.com; Thomson ONE Wealth.

BUSINESS SERVICES-MULTINATIONAL COMPANIES

U.S. Department of Commerce (DOC), Bureau of Economic Analysis (BEA), 4600 Silver Hill Rd., Washington, DC, 20233, USA, (301) 278-9004, customerservice@bea.gov, https://www.bea.gov; Survey of Current Business (SCB).

BUSINESS SERVICES-RECEIPTS

U.S. Census Bureau, 4600 Silver Hill Rd., Washington, DC, 20233, USA, (301) 763-4636, (800) 923-8282, https://www.census.gov; County Business Patterns (CBP) 2020.

U.S. Census Bureau, Center for Economic Studies (CES), 4600 Silver Hill Rd., Washington, DC, 20233, USA, (301) 763-6460, (301) 763-5935, ces.contacts@census.gov, https://www.census.gov/programs-surveys/ces.html; Professional, Scientific and Technical Services, 2017 Economic Census.

BUSINESS TAX

Tax Foundation, 1325 G St. NW, Ste. 950, Washington, DC, 20005, USA, (202) 464-6200, https://taxfoundation.org/; U.S. Businesses Pay or Remit 93 Percent of All Taxes Collected in America.

BUSINESS TRAVEL

Global Business Travel Association (GBTA), 107 S West St., Ste. 762, Alexandria, VA, 22314, USA, (703) 684-0836, (703) 783-8686, info@gbta.org, https://www.gbta.org/; unpublished data.

BUSINESS, TECHNOLOGY AND FINANCE

Consumer Technology Association (CTA), 1919 S Eads St., Arlington, VA, 22202, USA, (703) 907-7600, (866) 858-1555, (703) 907-7675, cta@cta.tech, https://www.cta.tech; Mobility and Auto Technology in the COVID-19 Era.

The Economist Group, 900 3rd Ave., 16th Fl., New York, NY, 10022, USA, (212) 541-0500, (202) 429-0890, customerhelp@economist.com, https://www.economistgroup.com; The Economist.

Gartner, Inc., 56 Top Gallant Rd., Stamford, CT, 06902, USA, (203) 964-0096, https://www.gartner.com; Digital Markets Insights.

Growth Intelligence, 25-27 Horsell Rd., London, N5 1XL, GBR, info@growthintelligence.com, https://growthintelligence.com/; unpublished data.

BUTTER

U.S. Department of Agriculture (USDA), Economic Research Service (ERS), 1400 Independence Ave. SW, Mail Stop 1800, Washington, DC, 20250-0002, USA, (202) 720-2791, https://www.ers.usda.gov/; Food Price Outlook.

U.S. Department of Agriculture (USDA), National Agricultural Statistics Service (USDA-NASS), 1400 Independence Ave. SW, Washington, DC, 20250,

USA, (800) 727-9540, nass@nass.usda.gov, https://www.nass.usda.gov; Dairy Products and Milk Production.

BUTTERFISH

National Oceanic and Atmospheric Administration (NOAA), National Marine Fisheries Service (NOAA Fisheries), 1315 East-West Hwy., 14th Fl., Silver Spring, MD, 20910, USA, (301) 427-8000, https://www.fisheries.noaa.gov/; Fisheries of the United States, 2020.

BUTTERFLIES

Xerces Society for Invertebrate Conservation, 628 NE Broadway, Ste. 200, Portland, OR, 97232, USA, (855) 232-6639, (503) 233-6794, info@xerces.org, https://xerces.org/; Drifting Toward Disaster: How Dicamba Herbicides are Harming Cultivated and Wild Landscapes and Wings: Essays on Invertebrate Conservation.

C

CABBAGE

U.S. Department of Agriculture (USDA), National Agricultural Statistics Service (USDA-NASS), 1400 Independence Ave. SW, Washington, DC, 20250, USA, (800) 727-9540, nass@nass.usda.gov, https://www.nass.usda.gov; Quick Stats and Vegetables Annual Summary.

CABLE TELEVISION

See SUBSCRIPTION TELEVISION

CADMIUM

U.S. Department of the Interior (DOI), U.S. Geological Survey (USGS), National Minerals Information Center (NMIC), 12201 Sunrise Valley Dr., Reston, VA, 20192, USA, (703) 648-4920, (703) 648-7971, (703) 648-4995, sfortier@usgs.gov, https://www.usgs.gov/centers/nmic; Mineral Commodity Summaries 2022 and Minerals Yearbook.

CAFETERIAS

CALCIUM-DIETARY

U.S. Department of Agriculture (USDA), Economic Research Service (ERS), 1400 Independence Ave. SW, Mail Stop 1800, Washington, DC, 20250-0002, USA, (202) 720-2791, https://www.ers.usda.gov/; Food Price Outlook.

CALCIUM CHLORIDE

U.S. Department of the Interior (DOI), U.S. Geological Survey (USGS), National Minerals Information Center (NMIC), 12201 Sunrise Valley Dr., Reston, VA, 20192, USA, (703) 648-4920, (703) 648-7971, (703) 648-4995, sfortier@usgs.gov, https://www.usgs.gov/centers/nmic; Mineral Commodity Summaries 2022 and Minerals Yearbook.

CALIFORNIA

See also-STATE DATA (FOR INDIVIDUAL STATES)

Blue Ribbon Panel on Transparency, Accountability, and Fairness in Law Enforcement (The Panel), San Francisco, CA, 94108, USA, info@sfblueribbonpanel.com, https://sfblueribbonpanel.com/; unpublished data.

California Air Resources Board (CARB), PO Box 2815 , Sacramento, CA, 95812, USA, (800) 242-4450, helpline@arb.ca.gov, https://ww2.arb.ca.gov/; iADAM: Air Quality Data Statistics.

California Department of Finance, 915 L St., Sacramento, CA, 95814, USA, (916) 445-3274, (916) 445-3878, https://dof.ca.gov/; Economic Indicators.

California Department of Forestry and Fire Protection (CAL FIRE), 1416 9th St., PO Box 944246, Sacramento, CA, 94244-2460, USA, (916) 653-5123, https://www.fire.ca.gov/; CAL Fire Incidents Overview and CAL FIRE Stats and Events.

California Department of Public Health (CDPH), PO Box 997377, MS 0500, Sacramento, CA, 95899-7377, USA, (916) 558-1784, https://www.cdph.ca.gov; COVID-19 by the Numbers.

California State University San Bernardino, Center for the Study of Hate and Extremism, 5500 University Pkwy., San Bernardino, CA, 92407, USA, (909) 537-7503, (909) 537-7711, blevin8@aol.com, https://csbs.csusb.edu/hate-and-extremism-center; Report to the Nation: Illustrated Almanac.

The 5 Gyres Institute, PO Box 5699, Santa Monica, CA, 90409, USA, info@5gyres.org, https://www.5gyres.org/; Understanding Microplastic Levels, Pathways, and Transport in the San Francisco Bay Region.

National Oceanic and Atmospheric Administration (NOAA), National Centers for Environmental Information (NCEI), National Integrated Drought Information System (NIDIS), 151 Patton Ave., Asheville, ND, 28801-5001, USA, drought.portal@noaa.gov, https://www.drought.gov; Drought Status Update for California-Nevada.

New York University School of Law, Institute for Policy Integrity, 139 MacDougal St., Wilf Hall, 3rd Fl., New York, NY, 10012, USA, (212) 992-8932, (212) 995-4592, https://policyintegrity.org/; No Turning Back: An Analysis of EPA's Authority to Withdraw California's Preemption Waiver Under Section 209 of the Clean Air Act.

Public Policy Institute of California (PPIC), 500 Washington St., Ste. 600, San Francisco, CA, 94111, USA, (415) 291-4400, (916) 440-1120, (415) 291-4401, https://www.ppic.org/; California's Population; Droughts in California; and Making the Most of Water for the Environment: A Functional Flows Approach for California's Rivers.

Public Policy Institute of California (PPIC) Water Policy Center, 500 Washington St., Ste. 600, San Francisco, CA, 94111, USA, (415) 291-4433, (415) 291-4400, (415) 291-4401, https://www.ppic.org/water/; Policy Brief: Drought and California's Agriculture.

Stanford Center on Poverty & Inequality (CPI), Bldg. 370, 450 Jane Stanford Way, Stanford, CA, 94305, USA, (650) 724-6912, (650) 736-9883, inequality@stanford.edu, https://inequality.stanford.edu/; California Poverty Measure (CPM) Index and Pathways: A Magazine on Poverty, Inequality, and Social Policy.

University of California Davis, Institute of Transportation Studies (ITS-Davis), 1605 Tilia St., Davis, CA, 95616, USA, (530) 752-6548, kcswayze@ucdavis.edu, https://its.ucdavis.edu; A Before and After Evaluation of Shared Mobility Projects in the San Joaquin Valley.

University of California Los Angeles (UCLA) School of Law, Covid-19 Behind Bars Data Project, 385 Charles E. Young Dr. E, Los Angeles, CA, 90095, USA, (310) 206-5568, covidbehindbars@law.ucla.edu, https://uclacovidbehindbars.org; In California Jails, Sherrifs Have Been Left in Charge of Covid Mitigation. The Results Have Been Disastrous..

University of California Los Angeles (UCLA), Center for Health Policy Research (CHPR), 10960 Wilshire Blvd., Ste. 1550, Campus Mail Code 714346, Los Angeles, CA, 90024, USA, (310) 794-0909, (310) 794-2686, healthpolicy@ucla.edu, https://healthpolicy.ucla.edu; AskCHIS Database; 3.6 Million Californians Would Benefit If California Takes Bold Action to Expand Coverage and Improve Affordability; and Coronavirus Disease 2019 and the Case to Cover Undocumented Immigrants in California (Health Equity).

University of California Los Angeles (UCLA), Luskin Center for Innovation, 3323 Public Affairs Bldg., PO Box 951656, Los Angeles, CA, 90095-1656, USA, (310) 267-5435, (310) 267-5443, https://innovation.luskin.ucla.edu/; Economic Benefits of Energy Efficiency Programs: A Case Study of Investments by the Los Angeles Department of Water & Power and Keeping the Lights and Heat On: COVID-19 Utility Debt in Communities Served by Pacific Gas and Electric Company.

World Weather Attribution (WWA), wwamedia@imperial.ac.uk, https://www.worldweatherattribution.org; Rapid Attribution Analysis of the Extraordinary Heatwave on the Pacific Coast of the US and Canada June 2021.

CALIFORNIA-STATE DATA CENTERS

Association of Bay Area Governments (ABAG), 375 Beale St., Ste. 700, San Francisco, CA, 94105-2066, USA, (415) 820-7900, (415) 660-3500, info@bayareametro.gov, https://abag.ca.gov/; State Data Reports (CA).

California Department of Finance, State Census Data Center, 915 L St., 8th Fl., Sacramento, CA, 95814, USA, (916) 323-4086, (916) 327-0222, ficalpop@dof.ca.gov, https://dof.ca.gov/forecasting/demographics/state-census-data-center/; State Data Reports (CA).

Sacramento Area Council of Governments (SACOG), 1415 L St., Ste. 300, Sacramento, CA, 95814, USA, (916) 321-9000, contact@sacog.org, https://www.sacog.org; State Data Reports (CA).

San Diego Association of Governments (SANDAG), 401 B St., Ste. 800, San Diego, CA, 92101, USA, (619) 699-1900, (619) 699-1904 (TTY), (619) 699-1009, pio@sandag.org, https://www.sandag.org/; State Data Reports (CA).

Southern California Association of Governments (SCAG), 900 Wilshire Blvd., Ste. 1700, Los Angeles, CA, 90017, USA, (213) 236-1800, https://scag.ca.gov/; State Data Reports (CA).

University of California, Berkeley, D-Lab, UC DATA, 350 Social Sciences Bldg., Berkeley, CA, 94720-3030, USA, (510) 664-7000, dlab@berkeley.edu, https://dlab.berkeley.edu/data/uc-data; State Data Reports (CA).

CALIFORNIA-PRIMARY STATISTICS SOURCES

California Department of Education (CDE), 1430 N St., Sacramento, CA, 95814-5901, USA, (916) 319-0800, (916) 445-4556 (TTY/TDD), (916) 445-4550, https://www.cde.ca.gov/; California School Dashboard.

California Department of Finance, 915 L St., Sacramento, CA, 95814, USA, (916) 445-3274, (916) 445-3878, https://dof.ca.gov/; Finance Bulletin.

California Department of Public Health (CDPH), PO Box 997377, MS 0500, Sacramento, CA, 95899-7377, USA, (916) 558-1784, https://www.cdph.ca.gov; Vital Records.

SAGE Publications, 2455 Teller Rd., Thousand Oaks, CA, 91320, USA, (800) 818-7243, (800) 583-2665, journals@sagepub.com, https://www.sagepub.com; Data Planet.

CALISTHENICS

National Sporting Goods Association (NSGA), 3041 Woodcreek Dr., Ste. 210, Downers Grove, IL, 60515, USA, (847) 296-6742, (847) 391-9827, info@nsga.org, https://www.nsga.org; Sports Participation in the United States 2022.

CALVES

U.S. Department of Agriculture (USDA), Economic Research Service (ERS), 1400 Independence Ave. SW, Mail Stop 1800, Washington, DC, 20250-0002, USA, (202) 720-2791, https://www.ers.usda.gov/; Food Price Outlook.

U.S. Department of Agriculture (USDA), National Agricultural Statistics Service (USDA-NASS), 1400 Independence Ave. SW, Washington, DC, 20250, USA, (800) 727-9540, nass@nass.usda.gov, https://www.nass.usda.gov; Cattle; Livestock Slaughter; and Meat Animals Production, Disposition, and Income Annual Summary.

CAMBODIA-NATIONAL STATISTICAL OFFICE

Cambodia Ministry of Planning, National Institute of Statistics, 386 Preah Monivong Blvd., Boeung Keng Kong 1, Chamkarmorn, Phnom Penh, CMB, info@nis.gov.kh, https://www.nis.gov.kh/; National Data Reports (Cambodia).

CAMBODIA-AGRICULTURE

The Economist Group: Economist Intelligence Unit (EIU), 900 3rd Ave., 16th Fl., New York, NY, 10022, USA, (212) 541-0500, americas@eiu.com, https://www.eiu.com; Cambodia Country Report.

Euromonitor International, Inc., 1 N Dearborn St., Ste. 1700, Chicago, IL, 60602, USA, (312) 922-1115, (312) 922-1157, info-usa@euromonitor.com, https://www.euromonitor.com/; Geographies.

Palgrave Macmillan, 1 New York Plaza, Ste. 4500, New York, NY, 10004-1562, USA, (800) 777-4643, orders@palgrave.com, https://www.palgrave.com/us; The Statesman's Yearbook, 2023.

Routledge - Taylor & Francis Group, 6000 Broken Sound Pkwy. NW, Ste. 300, Boca Raton, FL, 33487, USA, (800) 634-1420, (800) 634-7064, orders@taylorandfrancis.com, https://www.routledge.com/; The Europa World Year Book 2022.

United Nations Economic and Social Commission for Asia and the Pacific (ESCAP), United Nations Building, Rajadamnern Nok Ave., Bangkok, 10200, THA, https://www.unescap.org/; Asia-Pacific Development Journal and SDG Gateway Data Explorer.

United Nations Food and Agricultural Organization (FAO), 2121 K St., Ste. 800B, Washington, DC, 20037, USA, (202) 653-2400 (Dial from U.S.), (202) 653-5760 (Fax from U.S.), fao-hq@fao.org, https://www.fao.org; AQUASTAT and The State of Food and Agriculture (SOFA) 2022.

United Nations Statistics Division (UNSD), United Nations Plz., New York, NY, 10017, USA, (800) 253-9646, (212) 963-9851, statistics@un.org, https://unstats.un.org; Statistical Yearbook of the United Nations 2021.

The World Bank, 1818 H St. NW, Washington, DC, 20433, USA, (202) 473-1000, (202) 477-6391, eds03@worldbank.org, https://www.worldbank.org/; Cambodia (report).

CAMBODIA-AIRLINES

Palgrave Macmillan, 1 New York Plaza, Ste. 4500, New York, NY, 10004-1562, USA, (800) 777-4643, orders@palgrave.com, https://www.palgrave.com/us; The Statesman's Yearbook, 2023.

Routledge - Taylor & Francis Group, 6000 Broken Sound Pkwy. NW, Ste. 300, Boca Raton, FL, 33487, USA, (800) 634-1420, (800) 634-7064, orders@taylorandfrancis.com, https://www.routledge.com/; The Europa World Year Book 2022.

CAMBODIA-ARMED FORCES

Central Intelligence Agency (CIA), Office of Public Affairs, Washington, DC, 20505, USA, (703) 482-0623, https://www.cia.gov; The World Factbook.

International Institute for Strategic Studies (IISS) - Americas, 2121 K St. NW, Ste. 600, Washington, DC, 20037, USA, (202) 659-1490, (202) 659-1499, https://www.iiss.org/; Armed Conflict Survey 2021 and The Military Balance 2022.

Palgrave Macmillan, 1 New York Plaza, Ste. 4500, New York, NY, 10004-1562, USA, (800) 777-4643, orders@palgrave.com, https://www.palgrave.com/us; The Statesman's Yearbook, 2023.

Stockholm International Peace Research Institute (SIPRI), Signalistgatan 9, Stockholm, SE 169 72, SWE, https://www.sipri.org/; SIPRI Arms Transfers Database and SIPRI Military Expenditure Database.

CAMBODIA-BALANCE OF PAYMENTS

United Nations Conference on Trade and Development (UNCTAD), Palais des Nations, Geneva, 1211, SWI, (212) 963-6896, unctadinfo@unctad.org, https://unctad.org; Handbook of Statistics 2021.

The World Bank, 1818 H St. NW, Washington, DC, 20433, USA, (202) 473-1000, (202) 477-6391, eds03@worldbank.org, https://www.worldbank.org/; Cambodia (report).

CAMBODIA-BANKS AND BANKING

Euromonitor International, Inc., 1 N Dearborn St., Ste. 1700, Chicago, IL, 60602, USA, (312) 922-1115, (312) 922-1157, info-usa@euromonitor.com, https://www.euromonitor.com/; Geographies.

National Bank of Cambodia (NBC), 22-24 Norodom Blvd., Phnom Penh, CMB, info@nbc.org.kh, https://www.nbc.org.kh/english/; Annual Report 2021 and Economic and Monetary Statistics.

CAMBODIA-BROADCASTING

Central Intelligence Agency (CIA), Office of Public Affairs, Washington, DC, 20505, USA, (703) 482-0623, https://www.cia.gov; The World Factbook.

Euromonitor International, Inc., 1 N Dearborn St., Ste. 1700, Chicago, IL, 60602, USA, (312) 922-1115, (312) 922-1157, info-usa@euromonitor.com, https://www.euromonitor.com/; Geographies.

Palgrave Macmillan, 1 New York Plaza, Ste. 4500, New York, NY, 10004-1562, USA, (800) 777-4643, orders@palgrave.com, https://www.palgrave.com/us; The Statesman's Yearbook, 2023.

WRTH Publications Limited, PO Box 290, Oxford, OX2 7FT, GBR, sales@wrth.com, https://www.wrth.com; World Radio TV Handbook 2023.

CAMBODIA-BUDGET

Central Intelligence Agency (CIA), Office of Public Affairs, Washington, DC, 20505, USA, (703) 482-0623, https://www.cia.gov; The World Factbook.

CAMBODIA-BUSINESS

United Nations Economic and Social Commission for Asia and the Pacific (ESCAP), United Nations Building, Rajadamnern Nok Ave., Bangkok, 10200, THA, https://www.unescap.org/; SDG Gateway Data Explorer.

CAMBODIA-CHILDBIRTH-STATISTICS

United Nations Economic and Social Commission for Asia and the Pacific (ESCAP), United Nations Building, Rajadamnern Nok Ave., Bangkok, 10200, THA, https://www.unescap.org/; Asia-Pacific Development Journal.

CAMBODIA-CLIMATE

International Institute for Environment and Development (IIED), 235 High Holborn, London, WC1V 7DN, GBR, inforequest@iied.org, https://www.iied.org; Environment & Urbanization.

Palgrave Macmillan, 1 New York Plaza, Ste. 4500, New York, NY, 10004-1562, USA, (800) 777-4643, orders@palgrave.com, https://www.palgrave.com/us; The Statesman's Yearbook, 2023.

CAMBODIA-COAL PRODUCTION

See CAMBODIA-MINERAL INDUSTRIES

CAMBODIA-COMMERCE

Palgrave Macmillan, 1 New York Plaza, Ste. 4500, New York, NY, 10004-1562, USA, (800) 777-4643, orders@palgrave.com, https://www.palgrave.com/us; The Statesman's Yearbook, 2023.

UK Data Service, University of Essex, Wivenhoe Park, Colchester, Essex, CO4 3SQ, GBR, https://ukdataservice.ac.uk/; International Aggregate Data.

CAMBODIA-COMMODITY EXCHANGES

Barchart, 209 W Jackson Blvd., 2nd Fl., Chicago, IL, 60606, USA, (877) 247-4394, commodities@barchart.com, https://www.barchart.com/cmdty; The cmdty Yearbook 2023; cmdtyStats: Commodity Statistics and Fundamental Data; cmdtyView: Commodity Index; and Commodity Data and Prices.

International Monetary Fund (IMF), 700 19th St. NW, Washington, DC, 20431, USA, (202) 623-7000, (202) 623-4661, publications@imf.org, https://www.imf.org; IMF Primary Commodity Prices.

CAMBODIA-CONSUMER PRICE INDEXES

The World Bank, 1818 H St. NW, Washington, DC, 20433, USA, (202) 473-1000, (202) 477-6391, eds03@worldbank.org, https://www.worldbank.org/; Cambodia (report).

CAMBODIA-CORN INDUSTRY

See CAMBODIA-CROPS

CAMBODIA-COTTON

See CAMBODIA-CROPS

CAMBODIA-CROPS

Palgrave Macmillan, 1 New York Plaza, Ste. 4500, New York, NY, 10004-1562, USA, (800) 777-4643, orders@palgrave.com, https://www.palgrave.com/us; The Statesman's Yearbook, 2023.

United Nations Food and Agricultural Organization (FAO), 2121 K St., Ste. 800B, Washington, DC, 20037, USA, (202) 653-2400 (Dial from U.S.), (202) 653-5760 (Fax from U.S.), fao-hq@fao.org, https://www.fao.org; The State of Food and Agriculture (SOFA) 2022.

United Nations Statistics Division (UNSD), United Nations Plz., New York, NY, 10017, USA, (800) 253-9646, (212) 963-9851, statistics@un.org, https://unstats.un.org; Statistical Yearbook of the United Nations 2021.

CAMBODIA-DAIRY PROCESSING

Palgrave Macmillan, 1 New York Plaza, Ste. 4500, New York, NY, 10004-1562, USA, (800) 777-4643, orders@palgrave.com, https://www.palgrave.com/us; The Statesman's Yearbook, 2023.

United Nations Food and Agricultural Organization (FAO), 2121 K St., Ste. 800B, Washington, DC, 20037, USA, (202) 653-2400 (Dial from U.S.), (202) 653-5760 (Fax from U.S.), fao-hq@fao.org, https://www.fao.org; The State of Food and Agriculture (SOFA) 2022.

CAMBODIA-DEBTS, EXTERNAL

The World Bank, 1818 H St. NW, Washington, DC, 20433, USA, (202) 473-1000, (202) 477-6391, eds03@worldbank.org, https://www.worldbank.org/; Global Financial Development Report 2019-2020: Bank Regulation and Supervision a Decade after the Global Financial Crisis.

CAMBODIA-DEFENSE EXPENDITURES

See CAMBODIA-ARMED FORCES

CAMBODIA-ECONOMIC ASSISTANCE

United Nations Statistics Division (UNSD), United Nations Plz., New York, NY, 10017, USA, (800) 253-9646, (212) 963-9851, statistics@un.org, https://unstats.un.org; Statistical Yearbook of the United Nations 2021.

CAMBODIA-ECONOMIC CONDITIONS

Bernan Press, 15250 NBN Way, Bldg. C, Blue Ridge Summit, PA, 17214, USA, (301) 459-2255, (800) 865-3457, (800) 865-3450, customercare@bernan.com, https://rowman.com/Page/Bernan; World Economic Outlook, April 2022.

Central Intelligence Agency (CIA), Office of Public Affairs, Washington, DC, 20505, USA, (703) 482-0623, https://www.cia.gov; The World Factbook.

Council for the Development of Cambodia (CDC), Government Palace, Sisowath Quay, Wat Phnom, Phnom Penh, CMB, info@cdc.gov.kh, https://cdc.gov.kh/; unpublished data.

The Economist Group: Economist Intelligence Unit (EIU), 900 3rd Ave., 16th Fl., New York, NY, 10022, USA, (212) 541-0500, americas@eiu.com, https://www.eiu.com; Cambodia Country Report.

Euromonitor International, Inc., 1 N Dearborn St., Ste. 1700, Chicago, IL, 60602, USA, (312) 922-1115, (312) 922-1157, info-usa@euromonitor.com, https://www.euromonitor.com/; Geographies.

International Monetary Fund (IMF), 700 19th St. NW, Washington, DC, 20431, USA, (202) 623-7000, (202) 623-4661, publications@imf.org, https://www.imf.org; IMF Data and World Economic Outlook.

National Bank of Cambodia (NBC), 22-24 Norodom Blvd., Phnom Penh, CMB, info@nbc.org.kh, https://www.nbc.org.kh/english/; Annual Report 2021 and Economic and Monetary Statistics.

Palgrave Macmillan, 1 New York Plaza, Ste. 4500, New York, NY, 10004-1562, USA, (800) 777-4643, orders@palgrave.com, https://www.palgrave.com/us; The Statesman's Yearbook, 2023.

Routledge - Taylor & Francis Group, 6000 Broken Sound Pkwy. NW, Ste. 300, Boca Raton, FL, 33487, USA, (800) 634-1420, (800) 634-7064, orders@taylorandfrancis.com, https://www.routledge.com/; The Europa World Year Book 2022.

United Nations Statistics Division (UNSD), United Nations Plz., New York, NY, 10017, USA, (800) 253-9646, (212) 963-9851, statistics@un.org, https://unstats.un.org; World Statistics Pocketbook 2021.

The World Bank, 1818 H St. NW, Washington, DC, 20433, USA, (202) 473-1000, (202) 477-6391, eds03@worldbank.org, https://www.worldbank.org/; Cambodia (report); Global Economic Monitor (GEM); Global Economic Prospects, June 2022; and The Global Findex Database 2021.

CAMBODIA-EDUCATION

Euromonitor International, Inc., 1 N Dearborn St., Ste. 1700, Chicago, IL, 60602, USA, (312) 922-1115, (312) 922-1157, info-usa@euromonitor.com, https://www.euromonitor.com/; Geographies.

Infoplease, c/o Sandbox Networks, Inc., 1 Lincoln St., 24th Fl., Boston, MA, 02111, USA, https://www.infoplease.com; Countries of the World.

Palgrave Macmillan, 1 New York Plaza, Ste. 4500, New York, NY, 10004-1562, USA, (800) 777-4643, orders@palgrave.com, https://www.palgrave.com/us; The Statesman's Yearbook, 2023.

Routledge - Taylor & Francis Group, 6000 Broken Sound Pkwy. NW, Ste. 300, Boca Raton, FL, 33487, USA, (800) 634-1420, (800) 634-7064, orders@taylorandfrancis.com, https://www.routledge.com/; The Europa World Year Book 2022.

UNESCO Institute for Statistics, C.P 250 Succursale H, Montreal, QC, H3G 2K8, CAN, (514) 343-6880 (Dial from U.S.), (514) 343-5740 (Fax from U.S.), uis.publications@unesco.org, http://uis.unesco.org/; Literacy.

United Nations Economic and Social Commission for Asia and the Pacific (ESCAP), United Nations Building, Rajadamnern Nok Ave., Bangkok, 10200, THA, https://www.unescap.org/; Asia-Pacific Development Journal and SDG Gateway Data Explorer.

United Nations Statistics Division (UNSD), United Nations Plz., New York, NY, 10017, USA, (800) 253-9646, (212) 963-9851, statistics@un.org, https://unstats.un.org; Millennium Development Goal Indicators.

The World Bank, 1818 H St. NW, Washington, DC, 20433, USA, (202) 473-1000, (202) 477-6391, eds03@worldbank.org, https://www.worldbank.org/; Cambodia (report).

CAMBODIA-ELECTRICITY

Central Intelligence Agency (CIA), Office of Public Affairs, Washington, DC, 20505, USA, (703) 482-0623, https://www.cia.gov; The World Factbook.

United Nations Statistics Division (UNSD), United Nations Plz., New York, NY, 10017, USA, (800) 253-9646, (212) 963-9851, statistics@un.org, https://unstats.un.org; Statistical Yearbook of the United Nations 2021.

CAMBODIA-EMPLOYMENT

UK Data Service, University of Essex, Wivenhoe Park, Colchester, Essex, CO4 3SQ, GBR, https://ukdataservice.ac.uk/; International Aggregate Data.

United Nations Economic and Social Commission for Asia and the Pacific (ESCAP), United Nations Building, Rajadamnern Nok Ave., Bangkok, 10200, THA, https://www.unescap.org/; Asia-Pacific Development Journal.

The World Bank, 1818 H St. NW, Washington, DC, 20433, USA, (202) 473-1000, (202) 477-6391, eds03@worldbank.org, https://www.worldbank.org/; Cambodia (report).

CAMBODIA-ENVIRONMENTAL CONDITIONS

DSI Data Service & Information, Xantener Strasse 51a, Rheinberg, D-47495, GER, dsi@dsidata.com, https://www.dsidata.com/; Global Environmental Database.

The Economist Group: Economist Intelligence Unit (EIU), 900 3rd Ave., 16th Fl., New York, NY, 10022, USA, (212) 541-0500, americas@eiu.com, https://www.eiu.com; Cambodia Country Report.

International Institute for Environment and Development (IIED), 235 High Holborn, London, WC1V 7DN, GBR, inforequest@iied.org, https://www.iied.org; Environment & Urbanization.

United Nations Statistics Division (UNSD), United Nations Plz., New York, NY, 10017, USA, (800) 253-9646, (212) 963-9851, statistics@un.org, https://unstats.un.org; World Statistics Pocketbook 2021.

CAMBODIA-EXPORTS

Central Intelligence Agency (CIA), Office of Public Affairs, Washington, DC, 20505, USA, (703) 482-0623, https://www.cia.gov; The World Factbook.

The Economist Group: Economist Intelligence Unit (EIU), 900 3rd Ave., 16th Fl., New York, NY, 10022, USA, (212) 541-0500, americas@eiu.com, https://www.eiu.com; Cambodia Country Report.

International Monetary Fund (IMF), 700 19th St. NW, Washington, DC, 20431, USA, (202) 623-7000, (202) 623-4661, publications@imf.org, https://www.imf.org; Direction of Trade Statistics (DOTS).

S&P Global, IHS Markit, 15 Inverness Way E, Englewood, CO, 80112, USA, (800) 447-2273, (800) 854-7179, https://ihsmarkit.com; Global Trade Atlas (GTA).

United Nations Conference on Trade and Development (UNCTAD), Palais des Nations, Geneva, 1211, SWI, (212) 963-6896, unctadinfo@unctad.org, https://unctad.org; Handbook of Statistics 2021.

CAMBODIA-FEMALE WORKING POPULATION

See CAMBODIA-EMPLOYMENT

CAMBODIA-FERTILITY, HUMAN

Central Intelligence Agency (CIA), Office of Public Affairs, Washington, DC, 20505, USA, (703) 482-0623, https://www.cia.gov; The World Factbook.

CAMBODIA-FERTILIZER INDUSTRY

United Nations Food and Agricultural Organization (FAO), 2121 K St., Ste. 800B, Washington, DC, 20037, USA, (202) 653-2400 (Dial from U.S.), (202) 653-5760 (Fax from U.S.), fao-hq@fao.org, https://www.fao.org; The State of Food and Agriculture (SOFA) 2022.

CAMBODIA-FETAL MORTALITY

See CAMBODIA-MORTALITY

CAMBODIA-FINANCE

Council for the Development of Cambodia (CDC), Government Palace, Sisowath Quay, Wat Phnom, Phnom Penh, CMB, info@cdc.gov.kh, https://cdc.gov.kh/; unpublished data.

National Bank of Cambodia (NBC), 22-24 Norodom Blvd., Phnom Penh, CMB, info@nbc.org.kh, https://www.nbc.org.kh/english/; Annual Report 2021 and Economic and Monetary Statistics.

Stockholm International Peace Research Institute (SIPRI), Signalistgatan 9, Stockholm, SE 169 72, SWE, https://www.sipri.org/; SIPRI Arms Transfers Database and SIPRI Military Expenditure Database.

United Nations Economic and Social Commission for Asia and the Pacific (ESCAP), United Nations Building, Rajadamnern Nok Ave., Bangkok, 10200, THA, https://www.unescap.org/; Asia-Pacific Development Journal and SDG Gateway Data Explorer.

United Nations Statistics Division (UNSD), United Nations Plz., New York, NY, 10017, USA, (800) 253-9646, (212) 963-9851, statistics@un.org, https://unstats.un.org; Statistical Yearbook of the United Nations 2021.

The World Bank, 1818 H St. NW, Washington, DC, 20433, USA, (202) 473-1000, (202) 477-6391, eds03@worldbank.org, https://www.worldbank.org/; Cambodia (report).

CAMBODIA-FINANCE, PUBLIC

Bernan Press, 15250 NBN Way, Bldg. C, Blue Ridge Summit, PA, 17214, USA, (301) 459-2255, (800) 865-3457, (800) 865-3450, customercare@bernan.com, https://rowman.com/Page/Bernan; National Accounts Statistics: Analysis of Main Aggregates 2020.

The Economist Group: Economist Intelligence Unit (EIU), 900 3rd Ave., 16th Fl., New York, NY, 10022, USA, (212) 541-0500, americas@eiu.com, https://www.eiu.com; Cambodia Country Report.

International Monetary Fund (IMF), 700 19th St. NW, Washington, DC, 20431, USA, (202) 623-7000, (202) 623-4661, publications@imf.org, https://www.imf.org; Regional Economic Outlook.

Palgrave Macmillan, 1 New York Plaza, Ste. 4500, New York, NY, 10004-1562, USA, (800) 777-4643, orders@palgrave.com, https://www.palgrave.com/us; The Statesman's Yearbook, 2023.

Routledge - Taylor & Francis Group, 6000 Broken Sound Pkwy. NW, Ste. 300, Boca Raton, FL, 33487,

USA, (800) 634-1420, (800) 634-7064, orders@taylorandfrancis.com, https://www.routledge.com/; The Europa World Year Book 2022.

United Nations Economic and Social Commission for Asia and the Pacific (ESCAP), United Nations Building, Rajadamnern Nok Ave., Bangkok, 10200, THA, https://www.unescap.org/; SDG Gateway Data Explorer.

United Nations Statistics Division (UNSD), United Nations Plz., New York, NY, 10017, USA, (800) 253-9646, (212) 963-9851, statistics@un.org, https://unstats.un.org; National Accounts Main Aggregates Database and National Accounts Statistics: Main Aggregates and Detailed Tables.

The World Bank, 1818 H St. NW, Washington, DC, 20433, USA, (202) 473-1000, (202) 477-6391, eds03@worldbank.org, https://www.worldbank.org/; Cambodia (report).

CAMBODIA-FISHERIES

Palgrave Macmillan, 1 New York Plaza, Ste. 4500, New York, NY, 10004-1562, USA, (800) 777-4643, orders@palgrave.com, https://www.palgrave.com/us; The Statesman's Yearbook, 2023.

Routledge - Taylor & Francis Group, 6000 Broken Sound Pkwy. NW, Ste. 300, Boca Raton, FL, 33487, USA, (800) 634-1420, (800) 634-7064, orders@taylorandfrancis.com, https://www.routledge.com/; The Europa World Year Book 2022.

United Nations Food and Agricultural Organization (FAO), 2121 K St., Ste. 800B, Washington, DC, 20037, USA, (202) 653-2400 (Dial from U.S.), (202) 653-5760 (Fax from U.S.), fao-hq@fao.org, https://www.fao.org; The State of Food and Agriculture (SOFA) 2022.

United Nations Statistics Division (UNSD), United Nations Plz., New York, NY, 10017, USA, (800) 253-9646, (212) 963-9851, statistics@un.org, https://unstats.un.org; Statistical Yearbook of the United Nations 2021.

The World Bank, 1818 H St. NW, Washington, DC, 20433, USA, (202) 473-1000, (202) 477-6391, eds03@worldbank.org, https://www.worldbank.org/; Cambodia (report).

CAMBODIA-FOOD

United Nations Economic and Social Commission for Asia and the Pacific (ESCAP), United Nations Building, Rajadamnern Nok Ave., Bangkok, 10200, THA, https://www.unescap.org/; SDG Gateway Data Explorer.

United Nations Food and Agricultural Organization (FAO), 2121 K St., Ste. 800B, Washington, DC, 20037, USA, (202) 653-2400 (Dial from U.S.), (202) 653-5760 (Fax from U.S.), fao-hq@fao.org, https://www.fao.org; The State of Food and Agriculture (SOFA) 2022.

CAMBODIA-FORESTS AND FORESTRY

Palgrave Macmillan, 1 New York Plaza, Ste. 4500, New York, NY, 10004-1562, USA, (800) 777-4643, orders@palgrave.com, https://www.palgrave.com/us; The Statesman's Yearbook, 2023.

Routledge - Taylor & Francis Group, 6000 Broken Sound Pkwy. NW, Ste. 300, Boca Raton, FL, 33487, USA, (800) 634-1420, (800) 634-7064, orders@taylorandfrancis.com, https://www.routledge.com/; The Europa World Year Book 2022.

UNESCO Institute for Statistics, C.P 250 Succursale H, Montreal, QC, H3G 2K8, CAN, (514) 343-6880 (Dial from U.S.), (514) 343-5740 (Fax from U.S.), uis.publications@unesco.org, http://uis.unesco.org/; UIS.Stat.

United Nations Food and Agricultural Organization (FAO), 2121 K St., Ste. 800B, Washington, DC, 20037, USA, (202) 653-2400 (Dial from U.S.), (202) 653-5760 (Fax from U.S.), fao-hq@fao.org, https://www.fao.org; FAO Yearbook of Forest Products 2019 and The State of Food and Agriculture (SOFA) 2022.

United Nations Statistics Division (UNSD), United Nations Plz., New York, NY, 10017, USA, (800) 253-9646, (212) 963-9851, statistics@un.org, https://unstats.un.org; Statistical Yearbook of the United Nations 2021.

The World Bank, 1818 H St. NW, Washington, DC, 20433, USA, (202) 473-1000, (202) 477-6391, eds03@worldbank.org, https://www.worldbank.org/; Cambodia (report).

CAMBODIA-GROSS DOMESTIC PRODUCT

The Economist Group: Economist Intelligence Unit (EIU), 900 3rd Ave., 16th Fl., New York, NY, 10022, USA, (212) 541-0500, americas@eiu.com, https://www.eiu.com; Cambodia Country Report.

United Nations Statistics Division (UNSD), United Nations Plz., New York, NY, 10017, USA, (800) 253-9646, (212) 963-9851, statistics@un.org, https://unstats.un.org; Statistical Yearbook of the United Nations 2021.

CAMBODIA-GROSS NATIONAL PRODUCT

Palgrave Macmillan, 1 New York Plaza, Ste. 4500, New York, NY, 10004-1562, USA, (800) 777-4643, orders@palgrave.com, https://www.palgrave.com/us; The Statesman's Yearbook, 2023.

United Nations Statistics Division (UNSD), United Nations Plz., New York, NY, 10017, USA, (800) 253-9646, (212) 963-9851, statistics@un.org, https://unstats.un.org; Statistical Yearbook of the United Nations 2021.

CAMBODIA-HOUSING

Euromonitor International, Inc., 1 N Dearborn St., Ste. 1700, Chicago, IL, 60602, USA, (312) 922-1115, (312) 922-1157, info-usa@euromonitor.com, https://www.euromonitor.com/; Geographies.

CAMBODIA-ILLITERATE PERSONS

UNESCO Institute for Statistics, C.P 250 Succursale H, Montreal, QC, H3G 2K8, CAN, (514) 343-6880 (Dial from U.S.), (514) 343-5740 (Fax from U.S.), uis.publications@unesco.org, http://uis.unesco.org/; UIS.Stat.

United Nations Economic and Social Commission for Asia and the Pacific (ESCAP), United Nations Building, Rajadamnern Nok Ave., Bangkok, 10200, THA, https://www.unescap.org/; Asia-Pacific Development Journal.

CAMBODIA-IMPORTS

Central Intelligence Agency (CIA), Office of Public Affairs, Washington, DC, 20505, USA, (703) 482-0623, https://www.cia.gov; The World Factbook.

The Economist Group: Economist Intelligence Unit (EIU), 900 3rd Ave., 16th Fl., New York, NY, 10022, USA, (212) 541-0500, americas@eiu.com, https://www.eiu.com; Cambodia Country Report.

International Monetary Fund (IMF), 700 19th St. NW, Washington, DC, 20431, USA, (202) 623-7000, (202) 623-4661, publications@imf.org, https://www.imf.org; Direction of Trade Statistics (DOTS).

S&P Global, IHS Markit, 15 Inverness Way E, Englewood, CO, 80112, USA, (800) 447-2273, (800) 854-7179, https://ihsmarkit.com; Global Trade Atlas (GTA).

United Nations Conference on Trade and Development (UNCTAD), Palais des Nations, Geneva, 1211, SWI, (212) 963-6896, unctadinfo@unctad.org, https://unctad.org; Handbook of Statistics 2021.

CAMBODIA-INDUSTRIES

Central Intelligence Agency (CIA), Office of Public Affairs, Washington, DC, 20505, USA, (703) 482-0623, https://www.cia.gov; The World Factbook.

Council for the Development of Cambodia (CDC), Government Palace, Sisowath Quay, Wat Phnom, Phnom Penh, CMB, info@cdc.gov.kh, https://cdc.gov.kh/; unpublished data.

The Economist Group: Economist Intelligence Unit (EIU), 900 3rd Ave., 16th Fl., New York, NY, 10022, USA, (212) 541-0500, americas@eiu.com, https://www.eiu.com; Cambodia Country Report.

Euromonitor International, Inc., 1 N Dearborn St., Ste. 1700, Chicago, IL, 60602, USA, (312) 922-1115, (312) 922-1157, info-usa@euromonitor.com, https://www.euromonitor.com/; Geographies.

Palgrave Macmillan, 1 New York Plaza, Ste. 4500, New York, NY, 10004-1562, USA, (800) 777-4643, orders@palgrave.com, https://www.palgrave.com/us; The Statesman's Yearbook, 2023.

Routledge - Taylor & Francis Group, 6000 Broken Sound Pkwy. NW, Ste. 300, Boca Raton, FL, 33487, USA, (800) 634-1420, (800) 634-7064, orders@taylorandfrancis.com, https://www.routledge.com/; The Europa World Year Book 2022.

United Nations Economic and Social Commission for Asia and the Pacific (ESCAP), United Nations Building, Rajadamnern Nok Ave., Bangkok, 10200, THA, https://www.unescap.org/; Asia-Pacific Development Journal and SDG Gateway Data Explorer.

United Nations Industrial Development Organization (UNIDO), 1 United Nations Plz., Rm. DC1-1118, New York, NY, 10017, USA, (212) 963-6890, (212) 963 6885, (212) 963-7904, office.newyork@unido.org, https://www.unido.org/; Industrial Statistics Databases and International Yearbook of Industrial Statistics 2021.

The World Bank, 1818 H St. NW, Washington, DC, 20433, USA, (202) 473-1000, (202) 477-6391, eds03@worldbank.org, https://www.worldbank.org/; Cambodia (report).

CAMBODIA-INFANT AND MATERNAL MORTALITY

See CAMBODIA-MORTALITY

CAMBODIA-INTERNATIONAL TRADE

The Economist Group: Economist Intelligence Unit (EIU), 900 3rd Ave., 16th Fl., New York, NY, 10022, USA, (212) 541-0500, americas@eiu.com, https://www.eiu.com; Cambodia Country Report.

Euromonitor International, Inc., 1 N Dearborn St., Ste. 1700, Chicago, IL, 60602, USA, (312) 922-1115, (312) 922-1157, info-usa@euromonitor.com, https://www.euromonitor.com/; Geographies.

Palgrave Macmillan, 1 New York Plaza, Ste. 4500, New York, NY, 10004-1562, USA, (800) 777-4643, orders@palgrave.com, https://www.palgrave.com/us; The Statesman's Yearbook, 2023.

Routledge - Taylor & Francis Group, 6000 Broken Sound Pkwy. NW, Ste. 300, Boca Raton, FL, 33487, USA, (800) 634-1420, (800) 634-7064, orders@taylorandfrancis.com, https://www.routledge.com/; The Europa World Year Book 2022.

United Nations Conference on Trade and Development (UNCTAD), Palais des Nations, Geneva, 1211, SWI, (212) 963-6896, unctadinfo@unctad.org, https://unctad.org; Trade and Development Report 2021.

United Nations Economic and Social Commission for Asia and the Pacific (ESCAP), United Nations Building, Rajadamnern Nok Ave., Bangkok, 10200, THA, https://www.unescap.org/; Asia-Pacific Development Journal and SDG Gateway Data Explorer.

United Nations Food and Agricultural Organization (FAO), 2121 K St., Ste. 800B, Washington, DC, 20037, USA, (202) 653-2400 (Dial from U.S.), (202) 653-5760 (Fax from U.S.), fao-hq@fao.org, https://www.fao.org; The State of Food and Agriculture (SOFA) 2022.

United Nations Statistics Division (UNSD), United Nations Plz., New York, NY, 10017, USA, (800) 253-9646, (212) 963-9851, statistics@un.org, https://unstats.un.org; International Trade Statistics Yearbook 2020 and Statistical Yearbook of the United Nations 2021.

The World Bank, 1818 H St. NW, Washington, DC, 20433, USA, (202) 473-1000, (202) 477-6391, eds03@worldbank.org, https://www.worldbank.org/; Cambodia (report).

World Trade Organization (WTO), Ctre. William Rappard, Rue de Lausanne 154, Case postale, Geneva, CH-1211, SWI, enquiries@wto.org, https://www.wto.org; World Trade Statistical Review 2022.

CAMBODIA-INTERNET USERS

International Telecommunication Union (ITU), Place des Nations, Geneva, CH-1211, SWI, itumail@itu.int, https://www.itu.int; Global Connectivity Report 2022; World Telecommunication/ICT Indicators Database 2021; and Yearbook of Statistics 2019.

The World Bank, 1818 H St. NW, Washington, DC, 20433, USA, (202) 473-1000, (202) 477-6391, eds03@worldbank.org, https://www.worldbank.org/; Cambodia (report).

CAMBODIA-LABOR

Central Intelligence Agency (CIA), Office of Public Affairs, Washington, DC, 20505, USA, (703) 482-0623, https://www.cia.gov; The World Factbook.

Euromonitor International, Inc., 1 N Dearborn St., Ste. 1700, Chicago, IL, 60602, USA, (312) 922-1115, (312) 922-1157, info-usa@euromonitor.com, https://www.euromonitor.com/; Geographies.

Palgrave Macmillan, 1 New York Plaza, Ste. 4500, New York, NY, 10004-1562, USA, (800) 777-4643, orders@palgrave.com, https://www.palgrave.com/us; The Statesman's Yearbook, 2023.

United Nations Food and Agricultural Organization (FAO), 2121 K St., Ste. 800B, Washington, DC, 20037, USA, (202) 653-2400 (Dial from U.S.), (202) 653-5760 (Fax from U.S.), fao-hq@fao.org, https://www.fao.org; The State of Food and Agriculture (SOFA) 2022.

CAMBODIA-LAND USE

United Nations Statistics Division (UNSD), United Nations Plz., New York, NY, 10017, USA, (800) 253-9646, (212) 963-9851, statistics@un.org, https://unstats.un.org; Millennium Development Goal Indicators.

CAMBODIA-LIFE EXPECTANCY

Central Intelligence Agency (CIA), Office of Public Affairs, Washington, DC, 20505, USA, (703) 482-0623, https://www.cia.gov; The World Factbook.

United Nations Department of Economic and Social Affairs (DESA), Population Division, 2 United Nations Plz., Rm. DC2-1950, New York, NY, 10017, USA, (212) 963-3209, (212) 963-2147, population@un.org, https://www.un.org/development/desa/pd/; World Population Ageing 2020 Highlights.

United Nations Economic and Social Commission for Asia and the Pacific (ESCAP), United Nations Building, Rajadamnern Nok Ave., Bangkok, 10200, THA, https://www.unescap.org/; Asia-Pacific Development Journal.

United Nations Statistics Division (UNSD), United Nations Plz., New York, NY, 10017, USA, (800) 253-9646, (212) 963-9851, statistics@un.org, https://unstats.un.org; Millennium Development Goal Indicators.

CAMBODIA-LITERACY

Euromonitor International, Inc., 1 N Dearborn St., Ste. 1700, Chicago, IL, 60602, USA, (312) 922-1115, (312) 922-1157, info-usa@euromonitor.com, https://www.euromonitor.com/; Geographies.

UNESCO Institute for Statistics, C.P 250 Succursale H, Montreal, QC, H3G 2K8, CAN, (514) 343-6880 (Dial from U.S.), (514) 343-5740 (Fax from U.S.), uis.publications@unesco.org, http://uis.unesco.org/; Literacy.

CAMBODIA-LIVESTOCK

Palgrave Macmillan, 1 New York Plaza, Ste. 4500, New York, NY, 10004-1562, USA, (800) 777-4643, orders@palgrave.com, https://www.palgrave.com/us; The Statesman's Yearbook, 2023.

Routledge - Taylor & Francis Group, 6000 Broken Sound Pkwy. NW, Ste. 300, Boca Raton, FL, 33487, USA, (800) 634-1420, (800) 634-7064, orders@taylorandfrancis.com, https://www.routledge.com/; The Europa World Year Book 2022.

United Nations Food and Agricultural Organization (FAO), 2121 K St., Ste. 800B, Washington, DC, 20037, USA, (202) 653-2400 (Dial from U.S.), (202) 653-5760 (Fax from U.S.), fao-hq@fao.org, https://www.fao.org; The State of Food and Agriculture (SOFA) 2022.

United Nations Statistics Division (UNSD), United Nations Plz., New York, NY, 10017, USA, (800) 253-9646, (212) 963-9851, statistics@un.org, https://unstats.un.org; Statistical Yearbook of the United Nations 2021.

CAMBODIA-MANPOWER

United Nations Economic and Social Commission for Asia and the Pacific (ESCAP), United Nations Building, Rajadamnern Nok Ave., Bangkok, 10200, THA, https://www.unescap.org/; SDG Gateway Data Explorer.

CAMBODIA-MINERAL INDUSTRIES

Palgrave Macmillan, 1 New York Plaza, Ste. 4500, New York, NY, 10004-1562, USA, (800) 777-4643, orders@palgrave.com, https://www.palgrave.com/us; The Statesman's Yearbook, 2023.

Routledge - Taylor & Francis Group, 6000 Broken Sound Pkwy. NW, Ste. 300, Boca Raton, FL, 33487, USA, (800) 634-1420, (800) 634-7064, orders@taylorandfrancis.com, https://www.routledge.com/; The Europa World Year Book 2022.

United Nations Conference on Trade and Development (UNCTAD), Palais des Nations, Geneva, 1211, SWI, (212) 963-6896, unctadinfo@unctad.org, https://unctad.org; Trade and Development Report 2021.

United Nations Statistics Division (UNSD), United Nations Plz., New York, NY, 10017, USA, (800) 253-9646, (212) 963-9851, statistics@un.org, https://unstats.un.org; Statistical Yearbook of the United Nations 2021.

The World Bank, 1818 H St. NW, Washington, DC, 20433, USA, (202) 473-1000, (202) 477-6391, eds03@worldbank.org, https://www.worldbank.org/; Cambodia (report).

CAMBODIA-MONEY SUPPLY

The Economist Group: Economist Intelligence Unit (EIU), 900 3rd Ave., 16th Fl., New York, NY, 10022, USA, (212) 541-0500, americas@eiu.com, https://www.eiu.com; Cambodia Country Report.

The World Bank, 1818 H St. NW, Washington, DC, 20433, USA, (202) 473-1000, (202) 477-6391, eds03@worldbank.org, https://www.worldbank.org/; Cambodia (report).

CAMBODIA-MORTALITY

UNICEF, 3 United Nations Plz., New York, NY, 10017, USA, (212) 303-7984, (917) 244-2215, https://www.unicef.org; The State of the World's Children 2023.

United Nations Economic and Social Commission for Asia and the Pacific (ESCAP), United Nations Building, Rajadamnern Nok Ave., Bangkok, 10200, THA, https://www.unescap.org/; Asia-Pacific Development Journal.

United Nations Statistics Division (UNSD), United Nations Plz., New York, NY, 10017, USA, (800) 253-9646, (212) 963-9851, statistics@un.org, https://unstats.un.org; Millennium Development Goal Indicators; Statistical Yearbook of the United Nations 2021; and World Statistics Pocketbook 2021.

World Health Organization (WHO), Ave. Appia 20, Geneva, CH-1211, SWI, (202) 974-3000 (Telephone in U.S.), publications@who.int, https://www.who.int/; Global Health Observatory (GHO).

CAMBODIA-NUTRITION

United Nations Food and Agricultural Organization (FAO), 2121 K St., Ste. 800B, Washington, DC, 20037, USA, (202) 653-2400 (Dial from U.S.), (202) 653-5760 (Fax from U.S.), fao-hq@fao.org, https://www.fao.org; The State of Food and Agriculture (SOFA) 2022.

United Nations Statistics Division (UNSD), United Nations Plz., New York, NY, 10017, USA, (800) 253-9646, (212) 963-9851, statistics@un.org, https://unstats.un.org; Millennium Development Goal Indicators.

CAMBODIA-PAPER

See CAMBODIA-FORESTS AND FORESTRY

CAMBODIA-PESTICIDES

United Nations Food and Agricultural Organization (FAO), 2121 K St., Ste. 800B, Washington, DC, 20037, USA, (202) 653-2400 (Dial from U.S.), (202) 653-5760 (Fax from U.S.), fao-hq@fao.org, https://www.fao.org; The State of Food and Agriculture (SOFA) 2022.

CAMBODIA-PETROLEUM INDUSTRY AND TRADE

Palgrave Macmillan, 1 New York Plaza, Ste. 4500, New York, NY, 10004-1562, USA, (800) 777-4643, orders@palgrave.com, https://www.palgrave.com/us; The Statesman's Yearbook, 2023.

United Nations Food and Agricultural Organization (FAO), 2121 K St., Ste. 800B, Washington, DC, 20037, USA, (202) 653-2400 (Dial from U.S.), (202) 653-5760 (Fax from U.S.), fao-hq@fao.org, https://www.fao.org; The State of Food and Agriculture (SOFA) 2022.

United Nations Statistics Division (UNSD), United Nations Plz., New York, NY, 10017, USA, (800) 253-9646, (212) 963-9851, statistics@un.org, https://unstats.un.org; Statistical Yearbook of the United Nations 2021.

CAMBODIA-POPULATION

Central Intelligence Agency (CIA), Office of Public Affairs, Washington, DC, 20505, USA, (703) 482-0623, https://www.cia.gov; The World Factbook.

The Economist Group: Economist Intelligence Unit (EIU), 900 3rd Ave., 16th Fl., New York, NY, 10022, USA, (212) 541-0500, americas@eiu.com, https://www.eiu.com; Cambodia Country Report.

Infoplease, c/o Sandbox Networks, Inc., 1 Lincoln St., 24th Fl., Boston, MA, 02111, USA, https://www.infoplease.com; Countries of the World.

Palgrave Macmillan, 1 New York Plaza, Ste. 4500, New York, NY, 10004-1562, USA, (800) 777-4643, orders@palgrave.com, https://www.palgrave.com/us; The Statesman's Yearbook, 2023.

Routledge - Taylor & Francis Group, 6000 Broken Sound Pkwy. NW, Ste. 300, Boca Raton, FL, 33487, USA, (800) 634-1420, (800) 634-7064, orders@taylorandfrancis.com, https://www.routledge.com/; The Europa World Year Book 2022.

UK Data Service, University of Essex, Wivenhoe Park, Colchester, Essex, CO4 3SQ, GBR, https://ukdataservice.ac.uk/; International Aggregate Data.

United Nations Department of Economic and Social Affairs (DESA), Population Division, 2 United Nations Plz., Rm. DC2-1950, New York, NY, 10017, USA, (212) 963-3209, (212) 963-2147, population@un.org, https://www.un.org/development/desa/pd/; Revision of World Urbanization Prospects and World Population Ageing 2020 Highlights.

United Nations Development Programme (UNDP), One United Nations Plz., New York, NY, 10017, USA, (212) 906-5000, (212) 906-5001, https://www.undp.org; Human Development Report 2021-2022.

United Nations Economic and Social Commission for Asia and the Pacific (ESCAP), United Nations Building, Rajadamnern Nok Ave., Bangkok, 10200, THA, https://www.unescap.org/; Asia-Pacific Development Journal and SDG Gateway Data Explorer.

United Nations Statistics Division (UNSD), United Nations Plz., New York, NY, 10017, USA, (800) 253-

9646, (212) 963-9851, statistics@un.org, https://unstats.un.org; Statistical Yearbook of the United Nations 2021 and World Statistics Pocketbook 2021.

The World Bank, 1818 H St. NW, Washington, DC, 20433, USA, (202) 473-1000, (202) 477-6391, eds03@worldbank.org, https://www.worldbank.org/; Cambodia (report) and The Global Findex Database 2021.

CAMBODIA-POPULATION DENSITY

Central Intelligence Agency (CIA), Office of Public Affairs, Washington, DC, 20505, USA, (703) 482-0623, https://www.cia.gov; The World Factbook.

Palgrave Macmillan, 1 New York Plaza, Ste. 4500, New York, NY, 10004-1562, USA, (800) 777-4643, orders@palgrave.com, https://www.palgrave.com/us; The Statesman's Yearbook, 2023.

Routledge - Taylor & Francis Group, 6000 Broken Sound Pkwy. NW, Ste. 300, Boca Raton, FL, 33487, USA, (800) 634-1420, (800) 634-7064, orders@taylorandfrancis.com, https://www.routledge.com/; The Europa World Year Book 2022.

CAMBODIA-POULTRY

See CAMBODIA-LIVESTOCK

CAMBODIA-POWER RESOURCES

Euromonitor International, Inc., 1 N Dearborn St., Ste. 1700, Chicago, IL, 60602, USA, (312) 922-1115, (312) 922-1157, info-usa@euromonitor.com, https://www.euromonitor.com/; Geographies.

United Nations Economic and Social Commission for Asia and the Pacific (ESCAP), United Nations Building, Rajadamnern Nok Ave., Bangkok, 10200, THA, https://www.unescap.org/; Asia-Pacific Development Journal.

United Nations Food and Agricultural Organization (FAO), 2121 K St., Ste. 800B, Washington, DC, 20037, USA, (202) 653-2400 (Dial from U.S.), (202) 653-5760 (Fax from U.S.), fao-hq@fao.org, https://www.fao.org; The State of Food and Agriculture (SOFA) 2022.

United Nations Statistics Division (UNSD), United Nations Plz., New York, NY, 10017, USA, (800) 253-9646, (212) 963-9851, statistics@un.org, https://unstats.un.org; Energy Statistics Yearbook 2019; Statistical Yearbook of the United Nations 2021; and World Statistics Pocketbook 2021.

CAMBODIA-PRICES

Euromonitor International, Inc., 1 N Dearborn St., Ste. 1700, Chicago, IL, 60602, USA, (312) 922-1115, (312) 922-1157, info-usa@euromonitor.com, https://www.euromonitor.com/; Geographies.

The World Bank, 1818 H St. NW, Washington, DC, 20433, USA, (202) 473-1000, (202) 477-6391, eds03@worldbank.org, https://www.worldbank.org/; Cambodia (report).

CAMBODIA-PUBLIC HEALTH

Euromonitor International, Inc., 1 N Dearborn St., Ste. 1700, Chicago, IL, 60602, USA, (312) 922-1115, (312) 922-1157, info-usa@euromonitor.com, https://www.euromonitor.com/; Geographies.

Palgrave Macmillan, 1 New York Plaza, Ste. 4500, New York, NY, 10004-1562, USA, (800) 777-4643, orders@palgrave.com, https://www.palgrave.com/us; The Statesman's Yearbook, 2023.

U.S. Census Bureau, 4600 Silver Hill Rd., Washington, DC, 20233, USA, (301) 763-4636, (800) 923-8282, https://www.census.gov; HIV/AIDS Surveillance Data Base.

UNICEF, 3 United Nations Plz., New York, NY, 10017, USA, (212) 303-7984, (917) 244-2215, https://www.unicef.org; The State of the World's Children 2023.

United Nations Department of Economic and Social Affairs (DESA), Population Division, 2 United Nations Plz., Rm. DC2-1950, New York, NY, 10017, USA, (212) 963-3209, (212) 963-2147, population@un.org, https://www.un.org/development/desa/pd/; World Fertility Data 2019.

United Nations Development Programme (UNDP), One United Nations Plz., New York, NY, 10017, USA, (212) 906-5000, (212) 906-5001, https://www.undp.org; Human Development Report 2021-2022.

United Nations Economic and Social Commission for Asia and the Pacific (ESCAP), United Nations Building, Rajadamnern Nok Ave., Bangkok, 10200, THA, https://www.unescap.org/; Asia-Pacific Development Journal.

United Nations Statistics Division (UNSD), United Nations Plz., New York, NY, 10017, USA, (800) 253-9646, (212) 963-9851, statistics@un.org, https://unstats.un.org; Millennium Development Goal Indicators and Statistical Yearbook of the United Nations 2021.

The World Bank, 1818 H St. NW, Washington, DC, 20433, USA, (202) 473-1000, (202) 477-6391, eds03@worldbank.org, https://www.worldbank.org/; Cambodia (report).

World Health Organization (WHO), Ave. Appia 20, Geneva, CH-1211, SWI, (202) 974-3000 (Telephone in U.S.), publications@who.int, https://www.who.int/; Global Health Observatory (GHO).

CAMBODIA-RAILROADS

Janes, USA, (703) 574-7580, (888) 977-1519, customer.care@janes.com, https://www.janes.com; Janes World Railways 2021-2022.

Palgrave Macmillan, 1 New York Plaza, Ste. 4500, New York, NY, 10004-1562, USA, (800) 777-4643, orders@palgrave.com, https://www.palgrave.com/us; The Statesman's Yearbook, 2023.

Routledge - Taylor & Francis Group, 6000 Broken Sound Pkwy. NW, Ste. 300, Boca Raton, FL, 33487, USA, (800) 634-1420, (800) 634-7064, orders@taylorandfrancis.com, https://www.routledge.com/; The Europa World Year Book 2022.

United Nations Statistics Division (UNSD), United Nations Plz., New York, NY, 10017, USA, (800) 253-9646, (212) 963-9851, statistics@un.org, https://unstats.un.org; Statistical Yearbook of the United Nations 2021.

CAMBODIA-RELIGION

Central Intelligence Agency (CIA), Office of Public Affairs, Washington, DC, 20505, USA, (703) 482-0623, https://www.cia.gov; The World Factbook.

Palgrave Macmillan, 1 New York Plaza, Ste. 4500, New York, NY, 10004-1562, USA, (800) 777-4643, orders@palgrave.com, https://www.palgrave.com/us; The Statesman's Yearbook, 2023.

CAMBODIA-RETAIL TRADE

Euromonitor International, Inc., 1 N Dearborn St., Ste. 1700, Chicago, IL, 60602, USA, (312) 922-1115, (312) 922-1157, info-usa@euromonitor.com, https://www.euromonitor.com/; Geographies.

CAMBODIA-RICE PRODUCTION

See CAMBODIA-CROPS

CAMBODIA-RUBBER INDUSTRY AND TRADE

International Rubber Study Group (IRSG), 51 Changi Business Park Central 2, Unit No. 6, 486066, SGP, https://www.rubberstudy.org; Monthly Rubber Bulletin (MRB); Rubber Industry Report; Rubber Statistical Bulletin; and World Rubber Industry Report (WRIO).

United Nations Statistics Division (UNSD), United Nations Plz., New York, NY, 10017, USA, (800) 253-9646, (212) 963-9851, statistics@un.org, https://unstats.un.org; Statistical Yearbook of the United Nations 2021.

CAMBODIA-SHIPPING

Routledge - Taylor & Francis Group, 6000 Broken Sound Pkwy. NW, Ste. 300, Boca Raton, FL, 33487, USA, (800) 634-1420, (800) 634-7064, orders@taylorandfrancis.com, https://www.routledge.com/; The Europa World Year Book 2022.

United Nations Statistics Division (UNSD), United Nations Plz., New York, NY, 10017, USA, (800) 253-9646, (212) 963-9851, statistics@un.org, https://unstats.un.org; Statistical Yearbook of the United Nations 2021.

CAMBODIA-SOYBEAN PRODUCTION

See CAMBODIA-CROPS

CAMBODIA-STEEL PRODUCTION

See CAMBODIA-MINERAL INDUSTRIES

CAMBODIA-TELEPHONE

Palgrave Macmillan, 1 New York Plaza, Ste. 4500, New York, NY, 10004-1562, USA, (800) 777-4643, orders@palgrave.com, https://www.palgrave.com/us; The Statesman's Yearbook, 2023.

United Nations Statistics Division (UNSD), United Nations Plz., New York, NY, 10017, USA, (800) 253-9646, (212) 963-9851, statistics@un.org, https://unstats.un.org; World Statistics Pocketbook 2021.

CAMBODIA-TEXTILE FABRICS

United Nations Statistics Division (UNSD), United Nations Plz., New York, NY, 10017, USA, (800) 253-9646, (212) 963-9851, statistics@un.org, https://unstats.un.org; Statistical Yearbook of the United Nations 2021.

CAMBODIA-TOBACCO INDUSTRY

United Nations Statistics Division (UNSD), United Nations Plz., New York, NY, 10017, USA, (800) 253-9646, (212) 963-9851, statistics@un.org, https://unstats.un.org; Statistical Yearbook of the United Nations 2021.

CAMBODIA-TOURISM

Euromonitor International, Inc., 1 N Dearborn St., Ste. 1700, Chicago, IL, 60602, USA, (312) 922-1115, (312) 922-1157, info-usa@euromonitor.com, https://www.euromonitor.com/; Geographies.

The World Bank, 1818 H St. NW, Washington, DC, 20433, USA, (202) 473-1000, (202) 477-6391, eds03@worldbank.org, https://www.worldbank.org/; Cambodia (report).

CAMBODIA-TRADE

See CAMBODIA-INTERNATIONAL TRADE

CAMBODIA-TRANSPORTATION

Central Intelligence Agency (CIA), Office of Public Affairs, Washington, DC, 20505, USA, (703) 482-0623, https://www.cia.gov; The World Factbook.

Euromonitor International, Inc., 1 N Dearborn St., Ste. 1700, Chicago, IL, 60602, USA, (312) 922-1115, (312) 922-1157, info-usa@euromonitor.com, https://www.euromonitor.com/; Geographies.

Routledge - Taylor & Francis Group, 6000 Broken Sound Pkwy. NW, Ste. 300, Boca Raton, FL, 33487, USA, (800) 634-1420, (800) 634-7064, orders@taylorandfrancis.com, https://www.routledge.com/; The Europa World Year Book 2022.

United Nations Economic and Social Commission for Asia and the Pacific (ESCAP), United Nations Building, Rajadamnern Nok Ave., Bangkok, 10200, THA, https://www.unescap.org/; SDG Gateway Data Explorer.

The World Bank, 1818 H St. NW, Washington, DC, 20433, USA, (202) 473-1000, (202) 477-6391, eds03@worldbank.org, https://www.worldbank.org/; Cambodia (report).

CAMBODIA-UNEMPLOYMENT

United Nations Economic and Social Commission for Asia and the Pacific (ESCAP), United Nations Building, Rajadamnern Nok Ave., Bangkok, 10200, THA, https://www.unescap.org/; SDG Gateway Data Explorer.

The World Bank, 1818 H St. NW, Washington, DC, 20433, USA, (202) 473-1000, (202) 477-6391, eds03@worldbank.org, https://www.worldbank.org/; Cambodia (report).

CAMBODIA-VITAL STATISTICS

U.S. Census Bureau, 4600 Silver Hill Rd., Washington, DC, 20233, USA, (301) 763-4636, (800) 923-8282, https://www.census.gov; HIV/AIDS Surveillance Data Base.

United Nations Department of Economic and Social Affairs (DESA), Population Division, 2 United Nations Plz., Rm. DC2-1950, New York, NY, 10017, USA, (212) 963-3209, (212) 963-2147, population@un.org, https://www.un.org/development/desa/pd/; World Contraceptive Use 2021: Estimates and Projections of Family Planning Indicators and World Marriage Data 2019.

United Nations Statistics Division (UNSD), United Nations Plz., New York, NY, 10017, USA, (800) 253-9646, (212) 963-9851, statistics@un.org, https://unstats.un.org; Statistical Yearbook of the United Nations 2021.

CAMBODIA-WAGES

United Nations Economic and Social Commission for Asia and the Pacific (ESCAP), United Nations Building, Rajadamnern Nok Ave., Bangkok, 10200, THA, https://www.unescap.org/; SDG Gateway Data Explorer.

The World Bank, 1818 H St. NW, Washington, DC, 20433, USA, (202) 473-1000, (202) 477-6391, eds03@worldbank.org, https://www.worldbank.org/; Cambodia (report).

CAMEROON-NATIONAL STATISTICAL OFFICE

National Institute of Statistics of Cameroon, BP 134, Yaounde, CMR, infos@ins.cm, https://ins-cameroun.cm/en/; National Data Reports (Cameroon).

CAMEROON-AGRICULTURE

African Development Bank Group (AfDB), Avenue Joseph Anoma, 01 BP 1387, Abidjan, 01, COT, https://www.afdb.org; African Economic Outlook 2021 and Compendium of Statistics on Bank Group Operations 2019.

The Economist Group: Economist Intelligence Unit (EIU), 900 3rd Ave., 16th Fl., New York, NY, 10022, USA, (212) 541-0500, americas@eiu.com, https://www.eiu.com; Cameroon Country Report.

Euromonitor International, Inc., 1 N Dearborn St., Ste. 1700, Chicago, IL, 60602, USA, (312) 922-1115, (312) 922-1157, info-usa@euromonitor.com, https://www.euromonitor.com/; Geographies.

Organisation of Islamic Cooperation (OIC), Statistical, Economic and Social Research and Training Centre for Islamic Countries (SESRIC), Kudus Cad. No. 9, Diplomatik Site, Ankara, 06450, TUR, statistics@sesric.org, https://www.sesric.org/; OIC Statistics (OICStat) Database and OIC-Countries in Figures (OIC-CIF).

Palgrave Macmillan, 1 New York Plaza, Ste. 4500, New York, NY, 10004-1562, USA, (800) 777-4643, orders@palgrave.com, https://www.palgrave.com/us; The Statesman's Yearbook, 2023.

Routledge - Taylor & Francis Group, 6000 Broken Sound Pkwy. NW, Ste. 300, Boca Raton, FL, 33487, USA, (800) 634-1420, (800) 634-7064, orders@taylorandfrancis.com, https://www.routledge.com/; The Europa World Year Book 2022.

United Nations Economic Commission for Africa (UNECA), PO Box 3001, Addis Ababa, ETH, ecainfo@uneca.org, https://www.uneca.org/; African Statistical Yearbook 2020 and Economic Report on Africa 2021.

United Nations Food and Agricultural Organization (FAO), 2121 K St., Ste. 800B, Washington, DC, 20037, USA, (202) 653-2400 (Dial from U.S.), (202) 653-5760 (Fax from U.S.), fao-hq@fao.org, https://www.fao.org; AQUASTAT and The State of Food and Agriculture (SOFA) 2022.

United Nations Statistics Division (UNSD), United Nations Plz., New York, NY, 10017, USA, (800) 253-9646, (212) 963-9851, statistics@un.org, https://unstats.un.org; Statistical Yearbook of the United Nations 2021.

The World Bank, 1818 H St. NW, Washington, DC, 20433, USA, (202) 473-1000, (202) 477-6391, eds03@worldbank.org, https://www.worldbank.org/; Camaroon (report).

CAMEROON-AIRLINES

International Civil Aviation Organization (ICAO), 999 Robert-Bourassa Blvd., Montreal, QC, H3C 5H7, CAN, (514) 954-8219 (Dial from U.S.), (514) 954-6077 (Fax from U.S.), icaohq@icao.int, https://www.icao.int; ICAO Regional Reports.

Palgrave Macmillan, 1 New York Plaza, Ste. 4500, New York, NY, 10004-1562, USA, (800) 777-4643, orders@palgrave.com, https://www.palgrave.com/us; The Statesman's Yearbook, 2023.

Routledge - Taylor & Francis Group, 6000 Broken Sound Pkwy. NW, Ste. 300, Boca Raton, FL, 33487, USA, (800) 634-1420, (800) 634-7064, orders@taylorandfrancis.com, https://www.routledge.com/; The Europa World Year Book 2022.

United Nations Economic Commission for Africa (UNECA), PO Box 3001, Addis Ababa, ETH, ecainfo@uneca.org, https://www.uneca.org/; African Statistical Yearbook 2020.

CAMEROON-ALUMINUM PRODUCTION

See CAMEROON-MINERAL INDUSTRIES

CAMEROON-ARMED FORCES

Central Intelligence Agency (CIA), Office of Public Affairs, Washington, DC, 20505, USA, (703) 482-0623, https://www.cia.gov; The World Factbook.

International Institute for Strategic Studies (IISS) - Americas, 2121 K St. NW, Ste. 600, Washington, DC, 20037, USA, (202) 659-1490, (202) 659-1499, https://www.iiss.org/; The Military Balance 2022.

Palgrave Macmillan, 1 New York Plaza, Ste. 4500, New York, NY, 10004-1562, USA, (800) 777-4643, orders@palgrave.com, https://www.palgrave.com/us; The Statesman's Yearbook, 2023.

Stockholm International Peace Research Institute (SIPRI), Signalistgatan 9, Stockholm, SE 169 72, SWE, https://www.sipri.org/; SIPRI Arms Transfers Database and SIPRI Military Expenditure Database.

CAMEROON-BALANCE OF PAYMENTS

African Development Bank Group (AfDB), Avenue Joseph Anoma, 01 BP 1387, Abidjan, 01, COT, https://www.afdb.org; The AfDB Statistics Pocketbook 2019.

Routledge - Taylor & Francis Group, 6000 Broken Sound Pkwy. NW, Ste. 300, Boca Raton, FL, 33487, USA, (800) 634-1420, (800) 634-7064, orders@taylorandfrancis.com, https://www.routledge.com/; The Europa World Year Book 2022.

United Nations Conference on Trade and Development (UNCTAD), Palais des Nations, Geneva, 1211, SWI, (212) 963-6896, unctadinfo@unctad.org, https://unctad.org; Handbook of Statistics 2021.

United Nations Economic Commission for Africa (UNECA), PO Box 3001, Addis Ababa, ETH, ecainfo@uneca.org, https://www.uneca.org/; African Statistical Yearbook 2020.

The World Bank, 1818 H St. NW, Washington, DC, 20433, USA, (202) 473-1000, (202) 477-6391, eds03@worldbank.org, https://www.worldbank.org/; Camaroon (report).

CAMEROON-BANKS AND BANKING

Euromonitor International, Inc., 1 N Dearborn St., Ste. 1700, Chicago, IL, 60602, USA, (312) 922-1115, (312) 922-1157, info-usa@euromonitor.com, https://www.euromonitor.com/; Geographies.

International Monetary Fund (IMF), 700 19th St. NW, Washington, DC, 20431, USA, (202) 623-7000, (202) 623-4661, publications@imf.org, https://www.imf.org; International Financial Statistics (IFS).

Routledge - Taylor & Francis Group, 6000 Broken Sound Pkwy. NW, Ste. 300, Boca Raton, FL, 33487, USA, (800) 634-1420, (800) 634-7064, orders@taylorandfrancis.com, https://www.routledge.com/; The Europa World Year Book 2022.

United Nations Economic Commission for Africa (UNECA), PO Box 3001, Addis Ababa, ETH, ecainfo@uneca.org, https://www.uneca.org/; African Statistical Yearbook 2020.

CAMEROON-BARLEY PRODUCTION

See CAMEROON-CROPS

CAMEROON-BROADCASTING

Central Intelligence Agency (CIA), Office of Public Affairs, Washington, DC, 20505, USA, (703) 482-0623, https://www.cia.gov; The World Factbook.

Euromonitor International, Inc., 1 N Dearborn St., Ste. 1700, Chicago, IL, 60602, USA, (312) 922-1115, (312) 922-1157, info-usa@euromonitor.com, https://www.euromonitor.com/; Geographies.

Palgrave Macmillan, 1 New York Plaza, Ste. 4500, New York, NY, 10004-1562, USA, (800) 777-4643, orders@palgrave.com, https://www.palgrave.com/us; The Statesman's Yearbook, 2023.

WRTH Publications Limited, PO Box 290, Oxford, OX2 7FT, GBR, sales@wrth.com, https://www.wrth.com; World Radio TV Handbook 2023.

CAMEROON-BUDGET

Central Intelligence Agency (CIA), Office of Public Affairs, Washington, DC, 20505, USA, (703) 482-0623, https://www.cia.gov; The World Factbook.

CAMEROON-CACAO

See CAMEROON-CROPS

CAMEROON-CLIMATE

International Institute for Environment and Development (IIED), 235 High Holborn, London, WC1V 7DN, GBR, inforequest@iied.org, https://www.iied.org; Environment & Urbanization.

Palgrave Macmillan, 1 New York Plaza, Ste. 4500, New York, NY, 10004-1562, USA, (800) 777-4643, orders@palgrave.com, https://www.palgrave.com/us; The Statesman's Yearbook, 2023.

CAMEROON-COAL PRODUCTION

See CAMEROON-MINERAL INDUSTRIES

CAMEROON-COCOA PRODUCTION

See CAMEROON-CROPS

CAMEROON-COFFEE

See CAMEROON-CROPS

CAMEROON-COMMERCE

Palgrave Macmillan, 1 New York Plaza, Ste. 4500, New York, NY, 10004-1562, USA, (800) 777-4643, orders@palgrave.com, https://www.palgrave.com/us; The Statesman's Yearbook, 2023.

UK Data Service, University of Essex, Wivenhoe Park, Colchester, Essex, CO4 3SQ, GBR, https://ukdataservice.ac.uk/; International Aggregate Data.

CAMEROON-COMMODITY EXCHANGES

Barchart, 209 W Jackson Blvd., 2nd Fl., Chicago, IL, 60606, USA, (877) 247-4394, commodities@barchart.com, https://www.barchart.com/cmdty; The cmdty Yearbook 2023; cmdtyStats: Commodity Statistics and Fundamental Data; cmdtyView: Commodity Index; and Commodity Data and Prices.

International Monetary Fund (IMF), 700 19th St. NW, Washington, DC, 20431, USA, (202) 623-7000, (202) 623-4661, publications@imf.org, https://www.imf.org; IMF Primary Commodity Prices.

CAMEROON-CONSTRUCTION INDUSTRY

United Nations Economic Commission for Africa (UNECA), PO Box 3001, Addis Ababa, ETH, ecainfo@uneca.org, https://www.uneca.org/; African Statistical Yearbook 2020.

United Nations Statistics Division (UNSD), United Nations Plz., New York, NY, 10017, USA, (800) 253-9646, (212) 963-9851, statistics@un.org, https://unstats.un.org; Statistical Yearbook of the United Nations 2021.

CAMEROON-CONSUMER PRICE INDEXES

Routledge - Taylor & Francis Group, 6000 Broken Sound Pkwy. NW, Ste. 300, Boca Raton, FL, 33487, USA, (800) 634-1420, (800) 634-7064, orders@taylorandfrancis.com, https://www.routledge.com/; The Europa World Year Book 2022.

United Nations Economic Commission for Africa (UNECA), PO Box 3001, Addis Ababa, ETH, ecainfo@uneca.org, https://www.uneca.org/; African Statistical Yearbook 2020.

The World Bank, 1818 H St. NW, Washington, DC, 20433, USA, (202) 473-1000, (202) 477-6391, eds03@worldbank.org, https://www.worldbank.org/; Camaroon (report).

CAMEROON-CONSUMPTION (ECONOMICS)

African Development Bank Group (AfDB), Avenue Joseph Anoma, 01 BP 1387, Abidjan, 01, COT, https://www.afdb.org; The AfDB Statistics Pocketbook 2019.

CAMEROON-COPPER INDUSTRY AND TRADE

See CAMEROON-MINERAL INDUSTRIES

CAMEROON-CORN INDUSTRY

See CAMEROON-CROPS

CAMEROON-COTTON

See CAMEROON-CROPS

CAMEROON-CROPS

International Monetary Fund (IMF), 700 19th St. NW, Washington, DC, 20431, USA, (202) 623-7000, (202) 623-4661, publications@imf.org, https://www.imf.org; International Financial Statistics (IFS).

Palgrave Macmillan, 1 New York Plaza, Ste. 4500, New York, NY, 10004-1562, USA, (800) 777-4643, orders@palgrave.com, https://www.palgrave.com/us; The Statesman's Yearbook, 2023.

United Nations Economic Commission for Africa (UNECA), PO Box 3001, Addis Ababa, ETH, ecainfo@uneca.org, https://www.uneca.org/; African Statistical Yearbook 2020.

United Nations Food and Agricultural Organization (FAO), 2121 K St., Ste. 800B, Washington, DC, 20037, USA, (202) 653-2400 (Dial from U.S.), (202) 653-5760 (Fax from U.S.), fao-hq@fao.org, https://www.fao.org; The State of Food and Agriculture (SOFA) 2022.

United Nations Statistics Division (UNSD), United Nations Plz., New York, NY, 10017, USA, (800) 253-9646, (212) 963-9851, statistics@un.org, https://unstats.un.org; Statistical Yearbook of the United Nations 2021.

CAMEROON-DAIRY PROCESSING

Palgrave Macmillan, 1 New York Plaza, Ste. 4500, New York, NY, 10004-1562, USA, (800) 777-4643, orders@palgrave.com, https://www.palgrave.com/us; The Statesman's Yearbook, 2023.

United Nations Food and Agricultural Organization (FAO), 2121 K St., Ste. 800B, Washington, DC, 20037, USA, (202) 653-2400 (Dial from U.S.), (202) 653-5760 (Fax from U.S.), fao-hq@fao.org, https://www.fao.org; The State of Food and Agriculture (SOFA) 2022.

CAMEROON-DEBTS, EXTERNAL

African Development Bank Group (AfDB), Avenue Joseph Anoma, 01 BP 1387, Abidjan, 01, COT, https://www.afdb.org; The AfDB Statistics Pocketbook 2019; African Economic Outlook 2021; and Compendium of Statistics on Bank Group Operations 2019.

Palgrave Macmillan, 1 New York Plaza, Ste. 4500, New York, NY, 10004-1562, USA, (800) 777-4643, orders@palgrave.com, https://www.palgrave.com/us; The Statesman's Yearbook, 2023.

United Nations Economic Commission for Africa (UNECA), PO Box 3001, Addis Ababa, ETH, ecainfo@uneca.org, https://www.uneca.org/; Economic Report on Africa 2021.

The World Bank, 1818 H St. NW, Washington, DC, 20433, USA, (202) 473-1000, (202) 477-6391, eds03@worldbank.org, https://www.worldbank.org/; Global Financial Development Report 2019-2020: Bank Regulation and Supervision a Decade after the Global Financial Crisis; World Development Indicators (WDI) 2022; and World Development Report 2022: Finance for an Equitable Recovery.

CAMEROON-DEFENSE EXPENDITURES

See CAMEROON-ARMED FORCES

CAMEROON-DIAMONDS

See CAMEROON-MINERAL INDUSTRIES

CAMEROON-ECONOMIC ASSISTANCE

United Nations Statistics Division (UNSD), United Nations Plz., New York, NY, 10017, USA, (800) 253-9646, (212) 963-9851, statistics@un.org, https://unstats.un.org; Statistical Yearbook of the United Nations 2021.

CAMEROON-ECONOMIC CONDITIONS

African Development Bank Group (AfDB), Avenue Joseph Anoma, 01 BP 1387, Abidjan, 01, COT, https://www.afdb.org; The AfDB Statistics Pocketbook 2019; Africa Economic Brief - COVID-19 Pandemic Potential Risks for Trade and Trade Finance in Africa; African Economic Outlook 2021; The African Statistical Journal; Compendium of Statistics on Bank Group Operations 2019; and Gender, Poverty and Environmental Indicators on African Countries 2019.

Bernan Press, 15250 NBN Way, Bldg. C, Blue Ridge Summit, PA, 17214, USA, (301) 459-2255, (800) 865-3457, (800) 865-3450, customercare@bernan.com, https://rowman.com/Page/Bernan; World Economic Outlook, April 2022.

Central Intelligence Agency (CIA), Office of Public Affairs, Washington, DC, 20505, USA, (703) 482-0623, https://www.cia.gov; The World Factbook.

The Economist Group: Economist Intelligence Unit (EIU), 900 3rd Ave., 16th Fl., New York, NY, 10022, USA, (212) 541-0500, americas@eiu.com, https://www.eiu.com; Cameroon Country Report.

Euromonitor International, Inc., 1 N Dearborn St., Ste. 1700, Chicago, IL, 60602, USA, (312) 922-1115, (312) 922-1157, info-usa@euromonitor.com, https://www.euromonitor.com/; Geographies and Market Research on the Consumer Finance Industry.

International Monetary Fund (IMF), 700 19th St. NW, Washington, DC, 20431, USA, (202) 623-7000, (202) 623-4661, publications@imf.org, https://www.imf.org; IMF Data and World Economic Outlook.

Organisation of Islamic Cooperation (OIC), Statistical, Economic and Social Research and Training Centre for Islamic Countries (SESRIC), Kudus Cad. No. 9, Diplomatik Site, Ankara, 06450, TUR, statistics@sesric.org, https://www.sesric.org/; OIC Economic Outlook 2021; OIC Statistics (OICStat) Database; and OIC-Countries in Figures (OIC-CIF).

Palgrave Macmillan, 1 New York Plaza, Ste. 4500, New York, NY, 10004-1562, USA, (800) 777-4643, orders@palgrave.com, https://www.palgrave.com/us; The Statesman's Yearbook, 2023.

Routledge - Taylor & Francis Group, 6000 Broken Sound Pkwy. NW, Ste. 300, Boca Raton, FL, 33487, USA, (800) 634-1420, (800) 634-7064, orders@taylorandfrancis.com, https://www.routledge.com/; The Europa World Year Book 2022.

United Nations Economic Commission for Africa (UNECA), PO Box 3001, Addis Ababa, ETH, ecainfo@uneca.org, https://www.uneca.org/; Economic Report on Africa 2021.

United Nations Statistics Division (UNSD), United Nations Plz., New York, NY, 10017, USA, (800) 253-9646, (212) 963-9851, statistics@un.org, https://unstats.un.org; World Statistics Pocketbook 2021.

The World Bank, 1818 H St. NW, Washington, DC, 20433, USA, (202) 473-1000, (202) 477-6391, eds03@worldbank.org, https://www.worldbank.org/; Camaroon (report); Global Economic Monitor (GEM); Global Economic Prospects, June 2022; The Global Findex Database 2021; and World Development Report 2022: Finance for an Equitable Recovery.

CAMEROON-EDUCATION

African Development Bank Group (AfDB), Avenue Joseph Anoma, 01 BP 1387, Abidjan, 01, COT, https://www.afdb.org; The AfDB Statistics Pocketbook 2019.

Euromonitor International, Inc., 1 N Dearborn St., Ste. 1700, Chicago, IL, 60602, USA, (312) 922-1115, (312) 922-1157, info-usa@euromonitor.com, https://www.euromonitor.com/; Geographies.

Infoplease, c/o Sandbox Networks, Inc., 1 Lincoln St., 24th Fl., Boston, MA, 02111, USA, https://www.infoplease.com; Countries of the World.

Organisation of Islamic Cooperation (OIC), Statistical, Economic and Social Research and Training Centre for Islamic Countries (SESRIC), Kudus Cad. No. 9, Diplomatik Site, Ankara, 06450, TUR, statistics@sesric.org, https://www.sesric.org/; OIC Statistics (OICStat) Database.

Palgrave Macmillan, 1 New York Plaza, Ste. 4500, New York, NY, 10004-1562, USA, (800) 777-4643, orders@palgrave.com, https://www.palgrave.com/us; The Statesman's Yearbook, 2023.

Routledge - Taylor & Francis Group, 6000 Broken Sound Pkwy. NW, Ste. 300, Boca Raton, FL, 33487, USA, (800) 634-1420, (800) 634-7064, orders@taylorandfrancis.com, https://www.routledge.com/; The Europa World Year Book 2022.

UNESCO Institute for Statistics, C.P 250 Succursale H, Montreal, QC, H3G 2K8, CAN, (514) 343-6880 (Dial from U.S.), (514) 343-5740 (Fax from U.S.), uis.publications@unesco.org, http://uis.unesco.org/; Literacy and UIS.Stat.

United Nations Economic Commission for Africa (UNECA), PO Box 3001, Addis Ababa, ETH, ecainfo@uneca.org, https://www.uneca.org/; African Statistical Yearbook 2020.

United Nations Statistics Division (UNSD), United Nations Plz., New York, NY, 10017, USA, (800) 253-9646, (212) 963-9851, statistics@un.org, https://unstats.un.org; Millennium Development Goal Indicators.

The World Bank, 1818 H St. NW, Washington, DC, 20433, USA, (202) 473-1000, (202) 477-6391, eds03@worldbank.org, https://www.worldbank.org/; Camaroon (report); World Development Indicators (WDI) 2022; and World Development Report 2022: Finance for an Equitable Recovery.

CAMEROON-ELECTRICITY

International Energy Agency (IEA), 9 Rue de la Federation, Paris, 75739, FRA, info@iea.org, https://www.iea.org/; World Energy Outlook 2021.

U.S. Energy Information Administration (EIA), 1000 Independence Ave. SW, Washington, DC, 20585, USA, (202) 586-8800, infoctr@eia.gov, https://www.eia.gov; International Energy Outlook 2021.

United Nations Statistics Division (UNSD), United Nations Plz., New York, NY, 10017, USA, (800) 253-9646, (212) 963-9851, statistics@un.org, https://unstats.un.org; Statistical Yearbook of the United Nations 2021.

CAMEROON-EMPLOYMENT

International Labour Organization (ILO), 4 Rte. des Morillons, Geneva, CH-1211, SWI, ilo@ilo.org, https://www.ilo.org; NORMLEX Information System on International Labour Standards.

UK Data Service, University of Essex, Wivenhoe Park, Colchester, Essex, CO4 3SQ, GBR, https://ukdataservice.ac.uk/; International Aggregate Data.

United Nations Economic Commission for Africa (UNECA), PO Box 3001, Addis Ababa, ETH, ecainfo@uneca.org, https://www.uneca.org/; African Statistical Yearbook 2020.

United Nations Statistics Division (UNSD), United Nations Plz., New York, NY, 10017, USA, (800) 253-9646, (212) 963-9851, statistics@un.org, https://unstats.un.org; Statistical Yearbook of the United Nations 2021.

The World Bank, 1818 H St. NW, Washington, DC, 20433, USA, (202) 473-1000, (202) 477-6391, eds03@worldbank.org, https://www.worldbank.org/; Camaroon (report).

CAMEROON-ENVIRONMENTAL CONDITIONS

DSI Data Service & Information, Xantener Strasse 51a, Rheinberg, D-47495, GER, dsi@dsidata.com, https://www.dsidata.com/; Global Environmental Database.

The Economist Group: Economist Intelligence Unit (EIU), 900 3rd Ave., 16th Fl., New York, NY, 10022, USA, (212) 541-0500, americas@eiu.com, https://www.eiu.com; Cameroon Country Report.

International Institute for Environment and Development (IIED), 235 High Holborn, London, WC1V 7DN, GBR, inforequest@iied.org, https://www.iied.org; Environment & Urbanization.

Organisation of Islamic Cooperation (OIC), Statistical, Economic and Social Research and Training Centre for Islamic Countries (SESRIC), Kudus Cad. No. 9, Diplomatik Site, Ankara, 06450, TUR, statistics@sesric.org, https://www.sesric.org/; OIC Statistics (OICStat) Database and OIC-Countries in Figures (OIC-CIF).

United Nations Statistics Division (UNSD), United Nations Plz., New York, NY, 10017, USA, (800) 253-9646, (212) 963-9851, statistics@un.org, https://unstats.un.org; World Statistics Pocketbook 2021.

CAMEROON-EXPORTS

African Development Bank Group (AfDB), Avenue Joseph Anoma, 01 BP 1387, Abidjan, 01, COT, https://www.afdb.org; African Economic Outlook 2021.

Central Intelligence Agency (CIA), Office of Public Affairs, Washington, DC, 20505, USA, (703) 482-0623, https://www.cia.gov; The World Factbook.

The Economist Group: Economist Intelligence Unit (EIU), 900 3rd Ave., 16th Fl., New York, NY, 10022, USA, (212) 541-0500, americas@eiu.com, https://www.eiu.com; Cameroon Country Report.

International Monetary Fund (IMF), 700 19th St. NW, Washington, DC, 20431, USA, (202) 623-7000, (202) 623-4661, publications@imf.org, https://www.imf.org; Direction of Trade Statistics (DOTS).

Organisation of Islamic Cooperation (OIC), Statistical, Economic and Social Research and Training Centre for Islamic Countries (SESRIC), Kudus Cad. No. 9, Diplomatik Site, Ankara, 06450, TUR, statistics@sesric.org, https://www.sesric.org/; OIC Statistics (OICStat) Database.

S&P Global, IHS Markit, 15 Inverness Way E, Englewood, CO, 80112, USA, (800) 447-2273, (800) 854-7179, https://ihsmarkit.com; Global Trade Atlas (GTA).

United Nations Conference on Trade and Development (UNCTAD), Palais des Nations, Geneva, 1211, SWI, (212) 963-6896, unctadinfo@unctad.org, https://unctad.org; Handbook of Statistics 2021.

The World Bank, 1818 H St. NW, Washington, DC, 20433, USA, (202) 473-1000, (202) 477-6391, eds03@worldbank.org, https://www.worldbank.org/; World Development Report 2022: Finance for an Equitable Recovery.

CAMEROON-FEMALE WORKING POPULATION

See CAMEROON-EMPLOYMENT

CAMEROON-FERTILITY, HUMAN

Central Intelligence Agency (CIA), Office of Public Affairs, Washington, DC, 20505, USA, (703) 482-0623, https://www.cia.gov; The World Factbook.

CAMEROON-FERTILIZER INDUSTRY

United Nations Food and Agricultural Organization (FAO), 2121 K St., Ste. 800B, Washington, DC, 20037, USA, (202) 653-2400 (Dial from U.S.), (202) 653-5760 (Fax from U.S.), fao-hq@fao.org, https://www.fao.org; The State of Food and Agriculture (SOFA) 2022.

CAMEROON-FETAL MORTALITY

See CAMEROON-MORTALITY

CAMEROON-FINANCE

Stockholm International Peace Research Institute (SIPRI), Signalistgatan 9, Stockholm, SE 169 72, SWE, https://www.sipri.org/; SIPRI Arms Transfers Database and SIPRI Military Expenditure Database.

United Nations Economic Commission for Africa (UNECA), PO Box 3001, Addis Ababa, ETH, ecainfo@uneca.org, https://www.uneca.org/; African Statistical Yearbook 2020.

United Nations Statistics Division (UNSD), United Nations Plz., New York, NY, 10017, USA, (800) 253-9646, (212) 963-9851, statistics@un.org, https://unstats.un.org; Statistical Yearbook of the United Nations 2021.

The World Bank, 1818 H St. NW, Washington, DC, 20433, USA, (202) 473-1000, (202) 477-6391, eds03@worldbank.org, https://www.worldbank.org/; Camaroon (report).

CAMEROON-FINANCE, PUBLIC

African Development Bank Group (AfDB), Avenue Joseph Anoma, 01 BP 1387, Abidjan, 01, COT, https://www.afdb.org; The AfDB Statistics Pocketbook 2019.

Bernan Press, 15250 NBN Way, Bldg. C, Blue Ridge Summit, PA, 17214, USA, (301) 459-2255, (800) 865-3457, (800) 865-3450, customercare@bernan.com, https://rowman.com/Page/Bernan; National Accounts Statistics: Analysis of Main Aggregates 2020.

The Economist Group: Economist Intelligence Unit (EIU), 900 3rd Ave., 16th Fl., New York, NY, 10022, USA, (212) 541-0500, americas@eiu.com, https://www.eiu.com; Cameroon Country Report.

International Monetary Fund (IMF), 700 19th St. NW, Washington, DC, 20431, USA, (202) 623-7000, (202) 623-4661, publications@imf.org, https://www.imf.org; International Financial Statistics (IFS) and Regional Economic Outlook.

Palgrave Macmillan, 1 New York Plaza, Ste. 4500, New York, NY, 10004-1562, USA, (800) 777-4643, orders@palgrave.com, https://www.palgrave.com/us; The Statesman's Yearbook, 2023.

Routledge - Taylor & Francis Group, 6000 Broken Sound Pkwy. NW, Ste. 300, Boca Raton, FL, 33487, USA, (800) 634-1420, (800) 634-7064, orders@taylorandfrancis.com, https://www.routledge.com/; The Europa World Year Book 2022.

United Nations Economic Commission for Africa (UNECA), PO Box 3001, Addis Ababa, ETH, ecainfo@uneca.org, https://www.uneca.org/; African Statistical Yearbook 2020.

United Nations Statistics Division (UNSD), United Nations Plz., New York, NY, 10017, USA, (800) 253-9646, (212) 963-9851, statistics@un.org, https://unstats.un.org; National Accounts Main Aggregates Database and National Accounts Statistics: Main Aggregates and Detailed Tables.

The World Bank, 1818 H St. NW, Washington, DC, 20433, USA, (202) 473-1000, (202) 477-6391, eds03@worldbank.org, https://www.worldbank.org/; Camaroon (report).

CAMEROON-FISHERIES

Palgrave Macmillan, 1 New York Plaza, Ste. 4500, New York, NY, 10004-1562, USA, (800) 777-4643, orders@palgrave.com, https://www.palgrave.com/us; The Statesman's Yearbook, 2023.

Routledge - Taylor & Francis Group, 6000 Broken Sound Pkwy. NW, Ste. 300, Boca Raton, FL, 33487, USA, (800) 634-1420, (800) 634-7064, orders@taylorandfrancis.com, https://www.routledge.com/; The Europa World Year Book 2022.

United Nations Economic Commission for Africa (UNECA), PO Box 3001, Addis Ababa, ETH, ecainfo@uneca.org, https://www.uneca.org/; African Statistical Yearbook 2020.

United Nations Food and Agricultural Organization (FAO), 2121 K St., Ste. 800B, Washington, DC, 20037, USA, (202) 653-2400 (Dial from U.S.), (202) 653-5760 (Fax from U.S.), fao-hq@fao.org, https://www.fao.org; FAO Yearbook of Fishery and Aquaculture Statistics 2019; Fishery Statistical Collections Global Capture Production; FishStatJ; and The State of Food and Agriculture (SOFA) 2022.

United Nations Statistics Division (UNSD), United Nations Plz., New York, NY, 10017, USA, (800) 253-9646, (212) 963-9851, statistics@un.org, https://unstats.un.org; Statistical Yearbook of the United Nations 2021.

The World Bank, 1818 H St. NW, Washington, DC, 20433, USA, (202) 473-1000, (202) 477-6391, eds03@worldbank.org, https://www.worldbank.org/; Camaroon (report).

CAMEROON-FOOD

African Development Bank Group (AfDB), Avenue Joseph Anoma, 01 BP 1387, Abidjan, 01, COT, https://www.afdb.org; The AfDB Statistics Pocketbook 2019.

United Nations Food and Agricultural Organization (FAO), 2121 K St., Ste. 800B, Washington, DC, 20037, USA, (202) 653-2400 (Dial from U.S.), (202) 653-5760 (Fax from U.S.), fao-hq@fao.org, https://www.fao.org; The State of Food and Agriculture (SOFA) 2022.

CAMEROON-FOREIGN EXCHANGE RATES

African Development Bank Group (AfDB), Avenue Joseph Anoma, 01 BP 1387, Abidjan, 01, COT, https://www.afdb.org; The AfDB Statistics Pocketbook 2019 and African Economic Outlook 2021.

CAMEROON-FORESTS AND FORESTRY

International Monetary Fund (IMF), 700 19th St. NW, Washington, DC, 20431, USA, (202) 623-7000, (202) 623-4661, publications@imf.org, https://www.imf.org; International Financial Statistics (IFS).

Palgrave Macmillan, 1 New York Plaza, Ste. 4500, New York, NY, 10004-1562, USA, (800) 777-4643, orders@palgrave.com, https://www.palgrave.com/us; The Statesman's Yearbook, 2023.

Routledge - Taylor & Francis Group, 6000 Broken Sound Pkwy. NW, Ste. 300, Boca Raton, FL, 33487, USA, (800) 634-1420, (800) 634-7064, orders@taylorandfrancis.com, https://www.routledge.com/; The Europa World Year Book 2022.

UNESCO Institute for Statistics, C.P 250 Succursale H, Montreal, QC, H3G 2K8, CAN, (514) 343-6880 (Dial from U.S.), (514) 343-5740 (Fax from U.S.), uis.publications@unesco.org, http://uis.unesco.org/; UIS.Stat.

United Nations Economic Commission for Africa (UNECA), PO Box 3001, Addis Ababa, ETH,

ecainfo@uneca.org, https://www.uneca.org/; African Statistical Yearbook 2020.

United Nations Food and Agricultural Organization (FAO), 2121 K St., Ste. 800B, Washington, DC, 20037, USA, (202) 653-2400 (Dial from U.S.), (202) 653-5760 (Fax from U.S.), fao-hq@fao.org, https://www.fao.org; FAO Yearbook of Forest Products 2019 and The State of Food and Agriculture (SOFA) 2022.

United Nations Statistics Division (UNSD), United Nations Plz., New York, NY, 10017, USA, (800) 253-9646, (212) 963-9851, statistics@un.org, https://unstats.un.org; Statistical Yearbook of the United Nations 2021.

The World Bank, 1818 H St. NW, Washington, DC, 20433, USA, (202) 473-1000, (202) 477-6391, eds03@worldbank.org, https://www.worldbank.org/; Camaroon (report) and World Development Report 2022: Finance for an Equitable Recovery.

CAMEROON-GAS PRODUCTION

See CAMEROON-MINERAL INDUSTRIES

CAMEROON-GEOGRAPHIC INFORMATION SYSTEMS

The World Bank, 1818 H St. NW, Washington, DC, 20433, USA, (202) 473-1000, (202) 477-6391, eds03@worldbank.org, https://www.worldbank.org/; Camaroon (report).

CAMEROON-GOLD INDUSTRY

The World Bank, 1818 H St. NW, Washington, DC, 20433, USA, (202) 473-1000, (202) 477-6391, eds03@worldbank.org, https://www.worldbank.org/; World Development Indicators (WDI) 2022.

CAMEROON-GOLD PRODUCTION

See CAMEROON-MINERAL INDUSTRIES

CAMEROON-GROSS DOMESTIC PRODUCT

African Development Bank Group (AfDB), Avenue Joseph Anoma, 01 BP 1387, Abidjan, 01, COT, https://www.afdb.org; The AfDB Statistics Pocketbook 2019.

The Economist Group: Economist Intelligence Unit (EIU), 900 3rd Ave., 16th Fl., New York, NY, 10022, USA, (212) 541-0500, americas@eiu.com, https://www.eiu.com; Cameroon Country Report.

Routledge - Taylor & Francis Group, 6000 Broken Sound Pkwy. NW, Ste. 300, Boca Raton, FL, 33487, USA, (800) 634-1420, (800) 634-7064, orders@taylorandfrancis.com, https://www.routledge.com/; The Europa World Year Book 2022.

United Nations Economic Commission for Africa (UNECA), PO Box 3001, Addis Ababa, ETH, ecainfo@uneca.org, https://www.uneca.org/; African Statistical Yearbook 2020.

United Nations Statistics Division (UNSD), United Nations Plz., New York, NY, 10017, USA, (800) 253-9646, (212) 963-9851, statistics@un.org, https://unstats.un.org; Statistical Yearbook of the United Nations 2021.

The World Bank, 1818 H St. NW, Washington, DC, 20433, USA, (202) 473-1000, (202) 477-6391, eds03@worldbank.org, https://www.worldbank.org/; World Development Indicators (WDI) 2022 and World Development Report 2022: Finance for an Equitable Recovery.

CAMEROON-GROSS NATIONAL PRODUCT

Palgrave Macmillan, 1 New York Plaza, Ste. 4500, New York, NY, 10004-1562, USA, (800) 777-4643, orders@palgrave.com, https://www.palgrave.com/us; The Statesman's Yearbook, 2023.

Routledge - Taylor & Francis Group, 6000 Broken Sound Pkwy. NW, Ste. 300, Boca Raton, FL, 33487, USA, (800) 634-1420, (800) 634-7064, orders@taylorandfrancis.com, https://www.routledge.com/; The Europa World Year Book 2022.

United Nations Statistics Division (UNSD), United Nations Plz., New York, NY, 10017, USA, (800) 253-9646, (212) 963-9851, statistics@un.org, https://unstats.un.org; Statistical Yearbook of the United Nations 2021.

The World Bank, 1818 H St. NW, Washington, DC, 20433, USA, (202) 473-1000, (202) 477-6391, eds03@worldbank.org, https://www.worldbank.org/; World Development Indicators (WDI) 2022 and World Development Report 2022: Finance for an Equitable Recovery.

CAMEROON-HOUSING

Euromonitor International, Inc., 1 N Dearborn St., Ste. 1700, Chicago, IL, 60602, USA, (312) 922-1115, (312) 922-1157, info-usa@euromonitor.com, https://www.euromonitor.com/; Geographies.

United Nations Statistics Division (UNSD), United Nations Plz., New York, NY, 10017, USA, (800) 253-9646, (212) 963-9851, statistics@un.org, https://unstats.un.org; Statistical Yearbook of the United Nations 2021.

CAMEROON-ILLITERATE PERSONS

UNESCO Institute for Statistics, C.P 250 Succursale H, Montreal, QC, H3G 2K8, CAN, (514) 343-6880 (Dial from U.S.), (514) 343-5740 (Fax from U.S.), uis.publications@unesco.org, http://uis.unesco.org/; UIS.Stat.

CAMEROON-IMPORTS

African Development Bank Group (AfDB), Avenue Joseph Anoma, 01 BP 1387, Abidjan, 01, COT, https://www.afdb.org; African Economic Outlook 2021.

Central Intelligence Agency (CIA), Office of Public Affairs, Washington, DC, 20505, USA, (703) 482-0623, https://www.cia.gov; The World Factbook.

The Economist Group: Economist Intelligence Unit (EIU), 900 3rd Ave., 16th Fl., New York, NY, 10022, USA, (212) 541-0500, americas@eiu.com, https://www.eiu.com; Cameroon Country Report.

International Monetary Fund (IMF), 700 19th St. NW, Washington, DC, 20431, USA, (202) 623-7000, (202) 623-4661, publications@imf.org, https://www.imf.org; Direction of Trade Statistics (DOTS).

S&P Global, IHS Markit, 15 Inverness Way E, Englewood, CO, 80112, USA, (800) 447-2273, (800) 854-7179, https://ihsmarkit.com; Global Trade Atlas (GTA).

United Nations Conference on Trade and Development (UNCTAD), Palais des Nations, Geneva, 1211, SWI, (212) 963-6896, unctadinfo@unctad.org, https://unctad.org; Handbook of Statistics 2021.

The World Bank, 1818 H St. NW, Washington, DC, 20433, USA, (202) 473-1000, (202) 477-6391, eds03@worldbank.org, https://www.worldbank.org/; World Development Report 2022: Finance for an Equitable Recovery.

CAMEROON-INDUSTRIAL METALS PRODUCTION

See CAMEROON-MINERAL INDUSTRIES

CAMEROON-INDUSTRIES

Central Intelligence Agency (CIA), Office of Public Affairs, Washington, DC, 20505, USA, (703) 482-0623, https://www.cia.gov; The World Factbook.

The Economist Group: Economist Intelligence Unit (EIU), 900 3rd Ave., 16th Fl., New York, NY, 10022, USA, (212) 541-0500, americas@eiu.com, https://www.eiu.com; Cameroon Country Report.

Euromonitor International, Inc., 1 N Dearborn St., Ste. 1700, Chicago, IL, 60602, USA, (312) 922-1115, (312) 922-1157, info-usa@euromonitor.com, https://www.euromonitor.com/; Geographies.

International Labour Organization (ILO), 4 Rte. des Morillons, Geneva, CH-1211, SWI, ilo@ilo.org, https://www.ilo.org; NORMLEX Information System on International Labour Standards.

Routledge - Taylor & Francis Group, 6000 Broken Sound Pkwy. NW, Ste. 300, Boca Raton, FL, 33487, USA, (800) 634-1420, (800) 634-7064, orders@taylorandfrancis.com, https://www.routledge.com/; The Europa World Year Book 2022.

United Nations Economic Commission for Africa (UNECA), PO Box 3001, Addis Ababa, ETH, ecainfo@uneca.org, https://www.uneca.org/; African Statistical Yearbook 2020.

United Nations Industrial Development Organization (UNIDO), 1 United Nations Plz., Rm. DC1-1118, New York, NY, 10017, USA, (212) 963-6890, (212) 963 6885, (212) 963-7904, office.newyork@unido.org, https://www.unido.org/; Industrial Statistics Databases and International Yearbook of Industrial Statistics 2021.

The World Bank, 1818 H St. NW, Washington, DC, 20433, USA, (202) 473-1000, (202) 477-6391, eds03@worldbank.org, https://www.worldbank.org/; Camaroon (report) and World Development Indicators (WDI) 2022.

CAMEROON-INTERNATIONAL TRADE

African Development Bank Group (AfDB), Avenue Joseph Anoma, 01 BP 1387, Abidjan, 01, COT, https://www.afdb.org; The AfDB Statistics Pocketbook 2019 and African Economic Outlook 2021.

The Economist Group: Economist Intelligence Unit (EIU), 900 3rd Ave., 16th Fl., New York, NY, 10022, USA, (212) 541-0500, americas@eiu.com, https://www.eiu.com; Cameroon Country Report.

Euromonitor International, Inc., 1 N Dearborn St., Ste. 1700, Chicago, IL, 60602, USA, (312) 922-1115, (312) 922-1157, info-usa@euromonitor.com, https://www.euromonitor.com/; Geographies.

Organization for Economic Cooperation and Development (OECD), 2001 L St. NW, Ste. 650, Washington, DC, 20036-4922, USA, (202) 785-6323, (800) 456-6323, (202) 785-0350, washington.contact@oecd.org, https://www.oecd.org/; OECD Digital Economy Outlook 2020.

Palgrave Macmillan, 1 New York Plaza, Ste. 4500, New York, NY, 10004-1562, USA, (800) 777-4643, orders@palgrave.com, https://www.palgrave.com/us; The Statesman's Yearbook, 2023.

Routledge - Taylor & Francis Group, 6000 Broken Sound Pkwy. NW, Ste. 300, Boca Raton, FL, 33487, USA, (800) 634-1420, (800) 634-7064, orders@taylorandfrancis.com, https://www.routledge.com/; The Europa World Year Book 2022.

United Nations Conference on Trade and Development (UNCTAD), Palais des Nations, Geneva, 1211, SWI, (212) 963-6896, unctadinfo@unctad.org, https://unctad.org; Trade and Development Report 2021.

United Nations Economic Commission for Africa (UNECA), PO Box 3001, Addis Ababa, ETH, ecainfo@uneca.org, https://www.uneca.org/; African Statistical Yearbook 2020.

United Nations Food and Agricultural Organization (FAO), 2121 K St., Ste. 800B, Washington, DC, 20037, USA, (202) 653-2400 (Dial from U.S.), (202) 653-5760 (Fax from U.S.), fao-hq@fao.org, https://www.fao.org; The State of Food and Agriculture (SOFA) 2022.

United Nations Statistics Division (UNSD), United Nations Plz., New York, NY, 10017, USA, (800) 253-9646, (212) 963-9851, statistics@un.org, https://unstats.un.org; International Trade Statistics Yearbook 2020 and Statistical Yearbook of the United Nations 2021.

The World Bank, 1818 H St. NW, Washington, DC, 20433, USA, (202) 473-1000, (202) 477-6391, eds03@worldbank.org, https://www.worldbank.org/; Camaroon (report); World Development Indicators (WDI) 2022; and World Development Report 2022: Finance for an Equitable Recovery.

World Trade Organization (WTO), Ctre. William Rappard, Rue de Lausanne 154, Case postale, Geneva, CH-1211, SWI, enquiries@wto.org, https://www.wto.org; World Trade Statistical Review 2022.

CAMEROON-INTERNET USERS

International Telecommunication Union (ITU), Place des Nations, Geneva, CH-1211, SWI, itumail@itu.int, https://www.itu.int; Global Connectivity Report 2022; World Telecommunication/ICT Indicators Database 2021; and Yearbook of Statistics 2019.

The World Bank, 1818 H St. NW, Washington, DC, 20433, USA, (202) 473-1000, (202) 477-6391, eds03@worldbank.org, https://www.worldbank.org/; Camaroon (report).

CAMEROON-LABOR

African Development Bank Group (AfDB), Avenue Joseph Anoma, 01 BP 1387, Abidjan, 01, COT, https://www.afdb.org; The AfDB Statistics Pocketbook 2019.

Central Intelligence Agency (CIA), Office of Public Affairs, Washington, DC, 20505, USA, (703) 482-0623, https://www.cia.gov; The World Factbook.

Euromonitor International, Inc., 1 N Dearborn St., Ste. 1700, Chicago, IL, 60602, USA, (312) 922-1115, (312) 922-1157, info-usa@euromonitor.com, https://www.euromonitor.com/; Geographies.

International Labour Organization (ILO), 4 Rte. des Morillons, Geneva, CH-1211, SWI, ilo@ilo.org, https://www.ilo.org; NORMLEX Information System on International Labour Standards.

Organisation of Islamic Cooperation (OIC), Statistical, Economic and Social Research and Training Centre for Islamic Countries (SESRIC), Kudus Cad. No. 9, Diplomatik Site, Ankara, 06450, TUR, statistics@sesric.org, https://www.sesric.org/; OIC Statistics (OICStat) Database.

Palgrave Macmillan, 1 New York Plaza, Ste. 4500, New York, NY, 10004-1562, USA, (800) 777-4643, orders@palgrave.com, https://www.palgrave.com/us; The Statesman's Yearbook, 2023.

United Nations Food and Agricultural Organization (FAO), 2121 K St., Ste. 800B, Washington, DC, 20037, USA, (202) 653-2400 (Dial from U.S.), (202) 653-5760 (Fax from U.S.), fao-hq@fao.org, https://www.fao.org; The State of Food and Agriculture (SOFA) 2022.

The World Bank, 1818 H St. NW, Washington, DC, 20433, USA, (202) 473-1000, (202) 477-6391, eds03@worldbank.org, https://www.worldbank.org/; World Development Indicators (WDI) 2022 and World Development Report 2022: Finance for an Equitable Recovery.

CAMEROON-LAND USE

United Nations Statistics Division (UNSD), United Nations Plz., New York, NY, 10017, USA, (800) 253-9646, (212) 963-9851, statistics@un.org, https://unstats.un.org; Millennium Development Goal Indicators.

The World Bank, 1818 H St. NW, Washington, DC, 20433, USA, (202) 473-1000, (202) 477-6391, eds03@worldbank.org, https://www.worldbank.org/; World Development Report 2022: Finance for an Equitable Recovery.

CAMEROON-LIFE EXPECTANCY

African Development Bank Group (AfDB), Avenue Joseph Anoma, 01 BP 1387, Abidjan, 01, COT, https://www.afdb.org; The AfDB Statistics Pocketbook 2019.

Central Intelligence Agency (CIA), Office of Public Affairs, Washington, DC, 20505, USA, (703) 482-0623, https://www.cia.gov; The World Factbook.

United Nations Department of Economic and Social Affairs (DESA), Population Division, 2 United Nations Plz., Rm. DC2-1950, New York, NY, 10017, USA, (212) 963-3209, (212) 963-2147, population@un.org, https://www.un.org/development/desa/pd/; World Population Ageing 2020 Highlights.

United Nations Statistics Division (UNSD), United Nations Plz., New York, NY, 10017, USA, (800) 253-9646, (212) 963-9851, statistics@un.org, https://unstats.un.org; Millennium Development Goal Indicators.

CAMEROON-LITERACY

Euromonitor International, Inc., 1 N Dearborn St., Ste. 1700, Chicago, IL, 60602, USA, (312) 922-1115, (312) 922-1157, info-usa@euromonitor.com, https://www.euromonitor.com/; Geographies.

UNESCO Institute for Statistics, C.P 250 Succursale H, Montreal, QC, H3G 2K8, CAN, (514) 343-6880 (Dial from U.S.), (514) 343-5740 (Fax from U.S.), uis.publications@unesco.org, http://uis.unesco.org/; Literacy.

CAMEROON-LIVESTOCK

Palgrave Macmillan, 1 New York Plaza, Ste. 4500, New York, NY, 10004-1562, USA, (800) 777-4643, orders@palgrave.com, https://www.palgrave.com/us; The Statesman's Yearbook, 2023.

Routledge - Taylor & Francis Group, 6000 Broken Sound Pkwy. NW, Ste. 300, Boca Raton, FL, 33487, USA, (800) 634-1420, (800) 634-7064, orders@taylorandfrancis.com, https://www.routledge.com/; The Europa World Year Book 2022.

United Nations Economic Commission for Africa (UNECA), PO Box 3001, Addis Ababa, ETH, ecainfo@uneca.org, https://www.uneca.org/; African Statistical Yearbook 2020.

United Nations Food and Agricultural Organization (FAO), 2121 K St., Ste. 800B, Washington, DC, 20037, USA, (202) 653-2400 (Dial from U.S.), (202) 653-5760 (Fax from U.S.), fao-hq@fao.org, https://www.fao.org; The State of Food and Agriculture (SOFA) 2022.

United Nations Statistics Division (UNSD), United Nations Plz., New York, NY, 10017, USA, (800) 253-9646, (212) 963-9851, statistics@un.org, https://unstats.un.org; Statistical Yearbook of the United Nations 2021.

CAMEROON-MATERNAL AND INFANT WELFARE

United Nations Statistics Division (UNSD), United Nations Plz., New York, NY, 10017, USA, (800) 253-9646, (212) 963-9851, statistics@un.org, https://unstats.un.org; Statistical Yearbook of the United Nations 2021.

The World Bank, 1818 H St. NW, Washington, DC, 20433, USA, (202) 473-1000, (202) 477-6391, eds03@worldbank.org, https://www.worldbank.org/; World Development Indicators (WDI) 2022.

CAMEROON-MINERAL INDUSTRIES

Barchart, 209 W Jackson Blvd., 2nd Fl., Chicago, IL, 60606, USA, (877) 247-4394, commodities@barchart.com, https://www.barchart.com/cmdty; The cmdty Yearbook 2023; cmdtyStats: Commodity Statistics and Fundamental Data; cmdtyView: Commodity Index; and Commodity Data and Prices.

International Energy Agency (IEA), 9 Rue de la Federation, Paris, 75739, FRA, info@iea.org, https://www.iea.org/; World Energy Outlook 2021.

Palgrave Macmillan, 1 New York Plaza, Ste. 4500, New York, NY, 10004-1562, USA, (800) 777-4643, orders@palgrave.com, https://www.palgrave.com/us; The Statesman's Yearbook, 2023.

Routledge - Taylor & Francis Group, 6000 Broken Sound Pkwy. NW, Ste. 300, Boca Raton, FL, 33487, USA, (800) 634-1420, (800) 634-7064, orders@taylorandfrancis.com, https://www.routledge.com/; The Europa World Year Book 2022.

United Nations Conference on Trade and Development (UNCTAD), Palais des Nations, Geneva, 1211, SWI, (212) 963-6896, unctadinfo@unctad.org, https://unctad.org; Trade and Development Report 2021.

United Nations Economic Commission for Africa (UNECA), PO Box 3001, Addis Ababa, ETH, ecainfo@uneca.org, https://www.uneca.org/; African Statistical Yearbook 2020.

United Nations Statistics Division (UNSD), United Nations Plz., New York, NY, 10017, USA, (800) 253-9646, (212) 963-9851, statistics@un.org, https://unstats.un.org; Statistical Yearbook of the United Nations 2021.

CAMEROON-MONEY SUPPLY

The Economist Group: Economist Intelligence Unit (EIU), 900 3rd Ave., 16th Fl., New York, NY, 10022, USA, (212) 541-0500, americas@eiu.com, https://www.eiu.com; Cameroon Country Report.

Routledge - Taylor & Francis Group, 6000 Broken Sound Pkwy. NW, Ste. 300, Boca Raton, FL, 33487, USA, (800) 634-1420, (800) 634-7064, orders@taylorandfrancis.com, https://www.routledge.com/; The Europa World Year Book 2022.

The World Bank, 1818 H St. NW, Washington, DC, 20433, USA, (202) 473-1000, (202) 477-6391, eds03@worldbank.org, https://www.worldbank.org/; Camaroon (report).

CAMEROON-MORTALITY

UNICEF, 3 United Nations Plz., New York, NY, 10017, USA, (212) 303-7984, (917) 244-2215, https://www.unicef.org; The State of the World's Children 2023.

United Nations Statistics Division (UNSD), United Nations Plz., New York, NY, 10017, USA, (800) 253-9646, (212) 963-9851, statistics@un.org, https://unstats.un.org; Millennium Development Goal Indicators; Statistical Yearbook of the United Nations 2021; and World Statistics Pocketbook 2021.

World Health Organization (WHO), Ave. Appia 20, Geneva, CH-1211, SWI, (202) 974-3000 (Telephone in U.S.), publications@who.int, https://www.who.int/; Global Health Observatory (GHO).

CAMEROON-MOTION PICTURES

Palgrave Macmillan, 1 New York Plaza, Ste. 4500, New York, NY, 10004-1562, USA, (800) 777-4643, orders@palgrave.com, https://www.palgrave.com/us; The Statesman's Yearbook, 2023.

CAMEROON-MOTOR VEHICLES

International Road Federation (IRF), Madison Place, 500 Montgomery St., 5th Fl., Alexandria, VA, 22314, USA, (703) 535-1001, (703) 535-1007, info@irf.global, https://www.irf.global/; World Road Statistics (WRS).

CAMEROON-NATURAL GAS PRODUCTION

See CAMEROON-MINERAL INDUSTRIES

CAMEROON-NUTRITION

United Nations Food and Agricultural Organization (FAO), 2121 K St., Ste. 800B, Washington, DC, 20037, USA, (202) 653-2400 (Dial from U.S.), (202) 653-5760 (Fax from U.S.), fao-hq@fao.org, https://www.fao.org; The State of Food and Agriculture (SOFA) 2022.

United Nations Statistics Division (UNSD), United Nations Plz., New York, NY, 10017, USA, (800) 253-9646, (212) 963-9851, statistics@un.org, https://unstats.un.org; Millennium Development Goal Indicators.

CAMEROON-PAPER MANUFACTURING

UNESCO Institute for Statistics, C.P 250 Succursale H, Montreal, QC, H3G 2K8, CAN, (514) 343-6880 (Dial from U.S.), (514) 343-5740 (Fax from U.S.), uis.publications@unesco.org, http://uis.unesco.org/; UIS.Stat.

CAMEROON-PEANUT PRODUCTION

See CAMEROON-CROPS

CAMEROON-PESTICIDES

United Nations Food and Agricultural Organization (FAO), 2121 K St., Ste. 800B, Washington, DC, 20037, USA, (202) 653-2400 (Dial from U.S.), (202) 653-5760 (Fax from U.S.), fao-hq@fao.org, https://www.fao.org; The State of Food and Agriculture (SOFA) 2022.

CAMEROON-PETROLEUM INDUSTRY AND TRADE

International Energy Agency (IEA), 9 Rue de la Federation, Paris, 75739, FRA, info@iea.org, https://www.iea.org/; World Energy Outlook 2021.

Palgrave Macmillan, 1 New York Plaza, Ste. 4500, New York, NY, 10004-1562, USA, (800) 777-4643, orders@palgrave.com, https://www.palgrave.com/us; The Statesman's Yearbook, 2023.

U.S. Energy Information Administration (EIA), 1000 Independence Ave. SW, Washington, DC, 20585, USA, (202) 586-8800, infoctr@eia.gov, https://www.eia.gov; International Energy Outlook 2021.

United Nations Food and Agricultural Organization (FAO), 2121 K St., Ste. 800B, Washington, DC, 20037, USA, (202) 653-2400 (Dial from U.S.), (202) 653-5760 (Fax from U.S.), fao-hq@fao.org, https://www.fao.org; The State of Food and Agriculture (SOFA) 2022.

CAMEROON-POPULATION

African Development Bank Group (AfDB), Avenue Joseph Anoma, 01 BP 1387, Abidjan, 01, COT, https://www.afdb.org; The AfDB Statistics Pocketbook 2019; Africa Economic Brief - COVID-19 Pandemic Potential Risks for Trade and Trade Finance in Africa; The African Statistical Journal; and Gender, Poverty and Environmental Indicators on African Countries 2019.

Central Intelligence Agency (CIA), Office of Public Affairs, Washington, DC, 20505, USA, (703) 482-0623, https://www.cia.gov; The World Factbook.

The Economist Group: Economist Intelligence Unit (EIU), 900 3rd Ave., 16th Fl., New York, NY, 10022, USA, (212) 541-0500, americas@eiu.com, https://www.eiu.com; Cameroon Country Report.

European Commission, Eurostat, Luxembourg, 2920, LUX, https://ec.europa.eu/eurostat/; EU in the World 2020.

Infoplease, c/o Sandbox Networks, Inc., 1 Lincoln St., 24th Fl., Boston, MA, 02111, USA, https://www.infoplease.com; Countries of the World.

International Labour Organization (ILO), 4 Rte. des Morillons, Geneva, CH-1211, SWI, ilo@ilo.org, https://www.ilo.org; NORMLEX Information System on International Labour Standards.

Palgrave Macmillan, 1 New York Plaza, Ste. 4500, New York, NY, 10004-1562, USA, (800) 777-4643, orders@palgrave.com, https://www.palgrave.com/us; The Statesman's Yearbook, 2023.

Routledge - Taylor & Francis Group, 6000 Broken Sound Pkwy. NW, Ste. 300, Boca Raton, FL, 33487, USA, (800) 634-1420, (800) 634-7064, orders@taylorandfrancis.com, https://www.routledge.com/; The Europa World Year Book 2022.

UK Data Service, University of Essex, Wivenhoe Park, Colchester, Essex, CO4 3SQ, GBR, https://ukdataservice.ac.uk/; International Aggregate Data.

UNESCO Institute for Statistics, C.P 250 Succursale H, Montreal, QC, H3G 2K8, CAN, (514) 343-6880 (Dial from U.S.), (514) 343-5740 (Fax from U.S.), uis.publications@unesco.org, http://uis.unesco.org/; UIS.Stat.

United Nations Department of Economic and Social Affairs (DESA), Population Division, 2 United Nations Plz., Rm. DC2-1950, New York, NY, 10017, USA, (212) 963-3209, (212) 963-2147, population@un.org, https://www.un.org/development/desa/pd/; Revision of World Urbanization Prospects and World Population Ageing 2020 Highlights.

United Nations Development Programme (UNDP), One United Nations Plz., New York, NY, 10017, USA, (212) 906-5000, (212) 906-5001, https://www.undp.org; Human Development Report 2021-2022.

United Nations Statistics Division (UNSD), United Nations Plz., New York, NY, 10017, USA, (800) 253-9646, (212) 963-9851, statistics@un.org, https://unstats.un.org; Statistical Yearbook of the United Nations 2021 and World Statistics Pocketbook 2021.

The World Bank, 1818 H St. NW, Washington, DC, 20433, USA, (202) 473-1000, (202) 477-6391, eds03@worldbank.org, https://www.worldbank.org/; Camaroon (report); The Global Findex Database 2021; and World Development Report 2022: Finance for an Equitable Recovery.

CAMEROON-POPULATION DENSITY

African Development Bank Group (AfDB), Avenue Joseph Anoma, 01 BP 1387, Abidjan, 01, COT, https://www.afdb.org; The AfDB Statistics Pocketbook 2019.

Central Intelligence Agency (CIA), Office of Public Affairs, Washington, DC, 20505, USA, (703) 482-0623, https://www.cia.gov; The World Factbook.

Palgrave Macmillan, 1 New York Plaza, Ste. 4500, New York, NY, 10004-1562, USA, (800) 777-4643, orders@palgrave.com, https://www.palgrave.com/us; The Statesman's Yearbook, 2023.

Routledge - Taylor & Francis Group, 6000 Broken Sound Pkwy. NW, Ste. 300, Boca Raton, FL, 33487, USA, (800) 634-1420, (800) 634-7064, orders@taylorandfrancis.com, https://www.routledge.com/; The Europa World Year Book 2022.

UNESCO Institute for Statistics, C.P 250 Succursale H, Montreal, QC, H3G 2K8, CAN, (514) 343-6880 (Dial from U.S.), (514) 343-5740 (Fax from U.S.), uis.publications@unesco.org, http://uis.unesco.org/; UIS.Stat.

The World Bank, 1818 H St. NW, Washington, DC, 20433, USA, (202) 473-1000, (202) 477-6391, eds03@worldbank.org, https://www.worldbank.org/; Camaroon (report) and The Global Findex Database 2021.

CAMEROON-POWER RESOURCES

Euromonitor International, Inc., 1 N Dearborn St., Ste. 1700, Chicago, IL, 60602, USA, (312) 922-1115, (312) 922-1157, info-usa@euromonitor.com, https://www.euromonitor.com/; Geographies.

International Energy Agency (IEA), 9 Rue de la Federation, Paris, 75739, FRA, info@iea.org, https://www.iea.org/; World Energy Outlook 2021.

Palgrave Macmillan, 1 New York Plaza, Ste. 4500, New York, NY, 10004-1562, USA, (800) 777-4643, orders@palgrave.com, https://www.palgrave.com/us; The Statesman's Yearbook, 2023.

U.S. Energy Information Administration (EIA), 1000 Independence Ave. SW, Washington, DC, 20585, USA, (202) 586-8800, infoctr@eia.gov, https://www.eia.gov; International Energy Outlook 2021.

United Nations Economic Commission for Africa (UNECA), PO Box 3001, Addis Ababa, ETH, ecainfo@uneca.org, https://www.uneca.org/; African Statistical Yearbook 2020.

United Nations Food and Agricultural Organization (FAO), 2121 K St., Ste. 800B, Washington, DC, 20037, USA, (202) 653-2400 (Dial from U.S.), (202) 653-5760 (Fax from U.S.), fao-hq@fao.org, https://www.fao.org; The State of Food and Agriculture (SOFA) 2022.

United Nations Statistics Division (UNSD), United Nations Plz., New York, NY, 10017, USA, (800) 253-9646, (212) 963-9851, statistics@un.org, https://unstats.un.org; Statistical Yearbook of the United Nations 2021 and World Statistics Pocketbook 2021.

The World Bank, 1818 H St. NW, Washington, DC, 20433, USA, (202) 473-1000, (202) 477-6391, eds03@worldbank.org, https://www.worldbank.org/; World Development Report 2022: Finance for an Equitable Recovery.

CAMEROON-PRICES

Euromonitor International, Inc., 1 N Dearborn St., Ste. 1700, Chicago, IL, 60602, USA, (312) 922-1115, (312) 922-1157, info-usa@euromonitor.com, https://www.euromonitor.com/; Geographies.

International Monetary Fund (IMF), 700 19th St. NW, Washington, DC, 20431, USA, (202) 623-7000, (202) 623-4661, publications@imf.org, https://www.imf.org; International Financial Statistics (IFS).

United Nations Economic Commission for Africa (UNECA), PO Box 3001, Addis Ababa, ETH, ecainfo@uneca.org, https://www.uneca.org/; African Statistical Yearbook 2020.

The World Bank, 1818 H St. NW, Washington, DC, 20433, USA, (202) 473-1000, (202) 477-6391, eds03@worldbank.org, https://www.worldbank.org/; Camaroon (report).

CAMEROON-PUBLIC HEALTH

African Development Bank Group (AfDB), Avenue Joseph Anoma, 01 BP 1387, Abidjan, 01, COT, https://www.afdb.org; The AfDB Statistics Pocketbook 2019.

Euromonitor International, Inc., 1 N Dearborn St., Ste. 1700, Chicago, IL, 60602, USA, (312) 922-1115, (312) 922-1157, info-usa@euromonitor.com, https://www.euromonitor.com/; Geographies.

Organisation of Islamic Cooperation (OIC), Statistical, Economic and Social Research and Training Centre for Islamic Countries (SESRIC), Kudus Cad. No. 9, Diplomatik Site, Ankara, 06450, TUR, statistics@sesric.org, https://www.sesric.org/; OIC Statistics (OICStat) Database.

Palgrave Macmillan, 1 New York Plaza, Ste. 4500, New York, NY, 10004-1562, USA, (800) 777-4643, orders@palgrave.com, https://www.palgrave.com/us; The Statesman's Yearbook, 2023.

U.S. Census Bureau, 4600 Silver Hill Rd., Washington, DC, 20233, USA, (301) 763-4636, (800) 923-8282, https://www.census.gov; HIV/AIDS Surveillance Data Base.

UNICEF, 3 United Nations Plz., New York, NY, 10017, USA, (212) 303-7984, (917) 244-2215, https://www.unicef.org; The State of the World's Children 2023.

United Nations Department of Economic and Social Affairs (DESA), Population Division, 2 United Nations Plz., Rm. DC2-1950, New York, NY, 10017, USA, (212) 963-3209, (212) 963-2147, population@un.org, https://www.un.org/development/desa/pd/; World Fertility Data 2019.

United Nations Development Programme (UNDP), One United Nations Plz., New York, NY, 10017, USA, (212) 906-5000, (212) 906-5001, https://www.undp.org; Human Development Report 2021-2022.

United Nations Economic Commission for Africa (UNECA), PO Box 3001, Addis Ababa, ETH, ecainfo@uneca.org, https://www.uneca.org/; African Statistical Yearbook 2020.

United Nations Statistics Division (UNSD), United Nations Plz., New York, NY, 10017, USA, (800) 253-9646, (212) 963-9851, statistics@un.org, https://unstats.un.org; Millennium Development Goal Indicators and Statistical Yearbook of the United Nations 2021.

The World Bank, 1818 H St. NW, Washington, DC, 20433, USA, (202) 473-1000, (202) 477-6391, eds03@worldbank.org, https://www.worldbank.org/; Camaroon (report).

World Health Organization (WHO), Ave. Appia 20, Geneva, CH-1211, SWI, (202) 974-3000 (Telephone in U.S.), publications@who.int, https://www.who.int/; Global Health Observatory (GHO).

CAMEROON-PUBLISHERS AND PUBLISHING

UNESCO Institute for Statistics, C.P 250 Succursale H, Montreal, QC, H3G 2K8, CAN, (514) 343-6880 (Dial from U.S.), (514) 343-5740 (Fax from U.S.), uis.publications@unesco.org, http://uis.unesco.org/; UIS.Stat.

CAMEROON-RAILROADS

Janes, USA, (703) 574-7580, (888) 977-1519, customer.care@janes.com, https://www.janes.com; Janes World Railways 2021-2022.

Palgrave Macmillan, 1 New York Plaza, Ste. 4500, New York, NY, 10004-1562, USA, (800) 777-4643, orders@palgrave.com, https://www.palgrave.com/us; The Statesman's Yearbook, 2023.

Routledge - Taylor & Francis Group, 6000 Broken Sound Pkwy. NW, Ste. 300, Boca Raton, FL, 33487, USA, (800) 634-1420, (800) 634-7064, orders@taylorandfrancis.com, https://www.routledge.com/; The Europa World Year Book 2022.

United Nations Economic Commission for Africa (UNECA), PO Box 3001, Addis Ababa, ETH, ecainfo@uneca.org, https://www.uneca.org/; African Statistical Yearbook 2020.

United Nations Statistics Division (UNSD), United Nations Plz., New York, NY, 10017, USA, (800) 253-9646, (212) 963-9851, statistics@un.org, https://unstats.un.org; Statistical Yearbook of the United Nations 2021.

CAMEROON-RELIGION

Central Intelligence Agency (CIA), Office of Public Affairs, Washington, DC, 20505, USA, (703) 482-0623, https://www.cia.gov; The World Factbook.

Palgrave Macmillan, 1 New York Plaza, Ste. 4500, New York, NY, 10004-1562, USA, (800) 777-4643, orders@palgrave.com, https://www.palgrave.com/us; The Statesman's Yearbook, 2023.

CAMEROON-RETAIL TRADE

Euromonitor International, Inc., 1 N Dearborn St., Ste. 1700, Chicago, IL, 60602, USA, (312) 922-1115, (312) 922-1157, info-usa@euromonitor.com, https://www.euromonitor.com/; Geographies.

CAMEROON-RICE PRODUCTION

See CAMEROON-CROPS

CAMEROON-ROADS

International Road Federation (IRF), Madison Place, 500 Montgomery St., 5th Fl., Alexandria, VA, 22314, USA, (703) 535-1001, (703) 535-1007, info@irf.global, https://www.irf.global/; World Road Statistics (WRS).

United Nations Economic Commission for Africa (UNECA), PO Box 3001, Addis Ababa, ETH, ecainfo@uneca.org, https://www.uneca.org/; African Statistical Yearbook 2020.

CAMEROON-RUBBER INDUSTRY AND TRADE

International Rubber Study Group (IRSG), 51 Changi Business Park Central 2, Unit No. 6, 486066, SGP, https://www.rubberstudy.org; Monthly Rubber Bulletin (MRB); Rubber Industry Report; Rubber Statistical Bulletin; and World Rubber Industry Report (WRIO).

United Nations Statistics Division (UNSD), United Nations Plz., New York, NY, 10017, USA, (800) 253-9646, (212) 963-9851, statistics@un.org, https://unstats.un.org; Statistical Yearbook of the United Nations 2021.

CAMEROON-SHIPPING

Routledge - Taylor & Francis Group, 6000 Broken Sound Pkwy. NW, Ste. 300, Boca Raton, FL, 33487, USA, (800) 634-1420, (800) 634-7064, orders@taylorandfrancis.com, https://www.routledge.com/; The Europa World Year Book 2022.

United Nations Economic Commission for Africa (UNECA), PO Box 3001, Addis Ababa, ETH, ecainfo@uneca.org, https://www.uneca.org/; African Statistical Yearbook 2020.

United Nations Statistics Division (UNSD), United Nations Plz., New York, NY, 10017, USA, (800) 253-9646, (212) 963-9851, statistics@un.org, https://unstats.un.org; Statistical Yearbook of the United Nations 2021.

CAMEROON-STEEL PRODUCTION

See CAMEROON-MINERAL INDUSTRIES

CAMEROON-SUGAR PRODUCTION

See CAMEROON-CROPS

CAMEROON-TAXATION

International Road Federation (IRF), Madison Place, 500 Montgomery St., 5th Fl., Alexandria, VA, 22314, USA, (703) 535-1001, (703) 535-1007, info@irf.global, https://www.irf.global/; World Road Statistics (WRS).

The World Bank, 1818 H St. NW, Washington, DC, 20433, USA, (202) 473-1000, (202) 477-6391, eds03@worldbank.org, https://www.worldbank.org/; World Development Indicators (WDI) 2022.

CAMEROON-TEA PRODUCTION

See CAMEROON-CROPS

CAMEROON-TELEPHONE

Palgrave Macmillan, 1 New York Plaza, Ste. 4500, New York, NY, 10004-1562, USA, (800) 777-4643, orders@palgrave.com, https://www.palgrave.com/us; The Statesman's Yearbook, 2023.

Routledge - Taylor & Francis Group, 6000 Broken Sound Pkwy. NW, Ste. 300, Boca Raton, FL, 33487, USA, (800) 634-1420, (800) 634-7064, orders@taylorandfrancis.com, https://www.routledge.com/; The Europa World Year Book 2022.

United Nations Statistics Division (UNSD), United Nations Plz., New York, NY, 10017, USA, (800) 253-9646, (212) 963-9851, statistics@un.org, https://unstats.un.org; World Statistics Pocketbook 2021.

CAMEROON-THEATER

UNESCO Institute for Statistics, C.P 250 Succursale H, Montreal, QC, H3G 2K8, CAN, (514) 343-6880 (Dial from U.S.), (514) 343-5740 (Fax from U.S.), uis.publications@unesco.org, http://uis.unesco.org/; UIS.Stat.

CAMEROON-TOBACCO INDUSTRY

United Nations Statistics Division (UNSD), United Nations Plz., New York, NY, 10017, USA, (800) 253-9646, (212) 963-9851, statistics@un.org, https://unstats.un.org; Statistical Yearbook of the United Nations 2021.

CAMEROON-TOURISM

Euromonitor International, Inc., 1 N Dearborn St., Ste. 1700, Chicago, IL, 60602, USA, (312) 922-1115, (312) 922-1157, info-usa@euromonitor.com, https://www.euromonitor.com/; Geographies.

Organisation of Islamic Cooperation (OIC), Statistical, Economic and Social Research and Training Centre for Islamic Countries (SESRIC), Kudus Cad. No. 9, Diplomatik Site, Ankara, 06450, TUR, statistics@sesric.org, https://www.sesric.org/; International Tourism in the OIC Countries: Prospects and Challenges, 2020 and OIC Statistics (OICStat) Database.

Palgrave Macmillan, 1 New York Plaza, Ste. 4500, New York, NY, 10004-1562, USA, (800) 777-4643, orders@palgrave.com, https://www.palgrave.com/us; The Statesman's Yearbook, 2023.

Routledge - Taylor & Francis Group, 6000 Broken Sound Pkwy. NW, Ste. 300, Boca Raton, FL, 33487, USA, (800) 634-1420, (800) 634-7064, orders@taylorandfrancis.com, https://www.routledge.com/; The Europa World Year Book 2022.

United Nations Economic Commission for Africa (UNECA), PO Box 3001, Addis Ababa, ETH, ecainfo@uneca.org, https://www.uneca.org/; African Statistical Yearbook 2020.

United Nations Statistics Division (UNSD), United Nations Plz., New York, NY, 10017, USA, (800) 253-9646, (212) 963-9851, statistics@un.org, https://unstats.un.org; Statistical Yearbook of the United Nations 2021.

The World Bank, 1818 H St. NW, Washington, DC, 20433, USA, (202) 473-1000, (202) 477-6391, eds03@worldbank.org, https://www.worldbank.org/; Camaroon (report).

CAMEROON-TRADE

See CAMEROON-INTERNATIONAL TRADE

CAMEROON-TRANSPORTATION

African Development Bank Group (AfDB), Avenue Joseph Anoma, 01 BP 1387, Abidjan, 01, COT, https://www.afdb.org; African Economic Outlook 2021 and Compendium of Statistics on Bank Group Operations 2019.

Central Intelligence Agency (CIA), Office of Public Affairs, Washington, DC, 20505, USA, (703) 482-0623, https://www.cia.gov; The World Factbook.

Euromonitor International, Inc., 1 N Dearborn St., Ste. 1700, Chicago, IL, 60602, USA, (312) 922-1115, (312) 922-1157, info-usa@euromonitor.com, https://www.euromonitor.com/; Geographies.

Organisation of Islamic Cooperation (OIC), Statistical, Economic and Social Research and Training Centre for Islamic Countries (SESRIC), Kudus Cad. No. 9, Diplomatik Site, Ankara, 06450, TUR, statistics@sesric.org, https://www.sesric.org/; OIC Statistics (OICStat) Database.

Palgrave Macmillan, 1 New York Plaza, Ste. 4500, New York, NY, 10004-1562, USA, (800) 777-4643, orders@palgrave.com, https://www.palgrave.com/us; The Statesman's Yearbook, 2023.

Routledge - Taylor & Francis Group, 6000 Broken Sound Pkwy. NW, Ste. 300, Boca Raton, FL, 33487, USA, (800) 634-1420, (800) 634-7064, orders@taylorandfrancis.com, https://www.routledge.com/; The Europa World Year Book 2022.

United Nations Economic Commission for Africa (UNECA), PO Box 3001, Addis Ababa, ETH, ecainfo@uneca.org, https://www.uneca.org/; African Statistical Yearbook 2020 and Economic Report on Africa 2021.

The World Bank, 1818 H St. NW, Washington, DC, 20433, USA, (202) 473-1000, (202) 477-6391, eds03@worldbank.org, https://www.worldbank.org/; Camaroon (report).

CAMEROON-UNEMPLOYMENT

International Labour Organization (ILO), 4 Rte. des Morillons, Geneva, CH-1211, SWI, ilo@ilo.org, https://www.ilo.org; NORMLEX Information System on International Labour Standards.

United Nations Statistics Division (UNSD), United Nations Plz., New York, NY, 10017, USA, (800) 253-9646, (212) 963-9851, statistics@un.org, https://unstats.un.org; Statistical Yearbook of the United Nations 2021.

CAMEROON-VITAL STATISTICS

Palgrave Macmillan, 1 New York Plaza, Ste. 4500, New York, NY, 10004-1562, USA, (800) 777-4643, orders@palgrave.com, https://www.palgrave.com/us; The Statesman's Yearbook, 2023.

U.S. Census Bureau, 4600 Silver Hill Rd., Washington, DC, 20233, USA, (301) 763-4636, (800) 923-8282, https://www.census.gov; HIV/AIDS Surveillance Data Base.

United Nations Department of Economic and Social Affairs (DESA), Population Division, 2 United Nations Plz., Rm. DC2-1950, New York, NY, 10017, USA, (212) 963-3209, (212) 963-2147, population@un.org, https://www.un.org/development/desa/pd/; World Contraceptive Use 2021: Estimates and Projections of Family Planning Indicators and World Marriage Data 2019.

United Nations Statistics Division (UNSD), United Nations Plz., New York, NY, 10017, USA, (800) 253-9646, (212) 963-9851, statistics@un.org, https://unstats.un.org; Statistical Yearbook of the United Nations 2021.

CAMEROON-WAGES

International Labour Organization (ILO), 4 Rte. des Morillons, Geneva, CH-1211, SWI, ilo@ilo.org, https://www.ilo.org; NORMLEX Information System on International Labour Standards.

The World Bank, 1818 H St. NW, Washington, DC, 20433, USA, (202) 473-1000, (202) 477-6391, eds03@worldbank.org, https://www.worldbank.org/; Camaroon (report).

CAMEROON-WEATHER

See CAMEROON-CLIMATE

CAMEROON-WHEAT PRODUCTION

See CAMEROON-CROPS

CAMEROON-WOOD AND WOOD PULP

See CAMEROON-FORESTS AND FORESTRY

CAMEROON-WOOL PRODUCTION

See CAMEROON-TEXTILE INDUSTRY

CAMPAIGN FUNDS

CQ Press, An Imprint of SAGE Publication, 2455 Teller Rd., Thousand Oaks, CA, 91320, USA, (800) 818-7243, (805) 499-9774, (800) 583-2665, info@sagepub.com, https://us.sagepub.com/en-us/nam/cqpress; CQPress Congress Collection.

Federal Election Commission (FEC), 1050 1st St. NE, Washington, DC, 20463, USA, (800) 424-9530, (202) 694-1100, pubrec@fec.gov, https://www.fec.gov; Campaign Finance Data and FEC Congressional Budget Justification Fiscal Year 2022.

KFF Health News, 1330 G St. NW, Washington, DC, 20005, USA, (202) 347-5270, https://khn.org/; Campaign Contributions Tracker: Pharma Cash to Congress.

OpenSecrets, 1300 L St. NW , Ste. 200, Washington, DC, 20005, USA, (202) 857-0044, (202) 857-7809, info@crp.org, https://www.opensecrets.org/; Dozens of Members of Congress Up for Reelection in 2022 Midterms Received the Majority of Their Campaign Funds From PACs and GOP Candidates Who Participated in the Jan. 6 Rally Are Raising Millions.

CAMPAIGN MANAGEMENT

OpenSecrets, 1300 L St. NW , Ste. 200, Washington, DC, 20005, USA, (202) 857-0044, (202) 857-7809, info@crp.org, https://www.opensecrets.org/; Dozens of Members of Congress Up for Reelection in 2022 Midterms Received the Majority of Their Campaign Funds From PACs.

YouGov, 38 W 21st St., New York, NY, 10010, USA, (646) 213-7414, help.us@yougov.com, https://today.yougov.com/; Presidential Voting Intention 2020.

CAMPING, ETC

National Sporting Goods Association (NSGA), 3041 Woodcreek Dr., Ste. 210, Downers Grove, IL, 60515, USA, (847) 296-6742, (847) 391-9827, info@nsga.org, https://www.nsga.org; Sports Participation in the United States 2022 and Sports Participation: Historical Sports Participation 2022.

CAMPUS POLICE

Police Executive Research Forum (PERF), 1120 Connecticut Ave. NW, Ste. 930, Washington, DC, 20036, USA, (202) 466-7820, https://www.policeforum.org; Municipal and Campus Police: Strategies for Working Together During Turbulent Times.

CANADA-NATIONAL STATISTICAL OFFICE

Statistics Canada (StatCan), 150 Tunney's Pasture Driveway, Ottawa, ON, K1A 0T6, CAN, (800) 263-1136 (Dial from U.S.), (514) 283-8300 (Dial from U.S.), (514) 283-9350 (Fax from U.S.), infostats@statcan.gc.ca, https://www.statcan.gc.ca; National Data Reports (Canada).

CANADA-PRIMARY STATISTICS SOURCES

British Columbia Vital Statistics Agency, Stn Prov Govt, PO Box 9408, Victoria, BC, V8W 9V1, CAN, (250) 387-6121 (Dial from U.S.), (250) 952-4124 (Fax from U.S.), servicebc@gov.bc.ca, https://www2.gov.bc.ca/gov/content/family-social-supports/seniors/health-safety/health-care-programs-and-services/vital-statistics; Statistics and Reports.

Northwest Territories Bureau of Statistics, Government of the Northwest Territories, PO Box 1320, Yellowknife, NT, X1A 2L9, CAN, (867) 767-9169 (Dial from U.S.), (888) 782-8768, (867) 873-0275 (Fax from U.S.), info@stats.gov.nt.ca, https://www.statsnwt.ca/; Statistics Quarterly.

Nova Scotia Department of Finance and Treasury Board, Economics and Statistics Division, 1723 Hollis St., PO Box 187, Halifax, NS, B3J 2N3, CAN, (902) 424-5554 (Dial from U.S.), (902) 424-0635 (Fax from U.S.), financeweb@novascotia.ca, https://www.novascotia.ca/finance/statistics/; DailyStats and Nova Scotia Demographic Updates.

Nunavut Bureau of Statistics, Government of Nunavut, PO Box 1000 Station 200, Iqaluit, NU, X0A 0H0, CAN, (867) 975-6000 (Dial from U.S.), (867) 975-6099 (Dial from U.S.), info@gov.nu.ca, https://www.gov.nu.ca/eia/information/statistics-home; Population Data.

Service New Brunswick, PO Box 1998 , Fredericton, NB, E3B 5G4, CAN, (888) 762-8600 (Dial from U.S.), (506) 684-7901 (Dial from U.S.), (506) 444-4253 (Fax from U.S.), snb@snb.ca, https://www2.snb.ca/; 2020 Annual Statistics of New Brunswick.

Statistics Canada (StatCan), 150 Tunney's Pasture Driveway, Ottawa, ON, K1A 0T6, CAN, (800) 263-1136 (Dial from U.S.), (514) 283-8300 (Dial from U.S.), (514) 283-9350 (Fax from U.S.), infostats@statcan.gc.ca, https://www.statcan.gc.ca; Children and Youth Statistics; Gender, Diversity and Inclusion Statistics (GDIS) Hub; and Quarterly Demographic Estimates.

CANADA-DATABASES

The Conference Board of Canada, 135 Laurier Avenue W, Ottawa, ON, K1P 5J2, CAN, (866) 711-2262 (Dial from U.S.), (613) 526-3280 (Dial from U.S.), (613) 526-4857 (Fax from U.S.), contactcboc@conferenceboard.ca, https://www.conferenceboard.ca/; Canadian Economic Forecasts (5 Years) Database; Metropolitan Forecast Database; and Provincial Economic Forecast (5 Years) Database.

Institute de la statistique du Quebec, 200 Chemin Sainte-Foy, 3rd Fl., Quebec City, QC, G1R 5T4, CAN, (418) 691-2401 (Dial from U.S.), (800) 463-4090 (Dial from U.S.), (418) 643-4129 (Fax from U.S.), https://statistique.quebec.ca/en; Databank of Official Statistics on Quebec.

Statistics Canada (StatCan), 150 Tunney's Pasture Driveway, Ottawa, ON, K1A 0T6, CAN, (800) 263-1136 (Dial from U.S.), (514) 283-8300 (Dial from U.S.), (514) 283-9350 (Fax from U.S.), infostats@statcan.gc.ca, https://www.statcan.gc.ca; Canadian Socio-Economic Information Management System (CANSIM) Summary Reference Index.

CANADA-AGRICULTURE

The Economist Group: Economist Intelligence Unit (EIU), 900 3rd Ave., 16th Fl., New York, NY, 10022, USA, (212) 541-0500, americas@eiu.com, https://www.eiu.com; Canada Country Report.

Euromonitor International, Inc., 1 N Dearborn St., Ste. 1700, Chicago, IL, 60602, USA, (312) 922-1115, (312) 922-1157, info-usa@euromonitor.com, https://www.euromonitor.com/; Geographies.

Organization for Economic Cooperation and Development (OECD), 2001 L St. NW, Ste. 650, Washington, DC, 20036-4922, USA, (202) 785-6323, (800) 456-6323, (202) 785-0350, washington.contact@oecd.org, https://www.oecd.org/; Economic Survey of Canada 2023; OECD-FAO Agricultural Outlook 2022-2031; and STAN (STructural ANalysis) Database.

Palgrave Macmillan, 1 New York Plaza, Ste. 4500, New York, NY, 10004-1562, USA, (800) 777-4643, orders@palgrave.com, https://www.palgrave.com/us; The Statesman's Yearbook, 2023.

Routledge - Taylor & Francis Group, 6000 Broken Sound Pkwy. NW, Ste. 300, Boca Raton, FL, 33487, USA, (800) 634-1420, (800) 634-7064, orders@taylorandfrancis.com, https://www.routledge.com/; The Europa World Year Book 2022.

Statistics Canada (StatCan), 150 Tunney's Pasture Driveway, Ottawa, ON, K1A 0T6, CAN, (800) 263-1136 (Dial from U.S.), (514) 283-8300 (Dial from U.S.), (514) 283-9350 (Fax from U.S.), infostats@statcan.gc.ca, https://www.statcan.gc.ca; Net Income of Cannabis Authorities and Government Revenue from the Sale of Cannabis (x 1,000).

U.S. Department of Agriculture (USDA), Economic Research Service (ERS), 1400 Independence Ave. SW, Mail Stop 1800, Washington, DC, 20250-0002, USA, (202) 720-2791, https://www.ers.usda.gov/; Countries and Regions: The United States-Mexico-Canada Agreement (USMCA), Canada and Mexico.

United Nations Food and Agricultural Organization (FAO), 2121 K St., Ste. 800B, Washington, DC, 20037, USA, (202) 653-2400 (Dial from U.S.), (202) 653-5760 (Fax from U.S.), fao-hq@fao.org, https://www.fao.org; AQUASTAT and The State of Food and Agriculture (SOFA) 2022.

United Nations Statistics Division (UNSD), United Nations Plz., New York, NY, 10017, USA, (800) 253-9646, (212) 963-9851, statistics@un.org, https://unstats.un.org; Statistical Yearbook of the United Nations 2021.

The World Bank, 1818 H St. NW, Washington, DC, 20433, USA, (202) 473-1000, (202) 477-6391, eds03@worldbank.org, https://www.worldbank.org/; Canada (report) and World Development Indicators (WDI) 2022.

CANADA-AIRLINES

International Civil Aviation Organization (ICAO), 999 Robert-Bourassa Blvd., Montreal, QC, H3C 5H7, CAN, (514) 954-8219 (Dial from U.S.), (514) 954-6077 (Fax from U.S.), icaohq@icao.int, https://www.icao.int; ICAO Regional Reports.

Organization for Economic Cooperation and Development (OECD), 2001 L St. NW, Ste. 650, Washington, DC, 20036-4922, USA, (202) 785-6323, (800) 456-6323, (202) 785-0350, washington.contact@oecd.org, https://www.oecd.org/; OECD Tourism Trends and Policies 2022.

Palgrave Macmillan, 1 New York Plaza, Ste. 4500, New York, NY, 10004-1562, USA, (800) 777-4643, orders@palgrave.com, https://www.palgrave.com/us; The Statesman's Yearbook, 2023.

Routledge - Taylor & Francis Group, 6000 Broken Sound Pkwy. NW, Ste. 300, Boca Raton, FL, 33487, USA, (800) 634-1420, (800) 634-7064, orders@taylorandfrancis.com, https://www.routledge.com/; The Europa World Year Book 2022.

CANADA-ALUMINUM PRODUCTION

See CANADA-MINERAL INDUSTRIES

CANADA-ANIMAL FEEDING

United Nations Statistics Division (UNSD), United Nations Plz., New York, NY, 10017, USA, (800) 253-9646, (212) 963-9851, statistics@un.org, https://unstats.un.org; Statistical Yearbook of the United Nations 2021.

CANADA-ARMED FORCES

Central Intelligence Agency (CIA), Office of Public Affairs, Washington, DC, 20505, USA, (703) 482-0623, https://www.cia.gov; The World Factbook.

International Institute for Strategic Studies (IISS) - Americas, 2121 K St. NW, Ste. 600, Washington, DC, 20037, USA, (202) 659-1490, (202) 659-1499, https://www.iiss.org/; The Military Balance 2022.

Palgrave Macmillan, 1 New York Plaza, Ste. 4500, New York, NY, 10004-1562, USA, (800) 777-4643, orders@palgrave.com, https://www.palgrave.com/us; The Statesman's Yearbook, 2023.

Stockholm International Peace Research Institute (SIPRI), Signalistgatan 9, Stockholm, SE 169 72, SWE, https://www.sipri.org/; SIPRI Arms Transfers Database and SIPRI Military Expenditure Database.

CANADA-AUTOMOBILE INDUSTRY AND TRADE

Routledge - Taylor & Francis Group, 6000 Broken Sound Pkwy. NW, Ste. 300, Boca Raton, FL, 33487,

USA, (800) 634-1420, (800) 634-7064, orders@taylorandfrancis.com, https://www.routledge.com/; The Europa World Year Book 2022.

CANADA-BALANCE OF PAYMENTS

International Monetary Fund (IMF), 700 19th St. NW, Washington, DC, 20431, USA, (202) 623-7000, (202) 623-4661, publications@imf.org, https://www.imf.org; Balance of Payments Statistics: Annual Report 2021 and International Financial Statistics (IFS).

Organization for Economic Cooperation and Development (OECD), 2001 L St. NW, Ste. 650, Washington, DC, 20036-4922, USA, (202) 785-6323, (800) 456-6323, (202) 785-0350, washington.contact@oecd.org, https://www.oecd.org/; Economic Survey of Canada 2023; Geographical Distribution of Financial Flows to Developing Countries 2023; OECD Digital Economy Outlook 2020; and OECD Main Economic Indicators (MEI).

Routledge - Taylor & Francis Group, 6000 Broken Sound Pkwy. NW, Ste. 300, Boca Raton, FL, 33487, USA, (800) 634-1420, (800) 634-7064, orders@taylorandfrancis.com, https://www.routledge.com/; The Europa World Year Book 2022.

United Nations Conference on Trade and Development (UNCTAD), Palais des Nations, Geneva, 1211, SWI, (212) 963-6896, unctadinfo@unctad.org, https://unctad.org; Handbook of Statistics 2021.

The World Bank, 1818 H St. NW, Washington, DC, 20433, USA, (202) 473-1000, (202) 477-6391, eds03@worldbank.org, https://www.worldbank.org/; Canada (report); World Development Indicators (WDI) 2022; and World Development Report 2022: Finance for an Equitable Recovery.

CANADA-BANKS AND BANKING

Euromonitor International, Inc., 1 N Dearborn St., Ste. 1700, Chicago, IL, 60602, USA, (312) 922-1115, (312) 922-1157, info-usa@euromonitor.com, https://www.euromonitor.com/; Geographies.

International Monetary Fund (IMF), 700 19th St. NW, Washington, DC, 20431, USA, (202) 623-7000, (202) 623-4661, publications@imf.org, https://www.imf.org; International Financial Statistics (IFS).

Organization for Economic Cooperation and Development (OECD), 2001 L St. NW, Ste. 650, Washington, DC, 20036-4922, USA, (202) 785-6323, (800) 456-6323, (202) 785-0350, washington.contact@oecd.org, https://www.oecd.org/; Economic Survey of Canada 2023; OECD Business and Finance Outlook 2021; and OECD Digital Economy Outlook 2020.

Routledge - Taylor & Francis Group, 6000 Broken Sound Pkwy. NW, Ste. 300, Boca Raton, FL, 33487, USA, (800) 634-1420, (800) 634-7064, orders@taylorandfrancis.com, https://www.routledge.com/; The Europa World Year Book 2022.

United Nations Statistics Division (UNSD), United Nations Plz., New York, NY, 10017, USA, (800) 253-9646, (212) 963-9851, statistics@un.org, https://unstats.un.org; Statistical Yearbook of the United Nations 2021.

CANADA-BARLEY PRODUCTION

See CANADA-CROPS

CANADA-BEVERAGE INDUSTRY

United Nations Food and Agricultural Organization (FAO), 2121 K St., Ste. 800B, Washington, DC, 20037, USA, (202) 653-2400 (Dial from U.S.), (202) 653-5760 (Fax from U.S.), fao-hq@fao.org, https://www.fao.org; The State of Food and Agriculture (SOFA) 2022.

CANADA-BONDS

Organization for Economic Cooperation and Development (OECD), 2001 L St. NW, Ste. 650, Washington, DC, 20036-4922, USA, (202) 785-6323, (800) 456-6323, (202) 785-0350, washington.contact@oecd.org, https://www.oecd.org/; OECD Business and Finance Outlook 2021.

United Nations Statistics Division (UNSD), United Nations Plz., New York, NY, 10017, USA, (800) 253-9646, (212) 963-9851, statistics@un.org, https://unstats.un.org; Statistical Yearbook of the United Nations 2021.

CANADA-BROADCASTING

Central Intelligence Agency (CIA), Office of Public Affairs, Washington, DC, 20505, USA, (703) 482-0623, https://www.cia.gov; The World Factbook.

Euromonitor International, Inc., 1 N Dearborn St., Ste. 1700, Chicago, IL, 60602, USA, (312) 922-1115, (312) 922-1157, info-usa@euromonitor.com, https://www.euromonitor.com/; Geographies.

Palgrave Macmillan, 1 New York Plaza, Ste. 4500, New York, NY, 10004-1562, USA, (800) 777-4643, orders@palgrave.com, https://www.palgrave.com/us; The Statesman's Yearbook, 2023.

UNESCO Institute for Statistics, C.P 250 Succursale H, Montreal, QC, H3G 2K8, CAN, (514) 343-6880 (Dial from U.S.), (514) 343-5740 (Fax from U.S.), uis.publications@unesco.org, http://uis.unesco.org/; UIS.Stat.

WRTH Publications Limited, PO Box 290, Oxford, OX2 7FT, GBR, sales@wrth.com, https://www.wrth.com; World Radio TV Handbook 2023.

CANADA-BUDGET

Central Intelligence Agency (CIA), Office of Public Affairs, Washington, DC, 20505, USA, (703) 482-0623, https://www.cia.gov; The World Factbook.

CANADA-BUSINESS

Global Entrepreneurship Monitor (GEM), Babson College, 231 Forest St., Babson Park, MA, 02457, USA, (781) 235-1200, info@gemconsortium.org, https://www.gemconsortium.org/; Canada Economy Profile.

Government of Alberta, PO Box 1333, Edmonton, AB, T5J 2N2, CAN, (780) 427-2711 (Dial from U.S.), https://www.alberta.ca; Alberta Business and Economy.

Green Science Policy Institute, PO Box 9127, Berkeley, CA, 94709, USA, (510) 898-1739, info@greensciencepolicy.org, https://greensciencepolicy.org/; Fluorinated Compounds in North American Cosmetics.

International Council of Shopping Centers (ICSC), 1251 Avenue of the Americas, 45th Fl., New York, NY, 10020-1104, USA, (646) 728-3800, (844) 728-4272, (732) 694-1690, membership@icsc.org, https://www.icsc.org; Industry Benchmark Report.

Organization for Economic Cooperation and Development (OECD), 2001 L St. NW, Ste. 650, Washington, DC, 20036-4922, USA, (202) 785-6323, (800) 456-6323, (202) 785-0350, washington.contact@oecd.org, https://www.oecd.org/; OECD Main Economic Indicators (MEI).

CANADA-CAPITAL INVESTMENTS

Organization for Economic Cooperation and Development (OECD), 2001 L St. NW, Ste. 650, Washington, DC, 20036-4922, USA, (202) 785-6323, (800) 456-6323, (202) 785-0350, washington.contact@oecd.org, https://www.oecd.org/; OECD Business and Finance Outlook 2021.

CANADA-CHILDBIRTH-STATISTICS

The World Bank, 1818 H St. NW, Washington, DC, 20433, USA, (202) 473-1000, (202) 477-6391, eds03@worldbank.org, https://www.worldbank.org/; World Development Indicators (WDI) 2022.

CANADA-CHILDREN

Statistics Canada (StatCan), 150 Tunney's Pasture Driveway, Ottawa, ON, K1A 0T6, CAN, (800) 263-1136 (Dial from U.S.), (514) 283-8300 (Dial from U.S.), (514) 283-9350 (Fax from U.S.), infostats@statcan.gc.ca, https://www.statcan.gc.ca; Children and Youth Statistics.

CANADA-CLIMATE

Environment and Climate Change Canada, Fontaine Bldg., 200 Sacre-Coeur Blvd., 12th Fl., Gatineau, QC, K1A 0H3, CAN, (819) 938-3838 (Dial from U.S.), enviroinfo@ec.gc.ca, https://www.canada.ca/en/environment-climate-change.html; Canadian Environmental Sustainability Indicators (CESI).

Palgrave Macmillan, 1 New York Plaza, Ste. 4500, New York, NY, 10004-1562, USA, (800) 777-4643, orders@palgrave.com, https://www.palgrave.com/us; The Statesman's Yearbook, 2023.

Polaris Institute, 135 Laurier Ave. W, Ste. 630, Ottawa, ON, K1P 5J2, CAN, (613) 237-1717 (Dial from U.S.), polaris@polarisinstitute.org, https://www.polarisinstitute.org/; unpublished data.

World Weather Attribution (WWA), wwamedia@imperial.ac.uk, https://www.worldweatherattribution.org; Rapid Attribution Analysis of the Extraordinary Heatwave on the Pacific Coast of the US and Canada June 2021.

CANADA-COAL PRODUCTION

See CANADA-MINERAL INDUSTRIES

CANADA-COFFEE

See CANADA-CROPS

CANADA-COFFEE INDUSTRY

United Nations Statistics Division (UNSD), United Nations Plz., New York, NY, 10017, USA, (800) 253-9646, (212) 963-9851, statistics@un.org, https://unstats.un.org; Statistical Yearbook of the United Nations 2021.

CANADA-COMMERCE

Palgrave Macmillan, 1 New York Plaza, Ste. 4500, New York, NY, 10004-1562, USA, (800) 777-4643, orders@palgrave.com, https://www.palgrave.com/us; The Statesman's Yearbook, 2023.

Statistics Canada (StatCan), 150 Tunney's Pasture Driveway, Ottawa, ON, K1A 0T6, CAN, (800) 263-1136 (Dial from U.S.), (514) 283-8300 (Dial from U.S.), (514) 283-9350 (Fax from U.S.), infostats@statcan.gc.ca, https://www.statcan.gc.ca; Net Income of Cannabis Authorities and Government Revenue from the Sale of Cannabis (x 1,000).

UK Data Service, University of Essex, Wivenhoe Park, Colchester, Essex, CO4 3SQ, GBR, https://ukdataservice.ac.uk/; International Aggregate Data.

CANADA-COMMODITY EXCHANGES

Barchart, 209 W Jackson Blvd., 2nd Fl., Chicago, IL, 60606, USA, (877) 247-4394, commodities@barchart.com, https://www.barchart.com/cmdty; The cmdty Yearbook 2023; cmdtyStats: Commodity Statistics and Fundamental Data; cmdtyView: Commodity Index; and Commodity Data and Prices.

International Lead and Zinc Study Group (ILZSG), Rua Almirante Barroso 38, 5th Fl., Lisbon, 1000-013, PRT, sales@ilzsg.org, https://www.ilzsg.org; Interactive Statistical Database.

International Monetary Fund (IMF), 700 19th St. NW, Washington, DC, 20431, USA, (202) 623-7000, (202) 623-4661, publications@imf.org, https://www.imf.org; IMF Primary Commodity Prices.

United Nations Statistics Division (UNSD), United Nations Plz., New York, NY, 10017, USA, (800) 253-9646, (212) 963-9851, statistics@un.org, https://unstats.un.org; Statistical Yearbook of the United Nations 2021.

World Bureau of Metal Statistics (WBMS), 31 Star St., Ware, Hertfordshire, SG12 9BA, GBR, https://www.refinitiv.com/en/trading-solutions/world-bureau-metal-statistics; Annual Stainless Steel Statistics; Long Term Production/Consumption Series - All Metals; World Flow Charts; and World Metal Statistics.

CANADA-CONSTRUCTION INDUSTRY

Nova Scotia Department of Finance and Treasury Board, Economics and Statistics Division, 1723 Hollis St., PO Box 187, Halifax, NS, B3J 2N3, CAN, (902) 424-5554 (Dial from U.S.), (902) 424-0635

(Fax from U.S.), financeweb@novascotia.ca, https://www.novascotia.ca/finance/statistics/; Nova Scotia Economic Indicators.

Organization for Economic Cooperation and Development (OECD), 2001 L St. NW, Ste. 650, Washington, DC, 20036-4922, USA, (202) 785-6323, (800) 456-6323, (202) 785-0350, washington.contact@oecd.org, https://www.oecd.org/; Economic Survey of Canada 2023; OECD Main Economic Indicators (MEI); and STAN (STructural ANalysis) Database.

Palgrave Macmillan, 1 New York Plaza, Ste. 4500, New York, NY, 10004-1562, USA, (800) 777-4643, orders@palgrave.com, https://www.palgrave.com/us; The Statesman's Yearbook, 2023.

United Nations Statistics Division (UNSD), United Nations Plz., New York, NY, 10017, USA, (800) 253-9646, (212) 963-9851, statistics@un.org, https://unstats.un.org; Statistical Yearbook of the United Nations 2021.

CANADA-CONSUMER PRICE INDEXES

Nova Scotia Department of Finance and Treasury Board, Economics and Statistics Division, 1723 Hollis St., PO Box 187, Halifax, NS, B3J 2N3, CAN, (902) 424-5554 (Dial from U.S.), (902) 424-0635 (Fax from U.S.), financeweb@novascotia.ca, https://www.novascotia.ca/finance/statistics/; Nova Scotia Consumer Price Index and Nova Scotia Economic Indicators.

Organization for Economic Cooperation and Development (OECD), 2001 L St. NW, Ste. 650, Washington, DC, 20036-4922, USA, (202) 785-6323, (800) 456-6323, (202) 785-0350, washington.contact@oecd.org, https://www.oecd.org/; OECD Digital Economy Outlook 2020.

Routledge - Taylor & Francis Group, 6000 Broken Sound Pkwy. NW, Ste. 300, Boca Raton, FL, 33487, USA, (800) 634-1420, (800) 634-7064, orders@taylorandfrancis.com, https://www.routledge.com/; The Europa World Year Book 2022.

The World Bank, 1818 H St. NW, Washington, DC, 20433, USA, (202) 473-1000, (202) 477-6391, eds03@worldbank.org, https://www.worldbank.org/; Canada (report).

CANADA-CONSUMPTION (ECONOMICS)

International Monetary Fund (IMF), 700 19th St. NW, Washington, DC, 20431, USA, (202) 623-7000, (202) 623-4661, publications@imf.org, https://www.imf.org; International Financial Statistics (IFS).

Organization for Economic Cooperation and Development (OECD), 2001 L St. NW, Ste. 650, Washington, DC, 20036-4922, USA, (202) 785-6323, (800) 456-6323, (202) 785-0350, washington.contact@oecd.org, https://www.oecd.org/; OECD-FAO Agricultural Outlook 2022-2031 and Revenue Statistics 2022.

TAPPI - Technical Association of the Pulp and Paper Industry, 15 Technology Pkwy. S, Ste. 115, Peachtree Corners, GA, 30092, USA, (770) 446-1400, (800) 332-8686, (770) 446-6947, memberconnection@tappi.org, https://www.tappi.org/; TAPPI Journal.

World Steel Association (Worldsteel), Avenue de Tervueren 270, Brussels, B-1150, BEL, steel@worldsteel.org, https://www.worldsteel.org; Steel Statistical Yearbook 2021.

CANADA-COPPER INDUSTRY AND TRADE

See CANADA-MINERAL INDUSTRIES

CANADA-CORN INDUSTRY

See CANADA-CROPS

CANADA-COTTON

See CANADA-CROPS

CANADA-CRIME

Royal Canadian Mounted Police (RCMP), 73 Leikin Dr., Ottawa, ON, K1A 0R2, CAN, (613) 993-7267 (Dial from U.S.), (613) 825-1391 (TTY), (613) 993-0260 (Fax from U.S.), https://www.rcmp-grc.gc.ca/; unpublished data.

Statistics Canada (StatCan), 150 Tunney's Pasture Driveway, Ottawa, ON, K1A 0T6, CAN, (800) 263-1136 (Dial from U.S.), (514) 283-8300 (Dial from U.S.), (514) 283-9350 (Fax from U.S.), infostats@statcan.gc.ca, https://www.statcan.gc.ca; Family Violence in Canada: A Statistical Profile, 2019.

CANADA-CROPS

International Monetary Fund (IMF), 700 19th St. NW, Washington, DC, 20431, USA, (202) 623-7000, (202) 623-4661, publications@imf.org, https://www.imf.org; International Financial Statistics (IFS).

Organization for Economic Cooperation and Development (OECD), 2001 L St. NW, Ste. 650, Washington, DC, 20036-4922, USA, (202) 785-6323, (800) 456-6323, (202) 785-0350, washington.contact@oecd.org, https://www.oecd.org/; OECD-FAO Agricultural Outlook 2022-2031.

Palgrave Macmillan, 1 New York Plaza, Ste. 4500, New York, NY, 10004-1562, USA, (800) 777-4643, orders@palgrave.com, https://www.palgrave.com/us; The Statesman's Yearbook, 2023.

United Nations Food and Agricultural Organization (FAO), 2121 K St., Ste. 800B, Washington, DC, 20037, USA, (202) 653-2400 (Dial from U.S.), (202) 653-5760 (Fax from U.S.), fao-hq@fao.org, https://www.fao.org; The State of Food and Agriculture (SOFA) 2022.

United Nations Statistics Division (UNSD), United Nations Plz., New York, NY, 10017, USA, (800) 253-9646, (212) 963-9851, statistics@un.org, https://unstats.un.org; Statistical Yearbook of the United Nations 2021.

CANADA-CUSTOMS ADMINISTRATION

Western Washington University, Border Policy Research Institute (BPRI), 516 High St., Bellingham, WA, 98225, USA, (360) 650-3000, laurie.trautman@wwu.edu, https://bpri.wwu.edu/; COVID-19 and the US-Canada Border.

CANADA-DAIRY PROCESSING

Organization for Economic Cooperation and Development (OECD), 2001 L St. NW, Ste. 650, Washington, DC, 20036-4922, USA, (202) 785-6323, (800) 456-6323, (202) 785-0350, washington.contact@oecd.org, https://www.oecd.org/; OECD-FAO Agricultural Outlook 2022-2031.

Palgrave Macmillan, 1 New York Plaza, Ste. 4500, New York, NY, 10004-1562, USA, (800) 777-4643, orders@palgrave.com, https://www.palgrave.com/us; The Statesman's Yearbook, 2023.

United Nations Food and Agricultural Organization (FAO), 2121 K St., Ste. 800B, Washington, DC, 20037, USA, (202) 653-2400 (Dial from U.S.), (202) 653-5760 (Fax from U.S.), fao-hq@fao.org, https://www.fao.org; The State of Food and Agriculture (SOFA) 2022.

CANADA-DEBTS, EXTERNAL

Organization for Economic Cooperation and Development (OECD), 2001 L St. NW, Ste. 650, Washington, DC, 20036-4922, USA, (202) 785-6323, (800) 456-6323, (202) 785-0350, washington.contact@oecd.org, https://www.oecd.org/; Geographical Distribution of Financial Flows to Developing Countries 2023; OECD Business and Finance Outlook 2021; and OECD Digital Economy Outlook 2020.

Palgrave Macmillan, 1 New York Plaza, Ste. 4500, New York, NY, 10004-1562, USA, (800) 777-4643, orders@palgrave.com, https://www.palgrave.com/us; The Statesman's Yearbook, 2023.

The World Bank, 1818 H St. NW, Washington, DC, 20433, USA, (202) 473-1000, (202) 477-6391, eds03@worldbank.org, https://www.worldbank.org/; Global Financial Development Report 2019-2020: Bank Regulation and Supervision a Decade after the Global Financial Crisis; World Development Indicators (WDI) 2022; and World Development Report 2022: Finance for an Equitable Recovery.

CANADA-DEFENSE EXPENDITURES

See CANADA-ARMED FORCES

CANADA-DIAMONDS

See CANADA-MINERAL INDUSTRIES

CANADA-ECONOMIC ASSISTANCE

Organization for Economic Cooperation and Development (OECD), 2001 L St. NW, Ste. 650, Washington, DC, 20036-4922, USA, (202) 785-6323, (800) 456-6323, (202) 785-0350, washington.contact@oecd.org, https://www.oecd.org/; Geographical Distribution of Financial Flows to Developing Countries 2023.

United Nations Statistics Division (UNSD), United Nations Plz., New York, NY, 10017, USA, (800) 253-9646, (212) 963-9851, statistics@un.org, https://unstats.un.org; Statistical Yearbook of the United Nations 2021.

CANADA-ECONOMIC CONDITIONS

Bernan Press, 15250 NBN Way, Bldg. C, Blue Ridge Summit, PA, 17214, USA, (301) 459-2255, (800) 865-3457, (800) 865-3450, customercare@bernan.com, https://rowman.com/Page/Bernan; World Economic Outlook, April 2022.

Central Intelligence Agency (CIA), Office of Public Affairs, Washington, DC, 20505, USA, (703) 482-0623, https://www.cia.gov; The World Factbook.

Department of Finance, Government of the Northwest Territories (GNWT), PO Box 1320, Yellowknife, NT, X1A 2L9, CAN, (866) 475-8162 (Dial from U.S.), (867) 678-6625 (Dial from U.S.), hrhelpdesk@gov.nt.ca, https://www.fin.gov.nt.ca/; Budget Dialogue 2021 - Revenue Options.

The Economist Group: Economist Intelligence Unit (EIU), 900 3rd Ave., 16th Fl., New York, NY, 10022, USA, (212) 541-0500, americas@eiu.com, https://www.eiu.com; Canada Country Report.

Euromonitor International, Inc., 1 N Dearborn St., Ste. 1700, Chicago, IL, 60602, USA, (312) 922-1115, (312) 922-1157, info-usa@euromonitor.com, https://www.euromonitor.com/; Geographies and Market Research on the Consumer Finance Industry.

Federal Statistical Office Germany, Gustav-Stresemann-Ring 11, Wiesbaden, D-65189, GER, https://www.destatis.de; Basic Indicators: Canada.

Global Entrepreneurship Monitor (GEM), Babson College, 231 Forest St., Babson Park, MA, 02457, USA, (781) 235-1200, info@gemconsortium.org, https://www.gemconsortium.org/; Canada Economy Profile.

Government of Alberta, PO Box 1333, Edmonton, AB, T5J 2N2, CAN, (780) 427-2711 (Dial from U.S.), https://www.alberta.ca; Alberta Business and Economy.

International Monetary Fund (IMF), 700 19th St. NW, Washington, DC, 20431, USA, (202) 623-7000, (202) 623-4661, publications@imf.org, https://www.imf.org; IMF Data and World Economic Outlook.

Newfoundland and Labrador Statistics Agency (NLSA), Department of Finance, Economics and Statistics Branch, 5 Mews Pl., St. John's, NL, A1B 4J6, CAN, (709) 729-2913 (Dial from U.S.), (709) 729-0158 (Dial from U.S.), infostats@gov.nl.ca, https://www.stats.gov.nl.ca/; The Economy 2019.

Nova Scotia Department of Finance and Treasury Board, Economics and Statistics Division, 1723 Hollis St., PO Box 187, Halifax, NS, B3J 2N3, CAN, (902) 424-5554 (Dial from U.S.), (902) 424-0635 (Fax from U.S.), financeweb@novascotia.ca, https://www.novascotia.ca/finance/statistics/; Labour Market Report and Nova Scotia Economic Indicators.

Organization for Economic Cooperation and Development (OECD), 2001 L St. NW, Ste. 650, Washington, DC, 20036-4922, USA, (202) 785-6323, (800) 456-6323, (202) 785-0350, washington.contact@oecd.org, https://www.oecd.org/; Economic Survey of Canada 2023; Geographical Distribution of Financial Flows to Developing Countries 2023; OECD Composite Leading Indicator (CLI); OECD Digital Economy Outlook 2020; OECD Employment Outlook 2022: Building Back More Inclusive Labour Markets; OECD Labour Force Statistics 2022; and OECD Main Economic Indicators (MEI).

Palgrave Macmillan, 1 New York Plaza, Ste. 4500, New York, NY, 10004-1562, USA, (800) 777-4643, orders@palgrave.com, https://www.palgrave.com/us; The Statesman's Yearbook, 2023.

Prince Edward Island Department of Finance, PO Box 2000, Charlottetown, PE, C1A 7N8, CAN, (902) 368-4040 (Dial from U.S.), (902) 368-6575 (Fax from U.S.), deptfinance@gov.pe.ca, https://www.princeedwardisland.ca/en/topic/finance; Tourism Indicators of Prince Edward Island, 2020.

Routledge - Taylor & Francis Group, 6000 Broken Sound Pkwy. NW, Ste. 300, Boca Raton, FL, 33487, USA, (800) 634-1420, (800) 634-7064, orders@taylorandfrancis.com, https://www.routledge.com/; The Europa World Year Book 2022.

Saskatchewan Bureau of Statistics (SBS), 2350 Albert St., 9th Fl., Regina, SK, S4P 4A6, CAN, (306) 787-3251 (Dial from U.S.), vitalstatistics@ehealthsask.ca, https://www.saskatchewan.ca/government/government-data/bureau-of-statistics; 2021 Economic Review.

United Nations Statistics Division (UNSD), United Nations Plz., New York, NY, 10017, USA, (800) 253-9646, (212) 963-9851, statistics@un.org, https://unstats.un.org; World Statistics Pocketbook 2021.

Western Washington University, Border Policy Research Institute (BPRI), 516 High St., Bellingham, WA, 98225, USA, (360) 650-3000, laurie.trautman@wwu.edu, https://bpri.wwu.edu/; Border Barometer.

Women and Gender Equality Canada (WAGE), PO Box 8097, Station T CSC , Ottawa, ON, K1G 3H6, CAN, (855) 969-9922 (Dial from U.S.), (819) 420-6905 (Dial from U.S.), (819) 420-6906 (Fax from U.S.), wage.communications.fegc@wage-fegc.gc.ca, https://women-gender-equality.canada.ca/en.html; Equality Matters Newsletter.

The World Bank, 1818 H St. NW, Washington, DC, 20433, USA, (202) 473-1000, (202) 477-6391, eds03@worldbank.org, https://www.worldbank.org/; Canada (report); Global Economic Monitor (GEM); Global Economic Prospects, June 2022; The Global Findex Database 2021; and World Development Report 2022: Finance for an Equitable Recovery.

CANADA-EDUCATION

Euromonitor International, Inc., 1 N Dearborn St., Ste. 1700, Chicago, IL, 60602, USA, (312) 922-1115, (312) 922-1157, info-usa@euromonitor.com, https://www.euromonitor.com/; Geographies.

Infoplease, c/o Sandbox Networks, Inc., 1 Lincoln St., 24th Fl., Boston, MA, 02111, USA, https://www.infoplease.com; Countries of the World.

Organization for Economic Cooperation and Development (OECD), 2001 L St. NW, Ste. 650, Washington, DC, 20036-4922, USA, (202) 785-6323, (800) 456-6323, (202) 785-0350, washington.contact@oecd.org, https://www.oecd.org/; Education at a Glance 2022: OECD Indicators.

Palgrave Macmillan, 1 New York Plaza, Ste. 4500, New York, NY, 10004-1562, USA, (800) 777-4643, orders@palgrave.com, https://www.palgrave.com/us; The Statesman's Yearbook, 2023.

Routledge - Taylor & Francis Group, 6000 Broken Sound Pkwy. NW, Ste. 300, Boca Raton, FL, 33487, USA, (800) 634-1420, (800) 634-7064, orders@taylorandfrancis.com, https://www.routledge.com/; The Europa World Year Book 2022.

UNESCO Institute for Statistics, C.P 250 Succursale H, Montreal, QC, H3G 2K8, CAN, (514) 343-6880 (Dial from U.S.), (514) 343-5740 (Fax from U.S.), uis.publications@unesco.org, http://uis.unesco.org/; Literacy and UIS.Stat.

United Nations Statistics Division (UNSD), United Nations Plz., New York, NY, 10017, USA, (800) 253-9646, (212) 963-9851, statistics@un.org, https://unstats.un.org; Millennium Development Goal Indicators.

Women and Gender Equality Canada (WAGE), PO Box 8097, Station T CSC , Ottawa, ON, K1G 3H6, CAN, (855) 969-9922 (Dial from U.S.), (819) 420-6905 (Dial from U.S.), (819) 420-6906 (Fax from U.S.), wage.communications.fegc@wage-fegc.gc.ca, https://women-gender-equality.canada.ca/en.html; Equality Matters Newsletter.

The World Bank, 1818 H St. NW, Washington, DC, 20433, USA, (202) 473-1000, (202) 477-6391, eds03@worldbank.org, https://www.worldbank.org/; Canada (report); World Development Indicators (WDI) 2022; and World Development Report 2022: Finance for an Equitable Recovery.

CANADA-ELECTRICITY

International Energy Agency (IEA), 9 Rue de la Federation, Paris, 75739, FRA, info@iea.org, https://www.iea.org/; Coal 2021: Analysis and Forecast to 2024 and World Energy Outlook 2021.

Organization for Economic Cooperation and Development (OECD), 2001 L St. NW, Ste. 650, Washington, DC, 20036-4922, USA, (202) 785-6323, (800) 456-6323, (202) 785-0350, washington.contact@oecd.org, https://www.oecd.org/; Energy Prices and Taxes for OECD Countries 2020 and STAN (STructural ANalysis) Database.

PowerOutage.com, jrobinson@bluefirestudios.com, https://poweroutage.com/; Ukraine Power Outages.

U.S. Energy Information Administration (EIA), 1000 Independence Ave. SW, Washington, DC, 20585, USA, (202) 586-8800, infoctr@eia.gov, https://www.eia.gov; International Energy Outlook 2021.

United Nations Statistics Division (UNSD), United Nations Plz., New York, NY, 10017, USA, (800) 253-9646, (212) 963-9851, statistics@un.org, https://unstats.un.org; Statistical Yearbook of the United Nations 2021.

CANADA-EMPLOYMENT

Canadian Centre for Policy Alternatives (CCPA), 141 Laurier Ave. W, Ste. 1000, Ottawa, ON, K1P 5J3, CAN, (613) 563-1341 (Dial from U.S.), (844) 563-1341 (Dial from U.S.), (613) 233-1458 (Fax from U.S.), ccpa@policyalternatives.ca, https://www.policyalternatives.ca/; The Best and Worst Places to be a Woman in Canada 2019: The Gender Gap in Canada's 26 Biggest Cities and Heating Up, Backing Down Evaluating Recent Climate Policy Progress in Canada.

The Conference Board of Canada, 135 Laurier Avenue W, Ottawa, ON, K1P 5J2, CAN, (866) 711-2262 (Dial from U.S.), (613) 526-3280 (Dial from U.S.), (613) 526-4857 (Fax from U.S.), contactcboc@conferenceboard.ca, https://www.conferenceboard.ca/; Help-Wanted Index.

International Labour Organization (ILO), 4 Rte. des Morillons, Geneva, CH-1211, SWI, ilo@ilo.org, https://www.ilo.org; NORMLEX Information System on International Labour Standards.

Nova Scotia Department of Finance and Treasury Board, Economics and Statistics Division, 1723 Hollis St., PO Box 187, Halifax, NS, B3J 2N3, CAN, (902) 424-5554 (Dial from U.S.), (902) 424-0635 (Fax from U.S.), financeweb@novascotia.ca, https://www.novascotia.ca/finance/statistics/; Labour Market Report and Nova Scotia Economic Indicators.

Organization for Economic Cooperation and Development (OECD), 2001 L St. NW, Ste. 650, Washington, DC, 20036-4922, USA, (202) 785-6323, (800) 456-6323, (202) 785-0350, washington.contact@oecd.org, https://www.oecd.org/; Economic Survey of Canada 2023; OECD Composite Leading Indicator (CLI); OECD Digital Economy Outlook 2020; OECD Employment Outlook 2022: Building Back More Inclusive Labour Markets; and OECD Labour Force Statistics 2022.

UK Data Service, University of Essex, Wivenhoe Park, Colchester, Essex, CO4 3SQ, GBR, https://ukdataservice.ac.uk/; International Aggregate Data.

United Nations Statistics Division (UNSD), United Nations Plz., New York, NY, 10017, USA, (800) 253-9646, (212) 963-9851, statistics@un.org, https://unstats.un.org; Statistical Yearbook of the United Nations 2021.

Women and Gender Equality Canada (WAGE), PO Box 8097, Station T CSC , Ottawa, ON, K1G 3H6, CAN, (855) 969-9922 (Dial from U.S.), (819) 420-6905 (Dial from U.S.), (819) 420-6906 (Fax from U.S.), wage.communications.fegc@wage-fegc.gc.ca, https://women-gender-equality.canada.ca/en.html; Equality Matters Newsletter.

The World Bank, 1818 H St. NW, Washington, DC, 20433, USA, (202) 473-1000, (202) 477-6391, eds03@worldbank.org, https://www.worldbank.org/; Canada (report).

CANADA-ENERGY INDUSTRIES

Canadian Centre for Policy Alternatives (CCPA), 141 Laurier Ave. W, Ste. 1000, Ottawa, ON, K1P 5J3, CAN, (613) 563-1341 (Dial from U.S.), (844) 563-1341 (Dial from U.S.), (613) 233-1458 (Fax from U.S.), ccpa@policyalternatives.ca, https://www.policyalternatives.ca/; Heating Up, Backing Down Evaluating Recent Climate Policy Progress in Canada.

Enerdata, 47 avenue Alsace Lorraine, Grenoble, 38027, FRA, (332) 216-4534, research@enerdata.net, https://www.enerdata.net; World Refinery Database.

International Energy Agency (IEA), 9 Rue de la Federation, Paris, 75739, FRA, info@iea.org, https://www.iea.org/; Renewables Information and World Energy Statistics and Balances.

United Nations Statistics Division (UNSD), United Nations Plz., New York, NY, 10017, USA, (800) 253-9646, (212) 963-9851, statistics@un.org, https://unstats.un.org; Statistical Yearbook of the United Nations 2021.

CANADA-ENVIRONMENTAL CONDITIONS

Canadian Centre for Policy Alternatives (CCPA), 141 Laurier Ave. W, Ste. 1000, Ottawa, ON, K1P 5J3, CAN, (613) 563-1341 (Dial from U.S.), (844) 563-1341 (Dial from U.S.), (613) 233-1458 (Fax from U.S.), ccpa@policyalternatives.ca, https://www.policyalternatives.ca/; Heating Up, Backing Down Evaluating Recent Climate Policy Progress in Canada.

DSI Data Service & Information, Xantener Strasse 51a, Rheinberg, D-47495, GER, dsi@dsidata.com, https://www.dsidata.com/; Global Environmental Database.

The Economist Group: Economist Intelligence Unit (EIU), 900 3rd Ave., 16th Fl., New York, NY, 10022, USA, (212) 541-0500, americas@eiu.com, https://www.eiu.com; Canada Country Report.

Environment and Climate Change Canada, Fontaine Bldg., 200 Sacre-Coeur Blvd., 12th Fl., Gatineau, QC, K1A 0H3, CAN, (819) 938-3838 (Dial from U.S.), enviroinfo@ec.gc.ca, https://www.canada.ca/en/environment-climate-change.html; Air Pollutant Emissions and Canadian Environmental Sustainability Indicators (CESI).

Federal Statistical Office Germany, Gustav-Stresemann-Ring 11, Wiesbaden, D-65189, GER, https://www.destatis.de; Basic Indicators: Canada.

Organization for Economic Cooperation and Development (OECD), 2001 L St. NW, Ste. 650, Washington, DC, 20036-4922, USA, (202) 785-6323, (800) 456-6323, (202) 785-0350, washington.contact@oecd.org, https://www.oecd.org/; Environment Statistics.

United Nations Statistics Division (UNSD), United Nations Plz., New York, NY, 10017, USA, (800) 253-9646, (212) 963-9851, statistics@un.org, https://unstats.un.org; World Statistics Pocketbook 2021.

CANADA-ENVIRONMENTAL INDUSTRY

Canadian Centre for Policy Alternatives (CCPA), 141 Laurier Ave. W, Ste. 1000, Ottawa, ON, K1P 5J3, CAN, (613) 563-1341 (Dial from U.S.), (844) 563-1341 (Dial from U.S.), (613) 233-1458 (Fax from U.S.), ccpa@policyalternatives.ca, https://www.policyalternatives.ca/; Heating Up, Backing Down Evaluating Recent Climate Policy Progress in Canada.

CANADA-EXPENDITURES, PUBLIC

Organization for Economic Cooperation and Development (OECD), 2001 L St. NW, Ste. 650, Washington, DC, 20036-4922, USA, (202) 785-6323, (800) 456-6323, (202) 785-0350, washington.contact@oecd.org, https://www.oecd.org/; Revenue Statistics 2022.

CANADA-EXPORTS

Central Intelligence Agency (CIA), Office of Public Affairs, Washington, DC, 20505, USA, (703) 482-0623, https://www.cia.gov; The World Factbook.

The Economist Group: Economist Intelligence Unit (EIU), 900 3rd Ave., 16th Fl., New York, NY, 10022, USA, (212) 541-0500, americas@eiu.com, https://www.eiu.com; Canada Country Report.

International Monetary Fund (IMF), 700 19th St. NW, Washington, DC, 20431, USA, (202) 623-7000, (202) 623-4661, publications@imf.org, https://www.imf.org; Direction of Trade Statistics (DOTS) and International Financial Statistics (IFS).

Organization for Economic Cooperation and Development (OECD), 2001 L St. NW, Ste. 650, Washington, DC, 20036-4922, USA, (202) 785-6323, (800) 456-6323, (202) 785-0350, washington.contact@oecd.org, https://www.oecd.org/; Economic Survey of Canada 2023; Geographical Distribution of Financial Flows to Developing Countries 2023; OECD Digital Economy Outlook 2020; OECD Review of Fisheries 2022; OECD-FAO Agricultural Outlook 2022-2031; and STAN (STructural ANalysis) Database.

S&P Global, IHS Markit, 15 Inverness Way E, Englewood, CO, 80112, USA, (800) 447-2273, (800) 854-7179, https://ihsmarkit.com; Global Trade Atlas (GTA).

TAPPI - Technical Association of the Pulp and Paper Industry, 15 Technology Pkwy. S, Ste. 115, Peachtree Corners, GA, 30092, USA, (770) 446-1400, (800) 332-8686, (770) 446-6947, memberconnection@tappi.org, https://www.tappi.org/; TAPPI Journal.

United Nations Conference on Trade and Development (UNCTAD), Palais des Nations, Geneva, 1211, SWI, (212) 963-6896, unctadinfo@unctad.org, https://unctad.org; Handbook of Statistics 2021.

The World Bank, 1818 H St. NW, Washington, DC, 20433, USA, (202) 473-1000, (202) 477-6391, eds03@worldbank.org, https://www.worldbank.org/; World Development Report 2022: Finance for an Equitable Recovery.

World Steel Association (Worldsteel), Avenue de Tervueren 270, Brussels, B-1150, BEL, steel@worldsteel.org, https://www.worldsteel.org; Steel Statistical Yearbook 2021.

CANADA-FEMALE WORKING POPULATION

See CANADA-EMPLOYMENT

CANADA-FERTILITY, HUMAN

Central Intelligence Agency (CIA), Office of Public Affairs, Washington, DC, 20505, USA, (703) 482-0623, https://www.cia.gov; The World Factbook.

CANADA-FERTILIZER INDUSTRY

Organization for Economic Cooperation and Development (OECD), 2001 L St. NW, Ste. 650, Washington, DC, 20036-4922, USA, (202) 785-6323, (800) 456-6323, (202) 785-0350, washington.contact@oecd.org, https://www.oecd.org/; OECD-FAO Agricultural Outlook 2022-2031.

United Nations Food and Agricultural Organization (FAO), 2121 K St., Ste. 800B, Washington, DC, 20037, USA, (202) 653-2400 (Dial from U.S.), (202) 653-5760 (Fax from U.S.), fao-hq@fao.org, https://www.fao.org; The State of Food and Agriculture (SOFA) 2022.

CANADA-FETAL MORTALITY

See CANADA-MORTALITY

CANADA-FINANCE

International Monetary Fund (IMF), 700 19th St. NW, Washington, DC, 20431, USA, (202) 623-7000, (202) 623-4661, publications@imf.org, https://www.imf.org; International Financial Statistics (IFS).

Organization for Economic Cooperation and Development (OECD), 2001 L St. NW, Ste. 650, Washington, DC, 20036-4922, USA, (202) 785-6323, (800) 456-6323, (202) 785-0350, washington.contact@oecd.org, https://www.oecd.org/; OECD Digital Economy Outlook 2020.

Stockholm International Peace Research Institute (SIPRI), Signalistgatan 9, Stockholm, SE 169 72, SWE, https://www.sipri.org/; SIPRI Arms Transfers Database and SIPRI Military Expenditure Database.

United Nations Statistics Division (UNSD), United Nations Plz., New York, NY, 10017, USA, (800) 253-9646, (212) 963-9851, statistics@un.org, https://unstats.un.org; Statistical Yearbook of the United Nations 2021.

The World Bank, 1818 H St. NW, Washington, DC, 20433, USA, (202) 473-1000, (202) 477-6391, eds03@worldbank.org, https://www.worldbank.org/; Canada (report).

CANADA-FINANCE, PUBLIC

Bernan Press, 15250 NBN Way, Bldg. C, Blue Ridge Summit, PA, 17214, USA, (301) 459-2255, (800) 865-3457, (800) 865-3450, customercare@bernan.com, https://rowman.com/Page/Bernan; National Accounts Statistics: Analysis of Main Aggregates 2020.

The Economist Group: Economist Intelligence Unit (EIU), 900 3rd Ave., 16th Fl., New York, NY, 10022, USA, (212) 541-0500, americas@eiu.com, https://www.eiu.com; Canada Country Report.

International Monetary Fund (IMF), 700 19th St. NW, Washington, DC, 20431, USA, (202) 623-7000, (202) 623-4661, publications@imf.org, https://www.imf.org; International Financial Statistics (IFS) and Regional Economic Outlook.

Organization for Economic Cooperation and Development (OECD), 2001 L St. NW, Ste. 650, Washington, DC, 20036-4922, USA, (202) 785-6323, (800) 456-6323, (202) 785-0350, washington.contact@oecd.org, https://www.oecd.org/; Geographical Distribution of Financial Flows to Developing Countries 2023; OECD Business and Finance Outlook 2021; OECD Digital Economy Outlook 2020; and Revenue Statistics 2022.

Palgrave Macmillan, 1 New York Plaza, Ste. 4500, New York, NY, 10004-1562, USA, (800) 777-4643, orders@palgrave.com, https://www.palgrave.com/us; The Statesman's Yearbook, 2023.

Routledge - Taylor & Francis Group, 6000 Broken Sound Pkwy. NW, Ste. 300, Boca Raton, FL, 33487, USA, (800) 634-1420, (800) 634-7064, orders@taylorandfrancis.com, https://www.routledge.com/; The Europa World Year Book 2022.

United Nations Statistics Division (UNSD), United Nations Plz., New York, NY, 10017, USA, (800) 253-9646, (212) 963-9851, statistics@un.org, https://unstats.un.org; National Accounts Main Aggregates Database and National Accounts Statistics: Main Aggregates and Detailed Tables.

The World Bank, 1818 H St. NW, Washington, DC, 20433, USA, (202) 473-1000, (202) 477-6391, eds03@worldbank.org, https://www.worldbank.org/; Canada (report).

CANADA-FISHERIES

Organization for Economic Cooperation and Development (OECD), 2001 L St. NW, Ste. 650, Washington, DC, 20036-4922, USA, (202) 785-6323, (800) 456-6323, (202) 785-0350, washington.contact@oecd.org, https://www.oecd.org/; OECD Review of Fisheries 2022 and STAN (STructural ANalysis) Database.

Palgrave Macmillan, 1 New York Plaza, Ste. 4500, New York, NY, 10004-1562, USA, (800) 777-4643, orders@palgrave.com, https://www.palgrave.com/us; The Statesman's Yearbook, 2023.

Routledge - Taylor & Francis Group, 6000 Broken Sound Pkwy. NW, Ste. 300, Boca Raton, FL, 33487, USA, (800) 634-1420, (800) 634-7064, orders@taylorandfrancis.com, https://www.routledge.com/; The Europa World Year Book 2022.

United Nations Food and Agricultural Organization (FAO), 2121 K St., Ste. 800B, Washington, DC, 20037, USA, (202) 653-2400 (Dial from U.S.), (202) 653-5760 (Fax from U.S.), fao-hq@fao.org, https://www.fao.org; FAO Yearbook of Fishery and Aquaculture Statistics 2019; Fishery Statistical Collections Global Capture Production; FishStatJ; and The State of Food and Agriculture (SOFA) 2022.

United Nations Statistics Division (UNSD), United Nations Plz., New York, NY, 10017, USA, (800) 253-9646, (212) 963-9851, statistics@un.org, https://unstats.un.org; Statistical Yearbook of the United Nations 2021.

The World Bank, 1818 H St. NW, Washington, DC, 20433, USA, (202) 473-1000, (202) 477-6391, eds03@worldbank.org, https://www.worldbank.org/; Canada (report).

CANADA-FOOD

Euromonitor International, Inc., 1 N Dearborn St., Ste. 1700, Chicago, IL, 60602, USA, (312) 922-1115, (312) 922-1157, info-usa@euromonitor.com, https://www.euromonitor.com/; Market Research on the Retailing Industry.

United Nations Food and Agricultural Organization (FAO), 2121 K St., Ste. 800B, Washington, DC, 20037, USA, (202) 653-2400 (Dial from U.S.), (202) 653-5760 (Fax from U.S.), fao-hq@fao.org, https://www.fao.org; The State of Food and Agriculture (SOFA) 2022.

CANADA-FOREIGN EXCHANGE RATES

International Monetary Fund (IMF), 700 19th St. NW, Washington, DC, 20431, USA, (202) 623-7000, (202) 623-4661, publications@imf.org, https://www.imf.org; International Financial Statistics (IFS).

Organization for Economic Cooperation and Development (OECD), 2001 L St. NW, Ste. 650, Washington, DC, 20036-4922, USA, (202) 785-6323, (800) 456-6323, (202) 785-0350, washington.contact@oecd.org, https://www.oecd.org/; OECD Business and Finance Outlook 2021; OECD Digital Economy Outlook 2020; OECD Tourism Trends and Policies 2022; and Revenue Statistics 2022.

CANADA-FORESTS AND FORESTRY

International Monetary Fund (IMF), 700 19th St. NW, Washington, DC, 20431, USA, (202) 623-7000, (202) 623-4661, publications@imf.org, https://www.imf.org; International Financial Statistics (IFS).

Organization for Economic Cooperation and Development (OECD), 2001 L St. NW, Ste. 650, Washington, DC, 20036-4922, USA, (202) 785-6323, (800) 456-6323, (202) 785-0350, washington.contact@oecd.org, https://www.oecd.org/; STAN (STructural ANalysis) Database.

Palgrave Macmillan, 1 New York Plaza, Ste. 4500, New York, NY, 10004-1562, USA, (800) 777-4643, orders@palgrave.com, https://www.palgrave.com/us; The Statesman's Yearbook, 2023.

Routledge - Taylor & Francis Group, 6000 Broken Sound Pkwy. NW, Ste. 300, Boca Raton, FL, 33487, USA, (800) 634-1420, (800) 634-7064, orders@taylorandfrancis.com, https://www.routledge.com/; The Europa World Year Book 2022.

TAPPI - Technical Association of the Pulp and Paper Industry, 15 Technology Pkwy. S, Ste. 115, Peachtree Corners, GA, 30092, USA, (770) 446-

1400, (800) 332-8686, (770) 446-6947, memberconnection@tappi.org, https://www.tappi.org/; TAPPI Journal.

United Nations Food and Agricultural Organization (FAO), 2121 K St., Ste. 800B, Washington, DC, 20037, USA, (202) 653-2400 (Dial from U.S.), (202) 653-5760 (Fax from U.S.), fao-hq@fao.org, https://www.fao.org; FAO Yearbook of Forest Products 2019 and The State of Food and Agriculture (SOFA) 2022.

United Nations Statistics Division (UNSD), United Nations Plz., New York, NY, 10017, USA, (800) 253-9646, (212) 963-9851, statistics@un.org, https://unstats.un.org; Statistical Yearbook of the United Nations 2021.

The World Bank, 1818 H St. NW, Washington, DC, 20433, USA, (202) 473-1000, (202) 477-6391, eds03@worldbank.org, https://www.worldbank.org/; Canada (report) and World Development Report 2022: Finance for an Equitable Recovery.

CANADA-FRUIT PRODUCTION

See CANADA-CROPS

CANADA-GAS PRODUCTION

See CANADA-MINERAL INDUSTRIES

CANADA-GEOGRAPHIC INFORMATION SYSTEMS

The World Bank, 1818 H St. NW, Washington, DC, 20433, USA, (202) 473-1000, (202) 477-6391, eds03@worldbank.org, https://www.worldbank.org/; Canada (report).

CANADA-GOLD INDUSTRY

The World Bank, 1818 H St. NW, Washington, DC, 20433, USA, (202) 473-1000, (202) 477-6391, eds03@worldbank.org, https://www.worldbank.org/; World Development Indicators (WDI) 2022.

CANADA-GOLD PRODUCTION

See CANADA-MINERAL INDUSTRIES

CANADA-GRANTS-IN-AID

Global Affairs Canada, Enquiries Service (LOS), 125 Sussex Dr., Ottowa, ON, K1A 0G2, CAN, (613) 944-4000 (Dial from U.S.), (613) 996-9709 (Fax from U.S.), info@international.gc.ca, https://www.international.gc.ca/; Statistical Report on International Assistance, 2021-2022.

Organization for Economic Cooperation and Development (OECD), 2001 L St. NW, Ste. 650, Washington, DC, 20036-4922, USA, (202) 785-6323, (800) 456-6323, (202) 785-0350, washington.contact@oecd.org, https://www.oecd.org/; Geographical Distribution of Financial Flows to Developing Countries 2023.

CANADA-GROSS DOMESTIC PRODUCT

The Economist Group: Economist Intelligence Unit (EIU), 900 3rd Ave., 16th Fl., New York, NY, 10022, USA, (212) 541-0500, americas@eiu.com, https://www.eiu.com; Canada Country Report.

International Monetary Fund (IMF), 700 19th St. NW, Washington, DC, 20431, USA, (202) 623-7000, (202) 623-4661, publications@imf.org, https://www.imf.org; International Financial Statistics (IFS).

Nova Scotia Department of Finance and Treasury Board, Economics and Statistics Division, 1723 Hollis St., PO Box 187, Halifax, NS, B3J 2N3, CAN, (902) 424-5554 (Dial from U.S.), (902) 424-0635 (Fax from U.S.), financeweb@novascotia.ca, https://www.novascotia.ca/finance/statistics/; Labour Market Report.

Organization for Economic Cooperation and Development (OECD), 2001 L St. NW, Ste. 650, Washington, DC, 20036-4922, USA, (202) 785-6323, (800) 456-6323, (202) 785-0350, washington.contact@oecd.org, https://www.oecd.org/; Geographical Distribution of Financial Flows to Developing Countries 2023; OECD Digital Economy Outlook 2020; OECD Main Economic Indicators (MEI); and Revenue Statistics 2022.

Routledge - Taylor & Francis Group, 6000 Broken Sound Pkwy. NW, Ste. 300, Boca Raton, FL, 33487, USA, (800) 634-1420, (800) 634-7064, orders@taylorandfrancis.com, https://www.routledge.com/; The Europa World Year Book 2022.

United Nations Statistics Division (UNSD), United Nations Plz., New York, NY, 10017, USA, (800) 253-9646, (212) 963-9851, statistics@un.org, https://unstats.un.org; Statistical Yearbook of the United Nations 2021.

The World Bank, 1818 H St. NW, Washington, DC, 20433, USA, (202) 473-1000, (202) 477-6391, eds03@worldbank.org, https://www.worldbank.org/; World Development Indicators (WDI) 2022 and World Development Report 2022: Finance for an Equitable Recovery.

CANADA-GROSS NATIONAL PRODUCT

Organization for Economic Cooperation and Development (OECD), 2001 L St. NW, Ste. 650, Washington, DC, 20036-4922, USA, (202) 785-6323, (800) 456-6323, (202) 785-0350, washington.contact@oecd.org, https://www.oecd.org/; Geographical Distribution of Financial Flows to Developing Countries 2023; OECD Composite Leading Indicator (CLI); OECD Digital Economy Outlook 2020; and OECD Main Economic Indicators (MEI).

Palgrave Macmillan, 1 New York Plaza, Ste. 4500, New York, NY, 10004-1562, USA, (800) 777-4643, orders@palgrave.com, https://www.palgrave.com/us; The Statesman's Yearbook, 2023.

Routledge - Taylor & Francis Group, 6000 Broken Sound Pkwy. NW, Ste. 300, Boca Raton, FL, 33487, USA, (800) 634-1420, (800) 634-7064, orders@taylorandfrancis.com, https://www.routledge.com/; The Europa World Year Book 2022.

United Nations Statistics Division (UNSD), United Nations Plz., New York, NY, 10017, USA, (800) 253-9646, (212) 963-9851, statistics@un.org, https://unstats.un.org; Statistical Yearbook of the United Nations 2021.

The World Bank, 1818 H St. NW, Washington, DC, 20433, USA, (202) 473-1000, (202) 477-6391, eds03@worldbank.org, https://www.worldbank.org/; World Development Indicators (WDI) 2022 and World Development Report 2022: Finance for an Equitable Recovery.

CANADA-HOUSING

Euromonitor International, Inc., 1 N Dearborn St., Ste. 1700, Chicago, IL, 60602, USA, (312) 922-1115, (312) 922-1157, info-usa@euromonitor.com, https://www.euromonitor.com/; Geographies.

United Nations Statistics Division (UNSD), United Nations Plz., New York, NY, 10017, USA, (800) 253-9646, (212) 963-9851, statistics@un.org, https://unstats.un.org; Statistical Yearbook of the United Nations 2021.

CANADA-HOUSING-FINANCE

Organization for Economic Cooperation and Development (OECD), 2001 L St. NW, Ste. 650, Washington, DC, 20036-4922, USA, (202) 785-6323, (800) 456-6323, (202) 785-0350, washington.contact@oecd.org, https://www.oecd.org/; OECD Main Economic Indicators (MEI).

CANADA-HOUSING CONSTRUCTION

See CANADA-CONSTRUCTION INDUSTRY

CANADA-IMPORTS

Central Intelligence Agency (CIA), Office of Public Affairs, Washington, DC, 20505, USA, (703) 482-0623, https://www.cia.gov; The World Factbook.

The Economist Group: Economist Intelligence Unit (EIU), 900 3rd Ave., 16th Fl., New York, NY, 10022, USA, (212) 541-0500, americas@eiu.com, https://www.eiu.com; Canada Country Report.

International Monetary Fund (IMF), 700 19th St. NW, Washington, DC, 20431, USA, (202) 623-7000, (202) 623-4661, publications@imf.org, https://www.imf.org; Direction of Trade Statistics (DOTS) and International Financial Statistics (IFS).

Organization for Economic Cooperation and Development (OECD), 2001 L St. NW, Ste. 650, Washington, DC, 20036-4922, USA, (202) 785-6323, (800) 456-6323, (202) 785-0350, washington.contact@oecd.org, https://www.oecd.org/; Economic Survey of Canada 2023; OECD Digital Economy Outlook 2020; OECD Review of Fisheries 2022; OECD-FAO Agricultural Outlook 2022-2031; and STAN (STructural ANalysis) Database.

S&P Global, IHS Markit, 15 Inverness Way E, Englewood, CO, 80112, USA, (800) 447-2273, (800) 854-7179, https://ihsmarkit.com; Global Trade Atlas (GTA).

TAPPI - Technical Association of the Pulp and Paper Industry, 15 Technology Pkwy. S, Ste. 115, Peachtree Corners, GA, 30092, USA, (770) 446-1400, (800) 332-8686, (770) 446-6947, memberconnection@tappi.org, https://www.tappi.org/; TAPPI Journal.

United Nations Conference on Trade and Development (UNCTAD), Palais des Nations, Geneva, 1211, SWI, (212) 963-6896, unctadinfo@unctad.org, https://unctad.org; Handbook of Statistics 2021.

The World Bank, 1818 H St. NW, Washington, DC, 20433, USA, (202) 473-1000, (202) 477-6391, eds03@worldbank.org, https://www.worldbank.org/; World Development Report 2022: Finance for an Equitable Recovery.

World Steel Association (Worldsteel), Avenue de Tervueren 270, Brussels, B-1150, BEL, steel@worldsteel.org, https://www.worldsteel.org; Steel Statistical Yearbook 2021.

CANADA-INDUSTRIAL METALS PRODUCTION

See CANADA-MINERAL INDUSTRIES

CANADA-INDUSTRIAL PRODUCTIVITY

International Lead and Zinc Study Group (ILZSG), Rua Almirante Barroso 38, 5th Fl., Lisbon, 1000-013, PRT, sales@ilzsg.org, https://www.ilzsg.org; Interactive Statistical Database.

Nova Scotia Department of Finance and Treasury Board, Economics and Statistics Division, 1723 Hollis St., PO Box 187, Halifax, NS, B3J 2N3, CAN, (902) 424-5554 (Dial from U.S.), (902) 424-0635 (Fax from U.S.), financeweb@novascotia.ca, https://www.novascotia.ca/finance/statistics/; Nova Scotia Economic Indicators.

Organization for Economic Cooperation and Development (OECD), 2001 L St. NW, Ste. 650, Washington, DC, 20036-4922, USA, (202) 785-6323, (800) 456-6323, (202) 785-0350, washington.contact@oecd.org, https://www.oecd.org/; OECD Digital Economy Outlook 2020; OECD Main Economic Indicators (MEI); OECD-FAO Agricultural Outlook 2022-2031; and STAN (STructural ANalysis) Database.

TAPPI - Technical Association of the Pulp and Paper Industry, 15 Technology Pkwy. S, Ste. 115, Peachtree Corners, GA, 30092, USA, (770) 446-1400, (800) 332-8686, (770) 446-6947, memberconnection@tappi.org, https://www.tappi.org/; TAPPI Journal.

World Steel Association (Worldsteel), Avenue de Tervueren 270, Brussels, B-1150, BEL, steel@worldsteel.org, https://www.worldsteel.org; Steel Statistical Yearbook 2021.

CANADA-INDUSTRIAL PROPERTY

World Intellectual Property Organization (WIPO), 34, chemin des Colombettes, Geneva, CH-1211, SWI, https://www.wipo.int; Madrid Yearly Review 2022: International Registrations of Marks.

CANADA-INDUSTRIES

Central Intelligence Agency (CIA), Office of Public Affairs, Washington, DC, 20505, USA, (703) 482-0623, https://www.cia.gov; The World Factbook.

The Economist Group: Economist Intelligence Unit (EIU), 900 3rd Ave., 16th Fl., New York, NY, 10022, USA, (212) 541-0500, americas@eiu.com, https://www.eiu.com; Canada Country Report.

Euromonitor International, Inc., 1 N Dearborn St., Ste. 1700, Chicago, IL, 60602, USA, (312) 922-1115, (312) 922-1157, info-usa@euromonitor.com, https://www.euromonitor.com/; Geographies.

International Labour Organization (ILO), 4 Rte. des Morillons, Geneva, CH-1211, SWI, ilo@ilo.org, https://www.ilo.org; NORMLEX Information System on International Labour Standards.

Organization for Economic Cooperation and Development (OECD), 2001 L St. NW, Ste. 650, Washington, DC, 20036-4922, USA, (202) 785-6323, (800) 456-6323, (202) 785-0350, washington.contact@oecd.org, https://www.oecd.org/; Environment Statistics; OECD Digital Economy Outlook 2020; and STAN (STructural ANalysis) Database.

Palgrave Macmillan, 1 New York Plaza, Ste. 4500, New York, NY, 10004-1562, USA, (800) 777-4643, orders@palgrave.com, https://www.palgrave.com/us; The Statesman's Yearbook, 2023.

Polaris Institute, 135 Laurier Ave. W, Ste. 630, Ottawa, ON, K1P 5J2, CAN, (613) 237-1717 (Dial from U.S.), polaris@polarisinstitute.org, https://www.polarisinstitute.org/; unpublished data.

Routledge - Taylor & Francis Group, 6000 Broken Sound Pkwy. NW, Ste. 300, Boca Raton, FL, 33487, USA, (800) 634-1420, (800) 634-7064, orders@taylorandfrancis.com, https://www.routledge.com/; The Europa World Year Book 2022.

Statistics Canada (StatCan), 150 Tunney's Pasture Driveway, Ottawa, ON, K1A 0T6, CAN, (800) 263-1136 (Dial from U.S.), (514) 283-8300 (Dial from U.S.), (514) 283-9350 (Fax from U.S.), infostats@statcan.gc.ca, https://www.statcan.gc.ca; Net Income of Cannabis Authorities and Government Revenue from the Sale of Cannabis (x 1,000).

U.S. Department of Commerce (DOC), 1401 Constitution Ave. NW, Washington, DC, 20230, USA, (202) 482-2000, https://www.commerce.gov/; Digital Trade in North America.

United Nations Industrial Development Organization (UNIDO), 1 United Nations Plz., Rm. DC1-1118, New York, NY, 10017, USA, (212) 963-6890, (212) 963 6885, (212) 963-7904, office.newyork@unido.org, https://www.unido.org/; Industrial Statistics Databases and International Yearbook of Industrial Statistics 2021.

The World Bank, 1818 H St. NW, Washington, DC, 20433, USA, (202) 473-1000, (202) 477-6391, eds03@worldbank.org, https://www.worldbank.org/; Canada (report) and World Development Indicators (WDI) 2022.

World Intellectual Property Organization (WIPO), 34, chemin des Colombettes, Geneva, CH-1211, SWI, https://www.wipo.int; Madrid Yearly Review 2022: International Registrations of Marks.

CANADA-INFANT AND MATERNAL MORTALITY

See CANADA-MORTALITY

CANADA-INTEREST RATES

Organization for Economic Cooperation and Development (OECD), 2001 L St. NW, Ste. 650, Washington, DC, 20036-4922, USA, (202) 785-6323, (800) 456-6323, (202) 785-0350, washington.contact@oecd.org, https://www.oecd.org/; OECD Business and Finance Outlook 2021; OECD Digital Economy Outlook 2020; and OECD Main Economic Indicators (MEI).

United Nations Statistics Division (UNSD), United Nations Plz., New York, NY, 10017, USA, (800) 253-9646, (212) 963-9851, statistics@un.org, https://unstats.un.org; Statistical Yearbook of the United Nations 2021.

CANADA-INTERNAL REVENUE

Organization for Economic Cooperation and Development (OECD), 2001 L St. NW, Ste. 650, Washington, DC, 20036-4922, USA, (202) 785-6323, (800) 456-6323, (202) 785-0350, washington.contact@oecd.org, https://www.oecd.org/; Revenue Statistics 2022.

CANADA-INTERNATIONAL FINANCE

Global Affairs Canada, Enquiries Service (LOS), 125 Sussex Dr., Ottowa, ON, K1A 0G2, CAN, (613) 944-4000 (Dial from U.S.), (613) 996-9709 (Fax from U.S.), info@international.gc.ca, https://www.international.gc.ca/; Statistical Report on International Assistance, 2021-2022.

Organization for Economic Cooperation and Development (OECD), 2001 L St. NW, Ste. 650, Washington, DC, 20036-4922, USA, (202) 785-6323, (800) 456-6323, (202) 785-0350, washington.contact@oecd.org, https://www.oecd.org/; OECD Business and Finance Outlook 2021; OECD Digital Economy Outlook 2020; and OECD Main Economic Indicators (MEI).

Western Washington University, Border Policy Research Institute (BPRI), 516 High St., Bellingham, WA, 98225, USA, (360) 650-3000, laurie.trautman@wwu.edu, https://bpri.wwu.edu/; Border Barometer.

World Bank Group: International Finance Corporation (IFC), 2121 Pennsylvania Ave. NW, Washington, DC, 20433, USA, (202) 473-1000, (202) 473-7711, (202) 974-4384, https://www.ifc.org; Annual Report 2021: Meeting the Moment.

CANADA-INTERNATIONAL LIQUIDITY

Organization for Economic Cooperation and Development (OECD), 2001 L St. NW, Ste. 650, Washington, DC, 20036-4922, USA, (202) 785-6323, (800) 456-6323, (202) 785-0350, washington.contact@oecd.org, https://www.oecd.org/; OECD Business and Finance Outlook 2021.

CANADA-INTERNATIONAL TRADE

Asia Pacific Economic Cooperation (APEC), 35 Heng Mui Keng Terrace, 119616, SGP, info@apec.org, https://www.apec.org/; APEC Regional Trends Analysis - What Goes Around Comes Around: Pivoting to a Circular Economy; Uncertainty Tests APEC's Resilience amid COVID-19.

The Economist Group: Economist Intelligence Unit (EIU), 900 3rd Ave., 16th Fl., New York, NY, 10022, USA, (212) 541-0500, americas@eiu.com, https://www.eiu.com; Canada Country Report.

Euromonitor International, Inc., 1 N Dearborn St., Ste. 1700, Chicago, IL, 60602, USA, (312) 922-1115, (312) 922-1157, info-usa@euromonitor.com, https://www.euromonitor.com/; Geographies.

Organization for Economic Cooperation and Development (OECD), 2001 L St. NW, Ste. 650, Washington, DC, 20036-4922, USA, (202) 785-6323, (800) 456-6323, (202) 785-0350, washington.contact@oecd.org, https://www.oecd.org/; Economic Survey of Canada 2023; OECD Digital Economy Outlook 2020; OECD Main Economic Indicators (MEI); and OECD-FAO Agricultural Outlook 2022-2031.

Palgrave Macmillan, 1 New York Plaza, Ste. 4500, New York, NY, 10004-1562, USA, (800) 777-4643, orders@palgrave.com, https://www.palgrave.com/us; The Statesman's Yearbook, 2023.

Routledge - Taylor & Francis Group, 6000 Broken Sound Pkwy. NW, Ste. 300, Boca Raton, FL, 33487, USA, (800) 634-1420, (800) 634-7064, orders@taylorandfrancis.com, https://www.routledge.com/; The Europa World Year Book 2022.

U.S. Department of Commerce (DOC), 1401 Constitution Ave. NW, Washington, DC, 20230, USA, (202) 482-2000, https://www.commerce.gov/; Digital Trade in North America.

U.S. Department of Labor (DOL), Bureau of International Labor Affairs (ILAB), 200 Constitution Ave. NW, Washington, DC, 20210, USA, (202) 693-4770, contact-ilab@dol.gov, https://www.dol.gov/agencies/ilab; Report on the U.S. Employment Impact of the United States-Mexico-Canada Agreement and United States-Mexico-Canada Agreement (USMCA) Labor Rights Report.

U.S. Department of Labor (DOL), Bureau of Labor Statistics (BLS), Postal Square Bldg., 2 Massachusetts Ave. NE, Washington, DC, 20212-0001, USA, (202) 691-5200, (202) 691-7890, blsdata_staff@bls.gov, https://www.bls.gov; Import/Export Price Indexes (International Price Program - IPP).

United Nations Conference on Trade and Development (UNCTAD), Palais des Nations, Geneva, 1211, SWI, (212) 963-6896, unctadinfo@unctad.org, https://unctad.org; Trade and Development Report 2021.

United Nations Food and Agricultural Organization (FAO), 2121 K St., Ste. 800B, Washington, DC, 20037, USA, (202) 653-2400 (Dial from U.S.), (202) 653-5760 (Fax from U.S.), fao-hq@fao.org, https://www.fao.org; The State of Food and Agriculture (SOFA) 2022.

United Nations Statistics Division (UNSD), United Nations Plz., New York, NY, 10017, USA, (800) 253-9646, (212) 963-9851, statistics@un.org, https://unstats.un.org; International Trade Statistics Yearbook 2020 and Statistical Yearbook of the United Nations 2021.

Western Washington University, Border Policy Research Institute (BPRI), 516 High St., Bellingham, WA, 98225, USA, (360) 650-3000, laurie.trautman@wwu.edu, https://bpri.wwu.edu/; Border Barometer and COVID-19 and the US-Canada Border.

The World Bank, 1818 H St. NW, Washington, DC, 20433, USA, (202) 473-1000, (202) 477-6391, eds03@worldbank.org, https://www.worldbank.org/; Canada (report); World Development Indicators (WDI) 2022; and World Development Report 2022: Finance for an Equitable Recovery.

World Bureau of Metal Statistics (WBMS), 31 Star St., Ware, Hertfordshire, SG12 9BA, GBR, https://www.refinitiv.com/en/trading-solutions/world-bureau-metal-statistics; Long Term Production/Consumption Series - All Metals; World Flow Charts; and World Metal Statistics.

World Steel Association (Worldsteel), Avenue de Tervueren 270, Brussels, B-1150, BEL, steel@worldsteel.org, https://www.worldsteel.org; Steel Statistical Yearbook 2021.

World Trade Organization (WTO), Ctre. William Rappard, Rue de Lausanne 154, Case postale, Geneva, CH-1211, SWI, enquiries@wto.org, https://www.wto.org; World Trade Statistical Review 2022.

CANADA-INTERNET USERS

International Telecommunication Union (ITU), Place des Nations, Geneva, CH-1211, SWI, itumail@itu.int, https://www.itu.int; Global Connectivity Report 2022; World Telecommunication/ICT Indicators Database 2021; and Yearbook of Statistics 2019.

The World Bank, 1818 H St. NW, Washington, DC, 20433, USA, (202) 473-1000, (202) 477-6391, eds03@worldbank.org, https://www.worldbank.org/; Canada (report).

CANADA-INVESTMENTS

International Monetary Fund (IMF), 700 19th St. NW, Washington, DC, 20431, USA, (202) 623-7000, (202) 623-4661, publications@imf.org, https://www.imf.org; International Financial Statistics (IFS).

Organization for Economic Cooperation and Development (OECD), 2001 L St. NW, Ste. 650, Washington, DC, 20036-4922, USA, (202) 785-6323, (800) 456-6323, (202) 785-0350, washington.contact@oecd.org, https://www.oecd.org/; OECD Business and Finance Outlook 2021; OECD Digital Economy Outlook 2020; and STAN (STructural ANalysis) Database.

CANADA-LABOR

Central Intelligence Agency (CIA), Office of Public Affairs, Washington, DC, 20505, USA, (703) 482-0623, https://www.cia.gov; The World Factbook.

The Conference Board of Canada, 135 Laurier Avenue W, Ottawa, ON, K1P 5J2, CAN, (866) 711-

2262 (Dial from U.S.), (613) 526-3280 (Dial from U.S.), (613) 526-4857 (Fax from U.S.), contactcboc@conferenceboard.ca, https://www.conferenceboard.ca/; Help-Wanted Index.

Euromonitor International, Inc., 1 N Dearborn St., Ste. 1700, Chicago, IL, 60602, USA, (312) 922-1115, (312) 922-1157, info-usa@euromonitor.com, https://www.euromonitor.com/; Geographies.

Federal Statistical Office Germany, Gustav-Stresemann-Ring 11, Wiesbaden, D-65189, GER, https://www.destatis.de; Basic Indicators: Canada.

International Labour Organization (ILO), 4 Rte. des Morillons, Geneva, CH-1211, SWI, ilo@ilo.org, https://www.ilo.org; NORMLEX Information System on International Labour Standards.

Nova Scotia Department of Finance and Treasury Board, Economics and Statistics Division, 1723 Hollis St., PO Box 187, Halifax, NS, B3J 2N3, CAN, (902) 424-5554 (Dial from U.S.), (902) 424-0635 (Fax from U.S.), financeweb@novascotia.ca, https://www.novascotia.ca/finance/statistics/; Nova Scotia Economic Indicators.

Organization for Economic Cooperation and Development (OECD), 2001 L St. NW, Ste. 650, Washington, DC, 20036-4922, USA, (202) 785-6323, (800) 456-6323, (202) 785-0350, washington.contact@oecd.org, https://www.oecd.org/; Economic Survey of Canada 2023; OECD Digital Economy Outlook 2020; OECD Employment Outlook 2022: Building Back More Inclusive Labour Markets; and OECD Main Economic Indicators (MEI).

Palgrave Macmillan, 1 New York Plaza, Ste. 4500, New York, NY, 10004-1562, USA, (800) 777-4643, orders@palgrave.com, https://www.palgrave.com/us; The Statesman's Yearbook, 2023.

Statistics Canada (StatCan), 150 Tunney's Pasture Driveway, Ottawa, ON, K1A 0T6, CAN, (800) 263-1136 (Dial from U.S.), (514) 283-8300 (Dial from U.S.), (514) 283-9350 (Fax from U.S.), infostats@statcan.gc.ca, https://www.statcan.gc.ca; Children and Youth Statistics.

United Nations Food and Agricultural Organization (FAO), 2121 K St., Ste. 800B, Washington, DC, 20037, USA, (202) 653-2400 (Dial from U.S.), (202) 653-5760 (Fax from U.S.), fao-hq@fao.org, https://www.fao.org; The State of Food and Agriculture (SOFA) 2022.

The World Bank, 1818 H St. NW, Washington, DC, 20433, USA, (202) 473-1000, (202) 477-6391, eds03@worldbank.org, https://www.worldbank.org/; World Development Indicators (WDI) 2022 and World Development Report 2022: Finance for an Equitable Recovery.

CANADA-LAND USE

United Nations Statistics Division (UNSD), United Nations Plz., New York, NY, 10017, USA, (800) 253-9646, (212) 963-9851, statistics@un.org, https://unstats.un.org; Millennium Development Goal Indicators.

The World Bank, 1818 H St. NW, Washington, DC, 20433, USA, (202) 473-1000, (202) 477-6391, eds03@worldbank.org, https://www.worldbank.org/; World Development Report 2022: Finance for an Equitable Recovery.

CANADA-LIBRARIES

UNESCO Institute for Statistics, C.P 250 Succursale H, Montreal, QC, H3G 2K8, CAN, (514) 343-6880 (Dial from U.S.), (514) 343-5740 (Fax from U.S.), uis.publications@unesco.org, http://uis.unesco.org/; UIS.Stat.

CANADA-LIFE EXPECTANCY

Central Intelligence Agency (CIA), Office of Public Affairs, Washington, DC, 20505, USA, (703) 482-0623, https://www.cia.gov; The World Factbook.

United Nations Department of Economic and Social Affairs (DESA), Population Division, 2 United Nations Plz., Rm. DC2-1950, New York, NY, 10017, USA, (212) 963-3209, (212) 963-2147, population@un.org, https://www.un.org/development/desa/pd/; World Population Ageing 2020 Highlights.

United Nations Statistics Division (UNSD), United Nations Plz., New York, NY, 10017, USA, (800) 253-9646, (212) 963-9851, statistics@un.org, https://unstats.un.org; Millennium Development Goal Indicators.

CANADA-LITERACY

Euromonitor International, Inc., 1 N Dearborn St., Ste. 1700, Chicago, IL, 60602, USA, (312) 922-1115, (312) 922-1157, info-usa@euromonitor.com, https://www.euromonitor.com/; Geographies.

UNESCO Institute for Statistics, C.P 250 Succursale H, Montreal, QC, H3G 2K8, CAN, (514) 343-6880 (Dial from U.S.), (514) 343-5740 (Fax from U.S.), uis.publications@unesco.org, http://uis.unesco.org/; Literacy.

CANADA-LIVESTOCK

Organization for Economic Cooperation and Development (OECD), 2001 L St. NW, Ste. 650, Washington, DC, 20036-4922, USA, (202) 785-6323, (800) 456-6323, (202) 785-0350, washington.contact@oecd.org, https://www.oecd.org/; OECD-FAO Agricultural Outlook 2022-2031.

Palgrave Macmillan, 1 New York Plaza, Ste. 4500, New York, NY, 10004-1562, USA, (800) 777-4643, orders@palgrave.com, https://www.palgrave.com/us; The Statesman's Yearbook, 2023.

Routledge - Taylor & Francis Group, 6000 Broken Sound Pkwy. NW, Ste. 300, Boca Raton, FL, 33487, USA, (800) 634-1420, (800) 634-7064, orders@taylorandfrancis.com, https://www.routledge.com/; The Europa World Year Book 2022.

United Nations Food and Agricultural Organization (FAO), 2121 K St., Ste. 800B, Washington, DC, 20037, USA, (202) 653-2400 (Dial from U.S.), (202) 653-5760 (Fax from U.S.), fao-hq@fao.org, https://www.fao.org; The State of Food and Agriculture (SOFA) 2022.

United Nations Statistics Division (UNSD), United Nations Plz., New York, NY, 10017, USA, (800) 253-9646, (212) 963-9851, statistics@un.org, https://unstats.un.org; Statistical Yearbook of the United Nations 2021.

CANADA-MAGNESIUM PRODUCTION AND CONSUMPTION

See CANADA-MINERAL INDUSTRIES

CANADA-MANUFACTURES

Organization for Economic Cooperation and Development (OECD), 2001 L St. NW, Ste. 650, Washington, DC, 20036-4922, USA, (202) 785-6323, (800) 456-6323, (202) 785-0350, washington.contact@oecd.org, https://www.oecd.org/; Economic Survey of Canada 2023; OECD Main Economic Indicators (MEI); and STAN (STructural ANalysis) Database.

CANADA-MARRIAGE

Routledge - Taylor & Francis Group, 6000 Broken Sound Pkwy. NW, Ste. 300, Boca Raton, FL, 33487, USA, (800) 634-1420, (800) 634-7064, orders@taylorandfrancis.com, https://www.routledge.com/; The Europa World Year Book 2022.

CANADA-MEDICAL CARE, COST OF

Canadian Cancer Society, 55 St. Clair Avenue W, Ste. 500, Toronto, ON, M4V 2Y7, CAN, (888) 939-3333 (Dial from U.S.), (416) 961-7223 (Dial from U.S.), (416) 961-4189 (Fax from U.S.), connect@cancer.ca, https://www.cancer.ca/en; Canadian Cancer Statistics.

Canadian Medical Association (CMA), 1410 Blair Towers Place, Ste. 500, Ottawa, ON, K1J 9B9, CAN, (888) 855-2555 (Dial from U.S.), (613) 731-8610, (613) 236-8864 (Fax from U.S.), cmamsc@cma.ca, https://www.cma.ca; Canadian Journal of Surgery (CJS) and Canadian Medical Association Journal (CMAJ).

Institute of Health Economics (IHE), 1200 10405 Jasper Ave. NW, Edmonton, AB, T5J 3N4, CAN, (780) 448-4881 (Dial from U.S.), (780) 448-0018 (Fax from U.S.), info@ihe.ca, https://www.ihe.ca/; Association Between Strained ICU Capacity and Healthcare Costs in Canada: A Population-Based Cohort Study; The Diagonal Approach: A Theoretic Framework for Economic Evaluation of Vertical and Horizontal Interventions in Healthcare; and IHE Mental Health In Your Pocket 2019.

Public Health Agency of Canada, 130 Colonnade Rd., Ottawa, ON, K1A 0K9, CAN, (844) 280-5020 (Dial from U.S.), https://www.phac-aspc.gc.ca/; Public Health Agency of Canada 2022-23 Departmental Plan and Tuberculosis in Canada, 2020.

Society of Rural Physicians of Canada (SRPC), PO Box 893, 383 Rte. 148, Shawville, QC, J0X 2Y0, CAN, (877) 276-1949 (Dial from U.S.), (819) 647-7054 (Dial from U.S.), (819) 647-2485 (Fax from U.S.), info@srpc.ca, https://srpc.ca/; Canadian Journal of Rural Medicine (CJRM).

CANADA-MERCURY PRODUCTION

See CANADA-MINERAL INDUSTRIES

CANADA-MINERAL INDUSTRIES

Barchart, 209 W Jackson Blvd., 2nd Fl., Chicago, IL, 60606, USA, (877) 247-4394, commodities@barchart.com, https://www.barchart.com/cmdty; The cmdty Yearbook 2023; cmdtyStats: Commodity Statistics and Fundamental Data; cmdtyView: Commodity Index; and Commodity Data and Prices.

Canadian Centre for Policy Alternatives (CCPA), 141 Laurier Ave. W, Ste. 1000, Ottawa, ON, K1P 5J3, CAN, (613) 563-1341 (Dial from U.S.), (844) 563-1341 (Dial from U.S.), (613) 233-1458 (Fax from U.S.), ccpa@policyalternatives.ca, https://www.policyalternatives.ca/; Heating Up, Backing Down Evaluating Recent Climate Policy Progress in Canada.

International Energy Agency (IEA), 9 Rue de la Federation, Paris, 75739, FRA, info@iea.org, https://www.iea.org/; Coal 2021: Analysis and Forecast to 2024; World Energy Outlook 2021; and World Energy Statistics and Balances.

International Lead and Zinc Study Group (ILZSG), Rua Almirante Barroso 38, 5th Fl., Lisbon, 1000-013, PRT, sales@ilzsg.org, https://www.ilzsg.org; Interactive Statistical Database.

International Monetary Fund (IMF), 700 19th St. NW, Washington, DC, 20431, USA, (202) 623-7000, (202) 623-4661, publications@imf.org, https://www.imf.org; International Financial Statistics (IFS).

Organization for Economic Cooperation and Development (OECD), 2001 L St. NW, Ste. 650, Washington, DC, 20036-4922, USA, (202) 785-6323, (800) 456-6323, (202) 785-0350, washington.contact@oecd.org, https://www.oecd.org/; Energy Prices and Taxes for OECD Countries 2020 and STAN (STructural ANalysis) Database.

Palgrave Macmillan, 1 New York Plaza, Ste. 4500, New York, NY, 10004-1562, USA, (800) 777-4643, orders@palgrave.com, https://www.palgrave.com/us; The Statesman's Yearbook, 2023.

Routledge - Taylor & Francis Group, 6000 Broken Sound Pkwy. NW, Ste. 300, Boca Raton, FL, 33487, USA, (800) 634-1420, (800) 634-7064, orders@taylorandfrancis.com, https://www.routledge.com/; The Europa World Year Book 2022.

United Nations Conference on Trade and Development (UNCTAD), Palais des Nations, Geneva, 1211, SWI, (212) 963-6896, unctadinfo@unctad.org, https://unctad.org; Trade and Development Report 2021.

United Nations Statistics Division (UNSD), United Nations Plz., New York, NY, 10017, USA, (800) 253-9646, (212) 963-9851, statistics@un.org, https://unstats.un.org; Statistical Yearbook of the United Nations 2021.

World Bureau of Metal Statistics (WBMS), 31 Star St., Ware, Hertfordshire, SG12 9BA, GBR, https://

www.refinitiv.com/en/trading-solutions/world-bureau-metal-statistics; Annual Stainless Steel Statistics; Long Term Production/Consumption Series - All Metals; World Flow Charts; and World Metal Statistics.

World Steel Association (Worldsteel), Avenue de Tervueren 270, Brussels, B-1150, BEL, steel@worldsteel.org, https://www.worldsteel.org; Steel Statistical Yearbook 2021.

CANADA-MONEY SUPPLY

The Economist Group: Economist Intelligence Unit (EIU), 900 3rd Ave., 16th Fl., New York, NY, 10022, USA, (212) 541-0500, americas@eiu.com, https://www.eiu.com; Canada Country Report.

International Monetary Fund (IMF), 700 19th St. NW, Washington, DC, 20431, USA, (202) 623-7000, (202) 623-4661, publications@imf.org, https://www.imf.org; International Financial Statistics (IFS).

United Nations Statistics Division (UNSD), United Nations Plz., New York, NY, 10017, USA, (800) 253-9646, (212) 963-9851, statistics@un.org, https://unstats.un.org; Statistical Yearbook of the United Nations 2021.

The World Bank, 1818 H St. NW, Washington, DC, 20433, USA, (202) 473-1000, (202) 477-6391, eds03@worldbank.org, https://www.worldbank.org/; Canada (report).

CANADA-MONUMENTS AND HISTORIC SITES

UNESCO Institute for Statistics, C.P 250 Succursale H, Montreal, QC, H3G 2K8, CAN, (514) 343-6880 (Dial from U.S.), (514) 343-5740 (Fax from U.S.), uis.publications@unesco.org, http://uis.unesco.org/; UIS.Stat.

CANADA-MORTALITY

UNICEF, 3 United Nations Plz., New York, NY, 10017, USA, (212) 303-7984, (917) 244-2215, https://www.unicef.org; The State of the World's Children 2023.

United Nations Statistics Division (UNSD), United Nations Plz., New York, NY, 10017, USA, (800) 253-9646, (212) 963-9851, statistics@un.org, https://unstats.un.org; Millennium Development Goal Indicators; Statistical Yearbook of the United Nations 2021; and World Statistics Pocketbook 2021.

The World Bank, 1818 H St. NW, Washington, DC, 20433, USA, (202) 473-1000, (202) 477-6391, eds03@worldbank.org, https://www.worldbank.org/; World Development Indicators (WDI) 2022.

World Health Organization (WHO), Ave. Appia 20, Geneva, CH-1211, SWI, (202) 974-3000 (Telephone in U.S.), publications@who.int, https://www.who.int/; Global Health Observatory (GHO).

CANADA-MOTION PICTURES

Geena Davis Institute on Gender in Media, 4712 Admiralty Way, Ste. 455, Marina del Rey, CA, 90292, USA, https://seejane.org/; From Real to Reel: Representation and Inclusion in Film and Television Produced in British Columbia.

Palgrave Macmillan, 1 New York Plaza, Ste. 4500, New York, NY, 10004-1562, USA, (800) 777-4643, orders@palgrave.com, https://www.palgrave.com/us; The Statesman's Yearbook, 2023.

CANADA-MOTOR VEHICLES

International Road Federation (IRF), Madison Place, 500 Montgomery St., 5th Fl., Alexandria, VA, 22314, USA, (703) 535-1001, (703) 535-1007, info@irf.global, https://www.irf.global/; World Road Statistics (WRS).

CANADA-NATURAL GAS PRODUCTION

See CANADA-MINERAL INDUSTRIES

CANADA-NICKEL AND NICKEL ORE

See CANADA-MINERAL INDUSTRIES

CANADA-NUTRITION

United Nations Food and Agricultural Organization (FAO), 2121 K St., Ste. 800B, Washington, DC, 20037, USA, (202) 653-2400 (Dial from U.S.), (202) 653-5760 (Fax from U.S.), fao-hq@fao.org, https://www.fao.org; The State of Food and Agriculture (SOFA) 2022.

United Nations Statistics Division (UNSD), United Nations Plz., New York, NY, 10017, USA, (800) 253-9646, (212) 963-9851, statistics@un.org, https://unstats.un.org; Millennium Development Goal Indicators.

CANADA-OLDER PEOPLE

Statistics Canada (StatCan), 150 Tunney's Pasture Driveway, Ottawa, ON, K1A 0T6, CAN, (800) 263-1136 (Dial from U.S.), (514) 283-8300 (Dial from U.S.), (514) 283-9350 (Fax from U.S.), infostats@statcan.gc.ca, https://www.statcan.gc.ca; Older Adults and Population Aging Statistics.

CANADA-PAPER

See CANADA-FORESTS AND FORESTRY

CANADA-PEANUT PRODUCTION

See CANADA-CROPS

CANADA-PERIODICALS

The Canadian Journalism Project: J-Source, Toronto Metropolitan University, 350 Victoria St., Toronto, ON, M5B 2K3, CAN, info@j-source.ca, https://j-source.ca/; J-Source Newsletter.

CANADA-PESTICIDES

United Nations Food and Agricultural Organization (FAO), 2121 K St., Ste. 800B, Washington, DC, 20037, USA, (202) 653-2400 (Dial from U.S.), (202) 653-5760 (Fax from U.S.), fao-hq@fao.org, https://www.fao.org; The State of Food and Agriculture (SOFA) 2022.

CANADA-PETROLEUM INDUSTRY AND TRADE

International Energy Agency (IEA), 9 Rue de la Federation, Paris, 75739, FRA, info@iea.org, https://www.iea.org/; World Energy Outlook 2021 and World Energy Statistics and Balances.

International Monetary Fund (IMF), 700 19th St. NW, Washington, DC, 20431, USA, (202) 623-7000, (202) 623-4661, publications@imf.org, https://www.imf.org; International Financial Statistics (IFS).

Organization for Economic Cooperation and Development (OECD), 2001 L St. NW, Ste. 650, Washington, DC, 20036-4922, USA, (202) 785-6323, (800) 456-6323, (202) 785-0350, washington.contact@oecd.org, https://www.oecd.org/; Energy Prices and Taxes for OECD Countries 2020.

Palgrave Macmillan, 1 New York Plaza, Ste. 4500, New York, NY, 10004-1562, USA, (800) 777-4643, orders@palgrave.com, https://www.palgrave.com/us; The Statesman's Yearbook, 2023.

U.S. Energy Information Administration (EIA), 1000 Independence Ave. SW, Washington, DC, 20585, USA, (202) 586-8800, infoctr@eia.gov, https://www.eia.gov; International Energy Outlook 2021.

United Nations Food and Agricultural Organization (FAO), 2121 K St., Ste. 800B, Washington, DC, 20037, USA, (202) 653-2400 (Dial from U.S.), (202) 653-5760 (Fax from U.S.), fao-hq@fao.org, https://www.fao.org; The State of Food and Agriculture (SOFA) 2022.

United Nations Statistics Division (UNSD), United Nations Plz., New York, NY, 10017, USA, (800) 253-9646, (212) 963-9851, statistics@un.org, https://unstats.un.org; Statistical Yearbook of the United Nations 2021.

CANADA-PHOSPHATES PRODUCTION

See CANADA-MINERAL INDUSTRIES

CANADA-PLASTICS INDUSTRY AND TRADE

United Nations Statistics Division (UNSD), United Nations Plz., New York, NY, 10017, USA, (800) 253-9646, (212) 963-9851, statistics@un.org, https://unstats.un.org; Statistical Yearbook of the United Nations 2021.

CANADA-PLATINUM PRODUCTION

See CANADA-MINERAL INDUSTRIES

CANADA-POPULATION

Canadian Cancer Society, 55 St. Clair Avenue W, Ste. 500, Toronto, ON, M4V 2Y7, CAN, (888) 939-3333 (Dial from U.S.), (416) 961-7223 (Dial from U.S.), (416) 961-4189 (Fax from U.S.), connect@cancer.ca, https://www.cancer.ca/en; Canadian Cancer Statistics.

Canadian Centre for Policy Alternatives (CCPA), 141 Laurier Ave. W, Ste. 1000, Ottawa, ON, K1P 5J3, CAN, (613) 563-1341 (Dial from U.S.), (844) 563-1341 (Dial from U.S.), (613) 233-1458 (Fax from U.S.), ccpa@policyalternatives.ca, https://www.policyalternatives.ca/; The Best and Worst Places to be a Woman in Canada 2019: The Gender Gap in Canada's 26 Biggest Cities.

Canadian Institute for Health Information (CIHI), 495 Richmond Rd., Ste. 600, Ottawa, ON, K2A 4H6, CAN, (613) 241-7860 (Dial from U.S.), (613) 241-5543 (Dial from U.S.), (613) 241-8120 (Fax from U.S.), communications@cihi.ca, https://www.cihi.ca; Health Indicators e-Publication; National Trauma Registry (NTR) Metadata; Nursing in Canada, 2021: Data Tables; and Wait Times for Priority Procedures in Canada, 2022.

Canadian Medical Association (CMA), 1410 Blair Towers Place, Ste. 500, Ottawa, ON, K1J 9B9, CAN, (888) 855-2555 (Dial from U.S.), (613) 731-8610, (613) 236-8864 (Fax from U.S.), cmamsc@cma.ca, https://www.cma.ca; Canadian Journal of Surgery (CJS) and Canadian Medical Association Journal (CMAJ).

Central Intelligence Agency (CIA), Office of Public Affairs, Washington, DC, 20505, USA, (703) 482-0623, https://www.cia.gov; The World Factbook.

The Economist Group: Economist Intelligence Unit (EIU), 900 3rd Ave., 16th Fl., New York, NY, 10022, USA, (212) 541-0500, americas@eiu.com, https://www.eiu.com; Canada Country Report.

Federal Statistical Office Germany, Gustav-Stresemann-Ring 11, Wiesbaden, D-65189, GER, https://www.destatis.de; Basic Indicators: Canada.

Health Canada, Address Locator 1801B, Ottawa, ON, K1A 0K9, CAN, (613) 957-2991 (Dial from U.S.), (613) 941-5366 (Fax from U.S.), hcinfo.infosc@canada.ca, https://www.hc-sc.gc.ca/; Canadian Alcohol and Drugs Survey (CADS): Summary of Results for 2019; Health Product InfoWatch; and Smoking, Vaping and Tobacco.

Infoplease, c/o Sandbox Networks, Inc., 1 Lincoln St., 24th Fl., Boston, MA, 02111, USA, https://www.infoplease.com; Countries of the World.

Institute of Health Economics (IHE), 1200 10405 Jasper Ave. NW, Edmonton, AB, T5J 3N4, CAN, (780) 448-4881 (Dial from U.S.), (780) 448-0018 (Fax from U.S.), info@ihe.ca, https://www.ihe.ca/; Association Between Strained ICU Capacity and Healthcare Costs in Canada: A Population-Based Cohort Study; The Diagonal Approach: A Theoretic Framework for Economic Evaluation of Vertical and Horizontal Interventions in Healthcare; and IHE Mental Health In Your Pocket 2019.

International Labour Organization (ILO), 4 Rte. des Morillons, Geneva, CH-1211, SWI, ilo@ilo.org, https://www.ilo.org; NORMLEX Information System on International Labour Standards.

Northwest Territories Bureau of Statistics, Government of the Northwest Territories, PO Box 1320, Yellowknife, NT, X1A 2L9, CAN, (867) 767-9169 (Dial from U.S.), (888) 782-8768, (867) 873-0275 (Fax from U.S.), info@stats.gov.nt.ca, https://www.statsnwt.ca/; Northwest Territories Community Data and Summary of NWT Community Statistics, 2020.

Nova Scotia Department of Finance and Treasury Board, Economics and Statistics Division, 1723 Hollis St., PO Box 187, Halifax, NS, B3J 2N3, CAN,

(902) 424-5554 (Dial from U.S.), (902) 424-0635 (Fax from U.S.), financeweb@novascotia.ca, https://www.novascotia.ca/finance/statistics/; Nova Scotia Economic Indicators.

Organization for Economic Cooperation and Development (OECD), 2001 L St. NW, Ste. 650, Washington, DC, 20036-4922, USA, (202) 785-6323, (800) 456-6323, (202) 785-0350, washington.contact@oecd.org, https://www.oecd.org/; OECD Labour Force Statistics 2022 and OECD Tourism Trends and Policies 2022.

Palgrave Macmillan, 1 New York Plaza, Ste. 4500, New York, NY, 10004-1562, USA, (800) 777-4643, orders@palgrave.com, https://www.palgrave.com/us; The Statesman's Yearbook, 2023.

Public Health Agency of Canada, 130 Colonnade Rd., Ottawa, ON, K1A 0K9, CAN, (844) 280-5020 (Dial from U.S.), https://www.phac-aspc.gc.ca/; Mpox (Monkeypox) and Tuberculosis in Canada, 2020.

Routledge - Taylor & Francis Group, 6000 Broken Sound Pkwy. NW, Ste. 300, Boca Raton, FL, 33487, USA, (800) 634-1420, (800) 634-7064, orders@taylorandfrancis.com, https://www.routledge.com/; The Europa World Year Book 2022.

Society of Rural Physicians of Canada (SRPC), PO Box 893, 383 Rte. 148, Shawville, QC, J0X 2Y0, CAN, (877) 276-1949 (Dial from U.S.), (819) 647-7054 (Dial from U.S.), (819) 647-2485 (Fax from U.S.), info@srpc.ca, https://srpc.ca/; Canadian Journal of Rural Medicine (CJRM).

Statistics Canada (StatCan), 150 Tunney's Pasture Driveway, Ottawa, ON, K1A 0T6, CAN, (800) 263-1136 (Dial from U.S.), (514) 283-8300 (Dial from U.S.), (514) 283-9350 (Fax from U.S.), infostats@statcan.gc.ca, https://www.statcan.gc.ca; Children and Youth Statistics; Family Violence in Canada: A Statistical Profile, 2019; National Household Survey: Aboriginal Peoples; Net Income of Cannabis Authorities and Government Revenue from the Sale of Cannabis (x 1,000); Older Adults and Population Aging Statistics; and Quarterly Demographic Estimates.

UK Data Service, University of Essex, Wivenhoe Park, Colchester, Essex, CO4 3SQ, GBR, https://ukdataservice.ac.uk/; International Aggregate Data.

UNESCO Institute for Statistics, C.P 250 Succursale H, Montreal, QC, H3G 2K8, CAN, (514) 343-6880 (Dial from U.S.), (514) 343-5740 (Fax from U.S.), uis.publications@unesco.org, http://uis.unesco.org/; UIS.Stat.

United Nations Department of Economic and Social Affairs (DESA), Population Division, 2 United Nations Plz., Rm. DC2-1950, New York, NY, 10017, USA, (212) 963-3209, (212) 963-2147, population@un.org, https://www.un.org/development/desa/pd/; Revision of World Urbanization Prospects and World Population Ageing 2020 Highlights.

United Nations Development Programme (UNDP), One United Nations Plz., New York, NY, 10017, USA, (212) 906-5000, (212) 906-5001, https://www.undp.org; Human Development Report 2021-2022.

United Nations Statistics Division (UNSD), United Nations Plz., New York, NY, 10017, USA, (800) 253-9646, (212) 963-9851, statistics@un.org, https://unstats.un.org; Statistical Yearbook of the United Nations 2021 and World Statistics Pocketbook 2021.

Women and Gender Equality Canada (WAGE), PO Box 8097, Station T CSC , Ottawa, ON, K1G 3H6, CAN, (855) 969-9922 (Dial from U.S.), (819) 420-6905 (Dial from U.S.), (819) 420-6906 (Fax from U.S.), wage.communications.fegc@wage-fegc.gc.ca, https://women-gender-equality.canada.ca/en.html; Equality Matters Newsletter.

The World Bank, 1818 H St. NW, Washington, DC, 20433, USA, (202) 473-1000, (202) 477-6391, eds03@worldbank.org, https://www.worldbank.org/; Canada (report); The Global Findex Database 2021; and World Development Report 2022: Finance for an Equitable Recovery.

CANADA-POPULATION DENSITY

Central Intelligence Agency (CIA), Office of Public Affairs, Washington, DC, 20505, USA, (703) 482-0623, https://www.cia.gov; The World Factbook.

Palgrave Macmillan, 1 New York Plaza, Ste. 4500, New York, NY, 10004-1562, USA, (800) 777-4643, orders@palgrave.com, https://www.palgrave.com/us; The Statesman's Yearbook, 2023.

Routledge - Taylor & Francis Group, 6000 Broken Sound Pkwy. NW, Ste. 300, Boca Raton, FL, 33487, USA, (800) 634-1420, (800) 634-7064, orders@taylorandfrancis.com, https://www.routledge.com/; The Europa World Year Book 2022.

UNESCO Institute for Statistics, C.P 250 Succursale H, Montreal, QC, H3G 2K8, CAN, (514) 343-6880 (Dial from U.S.), (514) 343-5740 (Fax from U.S.), uis.publications@unesco.org, http://uis.unesco.org/; UIS.Stat.

The World Bank, 1818 H St. NW, Washington, DC, 20433, USA, (202) 473-1000, (202) 477-6391, eds03@worldbank.org, https://www.worldbank.org/; Canada (report) and World Development Report 2022: Finance for an Equitable Recovery.

CANADA-POSTAL SERVICE

Palgrave Macmillan, 1 New York Plaza, Ste. 4500, New York, NY, 10004-1562, USA, (800) 777-4643, orders@palgrave.com, https://www.palgrave.com/us; The Statesman's Yearbook, 2023.

CANADA-POWER RESOURCES

Euromonitor International, Inc., 1 N Dearborn St., Ste. 1700, Chicago, IL, 60602, USA, (312) 922-1115, (312) 922-1157, info-usa@euromonitor.com, https://www.euromonitor.com/; Geographies.

International Energy Agency (IEA), 9 Rue de la Federation, Paris, 75739, FRA, info@iea.org, https://www.iea.org/; Coal 2021: Analysis and Forecast to 2024 and World Energy Outlook 2021.

Organization for Economic Cooperation and Development (OECD), 2001 L St. NW, Ste. 650, Washington, DC, 20036-4922, USA, (202) 785-6323, (800) 456-6323, (202) 785-0350, washington.contact@oecd.org, https://www.oecd.org/; Energy Prices and Taxes for OECD Countries 2020 and Environment Statistics.

Palgrave Macmillan, 1 New York Plaza, Ste. 4500, New York, NY, 10004-1562, USA, (800) 777-4643, orders@palgrave.com, https://www.palgrave.com/us; The Statesman's Yearbook, 2023.

PowerOutage.com, jrobinson@bluefirestudios.com, https://poweroutage.com/; Canada Power Outages.

U.S. Energy Information Administration (EIA), 1000 Independence Ave. SW, Washington, DC, 20585, USA, (202) 586-8800, infoctr@eia.gov, https://www.eia.gov; International Energy Outlook 2021.

United Nations Statistics Division (UNSD), United Nations Plz., New York, NY, 10017, USA, (800) 253-9646, (212) 963-9851, statistics@un.org, https://unstats.un.org; Energy Statistics Yearbook 2019; Statistical Yearbook of the United Nations 2021; and World Statistics Pocketbook 2021.

The World Bank, 1818 H St. NW, Washington, DC, 20433, USA, (202) 473-1000, (202) 477-6391, eds03@worldbank.org, https://www.worldbank.org/; World Development Report 2022: Finance for an Equitable Recovery.

CANADA-PRICES

Euromonitor International, Inc., 1 N Dearborn St., Ste. 1700, Chicago, IL, 60602, USA, (312) 922-1115, (312) 922-1157, info-usa@euromonitor.com, https://www.euromonitor.com/; Geographies.

International Monetary Fund (IMF), 700 19th St. NW, Washington, DC, 20431, USA, (202) 623-7000, (202) 623-4661, publications@imf.org, https://www.imf.org; International Financial Statistics (IFS).

Organization for Economic Cooperation and Development (OECD), 2001 L St. NW, Ste. 650, Washington, DC, 20036-4922, USA, (202) 785-6323, (800) 456-6323, (202) 785-0350, washington.contact@oecd.org, https://www.oecd.org/; OECD Digital Economy Outlook 2020 and OECD Main Economic Indicators (MEI).

TAPPI - Technical Association of the Pulp and Paper Industry, 15 Technology Pkwy. S, Ste. 115, Peachtree Corners, GA, 30092, USA, (770) 446-1400, (800) 332-8686, (770) 446-6947, memberconnection@tappi.org, https://www.tappi.org/; TAPPI Journal.

The World Bank, 1818 H St. NW, Washington, DC, 20433, USA, (202) 473-1000, (202) 477-6391, eds03@worldbank.org, https://www.worldbank.org/; Canada (report).

World Bureau of Metal Statistics (WBMS), 31 Star St., Ware, Hertfordshire, SG12 9BA, GBR, https://www.refinitiv.com/en/trading-solutions/world-bureau-metal-statistics; Long Term Production/Consumption Series - All Metals; World Flow Charts; and World Metal Statistics.

CANADA-PROPERTY TAX

Organization for Economic Cooperation and Development (OECD), 2001 L St. NW, Ste. 650, Washington, DC, 20036-4922, USA, (202) 785-6323, (800) 456-6323, (202) 785-0350, washington.contact@oecd.org, https://www.oecd.org/; Revenue Statistics 2022.

CANADA-PUBLIC HEALTH

Canadian Institute for Health Information (CIHI), 495 Richmond Rd., Ste. 600, Ottawa, ON, K2A 4H6, CAN, (613) 241-7860 (Dial from U.S.), (613) 241-5543 (Dial from U.S.), (613) 241-8120 (Fax from U.S.), communications@cihi.ca, https://www.cihi.ca; Canadian Institute for Health Information Annual Report, 2021-2022; Canadian Management Information System Database (CMDB) Metadata; Health Indicators e-Publication; Health Workforce Database (HWDB) Metadata; National Health Expenditure Trends, 2022; National Trauma Registry (NTR) Metadata; Nursing in Canada, 2021: Data Tables; Organ Replacement in Canada: CORR Annual Statistics; and Wait Times for Priority Procedures in Canada, 2022.

Canadian Medical Association (CMA), 1410 Blair Towers Place, Ste. 500, Ottawa, ON, K1J 9B9, CAN, (888) 855-2555 (Dial from U.S.), (613) 731-8610, (613) 236-8864 (Fax from U.S.), cmamsc@cma.ca, https://www.cma.ca; Canadian Journal of Surgery (CJS); Canadian Medical Association Journal (CMAJ); and Journal of Psychiatry and Neuroscience.

Euromonitor International, Inc., 1 N Dearborn St., Ste. 1700, Chicago, IL, 60602, USA, (312) 922-1115, (312) 922-1157, info-usa@euromonitor.com, https://www.euromonitor.com/; Geographies and Market Research on the Health and Wellness Industry.

Health Canada, Address Locator 1801B, Ottawa, ON, K1A 0K9, CAN, (613) 957-2991 (Dial from U.S.), (613) 941-5366 (Fax from U.S.), hcinfo.infosc@canada.ca, https://www.hc-sc.gc.ca/; Canada Health Act Annual Report 2021-2022; Canadian Alcohol and Drugs Survey (CADS): Summary of Results for 2019; Health Product InfoWatch; and Smoking, Vaping and Tobacco.

Institute of Health Economics (IHE), 1200 10405 Jasper Ave. NW, Edmonton, AB, T5J 3N4, CAN, (780) 448-4881 (Dial from U.S.), (780) 448-0018 (Fax from U.S.), info@ihe.ca, https://www.ihe.ca/; Association Between Strained ICU Capacity and Healthcare Costs in Canada: A Population-Based Cohort Study; The Diagonal Approach: A Theoretic Framework for Economic Evaluation of Vertical and Horizontal Interventions in Healthcare; and IHE Mental Health In Your Pocket 2019.

Organization for Economic Cooperation and Development (OECD), 2001 L St. NW, Ste. 650, Washington, DC, 20036-4922, USA, (202) 785-6323, (800) 456-6323, (202) 785-0350, washington.contact@oecd.org, https://www.oecd.org/; Health at a Glance 2021.

Palgrave Macmillan, 1 New York Plaza, Ste. 4500, New York, NY, 10004-1562, USA, (800) 777-4643, orders@palgrave.com, https://www.palgrave.com/us; The Statesman's Yearbook, 2023.

Public Health Agency of Canada, 130 Colonnade Rd., Ottawa, ON, K1A 0K9, CAN, (844) 280-5020 (Dial from U.S.), https://www.phac-aspc.gc.ca/; Canada Communicable Disease Report (CCDR), 2023; Canadian Integrated Program for Antimicrobial Resistance Surveillance (CIPARS); Chief Public Health Officer's Annual Report on the State of Public Health in Canada, 2022; CHIRPP Injury Reports; Departmental Results Report, 2020-2021; FluWatch; Influenza Surveillance Resources; Mpox (Monkeypox); Perinatal Health Indicators (PHI); Public Health Agency of Canada 2022-23 Departmental Plan; Surveillance of Hepatitis C in Canada; Tuberculosis in Canada, 2020; and Victims of Police-Reported Family and Intimate Partner Violence in Canada, 2021.

Society of Rural Physicians of Canada (SRPC), PO Box 893, 383 Rte. 148, Shawville, QC, J0X 2Y0, CAN, (877) 276-1949 (Dial from U.S.), (819) 647-7054 (Dial from U.S.), (819) 647-2485 (Fax from U.S.), info@srpc.ca, https://srpc.ca/; Canadian Journal of Rural Medicine (CJRM).

U.S. Census Bureau, 4600 Silver Hill Rd., Washington, DC, 20233, USA, (301) 763-4636, (800) 923-8282, https://www.census.gov; HIV/AIDS Surveillance Data Base.

UNICEF, 3 United Nations Plz., New York, NY, 10017, USA, (212) 303-7984, (917) 244-2215, https://www.unicef.org; The State of the World's Children 2023.

United Nations Department of Economic and Social Affairs (DESA), Population Division, 2 United Nations Plz., Rm. DC2-1950, New York, NY, 10017, USA, (212) 963-3209, (212) 963-2147, population@un.org, https://www.un.org/development/desa/pd/; World Fertility Data 2019.

United Nations Development Programme (UNDP), One United Nations Plz., New York, NY, 10017, USA, (212) 906-5000, (212) 906-5001, https://www.undp.org; Human Development Report 2021-2022.

United Nations Statistics Division (UNSD), United Nations Plz., New York, NY, 10017, USA, (800) 253-9646, (212) 963-9851, statistics@un.org, https://unstats.un.org; Millennium Development Goal Indicators and Statistical Yearbook of the United Nations 2021.

The World Bank, 1818 H St. NW, Washington, DC, 20433, USA, (202) 473-1000, (202) 477-6391, eds03@worldbank.org, https://www.worldbank.org/; Canada (report).

World Health Organization (WHO), Ave. Appia 20, Geneva, CH-1211, SWI, (202) 974-3000 (Telephone in U.S.), publications@who.int, https://www.who.int/; Global Health Observatory (GHO) and Health Statistics and Information Systems.

CANADA-PUBLISHERS AND PUBLISHING

The Canadian Journalism Project: J-Source, Toronto Metropolitan University, 350 Victoria St., Toronto, ON, M5B 2K3, CAN, info@j-source.ca, https://j-source.ca/; J-Source Newsletter.

Palgrave Macmillan, 1 New York Plaza, Ste. 4500, New York, NY, 10004-1562, USA, (800) 777-4643, orders@palgrave.com, https://www.palgrave.com/us; The Statesman's Yearbook, 2023.

UNESCO Institute for Statistics, C.P 250 Succursale H, Montreal, QC, H3G 2K8, CAN, (514) 343-6880 (Dial from U.S.), (514) 343-5740 (Fax from U.S.), uis.publications@unesco.org, http://uis.unesco.org/; UIS.Stat.

CANADA-RAILROADS

Janes, USA, (703) 574-7580, (888) 977-1519, customer.care@janes.com, https://www.janes.com; Janes World Railways 2021-2022.

Palgrave Macmillan, 1 New York Plaza, Ste. 4500, New York, NY, 10004-1562, USA, (800) 777-4643, orders@palgrave.com, https://www.palgrave.com/us; The Statesman's Yearbook, 2023.

Routledge - Taylor & Francis Group, 6000 Broken Sound Pkwy. NW, Ste. 300, Boca Raton, FL, 33487, USA, (800) 634-1420, (800) 634-7064, orders@taylorandfrancis.com, https://www.routledge.com/; The Europa World Year Book 2022.

United Nations Statistics Division (UNSD), United Nations Plz., New York, NY, 10017, USA, (800) 253-9646, (212) 963-9851, statistics@un.org, https://unstats.un.org; Statistical Yearbook of the United Nations 2021.

CANADA-RELIGION

Central Intelligence Agency (CIA), Office of Public Affairs, Washington, DC, 20505, USA, (703) 482-0623, https://www.cia.gov; The World Factbook.

Palgrave Macmillan, 1 New York Plaza, Ste. 4500, New York, NY, 10004-1562, USA, (800) 777-4643, orders@palgrave.com, https://www.palgrave.com/us; The Statesman's Yearbook, 2023.

CANADA-RETAIL TRADE

Euromonitor International, Inc., 1 N Dearborn St., Ste. 1700, Chicago, IL, 60602, USA, (312) 922-1115, (312) 922-1157, info-usa@euromonitor.com, https://www.euromonitor.com/; Geographies.

Statistics Canada (StatCan), 150 Tunney's Pasture Driveway, Ottawa, ON, K1A 0T6, CAN, (800) 263-1136 (Dial from U.S.), (514) 283-8300 (Dial from U.S.), (514) 283-9350 (Fax from U.S.), infostats@statcan.gc.ca, https://www.statcan.gc.ca; Net Income of Cannabis Authorities and Government Revenue from the Sale of Cannabis (x 1,000).

United Nations Statistics Division (UNSD), United Nations Plz., New York, NY, 10017, USA, (800) 253-9646, (212) 963-9851, statistics@un.org, https://unstats.un.org; Statistical Yearbook of the United Nations 2021.

CANADA-RICE PRODUCTION

See CANADA-CROPS

CANADA-ROADS

International Road Federation (IRF), Madison Place, 500 Montgomery St., 5th Fl., Alexandria, VA, 22314, USA, (703) 535-1001, (703) 535-1007, info@irf.global, https://www.irf.global/; World Road Statistics (WRS).

CANADA-RUBBER INDUSTRY AND TRADE

International Rubber Study Group (IRSG), 51 Changi Business Park Central 2, Unit No. 6, 486066, SGP, https://www.rubberstudy.org; Monthly Rubber Bulletin (MRB); Rubber Industry Report; Rubber Statistical Bulletin; and World Rubber Industry Report (WRIO).

United Nations Statistics Division (UNSD), United Nations Plz., New York, NY, 10017, USA, (800) 253-9646, (212) 963-9851, statistics@un.org, https://unstats.un.org; Statistical Yearbook of the United Nations 2021.

CANADA-RYE PRODUCTION

See CANADA-CROPS

CANADA-SHIPPING

Routledge - Taylor & Francis Group, 6000 Broken Sound Pkwy. NW, Ste. 300, Boca Raton, FL, 33487, USA, (800) 634-1420, (800) 634-7064, orders@taylorandfrancis.com, https://www.routledge.com/; The Europa World Year Book 2022.

S&P Global, IHS Markit, 15 Inverness Way E, Englewood, CO, 80112, USA, (800) 447-2273, (800) 854-7179, https://ihsmarkit.com; IHS Maritime World Shipbuilding Statistics; Journal of Commerce; Lloyd's Register of Ships 2021-2022; and Maritime Portal Desktop.

United Nations Statistics Division (UNSD), United Nations Plz., New York, NY, 10017, USA, (800) 253-9646, (212) 963-9851, statistics@un.org, https://unstats.un.org; Statistical Yearbook of the United Nations 2021.

CANADA-SOYBEAN PRODUCTION

See CANADA-CROPS

CANADA-STEEL PRODUCTION

See CANADA-MINERAL INDUSTRIES

CANADA-SUGAR PRODUCTION

See CANADA-CROPS

CANADA-SULPHUR PRODUCTION

See CANADA-MINERAL INDUSTRIES

CANADA-TAXATION

International Road Federation (IRF), Madison Place, 500 Montgomery St., 5th Fl., Alexandria, VA, 22314, USA, (703) 535-1001, (703) 535-1007, info@irf.global, https://www.irf.global/; World Road Statistics (WRS).

Organization for Economic Cooperation and Development (OECD), 2001 L St. NW, Ste. 650, Washington, DC, 20036-4922, USA, (202) 785-6323, (800) 456-6323, (202) 785-0350, washington.contact@oecd.org, https://www.oecd.org/; Revenue Statistics 2022.

Palgrave Macmillan, 1 New York Plaza, Ste. 4500, New York, NY, 10004-1562, USA, (800) 777-4643, orders@palgrave.com, https://www.palgrave.com/us; The Statesman's Yearbook, 2023.

The World Bank, 1818 H St. NW, Washington, DC, 20433, USA, (202) 473-1000, (202) 477-6391, eds03@worldbank.org, https://www.worldbank.org/; World Development Indicators (WDI) 2022.

CANADA-TELEPHONE

Central Intelligence Agency (CIA), Office of Public Affairs, Washington, DC, 20505, USA, (703) 482-0623, https://www.cia.gov; The World Factbook.

Palgrave Macmillan, 1 New York Plaza, Ste. 4500, New York, NY, 10004-1562, USA, (800) 777-4643, orders@palgrave.com, https://www.palgrave.com/us; The Statesman's Yearbook, 2023.

Routledge - Taylor & Francis Group, 6000 Broken Sound Pkwy. NW, Ste. 300, Boca Raton, FL, 33487, USA, (800) 634-1420, (800) 634-7064, orders@taylorandfrancis.com, https://www.routledge.com/; The Europa World Year Book 2022.

United Nations Statistics Division (UNSD), United Nations Plz., New York, NY, 10017, USA, (800) 253-9646, (212) 963-9851, statistics@un.org, https://unstats.un.org; World Statistics Pocketbook 2021.

CANADA-TELEVISION

Geena Davis Institute on Gender in Media, 4712 Admiralty Way, Ste. 455, Marina del Rey, CA, 90292, USA, https://seejane.org/; From Real to Reel: Representation and Inclusion in Film and Television Produced in British Columbia.

CANADA-TEXTILE INDUSTRY

Euromonitor International, Inc., 1 N Dearborn St., Ste. 1700, Chicago, IL, 60602, USA, (312) 922-1115, (312) 922-1157, info-usa@euromonitor.com, https://www.euromonitor.com/; Geographies.

Organization for Economic Cooperation and Development (OECD), 2001 L St. NW, Ste. 650, Washington, DC, 20036-4922, USA, (202) 785-6323, (800) 456-6323, (202) 785-0350, washington.contact@oecd.org, https://www.oecd.org/; OECD-FAO Agricultural Outlook 2022-2031 and STAN (STructural ANalysis) Database.

Palgrave Macmillan, 1 New York Plaza, Ste. 4500, New York, NY, 10004-1562, USA, (800) 777-4643, orders@palgrave.com, https://www.palgrave.com/us; The Statesman's Yearbook, 2023.

United Nations Statistics Division (UNSD), United Nations Plz., New York, NY, 10017, USA, (800) 253-9646, (212) 963-9851, statistics@un.org, https://unstats.un.org; Statistical Yearbook of the United Nations 2021.

CANADA-THEATER

UNESCO Institute for Statistics, C.P 250 Succursale H, Montreal, QC, H3G 2K8, CAN, (514) 343-6880 (Dial from U.S.), (514) 343-5740 (Fax from U.S.), uis.publications@unesco.org, http://uis.unesco.org/; UIS.Stat.

CANADA-TOBACCO INDUSTRY

Organization for Economic Cooperation and Development (OECD), 2001 L St. NW, Ste. 650, Washington, DC, 20036-4922, USA, (202) 785-6323, (800) 456-6323, (202) 785-0350, washington.contact@oecd.org, https://www.oecd.org/; STAN (STructural ANalysis) Database.

United Nations Statistics Division (UNSD), United Nations Plz., New York, NY, 10017, USA, (800) 253-9646, (212) 963-9851, statistics@un.org, https://unstats.un.org; Statistical Yearbook of the United Nations 2021.

CANADA-TOURISM

Euromonitor International, Inc., 1 N Dearborn St., Ste. 1700, Chicago, IL, 60602, USA, (312) 922-1115, (312) 922-1157, info-usa@euromonitor.com, https://www.euromonitor.com/; Geographies.

Organization for Economic Cooperation and Development (OECD), 2001 L St. NW, Ste. 650, Washington, DC, 20036-4922, USA, (202) 785-6323, (800) 456-6323, (202) 785-0350, washington.contact@oecd.org, https://www.oecd.org/; OECD Tourism Trends and Policies 2022.

Prince Edward Island Department of Finance, PO Box 2000, Charlottetown, PE, C1A 7N8, CAN, (902) 368-4040 (Dial from U.S.), (902) 368-6575 (Fax from U.S.), deptfinance@gov.pe.ca, https://www.princeedwardisland.ca/en/topic/finance; Tourism Indicators of Prince Edward Island, 2020.

Routledge - Taylor & Francis Group, 6000 Broken Sound Pkwy. NW, Ste. 300, Boca Raton, FL, 33487, USA, (800) 634-1420, (800) 634-7064, orders@taylorandfrancis.com, https://www.routledge.com/; The Europa World Year Book 2022.

United Nations Statistics Division (UNSD), United Nations Plz., New York, NY, 10017, USA, (800) 253-9646, (212) 963-9851, statistics@un.org, https://unstats.un.org; Statistical Yearbook of the United Nations 2021.

United Nations World Tourism Organization (UNWTO), Calle Poeta Joan Maragall 42, Madrid, 28020, SPA, info@unwto.org, https://www.unwto.org/; Yearbook of Tourism Statistics, 2021 Edition.

The World Bank, 1818 H St. NW, Washington, DC, 20433, USA, (202) 473-1000, (202) 477-6391, eds03@worldbank.org, https://www.worldbank.org/; Canada (report).

CANADA-TRADE

See CANADA-INTERNATIONAL TRADE

CANADA-TRANSPORTATION

Central Intelligence Agency (CIA), Office of Public Affairs, Washington, DC, 20505, USA, (703) 482-0623, https://www.cia.gov; The World Factbook.

Euromonitor International, Inc., 1 N Dearborn St., Ste. 1700, Chicago, IL, 60602, USA, (312) 922-1115, (312) 922-1157, info-usa@euromonitor.com, https://www.euromonitor.com/; Geographies.

Palgrave Macmillan, 1 New York Plaza, Ste. 4500, New York, NY, 10004-1562, USA, (800) 777-4643, orders@palgrave.com, https://www.palgrave.com/us; The Statesman's Yearbook, 2023.

Routledge - Taylor & Francis Group, 6000 Broken Sound Pkwy. NW, Ste. 300, Boca Raton, FL, 33487, USA, (800) 634-1420, (800) 634-7064, orders@taylorandfrancis.com, https://www.routledge.com/; The Europa World Year Book 2022.

The World Bank, 1818 H St. NW, Washington, DC, 20433, USA, (202) 473-1000, (202) 477-6391, eds03@worldbank.org, https://www.worldbank.org/; Canada (report).

CANADA-UNEMPLOYMENT

International Labour Organization (ILO), 4 Rte. des Morillons, Geneva, CH-1211, SWI, ilo@ilo.org, https://www.ilo.org; NORMLEX Information System on International Labour Standards.

Organization for Economic Cooperation and Development (OECD), 2001 L St. NW, Ste. 650, Washington, DC, 20036-4922, USA, (202) 785-6323, (800) 456-6323, (202) 785-0350, washington.contact@oecd.org, https://www.oecd.org/; OECD Composite Leading Indicator (CLI); OECD Employment Outlook 2022: Building Back More Inclusive Labour Markets; and OECD Labour Force Statistics 2022.

Palgrave Macmillan, 1 New York Plaza, Ste. 4500, New York, NY, 10004-1562, USA, (800) 777-4643, orders@palgrave.com, https://www.palgrave.com/us; The Statesman's Yearbook, 2023.

United Nations Statistics Division (UNSD), United Nations Plz., New York, NY, 10017, USA, (800) 253-9646, (212) 963-9851, statistics@un.org, https://unstats.un.org; Statistical Yearbook of the United Nations 2021.

CANADA-URANIUM PRODUCTION AND CONSUMPTION

See CANADA-MINERAL INDUSTRIES

CANADA-VITAL STATISTICS

Canadian Cancer Society, 55 St. Clair Avenue W, Ste. 500, Toronto, ON, M4V 2Y7, CAN, (888) 939-3333 (Dial from U.S.), (416) 961-7223 (Dial from U.S.), (416) 961-4189 (Fax from U.S.), connect@cancer.ca, https://www.cancer.ca/en; Canadian Cancer Statistics.

Canadian Medical Association (CMA), 1410 Blair Towers Place, Ste. 500, Ottawa, ON, K1J 9B9, CAN, (888) 855-2555 (Dial from U.S.), (613) 731-8610, (613) 236-8864 (Fax from U.S.), cmamsc@cma.ca, https://www.cma.ca; Canadian Journal of Surgery (CJS); Canadian Medical Association Journal (CMAJ); and Journal of Psychiatry and Neuroscience.

Health Canada, Address Locator 1801B, Ottawa, ON, K1A 0K9, CAN, (613) 957-2991 (Dial from U.S.), (613) 941-5366 (Fax from U.S.), hcinfo.infosc@canada.ca, https://www.hc-sc.gc.ca/; Smoking, Vaping and Tobacco.

Manitoba Vital Statistics Branch, 254 Portage Ave., Winnipeg, MB, R3C 0B6, CAN, (204) 945-3701 (Dial from U.S.), (204) 948-3128 (Fax from U.S.), vitalstats@gov.mb.ca, http://vitalstats.gov.mb.ca; Manitoba Vital Statistics Database.

Northwest Territories Bureau of Statistics, Government of the Northwest Territories, PO Box 1320, Yellowknife, NT, X1A 2L9, CAN, (867) 767-9169 (Dial from U.S.), (888) 782-8768, (867) 873-0275 (Fax from U.S.), info@stats.gov.nt.ca, https://www.statsnwt.ca/; Northwest Territories Community Data and Summary of NWT Community Statistics, 2020.

Palgrave Macmillan, 1 New York Plaza, Ste. 4500, New York, NY, 10004-1562, USA, (800) 777-4643, orders@palgrave.com, https://www.palgrave.com/us; The Statesman's Yearbook, 2023.

Public Health Agency of Canada, 130 Colonnade Rd., Ottawa, ON, K1A 0K9, CAN, (844) 280-5020 (Dial from U.S.), https://www.phac-aspc.gc.ca/; Chief Public Health Officer's Annual Report on the State of Public Health in Canada, 2022 and Tuberculosis in Canada, 2020.

U.S. Census Bureau, 4600 Silver Hill Rd., Washington, DC, 20233, USA, (301) 763-4636, (800) 923-8282, https://www.census.gov; HIV/AIDS Surveillance Data Base.

United Nations Department of Economic and Social Affairs (DESA), Population Division, 2 United Nations Plz., Rm. DC2-1950, New York, NY, 10017, USA, (212) 963-3209, (212) 963-2147, population@un.org, https://www.un.org/development/desa/pd/; World Contraceptive Use 2021: Estimates and Projections of Family Planning Indicators and World Marriage Data 2019.

United Nations Statistics Division (UNSD), United Nations Plz., New York, NY, 10017, USA, (800) 253-9646, (212) 963-9851, statistics@un.org, https://unstats.un.org; Statistical Yearbook of the United Nations 2021.

CANADA-WAGES

International Labour Organization (ILO), 4 Rte. des Morillons, Geneva, CH-1211, SWI, ilo@ilo.org, https://www.ilo.org; NORMLEX Information System on International Labour Standards.

Organization for Economic Cooperation and Development (OECD), 2001 L St. NW, Ste. 650, Washington, DC, 20036-4922, USA, (202) 785-6323, (800) 456-6323, (202) 785-0350, washington.contact@oecd.org, https://www.oecd.org/; OECD Digital Economy Outlook 2020; OECD Main Economic Indicators (MEI); and STAN (STructural ANalysis) Database.

United Nations Statistics Division (UNSD), United Nations Plz., New York, NY, 10017, USA, (800) 253-9646, (212) 963-9851, statistics@un.org, https://unstats.un.org; Statistical Yearbook of the United Nations 2021.

The World Bank, 1818 H St. NW, Washington, DC, 20433, USA, (202) 473-1000, (202) 477-6391, eds03@worldbank.org, https://www.worldbank.org/; Canada (report).

CANADA-WEATHER

See CANADA-CLIMATE

CANADA-WHALES

See CANADA-FISHERIES

CANADA-WHEAT PRODUCTION

See CANADA-CROPS

CANADA-WHOLESALE TRADE

United Nations Statistics Division (UNSD), United Nations Plz., New York, NY, 10017, USA, (800) 253-9646, (212) 963-9851, statistics@un.org, https://unstats.un.org; Statistical Yearbook of the United Nations 2021.

CANADA-WOOD AND WOOD PULP

See CANADA-FORESTS AND FORESTRY

CANADA-WOOD PRODUCTS

Organization for Economic Cooperation and Development (OECD), 2001 L St. NW, Ste. 650, Washington, DC, 20036-4922, USA, (202) 785-6323, (800) 456-6323, (202) 785-0350, washington.contact@oecd.org, https://www.oecd.org/; STAN (STructural ANalysis) Database.

CANADA-WOOL PRODUCTION

See CANADA-TEXTILE INDUSTRY

CANADA-ZINC AND ZINC ORE

See CANADA-MINERAL INDUSTRIES

CANADA-ZOOS

UNESCO Institute for Statistics, C.P 250 Succursale H, Montreal, QC, H3G 2K8, CAN, (514) 343-6880 (Dial from U.S.), (514) 343-5740 (Fax from U.S.), uis.publications@unesco.org, http://uis.unesco.org/; UIS.Stat.

CANCER

American Cancer Society (ACS), 3380 Chastain Meadows Pkwy NW, Ste. 200, Kennesaw, GA, 30144, USA, (800) 227-2345, https://www.cancer.org; Breast Cancer Facts & Figures 2022-2024; Cancer Facts & Figures 2023; Cancer Facts & Figures for African American/Black People 2022-2024; Cancer Prevention & Early Detection Facts & Figures 2022; Cancer Treatment & Survivorship Facts & Figures 2022-2024; Colorectal Cancer Facts & Figures 2023-2025; and Global Cancer Facts & Figures.

American Society of Clinical Oncology (ASCO), 2318 Mill Rd., Ste. 800, Alexandria, VA, 22314, USA, (888) 282-2552, (703) 299-0158, (703) 299-0255, customerservice@asco.org, https://www.asco.org; 2020 National Cancer Opinion Survey and State of Cancer Care in America.

Bernan Press, 15250 NBN Way, Bldg. C, Blue Ridge Summit, PA, 17214, USA, (301) 459-2255, (800) 865-3457, (800) 865-3450, customercare@bernan.com, https://rowman.com/Page/Bernan; Vital Statistics of the United States 2022: Births, Life Expectancy, Deaths, and Selected Health Data.

Canadian Cancer Society, 55 St. Clair Avenue W, Ste. 500, Toronto, ON, M4V 2Y7, CAN, (888) 939-3333 (Dial from U.S.), (416) 961-7223 (Dial from U.S.), (416) 961-4189 (Fax from U.S.), connect@cancer.ca, https://www.cancer.ca/en; Canadian Cancer Statistics.

Cancer Treatment Centers of America Global, Inc. (CTCA), 5900 Broken Sound Pkwy NW, Boca Raton, FL, 33487, USA, (800) 234-7139, (844) 374-2443, https://www.cancercenter.com/; unpublished data.

The Lancet, 230 Park Ave., New York, NY, 10169, USA, (212) 633-3800, editorial@lancet.com, https://www.thelancet.com/; The Lancet Oncology.

Oral Cancer Foundation (OCF), 1211 E State St., Boise, ID, 83712, USA, (949) 723-4400, info@oralcancerfoundation.org, https://oralcancerfoundation.org/; unpublished data.

St Jude Children's Research Hospital, 262 Danny Thomas Pl., Memphis, TN, 38105, USA, (866) 278-5833, (901) 595-1040 (TTY), https://www.stjude.org/; The Scientific Report: Translating Science into Survival.

U.S. Department of Health and Human Services (HHS), National Institutes of Health (NIH), National Cancer Institute (NCI), 9609 Medical Center Dr., Bethesda, MD, 20850, USA, (800) 422-6237, nciinfo@nih.gov, https://www.cancer.gov; Annual Report to the Nation on the Status of Cancer; Cancer Stat Facts; State Cancer Profiles; Surveillance, Epidemiology, and End Results (SEER) Incidence Data, 1975-2020; and U.S. Atlas of Cancer Mortality 1950-1994.

U.S. Department of Health and Human Services (HHS), National Toxicology Program (NTP), PO Box 12233, MD K2-03, Research Triangle Park, NC, 27709, USA, (984) 287-3209, cdm@niehs.nih.gov, https://ntp.niehs.nih.gov; Chemical Effects in Biological Systems (CEBS).

U.S. Department of Health and Human Services, Centers for Disease Control and Prevention (CDC), 1600 Clifton Rd., Atlanta, GA, 30329-4027, USA, (800) 232-4636, (888) 232-6348 (TTY), cdcinfo@cdc.gov, https://www.cdc.gov; Behavioral Risk Factor Surveillance System (BRFSS) Data; CDC Wonder Databases; and United States Cancer Statistics (USCS): Data Visualizations.

U.S. Department of Health and Human Services, Centers for Disease Control and Prevention (CDC), National Center for Chronic Disease Prevention and Health Promotion (NCCDPHP), 1600 Clifton Rd., Atlanta, GA, 30329, USA, (800) 232-4636, (888) 232-6348 (TTY), https://www.cdc.gov/chronicdisease/; Leading Indicators for Chronic Diseases and Risk Factors Open Data Portal.

U.S. Department of Health and Human Services, Centers for Disease Control and Prevention (CDC), National Center for Health Statistics (NCHS), 3311 Toledo Rd., Hyattsville, MD, 20782-2064, USA, (800) 232-4636, (301) 458-4000, https://www.cdc.gov/nchs; FastStats - Statistics by Topic; Health, United States, 2020-2021; National Vital Statistics Reports (NVSR); and Vital Statistics Online Data Portal.

U.S. Preventive Services Task Force (USPSTF), 5600 Fishers Ln., Mail Stop 06E53A, Rockville, MD, 20857, USA, https://www.uspreventiveservicestaskforce.org/uspstf/; Annual Report to Congress on High-Priority Evidence Gaps for Clinical Preventive Services.

World Health Organization (WHO), Ave. Appia 20, Geneva, CH-1211, SWI, (202) 974-3000 (Telephone in U.S.), publications@who.int, https://www.who.int/; Global Health Observatory (GHO) Data.

CANCER-ALTERNATIVE TREATMENT

American Society of Clinical Oncology (ASCO), 2318 Mill Rd., Ste. 800, Alexandria, VA, 22314, USA, (888) 282-2552, (703) 299-0158, (703) 299-0255, customerservice@asco.org, https://www.asco.org; State of Cancer Care in America.

CANCER-CHEMOTHERAPY

American Society of Clinical Oncology (ASCO), 2318 Mill Rd., Ste. 800, Alexandria, VA, 22314, USA, (888) 282-2552, (703) 299-0158, (703) 299-0255, customerservice@asco.org, https://www.asco.org; Most Women With Early Stage Breast Cancer Can Forgo Chemotherapy When Guided by a Diagnostic Test.

CANCER-DIAGNOSIS

American Cancer Society (ACS), 3380 Chastain Meadows Pkwy NW, Ste. 200, Kennesaw, GA, 30144, USA, (800) 227-2345, https://www.cancer.org; Cancer Prevention & Early Detection Facts & Figures 2022.

American Society of Clinical Oncology (ASCO), 2318 Mill Rd., Ste. 800, Alexandria, VA, 22314, USA, (888) 282-2552, (703) 299-0158, (703) 299-0255, customerservice@asco.org, https://www.asco.org; Identification of Transgender People With Cancer in Electronic Health Records: Recommendations Based on CancerLinQ Observations; Most Women With Early Stage Breast Cancer Can Forgo Chemotherapy When Guided by a Diagnostic Test; and State of Cancer Care in America.

World Health Organization (WHO), International Agency for Research on Cancer (IARC), 25 Avenue Tony Garnier, CS 90627, Lyon, 69366, FRA, https://www.iarc.who.int; The Cancer Atlas; Global Cancer Observatory (GCO); and World Cancer Report: Cancer Research for Cancer Prevention.

CANCER-EPIDEMIOLOGY

U.S. Department of Health and Human Services (HHS), National Institutes of Health (NIH), National Cancer Institute (NCI), 9609 Medical Center Dr., Bethesda, MD, 20850, USA, (800) 422-6237, nciinfo@nih.gov, https://www.cancer.gov; Cancer Trends Progress Report and Surveillance, Epidemiology, and End Results (SEER) Explorer.

World Health Organization (WHO), International Agency for Research on Cancer (IARC), 25 Avenue Tony Garnier, CS 90627, Lyon, 69366, FRA, https://www.iarc.who.int; Global Cancer Observatory (GCO).

CANCER-MORTALITY

American Cancer Society (ACS), 3380 Chastain Meadows Pkwy NW, Ste. 200, Kennesaw, GA, 30144, USA, (800) 227-2345, https://www.cancer.org; Cancer Facts & Figures 2023; Cancer Treatment & Survivorship Facts & Figures 2022-2024; and Global Cancer Facts & Figures.

Bernan Press, 15250 NBN Way, Bldg. C, Blue Ridge Summit, PA, 17214, USA, (301) 459-2255, (800) 865-3457, (800) 865-3450, customercare@bernan.com, https://rowman.com/Page/Bernan; Vital Statistics of the United States 2022: Births, Life Expectancy, Deaths, and Selected Health Data.

Environmental Working Group (EWG), 1250 U St. NW, Ste. 1000, Washington, DC, 20005, USA, (202) 667-6982, https://www.ewg.org/; Nitrate in US Tap Water May Cause More than 12,500 Cancers a Year.

The Lancet, 230 Park Ave., New York, NY, 10169, USA, (212) 633-3800, editorial@lancet.com, https://www.thelancet.com/; The Lancet Oncology.

U.S. Department of Health and Human Services (HHS), National Institutes of Health (NIH), National Cancer Institute (NCI), 9609 Medical Center Dr., Bethesda, MD, 20850, USA, (800) 422-6237, nciinfo@nih.gov, https://www.cancer.gov; Annual Report to the Nation on the Status of Cancer; Cancer Trends Progress Report; NCI Cancer Atlas; Surveillance, Epidemiology, and End Results (SEER) Explorer; Surveillance, Epidemiology, and End Results (SEER) Incidence Data, 1975-2020; and U.S. Atlas of Cancer Mortality 1950-1994.

U.S. Department of Health and Human Services, Centers for Disease Control and Prevention (CDC), 1600 Clifton Rd., Atlanta, GA, 30329-4027, USA, (800) 232-4636, (888) 232-6348 (TTY), cdcinfo@cdc.gov, https://www.cdc.gov; CDC Wonder Databases.

U.S. Department of Health and Human Services, Centers for Disease Control and Prevention (CDC), National Center for Health Statistics (NCHS), 3311 Toledo Rd., Hyattsville, MD, 20782-2064, USA, (800) 232-4636, (301) 458-4000, https://www.cdc.gov/nchs; National Vital Statistics Reports (NVSR) and Vital Statistics Online Data Portal.

World Health Organization (WHO), International Agency for Research on Cancer (IARC), 25 Avenue Tony Garnier, CS 90627, Lyon, 69366, FRA, https://www.iarc.who.int; Global Cancer Observatory (GCO).

CANCER-PATIENTS

American Society of Clinical Oncology (ASCO), 2318 Mill Rd., Ste. 800, Alexandria, VA, 22314, USA, (888) 282-2552, (703) 299-0158, (703) 299-0255, customerservice@asco.org, https://www.asco.org; Identification of Transgender People With Cancer in Electronic Health Records: Recommendations Based on CancerLinQ Observations.

U.S. Department of Health and Human Services (HHS), National Institutes of Health (NIH), National Cancer Institute (NCI), 9609 Medical Center Dr., Bethesda, MD, 20850, USA, (800) 422-6237, nciinfo@nih.gov, https://www.cancer.gov; Surveillance, Epidemiology, and End Results (SEER) Explorer.

U.S. Department of Health and Human Services, Centers for Disease Control and Prevention (CDC), National Center for Health Statistics (NCHS), 3311 Toledo Rd., Hyattsville, MD, 20782-2064, USA, (800) 232-4636, (301) 458-4000, https://www.cdc.gov/nchs; HPV-Associated Cancer Statistics.

World Health Organization (WHO), International Agency for Research on Cancer (IARC), 25 Avenue Tony Garnier, CS 90627, Lyon, 69366, FRA, https://www.iarc.who.int; Global Cancer Observatory (GCO).

CANCER-PREVENTION

American Cancer Society (ACS), 3380 Chastain Meadows Pkwy NW, Ste. 200, Kennesaw, GA, 30144, USA, (800) 227-2345, https://www.cancer.org; Cancer Prevention & Early Detection Facts & Figures 2022.

American Society of Clinical Oncology (ASCO), 2318 Mill Rd., Ste. 800, Alexandria, VA, 22314, USA, (888) 282-2552, (703) 299-0158, (703) 299-0255, customerservice@asco.org, https://www.asco.org; National ASCO Survey Finds Major Gaps in Americans' Knowledge of Cancer Prevention, E-Cigarettes, and End-of-Life Care.

U.S. Department of Health and Human Services (HHS), National Institutes of Health (NIH), National Cancer Institute (NCI), 9609 Medical Center Dr., Bethesda, MD, 20850, USA, (800) 422-6237, nciinfo@nih.gov, https://www.cancer.gov; Cancer Trends Progress Report.

World Health Organization (WHO), International Agency for Research on Cancer (IARC), 25 Avenue Tony Garnier, CS 90627, Lyon, 69366, FRA, https://www.iarc.who.int; The Cancer Atlas and World Cancer Report: Cancer Research for Cancer Prevention.

CANCER-RISK FACTORS

U.S. Department of Health and Human Services (HHS), National Toxicology Program (NTP), PO Box 12233, MD K2-03, Research Triangle Park, NC,

27709, USA, (984) 287-3209, cdm@niehs.nih.gov, https://ntp.niehs.nih.gov; Chemical Effects in Biological Systems (CEBS).

U.S. Department of Health and Human Services, Centers for Disease Control and Prevention (CDC), 1600 Clifton Rd., Atlanta, GA, 30329-4027, USA, (800) 232-4636, (888) 232-6348 (TTY), cdcinfo@cdc.gov, https://www.cdc.gov; Behavioral Risk Factor Surveillance System (BRFSS) Data.

U.S. Department of Health and Human Services, Centers for Disease Control and Prevention (CDC), National Center for Health Statistics (NCHS), 3311 Toledo Rd., Hyattsville, MD, 20782-2064, USA, (800) 232-4636, (301) 458-4000, https://www.cdc.gov/nchs; HPV-Associated Cancer Statistics.

World Health Organization (WHO), International Agency for Research on Cancer (IARC), 25 Avenue Tony Garnier, CS 90627, Lyon, 69366, FRA, https://www.iarc.who.int; Global Cancer Observatory (GCO).

CANCER-SOCIAL ASPECTS

American Society of Clinical Oncology (ASCO), 2318 Mill Rd., Ste. 800, Alexandria, VA, 22314, USA, (888) 282-2552, (703) 299-0158, (703) 299-0255, customerservice@asco.org, https://www.asco.org; National ASCO Survey Finds Major Gaps in Americans' Knowledge of Cancer Prevention, E-Cigarettes, and End-of-Life Care and 2020 National Cancer Opinion Survey.

CANCER-SUSCEPTIBILITY

U.S. Department of Health and Human Services, Centers for Disease Control and Prevention (CDC), 1600 Clifton Rd., Atlanta, GA, 30329-4027, USA, (800) 232-4636, (888) 232-6348 (TTY), cdcinfo@cdc.gov, https://www.cdc.gov; Behavioral Risk Factor Surveillance System (BRFSS) Data.

U.S. Department of Health and Human Services, Centers for Disease Control and Prevention (CDC), National Center for Health Statistics (NCHS), 3311 Toledo Rd., Hyattsville, MD, 20782-2064, USA, (800) 232-4636, (301) 458-4000, https://www.cdc.gov/nchs; HPV-Associated Cancer Statistics.

CANCER-TREATMENT

American Cancer Society (ACS), 3380 Chastain Meadows Pkwy NW, Ste. 200, Kennesaw, GA, 30144, USA, (800) 227-2345, https://www.cancer.org; Cancer Treatment & Survivorship Facts & Figures 2022-2024.

American Society of Clinical Oncology (ASCO), 2318 Mill Rd., Ste. 800, Alexandria, VA, 22314, USA, (888) 282-2552, (703) 299-0158, (703) 299-0255, customerservice@asco.org, https://www.asco.org; Most Women With Early Stage Breast Cancer Can Forgo Chemotherapy When Guided by a Diagnostic Test and State of Cancer Care in America.

St Jude Children's Research Hospital, 262 Danny Thomas Pl., Memphis, TN, 38105, USA, (866) 278-5833, (901) 595-1040 (TTY), https://www.stjude.org/; The Scientific Report: Translating Science into Survival.

U.S. Department of Health and Human Services (HHS), National Institutes of Health (NIH), National Cancer Institute (NCI), 9609 Medical Center Dr., Bethesda, MD, 20850, USA, (800) 422-6237, nciinfo@nih.gov, https://www.cancer.gov; Surveillance, Epidemiology, and End Results (SEER) Explorer.

World Health Organization (WHO), International Agency for Research on Cancer (IARC), 25 Avenue Tony Garnier, CS 90627, Lyon, 69366, FRA, https://www.iarc.who.int; The Cancer Atlas and Global Cancer Observatory (GCO).

CANCER VACCINES

American Association for the Advancement of Science (AAAS), 1200 New York Ave. NW, Washington, DC, 20005, USA, (202) 326-6400, https://www.aaas.org; Science Immunology.

U.S. Department of Health and Human Services, Centers for Disease Control and Prevention (CDC), 1600 Clifton Rd., Atlanta, GA, 30329-4027, USA, (800) 232-4636, (888) 232-6348 (TTY), cdcinfo@cdc.gov, https://www.cdc.gov; Vaccine Adverse Event Reporting System (VAERS) Publications.

CANNABIDIOL (CBD)

ConsumerLab, 333 Mamaroneck Ave., White Plains, NY, 10605, USA, (914) 722-9149, info@consumerlab.com, https://www.consumerlab.com; Product Reviews: CBD and Hemp Extract Supplements, Lotions, and Balms Review.

CANNABIS

AAA Foundation for Traffic Safety (FTS), 607 14th St. NW, Ste. 201, Washington, DC, 20005, USA, (202) 638-5944, (202) 638-5943, info@aaafoundation.org, https://www.aaafoundation.org/; Cannabis Use Among Drivers in Fatal Crashes in Washington State Before and After Legalization.

American Academy of Pediatrics (AAP), 345 Park Blvd., Itasca, IL, 60143, USA, (800) 433-9016, (847) 434-8000, mcc@aap.org, https://www.aap.org; Pediatric Edible Cannabis Exposures and Acute Toxicity: 2017-2021.

National Cannabis Industry Association (NCIA), 126 C St. NW, Washington, DC, 20001, USA, (888) 683-5650, (888) 683-5670, info@thecannabisindustry.org, https://thecannabisindustry.org/; The Key to Consumer Safety: Displacing the Illicit Cannabis Market - Recommendations for Safe Vaping.

Statistics Canada (StatCan), 150 Tunney's Pasture Driveway, Ottawa, ON, K1A 0T6, CAN, (800) 263-1136 (Dial from U.S.), (514) 283-8300 (Dial from U.S.), (514) 283-9350 (Fax from U.S.), infostats@statcan.gc.ca, https://www.statcan.gc.ca; Net Income of Cannabis Authorities and Government Revenue from the Sale of Cannabis (x 1,000).

CANOLA

U.S. Department of Agriculture (USDA), National Agricultural Statistics Service (USDA-NASS), 1400 Independence Ave. SW, Washington, DC, 20250, USA, (800) 727-9540, nass@nass.usda.gov, https://www.nass.usda.gov; Quick Stats.

CANTALOUPE

U.S. Department of Health and Human Services (HHS), Centers for Medicare and Medicaid Services (CMS), 7500 Security Blvd., Baltimore, MD, 21244, USA, (410) 786-3000, (877) 267-2323, https://www.cms.gov; CMS Fast Facts.

CAPACITY UTILIZATION INDEX

Board of Governors of the Federal Reserve System, Constitution Ave. NW, Washington, DC, 20551, USA, (202) 452-3000, (202) 263-4869 (TDD), https://www.federalreserve.gov; Industrial Production and Capacity Utilization 2023.

CAPE VERDE-NATIONAL STATISTICAL OFFICE

Instituto Nacional de Estatistica, Cape Verde, C.P. 116, Praia, CPV, inecv@ine.gov.cv, https://ine.cv/; National Data Reports (Cape Verde).

CAPE VERDE-AGRICULTURE

African Development Bank Group (AfDB), Avenue Joseph Anoma, 01 BP 1387, Abidjan, 01, COT, https://www.afdb.org; African Economic Outlook 2021 and Compendium of Statistics on Bank Group Operations 2019.

The Economist Group: Economist Intelligence Unit (EIU), 900 3rd Ave., 16th Fl., New York, NY, 10022, USA, (212) 541-0500, americas@eiu.com, https://www.eiu.com; Cape Verde Country Report.

Euromonitor International, Inc., 1 N Dearborn St., Ste. 1700, Chicago, IL, 60602, USA, (312) 922-1115, (312) 922-1157, info-usa@euromonitor.com, https://www.euromonitor.com/; Geographies.

Palgrave Macmillan, 1 New York Plaza, Ste. 4500, New York, NY, 10004-1562, USA, (800) 777-4643, orders@palgrave.com, https://www.palgrave.com/us; The Statesman's Yearbook, 2023.

Routledge - Taylor & Francis Group, 6000 Broken Sound Pkwy. NW, Ste. 300, Boca Raton, FL, 33487, USA, (800) 634-1420, (800) 634-7064, orders@taylorandfrancis.com, https://www.routledge.com/; The Europa World Year Book 2022.

United Nations Economic Commission for Africa (UNECA), PO Box 3001, Addis Ababa, ETH, ecainfo@uneca.org, https://www.uneca.org/; African Statistical Yearbook 2020 and Economic Report on Africa 2021.

United Nations Food and Agricultural Organization (FAO), 2121 K St., Ste. 800B, Washington, DC, 20037, USA, (202) 653-2400 (Dial from U.S.), (202) 653-5760 (Fax from U.S.), fao-hq@fao.org, https://www.fao.org; AQUASTAT and The State of Food and Agriculture (SOFA) 2022.

United Nations Statistics Division (UNSD), United Nations Plz., New York, NY, 10017, USA, (800) 253-9646, (212) 963-9851, statistics@un.org, https://unstats.un.org; Statistical Yearbook of the United Nations 2021.

The World Bank, 1818 H St. NW, Washington, DC, 20433, USA, (202) 473-1000, (202) 477-6391, eds03@worldbank.org, https://www.worldbank.org/; Cabo Verde (report) and World Development Indicators (WDI) 2022.

CAPE VERDE-AIRLINES

Palgrave Macmillan, 1 New York Plaza, Ste. 4500, New York, NY, 10004-1562, USA, (800) 777-4643, orders@palgrave.com, https://www.palgrave.com/us; The Statesman's Yearbook, 2023.

Routledge - Taylor & Francis Group, 6000 Broken Sound Pkwy. NW, Ste. 300, Boca Raton, FL, 33487, USA, (800) 634-1420, (800) 634-7064, orders@taylorandfrancis.com, https://www.routledge.com/; The Europa World Year Book 2022.

United Nations Economic Commission for Africa (UNECA), PO Box 3001, Addis Ababa, ETH, ecainfo@uneca.org, https://www.uneca.org/; African Statistical Yearbook 2020.

CAPE VERDE-ARMED FORCES

Central Intelligence Agency (CIA), Office of Public Affairs, Washington, DC, 20505, USA, (703) 482-0623, https://www.cia.gov; The World Factbook.

International Institute for Strategic Studies (IISS) - Americas, 2121 K St. NW, Ste. 600, Washington, DC, 20037, USA, (202) 659-1490, (202) 659-1499, https://www.iiss.org/; The Military Balance 2022.

Palgrave Macmillan, 1 New York Plaza, Ste. 4500, New York, NY, 10004-1562, USA, (800) 777-4643, orders@palgrave.com, https://www.palgrave.com/us; The Statesman's Yearbook, 2023.

Stockholm International Peace Research Institute (SIPRI), Signalistgatan 9, Stockholm, SE 169 72, SWE, https://www.sipri.org/; SIPRI Arms Transfers Database and SIPRI Military Expenditure Database.

CAPE VERDE-BALANCE OF PAYMENTS

African Development Bank Group (AfDB), Avenue Joseph Anoma, 01 BP 1387, Abidjan, 01, COT, https://www.afdb.org; The AfDB Statistics Pocketbook 2019.

Routledge - Taylor & Francis Group, 6000 Broken Sound Pkwy. NW, Ste. 300, Boca Raton, FL, 33487, USA, (800) 634-1420, (800) 634-7064, orders@taylorandfrancis.com, https://www.routledge.com/; The Europa World Year Book 2022.

United Nations Conference on Trade and Development (UNCTAD), Palais des Nations, Geneva, 1211, SWI, (212) 963-6896, unctadinfo@unctad.org, https://unctad.org; Handbook of Statistics 2021.

United Nations Economic Commission for Africa (UNECA), PO Box 3001, Addis Ababa, ETH,

ecainfo@uneca.org, https://www.uneca.org/; African Statistical Yearbook 2020.

The World Bank, 1818 H St. NW, Washington, DC, 20433, USA, (202) 473-1000, (202) 477-6391, eds03@worldbank.org, https://www.worldbank.org/; Cabo Verde (report) and World Development Indicators (WDI) 2022.

CAPE VERDE-BANKS AND BANKING

Euromonitor International, Inc., 1 N Dearborn St., Ste. 1700, Chicago, IL, 60602, USA, (312) 922-1115, (312) 922-1157, info-usa@euromonitor.com, https://www.euromonitor.com/; Geographies.

Routledge - Taylor & Francis Group, 6000 Broken Sound Pkwy. NW, Ste. 300, Boca Raton, FL, 33487, USA, (800) 634-1420, (800) 634-7064, orders@taylorandfrancis.com, https://www.routledge.com/; The Europa World Year Book 2022.

United Nations Economic Commission for Africa (UNECA), PO Box 3001, Addis Ababa, ETH, ecainfo@uneca.org, https://www.uneca.org/; African Statistical Yearbook 2020.

CAPE VERDE-BROADCASTING

Central Intelligence Agency (CIA), Office of Public Affairs, Washington, DC, 20505, USA, (703) 482-0623, https://www.cia.gov; The World Factbook.

Euromonitor International, Inc., 1 N Dearborn St., Ste. 1700, Chicago, IL, 60602, USA, (312) 922-1115, (312) 922-1157, info-usa@euromonitor.com, https://www.euromonitor.com/; Geographies.

Palgrave Macmillan, 1 New York Plaza, Ste. 4500, New York, NY, 10004-1562, USA, (800) 777-4643, orders@palgrave.com, https://www.palgrave.com/us; The Statesman's Yearbook, 2023.

WRTH Publications Limited, PO Box 290, Oxford, OX2 7FT, GBR, sales@wrth.com, https://www.wrth.com; World Radio TV Handbook 2023.

CAPE VERDE-BUDGET

Central Intelligence Agency (CIA), Office of Public Affairs, Washington, DC, 20505, USA, (703) 482-0623, https://www.cia.gov; The World Factbook.

CAPE VERDE-CHILDBIRTH-STATISTICS

The World Bank, 1818 H St. NW, Washington, DC, 20433, USA, (202) 473-1000, (202) 477-6391, eds03@worldbank.org, https://www.worldbank.org/; World Development Indicators (WDI) 2022.

CAPE VERDE-CLIMATE

International Institute for Environment and Development (IIED), 235 High Holborn, London, WC1V 7DN, GBR, inforequest@iied.org, https://www.iied.org; Environment & Urbanization.

Palgrave Macmillan, 1 New York Plaza, Ste. 4500, New York, NY, 10004-1562, USA, (800) 777-4643, orders@palgrave.com, https://www.palgrave.com/us; The Statesman's Yearbook, 2023.

CAPE VERDE-COAL PRODUCTION

See CAPE VERDE-MINERAL INDUSTRIES

CAPE VERDE-COMMERCE

Palgrave Macmillan, 1 New York Plaza, Ste. 4500, New York, NY, 10004-1562, USA, (800) 777-4643, orders@palgrave.com, https://www.palgrave.com/us; The Statesman's Yearbook, 2023.

UK Data Service, University of Essex, Wivenhoe Park, Colchester, Essex, CO4 3SQ, GBR, https://ukdataservice.ac.uk/; International Aggregate Data.

CAPE VERDE-COMMODITY EXCHANGES

Barchart, 209 W Jackson Blvd., 2nd Fl., Chicago, IL, 60606, USA, (877) 247-4394, commodities@barchart.com, https://www.barchart.com/cmdty; The cmdty Yearbook 2023; cmdtyStats: Commodity Statistics and Fundamental Data; cmdtyView: Commodity Index; and Commodity Data and Prices.

International Monetary Fund (IMF), 700 19th St. NW, Washington, DC, 20431, USA, (202) 623-7000, (202) 623-4661, publications@imf.org, https://www.imf.org; IMF Primary Commodity Prices.

CAPE VERDE-CONSTRUCTION INDUSTRY

United Nations Economic Commission for Africa (UNECA), PO Box 3001, Addis Ababa, ETH, ecainfo@uneca.org, https://www.uneca.org/; African Statistical Yearbook 2020.

United Nations Statistics Division (UNSD), United Nations Plz., New York, NY, 10017, USA, (800) 253-9646, (212) 963-9851, statistics@un.org, https://unstats.un.org; Statistical Yearbook of the United Nations 2021.

CAPE VERDE-CONSUMER PRICE INDEXES

Routledge - Taylor & Francis Group, 6000 Broken Sound Pkwy. NW, Ste. 300, Boca Raton, FL, 33487, USA, (800) 634-1420, (800) 634-7064, orders@taylorandfrancis.com, https://www.routledge.com/; The Europa World Year Book 2022.

The World Bank, 1818 H St. NW, Washington, DC, 20433, USA, (202) 473-1000, (202) 477-6391, eds03@worldbank.org, https://www.worldbank.org/; Cabo Verde (report).

CAPE VERDE-CONSUMPTION (ECONOMICS)

African Development Bank Group (AfDB), Avenue Joseph Anoma, 01 BP 1387, Abidjan, 01, COT, https://www.afdb.org; The AfDB Statistics Pocketbook 2019.

CAPE VERDE-CORN INDUSTRY

See CAPE VERDE-CROPS

CAPE VERDE-CROPS

Palgrave Macmillan, 1 New York Plaza, Ste. 4500, New York, NY, 10004-1562, USA, (800) 777-4643, orders@palgrave.com, https://www.palgrave.com/us; The Statesman's Yearbook, 2023.

United Nations Economic Commission for Africa (UNECA), PO Box 3001, Addis Ababa, ETH, ecainfo@uneca.org, https://www.uneca.org/; African Statistical Yearbook 2020.

United Nations Food and Agricultural Organization (FAO), 2121 K St., Ste. 800B, Washington, DC, 20037, USA, (202) 653-2400 (Dial from U.S.), (202) 653-5760 (Fax from U.S.), fao-hq@fao.org, https://www.fao.org; The State of Food and Agriculture (SOFA) 2022.

United Nations Statistics Division (UNSD), United Nations Plz., New York, NY, 10017, USA, (800) 253-9646, (212) 963-9851, statistics@un.org, https://unstats.un.org; Statistical Yearbook of the United Nations 2021.

CAPE VERDE-DAIRY PROCESSING

Palgrave Macmillan, 1 New York Plaza, Ste. 4500, New York, NY, 10004-1562, USA, (800) 777-4643, orders@palgrave.com, https://www.palgrave.com/us; The Statesman's Yearbook, 2023.

United Nations Food and Agricultural Organization (FAO), 2121 K St., Ste. 800B, Washington, DC, 20037, USA, (202) 653-2400 (Dial from U.S.), (202) 653-5760 (Fax from U.S.), fao-hq@fao.org, https://www.fao.org; The State of Food and Agriculture (SOFA) 2022.

CAPE VERDE-DEBTS, EXTERNAL

African Development Bank Group (AfDB), Avenue Joseph Anoma, 01 BP 1387, Abidjan, 01, COT, https://www.afdb.org; The AfDB Statistics Pocketbook 2019; African Economic Outlook 2021; and Compendium of Statistics on Bank Group Operations 2019.

United Nations Economic Commission for Africa (UNECA), PO Box 3001, Addis Ababa, ETH, ecainfo@uneca.org, https://www.uneca.org/; Economic Report on Africa 2021.

The World Bank, 1818 H St. NW, Washington, DC, 20433, USA, (202) 473-1000, (202) 477-6391, eds03@worldbank.org, https://www.worldbank.org/; Global Financial Development Report 2019-2020: Bank Regulation and Supervision a Decade after the Global Financial Crisis.

CAPE VERDE-DEFENSE EXPENDITURES

See CAPE VERDE-ARMED FORCES

CAPE VERDE-ECONOMIC ASSISTANCE

United Nations Statistics Division (UNSD), United Nations Plz., New York, NY, 10017, USA, (800) 253-9646, (212) 963-9851, statistics@un.org, https://unstats.un.org; Statistical Yearbook of the United Nations 2021.

CAPE VERDE-ECONOMIC CONDITIONS

African Development Bank Group (AfDB), Avenue Joseph Anoma, 01 BP 1387, Abidjan, 01, COT, https://www.afdb.org; The AfDB Statistics Pocketbook 2019; Africa Economic Brief - COVID-19 Pandemic Potential Risks for Trade and Trade Finance in Africa; African Economic Outlook 2021; The African Statistical Journal; Compendium of Statistics on Bank Group Operations 2019; and Gender, Poverty and Environmental Indicators on African Countries 2019.

Bernan Press, 15250 NBN Way, Bldg. C, Blue Ridge Summit, PA, 17214, USA, (301) 459-2255, (800) 865-3457, (800) 865-3450, customercare@bernan.com, https://rowman.com/Page/Bernan; World Economic Outlook, April 2022.

Central Intelligence Agency (CIA), Office of Public Affairs, Washington, DC, 20505, USA, (703) 482-0623, https://www.cia.gov; The World Factbook.

The Economist Group: Economist Intelligence Unit (EIU), 900 3rd Ave., 16th Fl., New York, NY, 10022, USA, (212) 541-0500, americas@eiu.com, https://www.eiu.com; Cape Verde Country Report.

Euromonitor International, Inc., 1 N Dearborn St., Ste. 1700, Chicago, IL, 60602, USA, (312) 922-1115, (312) 922-1157, info-usa@euromonitor.com, https://www.euromonitor.com/; Geographies.

International Monetary Fund (IMF), 700 19th St. NW, Washington, DC, 20431, USA, (202) 623-7000, (202) 623-4661, publications@imf.org, https://www.imf.org; IMF Data and World Economic Outlook.

Palgrave Macmillan, 1 New York Plaza, Ste. 4500, New York, NY, 10004-1562, USA, (800) 777-4643, orders@palgrave.com, https://www.palgrave.com/us; The Statesman's Yearbook, 2023.

Routledge - Taylor & Francis Group, 6000 Broken Sound Pkwy. NW, Ste. 300, Boca Raton, FL, 33487, USA, (800) 634-1420, (800) 634-7064, orders@taylorandfrancis.com, https://www.routledge.com/; The Europa World Year Book 2022.

United Nations Economic Commission for Africa (UNECA), PO Box 3001, Addis Ababa, ETH, ecainfo@uneca.org, https://www.uneca.org/; Economic Report on Africa 2021.

United Nations Statistics Division (UNSD), United Nations Plz., New York, NY, 10017, USA, (800) 253-9646, (212) 963-9851, statistics@un.org, https://unstats.un.org; World Statistics Pocketbook 2021.

The World Bank, 1818 H St. NW, Washington, DC, 20433, USA, (202) 473-1000, (202) 477-6391, eds03@worldbank.org, https://www.worldbank.org/; Cabo Verde (report); Global Economic Monitor (GEM); Global Economic Prospects, June 2022; and The Global Findex Database 2021.

CAPE VERDE-EDUCATION

African Development Bank Group (AfDB), Avenue Joseph Anoma, 01 BP 1387, Abidjan, 01, COT, https://www.afdb.org; The AfDB Statistics Pocketbook 2019.

Euromonitor International, Inc., 1 N Dearborn St., Ste. 1700, Chicago, IL, 60602, USA, (312) 922-

1115, (312) 922-1157, info-usa@euromonitor.com, https://www.euromonitor.com/; Geographies.

Infoplease, c/o Sandbox Networks, Inc., 1 Lincoln St., 24th Fl., Boston, MA, 02111, USA, https://www.infoplease.com; Countries of the World.

Palgrave Macmillan, 1 New York Plaza, Ste. 4500, New York, NY, 10004-1562, USA, (800) 777-4643, orders@palgrave.com, https://www.palgrave.com/us; The Statesman's Yearbook, 2023.

Routledge - Taylor & Francis Group, 6000 Broken Sound Pkwy. NW, Ste. 300, Boca Raton, FL, 33487, USA, (800) 634-1420, (800) 634-7064, orders@taylorandfrancis.com, https://www.routledge.com/; The Europa World Year Book 2022.

UNESCO Institute for Statistics, C.P 250 Succursale H, Montreal, QC, H3G 2K8, CAN, (514) 343-6880 (Dial from U.S.), (514) 343-5740 (Fax from U.S.), uis.publications@unesco.org, http://uis.unesco.org/; Literacy and UIS.Stat.

United Nations Economic Commission for Africa (UNECA), PO Box 3001, Addis Ababa, ETH, ecainfo@uneca.org, https://www.uneca.org/; African Statistical Yearbook 2020.

United Nations Statistics Division (UNSD), United Nations Plz., New York, NY, 10017, USA, (800) 253-9646, (212) 963-9851, statistics@un.org, https://unstats.un.org; Millennium Development Goal Indicators.

The World Bank, 1818 H St. NW, Washington, DC, 20433, USA, (202) 473-1000, (202) 477-6391, eds03@worldbank.org, https://www.worldbank.org/; Cabo Verde (report) and World Development Indicators (WDI) 2022.

CAPE VERDE-EMPLOYMENT

International Labour Organization (ILO), 4 Rte. des Morillons, Geneva, CH-1211, SWI, ilo@ilo.org, https://www.ilo.org; NORMLEX Information System on International Labour Standards.

UK Data Service, University of Essex, Wivenhoe Park, Colchester, Essex, CO4 3SQ, GBR, https://ukdataservice.ac.uk/; International Aggregate Data.

United Nations Economic Commission for Africa (UNECA), PO Box 3001, Addis Ababa, ETH, ecainfo@uneca.org, https://www.uneca.org/; African Statistical Yearbook 2020.

The World Bank, 1818 H St. NW, Washington, DC, 20433, USA, (202) 473-1000, (202) 477-6391, eds03@worldbank.org, https://www.worldbank.org/; Cabo Verde (report).

CAPE VERDE-ENVIRONMENTAL CONDITIONS

DSI Data Service & Information, Xantener Strasse 51a, Rheinberg, D-47495, GER, dsi@dsidata.com, https://www.dsidata.com/; Global Environmental Database.

The Economist Group: Economist Intelligence Unit (EIU), 900 3rd Ave., 16th Fl., New York, NY, 10022, USA, (212) 541-0500, americas@eiu.com, https://www.eiu.com; Cape Verde Country Report.

International Institute for Environment and Development (IIED), 235 High Holborn, London, WC1V 7DN, GBR, inforequest@iied.org, https://www.iied.org; Environment & Urbanization.

United Nations Statistics Division (UNSD), United Nations Plz., New York, NY, 10017, USA, (800) 253-9646, (212) 963-9851, statistics@un.org, https://unstats.un.org; World Statistics Pocketbook 2021.

CAPE VERDE-EXPORTS

African Development Bank Group (AfDB), Avenue Joseph Anoma, 01 BP 1387, Abidjan, 01, COT, https://www.afdb.org; African Economic Outlook 2021.

Central Intelligence Agency (CIA), Office of Public Affairs, Washington, DC, 20505, USA, (703) 482-0623, https://www.cia.gov; The World Factbook.

The Economist Group: Economist Intelligence Unit (EIU), 900 3rd Ave., 16th Fl., New York, NY, 10022, USA, (212) 541-0500, americas@eiu.com, https://www.eiu.com; Cape Verde Country Report.

International Monetary Fund (IMF), 700 19th St. NW, Washington, DC, 20431, USA, (202) 623-7000, (202) 623-4661, publications@imf.org, https://www.imf.org; Direction of Trade Statistics (DOTS).

S&P Global, IHS Markit, 15 Inverness Way E, Englewood, CO, 80112, USA, (800) 447-2273, (800) 854-7179, https://ihsmarkit.com; Global Trade Atlas (GTA).

United Nations Conference on Trade and Development (UNCTAD), Palais des Nations, Geneva, 1211, SWI, (212) 963-6896, unctadinfo@unctad.org, https://unctad.org; Handbook of Statistics 2021.

CAPE VERDE-FERTILITY, HUMAN

Central Intelligence Agency (CIA), Office of Public Affairs, Washington, DC, 20505, USA, (703) 482-0623, https://www.cia.gov; The World Factbook.

CAPE VERDE-FERTILIZER INDUSTRY

United Nations Food and Agricultural Organization (FAO), 2121 K St., Ste. 800B, Washington, DC, 20037, USA, (202) 653-2400 (Dial from U.S.), (202) 653-5760 (Fax from U.S.), fao-hq@fao.org, https://www.fao.org; The State of Food and Agriculture (SOFA) 2022.

CAPE VERDE-FETAL MORTALITY

See CAPE VERDE-MORTALITY

CAPE VERDE-FINANCE

Stockholm International Peace Research Institute (SIPRI), Signalistgatan 9, Stockholm, SE 169 72, SWE, https://www.sipri.org/; SIPRI Arms Transfers Database and SIPRI Military Expenditure Database.

United Nations Economic Commission for Africa (UNECA), PO Box 3001, Addis Ababa, ETH, ecainfo@uneca.org, https://www.uneca.org/; African Statistical Yearbook 2020.

The World Bank, 1818 H St. NW, Washington, DC, 20433, USA, (202) 473-1000, (202) 477-6391, eds03@worldbank.org, https://www.worldbank.org/; Cabo Verde (report).

CAPE VERDE-FINANCE, PUBLIC

African Development Bank Group (AfDB), Avenue Joseph Anoma, 01 BP 1387, Abidjan, 01, COT, https://www.afdb.org; The AfDB Statistics Pocketbook 2019.

Bernan Press, 15250 NBN Way, Bldg. C, Blue Ridge Summit, PA, 17214, USA, (301) 459-2255, (800) 865-3457, (800) 865-3450, customercare@bernan.com, https://rowman.com/Page/Bernan; National Accounts Statistics: Analysis of Main Aggregates 2020.

The Economist Group: Economist Intelligence Unit (EIU), 900 3rd Ave., 16th Fl., New York, NY, 10022, USA, (212) 541-0500, americas@eiu.com, https://www.eiu.com; Cape Verde Country Report.

International Monetary Fund (IMF), 700 19th St. NW, Washington, DC, 20431, USA, (202) 623-7000, (202) 623-4661, publications@imf.org, https://www.imf.org; Regional Economic Outlook.

Palgrave Macmillan, 1 New York Plaza, Ste. 4500, New York, NY, 10004-1562, USA, (800) 777-4643, orders@palgrave.com, https://www.palgrave.com/us; The Statesman's Yearbook, 2023.

Routledge - Taylor & Francis Group, 6000 Broken Sound Pkwy. NW, Ste. 300, Boca Raton, FL, 33487, USA, (800) 634-1420, (800) 634-7064, orders@taylorandfrancis.com, https://www.routledge.com/; The Europa World Year Book 2022.

United Nations Economic Commission for Africa (UNECA), PO Box 3001, Addis Ababa, ETH, ecainfo@uneca.org, https://www.uneca.org/; African Statistical Yearbook 2020.

United Nations Statistics Division (UNSD), United Nations Plz., New York, NY, 10017, USA, (800) 253-9646, (212) 963-9851, statistics@un.org, https://unstats.un.org; National Accounts Main Aggregates Database and National Accounts Statistics: Main Aggregates and Detailed Tables.

The World Bank, 1818 H St. NW, Washington, DC, 20433, USA, (202) 473-1000, (202) 477-6391, eds03@worldbank.org, https://www.worldbank.org/; Cabo Verde (report).

CAPE VERDE-FISHERIES

Palgrave Macmillan, 1 New York Plaza, Ste. 4500, New York, NY, 10004-1562, USA, (800) 777-4643, orders@palgrave.com, https://www.palgrave.com/us; The Statesman's Yearbook, 2023.

Routledge - Taylor & Francis Group, 6000 Broken Sound Pkwy. NW, Ste. 300, Boca Raton, FL, 33487, USA, (800) 634-1420, (800) 634-7064, orders@taylorandfrancis.com, https://www.routledge.com/; The Europa World Year Book 2022.

United Nations Economic Commission for Africa (UNECA), PO Box 3001, Addis Ababa, ETH, ecainfo@uneca.org, https://www.uneca.org/; African Statistical Yearbook 2020.

United Nations Food and Agricultural Organization (FAO), 2121 K St., Ste. 800B, Washington, DC, 20037, USA, (202) 653-2400 (Dial from U.S.), (202) 653-5760 (Fax from U.S.), fao-hq@fao.org, https://www.fao.org; FAO Yearbook of Fishery and Aquaculture Statistics 2019; Fishery Statistical Collections Global Capture Production; FishStatJ; and The State of Food and Agriculture (SOFA) 2022.

United Nations Statistics Division (UNSD), United Nations Plz., New York, NY, 10017, USA, (800) 253-9646, (212) 963-9851, statistics@un.org, https://unstats.un.org; Statistical Yearbook of the United Nations 2021.

The World Bank, 1818 H St. NW, Washington, DC, 20433, USA, (202) 473-1000, (202) 477-6391, eds03@worldbank.org, https://www.worldbank.org/; Cabo Verde (report).

CAPE VERDE-FOOD

African Development Bank Group (AfDB), Avenue Joseph Anoma, 01 BP 1387, Abidjan, 01, COT, https://www.afdb.org; The AfDB Statistics Pocketbook 2019.

United Nations Food and Agricultural Organization (FAO), 2121 K St., Ste. 800B, Washington, DC, 20037, USA, (202) 653-2400 (Dial from U.S.), (202) 653-5760 (Fax from U.S.), fao-hq@fao.org, https://www.fao.org; The State of Food and Agriculture (SOFA) 2022.

CAPE VERDE-FOREIGN EXCHANGE RATES

African Development Bank Group (AfDB), Avenue Joseph Anoma, 01 BP 1387, Abidjan, 01, COT, https://www.afdb.org; The AfDB Statistics Pocketbook 2019 and African Economic Outlook 2021.

CAPE VERDE-FORESTS AND FORESTRY

United Nations Economic Commission for Africa (UNECA), PO Box 3001, Addis Ababa, ETH, ecainfo@uneca.org, https://www.uneca.org/; African Statistical Yearbook 2020.

United Nations Food and Agricultural Organization (FAO), 2121 K St., Ste. 800B, Washington, DC, 20037, USA, (202) 653-2400 (Dial from U.S.), (202) 653-5760 (Fax from U.S.), fao-hq@fao.org, https://www.fao.org; FAO Yearbook of Forest Products 2019 and The State of Food and Agriculture (SOFA) 2022.

The World Bank, 1818 H St. NW, Washington, DC, 20433, USA, (202) 473-1000, (202) 477-6391, eds03@worldbank.org, https://www.worldbank.org/; Cabo Verde (report).

CAPE VERDE-GEOGRAPHIC INFORMATION SYSTEMS

The World Bank, 1818 H St. NW, Washington, DC, 20433, USA, (202) 473-1000, (202) 477-6391, eds03@worldbank.org, https://www.worldbank.org/; Cabo Verde (report).

CAPE VERDE-GOLD INDUSTRY

The World Bank, 1818 H St. NW, Washington, DC, 20433, USA, (202) 473-1000, (202) 477-6391, eds03@worldbank.org, https://www.worldbank.org/; World Development Indicators (WDI) 2022.

CAPE VERDE-GROSS DOMESTIC PRODUCT

African Development Bank Group (AfDB), Avenue Joseph Anoma, 01 BP 1387, Abidjan, 01, COT, https://www.afdb.org; The AfDB Statistics Pocketbook 2019.

The Economist Group: Economist Intelligence Unit (EIU), 900 3rd Ave., 16th Fl., New York, NY, 10022, USA, (212) 541-0500, americas@eiu.com, https://www.eiu.com; Cape Verde Country Report.

Routledge - Taylor & Francis Group, 6000 Broken Sound Pkwy. NW, Ste. 300, Boca Raton, FL, 33487, USA, (800) 634-1420, (800) 634-7064, orders@taylorandfrancis.com, https://www.routledge.com/; The Europa World Year Book 2022.

United Nations Economic Commission for Africa (UNECA), PO Box 3001, Addis Ababa, ETH, ecainfo@uneca.org, https://www.uneca.org/; African Statistical Yearbook 2020.

The World Bank, 1818 H St. NW, Washington, DC, 20433, USA, (202) 473-1000, (202) 477-6391, eds03@worldbank.org, https://www.worldbank.org/; World Development Indicators (WDI) 2022.

CAPE VERDE-GROSS NATIONAL PRODUCT

Palgrave Macmillan, 1 New York Plaza, Ste. 4500, New York, NY, 10004-1562, USA, (800) 777-4643, orders@palgrave.com, https://www.palgrave.com/us; The Statesman's Yearbook, 2023.

The World Bank, 1818 H St. NW, Washington, DC, 20433, USA, (202) 473-1000, (202) 477-6391, eds03@worldbank.org, https://www.worldbank.org/; World Development Indicators (WDI) 2022.

CAPE VERDE-HOUSING

Euromonitor International, Inc., 1 N Dearborn St., Ste. 1700, Chicago, IL, 60602, USA, (312) 922-1115, (312) 922-1157, info-usa@euromonitor.com, https://www.euromonitor.com/; Geographies.

CAPE VERDE-ILLITERATE PERSONS

UNESCO Institute for Statistics, C.P 250 Succursale H, Montreal, QC, H3G 2K8, CAN, (514) 343-6880 (Dial from U.S.), (514) 343-5740 (Fax from U.S.), uis.publications@unesco.org, http://uis.unesco.org/; UIS.Stat.

CAPE VERDE-IMPORTS

African Development Bank Group (AfDB), Avenue Joseph Anoma, 01 BP 1387, Abidjan, 01, COT, https://www.afdb.org; African Economic Outlook 2021.

Central Intelligence Agency (CIA), Office of Public Affairs, Washington, DC, 20505, USA, (703) 482-0623, https://www.cia.gov; The World Factbook.

The Economist Group: Economist Intelligence Unit (EIU), 900 3rd Ave., 16th Fl., New York, NY, 10022, USA, (212) 541-0500, americas@eiu.com, https://www.eiu.com; Cape Verde Country Report.

International Monetary Fund (IMF), 700 19th St. NW, Washington, DC, 20431, USA, (202) 623-7000, (202) 623-4661, publications@imf.org, https://www.imf.org; Direction of Trade Statistics (DOTS).

S&P Global, IHS Markit, 15 Inverness Way E, Englewood, CO, 80112, USA, (800) 447-2273, (800) 854-7179, https://ihsmarkit.com; Global Trade Atlas (GTA).

United Nations Conference on Trade and Development (UNCTAD), Palais des Nations, Geneva, 1211, SWI, (212) 963-6896, unctadinfo@unctad.org, https://unctad.org; Handbook of Statistics 2021.

CAPE VERDE-INDUSTRIES

Central Intelligence Agency (CIA), Office of Public Affairs, Washington, DC, 20505, USA, (703) 482-0623, https://www.cia.gov; The World Factbook.

The Economist Group: Economist Intelligence Unit (EIU), 900 3rd Ave., 16th Fl., New York, NY, 10022, USA, (212) 541-0500, americas@eiu.com, https://www.eiu.com; Cape Verde Country Report.

Euromonitor International, Inc., 1 N Dearborn St., Ste. 1700, Chicago, IL, 60602, USA, (312) 922-1115, (312) 922-1157, info-usa@euromonitor.com, https://www.euromonitor.com/; Geographies.

International Labour Organization (ILO), 4 Rte. des Morillons, Geneva, CH-1211, SWI, ilo@ilo.org, https://www.ilo.org; NORMLEX Information System on International Labour Standards.

Palgrave Macmillan, 1 New York Plaza, Ste. 4500, New York, NY, 10004-1562, USA, (800) 777-4643, orders@palgrave.com, https://www.palgrave.com/us; The Statesman's Yearbook, 2023.

Routledge - Taylor & Francis Group, 6000 Broken Sound Pkwy. NW, Ste. 300, Boca Raton, FL, 33487, USA, (800) 634-1420, (800) 634-7064, orders@taylorandfrancis.com, https://www.routledge.com/; The Europa World Year Book 2022.

United Nations Economic Commission for Africa (UNECA), PO Box 3001, Addis Ababa, ETH, ecainfo@uneca.org, https://www.uneca.org/; African Statistical Yearbook 2020.

United Nations Industrial Development Organization (UNIDO), 1 United Nations Plz., Rm. DC1-1118, New York, NY, 10017, USA, (212) 963-6890, (212) 963 6885, (212) 963-7904, office.newyork@unido.org, https://www.unido.org/; Industrial Statistics Databases and International Yearbook of Industrial Statistics 2021.

The World Bank, 1818 H St. NW, Washington, DC, 20433, USA, (202) 473-1000, (202) 477-6391, eds03@worldbank.org, https://www.worldbank.org/; Cabo Verde (report) and World Development Indicators (WDI) 2022.

CAPE VERDE-INFANT AND MATERNAL MORTALITY

See CAPE VERDE-MORTALITY

CAPE VERDE-INTERNATIONAL TRADE

African Development Bank Group (AfDB), Avenue Joseph Anoma, 01 BP 1387, Abidjan, 01, COT, https://www.afdb.org; The AfDB Statistics Pocketbook 2019 and African Economic Outlook 2021.

The Economist Group: Economist Intelligence Unit (EIU), 900 3rd Ave., 16th Fl., New York, NY, 10022, USA, (212) 541-0500, americas@eiu.com, https://www.eiu.com; Cape Verde Country Report.

Euromonitor International, Inc., 1 N Dearborn St., Ste. 1700, Chicago, IL, 60602, USA, (312) 922-1115, (312) 922-1157, info-usa@euromonitor.com, https://www.euromonitor.com/; Geographies.

Palgrave Macmillan, 1 New York Plaza, Ste. 4500, New York, NY, 10004-1562, USA, (800) 777-4643, orders@palgrave.com, https://www.palgrave.com/us; The Statesman's Yearbook, 2023.

Routledge - Taylor & Francis Group, 6000 Broken Sound Pkwy. NW, Ste. 300, Boca Raton, FL, 33487, USA, (800) 634-1420, (800) 634-7064, orders@taylorandfrancis.com, https://www.routledge.com/; The Europa World Year Book 2022.

United Nations Conference on Trade and Development (UNCTAD), Palais des Nations, Geneva, 1211, SWI, (212) 963-6896, unctadinfo@unctad.org, https://unctad.org; Trade and Development Report 2021.

United Nations Economic Commission for Africa (UNECA), PO Box 3001, Addis Ababa, ETH, ecainfo@uneca.org, https://www.uneca.org/; African Statistical Yearbook 2020.

United Nations Food and Agricultural Organization (FAO), 2121 K St., Ste. 800B, Washington, DC, 20037, USA, (202) 653-2400 (Dial from U.S.), (202) 653-5760 (Fax from U.S.), fao-hq@fao.org, https://www.fao.org; The State of Food and Agriculture (SOFA) 2022.

United Nations Statistics Division (UNSD), United Nations Plz., New York, NY, 10017, USA, (800) 253-9646, (212) 963-9851, statistics@un.org, https://unstats.un.org; International Trade Statistics Yearbook 2020 and Statistical Yearbook of the United Nations 2021.

The World Bank, 1818 H St. NW, Washington, DC, 20433, USA, (202) 473-1000, (202) 477-6391, eds03@worldbank.org, https://www.worldbank.org/; Cabo Verde (report) and World Development Indicators (WDI) 2022.

World Trade Organization (WTO), Ctre. William Rappard, Rue de Lausanne 154, Case postale, Geneva, CH-1211, SWI, enquiries@wto.org, https://www.wto.org; World Trade Statistical Review 2022.

CAPE VERDE-INTERNET USERS

International Telecommunication Union (ITU), Place des Nations, Geneva, CH-1211, SWI, itumail@itu.int, https://www.itu.int; Global Connectivity Report 2022; World Telecommunication/ICT Indicators Database 2021; and Yearbook of Statistics 2019.

The World Bank, 1818 H St. NW, Washington, DC, 20433, USA, (202) 473-1000, (202) 477-6391, eds03@worldbank.org, https://www.worldbank.org/; Cabo Verde (report).

CAPE VERDE-LABOR

African Development Bank Group (AfDB), Avenue Joseph Anoma, 01 BP 1387, Abidjan, 01, COT, https://www.afdb.org; The AfDB Statistics Pocketbook 2019.

Central Intelligence Agency (CIA), Office of Public Affairs, Washington, DC, 20505, USA, (703) 482-0623, https://www.cia.gov; The World Factbook.

Euromonitor International, Inc., 1 N Dearborn St., Ste. 1700, Chicago, IL, 60602, USA, (312) 922-1115, (312) 922-1157, info-usa@euromonitor.com, https://www.euromonitor.com/; Geographies.

International Labour Organization (ILO), 4 Rte. des Morillons, Geneva, CH-1211, SWI, ilo@ilo.org, https://www.ilo.org; NORMLEX Information System on International Labour Standards.

Palgrave Macmillan, 1 New York Plaza, Ste. 4500, New York, NY, 10004-1562, USA, (800) 777-4643, orders@palgrave.com, https://www.palgrave.com/us; The Statesman's Yearbook, 2023.

United Nations Food and Agricultural Organization (FAO), 2121 K St., Ste. 800B, Washington, DC, 20037, USA, (202) 653-2400 (Dial from U.S.), (202) 653-5760 (Fax from U.S.), fao-hq@fao.org, https://www.fao.org; The State of Food and Agriculture (SOFA) 2022.

The World Bank, 1818 H St. NW, Washington, DC, 20433, USA, (202) 473-1000, (202) 477-6391, eds03@worldbank.org, https://www.worldbank.org/; World Development Indicators (WDI) 2022.

CAPE VERDE-LAND USE

United Nations Statistics Division (UNSD), United Nations Plz., New York, NY, 10017, USA, (800) 253-9646, (212) 963-9851, statistics@un.org, https://unstats.un.org; Millennium Development Goal Indicators.

CAPE VERDE-LIFE EXPECTANCY

African Development Bank Group (AfDB), Avenue Joseph Anoma, 01 BP 1387, Abidjan, 01, COT, https://www.afdb.org; The AfDB Statistics Pocketbook 2019.

Central Intelligence Agency (CIA), Office of Public Affairs, Washington, DC, 20505, USA, (703) 482-0623, https://www.cia.gov; The World Factbook.

United Nations Department of Economic and Social Affairs (DESA), Population Division, 2 United Nations Plz., Rm. DC2-1950, New York, NY, 10017, USA, (212) 963-3209, (212) 963-2147, population@un.org, https://www.un.org/development/desa/pd/; World Population Ageing 2020 Highlights.

United Nations Statistics Division (UNSD), United Nations Plz., New York, NY, 10017, USA, (800) 253-

9646, (212) 963-9851, statistics@un.org, https://unstats.un.org; Millennium Development Goal Indicators.

CAPE VERDE-LITERACY

Euromonitor International, Inc., 1 N Dearborn St., Ste. 1700, Chicago, IL, 60602, USA, (312) 922-1115, (312) 922-1157, info-usa@euromonitor.com, https://www.euromonitor.com/; Geographies.

UNESCO Institute for Statistics, C.P 250 Succursale H, Montreal, QC, H3G 2K8, CAN, (514) 343-6880 (Dial from U.S.), (514) 343-5740 (Fax from U.S.), uis.publications@unesco.org, http://uis.unesco.org/; Literacy.

CAPE VERDE-LIVESTOCK

Palgrave Macmillan, 1 New York Plaza, Ste. 4500, New York, NY, 10004-1562, USA, (800) 777-4643, orders@palgrave.com, https://www.palgrave.com/us; The Statesman's Yearbook, 2023.

Routledge - Taylor & Francis Group, 6000 Broken Sound Pkwy. NW, Ste. 300, Boca Raton, FL, 33487, USA, (800) 634-1420, (800) 634-7064, orders@taylorandfrancis.com, https://www.routledge.com/; The Europa World Year Book 2022.

United Nations Economic Commission for Africa (UNECA), PO Box 3001, Addis Ababa, ETH, ecainfo@uneca.org, https://www.uneca.org/; African Statistical Yearbook 2020.

United Nations Food and Agricultural Organization (FAO), 2121 K St., Ste. 800B, Washington, DC, 20037, USA, (202) 653-2400 (Dial from U.S.), (202) 653-5760 (Fax from U.S.), fao-hq@fao.org, https://www.fao.org; The State of Food and Agriculture (SOFA) 2022.

United Nations Statistics Division (UNSD), United Nations Plz., New York, NY, 10017, USA, (800) 253-9646, (212) 963-9851, statistics@un.org, https://unstats.un.org; Statistical Yearbook of the United Nations 2021.

CAPE VERDE-MARRIAGE

United Nations Statistics Division (UNSD), United Nations Plz., New York, NY, 10017, USA, (800) 253-9646, (212) 963-9851, statistics@un.org, https://unstats.un.org; Statistical Yearbook of the United Nations 2021.

CAPE VERDE-MINERAL INDUSTRIES

Palgrave Macmillan, 1 New York Plaza, Ste. 4500, New York, NY, 10004-1562, USA, (800) 777-4643, orders@palgrave.com, https://www.palgrave.com/us; The Statesman's Yearbook, 2023.

Routledge - Taylor & Francis Group, 6000 Broken Sound Pkwy. NW, Ste. 300, Boca Raton, FL, 33487, USA, (800) 634-1420, (800) 634-7064, orders@taylorandfrancis.com, https://www.routledge.com/; The Europa World Year Book 2022.

United Nations Conference on Trade and Development (UNCTAD), Palais des Nations, Geneva, 1211, SWI, (212) 963-6896, unctadinfo@unctad.org, https://unctad.org; Trade and Development Report 2021.

United Nations Economic Commission for Africa (UNECA), PO Box 3001, Addis Ababa, ETH, ecainfo@uneca.org, https://www.uneca.org/; African Statistical Yearbook 2020.

United Nations Statistics Division (UNSD), United Nations Plz., New York, NY, 10017, USA, (800) 253-9646, (212) 963-9851, statistics@un.org, https://unstats.un.org; Statistical Yearbook of the United Nations 2021.

CAPE VERDE-MONEY SUPPLY

The Economist Group: Economist Intelligence Unit (EIU), 900 3rd Ave., 16th Fl., New York, NY, 10022, USA, (212) 541-0500, americas@eiu.com, https://www.eiu.com; Cape Verde Country Report.

Routledge - Taylor & Francis Group, 6000 Broken Sound Pkwy. NW, Ste. 300, Boca Raton, FL, 33487, USA, (800) 634-1420, (800) 634-7064, orders@taylorandfrancis.com, https://www.routledge.com/; The Europa World Year Book 2022.

The World Bank, 1818 H St. NW, Washington, DC, 20433, USA, (202) 473-1000, (202) 477-6391, eds03@worldbank.org, https://www.worldbank.org/; Cabo Verde (report).

CAPE VERDE-MORTALITY

United Nations Statistics Division (UNSD), United Nations Plz., New York, NY, 10017, USA, (800) 253-9646, (212) 963-9851, statistics@un.org, https://unstats.un.org; Millennium Development Goal Indicators; Statistical Yearbook of the United Nations 2021; and World Statistics Pocketbook 2021.

The World Bank, 1818 H St. NW, Washington, DC, 20433, USA, (202) 473-1000, (202) 477-6391, eds03@worldbank.org, https://www.worldbank.org/; World Development Indicators (WDI) 2022.

World Health Organization (WHO), Ave. Appia 20, Geneva, CH-1211, SWI, (202) 974-3000 (Telephone in U.S.), publications@who.int, https://www.who.int/; Global Health Observatory (GHO).

CAPE VERDE-NUTRITION

United Nations Food and Agricultural Organization (FAO), 2121 K St., Ste. 800B, Washington, DC, 20037, USA, (202) 653-2400 (Dial from U.S.), (202) 653-5760 (Fax from U.S.), fao-hq@fao.org, https://www.fao.org; The State of Food and Agriculture (SOFA) 2022.

United Nations Statistics Division (UNSD), United Nations Plz., New York, NY, 10017, USA, (800) 253-9646, (212) 963-9851, statistics@un.org, https://unstats.un.org; Millennium Development Goal Indicators.

CAPE VERDE-PESTICIDES

United Nations Food and Agricultural Organization (FAO), 2121 K St., Ste. 800B, Washington, DC, 20037, USA, (202) 653-2400 (Dial from U.S.), (202) 653-5760 (Fax from U.S.), fao-hq@fao.org, https://www.fao.org; The State of Food and Agriculture (SOFA) 2022.

CAPE VERDE-PETROLEUM INDUSTRY AND TRADE

United Nations Food and Agricultural Organization (FAO), 2121 K St., Ste. 800B, Washington, DC, 20037, USA, (202) 653-2400 (Dial from U.S.), (202) 653-5760 (Fax from U.S.), fao-hq@fao.org, https://www.fao.org; The State of Food and Agriculture (SOFA) 2022.

CAPE VERDE-POPULATION

African Development Bank Group (AfDB), Avenue Joseph Anoma, 01 BP 1387, Abidjan, 01, COT, https://www.afdb.org; The AfDB Statistics Pocketbook 2019; Africa Economic Brief - COVID-19 Pandemic Potential Risks for Trade and Trade Finance in Africa; The African Statistical Journal; and Gender, Poverty and Environmental Indicators on African Countries 2019.

Central Intelligence Agency (CIA), Office of Public Affairs, Washington, DC, 20505, USA, (703) 482-0623, https://www.cia.gov; The World Factbook.

The Economist Group: Economist Intelligence Unit (EIU), 900 3rd Ave., 16th Fl., New York, NY, 10022, USA, (212) 541-0500, americas@eiu.com, https://www.eiu.com; Cape Verde Country Report.

European Commission, Eurostat, Luxembourg, 2920, LUX, https://ec.europa.eu/eurostat/; EU in the World 2020.

Infoplease, c/o Sandbox Networks, Inc., 1 Lincoln St., 24th Fl., Boston, MA, 02111, USA, https://www.infoplease.com; Countries of the World.

International Labour Organization (ILO), 4 Rte. des Morillons, Geneva, CH-1211, SWI, ilo@ilo.org, https://www.ilo.org; NORMLEX Information System on International Labour Standards.

Palgrave Macmillan, 1 New York Plaza, Ste. 4500, New York, NY, 10004-1562, USA, (800) 777-4643, orders@palgrave.com, https://www.palgrave.com/us; The Statesman's Yearbook, 2023.

Routledge - Taylor & Francis Group, 6000 Broken Sound Pkwy. NW, Ste. 300, Boca Raton, FL, 33487, USA, (800) 634-1420, (800) 634-7064, orders@taylorandfrancis.com, https://www.routledge.com/; The Europa World Year Book 2022.

UK Data Service, University of Essex, Wivenhoe Park, Colchester, Essex, CO4 3SQ, GBR, https://ukdataservice.ac.uk/; International Aggregate Data.

UNESCO Institute for Statistics, C.P 250 Succursale H, Montreal, QC, H3G 2K8, CAN, (514) 343-6880 (Dial from U.S.), (514) 343-5740 (Fax from U.S.), uis.publications@unesco.org, http://uis.unesco.org/; UIS.Stat.

United Nations Department of Economic and Social Affairs (DESA), Population Division, 2 United Nations Plz., Rm. DC2-1950, New York, NY, 10017, USA, (212) 963-3209, (212) 963-2147, population@un.org, https://www.un.org/development/desa/pd/; Revision of World Urbanization Prospects and World Population Ageing 2020 Highlights.

United Nations Development Programme (UNDP), One United Nations Plz., New York, NY, 10017, USA, (212) 906-5000, (212) 906-5001, https://www.undp.org; Human Development Report 2021-2022.

United Nations Statistics Division (UNSD), United Nations Plz., New York, NY, 10017, USA, (800) 253-9646, (212) 963-9851, statistics@un.org, https://unstats.un.org; Statistical Yearbook of the United Nations 2021 and World Statistics Pocketbook 2021.

The World Bank, 1818 H St. NW, Washington, DC, 20433, USA, (202) 473-1000, (202) 477-6391, eds03@worldbank.org, https://www.worldbank.org/; Cabo Verde (report) and The Global Findex Database 2021.

CAPE VERDE-POPULATION DENSITY

African Development Bank Group (AfDB), Avenue Joseph Anoma, 01 BP 1387, Abidjan, 01, COT, https://www.afdb.org; The AfDB Statistics Pocketbook 2019.

Central Intelligence Agency (CIA), Office of Public Affairs, Washington, DC, 20505, USA, (703) 482-0623, https://www.cia.gov; The World Factbook.

Palgrave Macmillan, 1 New York Plaza, Ste. 4500, New York, NY, 10004-1562, USA, (800) 777-4643, orders@palgrave.com, https://www.palgrave.com/us; The Statesman's Yearbook, 2023.

Routledge - Taylor & Francis Group, 6000 Broken Sound Pkwy. NW, Ste. 300, Boca Raton, FL, 33487, USA, (800) 634-1420, (800) 634-7064, orders@taylorandfrancis.com, https://www.routledge.com/; The Europa World Year Book 2022.

UNESCO Institute for Statistics, C.P 250 Succursale H, Montreal, QC, H3G 2K8, CAN, (514) 343-6880 (Dial from U.S.), (514) 343-5740 (Fax from U.S.), uis.publications@unesco.org, http://uis.unesco.org/; UIS.Stat.

The World Bank, 1818 H St. NW, Washington, DC, 20433, USA, (202) 473-1000, (202) 477-6391, eds03@worldbank.org, https://www.worldbank.org/; Cabo Verde (report).

CAPE VERDE-POWER RESOURCES

Euromonitor International, Inc., 1 N Dearborn St., Ste. 1700, Chicago, IL, 60602, USA, (312) 922-1115, (312) 922-1157, info-usa@euromonitor.com, https://www.euromonitor.com/; Geographies.

United Nations Economic Commission for Africa (UNECA), PO Box 3001, Addis Ababa, ETH, ecainfo@uneca.org, https://www.uneca.org/; African Statistical Yearbook 2020.

United Nations Food and Agricultural Organization (FAO), 2121 K St., Ste. 800B, Washington, DC, 20037, USA, (202) 653-2400 (Dial from U.S.), (202) 653-5760 (Fax from U.S.), fao-hq@fao.org, https://www.fao.org; The State of Food and Agriculture (SOFA) 2022.

United Nations Statistics Division (UNSD), United Nations Plz., New York, NY, 10017, USA, (800) 253-9646, (212) 963-9851, statistics@un.org, https://unstats.un.org; Energy Statistics Yearbook 2019 and World Statistics Pocketbook 2021.

CAPE VERDE-PRICES

Euromonitor International, Inc., 1 N Dearborn St., Ste. 1700, Chicago, IL, 60602, USA, (312) 922-1115, (312) 922-1157, info-usa@euromonitor.com, https://www.euromonitor.com/; Geographies.

The World Bank, 1818 H St. NW, Washington, DC, 20433, USA, (202) 473-1000, (202) 477-6391, eds03@worldbank.org, https://www.worldbank.org/; Cabo Verde (report).

CAPE VERDE-PUBLIC HEALTH

African Development Bank Group (AfDB), Avenue Joseph Anoma, 01 BP 1387, Abidjan, 01, COT, https://www.afdb.org; The AfDB Statistics Pocketbook 2019.

Euromonitor International, Inc., 1 N Dearborn St., Ste. 1700, Chicago, IL, 60602, USA, (312) 922-1115, (312) 922-1157, info-usa@euromonitor.com, https://www.euromonitor.com/; Geographies.

Palgrave Macmillan, 1 New York Plaza, Ste. 4500, New York, NY, 10004-1562, USA, (800) 777-4643, orders@palgrave.com, https://www.palgrave.com/us; The Statesman's Yearbook, 2023.

U.S. Census Bureau, 4600 Silver Hill Rd., Washington, DC, 20233, USA, (301) 763-4636, (800) 923-8282, https://www.census.gov; HIV/AIDS Surveillance Data Base.

United Nations Department of Economic and Social Affairs (DESA), Population Division, 2 United Nations Plz., Rm. DC2-1950, New York, NY, 10017, USA, (212) 963-3209, (212) 963-2147, population@un.org, https://www.un.org/development/desa/pd/; World Fertility Data 2019.

United Nations Development Programme (UNDP), One United Nations Plz., New York, NY, 10017, USA, (212) 906-5000, (212) 906-5001, https://www.undp.org; Human Development Report 2021-2022.

United Nations Economic Commission for Africa (UNECA), PO Box 3001, Addis Ababa, ETH, ecainfo@uneca.org, https://www.uneca.org/; African Statistical Yearbook 2020.

United Nations Statistics Division (UNSD), United Nations Plz., New York, NY, 10017, USA, (800) 253-9646, (212) 963-9851, statistics@un.org, https://unstats.un.org; Millennium Development Goal Indicators and Statistical Yearbook of the United Nations 2021.

The World Bank, 1818 H St. NW, Washington, DC, 20433, USA, (202) 473-1000, (202) 477-6391, eds03@worldbank.org, https://www.worldbank.org/; Cabo Verde (report).

World Health Organization (WHO), Ave. Appia 20, Geneva, CH-1211, SWI, (202) 974-3000 (Telephone in U.S.), publications@who.int, https://www.who.int/; Global Health Observatory (GHO) and Health Statistics and Information Systems.

CAPE VERDE-PUBLISHERS AND PUBLISHING

Routledge - Taylor & Francis Group, 6000 Broken Sound Pkwy. NW, Ste. 300, Boca Raton, FL, 33487, USA, (800) 634-1420, (800) 634-7064, orders@taylorandfrancis.com, https://www.routledge.com/; The Europa World Year Book 2022.

CAPE VERDE-RAILROADS

United Nations Economic Commission for Africa (UNECA), PO Box 3001, Addis Ababa, ETH, ecainfo@uneca.org, https://www.uneca.org/; African Statistical Yearbook 2020.

CAPE VERDE-RELIGION

Central Intelligence Agency (CIA), Office of Public Affairs, Washington, DC, 20505, USA, (703) 482-0623, https://www.cia.gov; The World Factbook.

Palgrave Macmillan, 1 New York Plaza, Ste. 4500, New York, NY, 10004-1562, USA, (800) 777-4643, orders@palgrave.com, https://www.palgrave.com/us; The Statesman's Yearbook, 2023.

CAPE VERDE-RETAIL TRADE

Euromonitor International, Inc., 1 N Dearborn St., Ste. 1700, Chicago, IL, 60602, USA, (312) 922-1115, (312) 922-1157, info-usa@euromonitor.com, https://www.euromonitor.com/; Geographies.

CAPE VERDE-ROADS

United Nations Economic Commission for Africa (UNECA), PO Box 3001, Addis Ababa, ETH, ecainfo@uneca.org, https://www.uneca.org/; African Statistical Yearbook 2020.

CAPE VERDE-SHIPPING

Routledge - Taylor & Francis Group, 6000 Broken Sound Pkwy. NW, Ste. 300, Boca Raton, FL, 33487, USA, (800) 634-1420, (800) 634-7064, orders@taylorandfrancis.com, https://www.routledge.com/; The Europa World Year Book 2022.

United Nations Economic Commission for Africa (UNECA), PO Box 3001, Addis Ababa, ETH, ecainfo@uneca.org, https://www.uneca.org/; African Statistical Yearbook 2020.

United Nations Statistics Division (UNSD), United Nations Plz., New York, NY, 10017, USA, (800) 253-9646, (212) 963-9851, statistics@un.org, https://unstats.un.org; Statistical Yearbook of the United Nations 2021.

CAPE VERDE-TAXATION

The World Bank, 1818 H St. NW, Washington, DC, 20433, USA, (202) 473-1000, (202) 477-6391, eds03@worldbank.org, https://www.worldbank.org/; World Development Indicators (WDI) 2022.

CAPE VERDE-TELEPHONE

Palgrave Macmillan, 1 New York Plaza, Ste. 4500, New York, NY, 10004-1562, USA, (800) 777-4643, orders@palgrave.com, https://www.palgrave.com/us; The Statesman's Yearbook, 2023.

Routledge - Taylor & Francis Group, 6000 Broken Sound Pkwy. NW, Ste. 300, Boca Raton, FL, 33487, USA, (800) 634-1420, (800) 634-7064, orders@taylorandfrancis.com, https://www.routledge.com/; The Europa World Year Book 2022.

United Nations Statistics Division (UNSD), United Nations Plz., New York, NY, 10017, USA, (800) 253-9646, (212) 963-9851, statistics@un.org, https://unstats.un.org; World Statistics Pocketbook 2021.

CAPE VERDE-TEXTILE INDUSTRY

Palgrave Macmillan, 1 New York Plaza, Ste. 4500, New York, NY, 10004-1562, USA, (800) 777-4643, orders@palgrave.com, https://www.palgrave.com/us; The Statesman's Yearbook, 2023.

CAPE VERDE-TOBACCO INDUSTRY

United Nations Statistics Division (UNSD), United Nations Plz., New York, NY, 10017, USA, (800) 253-9646, (212) 963-9851, statistics@un.org, https://unstats.un.org; Statistical Yearbook of the United Nations 2021.

CAPE VERDE-TOURISM

Euromonitor International, Inc., 1 N Dearborn St., Ste. 1700, Chicago, IL, 60602, USA, (312) 922-1115, (312) 922-1157, info-usa@euromonitor.com, https://www.euromonitor.com/; Geographies.

United Nations Economic Commission for Africa (UNECA), PO Box 3001, Addis Ababa, ETH, ecainfo@uneca.org, https://www.uneca.org/; African Statistical Yearbook 2020.

The World Bank, 1818 H St. NW, Washington, DC, 20433, USA, (202) 473-1000, (202) 477-6391, eds03@worldbank.org, https://www.worldbank.org/; Cabo Verde (report).

CAPE VERDE-TRADE

See CAPE VERDE-INTERNATIONAL TRADE

CAPE VERDE-TRANSPORTATION

Central Intelligence Agency (CIA), Office of Public Affairs, Washington, DC, 20505, USA, (703) 482-0623, https://www.cia.gov; The World Factbook.

Euromonitor International, Inc., 1 N Dearborn St., Ste. 1700, Chicago, IL, 60602, USA, (312) 922-1115, (312) 922-1157, info-usa@euromonitor.com, https://www.euromonitor.com/; Geographies.

Palgrave Macmillan, 1 New York Plaza, Ste. 4500, New York, NY, 10004-1562, USA, (800) 777-4643, orders@palgrave.com, https://www.palgrave.com/us; The Statesman's Yearbook, 2023.

Routledge - Taylor & Francis Group, 6000 Broken Sound Pkwy. NW, Ste. 300, Boca Raton, FL, 33487, USA, (800) 634-1420, (800) 634-7064, orders@taylorandfrancis.com, https://www.routledge.com/; The Europa World Year Book 2022.

United Nations Economic Commission for Africa (UNECA), PO Box 3001, Addis Ababa, ETH, ecainfo@uneca.org, https://www.uneca.org/; African Statistical Yearbook 2020.

The World Bank, 1818 H St. NW, Washington, DC, 20433, USA, (202) 473-1000, (202) 477-6391, eds03@worldbank.org, https://www.worldbank.org/; Cabo Verde (report).

CAPE VERDE-UNEMPLOYMENT

International Labour Organization (ILO), 4 Rte. des Morillons, Geneva, CH-1211, SWI, ilo@ilo.org, https://www.ilo.org; NORMLEX Information System on International Labour Standards.

CAPE VERDE-VITAL STATISTICS

Palgrave Macmillan, 1 New York Plaza, Ste. 4500, New York, NY, 10004-1562, USA, (800) 777-4643, orders@palgrave.com, https://www.palgrave.com/us; The Statesman's Yearbook, 2023.

U.S. Census Bureau, 4600 Silver Hill Rd., Washington, DC, 20233, USA, (301) 763-4636, (800) 923-8282, https://www.census.gov; HIV/AIDS Surveillance Data Base.

United Nations Department of Economic and Social Affairs (DESA), Population Division, 2 United Nations Plz., Rm. DC2-1950, New York, NY, 10017, USA, (212) 963-3209, (212) 963-2147, population@un.org, https://www.un.org/development/desa/pd/; World Contraceptive Use 2021: Estimates and Projections of Family Planning Indicators and World Marriage Data 2019.

United Nations Statistics Division (UNSD), United Nations Plz., New York, NY, 10017, USA, (800) 253-9646, (212) 963-9851, statistics@un.org, https://unstats.un.org; Statistical Yearbook of the United Nations 2021.

CAPE VERDE-WAGES

International Labour Organization (ILO), 4 Rte. des Morillons, Geneva, CH-1211, SWI, ilo@ilo.org, https://www.ilo.org; NORMLEX Information System on International Labour Standards.

The World Bank, 1818 H St. NW, Washington, DC, 20433, USA, (202) 473-1000, (202) 477-6391, eds03@worldbank.org, https://www.worldbank.org/; Cabo Verde (report).

CAPITAL

See also Individual industries

International Monetary Fund (IMF), 700 19th St. NW, Washington, DC, 20431, USA, (202) 623-7000, (202) 623-4661, publications@imf.org, https://www.imf.org; Fiscal Monitor and Global Financial Stability Report.

Organization for Economic Cooperation and Development (OECD), 2001 L St. NW, Ste. 650, Washington, DC, 20036-4922, USA, (202) 785-6323, (800) 456-6323, (202) 785-0350, washington.contact@oecd.org, https://www.oecd.org/; The

Future of Corporate Governance in Capital Markets Following the COVID-19 Crisis.

Refinitiv, 22 Thomson Pl., Boston, MA, 02210, USA, (857) 365-1200, https://www.refinitiv.com; International Financing Review (IFR).

Thomson Reuters, 3 Times Square, New York, NY, 10036, USA, (646) 540-3000, general.info@thomsonreuters.com, https://thomsonreuters.com/; Reuters News Agency.

CAPITAL-BANKS AND BANKING

Federal Deposit Insurance Corporation (FDIC), 550 17th St. NW, Washington, DC, 20429-9990, USA, (877) 275-3342, (800) 925-4618 (TTY), publicinfo@fdic.gov, https://www.fdic.gov; FDIC State Profiles and Quarterly Banking Profile (QBP).

Securities Industry and Financial Markets Association (SIFMA), 140 Broadway, 35th Fl., New York, NY, 10005, USA, (212) 313-1200, (212) 313-1000, research@sifma.org, https://www.sifma.org/; Capital Markets in the U.S. Database.

CAPITAL-EXPENDITURES

U.S. Census Bureau, 4600 Silver Hill Rd., Washington, DC, 20233, USA, (301) 763-4636, (800) 923-8282, https://www.census.gov; Annual Capital Expenditures Survey (ACES) 2020.

CAPITAL-NEW SECURITY ISSUES

Board of Governors of the Federal Reserve System, Constitution Ave. NW, Washington, DC, 20551, USA, (202) 452-3000, (202) 263-4869 (TDD), https://www.federalreserve.gov; Federal Reserve Bulletin.

CAPITAL-STOCKS-COMMODITY MARKET PRICE INDEXES

U.S. Department of Commerce (DOC), Bureau of Economic Analysis (BEA), 4600 Silver Hill Rd., Washington, DC, 20233, USA, (301) 278-9004, customerservice@bea.gov, https://www.bea.gov; Survey of Current Business (SCB).

CAPITAL-UTILITIES

American Gas Association (AGA), 400 N Capitol St. NW, Ste. 450, Washington, DC, 20001, USA, (202) 824-7000, https://www.aga.org; Natural Gas Market Indicators.

Edison Electric Institute (EEI), 701 Pennsylvania Ave. NW, Washington, DC, 20004-2696, USA, (202) 508-5000, eeiorders@eei.org, https://www.eei.org; Electric Perspectives.

U.S. Energy Information Administration (EIA), 1000 Independence Ave. SW, Washington, DC, 20585, USA, (202) 586-8800, infoctr@eia.gov, https://www.eia.gov; Electric Power Annual 2021.

CAPITAL EQUIPMENT-PRODUCER PRICE INDEXES

U.S. Department of Labor (DOL), Bureau of Labor Statistics (BLS), Postal Square Bldg., 2 Massachusetts Ave. NE, Washington, DC, 20212-0001, USA, (202) 691-5200, (202) 691-7890, blsdata_staff@bls.gov, https://www.bls.gov; Producer Price Indexes (PPI).

CAPITAL PUNISHMENT

Capital Punishment UK, GBR, cpuk3200@gmail.com, https://www.capitalpunishmentuk.org/; Capital Punishment UK.

Death Penalty Information Center (DPIC), 1701 K St. NW, Ste. 205, Washington, DC, 20006, USA, (202) 289-2275, dpic@deathpenaltyinfo.org, https://deathpenaltyinfo.org/; The Death Penalty in 2022: Year End Report; DPIC Analysis: At Least 1,300 Prisoners Are on U.S. Death Rows in Violation of U.S. Human Rights Obligations; DPIC Mid-Year Review: Pandemic and Continuing Historic Decline Produce Record-Low Death Penalty Use in First Half of 2020; Execution Database; and Study: Dehumanizing Belief Systems Linked to Support for Guns Rights, the Death Penalty, and Anti-Immigration Practices.

The Gallup Organization, 901 F St. NW, Washington, DC, 20004, USA, (202) 715-3030, (800) 204-1192, (202) 715-3045, https://www.gallup.com; Record-Low 54% in U.S. Say Death Penalty Morally Acceptable.

University of Michigan Institute for Social Research, Inter-University Consortium for Political and Social Science Research (ICPSR), National Archive of Criminal Justice Data (NACJD), PO Box 1248, Ann Arbor, MI, 48106-1248, USA, (734) 615-8400, nacjd@icpsr.umich.edu, https://www.icpsr.umich.edu/web/pages/NACJD/; Capital Punishment in the United States, 1973-2020.

CAPITOL RIOT, WASHINGTON, D.C., 2021

Institute for Strategic Dialogue (ISD), PO Box 75769, London, SW1P 9ER, GBR, info@isdglobal.org, https://www.isdglobal.org/; Inspiration and Influence: Discussions of the US Military in Extreme Right-Wing Telegram Channels.

OpenSecrets, 1300 L St. NW , Ste. 200, Washington, DC, 20005, USA, (202) 857-0044, (202) 857-7809, info@crp.org, https://www.opensecrets.org/; GOP Candidates Who Participated in the Jan. 6 Rally Are Raising Millions.

University of Maryland, National Consortium for the Study of Terrorism and Responses to Terrorism (START), PO Box 266, 5245 Greenbelt Rd., College Park, MD, 20740, USA, (301) 405-6600, (301) 314-1980, infostart@start.umd.edu, https://www.start.umd.edu; Proud Boys Crimes and Characteristics; QAnon Offenders in the United States; and Radicalization in the Ranks.

CARBON DIOXIDE EMISSIONS

Bipartisan Policy Center (BPC), 1225 Eye St. NW, Ste. 1000, Washington, DC, 20005, USA, (202) 204-2400, bipartisaninfo@bipartisanpolicy.org, https://bipartisanpolicy.org/; Carbon Removal: Comparing Historical Federal Research Investments with the National Academies' Recommended Future Funding Levels.

Carbon Brief, 180 Borough High St., London, SE1 1LB, GBR, info@carbonbrief.org, https://www.carbonbrief.org/; Global Planted Forests 1990-2015.

Carbon Tracker Initiative (CTI), 40 Bermondsey St., 2nd Fl., London, SE1 3UD, GBR, hello@carbontracker.org, https://www.carbontracker.org/; Closing the Gap to a Paris-Compliant EU-ETS.

Climate Analytics, 135 Madison Ave., 5th Fl., Ste. 05-115, New York, NY, 10016, USA, info.ny@climateanalytics.org, https://climateanalytics.org/; Climate Action Tracker (CAT).

Climate Change Committee (CCC), 151 Buckingham Palace Rd., London, SW1W 9SZ, GBR, https://www.theccc.org.uk/; Independent Assessment of UK Climate Risk and 2021 Progress Report to Parliament.

Environmental Defense Fund (EDF), 1875 Connecticut Ave. NW, Ste. 600, Washington, DC, 20009, USA, (202) 572-3298, (202) 387-3500, (202) 234-6049, https://www.edf.org; Solutions Newsletter.

European Centre for Medium-Range Weather Forecasts (ECMWF), Copernicus Climate Change Service (C3S), Shinfield Park, Reading, RG2 9AX, GBR, copernicus-support@ecmwf.int, https://climate.copernicus.eu/; Last Four Years Have Been the Warmest on Record - and CO2 Continues to Rise.

European Commission, Joint Research Centre, EU Science Hub, Brussels, B-1049, BEL, ies-contact@jrc.ec.europa.eu, https://ec.europa.eu/jrc/en; Emissions Database for Global Atmospheric Research (EDGAR).

The Global Carbon Project (GCP), c/o CSIRO Oceans and Atmosphere, GPO Box 1700, Canberra, ACT, 2601, AUS, info@globalcarbonproject.org, https://www.globalcarbonproject.org/; Global Carbon Atlas.

Harvard T.H. Chan School of Public Health, Center for Climate, Health, and the Global Environment (Harvard C-CHANGE), 401 Park Dr., 4th Fl. W, Ste. 415, Boston, MA, 02215, USA, (617) 384-8350, cchange@hsph.harvard.edu, https://www.hsph.harvard.edu/c-change/; Carbon Standards Re-Examined: An Analysis of Potential Emissions Outcomes for the Affordable Clean Energy Rule and the Clean Power Plan.

Intergovernmental Panel on Climate Change (IPCC), C/O World Meteorological Organization, 7 bis Avenue de la Paix, C.P. 2300, Geneva, CH-1211, SWI, ipcc-sec@wmo.int, https://www.ipcc.ch/; AR6 Synthesis Report: Climate Change 2023; Climate Change 2022: Mitigation of Climate Change; and Climate Change and Land.

International Energy Agency (IEA), 9 Rue de la Federation, Paris, 75739, FRA, info@iea.org, https://www.iea.org/; CO2 Emissions in 2022; Global Energy Review: CO2 Emissions in 2020; Government Energy Spending Tracker; Greenhouse Gas Emissions from Energy; and Net Zero by 2050: A Roadmap for the Global Energy Sector.

International Fund for Agricultural Development (IFAD), Via Paolo di Dono, 44, Rome, 00142, ITA, ifad@ifad.org, https://www.ifad.org/; Climate Change and Food System Activities - A Review of Emission Trends, Climate Impacts and the Effects of Dietary Change.

NewClimate Institute, Waidmarkt 11a, Cologne, D-50676, GER, info@newclimate.org, https://newclimate.org/; Exploring the Impact of the COVID-19 Pandemic on Global Emission Projections and Net Zero Stocktake 2022.

Oko-Institut e.V. (Institute for Applied Ecology), PO Box 17 71, Freiburg, D-79017, GER, info@oeko.de, https://www.oeko.de; E-Fuels Versus DACCS.

Oxford University Centre for the Environment, Centre for Research into Energy Demand Solutions (CREDS), South Parks Rd., Oxford, OX1 3QY, GBR, credsadmin@ouce.ox.ac.uk, https://www.creds.ac.uk; E-bike Carbon Savings - How Much and Where?.

S&P Global Commodity Insights, One World Trade Center, New York, NY, 10007, USA, (800) 752-8878, support@platts.com, https://www.spglobal.com/commodityinsights/en; Platts European Power Daily.

U.S. Energy Information Administration (EIA), 1000 Independence Ave. SW, Washington, DC, 20585, USA, (202) 586-8800, infoctr@eia.gov, https://www.eia.gov; International Energy Outlook 2021.

U.S. Global Change Research Program (USGCRP), 1800 G St. NW, Ste. 9100, Washington, DC, 20006, USA, (202) 223-6262, (202) 223-3065, https://www.globalchange.gov/; National Climate Assessment.

United Nations Environment Programme (UNEP) Copenhagen Climate Centre, Marmorvej 51, Copenhagen, DK-2100, DEN, unep@dtu.dk, https://unepdtu.org/; Emissions Gap Report 2021 and Reducing Consumer Food Waste Using Green and Digital Technologies.

United Nations Environment Programme (UNEP), 900 17th St. NW, Ste. 506, Washington, DC, 20006, USA, (202) 974-1300, publications@unep.org, https://www.unep.org/; Emissions Gap Report 2022 and UN Environment Open Data.

World Wildlife Fund (WWF), 1250 24th St. NW, Washington, DC, 20037-1193, USA, (202) 495-4800, (202) 495-4211, https://wwf.panda.org/; Living Planet Report 2022.

CARCINOGENS

Silent Spring Institute, 320 Nevada St., Ste. 302, Newton, MA, 02460, USA, (617) 332-4288, (617) 332-4284, info@silentspring.org, https://silentspring.org/; Identifying Toxic Consumer Products: A Novel Data Set Reveals Air Emissions of Potent Carcinogens, Reproductive Toxicants, and Developmental Toxicants.

U.S. Department of Health and Human Services (HHS), National Toxicology Program (NTP), PO Box 12233, MD K2-03, Research Triangle Park, NC, 27709, USA, (984) 287-3209, cdm@niehs.nih.gov, https://ntp.niehs.nih.gov; Chemical Effects in Biological Systems (CEBS).

CARDIAC ARREST

Cardiac Arrest Registry to Enhance Survival (CARES), 1599 Clifton Rd. NE, Woodruff Health Sciences Center, Mailstop 1599/001/1BQ, Atlanta, GA, 30322, USA, cares@emory.edu, https://mycares.net; Race/Ethnicity and Neighborhood Characteristics Are Associated With Bystander Cardiopulmonary Resuscitation in Pediatric Out-of-Hospital Cardiac Arrest in the United States.

CARDIOLOGY

American Medical Association (AMA), AMA Plaza, 330 N Wabash Ave., Ste. 39300, Chicago, IL, 60611-5885, USA, (312) 464-4782, amacatalog@ama-assn.org, https://www.ama-assn.org; JAMA Cardiology.

Cardiac Arrest Registry to Enhance Survival (CARES), 1599 Clifton Rd. NE, Woodruff Health Sciences Center, Mailstop 1599/001/1BQ, Atlanta, GA, 30322, USA, cares@emory.edu, https://mycares.net; Race/Ethnicity and Neighborhood Characteristics Are Associated With Bystander Cardiopulmonary Resuscitation in Pediatric Out-of-Hospital Cardiac Arrest in the United States.

CARDIOVASCULAR DISEASE

See HEART-DISEASES

CAREGIVERS

Alzheimer's Foundation of America (AFA), 322 8th Ave., 16th Fl., New York, NY, 10001, USA, (866) 232-8484, (646) 638-1542, (646) 638-1546, info@alzfdn.org, https://alzfdn.org; unpublished data.

Family Caregiver Alliance (FCA), 235 Montgomery St., Ste. 930, San Francisco, CA, 94104, USA, (415) 434-3388, (800) 445-8106, https://www.caregiver.org/; unpublished data.

National Alliance for Caregiving (NAC), 1730 Rhode Island Ave. NW, Ste. 812, Washington, DC, 20036, USA, (202) 918-1013, (202) 918-1014, info@caregiving.org, https://www.caregiving.org/; Caregiving in the U.S. 2020.

National Association for Regulatory Administration (NARA), 400 S 4th St., Ste. 754E, Minneapolis, MN, 55415, USA, (888) 674-7052, admin@naralicensing.org, https://www.naralicensing.org/; Key Indicators.

Southern Poverty Law Center (SPLC), 400 Washington Ave., Montgomery, AL, 36104, USA, (334) 956-8200, (888) 414-7752, https://www.splcenter.org/; Cut Off From Caregivers: The Children of Incarcerated Parents in Louisiana.

World Health Organization (WHO), Ave. Appia 20, Geneva, CH-1211, SWI, (202) 974-3000 (Telephone in U.S.), publications@who.int, https://www.who.int/; Whose Life Matters? Challenges, Barriers and Impact of COVID-19 Pandemic on Persons with Disability and Their Caregivers.

CARIBBEAN AREA

Caribbean Public Health Agency (CARPHA), Federation Park, 16-18 Jamaica Blvd., Port of Spain, TTO, (868) 622-4261 (Dial from U.S.), (868) 299-0820 (Dial from U.S.), postmaster@carpha.org, https://carpha.org/; unpublished data.

Centro del Agua del Tropico Humedo para America Latina y el Caribe (CATHALAC) (Water Center for the Humid Tropics of Latin America and the Caribbean), Ciudad del Saber , Edificio 111, Panama, 0843-03102, PAN, (507) 317-3200, cathalac@cathalac.int, https://cathalac.int/; unpublished data.

United Nations Economic and Social Council (ECOSOC), United Nations Plz., New York, NY, 10017, USA, (917) 367-5027, (212) 963-1259, ecosocinfo@un.org, https://www.un.org/ecosoc; Summary of the Work of the Economic Commission for Latin America and the Caribbean, 2021-2022.

United Nations Economic Commission for Latin America and the Caribbean (ECLAC), Casilla 179-D, Santiago, 7630412, CHL, (202) 596-3713, prensa@cepal.org, https://www.cepal.org/en; CEPALSTAT; Economic Survey of Latin America and the Caribbean 2019. The New Global Financial Context: Effects and Transmission Mechanisms in the Region; Economic Survey of Latin America and the Caribbean 2020: Main Conditioning Factors of Fiscal and Monetary Policies in the Post-COVID-19 Era; Economic Survey of Latin America and the Caribbean 2022: Trends and Challenges of Investing for a Sustainable and Inclusive Recovery; Latin American Economic Outlook 2022: Towards a Green and Just Transition; and Statistical Yearbook for Latin America and the Caribbean 2021.

The World Bank, 1818 H St. NW, Washington, DC, 20433, USA, (202) 473-1000, (202) 477-6391, eds03@worldbank.org, https://www.worldbank.org/; Caribbean (report).

World Health Organization (WHO), Pan American Health Organization (PAHO), 525 23rd St. NW, Washington, DC, 20037, USA, (202) 974-3000, (202) 974-3663, pubrights@paho.org, https://www.paho.org; A New Agenda for Mental Health in the Americas: Report of the Pan American Health Organization High-Level Commission on Mental Health and COVID-19; Core Indicators 2022; Country Profiles; Health in the Americas+; Pan American Journal of Public Health (PAJPH); Polio Weekly Bulletin; Report on Tobacco Control for the Region of the Americas 2022; and WHO Reveals Leading Causes of Death and Disability Worldwide: 2000-2019.

CARIBBEAN AREA-ECONOMIC CONDITIONS

Inter-American Development Bank (IDB), 1300 New York Ave. NW, Washington, DC, 20577, USA, (202) 623-1000, (202) 623-3096, https://www.iadb.org/en; Latin Macro Watch (LMW).

United Nations Economic and Social Council (ECOSOC), United Nations Plz., New York, NY, 10017, USA, (917) 367-5027, (212) 963-1259, ecosocinfo@un.org, https://www.un.org/ecosoc; Summary of the Work of the Economic Commission for Latin America and the Caribbean, 2021-2022.

United Nations Economic Commission for Latin America and the Caribbean (ECLAC), Casilla 179-D, Santiago, 7630412, CHL, (202) 596-3713, prensa@cepal.org, https://www.cepal.org/en; Economic Survey of Latin America and the Caribbean 2019. The New Global Financial Context: Effects and Transmission Mechanisms in the Region; Economic Survey of Latin America and the Caribbean 2020: Main Conditioning Factors of Fiscal and Monetary Policies in the Post-COVID-19 Era; Economic Survey of Latin America and the Caribbean 2021: Labour Dynamics and Employment Policies for Sustainable and Inclusive Recovery Beyond the COVID-19 Crisis; Economic Survey of Latin America and the Caribbean 2022: Trends and Challenges of Investing for a Sustainable and Inclusive Recovery; Foreign Direct Investment in Latin America and the Caribbean 2022; Latin American Economic Outlook 2022: Towards a Green and Just Transition; and Statistical Yearbook for Latin America and the Caribbean 2021.

CARIBBEAN AREA-SOCIAL CONDITIONS

UNICEF, 3 United Nations Plz., New York, NY, 10017, USA, (212) 303-7984, (917) 244-2215, https://www.unicef.org; A Statistical Profile of Violence Against Children in Latin America and the Caribbean.

CARJACKING

See CRIME-CARJACKING

CARROTS

U.S. Department of Agriculture (USDA), Economic Research Service (ERS), 1400 Independence Ave. SW, Mail Stop 1800, Washington, DC, 20250-0002, USA, (202) 720-2791, https://www.ers.usda.gov/; Food Price Outlook.

U.S. Department of Agriculture (USDA), National Agricultural Statistics Service (USDA-NASS), 1400 Independence Ave. SW, Washington, DC, 20250, USA, (800) 727-9540, nass@nass.usda.gov, https://www.nass.usda.gov; Quick Stats and Vegetables Annual Summary.

CARS

See AUTOMOBILES

CASUALTIES-MILITARY CONFLICT

Bulletin of the Atomic Scientists, PO Box 15461, Chicago, IL, 60615-5146, USA, (773) 834-3779, admin@thebulletin.org, https://thebulletin.org/; What Do Americans Really Think About Conflict with Nuclear North Korea? The Answer Is Both Reassuring and Disturbing.

CASUALTY INSURANCE

Insurance Information Institute (III), 110 William St., New York, NY, 10038, USA, (212) 346-5500, info@iii.org, https://www.iii.org/; Insurance Fact Book 2021.

CATALOG AND MAIL SALES

U.S. Census Bureau, Center for Economic Studies (CES), 4600 Silver Hill Rd., Washington, DC, 20233, USA, (301) 763-6460, (301) 763-5935, ces.contacts@census.gov, https://www.census.gov/programs-surveys/ces.html; Retail Trade, 2017 Economic Census and Wholesale Trade, 2017 Economic Census.

U.S. Department of Commerce (DOC), International Trade Administration (ITA), 1401 Constitution Ave. NW, Washington, DC, 20230, USA, (800) 872-8723, https://www.trade.gov/; TradeStats Express (TSE).

CATFISH

U.S. Department of Agriculture (USDA), National Agricultural Statistics Service (USDA-NASS), 1400 Independence Ave. SW, Washington, DC, 20250, USA, (800) 727-9540, nass@nass.usda.gov, https://www.nass.usda.gov; Catfish Processing; Catfish Production; and Quick Stats.

CATHOLIC POPULATION

See RELIGION

CATTLE-FARM MARKETINGS, SALES

U.S. Department of Agriculture (USDA), Economic Research Service (ERS), 1400 Independence Ave. SW, Mail Stop 1800, Washington, DC, 20250-0002, USA, (202) 720-2791, https://www.ers.usda.gov/; Agricultural Resource Management Survey (ARMS) Tailored Reports.

CATTLE-IMPORTS

U.S. Department of Agriculture (USDA), Economic Research Service (ERS), 1400 Independence Ave. SW, Mail Stop 1800, Washington, DC, 20250-0002, USA, (202) 720-2791, https://www.ers.usda.gov/; Foreign Agricultural Trade of the United States (FATUS) and Outlook for U.S. Agricultural Trade: May 2022.

CATTLE-NUMBER ON FARMS

U.S. Department of Agriculture (USDA), National Agricultural Statistics Service (USDA-NASS), 1400 Independence Ave. SW, Washington, DC, 20250, USA, (800) 727-9540, nass@nass.usda.gov, https://www.nass.usda.gov; Agricultural Statistics; Cattle; Cattle on Feed; Meat Animals Production, Disposition, and Income Annual Summary; and Milk Production.

CATTLE-ORGANIC

U.S. Department of Agriculture (USDA), Economic Research Service (ERS), 1400 Independence Ave. SW, Mail Stop 1800, Washington, DC, 20250-0002, USA, (202) 720-2791, https://www.ers.usda.gov/; Organic Market Summary and Trends.

CATTLE-PRICES

U.S. Department of Agriculture (USDA), National Agricultural Statistics Service (USDA-NASS), 1400

Independence Ave. SW, Washington, DC, 20250, USA, (800) 727-9540, nass@nass.usda.gov, https://www.nass.usda.gov; Cattle and Meat Animals Production, Disposition, and Income Annual Summary.

CATTLE-PRODUCTION

U.S. Department of Agriculture (USDA), National Agricultural Statistics Service (USDA-NASS), 1400 Independence Ave. SW, Washington, DC, 20250, USA, (800) 727-9540, nass@nass.usda.gov, https://www.nass.usda.gov; Agricultural Statistics; Cattle on Feed; Dairy Products; Meat Animals Production, Disposition, and Income Annual Summary; Milk Production; and Quick Stats.

CATTLE-SLAUGHTER

U.S. Department of Agriculture (USDA), National Agricultural Statistics Service (USDA-NASS), 1400 Independence Ave. SW, Washington, DC, 20250, USA, (800) 727-9540, nass@nass.usda.gov, https://www.nass.usda.gov; Livestock Slaughter and Meat Animals Production, Disposition, and Income Annual Summary.

CATTLE-VALUE ON FARMS

U.S. Department of Agriculture (USDA), National Agricultural Statistics Service (USDA-NASS), 1400 Independence Ave. SW, Washington, DC, 20250, USA, (800) 727-9540, nass@nass.usda.gov, https://www.nass.usda.gov; Meat Animals Production, Disposition, and Income Annual Summary.

CAULIFLOWER

U.S. Department of Agriculture (USDA), Economic Research Service (ERS), 1400 Independence Ave. SW, Mail Stop 1800, Washington, DC, 20250-0002, USA, (202) 720-2791, https://www.ers.usda.gov/; Food Price Outlook.

U.S. Department of Agriculture (USDA), National Agricultural Statistics Service (USDA-NASS), 1400 Independence Ave. SW, Washington, DC, 20250, USA, (800) 727-9540, nass@nass.usda.gov, https://www.nass.usda.gov; Quick Stats and Vegetables Annual Summary.

CAYMAN ISLANDS-NATIONAL STATISTICAL OFFICE

Economics and Statistics Office of the Cayman Islands, Government Administration Bldg., PO Box 127, George Town, Grand Cayman, KY1-9000, CYM, (345) 949-0940 (Dial from U.S.), (345) 949-8782 (Fax from U.S.), infostats@gov.ky, https://www.eso.ky/; National Data Reports (Cayman Islands).

CAYMAN ISLANDS-PRIMARY STATISTICS SOURCES

Economics and Statistics Office of the Cayman Islands, Government Administration Bldg., PO Box 127, George Town, Grand Cayman, KY1-9000, CYM, (345) 949-0940 (Dial from U.S.), (345) 949-8782 (Fax from U.S.), infostats@gov.ky, https://www.eso.ky/; Annual National Accounts Report 2020 and 2020 Compendium of Statistics.

CAYMAN ISLANDS-AGRICULTURE

The Economist Group: Economist Intelligence Unit (EIU), 900 3rd Ave., 16th Fl., New York, NY, 10022, USA, (212) 541-0500, americas@eiu.com, https://www.eiu.com; Cayman Islands Country Report.

Euromonitor International, Inc., 1 N Dearborn St., Ste. 1700, Chicago, IL, 60602, USA, (312) 922-1115, (312) 922-1157, info-usa@euromonitor.com, https://www.euromonitor.com/; Geographies.

Routledge - Taylor & Francis Group, 6000 Broken Sound Pkwy. NW, Ste. 300, Boca Raton, FL, 33487, USA, (800) 634-1420, (800) 634-7064, orders@taylorandfrancis.com, https://www.routledge.com/; The Europa World Year Book 2022.

United Nations Food and Agricultural Organization (FAO), 2121 K St., Ste. 800B, Washington, DC, 20037, USA, (202) 653-2400 (Dial from U.S.), (202) 653-5760 (Fax from U.S.), fao-hq@fao.org, https://www.fao.org; AQUASTAT and The State of Food and Agriculture (SOFA) 2022.

CAYMAN ISLANDS-AIRLINES

Palgrave Macmillan, 1 New York Plaza, Ste. 4500, New York, NY, 10004-1562, USA, (800) 777-4643, orders@palgrave.com, https://www.palgrave.com/us; The Statesman's Yearbook, 2023.

CAYMAN ISLANDS-ARMED FORCES

Central Intelligence Agency (CIA), Office of Public Affairs, Washington, DC, 20505, USA, (703) 482-0623, https://www.cia.gov; The World Factbook.

Stockholm International Peace Research Institute (SIPRI), Signalistgatan 9, Stockholm, SE 169 72, SWE, https://www.sipri.org/; SIPRI Arms Transfers Database and SIPRI Military Expenditure Database.

CAYMAN ISLANDS-BANKS AND BANKING

Euromonitor International, Inc., 1 N Dearborn St., Ste. 1700, Chicago, IL, 60602, USA, (312) 922-1115, (312) 922-1157, info-usa@euromonitor.com, https://www.euromonitor.com/; Geographies.

CAYMAN ISLANDS-BROADCASTING

Central Intelligence Agency (CIA), Office of Public Affairs, Washington, DC, 20505, USA, (703) 482-0623, https://www.cia.gov; The World Factbook.

Euromonitor International, Inc., 1 N Dearborn St., Ste. 1700, Chicago, IL, 60602, USA, (312) 922-1115, (312) 922-1157, info-usa@euromonitor.com, https://www.euromonitor.com/; Geographies.

Palgrave Macmillan, 1 New York Plaza, Ste. 4500, New York, NY, 10004-1562, USA, (800) 777-4643, orders@palgrave.com, https://www.palgrave.com/us; The Statesman's Yearbook, 2023.

UNESCO Institute for Statistics, C.P 250 Succursale H, Montreal, QC, H3G 2K8, CAN, (514) 343-6880 (Dial from U.S.), (514) 343-5740 (Fax from U.S.), uis.publications@unesco.org, http://uis.unesco.org/; UIS.Stat.

WRTH Publications Limited, PO Box 290, Oxford, OX2 7FT, GBR, sales@wrth.com, https://www.wrth.com; World Radio TV Handbook 2023.

CAYMAN ISLANDS-BUDGET

Central Intelligence Agency (CIA), Office of Public Affairs, Washington, DC, 20505, USA, (703) 482-0623, https://www.cia.gov; The World Factbook.

CAYMAN ISLANDS-CLIMATE

Palgrave Macmillan, 1 New York Plaza, Ste. 4500, New York, NY, 10004-1562, USA, (800) 777-4643, orders@palgrave.com, https://www.palgrave.com/us; The Statesman's Yearbook, 2023.

CAYMAN ISLANDS-COAL PRODUCTION

See CAYMAN ISLANDS-MINERAL INDUSTRIES

CAYMAN ISLANDS-COMMERCE

Palgrave Macmillan, 1 New York Plaza, Ste. 4500, New York, NY, 10004-1562, USA, (800) 777-4643, orders@palgrave.com, https://www.palgrave.com/us; The Statesman's Yearbook, 2023.

UK Data Service, University of Essex, Wivenhoe Park, Colchester, Essex, CO4 3SQ, GBR, https://ukdataservice.ac.uk/; International Aggregate Data.

CAYMAN ISLANDS-CONSUMER PRICE INDEXES

Routledge - Taylor & Francis Group, 6000 Broken Sound Pkwy. NW, Ste. 300, Boca Raton, FL, 33487, USA, (800) 634-1420, (800) 634-7064, orders@taylorandfrancis.com, https://www.routledge.com/; The Europa World Year Book 2022.

CAYMAN ISLANDS-CORN INDUSTRY

See CAYMAN ISLANDS-CROPS

CAYMAN ISLANDS-CROPS

United Nations Food and Agricultural Organization (FAO), 2121 K St., Ste. 800B, Washington, DC, 20037, USA, (202) 653-2400 (Dial from U.S.), (202) 653-5760 (Fax from U.S.), fao-hq@fao.org, https://www.fao.org; The State of Food and Agriculture (SOFA) 2022.

CAYMAN ISLANDS-DAIRY PROCESSING

United Nations Food and Agricultural Organization (FAO), 2121 K St., Ste. 800B, Washington, DC, 20037, USA, (202) 653-2400 (Dial from U.S.), (202) 653-5760 (Fax from U.S.), fao-hq@fao.org, https://www.fao.org; The State of Food and Agriculture (SOFA) 2022.

CAYMAN ISLANDS-ECONOMIC CONDITIONS

Bernan Press, 15250 NBN Way, Bldg. C, Blue Ridge Summit, PA, 17214, USA, (301) 459-2255, (800) 865-3457, (800) 865-3450, customercare@bernan.com, https://rowman.com/Page/Bernan; World Economic Outlook, April 2022.

Central Intelligence Agency (CIA), Office of Public Affairs, Washington, DC, 20505, USA, (703) 482-0623, https://www.cia.gov; The World Factbook.

The Economist Group: Economist Intelligence Unit (EIU), 900 3rd Ave., 16th Fl., New York, NY, 10022, USA, (212) 541-0500, americas@eiu.com, https://www.eiu.com; Cayman Islands Country Report.

Euromonitor International, Inc., 1 N Dearborn St., Ste. 1700, Chicago, IL, 60602, USA, (312) 922-1115, (312) 922-1157, info-usa@euromonitor.com, https://www.euromonitor.com/; Geographies.

Palgrave Macmillan, 1 New York Plaza, Ste. 4500, New York, NY, 10004-1562, USA, (800) 777-4643, orders@palgrave.com, https://www.palgrave.com/us; The Statesman's Yearbook, 2023.

United Nations Economic Commission for Latin America and the Caribbean (ECLAC), Casilla 179-D, Santiago, 7630412, CHL, (202) 596-3713, prensa@cepal.org, https://www.cepal.org/en; CEPALSTAT.

CAYMAN ISLANDS-EDUCATION

Euromonitor International, Inc., 1 N Dearborn St., Ste. 1700, Chicago, IL, 60602, USA, (312) 922-1115, (312) 922-1157, info-usa@euromonitor.com, https://www.euromonitor.com/; Geographies.

Palgrave Macmillan, 1 New York Plaza, Ste. 4500, New York, NY, 10004-1562, USA, (800) 777-4643, orders@palgrave.com, https://www.palgrave.com/us; The Statesman's Yearbook, 2023.

Routledge - Taylor & Francis Group, 6000 Broken Sound Pkwy. NW, Ste. 300, Boca Raton, FL, 33487, USA, (800) 634-1420, (800) 634-7064, orders@taylorandfrancis.com, https://www.routledge.com/; The Europa World Year Book 2022.

UNESCO Institute for Statistics, C.P 250 Succursale H, Montreal, QC, H3G 2K8, CAN, (514) 343-6880 (Dial from U.S.), (514) 343-5740 (Fax from U.S.), uis.publications@unesco.org, http://uis.unesco.org/; UIS.Stat.

CAYMAN ISLANDS-ELECTRICITY

United Nations Statistics Division (UNSD), United Nations Plz., New York, NY, 10017, USA, (800) 253-9646, (212) 963-9851, statistics@un.org, https://unstats.un.org; Statistical Yearbook of the United Nations 2021.

CAYMAN ISLANDS-EMPLOYMENT

UK Data Service, University of Essex, Wivenhoe Park, Colchester, Essex, CO4 3SQ, GBR, https://ukdataservice.ac.uk/; International Aggregate Data.

CAYMAN ISLANDS-ENVIRONMENTAL CONDITIONS

The Economist Group: Economist Intelligence Unit (EIU), 900 3rd Ave., 16th Fl., New York, NY, 10022, USA, (212) 541-0500, americas@eiu.com, https://www.eiu.com; Cayman Islands Country Report.

United Nations Economic Commission for Latin America and the Caribbean (ECLAC), Casilla 179-D, Santiago, 7630412, CHL, (202) 596-3713, prensa@cepal.org, https://www.cepal.org/en; CEPALSTAT.

CAYMAN ISLANDS-EXPORTS

Central Intelligence Agency (CIA), Office of Public Affairs, Washington, DC, 20505, USA, (703) 482-0623, https://www.cia.gov; The World Factbook.

The Economist Group: Economist Intelligence Unit (EIU), 900 3rd Ave., 16th Fl., New York, NY, 10022, USA, (212) 541-0500, americas@eiu.com, https://www.eiu.com; Cayman Islands Country Report.

CAYMAN ISLANDS-FERTILITY, HUMAN

Central Intelligence Agency (CIA), Office of Public Affairs, Washington, DC, 20505, USA, (703) 482-0623, https://www.cia.gov; The World Factbook.

CAYMAN ISLANDS-FERTILIZER INDUSTRY

United Nations Food and Agricultural Organization (FAO), 2121 K St., Ste. 800B, Washington, DC, 20037, USA, (202) 653-2400 (Dial from U.S.), (202) 653-5760 (Fax from U.S.), fao-hq@fao.org, https://www.fao.org; The State of Food and Agriculture (SOFA) 2022.

CAYMAN ISLANDS-FETAL MORTALITY

See CAYMAN ISLANDS-MORTALITY

CAYMAN ISLANDS-FINANCE, PUBLIC

The Economist Group: Economist Intelligence Unit (EIU), 900 3rd Ave., 16th Fl., New York, NY, 10022, USA, (212) 541-0500, americas@eiu.com, https://www.eiu.com; Cayman Islands Country Report.

Palgrave Macmillan, 1 New York Plaza, Ste. 4500, New York, NY, 10004-1562, USA, (800) 777-4643, orders@palgrave.com, https://www.palgrave.com/us; The Statesman's Yearbook, 2023.

Routledge - Taylor & Francis Group, 6000 Broken Sound Pkwy. NW, Ste. 300, Boca Raton, FL, 33487, USA, (800) 634-1420, (800) 634-7064, orders@taylorandfrancis.com, https://www.routledge.com/; The Europa World Year Book 2022.

United Nations Statistics Division (UNSD), United Nations Plz., New York, NY, 10017, USA, (800) 253-9646, (212) 963-9851, statistics@un.org, https://unstats.un.org; National Accounts Main Aggregates Database and National Accounts Statistics: Main Aggregates and Detailed Tables.

CAYMAN ISLANDS-FISHERIES

Routledge - Taylor & Francis Group, 6000 Broken Sound Pkwy. NW, Ste. 300, Boca Raton, FL, 33487, USA, (800) 634-1420, (800) 634-7064, orders@taylorandfrancis.com, https://www.routledge.com/; The Europa World Year Book 2022.

United Nations Food and Agricultural Organization (FAO), 2121 K St., Ste. 800B, Washington, DC, 20037, USA, (202) 653-2400 (Dial from U.S.), (202) 653-5760 (Fax from U.S.), fao-hq@fao.org, https://www.fao.org; FAO Yearbook of Fishery and Aquaculture Statistics 2019; Fishery Statistical Collections Global Capture Production; FishStatJ; and The State of Food and Agriculture (SOFA) 2022.

CAYMAN ISLANDS-FOOD

United Nations Food and Agricultural Organization (FAO), 2121 K St., Ste. 800B, Washington, DC, 20037, USA, (202) 653-2400 (Dial from U.S.), (202) 653-5760 (Fax from U.S.), fao-hq@fao.org, https://www.fao.org; The State of Food and Agriculture (SOFA) 2022.

CAYMAN ISLANDS-FORESTS AND FORESTRY

United Nations Food and Agricultural Organization (FAO), 2121 K St., Ste. 800B, Washington, DC, 20037, USA, (202) 653-2400 (Dial from U.S.), (202) 653-5760 (Fax from U.S.), fao-hq@fao.org, https://www.fao.org; The State of Food and Agriculture (SOFA) 2022.

United Nations Statistics Division (UNSD), United Nations Plz., New York, NY, 10017, USA, (800) 253-9646, (212) 963-9851, statistics@un.org, https://unstats.un.org; Statistical Yearbook of the United Nations 2021.

CAYMAN ISLANDS-GROSS DOMESTIC PRODUCT

The Economist Group: Economist Intelligence Unit (EIU), 900 3rd Ave., 16th Fl., New York, NY, 10022, USA, (212) 541-0500, americas@eiu.com, https://www.eiu.com; Cayman Islands Country Report.

Routledge - Taylor & Francis Group, 6000 Broken Sound Pkwy. NW, Ste. 300, Boca Raton, FL, 33487, USA, (800) 634-1420, (800) 634-7064, orders@taylorandfrancis.com, https://www.routledge.com/; The Europa World Year Book 2022.

CAYMAN ISLANDS-GROSS NATIONAL PRODUCT

Palgrave Macmillan, 1 New York Plaza, Ste. 4500, New York, NY, 10004-1562, USA, (800) 777-4643, orders@palgrave.com, https://www.palgrave.com/us; The Statesman's Yearbook, 2023.

CAYMAN ISLANDS-HOUSING

Euromonitor International, Inc., 1 N Dearborn St., Ste. 1700, Chicago, IL, 60602, USA, (312) 922-1115, (312) 922-1157, info-usa@euromonitor.com, https://www.euromonitor.com/; Geographies.

CAYMAN ISLANDS-ILLITERATE PERSONS

UNESCO Institute for Statistics, C.P 250 Succursale H, Montreal, QC, H3G 2K8, CAN, (514) 343-6880 (Dial from U.S.), (514) 343-5740 (Fax from U.S.), uis.publications@unesco.org, http://uis.unesco.org/; UIS.Stat.

CAYMAN ISLANDS-IMPORTS

Central Intelligence Agency (CIA), Office of Public Affairs, Washington, DC, 20505, USA, (703) 482-0623, https://www.cia.gov; The World Factbook.

The Economist Group: Economist Intelligence Unit (EIU), 900 3rd Ave., 16th Fl., New York, NY, 10022, USA, (212) 541-0500, americas@eiu.com, https://www.eiu.com; Cayman Islands Country Report.

CAYMAN ISLANDS-INDUSTRIES

Central Intelligence Agency (CIA), Office of Public Affairs, Washington, DC, 20505, USA, (703) 482-0623, https://www.cia.gov; The World Factbook.

The Economist Group: Economist Intelligence Unit (EIU), 900 3rd Ave., 16th Fl., New York, NY, 10022, USA, (212) 541-0500, americas@eiu.com, https://www.eiu.com; Cayman Islands Country Report.

Euromonitor International, Inc., 1 N Dearborn St., Ste. 1700, Chicago, IL, 60602, USA, (312) 922-1115, (312) 922-1157, info-usa@euromonitor.com, https://www.euromonitor.com/; Geographies.

Palgrave Macmillan, 1 New York Plaza, Ste. 4500, New York, NY, 10004-1562, USA, (800) 777-4643, orders@palgrave.com, https://www.palgrave.com/us; The Statesman's Yearbook, 2023.

Routledge - Taylor & Francis Group, 6000 Broken Sound Pkwy. NW, Ste. 300, Boca Raton, FL, 33487, USA, (800) 634-1420, (800) 634-7064, orders@taylorandfrancis.com, https://www.routledge.com/; The Europa World Year Book 2022.

CAYMAN ISLANDS-INFANT AND MATERNAL MORTALITY

See CAYMAN ISLANDS-MORTALITY

CAYMAN ISLANDS-INTERNATIONAL TRADE

The Economist Group: Economist Intelligence Unit (EIU), 900 3rd Ave., 16th Fl., New York, NY, 10022, USA, (212) 541-0500, americas@eiu.com, https://www.eiu.com; Cayman Islands Country Report.

Euromonitor International, Inc., 1 N Dearborn St., Ste. 1700, Chicago, IL, 60602, USA, (312) 922-1115, (312) 922-1157, info-usa@euromonitor.com, https://www.euromonitor.com/; Geographies.

Palgrave Macmillan, 1 New York Plaza, Ste. 4500, New York, NY, 10004-1562, USA, (800) 777-4643, orders@palgrave.com, https://www.palgrave.com/us; The Statesman's Yearbook, 2023.

United Nations Conference on Trade and Development (UNCTAD), Palais des Nations, Geneva, 1211, SWI, (212) 963-6896, unctadinfo@unctad.org, https://unctad.org; Trade and Development Report 2021.

United Nations Food and Agricultural Organization (FAO), 2121 K St., Ste. 800B, Washington, DC, 20037, USA, (202) 653-2400 (Dial from U.S.), (202) 653-5760 (Fax from U.S.), fao-hq@fao.org, https://www.fao.org; The State of Food and Agriculture (SOFA) 2022.

World Trade Organization (WTO), Ctre. William Rappard, Rue de Lausanne 154, Case postale, Geneva, CH-1211, SWI, enquiries@wto.org, https://www.wto.org; World Trade Statistical Review 2022.

CAYMAN ISLANDS-LABOR

Central Intelligence Agency (CIA), Office of Public Affairs, Washington, DC, 20505, USA, (703) 482-0623, https://www.cia.gov; The World Factbook.

Euromonitor International, Inc., 1 N Dearborn St., Ste. 1700, Chicago, IL, 60602, USA, (312) 922-1115, (312) 922-1157, info-usa@euromonitor.com, https://www.euromonitor.com/; Geographies.

United Nations Food and Agricultural Organization (FAO), 2121 K St., Ste. 800B, Washington, DC, 20037, USA, (202) 653-2400 (Dial from U.S.), (202) 653-5760 (Fax from U.S.), fao-hq@fao.org, https://www.fao.org; The State of Food and Agriculture (SOFA) 2022.

CAYMAN ISLANDS-LIFE EXPECTANCY

Central Intelligence Agency (CIA), Office of Public Affairs, Washington, DC, 20505, USA, (703) 482-0623, https://www.cia.gov; The World Factbook.

United Nations Department of Economic and Social Affairs (DESA), Population Division, 2 United Nations Plz., Rm. DC2-1950, New York, NY, 10017, USA, (212) 963-3209, (212) 963-2147, population@un.org, https://www.un.org/development/desa/pd/; World Population Ageing 2020 Highlights.

CAYMAN ISLANDS-LITERACY

Euromonitor International, Inc., 1 N Dearborn St., Ste. 1700, Chicago, IL, 60602, USA, (312) 922-1115, (312) 922-1157, info-usa@euromonitor.com, https://www.euromonitor.com/; Geographies.

CAYMAN ISLANDS-LIVESTOCK

Routledge - Taylor & Francis Group, 6000 Broken Sound Pkwy. NW, Ste. 300, Boca Raton, FL, 33487, USA, (800) 634-1420, (800) 634-7064, orders@taylorandfrancis.com, https://www.routledge.com/; The Europa World Year Book 2022.

United Nations Food and Agricultural Organization (FAO), 2121 K St., Ste. 800B, Washington, DC, 20037, USA, (202) 653-2400 (Dial from U.S.), (202) 653-5760 (Fax from U.S.), fao-hq@fao.org, https://www.fao.org; The State of Food and Agriculture (SOFA) 2022.

CAYMAN ISLANDS-MARRIAGE

Routledge - Taylor & Francis Group, 6000 Broken Sound Pkwy. NW, Ste. 300, Boca Raton, FL, 33487, USA, (800) 634-1420, (800) 634-7064, orders@taylorandfrancis.com, https://www.routledge.com/; The Europa World Year Book 2022.

United Nations Statistics Division (UNSD), United Nations Plz., New York, NY, 10017, USA, (800) 253-9646, (212) 963-9851, statistics@un.org, https://unstats.un.org; Statistical Yearbook of the United Nations 2021.

CAYMAN ISLANDS-MINERAL INDUSTRIES

United Nations Conference on Trade and Development (UNCTAD), Palais des Nations, Geneva, 1211, SWI, (212) 963-6896, unctadinfo@unctad.org, https://unctad.org; Trade and Development Report 2021.

United Nations Statistics Division (UNSD), United Nations Plz., New York, NY, 10017, USA, (800) 253-9646, (212) 963-9851, statistics@un.org, https://unstats.un.org; Statistical Yearbook of the United Nations 2021.

CAYMAN ISLANDS-MONEY SUPPLY

The Economist Group: Economist Intelligence Unit (EIU), 900 3rd Ave., 16th Fl., New York, NY, 10022, USA, (212) 541-0500, americas@eiu.com, https://www.eiu.com; Cayman Islands Country Report.

CAYMAN ISLANDS-MORTALITY

United Nations Statistics Division (UNSD), United Nations Plz., New York, NY, 10017, USA, (800) 253-9646, (212) 963-9851, statistics@un.org, https://unstats.un.org; Statistical Yearbook of the United Nations 2021.

CAYMAN ISLANDS-NUTRITION

United Nations Food and Agricultural Organization (FAO), 2121 K St., Ste. 800B, Washington, DC, 20037, USA, (202) 653-2400 (Dial from U.S.), (202) 653-5760 (Fax from U.S.), fao-hq@fao.org, https://www.fao.org; The State of Food and Agriculture (SOFA) 2022.

CAYMAN ISLANDS-PESTICIDES

United Nations Food and Agricultural Organization (FAO), 2121 K St., Ste. 800B, Washington, DC, 20037, USA, (202) 653-2400 (Dial from U.S.), (202) 653-5760 (Fax from U.S.), fao-hq@fao.org, https://www.fao.org; The State of Food and Agriculture (SOFA) 2022.

CAYMAN ISLANDS-PETROLEUM INDUSTRY AND TRADE

United Nations Food and Agricultural Organization (FAO), 2121 K St., Ste. 800B, Washington, DC, 20037, USA, (202) 653-2400 (Dial from U.S.), (202) 653-5760 (Fax from U.S.), fao-hq@fao.org, https://www.fao.org; The State of Food and Agriculture (SOFA) 2022.

CAYMAN ISLANDS-POPULATION

Caribbean Public Health Agency (CARPHA), Federation Park, 16-18 Jamaica Blvd., Port of Spain, TTO, (868) 622-4261 (Dial from U.S.), (868) 299-0820 (Dial from U.S.), postmaster@carpha.org, https://carpha.org/; unpublished data.

Central Intelligence Agency (CIA), Office of Public Affairs, Washington, DC, 20505, USA, (703) 482-0623, https://www.cia.gov; The World Factbook.

The Economist Group: Economist Intelligence Unit (EIU), 900 3rd Ave., 16th Fl., New York, NY, 10022, USA, (212) 541-0500, americas@eiu.com, https://www.eiu.com; Cayman Islands Country Report.

European Commission, Eurostat, Luxembourg, 2920, LUX, https://ec.europa.eu/eurostat/; EU in the World 2020.

Palgrave Macmillan, 1 New York Plaza, Ste. 4500, New York, NY, 10004-1562, USA, (800) 777-4643, orders@palgrave.com, https://www.palgrave.com/us; The Statesman's Yearbook, 2023.

Routledge - Taylor & Francis Group, 6000 Broken Sound Pkwy. NW, Ste. 300, Boca Raton, FL, 33487, USA, (800) 634-1420, (800) 634-7064, orders@taylorandfrancis.com, https://www.routledge.com/; The Europa World Year Book 2022.

UK Data Service, University of Essex, Wivenhoe Park, Colchester, Essex, CO4 3SQ, GBR, https://ukdataservice.ac.uk/; International Aggregate Data.

UNESCO Institute for Statistics, C.P 250 Succursale H, Montreal, QC, H3G 2K8, CAN, (514) 343-6880 (Dial from U.S.), (514) 343-5740 (Fax from U.S.), uis.publications@unesco.org, http://uis.unesco.org/; UIS.Stat.

United Nations Department of Economic and Social Affairs (DESA), Population Division, 2 United Nations Plz., Rm. DC2-1950, New York, NY, 10017, USA, (212) 963-3209, (212) 963-2147, population@un.org, https://www.un.org/development/desa/pd/; Revision of World Urbanization Prospects and World Population Ageing 2020 Highlights.

United Nations Economic Commission for Latin America and the Caribbean (ECLAC), Casilla 179-D, Santiago, 7630412, CHL, (202) 596-3713, prensa@cepal.org, https://www.cepal.org/en; CEPALSTAT.

United Nations Statistics Division (UNSD), United Nations Plz., New York, NY, 10017, USA, (800) 253-9646, (212) 963-9851, statistics@un.org, https://unstats.un.org; Statistical Yearbook of the United Nations 2021.

CAYMAN ISLANDS-POPULATION DENSITY

Central Intelligence Agency (CIA), Office of Public Affairs, Washington, DC, 20505, USA, (703) 482-0623, https://www.cia.gov; The World Factbook.

Palgrave Macmillan, 1 New York Plaza, Ste. 4500, New York, NY, 10004-1562, USA, (800) 777-4643, orders@palgrave.com, https://www.palgrave.com/us; The Statesman's Yearbook, 2023.

Routledge - Taylor & Francis Group, 6000 Broken Sound Pkwy. NW, Ste. 300, Boca Raton, FL, 33487, USA, (800) 634-1420, (800) 634-7064, orders@taylorandfrancis.com, https://www.routledge.com/; The Europa World Year Book 2022.

UNESCO Institute for Statistics, C.P 250 Succursale H, Montreal, QC, H3G 2K8, CAN, (514) 343-6880 (Dial from U.S.), (514) 343-5740 (Fax from U.S.), uis.publications@unesco.org, http://uis.unesco.org/; UIS.Stat.

CAYMAN ISLANDS-POWER RESOURCES

Euromonitor International, Inc., 1 N Dearborn St., Ste. 1700, Chicago, IL, 60602, USA, (312) 922-1115, (312) 922-1157, info-usa@euromonitor.com, https://www.euromonitor.com/; Geographies.

United Nations Food and Agricultural Organization (FAO), 2121 K St., Ste. 800B, Washington, DC, 20037, USA, (202) 653-2400 (Dial from U.S.), (202) 653-5760 (Fax from U.S.), fao-hq@fao.org, https://www.fao.org; The State of Food and Agriculture (SOFA) 2022.

United Nations Statistics Division (UNSD), United Nations Plz., New York, NY, 10017, USA, (800) 253-9646, (212) 963-9851, statistics@un.org, https://unstats.un.org; Energy Statistics Yearbook 2019.

CAYMAN ISLANDS-PRICES

Euromonitor International, Inc., 1 N Dearborn St., Ste. 1700, Chicago, IL, 60602, USA, (312) 922-1115, (312) 922-1157, info-usa@euromonitor.com, https://www.euromonitor.com/; Geographies.

CAYMAN ISLANDS-PUBLIC HEALTH

Euromonitor International, Inc., 1 N Dearborn St., Ste. 1700, Chicago, IL, 60602, USA, (312) 922-1115, (312) 922-1157, info-usa@euromonitor.com, https://www.euromonitor.com/; Geographies.

Palgrave Macmillan, 1 New York Plaza, Ste. 4500, New York, NY, 10004-1562, USA, (800) 777-4643, orders@palgrave.com, https://www.palgrave.com/us; The Statesman's Yearbook, 2023.

U.S. Census Bureau, 4600 Silver Hill Rd., Washington, DC, 20233, USA, (301) 763-4636, (800) 923-8282, https://www.census.gov; HIV/AIDS Surveillance Data Base.

United Nations Department of Economic and Social Affairs (DESA), Population Division, 2 United Nations Plz., Rm. DC2-1950, New York, NY, 10017, USA, (212) 963-3209, (212) 963-2147, population@un.org, https://www.un.org/development/desa/pd/; World Fertility Data 2019.

United Nations Statistics Division (UNSD), United Nations Plz., New York, NY, 10017, USA, (800) 253-9646, (212) 963-9851, statistics@un.org, https://unstats.un.org; Statistical Yearbook of the United Nations 2021.

World Health Organization (WHO), Ave. Appia 20, Geneva, CH-1211, SWI, (202) 974-3000 (Telephone in U.S.), publications@who.int, https://www.who.int/; Health Statistics and Information Systems.

CAYMAN ISLANDS-RELIGION

Central Intelligence Agency (CIA), Office of Public Affairs, Washington, DC, 20505, USA, (703) 482-0623, https://www.cia.gov; The World Factbook.

Palgrave Macmillan, 1 New York Plaza, Ste. 4500, New York, NY, 10004-1562, USA, (800) 777-4643, orders@palgrave.com, https://www.palgrave.com/us; The Statesman's Yearbook, 2023.

CAYMAN ISLANDS-RETAIL TRADE

Euromonitor International, Inc., 1 N Dearborn St., Ste. 1700, Chicago, IL, 60602, USA, (312) 922-1115, (312) 922-1157, info-usa@euromonitor.com, https://www.euromonitor.com/; Geographies.

CAYMAN ISLANDS-SHIPPING

Routledge - Taylor & Francis Group, 6000 Broken Sound Pkwy. NW, Ste. 300, Boca Raton, FL, 33487, USA, (800) 634-1420, (800) 634-7064, orders@taylorandfrancis.com, https://www.routledge.com/; The Europa World Year Book 2022.

United Nations Statistics Division (UNSD), United Nations Plz., New York, NY, 10017, USA, (800) 253-9646, (212) 963-9851, statistics@un.org, https://unstats.un.org; Statistical Yearbook of the United Nations 2021.

CAYMAN ISLANDS-TELEPHONE

Palgrave Macmillan, 1 New York Plaza, Ste. 4500, New York, NY, 10004-1562, USA, (800) 777-4643, orders@palgrave.com, https://www.palgrave.com/us; The Statesman's Yearbook, 2023.

Routledge - Taylor & Francis Group, 6000 Broken Sound Pkwy. NW, Ste. 300, Boca Raton, FL, 33487, USA, (800) 634-1420, (800) 634-7064, orders@taylorandfrancis.com, https://www.routledge.com/; The Europa World Year Book 2022.

CAYMAN ISLANDS-TEXTILE INDUSTRY

Palgrave Macmillan, 1 New York Plaza, Ste. 4500, New York, NY, 10004-1562, USA, (800) 777-4643, orders@palgrave.com, https://www.palgrave.com/us; The Statesman's Yearbook, 2023.

CAYMAN ISLANDS-TOURISM

Euromonitor International, Inc., 1 N Dearborn St., Ste. 1700, Chicago, IL, 60602, USA, (312) 922-1115, (312) 922-1157, info-usa@euromonitor.com, https://www.euromonitor.com/; Geographies.

Palgrave Macmillan, 1 New York Plaza, Ste. 4500, New York, NY, 10004-1562, USA, (800) 777-4643, orders@palgrave.com, https://www.palgrave.com/us; The Statesman's Yearbook, 2023.

Routledge - Taylor & Francis Group, 6000 Broken Sound Pkwy. NW, Ste. 300, Boca Raton, FL, 33487, USA, (800) 634-1420, (800) 634-7064, orders@taylorandfrancis.com, https://www.routledge.com/; The Europa World Year Book 2022.

United Nations Statistics Division (UNSD), United Nations Plz., New York, NY, 10017, USA, (800) 253-9646, (212) 963-9851, statistics@un.org, https://unstats.un.org; Statistical Yearbook of the United Nations 2021.

United Nations World Tourism Organization (UNWTO), Calle Poeta Joan Maragall 42, Madrid,

28020, SPA, info@unwto.org, https://www.unwto.org/; Yearbook of Tourism Statistics, 2021 Edition.

CAYMAN ISLANDS-TRADE

See CAYMAN ISLANDS-INTERNATIONAL TRADE

CAYMAN ISLANDS-TRANSPORTATION

Central Intelligence Agency (CIA), Office of Public Affairs, Washington, DC, 20505, USA, (703) 482-0623, https://www.cia.gov; The World Factbook.

Euromonitor International, Inc., 1 N Dearborn St., Ste. 1700, Chicago, IL, 60602, USA, (312) 922-1115, (312) 922-1157, info-usa@euromonitor.com, https://www.euromonitor.com/; Geographies.

Palgrave Macmillan, 1 New York Plaza, Ste. 4500, New York, NY, 10004-1562, USA, (800) 777-4643, orders@palgrave.com, https://www.palgrave.com/us; The Statesman's Yearbook, 2023.

Routledge - Taylor & Francis Group, 6000 Broken Sound Pkwy. NW, Ste. 300, Boca Raton, FL, 33487, USA, (800) 634-1420, (800) 634-7064, orders@taylorandfrancis.com, https://www.routledge.com/; The Europa World Year Book 2022.

CAYMAN ISLANDS-VITAL STATISTICS

Palgrave Macmillan, 1 New York Plaza, Ste. 4500, New York, NY, 10004-1562, USA, (800) 777-4643, orders@palgrave.com, https://www.palgrave.com/us; The Statesman's Yearbook, 2023.

U.S. Census Bureau, 4600 Silver Hill Rd., Washington, DC, 20233, USA, (301) 763-4636, (800) 923-8282, https://www.census.gov; HIV/AIDS Surveillance Data Base.

United Nations Department of Economic and Social Affairs (DESA), Population Division, 2 United Nations Plz., Rm. DC2-1950, New York, NY, 10017, USA, (212) 963-3209, (212) 963-2147, population@un.org, https://www.un.org/development/desa/pd/; World Contraceptive Use 2021: Estimates and Projections of Family Planning Indicators and World Marriage Data 2019.

United Nations Statistics Division (UNSD), United Nations Plz., New York, NY, 10017, USA, (800) 253-9646, (212) 963-9851, statistics@un.org, https://unstats.un.org; Statistical Yearbook of the United Nations 2021.

CELERY

U.S. Department of Agriculture (USDA), Economic Research Service (ERS), 1400 Independence Ave. SW, Mail Stop 1800, Washington, DC, 20250-0002, USA, (202) 720-2791, https://www.ers.usda.gov/; Food Price Outlook.

U.S. Department of Agriculture (USDA), National Agricultural Statistics Service (USDA-NASS), 1400 Independence Ave. SW, Washington, DC, 20250, USA, (800) 727-9540, nass@nass.usda.gov, https://www.nass.usda.gov; Quick Stats and Vegetables Annual Summary.

CELIAC DISEASE

Statistic Brain Research Institute, 1100 Glendon Ave., Los Angeles, CA, 90024, USA, https://www.statisticbrain.com/; Gluten/Celiac Disease Statistics.

CELL PHONE EQUIPMENT INDUSTRY

Kantar Worldpanel, 6 More London Place, London, SE1 2QY, GBR, https://www.kantarworldpanel.com; Android vs. iOS: Smartphone OS Sales Market Share Evolution.

CELL PHONE SERVICES INDUSTRY

Cellular Telecommunications and Internet Association (CTIA), 1400 16th St. NW, Ste. 600, Washington, DC, 20036, USA, (202) 736-3200, https://www.ctia.org; 2022 Annual Wireless Industry Survey.

Federal Communications Commission (FCC), Wireless Telecommunications Bureau (WTB), 45 L St. NE, Washington, DC, 20554, USA, (202) 418-0600, (888) 225-5322, (202) 418-0787, https://www.fcc.gov/wireless-telecommunications; unpublished data.

CELL PHONES

See also SMARTPHONES

Federal Communications Commission (FCC), Wireless Telecommunications Bureau (WTB), 45 L St. NE, Washington, DC, 20554, USA, (202) 418-0600, (888) 225-5322, (202) 418-0787, https://www.fcc.gov/wireless-telecommunications; unpublished data.

Kantar Worldpanel, 6 More London Place, London, SE1 2QY, GBR, https://www.kantarworldpanel.com; Android vs. iOS: Smartphone OS Sales Market Share Evolution.

Pew Research Center, Internet & Technology, 1615 L St. NW, Ste. 800, Washington, DC, 20036, USA, (202) 419-4300, (202) 857-8562, https://www.pewresearch.org/topic/internet-technology/; Activism in the Social Media Age; Mobile Divides in Emerging Economies; Mobile Technology and Home Broadband 2019; and Teens, Social Media & Technology 2022.

Rapid Intelligence, Sydney, NSW, 2001, AUS, https://www.rapint.com/; NationMaster.com.

University of California, Berkeley, Global Policy Lab, California Memorial Stadium, 2227 Piedmont Ave., Berkeley, CA, 94720, USA, (510) 643-5751, https://www.globalpolicy.science/; Public Mobility Data Enables COVID-19 Forecasting and Management at Local and Global Scales.

Worldometer, https://www.worldometers.info/; Worldometers.info.

CELL PHONES-SOCIAL ASPECTS

Center for Humane Technology (CHT), hello@humanetech.com, https://www.humanetech.com/; Ledger of Harms.

CELL PHONES AND TEENAGERS

Common Sense, 699 8th St., Ste. C150, San Francisco, CA, 94103, USA, (415) 863-0600, (415) 863-0601, https://www.commonsensemedia.org/; The New Normal: Parents, Teens, Screens, and Sleep in the United States and Teens and Mental Health: How Girls Really Feel About Social Media.

CELL PHONES AND TRAFFIC ACCIDENTS

Association for the Advancement of Automotive Medicine (AAAM), 35 E Wacker Dr., Ste. 850, Chicago, IL, 60601, USA, (847) 844-3880, info@aaam.org, https://www.aaam.org; unpublished data.

CELLULAR TELEPHONES

See CELL PHONES

CEMENT-CONSUMPTION

U.S. Department of the Interior (DOI), U.S. Geological Survey (USGS), National Minerals Information Center (NMIC), 12201 Sunrise Valley Dr., Reston, VA, 20192, USA, (703) 648-4920, (703) 648-7971, (703) 648-4995, sfortier@usgs.gov, https://www.usgs.gov/centers/nmic; Mineral Commodity Summaries 2022; Mineral Industry Surveys (MIS); and Minerals Yearbook.

CEMENT-EMPLOYMENT

U.S. Department of Labor (DOL), Bureau of Labor Statistics (BLS), Postal Square Bldg., 2 Massachusetts Ave. NE, Washington, DC, 20212-0001, USA, (202) 691-5200, (202) 691-7890, blsdata_staff@bls.gov, https://www.bls.gov; Industry-Occupation Matrix Data, By Occupation.

U.S. Department of the Interior (DOI), U.S. Geological Survey (USGS), National Minerals Information Center (NMIC), 12201 Sunrise Valley Dr., Reston, VA, 20192, USA, (703) 648-4920, (703) 648-7971, (703) 648-4995, sfortier@usgs.gov, https://www.usgs.gov/centers/nmic; Mineral Commodity Summaries 2022.

CEMENT-INTERNATIONAL TRADE

U.S. Department of the Interior (DOI), U.S. Geological Survey (USGS), National Minerals Information Center (NMIC), 12201 Sunrise Valley Dr., Reston, VA, 20192, USA, (703) 648-4920, (703) 648-7971, (703) 648-4995, sfortier@usgs.gov, https://www.usgs.gov/centers/nmic; Mineral Commodity Summaries 2022.

CEMENT-PRICE INDEXES

U.S. Department of Labor (DOL), Bureau of Labor Statistics (BLS), Postal Square Bldg., 2 Massachusetts Ave. NE, Washington, DC, 20212-0001, USA, (202) 691-5200, (202) 691-7890, blsdata_staff@bls.gov, https://www.bls.gov; Producer Price Indexes (PPI).

CEMENT-PRICES

U.S. Department of the Interior (DOI), U.S. Geological Survey (USGS), National Minerals Information Center (NMIC), 12201 Sunrise Valley Dr., Reston, VA, 20192, USA, (703) 648-4920, (703) 648-7971, (703) 648-4995, sfortier@usgs.gov, https://www.usgs.gov/centers/nmic; Mineral Commodity Summaries 2022.

CEMENT-PRODUCTION AND VALUE

U.S. Department of the Interior (DOI), U.S. Geological Survey (USGS), National Minerals Information Center (NMIC), 12201 Sunrise Valley Dr., Reston, VA, 20192, USA, (703) 648-4920, (703) 648-7971, (703) 648-4995, sfortier@usgs.gov, https://www.usgs.gov/centers/nmic; Mineral Commodity Summaries 2022 and Minerals Yearbook.

CEMENT-WORLD PRODUCTION

U.S. Department of the Interior (DOI), U.S. Geological Survey (USGS), National Minerals Information Center (NMIC), 12201 Sunrise Valley Dr., Reston, VA, 20192, USA, (703) 648-4920, (703) 648-7971, (703) 648-4995, sfortier@usgs.gov, https://www.usgs.gov/centers/nmic; Mineral Commodity Summaries 2022 and Minerals Yearbook.

CENSORSHIP

Committee to Protect Journalists (CPJ), PO Box 2675, New York, NY, 10108, USA, (212) 465-1004, (212) 214-0640, info@cpj.org, https://cpj.org; Database of Attacks on the Press: 1992-2023; Journalists Killed Since 1992; Record Number of Journalists Jailed Worldwide; and Ten Most Censored Countries.

Pew Research Center, Internet & Technology, 1615 L St. NW, Ste. 800, Washington, DC, 20036, USA, (202) 419-4300, (202) 857-8562, https://www.pewresearch.org/topic/internet-technology/; Most Americans Think Social Media Sites Censor Political Viewpoints.

CENTRAL AFRICAN REPUBLIC-NATIONAL STATISTICAL OFFICE

Institut Centrafricain des Statitistique et des Etudes Economiques et Sociales (ICASEES), BP 696, Bangui, CAF, info@icasees.cf, https://www.icasees.org/; National Data Reports (Central African Republic).

CENTRAL AFRICAN REPUBLIC-AGRICULTURE

African Development Bank Group (AfDB), Avenue Joseph Anoma, 01 BP 1387, Abidjan, 01, COT, https://www.afdb.org; African Economic Outlook 2021 and Compendium of Statistics on Bank Group Operations 2019.

The Economist Group: Economist Intelligence Unit (EIU), 900 3rd Ave., 16th Fl., New York, NY, 10022, USA, (212) 541-0500, americas@eiu.com, https://www.eiu.com; Central African Republic Country Report.

Euromonitor International, Inc., 1 N Dearborn St., Ste. 1700, Chicago, IL, 60602, USA, (312) 922-1115, (312) 922-1157, info-usa@euromonitor.com, https://www.euromonitor.com/; Geographies.

Palgrave Macmillan, 1 New York Plaza, Ste. 4500, New York, NY, 10004-1562, USA, (800) 777-4643, orders@palgrave.com, https://www.palgrave.com/us; The Statesman's Yearbook, 2023.

Routledge - Taylor & Francis Group, 6000 Broken Sound Pkwy. NW, Ste. 300, Boca Raton, FL, 33487, USA, (800) 634-1420, (800) 634-7064, orders@taylorandfrancis.com, https://www.routledge.com/; The Europa World Year Book 2022.

United Nations Economic Commission for Africa (UNECA), PO Box 3001, Addis Ababa, ETH, ecainfo@uneca.org, https://www.uneca.org/; African Statistical Yearbook 2020 and Economic Report on Africa 2021.

United Nations Food and Agricultural Organization (FAO), 2121 K St., Ste. 800B, Washington, DC, 20037, USA, (202) 653-2400 (Dial from U.S.), (202) 653-5760 (Fax from U.S.), fao-hq@fao.org, https://www.fao.org; AQUASTAT and The State of Food and Agriculture (SOFA) 2022.

United Nations Statistics Division (UNSD), United Nations Plz., New York, NY, 10017, USA, (800) 253-9646, (212) 963-9851, statistics@un.org, https://unstats.un.org; Statistical Yearbook of the United Nations 2021.

The World Bank, 1818 H St. NW, Washington, DC, 20433, USA, (202) 473-1000, (202) 477-6391, eds03@worldbank.org, https://www.worldbank.org/; Central African Republic (report) and World Development Indicators (WDI) 2022.

WRTH Publications Limited, PO Box 290, Oxford, OX2 7FT, GBR, sales@wrth.com, https://www.wrth.com; World Radio TV Handbook 2023.

CENTRAL AFRICAN REPUBLIC-AIRLINES

Palgrave Macmillan, 1 New York Plaza, Ste. 4500, New York, NY, 10004-1562, USA, (800) 777-4643, orders@palgrave.com, https://www.palgrave.com/us; The Statesman's Yearbook, 2023.

Routledge - Taylor & Francis Group, 6000 Broken Sound Pkwy. NW, Ste. 300, Boca Raton, FL, 33487, USA, (800) 634-1420, (800) 634-7064, orders@taylorandfrancis.com, https://www.routledge.com/; The Europa World Year Book 2022.

United Nations Economic Commission for Africa (UNECA), PO Box 3001, Addis Ababa, ETH, ecainfo@uneca.org, https://www.uneca.org/; African Statistical Yearbook 2020.

CENTRAL AFRICAN REPUBLIC-ALUMINUM PRODUCTION

See CENTRAL AFRICAN REPUBLIC-MINERAL INDUSTRIES

CENTRAL AFRICAN REPUBLIC-ARMED FORCES

Central Intelligence Agency (CIA), Office of Public Affairs, Washington, DC, 20505, USA, (703) 482-0623, https://www.cia.gov; The World Factbook.

International Institute for Strategic Studies (IISS) - Americas, 2121 K St. NW, Ste. 600, Washington, DC, 20037, USA, (202) 659-1490, (202) 659-1499, https://www.iiss.org/; Armed Conflict Survey 2021 and The Military Balance 2022.

Palgrave Macmillan, 1 New York Plaza, Ste. 4500, New York, NY, 10004-1562, USA, (800) 777-4643, orders@palgrave.com, https://www.palgrave.com/us; The Statesman's Yearbook, 2023.

Stockholm International Peace Research Institute (SIPRI), Signalistgatan 9, Stockholm, SE 169 72, SWE, https://www.sipri.org/; SIPRI Arms Transfers Database and SIPRI Military Expenditure Database.

CENTRAL AFRICAN REPUBLIC-BALANCE OF PAYMENTS

African Development Bank Group (AfDB), Avenue Joseph Anoma, 01 BP 1387, Abidjan, 01, COT, https://www.afdb.org; The AfDB Statistics Pocketbook 2019.

International Monetary Fund (IMF), 700 19th St. NW, Washington, DC, 20431, USA, (202) 623-7000, (202) 623-4661, publications@imf.org, https://www.imf.org; Balance of Payments Statistics: Annual Report 2021.

Routledge - Taylor & Francis Group, 6000 Broken Sound Pkwy. NW, Ste. 300, Boca Raton, FL, 33487, USA, (800) 634-1420, (800) 634-7064, orders@taylorandfrancis.com, https://www.routledge.com/; The Europa World Year Book 2022.

United Nations Conference on Trade and Development (UNCTAD), Palais des Nations, Geneva, 1211, SWI, (212) 963-6896, unctadinfo@unctad.org, https://unctad.org; Handbook of Statistics 2021.

United Nations Economic Commission for Africa (UNECA), PO Box 3001, Addis Ababa, ETH, ecainfo@uneca.org, https://www.uneca.org/; African Statistical Yearbook 2020.

The World Bank, 1818 H St. NW, Washington, DC, 20433, USA, (202) 473-1000, (202) 477-6391, eds03@worldbank.org, https://www.worldbank.org/; Central African Republic (report); World Development Indicators (WDI) 2022; and World Development Report 2022: Finance for an Equitable Recovery.

CENTRAL AFRICAN REPUBLIC-BANKS AND BANKING

Euromonitor International, Inc., 1 N Dearborn St., Ste. 1700, Chicago, IL, 60602, USA, (312) 922-1115, (312) 922-1157, info-usa@euromonitor.com, https://www.euromonitor.com/; Geographies.

International Monetary Fund (IMF), 700 19th St. NW, Washington, DC, 20431, USA, (202) 623-7000, (202) 623-4661, publications@imf.org, https://www.imf.org; International Financial Statistics (IFS).

Routledge - Taylor & Francis Group, 6000 Broken Sound Pkwy. NW, Ste. 300, Boca Raton, FL, 33487, USA, (800) 634-1420, (800) 634-7064, orders@taylorandfrancis.com, https://www.routledge.com/; The Europa World Year Book 2022.

United Nations Economic Commission for Africa (UNECA), PO Box 3001, Addis Ababa, ETH, ecainfo@uneca.org, https://www.uneca.org/; African Statistical Yearbook 2020.

CENTRAL AFRICAN REPUBLIC-BARLEY PRODUCTION

See CENTRAL AFRICAN REPUBLIC-CROPS

CENTRAL AFRICAN REPUBLIC-BROADCASTING

Central Intelligence Agency (CIA), Office of Public Affairs, Washington, DC, 20505, USA, (703) 482-0623, https://www.cia.gov; The World Factbook.

Euromonitor International, Inc., 1 N Dearborn St., Ste. 1700, Chicago, IL, 60602, USA, (312) 922-1115, (312) 922-1157, info-usa@euromonitor.com, https://www.euromonitor.com/; Geographies.

Palgrave Macmillan, 1 New York Plaza, Ste. 4500, New York, NY, 10004-1562, USA, (800) 777-4643, orders@palgrave.com, https://www.palgrave.com/us; The Statesman's Yearbook, 2023.

CENTRAL AFRICAN REPUBLIC-BUDGET

Central Intelligence Agency (CIA), Office of Public Affairs, Washington, DC, 20505, USA, (703) 482-0623, https://www.cia.gov; The World Factbook.

CENTRAL AFRICAN REPUBLIC-CHILDBIRTH-STATISTICS

The World Bank, 1818 H St. NW, Washington, DC, 20433, USA, (202) 473-1000, (202) 477-6391, eds03@worldbank.org, https://www.worldbank.org/; World Development Indicators (WDI) 2022.

CENTRAL AFRICAN REPUBLIC-CLIMATE

International Institute for Environment and Development (IIED), 235 High Holborn, London, WC1V 7DN, GBR, inforequest@iied.org, https://www.iied.org; Environment & Urbanization.

Palgrave Macmillan, 1 New York Plaza, Ste. 4500, New York, NY, 10004-1562, USA, (800) 777-4643, orders@palgrave.com, https://www.palgrave.com/us; The Statesman's Yearbook, 2023.

CENTRAL AFRICAN REPUBLIC-COAL PRODUCTION

See CENTRAL AFRICAN REPUBLIC-MINERAL INDUSTRIES

CENTRAL AFRICAN REPUBLIC-COCOA PRODUCTION

See CENTRAL AFRICAN REPUBLIC-CROPS

CENTRAL AFRICAN REPUBLIC-COFFEE

See CENTRAL AFRICAN REPUBLIC-CROPS

CENTRAL AFRICAN REPUBLIC-COMMERCE

Palgrave Macmillan, 1 New York Plaza, Ste. 4500, New York, NY, 10004-1562, USA, (800) 777-4643, orders@palgrave.com, https://www.palgrave.com/us; The Statesman's Yearbook, 2023.

UK Data Service, University of Essex, Wivenhoe Park, Colchester, Essex, CO4 3SQ, GBR, https://ukdataservice.ac.uk/; International Aggregate Data.

CENTRAL AFRICAN REPUBLIC-COMMODITY EXCHANGES

Barchart, 209 W Jackson Blvd., 2nd Fl., Chicago, IL, 60606, USA, (877) 247-4394, commodities@barchart.com, https://www.barchart.com/cmdty; The cmdty Yearbook 2023; cmdtyStats: Commodity Statistics and Fundamental Data; cmdtyView: Commodity Index; and Commodity Data and Prices.

International Monetary Fund (IMF), 700 19th St. NW, Washington, DC, 20431, USA, (202) 623-7000, (202) 623-4661, publications@imf.org, https://www.imf.org; IMF Primary Commodity Prices.

CENTRAL AFRICAN REPUBLIC-CONSTRUCTION INDUSTRY

United Nations Economic Commission for Africa (UNECA), PO Box 3001, Addis Ababa, ETH, ecainfo@uneca.org, https://www.uneca.org/; African Statistical Yearbook 2020.

CENTRAL AFRICAN REPUBLIC-CONSUMER PRICE INDEXES

Routledge - Taylor & Francis Group, 6000 Broken Sound Pkwy. NW, Ste. 300, Boca Raton, FL, 33487, USA, (800) 634-1420, (800) 634-7064, orders@taylorandfrancis.com, https://www.routledge.com/; The Europa World Year Book 2022.

United Nations Economic Commission for Africa (UNECA), PO Box 3001, Addis Ababa, ETH, ecainfo@uneca.org, https://www.uneca.org/; African Statistical Yearbook 2020.

The World Bank, 1818 H St. NW, Washington, DC, 20433, USA, (202) 473-1000, (202) 477-6391, eds03@worldbank.org, https://www.worldbank.org/; Central African Republic (report).

CENTRAL AFRICAN REPUBLIC-CONSUMPTION (ECONOMICS)

African Development Bank Group (AfDB), Avenue Joseph Anoma, 01 BP 1387, Abidjan, 01, COT, https://www.afdb.org; The AfDB Statistics Pocketbook 2019.

CENTRAL AFRICAN REPUBLIC-COPPER INDUSTRY AND TRADE

See CENTRAL AFRICAN REPUBLIC-MINERAL INDUSTRIES

CENTRAL AFRICAN REPUBLIC-CORN INDUSTRY

See CENTRAL AFRICAN REPUBLIC-CROPS

CENTRAL AFRICAN REPUBLIC-COTTON

See CENTRAL AFRICAN REPUBLIC-CROPS

CENTRAL AFRICAN REPUBLIC-CROPS

Palgrave Macmillan, 1 New York Plaza, Ste. 4500, New York, NY, 10004-1562, USA, (800) 777-4643, orders@palgrave.com, https://www.palgrave.com/us; The Statesman's Yearbook, 2023.

United Nations Economic Commission for Africa (UNECA), PO Box 3001, Addis Ababa, ETH, ecainfo@uneca.org, https://www.uneca.org/; African Statistical Yearbook 2020.

United Nations Food and Agricultural Organization (FAO), 2121 K St., Ste. 800B, Washington, DC, 20037, USA, (202) 653-2400 (Dial from U.S.), (202) 653-5760 (Fax from U.S.), fao-hq@fao.org, https://www.fao.org; The State of Food and Agriculture (SOFA) 2022.

United Nations Statistics Division (UNSD), United Nations Plz., New York, NY, 10017, USA, (800) 253-9646, (212) 963-9851, statistics@un.org, https://unstats.un.org; Statistical Yearbook of the United Nations 2021.

CENTRAL AFRICAN REPUBLIC-DAIRY PROCESSING

Palgrave Macmillan, 1 New York Plaza, Ste. 4500, New York, NY, 10004-1562, USA, (800) 777-4643, orders@palgrave.com, https://www.palgrave.com/us; The Statesman's Yearbook, 2023.

United Nations Food and Agricultural Organization (FAO), 2121 K St., Ste. 800B, Washington, DC, 20037, USA, (202) 653-2400 (Dial from U.S.), (202) 653-5760 (Fax from U.S.), fao-hq@fao.org, https://www.fao.org; The State of Food and Agriculture (SOFA) 2022.

CENTRAL AFRICAN REPUBLIC-DEBTS, EXTERNAL

African Development Bank Group (AfDB), Avenue Joseph Anoma, 01 BP 1387, Abidjan, 01, COT, https://www.afdb.org; The AfDB Statistics Pocketbook 2019; African Economic Outlook 2021; and Compendium of Statistics on Bank Group Operations 2019.

United Nations Economic Commission for Africa (UNECA), PO Box 3001, Addis Ababa, ETH, ecainfo@uneca.org, https://www.uneca.org/; Economic Report on Africa 2021.

The World Bank, 1818 H St. NW, Washington, DC, 20433, USA, (202) 473-1000, (202) 477-6391, eds03@worldbank.org, https://www.worldbank.org/; Global Financial Development Report 2019-2020: Bank Regulation and Supervision a Decade after the Global Financial Crisis; World Development Indicators (WDI) 2022; and World Development Report 2022: Finance for an Equitable Recovery.

CENTRAL AFRICAN REPUBLIC-DEFENSE EXPENDITURES

See CENTRAL AFRICAN REPUBLIC-ARMED FORCES

CENTRAL AFRICAN REPUBLIC-DIAMONDS

See CENTRAL AFRICAN REPUBLIC-MINERAL INDUSTRIES

CENTRAL AFRICAN REPUBLIC-ECONOMIC ASSISTANCE

United Nations Statistics Division (UNSD), United Nations Plz., New York, NY, 10017, USA, (800) 253-9646, (212) 963-9851, statistics@un.org, https://unstats.un.org; Statistical Yearbook of the United Nations 2021.

CENTRAL AFRICAN REPUBLIC-ECONOMIC CONDITIONS

African Development Bank Group (AfDB), Avenue Joseph Anoma, 01 BP 1387, Abidjan, 01, COT, https://www.afdb.org; The AfDB Statistics Pocketbook 2019; Africa Economic Brief - COVID-19 Pandemic Potential Risks for Trade and Trade Finance in Africa; African Economic Outlook 2021; The African Statistical Journal; Compendium of Statistics on Bank Group Operations 2019; and Gender, Poverty and Environmental Indicators on African Countries 2019.

Bernan Press, 15250 NBN Way, Bldg. C, Blue Ridge Summit, PA, 17214, USA, (301) 459-2255, (800) 865-3457, (800) 865-3450, customercare@bernan.com, https://rowman.com/Page/Bernan; World Economic Outlook, April 2022.

Central Intelligence Agency (CIA), Office of Public Affairs, Washington, DC, 20505, USA, (703) 482-0623, https://www.cia.gov; The World Factbook.

The Economist Group: Economist Intelligence Unit (EIU), 900 3rd Ave., 16th Fl., New York, NY, 10022, USA, (212) 541-0500, americas@eiu.com, https://www.eiu.com; Central African Republic Country Report.

Euromonitor International, Inc., 1 N Dearborn St., Ste. 1700, Chicago, IL, 60602, USA, (312) 922-1115, (312) 922-1157, info-usa@euromonitor.com, https://www.euromonitor.com/; Geographies.

International Monetary Fund (IMF), 700 19th St. NW, Washington, DC, 20431, USA, (202) 623-7000, (202) 623-4661, publications@imf.org, https://www.imf.org; IMF Data and World Economic Outlook.

Palgrave Macmillan, 1 New York Plaza, Ste. 4500, New York, NY, 10004-1562, USA, (800) 777-4643, orders@palgrave.com, https://www.palgrave.com/us; The Statesman's Yearbook, 2023.

Routledge - Taylor & Francis Group, 6000 Broken Sound Pkwy. NW, Ste. 300, Boca Raton, FL, 33487, USA, (800) 634-1420, (800) 634-7064, orders@taylorandfrancis.com, https://www.routledge.com/; The Europa World Year Book 2022.

United Nations Economic Commission for Africa (UNECA), PO Box 3001, Addis Ababa, ETH, ecainfo@uneca.org, https://www.uneca.org/; Economic Report on Africa 2021.

United Nations Statistics Division (UNSD), United Nations Plz., New York, NY, 10017, USA, (800) 253-9646, (212) 963-9851, statistics@un.org, https://unstats.un.org; World Statistics Pocketbook 2021.

The World Bank, 1818 H St. NW, Washington, DC, 20433, USA, (202) 473-1000, (202) 477-6391, eds03@worldbank.org, https://www.worldbank.org/; Central African Republic (report); Global Economic Monitor (GEM); Global Economic Prospects, June 2022; The Global Findex Database 2021; and World Development Report 2022: Finance for an Equitable Recovery.

CENTRAL AFRICAN REPUBLIC-EDUCATION

African Development Bank Group (AfDB), Avenue Joseph Anoma, 01 BP 1387, Abidjan, 01, COT, https://www.afdb.org; The AfDB Statistics Pocketbook 2019.

Euromonitor International, Inc., 1 N Dearborn St., Ste. 1700, Chicago, IL, 60602, USA, (312) 922-1115, (312) 922-1157, info-usa@euromonitor.com, https://www.euromonitor.com/; Geographies.

Infoplease, c/o Sandbox Networks, Inc., 1 Lincoln St., 24th Fl., Boston, MA, 02111, USA, https://www.infoplease.com; Countries of the World.

Palgrave Macmillan, 1 New York Plaza, Ste. 4500, New York, NY, 10004-1562, USA, (800) 777-4643, orders@palgrave.com, https://www.palgrave.com/us; The Statesman's Yearbook, 2023.

Routledge - Taylor & Francis Group, 6000 Broken Sound Pkwy. NW, Ste. 300, Boca Raton, FL, 33487, USA, (800) 634-1420, (800) 634-7064, orders@taylorandfrancis.com, https://www.routledge.com/; The Europa World Year Book 2022.

UNESCO Institute for Statistics, C.P 250 Succursale H, Montreal, QC, H3G 2K8, CAN, (514) 343-6880 (Dial from U.S.), (514) 343-5740 (Fax from U.S.), uis.publications@unesco.org, http://uis.unesco.org/; Literacy and UIS.Stat.

United Nations Economic Commission for Africa (UNECA), PO Box 3001, Addis Ababa, ETH, ecainfo@uneca.org, https://www.uneca.org/; African Statistical Yearbook 2020.

United Nations Statistics Division (UNSD), United Nations Plz., New York, NY, 10017, USA, (800) 253-9646, (212) 963-9851, statistics@un.org, https://unstats.un.org; Millennium Development Goal Indicators.

The World Bank, 1818 H St. NW, Washington, DC, 20433, USA, (202) 473-1000, (202) 477-6391, eds03@worldbank.org, https://www.worldbank.org/; Central African Republic (report); World Development Indicators (WDI) 2022; and World Development Report 2022: Finance for an Equitable Recovery.

CENTRAL AFRICAN REPUBLIC-ELECTRICITY

United Nations Statistics Division (UNSD), United Nations Plz., New York, NY, 10017, USA, (800) 253-9646, (212) 963-9851, statistics@un.org, https://unstats.un.org; Statistical Yearbook of the United Nations 2021.

CENTRAL AFRICAN REPUBLIC-EMPLOYMENT

International Labour Organization (ILO), 4 Rte. des Morillons, Geneva, CH-1211, SWI, ilo@ilo.org, https://www.ilo.org; NORMLEX Information System on International Labour Standards.

UK Data Service, University of Essex, Wivenhoe Park, Colchester, Essex, CO4 3SQ, GBR, https://ukdataservice.ac.uk/; International Aggregate Data.

United Nations Economic Commission for Africa (UNECA), PO Box 3001, Addis Ababa, ETH, ecainfo@uneca.org, https://www.uneca.org/; African Statistical Yearbook 2020.

United Nations Statistics Division (UNSD), United Nations Plz., New York, NY, 10017, USA, (800) 253-9646, (212) 963-9851, statistics@un.org, https://unstats.un.org; Statistical Yearbook of the United Nations 2021.

The World Bank, 1818 H St. NW, Washington, DC, 20433, USA, (202) 473-1000, (202) 477-6391, eds03@worldbank.org, https://www.worldbank.org/; Central African Republic (report).

CENTRAL AFRICAN REPUBLIC-ENVIRONMENTAL CONDITIONS

DSI Data Service & Information, Xantener Strasse 51a, Rheinberg, D-47495, GER, dsi@dsidata.com, https://www.dsidata.com/; Global Environmental Database.

The Economist Group: Economist Intelligence Unit (EIU), 900 3rd Ave., 16th Fl., New York, NY, 10022, USA, (212) 541-0500, americas@eiu.com, https://www.eiu.com; Central African Republic Country Report.

International Institute for Environment and Development (IIED), 235 High Holborn, London, WC1V 7DN, GBR, inforequest@iied.org, https://www.iied.org; Environment & Urbanization.

United Nations Statistics Division (UNSD), United Nations Plz., New York, NY, 10017, USA, (800) 253-9646, (212) 963-9851, statistics@un.org, https://unstats.un.org; World Statistics Pocketbook 2021.

CENTRAL AFRICAN REPUBLIC-EXPORTS

African Development Bank Group (AfDB), Avenue Joseph Anoma, 01 BP 1387, Abidjan, 01, COT, https://www.afdb.org; African Economic Outlook 2021.

Central Intelligence Agency (CIA), Office of Public Affairs, Washington, DC, 20505, USA, (703) 482-0623, https://www.cia.gov; The World Factbook.

The Economist Group: Economist Intelligence Unit (EIU), 900 3rd Ave., 16th Fl., New York, NY, 10022, USA, (212) 541-0500, americas@eiu.com, https://www.eiu.com; Central African Republic Country Report.

International Monetary Fund (IMF), 700 19th St. NW, Washington, DC, 20431, USA, (202) 623-7000, (202) 623-4661, publications@imf.org, https://www.imf.org; Direction of Trade Statistics (DOTS).

S&P Global, IHS Markit, 15 Inverness Way E, Englewood, CO, 80112, USA, (800) 447-2273, (800) 854-7179, https://ihsmarkit.com; Global Trade Atlas (GTA).

United Nations Conference on Trade and Development (UNCTAD), Palais des Nations, Geneva, 1211, SWI, (212) 963-6896, unctadinfo@unctad.org, https://unctad.org; Handbook of Statistics 2021.

The World Bank, 1818 H St. NW, Washington, DC, 20433, USA, (202) 473-1000, (202) 477-6391, eds03@worldbank.org, https://www.worldbank.org/; World Development Report 2022: Finance for an Equitable Recovery.

CENTRAL AFRICAN REPUBLIC-FERTILITY, HUMAN

Central Intelligence Agency (CIA), Office of Public Affairs, Washington, DC, 20505, USA, (703) 482-0623, https://www.cia.gov; The World Factbook.

CENTRAL AFRICAN REPUBLIC-FERTILIZER INDUSTRY

United Nations Food and Agricultural Organization (FAO), 2121 K St., Ste. 800B, Washington, DC, 20037, USA, (202) 653-2400 (Dial from U.S.), (202) 653-5760 (Fax from U.S.), fao-hq@fao.org, https://www.fao.org; The State of Food and Agriculture (SOFA) 2022.

CENTRAL AFRICAN REPUBLIC-FETAL MORTALITY

See CENTRAL AFRICAN REPUBLIC-MORTALITY

CENTRAL AFRICAN REPUBLIC-FINANCE

Stockholm International Peace Research Institute (SIPRI), Signalistgatan 9, Stockholm, SE 169 72, SWE, https://www.sipri.org/; SIPRI Arms Transfers Database and SIPRI Military Expenditure Database.

United Nations Economic Commission for Africa (UNECA), PO Box 3001, Addis Ababa, ETH, ecainfo@uneca.org, https://www.uneca.org/; African Statistical Yearbook 2020.

United Nations Statistics Division (UNSD), United Nations Plz., New York, NY, 10017, USA, (800) 253-9646, (212) 963-9851, statistics@un.org, https://unstats.un.org; Statistical Yearbook of the United Nations 2021.

The World Bank, 1818 H St. NW, Washington, DC, 20433, USA, (202) 473-1000, (202) 477-6391, eds03@worldbank.org, https://www.worldbank.org/; Central African Republic (report).

CENTRAL AFRICAN REPUBLIC-FINANCE, PUBLIC

African Development Bank Group (AfDB), Avenue Joseph Anoma, 01 BP 1387, Abidjan, 01, COT, https://www.afdb.org; The AfDB Statistics Pocketbook 2019.

Bernan Press, 15250 NBN Way, Bldg. C, Blue Ridge Summit, PA, 17214, USA, (301) 459-2255, (800) 865-3457, (800) 865-3450, customercare@bernan.com, https://rowman.com/Page/Bernan; National Accounts Statistics: Analysis of Main Aggregates 2020.

The Economist Group: Economist Intelligence Unit (EIU), 900 3rd Ave., 16th Fl., New York, NY, 10022, USA, (212) 541-0500, americas@eiu.com, https://www.eiu.com; Central African Republic Country Report.

International Monetary Fund (IMF), 700 19th St. NW, Washington, DC, 20431, USA, (202) 623-7000, (202) 623-4661, publications@imf.org, https://www.imf.org; International Financial Statistics (IFS) and Regional Economic Outlook.

Routledge - Taylor & Francis Group, 6000 Broken Sound Pkwy. NW, Ste. 300, Boca Raton, FL, 33487, USA, (800) 634-1420, (800) 634-7064, orders@taylorandfrancis.com, https://www.routledge.com/; The Europa World Year Book 2022.

United Nations Economic Commission for Africa (UNECA), PO Box 3001, Addis Ababa, ETH, ecainfo@uneca.org, https://www.uneca.org/; African Statistical Yearbook 2020.

United Nations Statistics Division (UNSD), United Nations Plz., New York, NY, 10017, USA, (800) 253-9646, (212) 963-9851, statistics@un.org, https://unstats.un.org; National Accounts Main Aggregates Database and National Accounts Statistics: Main Aggregates and Detailed Tables.

The World Bank, 1818 H St. NW, Washington, DC, 20433, USA, (202) 473-1000, (202) 477-6391, eds03@worldbank.org, https://www.worldbank.org/; Central African Republic (report).

CENTRAL AFRICAN REPUBLIC-FISHERIES

Palgrave Macmillan, 1 New York Plaza, Ste. 4500, New York, NY, 10004-1562, USA, (800) 777-4643, orders@palgrave.com, https://www.palgrave.com/us; The Statesman's Yearbook, 2023.

Routledge - Taylor & Francis Group, 6000 Broken Sound Pkwy. NW, Ste. 300, Boca Raton, FL, 33487, USA, (800) 634-1420, (800) 634-7064, orders@taylorandfrancis.com, https://www.routledge.com/; The Europa World Year Book 2022.

United Nations Economic Commission for Africa (UNECA), PO Box 3001, Addis Ababa, ETH, ecainfo@uneca.org, https://www.uneca.org/; African Statistical Yearbook 2020.

United Nations Food and Agricultural Organization (FAO), 2121 K St., Ste. 800B, Washington, DC, 20037, USA, (202) 653-2400 (Dial from U.S.), (202) 653-5760 (Fax from U.S.), fao-hq@fao.org, https://www.fao.org; FAO Yearbook of Fishery and Aquaculture Statistics 2019; Fishery Statistical Collections Global Capture Production; FishStatJ; and The State of Food and Agriculture (SOFA) 2022.

United Nations Statistics Division (UNSD), United Nations Plz., New York, NY, 10017, USA, (800) 253-9646, (212) 963-9851, statistics@un.org, https://unstats.un.org; Statistical Yearbook of the United Nations 2021.

The World Bank, 1818 H St. NW, Washington, DC, 20433, USA, (202) 473-1000, (202) 477-6391, eds03@worldbank.org, https://www.worldbank.org/; Central African Republic (report).

CENTRAL AFRICAN REPUBLIC-FOOD

African Development Bank Group (AfDB), Avenue Joseph Anoma, 01 BP 1387, Abidjan, 01, COT, https://www.afdb.org; The AfDB Statistics Pocketbook 2019.

United Nations Food and Agricultural Organization (FAO), 2121 K St., Ste. 800B, Washington, DC, 20037, USA, (202) 653-2400 (Dial from U.S.), (202) 653-5760 (Fax from U.S.), fao-hq@fao.org, https://www.fao.org; The State of Food and Agriculture (SOFA) 2022.

CENTRAL AFRICAN REPUBLIC-FOREIGN EXCHANGE RATES

African Development Bank Group (AfDB), Avenue Joseph Anoma, 01 BP 1387, Abidjan, 01, COT, https://www.afdb.org; The AfDB Statistics Pocketbook 2019 and African Economic Outlook 2021.

CENTRAL AFRICAN REPUBLIC-FORESTS AND FORESTRY

Palgrave Macmillan, 1 New York Plaza, Ste. 4500, New York, NY, 10004-1562, USA, (800) 777-4643, orders@palgrave.com, https://www.palgrave.com/us; The Statesman's Yearbook, 2023.

Routledge - Taylor & Francis Group, 6000 Broken Sound Pkwy. NW, Ste. 300, Boca Raton, FL, 33487, USA, (800) 634-1420, (800) 634-7064, orders@taylorandfrancis.com, https://www.routledge.com/; The Europa World Year Book 2022.

UNESCO Institute for Statistics, C.P 250 Succursale H, Montreal, QC, H3G 2K8, CAN, (514) 343-6880 (Dial from U.S.), (514) 343-5740 (Fax from U.S.), uis.publications@unesco.org, http://uis.unesco.org/; UIS.Stat.

United Nations Economic Commission for Africa (UNECA), PO Box 3001, Addis Ababa, ETH, ecainfo@uneca.org, https://www.uneca.org/; African Statistical Yearbook 2020.

United Nations Food and Agricultural Organization (FAO), 2121 K St., Ste. 800B, Washington, DC, 20037, USA, (202) 653-2400 (Dial from U.S.), (202) 653-5760 (Fax from U.S.), fao-hq@fao.org, https://www.fao.org; FAO Yearbook of Forest Products 2019 and The State of Food and Agriculture (SOFA) 2022.

United Nations Statistics Division (UNSD), United Nations Plz., New York, NY, 10017, USA, (800) 253-9646, (212) 963-9851, statistics@un.org, https://unstats.un.org; Statistical Yearbook of the United Nations 2021.

The World Bank, 1818 H St. NW, Washington, DC, 20433, USA, (202) 473-1000, (202) 477-6391, eds03@worldbank.org, https://www.worldbank.org/; Central African Republic (report) and World Development Report 2022: Finance for an Equitable Recovery.

CENTRAL AFRICAN REPUBLIC-GEOGRAPHIC INFORMATION SYSTEMS

The World Bank, 1818 H St. NW, Washington, DC, 20433, USA, (202) 473-1000, (202) 477-6391, eds03@worldbank.org, https://www.worldbank.org/; Central African Republic (report).

CENTRAL AFRICAN REPUBLIC-GOLD INDUSTRY

The World Bank, 1818 H St. NW, Washington, DC, 20433, USA, (202) 473-1000, (202) 477-6391, eds03@worldbank.org, https://www.worldbank.org/; World Development Indicators (WDI) 2022.

CENTRAL AFRICAN REPUBLIC-GOLD PRODUCTION

See CENTRAL AFRICAN REPUBLIC-MINERAL INDUSTRIES

CENTRAL AFRICAN REPUBLIC-GROSS DOMESTIC PRODUCT

African Development Bank Group (AfDB), Avenue Joseph Anoma, 01 BP 1387, Abidjan, 01, COT, https://www.afdb.org; The AfDB Statistics Pocketbook 2019.

The Economist Group: Economist Intelligence Unit (EIU), 900 3rd Ave., 16th Fl., New York, NY, 10022, USA, (212) 541-0500, americas@eiu.com, https://www.eiu.com; Central African Republic Country Report.

Routledge - Taylor & Francis Group, 6000 Broken Sound Pkwy. NW, Ste. 300, Boca Raton, FL, 33487, USA, (800) 634-1420, (800) 634-7064, orders@taylorandfrancis.com, https://www.routledge.com/; The Europa World Year Book 2022.

United Nations Economic Commission for Africa (UNECA), PO Box 3001, Addis Ababa, ETH, ecainfo@uneca.org, https://www.uneca.org/; African Statistical Yearbook 2020.

United Nations Statistics Division (UNSD), United Nations Plz., New York, NY, 10017, USA, (800) 253-9646, (212) 963-9851, statistics@un.org, https://unstats.un.org; Statistical Yearbook of the United Nations 2021.

The World Bank, 1818 H St. NW, Washington, DC, 20433, USA, (202) 473-1000, (202) 477-6391, eds03@worldbank.org, https://www.worldbank.org/; World Development Indicators (WDI) 2022 and World Development Report 2022: Finance for an Equitable Recovery.

CENTRAL AFRICAN REPUBLIC-GROSS NATIONAL PRODUCT

Palgrave Macmillan, 1 New York Plaza, Ste. 4500, New York, NY, 10004-1562, USA, (800) 777-4643, orders@palgrave.com, https://www.palgrave.com/us; The Statesman's Yearbook, 2023.

The World Bank, 1818 H St. NW, Washington, DC, 20433, USA, (202) 473-1000, (202) 477-6391, eds03@worldbank.org, https://www.worldbank.org/;

World Development Indicators (WDI) 2022 and World Development Report 2022: Finance for an Equitable Recovery.

CENTRAL AFRICAN REPUBLIC-HOUSING

Euromonitor International, Inc., 1 N Dearborn St., Ste. 1700, Chicago, IL, 60602, USA, (312) 922-1115, (312) 922-1157, info-usa@euromonitor.com, https://www.euromonitor.com/; Geographies.

CENTRAL AFRICAN REPUBLIC-ILLITERATE PERSONS

UNESCO Institute for Statistics, C.P 250 Succursale H, Montreal, QC, H3G 2K8, CAN, (514) 343-6880 (Dial from U.S.), (514) 343-5740 (Fax from U.S.), uis.publications@unesco.org, http://uis.unesco.org/; UIS.Stat.

CENTRAL AFRICAN REPUBLIC-IMPORTS

African Development Bank Group (AfDB), Avenue Joseph Anoma, 01 BP 1387, Abidjan, 01, COT, https://www.afdb.org; African Economic Outlook 2021.

Central Intelligence Agency (CIA), Office of Public Affairs, Washington, DC, 20505, USA, (703) 482-0623, https://www.cia.gov; The World Factbook.

The Economist Group: Economist Intelligence Unit (EIU), 900 3rd Ave., 16th Fl., New York, NY, 10022, USA, (212) 541-0500, americas@eiu.com, https://www.eiu.com; Central African Republic Country Report.

International Monetary Fund (IMF), 700 19th St. NW, Washington, DC, 20431, USA, (202) 623-7000, (202) 623-4661, publications@imf.org, https://www.imf.org; Direction of Trade Statistics (DOTS).

S&P Global, IHS Markit, 15 Inverness Way E, Englewood, CO, 80112, USA, (800) 447-2273, (800) 854-7179, https://ihsmarkit.com; Global Trade Atlas (GTA).

United Nations Conference on Trade and Development (UNCTAD), Palais des Nations, Geneva, 1211, SWI, (212) 963-6896, unctadinfo@unctad.org, https://unctad.org; Handbook of Statistics 2021.

The World Bank, 1818 H St. NW, Washington, DC, 20433, USA, (202) 473-1000, (202) 477-6391, eds03@worldbank.org, https://www.worldbank.org/; World Development Report 2022: Finance for an Equitable Recovery.

CENTRAL AFRICAN REPUBLIC-INDUSTRIES

Central Intelligence Agency (CIA), Office of Public Affairs, Washington, DC, 20505, USA, (703) 482-0623, https://www.cia.gov; The World Factbook.

The Economist Group: Economist Intelligence Unit (EIU), 900 3rd Ave., 16th Fl., New York, NY, 10022, USA, (212) 541-0500, americas@eiu.com, https://www.eiu.com; Central African Republic Country Report.

Euromonitor International, Inc., 1 N Dearborn St., Ste. 1700, Chicago, IL, 60602, USA, (312) 922-1115, (312) 922-1157, info-usa@euromonitor.com, https://www.euromonitor.com/; Geographies.

International Labour Organization (ILO), 4 Rte. des Morillons, Geneva, CH-1211, SWI, ilo@ilo.org, https://www.ilo.org; NORMLEX Information System on International Labour Standards.

Palgrave Macmillan, 1 New York Plaza, Ste. 4500, New York, NY, 10004-1562, USA, (800) 777-4643, orders@palgrave.com, https://www.palgrave.com/us; The Statesman's Yearbook, 2023.

Routledge - Taylor & Francis Group, 6000 Broken Sound Pkwy. NW, Ste. 300, Boca Raton, FL, 33487, USA, (800) 634-1420, (800) 634-7064, orders@taylorandfrancis.com, https://www.routledge.com/; The Europa World Year Book 2022.

United Nations Economic Commission for Africa (UNECA), PO Box 3001, Addis Ababa, ETH, ecainfo@uneca.org, https://www.uneca.org/; African Statistical Yearbook 2020.

United Nations Industrial Development Organization (UNIDO), 1 United Nations Plz., Rm. DC1-1118, New York, NY, 10017, USA, (212) 963-6890, (212) 963 6885, (212) 963-7904, office.newyork@unido.org, https://www.unido.org/; Industrial Statistics Databases and International Yearbook of Industrial Statistics 2021.

The World Bank, 1818 H St. NW, Washington, DC, 20433, USA, (202) 473-1000, (202) 477-6391, eds03@worldbank.org, https://www.worldbank.org/; Central African Republic (report) and World Development Indicators (WDI) 2022.

CENTRAL AFRICAN REPUBLIC-INFANT AND MATERNAL MORTALITY

See CENTRAL AFRICAN REPUBLIC-MORTALITY

CENTRAL AFRICAN REPUBLIC-INTERNATIONAL TRADE

African Development Bank Group (AfDB), Avenue Joseph Anoma, 01 BP 1387, Abidjan, 01, COT, https://www.afdb.org; The AfDB Statistics Pocketbook 2019 and African Economic Outlook 2021.

The Economist Group: Economist Intelligence Unit (EIU), 900 3rd Ave., 16th Fl., New York, NY, 10022, USA, (212) 541-0500, americas@eiu.com, https://www.eiu.com; Central African Republic Country Report.

Euromonitor International, Inc., 1 N Dearborn St., Ste. 1700, Chicago, IL, 60602, USA, (312) 922-1115, (312) 922-1157, info-usa@euromonitor.com, https://www.euromonitor.com/; Geographies.

Palgrave Macmillan, 1 New York Plaza, Ste. 4500, New York, NY, 10004-1562, USA, (800) 777-4643, orders@palgrave.com, https://www.palgrave.com/us; The Statesman's Yearbook, 2023.

Routledge - Taylor & Francis Group, 6000 Broken Sound Pkwy. NW, Ste. 300, Boca Raton, FL, 33487, USA, (800) 634-1420, (800) 634-7064, orders@taylorandfrancis.com, https://www.routledge.com/; The Europa World Year Book 2022.

United Nations Conference on Trade and Development (UNCTAD), Palais des Nations, Geneva, 1211, SWI, (212) 963-6896, unctadinfo@unctad.org, https://unctad.org; Trade and Development Report 2021.

United Nations Economic Commission for Africa (UNECA), PO Box 3001, Addis Ababa, ETH, ecainfo@uneca.org, https://www.uneca.org/; African Statistical Yearbook 2020.

United Nations Food and Agricultural Organization (FAO), 2121 K St., Ste. 800B, Washington, DC, 20037, USA, (202) 653-2400 (Dial from U.S.), (202) 653-5760 (Fax from U.S.), fao-hq@fao.org, https://www.fao.org; The State of Food and Agriculture (SOFA) 2022.

United Nations Statistics Division (UNSD), United Nations Plz., New York, NY, 10017, USA, (800) 253-9646, (212) 963-9851, statistics@un.org, https://unstats.un.org; Statistical Yearbook of the United Nations 2021.

The World Bank, 1818 H St. NW, Washington, DC, 20433, USA, (202) 473-1000, (202) 477-6391, eds03@worldbank.org, https://www.worldbank.org/; Central African Republic (report); World Development Indicators (WDI) 2022; and World Development Report 2022: Finance for an Equitable Recovery.

World Trade Organization (WTO), Ctre. William Rappard, Rue de Lausanne 154, Case postale, Geneva, CH-1211, SWI, enquiries@wto.org, https://www.wto.org; World Trade Statistical Review 2022.

CENTRAL AFRICAN REPUBLIC-INTERNET USERS

International Telecommunication Union (ITU), Place des Nations, Geneva, CH-1211, SWI, itumail@itu.int, https://www.itu.int; Global Connectivity Report 2022; World Telecommunication/ICT Indicators Database 2021; and Yearbook of Statistics 2019.

The World Bank, 1818 H St. NW, Washington, DC, 20433, USA, (202) 473-1000, (202) 477-6391, eds03@worldbank.org, https://www.worldbank.org/; Central African Republic (report).

CENTRAL AFRICAN REPUBLIC-LABOR

African Development Bank Group (AfDB), Avenue Joseph Anoma, 01 BP 1387, Abidjan, 01, COT, https://www.afdb.org; The AfDB Statistics Pocketbook 2019.

Central Intelligence Agency (CIA), Office of Public Affairs, Washington, DC, 20505, USA, (703) 482-0623, https://www.cia.gov; The World Factbook.

Euromonitor International, Inc., 1 N Dearborn St., Ste. 1700, Chicago, IL, 60602, USA, (312) 922-1115, (312) 922-1157, info-usa@euromonitor.com, https://www.euromonitor.com/; Geographies.

International Labour Organization (ILO), 4 Rte. des Morillons, Geneva, CH-1211, SWI, ilo@ilo.org, https://www.ilo.org; NORMLEX Information System on International Labour Standards.

Palgrave Macmillan, 1 New York Plaza, Ste. 4500, New York, NY, 10004-1562, USA, (800) 777-4643, orders@palgrave.com, https://www.palgrave.com/us; The Statesman's Yearbook, 2023.

United Nations Food and Agricultural Organization (FAO), 2121 K St., Ste. 800B, Washington, DC, 20037, USA, (202) 653-2400 (Dial from U.S.), (202) 653-5760 (Fax from U.S.), fao-hq@fao.org, https://www.fao.org; The State of Food and Agriculture (SOFA) 2022.

The World Bank, 1818 H St. NW, Washington, DC, 20433, USA, (202) 473-1000, (202) 477-6391, eds03@worldbank.org, https://www.worldbank.org/; World Development Indicators (WDI) 2022 and World Development Report 2022: Finance for an Equitable Recovery.

CENTRAL AFRICAN REPUBLIC-LAND USE

United Nations Statistics Division (UNSD), United Nations Plz., New York, NY, 10017, USA, (800) 253-9646, (212) 963-9851, statistics@un.org, https://unstats.un.org; Millennium Development Goal Indicators.

The World Bank, 1818 H St. NW, Washington, DC, 20433, USA, (202) 473-1000, (202) 477-6391, eds03@worldbank.org, https://www.worldbank.org/; World Development Report 2022: Finance for an Equitable Recovery.

CENTRAL AFRICAN REPUBLIC-LIFE EXPECTANCY

African Development Bank Group (AfDB), Avenue Joseph Anoma, 01 BP 1387, Abidjan, 01, COT, https://www.afdb.org; The AfDB Statistics Pocketbook 2019.

Central Intelligence Agency (CIA), Office of Public Affairs, Washington, DC, 20505, USA, (703) 482-0623, https://www.cia.gov; The World Factbook.

United Nations Department of Economic and Social Affairs (DESA), Population Division, 2 United Nations Plz., Rm. DC2-1950, New York, NY, 10017, USA, (212) 963-3209, (212) 963-2147, population@un.org, https://www.un.org/development/desa/pd/; World Population Ageing 2020 Highlights.

United Nations Statistics Division (UNSD), United Nations Plz., New York, NY, 10017, USA, (800) 253-9646, (212) 963-9851, statistics@un.org, https://unstats.un.org; Millennium Development Goal Indicators.

CENTRAL AFRICAN REPUBLIC-LITERACY

Euromonitor International, Inc., 1 N Dearborn St., Ste. 1700, Chicago, IL, 60602, USA, (312) 922-1115, (312) 922-1157, info-usa@euromonitor.com, https://www.euromonitor.com/; Geographies.

UNESCO Institute for Statistics, C.P 250 Succursale H, Montreal, QC, H3G 2K8, CAN, (514) 343-6880 (Dial from U.S.), (514) 343-5740 (Fax from U.S.), uis.publications@unesco.org, http://uis.unesco.org/; Literacy.

CENTRAL AFRICAN REPUBLIC-LIVESTOCK

Palgrave Macmillan, 1 New York Plaza, Ste. 4500, New York, NY, 10004-1562, USA, (800) 777-4643, orders@palgrave.com, https://www.palgrave.com/us; The Statesman's Yearbook, 2023.

Routledge - Taylor & Francis Group, 6000 Broken Sound Pkwy. NW, Ste. 300, Boca Raton, FL, 33487, USA, (800) 634-1420, (800) 634-7064, orders@taylorandfrancis.com, https://www.routledge.com/; The Europa World Year Book 2022.

United Nations Economic Commission for Africa (UNECA), PO Box 3001, Addis Ababa, ETH, ecainfo@uneca.org, https://www.uneca.org/; African Statistical Yearbook 2020.

United Nations Food and Agricultural Organization (FAO), 2121 K St., Ste. 800B, Washington, DC, 20037, USA, (202) 653-2400 (Dial from U.S.), (202) 653-5760 (Fax from U.S.), fao-hq@fao.org, https://www.fao.org; The State of Food and Agriculture (SOFA) 2022.

United Nations Statistics Division (UNSD), United Nations Plz., New York, NY, 10017, USA, (800) 253-9646, (212) 963-9851, statistics@un.org, https://unstats.un.org; Statistical Yearbook of the United Nations 2021.

CENTRAL AFRICAN REPUBLIC-MARRIAGE

Routledge - Taylor & Francis Group, 6000 Broken Sound Pkwy. NW, Ste. 300, Boca Raton, FL, 33487, USA, (800) 634-1420, (800) 634-7064, orders@taylorandfrancis.com, https://www.routledge.com/; The Europa World Year Book 2022.

CENTRAL AFRICAN REPUBLIC-MINERAL INDUSTRIES

Palgrave Macmillan, 1 New York Plaza, Ste. 4500, New York, NY, 10004-1562, USA, (800) 777-4643, orders@palgrave.com, https://www.palgrave.com/us; The Statesman's Yearbook, 2023.

Routledge - Taylor & Francis Group, 6000 Broken Sound Pkwy. NW, Ste. 300, Boca Raton, FL, 33487, USA, (800) 634-1420, (800) 634-7064, orders@taylorandfrancis.com, https://www.routledge.com/; The Europa World Year Book 2022.

United Nations Conference on Trade and Development (UNCTAD), Palais des Nations, Geneva, 1211, SWI, (212) 963-6896, unctadinfo@unctad.org, https://unctad.org; Trade and Development Report 2021.

United Nations Economic Commission for Africa (UNECA), PO Box 3001, Addis Ababa, ETH, ecainfo@uneca.org, https://www.uneca.org/; African Statistical Yearbook 2020.

United Nations Statistics Division (UNSD), United Nations Plz., New York, NY, 10017, USA, (800) 253-9646, (212) 963-9851, statistics@un.org, https://unstats.un.org; Statistical Yearbook of the United Nations 2021.

CENTRAL AFRICAN REPUBLIC-MONEY SUPPLY

The Economist Group: Economist Intelligence Unit (EIU), 900 3rd Ave., 16th Fl., New York, NY, 10022, USA, (212) 541-0500, americas@eiu.com, https://www.eiu.com; Central African Republic Country Report.

Routledge - Taylor & Francis Group, 6000 Broken Sound Pkwy. NW, Ste. 300, Boca Raton, FL, 33487, USA, (800) 634-1420, (800) 634-7064, orders@taylorandfrancis.com, https://www.routledge.com/; The Europa World Year Book 2022.

United Nations Statistics Division (UNSD), United Nations Plz., New York, NY, 10017, USA, (800) 253-9646, (212) 963-9851, statistics@un.org, https://unstats.un.org; Statistical Yearbook of the United Nations 2021.

The World Bank, 1818 H St. NW, Washington, DC, 20433, USA, (202) 473-1000, (202) 477-6391, eds03@worldbank.org, https://www.worldbank.org/; Central African Republic (report).

CENTRAL AFRICAN REPUBLIC-MONUMENTS AND HISTORIC SITES

UNESCO Institute for Statistics, C.P 250 Succursale H, Montreal, QC, H3G 2K8, CAN, (514) 343-6880 (Dial from U.S.), (514) 343-5740 (Fax from U.S.), uis.publications@unesco.org, http://uis.unesco.org/; UIS.Stat.

CENTRAL AFRICAN REPUBLIC-MORTALITY

UNICEF, 3 United Nations Plz., New York, NY, 10017, USA, (212) 303-7984, (917) 244-2215, https://www.unicef.org; The State of the World's Children 2023.

United Nations Statistics Division (UNSD), United Nations Plz., New York, NY, 10017, USA, (800) 253-9646, (212) 963-9851, statistics@un.org, https://unstats.un.org; Millennium Development Goal Indicators; Statistical Yearbook of the United Nations 2021; and World Statistics Pocketbook 2021.

The World Bank, 1818 H St. NW, Washington, DC, 20433, USA, (202) 473-1000, (202) 477-6391, eds03@worldbank.org, https://www.worldbank.org/; World Development Indicators (WDI) 2022.

World Health Organization (WHO), Ave. Appia 20, Geneva, CH-1211, SWI, (202) 974-3000 (Telephone in U.S.), publications@who.int, https://www.who.int/; Global Health Observatory (GHO) and Health Statistics and Information Systems.

CENTRAL AFRICAN REPUBLIC-MOTION PICTURES

Palgrave Macmillan, 1 New York Plaza, Ste. 4500, New York, NY, 10004-1562, USA, (800) 777-4643, orders@palgrave.com, https://www.palgrave.com/us; The Statesman's Yearbook, 2023.

CENTRAL AFRICAN REPUBLIC-MOTOR VEHICLES

International Road Federation (IRF), Madison Place, 500 Montgomery St., 5th Fl., Alexandria, VA, 22314, USA, (703) 535-1001, (703) 535-1007, info@irf.global, https://www.irf.global/; World Road Statistics (WRS).

CENTRAL AFRICAN REPUBLIC-NATURAL GAS PRODUCTION

See CENTRAL AFRICAN REPUBLIC-MINERAL INDUSTRIES

CENTRAL AFRICAN REPUBLIC-NUTRITION

United Nations Food and Agricultural Organization (FAO), 2121 K St., Ste. 800B, Washington, DC, 20037, USA, (202) 653-2400 (Dial from U.S.), (202) 653-5760 (Fax from U.S.), fao-hq@fao.org, https://www.fao.org; The State of Food and Agriculture (SOFA) 2022.

United Nations Statistics Division (UNSD), United Nations Plz., New York, NY, 10017, USA, (800) 253-9646, (212) 963-9851, statistics@un.org, https://unstats.un.org; Millennium Development Goal Indicators.

CENTRAL AFRICAN REPUBLIC-PAPER

See CENTRAL AFRICAN REPUBLIC-FORESTS AND FORESTRY

CENTRAL AFRICAN REPUBLIC-PEANUT PRODUCTION

See CENTRAL AFRICAN REPUBLIC-CROPS

CENTRAL AFRICAN REPUBLIC-PESTICIDES

United Nations Food and Agricultural Organization (FAO), 2121 K St., Ste. 800B, Washington, DC, 20037, USA, (202) 653-2400 (Dial from U.S.), (202) 653-5760 (Fax from U.S.), fao-hq@fao.org, https://www.fao.org; The State of Food and Agriculture (SOFA) 2022.

CENTRAL AFRICAN REPUBLIC-PETROLEUM INDUSTRY AND TRADE

United Nations Food and Agricultural Organization (FAO), 2121 K St., Ste. 800B, Washington, DC, 20037, USA, (202) 653-2400 (Dial from U.S.), (202) 653-5760 (Fax from U.S.), fao-hq@fao.org, https://www.fao.org; The State of Food and Agriculture (SOFA) 2022.

CENTRAL AFRICAN REPUBLIC-POPULATION

African Development Bank Group (AfDB), Avenue Joseph Anoma, 01 BP 1387, Abidjan, 01, COT, https://www.afdb.org; The AfDB Statistics Pocketbook 2019; Africa Economic Brief - COVID-19 Pandemic Potential Risks for Trade and Trade Finance in Africa; The African Statistical Journal; and Gender, Poverty and Environmental Indicators on African Countries 2019.

Central Intelligence Agency (CIA), Office of Public Affairs, Washington, DC, 20505, USA, (703) 482-0623, https://www.cia.gov; The World Factbook.

The Economist Group: Economist Intelligence Unit (EIU), 900 3rd Ave., 16th Fl., New York, NY, 10022, USA, (212) 541-0500, americas@eiu.com, https://www.eiu.com; Central African Republic Country Report.

European Commission, Eurostat, Luxembourg, 2920, LUX, https://ec.europa.eu/eurostat/; EU in the World 2020.

Infoplease, c/o Sandbox Networks, Inc., 1 Lincoln St., 24th Fl., Boston, MA, 02111, USA, https://www.infoplease.com; Countries of the World.

International Labour Organization (ILO), 4 Rte. des Morillons, Geneva, CH-1211, SWI, ilo@ilo.org, https://www.ilo.org; NORMLEX Information System on International Labour Standards.

Palgrave Macmillan, 1 New York Plaza, Ste. 4500, New York, NY, 10004-1562, USA, (800) 777-4643, orders@palgrave.com, https://www.palgrave.com/us; The Statesman's Yearbook, 2023.

Routledge - Taylor & Francis Group, 6000 Broken Sound Pkwy. NW, Ste. 300, Boca Raton, FL, 33487, USA, (800) 634-1420, (800) 634-7064, orders@taylorandfrancis.com, https://www.routledge.com/; The Europa World Year Book 2022.

UK Data Service, University of Essex, Wivenhoe Park, Colchester, Essex, CO4 3SQ, GBR, https://ukdataservice.ac.uk/; International Aggregate Data.

UNESCO Institute for Statistics, C.P 250 Succursale H, Montreal, QC, H3G 2K8, CAN, (514) 343-6880 (Dial from U.S.), (514) 343-5740 (Fax from U.S.), uis.publications@unesco.org, http://uis.unesco.org/; UIS.Stat.

United Nations Department of Economic and Social Affairs (DESA), Population Division, 2 United Nations Plz., Rm. DC2-1950, New York, NY, 10017, USA, (212) 963-3209, (212) 963-2147, population@un.org, https://www.un.org/development/desa/pd/; Revision of World Urbanization Prospects and World Population Ageing 2020 Highlights.

United Nations Development Programme (UNDP), One United Nations Plz., New York, NY, 10017, USA, (212) 906-5000, (212) 906-5001, https://www.undp.org; Human Development Report 2021-2022.

United Nations Statistics Division (UNSD), United Nations Plz., New York, NY, 10017, USA, (800) 253-9646, (212) 963-9851, statistics@un.org, https://unstats.un.org; Statistical Yearbook of the United Nations 2021 and World Statistics Pocketbook 2021.

The World Bank, 1818 H St. NW, Washington, DC, 20433, USA, (202) 473-1000, (202) 477-6391, eds03@worldbank.org, https://www.worldbank.org/; Central African Republic (report); The Global Findex Database 2021; and World Development Report 2022: Finance for an Equitable Recovery.

World Health Organization (WHO), Ave. Appia 20, Geneva, CH-1211, SWI, (202) 974-3000 (Telephone in U.S.), publications@who.int, https://www.who.int/; Health Statistics and Information Systems.

CENTRAL AFRICAN REPUBLIC-POPULATION DENSITY

African Development Bank Group (AfDB), Avenue Joseph Anoma, 01 BP 1387, Abidjan, 01, COT, https://www.afdb.org; The AfDB Statistics Pocketbook 2019.

Central Intelligence Agency (CIA), Office of Public Affairs, Washington, DC, 20505, USA, (703) 482-0623, https://www.cia.gov; The World Factbook.

Palgrave Macmillan, 1 New York Plaza, Ste. 4500, New York, NY, 10004-1562, USA, (800) 777-4643, orders@palgrave.com, https://www.palgrave.com/us; The Statesman's Yearbook, 2023.

Routledge - Taylor & Francis Group, 6000 Broken Sound Pkwy. NW, Ste. 300, Boca Raton, FL, 33487, USA, (800) 634-1420, (800) 634-7064, orders@taylorandfrancis.com, https://www.routledge.com/; The Europa World Year Book 2022.

UNESCO Institute for Statistics, C.P 250 Succursale H, Montreal, QC, H3G 2K8, CAN, (514) 343-6880 (Dial from U.S.), (514) 343-5740 (Fax from U.S.), uis.publications@unesco.org, http://uis.unesco.org/; UIS.Stat.

The World Bank, 1818 H St. NW, Washington, DC, 20433, USA, (202) 473-1000, (202) 477-6391, eds03@worldbank.org, https://www.worldbank.org/; Central African Republic (report) and World Development Report 2022: Finance for an Equitable Recovery.

CENTRAL AFRICAN REPUBLIC-POWER RESOURCES

Euromonitor International, Inc., 1 N Dearborn St., Ste. 1700, Chicago, IL, 60602, USA, (312) 922-1115, (312) 922-1157, info-usa@euromonitor.com, https://www.euromonitor.com/; Geographies.

Palgrave Macmillan, 1 New York Plaza, Ste. 4500, New York, NY, 10004-1562, USA, (800) 777-4643, orders@palgrave.com, https://www.palgrave.com/us; The Statesman's Yearbook, 2023.

United Nations Economic Commission for Africa (UNECA), PO Box 3001, Addis Ababa, ETH, ecainfo@uneca.org, https://www.uneca.org/; African Statistical Yearbook 2020.

United Nations Food and Agricultural Organization (FAO), 2121 K St., Ste. 800B, Washington, DC, 20037, USA, (202) 653-2400 (Dial from U.S.), (202) 653-5760 (Fax from U.S.), fao-hq@fao.org, https://www.fao.org; The State of Food and Agriculture (SOFA) 2022.

United Nations Statistics Division (UNSD), United Nations Plz., New York, NY, 10017, USA, (800) 253-9646, (212) 963-9851, statistics@un.org, https://unstats.un.org; Energy Statistics Yearbook 2019; Statistical Yearbook of the United Nations 2021; and World Statistics Pocketbook 2021.

The World Bank, 1818 H St. NW, Washington, DC, 20433, USA, (202) 473-1000, (202) 477-6391, eds03@worldbank.org, https://www.worldbank.org/; World Development Report 2022: Finance for an Equitable Recovery.

CENTRAL AFRICAN REPUBLIC-PRICES

Euromonitor International, Inc., 1 N Dearborn St., Ste. 1700, Chicago, IL, 60602, USA, (312) 922-1115, (312) 922-1157, info-usa@euromonitor.com, https://www.euromonitor.com/; Geographies.

International Monetary Fund (IMF), 700 19th St. NW, Washington, DC, 20431, USA, (202) 623-7000, (202) 623-4661, publications@imf.org, https://www.imf.org; International Financial Statistics (IFS).

United Nations Economic Commission for Africa (UNECA), PO Box 3001, Addis Ababa, ETH, ecainfo@uneca.org, https://www.uneca.org/; African Statistical Yearbook 2020.

The World Bank, 1818 H St. NW, Washington, DC, 20433, USA, (202) 473-1000, (202) 477-6391, eds03@worldbank.org, https://www.worldbank.org/; Central African Republic (report).

CENTRAL AFRICAN REPUBLIC-PUBLIC HEALTH

African Development Bank Group (AfDB), Avenue Joseph Anoma, 01 BP 1387, Abidjan, 01, COT, https://www.afdb.org; The AfDB Statistics Pocketbook 2019.

Euromonitor International, Inc., 1 N Dearborn St., Ste. 1700, Chicago, IL, 60602, USA, (312) 922-1115, (312) 922-1157, info-usa@euromonitor.com, https://www.euromonitor.com/; Geographies.

Palgrave Macmillan, 1 New York Plaza, Ste. 4500, New York, NY, 10004-1562, USA, (800) 777-4643, orders@palgrave.com, https://www.palgrave.com/us; The Statesman's Yearbook, 2023.

U.S. Census Bureau, 4600 Silver Hill Rd., Washington, DC, 20233, USA, (301) 763-4636, (800) 923-8282, https://www.census.gov; HIV/AIDS Surveillance Data Base.

UNICEF, 3 United Nations Plz., New York, NY, 10017, USA, (212) 303-7984, (917) 244-2215, https://www.unicef.org; The State of the World's Children 2023.

United Nations Department of Economic and Social Affairs (DESA), Population Division, 2 United Nations Plz., Rm. DC2-1950, New York, NY, 10017, USA, (212) 963-3209, (212) 963-2147, population@un.org, https://www.un.org/development/desa/pd/; World Fertility Data 2019.

United Nations Development Programme (UNDP), One United Nations Plz., New York, NY, 10017, USA, (212) 906-5000, (212) 906-5001, https://www.undp.org; Human Development Report 2021-2022.

United Nations Economic Commission for Africa (UNECA), PO Box 3001, Addis Ababa, ETH, ecainfo@uneca.org, https://www.uneca.org/; African Statistical Yearbook 2020.

United Nations Statistics Division (UNSD), United Nations Plz., New York, NY, 10017, USA, (800) 253-9646, (212) 963-9851, statistics@un.org, https://unstats.un.org; Millennium Development Goal Indicators and Statistical Yearbook of the United Nations 2021.

The World Bank, 1818 H St. NW, Washington, DC, 20433, USA, (202) 473-1000, (202) 477-6391, eds03@worldbank.org, https://www.worldbank.org/; Central African Republic (report).

World Health Organization (WHO), Ave. Appia 20, Geneva, CH-1211, SWI, (202) 974-3000 (Telephone in U.S.), publications@who.int, https://www.who.int/; Global Health Observatory (GHO) and Health Statistics and Information Systems.

CENTRAL AFRICAN REPUBLIC-RAILROADS

United Nations Economic Commission for Africa (UNECA), PO Box 3001, Addis Ababa, ETH, ecainfo@uneca.org, https://www.uneca.org/; African Statistical Yearbook 2020.

CENTRAL AFRICAN REPUBLIC-RELIGION

Central Intelligence Agency (CIA), Office of Public Affairs, Washington, DC, 20505, USA, (703) 482-0623, https://www.cia.gov; The World Factbook.

Palgrave Macmillan, 1 New York Plaza, Ste. 4500, New York, NY, 10004-1562, USA, (800) 777-4643, orders@palgrave.com, https://www.palgrave.com/us; The Statesman's Yearbook, 2023.

CENTRAL AFRICAN REPUBLIC-RETAIL TRADE

Euromonitor International, Inc., 1 N Dearborn St., Ste. 1700, Chicago, IL, 60602, USA, (312) 922-1115, (312) 922-1157, info-usa@euromonitor.com, https://www.euromonitor.com/; Geographies.

CENTRAL AFRICAN REPUBLIC-RICE PRODUCTION

See CENTRAL AFRICAN REPUBLIC-CROPS

CENTRAL AFRICAN REPUBLIC-ROADS

International Road Federation (IRF), Madison Place, 500 Montgomery St., 5th Fl., Alexandria, VA, 22314, USA, (703) 535-1001, (703) 535-1007, info@irf.global, https://www.irf.global/; World Road Statistics (WRS).

United Nations Economic Commission for Africa (UNECA), PO Box 3001, Addis Ababa, ETH, ecainfo@uneca.org, https://www.uneca.org/; African Statistical Yearbook 2020.

CENTRAL AFRICAN REPUBLIC-RUBBER INDUSTRY AND TRADE

International Rubber Study Group (IRSG), 51 Changi Business Park Central 2, Unit No. 6, 486066, SGP, https://www.rubberstudy.org; Monthly Rubber Bulletin (MRB); Rubber Industry Report; Rubber Statistical Bulletin; and World Rubber Industry Report (WRIO).

United Nations Statistics Division (UNSD), United Nations Plz., New York, NY, 10017, USA, (800) 253-9646, (212) 963-9851, statistics@un.org, https://unstats.un.org; Statistical Yearbook of the United Nations 2021.

CENTRAL AFRICAN REPUBLIC-SHIPPING

Routledge - Taylor & Francis Group, 6000 Broken Sound Pkwy. NW, Ste. 300, Boca Raton, FL, 33487, USA, (800) 634-1420, (800) 634-7064, orders@taylorandfrancis.com, https://www.routledge.com/; The Europa World Year Book 2022.

United Nations Economic Commission for Africa (UNECA), PO Box 3001, Addis Ababa, ETH, ecainfo@uneca.org, https://www.uneca.org/; African Statistical Yearbook 2020.

CENTRAL AFRICAN REPUBLIC-STEEL PRODUCTION

See CENTRAL AFRICAN REPUBLIC-MINERAL INDUSTRIES

CENTRAL AFRICAN REPUBLIC-SUGAR PRODUCTION

See CENTRAL AFRICAN REPUBLIC-CROPS

CENTRAL AFRICAN REPUBLIC-TAXATION

International Road Federation (IRF), Madison Place, 500 Montgomery St., 5th Fl., Alexandria, VA, 22314, USA, (703) 535-1001, (703) 535-1007, info@irf.global, https://www.irf.global/; World Road Statistics (WRS).

The World Bank, 1818 H St. NW, Washington, DC, 20433, USA, (202) 473-1000, (202) 477-6391, eds03@worldbank.org, https://www.worldbank.org/; World Development Indicators (WDI) 2022.

CENTRAL AFRICAN REPUBLIC-TELEPHONE

Palgrave Macmillan, 1 New York Plaza, Ste. 4500, New York, NY, 10004-1562, USA, (800) 777-4643, orders@palgrave.com, https://www.palgrave.com/us; The Statesman's Yearbook, 2023.

Routledge - Taylor & Francis Group, 6000 Broken Sound Pkwy. NW, Ste. 300, Boca Raton, FL, 33487, USA, (800) 634-1420, (800) 634-7064, orders@taylorandfrancis.com, https://www.routledge.com/; The Europa World Year Book 2022.

United Nations Statistics Division (UNSD), United Nations Plz., New York, NY, 10017, USA, (800) 253-9646, (212) 963-9851, statistics@un.org, https://unstats.un.org; World Statistics Pocketbook 2021.

CENTRAL AFRICAN REPUBLIC-TEXTILE INDUSTRY

Palgrave Macmillan, 1 New York Plaza, Ste. 4500, New York, NY, 10004-1562, USA, (800) 777-4643, orders@palgrave.com, https://www.palgrave.com/us; The Statesman's Yearbook, 2023.

United Nations Statistics Division (UNSD), United Nations Plz., New York, NY, 10017, USA, (800) 253-9646, (212) 963-9851, statistics@un.org, https://unstats.un.org; Statistical Yearbook of the United Nations 2021.

CENTRAL AFRICAN REPUBLIC-TOBACCO INDUSTRY

United Nations Statistics Division (UNSD), United Nations Plz., New York, NY, 10017, USA, (800) 253-9646, (212) 963-9851, statistics@un.org, https://unstats.un.org; Statistical Yearbook of the United Nations 2021.

CENTRAL AFRICAN REPUBLIC-TOURISM

Euromonitor International, Inc., 1 N Dearborn St., Ste. 1700, Chicago, IL, 60602, USA, (312) 922-1115, (312) 922-1157, info-usa@euromonitor.com, https://www.euromonitor.com/; Geographies.

Routledge - Taylor & Francis Group, 6000 Broken Sound Pkwy. NW, Ste. 300, Boca Raton, FL, 33487, USA, (800) 634-1420, (800) 634-7064, orders@taylorandfrancis.com, https://www.routledge.com/; The Europa World Year Book 2022.

United Nations Economic Commission for Africa (UNECA), PO Box 3001, Addis Ababa, ETH, ecainfo@uneca.org, https://www.uneca.org/; African Statistical Yearbook 2020.

United Nations Statistics Division (UNSD), United Nations Plz., New York, NY, 10017, USA, (800) 253-9646, (212) 963-9851, statistics@un.org, https://unstats.un.org; Statistical Yearbook of the United Nations 2021.

The World Bank, 1818 H St. NW, Washington, DC, 20433, USA, (202) 473-1000, (202) 477-6391, eds03@worldbank.org, https://www.worldbank.org/; Central African Republic (report).

CENTRAL AFRICAN REPUBLIC-TRADE

See CENTRAL AFRICAN REPUBLIC-INTERNATIONAL TRADE

CENTRAL AFRICAN REPUBLIC-TRANSPORTATION

Central Intelligence Agency (CIA), Office of Public Affairs, Washington, DC, 20505, USA, (703) 482-0623, https://www.cia.gov; The World Factbook.

Euromonitor International, Inc., 1 N Dearborn St., Ste. 1700, Chicago, IL, 60602, USA, (312) 922-1115, (312) 922-1157, info-usa@euromonitor.com, https://www.euromonitor.com/; Geographies.

Palgrave Macmillan, 1 New York Plaza, Ste. 4500, New York, NY, 10004-1562, USA, (800) 777-4643, orders@palgrave.com, https://www.palgrave.com/us; The Statesman's Yearbook, 2023.

Routledge - Taylor & Francis Group, 6000 Broken Sound Pkwy. NW, Ste. 300, Boca Raton, FL, 33487, USA, (800) 634-1420, (800) 634-7064, orders@taylorandfrancis.com, https://www.routledge.com/; The Europa World Year Book 2022.

United Nations Economic Commission for Africa (UNECA), PO Box 3001, Addis Ababa, ETH, ecainfo@uneca.org, https://www.uneca.org/; African Statistical Yearbook 2020.

The World Bank, 1818 H St. NW, Washington, DC, 20433, USA, (202) 473-1000, (202) 477-6391, eds03@worldbank.org, https://www.worldbank.org/; Central African Republic (report).

CENTRAL AFRICAN REPUBLIC-UNEMPLOYMENT

International Labour Organization (ILO), 4 Rte. des Morillons, Geneva, CH-1211, SWI, ilo@ilo.org, https://www.ilo.org; NORMLEX Information System on International Labour Standards.

United Nations Statistics Division (UNSD), United Nations Plz., New York, NY, 10017, USA, (800) 253-9646, (212) 963-9851, statistics@un.org, https://unstats.un.org; Statistical Yearbook of the United Nations 2021.

CENTRAL AFRICAN REPUBLIC-URANIUM PRODUCTION AND CONSUMPTION

See CENTRAL AFRICAN REPUBLIC-MINERAL INDUSTRIES

CENTRAL AFRICAN REPUBLIC-VITAL STATISTICS

U.S. Census Bureau, 4600 Silver Hill Rd., Washington, DC, 20233, USA, (301) 763-4636, (800) 923-8282, https://www.census.gov; HIV/AIDS Surveillance Data Base.

United Nations Department of Economic and Social Affairs (DESA), Population Division, 2 United Nations Plz., Rm. DC2-1950, New York, NY, 10017, USA, (212) 963-3209, (212) 963-2147, population@un.org, https://www.un.org/development/desa/pd/; World Contraceptive Use 2021: Estimates and Projections of Family Planning Indicators and World Marriage Data 2019.

United Nations Statistics Division (UNSD), United Nations Plz., New York, NY, 10017, USA, (800) 253-9646, (212) 963-9851, statistics@un.org, https://unstats.un.org; Statistical Yearbook of the United Nations 2021.

World Health Organization (WHO), Ave. Appia 20, Geneva, CH-1211, SWI, (202) 974-3000 (Telephone in U.S.), publications@who.int, https://www.who.int/; Health Statistics and Information Systems.

CENTRAL AFRICAN REPUBLIC-WAGES

International Labour Organization (ILO), 4 Rte. des Morillons, Geneva, CH-1211, SWI, ilo@ilo.org, https://www.ilo.org; NORMLEX Information System on International Labour Standards.

The World Bank, 1818 H St. NW, Washington, DC, 20433, USA, (202) 473-1000, (202) 477-6391, eds03@worldbank.org, https://www.worldbank.org/; Central African Republic (report).

CENTRAL AFRICAN REPUBLIC-WEATHER

See CENTRAL AFRICAN REPUBLIC-CLIMATE

CENTRAL AFRICAN REPUBLIC-WHEAT PRODUCTION

See CENTRAL AFRICAN REPUBLIC-CROPS

CENTRAL AFRICAN REPUBLIC-WHOLESALE PRICE INDEXES

International Monetary Fund (IMF), 700 19th St. NW, Washington, DC, 20431, USA, (202) 623-7000, (202) 623-4661, publications@imf.org, https://www.imf.org; International Financial Statistics (IFS).

CENTRAL AFRICAN REPUBLIC-WOOL PRODUCTION

See CENTRAL AFRICAN REPUBLIC-TEXTILE INDUSTRY

CENTRAL AMERICA

Migration Policy Institute (MPI), 1275 K St. NW, Ste. 800, Washington, DC, 20005, USA, (202) 266-1940, (202) 266-1900, info@migrationpolicy.org, https://www.migrationpolicy.org/; From Control to Crisis: Changing Trends and Policies Reshaping U.S.-Mexico Border Enforcement.

World Health Organization (WHO), Pan American Health Organization (PAHO), 525 23rd St. NW, Washington, DC, 20037, USA, (202) 974-3000, (202) 974-3663, pubrights@paho.org, https://www.paho.org; A New Agenda for Mental Health in the Americas: Report of the Pan American Health Organization High-Level Commission on Mental Health and COVID-19; Core Indicators 2022; Country Profiles; Health in the Americas+; Pan American Journal of Public Health (PAJPH); Polio Weekly Bulletin; Report on Tobacco Control for the Region of the Americas 2022; and WHO Reveals Leading Causes of Death and Disability Worldwide: 2000-2019.

CENTRAL AND SOUTH AMERICAN POPULATION (HISPANIC ORIGIN)

Bernan Press, 15250 NBN Way, Bldg. C, Blue Ridge Summit, PA, 17214, USA, (301) 459-2255, (800) 865-3457, (800) 865-3450, customercare@bernan.com, https://rowman.com/Page/Bernan; Vital Statistics of the United States 2022: Births, Life Expectancy, Deaths, and Selected Health Data.

U.S. Department of Health and Human Services, Centers for Disease Control and Prevention (CDC), National Center for Health Statistics (NCHS), 3311 Toledo Rd., Hyattsville, MD, 20782-2064, USA, (800) 232-4636, (301) 458-4000, https://www.cdc.gov/nchs; National Vital Statistics Reports (NVSR) and Vital Statistics Online Data Portal.

World Health Organization (WHO), Pan American Health Organization (PAHO), 525 23rd St. NW, Washington, DC, 20037, USA, (202) 974-3000, (202) 974-3663, pubrights@paho.org, https://www.paho.org; A New Agenda for Mental Health in the Americas: Report of the Pan American Health Organization High-Level Commission on Mental Health and COVID-19; Core Indicators 2022; Country Profiles; Health in the Americas+; Pan American Journal of Public Health (PAJPH); Polio Weekly Bulletin; Report on Tobacco Control for the Region of the Americas 2022; and WHO Reveals Leading Causes of Death and Disability Worldwide: 2000-2019.

CEREAL AND BAKERY PRODUCTS-EXPENDITURES-PRICES

U.S. Department of Agriculture (USDA), Economic Research Service (ERS), 1400 Independence Ave. SW, Mail Stop 1800, Washington, DC, 20250-0002, USA, (202) 720-2791, https://www.ers.usda.gov/; Food Price Outlook.

U.S. Department of Labor (DOL), Bureau of Labor Statistics (BLS), Postal Square Bldg., 2 Massachusetts Ave. NE, Washington, DC, 20212-0001, USA, (202) 691-5200, (202) 691-7890, blsdata_staff@bls.gov, https://www.bls.gov; Consumer Expenditure Survey (CE); Consumer Price Index (CPI) Databases; and Monthly Labor Review.

CEREAL AND BAKERY PRODUCTS-INTERNATIONAL TRADE

U.S. Census Bureau, International Trade Program, 4600 Silver Hill Rd., Washington, DC, 20233, USA, (800) 549-0595, eid.international.trade.data@census.gov, https://www.census.gov/foreign-trade; International Trade Data.

CEREBROVASCULAR DISEASE

American Heart Association (AHA), 7272 Greenville Ave., Dallas, TX, 75231, USA, (800) 242-8721, (214) 570-5943, https://www.heart.org; AHA/ACC/HRS Guideline for the Management of Patients with Atrial Fibrillation and Heart Disease and Stroke Statistics.

U.S. Department of Health and Human Services, Centers for Disease Control and Prevention (CDC), 1600 Clifton Rd., Atlanta, GA, 30329-4027, USA, (800) 232-4636, (888) 232-6348 (TTY), cdcinfo@cdc.gov, https://www.cdc.gov; Heart Disease Facts.

CEREBROVASCULAR DISEASE-DEATHS

Bernan Press, 15250 NBN Way, Bldg. C, Blue Ridge Summit, PA, 17214, USA, (301) 459-2255, (800) 865-3457, (800) 865-3450, customercare@bernan.com, https://rowman.com/Page/Bernan; Vital Statistics of the United States 2022: Births, Life Expectancy, Deaths, and Selected Health Data.

U.S. Department of Health and Human Services, Centers for Disease Control and Prevention (CDC), National Center for Health Statistics (NCHS), 3311 Toledo Rd., Hyattsville, MD, 20782-2064, USA, (800) 232-4636, (301) 458-4000, https://www.cdc.gov/nchs; National Vital Statistics Reports (NVSR) and Vital Statistics Online Data Portal.

CERTIFICATES OF DEPOSIT

Board of Governors of the Federal Reserve System, Constitution Ave. NW, Washington, DC, 20551, USA, (202) 452-3000, (202) 263-4869 (TDD), https://www.federalreserve.gov; Federal Reserve Bulletin.

CERVIX UTERI-CANCER

American Cancer Society (ACS), 3380 Chastain Meadows Pkwy NW, Ste. 200, Kennesaw, GA,

30144, USA, (800) 227-2345, https://www.cancer.org; Cancer Facts & Figures 2023; Cancer Treatment & Survivorship Facts & Figures 2022-2024; and Global Cancer Facts & Figures.

Canadian Cancer Society, 55 St. Clair Avenue W, Ste. 500, Toronto, ON, M4V 2Y7, CAN, (888) 939-3333 (Dial from U.S.), (416) 961-7223 (Dial from U.S.), (416) 961-4189 (Fax from U.S.), connect@cancer.ca, https://www.cancer.ca/en; Canadian Cancer Statistics.

Cancer Treatment Centers of America Global, Inc. (CTCA), 5900 Broken Sound Pkwy NW, Boca Raton, FL, 33487, USA, (800) 234-7139, (844) 374-2443, https://www.cancercenter.com/; unpublished data.

The Lancet, 230 Park Ave., New York, NY, 10169, USA, (212) 633-3800, editorial@lancet.com, https://www.thelancet.com/; The Lancet Oncology.

U.S. Department of Health and Human Services (HHS), National Institutes of Health (NIH), National Cancer Institute (NCI), 9609 Medical Center Dr., Bethesda, MD, 20850, USA, (800) 422-6237, nciinfo@nih.gov, https://www.cancer.gov; Annual Report to the Nation on the Status of Cancer; Cancer Stat Facts; and Surveillance, Epidemiology, and End Results (SEER) Incidence Data, 1975-2020.

CESAREAN SECTION DELIVERIES

See CHILDBIRTH-CESAREAN SECTION DELIVERIES

CESIUM

U.S. Department of the Interior (DOI), U.S. Geological Survey (USGS), National Minerals Information Center (NMIC), 12201 Sunrise Valley Dr., Reston, VA, 20192, USA, (703) 648-4920, (703) 648-7971, (703) 648-4995, sfortier@usgs.gov, https://www.usgs.gov/centers/nmic; Mineral Commodity Summaries 2022.

CHAD-NATIONAL STATISTICAL OFFICE

Institut National de la Statistique, des Etudes Economiques et Demographiques Chad (INSEED), BO Box 453, N'Djamena, CHD, info@inseed-td.net, https://www.inseed.td/; National Data Reports (Chad).

CHAD-AGRICULTURE

African Development Bank Group (AfDB), Avenue Joseph Anoma, 01 BP 1387, Abidjan, 01, COT, https://www.afdb.org; African Economic Outlook 2021 and Compendium of Statistics on Bank Group Operations 2019.

The Economist Group: Economist Intelligence Unit (EIU), 900 3rd Ave., 16th Fl., New York, NY, 10022, USA, (212) 541-0500, americas@eiu.com, https://www.eiu.com; Chad Country Report.

Euromonitor International, Inc., 1 N Dearborn St., Ste. 1700, Chicago, IL, 60602, USA, (312) 922-1115, (312) 922-1157, info-usa@euromonitor.com, https://www.euromonitor.com/; Geographies.

Organisation of Islamic Cooperation (OIC), Statistical, Economic and Social Research and Training Centre for Islamic Countries (SESRIC), Kudus Cad. No. 9, Diplomatik Site, Ankara, 06450, TUR, statistics@sesric.org, https://www.sesric.org/; OIC Statistics (OICStat) Database and OIC-Countries in Figures (OIC-CIF).

Palgrave Macmillan, 1 New York Plaza, Ste. 4500, New York, NY, 10004-1562, USA, (800) 777-4643, orders@palgrave.com, https://www.palgrave.com/us; The Statesman's Yearbook, 2023.

Routledge - Taylor & Francis Group, 6000 Broken Sound Pkwy. NW, Ste. 300, Boca Raton, FL, 33487, USA, (800) 634-1420, (800) 634-7064, orders@taylorandfrancis.com, https://www.routledge.com/; The Europa World Year Book 2022.

United Nations Economic Commission for Africa (UNECA), PO Box 3001, Addis Ababa, ETH, ecainfo@uneca.org, https://www.uneca.org/; African Statistical Yearbook 2020 and Economic Report on Africa 2021.

United Nations Food and Agricultural Organization (FAO), 2121 K St., Ste. 800B, Washington, DC, 20037, USA, (202) 653-2400 (Dial from U.S.), (202) 653-5760 (Fax from U.S.), fao-hq@fao.org, https://www.fao.org; AQUASTAT and The State of Food and Agriculture (SOFA) 2022.

United Nations Statistics Division (UNSD), United Nations Plz., New York, NY, 10017, USA, (800) 253-9646, (212) 963-9851, statistics@un.org, https://unstats.un.org; Statistical Yearbook of the United Nations 2021.

The World Bank, 1818 H St. NW, Washington, DC, 20433, USA, (202) 473-1000, (202) 477-6391, eds03@worldbank.org, https://www.worldbank.org/; Chad (report) and World Development Indicators (WDI) 2022.

WRTH Publications Limited, PO Box 290, Oxford, OX2 7FT, GBR, sales@wrth.com, https://www.wrth.com; World Radio TV Handbook 2023.

CHAD-AIRLINES

Palgrave Macmillan, 1 New York Plaza, Ste. 4500, New York, NY, 10004-1562, USA, (800) 777-4643, orders@palgrave.com, https://www.palgrave.com/us; The Statesman's Yearbook, 2023.

Routledge - Taylor & Francis Group, 6000 Broken Sound Pkwy. NW, Ste. 300, Boca Raton, FL, 33487, USA, (800) 634-1420, (800) 634-7064, orders@taylorandfrancis.com, https://www.routledge.com/; The Europa World Year Book 2022.

United Nations Economic Commission for Africa (UNECA), PO Box 3001, Addis Ababa, ETH, ecainfo@uneca.org, https://www.uneca.org/; African Statistical Yearbook 2020.

CHAD-ALUMINUM PRODUCTION

See CHAD-MINERAL INDUSTRIES

CHAD-ARMED FORCES

Central Intelligence Agency (CIA), Office of Public Affairs, Washington, DC, 20505, USA, (703) 482-0623, https://www.cia.gov; The World Factbook.

International Institute for Strategic Studies (IISS) - Americas, 2121 K St. NW, Ste. 600, Washington, DC, 20037, USA, (202) 659-1490, (202) 659-1499, https://www.iiss.org/; Armed Conflict Survey 2021 and The Military Balance 2022.

Palgrave Macmillan, 1 New York Plaza, Ste. 4500, New York, NY, 10004-1562, USA, (800) 777-4643, orders@palgrave.com, https://www.palgrave.com/us; The Statesman's Yearbook, 2023.

Stockholm International Peace Research Institute (SIPRI), Signalistgatan 9, Stockholm, SE 169 72, SWE, https://www.sipri.org/; SIPRI Arms Transfers Database and SIPRI Military Expenditure Database.

CHAD-BALANCE OF PAYMENTS

African Development Bank Group (AfDB), Avenue Joseph Anoma, 01 BP 1387, Abidjan, 01, COT, https://www.afdb.org; The AfDB Statistics Pocketbook 2019.

International Monetary Fund (IMF), 700 19th St. NW, Washington, DC, 20431, USA, (202) 623-7000, (202) 623-4661, publications@imf.org, https://www.imf.org; Balance of Payments Statistics: Annual Report 2021.

Routledge - Taylor & Francis Group, 6000 Broken Sound Pkwy. NW, Ste. 300, Boca Raton, FL, 33487, USA, (800) 634-1420, (800) 634-7064, orders@taylorandfrancis.com, https://www.routledge.com/; The Europa World Year Book 2022.

United Nations Conference on Trade and Development (UNCTAD), Palais des Nations, Geneva, 1211, SWI, (212) 963-6896, unctadinfo@unctad.org, https://unctad.org; Handbook of Statistics 2021.

United Nations Economic Commission for Africa (UNECA), PO Box 3001, Addis Ababa, ETH, ecainfo@uneca.org, https://www.uneca.org/; African Statistical Yearbook 2020.

The World Bank, 1818 H St. NW, Washington, DC, 20433, USA, (202) 473-1000, (202) 477-6391, eds03@worldbank.org, https://www.worldbank.org/; Chad (report); World Development Indicators (WDI) 2022; and World Development Report 2022: Finance for an Equitable Recovery.

CHAD-BANKS AND BANKING

Euromonitor International, Inc., 1 N Dearborn St., Ste. 1700, Chicago, IL, 60602, USA, (312) 922-1115, (312) 922-1157, info-usa@euromonitor.com, https://www.euromonitor.com/; Geographies.

International Monetary Fund (IMF), 700 19th St. NW, Washington, DC, 20431, USA, (202) 623-7000, (202) 623-4661, publications@imf.org, https://www.imf.org; International Financial Statistics (IFS).

Routledge - Taylor & Francis Group, 6000 Broken Sound Pkwy. NW, Ste. 300, Boca Raton, FL, 33487, USA, (800) 634-1420, (800) 634-7064, orders@taylorandfrancis.com, https://www.routledge.com/; The Europa World Year Book 2022.

United Nations Economic Commission for Africa (UNECA), PO Box 3001, Addis Ababa, ETH, ecainfo@uneca.org, https://www.uneca.org/; African Statistical Yearbook 2020.

CHAD-BARLEY PRODUCTION

See CHAD-CROPS

CHAD-BROADCASTING

Central Intelligence Agency (CIA), Office of Public Affairs, Washington, DC, 20505, USA, (703) 482-0623, https://www.cia.gov; The World Factbook.

Euromonitor International, Inc., 1 N Dearborn St., Ste. 1700, Chicago, IL, 60602, USA, (312) 922-1115, (312) 922-1157, info-usa@euromonitor.com, https://www.euromonitor.com/; Geographies.

Palgrave Macmillan, 1 New York Plaza, Ste. 4500, New York, NY, 10004-1562, USA, (800) 777-4643, orders@palgrave.com, https://www.palgrave.com/us; The Statesman's Yearbook, 2023.

CHAD-BUDGET

Central Intelligence Agency (CIA), Office of Public Affairs, Washington, DC, 20505, USA, (703) 482-0623, https://www.cia.gov; The World Factbook.

CHAD-CHILDBIRTH-STATISTICS

The World Bank, 1818 H St. NW, Washington, DC, 20433, USA, (202) 473-1000, (202) 477-6391, eds03@worldbank.org, https://www.worldbank.org/; World Development Indicators (WDI) 2022.

CHAD-CLIMATE

International Institute for Environment and Development (IIED), 235 High Holborn, London, WC1V 7DN, GBR, inforequest@iied.org, https://www.iied.org; Environment & Urbanization.

Palgrave Macmillan, 1 New York Plaza, Ste. 4500, New York, NY, 10004-1562, USA, (800) 777-4643, orders@palgrave.com, https://www.palgrave.com/us; The Statesman's Yearbook, 2023.

CHAD-COAL PRODUCTION

See CHAD-MINERAL INDUSTRIES

CHAD-COFFEE

See CHAD-CROPS

CHAD-COMMERCE

Palgrave Macmillan, 1 New York Plaza, Ste. 4500, New York, NY, 10004-1562, USA, (800) 777-4643, orders@palgrave.com, https://www.palgrave.com/us; The Statesman's Yearbook, 2023.

UK Data Service, University of Essex, Wivenhoe Park, Colchester, Essex, CO4 3SQ, GBR, https://ukdataservice.ac.uk/; International Aggregate Data.

CHAD-COMMODITY EXCHANGES

Barchart, 209 W Jackson Blvd., 2nd Fl., Chicago, IL, 60606, USA, (877) 247-4394, commodities@barchart.com, https://www.barchart.com/cmdty; The cmdty Yearbook 2023; cmdtyStats: Commodity Statistics and Fundamental Data; cmdtyView: Commodity Index; and Commodity Data and Prices.

International Monetary Fund (IMF), 700 19th St. NW, Washington, DC, 20431, USA, (202) 623-7000, (202) 623-4661, publications@imf.org, https://www.imf.org; IMF Primary Commodity Prices.

CHAD-CONSTRUCTION INDUSTRY

United Nations Economic Commission for Africa (UNECA), PO Box 3001, Addis Ababa, ETH, ecainfo@uneca.org, https://www.uneca.org/; African Statistical Yearbook 2020.

CHAD-CONSUMER PRICE INDEXES

Routledge - Taylor & Francis Group, 6000 Broken Sound Pkwy. NW, Ste. 300, Boca Raton, FL, 33487, USA, (800) 634-1420, (800) 634-7064, orders@taylorandfrancis.com, https://www.routledge.com/; The Europa World Year Book 2022.

United Nations Economic Commission for Africa (UNECA), PO Box 3001, Addis Ababa, ETH, ecainfo@uneca.org, https://www.uneca.org/; African Statistical Yearbook 2020.

CHAD-CONSUMPTION (ECONOMICS)

African Development Bank Group (AfDB), Avenue Joseph Anoma, 01 BP 1387, Abidjan, 01, COT, https://www.afdb.org; The AfDB Statistics Pocketbook 2019.

CHAD-COPPER INDUSTRY AND TRADE

See CHAD-MINERAL INDUSTRIES

CHAD-CORN INDUSTRY

See CHAD-CROPS

CHAD-COTTON

See CHAD-CROPS

CHAD-CROPS

International Monetary Fund (IMF), 700 19th St. NW, Washington, DC, 20431, USA, (202) 623-7000, (202) 623-4661, publications@imf.org, https://www.imf.org; International Financial Statistics (IFS).

Palgrave Macmillan, 1 New York Plaza, Ste. 4500, New York, NY, 10004-1562, USA, (800) 777-4643, orders@palgrave.com, https://www.palgrave.com/us; The Statesman's Yearbook, 2023.

United Nations Economic Commission for Africa (UNECA), PO Box 3001, Addis Ababa, ETH, ecainfo@uneca.org, https://www.uneca.org/; African Statistical Yearbook 2020.

United Nations Food and Agricultural Organization (FAO), 2121 K St., Ste. 800B, Washington, DC, 20037, USA, (202) 653-2400 (Dial from U.S.), (202) 653-5760 (Fax from U.S.), fao-hq@fao.org, https://www.fao.org; The State of Food and Agriculture (SOFA) 2022.

United Nations Statistics Division (UNSD), United Nations Plz., New York, NY, 10017, USA, (800) 253-9646, (212) 963-9851, statistics@un.org, https://unstats.un.org; Statistical Yearbook of the United Nations 2021.

CHAD-DAIRY PROCESSING

Palgrave Macmillan, 1 New York Plaza, Ste. 4500, New York, NY, 10004-1562, USA, (800) 777-4643, orders@palgrave.com, https://www.palgrave.com/us; The Statesman's Yearbook, 2023.

United Nations Food and Agricultural Organization (FAO), 2121 K St., Ste. 800B, Washington, DC, 20037, USA, (202) 653-2400 (Dial from U.S.), (202) 653-5760 (Fax from U.S.), fao-hq@fao.org, https://www.fao.org; The State of Food and Agriculture (SOFA) 2022.

CHAD-DEBTS, EXTERNAL

African Development Bank Group (AfDB), Avenue Joseph Anoma, 01 BP 1387, Abidjan, 01, COT, https://www.afdb.org; The AfDB Statistics Pocketbook 2019; African Economic Outlook 2021; and Compendium of Statistics on Bank Group Operations 2019.

United Nations Economic Commission for Africa (UNECA), PO Box 3001, Addis Ababa, ETH, ecainfo@uneca.org, https://www.uneca.org/; Economic Report on Africa 2021.

The World Bank, 1818 H St. NW, Washington, DC, 20433, USA, (202) 473-1000, (202) 477-6391, eds03@worldbank.org, https://www.worldbank.org/; Global Financial Development Report 2019-2020: Bank Regulation and Supervision a Decade after the Global Financial Crisis; World Development Indicators (WDI) 2022; and World Development Report 2022: Finance for an Equitable Recovery.

CHAD-DEFENSE EXPENDITURES

See CHAD-ARMED FORCES

CHAD-DIAMONDS

See CHAD-MINERAL INDUSTRIES

CHAD-ECONOMIC ASSISTANCE

United Nations Statistics Division (UNSD), United Nations Plz., New York, NY, 10017, USA, (800) 253-9646, (212) 963-9851, statistics@un.org, https://unstats.un.org; Statistical Yearbook of the United Nations 2021.

CHAD-ECONOMIC CONDITIONS

African Development Bank Group (AfDB), Avenue Joseph Anoma, 01 BP 1387, Abidjan, 01, COT, https://www.afdb.org; The AfDB Statistics Pocketbook 2019; Africa Economic Brief - COVID-19 Pandemic Potential Risks for Trade and Trade Finance in Africa; African Economic Outlook 2021; The African Statistical Journal; Compendium of Statistics on Bank Group Operations 2019; and Gender, Poverty and Environmental Indicators on African Countries 2019.

Bernan Press, 15250 NBN Way, Bldg. C, Blue Ridge Summit, PA, 17214, USA, (301) 459-2255, (800) 865-3457, (800) 865-3450, customercare@bernan.com, https://rowman.com/Page/Bernan; World Economic Outlook, April 2022.

Central Intelligence Agency (CIA), Office of Public Affairs, Washington, DC, 20505, USA, (703) 482-0623, https://www.cia.gov; The World Factbook.

The Economist Group: Economist Intelligence Unit (EIU), 900 3rd Ave., 16th Fl., New York, NY, 10022, USA, (212) 541-0500, americas@eiu.com, https://www.eiu.com; Chad Country Report.

Euromonitor International, Inc., 1 N Dearborn St., Ste. 1700, Chicago, IL, 60602, USA, (312) 922-1115, (312) 922-1157, info-usa@euromonitor.com, https://www.euromonitor.com/; Geographies.

International Monetary Fund (IMF), 700 19th St. NW, Washington, DC, 20431, USA, (202) 623-7000, (202) 623-4661, publications@imf.org, https://www.imf.org; IMF Data and World Economic Outlook.

Organisation of Islamic Cooperation (OIC), Statistical, Economic and Social Research and Training Centre for Islamic Countries (SESRIC), Kudus Cad. No. 9, Diplomatik Site, Ankara, 06450, TUR, statistics@sesric.org, https://www.sesric.org/; OIC Economic Outlook 2021; OIC Statistics (OICStat) Database; and OIC-Countries in Figures (OIC-CIF).

Palgrave Macmillan, 1 New York Plaza, Ste. 4500, New York, NY, 10004-1562, USA, (800) 777-4643, orders@palgrave.com, https://www.palgrave.com/us; The Statesman's Yearbook, 2023.

Routledge - Taylor & Francis Group, 6000 Broken Sound Pkwy. NW, Ste. 300, Boca Raton, FL, 33487, USA, (800) 634-1420, (800) 634-7064, orders@taylorandfrancis.com, https://www.routledge.com/; The Europa World Year Book 2022.

United Nations Economic Commission for Africa (UNECA), PO Box 3001, Addis Ababa, ETH, ecainfo@uneca.org, https://www.uneca.org/; Economic Report on Africa 2021.

United Nations Statistics Division (UNSD), United Nations Plz., New York, NY, 10017, USA, (800) 253-9646, (212) 963-9851, statistics@un.org, https://unstats.un.org; World Statistics Pocketbook 2021.

The World Bank, 1818 H St. NW, Washington, DC, 20433, USA, (202) 473-1000, (202) 477-6391, eds03@worldbank.org, https://www.worldbank.org/; Chad (report); Global Economic Monitor (GEM); Global Economic Prospects, June 2022; The Global Findex Database 2021; and World Development Report 2022: Finance for an Equitable Recovery.

CHAD-EDUCATION

African Development Bank Group (AfDB), Avenue Joseph Anoma, 01 BP 1387, Abidjan, 01, COT, https://www.afdb.org; The AfDB Statistics Pocketbook 2019.

Euromonitor International, Inc., 1 N Dearborn St., Ste. 1700, Chicago, IL, 60602, USA, (312) 922-1115, (312) 922-1157, info-usa@euromonitor.com, https://www.euromonitor.com/; Geographies.

Infoplease, c/o Sandbox Networks, Inc., 1 Lincoln St., 24th Fl., Boston, MA, 02111, USA, https://www.infoplease.com; Countries of the World.

Organisation of Islamic Cooperation (OIC), Statistical, Economic and Social Research and Training Centre for Islamic Countries (SESRIC), Kudus Cad. No. 9, Diplomatik Site, Ankara, 06450, TUR, statistics@sesric.org, https://www.sesric.org/; OIC Statistics (OICStat) Database.

Palgrave Macmillan, 1 New York Plaza, Ste. 4500, New York, NY, 10004-1562, USA, (800) 777-4643, orders@palgrave.com, https://www.palgrave.com/us; The Statesman's Yearbook, 2023.

Routledge - Taylor & Francis Group, 6000 Broken Sound Pkwy. NW, Ste. 300, Boca Raton, FL, 33487, USA, (800) 634-1420, (800) 634-7064, orders@taylorandfrancis.com, https://www.routledge.com/; The Europa World Year Book 2022.

UNESCO Institute for Statistics, C.P 250 Succursale H, Montreal, QC, H3G 2K8, CAN, (514) 343-6880 (Dial from U.S.), (514) 343-5740 (Fax from U.S.), uis.publications@unesco.org, http://uis.unesco.org/; Literacy and UIS.Stat.

United Nations Economic Commission for Africa (UNECA), PO Box 3001, Addis Ababa, ETH, ecainfo@uneca.org, https://www.uneca.org/; African Statistical Yearbook 2020.

United Nations Statistics Division (UNSD), United Nations Plz., New York, NY, 10017, USA, (800) 253-9646, (212) 963-9851, statistics@un.org, https://unstats.un.org; Millennium Development Goal Indicators.

The World Bank, 1818 H St. NW, Washington, DC, 20433, USA, (202) 473-1000, (202) 477-6391, eds03@worldbank.org, https://www.worldbank.org/; Chad (report); World Development Indicators (WDI) 2022; and World Development Report 2022: Finance for an Equitable Recovery.

CHAD-ELECTRICITY

United Nations Statistics Division (UNSD), United Nations Plz., New York, NY, 10017, USA, (800) 253-9646, (212) 963-9851, statistics@un.org, https://unstats.un.org; Statistical Yearbook of the United Nations 2021.

CHAD-EMPLOYMENT

International Labour Organization (ILO), 4 Rte. des Morillons, Geneva, CH-1211, SWI, ilo@ilo.org, https://www.ilo.org; NORMLEX Information System on International Labour Standards.

UK Data Service, University of Essex, Wivenhoe Park, Colchester, Essex, CO4 3SQ, GBR, https://ukdataservice.ac.uk/; International Aggregate Data.

United Nations Economic Commission for Africa (UNECA), PO Box 3001, Addis Ababa, ETH, ecainfo@uneca.org, https://www.uneca.org/; African Statistical Yearbook 2020.

The World Bank, 1818 H St. NW, Washington, DC, 20433, USA, (202) 473-1000, (202) 477-6391, eds03@worldbank.org, https://www.worldbank.org/; Chad (report).

CHAD-ENVIRONMENTAL CONDITIONS

DSI Data Service & Information, Xantener Strasse 51a, Rheinberg, D-47495, GER, dsi@dsidata.com, https://www.dsidata.com/; Global Environmental Database.

The Economist Group: Economist Intelligence Unit (EIU), 900 3rd Ave., 16th Fl., New York, NY, 10022, USA, (212) 541-0500, americas@eiu.com, https://www.eiu.com; Chad Country Report.

International Institute for Environment and Development (IIED), 235 High Holborn, London, WC1V 7DN, GBR, inforequest@iied.org, https://www.iied.org; Environment & Urbanization.

Organisation of Islamic Cooperation (OIC), Statistical, Economic and Social Research and Training Centre for Islamic Countries (SESRIC), Kudus Cad. No. 9, Diplomatik Site, Ankara, 06450, TUR, statistics@sesric.org, https://www.sesric.org/; OIC Statistics (OICStat) Database and OIC-Countries in Figures (OIC-CIF).

United Nations Statistics Division (UNSD), United Nations Plz., New York, NY, 10017, USA, (800) 253-9646, (212) 963-9851, statistics@un.org, https://unstats.un.org; World Statistics Pocketbook 2021.

CHAD-EXPORTS

African Development Bank Group (AfDB), Avenue Joseph Anoma, 01 BP 1387, Abidjan, 01, COT, https://www.afdb.org; African Economic Outlook 2021.

Central Intelligence Agency (CIA), Office of Public Affairs, Washington, DC, 20505, USA, (703) 482-0623, https://www.cia.gov; The World Factbook.

The Economist Group: Economist Intelligence Unit (EIU), 900 3rd Ave., 16th Fl., New York, NY, 10022, USA, (212) 541-0500, americas@eiu.com, https://www.eiu.com; Chad Country Report.

International Monetary Fund (IMF), 700 19th St. NW, Washington, DC, 20431, USA, (202) 623-7000, (202) 623-4661, publications@imf.org, https://www.imf.org; Direction of Trade Statistics (DOTS).

Organisation of Islamic Cooperation (OIC), Statistical, Economic and Social Research and Training Centre for Islamic Countries (SESRIC), Kudus Cad. No. 9, Diplomatik Site, Ankara, 06450, TUR, statistics@sesric.org, https://www.sesric.org/; OIC Statistics (OICStat) Database.

S&P Global, IHS Markit, 15 Inverness Way E, Englewood, CO, 80112, USA, (800) 447-2273, (800) 854-7179, https://ihsmarkit.com; Global Trade Atlas (GTA).

United Nations Conference on Trade and Development (UNCTAD), Palais des Nations, Geneva, 1211, SWI, (212) 963-6896, unctadinfo@unctad.org, https://unctad.org; Handbook of Statistics 2021.

The World Bank, 1818 H St. NW, Washington, DC, 20433, USA, (202) 473-1000, (202) 477-6391, eds03@worldbank.org, https://www.worldbank.org/; World Development Report 2022: Finance for an Equitable Recovery.

CHAD-FEMALE WORKING POPULATION

See CHAD-EMPLOYMENT

CHAD-FERTILITY, HUMAN

Central Intelligence Agency (CIA), Office of Public Affairs, Washington, DC, 20505, USA, (703) 482-0623, https://www.cia.gov; The World Factbook.

CHAD-FERTILIZER INDUSTRY

United Nations Food and Agricultural Organization (FAO), 2121 K St., Ste. 800B, Washington, DC, 20037, USA, (202) 653-2400 (Dial from U.S.), (202) 653-5760 (Fax from U.S.), fao-hq@fao.org, https://www.fao.org; The State of Food and Agriculture (SOFA) 2022.

CHAD-FETAL MORTALITY

See CHAD-MORTALITY

CHAD-FINANCE

Stockholm International Peace Research Institute (SIPRI), Signalistgatan 9, Stockholm, SE 169 72, SWE, https://www.sipri.org/; SIPRI Arms Transfers Database and SIPRI Military Expenditure Database.

United Nations Economic Commission for Africa (UNECA), PO Box 3001, Addis Ababa, ETH, ecainfo@uneca.org, https://www.uneca.org/; African Statistical Yearbook 2020.

United Nations Statistics Division (UNSD), United Nations Plz., New York, NY, 10017, USA, (800) 253-9646, (212) 963-9851, statistics@un.org, https://unstats.un.org; Statistical Yearbook of the United Nations 2021.

The World Bank, 1818 H St. NW, Washington, DC, 20433, USA, (202) 473-1000, (202) 477-6391, eds03@worldbank.org, https://www.worldbank.org/; Chad (report).

CHAD-FINANCE, PUBLIC

African Development Bank Group (AfDB), Avenue Joseph Anoma, 01 BP 1387, Abidjan, 01, COT, https://www.afdb.org; The AfDB Statistics Pocketbook 2019.

Bernan Press, 15250 NBN Way, Bldg. C, Blue Ridge Summit, PA, 17214, USA, (301) 459-2255, (800) 865-3457, (800) 865-3450, customercare@bernan.com, https://rowman.com/Page/Bernan; National Accounts Statistics: Analysis of Main Aggregates 2020.

The Economist Group: Economist Intelligence Unit (EIU), 900 3rd Ave., 16th Fl., New York, NY, 10022, USA, (212) 541-0500, americas@eiu.com, https://www.eiu.com; Chad Country Report.

International Monetary Fund (IMF), 700 19th St. NW, Washington, DC, 20431, USA, (202) 623-7000, (202) 623-4661, publications@imf.org, https://www.imf.org; International Financial Statistics (IFS) and Regional Economic Outlook.

Palgrave Macmillan, 1 New York Plaza, Ste. 4500, New York, NY, 10004-1562, USA, (800) 777-4643, orders@palgrave.com, https://www.palgrave.com/us; The Statesman's Yearbook, 2023.

Routledge - Taylor & Francis Group, 6000 Broken Sound Pkwy. NW, Ste. 300, Boca Raton, FL, 33487, USA, (800) 634-1420, (800) 634-7064, orders@taylorandfrancis.com, https://www.routledge.com/; The Europa World Year Book 2022.

United Nations Economic Commission for Africa (UNECA), PO Box 3001, Addis Ababa, ETH, ecainfo@uneca.org, https://www.uneca.org/; African Statistical Yearbook 2020.

United Nations Statistics Division (UNSD), United Nations Plz., New York, NY, 10017, USA, (800) 253-9646, (212) 963-9851, statistics@un.org, https://unstats.un.org; National Accounts Main Aggregates Database and National Accounts Statistics: Main Aggregates and Detailed Tables.

The World Bank, 1818 H St. NW, Washington, DC, 20433, USA, (202) 473-1000, (202) 477-6391, eds03@worldbank.org, https://www.worldbank.org/; Chad (report).

CHAD-FISHERIES

Palgrave Macmillan, 1 New York Plaza, Ste. 4500, New York, NY, 10004-1562, USA, (800) 777-4643, orders@palgrave.com, https://www.palgrave.com/us; The Statesman's Yearbook, 2023.

Routledge - Taylor & Francis Group, 6000 Broken Sound Pkwy. NW, Ste. 300, Boca Raton, FL, 33487, USA, (800) 634-1420, (800) 634-7064, orders@taylorandfrancis.com, https://www.routledge.com/; The Europa World Year Book 2022.

United Nations Economic Commission for Africa (UNECA), PO Box 3001, Addis Ababa, ETH, ecainfo@uneca.org, https://www.uneca.org/; African Statistical Yearbook 2020.

United Nations Food and Agricultural Organization (FAO), 2121 K St., Ste. 800B, Washington, DC, 20037, USA, (202) 653-2400 (Dial from U.S.), (202) 653-5760 (Fax from U.S.), fao-hq@fao.org, https://www.fao.org; FAO Yearbook of Fishery and Aquaculture Statistics 2019; Fishery Statistical Collections Global Capture Production; FishStatJ; and The State of Food and Agriculture (SOFA) 2022.

United Nations Statistics Division (UNSD), United Nations Plz., New York, NY, 10017, USA, (800) 253-9646, (212) 963-9851, statistics@un.org, https://unstats.un.org; Statistical Yearbook of the United Nations 2021.

The World Bank, 1818 H St. NW, Washington, DC, 20433, USA, (202) 473-1000, (202) 477-6391, eds03@worldbank.org, https://www.worldbank.org/; Chad (report).

CHAD-FOOD

African Development Bank Group (AfDB), Avenue Joseph Anoma, 01 BP 1387, Abidjan, 01, COT, https://www.afdb.org; The AfDB Statistics Pocketbook 2019.

United Nations Food and Agricultural Organization (FAO), 2121 K St., Ste. 800B, Washington, DC, 20037, USA, (202) 653-2400 (Dial from U.S.), (202) 653-5760 (Fax from U.S.), fao-hq@fao.org, https://www.fao.org; The State of Food and Agriculture (SOFA) 2022.

CHAD-FOREIGN EXCHANGE RATES

African Development Bank Group (AfDB), Avenue Joseph Anoma, 01 BP 1387, Abidjan, 01, COT, https://www.afdb.org; The AfDB Statistics Pocketbook 2019 and African Economic Outlook 2021.

CHAD-FORESTS AND FORESTRY

Routledge - Taylor & Francis Group, 6000 Broken Sound Pkwy. NW, Ste. 300, Boca Raton, FL, 33487, USA, (800) 634-1420, (800) 634-7064, orders@taylorandfrancis.com, https://www.routledge.com/; The Europa World Year Book 2022.

United Nations Economic Commission for Africa (UNECA), PO Box 3001, Addis Ababa, ETH, ecainfo@uneca.org, https://www.uneca.org/; African Statistical Yearbook 2020.

United Nations Food and Agricultural Organization (FAO), 2121 K St., Ste. 800B, Washington, DC, 20037, USA, (202) 653-2400 (Dial from U.S.), (202) 653-5760 (Fax from U.S.), fao-hq@fao.org, https://www.fao.org; FAO Yearbook of Forest Products 2019 and The State of Food and Agriculture (SOFA) 2022.

The World Bank, 1818 H St. NW, Washington, DC, 20433, USA, (202) 473-1000, (202) 477-6391, eds03@worldbank.org, https://www.worldbank.org/; Chad (report) and World Development Report 2022: Finance for an Equitable Recovery.

CHAD-GOLD INDUSTRY

The World Bank, 1818 H St. NW, Washington, DC, 20433, USA, (202) 473-1000, (202) 477-6391, eds03@worldbank.org, https://www.worldbank.org/; World Development Indicators (WDI) 2022.

CHAD-GOLD PRODUCTION

See CHAD-MINERAL INDUSTRIES

CHAD-GROSS DOMESTIC PRODUCT

African Development Bank Group (AfDB), Avenue Joseph Anoma, 01 BP 1387, Abidjan, 01, COT, https://www.afdb.org; The AfDB Statistics Pocketbook 2019.

The Economist Group: Economist Intelligence Unit (EIU), 900 3rd Ave., 16th Fl., New York, NY, 10022, USA, (212) 541-0500, americas@eiu.com, https://www.eiu.com; Chad Country Report.

Routledge - Taylor & Francis Group, 6000 Broken Sound Pkwy. NW, Ste. 300, Boca Raton, FL, 33487, USA, (800) 634-1420, (800) 634-7064, orders@taylorandfrancis.com, https://www.routledge.com/; The Europa World Year Book 2022.

United Nations Economic Commission for Africa (UNECA), PO Box 3001, Addis Ababa, ETH,

ecainfo@uneca.org, https://www.uneca.org/; African Statistical Yearbook 2020.

United Nations Statistics Division (UNSD), United Nations Plz., New York, NY, 10017, USA, (800) 253-9646, (212) 963-9851, statistics@un.org, https://unstats.un.org; Statistical Yearbook of the United Nations 2021.

The World Bank, 1818 H St. NW, Washington, DC, 20433, USA, (202) 473-1000, (202) 477-6391, eds03@worldbank.org, https://www.worldbank.org/; World Development Indicators (WDI) 2022 and World Development Report 2022: Finance for an Equitable Recovery.

CHAD-GROSS NATIONAL PRODUCT

Palgrave Macmillan, 1 New York Plaza, Ste. 4500, New York, NY, 10004-1562, USA, (800) 777-4643, orders@palgrave.com, https://www.palgrave.com/us; The Statesman's Yearbook, 2023.

United Nations Statistics Division (UNSD), United Nations Plz., New York, NY, 10017, USA, (800) 253-9646, (212) 963-9851, statistics@un.org, https://unstats.un.org; Statistical Yearbook of the United Nations 2021.

The World Bank, 1818 H St. NW, Washington, DC, 20433, USA, (202) 473-1000, (202) 477-6391, eds03@worldbank.org, https://www.worldbank.org/; World Development Indicators (WDI) 2022 and World Development Report 2022: Finance for an Equitable Recovery.

CHAD-HOUSING

Euromonitor International, Inc., 1 N Dearborn St., Ste. 1700, Chicago, IL, 60602, USA, (312) 922-1115, (312) 922-1157, info-usa@euromonitor.com, https://www.euromonitor.com/; Geographies.

CHAD-ILLITERATE PERSONS

UNESCO Institute for Statistics, C.P 250 Succursale H, Montreal, QC, H3G 2K8, CAN, (514) 343-6880 (Dial from U.S.), (514) 343-5740 (Fax from U.S.), uis.publications@unesco.org, http://uis.unesco.org/; UIS.Stat.

CHAD-IMPORTS

African Development Bank Group (AfDB), Avenue Joseph Anoma, 01 BP 1387, Abidjan, 01, COT, https://www.afdb.org; African Economic Outlook 2021.

Central Intelligence Agency (CIA), Office of Public Affairs, Washington, DC, 20505, USA, (703) 482-0623, https://www.cia.gov; The World Factbook.

The Economist Group: Economist Intelligence Unit (EIU), 900 3rd Ave., 16th Fl., New York, NY, 10022, USA, (212) 541-0500, americas@eiu.com, https://www.eiu.com; Chad Country Report.

International Monetary Fund (IMF), 700 19th St. NW, Washington, DC, 20431, USA, (202) 623-7000, (202) 623-4661, publications@imf.org, https://www.imf.org; Direction of Trade Statistics (DOTS).

S&P Global, IHS Markit, 15 Inverness Way E, Englewood, CO, 80112, USA, (800) 447-2273, (800) 854-7179, https://ihsmarkit.com; Global Trade Atlas (GTA).

United Nations Conference on Trade and Development (UNCTAD), Palais des Nations, Geneva, 1211, SWI, (212) 963-6896, unctadinfo@unctad.org, https://unctad.org; Handbook of Statistics 2021.

The World Bank, 1818 H St. NW, Washington, DC, 20433, USA, (202) 473-1000, (202) 477-6391, eds03@worldbank.org, https://www.worldbank.org/; World Development Report 2022: Finance for an Equitable Recovery.

CHAD-INDUSTRIES

Central Intelligence Agency (CIA), Office of Public Affairs, Washington, DC, 20505, USA, (703) 482-0623, https://www.cia.gov; The World Factbook.

The Economist Group: Economist Intelligence Unit (EIU), 900 3rd Ave., 16th Fl., New York, NY, 10022, USA, (212) 541-0500, americas@eiu.com, https://www.eiu.com; Chad Country Report.

Euromonitor International, Inc., 1 N Dearborn St., Ste. 1700, Chicago, IL, 60602, USA, (312) 922-1115, (312) 922-1157, info-usa@euromonitor.com, https://www.euromonitor.com/; Geographies.

International Labour Organization (ILO), 4 Rte. des Morillons, Geneva, CH-1211, SWI, ilo@ilo.org, https://www.ilo.org; NORMLEX Information System on International Labour Standards.

Palgrave Macmillan, 1 New York Plaza, Ste. 4500, New York, NY, 10004-1562, USA, (800) 777-4643, orders@palgrave.com, https://www.palgrave.com/us; The Statesman's Yearbook, 2023.

Routledge - Taylor & Francis Group, 6000 Broken Sound Pkwy. NW, Ste. 300, Boca Raton, FL, 33487, USA, (800) 634-1420, (800) 634-7064, orders@taylorandfrancis.com, https://www.routledge.com/; The Europa World Year Book 2022.

United Nations Economic Commission for Africa (UNECA), PO Box 3001, Addis Ababa, ETH, ecainfo@uneca.org, https://www.uneca.org/; African Statistical Yearbook 2020.

United Nations Industrial Development Organization (UNIDO), 1 United Nations Plz., Rm. DC1-1118, New York, NY, 10017, USA, (212) 963-6890, (212) 963 6885, (212) 963-7904, office.newyork@unido.org, https://www.unido.org/; Industrial Statistics Databases and International Yearbook of Industrial Statistics 2021.

The World Bank, 1818 H St. NW, Washington, DC, 20433, USA, (202) 473-1000, (202) 477-6391, eds03@worldbank.org, https://www.worldbank.org/; Chad (report) and World Development Indicators (WDI) 2022.

CHAD-INFANT AND MATERNAL MORTALITY

See CHAD-MORTALITY

CHAD-INTERNATIONAL TRADE

African Development Bank Group (AfDB), Avenue Joseph Anoma, 01 BP 1387, Abidjan, 01, COT, https://www.afdb.org; The AfDB Statistics Pocketbook 2019 and African Economic Outlook 2021.

The Economist Group: Economist Intelligence Unit (EIU), 900 3rd Ave., 16th Fl., New York, NY, 10022, USA, (212) 541-0500, americas@eiu.com, https://www.eiu.com; Chad Country Report.

Euromonitor International, Inc., 1 N Dearborn St., Ste. 1700, Chicago, IL, 60602, USA, (312) 922-1115, (312) 922-1157, info-usa@euromonitor.com, https://www.euromonitor.com/; Geographies.

Palgrave Macmillan, 1 New York Plaza, Ste. 4500, New York, NY, 10004-1562, USA, (800) 777-4643, orders@palgrave.com, https://www.palgrave.com/us; The Statesman's Yearbook, 2023.

Routledge - Taylor & Francis Group, 6000 Broken Sound Pkwy. NW, Ste. 300, Boca Raton, FL, 33487, USA, (800) 634-1420, (800) 634-7064, orders@taylorandfrancis.com, https://www.routledge.com/; The Europa World Year Book 2022.

United Nations Conference on Trade and Development (UNCTAD), Palais des Nations, Geneva, 1211, SWI, (212) 963-6896, unctadinfo@unctad.org, https://unctad.org; Trade and Development Report 2021.

United Nations Economic Commission for Africa (UNECA), PO Box 3001, Addis Ababa, ETH, ecainfo@uneca.org, https://www.uneca.org/; African Statistical Yearbook 2020.

United Nations Food and Agricultural Organization (FAO), 2121 K St., Ste. 800B, Washington, DC, 20037, USA, (202) 653-2400 (Dial from U.S.), (202) 653-5760 (Fax from U.S.), fao-hq@fao.org, https://www.fao.org; The State of Food and Agriculture (SOFA) 2022.

United Nations Statistics Division (UNSD), United Nations Plz., New York, NY, 10017, USA, (800) 253-9646, (212) 963-9851, statistics@un.org, https://unstats.un.org; International Trade Statistics Yearbook 2020 and Statistical Yearbook of the United Nations 2021.

The World Bank, 1818 H St. NW, Washington, DC, 20433, USA, (202) 473-1000, (202) 477-6391, eds03@worldbank.org, https://www.worldbank.org/; Chad (report); World Development Indicators (WDI) 2022; and World Development Report 2022: Finance for an Equitable Recovery.

World Trade Organization (WTO), Ctre. William Rappard, Rue de Lausanne 154, Case postale, Geneva, CH-1211, SWI, enquiries@wto.org, https://www.wto.org; World Trade Statistical Review 2022.

CHAD-INTERNET USERS

International Telecommunication Union (ITU), Place des Nations, Geneva, CH-1211, SWI, itumail@itu.int, https://www.itu.int; Global Connectivity Report 2022; World Telecommunication/ICT Indicators Database 2021; and Yearbook of Statistics 2019.

The World Bank, 1818 H St. NW, Washington, DC, 20433, USA, (202) 473-1000, (202) 477-6391, eds03@worldbank.org, https://www.worldbank.org/; Chad (report).

CHAD-LABOR

African Development Bank Group (AfDB), Avenue Joseph Anoma, 01 BP 1387, Abidjan, 01, COT, https://www.afdb.org; The AfDB Statistics Pocketbook 2019.

Central Intelligence Agency (CIA), Office of Public Affairs, Washington, DC, 20505, USA, (703) 482-0623, https://www.cia.gov; The World Factbook.

Euromonitor International, Inc., 1 N Dearborn St., Ste. 1700, Chicago, IL, 60602, USA, (312) 922-1115, (312) 922-1157, info-usa@euromonitor.com, https://www.euromonitor.com/; Geographies.

International Labour Organization (ILO), 4 Rte. des Morillons, Geneva, CH-1211, SWI, ilo@ilo.org, https://www.ilo.org; NORMLEX Information System on International Labour Standards.

Organisation of Islamic Cooperation (OIC), Statistical, Economic and Social Research and Training Centre for Islamic Countries (SESRIC), Kudus Cad. No. 9, Diplomatik Site, Ankara, 06450, TUR, statistics@sesric.org, https://www.sesric.org/; OIC Statistics (OICStat) Database.

Palgrave Macmillan, 1 New York Plaza, Ste. 4500, New York, NY, 10004-1562, USA, (800) 777-4643, orders@palgrave.com, https://www.palgrave.com/us; The Statesman's Yearbook, 2023.

United Nations Food and Agricultural Organization (FAO), 2121 K St., Ste. 800B, Washington, DC, 20037, USA, (202) 653-2400 (Dial from U.S.), (202) 653-5760 (Fax from U.S.), fao-hq@fao.org, https://www.fao.org; The State of Food and Agriculture (SOFA) 2022.

The World Bank, 1818 H St. NW, Washington, DC, 20433, USA, (202) 473-1000, (202) 477-6391, eds03@worldbank.org, https://www.worldbank.org/; World Development Indicators (WDI) 2022 and World Development Report 2022: Finance for an Equitable Recovery.

CHAD-LAND USE

United Nations Statistics Division (UNSD), United Nations Plz., New York, NY, 10017, USA, (800) 253-9646, (212) 963-9851, statistics@un.org, https://unstats.un.org; Millennium Development Goal Indicators.

The World Bank, 1818 H St. NW, Washington, DC, 20433, USA, (202) 473-1000, (202) 477-6391, eds03@worldbank.org, https://www.worldbank.org/; World Development Report 2022: Finance for an Equitable Recovery.

CHAD-LIFE EXPECTANCY

African Development Bank Group (AfDB), Avenue Joseph Anoma, 01 BP 1387, Abidjan, 01, COT, https://www.afdb.org; The AfDB Statistics Pocketbook 2019.

Central Intelligence Agency (CIA), Office of Public Affairs, Washington, DC, 20505, USA, (703) 482-0623, https://www.cia.gov; The World Factbook.

United Nations Department of Economic and Social Affairs (DESA), Population Division, 2 United Nations Plz., Rm. DC2-1950, New York, NY, 10017, USA, (212) 963-3209, (212) 963-2147, population@un.org, https://www.un.org/development/desa/pd/; World Population Ageing 2020 Highlights.

United Nations Statistics Division (UNSD), United Nations Plz., New York, NY, 10017, USA, (800) 253-9646, (212) 963-9851, statistics@un.org, https://unstats.un.org; Millennium Development Goal Indicators.

CHAD-LITERACY

Euromonitor International, Inc., 1 N Dearborn St., Ste. 1700, Chicago, IL, 60602, USA, (312) 922-1115, (312) 922-1157, info-usa@euromonitor.com, https://www.euromonitor.com/; Geographies.

UNESCO Institute for Statistics, C.P 250 Succursale H, Montreal, QC, H3G 2K8, CAN, (514) 343-6880 (Dial from U.S.), (514) 343-5740 (Fax from U.S.), uis.publications@unesco.org, http://uis.unesco.org/; Literacy.

CHAD-LIVESTOCK

Palgrave Macmillan, 1 New York Plaza, Ste. 4500, New York, NY, 10004-1562, USA, (800) 777-4643, orders@palgrave.com, https://www.palgrave.com/us; The Statesman's Yearbook, 2023.

Routledge - Taylor & Francis Group, 6000 Broken Sound Pkwy. NW, Ste. 300, Boca Raton, FL, 33487, USA, (800) 634-1420, (800) 634-7064, orders@taylorandfrancis.com, https://www.routledge.com/; The Europa World Year Book 2022.

United Nations Economic Commission for Africa (UNECA), PO Box 3001, Addis Ababa, ETH, ecainfo@uneca.org, https://www.uneca.org/; African Statistical Yearbook 2020.

United Nations Food and Agricultural Organization (FAO), 2121 K St., Ste. 800B, Washington, DC, 20037, USA, (202) 653-2400 (Dial from U.S.), (202) 653-5760 (Fax from U.S.), fao-hq@fao.org, https://www.fao.org; The State of Food and Agriculture (SOFA) 2022.

United Nations Statistics Division (UNSD), United Nations Plz., New York, NY, 10017, USA, (800) 253-9646, (212) 963-9851, statistics@un.org, https://unstats.un.org; Statistical Yearbook of the United Nations 2021.

CHAD-MINERAL INDUSTRIES

Palgrave Macmillan, 1 New York Plaza, Ste. 4500, New York, NY, 10004-1562, USA, (800) 777-4643, orders@palgrave.com, https://www.palgrave.com/us; The Statesman's Yearbook, 2023.

United Nations Conference on Trade and Development (UNCTAD), Palais des Nations, Geneva, 1211, SWI, (212) 963-6896, unctadinfo@unctad.org, https://unctad.org; Trade and Development Report 2021.

United Nations Economic Commission for Africa (UNECA), PO Box 3001, Addis Ababa, ETH, ecainfo@uneca.org, https://www.uneca.org/; African Statistical Yearbook 2020.

The World Bank, 1818 H St. NW, Washington, DC, 20433, USA, (202) 473-1000, (202) 477-6391, eds03@worldbank.org, https://www.worldbank.org/; Chad (report).

CHAD-MONEY SUPPLY

The Economist Group: Economist Intelligence Unit (EIU), 900 3rd Ave., 16th Fl., New York, NY, 10022, USA, (212) 541-0500, americas@eiu.com, https://www.eiu.com; Chad Country Report.

Routledge - Taylor & Francis Group, 6000 Broken Sound Pkwy. NW, Ste. 300, Boca Raton, FL, 33487, USA, (800) 634-1420, (800) 634-7064, orders@taylorandfrancis.com, https://www.routledge.com/; The Europa World Year Book 2022.

United Nations Statistics Division (UNSD), United Nations Plz., New York, NY, 10017, USA, (800) 253-9646, (212) 963-9851, statistics@un.org, https://unstats.un.org; Statistical Yearbook of the United Nations 2021.

The World Bank, 1818 H St. NW, Washington, DC, 20433, USA, (202) 473-1000, (202) 477-6391, eds03@worldbank.org, https://www.worldbank.org/; Chad (report).

CHAD-MORTALITY

United Nations Statistics Division (UNSD), United Nations Plz., New York, NY, 10017, USA, (800) 253-9646, (212) 963-9851, statistics@un.org, https://unstats.un.org; Millennium Development Goal Indicators; Statistical Yearbook of the United Nations 2021; and World Statistics Pocketbook 2021.

The World Bank, 1818 H St. NW, Washington, DC, 20433, USA, (202) 473-1000, (202) 477-6391, eds03@worldbank.org, https://www.worldbank.org/; World Development Indicators (WDI) 2022.

World Health Organization (WHO), Ave. Appia 20, Geneva, CH-1211, SWI, (202) 974-3000 (Telephone in U.S.), publications@who.int, https://www.who.int/; Global Health Observatory (GHO).

CHAD-MOTOR VEHICLES

International Road Federation (IRF), Madison Place, 500 Montgomery St., 5th Fl., Alexandria, VA, 22314, USA, (703) 535-1001, (703) 535-1007, info@irf.global, https://www.irf.global/; World Road Statistics (WRS).

CHAD-NATURAL GAS PRODUCTION

See CHAD-MINERAL INDUSTRIES

CHAD-NUTRITION

United Nations Food and Agricultural Organization (FAO), 2121 K St., Ste. 800B, Washington, DC, 20037, USA, (202) 653-2400 (Dial from U.S.), (202) 653-5760 (Fax from U.S.), fao-hq@fao.org, https://www.fao.org; The State of Food and Agriculture (SOFA) 2022.

United Nations Statistics Division (UNSD), United Nations Plz., New York, NY, 10017, USA, (800) 253-9646, (212) 963-9851, statistics@un.org, https://unstats.un.org; Millennium Development Goal Indicators.

CHAD-PAPER

See CHAD-FORESTS AND FORESTRY

CHAD-PAPER PRODUCTS INDUSTRY

UNESCO Institute for Statistics, C.P 250 Succursale H, Montreal, QC, H3G 2K8, CAN, (514) 343-6880 (Dial from U.S.), (514) 343-5740 (Fax from U.S.), uis.publications@unesco.org, http://uis.unesco.org/; UIS.Stat.

CHAD-PEANUT PRODUCTION

See CHAD-CROPS

CHAD-PESTICIDES

United Nations Food and Agricultural Organization (FAO), 2121 K St., Ste. 800B, Washington, DC, 20037, USA, (202) 653-2400 (Dial from U.S.), (202) 653-5760 (Fax from U.S.), fao-hq@fao.org, https://www.fao.org; The State of Food and Agriculture (SOFA) 2022.

CHAD-PETROLEUM INDUSTRY AND TRADE

United Nations Food and Agricultural Organization (FAO), 2121 K St., Ste. 800B, Washington, DC, 20037, USA, (202) 653-2400 (Dial from U.S.), (202) 653-5760 (Fax from U.S.), fao-hq@fao.org, https://www.fao.org; The State of Food and Agriculture (SOFA) 2022.

CHAD-POPULATION

African Development Bank Group (AfDB), Avenue Joseph Anoma, 01 BP 1387, Abidjan, 01, COT, https://www.afdb.org; The AfDB Statistics Pocketbook 2019; Africa Economic Brief - COVID-19 Pandemic Potential Risks for Trade and Trade Finance in Africa; The African Statistical Journal; and Gender, Poverty and Environmental Indicators on African Countries 2019.

Central Intelligence Agency (CIA), Office of Public Affairs, Washington, DC, 20505, USA, (703) 482-0623, https://www.cia.gov; The World Factbook.

The Economist Group: Economist Intelligence Unit (EIU), 900 3rd Ave., 16th Fl., New York, NY, 10022, USA, (212) 541-0500, americas@eiu.com, https://www.eiu.com; Chad Country Report.

European Commission, Eurostat, Luxembourg, 2920, LUX, https://ec.europa.eu/eurostat/; EU in the World 2020.

Infoplease, c/o Sandbox Networks, Inc., 1 Lincoln St., 24th Fl., Boston, MA, 02111, USA, https://www.infoplease.com; Countries of the World.

International Labour Organization (ILO), 4 Rte. des Morillons, Geneva, CH-1211, SWI, ilo@ilo.org, https://www.ilo.org; NORMLEX Information System on International Labour Standards.

Palgrave Macmillan, 1 New York Plaza, Ste. 4500, New York, NY, 10004-1562, USA, (800) 777-4643, orders@palgrave.com, https://www.palgrave.com/us; The Statesman's Yearbook, 2023.

Routledge - Taylor & Francis Group, 6000 Broken Sound Pkwy. NW, Ste. 300, Boca Raton, FL, 33487, USA, (800) 634-1420, (800) 634-7064, orders@taylorandfrancis.com, https://www.routledge.com/; The Europa World Year Book 2022.

UK Data Service, University of Essex, Wivenhoe Park, Colchester, Essex, CO4 3SQ, GBR, https://ukdataservice.ac.uk/; International Aggregate Data.

UNESCO Institute for Statistics, C.P 250 Succursale H, Montreal, QC, H3G 2K8, CAN, (514) 343-6880 (Dial from U.S.), (514) 343-5740 (Fax from U.S.), uis.publications@unesco.org, http://uis.unesco.org/; UIS.Stat.

United Nations Department of Economic and Social Affairs (DESA), Population Division, 2 United Nations Plz., Rm. DC2-1950, New York, NY, 10017, USA, (212) 963-3209, (212) 963-2147, population@un.org, https://www.un.org/development/desa/pd/; Revision of World Urbanization Prospects and World Population Ageing 2020 Highlights.

United Nations Development Programme (UNDP), One United Nations Plz., New York, NY, 10017, USA, (212) 906-5000, (212) 906-5001, https://www.undp.org; Human Development Report 2021-2022.

United Nations Statistics Division (UNSD), United Nations Plz., New York, NY, 10017, USA, (800) 253-9646, (212) 963-9851, statistics@un.org, https://unstats.un.org; Statistical Yearbook of the United Nations 2021 and World Statistics Pocketbook 2021.

The World Bank, 1818 H St. NW, Washington, DC, 20433, USA, (202) 473-1000, (202) 477-6391, eds03@worldbank.org, https://www.worldbank.org/; Chad (report); The Global Findex Database 2021; and World Development Report 2022: Finance for an Equitable Recovery.

CHAD-POPULATION DENSITY

African Development Bank Group (AfDB), Avenue Joseph Anoma, 01 BP 1387, Abidjan, 01, COT, https://www.afdb.org; The AfDB Statistics Pocketbook 2019.

Central Intelligence Agency (CIA), Office of Public Affairs, Washington, DC, 20505, USA, (703) 482-0623, https://www.cia.gov; The World Factbook.

Palgrave Macmillan, 1 New York Plaza, Ste. 4500, New York, NY, 10004-1562, USA, (800) 777-4643, orders@palgrave.com, https://www.palgrave.com/us; The Statesman's Yearbook, 2023.

Routledge - Taylor & Francis Group, 6000 Broken Sound Pkwy. NW, Ste. 300, Boca Raton, FL, 33487, USA, (800) 634-1420, (800) 634-7064, orders@taylorandfrancis.com, https://www.routledge.com/; The Europa World Year Book 2022.

UNESCO Institute for Statistics, C.P 250 Succursale H, Montreal, QC, H3G 2K8, CAN, (514) 343-6880 (Dial from U.S.), (514) 343-5740 (Fax from U.S.), uis.publications@unesco.org, http://uis.unesco.org/; UIS.Stat.

The World Bank, 1818 H St. NW, Washington, DC, 20433, USA, (202) 473-1000, (202) 477-6391, eds03@worldbank.org, https://www.worldbank.org/; Chad (report) and World Development Report 2022: Finance for an Equitable Recovery.

CHAD-POWER RESOURCES

Euromonitor International, Inc., 1 N Dearborn St., Ste. 1700, Chicago, IL, 60602, USA, (312) 922-1115, (312) 922-1157, info-usa@euromonitor.com, https://www.euromonitor.com/; Geographies.

Palgrave Macmillan, 1 New York Plaza, Ste. 4500, New York, NY, 10004-1562, USA, (800) 777-4643, orders@palgrave.com, https://www.palgrave.com/us; The Statesman's Yearbook, 2023.

United Nations Economic Commission for Africa (UNECA), PO Box 3001, Addis Ababa, ETH, ecainfo@uneca.org, https://www.uneca.org/; African Statistical Yearbook 2020.

United Nations Food and Agricultural Organization (FAO), 2121 K St., Ste. 800B, Washington, DC, 20037, USA, (202) 653-2400 (Dial from U.S.), (202) 653-5760 (Fax from U.S.), fao-hq@fao.org, https://www.fao.org; The State of Food and Agriculture (SOFA) 2022.

United Nations Statistics Division (UNSD), United Nations Plz., New York, NY, 10017, USA, (800) 253-9646, (212) 963-9851, statistics@un.org, https://unstats.un.org; Energy Statistics Yearbook 2019 and World Statistics Pocketbook 2021.

The World Bank, 1818 H St. NW, Washington, DC, 20433, USA, (202) 473-1000, (202) 477-6391, eds03@worldbank.org, https://www.worldbank.org/; World Development Report 2022: Finance for an Equitable Recovery.

CHAD-PRICES

Euromonitor International, Inc., 1 N Dearborn St., Ste. 1700, Chicago, IL, 60602, USA, (312) 922-1115, (312) 922-1157, info-usa@euromonitor.com, https://www.euromonitor.com/; Geographies.

International Monetary Fund (IMF), 700 19th St. NW, Washington, DC, 20431, USA, (202) 623-7000, (202) 623-4661, publications@imf.org, https://www.imf.org; International Financial Statistics (IFS).

United Nations Economic Commission for Africa (UNECA), PO Box 3001, Addis Ababa, ETH, ecainfo@uneca.org, https://www.uneca.org/; African Statistical Yearbook 2020.

The World Bank, 1818 H St. NW, Washington, DC, 20433, USA, (202) 473-1000, (202) 477-6391, eds03@worldbank.org, https://www.worldbank.org/; Chad (report).

CHAD-PUBLIC HEALTH

African Development Bank Group (AfDB), Avenue Joseph Anoma, 01 BP 1387, Abidjan, 01, COT, https://www.afdb.org; The AfDB Statistics Pocketbook 2019.

Euromonitor International, Inc., 1 N Dearborn St., Ste. 1700, Chicago, IL, 60602, USA, (312) 922-1115, (312) 922-1157, info-usa@euromonitor.com, https://www.euromonitor.com/; Geographies.

Organisation of Islamic Cooperation (OIC), Statistical, Economic and Social Research and Training Centre for Islamic Countries (SESRIC), Kudus Cad. No. 9, Diplomatik Site, Ankara, 06450, TUR, statistics@sesric.org, https://www.sesric.org/; OIC Statistics (OICStat) Database.

Palgrave Macmillan, 1 New York Plaza, Ste. 4500, New York, NY, 10004-1562, USA, (800) 777-4643, orders@palgrave.com, https://www.palgrave.com/us; The Statesman's Yearbook, 2023.

U.S. Census Bureau, 4600 Silver Hill Rd., Washington, DC, 20233, USA, (301) 763-4636, (800) 923-8282, https://www.census.gov; HIV/AIDS Surveillance Data Base.

UNICEF, 3 United Nations Plz., New York, NY, 10017, USA, (212) 303-7984, (917) 244-2215, https://www.unicef.org; The State of the World's Children 2023.

United Nations Department of Economic and Social Affairs (DESA), Population Division, 2 United Nations Plz., Rm. DC2-1950, New York, NY, 10017, USA, (212) 963-3209, (212) 963-2147, population@un.org, https://www.un.org/development/desa/pd/; World Fertility Data 2019.

United Nations Economic Commission for Africa (UNECA), PO Box 3001, Addis Ababa, ETH, ecainfo@uneca.org, https://www.uneca.org/; African Statistical Yearbook 2020.

United Nations Statistics Division (UNSD), United Nations Plz., New York, NY, 10017, USA, (800) 253-9646, (212) 963-9851, statistics@un.org, https://unstats.un.org; Millennium Development Goal Indicators and Statistical Yearbook of the United Nations 2021.

The World Bank, 1818 H St. NW, Washington, DC, 20433, USA, (202) 473-1000, (202) 477-6391, eds03@worldbank.org, https://www.worldbank.org/; Chad (report).

World Health Organization (WHO), Ave. Appia 20, Geneva, CH-1211, SWI, (202) 974-3000 (Telephone in U.S.), publications@who.int, https://www.who.int/; Global Health Observatory (GHO) and Health Statistics and Information Systems.

CHAD-RAILROADS

United Nations Economic Commission for Africa (UNECA), PO Box 3001, Addis Ababa, ETH, ecainfo@uneca.org, https://www.uneca.org/; African Statistical Yearbook 2020.

CHAD-RELIGION

Central Intelligence Agency (CIA), Office of Public Affairs, Washington, DC, 20505, USA, (703) 482-0623, https://www.cia.gov; The World Factbook.

Palgrave Macmillan, 1 New York Plaza, Ste. 4500, New York, NY, 10004-1562, USA, (800) 777-4643, orders@palgrave.com, https://www.palgrave.com/us; The Statesman's Yearbook, 2023.

CHAD-RETAIL TRADE

Euromonitor International, Inc., 1 N Dearborn St., Ste. 1700, Chicago, IL, 60602, USA, (312) 922-1115, (312) 922-1157, info-usa@euromonitor.com, https://www.euromonitor.com/; Geographies.

CHAD-RICE PRODUCTION

See CHAD-CROPS

CHAD-ROADS

International Road Federation (IRF), Madison Place, 500 Montgomery St., 5th Fl., Alexandria, VA, 22314, USA, (703) 535-1001, (703) 535-1007, info@irf.global, https://www.irf.global/; World Road Statistics (WRS).

United Nations Economic Commission for Africa (UNECA), PO Box 3001, Addis Ababa, ETH, ecainfo@uneca.org, https://www.uneca.org/; African Statistical Yearbook 2020.

CHAD-RUBBER INDUSTRY AND TRADE

International Rubber Study Group (IRSG), 51 Changi Business Park Central 2, Unit No. 6, 486066, SGP, https://www.rubberstudy.org; Monthly Rubber Bulletin (MRB); Rubber Industry Report; Rubber Statistical Bulletin; and World Rubber Industry Report (WRIO).

CHAD-SHIPPING

United Nations Economic Commission for Africa (UNECA), PO Box 3001, Addis Ababa, ETH, ecainfo@uneca.org, https://www.uneca.org/; African Statistical Yearbook 2020.

CHAD-STEEL PRODUCTION

See CHAD-MINERAL INDUSTRIES

CHAD-SUGAR PRODUCTION

See CHAD-CROPS

CHAD-TAXATION

International Road Federation (IRF), Madison Place, 500 Montgomery St., 5th Fl., Alexandria, VA, 22314, USA, (703) 535-1001, (703) 535-1007, info@irf.global, https://www.irf.global/; World Road Statistics (WRS).

Palgrave Macmillan, 1 New York Plaza, Ste. 4500, New York, NY, 10004-1562, USA, (800) 777-4643, orders@palgrave.com, https://www.palgrave.com/us; The Statesman's Yearbook, 2023.

The World Bank, 1818 H St. NW, Washington, DC, 20433, USA, (202) 473-1000, (202) 477-6391, eds03@worldbank.org, https://www.worldbank.org/; World Development Indicators (WDI) 2022.

CHAD-TELEPHONE

Palgrave Macmillan, 1 New York Plaza, Ste. 4500, New York, NY, 10004-1562, USA, (800) 777-4643, orders@palgrave.com, https://www.palgrave.com/us; The Statesman's Yearbook, 2023.

Routledge - Taylor & Francis Group, 6000 Broken Sound Pkwy. NW, Ste. 300, Boca Raton, FL, 33487, USA, (800) 634-1420, (800) 634-7064, orders@taylorandfrancis.com, https://www.routledge.com/; The Europa World Year Book 2022.

United Nations Statistics Division (UNSD), United Nations Plz., New York, NY, 10017, USA, (800) 253-9646, (212) 963-9851, statistics@un.org, https://unstats.un.org; World Statistics Pocketbook 2021.

CHAD-TEXTILE INDUSTRY

United Nations Statistics Division (UNSD), United Nations Plz., New York, NY, 10017, USA, (800) 253-9646, (212) 963-9851, statistics@un.org, https://unstats.un.org; Statistical Yearbook of the United Nations 2021.

CHAD-THEATER

UNESCO Institute for Statistics, C.P 250 Succursale H, Montreal, QC, H3G 2K8, CAN, (514) 343-6880 (Dial from U.S.), (514) 343-5740 (Fax from U.S.), uis.publications@unesco.org, http://uis.unesco.org/; UIS.Stat.

CHAD-TOBACCO INDUSTRY

United Nations Statistics Division (UNSD), United Nations Plz., New York, NY, 10017, USA, (800) 253-9646, (212) 963-9851, statistics@un.org, https://unstats.un.org; Statistical Yearbook of the United Nations 2021.

CHAD-TOURISM

Euromonitor International, Inc., 1 N Dearborn St., Ste. 1700, Chicago, IL, 60602, USA, (312) 922-1115, (312) 922-1157, info-usa@euromonitor.com, https://www.euromonitor.com/; Geographies.

Organisation of Islamic Cooperation (OIC), Statistical, Economic and Social Research and Training Centre for Islamic Countries (SESRIC), Kudus Cad. No. 9, Diplomatik Site, Ankara, 06450, TUR, statistics@sesric.org, https://www.sesric.org/; International Tourism in the OIC Countries: Prospects and Challenges, 2020 and OIC Statistics (OICStat) Database.

Routledge - Taylor & Francis Group, 6000 Broken Sound Pkwy. NW, Ste. 300, Boca Raton, FL, 33487, USA, (800) 634-1420, (800) 634-7064, orders@taylorandfrancis.com, https://www.routledge.com/; The Europa World Year Book 2022.

United Nations Economic Commission for Africa (UNECA), PO Box 3001, Addis Ababa, ETH, ecainfo@uneca.org, https://www.uneca.org/; African Statistical Yearbook 2020.

United Nations Statistics Division (UNSD), United Nations Plz., New York, NY, 10017, USA, (800) 253-9646, (212) 963-9851, statistics@un.org, https://unstats.un.org; Statistical Yearbook of the United Nations 2021.

United Nations World Tourism Organization (UNWTO), Calle Poeta Joan Maragall 42, Madrid, 28020, SPA, info@unwto.org, https://www.unwto.org/; Yearbook of Tourism Statistics, 2021 Edition.

The World Bank, 1818 H St. NW, Washington, DC, 20433, USA, (202) 473-1000, (202) 477-6391, eds03@worldbank.org, https://www.worldbank.org/; Chad (report).

CHAD-TRADE

See CHAD-INTERNATIONAL TRADE

CHAD-TRANSPORTATION

Central Intelligence Agency (CIA), Office of Public Affairs, Washington, DC, 20505, USA, (703) 482-0623, https://www.cia.gov; The World Factbook.

Euromonitor International, Inc., 1 N Dearborn St., Ste. 1700, Chicago, IL, 60602, USA, (312) 922-1115, (312) 922-1157, info-usa@euromonitor.com, https://www.euromonitor.com/; Geographies.

Organisation of Islamic Cooperation (OIC), Statistical, Economic and Social Research and Training Centre for Islamic Countries (SESRIC), Kudus Cad. No. 9, Diplomatik Site, Ankara, 06450, TUR, statistics@sesric.org, https://www.sesric.org/; OIC Statistics (OICStat) Database.

Palgrave Macmillan, 1 New York Plaza, Ste. 4500, New York, NY, 10004-1562, USA, (800) 777-4643, orders@palgrave.com, https://www.palgrave.com/us; The Statesman's Yearbook, 2023.

Routledge - Taylor & Francis Group, 6000 Broken Sound Pkwy. NW, Ste. 300, Boca Raton, FL, 33487, USA, (800) 634-1420, (800) 634-7064, orders@taylorandfrancis.com, https://www.routledge.com/; The Europa World Year Book 2022.

United Nations Economic Commission for Africa (UNECA), PO Box 3001, Addis Ababa, ETH, ecainfo@uneca.org, https://www.uneca.org/; African Statistical Yearbook 2020.

The World Bank, 1818 H St. NW, Washington, DC, 20433, USA, (202) 473-1000, (202) 477-6391, eds03@worldbank.org, https://www.worldbank.org/; Chad (report).

CHAD-UNEMPLOYMENT

International Labour Organization (ILO), 4 Rte. des Morillons, Geneva, CH-1211, SWI, ilo@ilo.org, https://www.ilo.org; NORMLEX Information System on International Labour Standards.

The World Bank, 1818 H St. NW, Washington, DC, 20433, USA, (202) 473-1000, (202) 477-6391, eds03@worldbank.org, https://www.worldbank.org/; Chad (report).

CHAD-VITAL STATISTICS

U.S. Census Bureau, 4600 Silver Hill Rd., Washington, DC, 20233, USA, (301) 763-4636, (800) 923-8282, https://www.census.gov; HIV/AIDS Surveillance Data Base.

United Nations Department of Economic and Social Affairs (DESA), Population Division, 2 United Nations Plz., Rm. DC2-1950, New York, NY, 10017, USA, (212) 963-3209, (212) 963-2147, population@un.org, https://www.un.org/development/desa/pd/; World Contraceptive Use 2021: Estimates and Projections of Family Planning Indicators and World Marriage Data 2019.

United Nations Statistics Division (UNSD), United Nations Plz., New York, NY, 10017, USA, (800) 253-9646, (212) 963-9851, statistics@un.org, https://unstats.un.org; Statistical Yearbook of the United Nations 2021.

CHAD-WAGES

International Labour Organization (ILO), 4 Rte. des Morillons, Geneva, CH-1211, SWI, ilo@ilo.org, https://www.ilo.org; NORMLEX Information System on International Labour Standards.

The World Bank, 1818 H St. NW, Washington, DC, 20433, USA, (202) 473-1000, (202) 477-6391, eds03@worldbank.org, https://www.worldbank.org/; Chad (report).

CHAD-WEATHER

See CHAD-CLIMATE

CHAD-WHEAT PRODUCTION

See CHAD-CROPS

CHAD-WOOL PRODUCTION

See CHAD-TEXTILE INDUSTRY

CHARITABLE CONTRIBUTIONS

See also PHILANTHROPY

American Academy of Arts & Sciences, 136 Irving St., Cambridge, MA, 02138, USA, (617) 576-5000, https://www.amacad.org/; Humanities Indicators.

Charities Aid Foundation (CAF), 25 Kings Hill Ave., Kings Hill, West Malling, Kent, ME19 4TA, GBR, cafbank@cafonline.org, https://www.cafonline.org/; Charity Search; The Global Response to the COVID-19 Pandemic: Lessons in Compassion, Innovation and Resilience; UK Giving Report 2020: COVID-19 Special Report; UK Giving Report 2022; and World Giving Index 2022.

Charities Aid Foundation of America (CAF America), 225 Reinekers Ln., Ste. 375, Alexandria, VA, 22314, USA, (202) 793-2232, (703) 549-8934, info@cafamerica.org, https://www.cafamerica.org/; Charitable Giving in the USA 2019 and COVID-19 Reports Series.

Charity Navigator, 299 Market St., Ste. 250, Saddle Brook, NJ, 07663, USA, helpandsupport@charitynavigator.org, https://www.charitynavigator.org/; Charities with Perfect Scores and Charity Navigator Search.

CharityWatch, PO Box 578460, Chicago, IL, 60657, USA, (773) 529-2300, https://www.charitywatch.org/; Top Rated Charities.

The Chronicle of Philanthropy, 1255 23rd St. NW, 7th Fl., Washington, DC, 20037, USA, (202) 466-1200, philanthropy@pubservice.com, https://www.philanthropy.com/; America's Favorite Charities 2021; The Chronicle of Philanthropy; and Data & Research.

Council on American-Islamic Relations (CAIR), 453 New Jersey Ave. SE, Washington, DC, 20003, USA, (202) 488-8787, (202) 488-0833, info@cair.com, https://www.islamophobia.org/; Hijacked by Hate: American Philanthropy and the Islamophobia Network.

Giving Institute, 7918 Jones Branch Dr., No. 300, McLean, VA, 22102, USA, (312) 981-6794, (312) 265-2908, info@givinginstitute.org, https://www.givinginstitute.org/; Giving USA 2021: The Annual Report on Philanthropy for the Year 2020.

GuideStar by Candid, 1250 H St. NW, Ste. 1150, Washington, DC, 20005, USA, (800) 421-8656, support@candid.org, https://www2.guidestar.org/; 2022 Nonprofit Compensation Report.

Independent Sector, 1602 L St. NW, Ste. 900, Washington, DC, 20036, USA, (202) 467-6100, (202) 467-6101, info@independentsector.org, https://independentsector.org/; Health of the U.S. Nonprofit Sector Quarterly Review.

Indiana University Lilly Family School of Philanthropy, Women's Philanthropy Institute (WPI), 301 University Blvd., University Hall, Ste. 3000, Indianapolis, IN, 46202-5146, USA, (317) 278-8990, (317) 274-4200, (317) 278-8999, wpiinfo@iupui.edu, https://philanthropy.iupui.edu/institutes/womens-philanthropy-institute/; Women Give 2022: Racial Justice, Gender and Generosity.

Internal Revenue Service (IRS), Statistics of Income Division (SOI), 1111 Constitution Ave. NW, K-Room 4100-123, Washington, DC, 20224-0002, USA, (202) 874-0410, (202) 874-0964, sis@irs.gov, https://www.irs.gov/uac/soi-tax-stats-statistics-of-income; Statistics of Income Bulletin and Tax Stats - Individual Tax Statistics.

The Urban Institute, 500 L'Enfant Plaza SW, Washington, DC, 20024, USA, (202) 833-7200, https://www.urban.org/; The Nonprofit Sector in Brief 2019.

The Urban Institute, National Center for Charitable Statistics (NCCS), 500 L'Enfant Plaza SW, Washington, DC, 20024, USA, (202) 833-7200, https://nccs.urban.org/; National Center for Charitable Statistics (NCCS) Data Archive and The Nonprofit Sector in Brief.

The Wallace Foundation, 140 Broadway, 49th Fl., New York, NY, 10005, USA, (212) 251-9700, (212) 679-6990, https://www.wallacefoundation.org; Knowledge Center.

CHARITIES

Bill and Melinda Gates Foundation, 440 5th Ave. N, Seattle, WA, 98109, USA, (206) 709-3100, info@gatesfoundation.org, https://www.gatesfoundation.org/; 2020 Annual Report of the Bill and Melinda Gates Foundation.

Charities Aid Foundation of America (CAF America), 225 Reinekers Ln., Ste. 375, Alexandria, VA, 22314, USA, (202) 793-2232, (703) 549-8934, info@cafamerica.org, https://www.cafamerica.org/; Charitable Giving in the USA 2019 and COVID-19 Reports Series.

CHARTER SCHOOLS

See SCHOOLS-CHARTER SCHOOLS

CHAUVINISM AND JINGOISM

University of Maryland, National Consortium for the Study of Terrorism and Responses to Terrorism (START), PO Box 266, 5245 Greenbelt Rd., College Park, MD, 20740, USA, (301) 405-6600, (301) 314-1980, infostart@start.umd.edu, https://www.start.umd.edu; Proud Boys Crimes and Characteristics.

CHECKING ACCOUNTS

See BANKS, COMMERCIAL-CHECKING ACCOUNTS

CHEESE

See also DAIRY PRODUCTS

U.S. Department of Agriculture (USDA), Economic Research Service (ERS), 1400 Independence Ave. SW, Mail Stop 1800, Washington, DC, 20250-0002, USA, (202) 720-2791, https://www.ers.usda.gov/; Food Price Outlook.

U.S. Department of Agriculture (USDA), Foreign Agricultural Service (FAS), 1400 Independence Ave. SW, Mail Stop 1001, Washington, DC, 20250, USA, (202) 720-3935, https://www.fas.usda.gov/; Production, Supply and Distribution Online (PSD) Online.

U.S. Department of Agriculture (USDA), National Agricultural Statistics Service (USDA-NASS), 1400 Independence Ave. SW, Washington, DC, 20250, USA, (800) 727-9540, nass@nass.usda.gov, https://www.nass.usda.gov; Dairy Products; Milk Production; and Quick Stats.

U.S. Department of Labor (DOL), Bureau of Labor Statistics (BLS), Postal Square Bldg., 2 Massachusetts Ave. NE, Washington, DC, 20212-0001, USA, (202) 691-5200, (202) 691-7890, blsdata_staff@bls.gov, https://www.bls.gov; Consumer Price Index (CPI) Databases.

CHEFS

American Personal and Private Chef Association (APCA), 4572 Delaware St., San Diego, CA, 92116, USA, (619) 294-2436, (800) 644-8389, https://www.personalchef.com/; unpublished data.

CHEMICALS

Green Science Policy Institute, PO Box 9127, Berkeley, CA, 94709, USA, (510) 898-1739, info@greensciencepolicy.org, https://greensciencepolicy.org/; Fluorinated Compounds in North American Cosmetics.

U.S. Census Bureau, International Trade Program, 4600 Silver Hill Rd., Washington, DC, 20233, USA, (800) 549-0595, eid.international.trade.data@census.gov, https://www.census.gov/foreign-trade; International Trade Data.

U.S. Department of Health and Human Services (HHS), National Toxicology Program (NTP), PO Box 12233, MD K2-03, Research Triangle Park, NC, 27709, USA, (984) 287-3209, cdm@niehs.nih.gov, https://ntp.niehs.nih.gov; Systematic Review of Flouride Exposure and Neurodevelopmental and Cognitive Health Effects.

CHEMICALS-PRODUCER PRICE INDEXES

U.S. Department of Labor (DOL), Bureau of Labor Statistics (BLS), Postal Square Bldg., 2 Massachusetts Ave. NE, Washington, DC, 20212-0001, USA, (202) 691-5200, (202) 691-7890, blsdata_staff@bls.gov, https://www.bls.gov; Consumer Price Index (CPI) Databases and Industry Data (Producer Price Index - PPI).

CHEMICALS-TOXIC CHEMICAL RELEASES

American Chemical Society (ACS), 1155 16th St. NW, Washington, DC, 20036, USA, (800) 227-5558, (202) 872-4600, help@services.acs.org, https://www.acs.org; Population-Wide Exposure to Per- and Polyfluoroalkyl Substances from Drinking Water in the United States.

Bernan Press, 15250 NBN Way, Bldg. C, Blue Ridge Summit, PA, 17214, USA, (301) 459-2255, (800) 865-3457, (800) 865-3450, customercare@bernan.com, https://rowman.com/Page/Bernan; Pesticide Residues in Food 2021 - Joint FAO/WHO Meeting on Pesticide Residues.

Environmental Working Group (EWG), 1250 U St. NW, Ste. 1000, Washington, DC, 20005, USA, (202) 667-6982, https://www.ewg.org/; PFAS Contamination in the U.S..

Greenpeace, 1300 I St. NW, Ste. 1100 E, Washington, DC, 20001, USA, (800) 722-6995, (202) 462-1177, (202) 462-4507, connect@greenpeace.us, https://www.greenpeace.org; Research Brief: Environmental Justice Across Industrial Sectors.

International Tanker Owners Pollution Federation (ITOPF), 55 City Rd., 1 Oliver's Yard, London, EC1Y 1DT, GBR, central@itopf.com, https://www.itopf.org; ITOPF Handbook 2022-2023.

Silent Spring Institute, 320 Nevada St., Ste. 302, Newton, MA, 02460, USA, (617) 332-4288, (617) 332-4284, info@silentspring.org, https://silentspring.org/; Identifying Toxic Consumer Products: A Novel Data Set Reveals Air Emissions of Potent Carcinogens, Reproductive Toxicants, and Developmental Toxicants.

U.S. Department of Health and Human Services (HHS), National Toxicology Program (NTP), PO Box 12233, MD K2-03, Research Triangle Park, NC, 27709, USA, (984) 287-3209, cdm@niehs.nih.gov, https://ntp.niehs.nih.gov; Chemical Effects in Biological Systems (CEBS).

U.S. Department of the Interior (DOI), U.S. Geological Survey (USGS), 12201 Sunrise Valley Dr., Reston, VA, 20192, USA, (888) 392-8545, https://www.usgs.gov/; Per- and Polyfluoroalkyl Substances (PFAS) in United States Tapwater: Comparison of Underserved Private-Well and Public-Supply Exposures and Associated Health Implications.

U.S. Department of the Interior (DOI), U.S. Geological Survey (USGS), National Water-Quality Assessment (NAWQA) Project, 12201 Sunrise Valley Dr., Reston, VA, 20192, USA, (888) 392-8545, (770) 283-9728, msdalton@usgs.gov, https://water.usgs.gov/nawqa/; Is There an Urban Pesticide Signature? Urban Streams in Five U.S. Regions Share Common Dissolved-Phase Pesticides But Differ in Predicted Aquatic Toxicity.

U.S. Environmental Protection Agency (EPA), 1200 Pennsylvania Ave. NW, Washington, DC, 20460, USA, (202) 564-4700, https://www.epa.gov/; Integrated Risk Information System (IRIS) and Toxics Release Inventory (TRI) Program.

CHEMICALS MANUFACTURING-EARNINGS

U.S. Census Bureau, 4600 Silver Hill Rd., Washington, DC, 20233, USA, (301) 763-4636, (800) 923-8282, https://www.census.gov; County Business Patterns (CBP) 2020.

U.S. Department of Labor (DOL), Bureau of Labor Statistics (BLS), Postal Square Bldg., 2 Massachusetts Ave. NE, Washington, DC, 20212-0001, USA, (202) 691-5200, (202) 691-7890, blsdata_staff@bls.gov, https://www.bls.gov; Current Employment Statistics (CES).

CHEMICALS MANUFACTURING-EMPLOYEES

U.S. Census Bureau, 4600 Silver Hill Rd., Washington, DC, 20233, USA, (301) 763-4636, (800) 923-8282, https://www.census.gov; County Business Patterns (CBP) 2020.

U.S. Department of Commerce (DOC), Bureau of Economic Analysis (BEA), 4600 Silver Hill Rd., Washington, DC, 20233, USA, (301) 278-9004, customerservice@bea.gov, https://www.bea.gov; Survey of Current Business (SCB).

U.S. Department of Labor (DOL), Bureau of Labor Statistics (BLS), Postal Square Bldg., 2 Massachusetts Ave. NE, Washington, DC, 20212-0001, USA, (202) 691-5200, (202) 691-7890, blsdata_staff@bls.gov, https://www.bls.gov; Current Employment Statistics (CES) and Industry-Occupation Matrix Data, By Occupation.

CHEMICALS MANUFACTURING-GROSS DOMESTIC PRODUCT

U.S. Department of Commerce (DOC), Bureau of Economic Analysis (BEA), 4600 Silver Hill Rd., Washington, DC, 20233, USA, (301) 278-9004, customerservice@bea.gov, https://www.bea.gov; Survey of Current Business (SCB).

CHEMICALS MANUFACTURING-INDUSTRIAL SAFETY

U.S. Department of Labor (DOL), Bureau of Labor Statistics (BLS), Postal Square Bldg., 2 Massachusetts Ave. NE, Washington, DC, 20212-0001, USA, (202) 691-5200, (202) 691-7890, blsdata_staff@bls.gov, https://www.bls.gov; Injuries, Illnesses, and Fatalities (IIF).

U.S. Environmental Protection Agency (EPA), 1200 Pennsylvania Ave. NW, Washington, DC, 20460, USA, (202) 564-4700, https://www.epa.gov/; Integrated Risk Information System (IRIS).

CHEMICALS MANUFACTURING-INTERNATIONAL TRADE

Directorate-General of Budget, Accounting and Statistics (DGBAS), Republic of China (Taiwan), Jhongsiao East Rd., 1, Section 1, Taipei, 10058, TWN, https://eng.dgbas.gov.tw; Statistical Yearbook of the Republic of China 2020.

U.S. Census Bureau, International Trade Program, 4600 Silver Hill Rd., Washington, DC, 20233, USA, (800) 549-0595, eid.international.trade.data@census.gov, https://www.census.gov/foreign-trade; International Trade Data.

CHEMICALS MANUFACTURING-INVENTORIES

U.S. Census Bureau, 4600 Silver Hill Rd., Washington, DC, 20233, USA, (301) 763-4636, (800) 923-8282, https://www.census.gov; Manufacturers' Shipments, Inventories and Orders.

CHEMICALS MANUFACTURING-MULTINATIONAL COMPANIES

U.S. Department of Commerce (DOC), Bureau of Economic Analysis (BEA), 4600 Silver Hill Rd., Washington, DC, 20233, USA, (301) 278-9004, customerservice@bea.gov, https://www.bea.gov; Survey of Current Business (SCB).

CHEMICALS MANUFACTURING-PATENTS

U.S. Patent and Trademark Office (USPTO), Madison Bldg., 600 Dulany St., Alexandria, VA, 22314, USA, (571) 272-1000, (800) 786-9199, https://www.uspto.gov; Patent Trial and Appeal Board (PTAB) Performance Benchmarks for Dispositions, Pendency, Inventory, and Other Tracking Measures and Patents Data, at a Glance.

CHEMICALS MANUFACTURING-PRODUCTIVITY

U.S. Department of Labor (DOL), Bureau of Labor Statistics (BLS), Postal Square Bldg., 2 Massachusetts Ave. NE, Washington, DC, 20212-0001, USA, (202) 691-5200, (202) 691-7890, blsdata_staff@bls.gov, https://www.bls.gov; Productivity.

CHEMICALS MANUFACTURING-PROFITS

U.S. Census Bureau, 4600 Silver Hill Rd., Washington, DC, 20233, USA, (301) 763-4636, (800) 923-8282, https://www.census.gov; Quarterly Financial Report for Manufacturing, Mining, Trade, and Selected Service Industries.

U.S. Department of Commerce (DOC), Bureau of Economic Analysis (BEA), 4600 Silver Hill Rd., Washington, DC, 20233, USA, (301) 278-9004, customerservice@bea.gov, https://www.bea.gov; National Income and Product Accounts (NIPA): 2022 Update and Survey of Current Business (SCB).

CHEMICALS MANUFACTURING-SHIPMENTS

Association of American Railroads (AAR), 425 3rd St. SW, Washington, DC, 20024, USA, (202) 639-2100, https://www.aar.org; Rail Transportation of Chemicals.

International Tanker Owners Pollution Federation (ITOPF), 55 City Rd., 1 Oliver's Yard, London, EC1Y 1DT, GBR, central@itopf.com, https://www.itopf.org; ITOPF Handbook 2022-2023.

U.S. Census Bureau, 4600 Silver Hill Rd., Washington, DC, 20233, USA, (301) 763-4636, (800) 923-8282, https://www.census.gov; Manufacturers' Shipments, Inventories and Orders.

CHEMICALS MANUFACTURING-TOXIC CHEMICAL RELEASES

U.S. Department of Health and Human Services (HHS), National Toxicology Program (NTP), PO Box 12233, MD K2-03, Research Triangle Park, NC, 27709, USA, (984) 287-3209, cdm@niehs.nih.gov, https://ntp.niehs.nih.gov; Chemical Effects in Biological Systems (CEBS).

U.S. Environmental Protection Agency (EPA), 1200 Pennsylvania Ave. NW, Washington, DC, 20460, USA, (202) 564-4700, https://www.epa.gov/; Integrated Risk Information System (IRIS) and Toxics Release Inventory (TRI) Program.

CHEMISTRY

See also PHYSICAL SCIENCES

American Association for the Advancement of Science (AAAS), 1200 New York Ave. NW, Washington, DC, 20005, USA, (202) 326-6400, https://www.aaas.org; Science and Science Advances.

Elsevier, Radarweg 29, Amsterdam, 1043 NX, NLD, https://www.elsevier.com; ScienceDirect.

CHEMISTRY-EMPLOYMENT

U.S. Department of Labor (DOL), Bureau of Labor Statistics (BLS), Postal Square Bldg., 2 Massachusetts Ave. NE, Washington, DC, 20212-0001, USA, (202) 691-5200, (202) 691-7890, blsdata_staff@bls.gov, https://www.bls.gov; Monthly Labor Review.

CHEMISTRY-SALARY OFFERS

National Association of Colleges and Employers (NACE), 1 E Broad St., Ste 130-1005, Bethlehem,

PA, 18018, USA, (610) 868-1421, customerservice@naceweb.org, https://www.naceweb.org/; Salary Survey.

CHEMOTHERAPY

American Society of Clinical Oncology (ASCO), 2318 Mill Rd., Ste. 800, Alexandria, VA, 22314, USA, (888) 282-2552, (703) 299-0158, (703) 299-0255, customerservice@asco.org, https://www.asco.org; Most Women With Early Stage Breast Cancer Can Forgo Chemotherapy When Guided by a Diagnostic Test and State of Cancer Care in America.

CHERRIES

U.S. Department of Agriculture (USDA), National Agricultural Statistics Service (USDA-NASS), 1400 Independence Ave. SW, Washington, DC, 20250, USA, (800) 727-9540, nass@nass.usda.gov, https://www.nass.usda.gov; Quick Stats.

CHESS

Unites States Chess Federation (USCF), PO Box 3967, Crossville, TN, 38557-3967, USA, (931) 787-1234, https://www.uschess.org; unpublished data.

CHICKEN POX

U.S. Department of Health and Human Services, Centers for Disease Control and Prevention (CDC), 1600 Clifton Rd., Atlanta, GA, 30329-4027, USA, (800) 232-4636, (888) 232-6348 (TTY), cdcinfo@cdc.gov, https://www.cdc.gov; Morbidity and Mortality Weekly Report (MMWR) and National Notifiable Diseases Surveillance System (NNDSS).

CHICKENS

See LIVESTOCK AND LIVESTOCK PRODUCTS

CHIEF EXECUTIVE OFFICERS

GuideStar by Candid, 1250 H St. NW, Ste. 1150, Washington, DC, 20005, USA, (800) 421-8656, support@candid.org, https://www2.guidestar.org/; 2022 Nonprofit Compensation Report.

PricewaterhouseCoopers (PwC) Strategy&, 90 Park Ave., Ste. 400, New York, NY, 10016, USA, (212) 697-1900, (212) 551-6732, https://www.strategyand.pwc.com/gx/en/; 2019 Chief Digital Officer Study.

CHILD ABUSE

Australian Institute of Family Studies, Child Family Community Australia (CFCA), 40 City Rd., Level 4, Southbank, VIC, 3006, AUS, enquiries@aifs.gov.au, https://aifs.gov.au/research_programs/child-family-community-australia; Alcohol-Related Harm in Families and Alcohol Consumption During COVID-19.

Australian Institute of Health and Welfare (AIHW), GPO Box 570, Canberra, ACT, 2601, AUS, info@aihw.gov.au, https://www.aihw.gov.au/; Child Protection Australia 2020-2021.

Childhelp, 6730 N Scottsdale Rd., Ste. 150, Scottsdale, AZ, 85253, USA, (480) 922-8212, https://www.childhelp.org/; Child Abuse Statistics.

Free the Slaves, 1320 19th St. NW, Ste. 600, Washington, DC, 20036, USA, (202) 775-7480, (202) 775-7485, info@freetheslaves.net, https://www.freetheslaves.net/; Learning From NGOs' Approaches to Modern Slavery in Southeast Asia.

Human Rights Watch, 350 5th Ave., 34th Fl., New York, NY, 10118-3299, USA, (212) 290-4700, (212) 736-1300, https://www.hrw.org; Like I'm Drowning: Children and Families Sent to Harm by the US 'Remain in Mexico' Program.

Institute on Violence, Abuse and Trauma (IVAT), 10065 Old Grove Rd. , Ste. 101, San Diego, CA, 92131, USA, (858) 527-1860, (858) 527-1743, https://www.ivatcenters.org/; Journal of Child Sexual Abuse (JCSA) and Journal of Family Trauma, Child Custody, and Child Development (JFT).

International Criminal Police Organization (INTERPOL), General Secretariat, 200 quai Charles de Gaulle, Lyon, 69006, FRA, https://www.interpol.int; International Child Sexual Exploitation ((ICSE)) Database.

National Indian Child Welfare Association (NICWA), 5100 SW Macadam Ave., Ste. 300, Portland, OR, 97239, USA, (503) 222-4044, info@nicwa.org, https://www.nicwa.org/; unpublished data.

National Sexual Violence Resource Center (NSVRC), Governor's Plaza N, Bldg. 2, 2101 N Front St., Harrisburg, PA, 17110, USA, (877) 739-3895, (717) 909-0715 (TTY), (717) 909-0714, https://www.nsvrc.org/resources@nsvrc.org, https://www.nsvrc.org/; National Sexual Violence Resource Center Library Catalog and Serving Teen Survivors: A Manual for Advocates.

Public Health Agency of Canada, 130 Colonnade Rd., Ottawa, ON, K1A 0K9, CAN, (844) 280-5020 (Dial from U.S.), https://www.phac-aspc.gc.ca/; Victims of Police-Reported Family and Intimate Partner Violence in Canada, 2021.

The Stimson Center, 1211 Connecticut Ave. NW, 8th Fl., Washington, DC, 20036, USA, (202) 223-5956, (202) 238-9604, communications@stimson.org, https://www.stimson.org/; 2022 Human Rights Reports: Insights Into Global Child Soldier Recruitment and Use.

U.S. Department of Health and Human Services (HHS), Administration for Children and Families (ACF), Children's Bureau, 330 C St. SW, Washington, DC, 20201, USA, https://www.acf.hhs.gov/cb; The Adoption and Foster Care Analysis and Reporting System (AFCARS); Child Maltreatment 2020; and Child Welfare Outcomes: Report to Congress Executive Summary.

U.S. Department of Health and Human Services (HHS), Administration for Children and Families (ACF), Office of Planning, Research & Evaluation (OPRE), 330 C St. SW, Washington, DC, 20201, USA, https://www.acf.hhs.gov/opre; National Survey of Child and Adolescent Well-Being (NSCAW), 1997-2014 and 2015-2024.

U.S. Government Accountablity Office (GAO), 441 G St. NW, Washington, DC, 20548, USA, (202) 512-3000, contact@gao.gov, https://www.gao.gov/; Human Trafficking: Department of State Collaborates with Partner Governments on Child Protection Compacts but Should Strengthen Oversight.

UNICEF, 3 United Nations Plz., New York, NY, 10017, USA, (212) 303-7984, (917) 244-2215, https://www.unicef.org; A Statistical Profile of Violence Against Children in Latin America and the Caribbean.

CHILD AGRICULTURAL LABORERS

Marshfield Clinic Research Institute (MCRI), National Children's Center for Rural and Agricultural Health and Safety (NCCRAHS), 1000 N Oak Ave., Marshfield, WI, 54449-5790, USA, (800) 662-6900, (715) 389-4999, nccrahs@mcrf.mfldclin.edu, https://www.marshfieldresearch.org/nccrahs; Childhood Agricultural Injuries: 2022 Fact Sheet.

CHILD CARE

U.S. Census Bureau, 4600 Silver Hill Rd., Washington, DC, 20233, USA, (301) 763-4636, (800) 923-8282, https://www.census.gov; American Community Survey (ACS) 2020 and American Housing Survey (AHS) 2019.

U.S. Department of Education (ED), Institute of Education Sciences (IES), National Center for Education Statistics (NCES), Potomac Center Plaza, 550 12th St. SW, Washington, DC, 20202, USA, (202) 403-5551, https://nces.ed.gov/; Digest of Education Statistics, 2020.

U.S. Department of Labor (DOL), Bureau of Labor Statistics (BLS), Postal Square Bldg., 2 Massachusetts Ave. NE, Washington, DC, 20212-0001, USA, (202) 691-5200, (202) 691-7890, blsdata_staff@bls.gov, https://www.bls.gov; Consumer Price Index (CPI) Databases.

CHILD CARE-COSTS

U.S. Department of Agriculture (USDA), Food and Nutrition Service (FNS), Braddock Metro Center II, 1320 Braddock Pl., Alexandria, VA, 22314, USA, (703) 305-2062, https://www.fns.usda.gov/; WIC Infant and Toddler Feeding Practices Study - 2: Fourth Year Report.

CHILD DAY CARE SERVICES

National Association for Regulatory Administration (NARA), 400 S 4th St., Ste. 754E, Minneapolis, MN, 55415, USA, (888) 674-7052, admin@naralicensing.org, https://www.naralicensing.org/; Key Indicators.

U.S. Census Bureau, 4600 Silver Hill Rd., Washington, DC, 20233, USA, (301) 763-4636, (800) 923-8282, https://www.census.gov; Economic Census, Nonemployer Statistics (NES) 2019.

CHILD DAY CARE SERVICES-EARNINGS

U.S. Census Bureau, 4600 Silver Hill Rd., Washington, DC, 20233, USA, (301) 763-4636, (800) 923-8282, https://www.census.gov; Economic Census, Nonemployer Statistics (NES) 2019.

CHILD DAY CARE SERVICES-EMPLOYEES

U.S. Census Bureau, 4600 Silver Hill Rd., Washington, DC, 20233, USA, (301) 763-4636, (800) 923-8282, https://www.census.gov; Economic Census, Nonemployer Statistics (NES) 2019.

CHILD DAY CARE SERVICES-FINANCES

U.S. Census Bureau, 4600 Silver Hill Rd., Washington, DC, 20233, USA, (301) 763-4636, (800) 923-8282, https://www.census.gov; Economic Census, Nonemployer Statistics (NES) 2019.

CHILD HEALTH

Children's Defense Fund (CDF), 840 1st St. NE, Ste. 300, Washington, DC, 20002, USA, (202) 628-8787, cdfinfo@childrensdefense.org, https://www.childrensdefense.org/; Child Poverty in America 2019.

The Henry J. Kaiser Family Foundation (KFF), 185 Berry St., Ste. 2000, San Francisco, CA, 94107, USA, (650) 854-9400, (650) 854-4800, https://www.kff.org; Medicaid and CHIP Eligibility and Enrollment Policies as of January 2022: Findings from a 50-State Survey.

PLOS, 1265 Battery St., Ste. 200, San Francisco, CA, 94111, USA, (415) 624-1200, (415) 795-1584, plos@plos.org, https://www.plos.org/; Towards a Further Understanding of Measles Vaccine Hesitancy in Khartoum State, Sudan: A Qualitative Study.

U.S. Department of Health and Human Services (HHS), Health Resources and Services Administration (HRSA), 5600 Fishers Ln., Rockville, MD, 20857, USA, (877) 464-4772, (877) 897-9910 (TTY), https://bhw.hrsa.gov/; Vaccine Injury Compensation Program Data Report.

U.S. Department of Health and Human Services (HHS), Health Resources and Services Administration (HRSA), Maternal and Child Health Bureau (MCHB), U.S. Department of Health and Human Services, 5600 Fishers Ln., Rockville, MD, 20857, USA, (877) 464-4772, (877) 897-9910 (TTY), https://mchb.hrsa.gov/; 2020 National Survey of Children's Health (NSCH).

U.S. Department of the Interior (DOI), Office of the Secretary, 1849 C St. NW, Washington, DC, 20240, USA, (202) 208-3100, https://www.doi.gov/office-of-the-secretary; Federal Indian Boarding School Initiative Investigative Report.

CHILD LABOR

Human Rights Watch, 350 5th Ave., 34th Fl., New York, NY, 10118-3299, USA, (212) 290-4700, (212) 736-1300, https://www.hrw.org; I Must Work to Eat: Covid-19, Poverty, and Child Labor in Ghana, Nepal, and Uganda.

International Labour Organization (ILO), 4 Rte. des Morillons, Geneva, CH-1211, SWI, ilo@ilo.org, https://www.ilo.org; SIMPOC - Statistical Information and Monitoring Programme on Child Labour.

Kenya National Bureau of Statistics (KHBS), PO Box 30266-00100, Nairobi, 00100, KEN, datarequest@knbs.or.ke, https://www.knbs.or.ke/; Economic Survey of Kenya, 2022.

Marshfield Clinic Research Institute (MCRI), National Children's Center for Rural and Agricultural Health and Safety (NCCRAHS), 1000 N Oak Ave., Marshfield, WI, 54449-5790, USA, (800) 662-6900, (715) 389-4999, nccrahs@mcrf.mfldclin.edu, https://www.marshfieldresearch.org/nccrahs; Childhood Agricultural Injuries: 2022 Fact Sheet.

U.S. Department of Labor (DOL), Bureau of International Labor Affairs (ILAB), 200 Constitution Ave. NW, Washington, DC, 20210, USA, (202) 693-4770, contact-ilab@dol.gov, https://www.dol.gov/agencies/ilab; Findings on the Worst Forms of Child Labor 2020.

World Vision, PO Box 9716, Federal Way, WA, 98063, USA, (888) 511-6548, https://www.worldvision.org/; unpublished data.

CHILD MARRIAGE

United Kingdom Foreign, Commonwealth & Development Office (FCDO), Forced Marriage Unit (FMU), King Charles St., London, SW1A 2AH, GBR, fmu@fcdo.gov.uk, https://www.gov.uk/guidance/forced-marriage; Forced Marriage Unit Statistics 2021.

CHILD SOLDIERS

The Stimson Center, 1211 Connecticut Ave. NW, 8th Fl., Washington, DC, 20036, USA, (202) 223-5956, (202) 238-9604, communications@stimson.org, https://www.stimson.org/; 2022 Human Rights Reports: Insights Into Global Child Soldier Recruitment and Use.

CHILD SUPPORT

U.S. Department of Health and Human Services (HHS), Administration for Children and Families (ACF), Office of Child Support Enforcement (OCSE), 330 C St. SW, Washington, DC, 20201, USA, https://www.acf.hhs.gov/css; Child Support Enforcement FY 2020 Preliminary Report.

CHILD WELFARE-NORTH AMERICA

American Civil Liberties Union (ACLU), 125 Broad St. , 18th Fl., New York, NY, 10004, USA, (212) 549-2500, https://www.aclu.org/; 'If I Wasn't Poor, I Wouldn't Be Unfit': The Family Separation Crisis in the US Child Welfare System.

Child Welfare League of America (CWLA), 727 15th St. NW, Ste. 1200, Washington, DC, 20005, USA, (202) 688-4200, cwla@cwla.org, https://www.cwla.org/; Child Welfare Journal.

Children's Defense Fund (CDF), 840 1st St. NE, Ste. 300, Washington, DC, 20002, USA, (202) 628-8787, cdfinfo@childrensdefense.org, https://www.childrensdefense.org/; Child Poverty in America 2019.

Public Health Agency of Canada, 130 Colonnade Rd., Ottawa, ON, K1A 0K9, CAN, (844) 280-5020 (Dial from U.S.), https://www.phac-aspc.gc.ca/; CHIRPP Injury Reports.

U.S. Department of Health and Human Services (HHS), Administration for Children and Families (ACF), Children's Bureau, Child Welfare Information Gateway, 330 C St. SW, Washington, DC, 20201, USA, (800) 394-3366, info@childwelfare.gov, https://www.childwelfare.gov/; Adoption Statistics; Child Abuse & Neglect Statistics; Child and Family Well-Being Statistics; and Foster Care Statistics.

U.S. Department of Health and Human Services (HHS), Health Resources and Services Administration (HRSA), Maternal and Child Health Bureau (MCHB), U.S. Department of Health and Human Services, 5600 Fishers Ln., Rockville, MD, 20857, USA, (877) 464-4772, (877) 897-9910 (TTY), https://mchb.hrsa.gov; 2020 National Survey of Children's Health (NSCH).

U.S. Department of the Interior (DOI), Office of the Secretary, 1849 C St. NW, Washington, DC, 20240, USA, (202) 208-3100, https://www.doi.gov/office-of-the-secretary; Federal Indian Boarding School Initiative Investigative Report.

The Urban Institute, 500 L'Enfant Plaza SW, Washington, DC, 20024, USA, (202) 833-7200, https://www.urban.org/; Kids' Share 2022: Report on Federal Expenditures on Children through 2021 and Future Projections.

CHILDBIRTH

Bernan Press, 15250 NBN Way, Bldg. C, Blue Ridge Summit, PA, 17214, USA, (301) 459-2255, (800) 865-3457, (800) 865-3450, customercare@bernan.com, https://rowman.com/Page/Bernan; Vital Statistics of the United States 2022: Births, Life Expectancy, Deaths, and Selected Health Data.

Guttmacher Institute, 125 Maiden Ln., 7th Fl., New York, NY, 10038, USA, (212) 248-1111, (800) 355-0244, (212) 248-1951, info@guttmacher.org, https://www.guttmacher.org/; Adolescent Sexual and Reproductive Health in the United States and Anti-Abortion Judge Attempts to Ban Mifepristone Nationwide, Ignoring Science and More than Two Decades of the Drug's Safe Use in the United States.

March of Dimes Perinatal Data Center (PeriStats), 1550 Crystal Dr., Ste. 1300, Arlington, VA, 22202, USA, (888) 663-4637, https://www.marchofdimes.org/peristats; PeriStats.

U.S. Department of Health and Human Services, Centers for Disease Control and Prevention (CDC), 1600 Clifton Rd., Atlanta, GA, 30329-4027, USA, (800) 232-4636, (888) 232-6348 (TTY), cdcinfo@cdc.gov, https://www.cdc.gov; State-Specific Assisted Reproductive Technology Surveillance.

U.S. Department of Health and Human Services, Centers for Disease Control and Prevention (CDC), National Center for Health Statistics (NCHS), 3311 Toledo Rd., Hyattsville, MD, 20782-2064, USA, (800) 232-4636, (301) 458-4000, https://www.cdc.gov/nchs; FastStats - Statistics by Topic; National Vital Statistics Reports (NVSR); and Vital Statistics Online Data Portal.

United Nations Statistics Division (UNSD), United Nations Plz., New York, NY, 10017, USA, (800) 253-9646, (212) 963-9851, statistics@un.org, https://unstats.un.org; Millennium Development Goal Indicators.

CHILDBIRTH-AMERICAN INDIAN, ESKIMO, AND ALEUT POPULATION

Bernan Press, 15250 NBN Way, Bldg. C, Blue Ridge Summit, PA, 17214, USA, (301) 459-2255, (800) 865-3457, (800) 865-3450, customercare@bernan.com, https://rowman.com/Page/Bernan; Vital Statistics of the United States 2022: Births, Life Expectancy, Deaths, and Selected Health Data.

U.S. Department of Health and Human Services, Centers for Disease Control and Prevention (CDC), National Center for Health Statistics (NCHS), 3311 Toledo Rd., Hyattsville, MD, 20782-2064, USA, (800) 232-4636, (301) 458-4000, https://www.cdc.gov/nchs; National Vital Statistics Reports (NVSR) and Vital Statistics Online Data Portal.

CHILDBIRTH-ASIAN AND PACIFIC ISLANDER POPULATION

Bernan Press, 15250 NBN Way, Bldg. C, Blue Ridge Summit, PA, 17214, USA, (301) 459-2255, (800) 865-3457, (800) 865-3450, customercare@bernan.com, https://rowman.com/Page/Bernan; Vital Statistics of the United States 2022: Births, Life Expectancy, Deaths, and Selected Health Data.

U.S. Department of Health and Human Services, Centers for Disease Control and Prevention (CDC), National Center for Health Statistics (NCHS), 3311 Toledo Rd., Hyattsville, MD, 20782-2064, USA, (800) 232-4636, (301) 458-4000, https://www.cdc.gov/nchs; National Vital Statistics Reports (NVSR) and Vital Statistics Online Data Portal.

CHILDBIRTH-BIRTH WEIGHT

Bernan Press, 15250 NBN Way, Bldg. C, Blue Ridge Summit, PA, 17214, USA, (301) 459-2255, (800) 865-3457, (800) 865-3450, customercare@bernan.com, https://rowman.com/Page/Bernan; Vital Statistics of the United States 2022: Births, Life Expectancy, Deaths, and Selected Health Data.

U.S. Department of Health and Human Services, Centers for Disease Control and Prevention (CDC), National Center for Health Statistics (NCHS), 3311 Toledo Rd., Hyattsville, MD, 20782-2064, USA, (800) 232-4636, (301) 458-4000, https://www.cdc.gov/nchs; National Vital Statistics Reports (NVSR) and Vital Statistics Online Data Portal.

CHILDBIRTH-BIRTHS TO MOTHERS WHO SMOKED

Bernan Press, 15250 NBN Way, Bldg. C, Blue Ridge Summit, PA, 17214, USA, (301) 459-2255, (800) 865-3457, (800) 865-3450, customercare@bernan.com, https://rowman.com/Page/Bernan; Vital Statistics of the United States 2022: Births, Life Expectancy, Deaths, and Selected Health Data.

U.S. Department of Health and Human Services, Centers for Disease Control and Prevention (CDC), National Center for Health Statistics (NCHS), 3311 Toledo Rd., Hyattsville, MD, 20782-2064, USA, (800) 232-4636, (301) 458-4000, https://www.cdc.gov/nchs; National Vital Statistics Reports (NVSR).

CHILDBIRTH-BIRTHS TO SINGLE OR UNMARRIED WOMEN

Bernan Press, 15250 NBN Way, Bldg. C, Blue Ridge Summit, PA, 17214, USA, (301) 459-2255, (800) 865-3457, (800) 865-3450, customercare@bernan.com, https://rowman.com/Page/Bernan; Vital Statistics of the United States 2022: Births, Life Expectancy, Deaths, and Selected Health Data.

Guttmacher Institute, 125 Maiden Ln., 7th Fl., New York, NY, 10038, USA, (212) 248-1111, (800) 355-0244, (212) 248-1951, info@guttmacher.org, https://www.guttmacher.org/; Adolescent Sexual and Reproductive Health in the United States.

U.S. Department of Health and Human Services, Centers for Disease Control and Prevention (CDC), National Center for Health Statistics (NCHS), 3311 Toledo Rd., Hyattsville, MD, 20782-2064, USA, (800) 232-4636, (301) 458-4000, https://www.cdc.gov/nchs; National Vital Statistics Reports (NVSR) and Vital Statistics Online Data Portal.

CHILDBIRTH-BIRTHS TO TEENAGE MOTHERS

Bernan Press, 15250 NBN Way, Bldg. C, Blue Ridge Summit, PA, 17214, USA, (301) 459-2255, (800) 865-3457, (800) 865-3450, customercare@bernan.com, https://rowman.com/Page/Bernan; Vital Statistics of the United States 2022: Births, Life Expectancy, Deaths, and Selected Health Data.

Guttmacher Institute, 125 Maiden Ln., 7th Fl., New York, NY, 10038, USA, (212) 248-1111, (800) 355-0244, (212) 248-1951, info@guttmacher.org, https://www.guttmacher.org/; Adolescent Sexual and Reproductive Health in the United States.

U.S. Department of Health and Human Services, Centers for Disease Control and Prevention (CDC), National Center for Health Statistics (NCHS), 3311 Toledo Rd., Hyattsville, MD, 20782-2064, USA, (800) 232-4636, (301) 458-4000, https://www.cdc.gov/nchs; National Vital Statistics Reports (NVSR) and Vital Statistics Online Data Portal.

CHILDBIRTH-BLACK POPULATION

Bernan Press, 15250 NBN Way, Bldg. C, Blue Ridge Summit, PA, 17214, USA, (301) 459-2255, (800) 865-3457, (800) 865-3450, customercare@bernan.com, https://rowman.com/Page/Bernan; Vital Statistics of the United States 2022: Births, Life Expectancy, Deaths, and Selected Health Data.

Guttmacher Institute, 125 Maiden Ln., 7th Fl., New York, NY, 10038, USA, (212) 248-1111, (800) 355-0244, (212) 248-1951, info@guttmacher.org, https://www.guttmacher.org/; Adolescent Sexual and Reproductive Health in the United States.

U.S. Commission on Civil Rights (USCCR), 1331 Pennsylvania Ave. NW, Ste. 1150, Washington, DC,

20425, USA, (202) 376-7700, (202) 376-8116 (TTY), publications@usccr.gov, https://www.usccr.gov/; 2021 Statutory Enforcement Report: Racial Disparities in Maternal Health.

U.S. Department of Health and Human Services, Centers for Disease Control and Prevention (CDC), National Center for Health Statistics (NCHS), 3311 Toledo Rd., Hyattsville, MD, 20782-2064, USA, (800) 232-4636, (301) 458-4000, https://www.cdc.gov/nchs; National Vital Statistics Reports (NVSR) and Vital Statistics Online Data Portal.

CHILDBIRTH-CESAREAN SECTION DELIVERIES

Public Health Agency of Canada, 130 Colonnade Rd., Ottawa, ON, K1A 0K9, CAN, (844) 280-5020 (Dial from U.S.), https://www.phac-aspc.gc.ca/; Perinatal Health Indicators (PHI).

U.S. Department of Health and Human Services, Centers for Disease Control and Prevention (CDC), National Center for Health Statistics (NCHS), 3311 Toledo Rd., Hyattsville, MD, 20782-2064, USA, (800) 232-4636, (301) 458-4000, https://www.cdc.gov/nchs; FastStats - Statistics by Topic and Vital Statistics Online Data Portal.

CHILDBIRTH-CHARACTERISTICS OF MOTHER

Bernan Press, 15250 NBN Way, Bldg. C, Blue Ridge Summit, PA, 17214, USA, (301) 459-2255, (800) 865-3457, (800) 865-3450, customercare@bernan.com, https://rowman.com/Page/Bernan; Vital Statistics of the United States 2022: Births, Life Expectancy, Deaths, and Selected Health Data.

Guttmacher Institute, 125 Maiden Ln., 7th Fl., New York, NY, 10038, USA, (212) 248-1111, (800) 355-0244, (212) 248-1951, info@guttmacher.org, https://www.guttmacher.org/; Adolescent Sexual and Reproductive Health in the United States.

The Henry J. Kaiser Family Foundation (KFF), 185 Berry St., Ste. 2000, San Francisco, CA, 94107, USA, (650) 854-9400, (650) 854-4800, https://www.kff.org; Racial Disparities in Maternal and Infant Health: Current Status and Efforts to Address Them.

National Bureau of Economic Research (NBER), 1050 Massachusetts Ave., Cambridge, MA, 02138, USA, (617) 868-3900, info@nber.org, https://www.nber.org/; Maternal and Infant Health Inequality: New Evidence from Linked Administrative Data.

Public Health Agency of Canada, 130 Colonnade Rd., Ottawa, ON, K1A 0K9, CAN, (844) 280-5020 (Dial from U.S.), https://www.phac-aspc.gc.ca/; Perinatal Health Indicators (PHI).

U.S. Department of Health and Human Services, Centers for Disease Control and Prevention (CDC), National Center for Health Statistics (NCHS), 3311 Toledo Rd., Hyattsville, MD, 20782-2064, USA, (800) 232-4636, (301) 458-4000, https://www.cdc.gov/nchs; National Vital Statistics Reports (NVSR) and Vital Statistics Online Data Portal.

CHILDBIRTH-COMPLICATIONS

March of Dimes Perinatal Data Center (PeriStats), 1550 Crystal Dr., Ste. 1300, Arlington, VA, 22202, USA, (888) 663-4637, https://www.marchofdimes.org/peristats; PeriStats.

Public Health Agency of Canada, 130 Colonnade Rd., Ottawa, ON, K1A 0K9, CAN, (844) 280-5020 (Dial from U.S.), https://www.phac-aspc.gc.ca/; Perinatal Health Indicators (PHI).

U.S. Department of Health and Human Services, Centers for Disease Control and Prevention (CDC), National Center for Health Statistics (NCHS), 3311 Toledo Rd., Hyattsville, MD, 20782-2064, USA, (800) 232-4636, (301) 458-4000, https://www.cdc.gov/nchs; FastStats - Statistics by Topic and Vital Statistics Online Data Portal.

CHILDBIRTH-EDUCATIONAL ATTAINMENT OF MOTHER

Bernan Press, 15250 NBN Way, Bldg. C, Blue Ridge Summit, PA, 17214, USA, (301) 459-2255, (800) 865-3457, (800) 865-3450, customercare@bernan.com, https://rowman.com/Page/Bernan; Vital Statistics of the United States 2022: Births, Life Expectancy, Deaths, and Selected Health Data.

Guttmacher Institute, 125 Maiden Ln., 7th Fl., New York, NY, 10038, USA, (212) 248-1111, (800) 355-0244, (212) 248-1951, info@guttmacher.org, https://www.guttmacher.org/; Adolescent Sexual and Reproductive Health in the United States.

U.S. Department of Health and Human Services, Centers for Disease Control and Prevention (CDC), National Center for Health Statistics (NCHS), 3311 Toledo Rd., Hyattsville, MD, 20782-2064, USA, (800) 232-4636, (301) 458-4000, https://www.cdc.gov/nchs; National Vital Statistics Reports (NVSR).

CHILDBIRTH-FOREIGN COUNTRIES

U.S. Census Bureau, 4600 Silver Hill Rd., Washington, DC, 20233, USA, (301) 763-4636, (800) 923-8282, https://www.census.gov; International Database: World Population Estimates and Projections.

CHILDBIRTH-HISPANIC ORIGIN POPULATION

Bernan Press, 15250 NBN Way, Bldg. C, Blue Ridge Summit, PA, 17214, USA, (301) 459-2255, (800) 865-3457, (800) 865-3450, customercare@bernan.com, https://rowman.com/Page/Bernan; Vital Statistics of the United States 2022: Births, Life Expectancy, Deaths, and Selected Health Data.

Guttmacher Institute, 125 Maiden Ln., 7th Fl., New York, NY, 10038, USA, (212) 248-1111, (800) 355-0244, (212) 248-1951, info@guttmacher.org, https://www.guttmacher.org/; Adolescent Sexual and Reproductive Health in the United States.

U.S. Department of Health and Human Services, Centers for Disease Control and Prevention (CDC), National Center for Health Statistics (NCHS), 3311 Toledo Rd., Hyattsville, MD, 20782-2064, USA, (800) 232-4636, (301) 458-4000, https://www.cdc.gov/nchs; National Vital Statistics Reports (NVSR) and Vital Statistics Online Data Portal.

CHILDBIRTH-LOW BIRTH WEIGHT BY SMOKING STATUS

Bernan Press, 15250 NBN Way, Bldg. C, Blue Ridge Summit, PA, 17214, USA, (301) 459-2255, (800) 865-3457, (800) 865-3450, customercare@bernan.com, https://rowman.com/Page/Bernan; Vital Statistics of the United States 2022: Births, Life Expectancy, Deaths, and Selected Health Data.

U.S. Department of Health and Human Services, Centers for Disease Control and Prevention (CDC), National Center for Health Statistics (NCHS), 3311 Toledo Rd., Hyattsville, MD, 20782-2064, USA, (800) 232-4636, (301) 458-4000, https://www.cdc.gov/nchs; National Vital Statistics Reports (NVSR).

CHILDBIRTH-OUTLYING AREAS OF THE UNITED STATES

U.S. Department of Health and Human Services, Centers for Disease Control and Prevention (CDC), National Center for Health Statistics (NCHS), 3311 Toledo Rd., Hyattsville, MD, 20782-2064, USA, (800) 232-4636, (301) 458-4000, https://www.cdc.gov/nchs; Vital Statistics Online Data Portal.

CHILDBIRTH-PRENATAL CARE

Bernan Press, 15250 NBN Way, Bldg. C, Blue Ridge Summit, PA, 17214, USA, (301) 459-2255, (800) 865-3457, (800) 865-3450, customercare@bernan.com, https://rowman.com/Page/Bernan; Vital Statistics of the United States 2022: Births, Life Expectancy, Deaths, and Selected Health Data.

March of Dimes Perinatal Data Center (PeriStats), 1550 Crystal Dr., Ste. 1300, Arlington, VA, 22202, USA, (888) 663-4637, https://www.marchofdimes.org/peristats; PeriStats.

Public Health Agency of Canada, 130 Colonnade Rd., Ottawa, ON, K1A 0K9, CAN, (844) 280-5020 (Dial from U.S.), https://www.phac-aspc.gc.ca/; Perinatal Health Indicators (PHI).

U.S. Department of Health and Human Services, Centers for Disease Control and Prevention (CDC), National Center for Health Statistics (NCHS), 3311 Toledo Rd., Hyattsville, MD, 20782-2064, USA, (800) 232-4636, (301) 458-4000, https://www.cdc.gov/nchs; National Vital Statistics Reports (NVSR) and Vital Statistics Online Data Portal.

CHILDBIRTH-RACE

Bernan Press, 15250 NBN Way, Bldg. C, Blue Ridge Summit, PA, 17214, USA, (301) 459-2255, (800) 865-3457, (800) 865-3450, customercare@bernan.com, https://rowman.com/Page/Bernan; Vital Statistics of the United States 2022: Births, Life Expectancy, Deaths, and Selected Health Data.

Guttmacher Institute, 125 Maiden Ln., 7th Fl., New York, NY, 10038, USA, (212) 248-1111, (800) 355-0244, (212) 248-1951, info@guttmacher.org, https://www.guttmacher.org/; Adolescent Sexual and Reproductive Health in the United States.

U.S. Commission on Civil Rights (USCCR), 1331 Pennsylvania Ave. NW, Ste. 1150, Washington, DC, 20425, USA, (202) 376-7700, (202) 376-8116 (TTY), publications@usccr.gov, https://www.usccr.gov/; 2021 Statutory Enforcement Report: Racial Disparities in Maternal Health.

U.S. Department of Health and Human Services, Centers for Disease Control and Prevention (CDC), National Center for Health Statistics (NCHS), 3311 Toledo Rd., Hyattsville, MD, 20782-2064, USA, (800) 232-4636, (301) 458-4000, https://www.cdc.gov/nchs; National Vital Statistics Reports (NVSR) and Vital Statistics Online Data Portal.

CHILDREN

See also POPULATION and VITAL STATISTICS

The Annie E. Casey Foundation, 701 Saint Paul St., Baltimore, MD, 21202, USA, (410) 547-6600, (410) 547-6624, https://www.aecf.org/; 2021 KIDS COUNT Data Book: State Trends in Child Well-Being and KIDS COUNT Database.

Common Sense, 699 8th St., Ste. C150, San Francisco, CA, 94103, USA, (415) 863-0600, (415) 863-0601, https://www.commonsensemedia.org/; 2023 State of Kids' Privacy.

Federal Interagency Forum on Child and Family Statistics (The Forum), USA, childstats@ed.gov, https://www.childstats.gov; America's Children: Key National Indicators of Well-Being, 2021.

Girl Scouts of the USA, 420 Fifth Ave., New York, NY, 10018, USA, (212) 852-8000, (800) 478-7248, https://www.girlscouts.org/; Decoding the Digital Girl: Defining and Supporting Girls' Digital Leadership and A New Decade of Girls' Leadership: Part 1.

National Highway Traffic Safety Administration (NHTSA), National Center for Statistics and Analysis (NCSA), 1200 New Jersey Ave. SE, West Bldg., Washington, DC, 20590, USA, (800) 934-8517, (202) 366-2746, ncsarequests@dot.gov, https://www.nhtsa.gov/research-data/national-center-statistics-and-analysis-ncsa; Traffic Safety Facts, 2011-2020 Data - School-Transportation-Related Crashes and Traffic Safety Facts, 2020 Data - Children.

St Jude Children's Research Hospital, 262 Danny Thomas Pl., Memphis, TN, 38105, USA, (866) 278-5833, (901) 595-1040 (TTY), https://www.stjude.org/; The Scientific Report: Translating Science into Survival.

Statistics Canada (StatCan), 150 Tunney's Pasture Driveway, Ottawa, ON, K1A 0T6, CAN, (800) 263-1136 (Dial from U.S.), (514) 283-8300 (Dial from U.S.), (514) 283-9350 (Fax from U.S.), infostats@statcan.gc.ca, https://www.statcan.gc.ca; Children and Youth Statistics.

U.S. Census Bureau, 4600 Silver Hill Rd., Washington, DC, 20233, USA, (301) 763-4636, (800) 923-8282, https://www.census.gov; Explore Census Data and United States QuickFacts.

U.S. Department of Health and Human Services (HHS), Health Resources and Services Administration (HRSA), Maternal and Child Health Bureau

(MCHB), U.S. Department of Health and Human Services, 5600 Fishers Ln., Rockville, MD, 20857, USA, (877) 464-4772, (877) 897-9910 (TTY), https://mchb.hrsa.gov; Explore the Title V Federal-State Partnership.

U.S. Department of State (DOS), Bureau of Consular Affairs, Office of Children's Issues, 2201 C. St. NW, SA-17, 9th Fl., Washington, DC, 20522-1709, USA, (888) 407-4747, (202) 501-4444, adoption@state.gov, https://travel.state.gov/content/travel/en/Intercountry-Adoption.html; Annual Report on Intercountry Adoption, Fiscal Year 2021 and Country Information.

U.S. Department of the Interior (DOI), Office of the Secretary, 1849 C St. NW, Washington, DC, 20240, USA, (202) 208-3100, https://www.doi.gov/office-of-the-secretary; Federal Indian Boarding School Initiative Investigative Report.

UNICEF, 3 United Nations Plz., New York, NY, 10017, USA, (212) 303-7984, (917) 244-2215, https://www.unicef.org; Adolescent Girls in West and Central Africa: Data Brief.

CHILDREN-ACTIVITY LIMITATION

U.S. Department of Health and Human Services, Centers for Disease Control and Prevention (CDC), National Center for Health Statistics (NCHS), 3311 Toledo Rd., Hyattsville, MD, 20782-2064, USA, (800) 232-4636, (301) 458-4000, https://www.cdc.gov/nchs; Health, United States, 2020-2021.

CHILDREN-AGE AND/OR SEX

Girl Scouts of the USA, 420 Fifth Ave., New York, NY, 10018, USA, (212) 852-8000, (800) 478-7248, https://www.girlscouts.org/; Girl Scout Alums by the Numbers.

CHILDREN-AIDS

U.S. Department of Health and Human Services, Centers for Disease Control and Prevention (CDC), 1600 Clifton Rd., Atlanta, GA, 30329-4027, USA, (800) 232-4636, (888) 232-6348 (TTY), cdcinfo@cdc.gov, https://www.cdc.gov; HIV Surveillance Reports.

UNICEF, 3 United Nations Plz., New York, NY, 10017, USA, (212) 303-7984, (917) 244-2215, https://www.unicef.org; Country Profiles.

World Health Organization (WHO), Ave. Appia 20, Geneva, CH-1211, SWI, (202) 974-3000 (Telephone in U.S.), publications@who.int, https://www.who.int/; HIV/AIDS Surveillance in Europe 2022.

CHILDREN-ALCOHOL USE

Montana Office of Public Instruction, PO Box 202501, Helena, MT, 59620-2501, USA, (406) 444-3680, (406) 444-3693, https://opi.mt.gov/; Culture and Schools: American Indian Stakeholder Perspectives on the American Indian Student Achievement Gap.

Substance Abuse and Mental Health Services Administration (SAMHSA), 5600 Fishers Ln., Rockville, MD, 20857, USA, (877) 726-4727, (800) 487-4889 (TTY), samhsainfo@samhsa.hhs.gov, https://www.samhsa.gov/; 2020 National Survey of Substance Abuse Treatment Services (N-SSATS) and 2019-2020 National Survey on Drug Use and Health (NSDUH).

U.S. Department of Health and Human Services (HHS), National Institutes of Health (NIH), National Institute on Alcohol Abuse and Alcoholism (NIAAA), 9000 Rockville Pike, Bethesda, MD, 20892, USA, (888) 696-4222, (301) 443-3860, askniaaa@nih.gov, https://www.niaaa.nih.gov/; Alcohol Facts and Statistics; Alcohol Policy Information System (APIS); and Surveillance Reports.

CHILDREN-CHILD ABUSE

See CHILD ABUSE

CHILDREN-CHILD CASE WORKERS

Australian Institute of Health and Welfare (AIHW), GPO Box 570, Canberra, ACT, 2601, AUS, info@aihw.gov.au, https://www.aihw.gov.au/; Child Protection Australia 2020-2021.

CHILDREN-CHILD DAY CARE

U.S. Department of Education (ED), Institute of Education Sciences (IES), National Center for Education Statistics (NCES), Potomac Center Plaza, 550 12th St. SW, Washington, DC, 20202, USA, (202) 403-5551, https://nces.ed.gov/; Digest of Education Statistics, 2020.

U.S. Department of Labor (DOL), Bureau of Labor Statistics (BLS), Postal Square Bldg., 2 Massachusetts Ave. NE, Washington, DC, 20212-0001, USA, (202) 691-5200, (202) 691-7890, blsdata_staff@bls.gov, https://www.bls.gov; Consumer Price Index (CPI) Databases.

CHILDREN-CHILD SUPPORT

U.S. Department of Health and Human Services (HHS), Administration for Children and Families (ACF), Office of Child Support Enforcement (OCSE), 330 C St. SW, Washington, DC, 20201, USA, https://www.acf.hhs.gov/css; Child Support Enforcement FY 2020 Preliminary Report.

CHILDREN-CIGARETTE SMOKING

Health Canada, Address Locator 1801B, Ottawa, ON, K1A 0K9, CAN, (613) 957-2991 (Dial from U.S.), (613) 941-5366 (Fax from U.S.), hcinfo.infosc@canada.ca, https://www.hc-sc.gc.ca/; Smoking, Vaping and Tobacco.

Substance Abuse and Mental Health Services Administration (SAMHSA), 5600 Fishers Ln., Rockville, MD, 20857, USA, (877) 726-4727, (800) 487-4889 (TTY), samhsainfo@samhsa.hhs.gov, https://www.samhsa.gov/; 2019-2020 National Survey on Drug Use and Health (NSDUH).

CHILDREN-COLLEGE ENROLLMENT

U.S. Census Bureau, 4600 Silver Hill Rd., Washington, DC, 20233, USA, (301) 763-4636, (800) 923-8282, https://www.census.gov; School Enrollment in the United States: 2020.

U.S. Department of Education (ED), Institute of Education Sciences (IES), National Center for Education Statistics (NCES), Potomac Center Plaza, 550 12th St. SW, Washington, DC, 20202, USA, (202) 403-5551, https://nces.ed.gov/; Digest of Education Statistics, 2020.

CHILDREN-COMPUTER USE

U.S. Department of Education (ED), Institute of Education Sciences (IES), National Center for Education Statistics (NCES), Potomac Center Plaza, 550 12th St. SW, Washington, DC, 20202, USA, (202) 403-5551, https://nces.ed.gov/; Digest of Education Statistics, 2020.

CHILDREN-CONGENITAL ABNORMALITIES

U.S. Department of Health and Human Services, Centers for Disease Control and Prevention (CDC), National Center for Health Statistics (NCHS), 3311 Toledo Rd., Hyattsville, MD, 20782-2064, USA, (800) 232-4636, (301) 458-4000, https://www.cdc.gov/nchs; Health, United States, 2020-2021.

CHILDREN-COST OF RAISING

U.S. Department of Agriculture (USDA), Food and Nutrition Service (FNS), Braddock Metro Center II, 1320 Braddock Pl., Alexandria, VA, 22314, USA, (703) 305-2062, https://www.fns.usda.gov/; WIC Infant and Toddler Feeding Practices Study - 2: Fourth Year Report.

CHILDREN-CRIMES AGAINST

Amnesty International USA, 311 W 43rd St., 7th Fl., New York, NY, 10036, USA, (212) 807-8400, (800) 266-3789, (212) 627-1451, aimember@aiusa.org, https://www.amnestyusa.org/; Hunger for Justice: Crimes Against Humanity in Venezuela.

Children's Defense Fund (CDF), 840 1st St. NE, Ste. 300, Washington, DC, 20002, USA, (202) 628-8787, cdfinfo@childrensdefense.org, https://www.childrensdefense.org/; Protect Children, Not Guns 2019.

Human Rights Watch, 350 5th Ave., 34th Fl., New York, NY, 10118-3299, USA, (212) 290-4700, (212) 736-1300, https://www.hrw.org; Like I'm Drowning: Children and Families Sent to Harm by the US 'Remain in Mexico' Program.

Naval Postgraduate School, Center for Homeland Defense and Security (CHDS), 1 University Cir., Bldg. 220, Rm. 064, Monteray, CA, 93943, USA, (831) 656-2356 , mccolgan@nps.edu, https://www.chds.us; K-12 School Shooting Database.

Plan International UK, Finsgate , 5-7 Cranwood St., London, EC1V 9LH, GBR, https://www.plan-uk.org/; What Works for Ending Public Sexual Harassment?.

Statistic Brain Research Institute, 1100 Glendon Ave., Los Angeles, CA, 90024, USA, https://www.statisticbrain.com/; AMBER Alert Statistics.

The Stimson Center, 1211 Connecticut Ave. NW, 8th Fl., Washington, DC, 20036, USA, (202) 223-5956, (202) 238-9604, communications@stimson.org, https://www.stimson.org/; 2022 Human Rights Reports: Insights Into Global Child Soldier Recruitment and Use.

U.S. Government Accountablity Office (GAO), 441 G St. NW, Washington, DC, 20548, USA, (202) 512-3000, contact@gao.gov, https://www.gao.gov/; Human Trafficking: Department of State Collaborates with Partner Governments on Child Protection Compacts but Should Strengthen Oversight.

United Kingdom Foreign, Commonwealth & Development Office (FCDO), Forced Marriage Unit (FMU), King Charles St., London, SW1A 2AH, GBR, fmu@fcdo.gov.uk, https://www.gov.uk/guidance/forced-marriage; Forced Marriage Unit Statistics 2021.

University of New Hampshire, Crimes Against Children Research Center (CCRC), 125 McConnell Hall, 15 Academic Way, Durham, NH, 03824, USA, (603) 862-3541, (603) 862-1122, david.finkelhor@unh.edu, https://www.unh.edu/ccrc/; unpublished data.

Youth Pride, Inc. (YPI), 743 Westminster St., Providence, RI, 02903, USA, (401) 421-5626, (401) 274-1990, info@youthprideri.org, https://www.youthprideri.org/; unpublished data.

CHILDREN-CRIMINAL STATISTICS

U.S. Department of Justice (DOJ), Bureau of Justice Statistics (BJS), 810 7th St. NW, Washington, DC, 20531, USA, (202) 307-0765, askbjs@usdoj.gov, https://www.bjs.gov/; Criminal Victimization, 2020.

CHILDREN-DEATHS AND DEATH RATES

Bernan Press, 15250 NBN Way, Bldg. C, Blue Ridge Summit, PA, 17214, USA, (301) 459-2255, (800) 865-3457, (800) 865-3450, customercare@bernan.com, https://rowman.com/Page/Bernan; Vital Statistics of the United States 2022: Births, Life Expectancy, Deaths, and Selected Health Data.

Child Trends, 7315 Wisconsin Ave., Ste. 1200W, Bethesda, MD, 20814, USA, (240) 223-9200, https://www.childtrends.org/; Teen Suicide Databank Indicator.

Children's Defense Fund (CDF), 840 1st St. NE, Ste. 300, Washington, DC, 20002, USA, (202) 628-8787, cdfinfo@childrensdefense.org, https://www.childrensdefense.org/; Protect Children, Not Guns 2019.

International Food Policy Research Institute (IFPRI), 1201 Eye St. NW, Washington, DC, 20005-3915, USA, (202) 862-5600, (202) 862-5606, ifpri@cgiar.org, https://www.ifpri.org/; The COVID-19 Crisis Will Exacerbate Maternal and Child Undernutrition and Child Mortality in Low- and Middle-Income Countries.

Kids and Cars, Kansas City, MO, 64114, USA, (913) 732-2792, (913) 205-6973, amber@kidsandcars.org, https://www.kidsandcars.org/; www.kidsandcars.org.

Marshfield Clinic Research Institute (MCRI), National Children's Center for Rural and Agricultural Health and Safety (NCCRAHS), 1000 N Oak Ave., Marshfield, WI, 54449-5790, USA, (800) 662-6900, (715) 389-4999, nccrahs@mcrf.mfldclin.edu, https://www.marshfieldresearch.org/nccrahs; Childhood Agricultural Injuries: 2022 Fact Sheet.

National Highway Traffic Safety Administration (NHTSA), National Center for Statistics and Analysis (NCSA), 1200 New Jersey Ave. SE, West Bldg., Washington, DC, 20590, USA, (800) 934-8517, (202) 366-2746, ncsarequests@dot.gov, https://www.nhtsa.gov/research-data/national-center-statistics-and-analysis-ncsa; Traffic Safety Facts, 2011-2020 Data - School-Transportation-Related Crashes and Traffic Safety Facts, 2020 Data - Children.

Naval Postgraduate School, Center for Homeland Defense and Security (CHDS), 1 University Cir., Bldg. 220, Rm. 064, Monteray, CA, 93943, USA, (831) 656-2356 , mccolgan@nps.edu, https://www.chds.us; K-12 School Shooting Database.

Public Health Agency of Canada, 130 Colonnade Rd., Ottawa, ON, K1A 0K9, CAN, (844) 280-5020 (Dial from U.S.), https://www.phac-aspc.gc.ca/; CHIRPP Injury Reports.

Save the Children, 501 Kings Hwy. E, Ste. 400, Fairfield, CT, 06825, USA, (203) 221-4000, (800) 728-3843, https://www.savethechildren.org/; Childhood in the Time of COVID: U.S. Complement to the Global Childhood Report 2021; Global Childhood Report 2021: The Toughest Places to Be a Child; Global Girlhood Report 2022: Girls on the Frontline; and Stop the War on Children: Gender Matters.

U.S. Department of Health and Human Services, Centers for Disease Control and Prevention (CDC), 1600 Clifton Rd., Atlanta, GA, 30329-4027, USA, (800) 232-4636, (888) 232-6348 (TTY), cdcinfo@cdc.gov, https://www.cdc.gov; HIV Surveillance Reports.

U.S. Department of Health and Human Services, Centers for Disease Control and Prevention (CDC), National Center for Health Statistics (NCHS), 3311 Toledo Rd., Hyattsville, MD, 20782-2064, USA, (800) 232-4636, (301) 458-4000, https://www.cdc.gov/nchs; National Vital Statistics Reports (NVSR) and Vital Statistics Online Data Portal.

U.S. Department of the Interior (DOI), Office of the Secretary, 1849 C St. NW, Washington, DC, 20240, USA, (202) 208-3100, https://www.doi.gov/office-of-the-secretary; Federal Indian Boarding School Initiative Investigative Report.

UNICEF, 3 United Nations Plz., New York, NY, 10017, USA, (212) 303-7984, (917) 244-2215, https://www.unicef.org; COVID-19 and Children: UNICEF Data Hub.

United Nations Statistics Division (UNSD), United Nations Plz., New York, NY, 10017, USA, (800) 253-9646, (212) 963-9851, statistics@un.org, https://unstats.un.org; Millennium Development Goal Indicators.

United Nations UN Women, 405 E 42nd St., New York, NY, 10017-3599, USA, (646) 781-4400, (646) 781-4444, https://www.unwomen.org; Progress on the Sustainable Development Goals: The Gender Snapshot 2021.

World Health Organization (WHO), Ave. Appia 20, Geneva, CH-1211, SWI, (202) 974-3000 (Telephone in U.S.), publications@who.int, https://www.who.int/; HIV/AIDS Surveillance in Europe 2022.

CHILDREN-DISABILITY STATUS

U.S. Department of Education (ED), Institute of Education Sciences (IES), National Center for Education Statistics (NCES), Potomac Center Plaza, 550 12th St. SW, Washington, DC, 20202, USA, (202) 403-5551, https://nces.ed.gov/; DataLab.

CHILDREN-DISEASES

Human Cell Atlas (HCA), hca@humancellatlas.org, https://www.humancellatlas.org/; The Local and Systemic Response to SARS-CoV-2 Infection in Children and Adults and Pre-Activated Anti-Viral Innate Immunity in the Upper Airways Controls Early SARS-CoV-2 Infection in Children.

Rockefeller Foundation, 420 5th Ave., New York, NY, 10018, USA, (212) 869-8500, https://www.rockefellerfoundation.org; Implementing Covid-19 Routine Testing in K-12 Schools: Lessons and Recommendations from Pilot Sites.

Save the Children, 501 Kings Hwy. E, Ste. 400, Fairfield, CT, 06825, USA, (203) 221-4000, (800) 728-3843, https://www.savethechildren.org/; Childhood in the Time of COVID: U.S. Complement to the Global Childhood Report 2021; Global Childhood Report 2021: The Toughest Places to Be a Child; Global Girlhood Report 2022: Girls on the Frontline; and Stop the War on Children: Gender Matters.

U.S. Department of Health and Human Services (HHS), Health Resources and Services Administration (HRSA), Maternal and Child Health Bureau (MCHB), U.S. Department of Health and Human Services, 5600 Fishers Ln., Rockville, MD, 20857, USA, (877) 464-4772, (877) 897-9910 (TTY), https://mchb.hrsa.gov; 2020 National Survey of Children's Health (NSCH).

U.S. Department of Health and Human Services (HHS), National Institutes of Health (NIH), Researching COVID to Enhance Recovery (RECOVER), 9000 Rockville Pike, Bethesda, MD, 20892, USA, (301) 496-4000, (301) 402-9612 (TTY), https://recovercovid.org; Can Multisystem Inflammatory Syndrome in Children Be Managed in the Outpatient Setting? An EHR-Based Cohort Study From the RECOVER Program.

UNICEF, 3 United Nations Plz., New York, NY, 10017, USA, (212) 303-7984, (917) 244-2215, https://www.unicef.org; COVID-19 and Children: UNICEF Data Hub.

University of Washington, Institute for Health Metrics and Evaluation (IHME), Population Health Building/Hans Rosling Center, UW Campus Box 351615, 3980 15th Ave. NE, Seattle, WA, 98195, USA, (206) 897-2800, (206) 897-2899, engage@healthdata.org, https://www.healthdata.org; Global Burden of Disease (GBD).

CHILDREN-DRUG USE

American Academy of Pediatrics (AAP), 345 Park Blvd., Itasca, IL, 60143, USA, (800) 433-9016, (847) 434-8000, mcc@aap.org, https://www.aap.org; Pediatric Edible Cannabis Exposures and Acute Toxicity: 2017-2021.

Substance Abuse and Mental Health Services Administration (SAMHSA), 5600 Fishers Ln., Rockville, MD, 20857, USA, (877) 726-4727, (800) 487-4889 (TTY), samhsainfo@samhsa.hhs.gov, https://www.samhsa.gov/; 2019-2020 National Survey on Drug Use and Health (NSDUH).

CHILDREN-EDUCATION

Alabama State Department of Education, 50 N Ripley St., PO Box 302101, Montgomery, AL, 36104, USA, (334) 694-4900, comm@alsde.edu, https://www.alabamaachieves.org/; Alabama Education Report Card and Education Report Card: Supporting Data.

Bernan Press, 15250 NBN Way, Bldg. C, Blue Ridge Summit, PA, 17214, USA, (301) 459-2255, (800) 865-3457, (800) 865-3450, customercare@bernan.com, https://rowman.com/Page/Bernan; Digest of Education Statistics 2020.

Center for Education Reform (CER), Willard Office Bldg., 1455 Pennsylvania Ave. NW, Ste. 403, Washington, DC, 20004, USA, (202) 750-0016, https://edreform.com/; Just the FAQs - Charter Schools.

Colorado Department of Education, 201 E Colfax Ave., Denver, CO, 80203, USA, (303) 866-6600, (303) 830-0793, https://www.cde.state.co.us/; CSAP (Colorado Student Assessment Program) and TCAP (Transitional Colorado Assessment Program) Data and Results.

Connecticut State Department of Education, 450 Columbus Blvd., Hartford, CT, 06103, USA, (860) 713-6543, https://portal.ct.gov/SDE; Connecticut Report Cards.

Delaware Department of Education, The Townsend Bldg., 401 Federal St., Ste. 2, Dover, DE, 19901-3639, USA, (302) 735-4000, (302) 739-4654, dedoe@doe.k12.de.us, https://education.delaware.gov/; Delaware Educator Data System (DEEDS) and Delaware Report Card.

District of Columbia, Public Schools, 1200 First St. NE, Washington, DC, 20002, USA, (202) 442-5885, (202) 442-5026, https://dcps.dc.gov/; District of Columbia Public Schools.

Florida Department of Education, Turlington Building, 325 W Gaines St., Ste. 1514, Tallahassee, FL, 32399, USA, (850) 245-0505, (850) 245-9667, commissioner@fldoe.org, https://www.fldoe.org/; 2021 School Accountability Updates.

The Gallup Organization, 901 F St. NW, Washington, DC, 20004, USA, (202) 715-3030, (800) 204-1192, (202) 715-3045, https://www.gallup.com; Gallup Student Poll.

Georgia Department of Education, 205 Jesse Hill Jr. Dr. SE, Atlanta, GA, 30334, USA, (404) 656-2800, (800) 311-3627, (404) 651-8737, askdoe@gadoe.org, https://www.gadoe.org; College and Career Ready Performance Index.

Hawaii State Department of Education, 1390 Miller St., Honolulu, HI, 96813, USA, (808) 784-6200, doe_info@hawaiidoe.org, https://www.hawaiipublicschools.org/; Hawaii Department of Education Data Book: School Year 2021-2022.

Idaho State Department of Education, PO Box 83720, Boise, ID, 83720-0027, USA, (208) 332-6800, (208) 334-2228, info@sde.idaho.gov, https://www.sde.idaho.gov/; Idaho School Finder and Report Card.

Illinois State Board of Education, 100 N 1st St., Springfield, IL, 62777, USA, (866) 262-6663, (217) 782-4321, https://www.isbe.net/; Illinois Report Card 2021-2022 and Illinois Report Card Data Library.

Indiana Department of Education, Indiana Government Center N, 100 N Senate Ave, 9th Fl., Indianapolis, IN, 46204, USA, (317) 232-6610, https://www.in.gov/doe/; Annual School Performance Reports.

Iowa Department of Education, Grimes State Office Bldg., 400 E 14th St., Des Moines, IA, 50319-0146, USA, (512) 281-5294, (512) 242-5988, https://educateiowa.gov/; Education Statistics - PK-12.

Kansas State Department of Education, 900 SW Jackson St., Topeka, KS, 66612, USA, (785) 296-3201, (785) 296-7933, https://www.ksde.org/; Kansas K-12 Reports.

Kentucky Department of Education, 300 Sower Blvd., 5th Fl., Frankfort, KY, 40601, USA, (502) 564-3141, https://education.ky.gov; Kentucky School Report Card.

Louisiana Department of Education, PO Box 94064, Baton Rouge, LA, 70804-9064, USA, (877) 453-2721, https://www.louisianabelieves.com/; Louisiana School Report Cards.

Maine Department of Education, 23 State House Station, Augusta, ME, 04333-0023, USA, (207) 624-6600, (207) 624-6896, (207) 624-6700, medms.helpdesk@maine.gov, https://www.maine.gov/doe; Every Student Succeeds Act (ESSA) Dashboard; Maine Comprehensive Assessment System (MECAS); and MEA (Maine Educational Assessment) Science Family Resources.

Maryland State Department of Education, 200 W Baltimore St., Baltimore, MD, 21201-2595, USA, (410) 767-0100, info.msde@maryland.gov, https://www.marylandpublicschools.org/; 2022 Maryland School Report Cards.

Massachusetts Department of Elementary and Secondary Education, 75 Pleasant St., Malden, MA, 02148-4906, USA, (781) 338-3000, (800) 439-2370

(TTY), https://www.doe.mass.edu/; Massachusetts School and District Profiles and 2022 Massachusetts State Report Card.

Michigan Department of Education, 608 W Allegan St., PO Box 30008, Lansing, MI, 48909, USA, (833) 633-5788, (517) 355-4565, https://www.michigan.gov/mde/; Michigan School Index Report.

Minnesota Department of Education, 400 NE Stinson Blvd., Minneapolis, MN, 55413, USA, (651) 582-8200, mde.commissioner@state.mn.us, https://education.mn.gov/MDE; Data Reports and Analytics and Minnesota School Report Card.

Mississippi Department of Education, PO Box 771, Jackson, MS, 39205-0771, USA, (601) 359-3513, https://www.mdek12.org/; Mississippi Succeeds Report Card.

Missouri Department of Elementary and Secondary Education, PO Box 480, Jefferson City, MO, 65102-0480, USA, (573) 751-4212, https://dese.mo.gov/; Missouri Comprehensive Data System.

Montana Office of Public Instruction, PO Box 202501, Helena, MT, 59620-2501, USA, (406) 444-3680, (406) 444-3693, https://opi.mt.gov/; Consolidated State Performance Report (CSPR) and ESSA (Every Student Succeeds Act) Info & Documents.

National Association of Charter School Authorizers (NACSA), 1 E Erie St., Ste. 525, Chicago, IL, 60611, USA, (312) 376-2300, https://qualitycharters.org/; Authorizing by the Numbers.

Nebraska Department of Education, PO Box 94987, Lincoln, NE, 68509-4987, USA, (402) 471-2295, (402) 471-0117, https://www.education.ne.gov/; Nebraska State Accountability.

Nevada Department of Education, 700 E 5th St., Carson City, NV, 89701, USA, (775) 687-9115, ndeinfo@doe.nv.gov, https://doe.nv.gov/; Nevada Annual Reports of Accountability.

New Hampshire Department of Education, 101 Pleasant St., Concord, NH, 03301-3860, USA, (603) 271-3494, (603) 271-1953, info@doe.nh.gov, https://www.education.nh.gov/; Assessment Data.

New Jersey Department of Education, PO Box 500, Trenton, NJ, 08625-0500, USA, (609) 376-3500, https://www.state.nj.us/education/; Department of Education Data & Reports Portal.

New Mexico Public Education Department, Jerry Apodaca Education Building, 300 Don Gaspar, Santa Fe, NM, 87501, USA, (505) 827-5800, ped.helpdesk@state.nm.us, https://webnew.ped.state.nm.us/; Graduation Data.

New York State Education Department (NYSED), 89 Washington Ave., Albany, NY, 12234, USA, (518) 474-3852, http://www.nysed.gov/; New York State Education Data.

North Carolina Department of Public Instruction (NCDPI), 6301 Mail Service Center, Raleigh, NC, 27699-6301, USA, (987) 236-2100, information@dpi.nc.gov, https://www.dpi.nc.gov/; North Carolina School Report Cards.

North Dakota Department of Public Instruction, 600 E Boulevard Ave., Dept. 201, Bismarck, ND, 58505-0440, USA, (701) 328-2260, (701) 328-4770, dpi@nd.gov, https://www.nd.gov/dpi; unpublished data.

Ohio Department of Education, 25 S Front St., Columbus, OH, 43215-4183, USA, (877) 644-6338, contact.center@education.ohio.gov, https://education.ohio.gov/; Ohio School Report Cards.

Oklahoma State Department of Education, Oliver Hodge Bldg., 2500 N Lincoln Blvd., Oklahoma City, OK, 73105-4599, USA, (405) 521-3308, sdeservicedesk@sde.ok.gov, https://sde.ok.gov/; OSDE Public Records.

Oregon Department of Education, 255 Capitol St. NE, Salem, OR, 97310-0203, USA, (503) 947-5600, (503) 378-5156, https://www.oregon.gov/ode; School and District Profiles and Reports.

Pennsylvania Department of Education, 333 Market St., Harrisburg, PA, 17126, USA, (717) 783-6788, https://www.education.pa.gov; Pennsylvania System of School Assessment (PSSA).

Rhode Island Department of Education (RIDE), 255 Westminster St., Providence, RI, 02903, USA, (401) 222-4600, https://www.ride.ri.gov/; Rhode Island School and District Report Cards.

South Carolina Department of Education, 1429 Senate St., Columbia, SC, 29201, USA, (803) 734-8500, info@ed.sc.gov, https://ed.sc.gov/; Reading Partners 2019 Outcomes Report and South Carolina District School Report Cards.

State of Alaska Department of Education and Early Development, PO Box 110500, Juneau, AK, 99811-0500, USA, (907) 465-2800, (800) 770-8973 (TTY), (907) 465-2441, eed.webmaster@alaska.gov, https://education.alaska.gov/; Data Center.

Tennessee Department of Education, 710 James Robertson Pkwy., Nashville, TN, 37243, USA, (615) 741-5158, https://www.tn.gov/education/; Tennessee State Report Card and Tennessee Value-Added Assessment System - TVAAS.

Texas Education Agency (TEA), William B. Travis Bldg., 1701 N Congress Ave., Austin, TX, 78701, USA, (512) 463-9734, (512) 463-9838, generalinquiry@tea.texas.gov, https://tea.texas.gov; 2022 Comprehensive Biennial Report on Texas Public Schools and Texas Academic Performance Reports 2021-2022.

U.S. Department of the Interior (DOI), Office of the Secretary, 1849 C St. NW, Washington, DC, 20240, USA, (202) 208-3100, https://www.doi.gov/office-of-the-secretary; Federal Indian Boarding School Initiative Investigative Report.

U.S. Government Accountablity Office (GAO), 441 G St. NW, Washington, DC, 20548, USA, (202) 512-3000, contact@gao.gov, https://www.gao.gov/; School Meals Program: USDA Has Reported Taking Some Steps to Reduce Improper Payments but Should Comprehensively Assess Fraud Risks.

UNESCO Institute for Statistics, C.P 250 Succursale H, Montreal, QC, H3G 2K8, CAN, (514) 343-6880 (Dial from U.S.), (514) 343-5740 (Fax from U.S.), uis.publications@unesco.org, http://uis.unesco.org/; Global Education Monitoring Report 2019 - Migration, Displacement and Education: Building Bridges, Not Walls; Global Education Monitoring Report 2020 - Inclusion and Education; and Global Education Monitoring Report 2021-2022: Non-State Actors in Education.

UNICEF, 3 United Nations Plz., New York, NY, 10017, USA, (212) 303-7984, (917) 244-2215, https://www.unicef.org; Country Profiles.

United Nations Statistics Division (UNSD), United Nations Plz., New York, NY, 10017, USA, (800) 253-9646, (212) 963-9851, statistics@un.org, https://unstats.un.org; Millennium Development Goal Indicators.

University of California Los Angeles (UCLA), Luskin Center for Innovation, 3323 Public Affairs Bldg., PO Box 951656, Los Angeles, CA, 90095-1656, USA, (310) 267-5435, (310) 267-5443, https://innovation.luskin.ucla.edu/; Heat and Learning.

Utah State Board of Education, PO Box 144200, Salt Lake City, UT, 84114-4200, USA, (801) 538-7500, ryan.bartlett@schools.utah.gov, https://www.schools.utah.gov/; Utah Schools Data and Statistics and Utah Schools Special Education Services.

Vermont Agency of Education, 1 National Life Dr., Davis 5, Montpelier, VT, 05620-2501, USA, (802) 828-1130, (802) 828-6430, aoe.edinfo@vermont.gov, https://education.vermont.gov/; State Report Card.

Virginia Department of Education (VDOE), PO Box 2120, Richmond, VA, 23218, USA, (800) 292-3820, https://www.doe.virginia.gov/; State Assessment Results and Statistics & Reports.

Washington Office of Superintendent of Public Instruction (OSPI), Old Capitol Bldg., PO Box 47200, Olympia, WA, 98504-7200, USA, (360) 725-6000, (360) 664-3631 (TTY), https://www.k12.wa.us/; Washington State Report Card.

West Virginia Department of Education, 1900 Kanawha Blvd. E, Charleston, WV, 25305, USA, (304) 558-2681, (833) 627-2833, https://wvde.us/; West Virginia Education Information System (WVEIS).

Wisconsin Department of Public Instruction, 125 S Webster St., Madison, WI, 53703, USA, (800) 441-4563, (608) 266-3390, https://dpi.wi.gov/; Wisconsin School Performance Report (SPR).

Wyoming Department of Education (WDE), 122 W 25th St., Ste. E200, Cheyenne, WY, 82002, USA, (307) 777-7675, (307) 777-6234, https://edu.wyoming.gov/; Wyoming Statewide Assessment System.

CHILDREN-FAMILIES WITH

The Annie E. Casey Foundation, 701 Saint Paul St., Baltimore, MD, 21202, USA, (410) 547-6600, (410) 547-6624, https://www.aecf.org/; 2021 KIDS COUNT Data Book: State Trends in Child Well-Being and KIDS COUNT Database.

Casey Family Programs, 2001 8th Ave., Ste. 2700, Seattle, WA, 98121, USA, (206) 282-7300, (206) 282-3555, info@casey.org, https://www.casey.org/; Creating a Better Future for Children and Families in a Time of Crisis and State-by-State Data: Foster Care.

The Henry J. Kaiser Family Foundation (KFF), 185 Berry St., Ste. 2000, San Francisco, CA, 94107, USA, (650) 854-9400, (650) 854-4800, https://www.kff.org; More Than 3 Million People Age 65 or Older Live with School-Age Children, and Could Be at Heightened Risk of COVID-19 Infection if Children Bring the Virus Home from School.

The Lancet, 230 Park Ave., New York, NY, 10169, USA, (212) 633-3800, editorial@lancet.com, https://www.thelancet.com/; Global, Regional, and National Minimum Estimates of Children Affected by COVID-19-Associated Orphanhood and Caregiver Death, by Age and Family Circumstance up to Oct 31, 2021: An Updated Modelling Study.

Southern Poverty Law Center (SPLC), 400 Washington Ave., Montgomery, AL, 36104, USA, (334) 956-8200, (888) 414-7752, https://www.splcenter.org/; Cut Off From Caregivers: The Children of Incarcerated Parents in Louisiana.

U.S. Department of Health and Human Services (HHS), Health Resources and Services Administration (HRSA), Maternal and Child Health Bureau (MCHB), U.S. Department of Health and Human Services, 5600 Fishers Ln., Rockville, MD, 20857, USA, (877) 464-4772, (877) 897-9910 (TTY), https://mchb.hrsa.gov; Explore the Title V Federal-State Partnership.

CHILDREN-FOOD SECURITY

The Economist Group: Economist Intelligence Unit (EIU), 900 3rd Ave., 16th Fl., New York, NY, 10022, USA, (212) 541-0500, americas@eiu.com, https://www.eiu.com; Global Food Security Index 2022.

Rockefeller Foundation, 420 5th Ave., New York, NY, 10018, USA, (212) 869-8500, https://www.rockefellerfoundation.org; Reset the Table: Meeting the Moment to Transform the U.S. Food System.

Save the Children, 501 Kings Hwy. E, Ste. 400, Fairfield, CT, 06825, USA, (203) 221-4000, (800) 728-3843, https://www.savethechildren.org/; Childhood in the Time of COVID: U.S. Complement to the Global Childhood Report 2021; Global Childhood Report 2021: The Toughest Places to Be a Child; Global Girlhood Report 2022: Girls on the Frontline; and Stop the War on Children: Gender Matters.

U.S. Department of Agriculture (USDA), Economic Research Service (ERS), 1400 Independence Ave. SW, Mail Stop 1800, Washington, DC, 20250-0002, USA, (202) 720-2791, https://www.ers.usda.gov/; The Food and Nutrition Assistance Landscape: Fiscal Year 2021 Annual Report; Food and Nutrition Assistance Research Reports Database; Food Environment Atlas; and Household Food Security in the United States in 2020.

U.S. Department of Agriculture (USDA), Food and Nutrition Service (FNS), Braddock Metro Center II, 1320 Braddock Pl., Alexandria, VA, 22314, USA,

(703) 305-2062, https://www.fns.usda.gov/; Direct Certification in the National School Lunch Program: State Implementation Progress and SNAP Data Tables.

U.S. Government Accountablity Office (GAO), 441 G St. NW, Washington, DC, 20548, USA, (202) 512-3000, contact@gao.gov, https://www.gao.gov/; School Meals Program: USDA Has Reported Taking Some Steps to Reduce Improper Payments but Should Comprehensively Assess Fraud Risks.

United Nations Statistics Division (UNSD), United Nations Plz., New York, NY, 10017, USA, (800) 253-9646, (212) 963-9851, statistics@un.org, https://unstats.un.org; Millennium Development Goal Indicators.

UrbanFootprint, 2095 Rose St., Ste. 21, Berkeley, CA, 94709, USA, https://urbanfootprint.com; Food Security Insights.

CHILDREN-FOOD STAMP PROGRAM

U.S. Department of Agriculture (USDA), Food and Nutrition Service (FNS), Braddock Metro Center II, 1320 Braddock Pl., Alexandria, VA, 22314, USA, (703) 305-2062, https://www.fns.usda.gov/; Characteristics of SNAP Households: FY 2019 and SNAP Data Tables.

CHILDREN-FOREIGN BORN POPULATION

Migration Policy Institute (MPI), 1275 K St. NW, Ste. 800, Washington, DC, 20005, USA, (202) 266-1940, (202) 266-1900, info@migrationpolicy.org, https://www.migrationpolicy.org/; U.S. Immigration Policy under Trump: Deep Changes and Lasting Impacts.

CHILDREN-FRACTURES

U.S. Department of Health and Human Services, Centers for Disease Control and Prevention (CDC), National Center for Health Statistics (NCHS), 3311 Toledo Rd., Hyattsville, MD, 20782-2064, USA, (800) 232-4636, (301) 458-4000, https://www.cdc.gov/nchs; Health, United States, 2020-2021.

CHILDREN-HEALTH AND HYGIENE

American Academy of Pediatrics (AAP), 345 Park Blvd., Itasca, IL, 60143, USA, (800) 433-9016, (847) 434-8000, mcc@aap.org, https://www.aap.org; Children and COVID-19: State-Level Data Report and Pediatric Edible Cannabis Exposures and Acute Toxicity: 2017-2021.

Amnesty International USA, 311 W 43rd St., 7th Fl., New York, NY, 10036, USA, (212) 807-8400, (800) 266-3789, (212) 627-1451, aimember@aiusa.org, https://www.amnestyusa.org/; No Home for Children: The Homestead 'Temporary Emergency' Facility.

The Annie E. Casey Foundation, 701 Saint Paul St., Baltimore, MD, 21202, USA, (410) 547-6600, (410) 547-6624, https://www.aecf.org/; Kids, Families and COVID-19: Pandemic Pain Points and the Urgent Need to Respond.

Australian Government Department of Social Services, 71 Athllon Dr., Canberra, ACT, 2900, AUS, https://www.dss.gov.au/; Growing Up in Australia: The Longitudinal Study of Australian Children Annual Statistical Report.

Australian Institute of Family Studies, Child Family Community Australia (CFCA), 40 City Rd., Level 4, Southbank, VIC, 3006, AUS, enquiries@aifs.gov.au, https://aifs.gov.au/research_programs/child-family-community-australia; Child Wellbeing During the COVID Pandemic: Parental Concerns.

Children's Defense Fund (CDF), 840 1st St. NE, Ste. 300, Washington, DC, 20002, USA, (202) 628-8787, cdfinfo@childrensdefense.org, https://www.childrensdefense.org/; Child Poverty in America 2019.

Every Texan, 7020 Easy Wind Dr., Ste. 200, Austin, TX, 78752, USA, (512) 320-0222, (512) 320-0227, info@everytexan.org, https://everytexan.org/; 2022 Texas KIDS COUNT Data Book.

The Henry J. Kaiser Family Foundation (KFF), 185 Berry St., Ste. 2000, San Francisco, CA, 94107, USA, (650) 854-9400, (650) 854-4800, https://www.kff.org; KFF COVID-19 Vaccine Monitor: January 2022 Parents and Kids Update.

Human Cell Atlas (HCA), hca@humancellatlas.org, https://www.humancellatlas.org/; The Local and Systemic Response to SARS-CoV-2 Infection in Children and Adults and Pre-Activated Anti-Viral Innate Immunity in the Upper Airways Controls Early SARS-CoV-2 Infection in Children.

NewsGuard, 25 W 52nd St., 15th Fl., New York, NY, 10019, USA, https://www.newsguardtech.com/; COVID-19 Vaccine Misinformation Targeting Children, Teenagers and Parents on Social Media: A Report for Governments and the WHO.

Plan International UK, Finsgate , 5-7 Cranwood St., London, EC1V 9LH, GBR, https://www.plan-uk.org/; What Works for Ending Public Sexual Harassment?.

Robert Wood Johnson Foundation (RWJF), 50 College Rd. E, Princeton, NJ, 08540-6614, USA, (877) 843-7953, (609) 627-6000, https://www.rwjf.org/; From Crisis to Opportunity: Reforming Our Nation's Policies to Help All Children Grow Up Healthy.

Rockefeller Foundation, 420 5th Ave., New York, NY, 10018, USA, (212) 869-8500, https://www.rockefellerfoundation.org; Implementing Covid-19 Routine Testing in K-12 Schools: Lessons and Recommendations from Pilot Sites.

Southern Poverty Law Center (SPLC), 400 Washington Ave., Montgomery, AL, 36104, USA, (334) 956-8200, (888) 414-7752, https://www.splcenter.org/; Cut Off From Caregivers: The Children of Incarcerated Parents in Louisiana.

St Jude Children's Research Hospital, 262 Danny Thomas Pl., Memphis, TN, 38105, USA, (866) 278-5833, (901) 595-1040 (TTY), https://www.stjude.org/; The Scientific Report: Translating Science into Survival.

U.S. Department of Health and Human Services (HHS), Health Resources and Services Administration (HRSA), Maternal and Child Health Bureau (MCHB), U.S. Department of Health and Human Services, 5600 Fishers Ln., Rockville, MD, 20857, USA, (877) 464-4772, (877) 897-9910 (TTY), https://mchb.hrsa.gov; 2020 National Survey of Children's Health (NSCH).

U.S. Department of Health and Human Services (HHS), Office of Inspector General (OIG), 330 Independence Ave. SW, Washington, DC, 20201, USA, (877) 696-6775, public.affairs@oig.hhs.gov, https://oig.hhs.gov/; Care Provider Facilities Described Challenges Addressing Mental Health Needs of Children in HHS Custody.

UNICEF, 3 United Nations Plz., New York, NY, 10017, USA, (212) 303-7984, (917) 244-2215, https://www.unicef.org; Children's Climate Risk Index (CCRI) and COVID-19 and Children: UNICEF Data Hub.

United Health Foundation, America's Health Rankings, PO Box 1459, Minneapolis, MN, 55440-1459, USA, (952) 936-1917, jenifer_mccormick@uhg.com, https://www.americashealthrankings.org/; 2022 Health of Women and Children Report.

United States Public Interest Research Group (U.S. PIRG), 1543 Wazee St., Ste. 460, Denver, MA, 80202, USA, (303) 801-0582, https://uspirg.org; Trouble in Toyland 2021: The 36th Annual Toy Safety Report.

University of California Los Angeles (UCLA), Center for Health Policy Research (CHPR), 10960 Wilshire Blvd., Ste. 1550, Campus Mail Code 714346, Los Angeles, CA, 90024, USA, (310) 794-0909, (310) 794-2686, healthpolicy@ucla.edu, https://healthpolicy.ucla.edu; AskCHIS Database.

CHILDREN-HEALTH INSURANCE COVERAGE

The Annie E. Casey Foundation, 701 Saint Paul St., Baltimore, MD, 21202, USA, (410) 547-6600, (410) 547-6624, https://www.aecf.org/; Kids, Families and COVID-19: Pandemic Pain Points and the Urgent Need to Respond.

Federal Interagency Forum on Child and Family Statistics (The Forum), USA, childstats@ed.gov, https://www.childstats.gov; America's Children: Key National Indicators of Well-Being, 2021.

The Henry J. Kaiser Family Foundation (KFF), 185 Berry St., Ste. 2000, San Francisco, CA, 94107, USA, (650) 854-9400, (650) 854-4800, https://www.kff.org; Medicaid and CHIP Eligibility and Enrollment Policies as of January 2022: Findings from a 50-State Survey.

National Governors Association (NGA), 444 N Capitol St., Ste. 267, Washington, DC, 20001, USA, (202) 624-5300, (202) 624-5313, info@nga.org, https://www.nga.org; Maternal and Child Health Update 2020.

U.S. Census Bureau, 4600 Silver Hill Rd., Washington, DC, 20233, USA, (301) 763-4636, (800) 923-8282, https://www.census.gov; Health Insurance Coverage in the United States: 2021.

U.S. Department of Health and Human Services (HHS), Health Resources and Services Administration (HRSA), Maternal and Child Health Bureau (MCHB), U.S. Department of Health and Human Services, 5600 Fishers Ln., Rockville, MD, 20857, USA, (877) 464-4772, (877) 897-9910 (TTY), https://mchb.hrsa.gov; Explore the Title V Federal-State Partnership and 2020 National Survey of Children's Health (NSCH).

United Health Foundation, America's Health Rankings, PO Box 1459, Minneapolis, MN, 55440-1459, USA, (952) 936-1917, jenifer_mccormick@uhg.com, https://www.americashealthrankings.org/; 2022 Health of Women and Children Report.

CHILDREN-HIGH SCHOOL DROPOUTS

U.S. Department of Education (ED), Institute of Education Sciences (IES), 550 12th St. SW, Washington, DC, 20024, USA, (202) 245-6940, contact.ies@ed.gov, https://ies.ed.gov/; What Works Clearinghouse (WWC).

CHILDREN-HIGH SCHOOL GRADUATES

U.S. Department of Education (ED), Institute of Education Sciences (IES), National Center for Education Statistics (NCES), Potomac Center Plaza, 550 12th St. SW, Washington, DC, 20202, USA, (202) 403-5551, https://nces.ed.gov/; Digest of Education Statistics, 2020.

CHILDREN-HISPANIC ORIGIN POPULATION

Child Trends, 7315 Wisconsin Ave., Ste. 1200W, Bethesda, MD, 20814, USA, (240) 223-9200, https://www.childtrends.org/; Undercounting Hispanics in the 2020 Census Will Result in a Loss in Federal Funding to Many States for Child and Family Assistance Programs.

Children's Defense Fund (CDF), 840 1st St. NE, Ste. 300, Washington, DC, 20002, USA, (202) 628-8787, cdfinfo@childrensdefense.org, https://www.childrensdefense.org/; Ending Child Poverty Now and The State of America's Children 2021.

U.S. Census Bureau, 4600 Silver Hill Rd., Washington, DC, 20233, USA, (301) 763-4636, (800) 923-8282, https://www.census.gov; Racial Identification for the Self-Reported Hispanic or Latino Population: 2010 and 2020 Census.

CHILDREN-HOSPITAL UTILIZATION

U.S. Department of Health and Human Services (HHS), Health Resources and Services Administration (HRSA), Maternal and Child Health Bureau (MCHB), U.S. Department of Health and Human Services, 5600 Fishers Ln., Rockville, MD, 20857, USA, (877) 464-4772, (877) 897-9910 (TTY), https://mchb.hrsa.gov; 2020 National Survey of Children's Health (NSCH).

U.S. Department of Health and Human Services, Centers for Disease Control and Prevention (CDC), National Center for Health Statistics (NCHS), 3311 Toledo Rd., Hyattsville, MD, 20782-2064, USA, (800) 232-4636, (301) 458-4000, https://www.cdc.

gov/nchs; FastStats - Statistics by Topic and Health, United States, 2020-2021.

CHILDREN-HUNGER

Concern Worldwide U.S., 355 Lexington Ave., 16th Fl., New York, NY, 10017, USA, (212) 557-8000, (212) 692-0415, info.usa@concern.net, https://www.concernusa.org/; Global Hunger Index 2022.

Federal Interagency Forum on Child and Family Statistics (The Forum), USA, childstats@ed.gov, https://www.childstats.gov; America's Children: Key National Indicators of Well-Being, 2021.

Rockefeller Foundation, 420 5th Ave., New York, NY, 10018, USA, (212) 869-8500, https://www.rockefellerfoundation.org; Reset the Table: Meeting the Moment to Transform the U.S. Food System.

Save the Children, 501 Kings Hwy. E, Ste. 400, Fairfield, CT, 06825, USA, (203) 221-4000, (800) 728-3843, https://www.savethechildren.org/; Childhood in the Time of COVID: U.S. Complement to the Global Childhood Report 2021; Global Childhood Report 2021: The Toughest Places to Be a Child; Global Girlhood Report 2022: Girls on the Frontline; and Stop the War on Children: Gender Matters.

U.S. Department of Agriculture (USDA), Economic Research Service (ERS), 1400 Independence Ave. SW, Mail Stop 1800, Washington, DC, 20250-0002, USA, (202) 720-2791, https://www.ers.usda.gov/; The Food and Nutrition Assistance Landscape: Fiscal Year 2021 Annual Report; Food and Nutrition Assistance Research Reports Database; and Food Environment Atlas.

UNICEF, 3 United Nations Plz., New York, NY, 10017, USA, (212) 303-7984, (917) 244-2215, https://www.unicef.org; Children's Climate Risk Index (CCRI).

United Nations Statistics Division (UNSD), United Nations Plz., New York, NY, 10017, USA, (800) 253-9646, (212) 963-9851, statistics@un.org, https://unstats.un.org; Millennium Development Goal Indicators.

CHILDREN-IMMIGRANTS

American Immigration Council, 1331 G St. NW , Ste. 200, Washington, DC, 20005, USA, (202) 507-7500, info@immcouncil.org, https://www.americanimmigrationcouncil.org/; U.S. Citizen Children Impacted by Immigration Enforcement.

Amnesty International USA, 311 W 43rd St., 7th Fl., New York, NY, 10036, USA, (212) 807-8400, (800) 266-3789, (212) 627-1451, aimember@aiusa.org, https://www.amnestyusa.org/; No Home for Children: The Homestead 'Temporary Emergency' Facility.

Human Rights Watch, 350 5th Ave., 34th Fl., New York, NY, 10118-3299, USA, (212) 290-4700, (212) 736-1300, https://www.hrw.org; Like I'm Drowning: Children and Families Sent to Harm by the US 'Remain in Mexico' Program.

Ipsos, 360 Park Ave. S, 17th Fl., New York, NY, 10010, USA, (212) 265-3200, https://www.ipsos.com/en-us; A Majority of Americans Do Not Support Separating Immigrant Families.

U.S. Department of Health and Human Services (HHS), Office of Inspector General (OIG), 330 Independence Ave. SW, Washington, DC, 20201, USA, (877) 696-6775, public.affairs@oig.hhs.gov, https://oig.hhs.gov/; Care Provider Facilities Described Challenges Addressing Mental Health Needs of Children in HHS Custody.

U.S. Department of Homeland Security (DHS), Office of Immigration Statistics (OIS), 2707 Martin Luther King Jr. Ave. SE, Washington, DC, 20528-0525, USA, (202) 282-8000, immigrationstatistics@hq.dhs.gov, https://www.dhs.gov/office-immigration-statistics; Estimates of the Lawful Permanent Resident Population in the United States: January 2019-2021 and Yearbook of Immigration Statistics 2020.

CHILDREN-IMMUNIZATION AGAINST DISEASES

U.S. Department of Health and Human Services, Centers for Disease Control and Prevention (CDC), 1600 Clifton Rd., Atlanta, GA, 30329-4027, USA, (800) 232-4636, (888) 232-6348 (TTY), cdcinfo@cdc.gov, https://www.cdc.gov; Morbidity and Mortality Weekly Report (MMWR).

UNICEF, 3 United Nations Plz., New York, NY, 10017, USA, (212) 303-7984, (917) 244-2215, https://www.unicef.org; Country Profiles.

CHILDREN-INCOME-FAMILIES WITH CHILDREN

The Annie E. Casey Foundation, 701 Saint Paul St., Baltimore, MD, 21202, USA, (410) 547-6600, (410) 547-6624, https://www.aecf.org/; 2021 KIDS COUNT Data Book: State Trends in Child Well-Being.

Bank Street Graduate School of Education, National Center for Children in Poverty (NCCP), 475 Riverside Dr., Ste. 1400, New York, NY, 10115, USA, info@nccp.org, https://www.nccp.org/; 50-State Demographics Data Generator.

Federal Interagency Forum on Child and Family Statistics (The Forum), USA, childstats@ed.gov, https://www.childstats.gov; America's Children: Key National Indicators of Well-Being, 2021.

CHILDREN-INJURIES

Children's Defense Fund (CDF), 840 1st St. NE, Ste. 300, Washington, DC, 20002, USA, (202) 628-8787, cdfinfo@childrensdefense.org, https://www.childrensdefense.org/; Protect Children, Not Guns 2019.

Kids and Cars, Kansas City, MO, 64114, USA, (913) 732-2792, (913) 205-6973, amber@kidsandcars.org, https://www.kidsandcars.org/; www.kidsandcars.org.

Marshfield Clinic Research Institute (MCRI), National Children's Center for Rural and Agricultural Health and Safety (NCCRAHS), 1000 N Oak Ave., Marshfield, WI, 54449-5790, USA, (800) 662-6900, (715) 389-4999, nccrahs@mcrf.mfldclin.edu, https://www.marshfieldresearch.org/nccrahs; Childhood Agricultural Injuries: 2022 Fact Sheet.

Naval Postgraduate School, Center for Homeland Defense and Security (CHDS), 1 University Cir., Bldg. 220, Rm. 064, Monteray, CA, 93943, USA, (831) 656-2356 , mccolgan@nps.edu, https://www.chds.us; K-12 School Shooting Database.

Public Health Agency of Canada, 130 Colonnade Rd., Ottawa, ON, K1A 0K9, CAN, (844) 280-5020 (Dial from U.S.), https://www.phac-aspc.gc.ca/; Victims of Police-Reported Family and Intimate Partner Violence in Canada, 2021.

U.S. Department of Health and Human Services, Centers for Disease Control and Prevention (CDC), National Center for Health Statistics (NCHS), 3311 Toledo Rd., Hyattsville, MD, 20782-2064, USA, (800) 232-4636, (301) 458-4000, https://www.cdc.gov/nchs; FastStats - Statistics by Topic.

United States Public Interest Research Group (U.S. PIRG), 1543 Wazee St., Ste. 460, Denver, MA, 80202, USA, (303) 801-0582, https://uspirg.org; Trouble in Toyland 2021: The 36th Annual Toy Safety Report.

University of Virginia School of Engineering and Applied Science, Center for Applied Biomechanics (CAB), 4040 Lewis and Clark Dr., Charlottesville, VA, 22911, USA, (434) 297-8001, https://engineering.virginia.edu/research/centers-institutes/center-applied-biomechanics/research; unpublished data.

CHILDREN-INTERNET ACCESS

National Alliance for Public Charter Schools, 800 Connecticut Ave. NW, Ste. 300, Washington, DC, 20006, USA, (202) 289-2700, (202) 289-4009, datarequest@publiccharters.org, https://www.publiccharters.org/; Closing the Digital Divide.

CHILDREN-JUVENILE DELINQUENCY

Bureau of Alcohol, Tobacco, Firearms and Explosives (ATF), United States Bomb Data Center (USBDC), 3750 Corporal Rd., Huntsville, AL, 35898 , USA, (800) 461-8841, usbdc@atf.gov, https://www.atf.gov/explosives/us-bomb-data-center; 2019 Juvenile Offender (Fire) Incident Report.

Justice Policy Institute (JPI), 1012 14th St. NW, Ste. 600, Washington, DC, 20005, USA, (202) 558-7974, (202) 558-7978, info@justicepolicy.org, https://www.justicepolicy.org; Sticker Shock: The Cost of New York's Youth Prisons Approaches $1 Million Per Kid.

National Center for Juvenile Justice (NCJJ), 3700 S Water St., Ste. 200, Pittsburgh, PA, 15203, USA, (412) 227-6950, (412) 227-6955, ncjj@ncjfcj.org, https://www.ncjj.org/; Criminological Highlights: Children and Youth and Trends and Characteristics of Delinquency Cases Handled in Juvenile Court, 2019.

U.S. Department of Justice (DOJ), Office of Juvenile Justice and Delinquency Prevention (OJJDP), 810 7th St. NW, Washington, DC, 20531, USA, (202) 307-5911, https://www.ojjdp.gov/; Statistical Briefing Book (SBB).

CHILDREN-LABOR FORCE (16 TO 19 YEARS OLD)-EMPLOYED

Marshfield Clinic Research Institute (MCRI), National Children's Center for Rural and Agricultural Health and Safety (NCCRAHS), 1000 N Oak Ave., Marshfield, WI, 54449-5790, USA, (800) 662-6900, (715) 389-4999, nccrahs@mcrf.mfldclin.edu, https://www.marshfieldresearch.org/nccrahs; Childhood Agricultural Injuries: 2022 Fact Sheet.

U.S. Department of Labor (DOL), Bureau of Labor Statistics (BLS), Postal Square Bldg., 2 Massachusetts Ave. NE, Washington, DC, 20212-0001, USA, (202) 691-5200, (202) 691-7890, blsdata_staff@bls.gov, https://www.bls.gov; Labor Force Statistics from the Current Population Survey (CPS) and Monthly Labor Review.

CHILDREN-LABOR FORCE (16 TO 19 YEARS OLD)-EMPLOYMENT STATUS

U.S. Department of Labor (DOL), Bureau of Labor Statistics (BLS), Postal Square Bldg., 2 Massachusetts Ave. NE, Washington, DC, 20212-0001, USA, (202) 691-5200, (202) 691-7890, blsdata_staff@bls.gov, https://www.bls.gov; Labor Force Statistics from the Current Population Survey (CPS) and Monthly Labor Review.

CHILDREN-LABOR FORCE (16 TO 19 YEARS OLD)-PARTICIPATION RATES

U.S. Department of Labor (DOL), Bureau of Labor Statistics (BLS), Postal Square Bldg., 2 Massachusetts Ave. NE, Washington, DC, 20212-0001, USA, (202) 691-5200, (202) 691-7890, blsdata_staff@bls.gov, https://www.bls.gov; Monthly Labor Review.

CHILDREN-LABOR FORCE (16 TO 19 YEARS OLD)-SEX

U.S. Department of Labor (DOL), Bureau of Labor Statistics (BLS), Postal Square Bldg., 2 Massachusetts Ave. NE, Washington, DC, 20212-0001, USA, (202) 691-5200, (202) 691-7890, blsdata_staff@bls.gov, https://www.bls.gov; Labor Force Statistics from the Current Population Survey (CPS) and Monthly Labor Review.

CHILDREN-LABOR FORCE (16 TO 19 YEARS OLD)-UNEMPLOYED

U.S. Department of Labor (DOL), Bureau of Labor Statistics (BLS), Postal Square Bldg., 2 Massachusetts Ave. NE, Washington, DC, 20212-0001, USA, (202) 691-5200, (202) 691-7890, blsdata_staff@bls.gov, https://www.bls.gov; Monthly Labor Review.

CHILDREN-LITERACY

UNESCO Institute for Statistics, C.P 250 Succursale H, Montreal, QC, H3G 2K8, CAN, (514) 343-6880 (Dial from U.S.), (514) 343-5740 (Fax from U.S.), uis.publications@unesco.org, http://uis.unesco.org/; Global Education Monitoring Report 2019 - Migration, Displacement and Education: Building Bridges, Not Walls; Global Education Monitoring Report 2020 - Inclusion and Education;

and Global Education Monitoring Report 2021-2022: Non-State Actors in Education.

CHILDREN-MEDICAL CARE

Cardiac Arrest Registry to Enhance Survival (CARES), 1599 Clifton Rd. NE, Woodruff Health Sciences Center, Mailstop 1599/001/1BQ, Atlanta, GA, 30322, USA, cares@emory.edu, https://mycares.net; Race/Ethnicity and Neighborhood Characteristics Are Associated With Bystander Cardiopulmonary Resuscitation in Pediatric Out-of-Hospital Cardiac Arrest in the United States.

The Henry J. Kaiser Family Foundation (KFF), 185 Berry St., Ste. 2000, San Francisco, CA, 94107, USA, (650) 854-9400, (650) 854-4800, https://www.kff.org; KFF COVID-19 Vaccine Monitor: January 2022 Parents and Kids Update.

Rockefeller Foundation, 420 5th Ave., New York, NY, 10018, USA, (212) 869-8500, https://www.rockefellerfoundation.org; Implementing Covid-19 Routine Testing in K-12 Schools: Lessons and Recommendations from Pilot Sites.

U.S. Department of Health and Human Services, Centers for Disease Control and Prevention (CDC), Coronavirus Disease 2019 (COVID-19)-Associated Hospitalization Surveillance Network (COVID-NET), 1600 Clifton Rd., Atlanta, GA, 30329-4027, USA, (800) 232-4636, cdcinfo@cdc.gov, https://www.cdc.gov/coronavirus/2019-ncov/covid-data/covid-net/purpose-methods.html; Hospitalization Rates and Characteristics of Children Aged Less than 18 Years Hospitalized with Laboratory-Confirmed COVID-19 - COVID-NET, 14 States, March 1-July 25, 2020 and Hospitalizations of Children and Adolescents with Laboratory-Confirmed COVID-19 - COVID-NET, 14 States, July 2021-January 2022.

CHILDREN-MENTAL HEALTH

American Immigration Council, 1331 G St. NW , Ste. 200, Washington, DC, 20005, USA, (202) 507-7500, info@immcouncil.org, https://www.americanimmigrationcouncil.org/; U.S. Citizen Children Impacted by Immigration Enforcement.

American Psychological Association (APA), 750 First St. NE, Washington, DC, 20002-4242, USA, (800) 374-2721, (202) 336-5500, https://www.apa.org/; The Young People Feel It: A Look at the Mental Health Impact of Antitrans Legislation.

Australian Institute of Family Studies, Child Family Community Australia (CFCA), 40 City Rd., Level 4, Southbank, VIC, 3006, AUS, enquiries@aifs.gov.au, https://aifs.gov.au/research_programs/child-family-community-australia; Child Wellbeing During the COVID Pandemic: Parental Concerns.

Center for Humane Technology (CHT), hello@humanetech.com, https://www.humanetech.com/; Ledger of Harms.

Child Trends, 7315 Wisconsin Ave., Ste. 1200W, Bethesda, MD, 20814, USA, (240) 223-9200, https://www.childtrends.org/; Family Instability and Children's Social Development.

Cyberbullying Research Center, USA, hinduja@cyberbullying.org, https://cyberbullying.org; 2021 Cyberbullying Data; Summary of Our Cyberbullying Research (2007-2021); and Tween Cyberbullying in 2020.

Federal Interagency Forum on Child and Family Statistics (The Forum), USA, childstats@ed.gov, https://www.childstats.gov; America's Children: Key National Indicators of Well-Being, 2021.

The Gallup Organization, 901 F St. NW, Washington, DC, 20004, USA, (202) 715-3030, (800) 204-1192, (202) 715-3045, https://www.gallup.com; Gallup Student Poll.

Girl Scouts of the USA, 420 Fifth Ave., New York, NY, 10018, USA, (212) 852-8000, (800) 478-7248, https://www.girlscouts.org/; Girls Speak Out About Mental Health.

Human Rights Watch, 350 5th Ave., 34th Fl., New York, NY, 10118-3299, USA, (212) 290-4700, (212) 736-1300, https://www.hrw.org; Like I'm Drowning: Children and Families Sent to Harm by the US 'Remain in Mexico' Program.

Montana Office of Public Instruction, PO Box 202501, Helena, MT, 59620-2501, USA, (406) 444-3680, (406) 444-3693, https://opi.mt.gov/; Culture and Schools: American Indian Stakeholder Perspectives on the American Indian Student Achievement Gap.

Save the Children, 501 Kings Hwy. E, Ste. 400, Fairfield, CT, 06825, USA, (203) 221-4000, (800) 728-3843, https://www.savethechildren.org/; Childhood in the Time of COVID: U.S. Complement to the Global Childhood Report 2021; Global Childhood Report 2021: The Toughest Places to Be a Child; Global Girlhood Report 2022: Girls on the Frontline; and Stop the War on Children: Gender Matters.

The Trevor Project, PO Box 69232, West Hollywood, CA, 90069, USA, (212) 695-8650, info@thetrevorproject.org, https://www.thetrevorproject.org/; Facts About LGBTQ Youth Suicide and 2022 National Survey on LGBTQ Youth Mental Health.

U.S. Department of Health and Human Services (HHS), National Institutes of Health (NIH), National Institute of Mental Health (NIMH), 6001 Executive Blvd., Room 6200, MSC 9663, Bethesda, MD, 20892-9663, USA, (866) 615-6464, (301) 443-8431 (TTY), (301) 443-4279, nimhinfo@nih.gov, https://www.nimh.nih.gov/; Mental Health Statistics.

U.S. Department of Health and Human Services (HHS), Office of Inspector General (OIG), 330 Independence Ave. SW, Washington, DC, 20201, USA, (877) 696-6775, public.affairs@oig.hhs.gov, https://oig.hhs.gov/; Care Provider Facilities Described Challenges Addressing Mental Health Needs of Children in HHS Custody.

U.S. Department of Health and Human Services (HHS), Office of the Surgeon General (OSG), Humphrey Bldg., 200 Independence Ave. SW, Ste. 701H, Washington, DC, 20201, USA, (202) 401-7529, surgeongeneral@hhs.gov, https://www.hhs.gov/surgeongeneral; The Mental Health of Minority and Marginalized Young People: An Opportunity for Action.

U.S. Department of Health and Human Services, Centers for Disease Control and Prevention (CDC), National Center for Health Statistics (NCHS), 3311 Toledo Rd., Hyattsville, MD, 20782-2064, USA, (800) 232-4636, (301) 458-4000, https://www.cdc.gov/nchs; NCHS Survey Measures Catalog: Child and Adolescent Mental Health.

U.S. Department of the Interior (DOI), Office of the Secretary, 1849 C St. NW, Washington, DC, 20240, USA, (202) 208-3100, https://www.doi.gov/office-of-the-secretary; Federal Indian Boarding School Initiative Investigative Report.

UNICEF, 3 United Nations Plz., New York, NY, 10017, USA, (212) 303-7984, (917) 244-2215, https://www.unicef.org; COVID-19 and Children: UNICEF Data Hub.

United Nations Sustainable Development Solutions Network (UNSDSN), 475 Riverside Dr., Ste. 530, New York, NY, 10115, USA, (212) 870-3920, info@unsdsn.org, https://www.unsdsn.org; World Happiness Report 2023.

World Health Organization (WHO), Ave. Appia 20, Geneva, CH-1211, SWI, (202) 974-3000 (Telephone in U.S.), publications@who.int, https://www.who.int/; Mental Health Atlas 2020.

Yale School of Medicine, Yale Child Study Center, 230 S Frontage Rd., New Haven, CT, 06520, USA, (844) 362-9272, https://medicine.yale.edu/childstudy; unpublished data.

Youth Pride, Inc. (YPI), 743 Westminster St., Providence, RI, 02903, USA, (401) 421-5626, (401) 274-1990, info@youthprideri.org, https://www.youthprideri.org/; unpublished data.

CHILDREN-MOTHERS IN LABOR FORCE-BY AGE OF CHILDREN

U.S. Department of Labor (DOL), Bureau of Labor Statistics (BLS), Postal Square Bldg., 2 Massachusetts Ave. NE, Washington, DC, 20212-0001, USA, (202) 691-5200, (202) 691-7890, blsdata_staff@bls.gov, https://www.bls.gov; Labor Force Statistics from the Current Population Survey (CPS) and Monthly Labor Review.

CHILDREN-NUTRITION

Australian Government Department of Social Services, 71 Athllon Dr., Canberra, ACT, 2900, AUS, https://www.dss.gov.au/; Growing Up in Australia: The Longitudinal Study of Australian Children Annual Statistical Report.

Datasembly, 1775 Tysons Blvd., Tysons, VA, 22102, USA, (833) 328-2736, https://datasembly.com/; Datasembly Releases Latest Numbers on Baby Formula.

International Food Policy Research Institute (IFPRI), 1201 Eye St. NW, Washington, DC, 20005-3915, USA, (202) 862-5600, (202) 862-5606, ifpri@cgiar.org, https://www.ifpri.org/; The COVID-19 Crisis Will Exacerbate Maternal and Child Undernutrition and Child Mortality in Low- and Middle-Income Countries.

Kantar, 3 World Trade Center, 35th Fl., New York, NY, 10007, USA, (866) 471-1399, https://www.kantar.com/; Improving Child Nutrition in Myanmar.

United Nations Statistics Division (UNSD), United Nations Plz., New York, NY, 10017, USA, (800) 253-9646, (212) 963-9851, statistics@un.org, https://unstats.un.org; Millennium Development Goal Indicators.

CHILDREN-OVERWEIGHT

Robert Wood Johnson Foundation (RWJF), 50 College Rd. E, Princeton, NJ, 08540-6614, USA, (877) 843-7953, (609) 627-6000, https://www.rwjf.org/; From Crisis to Opportunity: Reforming Our Nation's Policies to Help All Children Grow Up Healthy.

Trust for America's Health (TFAH), 1730 M St. NW, Ste. 900, Washington, DC, 20036, USA, (202) 223-9870, (202) 223-9871, info@tfah.org, https://www.tfah.org/; National Obesity Monitor and State of Obesity 2022: Better Policies for a Healthier America.

University of California Los Angeles (UCLA), Center for Health Policy Research (CHPR), 10960 Wilshire Blvd., Ste. 1550, Campus Mail Code 714346, Los Angeles, CA, 90024, USA, (310) 794-0909, (310) 794-2686, healthpolicy@ucla.edu, https://healthpolicy.ucla.edu; Racial/Ethnic Variations in Weight Management Among Patients with Overweight and Obesity Status Who Are Served by Health Centres (Clinical Obesity).

CHILDREN-PARENTAL INVOLVEMENT

Child Trends, 7315 Wisconsin Ave., Ste. 1200W, Bethesda, MD, 20814, USA, (240) 223-9200, https://www.childtrends.org/; Family Instability and Children's Social Development.

U.S. Department of Education (ED), Institute of Education Sciences (IES), National Center for Education Statistics (NCES), Potomac Center Plaza, 550 12th St. SW, Washington, DC, 20202, USA, (202) 403-5551, https://nces.ed.gov/; The National Household Education Surveys Program (NHES) Data.

CHILDREN-PHYSICIAN VISITS

U.S. Department of Health and Human Services, Centers for Disease Control and Prevention (CDC), National Center for Health Statistics (NCHS), 3311 Toledo Rd., Hyattsville, MD, 20782-2064, USA, (800) 232-4636, (301) 458-4000, https://www.cdc.gov/nchs; FastStats - Statistics by Topic and Health, United States, 2020-2021.

CHILDREN-PNEUMONIA

U.S. Department of Health and Human Services, Centers for Disease Control and Prevention (CDC), National Center for Health Statistics (NCHS), 3311 Toledo Rd., Hyattsville, MD, 20782-2064, USA, (800) 232-4636, (301) 458-4000, https://www.cdc.gov/nchs; Health, United States, 2020-2021.

CHILDREN-POVERTY

American Civil Liberties Union (ACLU), 125 Broad St. , 18th Fl., New York, NY, 10004, USA, (212) 549-

2500, https://www.aclu.org/; 'If I Wasn't Poor, I Wouldn't Be Unfit': The Family Separation Crisis in the US Child Welfare System.

The Annie E. Casey Foundation, 701 Saint Paul St., Baltimore, MD, 21202, USA, (410) 547-6600, (410) 547-6624, https://www.aecf.org/; Children Living in High-Poverty, Low-Opportunity Neighborhoods; 2021 KIDS COUNT Data Book: State Trends in Child Well-Being; and KIDS COUNT Database.

Bank Street Graduate School of Education, National Center for Children in Poverty (NCCP), 475 Riverside Dr., Ste. 1400, New York, NY, 10115, USA, info@nccp.org, https://www.nccp.org/; 50-State Demographics Data Generator.

Children's Defense Fund (CDF), 840 1st St. NE, Ste. 300, Washington, DC, 20002, USA, (202) 628-8787, cdfinfo@childrensdefense.org, https://www.childrensdefense.org/; Child Poverty in America 2019; Ending Child Poverty Now; and The State of America's Children 2021.

Every Texan, 7020 Easy Wind Dr., Ste. 200, Austin, TX, 78752, USA, (512) 320-0222, (512) 320-0227, info@everytexan.org, https://everytexan.org/; 2022 Texas KIDS COUNT Data Book.

Federal Interagency Forum on Child and Family Statistics (The Forum), USA, childstats@ed.gov, https://www.childstats.gov; America's Children: Key National Indicators of Well-Being, 2021.

Montana Office of Public Instruction, PO Box 202501, Helena, MT, 59620-2501, USA, (406) 444-3680, (406) 444-3693, https://opi.mt.gov/; Culture and Schools: American Indian Stakeholder Perspectives on the American Indian Student Achievement Gap.

Save the Children, 501 Kings Hwy. E, Ste. 400, Fairfield, CT, 06825, USA, (203) 221-4000, (800) 728-3843, https://www.savethechildren.org/; Childhood in the Time of COVID: U.S. Complement to the Global Childhood Report 2021; Global Childhood Report 2021: The Toughest Places to Be a Child; Global Girlhood Report 2022: Girls on the Frontline; and Stop the War on Children: Gender Matters.

U.S. Census Bureau, 4600 Silver Hill Rd., Washington, DC, 20233, USA, (301) 763-4636, (800) 923-8282, https://www.census.gov; Income and Poverty in the United States: 2020.

U.S. Department of Agriculture (USDA), Economic Research Service (ERS), 1400 Independence Ave. SW, Mail Stop 1800, Washington, DC, 20250-0002, USA, (202) 720-2791, https://www.ers.usda.gov/; Food Environment Atlas.

United Nations Population Fund (UNFPA), 605 3rd Ave., New York, NY, 10158, USA, https://www.unfpa.org/; Humanitarian Action Overview Report 2023.

University of Michigan, Poverty Solutions, 735 S State St., Ste. 5100, Ann Arbor, MI, 48109-3091, USA, povertysolutions@umich.edu, https://poverty.umich.edu/; Housing and Health Inequities During COVID-19: Findings from the National Household Pulse Survey.

The Urban Institute, 500 L'Enfant Plaza SW, Washington, DC, 20024, USA, (202) 833-7200, https://www.urban.org/; 2021 Poverty Projections: Assessing the Impact of Benefits and Stimulus Measures.

World Vision, PO Box 9716, Federal Way, WA, 98063, USA, (888) 511-6548, https://www.worldvision.org/; unpublished data.

CHILDREN-RESPIRATORY INFECTION

The Henry J. Kaiser Family Foundation (KFF), 185 Berry St., Ste. 2000, San Francisco, CA, 94107, USA, (650) 854-9400, (650) 854-4800, https://www.kff.org; More Than 3 Million People Age 65 or Older Live with School-Age Children, and Could Be at Heightened Risk of COVID-19 Infection if Children Bring the Virus Home from School.

U.S. Department of Health and Human Services, Centers for Disease Control and Prevention (CDC), 1600 Clifton Rd., Atlanta, GA, 30329-4027, USA, (800) 232-4636, (888) 232-6348 (TTY), cdcinfo@cdc.gov, https://www.cdc.gov; Mask Use and Ventilation Improvements to Reduce COVID-19 Incidence in Elementary Schools - Georgia, November 16 - December 11, 2020.

U.S. Department of Health and Human Services, Centers for Disease Control and Prevention (CDC), National Center for Health Statistics (NCHS), 3311 Toledo Rd., Hyattsville, MD, 20782-2064, USA, (800) 232-4636, (301) 458-4000, https://www.cdc.gov/nchs; Health, United States, 2020-2021.

CHILDREN-SCHOOL CRIMES

U.S. Department of Education (ED), Institute of Education Sciences (IES), National Center for Education Statistics (NCES), Potomac Center Plaza, 550 12th St. SW, Washington, DC, 20202, USA, (202) 403-5551, https://nces.ed.gov/; Indicators of School Crime and Safety: 2021.

Youth Pride, Inc. (YPI), 743 Westminster St., Providence, RI, 02903, USA, (401) 421-5626, (401) 274-1990, info@youthprideri.org, https://www.youthprideri.org/; unpublished data.

CHILDREN-SCHOOL ENROLLMENT

Market Data Retrieval (MDR), A Dun & Bradstreet Division, 5335 Gate Pkwy., Jacksonville, FL, 32256, USA, (973) 921-5500, (800) 333-8802, mdrinfo@dnb.com, https://mdreducation.com/; Education MarketView.

U.S. Census Bureau, 4600 Silver Hill Rd., Washington, DC, 20233, USA, (301) 763-4636, (800) 923-8282, https://www.census.gov; School Enrollment in the United States: 2020.

U.S. Department of Education (ED), Institute of Education Sciences (IES), National Center for Education Statistics (NCES), Potomac Center Plaza, 550 12th St. SW, Washington, DC, 20202, USA, (202) 403-5551, https://nces.ed.gov/; Digest of Education Statistics, 2020 and Projections of Education Statistics to 2028.

U.S. Department of the Interior (DOI), Office of the Secretary, 1849 C St. NW, Washington, DC, 20240, USA, (202) 208-3100, https://www.doi.gov/office-of-the-secretary; Federal Indian Boarding School Initiative Investigative Report.

UNESCO Institute for Statistics, C.P 250 Succursale H, Montreal, QC, H3G 2K8, CAN, (514) 343-6880 (Dial from U.S.), (514) 343-5740 (Fax from U.S.), uis.publications@unesco.org, http://uis.unesco.org/; Global Education Monitoring Report 2020 - Inclusion and Education and Global Education Monitoring Report 2021-2022: Non-State Actors in Education.

CHILDREN-SCHOOL ENROLLMENT-PREPRIMARY SCHOOL ENROLLMENT

U.S. Census Bureau, 4600 Silver Hill Rd., Washington, DC, 20233, USA, (301) 763-4636, (800) 923-8282, https://www.census.gov; School Enrollment in the United States: 2020.

CHILDREN-SCHOOL ENROLLMENT-PROJECTIONS

U.S. Department of Education (ED), Institute of Education Sciences (IES), National Center for Education Statistics (NCES), Potomac Center Plaza, 550 12th St. SW, Washington, DC, 20202, USA, (202) 403-5551, https://nces.ed.gov/; Digest of Education Statistics, 2020 and Projections of Education Statistics to 2028.

CHILDREN-SOCIAL SECURITY BENEFICIARIES AND PAYMENTS

Social Security Administration (SSA), Office of Public Inquiries and Communications Support, 1100 W High Rise, 6401 Security Blvd., Baltimore, MD, 21235, USA, (800) 772-1213, (800) 325-0778 (TTY), https://www.ssa.gov; Annual Statistical Supplement, 2021 and SSI Monthly Statistics.

CHILDREN-SOCIAL WELFARE PROGRAMS

American Civil Liberties Union (ACLU), 125 Broad St. , 18th Fl., New York, NY, 10004, USA, (212) 549-2500, https://www.aclu.org/; 'If I Wasn't Poor, I Wouldn't Be Unfit': The Family Separation Crisis in the US Child Welfare System.

Australian Government Department of Social Services, 71 Athllon Dr., Canberra, ACT, 2900, AUS, https://www.dss.gov.au/; Growing Up in Australia: The Longitudinal Study of Australian Children Annual Statistical Report.

Bank Street Graduate School of Education, National Center for Children in Poverty (NCCP), 475 Riverside Dr., Ste. 1400, New York, NY, 10115, USA, info@nccp.org, https://www.nccp.org/; 50-State Demographics Data Generator.

Casey Family Programs, 2001 8th Ave., Ste. 2700, Seattle, WA, 98121, USA, (206) 282-7300, (206) 282-3555, info@casey.org, https://www.casey.org/; Creating a Better Future for Children and Families in a Time of Crisis and State-by-State Data: Foster Care.

Child Welfare League of America (CWLA), 727 15th St. NW, Ste. 1200, Washington, DC, 20005, USA, (202) 688-4200, cwla@cwla.org, https://www.cwla.org/; Child Welfare Journal.

Federal Interagency Forum on Child and Family Statistics (The Forum), USA, childstats@ed.gov, https://www.childstats.gov; America's Children: Key National Indicators of Well-Being, 2021.

U.S. Department of Agriculture (USDA), Economic Research Service (ERS), 1400 Independence Ave. SW, Mail Stop 1800, Washington, DC, 20250-0002, USA, (202) 720-2791, https://www.ers.usda.gov/; Food Environment Atlas.

U.S. Department of Agriculture (USDA), Food and Nutrition Service (FNS), Braddock Metro Center II, 1320 Braddock Pl., Alexandria, VA, 22314, USA, (703) 305-2062, https://www.fns.usda.gov/; Direct Certification in the National School Lunch Program: State Implementation Progress and SNAP Data Tables.

U.S. Department of Health and Human Services (HHS), Administration for Children and Families (ACF), Children's Bureau, Child Welfare Information Gateway, 330 C St. SW, Washington, DC, 20201, USA, (800) 394-3366, info@childwelfare.gov, https://www.childwelfare.gov/; Foster Care Statistics.

CHILDREN-SUICIDE

American Academy of Pediatrics (AAP), 345 Park Blvd., Itasca, IL, 60143, USA, (800) 433-9016, (847) 434-8000, mcc@aap.org, https://www.aap.org; Pubertal Suppression for Transgender Youth and Risk of Suicidal Ideation.

American Association of Suicidology (AAS), 448 Walton Ave., No. 790, Hummelstown, PA, 17036, USA, (202) 237-2280, (202) 237-2282, info@suicidology.org, https://suicidology.org; U.S.A. Suicide: 2019 Official Final Data.

Bernan Press, 15250 NBN Way, Bldg. C, Blue Ridge Summit, PA, 17214, USA, (301) 459-2255, (800) 865-3457, (800) 865-3450, customercare@bernan.com, https://rowman.com/Page/Bernan; Vital Statistics of the United States 2022: Births, Life Expectancy, Deaths, and Selected Health Data.

Child Trends, 7315 Wisconsin Ave., Ste. 1200W, Bethesda, MD, 20814, USA, (240) 223-9200, https://www.childtrends.org/; Teen Suicide Databank Indicator.

Children's Defense Fund (CDF), 840 1st St. NE, Ste. 300, Washington, DC, 20002, USA, (202) 628-8787, cdfinfo@childrensdefense.org, https://www.childrensdefense.org/; Protect Children, Not Guns 2019.

Montana Office of Public Instruction, PO Box 202501, Helena, MT, 59620-2501, USA, (406) 444-3680, (406) 444-3693, https://opi.mt.gov/; Culture and Schools: American Indian Stakeholder Perspectives on the American Indian Student Achievement Gap.

The Trevor Project, PO Box 69232, West Hollywood, CA, 90069, USA, (212) 695-8650, info@thetrevorproject.org, https://www.

thetrevorproject.org/; Facts About LGBTQ Youth Suicide and 2022 National Survey on LGBTQ Youth Mental Health.

U.S. Department of Health and Human Services, Centers for Disease Control and Prevention (CDC), 1600 Clifton Rd., Atlanta, GA, 30329-4027, USA, (800) 232-4636, (888) 232-6348 (TTY), cdcinfo@cdc.gov, https://www.cdc.gov; Emergency Department Visits for Suspected Suicide Attempts Among Persons Aged 12-25 Years Before and During the COVID-19 Pandemic - United States, January 2019 - May 2021 and Notes from the Field: Recent Changes in Suicide Rates, by Race and Ethnicity and Age Group - United States, 2021.

U.S. Department of Health and Human Services, Centers for Disease Control and Prevention (CDC), National Center for Health Statistics (NCHS), 3311 Toledo Rd., Hyattsville, MD, 20782-2064, USA, (800) 232-4636, (301) 458-4000, https://www.cdc.gov/nchs; National Vital Statistics Reports (NVSR) and Vital Statistics Online Data Portal.

CHILDREN AND VIOLENCE

Issue Lab by Candid, 32 Old Slip, 24th Fl., New York, NY, 10003, USA, (800) 424-9836, https://www.issuelab.org/; Issue Lab Special Collection: Gun Violence.

Naval Postgraduate School, Center for Homeland Defense and Security (CHDS), 1 University Cir., Bldg. 220, Rm. 064, Monteray, CA, 93943, USA, (831) 656-2356 , mccolgan@nps.edu, https://www.chds.us; K-12 School Shooting Database.

Save the Children, 501 Kings Hwy. E, Ste. 400, Fairfield, CT, 06825, USA, (203) 221-4000, (800) 728-3843, https://www.savethechildren.org/; Childhood in the Time of COVID: U.S. Complement to the Global Childhood Report 2021; Global Childhood Report 2021: The Toughest Places to Be a Child; Global Girlhood Report 2022: Girls on the Frontline; and Stop the War on Children: Gender Matters.

U.S. Department of Justice (DOJ), Office of Juvenile Justice and Delinquency Prevention (OJJDP), 810 7th St. NW, Washington, DC, 20531, USA, (202) 307-5911, https://www.ojjdp.gov/; Statistical Briefing Book (SBB).

UNICEF, 3 United Nations Plz., New York, NY, 10017, USA, (212) 303-7984, (917) 244-2215, https://www.unicef.org; A Statistical Profile of Violence Against Children in Latin America and the Caribbean.

CHILDREN AND WAR

Save the Children, 501 Kings Hwy. E, Ste. 400, Fairfield, CT, 06825, USA, (203) 221-4000, (800) 728-3843, https://www.savethechildren.org/; Childhood in the Time of COVID: U.S. Complement to the Global Childhood Report 2021; Global Childhood Report 2021: The Toughest Places to Be a Child; Global Girlhood Report 2022: Girls on the Frontline; and Stop the War on Children: Gender Matters.

CHILDREN'S HEALTH INSURANCE PROGRAM (CHIP)

Center on Budget and Policy Priorities, 1275 First St. NE, Ste. 1200, Washington, DC, 20002, USA, (202) 408-1080, (202) 408-1056, center@cbpp.org, https://www.cbpp.org/; Medicaid Enrollment Decline Among Adults and Children Too Large to Be Explained by Falling Unemployment.

The Henry J. Kaiser Family Foundation (KFF), 185 Berry St., Ste. 2000, San Francisco, CA, 94107, USA, (650) 854-9400, (650) 854-4800, https://www.kff.org; Medicaid and CHIP Eligibility and Enrollment Policies as of January 2022: Findings from a 50-State Survey.

National Governors Association (NGA), 444 N Capitol St., Ste. 267, Washington, DC, 20001, USA, (202) 624-5300, (202) 624-5313, info@nga.org, https://www.nga.org; Maternal and Child Health Update 2020.

CHILE-NATIONAL STATISTICAL OFFICE

Instituto Nacional de Estadisticas, Chile, Morande No. 801, Piso 22, Santiago, 8340148, CHL, ine@ine.cl, https://www.ine.cl/; National Data Reports (Chile).

CHILE-AGRICULTURE

The Economist Group: Economist Intelligence Unit (EIU), 900 3rd Ave., 16th Fl., New York, NY, 10022, USA, (212) 541-0500, americas@eiu.com, https://www.eiu.com; Chile Country Report.

Euromonitor International, Inc., 1 N Dearborn St., Ste. 1700, Chicago, IL, 60602, USA, (312) 922-1115, (312) 922-1157, info-usa@euromonitor.com, https://www.euromonitor.com/; Geographies.

Inter-American Development Bank (IDB), 1300 New York Ave. NW, Washington, DC, 20577, USA, (202) 623-1000, (202) 623-3096, https://www.iadb.org/en; Latin Macro Watch (LMW).

Organization for Economic Cooperation and Development (OECD), 2001 L St. NW, Ste. 650, Washington, DC, 20036-4922, USA, (202) 785-6323, (800) 456-6323, (202) 785-0350, washington.contact@oecd.org, https://www.oecd.org/; Economic Survey of Chile 2022.

Palgrave Macmillan, 1 New York Plaza, Ste. 4500, New York, NY, 10004-1562, USA, (800) 777-4643, orders@palgrave.com, https://www.palgrave.com/us; The Statesman's Yearbook, 2023.

Routledge - Taylor & Francis Group, 6000 Broken Sound Pkwy. NW, Ste. 300, Boca Raton, FL, 33487, USA, (800) 634-1420, (800) 634-7064, orders@taylorandfrancis.com, https://www.routledge.com/; The Europa World Year Book 2022.

United Nations Food and Agricultural Organization (FAO), 2121 K St., Ste. 800B, Washington, DC, 20037, USA, (202) 653-2400 (Dial from U.S.), (202) 653-5760 (Fax from U.S.), fao-hq@fao.org, https://www.fao.org; AQUASTAT and The State of Food and Agriculture (SOFA) 2022.

United Nations Statistics Division (UNSD), United Nations Plz., New York, NY, 10017, USA, (800) 253-9646, (212) 963-9851, statistics@un.org, https://unstats.un.org; Statistical Yearbook of the United Nations 2021.

University of California Los Angeles (UCLA), Latin American Institute (LAI), 10343 Bunche Hall, 315 Portola Plaza, Los Angeles, CA, 90095-1447, USA, (310) 825-4571, lai@international.ucla.edu, https://www.international.ucla.edu/lai; unpublished data.

The World Bank, 1818 H St. NW, Washington, DC, 20433, USA, (202) 473-1000, (202) 477-6391, eds03@worldbank.org, https://www.worldbank.org/; Chile (report) and World Development Indicators (WDI) 2022.

CHILE-AIRLINES

International Civil Aviation Organization (ICAO), 999 Robert-Bourassa Blvd., Montreal, QC, H3C 5H7, CAN, (514) 954-8219 (Dial from U.S.), (514) 954-6077 (Fax from U.S.), icaohq@icao.int, https://www.icao.int; ICAO Regional Reports.

Palgrave Macmillan, 1 New York Plaza, Ste. 4500, New York, NY, 10004-1562, USA, (800) 777-4643, orders@palgrave.com, https://www.palgrave.com/us; The Statesman's Yearbook, 2023.

Routledge - Taylor & Francis Group, 6000 Broken Sound Pkwy. NW, Ste. 300, Boca Raton, FL, 33487, USA, (800) 634-1420, (800) 634-7064, orders@taylorandfrancis.com, https://www.routledge.com/; The Europa World Year Book 2022.

CHILE-ALUMINUM PRODUCTION

See CHILE-MINERAL INDUSTRIES

CHILE-ANIMAL FEEDING

United Nations Statistics Division (UNSD), United Nations Plz., New York, NY, 10017, USA, (800) 253-9646, (212) 963-9851, statistics@un.org, https://unstats.un.org; Statistical Yearbook of the United Nations 2021.

CHILE-ARMED FORCES

Central Intelligence Agency (CIA), Office of Public Affairs, Washington, DC, 20505, USA, (703) 482-0623, https://www.cia.gov; The World Factbook.

International Institute for Strategic Studies (IISS) - Americas, 2121 K St. NW, Ste. 600, Washington, DC, 20037, USA, (202) 659-1490, (202) 659-1499, https://www.iiss.org/; The Military Balance 2022.

Palgrave Macmillan, 1 New York Plaza, Ste. 4500, New York, NY, 10004-1562, USA, (800) 777-4643, orders@palgrave.com, https://www.palgrave.com/us; The Statesman's Yearbook, 2023.

Stockholm International Peace Research Institute (SIPRI), Signalistgatan 9, Stockholm, SE 169 72, SWE, https://www.sipri.org/; SIPRI Arms Transfers Database and SIPRI Military Expenditure Database.

CHILE-ARTICHOKE PRODUCTION

See CHILE-CROPS

CHILE-BALANCE OF PAYMENTS

Inter-American Development Bank (IDB), 1300 New York Ave. NW, Washington, DC, 20577, USA, (202) 623-1000, (202) 623-3096, https://www.iadb.org/en; Latin Macro Watch (LMW).

International Monetary Fund (IMF), 700 19th St. NW, Washington, DC, 20431, USA, (202) 623-7000, (202) 623-4661, publications@imf.org, https://www.imf.org; Balance of Payments Statistics: Annual Report 2021.

Organization for Economic Cooperation and Development (OECD), 2001 L St. NW, Ste. 650, Washington, DC, 20036-4922, USA, (202) 785-6323, (800) 456-6323, (202) 785-0350, washington.contact@oecd.org, https://www.oecd.org/; Economic Survey of Chile 2022.

Routledge - Taylor & Francis Group, 6000 Broken Sound Pkwy. NW, Ste. 300, Boca Raton, FL, 33487, USA, (800) 634-1420, (800) 634-7064, orders@taylorandfrancis.com, https://www.routledge.com/; The Europa World Year Book 2022.

United Nations Conference on Trade and Development (UNCTAD), Palais des Nations, Geneva, 1211, SWI, (212) 963-6896, unctadinfo@unctad.org, https://unctad.org; Handbook of Statistics 2021.

United Nations Economic Commission for Latin America and the Caribbean (ECLAC), Casilla 179-D, Santiago, 7630412, CHL, (202) 596-3713, prensa@cepal.org, https://www.cepal.org/en; Economic Survey of Latin America and the Caribbean 2021: Labour Dynamics and Employment Policies for Sustainable and Inclusive Recovery Beyond the COVID-19 Crisis.

The World Bank, 1818 H St. NW, Washington, DC, 20433, USA, (202) 473-1000, (202) 477-6391, eds03@worldbank.org, https://www.worldbank.org/; Chile (report); World Development Indicators (WDI) 2022; and World Development Report 2022: Finance for an Equitable Recovery.

CHILE-BANKS AND BANKING

Euromonitor International, Inc., 1 N Dearborn St., Ste. 1700, Chicago, IL, 60602, USA, (312) 922-1115, (312) 922-1157, info-usa@euromonitor.com, https://www.euromonitor.com/; Geographies.

Inter-American Development Bank (IDB), 1300 New York Ave. NW, Washington, DC, 20577, USA, (202) 623-1000, (202) 623-3096, https://www.iadb.org/en; Latin Macro Watch (LMW).

International Monetary Fund (IMF), 700 19th St. NW, Washington, DC, 20431, USA, (202) 623-7000, (202) 623-4661, publications@imf.org, https://www.imf.org; International Financial Statistics (IFS).

Organization for Economic Cooperation and Development (OECD), 2001 L St. NW, Ste. 650, Washington, DC, 20036-4922, USA, (202) 785-6323, (800) 456-6323, (202) 785-0350, washington.contact@oecd.org, https://www.oecd.org/; Economic Survey of Chile 2022.

Routledge - Taylor & Francis Group, 6000 Broken Sound Pkwy. NW, Ste. 300, Boca Raton, FL, 33487,

USA, (800) 634-1420, (800) 634-7064, orders@taylorandfrancis.com, https://www.routledge.com/; The Europa World Year Book 2022.

CHILE-BARLEY PRODUCTION

See CHILE-CROPS

CHILE-BONDS

Inter-American Development Bank (IDB), 1300 New York Ave. NW, Washington, DC, 20577, USA, (202) 623-1000, (202) 623-3096, https://www.iadb.org/en; Latin Macro Watch (LMW).

CHILE-BROADCASTING

Central Intelligence Agency (CIA), Office of Public Affairs, Washington, DC, 20505, USA, (703) 482-0623, https://www.cia.gov; The World Factbook.

Euromonitor International, Inc., 1 N Dearborn St., Ste. 1700, Chicago, IL, 60602, USA, (312) 922-1115, (312) 922-1157, info-usa@euromonitor.com, https://www.euromonitor.com/; Geographies.

Palgrave Macmillan, 1 New York Plaza, Ste. 4500, New York, NY, 10004-1562, USA, (800) 777-4643, orders@palgrave.com, https://www.palgrave.com/us; The Statesman's Yearbook, 2023.

WRTH Publications Limited, PO Box 290, Oxford, OX2 7FT, GBR, sales@wrth.com, https://www.wrth.com; World Radio TV Handbook 2023.

CHILE-BUDGET

Central Intelligence Agency (CIA), Office of Public Affairs, Washington, DC, 20505, USA, (703) 482-0623, https://www.cia.gov; The World Factbook.

CHILE-BUSINESS

Global Entrepreneurship Monitor (GEM), Babson College, 231 Forest St., Babson Park, MA, 02457, USA, (781) 235-1200, info@gemconsortium.org, https://www.gemconsortium.org/; Chile Economy Profile and GEM 2022-2023 Global Report.

Inter-American Development Bank (IDB), 1300 New York Ave. NW, Washington, DC, 20577, USA, (202) 623-1000, (202) 623-3096, https://www.iadb.org/en; Latin Macro Watch (LMW).

CHILE-CAPITAL INVESTMENTS

Inter-American Development Bank (IDB), 1300 New York Ave. NW, Washington, DC, 20577, USA, (202) 623-1000, (202) 623-3096, https://www.iadb.org/en; Latin Macro Watch (LMW).

CHILE-CHILDBIRTH-STATISTICS

The World Bank, 1818 H St. NW, Washington, DC, 20433, USA, (202) 473-1000, (202) 477-6391, eds03@worldbank.org, https://www.worldbank.org/; World Development Indicators (WDI) 2022.

CHILE-CLIMATE

Palgrave Macmillan, 1 New York Plaza, Ste. 4500, New York, NY, 10004-1562, USA, (800) 777-4643, orders@palgrave.com, https://www.palgrave.com/us; The Statesman's Yearbook, 2023.

University of California Los Angeles (UCLA), Latin American Institute (LAI), 10343 Bunche Hall, 315 Portola Plaza, Los Angeles, CA, 90095-1447, USA, (310) 825-4571, lai@international.ucla.edu, https://www.international.ucla.edu/lai; unpublished data.

CHILE-COAL PRODUCTION

See CHILE-MINERAL INDUSTRIES

CHILE-COFFEE

See CHILE-CROPS

CHILE-COMMERCE

Palgrave Macmillan, 1 New York Plaza, Ste. 4500, New York, NY, 10004-1562, USA, (800) 777-4643, orders@palgrave.com, https://www.palgrave.com/us; The Statesman's Yearbook, 2023.

UK Data Service, University of Essex, Wivenhoe Park, Colchester, Essex, CO4 3SQ, GBR, https://ukdataservice.ac.uk/; International Aggregate Data.

CHILE-COMMODITY EXCHANGES

Barchart, 209 W Jackson Blvd., 2nd Fl., Chicago, IL, 60606, USA, (877) 247-4394, commodities@barchart.com, https://www.barchart.com/cmdty; The cmdty Yearbook 2023; cmdtyStats: Commodity Statistics and Fundamental Data; cmdtyView: Commodity Index; and Commodity Data and Prices.

International Monetary Fund (IMF), 700 19th St. NW, Washington, DC, 20431, USA, (202) 623-7000, (202) 623-4661, publications@imf.org, https://www.imf.org; IMF Primary Commodity Prices.

United Nations Statistics Division (UNSD), United Nations Plz., New York, NY, 10017, USA, (800) 253-9646, (212) 963-9851, statistics@un.org, https://unstats.un.org; Statistical Yearbook of the United Nations 2021.

World Bureau of Metal Statistics (WBMS), 31 Star St., Ware, Hertfordshire, SG12 9BA, GBR, https://www.refinitiv.com/en/trading-solutions/world-bureau-metal-statistics; Annual Stainless Steel Statistics; Long Term Production/Consumption Series - All Metals; World Flow Charts; and World Metal Statistics.

CHILE-CONSTRUCTION INDUSTRY

Inter-American Development Bank (IDB), 1300 New York Ave. NW, Washington, DC, 20577, USA, (202) 623-1000, (202) 623-3096, https://www.iadb.org/en; Latin Macro Watch (LMW).

Organization for Economic Cooperation and Development (OECD), 2001 L St. NW, Ste. 650, Washington, DC, 20036-4922, USA, (202) 785-6323, (800) 456-6323, (202) 785-0350, washington.contact@oecd.org, https://www.oecd.org/; Economic Survey of Chile 2022.

Palgrave Macmillan, 1 New York Plaza, Ste. 4500, New York, NY, 10004-1562, USA, (800) 777-4643, orders@palgrave.com, https://www.palgrave.com/us; The Statesman's Yearbook, 2023.

United Nations Statistics Division (UNSD), United Nations Plz., New York, NY, 10017, USA, (800) 253-9646, (212) 963-9851, statistics@un.org, https://unstats.un.org; Statistical Yearbook of the United Nations 2021.

CHILE-CONSUMER PRICE INDEXES

Routledge - Taylor & Francis Group, 6000 Broken Sound Pkwy. NW, Ste. 300, Boca Raton, FL, 33487, USA, (800) 634-1420, (800) 634-7064, orders@taylorandfrancis.com, https://www.routledge.com/; The Europa World Year Book 2022.

The World Bank, 1818 H St. NW, Washington, DC, 20433, USA, (202) 473-1000, (202) 477-6391, eds03@worldbank.org, https://www.worldbank.org/; Chile (report).

CHILE-CONSUMPTION (ECONOMICS)

Inter-American Development Bank (IDB), 1300 New York Ave. NW, Washington, DC, 20577, USA, (202) 623-1000, (202) 623-3096, https://www.iadb.org/en; Latin Macro Watch (LMW).

CHILE-COPPER INDUSTRY AND TRADE

See CHILE-MINERAL INDUSTRIES

CHILE-CORN INDUSTRY

See CHILE-CROPS

CHILE-COTTON

See CHILE-CROPS

CHILE-CROPS

Palgrave Macmillan, 1 New York Plaza, Ste. 4500, New York, NY, 10004-1562, USA, (800) 777-4643, orders@palgrave.com, https://www.palgrave.com/us; The Statesman's Yearbook, 2023.

United Nations Food and Agricultural Organization (FAO), 2121 K St., Ste. 800B, Washington, DC, 20037, USA, (202) 653-2400 (Dial from U.S.), (202) 653-5760 (Fax from U.S.), fao-hq@fao.org, https://www.fao.org; The State of Food and Agriculture (SOFA) 2022.

United Nations Statistics Division (UNSD), United Nations Plz., New York, NY, 10017, USA, (800) 253-9646, (212) 963-9851, statistics@un.org, https://unstats.un.org; Statistical Yearbook of the United Nations 2021.

CHILE-CUSTOMS ADMINISTRATION

Inter-American Development Bank (IDB), 1300 New York Ave. NW, Washington, DC, 20577, USA, (202) 623-1000, (202) 623-3096, https://www.iadb.org/en; Latin Macro Watch (LMW).

CHILE-DAIRY PROCESSING

Palgrave Macmillan, 1 New York Plaza, Ste. 4500, New York, NY, 10004-1562, USA, (800) 777-4643, orders@palgrave.com, https://www.palgrave.com/us; The Statesman's Yearbook, 2023.

United Nations Food and Agricultural Organization (FAO), 2121 K St., Ste. 800B, Washington, DC, 20037, USA, (202) 653-2400 (Dial from U.S.), (202) 653-5760 (Fax from U.S.), fao-hq@fao.org, https://www.fao.org; The State of Food and Agriculture (SOFA) 2022.

CHILE-DEBT

The World Bank, 1818 H St. NW, Washington, DC, 20433, USA, (202) 473-1000, (202) 477-6391, eds03@worldbank.org, https://www.worldbank.org/; Global Financial Development Report 2019-2020: Bank Regulation and Supervision a Decade after the Global Financial Crisis.

CHILE-DEBTS, EXTERNAL

Inter-American Development Bank (IDB), 1300 New York Ave. NW, Washington, DC, 20577, USA, (202) 623-1000, (202) 623-3096, https://www.iadb.org/en; Latin Macro Watch (LMW).

Palgrave Macmillan, 1 New York Plaza, Ste. 4500, New York, NY, 10004-1562, USA, (800) 777-4643, orders@palgrave.com, https://www.palgrave.com/us; The Statesman's Yearbook, 2023.

United Nations Economic Commission for Latin America and the Caribbean (ECLAC), Casilla 179-D, Santiago, 7630412, CHL, (202) 596-3713, prensa@cepal.org, https://www.cepal.org/en; Economic Survey of Latin America and the Caribbean 2021: Labour Dynamics and Employment Policies for Sustainable and Inclusive Recovery Beyond the COVID-19 Crisis.

The World Bank, 1818 H St. NW, Washington, DC, 20433, USA, (202) 473-1000, (202) 477-6391, eds03@worldbank.org, https://www.worldbank.org/; Global Financial Development Report 2019-2020: Bank Regulation and Supervision a Decade after the Global Financial Crisis; World Development Indicators (WDI) 2022; and World Development Report 2022: Finance for an Equitable Recovery.

CHILE-DEFENSE EXPENDITURES

See CHILE-ARMED FORCES

CHILE-DIAMONDS

See CHILE-MINERAL INDUSTRIES

CHILE-DISPOSABLE INCOME

Inter-American Development Bank (IDB), 1300 New York Ave. NW, Washington, DC, 20577, USA, (202) 623-1000, (202) 623-3096, https://www.iadb.org/en; Latin Macro Watch (LMW).

CHILE-ECONOMIC ASSISTANCE

Inter-American Development Bank (IDB), 1300 New York Ave. NW, Washington, DC, 20577, USA, (202) 623-1000, (202) 623-3096, https://www.iadb.org/en; Latin Macro Watch (LMW).

United Nations Statistics Division (UNSD), United Nations Plz., New York, NY, 10017, USA, (800) 253-9646, (212) 963-9851, statistics@un.org, https://unstats.un.org; Statistical Yearbook of the United Nations 2021.

CHILE-ECONOMIC CONDITIONS

Bernan Press, 15250 NBN Way, Bldg. C, Blue Ridge Summit, PA, 17214, USA, (301) 459-2255, (800) 865-3457, (800) 865-3450, customercare@bernan.com, https://rowman.com/Page/Bernan; World Economic Outlook, April 2022.

Central Intelligence Agency (CIA), Office of Public Affairs, Washington, DC, 20505, USA, (703) 482-0623, https://www.cia.gov; The World Factbook.

The Economist Group: Economist Intelligence Unit (EIU), 900 3rd Ave., 16th Fl., New York, NY, 10022, USA, (212) 541-0500, americas@eiu.com, https://www.eiu.com; Chile Country Report.

Euromonitor International, Inc., 1 N Dearborn St., Ste. 1700, Chicago, IL, 60602, USA, (312) 922-1115, (312) 922-1157, info-usa@euromonitor.com, https://www.euromonitor.com/; Geographies and Market Research on the Consumer Finance Industry.

Global Entrepreneurship Monitor (GEM), Babson College, 231 Forest St., Babson Park, MA, 02457, USA, (781) 235-1200, info@gemconsortium.org, https://www.gemconsortium.org/; Chile Economy Profile and GEM 2022-2023 Global Report.

Inter-American Development Bank (IDB), 1300 New York Ave. NW, Washington, DC, 20577, USA, (202) 623-1000, (202) 623-3096, https://www.iadb.org/en; Latin Macro Watch (LMW).

International Monetary Fund (IMF), 700 19th St. NW, Washington, DC, 20431, USA, (202) 623-7000, (202) 623-4661, publications@imf.org, https://www.imf.org; IMF Data and World Economic Outlook.

Organization for Economic Cooperation and Development (OECD), 2001 L St. NW, Ste. 650, Washington, DC, 20036-4922, USA, (202) 785-6323, (800) 456-6323, (202) 785-0350, washington.contact@oecd.org, https://www.oecd.org/; Economic Survey of Chile 2022.

Palgrave Macmillan, 1 New York Plaza, Ste. 4500, New York, NY, 10004-1562, USA, (800) 777-4643, orders@palgrave.com, https://www.palgrave.com/us; The Statesman's Yearbook, 2023.

Routledge - Taylor & Francis Group, 6000 Broken Sound Pkwy. NW, Ste. 300, Boca Raton, FL, 33487, USA, (800) 634-1420, (800) 634-7064, orders@taylorandfrancis.com, https://www.routledge.com/; The Europa World Year Book 2022.

United Nations Economic Commission for Latin America and the Caribbean (ECLAC), Casilla 179-D, Santiago, 7630412, CHL, (202) 596-3713, prensa@cepal.org, https://www.cepal.org/en; CEPALSTAT; Economic Survey of Latin America and the Caribbean 2021: Labour Dynamics and Employment Policies for Sustainable and Inclusive Recovery Beyond the COVID-19 Crisis; Foreign Direct Investment in Latin America and the Caribbean 2022; and Social Panorama of Latin America and the Caribbean 2022: Transforming Education as a Basis for Sustainable Development.

United Nations Statistics Division (UNSD), United Nations Plz., New York, NY, 10017, USA, (800) 253-9646, (212) 963-9851, statistics@un.org, https://unstats.un.org; World Statistics Pocketbook 2021.

University of California Los Angeles (UCLA), Latin American Institute (LAI), 10343 Bunche Hall, 315 Portola Plaza, Los Angeles, CA, 90095-1447, USA, (310) 825-4571, lai@international.ucla.edu, https://www.international.ucla.edu/lai; unpublished data.

The World Bank, 1818 H St. NW, Washington, DC, 20433, USA, (202) 473-1000, (202) 477-6391, eds03@worldbank.org, https://www.worldbank.org/; Chile (report); Global Economic Monitor (GEM); Global Economic Prospects, June 2022; The Global Findex Database 2021; and World Development Report 2022: Finance for an Equitable Recovery.

CHILE-EDUCATION

Euromonitor International, Inc., 1 N Dearborn St., Ste. 1700, Chicago, IL, 60602, USA, (312) 922-1115, (312) 922-1157, info-usa@euromonitor.com, https://www.euromonitor.com/; Geographies.

Infoplease, c/o Sandbox Networks, Inc., 1 Lincoln St., 24th Fl., Boston, MA, 02111, USA, https://www.infoplease.com; Countries of the World.

Palgrave Macmillan, 1 New York Plaza, Ste. 4500, New York, NY, 10004-1562, USA, (800) 777-4643, orders@palgrave.com, https://www.palgrave.com/us; The Statesman's Yearbook, 2023.

Routledge - Taylor & Francis Group, 6000 Broken Sound Pkwy. NW, Ste. 300, Boca Raton, FL, 33487, USA, (800) 634-1420, (800) 634-7064, orders@taylorandfrancis.com, https://www.routledge.com/; The Europa World Year Book 2022.

UNESCO Institute for Statistics, C.P 250 Succursale H, Montreal, QC, H3G 2K8, CAN, (514) 343-6880 (Dial from U.S.), (514) 343-5740 (Fax from U.S.), uis.publications@unesco.org, http://uis.unesco.org/; Literacy and UIS.Stat.

United Nations Statistics Division (UNSD), United Nations Plz., New York, NY, 10017, USA, (800) 253-9646, (212) 963-9851, statistics@un.org, https://unstats.un.org; Millennium Development Goal Indicators.

The World Bank, 1818 H St. NW, Washington, DC, 20433, USA, (202) 473-1000, (202) 477-6391, eds03@worldbank.org, https://www.worldbank.org/; Chile (report); World Development Indicators (WDI) 2022; and World Development Report 2022: Finance for an Equitable Recovery.

CHILE-ELECTRICITY

Inter-American Development Bank (IDB), 1300 New York Ave. NW, Washington, DC, 20577, USA, (202) 623-1000, (202) 623-3096, https://www.iadb.org/en; Latin Macro Watch (LMW).

International Energy Agency (IEA), 9 Rue de la Federation, Paris, 75739, FRA, info@iea.org, https://www.iea.org/; World Energy Outlook 2021.

U.S. Energy Information Administration (EIA), 1000 Independence Ave. SW, Washington, DC, 20585, USA, (202) 586-8800, infoctr@eia.gov, https://www.eia.gov; International Energy Outlook 2021.

United Nations Statistics Division (UNSD), United Nations Plz., New York, NY, 10017, USA, (800) 253-9646, (212) 963-9851, statistics@un.org, https://unstats.un.org; Statistical Yearbook of the United Nations 2021.

CHILE-EMPLOYMENT

International Labour Organization (ILO), 4 Rte. des Morillons, Geneva, CH-1211, SWI, ilo@ilo.org, https://www.ilo.org; NORMLEX Information System on International Labour Standards.

Organization for Economic Cooperation and Development (OECD), 2001 L St. NW, Ste. 650, Washington, DC, 20036-4922, USA, (202) 785-6323, (800) 456-6323, (202) 785-0350, washington.contact@oecd.org, https://www.oecd.org/; Economic Survey of Chile 2022.

UK Data Service, University of Essex, Wivenhoe Park, Colchester, Essex, CO4 3SQ, GBR, https://ukdataservice.ac.uk/; International Aggregate Data.

The World Bank, 1818 H St. NW, Washington, DC, 20433, USA, (202) 473-1000, (202) 477-6391, eds03@worldbank.org, https://www.worldbank.org/; Chile (report).

CHILE-ENVIRONMENTAL CONDITIONS

DSI Data Service & Information, Xantener Strasse 51a, Rheinberg, D-47495, GER, dsi@dsidata.com, https://www.dsidata.com/; Global Environmental Database.

The Economist Group: Economist Intelligence Unit (EIU), 900 3rd Ave., 16th Fl., New York, NY, 10022, USA, (212) 541-0500, americas@eiu.com, https://www.eiu.com; Chile Country Report.

United Nations Economic Commission for Latin America and the Caribbean (ECLAC), Casilla 179-D, Santiago, 7630412, CHL, (202) 596-3713, prensa@cepal.org, https://www.cepal.org/en; CEPALSTAT.

United Nations Statistics Division (UNSD), United Nations Plz., New York, NY, 10017, USA, (800) 253-9646, (212) 963-9851, statistics@un.org, https://unstats.un.org; World Statistics Pocketbook 2021.

CHILE-EXPENDITURES, PUBLIC

Inter-American Development Bank (IDB), 1300 New York Ave. NW, Washington, DC, 20577, USA, (202) 623-1000, (202) 623-3096, https://www.iadb.org/en; Latin Macro Watch (LMW).

CHILE-EXPORTS

BC Stats, Stn Prov Govt, PO Box 9410, Victoria, BC, V8W 9V1, CAN, (250) 387-6121 (Dial from U.S.), bc.stats@gov.bc.ca, https://www2.gov.bc.ca/gov/content/data/about-data-management/bc-stats; Country Trade Profile - Chile.

Central Intelligence Agency (CIA), Office of Public Affairs, Washington, DC, 20505, USA, (703) 482-0623, https://www.cia.gov; The World Factbook.

The Economist Group: Economist Intelligence Unit (EIU), 900 3rd Ave., 16th Fl., New York, NY, 10022, USA, (212) 541-0500, americas@eiu.com, https://www.eiu.com; Chile Country Report.

Inter-American Development Bank (IDB), 1300 New York Ave. NW, Washington, DC, 20577, USA, (202) 623-1000, (202) 623-3096, https://www.iadb.org/en; Latin Macro Watch (LMW).

International Monetary Fund (IMF), 700 19th St. NW, Washington, DC, 20431, USA, (202) 623-7000, (202) 623-4661, publications@imf.org, https://www.imf.org; Direction of Trade Statistics (DOTS) and International Financial Statistics (IFS).

Organization for Economic Cooperation and Development (OECD), 2001 L St. NW, Ste. 650, Washington, DC, 20036-4922, USA, (202) 785-6323, (800) 456-6323, (202) 785-0350, washington.contact@oecd.org, https://www.oecd.org/; Economic Survey of Chile 2022.

S&P Global, IHS Markit, 15 Inverness Way E, Englewood, CO, 80112, USA, (800) 447-2273, (800) 854-7179, https://ihsmarkit.com; Global Trade Atlas (GTA).

United Nations Conference on Trade and Development (UNCTAD), Palais des Nations, Geneva, 1211, SWI, (212) 963-6896, unctadinfo@unctad.org, https://unctad.org; Handbook of Statistics 2021.

The World Bank, 1818 H St. NW, Washington, DC, 20433, USA, (202) 473-1000, (202) 477-6391, eds03@worldbank.org, https://www.worldbank.org/; World Development Report 2022: Finance for an Equitable Recovery.

CHILE-FEMALE WORKING POPULATION

See CHILE-EMPLOYMENT

CHILE-FERTILITY, HUMAN

Central Intelligence Agency (CIA), Office of Public Affairs, Washington, DC, 20505, USA, (703) 482-0623, https://www.cia.gov; The World Factbook.

CHILE-FERTILIZER INDUSTRY

United Nations Food and Agricultural Organization (FAO), 2121 K St., Ste. 800B, Washington, DC, 20037, USA, (202) 653-2400 (Dial from U.S.), (202) 653-5760 (Fax from U.S.), fao-hq@fao.org, https://www.fao.org; The State of Food and Agriculture (SOFA) 2022.

CHILE-FETAL MORTALITY

See CHILE-MORTALITY

CHILE-FINANCE

Inter-American Development Bank (IDB), 1300 New York Ave. NW, Washington, DC, 20577, USA, (202)

623-1000, (202) 623-3096, https://www.iadb.org/en; Latin Macro Watch (LMW).

Stockholm International Peace Research Institute (SIPRI), Signalistgatan 9, Stockholm, SE 169 72, SWE, https://www.sipri.org/; SIPRI Arms Transfers Database and SIPRI Military Expenditure Database.

United Nations Statistics Division (UNSD), United Nations Plz., New York, NY, 10017, USA, (800) 253-9646, (212) 963-9851, statistics@un.org, https://unstats.un.org; Statistical Yearbook of the United Nations 2021.

The World Bank, 1818 H St. NW, Washington, DC, 20433, USA, (202) 473-1000, (202) 477-6391, eds03@worldbank.org, https://www.worldbank.org/; Chile (report).

CHILE-FINANCE, PUBLIC

Bernan Press, 15250 NBN Way, Bldg. C, Blue Ridge Summit, PA, 17214, USA, (301) 459-2255, (800) 865-3457, (800) 865-3450, customercare@bernan.com, https://rowman.com/Page/Bernan; National Accounts Statistics: Analysis of Main Aggregates 2020.

The Economist Group: Economist Intelligence Unit (EIU), 900 3rd Ave., 16th Fl., New York, NY, 10022, USA, (212) 541-0500, americas@eiu.com, https://www.eiu.com; Chile Country Report.

Inter-American Development Bank (IDB), 1300 New York Ave. NW, Washington, DC, 20577, USA, (202) 623-1000, (202) 623-3096, https://www.iadb.org/en; Latin Macro Watch (LMW).

International Monetary Fund (IMF), 700 19th St. NW, Washington, DC, 20431, USA, (202) 623-7000, (202) 623-4661, publications@imf.org, https://www.imf.org; International Financial Statistics (IFS) and Regional Economic Outlook.

Palgrave Macmillan, 1 New York Plaza, Ste. 4500, New York, NY, 10004-1562, USA, (800) 777-4643, orders@palgrave.com, https://www.palgrave.com/us; The Statesman's Yearbook, 2023.

Routledge - Taylor & Francis Group, 6000 Broken Sound Pkwy. NW, Ste. 300, Boca Raton, FL, 33487, USA, (800) 634-1420, (800) 634-7064, orders@taylorandfrancis.com, https://www.routledge.com/; The Europa World Year Book 2022.

United Nations Statistics Division (UNSD), United Nations Plz., New York, NY, 10017, USA, (800) 253-9646, (212) 963-9851, statistics@un.org, https://unstats.un.org; National Accounts Main Aggregates Database and National Accounts Statistics: Main Aggregates and Detailed Tables.

The World Bank, 1818 H St. NW, Washington, DC, 20433, USA, (202) 473-1000, (202) 477-6391, eds03@worldbank.org, https://www.worldbank.org/; Chile (report).

CHILE-FISHERIES

Inter-American Development Bank (IDB), 1300 New York Ave. NW, Washington, DC, 20577, USA, (202) 623-1000, (202) 623-3096, https://www.iadb.org/en; Latin Macro Watch (LMW).

Palgrave Macmillan, 1 New York Plaza, Ste. 4500, New York, NY, 10004-1562, USA, (800) 777-4643, orders@palgrave.com, https://www.palgrave.com/us; The Statesman's Yearbook, 2023.

Routledge - Taylor & Francis Group, 6000 Broken Sound Pkwy. NW, Ste. 300, Boca Raton, FL, 33487, USA, (800) 634-1420, (800) 634-7064, orders@taylorandfrancis.com, https://www.routledge.com/; The Europa World Year Book 2022.

United Nations Food and Agricultural Organization (FAO), 2121 K St., Ste. 800B, Washington, DC, 20037, USA, (202) 653-2400 (Dial from U.S.), (202) 653-5760 (Fax from U.S.), fao-hq@fao.org, https://www.fao.org; FAO Yearbook of Fishery and Aquaculture Statistics 2019; Fishery Statistical Collections Global Capture Production; FishStatJ; and The State of Food and Agriculture (SOFA) 2022.

United Nations Statistics Division (UNSD), United Nations Plz., New York, NY, 10017, USA, (800) 253-9646, (212) 963-9851, statistics@un.org, https://unstats.un.org; Statistical Yearbook of the United Nations 2021.

The World Bank, 1818 H St. NW, Washington, DC, 20433, USA, (202) 473-1000, (202) 477-6391, eds03@worldbank.org, https://www.worldbank.org/; Chile (report).

CHILE-FOOD

Euromonitor International, Inc., 1 N Dearborn St., Ste. 1700, Chicago, IL, 60602, USA, (312) 922-1115, (312) 922-1157, info-usa@euromonitor.com, https://www.euromonitor.com/; Market Research on the Retailing Industry.

United Nations Food and Agricultural Organization (FAO), 2121 K St., Ste. 800B, Washington, DC, 20037, USA, (202) 653-2400 (Dial from U.S.), (202) 653-5760 (Fax from U.S.), fao-hq@fao.org, https://www.fao.org; The State of Food and Agriculture (SOFA) 2022.

CHILE-FOREIGN EXCHANGE RATES

Inter-American Development Bank (IDB), 1300 New York Ave. NW, Washington, DC, 20577, USA, (202) 623-1000, (202) 623-3096, https://www.iadb.org/en; Latin Macro Watch (LMW).

International Monetary Fund (IMF), 700 19th St. NW, Washington, DC, 20431, USA, (202) 623-7000, (202) 623-4661, publications@imf.org, https://www.imf.org; International Financial Statistics (IFS).

CHILE-FORESTS AND FORESTRY

Inter-American Development Bank (IDB), 1300 New York Ave. NW, Washington, DC, 20577, USA, (202) 623-1000, (202) 623-3096, https://www.iadb.org/en; Latin Macro Watch (LMW).

Palgrave Macmillan, 1 New York Plaza, Ste. 4500, New York, NY, 10004-1562, USA, (800) 777-4643, orders@palgrave.com, https://www.palgrave.com/us; The Statesman's Yearbook, 2023.

Routledge - Taylor & Francis Group, 6000 Broken Sound Pkwy. NW, Ste. 300, Boca Raton, FL, 33487, USA, (800) 634-1420, (800) 634-7064, orders@taylorandfrancis.com, https://www.routledge.com/; The Europa World Year Book 2022.

UNESCO Institute for Statistics, C.P 250 Succursale H, Montreal, QC, H3G 2K8, CAN, (514) 343-6880 (Dial from U.S.), (514) 343-5740 (Fax from U.S.), uis.publications@unesco.org, http://uis.unesco.org/; UIS.Stat.

United Nations Food and Agricultural Organization (FAO), 2121 K St., Ste. 800B, Washington, DC, 20037, USA, (202) 653-2400 (Dial from U.S.), (202) 653-5760 (Fax from U.S.), fao-hq@fao.org, https://www.fao.org; FAO Yearbook of Forest Products 2019 and The State of Food and Agriculture (SOFA) 2022.

United Nations Statistics Division (UNSD), United Nations Plz., New York, NY, 10017, USA, (800) 253-9646, (212) 963-9851, statistics@un.org, https://unstats.un.org; Statistical Yearbook of the United Nations 2021.

The World Bank, 1818 H St. NW, Washington, DC, 20433, USA, (202) 473-1000, (202) 477-6391, eds03@worldbank.org, https://www.worldbank.org/; Chile (report) and World Development Report 2022: Finance for an Equitable Recovery.

CHILE-GAS PRODUCTION

See CHILE-MINERAL INDUSTRIES

CHILE-GEOGRAPHIC INFORMATION SYSTEMS

The World Bank, 1818 H St. NW, Washington, DC, 20433, USA, (202) 473-1000, (202) 477-6391, eds03@worldbank.org, https://www.worldbank.org/; Chile (report).

CHILE-GOLD INDUSTRY

The World Bank, 1818 H St. NW, Washington, DC, 20433, USA, (202) 473-1000, (202) 477-6391, eds03@worldbank.org, https://www.worldbank.org/; World Development Indicators (WDI) 2022.

CHILE-GOLD PRODUCTION

See CHILE-MINERAL INDUSTRIES

CHILE-GROSS DOMESTIC PRODUCT

The Economist Group: Economist Intelligence Unit (EIU), 900 3rd Ave., 16th Fl., New York, NY, 10022, USA, (212) 541-0500, americas@eiu.com, https://www.eiu.com; Chile Country Report.

Inter-American Development Bank (IDB), 1300 New York Ave. NW, Washington, DC, 20577, USA, (202) 623-1000, (202) 623-3096, https://www.iadb.org/en; Latin Macro Watch (LMW).

Routledge - Taylor & Francis Group, 6000 Broken Sound Pkwy. NW, Ste. 300, Boca Raton, FL, 33487, USA, (800) 634-1420, (800) 634-7064, orders@taylorandfrancis.com, https://www.routledge.com/; The Europa World Year Book 2022.

United Nations Statistics Division (UNSD), United Nations Plz., New York, NY, 10017, USA, (800) 253-9646, (212) 963-9851, statistics@un.org, https://unstats.un.org; Statistical Yearbook of the United Nations 2021.

The World Bank, 1818 H St. NW, Washington, DC, 20433, USA, (202) 473-1000, (202) 477-6391, eds03@worldbank.org, https://www.worldbank.org/; World Development Indicators (WDI) 2022 and World Development Report 2022: Finance for an Equitable Recovery.

CHILE-GROSS NATIONAL PRODUCT

Inter-American Development Bank (IDB), 1300 New York Ave. NW, Washington, DC, 20577, USA, (202) 623-1000, (202) 623-3096, https://www.iadb.org/en; Latin Macro Watch (LMW).

Palgrave Macmillan, 1 New York Plaza, Ste. 4500, New York, NY, 10004-1562, USA, (800) 777-4643, orders@palgrave.com, https://www.palgrave.com/us; The Statesman's Yearbook, 2023.

United Nations Statistics Division (UNSD), United Nations Plz., New York, NY, 10017, USA, (800) 253-9646, (212) 963-9851, statistics@un.org, https://unstats.un.org; Statistical Yearbook of the United Nations 2021.

The World Bank, 1818 H St. NW, Washington, DC, 20433, USA, (202) 473-1000, (202) 477-6391, eds03@worldbank.org, https://www.worldbank.org/; World Development Indicators (WDI) 2022 and World Development Report 2022: Finance for an Equitable Recovery.

CHILE-HOUSING

Euromonitor International, Inc., 1 N Dearborn St., Ste. 1700, Chicago, IL, 60602, USA, (312) 922-1115, (312) 922-1157, info-usa@euromonitor.com, https://www.euromonitor.com/; Geographies.

CHILE-ILLITERATE PERSONS

Central Intelligence Agency (CIA), Office of Public Affairs, Washington, DC, 20505, USA, (703) 482-0623, https://www.cia.gov; The World Factbook.

UNESCO Institute for Statistics, C.P 250 Succursale H, Montreal, QC, H3G 2K8, CAN, (514) 343-6880 (Dial from U.S.), (514) 343-5740 (Fax from U.S.), uis.publications@unesco.org, http://uis.unesco.org/; UIS.Stat.

CHILE-IMPORTS

BC Stats, Stn Prov Govt, PO Box 9410, Victoria, BC, V8W 9V1, CAN, (250) 387-6121 (Dial from U.S.), bc.stats@gov.bc.ca, https://www2.gov.bc.ca/gov/content/data/about-data-management/bc-stats; Country Trade Profile - Chile.

Central Intelligence Agency (CIA), Office of Public Affairs, Washington, DC, 20505, USA, (703) 482-0623, https://www.cia.gov; The World Factbook.

The Economist Group: Economist Intelligence Unit (EIU), 900 3rd Ave., 16th Fl., New York, NY, 10022, USA, (212) 541-0500, americas@eiu.com, https://www.eiu.com; Chile Country Report.

Inter-American Development Bank (IDB), 1300 New York Ave. NW, Washington, DC, 20577, USA, (202) 623-1000, (202) 623-3096, https://www.iadb.org/en; Latin Macro Watch (LMW).

International Monetary Fund (IMF), 700 19th St. NW, Washington, DC, 20431, USA, (202) 623-7000, (202) 623-4661, publications@imf.org, https://www.imf.org; Direction of Trade Statistics (DOTS) and International Financial Statistics (IFS).

Organization for Economic Cooperation and Development (OECD), 2001 L St. NW, Ste. 650, Washington, DC, 20036-4922, USA, (202) 785-6323, (800) 456-6323, (202) 785-0350, washington.contact@oecd.org, https://www.oecd.org/; Economic Survey of Chile 2022.

S&P Global, IHS Markit, 15 Inverness Way E, Englewood, CO, 80112, USA, (800) 447-2273, (800) 854-7179, https://ihsmarkit.com; Global Trade Atlas (GTA).

United Nations Conference on Trade and Development (UNCTAD), Palais des Nations, Geneva, 1211, SWI, (212) 963-6896, unctadinfo@unctad.org, https://unctad.org; Handbook of Statistics 2021.

The World Bank, 1818 H St. NW, Washington, DC, 20433, USA, (202) 473-1000, (202) 477-6391, eds03@worldbank.org, https://www.worldbank.org/; World Development Report 2022: Finance for an Equitable Recovery.

CHILE-INDUSTRIAL METALS PRODUCTION

See CHILE-MINERAL INDUSTRIES

CHILE-INDUSTRIAL PROPERTY

International Energy Agency (IEA), 9 Rue de la Federation, Paris, 75739, FRA, info@iea.org, https://www.iea.org/; World Energy Outlook 2021.

World Intellectual Property Organization (WIPO), 34, chemin des Colombettes, Geneva, CH-1211, SWI, https://www.wipo.int; Madrid Yearly Review 2022: International Registrations of Marks.

CHILE-INDUSTRIES

Central Intelligence Agency (CIA), Office of Public Affairs, Washington, DC, 20505, USA, (703) 482-0623, https://www.cia.gov; The World Factbook.

The Economist Group: Economist Intelligence Unit (EIU), 900 3rd Ave., 16th Fl., New York, NY, 10022, USA, (212) 541-0500, americas@eiu.com, https://www.eiu.com; Chile Country Report.

Euromonitor International, Inc., 1 N Dearborn St., Ste. 1700, Chicago, IL, 60602, USA, (312) 922-1115, (312) 922-1157, info-usa@euromonitor.com, https://www.euromonitor.com/; Geographies.

International Energy Agency (IEA), 9 Rue de la Federation, Paris, 75739, FRA, info@iea.org, https://www.iea.org/; World Energy Outlook 2021.

Palgrave Macmillan, 1 New York Plaza, Ste. 4500, New York, NY, 10004-1562, USA, (800) 777-4643, orders@palgrave.com, https://www.palgrave.com/us; The Statesman's Yearbook, 2023.

Routledge - Taylor & Francis Group, 6000 Broken Sound Pkwy. NW, Ste. 300, Boca Raton, FL, 33487, USA, (800) 634-1420, (800) 634-7064, orders@taylorandfrancis.com, https://www.routledge.com/; The Europa World Year Book 2022.

United Nations Economic Commission for Latin America and the Caribbean (ECLAC), Casilla 179-D, Santiago, 7630412, CHL, (202) 596-3713, prensa@cepal.org, https://www.cepal.org/en; Economic Survey of Latin America and the Caribbean 2021: Labour Dynamics and Employment Policies for Sustainable and Inclusive Recovery Beyond the COVID-19 Crisis.

United Nations Industrial Development Organization (UNIDO), 1 United Nations Plz., Rm. DC1-1118, New York, NY, 10017, USA, (212) 963-6890, (212) 963 6885, (212) 963-7904, office.newyork@unido.org, https://www.unido.org/; Industrial Statistics Databases and International Yearbook of Industrial Statistics 2021.

The World Bank, 1818 H St. NW, Washington, DC, 20433, USA, (202) 473-1000, (202) 477-6391, eds03@worldbank.org, https://www.worldbank.org/; Chile (report) and World Development Indicators (WDI) 2022.

CHILE-INFANT AND MATERNAL MORTALITY

See CHILE-MORTALITY

CHILE-INFLATION (FINANCE)

United Nations Economic Commission for Latin America and the Caribbean (ECLAC), Casilla 179-D, Santiago, 7630412, CHL, (202) 596-3713, prensa@cepal.org, https://www.cepal.org/en; Economic Survey of Latin America and the Caribbean 2021: Labour Dynamics and Employment Policies for Sustainable and Inclusive Recovery Beyond the COVID-19 Crisis.

CHILE-INTEREST RATES

Inter-American Development Bank (IDB), 1300 New York Ave. NW, Washington, DC, 20577, USA, (202) 623-1000, (202) 623-3096, https://www.iadb.org/en; Latin Macro Watch (LMW).

CHILE-INTERNAL REVENUE

Inter-American Development Bank (IDB), 1300 New York Ave. NW, Washington, DC, 20577, USA, (202) 623-1000, (202) 623-3096, https://www.iadb.org/en; Latin Macro Watch (LMW).

CHILE-INTERNATIONAL FINANCE

Inter-American Development Bank (IDB), 1300 New York Ave. NW, Washington, DC, 20577, USA, (202) 623-1000, (202) 623-3096, https://www.iadb.org/en; Latin Macro Watch (LMW).

CHILE-INTERNATIONAL LIQUIDITY

Inter-American Development Bank (IDB), 1300 New York Ave. NW, Washington, DC, 20577, USA, (202) 623-1000, (202) 623-3096, https://www.iadb.org/en; Latin Macro Watch (LMW).

CHILE-INTERNATIONAL TRADE

The Economist Group: Economist Intelligence Unit (EIU), 900 3rd Ave., 16th Fl., New York, NY, 10022, USA, (212) 541-0500, americas@eiu.com, https://www.eiu.com; Chile Country Report.

Euromonitor International, Inc., 1 N Dearborn St., Ste. 1700, Chicago, IL, 60602, USA, (312) 922-1115, (312) 922-1157, info-usa@euromonitor.com, https://www.euromonitor.com/; Geographies.

Inter-American Development Bank (IDB), 1300 New York Ave. NW, Washington, DC, 20577, USA, (202) 623-1000, (202) 623-3096, https://www.iadb.org/en; Latin Macro Watch (LMW).

International Monetary Fund (IMF), 700 19th St. NW, Washington, DC, 20431, USA, (202) 623-7000, (202) 623-4661, publications@imf.org, https://www.imf.org; International Financial Statistics (IFS).

Organization for Economic Cooperation and Development (OECD), 2001 L St. NW, Ste. 650, Washington, DC, 20036-4922, USA, (202) 785-6323, (800) 456-6323, (202) 785-0350, washington.contact@oecd.org, https://www.oecd.org/; Economic Survey of Chile 2022.

Palgrave Macmillan, 1 New York Plaza, Ste. 4500, New York, NY, 10004-1562, USA, (800) 777-4643, orders@palgrave.com, https://www.palgrave.com/us; The Statesman's Yearbook, 2023.

Routledge - Taylor & Francis Group, 6000 Broken Sound Pkwy. NW, Ste. 300, Boca Raton, FL, 33487, USA, (800) 634-1420, (800) 634-7064, orders@taylorandfrancis.com, https://www.routledge.com/; The Europa World Year Book 2022.

United Nations Conference on Trade and Development (UNCTAD), Palais des Nations, Geneva, 1211, SWI, (212) 963-6896, unctadinfo@unctad.org, https://unctad.org; Trade and Development Report 2021.

United Nations Economic Commission for Latin America and the Caribbean (ECLAC), Casilla 179-D, Santiago, 7630412, CHL, (202) 596-3713, prensa@cepal.org, https://www.cepal.org/en; Economic Survey of Latin America and the Caribbean 2021: Labour Dynamics and Employment Policies for Sustainable and Inclusive Recovery Beyond the COVID-19 Crisis.

United Nations Food and Agricultural Organization (FAO), 2121 K St., Ste. 800B, Washington, DC, 20037, USA, (202) 653-2400 (Dial from U.S.), (202) 653-5760 (Fax from U.S.), fao-hq@fao.org, https://www.fao.org; The State of Food and Agriculture (SOFA) 2022.

United Nations Statistics Division (UNSD), United Nations Plz., New York, NY, 10017, USA, (800) 253-9646, (212) 963-9851, statistics@un.org, https://unstats.un.org; International Trade Statistics Yearbook 2020 and Statistical Yearbook of the United Nations 2021.

The World Bank, 1818 H St. NW, Washington, DC, 20433, USA, (202) 473-1000, (202) 477-6391, eds03@worldbank.org, https://www.worldbank.org/; Chile (report); World Development Indicators (WDI) 2022; and World Development Report 2022: Finance for an Equitable Recovery.

World Bureau of Metal Statistics (WBMS), 31 Star St., Ware, Hertfordshire, SG12 9BA, GBR, https://www.refinitiv.com/en/trading-solutions/world-bureau-metal-statistics; Long Term Production/Consumption Series - All Metals; World Flow Charts; and World Metal Statistics.

World Trade Organization (WTO), Ctre. William Rappard, Rue de Lausanne 154, Case postale, Geneva, CH-1211, SWI, enquiries@wto.org, https://www.wto.org; World Trade Statistical Review 2022.

CHILE-INTERNET USERS

International Telecommunication Union (ITU), Place des Nations, Geneva, CH-1211, SWI, itumail@itu.int, https://www.itu.int; Global Connectivity Report 2022; World Telecommunication/ICT Indicators Database 2021; and Yearbook of Statistics 2019.

The World Bank, 1818 H St. NW, Washington, DC, 20433, USA, (202) 473-1000, (202) 477-6391, eds03@worldbank.org, https://www.worldbank.org/; Chile (report).

CHILE-INVESTMENTS

Inter-American Development Bank (IDB), 1300 New York Ave. NW, Washington, DC, 20577, USA, (202) 623-1000, (202) 623-3096, https://www.iadb.org/en; Latin Macro Watch (LMW).

CHILE-IRRIGATION

Inter-American Development Bank (IDB), 1300 New York Ave. NW, Washington, DC, 20577, USA, (202) 623-1000, (202) 623-3096, https://www.iadb.org/en; Latin Macro Watch (LMW).

CHILE-LABOR

Central Intelligence Agency (CIA), Office of Public Affairs, Washington, DC, 20505, USA, (703) 482-0623, https://www.cia.gov; The World Factbook.

Euromonitor International, Inc., 1 N Dearborn St., Ste. 1700, Chicago, IL, 60602, USA, (312) 922-1115, (312) 922-1157, info-usa@euromonitor.com, https://www.euromonitor.com/; Geographies.

International Labour Organization (ILO), 4 Rte. des Morillons, Geneva, CH-1211, SWI, ilo@ilo.org, https://www.ilo.org; NORMLEX Information System on International Labour Standards.

Organization for Economic Cooperation and Development (OECD), 2001 L St. NW, Ste. 650, Washington, DC, 20036-4922, USA, (202) 785-6323, (800) 456-6323, (202) 785-0350, washington.contact@oecd.org, https://www.oecd.org/; Economic Survey of Chile 2022.

Palgrave Macmillan, 1 New York Plaza, Ste. 4500, New York, NY, 10004-1562, USA, (800) 777-4643, orders@palgrave.com, https://www.palgrave.com/us; The Statesman's Yearbook, 2023.

United Nations Food and Agricultural Organization (FAO), 2121 K St., Ste. 800B, Washington, DC, 20037, USA, (202) 653-2400 (Dial from U.S.), (202) 653-5760 (Fax from U.S.), fao-hq@fao.org, https://www.fao.org; The State of Food and Agriculture (SOFA) 2022.

The World Bank, 1818 H St. NW, Washington, DC, 20433, USA, (202) 473-1000, (202) 477-6391, eds03@worldbank.org, https://www.worldbank.org/; World Development Indicators (WDI) 2022 and World Development Report 2022: Finance for an Equitable Recovery.

CHILE-LAND USE

Inter-American Development Bank (IDB), 1300 New York Ave. NW, Washington, DC, 20577, USA, (202) 623-1000, (202) 623-3096, https://www.iadb.org/en; Latin Macro Watch (LMW).

United Nations Statistics Division (UNSD), United Nations Plz., New York, NY, 10017, USA, (800) 253-9646, (212) 963-9851, statistics@un.org, https://unstats.un.org; Millennium Development Goal Indicators.

The World Bank, 1818 H St. NW, Washington, DC, 20433, USA, (202) 473-1000, (202) 477-6391, eds03@worldbank.org, https://www.worldbank.org/; World Development Report 2022: Finance for an Equitable Recovery.

CHILE-LIBRARIES

UNESCO Institute for Statistics, C.P 250 Succursale H, Montreal, QC, H3G 2K8, CAN, (514) 343-6880 (Dial from U.S.), (514) 343-5740 (Fax from U.S.), uis.publications@unesco.org, http://uis.unesco.org/; UIS.Stat.

CHILE-LIFE EXPECTANCY

Central Intelligence Agency (CIA), Office of Public Affairs, Washington, DC, 20505, USA, (703) 482-0623, https://www.cia.gov; The World Factbook.

United Nations Department of Economic and Social Affairs (DESA), Population Division, 2 United Nations Plz., Rm. DC2-1950, New York, NY, 10017, USA, (212) 963-3209, (212) 963-2147, population@un.org, https://www.un.org/development/desa/pd/; World Population Ageing 2020 Highlights.

United Nations Statistics Division (UNSD), United Nations Plz., New York, NY, 10017, USA, (800) 253-9646, (212) 963-9851, statistics@un.org, https://unstats.un.org; Millennium Development Goal Indicators.

CHILE-LITERACY

Euromonitor International, Inc., 1 N Dearborn St., Ste. 1700, Chicago, IL, 60602, USA, (312) 922-1115, (312) 922-1157, info-usa@euromonitor.com, https://www.euromonitor.com/; Geographies.

UNESCO Institute for Statistics, C.P 250 Succursale H, Montreal, QC, H3G 2K8, CAN, (514) 343-6880 (Dial from U.S.), (514) 343-5740 (Fax from U.S.), uis.publications@unesco.org, http://uis.unesco.org/; Literacy.

CHILE-LIVESTOCK

Palgrave Macmillan, 1 New York Plaza, Ste. 4500, New York, NY, 10004-1562, USA, (800) 777-4643, orders@palgrave.com, https://www.palgrave.com/us; The Statesman's Yearbook, 2023.

Routledge - Taylor & Francis Group, 6000 Broken Sound Pkwy. NW, Ste. 300, Boca Raton, FL, 33487, USA, (800) 634-1420, (800) 634-7064, orders@taylorandfrancis.com, https://www.routledge.com/; The Europa World Year Book 2022.

United Nations Food and Agricultural Organization (FAO), 2121 K St., Ste. 800B, Washington, DC, 20037, USA, (202) 653-2400 (Dial from U.S.), (202) 653-5760 (Fax from U.S.), fao-hq@fao.org, https://www.fao.org; The State of Food and Agriculture (SOFA) 2022.

United Nations Statistics Division (UNSD), United Nations Plz., New York, NY, 10017, USA, (800) 253-9646, (212) 963-9851, statistics@un.org, https://unstats.un.org; Statistical Yearbook of the United Nations 2021.

CHILE-MANUFACTURES

Inter-American Development Bank (IDB), 1300 New York Ave. NW, Washington, DC, 20577, USA, (202) 623-1000, (202) 623-3096, https://www.iadb.org/en; Latin Macro Watch (LMW).

International Monetary Fund (IMF), 700 19th St. NW, Washington, DC, 20431, USA, (202) 623-7000, (202) 623-4661, publications@imf.org, https://www.imf.org; International Financial Statistics (IFS).

Organization for Economic Cooperation and Development (OECD), 2001 L St. NW, Ste. 650, Washington, DC, 20036-4922, USA, (202) 785-6323, (800) 456-6323, (202) 785-0350, washington.contact@oecd.org, https://www.oecd.org/; Economic Survey of Chile 2022.

CHILE-MARRIAGE

Routledge - Taylor & Francis Group, 6000 Broken Sound Pkwy. NW, Ste. 300, Boca Raton, FL, 33487, USA, (800) 634-1420, (800) 634-7064, orders@taylorandfrancis.com, https://www.routledge.com/; The Europa World Year Book 2022.

United Nations Statistics Division (UNSD), United Nations Plz., New York, NY, 10017, USA, (800) 253-9646, (212) 963-9851, statistics@un.org, https://unstats.un.org; Statistical Yearbook of the United Nations 2021.

CHILE-MERCURY PRODUCTION

See CHILE-MINERAL INDUSTRIES

CHILE-MINERAL INDUSTRIES

Barchart, 209 W Jackson Blvd., 2nd Fl., Chicago, IL, 60606, USA, (877) 247-4394, commodities@barchart.com, https://www.barchart.com/cmdty; The cmdty Yearbook 2023; cmdtyStats: Commodity Statistics and Fundamental Data; cmdtyView: Commodity Index; and Commodity Data and Prices.

Inter-American Development Bank (IDB), 1300 New York Ave. NW, Washington, DC, 20577, USA, (202) 623-1000, (202) 623-3096, https://www.iadb.org/en; Latin Macro Watch (LMW).

International Energy Agency (IEA), 9 Rue de la Federation, Paris, 75739, FRA, info@iea.org, https://www.iea.org/; World Energy Outlook 2021.

International Monetary Fund (IMF), 700 19th St. NW, Washington, DC, 20431, USA, (202) 623-7000, (202) 623-4661, publications@imf.org, https://www.imf.org; International Financial Statistics (IFS).

Organization for Economic Cooperation and Development (OECD), 2001 L St. NW, Ste. 650, Washington, DC, 20036-4922, USA, (202) 785-6323, (800) 456-6323, (202) 785-0350, washington.contact@oecd.org, https://www.oecd.org/; Economic Survey of Chile 2022.

Palgrave Macmillan, 1 New York Plaza, Ste. 4500, New York, NY, 10004-1562, USA, (800) 777-4643, orders@palgrave.com, https://www.palgrave.com/us; The Statesman's Yearbook, 2023.

Routledge - Taylor & Francis Group, 6000 Broken Sound Pkwy. NW, Ste. 300, Boca Raton, FL, 33487, USA, (800) 634-1420, (800) 634-7064, orders@taylorandfrancis.com, https://www.routledge.com/; The Europa World Year Book 2022.

United Nations Conference on Trade and Development (UNCTAD), Palais des Nations, Geneva, 1211, SWI, (212) 963-6896, unctadinfo@unctad.org, https://unctad.org; Trade and Development Report 2021.

United Nations Statistics Division (UNSD), United Nations Plz., New York, NY, 10017, USA, (800) 253-9646, (212) 963-9851, statistics@un.org, https://unstats.un.org; Statistical Yearbook of the United Nations 2021.

World Bureau of Metal Statistics (WBMS), 31 Star St., Ware, Hertfordshire, SG12 9BA, GBR, https://www.refinitiv.com/en/trading-solutions/world-bureau-metal-statistics; Annual Stainless Steel Statistics; Long Term Production/Consumption Series - All Metals; World Flow Charts; and World Metal Statistics.

CHILE-MONEY SUPPLY

The Economist Group: Economist Intelligence Unit (EIU), 900 3rd Ave., 16th Fl., New York, NY, 10022, USA, (212) 541-0500, americas@eiu.com, https://www.eiu.com; Chile Country Report.

Inter-American Development Bank (IDB), 1300 New York Ave. NW, Washington, DC, 20577, USA, (202) 623-1000, (202) 623-3096, https://www.iadb.org/en; Latin Macro Watch (LMW).

International Monetary Fund (IMF), 700 19th St. NW, Washington, DC, 20431, USA, (202) 623-7000, (202) 623-4661, publications@imf.org, https://www.imf.org; International Financial Statistics (IFS).

Organization for Economic Cooperation and Development (OECD), 2001 L St. NW, Ste. 650, Washington, DC, 20036-4922, USA, (202) 785-6323, (800) 456-6323, (202) 785-0350, washington.contact@oecd.org, https://www.oecd.org/; Economic Survey of Chile 2022.

Routledge - Taylor & Francis Group, 6000 Broken Sound Pkwy. NW, Ste. 300, Boca Raton, FL, 33487, USA, (800) 634-1420, (800) 634-7064, orders@taylorandfrancis.com, https://www.routledge.com/; The Europa World Year Book 2022.

United Nations Statistics Division (UNSD), United Nations Plz., New York, NY, 10017, USA, (800) 253-9646, (212) 963-9851, statistics@un.org, https://unstats.un.org; Statistical Yearbook of the United Nations 2021.

The World Bank, 1818 H St. NW, Washington, DC, 20433, USA, (202) 473-1000, (202) 477-6391, eds03@worldbank.org, https://www.worldbank.org/; Chile (report).

CHILE-MORTALITY

UNICEF, 3 United Nations Plz., New York, NY, 10017, USA, (212) 303-7984, (917) 244-2215, https://www.unicef.org; The State of the World's Children 2023.

United Nations Statistics Division (UNSD), United Nations Plz., New York, NY, 10017, USA, (800) 253-9646, (212) 963-9851, statistics@un.org, https://unstats.un.org; Millennium Development Goal Indicators; Statistical Yearbook of the United Nations 2021; and World Statistics Pocketbook 2021.

The World Bank, 1818 H St. NW, Washington, DC, 20433, USA, (202) 473-1000, (202) 477-6391, eds03@worldbank.org, https://www.worldbank.org/; World Development Indicators (WDI) 2022.

World Health Organization (WHO), Ave. Appia 20, Geneva, CH-1211, SWI, (202) 974-3000 (Telephone in U.S.), publications@who.int, https://www.who.int/; Global Health Observatory (GHO).

CHILE-MOTION PICTURES

Palgrave Macmillan, 1 New York Plaza, Ste. 4500, New York, NY, 10004-1562, USA, (800) 777-4643, orders@palgrave.com, https://www.palgrave.com/us; The Statesman's Yearbook, 2023.

CHILE-MOTOR VEHICLES

International Road Federation (IRF), Madison Place, 500 Montgomery St., 5th Fl., Alexandria, VA, 22314, USA, (703) 535-1001, (703) 535-1007, info@irf.global, https://www.irf.global/; World Road Statistics (WRS).

CHILE-NATURAL GAS PRODUCTION

See CHILE-MINERAL INDUSTRIES

CHILE-NICKEL AND NICKEL ORE

See CHILE-MINERAL INDUSTRIES

CHILE-NUTRITION

United Nations Food and Agricultural Organization (FAO), 2121 K St., Ste. 800B, Washington, DC, 20037, USA, (202) 653-2400 (Dial from U.S.), (202) 653-5760 (Fax from U.S.), fao-hq@fao.org, https://www.fao.org; The State of Food and Agriculture (SOFA) 2022.

United Nations Statistics Division (UNSD), United Nations Plz., New York, NY, 10017, USA, (800) 253-9646, (212) 963-9851, statistics@un.org, https://unstats.un.org; Millennium Development Goal Indicators.

CHILE-PAPER

See CHILE-FORESTS AND FORESTRY

CHILE-PEANUT PRODUCTION

See CHILE-CROPS

CHILE-PESTICIDES

United Nations Food and Agricultural Organization (FAO), 2121 K St., Ste. 800B, Washington, DC, 20037, USA, (202) 653-2400 (Dial from U.S.), (202) 653-5760 (Fax from U.S.), fao-hq@fao.org, https://www.fao.org; The State of Food and Agriculture (SOFA) 2022.

CHILE-PETROLEUM INDUSTRY AND TRADE

Inter-American Development Bank (IDB), 1300 New York Ave. NW, Washington, DC, 20577, USA, (202) 623-1000, (202) 623-3096, https://www.iadb.org/en; Latin Macro Watch (LMW).

International Energy Agency (IEA), 9 Rue de la Federation, Paris, 75739, FRA, info@iea.org, https://www.iea.org/; World Energy Outlook 2021.

Palgrave Macmillan, 1 New York Plaza, Ste. 4500, New York, NY, 10004-1562, USA, (800) 777-4643, orders@palgrave.com, https://www.palgrave.com/us; The Statesman's Yearbook, 2023.

U.S. Energy Information Administration (EIA), 1000 Independence Ave. SW, Washington, DC, 20585, USA, (202) 586-8800, infoctr@eia.gov, https://www.eia.gov; International Energy Outlook 2021.

United Nations Food and Agricultural Organization (FAO), 2121 K St., Ste. 800B, Washington, DC, 20037, USA, (202) 653-2400 (Dial from U.S.), (202) 653-5760 (Fax from U.S.), fao-hq@fao.org, https://www.fao.org; The State of Food and Agriculture (SOFA) 2022.

United Nations Statistics Division (UNSD), United Nations Plz., New York, NY, 10017, USA, (800) 253-9646, (212) 963-9851, statistics@un.org, https://unstats.un.org; Statistical Yearbook of the United Nations 2021.

CHILE-PLASTICS INDUSTRY AND TRADE

United Nations Statistics Division (UNSD), United Nations Plz., New York, NY, 10017, USA, (800) 253-9646, (212) 963-9851, statistics@un.org, https://unstats.un.org; Statistical Yearbook of the United Nations 2021.

CHILE-POPULATION

Central Intelligence Agency (CIA), Office of Public Affairs, Washington, DC, 20505, USA, (703) 482-0623, https://www.cia.gov; The World Factbook.

The Economist Group: Economist Intelligence Unit (EIU), 900 3rd Ave., 16th Fl., New York, NY, 10022, USA, (212) 541-0500, americas@eiu.com, https://www.eiu.com; Chile Country Report.

Infoplease, c/o Sandbox Networks, Inc., 1 Lincoln St., 24th Fl., Boston, MA, 02111, USA, https://www.infoplease.com; Countries of the World.

Inter-American Development Bank (IDB), 1300 New York Ave. NW, Washington, DC, 20577, USA, (202) 623-1000, (202) 623-3096, https://www.iadb.org/en; Latin Macro Watch (LMW).

International Labour Organization (ILO), 4 Rte. des Morillons, Geneva, CH-1211, SWI, ilo@ilo.org, https://www.ilo.org; NORMLEX Information System on International Labour Standards.

Palgrave Macmillan, 1 New York Plaza, Ste. 4500, New York, NY, 10004-1562, USA, (800) 777-4643, orders@palgrave.com, https://www.palgrave.com/us; The Statesman's Yearbook, 2023.

Routledge - Taylor & Francis Group, 6000 Broken Sound Pkwy. NW, Ste. 300, Boca Raton, FL, 33487, USA, (800) 634-1420, (800) 634-7064, orders@taylorandfrancis.com, https://www.routledge.com/; The Europa World Year Book 2022.

UK Data Service, University of Essex, Wivenhoe Park, Colchester, Essex, CO4 3SQ, GBR, https://ukdataservice.ac.uk/; International Aggregate Data.

UNESCO Institute for Statistics, C.P 250 Succursale H, Montreal, QC, H3G 2K8, CAN, (514) 343-6880 (Dial from U.S.), (514) 343-5740 (Fax from U.S.), uis.publications@unesco.org, http://uis.unesco.org/; UIS.Stat.

United Nations Department of Economic and Social Affairs (DESA), Population Division, 2 United Nations Plz., Rm. DC2-1950, New York, NY, 10017, USA, (212) 963-3209, (212) 963-2147, population@un.org, https://www.un.org/development/desa/pd/; Revision of World Urbanization Prospects and World Population Ageing 2020 Highlights.

United Nations Development Programme (UNDP), One United Nations Plz., New York, NY, 10017, USA, (212) 906-5000, (212) 906-5001, https://www.undp.org; Human Development Report 2021-2022.

United Nations Economic Commission for Latin America and the Caribbean (ECLAC), Casilla 179-D, Santiago, 7630412, CHL, (202) 596-3713, prensa@cepal.org, https://www.cepal.org/en; CEPALSTAT and Social Panorama of Latin America and the Caribbean 2022: Transforming Education as a Basis for Sustainable Development.

United Nations Statistics Division (UNSD), United Nations Plz., New York, NY, 10017, USA, (800) 253-9646, (212) 963-9851, statistics@un.org, https://unstats.un.org; Statistical Yearbook of the United Nations 2021 and World Statistics Pocketbook 2021.

University of California Los Angeles (UCLA), Latin American Institute (LAI), 10343 Bunche Hall, 315 Portola Plaza, Los Angeles, CA, 90095-1447, USA, (310) 825-4571, lai@international.ucla.edu, https://www.international.ucla.edu/lai; unpublished data.

The World Bank, 1818 H St. NW, Washington, DC, 20433, USA, (202) 473-1000, (202) 477-6391, eds03@worldbank.org, https://www.worldbank.org/; Chile (report); The Global Findex Database 2021; and World Development Report 2022: Finance for an Equitable Recovery.

CHILE-POPULATION DENSITY

Central Intelligence Agency (CIA), Office of Public Affairs, Washington, DC, 20505, USA, (703) 482-0623, https://www.cia.gov; The World Factbook.

Inter-American Development Bank (IDB), 1300 New York Ave. NW, Washington, DC, 20577, USA, (202) 623-1000, (202) 623-3096, https://www.iadb.org/en; Latin Macro Watch (LMW).

Palgrave Macmillan, 1 New York Plaza, Ste. 4500, New York, NY, 10004-1562, USA, (800) 777-4643, orders@palgrave.com, https://www.palgrave.com/us; The Statesman's Yearbook, 2023.

Routledge - Taylor & Francis Group, 6000 Broken Sound Pkwy. NW, Ste. 300, Boca Raton, FL, 33487, USA, (800) 634-1420, (800) 634-7064, orders@taylorandfrancis.com, https://www.routledge.com/; The Europa World Year Book 2022.

UNESCO Institute for Statistics, C.P 250 Succursale H, Montreal, QC, H3G 2K8, CAN, (514) 343-6880 (Dial from U.S.), (514) 343-5740 (Fax from U.S.), uis.publications@unesco.org, http://uis.unesco.org/; UIS.Stat.

The World Bank, 1818 H St. NW, Washington, DC, 20433, USA, (202) 473-1000, (202) 477-6391, eds03@worldbank.org, https://www.worldbank.org/; Chile (report) and World Development Report 2022: Finance for an Equitable Recovery.

CHILE-POSTAL SERVICE

Palgrave Macmillan, 1 New York Plaza, Ste. 4500, New York, NY, 10004-1562, USA, (800) 777-4643, orders@palgrave.com, https://www.palgrave.com/us; The Statesman's Yearbook, 2023.

CHILE-POWER RESOURCES

Euromonitor International, Inc., 1 N Dearborn St., Ste. 1700, Chicago, IL, 60602, USA, (312) 922-1115, (312) 922-1157, info-usa@euromonitor.com, https://www.euromonitor.com/; Geographies.

International Energy Agency (IEA), 9 Rue de la Federation, Paris, 75739, FRA, info@iea.org, https://www.iea.org/; World Energy Outlook 2021.

Palgrave Macmillan, 1 New York Plaza, Ste. 4500, New York, NY, 10004-1562, USA, (800) 777-4643, orders@palgrave.com, https://www.palgrave.com/us; The Statesman's Yearbook, 2023.

U.S. Energy Information Administration (EIA), 1000 Independence Ave. SW, Washington, DC, 20585, USA, (202) 586-8800, infoctr@eia.gov, https://www.eia.gov; International Energy Outlook 2021.

United Nations Food and Agricultural Organization (FAO), 2121 K St., Ste. 800B, Washington, DC, 20037, USA, (202) 653-2400 (Dial from U.S.), (202) 653-5760 (Fax from U.S.), fao-hq@fao.org, https://www.fao.org; The State of Food and Agriculture (SOFA) 2022.

United Nations Statistics Division (UNSD), United Nations Plz., New York, NY, 10017, USA, (800) 253-9646, (212) 963-9851, statistics@un.org, https://unstats.un.org; Energy Statistics Yearbook 2019 and World Statistics Pocketbook 2021.

The World Bank, 1818 H St. NW, Washington, DC, 20433, USA, (202) 473-1000, (202) 477-6391, eds03@worldbank.org, https://www.worldbank.org/; World Development Report 2022: Finance for an Equitable Recovery.

CHILE-PRICES

Euromonitor International, Inc., 1 N Dearborn St., Ste. 1700, Chicago, IL, 60602, USA, (312) 922-1115, (312) 922-1157, info-usa@euromonitor.com, https://www.euromonitor.com/; Geographies.

International Monetary Fund (IMF), 700 19th St. NW, Washington, DC, 20431, USA, (202) 623-7000, (202) 623-4661, publications@imf.org, https://www.imf.org; International Financial Statistics (IFS).

The World Bank, 1818 H St. NW, Washington, DC, 20433, USA, (202) 473-1000, (202) 477-6391, eds03@worldbank.org, https://www.worldbank.org/; Chile (report).

World Bureau of Metal Statistics (WBMS), 31 Star St., Ware, Hertfordshire, SG12 9BA, GBR, https://www.refinitiv.com/en/trading-solutions/world-bureau-metal-statistics; Long Term Production/Consumption Series - All Metals; World Flow Charts; and World Metal Statistics.

CHILE-PUBLIC HEALTH

Euromonitor International, Inc., 1 N Dearborn St., Ste. 1700, Chicago, IL, 60602, USA, (312) 922-1115, (312) 922-1157, info-usa@euromonitor.com, https://www.euromonitor.com/; Geographies and Market Research on the Health and Wellness Industry.

Palgrave Macmillan, 1 New York Plaza, Ste. 4500, New York, NY, 10004-1562, USA, (800) 777-4643, orders@palgrave.com, https://www.palgrave.com/us; The Statesman's Yearbook, 2023.

U.S. Census Bureau, 4600 Silver Hill Rd., Washington, DC, 20233, USA, (301) 763-4636, (800) 923-8282, https://www.census.gov; HIV/AIDS Surveillance Data Base.

UNICEF, 3 United Nations Plz., New York, NY, 10017, USA, (212) 303-7984, (917) 244-2215, https://www.unicef.org; The State of the World's Children 2023.

United Nations Department of Economic and Social Affairs (DESA), Population Division, 2 United Nations Plz., Rm. DC2-1950, New York, NY, 10017, USA, (212) 963-3209, (212) 963-2147, population@un.org, https://www.un.org/development/desa/pd/; World Fertility Data 2019.

United Nations Development Programme (UNDP), One United Nations Plz., New York, NY, 10017, USA, (212) 906-5000, (212) 906-5001, https://www.undp.org; Human Development Report 2021-2022.

United Nations Statistics Division (UNSD), United Nations Plz., New York, NY, 10017, USA, (800) 253-9646, (212) 963-9851, statistics@un.org, https://unstats.un.org; Millennium Development Goal Indicators and Statistical Yearbook of the United Nations 2021.

The World Bank, 1818 H St. NW, Washington, DC, 20433, USA, (202) 473-1000, (202) 477-6391, eds03@worldbank.org, https://www.worldbank.org/; Chile (report).

World Health Organization (WHO), Ave. Appia 20, Geneva, CH-1211, SWI, (202) 974-3000 (Telephone in U.S.), publications@who.int, https://www.who.int/; Global Health Observatory (GHO) and Health Statistics and Information Systems.

CHILE-PUBLISHERS AND PUBLISHING

Routledge - Taylor & Francis Group, 6000 Broken Sound Pkwy. NW, Ste. 300, Boca Raton, FL, 33487, USA, (800) 634-1420, (800) 634-7064, orders@taylorandfrancis.com, https://www.routledge.com/; The Europa World Year Book 2022.

UNESCO Institute for Statistics, C.P 250 Succursale H, Montreal, QC, H3G 2K8, CAN, (514) 343-6880 (Dial from U.S.), (514) 343-5740 (Fax from U.S.), uis.publications@unesco.org, http://uis.unesco.org/; UIS.Stat.

CHILE-RAILROADS

Janes, USA, (703) 574-7580, (888) 977-1519, customer.care@janes.com, https://www.janes.com; Janes World Railways 2021-2022.

Palgrave Macmillan, 1 New York Plaza, Ste. 4500, New York, NY, 10004-1562, USA, (800) 777-4643, orders@palgrave.com, https://www.palgrave.com/us; The Statesman's Yearbook, 2023.

Routledge - Taylor & Francis Group, 6000 Broken Sound Pkwy. NW, Ste. 300, Boca Raton, FL, 33487, USA, (800) 634-1420, (800) 634-7064, orders@taylorandfrancis.com, https://www.routledge.com/; The Europa World Year Book 2022.

United Nations Statistics Division (UNSD), United Nations Plz., New York, NY, 10017, USA, (800) 253-9646, (212) 963-9851, statistics@un.org, https://unstats.un.org; Statistical Yearbook of the United Nations 2021.

CHILE-RELIGION

Central Intelligence Agency (CIA), Office of Public Affairs, Washington, DC, 20505, USA, (703) 482-0623, https://www.cia.gov; The World Factbook.

Palgrave Macmillan, 1 New York Plaza, Ste. 4500, New York, NY, 10004-1562, USA, (800) 777-4643, orders@palgrave.com, https://www.palgrave.com/us; The Statesman's Yearbook, 2023.

CHILE-RETAIL TRADE

Euromonitor International, Inc., 1 N Dearborn St., Ste. 1700, Chicago, IL, 60602, USA, (312) 922-1115, (312) 922-1157, info-usa@euromonitor.com, https://www.euromonitor.com/; Geographies and Market Research on the Retailing Industry.

Inter-American Development Bank (IDB), 1300 New York Ave. NW, Washington, DC, 20577, USA, (202) 623-1000, (202) 623-3096, https://www.iadb.org/en; Latin Macro Watch (LMW).

CHILE-RICE PRODUCTION

See CHILE-CROPS

CHILE-ROADS

International Road Federation (IRF), Madison Place, 500 Montgomery St., 5th Fl., Alexandria, VA, 22314, USA, (703) 535-1001, (703) 535-1007, info@irf.global, https://www.irf.global/; World Road Statistics (WRS).

CHILE-RUBBER INDUSTRY AND TRADE

International Rubber Study Group (IRSG), 51 Changi Business Park Central 2, Unit No. 6, 486066, SGP, https://www.rubberstudy.org; Monthly Rubber Bulletin (MRB); Rubber Industry Report; Rubber Statistical Bulletin; and World Rubber Industry Report (WRIO).

CHILE-SHIPPING

Routledge - Taylor & Francis Group, 6000 Broken Sound Pkwy. NW, Ste. 300, Boca Raton, FL, 33487, USA, (800) 634-1420, (800) 634-7064, orders@taylorandfrancis.com, https://www.routledge.com/; The Europa World Year Book 2022.

S&P Global, IHS Markit, 15 Inverness Way E, Englewood, CO, 80112, USA, (800) 447-2273, (800) 854-7179, https://ihsmarkit.com; IHS Maritime World Shipbuilding Statistics; Journal of Commerce; Lloyd's Register of Ships 2021-2022; and Maritime Portal Desktop.

United Nations Statistics Division (UNSD), United Nations Plz., New York, NY, 10017, USA, (800) 253-9646, (212) 963-9851, statistics@un.org, https://unstats.un.org; Statistical Yearbook of the United Nations 2021.

CHILE-SOYBEAN PRODUCTION

See CHILE-CROPS

CHILE-STEEL PRODUCTION

See CHILE-MINERAL INDUSTRIES

CHILE-SUGAR PRODUCTION

See CHILE-CROPS

CHILE-SULPHUR PRODUCTION

See CHILE-MINERAL INDUSTRIES

CHILE-TAXATION

Inter-American Development Bank (IDB), 1300 New York Ave. NW, Washington, DC, 20577, USA, (202) 623-1000, (202) 623-3096, https://www.iadb.org/en; Latin Macro Watch (LMW).

International Road Federation (IRF), Madison Place, 500 Montgomery St., 5th Fl., Alexandria, VA, 22314, USA, (703) 535-1001, (703) 535-1007, info@irf.global, https://www.irf.global/; World Road Statistics (WRS).

The World Bank, 1818 H St. NW, Washington, DC, 20433, USA, (202) 473-1000, (202) 477-6391, eds03@worldbank.org, https://www.worldbank.org/; World Development Indicators (WDI) 2022.

CHILE-TEA PRODUCTION

See CHILE-CROPS

CHILE-TELEPHONE

Palgrave Macmillan, 1 New York Plaza, Ste. 4500, New York, NY, 10004-1562, USA, (800) 777-4643, orders@palgrave.com, https://www.palgrave.com/us; The Statesman's Yearbook, 2023.

Routledge - Taylor & Francis Group, 6000 Broken Sound Pkwy. NW, Ste. 300, Boca Raton, FL, 33487, USA, (800) 634-1420, (800) 634-7064, orders@taylorandfrancis.com, https://www.routledge.com/; The Europa World Year Book 2022.

United Nations Statistics Division (UNSD), United Nations Plz., New York, NY, 10017, USA, (800) 253-9646, (212) 963-9851, statistics@un.org, https://unstats.un.org; World Statistics Pocketbook 2021.

CHILE-TEXTILE INDUSTRY

Euromonitor International, Inc., 1 N Dearborn St., Ste. 1700, Chicago, IL, 60602, USA, (312) 922-1115, (312) 922-1157, info-usa@euromonitor.com, https://www.euromonitor.com/; Market Research on the Retailing Industry.

United Nations Statistics Division (UNSD), United Nations Plz., New York, NY, 10017, USA, (800) 253-9646, (212) 963-9851, statistics@un.org, https://unstats.un.org; Statistical Yearbook of the United Nations 2021.

CHILE-THEATER

UNESCO Institute for Statistics, C.P 250 Succursale H, Montreal, QC, H3G 2K8, CAN, (514) 343-6880 (Dial from U.S.), (514) 343-5740 (Fax from U.S.), uis.publications@unesco.org, http://uis.unesco.org/; UIS.Stat.

CHILE-TOBACCO INDUSTRY

United Nations Statistics Division (UNSD), United Nations Plz., New York, NY, 10017, USA, (800) 253-9646, (212) 963-9851, statistics@un.org, https://unstats.un.org; Statistical Yearbook of the United Nations 2021.

CHILE-TOURISM

Euromonitor International, Inc., 1 N Dearborn St., Ste. 1700, Chicago, IL, 60602, USA, (312) 922-1115, (312) 922-1157, info-usa@euromonitor.com, https://www.euromonitor.com/; Geographies.

Palgrave Macmillan, 1 New York Plaza, Ste. 4500, New York, NY, 10004-1562, USA, (800) 777-4643, orders@palgrave.com, https://www.palgrave.com/us; The Statesman's Yearbook, 2023.

Routledge - Taylor & Francis Group, 6000 Broken Sound Pkwy. NW, Ste. 300, Boca Raton, FL, 33487, USA, (800) 634-1420, (800) 634-7064, orders@taylorandfrancis.com, https://www.routledge.com/; The Europa World Year Book 2022.

United Nations Statistics Division (UNSD), United Nations Plz., New York, NY, 10017, USA, (800) 253-9646, (212) 963-9851, statistics@un.org, https://unstats.un.org; Statistical Yearbook of the United Nations 2021.

United Nations World Tourism Organization (UNWTO), Calle Poeta Joan Maragall 42, Madrid, 28020, SPA, info@unwto.org, https://www.unwto.org/; Yearbook of Tourism Statistics, 2021 Edition.

The World Bank, 1818 H St. NW, Washington, DC, 20433, USA, (202) 473-1000, (202) 477-6391, eds03@worldbank.org, https://www.worldbank.org/; Chile (report).

CHILE-TRADE

See CHILE-INTERNATIONAL TRADE

CHILE-TRANSPORTATION

Central Intelligence Agency (CIA), Office of Public Affairs, Washington, DC, 20505, USA, (703) 482-0623, https://www.cia.gov; The World Factbook.

Euromonitor International, Inc., 1 N Dearborn St., Ste. 1700, Chicago, IL, 60602, USA, (312) 922-1115, (312) 922-1157, info-usa@euromonitor.com, https://www.euromonitor.com/; Geographies.

Inter-American Development Bank (IDB), 1300 New York Ave. NW, Washington, DC, 20577, USA, (202) 623-1000, (202) 623-3096, https://www.iadb.org/en; Latin Macro Watch (LMW).

Palgrave Macmillan, 1 New York Plaza, Ste. 4500, New York, NY, 10004-1562, USA, (800) 777-4643, orders@palgrave.com, https://www.palgrave.com/us; The Statesman's Yearbook, 2023.

Routledge - Taylor & Francis Group, 6000 Broken Sound Pkwy. NW, Ste. 300, Boca Raton, FL, 33487, USA, (800) 634-1420, (800) 634-7064, orders@taylorandfrancis.com, https://www.routledge.com/; The Europa World Year Book 2022.

The World Bank, 1818 H St. NW, Washington, DC, 20433, USA, (202) 473-1000, (202) 477-6391, eds03@worldbank.org, https://www.worldbank.org/; Chile (report).

CHILE-UNEMPLOYMENT

International Labour Organization (ILO), 4 Rte. des Morillons, Geneva, CH-1211, SWI, ilo@ilo.org, https://www.ilo.org; NORMLEX Information System on International Labour Standards.

Organization for Economic Cooperation and Development (OECD), 2001 L St. NW, Ste. 650, Washington, DC, 20036-4922, USA, (202) 785-6323, (800) 456-6323, (202) 785-0350, washington.contact@oecd.org, https://www.oecd.org/; Economic Survey of Chile 2022.

Palgrave Macmillan, 1 New York Plaza, Ste. 4500, New York, NY, 10004-1562, USA, (800) 777-4643, orders@palgrave.com, https://www.palgrave.com/us; The Statesman's Yearbook, 2023.

United Nations Statistics Division (UNSD), United Nations Plz., New York, NY, 10017, USA, (800) 253-9646, (212) 963-9851, statistics@un.org, https://unstats.un.org; Statistical Yearbook of the United Nations 2021.

CHILE-VITAL STATISTICS

Palgrave Macmillan, 1 New York Plaza, Ste. 4500, New York, NY, 10004-1562, USA, (800) 777-4643, orders@palgrave.com, https://www.palgrave.com/us; The Statesman's Yearbook, 2023.

U.S. Census Bureau, 4600 Silver Hill Rd., Washington, DC, 20233, USA, (301) 763-4636, (800) 923-8282, https://www.census.gov; HIV/AIDS Surveillance Data Base.

United Nations Department of Economic and Social Affairs (DESA), Population Division, 2 United Nations Plz., Rm. DC2-1950, New York, NY, 10017, USA, (212) 963-3209, (212) 963-2147, population@un.org, https://www.un.org/development/desa/pd/; World Contraceptive Use 2021: Estimates and Projections of Family Planning Indicators and World Marriage Data 2019.

United Nations Statistics Division (UNSD), United Nations Plz., New York, NY, 10017, USA, (800) 253-9646, (212) 963-9851, statistics@un.org, https://unstats.un.org; Statistical Yearbook of the United Nations 2021.

CHILE-WAGES

International Labour Organization (ILO), 4 Rte. des Morillons, Geneva, CH-1211, SWI, ilo@ilo.org, https://www.ilo.org; NORMLEX Information System on International Labour Standards.

United Nations Statistics Division (UNSD), United Nations Plz., New York, NY, 10017, USA, (800) 253-9646, (212) 963-9851, statistics@un.org, https://unstats.un.org; Statistical Yearbook of the United Nations 2021.

The World Bank, 1818 H St. NW, Washington, DC, 20433, USA, (202) 473-1000, (202) 477-6391, eds03@worldbank.org, https://www.worldbank.org/; Chile (report).

CHILE-WHALES

See CHILE-FISHERIES

CHILE-WHEAT PRODUCTION

See CHILE-CROPS

CHILE-WHOLESALE PRICE INDEXES

Inter-American Development Bank (IDB), 1300 New York Ave. NW, Washington, DC, 20577, USA, (202) 623-1000, (202) 623-3096, https://www.iadb.org/en; Latin Macro Watch (LMW).

CHILE-WHOLESALE TRADE

Inter-American Development Bank (IDB), 1300 New York Ave. NW, Washington, DC, 20577, USA, (202) 623-1000, (202) 623-3096, https://www.iadb.org/en; Latin Macro Watch (LMW).

United Nations Statistics Division (UNSD), United Nations Plz., New York, NY, 10017, USA, (800) 253-9646, (212) 963-9851, statistics@un.org, https://unstats.un.org; Statistical Yearbook of the United Nations 2021.

CHILE-WOOD AND WOOD PULP

See CHILE-FORESTS AND FORESTRY

CHILE-WOOL PRODUCTION

See CHILE-TEXTILE INDUSTRY

CHILE-ZINC AND ZINC ORE

See CHILE-MINERAL INDUSTRIES

CHINA-NATIONAL STATISTICAL OFFICE

National Bureau of Statistics of China (NBS), No. 57, Yuetan Nanjie, Sanlihe, Xicheng District, Beijing, 100826, CHN, info@gj.stats.cn, http://www.stats.gov.cn/english/; National Data Reports (China).

CHINA-PRIMARY STATISTICS SOURCES

National Bureau of Statistics of China (NBS), No. 57, Yuetan Nanjie, Sanlihe, Xicheng District, Beijing, 100826, CHN, info@gj.stats.cn, http://www.stats.gov.cn/english/; China Statistical Yearbook, 2021.

CHINA-AGRICULTURAL MACHINERY

National Bureau of Statistics of China (NBS), No. 57, Yuetan Nanjie, Sanlihe, Xicheng District, Beijing, 100826, CHN, info@gj.stats.cn, http://www.stats.gov.cn/english/; China Statistical Yearbook, 2021.

CHINA-AGRICULTURE

Asian Development Bank (ADB), 6 ADB Ave., Mandaluyong City, 1550, PHL, information@adb.org, https://www.adb.org/; Key Indicators for Asia and the Pacific 2022.

The Economist Group: Economist Intelligence Unit (EIU), 900 3rd Ave., 16th Fl., New York, NY, 10022, USA, (212) 541-0500, americas@eiu.com, https://www.eiu.com; China Country Report.

Euromonitor International, Inc., 1 N Dearborn St., Ste. 1700, Chicago, IL, 60602, USA, (312) 922-1115, (312) 922-1157, info-usa@euromonitor.com, https://www.euromonitor.com/; Geographies.

Federal Statistical Office Germany, Gustav-Stresemann-Ring 11, Wiesbaden, D-65189, GER, https://www.destatis.de; Basic Indicators: China.

National Bureau of Statistics of China (NBS), No. 57, Yuetan Nanjie, Sanlihe, Xicheng District, Beijing, 100826, CHN, info@gj.stats.cn, http://www.stats.gov.cn/english/; China Statistical Yearbook, 2021.

Palgrave Macmillan, 1 New York Plaza, Ste. 4500, New York, NY, 10004-1562, USA, (800) 777-4643, orders@palgrave.com, https://www.palgrave.com/us; The Statesman's Yearbook, 2023.

Routledge - Taylor & Francis Group, 6000 Broken Sound Pkwy. NW, Ste. 300, Boca Raton, FL, 33487, USA, (800) 634-1420, (800) 634-7064, orders@taylorandfrancis.com, https://www.routledge.com/; The Europa World Year Book 2022.

U.S. Department of Agriculture (USDA), Economic Research Service (ERS), 1400 Independence Ave. SW, Mail Stop 1800, Washington, DC, 20250-0002, USA, (202) 720-2791, https://www.ers.usda.gov/; Countries and Regions: China.

United Nations Economic and Social Commission for Asia and the Pacific (ESCAP), United Nations Building, Rajadamnern Nok Ave., Bangkok, 10200, THA, https://www.unescap.org/; Asia-Pacific Development Journal and SDG Gateway Data Explorer.

United Nations Food and Agricultural Organization (FAO), 2121 K St., Ste. 800B, Washington, DC, 20037, USA, (202) 653-2400 (Dial from U.S.), (202) 653-5760 (Fax from U.S.), fao-hq@fao.org, https://www.fao.org; AQUASTAT and The State of Food and Agriculture (SOFA) 2022.

United Nations Statistics Division (UNSD), United Nations Plz., New York, NY, 10017, USA, (800) 253-9646, (212) 963-9851, statistics@un.org, https://unstats.un.org; Statistical Yearbook of the United Nations 2021.

The World Bank, 1818 H St. NW, Washington, DC, 20433, USA, (202) 473-1000, (202) 477-6391, eds03@worldbank.org, https://www.worldbank.org/; World Development Indicators (WDI) 2022.

CHINA-AIRLINES

Palgrave Macmillan, 1 New York Plaza, Ste. 4500, New York, NY, 10004-1562, USA, (800) 777-4643, orders@palgrave.com, https://www.palgrave.com/us; The Statesman's Yearbook, 2023.

Routledge - Taylor & Francis Group, 6000 Broken Sound Pkwy. NW, Ste. 300, Boca Raton, FL, 33487, USA, (800) 634-1420, (800) 634-7064, orders@taylorandfrancis.com, https://www.routledge.com/; The Europa World Year Book 2022.

CHINA-ALUMINUM PRODUCTION

See CHINA-MINERAL INDUSTRIES

CHINA-ARMED FORCES

Central Intelligence Agency (CIA), Office of Public Affairs, Washington, DC, 20505, USA, (703) 482-0623, https://www.cia.gov; The World Factbook.

Human Rights Watch, 350 5th Ave., 34th Fl., New York, NY, 10118-3299, USA, (212) 290-4700, (212) 736-1300, https://www.hrw.org; Break Their Lineage, Break Their Roots: China's Crimes against Humanity Targeting Uyghurs and Other Turkic Muslims.

International Institute for Strategic Studies (IISS) - Americas, 2121 K St. NW, Ste. 600, Washington, DC, 20037, USA, (202) 659-1490, (202) 659-1499, https://www.iiss.org/; Armed Conflict Survey 2021 and The Military Balance 2022.

Palgrave Macmillan, 1 New York Plaza, Ste. 4500, New York, NY, 10004-1562, USA, (800) 777-4643, orders@palgrave.com, https://www.palgrave.com/us; The Statesman's Yearbook, 2023.

Stockholm International Peace Research Institute (SIPRI), Signalistgatan 9, Stockholm, SE 169 72, SWE, https://www.sipri.org/; SIPRI Arms Transfers Database and SIPRI Military Expenditure Database.

U.S. Department of Defense (DOD), 1400 Defense Pentagon, Washington, DC, 20301-1400, USA, (703) 571-3343, https://www.defense.gov; Military and Security Developments Involving the People's Republic of China 2021: Annual Report to Congress.

CHINA-AUTOMOBILE INDUSTRY AND TRADE

Bain & Company, 131 Dartmouth St., Boston, MA, 02116, USA, (617) 572-2000, (617) 572-2427, https://www.bain.com/; The Coronavirus Demand Challenge Awaiting China's Auto Industry.

International Council on Clean Transportation (ICCT), 1500 K St. NW, Ste. 650, Washington, DC, 20005, USA, (202) 798-3986, https://theicct.org; Real-World Performance of Battery Electric Passenger Cars in China: Energy Consumption, Range, and Charging Patterns.

National Bureau of Statistics of China (NBS), No. 57, Yuetan Nanjie, Sanlihe, Xicheng District, Beijing, 100826, CHN, info@gj.stats.cn, http://www.stats.gov.cn/english/; China Statistical Yearbook, 2021.

CHINA-BALANCE OF PAYMENTS

International Monetary Fund (IMF), 700 19th St. NW, Washington, DC, 20431, USA, (202) 623-7000, (202) 623-4661, publications@imf.org, https://www.imf.org; Balance of Payments Statistics: Annual Report 2021.

National Bureau of Statistics of China (NBS), No. 57, Yuetan Nanjie, Sanlihe, Xicheng District, Beijing, 100826, CHN, info@gj.stats.cn, http://www.stats.gov.cn/english/; China Statistical Yearbook, 2021.

Routledge - Taylor & Francis Group, 6000 Broken Sound Pkwy. NW, Ste. 300, Boca Raton, FL, 33487, USA, (800) 634-1420, (800) 634-7064, orders@taylorandfrancis.com, https://www.routledge.com/; The Europa World Year Book 2022.

United Nations Conference on Trade and Development (UNCTAD), Palais des Nations, Geneva, 1211, SWI, (212) 963-6896, unctadinfo@unctad.org, https://unctad.org; Handbook of Statistics 2021.

The World Bank, 1818 H St. NW, Washington, DC, 20433, USA, (202) 473-1000, (202) 477-6391, eds03@worldbank.org, https://www.worldbank.org/; World Development Indicators (WDI) 2022 and World Development Report 2022: Finance for an Equitable Recovery.

CHINA-BANKS AND BANKING

Asian Development Bank (ADB), 6 ADB Ave., Mandaluyong City, 1550, PHL, information@adb.org, https://www.adb.org/; Key Indicators for Asia and the Pacific 2022.

Euromonitor International, Inc., 1 N Dearborn St., Ste. 1700, Chicago, IL, 60602, USA, (312) 922-1115, (312) 922-1157, info-usa@euromonitor.com, https://www.euromonitor.com/; Geographies.

National Bureau of Statistics of China (NBS), No. 57, Yuetan Nanjie, Sanlihe, Xicheng District, Beijing, 100826, CHN, info@gj.stats.cn, http://www.stats.gov.cn/english/; China Statistical Yearbook, 2021.

People's Bank of China, 32 Chengfang St., Beijing, 100800, CHN, webbox@pbc.gov.cn, http://www.pbc.gov.cn/en/3688006/index.html; unpublished data.

Routledge - Taylor & Francis Group, 6000 Broken Sound Pkwy. NW, Ste. 300, Boca Raton, FL, 33487, USA, (800) 634-1420, (800) 634-7064, orders@taylorandfrancis.com, https://www.routledge.com/; The Europa World Year Book 2022.

CHINA-BARLEY PRODUCTION

See CHINA-CROPS

CHINA-BEVERAGE INDUSTRY

National Bureau of Statistics of China (NBS), No. 57, Yuetan Nanjie, Sanlihe, Xicheng District, Beijing, 100826, CHN, info@gj.stats.cn, http://www.stats.gov.cn/english/; China Statistical Yearbook, 2021.

CHINA-BROADCASTING

Central Intelligence Agency (CIA), Office of Public Affairs, Washington, DC, 20505, USA, (703) 482-0623, https://www.cia.gov; The World Factbook.

Euromonitor International, Inc., 1 N Dearborn St., Ste. 1700, Chicago, IL, 60602, USA, (312) 922-1115, (312) 922-1157, info-usa@euromonitor.com, https://www.euromonitor.com/; Geographies.

Palgrave Macmillan, 1 New York Plaza, Ste. 4500, New York, NY, 10004-1562, USA, (800) 777-4643, orders@palgrave.com, https://www.palgrave.com/us; The Statesman's Yearbook, 2023.

WRTH Publications Limited, PO Box 290, Oxford, OX2 7FT, GBR, sales@wrth.com, https://www.wrth.com; World Radio TV Handbook 2023.

CHINA-BUDGET

Central Intelligence Agency (CIA), Office of Public Affairs, Washington, DC, 20505, USA, (703) 482-0623, https://www.cia.gov; The World Factbook.

CHINA-BUSINESS

Bain & Company, 131 Dartmouth St., Boston, MA, 02116, USA, (617) 572-2000, (617) 572-2427, https://www.bain.com/; China Internet Report: How to Embrace the Unique Platform Business Model in China.

Global Entrepreneurship Monitor (GEM), Babson College, 231 Forest St., Babson Park, MA, 02457, USA, (781) 235-1200, info@gemconsortium.org, https://www.gemconsortium.org/; GEM 2022-2023 Global Report.

Japan Center for Economic Research (JCER), Nikkei Inc. Bldg. 11F, 1-3-7 Otemachi, Chiyoda-ku, Tokyo, 100-8066, JPN, https://www.jcer.or.jp/en; East Asia Risk and Japan-China Relations.

Kantar Worldpanel, 6 More London Place, London, SE1 2QY, GBR, https://www.kantarworldpanel.com; Grocery Market Share.

National Bureau of Statistics of China (NBS), No. 57, Yuetan Nanjie, Sanlihe, Xicheng District, Beijing, 100826, CHN, info@gj.stats.cn, http://www.stats.gov.cn/english/; China Statistical Yearbook, 2021.

United Nations Economic and Social Commission for Asia and the Pacific (ESCAP), United Nations Building, Rajadamnern Nok Ave., Bangkok, 10200, THA, https://www.unescap.org/; SDG Gateway Data Explorer.

CHINA-CAPITAL INVESTMENTS

National Bureau of Statistics of China (NBS), No. 57, Yuetan Nanjie, Sanlihe, Xicheng District, Beijing, 100826, CHN, info@gj.stats.cn, http://www.stats.gov.cn/english/; China Statistical Yearbook, 2021.

CHINA-CHESTNUT PRODUCTION

See CHINA-CROPS

CHINA-CHILDBIRTH-STATISTICS

National Bureau of Statistics of China (NBS), No. 57, Yuetan Nanjie, Sanlihe, Xicheng District, Beijing, 100826, CHN, info@gj.stats.cn, http://www.stats.gov.cn/english/; China Statistical Yearbook, 2021.

United Nations Economic and Social Commission for Asia and the Pacific (ESCAP), United Nations Building, Rajadamnern Nok Ave., Bangkok, 10200, THA, https://www.unescap.org/; Asia-Pacific Development Journal.

The World Bank, 1818 H St. NW, Washington, DC, 20433, USA, (202) 473-1000, (202) 477-6391, eds03@worldbank.org, https://www.worldbank.org/; World Development Indicators (WDI) 2022.

CHINA-CLIMATE

International Institute for Environment and Development (IIED), 235 High Holborn, London, WC1V 7DN, GBR, inforequest@iied.org, https://www.iied.org; Environment & Urbanization.

Palgrave Macmillan, 1 New York Plaza, Ste. 4500, New York, NY, 10004-1562, USA, (800) 777-4643, orders@palgrave.com, https://www.palgrave.com/us; The Statesman's Yearbook, 2023.

CHINA-COAL PRODUCTION

See CHINA-MINERAL INDUSTRIES

CHINA-COFFEE

See CHINA-CROPS

CHINA-COMMERCE

Palgrave Macmillan, 1 New York Plaza, Ste. 4500, New York, NY, 10004-1562, USA, (800) 777-4643, orders@palgrave.com, https://www.palgrave.com/us; The Statesman's Yearbook, 2023.

UK Data Service, University of Essex, Wivenhoe Park, Colchester, Essex, CO4 3SQ, GBR, https://ukdataservice.ac.uk/; International Aggregate Data.

CHINA-COMMODITY EXCHANGES

Barchart, 209 W Jackson Blvd., 2nd Fl., Chicago, IL, 60606, USA, (877) 247-4394, commodities@barchart.com, https://www.barchart.com/cmdty; The cmdty Yearbook 2023; cmdtyStats: Commodity Statistics and Fundamental Data; cmdtyView: Commodity Index; and Commodity Data and Prices.

International Monetary Fund (IMF), 700 19th St. NW, Washington, DC, 20431, USA, (202) 623-7000, (202) 623-4661, publications@imf.org, https://www.imf.org; IMF Primary Commodity Prices.

National Bureau of Statistics of China (NBS), No. 57, Yuetan Nanjie, Sanlihe, Xicheng District, Beijing, 100826, CHN, info@gj.stats.cn, http://www.stats.gov.cn/english/; China Statistical Yearbook, 2021.

CHINA-CONSTRUCTION INDUSTRY

National Bureau of Statistics of China (NBS), No. 57, Yuetan Nanjie, Sanlihe, Xicheng District, Beijing, 100826, CHN, info@gj.stats.cn, http://www.stats.gov.cn/english/; China Statistical Yearbook, 2021.

Palgrave Macmillan, 1 New York Plaza, Ste. 4500, New York, NY, 10004-1562, USA, (800) 777-4643, orders@palgrave.com, https://www.palgrave.com/us; The Statesman's Yearbook, 2023.

CHINA-CONSUMER GOODS

International Council on Clean Transportation (ICCT), 1500 K St. NW, Ste. 650, Washington, DC, 20005, USA, (202) 798-3986, https://theicct.org; Real-World Performance of Battery Electric Passenger Cars in China: Energy Consumption, Range, and Charging Patterns.

Kantar, 3 World Trade Center, 35th Fl., New York, NY, 10007, USA, (866) 471-1399, https://www.kantar.com/; 2022 China Shoppers Report.

CHINA-CONSUMER PRICE INDEXES

Asian Development Bank (ADB), 6 ADB Ave., Mandaluyong City, 1550, PHL, information@adb.org, https://www.adb.org/; Key Indicators for Asia and the Pacific 2022.

Routledge - Taylor & Francis Group, 6000 Broken Sound Pkwy. NW, Ste. 300, Boca Raton, FL, 33487, USA, (800) 634-1420, (800) 634-7064, orders@taylorandfrancis.com, https://www.routledge.com/; The Europa World Year Book 2022.

CHINA-COPPER INDUSTRY AND TRADE

See CHINA-MINERAL INDUSTRIES

CHINA-CORN INDUSTRY

See CHINA-CROPS

CHINA-COTTON

See CHINA-CROPS

CHINA-CRIME

National Bureau of Statistics of China (NBS), No. 57, Yuetan Nanjie, Sanlihe, Xicheng District, Beijing, 100826, CHN, info@gj.stats.cn, http://www.stats.gov.cn/english/; China Statistical Yearbook, 2021.

CHINA-CROPS

National Bureau of Statistics of China (NBS), No. 57, Yuetan Nanjie, Sanlihe, Xicheng District, Beijing, 100826, CHN, info@gj.stats.cn, http://www.stats.gov.cn/english/; China Statistical Yearbook, 2021.

Palgrave Macmillan, 1 New York Plaza, Ste. 4500, New York, NY, 10004-1562, USA, (800) 777-4643, orders@palgrave.com, https://www.palgrave.com/us; The Statesman's Yearbook, 2023.

United Nations Food and Agricultural Organization (FAO), 2121 K St., Ste. 800B, Washington, DC, 20037, USA, (202) 653-2400 (Dial from U.S.), (202) 653-5760 (Fax from U.S.), fao-hq@fao.org, https://www.fao.org; The State of Food and Agriculture (SOFA) 2022.

United Nations Statistics Division (UNSD), United Nations Plz., New York, NY, 10017, USA, (800) 253-9646, (212) 963-9851, statistics@un.org, https://unstats.un.org; Statistical Yearbook of the United Nations 2021.

CHINA-DAIRY PROCESSING

National Bureau of Statistics of China (NBS), No. 57, Yuetan Nanjie, Sanlihe, Xicheng District, Beijing, 100826, CHN, info@gj.stats.cn, http://www.stats.gov.cn/english/; China Statistical Yearbook, 2021.

Palgrave Macmillan, 1 New York Plaza, Ste. 4500, New York, NY, 10004-1562, USA, (800) 777-4643, orders@palgrave.com, https://www.palgrave.com/us; The Statesman's Yearbook, 2023.

United Nations Food and Agricultural Organization (FAO), 2121 K St., Ste. 800B, Washington, DC, 20037, USA, (202) 653-2400 (Dial from U.S.), (202) 653-5760 (Fax from U.S.), fao-hq@fao.org, https://www.fao.org; The State of Food and Agriculture (SOFA) 2022.

CHINA-DEBTS, EXTERNAL

Asian Development Bank (ADB), 6 ADB Ave., Mandaluyong City, 1550, PHL, information@adb.org, https://www.adb.org/; Key Indicators for Asia and the Pacific 2022.

Palgrave Macmillan, 1 New York Plaza, Ste. 4500, New York, NY, 10004-1562, USA, (800) 777-4643, orders@palgrave.com, https://www.palgrave.com/us; The Statesman's Yearbook, 2023.

The World Bank, 1818 H St. NW, Washington, DC, 20433, USA, (202) 473-1000, (202) 477-6391, eds03@worldbank.org, https://www.worldbank.org/; Global Financial Development Report 2019-2020: Bank Regulation and Supervision a Decade after the Global Financial Crisis; World Development Indicators (WDI) 2022; and World Development Report 2022: Finance for an Equitable Recovery.

CHINA-DEFENSE EXPENDITURES

See CHINA-ARMED FORCES

CHINA-DIAMONDS

See CHINA-MINERAL INDUSTRIES

CHINA-DIVORCE

National Bureau of Statistics of China (NBS), No. 57, Yuetan Nanjie, Sanlihe, Xicheng District, Beijing, 100826, CHN, info@gj.stats.cn, http://www.stats.gov.cn/english/; China Statistical Yearbook, 2021.

CHINA-ECONOMIC ASSISTANCE

AidData, William & Mary Global Research Institute, 427 Scotland St., Williamsburg, VA, 23185, USA, (757) 221-1468, info@aiddata.org, https://www.aiddata.org/; Ties That Bind: Quantifying China's Public Diplomacy and Its 'Good Neighbor' Effect.

National Bureau of Statistics of China (NBS), No. 57, Yuetan Nanjie, Sanlihe, Xicheng District, Beijing, 100826, CHN, info@gj.stats.cn, http://www.stats.gov.cn/english/; China Statistical Yearbook, 2021.

United Nations Statistics Division (UNSD), United Nations Plz., New York, NY, 10017, USA, (800) 253-9646, (212) 963-9851, statistics@un.org, https://unstats.un.org; Statistical Yearbook of the United Nations 2021.

CHINA-ECONOMIC CONDITIONS

AidData, William & Mary Global Research Institute, 427 Scotland St., Williamsburg, VA, 23185, USA, (757) 221-1468, info@aiddata.org, https://www.aiddata.org/; Ties That Bind: Quantifying China's Public Diplomacy and Its 'Good Neighbor' Effect.

Asian Development Bank (ADB), 6 ADB Ave., Mandaluyong City, 1550, PHL, information@adb.org, https://www.adb.org/; Key Indicators for Asia and the Pacific 2022.

Bain & Company, 131 Dartmouth St., Boston, MA, 02116, USA, (617) 572-2000, (617) 572-2427, https://www.bain.com/; China Internet Report: How to Embrace the Unique Platform Business Model in China; China's Unstoppable 2020 Luxury Market; and The Coronavirus Demand Challenge Awaiting China's Auto Industry.

Bernan Press, 15250 NBN Way, Bldg. C, Blue Ridge Summit, PA, 17214, USA, (301) 459-2255, (800) 865-3457, (800) 865-3450, customercare@bernan.com, https://rowman.com/Page/Bernan; World Economic Outlook, April 2022.

Central Intelligence Agency (CIA), Office of Public Affairs, Washington, DC, 20505, USA, (703) 482-0623, https://www.cia.gov; The World Factbook.

Climate Analytics, 135 Madison Ave., 5th Fl., Ste. 05-115, New York, NY, 10016, USA, info.ny@climateanalytics.org, https://climateanalytics.org/; Exploring New Electric Vehicle Roadmaps for China in a Post-COVID-19 Era.

The Economist Group: Economist Intelligence Unit (EIU), 900 3rd Ave., 16th Fl., New York, NY, 10022, USA, (212) 541-0500, americas@eiu.com, https://www.eiu.com; China Country Report and China's Emerging Cities 2021: Southeast China Takes the Lead.

Euromonitor International, Inc., 1 N Dearborn St., Ste. 1700, Chicago, IL, 60602, USA, (312) 922-1115, (312) 922-1157, info-usa@euromonitor.com, https://www.euromonitor.com/; Geographies and Market Research on the Consumer Finance Industry.

Federal Statistical Office Germany, Gustav-Stresemann-Ring 11, Wiesbaden, D-65189, GER, https://www.destatis.de; Basic Indicators: China.

Global Entrepreneurship Monitor (GEM), Babson College, 231 Forest St., Babson Park, MA, 02457, USA, (781) 235-1200, info@gemconsortium.org, https://www.gemconsortium.org/; GEM 2022-2023 Global Report.

Government of the Hong Kong Special Administrative Region of the People's Republic of China: Census and Statistics Department, Wanchai Tower, 12 Harbour Road, Wan Chai, Hong Kong, CHN, gen-enquiry@censtatd.gov.hk, https://www.censtatd.gov.hk; Annual Report on the Consumer Price Index and Quarterly Report of Wage and Payroll Statistics.

International Monetary Fund (IMF), 700 19th St. NW, Washington, DC, 20431, USA, (202) 623-7000, (202) 623-4661, publications@imf.org, https://www.imf.org; IMF Data and World Economic Outlook.

Japan Center for Economic Research (JCER), Nikkei Inc. Bldg. 11F, 1-3-7 Otemachi, Chiyoda-ku, Tokyo, 100-8066, JPN, https://www.jcer.or.jp/en; East Asia Risk and Japan-China Relations.

Kantar, 3 World Trade Center, 35th Fl., New York, NY, 10007, USA, (866) 471-1399, https://www.kantar.com/; 2022 China Shoppers Report.

National Bureau of Statistics of China (NBS), No. 57, Yuetan Nanjie, Sanlihe, Xicheng District, Beijing, 100826, CHN, info@gj.stats.cn, http://www.stats.gov.cn/english/; China Statistical Yearbook, 2021.

Nikkei Inc., 1-3-7 Ohtemachi Chiyoda-ku, Tokyo, 100-8066, JPN, https://www.nikkei.co.jp/nikkeiinfo/en/; Nikkei Asia.

Palgrave Macmillan, 1 New York Plaza, Ste. 4500, New York, NY, 10004-1562, USA, (800) 777-4643, orders@palgrave.com, https://www.palgrave.com/us; The Statesman's Yearbook, 2023.

Routledge - Taylor & Francis Group, 6000 Broken Sound Pkwy. NW, Ste. 300, Boca Raton, FL, 33487, USA, (800) 634-1420, (800) 634-7064, orders@taylorandfrancis.com, https://www.routledge.com/; The Europa World Year Book 2022.

United Nations Statistics Division (UNSD), United Nations Plz., New York, NY, 10017, USA, (800) 253-9646, (212) 963-9851, statistics@un.org, https://unstats.un.org; World Statistics Pocketbook 2021.

The World Bank, 1818 H St. NW, Washington, DC, 20433, USA, (202) 473-1000, (202) 477-6391, eds03@worldbank.org, https://www.worldbank.org/; Global Economic Monitor (GEM); Global Economic Prospects, June 2022; The Global Findex Database 2021; and World Development Report 2022: Finance for an Equitable Recovery.

CHINA-EDUCATION

Euromonitor International, Inc., 1 N Dearborn St., Ste. 1700, Chicago, IL, 60602, USA, (312) 922-1115, (312) 922-1157, info-usa@euromonitor.com, https://www.euromonitor.com/; Geographies.

Infoplease, c/o Sandbox Networks, Inc., 1 Lincoln St., 24th Fl., Boston, MA, 02111, USA, https://www.infoplease.com; Countries of the World.

National Bureau of Statistics of China (NBS), No. 57, Yuetan Nanjie, Sanlihe, Xicheng District, Beijing, 100826, CHN, info@gj.stats.cn, http://www.stats.gov.cn/english/; China Statistical Yearbook, 2021.

Palgrave Macmillan, 1 New York Plaza, Ste. 4500, New York, NY, 10004-1562, USA, (800) 777-4643, orders@palgrave.com, https://www.palgrave.com/us; The Statesman's Yearbook, 2023.

Routledge - Taylor & Francis Group, 6000 Broken Sound Pkwy. NW, Ste. 300, Boca Raton, FL, 33487, USA, (800) 634-1420, (800) 634-7064, orders@taylorandfrancis.com, https://www.routledge.com/; The Europa World Year Book 2022.

UNESCO Institute for Statistics, C.P 250 Succursale H, Montreal, QC, H3G 2K8, CAN, (514) 343-6880 (Dial from U.S.), (514) 343-5740 (Fax from U.S.), uis.publications@unesco.org, http://uis.unesco.org/; Literacy and UIS.Stat.

United Nations Economic and Social Commission for Asia and the Pacific (ESCAP), United Nations Building, Rajadamnern Nok Ave., Bangkok, 10200, THA, https://www.unescap.org/; Asia-Pacific Development Journal and SDG Gateway Data Explorer.

United Nations Statistics Division (UNSD), United Nations Plz., New York, NY, 10017, USA, (800) 253-9646, (212) 963-9851, statistics@un.org, https://unstats.un.org; Millennium Development Goal Indicators.

The World Bank, 1818 H St. NW, Washington, DC, 20433, USA, (202) 473-1000, (202) 477-6391, eds03@worldbank.org, https://www.worldbank.org/; World Development Indicators (WDI) 2022 and World Development Report 2022: Finance for an Equitable Recovery.

CHINA-ELECTRICITY

International Energy Agency (IEA), 9 Rue de la Federation, Paris, 75739, FRA, info@iea.org, https://www.iea.org/; World Energy Outlook 2021.

National Bureau of Statistics of China (NBS), No. 57, Yuetan Nanjie, Sanlihe, Xicheng District, Beijing, 100826, CHN, info@gj.stats.cn, http://www.stats.gov.cn/english/; China Statistical Yearbook, 2021.

S&P Global Commodity Insights, One World Trade Center, New York, NY, 10007, USA, (800) 752-8878, support@platts.com, https://www.spglobal.com/commodityinsights/en; Platts Asia Pacific / Arab Gulf Marketscan (APAG Marketscan).

U.S. Energy Information Administration (EIA), 1000 Independence Ave. SW, Washington, DC, 20585, USA, (202) 586-8800, infoctr@eia.gov, https://www.eia.gov; International Energy Outlook 2021.

United Nations Statistics Division (UNSD), United Nations Plz., New York, NY, 10017, USA, (800) 253-9646, (212) 963-9851, statistics@un.org, https://unstats.un.org; Statistical Yearbook of the United Nations 2021.

The World Bank, 1818 H St. NW, Washington, DC, 20433, USA, (202) 473-1000, (202) 477-6391, eds03@worldbank.org, https://www.worldbank.org/; World Development Indicators (WDI) 2022.

CHINA-EMPLOYMENT

Brown University, Population Studies and Training Center (PSTC), 68 Waterman St., PO Box 1836, Providence, RI, 02912, USA, (401) 863-2668, (401) 863-3351, population_studies@brown.edu, https://www.brown.edu/academics/population-studies/; Women's Political Leadership and Adult Health: Evidence from Rural and Urban China.

National Bureau of Statistics of China (NBS), No. 57, Yuetan Nanjie, Sanlihe, Xicheng District, Beijing, 100826, CHN, info@gj.stats.cn, http://www.stats.gov.cn/english/; China Statistical Yearbook, 2021.

UK Data Service, University of Essex, Wivenhoe Park, Colchester, Essex, CO4 3SQ, GBR, https://ukdataservice.ac.uk/; International Aggregate Data.

United Nations Economic and Social Commission for Asia and the Pacific (ESCAP), United Nations Building, Rajadamnern Nok Ave., Bangkok, 10200, THA, https://www.unescap.org/; Asia-Pacific Development Journal.

The World Bank, 1818 H St. NW, Washington, DC, 20433, USA, (202) 473-1000, (202) 477-6391, eds03@worldbank.org, https://www.worldbank.org/; World Development Indicators (WDI) 2022.

CHINA-ENERGY INDUSTRIES

Enerdata, 47 avenue Alsace Lorraine, Grenoble, 38027, FRA, (332) 216-4534, research@enerdata.net, https://www.enerdata.net; World Refinery Database.

National Bureau of Statistics of China (NBS), No. 57, Yuetan Nanjie, Sanlihe, Xicheng District, Beijing, 100826, CHN, info@gj.stats.cn, http://www.stats.gov.cn/english/; China Statistical Yearbook, 2021.

S&P Global Commodity Insights, One World Trade Center, New York, NY, 10007, USA, (800) 752-8878, support@platts.com, https://www.spglobal.com/commodityinsights/en; Platts Asia Pacific / Arab Gulf Marketscan (APAG Marketscan).

CHINA-ENVIRONMENTAL CONDITIONS

DSI Data Service & Information, Xantener Strasse 51a, Rheinberg, D-47495, GER, dsi@dsidata.com, https://www.dsidata.com/; Global Environmental Database.

The Economist Group: Economist Intelligence Unit (EIU), 900 3rd Ave., 16th Fl., New York, NY, 10022, USA, (212) 541-0500, americas@eiu.com, https://www.eiu.com; China Country Report.

Federal Statistical Office Germany, Gustav-Stresemann-Ring 11, Wiesbaden, D-65189, GER, https://www.destatis.de; Basic Indicators: China.

International Institute for Environment and Development (IIED), 235 High Holborn, London, WC1V

7DN, GBR, inforequest@iied.org, https://www.iied.org; Environment & Urbanization.

United Nations Statistics Division (UNSD), United Nations Plz., New York, NY, 10017, USA, (800) 253-9646, (212) 963-9851, statistics@un.org, https://unstats.un.org; World Statistics Pocketbook 2021.

CHINA-EXPORTS

Asian Development Bank (ADB), 6 ADB Ave., Mandaluyong City, 1550, PHL, information@adb.org, https://www.adb.org/; Key Indicators for Asia and the Pacific 2022.

BC Stats, Stn Prov Govt, PO Box 9410, Victoria, BC, V8W 9V1, CAN, (250) 387-6121 (Dial from U.S.), bc.stats@gov.bc.ca, https://www2.gov.bc.ca/gov/content/data/about-data-management/bc-stats; Country Trade Profile - China (Mainland).

Central Intelligence Agency (CIA), Office of Public Affairs, Washington, DC, 20505, USA, (703) 482-0623, https://www.cia.gov; The World Factbook.

The Economist Group: Economist Intelligence Unit (EIU), 900 3rd Ave., 16th Fl., New York, NY, 10022, USA, (212) 541-0500, americas@eiu.com, https://www.eiu.com; China Country Report.

Federal Statistical Office Germany, Gustav-Stresemann-Ring 11, Wiesbaden, D-65189, GER, https://www.destatis.de; Basic Indicators: China.

International Monetary Fund (IMF), 700 19th St. NW, Washington, DC, 20431, USA, (202) 623-7000, (202) 623-4661, publications@imf.org, https://www.imf.org; Direction of Trade Statistics (DOTS) and International Financial Statistics (IFS).

National Bureau of Statistics of China (NBS), No. 57, Yuetan Nanjie, Sanlihe, Xicheng District, Beijing, 100826, CHN, info@gj.stats.cn, http://www.stats.gov.cn/english/; China Statistical Yearbook, 2021.

S&P Global, IHS Markit, 15 Inverness Way E, Englewood, CO, 80112, USA, (800) 447-2273, (800) 854-7179, https://ihsmarkit.com; Global Trade Atlas (GTA).

United Nations Conference on Trade and Development (UNCTAD), Palais des Nations, Geneva, 1211, SWI, (212) 963-6896, unctadinfo@unctad.org, https://unctad.org; Handbook of Statistics 2021.

The World Bank, 1818 H St. NW, Washington, DC, 20433, USA, (202) 473-1000, (202) 477-6391, eds03@worldbank.org, https://www.worldbank.org/; World Development Report 2022: Finance for an Equitable Recovery.

CHINA-FEMALE WORKING POPULATION

See CHINA-EMPLOYMENT

CHINA-FERTILITY, HUMAN

Central Intelligence Agency (CIA), Office of Public Affairs, Washington, DC, 20505, USA, (703) 482-0623, https://www.cia.gov; The World Factbook.

CHINA-FERTILIZER INDUSTRY

National Bureau of Statistics of China (NBS), No. 57, Yuetan Nanjie, Sanlihe, Xicheng District, Beijing, 100826, CHN, info@gj.stats.cn, http://www.stats.gov.cn/english/; China Statistical Yearbook, 2021.

United Nations Food and Agricultural Organization (FAO), 2121 K St., Ste. 800B, Washington, DC, 20037, USA, (202) 653-2400 (Dial from U.S.), (202) 653-5760 (Fax from U.S.), fao-hq@fao.org, https://www.fao.org; The State of Food and Agriculture (SOFA) 2022.

CHINA-FETAL DEATH

National Bureau of Statistics of China (NBS), No. 57, Yuetan Nanjie, Sanlihe, Xicheng District, Beijing, 100826, CHN, info@gj.stats.cn, http://www.stats.gov.cn/english/; China Statistical Yearbook, 2021.

CHINA-FINANCE

International Monetary Fund (IMF), 700 19th St. NW, Washington, DC, 20431, USA, (202) 623-7000, (202) 623-4661, publications@imf.org, https://www.imf.org; International Financial Statistics (IFS).

National Bureau of Statistics of China (NBS), No. 57, Yuetan Nanjie, Sanlihe, Xicheng District, Beijing, 100826, CHN, info@gj.stats.cn, http://www.stats.gov.cn/english/; China Statistical Yearbook, 2021.

People's Bank of China, 32 Chengfang St., Beijing, 100800, CHN, webbox@pbc.gov.cn, http://www.pbc.gov.cn/en/3688006/index.html; unpublished data.

Stockholm International Peace Research Institute (SIPRI), Signalistgatan 9, Stockholm, SE 169 72, SWE, https://www.sipri.org/; SIPRI Arms Transfers Database and SIPRI Military Expenditure Database.

United Nations Economic and Social Commission for Asia and the Pacific (ESCAP), United Nations Building, Rajadamnern Nok Ave., Bangkok, 10200, THA, https://www.unescap.org/; Asia-Pacific Development Journal and SDG Gateway Data Explorer.

CHINA-FINANCE, PUBLIC

Asian Development Bank (ADB), 6 ADB Ave., Mandaluyong City, 1550, PHL, information@adb.org, https://www.adb.org/; Key Indicators for Asia and the Pacific 2022.

Bernan Press, 15250 NBN Way, Bldg. C, Blue Ridge Summit, PA, 17214, USA, (301) 459-2255, (800) 865-3457, (800) 865-3450, customercare@bernan.com, https://rowman.com/Page/Bernan; National Accounts Statistics: Analysis of Main Aggregates 2020.

The Economist Group: Economist Intelligence Unit (EIU), 900 3rd Ave., 16th Fl., New York, NY, 10022, USA, (212) 541-0500, americas@eiu.com, https://www.eiu.com; China Country Report.

Federal Statistical Office Germany, Gustav-Stresemann-Ring 11, Wiesbaden, D-65189, GER, https://www.destatis.de; Basic Indicators: China.

International Monetary Fund (IMF), 700 19th St. NW, Washington, DC, 20431, USA, (202) 623-7000, (202) 623-4661, publications@imf.org, https://www.imf.org; International Financial Statistics (IFS) and Regional Economic Outlook.

National Bureau of Statistics of China (NBS), No. 57, Yuetan Nanjie, Sanlihe, Xicheng District, Beijing, 100826, CHN, info@gj.stats.cn, http://www.stats.gov.cn/english/; China Statistical Yearbook, 2021.

Palgrave Macmillan, 1 New York Plaza, Ste. 4500, New York, NY, 10004-1562, USA, (800) 777-4643, orders@palgrave.com, https://www.palgrave.com/us; The Statesman's Yearbook, 2023.

Routledge - Taylor & Francis Group, 6000 Broken Sound Pkwy. NW, Ste. 300, Boca Raton, FL, 33487, USA, (800) 634-1420, (800) 634-7064, orders@taylorandfrancis.com, https://www.routledge.com/; The Europa World Year Book 2022.

United Nations Economic and Social Commission for Asia and the Pacific (ESCAP), United Nations Building, Rajadamnern Nok Ave., Bangkok, 10200, THA, https://www.unescap.org/; SDG Gateway Data Explorer.

United Nations Statistics Division (UNSD), United Nations Plz., New York, NY, 10017, USA, (800) 253-9646, (212) 963-9851, statistics@un.org, https://unstats.un.org; National Accounts Main Aggregates Database and National Accounts Statistics: Main Aggregates and Detailed Tables.

CHINA-FISHERIES

National Bureau of Statistics of China (NBS), No. 57, Yuetan Nanjie, Sanlihe, Xicheng District, Beijing, 100826, CHN, info@gj.stats.cn, http://www.stats.gov.cn/english/; China Statistical Yearbook, 2021.

Palgrave Macmillan, 1 New York Plaza, Ste. 4500, New York, NY, 10004-1562, USA, (800) 777-4643, orders@palgrave.com, https://www.palgrave.com/us; The Statesman's Yearbook, 2023.

Routledge - Taylor & Francis Group, 6000 Broken Sound Pkwy. NW, Ste. 300, Boca Raton, FL, 33487, USA, (800) 634-1420, (800) 634-7064, orders@taylorandfrancis.com, https://www.routledge.com/; The Europa World Year Book 2022.

United Nations Food and Agricultural Organization (FAO), 2121 K St., Ste. 800B, Washington, DC, 20037, USA, (202) 653-2400 (Dial from U.S.), (202) 653-5760 (Fax from U.S.), fao-hq@fao.org, https://www.fao.org; FAO Yearbook of Fishery and Aquaculture Statistics 2019; Fishery Statistical Collections Global Capture Production; FishStatJ; and The State of Food and Agriculture (SOFA) 2022.

United Nations Statistics Division (UNSD), United Nations Plz., New York, NY, 10017, USA, (800) 253-9646, (212) 963-9851, statistics@un.org, https://unstats.un.org; Statistical Yearbook of the United Nations 2021.

CHINA-FOOD

Euromonitor International, Inc., 1 N Dearborn St., Ste. 1700, Chicago, IL, 60602, USA, (312) 922-1115, (312) 922-1157, info-usa@euromonitor.com, https://www.euromonitor.com/; Market Research on the Retailing Industry.

National Bureau of Statistics of China (NBS), No. 57, Yuetan Nanjie, Sanlihe, Xicheng District, Beijing, 100826, CHN, info@gj.stats.cn, http://www.stats.gov.cn/english/; China Statistical Yearbook, 2021.

United Nations Economic and Social Commission for Asia and the Pacific (ESCAP), United Nations Building, Rajadamnern Nok Ave., Bangkok, 10200, THA, https://www.unescap.org/; SDG Gateway Data Explorer.

United Nations Food and Agricultural Organization (FAO), 2121 K St., Ste. 800B, Washington, DC, 20037, USA, (202) 653-2400 (Dial from U.S.), (202) 653-5760 (Fax from U.S.), fao-hq@fao.org, https://www.fao.org; The State of Food and Agriculture (SOFA) 2022.

CHINA-FOREIGN EXCHANGE RATES

Asian Development Bank (ADB), 6 ADB Ave., Mandaluyong City, 1550, PHL, information@adb.org, https://www.adb.org/; Key Indicators for Asia and the Pacific 2022.

International Monetary Fund (IMF), 700 19th St. NW, Washington, DC, 20431, USA, (202) 623-7000, (202) 623-4661, publications@imf.org, https://www.imf.org; International Financial Statistics (IFS).

National Bureau of Statistics of China (NBS), No. 57, Yuetan Nanjie, Sanlihe, Xicheng District, Beijing, 100826, CHN, info@gj.stats.cn, http://www.stats.gov.cn/english/; China Statistical Yearbook, 2021.

CHINA-FORESTS AND FORESTRY

National Bureau of Statistics of China (NBS), No. 57, Yuetan Nanjie, Sanlihe, Xicheng District, Beijing, 100826, CHN, info@gj.stats.cn, http://www.stats.gov.cn/english/; China Statistical Yearbook, 2021.

Palgrave Macmillan, 1 New York Plaza, Ste. 4500, New York, NY, 10004-1562, USA, (800) 777-4643, orders@palgrave.com, https://www.palgrave.com/us; The Statesman's Yearbook, 2023.

Routledge - Taylor & Francis Group, 6000 Broken Sound Pkwy. NW, Ste. 300, Boca Raton, FL, 33487, USA, (800) 634-1420, (800) 634-7064, orders@taylorandfrancis.com, https://www.routledge.com/; The Europa World Year Book 2022.

UNESCO Institute for Statistics, C.P 250 Succursale H, Montreal, QC, H3G 2K8, CAN, (514) 343-6880 (Dial from U.S.), (514) 343-5740 (Fax from U.S.), uis.publications@unesco.org, http://uis.unesco.org/; UIS.Stat.

United Nations Food and Agricultural Organization (FAO), 2121 K St., Ste. 800B, Washington, DC, 20037, USA, (202) 653-2400 (Dial from U.S.), (202) 653-5760 (Fax from U.S.), fao-hq@fao.org, https://www.fao.org; FAO Yearbook of Forest Products 2019 and The State of Food and Agriculture (SOFA) 2022.

The World Bank, 1818 H St. NW, Washington, DC, 20433, USA, (202) 473-1000, (202) 477-6391, eds03@worldbank.org, https://www.worldbank.org/; World Development Report 2022: Finance for an Equitable Recovery.

CHINA-FRUIT PRODUCTION

See CHINA-CROPS

CHINA-GAS PRODUCTION

See CHINA-MINERAL INDUSTRIES

CHINA-GOLD INDUSTRY

National Bureau of Statistics of China (NBS), No. 57, Yuetan Nanjie, Sanlihe, Xicheng District, Beijing, 100826, CHN, info@gj.stats.cn, http://www.stats.gov.cn/english/; China Statistical Yearbook, 2021.

The World Bank, 1818 H St. NW, Washington, DC, 20433, USA, (202) 473-1000, (202) 477-6391, eds03@worldbank.org, https://www.worldbank.org/; World Development Indicators (WDI) 2022.

CHINA-GOLD PRODUCTION

See CHINA-MINERAL INDUSTRIES

CHINA-GROSS DOMESTIC PRODUCT

Asian Development Bank (ADB), 6 ADB Ave., Mandaluyong City, 1550, PHL, information@adb.org, https://www.adb.org/; Key Indicators for Asia and the Pacific 2022.

The Economist Group: Economist Intelligence Unit (EIU), 900 3rd Ave., 16th Fl., New York, NY, 10022, USA, (212) 541-0500, americas@eiu.com, https://www.eiu.com; China Country Report.

Federal Statistical Office Germany, Gustav-Stresemann-Ring 11, Wiesbaden, D-65189, GER, https://www.destatis.de; Basic Indicators: China.

The World Bank, 1818 H St. NW, Washington, DC, 20433, USA, (202) 473-1000, (202) 477-6391, eds03@worldbank.org, https://www.worldbank.org/; World Development Indicators (WDI) 2022 and World Development Report 2022: Finance for an Equitable Recovery.

CHINA-GROSS NATIONAL PRODUCT

Asian Development Bank (ADB), 6 ADB Ave., Mandaluyong City, 1550, PHL, information@adb.org, https://www.adb.org/; Key Indicators for Asia and the Pacific 2022.

National Bureau of Statistics of China (NBS), No. 57, Yuetan Nanjie, Sanlihe, Xicheng District, Beijing, 100826, CHN, info@gj.stats.cn, http://www.stats.gov.cn/english/; China Statistical Yearbook, 2021.

Palgrave Macmillan, 1 New York Plaza, Ste. 4500, New York, NY, 10004-1562, USA, (800) 777-4643, orders@palgrave.com, https://www.palgrave.com/us; The Statesman's Yearbook, 2023.

The World Bank, 1818 H St. NW, Washington, DC, 20433, USA, (202) 473-1000, (202) 477-6391, eds03@worldbank.org, https://www.worldbank.org/; World Development Indicators (WDI) 2022 and World Development Report 2022: Finance for an Equitable Recovery.

CHINA-HEMP FIBRE PRODUCTION

See CHINA-TEXTILE INDUSTRY

CHINA-HIDES AND SKINS INDUSTRY

National Bureau of Statistics of China (NBS), No. 57, Yuetan Nanjie, Sanlihe, Xicheng District, Beijing, 100826, CHN, info@gj.stats.cn, http://www.stats.gov.cn/english/; China Statistical Yearbook, 2021.

CHINA-HONEY TRADE

National Bureau of Statistics of China (NBS), No. 57, Yuetan Nanjie, Sanlihe, Xicheng District, Beijing, 100826, CHN, info@gj.stats.cn, http://www.stats.gov.cn/english/; China Statistical Yearbook, 2021.

CHINA-HOUSING

Euromonitor International, Inc., 1 N Dearborn St., Ste. 1700, Chicago, IL, 60602, USA, (312) 922-1115, (312) 922-1157, info-usa@euromonitor.com, https://www.euromonitor.com/; Geographies.

National Bureau of Statistics of China (NBS), No. 57, Yuetan Nanjie, Sanlihe, Xicheng District, Beijing, 100826, CHN, info@gj.stats.cn, http://www.stats.gov.cn/english/; China Statistical Yearbook, 2021.

CHINA-ILLITERATE PERSONS

United Nations Economic and Social Commission for Asia and the Pacific (ESCAP), United Nations Building, Rajadamnern Nok Ave., Bangkok, 10200, THA, https://www.unescap.org/; Asia-Pacific Development Journal.

CHINA-IMPORTS

Asian Development Bank (ADB), 6 ADB Ave., Mandaluyong City, 1550, PHL, information@adb.org, https://www.adb.org/; Key Indicators for Asia and the Pacific 2022.

BC Stats, Stn Prov Govt, PO Box 9410, Victoria, BC, V8W 9V1, CAN, (250) 387-6121 (Dial from U.S.), bc.stats@gov.bc.ca, https://www2.gov.bc.ca/gov/content/data/about-data-management/bc-stats; Country Trade Profile - China (Mainland).

Central Intelligence Agency (CIA), Office of Public Affairs, Washington, DC, 20505, USA, (703) 482-0623, https://www.cia.gov; The World Factbook.

The Economist Group: Economist Intelligence Unit (EIU), 900 3rd Ave., 16th Fl., New York, NY, 10022, USA, (212) 541-0500, americas@eiu.com, https://www.eiu.com; China Country Report.

Euromonitor International, Inc., 1 N Dearborn St., Ste. 1700, Chicago, IL, 60602, USA, (312) 922-1115, (312) 922-1157, info-usa@euromonitor.com, https://www.euromonitor.com/; Geographies.

Federal Statistical Office Germany, Gustav-Stresemann-Ring 11, Wiesbaden, D-65189, GER, https://www.destatis.de; Basic Indicators: China.

International Monetary Fund (IMF), 700 19th St. NW, Washington, DC, 20431, USA, (202) 623-7000, (202) 623-4661, publications@imf.org, https://www.imf.org; Direction of Trade Statistics (DOTS) and International Financial Statistics (IFS).

National Bureau of Statistics of China (NBS), No. 57, Yuetan Nanjie, Sanlihe, Xicheng District, Beijing, 100826, CHN, info@gj.stats.cn, http://www.stats.gov.cn/english/; China Statistical Yearbook, 2021.

S&P Global, IHS Markit, 15 Inverness Way E, Englewood, CO, 80112, USA, (800) 447-2273, (800) 854-7179, https://ihsmarkit.com; Global Trade Atlas (GTA).

The World Bank, 1818 H St. NW, Washington, DC, 20433, USA, (202) 473-1000, (202) 477-6391, eds03@worldbank.org, https://www.worldbank.org/; World Development Report 2022: Finance for an Equitable Recovery.

CHINA-INDUSTRIAL METALS PRODUCTION

See CHINA-MINERAL INDUSTRIES

CHINA-INDUSTRIAL PRODUCTIVITY

National Bureau of Statistics of China (NBS), No. 57, Yuetan Nanjie, Sanlihe, Xicheng District, Beijing, 100826, CHN, info@gj.stats.cn, http://www.stats.gov.cn/english/; China Statistical Yearbook, 2021.

CHINA-INDUSTRIAL PROPERTY

World Intellectual Property Organization (WIPO), 34, chemin des Colombettes, Geneva, CH-1211, SWI, https://www.wipo.int; Madrid Yearly Review 2022: International Registrations of Marks.

CHINA-INDUSTRIES

Central Intelligence Agency (CIA), Office of Public Affairs, Washington, DC, 20505, USA, (703) 482-0623, https://www.cia.gov; The World Factbook.

The Economist Group: Economist Intelligence Unit (EIU), 900 3rd Ave., 16th Fl., New York, NY, 10022, USA, (212) 541-0500, americas@eiu.com, https://www.eiu.com; China Country Report.

Euromonitor International, Inc., 1 N Dearborn St., Ste. 1700, Chicago, IL, 60602, USA, (312) 922-1115, (312) 922-1157, info-usa@euromonitor.com, https://www.euromonitor.com/; Geographies.

National Bureau of Statistics of China (NBS), No. 57, Yuetan Nanjie, Sanlihe, Xicheng District, Beijing, 100826, CHN, info@gj.stats.cn, http://www.stats.gov.cn/english/; China Statistical Yearbook, 2021.

Palgrave Macmillan, 1 New York Plaza, Ste. 4500, New York, NY, 10004-1562, USA, (800) 777-4643, orders@palgrave.com, https://www.palgrave.com/us; The Statesman's Yearbook, 2023.

Routledge - Taylor & Francis Group, 6000 Broken Sound Pkwy. NW, Ste. 300, Boca Raton, FL, 33487, USA, (800) 634-1420, (800) 634-7064, orders@taylorandfrancis.com, https://www.routledge.com/; The Europa World Year Book 2022.

United Nations Economic and Social Commission for Asia and the Pacific (ESCAP), United Nations Building, Rajadamnern Nok Ave., Bangkok, 10200, THA, https://www.unescap.org/; Asia-Pacific Development Journal and SDG Gateway Data Explorer.

United Nations Industrial Development Organization (UNIDO), 1 United Nations Plz., Rm. DC1-1118, New York, NY, 10017, USA, (212) 963-6890, (212) 963 6885, (212) 963-7904, office.newyork@unido.org, https://www.unido.org/; Industrial Statistics Databases and International Yearbook of Industrial Statistics 2021.

The World Bank, 1818 H St. NW, Washington, DC, 20433, USA, (202) 473-1000, (202) 477-6391, eds03@worldbank.org, https://www.worldbank.org/; World Development Indicators (WDI) 2022.

World Intellectual Property Organization (WIPO), 34, chemin des Colombettes, Geneva, CH-1211, SWI, https://www.wipo.int; Madrid Yearly Review 2022: International Registrations of Marks.

CHINA-INFANT AND MATERNAL MORTALITY

See CHINA-MORTALITY

CHINA-INTERNATIONAL FINANCE

Asian Development Bank (ADB), 6 ADB Ave., Mandaluyong City, 1550, PHL, information@adb.org, https://www.adb.org/; Key Indicators for Asia and the Pacific 2022.

Japan Center for Economic Research (JCER), Nikkei Inc. Bldg. 11F, 1-3-7 Otemachi, Chiyoda-ku, Tokyo, 100-8066, JPN, https://www.jcer.or.jp/en; East Asia Risk and Japan-China Relations.

CHINA-INTERNATIONAL TRADE

Asia Pacific Economic Cooperation (APEC), 35 Heng Mui Keng Terrace, 119616, SGP, info@apec.org, https://www.apec.org/; APEC Regional Trends Analysis - What Goes Around Comes Around: Pivoting to a Circular Economy; Uncertainty Tests APEC's Resilience amid COVID-19.

Asian Development Bank (ADB), 6 ADB Ave., Mandaluyong City, 1550, PHL, information@adb.org, https://www.adb.org/; Key Indicators for Asia and the Pacific 2022.

Cato Institute, 1000 Massachusetts Ave. NW, Washington, DC, 20001-5403, USA, (202) 842-0200, https://www.cato.org/; Course Correction: Charting a More Effective Approach to U.S.-China Trade.

The Economist Group: Economist Intelligence Unit (EIU), 900 3rd Ave., 16th Fl., New York, NY, 10022, USA, (212) 541-0500, americas@eiu.com, https://www.eiu.com; China Country Report.

Euromonitor International, Inc., 1 N Dearborn St., Ste. 1700, Chicago, IL, 60602, USA, (312) 922-1115, (312) 922-1157, info-usa@euromonitor.com, https://www.euromonitor.com/; Geographies.

Federal Statistical Office Germany, Gustav-Stresemann-Ring 11, Wiesbaden, D-65189, GER, https://www.destatis.de; Basic Indicators: China.

Japan Center for Economic Research (JCER), Nikkei Inc. Bldg. 11F, 1-3-7 Otemachi, Chiyoda-ku, Tokyo, 100-8066, JPN, https://www.jcer.or.jp/en; East Asia Risk and Japan-China Relations.

National Bureau of Statistics of China (NBS), No. 57, Yuetan Nanjie, Sanlihe, Xicheng District, Beijing, 100826, CHN, info@gj.stats.cn, http://www.stats.gov.cn/english/; China Statistical Yearbook, 2021.

Palgrave Macmillan, 1 New York Plaza, Ste. 4500, New York, NY, 10004-1562, USA, (800) 777-4643, orders@palgrave.com, https://www.palgrave.com/us; The Statesman's Yearbook, 2023.

Pew Research Center, 1615 L St. NW, Ste. 800, Washington, DC, 20036, USA, (202) 419-4300, (202) 857-8562, info@pewresearch.org, https://www.pewresearch.org/; How Global Public Opinion of China Has Shifted in the Xi Era.

Pew Research Center, Politics & Policy, 1615 L St. NW, Ste. 800, Washington, DC, 20036, USA, (202) 419-4300, (202) 857-8562, https://www.pewresearch.org/topic/politics-policy/; Americans Are Critical of China's Global Role - as Well as Its Relationship With Russia.

Routledge - Taylor & Francis Group, 6000 Broken Sound Pkwy. NW, Ste. 300, Boca Raton, FL, 33487, USA, (800) 634-1420, (800) 634-7064, orders@taylorandfrancis.com, https://www.routledge.com/; The Europa World Year Book 2022.

U.S. Department of Labor (DOL), Bureau of Labor Statistics (BLS), Postal Square Bldg., 2 Massachusetts Ave. NE, Washington, DC, 20212-0001, USA, (202) 691-5200, (202) 691-7890, blsdata_staff@bls.gov, https://www.bls.gov; Import/Export Price Indexes (International Price Program - IPP).

United Nations Conference on Trade and Development (UNCTAD), Palais des Nations, Geneva, 1211, SWI, (212) 963-6896, unctadinfo@unctad.org, https://unctad.org; Trade and Development Report 2021.

United Nations Economic and Social Commission for Asia and the Pacific (ESCAP), United Nations Building, Rajadamnern Nok Ave., Bangkok, 10200, THA, https://www.unescap.org/; Asia-Pacific Development Journal and SDG Gateway Data Explorer.

United Nations Food and Agricultural Organization (FAO), 2121 K St., Ste. 800B, Washington, DC, 20037, USA, (202) 653-2400 (Dial from U.S.), (202) 653-5760 (Fax from U.S.), fao-hq@fao.org, https://www.fao.org; The State of Food and Agriculture (SOFA) 2022.

United Nations Statistics Division (UNSD), United Nations Plz., New York, NY, 10017, USA, (800) 253-9646, (212) 963-9851, statistics@un.org, https://unstats.un.org; Statistical Yearbook of the United Nations 2021.

The World Bank, 1818 H St. NW, Washington, DC, 20433, USA, (202) 473-1000, (202) 477-6391, eds03@worldbank.org, https://www.worldbank.org/; World Development Indicators (WDI) 2022 and World Development Report 2022: Finance for an Equitable Recovery.

World Trade Organization (WTO), Ctre. William Rappard, Rue de Lausanne 154, Case postale, Geneva, CH-1211, SWI, enquiries@wto.org, https://www.wto.org; World Trade Statistical Review 2022.

CHINA-INTERNET USERS

Bain & Company, 131 Dartmouth St., Boston, MA, 02116, USA, (617) 572-2000, (617) 572-2427, https://www.bain.com/; China Internet Report: How to Embrace the Unique Platform Business Model in China.

Federal Statistical Office Germany, Gustav-Stresemann-Ring 11, Wiesbaden, D-65189, GER, https://www.destatis.de; Basic Indicators: China.

International Telecommunication Union (ITU), Place des Nations, Geneva, CH-1211, SWI, itumail@itu.int, https://www.itu.int; Global Connectivity Report 2022; World Telecommunication/ICT Indicators Database 2021; and Yearbook of Statistics 2019.

Reporters Without Borders/Reporters sans frontieres (RSF), General Secretariat, CS 90247, Paris, 75083, FRA, secretariat@rsf.org, https://rsf.org/en; China's Pursuit of a New World Media Order.

CHINA-LABOR

Brown University, Population Studies and Training Center (PSTC), 68 Waterman St., PO Box 1836, Providence, RI, 02912, USA, (401) 863-2668, (401) 863-3351, population_studies@brown.edu, https://www.brown.edu/academics/population-studies/; Women's Political Leadership and Adult Health: Evidence from Rural and Urban China.

Central Intelligence Agency (CIA), Office of Public Affairs, Washington, DC, 20505, USA, (703) 482-0623, https://www.cia.gov; The World Factbook.

Euromonitor International, Inc., 1 N Dearborn St., Ste. 1700, Chicago, IL, 60602, USA, (312) 922-1115, (312) 922-1157, info-usa@euromonitor.com, https://www.euromonitor.com/; Geographies.

Federal Statistical Office Germany, Gustav-Stresemann-Ring 11, Wiesbaden, D-65189, GER, https://www.destatis.de; Basic Indicators: China.

National Bureau of Statistics of China (NBS), No. 57, Yuetan Nanjie, Sanlihe, Xicheng District, Beijing, 100826, CHN, info@gj.stats.cn, http://www.stats.gov.cn/english/; China Statistical Yearbook, 2021.

Palgrave Macmillan, 1 New York Plaza, Ste. 4500, New York, NY, 10004-1562, USA, (800) 777-4643, orders@palgrave.com, https://www.palgrave.com/us; The Statesman's Yearbook, 2023.

United Nations Food and Agricultural Organization (FAO), 2121 K St., Ste. 800B, Washington, DC, 20037, USA, (202) 653-2400 (Dial from U.S.), (202) 653-5760 (Fax from U.S.), fao-hq@fao.org, https://www.fao.org; The State of Food and Agriculture (SOFA) 2022.

The World Bank, 1818 H St. NW, Washington, DC, 20433, USA, (202) 473-1000, (202) 477-6391, eds03@worldbank.org, https://www.worldbank.org/; World Development Indicators (WDI) 2022 and World Development Report 2022: Finance for an Equitable Recovery.

CHINA-LAND USE

National Bureau of Statistics of China (NBS), No. 57, Yuetan Nanjie, Sanlihe, Xicheng District, Beijing, 100826, CHN, info@gj.stats.cn, http://www.stats.gov.cn/english/; China Statistical Yearbook, 2021.

United Nations Statistics Division (UNSD), United Nations Plz., New York, NY, 10017, USA, (800) 253-9646, (212) 963-9851, statistics@un.org, https://unstats.un.org; Millennium Development Goal Indicators.

The World Bank, 1818 H St. NW, Washington, DC, 20433, USA, (202) 473-1000, (202) 477-6391, eds03@worldbank.org, https://www.worldbank.org/; World Development Report 2022: Finance for an Equitable Recovery.

CHINA-LIFE EXPECTANCY

Central Intelligence Agency (CIA), Office of Public Affairs, Washington, DC, 20505, USA, (703) 482-0623, https://www.cia.gov; The World Factbook.

United Nations Department of Economic and Social Affairs (DESA), Population Division, 2 United Nations Plz., Rm. DC2-1950, New York, NY, 10017, USA, (212) 963-3209, (212) 963-2147, population@un.org, https://www.un.org/development/desa/pd/; World Population Ageing 2020 Highlights.

United Nations Economic and Social Commission for Asia and the Pacific (ESCAP), United Nations Building, Rajadamnern Nok Ave., Bangkok, 10200, THA, https://www.unescap.org/; Asia-Pacific Development Journal.

United Nations Statistics Division (UNSD), United Nations Plz., New York, NY, 10017, USA, (800) 253-9646, (212) 963-9851, statistics@un.org, https://unstats.un.org; Millennium Development Goal Indicators.

CHINA-LITERACY

Euromonitor International, Inc., 1 N Dearborn St., Ste. 1700, Chicago, IL, 60602, USA, (312) 922-1115, (312) 922-1157, info-usa@euromonitor.com, https://www.euromonitor.com/; Geographies.

UNESCO Institute for Statistics, C.P 250 Succursale H, Montreal, QC, H3G 2K8, CAN, (514) 343-6880 (Dial from U.S.), (514) 343-5740 (Fax from U.S.), uis.publications@unesco.org, http://uis.unesco.org/; Literacy.

CHINA-LIVESTOCK

National Bureau of Statistics of China (NBS), No. 57, Yuetan Nanjie, Sanlihe, Xicheng District, Beijing, 100826, CHN, info@gj.stats.cn, http://www.stats.gov.cn/english/; China Statistical Yearbook, 2021.

Palgrave Macmillan, 1 New York Plaza, Ste. 4500, New York, NY, 10004-1562, USA, (800) 777-4643, orders@palgrave.com, https://www.palgrave.com/us; The Statesman's Yearbook, 2023.

Routledge - Taylor & Francis Group, 6000 Broken Sound Pkwy. NW, Ste. 300, Boca Raton, FL, 33487, USA, (800) 634-1420, (800) 634-7064, orders@taylorandfrancis.com, https://www.routledge.com/; The Europa World Year Book 2022.

United Nations Food and Agricultural Organization (FAO), 2121 K St., Ste. 800B, Washington, DC, 20037, USA, (202) 653-2400 (Dial from U.S.), (202) 653-5760 (Fax from U.S.), fao-hq@fao.org, https://www.fao.org; The State of Food and Agriculture (SOFA) 2022.

United Nations Statistics Division (UNSD), United Nations Plz., New York, NY, 10017, USA, (800) 253-9646, (212) 963-9851, statistics@un.org, https://unstats.un.org; Statistical Yearbook of the United Nations 2021.

CHINA-MAGNESIUM PRODUCTION AND CONSUMPTION

See CHINA-MINERAL INDUSTRIES

CHINA-MANPOWER

National Bureau of Statistics of China (NBS), No. 57, Yuetan Nanjie, Sanlihe, Xicheng District, Beijing, 100826, CHN, info@gj.stats.cn, http://www.stats.gov.cn/english/; China Statistical Yearbook, 2021.

United Nations Economic and Social Commission for Asia and the Pacific (ESCAP), United Nations Building, Rajadamnern Nok Ave., Bangkok, 10200, THA, https://www.unescap.org/; SDG Gateway Data Explorer.

CHINA-MANUFACTURES

Asian Development Bank (ADB), 6 ADB Ave., Mandaluyong City, 1550, PHL, information@adb.org, https://www.adb.org/; Key Indicators for Asia and the Pacific 2022.

National Bureau of Statistics of China (NBS), No. 57, Yuetan Nanjie, Sanlihe, Xicheng District, Beijing, 100826, CHN, info@gj.stats.cn, http://www.stats.gov.cn/english/; China Statistical Yearbook, 2021.

CHINA-MARRIAGE

National Bureau of Statistics of China (NBS), No. 57, Yuetan Nanjie, Sanlihe, Xicheng District, Beijing, 100826, CHN, info@gj.stats.cn, http://www.stats.gov.cn/english/; China Statistical Yearbook, 2021.

CHINA-MERCURY PRODUCTION

See CHINA-MINERAL INDUSTRIES

CHINA-MILITARY POLICY

Human Rights Watch, 350 5th Ave., 34th Fl., New York, NY, 10118-3299, USA, (212) 290-4700, (212) 736-1300, https://www.hrw.org; Break Their Lineage, Break Their Roots: China's Crimes against Humanity Targeting Uyghurs and Other Turkic Muslims.

U.S. Department of Defense (DOD), 1400 Defense Pentagon, Washington, DC, 20301-1400, USA, (703) 571-3343, https://www.defense.gov; Military and Security Developments Involving the People's Republic of China 2021: Annual Report to Congress.

CHINA-MINERAL INDUSTRIES

Asian Development Bank (ADB), 6 ADB Ave., Mandaluyong City, 1550, PHL, information@adb.org, https://www.adb.org/; Key Indicators for Asia and the Pacific 2022.

Barchart, 209 W Jackson Blvd., 2nd Fl., Chicago, IL, 60606, USA, (877) 247-4394, commodities@barchart.com, https://www.barchart.com/cmdty; The cmdty Yearbook 2023; cmdtyStats: Commodity Statistics and Fundamental Data; cmdtyView: Commodity Index; and Commodity Data and Prices.

International Energy Agency (IEA), 9 Rue de la Federation, Paris, 75739, FRA, info@iea.org, https://www.iea.org/; World Energy Outlook 2021.

National Bureau of Statistics of China (NBS), No. 57, Yuetan Nanjie, Sanlihe, Xicheng District, Beijing, 100826, CHN, info@gj.stats.cn, http://www.stats.gov.cn/english/; China Statistical Yearbook, 2021.

Palgrave Macmillan, 1 New York Plaza, Ste. 4500, New York, NY, 10004-1562, USA, (800) 777-4643, orders@palgrave.com, https://www.palgrave.com/us; The Statesman's Yearbook, 2023.

Routledge - Taylor & Francis Group, 6000 Broken Sound Pkwy. NW, Ste. 300, Boca Raton, FL, 33487, USA, (800) 634-1420, (800) 634-7064, orders@taylorandfrancis.com, https://www.routledge.com/; The Europa World Year Book 2022.

United Nations Conference on Trade and Development (UNCTAD), Palais des Nations, Geneva, 1211, SWI, (212) 963-6896, unctadinfo@unctad.org, https://unctad.org; Trade and Development Report 2021.

United Nations Statistics Division (UNSD), United Nations Plz., New York, NY, 10017, USA, (800) 253-9646, (212) 963-9851, statistics@un.org, https://unstats.un.org; Statistical Yearbook of the United Nations 2021.

CHINA-MONEY SUPPLY

The Economist Group: Economist Intelligence Unit (EIU), 900 3rd Ave., 16th Fl., New York, NY, 10022, USA, (212) 541-0500, americas@eiu.com, https://www.eiu.com; China Country Report.

Federal Statistical Office Germany, Gustav-Stresemann-Ring 11, Wiesbaden, D-65189, GER, https://www.destatis.de; Basic Indicators: China.

International Monetary Fund (IMF), 700 19th St. NW, Washington, DC, 20431, USA, (202) 623-7000, (202) 623-4661, publications@imf.org, https://www.imf.org; International Financial Statistics (IFS).

National Bureau of Statistics of China (NBS), No. 57, Yuetan Nanjie, Sanlihe, Xicheng District, Beijing, 100826, CHN, info@gj.stats.cn, http://www.stats.gov.cn/english/; China Statistical Yearbook, 2021.

Routledge - Taylor & Francis Group, 6000 Broken Sound Pkwy. NW, Ste. 300, Boca Raton, FL, 33487, USA, (800) 634-1420, (800) 634-7064, orders@taylorandfrancis.com, https://www.routledge.com/; The Europa World Year Book 2022.

CHINA-MORTALITY

National Bureau of Statistics of China (NBS), No. 57, Yuetan Nanjie, Sanlihe, Xicheng District, Beijing, 100826, CHN, info@gj.stats.cn, http://www.stats.gov.cn/english/; China Statistical Yearbook, 2021.

UNICEF, 3 United Nations Plz., New York, NY, 10017, USA, (212) 303-7984, (917) 244-2215, https://www.unicef.org; The State of the World's Children 2023.

United Nations Economic and Social Commission for Asia and the Pacific (ESCAP), United Nations Building, Rajadamnern Nok Ave., Bangkok, 10200, THA, https://www.unescap.org/; Asia-Pacific Development Journal.

United Nations Statistics Division (UNSD), United Nations Plz., New York, NY, 10017, USA, (800) 253-9646, (212) 963-9851, statistics@un.org, https://unstats.un.org; Millennium Development Goal Indicators; Statistical Yearbook of the United Nations 2021; and World Statistics Pocketbook 2021.

University of Texas at Austin, COVID-19 Modeling Consortium, 1 University Station C0930, Austin, TX, 78712, USA, utpandemics@austin.utexas.edu, https://covid-19.tacc.utexas.edu/; Estimated COVID-19 Mortality in China, December 16, 2022 - January 19, 2023.

The World Bank, 1818 H St. NW, Washington, DC, 20433, USA, (202) 473-1000, (202) 477-6391, eds03@worldbank.org, https://www.worldbank.org/; World Development Indicators (WDI) 2022.

World Health Organization (WHO), Ave. Appia 20, Geneva, CH-1211, SWI, (202) 974-3000 (Telephone in U.S.), publications@who.int, https://www.who.int/; Global Health Observatory (GHO).

CHINA-MOTION PICTURES

Palgrave Macmillan, 1 New York Plaza, Ste. 4500, New York, NY, 10004-1562, USA, (800) 777-4643, orders@palgrave.com, https://www.palgrave.com/us; The Statesman's Yearbook, 2023.

CHINA-NATURAL GAS PRODUCTION

See CHINA-MINERAL INDUSTRIES

CHINA-NUTRITION

Asian Development Bank (ADB), 6 ADB Ave., Mandaluyong City, 1550, PHL, information@adb.org, https://www.adb.org/; Key Indicators for Asia and the Pacific 2022.

United Nations Food and Agricultural Organization (FAO), 2121 K St., Ste. 800B, Washington, DC, 20037, USA, (202) 653-2400 (Dial from U.S.), (202) 653-5760 (Fax from U.S.), fao-hq@fao.org, https://www.fao.org; The State of Food and Agriculture (SOFA) 2022.

United Nations Statistics Division (UNSD), United Nations Plz., New York, NY, 10017, USA, (800) 253-9646, (212) 963-9851, statistics@un.org, https://unstats.un.org; Millennium Development Goal Indicators.

CHINA-PAPER

See CHINA-FORESTS AND FORESTRY

CHINA-PEANUT PRODUCTION

See CHINA-CROPS

CHINA-PERIODICALS

National Bureau of Statistics of China (NBS), No. 57, Yuetan Nanjie, Sanlihe, Xicheng District, Beijing, 100826, CHN, info@gj.stats.cn, http://www.stats.gov.cn/english/; China Statistical Yearbook, 2021.

CHINA-PESTICIDES

United Nations Food and Agricultural Organization (FAO), 2121 K St., Ste. 800B, Washington, DC, 20037, USA, (202) 653-2400 (Dial from U.S.), (202) 653-5760 (Fax from U.S.), fao-hq@fao.org, https://www.fao.org; The State of Food and Agriculture (SOFA) 2022.

CHINA-PETROLEUM INDUSTRY AND TRADE

Asian Development Bank (ADB), 6 ADB Ave., Mandaluyong City, 1550, PHL, information@adb.org, https://www.adb.org/; Key Indicators for Asia and the Pacific 2022.

International Energy Agency (IEA), 9 Rue de la Federation, Paris, 75739, FRA, info@iea.org, https://www.iea.org/; World Energy Outlook 2021.

National Bureau of Statistics of China (NBS), No. 57, Yuetan Nanjie, Sanlihe, Xicheng District, Beijing, 100826, CHN, info@gj.stats.cn, http://www.stats.gov.cn/english/; China Statistical Yearbook, 2021.

Palgrave Macmillan, 1 New York Plaza, Ste. 4500, New York, NY, 10004-1562, USA, (800) 777-4643, orders@palgrave.com, https://www.palgrave.com/us; The Statesman's Yearbook, 2023.

U.S. Energy Information Administration (EIA), 1000 Independence Ave. SW, Washington, DC, 20585, USA, (202) 586-8800, infoctr@eia.gov, https://www.eia.gov; International Energy Outlook 2021.

United Nations Food and Agricultural Organization (FAO), 2121 K St., Ste. 800B, Washington, DC, 20037, USA, (202) 653-2400 (Dial from U.S.), (202) 653-5760 (Fax from U.S.), fao-hq@fao.org, https://www.fao.org; The State of Food and Agriculture (SOFA) 2022.

United Nations Statistics Division (UNSD), United Nations Plz., New York, NY, 10017, USA, (800) 253-9646, (212) 963-9851, statistics@un.org, https://unstats.un.org; Statistical Yearbook of the United Nations 2021.

CHINA-PHOSPHATES PRODUCTION

See CHINA-MINERAL INDUSTRIES

CHINA-PLASTICS INDUSTRY AND TRADE

National Bureau of Statistics of China (NBS), No. 57, Yuetan Nanjie, Sanlihe, Xicheng District, Beijing, 100826, CHN, info@gj.stats.cn, http://www.stats.gov.cn/english/; China Statistical Yearbook, 2021.

CHINA-POPULATION

Asian Development Bank (ADB), 6 ADB Ave., Mandaluyong City, 1550, PHL, information@adb.org, https://www.adb.org/; Key Indicators for Asia and the Pacific 2022.

Brown University, Population Studies and Training Center (PSTC), 68 Waterman St., PO Box 1836, Providence, RI, 02912, USA, (401) 863-2668, (401) 863-3351, population_studies@brown.edu, https://www.brown.edu/academics/population-studies/; Women's Political Leadership and Adult Health: Evidence from Rural and Urban China.

Central Intelligence Agency (CIA), Office of Public Affairs, Washington, DC, 20505, USA, (703) 482-0623, https://www.cia.gov; The World Factbook.

The Economist Group: Economist Intelligence Unit (EIU), 900 3rd Ave., 16th Fl., New York, NY, 10022, USA, (212) 541-0500, americas@eiu.com, https://www.eiu.com; China Country Report and China's Emerging Cities 2021: Southeast China Takes the Lead.

Federal Statistical Office Germany, Gustav-Stresemann-Ring 11, Wiesbaden, D-65189, GER, https://www.destatis.de; Basic Indicators: China.

Human Rights Watch, 350 5th Ave., 34th Fl., New York, NY, 10118-3299, USA, (212) 290-4700, (212) 736-1300, https://www.hrw.org; Break Their Lineage, Break Their Roots: China's Crimes against Humanity Targeting Uyghurs and Other Turkic Muslims.

Infoplease, c/o Sandbox Networks, Inc., 1 Lincoln St., 24th Fl., Boston, MA, 02111, USA, https://www.infoplease.com; Countries of the World.

National Bureau of Statistics of China (NBS), No. 57, Yuetan Nanjie, Sanlihe, Xicheng District, Beijing, 100826, CHN, info@gj.stats.cn, http://www.stats.gov.cn/english/; China Statistical Yearbook, 2021.

Palgrave Macmillan, 1 New York Plaza, Ste. 4500, New York, NY, 10004-1562, USA, (800) 777-4643, orders@palgrave.com, https://www.palgrave.com/us; The Statesman's Yearbook, 2023.

Reporters Without Borders/Reporters sans frontieres (RSF), General Secretariat, CS 90247, Paris, 75083, FRA, secretariat@rsf.org, https://rsf.org/en; China's Pursuit of a New World Media Order.

Routledge - Taylor & Francis Group, 6000 Broken Sound Pkwy. NW, Ste. 300, Boca Raton, FL, 33487, USA, (800) 634-1420, (800) 634-7064, orders@taylorandfrancis.com, https://www.routledge.com/; The Europa World Year Book 2022.

UK Data Service, University of Essex, Wivenhoe Park, Colchester, Essex, CO4 3SQ, GBR, https://ukdataservice.ac.uk/; International Aggregate Data.

UNESCO Institute for Statistics, C.P 250 Succursale H, Montreal, QC, H3G 2K8, CAN, (514) 343-6880 (Dial from U.S.), (514) 343-5740 (Fax from U.S.), uis.publications@unesco.org, http://uis.unesco.org/; UIS.Stat.

United Nations Department of Economic and Social Affairs (DESA), Population Division, 2 United Nations Plz., Rm. DC2-1950, New York, NY, 10017, USA, (212) 963-3209, (212) 963-2147, population@un.org, https://www.un.org/

development/desa/pd/; Revision of World Urbanization Prospects and World Population Ageing 2020 Highlights.

United Nations Development Programme (UNDP), One United Nations Plz., New York, NY, 10017, USA, (212) 906-5000, (212) 906-5001, https://www.undp.org; Human Development Report 2021-2022.

United Nations Economic and Social Commission for Asia and the Pacific (ESCAP), United Nations Building, Rajadamnern Nok Ave., Bangkok, 10200, THA, https://www.unescap.org/; Asia-Pacific Development Journal and SDG Gateway Data Explorer.

United Nations Statistics Division (UNSD), United Nations Plz., New York, NY, 10017, USA, (800) 253-9646, (212) 963-9851, statistics@un.org, https://unstats.un.org; Statistical Yearbook of the United Nations 2021 and World Statistics Pocketbook 2021.

University of Texas at Austin, COVID-19 Modeling Consortium, 1 University Station C0930, Austin, TX, 78712, USA, utpandemics@austin.utexas.edu, https://covid-19.tacc.utexas.edu/; Estimated COVID-19 Mortality in China, December 16, 2022 - January 19, 2023.

The World Bank, 1818 H St. NW, Washington, DC, 20433, USA, (202) 473-1000, (202) 477-6391, eds03@worldbank.org, https://www.worldbank.org/; The Global Findex Database 2021 and World Development Report 2022: Finance for an Equitable Recovery.

CHINA-POPULATION DENSITY

Central Intelligence Agency (CIA), Office of Public Affairs, Washington, DC, 20505, USA, (703) 482-0623, https://www.cia.gov; The World Factbook.

National Bureau of Statistics of China (NBS), No. 57, Yuetan Nanjie, Sanlihe, Xicheng District, Beijing, 100826, CHN, info@gj.stats.cn, http://www.stats.gov.cn/english/; China Statistical Yearbook, 2021.

Palgrave Macmillan, 1 New York Plaza, Ste. 4500, New York, NY, 10004-1562, USA, (800) 777-4643, orders@palgrave.com, https://www.palgrave.com/us; The Statesman's Yearbook, 2023.

Routledge - Taylor & Francis Group, 6000 Broken Sound Pkwy. NW, Ste. 300, Boca Raton, FL, 33487, USA, (800) 634-1420, (800) 634-7064, orders@taylorandfrancis.com, https://www.routledge.com/; The Europa World Year Book 2022.

UNESCO Institute for Statistics, C.P 250 Succursale H, Montreal, QC, H3G 2K8, CAN, (514) 343-6880 (Dial from U.S.), (514) 343-5740 (Fax from U.S.), uis.publications@unesco.org, http://uis.unesco.org/; UIS.Stat.

The World Bank, 1818 H St. NW, Washington, DC, 20433, USA, (202) 473-1000, (202) 477-6391, eds03@worldbank.org, https://www.worldbank.org/; World Development Report 2022: Finance for an Equitable Recovery.

CHINA-POSTAL SERVICE

National Bureau of Statistics of China (NBS), No. 57, Yuetan Nanjie, Sanlihe, Xicheng District, Beijing, 100826, CHN, info@gj.stats.cn, http://www.stats.gov.cn/english/; China Statistical Yearbook, 2021.

Palgrave Macmillan, 1 New York Plaza, Ste. 4500, New York, NY, 10004-1562, USA, (800) 777-4643, orders@palgrave.com, https://www.palgrave.com/us; The Statesman's Yearbook, 2023.

CHINA-POWER RESOURCES

International Energy Agency (IEA), 9 Rue de la Federation, Paris, 75739, FRA, info@iea.org, https://www.iea.org/; World Energy Outlook 2021.

National Bureau of Statistics of China (NBS), No. 57, Yuetan Nanjie, Sanlihe, Xicheng District, Beijing, 100826, CHN, info@gj.stats.cn, http://www.stats.gov.cn/english/; China Statistical Yearbook, 2021.

Palgrave Macmillan, 1 New York Plaza, Ste. 4500, New York, NY, 10004-1562, USA, (800) 777-4643, orders@palgrave.com, https://www.palgrave.com/us; The Statesman's Yearbook, 2023.

S&P Global Commodity Insights, One World Trade Center, New York, NY, 10007, USA, (800) 752-8878, support@platts.com, https://www.spglobal.com/commodityinsights/en; Platts Asia Pacific / Arab Gulf Marketscan (APAG Marketscan).

U.S. Energy Information Administration (EIA), 1000 Independence Ave. SW, Washington, DC, 20585, USA, (202) 586-8800, infoctr@eia.gov, https://www.eia.gov; International Energy Outlook 2021.

United Nations Economic and Social Commission for Asia and the Pacific (ESCAP), United Nations Building, Rajadamnern Nok Ave., Bangkok, 10200, THA, https://www.unescap.org/; Asia-Pacific Development Journal.

United Nations Statistics Division (UNSD), United Nations Plz., New York, NY, 10017, USA, (800) 253-9646, (212) 963-9851, statistics@un.org, https://unstats.un.org; Statistical Yearbook of the United Nations 2021 and World Statistics Pocketbook 2021.

The World Bank, 1818 H St. NW, Washington, DC, 20433, USA, (202) 473-1000, (202) 477-6391, eds03@worldbank.org, https://www.worldbank.org/; World Development Report 2022: Finance for an Equitable Recovery.

CHINA-PRICES

Asian Development Bank (ADB), 6 ADB Ave., Mandaluyong City, 1550, PHL, information@adb.org, https://www.adb.org/; Key Indicators for Asia and the Pacific 2022.

Euromonitor International, Inc., 1 N Dearborn St., Ste. 1700, Chicago, IL, 60602, USA, (312) 922-1115, (312) 922-1157, info-usa@euromonitor.com, https://www.euromonitor.com/; Geographies.

International Monetary Fund (IMF), 700 19th St. NW, Washington, DC, 20431, USA, (202) 623-7000, (202) 623-4661, publications@imf.org, https://www.imf.org; International Financial Statistics (IFS).

National Bureau of Statistics of China (NBS), No. 57, Yuetan Nanjie, Sanlihe, Xicheng District, Beijing, 100826, CHN, info@gj.stats.cn, http://www.stats.gov.cn/english/; China Statistical Yearbook, 2021.

CHINA-PUBLIC HEALTH

Euromonitor International, Inc., 1 N Dearborn St., Ste. 1700, Chicago, IL, 60602, USA, (312) 922-1115, (312) 922-1157, info-usa@euromonitor.com, https://www.euromonitor.com/; Geographies and Market Research on the Health and Wellness Industry.

National Bureau of Statistics of China (NBS), No. 57, Yuetan Nanjie, Sanlihe, Xicheng District, Beijing, 100826, CHN, info@gj.stats.cn, http://www.stats.gov.cn/english/; China Statistical Yearbook, 2021.

Palgrave Macmillan, 1 New York Plaza, Ste. 4500, New York, NY, 10004-1562, USA, (800) 777-4643, orders@palgrave.com, https://www.palgrave.com/us; The Statesman's Yearbook, 2023.

PLOS, 1265 Battery St., Ste. 200, San Francisco, CA, 94111, USA, (415) 624-1200, (415) 795-1584, plos@plos.org, https://www.plos.org/; Outbreak Analysis with a Logistic Growth Model Shows COVID-19 Suppression Dynamics in China.

U.S. Census Bureau, 4600 Silver Hill Rd., Washington, DC, 20233, USA, (301) 763-4636, (800) 923-8282, https://www.census.gov; HIV/AIDS Surveillance Data Base.

UNICEF, 3 United Nations Plz., New York, NY, 10017, USA, (212) 303-7984, (917) 244-2215, https://www.unicef.org; The State of the World's Children 2023.

United Nations Department of Economic and Social Affairs (DESA), Population Division, 2 United Nations Plz., Rm. DC2-1950, New York, NY, 10017, USA, (212) 963-3209, (212) 963-2147, population@un.org, https://www.un.org/development/desa/pd/; World Fertility Data 2019.

United Nations Development Programme (UNDP), One United Nations Plz., New York, NY, 10017, USA, (212) 906-5000, (212) 906-5001, https://www.undp.org; Human Development Report 2021-2022.

United Nations Economic and Social Commission for Asia and the Pacific (ESCAP), United Nations Building, Rajadamnern Nok Ave., Bangkok, 10200, THA, https://www.unescap.org/; Asia-Pacific Development Journal.

United Nations Statistics Division (UNSD), United Nations Plz., New York, NY, 10017, USA, (800) 253-9646, (212) 963-9851, statistics@un.org, https://unstats.un.org; Millennium Development Goal Indicators and Statistical Yearbook of the United Nations 2021.

World Health Organization (WHO), Ave. Appia 20, Geneva, CH-1211, SWI, (202) 974-3000 (Telephone in U.S.), publications@who.int, https://www.who.int/; Global Health Observatory (GHO) and Health Statistics and Information Systems.

CHINA-PUBLIC UTILITIES

National Bureau of Statistics of China (NBS), No. 57, Yuetan Nanjie, Sanlihe, Xicheng District, Beijing, 100826, CHN, info@gj.stats.cn, http://www.stats.gov.cn/english/; China Statistical Yearbook, 2021.

CHINA-PUBLISHERS AND PUBLISHING

National Bureau of Statistics of China (NBS), No. 57, Yuetan Nanjie, Sanlihe, Xicheng District, Beijing, 100826, CHN, info@gj.stats.cn, http://www.stats.gov.cn/english/; China Statistical Yearbook, 2021.

Palgrave Macmillan, 1 New York Plaza, Ste. 4500, New York, NY, 10004-1562, USA, (800) 777-4643, orders@palgrave.com, https://www.palgrave.com/us; The Statesman's Yearbook, 2023.

Routledge - Taylor & Francis Group, 6000 Broken Sound Pkwy. NW, Ste. 300, Boca Raton, FL, 33487, USA, (800) 634-1420, (800) 634-7064, orders@taylorandfrancis.com, https://www.routledge.com/; The Europa World Year Book 2022.

UNESCO Institute for Statistics, C.P 250 Succursale H, Montreal, QC, H3G 2K8, CAN, (514) 343-6880 (Dial from U.S.), (514) 343-5740 (Fax from U.S.), uis.publications@unesco.org, http://uis.unesco.org/; UIS.Stat.

CHINA-RAILROADS

Janes, USA, (703) 574-7580, (888) 977-1519, customer.care@janes.com, https://www.janes.com; Janes World Railways 2021-2022.

National Bureau of Statistics of China (NBS), No. 57, Yuetan Nanjie, Sanlihe, Xicheng District, Beijing, 100826, CHN, info@gj.stats.cn, http://www.stats.gov.cn/english/; China Statistical Yearbook, 2021.

Palgrave Macmillan, 1 New York Plaza, Ste. 4500, New York, NY, 10004-1562, USA, (800) 777-4643, orders@palgrave.com, https://www.palgrave.com/us; The Statesman's Yearbook, 2023.

Routledge - Taylor & Francis Group, 6000 Broken Sound Pkwy. NW, Ste. 300, Boca Raton, FL, 33487, USA, (800) 634-1420, (800) 634-7064, orders@taylorandfrancis.com, https://www.routledge.com/; The Europa World Year Book 2022.

United Nations Statistics Division (UNSD), United Nations Plz., New York, NY, 10017, USA, (800) 253-9646, (212) 963-9851, statistics@un.org, https://unstats.un.org; Statistical Yearbook of the United Nations 2021.

CHINA-RELIGION

Central Intelligence Agency (CIA), Office of Public Affairs, Washington, DC, 20505, USA, (703) 482-0623, https://www.cia.gov; The World Factbook.

Palgrave Macmillan, 1 New York Plaza, Ste. 4500, New York, NY, 10004-1562, USA, (800) 777-4643, orders@palgrave.com, https://www.palgrave.com/us; The Statesman's Yearbook, 2023.

CHINA-RETAIL TRADE

Euromonitor International, Inc., 1 N Dearborn St., Ste. 1700, Chicago, IL, 60602, USA, (312) 922-1115, (312) 922-1157, info-usa@euromonitor.com, https://www.euromonitor.com/; Geographies and Market Research on the Retailing Industry.

National Bureau of Statistics of China (NBS), No. 57, Yuetan Nanjie, Sanlihe, Xicheng District, Beijing,

100826, CHN, info@gj.stats.cn, http://www.stats.gov.cn/english/; China Statistical Yearbook, 2021.

CHINA-RICE PRODUCTION

See CHINA-CROPS

CHINA-RUBBER INDUSTRY AND TRADE

International Rubber Study Group (IRSG), 51 Changi Business Park Central 2, Unit No. 6, 486066, SGP, https://www.rubberstudy.org; Monthly Rubber Bulletin (MRB); Rubber Industry Report; Rubber Statistical Bulletin; and World Rubber Industry Report (WRIO).

National Bureau of Statistics of China (NBS), No. 57, Yuetan Nanjie, Sanlihe, Xicheng District, Beijing, 100826, CHN, info@gj.stats.cn, http://www.stats.gov.cn/english/; China Statistical Yearbook, 2021.

United Nations Statistics Division (UNSD), United Nations Plz., New York, NY, 10017, USA, (800) 253-9646, (212) 963-9851, statistics@un.org, https://unstats.un.org; Statistical Yearbook of the United Nations 2021.

CHINA-SHIPPING

National Bureau of Statistics of China (NBS), No. 57, Yuetan Nanjie, Sanlihe, Xicheng District, Beijing, 100826, CHN, info@gj.stats.cn, http://www.stats.gov.cn/english/; China Statistical Yearbook, 2021.

Routledge - Taylor & Francis Group, 6000 Broken Sound Pkwy. NW, Ste. 300, Boca Raton, FL, 33487, USA, (800) 634-1420, (800) 634-7064, orders@taylorandfrancis.com, https://www.routledge.com/; The Europa World Year Book 2022.

S&P Global, IHS Markit, 15 Inverness Way E, Englewood, CO, 80112, USA, (800) 447-2273, (800) 854-7179, https://ihsmarkit.com; IHS Maritime World Shipbuilding Statistics; Journal of Commerce; Lloyd's Register of Ships 2021-2022; and Maritime Portal Desktop.

United Nations Statistics Division (UNSD), United Nations Plz., New York, NY, 10017, USA, (800) 253-9646, (212) 963-9851, statistics@un.org, https://unstats.un.org; Statistical Yearbook of the United Nations 2021.

CHINA-SOYBEAN PRODUCTION

See CHINA-CROPS

CHINA-STEEL PRODUCTION

See CHINA-MINERAL INDUSTRIES

CHINA-SUGAR PRODUCTION

See CHINA-CROPS

CHINA-SULPHUR PRODUCTION

See CHINA-MINERAL INDUSTRIES

CHINA-TAXATION

Palgrave Macmillan, 1 New York Plaza, Ste. 4500, New York, NY, 10004-1562, USA, (800) 777-4643, orders@palgrave.com, https://www.palgrave.com/us; The Statesman's Yearbook, 2023.

The World Bank, 1818 H St. NW, Washington, DC, 20433, USA, (202) 473-1000, (202) 477-6391, eds03@worldbank.org, https://www.worldbank.org/; World Development Indicators (WDI) 2022.

CHINA-TEA PRODUCTION

See CHINA-CROPS

CHINA-TELEPHONE

Palgrave Macmillan, 1 New York Plaza, Ste. 4500, New York, NY, 10004-1562, USA, (800) 777-4643, orders@palgrave.com, https://www.palgrave.com/us; The Statesman's Yearbook, 2023.

United Nations Statistics Division (UNSD), United Nations Plz., New York, NY, 10017, USA, (800) 253-9646, (212) 963-9851, statistics@un.org, https://unstats.un.org; World Statistics Pocketbook 2021.

CHINA-TEXTILE INDUSTRY

Euromonitor International, Inc., 1 N Dearborn St., Ste. 1700, Chicago, IL, 60602, USA, (312) 922-1115, (312) 922-1157, info-usa@euromonitor.com, https://www.euromonitor.com/; Market Research on the Retailing Industry.

National Bureau of Statistics of China (NBS), No. 57, Yuetan Nanjie, Sanlihe, Xicheng District, Beijing, 100826, CHN, info@gj.stats.cn, http://www.stats.gov.cn/english/; China Statistical Yearbook, 2021.

Palgrave Macmillan, 1 New York Plaza, Ste. 4500, New York, NY, 10004-1562, USA, (800) 777-4643, orders@palgrave.com, https://www.palgrave.com/us; The Statesman's Yearbook, 2023.

United Nations Statistics Division (UNSD), United Nations Plz., New York, NY, 10017, USA, (800) 253-9646, (212) 963-9851, statistics@un.org, https://unstats.un.org; Statistical Yearbook of the United Nations 2021.

CHINA-TOBACCO INDUSTRY

National Bureau of Statistics of China (NBS), No. 57, Yuetan Nanjie, Sanlihe, Xicheng District, Beijing, 100826, CHN, info@gj.stats.cn, http://www.stats.gov.cn/english/; China Statistical Yearbook, 2021.

United Nations Statistics Division (UNSD), United Nations Plz., New York, NY, 10017, USA, (800) 253-9646, (212) 963-9851, statistics@un.org, https://unstats.un.org; Statistical Yearbook of the United Nations 2021.

CHINA-TOURISM

Euromonitor International, Inc., 1 N Dearborn St., Ste. 1700, Chicago, IL, 60602, USA, (312) 922-1115, (312) 922-1157, info-usa@euromonitor.com, https://www.euromonitor.com/; Geographies.

National Bureau of Statistics of China (NBS), No. 57, Yuetan Nanjie, Sanlihe, Xicheng District, Beijing, 100826, CHN, info@gj.stats.cn, http://www.stats.gov.cn/english/; China Statistical Yearbook, 2021.

Palgrave Macmillan, 1 New York Plaza, Ste. 4500, New York, NY, 10004-1562, USA, (800) 777-4643, orders@palgrave.com, https://www.palgrave.com/us; The Statesman's Yearbook, 2023.

Routledge - Taylor & Francis Group, 6000 Broken Sound Pkwy. NW, Ste. 300, Boca Raton, FL, 33487, USA, (800) 634-1420, (800) 634-7064, orders@taylorandfrancis.com, https://www.routledge.com/; The Europa World Year Book 2022.

United Nations World Tourism Organization (UNWTO), Calle Poeta Joan Maragall 42, Madrid, 28020, SPA, info@unwto.org, https://www.unwto.org/; Yearbook of Tourism Statistics, 2021 Edition.

CHINA-TRADE

See CHINA-INTERNATIONAL TRADE

CHINA-TRANSPORTATION

Central Intelligence Agency (CIA), Office of Public Affairs, Washington, DC, 20505, USA, (703) 482-0623, https://www.cia.gov; The World Factbook.

Euromonitor International, Inc., 1 N Dearborn St., Ste. 1700, Chicago, IL, 60602, USA, (312) 922-1115, (312) 922-1157, info-usa@euromonitor.com, https://www.euromonitor.com/; Geographies.

National Bureau of Statistics of China (NBS), No. 57, Yuetan Nanjie, Sanlihe, Xicheng District, Beijing, 100826, CHN, info@gj.stats.cn, http://www.stats.gov.cn/english/; China Statistical Yearbook, 2021.

Palgrave Macmillan, 1 New York Plaza, Ste. 4500, New York, NY, 10004-1562, USA, (800) 777-4643, orders@palgrave.com, https://www.palgrave.com/us; The Statesman's Yearbook, 2023.

Routledge - Taylor & Francis Group, 6000 Broken Sound Pkwy. NW, Ste. 300, Boca Raton, FL, 33487, USA, (800) 634-1420, (800) 634-7064, orders@taylorandfrancis.com, https://www.routledge.com/; The Europa World Year Book 2022.

United Nations Economic and Social Commission for Asia and the Pacific (ESCAP), United Nations Building, Rajadamnern Nok Ave., Bangkok, 10200, THA, https://www.unescap.org/; SDG Gateway Data Explorer.

CHINA-UNEMPLOYMENT

National Bureau of Statistics of China (NBS), No. 57, Yuetan Nanjie, Sanlihe, Xicheng District, Beijing, 100826, CHN, info@gj.stats.cn, http://www.stats.gov.cn/english/; China Statistical Yearbook, 2021.

Palgrave Macmillan, 1 New York Plaza, Ste. 4500, New York, NY, 10004-1562, USA, (800) 777-4643, orders@palgrave.com, https://www.palgrave.com/us; The Statesman's Yearbook, 2023.

CHINA-VITAL STATISTICS

National Bureau of Statistics of China (NBS), No. 57, Yuetan Nanjie, Sanlihe, Xicheng District, Beijing, 100826, CHN, info@gj.stats.cn, http://www.stats.gov.cn/english/; China Statistical Yearbook, 2021.

Palgrave Macmillan, 1 New York Plaza, Ste. 4500, New York, NY, 10004-1562, USA, (800) 777-4643, orders@palgrave.com, https://www.palgrave.com/us; The Statesman's Yearbook, 2023.

U.S. Census Bureau, 4600 Silver Hill Rd., Washington, DC, 20233, USA, (301) 763-4636, (800) 923-8282, https://www.census.gov; HIV/AIDS Surveillance Data Base.

United Nations Department of Economic and Social Affairs (DESA), Population Division, 2 United Nations Plz., Rm. DC2-1950, New York, NY, 10017, USA, (212) 963-3209, (212) 963-2147, population@un.org, https://www.un.org/development/desa/pd/; World Contraceptive Use 2021: Estimates and Projections of Family Planning Indicators and World Marriage Data 2019.

United Nations Statistics Division (UNSD), United Nations Plz., New York, NY, 10017, USA, (800) 253-9646, (212) 963-9851, statistics@un.org, https://unstats.un.org; Statistical Yearbook of the United Nations 2021.

CHINA-WAGES

Government of the Hong Kong Special Administrative Region of the People's Republic of China: Census and Statistics Department, Wanchai Tower, 12 Harbour Road, Wan Chai, Hong Kong, CHN, gen-enquiry@censtatd.gov.hk, https://www.censtatd.gov.hk; Quarterly Report of Wage and Payroll Statistics.

National Bureau of Statistics of China (NBS), No. 57, Yuetan Nanjie, Sanlihe, Xicheng District, Beijing, 100826, CHN, info@gj.stats.cn, http://www.stats.gov.cn/english/; China Statistical Yearbook, 2021.

United Nations Economic and Social Commission for Asia and the Pacific (ESCAP), United Nations Building, Rajadamnern Nok Ave., Bangkok, 10200, THA, https://www.unescap.org/; SDG Gateway Data Explorer.

CHINA-WEATHER

See CHINA-CLIMATE

CHINA-WHEAT PRODUCTION

See CHINA-CROPS

CHINA-WOOD AND WOOD PULP

See CHINA-FORESTS AND FORESTRY

CHINA-WOOL PRODUCTION

See CHINA-TEXTILE INDUSTRY

CHINA-ZINC AND ZINC ORE

See CHINA-MINERAL INDUSTRIES

CHINA, REPUBLIC OF (TAIWAN)

See TAIWAN

CHIROPRACTOR'S OFFICES

U.S. Census Bureau, 4600 Silver Hill Rd., Washington, DC, 20233, USA, (301) 763-4636, (800) 923-

8282, https://www.census.gov; Economic Census, Nonemployer Statistics (NES) 2019.

CHOLELITHIASIS-DEATHS

Bernan Press, 15250 NBN Way, Bldg. C, Blue Ridge Summit, PA, 17214, USA, (301) 459-2255, (800) 865-3457, (800) 865-3450, customercare@bernan.com, https://rowman.com/Page/Bernan; Vital Statistics of the United States 2022: Births, Life Expectancy, Deaths, and Selected Health Data.

U.S. Department of Health and Human Services, Centers for Disease Control and Prevention (CDC), National Center for Health Statistics (NCHS), 3311 Toledo Rd., Hyattsville, MD, 20782-2064, USA, (800) 232-4636, (301) 458-4000, https://www.cdc.gov/nchs; National Vital Statistics Reports (NVSR) and Vital Statistics Online Data Portal.

CHOLERA

Bulletin of the Atomic Scientists, PO Box 15461, Chicago, IL, 60615-5146, USA, (773) 834-3779, admin@thebulletin.org, https://thebulletin.org/; An Illustrated History of the World's Deadliest Epidemics, from Ancient Rome to Covid-19.

U.S. Department of Health and Human Services, Centers for Disease Control and Prevention (CDC), 1600 Clifton Rd., Atlanta, GA, 30329-4027, USA, (800) 232-4636, (888) 232-6348 (TTY), cdcinfo@cdc.gov, https://www.cdc.gov; Morbidity and Mortality Weekly Report (MMWR) and National Notifiable Diseases Surveillance System (NNDSS).

CHOLESTEROL

U.S. Department of Health and Human Services, Centers for Disease Control and Prevention (CDC), 1600 Clifton Rd., Atlanta, GA, 30329-4027, USA, (800) 232-4636, (888) 232-6348 (TTY), cdcinfo@cdc.gov, https://www.cdc.gov; Behavioral Risk Factor Surveillance System (BRFSS) Data.

U.S. Department of Health and Human Services, Centers for Disease Control and Prevention (CDC), National Center for Health Statistics (NCHS), 3311 Toledo Rd., Hyattsville, MD, 20782-2064, USA, (800) 232-4636, (301) 458-4000, https://www.cdc.gov/nchs; FastStats - Statistics by Topic.

CHRISTIAN POPULATION

See RELIGION

CHRISTMAS

INRIX, 10210 NE Points Dr., No. 400, Kirkland, WA, 98033, USA, (425) 284-3800, https://inrix.com; Holiday Shopping Update.

CHRISTMAS ISLAND-AGRICULTURE

United Nations Food and Agricultural Organization (FAO), 2121 K St., Ste. 800B, Washington, DC, 20037, USA, (202) 653-2400 (Dial from U.S.), (202) 653-5760 (Fax from U.S.), fao-hq@fao.org, https://www.fao.org; AQUASTAT and The State of Food and Agriculture (SOFA) 2022.

CHRISTMAS ISLAND-AIRLINES

Palgrave Macmillan, 1 New York Plaza, Ste. 4500, New York, NY, 10004-1562, USA, (800) 777-4643, orders@palgrave.com, https://www.palgrave.com/us; The Statesman's Yearbook, 2023.

CHRISTMAS ISLAND-ARMED FORCES

Central Intelligence Agency (CIA), Office of Public Affairs, Washington, DC, 20505, USA, (703) 482-0623, https://www.cia.gov; The World Factbook.

Stockholm International Peace Research Institute (SIPRI), Signalistgatan 9, Stockholm, SE 169 72, SWE, https://www.sipri.org/; SIPRI Arms Transfers Database and SIPRI Military Expenditure Database.

CHRISTMAS ISLAND-BROADCASTING

Central Intelligence Agency (CIA), Office of Public Affairs, Washington, DC, 20505, USA, (703) 482-0623, https://www.cia.gov; The World Factbook.

WRTH Publications Limited, PO Box 290, Oxford, OX2 7FT, GBR, sales@wrth.com, https://www.wrth.com; World Radio TV Handbook 2023.

CHRISTMAS ISLAND-BUDGET

Central Intelligence Agency (CIA), Office of Public Affairs, Washington, DC, 20505, USA, (703) 482-0623, https://www.cia.gov; The World Factbook.

CHRISTMAS ISLAND-CLIMATE

Palgrave Macmillan, 1 New York Plaza, Ste. 4500, New York, NY, 10004-1562, USA, (800) 777-4643, orders@palgrave.com, https://www.palgrave.com/us; The Statesman's Yearbook, 2023.

CHRISTMAS ISLAND-CORN INDUSTRY

See CHRISTMAS ISLAND-CROPS

CHRISTMAS ISLAND-CROPS

United Nations Food and Agricultural Organization (FAO), 2121 K St., Ste. 800B, Washington, DC, 20037, USA, (202) 653-2400 (Dial from U.S.), (202) 653-5760 (Fax from U.S.), fao-hq@fao.org, https://www.fao.org; The State of Food and Agriculture (SOFA) 2022.

CHRISTMAS ISLAND-DAIRY PROCESSING

United Nations Food and Agricultural Organization (FAO), 2121 K St., Ste. 800B, Washington, DC, 20037, USA, (202) 653-2400 (Dial from U.S.), (202) 653-5760 (Fax from U.S.), fao-hq@fao.org, https://www.fao.org; The State of Food and Agriculture (SOFA) 2022.

CHRISTMAS ISLAND-ECONOMIC CONDITIONS

Bernan Press, 15250 NBN Way, Bldg. C, Blue Ridge Summit, PA, 17214, USA, (301) 459-2255, (800) 865-3457, (800) 865-3450, customercare@bernan.com, https://rowman.com/Page/Bernan; World Economic Outlook, April 2022.

Central Intelligence Agency (CIA), Office of Public Affairs, Washington, DC, 20505, USA, (703) 482-0623, https://www.cia.gov; The World Factbook.

CHRISTMAS ISLAND-EDUCATION

Palgrave Macmillan, 1 New York Plaza, Ste. 4500, New York, NY, 10004-1562, USA, (800) 777-4643, orders@palgrave.com, https://www.palgrave.com/us; The Statesman's Yearbook, 2023.

CHRISTMAS ISLAND-EXPORTS

Central Intelligence Agency (CIA), Office of Public Affairs, Washington, DC, 20505, USA, (703) 482-0623, https://www.cia.gov; The World Factbook.

CHRISTMAS ISLAND-FERTILITY, HUMAN

Central Intelligence Agency (CIA), Office of Public Affairs, Washington, DC, 20505, USA, (703) 482-0623, https://www.cia.gov; The World Factbook.

CHRISTMAS ISLAND-FERTILIZER INDUSTRY

United Nations Food and Agricultural Organization (FAO), 2121 K St., Ste. 800B, Washington, DC, 20037, USA, (202) 653-2400 (Dial from U.S.), (202) 653-5760 (Fax from U.S.), fao-hq@fao.org, https://www.fao.org; The State of Food and Agriculture (SOFA) 2022.

CHRISTMAS ISLAND-FETAL MORTALITY

See CHRISTMAS ISLAND-MORTALITY

CHRISTMAS ISLAND-FINANCE, PUBLIC

Routledge - Taylor & Francis Group, 6000 Broken Sound Pkwy. NW, Ste. 300, Boca Raton, FL, 33487, USA, (800) 634-1420, (800) 634-7064, orders@taylorandfrancis.com, https://www.routledge.com/; The Europa World Year Book 2022.

United Nations Statistics Division (UNSD), United Nations Plz., New York, NY, 10017, USA, (800) 253-9646, (212) 963-9851, statistics@un.org, https://unstats.un.org; National Accounts Main Aggregates Database and National Accounts Statistics: Main Aggregates and Detailed Tables.

CHRISTMAS ISLAND-FISHERIES

United Nations Food and Agricultural Organization (FAO), 2121 K St., Ste. 800B, Washington, DC, 20037, USA, (202) 653-2400 (Dial from U.S.), (202) 653-5760 (Fax from U.S.), fao-hq@fao.org, https://www.fao.org; FAO Yearbook of Fishery and Aquaculture Statistics 2019; Fishery Statistical Collections Global Capture Production; FishStatJ; and The State of Food and Agriculture (SOFA) 2022.

CHRISTMAS ISLAND-FOOD

United Nations Food and Agricultural Organization (FAO), 2121 K St., Ste. 800B, Washington, DC, 20037, USA, (202) 653-2400 (Dial from U.S.), (202) 653-5760 (Fax from U.S.), fao-hq@fao.org, https://www.fao.org; The State of Food and Agriculture (SOFA) 2022.

CHRISTMAS ISLAND-FORESTS AND FORESTRY

United Nations Food and Agricultural Organization (FAO), 2121 K St., Ste. 800B, Washington, DC, 20037, USA, (202) 653-2400 (Dial from U.S.), (202) 653-5760 (Fax from U.S.), fao-hq@fao.org, https://www.fao.org; The State of Food and Agriculture (SOFA) 2022.

CHRISTMAS ISLAND-IMPORTS

Central Intelligence Agency (CIA), Office of Public Affairs, Washington, DC, 20505, USA, (703) 482-0623, https://www.cia.gov; The World Factbook.

CHRISTMAS ISLAND-INDUSTRIES

Central Intelligence Agency (CIA), Office of Public Affairs, Washington, DC, 20505, USA, (703) 482-0623, https://www.cia.gov; The World Factbook.

Palgrave Macmillan, 1 New York Plaza, Ste. 4500, New York, NY, 10004-1562, USA, (800) 777-4643, orders@palgrave.com, https://www.palgrave.com/us; The Statesman's Yearbook, 2023.

CHRISTMAS ISLAND-INTERNATIONAL TRADE

Routledge - Taylor & Francis Group, 6000 Broken Sound Pkwy. NW, Ste. 300, Boca Raton, FL, 33487, USA, (800) 634-1420, (800) 634-7064, orders@taylorandfrancis.com, https://www.routledge.com/; The Europa World Year Book 2022.

United Nations Conference on Trade and Development (UNCTAD), Palais des Nations, Geneva, 1211, SWI, (212) 963-6896, unctadinfo@unctad.org, https://unctad.org; Trade and Development Report 2021.

United Nations Food and Agricultural Organization (FAO), 2121 K St., Ste. 800B, Washington, DC, 20037, USA, (202) 653-2400 (Dial from U.S.), (202) 653-5760 (Fax from U.S.), fao-hq@fao.org, https://www.fao.org; The State of Food and Agriculture (SOFA) 2022.

World Trade Organization (WTO), Ctre. William Rappard, Rue de Lausanne 154, Case postale, Geneva, CH-1211, SWI, enquiries@wto.org, https://www.wto.org; World Trade Statistical Review 2022.

CHRISTMAS ISLAND-LABOR

Central Intelligence Agency (CIA), Office of Public Affairs, Washington, DC, 20505, USA, (703) 482-0623, https://www.cia.gov; The World Factbook.

United Nations Food and Agricultural Organization (FAO), 2121 K St., Ste. 800B, Washington, DC, 20037, USA, (202) 653-2400 (Dial from U.S.), (202) 653-5760 (Fax from U.S.), fao-hq@fao.org, https://www.fao.org; The State of Food and Agriculture (SOFA) 2022.

CHRISTMAS ISLAND-LIFE EXPECTANCY

Central Intelligence Agency (CIA), Office of Public Affairs, Washington, DC, 20505, USA, (703) 482-0623, https://www.cia.gov; The World Factbook.

United Nations Department of Economic and Social Affairs (DESA), Population Division, 2 United Nations Plz., Rm. DC2-1950, New York, NY, 10017, USA, (212) 963-3209, (212) 963-2147, population@un.org, https://www.un.org/development/desa/pd/; World Population Ageing 2020 Highlights.

CHRISTMAS ISLAND-LIVESTOCK

United Nations Food and Agricultural Organization (FAO), 2121 K St., Ste. 800B, Washington, DC, 20037, USA, (202) 653-2400 (Dial from U.S.), (202) 653-5760 (Fax from U.S.), fao-hq@fao.org, https://www.fao.org; The State of Food and Agriculture (SOFA) 2022.

CHRISTMAS ISLAND-MARRIAGE

United Nations Statistics Division (UNSD), United Nations Plz., New York, NY, 10017, USA, (800) 253-9646, (212) 963-9851, statistics@un.org, https://unstats.un.org; Statistical Yearbook of the United Nations 2021.

CHRISTMAS ISLAND-MINERAL INDUSTRIES

Palgrave Macmillan, 1 New York Plaza, Ste. 4500, New York, NY, 10004-1562, USA, (800) 777-4643, orders@palgrave.com, https://www.palgrave.com/us; The Statesman's Yearbook, 2023.

Routledge - Taylor & Francis Group, 6000 Broken Sound Pkwy. NW, Ste. 300, Boca Raton, FL, 33487, USA, (800) 634-1420, (800) 634-7064, orders@taylorandfrancis.com, https://www.routledge.com/; The Europa World Year Book 2022.

United Nations Conference on Trade and Development (UNCTAD), Palais des Nations, Geneva, 1211, SWI, (212) 963-6896, unctadinfo@unctad.org, https://unctad.org; Trade and Development Report 2021.

CHRISTMAS ISLAND-MORTALITY

United Nations Statistics Division (UNSD), United Nations Plz., New York, NY, 10017, USA, (800) 253-9646, (212) 963-9851, statistics@un.org, https://unstats.un.org; Statistical Yearbook of the United Nations 2021.

CHRISTMAS ISLAND-NUTRITION

United Nations Food and Agricultural Organization (FAO), 2121 K St., Ste. 800B, Washington, DC, 20037, USA, (202) 653-2400 (Dial from U.S.), (202) 653-5760 (Fax from U.S.), fao-hq@fao.org, https://www.fao.org; The State of Food and Agriculture (SOFA) 2022.

CHRISTMAS ISLAND-PESTICIDES

United Nations Food and Agricultural Organization (FAO), 2121 K St., Ste. 800B, Washington, DC, 20037, USA, (202) 653-2400 (Dial from U.S.), (202) 653-5760 (Fax from U.S.), fao-hq@fao.org, https://www.fao.org; The State of Food and Agriculture (SOFA) 2022.

CHRISTMAS ISLAND-PETROLEUM INDUSTRY AND TRADE

United Nations Food and Agricultural Organization (FAO), 2121 K St., Ste. 800B, Washington, DC, 20037, USA, (202) 653-2400 (Dial from U.S.), (202) 653-5760 (Fax from U.S.), fao-hq@fao.org, https://www.fao.org; The State of Food and Agriculture (SOFA) 2022.

CHRISTMAS ISLAND-POPULATION

Central Intelligence Agency (CIA), Office of Public Affairs, Washington, DC, 20505, USA, (703) 482-0623, https://www.cia.gov; The World Factbook.

Palgrave Macmillan, 1 New York Plaza, Ste. 4500, New York, NY, 10004-1562, USA, (800) 777-4643, orders@palgrave.com, https://www.palgrave.com/us; The Statesman's Yearbook, 2023.

Routledge - Taylor & Francis Group, 6000 Broken Sound Pkwy. NW, Ste. 300, Boca Raton, FL, 33487, USA, (800) 634-1420, (800) 634-7064, orders@taylorandfrancis.com, https://www.routledge.com/; The Europa World Year Book 2022.

UK Data Service, University of Essex, Wivenhoe Park, Colchester, Essex, CO4 3SQ, GBR, https://ukdataservice.ac.uk/; International Aggregate Data.

UNESCO Institute for Statistics, C.P 250 Succursale H, Montreal, QC, H3G 2K8, CAN, (514) 343-6880 (Dial from U.S.), (514) 343-5740 (Fax from U.S.), uis.publications@unesco.org, http://uis.unesco.org/; UIS.Stat.

United Nations Department of Economic and Social Affairs (DESA), Population Division, 2 United Nations Plz., Rm. DC2-1950, New York, NY, 10017, USA, (212) 963-3209, (212) 963-2147, population@un.org, https://www.un.org/development/desa/pd/; Revision of World Urbanization Prospects and World Population Ageing 2020 Highlights.

United Nations Statistics Division (UNSD), United Nations Plz., New York, NY, 10017, USA, (800) 253-9646, (212) 963-9851, statistics@un.org, https://unstats.un.org; Statistical Yearbook of the United Nations 2021.

CHRISTMAS ISLAND-POPULATION DENSITY

Central Intelligence Agency (CIA), Office of Public Affairs, Washington, DC, 20505, USA, (703) 482-0623, https://www.cia.gov; The World Factbook.

Routledge - Taylor & Francis Group, 6000 Broken Sound Pkwy. NW, Ste. 300, Boca Raton, FL, 33487, USA, (800) 634-1420, (800) 634-7064, orders@taylorandfrancis.com, https://www.routledge.com/; The Europa World Year Book 2022.

UNESCO Institute for Statistics, C.P 250 Succursale H, Montreal, QC, H3G 2K8, CAN, (514) 343-6880 (Dial from U.S.), (514) 343-5740 (Fax from U.S.), uis.publications@unesco.org, http://uis.unesco.org/; UIS.Stat.

CHRISTMAS ISLAND-POWER RESOURCES

United Nations Food and Agricultural Organization (FAO), 2121 K St., Ste. 800B, Washington, DC, 20037, USA, (202) 653-2400 (Dial from U.S.), (202) 653-5760 (Fax from U.S.), fao-hq@fao.org, https://www.fao.org; The State of Food and Agriculture (SOFA) 2022.

United Nations Statistics Division (UNSD), United Nations Plz., New York, NY, 10017, USA, (800) 253-9646, (212) 963-9851, statistics@un.org, https://unstats.un.org; Statistical Yearbook of the United Nations 2021.

CHRISTMAS ISLAND-PUBLIC HEALTH

Palgrave Macmillan, 1 New York Plaza, Ste. 4500, New York, NY, 10004-1562, USA, (800) 777-4643, orders@palgrave.com, https://www.palgrave.com/us; The Statesman's Yearbook, 2023.

U.S. Census Bureau, 4600 Silver Hill Rd., Washington, DC, 20233, USA, (301) 763-4636, (800) 923-8282, https://www.census.gov; HIV/AIDS Surveillance Data Base.

United Nations Department of Economic and Social Affairs (DESA), Population Division, 2 United Nations Plz., Rm. DC2-1950, New York, NY, 10017, USA, (212) 963-3209, (212) 963-2147, population@un.org, https://www.un.org/development/desa/pd/; World Fertility Data 2019.

CHRISTMAS ISLAND-RELIGION

Central Intelligence Agency (CIA), Office of Public Affairs, Washington, DC, 20505, USA, (703) 482-0623, https://www.cia.gov; The World Factbook.

Palgrave Macmillan, 1 New York Plaza, Ste. 4500, New York, NY, 10004-1562, USA, (800) 777-4643, orders@palgrave.com, https://www.palgrave.com/us; The Statesman's Yearbook, 2023.

CHRISTMAS ISLAND-SHIPPING

Routledge - Taylor & Francis Group, 6000 Broken Sound Pkwy. NW, Ste. 300, Boca Raton, FL, 33487, USA, (800) 634-1420, (800) 634-7064, orders@taylorandfrancis.com, https://www.routledge.com/; The Europa World Year Book 2022.

United Nations Statistics Division (UNSD), United Nations Plz., New York, NY, 10017, USA, (800) 253-9646, (212) 963-9851, statistics@un.org, https://unstats.un.org; Statistical Yearbook of the United Nations 2021.

CHRISTMAS ISLAND-TOURISM

Palgrave Macmillan, 1 New York Plaza, Ste. 4500, New York, NY, 10004-1562, USA, (800) 777-4643, orders@palgrave.com, https://www.palgrave.com/us; The Statesman's Yearbook, 2023.

CHRISTMAS ISLAND-TRADE

See CHRISTMAS ISLAND-INTERNATIONAL TRADE

CHRISTMAS ISLAND-TRANSPORTATION

Central Intelligence Agency (CIA), Office of Public Affairs, Washington, DC, 20505, USA, (703) 482-0623, https://www.cia.gov; The World Factbook.

Palgrave Macmillan, 1 New York Plaza, Ste. 4500, New York, NY, 10004-1562, USA, (800) 777-4643, orders@palgrave.com, https://www.palgrave.com/us; The Statesman's Yearbook, 2023.

Routledge - Taylor & Francis Group, 6000 Broken Sound Pkwy. NW, Ste. 300, Boca Raton, FL, 33487, USA, (800) 634-1420, (800) 634-7064, orders@taylorandfrancis.com, https://www.routledge.com/; The Europa World Year Book 2022.

CHRISTMAS ISLAND-VITAL STATISTICS

U.S. Census Bureau, 4600 Silver Hill Rd., Washington, DC, 20233, USA, (301) 763-4636, (800) 923-8282, https://www.census.gov; HIV/AIDS Surveillance Data Base.

United Nations Department of Economic and Social Affairs (DESA), Population Division, 2 United Nations Plz., Rm. DC2-1950, New York, NY, 10017, USA, (212) 963-3209, (212) 963-2147, population@un.org, https://www.un.org/development/desa/pd/; World Contraceptive Use 2021: Estimates and Projections of Family Planning Indicators and World Marriage Data 2019.

United Nations Statistics Division (UNSD), United Nations Plz., New York, NY, 10017, USA, (800) 253-9646, (212) 963-9851, statistics@un.org, https://unstats.un.org; Statistical Yearbook of the United Nations 2021.

CHROMITE

U.S. Department of the Interior (DOI), U.S. Geological Survey (USGS), National Minerals Information Center (NMIC), 12201 Sunrise Valley Dr., Reston, VA, 20192, USA, (703) 648-4920, (703) 648-7971, (703) 648-4995, sfortier@usgs.gov, https://www.usgs.gov/centers/nmic; Mineral Commodity Summaries 2022 and Minerals Yearbook.

CHROMIUM

U.S. Census Bureau, International Trade Program, 4600 Silver Hill Rd., Washington, DC, 20233, USA, (800) 549-0595, eid.international.trade.data@census.gov, https://www.census.gov/foreign-trade; International Trade Data.

U.S. Department of the Interior (DOI), U.S. Geological Survey (USGS), National Minerals Information Center (NMIC), 12201 Sunrise Valley Dr., Reston, VA, 20192, USA, (703) 648-4920, (703) 648-7971, (703) 648-4995, sfortier@usgs.gov, https://www.usgs.gov/centers/nmic; Mineral Commodity Summaries 2022 and Mineral Industry Surveys (MIS).

CHRONIC DISEASES

Australian Institute of Health and Welfare (AIHW), GPO Box 570, Canberra, ACT, 2601, AUS, info@aihw.gov.au, https://www.aihw.gov.au/; Heart, Stroke and Vascular Disease: Australian Facts.

National Foundation for Infectious Diseases (NFID), 1629 K St. NW, Ste. 300, Washington, DC, 20006, USA, (301) 656-0003, https://www.nfid.org/; 2021 Chronic Health Conditions Surveys: Gaps between Healthcare Professionals and Adult Patients.

SAGE Publications, 2455 Teller Rd., Thousand Oaks, CA, 91320, USA, (800) 818-7243, (800) 583-2665, journals@sagepub.com, https://www.sagepub.com; American Journal of Alzheimer's Disease and Other Dementias.

U.S. Department of Health and Human Services (HHS), National Institutes of Health (NIH), National Center for Advancing Translational Sciences (NCATS), Genetic and Rare Diseases Information Center (GARD), PO Box 8126, Gaithersburg, MD, 20898-8126, USA, (888) 205-2311, info@ncats.nih.gov, https://rarediseases.info.nih.gov/; Genetic and Rare Diseases Information Center (GARD).

U.S. Department of Health and Human Services (HHS), National Institutes of Health (NIH), Researching COVID to Enhance Recovery (RECOVER), 9000 Rockville Pike, Bethesda, MD, 20892, USA, (301) 496-4000, (301) 402-9612 (TTY), https://recovercovid.org; Can Multisystem Inflammatory Syndrome in Children Be Managed in the Outpatient Setting? An EHR-Based Cohort Study From the RECOVER Program; Development of a Definition of Postacute Sequelae of SARS-CoV-2 Infection; Racial/Ethnic Disparities in Post-Acute Sequelae of SARS-CoV-2 Infection in New York: An EHR-Based Cohort Study from the RECOVER Program; and Risk of Post-Acute Sequelae of SARS-CoV-2 Infection Associated with Pre-Coronavirus Disease Obstructive Sleep Apnea Diagnoses: An Electronic Health Record-Based Analysis from the RECOVER Initiative.

U.S. Department of Health and Human Services, Centers for Disease Control and Prevention (CDC), 1600 Clifton Rd., Atlanta, GA, 30329-4027, USA, (800) 232-4636, (888) 232-6348 (TTY), cdcinfo@cdc.gov, https://www.cdc.gov; Chronic Disease Indicators; Emerging Infectious Diseases; Health-Related Quality of Life (HRQOL); and Preventing Chronic Disease: Public Health Research, Practice, and Policy.

U.S. Department of Health and Human Services, Centers for Disease Control and Prevention (CDC), National Center for Chronic Disease Prevention and Health Promotion (NCCDPHP), 1600 Clifton Rd., Atlanta, GA, 30329, USA, (800) 232-4636, (888) 232-6348 (TTY), https://www.cdc.gov/chronicdisease/; Leading Indicators for Chronic Diseases and Risk Factors Open Data Portal.

University of Washington, Institute for Health Metrics and Evaluation (IHME), Population Health Building/Hans Rosling Center, UW Campus Box 351615, 3980 15th Ave. NE, Seattle, WA, 98195, USA, (206) 897-2800, (206) 897-2899, engage@healthdata.org, https://www.healthdata.org; Estimated Global Proportions of Individuals With Persistent Fatigue, Cognitive, and Respiratory Symptom Clusters Following Symptomatic COVID-19 in 2020 and 2021.

World Health Organization (WHO), Ave. Appia 20, Geneva, CH-1211, SWI, (202) 974-3000 (Telephone in U.S.), publications@who.int, https://www.who.int/; Noncommunicable Diseases Progress Monitor 2022 and WHO Report on the Global Tobacco Epidemic 2021.

CHURCH ATTENDANCE

See also PUBLIC WORSHIP

Hartford Seminary, Hartford Institute for Religion Research, 77 Sherman St., Hartford, CT, 06105-2260, USA, (860) 509-9542, hirr@hartsem.edu, http://hirr.hartsem.edu/; Database of Megachurches in the U.S..

CHURCH BUILDINGS

Bureau of Alcohol, Tobacco, Firearms and Explosives (ATF), United States Bomb Data Center (USBDC), 3750 Corporal Rd., Huntsville, AL, 35898 , USA, (800) 461-8841, usbdc@atf.gov, https://www.atf.gov/explosives/us-bomb-data-center; 2019 House of Worship Incidents in the United States.

Hartford Seminary, Hartford Institute for Religion Research, 77 Sherman St., Hartford, CT, 06105-2260, USA, (860) 509-9542, hirr@hartsem.edu, http://hirr.hartsem.edu/; Research on Orthodox Christian Communities in the United States.

U.S. Department of Justice (DOJ), Federal Bureau of Investigation (FBI), 935 Pennsylvania Ave. NW, Washington, DC, 20535-0001, USA, (202) 324-3000, https://www.fbi.gov/; Active Shooter Incidents in the United States in 2021.

CHURCH BUILDINGS-CONSTRUCTION VALUE

Dodge Construction Network, 300 American Metro Blvd., Ste. 185, Hamilton, NJ, 08619, USA, (877) 784-9556, support@construction.com, https://www.construction.com/; Mid-Year 2023 Construction Outlook.

CIGAR USAGE

Substance Abuse and Mental Health Services Administration (SAMHSA), 5600 Fishers Ln., Rockville, MD, 20857, USA, (877) 726-4727, (800) 487-4889 (TTY), samhsainfo@samhsa.hhs.gov, https://www.samhsa.gov/; 2019-2020 National Survey on Drug Use and Health (NSDUH).

CIGARETTES

See also TOBACCO INDUSTRY

CIGARETTES-ADVERTISING

Magazine Publishers of America (MPA) - The Association of Magazine Media, 1211 Connecticut Ave. NW, Ste. 610, Washington, DC, 20036, USA, (202) 296-7277, mpa@magazine.org, https://www.magazine.org/; Magazine Media Factbook 2021.

CIGARETTES-INTERNATIONAL TRADE

U.S. Census Bureau, International Trade Program, 4600 Silver Hill Rd., Washington, DC, 20233, USA, (800) 549-0595, eid.international.trade.data@census.gov, https://www.census.gov/foreign-trade; International Trade Data.

CIGARETTES-SMOKERS AND USE

American Lung Association, 55 W Wacker Dr., Ste. 1150, Chicago, IL, 60601, USA, (800) 586-4872, info@lung.org, https://www.lung.org/; State of Tobacco Control Report 2022 and Tobacco Cessation Coverage: Factsheets and Reports.

Substance Abuse and Mental Health Services Administration (SAMHSA), 5600 Fishers Ln., Rockville, MD, 20857, USA, (877) 726-4727, (800) 487-4889 (TTY), samhsainfo@samhsa.hhs.gov, https://www.samhsa.gov/; 2019-2020 National Survey on Drug Use and Health (NSDUH).

Truth Initiative, 900 G St. NW, 4th Fl., Washington, DC, 20001, USA, (202) 454-5555, https://truthinitiative.org; Local Restrictions on Flavored Tobacco and E-cigarette Products.

U.S. Department of Health and Human Services (HHS), National Institutes of Health (NIH), National Institute on Drug Abuse (NIDA), Office of Science Policy and Communications, 3WFN MSC 6024, 16071 Industrial Dr - Dock 11, Bethesda, MD, 20892, USA, (301) 443-6441, https://www.drugabuse.gov/; Vaping Devices (Electronic Cigarettes) DrugFacts.

U.S. Department of Health and Human Services, Centers for Disease Control and Prevention (CDC), 1600 Clifton Rd., Atlanta, GA, 30329-4027, USA, (800) 232-4636, (888) 232-6348 (TTY), cdcinfo@cdc.gov, https://www.cdc.gov; Morbidity and Mortality Weekly Report (MMWR); National Youth Tobacco Survey (NYTS); and State Tobacco Activities Tracking and Evaluation (STATE) System.

U.S. Department of Health and Human Services, Centers for Disease Control and Prevention (CDC), National Center for Health Statistics (NCHS), 3311 Toledo Rd., Hyattsville, MD, 20782-2064, USA, (800) 232-4636, (301) 458-4000, https://www.cdc.gov/nchs; Health, United States, 2020-2021.

CIRCUMCISION

University of Washington, Institute for Health Metrics and Evaluation (IHME), Population Health Building/Hans Rosling Center, UW Campus Box 351615, 3980 15th Ave. NE, Seattle, WA, 98195, USA, (206) 897-2800, (206) 897-2899, engage@healthdata.org, https://www.healthdata.org; Mapping Male Circumcision for HIV Prevention Efforts in Sub-Saharan Africa.

CIRRHOSIS OF THE LIVER

U.S. Department of Health and Human Services (HHS), National Institutes of Health (NIH), National Institute on Alcohol Abuse and Alcoholism (NIAAA), 9000 Rockville Pike, Bethesda, MD, 20892, USA, (888) 696-4222, (301) 443-3860, askniaaa@nih.gov, https://www.niaaa.nih.gov/; Surveillance Reports.

U.S. Department of Health and Human Services, Centers for Disease Control and Prevention (CDC), National Center for Health Statistics (NCHS), 3311 Toledo Rd., Hyattsville, MD, 20782-2064, USA, (800) 232-4636, (301) 458-4000, https://www.cdc.gov/nchs; FastStats - Statistics by Topic.

CIRRHOSIS OF THE LIVER-DEATHS

Bernan Press, 15250 NBN Way, Bldg. C, Blue Ridge Summit, PA, 17214, USA, (301) 459-2255, (800) 865-3457, (800) 865-3450, customercare@bernan.com, https://rowman.com/Page/Bernan; Vital Statistics of the United States 2022: Births, Life Expectancy, Deaths, and Selected Health Data.

U.S. Department of Health and Human Services, Centers for Disease Control and Prevention (CDC), National Center for Health Statistics (NCHS), 3311 Toledo Rd., Hyattsville, MD, 20782-2064, USA, (800) 232-4636, (301) 458-4000, https://www.cdc.gov/nchs; National Vital Statistics Reports (NVSR) and Vital Statistics Online Data Portal.

CITIES

The Annie E. Casey Foundation, 701 Saint Paul St., Baltimore, MD, 21202, USA, (410) 547-6600, (410) 547-6624, https://www.aecf.org/; KIDS COUNT Database.

Bernan Press, 15250 NBN Way, Bldg. C, Blue Ridge Summit, PA, 17214, USA, (301) 459-2255, (800) 865-3457, (800) 865-3450, customercare@bernan.com, https://rowman.com/Page/Bernan; Places, Towns and Townships 2021.

CDP, 60 Great Tower St., 4th Fl., London, EC3R 5AZ, GBR, https://www.cdp.net; CDP Cities, States and Regions Open Data Portal.

Infoplease, c/o Sandbox Networks, Inc., 1 Lincoln St., 24th Fl., Boston, MA, 02111, USA, https://www.infoplease.com; Compendium of U.S. Statistics and The 50 States of America: U.S. State Information.

National Highway Traffic Safety Administration (NHTSA), National Center for Statistics and Analysis (NCSA), 1200 New Jersey Ave. SE, West Bldg., Washington, DC, 20590, USA, (800) 934-8517, (202) 366-2746, ncsarequests@dot.gov, https://www.nhtsa.gov/research-data/national-center-statistics-and-analysis-ncsa; Traffic Safety Facts, 2019 Data - Rural/Urban Comparison of Traffic Fatalities.

SAGE Publications, 2455 Teller Rd., Thousand Oaks, CA, 91320, USA, (800) 818-7243, (800) 583-2665, journals@sagepub.com, https://www.sagepub.com; Environment and Urbanization.

U.S. Department of Energy (DOE), Office of Energy Efficiency and Renewable Energy (EERE), Alternative Fuels Data Center (AFDC), Mail Stop EE-1, Washington, DC, 20585, USA, (202) 586-5000, https://www.afdc.energy.gov/; Clean Cities.

U.S. National Archives and Records Administration, 8601 Adelphi Rd., College Park, MD, 20740-6001, USA, (866) 272-6272, (301) 837-0483, https://www.archives.gov; Access to Archival Databases (AAD).

CITIES-AMERICAN INDIAN POPULATION

U.S. Census Bureau, 4600 Silver Hill Rd., Washington, DC, 20233, USA, (301) 763-4636, (800) 923-8282, https://www.census.gov; Explore Census Data and United States QuickFacts.

CITIES-ASIAN POPULATION

U.S. Census Bureau, 4600 Silver Hill Rd., Washington, DC, 20233, USA, (301) 763-4636, (800) 923-8282, https://www.census.gov; Explore Census Data and United States QuickFacts.

CITIES-BLACK POPULATION

U.S. Census Bureau, 4600 Silver Hill Rd., Washington, DC, 20233, USA, (301) 763-4636, (800) 923-8282, https://www.census.gov; Explore Census Data and United States QuickFacts.

CITIES-CLIMATE

CDP, 60 Great Tower St., 4th Fl., London, EC3R 5AZ, GBR, https://www.cdp.net; CDP Cities, States and Regions Open Data Portal.

National Oceanic and Atmospheric Administration (NOAA), National Centers for Environmental Information (NCEI), Federal Bldg., 151 Patton Ave., Asheville, NC, 28801-5001, USA, (828) 271-4800, (828) 271-4010 (TTY), (828) 271-4876, ncei.info@noaa.gov, https://www.ncei.noaa.gov/; Climatological Data Publications and Comparative Climatic Data (CCD).

World Meteorological Organization (WMO), 7bis, ave. de la Paix, PO Box 2300, Geneva, CH-1211, SWI, wmo@wmo.int, https://public.wmo.int/en; WMO Bulletin.

World Resources Institute (WRI), 10 G St. NE, Ste. 800, Washington, DC, 20002, USA, (202) 729-7600, (202) 280-1314, https://www.wri.org/; World Resources Report: Towards a More Equal City.

CITIES-CLIMATE-FOREIGN COUNTRIES

University of Washington, Institute for Health Metrics and Evaluation (IHME), Population Health Building/Hans Rosling Center, UW Campus Box 351615, 3980 15th Ave. NE, Seattle, WA, 98195, USA, (206) 897-2800, (206) 897-2899, engage@healthdata.org, https://www.healthdata.org; Air Quality and Health in Cities.

CITIES-COMMUTING TO WORK

U.S. Census Bureau, 4600 Silver Hill Rd., Washington, DC, 20233, USA, (301) 763-4636, (800) 923-8282, https://www.census.gov; Explore Census Data and United States QuickFacts.

CITIES-CRIME

Bernan Press, 15250 NBN Way, Bldg. C, Blue Ridge Summit, PA, 17214, USA, (301) 459-2255, (800) 865-3457, (800) 865-3450, customercare@bernan.com, https://rowman.com/Page/Bernan; Crime in the United States 2022 and Justice Statistics: An Extended Look at Crime in the United States 2021.

California State University San Bernardino, Center for the Study of Hate and Extremism, 5500 University Pkwy., San Bernardino, CA, 92407, USA, (909) 537-7503, (909) 537-7711, blevin8@aol.com, https://csbs.csusb.edu/hate-and-extremism-center; Report to the Nation: Factbook on Hate and Extremism in the U.S. and Internationally and Report to the Nation: Illustrated Almanac.

Major Cities Chiefs Association (MCCA), PO Box 71690, Salt Lake City, UT, 84171, USA, (801) 209-1815, patricia@majorcitieschiefs.com, https://majorcitieschiefs.com/; MCCA Report on the 2020 Protest and Civil Unrest.

U.S. Department of Justice (DOJ), Federal Bureau of Investigation (FBI), 935 Pennsylvania Ave. NW, Washington, DC, 20535-0001, USA, (202) 324-3000, https://www.fbi.gov/; Crime in the United States 2019.

University of California Davis, Violence Prevention Research Program (VPRP), 2315 Stockton Blvd., Sacramento, CA, 95817, USA, (916) 734-3539 , hs-vprp@ucdavis.edu, https://health.ucdavis.edu/vprp/; Physical Distancing, Violence, and Crime in US Cities during the Coronavirus Pandemic.

The Urban Institute, Greater D.C. (Urban-Greater D.C), 500 L'Enfant Plaza SW, Washington, DC, 20024, USA, (202) 833-7200, https://greaterdc.urban.org/; Strengthening Nonpolice Safety Infrastructure in DC.

Wayne State University, Center for Urban Studies (CUS), 5700 Cass, 2207 A/AB, Detroit, MI, 48202, USA, (313) 577-2208, (313) 577-1274, cusinfo@wayne.edu, http://www.cus.wayne.edu/; unpublished data.

CITIES-DEBT

U.S. Census Bureau, Public Sector, 4600 Silver Hill Rd., Washington, DC, 20233, USA, (800) 923-8282, (301) 763-4636, ewd.outreach@census.gov, https://www.census.gov/topics/public-sector.html; Annual Survey of State and Local Government Finances.

CITIES-DISABILITY POPULATION

U.S. Census Bureau, 4600 Silver Hill Rd., Washington, DC, 20233, USA, (301) 763-4636, (800) 923-8282, https://www.census.gov; Explore Census Data and United States QuickFacts.

CITIES-DRUG USE

U.S. Department of Justice (DOJ), National Institute of Justice (NIJ), 810 7th St. NW, Washington, DC, 20531, USA, (202) 307-2942, (800) 851-3420, https://www.nij.gov/; 2021 Annual Report to Congress.

CITIES-ECONOMIC INDICATORS

The Brookings Institution, 1775 Massachusetts Ave. NW, Washington, DC, 20036, USA, (202) 797-6000, communications@brookings.edu, https://www.brookings.edu/; Metro Monitor 2023 and Metro Recovery Index.

CDP, 60 Great Tower St., 4th Fl., London, EC3R 5AZ, GBR, https://www.cdp.net; CDP Cities, States and Regions Open Data Portal.

The Economist Group: Economist Intelligence Unit (EIU), 900 3rd Ave., 16th Fl., New York, NY, 10022, USA, (212) 541-0500, americas@eiu.com, https://www.eiu.com; China's Emerging Cities 2021: Southeast China Takes the Lead.

PeoplePerHour, London, GBR, https://www.peopleperhour.com/; Start-up Cities: The World's Best 25 Cities to Start a Business.

United Nations Human Settlements Programme (UN-HABITAT), PO Box 30030, Nairobi, 00100, KEN, unhabitat-info@un.org, https://unhabitat.org/; Cities and Pandemics: Towards a More Just, Green and Healthy Future.

Wayne State University, Center for Urban Studies (CUS), 5700 Cass, 2207 A/AB, Detroit, MI, 48202, USA, (313) 577-2208, (313) 577-1274, cusinfo@wayne.edu, http://www.cus.wayne.edu/; unpublished data.

CITIES-EMPLOYEES, EARNINGS, PAYROLLS

The Annie E. Casey Foundation, 701 Saint Paul St., Baltimore, MD, 21202, USA, (410) 547-6600, (410) 547-6624, https://www.aecf.org/; Working Hard for the Money: Trends in Women's Employment: 1970 to 2007.

U.S. Census Bureau, Public Sector, 4600 Silver Hill Rd., Washington, DC, 20233, USA, (800) 923-8282, (301) 763-4636, ewd.outreach@census.gov, https://www.census.gov/topics/public-sector.html; Annual Survey of Public Employment & Payroll (ASPEP).

U.S. Department of Labor (DOL), Bureau of Labor Statistics (BLS), Postal Square Bldg., 2 Massachusetts Ave. NE, Washington, DC, 20212-0001, USA, (202) 691-5200, (202) 691-7890, blsdata_staff@bls.gov, https://www.bls.gov; Overview of BLS Wage Data by Area and Occupation.

CITIES-FINANCES OF CITY GOVERNMENTS

U.S. Census Bureau, Public Sector, 4600 Silver Hill Rd., Washington, DC, 20233, USA, (800) 923-8282, (301) 763-4636, ewd.outreach@census.gov, https://www.census.gov/topics/public-sector.html; Annual Survey of State and Local Government Finances.

CITIES-HAWAIIAN POPULATION

U.S. Census Bureau, 4600 Silver Hill Rd., Washington, DC, 20233, USA, (301) 763-4636, (800) 923-8282, https://www.census.gov; Explore Census Data and United States QuickFacts.

CITIES-HISPANIC ORIGIN POPULATION

U.S. Census Bureau, 4600 Silver Hill Rd., Washington, DC, 20233, USA, (301) 763-4636, (800) 923-8282, https://www.census.gov; Explore Census Data and United States QuickFacts.

CITIES-HOUSEHOLDS

U.S. Census Bureau, 4600 Silver Hill Rd., Washington, DC, 20233, USA, (301) 763-4636, (800) 923-8282, https://www.census.gov; Explore Census Data and United States QuickFacts.

United Nations Human Settlements Programme (UN-HABITAT), PO Box 30030, Nairobi, 00100, KEN, unhabitat-info@un.org, https://unhabitat.org/; Cities and Pandemics: Towards a More Just, Green and Healthy Future; The Future of Asian & Pacific Cities 2019; and World Cities Report 2022: Envisaging the Future of Cities.

CITIES-HOUSING

Harvard Joint Center for Housing Studies (JCHS), 1 Bow St., Ste. 400, Cambridge, MA, 02138, USA, (617) 495-7908, (617) 496-9957, jchs@harvard.edu, https://www.jchs.harvard.edu/; Improving America's Housing 2021.

Robert Charles Lesser & Co. (RCLCO), 7200 Wisconsin Ave., Ste. 1110, Bethesda, MD, 20814, USA, (240) 644-1300, (240) 644-1311, https://www.rclco.com/; Top-Selling Master-Planned Communities of 2021.

U.S. Census Bureau, 4600 Silver Hill Rd., Washington, DC, 20233, USA, (301) 763-4636, (800) 923-8282, https://www.census.gov; Explore Census Data and United States QuickFacts.

U.S. Department of Housing and Urban Development (HUD), Office of Policy Development and Research (PD&R), PO Box 23268, Washington, DC, 20026-3268, USA, (800) 245-2691, (800) 927-7589 (TDD), (202) 708-9981, helpdesk@huduser.gov, https://www.huduser.gov; HUD User.

The Urban Institute, Greater D.C. (Urban-Greater D.C), 500 L'Enfant Plaza SW, Washington, DC, 20024, USA, (202) 833-7200, https://greaterdc.urban.org/; DC Flexible Rent Subsidy Program: Findings from the Program's First Year.

Urban Land Institute (ULI), 2001 L St. NW, Ste. 200, Washington, DC, 20036, USA, (202) 624-7000, (800) 321-5011, (202) 403-3849, customerservice@uli.org, https://uli.org/; ULI Case Studies and Urban Land Magazine.

CITIES-LANGUAGE SPOKEN AT HOME

U.S. Census Bureau, 4600 Silver Hill Rd., Washington, DC, 20233, USA, (301) 763-4636, (800) 923-8282, https://www.census.gov; Explore Census Data and United States QuickFacts.

CITIES-POPULATION

The Annie E. Casey Foundation, 701 Saint Paul St., Baltimore, MD, 21202, USA, (410) 547-6600, (410) 547-6624, https://www.aecf.org/; KIDS COUNT Database.

Bernan Press, 15250 NBN Way, Bldg. C, Blue Ridge Summit, PA, 17214, USA, (301) 459-2255, (800) 865-3457, (800) 865-3450, customercare@bernan.com, https://rowman.com/Page/Bernan; The Who, What, and Where of America: Understanding the American Community Survey.

The Brookings Institution, 1775 Massachusetts Ave. NW, Washington, DC, 20036, USA, (202) 797-6000, communications@brookings.edu, https://www.brookings.edu/; Metro Monitor 2023 and Metro Recovery Index.

Migration Policy Institute (MPI), 1275 K St. NW, Ste. 800, Washington, DC, 20005, USA, (202) 266-1940, (202) 266-1900, info@migrationpolicy.org, https://www.migrationpolicy.org/; International Migrant Population by Country of Destination, 1960-2020.

National Highway Traffic Safety Administration (NHTSA), National Center for Statistics and Analysis (NCSA), 1200 New Jersey Ave. SE, West Bldg., Washington, DC, 20590, USA, (800) 934-8517, (202) 366-2746, ncsarequests@dot.gov, https://www.nhtsa.gov/research-data/national-center-statistics-and-analysis-ncsa; Traffic Safety Facts, 2019 Data - Rural/Urban Comparison of Traffic Fatalities.

PeoplePerHour, London, GBR, https://www.peopleperhour.com/; Start-up Cities: The World's Best 25 Cities to Start a Business.

U.S. Census Bureau, 4600 Silver Hill Rd., Washington, DC, 20233, USA, (301) 763-4636, (800) 923-8282, https://www.census.gov; Explore Census Data and United States QuickFacts.

United Nations Human Settlements Programme (UN-HABITAT), PO Box 30030, Nairobi, 00100, KEN, unhabitat-info@un.org, https://unhabitat.org/; Cities and Pandemics: Towards a More Just, Green and Healthy Future.

The Urban Institute, Greater D.C. (Urban-Greater D.C), 500 L'Enfant Plaza SW, Washington, DC, 20024, USA, (202) 833-7200, https://greaterdc.urban.org/; Strengthening Nonpolice Safety Infrastructure in DC.

Wayne State University, Center for Urban Studies (CUS), 5700 Cass, 2207 A/AB, Detroit, MI, 48202, USA, (313) 577-2208, (313) 577-1274, cusinfo@wayne.edu, http://www.cus.wayne.edu/; unpublished data.

World Resources Institute (WRI), 10 G St. NE, Ste. 800, Washington, DC, 20002, USA, (202) 729-7600, (202) 280-1314, https://www.wri.org/; World Resources Report: Towards a More Equal City.

CITIES-POPULATION-RANKINGS AND RATINGS

Canadian Centre for Policy Alternatives (CCPA), 141 Laurier Ave. W, Ste. 1000, Ottawa, ON, K1P 5J3, CAN, (613) 563-1341 (Dial from U.S.), (844) 563-1341 (Dial from U.S.), (613) 233-1458 (Fax from U.S.), ccpa@policyalternatives.ca, https://www.policyalternatives.ca/; The Best and Worst Places to be a Woman in Canada 2019: The Gender Gap in Canada's 26 Biggest Cities.

U.S. Census Bureau, 4600 Silver Hill Rd., Washington, DC, 20233, USA, (301) 763-4636, (800) 923-8282, https://www.census.gov; Decennial Census of Population and Housing Data.

CITIES-PROPERTY TAX RATES

District of Columbia, Office of the Chief Financial Officer, 1350 Pennsylvania Ave. NW, Ste. 203, Washington, DC, 20004, USA, (202) 727-2476, (202) 727-1643, ocfo@dc.gov, https://cfo.dc.gov/; Tax Rates and Tax Burdens 2020: A Nationwide Comparison.

Nestpick Global Services, GmbH, Neue Schonhauser Strasse 3-5, Berlin, D-10178, GER, info@nestpick.com, https://www.nestpick.com; Best Cities for Startup Employees.

CITIES-PROPERTY TAX RATES-RANKINGS AND RATINGS

District of Columbia, Office of the Chief Financial Officer, 1350 Pennsylvania Ave. NW, Ste. 203, Washington, DC, 20004, USA, (202) 727-2476, (202) 727-1643, ocfo@dc.gov, https://cfo.dc.gov/; Tax Rates and Tax Burdens 2020: A Nationwide Comparison.

CITIES-TAXES PAID-BY FAMILY INCOME LEVEL

District of Columbia, Office of the Chief Financial Officer, 1350 Pennsylvania Ave. NW, Ste. 203, Washington, DC, 20004, USA, (202) 727-2476, (202) 727-1643, ocfo@dc.gov, https://cfo.dc.gov/; Tax Rates and Tax Burdens 2020: A Nationwide Comparison.

CITIZENSHIP

Civiqs, PO Box 70008, Oakland, CA, 94612, USA, (510) 394-5664, inquiries@civiqs.com, https://civiqs.com/; Should the United States Deport Immigrants Living Here Illegally, or Offer Them a Path to Citizenship?.

U.S. Citizenship and Immigration Services (USCIS), 2675 Prosperity Ave., MS 2480, Fairfax, VA, 20598, USA, (800) 375-5283, (800) 767-1833 (TTY), https://www.uscis.gov/; Naturalization Test Performance.

CITRUS FRUITS-CONSUMPTION

U.S. Department of Agriculture (USDA), Economic Research Service (ERS), 1400 Independence Ave. SW, Mail Stop 1800, Washington, DC, 20250-0002, USA, (202) 720-2791, https://www.ers.usda.gov/; Food Price Outlook.

CITRUS FRUITS-INTERNATIONAL TRADE

U.S. Department of Agriculture (USDA), Economic Research Service (ERS), 1400 Independence Ave. SW, Mail Stop 1800, Washington, DC, 20250-0002, USA, (202) 720-2791, https://www.ers.usda.gov/; Food Price Outlook and Fruit & Tree Nuts.

CITRUS FRUITS-PESTICIDES

U.S. Department of Agriculture (USDA), Foreign Agricultural Service (FAS), 1400 Independence Ave. SW, Mail Stop 1001, Washington, DC, 20250, USA, (202) 720-3935, https://www.fas.usda.gov/; Production, Supply and Distribution Online (PSD) Online.

CITRUS FRUITS-PRODUCTION

U.S. Department of Agriculture (USDA), Economic Research Service (ERS), 1400 Independence Ave. SW, Mail Stop 1800, Washington, DC, 20250-0002, USA, (202) 720-2791, https://www.ers.usda.gov/; Food Price Outlook and Fruit & Tree Nuts.

U.S. Department of Agriculture (USDA), National Agricultural Statistics Service (USDA-NASS), 1400 Independence Ave. SW, Washington, DC, 20250, USA, (800) 727-9540, nass@nass.usda.gov, https://www.nass.usda.gov; Citrus Fruits; Cold Storage; and Quick Stats.

CIVICS

American Academy of Arts & Sciences, 136 Irving St., Cambridge, MA, 02138, USA, (617) 576-5000, https://www.amacad.org/; Humanities Indicators.

National Conference on Citizenship (NCoC), 1920 L St. NW, Ste. 450, Washington, DC, 20036, USA, (202) 601-7096, ncocadmin@ncoc.org, https://ncoc.org/; Civic Health Index (CHI).

Tufts University, Tisch College of Civic Life, Center for Information and Research on Civic Learning and Engagement (CIRCLE), Barnum Hall, Medford, MA, 02155, USA, (617) 627-2593, circle@tufts.edu, https://circle.tufts.edu/; The Youth Vote in 2022.

U.S. Citizenship and Immigration Services (USCIS), 2675 Prosperity Ave., MS 2480, Fairfax, VA, 20598, USA, (800) 375-5283, (800) 767-1833 (TTY), https://www.uscis.gov/; Naturalization Test Performance.

U.S. Department of Education (ED), Institute of Education Sciences (IES), National Center for Education Statistics (NCES), Potomac Center Plaza, 550 12th St. SW, Washington, DC, 20202, USA, (202) 403-5551, https://nces.ed.gov/; Nation's Report Card: Civics 2022.

CIVIL AVIATION

See AERONAUTICS, COMMERCIAL

CIVIL CASES-U.S. DISTRICT COURTS

Administrative Office of the United States Courts, One Columbus Cir. NE, Washington, DC, 20544, USA, (202) 502-2600, https://www.uscourts.gov; Civil Justice Reform Act Report 2022; Federal Judicial Caseload Statistics 2022; and Statistical Tables for the Federal Judiciary 2022.

CIVIL DISOBEDIENCE

Major Cities Chiefs Association (MCCA), PO Box 71690, Salt Lake City, UT, 84171, USA, (801) 209-1815, patricia@majorcitieschiefs.com, https://majorcitieschiefs.com/; MCCA Report on the 2020 Protest and Civil Unrest.

CIVIL RIGHTS

Freedom House, 1850 M St. NW, 11th Fl., Washington, DC, 20036, USA, (202) 296-5101, info@freedomhouse.org, https://freedomhouse.org; The Democracy Project and Freedom in the World 2022: The Global Expansion of Authoritarian Rule.

John S. and James L. Knight Foundation, 2850 Tigertail Ave., Ste. 600, Miami, FL, 33133, USA, (305) 908-2600, (305) 908-2698, https://knightfoundation.org; College Student Views on Free Expression and Campus Speech 2022.

New York Civil Liberties Union (NYCLU, 125 Broad St., 19th Fl., New York, NY, 10004, USA, (212) 607-3300, (212) 607-3318, https://www.nyclu.org/; unpublished data.

Pew Research Center, Politics & Policy, 1615 L St. NW, Ste. 800, Washington, DC, 20036, USA, (202) 419-4300, (202) 857-8562, https://www.pewresearch.org/topic/politics-policy/; Majority of Public Favors Giving Civilians the Power to Sue Police Officers for Misconduct.

U.S. Department of Labor (DOL), Bureau of International Labor Affairs (ILAB), 200 Constitution Ave. NW, Washington, DC, 20210, USA, (202) 693-4770, contact-ilab@dol.gov, https://www.dol.gov/agencies/ilab; United States-Mexico-Canada Agreement (USMCA) Labor Rights Report.

CIVIL RIGHTS-ISRAEL

Human Rights Watch, 350 5th Ave., 34th Fl., New York, NY, 10118-3299, USA, (212) 290-4700, (212) 736-1300, https://www.hrw.org; A Threshold Crossed: Israeli Authorities and the Crimes of Apartheid and Persecution.

CIVIL RIGHTS-RELIGIOUS ASPECTS

Public Religion Research Institute (PRRI), 1023 15th St. NW, 9th Fl., Washington, DC, 20005, USA, (202) 238-9424, info@prri.org, https://www.prri.org/; Wedding Cakes, Same-Sex Marriage, and the Future of LGBT Rights in America.

CIVIL RIGHTS-UNITED STATES

American Civil Liberties Union (ACLU), 125 Broad St. , 18th Fl., New York, NY, 10004, USA, (212) 549-2500, https://www.aclu.org/; License to Abuse: How ICE's 287(g) Program Empowers Racist Sheriffs and Civil Rights Violations.

American Medical Association (AMA), AMA Plaza, 330 N Wabash Ave., Ste. 39300, Chicago, IL, 60611-5885, USA, (312) 464-4782, amacatalog@ama-assn.org, https://www.ama-assn.org; Transgender Individuals' Access to Public Facilities.

Council on American-Islamic Relations (CAIR), 453 New Jersey Ave. SE, Washington, DC, 20003, USA, (202) 488-8787, (202) 488-0833, info@cair.com, https://www.islamophobia.org/; 2023 Civil Rights Report: Progress in the Shadow of Prejudice.

Institute for Strategic Dialogue (ISD), PO Box 75769, London, SW1P 9ER, GBR, info@isdglobal.org, https://www.isdglobal.org/; 'Climate Lockdown' and the Culture Wars: How COVID-19 Sparked a New Narrative Against Climate Action.

Ipsos, 360 Park Ave. S, 17th Fl., New York, NY, 10010, USA, (212) 265-3200, https://www.ipsos.

com/en-us; A Majority of Americans Do Not Support Separating Immigrant Families.

Marist College Institute for Public Opinion, 3399 North Rd., Poughkeepsie, NY, 12601, USA, (845) 575-5050, https://maristpoll.marist.edu; Abortion Rights, May 2022.

New York University School of Law, Brennan Center for Justice, 120 Broadway, Ste. 1750, New York, NY, 10271, USA, (646) 292-8310, (202) 249-7190, (212) 463-7308, brennancenter@nyu.edu, https://www.brennancenter.org; Voter Purge Rates Remain High, Analysis Finds.

Pew Research Center, Internet & Technology, 1615 L St. NW, Ste. 800, Washington, DC, 20036, USA, (202) 419-4300, (202) 857-8562, https://www.pewresearch.org/topic/internet-technology/; Most Americans Think Social Media Sites Censor Political Viewpoints.

Public Religion Research Institute (PRRI), 1023 15th St. NW, 9th Fl., Washington, DC, 20005, USA, (202) 238-9424, info@prri.org, https://www.prri.org/; America's Growing Support for Transgender Rights; Americans Overwhelmingly Oppose Allowing Business Owners to Refuse Service to Gay and Lesbian People for Religious Reasons; Americans' Support for Key LGBTQ Rights Continues to Tick Upward; and Support for Transgender Rights Is Generally High Across the U.S..

U.S. Commission on Civil Rights (USCCR), 1331 Pennsylvania Ave. NW, Ste. 1150, Washington, DC, 20425, USA, (202) 376-7700, (202) 376-8116 (TTY), publications@usccr.gov, https://www.usccr.gov/; 2019 Statutory Enforcement Report: Are Rights A Reality? Evaluating Federal Civil Rights Enforcement; 2022 Statutory Enforcement Report: Civil Rights and Protections During the Federal Response to Hurricanes Harvey and Maria; and 2020 Statutory Enforcement Report: Subminimum Wages: Impacts on the Civil Rights of People with Disabilities.

U.S. Department of Education (ED), Office for Civil Rights (OCR), Lyndon Baines Johnson Bldg., 400 Maryland Ave. SW, Washington, DC, 20202-1100, USA, (800) 421-3481, (202) 453-6012, ocr@ed.gov, https://www2.ed.gov/about/offices/list/ocr; Annual Report to the Secretary, the President, and the Congress Fiscal Year 2020.

U.S. Department of Justice (DOJ), Civil Rights Division, 950 Pennsylvania Ave. NW, Washington, DC, 20530, USA, (202) 514-3847, (202) 514-0716 (TTY), https://www.justice.gov/crt; unpublished data.

University of California, Berkeley, Othering & Belonging Institute, 460 Stephens Hall, Berkeley, CA, 94720-2330, USA, (510) 642-3326, belonging@berkeley.edu, https://belonging.berkeley.edu; Consequences of Islamophobia on Civil Liberties and Rights in the United States and The Pervasiveness of Islamophobia in the United States.

CIVIL RIGHTS DEMONSTRATIONS

Major Cities Chiefs Association (MCCA), PO Box 71690, Salt Lake City, UT, 84171, USA, (801) 209-1815, patricia@majorcitieschiefs.com, https://majorcitieschiefs.com/; MCCA Report on the 2020 Protest and Civil Unrest.

CIVIL RIGHTS STRUGGLES AROUND THE WORLD

Human Rights Watch, 350 5th Ave., 34th Fl., New York, NY, 10118-3299, USA, (212) 290-4700, (212) 736-1300, https://www.hrw.org; World Report 2023: Our Annual Review of Human Rights Around the Globe.

CIVIL SERVICE EMPLOYEES

See GOVERNMENT

CIVILIAN REVIEW BOARDS (POLICE ADMINISTRATION)

Council on Criminal Justice (CCJ), Task Force on Policing, 700 Pennsylvania Ave. SE, Washington, DC, 20020, USA, info@counciloncj.org, https://counciloncj.org/tfp/; Policy Assessment: Civilian Oversight.

CLAMS

National Oceanic and Atmospheric Administration (NOAA), National Marine Fisheries Service (NOAA Fisheries), 1315 East-West Hwy., 14th Fl., Silver Spring, MD, 20910, USA, (301) 427-8000, https://www.fisheries.noaa.gov/; Fisheries of the United States, 2020.

CLAY CONSTRUCTION PRODUCTS

U.S. Department of the Interior (DOI), U.S. Geological Survey (USGS), National Minerals Information Center (NMIC), 12201 Sunrise Valley Dr., Reston, VA, 20192, USA, (703) 648-4920, (703) 648-7971, (703) 648-4995, sfortier@usgs.gov, https://www.usgs.gov/centers/nmic; Mineral Industry Surveys (MIS).

CLERGYMEN

National Council of the Churches of Christ in the USA, 110 Maryland Ave. NE, Ste. 108, Washington, DC, 20002, USA, (202) 544-2350, info@nationalcouncilofchurches.us, https://www.nationalcouncilofchurches.us/; unpublished data.

CLERGYMEN-EMPLOYMENT

U.S. Department of Labor (DOL), Bureau of Labor Statistics (BLS), Postal Square Bldg., 2 Massachusetts Ave. NE, Washington, DC, 20212-0001, USA, (202) 691-5200, (202) 691-7890, blsdata_staff@bls.gov, https://www.bls.gov; Monthly Labor Review.

CLIMATE

American Meteorological Society (AMS), 45 Beacon St., Boston, MA, 02108-3693, USA, (617) 227-2425, (617) 742-8718, amsinfo@ametsoc.org, https://www.ametsoc.org/ams/; Bulletin of the American Meteorological Society (BAMS); Earth Interactions; Journal of Applied Meteorology and Climatology; Journal of Atmospheric and Oceanic Technology; Journal of Climate; Journal of Hydrometeorology; Journal of Physical Oceanography; Journal of the Atmospheric Sciences; Meteorological Monographs; Monthly Weather Review; State of the Climate in 2020; Weather and Forecasting; and Weather, Climate, and Society.

Aspen Global Change Institute (AGCI), 104 Midland Ave., Ste. 205, Basalt, CO, 81621, USA, (970) 925-7376, https://www.agci.org/; Climate Change Portals and Related Resources.

Aspen Global Change Institute (AGCI), Climate Communication, 104 Midland Ave., Ste. 205, Basalt, CO, 81621, USA, (970) 925-7376, info@agci.org, https://climatecommunication.org/; unpublished data.

Carbon Brief, 180 Borough High St., London, SE1 1LB, GBR, info@carbonbrief.org, https://www.carbonbrief.org/; Carbon Brief.

Environment and Climate Change Canada, Fontaine Bldg., 200 Sacre-Coeur Blvd., 12th Fl., Gatineau, QC, K1A 0H3, CAN, (819) 938-3838 (Dial from U.S.), enviroinfo@ec.gc.ca, https://www.canada.ca/en/environment-climate-change.html; Canadian Environmental Sustainability Indicators (CESI).

Environmental Business International, Inc. (EBI), 4452 Park Blvd., Ste. 306, San Diego, CA, 92116, USA, (619) 295-7685, info@ebionline.org, https://ebionline.org/; Climate Change Business Journal (CCBJ).

European Severe Storms Laboratory (ESSL), c/o DLR, Muenchener Str. 20, Wessling, D-82234, GER, https://www.essl.org/, https://www.essl.org/cms/; European Severe Weather Database (ESWD).

Global Environmental Facility (GEF), 1818 H St. NW, Washington, DC, 20433, USA, (202) 473-0508, (202) 522-3240, communications@thegef.org, https://www.thegef.org/; Beyond the Numbers: Actions by the GEF Partnership to Safeguard the Global Environment and The Restoration Initiative: 2021 Year in Review.

Intergovernmental Panel on Climate Change (IPCC), C/O World Meteorological Organization, 7 bis Avenue de la Paix, C.P. 2300, Geneva, CH-1211, SWI, ipcc-sec@wmo.int, https://www.ipcc.ch/; Climate Change 2022: Mitigation of Climate Change and Climate Change and Land.

National Bureau of Economic Research (NBER), 1050 Massachusetts Ave., Cambridge, MA, 02138, USA, (617) 868-3900, info@nber.org, https://www.nber.org/; The Urban Crime and Heat Gradient in High and Low Poverty Areas.

National Oceanic and Atmospheric Administration (NOAA), 1401 Constitution Ave. NW, Rm. 5128, Washington, DC, 20230, USA, https://www.noaa.gov/; unpublished data.

National Oceanic and Atmospheric Administration (NOAA), National Centers for Environmental Information (NCEI), Federal Bldg., 151 Patton Ave., Asheville, NC, 28801-5001, USA, (828) 271-4800, (828) 271-4010 (TTY), (828) 271-4876, ncei.info@noaa.gov, https://www.ncei.noaa.gov/; Climate at a Glance; Climate Data Online (CDO); Climate Monitoring; Global Historical Climatology Network Daily (GHCNd); Global Ocean Heat Content Climate Data Record (CDR); U.S. Climate Extremes Index (CEI); and Warming of the World Ocean, 1955-2003.

National Oceanic and Atmospheric Administration (NOAA), National Centers for Environmental Information (NCEI), National Integrated Drought Information System (NIDIS), 151 Patton Ave., Asheville, ND, 28801-5001, USA, drought.portal@noaa.gov, https://www.drought.gov; Drought Status Update for California-Nevada; Drought Status Update for the Pacific Northwest; Drought.gov; and National Current Conditions.

Pennsylvania State University, College of Earth and Mineral Sciences, Earth System Science Center (ESSC), Earth-Engineering Sciences Bldg., University Park, PA, 16802, USA, (814) 865-4177, (814) 865-9429, mann@psu.edu, http://www.essc.psu.edu/; The 2022 North Atlantic Hurricane Season: Penn State ESSC Forecast.

Pennsylvania State University, Earth and Environmental Systems Institute (EESI), 2217 Earth-Engineering Sciences Bldg., University Park, PA, 16802-6813, USA, (814) 863-7091, (814) 865-3191, info@eesi.psu.edu, https://www.eesi.psu.edu/; unpublished data.

United Nations Environment Programme (UNEP), 900 17th St. NW, Ste. 506, Washington, DC, 20006, USA, (202) 974-1300, publications@unep.org, https://www.unep.org/; Protected Planet Report 2020 and Scientific Assessment of Ozone Depletion 2022.

World Meteorological Organization (WMO), 7bis, ave. de la Paix, PO Box 2300, Geneva, CH-1211, SWI, wmo@wmo.int, https://public.wmo.int/en; State of the Global Climate 2022 and WMO Bulletin.

World Weather Attribution (WWA), wwamedia@imperial.ac.uk, https://www.worldweatherattribution.org; Human Influence on Growing Period Frosts Like the Early April 2021 in Central France and Rapid Attribution Analysis of the Extraordinary Heatwave on the Pacific Coast of the US and Canada June 2021.

CLIMATE-SELECTED CITIES

Berkeley Earth, admin@berkeleyearth.org, https://berkeleyearth.org; Global Warming Statistics: City Selection.

CDP, 60 Great Tower St., 4th Fl., London, EC3R 5AZ, GBR, https://www.cdp.net; CDP Cities, States and Regions Open Data Portal.

National Oceanic and Atmospheric Administration (NOAA), National Centers for Environmental Information (NCEI), Federal Bldg., 151 Patton Ave., Asheville, NC, 28801-5001, USA, (828) 271-4800, (828) 271-4010 (TTY), (828) 271-4876, ncei.info@noaa.gov, https://www.ncei.noaa.gov/; Climatological Data Publications and Comparative Climatic Data (CCD).

CLIMATE-SELECTED CITIES-PRECIPITATION

National Oceanic and Atmospheric Administration (NOAA), National Centers for Environmental Information (NCEI), Federal Bldg., 151 Patton Ave., Asheville, NC, 28801-5001, USA, (828) 271-4800, (828) 271-4010 (TTY), (828) 271-4876, ncei.info@noaa.gov, https://www.ncei.noaa.gov/; Climatological Data Publications and Comparative Climatic Data (CCD).

CLIMATE-SELECTED CITIES-TEMPERATURE

National Oceanic and Atmospheric Administration (NOAA), National Centers for Environmental Information (NCEI), Federal Bldg., 151 Patton Ave., Asheville, NC, 28801-5001, USA, (828) 271-4800, (828) 271-4010 (TTY), (828) 271-4876, ncei.info@noaa.gov, https://www.ncei.noaa.gov/; Climatological Data Publications and Comparative Climatic Data (CCD).

CLIMATE CHANGE

See also GLOBAL WARMING

Act Now Coalition, USA, https://www.actnowcoalition.org/; unpublished data.

American Meteor Society (AMS), USA, https://www.amsmeteors.org; Localized Climate Reporting by TV Weathercasters Enhances Public Understanding of Climate Change as a Local Problem: Evidence from a Randomized Controlled Experiment and Reporting on Climate Change by Broadcast Meteorologists: A National Assessment.

American Meteorological Society (AMS), 45 Beacon St., Boston, MA, 02108-3693, USA, (617) 227-2425, (617) 742-8718, amsinfo@ametsoc.org, https://www.ametsoc.org/ams/; Explaining Extreme Events in 2021 and 2022 from a Climate Perspective; Journal of Climate; State of the Climate in 2020; and Weather, Climate, and Society.

American Public Health Association (APHA), 800 I St. NW, Washington, DC, 20001, USA, (202) 777-2742, (202) 777-2500 (TTY), (202) 777-2534, membership.mail@apha.org, https://www.apha.org/; Climate Change, Health, and Equity: A Guide for Local Health Departments.

Aspen Global Change Institute (AGCI), 104 Midland Ave., Ste. 205, Basalt, CO, 81621, USA, (970) 925-7376, https://www.agci.org/; Climate Change Portals and Related Resources.

Aspen Global Change Institute (AGCI), Climate Communication, 104 Midland Ave., Ste. 205, Basalt, CO, 81621, USA, (970) 925-7376, info@agci.org, https://climatecommunication.org/; unpublished data.

Berkeley Earth, admin@berkeleyearth.org, https://berkeleyearth.org; Global Temperature Report for 2022; Global Warming Data Visualization; and Global Warming Statistics: City Selection.

Bipartisan Policy Center (BPC), 1225 Eye St. NW, Ste. 1000, Washington, DC, 20005, USA, (202) 204-2400, bipartisaninfo@bipartisanpolicy.org, https://bipartisanpolicy.org/; Carbon Removal: Comparing Historical Federal Research Investments with the National Academies' Recommended Future Funding Levels.

Carbon Brief, 180 Borough High St., London, SE1 1LB, GBR, info@carbonbrief.org, https://www.carbonbrief.org/; Carbon Brief and Global Planted Forests 1990-2015.

Carbon Tracker Initiative (CTI), 40 Bermondsey St., 2nd Fl., London, SE1 3UD, GBR, hello@carbontracker.org, https://www.carbontracker.org/; Global Registry of Fossil Fuels.

Centro del Agua del Tropico Humedo para America Latina y el Caribe (CATHALAC) (Water Center for the Humid Tropics of Latin America and the Caribbean), Ciudad del Saber , Edificio 111, Panama, 0843-03102, PAN, (507) 317-3200, cathalac@cathalac.int, https://cathalac.int/; unpublished data.

Climate Analytics, 135 Madison Ave., 5th Fl., Ste. 05-115, New York, NY, 10016, USA, info.ny@climateanalytics.org, https://climateanalytics.org/; Climate Action Tracker (CAT); Extreme Atlantic Hurricane Seasons Made Twice as Likely by Ocean Warming; Incremental Improvements of 2030 Targets Insufficient to Achieve the Paris Agreement Goals; and 2 Steps Down the Debt Spiral: COVID-19 and Tropical Cyclones Severely Limit the Fiscal Space of Many Small Island Developing States.

CoreLogic, 40 Pacifica, Ste. 900, Irvine, CA, 92618, USA, (800) 426-1466, (949) 214-1000, https://www.corelogic.com/; 2021 Climate Change Catastrophe Report.

Democracy Fund Voter Study Group, 1200 17th St. NW, Ste. 300, Washington, DC, 20036, USA, (202) 420-7900, https://www.voterstudygroup.org/; Degrees of Change: Americans' Shifting Views on Global Warming.

Environmental Business International, Inc. (EBI), 4452 Park Blvd., Ste. 306, San Diego, CA, 92116, USA, (619) 295-7685, info@ebionline.org, https://ebionline.org/; Climate Change Business Journal (CCBJ).

Environmental Working Group (EWG), 1250 U St. NW, Ste. 1000, Washington, DC, 20005, USA, (202) 667-6982, https://www.ewg.org/; EWG's Quick Tips for Reducing Your Diet's Climate Footprint.

European Centre for Medium-Range Weather Forecasts (ECMWF), Copernicus Climate Change Service (C3S), Shinfield Park, Reading, RG2 9AX, GBR, copernicus-support@ecmwf.int, https://climate.copernicus.eu/; CAMS and C3S Knowledge Base (CKB); Climate Datasets; Investigating an Unusually Mild Winter and Spring in Siberia; Last Four Years Have Been the Warmest on Record - and CO2 Continues to Rise; and Surface Air Temperature for May 2020.

European Commission, Joint Research Centre, EU Science Hub, Brussels, B-1049, BEL, ies-contact@jrc.ec.europa.eu, https://ec.europa.eu/jrc/en; Emissions Database for Global Atmospheric Research (EDGAR).

The Global Carbon Project (GCP), c/o CSIRO Oceans and Atmosphere, GPO Box 1700, Canberra, ACT, 2601, AUS, info@globalcarbonproject.org, https://www.globalcarbonproject.org/; Global Carbon Atlas.

Global Center on Adaptation (GCA), Antoine Platekade 1006, Rotterdam, 3072 ME, NLD, info@gca.org, https://gca.org/; Adapt Now: A Global Call for Leadership on Climate Resilience.

Global Environmental Facility (GEF), 1818 H St. NW, Washington, DC, 20433, USA, (202) 473-0508, (202) 522-3240, communications@thegef.org, https://www.thegef.org/; Beyond the Numbers: Actions by the GEF Partnership to Safeguard the Global Environment and The Restoration Initiative: 2021 Year in Review.

Home Office of the Government of the United Kingdom, Direct Communications Unit, 2 Marsham St., London, SW1P 4DF, GBR, public.enquiries@homeoffice.gov.uk, https://www.gov.uk/government/organisations/home-office; Agricultural Statistics and Climate Change: 10th Edition.

Intergovernmental Panel on Climate Change (IPCC), C/O World Meteorological Organization, 7 bis Avenue de la Paix, C.P. 2300, Geneva, CH-1211, SWI, ipcc-sec@wmo.int, https://www.ipcc.ch/; AR6 Synthesis Report: Climate Change 2023 and The Ocean and Cryosphere in a Changing Climate.

International Energy Agency (IEA), 9 Rue de la Federation, Paris, 75739, FRA, info@iea.org, https://www.iea.org/; Global Energy Review 2021 and Government Energy Spending Tracker.

International Fund for Agricultural Development (IFAD), Via Paolo di Dono, 44, Rome, 00142, ITA, ifad@ifad.org, https://www.ifad.org/; Climate Change and Food System Activities - A Review of Emission Trends, Climate Impacts and the Effects of Dietary Change.

Media Matters for America, PO Box 44811, Washington, DC, 20026, USA, (202) 756-4100, action@mediamatters.org, https://www.mediamatters.org; Broadcast TV News Shows Link Western Heat Wave and Drought to Climate Change in 27% of Segments.

Met Office, FitzRoy Rd., Exeter, EX1 3PB, GBR, enquiries@metoffice.gov.uk, https://www.metoffice.gov.uk; Met Office DataPoint.

National Aeronautics and Space Administration (NASA), NASA Headquarters, 300 E St. SW, Ste. 5R30, Washington, DC, 20546, USA, (202) 358-0001, (202) 358-4338, https://www.nasa.gov; NASA Earth Exchange (NEX).

National Bureau of Economic Research (NBER), 1050 Massachusetts Ave., Cambridge, MA, 02138, USA, (617) 868-3900, info@nber.org, https://www.nber.org/; The Urban Crime and Heat Gradient in High and Low Poverty Areas.

National Oceanic and Atmospheric Administration (NOAA), National Centers for Environmental Information (NCEI), Federal Bldg., 151 Patton Ave., Asheville, NC, 28801-5001, USA, (828) 271-4800, (828) 271-4010 (TTY), (828) 271-4876, ncei.info@noaa.gov, https://www.ncei.noaa.gov/; Global Climate Report, June 2021; Global Historical Climatology Network Daily (GHCNd); and U.S. Climate Extremes Index (CEI).

Natural England, County Hall, Spetchley Rd., Worcester, WR5 2NP, GBR, enquiries@naturalengland.org.uk, https://www.gov.uk/government/organisations/natural-england; Designated Sites View.

New York University School of Law, Institute for Policy Integrity, 139 MacDougal St., Wilf Hall, 3rd Fl., New York, NY, 10012, USA, (212) 992-8932, (212) 995-4592, https://policyintegrity.org/; How the Trump Administration Is Obscuring the Costs of Climate Change.

NewClimate Institute, Waidmarkt 11a, Cologne, D-50676, GER, info@newclimate.org, https://newclimate.org/; Net Zero Stocktake 2022.

Pennsylvania State University, Earth and Environmental Systems Institute (EESI), 2217 Earth-Engineering Sciences Bldg., University Park, PA, 16802-6813, USA, (814) 863-7091, (814) 865-3191, info@eesi.psu.edu, https://www.eesi.psu.edu/; unpublished data.

Polaris Institute, 135 Laurier Ave. W, Ste. 630, Ottawa, ON, K1P 5J2, CAN, (613) 237-1717 (Dial from U.S.), polaris@polarisinstitute.org, https://www.polarisinstitute.org/; unpublished data.

Proceedings of the National Academy of Sciences (PNAS), 500 Fifth St. NW, NAS 338, Washington, DC, 20001, USA, (202) 334-2679, pnas@nas.edu, https://www.pnas.org; Global Increase in Major Tropical Cyclone Exceedance Probability Over the Past Four Decades and Pre-Columbian Fire Management and Control of Climate-Driven Floodwaters Over 3,500 Years in Southwestern Amazonia.

Public Agenda, 1 Dock 72 Way, No. 6101, Brooklyn, NY, 11205-1242, USA, (212) 686-6610, info@publicagenda.org, https://www.publicagenda.org/; America's Hidden Common Ground on Climate Change.

Rainforest Action Network (RAN), 425 Bush St., Ste. 300, San Francisco, CA, 94108, USA, (415) 398-4404, (415) 398-2732, answers@ran.org, https://www.ran.org/; Banking on Climate Chaos: Fossil Fuel Finance Report, 2021 and Fracking Fiasco: The Banks that Fueled the U.S. Shale Bust.

U.S. Department of Commerce (DOC), National Institute of Standards and Technology (NIST), 100 Bureau Dr., Gaithersburg, MD, 20899, USA, (301) 975-2000, https://www.nist.gov; Data-Based Models for Hurricane Evolution Prediction: A Deep Learning Approach.

U.S. Global Change Research Program (USGCRP), 1800 G St. NW, Ste. 9100, Washington, DC, 20006, USA, (202) 223-6262, (202) 223-3065, https://www.globalchange.gov/; National Climate Assessment.

United Nations Department of Economic and Social Affairs (DESA), United Nations Plz., New York, NY, 10017, USA, (212) 963-4849, statistics@un.org, https://www.un.org/en/desa; The Sustainable Development Goals Report 2022.

United Nations Educational, Scientific and Cultural Organization (UNESCO), 7, place de Fontenoy, Paris, 75007, FRA, https://www.unesco.org; World Water Development Report (WWDR) 2023: Partnerships and Cooperation for Water.

United Nations Environment Programme (UNEP) Copenhagen Climate Centre, Marmorvej 51, Copenhagen, DK-2100, DEN, unep@dtu.dk, https://unepdtu.org/; Emissions Gap Report 2021 and Reducing Consumer Food Waste Using Green and Digital Technologies.

United Nations Environment Programme (UNEP), 900 17th St. NW, Ste. 506, Washington, DC, 20006, USA, (202) 974-1300, publications@unep.org, https://www.unep.org/; Emissions Gap Report 2022; Frontiers 2022: Noise, Blazes and Mismatches; and UN Environment Open Data.

United Nations Intergovernmental Science-Policy Platform on Biodiversity and Ecosystem Services (IPBES), Platz der Vereinten Nationen 1, 10th Fl., Bonn, D-53113, GER, secretariat@ipbes.net, https://www.ipbes.net/; Global Assessment Report on Biodiversity and Ecosystem Services.

University of California San Diego, U.S. Immigration Policy Center (USIPC), 9500 Gilman Dr., La Jolla, CA, 92093, USA, (858) 534-2230, usipc@ucsd.edu, https://usipc.ucsd.edu/; Public Preferences for Admitting Migrants Displaced by Climate Change.

University of Colorado Boulder, National Snow & Ice Data Center (NSIDC), CIRES, 449 UCB, Boulder, CO, 80309-0449, USA, (303) 492-6199, (303) 492-2468, nsidc@nsidc.org, https://nsidc.org/; EASE-Grid Sea Ice Age, Version 4 and Sea Ice Index.

University of Vienna Department of Demography, Wittgenstein Centre for Demography and Global Human Capital, Dr. Ignaz Seipel-Platz 2, Vienna, A-1010, AUT, heike.barakat@univie.ac.at, https://www.wittgensteincentre.org/en/; The Role of Education in Enabling the Sustainable Development Agenda.

The Washington Post, 1301 K St. NW, Washington, DC, 20071, USA, (800) 477-4679, https://www.washingtonpost.com/; Beyond the Limit: 2 Degrees C: Extreme Climate Change Has Arrived in America; Gone in a Generation: Across America, Climate Change Is Already Disrupting Lives; and 2020 Rivals Hottest Year on Record, Pushing Earth Closer to a Critical Climate Threshold.

The World Bank, 1818 H St. NW, Washington, DC, 20433, USA, (202) 473-1000, (202) 477-6391, eds03@worldbank.org, https://www.worldbank.org/; Atlas of Sustainable Development Goals 2020: From World Development Indicators.

World Economic Forum (WEF), 350 Madison Ave., 11th Fl., New York, NY, 10017, USA, (212) 703-2300, forumusa@weforum.org, https://www.weforum.org/; The Global Risks Report 2022.

World Food Programme, Via Cesare Giulio Viola 68, Parco dei Medici, Rome, 00148, ITA, https://www.wfp.org/; HungerMap.

World Meteorological Organization (WMO), 7bis, ave. de la Paix, PO Box 2300, Geneva, CH-1211, SWI, wmo@wmo.int, https://public.wmo.int/en; WMO Global Annual to Decadal Climate Update (Target years: 2023-2027) and WMO Greenhouse Gas Bulletin.

World Resources Institute (WRI), 10 G St. NE, Ste. 800, Washington, DC, 20002, USA, (202) 729-7600, (202) 280-1314, https://www.wri.org/; World Resources Report: Towards a More Equal City.

World Weather Attribution (WWA), wwamedia@imperial.ac.uk, https://www.worldweatherattribution.org; Attribution of the Australian Bushfire Risk to Anthropogenic Climate Change; Human Contribution to the Record-Breaking July 2019 Heat Wave in Western Europe; Human Influence on Growing Period Frosts Like the Early April 2021 in Central France; Prolonged Siberian Heat of 2020; Rapid Attribution Analysis of the Extraordinary Heatwave on the Pacific Coast of the US and Canada June 2021; and Rapid Attribution of the Extreme Rainfall in Texas from Tropical Storm Imelda.

Worldometer, https://www.worldometers.info/; Worldometers.info.

Yale Project on Climate Change Communication (YPCCC), Yale School of the Environment, 195 Prospect St., New Haven, CT, 06511, USA, (203) 432-5055, climatechange@yale.edu, https://climatecommunication.yale.edu/; Changes in Awareness of and Support for the Green New Deal; Climate Change in the American Mind: Beliefs & Attitudes, Spring 2023; Climate Change in the Indian Mind, 2022; Global Warming's Six Americas Across Age, Race/Ethnicity, and Gender; Politics & Global Warming, April 2022; and Yale Climate Opinion Maps 2021.

CLIMATE CHANGE AND FOOD PRODUCTION

Project Drawdown, 3450 Sacramento St., No. 506, San Francisco, CA, 94118, USA, https://drawdown.org; Farming Our Way Out of the Climate Crisis.

Union of Concerned Scientists (UCS), 2 Brattle Sq., Cambridge, MA, 02138-3780, USA, (617) 547-5552, (617) 864-9405, https://www.ucsusa.org/; Too Hot to Work: Assessing the Threats Climate Change Poses to Outdoor Workers.

United Nations Environment Programme (UNEP) Copenhagen Climate Centre, Marmorvej 51, Copenhagen, DK-2100, DEN, unep@dtu.dk, https://unepdtu.org/; Reducing Consumer Food Waste Using Green and Digital Technologies.

CLIMATE CHANGE AND HEALTH

Center for Biological Diversity, PO Box 710, Tucson, AZ, 85702-0710, USA, (520) 623-5252, (866) 357-3349, (520) 623-9797, center@biologicaldiversity.org, https://www.biologicaldiversity.org/; Gender and the Climate Crisis: Equitable Solutions for Climate Plans.

Climate Central, One Palmer Square, Ste. 402, Princeton, NJ, 08542, USA, (609) 924-3800, (877) 425-4724, https://www.climatecentral.org/; Climate Change Is Threatening Air Quality Across the Country; Extreme Heat: When Outdoor Sports Become Risky; Flooded Future: Global Vulnerability to Sea Level Rise Worse than Previously Understood; and Seniors at Risk: Heat and Climate Change.

Imperial College London, South Kensington Campus, London, SW7 2AZ, GBR, https://www.imperial.ac.uk/; The Effect of Climate Change on Yellow Fever Disease Burden in Africa.

The Lancet Countdown: Tracking the Connections Between Public Health and Climate Change, 90 Tottenham Court Rd., 2nd Fl., London, W1T 4TJ, GBR, info@lancetcountdown.org, https://www.lancetcountdown.org/; The Lancet Countdown on Health and Climate Change: 2022 Report.

UNICEF, 3 United Nations Plz., New York, NY, 10017, USA, (212) 303-7984, (917) 244-2215, https://www.unicef.org; Children's Climate Risk Index (CCRI).

University of California Los Angeles (UCLA), Luskin Center for Innovation, 3323 Public Affairs Bldg., PO Box 951656, Los Angeles, CA, 90095-1656, USA, (310) 267-5435, (310) 267-5443, https://innovation.luskin.ucla.edu/; Heat and Learning.

CLIMATE CHANGE, ECONOMIES, AND SOCIETY

BloombergNEF, New York, NY, 10022, USA, (212) 617-4050, https://about.bnef.com; Climatescope 2022.

CDP, 60 Great Tower St., 4th Fl., London, EC3R 5AZ, GBR, https://www.cdp.net; CDP Cities, States and Regions Open Data Portal; Engaging the Chain: Driving Speed and Scale; The TIme to Green Finance; and Working Together to Beat the Climate Crisis.

Center for Biological Diversity, PO Box 710, Tucson, AZ, 85702-0710, USA, (520) 623-5252, (866) 357-3349, (520) 623-9797, center@biologicaldiversity.org, https://www.biologicaldiversity.org/; Gender and the Climate Crisis: Equitable Solutions for Climate Plans.

Center for Global Development (CDG), 1800 Massachusetts Ave. NW, Washington, DC, 20036, USA, (202) 416-4000, (202) 416-4050, https://www.cgdev.org/; Climate Change and Migration: An Overview for Policymakers and Development Practitioners.

Climate Analytics, 135 Madison Ave., 5th Fl., Ste. 05-115, New York, NY, 10016, USA, info.ny@climateanalytics.org, https://climateanalytics.org/; 1.5 Degree C National Pathway Explorer; Climate Action Tracker: How a Renewable Energy COVID-19 Recovery Creates Opportunities for India; Exploring New Electric Vehicle Roadmaps for China in a Post-COVID-19 Era; and Why Gas Is the New Coal.

Climate Central, One Palmer Square, Ste. 402, Princeton, NJ, 08542, USA, (609) 924-3800, (877) 425-4724, https://www.climatecentral.org/; Climate Change Is Threatening Air Quality Across the Country; Extreme Heat: When Outdoor Sports Become Risky; Flooded Future: Global Vulnerability to Sea Level Rise Worse than Previously Understood; and Seniors at Risk: Heat and Climate Change.

Germanwatch, Kaiserstrasse 201, Bonn, D-53113, GER, info@germanwatch.org, https://germanwatch.org; Global Climate Risk Index 2021.

Global Center on Adaptation (GCA), Antoine Platekade 1006, Rotterdam, 3072 ME, NLD, info@gca.org, https://gca.org/; Adapt Now: A Global Call for Leadership on Climate Resilience.

Global Change Data Lab, Our World in Data, GBR, info@ourworldindata.org, https://ourworldindata.org; Measuring Progress Towards the Sustainable Development Goals.

Global Facility for Disaster Reduction and Recovery (GFDRR), 1818 H St. NW, Washington, DC, 20433, USA, (202) 473-1000, gfdrr@worldbank.org, https://www.gfdrr.org/; Overlooked : Examining the Impact of Disasters and Climate Shocks on Poverty in the Europe and Central Asia Region.

Greenpeace, 1300 I St. NW, Ste. 1100 E, Washington, DC, 20001, USA, (800) 722-6995, (202) 462-1177, (202) 462-4507, connect@greenpeace.us, https://www.greenpeace.org; In the Dark: How Social Media Companies' Climate Disinformation Problem is Hidden from the Public.

The 5 Gyres Institute, PO Box 5699, Santa Monica, CA, 90409, USA, info@5gyres.org, https://www.5gyres.org/; Plastic & Climate Change: The Hidden Costs of a Plastic Planet.

Imperial College London, South Kensington Campus, London, SW7 2AZ, GBR, https://www.imperial.ac.uk/; The Effect of Climate Change on Yellow Fever Disease Burden in Africa.

INRIX, 10210 NE Points Dr., No. 400, Kirkland, WA, 98033, USA, (425) 284-3800, https://inrix.com; Signal Optimization and Climate Outcomes.

Institute for Strategic Dialogue (ISD), PO Box 75769, London, SW1P 9ER, GBR, info@isdglobal.org, https://www.isdglobal.org/; 'Climate Lockdown' and the Culture Wars: How COVID-19 Sparked a New Narrative Against Climate Action.

International Energy Agency (IEA), 9 Rue de la Federation, Paris, 75739, FRA, info@iea.org, https://www.iea.org/; Global Energy Review: CO2 Emissions in 2020.

International Institute for Environment and Development (IIED), 235 High Holborn, London, WC1V 7DN, GBR, inforequest@iied.org, https://www.iied.org; Redesigning Debt: Lessons from HIPC for COVID, Climate and Nature.

International Renewable Energy Agency (IRENA), PO Box 236, Abu Dhabi, UAE, info@irena.org, https://www.irena.org/; World Energy Transitions Outlook: 1.5 Degree C Pathway.

The Lancet Countdown: Tracking the Connections Between Public Health and Climate Change, 90 Tottenham Court Rd., 2nd Fl., London, W1T 4TJ, GBR, info@lancetcountdown.org, https://www.lancetcountdown.org/; The Lancet Countdown on Health and Climate Change: 2022 Report.

National Bureau of Economic Research (NBER), 1050 Massachusetts Ave., Cambridge, MA, 02138, USA, (617) 868-3900, info@nber.org, https://www.nber.org/; Valuing the Global Mortality Consequences of Climate Change Accounting for Adaptation Costs and Benefits.

Natural Resources Defence Council (NRDC), 40 W 20th St., 11th Fl., New York, NY, 10011, USA, (212) 727-2700, (202) 289-6868, nrdcinfo@nrdc.org, https://www.nrdc.org; 2023 Farm Bill Can Help Address Climate Crisis.

Oceana, 1025 Connecticut Ave. NW, Washington, DC, 20036, USA, (202) 833-3900, (877) 762-3262, (202) 833-2070, info@oceana.org, https://oceana.org/; Permanent Protections From Offshore Drilling Benefit Coastal Economies and Help Fight Climate Change.

Potsdam Institute for Climate Impact Research (PIK), PO Box 60 12 03, Potsdam, D-14412, GER, presse@pik-potsdam.de, https://www.pik-potsdam.de/; ClimateImpactsOnline.

Project Drawdown, 3450 Sacramento St., No. 506, San Francisco, CA, 94118, USA, https://drawdown.org; Farming Our Way Out of the Climate Crisis.

Roosevelt Institute, 570 Lexington Ave., 5th Fl., New York, NY, 10022, USA, (212) 444-9130, info@rooseveltinstitute.org, https://rooseveltinstitute.org/; Clean Energy Neoliberalism: Climate, Tax Credits, and Racial Justice.

Swedish International Development Cooperation Agency (SIDA), Box 2025, Sundbyberg, SE-174 02, SWE, sida@sida.se, https://www.sida.se/en; Environment and Climate Change 2020: Towards Environmental Sustainability and Resilience.

U.S. Army War College, Public Affairs Office, 122 Forbes Ave., Carlisle, PA, 17013-5234, USA, usarmy.carlisle.awc.mbx.atwc-cpa@mail.mil, https://www.armywarcollege.edu/; Implications of Climate Change for the U.S. Army.

UNICEF, 3 United Nations Plz., New York, NY, 10017, USA, (212) 303-7984, (917) 244-2215, https://www.unicef.org; Children's Climate Risk Index (CCRI).

Union of Concerned Scientists (UCS), 2 Brattle Sq., Cambridge, MA, 02138-3780, USA, (617) 547-5552, (617) 864-9405, https://www.ucsusa.org/; Too Hot to Work: Assessing the Threats Climate Change Poses to Outdoor Workers.

United Nations Environment Programme (UNEP), 900 17th St. NW, Ste. 506, Washington, DC, 20006, USA, (202) 974-1300, publications@unep.org, https://www.unep.org/; Spreading like Wildfire: The Rising Threat of Extraordinary Landscape Fires.

United Nations Human Settlements Programme (UN-HABITAT), PO Box 30030, Nairobi, 00100, KEN, unhabitat-info@un.org, https://unhabitat.org/; Cities and Pandemics: Towards a More Just, Green and Healthy Future.

University of California Los Angeles (UCLA), Luskin Center for Innovation, 3323 Public Affairs Bldg., PO Box 951656, Los Angeles, CA, 90095-1656, USA, (310) 267-5435, (310) 267-5443, https://innovation.luskin.ucla.edu/; Heat and Learning.

University of California San Diego, U.S. Immigration Policy Center (USIPC), 9500 Gilman Dr., La Jolla, CA, 92093, USA, (858) 534-2230, usipc@ucsd.edu, https://usipc.ucsd.edu/; Public Preferences for Admitting Migrants Displaced by Climate Change.

University of California, Berkeley, Global Policy Lab, California Memorial Stadium, 2227 Piedmont Ave., Berkeley, CA, 94720, USA, (510) 643-5751, https://www.globalpolicy.science/; Clear, Present and Underpriced: The Physical Risks of Climate Change.

The Washington Post, 1301 K St. NW, Washington, DC, 20071, USA, (800) 477-4679, https://www.washingtonpost.com/; 2020 Rivals Hottest Year on Record, Pushing Earth Closer to a Critical Climate Threshold.

World Meteorological Organization (WMO), 7bis, ave. de la Paix, PO Box 2300, Geneva, CH-1211, SWI, wmo@wmo.int, https://public.wmo.int/en; Atlas of Mortality and Economic Losses from Weather, Climate and Water Extremes (1970-2019).

World Resources Institute (WRI), 10 G St. NE, Ste. 800, Washington, DC, 20002, USA, (202) 729-7600, (202) 280-1314, https://www.wri.org/; America's New Climate Economy: A Comprehensive Guide to the Economic Benefits of Climate Policy in the United States and State of Climate Action 2021: Systems Transformations Required to Limit Global Warming to 1.5 Degree C.

World Wildlife Fund (WWF), 1250 24th St. NW, Washington, DC, 20037-1193, USA, (202) 495-4800, (202) 495-4211, https://wwf.panda.org/; An Eco-wakening: Measuring Global Awareness, Engagement and Action for Nature.

CLOCKS AND WATCHES

U.S. Census Bureau, International Trade Program, 4600 Silver Hill Rd., Washington, DC, 20233, USA, (800) 549-0595, eid.international.trade.data@census.gov, https://www.census.gov/foreign-trade; International Trade Data.

CLOTHING AND ACCESSORY STORES-RETAIL-CONSUMER PRICE INDEXES

The NPD Group, 900 W Shore Rd., Port Washington, NY, 11050, USA, (516) 625-0700, contactnpd@npd.com, https://www.npd.com; Fashion Accessories.

U.S. Department of Labor (DOL), Bureau of Labor Statistics (BLS), Postal Square Bldg., 2 Massachusetts Ave. NE, Washington, DC, 20212-0001, USA, (202) 691-5200, (202) 691-7890, blsdata_staff@bls.gov, https://www.bls.gov; Consumer Price Indexe (CPI) Publications.

CLOTHING AND ACCESSORY STORES-RETAIL-EARNINGS

Euromonitor International, Inc., 1 N Dearborn St., Ste. 1700, Chicago, IL, 60602, USA, (312) 922-1115, (312) 922-1157, info-usa@euromonitor.com, https://www.euromonitor.com/; Strategic Analysis of the World's Largest Companies.

The NPD Group, 900 W Shore Rd., Port Washington, NY, 11050, USA, (516) 625-0700, contactnpd@npd.com, https://www.npd.com; Fashion Accessories.

U.S. Census Bureau, 4600 Silver Hill Rd., Washington, DC, 20233, USA, (301) 763-4636, (800) 923-8282, https://www.census.gov; County Business Patterns (CBP) 2020.

U.S. Census Bureau, Center for Economic Studies (CES), 4600 Silver Hill Rd., Washington, DC, 20233, USA, (301) 763-6460, (301) 763-5935, ces.contacts@census.gov, https://www.census.gov/programs-surveys/ces.html; Retail Trade, 2017 Economic Census and Wholesale Trade, 2017 Economic Census.

U.S. Department of Commerce (DOC), International Trade Administration (ITA), 1401 Constitution Ave. NW, Washington, DC, 20230, USA, (800) 872-8723, https://www.trade.gov/; TradeStats Express (TSE).

U.S. Department of Labor (DOL), Bureau of Labor Statistics (BLS), Postal Square Bldg., 2 Massachusetts Ave. NE, Washington, DC, 20212-0001, USA, (202) 691-5200, (202) 691-7890, blsdata_staff@bls.gov, https://www.bls.gov; Current Employment Statistics (CES).

CLOTHING AND ACCESSORY STORES-RETAIL-ELECTRONIC COMMERCE

U.S. Census Bureau, 4600 Silver Hill Rd., Washington, DC, 20233, USA, (301) 763-4636, (800) 923-8282, https://www.census.gov; 2019 E-Stats Report: Measuring the Electronic Economy.

CLOTHING AND ACCESSORY STORES-RETAIL-EMPLOYEES

U.S. Census Bureau, 4600 Silver Hill Rd., Washington, DC, 20233, USA, (301) 763-4636, (800) 923-8282, https://www.census.gov; County Business Patterns (CBP) 2020.

U.S. Census Bureau, Center for Economic Studies (CES), 4600 Silver Hill Rd., Washington, DC, 20233, USA, (301) 763-6460, (301) 763-5935, ces.contacts@census.gov, https://www.census.gov/programs-surveys/ces.html; Retail Trade, 2017 Economic Census and Wholesale Trade, 2017 Economic Census.

U.S. Department of Labor (DOL), Bureau of Labor Statistics (BLS), Postal Square Bldg., 2 Massachusetts Ave. NE, Washington, DC, 20212-0001, USA, (202) 691-5200, (202) 691-7890, blsdata_staff@bls.gov, https://www.bls.gov; Current Employment Statistics (CES).

CLOTHING AND ACCESSORY STORES-RETAIL-ESTABLISHMENTS

U.S. Census Bureau, 4600 Silver Hill Rd., Washington, DC, 20233, USA, (301) 763-4636, (800) 923-8282, https://www.census.gov; County Business Patterns (CBP) 2020 and Economic Census, Nonemployer Statistics (NES) 2019.

U.S. Census Bureau, Center for Economic Studies (CES), 4600 Silver Hill Rd., Washington, DC, 20233, USA, (301) 763-6460, (301) 763-5935, ces.contacts@census.gov, https://www.census.gov/programs-surveys/ces.html; Retail Trade, 2017 Economic Census and Wholesale Trade, 2017 Economic Census.

U.S. Department of Commerce (DOC), International Trade Administration (ITA), 1401 Constitution Ave. NW, Washington, DC, 20230, USA, (800) 872-8723, https://www.trade.gov/; TradeStats Express (TSE).

CLOTHING AND ACCESSORY STORES-RETAIL-INVENTORIES

U.S. Census Bureau, Center for Economic Studies (CES), 4600 Silver Hill Rd., Washington, DC, 20233, USA, (301) 763-6460, (301) 763-5935, ces.contacts@census.gov, https://www.census.gov/programs-surveys/ces.html; Retail Trade, 2017 Economic Census and Wholesale Trade, 2017 Economic Census.

U.S. Department of Commerce (DOC), International Trade Administration (ITA), 1401 Constitution Ave. NW, Washington, DC, 20230, USA, (800) 872-8723, https://www.trade.gov/; TradeStats Express (TSE).

CLOTHING AND ACCESSORY STORES-RETAIL-NONEMPLOYERS

U.S. Census Bureau, 4600 Silver Hill Rd., Washington, DC, 20233, USA, (301) 763-4636, (800) 923-8282, https://www.census.gov; Economic Census, Nonemployer Statistics (NES) 2019.

CLOTHING AND ACCESSORY STORES-RETAIL-PRODUCTIVITY

U.S. Department of Labor (DOL), Bureau of Labor Statistics (BLS), Postal Square Bldg., 2 Massachusetts Ave. NE, Washington, DC, 20212-0001, USA, (202) 691-5200, (202) 691-7890, blsdata_staff@bls.gov, https://www.bls.gov; Productivity.

CLOTHING AND ACCESSORY STORES-RETAIL-PURCHASES

U.S. Census Bureau, Center for Economic Studies (CES), 4600 Silver Hill Rd., Washington, DC, 20233, USA, (301) 763-6460, (301) 763-5935, ces.contacts@census.gov, https://www.census.gov/programs-surveys/ces.html; Retail Trade, 2017 Economic Census and Wholesale Trade, 2017 Economic Census.

U.S. Department of Commerce (DOC), International Trade Administration (ITA), 1401 Constitution Ave. NW, Washington, DC, 20230, USA, (800) 872-8723, https://www.trade.gov/; TradeStats Express (TSE).

CLOTHING AND ACCESSORY STORES-RETAIL-SALES

International Council of Shopping Centers (ICSC), 1251 Avenue of the Americas, 45th Fl., New York, NY, 10020-1104, USA, (646) 728-3800, (844) 728-4272, (732) 694-1690, membership@icsc.org, https://www.icsc.org; The Halo Effect II: Quantifying the Impact of Omnichannel.

The NPD Group, 900 W Shore Rd., Port Washington, NY, 11050, USA, (516) 625-0700, contactnpd@npd.com, https://www.npd.com; Fashion Accessories.

U.S. Census Bureau, 4600 Silver Hill Rd., Washington, DC, 20233, USA, (301) 763-4636, (800) 923-8282, https://www.census.gov; Economic Census, Nonemployer Statistics (NES) 2019.

U.S. Census Bureau, Center for Economic Studies (CES), 4600 Silver Hill Rd., Washington, DC, 20233, USA, (301) 763-6460, (301) 763-5935, ces.contacts@census.gov, https://www.census.gov/programs-surveys/ces.html; Retail Trade, 2017 Economic Census and Wholesale Trade, 2017 Economic Census.

U.S. Department of Commerce (DOC), International Trade Administration (ITA), 1401 Constitution Ave. NW, Washington, DC, 20230, USA, (800) 872-8723, https://www.trade.gov/; TradeStats Express (TSE).

COAL

See also PETROLEUM INDUSTRY AND TRADE

U.S. Library of Congress (LOC), Congressional Research Service (CRS), 101 Independence Ave. SE, Washington, DC, 20540, USA, (202) 707-5000, https://www.loc.gov/crsinfo/; Renewable Energy and Energy Efficiency Incentives: A Summary of Federal Programs.

COAL-CAR LOADINGS

Association of American Railroads (AAR), 425 3rd St. SW, Washington, DC, 20024, USA, (202) 639-2100, https://www.aar.org; Freight Commodity Statistics 2022 and Weekly Railroad Traffic Online.

COAL-CONSUMPTION

U.S. Energy Information Administration (EIA), 1000 Independence Ave. SW, Washington, DC, 20585, USA, (202) 586-8800, infoctr@eia.gov, https://www.eia.gov; Annual Energy Outlook 2022; Monthly Energy Review (MER); and State Energy Data System (SEDS).

COAL-CONSUMPTION-ELECTRIC UTILITIES

Edison Electric Institute (EEI), 701 Pennsylvania Ave. NW, Washington, DC, 20004-2696, USA, (202) 508-5000, eeiorders@eei.org, https://www.eei.org; Electric Perspectives.

U.S. Energy Information Administration (EIA), 1000 Independence Ave. SW, Washington, DC, 20585, USA, (202) 586-8800, infoctr@eia.gov, https://www.eia.gov; Electric Power Annual 2021 and Electric Power Monthly.

COAL-INTERNATIONAL TRADE

U.S. Census Bureau, International Trade Program, 4600 Silver Hill Rd., Washington, DC, 20233, USA, (800) 549-0595, eid.international.trade.data@census.gov, https://www.census.gov/foreign-trade; International Trade Data.

U.S. Energy Information Administration (EIA), 1000 Independence Ave. SW, Washington, DC, 20585, USA, (202) 586-8800, infoctr@eia.gov, https://www.eia.gov; Annual Coal Report 2020; Annual Energy Outlook 2022; and Monthly Energy Review (MER).

COAL-PRICES

U.S. Energy Information Administration (EIA), 1000 Independence Ave. SW, Washington, DC, 20585, USA, (202) 586-8800, infoctr@eia.gov, https://www.eia.gov; Monthly Energy Review (MER).

COAL-PRODUCTION

International Energy Agency (IEA), 9 Rue de la Federation, Paris, 75739, FRA, info@iea.org, https://www.iea.org/; World Energy Statistics and Balances.

U.S. Energy Information Administration (EIA), 1000 Independence Ave. SW, Washington, DC, 20585, USA, (202) 586-8800, infoctr@eia.gov, https://www.eia.gov; Annual Coal Report 2020; Annual Energy Outlook 2022; Monthly Energy Review (MER); and Weekly Coal Production.

COAL-PRODUCTION-WORLD

International Energy Agency (IEA), 9 Rue de la Federation, Paris, 75739, FRA, info@iea.org, https://www.iea.org/; World Energy Statistics and Balances.

U.S. Department of the Interior (DOI), U.S. Geological Survey (USGS), National Minerals Information Center (NMIC), 12201 Sunrise Valley Dr., Reston, VA, 20192, USA, (703) 648-4920, (703) 648-7971, (703) 648-4995, sfortier@usgs.gov, https://www.usgs.gov/centers/nmic; Mineral Commodity Summaries 2022 and Minerals Yearbook.

U.S. Energy Information Administration (EIA), 1000 Independence Ave. SW, Washington, DC, 20585, USA, (202) 586-8800, infoctr@eia.gov, https://www.eia.gov; International Energy Outlook 2021.

COAL-RESERVES

U.S. Energy Information Administration (EIA), 1000 Independence Ave. SW, Washington, DC, 20585, USA, (202) 586-8800, infoctr@eia.gov, https://www.eia.gov; Annual Coal Report 2020.

COAL MINING INDUSTRY-CAPITAL

U.S. Census Bureau, Center for Economic Studies (CES), 4600 Silver Hill Rd., Washington, DC, 20233, USA, (301) 763-6460, (301) 763-5935, ces.contacts@census.gov, https://www.census.gov/programs-surveys/ces.html; Mining, Quarrying and Oil and Gas Extraction, 2017 Economic Census.

COAL MINING INDUSTRY-EARNINGS

U.S. Department of Labor (DOL), Bureau of Labor Statistics (BLS), Postal Square Bldg., 2 Massachusetts Ave. NE, Washington, DC, 20212-0001, USA, (202) 691-5200, (202) 691-7890, blsdata_staff@bls.gov, https://www.bls.gov; Current Employment Statistics (CES).

COAL MINING INDUSTRY-EMPLOYMENT

U.S. Department of Labor (DOL), Bureau of Labor Statistics (BLS), Postal Square Bldg., 2 Massachusetts Ave. NE, Washington, DC, 20212-0001, USA, (202) 691-5200, (202) 691-7890, blsdata_staff@bls.gov, https://www.bls.gov; Current Employment Statistics (CES) and Industry-Occupation Matrix Data, By Occupation.

U.S. Energy Information Administration (EIA), 1000 Independence Ave. SW, Washington, DC, 20585, USA, (202) 586-8800, infoctr@eia.gov, https://www.eia.gov; Annual Coal Report 2020.

COAL MINING INDUSTRY-ESTABLISHMENTS

U.S. Census Bureau, Center for Economic Studies (CES), 4600 Silver Hill Rd., Washington, DC, 20233, USA, (301) 763-6460, (301) 763-5935, ces.contacts@census.gov, https://www.census.gov/programs-surveys/ces.html; Mining, Quarrying and Oil and Gas Extraction, 2017 Economic Census.

COAL MINING INDUSTRY-INDUSTRIAL SAFETY

U.S. Department of Labor (DOL), Bureau of Labor Statistics (BLS), Postal Square Bldg., 2 Massachusetts Ave. NE, Washington, DC, 20212-0001, USA, (202) 691-5200, (202) 691-7890, blsdata_staff@bls.gov, https://www.bls.gov; Injuries, Illnesses, and Fatalities (IIF).

U.S. Department of Labor (DOL), Mine Safety and Health Administration (MSHA), 201 12th St. S, Ste. 401, Arlington, VA, 22202-5450, USA, (202) 693-9400, askmsha@dol.gov, https://www.msha.gov; Mine Safety and Health at a Glance; Mining Industry Accident, Injuries, Employment, and Production Statistics and Reports; MSHA Fatality Reports; and Statistics Single Source Page.

COAL MINING INDUSTRY-MINES

U.S. Energy Information Administration (EIA), 1000 Independence Ave. SW, Washington, DC, 20585, USA, (202) 586-8800, infoctr@eia.gov, https://www.eia.gov; Annual Coal Report 2020 and International Energy Outlook 2021.

COAL MINING INDUSTRY-OUTPUT

Board of Governors of the Federal Reserve System, Constitution Ave. NW, Washington, DC, 20551, USA, (202) 452-3000, (202) 263-4869 (TDD), https://www.federalreserve.gov; Federal Reserve Bulletin and Industrial Production and Capacity Utilization 2023.

International Energy Agency (IEA), 9 Rue de la Federation, Paris, 75739, FRA, info@iea.org, https://www.iea.org/; World Energy Statistics and Balances.

U.S. Energy Information Administration (EIA), 1000 Independence Ave. SW, Washington, DC, 20585, USA, (202) 586-8800, infoctr@eia.gov, https://www.eia.gov; Monthly Energy Review (MER) and State Energy Data System (SEDS).

U.S. Library of Congress (LOC), Congressional Research Service (CRS), 101 Independence Ave. SE, Washington, DC, 20540, USA, (202) 707-5000, https://www.loc.gov/crsinfo/; Renewable Energy and Energy Efficiency Incentives: A Summary of Federal Programs.

COAL MINING INDUSTRY-PRODUCTIVITY

U.S. Department of Labor (DOL), Bureau of Labor Statistics (BLS), Postal Square Bldg., 2 Massachusetts Ave. NE, Washington, DC, 20212-0001, USA, (202) 691-5200, (202) 691-7890, blsdata_staff@bls.gov, https://www.bls.gov; Productivity.

U.S. Energy Information Administration (EIA), 1000 Independence Ave. SW, Washington, DC, 20585, USA, (202) 586-8800, infoctr@eia.gov, https://www.eia.gov; Annual Coal Report 2020.

COAL MINING INDUSTRY-SHIPMENTS

Association of American Railroads (AAR), 425 3rd St. SW, Washington, DC, 20024, USA, (202) 639-2100, https://www.aar.org; Rail Transportation of Coal.

U.S. Census Bureau, Center for Economic Studies (CES), 4600 Silver Hill Rd., Washington, DC, 20233, USA, (301) 763-6460, (301) 763-5935, ces.contacts@census.gov, https://www.census.gov/programs-surveys/ces.html; Mining, Quarrying and Oil and Gas Extraction, 2017 Economic Census.

COAL MINING INDUSTRY-VALUE ADDED

U.S. Census Bureau, Center for Economic Studies (CES), 4600 Silver Hill Rd., Washington, DC, 20233, USA, (301) 763-6460, (301) 763-5935, ces.contacts@census.gov, https://www.census.gov/programs-surveys/ces.html; Mining, Quarrying and Oil and Gas Extraction, 2017 Economic Census.

COAST GUARD PERSONNEL

U.S. Department of Homeland Security (DHS), U.S. Coast Guard (USCG), Attn. National Command Center, U.S. Coastguard Stop 7318, 2703 Martin Luther King Jr. Ave. SE, Washington, DC, 20593-7318, USA, (202) 372-2100, nationalcommandcenter@uscg.mil, https://www.uscg.mil/; United States Coast Guard Annual Performance Report.

COASTAL POPULATION

Harvard T.H. Chan School of Public Health, Center for Climate, Health, and the Global Environment (Harvard C-CHANGE), 401 Park Dr., 4th Fl. W, Ste. 415, Boston, MA, 02215, USA, (617) 384-8350, cchange@hsph.harvard.edu, https://www.hsph.harvard.edu/c-change/; Flood Risk to Hospitals on the United States Atlantic and Gulf Coasts From Hurricanes and Sea Level Rise.

Oceana, 1025 Connecticut Ave. NW, Washington, DC, 20036, USA, (202) 833-3900, (877) 762-3262,

(202) 833-2070, info@oceana.org, https://oceana.org/; Permanent Protections From Offshore Drilling Benefit Coastal Economies and Help Fight Climate Change.

Yale Project on Climate Change Communication (YPCCC), Yale School of the Environment, 195 Prospect St., New Haven, CT, 06511, USA, (203) 432-5055, climatechange@yale.edu, https://climatecommunication.yale.edu/; Are Hurricane-prone States More Concerned about Climate Change?.

COBALT

U.S. Census Bureau, International Trade Program, 4600 Silver Hill Rd., Washington, DC, 20233, USA, (800) 549-0595, eid.international.trade.data@census.gov, https://www.census.gov/foreign-trade; International Trade Data.

U.S. Department of the Interior (DOI), U.S. Geological Survey (USGS), National Minerals Information Center (NMIC), 12201 Sunrise Valley Dr., Reston, VA, 20192, USA, (703) 648-4920, (703) 648-7971, (703) 648-4995, sfortier@usgs.gov, https://www.usgs.gov/centers/nmic; Mineral Commodity Summaries 2022 and Mineral Industry Surveys (MIS).

World Bureau of Metal Statistics (WBMS), 31 Star St., Ware, Hertfordshire, SG12 9BA, GBR, https://www.refinitiv.com/en/trading-solutions/world-bureau-metal-statistics; Cobalt/Stainless Steel Trade Statistics.

COCAINE

Drug Policy Alliance (DPA), 131 W 33rd St., 15th Fl., New York, NY, 10001, USA, (212) 613-8020, (212) 613-8021, contact@drugpolicy.org, https://drugpolicy.org/; Drug Facts.

U.S. Department of Justice (DOJ), Drug Enforcement Administration (DEA), 8701 Morrissette Dr., Springfield, VA, 22152, USA, (202) 307-1000, info@dea.gov, https://www.dea.gov; Drugs of Abuse: A DEA Resource Guide 2020.

COCAINE-ARRESTS

Substance Abuse and Mental Health Services Administration (SAMHSA), 5600 Fishers Ln., Rockville, MD, 20857, USA, (877) 726-4727, (800) 487-4889 (TTY), samhsainfo@samhsa.hhs.gov, https://www.samhsa.gov/; 2019-2020 National Survey on Drug Use and Health (NSDUH).

U.S. Department of Justice (DOJ), Drug Enforcement Administration (DEA), 8701 Morrissette Dr., Springfield, VA, 22152, USA, (202) 307-1000, info@dea.gov, https://www.dea.gov; 2020 National Drug Threat Assessment.

U.S. Department of Justice (DOJ), Federal Bureau of Investigation (FBI), 935 Pennsylvania Ave. NW, Washington, DC, 20535-0001, USA, (202) 324-3000, https://www.fbi.gov/; Crime in the United States 2019.

COCOA

U.S. Department of Agriculture (USDA), Economic Research Service (ERS), 1400 Independence Ave. SW, Mail Stop 1800, Washington, DC, 20250-0002, USA, (202) 720-2791, https://www.ers.usda.gov/; Food Price Outlook and Foreign Agricultural Trade of the United States (FATUS).

COCOS (KEELING) ISLANDS-AGRICULTURE

Routledge - Taylor & Francis Group, 6000 Broken Sound Pkwy. NW, Ste. 300, Boca Raton, FL, 33487, USA, (800) 634-1420, (800) 634-7064, orders@taylorandfrancis.com, https://www.routledge.com/; The Europa World Year Book 2022.

United Nations Food and Agricultural Organization (FAO), 2121 K St., Ste. 800B, Washington, DC, 20037, USA, (202) 653-2400 (Dial from U.S.), (202) 653-5760 (Fax from U.S.), fao-hq@fao.org, https://www.fao.org; AQUASTAT and The State of Food and Agriculture (SOFA) 2022.

COCOS (KEELING) ISLANDS-AIRLINES

Palgrave Macmillan, 1 New York Plaza, Ste. 4500, New York, NY, 10004-1562, USA, (800) 777-4643, orders@palgrave.com, https://www.palgrave.com/us; The Statesman's Yearbook, 2023.

COCOS (KEELING) ISLANDS-ARMED FORCES

Central Intelligence Agency (CIA), Office of Public Affairs, Washington, DC, 20505, USA, (703) 482-0623, https://www.cia.gov; The World Factbook.

Stockholm International Peace Research Institute (SIPRI), Signalistgatan 9, Stockholm, SE 169 72, SWE, https://www.sipri.org/; SIPRI Arms Transfers Database and SIPRI Military Expenditure Database.

COCOS (KEELING) ISLANDS-BROADCASTING

Central Intelligence Agency (CIA), Office of Public Affairs, Washington, DC, 20505, USA, (703) 482-0623, https://www.cia.gov; The World Factbook.

WRTH Publications Limited, PO Box 290, Oxford, OX2 7FT, GBR, sales@wrth.com, https://www.wrth.com; World Radio TV Handbook 2023.

COCOS (KEELING) ISLANDS-BUDGET

Central Intelligence Agency (CIA), Office of Public Affairs, Washington, DC, 20505, USA, (703) 482-0623, https://www.cia.gov; The World Factbook.

COCOS (KEELING) ISLANDS-CLIMATE

Palgrave Macmillan, 1 New York Plaza, Ste. 4500, New York, NY, 10004-1562, USA, (800) 777-4643, orders@palgrave.com, https://www.palgrave.com/us; The Statesman's Yearbook, 2023.

COCOS (KEELING) ISLANDS-CORN INDUSTRY

See COCOS (KEELING) ISLANDS-CROPS

COCOS (KEELING) ISLANDS-CROPS

United Nations Food and Agricultural Organization (FAO), 2121 K St., Ste. 800B, Washington, DC, 20037, USA, (202) 653-2400 (Dial from U.S.), (202) 653-5760 (Fax from U.S.), fao-hq@fao.org, https://www.fao.org; The State of Food and Agriculture (SOFA) 2022.

COCOS (KEELING) ISLANDS-DAIRY PROCESSING

United Nations Food and Agricultural Organization (FAO), 2121 K St., Ste. 800B, Washington, DC, 20037, USA, (202) 653-2400 (Dial from U.S.), (202) 653-5760 (Fax from U.S.), fao-hq@fao.org, https://www.fao.org; The State of Food and Agriculture (SOFA) 2022.

COCOS (KEELING) ISLANDS-ECONOMIC CONDITIONS

Bernan Press, 15250 NBN Way, Bldg. C, Blue Ridge Summit, PA, 17214, USA, (301) 459-2255, (800) 865-3457, (800) 865-3450, customercare@bernan.com, https://rowman.com/Page/Bernan; World Economic Outlook, April 2022.

Central Intelligence Agency (CIA), Office of Public Affairs, Washington, DC, 20505, USA, (703) 482-0623, https://www.cia.gov; The World Factbook.

COCOS (KEELING) ISLANDS-EDUCATION

Palgrave Macmillan, 1 New York Plaza, Ste. 4500, New York, NY, 10004-1562, USA, (800) 777-4643, orders@palgrave.com, https://www.palgrave.com/us; The Statesman's Yearbook, 2023.

COCOS (KEELING) ISLANDS-EXPORTS

Central Intelligence Agency (CIA), Office of Public Affairs, Washington, DC, 20505, USA, (703) 482-0623, https://www.cia.gov; The World Factbook.

COCOS (KEELING) ISLANDS-FERTILITY, HUMAN

Central Intelligence Agency (CIA), Office of Public Affairs, Washington, DC, 20505, USA, (703) 482-0623, https://www.cia.gov; The World Factbook.

COCOS (KEELING) ISLANDS-FERTILIZER INDUSTRY

United Nations Food and Agricultural Organization (FAO), 2121 K St., Ste. 800B, Washington, DC, 20037, USA, (202) 653-2400 (Dial from U.S.), (202) 653-5760 (Fax from U.S.), fao-hq@fao.org, https://www.fao.org; The State of Food and Agriculture (SOFA) 2022.

COCOS (KEELING) ISLANDS-FETAL MORTALITY

See COCOS (KEELING) ISLANDS-MORTALITY

COCOS (KEELING) ISLANDS-FINANCE, PUBLIC

Routledge - Taylor & Francis Group, 6000 Broken Sound Pkwy. NW, Ste. 300, Boca Raton, FL, 33487, USA, (800) 634-1420, (800) 634-7064, orders@taylorandfrancis.com, https://www.routledge.com/; The Europa World Year Book 2022.

United Nations Statistics Division (UNSD), United Nations Plz., New York, NY, 10017, USA, (800) 253-9646, (212) 963-9851, statistics@un.org, https://unstats.un.org; National Accounts Main Aggregates Database and National Accounts Statistics: Main Aggregates and Detailed Tables.

COCOS (KEELING) ISLANDS-FISHERIES

United Nations Food and Agricultural Organization (FAO), 2121 K St., Ste. 800B, Washington, DC, 20037, USA, (202) 653-2400 (Dial from U.S.), (202) 653-5760 (Fax from U.S.), fao-hq@fao.org, https://www.fao.org; FAO Yearbook of Fishery and Aquaculture Statistics 2019; Fishery Statistical Collections Global Capture Production; FishStatJ; and The State of Food and Agriculture (SOFA) 2022.

COCOS (KEELING) ISLANDS-FOOD

United Nations Food and Agricultural Organization (FAO), 2121 K St., Ste. 800B, Washington, DC, 20037, USA, (202) 653-2400 (Dial from U.S.), (202) 653-5760 (Fax from U.S.), fao-hq@fao.org, https://www.fao.org; The State of Food and Agriculture (SOFA) 2022.

COCOS (KEELING) ISLANDS-FORESTS AND FORESTRY

United Nations Food and Agricultural Organization (FAO), 2121 K St., Ste. 800B, Washington, DC, 20037, USA, (202) 653-2400 (Dial from U.S.), (202) 653-5760 (Fax from U.S.), fao-hq@fao.org, https://www.fao.org; The State of Food and Agriculture (SOFA) 2022.

COCOS (KEELING) ISLANDS-IMPORTS

Central Intelligence Agency (CIA), Office of Public Affairs, Washington, DC, 20505, USA, (703) 482-0623, https://www.cia.gov; The World Factbook.

COCOS (KEELING) ISLANDS-INDUSTRIES

Central Intelligence Agency (CIA), Office of Public Affairs, Washington, DC, 20505, USA, (703) 482-0623, https://www.cia.gov; The World Factbook.

COCOS (KEELING) ISLANDS-INFANT AND MATERNAL MORTALITY

See COCOS (KEELING) ISLANDS-MORTALITY

COCOS (KEELING) ISLANDS-INTERNATIONAL TRADE

Routledge - Taylor & Francis Group, 6000 Broken Sound Pkwy. NW, Ste. 300, Boca Raton, FL, 33487, USA, (800) 634-1420, (800) 634-7064, orders@taylorandfrancis.com, https://www.routledge.com/; The Europa World Year Book 2022.

United Nations Food and Agricultural Organization (FAO), 2121 K St., Ste. 800B, Washington, DC, 20037, USA, (202) 653-2400 (Dial from U.S.), (202) 653-5760 (Fax from U.S.), fao-hq@fao.org, https://www.fao.org; The State of Food and Agriculture (SOFA) 2022.

World Trade Organization (WTO), Ctre. William Rappard, Rue de Lausanne 154, Case postale, Geneva, CH-1211, SWI, enquiries@wto.org, https://www.wto.org; World Trade Statistical Review 2022.

COCOS (KEELING) ISLANDS-LABOR

Central Intelligence Agency (CIA), Office of Public Affairs, Washington, DC, 20505, USA, (703) 482-0623, https://www.cia.gov; The World Factbook.

United Nations Food and Agricultural Organization (FAO), 2121 K St., Ste. 800B, Washington, DC, 20037, USA, (202) 653-2400 (Dial from U.S.), (202) 653-5760 (Fax from U.S.), fao-hq@fao.org, https://www.fao.org; The State of Food and Agriculture (SOFA) 2022.

COCOS (KEELING) ISLANDS-LIFE EXPECTANCY

Central Intelligence Agency (CIA), Office of Public Affairs, Washington, DC, 20505, USA, (703) 482-0623, https://www.cia.gov; The World Factbook.

United Nations Department of Economic and Social Affairs (DESA), Population Division, 2 United Nations Plz., Rm. DC2-1950, New York, NY, 10017, USA, (212) 963-3209, (212) 963-2147, population@un.org, https://www.un.org/development/desa/pd/; World Population Ageing 2020 Highlights.

COCOS (KEELING) ISLANDS-LIVESTOCK

United Nations Food and Agricultural Organization (FAO), 2121 K St., Ste. 800B, Washington, DC, 20037, USA, (202) 653-2400 (Dial from U.S.), (202) 653-5760 (Fax from U.S.), fao-hq@fao.org, https://www.fao.org; The State of Food and Agriculture (SOFA) 2022.

COCOS (KEELING) ISLANDS-MARRIAGE

United Nations Statistics Division (UNSD), United Nations Plz., New York, NY, 10017, USA, (800) 253-9646, (212) 963-9851, statistics@un.org, https://unstats.un.org; Statistical Yearbook of the United Nations 2021.

COCOS (KEELING) ISLANDS-NUTRITION

United Nations Food and Agricultural Organization (FAO), 2121 K St., Ste. 800B, Washington, DC, 20037, USA, (202) 653-2400 (Dial from U.S.), (202) 653-5760 (Fax from U.S.), fao-hq@fao.org, https://www.fao.org; The State of Food and Agriculture (SOFA) 2022.

COCOS (KEELING) ISLANDS-PESTICIDES

United Nations Food and Agricultural Organization (FAO), 2121 K St., Ste. 800B, Washington, DC, 20037, USA, (202) 653-2400 (Dial from U.S.), (202) 653-5760 (Fax from U.S.), fao-hq@fao.org, https://www.fao.org; The State of Food and Agriculture (SOFA) 2022.

COCOS (KEELING) ISLANDS-PETROLEUM INDUSTRY AND TRADE

United Nations Food and Agricultural Organization (FAO), 2121 K St., Ste. 800B, Washington, DC, 20037, USA, (202) 653-2400 (Dial from U.S.), (202) 653-5760 (Fax from U.S.), fao-hq@fao.org, https://www.fao.org; The State of Food and Agriculture (SOFA) 2022.

COCOS (KEELING) ISLANDS-POPULATION

Central Intelligence Agency (CIA), Office of Public Affairs, Washington, DC, 20505, USA, (703) 482-0623, https://www.cia.gov; The World Factbook.

Palgrave Macmillan, 1 New York Plaza, Ste. 4500, New York, NY, 10004-1562, USA, (800) 777-4643, orders@palgrave.com, https://www.palgrave.com/us; The Statesman's Yearbook, 2023.

Routledge - Taylor & Francis Group, 6000 Broken Sound Pkwy. NW, Ste. 300, Boca Raton, FL, 33487, USA, (800) 634-1420, (800) 634-7064, orders@taylorandfrancis.com, https://www.routledge.com/; The Europa World Year Book 2022.

UK Data Service, University of Essex, Wivenhoe Park, Colchester, Essex, CO4 3SQ, GBR, https://ukdataservice.ac.uk/; International Aggregate Data.

UNESCO Institute for Statistics, C.P 250 Succursale H, Montreal, QC, H3G 2K8, CAN, (514) 343-6880 (Dial from U.S.), (514) 343-5740 (Fax from U.S.), uis.publications@unesco.org, http://uis.unesco.org/; UIS.Stat.

United Nations Department of Economic and Social Affairs (DESA), Population Division, 2 United Nations Plz., Rm. DC2-1950, New York, NY, 10017, USA, (212) 963-3209, (212) 963-2147, population@un.org, https://www.un.org/development/desa/pd/; Revision of World Urbanization Prospects and World Population Ageing 2020 Highlights.

United Nations Statistics Division (UNSD), United Nations Plz., New York, NY, 10017, USA, (800) 253-9646, (212) 963-9851, statistics@un.org, https://unstats.un.org; Statistical Yearbook of the United Nations 2021.

COCOS (KEELING) ISLANDS-POPULATION DENSITY

Central Intelligence Agency (CIA), Office of Public Affairs, Washington, DC, 20505, USA, (703) 482-0623, https://www.cia.gov; The World Factbook.

Routledge - Taylor & Francis Group, 6000 Broken Sound Pkwy. NW, Ste. 300, Boca Raton, FL, 33487, USA, (800) 634-1420, (800) 634-7064, orders@taylorandfrancis.com, https://www.routledge.com/; The Europa World Year Book 2022.

COCOS (KEELING) ISLANDS-POSTAL SERVICE

Palgrave Macmillan, 1 New York Plaza, Ste. 4500, New York, NY, 10004-1562, USA, (800) 777-4643, orders@palgrave.com, https://www.palgrave.com/us; The Statesman's Yearbook, 2023.

COCOS (KEELING) ISLANDS-POWER RESOURCES

United Nations Food and Agricultural Organization (FAO), 2121 K St., Ste. 800B, Washington, DC, 20037, USA, (202) 653-2400 (Dial from U.S.), (202) 653-5760 (Fax from U.S.), fao-hq@fao.org, https://www.fao.org; The State of Food and Agriculture (SOFA) 2022.

COCOS (KEELING) ISLANDS-PUBLIC HEALTH

Palgrave Macmillan, 1 New York Plaza, Ste. 4500, New York, NY, 10004-1562, USA, (800) 777-4643, orders@palgrave.com, https://www.palgrave.com/us; The Statesman's Yearbook, 2023.

U.S. Census Bureau, 4600 Silver Hill Rd., Washington, DC, 20233, USA, (301) 763-4636, (800) 923-8282, https://www.census.gov; HIV/AIDS Surveillance Data Base.

United Nations Department of Economic and Social Affairs (DESA), Population Division, 2 United Nations Plz., Rm. DC2-1950, New York, NY, 10017, USA, (212) 963-3209, (212) 963-2147, population@un.org, https://www.un.org/development/desa/pd/; World Fertility Data 2019.

COCOS (KEELING) ISLANDS-RELIGION

Central Intelligence Agency (CIA), Office of Public Affairs, Washington, DC, 20505, USA, (703) 482-0623, https://www.cia.gov; The World Factbook.

Palgrave Macmillan, 1 New York Plaza, Ste. 4500, New York, NY, 10004-1562, USA, (800) 777-4643, orders@palgrave.com, https://www.palgrave.com/us; The Statesman's Yearbook, 2023.

COCOS (KEELING) ISLANDS-TELEPHONE

Palgrave Macmillan, 1 New York Plaza, Ste. 4500, New York, NY, 10004-1562, USA, (800) 777-4643, orders@palgrave.com, https://www.palgrave.com/us; The Statesman's Yearbook, 2023.

COCOS (KEELING) ISLANDS-TRADE

See COCOS (KEELING) ISLANDS-INTERNATIONAL TRADE

COCOS (KEELING) ISLANDS-TRANSPORTATION

Central Intelligence Agency (CIA), Office of Public Affairs, Washington, DC, 20505, USA, (703) 482-0623, https://www.cia.gov; The World Factbook.

Palgrave Macmillan, 1 New York Plaza, Ste. 4500, New York, NY, 10004-1562, USA, (800) 777-4643, orders@palgrave.com, https://www.palgrave.com/us; The Statesman's Yearbook, 2023.

COCOS (KEELING) ISLANDS-VITAL STATISTICS

U.S. Census Bureau, 4600 Silver Hill Rd., Washington, DC, 20233, USA, (301) 763-4636, (800) 923-8282, https://www.census.gov; HIV/AIDS Surveillance Data Base.

United Nations Department of Economic and Social Affairs (DESA), Population Division, 2 United Nations Plz., Rm. DC2-1950, New York, NY, 10017, USA, (212) 963-3209, (212) 963-2147, population@un.org, https://www.un.org/development/desa/pd/; World Contraceptive Use 2021: Estimates and Projections of Family Planning Indicators and World Marriage Data 2019.

United Nations Statistics Division (UNSD), United Nations Plz., New York, NY, 10017, USA, (800) 253-9646, (212) 963-9851, statistics@un.org, https://unstats.un.org; Statistical Yearbook of the United Nations 2021.

COD

National Oceanic and Atmospheric Administration (NOAA), National Marine Fisheries Service (NOAA Fisheries), 1315 East-West Hwy., 14th Fl., Silver Spring, MD, 20910, USA, (301) 427-8000, https://www.fisheries.noaa.gov/; Fisheries of the United States, 2020.

COFFEE-CONSUMPTION

National Coffee Association (NCA), 45 Broadway, Ste. 1140, New York, NY, 10006, USA, (212) 766-4007, (212) 766-5815, https://www.ncausa.org; Coffee, Consumers, & COVID-19: Road Map to Recovery and National Coffee Data Trends (NCDT) 2022.

U.S. Department of Agriculture (USDA), Economic Research Service (ERS), 1400 Independence Ave. SW, Mail Stop 1800, Washington, DC, 20250-0002, USA, (202) 720-2791, https://www.ers.usda.gov/; Food Price Outlook.

COFFEE-INTERNATIONAL TRADE

U.S. Census Bureau, International Trade Program, 4600 Silver Hill Rd., Washington, DC, 20233, USA, (800) 549-0595, eid.international.trade.data@census.gov, https://www.census.gov/foreign-trade; International Trade Data.

U.S. Department of Agriculture (USDA), Economic Research Service (ERS), 1400 Independence Ave. SW, Mail Stop 1800, Washington, DC, 20250-0002, USA, (202) 720-2791, https://www.ers.usda.gov/; Foreign Agricultural Trade of the United States (FATUS) and Outlook for U.S. Agricultural Trade: May 2022.

U.S. Department of Agriculture (USDA), Foreign Agricultural Service (FAS), 1400 Independence Ave. SW, Mail Stop 1001, Washington, DC, 20250, USA, (202) 720-3935, https://www.fas.usda.gov/; Coffee: World Markets and Trade.

COFFEE-PRICE INDEXES

U.S. Department of Labor (DOL), Bureau of Labor Statistics (BLS), Postal Square Bldg., 2 Massachusetts Ave. NE, Washington, DC, 20212-0001, USA, (202) 691-5200, (202) 691-7890, blsdata_staff@bls.gov, https://www.bls.gov; Consumer Price Index (CPI) Databases.

COFFEE-PRICES

U.S. Department of Labor (DOL), Bureau of Labor Statistics (BLS), Postal Square Bldg., 2 Massachusetts Ave. NE, Washington, DC, 20212-0001, USA, (202) 691-5200, (202) 691-7890, blsdata_staff@bls.gov, https://www.bls.gov; Consumer Price Index (CPI) Databases.

COFFEE-WORLD PRODUCTION

U.S. Department of Agriculture (USDA), National Agricultural Statistics Service (USDA-NASS), 1400 Independence Ave. SW, Washington, DC, 20250, USA, (800) 727-9540, nass@nass.usda.gov, https://www.nass.usda.gov; Quick Stats.

United Nations Statistics Division (UNSD), United Nations Plz., New York, NY, 10017, USA, (800) 253-9646, (212) 963-9851, statistics@un.org, https://unstats.un.org; Monthly Bulletin of Statistics Online.

COGENERATION OF ELECTRICITY

Edison Electric Institute (EEI), 701 Pennsylvania Ave. NW, Washington, DC, 20004-2696, USA, (202) 508-5000, eeiorders@eei.org, https://www.eei.org; Electric Perspectives.

U.S. Energy Information Administration (EIA), 1000 Independence Ave. SW, Washington, DC, 20585, USA, (202) 586-8800, infoctr@eia.gov, https://www.eia.gov; Electric Power Annual 2021.

COGNITION

U.S. Department of Health and Human Services (HHS), National Toxicology Program (NTP), PO Box 12233, MD K2-03, Research Triangle Park, NC, 27709, USA, (984) 287-3209, cdm@niehs.nih.gov, https://ntp.niehs.nih.gov; Systematic Review of Flouride Exposure and Neurodevelopmental and Cognitive Health Effects.

COLLEGE GRADUATES

The Brookings Institution, 1775 Massachusetts Ave. NW, Washington, DC, 20036, USA, (202) 797-6000, communications@brookings.edu, https://www.brookings.edu/; Policies and Payoffs to Addressing America's College Graduation Deficit.

National Student Clearinghouse Research Center, 2300 Dulles Station Blvd., Ste. 220, Herndon, VA, 21071, USA, https://nscresearchcenter.org; Completing College: National and State Reports.

U.S. Government Accountablity Office (GAO), 441 G St. NW, Washington, DC, 20548, USA, (202) 512-3000, contact@gao.gov, https://www.gao.gov/; Public Service Loan Forgiveness: Improving the Temporary Expanded Process Could Help Reduce Borrower Confusion.

University of California Los Angeles (UCLA) School of Law, The Williams Institute, 1060 Veteran Ave., Ste. 134, PO Box 957092, Los Angeles, CA, 90095-7092, USA, (310) 267-4382, (310) 825-7270, williamsinstitute@law.ucla.edu, https://williamsinstitute.law.ucla.edu/; Educational Experiences of Transgender People: Findings from a National Probability Survey.

COLLEGE GRADUATES-EMPLOYMENT

Association of American Colleges & Universitites (AAC&U), 1818 R St. NW, Washington, DC, 20009, USA, (202) 387-3760, information@aacu.org, https://www.aacu.org/; Peer Review: Faculty Development for Self-Renewal.

Michigan State University (MSU) Career Services Network, Collegiate Employment Research Institute (CERI), Student Services Bldg., 556 E Circle Dr., Rm. 113, East Lansing, MI, 48824, USA, (517) 355-2211, gardnerp@msu.edu, https://ceri.msu.edu/; College Hiring Outlook 2023 and Recruiting Trends 2020-2021.

COLLEGE STUDENTS

Alliance for Excellent Education (All4Ed), 1425 K St. NW, Ste. 700, Washington, DC, 20005, USA, (202) 828-0828, (202) 828-0821, https://all4ed.org; Undermeasuring: College and Career Readiness Indicators May Not Reflect College and Career Outcomes.

Association of American Universities (AAU), 1200 New York Ave. NW, Ste. 550, Washington, DC, 20005, USA, (202) 408-7500, (202) 408-8184, https://www.aau.edu; AAU Campus Climate Survey.

The Brookings Institution, 1775 Massachusetts Ave. NW, Washington, DC, 20036, USA, (202) 797-6000, communications@brookings.edu, https://www.brookings.edu/; Policies and Payoffs to Addressing America's College Graduation Deficit.

The Chronicle of Higher Education, 1255 23rd St. NW, Washington, DC, 20037, USA, (202) 466-1000, circulation@chronicle.com, https://www.chronicle.com/; Almanac of Higher Education, 2021 and The Chronicle of Higher Education.

College Board, 250 Vesey St., New York, NY, 10281, USA, (212) 713-8000, (800) 323-7155, (212) 713-8143, store_help@collegeboard.org, https://www.collegeboard.com; Living Expense Budget 2021-2022.

Foundation for Individual Rights and Expression (FIRE), 510 Walnut St., Ste. 1250, Philadelphia, PA, 19106, USA, (215) 717-3473, fire@thefire.org, https://www.thefire.org/; 2023 College Free Speech Rankings and Spotlight on Speech Codes 2023.

Gap Year Association (GYA), PO Box 17427, Portland, OR, 97217, USA, (503) 206-7336, info@gapyearassociation.org, https://gapyearassociation.org/; Annual State of the Field Survey 2020-2021 and National Alumni Survey 2020 Report.

GreatSchools, 2201 Broadway, 4th Fl., Oakland, CA, 94612, USA, https://www.greatschools.org/; Success without Selection: Identifying District High Schools that Help Underserved Students Enroll and Persist in College.

Indiana University Center for Postsecondary Research, National Survey of Student Engagement (NSSE), 201 N Rose Ave., Bloomington, IN, 47405, USA, (812) 856-5824, nsse@indiana.edu, https://nsse.indiana.edu/; Engagement Insights 2022: Survey Findings on the Quality of Undergraduate Education.

Inside Higher Ed, 1150 Connecticut Ave. NW, Ste. 400, Washington, DC, 20036, USA, (202) 659-9208, (202) 659-9381, info@insidehighered.com, https://www.insidehighered.com/; Survey of College and University Admissions Directors, 2022.

Institute of International Education (IIE), 1 World Trade Center, 36th Fl., New York, NY, 10007, USA, (212) 883-8200, (212) 984-5452, iieresearch@iie.org, https://www.iie.org; International Student Enrollment Survey, November 2022 and Open Doors Data Portal for International Students.

National Bureau of Economic Research (NBER), 1050 Massachusetts Ave., Cambridge, MA, 02138, USA, (617) 868-3900, info@nber.org, https://www.nber.org/; Legacy and Athlete Preferences at Harvard.

Temple University, Hope Center for College, Community, and Justice, Medical Education & Research Bldg., 3500N Broad St., Philadelphia, PA, 19140, USA, (215) 204-7000, hopectr@temple.edu, https://hope4college.com/; The Hope Center Survey 2021: Basic Needs Insecurity During the Ongoing Pandemic.

U.S. Department of Education (ED), Institute of Education Sciences (IES), National Center for Education Statistics (NCES), Potomac Center Plaza, 550 12th St. SW, Washington, DC, 20202, USA, (202) 403-5551, https://nces.ed.gov/; Postsecondary Institutions and Cost of Attendance in 2021-2022; Degrees and Other Awards Conferred: 2020-2021, and 12-Month Enrollment: 2020-2021 and Trends Among Young Adults Over Three Decades, 1974-2006.

U.S. Department of Education (ED), Office of Postsecondary Education (OPE), Lyndon Baines Johnson Bldg., 400 Maryland Ave. SW, Washington, DC, 20202, USA, (202) 453-6914, https://www2.ed.gov/about/offices/list/ope; The Campus Safety and Security Data Analysis Cutting Tool.

U.S. Department of Justice (DOJ), Bureau of Justice Statistics (BJS), 810 7th St. NW, Washington, DC, 20531, USA, (202) 307-0765, askbjs@usdoj.gov, https://www.bjs.gov/; Rape and Sexual Assault Among College-Age Females, 1995-2013.

University of California Los Angeles (UCLA) School of Law, The Williams Institute, 1060 Veteran Ave., Ste. 134, PO Box 957092, Los Angeles, CA, 90095-7092, USA, (310) 267-4382, (310) 825-7270, williamsinstitute@law.ucla.edu, https://williamsinstitute.law.ucla.edu/; Educational Experiences of Transgender People: Findings from a National Probability Survey.

University of California Los Angeles (UCLA), Higher Education Research Institute (HERI), SEIS Bldg., 300 Charles E. Young Dr. N, Los Angeles, CA, 90095-1522, USA, (310) 825-1925, heri@ucla.edu, https://heri.ucla.edu/; 2022 Your First College Year (YFCY) Survey.

University of California Los Angeles (UCLA), The Civil Rights Project, 8370 Math Sciences, PO Box 951521, Los Angeles, CA, 90095-1521, USA, crp@ucla.edu, https://www.civilrightsproject.ucla.edu/; The Walls Around Opportunity: The Failure of Colorblind Policy for Higher Education.

COLLEGE STUDENTS-ATTITUDES

John S. and James L. Knight Foundation, 2850 Tigertail Ave., Ste. 600, Miami, FL, 33133, USA, (305) 908-2600, (305) 908-2698, https://knightfoundation.org; College Student Views on Free Expression and Campus Speech 2022.

COLLEGE TUITION

The Brookings Institution, 1775 Massachusetts Ave. NW, Washington, DC, 20036, USA, (202) 797-6000, communications@brookings.edu, https://www.brookings.edu/; Policies and Payoffs to Addressing America's College Graduation Deficit.

College Board, 250 Vesey St., New York, NY, 10281, USA, (212) 713-8000, (800) 323-7155, (212) 713-8143, store_help@collegeboard.org, https://www.collegeboard.com; Trends in College Pricing and Student Aid 2022 and Trends in Student Aid 2022: Data in Excel.

Inside Higher Ed, 1150 Connecticut Ave. NW, Ste. 400, Washington, DC, 20036, USA, (202) 659-9208, (202) 659-9381, info@insidehighered.com, https://www.insidehighered.com/; Survey of College and University Admissions Directors, 2022.

Investment Company Institute (ICI), 1401 H St. NW, Ste. 1200, Washington, DC, 20005, USA, (202) 326-5800, doug.richardson@ici.org, https://www.ici.org/; Quarterly 529 Plan Program Statistics.

U.S. Department of Education (ED), Institute of Education Sciences (IES), 550 12th St. SW, Washington, DC, 20024, USA, (202) 245-6940, contact.ies@ed.gov, https://ies.ed.gov/; College Affordability and Transparency Center.

U.S. Department of Education (ED), Institute of Education Sciences (IES), National Center for Education Statistics (NCES), Potomac Center Plaza, 550 12th St. SW, Washington, DC, 20202, USA, (202) 403-5551, https://nces.ed.gov/; Digest of Education Statistics, 2020 and Postsecondary Institutions and Cost of Attendance in 2021-2022; Degrees and Other Awards Conferred: 2020-2021, and 12-Month Enrollment: 2020-2021.

COLLEGE TUITION-PRICE INDEXES

U.S. Department of Labor (DOL), Bureau of Labor Statistics (BLS), Postal Square Bldg., 2 Massachusetts Ave. NE, Washington, DC, 20212-0001, USA, (202) 691-5200, (202) 691-7890, blsdata_staff@bls.gov, https://www.bls.gov; Consumer Price Index (CPI) Databases.

COLLEGES AND UNIVERSITIES

See EDUCATION-HIGHER EDUCATION INSTITUTIONS

COLOMBIA-NATIONAL STATISTICAL OFFICE

Departamento Administrativo Nacional de Estadisticas of Colombia (National Administrative Department of Statistics of Colombia), Carrera 59 No.26-70, Bogota, 111321, COL, contacto@dane.gov.co, https://www.dane.gov.co/; National Data Reports (Colombia).

COLOMBIA-AGRICULTURE

The Economist Group: Economist Intelligence Unit (EIU), 900 3rd Ave., 16th Fl., New York, NY, 10022, USA, (212) 541-0500, americas@eiu.com, https://www.eiu.com; Colombia Country Report.

Euromonitor International, Inc., 1 N Dearborn St., Ste. 1700, Chicago, IL, 60602, USA, (312) 922-1115, (312) 922-1157, info-usa@euromonitor.com, https://www.euromonitor.com/; Geographies.

Inter-American Development Bank (IDB), 1300 New York Ave. NW, Washington, DC, 20577, USA, (202) 623-1000, (202) 623-3096, https://www.iadb.org/en; Latin Macro Watch (LMW).

Palgrave Macmillan, 1 New York Plaza, Ste. 4500, New York, NY, 10004-1562, USA, (800) 777-4643, orders@palgrave.com, https://www.palgrave.com/us; The Statesman's Yearbook, 2023.

Routledge - Taylor & Francis Group, 6000 Broken Sound Pkwy. NW, Ste. 300, Boca Raton, FL, 33487, USA, (800) 634-1420, (800) 634-7064, orders@taylorandfrancis.com, https://www.routledge.com/; The Europa World Year Book 2022.

United Nations Food and Agricultural Organization (FAO), 2121 K St., Ste. 800B, Washington, DC, 20037, USA, (202) 653-2400 (Dial from U.S.), (202) 653-5760 (Fax from U.S.), fao-hq@fao.org, https://www.fao.org; AQUASTAT and The State of Food and Agriculture (SOFA) 2022.

United Nations Statistics Division (UNSD), United Nations Plz., New York, NY, 10017, USA, (800) 253-9646, (212) 963-9851, statistics@un.org, https://unstats.un.org; Statistical Yearbook of the United Nations 2021.

The World Bank, 1818 H St. NW, Washington, DC, 20433, USA, (202) 473-1000, (202) 477-6391, eds03@worldbank.org, https://www.worldbank.org/; Colombia (report).

COLOMBIA-AIRLINES

International Civil Aviation Organization (ICAO), 999 Robert-Bourassa Blvd., Montreal, QC, H3C 5H7, CAN, (514) 954-8219 (Dial from U.S.), (514) 954-6077 (Fax from U.S.), icaohq@icao.int, https://www.icao.int; ICAO Regional Reports.

Palgrave Macmillan, 1 New York Plaza, Ste. 4500, New York, NY, 10004-1562, USA, (800) 777-4643, orders@palgrave.com, https://www.palgrave.com/us; The Statesman's Yearbook, 2023.

Routledge - Taylor & Francis Group, 6000 Broken Sound Pkwy. NW, Ste. 300, Boca Raton, FL, 33487, USA, (800) 634-1420, (800) 634-7064, orders@taylorandfrancis.com, https://www.routledge.com/; The Europa World Year Book 2022.

COLOMBIA-ALUMINUM PRODUCTION

See COLOMBIA-MINERAL INDUSTRIES

COLOMBIA-ARMED FORCES

Central Intelligence Agency (CIA), Office of Public Affairs, Washington, DC, 20505, USA, (703) 482-0623, https://www.cia.gov; The World Factbook.

International Institute for Strategic Studies (IISS) - Americas, 2121 K St. NW, Ste. 600, Washington, DC, 20037, USA, (202) 659-1490, (202) 659-1499, https://www.iiss.org/; Armed Conflict Survey 2021 and The Military Balance 2022.

Palgrave Macmillan, 1 New York Plaza, Ste. 4500, New York, NY, 10004-1562, USA, (800) 777-4643, orders@palgrave.com, https://www.palgrave.com/us; The Statesman's Yearbook, 2023.

Stockholm International Peace Research Institute (SIPRI), Signalistgatan 9, Stockholm, SE 169 72, SWE, https://www.sipri.org/; SIPRI Arms Transfers Database and SIPRI Military Expenditure Database.

COLOMBIA-BALANCE OF PAYMENTS

Inter-American Development Bank (IDB), 1300 New York Ave. NW, Washington, DC, 20577, USA, (202) 623-1000, (202) 623-3096, https://www.iadb.org/en; Latin Macro Watch (LMW).

International Monetary Fund (IMF), 700 19th St. NW, Washington, DC, 20431, USA, (202) 623-7000, (202) 623-4661, publications@imf.org, https://www.imf.org; Balance of Payments Statistics: Annual Report 2021.

Routledge - Taylor & Francis Group, 6000 Broken Sound Pkwy. NW, Ste. 300, Boca Raton, FL, 33487, USA, (800) 634-1420, (800) 634-7064, orders@taylorandfrancis.com, https://www.routledge.com/; The Europa World Year Book 2022.

United Nations Conference on Trade and Development (UNCTAD), Palais des Nations, Geneva, 1211, SWI, (212) 963-6896, unctadinfo@unctad.org, https://unctad.org; Handbook of Statistics 2021.

United Nations Economic Commission for Latin America and the Caribbean (ECLAC), Casilla 179-D, Santiago, 7630412, CHL, (202) 596-3713, prensa@cepal.org, https://www.cepal.org/en; Economic Survey of Latin America and the Caribbean 2021: Labour Dynamics and Employment Policies for Sustainable and Inclusive Recovery Beyond the COVID-19 Crisis.

The World Bank, 1818 H St. NW, Washington, DC, 20433, USA, (202) 473-1000, (202) 477-6391, eds03@worldbank.org, https://www.worldbank.org/; Colombia (report) and World Development Report 2022: Finance for an Equitable Recovery.

COLOMBIA-BANKS AND BANKING

Euromonitor International, Inc., 1 N Dearborn St., Ste. 1700, Chicago, IL, 60602, USA, (312) 922-1115, (312) 922-1157, info-usa@euromonitor.com, https://www.euromonitor.com/; Geographies.

Inter-American Development Bank (IDB), 1300 New York Ave. NW, Washington, DC, 20577, USA, (202) 623-1000, (202) 623-3096, https://www.iadb.org/en; Latin Macro Watch (LMW).

International Monetary Fund (IMF), 700 19th St. NW, Washington, DC, 20431, USA, (202) 623-7000, (202) 623-4661, publications@imf.org, https://www.imf.org; International Financial Statistics (IFS).

Routledge - Taylor & Francis Group, 6000 Broken Sound Pkwy. NW, Ste. 300, Boca Raton, FL, 33487, USA, (800) 634-1420, (800) 634-7064, orders@taylorandfrancis.com, https://www.routledge.com/; The Europa World Year Book 2022.

United Nations Statistics Division (UNSD), United Nations Plz., New York, NY, 10017, USA, (800) 253-9646, (212) 963-9851, statistics@un.org, https://unstats.un.org; Statistical Yearbook of the United Nations 2021.

COLOMBIA-BARLEY PRODUCTION

See COLOMBIA-CROPS

COLOMBIA-BONDS

Inter-American Development Bank (IDB), 1300 New York Ave. NW, Washington, DC, 20577, USA, (202) 623-1000, (202) 623-3096, https://www.iadb.org/en; Latin Macro Watch (LMW).

COLOMBIA-BROADCASTING

Central Intelligence Agency (CIA), Office of Public Affairs, Washington, DC, 20505, USA, (703) 482-0623, https://www.cia.gov; The World Factbook.

Euromonitor International, Inc., 1 N Dearborn St., Ste. 1700, Chicago, IL, 60602, USA, (312) 922-1115, (312) 922-1157, info-usa@euromonitor.com, https://www.euromonitor.com/; Geographies.

Palgrave Macmillan, 1 New York Plaza, Ste. 4500, New York, NY, 10004-1562, USA, (800) 777-4643, orders@palgrave.com, https://www.palgrave.com/us; The Statesman's Yearbook, 2023.

UNESCO Institute for Statistics, C.P 250 Succursale H, Montreal, QC, H3G 2K8, CAN, (514) 343-6880 (Dial from U.S.), (514) 343-5740 (Fax from U.S.), uis.publications@unesco.org, http://uis.unesco.org/; UIS.Stat.

WRTH Publications Limited, PO Box 290, Oxford, OX2 7FT, GBR, sales@wrth.com, https://www.wrth.com; World Radio TV Handbook 2023.

COLOMBIA-BUDGET

Central Intelligence Agency (CIA), Office of Public Affairs, Washington, DC, 20505, USA, (703) 482-0623, https://www.cia.gov; The World Factbook.

COLOMBIA-BUSINESS

Global Entrepreneurship Monitor (GEM), Babson College, 231 Forest St., Babson Park, MA, 02457, USA, (781) 235-1200, info@gemconsortium.org, https://www.gemconsortium.org/; Colombia Economy Profile and GEM 2022-2023 Global Report.

Inter-American Development Bank (IDB), 1300 New York Ave. NW, Washington, DC, 20577, USA, (202) 623-1000, (202) 623-3096, https://www.iadb.org/en; Latin Macro Watch (LMW).

COLOMBIA-CAPITAL INVESTMENTS

Inter-American Development Bank (IDB), 1300 New York Ave. NW, Washington, DC, 20577, USA, (202) 623-1000, (202) 623-3096, https://www.iadb.org/en; Latin Macro Watch (LMW).

COLOMBIA-CLIMATE

Palgrave Macmillan, 1 New York Plaza, Ste. 4500, New York, NY, 10004-1562, USA, (800) 777-4643, orders@palgrave.com, https://www.palgrave.com/us; The Statesman's Yearbook, 2023.

COLOMBIA-COAL PRODUCTION

See COLOMBIA-MINERAL INDUSTRIES

COLOMBIA-COCOA PRODUCTION

See COLOMBIA-CROPS

COLOMBIA-COFFEE

See COLOMBIA-CROPS

COLOMBIA-COMMERCE

Palgrave Macmillan, 1 New York Plaza, Ste. 4500, New York, NY, 10004-1562, USA, (800) 777-4643, orders@palgrave.com, https://www.palgrave.com/us; The Statesman's Yearbook, 2023.

UK Data Service, University of Essex, Wivenhoe Park, Colchester, Essex, CO4 3SQ, GBR, https://ukdataservice.ac.uk/; International Aggregate Data.

COLOMBIA-COMMODITY EXCHANGES

Barchart, 209 W Jackson Blvd., 2nd Fl., Chicago, IL, 60606, USA, (877) 247-4394, commodities@barchart.com, https://www.barchart.com/cmdty; The cmdty Yearbook 2023; cmdtyStats: Commodity Statistics and Fundamental Data; cmdtyView: Commodity Index; and Commodity Data and Prices.

International Monetary Fund (IMF), 700 19th St. NW, Washington, DC, 20431, USA, (202) 623-7000, (202) 623-4661, publications@imf.org, https://www.imf.org; IMF Primary Commodity Prices.

United Nations Statistics Division (UNSD), United Nations Plz., New York, NY, 10017, USA, (800) 253-9646, (212) 963-9851, statistics@un.org, https://unstats.un.org; Statistical Yearbook of the United Nations 2021.

COLOMBIA-CONSTRUCTION INDUSTRY

Inter-American Development Bank (IDB), 1300 New York Ave. NW, Washington, DC, 20577, USA, (202)

623-1000, (202) 623-3096, https://www.iadb.org/en; Latin Macro Watch (LMW).

United Nations Statistics Division (UNSD), United Nations Plz., New York, NY, 10017, USA, (800) 253-9646, (212) 963-9851, statistics@un.org, https://unstats.un.org; Statistical Yearbook of the United Nations 2021.

COLOMBIA-CONSUMER PRICE INDEXES

Routledge - Taylor & Francis Group, 6000 Broken Sound Pkwy. NW, Ste. 300, Boca Raton, FL, 33487, USA, (800) 634-1420, (800) 634-7064, orders@taylorandfrancis.com, https://www.routledge.com/; The Europa World Year Book 2022.

The World Bank, 1818 H St. NW, Washington, DC, 20433, USA, (202) 473-1000, (202) 477-6391, eds03@worldbank.org, https://www.worldbank.org/; Colombia (report).

COLOMBIA-CONSUMPTION (ECONOMICS)

Inter-American Development Bank (IDB), 1300 New York Ave. NW, Washington, DC, 20577, USA, (202) 623-1000, (202) 623-3096, https://www.iadb.org/en; Latin Macro Watch (LMW).

COLOMBIA-COPPER INDUSTRY AND TRADE

See COLOMBIA-MINERAL INDUSTRIES

COLOMBIA-CORN INDUSTRY

See COLOMBIA-CROPS

COLOMBIA-COTTON

See COLOMBIA-CROPS

COLOMBIA-CROPS

International Monetary Fund (IMF), 700 19th St. NW, Washington, DC, 20431, USA, (202) 623-7000, (202) 623-4661, publications@imf.org, https://www.imf.org; International Financial Statistics (IFS).

Palgrave Macmillan, 1 New York Plaza, Ste. 4500, New York, NY, 10004-1562, USA, (800) 777-4643, orders@palgrave.com, https://www.palgrave.com/us; The Statesman's Yearbook, 2023.

United Nations Food and Agricultural Organization (FAO), 2121 K St., Ste. 800B, Washington, DC, 20037, USA, (202) 653-2400 (Dial from U.S.), (202) 653-5760 (Fax from U.S.), fao-hq@fao.org, https://www.fao.org; The State of Food and Agriculture (SOFA) 2022.

United Nations Statistics Division (UNSD), United Nations Plz., New York, NY, 10017, USA, (800) 253-9646, (212) 963-9851, statistics@un.org, https://unstats.un.org; Statistical Yearbook of the United Nations 2021.

COLOMBIA-CUSTOMS ADMINISTRATION

Inter-American Development Bank (IDB), 1300 New York Ave. NW, Washington, DC, 20577, USA, (202) 623-1000, (202) 623-3096, https://www.iadb.org/en; Latin Macro Watch (LMW).

COLOMBIA-DAIRY PROCESSING

Palgrave Macmillan, 1 New York Plaza, Ste. 4500, New York, NY, 10004-1562, USA, (800) 777-4643, orders@palgrave.com, https://www.palgrave.com/us; The Statesman's Yearbook, 2023.

United Nations Food and Agricultural Organization (FAO), 2121 K St., Ste. 800B, Washington, DC, 20037, USA, (202) 653-2400 (Dial from U.S.), (202) 653-5760 (Fax from U.S.), fao-hq@fao.org, https://www.fao.org; The State of Food and Agriculture (SOFA) 2022.

COLOMBIA-DEBT

The World Bank, 1818 H St. NW, Washington, DC, 20433, USA, (202) 473-1000, (202) 477-6391, eds03@worldbank.org, https://www.worldbank.org/; Global Financial Development Report 2019-2020: Bank Regulation and Supervision a Decade after the Global Financial Crisis.

COLOMBIA-DEBTS, EXTERNAL

Inter-American Development Bank (IDB), 1300 New York Ave. NW, Washington, DC, 20577, USA, (202) 623-1000, (202) 623-3096, https://www.iadb.org/en; Latin Macro Watch (LMW).

Palgrave Macmillan, 1 New York Plaza, Ste. 4500, New York, NY, 10004-1562, USA, (800) 777-4643, orders@palgrave.com, https://www.palgrave.com/us; The Statesman's Yearbook, 2023.

United Nations Economic Commission for Latin America and the Caribbean (ECLAC), Casilla 179-D, Santiago, 7630412, CHL, (202) 596-3713, prensa@cepal.org, https://www.cepal.org/en; Economic Survey of Latin America and the Caribbean 2021: Labour Dynamics and Employment Policies for Sustainable and Inclusive Recovery Beyond the COVID-19 Crisis.

The World Bank, 1818 H St. NW, Washington, DC, 20433, USA, (202) 473-1000, (202) 477-6391, eds03@worldbank.org, https://www.worldbank.org/; Global Financial Development Report 2019-2020: Bank Regulation and Supervision a Decade after the Global Financial Crisis and World Development Report 2022: Finance for an Equitable Recovery.

COLOMBIA-DEFENSE EXPENDITURES

See COLOMBIA-ARMED FORCES

COLOMBIA-DIAMONDS

See COLOMBIA-MINERAL INDUSTRIES

COLOMBIA-DISPOSABLE INCOME

Inter-American Development Bank (IDB), 1300 New York Ave. NW, Washington, DC, 20577, USA, (202) 623-1000, (202) 623-3096, https://www.iadb.org/en; Latin Macro Watch (LMW).

COLOMBIA-ECONOMIC ASSISTANCE

Inter-American Development Bank (IDB), 1300 New York Ave. NW, Washington, DC, 20577, USA, (202) 623-1000, (202) 623-3096, https://www.iadb.org/en; Latin Macro Watch (LMW).

United Nations Statistics Division (UNSD), United Nations Plz., New York, NY, 10017, USA, (800) 253-9646, (212) 963-9851, statistics@un.org, https://unstats.un.org; Statistical Yearbook of the United Nations 2021.

COLOMBIA-ECONOMIC CONDITIONS

Bernan Press, 15250 NBN Way, Bldg. C, Blue Ridge Summit, PA, 17214, USA, (301) 459-2255, (800) 865-3457, (800) 865-3450, customercare@bernan.com, https://rowman.com/Page/Bernan; World Economic Outlook, April 2022.

Central Intelligence Agency (CIA), Office of Public Affairs, Washington, DC, 20505, USA, (703) 482-0623, https://www.cia.gov; The World Factbook.

The Economist Group: Economist Intelligence Unit (EIU), 900 3rd Ave., 16th Fl., New York, NY, 10022, USA, (212) 541-0500, americas@eiu.com, https://www.eiu.com; Colombia Country Report.

Euromonitor International, Inc., 1 N Dearborn St., Ste. 1700, Chicago, IL, 60602, USA, (312) 922-1115, (312) 922-1157, info-usa@euromonitor.com, https://www.euromonitor.com/; Geographies and Market Research on the Consumer Finance Industry.

Global Entrepreneurship Monitor (GEM), Babson College, 231 Forest St., Babson Park, MA, 02457, USA, (781) 235-1200, info@gemconsortium.org, https://www.gemconsortium.org/; Colombia Economy Profile and GEM 2022-2023 Global Report.

Inter-American Development Bank (IDB), 1300 New York Ave. NW, Washington, DC, 20577, USA, (202) 623-1000, (202) 623-3096, https://www.iadb.org/en; Latin Macro Watch (LMW).

International Monetary Fund (IMF), 700 19th St. NW, Washington, DC, 20431, USA, (202) 623-7000, (202) 623-4661, publications@imf.org, https://www.imf.org; IMF Data and World Economic Outlook.

Palgrave Macmillan, 1 New York Plaza, Ste. 4500, New York, NY, 10004-1562, USA, (800) 777-4643, orders@palgrave.com, https://www.palgrave.com/us; The Statesman's Yearbook, 2023.

Routledge - Taylor & Francis Group, 6000 Broken Sound Pkwy. NW, Ste. 300, Boca Raton, FL, 33487, USA, (800) 634-1420, (800) 634-7064, orders@taylorandfrancis.com, https://www.routledge.com/; The Europa World Year Book 2022.

United Nations Economic Commission for Latin America and the Caribbean (ECLAC), Casilla 179-D, Santiago, 7630412, CHL, (202) 596-3713, prensa@cepal.org, https://www.cepal.org/en; CEPALSTAT; Economic Survey of Latin America and the Caribbean 2021: Labour Dynamics and Employment Policies for Sustainable and Inclusive Recovery Beyond the COVID-19 Crisis; Foreign Direct Investment in Latin America and the Caribbean 2022; and Social Panorama of Latin America and the Caribbean 2022: Transforming Education as a Basis for Sustainable Development.

United Nations Statistics Division (UNSD), United Nations Plz., New York, NY, 10017, USA, (800) 253-9646, (212) 963-9851, statistics@un.org, https://unstats.un.org; World Statistics Pocketbook 2021.

The World Bank, 1818 H St. NW, Washington, DC, 20433, USA, (202) 473-1000, (202) 477-6391, eds03@worldbank.org, https://www.worldbank.org/; Colombia (report); Global Economic Monitor (GEM); Global Economic Prospects, June 2022; The Global Findex Database 2021; and World Development Report 2022: Finance for an Equitable Recovery.

COLOMBIA-EDUCATION

Euromonitor International, Inc., 1 N Dearborn St., Ste. 1700, Chicago, IL, 60602, USA, (312) 922-1115, (312) 922-1157, info-usa@euromonitor.com, https://www.euromonitor.com/; Geographies.

Infoplease, c/o Sandbox Networks, Inc., 1 Lincoln St., 24th Fl., Boston, MA, 02111, USA, https://www.infoplease.com; Countries of the World.

Palgrave Macmillan, 1 New York Plaza, Ste. 4500, New York, NY, 10004-1562, USA, (800) 777-4643, orders@palgrave.com, https://www.palgrave.com/us; The Statesman's Yearbook, 2023.

Routledge - Taylor & Francis Group, 6000 Broken Sound Pkwy. NW, Ste. 300, Boca Raton, FL, 33487, USA, (800) 634-1420, (800) 634-7064, orders@taylorandfrancis.com, https://www.routledge.com/; The Europa World Year Book 2022.

UNESCO Institute for Statistics, C.P 250 Succursale H, Montreal, QC, H3G 2K8, CAN, (514) 343-6880 (Dial from U.S.), (514) 343-5740 (Fax from U.S.), uis.publications@unesco.org, http://uis.unesco.org/; Literacy and UIS.Stat.

United Nations Statistics Division (UNSD), United Nations Plz., New York, NY, 10017, USA, (800) 253-9646, (212) 963-9851, statistics@un.org, https://unstats.un.org; Millennium Development Goal Indicators.

The World Bank, 1818 H St. NW, Washington, DC, 20433, USA, (202) 473-1000, (202) 477-6391, eds03@worldbank.org, https://www.worldbank.org/; Colombia (report) and World Development Report 2022: Finance for an Equitable Recovery.

COLOMBIA-ELECTRICITY

Inter-American Development Bank (IDB), 1300 New York Ave. NW, Washington, DC, 20577, USA, (202) 623-1000, (202) 623-3096, https://www.iadb.org/en; Latin Macro Watch (LMW).

International Energy Agency (IEA), 9 Rue de la Federation, Paris, 75739, FRA, info@iea.org, https://www.iea.org/; World Energy Outlook 2021.

U.S. Energy Information Administration (EIA), 1000 Independence Ave. SW, Washington, DC, 20585, USA, (202) 586-8800, infoctr@eia.gov, https://www.eia.gov; International Energy Outlook 2021.

United Nations Statistics Division (UNSD), United Nations Plz., New York, NY, 10017, USA, (800) 253-9646, (212) 963-9851, statistics@un.org, https://unstats.un.org; Statistical Yearbook of the United Nations 2021.

COLOMBIA-EMPLOYMENT

International Labour Organization (ILO), 4 Rte. des Morillons, Geneva, CH-1211, SWI, ilo@ilo.org, https://www.ilo.org; NORMLEX Information System on International Labour Standards.

UK Data Service, University of Essex, Wivenhoe Park, Colchester, Essex, CO4 3SQ, GBR, https://ukdataservice.ac.uk/; International Aggregate Data.

The World Bank, 1818 H St. NW, Washington, DC, 20433, USA, (202) 473-1000, (202) 477-6391, eds03@worldbank.org, https://www.worldbank.org/; Colombia (report).

COLOMBIA-ENVIRONMENTAL CONDITIONS

DSI Data Service & Information, Xantener Strasse 51a, Rheinberg, D-47495, GER, dsi@dsidata.com, https://www.dsidata.com/; Global Environmental Database.

The Economist Group: Economist Intelligence Unit (EIU), 900 3rd Ave., 16th Fl., New York, NY, 10022, USA, (212) 541-0500, americas@eiu.com, https://www.eiu.com; Colombia Country Report.

United Nations Economic Commission for Latin America and the Caribbean (ECLAC), Casilla 179-D, Santiago, 7630412, CHL, (202) 596-3713, prensa@cepal.org, https://www.cepal.org/en; CEPALSTAT.

United Nations Statistics Division (UNSD), United Nations Plz., New York, NY, 10017, USA, (800) 253-9646, (212) 963-9851, statistics@un.org, https://unstats.un.org; World Statistics Pocketbook 2021.

COLOMBIA-EXCISE TAX

Inter-American Development Bank (IDB), 1300 New York Ave. NW, Washington, DC, 20577, USA, (202) 623-1000, (202) 623-3096, https://www.iadb.org/en; Latin Macro Watch (LMW).

COLOMBIA-EXPENDITURES, PUBLIC

Inter-American Development Bank (IDB), 1300 New York Ave. NW, Washington, DC, 20577, USA, (202) 623-1000, (202) 623-3096, https://www.iadb.org/en; Latin Macro Watch (LMW).

COLOMBIA-EXPORTS

Central Intelligence Agency (CIA), Office of Public Affairs, Washington, DC, 20505, USA, (703) 482-0623, https://www.cia.gov; The World Factbook.

The Economist Group: Economist Intelligence Unit (EIU), 900 3rd Ave., 16th Fl., New York, NY, 10022, USA, (212) 541-0500, americas@eiu.com, https://www.eiu.com; Colombia Country Report.

Inter-American Development Bank (IDB), 1300 New York Ave. NW, Washington, DC, 20577, USA, (202) 623-1000, (202) 623-3096, https://www.iadb.org/en; Latin Macro Watch (LMW).

International Monetary Fund (IMF), 700 19th St. NW, Washington, DC, 20431, USA, (202) 623-7000, (202) 623-4661, publications@imf.org, https://www.imf.org; Direction of Trade Statistics (DOTS) and International Financial Statistics (IFS).

S&P Global, IHS Markit, 15 Inverness Way E, Englewood, CO, 80112, USA, (800) 447-2273, (800) 854-7179, https://ihsmarkit.com; Global Trade Atlas (GTA).

The World Bank, 1818 H St. NW, Washington, DC, 20433, USA, (202) 473-1000, (202) 477-6391, eds03@worldbank.org, https://www.worldbank.org/; World Development Report 2022: Finance for an Equitable Recovery.

COLOMBIA-FEMALE WORKING POPULATION

See COLOMBIA-EMPLOYMENT

COLOMBIA-FERTILITY, HUMAN

Central Intelligence Agency (CIA), Office of Public Affairs, Washington, DC, 20505, USA, (703) 482-0623, https://www.cia.gov; The World Factbook.

COLOMBIA-FERTILIZER INDUSTRY

United Nations Food and Agricultural Organization (FAO), 2121 K St., Ste. 800B, Washington, DC, 20037, USA, (202) 653-2400 (Dial from U.S.), (202) 653-5760 (Fax from U.S.), fao-hq@fao.org, https://www.fao.org; The State of Food and Agriculture (SOFA) 2022.

COLOMBIA-FETAL MORTALITY

See COLOMBIA-MORTALITY

COLOMBIA-FINANCE

Inter-American Development Bank (IDB), 1300 New York Ave. NW, Washington, DC, 20577, USA, (202) 623-1000, (202) 623-3096, https://www.iadb.org/en; Latin Macro Watch (LMW).

Stockholm International Peace Research Institute (SIPRI), Signalistgatan 9, Stockholm, SE 169 72, SWE, https://www.sipri.org/; SIPRI Arms Transfers Database and SIPRI Military Expenditure Database.

United Nations Statistics Division (UNSD), United Nations Plz., New York, NY, 10017, USA, (800) 253-9646, (212) 963-9851, statistics@un.org, https://unstats.un.org; Statistical Yearbook of the United Nations 2021.

The World Bank, 1818 H St. NW, Washington, DC, 20433, USA, (202) 473-1000, (202) 477-6391, eds03@worldbank.org, https://www.worldbank.org/; Colombia (report).

COLOMBIA-FINANCE, PUBLIC

Bernan Press, 15250 NBN Way, Bldg. C, Blue Ridge Summit, PA, 17214, USA, (301) 459-2255, (800) 865-3457, (800) 865-3450, customercare@bernan.com, https://rowman.com/Page/Bernan; National Accounts Statistics: Analysis of Main Aggregates 2020.

The Economist Group: Economist Intelligence Unit (EIU), 900 3rd Ave., 16th Fl., New York, NY, 10022, USA, (212) 541-0500, americas@eiu.com, https://www.eiu.com; Colombia Country Report.

Inter-American Development Bank (IDB), 1300 New York Ave. NW, Washington, DC, 20577, USA, (202) 623-1000, (202) 623-3096, https://www.iadb.org/en; Latin Macro Watch (LMW).

International Monetary Fund (IMF), 700 19th St. NW, Washington, DC, 20431, USA, (202) 623-7000, (202) 623-4661, publications@imf.org, https://www.imf.org; International Financial Statistics (IFS) and Regional Economic Outlook.

Palgrave Macmillan, 1 New York Plaza, Ste. 4500, New York, NY, 10004-1562, USA, (800) 777-4643, orders@palgrave.com, https://www.palgrave.com/us; The Statesman's Yearbook, 2023.

Routledge - Taylor & Francis Group, 6000 Broken Sound Pkwy. NW, Ste. 300, Boca Raton, FL, 33487, USA, (800) 634-1420, (800) 634-7064, orders@taylorandfrancis.com, https://www.routledge.com/; The Europa World Year Book 2022.

United Nations Statistics Division (UNSD), United Nations Plz., New York, NY, 10017, USA, (800) 253-9646, (212) 963-9851, statistics@un.org, https://unstats.un.org; National Accounts Main Aggregates Database and National Accounts Statistics: Main Aggregates and Detailed Tables.

The World Bank, 1818 H St. NW, Washington, DC, 20433, USA, (202) 473-1000, (202) 477-6391, eds03@worldbank.org, https://www.worldbank.org/; Colombia (report).

COLOMBIA-FISHERIES

Inter-American Development Bank (IDB), 1300 New York Ave. NW, Washington, DC, 20577, USA, (202) 623-1000, (202) 623-3096, https://www.iadb.org/en; Latin Macro Watch (LMW).

Palgrave Macmillan, 1 New York Plaza, Ste. 4500, New York, NY, 10004-1562, USA, (800) 777-4643, orders@palgrave.com, https://www.palgrave.com/us; The Statesman's Yearbook, 2023.

Routledge - Taylor & Francis Group, 6000 Broken Sound Pkwy. NW, Ste. 300, Boca Raton, FL, 33487, USA, (800) 634-1420, (800) 634-7064, orders@taylorandfrancis.com, https://www.routledge.com/; The Europa World Year Book 2022.

United Nations Food and Agricultural Organization (FAO), 2121 K St., Ste. 800B, Washington, DC, 20037, USA, (202) 653-2400 (Dial from U.S.), (202) 653-5760 (Fax from U.S.), fao-hq@fao.org, https://www.fao.org; FAO Yearbook of Fishery and Aquaculture Statistics 2019; Fishery Statistical Collections Global Capture Production; FishStatJ; and The State of Food and Agriculture (SOFA) 2022.

United Nations Statistics Division (UNSD), United Nations Plz., New York, NY, 10017, USA, (800) 253-9646, (212) 963-9851, statistics@un.org, https://unstats.un.org; Statistical Yearbook of the United Nations 2021.

The World Bank, 1818 H St. NW, Washington, DC, 20433, USA, (202) 473-1000, (202) 477-6391, eds03@worldbank.org, https://www.worldbank.org/; Colombia (report).

COLOMBIA-FOOD

Euromonitor International, Inc., 1 N Dearborn St., Ste. 1700, Chicago, IL, 60602, USA, (312) 922-1115, (312) 922-1157, info-usa@euromonitor.com, https://www.euromonitor.com/; Market Research on the Retailing Industry.

United Nations Food and Agricultural Organization (FAO), 2121 K St., Ste. 800B, Washington, DC, 20037, USA, (202) 653-2400 (Dial from U.S.), (202) 653-5760 (Fax from U.S.), fao-hq@fao.org, https://www.fao.org; The State of Food and Agriculture (SOFA) 2022.

COLOMBIA-FOREIGN EXCHANGE RATES

Inter-American Development Bank (IDB), 1300 New York Ave. NW, Washington, DC, 20577, USA, (202) 623-1000, (202) 623-3096, https://www.iadb.org/en; Latin Macro Watch (LMW).

International Monetary Fund (IMF), 700 19th St. NW, Washington, DC, 20431, USA, (202) 623-7000, (202) 623-4661, publications@imf.org, https://www.imf.org; International Financial Statistics (IFS).

COLOMBIA-FORESTS AND FORESTRY

Inter-American Development Bank (IDB), 1300 New York Ave. NW, Washington, DC, 20577, USA, (202) 623-1000, (202) 623-3096, https://www.iadb.org/en; Latin Macro Watch (LMW).

Routledge - Taylor & Francis Group, 6000 Broken Sound Pkwy. NW, Ste. 300, Boca Raton, FL, 33487, USA, (800) 634-1420, (800) 634-7064, orders@taylorandfrancis.com, https://www.routledge.com/; The Europa World Year Book 2022.

UNESCO Institute for Statistics, C.P 250 Succursale H, Montreal, QC, H3G 2K8, CAN, (514) 343-6880 (Dial from U.S.), (514) 343-5740 (Fax from U.S.), uis.publications@unesco.org, http://uis.unesco.org/; UIS.Stat.

United Nations Food and Agricultural Organization (FAO), 2121 K St., Ste. 800B, Washington, DC, 20037, USA, (202) 653-2400 (Dial from U.S.), (202) 653-5760 (Fax from U.S.), fao-hq@fao.org, https://www.fao.org; FAO Yearbook of Forest Products 2019 and The State of Food and Agriculture (SOFA) 2022.

United Nations Statistics Division (UNSD), United Nations Plz., New York, NY, 10017, USA, (800) 253-9646, (212) 963-9851, statistics@un.org, https://unstats.un.org; Statistical Yearbook of the United Nations 2021.

The World Bank, 1818 H St. NW, Washington, DC, 20433, USA, (202) 473-1000, (202) 477-6391, eds03@worldbank.org, https://www.worldbank.org/; Colombia (report) and World Development Report 2022: Finance for an Equitable Recovery.

COLOMBIA-GAS PRODUCTION

See COLOMBIA-MINERAL INDUSTRIES

COLOMBIA-GEOGRAPHIC INFORMATION SYSTEMS

The World Bank, 1818 H St. NW, Washington, DC, 20433, USA, (202) 473-1000, (202) 477-6391, eds03@worldbank.org, https://www.worldbank.org/; Colombia (report).

COLOMBIA-GOLD PRODUCTION

See COLOMBIA-MINERAL INDUSTRIES

COLOMBIA-GROSS DOMESTIC PRODUCT

The Economist Group: Economist Intelligence Unit (EIU), 900 3rd Ave., 16th Fl., New York, NY, 10022, USA, (212) 541-0500, americas@eiu.com, https://www.eiu.com; Colombia Country Report.

Inter-American Development Bank (IDB), 1300 New York Ave. NW, Washington, DC, 20577, USA, (202) 623-1000, (202) 623-3096, https://www.iadb.org/en; Latin Macro Watch (LMW).

Routledge - Taylor & Francis Group, 6000 Broken Sound Pkwy. NW, Ste. 300, Boca Raton, FL, 33487, USA, (800) 634-1420, (800) 634-7064, orders@taylorandfrancis.com, https://www.routledge.com/; The Europa World Year Book 2022.

United Nations Statistics Division (UNSD), United Nations Plz., New York, NY, 10017, USA, (800) 253-9646, (212) 963-9851, statistics@un.org, https://unstats.un.org; Statistical Yearbook of the United Nations 2021.

The World Bank, 1818 H St. NW, Washington, DC, 20433, USA, (202) 473-1000, (202) 477-6391, eds03@worldbank.org, https://www.worldbank.org/; World Development Report 2022: Finance for an Equitable Recovery.

COLOMBIA-GROSS NATIONAL PRODUCT

Inter-American Development Bank (IDB), 1300 New York Ave. NW, Washington, DC, 20577, USA, (202) 623-1000, (202) 623-3096, https://www.iadb.org/en; Latin Macro Watch (LMW).

Palgrave Macmillan, 1 New York Plaza, Ste. 4500, New York, NY, 10004-1562, USA, (800) 777-4643, orders@palgrave.com, https://www.palgrave.com/us; The Statesman's Yearbook, 2023.

United Nations Statistics Division (UNSD), United Nations Plz., New York, NY, 10017, USA, (800) 253-9646, (212) 963-9851, statistics@un.org, https://unstats.un.org; Statistical Yearbook of the United Nations 2021.

The World Bank, 1818 H St. NW, Washington, DC, 20433, USA, (202) 473-1000, (202) 477-6391, eds03@worldbank.org, https://www.worldbank.org/; World Development Report 2022: Finance for an Equitable Recovery.

COLOMBIA-HOUSING

Euromonitor International, Inc., 1 N Dearborn St., Ste. 1700, Chicago, IL, 60602, USA, (312) 922-1115, (312) 922-1157, info-usa@euromonitor.com, https://www.euromonitor.com/; Geographies.

COLOMBIA-ILLITERATE PERSONS

UNESCO Institute for Statistics, C.P 250 Succursale H, Montreal, QC, H3G 2K8, CAN, (514) 343-6880 (Dial from U.S.), (514) 343-5740 (Fax from U.S.), uis.publications@unesco.org, http://uis.unesco.org/; UIS.Stat.

COLOMBIA-IMPORTS

Central Intelligence Agency (CIA), Office of Public Affairs, Washington, DC, 20505, USA, (703) 482-0623, https://www.cia.gov; The World Factbook.

The Economist Group: Economist Intelligence Unit (EIU), 900 3rd Ave., 16th Fl., New York, NY, 10022, USA, (212) 541-0500, americas@eiu.com, https://www.eiu.com; Colombia Country Report.

Inter-American Development Bank (IDB), 1300 New York Ave. NW, Washington, DC, 20577, USA, (202) 623-1000, (202) 623-3096, https://www.iadb.org/en; Latin Macro Watch (LMW).

International Monetary Fund (IMF), 700 19th St. NW, Washington, DC, 20431, USA, (202) 623-7000, (202) 623-4661, publications@imf.org, https://www.imf.org; Direction of Trade Statistics (DOTS) and International Financial Statistics (IFS).

S&P Global, IHS Markit, 15 Inverness Way E, Englewood, CO, 80112, USA, (800) 447-2273, (800) 854-7179, https://ihsmarkit.com; Global Trade Atlas (GTA).

The World Bank, 1818 H St. NW, Washington, DC, 20433, USA, (202) 473-1000, (202) 477-6391, eds03@worldbank.org, https://www.worldbank.org/; World Development Report 2022: Finance for an Equitable Recovery.

COLOMBIA-INCOME TAX

Inter-American Development Bank (IDB), 1300 New York Ave. NW, Washington, DC, 20577, USA, (202) 623-1000, (202) 623-3096, https://www.iadb.org/en; Latin Macro Watch (LMW).

COLOMBIA-INDUSTRIAL METALS PRODUCTIONS

See COLOMBIA-MINERAL INDUSTRIES

COLOMBIA-INDUSTRIAL PROPERTY

World Intellectual Property Organization (WIPO), 34, chemin des Colombettes, Geneva, CH-1211, SWI, https://www.wipo.int; Madrid Yearly Review 2022: International Registrations of Marks.

COLOMBIA-INDUSTRIES

Central Intelligence Agency (CIA), Office of Public Affairs, Washington, DC, 20505, USA, (703) 482-0623, https://www.cia.gov; The World Factbook.

The Economist Group: Economist Intelligence Unit (EIU), 900 3rd Ave., 16th Fl., New York, NY, 10022, USA, (212) 541-0500, americas@eiu.com, https://www.eiu.com; Colombia Country Report.

Euromonitor International, Inc., 1 N Dearborn St., Ste. 1700, Chicago, IL, 60602, USA, (312) 922-1115, (312) 922-1157, info-usa@euromonitor.com, https://www.euromonitor.com/; Geographies.

International Labour Organization (ILO), 4 Rte. des Morillons, Geneva, CH-1211, SWI, ilo@ilo.org, https://www.ilo.org; NORMLEX Information System on International Labour Standards.

Palgrave Macmillan, 1 New York Plaza, Ste. 4500, New York, NY, 10004-1562, USA, (800) 777-4643, orders@palgrave.com, https://www.palgrave.com/us; The Statesman's Yearbook, 2023.

Routledge - Taylor & Francis Group, 6000 Broken Sound Pkwy. NW, Ste. 300, Boca Raton, FL, 33487, USA, (800) 634-1420, (800) 634-7064, orders@taylorandfrancis.com, https://www.routledge.com/; The Europa World Year Book 2022.

United Nations Economic Commission for Latin America and the Caribbean (ECLAC), Casilla 179-D, Santiago, 7630412, CHL, (202) 596-3713, prensa@cepal.org, https://www.cepal.org/en; Economic Survey of Latin America and the Caribbean 2021: Labour Dynamics and Employment Policies for Sustainable and Inclusive Recovery Beyond the COVID-19 Crisis.

United Nations Industrial Development Organization (UNIDO), 1 United Nations Plz., Rm. DC1-1118, New York, NY, 10017, USA, (212) 963-6890, (212) 963 6885, (212) 963-7904, office.newyork@unido.org, https://www.unido.org/; Industrial Statistics Databases and International Yearbook of Industrial Statistics 2021.

The World Bank, 1818 H St. NW, Washington, DC, 20433, USA, (202) 473-1000, (202) 477-6391, eds03@worldbank.org, https://www.worldbank.org/; Colombia (report).

World Intellectual Property Organization (WIPO), 34, chemin des Colombettes, Geneva, CH-1211, SWI, https://www.wipo.int; Madrid Yearly Review 2022: International Registrations of Marks.

COLOMBIA-INFANT AND MATERNAL MORTALITY

See COLOMBIA-MORTALITY

COLOMBIA-INFLATION (FINANCE)

United Nations Economic Commission for Latin America and the Caribbean (ECLAC), Casilla 179-D, Santiago, 7630412, CHL, (202) 596-3713, prensa@cepal.org, https://www.cepal.org/en; Economic Survey of Latin America and the Caribbean 2021: Labour Dynamics and Employment Policies for Sustainable and Inclusive Recovery Beyond the COVID-19 Crisis.

COLOMBIA-INTEREST RATES

Inter-American Development Bank (IDB), 1300 New York Ave. NW, Washington, DC, 20577, USA, (202) 623-1000, (202) 623-3096, https://www.iadb.org/en; Latin Macro Watch (LMW).

COLOMBIA-INTERNAL REVENUE

Inter-American Development Bank (IDB), 1300 New York Ave. NW, Washington, DC, 20577, USA, (202) 623-1000, (202) 623-3096, https://www.iadb.org/en; Latin Macro Watch (LMW).

COLOMBIA-INTERNATIONAL FINANCE

Inter-American Development Bank (IDB), 1300 New York Ave. NW, Washington, DC, 20577, USA, (202) 623-1000, (202) 623-3096, https://www.iadb.org/en; Latin Macro Watch (LMW).

COLOMBIA-INTERNATIONAL LIQUIDITY

Inter-American Development Bank (IDB), 1300 New York Ave. NW, Washington, DC, 20577, USA, (202) 623-1000, (202) 623-3096, https://www.iadb.org/en; Latin Macro Watch (LMW).

COLOMBIA-INTERNATIONAL TRADE

The Economist Group: Economist Intelligence Unit (EIU), 900 3rd Ave., 16th Fl., New York, NY, 10022, USA, (212) 541-0500, americas@eiu.com, https://www.eiu.com; Colombia Country Report.

Euromonitor International, Inc., 1 N Dearborn St., Ste. 1700, Chicago, IL, 60602, USA, (312) 922-1115, (312) 922-1157, info-usa@euromonitor.com, https://www.euromonitor.com/; Geographies.

Inter-American Development Bank (IDB), 1300 New York Ave. NW, Washington, DC, 20577, USA, (202) 623-1000, (202) 623-3096, https://www.iadb.org/en; Latin Macro Watch (LMW).

International Monetary Fund (IMF), 700 19th St. NW, Washington, DC, 20431, USA, (202) 623-7000, (202) 623-4661, publications@imf.org, https://www.imf.org; International Financial Statistics (IFS).

Palgrave Macmillan, 1 New York Plaza, Ste. 4500, New York, NY, 10004-1562, USA, (800) 777-4643, orders@palgrave.com, https://www.palgrave.com/us; The Statesman's Yearbook, 2023.

Routledge - Taylor & Francis Group, 6000 Broken Sound Pkwy. NW, Ste. 300, Boca Raton, FL, 33487, USA, (800) 634-1420, (800) 634-7064, orders@taylorandfrancis.com, https://www.routledge.com/; The Europa World Year Book 2022.

United Nations Conference on Trade and Development (UNCTAD), Palais des Nations, Geneva, 1211, SWI, (212) 963-6896, unctadinfo@unctad.org, https://unctad.org; Trade and Development Report 2021.

United Nations Economic Commission for Latin America and the Caribbean (ECLAC), Casilla 179-D, Santiago, 7630412, CHL, (202) 596-3713, prensa@cepal.org, https://www.cepal.org/en; Economic Survey of Latin America and the Caribbean 2021: Labour Dynamics and Employment Policies for Sustainable and Inclusive Recovery Beyond the COVID-19 Crisis.

United Nations Food and Agricultural Organization (FAO), 2121 K St., Ste. 800B, Washington, DC, 20037, USA, (202) 653-2400 (Dial from U.S.), (202) 653-5760 (Fax from U.S.), fao-hq@fao.org, https://www.fao.org; The State of Food and Agriculture (SOFA) 2022.

United Nations Statistics Division (UNSD), United Nations Plz., New York, NY, 10017, USA, (800) 253-

9646, (212) 963-9851, statistics@un.org, https://unstats.un.org; International Trade Statistics Yearbook 2020 and Statistical Yearbook of the United Nations 2021.

The World Bank, 1818 H St. NW, Washington, DC, 20433, USA, (202) 473-1000, (202) 477-6391, eds03@worldbank.org, https://www.worldbank.org/; Colombia (report) and World Development Report 2022: Finance for an Equitable Recovery.

World Trade Organization (WTO), Ctre. William Rappard, Rue de Lausanne 154, Case postale, Geneva, CH-1211, SWI, enquiries@wto.org, https://www.wto.org; World Trade Statistical Review 2022.

COLOMBIA-INTERNET USERS

International Telecommunication Union (ITU), Place des Nations, Geneva, CH-1211, SWI, itumail@itu.int, https://www.itu.int; Global Connectivity Report 2022; World Telecommunication/ICT Indicators Database 2021; and Yearbook of Statistics 2019.

The World Bank, 1818 H St. NW, Washington, DC, 20433, USA, (202) 473-1000, (202) 477-6391, eds03@worldbank.org, https://www.worldbank.org/; Colombia (report).

COLOMBIA-INVESTMENTS

Inter-American Development Bank (IDB), 1300 New York Ave. NW, Washington, DC, 20577, USA, (202) 623-1000, (202) 623-3096, https://www.iadb.org/en; Latin Macro Watch (LMW).

COLOMBIA-IRRIGATION

Inter-American Development Bank (IDB), 1300 New York Ave. NW, Washington, DC, 20577, USA, (202) 623-1000, (202) 623-3096, https://www.iadb.org/en; Latin Macro Watch (LMW).

COLOMBIA-LABOR

Central Intelligence Agency (CIA), Office of Public Affairs, Washington, DC, 20505, USA, (703) 482-0623, https://www.cia.gov; The World Factbook.

Euromonitor International, Inc., 1 N Dearborn St., Ste. 1700, Chicago, IL, 60602, USA, (312) 922-1115, (312) 922-1157, info-usa@euromonitor.com, https://www.euromonitor.com/; Geographies.

International Labour Organization (ILO), 4 Rte. des Morillons, Geneva, CH-1211, SWI, ilo@ilo.org, https://www.ilo.org; NORMLEX Information System on International Labour Standards.

Palgrave Macmillan, 1 New York Plaza, Ste. 4500, New York, NY, 10004-1562, USA, (800) 777-4643, orders@palgrave.com, https://www.palgrave.com/us; The Statesman's Yearbook, 2023.

United Nations Food and Agricultural Organization (FAO), 2121 K St., Ste. 800B, Washington, DC, 20037, USA, (202) 653-2400 (Dial from U.S.), (202) 653-5760 (Fax from U.S.), fao-hq@fao.org, https://www.fao.org; The State of Food and Agriculture (SOFA) 2022.

The World Bank, 1818 H St. NW, Washington, DC, 20433, USA, (202) 473-1000, (202) 477-6391, eds03@worldbank.org, https://www.worldbank.org/; World Development Report 2022: Finance for an Equitable Recovery.

COLOMBIA-LAND USE

Inter-American Development Bank (IDB), 1300 New York Ave. NW, Washington, DC, 20577, USA, (202) 623-1000, (202) 623-3096, https://www.iadb.org/en; Latin Macro Watch (LMW).

United Nations Statistics Division (UNSD), United Nations Plz., New York, NY, 10017, USA, (800) 253-9646, (212) 963-9851, statistics@un.org, https://unstats.un.org; Millennium Development Goal Indicators.

The World Bank, 1818 H St. NW, Washington, DC, 20433, USA, (202) 473-1000, (202) 477-6391, eds03@worldbank.org, https://www.worldbank.org/; World Development Report 2022: Finance for an Equitable Recovery.

COLOMBIA-LIBRARIES

UNESCO Institute for Statistics, C.P 250 Succursale H, Montreal, QC, H3G 2K8, CAN, (514) 343-6880 (Dial from U.S.), (514) 343-5740 (Fax from U.S.), uis.publications@unesco.org, http://uis.unesco.org/; UIS.Stat.

COLOMBIA-LIFE EXPECTANCY

Central Intelligence Agency (CIA), Office of Public Affairs, Washington, DC, 20505, USA, (703) 482-0623, https://www.cia.gov; The World Factbook.

United Nations Department of Economic and Social Affairs (DESA), Population Division, 2 United Nations Plz., Rm. DC2-1950, New York, NY, 10017, USA, (212) 963-3209, (212) 963-2147, population@un.org, https://www.un.org/development/desa/pd/; World Population Ageing 2020 Highlights.

United Nations Statistics Division (UNSD), United Nations Plz., New York, NY, 10017, USA, (800) 253-9646, (212) 963-9851, statistics@un.org, https://unstats.un.org; Millennium Development Goal Indicators.

COLOMBIA-LITERACY

Euromonitor International, Inc., 1 N Dearborn St., Ste. 1700, Chicago, IL, 60602, USA, (312) 922-1115, (312) 922-1157, info-usa@euromonitor.com, https://www.euromonitor.com/; Geographies.

UNESCO Institute for Statistics, C.P 250 Succursale H, Montreal, QC, H3G 2K8, CAN, (514) 343-6880 (Dial from U.S.), (514) 343-5740 (Fax from U.S.), uis.publications@unesco.org, http://uis.unesco.org/; Literacy.

COLOMBIA-LIVESTOCK

Palgrave Macmillan, 1 New York Plaza, Ste. 4500, New York, NY, 10004-1562, USA, (800) 777-4643, orders@palgrave.com, https://www.palgrave.com/us; The Statesman's Yearbook, 2023.

Routledge - Taylor & Francis Group, 6000 Broken Sound Pkwy. NW, Ste. 300, Boca Raton, FL, 33487, USA, (800) 634-1420, (800) 634-7064, orders@taylorandfrancis.com, https://www.routledge.com/; The Europa World Year Book 2022.

United Nations Food and Agricultural Organization (FAO), 2121 K St., Ste. 800B, Washington, DC, 20037, USA, (202) 653-2400 (Dial from U.S.), (202) 653-5760 (Fax from U.S.), fao-hq@fao.org, https://www.fao.org; The State of Food and Agriculture (SOFA) 2022.

United Nations Statistics Division (UNSD), United Nations Plz., New York, NY, 10017, USA, (800) 253-9646, (212) 963-9851, statistics@un.org, https://unstats.un.org; Statistical Yearbook of the United Nations 2021.

COLOMBIA-MANUFACTURES

Inter-American Development Bank (IDB), 1300 New York Ave. NW, Washington, DC, 20577, USA, (202) 623-1000, (202) 623-3096, https://www.iadb.org/en; Latin Macro Watch (LMW).

COLOMBIA-MARRIAGE

Routledge - Taylor & Francis Group, 6000 Broken Sound Pkwy. NW, Ste. 300, Boca Raton, FL, 33487, USA, (800) 634-1420, (800) 634-7064, orders@taylorandfrancis.com, https://www.routledge.com/; The Europa World Year Book 2022.

United Nations Statistics Division (UNSD), United Nations Plz., New York, NY, 10017, USA, (800) 253-9646, (212) 963-9851, statistics@un.org, https://unstats.un.org; Statistical Yearbook of the United Nations 2021.

COLOMBIA-MERCURY PRODUCTION

See COLOMBIA-MINERAL INDUSTRIES

COLOMBIA-MINERAL INDUSTRIES

Barchart, 209 W Jackson Blvd., 2nd Fl., Chicago, IL, 60606, USA, (877) 247-4394, commodities@barchart.com, https://www.barchart.com/cmdty; The cmdty Yearbook 2023; cmdtyStats: Commodity Statistics and Fundamental Data; cmdtyView: Commodity Index; and Commodity Data and Prices.

Inter-American Development Bank (IDB), 1300 New York Ave. NW, Washington, DC, 20577, USA, (202) 623-1000, (202) 623-3096, https://www.iadb.org/en; Latin Macro Watch (LMW).

International Energy Agency (IEA), 9 Rue de la Federation, Paris, 75739, FRA, info@iea.org, https://www.iea.org/; World Energy Outlook 2021.

Palgrave Macmillan, 1 New York Plaza, Ste. 4500, New York, NY, 10004-1562, USA, (800) 777-4643, orders@palgrave.com, https://www.palgrave.com/us; The Statesman's Yearbook, 2023.

Routledge - Taylor & Francis Group, 6000 Broken Sound Pkwy. NW, Ste. 300, Boca Raton, FL, 33487, USA, (800) 634-1420, (800) 634-7064, orders@taylorandfrancis.com, https://www.routledge.com/; The Europa World Year Book 2022.

United Nations Conference on Trade and Development (UNCTAD), Palais des Nations, Geneva, 1211, SWI, (212) 963-6896, unctadinfo@unctad.org, https://unctad.org; Trade and Development Report 2021.

United Nations Statistics Division (UNSD), United Nations Plz., New York, NY, 10017, USA, (800) 253-9646, (212) 963-9851, statistics@un.org, https://unstats.un.org; Statistical Yearbook of the United Nations 2021.

COLOMBIA-MONEY SUPPLY

The Economist Group: Economist Intelligence Unit (EIU), 900 3rd Ave., 16th Fl., New York, NY, 10022, USA, (212) 541-0500, americas@eiu.com, https://www.eiu.com; Colombia Country Report.

Inter-American Development Bank (IDB), 1300 New York Ave. NW, Washington, DC, 20577, USA, (202) 623-1000, (202) 623-3096, https://www.iadb.org/en; Latin Macro Watch (LMW).

International Monetary Fund (IMF), 700 19th St. NW, Washington, DC, 20431, USA, (202) 623-7000, (202) 623-4661, publications@imf.org, https://www.imf.org; International Financial Statistics (IFS).

Routledge - Taylor & Francis Group, 6000 Broken Sound Pkwy. NW, Ste. 300, Boca Raton, FL, 33487, USA, (800) 634-1420, (800) 634-7064, orders@taylorandfrancis.com, https://www.routledge.com/; The Europa World Year Book 2022.

United Nations Statistics Division (UNSD), United Nations Plz., New York, NY, 10017, USA, (800) 253-9646, (212) 963-9851, statistics@un.org, https://unstats.un.org; Statistical Yearbook of the United Nations 2021.

The World Bank, 1818 H St. NW, Washington, DC, 20433, USA, (202) 473-1000, (202) 477-6391, eds03@worldbank.org, https://www.worldbank.org/; Colombia (report).

COLOMBIA-MONUMENTS AND HISTORIC SITES

UNESCO Institute for Statistics, C.P 250 Succursale H, Montreal, QC, H3G 2K8, CAN, (514) 343-6880 (Dial from U.S.), (514) 343-5740 (Fax from U.S.), uis.publications@unesco.org, http://uis.unesco.org/; UIS.Stat.

COLOMBIA-MORTALITY

UNICEF, 3 United Nations Plz., New York, NY, 10017, USA, (212) 303-7984, (917) 244-2215, https://www.unicef.org; The State of the World's Children 2023.

United Nations Statistics Division (UNSD), United Nations Plz., New York, NY, 10017, USA, (800) 253-9646, (212) 963-9851, statistics@un.org, https://unstats.un.org; Millennium Development Goal Indicators; Statistical Yearbook of the United Nations 2021; and World Statistics Pocketbook 2021.

World Health Organization (WHO), Ave. Appia 20, Geneva, CH-1211, SWI, (202) 974-3000 (Telephone in U.S.), publications@who.int, https://www.who.int/; Global Health Observatory (GHO).

COLOMBIA-MOTION PICTURES

Palgrave Macmillan, 1 New York Plaza, Ste. 4500, New York, NY, 10004-1562, USA, (800) 777-4643, orders@palgrave.com, https://www.palgrave.com/us; The Statesman's Yearbook, 2023.

COLOMBIA-MOTOR VEHICLES

International Road Federation (IRF), Madison Place, 500 Montgomery St., 5th Fl., Alexandria, VA, 22314, USA, (703) 535-1001, (703) 535-1007, info@irf.global, https://www.irf.global/; World Road Statistics (WRS).

COLOMBIA-NATURAL GAS PRODUCTION

See COLOMBIA-MINERAL INDUSTRIES

COLOMBIA-NUTRITION

United Nations Food and Agricultural Organization (FAO), 2121 K St., Ste. 800B, Washington, DC, 20037, USA, (202) 653-2400 (Dial from U.S.), (202) 653-5760 (Fax from U.S.), fao-hq@fao.org, https://www.fao.org; The State of Food and Agriculture (SOFA) 2022.

United Nations Statistics Division (UNSD), United Nations Plz., New York, NY, 10017, USA, (800) 253-9646, (212) 963-9851, statistics@un.org, https://unstats.un.org; Millennium Development Goal Indicators.

COLOMBIA-OIL INDUSTRIES

International Monetary Fund (IMF), 700 19th St. NW, Washington, DC, 20431, USA, (202) 623-7000, (202) 623-4661, publications@imf.org, https://www.imf.org; International Financial Statistics (IFS).

COLOMBIA-PAPER

See COLOMBIA-FORESTS AND FORESTRY

COLOMBIA-PEANUT PRODUCTION

See COLOMBIA-CROPS

COLOMBIA-PESTICIDES

United Nations Food and Agricultural Organization (FAO), 2121 K St., Ste. 800B, Washington, DC, 20037, USA, (202) 653-2400 (Dial from U.S.), (202) 653-5760 (Fax from U.S.), fao-hq@fao.org, https://www.fao.org; The State of Food and Agriculture (SOFA) 2022.

COLOMBIA-PETROLEUM INDUSTRY AND TRADE

Inter-American Development Bank (IDB), 1300 New York Ave. NW, Washington, DC, 20577, USA, (202) 623-1000, (202) 623-3096, https://www.iadb.org/en; Latin Macro Watch (LMW).

International Energy Agency (IEA), 9 Rue de la Federation, Paris, 75739, FRA, info@iea.org, https://www.iea.org/; World Energy Outlook 2021.

International Monetary Fund (IMF), 700 19th St. NW, Washington, DC, 20431, USA, (202) 623-7000, (202) 623-4661, publications@imf.org, https://www.imf.org; International Financial Statistics (IFS).

U.S. Energy Information Administration (EIA), 1000 Independence Ave. SW, Washington, DC, 20585, USA, (202) 586-8800, infoctr@eia.gov, https://www.eia.gov; International Energy Outlook 2021.

United Nations Food and Agricultural Organization (FAO), 2121 K St., Ste. 800B, Washington, DC, 20037, USA, (202) 653-2400 (Dial from U.S.), (202) 653-5760 (Fax from U.S.), fao-hq@fao.org, https://www.fao.org; The State of Food and Agriculture (SOFA) 2022.

United Nations Statistics Division (UNSD), United Nations Plz., New York, NY, 10017, USA, (800) 253-9646, (212) 963-9851, statistics@un.org, https://unstats.un.org; Statistical Yearbook of the United Nations 2021.

COLOMBIA-PHOSPHATES PRODUCTION

See COLOMBIA-MINERAL INDUSTRIES

COLOMBIA-PLASTICS INDUSTRY AND TRADE

United Nations Statistics Division (UNSD), United Nations Plz., New York, NY, 10017, USA, (800) 253-9646, (212) 963-9851, statistics@un.org, https://unstats.un.org; Statistical Yearbook of the United Nations 2021.

COLOMBIA-PLATINUM PRODUCTION

See COLOMBIA-MINERAL INDUSTRIES

COLOMBIA-POPULATION

Central Intelligence Agency (CIA), Office of Public Affairs, Washington, DC, 20505, USA, (703) 482-0623, https://www.cia.gov; The World Factbook.

Departamento Administrativo Nacional de Estadisticas of Colombia (National Administrative Department of Statistics of Colombia), Carrera 59 No.26-70, Bogota, 111321, COL, contacto@dane.gov.co, https://www.dane.gov.co/; Population Series 1985-2020.

The Economist Group: Economist Intelligence Unit (EIU), 900 3rd Ave., 16th Fl., New York, NY, 10022, USA, (212) 541-0500, americas@eiu.com, https://www.eiu.com; Colombia Country Report.

Infoplease, c/o Sandbox Networks, Inc., 1 Lincoln St., 24th Fl., Boston, MA, 02111, USA, https://www.infoplease.com; Countries of the World.

Inter-American Development Bank (IDB), 1300 New York Ave. NW, Washington, DC, 20577, USA, (202) 623-1000, (202) 623-3096, https://www.iadb.org/en; Latin Macro Watch (LMW).

International Labour Organization (ILO), 4 Rte. des Morillons, Geneva, CH-1211, SWI, ilo@ilo.org, https://www.ilo.org; NORMLEX Information System on International Labour Standards.

Palgrave Macmillan, 1 New York Plaza, Ste. 4500, New York, NY, 10004-1562, USA, (800) 777-4643, orders@palgrave.com, https://www.palgrave.com/us; The Statesman's Yearbook, 2023.

Routledge - Taylor & Francis Group, 6000 Broken Sound Pkwy. NW, Ste. 300, Boca Raton, FL, 33487, USA, (800) 634-1420, (800) 634-7064, orders@taylorandfrancis.com, https://www.routledge.com/; The Europa World Year Book 2022.

UK Data Service, University of Essex, Wivenhoe Park, Colchester, Essex, CO4 3SQ, GBR, https://ukdataservice.ac.uk/; International Aggregate Data.

UNESCO Institute for Statistics, C.P 250 Succursale H, Montreal, QC, H3G 2K8, CAN, (514) 343-6880 (Dial from U.S.), (514) 343-5740 (Fax from U.S.), uis.publications@unesco.org, http://uis.unesco.org/; UIS.Stat.

United Nations Department of Economic and Social Affairs (DESA), Population Division, 2 United Nations Plz., Rm. DC2-1950, New York, NY, 10017, USA, (212) 963-3209, (212) 963-2147, population@un.org, https://www.un.org/development/desa/pd/; Revision of World Urbanization Prospects and World Population Ageing 2020 Highlights.

United Nations Development Programme (UNDP), One United Nations Plz., New York, NY, 10017, USA, (212) 906-5000, (212) 906-5001, https://www.undp.org; Human Development Report 2021-2022.

United Nations Economic Commission for Latin America and the Caribbean (ECLAC), Casilla 179-D, Santiago, 7630412, CHL, (202) 596-3713, prensa@cepal.org, https://www.cepal.org/en; CEPALSTAT and Social Panorama of Latin America and the Caribbean 2022: Transforming Education as a Basis for Sustainable Development.

United Nations Statistics Division (UNSD), United Nations Plz., New York, NY, 10017, USA, (800) 253-9646, (212) 963-9851, statistics@un.org, https://unstats.un.org; Statistical Yearbook of the United Nations 2021 and World Statistics Pocketbook 2021.

The World Bank, 1818 H St. NW, Washington, DC, 20433, USA, (202) 473-1000, (202) 477-6391, eds03@worldbank.org, https://www.worldbank.org/; Colombia (report); The Global Findex Database 2021; and World Development Report 2022: Finance for an Equitable Recovery.

COLOMBIA-POPULATION DENSITY

Central Intelligence Agency (CIA), Office of Public Affairs, Washington, DC, 20505, USA, (703) 482-0623, https://www.cia.gov; The World Factbook.

Inter-American Development Bank (IDB), 1300 New York Ave. NW, Washington, DC, 20577, USA, (202) 623-1000, (202) 623-3096, https://www.iadb.org/en; Latin Macro Watch (LMW).

Palgrave Macmillan, 1 New York Plaza, Ste. 4500, New York, NY, 10004-1562, USA, (800) 777-4643, orders@palgrave.com, https://www.palgrave.com/us; The Statesman's Yearbook, 2023.

Routledge - Taylor & Francis Group, 6000 Broken Sound Pkwy. NW, Ste. 300, Boca Raton, FL, 33487, USA, (800) 634-1420, (800) 634-7064, orders@taylorandfrancis.com, https://www.routledge.com/; The Europa World Year Book 2022.

UNESCO Institute for Statistics, C.P 250 Succursale H, Montreal, QC, H3G 2K8, CAN, (514) 343-6880 (Dial from U.S.), (514) 343-5740 (Fax from U.S.), uis.publications@unesco.org, http://uis.unesco.org/; UIS.Stat.

The World Bank, 1818 H St. NW, Washington, DC, 20433, USA, (202) 473-1000, (202) 477-6391, eds03@worldbank.org, https://www.worldbank.org/; Colombia (report) and World Development Report 2022: Finance for an Equitable Recovery.

COLOMBIA-POWER RESOURCES

Euromonitor International, Inc., 1 N Dearborn St., Ste. 1700, Chicago, IL, 60602, USA, (312) 922-1115, (312) 922-1157, info-usa@euromonitor.com, https://www.euromonitor.com/; Geographies.

International Energy Agency (IEA), 9 Rue de la Federation, Paris, 75739, FRA, info@iea.org, https://www.iea.org/; World Energy Outlook 2021.

Palgrave Macmillan, 1 New York Plaza, Ste. 4500, New York, NY, 10004-1562, USA, (800) 777-4643, orders@palgrave.com, https://www.palgrave.com/us; The Statesman's Yearbook, 2023.

U.S. Energy Information Administration (EIA), 1000 Independence Ave. SW, Washington, DC, 20585, USA, (202) 586-8800, infoctr@eia.gov, https://www.eia.gov; International Energy Outlook 2021.

United Nations Food and Agricultural Organization (FAO), 2121 K St., Ste. 800B, Washington, DC, 20037, USA, (202) 653-2400 (Dial from U.S.), (202) 653-5760 (Fax from U.S.), fao-hq@fao.org, https://www.fao.org; The State of Food and Agriculture (SOFA) 2022.

United Nations Statistics Division (UNSD), United Nations Plz., New York, NY, 10017, USA, (800) 253-9646, (212) 963-9851, statistics@un.org, https://unstats.un.org; Energy Statistics Yearbook 2019; Statistical Yearbook of the United Nations 2021; and World Statistics Pocketbook 2021.

The World Bank, 1818 H St. NW, Washington, DC, 20433, USA, (202) 473-1000, (202) 477-6391, eds03@worldbank.org, https://www.worldbank.org/; World Development Report 2022: Finance for an Equitable Recovery.

COLOMBIA-PRICES

Euromonitor International, Inc., 1 N Dearborn St., Ste. 1700, Chicago, IL, 60602, USA, (312) 922-1115, (312) 922-1157, info-usa@euromonitor.com, https://www.euromonitor.com/; Geographies.

International Monetary Fund (IMF), 700 19th St. NW, Washington, DC, 20431, USA, (202) 623-7000, (202) 623-4661, publications@imf.org, https://www.imf.org; International Financial Statistics (IFS).

United Nations Economic Commission for Latin America and the Caribbean (ECLAC), Casilla 179-D, Santiago, 7630412, CHL, (202) 596-3713, prensa@cepal.org, https://www.cepal.org/en; Economic Survey of Latin America and the Caribbean

2021: Labour Dynamics and Employment Policies for Sustainable and Inclusive Recovery Beyond the COVID-19 Crisis.

The World Bank, 1818 H St. NW, Washington, DC, 20433, USA, (202) 473-1000, (202) 477-6391, eds03@worldbank.org, https://www.worldbank.org/; Colombia (report).

COLOMBIA-PUBLIC HEALTH

Euromonitor International, Inc., 1 N Dearborn St., Ste. 1700, Chicago, IL, 60602, USA, (312) 922-1115, (312) 922-1157, info-usa@euromonitor.com, https://www.euromonitor.com/; Geographies and Market Research on the Health and Wellness Industry.

Palgrave Macmillan, 1 New York Plaza, Ste. 4500, New York, NY, 10004-1562, USA, (800) 777-4643, orders@palgrave.com, https://www.palgrave.com/us; The Statesman's Yearbook, 2023.

U.S. Census Bureau, 4600 Silver Hill Rd., Washington, DC, 20233, USA, (301) 763-4636, (800) 923-8282, https://www.census.gov; HIV/AIDS Surveillance Data Base.

UNICEF, 3 United Nations Plz., New York, NY, 10017, USA, (212) 303-7984, (917) 244-2215, https://www.unicef.org; The State of the World's Children 2023.

United Nations Department of Economic and Social Affairs (DESA), Population Division, 2 United Nations Plz., Rm. DC2-1950, New York, NY, 10017, USA, (212) 963-3209, (212) 963-2147, population@un.org, https://www.un.org/development/desa/pd/; World Fertility Data 2019.

United Nations Development Programme (UNDP), One United Nations Plz., New York, NY, 10017, USA, (212) 906-5000, (212) 906-5001, https://www.undp.org; Human Development Report 2021-2022.

United Nations Statistics Division (UNSD), United Nations Plz., New York, NY, 10017, USA, (800) 253-9646, (212) 963-9851, statistics@un.org, https://unstats.un.org; Millennium Development Goal Indicators and Statistical Yearbook of the United Nations 2021.

The World Bank, 1818 H St. NW, Washington, DC, 20433, USA, (202) 473-1000, (202) 477-6391, eds03@worldbank.org, https://www.worldbank.org/; Colombia (report).

World Health Organization (WHO), Ave. Appia 20, Geneva, CH-1211, SWI, (202) 974-3000 (Telephone in U.S.), publications@who.int, https://www.who.int/; Global Health Observatory (GHO) and Health Statistics and Information Systems.

COLOMBIA-PUBLISHERS AND PUBLISHING

Routledge - Taylor & Francis Group, 6000 Broken Sound Pkwy. NW, Ste. 300, Boca Raton, FL, 33487, USA, (800) 634-1420, (800) 634-7064, orders@taylorandfrancis.com, https://www.routledge.com/; The Europa World Year Book 2022.

UNESCO Institute for Statistics, C.P 250 Succursale H, Montreal, QC, H3G 2K8, CAN, (514) 343-6880 (Dial from U.S.), (514) 343-5740 (Fax from U.S.), uis.publications@unesco.org, http://uis.unesco.org/; UIS.Stat.

COLOMBIA-RAILROADS

Janes, USA, (703) 574-7580, (888) 977-1519, customer.care@janes.com, https://www.janes.com; Janes World Railways 2021-2022.

Palgrave Macmillan, 1 New York Plaza, Ste. 4500, New York, NY, 10004-1562, USA, (800) 777-4643, orders@palgrave.com, https://www.palgrave.com/us; The Statesman's Yearbook, 2023.

Routledge - Taylor & Francis Group, 6000 Broken Sound Pkwy. NW, Ste. 300, Boca Raton, FL, 33487, USA, (800) 634-1420, (800) 634-7064, orders@taylorandfrancis.com, https://www.routledge.com/; The Europa World Year Book 2022.

United Nations Statistics Division (UNSD), United Nations Plz., New York, NY, 10017, USA, (800) 253-9646, (212) 963-9851, statistics@un.org, https://unstats.un.org; Statistical Yearbook of the United Nations 2021.

COLOMBIA-RELIGION

Central Intelligence Agency (CIA), Office of Public Affairs, Washington, DC, 20505, USA, (703) 482-0623, https://www.cia.gov; The World Factbook.

Palgrave Macmillan, 1 New York Plaza, Ste. 4500, New York, NY, 10004-1562, USA, (800) 777-4643, orders@palgrave.com, https://www.palgrave.com/us; The Statesman's Yearbook, 2023.

COLOMBIA-RETAIL TRADE

Euromonitor International, Inc., 1 N Dearborn St., Ste. 1700, Chicago, IL, 60602, USA, (312) 922-1115, (312) 922-1157, info-usa@euromonitor.com, https://www.euromonitor.com/; Geographies.

Inter-American Development Bank (IDB), 1300 New York Ave. NW, Washington, DC, 20577, USA, (202) 623-1000, (202) 623-3096, https://www.iadb.org/en; Latin Macro Watch (LMW).

United Nations Statistics Division (UNSD), United Nations Plz., New York, NY, 10017, USA, (800) 253-9646, (212) 963-9851, statistics@un.org, https://unstats.un.org; Statistical Yearbook of the United Nations 2021.

COLOMBIA-RICE PRODUCTION

See COLOMBIA-CROPS

COLOMBIA-ROADS

International Road Federation (IRF), Madison Place, 500 Montgomery St., 5th Fl., Alexandria, VA, 22314, USA, (703) 535-1001, (703) 535-1007, info@irf.global, https://www.irf.global/; World Road Statistics (WRS).

COLOMBIA-RUBBER INDUSTRY AND TRADE

International Rubber Study Group (IRSG), 51 Changi Business Park Central 2, Unit No. 6, 486066, SGP, https://www.rubberstudy.org; Monthly Rubber Bulletin (MRB); Rubber Industry Report; Rubber Statistical Bulletin; and World Rubber Industry Report (WRIO).

COLOMBIA-SHIPPING

Routledge - Taylor & Francis Group, 6000 Broken Sound Pkwy. NW, Ste. 300, Boca Raton, FL, 33487, USA, (800) 634-1420, (800) 634-7064, orders@taylorandfrancis.com, https://www.routledge.com/; The Europa World Year Book 2022.

S&P Global, IHS Markit, 15 Inverness Way E, Englewood, CO, 80112, USA, (800) 447-2273, (800) 854-7179, https://ihsmarkit.com; IHS Maritime World Shipbuilding Statistics; Journal of Commerce; Lloyd's Register of Ships 2021-2022; and Maritime Portal Desktop.

United Nations Statistics Division (UNSD), United Nations Plz., New York, NY, 10017, USA, (800) 253-9646, (212) 963-9851, statistics@un.org, https://unstats.un.org; Statistical Yearbook of the United Nations 2021.

COLOMBIA-SOYBEAN PRODUCTION

See COLOMBIA-CROPS

COLOMBIA-STEEL PRODUCTION

See COLOMBIA-MINERAL INDUSTRIES

COLOMBIA-SUGAR PRODUCTION

See COLOMBIA-CROPS

COLOMBIA-SULPHUR PRODUCTION

See COLOMBIA-MINERAL INDUSTRIES

COLOMBIA-TAXATION

Inter-American Development Bank (IDB), 1300 New York Ave. NW, Washington, DC, 20577, USA, (202) 623-1000, (202) 623-3096, https://www.iadb.org/en; Latin Macro Watch (LMW).

International Road Federation (IRF), Madison Place, 500 Montgomery St., 5th Fl., Alexandria, VA, 22314, USA, (703) 535-1001, (703) 535-1007, info@irf.global, https://www.irf.global/; World Road Statistics (WRS).

COLOMBIA-TELEPHONE

Central Intelligence Agency (CIA), Office of Public Affairs, Washington, DC, 20505, USA, (703) 482-0623, https://www.cia.gov; The World Factbook.

Palgrave Macmillan, 1 New York Plaza, Ste. 4500, New York, NY, 10004-1562, USA, (800) 777-4643, orders@palgrave.com, https://www.palgrave.com/us; The Statesman's Yearbook, 2023.

Routledge - Taylor & Francis Group, 6000 Broken Sound Pkwy. NW, Ste. 300, Boca Raton, FL, 33487, USA, (800) 634-1420, (800) 634-7064, orders@taylorandfrancis.com, https://www.routledge.com/; The Europa World Year Book 2022.

United Nations Statistics Division (UNSD), United Nations Plz., New York, NY, 10017, USA, (800) 253-9646, (212) 963-9851, statistics@un.org, https://unstats.un.org; World Statistics Pocketbook 2021.

COLOMBIA-TEXTILE INDUSTRY

Euromonitor International, Inc., 1 N Dearborn St., Ste. 1700, Chicago, IL, 60602, USA, (312) 922-1115, (312) 922-1157, info-usa@euromonitor.com, https://www.euromonitor.com/; Market Research on the Retailing Industry.

United Nations Statistics Division (UNSD), United Nations Plz., New York, NY, 10017, USA, (800) 253-9646, (212) 963-9851, statistics@un.org, https://unstats.un.org; Statistical Yearbook of the United Nations 2021.

COLOMBIA-THEATER

UNESCO Institute for Statistics, C.P 250 Succursale H, Montreal, QC, H3G 2K8, CAN, (514) 343-6880 (Dial from U.S.), (514) 343-5740 (Fax from U.S.), uis.publications@unesco.org, http://uis.unesco.org/; UIS.Stat.

COLOMBIA-TOBACCO INDUSTRY

United Nations Statistics Division (UNSD), United Nations Plz., New York, NY, 10017, USA, (800) 253-9646, (212) 963-9851, statistics@un.org, https://unstats.un.org; Statistical Yearbook of the United Nations 2021.

COLOMBIA-TOURISM

Euromonitor International, Inc., 1 N Dearborn St., Ste. 1700, Chicago, IL, 60602, USA, (312) 922-1115, (312) 922-1157, info-usa@euromonitor.com, https://www.euromonitor.com/; Geographies.

Palgrave Macmillan, 1 New York Plaza, Ste. 4500, New York, NY, 10004-1562, USA, (800) 777-4643, orders@palgrave.com, https://www.palgrave.com/us; The Statesman's Yearbook, 2023.

Routledge - Taylor & Francis Group, 6000 Broken Sound Pkwy. NW, Ste. 300, Boca Raton, FL, 33487, USA, (800) 634-1420, (800) 634-7064, orders@taylorandfrancis.com, https://www.routledge.com/; The Europa World Year Book 2022.

United Nations Statistics Division (UNSD), United Nations Plz., New York, NY, 10017, USA, (800) 253-9646, (212) 963-9851, statistics@un.org, https://unstats.un.org; Statistical Yearbook of the United Nations 2021.

United Nations World Tourism Organization (UNWTO), Calle Poeta Joan Maragall 42, Madrid, 28020, SPA, info@unwto.org, https://www.unwto.org/; Yearbook of Tourism Statistics, 2021 Edition.

The World Bank, 1818 H St. NW, Washington, DC, 20433, USA, (202) 473-1000, (202) 477-6391, eds03@worldbank.org, https://www.worldbank.org/; Colombia (report).

COLOMBIA-TRADE

See COLOMBIA-INTERNATIONAL TRADE

COLOMBIA-TRANSPORTATION

Central Intelligence Agency (CIA), Office of Public Affairs, Washington, DC, 20505, USA, (703) 482-0623, https://www.cia.gov; The World Factbook.

Euromonitor International, Inc., 1 N Dearborn St., Ste. 1700, Chicago, IL, 60602, USA, (312) 922-1115, (312) 922-1157, info-usa@euromonitor.com, https://www.euromonitor.com/; Geographies.

Inter-American Development Bank (IDB), 1300 New York Ave. NW, Washington, DC, 20577, USA, (202) 623-1000, (202) 623-3096, https://www.iadb.org/en; Latin Macro Watch (LMW).

Palgrave Macmillan, 1 New York Plaza, Ste. 4500, New York, NY, 10004-1562, USA, (800) 777-4643, orders@palgrave.com, https://www.palgrave.com/us; The Statesman's Yearbook, 2023.

Routledge - Taylor & Francis Group, 6000 Broken Sound Pkwy. NW, Ste. 300, Boca Raton, FL, 33487, USA, (800) 634-1420, (800) 634-7064, orders@taylorandfrancis.com, https://www.routledge.com/; The Europa World Year Book 2022.

The World Bank, 1818 H St. NW, Washington, DC, 20433, USA, (202) 473-1000, (202) 477-6391, eds03@worldbank.org, https://www.worldbank.org/; Colombia (report).

COLOMBIA-UNEMPLOYMENT

International Labour Organization (ILO), 4 Rte. des Morillons, Geneva, CH-1211, SWI, ilo@ilo.org, https://www.ilo.org; NORMLEX Information System on International Labour Standards.

United Nations Statistics Division (UNSD), United Nations Plz., New York, NY, 10017, USA, (800) 253-9646, (212) 963-9851, statistics@un.org, https://unstats.un.org; Statistical Yearbook of the United Nations 2021.

COLOMBIA-VITAL STATISTICS

Palgrave Macmillan, 1 New York Plaza, Ste. 4500, New York, NY, 10004-1562, USA, (800) 777-4643, orders@palgrave.com, https://www.palgrave.com/us; The Statesman's Yearbook, 2023.

U.S. Census Bureau, 4600 Silver Hill Rd., Washington, DC, 20233, USA, (301) 763-4636, (800) 923-8282, https://www.census.gov; HIV/AIDS Surveillance Data Base.

United Nations Department of Economic and Social Affairs (DESA), Population Division, 2 United Nations Plz., Rm. DC2-1950, New York, NY, 10017, USA, (212) 963-3209, (212) 963-2147, population@un.org, https://www.un.org/development/desa/pd/; World Contraceptive Use 2021: Estimates and Projections of Family Planning Indicators and World Marriage Data 2019.

United Nations Statistics Division (UNSD), United Nations Plz., New York, NY, 10017, USA, (800) 253-9646, (212) 963-9851, statistics@un.org, https://unstats.un.org; Statistical Yearbook of the United Nations 2021.

COLOMBIA-WAGES

International Labour Organization (ILO), 4 Rte. des Morillons, Geneva, CH-1211, SWI, ilo@ilo.org, https://www.ilo.org; NORMLEX Information System on International Labour Standards.

United Nations Statistics Division (UNSD), United Nations Plz., New York, NY, 10017, USA, (800) 253-9646, (212) 963-9851, statistics@un.org, https://unstats.un.org; Statistical Yearbook of the United Nations 2021.

The World Bank, 1818 H St. NW, Washington, DC, 20433, USA, (202) 473-1000, (202) 477-6391, eds03@worldbank.org, https://www.worldbank.org/; Colombia (report).

COLOMBIA-WEATHER

See COLOMBIA-CLIMATE

COLOMBIA-WHEAT PRODUCTION

See COLOMBIA-CROPS

COLOMBIA-WHOLESALE PRICE INDEXES

Inter-American Development Bank (IDB), 1300 New York Ave. NW, Washington, DC, 20577, USA, (202) 623-1000, (202) 623-3096, https://www.iadb.org/en; Latin Macro Watch (LMW).

International Monetary Fund (IMF), 700 19th St. NW, Washington, DC, 20431, USA, (202) 623-7000, (202) 623-4661, publications@imf.org, https://www.imf.org; International Financial Statistics (IFS).

COLOMBIA-WHOLESALE TRADE

Inter-American Development Bank (IDB), 1300 New York Ave. NW, Washington, DC, 20577, USA, (202) 623-1000, (202) 623-3096, https://www.iadb.org/en; Latin Macro Watch (LMW).

United Nations Statistics Division (UNSD), United Nations Plz., New York, NY, 10017, USA, (800) 253-9646, (212) 963-9851, statistics@un.org, https://unstats.un.org; Statistical Yearbook of the United Nations 2021.

COLOMBIA-WOOD AND WOOD PULP

See COLOMBIA-FORESTS AND FORESTRY

COLOMBIA-WOOL PRODUCTION

See COLOMBIA-TEXTILE INDUSTRY

COLOMBIA-ZINC AND ZINC ORE

See COLOMBIA-MINERAL INDUSTRIES

COLOMBIA-ZOOS

UNESCO Institute for Statistics, C.P 250 Succursale H, Montreal, QC, H3G 2K8, CAN, (514) 343-6880 (Dial from U.S.), (514) 343-5740 (Fax from U.S.), uis.publications@unesco.org, http://uis.unesco.org/; UIS.Stat.

COLON (ANATOMY)-CANCER

American Cancer Society (ACS), 3380 Chastain Meadows Pkwy NW, Ste. 200, Kennesaw, GA, 30144, USA, (800) 227-2345, https://www.cancer.org; Colorectal Cancer Facts & Figures 2023-2025.

Cancer Treatment Centers of America Global, Inc. (CTCA), 5900 Broken Sound Pkwy NW, Boca Raton, FL, 33487, USA, (800) 234-7139, (844) 374-2443, https://www.cancercenter.com/; unpublished data.

COLONY COLLAPSE DISORDER OF HONEYBEES

Bee Informed Partnership (BIP), 4112 Plant Sciences Bldg., College Park, MD, 20742, USA, (443) 296-2470, https://beeinformed.org/; Loss & Management Survey and 2021-2022 Weighted Average Winter All Colony Loss.

COLORADO

See also-STATE DATA (FOR INDIVIDUAL STATES)

Colorado Avalanche Information Center (CAIC), 1313 Sherman St., Rm. 423, Denver, CO, 80203, USA, (303) 499-9650, help@caic.com, https://www.avalanche.state.co.us; US Avalanche Accidents 2022.

The Urban Institute, 500 L'Enfant Plaza SW, Washington, DC, 20024, USA, (202) 833-7200, https://www.urban.org/; Housing First Breaks the Homelessness-Jail Cycle.

COLORADO-STATE DATA CENTERS

Colorado State Demography Office, 1313 Sherman St., Rm. 521, Denver, CO, 80203, USA, (303) 864-7753, (303) 864-7750, adam.bickford@state.co.us, https://demography.dola.colorado.gov; State Data Reports (CO).

COLORADO-PRIMARY STATISTICS SOURCES

Colorado Department of Education, 201 E Colfax Ave., Denver, CO, 80203, USA, (303) 866-6600, (303) 830-0793, https://www.cde.state.co.us/; CSAP (Colorado Student Assessment Program) and TCAP (Transitional Colorado Assessment Program) Data and Results.

SAGE Publications, 2455 Teller Rd., Thousand Oaks, CA, 91320, USA, (800) 818-7243, (800) 583-2665, journals@sagepub.com, https://www.sagepub.com; Data Planet.

University of Colorado Boulder Libraries, Rare and Distinctive Collections, Government Information Library, 1720 Pleasant St., 184 UCB, Boulder, CO, 80309-0184, USA, (303) 492-8705, rad@colorado.edu, https://www.colorado.edu/libraries/libraries-collections/rare-distinctive/government-info; unpublished data.

University of Colorado Boulder, Leeds School of Business, Business Research Division, 995 Regent Dr., 419 UCB, Boulder, CO, 80309, USA, (303) 492-1811, https://www.colorado.edu/business/business-research-division; Colorado Business Economic Outlook 2023.

COLUMBIUM-TANTALUM

U.S. Department of the Interior (DOI), U.S. Geological Survey (USGS), National Minerals Information Center (NMIC), 12201 Sunrise Valley Dr., Reston, VA, 20192, USA, (703) 648-4920, (703) 648-7971, (703) 648-4995, sfortier@usgs.gov, https://www.usgs.gov/centers/nmic; Mineral Commodity Summaries 2022 and Minerals Yearbook.

COMBAT

Center for a New American Security (CNAS), 1152 15th St. NW, Ste. 950, Washington, DC, 20005, USA, (202) 457-9400, (202) 457-9401, info@cnas.org, https://www.cnas.org/; Women in Combat: Five-Year Status Update.

COMMERCE-DOMESTIC

U.S. Census Bureau, 4600 Silver Hill Rd., Washington, DC, 20233, USA, (301) 763-4636, (800) 923-8282, https://www.census.gov; 2019 E-Stats Report: Measuring the Electronic Economy.

COMMERCE-DOMESTIC-BY RAIL

Association of American Railroads (AAR), 425 3rd St. SW, Washington, DC, 20024, USA, (202) 639-2100, https://www.aar.org; Weekly Railroad Traffic Online.

COMMERCE-DOMESTIC-BY WATER

U.S. Army Corps of Engineers (USACE), Institute for Water Resources (IWR), Waterborne Commerce Statistics Center (WCSC), 7701 Telegraph Rd., Alexandria, VA, 22315, USA, (703) 428-8015, (703) 428-8171, iwr@usace.army.mil, https://www.iwr.usace.army.mil/About/Technical-Centers/WCSC-Waterborne-Commerce-Statistics-Center-2/; Transportation Operational Waterborne Statistics (TOWS) Database; Waterborne Commerce Monthly Commodity Indicators; Waterborne Container Traffic; and Waterborne Tonnage for Principal U.S. Ports and All 50 States and U.S. Territories, 2021.

COMMERCE-FOREIGN

See INTERNATIONAL TRADE

COMMERCE AND HOUSING CREDIT

U.S. Office of Management and Budget (OMB), 725 17th St. NW, Washington, DC, 20503, USA, (202) 395-3080, https://www.whitehouse.gov/omb/; Historical Tables.

COMMERCIAL BUILDINGS-CONSTRUCTION VALUE

Dodge Construction Network, 300 American Metro Blvd., Ste. 185, Hamilton, NJ, 08619, USA, (877) 784-9556, support@construction.com, https://www.construction.com/; Mid-Year 2023 Construction Outlook.

COMMERCIAL BUILDINGS-CRIMINAL STATISTICS

U.S. Department of Justice (DOJ), Bureau of Justice Statistics (BJS), 810 7th St. NW, Washington, DC,

20531, USA, (202) 307-0765, askbjs@usdoj.gov, https://www.bjs.gov/; Criminal Victimization, 2020.

COMMERCIAL BUILDINGS-ELECTRICITY

U.S. Census Bureau, Center for Economic Studies (CES), 4600 Silver Hill Rd., Washington, DC, 20233, USA, (301) 763-6460, (301) 763-5935, ces.contacts@census.gov, https://www.census.gov/programs-surveys/ces.html; Construction, 2017 Economic Census.

COMMERCIAL BUILDINGS-ENERGY CHARACTERISTICS

Dodge Construction Network, 300 American Metro Blvd., Ste. 185, Hamilton, NJ, 08619, USA, (877) 784-9556, support@construction.com, https://www.construction.com/; Dodge MarketShare.

U.S. Energy Information Administration (EIA), 1000 Independence Ave. SW, Washington, DC, 20585, USA, (202) 586-8800, infoctr@eia.gov, https://www.eia.gov; Residential Energy Consumption Survey (RECS).

COMMERCIAL BUILDINGS-FLOOR SPACE

Dodge Construction Network, 300 American Metro Blvd., Ste. 185, Hamilton, NJ, 08619, USA, (877) 784-9556, support@construction.com, https://www.construction.com/; Mid-Year 2023 Construction Outlook.

COMMERCIAL PAPER

Board of Governors of the Federal Reserve System, Constitution Ave. NW, Washington, DC, 20551, USA, (202) 452-3000, (202) 263-4869 (TDD), https://www.federalreserve.gov; Federal Reserve Bulletin.

COMMERCIAL TREATIES

Center for Economic and Policy Research (CEPR), 1611 Connecticut Ave. NW, Ste. 400, Washington, DC, 20009, USA, (202) 293-5380, (202) 588-1356, info@cepr.net, https://cepr.net/; Realism About Investment Treaties.

COMMODITIES

See Individual commodities

COMMODITY FLOW

Barchart, 209 W Jackson Blvd., 2nd Fl., Chicago, IL, 60606, USA, (877) 247-4394, commodities@barchart.com, https://www.barchart.com/cmdty; The cmdty Yearbook 2023; cmdtyStats: Commodity Statistics and Fundamental Data; cmdtyView: Commodity Index; and Commodity Data and Prices.

U.S. Census Bureau, Center for Economic Studies (CES), 4600 Silver Hill Rd., Washington, DC, 20233, USA, (301) 763-6460, (301) 763-5935, ces.contacts@census.gov, https://www.census.gov/programs-surveys/ces.html; Transportation and Warehousing, 2017 Economic Census.

COMMON FALLACIES

Harvard John F. Kennedy School of Government, 79 John F. Kennedy St., Cambridge, MA, 02138, USA, (617) 495-1100, https://www.hks.harvard.edu/; Harvard Kennedy School Misinformation Review; Harvard Kennedy School Misinformation Review - The Causes and Consequences of COVID-19 Misperceptions: Understanding the Role of News and Social Media; and Harvard Kennedy School Misinformation Review - The Relation between Media Consumption and Misinformation at the Outset of the SARS-CoV-2 Pandemic in the US.

National Bureau of Economic Research (NBER), 1050 Massachusetts Ave., Cambridge, MA, 02138, USA, (617) 868-3900, info@nber.org, https://www.nber.org/; Misinformation During a Pandemic and The Persuasive Effect of Fox News: Non-Compliance with Social Distancing During the Covid-19 Pandemic.

COMMUNICABLE DISEASES

American Chemical Society (ACS), 1155 16th St. NW, Washington, DC, 20036, USA, (800) 227-5558, (202) 872-4600, help@services.acs.org, https://www.acs.org; Aerosol Filtration Efficiency of Common Fabrics Used in Respiratory Cloth Masks; Filtration Efficiencies of Nanoscale Aerosol by Cloth Mask Materials Used to Slow the Spread of SARS-CoV-2; and Household Materials Selection for Homemade Cloth Face Coverings and Their Filtration Efficiency Enhancement with Triboelectric Charging.

BNO News, Hertensprong 29, Tilburg, 5042LG, NLD, contact@bnonews.com, https://bnonews.com; Monkeypox Tracker.

Commonwealth Fund, 1 E 75th St., New York, NY, 10021, USA, (212) 606-3800 , info@cmwf.org, https://www.commonwealthfund.org/; Two Years of U.S. COVID-19 Vaccines Have Prevented Millions of Hospitalizations and Deaths.

European Centre for Disease Prevention and Control (ECDC), Stockholm, SE 171 83, SWE, ecdc.info@ecdc.europa.eu, https://ecdc.europa.eu; Annual Epidemiological Reports (AERs) and Disease Surveillance Reports.

Imperial College London, South Kensington Campus, London, SW7 2AZ, GBR, https://www.imperial.ac.uk/; Estimating the Effects of Non-Pharmaceutical Interventions on COVID-19 in Europe.

Imperial College London, School of Public Health, MRC Centre for Global Infectious Disease Analysis, Medical School Bldg., Norfolk Place, London, W2 1PG, GBR, mrc.gida@imperial.ac.uk, https://www.imperial.ac.uk/mrc-global-infectious-disease-analysis/; Evaluation of Individual and Ensemble Probabilistic Forecasts of COVID-19 Mortality in the United States and Genetic Evidence for the Association Between COVID-19 Epidemic Severity and Timing of Non-Pharmaceutical Interventions.

Johns Hopkins Coronavirus Resource Center, 3400 N Charles St., Baltimore, MD, 21218, USA, https://coronavirus.jhu.edu/; COVID-19 Testing Insights Initiative and Testing Trends Tool: Track Trends in COVID-19 Cases and Tests.

Physicians for Human Rights (PHR), 256 W 38th St., 9th Fl., New York, NY, 10018, USA, (646) 564-3720, (646) 564-3750, https://phr.org/; Silenced and Endangered: Clinicians' Human Rights and Health Concerns about Their Facilities' Response to COVID-19.

Public Health Agency of Canada, 130 Colonnade Rd., Ottawa, ON, K1A 0K9, CAN, (844) 280-5020 (Dial from U.S.), https://www.phac-aspc.gc.ca/; Canada Communicable Disease Report (CCDR), 2023.

U.S. Department of Health and Human Services (HHS), National Institutes of Health (NIH), National Institute of Allergy and Infectious Diseases (NIAID), Office of Communications and Government Relations, 5601 Fishers Ln., MSC 9806, Bethesda, MD, 20892-9806, USA, (866) 284-4107, (301) 496-5717, (301) 402-3573, ocpostoffice@niaid.nih.gov, https://www.niaid.nih.gov; Diseases & Conditions.

U.S. Department of Health and Human Services (HHS), National Institutes of Health (NIH), Researching COVID to Enhance Recovery (RECOVER), 9000 Rockville Pike, Bethesda, MD, 20892, USA, (301) 496-4000, (301) 402-9612 (TTY), https://recovercovid.org; Development of a Definition of Postacute Sequelae of SARS-CoV-2 Infection.

U.S. Department of Health and Human Services, Centers for Disease Control and Prevention (CDC), 1600 Clifton Rd., Atlanta, GA, 30329-4027, USA, (800) 232-4636, (888) 232-6348 (TTY), cdcinfo@cdc.gov, https://www.cdc.gov; Early Estimates of Bivalent mRNA Vaccine Effectiveness in Preventing COVID-19-Associated Emergency Department or Urgent Care Encounters and Hospitalizations Among Immunocompetent Adults - VISION Network, Nine States, September-November 2022; FluSight: Flu Forecasting; 2022 Monkeypox and Orthopoxvirus Outbreak Global Map; Monkeypox: 2022 U.S. Map & Case Count; Morbidity and Mortality Weekly Report (MMWR); National Notifiable Diseases Surveillance System (NNDSS); and Rates of COVID-19 Cases or Deaths by Age Group and Vaccination Status and Booster Dose.

U.S. Department of Health and Human Services, Centers for Disease Control and Prevention (CDC), National Center for Health Statistics (NCHS), 3311 Toledo Rd., Hyattsville, MD, 20782-2064, USA, (800) 232-4636, (301) 458-4000, https://www.cdc.gov/nchs; HPV-Associated Cancer Statistics.

U.S. Department of Health and Human Services, Centers for Disease Control and Prevention (CDC), National Center for HIV, Viral Hepatitis, STD, and TB Prevention (NCHHSTP), 1600 Clifton Rd., Atlanta, GA, 30329-4027, USA, (800) 232-4636, (888) 232-6348 (TTY), https://www.cdc.gov/nchhstp/; NCHHSTP AtlasPlus.

UK Health Security Agency (UKHSA), Nobel House, 17 Smith Sq., London, SW1P 3JR, GBR, enquiries@ukhsa.gov.uk, https://www.gov.uk/government/organisations/uk-health-security-agency; Monkeypox Outbreak: Epidemiological Overview and Trends in HIV Testing, New Diagnoses and People Receiving HIV-Related Care in the United Kingdom: Data to the End of December 2019.

University of California San Diego, U.S. Immigration Policy Center (USIPC), 9500 Gilman Dr., La Jolla, CA, 92093, USA, (858) 534-2230, usipc@ucsd.edu, https://usipc.ucsd.edu/; COVID-19 and the Remaking of U.S. Immigration Policy? Empirically Evaluating the Myth of Immigration and Disease.

University of California, Berkeley, Global Policy Lab, California Memorial Stadium, 2227 Piedmont Ave., Berkeley, CA, 94720, USA, (510) 643-5751, https://www.globalpolicy.science/; The Effect of Large-Scale Anti-Contagion Policies on the COVID-19 Pandemic.

World Health Organization (WHO), Ave. Appia 20, Geneva, CH-1211, SWI, (202) 974-3000 (Telephone in U.S.), publications@who.int, https://www.who.int/; Advice on the Use of Masks in the Context of COVID-19; Global Health Observatory (GHO); Mpox (Monkeypox) Outbreak; Weekly Epidemiological Record (WER); and Western Pacific Surveillance and Response Journal.

COMMUNICATIONS-DEGREES CONFERRED

U.S. Department of Education (ED), Institute of Education Sciences (IES), National Center for Education Statistics (NCES), Potomac Center Plaza, 550 12th St. SW, Washington, DC, 20202, USA, (202) 403-5551, https://nces.ed.gov/; Digest of Education Statistics, 2020.

COMMUNICATIONS EQUIPMENT-MANUFACTURING-EARNINGS

U.S. Census Bureau, 4600 Silver Hill Rd., Washington, DC, 20233, USA, (301) 763-4636, (800) 923-8282, https://www.census.gov; Annual Survey of Manufactures (ASM) 2021.

U.S. Department of Labor (DOL), Bureau of Labor Statistics (BLS), Postal Square Bldg., 2 Massachusetts Ave. NE, Washington, DC, 20212-0001, USA, (202) 691-5200, (202) 691-7890, blsdata_staff@bls.gov, https://www.bls.gov; Current Employment Statistics (CES).

COMMUNICATIONS EQUIPMENT-MANUFACTURING-EMPLOYEES

U.S. Census Bureau, 4600 Silver Hill Rd., Washington, DC, 20233, USA, (301) 763-4636, (800) 923-8282, https://www.census.gov; Annual Survey of Manufactures (ASM) 2021.

U.S. Department of Labor (DOL), Bureau of Labor Statistics (BLS), Postal Square Bldg., 2 Massachusetts Ave. NE, Washington, DC, 20212-0001, USA, (202) 691-5200, (202) 691-7890, blsdata_staff@bls.gov, https://www.bls.gov; Current Employment Statistics (CES) and Industry-Occupation Matrix Data, By Occupation.

COMMUNICATIONS EQUIPMENT-MANUFACTURING-ESTABLISHMENTS

U.S. Census Bureau, 4600 Silver Hill Rd., Washington, DC, 20233, USA, (301) 763-4636, (800) 923-8282, https://www.census.gov; Annual Survey of Manufactures (ASM) 2021.

COMMUNICATIONS EQUIPMENT-MANUFACTURING-INVENTORIES

U.S. Census Bureau, 4600 Silver Hill Rd., Washington, DC, 20233, USA, (301) 763-4636, (800) 923-8282, https://www.census.gov; Manufacturers' Shipments, Inventories and Orders.

COMMUNICATIONS EQUIPMENT-MANUFACTURING-PRODUCTIVITY

U.S. Department of Labor (DOL), Bureau of Labor Statistics (BLS), Postal Square Bldg., 2 Massachusetts Ave. NE, Washington, DC, 20212-0001, USA, (202) 691-5200, (202) 691-7890, blsdata_staff@bls.gov, https://www.bls.gov; Productivity.

COMMUNICATIONS EQUIPMENT-MANUFACTURING-SHIPMENTS

U.S. Census Bureau, 4600 Silver Hill Rd., Washington, DC, 20233, USA, (301) 763-4636, (800) 923-8282, https://www.census.gov; Annual Survey of Manufactures (ASM) 2021 and Manufacturers' Shipments, Inventories and Orders.

COMMUNICATIONS INDUSTRY

See INFORMATION INDUSTRY; TELECOMMUNICATION INDUSTRY

COMMUNITY CARE FACILITIES FOR THE ELDERLY-INDUSTRY

U.S. Census Bureau, 4600 Silver Hill Rd., Washington, DC, 20233, USA, (301) 763-4636, (800) 923-8282, https://www.census.gov; Economic Census, Nonemployer Statistics (NES) 2019.

COMMUNITY COLLEGE STUDENTS

The Brookings Institution, 1775 Massachusetts Ave. NW, Washington, DC, 20036, USA, (202) 797-6000, communications@brookings.edu, https://www.brookings.edu/; Policies and Payoffs to Addressing America's College Graduation Deficit.

Monmouth University Polling Institute, 400 Cedar Ave., West Long Branch, NJ, 07764, USA, (732) 263-5860, polling@monmouth.edu, https://www.monmouth.edu/polling-institute/; Support for Illegal Immigrant Access to Licenses, State Colleges Rises Over Past Decade.

COMMUNITY DEVELOPMENT

Ewing Marion Kauffman Foundation, 4801 Rockhill Rd., Kansas City, MO, 64110, USA, (816) 932-1000, https://www.kauffman.org/; Community-Engaged Entrepreneurship Research: Methodologies to Advance Equity and Inclusion.

Harvard Joint Center for Housing Studies (JCHS), 1 Bow St., Ste. 400, Cambridge, MA, 02138, USA, (617) 495-7908, (617) 496-9957, jchs@harvard.edu, https://www.jchs.harvard.edu/; Improving America's Housing 2021.

U.S. Department of Housing and Urban Development (HUD), Office of Policy Development and Research (PD&R), PO Box 23268, Washington, DC, 20026-3268, USA, (800) 245-2691, (800) 927-7589 (TDD), (202) 708-9981, helpdesk@huduser.gov, https://www.huduser.gov; HUD User.

COMMUNITY DEVELOPMENT-FEDERAL OUTLAYS

U.S. Office of Management and Budget (OMB), 725 17th St. NW, Washington, DC, 20503, USA, (202) 395-3080, https://www.whitehouse.gov/omb/; Historical Tables.

COMMUNITY FOOD, HOUSING SERVICES

U.S. Census Bureau, 4600 Silver Hill Rd., Washington, DC, 20233, USA, (301) 763-4636, (800) 923-8282, https://www.census.gov; Economic Census, Nonemployer Statistics (NES) 2019.

United Way of Rhode Island (UWRI), 50 Valley St., Providence, RI, 02909, USA, (401) 444-0600, (401) 444-0635, info@uwri.org, https://www.unitedwayri.org/; 2021-2022 Community Impact Report.

COMMUNITY RELATIONS

Ewing Marion Kauffman Foundation, 4801 Rockhill Rd., Kansas City, MO, 64110, USA, (816) 932-1000, https://www.kauffman.org/; Community-Engaged Entrepreneurship Research: Methodologies to Advance Equity and Inclusion.

Indiana University Lilly Family School of Philanthropy, Women's Philanthropy Institute (WPI), 301 University Blvd., University Hall, Ste. 3000, Indianapolis, IN, 46202-5146, USA, (317) 278-8990, (317) 274-4200, (317) 278-8999, wpiinfo@iupui.edu, https://philanthropy.iupui.edu/institutes/womens-philanthropy-institute/; Women Give 2022: Racial Justice, Gender and Generosity.

National Academies of Sciences, Engineering, and Medicine (The National Academies), 500 5th St. NW, Washington, DC, 20001, USA, (202) 334-2000, contact@nas.edu, https://www.nationalacademies.org/; Proactive Policing: Effects on Crime and Communities.

Pew Research Center, 1615 L St. NW, Ste. 800, Washington, DC, 20036, USA, (202) 419-4300, (202) 857-8562, info@pewresearch.org, https://www.pewresearch.org/; For Local News, Americans Embrace Digital but Still Want Strong Community Connection and Local News Is Playing an Important Role for Americans During COVID-19 Outbreak.

Public Agenda, 1 Dock 72 Way, No. 6101, Brooklyn, NY, 11205-1242, USA, (212) 686-6610, info@publicagenda.org, https://www.publicagenda.org/; America's Hidden Common Ground on the Coronavirus Crisis: Results from a Public Agenda/USA Today/Ipsos Snapshot Survey on How Communities Are Responding and the Policies People Support and America's Hidden Common Ground on the Coronavirus Crisis: Results from a Public Agenda/USA Today/Ipsos Survey of Americans' Views on Reopening Their Communities.

RAND Corporation, PO Box 2138, 1776 Main St., Santa Monica, CA, 90407-2138, USA, (310) 451-7002, (412) 802-4981, order@rand.org, https://www.rand.org/; Would Law Enforcement Leaders Support Defunding the Police? Probably - If Communities Ask Police to Solve Fewer Problems.

Stop AAPI Hate, C/O Chinese for Affirmative Action, 17 Walter U. Lum Place, San Francisco, CA, 94108, USA, (415) 274-6750, (415) 397-8770, community@stopaapihate.org, https://stopaapihate.org; Two Years and Thousands of Voices: What Community-Generated Data Tells Us About Anti-AAPI Hate.

COMMUTING TO WORK

U.S. Census Bureau, 4600 Silver Hill Rd., Washington, DC, 20233, USA, (301) 763-4636, (800) 923-8282, https://www.census.gov; Explore Census Data and United States QuickFacts.

COMORBIDITY

U.S. Department of Health and Human Services, Centers for Disease Control and Prevention (CDC), National Center for Health Statistics (NCHS), 3311 Toledo Rd., Hyattsville, MD, 20782-2064, USA, (800) 232-4636, (301) 458-4000, https://www.cdc.gov/nchs; Excess Deaths Associated with COVID-19.

COMOROS-NATIONAL STATISTICAL OFFICE

Institut Nationale de la Statistique et des Etudes Economiques et Demographiques Comoros (INSEED), BP 131, Moroni, COM, secrcom@inseed.km, http://www.inseed.km/; National Data Reports (Comoros).

COMOROS-AGRICULTURE

African Development Bank Group (AfDB), Avenue Joseph Anoma, 01 BP 1387, Abidjan, 01, COT, https://www.afdb.org; African Economic Outlook 2021 and Compendium of Statistics on Bank Group Operations 2019.

The Economist Group: Economist Intelligence Unit (EIU), 900 3rd Ave., 16th Fl., New York, NY, 10022, USA, (212) 541-0500, americas@eiu.com, https://www.eiu.com; Comoros Country Report.

Euromonitor International, Inc., 1 N Dearborn St., Ste. 1700, Chicago, IL, 60602, USA, (312) 922-1115, (312) 922-1157, info-usa@euromonitor.com, https://www.euromonitor.com/; Geographies.

Organisation of Islamic Cooperation (OIC), Statistical, Economic and Social Research and Training Centre for Islamic Countries (SESRIC), Kudus Cad. No. 9, Diplomatik Site, Ankara, 06450, TUR, statistics@sesric.org, https://www.sesric.org/; OIC Statistics (OICStat) Database and OIC-Countries in Figures (OIC-CIF).

Palgrave Macmillan, 1 New York Plaza, Ste. 4500, New York, NY, 10004-1562, USA, (800) 777-4643, orders@palgrave.com, https://www.palgrave.com/us; The Statesman's Yearbook, 2023.

Routledge - Taylor & Francis Group, 6000 Broken Sound Pkwy. NW, Ste. 300, Boca Raton, FL, 33487, USA, (800) 634-1420, (800) 634-7064, orders@taylorandfrancis.com, https://www.routledge.com/; The Europa World Year Book 2022.

United Nations Economic Commission for Africa (UNECA), PO Box 3001, Addis Ababa, ETH, ecainfo@uneca.org, https://www.uneca.org/; African Statistical Yearbook 2020 and Economic Report on Africa 2021.

United Nations Food and Agricultural Organization (FAO), 2121 K St., Ste. 800B, Washington, DC, 20037, USA, (202) 653-2400 (Dial from U.S.), (202) 653-5760 (Fax from U.S.), fao-hq@fao.org, https://www.fao.org; AQUASTAT and The State of Food and Agriculture (SOFA) 2022.

The World Bank, 1818 H St. NW, Washington, DC, 20433, USA, (202) 473-1000, (202) 477-6391, eds03@worldbank.org, https://www.worldbank.org/; Comoros (report).

COMOROS-AIRLINES

Palgrave Macmillan, 1 New York Plaza, Ste. 4500, New York, NY, 10004-1562, USA, (800) 777-4643, orders@palgrave.com, https://www.palgrave.com/us; The Statesman's Yearbook, 2023.

Routledge - Taylor & Francis Group, 6000 Broken Sound Pkwy. NW, Ste. 300, Boca Raton, FL, 33487, USA, (800) 634-1420, (800) 634-7064, orders@taylorandfrancis.com, https://www.routledge.com/; The Europa World Year Book 2022.

United Nations Economic Commission for Africa (UNECA), PO Box 3001, Addis Ababa, ETH, ecainfo@uneca.org, https://www.uneca.org/; African Statistical Yearbook 2020.

COMOROS-ARMED FORCES

Central Intelligence Agency (CIA), Office of Public Affairs, Washington, DC, 20505, USA, (703) 482-0623, https://www.cia.gov; The World Factbook.

Palgrave Macmillan, 1 New York Plaza, Ste. 4500, New York, NY, 10004-1562, USA, (800) 777-4643, orders@palgrave.com, https://www.palgrave.com/us; The Statesman's Yearbook, 2023.

Stockholm International Peace Research Institute (SIPRI), Signalistgatan 9, Stockholm, SE 169 72, SWE, https://www.sipri.org/; SIPRI Arms Transfers Database and SIPRI Military Expenditure Database.

COMOROS-BALANCE OF PAYMENTS

African Development Bank Group (AfDB), Avenue Joseph Anoma, 01 BP 1387, Abidjan, 01, COT, https://www.afdb.org; The AfDB Statistics Pocketbook 2019.

Routledge - Taylor & Francis Group, 6000 Broken Sound Pkwy. NW, Ste. 300, Boca Raton, FL, 33487,

USA, (800) 634-1420, (800) 634-7064, orders@taylorandfrancis.com, https://www.routledge.com/; The Europa World Year Book 2022.

United Nations Conference on Trade and Development (UNCTAD), Palais des Nations, Geneva, 1211, SWI, (212) 963-6896, unctadinfo@unctad.org, https://unctad.org; Handbook of Statistics 2021.

United Nations Economic Commission for Africa (UNECA), PO Box 3001, Addis Ababa, ETH, ecainfo@uneca.org, https://www.uneca.org/; African Statistical Yearbook 2020.

The World Bank, 1818 H St. NW, Washington, DC, 20433, USA, (202) 473-1000, (202) 477-6391, eds03@worldbank.org, https://www.worldbank.org/; Comoros (report).

COMOROS-BANKS AND BANKING

Euromonitor International, Inc., 1 N Dearborn St., Ste. 1700, Chicago, IL, 60602, USA, (312) 922-1115, (312) 922-1157, info-usa@euromonitor.com, https://www.euromonitor.com/; Geographies.

Routledge - Taylor & Francis Group, 6000 Broken Sound Pkwy. NW, Ste. 300, Boca Raton, FL, 33487, USA, (800) 634-1420, (800) 634-7064, orders@taylorandfrancis.com, https://www.routledge.com/; The Europa World Year Book 2022.

United Nations Economic Commission for Africa (UNECA), PO Box 3001, Addis Ababa, ETH, ecainfo@uneca.org, https://www.uneca.org/; African Statistical Yearbook 2020.

COMOROS-BROADCASTING

Central Intelligence Agency (CIA), Office of Public Affairs, Washington, DC, 20505, USA, (703) 482-0623, https://www.cia.gov; The World Factbook.

Euromonitor International, Inc., 1 N Dearborn St., Ste. 1700, Chicago, IL, 60602, USA, (312) 922-1115, (312) 922-1157, info-usa@euromonitor.com, https://www.euromonitor.com/; Geographies.

Palgrave Macmillan, 1 New York Plaza, Ste. 4500, New York, NY, 10004-1562, USA, (800) 777-4643, orders@palgrave.com, https://www.palgrave.com/us; The Statesman's Yearbook, 2023.

WRTH Publications Limited, PO Box 290, Oxford, OX2 7FT, GBR, sales@wrth.com, https://www.wrth.com; World Radio TV Handbook 2023.

COMOROS-BUDGET

Central Intelligence Agency (CIA), Office of Public Affairs, Washington, DC, 20505, USA, (703) 482-0623, https://www.cia.gov; The World Factbook.

COMOROS-CLIMATE

International Institute for Environment and Development (IIED), 235 High Holborn, London, WC1V 7DN, GBR, inforequest@iied.org, https://www.iied.org; Environment & Urbanization.

Palgrave Macmillan, 1 New York Plaza, Ste. 4500, New York, NY, 10004-1562, USA, (800) 777-4643, orders@palgrave.com, https://www.palgrave.com/us; The Statesman's Yearbook, 2023.

COMOROS-COAL PRODUCTION

See COMOROS-MINERAL INDUSTRIES

COMOROS-COCOA PRODUCTION

See COMOROS-CROPS

COMOROS-COMMERCE

Palgrave Macmillan, 1 New York Plaza, Ste. 4500, New York, NY, 10004-1562, USA, (800) 777-4643, orders@palgrave.com, https://www.palgrave.com/us; The Statesman's Yearbook, 2023.

UK Data Service, University of Essex, Wivenhoe Park, Colchester, Essex, CO4 3SQ, GBR, https://ukdataservice.ac.uk/; International Aggregate Data.

COMOROS-CONSTRUCTION INDUSTRY

United Nations Economic Commission for Africa (UNECA), PO Box 3001, Addis Ababa, ETH, ecainfo@uneca.org, https://www.uneca.org/; African Statistical Yearbook 2020.

COMOROS-CONSUMER PRICE INDEXES

The World Bank, 1818 H St. NW, Washington, DC, 20433, USA, (202) 473-1000, (202) 477-6391, eds03@worldbank.org, https://www.worldbank.org/; Comoros (report).

COMOROS-CONSUMPTION (ECONOMICS)

African Development Bank Group (AfDB), Avenue Joseph Anoma, 01 BP 1387, Abidjan, 01, COT, https://www.afdb.org; The AfDB Statistics Pocketbook 2019.

COMOROS-CORN INDUSTRY

See COMOROS-CROPS

COMOROS-CROPS

Palgrave Macmillan, 1 New York Plaza, Ste. 4500, New York, NY, 10004-1562, USA, (800) 777-4643, orders@palgrave.com, https://www.palgrave.com/us; The Statesman's Yearbook, 2023.

United Nations Economic Commission for Africa (UNECA), PO Box 3001, Addis Ababa, ETH, ecainfo@uneca.org, https://www.uneca.org/; African Statistical Yearbook 2020.

United Nations Food and Agricultural Organization (FAO), 2121 K St., Ste. 800B, Washington, DC, 20037, USA, (202) 653-2400 (Dial from U.S.), (202) 653-5760 (Fax from U.S.), fao-hq@fao.org, https://www.fao.org; The State of Food and Agriculture (SOFA) 2022.

United Nations Statistics Division (UNSD), United Nations Plz., New York, NY, 10017, USA, (800) 253-9646, (212) 963-9851, statistics@un.org, https://unstats.un.org; Statistical Yearbook of the United Nations 2021.

COMOROS-DAIRY PROCESSING

Palgrave Macmillan, 1 New York Plaza, Ste. 4500, New York, NY, 10004-1562, USA, (800) 777-4643, orders@palgrave.com, https://www.palgrave.com/us; The Statesman's Yearbook, 2023.

United Nations Food and Agricultural Organization (FAO), 2121 K St., Ste. 800B, Washington, DC, 20037, USA, (202) 653-2400 (Dial from U.S.), (202) 653-5760 (Fax from U.S.), fao-hq@fao.org, https://www.fao.org; The State of Food and Agriculture (SOFA) 2022.

COMOROS-DEBTS, EXTERNAL

African Development Bank Group (AfDB), Avenue Joseph Anoma, 01 BP 1387, Abidjan, 01, COT, https://www.afdb.org; The AfDB Statistics Pocketbook 2019; African Economic Outlook 2021; and Compendium of Statistics on Bank Group Operations 2019.

United Nations Economic Commission for Africa (UNECA), PO Box 3001, Addis Ababa, ETH, ecainfo@uneca.org, https://www.uneca.org/; Economic Report on Africa 2021.

COMOROS-ECONOMIC ASSISTANCE

United Nations Statistics Division (UNSD), United Nations Plz., New York, NY, 10017, USA, (800) 253-9646, (212) 963-9851, statistics@un.org, https://unstats.un.org; Statistical Yearbook of the United Nations 2021.

COMOROS-ECONOMIC CONDITIONS

African Development Bank Group (AfDB), Avenue Joseph Anoma, 01 BP 1387, Abidjan, 01, COT, https://www.afdb.org; The AfDB Statistics Pocketbook 2019; Africa Economic Brief - COVID-19 Pandemic Potential Risks for Trade and Trade Finance in Africa; African Economic Outlook 2021; The African Statistical Journal; Compendium of Statistics on Bank Group Operations 2019; and Gender, Poverty and Environmental Indicators on African Countries 2019.

Bernan Press, 15250 NBN Way, Bldg. C, Blue Ridge Summit, PA, 17214, USA, (301) 459-2255, (800) 865-3457, (800) 865-3450, customercare@bernan.com, https://rowman.com/Page/Bernan; World Economic Outlook, April 2022.

Central Intelligence Agency (CIA), Office of Public Affairs, Washington, DC, 20505, USA, (703) 482-0623, https://www.cia.gov; The World Factbook.

The Economist Group: Economist Intelligence Unit (EIU), 900 3rd Ave., 16th Fl., New York, NY, 10022, USA, (212) 541-0500, americas@eiu.com, https://www.eiu.com; Comoros Country Report.

Euromonitor International, Inc., 1 N Dearborn St., Ste. 1700, Chicago, IL, 60602, USA, (312) 922-1115, (312) 922-1157, info-usa@euromonitor.com, https://www.euromonitor.com/; Geographies.

Organisation of Islamic Cooperation (OIC), Statistical, Economic and Social Research and Training Centre for Islamic Countries (SESRIC), Kudus Cad. No. 9, Diplomatik Site, Ankara, 06450, TUR, statistics@sesric.org, https://www.sesric.org/; OIC Economic Outlook 2021; OIC Statistics (OICStat) Database; and OIC-Countries in Figures (OIC-CIF).

Routledge - Taylor & Francis Group, 6000 Broken Sound Pkwy. NW, Ste. 300, Boca Raton, FL, 33487, USA, (800) 634-1420, (800) 634-7064, orders@taylorandfrancis.com, https://www.routledge.com/; The Europa World Year Book 2022.

United Nations Economic Commission for Africa (UNECA), PO Box 3001, Addis Ababa, ETH, ecainfo@uneca.org, https://www.uneca.org/; Economic Report on Africa 2021.

United Nations Statistics Division (UNSD), United Nations Plz., New York, NY, 10017, USA, (800) 253-9646, (212) 963-9851, statistics@un.org, https://unstats.un.org; World Statistics Pocketbook 2021.

The World Bank, 1818 H St. NW, Washington, DC, 20433, USA, (202) 473-1000, (202) 477-6391, eds03@worldbank.org, https://www.worldbank.org/; Comoros (report) and The Global Findex Database 2021.

COMOROS-EDUCATION

African Development Bank Group (AfDB), Avenue Joseph Anoma, 01 BP 1387, Abidjan, 01, COT, https://www.afdb.org; The AfDB Statistics Pocketbook 2019.

Euromonitor International, Inc., 1 N Dearborn St., Ste. 1700, Chicago, IL, 60602, USA, (312) 922-1115, (312) 922-1157, info-usa@euromonitor.com, https://www.euromonitor.com/; Geographies.

Organisation of Islamic Cooperation (OIC), Statistical, Economic and Social Research and Training Centre for Islamic Countries (SESRIC), Kudus Cad. No. 9, Diplomatik Site, Ankara, 06450, TUR, statistics@sesric.org, https://www.sesric.org/; OIC Statistics (OICStat) Database.

Palgrave Macmillan, 1 New York Plaza, Ste. 4500, New York, NY, 10004-1562, USA, (800) 777-4643, orders@palgrave.com, https://www.palgrave.com/us; The Statesman's Yearbook, 2023.

Routledge - Taylor & Francis Group, 6000 Broken Sound Pkwy. NW, Ste. 300, Boca Raton, FL, 33487, USA, (800) 634-1420, (800) 634-7064, orders@taylorandfrancis.com, https://www.routledge.com/; The Europa World Year Book 2022.

United Nations Economic Commission for Africa (UNECA), PO Box 3001, Addis Ababa, ETH, ecainfo@uneca.org, https://www.uneca.org/; African Statistical Yearbook 2020.

The World Bank, 1818 H St. NW, Washington, DC, 20433, USA, (202) 473-1000, (202) 477-6391, eds03@worldbank.org, https://www.worldbank.org/; Comoros (report).

COMOROS-EMPLOYMENT

UK Data Service, University of Essex, Wivenhoe Park, Colchester, Essex, CO4 3SQ, GBR, https://ukdataservice.ac.uk/; International Aggregate Data.

United Nations Economic Commission for Africa (UNECA), PO Box 3001, Addis Ababa, ETH,

ecainfo@uneca.org, https://www.uneca.org/; African Statistical Yearbook 2020.

The World Bank, 1818 H St. NW, Washington, DC, 20433, USA, (202) 473-1000, (202) 477-6391, eds03@worldbank.org, https://www.worldbank.org/; Comoros (report).

COMOROS-ENVIRONMENTAL CONDITIONS

The Economist Group: Economist Intelligence Unit (EIU), 900 3rd Ave., 16th Fl., New York, NY, 10022, USA, (212) 541-0500, americas@eiu.com, https://www.eiu.com; Comoros Country Report.

International Institute for Environment and Development (IIED), 235 High Holborn, London, WC1V 7DN, GBR, inforequest@iied.org, https://www.iied.org; Environment & Urbanization.

Organisation of Islamic Cooperation (OIC), Statistical, Economic and Social Research and Training Centre for Islamic Countries (SESRIC), Kudus Cad. No. 9, Diplomatik Site, Ankara, 06450, TUR, statistics@sesric.org, https://www.sesric.org/; OIC Statistics (OICStat) Database and OIC-Countries in Figures (OIC-CIF).

United Nations Statistics Division (UNSD), United Nations Plz., New York, NY, 10017, USA, (800) 253-9646, (212) 963-9851, statistics@un.org, https://unstats.un.org; World Statistics Pocketbook 2021.

COMOROS-EXPORTS

Central Intelligence Agency (CIA), Office of Public Affairs, Washington, DC, 20505, USA, (703) 482-0623, https://www.cia.gov; The World Factbook.

The Economist Group: Economist Intelligence Unit (EIU), 900 3rd Ave., 16th Fl., New York, NY, 10022, USA, (212) 541-0500, americas@eiu.com, https://www.eiu.com; Comoros Country Report.

International Monetary Fund (IMF), 700 19th St. NW, Washington, DC, 20431, USA, (202) 623-7000, (202) 623-4661, publications@imf.org, https://www.imf.org; Direction of Trade Statistics (DOTS).

Organisation of Islamic Cooperation (OIC), Statistical, Economic and Social Research and Training Centre for Islamic Countries (SESRIC), Kudus Cad. No. 9, Diplomatik Site, Ankara, 06450, TUR, statistics@sesric.org, https://www.sesric.org/; OIC Statistics (OICStat) Database.

S&P Global, IHS Markit, 15 Inverness Way E, Englewood, CO, 80112, USA, (800) 447-2273, (800) 854-7179, https://ihsmarkit.com; Global Trade Atlas (GTA).

United Nations Conference on Trade and Development (UNCTAD), Palais des Nations, Geneva, 1211, SWI, (212) 963-6896, unctadinfo@unctad.org, https://unctad.org; Handbook of Statistics 2021.

COMOROS-FERTILITY, HUMAN

Central Intelligence Agency (CIA), Office of Public Affairs, Washington, DC, 20505, USA, (703) 482-0623, https://www.cia.gov; The World Factbook.

COMOROS-FERTILIZER INDUSTRY

United Nations Food and Agricultural Organization (FAO), 2121 K St., Ste. 800B, Washington, DC, 20037, USA, (202) 653-2400 (Dial from U.S.), (202) 653-5760 (Fax from U.S.), fao-hq@fao.org, https://www.fao.org; The State of Food and Agriculture (SOFA) 2022.

COMOROS-FETAL MORTALITY

See COMOROS-MORTALITY

COMOROS-FINANCE

Stockholm International Peace Research Institute (SIPRI), Signalistgatan 9, Stockholm, SE 169 72, SWE, https://www.sipri.org/; SIPRI Arms Transfers Database and SIPRI Military Expenditure Database.

United Nations Economic Commission for Africa (UNECA), PO Box 3001, Addis Ababa, ETH, ecainfo@uneca.org, https://www.uneca.org/; African Statistical Yearbook 2020.

United Nations Statistics Division (UNSD), United Nations Plz., New York, NY, 10017, USA, (800) 253-9646, (212) 963-9851, statistics@un.org, https://unstats.un.org; Statistical Yearbook of the United Nations 2021.

The World Bank, 1818 H St. NW, Washington, DC, 20433, USA, (202) 473-1000, (202) 477-6391, eds03@worldbank.org, https://www.worldbank.org/; Comoros (report).

COMOROS-FINANCE, PUBLIC

African Development Bank Group (AfDB), Avenue Joseph Anoma, 01 BP 1387, Abidjan, 01, COT, https://www.afdb.org; The AfDB Statistics Pocketbook 2019.

The Economist Group: Economist Intelligence Unit (EIU), 900 3rd Ave., 16th Fl., New York, NY, 10022, USA, (212) 541-0500, americas@eiu.com, https://www.eiu.com; Comoros Country Report.

Palgrave Macmillan, 1 New York Plaza, Ste. 4500, New York, NY, 10004-1562, USA, (800) 777-4643, orders@palgrave.com, https://www.palgrave.com/us; The Statesman's Yearbook, 2023.

Routledge - Taylor & Francis Group, 6000 Broken Sound Pkwy. NW, Ste. 300, Boca Raton, FL, 33487, USA, (800) 634-1420, (800) 634-7064, orders@taylorandfrancis.com, https://www.routledge.com/; The Europa World Year Book 2022.

United Nations Economic Commission for Africa (UNECA), PO Box 3001, Addis Ababa, ETH, ecainfo@uneca.org, https://www.uneca.org/; African Statistical Yearbook 2020.

United Nations Statistics Division (UNSD), United Nations Plz., New York, NY, 10017, USA, (800) 253-9646, (212) 963-9851, statistics@un.org, https://unstats.un.org; National Accounts Main Aggregates Database and National Accounts Statistics: Main Aggregates and Detailed Tables.

The World Bank, 1818 H St. NW, Washington, DC, 20433, USA, (202) 473-1000, (202) 477-6391, eds03@worldbank.org, https://www.worldbank.org/; Comoros (report).

COMOROS-FISHERIES

Routledge - Taylor & Francis Group, 6000 Broken Sound Pkwy. NW, Ste. 300, Boca Raton, FL, 33487, USA, (800) 634-1420, (800) 634-7064, orders@taylorandfrancis.com, https://www.routledge.com/; The Europa World Year Book 2022.

United Nations Economic Commission for Africa (UNECA), PO Box 3001, Addis Ababa, ETH, ecainfo@uneca.org, https://www.uneca.org/; African Statistical Yearbook 2020.

United Nations Food and Agricultural Organization (FAO), 2121 K St., Ste. 800B, Washington, DC, 20037, USA, (202) 653-2400 (Dial from U.S.), (202) 653-5760 (Fax from U.S.), fao-hq@fao.org, https://www.fao.org; FAO Yearbook of Fishery and Aquaculture Statistics 2019; Fishery Statistical Collections Global Capture Production; FishStatJ; and The State of Food and Agriculture (SOFA) 2022.

United Nations Statistics Division (UNSD), United Nations Plz., New York, NY, 10017, USA, (800) 253-9646, (212) 963-9851, statistics@un.org, https://unstats.un.org; Statistical Yearbook of the United Nations 2021.

The World Bank, 1818 H St. NW, Washington, DC, 20433, USA, (202) 473-1000, (202) 477-6391, eds03@worldbank.org, https://www.worldbank.org/; Comoros (report).

COMOROS-FOOD

African Development Bank Group (AfDB), Avenue Joseph Anoma, 01 BP 1387, Abidjan, 01, COT, https://www.afdb.org; The AfDB Statistics Pocketbook 2019.

United Nations Food and Agricultural Organization (FAO), 2121 K St., Ste. 800B, Washington, DC, 20037, USA, (202) 653-2400 (Dial from U.S.), (202) 653-5760 (Fax from U.S.), fao-hq@fao.org, https://www.fao.org; The State of Food and Agriculture (SOFA) 2022.

COMOROS-FOREIGN EXCHANGE RATES

African Development Bank Group (AfDB), Avenue Joseph Anoma, 01 BP 1387, Abidjan, 01, COT, https://www.afdb.org; The AfDB Statistics Pocketbook 2019.

COMOROS-FORESTS AND FORESTRY

Palgrave Macmillan, 1 New York Plaza, Ste. 4500, New York, NY, 10004-1562, USA, (800) 777-4643, orders@palgrave.com, https://www.palgrave.com/us; The Statesman's Yearbook, 2023.

United Nations Economic Commission for Africa (UNECA), PO Box 3001, Addis Ababa, ETH, ecainfo@uneca.org, https://www.uneca.org/; African Statistical Yearbook 2020.

United Nations Food and Agricultural Organization (FAO), 2121 K St., Ste. 800B, Washington, DC, 20037, USA, (202) 653-2400 (Dial from U.S.), (202) 653-5760 (Fax from U.S.), fao-hq@fao.org, https://www.fao.org; The State of Food and Agriculture (SOFA) 2022.

The World Bank, 1818 H St. NW, Washington, DC, 20433, USA, (202) 473-1000, (202) 477-6391, eds03@worldbank.org, https://www.worldbank.org/; Comoros (report).

COMOROS-GROSS DOMESTIC PRODUCT

African Development Bank Group (AfDB), Avenue Joseph Anoma, 01 BP 1387, Abidjan, 01, COT, https://www.afdb.org; The AfDB Statistics Pocketbook 2019.

The Economist Group: Economist Intelligence Unit (EIU), 900 3rd Ave., 16th Fl., New York, NY, 10022, USA, (212) 541-0500, americas@eiu.com, https://www.eiu.com; Comoros Country Report.

Routledge - Taylor & Francis Group, 6000 Broken Sound Pkwy. NW, Ste. 300, Boca Raton, FL, 33487, USA, (800) 634-1420, (800) 634-7064, orders@taylorandfrancis.com, https://www.routledge.com/; The Europa World Year Book 2022.

United Nations Economic Commission for Africa (UNECA), PO Box 3001, Addis Ababa, ETH, ecainfo@uneca.org, https://www.uneca.org/; African Statistical Yearbook 2020.

United Nations Statistics Division (UNSD), United Nations Plz., New York, NY, 10017, USA, (800) 253-9646, (212) 963-9851, statistics@un.org, https://unstats.un.org; Statistical Yearbook of the United Nations 2021.

COMOROS-GROSS NATIONAL PRODUCT

Palgrave Macmillan, 1 New York Plaza, Ste. 4500, New York, NY, 10004-1562, USA, (800) 777-4643, orders@palgrave.com, https://www.palgrave.com/us; The Statesman's Yearbook, 2023.

COMOROS-HOUSING

Euromonitor International, Inc., 1 N Dearborn St., Ste. 1700, Chicago, IL, 60602, USA, (312) 922-1115, (312) 922-1157, info-usa@euromonitor.com, https://www.euromonitor.com/; Geographies.

COMOROS-ILLITERATE PERSONS

UNESCO Institute for Statistics, C.P 250 Succursale H, Montreal, QC, H3G 2K8, CAN, (514) 343-6880 (Dial from U.S.), (514) 343-5740 (Fax from U.S.), uis.publications@unesco.org, http://uis.unesco.org/; UIS.Stat.

COMOROS-IMPORTS

Central Intelligence Agency (CIA), Office of Public Affairs, Washington, DC, 20505, USA, (703) 482-0623, https://www.cia.gov; The World Factbook.

The Economist Group: Economist Intelligence Unit (EIU), 900 3rd Ave., 16th Fl., New York, NY, 10022, USA, (212) 541-0500, americas@eiu.com, https://www.eiu.com; Comoros Country Report.

International Monetary Fund (IMF), 700 19th St. NW, Washington, DC, 20431, USA, (202) 623-7000, (202) 623-4661, publications@imf.org, https://www.imf.org; Direction of Trade Statistics (DOTS).

S&P Global, IHS Markit, 15 Inverness Way E, Englewood, CO, 80112, USA, (800) 447-2273, (800) 854-7179, https://ihsmarkit.com; Global Trade Atlas (GTA).

United Nations Conference on Trade and Development (UNCTAD), Palais des Nations, Geneva, 1211, SWI, (212) 963-6896, unctadinfo@unctad.org, https://unctad.org; Handbook of Statistics 2021.

COMOROS-INDUSTRIES

Central Intelligence Agency (CIA), Office of Public Affairs, Washington, DC, 20505, USA, (703) 482-0623, https://www.cia.gov; The World Factbook.

The Economist Group: Economist Intelligence Unit (EIU), 900 3rd Ave., 16th Fl., New York, NY, 10022, USA, (212) 541-0500, americas@eiu.com, https://www.eiu.com; Comoros Country Report.

Euromonitor International, Inc., 1 N Dearborn St., Ste. 1700, Chicago, IL, 60602, USA, (312) 922-1115, (312) 922-1157, info-usa@euromonitor.com, https://www.euromonitor.com/; Geographies.

Palgrave Macmillan, 1 New York Plaza, Ste. 4500, New York, NY, 10004-1562, USA, (800) 777-4643, orders@palgrave.com, https://www.palgrave.com/us; The Statesman's Yearbook, 2023.

Routledge - Taylor & Francis Group, 6000 Broken Sound Pkwy. NW, Ste. 300, Boca Raton, FL, 33487, USA, (800) 634-1420, (800) 634-7064, orders@taylorandfrancis.com, https://www.routledge.com/; The Europa World Year Book 2022.

United Nations Economic Commission for Africa (UNECA), PO Box 3001, Addis Ababa, ETH, ecainfo@uneca.org, https://www.uneca.org/; African Statistical Yearbook 2020.

The World Bank, 1818 H St. NW, Washington, DC, 20433, USA, (202) 473-1000, (202) 477-6391, eds03@worldbank.org, https://www.worldbank.org/; Comoros (report).

COMOROS-INFANT AND MATERNAL MORTALITY

See COMOROS-MORTALITY

COMOROS-INTERNATIONAL TRADE

African Development Bank Group (AfDB), Avenue Joseph Anoma, 01 BP 1387, Abidjan, 01, COT, https://www.afdb.org; The AfDB Statistics Pocketbook 2019.

The Economist Group: Economist Intelligence Unit (EIU), 900 3rd Ave., 16th Fl., New York, NY, 10022, USA, (212) 541-0500, americas@eiu.com, https://www.eiu.com; Comoros Country Report.

Euromonitor International, Inc., 1 N Dearborn St., Ste. 1700, Chicago, IL, 60602, USA, (312) 922-1115, (312) 922-1157, info-usa@euromonitor.com, https://www.euromonitor.com/; Geographies.

Palgrave Macmillan, 1 New York Plaza, Ste. 4500, New York, NY, 10004-1562, USA, (800) 777-4643, orders@palgrave.com, https://www.palgrave.com/us; The Statesman's Yearbook, 2023.

Routledge - Taylor & Francis Group, 6000 Broken Sound Pkwy. NW, Ste. 300, Boca Raton, FL, 33487, USA, (800) 634-1420, (800) 634-7064, orders@taylorandfrancis.com, https://www.routledge.com/; The Europa World Year Book 2022.

United Nations Conference on Trade and Development (UNCTAD), Palais des Nations, Geneva, 1211, SWI, (212) 963-6896, unctadinfo@unctad.org, https://unctad.org; Trade and Development Report 2021.

United Nations Economic Commission for Africa (UNECA), PO Box 3001, Addis Ababa, ETH, ecainfo@uneca.org, https://www.uneca.org/; African Statistical Yearbook 2020.

United Nations Food and Agricultural Organization (FAO), 2121 K St., Ste. 800B, Washington, DC, 20037, USA, (202) 653-2400 (Dial from U.S.), (202) 653-5760 (Fax from U.S.), fao-hq@fao.org, https://www.fao.org; The State of Food and Agriculture (SOFA) 2022.

United Nations Statistics Division (UNSD), United Nations Plz., New York, NY, 10017, USA, (800) 253-9646, (212) 963-9851, statistics@un.org, https://unstats.un.org; International Trade Statistics Yearbook 2020.

The World Bank, 1818 H St. NW, Washington, DC, 20433, USA, (202) 473-1000, (202) 477-6391, eds03@worldbank.org, https://www.worldbank.org/; Comoros (report).

World Trade Organization (WTO), Ctre. William Rappard, Rue de Lausanne 154, Case postale, Geneva, CH-1211, SWI, enquiries@wto.org, https://www.wto.org; World Trade Statistical Review 2022.

COMOROS-LABOR

African Development Bank Group (AfDB), Avenue Joseph Anoma, 01 BP 1387, Abidjan, 01, COT, https://www.afdb.org; The AfDB Statistics Pocketbook 2019.

Central Intelligence Agency (CIA), Office of Public Affairs, Washington, DC, 20505, USA, (703) 482-0623, https://www.cia.gov; The World Factbook.

Euromonitor International, Inc., 1 N Dearborn St., Ste. 1700, Chicago, IL, 60602, USA, (312) 922-1115, (312) 922-1157, info-usa@euromonitor.com, https://www.euromonitor.com/; Geographies.

Organisation of Islamic Cooperation (OIC), Statistical, Economic and Social Research and Training Centre for Islamic Countries (SESRIC), Kudus Cad. No. 9, Diplomatik Site, Ankara, 06450, TUR, statistics@sesric.org, https://www.sesric.org/; OIC Statistics (OICStat) Database.

United Nations Food and Agricultural Organization (FAO), 2121 K St., Ste. 800B, Washington, DC, 20037, USA, (202) 653-2400 (Dial from U.S.), (202) 653-5760 (Fax from U.S.), fao-hq@fao.org, https://www.fao.org; The State of Food and Agriculture (SOFA) 2022.

COMOROS-LIBRARIES

UNESCO Institute for Statistics, C.P 250 Succursale H, Montreal, QC, H3G 2K8, CAN, (514) 343-6880 (Dial from U.S.), (514) 343-5740 (Fax from U.S.), uis.publications@unesco.org, http://uis.unesco.org/; UIS.Stat.

COMOROS-LIFE EXPECTANCY

African Development Bank Group (AfDB), Avenue Joseph Anoma, 01 BP 1387, Abidjan, 01, COT, https://www.afdb.org; The AfDB Statistics Pocketbook 2019.

Central Intelligence Agency (CIA), Office of Public Affairs, Washington, DC, 20505, USA, (703) 482-0623, https://www.cia.gov; The World Factbook.

United Nations Department of Economic and Social Affairs (DESA), Population Division, 2 United Nations Plz., Rm. DC2-1950, New York, NY, 10017, USA, (212) 963-3209, (212) 963-2147, population@un.org, https://www.un.org/development/desa/pd/; World Population Ageing 2020 Highlights.

COMOROS-LITERACY

Euromonitor International, Inc., 1 N Dearborn St., Ste. 1700, Chicago, IL, 60602, USA, (312) 922-1115, (312) 922-1157, info-usa@euromonitor.com, https://www.euromonitor.com/; Geographies.

COMOROS-LIVESTOCK

Palgrave Macmillan, 1 New York Plaza, Ste. 4500, New York, NY, 10004-1562, USA, (800) 777-4643, orders@palgrave.com, https://www.palgrave.com/us; The Statesman's Yearbook, 2023.

Routledge - Taylor & Francis Group, 6000 Broken Sound Pkwy. NW, Ste. 300, Boca Raton, FL, 33487, USA, (800) 634-1420, (800) 634-7064, orders@taylorandfrancis.com, https://www.routledge.com/; The Europa World Year Book 2022.

United Nations Economic Commission for Africa (UNECA), PO Box 3001, Addis Ababa, ETH, ecainfo@uneca.org, https://www.uneca.org/; African Statistical Yearbook 2020.

United Nations Food and Agricultural Organization (FAO), 2121 K St., Ste. 800B, Washington, DC, 20037, USA, (202) 653-2400 (Dial from U.S.), (202) 653-5760 (Fax from U.S.), fao-hq@fao.org, https://www.fao.org; The State of Food and Agriculture (SOFA) 2022.

United Nations Statistics Division (UNSD), United Nations Plz., New York, NY, 10017, USA, (800) 253-9646, (212) 963-9851, statistics@un.org, https://unstats.un.org; Statistical Yearbook of the United Nations 2021.

COMOROS-MARRIAGE

United Nations Statistics Division (UNSD), United Nations Plz., New York, NY, 10017, USA, (800) 253-9646, (212) 963-9851, statistics@un.org, https://unstats.un.org; Statistical Yearbook of the United Nations 2021.

COMOROS-MINERAL INDUSTRIES

United Nations Conference on Trade and Development (UNCTAD), Palais des Nations, Geneva, 1211, SWI, (212) 963-6896, unctadinfo@unctad.org, https://unctad.org; Trade and Development Report 2021.

United Nations Economic Commission for Africa (UNECA), PO Box 3001, Addis Ababa, ETH, ecainfo@uneca.org, https://www.uneca.org/; African Statistical Yearbook 2020.

The World Bank, 1818 H St. NW, Washington, DC, 20433, USA, (202) 473-1000, (202) 477-6391, eds03@worldbank.org, https://www.worldbank.org/; Comoros (report).

COMOROS-MONEY SUPPLY

The Economist Group: Economist Intelligence Unit (EIU), 900 3rd Ave., 16th Fl., New York, NY, 10022, USA, (212) 541-0500, americas@eiu.com, https://www.eiu.com; Comoros Country Report.

The World Bank, 1818 H St. NW, Washington, DC, 20433, USA, (202) 473-1000, (202) 477-6391, eds03@worldbank.org, https://www.worldbank.org/; Comoros (report).

COMOROS-MORTALITY

United Nations Statistics Division (UNSD), United Nations Plz., New York, NY, 10017, USA, (800) 253-9646, (212) 963-9851, statistics@un.org, https://unstats.un.org; Statistical Yearbook of the United Nations 2021 and World Statistics Pocketbook 2021.

COMOROS-NUTRITION

United Nations Food and Agricultural Organization (FAO), 2121 K St., Ste. 800B, Washington, DC, 20037, USA, (202) 653-2400 (Dial from U.S.), (202) 653-5760 (Fax from U.S.), fao-hq@fao.org, https://www.fao.org; The State of Food and Agriculture (SOFA) 2022.

COMOROS-PESTICIDES

United Nations Food and Agricultural Organization (FAO), 2121 K St., Ste. 800B, Washington, DC, 20037, USA, (202) 653-2400 (Dial from U.S.), (202) 653-5760 (Fax from U.S.), fao-hq@fao.org, https://www.fao.org; The State of Food and Agriculture (SOFA) 2022.

COMOROS-PETROLEUM INDUSTRY AND TRADE

United Nations Food and Agricultural Organization (FAO), 2121 K St., Ste. 800B, Washington, DC, 20037, USA, (202) 653-2400 (Dial from U.S.), (202) 653-5760 (Fax from U.S.), fao-hq@fao.org, https://www.fao.org; The State of Food and Agriculture (SOFA) 2022.

COMOROS-POPULATION

African Development Bank Group (AfDB), Avenue Joseph Anoma, 01 BP 1387, Abidjan, 01, COT, https://www.afdb.org; The AfDB Statistics Pocketbook 2019; Africa Economic Brief - COVID-19 Pandemic Potential Risks for Trade and Trade

Finance in Africa; The African Statistical Journal; and Gender, Poverty and Environmental Indicators on African Countries 2019.

Central Intelligence Agency (CIA), Office of Public Affairs, Washington, DC, 20505, USA, (703) 482-0623, https://www.cia.gov; The World Factbook.

The Economist Group: Economist Intelligence Unit (EIU), 900 3rd Ave., 16th Fl., New York, NY, 10022, USA, (212) 541-0500, americas@eiu.com, https://www.eiu.com; Comoros Country Report.

European Commission, Eurostat, Luxembourg, 2920, LUX, https://ec.europa.eu/eurostat/; EU in the World 2020.

Palgrave Macmillan, 1 New York Plaza, Ste. 4500, New York, NY, 10004-1562, USA, (800) 777-4643, orders@palgrave.com, https://www.palgrave.com/us; The Statesman's Yearbook, 2023.

Routledge - Taylor & Francis Group, 6000 Broken Sound Pkwy. NW, Ste. 300, Boca Raton, FL, 33487, USA, (800) 634-1420, (800) 634-7064, orders@taylorandfrancis.com, https://www.routledge.com/; The Europa World Year Book 2022.

UK Data Service, University of Essex, Wivenhoe Park, Colchester, Essex, CO4 3SQ, GBR, https://ukdataservice.ac.uk/; International Aggregate Data.

UNESCO Institute for Statistics, C.P 250 Succursale H, Montreal, QC, H3G 2K8, CAN, (514) 343-6880 (Dial from U.S.), (514) 343-5740 (Fax from U.S.), uis.publications@unesco.org, http://uis.unesco.org/; UIS.Stat.

United Nations Department of Economic and Social Affairs (DESA), Population Division, 2 United Nations Plz., Rm. DC2-1950, New York, NY, 10017, USA, (212) 963-3209, (212) 963-2147, population@un.org, https://www.un.org/development/desa/pd/; Revision of World Urbanization Prospects and World Population Ageing 2020 Highlights.

United Nations Development Programme (UNDP), One United Nations Plz., New York, NY, 10017, USA, (212) 906-5000, (212) 906-5001, https://www.undp.org; Human Development Report 2021-2022.

United Nations Statistics Division (UNSD), United Nations Plz., New York, NY, 10017, USA, (800) 253-9646, (212) 963-9851, statistics@un.org, https://unstats.un.org; Statistical Yearbook of the United Nations 2021 and World Statistics Pocketbook 2021.

The World Bank, 1818 H St. NW, Washington, DC, 20433, USA, (202) 473-1000, (202) 477-6391, eds03@worldbank.org, https://www.worldbank.org/; Comoros (report) and The Global Findex Database 2021.

COMOROS-POPULATION DENSITY

African Development Bank Group (AfDB), Avenue Joseph Anoma, 01 BP 1387, Abidjan, 01, COT, https://www.afdb.org; The AfDB Statistics Pocketbook 2019.

Central Intelligence Agency (CIA), Office of Public Affairs, Washington, DC, 20505, USA, (703) 482-0623, https://www.cia.gov; The World Factbook.

Palgrave Macmillan, 1 New York Plaza, Ste. 4500, New York, NY, 10004-1562, USA, (800) 777-4643, orders@palgrave.com, https://www.palgrave.com/us; The Statesman's Yearbook, 2023.

Routledge - Taylor & Francis Group, 6000 Broken Sound Pkwy. NW, Ste. 300, Boca Raton, FL, 33487, USA, (800) 634-1420, (800) 634-7064, orders@taylorandfrancis.com, https://www.routledge.com/; The Europa World Year Book 2022.

UNESCO Institute for Statistics, C.P 250 Succursale H, Montreal, QC, H3G 2K8, CAN, (514) 343-6880 (Dial from U.S.), (514) 343-5740 (Fax from U.S.), uis.publications@unesco.org, http://uis.unesco.org/; UIS.Stat.

The World Bank, 1818 H St. NW, Washington, DC, 20433, USA, (202) 473-1000, (202) 477-6391, eds03@worldbank.org, https://www.worldbank.org/; Comoros (report).

COMOROS-POWER RESOURCES

Euromonitor International, Inc., 1 N Dearborn St., Ste. 1700, Chicago, IL, 60602, USA, (312) 922-1115, (312) 922-1157, info-usa@euromonitor.com, https://www.euromonitor.com/; Geographies.

United Nations Economic Commission for Africa (UNECA), PO Box 3001, Addis Ababa, ETH, ecainfo@uneca.org, https://www.uneca.org/; African Statistical Yearbook 2020.

United Nations Food and Agricultural Organization (FAO), 2121 K St., Ste. 800B, Washington, DC, 20037, USA, (202) 653-2400 (Dial from U.S.), (202) 653-5760 (Fax from U.S.), fao-hq@fao.org, https://www.fao.org; The State of Food and Agriculture (SOFA) 2022.

United Nations Statistics Division (UNSD), United Nations Plz., New York, NY, 10017, USA, (800) 253-9646, (212) 963-9851, statistics@un.org, https://unstats.un.org; Energy Statistics Yearbook 2019; Statistical Yearbook of the United Nations 2021; and World Statistics Pocketbook 2021.

COMOROS-PRICES

Euromonitor International, Inc., 1 N Dearborn St., Ste. 1700, Chicago, IL, 60602, USA, (312) 922-1115, (312) 922-1157, info-usa@euromonitor.com, https://www.euromonitor.com/; Geographies.

United Nations Economic Commission for Africa (UNECA), PO Box 3001, Addis Ababa, ETH, ecainfo@uneca.org, https://www.uneca.org/; African Statistical Yearbook 2020.

The World Bank, 1818 H St. NW, Washington, DC, 20433, USA, (202) 473-1000, (202) 477-6391, eds03@worldbank.org, https://www.worldbank.org/; Comoros (report).

COMOROS-PUBLIC HEALTH

African Development Bank Group (AfDB), Avenue Joseph Anoma, 01 BP 1387, Abidjan, 01, COT, https://www.afdb.org; The AfDB Statistics Pocketbook 2019.

Euromonitor International, Inc., 1 N Dearborn St., Ste. 1700, Chicago, IL, 60602, USA, (312) 922-1115, (312) 922-1157, info-usa@euromonitor.com, https://www.euromonitor.com/; Geographies.

Organisation of Islamic Cooperation (OIC), Statistical, Economic and Social Research and Training Centre for Islamic Countries (SESRIC), Kudus Cad. No. 9, Diplomatik Site, Ankara, 06450, TUR, statistics@sesric.org, https://www.sesric.org/; OIC Statistics (OICStat) Database.

Palgrave Macmillan, 1 New York Plaza, Ste. 4500, New York, NY, 10004-1562, USA, (800) 777-4643, orders@palgrave.com, https://www.palgrave.com/us; The Statesman's Yearbook, 2023.

U.S. Census Bureau, 4600 Silver Hill Rd., Washington, DC, 20233, USA, (301) 763-4636, (800) 923-8282, https://www.census.gov; HIV/AIDS Surveillance Data Base.

United Nations Department of Economic and Social Affairs (DESA), Population Division, 2 United Nations Plz., Rm. DC2-1950, New York, NY, 10017, USA, (212) 963-3209, (212) 963-2147, population@un.org, https://www.un.org/development/desa/pd/; World Fertility Data 2019.

United Nations Development Programme (UNDP), One United Nations Plz., New York, NY, 10017, USA, (212) 906-5000, (212) 906-5001, https://www.undp.org; Human Development Report 2021-2022.

United Nations Economic Commission for Africa (UNECA), PO Box 3001, Addis Ababa, ETH, ecainfo@uneca.org, https://www.uneca.org/; African Statistical Yearbook 2020.

United Nations Statistics Division (UNSD), United Nations Plz., New York, NY, 10017, USA, (800) 253-9646, (212) 963-9851, statistics@un.org, https://unstats.un.org; Statistical Yearbook of the United Nations 2021.

The World Bank, 1818 H St. NW, Washington, DC, 20433, USA, (202) 473-1000, (202) 477-6391, eds03@worldbank.org, https://www.worldbank.org/; Comoros (report).

COMOROS-RAILROADS

United Nations Economic Commission for Africa (UNECA), PO Box 3001, Addis Ababa, ETH, ecainfo@uneca.org, https://www.uneca.org/; African Statistical Yearbook 2020.

COMOROS-RELIGION

Central Intelligence Agency (CIA), Office of Public Affairs, Washington, DC, 20505, USA, (703) 482-0623, https://www.cia.gov; The World Factbook.

Palgrave Macmillan, 1 New York Plaza, Ste. 4500, New York, NY, 10004-1562, USA, (800) 777-4643, orders@palgrave.com, https://www.palgrave.com/us; The Statesman's Yearbook, 2023.

COMOROS-RETAIL TRADE

Euromonitor International, Inc., 1 N Dearborn St., Ste. 1700, Chicago, IL, 60602, USA, (312) 922-1115, (312) 922-1157, info-usa@euromonitor.com, https://www.euromonitor.com/; Geographies.

COMOROS-RICE PRODUCTION

See COMOROS-CROPS

COMOROS-ROADS

United Nations Economic Commission for Africa (UNECA), PO Box 3001, Addis Ababa, ETH, ecainfo@uneca.org, https://www.uneca.org/; African Statistical Yearbook 2020.

COMOROS-SHIPPING

Routledge - Taylor & Francis Group, 6000 Broken Sound Pkwy. NW, Ste. 300, Boca Raton, FL, 33487, USA, (800) 634-1420, (800) 634-7064, orders@taylorandfrancis.com, https://www.routledge.com/; The Europa World Year Book 2022.

S&P Global, IHS Markit, 15 Inverness Way E, Englewood, CO, 80112, USA, (800) 447-2273, (800) 854-7179, https://ihsmarkit.com; IHS Maritime World Shipbuilding Statistics; Journal of Commerce; Lloyd's Register of Ships 2021-2022; and Maritime Portal Desktop.

United Nations Economic Commission for Africa (UNECA), PO Box 3001, Addis Ababa, ETH, ecainfo@uneca.org, https://www.uneca.org/; African Statistical Yearbook 2020.

United Nations Statistics Division (UNSD), United Nations Plz., New York, NY, 10017, USA, (800) 253-9646, (212) 963-9851, statistics@un.org, https://unstats.un.org; Statistical Yearbook of the United Nations 2021.

COMOROS-TELEPHONE

Palgrave Macmillan, 1 New York Plaza, Ste. 4500, New York, NY, 10004-1562, USA, (800) 777-4643, orders@palgrave.com, https://www.palgrave.com/us; The Statesman's Yearbook, 2023.

Routledge - Taylor & Francis Group, 6000 Broken Sound Pkwy. NW, Ste. 300, Boca Raton, FL, 33487, USA, (800) 634-1420, (800) 634-7064, orders@taylorandfrancis.com, https://www.routledge.com/; The Europa World Year Book 2022.

United Nations Statistics Division (UNSD), United Nations Plz., New York, NY, 10017, USA, (800) 253-9646, (212) 963-9851, statistics@un.org, https://unstats.un.org; World Statistics Pocketbook 2021.

COMOROS-TOURISM

Euromonitor International, Inc., 1 N Dearborn St., Ste. 1700, Chicago, IL, 60602, USA, (312) 922-1115, (312) 922-1157, info-usa@euromonitor.com, https://www.euromonitor.com/; Geographies.

Organisation of Islamic Cooperation (OIC), Statistical, Economic and Social Research and Training Centre for Islamic Countries (SESRIC), Kudus Cad. No. 9, Diplomatik Site, Ankara, 06450, TUR, statistics@sesric.org, https://www.sesric.org/; International Tourism in the OIC Countries: Prospects and Challenges, 2020 and OIC Statistics (OICStat) Database.

United Nations Economic Commission for Africa (UNECA), PO Box 3001, Addis Ababa, ETH, ecainfo@uneca.org, https://www.uneca.org/; African Statistical Yearbook 2020.

United Nations World Tourism Organization (UNWTO), Calle Poeta Joan Maragall 42, Madrid, 28020, SPA, info@unwto.org, https://www.unwto.org/; Yearbook of Tourism Statistics, 2021 Edition.

The World Bank, 1818 H St. NW, Washington, DC, 20433, USA, (202) 473-1000, (202) 477-6391, eds03@worldbank.org, https://www.worldbank.org/; Comoros (report).

COMOROS-TRADE

See COMOROS-INTERNATIONAL TRADE

COMOROS-TRANSPORTATION

Central Intelligence Agency (CIA), Office of Public Affairs, Washington, DC, 20505, USA, (703) 482-0623, https://www.cia.gov; The World Factbook.

Euromonitor International, Inc., 1 N Dearborn St., Ste. 1700, Chicago, IL, 60602, USA, (312) 922-1115, (312) 922-1157, info-usa@euromonitor.com, https://www.euromonitor.com/; Geographies.

Organisation of Islamic Cooperation (OIC), Statistical, Economic and Social Research and Training Centre for Islamic Countries (SESRIC), Kudus Cad. No. 9, Diplomatik Site, Ankara, 06450, TUR, statistics@sesric.org, https://www.sesric.org/; OIC Statistics (OICStat) Database.

Palgrave Macmillan, 1 New York Plaza, Ste. 4500, New York, NY, 10004-1562, USA, (800) 777-4643, orders@palgrave.com, https://www.palgrave.com/us; The Statesman's Yearbook, 2023.

Routledge - Taylor & Francis Group, 6000 Broken Sound Pkwy. NW, Ste. 300, Boca Raton, FL, 33487, USA, (800) 634-1420, (800) 634-7064, orders@taylorandfrancis.com, https://www.routledge.com/; The Europa World Year Book 2022.

United Nations Economic Commission for Africa (UNECA), PO Box 3001, Addis Ababa, ETH, ecainfo@uneca.org, https://www.uneca.org/; African Statistical Yearbook 2020.

The World Bank, 1818 H St. NW, Washington, DC, 20433, USA, (202) 473-1000, (202) 477-6391, eds03@worldbank.org, https://www.worldbank.org/; Comoros (report).

COMOROS-UNEMPLOYMENT

The World Bank, 1818 H St. NW, Washington, DC, 20433, USA, (202) 473-1000, (202) 477-6391, eds03@worldbank.org, https://www.worldbank.org/; Comoros (report).

COMOROS-VITAL STATISTICS

Palgrave Macmillan, 1 New York Plaza, Ste. 4500, New York, NY, 10004-1562, USA, (800) 777-4643, orders@palgrave.com, https://www.palgrave.com/us; The Statesman's Yearbook, 2023.

U.S. Census Bureau, 4600 Silver Hill Rd., Washington, DC, 20233, USA, (301) 763-4636, (800) 923-8282, https://www.census.gov; HIV/AIDS Surveillance Data Base.

United Nations Department of Economic and Social Affairs (DESA), Population Division, 2 United Nations Plz., Rm. DC2-1950, New York, NY, 10017, USA, (212) 963-3209, (212) 963-2147, population@un.org, https://www.un.org/development/desa/pd/; World Contraceptive Use 2021: Estimates and Projections of Family Planning Indicators and World Marriage Data 2019.

United Nations Statistics Division (UNSD), United Nations Plz., New York, NY, 10017, USA, (800) 253-9646, (212) 963-9851, statistics@un.org, https://unstats.un.org; Statistical Yearbook of the United Nations 2021.

COMOROS-WAGES

The World Bank, 1818 H St. NW, Washington, DC, 20433, USA, (202) 473-1000, (202) 477-6391, eds03@worldbank.org, https://www.worldbank.org/; Comoros (report).

COMPOSERS

University of Southern California (USC), Annenberg School for Communication and Journalism, Annenberg Inclusion Initiative, 3630 Watt Way, Ste. 402, Los Angeles, CA, 90089, USA, (213) 740-6180, (213) 740-3772, aii@usc.edu, https://annenberg.usc.edu/research/aii; Inclusion in the Recording Studio? Gender and Race/Ethnicity of Artists, Songwriters & Producers Across 900 Popular Songs from 2012-2020.

COMPUTER CRIMES

Common Sense, 699 8th St., Ste. C150, San Francisco, CA, 94103, USA, (415) 863-0600, (415) 863-0601, https://www.commonsensemedia.org/; 2023 State of Kids' Privacy.

Cyberbullying Research Center, USA, hinduja@cyberbullying.org, https://cyberbullying.org; Bullying, Cyberbullying, and Sexting by State; 2021 Cyberbullying Data; and Summary of Our Cyberbullying Research (2007-2021).

Identity Theft Resource Center (ITRC), 2514 Jamacha Rd., Ste. 502-525, El Cajon, CA, 92019-4492, USA, (888) 400-5530, itrc@idtheftcenter.org, https://www.idtheftcenter.org/; notified: Data Breach Information.

U.S. Department of Justice (DOJ), Federal Bureau of Investigation (FBI), 935 Pennsylvania Ave. NW, Washington, DC, 20535-0001, USA, (202) 324-3000, https://www.fbi.gov/; Crime in the United States 2019.

YouGov, 38 W 21st St., New York, NY, 10010, USA, (646) 213-7414, help.us@yougov.com, https://today.yougov.com/; Smart Appliances: Awareness Is High, But Knowledge Is Low.

COMPUTER GAMES

Newzoo, Danzigerkade 2F, Amsterdam, 1013 AP, NLD, https://newzoo.com; Global Cloud Gaming Report 2022 and Global Gamer Study.

The NPD Group, 900 W Shore Rd., Port Washington, NY, 11050, USA, (516) 625-0700, contactnpd@npd.com, https://www.npd.com; Media Entertainment.

COMPUTER PROGRAMMING

Gartner, Inc., 56 Top Gallant Rd., Stamford, CT, 06902, USA, (203) 964-0096, https://www.gartner.com; IDEAS Competitive Profiles.

COMPUTER PROGRAMMING-EARNINGS

U.S. Census Bureau, 4600 Silver Hill Rd., Washington, DC, 20233, USA, (301) 763-4636, (800) 923-8282, https://www.census.gov; Service Annual Survey 2021.

U.S. Department of Labor (DOL), Bureau of Labor Statistics (BLS), Postal Square Bldg., 2 Massachusetts Ave. NE, Washington, DC, 20212-0001, USA, (202) 691-5200, (202) 691-7890, blsdata_staff@bls.gov, https://www.bls.gov; Current Employment Statistics (CES).

COMPUTER PROGRAMMING-EMPLOYEES

U.S. Census Bureau, 4600 Silver Hill Rd., Washington, DC, 20233, USA, (301) 763-4636, (800) 923-8282, https://www.census.gov; Service Annual Survey 2021.

U.S. Department of Labor (DOL), Bureau of Labor Statistics (BLS), Postal Square Bldg., 2 Massachusetts Ave. NE, Washington, DC, 20212-0001, USA, (202) 691-5200, (202) 691-7890, blsdata_staff@bls.gov, https://www.bls.gov; Current Employment Statistics (CES) and Industry-Occupation Matrix Data, By Occupation.

COMPUTER SECURITY

Princeton University Center for Information Technology Policy (CITP), Princeton Web Transparency & Accountability Project (WebTAP), 308 Sherrerd Hall, Princeton, NJ, 08544, USA, (609) 258-9302, arvindn@cs.princeton.edu, https://webtap.princeton.edu/; Dark Patterns at Scale: Findings from a Crawl of 11K Shopping Websites and The Impact of User Location on Cookie Notices (Inside and Outside of the European Union).

SAE International, 400 Commonwealth Dr., Warrendale, PA, 15096, USA, (724) 776-4790, (724) 776-4841, (724) 776-0790, customerservice@sae.org, https://www.sae.org/; SAE International Journal of Transportation Cybersecurity and Privacy.

U.S. Department of Homeland Security (DHS), 2707 Martin Luther King Jr. Ave. SE, Washington, DC, 20528-0525, USA, (202) 282-8000, https://www.dhs.gov; Privacy Office Annual Report to Congress, July 2019 to September 2021.

COMPUTER SPECIALISTS-DEGREES CONFERRED

National Science Foundation, National Center for Science and Engineering Statistics (NCSES), 2415 Eisenhower Ave., Ste. W14200, Arlington, VA, 22314, USA, (703) 292-8780, (703) 292-9092, info@nsf.gov, https://www.nsf.gov/statistics/; Survey of Doctorate Recipients.

U.S. Department of Education (ED), Institute of Education Sciences (IES), National Center for Education Statistics (NCES), Potomac Center Plaza, 550 12th St. SW, Washington, DC, 20202, USA, (202) 403-5551, https://nces.ed.gov/; Digest of Education Statistics, 2020.

COMPUTER SPECIALISTS-LABOR FORCE

National Association of Colleges and Employers (NACE), 1 E Broad St., Ste 130-1005, Bethlehem, PA, 18018, USA, (610) 868-1421, customerservice@naceweb.org, https://www.naceweb.org/; Salary Survey.

COMPUTER USE

Campus Computing Project, PO Box 261242, Encino, CA, 91426-1242, USA, (818) 990-2212, (818) 979-6113, cgreen@campuscomputing.net, https://www.campuscomputing.net/; 2019 Campus Computing Survey.

The Chronicle of Higher Education, 1255 23rd St. NW, Washington, DC, 20037, USA, (202) 466-1000, circulation@chronicle.com, https://www.chronicle.com/; The Digital Campus.

Colorado Department of Education, Colorado State Library, Library Research Service (LRS), 201 E Colfax Ave., Rm. 309, Denver, CO, 80203, USA, (303) 866-6900, lrs@lrs.org, https://www.lrs.org; Colorado Public Library Statistics and Profiles: Totals, Averages, and Ratios.

Common Sense, 699 8th St., Ste. C150, San Francisco, CA, 94103, USA, (415) 863-0600, (415) 863-0601, https://www.commonsensemedia.org/; 2023 State of Kids' Privacy.

Inside Higher Ed, 1150 Connecticut Ave. NW, Ste. 400, Washington, DC, 20036, USA, (202) 659-9208, (202) 659-9381, info@insidehighered.com, https://www.insidehighered.com/; Survey of Faculty Attitudes on Technology, 2020.

Microsoft Research, 14820 NE 36th St., Bldg. 99, Redmond, WA, 98052, USA, https://research.microsoft.com; Assessing Human-AI Interaction Early through Factorial Surveys: A Study on the Guidelines for Human-AI Interaction.

MRI Simmons, 200 Liberty St., 4th Fl., New York, NY, 10281, USA, (866) 256-4468, info.ms@mrisimmons.com, https://www.mrisimmons.com/; MRI-Simmons USA.

Pew Research Center, Internet & Technology, 1615 L St. NW, Ste. 800, Washington, DC, 20036, USA, (202) 419-4300, (202) 857-8562, https://www.pewresearch.org/topic/internet-technology/; Mobile

Technology and Home Broadband 2019; Share of U.S. Adults Using Social Media, Including Facebook, Is Mostly Unchanged Since 2018; Social Media Use in 2021; and Teens, Social Media & Technology 2022.

Trustwave, 70 W Madison St., Ste. 600, Chicago, IL, 60602, USA, (312) 873-7500, https://www.trustwave.com; 2020 Trustwave Global Security Report.

U.S. Department of Education (ED), Institute of Education Sciences (IES), National Center for Education Statistics (NCES), Potomac Center Plaza, 550 12th St. SW, Washington, DC, 20202, USA, (202) 403-5551, https://nces.ed.gov/; Digest of Education Statistics, 2020.

YouGov, 38 W 21st St., New York, NY, 10010, USA, (646) 213-7414, help.us@yougov.com, https://today.yougov.com/; Smart Appliances: Awareness Is High, But Knowledge Is Low.

COMPUTERS

Microsoft Research, 14820 NE 36th St., Bldg. 99, Redmond, WA, 98052, USA, https://research.microsoft.com; Ultra Fast Speech Separation Model with Teacher Student Learning.

COMPUTERS-ACCESS CONTROL-PASSWORDS

Trustwave, 70 W Madison St., Ste. 600, Chicago, IL, 60602, USA, (312) 873-7500, https://www.trustwave.com; 2020 Trustwave Global Security Report.

Verizon, 1095 Avenue of the Americas, New York, NY, 10036, USA, (212) 395-1000, https://enterprise.verizon.com/resources/reports; Data Breach Investigations Report (DBIR) 2023.

YouGov, 38 W 21st St., New York, NY, 10010, USA, (646) 213-7414, help.us@yougov.com, https://today.yougov.com/; Smart Appliances: Awareness Is High, But Knowledge Is Low.

COMPUTERS-SOCIAL ASPECTS

Microsoft Research, 14820 NE 36th St., Bldg. 99, Redmond, WA, 98052, USA, https://research.microsoft.com; Assessing Human-AI Interaction Early through Factorial Surveys: A Study on the Guidelines for Human-AI Interaction.

COMPUTERS AND CHILDREN

Common Sense, 699 8th St., Ste. C150, San Francisco, CA, 94103, USA, (415) 863-0600, (415) 863-0601, https://www.commonsensemedia.org/; 2023 State of Kids' Privacy.

COMPUTERS AND ELECTRONIC EQUIPMENT, MANUFACTURING

U.S. Census Bureau, 4600 Silver Hill Rd., Washington, DC, 20233, USA, (301) 763-4636, (800) 923-8282, https://www.census.gov; County Business Patterns (CBP) 2020.

COMPUTERS AND ELECTRONIC EQUIPMENT, MANUFACTURING-EARNINGS

U.S. Census Bureau, 4600 Silver Hill Rd., Washington, DC, 20233, USA, (301) 763-4636, (800) 923-8282, https://www.census.gov; Annual Survey of Manufactures (ASM) 2021.

COMPUTERS AND ELECTRONIC EQUIPMENT, MANUFACTURING-EMPLOYEES

U.S. Census Bureau, 4600 Silver Hill Rd., Washington, DC, 20233, USA, (301) 763-4636, (800) 923-8282, https://www.census.gov; Annual Survey of Manufactures (ASM) 2021.

U.S. Department of Labor (DOL), Bureau of Labor Statistics (BLS), Postal Square Bldg., 2 Massachusetts Ave. NE, Washington, DC, 20212-0001, USA, (202) 691-5200, (202) 691-7890, blsdata_staff@bls.gov, https://www.bls.gov; Current Employment Statistics (CES) and Industry-Occupation Matrix Data, By Occupation.

COMPUTERS AND ELECTRONIC EQUIPMENT, MANUFACTURING-INVENTORIES

U.S. Census Bureau, 4600 Silver Hill Rd., Washington, DC, 20233, USA, (301) 763-4636, (800) 923-8282, https://www.census.gov; Manufacturers' Shipments, Inventories and Orders.

COMPUTERS AND ELECTRONIC EQUIPMENT, MANUFACTURING-SALES

Consumer Technology Association (CTA), 1919 S Eads St., Arlington, VA, 22202, USA, (703) 907-7600, (866) 858-1555, (703) 907-7675, cta@cta.tech, https://www.cta.tech; CTA U.S. Consumer Technology Five-Year Industry Forecast, 2021-2026 (July 2022).

Gartner, Inc., 56 Top Gallant Rd., Stamford, CT, 06902, USA, (203) 964-0096, https://www.gartner.com; Digital Markets Insights and IDEAS Competitive Profiles.

The NPD Group, 900 W Shore Rd., Port Washington, NY, 11050, USA, (516) 625-0700, contactnpd@npd.com, https://www.npd.com; B2B Technology; Consumer Technology; Media Entertainment; and Mobile.

Worldometer, https://www.worldometers.info/; Worldometers.info.

COMPUTERS AND ELECTRONIC EQUIPMENT, MANUFACTURING-SHIPMENTS

U.S. Census Bureau, 4600 Silver Hill Rd., Washington, DC, 20233, USA, (301) 763-4636, (800) 923-8282, https://www.census.gov; Annual Survey of Manufactures (ASM) 2021.

U.S. Census Bureau, International Trade Program, 4600 Silver Hill Rd., Washington, DC, 20233, USA, (800) 549-0595, eid.international.trade.data@census.gov, https://www.census.gov/foreign-trade; International Trade Data.

CONCEALED CARRY OF FIREARMS

Violence Policy Center (VPC), 1025 Connecticut Ave. NW, Ste. 1210, Washington, DC, 20036, USA, (202) 822-8200, https://vpc.org/; Concealed Carry Killers.

CONCERTS-SYMPHONY ORCHESTRAS

League of American Orchestras, 520 8th Ave., Ste. 2005, New York, NY, 10018, USA, (212) 262-5161, (212) 262-5198, knowledge@americanorchestras.org, https://americanorchestras.org/; A Youth Orchestra's Approach to EDI: Catalyst Snapshot of Chicago Youth Symphony Orchestra and The League's COVID-19 Impact Survey.

CONDENSED AND EVAPORATED MILK

U.S. Department of Agriculture (USDA), Economic Research Service (ERS), 1400 Independence Ave. SW, Mail Stop 1800, Washington, DC, 20250-0002, USA, (202) 720-2791, https://www.ers.usda.gov/; Food Price Outlook.

U.S. Department of Agriculture (USDA), National Agricultural Statistics Service (USDA-NASS), 1400 Independence Ave. SW, Washington, DC, 20250, USA, (800) 727-9540, nass@nass.usda.gov, https://www.nass.usda.gov; Dairy Products and Milk Production.

CONDOMINIUMS

National Association of Realtors (NAR), 430 N Michigan Ave., Chicago, IL, 60611-4087, USA, (800) 874-6500, (202) 383-1000, https://www.nar.realtor; Monthly Housing Affordability Index.

CONFERENCE OF THE PARTIES (UNITED NATIONS FRAMEWORK CONVENTION ON CLIMATE CHANGE (21ST, 2015, PARIS, FRANCE)

Climate Analytics, 135 Madison Ave., 5th Fl., Ste. 05-115, New York, NY, 10016, USA, info.ny@climateanalytics.org, https://climateanalytics.org/; 1.5 Degree C National Pathway Explorer and Why Gas Is the New Coal.

International Renewable Energy Agency (IRENA), PO Box 236, Abu Dhabi, UAE, info@irena.org, https://www.irena.org/; World Energy Transitions Outlook: 1.5 Degree C Pathway.

World Resources Institute (WRI), 10 G St. NE, Ste. 800, Washington, DC, 20002, USA, (202) 729-7600, (202) 280-1314, https://www.wri.org/; State of Climate Action 2021: Systems Transformations Required to Limit Global Warming to 1.5 Degree C.

CONFLICT MANAGEMENT

Mercy Corps, 45 SW Ankeny St., Portland, OR, 97204, USA, (800) 292-3355, (503) 896-5000, https://www.mercycorps.org/; Time to Turn Around: The Decline of UK Peacebuilding.

National Bureau of Economic Research (NBER), 1050 Massachusetts Ave., Cambridge, MA, 02138, USA, (617) 868-3900, info@nber.org, https://www.nber.org/; Destructive Behavior, Judgment, and Economic Decision-Making Under Thermal Stress.

CONGO-ALUMINUM PRODUCTION

See CONGO, REPUBLIC OF THE-MINERAL INDUSTRIES

CONGO-BARLEY PRODUCTION

See CONGO, REPUBLIC OF THE-CROPS

CONGO-COAL PRODUCTION

See CONGO, REPUBLIC OF THE-MINERAL INDUSTRIES

CONGO-COCOA PRODUCTION

See CONGO, REPUBLIC OF THE-CROPS

CONGO-COFFEE

See CONGO, REPUBLIC OF THE-CROPS

CONGO-COPPER INDUSTRY AND TRADE

See CONGO, REPUBLIC OF THE-MINERAL INDUSTRIES

CONGO-CORN INDUSTRY

See CONGO, REPUBLIC OF THE-CROPS

CONGO-COTTON

See CONGO, REPUBLIC OF THE-CROPS

CONGO-DEFENSE EXPENDITURES

See CONGO, REPUBLIC OF THE-ARMED FORCES

CONGO-DIAMONDS

See CONGO, REPUBLIC OF THE-MINERAL INDUSTRIES

CONGO-FETAL MORTALITY

See CONGO, REPUBLIC OF THE-MORTALITY

CONGO-GAS PRODUCTION

See CONGO, REPUBLIC OF THE-MINERAL INDUSTRIES

CONGO-GOLD PRODUCTION

See CONGO, REPUBLIC OF THE-MINERAL INDUSTRIES

CONGO-INFANT AND MATERNAL MORTALITY

See CONGO, REPUBLIC OF THE-MORTALITY

CONGO-NATURAL GAS PRODUCTION

See CONGO, REPUBLIC OF THE-MINERAL INDUSTRIES

CONGO-PAPER

See CONGO, REPUBLIC OF THE-FORESTS AND FORESTRY

CONGO-PEANUT PRODUCTION

See CONGO, REPUBLIC OF THE-CROPS

CONGO-RICE PRODUCTION

See CONGO, REPUBLIC OF THE-CROPS

CONGO-STEEL PRODUCTION

See CONGO, REPUBLIC OF THE-MINERAL INDUSTRIES

CONGO-SUGAR PRODUCTION

See CONGO, REPUBLIC OF THE-CROPS

CONGO-TRADE

See CONGO, REPUBLIC OF THE-INTERNATIONAL TRADE

CONGO-WEATHER

See CONGO, REPUBLIC OF THE-CLIMATE

CONGO-WHEAT PRODUCTION

See CONGO, REPUBLIC OF THE-CROPS

CONGO-WOOD AND WOOD PULP

See CONGO, REPUBLIC OF THE-FORESTS AND FORESTRY

CONGO-WOOL PRODUCTION

See CONGO, REPUBLIC OF THE-TEXTILE INDUSTRY

CONGO-ZINC AND ZINC ORE

See CONGO, REPUBLIC OF THE-MINERAL INDUSTRIES

CONGO, DEMOCRATIC REPUBLIC OF THE-NATIONAL STATISTICAL OFFICE

Centre National de la Statistique et des Etudes Economiques (CNSEE), Brazzaville, COG, cnsee@hotmail.fr, https://www.cnsee.org/; National Data Reports (Republic of the Congo).

Institut National de la Statistique, Republique du Congo (INS), Avenue de Foch en face de la radio , Brazzaville, ZAR, contact@ins-congo.cg, https://ins-congo.cg; National Data Reports (Republic of the Congo).

CONGO, DEMOCRATIC REPUBLIC OF THE-AGRICULTURE

African Development Bank Group (AfDB), Avenue Joseph Anoma, 01 BP 1387, Abidjan, 01, COT, https://www.afdb.org; African Economic Outlook 2021 and Compendium of Statistics on Bank Group Operations 2019.

The Economist Group: Economist Intelligence Unit (EIU), 900 3rd Ave., 16th Fl., New York, NY, 10022, USA, (212) 541-0500, americas@eiu.com, https://www.eiu.com; Congo (Democratic Republic) Country Report.

Palgrave Macmillan, 1 New York Plaza, Ste. 4500, New York, NY, 10004-1562, USA, (800) 777-4643, orders@palgrave.com, https://www.palgrave.com/us; The Statesman's Yearbook, 2023.

Routledge - Taylor & Francis Group, 6000 Broken Sound Pkwy. NW, Ste. 300, Boca Raton, FL, 33487, USA, (800) 634-1420, (800) 634-7064, orders@taylorandfrancis.com, https://www.routledge.com/; The Europa World Year Book 2022.

United Nations Economic Commission for Africa (UNECA), PO Box 3001, Addis Ababa, ETH, ecainfo@uneca.org, https://www.uneca.org/; African Statistical Yearbook 2020 and Economic Report on Africa 2021.

United Nations Food and Agricultural Organization (FAO), 2121 K St., Ste. 800B, Washington, DC, 20037, USA, (202) 653-2400 (Dial from U.S.), (202) 653-5760 (Fax from U.S.), fao-hq@fao.org, https://www.fao.org; AQUASTAT and The State of Food and Agriculture (SOFA) 2022.

United Nations Statistics Division (UNSD), United Nations Plz., New York, NY, 10017, USA, (800) 253-9646, (212) 963-9851, statistics@un.org, https://unstats.un.org; Statistical Yearbook of the United Nations 2021.

The World Bank, 1818 H St. NW, Washington, DC, 20433, USA, (202) 473-1000, (202) 477-6391, eds03@worldbank.org, https://www.worldbank.org/; Congo, Democratic Republic of (report) and World Development Indicators (WDI) 2022.

CONGO, DEMOCRATIC REPUBLIC OF THE-AIRLINES

Palgrave Macmillan, 1 New York Plaza, Ste. 4500, New York, NY, 10004-1562, USA, (800) 777-4643, orders@palgrave.com, https://www.palgrave.com/us; The Statesman's Yearbook, 2023.

Routledge - Taylor & Francis Group, 6000 Broken Sound Pkwy. NW, Ste. 300, Boca Raton, FL, 33487, USA, (800) 634-1420, (800) 634-7064, orders@taylorandfrancis.com, https://www.routledge.com/; The Europa World Year Book 2022.

United Nations Economic Commission for Africa (UNECA), PO Box 3001, Addis Ababa, ETH, ecainfo@uneca.org, https://www.uneca.org/; African Statistical Yearbook 2020.

CONGO, DEMOCRATIC REPUBLIC OF THE-ARMED FORCES

Central Intelligence Agency (CIA), Office of Public Affairs, Washington, DC, 20505, USA, (703) 482-0623, https://www.cia.gov; The World Factbook.

International Institute for Strategic Studies (IISS) - Americas, 2121 K St. NW, Ste. 600, Washington, DC, 20037, USA, (202) 659-1490, (202) 659-1499, https://www.iiss.org/; Armed Conflict Survey 2021 and The Military Balance 2022.

Palgrave Macmillan, 1 New York Plaza, Ste. 4500, New York, NY, 10004-1562, USA, (800) 777-4643, orders@palgrave.com, https://www.palgrave.com/us; The Statesman's Yearbook, 2023.

Stockholm International Peace Research Institute (SIPRI), Signalistgatan 9, Stockholm, SE 169 72, SWE, https://www.sipri.org/; SIPRI Arms Transfers Database and SIPRI Military Expenditure Database.

CONGO, DEMOCRATIC REPUBLIC OF THE-AUTOMOBILE INDUSTRY AND TRADE

Routledge - Taylor & Francis Group, 6000 Broken Sound Pkwy. NW, Ste. 300, Boca Raton, FL, 33487, USA, (800) 634-1420, (800) 634-7064, orders@taylorandfrancis.com, https://www.routledge.com/; The Europa World Year Book 2022.

CONGO, DEMOCRATIC REPUBLIC OF THE-BALANCE OF PAYMENTS

African Development Bank Group (AfDB), Avenue Joseph Anoma, 01 BP 1387, Abidjan, 01, COT, https://www.afdb.org; The AfDB Statistics Pocketbook 2019.

International Monetary Fund (IMF), 700 19th St. NW, Washington, DC, 20431, USA, (202) 623-7000, (202) 623-4661, publications@imf.org, https://www.imf.org; Balance of Payments Statistics: Annual Report 2021.

Palgrave Macmillan, 1 New York Plaza, Ste. 4500, New York, NY, 10004-1562, USA, (800) 777-4643, orders@palgrave.com, https://www.palgrave.com/us; The Statesman's Yearbook, 2023.

Routledge - Taylor & Francis Group, 6000 Broken Sound Pkwy. NW, Ste. 300, Boca Raton, FL, 33487, USA, (800) 634-1420, (800) 634-7064, orders@taylorandfrancis.com, https://www.routledge.com/; The Europa World Year Book 2022.

United Nations Conference on Trade and Development (UNCTAD), Palais des Nations, Geneva, 1211, SWI, (212) 963-6896, unctadinfo@unctad.org, https://unctad.org; Handbook of Statistics 2021.

United Nations Economic Commission for Africa (UNECA), PO Box 3001, Addis Ababa, ETH, ecainfo@uneca.org, https://www.uneca.org/; African Statistical Yearbook 2020.

The World Bank, 1818 H St. NW, Washington, DC, 20433, USA, (202) 473-1000, (202) 477-6391, eds03@worldbank.org, https://www.worldbank.org/; Congo, Democratic Republic of (report) and World Development Indicators (WDI) 2022.

CONGO, DEMOCRATIC REPUBLIC OF THE-BANKS AND BANKING

International Monetary Fund (IMF), 700 19th St. NW, Washington, DC, 20431, USA, (202) 623-7000, (202) 623-4661, publications@imf.org, https://www.imf.org; International Financial Statistics (IFS).

Routledge - Taylor & Francis Group, 6000 Broken Sound Pkwy. NW, Ste. 300, Boca Raton, FL, 33487, USA, (800) 634-1420, (800) 634-7064, orders@taylorandfrancis.com, https://www.routledge.com/; The Europa World Year Book 2022.

CONGO, DEMOCRATIC REPUBLIC OF THE-BARLEY PRODUCTION

See CONGO, DEMOCRATIC REPUBLIC OF THE-CROPS

CONGO, DEMOCRATIC REPUBLIC OF THE-BROADCASTING

Central Intelligence Agency (CIA), Office of Public Affairs, Washington, DC, 20505, USA, (703) 482-0623, https://www.cia.gov; The World Factbook.

Palgrave Macmillan, 1 New York Plaza, Ste. 4500, New York, NY, 10004-1562, USA, (800) 777-4643, orders@palgrave.com, https://www.palgrave.com/us; The Statesman's Yearbook, 2023.

WRTH Publications Limited, PO Box 290, Oxford, OX2 7FT, GBR, sales@wrth.com, https://www.wrth.com; World Radio TV Handbook 2023.

CONGO, DEMOCRATIC REPUBLIC OF THE-BUDGET

Central Intelligence Agency (CIA), Office of Public Affairs, Washington, DC, 20505, USA, (703) 482-0623, https://www.cia.gov; The World Factbook.

CONGO, DEMOCRATIC REPUBLIC OF THE-CHILDBIRTH-STATISTICS

The World Bank, 1818 H St. NW, Washington, DC, 20433, USA, (202) 473-1000, (202) 477-6391, eds03@worldbank.org, https://www.worldbank.org/; World Development Indicators (WDI) 2022.

CONGO, DEMOCRATIC REPUBLIC OF THE-CLIMATE

International Institute for Environment and Development (IIED), 235 High Holborn, London, WC1V 7DN, GBR, inforequest@iied.org, https://www.iied.org; Environment & Urbanization.

Palgrave Macmillan, 1 New York Plaza, Ste. 4500, New York, NY, 10004-1562, USA, (800) 777-4643, orders@palgrave.com, https://www.palgrave.com/us; The Statesman's Yearbook, 2023.

CONGO, DEMOCRATIC REPUBLIC OF THE-COAL PRODUCTION

See CONGO, DEMOCRATIC REPUBLIC OF THE-MINERAL INDUSTRIES

CONGO, DEMOCRATIC REPUBLIC OF THE-COCOA PRODUCTION

See CONGO, DEMOCRATIC REPUBLIC OF THE-CROPS

CONGO, DEMOCRATIC REPUBLIC OF THE-COMMERCE

Palgrave Macmillan, 1 New York Plaza, Ste. 4500, New York, NY, 10004-1562, USA, (800) 777-4643, orders@palgrave.com, https://www.palgrave.com/us; The Statesman's Yearbook, 2023.

UK Data Service, University of Essex, Wivenhoe Park, Colchester, Essex, CO4 3SQ, GBR, https://ukdataservice.ac.uk/; International Aggregate Data.

CONGO, DEMOCRATIC REPUBLIC OF THE-COMMODITY EXCHANGES

Barchart, 209 W Jackson Blvd., 2nd Fl., Chicago, IL, 60606, USA, (877) 247-4394, commodities@barchart.com, https://www.barchart.com/cmdty; The cmdty Yearbook 2023; cmdtyStats: Commodity Statistics and Fundamental Data; cmdtyView: Commodity Index; and Commodity Data and Prices.

International Monetary Fund (IMF), 700 19th St. NW, Washington, DC, 20431, USA, (202) 623-7000, (202) 623-4661, publications@imf.org, https://www.imf.org; IMF Primary Commodity Prices.

World Bureau of Metal Statistics (WBMS), 31 Star St., Ware, Hertfordshire, SG12 9BA, GBR, https://www.refinitiv.com/en/trading-solutions/world-bureau-metal-statistics; Annual Stainless Steel Statistics; Long Term Production/Consumption Series - All Metals; World Flow Charts; and World Metal Statistics.

CONGO, DEMOCRATIC REPUBLIC OF THE-CONSTRUCTION INDUSTRY

United Nations Economic Commission for Africa (UNECA), PO Box 3001, Addis Ababa, ETH, ecainfo@uneca.org, https://www.uneca.org/; African Statistical Yearbook 2020.

United Nations Statistics Division (UNSD), United Nations Plz., New York, NY, 10017, USA, (800) 253-9646, (212) 963-9851, statistics@un.org, https://unstats.un.org; Statistical Yearbook of the United Nations 2021.

CONGO, DEMOCRATIC REPUBLIC OF THE-CONSUMER PRICE INDEXES

Routledge - Taylor & Francis Group, 6000 Broken Sound Pkwy. NW, Ste. 300, Boca Raton, FL, 33487, USA, (800) 634-1420, (800) 634-7064, orders@taylorandfrancis.com, https://www.routledge.com/; The Europa World Year Book 2022.

United Nations Economic Commission for Africa (UNECA), PO Box 3001, Addis Ababa, ETH, ecainfo@uneca.org, https://www.uneca.org/; African Statistical Yearbook 2020.

The World Bank, 1818 H St. NW, Washington, DC, 20433, USA, (202) 473-1000, (202) 477-6391, eds03@worldbank.org, https://www.worldbank.org/; Congo, Democratic Republic of (report).

CONGO, DEMOCRATIC REPUBLIC OF THE-CONSUMPTION (ECONOMICS)

African Development Bank Group (AfDB), Avenue Joseph Anoma, 01 BP 1387, Abidjan, 01, COT, https://www.afdb.org; The AfDB Statistics Pocketbook 2019.

CONGO, DEMOCRATIC REPUBLIC OF THE-CORN INDUSTRY

See CONGO, DEMOCRATIC REPUBLIC OF THE-CROPS

CONGO, DEMOCRATIC REPUBLIC OF THE-COTTON

See CONGO, DEMOCRATIC REPUBLIC OF THE-CROPS

CONGO, DEMOCRATIC REPUBLIC OF THE-CROPS

Palgrave Macmillan, 1 New York Plaza, Ste. 4500, New York, NY, 10004-1562, USA, (800) 777-4643, orders@palgrave.com, https://www.palgrave.com/us; The Statesman's Yearbook, 2023.

United Nations Economic Commission for Africa (UNECA), PO Box 3001, Addis Ababa, ETH, ecainfo@uneca.org, https://www.uneca.org/; African Statistical Yearbook 2020.

United Nations Statistics Division (UNSD), United Nations Plz., New York, NY, 10017, USA, (800) 253-9646, (212) 963-9851, statistics@un.org, https://unstats.un.org; Statistical Yearbook of the United Nations 2021.

CONGO, DEMOCRATIC REPUBLIC OF THE-DAIRY PROCESSING

Palgrave Macmillan, 1 New York Plaza, Ste. 4500, New York, NY, 10004-1562, USA, (800) 777-4643, orders@palgrave.com, https://www.palgrave.com/us; The Statesman's Yearbook, 2023.

United Nations Food and Agricultural Organization (FAO), 2121 K St., Ste. 800B, Washington, DC, 20037, USA, (202) 653-2400 (Dial from U.S.), (202) 653-5760 (Fax from U.S.), fao-hq@fao.org, https://www.fao.org; The State of Food and Agriculture (SOFA) 2022.

CONGO, DEMOCRATIC REPUBLIC OF THE-DEBTS, EXTERNAL

African Development Bank Group (AfDB), Avenue Joseph Anoma, 01 BP 1387, Abidjan, 01, COT, https://www.afdb.org; The AfDB Statistics Pocketbook 2019; African Economic Outlook 2021; and Compendium of Statistics on Bank Group Operations 2019.

United Nations Economic Commission for Africa (UNECA), PO Box 3001, Addis Ababa, ETH, ecainfo@uneca.org, https://www.uneca.org/; Economic Report on Africa 2021.

The World Bank, 1818 H St. NW, Washington, DC, 20433, USA, (202) 473-1000, (202) 477-6391, eds03@worldbank.org, https://www.worldbank.org/; Global Financial Development Report 2019-2020: Bank Regulation and Supervision a Decade after the Global Financial Crisis and World Development Indicators (WDI) 2022.

CONGO, DEMOCRATIC REPUBLIC OF THE-DEFENSE EXPENDITURES

See CONGO, DEMOCRATIC REPUBLIC OF THE-ARMED FORCES

CONGO, DEMOCRATIC REPUBLIC OF THE-DIAMONDS

See CONGO, DEMOCRATIC REPUBLIC OF THE-MINERAL INDUSTRIES

CONGO, DEMOCRATIC REPUBLIC OF THE-DISPOSABLE INCOME

African Development Bank Group (AfDB), Avenue Joseph Anoma, 01 BP 1387, Abidjan, 01, COT, https://www.afdb.org; The AfDB Statistics Pocketbook 2019.

CONGO, DEMOCRATIC REPUBLIC OF THE-ECONOMIC ASSISTANCE

United Nations Statistics Division (UNSD), United Nations Plz., New York, NY, 10017, USA, (800) 253-9646, (212) 963-9851, statistics@un.org, https://unstats.un.org; Statistical Yearbook of the United Nations 2021.

CONGO, DEMOCRATIC REPUBLIC OF THE-ECONOMIC CONDITIONS

African Development Bank Group (AfDB), Avenue Joseph Anoma, 01 BP 1387, Abidjan, 01, COT, https://www.afdb.org; The AfDB Statistics Pocketbook 2019; Africa Economic Brief - COVID-19 Pandemic Potential Risks for Trade and Trade Finance in Africa; African Economic Outlook 2021; The African Statistical Journal; Compendium of Statistics on Bank Group Operations 2019; and Gender, Poverty and Environmental Indicators on African Countries 2019.

Bernan Press, 15250 NBN Way, Bldg. C, Blue Ridge Summit, PA, 17214, USA, (301) 459-2255, (800) 865-3457, (800) 865-3450, customercare@bernan.com, https://rowman.com/Page/Bernan; World Economic Outlook, April 2022.

Central Intelligence Agency (CIA), Office of Public Affairs, Washington, DC, 20505, USA, (703) 482-0623, https://www.cia.gov; The World Factbook.

The Economist Group: Economist Intelligence Unit (EIU), 900 3rd Ave., 16th Fl., New York, NY, 10022, USA, (212) 541-0500, americas@eiu.com, https://www.eiu.com; Congo (Democratic Republic) Country Report.

International Monetary Fund (IMF), 700 19th St. NW, Washington, DC, 20431, USA, (202) 623-7000, (202) 623-4661, publications@imf.org, https://www.imf.org; IMF Data and World Economic Outlook.

Palgrave Macmillan, 1 New York Plaza, Ste. 4500, New York, NY, 10004-1562, USA, (800) 777-4643, orders@palgrave.com, https://www.palgrave.com/us; The Statesman's Yearbook, 2023.

Routledge - Taylor & Francis Group, 6000 Broken Sound Pkwy. NW, Ste. 300, Boca Raton, FL, 33487, USA, (800) 634-1420, (800) 634-7064, orders@taylorandfrancis.com, https://www.routledge.com/; The Europa World Year Book 2022.

United Nations Economic Commission for Africa (UNECA), PO Box 3001, Addis Ababa, ETH, ecainfo@uneca.org, https://www.uneca.org/; Economic Report on Africa 2021.

The World Bank, 1818 H St. NW, Washington, DC, 20433, USA, (202) 473-1000, (202) 477-6391, eds03@worldbank.org, https://www.worldbank.org/; Congo, Democratic Republic of (report); Global Economic Monitor (GEM); Global Economic Prospects, June 2022; and The Global Findex Database 2021.

CONGO, DEMOCRATIC REPUBLIC OF THE-EDUCATION

African Development Bank Group (AfDB), Avenue Joseph Anoma, 01 BP 1387, Abidjan, 01, COT, https://www.afdb.org; The AfDB Statistics Pocketbook 2019.

Infoplease, c/o Sandbox Networks, Inc., 1 Lincoln St., 24th Fl., Boston, MA, 02111, USA, https://www.infoplease.com; Countries of the World.

Palgrave Macmillan, 1 New York Plaza, Ste. 4500, New York, NY, 10004-1562, USA, (800) 777-4643, orders@palgrave.com, https://www.palgrave.com/us; The Statesman's Yearbook, 2023.

Routledge - Taylor & Francis Group, 6000 Broken Sound Pkwy. NW, Ste. 300, Boca Raton, FL, 33487, USA, (800) 634-1420, (800) 634-7064, orders@taylorandfrancis.com, https://www.routledge.com/; The Europa World Year Book 2022.

UNESCO Institute for Statistics, C.P 250 Succursale H, Montreal, QC, H3G 2K8, CAN, (514) 343-6880 (Dial from U.S.), (514) 343-5740 (Fax from U.S.), uis.publications@unesco.org, http://uis.unesco.org/; Literacy and UIS.Stat.

United Nations Economic Commission for Africa (UNECA), PO Box 3001, Addis Ababa, ETH, ecainfo@uneca.org, https://www.uneca.org/; African Statistical Yearbook 2020.

United Nations Statistics Division (UNSD), United Nations Plz., New York, NY, 10017, USA, (800) 253-9646, (212) 963-9851, statistics@un.org, https://unstats.un.org; Millennium Development Goal Indicators.

The World Bank, 1818 H St. NW, Washington, DC, 20433, USA, (202) 473-1000, (202) 477-6391, eds03@worldbank.org, https://www.worldbank.org/; Congo, Democratic Republic of (report) and World Development Indicators (WDI) 2022.

CONGO, DEMOCRATIC REPUBLIC OF THE-ELECTRICITY

International Energy Agency (IEA), 9 Rue de la Federation, Paris, 75739, FRA, info@iea.org, https://www.iea.org/; World Energy Outlook 2021.

U.S. Energy Information Administration (EIA), 1000 Independence Ave. SW, Washington, DC, 20585, USA, (202) 586-8800, infoctr@eia.gov, https://www.eia.gov; International Energy Outlook 2021.

United Nations Statistics Division (UNSD), United Nations Plz., New York, NY, 10017, USA, (800) 253-9646, (212) 963-9851, statistics@un.org, https://unstats.un.org; Statistical Yearbook of the United Nations 2021.

CONGO, DEMOCRATIC REPUBLIC OF THE-EMPLOYMENT

International Labour Organization (ILO), 4 Rte. des Morillons, Geneva, CH-1211, SWI, ilo@ilo.org, https://www.ilo.org; NORMLEX Information System on International Labour Standards.

UK Data Service, University of Essex, Wivenhoe Park, Colchester, Essex, CO4 3SQ, GBR, https://ukdataservice.ac.uk/; International Aggregate Data.

United Nations Economic Commission for Africa (UNECA), PO Box 3001, Addis Ababa, ETH, ecainfo@uneca.org, https://www.uneca.org/; African Statistical Yearbook 2020.

United Nations Statistics Division (UNSD), United Nations Plz., New York, NY, 10017, USA, (800) 253-9646, (212) 963-9851, statistics@un.org, https://unstats.un.org; Statistical Yearbook of the United Nations 2021.

The World Bank, 1818 H St. NW, Washington, DC, 20433, USA, (202) 473-1000, (202) 477-6391, eds03@worldbank.org, https://www.worldbank.org/; Congo, Democratic Republic of (report).

CONGO, DEMOCRATIC REPUBLIC OF THE-ENERGY INDUSTRIES

Enerdata, 47 avenue Alsace Lorraine, Grenoble, 38027, FRA, (332) 216-4534, research@enerdata.net, https://www.enerdata.net; World Refinery Database.

United Nations Statistics Division (UNSD), United Nations Plz., New York, NY, 10017, USA, (800) 253-9646, (212) 963-9851, statistics@un.org, https://unstats.un.org; Statistical Yearbook of the United Nations 2021.

CONGO, DEMOCRATIC REPUBLIC OF THE-ENVIRONMENTAL CONDITIONS

DSI Data Service & Information, Xantener Strasse 51a, Rheinberg, D-47495, GER, dsi@dsidata.com, https://www.dsidata.com/; Global Environmental Database.

The Economist Group: Economist Intelligence Unit (EIU), 900 3rd Ave., 16th Fl., New York, NY, 10022, USA, (212) 541-0500, americas@eiu.com, https://www.eiu.com; Congo (Democratic Republic) Country Report.

International Institute for Environment and Development (IIED), 235 High Holborn, London, WC1V 7DN, GBR, inforequest@iied.org, https://www.iied.org; Environment & Urbanization.

CONGO, DEMOCRATIC REPUBLIC OF THE-EXPORTS

African Development Bank Group (AfDB), Avenue Joseph Anoma, 01 BP 1387, Abidjan, 01, COT, https://www.afdb.org; African Economic Outlook 2021.

Central Intelligence Agency (CIA), Office of Public Affairs, Washington, DC, 20505, USA, (703) 482-0623, https://www.cia.gov; The World Factbook.

The Economist Group: Economist Intelligence Unit (EIU), 900 3rd Ave., 16th Fl., New York, NY, 10022, USA, (212) 541-0500, americas@eiu.com, https://www.eiu.com; Congo (Democratic Republic) Country Report.

International Monetary Fund (IMF), 700 19th St. NW, Washington, DC, 20431, USA, (202) 623-7000, (202) 623-4661, publications@imf.org, https://www.imf.org; Direction of Trade Statistics (DOTS).

S&P Global, IHS Markit, 15 Inverness Way E, Englewood, CO, 80112, USA, (800) 447-2273, (800) 854-7179, https://ihsmarkit.com; Global Trade Atlas (GTA).

United Nations Conference on Trade and Development (UNCTAD), Palais des Nations, Geneva, 1211, SWI, (212) 963-6896, unctadinfo@unctad.org, https://unctad.org; Handbook of Statistics 2021.

CONGO, DEMOCRATIC REPUBLIC OF THE-FEMALE WORKING POPULATION

See CONGO, DEMOCRATIC REPUBLIC OF THE-EMPLOYMENT

CONGO, DEMOCRATIC REPUBLIC OF THE-FERTILITY, HUMAN

Central Intelligence Agency (CIA), Office of Public Affairs, Washington, DC, 20505, USA, (703) 482-0623, https://www.cia.gov; The World Factbook.

CONGO, DEMOCRATIC REPUBLIC OF THE-FERTILIZER INDUSTRY

United Nations Food and Agricultural Organization (FAO), 2121 K St., Ste. 800B, Washington, DC, 20037, USA, (202) 653-2400 (Dial from U.S.), (202) 653-5760 (Fax from U.S.), fao-hq@fao.org, https://www.fao.org; The State of Food and Agriculture (SOFA) 2022.

CONGO, DEMOCRATIC REPUBLIC OF THE-FETAL MORTALITY

See CONGO, DEMOCRATIC REPUBLIC OF THE-MORTALITY

CONGO, DEMOCRATIC REPUBLIC OF THE-FINANCE

International Monetary Fund (IMF), 700 19th St. NW, Washington, DC, 20431, USA, (202) 623-7000, (202) 623-4661, publications@imf.org, https://www.imf.org; International Financial Statistics (IFS).

Stockholm International Peace Research Institute (SIPRI), Signalistgatan 9, Stockholm, SE 169 72, SWE, https://www.sipri.org/; SIPRI Arms Transfers Database and SIPRI Military Expenditure Database.

United Nations Economic Commission for Africa (UNECA), PO Box 3001, Addis Ababa, ETH, ecainfo@uneca.org, https://www.uneca.org/; African Statistical Yearbook 2020.

United Nations Statistics Division (UNSD), United Nations Plz., New York, NY, 10017, USA, (800) 253-9646, (212) 963-9851, statistics@un.org, https://unstats.un.org; Statistical Yearbook of the United Nations 2021.

The World Bank, 1818 H St. NW, Washington, DC, 20433, USA, (202) 473-1000, (202) 477-6391, eds03@worldbank.org, https://www.worldbank.org/; Congo, Democratic Republic of (report).

CONGO, DEMOCRATIC REPUBLIC OF THE-FINANCE, PUBLIC

African Development Bank Group (AfDB), Avenue Joseph Anoma, 01 BP 1387, Abidjan, 01, COT, https://www.afdb.org; The AfDB Statistics Pocketbook 2019.

Bernan Press, 15250 NBN Way, Bldg. C, Blue Ridge Summit, PA, 17214, USA, (301) 459-2255, (800) 865-3457, (800) 865-3450, customercare@bernan.com, https://rowman.com/Page/Bernan; National Accounts Statistics: Analysis of Main Aggregates 2020.

The Economist Group: Economist Intelligence Unit (EIU), 900 3rd Ave., 16th Fl., New York, NY, 10022, USA, (212) 541-0500, americas@eiu.com, https://www.eiu.com; Congo (Democratic Republic) Country Report.

International Monetary Fund (IMF), 700 19th St. NW, Washington, DC, 20431, USA, (202) 623-7000, (202) 623-4661, publications@imf.org, https://www.imf.org; International Financial Statistics (IFS) and Regional Economic Outlook.

Palgrave Macmillan, 1 New York Plaza, Ste. 4500, New York, NY, 10004-1562, USA, (800) 777-4643, orders@palgrave.com, https://www.palgrave.com/us; The Statesman's Yearbook, 2023.

Routledge - Taylor & Francis Group, 6000 Broken Sound Pkwy. NW, Ste. 300, Boca Raton, FL, 33487, USA, (800) 634-1420, (800) 634-7064, orders@taylorandfrancis.com, https://www.routledge.com/; The Europa World Year Book 2022.

United Nations Economic Commission for Africa (UNECA), PO Box 3001, Addis Ababa, ETH, ecainfo@uneca.org, https://www.uneca.org/; African Statistical Yearbook 2020.

United Nations Statistics Division (UNSD), United Nations Plz., New York, NY, 10017, USA, (800) 253-9646, (212) 963-9851, statistics@un.org, https://unstats.un.org; National Accounts Main Aggregates Database and National Accounts Statistics: Main Aggregates and Detailed Tables.

The World Bank, 1818 H St. NW, Washington, DC, 20433, USA, (202) 473-1000, (202) 477-6391, eds03@worldbank.org, https://www.worldbank.org/; Congo, Democratic Republic of (report).

CONGO, DEMOCRATIC REPUBLIC OF THE-FISHERIES

Palgrave Macmillan, 1 New York Plaza, Ste. 4500, New York, NY, 10004-1562, USA, (800) 777-4643, orders@palgrave.com, https://www.palgrave.com/us; The Statesman's Yearbook, 2023.

Routledge - Taylor & Francis Group, 6000 Broken Sound Pkwy. NW, Ste. 300, Boca Raton, FL, 33487, USA, (800) 634-1420, (800) 634-7064, orders@taylorandfrancis.com, https://www.routledge.com/; The Europa World Year Book 2022.

United Nations Economic Commission for Africa (UNECA), PO Box 3001, Addis Ababa, ETH, ecainfo@uneca.org, https://www.uneca.org/; African Statistical Yearbook 2020.

United Nations Food and Agricultural Organization (FAO), 2121 K St., Ste. 800B, Washington, DC, 20037, USA, (202) 653-2400 (Dial from U.S.), (202) 653-5760 (Fax from U.S.), fao-hq@fao.org, https://www.fao.org; FAO Yearbook of Fishery and Aquaculture Statistics 2019; Fishery Statistical Collections Global Capture Production; FishStatJ; and The State of Food and Agriculture (SOFA) 2022.

United Nations Statistics Division (UNSD), United Nations Plz., New York, NY, 10017, USA, (800) 253-9646, (212) 963-9851, statistics@un.org, https://unstats.un.org; Statistical Yearbook of the United Nations 2021.

The World Bank, 1818 H St. NW, Washington, DC, 20433, USA, (202) 473-1000, (202) 477-6391, eds03@worldbank.org, https://www.worldbank.org/; Congo, Democratic Republic of (report).

CONGO, DEMOCRATIC REPUBLIC OF THE-FOOD

African Development Bank Group (AfDB), Avenue Joseph Anoma, 01 BP 1387, Abidjan, 01, COT, https://www.afdb.org; The AfDB Statistics Pocketbook 2019.

United Nations Food and Agricultural Organization (FAO), 2121 K St., Ste. 800B, Washington, DC, 20037, USA, (202) 653-2400 (Dial from U.S.), (202) 653-5760 (Fax from U.S.), fao-hq@fao.org, https://www.fao.org; The State of Food and Agriculture (SOFA) 2022.

CONGO, DEMOCRATIC REPUBLIC OF THE-FOREIGN EXCHANGE RATES

African Development Bank Group (AfDB), Avenue Joseph Anoma, 01 BP 1387, Abidjan, 01, COT, https://www.afdb.org; The AfDB Statistics Pocketbook 2019 and African Economic Outlook 2021.

CONGO, DEMOCRATIC REPUBLIC OF THE-FORESTS AND FORESTRY

Palgrave Macmillan, 1 New York Plaza, Ste. 4500, New York, NY, 10004-1562, USA, (800) 777-4643, orders@palgrave.com, https://www.palgrave.com/us; The Statesman's Yearbook, 2023.

Routledge - Taylor & Francis Group, 6000 Broken Sound Pkwy. NW, Ste. 300, Boca Raton, FL, 33487, USA, (800) 634-1420, (800) 634-7064, orders@taylorandfrancis.com, https://www.routledge.com/; The Europa World Year Book 2022.

UNESCO Institute for Statistics, C.P 250 Succursale H, Montreal, QC, H3G 2K8, CAN, (514) 343-6880 (Dial from U.S.), (514) 343-5740 (Fax from U.S.), uis.publications@unesco.org, http://uis.unesco.org/; UIS.Stat.

United Nations Economic Commission for Africa (UNECA), PO Box 3001, Addis Ababa, ETH, ecainfo@uneca.org, https://www.uneca.org/; African Statistical Yearbook 2020.

United Nations Food and Agricultural Organization (FAO), 2121 K St., Ste. 800B, Washington, DC, 20037, USA, (202) 653-2400 (Dial from U.S.), (202) 653-5760 (Fax from U.S.), fao-hq@fao.org, https://www.fao.org; FAO Yearbook of Forest Products 2019 and The State of Food and Agriculture (SOFA) 2022.

United Nations Statistics Division (UNSD), United Nations Plz., New York, NY, 10017, USA, (800) 253-

9646, (212) 963-9851, statistics@un.org, https://unstats.un.org; Statistical Yearbook of the United Nations 2021.

The World Bank, 1818 H St. NW, Washington, DC, 20433, USA, (202) 473-1000, (202) 477-6391, eds03@worldbank.org, https://www.worldbank.org/; Congo, Democratic Republic of (report).

CONGO, DEMOCRATIC REPUBLIC OF THE-GAS PRODUCTION

See CONGO, DEMOCRATIC REPUBLIC OF THE-MINERAL INDUSTRIES

CONGO, DEMOCRATIC REPUBLIC OF THE-GEOGRAPHIC INFORMATION SYSTEMS

The World Bank, 1818 H St. NW, Washington, DC, 20433, USA, (202) 473-1000, (202) 477-6391, eds03@worldbank.org, https://www.worldbank.org/; Congo, Democratic Republic of (report).

CONGO, DEMOCRATIC REPUBLIC OF THE-GOLD INDUSTRY

The World Bank, 1818 H St. NW, Washington, DC, 20433, USA, (202) 473-1000, (202) 477-6391, eds03@worldbank.org, https://www.worldbank.org/; World Development Indicators (WDI) 2022.

CONGO, DEMOCRATIC REPUBLIC OF THE-GOLD PRODUCTION

See CONGO, DEMOCRATIC REPUBLIC OF THE-MINERAL INDUSTRIES

CONGO, DEMOCRATIC REPUBLIC OF THE-GROSS DOMESTIC PRODUCT

African Development Bank Group (AfDB), Avenue Joseph Anoma, 01 BP 1387, Abidjan, 01, COT, https://www.afdb.org; The AfDB Statistics Pocketbook 2019.

The Economist Group: Economist Intelligence Unit (EIU), 900 3rd Ave., 16th Fl., New York, NY, 10022, USA, (212) 541-0500, americas@eiu.com, https://www.eiu.com; Congo (Democratic Republic) Country Report.

Routledge - Taylor & Francis Group, 6000 Broken Sound Pkwy. NW, Ste. 300, Boca Raton, FL, 33487, USA, (800) 634-1420, (800) 634-7064, orders@taylorandfrancis.com, https://www.routledge.com/; The Europa World Year Book 2022.

United Nations Economic Commission for Africa (UNECA), PO Box 3001, Addis Ababa, ETH, ecainfo@uneca.org, https://www.uneca.org/; African Statistical Yearbook 2020.

United Nations Statistics Division (UNSD), United Nations Plz., New York, NY, 10017, USA, (800) 253-9646, (212) 963-9851, statistics@un.org, https://unstats.un.org; Statistical Yearbook of the United Nations 2021.

The World Bank, 1818 H St. NW, Washington, DC, 20433, USA, (202) 473-1000, (202) 477-6391, eds03@worldbank.org, https://www.worldbank.org/; World Development Indicators (WDI) 2022.

CONGO, DEMOCRATIC REPUBLIC OF THE-GROSS NATIONAL PRODUCT

Palgrave Macmillan, 1 New York Plaza, Ste. 4500, New York, NY, 10004-1562, USA, (800) 777-4643, orders@palgrave.com, https://www.palgrave.com/us; The Statesman's Yearbook, 2023.

United Nations Statistics Division (UNSD), United Nations Plz., New York, NY, 10017, USA, (800) 253-9646, (212) 963-9851, statistics@un.org, https://unstats.un.org; Statistical Yearbook of the United Nations 2021.

The World Bank, 1818 H St. NW, Washington, DC, 20433, USA, (202) 473-1000, (202) 477-6391, eds03@worldbank.org, https://www.worldbank.org/; World Development Indicators (WDI) 2022.

CONGO, DEMOCRATIC REPUBLIC OF THE-ILLITERATE PERSONS

UNESCO Institute for Statistics, C.P 250 Succursale H, Montreal, QC, H3G 2K8, CAN, (514) 343-6880 (Dial from U.S.), (514) 343-5740 (Fax from U.S.), uis.publications@unesco.org, http://uis.unesco.org/; UIS.Stat.

CONGO, DEMOCRATIC REPUBLIC OF THE-IMPORTS

African Development Bank Group (AfDB), Avenue Joseph Anoma, 01 BP 1387, Abidjan, 01, COT, https://www.afdb.org; African Economic Outlook 2021.

Central Intelligence Agency (CIA), Office of Public Affairs, Washington, DC, 20505, USA, (703) 482-0623, https://www.cia.gov; The World Factbook.

The Economist Group: Economist Intelligence Unit (EIU), 900 3rd Ave., 16th Fl., New York, NY, 10022, USA, (212) 541-0500, americas@eiu.com, https://www.eiu.com; Congo (Democratic Republic) Country Report.

Euromonitor International, Inc., 1 N Dearborn St., Ste. 1700, Chicago, IL, 60602, USA, (312) 922-1115, (312) 922-1157, info-usa@euromonitor.com, https://www.euromonitor.com/; Geographies.

International Monetary Fund (IMF), 700 19th St. NW, Washington, DC, 20431, USA, (202) 623-7000, (202) 623-4661, publications@imf.org, https://www.imf.org; Direction of Trade Statistics (DOTS).

S&P Global, IHS Markit, 15 Inverness Way E, Englewood, CO, 80112, USA, (800) 447-2273, (800) 854-7179, https://ihsmarkit.com; Global Trade Atlas (GTA).

CONGO, DEMOCRATIC REPUBLIC OF THE-INDUSTRIAL METALS PRODUCTION

See CONGO, DEMOCRATIC REPUBLIC OF THE-MINERAL INDUSTRIES

CONGO, DEMOCRATIC REPUBLIC OF THE-INDUSTRIES

Central Intelligence Agency (CIA), Office of Public Affairs, Washington, DC, 20505, USA, (703) 482-0623, https://www.cia.gov; The World Factbook.

The Economist Group: Economist Intelligence Unit (EIU), 900 3rd Ave., 16th Fl., New York, NY, 10022, USA, (212) 541-0500, americas@eiu.com, https://www.eiu.com; Congo (Democratic Republic) Country Report.

International Labour Organization (ILO), 4 Rte. des Morillons, Geneva, CH-1211, SWI, ilo@ilo.org, https://www.ilo.org; NORMLEX Information System on International Labour Standards.

Palgrave Macmillan, 1 New York Plaza, Ste. 4500, New York, NY, 10004-1562, USA, (800) 777-4643, orders@palgrave.com, https://www.palgrave.com/us; The Statesman's Yearbook, 2023.

Routledge - Taylor & Francis Group, 6000 Broken Sound Pkwy. NW, Ste. 300, Boca Raton, FL, 33487, USA, (800) 634-1420, (800) 634-7064, orders@taylorandfrancis.com, https://www.routledge.com/; The Europa World Year Book 2022.

United Nations Industrial Development Organization (UNIDO), 1 United Nations Plz., Rm. DC1-1118, New York, NY, 10017, USA, (212) 963-6890, (212) 963 6885, (212) 963-7904, office.newyork@unido.org, https://www.unido.org/; Industrial Statistics Databases and International Yearbook of Industrial Statistics 2021.

The World Bank, 1818 H St. NW, Washington, DC, 20433, USA, (202) 473-1000, (202) 477-6391, eds03@worldbank.org, https://www.worldbank.org/; Congo, Democratic Republic of (report) and World Development Indicators (WDI) 2022.

CONGO, DEMOCRATIC REPUBLIC OF THE-INFANT AND MATERNAL MORTALITY

See CONGO, DEMOCRATIC REPUBLIC OF THE-MORTALITY

CONGO, DEMOCRATIC REPUBLIC OF THE-INTERNATIONAL TRADE

African Development Bank Group (AfDB), Avenue Joseph Anoma, 01 BP 1387, Abidjan, 01, COT, https://www.afdb.org; The AfDB Statistics Pocketbook 2019 and African Economic Outlook 2021.

The Economist Group: Economist Intelligence Unit (EIU), 900 3rd Ave., 16th Fl., New York, NY, 10022, USA, (212) 541-0500, americas@eiu.com, https://www.eiu.com; Congo (Democratic Republic) Country Report.

International Monetary Fund (IMF), 700 19th St. NW, Washington, DC, 20431, USA, (202) 623-7000, (202) 623-4661, publications@imf.org, https://www.imf.org; International Financial Statistics (IFS).

Palgrave Macmillan, 1 New York Plaza, Ste. 4500, New York, NY, 10004-1562, USA, (800) 777-4643, orders@palgrave.com, https://www.palgrave.com/us; The Statesman's Yearbook, 2023.

Routledge - Taylor & Francis Group, 6000 Broken Sound Pkwy. NW, Ste. 300, Boca Raton, FL, 33487, USA, (800) 634-1420, (800) 634-7064, orders@taylorandfrancis.com, https://www.routledge.com/; The Europa World Year Book 2022.

United Nations Conference on Trade and Development (UNCTAD), Palais des Nations, Geneva, 1211, SWI, (212) 963-6896, unctadinfo@unctad.org, https://unctad.org; Trade and Development Report 2021.

United Nations Economic Commission for Africa (UNECA), PO Box 3001, Addis Ababa, ETH, ecainfo@uneca.org, https://www.uneca.org/; African Statistical Yearbook 2020.

United Nations Food and Agricultural Organization (FAO), 2121 K St., Ste. 800B, Washington, DC, 20037, USA, (202) 653-2400 (Dial from U.S.), (202) 653-5760 (Fax from U.S.), fao-hq@fao.org, https://www.fao.org; The State of Food and Agriculture (SOFA) 2022.

United Nations Statistics Division (UNSD), United Nations Plz., New York, NY, 10017, USA, (800) 253-9646, (212) 963-9851, statistics@un.org, https://unstats.un.org; International Trade Statistics Yearbook 2020 and Statistical Yearbook of the United Nations 2021.

The World Bank, 1818 H St. NW, Washington, DC, 20433, USA, (202) 473-1000, (202) 477-6391, eds03@worldbank.org, https://www.worldbank.org/; Congo, Democratic Republic of (report) and World Development Indicators (WDI) 2022.

World Bureau of Metal Statistics (WBMS), 31 Star St., Ware, Hertfordshire, SG12 9BA, GBR, https://www.refinitiv.com/en/trading-solutions/world-bureau-metal-statistics; Long Term Production/Consumption Series - All Metals; World Flow Charts; and World Metal Statistics.

World Trade Organization (WTO), Ctre. William Rappard, Rue de Lausanne 154, Case postale, Geneva, CH-1211, SWI, enquiries@wto.org, https://www.wto.org; World Trade Statistical Review 2022.

CONGO, DEMOCRATIC REPUBLIC OF THE-INTERNET USERS

International Telecommunication Union (ITU), Place des Nations, Geneva, CH-1211, SWI, itumail@itu.int, https://www.itu.int; Global Connectivity Report 2022; World Telecommunication/ICT Indicators Database 2021; and Yearbook of Statistics 2019.

The World Bank, 1818 H St. NW, Washington, DC, 20433, USA, (202) 473-1000, (202) 477-6391, eds03@worldbank.org, https://www.worldbank.org/; Congo, Democratic Republic of (report).

CONGO, DEMOCRATIC REPUBLIC OF THE-INVESTMENTS

International Monetary Fund (IMF), 700 19th St. NW, Washington, DC, 20431, USA, (202) 623-7000, (202) 623-4661, publications@imf.org, https://www.imf.org; International Financial Statistics (IFS).

CONGO, DEMOCRATIC REPUBLIC OF THE-LABOR

African Development Bank Group (AfDB), Avenue Joseph Anoma, 01 BP 1387, Abidjan, 01, COT, https://www.afdb.org; The AfDB Statistics Pocketbook 2019.

Central Intelligence Agency (CIA), Office of Public Affairs, Washington, DC, 20505, USA, (703) 482-0623, https://www.cia.gov; The World Factbook.

International Labour Organization (ILO), 4 Rte. des Morillons, Geneva, CH-1211, SWI, ilo@ilo.org, https://www.ilo.org; NORMLEX Information System on International Labour Standards.

Palgrave Macmillan, 1 New York Plaza, Ste. 4500, New York, NY, 10004-1562, USA, (800) 777-4643, orders@palgrave.com, https://www.palgrave.com/us; The Statesman's Yearbook, 2023.

United Nations Food and Agricultural Organization (FAO), 2121 K St., Ste. 800B, Washington, DC, 20037, USA, (202) 653-2400 (Dial from U.S.), (202) 653-5760 (Fax from U.S.), fao-hq@fao.org, https://www.fao.org; The State of Food and Agriculture (SOFA) 2022.

The World Bank, 1818 H St. NW, Washington, DC, 20433, USA, (202) 473-1000, (202) 477-6391, eds03@worldbank.org, https://www.worldbank.org/; World Development Indicators (WDI) 2022.

CONGO, DEMOCRATIC REPUBLIC OF THE-LAND USE

United Nations Statistics Division (UNSD), United Nations Plz., New York, NY, 10017, USA, (800) 253-9646, (212) 963-9851, statistics@un.org, https://unstats.un.org; Millennium Development Goal Indicators.

CONGO, DEMOCRATIC REPUBLIC OF THE-LIBRARIES

UNESCO Institute for Statistics, C.P 250 Succursale H, Montreal, QC, H3G 2K8, CAN, (514) 343-6880 (Dial from U.S.), (514) 343-5740 (Fax from U.S.), uis.publications@unesco.org, http://uis.unesco.org/; UIS.Stat.

CONGO, DEMOCRATIC REPUBLIC OF THE-LIFE EXPECTANCY

African Development Bank Group (AfDB), Avenue Joseph Anoma, 01 BP 1387, Abidjan, 01, COT, https://www.afdb.org; The AfDB Statistics Pocketbook 2019.

Central Intelligence Agency (CIA), Office of Public Affairs, Washington, DC, 20505, USA, (703) 482-0623, https://www.cia.gov; The World Factbook.

United Nations Department of Economic and Social Affairs (DESA), Population Division, 2 United Nations Plz., Rm. DC2-1950, New York, NY, 10017, USA, (212) 963-3209, (212) 963-2147, population@un.org, https://www.un.org/development/desa/pd/; World Population Ageing 2020 Highlights.

United Nations Statistics Division (UNSD), United Nations Plz., New York, NY, 10017, USA, (800) 253-9646, (212) 963-9851, statistics@un.org, https://unstats.un.org; Millennium Development Goal Indicators.

CONGO, DEMOCRATIC REPUBLIC OF THE-LITERACY

UNESCO Institute for Statistics, C.P 250 Succursale H, Montreal, QC, H3G 2K8, CAN, (514) 343-6880 (Dial from U.S.), (514) 343-5740 (Fax from U.S.), uis.publications@unesco.org, http://uis.unesco.org/; Literacy.

CONGO, DEMOCRATIC REPUBLIC OF THE-LIVESTOCK

Palgrave Macmillan, 1 New York Plaza, Ste. 4500, New York, NY, 10004-1562, USA, (800) 777-4643, orders@palgrave.com, https://www.palgrave.com/us; The Statesman's Yearbook, 2023.

Routledge - Taylor & Francis Group, 6000 Broken Sound Pkwy. NW, Ste. 300, Boca Raton, FL, 33487, USA, (800) 634-1420, (800) 634-7064, orders@taylorandfrancis.com, https://www.routledge.com/; The Europa World Year Book 2022.

United Nations Economic Commission for Africa (UNECA), PO Box 3001, Addis Ababa, ETH, ecainfo@uneca.org, https://www.uneca.org/; African Statistical Yearbook 2020.

United Nations Food and Agricultural Organization (FAO), 2121 K St., Ste. 800B, Washington, DC, 20037, USA, (202) 653-2400 (Dial from U.S.), (202) 653-5760 (Fax from U.S.), fao-hq@fao.org, https://www.fao.org; The State of Food and Agriculture (SOFA) 2022.

United Nations Statistics Division (UNSD), United Nations Plz., New York, NY, 10017, USA, (800) 253-9646, (212) 963-9851, statistics@un.org, https://unstats.un.org; Statistical Yearbook of the United Nations 2021.

CONGO, DEMOCRATIC REPUBLIC OF THE-MINERAL INDUSTRIES

Barchart, 209 W Jackson Blvd., 2nd Fl., Chicago, IL, 60606, USA, (877) 247-4394, commodities@barchart.com, https://www.barchart.com/cmdty; The cmdty Yearbook 2023; cmdtyStats: Commodity Statistics and Fundamental Data; cmdtyView: Commodity Index; and Commodity Data and Prices.

International Energy Agency (IEA), 9 Rue de la Federation, Paris, 75739, FRA, info@iea.org, https://www.iea.org/; World Energy Outlook 2021.

International Monetary Fund (IMF), 700 19th St. NW, Washington, DC, 20431, USA, (202) 623-7000, (202) 623-4661, publications@imf.org, https://www.imf.org; International Financial Statistics (IFS).

Palgrave Macmillan, 1 New York Plaza, Ste. 4500, New York, NY, 10004-1562, USA, (800) 777-4643, orders@palgrave.com, https://www.palgrave.com/us; The Statesman's Yearbook, 2023.

Routledge - Taylor & Francis Group, 6000 Broken Sound Pkwy. NW, Ste. 300, Boca Raton, FL, 33487, USA, (800) 634-1420, (800) 634-7064, orders@taylorandfrancis.com, https://www.routledge.com/; The Europa World Year Book 2022.

United Nations Conference on Trade and Development (UNCTAD), Palais des Nations, Geneva, 1211, SWI, (212) 963-6896, unctadinfo@unctad.org, https://unctad.org; Trade and Development Report 2021.

United Nations Economic Commission for Africa (UNECA), PO Box 3001, Addis Ababa, ETH, ecainfo@uneca.org, https://www.uneca.org/; African Statistical Yearbook 2020.

United Nations Statistics Division (UNSD), United Nations Plz., New York, NY, 10017, USA, (800) 253-9646, (212) 963-9851, statistics@un.org, https://unstats.un.org; Statistical Yearbook of the United Nations 2021.

World Bureau of Metal Statistics (WBMS), 31 Star St., Ware, Hertfordshire, SG12 9BA, GBR, https://www.refinitiv.com/en/trading-solutions/world-bureau-metal-statistics; Annual Stainless Steel Statistics; Long Term Production/Consumption Series - All Metals; World Flow Charts; and World Metal Statistics.

CONGO, DEMOCRATIC REPUBLIC OF THE-MONEY SUPPLY

The Economist Group: Economist Intelligence Unit (EIU), 900 3rd Ave., 16th Fl., New York, NY, 10022, USA, (212) 541-0500, americas@eiu.com, https://www.eiu.com; Congo (Democratic Republic) Country Report.

Routledge - Taylor & Francis Group, 6000 Broken Sound Pkwy. NW, Ste. 300, Boca Raton, FL, 33487, USA, (800) 634-1420, (800) 634-7064, orders@taylorandfrancis.com, https://www.routledge.com/; The Europa World Year Book 2022.

United Nations Statistics Division (UNSD), United Nations Plz., New York, NY, 10017, USA, (800) 253-9646, (212) 963-9851, statistics@un.org, https://unstats.un.org; Statistical Yearbook of the United Nations 2021.

The World Bank, 1818 H St. NW, Washington, DC, 20433, USA, (202) 473-1000, (202) 477-6391, eds03@worldbank.org, https://www.worldbank.org/; Congo, Democratic Republic of (report).

CONGO, DEMOCRATIC REPUBLIC OF THE-MORTALITY

UNICEF, 3 United Nations Plz., New York, NY, 10017, USA, (212) 303-7984, (917) 244-2215, https://www.unicef.org; The State of the World's Children 2023.

United Nations Statistics Division (UNSD), United Nations Plz., New York, NY, 10017, USA, (800) 253-9646, (212) 963-9851, statistics@un.org, https://unstats.un.org; Millennium Development Goal Indicators and Statistical Yearbook of the United Nations 2021.

The World Bank, 1818 H St. NW, Washington, DC, 20433, USA, (202) 473-1000, (202) 477-6391, eds03@worldbank.org, https://www.worldbank.org/; World Development Indicators (WDI) 2022.

World Health Organization (WHO), Ave. Appia 20, Geneva, CH-1211, SWI, (202) 974-3000 (Telephone in U.S.), publications@who.int, https://www.who.int/; Global Health Observatory (GHO).

CONGO, DEMOCRATIC REPUBLIC OF THE-MOTOR VEHICLES

International Road Federation (IRF), Madison Place, 500 Montgomery St., 5th Fl., Alexandria, VA, 22314, USA, (703) 535-1001, (703) 535-1007, info@irf.global, https://www.irf.global/; World Road Statistics (WRS).

CONGO, DEMOCRATIC REPUBLIC OF THE-NATURAL GAS PRODUCTION

See CONGO, DEMOCRATIC REPUBLIC OF THE-MINERAL INDUSTRIES

CONGO, DEMOCRATIC REPUBLIC OF THE-NUTRITION

United Nations Food and Agricultural Organization (FAO), 2121 K St., Ste. 800B, Washington, DC, 20037, USA, (202) 653-2400 (Dial from U.S.), (202) 653-5760 (Fax from U.S.), fao-hq@fao.org, https://www.fao.org; The State of Food and Agriculture (SOFA) 2022.

United Nations Statistics Division (UNSD), United Nations Plz., New York, NY, 10017, USA, (800) 253-9646, (212) 963-9851, statistics@un.org, https://unstats.un.org; Millennium Development Goal Indicators.

CONGO, DEMOCRATIC REPUBLIC OF THE-PAPER

See CONGO, DEMOCRATIC REPUBLIC OF THE-FORESTS AND FORESTRY

CONGO, DEMOCRATIC REPUBLIC OF THE-PEANUT PRODUCTION

See CONGO, DEMOCRATIC REPUBLIC OF THE-CROPS

CONGO, DEMOCRATIC REPUBLIC OF THE-PESTICIDES

United Nations Food and Agricultural Organization (FAO), 2121 K St., Ste. 800B, Washington, DC, 20037, USA, (202) 653-2400 (Dial from U.S.), (202) 653-5760 (Fax from U.S.), fao-hq@fao.org, https://www.fao.org; The State of Food and Agriculture (SOFA) 2022.

CONGO, DEMOCRATIC REPUBLIC OF THE-PETROLEUM INDUSTRY AND TRADE

International Energy Agency (IEA), 9 Rue de la Federation, Paris, 75739, FRA, info@iea.org, https://www.iea.org/; World Energy Outlook 2021.

Palgrave Macmillan, 1 New York Plaza, Ste. 4500, New York, NY, 10004-1562, USA, (800) 777-4643, orders@palgrave.com, https://www.palgrave.com/us; The Statesman's Yearbook, 2023.

U.S. Energy Information Administration (EIA), 1000 Independence Ave. SW, Washington, DC, 20585, USA, (202) 586-8800, infoctr@eia.gov, https://www.eia.gov; International Energy Outlook 2021.

United Nations Food and Agricultural Organization (FAO), 2121 K St., Ste. 800B, Washington, DC, 20037, USA, (202) 653-2400 (Dial from U.S.), (202) 653-5760 (Fax from U.S.), fao-hq@fao.org, https://www.fao.org; The State of Food and Agriculture (SOFA) 2022.

United Nations Statistics Division (UNSD), United Nations Plz., New York, NY, 10017, USA, (800) 253-9646, (212) 963-9851, statistics@un.org, https://unstats.un.org; Statistical Yearbook of the United Nations 2021.

CONGO, DEMOCRATIC REPUBLIC OF THE-POPULATION

African Development Bank Group (AfDB), Avenue Joseph Anoma, 01 BP 1387, Abidjan, 01, COT, https://www.afdb.org; The AfDB Statistics Pocketbook 2019; Africa Economic Brief - COVID-19 Pandemic Potential Risks for Trade and Trade Finance in Africa; The African Statistical Journal; and Gender, Poverty and Environmental Indicators on African Countries 2019.

Central Intelligence Agency (CIA), Office of Public Affairs, Washington, DC, 20505, USA, (703) 482-0623, https://www.cia.gov; The World Factbook.

The Economist Group: Economist Intelligence Unit (EIU), 900 3rd Ave., 16th Fl., New York, NY, 10022, USA, (212) 541-0500, americas@eiu.com, https://www.eiu.com; Congo (Democratic Republic) Country Report.

European Commission, Eurostat, Luxembourg, 2920, LUX, https://ec.europa.eu/eurostat/; EU in the World 2020.

Infoplease, c/o Sandbox Networks, Inc., 1 Lincoln St., 24th Fl., Boston, MA, 02111, USA, https://www.infoplease.com; Countries of the World.

International Labour Organization (ILO), 4 Rte. des Morillons, Geneva, CH-1211, SWI, ilo@ilo.org, https://www.ilo.org; NORMLEX Information System on International Labour Standards.

Palgrave Macmillan, 1 New York Plaza, Ste. 4500, New York, NY, 10004-1562, USA, (800) 777-4643, orders@palgrave.com, https://www.palgrave.com/us; The Statesman's Yearbook, 2023.

Routledge - Taylor & Francis Group, 6000 Broken Sound Pkwy. NW, Ste. 300, Boca Raton, FL, 33487, USA, (800) 634-1420, (800) 634-7064, orders@taylorandfrancis.com, https://www.routledge.com/; The Europa World Year Book 2022.

UK Data Service, University of Essex, Wivenhoe Park, Colchester, Essex, CO4 3SQ, GBR, https://ukdataservice.ac.uk/; International Aggregate Data.

UNESCO Institute for Statistics, C.P 250 Succursale H, Montreal, QC, H3G 2K8, CAN, (514) 343-6880 (Dial from U.S.), (514) 343-5740 (Fax from U.S.), uis.publications@unesco.org, http://uis.unesco.org/; UIS.Stat.

United Nations Department of Economic and Social Affairs (DESA), Population Division, 2 United Nations Plz., Rm. DC2-1950, New York, NY, 10017, USA, (212) 963-3209, (212) 963-2147, population@un.org, https://www.un.org/development/desa/pd/; Revision of World Urbanization Prospects and World Population Ageing 2020 Highlights.

United Nations Development Programme (UNDP), One United Nations Plz., New York, NY, 10017, USA, (212) 906-5000, (212) 906-5001, https://www.undp.org; Human Development Report 2021-2022.

United Nations Statistics Division (UNSD), United Nations Plz., New York, NY, 10017, USA, (800) 253-9646, (212) 963-9851, statistics@un.org, https://unstats.un.org; Statistical Yearbook of the United Nations 2021.

The World Bank, 1818 H St. NW, Washington, DC, 20433, USA, (202) 473-1000, (202) 477-6391, eds03@worldbank.org, https://www.worldbank.org/; Congo, Democratic Republic of (report) and The Global Findex Database 2021.

World Health Organization (WHO), Ave. Appia 20, Geneva, CH-1211, SWI, (202) 974-3000 (Telephone in U.S.), publications@who.int, https://www.who.int/; Health Statistics and Information Systems.

CONGO, DEMOCRATIC REPUBLIC OF THE-POPULATION DENSITY

African Development Bank Group (AfDB), Avenue Joseph Anoma, 01 BP 1387, Abidjan, 01, COT, https://www.afdb.org; The AfDB Statistics Pocketbook 2019.

Central Intelligence Agency (CIA), Office of Public Affairs, Washington, DC, 20505, USA, (703) 482-0623, https://www.cia.gov; The World Factbook.

Palgrave Macmillan, 1 New York Plaza, Ste. 4500, New York, NY, 10004-1562, USA, (800) 777-4643, orders@palgrave.com, https://www.palgrave.com/us; The Statesman's Yearbook, 2023.

Routledge - Taylor & Francis Group, 6000 Broken Sound Pkwy. NW, Ste. 300, Boca Raton, FL, 33487, USA, (800) 634-1420, (800) 634-7064, orders@taylorandfrancis.com, https://www.routledge.com/; The Europa World Year Book 2022.

UNESCO Institute for Statistics, C.P 250 Succursale H, Montreal, QC, H3G 2K8, CAN, (514) 343-6880 (Dial from U.S.), (514) 343-5740 (Fax from U.S.), uis.publications@unesco.org, http://uis.unesco.org/; UIS.Stat.

The World Bank, 1818 H St. NW, Washington, DC, 20433, USA, (202) 473-1000, (202) 477-6391, eds03@worldbank.org, https://www.worldbank.org/; Congo, Democratic Republic of (report).

CONGO, DEMOCRATIC REPUBLIC OF THE-POSTAL SERVICE

Palgrave Macmillan, 1 New York Plaza, Ste. 4500, New York, NY, 10004-1562, USA, (800) 777-4643, orders@palgrave.com, https://www.palgrave.com/us; The Statesman's Yearbook, 2023.

CONGO, DEMOCRATIC REPUBLIC OF THE-POWER RESOURCES

International Energy Agency (IEA), 9 Rue de la Federation, Paris, 75739, FRA, info@iea.org, https://www.iea.org/; World Energy Outlook 2021.

Palgrave Macmillan, 1 New York Plaza, Ste. 4500, New York, NY, 10004-1562, USA, (800) 777-4643, orders@palgrave.com, https://www.palgrave.com/us; The Statesman's Yearbook, 2023.

U.S. Energy Information Administration (EIA), 1000 Independence Ave. SW, Washington, DC, 20585, USA, (202) 586-8800, infoctr@eia.gov, https://www.eia.gov; International Energy Outlook 2021.

United Nations Economic Commission for Africa (UNECA), PO Box 3001, Addis Ababa, ETH, ecainfo@uneca.org, https://www.uneca.org/; African Statistical Yearbook 2020.

United Nations Food and Agricultural Organization (FAO), 2121 K St., Ste. 800B, Washington, DC, 20037, USA, (202) 653-2400 (Dial from U.S.), (202) 653-5760 (Fax from U.S.), fao-hq@fao.org, https://www.fao.org; The State of Food and Agriculture (SOFA) 2022.

United Nations Statistics Division (UNSD), United Nations Plz., New York, NY, 10017, USA, (800) 253-9646, (212) 963-9851, statistics@un.org, https://unstats.un.org; Energy Statistics Yearbook 2019 and Statistical Yearbook of the United Nations 2021.

CONGO, DEMOCRATIC REPUBLIC OF THE-PRICES

International Monetary Fund (IMF), 700 19th St. NW, Washington, DC, 20431, USA, (202) 623-7000, (202) 623-4661, publications@imf.org, https://www.imf.org; International Financial Statistics (IFS).

United Nations Economic Commission for Africa (UNECA), PO Box 3001, Addis Ababa, ETH, ecainfo@uneca.org, https://www.uneca.org/; African Statistical Yearbook 2020.

The World Bank, 1818 H St. NW, Washington, DC, 20433, USA, (202) 473-1000, (202) 477-6391, eds03@worldbank.org, https://www.worldbank.org/; Congo, Democratic Republic of (report).

World Bureau of Metal Statistics (WBMS), 31 Star St., Ware, Hertfordshire, SG12 9BA, GBR, https://www.refinitiv.com/en/trading-solutions/world-bureau-metal-statistics; Long Term Production/Consumption Series - All Metals; World Flow Charts; and World Metal Statistics.

CONGO, DEMOCRATIC REPUBLIC OF THE-PUBLIC HEALTH

African Development Bank Group (AfDB), Avenue Joseph Anoma, 01 BP 1387, Abidjan, 01, COT, https://www.afdb.org; The AfDB Statistics Pocketbook 2019.

Palgrave Macmillan, 1 New York Plaza, Ste. 4500, New York, NY, 10004-1562, USA, (800) 777-4643, orders@palgrave.com, https://www.palgrave.com/us; The Statesman's Yearbook, 2023.

U.S. Census Bureau, 4600 Silver Hill Rd., Washington, DC, 20233, USA, (301) 763-4636, (800) 923-8282, https://www.census.gov; HIV/AIDS Surveillance Data Base.

UNICEF, 3 United Nations Plz., New York, NY, 10017, USA, (212) 303-7984, (917) 244-2215, https://www.unicef.org; The State of the World's Children 2023.

United Nations Department of Economic and Social Affairs (DESA), Population Division, 2 United Nations Plz., Rm. DC2-1950, New York, NY, 10017, USA, (212) 963-3209, (212) 963-2147, population@un.org, https://www.un.org/development/desa/pd/; World Fertility Data 2019.

United Nations Economic Commission for Africa (UNECA), PO Box 3001, Addis Ababa, ETH, ecainfo@uneca.org, https://www.uneca.org/; African Statistical Yearbook 2020.

United Nations Statistics Division (UNSD), United Nations Plz., New York, NY, 10017, USA, (800) 253-9646, (212) 963-9851, statistics@un.org, https://unstats.un.org; Millennium Development Goal Indicators and Statistical Yearbook of the United Nations 2021.

The World Bank, 1818 H St. NW, Washington, DC, 20433, USA, (202) 473-1000, (202) 477-6391, eds03@worldbank.org, https://www.worldbank.org/; Congo, Democratic Republic of (report).

World Health Organization (WHO), Ave. Appia 20, Geneva, CH-1211, SWI, (202) 974-3000 (Telephone in U.S.), publications@who.int, https://www.who.int/; Global Health Observatory (GHO) and Health Statistics and Information Systems.

CONGO, DEMOCRATIC REPUBLIC OF THE-PUBLISHERS AND PUBLISHING

UNESCO Institute for Statistics, C.P 250 Succursale H, Montreal, QC, H3G 2K8, CAN, (514) 343-6880 (Dial from U.S.), (514) 343-5740 (Fax from U.S.), uis.publications@unesco.org, http://uis.unesco.org/; UIS.Stat.

CONGO, DEMOCRATIC REPUBLIC OF THE-RAILROADS

Janes, USA, (703) 574-7580, (888) 977-1519, customer.care@janes.com, https://www.janes.com; Janes World Railways 2021-2022.

Palgrave Macmillan, 1 New York Plaza, Ste. 4500, New York, NY, 10004-1562, USA, (800) 777-4643, orders@palgrave.com, https://www.palgrave.com/us; The Statesman's Yearbook, 2023.

Routledge - Taylor & Francis Group, 6000 Broken Sound Pkwy. NW, Ste. 300, Boca Raton, FL, 33487, USA, (800) 634-1420, (800) 634-7064, orders@taylorandfrancis.com, https://www.routledge.com/; The Europa World Year Book 2022.

United Nations Economic Commission for Africa (UNECA), PO Box 3001, Addis Ababa, ETH, ecainfo@uneca.org, https://www.uneca.org/; African Statistical Yearbook 2020.

United Nations Statistics Division (UNSD), United Nations Plz., New York, NY, 10017, USA, (800) 253-9646, (212) 963-9851, statistics@un.org, https://unstats.un.org; Statistical Yearbook of the United Nations 2021.

CONGO, DEMOCRATIC REPUBLIC OF THE-RELIGION

Central Intelligence Agency (CIA), Office of Public Affairs, Washington, DC, 20505, USA, (703) 482-0623, https://www.cia.gov; The World Factbook.

Palgrave Macmillan, 1 New York Plaza, Ste. 4500, New York, NY, 10004-1562, USA, (800) 777-4643, orders@palgrave.com, https://www.palgrave.com/us; The Statesman's Yearbook, 2023.

CONGO, DEMOCRATIC REPUBLIC OF THE-RICE PRODUCTION

See CONGO, DEMOCRATIC REPUBLIC OF THE-CROPS

CONGO, DEMOCRATIC REPUBLIC OF THE-ROADS

International Road Federation (IRF), Madison Place, 500 Montgomery St., 5th Fl., Alexandria, VA, 22314, USA, (703) 535-1001, (703) 535-1007, info@irf.global, https://www.irf.global/; World Road Statistics (WRS).

United Nations Economic Commission for Africa (UNECA), PO Box 3001, Addis Ababa, ETH, ecainfo@uneca.org, https://www.uneca.org/; African Statistical Yearbook 2020.

CONGO, DEMOCRATIC REPUBLIC OF THE-RUBBER INDUSTRY AND TRADE

International Rubber Study Group (IRSG), 51 Changi Business Park Central 2, Unit No. 6, 486066, SGP, https://www.rubberstudy.org; Monthly Rubber Bulletin (MRB); Rubber Industry Report; Rubber Statistical Bulletin; and World Rubber Industry Report (WRIO).

United Nations Statistics Division (UNSD), United Nations Plz., New York, NY, 10017, USA, (800) 253-9646, (212) 963-9851, statistics@un.org, https://unstats.un.org; Statistical Yearbook of the United Nations 2021.

CONGO, DEMOCRATIC REPUBLIC OF THE-SHIPPING

Routledge - Taylor & Francis Group, 6000 Broken Sound Pkwy. NW, Ste. 300, Boca Raton, FL, 33487, USA, (800) 634-1420, (800) 634-7064, orders@taylorandfrancis.com, https://www.routledge.com/; The Europa World Year Book 2022.

United Nations Economic Commission for Africa (UNECA), PO Box 3001, Addis Ababa, ETH, ecainfo@uneca.org, https://www.uneca.org/; African Statistical Yearbook 2020.

United Nations Statistics Division (UNSD), United Nations Plz., New York, NY, 10017, USA, (800) 253-9646, (212) 963-9851, statistics@un.org, https://unstats.un.org; Statistical Yearbook of the United Nations 2021.

CONGO, DEMOCRATIC REPUBLIC OF THE-SOYBEAN PRODUCTION

See CONGO, DEMOCRATIC REPUBLIC OF THE-CROPS

CONGO, DEMOCRATIC REPUBLIC OF THE-STEEL PRODUCTION

See CONGO, DEMOCRATIC REPUBLIC OF THE-MINERAL INDUSTRIES

CONGO, DEMOCRATIC REPUBLIC OF THE-SUGAR PRODUCTION

See CONGO, DEMOCRATIC REPUBLIC OF THE-CROPS

CONGO, DEMOCRATIC REPUBLIC OF THE-SULPHUR PRODUCTION

See CONGO, DEMOCRATIC REPUBLIC OF THE-MINERAL INDUSTRIES

CONGO, DEMOCRATIC REPUBLIC OF THE-TAXATION

The World Bank, 1818 H St. NW, Washington, DC, 20433, USA, (202) 473-1000, (202) 477-6391, eds03@worldbank.org, https://www.worldbank.org/; World Development Indicators (WDI) 2022.

CONGO, DEMOCRATIC REPUBLIC OF THE-TEA PRODUCTION

See CONGO, DEMOCRATIC REPUBLIC OF THE-CROPS

CONGO, DEMOCRATIC REPUBLIC OF THE-TELEPHONE

Palgrave Macmillan, 1 New York Plaza, Ste. 4500, New York, NY, 10004-1562, USA, (800) 777-4643, orders@palgrave.com, https://www.palgrave.com/us; The Statesman's Yearbook, 2023.

Routledge - Taylor & Francis Group, 6000 Broken Sound Pkwy. NW, Ste. 300, Boca Raton, FL, 33487, USA, (800) 634-1420, (800) 634-7064, orders@taylorandfrancis.com, https://www.routledge.com/; The Europa World Year Book 2022.

CONGO, DEMOCRATIC REPUBLIC OF THE-TEXTILE INDUSTRY

Palgrave Macmillan, 1 New York Plaza, Ste. 4500, New York, NY, 10004-1562, USA, (800) 777-4643, orders@palgrave.com, https://www.palgrave.com/us; The Statesman's Yearbook, 2023.

United Nations Statistics Division (UNSD), United Nations Plz., New York, NY, 10017, USA, (800) 253-9646, (212) 963-9851, statistics@un.org, https://unstats.un.org; Statistical Yearbook of the United Nations 2021.

CONGO, DEMOCRATIC REPUBLIC OF THE-THEATER

UNESCO Institute for Statistics, C.P 250 Succursale H, Montreal, QC, H3G 2K8, CAN, (514) 343-6880 (Dial from U.S.), (514) 343-5740 (Fax from U.S.), uis.publications@unesco.org, http://uis.unesco.org/; UIS.Stat.

CONGO, DEMOCRATIC REPUBLIC OF THE-TOBACCO INDUSTRY

United Nations Statistics Division (UNSD), United Nations Plz., New York, NY, 10017, USA, (800) 253-9646, (212) 963-9851, statistics@un.org, https://unstats.un.org; Statistical Yearbook of the United Nations 2021.

CONGO, DEMOCRATIC REPUBLIC OF THE-TOURISM

Palgrave Macmillan, 1 New York Plaza, Ste. 4500, New York, NY, 10004-1562, USA, (800) 777-4643, orders@palgrave.com, https://www.palgrave.com/us; The Statesman's Yearbook, 2023.

Routledge - Taylor & Francis Group, 6000 Broken Sound Pkwy. NW, Ste. 300, Boca Raton, FL, 33487, USA, (800) 634-1420, (800) 634-7064, orders@taylorandfrancis.com, https://www.routledge.com/; The Europa World Year Book 2022.

United Nations Economic Commission for Africa (UNECA), PO Box 3001, Addis Ababa, ETH, ecainfo@uneca.org, https://www.uneca.org/; African Statistical Yearbook 2020.

United Nations Statistics Division (UNSD), United Nations Plz., New York, NY, 10017, USA, (800) 253-9646, (212) 963-9851, statistics@un.org, https://unstats.un.org; Statistical Yearbook of the United Nations 2021.

United Nations World Tourism Organization (UNWTO), Calle Poeta Joan Maragall 42, Madrid, 28020, SPA, info@unwto.org, https://www.unwto.org/; Yearbook of Tourism Statistics, 2021 Edition.

The World Bank, 1818 H St. NW, Washington, DC, 20433, USA, (202) 473-1000, (202) 477-6391, eds03@worldbank.org, https://www.worldbank.org/; Congo, Democratic Republic of (report).

CONGO, DEMOCRATIC REPUBLIC OF THE-TRADE

See CONGO, DEMOCRATIC REPUBLIC OF THE-INTERNATIONAL TRADE

CONGO, DEMOCRATIC REPUBLIC OF THE-TRANSPORTATION

Central Intelligence Agency (CIA), Office of Public Affairs, Washington, DC, 20505, USA, (703) 482-0623, https://www.cia.gov; The World Factbook.

Palgrave Macmillan, 1 New York Plaza, Ste. 4500, New York, NY, 10004-1562, USA, (800) 777-4643, orders@palgrave.com, https://www.palgrave.com/us; The Statesman's Yearbook, 2023.

Routledge - Taylor & Francis Group, 6000 Broken Sound Pkwy. NW, Ste. 300, Boca Raton, FL, 33487, USA, (800) 634-1420, (800) 634-7064, orders@taylorandfrancis.com, https://www.routledge.com/; The Europa World Year Book 2022.

United Nations Economic Commission for Africa (UNECA), PO Box 3001, Addis Ababa, ETH, ecainfo@uneca.org, https://www.uneca.org/; African Statistical Yearbook 2020.

The World Bank, 1818 H St. NW, Washington, DC, 20433, USA, (202) 473-1000, (202) 477-6391, eds03@worldbank.org, https://www.worldbank.org/; Congo, Democratic Republic of (report).

CONGO, DEMOCRATIC REPUBLIC OF THE-UNEMPLOYMENT

International Labour Organization (ILO), 4 Rte. des Morillons, Geneva, CH-1211, SWI, ilo@ilo.org, https://www.ilo.org; NORMLEX Information System on International Labour Standards.

CONGO, DEMOCRATIC REPUBLIC OF THE-VITAL STATISTICS

U.S. Census Bureau, 4600 Silver Hill Rd., Washington, DC, 20233, USA, (301) 763-4636, (800) 923-8282, https://www.census.gov; HIV/AIDS Surveillance Data Base.

United Nations Department of Economic and Social Affairs (DESA), Population Division, 2 United Nations Plz., Rm. DC2-1950, New York, NY, 10017, USA, (212) 963-3209, (212) 963-2147, population@un.org, https://www.un.org/development/desa/pd/; World Contraceptive Use 2021: Estimates and Projections of Family Planning Indicators and World Marriage Data 2019.

United Nations Statistics Division (UNSD), United Nations Plz., New York, NY, 10017, USA, (800) 253-9646, (212) 963-9851, statistics@un.org, https://unstats.un.org; Statistical Yearbook of the United Nations 2021.

World Health Organization (WHO), Ave. Appia 20, Geneva, CH-1211, SWI, (202) 974-3000 (Telephone in U.S.), publications@who.int, https://www.who.int/; Health Statistics and Information Systems.

CONGO, DEMOCRATIC REPUBLIC OF THE-WAGES

International Labour Organization (ILO), 4 Rte. des Morillons, Geneva, CH-1211, SWI, ilo@ilo.org, https://www.ilo.org; NORMLEX Information System on International Labour Standards.

The World Bank, 1818 H St. NW, Washington, DC, 20433, USA, (202) 473-1000, (202) 477-6391, eds03@worldbank.org, https://www.worldbank.org/; Congo, Democratic Republic of (report).

CONGO, DEMOCRATIC REPUBLIC OF THE-WEATHER

See CONGO, DEMOCRATIC REPUBLIC OF THE-CLIMATE

CONGO, DEMOCRATIC REPUBLIC OF THE-WHEAT PRODUCTION

See CONGO, DEMOCRATIC REPUBLIC OF THE-CROPS

CONGO, DEMOCRATIC REPUBLIC OF THE-WOOL PRODUCTION

See CONGO, DEMOCRATIC REPUBLIC OF THE-TEXTILE INDUSTRY

CONGO, REPUBLIC OF THE-AGRICULTURE

African Development Bank Group (AfDB), Avenue Joseph Anoma, 01 BP 1387, Abidjan, 01, COT, https://www.afdb.org; African Economic Outlook 2021 and Compendium of Statistics on Bank Group Operations 2019.

The Economist Group: Economist Intelligence Unit (EIU), 900 3rd Ave., 16th Fl., New York, NY, 10022, USA, (212) 541-0500, americas@eiu.com, https://www.eiu.com; Congo (Brazzaville) Country Report.

Euromonitor International, Inc., 1 N Dearborn St., Ste. 1700, Chicago, IL, 60602, USA, (312) 922-1115, (312) 922-1157, info-usa@euromonitor.com, https://www.euromonitor.com/; Geographies.

Palgrave Macmillan, 1 New York Plaza, Ste. 4500, New York, NY, 10004-1562, USA, (800) 777-4643, orders@palgrave.com, https://www.palgrave.com/us; The Statesman's Yearbook, 2023.

Routledge - Taylor & Francis Group, 6000 Broken Sound Pkwy. NW, Ste. 300, Boca Raton, FL, 33487, USA, (800) 634-1420, (800) 634-7064, orders@taylorandfrancis.com, https://www.routledge.com/; The Europa World Year Book 2022.

United Nations Economic Commission for Africa (UNECA), PO Box 3001, Addis Ababa, ETH, ecainfo@uneca.org, https://www.uneca.org/; African Statistical Yearbook 2020 and Economic Report on Africa 2021.

United Nations Food and Agricultural Organization (FAO), 2121 K St., Ste. 800B, Washington, DC, 20037, USA, (202) 653-2400 (Dial from U.S.), (202) 653-5760 (Fax from U.S.), fao-hq@fao.org, https://www.fao.org; AQUASTAT and The State of Food and Agriculture (SOFA) 2022.

United Nations Statistics Division (UNSD), United Nations Plz., New York, NY, 10017, USA, (800) 253-9646, (212) 963-9851, statistics@un.org, https://unstats.un.org; Statistical Yearbook of the United Nations 2021.

The World Bank, 1818 H St. NW, Washington, DC, 20433, USA, (202) 473-1000, (202) 477-6391, eds03@worldbank.org, https://www.worldbank.org/; Congo, Republic of the (report) and World Development Indicators (WDI) 2022.

CONGO, REPUBLIC OF THE-AIRLINES

Palgrave Macmillan, 1 New York Plaza, Ste. 4500, New York, NY, 10004-1562, USA, (800) 777-4643, orders@palgrave.com, https://www.palgrave.com/us; The Statesman's Yearbook, 2023.

Routledge - Taylor & Francis Group, 6000 Broken Sound Pkwy. NW, Ste. 300, Boca Raton, FL, 33487, USA, (800) 634-1420, (800) 634-7064, orders@taylorandfrancis.com, https://www.routledge.com/; The Europa World Year Book 2022.

United Nations Economic Commission for Africa (UNECA), PO Box 3001, Addis Ababa, ETH, ecainfo@uneca.org, https://www.uneca.org/; African Statistical Yearbook 2020.

CONGO, REPUBLIC OF THE-ARMED FORCES

Central Intelligence Agency (CIA), Office of Public Affairs, Washington, DC, 20505, USA, (703) 482-0623, https://www.cia.gov; The World Factbook.

International Institute for Strategic Studies (IISS) - Americas, 2121 K St. NW, Ste. 600, Washington, DC, 20037, USA, (202) 659-1490, (202) 659-1499, https://www.iiss.org/; The Military Balance 2022.

Palgrave Macmillan, 1 New York Plaza, Ste. 4500, New York, NY, 10004-1562, USA, (800) 777-4643, orders@palgrave.com, https://www.palgrave.com/us; The Statesman's Yearbook, 2023.

Stockholm International Peace Research Institute (SIPRI), Signalistgatan 9, Stockholm, SE 169 72, SWE, https://www.sipri.org/; SIPRI Arms Transfers Database and SIPRI Military Expenditure Database.

CONGO, REPUBLIC OF THE-BALANCE OF PAYMENTS

African Development Bank Group (AfDB), Avenue Joseph Anoma, 01 BP 1387, Abidjan, 01, COT, https://www.afdb.org; The AfDB Statistics Pocketbook 2019.

International Monetary Fund (IMF), 700 19th St. NW, Washington, DC, 20431, USA, (202) 623-7000, (202) 623-4661, publications@imf.org, https://www.imf.org; Balance of Payments Statistics: Annual Report 2021.

Routledge - Taylor & Francis Group, 6000 Broken Sound Pkwy. NW, Ste. 300, Boca Raton, FL, 33487, USA, (800) 634-1420, (800) 634-7064, orders@taylorandfrancis.com, https://www.routledge.com/; The Europa World Year Book 2022.

United Nations Conference on Trade and Development (UNCTAD), Palais des Nations, Geneva, 1211, SWI, (212) 963-6896, unctadinfo@unctad.org, https://unctad.org; Handbook of Statistics 2021.

United Nations Economic Commission for Africa (UNECA), PO Box 3001, Addis Ababa, ETH, ecainfo@uneca.org, https://www.uneca.org/; African Statistical Yearbook 2020.

The World Bank, 1818 H St. NW, Washington, DC, 20433, USA, (202) 473-1000, (202) 477-6391, eds03@worldbank.org, https://www.worldbank.org/; Congo, Republic of the (report); World Development Indicators (WDI) 2022; and World Development Report 2022: Finance for an Equitable Recovery.

CONGO, REPUBLIC OF THE-BANKS AND BANKING

Euromonitor International, Inc., 1 N Dearborn St., Ste. 1700, Chicago, IL, 60602, USA, (312) 922-1115, (312) 922-1157, info-usa@euromonitor.com, https://www.euromonitor.com/; Geographies.

International Monetary Fund (IMF), 700 19th St. NW, Washington, DC, 20431, USA, (202) 623-7000, (202) 623-4661, publications@imf.org, https://www.imf.org; International Financial Statistics (IFS).

Routledge - Taylor & Francis Group, 6000 Broken Sound Pkwy. NW, Ste. 300, Boca Raton, FL, 33487, USA, (800) 634-1420, (800) 634-7064, orders@taylorandfrancis.com, https://www.routledge.com/; The Europa World Year Book 2022.

United Nations Economic Commission for Africa (UNECA), PO Box 3001, Addis Ababa, ETH, ecainfo@uneca.org, https://www.uneca.org/; African Statistical Yearbook 2020.

CONGO, REPUBLIC OF THE-BROADCASTING

Central Intelligence Agency (CIA), Office of Public Affairs, Washington, DC, 20505, USA, (703) 482-0623, https://www.cia.gov; The World Factbook.

Euromonitor International, Inc., 1 N Dearborn St., Ste. 1700, Chicago, IL, 60602, USA, (312) 922-1115, (312) 922-1157, info-usa@euromonitor.com, https://www.euromonitor.com/; Geographies.

Palgrave Macmillan, 1 New York Plaza, Ste. 4500, New York, NY, 10004-1562, USA, (800) 777-4643, orders@palgrave.com, https://www.palgrave.com/us; The Statesman's Yearbook, 2023.

WRTH Publications Limited, PO Box 290, Oxford, OX2 7FT, GBR, sales@wrth.com, https://www.wrth.com; World Radio TV Handbook 2023.

CONGO, REPUBLIC OF THE-BUDGET

Central Intelligence Agency (CIA), Office of Public Affairs, Washington, DC, 20505, USA, (703) 482-0623, https://www.cia.gov; The World Factbook.

CONGO, REPUBLIC OF THE-CHILDBIRTH-STATISTICS

The World Bank, 1818 H St. NW, Washington, DC, 20433, USA, (202) 473-1000, (202) 477-6391, eds03@worldbank.org, https://www.worldbank.org/; World Development Indicators (WDI) 2022.

CONGO, REPUBLIC OF THE-CLIMATE

Palgrave Macmillan, 1 New York Plaza, Ste. 4500, New York, NY, 10004-1562, USA, (800) 777-4643, orders@palgrave.com, https://www.palgrave.com/us; The Statesman's Yearbook, 2023.

CONGO, REPUBLIC OF THE-COMMERCE

Palgrave Macmillan, 1 New York Plaza, Ste. 4500, New York, NY, 10004-1562, USA, (800) 777-4643, orders@palgrave.com, https://www.palgrave.com/us; The Statesman's Yearbook, 2023.

UK Data Service, University of Essex, Wivenhoe Park, Colchester, Essex, CO4 3SQ, GBR, https://ukdataservice.ac.uk/; International Aggregate Data.

CONGO, REPUBLIC OF THE-COMMODITY EXCHANGES

Barchart, 209 W Jackson Blvd., 2nd Fl., Chicago, IL, 60606, USA, (877) 247-4394, commodities@barchart.com, https://www.barchart.com/cmdty; The cmdty Yearbook 2023; cmdtyStats: Commodity Statistics and Fundamental Data; cmdtyView: Commodity Index; and Commodity Data and Prices.

International Monetary Fund (IMF), 700 19th St. NW, Washington, DC, 20431, USA, (202) 623-7000, (202) 623-4661, publications@imf.org, https://www.imf.org; IMF Primary Commodity Prices.

CONGO, REPUBLIC OF THE-CONSTRUCTION INDUSTRY

United Nations Economic Commission for Africa (UNECA), PO Box 3001, Addis Ababa, ETH, ecainfo@uneca.org, https://www.uneca.org/; African Statistical Yearbook 2020.

CONGO, REPUBLIC OF THE-CONSUMER PRICE INDEXES

Routledge - Taylor & Francis Group, 6000 Broken Sound Pkwy. NW, Ste. 300, Boca Raton, FL, 33487, USA, (800) 634-1420, (800) 634-7064, orders@taylorandfrancis.com, https://www.routledge.com/; The Europa World Year Book 2022.

United Nations Economic Commission for Africa (UNECA), PO Box 3001, Addis Ababa, ETH, ecainfo@uneca.org, https://www.uneca.org/; African Statistical Yearbook 2020.

The World Bank, 1818 H St. NW, Washington, DC, 20433, USA, (202) 473-1000, (202) 477-6391, eds03@worldbank.org, https://www.worldbank.org/; Congo, Republic of the (report).

CONGO, REPUBLIC OF THE-CONSUMPTION (ECONOMICS)

African Development Bank Group (AfDB), Avenue Joseph Anoma, 01 BP 1387, Abidjan, 01, COT, https://www.afdb.org; The AfDB Statistics Pocketbook 2019.

CONGO, REPUBLIC OF THE-CROPS

Palgrave Macmillan, 1 New York Plaza, Ste. 4500, New York, NY, 10004-1562, USA, (800) 777-4643, orders@palgrave.com, https://www.palgrave.com/us; The Statesman's Yearbook, 2023.

United Nations Economic Commission for Africa (UNECA), PO Box 3001, Addis Ababa, ETH, ecainfo@uneca.org, https://www.uneca.org/; African Statistical Yearbook 2020.

United Nations Food and Agricultural Organization (FAO), 2121 K St., Ste. 800B, Washington, DC, 20037, USA, (202) 653-2400 (Dial from U.S.), (202) 653-5760 (Fax from U.S.), fao-hq@fao.org, https://www.fao.org; The State of Food and Agriculture (SOFA) 2022.

United Nations Statistics Division (UNSD), United Nations Plz., New York, NY, 10017, USA, (800) 253-9646, (212) 963-9851, statistics@un.org, https://unstats.un.org; Statistical Yearbook of the United Nations 2021.

CONGO, REPUBLIC OF THE-DAIRY PROCESSING

Palgrave Macmillan, 1 New York Plaza, Ste. 4500, New York, NY, 10004-1562, USA, (800) 777-4643, orders@palgrave.com, https://www.palgrave.com/us; The Statesman's Yearbook, 2023.

United Nations Food and Agricultural Organization (FAO), 2121 K St., Ste. 800B, Washington, DC, 20037, USA, (202) 653-2400 (Dial from U.S.), (202) 653-5760 (Fax from U.S.), fao-hq@fao.org, https://www.fao.org; The State of Food and Agriculture (SOFA) 2022.

CONGO, REPUBLIC OF THE-DEBTS, EXTERNAL

African Development Bank Group (AfDB), Avenue Joseph Anoma, 01 BP 1387, Abidjan, 01, COT, https://www.afdb.org; The AfDB Statistics Pocketbook 2019; African Economic Outlook 2021; and Compendium of Statistics on Bank Group Operations 2019.

Palgrave Macmillan, 1 New York Plaza, Ste. 4500, New York, NY, 10004-1562, USA, (800) 777-4643, orders@palgrave.com, https://www.palgrave.com/us; The Statesman's Yearbook, 2023.

United Nations Economic Commission for Africa (UNECA), PO Box 3001, Addis Ababa, ETH, ecainfo@uneca.org, https://www.uneca.org/; Economic Report on Africa 2021.

The World Bank, 1818 H St. NW, Washington, DC, 20433, USA, (202) 473-1000, (202) 477-6391, eds03@worldbank.org, https://www.worldbank.org/; Global Financial Development Report 2019-2020: Bank Regulation and Supervision a Decade after the Global Financial Crisis; World Development Indicators (WDI) 2022; and World Development Report 2022: Finance for an Equitable Recovery.

CONGO, REPUBLIC OF THE-ECONOMIC ASSISTANCE

United Nations Statistics Division (UNSD), United Nations Plz., New York, NY, 10017, USA, (800) 253-9646, (212) 963-9851, statistics@un.org, https://unstats.un.org; Statistical Yearbook of the United Nations 2021.

CONGO, REPUBLIC OF THE-ECONOMIC CONDITIONS

African Development Bank Group (AfDB), Avenue Joseph Anoma, 01 BP 1387, Abidjan, 01, COT, https://www.afdb.org; The AfDB Statistics Pocketbook 2019; Africa Economic Brief - COVID-19 Pandemic Potential Risks for Trade and Trade Finance in Africa; African Economic Outlook 2021; The African Statistical Journal; Compendium of Statistics on Bank Group Operations 2019; and Gender, Poverty and Environmental Indicators on African Countries 2019.

Bernan Press, 15250 NBN Way, Bldg. C, Blue Ridge Summit, PA, 17214, USA, (301) 459-2255, (800) 865-3457, (800) 865-3450, customercare@bernan.com, https://rowman.com/Page/Bernan; World Economic Outlook, April 2022.

Central Intelligence Agency (CIA), Office of Public Affairs, Washington, DC, 20505, USA, (703) 482-0623, https://www.cia.gov; The World Factbook.

The Economist Group: Economist Intelligence Unit (EIU), 900 3rd Ave., 16th Fl., New York, NY, 10022, USA, (212) 541-0500, americas@eiu.com, https://www.eiu.com; Congo (Brazzaville) Country Report.

Euromonitor International, Inc., 1 N Dearborn St., Ste. 1700, Chicago, IL, 60602, USA, (312) 922-1115, (312) 922-1157, info-usa@euromonitor.com, https://www.euromonitor.com/; Geographies.

International Monetary Fund (IMF), 700 19th St. NW, Washington, DC, 20431, USA, (202) 623-7000, (202) 623-4661, publications@imf.org, https://www.imf.org; IMF Data and World Economic Outlook.

Palgrave Macmillan, 1 New York Plaza, Ste. 4500, New York, NY, 10004-1562, USA, (800) 777-4643, orders@palgrave.com, https://www.palgrave.com/us; The Statesman's Yearbook, 2023.

Routledge - Taylor & Francis Group, 6000 Broken Sound Pkwy. NW, Ste. 300, Boca Raton, FL, 33487, USA, (800) 634-1420, (800) 634-7064, orders@taylorandfrancis.com, https://www.routledge.com/; The Europa World Year Book 2022.

United Nations Economic Commission for Africa (UNECA), PO Box 3001, Addis Ababa, ETH, ecainfo@uneca.org, https://www.uneca.org/; Economic Report on Africa 2021.

United Nations Statistics Division (UNSD), United Nations Plz., New York, NY, 10017, USA, (800) 253-9646, (212) 963-9851, statistics@un.org, https://unstats.un.org; World Statistics Pocketbook 2021.

The World Bank, 1818 H St. NW, Washington, DC, 20433, USA, (202) 473-1000, (202) 477-6391, eds03@worldbank.org, https://www.worldbank.org/; Congo, Republic of the (report); Global Economic Monitor (GEM); Global Economic Prospects, June 2022; The Global Findex Database 2021; and World Development Report 2022: Finance for an Equitable Recovery.

CONGO, REPUBLIC OF THE-EDUCATION

African Development Bank Group (AfDB), Avenue Joseph Anoma, 01 BP 1387, Abidjan, 01, COT, https://www.afdb.org; The AfDB Statistics Pocketbook 2019.

Euromonitor International, Inc., 1 N Dearborn St., Ste. 1700, Chicago, IL, 60602, USA, (312) 922-1115, (312) 922-1157, info-usa@euromonitor.com, https://www.euromonitor.com/; Geographies.

Infoplease, c/o Sandbox Networks, Inc., 1 Lincoln St., 24th Fl., Boston, MA, 02111, USA, https://www.infoplease.com; Countries of the World.

Palgrave Macmillan, 1 New York Plaza, Ste. 4500, New York, NY, 10004-1562, USA, (800) 777-4643, orders@palgrave.com, https://www.palgrave.com/us; The Statesman's Yearbook, 2023.

Routledge - Taylor & Francis Group, 6000 Broken Sound Pkwy. NW, Ste. 300, Boca Raton, FL, 33487, USA, (800) 634-1420, (800) 634-7064, orders@taylorandfrancis.com, https://www.routledge.com/; The Europa World Year Book 2022.

UNESCO Institute for Statistics, C.P 250 Succursale H, Montreal, QC, H3G 2K8, CAN, (514) 343-6880 (Dial from U.S.), (514) 343-5740 (Fax from U.S.), uis.publications@unesco.org, http://uis.unesco.org/; Literacy and UIS.Stat.

United Nations Economic Commission for Africa (UNECA), PO Box 3001, Addis Ababa, ETH, ecainfo@uneca.org, https://www.uneca.org/; African Statistical Yearbook 2020.

United Nations Statistics Division (UNSD), United Nations Plz., New York, NY, 10017, USA, (800) 253-9646, (212) 963-9851, statistics@un.org, https://unstats.un.org; Millennium Development Goal Indicators.

The World Bank, 1818 H St. NW, Washington, DC, 20433, USA, (202) 473-1000, (202) 477-6391, eds03@worldbank.org, https://www.worldbank.org/; Congo, Republic of the (report); World Development Indicators (WDI) 2022; and World Development Report 2022: Finance for an Equitable Recovery.

CONGO, REPUBLIC OF THE-ELECTRICITY

International Energy Agency (IEA), 9 Rue de la Federation, Paris, 75739, FRA, info@iea.org, https://www.iea.org/; World Energy Outlook 2021.

U.S. Energy Information Administration (EIA), 1000 Independence Ave. SW, Washington, DC, 20585, USA, (202) 586-8800, infoctr@eia.gov, https://www.eia.gov; International Energy Outlook 2021.

United Nations Statistics Division (UNSD), United Nations Plz., New York, NY, 10017, USA, (800) 253-9646, (212) 963-9851, statistics@un.org, https://unstats.un.org; Statistical Yearbook of the United Nations 2021.

CONGO, REPUBLIC OF THE-EMPLOYMENT

International Labour Organization (ILO), 4 Rte. des Morillons, Geneva, CH-1211, SWI, ilo@ilo.org, https://www.ilo.org; NORMLEX Information System on International Labour Standards.

UK Data Service, University of Essex, Wivenhoe Park, Colchester, Essex, CO4 3SQ, GBR, https://ukdataservice.ac.uk/; International Aggregate Data.

United Nations Economic Commission for Africa (UNECA), PO Box 3001, Addis Ababa, ETH, ecainfo@uneca.org, https://www.uneca.org/; African Statistical Yearbook 2020.

United Nations Statistics Division (UNSD), United Nations Plz., New York, NY, 10017, USA, (800) 253-9646, (212) 963-9851, statistics@un.org, https://unstats.un.org; Statistical Yearbook of the United Nations 2021.

The World Bank, 1818 H St. NW, Washington, DC, 20433, USA, (202) 473-1000, (202) 477-6391, eds03@worldbank.org, https://www.worldbank.org/; Congo, Republic of the (report).

CONGO, REPUBLIC OF THE-ENVIRONMENTAL CONDITIONS

DSI Data Service & Information, Xantener Strasse 51a, Rheinberg, D-47495, GER, dsi@dsidata.com, https://www.dsidata.com/; Global Environmental Database.

The Economist Group: Economist Intelligence Unit (EIU), 900 3rd Ave., 16th Fl., New York, NY, 10022, USA, (212) 541-0500, americas@eiu.com, https://www.eiu.com; Congo (Brazzaville) Country Report.

United Nations Statistics Division (UNSD), United Nations Plz., New York, NY, 10017, USA, (800) 253-9646, (212) 963-9851, statistics@un.org, https://unstats.un.org; World Statistics Pocketbook 2021.

CONGO, REPUBLIC OF THE-EXPORTS

African Development Bank Group (AfDB), Avenue Joseph Anoma, 01 BP 1387, Abidjan, 01, COT, https://www.afdb.org; African Economic Outlook 2021.

Central Intelligence Agency (CIA), Office of Public Affairs, Washington, DC, 20505, USA, (703) 482-0623, https://www.cia.gov; The World Factbook.

The Economist Group: Economist Intelligence Unit (EIU), 900 3rd Ave., 16th Fl., New York, NY, 10022, USA, (212) 541-0500, americas@eiu.com, https://www.eiu.com; Congo (Brazzaville) Country Report.

International Monetary Fund (IMF), 700 19th St. NW, Washington, DC, 20431, USA, (202) 623-7000, (202) 623-4661, publications@imf.org, https://www.imf.org; Direction of Trade Statistics (DOTS).

S&P Global, IHS Markit, 15 Inverness Way E, Englewood, CO, 80112, USA, (800) 447-2273, (800) 854-7179, https://ihsmarkit.com; Global Trade Atlas (GTA).

United Nations Conference on Trade and Development (UNCTAD), Palais des Nations, Geneva, 1211, SWI, (212) 963-6896, unctadinfo@unctad.org, https://unctad.org; Handbook of Statistics 2021.

The World Bank, 1818 H St. NW, Washington, DC, 20433, USA, (202) 473-1000, (202) 477-6391, eds03@worldbank.org, https://www.worldbank.org/; World Development Report 2022: Finance for an Equitable Recovery.

CONGO, REPUBLIC OF THE-FERTILITY, HUMAN

Central Intelligence Agency (CIA), Office of Public Affairs, Washington, DC, 20505, USA, (703) 482-0623, https://www.cia.gov; The World Factbook.

CONGO, REPUBLIC OF THE-FERTILIZER INDUSTRY

United Nations Food and Agricultural Organization (FAO), 2121 K St., Ste. 800B, Washington, DC, 20037, USA, (202) 653-2400 (Dial from U.S.), (202) 653-5760 (Fax from U.S.), fao-hq@fao.org, https://www.fao.org; The State of Food and Agriculture (SOFA) 2022.

CONGO, REPUBLIC OF THE-FINANCE

Stockholm International Peace Research Institute (SIPRI), Signalistgatan 9, Stockholm, SE 169 72, SWE, https://www.sipri.org/; SIPRI Arms Transfers Database and SIPRI Military Expenditure Database.

United Nations Economic Commission for Africa (UNECA), PO Box 3001, Addis Ababa, ETH, ecainfo@uneca.org, https://www.uneca.org/; African Statistical Yearbook 2020.

United Nations Statistics Division (UNSD), United Nations Plz., New York, NY, 10017, USA, (800) 253-9646, (212) 963-9851, statistics@un.org, https://unstats.un.org; Statistical Yearbook of the United Nations 2021.

The World Bank, 1818 H St. NW, Washington, DC, 20433, USA, (202) 473-1000, (202) 477-6391, eds03@worldbank.org, https://www.worldbank.org/; Congo, Republic of the (report).

CONGO, REPUBLIC OF THE-FINANCE, PUBLIC

African Development Bank Group (AfDB), Avenue Joseph Anoma, 01 BP 1387, Abidjan, 01, COT, https://www.afdb.org; The AfDB Statistics Pocketbook 2019.

Bernan Press, 15250 NBN Way, Bldg. C, Blue Ridge Summit, PA, 17214, USA, (301) 459-2255, (800) 865-3457, (800) 865-3450, customercare@bernan.com, https://rowman.com/Page/Bernan; National Accounts Statistics: Analysis of Main Aggregates 2020.

The Economist Group: Economist Intelligence Unit (EIU), 900 3rd Ave., 16th Fl., New York, NY, 10022, USA, (212) 541-0500, americas@eiu.com, https://www.eiu.com; Congo (Brazzaville) Country Report.

International Monetary Fund (IMF), 700 19th St. NW, Washington, DC, 20431, USA, (202) 623-7000, (202) 623-4661, publications@imf.org, https://www.imf.org; International Financial Statistics (IFS) and Regional Economic Outlook.

Palgrave Macmillan, 1 New York Plaza, Ste. 4500, New York, NY, 10004-1562, USA, (800) 777-4643, orders@palgrave.com, https://www.palgrave.com/us; The Statesman's Yearbook, 2023.

Routledge - Taylor & Francis Group, 6000 Broken Sound Pkwy. NW, Ste. 300, Boca Raton, FL, 33487, USA, (800) 634-1420, (800) 634-7064, orders@taylorandfrancis.com, https://www.routledge.com/; The Europa World Year Book 2022.

United Nations Economic Commission for Africa (UNECA), PO Box 3001, Addis Ababa, ETH, ecainfo@uneca.org, https://www.uneca.org/; African Statistical Yearbook 2020.

United Nations Statistics Division (UNSD), United Nations Plz., New York, NY, 10017, USA, (800) 253-9646, (212) 963-9851, statistics@un.org, https://unstats.un.org; National Accounts Main Aggregates Database and National Accounts Statistics: Main Aggregates and Detailed Tables.

The World Bank, 1818 H St. NW, Washington, DC, 20433, USA, (202) 473-1000, (202) 477-6391, eds03@worldbank.org, https://www.worldbank.org/; Congo, Republic of the (report).

CONGO, REPUBLIC OF THE-FISHERIES

Palgrave Macmillan, 1 New York Plaza, Ste. 4500, New York, NY, 10004-1562, USA, (800) 777-4643, orders@palgrave.com, https://www.palgrave.com/us; The Statesman's Yearbook, 2023.

Routledge - Taylor & Francis Group, 6000 Broken Sound Pkwy. NW, Ste. 300, Boca Raton, FL, 33487, USA, (800) 634-1420, (800) 634-7064, orders@taylorandfrancis.com, https://www.routledge.com/; The Europa World Year Book 2022.

United Nations Economic Commission for Africa (UNECA), PO Box 3001, Addis Ababa, ETH, ecainfo@uneca.org, https://www.uneca.org/; African Statistical Yearbook 2020.

United Nations Food and Agricultural Organization (FAO), 2121 K St., Ste. 800B, Washington, DC, 20037, USA, (202) 653-2400 (Dial from U.S.), (202) 653-5760 (Fax from U.S.), fao-hq@fao.org, https://www.fao.org; FAO Yearbook of Fishery and Aquaculture Statistics 2019; Fishery Statistical Collections Global Capture Production; FishStatJ; and The State of Food and Agriculture (SOFA) 2022.

United Nations Statistics Division (UNSD), United Nations Plz., New York, NY, 10017, USA, (800) 253-9646, (212) 963-9851, statistics@un.org, https://unstats.un.org; Statistical Yearbook of the United Nations 2021.

The World Bank, 1818 H St. NW, Washington, DC, 20433, USA, (202) 473-1000, (202) 477-6391, eds03@worldbank.org, https://www.worldbank.org/; Congo, Republic of the (report).

CONGO, REPUBLIC OF THE-FOOD

African Development Bank Group (AfDB), Avenue Joseph Anoma, 01 BP 1387, Abidjan, 01, COT, https://www.afdb.org; The AfDB Statistics Pocketbook 2019.

United Nations Food and Agricultural Organization (FAO), 2121 K St., Ste. 800B, Washington, DC, 20037, USA, (202) 653-2400 (Dial from U.S.), (202) 653-5760 (Fax from U.S.), fao-hq@fao.org, https://www.fao.org; The State of Food and Agriculture (SOFA) 2022.

CONGO, REPUBLIC OF THE-FOREIGN EXCHANGE RATES

African Development Bank Group (AfDB), Avenue Joseph Anoma, 01 BP 1387, Abidjan, 01, COT, https://www.afdb.org; The AfDB Statistics Pocketbook 2019 and African Economic Outlook 2021.

CONGO, REPUBLIC OF THE-FORESTS AND FORESTRY

International Monetary Fund (IMF), 700 19th St. NW, Washington, DC, 20431, USA, (202) 623-7000, (202) 623-4661, publications@imf.org, https://www.imf.org; International Financial Statistics (IFS).

Palgrave Macmillan, 1 New York Plaza, Ste. 4500, New York, NY, 10004-1562, USA, (800) 777-4643, orders@palgrave.com, https://www.palgrave.com/us; The Statesman's Yearbook, 2023.

Routledge - Taylor & Francis Group, 6000 Broken Sound Pkwy. NW, Ste. 300, Boca Raton, FL, 33487, USA, (800) 634-1420, (800) 634-7064, orders@taylorandfrancis.com, https://www.routledge.com/; The Europa World Year Book 2022.

UNESCO Institute for Statistics, C.P 250 Succursale H, Montreal, QC, H3G 2K8, CAN, (514) 343-6880 (Dial from U.S.), (514) 343-5740 (Fax from U.S.), uis.publications@unesco.org, http://uis.unesco.org/; UIS.Stat.

United Nations Economic Commission for Africa (UNECA), PO Box 3001, Addis Ababa, ETH, ecainfo@uneca.org, https://www.uneca.org/; African Statistical Yearbook 2020.

United Nations Food and Agricultural Organization (FAO), 2121 K St., Ste. 800B, Washington, DC, 20037, USA, (202) 653-2400 (Dial from U.S.), (202) 653-5760 (Fax from U.S.), fao-hq@fao.org, https://www.fao.org; FAO Yearbook of Forest Products 2019 and The State of Food and Agriculture (SOFA) 2022.

The World Bank, 1818 H St. NW, Washington, DC, 20433, USA, (202) 473-1000, (202) 477-6391, eds03@worldbank.org, https://www.worldbank.org/; Congo, Republic of the (report) and World Development Report 2022: Finance for an Equitable Recovery.

CONGO, REPUBLIC OF THE-GEOGRAPHIC INFORMATION SYSTEMS

The World Bank, 1818 H St. NW, Washington, DC, 20433, USA, (202) 473-1000, (202) 477-6391, eds03@worldbank.org, https://www.worldbank.org/; Congo, Republic of the (report).

CONGO, REPUBLIC OF THE-GOLD INDUSTRY

The World Bank, 1818 H St. NW, Washington, DC, 20433, USA, (202) 473-1000, (202) 477-6391, eds03@worldbank.org, https://www.worldbank.org/; World Development Indicators (WDI) 2022.

CONGO, REPUBLIC OF THE-GROSS DOMESTIC PRODUCT

African Development Bank Group (AfDB), Avenue Joseph Anoma, 01 BP 1387, Abidjan, 01, COT, https://www.afdb.org; The AfDB Statistics Pocketbook 2019.

The Economist Group: Economist Intelligence Unit (EIU), 900 3rd Ave., 16th Fl., New York, NY, 10022, USA, (212) 541-0500, americas@eiu.com, https://www.eiu.com; Congo (Brazzaville) Country Report.

Routledge - Taylor & Francis Group, 6000 Broken Sound Pkwy. NW, Ste. 300, Boca Raton, FL, 33487, USA, (800) 634-1420, (800) 634-7064, orders@taylorandfrancis.com, https://www.routledge.com/; The Europa World Year Book 2022.

United Nations Economic Commission for Africa (UNECA), PO Box 3001, Addis Ababa, ETH, ecainfo@uneca.org, https://www.uneca.org/; African Statistical Yearbook 2020.

United Nations Statistics Division (UNSD), United Nations Plz., New York, NY, 10017, USA, (800) 253-9646, (212) 963-9851, statistics@un.org, https://unstats.un.org; Statistical Yearbook of the United Nations 2021.

The World Bank, 1818 H St. NW, Washington, DC, 20433, USA, (202) 473-1000, (202) 477-6391, eds03@worldbank.org, https://www.worldbank.org/; World Development Indicators (WDI) 2022 and World Development Report 2022: Finance for an Equitable Recovery.

CONGO, REPUBLIC OF THE-GROSS NATIONAL PRODUCT

Palgrave Macmillan, 1 New York Plaza, Ste. 4500, New York, NY, 10004-1562, USA, (800) 777-4643, orders@palgrave.com, https://www.palgrave.com/us; The Statesman's Yearbook, 2023.

Routledge - Taylor & Francis Group, 6000 Broken Sound Pkwy. NW, Ste. 300, Boca Raton, FL, 33487, USA, (800) 634-1420, (800) 634-7064, orders@taylorandfrancis.com, https://www.routledge.com/; The Europa World Year Book 2022.

The World Bank, 1818 H St. NW, Washington, DC, 20433, USA, (202) 473-1000, (202) 477-6391, eds03@worldbank.org, https://www.worldbank.org/; World Development Indicators (WDI) 2022 and World Development Report 2022: Finance for an Equitable Recovery.

CONGO, REPUBLIC OF THE-HOUSING

Euromonitor International, Inc., 1 N Dearborn St., Ste. 1700, Chicago, IL, 60602, USA, (312) 922-1115, (312) 922-1157, info-usa@euromonitor.com, https://www.euromonitor.com/; Geographies.

United Nations Statistics Division (UNSD), United Nations Plz., New York, NY, 10017, USA, (800) 253-9646, (212) 963-9851, statistics@un.org, https://unstats.un.org; Statistical Yearbook of the United Nations 2021.

CONGO, REPUBLIC OF THE-ILLITERATE PERSONS

UNESCO Institute for Statistics, C.P 250 Succursale H, Montreal, QC, H3G 2K8, CAN, (514) 343-6880 (Dial from U.S.), (514) 343-5740 (Fax from U.S.), uis.publications@unesco.org, http://uis.unesco.org/; UIS.Stat.

CONGO, REPUBLIC OF THE-IMPORTS

African Development Bank Group (AfDB), Avenue Joseph Anoma, 01 BP 1387, Abidjan, 01, COT, https://www.afdb.org; African Economic Outlook 2021.

Central Intelligence Agency (CIA), Office of Public Affairs, Washington, DC, 20505, USA, (703) 482-0623, https://www.cia.gov; The World Factbook.

The Economist Group: Economist Intelligence Unit (EIU), 900 3rd Ave., 16th Fl., New York, NY, 10022, USA, (212) 541-0500, americas@eiu.com, https://www.eiu.com; Congo (Brazzaville) Country Report.

Euromonitor International, Inc., 1 N Dearborn St., Ste. 1700, Chicago, IL, 60602, USA, (312) 922-1115, (312) 922-1157, info-usa@euromonitor.com, https://www.euromonitor.com/; Geographies.

International Monetary Fund (IMF), 700 19th St. NW, Washington, DC, 20431, USA, (202) 623-7000, (202) 623-4661, publications@imf.org, https://www.imf.org; Direction of Trade Statistics (DOTS).

S&P Global, IHS Markit, 15 Inverness Way E, Englewood, CO, 80112, USA, (800) 447-2273, (800) 854-7179, https://ihsmarkit.com; Global Trade Atlas (GTA).

The World Bank, 1818 H St. NW, Washington, DC, 20433, USA, (202) 473-1000, (202) 477-6391, eds03@worldbank.org, https://www.worldbank.org/; World Development Report 2022: Finance for an Equitable Recovery.

CONGO, REPUBLIC OF THE-INDUSTRIES

Central Intelligence Agency (CIA), Office of Public Affairs, Washington, DC, 20505, USA, (703) 482-0623, https://www.cia.gov; The World Factbook.

The Economist Group: Economist Intelligence Unit (EIU), 900 3rd Ave., 16th Fl., New York, NY, 10022, USA, (212) 541-0500, americas@eiu.com, https://www.eiu.com; Congo (Brazzaville) Country Report.

Euromonitor International, Inc., 1 N Dearborn St., Ste. 1700, Chicago, IL, 60602, USA, (312) 922-1115, (312) 922-1157, info-usa@euromonitor.com, https://www.euromonitor.com/; Geographies.

International Labour Organization (ILO), 4 Rte. des Morillons, Geneva, CH-1211, SWI, ilo@ilo.org, https://www.ilo.org; NORMLEX Information System on International Labour Standards.

Palgrave Macmillan, 1 New York Plaza, Ste. 4500, New York, NY, 10004-1562, USA, (800) 777-4643, orders@palgrave.com, https://www.palgrave.com/us; The Statesman's Yearbook, 2023.

Routledge - Taylor & Francis Group, 6000 Broken Sound Pkwy. NW, Ste. 300, Boca Raton, FL, 33487, USA, (800) 634-1420, (800) 634-7064, orders@taylorandfrancis.com, https://www.routledge.com/; The Europa World Year Book 2022.

United Nations Economic Commission for Africa (UNECA), PO Box 3001, Addis Ababa, ETH, ecainfo@uneca.org, https://www.uneca.org/; African Statistical Yearbook 2020.

United Nations Industrial Development Organization (UNIDO), 1 United Nations Plz., Rm. DC1-1118, New York, NY, 10017, USA, (212) 963-6890, (212) 963 6885, (212) 963-7904, office.newyork@unido.org, https://www.unido.org/; Industrial Statistics Databases and International Yearbook of Industrial Statistics 2021.

The World Bank, 1818 H St. NW, Washington, DC, 20433, USA, (202) 473-1000, (202) 477-6391, eds03@worldbank.org, https://www.worldbank.org/; Congo, Republic of the (report) and World Development Indicators (WDI) 2022.

CONGO, REPUBLIC OF THE-INTERNATIONAL TRADE

African Development Bank Group (AfDB), Avenue Joseph Anoma, 01 BP 1387, Abidjan, 01, COT, https://www.afdb.org; The AfDB Statistics Pocketbook 2019 and African Economic Outlook 2021.

The Economist Group: Economist Intelligence Unit (EIU), 900 3rd Ave., 16th Fl., New York, NY, 10022, USA, (212) 541-0500, americas@eiu.com, https://www.eiu.com; Congo (Brazzaville) Country Report.

Euromonitor International, Inc., 1 N Dearborn St., Ste. 1700, Chicago, IL, 60602, USA, (312) 922-1115, (312) 922-1157, info-usa@euromonitor.com, https://www.euromonitor.com/; Geographies.

Palgrave Macmillan, 1 New York Plaza, Ste. 4500, New York, NY, 10004-1562, USA, (800) 777-4643, orders@palgrave.com, https://www.palgrave.com/us; The Statesman's Yearbook, 2023.

Routledge - Taylor & Francis Group, 6000 Broken Sound Pkwy. NW, Ste. 300, Boca Raton, FL, 33487, USA, (800) 634-1420, (800) 634-7064, orders@taylorandfrancis.com, https://www.routledge.com/; The Europa World Year Book 2022.

United Nations Conference on Trade and Development (UNCTAD), Palais des Nations, Geneva, 1211, SWI, (212) 963-6896, unctadinfo@unctad.org, https://unctad.org; Trade and Development Report 2021.

United Nations Economic Commission for Africa (UNECA), PO Box 3001, Addis Ababa, ETH, ecainfo@uneca.org, https://www.uneca.org/; African Statistical Yearbook 2020.

United Nations Food and Agricultural Organization (FAO), 2121 K St., Ste. 800B, Washington, DC, 20037, USA, (202) 653-2400 (Dial from U.S.), (202) 653-5760 (Fax from U.S.), fao-hq@fao.org, https://www.fao.org; The State of Food and Agriculture (SOFA) 2022.

United Nations Statistics Division (UNSD), United Nations Plz., New York, NY, 10017, USA, (800) 253-9646, (212) 963-9851, statistics@un.org, https://unstats.un.org; International Trade Statistics Yearbook 2020 and Statistical Yearbook of the United Nations 2021.

The World Bank, 1818 H St. NW, Washington, DC, 20433, USA, (202) 473-1000, (202) 477-6391, eds03@worldbank.org, https://www.worldbank.org/; Congo, Republic of the (report); World Development Indicators (WDI) 2022; and World Development Report 2022: Finance for an Equitable Recovery.

World Trade Organization (WTO), Ctre. William Rappard, Rue de Lausanne 154, Case postale, Geneva, CH-1211, SWI, enquiries@wto.org, https://www.wto.org; World Trade Statistical Review 2022.

CONGO, REPUBLIC OF THE-INTERNET USERS

International Telecommunication Union (ITU), Place des Nations, Geneva, CH-1211, SWI, itumail@itu.int, https://www.itu.int; Global Connectivity Report 2022; World Telecommunication/ICT Indicators Database 2021; and Yearbook of Statistics 2019.

The World Bank, 1818 H St. NW, Washington, DC, 20433, USA, (202) 473-1000, (202) 477-6391, eds03@worldbank.org, https://www.worldbank.org/; Congo, Republic of the (report).

CONGO, REPUBLIC OF THE-LABOR

African Development Bank Group (AfDB), Avenue Joseph Anoma, 01 BP 1387, Abidjan, 01, COT, https://www.afdb.org; The AfDB Statistics Pocketbook 2019.

Central Intelligence Agency (CIA), Office of Public Affairs, Washington, DC, 20505, USA, (703) 482-0623, https://www.cia.gov; The World Factbook.

Euromonitor International, Inc., 1 N Dearborn St., Ste. 1700, Chicago, IL, 60602, USA, (312) 922-1115, (312) 922-1157, info-usa@euromonitor.com, https://www.euromonitor.com/; Geographies.

International Labour Organization (ILO), 4 Rte. des Morillons, Geneva, CH-1211, SWI, ilo@ilo.org, https://www.ilo.org; NORMLEX Information System on International Labour Standards.

Palgrave Macmillan, 1 New York Plaza, Ste. 4500, New York, NY, 10004-1562, USA, (800) 777-4643, orders@palgrave.com, https://www.palgrave.com/us; The Statesman's Yearbook, 2023.

United Nations Food and Agricultural Organization (FAO), 2121 K St., Ste. 800B, Washington, DC, 20037, USA, (202) 653-2400 (Dial from U.S.), (202) 653-5760 (Fax from U.S.), fao-hq@fao.org, https://www.fao.org; The State of Food and Agriculture (SOFA) 2022.

The World Bank, 1818 H St. NW, Washington, DC, 20433, USA, (202) 473-1000, (202) 477-6391, eds03@worldbank.org, https://www.worldbank.org/; World Development Indicators (WDI) 2022 and World Development Report 2022: Finance for an Equitable Recovery.

CONGO, REPUBLIC OF THE-LAND USE

United Nations Statistics Division (UNSD), United Nations Plz., New York, NY, 10017, USA, (800) 253-9646, (212) 963-9851, statistics@un.org, https://unstats.un.org; Millennium Development Goal Indicators.

The World Bank, 1818 H St. NW, Washington, DC, 20433, USA, (202) 473-1000, (202) 477-6391, eds03@worldbank.org, https://www.worldbank.org/; World Development Report 2022: Finance for an Equitable Recovery.

CONGO, REPUBLIC OF THE-LIFE EXPECTANCY

African Development Bank Group (AfDB), Avenue Joseph Anoma, 01 BP 1387, Abidjan, 01, COT, https://www.afdb.org; The AfDB Statistics Pocketbook 2019.

Central Intelligence Agency (CIA), Office of Public Affairs, Washington, DC, 20505, USA, (703) 482-0623, https://www.cia.gov; The World Factbook.

United Nations Department of Economic and Social Affairs (DESA), Population Division, 2 United Nations Plz., Rm. DC2-1950, New York, NY, 10017, USA, (212) 963-3209, (212) 963-2147, population@un.org, https://www.un.org/development/desa/pd/; World Population Ageing 2020 Highlights.

United Nations Statistics Division (UNSD), United Nations Plz., New York, NY, 10017, USA, (800) 253-9646, (212) 963-9851, statistics@un.org, https://unstats.un.org; Millennium Development Goal Indicators.

CONGO, REPUBLIC OF THE-LITERACY

Euromonitor International, Inc., 1 N Dearborn St., Ste. 1700, Chicago, IL, 60602, USA, (312) 922-1115, (312) 922-1157, info-usa@euromonitor.com, https://www.euromonitor.com/; Geographies.

UNESCO Institute for Statistics, C.P 250 Succursale H, Montreal, QC, H3G 2K8, CAN, (514) 343-6880 (Dial from U.S.), (514) 343-5740 (Fax from U.S.), uis.publications@unesco.org, http://uis.unesco.org/; Literacy.

CONGO, REPUBLIC OF THE-LIVESTOCK

Palgrave Macmillan, 1 New York Plaza, Ste. 4500, New York, NY, 10004-1562, USA, (800) 777-4643, orders@palgrave.com, https://www.palgrave.com/us; The Statesman's Yearbook, 2023.

Routledge - Taylor & Francis Group, 6000 Broken Sound Pkwy. NW, Ste. 300, Boca Raton, FL, 33487, USA, (800) 634-1420, (800) 634-7064, orders@taylorandfrancis.com, https://www.routledge.com/; The Europa World Year Book 2022.

United Nations Economic Commission for Africa (UNECA), PO Box 3001, Addis Ababa, ETH, ecainfo@uneca.org, https://www.uneca.org/; African Statistical Yearbook 2020.

United Nations Food and Agricultural Organization (FAO), 2121 K St., Ste. 800B, Washington, DC, 20037, USA, (202) 653-2400 (Dial from U.S.), (202) 653-5760 (Fax from U.S.), fao-hq@fao.org, https://www.fao.org; The State of Food and Agriculture (SOFA) 2022.

United Nations Statistics Division (UNSD), United Nations Plz., New York, NY, 10017, USA, (800) 253-9646, (212) 963-9851, statistics@un.org, https://unstats.un.org; Statistical Yearbook of the United Nations 2021.

CONGO, REPUBLIC OF THE-MARRIAGE

United Nations Statistics Division (UNSD), United Nations Plz., New York, NY, 10017, USA, (800) 253-9646, (212) 963-9851, statistics@un.org, https://unstats.un.org; Statistical Yearbook of the United Nations 2021.

CONGO, REPUBLIC OF THE-MINERAL INDUSTRIES

International Energy Agency (IEA), 9 Rue de la Federation, Paris, 75739, FRA, info@iea.org, https://www.iea.org/; World Energy Outlook 2021.

Palgrave Macmillan, 1 New York Plaza, Ste. 4500, New York, NY, 10004-1562, USA, (800) 777-4643, orders@palgrave.com, https://www.palgrave.com/us; The Statesman's Yearbook, 2023.

Routledge - Taylor & Francis Group, 6000 Broken Sound Pkwy. NW, Ste. 300, Boca Raton, FL, 33487, USA, (800) 634-1420, (800) 634-7064, orders@taylorandfrancis.com, https://www.routledge.com/; The Europa World Year Book 2022.

United Nations Conference on Trade and Development (UNCTAD), Palais des Nations, Geneva, 1211,

SWI, (212) 963-6896, unctadinfo@unctad.org, https://unctad.org; Trade and Development Report 2021.

United Nations Economic Commission for Africa (UNECA), PO Box 3001, Addis Ababa, ETH, ecainfo@uneca.org, https://www.uneca.org/; African Statistical Yearbook 2020.

United Nations Statistics Division (UNSD), United Nations Plz., New York, NY, 10017, USA, (800) 253-9646, (212) 963-9851, statistics@un.org, https://unstats.un.org; Statistical Yearbook of the United Nations 2021.

CONGO, REPUBLIC OF THE-MONEY SUPPLY

The Economist Group: Economist Intelligence Unit (EIU), 900 3rd Ave., 16th Fl., New York, NY, 10022, USA, (212) 541-0500, americas@eiu.com, https://www.eiu.com; Congo (Brazzaville) Country Report.

Routledge - Taylor & Francis Group, 6000 Broken Sound Pkwy. NW, Ste. 300, Boca Raton, FL, 33487, USA, (800) 634-1420, (800) 634-7064, orders@taylorandfrancis.com, https://www.routledge.com/; The Europa World Year Book 2022.

United Nations Statistics Division (UNSD), United Nations Plz., New York, NY, 10017, USA, (800) 253-9646, (212) 963-9851, statistics@un.org, https://unstats.un.org; Statistical Yearbook of the United Nations 2021.

The World Bank, 1818 H St. NW, Washington, DC, 20433, USA, (202) 473-1000, (202) 477-6391, eds03@worldbank.org, https://www.worldbank.org/; Congo, Republic of the (report).

CONGO, REPUBLIC OF THE-MORTALITY

UNICEF, 3 United Nations Plz., New York, NY, 10017, USA, (212) 303-7984, (917) 244-2215, https://www.unicef.org; The State of the World's Children 2023.

United Nations Statistics Division (UNSD), United Nations Plz., New York, NY, 10017, USA, (800) 253-9646, (212) 963-9851, statistics@un.org, https://unstats.un.org; Millennium Development Goal Indicators; Statistical Yearbook of the United Nations 2021; and World Statistics Pocketbook 2021.

The World Bank, 1818 H St. NW, Washington, DC, 20433, USA, (202) 473-1000, (202) 477-6391, eds03@worldbank.org, https://www.worldbank.org/; World Development Indicators (WDI) 2022.

World Health Organization (WHO), Ave. Appia 20, Geneva, CH-1211, SWI, (202) 974-3000 (Telephone in U.S.), publications@who.int, https://www.who.int/; Global Health Observatory (GHO) and Health Statistics and Information Systems.

CONGO, REPUBLIC OF THE-MOTOR VEHICLES

International Road Federation (IRF), Madison Place, 500 Montgomery St., 5th Fl., Alexandria, VA, 22314, USA, (703) 535-1001, (703) 535-1007, info@irf.global, https://www.irf.global/; World Road Statistics (WRS).

CONGO, REPUBLIC OF THE-NUTRITION

United Nations Food and Agricultural Organization (FAO), 2121 K St., Ste. 800B, Washington, DC, 20037, USA, (202) 653-2400 (Dial from U.S.), (202) 653-5760 (Fax from U.S.), fao-hq@fao.org, https://www.fao.org; The State of Food and Agriculture (SOFA) 2022.

United Nations Statistics Division (UNSD), United Nations Plz., New York, NY, 10017, USA, (800) 253-9646, (212) 963-9851, statistics@un.org, https://unstats.un.org; Millennium Development Goal Indicators.

CONGO, REPUBLIC OF THE-PESTICIDES

United Nations Food and Agricultural Organization (FAO), 2121 K St., Ste. 800B, Washington, DC, 20037, USA, (202) 653-2400 (Dial from U.S.), (202) 653-5760 (Fax from U.S.), fao-hq@fao.org, https://www.fao.org; The State of Food and Agriculture (SOFA) 2022.

CONGO, REPUBLIC OF THE-PETROLEUM INDUSTRY AND TRADE

International Energy Agency (IEA), 9 Rue de la Federation, Paris, 75739, FRA, info@iea.org, https://www.iea.org/; World Energy Outlook 2021.

International Monetary Fund (IMF), 700 19th St. NW, Washington, DC, 20431, USA, (202) 623-7000, (202) 623-4661, publications@imf.org, https://www.imf.org; International Financial Statistics (IFS).

U.S. Energy Information Administration (EIA), 1000 Independence Ave. SW, Washington, DC, 20585, USA, (202) 586-8800, infoctr@eia.gov, https://www.eia.gov; International Energy Outlook 2021.

United Nations Food and Agricultural Organization (FAO), 2121 K St., Ste. 800B, Washington, DC, 20037, USA, (202) 653-2400 (Dial from U.S.), (202) 653-5760 (Fax from U.S.), fao-hq@fao.org, https://www.fao.org; The State of Food and Agriculture (SOFA) 2022.

United Nations Statistics Division (UNSD), United Nations Plz., New York, NY, 10017, USA, (800) 253-9646, (212) 963-9851, statistics@un.org, https://unstats.un.org; Statistical Yearbook of the United Nations 2021.

CONGO, REPUBLIC OF THE-POPULATION

African Development Bank Group (AfDB), Avenue Joseph Anoma, 01 BP 1387, Abidjan, 01, COT, https://www.afdb.org; The AfDB Statistics Pocketbook 2019; Africa Economic Brief - COVID-19 Pandemic Potential Risks for Trade and Trade Finance in Africa; The African Statistical Journal; and Gender, Poverty and Environmental Indicators on African Countries 2019.

Central Intelligence Agency (CIA), Office of Public Affairs, Washington, DC, 20505, USA, (703) 482-0623, https://www.cia.gov; The World Factbook.

The Economist Group: Economist Intelligence Unit (EIU), 900 3rd Ave., 16th Fl., New York, NY, 10022, USA, (212) 541-0500, americas@eiu.com, https://www.eiu.com; Congo (Brazzaville) Country Report.

European Commission, Eurostat, Luxembourg, 2920, LUX, https://ec.europa.eu/eurostat/; EU in the World 2020.

Infoplease, c/o Sandbox Networks, Inc., 1 Lincoln St., 24th Fl., Boston, MA, 02111, USA, https://www.infoplease.com; Countries of the World.

International Labour Organization (ILO), 4 Rte. des Morillons, Geneva, CH-1211, SWI, ilo@ilo.org, https://www.ilo.org; NORMLEX Information System on International Labour Standards.

Palgrave Macmillan, 1 New York Plaza, Ste. 4500, New York, NY, 10004-1562, USA, (800) 777-4643, orders@palgrave.com, https://www.palgrave.com/us; The Statesman's Yearbook, 2023.

Routledge - Taylor & Francis Group, 6000 Broken Sound Pkwy. NW, Ste. 300, Boca Raton, FL, 33487, USA, (800) 634-1420, (800) 634-7064, orders@taylorandfrancis.com, https://www.routledge.com/; The Europa World Year Book 2022.

UK Data Service, University of Essex, Wivenhoe Park, Colchester, Essex, CO4 3SQ, GBR, https://ukdataservice.ac.uk/; International Aggregate Data.

UNESCO Institute for Statistics, C.P 250 Succursale H, Montreal, QC, H3G 2K8, CAN, (514) 343-6880 (Dial from U.S.), (514) 343-5740 (Fax from U.S.), uis.publications@unesco.org, http://uis.unesco.org/; UIS.Stat.

United Nations Department of Economic and Social Affairs (DESA), Population Division, 2 United Nations Plz., Rm. DC2-1950, New York, NY, 10017, USA, (212) 963-3209, (212) 963-2147, population@un.org, https://www.un.org/development/desa/pd/; Revision of World Urbanization Prospects and World Population Ageing 2020 Highlights.

United Nations Development Programme (UNDP), One United Nations Plz., New York, NY, 10017, USA, (212) 906-5000, (212) 906-5001, https://www.undp.org; Human Development Report 2021-2022.

United Nations Statistics Division (UNSD), United Nations Plz., New York, NY, 10017, USA, (800) 253-9646, (212) 963-9851, statistics@un.org, https://unstats.un.org; Statistical Yearbook of the United Nations 2021 and World Statistics Pocketbook 2021.

The World Bank, 1818 H St. NW, Washington, DC, 20433, USA, (202) 473-1000, (202) 477-6391, eds03@worldbank.org, https://www.worldbank.org/; Congo, Republic of the (report); The Global Findex Database 2021; and World Development Report 2022: Finance for an Equitable Recovery.

World Health Organization (WHO), Ave. Appia 20, Geneva, CH-1211, SWI, (202) 974-3000 (Telephone in U.S.), publications@who.int, https://www.who.int/; Health Statistics and Information Systems.

CONGO, REPUBLIC OF THE-POPULATION DENSITY

African Development Bank Group (AfDB), Avenue Joseph Anoma, 01 BP 1387, Abidjan, 01, COT, https://www.afdb.org; The AfDB Statistics Pocketbook 2019.

Central Intelligence Agency (CIA), Office of Public Affairs, Washington, DC, 20505, USA, (703) 482-0623, https://www.cia.gov; The World Factbook.

Palgrave Macmillan, 1 New York Plaza, Ste. 4500, New York, NY, 10004-1562, USA, (800) 777-4643, orders@palgrave.com, https://www.palgrave.com/us; The Statesman's Yearbook, 2023.

Routledge - Taylor & Francis Group, 6000 Broken Sound Pkwy. NW, Ste. 300, Boca Raton, FL, 33487, USA, (800) 634-1420, (800) 634-7064, orders@taylorandfrancis.com, https://www.routledge.com/; The Europa World Year Book 2022.

UNESCO Institute for Statistics, C.P 250 Succursale H, Montreal, QC, H3G 2K8, CAN, (514) 343-6880 (Dial from U.S.), (514) 343-5740 (Fax from U.S.), uis.publications@unesco.org, http://uis.unesco.org/; UIS.Stat.

The World Bank, 1818 H St. NW, Washington, DC, 20433, USA, (202) 473-1000, (202) 477-6391, eds03@worldbank.org, https://www.worldbank.org/; Congo, Republic of the (report) and World Development Report 2022: Finance for an Equitable Recovery.

CONGO, REPUBLIC OF THE-POWER RESOURCES

Euromonitor International, Inc., 1 N Dearborn St., Ste. 1700, Chicago, IL, 60602, USA, (312) 922-1115, (312) 922-1157, info-usa@euromonitor.com, https://www.euromonitor.com/; Geographies.

International Energy Agency (IEA), 9 Rue de la Federation, Paris, 75739, FRA, info@iea.org, https://www.iea.org/; World Energy Outlook 2021.

Palgrave Macmillan, 1 New York Plaza, Ste. 4500, New York, NY, 10004-1562, USA, (800) 777-4643, orders@palgrave.com, https://www.palgrave.com/us; The Statesman's Yearbook, 2023.

U.S. Energy Information Administration (EIA), 1000 Independence Ave. SW, Washington, DC, 20585, USA, (202) 586-8800, infoctr@eia.gov, https://www.eia.gov; International Energy Outlook 2021.

United Nations Economic Commission for Africa (UNECA), PO Box 3001, Addis Ababa, ETH, ecainfo@uneca.org, https://www.uneca.org/; African Statistical Yearbook 2020.

United Nations Food and Agricultural Organization (FAO), 2121 K St., Ste. 800B, Washington, DC, 20037, USA, (202) 653-2400 (Dial from U.S.), (202) 653-5760 (Fax from U.S.), fao-hq@fao.org, https://www.fao.org; The State of Food and Agriculture (SOFA) 2022.

United Nations Statistics Division (UNSD), United Nations Plz., New York, NY, 10017, USA, (800) 253-9646, (212) 963-9851, statistics@un.org, https://unstats.un.org; Energy Statistics Yearbook 2019; Statistical Yearbook of the United Nations 2021; and World Statistics Pocketbook 2021.

The World Bank, 1818 H St. NW, Washington, DC, 20433, USA, (202) 473-1000, (202) 477-6391,

eds03@worldbank.org, https://www.worldbank.org/; World Development Report 2022: Finance for an Equitable Recovery.

CONGO, REPUBLIC OF THE-PRICES

Euromonitor International, Inc., 1 N Dearborn St., Ste. 1700, Chicago, IL, 60602, USA, (312) 922-1115, (312) 922-1157, info-usa@euromonitor.com, https://www.euromonitor.com/; Geographies.

International Monetary Fund (IMF), 700 19th St. NW, Washington, DC, 20431, USA, (202) 623-7000, (202) 623-4661, publications@imf.org, https://www.imf.org; International Financial Statistics (IFS).

United Nations Economic Commission for Africa (UNECA), PO Box 3001, Addis Ababa, ETH, ecainfo@uneca.org, https://www.uneca.org/; African Statistical Yearbook 2020.

The World Bank, 1818 H St. NW, Washington, DC, 20433, USA, (202) 473-1000, (202) 477-6391, eds03@worldbank.org, https://www.worldbank.org/; Congo, Republic of the (report).

CONGO, REPUBLIC OF THE-PUBLIC HEALTH

African Development Bank Group (AfDB), Avenue Joseph Anoma, 01 BP 1387, Abidjan, 01, COT, https://www.afdb.org; The AfDB Statistics Pocketbook 2019.

Palgrave Macmillan, 1 New York Plaza, Ste. 4500, New York, NY, 10004-1562, USA, (800) 777-4643, orders@palgrave.com, https://www.palgrave.com/us; The Statesman's Yearbook, 2023.

U.S. Census Bureau, 4600 Silver Hill Rd., Washington, DC, 20233, USA, (301) 763-4636, (800) 923-8282, https://www.census.gov; HIV/AIDS Surveillance Data Base.

UNICEF, 3 United Nations Plz., New York, NY, 10017, USA, (212) 303-7984, (917) 244-2215, https://www.unicef.org; The State of the World's Children 2023.

United Nations Department of Economic and Social Affairs (DESA), Population Division, 2 United Nations Plz., Rm. DC2-1950, New York, NY, 10017, USA, (212) 963-3209, (212) 963-2147, population@un.org, https://www.un.org/development/desa/pd/; World Fertility Data 2019.

United Nations Development Programme (UNDP), One United Nations Plz., New York, NY, 10017, USA, (212) 906-5000, (212) 906-5001, https://www.undp.org; Human Development Report 2021-2022.

United Nations Economic Commission for Africa (UNECA), PO Box 3001, Addis Ababa, ETH, ecainfo@uneca.org, https://www.uneca.org/; African Statistical Yearbook 2020.

United Nations Statistics Division (UNSD), United Nations Plz., New York, NY, 10017, USA, (800) 253-9646, (212) 963-9851, statistics@un.org, https://unstats.un.org; Millennium Development Goal Indicators and Statistical Yearbook of the United Nations 2021.

The World Bank, 1818 H St. NW, Washington, DC, 20433, USA, (202) 473-1000, (202) 477-6391, eds03@worldbank.org, https://www.worldbank.org/; Congo, Republic of the (report).

World Health Organization (WHO), Ave. Appia 20, Geneva, CH-1211, SWI, (202) 974-3000 (Telephone in U.S.), publications@who.int, https://www.who.int/; Global Health Observatory (GHO) and Health Statistics and Information Systems.

CONGO, REPUBLIC OF THE-PUBLISHERS AND PUBLISHING

UNESCO Institute for Statistics, C.P 250 Succursale H, Montreal, QC, H3G 2K8, CAN, (514) 343-6880 (Dial from U.S.), (514) 343-5740 (Fax from U.S.), uis.publications@unesco.org, http://uis.unesco.org/; UIS.Stat.

CONGO, REPUBLIC OF THE-RAILROADS

Janes, USA, (703) 574-7580, (888) 977-1519, customer.care@janes.com, https://www.janes.com; Janes World Railways 2021-2022.

Palgrave Macmillan, 1 New York Plaza, Ste. 4500, New York, NY, 10004-1562, USA, (800) 777-4643, orders@palgrave.com, https://www.palgrave.com/us; The Statesman's Yearbook, 2023.

Routledge - Taylor & Francis Group, 6000 Broken Sound Pkwy. NW, Ste. 300, Boca Raton, FL, 33487, USA, (800) 634-1420, (800) 634-7064, orders@taylorandfrancis.com, https://www.routledge.com/; The Europa World Year Book 2022.

United Nations Economic Commission for Africa (UNECA), PO Box 3001, Addis Ababa, ETH, ecainfo@uneca.org, https://www.uneca.org/; African Statistical Yearbook 2020.

United Nations Statistics Division (UNSD), United Nations Plz., New York, NY, 10017, USA, (800) 253-9646, (212) 963-9851, statistics@un.org, https://unstats.un.org; Statistical Yearbook of the United Nations 2021.

CONGO, REPUBLIC OF THE-RELIGION

Central Intelligence Agency (CIA), Office of Public Affairs, Washington, DC, 20505, USA, (703) 482-0623, https://www.cia.gov; The World Factbook.

Palgrave Macmillan, 1 New York Plaza, Ste. 4500, New York, NY, 10004-1562, USA, (800) 777-4643, orders@palgrave.com, https://www.palgrave.com/us; The Statesman's Yearbook, 2023.

CONGO, REPUBLIC OF THE-RETAIL TRADE

Euromonitor International, Inc., 1 N Dearborn St., Ste. 1700, Chicago, IL, 60602, USA, (312) 922-1115, (312) 922-1157, info-usa@euromonitor.com, https://www.euromonitor.com/; Geographies.

CONGO, REPUBLIC OF THE-ROADS

International Road Federation (IRF), Madison Place, 500 Montgomery St., 5th Fl., Alexandria, VA, 22314, USA, (703) 535-1001, (703) 535-1007, info@irf.global, https://www.irf.global/; World Road Statistics (WRS).

United Nations Economic Commission for Africa (UNECA), PO Box 3001, Addis Ababa, ETH, ecainfo@uneca.org, https://www.uneca.org/; African Statistical Yearbook 2020.

CONGO, REPUBLIC OF THE-RUBBER INDUSTRY AND TRADE

International Rubber Study Group (IRSG), 51 Changi Business Park Central 2, Unit No. 6, 486066, SGP, https://www.rubberstudy.org; Monthly Rubber Bulletin (MRB); Rubber Industry Report; Rubber Statistical Bulletin; and World Rubber Industry Report (WRIO).

CONGO, REPUBLIC OF THE-SHIPPING

Routledge - Taylor & Francis Group, 6000 Broken Sound Pkwy. NW, Ste. 300, Boca Raton, FL, 33487, USA, (800) 634-1420, (800) 634-7064, orders@taylorandfrancis.com, https://www.routledge.com/; The Europa World Year Book 2022.

S&P Global, IHS Markit, 15 Inverness Way E, Englewood, CO, 80112, USA, (800) 447-2273, (800) 854-7179, https://ihsmarkit.com; IHS Maritime World Shipbuilding Statistics; Journal of Commerce; Lloyd's Register of Ships 2021-2022; and Maritime Portal Desktop.

United Nations Economic Commission for Africa (UNECA), PO Box 3001, Addis Ababa, ETH, ecainfo@uneca.org, https://www.uneca.org/; African Statistical Yearbook 2020.

United Nations Statistics Division (UNSD), United Nations Plz., New York, NY, 10017, USA, (800) 253-9646, (212) 963-9851, statistics@un.org, https://unstats.un.org; Statistical Yearbook of the United Nations 2021.

CONGO, REPUBLIC OF THE-TAXATION

International Road Federation (IRF), Madison Place, 500 Montgomery St., 5th Fl., Alexandria, VA, 22314, USA, (703) 535-1001, (703) 535-1007, info@irf.global, https://www.irf.global/; World Road Statistics (WRS).

The World Bank, 1818 H St. NW, Washington, DC, 20433, USA, (202) 473-1000, (202) 477-6391, eds03@worldbank.org, https://www.worldbank.org/; World Development Indicators (WDI) 2022.

CONGO, REPUBLIC OF THE-TELEPHONE

Palgrave Macmillan, 1 New York Plaza, Ste. 4500, New York, NY, 10004-1562, USA, (800) 777-4643, orders@palgrave.com, https://www.palgrave.com/us; The Statesman's Yearbook, 2023.

Routledge - Taylor & Francis Group, 6000 Broken Sound Pkwy. NW, Ste. 300, Boca Raton, FL, 33487, USA, (800) 634-1420, (800) 634-7064, orders@taylorandfrancis.com, https://www.routledge.com/; The Europa World Year Book 2022.

United Nations Statistics Division (UNSD), United Nations Plz., New York, NY, 10017, USA, (800) 253-9646, (212) 963-9851, statistics@un.org, https://unstats.un.org; World Statistics Pocketbook 2021.

CONGO, REPUBLIC OF THE-TEXTILE INDUSTRY

Palgrave Macmillan, 1 New York Plaza, Ste. 4500, New York, NY, 10004-1562, USA, (800) 777-4643, orders@palgrave.com, https://www.palgrave.com/us; The Statesman's Yearbook, 2023.

CONGO, REPUBLIC OF THE-THEATER

UNESCO Institute for Statistics, C.P 250 Succursale H, Montreal, QC, H3G 2K8, CAN, (514) 343-6880 (Dial from U.S.), (514) 343-5740 (Fax from U.S.), uis.publications@unesco.org, http://uis.unesco.org/; UIS.Stat.

CONGO, REPUBLIC OF THE-TOBACCO INDUSTRY

United Nations Statistics Division (UNSD), United Nations Plz., New York, NY, 10017, USA, (800) 253-9646, (212) 963-9851, statistics@un.org, https://unstats.un.org; Statistical Yearbook of the United Nations 2021.

CONGO, REPUBLIC OF THE-TOURISM

Euromonitor International, Inc., 1 N Dearborn St., Ste. 1700, Chicago, IL, 60602, USA, (312) 922-1115, (312) 922-1157, info-usa@euromonitor.com, https://www.euromonitor.com/; Geographies.

Palgrave Macmillan, 1 New York Plaza, Ste. 4500, New York, NY, 10004-1562, USA, (800) 777-4643, orders@palgrave.com, https://www.palgrave.com/us; The Statesman's Yearbook, 2023.

Routledge - Taylor & Francis Group, 6000 Broken Sound Pkwy. NW, Ste. 300, Boca Raton, FL, 33487, USA, (800) 634-1420, (800) 634-7064, orders@taylorandfrancis.com, https://www.routledge.com/; The Europa World Year Book 2022.

United Nations Economic Commission for Africa (UNECA), PO Box 3001, Addis Ababa, ETH, ecainfo@uneca.org, https://www.uneca.org/; African Statistical Yearbook 2020.

United Nations Statistics Division (UNSD), United Nations Plz., New York, NY, 10017, USA, (800) 253-9646, (212) 963-9851, statistics@un.org, https://unstats.un.org; Statistical Yearbook of the United Nations 2021.

United Nations World Tourism Organization (UNWTO), Calle Poeta Joan Maragall 42, Madrid, 28020, SPA, info@unwto.org, https://www.unwto.org/; Yearbook of Tourism Statistics, 2021 Edition.

The World Bank, 1818 H St. NW, Washington, DC, 20433, USA, (202) 473-1000, (202) 477-6391, eds03@worldbank.org, https://www.worldbank.org/; Congo, Republic of the (report).

CONGO, REPUBLIC OF THE-TRANSPORTATION

Central Intelligence Agency (CIA), Office of Public Affairs, Washington, DC, 20505, USA, (703) 482-0623, https://www.cia.gov; The World Factbook.

Euromonitor International, Inc., 1 N Dearborn St., Ste. 1700, Chicago, IL, 60602, USA, (312) 922-

1115, (312) 922-1157, info-usa@euromonitor.com, https://www.euromonitor.com/; Geographies.

Palgrave Macmillan, 1 New York Plaza, Ste. 4500, New York, NY, 10004-1562, USA, (800) 777-4643, orders@palgrave.com, https://www.palgrave.com/us; The Statesman's Yearbook, 2023.

Routledge - Taylor & Francis Group, 6000 Broken Sound Pkwy. NW, Ste. 300, Boca Raton, FL, 33487, USA, (800) 634-1420, (800) 634-7064, orders@taylorandfrancis.com, https://www.routledge.com/; The Europa World Year Book 2022.

United Nations Economic Commission for Africa (UNECA), PO Box 3001, Addis Ababa, ETH, ecainfo@uneca.org, https://www.uneca.org/; African Statistical Yearbook 2020.

The World Bank, 1818 H St. NW, Washington, DC, 20433, USA, (202) 473-1000, (202) 477-6391, eds03@worldbank.org, https://www.worldbank.org/; Congo, Republic of the (report).

CONGO, REPUBLIC OF THE-UNEMPLOYMENT

International Labour Organization (ILO), 4 Rte. des Morillons, Geneva, CH-1211, SWI, ilo@ilo.org, https://www.ilo.org; NORMLEX Information System on International Labour Standards.

CONGO, REPUBLIC OF THE-VITAL STATISTICS

Palgrave Macmillan, 1 New York Plaza, Ste. 4500, New York, NY, 10004-1562, USA, (800) 777-4643, orders@palgrave.com, https://www.palgrave.com/us; The Statesman's Yearbook, 2023.

U.S. Census Bureau, 4600 Silver Hill Rd., Washington, DC, 20233, USA, (301) 763-4636, (800) 923-8282, https://www.census.gov; HIV/AIDS Surveillance Data Base.

United Nations Department of Economic and Social Affairs (DESA), Population Division, 2 United Nations Plz., Rm. DC2-1950, New York, NY, 10017, USA, (212) 963-3209, (212) 963-2147, population@un.org, https://www.un.org/development/desa/pd/; World Contraceptive Use 2021: Estimates and Projections of Family Planning Indicators and World Marriage Data 2019.

United Nations Statistics Division (UNSD), United Nations Plz., New York, NY, 10017, USA, (800) 253-9646, (212) 963-9851, statistics@un.org, https://unstats.un.org; Statistical Yearbook of the United Nations 2021.

World Health Organization (WHO), Ave. Appia 20, Geneva, CH-1211, SWI, (202) 974-3000 (Telephone in U.S.), publications@who.int, https://www.who.int/; Health Statistics and Information Systems.

CONGO, REPUBLIC OF THE-WAGES

International Labour Organization (ILO), 4 Rte. des Morillons, Geneva, CH-1211, SWI, ilo@ilo.org, https://www.ilo.org; NORMLEX Information System on International Labour Standards.

United Nations Statistics Division (UNSD), United Nations Plz., New York, NY, 10017, USA, (800) 253-9646, (212) 963-9851, statistics@un.org, https://unstats.un.org; Statistical Yearbook of the United Nations 2021.

The World Bank, 1818 H St. NW, Washington, DC, 20433, USA, (202) 473-1000, (202) 477-6391, eds03@worldbank.org, https://www.worldbank.org/; Congo, Republic of the (report).

CONGO, REPUBLIC OF THE-WHOLESALE PRICE INDEXES

International Monetary Fund (IMF), 700 19th St. NW, Washington, DC, 20431, USA, (202) 623-7000, (202) 623-4661, publications@imf.org, https://www.imf.org; International Financial Statistics (IFS).

CONGRESS, UNITED STATES

CQ Press, An Imprint of SAGE Publication, 2455 Teller Rd., Thousand Oaks, CA, 91320, USA, (800) 818-7243, (805) 499-9774, (800) 583-2665, info@sagepub.com, https://us.sagepub.com/en-us/nam/cqpress; CQPress Congress Collection.

FiveThirtyEight, 47 W 66th St., 2nd Fl., New York, NY, 10023, USA, contact@fivethirtyeight.com, https://fivethirtyeight.com/; 2020 Election Forecast.

Public Policy Polling (PPP), 2900 Highwoods Blvd., Ste. 201, Raleigh, NC, 27604, USA, (919) 866-4950, information@publicpolicypolling.com, https://www.publicpolicypolling.com/; Trump and Mastriano Have Big Leads in Pennsylvania Republican Primary for President and Senate.

U.S. Government Publishing Office (GPO),, 732 N Capitol St. NW, Washington, DC, 20401-0001, USA, (202) 512-1800, (866) 512-1800, (202) 512-2104, contactcenter@gpo.gov, https://www.gpo.gov/; Catalog of U.S. Government Publications (CGP) and Congressional Directory.

The Washington Post, 1301 K St. NW, Washington, DC, 20071, USA, (800) 477-4679, https://www.washingtonpost.com/; Fact Checker and The N.R.A. Has Trump. But It Has Lost Allies in Congress..

CONGRESS, UNITED STATES-ASIAN, PACIFIC ISLANDER MEMBERS

Joint Center for Political and Economic Studies, 633 Pennsylvania Ave. NW, Washington, DC, 20004, USA, (202) 789-3500, info@jointcenter.org, https://jointcenter.org/; Racial Diversity Among Top House Staff and Racial Diversity Among Top Staff in Senate Personal Offices.

OpenSecrets, 1300 L St. NW , Ste. 200, Washington, DC, 20005, USA, (202) 857-0044, (202) 857-7809, info@crp.org, https://www.opensecrets.org/; Racial and Gender Diversity in the 117th Congress.

U.S. Government Publishing Office (GPO),, 732 N Capitol St. NW, Washington, DC, 20401-0001, USA, (202) 512-1800, (866) 512-1800, (202) 512-2104, contactcenter@gpo.gov, https://www.gpo.gov/; Congressional Directory.

CONGRESS, UNITED STATES-BILLS, ACTS, RESOLUTIONS

FiveThirtyEight, 47 W 66th St., 2nd Fl., New York, NY, 10023, USA, contact@fivethirtyeight.com, https://fivethirtyeight.com/; Does Your Member of Congress Vote With or Against Biden? and Tracking Congress In the Age Of Trump.

U.S. Department of Education (ED), Office of Special Education and Rehabilitative Services (OSERS), 400 Maryland Ave. SW, Washington, DC, 20202-7100, USA, (202) 245-7468, https://www2.ed.gov/about/offices/list/osers; Annual Reports to Congress on the Implementation of the Individuals with Disabilities Education Act (IDEA).

U.S. Government Publishing Office (GPO),, 732 N Capitol St. NW, Washington, DC, 20401-0001, USA, (202) 512-1800, (866) 512-1800, (202) 512-2104, contactcenter@gpo.gov, https://www.gpo.gov/; Congressional Record.

University of California, Berkeley, Othering & Belonging Institute, 460 Stephens Hall, Berkeley, CA, 94720-2330, USA, (510) 642-3326, belonging@berkeley.edu, https://belonging.berkeley.edu; Consequences of Islamophobia on Civil Liberties and Rights in the United States.

CONGRESS, UNITED STATES-BLACK MEMBERS

Joint Center for Political and Economic Studies, 633 Pennsylvania Ave. NW, Washington, DC, 20004, USA, (202) 789-3500, info@jointcenter.org, https://jointcenter.org/; Racial Diversity Among Top House Staff and Racial Diversity Among Top Staff in Senate Personal Offices.

OpenSecrets, 1300 L St. NW , Ste. 200, Washington, DC, 20005, USA, (202) 857-0044, (202) 857-7809, info@crp.org, https://www.opensecrets.org/; Racial and Gender Diversity in the 117th Congress.

U.S. Government Publishing Office (GPO),, 732 N Capitol St. NW, Washington, DC, 20401-0001, USA, (202) 512-1800, (866) 512-1800, (202) 512-2104, contactcenter@gpo.gov, https://www.gpo.gov/; Congressional Directory.

U.S. House of Representatives, Office of the Clerk, U.S. Capitol, Rm. H154, Washington, DC, 20515-6601, USA, (202) 225-7000, (202) 228-2125, https://clerk.house.gov/; Black Americans in Congress.

CONGRESS, UNITED STATES-CAMPAIGN FINANCES

Federal Election Commission (FEC), 1050 1st St. NE, Washington, DC, 20463, USA, (800) 424-9530, (202) 694-1100, pubrec@fec.gov, https://www.fec.gov; Campaign Finance Data and FEC Congressional Budget Justification Fiscal Year 2022.

KFF Health News, 1330 G St. NW, Washington, DC, 20005, USA, (202) 347-5270, https://khn.org/; Campaign Contributions Tracker: Pharma Cash to Congress.

OpenSecrets, 1300 L St. NW , Ste. 200, Washington, DC, 20005, USA, (202) 857-0044, (202) 857-7809, info@crp.org, https://www.opensecrets.org/; Dozens of Members of Congress Up for Reelection in 2022 Midterms Received the Majority of Their Campaign Funds From PACs and GOP Candidates Who Participated in the Jan. 6 Rally Are Raising Millions.

CONGRESS, UNITED STATES-COMPOSITION

Joint Center for Political and Economic Studies, 633 Pennsylvania Ave. NW, Washington, DC, 20004, USA, (202) 789-3500, info@jointcenter.org, https://jointcenter.org/; Racial Diversity Among Top House Staff and Racial Diversity Among Top Staff in Senate Personal Offices.

OpenSecrets, 1300 L St. NW , Ste. 200, Washington, DC, 20005, USA, (202) 857-0044, (202) 857-7809, info@crp.org, https://www.opensecrets.org/; Racial and Gender Diversity in the 117th Congress.

Pew Research Center, 1615 L St. NW, Ste. 800, Washington, DC, 20036, USA, (202) 419-4300, (202) 857-8562, info@pewresearch.org, https://www.pewresearch.org/; House Gets Younger, Senate Gets Older: A Look at the Age and Generation of Lawmakers in the 118th Congress.

U.S. Government Publishing Office (GPO),, 732 N Capitol St. NW, Washington, DC, 20401-0001, USA, (202) 512-1800, (866) 512-1800, (202) 512-2104, contactcenter@gpo.gov, https://www.gpo.gov/; Congressional Directory.

CONGRESS, UNITED STATES-CONGRESSIONAL APPORTIONMENT

FiveThirtyEight, 47 W 66th St., 2nd Fl., New York, NY, 10023, USA, contact@fivethirtyeight.com, https://fivethirtyeight.com/; What Redistricting Looks Like In Every State.

U.S. House of Representatives, Office of the Clerk, U.S. Capitol, Rm. H154, Washington, DC, 20515-6601, USA, (202) 225-7000, (202) 228-2125, https://clerk.house.gov/; Representatives Apportioned to Each State 1st to 23rd Census (1790-2010).

CONGRESS, UNITED STATES-CONGRESSIONAL DISTRICTS-CANDIDATES, VOTES CAST

CQ Press, An Imprint of SAGE Publication, 2455 Teller Rd., Thousand Oaks, CA, 91320, USA, (800) 818-7243, (805) 499-9774, (800) 583-2665, info@sagepub.com, https://us.sagepub.com/en-us/nam/cqpress; America Votes 34: 2019-2020, Election Returns by State.

CONGRESS, UNITED STATES-HISPANIC MEMBERS

Joint Center for Political and Economic Studies, 633 Pennsylvania Ave. NW, Washington, DC, 20004, USA, (202) 789-3500, info@jointcenter.org, https://jointcenter.org/; Racial Diversity Among Top House Staff and Racial Diversity Among Top Staff in Senate Personal Offices.

National Association of Latino Elected and Appointed Officials (NALEO) Educational Fund, 1000 Corporate Center Dr., Ste. 310, Los Angeles, CA, 90015, USA, (213) 747-7606, (213) 747-7664, avargas@naleo.org, https://naleo.org/; National Directory of Latino Elected Officials 2021.

OpenSecrets, 1300 L St. NW , Ste. 200, Washington, DC, 20005, USA, (202) 857-0044, (202) 857-7809, info@crp.org, https://www.opensecrets.org/; Racial and Gender Diversity in the 117th Congress.

U.S. Government Publishing Office (GPO),, 732 N Capitol St. NW, Washington, DC, 20401-0001, USA, (202) 512-1800, (866) 512-1800, (202) 512-2104, contactcenter@gpo.gov, https://www.gpo.gov/; Congressional Directory.

CONGRESS, UNITED STATES-PUBLIC CONFIDENCE

PollingReport.com, USA, https://www.pollingreport.com/; State of the Union.

YouGov, 38 W 21st St., New York, NY, 10010, USA, (646) 213-7414, help.us@yougov.com, https://today.yougov.com/; US Congress Approval Rating.

CONGRESS, UNITED STATES-REPRESENTATIVES

FiveThirtyEight, 47 W 66th St., 2nd Fl., New York, NY, 10023, USA, contact@fivethirtyeight.com, https://fivethirtyeight.com/; Do Voters Want Democrats or Republicans In Congress?.

Joint Center for Political and Economic Studies, 633 Pennsylvania Ave. NW, Washington, DC, 20004, USA, (202) 789-3500, info@jointcenter.org, https://jointcenter.org/; Racial Diversity Among Top House Staff.

Pew Research Center, 1615 L St. NW, Ste. 800, Washington, DC, 20036, USA, (202) 419-4300, (202) 857-8562, info@pewresearch.org, https://www.pewresearch.org/; House Gets Younger, Senate Gets Older: A Look at the Age and Generation of Lawmakers in the 118th Congress.

CONGRESS, UNITED STATES-REPRESENTATIVES-VOTE CAST

CQ Press, An Imprint of SAGE Publication, 2455 Teller Rd., Thousand Oaks, CA, 91320, USA, (800) 818-7243, (805) 499-9774, (800) 583-2665, info@sagepub.com, https://us.sagepub.com/en-us/nam/cqpress; America Votes 34: 2019-2020, Election Returns by State and CQ Magazine.

FiveThirtyEight, 47 W 66th St., 2nd Fl., New York, NY, 10023, USA, contact@fivethirtyeight.com, https://fivethirtyeight.com/; Does Your Member of Congress Vote With or Against Biden? and Tracking Congress In the Age Of Trump.

CONGRESS, UNITED STATES-SENATORS

FiveThirtyEight, 47 W 66th St., 2nd Fl., New York, NY, 10023, USA, contact@fivethirtyeight.com, https://fivethirtyeight.com/; Do Voters Want Democrats or Republicans In Congress?.

Pew Research Center, 1615 L St. NW, Ste. 800, Washington, DC, 20036, USA, (202) 419-4300, (202) 857-8562, info@pewresearch.org, https://www.pewresearch.org/; House Gets Younger, Senate Gets Older: A Look at the Age and Generation of Lawmakers in the 118th Congress.

CONGRESS, UNITED STATES-SENATORS-VOTE CAST

CQ Press, An Imprint of SAGE Publication, 2455 Teller Rd., Thousand Oaks, CA, 91320, USA, (800) 818-7243, (805) 499-9774, (800) 583-2665, info@sagepub.com, https://us.sagepub.com/en-us/nam/cqpress; America Votes 34: 2019-2020, Election Returns by State.

FiveThirtyEight, 47 W 66th St., 2nd Fl., New York, NY, 10023, USA, contact@fivethirtyeight.com, https://fivethirtyeight.com/; Does Your Member of Congress Vote With or Against Biden? and Tracking Congress In the Age Of Trump.

CONGRESS, UNITED STATES-SENIORITY

U.S. Government Publishing Office (GPO),, 732 N Capitol St. NW, Washington, DC, 20401-0001, USA, (202) 512-1800, (866) 512-1800, (202) 512-2104, contactcenter@gpo.gov, https://www.gpo.gov/; Congressional Directory.

CONGRESS, UNITED STATES-TIME IN SESSION

U.S. Government Publishing Office (GPO),, 732 N Capitol St. NW, Washington, DC, 20401-0001, USA, (202) 512-1800, (866) 512-1800, (202) 512-2104, contactcenter@gpo.gov, https://www.gpo.gov/; Congressional Record.

CONGRESS, UNITED STATES-WOMEN MEMBERS

OpenSecrets, 1300 L St. NW , Ste. 200, Washington, DC, 20005, USA, (202) 857-0044, (202) 857-7809, info@crp.org, https://www.opensecrets.org/; Racial and Gender Diversity in the 117th Congress.

Rutgers University, Eagleton Institute of Politics, Center for American Women and Politics (CAWP), 191 Ryders Ln., New Brunswick, NJ, 08901-8557, USA, (848) 932-8179, (848) 932-9384, chelsea.hill@eagleton.rutgers.edu, https://cawp.rutgers.edu/; Black Women in Elective Office; By the Numbers: Black Women in the 117th Congress; Congress; and Election Watch.

U.S. Government Publishing Office (GPO),, 732 N Capitol St. NW, Washington, DC, 20401-0001, USA, (202) 512-1800, (866) 512-1800, (202) 512-2104, contactcenter@gpo.gov, https://www.gpo.gov/; Congressional Directory.

U.S. House of Representatives, Office of the Clerk, U.S. Capitol, Rm. H154, Washington, DC, 20515-6601, USA, (202) 225-7000, (202) 228-2125, https://clerk.house.gov/; Women in Congress: Historical Data.

CONNECTICUT

See also-STATE DATA (FOR INDIVIDUAL STATES)

Capitol Region Council of Governments (CRCOG), 241 Main St., Hartford, CT, 06106-5310, USA, (860) 522-2217, (860) 724-1274, info@crcog.org, https://crcog.org/; unpublished data.

Connecticut Department of Economic and Community Development (DECD), 450 Columbus Blvd., Hartford, CT, 06103, USA, (860) 500-2300, https://portal.ct.gov/DECD; Connecticut Economic Digest.

Connecticut Office of Policy and Management (OPM), 450 Capitol Ave., Hartford, CT, 06106, USA, (860) 418-6500, (860) 418-6487, https://portal.ct.gov/opm; unpublished data.

Yale Project on Climate Change Communication (YPCCC), Yale School of the Environment, 195 Prospect St., New Haven, CT, 06511, USA, (203) 432-5055, climatechange@yale.edu, https://climatecommunication.yale.edu/; Are Hurricane-prone States More Concerned about Climate Change?.

CONNECTICUT-STATE DATA CENTERS

Connecticut Data Collaborative (CTData), Connecticut Census State Data Center, 10 Constitution Plaza, Hartford, CT, 06103, USA, (860) 500-1983, info@ctdata.org, https://www.ctdata.org/census/; State Data Reports (CT).

CONNECTICUT-PRIMARY STATISTICS SOURCES

Connecticut State Department of Education, 450 Columbus Blvd., Hartford, CT, 06103, USA, (860) 713-6543, https://portal.ct.gov/SDE; Connecticut Report Cards.

Connecticut State Library, 231 Capitol Ave., Hartford, CT, 06106, USA, (860) 757-6500, (866) 886-4478, (860) 757-6542, csl.isref@ct.gov, https://ctstatelibrary.org; unpublished data.

SAGE Publications, 2455 Teller Rd., Thousand Oaks, CA, 91320, USA, (800) 818-7243, (800) 583-2665, journals@sagepub.com, https://www.sagepub.com; Data Planet.

CONSERVATION OF NATURAL RESOURCES

Sustainable Forestry Initiative (SFI), 2121 K St. NW, Ste. 750, Washington, DC, 20037, USA, (202) 596-3450, https://www.forests.org/; Growing Solutions for 25 Years: Better Choices for the Planet.

United Nations Economic Commission for Africa (UNECA), PO Box 3001, Addis Ababa, ETH, ecainfo@uneca.org, https://www.uneca.org/; African Governance Report VI.

Xerces Society for Invertebrate Conservation, 628 NE Broadway, Ste. 200, Portland, OR, 97232, USA, (855) 232-6639, (503) 233-6794, info@xerces.org, https://xerces.org/; Drifting Toward Disaster: How Dicamba Herbicides are Harming Cultivated and Wild Landscapes and Wings: Essays on Invertebrate Conservation.

CONSERVATISM

Center for American Progress Action Fund (CAP Action), 1333 H St. NW, 10th Fl., Washington, DC, 20005, USA, (202) 682-1611, https://www.americanprogressaction.org; Debunking Sen. Rick Scott's Claims About Taxpaying Americans and Facebook Engagement Patterns for Progressive- and Conservative-Leaning Pages.

Democracy Fund Voter Study Group, 1200 17th St. NW, Ste. 300, Washington, DC, 20036, USA, (202) 420-7900, https://www.voterstudygroup.org/; Theft Perception: Examining the Views of Americans Who Believe the 2020 Election was Stolen.

FiveThirtyEight, 47 W 66th St., 2nd Fl., New York, NY, 10023, USA, contact@fivethirtyeight.com, https://fivethirtyeight.com/; What Redistricting Looks Like In Every State and Where Americans Stand on Abortion, in 5 Charts.

The Gallup Organization, 901 F St. NW, Washington, DC, 20004, USA, (202) 715-3030, (800) 204-1192, (202) 715-3045, https://www.gallup.com; Mixed Views Among Americans on Transgender Issues and Social Conservatism in U.S. Highest in About a Decade.

Institute for Strategic Dialogue (ISD), PO Box 75769, London, SW1P 9ER, GBR, info@isdglobal.org, https://www.isdglobal.org/; 'Climate Lockdown' and the Culture Wars: How COVID-19 Sparked a New Narrative Against Climate Action.

OpenSecrets, 1300 L St. NW , Ste. 200, Washington, DC, 20005, USA, (202) 857-0044, (202) 857-7809, info@crp.org, https://www.opensecrets.org/; GOP Candidates Who Participated in the Jan. 6 Rally Are Raising Millions.

Pew Research Center, 1615 L St. NW, Ste. 800, Washington, DC, 20036, USA, (202) 419-4300, (202) 857-8562, info@pewresearch.org, https://www.pewresearch.org/; Beyond Red vs. Blue: The Political Typology and Deep Partisan Divide on Whether Greater Acceptance of Transgender People Is Good for Society.

Public Policy Polling (PPP), 2900 Highwoods Blvd., Ste. 201, Raleigh, NC, 27604, USA, (919) 866-4950, information@publicpolicypolling.com, https://www.publicpolicypolling.com/; The GOP Is Still Trump's Party, and There May Be a Price to Pay.

Public Religion Research Institute (PRRI), 1023 15th St. NW, 9th Fl., Washington, DC, 20005, USA, (202) 238-9424, info@prri.org, https://www.prri.org/; Four Myths About QAnon and the Movement's Impact on American Politics in 2022.

University of Washington, Center for an Informed Public (CIP), Seattle, WA, USA, uwcip@uw.edu, https://www.cip.uw.edu/; Recognize the Bias? News Media Partisanship Shapes the Coverage of Facial Recognition Technology in the United States.

YouGov, 38 W 21st St., New York, NY, 10010, USA, (646) 213-7414, help.us@yougov.com, https://today.yougov.com/; On Issues Relating to Transgender Youth, Democrats and Republicans Are Far Apart.

CONSPIRACY THEORIES

Civiqs, PO Box 70008, Oakland, CA, 94612, USA, (510) 394-5664, inquiries@civiqs.com, https://civiqs.com/; Are You a Supporter of QAnon?.

Institute for Strategic Dialogue (ISD), PO Box 75769, London, SW1P 9ER, GBR, info@isdglobal.org, https://www.isdglobal.org/; The Boom Before the Ban: QAnon and Facebook; The Conspiracy Consortium: Examining Discussions of COVID-19 Among Right-Wing Extremist Telegram Channels; and Ill Advice: A Case Study in Facebook's Failure to Tackle COVID-19 Disinformation.

Public Religion Research Institute (PRRI), 1023 15th St. NW, 9th Fl., Washington, DC, 20005, USA, (202) 238-9424, info@prri.org, https://www.prri.org/; Four Myths About QAnon and the Movement's Impact on American Politics in 2022 and Understanding QAnon's Connection to American Politics, Religion, and Media Consumption.

University of Maryland, National Consortium for the Study of Terrorism and Responses to Terrorism (START), PO Box 266, 5245 Greenbelt Rd., College Park, MD, 20740, USA, (301) 405-6600, (301) 314-1980, infostart@start.umd.edu, https://www.start.umd.edu; QAnon Offenders in the United States.

CONSTRUCTION INDUSTRY

Building Societies Association (BSA), York House, 23 Kingsway, 6th Fl., London, WC2B 6UJ, GBR, simon.rex@bsa.org.uk, https://www.bsa.org.uk; BSA Statistics.

Dodge Construction Network, 300 American Metro Blvd., Ste. 185, Hamilton, NJ, 08619, USA, (877) 784-9556, support@construction.com, https://www.construction.com/; Dodge MarketShare.

U.S. Census Bureau, 4600 Silver Hill Rd., Washington, DC, 20233, USA, (301) 763-4636, (800) 923-8282, https://www.census.gov; County Business Patterns (CBP) 2020; Economic Indicators; and Statistics of U.S. Businesses (SUSB).

U.S. Census Bureau, Center for Economic Studies (CES), 4600 Silver Hill Rd., Washington, DC, 20233, USA, (301) 763-6460, (301) 763-5935, ces.contacts@census.gov, https://www.census.gov/programs-surveys/ces.html; 2017 Economic Census Data and Selected Findings from the 2017 Economic Census of Island Areas.

U.S. Department of Labor (DOL), Bureau of Labor Statistics (BLS), Postal Square Bldg., 2 Massachusetts Ave. NE, Washington, DC, 20212-0001, USA, (202) 691-5200, (202) 691-7890, blsdata_staff@bls.gov, https://www.bls.gov; Industries at a Glance.

United Nations Conference on Trade and Development (UNCTAD), Palais des Nations, Geneva, 1211, SWI, (212) 963-6896, unctadinfo@unctad.org, https://unctad.org; Ships Built by Country of Building.

United Nations Statistics Division (UNSD), United Nations Plz., New York, NY, 10017, USA, (800) 253-9646, (212) 963-9851, statistics@un.org, https://unstats.un.org; UNdata.

The Urban Institute, Greater D.C. (Urban-Greater D.C), 500 L'Enfant Plaza SW, Washington, DC, 20024, USA, (202) 833-7200, https://greaterdc.urban.org/; DC Flexible Rent Subsidy Program: Findings from the Program's First Year.

Urban Land Institute (ULI), 2001 L St. NW, Ste. 200, Washington, DC, 20036, USA, (202) 624-7000, (800) 321-5011, (202) 403-3849, customerservice@uli.org, https://uli.org/; ULI Case Studies and Urban Land Magazine.

CONSTRUCTION INDUSTRY-BUILDING AUTHORIZED

U.S. Census Bureau, 4600 Silver Hill Rd., Washington, DC, 20233, USA, (301) 763-4636, (800) 923-8282, https://www.census.gov; Building Permits Survey.

CONSTRUCTION INDUSTRY-BUILDING PERMITS-VALUE

U.S. Census Bureau, 4600 Silver Hill Rd., Washington, DC, 20233, USA, (301) 763-4636, (800) 923-8282, https://www.census.gov; Building Permits Survey.

CONSTRUCTION INDUSTRY-CAPITAL

U.S. Census Bureau, Center for Economic Studies (CES), 4600 Silver Hill Rd., Washington, DC, 20233, USA, (301) 763-6460, (301) 763-5935, ces.contacts@census.gov, https://www.census.gov/programs-surveys/ces.html; Construction, 2017 Economic Census.

U.S. Department of Commerce (DOC), Bureau of Economic Analysis (BEA), 4600 Silver Hill Rd., Washington, DC, 20233, USA, (301) 278-9004, customerservice@bea.gov, https://www.bea.gov; Survey of Current Business (SCB).

CONSTRUCTION INDUSTRY-CONSTRUCTION CONTRACTS

Dodge Construction Network, 300 American Metro Blvd., Ste. 185, Hamilton, NJ, 08619, USA, (877) 784-9556, support@construction.com, https://www.construction.com/; Mid-Year 2023 Construction Outlook.

CONSTRUCTION INDUSTRY-COST

HVS Global Hospitality Services, 1400 Old Country Rd., Ste. 105N, Westbury, NY, 11590, USA, (516) 248-8828, (516) 742-3059, https://www.hvs.com/; HVS Hotel Valuation Index.

U.S. Census Bureau, Center for Economic Studies (CES), 4600 Silver Hill Rd., Washington, DC, 20233, USA, (301) 763-6460, (301) 763-5935, ces.contacts@census.gov, https://www.census.gov/programs-surveys/ces.html; Construction, 2017 Economic Census.

CONSTRUCTION INDUSTRY-EARNINGS

U.S. Census Bureau, 4600 Silver Hill Rd., Washington, DC, 20233, USA, (301) 763-4636, (800) 923-8282, https://www.census.gov; County Business Patterns (CBP) 2020 and Statistics of U.S. Businesses (SUSB).

U.S. Census Bureau, Center for Economic Studies (CES), 4600 Silver Hill Rd., Washington, DC, 20233, USA, (301) 763-6460, (301) 763-5935, ces.contacts@census.gov, https://www.census.gov/programs-surveys/ces.html; Construction, 2017 Economic Census and Selected Findings from the 2017 Economic Census of Island Areas.

U.S. Department of Commerce (DOC), Bureau of Economic Analysis (BEA), 4600 Silver Hill Rd., Washington, DC, 20233, USA, (301) 278-9004, customerservice@bea.gov, https://www.bea.gov; National Income and Product Accounts (NIPA): 2022 Update and Survey of Current Business (SCB).

U.S. Department of Labor (DOL), Bureau of Labor Statistics (BLS), Postal Square Bldg., 2 Massachusetts Ave. NE, Washington, DC, 20212-0001, USA, (202) 691-5200, (202) 691-7890, blsdata_staff@bls.gov, https://www.bls.gov; Current Employment Statistics (CES).

CONSTRUCTION INDUSTRY-EMPLOYEES

Institute for Supply Management (ISM), 309 W Elliot Rd. , Ste. 113, Tempe, AZ, 85284-1556, USA, (480) 752-6276, (480) 752-7890, membersvcs@ismworld.org, https://www.ismworld.org/; 2022 Salary Survey.

Institute for Women's Policy Research (IWPR), 1200 18th St. NW, Ste. 301, Washington, DC, 20036, USA, (202) 785-5100, (202) 833-4362, iwpr@iwpr.org, https://iwpr.org/; Women Gain Jobs in Construction Trades but Remain Underrepresented in the Field.

U.S. Census Bureau, 4600 Silver Hill Rd., Washington, DC, 20233, USA, (301) 763-4636, (800) 923-8282, https://www.census.gov; County Business Patterns (CBP) 2020 and Statistics of U.S. Businesses (SUSB).

U.S. Census Bureau, Center for Economic Studies (CES), 4600 Silver Hill Rd., Washington, DC, 20233, USA, (301) 763-6460, (301) 763-5935, ces.contacts@census.gov, https://www.census.gov/programs-surveys/ces.html; Selected Findings from the 2017 Economic Census of Island Areas.

U.S. Department of Labor (DOL), Bureau of Labor Statistics (BLS), Postal Square Bldg., 2 Massachusetts Ave. NE, Washington, DC, 20212-0001, USA, (202) 691-5200, (202) 691-7890, blsdata_staff@bls.gov, https://www.bls.gov; Current Employment Statistics (CES); Industry-Occupation Matrix Data, By Occupation; and Monthly Labor Review.

CONSTRUCTION INDUSTRY-FINANCES

Internal Revenue Service (IRS), Statistics of Income Division (SOI), 1111 Constitution Ave. NW, K-Room 4100-123, Washington, DC, 20224-0002, USA, (202) 874-0410, (202) 874-0964, sis@irs.gov, https://www.irs.gov/uac/soi-tax-stats-statistics-of-income; SOI Tax Stats - Business Tax Statistics and Statistics of Income Bulletin.

U.S. Census Bureau, 4600 Silver Hill Rd., Washington, DC, 20233, USA, (301) 763-4636, (800) 923-8282, https://www.census.gov; Construction Price Indexes and Construction Spending.

U.S. Census Bureau, Center for Economic Studies (CES), 4600 Silver Hill Rd., Washington, DC, 20233, USA, (301) 763-6460, (301) 763-5935, ces.contacts@census.gov, https://www.census.gov/programs-surveys/ces.html; Construction, 2017 Economic Census.

CONSTRUCTION INDUSTRY-GROSS DOMESTIC PRODUCT

U.S. Department of Commerce (DOC), Bureau of Economic Analysis (BEA), 4600 Silver Hill Rd., Washington, DC, 20233, USA, (301) 278-9004, customerservice@bea.gov, https://www.bea.gov; Survey of Current Business (SCB).

CONSTRUCTION INDUSTRY-INDUSTRIAL SAFETY

National Safety Council (NSC), 1121 Spring Lake Dr., Itasca, IL, 60143-3201, USA, (630) 285-1121, (800) 621-7615, customerservice@nsc.org, https://www.nsc.org/; National Safety Council Injury Facts.

U.S. Department of Labor (DOL), Bureau of Labor Statistics (BLS), Postal Square Bldg., 2 Massachusetts Ave. NE, Washington, DC, 20212-0001, USA, (202) 691-5200, (202) 691-7890, blsdata_staff@bls.gov, https://www.bls.gov; Injuries, Illnesses, and Fatalities (IIF).

CONSTRUCTION INDUSTRY-NONEMPLOYER

U.S. Census Bureau, 4600 Silver Hill Rd., Washington, DC, 20233, USA, (301) 763-4636, (800) 923-8282, https://www.census.gov; Economic Census, Nonemployer Statistics (NES) 2019.

CONSTRUCTION INDUSTRY-PRODUCER PRICE INDEXES

U.S. Department of Labor (DOL), Bureau of Labor Statistics (BLS), Postal Square Bldg., 2 Massachusetts Ave. NE, Washington, DC, 20212-0001, USA, (202) 691-5200, (202) 691-7890, blsdata_staff@bls.gov, https://www.bls.gov; Commodity Data Including 'Headline' FD-ID Indexes (Producer Price Index - PPI); Industry Data (Producer Price Index - PPI); and Producer Price Indexes (PPI).

CONSTRUCTION INDUSTRY-PROFITS

Forbes, Inc., 499 Washington Blvd., Jersey City, NJ, 07310, USA, (800) 295-0893, https://www.forbes.com; America's Largest Private Companies 2021.

Internal Revenue Service (IRS), Statistics of Income Division (SOI), 1111 Constitution Ave. NW, K-Room 4100-123, Washington, DC, 20224-0002, USA, (202) 874-0410, (202) 874-0964, sis@irs.gov, https://www.irs.gov/uac/soi-tax-stats-statistics-of-income; SOI Tax Stats - Business Tax Statistics; SOI Tax Stats - Historical Data Tables; and Statistics of Income Bulletin.

U.S. Census Bureau, Center for Economic Studies (CES), 4600 Silver Hill Rd., Washington, DC, 20233, USA, (301) 763-6460, (301) 763-5935, ces.contacts@census.gov, https://www.census.gov/programs-surveys/ces.html; Construction, 2017 Economic Census.

U.S. Department of Commerce (DOC), Bureau of Economic Analysis (BEA), 4600 Silver Hill Rd., Washington, DC, 20233, USA, (301) 278-9004, customerservice@bea.gov, https://www.bea.gov; National Income and Product Accounts (NIPA): 2022 Update and Survey of Current Business (SCB).

CONSTRUCTION INDUSTRY-RESIDENTIAL

Harvard Joint Center for Housing Studies (JCHS), 1 Bow St., Ste. 400, Cambridge, MA, 02138, USA, (617) 495-7908, (617) 496-9957, jchs@harvard.edu, https://www.jchs.harvard.edu/; America's Rental Housing 2022; Improving America's Housing 2021; Leading Indicator of Remodeling Activity (LIRA); and The State of the Nation's Housing 2022.

National Association of Home Builders (NAHB), 1201 15th St. NW, Washington, DC, 20005, USA, (800) 368-5242, info@nahb.org, https://www.nahb.org/; Housing Economics PLUS and National Statistics.

U.S. Census Bureau, 4600 Silver Hill Rd., Washington, DC, 20233, USA, (301) 763-4636, (800) 923-8282, https://www.census.gov; Building Permits Survey and Characteristics of New Housing.

U.S. Department of Housing and Urban Development (HUD), Office of Policy Development and Research (PD&R), PO Box 23268, Washington, DC, 20026-3268, USA, (800) 245-2691, (800) 927-7589 (TDD), (202) 708-9981, helpdesk@huduser.gov, https://www.huduser.gov; Comprehensive Housing Market Analyses and U.S. Housing Market Conditions.

CONSTRUCTION INDUSTRY-SHIPMENTS, RECEIPTS

Forbes, Inc., 499 Washington Blvd., Jersey City, NJ, 07310, USA, (800) 295-0893, https://www.forbes.com; America's Largest Private Companies 2021.

Internal Revenue Service (IRS), Statistics of Income Division (SOI), 1111 Constitution Ave. NW, K-Room 4100-123, Washington, DC, 20224-0002, USA, (202) 874-0410, (202) 874-0964, sis@irs.gov, https://www.irs.gov/uac/soi-tax-stats-statistics-of-income; SOI Tax Stats - Historical Data Tables and Statistics of Income Bulletin.

U.S. Census Bureau, Center for Economic Studies (CES), 4600 Silver Hill Rd., Washington, DC, 20233, USA, (301) 763-6460, (301) 763-5935, ces.contacts@census.gov, https://www.census.gov/programs-surveys/ces.html; Construction, 2017 Economic Census.

CONSTRUCTION MACHINERY-MANUFACTURING-EARNINGS

U.S. Census Bureau, 4600 Silver Hill Rd., Washington, DC, 20233, USA, (301) 763-4636, (800) 923-8282, https://www.census.gov; Annual Survey of Manufactures (ASM) 2021.

U.S. Department of Labor (DOL), Bureau of Labor Statistics (BLS), Postal Square Bldg., 2 Massachusetts Ave. NE, Washington, DC, 20212-0001, USA, (202) 691-5200, (202) 691-7890, blsdata_staff@bls.gov, https://www.bls.gov; Current Employment Statistics (CES).

CONSTRUCTION MACHINERY-MANUFACTURING-EMPLOYEES

U.S. Census Bureau, 4600 Silver Hill Rd., Washington, DC, 20233, USA, (301) 763-4636, (800) 923-8282, https://www.census.gov; Annual Survey of Manufactures (ASM) 2021.

U.S. Department of Labor (DOL), Bureau of Labor Statistics (BLS), Postal Square Bldg., 2 Massachusetts Ave. NE, Washington, DC, 20212-0001, USA, (202) 691-5200, (202) 691-7890, blsdata_staff@bls.gov, https://www.bls.gov; Current Employment Statistics (CES).

CONSTRUCTION MACHINERY-MANUFACTURING-SHIPMENTS

U.S. Census Bureau, 4600 Silver Hill Rd., Washington, DC, 20233, USA, (301) 763-4636, (800) 923-8282, https://www.census.gov; Annual Survey of Manufactures (ASM) 2021 and Manufacturers' Shipments, Inventories and Orders.

CONSTRUCTION MATERIALS

See BUILDING MATERIALS AND GARDEN SUPPLIES

CONSUMER BEHAVIOR

American Customer Satisfaction Index (ACSI), 3916 Ranchero Dr., Ann Arbor, MI, 48108, USA, (734) 913-0788, (734) 913-0790, info@theacsi.org, https://www.theacsi.org; Benchmarks by Company and Benchmarks by Industry.

Apartment List, USA, https://www.apartmentlist.com; Renter Stigma: Social and Economic Pressure in the Housing Market.

Bain & Company, 131 Dartmouth St., Boston, MA, 02116, USA, (617) 572-2000, (617) 572-2427, https://www.bain.com/; China's Unstoppable 2020 Luxury Market; The Coronavirus Demand Challenge Awaiting China's Auto Industry; and The Future of Retail: Winning Models for a New Era.

Civis Analytics, 200 W Monroe St., 22nd Fl., Chicago, IL, 60606, USA, https://www.civisanalytics.com/; Coronavirus Pulse Survey Research; COVID-19 Impact Research; and COVID-19 in the U.S.: Consumer Insights for Business.

Community Marketing & Insights (CMI), 611 S Palm Canyon Dr., Nos. 7-244, Palm Springs, CA, 92264, USA, (415) 343-4656, info@cmi.info, https://cmi.info/; LGBTQ Consumer Products Survey 2019 Report.

Consumer Technology Association (CTA), 1919 S Eads St., Arlington, VA, 22202, USA, (703) 907-7600, (866) 858-1555, (703) 907-7675, cta@cta.tech, https://www.cta.tech; Mobility and Auto Technology in the COVID-19 Era.

Deloitte, 30 Rockefeller Plaza, 41st Fl., New York, NY, 10112-0015, USA, (212) 492-4000, (212) 489-1687 , https://www2.deloitte.com; Tech Trends 2023 and Technology, Media, and Telecommunications Predictions 2023.

Euromonitor International, Inc., 1 N Dearborn St., Ste. 1700, Chicago, IL, 60602, USA, (312) 922-1115, (312) 922-1157, info-usa@euromonitor.com, https://www.euromonitor.com/; The Impact of Coronavirus on Consumer Finance; The Impact of Coronavirus on Consumer Goods and Services in the Middle East; The Impact of Coronavirus on Top 10 Global Consumer Trends 2020; Income and Expenditure Country Reports; Market Research on the Consumer Finance Industry; Passport Database; and Top 10 Global Consumer Trends for 2021.

Experian, 475 Anton Blvd., Costa Mesa, CA, 92626, USA, (714) 830-7000, https://www.experian.com/; Credit Scores Steady as Consumer Debt Balances Rise in 2022.

Forrester Research, Inc., 60 Acorn Park Dr., Cambridge, MA, 02140, USA, (617) 613-5730, https://www.forrester.com; The State of Consumers and Technology, 2019.

Frontier Group, 1129 State St., No. 10, Santa Barbara, CA, 93101, USA, (805) 730-1391, https://frontiergroup.org/; Trash in America: Moving from Destructive Consumption towards a Zero-Waste System.

Gartner, Inc., 56 Top Gallant Rd., Stamford, CT, 06902, USA, (203) 964-0096, https://www.gartner.com; Digital Markets Insights.

The Good Food Institute (GFI), PO Box 96503, PMB 42019, Washington, DC, 20090-6503, USA, (866) 849-4457, https://www.gfi.org/; Consumer Insights.

Growth from Knowledge (GfK), 200 Liberty St., 4th Fl., New York, NY, 10281, USA, (212) 240-5300, https://www.gfk.com/; Insights.

Harris Interactive, 85 Uxbridge Rd., 11th Fl., Ealing, W5 5TH, GBR, https://harris-interactive.co.uk/; The Grocer: Ethical Trading.

INRIX, 10210 NE Points Dr., No. 400, Kirkland, WA, 98033, USA, (425) 284-3800, https://inrix.com; Holiday Shopping Update.

International Food Information Council Foundation (IFIC), 1100 Connecticut Ave. NW, Ste. 430, Washington, DC, 20036, USA, (202) 296-6540, info@foodinsight.org, https://foodinsight.org/; 2022 Food and Health Survey and Food Insight.

Ipsos, 360 Park Ave. S, 17th Fl., New York, NY, 10010, USA, (212) 265-3200, https://www.ipsos.com/en-us; U.S. Consumer Confidence Takes a Small Step Back: Expectations Dampen with Surge of New Coronavirus Cases.

Kantar, 3 World Trade Center, 35th Fl., New York, NY, 10007, USA, (866) 471-1399, https://www.kantar.com/; Brand Footprint 2023 and 2022 China Shoppers Report.

Morning Consult, 729 15th St. NW, Washington, DC, 20005, USA, (202) 506-1957, contact@morningconsult.com, https://morningconsult.com; How 2020 Is Impacting Gen Z's Worldview: A Tracking Report Dedicated to Understanding How a Tumultuous Year Is Altering the Young Generation's Habits, Values, and Outlook; Most Trusted Brands 2022; The U.S. Consumer Confidence Dashboard; and When Will Consumers Feel Safe? Weekly Updates on Consumers' Comfort Level with Various Pastimes.

MRI Simmons, 200 Liberty St., 4th Fl., New York, NY, 10281, USA, (866) 256-4468, info.ms@mrisimmons.com, https://www.mrisimmons.com/; MRI-Simmons USA.

National Coffee Association (NCA), 45 Broadway, Ste. 1140, New York, NY, 10006, USA, (212) 766-4007, (212) 766-5815, https://www.ncausa.org; Coffee, Consumers, & COVID-19: Road Map to Recovery and National Coffee Data Trends (NCDT) 2022.

NielsenIQ (NIQ), 200 W Jackson Blvd., Chicago, IL, 60606, USA, https://nielseniq.com; Covid-Positive Households Are Altering Their Eating Habits; The F Word: Flexitarian Is Not a Curse to the Meat Industry; and Multicultural Consumers Are Set to Drive Beauty Growth Amid Continued Category Shifts in 2021.

The NPD Group, 900 W Shore Rd., Port Washington, NY, 11050, USA, (516) 625-0700, contactnpd@npd.com, https://www.npd.com; Automotive; Beauty; Consumer Technology; Fashion Accessories; Food Consumption; Foodservice; Home; Media Entertainment; and Toys.

Numerator, 24 E Washington St., Ste. 1200, Chicago, IL, 60602, USA, (312) 585-3927, https://www.numerator.com; The Real Deal with Fake Meat: Understanding the Plant-Based Meat Alternative Buyer and Shopping Behavior Index.

Ofcom, Riverside House , 2a Southwark Bridge Rd., London, SE1 9HA, GBR, https://www.ofcom.org.uk/; Open Data.

PeopleForBikes, PO Box 2359, Boulder, CO, 80306, USA, (303) 449-4893, info@peopleforbikes.org, https://www.peopleforbikes.org; COVID Participation Study.

Produce for Better Health (PBH) Foundation, USA, https://fruitsandveggies.org/; 2020 State of the Plate.

RAC Motoring Services, RAC House, Brockhurst Crescent, Walsall, WS5 4AW, GBR, https://www.rac.co.uk; More Drivers than Ever Plan to 'Go Electric' When They Next Change Their Cars and RAC Report on Motoring 2022.

Statista, 3 World Trade Center, 175 Greenwich St., 36th Fl., New York, NY, 10007, USA, (212) 433-2270, support@statista.com, https://www.statista.com; Statista: The Statistics Portal.

Tinuiti, 701 B St., Ste. 1225, San Diego, CA, 92101, USA, (833) 846-8484, hello@tinuiti.com, https://tinuiti.com; unpublished data.

U.S. Department of Justice (DOJ), Federal Bureau of Investigation (FBI), 935 Pennsylvania Ave. NW, Washington, DC, 20535-0001, USA, (202) 324-3000, https://www.fbi.gov/; NICS Firearm Checks: Month/Year.

University of California Davis, Institute of Transportation Studies (ITS-Davis), 1605 Tilia St., Davis, CA, 95616, USA, (530) 752-6548, kcswayze@ucdavis.edu, https://its.ucdavis.edu; Evaluating the Environmental Impacts of Online Shopping: A Behavioral and Transportation Approach.

University of Georgia, Terry College of Business, Selig Center for Economic Growth, E201 Ivester Hall, 650 S Lumpkin St., Athens, GA, 30602, USA, (706) 425-9782, jhumphre@uga.edu, https://www.terry.uga.edu/about/selig//; The Multicultural Economy 2021.

University of Michigan Surveys of Consumers, Survey Research Center, PO Box 1248, Ann Arbor, MI, 48106, USA, (734) 763-5224, (734) 764-3488, umsurvey@umich.edu, http://www.sca.isr.umich.edu/; University of Michigan Surveys of Consumers.

USAFacts, USA, info@usafacts.org, https://usafacts.org/; COVID-19 Recovery Indicators.

World Wildlife Fund (WWF), 1250 24th St. NW, Washington, DC, 20037-1193, USA, (202) 495-4800, (202) 495-4211, https://wwf.panda.org/; An Eco-wakening: Measuring Global Awareness, Engagement and Action for Nature.

CONSUMER COMPLAINTS

Federal Communications Commission (FCC), Consumer and Governmental Affairs Bureau (CGB), 45 L St. NE, Washington, DC, 20554, USA, (888) 225-5322, (844) 432-2275 (ASL Video Call), (866) 418-0232, https://www.fcc.gov/consumer-governmental-affairs; Consumer Complaint Data Center.

Identity Theft Resource Center (ITRC), 2514 Jamacha Rd., Ste. 502-525, El Cajon, CA, 92019-4492, USA, (888) 400-5530, itrc@idtheftcenter.org, https://www.idtheftcenter.org/; notified: Data Breach Information.

CONSUMER COMPLAINTS AGAINST AIRLINES

U.S. Department of Transportation (DOT), Office of Aviation Consumer Protection, 1200 New Jersey Ave. SE, Washington, DC, 20590, USA, (202) 366-2220, https://www.transportation.gov/airconsumer; Air Travel Consumer Report.

CONSUMER CREDIT

Board of Governors of the Federal Reserve System, Constitution Ave. NW, Washington, DC, 20551, USA, (202) 452-3000, (202) 263-4869 (TDD), https://www.federalreserve.gov; Federal Reserve Bulletin; Financial Accounts of the United States 2023; and Household Debt Service and Financial Obligations Ratios 2022.

Federal Financial Institutions Examination Council (FFIEC), 3501 Fairfax Dr., L. William Seidman Center, Mail Stop: B-7081a, Arlington, VA, 22226-3550 , USA, (703) 516-5590, https://www.ffiec.gov/; Uniform Bank Performance Report (UBPR).

CONSUMER CREDIT-DELINQUENCY RATES

Federal Financial Institutions Examination Council (FFIEC), 3501 Fairfax Dr., L. William Seidman Center, Mail Stop: B-7081a, Arlington, VA, 22226-3550 , USA, (703) 516-5590, https://www.ffiec.gov/; Uniform Bank Performance Report (UBPR).

CONSUMER GOODS

Cato Institute, 1000 Massachusetts Ave. NW, Washington, DC, 20001-5403, USA, (202) 842-0200, https://www.cato.org/; Has Fed Policy Mattered for Inflation?.

Community Marketing & Insights (CMI), 611 S Palm Canyon Dr., Nos. 7-244, Palm Springs, CA, 92264, USA, (415) 343-4656, info@cmi.info, https://cmi.info/; LGBTQ Consumer Products Survey 2019 Report.

Consumer Technology Association (CTA), 1919 S Eads St., Arlington, VA, 22202, USA, (703) 907-7600, (866) 858-1555, (703) 907-7675, cta@cta.tech, https://www.cta.tech; Mobility and Auto Technology in the COVID-19 Era.

Deloitte, 30 Rockefeller Plaza, 41st Fl., New York, NY, 10112-0015, USA, (212) 492-4000, (212) 489-1687 , https://www2.deloitte.com; Tech Trends 2023 and Technology, Media, and Telecommunications Predictions 2023.

Euromonitor International, Inc., 1 N Dearborn St., Ste. 1700, Chicago, IL, 60602, USA, (312) 922-1115, (312) 922-1157, info-usa@euromonitor.com, https://www.euromonitor.com/; The Impact of Coronavirus on Consumer Finance; The Impact of Coronavirus on Consumer Goods and Services in the Middle East; and The Impact of Coronavirus on Top 10 Global Consumer Trends 2020.

Federal Housing Finance Agency (FHFA), 400 7th St. SW, Washington, DC, 20019, USA, (202) 649-3800, (202) 649-1071, https://www.fhfa.gov/; House Price Index.

Gartner, Inc., 56 Top Gallant Rd., Stamford, CT, 06902, USA, (203) 964-0096, https://www.gartner.com; Digital Markets Insights.

Green Science Policy Institute, PO Box 9127, Berkeley, CA, 94709, USA, (510) 898-1739, info@greensciencepolicy.org, https://greensciencepolicy.org/; Fluorinated Compounds in North American Cosmetics.

Harris Interactive, 85 Uxbridge Rd., 11th Fl., Ealing, W5 5TH, GBR, https://harris-interactive.co.uk/; The Grocer: Ethical Trading.

Morning Consult, 729 15th St. NW, Washington, DC, 20005, USA, (202) 506-1957, contact@morningconsult.com, https://morningconsult.com; Most Trusted Brands 2022.

MRI Simmons, 200 Liberty St., 4th Fl., New York, NY, 10281, USA, (866) 256-4468, info.ms@mrisimmons.com, https://www.mrisimmons.com/; MRI-Simmons USA.

National Cannabis Industry Association (NCIA), 126 C St. NW, Washington, DC, 20001, USA, (888) 683-5650, (888) 683-5670, info@thecannabisindustry.org, https://thecannabisindustry.org/; The Key to Consumer Safety: Displacing the Illicit Cannabis Market - Recommendations for Safe Vaping.

RAC Motoring Services, RAC House, Brockhurst Crescent, Walsall, WS5 4AW, GBR, https://www.rac.co.uk; RAC Report on Motoring 2022.

Recording Industry Association of America (RIAA), 1000 F St. NW, 2nd Fl., Washington, DC, 20004, USA, (202) 775-0101, riaamembership@riaa.com, https://www.riaa.com/; U.S. Sales Database.

Silent Spring Institute, 320 Nevada St., Ste. 302, Newton, MA, 02460, USA, (617) 332-4288, (617) 332-4284, info@silentspring.org, https://silentspring.org/; Identifying Toxic Consumer Products: A Novel Data Set Reveals Air Emissions of Potent Carcinogens, Reproductive Toxicants, and Developmental Toxicants and Influence of Living in the Same Home on Biomonitored Levels of Consumer Product Chemicals.

U.S. Department of Justice (DOJ), Federal Bureau of Investigation (FBI), 935 Pennsylvania Ave. NW, Washington, DC, 20535-0001, USA, (202) 324-3000, https://www.fbi.gov/; NICS Firearm Checks: Month/Year.

CONSUMER GOODS-BOOKS

Book Industry Study Group (BISG), 232 Madison Ave., Ste. 1400, New York, NY, 10016, USA, (646) 336-7141, info@bisg.org, https://bisg.org/; unpublished data.

CONSUMER GOODS-COMMUNICATIONS

VSS, 400 Park Ave., 17th Fl., New York, NY, 10022, USA, (212) 935-4990, stevensonj@vss.com, https://www.vss.com/; unpublished data.

CONSUMER GOODS-ENTERTAINMENT

Euromonitor International, Inc., 1 N Dearborn St., Ste. 1700, Chicago, IL, 60602, USA, (312) 922-1115, (312) 922-1157, info-usa@euromonitor.com, https://www.euromonitor.com/; Income and Expenditure Country Reports and Market Research on the Consumer Finance Industry.

Newzoo, Danzigerkade 2F, Amsterdam, 1013 AP, NLD, https://newzoo.com; Global Cloud Gaming Report 2022 and Global Gamer Study.

U.S. Department of Labor (DOL), Bureau of Labor Statistics (BLS), Postal Square Bldg., 2 Massachusetts Ave. NE, Washington, DC, 20212-0001, USA, (202) 691-5200, (202) 691-7890, blsdata_staff@bls.gov, https://www.bls.gov; Consumer Expenditure Survey (CE).

CONSUMER GOODS-EXPENDITURES

Bain & Company, 131 Dartmouth St., Boston, MA, 02116, USA, (617) 572-2000, (617) 572-2427, https://www.bain.com/; The Coronavirus Demand Challenge Awaiting China's Auto Industry and The Future of Retail: Winning Models for a New Era.

Community Marketing & Insights (CMI), 611 S Palm Canyon Dr., Nos. 7-244, Palm Springs, CA, 92264, USA, (415) 343-4656, info@cmi.info, https://cmi.info/; LGBTQ Consumer Products Survey 2019 Report.

Consumer Technology Association (CTA), 1919 S Eads St., Arlington, VA, 22202, USA, (703) 907-7600, (866) 858-1555, (703) 907-7675, cta@cta.tech, https://www.cta.tech; CTA U.S. Consumer Technology One-Year Industry Forecast, 2018-2023 (July 2022).

Datasembly, 1775 Tysons Blvd., Tysons, VA, 22102, USA, (833) 328-2736, https://datasembly.com/; Grocery Price Index.

EnsembleIQ, 8550 W Bryn Mawr Ave., Ste. 200, Chicago, IL, 60631, USA, (877) 687-7321, https://ensembleiq.com/; 2021 Consumer Expenditures Report.

Euromonitor International, Inc., 1 N Dearborn St., Ste. 1700, Chicago, IL, 60602, USA, (312) 922-1115, (312) 922-1157, info-usa@euromonitor.com, https://www.euromonitor.com/; The Impact of Coronavirus on Consumer Finance; The Impact of Coronavirus on Consumer Goods and Services in the Middle East; The Impact of Coronavirus on Top 10 Global Consumer Trends 2020; Income and Expenditure Country Reports; Market Research on the Consumer Finance Industry; and Passport Database.

Forrester Research, Inc., 60 Acorn Park Dr., Cambridge, MA, 02140, USA, (617) 613-5730, https://www.forrester.com; Consumer Technographics.

Growth from Knowledge (GfK), 200 Liberty St., 4th Fl., New York, NY, 10281, USA, (212) 240-5300, https://www.gfk.com/; Insights.

Kantar, 3 World Trade Center, 35th Fl., New York, NY, 10007, USA, (866) 471-1399, https://www.kantar.com/; Brand Footprint 2023 and 2022 China Shoppers Report.

Kantar Worldpanel, 6 More London Place, London, SE1 2QY, GBR, https://www.kantarworldpanel.com; Android vs. iOS: Smartphone OS Sales Market Share Evolution.

The NPD Group, 900 W Shore Rd., Port Washington, NY, 11050, USA, (516) 625-0700, contactnpd@npd.com, https://www.npd.com; Automotive; Beauty; Consumer Technology; Fashion Accessories; Food Consumption; Foodservice; Home; Media Entertainment; Mobile; and Toys.

Numerator, 24 E Washington St., Ste. 1200, Chicago, IL, 60602, USA, (312) 585-3927, https://www.numerator.com; Shopping Behavior Index.

U.S. Department of Labor (DOL), Bureau of Labor Statistics (BLS), Postal Square Bldg., 2 Massachusetts Ave. NE, Washington, DC, 20212-0001, USA, (202) 691-5200, (202) 691-7890, blsdata_staff@bls.gov, https://www.bls.gov; Consumer Expenditure Survey (CE).

University of Georgia, Terry College of Business, Selig Center for Economic Growth, E201 Ivester Hall, 650 S Lumpkin St., Athens, GA, 30602, USA, (706) 425-9782, jhumphre@uga.edu, https://www.terry.uga.edu/about/selig//; The Multicultural Economy 2021.

University of Michigan Surveys of Consumers, Survey Research Center, PO Box 1248, Ann Arbor, MI, 48106, USA, (734) 763-5224, (734) 764-3488, umsurvey@umich.edu, http://www.sca.isr.umich.edu/; University of Michigan Surveys of Consumers.

CONSUMER GOODS-FOOD

Datasembly, 1775 Tysons Blvd., Tysons, VA, 22102, USA, (833) 328-2736, https://datasembly.com/; Grocery Price Index.

EnsembleIQ, 8550 W Bryn Mawr Ave., Ste. 200, Chicago, IL, 60631, USA, (877) 687-7321, https://ensembleiq.com/; 2021 Consumer Expenditures Report and Progressive Grocer's 87th Annual Report of the Grocery Industry.

Euromonitor International, Inc., 1 N Dearborn St., Ste. 1700, Chicago, IL, 60602, USA, (312) 922-1115, (312) 922-1157, info-usa@euromonitor.com, https://www.euromonitor.com/; Income and Expenditure Country Reports and Market Research on the Consumer Finance Industry.

Greenpeace, 1300 I St. NW, Ste. 1100 E, Washington, DC, 20001, USA, (800) 722-6995, (202) 462-1177, (202) 462-4507, connect@greenpeace.us, https://www.greenpeace.org; The High Cost of Cheap Tuna: US Supermarkets, Sustainability, and Human Rights at Sea.

U.S. Department of Agriculture (USDA), Economic Research Service (ERS), 1400 Independence Ave. SW, Mail Stop 1800, Washington, DC, 20250-0002, USA, (202) 720-2791, https://www.ers.usda.gov/; Amber Waves: The Economics of Food, Farming, Natural Resources, and Rural America and Food Price Outlook.

U.S. Department of Agriculture (USDA), National Agricultural Statistics Service (USDA-NASS), 1400 Independence Ave. SW, Washington, DC, 20250, USA, (800) 727-9540, nass@nass.usda.gov, https://www.nass.usda.gov; Agricultural Statistics.

U.S. Department of Labor (DOL), Bureau of Labor Statistics (BLS), Postal Square Bldg., 2 Massachusetts Ave. NE, Washington, DC, 20212-0001, USA, (202) 691-5200, (202) 691-7890, blsdata_staff@bls.gov, https://www.bls.gov; Consumer Expenditure Survey (CE).

CONSUMER GOODS-HOUSING

Euromonitor International, Inc., 1 N Dearborn St., Ste. 1700, Chicago, IL, 60602, USA, (312) 922-1115, (312) 922-1157, info-usa@euromonitor.com, https://www.euromonitor.com/; Market Research on the Consumer Finance Industry.

U.S. Department of Labor (DOL), Bureau of Labor Statistics (BLS), Postal Square Bldg., 2 Massachusetts Ave. NE, Washington, DC, 20212-0001, USA, (202) 691-5200, (202) 691-7890, blsdata_staff@bls.gov, https://www.bls.gov; Consumer Expenditure Survey (CE).

Zillow Real Estate Research, 1301 Second Ave., 31st Fl., Seattle, WA, 98101, USA, (877) 313-8601, https://www.zillow.com/research/; Zillow Home Value Index (ZHVI) Data and Zillow Observed Rent Index (ZORI) Data.

CONSUMER GOODS-MEDICAL CARE

U.S. Department of Labor (DOL), Bureau of Labor Statistics (BLS), Postal Square Bldg., 2 Massachusetts Ave. NE, Washington, DC, 20212-0001, USA, (202) 691-5200, (202) 691-7890, blsdata_staff@bls.gov, https://www.bls.gov; Consumer Expenditure Survey (CE).

CONSUMER GOODS-METROPOLITAN AREAS

U.S. Department of Labor (DOL), Bureau of Labor Statistics (BLS), Postal Square Bldg., 2 Massachusetts Ave. NE, Washington, DC, 20212-0001, USA, (202) 691-5200, (202) 691-7890, blsdata_staff@bls.gov, https://www.bls.gov; Consumer Expenditure Survey (CE).

CONSUMER GOODS-PRODUCER PRICES

Datasembly, 1775 Tysons Blvd., Tysons, VA, 22102, USA, (833) 328-2736, https://datasembly.com/; Grocery Price Index.

The NPD Group, 900 W Shore Rd., Port Washington, NY, 11050, USA, (516) 625-0700, contactnpd@npd.com, https://www.npd.com; Automotive; Beauty; Consumer Technology; Fashion Accessories; Food Consumption; Foodservice; Home; Media Entertainment; and Toys.

U.S. Department of Labor (DOL), Bureau of Labor Statistics (BLS), Postal Square Bldg., 2 Massachusetts Ave. NE, Washington, DC, 20212-0001, USA, (202) 691-5200, (202) 691-7890, blsdata_staff@bls.gov, https://www.bls.gov; Producer Price Indexes (PPI).

CONSUMER GOODS-READING MATERIALS

U.S. Department of Labor (DOL), Bureau of Labor Statistics (BLS), Postal Square Bldg., 2 Massachusetts Ave. NE, Washington, DC, 20212-0001, USA, (202) 691-5200, (202) 691-7890, blsdata_staff@bls.gov, https://www.bls.gov; Consumer Expenditure Survey (CE).

CONSUMER GOODS-SPORTING GOODS

Euromonitor International, Inc., 1 N Dearborn St., Ste. 1700, Chicago, IL, 60602, USA, (312) 922-1115, (312) 922-1157, info-usa@euromonitor.com, https://www.euromonitor.com/; Income and Expenditure Country Reports.

National Shooting Sports Foundation (NSSF), Newtown, CT, USA, (203) 426-1320, (203) 426-1087, https://www.nssf.org; 2021 Firearms Retailer Survey and NSGA Shooting Sports Participation Report 2021 Edition.

National Sporting Goods Association (NSGA), 3041 Woodcreek Dr., Ste. 210, Downers Grove, IL, 60515, USA, (847) 296-6742, (847) 391-9827, info@nsga.org, https://www.nsga.org; Sports Participation: Historical Sports Participation 2022.

Newzoo, Danzigerkade 2F, Amsterdam, 1013 AP, NLD, https://newzoo.com; Global Cloud Gaming Report 2022 and Global Gamer Study.

CONSUMER ISSUES

Experian, 475 Anton Blvd., Costa Mesa, CA, 92626, USA, (714) 830-7000, https://www.experian.com/; Credit Scores Steady as Consumer Debt Balances Rise in 2022.

Federal Communications Commission (FCC), Consumer and Governmental Affairs Bureau (CGB), 45 L St. NE, Washington, DC, 20554, USA, (888) 225-5322, (844) 432-2275 (ASL Video Call), (866) 418-0232, https://www.fcc.gov/consumer-governmental-affairs; Consumer Complaint Data Center.

Silent Spring Institute, 320 Nevada St., Ste. 302, Newton, MA, 02460, USA, (617) 332-4288, (617) 332-4284, info@silentspring.org, https://silentspring.org/; Identifying Toxic Consumer Products: A Novel Data Set Reveals Air Emissions of Potent Carcinogens, Reproductive Toxicants, and Developmental Toxicants.

CONSUMER PAYMENT SYSTEMS

The Nilson Report, PO Box 50539, Santa Barbara, CA, 93150, USA, (805) 684-8800, (805) 684-8825, info@nilsonreport.com, https://www.nilsonreport.com; The Nilson Report and The World's Top Card Issuers and Merchant Acquirers.

CONSUMER PRICE INDEXES

Cato Institute, 1000 Massachusetts Ave. NW, Washington, DC, 20001-5403, USA, (202) 842-0200, https://www.cato.org/; Has Fed Policy Mattered for Inflation?.

Council for Community and Economic Research (C2ER), PO Box 12546, Arlington, VA, 22210, USA, (571) 397-2362, (703) 832-8663, info@c2er.org, https://www.c2er.org; Cost of Living Index (COLI).

Datasembly, 1775 Tysons Blvd., Tysons, VA, 22102, USA, (833) 328-2736, https://datasembly.com/; Grocery Price Index.

Euromonitor International, Inc., 1 N Dearborn St., Ste. 1700, Chicago, IL, 60602, USA, (312) 922-1115, (312) 922-1157, info-usa@euromonitor.com, https://www.euromonitor.com/; The Impact of Coronavirus on Consumer Finance; The Impact of Coronavirus on Consumer Goods and Services in the Middle East; and The Impact of Coronavirus on Top 10 Global Consumer Trends 2020.

Forrester Research, Inc., 60 Acorn Park Dr., Cambridge, MA, 02140, USA, (617) 613-5730, https://www.forrester.com; Consumer Technographics.

Google Public Data Directory, USA, https://www.google.com/publicdata/directory; Google Public Data Directory.

Massachusetts Institute of Technology (MIT), Living Wage Calculator, 77 Massachusetts Ave., Cambridge, MA, 02139, USA, (617) 324-6565, (617) 253-1000, amyglas@mit.edu, https://livingwage.mit.edu; Living Wage Calculator.

U.S. Department of Commerce (DOC), Bureau of Economic Analysis (BEA), 4600 Silver Hill Rd., Washington, DC, 20233, USA, (301) 278-9004, customerservice@bea.gov, https://www.bea.gov; Survey of Current Business (SCB).

U.S. Department of Labor (DOL), Bureau of Labor Statistics (BLS), Postal Square Bldg., 2 Massachusetts Ave. NE, Washington, DC, 20212-0001, USA, (202) 691-5200, (202) 691-7890, blsdata_staff@bls.gov, https://www.bls.gov; All Urban Consumers (Chained CPI) (Consumer Price Index - CPI); All Urban Consumers (Current Series) (Consumer Price Index - CPI); Average Price Data (Consumer Price Index - CPI); Consumer Price Index (CPI) Databases; and Consumer Price Indexe (CPI) Publications.

CONSUMER PRICE INDEXES-BY COMMODITY GROUPS

Consumer Technology Association (CTA), 1919 S Eads St., Arlington, VA, 22202, USA, (703) 907-7600, (866) 858-1555, (703) 907-7675, cta@cta.tech, https://www.cta.tech; CTA U.S. Consumer Technology One-Year Industry Forecast, 2018-2023 (July 2022).

U.S. Department of Labor (DOL), Bureau of Labor Statistics (BLS), Postal Square Bldg., 2 Massachusetts Ave. NE, Washington, DC, 20212-0001, USA, (202) 691-5200, (202) 691-7890, blsdata_staff@bls.gov, https://www.bls.gov; All Urban Consumers (Chained CPI) (Consumer Price Index - CPI); All Urban Consumers (Current Series) (Consumer Price Index - CPI); Consumer Price Index (CPI) Databases; and Urban Wage Earners and Clerical Workers (Current Series) (Consumer Price Index - CPI).

CONSUMER PRICE INDEXES-FOREIGN COUNTRIES

The Economist Group: Economist Intelligence Unit (EIU), 900 3rd Ave., 16th Fl., New York, NY, 10022, USA, (212) 541-0500, americas@eiu.com, https://www.eiu.com; Worldwide Cost of Living 2021.

International Monetary Fund (IMF), 700 19th St. NW, Washington, DC, 20431, USA, (202) 623-7000, (202) 623-4661, publications@imf.org, https://www.imf.org; International Financial Statistics (IFS).

Organization for Economic Cooperation and Development (OECD), 2001 L St. NW, Ste. 650, Washington, DC, 20036-4922, USA, (202) 785-6323, (800) 456-6323, (202) 785-0350, washington.contact@oecd.org, https://www.oecd.org/; OECD Main Economic Indicators (MEI).

CONSUMER PRICE INDEXES-MEDICAL CARE

U.S. Department of Labor (DOL), Bureau of Labor Statistics (BLS), Postal Square Bldg., 2 Massachusetts Ave. NE, Washington, DC, 20212-0001, USA, (202) 691-5200, (202) 691-7890, blsdata_staff@bls.gov, https://www.bls.gov; Consumer Price Index (CPI) Databases.

CONSUMER PRICE INDEXES-PURCHASING POWER OF THE DOLLAR

U.S. Department of Commerce (DOC), Bureau of Economic Analysis (BEA), 4600 Silver Hill Rd., Washington, DC, 20233, USA, (301) 278-9004, customerservice@bea.gov, https://www.bea.gov; Survey of Current Business (SCB).

CONSUMER PRICE INDEXES-YEAR TO YEAR CHANGES

U.S. Department of Labor (DOL), Bureau of Labor Statistics (BLS), Postal Square Bldg., 2 Massachusetts Ave. NE, Washington, DC, 20212-0001, USA, (202) 691-5200, (202) 691-7890, blsdata_staff@bls.gov, https://www.bls.gov; Productivity.

CONSUMER PROTECTION

Administrative Office of the United States Courts, One Columbus Cir. NE, Washington, DC, 20544, USA, (202) 502-2600, https://www.uscourts.gov; Bankruptcy Abuse Prevention and Consumer Protection Act Report 2021.

American Association of Retired Persons (AARP), 601 E St. NW, Washington, DC, 20049, USA, (202) 434-3525, (888) 687-2277, member@aarp.org, https://www.aarp.org/; 2019 Survey on Prescription Drugs.

Federal Trade Commission (FTC), 600 Pennsylvania Ave. NW, Washington, DC, 20580, USA, (202) 326-2222, https://www.ftc.gov; FTC Annual Highlights 2020.

National Cannabis Industry Association (NCIA), 126 C St. NW, Washington, DC, 20001, USA, (888) 683-5650, (888) 683-5670, info@thecannabisindustry.org, https://thecannabisindustry.org/; The Key to Consumer Safety: Displacing the Illicit Cannabis Market - Recommendations for Safe Vaping.

Public Health Agency of Canada, 130 Colonnade Rd., Ottawa, ON, K1A 0K9, CAN, (844) 280-5020 (Dial from U.S.), https://www.phac-aspc.gc.ca/; CHIRPP Injury Reports.

Silent Spring Institute, 320 Nevada St., Ste. 302, Newton, MA, 02460, USA, (617) 332-4288, (617) 332-4284, info@silentspring.org, https://silentspring.org/; Influence of Living in the Same Home on Biomonitored Levels of Consumer Product Chemicals.

U.S. Department of Commerce (DOC), National Telecommunications and Information Administration (NTIA), Herbert C. Hoover Bldg., 1401 Constitution Ave. NW, Washington, DC, 20230, USA, (202) 482-2000, https://www.ntia.doc.gov; Data Central.

CONSUMPTION (ECONOMICS)

See also individual commodities

Frontier Group, 1129 State St., No. 10, Santa Barbara, CA, 93101, USA, (805) 730-1391, https://frontiergroup.org/; Trash in America: Moving from Destructive Consumption towards a Zero-Waste System.

CONTRACEPTIVE USE

Guttmacher Institute, 125 Maiden Ln., 7th Fl., New York, NY, 10038, USA, (212) 248-1111, (800) 355-0244, (212) 248-1951, info@guttmacher.org, https://www.guttmacher.org/; Contraceptive Use in the United States; Data Center; Induced Abortion in the United States; and Unintended Pregnancy in the United States.

National Organization for Women (NOW), 1100 H St. NW, Ste. 300, Washington, DC, 20005, USA, (202) 628-8669, (202) 331-9002 (TTY), https://now.org/; unpublished data.

U.S. Census Bureau, 4600 Silver Hill Rd., Washington, DC, 20233, USA, (301) 763-4636, (800) 923-8282, https://www.census.gov; HIV/AIDS Surveillance Data Base.

U.S. Department of Health and Human Services, Centers for Disease Control and Prevention (CDC), National Center for Health Statistics (NCHS), 3311 Toledo Rd., Hyattsville, MD, 20782-2064, USA, (800) 232-4636, (301) 458-4000, https://www.cdc.gov/nchs; FastStats - Statistics by Topic.

United Nations Department of Economic and Social Affairs (DESA), Population Division, 2 United Nations Plz., Rm. DC2-1950, New York, NY, 10017, USA, (212) 963-3209, (212) 963-2147, population@un.org, https://www.un.org/development/desa/pd/; Family Planning Indicators: Estimates and Projections of Family Planning Indicators 2022; World Contraceptive Use 2021: Estimates and Projections of Family Planning Indicators; World Family Planning 2022; and World Fertility and Family Planning 2020.

CONVENIENCE STORES

U.S. Department of Agriculture (USDA), Economic Research Service (ERS), 1400 Independence Ave. SW, Mail Stop 1800, Washington, DC, 20250-0002, USA, (202) 720-2791, https://www.ers.usda.gov/; Food Processing & Marketing.

CONVERSION

Pew Research Center, 1615 L St. NW, Ste. 800, Washington, DC, 20036, USA, (202) 419-4300, (202) 857-8562, info@pewresearch.org, https://www.pewresearch.org/; Black Muslims Account for a Fifth of All U.S. Muslims, and About Half Are Converts to Islam.

COOK ISLANDS-NATIONAL STATISTICAL OFFICE

Ministry of Finance and Economic Management (MFEM), Cook Islands Statistics Office (CISO), PO Box 120, Avarua, COK, statistics@cookislands.gov.ck, https://www.mfem.gov.ck/oldsite/index.php/statistics; National Data Reports (Cook Islands).

COOK ISLANDS-PRIMARY STATISTICS SOURCES

Ministry of Finance and Economic Management (MFEM), Cook Islands Statistics Office (CISO), PO Box 120, Avarua, COK, statistics@cookislands.gov.ck, https://www.mfem.gov.ck/oldsite/index.php/statistics; Vital Statistics and Population Estimates.

COOK ISLANDS-AGRICULTURE

Asian Development Bank (ADB), 6 ADB Ave., Mandaluyong City, 1550, PHL, information@adb.org, https://www.adb.org/; Key Indicators for Asia and the Pacific 2022.

Palgrave Macmillan, 1 New York Plaza, Ste. 4500, New York, NY, 10004-1562, USA, (800) 777-4643, orders@palgrave.com, https://www.palgrave.com/us; The Statesman's Yearbook, 2023.

Routledge - Taylor & Francis Group, 6000 Broken Sound Pkwy. NW, Ste. 300, Boca Raton, FL, 33487, USA, (800) 634-1420, (800) 634-7064, orders@taylorandfrancis.com, https://www.routledge.com/; The Europa World Year Book 2022.

United Nations Economic and Social Commission for Asia and the Pacific (ESCAP), United Nations Building, Rajadamnern Nok Ave., Bangkok, 10200, THA, https://www.unescap.org/; Asia-Pacific Development Journal and SDG Gateway Data Explorer.

United Nations Food and Agricultural Organization (FAO), 2121 K St., Ste. 800B, Washington, DC, 20037, USA, (202) 653-2400 (Dial from U.S.), (202) 653-5760 (Fax from U.S.), fao-hq@fao.org, https://www.fao.org; AQUASTAT and The State of Food and Agriculture (SOFA) 2022.

United Nations Statistics Division (UNSD), United Nations Plz., New York, NY, 10017, USA, (800) 253-9646, (212) 963-9851, statistics@un.org, https://unstats.un.org; Statistical Yearbook of the United Nations 2021.

COOK ISLANDS-AIRLINES

Palgrave Macmillan, 1 New York Plaza, Ste. 4500, New York, NY, 10004-1562, USA, (800) 777-4643, orders@palgrave.com, https://www.palgrave.com/us; The Statesman's Yearbook, 2023.

Routledge - Taylor & Francis Group, 6000 Broken Sound Pkwy. NW, Ste. 300, Boca Raton, FL, 33487, USA, (800) 634-1420, (800) 634-7064, orders@taylorandfrancis.com, https://www.routledge.com/; The Europa World Year Book 2022.

COOK ISLANDS-ARMED FORCES

Central Intelligence Agency (CIA), Office of Public Affairs, Washington, DC, 20505, USA, (703) 482-0623, https://www.cia.gov; The World Factbook.

Stockholm International Peace Research Institute (SIPRI), Signalistgatan 9, Stockholm, SE 169 72, SWE, https://www.sipri.org/; SIPRI Arms Transfers Database and SIPRI Military Expenditure Database.

COOK ISLANDS-BANKS AND BANKING

Asian Development Bank (ADB), 6 ADB Ave., Mandaluyong City, 1550, PHL, information@adb.org, https://www.adb.org/; Key Indicators for Asia and the Pacific 2022.

COOK ISLANDS-BROADCASTING

Central Intelligence Agency (CIA), Office of Public Affairs, Washington, DC, 20505, USA, (703) 482-0623, https://www.cia.gov; The World Factbook.

Palgrave Macmillan, 1 New York Plaza, Ste. 4500, New York, NY, 10004-1562, USA, (800) 777-4643, orders@palgrave.com, https://www.palgrave.com/us; The Statesman's Yearbook, 2023.

UNESCO Institute for Statistics, C.P 250 Succursale H, Montreal, QC, H3G 2K8, CAN, (514) 343-6880 (Dial from U.S.), (514) 343-5740 (Fax from U.S.), uis.publications@unesco.org, http://uis.unesco.org/; UIS.Stat.

WRTH Publications Limited, PO Box 290, Oxford, OX2 7FT, GBR, sales@wrth.com, https://www.wrth.com; World Radio TV Handbook 2023.

COOK ISLANDS-BUDGET

Central Intelligence Agency (CIA), Office of Public Affairs, Washington, DC, 20505, USA, (703) 482-0623, https://www.cia.gov; The World Factbook.

COOK ISLANDS-BUSINESS

United Nations Economic and Social Commission for Asia and the Pacific (ESCAP), United Nations Building, Rajadamnern Nok Ave., Bangkok, 10200, THA, https://www.unescap.org/; SDG Gateway Data Explorer.

COOK ISLANDS-CHILDBIRTH-STATISTICS

United Nations Economic and Social Commission for Asia and the Pacific (ESCAP), United Nations Building, Rajadamnern Nok Ave., Bangkok, 10200, THA, https://www.unescap.org/; Asia-Pacific Development Journal.

COOK ISLANDS-COAL PRODUCTION

See COOK ISLANDS-MINERAL INDUSTRIES

COOK ISLANDS-COMMERCE

Palgrave Macmillan, 1 New York Plaza, Ste. 4500, New York, NY, 10004-1562, USA, (800) 777-4643, orders@palgrave.com, https://www.palgrave.com/us; The Statesman's Yearbook, 2023.

UK Data Service, University of Essex, Wivenhoe Park, Colchester, Essex, CO4 3SQ, GBR, https://ukdataservice.ac.uk/; International Aggregate Data.

COOK ISLANDS-CONSUMER PRICE INDEXES

Asian Development Bank (ADB), 6 ADB Ave., Mandaluyong City, 1550, PHL, information@adb.org, https://www.adb.org/; Key Indicators for Asia and the Pacific 2022.

Routledge - Taylor & Francis Group, 6000 Broken Sound Pkwy. NW, Ste. 300, Boca Raton, FL, 33487, USA, (800) 634-1420, (800) 634-7064, orders@taylorandfrancis.com, https://www.routledge.com/; The Europa World Year Book 2022.

COOK ISLANDS-CORN INDUSTRY

See COOK ISLANDS-CROPS

COOK ISLANDS-CROPS

Palgrave Macmillan, 1 New York Plaza, Ste. 4500, New York, NY, 10004-1562, USA, (800) 777-4643, orders@palgrave.com, https://www.palgrave.com/us; The Statesman's Yearbook, 2023.

United Nations Food and Agricultural Organization (FAO), 2121 K St., Ste. 800B, Washington, DC, 20037, USA, (202) 653-2400 (Dial from U.S.), (202) 653-5760 (Fax from U.S.), fao-hq@fao.org, https://www.fao.org; The State of Food and Agriculture (SOFA) 2022.

COOK ISLANDS-DAIRY PROCESSING

United Nations Food and Agricultural Organization (FAO), 2121 K St., Ste. 800B, Washington, DC, 20037, USA, (202) 653-2400 (Dial from U.S.), (202) 653-5760 (Fax from U.S.), fao-hq@fao.org, https://www.fao.org; The State of Food and Agriculture (SOFA) 2022.

COOK ISLANDS-DEBTS, EXTERNAL

Asian Development Bank (ADB), 6 ADB Ave., Mandaluyong City, 1550, PHL, information@adb.org, https://www.adb.org/; Key Indicators for Asia and the Pacific 2022.

COOK ISLANDS-ECONOMIC ASSISTANCE

United Nations Statistics Division (UNSD), United Nations Plz., New York, NY, 10017, USA, (800) 253-9646, (212) 963-9851, statistics@un.org, https://unstats.un.org; Statistical Yearbook of the United Nations 2021.

COOK ISLANDS-ECONOMIC CONDITIONS

Asian Development Bank (ADB), 6 ADB Ave., Mandaluyong City, 1550, PHL, information@adb.org, https://www.adb.org/; Key Indicators for Asia and the Pacific 2022.

Bernan Press, 15250 NBN Way, Bldg. C, Blue Ridge Summit, PA, 17214, USA, (301) 459-2255, (800) 865-3457, (800) 865-3450, customercare@bernan.com, https://rowman.com/Page/Bernan; World Economic Outlook, April 2022.

Central Intelligence Agency (CIA), Office of Public Affairs, Washington, DC, 20505, USA, (703) 482-0623, https://www.cia.gov; The World Factbook.

Palgrave Macmillan, 1 New York Plaza, Ste. 4500, New York, NY, 10004-1562, USA, (800) 777-4643, orders@palgrave.com, https://www.palgrave.com/us; The Statesman's Yearbook, 2023.

Secretariat of the Pacific Community (SPC), Statistics for Development Division (SDD), 95 Promenade Roger Laroque, Anse Vata , BP D5, Noumea, 98848, NCL, spc@spc.int, https://sdd.spc.int/; The Economic and Social Impact of the COVID-19 Pandemic on the Pacific Island Economies and Statistics for Development Division Data.

United Nations Statistics Division (UNSD), United Nations Plz., New York, NY, 10017, USA, (800) 253-9646, (212) 963-9851, statistics@un.org, https://unstats.un.org; World Statistics Pocketbook 2021.

COOK ISLANDS-EDUCATION

Palgrave Macmillan, 1 New York Plaza, Ste. 4500, New York, NY, 10004-1562, USA, (800) 777-4643, orders@palgrave.com, https://www.palgrave.com/us; The Statesman's Yearbook, 2023.

Routledge - Taylor & Francis Group, 6000 Broken Sound Pkwy. NW, Ste. 300, Boca Raton, FL, 33487, USA, (800) 634-1420, (800) 634-7064, orders@taylorandfrancis.com, https://www.routledge.com/; The Europa World Year Book 2022.

UNESCO Institute for Statistics, C.P 250 Succursale H, Montreal, QC, H3G 2K8, CAN, (514) 343-6880 (Dial from U.S.), (514) 343-5740 (Fax from U.S.), uis.publications@unesco.org, http://uis.unesco.org/; UIS.Stat.

United Nations Economic and Social Commission for Asia and the Pacific (ESCAP), United Nations Building, Rajadamnern Nok Ave., Bangkok, 10200, THA, https://www.unescap.org/; Asia-Pacific Development Journal and SDG Gateway Data Explorer.

COOK ISLANDS-EMPLOYMENT

International Labour Organization (ILO), 4 Rte. des Morillons, Geneva, CH-1211, SWI, ilo@ilo.org, https://www.ilo.org; NORMLEX Information System on International Labour Standards.

UK Data Service, University of Essex, Wivenhoe Park, Colchester, Essex, CO4 3SQ, GBR, https://ukdataservice.ac.uk/; International Aggregate Data.

United Nations Economic and Social Commission for Asia and the Pacific (ESCAP), United Nations Building, Rajadamnern Nok Ave., Bangkok, 10200, THA, https://www.unescap.org/; Asia-Pacific Development Journal.

COOK ISLANDS-ENVIRONMENTAL CONDITIONS

United Nations Statistics Division (UNSD), United Nations Plz., New York, NY, 10017, USA, (800) 253-9646, (212) 963-9851, statistics@un.org, https://unstats.un.org; World Statistics Pocketbook 2021.

COOK ISLANDS-EXPORTS

Asian Development Bank (ADB), 6 ADB Ave., Mandaluyong City, 1550, PHL, information@adb.org, https://www.adb.org/; Key Indicators for Asia and the Pacific 2022.

Central Intelligence Agency (CIA), Office of Public Affairs, Washington, DC, 20505, USA, (703) 482-0623, https://www.cia.gov; The World Factbook.

COOK ISLANDS-FERTILITY, HUMAN

Central Intelligence Agency (CIA), Office of Public Affairs, Washington, DC, 20505, USA, (703) 482-0623, https://www.cia.gov; The World Factbook.

COOK ISLANDS-FERTILIZER INDUSTRY

United Nations Food and Agricultural Organization (FAO), 2121 K St., Ste. 800B, Washington, DC, 20037, USA, (202) 653-2400 (Dial from U.S.), (202) 653-5760 (Fax from U.S.), fao-hq@fao.org, https://www.fao.org; The State of Food and Agriculture (SOFA) 2022.

COOK ISLANDS-FETAL MORTALITY

See COOK ISLANDS-MORTALITY

COOK ISLANDS-FINANCE

Stockholm International Peace Research Institute (SIPRI), Signalistgatan 9, Stockholm, SE 169 72, SWE, https://www.sipri.org/; SIPRI Arms Transfers Database and SIPRI Military Expenditure Database.

United Nations Economic and Social Commission for Asia and the Pacific (ESCAP), United Nations Building, Rajadamnern Nok Ave., Bangkok, 10200, THA, https://www.unescap.org/; Asia-Pacific Development Journal and SDG Gateway Data Explorer.

United Nations Statistics Division (UNSD), United Nations Plz., New York, NY, 10017, USA, (800) 253-9646, (212) 963-9851, statistics@un.org, https://unstats.un.org; Statistical Yearbook of the United Nations 2021.

COOK ISLANDS-FINANCE, PUBLIC

Asian Development Bank (ADB), 6 ADB Ave., Mandaluyong City, 1550, PHL, information@adb.org, https://www.adb.org/; Key Indicators for Asia and the Pacific 2022.

Palgrave Macmillan, 1 New York Plaza, Ste. 4500, New York, NY, 10004-1562, USA, (800) 777-4643, orders@palgrave.com, https://www.palgrave.com/us; The Statesman's Yearbook, 2023.

Routledge - Taylor & Francis Group, 6000 Broken Sound Pkwy. NW, Ste. 300, Boca Raton, FL, 33487, USA, (800) 634-1420, (800) 634-7064, orders@taylorandfrancis.com, https://www.routledge.com/; The Europa World Year Book 2022.

United Nations Economic and Social Commission for Asia and the Pacific (ESCAP), United Nations Building, Rajadamnern Nok Ave., Bangkok, 10200, THA, https://www.unescap.org/; SDG Gateway Data Explorer.

United Nations Statistics Division (UNSD), United Nations Plz., New York, NY, 10017, USA, (800) 253-9646, (212) 963-9851, statistics@un.org, https://unstats.un.org; National Accounts Main Aggregates Database and National Accounts Statistics: Main Aggregates and Detailed Tables.

COOK ISLANDS-FISHERIES

Palgrave Macmillan, 1 New York Plaza, Ste. 4500, New York, NY, 10004-1562, USA, (800) 777-4643, orders@palgrave.com, https://www.palgrave.com/us; The Statesman's Yearbook, 2023.

Routledge - Taylor & Francis Group, 6000 Broken Sound Pkwy. NW, Ste. 300, Boca Raton, FL, 33487, USA, (800) 634-1420, (800) 634-7064, orders@taylorandfrancis.com, https://www.routledge.com/; The Europa World Year Book 2022.

United Nations Food and Agricultural Organization (FAO), 2121 K St., Ste. 800B, Washington, DC, 20037, USA, (202) 653-2400 (Dial from U.S.), (202) 653-5760 (Fax from U.S.), fao-hq@fao.org, https://www.fao.org; FAO Yearbook of Fishery and Aquaculture Statistics 2019; Fishery Statistical Collections Global Capture Production; FishStatJ; and The State of Food and Agriculture (SOFA) 2022.

United Nations Statistics Division (UNSD), United Nations Plz., New York, NY, 10017, USA, (800) 253-9646, (212) 963-9851, statistics@un.org, https://unstats.un.org; Statistical Yearbook of the United Nations 2021.

COOK ISLANDS-FOOD

United Nations Economic and Social Commission for Asia and the Pacific (ESCAP), United Nations Building, Rajadamnern Nok Ave., Bangkok, 10200, THA, https://www.unescap.org/; SDG Gateway Data Explorer.

United Nations Food and Agricultural Organization (FAO), 2121 K St., Ste. 800B, Washington, DC, 20037, USA, (202) 653-2400 (Dial from U.S.), (202) 653-5760 (Fax from U.S.), fao-hq@fao.org, https://www.fao.org; The State of Food and Agriculture (SOFA) 2022.

COOK ISLANDS-FOREIGN EXCHANGE RATES

Asian Development Bank (ADB), 6 ADB Ave., Mandaluyong City, 1550, PHL, information@adb.org, https://www.adb.org/; Key Indicators for Asia and the Pacific 2022.

COOK ISLANDS-FORESTS AND FORESTRY

UNESCO Institute for Statistics, C.P 250 Succursale H, Montreal, QC, H3G 2K8, CAN, (514) 343-6880 (Dial from U.S.), (514) 343-5740 (Fax from U.S.), uis.publications@unesco.org, http://uis.unesco.org/; UIS.Stat.

United Nations Food and Agricultural Organization (FAO), 2121 K St., Ste. 800B, Washington, DC, 20037, USA, (202) 653-2400 (Dial from U.S.), (202) 653-5760 (Fax from U.S.), fao-hq@fao.org, https://www.fao.org; The State of Food and Agriculture (SOFA) 2022.

United Nations Statistics Division (UNSD), United Nations Plz., New York, NY, 10017, USA, (800) 253-9646, (212) 963-9851, statistics@un.org, https://unstats.un.org; Statistical Yearbook of the United Nations 2021.

COOK ISLANDS-GROSS DOMESTIC PRODUCT

Asian Development Bank (ADB), 6 ADB Ave., Mandaluyong City, 1550, PHL, information@adb.org, https://www.adb.org/; Key Indicators for Asia and the Pacific 2022.

Routledge - Taylor & Francis Group, 6000 Broken Sound Pkwy. NW, Ste. 300, Boca Raton, FL, 33487, USA, (800) 634-1420, (800) 634-7064, orders@taylorandfrancis.com, https://www.routledge.com/; The Europa World Year Book 2022.

United Nations Statistics Division (UNSD), United Nations Plz., New York, NY, 10017, USA, (800) 253-9646, (212) 963-9851, statistics@un.org, https://unstats.un.org; Statistical Yearbook of the United Nations 2021.

COOK ISLANDS-GROSS NATIONAL PRODUCT

Asian Development Bank (ADB), 6 ADB Ave., Mandaluyong City, 1550, PHL, information@adb.org, https://www.adb.org/; Key Indicators for Asia and the Pacific 2022.

United Nations Statistics Division (UNSD), United Nations Plz., New York, NY, 10017, USA, (800) 253-9646, (212) 963-9851, statistics@un.org, https://unstats.un.org; Statistical Yearbook of the United Nations 2021.

COOK ISLANDS-HOUSING

United Nations Statistics Division (UNSD), United Nations Plz., New York, NY, 10017, USA, (800) 253-9646, (212) 963-9851, statistics@un.org, https://unstats.un.org; Statistical Yearbook of the United Nations 2021.

COOK ISLANDS-ILLITERATE PERSONS

UNESCO Institute for Statistics, C.P 250 Succursale H, Montreal, QC, H3G 2K8, CAN, (514) 343-6880 (Dial from U.S.), (514) 343-5740 (Fax from U.S.), uis.publications@unesco.org, http://uis.unesco.org/; UIS.Stat.

United Nations Economic and Social Commission for Asia and the Pacific (ESCAP), United Nations Building, Rajadamnern Nok Ave., Bangkok, 10200, THA, https://www.unescap.org/; Asia-Pacific Development Journal.

COOK ISLANDS-IMPORTS

Asian Development Bank (ADB), 6 ADB Ave., Mandaluyong City, 1550, PHL, information@adb.org, https://www.adb.org/; Key Indicators for Asia and the Pacific 2022.

Central Intelligence Agency (CIA), Office of Public Affairs, Washington, DC, 20505, USA, (703) 482-0623, https://www.cia.gov; The World Factbook.

COOK ISLANDS-INDUSTRIES

Central Intelligence Agency (CIA), Office of Public Affairs, Washington, DC, 20505, USA, (703) 482-0623, https://www.cia.gov; The World Factbook.

International Labour Organization (ILO), 4 Rte. des Morillons, Geneva, CH-1211, SWI, ilo@ilo.org, https://www.ilo.org; NORMLEX Information System on International Labour Standards.

Palgrave Macmillan, 1 New York Plaza, Ste. 4500, New York, NY, 10004-1562, USA, (800) 777-4643, orders@palgrave.com, https://www.palgrave.com/us; The Statesman's Yearbook, 2023.

United Nations Economic and Social Commission for Asia and the Pacific (ESCAP), United Nations Building, Rajadamnern Nok Ave., Bangkok, 10200, THA, https://www.unescap.org/; Asia-Pacific Development Journal and SDG Gateway Data Explorer.

COOK ISLANDS-INFANT AND MATERNAL MORTALITY

See COOK ISLANDS-MORTALITY

COOK ISLANDS-INTERNATIONAL FINANCE

Asian Development Bank (ADB), 6 ADB Ave., Mandaluyong City, 1550, PHL, information@adb.org, https://www.adb.org/; Key Indicators for Asia and the Pacific 2022.

COOK ISLANDS-INTERNATIONAL TRADE

Asian Development Bank (ADB), 6 ADB Ave., Mandaluyong City, 1550, PHL, information@adb.org, https://www.adb.org/; Key Indicators for Asia and the Pacific 2022.

Mercy Corps, 45 SW Ankeny St., Portland, OR, 97204, USA, (800) 292-3355, (503) 896-5000, https://www.mercycorps.org/; Time to Turn Around: The Decline of UK Peacebuilding.

Palgrave Macmillan, 1 New York Plaza, Ste. 4500, New York, NY, 10004-1562, USA, (800) 777-4643, orders@palgrave.com, https://www.palgrave.com/us; The Statesman's Yearbook, 2023.

Routledge - Taylor & Francis Group, 6000 Broken Sound Pkwy. NW, Ste. 300, Boca Raton, FL, 33487, USA, (800) 634-1420, (800) 634-7064, orders@taylorandfrancis.com, https://www.routledge.com/; The Europa World Year Book 2022.

United Nations Conference on Trade and Development (UNCTAD), Palais des Nations, Geneva, 1211, SWI, (212) 963-6896, unctadinfo@unctad.org, https://unctad.org; Trade and Development Report 2021.

United Nations Economic and Social Commission for Asia and the Pacific (ESCAP), United Nations Building, Rajadamnern Nok Ave., Bangkok, 10200, THA, https://www.unescap.org/; Asia-Pacific Development Journal and SDG Gateway Data Explorer.

United Nations Food and Agricultural Organization (FAO), 2121 K St., Ste. 800B, Washington, DC, 20037, USA, (202) 653-2400 (Dial from U.S.), (202) 653-5760 (Fax from U.S.), fao-hq@fao.org, https://www.fao.org; The State of Food and Agriculture (SOFA) 2022.

United Nations Statistics Division (UNSD), United Nations Plz., New York, NY, 10017, USA, (800) 253-9646, (212) 963-9851, statistics@un.org, https://unstats.un.org; International Trade Statistics Yearbook 2020 and Statistical Yearbook of the United Nations 2021.

World Trade Organization (WTO), Ctre. William Rappard, Rue de Lausanne 154, Case postale, Geneva, CH-1211, SWI, enquiries@wto.org, https://www.wto.org; World Trade Statistical Review 2022.

COOK ISLANDS-LABOR

Central Intelligence Agency (CIA), Office of Public Affairs, Washington, DC, 20505, USA, (703) 482-0623, https://www.cia.gov; The World Factbook.

International Labour Organization (ILO), 4 Rte. des Morillons, Geneva, CH-1211, SWI, ilo@ilo.org, https://www.ilo.org; NORMLEX Information System on International Labour Standards.

Palgrave Macmillan, 1 New York Plaza, Ste. 4500, New York, NY, 10004-1562, USA, (800) 777-4643, orders@palgrave.com, https://www.palgrave.com/us; The Statesman's Yearbook, 2023.

United Nations Food and Agricultural Organization (FAO), 2121 K St., Ste. 800B, Washington, DC, 20037, USA, (202) 653-2400 (Dial from U.S.), (202) 653-5760 (Fax from U.S.), fao-hq@fao.org, https://www.fao.org; The State of Food and Agriculture (SOFA) 2022.

COOK ISLANDS-LIBRARIES

UNESCO Institute for Statistics, C.P 250 Succursale H, Montreal, QC, H3G 2K8, CAN, (514) 343-6880 (Dial from U.S.), (514) 343-5740 (Fax from U.S.), uis.publications@unesco.org, http://uis.unesco.org/; UIS.Stat.

COOK ISLANDS-LIFE EXPECTANCY

Central Intelligence Agency (CIA), Office of Public Affairs, Washington, DC, 20505, USA, (703) 482-0623, https://www.cia.gov; The World Factbook.

United Nations Department of Economic and Social Affairs (DESA), Population Division, 2 United Nations Plz., Rm. DC2-1950, New York, NY, 10017, USA, (212) 963-3209, (212) 963-2147, population@un.org, https://www.un.org/development/desa/pd/; World Population Ageing 2020 Highlights.

United Nations Economic and Social Commission for Asia and the Pacific (ESCAP), United Nations Building, Rajadamnern Nok Ave., Bangkok, 10200, THA, https://www.unescap.org/; Asia-Pacific Development Journal.

COOK ISLANDS-LIVESTOCK

Palgrave Macmillan, 1 New York Plaza, Ste. 4500, New York, NY, 10004-1562, USA, (800) 777-4643, orders@palgrave.com, https://www.palgrave.com/us; The Statesman's Yearbook, 2023.

Routledge - Taylor & Francis Group, 6000 Broken Sound Pkwy. NW, Ste. 300, Boca Raton, FL, 33487, USA, (800) 634-1420, (800) 634-7064, orders@taylorandfrancis.com, https://www.routledge.com/; The Europa World Year Book 2022.

United Nations Food and Agricultural Organization (FAO), 2121 K St., Ste. 800B, Washington, DC, 20037, USA, (202) 653-2400 (Dial from U.S.), (202) 653-5760 (Fax from U.S.), fao-hq@fao.org, https://www.fao.org; The State of Food and Agriculture (SOFA) 2022.

United Nations Statistics Division (UNSD), United Nations Plz., New York, NY, 10017, USA, (800) 253-9646, (212) 963-9851, statistics@un.org, https://unstats.un.org; Statistical Yearbook of the United Nations 2021.

COOK ISLANDS-MANPOWER

United Nations Economic and Social Commission for Asia and the Pacific (ESCAP), United Nations Building, Rajadamnern Nok Ave., Bangkok, 10200, THA, https://www.unescap.org/; SDG Gateway Data Explorer.

COOK ISLANDS-MANUFACTURES

Asian Development Bank (ADB), 6 ADB Ave., Mandaluyong City, 1550, PHL, information@adb.org, https://www.adb.org/; Key Indicators for Asia and the Pacific 2022.

COOK ISLANDS-MARRIAGE

Routledge - Taylor & Francis Group, 6000 Broken Sound Pkwy. NW, Ste. 300, Boca Raton, FL, 33487, USA, (800) 634-1420, (800) 634-7064, orders@taylorandfrancis.com, https://www.routledge.com/; The Europa World Year Book 2022.

United Nations Statistics Division (UNSD), United Nations Plz., New York, NY, 10017, USA, (800) 253-9646, (212) 963-9851, statistics@un.org, https://unstats.un.org; Statistical Yearbook of the United Nations 2021.

COOK ISLANDS-MINERAL INDUSTRIES

Asian Development Bank (ADB), 6 ADB Ave., Mandaluyong City, 1550, PHL, information@adb.org, https://www.adb.org/; Key Indicators for Asia and the Pacific 2022.

United Nations Conference on Trade and Development (UNCTAD), Palais des Nations, Geneva, 1211, SWI, (212) 963-6896, unctadinfo@unctad.org, https://unctad.org; Trade and Development Report 2021.

COOK ISLANDS-MORTALITY

United Nations Economic and Social Commission for Asia and the Pacific (ESCAP), United Nations Building, Rajadamnern Nok Ave., Bangkok, 10200, THA, https://www.unescap.org/; Asia-Pacific Development Journal.

United Nations Statistics Division (UNSD), United Nations Plz., New York, NY, 10017, USA, (800) 253-9646, (212) 963-9851, statistics@un.org, https://unstats.un.org; Statistical Yearbook of the United Nations 2021 and World Statistics Pocketbook 2021.

COOK ISLANDS-NUTRITION

Asian Development Bank (ADB), 6 ADB Ave., Mandaluyong City, 1550, PHL, information@adb.org, https://www.adb.org/; Key Indicators for Asia and the Pacific 2022.

United Nations Food and Agricultural Organization (FAO), 2121 K St., Ste. 800B, Washington, DC, 20037, USA, (202) 653-2400 (Dial from U.S.), (202) 653-5760 (Fax from U.S.), fao-hq@fao.org, https://www.fao.org; The State of Food and Agriculture (SOFA) 2022.

COOK ISLANDS-PESTICIDES

United Nations Food and Agricultural Organization (FAO), 2121 K St., Ste. 800B, Washington, DC, 20037, USA, (202) 653-2400 (Dial from U.S.), (202) 653-5760 (Fax from U.S.), fao-hq@fao.org, https://www.fao.org; The State of Food and Agriculture (SOFA) 2022.

COOK ISLANDS-PETROLEUM INDUSTRY AND TRADE

Asian Development Bank (ADB), 6 ADB Ave., Mandaluyong City, 1550, PHL, information@adb.org, https://www.adb.org/; Key Indicators for Asia and the Pacific 2022.

United Nations Food and Agricultural Organization (FAO), 2121 K St., Ste. 800B, Washington, DC, 20037, USA, (202) 653-2400 (Dial from U.S.), (202) 653-5760 (Fax from U.S.), fao-hq@fao.org, https://www.fao.org; The State of Food and Agriculture (SOFA) 2022.

COOK ISLANDS-POPULATION

Asian Development Bank (ADB), 6 ADB Ave., Mandaluyong City, 1550, PHL, information@adb.org, https://www.adb.org/; Key Indicators for Asia and the Pacific 2022.

Central Intelligence Agency (CIA), Office of Public Affairs, Washington, DC, 20505, USA, (703) 482-0623, https://www.cia.gov; The World Factbook.

International Labour Organization (ILO), 4 Rte. des Morillons, Geneva, CH-1211, SWI, ilo@ilo.org, https://www.ilo.org; NORMLEX Information System on International Labour Standards.

Palgrave Macmillan, 1 New York Plaza, Ste. 4500, New York, NY, 10004-1562, USA, (800) 777-4643, orders@palgrave.com, https://www.palgrave.com/us; The Statesman's Yearbook, 2023.

Routledge - Taylor & Francis Group, 6000 Broken Sound Pkwy. NW, Ste. 300, Boca Raton, FL, 33487, USA, (800) 634-1420, (800) 634-7064, orders@taylorandfrancis.com, https://www.routledge.com/; The Europa World Year Book 2022.

UK Data Service, University of Essex, Wivenhoe Park, Colchester, Essex, CO4 3SQ, GBR, https://ukdataservice.ac.uk/; International Aggregate Data.

UNESCO Institute for Statistics, C.P 250 Succursale H, Montreal, QC, H3G 2K8, CAN, (514) 343-6880 (Dial from U.S.), (514) 343-5740 (Fax from U.S.), uis.publications@unesco.org, http://uis.unesco.org/; UIS.Stat.

United Nations Department of Economic and Social Affairs (DESA), Population Division, 2 United Nations Plz., Rm. DC2-1950, New York, NY, 10017, USA, (212) 963-3209, (212) 963-2147, population@un.org, https://www.un.org/development/desa/pd/; Revision of World Urbanization Prospects and World Population Ageing 2020 Highlights.

United Nations Economic and Social Commission for Asia and the Pacific (ESCAP), United Nations Building, Rajadamnern Nok Ave., Bangkok, 10200, THA, https://www.unescap.org/; Asia-Pacific Development Journal and SDG Gateway Data Explorer.

United Nations Statistics Division (UNSD), United Nations Plz., New York, NY, 10017, USA, (800) 253-9646, (212) 963-9851, statistics@un.org, https://unstats.un.org; Statistical Yearbook of the United Nations 2021 and World Statistics Pocketbook 2021.

COOK ISLANDS-POPULATION DENSITY

Central Intelligence Agency (CIA), Office of Public Affairs, Washington, DC, 20505, USA, (703) 482-0623, https://www.cia.gov; The World Factbook.

Palgrave Macmillan, 1 New York Plaza, Ste. 4500, New York, NY, 10004-1562, USA, (800) 777-4643, orders@palgrave.com, https://www.palgrave.com/us; The Statesman's Yearbook, 2023.

Routledge - Taylor & Francis Group, 6000 Broken Sound Pkwy. NW, Ste. 300, Boca Raton, FL, 33487, USA, (800) 634-1420, (800) 634-7064, orders@taylorandfrancis.com, https://www.routledge.com/; The Europa World Year Book 2022.

UNESCO Institute for Statistics, C.P 250 Succursale H, Montreal, QC, H3G 2K8, CAN, (514) 343-6880 (Dial from U.S.), (514) 343-5740 (Fax from U.S.), uis.publications@unesco.org, http://uis.unesco.org/; UIS.Stat.

COOK ISLANDS-POWER RESOURCES

Palgrave Macmillan, 1 New York Plaza, Ste. 4500, New York, NY, 10004-1562, USA, (800) 777-4643, orders@palgrave.com, https://www.palgrave.com/us; The Statesman's Yearbook, 2023.

United Nations Economic and Social Commission for Asia and the Pacific (ESCAP), United Nations Building, Rajadamnern Nok Ave., Bangkok, 10200, THA, https://www.unescap.org/; Asia-Pacific Development Journal and SDG Gateway Data Explorer.

United Nations Food and Agricultural Organization (FAO), 2121 K St., Ste. 800B, Washington, DC, 20037, USA, (202) 653-2400 (Dial from U.S.), (202) 653-5760 (Fax from U.S.), fao-hq@fao.org, https://www.fao.org; The State of Food and Agriculture (SOFA) 2022.

United Nations Statistics Division (UNSD), United Nations Plz., New York, NY, 10017, USA, (800) 253-9646, (212) 963-9851, statistics@un.org, https://unstats.un.org; Energy Statistics Yearbook 2019; Statistical Yearbook of the United Nations 2021; and World Statistics Pocketbook 2021.

COOK ISLANDS-PRICES

Asian Development Bank (ADB), 6 ADB Ave., Mandaluyong City, 1550, PHL, information@adb.org, https://www.adb.org/; Key Indicators for Asia and the Pacific 2022.

COOK ISLANDS-PUBLIC HEALTH

Palgrave Macmillan, 1 New York Plaza, Ste. 4500, New York, NY, 10004-1562, USA, (800) 777-4643, orders@palgrave.com, https://www.palgrave.com/us; The Statesman's Yearbook, 2023.

U.S. Census Bureau, 4600 Silver Hill Rd., Washington, DC, 20233, USA, (301) 763-4636, (800) 923-8282, https://www.census.gov; HIV/AIDS Surveillance Data Base.

United Nations Department of Economic and Social Affairs (DESA), Population Division, 2 United Nations Plz., Rm. DC2-1950, New York, NY, 10017, USA, (212) 963-3209, (212) 963-2147, population@un.org, https://www.un.org/development/desa/pd/; World Fertility Data 2019.

United Nations Economic and Social Commission for Asia and the Pacific (ESCAP), United Nations Building, Rajadamnern Nok Ave., Bangkok, 10200, THA, https://www.unescap.org/; Asia-Pacific Development Journal.

United Nations Statistics Division (UNSD), United Nations Plz., New York, NY, 10017, USA, (800) 253-9646, (212) 963-9851, statistics@un.org, https://unstats.un.org; Statistical Yearbook of the United Nations 2021.

World Health Organization (WHO), Ave. Appia 20, Geneva, CH-1211, SWI, (202) 974-3000 (Telephone in U.S.), publications@who.int, https://www.who.int/; Health Statistics and Information Systems.

COOK ISLANDS-RELIGION

Central Intelligence Agency (CIA), Office of Public Affairs, Washington, DC, 20505, USA, (703) 482-0623, https://www.cia.gov; The World Factbook.

Palgrave Macmillan, 1 New York Plaza, Ste. 4500, New York, NY, 10004-1562, USA, (800) 777-4643, orders@palgrave.com, https://www.palgrave.com/us; The Statesman's Yearbook, 2023.

COOK ISLANDS-RICE PRODUCTION

See COOK ISLANDS-CROPS

COOK ISLANDS-SHIPPING

Routledge - Taylor & Francis Group, 6000 Broken Sound Pkwy. NW, Ste. 300, Boca Raton, FL, 33487, USA, (800) 634-1420, (800) 634-7064, orders@taylorandfrancis.com, https://www.routledge.com/; The Europa World Year Book 2022.

United Nations Statistics Division (UNSD), United Nations Plz., New York, NY, 10017, USA, (800) 253-9646, (212) 963-9851, statistics@un.org, https://unstats.un.org; Statistical Yearbook of the United Nations 2021.

COOK ISLANDS-TAXATION

Inter-American Development Bank (IDB), 1300 New York Ave. NW, Washington, DC, 20577, USA, (202) 623-1000, (202) 623-3096, https://www.iadb.org/en; Latin Macro Watch (LMW).

Palgrave Macmillan, 1 New York Plaza, Ste. 4500, New York, NY, 10004-1562, USA, (800) 777-4643, orders@palgrave.com, https://www.palgrave.com/us; The Statesman's Yearbook, 2023.

COOK ISLANDS-TELEPHONE

Palgrave Macmillan, 1 New York Plaza, Ste. 4500, New York, NY, 10004-1562, USA, (800) 777-4643, orders@palgrave.com, https://www.palgrave.com/us; The Statesman's Yearbook, 2023.

Routledge - Taylor & Francis Group, 6000 Broken Sound Pkwy. NW, Ste. 300, Boca Raton, FL, 33487, USA, (800) 634-1420, (800) 634-7064, orders@taylorandfrancis.com, https://www.routledge.com/; The Europa World Year Book 2022.

United Nations Statistics Division (UNSD), United Nations Plz., New York, NY, 10017, USA, (800) 253-9646, (212) 963-9851, statistics@un.org, https://unstats.un.org; World Statistics Pocketbook 2021.

COOK ISLANDS-TEXTILE INDUSTRY

Palgrave Macmillan, 1 New York Plaza, Ste. 4500, New York, NY, 10004-1562, USA, (800) 777-4643, orders@palgrave.com, https://www.palgrave.com/us; The Statesman's Yearbook, 2023.

COOK ISLANDS-TOURISM

Routledge - Taylor & Francis Group, 6000 Broken Sound Pkwy. NW, Ste. 300, Boca Raton, FL, 33487, USA, (800) 634-1420, (800) 634-7064, orders@taylorandfrancis.com, https://www.routledge.com/; The Europa World Year Book 2022.

United Nations Statistics Division (UNSD), United Nations Plz., New York, NY, 10017, USA, (800) 253-9646, (212) 963-9851, statistics@un.org, https://unstats.un.org; Statistical Yearbook of the United Nations 2021.

United Nations World Tourism Organization (UNWTO), Calle Poeta Joan Maragall 42, Madrid, 28020, SPA, info@unwto.org, https://www.unwto.org/; Yearbook of Tourism Statistics, 2021 Edition.

COOK ISLANDS-TRADE

See COOK ISLANDS-INTERNATIONAL TRADE

COOK ISLANDS-TRANSPORTATION

Central Intelligence Agency (CIA), Office of Public Affairs, Washington, DC, 20505, USA, (703) 482-0623, https://www.cia.gov; The World Factbook.

Palgrave Macmillan, 1 New York Plaza, Ste. 4500, New York, NY, 10004-1562, USA, (800) 777-4643, orders@palgrave.com, https://www.palgrave.com/us; The Statesman's Yearbook, 2023.

Routledge - Taylor & Francis Group, 6000 Broken Sound Pkwy. NW, Ste. 300, Boca Raton, FL, 33487,

USA, (800) 634-1420, (800) 634-7064, orders@taylorandfrancis.com, https://www.routledge.com/; The Europa World Year Book 2022.

United Nations Economic and Social Commission for Asia and the Pacific (ESCAP), United Nations Building, Rajadamnern Nok Ave., Bangkok, 10200, THA, https://www.unescap.org/; SDG Gateway Data Explorer.

COOK ISLANDS-UNEMPLOYMENT

International Labour Organization (ILO), 4 Rte. des Morillons, Geneva, CH-1211, SWI, ilo@ilo.org, https://www.ilo.org; NORMLEX Information System on International Labour Standards.

COOK ISLANDS-VITAL STATISTICS

Palgrave Macmillan, 1 New York Plaza, Ste. 4500, New York, NY, 10004-1562, USA, (800) 777-4643, orders@palgrave.com, https://www.palgrave.com/us; The Statesman's Yearbook, 2023.

U.S. Census Bureau, 4600 Silver Hill Rd., Washington, DC, 20233, USA, (301) 763-4636, (800) 923-8282, https://www.census.gov; HIV/AIDS Surveillance Data Base.

United Nations Department of Economic and Social Affairs (DESA), Population Division, 2 United Nations Plz., Rm. DC2-1950, New York, NY, 10017, USA, (212) 963-3209, (212) 963-2147, population@un.org, https://www.un.org/development/desa/pd/; World Contraceptive Use 2021: Estimates and Projections of Family Planning Indicators and World Marriage Data 2019.

COOK ISLANDS-WAGES

International Labour Organization (ILO), 4 Rte. des Morillons, Geneva, CH-1211, SWI, ilo@ilo.org, https://www.ilo.org; NORMLEX Information System on International Labour Standards.

United Nations Economic and Social Commission for Asia and the Pacific (ESCAP), United Nations Building, Rajadamnern Nok Ave., Bangkok, 10200, THA, https://www.unescap.org/; SDG Gateway Data Explorer.

COOKIES

U.S. Department of Labor (DOL), Bureau of Labor Statistics (BLS), Postal Square Bldg., 2 Massachusetts Ave. NE, Washington, DC, 20212-0001, USA, (202) 691-5200, (202) 691-7890, blsdata_staff@bls.gov, https://www.bls.gov; Consumer Price Index (CPI) Databases.

COOKIES (COMPUTER SCIENCE)

Princeton University Center for Information Technology Policy (CITP), Princeton Web Transparency & Accountability Project (WebTAP), 308 Sherrerd Hall, Princeton, NJ, 08544, USA, (609) 258-9302, arvindn@cs.princeton.edu, https://webtap.princeton.edu/; The Impact of User Location on Cookie Notices (Inside and Outside of the European Union).

COOKING (TURMERIC)

ConsumerLab, 333 Mamaroneck Ave., White Plains, NY, 10605, USA, (914) 722-9149, info@consumerlab.com, https://www.consumerlab.com; Product Review: Turmeric and Curcumin Supplements and Spices.

COOKING OILS CONSUMPTION

U.S. Department of Agriculture (USDA), Economic Research Service (ERS), 1400 Independence Ave. SW, Mail Stop 1800, Washington, DC, 20250-0002, USA, (202) 720-2791, https://www.ers.usda.gov/; Food Price Outlook.

COOPERATION

Brown University, Population Studies and Training Center (PSTC), 68 Waterman St., PO Box 1836, Providence, RI, 02912, USA, (401) 863-2668, (401) 863-3351, population_studies@brown.edu, https://www.brown.edu/academics/population-studies/; The Determinants of Efficient Behavior in Coordination Games.

COPPER-CONSUMPTION

U.S. Department of the Interior (DOI), U.S. Geological Survey (USGS), National Minerals Information Center (NMIC), 12201 Sunrise Valley Dr., Reston, VA, 20192, USA, (703) 648-4920, (703) 648-7971, (703) 648-4995, sfortier@usgs.gov, https://www.usgs.gov/centers/nmic; Mineral Commodity Summaries 2022 and Mineral Industry Surveys (MIS).

World Bureau of Metal Statistics (WBMS), 31 Star St., Ware, Hertfordshire, SG12 9BA, GBR, https://www.refinitiv.com/en/trading-solutions/world-bureau-metal-statistics; Long Term Production/Consumption Series - Copper.

COPPER-INTERNATIONAL TRADE

U.S. Department of the Interior (DOI), U.S. Geological Survey (USGS), National Minerals Information Center (NMIC), 12201 Sunrise Valley Dr., Reston, VA, 20192, USA, (703) 648-4920, (703) 648-7971, (703) 648-4995, sfortier@usgs.gov, https://www.usgs.gov/centers/nmic; Mineral Commodity Summaries 2022.

World Bureau of Metal Statistics (WBMS), 31 Star St., Ware, Hertfordshire, SG12 9BA, GBR, https://www.refinitiv.com/en/trading-solutions/world-bureau-metal-statistics; Long Term Production/Consumption Series - Copper.

COPPER-PRICES

U.S. Department of the Interior (DOI), U.S. Geological Survey (USGS), National Minerals Information Center (NMIC), 12201 Sunrise Valley Dr., Reston, VA, 20192, USA, (703) 648-4920, (703) 648-7971, (703) 648-4995, sfortier@usgs.gov, https://www.usgs.gov/centers/nmic; Mineral Commodity Summaries 2022.

World Bureau of Metal Statistics (WBMS), 31 Star St., Ware, Hertfordshire, SG12 9BA, GBR, https://www.refinitiv.com/en/trading-solutions/world-bureau-metal-statistics; Long Term Production/Consumption Series - Copper.

COPPER-PRODUCTION-WORLD

U.S. Department of the Interior (DOI), U.S. Geological Survey (USGS), National Minerals Information Center (NMIC), 12201 Sunrise Valley Dr., Reston, VA, 20192, USA, (703) 648-4920, (703) 648-7971, (703) 648-4995, sfortier@usgs.gov, https://www.usgs.gov/centers/nmic; Mineral Commodity Summaries 2022.

World Bureau of Metal Statistics (WBMS), 31 Star St., Ware, Hertfordshire, SG12 9BA, GBR, https://www.refinitiv.com/en/trading-solutions/world-bureau-metal-statistics; Long Term Production/Consumption Series - Copper.

COPPER-PRODUCTION AND VALUE

U.S. Department of the Interior (DOI), U.S. Geological Survey (USGS), National Minerals Information Center (NMIC), 12201 Sunrise Valley Dr., Reston, VA, 20192, USA, (703) 648-4920, (703) 648-7971, (703) 648-4995, sfortier@usgs.gov, https://www.usgs.gov/centers/nmic; Metal Industry Indicators (MII) and Mineral Commodity Summaries 2022.

COPYRIGHTS

World Intellectual Property Organization (WIPO), 34, chemin des Colombettes, Geneva, CH-1211, SWI, https://www.wipo.int; IP Facts and Figures 2022.

COPYRIGHTS-REGISTRATION

U.S. Copyright Office, 101 Independence Ave. SE, Washington, DC, 20559-6000, USA, (202) 707-3000, (877) 476-0778, https://www.copyright.gov/; United States Copyright Office Annual Report for Fiscal 2020.

CORAL REEFS AND ISLANDS

International Coral Reef Initiative (ICRI), https://www.icriforum.org/; Noise Pollution in Coral Reefs.

CORN-ACREAGE

U.S. Department of Agriculture (USDA), National Agricultural Statistics Service (USDA-NASS), 1400 Independence Ave. SW, Washington, DC, 20250, USA, (800) 727-9540, nass@nass.usda.gov, https://www.nass.usda.gov; Crop Production and Crop Values Annual Summary.

CORN-ACREAGE-ORGANIC

U.S. Department of Agriculture (USDA), Economic Research Service (ERS), 1400 Independence Ave. SW, Mail Stop 1800, Washington, DC, 20250-0002, USA, (202) 720-2791, https://www.ers.usda.gov/; Organic Market Summary and Trends.

CORN-CONSUMPTION

U.S. Department of Agriculture (USDA), Economic Research Service (ERS), 1400 Independence Ave. SW, Mail Stop 1800, Washington, DC, 20250-0002, USA, (202) 720-2791, https://www.ers.usda.gov/; Food Price Outlook.

CORN-GENETIC ENGINEERING

U.S. Department of Agriculture (USDA), National Agricultural Statistics Service (USDA-NASS), 1400 Independence Ave. SW, Washington, DC, 20250, USA, (800) 727-9540, nass@nass.usda.gov, https://www.nass.usda.gov; Acreage.

CORN-INTERNATIONAL TRADE

U.S. Census Bureau, International Trade Program, 4600 Silver Hill Rd., Washington, DC, 20233, USA, (800) 549-0595, eid.international.trade.data@census.gov, https://www.census.gov/foreign-trade; International Trade Data.

U.S. Department of Agriculture (USDA), Economic Research Service (ERS), 1400 Independence Ave. SW, Mail Stop 1800, Washington, DC, 20250-0002, USA, (202) 720-2791, https://www.ers.usda.gov/; Foreign Agricultural Trade of the United States (FATUS).

U.S. Department of Agriculture (USDA), Foreign Agricultural Service (FAS), 1400 Independence Ave. SW, Mail Stop 1001, Washington, DC, 20250, USA, (202) 720-3935, https://www.fas.usda.gov/; Production, Supply and Distribution Online (PSD) Online.

CORN-PESTICIDES

U.S. Department of Agriculture (USDA), Foreign Agricultural Service (FAS), 1400 Independence Ave. SW, Mail Stop 1001, Washington, DC, 20250, USA, (202) 720-3935, https://www.fas.usda.gov/; Production, Supply and Distribution Online (PSD) Online.

CORN-PRICES

U.S. Department of Agriculture (USDA), National Agricultural Statistics Service (USDA-NASS), 1400 Independence Ave. SW, Washington, DC, 20250, USA, (800) 727-9540, nass@nass.usda.gov, https://www.nass.usda.gov; Crop Production and Crop Values Annual Summary.

CORN-PRODUCTION

U.S. Department of Agriculture (USDA), Economic Research Service (ERS), 1400 Independence Ave. SW, Mail Stop 1800, Washington, DC, 20250-0002, USA, (202) 720-2791, https://www.ers.usda.gov/; Feed Yearbook: Report.

U.S. Department of Agriculture (USDA), National Agricultural Statistics Service (USDA-NASS), 1400 Independence Ave. SW, Washington, DC, 20250, USA, (800) 727-9540, nass@nass.usda.gov, https://www.nass.usda.gov; Crop Production; Crop Progress; Crop Values Annual Summary; Grain Stocks; Quick Stats; and Vegetables Annual Summary.

U.S. Department of Agriculture (USDA), World Agricultural Outlook Board, (WAOB), 1400 Independence Ave. SW, Mail Stop 3812, Washington, DC, 20250, USA, (202) 720-9805, mark.jekanowski@usda.gov, https://www.usda.gov/oce/commodity-markets/waob; World Agricultural Supply and Demand Estimates (WASDE) Report.

CORN-PRODUCTION-WORLD

International Grains Council (IGC), 1 Canada Sq., Canary Wharf, London, E14 5AE, GBR, igc@igc.int, https://www.igc.int/en/; Grain Market Report and World Grain Statistics.

U.S. Department of Agriculture (USDA), Foreign Agricultural Service (FAS), 1400 Independence Ave. SW, Mail Stop 1001, Washington, DC, 20250, USA, (202) 720-3935, https://www.fas.usda.gov/; Production, Supply and Distribution Online (PSD) Online.

CORN-SUPPLY AND DISAPPEARANCE

U.S. Department of Agriculture (USDA), Economic Research Service (ERS), 1400 Independence Ave. SW, Mail Stop 1800, Washington, DC, 20250-0002, USA, (202) 720-2791, https://www.ers.usda.gov/; Feed Yearbook: Report.

U.S. Department of Agriculture (USDA), World Agricultural Outlook Board, (WAOB), 1400 Independence Ave. SW, Mail Stop 3812, Washington, DC, 20250, USA, (202) 720-9805, mark.jekanowski@usda.gov, https://www.usda.gov/oce/commodity-markets/waob; World Agricultural Supply and Demand Estimates (WASDE) Report.

CORONAVIRUS INFECTIONS

Act Now Coalition, USA, https://www.actnowcoalition.org/; unpublished data.

Act Now Coalition: COVID Act Now, USA, info@covidactnow.org, https://covidactnow.org; U.S. COVID Tracker.

American Academy of Pediatrics (AAP), 345 Park Blvd., Itasca, IL, 60143, USA, (800) 433-9016, (847) 434-8000, mcc@aap.org, https://www.aap.org; Children and COVID-19: State-Level Data Report.

American Chemical Society (ACS), 1155 16th St. NW, Washington, DC, 20036, USA, (800) 227-5558, (202) 872-4600, help@services.acs.org, https://www.acs.org; Aerosol Filtration Efficiency of Common Fabrics Used in Respiratory Cloth Masks; Filtration Efficiencies of Nanoscale Aerosol by Cloth Mask Materials Used to Slow the Spread of SARS-CoV-2; and Household Materials Selection for Homemade Cloth Face Coverings and Their Filtration Efficiency Enhancement with Triboelectric Charging.

American Immigration Council, 1331 G St. NW , Ste. 200, Washington, DC, 20005, USA, (202) 507-7500, info@immcouncil.org, https://www.americanimmigrationcouncil.org/; Immigration and Covid-19 and Undocumented Immigrants and the Covid-19 Crisis.

American Psychological Association (APA), 750 First St. NE, Washington, DC, 20002-4242, USA, (800) 374-2721, (202) 336-5500, https://www.apa.org/; One Year On: Unhealthy Weight Gains, Increased Drinking Reported by Americans Coping with Pandemic Stress.

American Sociological Association (ASA), 1430 K St. NW, Ste. 600, Washington, DC, 20005, USA, (202) 383-9005, (202) 638-0882, publications@asanet.org, https://www.asanet.org/; Footnotes: Sociologists and Sociology During COVID-19.

American Water Works Association (AWWA), 6666 W Quincy Ave., Denver, CO, 80235, USA, (303) 794-7711, (800) 926-7337, (303) 347-0804, https://www.awwa.org/; COVID-19 Utility and Water Sector Organization Impact Survey.

Biotechnology Innovation Organization (BIO), 1201 New York NW, Ste. 1300, Washington, DC, 20005, USA, (202) 962-9200, info@bio.org, https://www.bio.org/; BIO COVID-19 Therapeutic Development Tracker.

The Brookings Institution, 1775 Massachusetts Ave. NW, Washington, DC, 20036, USA, (202) 797-6000, communications@brookings.edu, https://www.brookings.edu/; Metro Recovery Index and Three Million More Guns: The Spring 2020 Spike in Firearm Sales.

California Department of Public Health (CDPH), PO Box 997377, MS 0500, Sacramento, CA, 95899-7377, USA, (916) 558-1784, https://www.cdph.ca.gov; COVID-19 by the Numbers.

Center for Economic and Policy Research (CEPR), 1611 Connecticut Ave. NW, Ste. 400, Washington, DC, 20009, USA, (202) 293-5380, (202) 588-1356, info@cepr.net, https://cepr.net/; A Basic Demographic Profile of Workers in Frontline Industries.

Civiqs, PO Box 70008, Oakland, CA, 94612, USA, (510) 394-5664, inquiries@civiqs.com, https://civiqs.com/; How Satisfied Are You With the U.S. Government's Current Response to the Coronavirus Outbreak?.

Civis Analytics, 200 W Monroe St., 22nd Fl., Chicago, IL, 60606, USA, https://www.civisanalytics.com/; Coronavirus Pulse Survey Research; COVID-19 Impact Research; and COVID-19 in the U.S.: Consumer Insights for Business.

Climate Analytics, 135 Madison Ave., 5th Fl., Ste. 05-115, New York, NY, 10016, USA, info.ny@climateanalytics.org, https://climateanalytics.org/; 2 Steps Down the Debt Spiral: COVID-19 and Tropical Cyclones Severely Limit the Fiscal Space of Many Small Island Developing States.

The COVID Tracking Project at The Atlantic, support@covidtracking.com, https://covidtracking.com; The COVID Racial Data Tracker and COVID Tracking Project Data.

Death Penalty Information Center (DPIC), 1701 K St. NW, Ste. 205, Washington, DC, 20006, USA, (202) 289-2275, dpic@deathpenaltyinfo.org, https://deathpenaltyinfo.org/; DPIC Mid-Year Review: Pandemic and Continuing Historic Decline Produce Record-Low Death Penalty Use in First Half of 2020.

Democracy Fund Voter Study Group, 1200 17th St. NW, Ste. 300, Washington, DC, 20036, USA, (202) 420-7900, https://www.voterstudygroup.org/; COVID-19: Tracking American Perspectives.

The Economist Group, 900 3rd Ave., 16th Fl., New York, NY, 10022, USA, (212) 541-0500, (202) 429-0890, customerhelp@economist.com, https://www.economistgroup.com; Covid-19 Data: The Global Normalcy Index.

Elsevier, Radarweg 29, Amsterdam, 1043 NX, NLD, https://www.elsevier.com; Novel Coronavirus Information Center.

Euromonitor International, Inc., 1 N Dearborn St., Ste. 1700, Chicago, IL, 60602, USA, (312) 922-1115, (312) 922-1157, info-usa@euromonitor.com, https://www.euromonitor.com/; The Impact of Coronavirus on Consumer Finance; The Impact of Coronavirus on Consumer Goods and Services in the Middle East; and The Impact of Coronavirus on Top 10 Global Consumer Trends 2020.

European Centre for Disease Prevention and Control (ECDC), Stockholm, SE 171 83, SWE, ecdc.info@ecdc.europa.eu, https://ecdc.europa.eu; COVID-19: Country Overview Report.

Federal Bureau of Prisons (BOP), 320 First St. NW, Washington, DC, 20534 , USA, (202) 307-3198, https://www.bop.gov/; Inmate COVID-19 Data: A Look at the Impact of COVID-19 on Individuals in Federal Custody.

FiveThirtyEight, 47 W 66th St., 2nd Fl., New York, NY, 10023, USA, contact@fivethirtyeight.com, https://fivethirtyeight.com/; Where the Latest COVID-19 Models Think We're Headed - And Why They Disagree.

Global Change Data Lab, Our World in Data, GBR, info@ourworldindata.org, https://ourworldindata.org; Coronavirus Pandemic (COVID-19); COVID-19 Database; and Which Countries Have Protected Both Health and the Economy in the Pandemic?.

Guttmacher Institute, 125 Maiden Ln., 7th Fl., New York, NY, 10038, USA, (212) 248-1111, (800) 355-0244, (212) 248-1951, info@guttmacher.org, https://www.guttmacher.org/; Early Impacts of the COVID-19 Pandemic: Findings from the 2020 Guttmacher Survey of Reproductive Health Experiences and State Policy Trends at Midyear 2022: With Roe About to Be Overturned, Some States Double Down on Abortion Restrictions.

Harvard Global Health Institute (HGHI), 42 Church St., Cambridge, MA, 02138, USA, (617) 384-5431, globalhealth@harvard.edu, https://globalhealth.harvard.edu/; COVID Risk Levels Dashboard and COVID-19 Hospital Capacity Estimates 2020.

Harvard John F. Kennedy School of Government, 79 John F. Kennedy St., Cambridge, MA, 02138, USA, (617) 495-1100, https://www.hks.harvard.edu/; Harvard Kennedy School Misinformation Review - The Causes and Consequences of COVID-19 Misperceptions: Understanding the Role of News and Social Media and Harvard Kennedy School Misinformation Review - The Relation between Media Consumption and Misinformation at the Outset of the SARS-CoV-2 Pandemic in the US.

Harvard T.H. Chan School of Public Health, 677 Huntington Ave., Boston, MA, 02115, USA, (617) 495-1000, https://www.hsph.harvard.edu/; Air Pollution and COVID-19 Mortality in the United States: Strengths and Limitations of an Ecological Regression Analysis.

hc1, 6100 Technology Center Dr., Indianapolis, IN, 46278, USA, (317) 219-4646, info@hc1.com, https://www.hc1.com; CV19 Lab Testing Dashboard.

The Hechinger Report, 525 W 120th St., Ste. 127, New York, NY, 10027, USA, (212) 678-7556, (212) 678-7556, hechinger@hechingerreport.org, https://hechingerreport.org; Analysis: Hundreds of Colleges and Universities Show Financial Warning Signs; How Higher Education's Own Choices Left it Vulnerable to the Pandemic Crisis; and What Has Happened When Campuses Shut Down for Other Disasters? A Coronavirus Case Study.

The Henry J. Kaiser Family Foundation (KFF), 185 Berry St., Ste. 2000, San Francisco, CA, 94107, USA, (650) 854-9400, (650) 854-4800, https://www.kff.org; About 1.5 Million Teachers Are at Higher Risk of Serious Illness From COVID-19; Almost One in Four Adult Workers Is Vulnerable to Severe Illness from COVID-19; KFF Health Tracking Poll: Coronavirus, Delayed Care and 2020 Election; KFF Health Tracking Poll: Coronavirus: Reopening, Schools, and the Government Response; More Than 3 Million People Age 65 or Older Live with School-Age Children, and Could Be at Heightened Risk of COVID-19 Infection if Children Bring the Virus Home from School; Rising Cases in Long-term Care Facilities Are Cause for Concern; State COVID-19 Data and Policy Actions; Temporary Enhanced Federal Medicaid Funding Can Soften the Economic Blow of the COVID-19 Pandemic on States, But Is Unlikely to Fully Offset State Revenue Declines or Forestall Budget Shortfalls; and Where are the COVID-19 Hotspots? Tracking State Outbreaks.

Human Cell Atlas (HCA), hca@humancellatlas.org, https://www.humancellatlas.org/; The Local and Systemic Response to SARS-CoV-2 Infection in Children and Adults and Pre-Activated Anti-Viral Innate Immunity in the Upper Airways Controls Early SARS-CoV-2 Infection in Children.

The Immigrant Learning Center (ILC), 442 Main St., Malden, MA, 02148-5177, USA, (781) 322-9777, (800) 439-2370 (TTY), (781) 321-1963, info@ilctr.org, https://www.ilctr.org/; Health and Financial Risks for Noncitizen Immigrants due to the COVID-19 Pandemic; Immigrant Detention and COVID-19: How a Pandemic Exploited and Spread through the US Immigrant Detention System; and Latinx Workers - Particularly Women - Face Devastating Job Losses in the COVID-19 Recession.

Imperial College London, South Kensington Campus, London, SW7 2AZ, GBR, https://www.imperial.ac.uk/; Estimating the Effects of Non-Pharmaceutical Interventions on COVID-19 in Europe.

Ipsos, 360 Park Ave. S, 17th Fl., New York, NY, 10010, USA, (212) 265-3200, https://www.ipsos.com/en-us; COVID-19, Racial Inequality Among Top Political Issues for Americans and U.S. Consumer Confidence Takes a Small Step Back: Expectations Dampen with Surge of New Coronavirus Cases.

Johns Hopkins Center for Health Security, 621 E Pratt St., Ste. 210, Baltimore, MD, 21202, USA, (443) 573-3304, (443) 573-3305, centerhealthsecurity@jhu.edu, https://www.centerforhealthsecurity.org/; COVID-19 Situation Reports.

Johns Hopkins Coronavirus Resource Center, 3400 N Charles St., Baltimore, MD, 21218, USA, https://coronavirus.jhu.edu/; COVID-19 Testing Insights Initiative and Testing Trends Tool: Track Trends in COVID-19 Cases and Tests.

The Lancet, 230 Park Ave., New York, NY, 10169, USA, (212) 633-3800, editorial@lancet.com, https://www.thelancet.com/; COVID-19 Resource Centre.

The Marshall Project, 156 W 56th St., 3rd Fl., New York, NY, 10019, USA, (212) 803-5200, info@themarshallproject.org, https://www.themarshallproject.org/; COVID Cases in Prisons and A State-By-State Look at 15 Months of Coronavirus in Prisons.

Massachusetts Institute of Technology (MIT), Living Wage Calculator, 77 Massachusetts Ave., Cambridge, MA, 02139, USA, (617) 324-6565, (617) 253-1000, amyglas@mit.edu, https://livingwage.mit.edu; Double Whammy: Essential Workers Threatened by Job Loss While Facing the Highest Risk of COVID Infection and Nothing New Under the Sun: Covid-19 Brings to Light Persistent Issues in the Navajo Nation.

Morning Consult, 729 15th St. NW, Washington, DC, 20005, USA, (202) 506-1957, contact@morningconsult.com, https://morningconsult.com; How 2020 Is Impacting Gen Z's Worldview: A Tracking Report Dedicated to Understanding How a Tumultuous Year Is Altering the Young Generation's Habits, Values, and Outlook; The U.S. Consumer Confidence Dashboard; and When Will Consumers Feel Safe? Weekly Updates on Consumers' Comfort Level with Various Pastimes.

National Academies of Sciences, Engineering, and Medicine (The National Academies), 500 5th St. NW, Washington, DC, 20001, USA, (202) 334-2000, contact@nas.edu, https://www.nationalacademies.org/; Rapid Expert Consultation on SARS-CoV-2 Viral Shedding and Antibody Response for the COVID-19 Pandemic; Rapid Expert Consultation on the Effectiveness of Fabric Masks for the COVID-19 Pandemic; and Rapid Expert Consultation on the Possibility of Bioaerosol Spread of SARS-CoV-2 for the COVID-19 Pandemic.

National Academy of Social Insurance (NASI), 1441 L St. NW, Ste. 530, Washington, DC, 20005, USA, (202) 452-8097, (202) 452-8111, nasi@nasi.org, https://www.nasi.org; The Impact of the COVID-19 Pandemic on Access to Health Care.

National Alliance for Public Charter Schools, 800 Connecticut Ave. NW, Ste. 300, Washington, DC, 20006, USA, (202) 289-2700, (202) 289-4009, datarequest@publiccharters.org, https://www.publiccharters.org/; Learning in Real Time: How Charter Schools Served Students During COVID-19 Closures.

National Bureau of Economic Research (NBER), 1050 Massachusetts Ave., Cambridge, MA, 02138, USA, (617) 868-3900, info@nber.org, https://www.nber.org/; Misinformation During a Pandemic and The Persuasive Effect of Fox News: Non-Compliance with Social Distancing During the Covid-19 Pandemic.

National Law Enforcement Officers Memorial Fund (NLEOMF), 444 E St. NW, Washington, DC, 20001, USA, (202) 737-3400, (202) 737-3405, info@nleomf.org, https://nleomf.org/; 2021 End-of-Year Preliminary Law Enforcement Officers Fatalities Report and The Takeaway: Covid-19 Fatalities.

National Student Clearinghouse Research Center, 2300 Dulles Station Blvd., Ste. 220, Herndon, VA, 21071, USA, https://nscresearchcenter.org; Spring 2022 Current Term Enrollment Estimates.

New York University School of Law, Institute for Policy Integrity, 139 MacDougal St., Wilf Hall, 3rd Fl., New York, NY, 10012, USA, (212) 992-8932, (212) 995-4592, https://policyintegrity.org/; Weakening Our Defenses: How the Trump Administration's Deregulatory Push Has Exacerbated the Covid-19 Pandemic.

NewClimate Institute, Waidmarkt 11a, Cologne, D-50676, GER, info@newclimate.org, https://newclimate.org/; Exploring the Impact of the COVID-19 Pandemic on Global Emission Projections.

Pew Research Center, 1615 L St. NW, Ste. 800, Washington, DC, 20036, USA, (202) 419-4300, (202) 857-8562, info@pewresearch.org, https://www.pewresearch.org/; American News Pathways Data Tool; Americans Are Following News about Presidential Candidates Much Less Closely than COVID-19 News; Local News Is Playing an Important Role for Americans During COVID-19 Outbreak; Many Black and Asian Americans Say They Have Experienced Discrimination Amid the COVID-19 Outbreak; Three Months In, Many Americans See Exaggeration, Conspiracy Theories and Partisanship in COVID-19 News; and Younger Adults Differ from Older Ones in Perceptions of News about COVID-19, George Floyd Protests.

Pew Research Center, Politics & Policy, 1615 L St. NW, Ste. 800, Washington, DC, 20036, USA, (202) 419-4300, (202) 857-8562, https://www.pewresearch.org/topic/politics-policy/; Republicans, Democrats Move Even Further Apart in Coronavirus Concerns: Growing Share of Republicans Say 'The Worst Is Behind Us'.

PLOS, 1265 Battery St., Ste. 200, San Francisco, CA, 94111, USA, (415) 624-1200, (415) 795-1584, plos@plos.org, https://www.plos.org/; Outbreak Analysis with a Logistic Growth Model Shows COVID-19 Suppression Dynamics in China.

ProPublica, 155 Avenue of the Americas, 13th Fl., New York, NY, 10013, USA, (212) 514-5250, (212) 785-2634, hello@propublica.org, https://www.propublica.org/; Hazardous Air Pollutant Exposure as a Contributing Factor to COVID-19 Mortality in the United States.

Public Agenda, 1 Dock 72 Way, No. 6101, Brooklyn, NY, 11205-1242, USA, (212) 686-6610, info@publicagenda.org, https://www.publicagenda.org/; America's Hidden Common Ground on the Coronavirus Crisis: Results from a Public Agenda/USA Today/Ipsos Snapshot Survey on How Communities Are Responding and the Policies People Support and America's Hidden Common Ground on the Coronavirus Crisis: Results from a Public Agenda/USA Today/Ipsos Survey of Americans' Views on Reopening Their Communities.

Resolve to Save Lives, 100 Broadway, 4th Fl., New York, NY, 10005, USA, info@resolvetosavelives.org, https://resolvetosavelives.org/; Tracking COVID-19 in the United States: From Information Catastrophe to Empowered Communities.

SAGE Publications, 2455 Teller Rd., Thousand Oaks, CA, 91320, USA, (800) 818-7243, (800) 583-2665, journals@sagepub.com, https://www.sagepub.com; Dialogues in Human Geography - Geographies of the COVID-19 Pandemic; Experimental Biology and Medicine - The Role of Chest Computed Tomography in the Management of COVID-19: A Review of Results and Recommendations; and Palliative Medicine - End-of-Life Care in COVID-19: An Audit of Pharmacological Management in Hospital Inpatients.

State Health Access Data Assistance Center (SHADAC), 2221 University Ave. SE, Ste. 345, Minneapolis, MN, 55414, USA, (612) 624-4802, (612) 624-1493, shadac@umn.edu, https://www.shadac.org/; 90 Percent of U.S. Adults Report Increased Stress Due to Coronavirus Pandemic; Coronavirus Pandemic Caused More than 10 million U.S. Adults to Lose Health Insurance; and Emergency Flexibility for States to Increase and Maintain Medicaid Eligibility for LTSS under COVID-19.

U.S. Census Bureau, 4600 Silver Hill Rd., Washington, DC, 20233, USA, (301) 763-4636, (800) 923-8282, https://www.census.gov; Measuring Household Experiences During the Coronavirus Pandemic: Household Pulse Survey.

U.S. Department of Health and Human Services (HHS), National Institutes of Health (NIH), National Center for Advancing Translational Sciences (NCATS), 31 Center Dr., Ste. 3B11, Bethesda, MD, 20892-2128, USA, (301) 594-8966, info@ncats.nih.gov, https://ncats.nih.gov/; OpenData COVID-19 Portal.

U.S. Department of Health and Human Services (HHS), National Institutes of Health (NIH), Office of Data Science Strategy (ODSS), 9000 Rockville Pike, Bethesda, MD, 20892, USA, (301) 827-7212, datascience@nih.gov, https://datascience.nih.gov/; Open-Access Data and Computational Resources to Address COVID-19.

U.S. Department of Health and Human Services (HHS), U.S. National Library of Medicine (NLM), National Center for Biotechnology Information (NCBI), 8600 Rockville Pike, Bethesda, MD, 20894, USA, info@ncbi.nlm.nih.gov, https://www.ncbi.nlm.nih.gov; NCBI SARS-CoV-2 Resources.

U.S. Department of Health and Human Services, Centers for Disease Control and Prevention (CDC), 1600 Clifton Rd., Atlanta, GA, 30329-4027, USA, (800) 232-4636, (888) 232-6348 (TTY), cdcinfo@cdc.gov, https://www.cdc.gov; COVID Data Tracker Weekly Review; COVID-19 Case Surveillance Public Use Data Profile; COVID-19 Vaccine Breakthrough Infections Reported to CDC - United States, January 1-April 30, 2021; Detection of Severe Acute Respiratory Syndrome Coronavirus 2 RNA on Surfaces in Quarantine Rooms; Effectiveness of a COVID-19 Additional Primary or Booster Vaccine Dose in Preventing SARS-CoV-2 Infection Among Nursing Home Residents During Widespread Circulation of the Omicron Variant - United States, February 14 - March 27, 2022; and Mask Use and Ventilation Improvements to Reduce COVID-19 Incidence in Elementary Schools - Georgia, November 16 - December 11, 2020.

U.S. Department of Health and Human Services, Centers for Disease Control and Prevention (CDC), National Center for Health Statistics (NCHS), 3311 Toledo Rd., Hyattsville, MD, 20782-2064, USA, (800) 232-4636, (301) 458-4000, https://www.cdc.gov/nchs; Household Pulse Survey: Anxiety and Depression.

U.S. Department of State (DOS), 2201 C St. NW, Washington, DC, 20520, USA, (202) 647-4000, ofm-info@state.gov, https://www.state.gov; Update: The United States Continues to Lead the Global Response to COVID-19.

U.S. Department of Transportation (DOT), Federal Railroad Administration (FRA), 1200 New Jersey Ave. SE, Washington, DC, 20590, USA, (202) 366-4000, (202) 493-6014, (202) 493-6481, frapa@dot.gov, https://railroads.dot.gov/; Coronavirus (COVID-19) Information from the FRA.

U.S. Government Accountablity Office (GAO), 441 G St. NW, Washington, DC, 20548, USA, (202) 512-3000, contact@gao.gov, https://www.gao.gov/; COVID-19: Opportunities to Improve Federal Response and Recovery Efforts.

UK Health Security Agency (UKHSA), Nobel House, 17 Smith Sq., London, SW1P 3JR, GBR, enquiries@ukhsa.gov.uk, https://www.gov.uk/government/organisations/uk-health-security-agency; COVID-19 Variants: Genomically Confirmed Case Numbers and Effectiveness of COVID-19 Vaccines Against the B.1.617.2 Variant.

UNESCO Institute for Statistics, C.P 250 Succursale H, Montreal, QC, H3G 2K8, CAN, (514) 343-6880 (Dial from U.S.), (514) 343-5740 (Fax from U.S.), uis.publications@unesco.org, http://uis.unesco.org/; COVID-19 Is a Serious Threat to Aid to Education Recovery and COVID-19 Recovery: Education.

Uniformed Services University, Department of Psychiatry, Center for the Study of Traumatic Stress (CSTS), 4301 Jones Bridge Rd., Bethesda, MD, 20814-4799, USA, cstsinfo@usuhs.edu, https://www.cstsonline.org/; Annals for Hospitalists Inpatient Notes - Preparing for Battle: How Hospitalists Can Manage the Stress of COVID-19.

United Kingdom Office for National Statistics (ONS), Cardiff Rd., Government Bldgs., Rm. D265 , Newport, NP10 8XG, GBR, info@ons.gsi.gov.uk, https://www.ons.gov.uk/; COVID-19 Infection Survey.

United Nations UN Women, 405 E 42nd St., New York, NY, 10017-3599, USA, (646) 781-4400, (646) 781-4444, https://www.unwomen.org; COVID-19: Emerging Gender Data and Why it Matters.

University of California Los Angeles (UCLA) School of Law, Covid-19 Behind Bars Data Project, 385 Charles E. Young Dr. E, Los Angeles, CA, 90095, USA, (310) 206-5568, covidbehindbars@law.ucla.edu, https://uclacovidbehindbars.org; Covid Behind Bars Data Project; In California Jails, Sherrifs Have Been Left in Charge of Covid Mitigation. The Results Have Been Disastrous.; and What We Won't Know When the Next Surge Arrives.

University of California, Berkeley, Global Policy Lab, California Memorial Stadium, 2227 Piedmont Ave., Berkeley, CA, 94720, USA, (510) 643-5751, https://www.globalpolicy.science/; The Effect of Large-Scale Anti-Contagion Policies on the COVID-19 Pandemic.

University of Minnesota, Center for Infectious Disease Research and Policy (CIDRAP), Office of the Vice President for Research, 420 Delaware St. SE, MMC 263, C315 Mayo, Minneapolis, MN, 55455, USA, (612) 626-6770, (612) 626-6783, https://www.cidrap.umn.edu/; Novel Coronavirus (COVID-19) Resource Center.

University of Washington, Institute for Health Metrics and Evaluation (IHME), Population Health Building/ Hans Rosling Center, UW Campus Box 351615, 3980 15th Ave. NE, Seattle, WA, 98195, USA, (206) 897-2800, (206) 897-2899, engage@healthdata.org, https://www.healthdata.org; Global Access to Handwashing: Implications for COVID-19 Control in Low-Income Countries.

The Urban Institute, 500 L'Enfant Plaza SW, Washington, DC, 20024, USA, (202) 833-7200, https://www.urban.org/; Local Government Efforts to Mitigate the Novel Coronavirus Pandemic Among Older Adults.

World Health Organization (WHO), Ave. Appia 20, Geneva, CH-1211, SWI, (202) 974-3000 (Telephone in U.S.), publications@who.int, https://www.who.int/; Advice on the Use of Masks in the Context of COVID-19; Coronavirus Disease (COVID-19) Situation Report; and Global Research on Coronavirus Disease (COVID-19).

Worldometer, https://www.worldometers.info/; COVID-19 Coronavirus Pandemic.

CORONAVIRUSES-GENETICS

GISAID Initiative, Munich, GER, https://www.gisaid.org; Tracking of hCoV-19 Variants.

CORPORATE BUSINESS SECTOR

Board of Governors of the Federal Reserve System, Constitution Ave. NW, Washington, DC, 20551, USA, (202) 452-3000, (202) 263-4869 (TDD), https://www.federalreserve.gov; Financial Accounts of the United States 2023.

CDP, 60 Great Tower St., 4th Fl., London, EC3R 5AZ, GBR, https://www.cdp.net; Engaging the Chain: Driving Speed and Scale.

The Conference Board, 845 3rd Ave., New York, NY, 10022-6660, USA, (212) 759-0900, (212) 339-0345, customer.service@conferenceboard.org, https://www.conference-board.org; CEO Confidence Survey.

OpenSecrets, 1300 L St. NW , Ste. 200, Washington, DC, 20005, USA, (202) 857-0044, (202) 857-7809, info@crp.org, https://www.opensecrets.org/; Blue Origin and SpaceX Lobby for Dominance and Government Contracts in Billionaire Space Race and Elon Musk's Twitter Takeover Adds to His Corporate Political Influence and Lobbying Power.

Organization for Economic Cooperation and Development (OECD), 2001 L St. NW, Ste. 650, Washington, DC, 20036-4922, USA, (202) 785-6323, (800) 456-6323, (202) 785-0350, washington.contact@oecd.org, https://www.oecd.org/; The Future of Corporate Governance in Capital Markets Following the COVID-19 Crisis; OECD Science, Technology and Industry Scoreboard; and OECD Science, Technology and R&D Statistics Database.

CORPORATE BUSINESS SECTOR-POLITICAL ACTION COMMITTEES (PACS)

Federal Election Commission (FEC), 1050 1st St. NE, Washington, DC, 20463, USA, (800) 424-9530, (202) 694-1100, pubrec@fec.gov, https://www.fec.gov; FEC Congressional Budget Justification Fiscal Year 2022.

CORPORATE GOVERNANCE

Organization for Economic Cooperation and Development (OECD), 2001 L St. NW, Ste. 650, Washington, DC, 20036-4922, USA, (202) 785-6323, (800) 456-6323, (202) 785-0350, washington.contact@oecd.org, https://www.oecd.org/; The Future of Corporate Governance in Capital Markets Following the COVID-19 Crisis.

CORPORATIONS-CAPITAL

Internal Revenue Service (IRS), Statistics of Income Division (SOI), 1111 Constitution Ave. NW, K-Room 4100-123, Washington, DC, 20224-0002, USA, (202) 874-0410, (202) 874-0964, sis@irs.gov, https://www.irs.gov/uac/soi-tax-stats-statistics-of-income; SOI Tax Stats - Business Tax Statistics.

CORPORATIONS-DIVIDEND PAYMENTS

U.S. Department of Commerce (DOC), Bureau of Economic Analysis (BEA), 4600 Silver Hill Rd., Washington, DC, 20233, USA, (301) 278-9004, customerservice@bea.gov, https://www.bea.gov; National Income and Product Accounts (NIPA): 2022 Update and Survey of Current Business (SCB).

CORPORATIONS-FINANCES

Board of Governors of the Federal Reserve System, Constitution Ave. NW, Washington, DC, 20551, USA, (202) 452-3000, (202) 263-4869 (TDD), https://www.federalreserve.gov; Financial Accounts of the United States 2023.

Environmental Business International, Inc. (EBI), 4452 Park Blvd., Ste. 306, San Diego, CA, 92116, USA, (619) 295-7685, info@ebionline.org, https://ebionline.org/; U.S. Environmental Industry Overview.

European Central Bank (ECB), Frankfurt am Main, D-60640, GER, info@ecb.europa.eu, https://www.ecb.europa.eu; Monetary Financial Institutions (MFI) Interest Rate Statistics.

Internal Revenue Service (IRS), Statistics of Income Division (SOI), 1111 Constitution Ave. NW, K-Room 4100-123, Washington, DC, 20224-0002, USA, (202) 874-0410, (202) 874-0964, sis@irs.gov, https://www.irs.gov/uac/soi-tax-stats-statistics-of-income; SOI Tax Stats - Business Tax Statistics; SOI Tax Stats - Historical Data Tables; and Statistics of Income Bulletin.

International Consortium of Investigative Journalists (ICIJ), 1730 Rhode Island Ave. NW, Ste. 317, Washington, DC, 20036, USA, (202) 808-3310, contact@icij.org, https://www.icij.org/; Offshore Leaks Database.

U.S. Census Bureau, Center for Economic Studies (CES), 4600 Silver Hill Rd., Washington, DC, 20233, USA, (301) 763-6460, (301) 763-5935, ces.contacts@census.gov, https://www.census.gov/programs-surveys/ces.html; Management of Companies and Enterprises, 2017 Economic Census.

U.S. Department of Labor (DOL), Bureau of Labor Statistics (BLS), Postal Square Bldg., 2 Massachusetts Ave. NE, Washington, DC, 20212-0001, USA, (202) 691-5200, (202) 691-7890, blsdata_staff@bls.gov, https://www.bls.gov; Employer Costs for Employee Compensation.

U.S. Securities and Exchange Commission (SEC), 100 F St. NE, Washington, DC, 20549, USA, (202) 551-6551, (202) 551-4119, https://www.sec.gov; Electronic Data Gathering, Analysis, and Retrieval (EDGAR) System.

The World Bank, 1818 H St. NW, Washington, DC, 20433, USA, (202) 473-1000, (202) 477-6391, eds03@worldbank.org, https://www.worldbank.org/; Doing Business 2019: Training for Reform and Doing Business 2020: Comparing Business Regulation in 190 Economies.

World Intellectual Property Organization (WIPO), 34, chemin des Colombettes, Geneva, CH-1211, SWI, https://www.wipo.int; IP Facts and Figures 2022.

CORPORATIONS-MANUFACTURING

U.S. Census Bureau, 4600 Silver Hill Rd., Washington, DC, 20233, USA, (301) 763-4636, (800) 923-8282, https://www.census.gov; Quarterly Financial Report for Manufacturing, Mining, Trade, and Selected Service Industries.

CORPORATIONS-NONFINANCIAL

Board of Governors of the Federal Reserve System, Constitution Ave. NW, Washington, DC, 20551, USA, (202) 452-3000, (202) 263-4869 (TDD), https://www.federalreserve.gov; Financial Accounts of the United States 2023.

CORPORATIONS-PHILANTHROPY

The Chronicle of Philanthropy, 1255 23rd St. NW, 7th Fl., Washington, DC, 20037, USA, (202) 466-1200, philanthropy@pubservice.com, https://www.philanthropy.com/; America's Favorite Charities 2021; The Chronicle of Philanthropy; and Data & Research.

Giving Institute, 7918 Jones Branch Dr., No. 300, McLean, VA, 22102, USA, (312) 981-6794, (312) 265-2908, info@givinginstitute.org, https://www.givinginstitute.org/; Giving USA 2021: The Annual Report on Philanthropy for the Year 2020.

Independent Sector, 1602 L St. NW, Ste. 900, Washington, DC, 20036, USA, (202) 467-6100, (202) 467-6101, info@independentsector.org, https://independentsector.org/; Health of the U.S. Nonprofit Sector Quarterly Review.

CORPORATIONS-PROFITS

Forbes, Inc., 499 Washington Blvd., Jersey City, NJ, 07310, USA, (800) 295-0893, https://www.forbes.com; America's Largest Private Companies 2021.

Internal Revenue Service (IRS), Statistics of Income Division (SOI), 1111 Constitution Ave. NW, K-Room 4100-123, Washington, DC, 20224-0002, USA, (202) 874-0410, (202) 874-0964, sis@irs.gov, https://www.irs.gov/uac/soi-tax-stats-statistics-of-income; SOI Tax Stats - Business Tax Statistics and Statistics of Income Bulletin.

U.S. Census Bureau, 4600 Silver Hill Rd., Washington, DC, 20233, USA, (301) 763-4636, (800) 923-8282, https://www.census.gov; Quarterly Financial Report for Manufacturing, Mining, Trade, and Selected Service Industries.

U.S. Department of Commerce (DOC), Bureau of Economic Analysis (BEA), 4600 Silver Hill Rd., Washington, DC, 20233, USA, (301) 278-9004, customerservice@bea.gov, https://www.bea.gov; National Income and Product Accounts (NIPA): 2022 Update and Survey of Current Business (SCB).

CORPORATIONS-RECEIPTS

Internal Revenue Service (IRS), Statistics of Income Division (SOI), 1111 Constitution Ave. NW, K-Room 4100-123, Washington, DC, 20224-0002, USA, (202) 874-0410, (202) 874-0964, sis@irs.gov, https://www.irs.gov/uac/soi-tax-stats-statistics-of-income; SOI Tax Stats - Business Tax Statistics and Statistics of Income Bulletin.

CORPORATIONS-SALES

Forbes, Inc., 499 Washington Blvd., Jersey City, NJ, 07310, USA, (800) 295-0893, https://www.forbes.com; America's Largest Private Companies 2021.

U.S. Census Bureau, 4600 Silver Hill Rd., Washington, DC, 20233, USA, (301) 763-4636, (800) 923-8282, https://www.census.gov; Quarterly Financial Report for Manufacturing, Mining, Trade, and Selected Service Industries.

CORPORATIONS-STOCKS AND BONDS

Board of Governors of the Federal Reserve System, Constitution Ave. NW, Washington, DC, 20551,

USA, (202) 452-3000, (202) 263-4869 (TDD), https://www.federalreserve.gov; Federal Reserve Bulletin.

United Nations Conference on Trade and Development (UNCTAD), Palais des Nations, Geneva, 1211, SWI, (212) 963-6896, unctadinfo@unctad.org, https://unctad.org; Global Foreign Direct Investment Flows Over the Last 30 Years.

CORPORATIONS-TAXES-CORPORATE INCOME TAX

Internal Revenue Service (IRS), Statistics of Income Division (SOI), 1111 Constitution Ave. NW, K-Room 4100-123, Washington, DC, 20224-0002, USA, (202) 874-0410, (202) 874-0964, sis@irs.gov, https://www.irs.gov/uac/soi-tax-stats-statistics-of-income; Tax Stats.

International Consortium of Investigative Journalists (ICIJ), 1730 Rhode Island Ave. NW, Ste. 317, Washington, DC, 20036, USA, (202) 808-3310, contact@icij.org, https://www.icij.org/; Offshore Leaks Database.

U.S. Department of Commerce (DOC), Bureau of Economic Analysis (BEA), 4600 Silver Hill Rd., Washington, DC, 20233, USA, (301) 278-9004, customerservice@bea.gov, https://www.bea.gov; National Income and Product Accounts (NIPA): 2022 Update and Survey of Current Business (SCB).

University of Missouri, Economic and Policy Analysis Research Center (EPARC), 10 Professional Bldg., Columbia, MO, 65211, USA, (573) 882-4805, (573) 882-5563, eparc@missouri.edu, https://eparc.missouri.edu/; Missouri Historical Tax Summary 1975-2019.

CORPORATIONS-TAXES-RETURNS

Internal Revenue Service (IRS), Statistics of Income Division (SOI), 1111 Constitution Ave. NW, K-Room 4100-123, Washington, DC, 20224-0002, USA, (202) 874-0410, (202) 874-0964, sis@irs.gov, https://www.irs.gov/uac/soi-tax-stats-statistics-of-income; SOI Tax Stats - Business Tax Statistics; SOI Tax Stats - Historical Data Tables; and Statistics of Income Bulletin.

CORRECTIONAL INSTITUTIONS

See also PRISONS AND PRISONERS

American Federation of Teachers (AFT), 555 New Jersey Ave. NW, Washington, DC, 20001, USA, (202) 879-4400, https://www.aft.org/; Private Prisons, Immigrant Detention and Investment Risks.

Australian Institute of Criminology (AIC), GPO Box 1936, Canberra, ACT, 2601, AUS, front.desk@aic.gov.au, https://www.aic.gov.au/; Deaths in Custody in Australia 2021-2022.

Federal Bureau of Prisons (BOP), 320 First St. NW, Washington, DC, 20534 , USA, (202) 307-3198, https://www.bop.gov/; By the Numbers: Inmate Statistics, Population Statistics, Staff Statistics.

Justice Research and Statistics Association (JRSA), 1000 Vermont Ave. NW, Ste. 450, Washington, DC, 20005, USA, (202) 842-9330, (202) 304-1417, cjinfo@jrsa.org, https://www.jrsa.org; SAC Publication Digest 2022.

The Leadership Conference Education Fund (The Education Fund), 1620 L St. NW, Ste. 1100, Washington, DC, 20036, USA, (202) 466-3311, https://civilrights.org/edfund/#; A Matter of Life and Death: The Importance of the Death in Custody Reporting Act.

National Correctional Industries Association (NCIA), 800 N Charles St., Ste. 550B, Baltimore, MD, 21201, USA, (410) 230-3972, memberservices@nationalcia.org, https://www.nationalcia.org/; unpublished data.

Prison Policy Initiative, PO Box 127, Northampton, MA, 01061, USA, https://www.prisonpolicy.org/; Does Our County Really Need a Bigger Jail? A Guide for Avoiding Unnecessary Jail Expansion; Grading the Parole Release Systems of All 50 States; and State of Phone Justice 2022: The Problem, the Progress, and What's Next.

The Sentencing Project, 1705 DeSales St. NW, 8th Fl., Washington, DC, 20036, USA, (202) 628-0871, staff@sentencingproject.org, https://www.sentencingproject.org; Growth in Mass Incarceration; Mass Incarceration Trends; and U.S. Criminal Justice Data.

U.S. Department of Justice (DOJ), Bureau of Justice Statistics (BJS), 810 7th St. NW, Washington, DC, 20531, USA, (202) 307-0765, askbjs@usdoj.gov, https://www.bjs.gov/; Annual Survey of Jails, 2019; Data Collection: National Corrections Reporting Program (NCRP); and Jails in Indian Country, 2019-2020 and the Impact of COVID-19 on the Tribal Jail Population.

CORRECTIONAL INSTITUTIONS-EMPLOYMENT

Federal Bureau of Prisons (BOP), 320 First St. NW, Washington, DC, 20534 , USA, (202) 307-3198, https://www.bop.gov/; By the Numbers: Inmate Statistics, Population Statistics, Staff Statistics.

U.S. Department of Labor (DOL), Bureau of Labor Statistics (BLS), Postal Square Bldg., 2 Massachusetts Ave. NE, Washington, DC, 20212-0001, USA, (202) 691-5200, (202) 691-7890, blsdata_staff@bls.gov, https://www.bls.gov; Monthly Labor Review.

CORRECTIONAL INSTITUTIONS-EXPENDITURES

Justice Policy Institute (JPI), 1012 14th St. NW, Ste. 600, Washington, DC, 20005, USA, (202) 558-7974, (202) 558-7978, info@justicepolicy.org, https://www.justicepolicy.org; Sticker Shock: The Cost of New York's Youth Prisons Approaches $1 Million Per Kid.

U.S. Census Bureau, Public Sector, 4600 Silver Hill Rd., Washington, DC, 20233, USA, (800) 923-8282, (301) 763-4636, ewd.outreach@census.gov, https://www.census.gov/topics/public-sector.html; Annual Survey of State and Local Government Finances.

CORRECTIONAL INSTITUTIONS-FACILITIES

U.S. Department of Justice (DOJ), Bureau of Justice Statistics (BJS), 810 7th St. NW, Washington, DC, 20531, USA, (202) 307-0765, askbjs@usdoj.gov, https://www.bjs.gov/; Jail Inmates in 2020 and Jails in Indian Country, 2019-2020 and the Impact of COVID-19 on the Tribal Jail Population.

CORRECTIONAL INSTITUTIONS-PRISONERS

American Civil Liberties Union (ACLU), 125 Broad St. , 18th Fl., New York, NY, 10004, USA, (212) 549-2500, https://www.aclu.org/; COVID-19 Model Finds Nearly 100,000 More Deaths Than Current Estimates, Due to Failures to Reduce Jails.

Australian Institute of Criminology (AIC), GPO Box 1936, Canberra, ACT, 2601, AUS, front.desk@aic.gov.au, https://www.aic.gov.au/; Deaths in Custody in Australia 2021-2022.

Council on Criminal Justice (CCJ), 700 Pennsylvania Ave. SE, Washington, DC, 20003, USA, info@counciloncj.org, https://counciloncj.org; Justice System Disparities: Black-White National Imprisonment Trends, 2000 to 2020 and The 1994 Crime Bill: Legacy and Lessons.

Council on Criminal Justice (CCJ), National Commission on COVID-19 and Criminal Justice, 700 Pennsylvania Ave. SE, Washington, DC, 20020, USA, info@counciloncj.org, https://counciloncj.org/covid-19/; COVID-19 in U.S. State and Federal Prisons; Experience to Action: Reshaping Criminal Justice After COVID-19; Impact Report: COVID-19 and Prisons; and Impact Report: COVID-19 Testing in State Prisons.

Federal Bureau of Prisons (BOP), 320 First St. NW, Washington, DC, 20534 , USA, (202) 307-3198, https://www.bop.gov/; Inmate COVID-19 Data: A Look at the Impact of COVID-19 on Individuals in Federal Custody.

The Marshall Project, 156 W 56th St., 3rd Fl., New York, NY, 10019, USA, (212) 803-5200, info@themarshallproject.org, https://www.themarshallproject.org/; COVID Cases in Prisons and A State-By-State Look at 15 Months of Coronavirus in Prisons.

Pew Research Center, 1615 L St. NW, Ste. 800, Washington, DC, 20036, USA, (202) 419-4300, (202) 857-8562, info@pewresearch.org, https://www.pewresearch.org/; Black Imprisonment Rate in the U.S. Has Fallen by a Third Since 2006.

Prison Policy Initiative, PO Box 127, Northampton, MA, 01061, USA, https://www.prisonpolicy.org/; Grading the Parole Release Systems of All 50 States; Mass Incarceration, COVID-19, and Community Spread; Mass Incarceration: The Whole Pie 2023; States of Incarceration: The Global Context 2021; Where People in Prison Come From: The Geography of Mass Incarceration; and Women's Mass Incarceration: The Whole Pie 2023.

Southern Poverty Law Center (SPLC), 400 Washington Ave., Montgomery, AL, 36104, USA, (334) 956-8200, (888) 414-7752, https://www.splcenter.org/; Solitary Confinement: Inhumane, Ineffective, and Wasteful.

U.S. Department of Justice (DOJ), Bureau of Justice Statistics (BJS), 810 7th St. NW, Washington, DC, 20531, USA, (202) 307-0765, askbjs@usdoj.gov, https://www.bjs.gov/; Annual Survey of Jails, 2019; Data Collection: National Corrections Reporting Program (NCRP); Jail Inmates in 2020; PREA (Prison Rape Elimination Act) Data Collection Activities, 2021; Prisoners in 2020; and Probation and Parole in the United States, 2020.

University of California Los Angeles (UCLA) School of Law, Covid-19 Behind Bars Data Project, 385 Charles E. Young Dr. E, Los Angeles, CA, 90095, USA, (310) 206-5568, covidbehindbars@law.ucla.edu, https://uclacovidbehindbars.org; Georgia Custodial Death Records Summary Report and Racial And Ethnic Inequalities in COVID-19 Mortality Within Carceral Settings: An Analysis of Texas Prisons.

Vera Institute of Justice, 34 35th St., Ste. 4-2A, Brooklyn, NY, 11232, USA, (212) 334-1300, (212) 941-9407, contactvera@vera.org, https://www.vera.org/; The New Dynamics of Mass Incarceration and An Unjust Burden: The Disparate Treatment of Black Americans in the Criminal Justice System.

CORRUPTION

Amnesty International USA, 311 W 43rd St., 7th Fl., New York, NY, 10036, USA, (212) 807-8400, (800) 266-3789, (212) 627-1451, aimember@aiusa.org, https://www.amnestyusa.org/; Hunger for Justice: Crimes Against Humanity in Venezuela.

Center for American Progress Action Fund (CAP Action), 1333 H St. NW, 10th Fl., Washington, DC, 20005, USA, (202) 682-1611, https://www.americanprogressaction.org; Costs of Corruption: Tax Bill Leads to Higher Health Premiums and Big Tax Cuts for the Rich and Tracking Waste and Abuse in Trump's Cabinet.

The European Institute for Crime Prevention and Control, Affiliated with the United Nations (HEUNI), Vilhonkatu 4 B 19, Helsinki, FI-00101, FIN, heuni@om.fi, https://heuni.fi/; Trafficking of Children and Young Persons in Finland.

Global Integrity, 1110 Vermont Ave. NW, Ste. 500, Washington, DC, 20005, USA, (202) 449-4100, info@globalintegrity.org, https://www.globalintegrity.org/; Africa Integrity Indicators.

International Consortium of Investigative Journalists (ICIJ), 1730 Rhode Island Ave. NW, Ste. 317, Washington, DC, 20036, USA, (202) 808-3310, contact@icij.org, https://www.icij.org/; Offshore Leaks Database.

Internet Center for Corruption Research (ICCR), Innstrasse 27, Passau, D-94032, GER, johann.graflambsdorff@uni-passau.de, https://www.icgg.org/; unpublished data.

Transparency International, Alt-Moabit 96, Berlin, D-10559, GER, ti@transparency.org, https://www.transparency.org; Corruption Perceptions Index 2022 and Global Corruption Barometer.

U.S. Department of Justice (DOJ), Criminal Division, 950 Pennsylvania Ave. NW, Washington, DC, 20530-0001, USA, (202) 514-2000, criminal.division@usdoj.gov, https://www.justice.gov/criminal; Report to Congress on the Activities and Operations of the Public Integrity Section for 2020.

COSMETICS

Green Science Policy Institute, PO Box 9127, Berkeley, CA, 94709, USA, (510) 898-1739, info@greensciencepolicy.org, https://greensciencepolicy.org/; Fluorinated Compounds in North American Cosmetics.

COSMETICS INDUSTRY

NielsenIQ (NIQ), 200 W Jackson Blvd., Chicago, IL, 60606, USA, https://nielseniq.com; Multicultural Consumers Are Set to Drive Beauty Growth Amid Continued Category Shifts in 2021.

The NPD Group, 900 W Shore Rd., Port Washington, NY, 11050, USA, (516) 625-0700, contactnpd@npd.com, https://www.npd.com; Beauty.

U.S. Census Bureau, Center for Economic Studies (CES), 4600 Silver Hill Rd., Washington, DC, 20233, USA, (301) 763-6460, (301) 763-5935, ces.contacts@census.gov, https://www.census.gov/programs-surveys/ces.html; Retail Trade, 2017 Economic Census and Wholesale Trade, 2017 Economic Census.

U.S. Census Bureau, International Trade Program, 4600 Silver Hill Rd., Washington, DC, 20233, USA, (800) 549-0595, eid.international.trade.data@census.gov, https://www.census.gov/foreign-trade; International Trade Data.

U.S. Department of Commerce (DOC), International Trade Administration (ITA), 1401 Constitution Ave. NW, Washington, DC, 20230, USA, (800) 872-8723, https://www.trade.gov/; TradeStats Express (TSE).

COST AND STANDARD OF LIVING

Center for Economic and Policy Research (CEPR), 1611 Connecticut Ave. NW, Ste. 400, Washington, DC, 20009, USA, (202) 293-5380, (202) 588-1356, info@cepr.net, https://cepr.net/; The Human Consequences of Economic Sanctions.

COST OF LIVING INDEXES

See CONSUMER PRICE INDEXES

COSTA RICA-NATIONAL STATISTICAL OFFICE

Instituto Nacional de Estadistica y Censos (INEC), Costa Rica, Rotonda de La Bandera, Calle Los Negritos Edificio Ana Lorena, Mercedes de Montes de Oca, San Jose, CRI, informacion@inec.go.cr, https://inec.cr/; National Data Reports (Costa Rica).

COSTA RICA-AGRICULTURE

The Economist Group: Economist Intelligence Unit (EIU), 900 3rd Ave., 16th Fl., New York, NY, 10022, USA, (212) 541-0500, americas@eiu.com, https://www.eiu.com; Costa Rica Country Report.

Euromonitor International, Inc., 1 N Dearborn St., Ste. 1700, Chicago, IL, 60602, USA, (312) 922-1115, (312) 922-1157, info-usa@euromonitor.com, https://www.euromonitor.com/; Geographies.

Inter-American Development Bank (IDB), 1300 New York Ave. NW, Washington, DC, 20577, USA, (202) 623-1000, (202) 623-3096, https://www.iadb.org/en; Latin Macro Watch (LMW).

Palgrave Macmillan, 1 New York Plaza, Ste. 4500, New York, NY, 10004-1562, USA, (800) 777-4643, orders@palgrave.com, https://www.palgrave.com/us; The Statesman's Yearbook, 2023.

Routledge - Taylor & Francis Group, 6000 Broken Sound Pkwy. NW, Ste. 300, Boca Raton, FL, 33487, USA, (800) 634-1420, (800) 634-7064, orders@taylorandfrancis.com, https://www.routledge.com/; The Europa World Year Book 2022.

United Nations Food and Agricultural Organization (FAO), 2121 K St., Ste. 800B, Washington, DC, 20037, USA, (202) 653-2400 (Dial from U.S.), (202) 653-5760 (Fax from U.S.), fao-hq@fao.org, https://www.fao.org; AQUASTAT and The State of Food and Agriculture (SOFA) 2022.

United Nations Statistics Division (UNSD), United Nations Plz., New York, NY, 10017, USA, (800) 253-9646, (212) 963-9851, statistics@un.org, https://unstats.un.org; Statistical Yearbook of the United Nations 2021.

The World Bank, 1818 H St. NW, Washington, DC, 20433, USA, (202) 473-1000, (202) 477-6391, eds03@worldbank.org, https://www.worldbank.org/; Costa Rica (report) and World Development Indicators (WDI) 2022.

COSTA RICA-AIRLINES

International Civil Aviation Organization (ICAO), 999 Robert-Bourassa Blvd., Montreal, QC, H3C 5H7, CAN, (514) 954-8219 (Dial from U.S.), (514) 954-6077 (Fax from U.S.), icaohq@icao.int, https://www.icao.int; ICAO Regional Reports.

Palgrave Macmillan, 1 New York Plaza, Ste. 4500, New York, NY, 10004-1562, USA, (800) 777-4643, orders@palgrave.com, https://www.palgrave.com/us; The Statesman's Yearbook, 2023.

Routledge - Taylor & Francis Group, 6000 Broken Sound Pkwy. NW, Ste. 300, Boca Raton, FL, 33487, USA, (800) 634-1420, (800) 634-7064, orders@taylorandfrancis.com, https://www.routledge.com/; The Europa World Year Book 2022.

COSTA RICA-ALUMINUM PRODUCTION

See COSTA RICA-MINERAL INDUSTRIES

COSTA RICA-ARMED FORCES

Central Intelligence Agency (CIA), Office of Public Affairs, Washington, DC, 20505, USA, (703) 482-0623, https://www.cia.gov; The World Factbook.

International Institute for Strategic Studies (IISS) - Americas, 2121 K St. NW, Ste. 600, Washington, DC, 20037, USA, (202) 659-1490, (202) 659-1499, https://www.iiss.org/; The Military Balance 2022.

Palgrave Macmillan, 1 New York Plaza, Ste. 4500, New York, NY, 10004-1562, USA, (800) 777-4643, orders@palgrave.com, https://www.palgrave.com/us; The Statesman's Yearbook, 2023.

Stockholm International Peace Research Institute (SIPRI), Signalistgatan 9, Stockholm, SE 169 72, SWE, https://www.sipri.org/; SIPRI Arms Transfers Database and SIPRI Military Expenditure Database.

COSTA RICA-BALANCE OF PAYMENTS

Inter-American Development Bank (IDB), 1300 New York Ave. NW, Washington, DC, 20577, USA, (202) 623-1000, (202) 623-3096, https://www.iadb.org/en; Latin Macro Watch (LMW).

International Monetary Fund (IMF), 700 19th St. NW, Washington, DC, 20431, USA, (202) 623-7000, (202) 623-4661, publications@imf.org, https://www.imf.org; Balance of Payments Statistics: Annual Report 2021.

Routledge - Taylor & Francis Group, 6000 Broken Sound Pkwy. NW, Ste. 300, Boca Raton, FL, 33487, USA, (800) 634-1420, (800) 634-7064, orders@taylorandfrancis.com, https://www.routledge.com/; The Europa World Year Book 2022.

United Nations Conference on Trade and Development (UNCTAD), Palais des Nations, Geneva, 1211, SWI, (212) 963-6896, unctadinfo@unctad.org, https://unctad.org; Handbook of Statistics 2021.

United Nations Economic Commission for Latin America and the Caribbean (ECLAC), Casilla 179-D, Santiago, 7630412, CHL, (202) 596-3713, prensa@cepal.org, https://www.cepal.org/en; Economic Survey of Latin America and the Caribbean 2021: Labour Dynamics and Employment Policies for Sustainable and Inclusive Recovery Beyond the COVID-19 Crisis.

The World Bank, 1818 H St. NW, Washington, DC, 20433, USA, (202) 473-1000, (202) 477-6391, eds03@worldbank.org, https://www.worldbank.org/; Costa Rica (report); World Development Indicators (WDI) 2022; and World Development Report 2022: Finance for an Equitable Recovery.

COSTA RICA-BANANAS

See COSTA RICA-CROPS

COSTA RICA-BANKS AND BANKING

Euromonitor International, Inc., 1 N Dearborn St., Ste. 1700, Chicago, IL, 60602, USA, (312) 922-1115, (312) 922-1157, info-usa@euromonitor.com, https://www.euromonitor.com/; Geographies.

Inter-American Development Bank (IDB), 1300 New York Ave. NW, Washington, DC, 20577, USA, (202) 623-1000, (202) 623-3096, https://www.iadb.org/en; Latin Macro Watch (LMW).

International Monetary Fund (IMF), 700 19th St. NW, Washington, DC, 20431, USA, (202) 623-7000, (202) 623-4661, publications@imf.org, https://www.imf.org; International Financial Statistics (IFS).

Routledge - Taylor & Francis Group, 6000 Broken Sound Pkwy. NW, Ste. 300, Boca Raton, FL, 33487, USA, (800) 634-1420, (800) 634-7064, orders@taylorandfrancis.com, https://www.routledge.com/; The Europa World Year Book 2022.

United Nations Statistics Division (UNSD), United Nations Plz., New York, NY, 10017, USA, (800) 253-9646, (212) 963-9851, statistics@un.org, https://unstats.un.org; Statistical Yearbook of the United Nations 2021.

COSTA RICA-BARLEY PRODUCTION

See COSTA RICA-CROPS

COSTA RICA-BONDS

Inter-American Development Bank (IDB), 1300 New York Ave. NW, Washington, DC, 20577, USA, (202) 623-1000, (202) 623-3096, https://www.iadb.org/en; Latin Macro Watch (LMW).

COSTA RICA-BROADCASTING

Central Intelligence Agency (CIA), Office of Public Affairs, Washington, DC, 20505, USA, (703) 482-0623, https://www.cia.gov; The World Factbook.

Euromonitor International, Inc., 1 N Dearborn St., Ste. 1700, Chicago, IL, 60602, USA, (312) 922-1115, (312) 922-1157, info-usa@euromonitor.com, https://www.euromonitor.com/; Geographies.

Palgrave Macmillan, 1 New York Plaza, Ste. 4500, New York, NY, 10004-1562, USA, (800) 777-4643, orders@palgrave.com, https://www.palgrave.com/us; The Statesman's Yearbook, 2023.

WRTH Publications Limited, PO Box 290, Oxford, OX2 7FT, GBR, sales@wrth.com, https://www.wrth.com; World Radio TV Handbook 2023.

COSTA RICA-BUDGET

Central Intelligence Agency (CIA), Office of Public Affairs, Washington, DC, 20505, USA, (703) 482-0623, https://www.cia.gov; The World Factbook.

COSTA RICA-BUSINESS

Global Entrepreneurship Monitor (GEM), Babson College, 231 Forest St., Babson Park, MA, 02457, USA, (781) 235-1200, info@gemconsortium.org, https://www.gemconsortium.org/; Costa Rica Economy Profile.

Inter-American Development Bank (IDB), 1300 New York Ave. NW, Washington, DC, 20577, USA, (202) 623-1000, (202) 623-3096, https://www.iadb.org/en; Latin Macro Watch (LMW).

COSTA RICA-CAPITAL INVESTMENTS

Inter-American Development Bank (IDB), 1300 New York Ave. NW, Washington, DC, 20577, USA, (202) 623-1000, (202) 623-3096, https://www.iadb.org/en; Latin Macro Watch (LMW).

COSTA RICA-CHILDBIRTH-STATISTICS

The World Bank, 1818 H St. NW, Washington, DC, 20433, USA, (202) 473-1000, (202) 477-6391,

eds03@worldbank.org, https://www.worldbank.org/; World Development Indicators (WDI) 2022.

COSTA RICA-CLIMATE

Palgrave Macmillan, 1 New York Plaza, Ste. 4500, New York, NY, 10004-1562, USA, (800) 777-4643, orders@palgrave.com, https://www.palgrave.com/us; The Statesman's Yearbook, 2023.

COSTA RICA-COAL PRODUCTION

See COSTA RICA-MINERAL INDUSTRIES

COSTA RICA-COCOA PRODUCTION

See COSTA RICA-CROPS

COSTA RICA-COFFEE

See COSTA RICA-CROPS

COSTA RICA-COMMERCE

Palgrave Macmillan, 1 New York Plaza, Ste. 4500, New York, NY, 10004-1562, USA, (800) 777-4643, orders@palgrave.com, https://www.palgrave.com/us; The Statesman's Yearbook, 2023.

UK Data Service, University of Essex, Wivenhoe Park, Colchester, Essex, CO4 3SQ, GBR, https://ukdataservice.ac.uk/; International Aggregate Data.

COSTA RICA-COMMODITY EXCHANGES

Barchart, 209 W Jackson Blvd., 2nd Fl., Chicago, IL, 60606, USA, (877) 247-4394, commodities@barchart.com, https://www.barchart.com/cmdty; The cmdty Yearbook 2023; cmdtyStats: Commodity Statistics and Fundamental Data; cmdtyView: Commodity Index; and Commodity Data and Prices.

International Monetary Fund (IMF), 700 19th St. NW, Washington, DC, 20431, USA, (202) 623-7000, (202) 623-4661, publications@imf.org, https://www.imf.org; IMF Primary Commodity Prices.

COSTA RICA-CONSTRUCTION INDUSTRY

Inter-American Development Bank (IDB), 1300 New York Ave. NW, Washington, DC, 20577, USA, (202) 623-1000, (202) 623-3096, https://www.iadb.org/en; Latin Macro Watch (LMW).

COSTA RICA-CONSUMER PRICE INDEXES

Routledge - Taylor & Francis Group, 6000 Broken Sound Pkwy. NW, Ste. 300, Boca Raton, FL, 33487, USA, (800) 634-1420, (800) 634-7064, orders@taylorandfrancis.com, https://www.routledge.com/; The Europa World Year Book 2022.

The World Bank, 1818 H St. NW, Washington, DC, 20433, USA, (202) 473-1000, (202) 477-6391, eds03@worldbank.org, https://www.worldbank.org/; Costa Rica (report).

COSTA RICA-CONSUMPTION (ECONOMICS)

Inter-American Development Bank (IDB), 1300 New York Ave. NW, Washington, DC, 20577, USA, (202) 623-1000, (202) 623-3096, https://www.iadb.org/en; Latin Macro Watch (LMW).

COSTA RICA-COPPER INDUSTRY AND TRADE

See COSTA RICA-MINERAL INDUSTRIES

COSTA RICA-CORN INDUSTRY

See COSTA RICA-CROPS

COSTA RICA-COTTON

See COSTA RICA-CROPS

COSTA RICA-CROPS

International Monetary Fund (IMF), 700 19th St. NW, Washington, DC, 20431, USA, (202) 623-7000, (202) 623-4661, publications@imf.org, https://www.imf.org; International Financial Statistics (IFS).

Palgrave Macmillan, 1 New York Plaza, Ste. 4500, New York, NY, 10004-1562, USA, (800) 777-4643, orders@palgrave.com, https://www.palgrave.com/us; The Statesman's Yearbook, 2023.

United Nations Food and Agricultural Organization (FAO), 2121 K St., Ste. 800B, Washington, DC, 20037, USA, (202) 653-2400 (Dial from U.S.), (202) 653-5760 (Fax from U.S.), fao-hq@fao.org, https://www.fao.org; The State of Food and Agriculture (SOFA) 2022.

United Nations Statistics Division (UNSD), United Nations Plz., New York, NY, 10017, USA, (800) 253-9646, (212) 963-9851, statistics@un.org, https://unstats.un.org; Statistical Yearbook of the United Nations 2021.

COSTA RICA-CUSTOMS ADMINISTRATION

Inter-American Development Bank (IDB), 1300 New York Ave. NW, Washington, DC, 20577, USA, (202) 623-1000, (202) 623-3096, https://www.iadb.org/en; Latin Macro Watch (LMW).

COSTA RICA-DAIRY PROCESSING

Palgrave Macmillan, 1 New York Plaza, Ste. 4500, New York, NY, 10004-1562, USA, (800) 777-4643, orders@palgrave.com, https://www.palgrave.com/us; The Statesman's Yearbook, 2023.

United Nations Food and Agricultural Organization (FAO), 2121 K St., Ste. 800B, Washington, DC, 20037, USA, (202) 653-2400 (Dial from U.S.), (202) 653-5760 (Fax from U.S.), fao-hq@fao.org, https://www.fao.org; The State of Food and Agriculture (SOFA) 2022.

COSTA RICA-DEBT

The World Bank, 1818 H St. NW, Washington, DC, 20433, USA, (202) 473-1000, (202) 477-6391, eds03@worldbank.org, https://www.worldbank.org/; Global Financial Development Report 2019-2020: Bank Regulation and Supervision a Decade after the Global Financial Crisis.

COSTA RICA-DEBTS, EXTERNAL

Inter-American Development Bank (IDB), 1300 New York Ave. NW, Washington, DC, 20577, USA, (202) 623-1000, (202) 623-3096, https://www.iadb.org/en; Latin Macro Watch (LMW).

United Nations Economic Commission for Latin America and the Caribbean (ECLAC), Casilla 179-D, Santiago, 7630412, CHL, (202) 596-3713, prensa@cepal.org, https://www.cepal.org/en; Economic Survey of Latin America and the Caribbean 2021: Labour Dynamics and Employment Policies for Sustainable and Inclusive Recovery Beyond the COVID-19 Crisis.

The World Bank, 1818 H St. NW, Washington, DC, 20433, USA, (202) 473-1000, (202) 477-6391, eds03@worldbank.org, https://www.worldbank.org/; Global Financial Development Report 2019-2020: Bank Regulation and Supervision a Decade after the Global Financial Crisis; World Development Indicators (WDI) 2022; and World Development Report 2022: Finance for an Equitable Recovery.

COSTA RICA-DEBTS, PUBLIC

United Nations Statistics Division (UNSD), United Nations Plz., New York, NY, 10017, USA, (800) 253-9646, (212) 963-9851, statistics@un.org, https://unstats.un.org; Statistical Yearbook of the United Nations 2021.

The World Bank, 1818 H St. NW, Washington, DC, 20433, USA, (202) 473-1000, (202) 477-6391, eds03@worldbank.org, https://www.worldbank.org/; Global Financial Development Report 2019-2020: Bank Regulation and Supervision a Decade after the Global Financial Crisis.

COSTA RICA-DEFENSE EXPENDITURES

See COSTA RICA-ARMED FORCES

COSTA RICA-DIAMONDS

See COSTA RICA-MINERAL INDUSTRIES

COSTA RICA-DISPOSABLE INCOME

Inter-American Development Bank (IDB), 1300 New York Ave. NW, Washington, DC, 20577, USA, (202) 623-1000, (202) 623-3096, https://www.iadb.org/en; Latin Macro Watch (LMW).

COSTA RICA-ECONOMIC ASSISTANCE

Inter-American Development Bank (IDB), 1300 New York Ave. NW, Washington, DC, 20577, USA, (202) 623-1000, (202) 623-3096, https://www.iadb.org/en; Latin Macro Watch (LMW).

United Nations Statistics Division (UNSD), United Nations Plz., New York, NY, 10017, USA, (800) 253-9646, (212) 963-9851, statistics@un.org, https://unstats.un.org; Statistical Yearbook of the United Nations 2021.

COSTA RICA-ECONOMIC CONDITIONS

Bernan Press, 15250 NBN Way, Bldg. C, Blue Ridge Summit, PA, 17214, USA, (301) 459-2255, (800) 865-3457, (800) 865-3450, customercare@bernan.com, https://rowman.com/Page/Bernan; World Economic Outlook, April 2022.

Central Intelligence Agency (CIA), Office of Public Affairs, Washington, DC, 20505, USA, (703) 482-0623, https://www.cia.gov; The World Factbook.

The Economist Group: Economist Intelligence Unit (EIU), 900 3rd Ave., 16th Fl., New York, NY, 10022, USA, (212) 541-0500, americas@eiu.com, https://www.eiu.com; Costa Rica Country Report.

Euromonitor International, Inc., 1 N Dearborn St., Ste. 1700, Chicago, IL, 60602, USA, (312) 922-1115, (312) 922-1157, info-usa@euromonitor.com, https://www.euromonitor.com/; Geographies.

Global Entrepreneurship Monitor (GEM), Babson College, 231 Forest St., Babson Park, MA, 02457, USA, (781) 235-1200, info@gemconsortium.org, https://www.gemconsortium.org/; Costa Rica Economy Profile.

Inter-American Development Bank (IDB), 1300 New York Ave. NW, Washington, DC, 20577, USA, (202) 623-1000, (202) 623-3096, https://www.iadb.org/en; Latin Macro Watch (LMW).

International Monetary Fund (IMF), 700 19th St. NW, Washington, DC, 20431, USA, (202) 623-7000, (202) 623-4661, publications@imf.org, https://www.imf.org; IMF Data and World Economic Outlook.

Palgrave Macmillan, 1 New York Plaza, Ste. 4500, New York, NY, 10004-1562, USA, (800) 777-4643, orders@palgrave.com, https://www.palgrave.com/us; The Statesman's Yearbook, 2023.

Routledge - Taylor & Francis Group, 6000 Broken Sound Pkwy. NW, Ste. 300, Boca Raton, FL, 33487, USA, (800) 634-1420, (800) 634-7064, orders@taylorandfrancis.com, https://www.routledge.com/; The Europa World Year Book 2022.

United Nations Economic Commission for Latin America and the Caribbean (ECLAC), Casilla 179-D, Santiago, 7630412, CHL, (202) 596-3713, prensa@cepal.org, https://www.cepal.org/en; CEPALSTAT; Economic Survey of Latin America and the Caribbean 2021: Labour Dynamics and Employment Policies for Sustainable and Inclusive Recovery Beyond the COVID-19 Crisis; Foreign Direct Investment in Latin America and the Caribbean 2022; and Social Panorama of Latin America and the Caribbean 2022: Transforming Education as a Basis for Sustainable Development.

United Nations Statistics Division (UNSD), United Nations Plz., New York, NY, 10017, USA, (800) 253-9646, (212) 963-9851, statistics@un.org, https://unstats.un.org; World Statistics Pocketbook 2021.

The World Bank, 1818 H St. NW, Washington, DC, 20433, USA, (202) 473-1000, (202) 477-6391, eds03@worldbank.org, https://www.worldbank.org/; Costa Rica (report); Global Economic Monitor (GEM); Global Economic Prospects, June 2022; The Global Findex Database 2021; and World Development Report 2022: Finance for an Equitable Recovery.

COSTA RICA-EDUCATION

Euromonitor International, Inc., 1 N Dearborn St., Ste. 1700, Chicago, IL, 60602, USA, (312) 922-1115, (312) 922-1157, info-usa@euromonitor.com, https://www.euromonitor.com/; Geographies.

Infoplease, c/o Sandbox Networks, Inc., 1 Lincoln St., 24th Fl., Boston, MA, 02111, USA, https://www.infoplease.com; Countries of the World.

Palgrave Macmillan, 1 New York Plaza, Ste. 4500, New York, NY, 10004-1562, USA, (800) 777-4643, orders@palgrave.com, https://www.palgrave.com/us; The Statesman's Yearbook, 2023.

Routledge - Taylor & Francis Group, 6000 Broken Sound Pkwy. NW, Ste. 300, Boca Raton, FL, 33487, USA, (800) 634-1420, (800) 634-7064, orders@taylorandfrancis.com, https://www.routledge.com/; The Europa World Year Book 2022.

UNESCO Institute for Statistics, C.P 250 Succursale H, Montreal, QC, H3G 2K8, CAN, (514) 343-6880 (Dial from U.S.), (514) 343-5740 (Fax from U.S.), uis.publications@unesco.org, http://uis.unesco.org/; Literacy and UIS.Stat.

United Nations Statistics Division (UNSD), United Nations Plz., New York, NY, 10017, USA, (800) 253-9646, (212) 963-9851, statistics@un.org, https://unstats.un.org; Millennium Development Goal Indicators.

The World Bank, 1818 H St. NW, Washington, DC, 20433, USA, (202) 473-1000, (202) 477-6391, eds03@worldbank.org, https://www.worldbank.org/; Costa Rica (report); World Development Indicators (WDI) 2022; and World Development Report 2022: Finance for an Equitable Recovery.

COSTA RICA-ELECTRICITY

Inter-American Development Bank (IDB), 1300 New York Ave. NW, Washington, DC, 20577, USA, (202) 623-1000, (202) 623-3096, https://www.iadb.org/en; Latin Macro Watch (LMW).

U.S. Energy Information Administration (EIA), 1000 Independence Ave. SW, Washington, DC, 20585, USA, (202) 586-8800, infoctr@eia.gov, https://www.eia.gov; International Energy Outlook 2021.

United Nations Statistics Division (UNSD), United Nations Plz., New York, NY, 10017, USA, (800) 253-9646, (212) 963-9851, statistics@un.org, https://unstats.un.org; Statistical Yearbook of the United Nations 2021.

COSTA RICA-EMPLOYMENT

International Labour Organization (ILO), 4 Rte. des Morillons, Geneva, CH-1211, SWI, ilo@ilo.org, https://www.ilo.org; NORMLEX Information System on International Labour Standards.

UK Data Service, University of Essex, Wivenhoe Park, Colchester, Essex, CO4 3SQ, GBR, https://ukdataservice.ac.uk/; International Aggregate Data.

The World Bank, 1818 H St. NW, Washington, DC, 20433, USA, (202) 473-1000, (202) 477-6391, eds03@worldbank.org, https://www.worldbank.org/; Costa Rica (report).

COSTA RICA-ENVIRONMENTAL CONDITIONS

DSI Data Service & Information, Xantener Strasse 51a, Rheinberg, D-47495, GER, dsi@dsidata.com, https://www.dsidata.com/; Global Environmental Database.

The Economist Group: Economist Intelligence Unit (EIU), 900 3rd Ave., 16th Fl., New York, NY, 10022, USA, (212) 541-0500, americas@eiu.com, https://www.eiu.com; Costa Rica Country Report.

United Nations Economic Commission for Latin America and the Caribbean (ECLAC), Casilla 179-D, Santiago, 7630412, CHL, (202) 596-3713, prensa@cepal.org, https://www.cepal.org/en; CEPALSTAT.

United Nations Statistics Division (UNSD), United Nations Plz., New York, NY, 10017, USA, (800) 253-9646, (212) 963-9851, statistics@un.org, https://unstats.un.org; World Statistics Pocketbook 2021.

COSTA RICA-EXPENDITURES, PUBLIC

Inter-American Development Bank (IDB), 1300 New York Ave. NW, Washington, DC, 20577, USA, (202) 623-1000, (202) 623-3096, https://www.iadb.org/en; Latin Macro Watch (LMW).

COSTA RICA-EXPORTS

Central Intelligence Agency (CIA), Office of Public Affairs, Washington, DC, 20505, USA, (703) 482-0623, https://www.cia.gov; The World Factbook.

The Economist Group: Economist Intelligence Unit (EIU), 900 3rd Ave., 16th Fl., New York, NY, 10022, USA, (212) 541-0500, americas@eiu.com, https://www.eiu.com; Costa Rica Country Report.

Inter-American Development Bank (IDB), 1300 New York Ave. NW, Washington, DC, 20577, USA, (202) 623-1000, (202) 623-3096, https://www.iadb.org/en; Latin Macro Watch (LMW).

International Monetary Fund (IMF), 700 19th St. NW, Washington, DC, 20431, USA, (202) 623-7000, (202) 623-4661, publications@imf.org, https://www.imf.org; Direction of Trade Statistics (DOTS) and International Financial Statistics (IFS).

S&P Global, IHS Markit, 15 Inverness Way E, Englewood, CO, 80112, USA, (800) 447-2273, (800) 854-7179, https://ihsmarkit.com; Global Trade Atlas (GTA).

United Nations Conference on Trade and Development (UNCTAD), Palais des Nations, Geneva, 1211, SWI, (212) 963-6896, unctadinfo@unctad.org, https://unctad.org; Handbook of Statistics 2021.

The World Bank, 1818 H St. NW, Washington, DC, 20433, USA, (202) 473-1000, (202) 477-6391, eds03@worldbank.org, https://www.worldbank.org/; World Development Report 2022: Finance for an Equitable Recovery.

COSTA RICA-FEMALE WORKING POPULATION

See COSTA RICA-EMPLOYMENT

COSTA RICA-FERTILITY, HUMAN

Central Intelligence Agency (CIA), Office of Public Affairs, Washington, DC, 20505, USA, (703) 482-0623, https://www.cia.gov; The World Factbook.

COSTA RICA-FERTILIZER INDUSTRY

United Nations Food and Agricultural Organization (FAO), 2121 K St., Ste. 800B, Washington, DC, 20037, USA, (202) 653-2400 (Dial from U.S.), (202) 653-5760 (Fax from U.S.), fao-hq@fao.org, https://www.fao.org; The State of Food and Agriculture (SOFA) 2022.

COSTA RICA-FETAL MORTALITY

See COSTA RICA-MORTALITY

COSTA RICA-FINANCE

Inter-American Development Bank (IDB), 1300 New York Ave. NW, Washington, DC, 20577, USA, (202) 623-1000, (202) 623-3096, https://www.iadb.org/en; Latin Macro Watch (LMW).

Stockholm International Peace Research Institute (SIPRI), Signalistgatan 9, Stockholm, SE 169 72, SWE, https://www.sipri.org/; SIPRI Arms Transfers Database and SIPRI Military Expenditure Database.

United Nations Statistics Division (UNSD), United Nations Plz., New York, NY, 10017, USA, (800) 253-9646, (212) 963-9851, statistics@un.org, https://unstats.un.org; Statistical Yearbook of the United Nations 2021.

The World Bank, 1818 H St. NW, Washington, DC, 20433, USA, (202) 473-1000, (202) 477-6391, eds03@worldbank.org, https://www.worldbank.org/; Costa Rica (report).

COSTA RICA-FINANCE, PUBLIC

Bernan Press, 15250 NBN Way, Bldg. C, Blue Ridge Summit, PA, 17214, USA, (301) 459-2255, (800) 865-3457, (800) 865-3450, customercare@bernan.com, https://rowman.com/Page/Bernan; National Accounts Statistics: Analysis of Main Aggregates 2020.

The Economist Group: Economist Intelligence Unit (EIU), 900 3rd Ave., 16th Fl., New York, NY, 10022, USA, (212) 541-0500, americas@eiu.com, https://www.eiu.com; Costa Rica Country Report.

Inter-American Development Bank (IDB), 1300 New York Ave. NW, Washington, DC, 20577, USA, (202) 623-1000, (202) 623-3096, https://www.iadb.org/en; Latin Macro Watch (LMW).

International Monetary Fund (IMF), 700 19th St. NW, Washington, DC, 20431, USA, (202) 623-7000, (202) 623-4661, publications@imf.org, https://www.imf.org; International Financial Statistics (IFS) and Regional Economic Outlook.

Palgrave Macmillan, 1 New York Plaza, Ste. 4500, New York, NY, 10004-1562, USA, (800) 777-4643, orders@palgrave.com, https://www.palgrave.com/us; The Statesman's Yearbook, 2023.

Routledge - Taylor & Francis Group, 6000 Broken Sound Pkwy. NW, Ste. 300, Boca Raton, FL, 33487, USA, (800) 634-1420, (800) 634-7064, orders@taylorandfrancis.com, https://www.routledge.com/; The Europa World Year Book 2022.

United Nations Statistics Division (UNSD), United Nations Plz., New York, NY, 10017, USA, (800) 253-9646, (212) 963-9851, statistics@un.org, https://unstats.un.org; National Accounts Main Aggregates Database and National Accounts Statistics: Main Aggregates and Detailed Tables.

The World Bank, 1818 H St. NW, Washington, DC, 20433, USA, (202) 473-1000, (202) 477-6391, eds03@worldbank.org, https://www.worldbank.org/; Costa Rica (report).

COSTA RICA-FISHERIES

Inter-American Development Bank (IDB), 1300 New York Ave. NW, Washington, DC, 20577, USA, (202) 623-1000, (202) 623-3096, https://www.iadb.org/en; Latin Macro Watch (LMW).

Palgrave Macmillan, 1 New York Plaza, Ste. 4500, New York, NY, 10004-1562, USA, (800) 777-4643, orders@palgrave.com, https://www.palgrave.com/us; The Statesman's Yearbook, 2023.

Routledge - Taylor & Francis Group, 6000 Broken Sound Pkwy. NW, Ste. 300, Boca Raton, FL, 33487, USA, (800) 634-1420, (800) 634-7064, orders@taylorandfrancis.com, https://www.routledge.com/; The Europa World Year Book 2022.

United Nations Food and Agricultural Organization (FAO), 2121 K St., Ste. 800B, Washington, DC, 20037, USA, (202) 653-2400 (Dial from U.S.), (202) 653-5760 (Fax from U.S.), fao-hq@fao.org, https://www.fao.org; FAO Yearbook of Fishery and Aquaculture Statistics 2019; Fishery Statistical Collections Global Capture Production; FishStatJ; and The State of Food and Agriculture (SOFA) 2022.

United Nations Statistics Division (UNSD), United Nations Plz., New York, NY, 10017, USA, (800) 253-9646, (212) 963-9851, statistics@un.org, https://unstats.un.org; Statistical Yearbook of the United Nations 2021.

The World Bank, 1818 H St. NW, Washington, DC, 20433, USA, (202) 473-1000, (202) 477-6391, eds03@worldbank.org, https://www.worldbank.org/; Costa Rica (report).

COSTA RICA-FOOD

United Nations Food and Agricultural Organization (FAO), 2121 K St., Ste. 800B, Washington, DC, 20037, USA, (202) 653-2400 (Dial from U.S.), (202) 653-5760 (Fax from U.S.), fao-hq@fao.org, https://www.fao.org; The State of Food and Agriculture (SOFA) 2022.

COSTA RICA-FOREIGN EXCHANGE RATES

Inter-American Development Bank (IDB), 1300 New York Ave. NW, Washington, DC, 20577, USA, (202) 623-1000, (202) 623-3096, https://www.iadb.org/en; Latin Macro Watch (LMW).

International Monetary Fund (IMF), 700 19th St. NW, Washington, DC, 20431, USA, (202) 623-7000, (202) 623-4661, publications@imf.org, https://www.imf.org; International Financial Statistics (IFS).

COSTA RICA-FORESTS AND FORESTRY

Inter-American Development Bank (IDB), 1300 New York Ave. NW, Washington, DC, 20577, USA, (202) 623-1000, (202) 623-3096, https://www.iadb.org/en; Latin Macro Watch (LMW).

Palgrave Macmillan, 1 New York Plaza, Ste. 4500, New York, NY, 10004-1562, USA, (800) 777-4643, orders@palgrave.com, https://www.palgrave.com/us; The Statesman's Yearbook, 2023.

Routledge - Taylor & Francis Group, 6000 Broken Sound Pkwy. NW, Ste. 300, Boca Raton, FL, 33487, USA, (800) 634-1420, (800) 634-7064, orders@taylorandfrancis.com, https://www.routledge.com/; The Europa World Year Book 2022.

UNESCO Institute for Statistics, C.P 250 Succursale H, Montreal, QC, H3G 2K8, CAN, (514) 343-6880 (Dial from U.S.), (514) 343-5740 (Fax from U.S.), uis.publications@unesco.org, http://uis.unesco.org/; UIS.Stat.

United Nations Food and Agricultural Organization (FAO), 2121 K St., Ste. 800B, Washington, DC, 20037, USA, (202) 653-2400 (Dial from U.S.), (202) 653-5760 (Fax from U.S.), fao-hq@fao.org, https://www.fao.org; FAO Yearbook of Forest Products 2019 and The State of Food and Agriculture (SOFA) 2022.

United Nations Statistics Division (UNSD), United Nations Plz., New York, NY, 10017, USA, (800) 253-9646, (212) 963-9851, statistics@un.org, https://unstats.un.org; Statistical Yearbook of the United Nations 2021.

The World Bank, 1818 H St. NW, Washington, DC, 20433, USA, (202) 473-1000, (202) 477-6391, eds03@worldbank.org, https://www.worldbank.org/; Costa Rica (report) and World Development Report 2022: Finance for an Equitable Recovery.

COSTA RICA-GAS PRODUCTION

See COSTA RICA-MINERAL INDUSTRIES

COSTA RICA-GEOGRAPHIC INFORMATION SYSTEMS

The World Bank, 1818 H St. NW, Washington, DC, 20433, USA, (202) 473-1000, (202) 477-6391, eds03@worldbank.org, https://www.worldbank.org/; Costa Rica (report).

COSTA RICA-GOLD INDUSTRY

The World Bank, 1818 H St. NW, Washington, DC, 20433, USA, (202) 473-1000, (202) 477-6391, eds03@worldbank.org, https://www.worldbank.org/; World Development Indicators (WDI) 2022.

COSTA RICA-GOLD PRODUCTION

See COSTA RICA-MINERAL INDUSTRIES

COSTA RICA-GROSS DOMESTIC PRODUCT

The Economist Group: Economist Intelligence Unit (EIU), 900 3rd Ave., 16th Fl., New York, NY, 10022, USA, (212) 541-0500, americas@eiu.com, https://www.eiu.com; Costa Rica Country Report.

Inter-American Development Bank (IDB), 1300 New York Ave. NW, Washington, DC, 20577, USA, (202) 623-1000, (202) 623-3096, https://www.iadb.org/en; Latin Macro Watch (LMW).

Routledge - Taylor & Francis Group, 6000 Broken Sound Pkwy. NW, Ste. 300, Boca Raton, FL, 33487, USA, (800) 634-1420, (800) 634-7064, orders@taylorandfrancis.com, https://www.routledge.com/; The Europa World Year Book 2022.

United Nations Statistics Division (UNSD), United Nations Plz., New York, NY, 10017, USA, (800) 253-9646, (212) 963-9851, statistics@un.org, https://unstats.un.org; Statistical Yearbook of the United Nations 2021.

The World Bank, 1818 H St. NW, Washington, DC, 20433, USA, (202) 473-1000, (202) 477-6391, eds03@worldbank.org, https://www.worldbank.org/; World Development Indicators (WDI) 2022 and World Development Report 2022: Finance for an Equitable Recovery.

COSTA RICA-GROSS NATIONAL PRODUCT

Inter-American Development Bank (IDB), 1300 New York Ave. NW, Washington, DC, 20577, USA, (202) 623-1000, (202) 623-3096, https://www.iadb.org/en; Latin Macro Watch (LMW).

Palgrave Macmillan, 1 New York Plaza, Ste. 4500, New York, NY, 10004-1562, USA, (800) 777-4643, orders@palgrave.com, https://www.palgrave.com/us; The Statesman's Yearbook, 2023.

United Nations Statistics Division (UNSD), United Nations Plz., New York, NY, 10017, USA, (800) 253-9646, (212) 963-9851, statistics@un.org, https://unstats.un.org; Statistical Yearbook of the United Nations 2021.

The World Bank, 1818 H St. NW, Washington, DC, 20433, USA, (202) 473-1000, (202) 477-6391, eds03@worldbank.org, https://www.worldbank.org/; World Development Indicators (WDI) 2022 and World Development Report 2022: Finance for an Equitable Recovery.

COSTA RICA-HOUSING

Euromonitor International, Inc., 1 N Dearborn St., Ste. 1700, Chicago, IL, 60602, USA, (312) 922-1115, (312) 922-1157, info-usa@euromonitor.com, https://www.euromonitor.com/; Geographies.

COSTA RICA-ILLITERATE PERSONS

UNESCO Institute for Statistics, C.P 250 Succursale H, Montreal, QC, H3G 2K8, CAN, (514) 343-6880 (Dial from U.S.), (514) 343-5740 (Fax from U.S.), uis.publications@unesco.org, http://uis.unesco.org/; UIS.Stat.

COSTA RICA-IMPORTS

Central Intelligence Agency (CIA), Office of Public Affairs, Washington, DC, 20505, USA, (703) 482-0623, https://www.cia.gov; The World Factbook.

The Economist Group: Economist Intelligence Unit (EIU), 900 3rd Ave., 16th Fl., New York, NY, 10022, USA, (212) 541-0500, americas@eiu.com, https://www.eiu.com; Costa Rica Country Report.

Inter-American Development Bank (IDB), 1300 New York Ave. NW, Washington, DC, 20577, USA, (202) 623-1000, (202) 623-3096, https://www.iadb.org/en; Latin Macro Watch (LMW).

International Monetary Fund (IMF), 700 19th St. NW, Washington, DC, 20431, USA, (202) 623-7000, (202) 623-4661, publications@imf.org, https://www.imf.org; Direction of Trade Statistics (DOTS) and International Financial Statistics (IFS).

S&P Global, IHS Markit, 15 Inverness Way E, Englewood, CO, 80112, USA, (800) 447-2273, (800) 854-7179, https://ihsmarkit.com; Global Trade Atlas (GTA).

United Nations Conference on Trade and Development (UNCTAD), Palais des Nations, Geneva, 1211, SWI, (212) 963-6896, unctadinfo@unctad.org, https://unctad.org; Handbook of Statistics 2021.

The World Bank, 1818 H St. NW, Washington, DC, 20433, USA, (202) 473-1000, (202) 477-6391, eds03@worldbank.org, https://www.worldbank.org/; World Development Report 2022: Finance for an Equitable Recovery.

COSTA RICA-INDUSTRIES

Central Intelligence Agency (CIA), Office of Public Affairs, Washington, DC, 20505, USA, (703) 482-0623, https://www.cia.gov; The World Factbook.

The Economist Group: Economist Intelligence Unit (EIU), 900 3rd Ave., 16th Fl., New York, NY, 10022, USA, (212) 541-0500, americas@eiu.com, https://www.eiu.com; Costa Rica Country Report.

Euromonitor International, Inc., 1 N Dearborn St., Ste. 1700, Chicago, IL, 60602, USA, (312) 922-1115, (312) 922-1157, info-usa@euromonitor.com, https://www.euromonitor.com/; Geographies.

International Labour Organization (ILO), 4 Rte. des Morillons, Geneva, CH-1211, SWI, ilo@ilo.org, https://www.ilo.org; NORMLEX Information System on International Labour Standards.

Palgrave Macmillan, 1 New York Plaza, Ste. 4500, New York, NY, 10004-1562, USA, (800) 777-4643, orders@palgrave.com, https://www.palgrave.com/us; The Statesman's Yearbook, 2023.

Routledge - Taylor & Francis Group, 6000 Broken Sound Pkwy. NW, Ste. 300, Boca Raton, FL, 33487, USA, (800) 634-1420, (800) 634-7064, orders@taylorandfrancis.com, https://www.routledge.com/; The Europa World Year Book 2022.

United Nations Economic Commission for Latin America and the Caribbean (ECLAC), Casilla 179-D, Santiago, 7630412, CHL, (202) 596-3713, prensa@cepal.org, https://www.cepal.org/en; Economic Survey of Latin America and the Caribbean 2021: Labour Dynamics and Employment Policies for Sustainable and Inclusive Recovery Beyond the COVID-19 Crisis.

United Nations Industrial Development Organization (UNIDO), 1 United Nations Plz., Rm. DC1-1118, New York, NY, 10017, USA, (212) 963-6890, (212) 963 6885, (212) 963-7904, office.newyork@unido.org, https://www.unido.org/; Industrial Statistics Databases and International Yearbook of Industrial Statistics 2021.

The World Bank, 1818 H St. NW, Washington, DC, 20433, USA, (202) 473-1000, (202) 477-6391, eds03@worldbank.org, https://www.worldbank.org/; Costa Rica (report) and World Development Indicators (WDI) 2022.

COSTA RICA-INFANT AND MATERNAL MORTALITY

See COSTA RICA-MORTALITY

COSTA RICA-INFLATION (FINANCE)

United Nations Economic Commission for Latin America and the Caribbean (ECLAC), Casilla 179-D, Santiago, 7630412, CHL, (202) 596-3713, prensa@cepal.org, https://www.cepal.org/en; Economic Survey of Latin America and the Caribbean 2021: Labour Dynamics and Employment Policies for Sustainable and Inclusive Recovery Beyond the COVID-19 Crisis.

COSTA RICA-INTEREST RATES

Inter-American Development Bank (IDB), 1300 New York Ave. NW, Washington, DC, 20577, USA, (202) 623-1000, (202) 623-3096, https://www.iadb.org/en; Latin Macro Watch (LMW).

COSTA RICA-INTERNAL REVENUE

Inter-American Development Bank (IDB), 1300 New York Ave. NW, Washington, DC, 20577, USA, (202) 623-1000, (202) 623-3096, https://www.iadb.org/en; Latin Macro Watch (LMW).

COSTA RICA-INTERNATIONAL FINANCE

Inter-American Development Bank (IDB), 1300 New York Ave. NW, Washington, DC, 20577, USA, (202) 623-1000, (202) 623-3096, https://www.iadb.org/en; Latin Macro Watch (LMW).

COSTA RICA-INTERNATIONAL LIQUIDITY

Inter-American Development Bank (IDB), 1300 New York Ave. NW, Washington, DC, 20577, USA, (202) 623-1000, (202) 623-3096, https://www.iadb.org/en; Latin Macro Watch (LMW).

COSTA RICA-INTERNATIONAL TRADE

Banque de France, 31 rue Croix des Petits-Champs, Paris, 75049, FRA, infos@banque-france.fr, https://www.banque-france.fr/en; Key Figures France and Abroad.

The Economist Group: Economist Intelligence Unit (EIU), 900 3rd Ave., 16th Fl., New York, NY, 10022, USA, (212) 541-0500, americas@eiu.com, https://www.eiu.com; Costa Rica Country Report.

Euromonitor International, Inc., 1 N Dearborn St., Ste. 1700, Chicago, IL, 60602, USA, (312) 922-1115, (312) 922-1157, info-usa@euromonitor.com, https://www.euromonitor.com/; Geographies.

Inter-American Development Bank (IDB), 1300 New York Ave. NW, Washington, DC, 20577, USA, (202) 623-1000, (202) 623-3096, https://www.iadb.org/en; Latin Macro Watch (LMW).

International Monetary Fund (IMF), 700 19th St. NW, Washington, DC, 20431, USA, (202) 623-7000, (202) 623-4661, publications@imf.org, https://www.imf.org; International Financial Statistics (IFS).

Palgrave Macmillan, 1 New York Plaza, Ste. 4500, New York, NY, 10004-1562, USA, (800) 777-4643, orders@palgrave.com, https://www.palgrave.com/us; The Statesman's Yearbook, 2023.

Routledge - Taylor & Francis Group, 6000 Broken Sound Pkwy. NW, Ste. 300, Boca Raton, FL, 33487, USA, (800) 634-1420, (800) 634-7064, orders@taylorandfrancis.com, https://www.routledge.com/; The Europa World Year Book 2022.

United Nations Conference on Trade and Development (UNCTAD), Palais des Nations, Geneva, 1211, SWI, (212) 963-6896, unctadinfo@unctad.org, https://unctad.org; Trade and Development Report 2021.

United Nations Economic Commission for Latin America and the Caribbean (ECLAC), Casilla 179-D, Santiago, 7630412, CHL, (202) 596-3713, prensa@cepal.org, https://www.cepal.org/en; Economic Survey of Latin America and the Caribbean 2021: Labour Dynamics and Employment Policies for Sustainable and Inclusive Recovery Beyond the COVID-19 Crisis.

United Nations Food and Agricultural Organization (FAO), 2121 K St., Ste. 800B, Washington, DC, 20037, USA, (202) 653-2400 (Dial from U.S.), (202) 653-5760 (Fax from U.S.), fao-hq@fao.org, https://www.fao.org; The State of Food and Agriculture (SOFA) 2022.

United Nations Statistics Division (UNSD), United Nations Plz., New York, NY, 10017, USA, (800) 253-9646, (212) 963-9851, statistics@un.org, https://unstats.un.org; International Trade Statistics Yearbook 2020 and Statistical Yearbook of the United Nations 2021.

The World Bank, 1818 H St. NW, Washington, DC, 20433, USA, (202) 473-1000, (202) 477-6391, eds03@worldbank.org, https://www.worldbank.org/; Costa Rica (report); World Development Indicators (WDI) 2022; and World Development Report 2022: Finance for an Equitable Recovery.

World Trade Organization (WTO), Ctre. William Rappard, Rue de Lausanne 154, Case postale, Geneva, CH-1211, SWI, enquiries@wto.org, https://www.wto.org; World Trade Statistical Review 2022.

COSTA RICA-INTERNET USERS

International Telecommunication Union (ITU), Place des Nations, Geneva, CH-1211, SWI, itumail@itu.int, https://www.itu.int; Global Connectivity Report 2022; World Telecommunication/ICT Indicators Database 2021; and Yearbook of Statistics 2019.

The World Bank, 1818 H St. NW, Washington, DC, 20433, USA, (202) 473-1000, (202) 477-6391, eds03@worldbank.org, https://www.worldbank.org/; Costa Rica (report).

COSTA RICA-INVESTMENTS

Inter-American Development Bank (IDB), 1300 New York Ave. NW, Washington, DC, 20577, USA, (202) 623-1000, (202) 623-3096, https://www.iadb.org/en; Latin Macro Watch (LMW).

COSTA RICA-IRRIGATION

Inter-American Development Bank (IDB), 1300 New York Ave. NW, Washington, DC, 20577, USA, (202) 623-1000, (202) 623-3096, https://www.iadb.org/en; Latin Macro Watch (LMW).

COSTA RICA-LABOR

Central Intelligence Agency (CIA), Office of Public Affairs, Washington, DC, 20505, USA, (703) 482-0623, https://www.cia.gov; The World Factbook.

Euromonitor International, Inc., 1 N Dearborn St., Ste. 1700, Chicago, IL, 60602, USA, (312) 922-1115, (312) 922-1157, info-usa@euromonitor.com, https://www.euromonitor.com/; Geographies.

International Labour Organization (ILO), 4 Rte. des Morillons, Geneva, CH-1211, SWI, ilo@ilo.org, https://www.ilo.org; NORMLEX Information System on International Labour Standards.

Palgrave Macmillan, 1 New York Plaza, Ste. 4500, New York, NY, 10004-1562, USA, (800) 777-4643, orders@palgrave.com, https://www.palgrave.com/us; The Statesman's Yearbook, 2023.

United Nations Food and Agricultural Organization (FAO), 2121 K St., Ste. 800B, Washington, DC, 20037, USA, (202) 653-2400 (Dial from U.S.), (202) 653-5760 (Fax from U.S.), fao-hq@fao.org, https://www.fao.org; The State of Food and Agriculture (SOFA) 2022.

The World Bank, 1818 H St. NW, Washington, DC, 20433, USA, (202) 473-1000, (202) 477-6391, eds03@worldbank.org, https://www.worldbank.org/; World Development Indicators (WDI) 2022 and World Development Report 2022: Finance for an Equitable Recovery.

COSTA RICA-LAND USE

Inter-American Development Bank (IDB), 1300 New York Ave. NW, Washington, DC, 20577, USA, (202) 623-1000, (202) 623-3096, https://www.iadb.org/en; Latin Macro Watch (LMW).

United Nations Statistics Division (UNSD), United Nations Plz., New York, NY, 10017, USA, (800) 253-9646, (212) 963-9851, statistics@un.org, https://unstats.un.org; Millennium Development Goal Indicators.

The World Bank, 1818 H St. NW, Washington, DC, 20433, USA, (202) 473-1000, (202) 477-6391, eds03@worldbank.org, https://www.worldbank.org/; World Development Report 2022: Finance for an Equitable Recovery.

COSTA RICA-LIBRARIES

UNESCO Institute for Statistics, C.P 250 Succursale H, Montreal, QC, H3G 2K8, CAN, (514) 343-6880 (Dial from U.S.), (514) 343-5740 (Fax from U.S.), uis.publications@unesco.org, http://uis.unesco.org/; UIS.Stat.

COSTA RICA-LIFE EXPECTANCY

Central Intelligence Agency (CIA), Office of Public Affairs, Washington, DC, 20505, USA, (703) 482-0623, https://www.cia.gov; The World Factbook.

United Nations Department of Economic and Social Affairs (DESA), Population Division, 2 United Nations Plz., Rm. DC2-1950, New York, NY, 10017, USA, (212) 963-3209, (212) 963-2147, population@un.org, https://www.un.org/development/desa/pd/; World Population Ageing 2020 Highlights.

United Nations Statistics Division (UNSD), United Nations Plz., New York, NY, 10017, USA, (800) 253-9646, (212) 963-9851, statistics@un.org, https://unstats.un.org; Millennium Development Goal Indicators.

COSTA RICA-LITERACY

Euromonitor International, Inc., 1 N Dearborn St., Ste. 1700, Chicago, IL, 60602, USA, (312) 922-1115, (312) 922-1157, info-usa@euromonitor.com, https://www.euromonitor.com/; Geographies.

UNESCO Institute for Statistics, C.P 250 Succursale H, Montreal, QC, H3G 2K8, CAN, (514) 343-6880 (Dial from U.S.), (514) 343-5740 (Fax from U.S.), uis.publications@unesco.org, http://uis.unesco.org/; Literacy.

COSTA RICA-LIVESTOCK

Palgrave Macmillan, 1 New York Plaza, Ste. 4500, New York, NY, 10004-1562, USA, (800) 777-4643, orders@palgrave.com, https://www.palgrave.com/us; The Statesman's Yearbook, 2023.

Routledge - Taylor & Francis Group, 6000 Broken Sound Pkwy. NW, Ste. 300, Boca Raton, FL, 33487, USA, (800) 634-1420, (800) 634-7064, orders@taylorandfrancis.com, https://www.routledge.com/; The Europa World Year Book 2022.

United Nations Food and Agricultural Organization (FAO), 2121 K St., Ste. 800B, Washington, DC, 20037, USA, (202) 653-2400 (Dial from U.S.), (202) 653-5760 (Fax from U.S.), fao-hq@fao.org, https://www.fao.org; The State of Food and Agriculture (SOFA) 2022.

United Nations Statistics Division (UNSD), United Nations Plz., New York, NY, 10017, USA, (800) 253-9646, (212) 963-9851, statistics@un.org, https://unstats.un.org; Statistical Yearbook of the United Nations 2021.

COSTA RICA-MANUFACTURES

Inter-American Development Bank (IDB), 1300 New York Ave. NW, Washington, DC, 20577, USA, (202) 623-1000, (202) 623-3096, https://www.iadb.org/en; Latin Macro Watch (LMW).

COSTA RICA-MARRIAGE

Routledge - Taylor & Francis Group, 6000 Broken Sound Pkwy. NW, Ste. 300, Boca Raton, FL, 33487, USA, (800) 634-1420, (800) 634-7064, orders@taylorandfrancis.com, https://www.routledge.com/; The Europa World Year Book 2022.

United Nations Statistics Division (UNSD), United Nations Plz., New York, NY, 10017, USA, (800) 253-9646, (212) 963-9851, statistics@un.org, https://unstats.un.org; Statistical Yearbook of the United Nations 2021.

COSTA RICA-MEAT INDUSTRY AND TRADE

International Monetary Fund (IMF), 700 19th St. NW, Washington, DC, 20431, USA, (202) 623-7000, (202) 623-4661, publications@imf.org, https://www.imf.org; International Financial Statistics (IFS).

COSTA RICA-MINERAL INDUSTRIES

Inter-American Development Bank (IDB), 1300 New York Ave. NW, Washington, DC, 20577, USA, (202) 623-1000, (202) 623-3096, https://www.iadb.org/en; Latin Macro Watch (LMW).

Palgrave Macmillan, 1 New York Plaza, Ste. 4500, New York, NY, 10004-1562, USA, (800) 777-4643, orders@palgrave.com, https://www.palgrave.com/us; The Statesman's Yearbook, 2023.

Routledge - Taylor & Francis Group, 6000 Broken Sound Pkwy. NW, Ste. 300, Boca Raton, FL, 33487, USA, (800) 634-1420, (800) 634-7064, orders@taylorandfrancis.com, https://www.routledge.com/; The Europa World Year Book 2022.

United Nations Conference on Trade and Development (UNCTAD), Palais des Nations, Geneva, 1211, SWI, (212) 963-6896, unctadinfo@unctad.org, https://unctad.org; Trade and Development Report 2021.

COSTA RICA-MONEY SUPPLY

The Economist Group: Economist Intelligence Unit (EIU), 900 3rd Ave., 16th Fl., New York, NY, 10022, USA, (212) 541-0500, americas@eiu.com, https://www.eiu.com; Costa Rica Country Report.

Inter-American Development Bank (IDB), 1300 New York Ave. NW, Washington, DC, 20577, USA, (202) 623-1000, (202) 623-3096, https://www.iadb.org/en; Latin Macro Watch (LMW).

International Monetary Fund (IMF), 700 19th St. NW, Washington, DC, 20431, USA, (202) 623-7000, (202) 623-4661, publications@imf.org, https://www.imf.org; International Financial Statistics (IFS).

Routledge - Taylor & Francis Group, 6000 Broken Sound Pkwy. NW, Ste. 300, Boca Raton, FL, 33487,

USA, (800) 634-1420, (800) 634-7064, orders@taylorandfrancis.com, https://www.routledge.com/; The Europa World Year Book 2022.

United Nations Statistics Division (UNSD), United Nations Plz., New York, NY, 10017, USA, (800) 253-9646, (212) 963-9851, statistics@un.org, https://unstats.un.org; Statistical Yearbook of the United Nations 2021.

The World Bank, 1818 H St. NW, Washington, DC, 20433, USA, (202) 473-1000, (202) 477-6391, eds03@worldbank.org, https://www.worldbank.org/; Costa Rica (report).

COSTA RICA-MORTALITY

UNICEF, 3 United Nations Plz., New York, NY, 10017, USA, (212) 303-7984, (917) 244-2215, https://www.unicef.org; The State of the World's Children 2023.

United Nations Statistics Division (UNSD), United Nations Plz., New York, NY, 10017, USA, (800) 253-9646, (212) 963-9851, statistics@un.org, https://unstats.un.org; Millennium Development Goal Indicators; Statistical Yearbook of the United Nations 2021; and World Statistics Pocketbook 2021.

The World Bank, 1818 H St. NW, Washington, DC, 20433, USA, (202) 473-1000, (202) 477-6391, eds03@worldbank.org, https://www.worldbank.org/; World Development Indicators (WDI) 2022.

World Health Organization (WHO), Ave. Appia 20, Geneva, CH-1211, SWI, (202) 974-3000 (Telephone in U.S.), publications@who.int, https://www.who.int/; Global Health Observatory (GHO).

COSTA RICA-MOTION PICTURES

Palgrave Macmillan, 1 New York Plaza, Ste. 4500, New York, NY, 10004-1562, USA, (800) 777-4643, orders@palgrave.com, https://www.palgrave.com/us; The Statesman's Yearbook, 2023.

COSTA RICA-NATURAL GAS PRODUCTION

See COSTA RICA-MINERAL INDUSTRIES

COSTA RICA-NUTRITION

United Nations Food and Agricultural Organization (FAO), 2121 K St., Ste. 800B, Washington, DC, 20037, USA, (202) 653-2400 (Dial from U.S.), (202) 653-5760 (Fax from U.S.), fao-hq@fao.org, https://www.fao.org; The State of Food and Agriculture (SOFA) 2022.

United Nations Statistics Division (UNSD), United Nations Plz., New York, NY, 10017, USA, (800) 253-9646, (212) 963-9851, statistics@un.org, https://unstats.un.org; Millennium Development Goal Indicators.

COSTA RICA-PAPER

See COSTA RICA-FORESTS AND FORESTRY

COSTA RICA-PEANUT PRODUCTION

See COSTA RICA-CROPS

COSTA RICA-PESTICIDES

United Nations Food and Agricultural Organization (FAO), 2121 K St., Ste. 800B, Washington, DC, 20037, USA, (202) 653-2400 (Dial from U.S.), (202) 653-5760 (Fax from U.S.), fao-hq@fao.org, https://www.fao.org; The State of Food and Agriculture (SOFA) 2022.

COSTA RICA-PETROLEUM INDUSTRY AND TRADE

Inter-American Development Bank (IDB), 1300 New York Ave. NW, Washington, DC, 20577, USA, (202) 623-1000, (202) 623-3096, https://www.iadb.org/en; Latin Macro Watch (LMW).

U.S. Energy Information Administration (EIA), 1000 Independence Ave. SW, Washington, DC, 20585, USA, (202) 586-8800, infoctr@eia.gov, https://www.eia.gov; International Energy Outlook 2021.

United Nations Food and Agricultural Organization (FAO), 2121 K St., Ste. 800B, Washington, DC, 20037, USA, (202) 653-2400 (Dial from U.S.), (202) 653-5760 (Fax from U.S.), fao-hq@fao.org, https://www.fao.org; The State of Food and Agriculture (SOFA) 2022.

United Nations Statistics Division (UNSD), United Nations Plz., New York, NY, 10017, USA, (800) 253-9646, (212) 963-9851, statistics@un.org, https://unstats.un.org; Statistical Yearbook of the United Nations 2021.

COSTA RICA-POPULATION

Central Intelligence Agency (CIA), Office of Public Affairs, Washington, DC, 20505, USA, (703) 482-0623, https://www.cia.gov; The World Factbook.

The Economist Group: Economist Intelligence Unit (EIU), 900 3rd Ave., 16th Fl., New York, NY, 10022, USA, (212) 541-0500, americas@eiu.com, https://www.eiu.com; Costa Rica Country Report.

Infoplease, c/o Sandbox Networks, Inc., 1 Lincoln St., 24th Fl., Boston, MA, 02111, USA, https://www.infoplease.com; Countries of the World.

Inter-American Development Bank (IDB), 1300 New York Ave. NW, Washington, DC, 20577, USA, (202) 623-1000, (202) 623-3096, https://www.iadb.org/en; Latin Macro Watch (LMW).

International Labour Organization (ILO), 4 Rte. des Morillons, Geneva, CH-1211, SWI, ilo@ilo.org, https://www.ilo.org; NORMLEX Information System on International Labour Standards.

Palgrave Macmillan, 1 New York Plaza, Ste. 4500, New York, NY, 10004-1562, USA, (800) 777-4643, orders@palgrave.com, https://www.palgrave.com/us; The Statesman's Yearbook, 2023.

Routledge - Taylor & Francis Group, 6000 Broken Sound Pkwy. NW, Ste. 300, Boca Raton, FL, 33487, USA, (800) 634-1420, (800) 634-7064, orders@taylorandfrancis.com, https://www.routledge.com/; The Europa World Year Book 2022.

UK Data Service, University of Essex, Wivenhoe Park, Colchester, Essex, CO4 3SQ, GBR, https://ukdataservice.ac.uk/; International Aggregate Data.

United Nations Department of Economic and Social Affairs (DESA), Population Division, 2 United Nations Plz., Rm. DC2-1950, New York, NY, 10017, USA, (212) 963-3209, (212) 963-2147, population@un.org, https://www.un.org/development/desa/pd/; Revision of World Urbanization Prospects and World Population Ageing 2020 Highlights.

United Nations Development Programme (UNDP), One United Nations Plz., New York, NY, 10017, USA, (212) 906-5000, (212) 906-5001, https://www.undp.org; Human Development Report 2021-2022.

United Nations Economic Commission for Latin America and the Caribbean (ECLAC), Casilla 179-D, Santiago, 7630412, CHL, (202) 596-3713, prensa@cepal.org, https://www.cepal.org/en; CEPALSTAT and Social Panorama of Latin America and the Caribbean 2022: Transforming Education as a Basis for Sustainable Development.

United Nations Statistics Division (UNSD), United Nations Plz., New York, NY, 10017, USA, (800) 253-9646, (212) 963-9851, statistics@un.org, https://unstats.un.org; Statistical Yearbook of the United Nations 2021 and World Statistics Pocketbook 2021.

The World Bank, 1818 H St. NW, Washington, DC, 20433, USA, (202) 473-1000, (202) 477-6391, eds03@worldbank.org, https://www.worldbank.org/; Costa Rica (report); The Global Findex Database 2021; and World Development Report 2022: Finance for an Equitable Recovery.

COSTA RICA-POPULATION DENSITY

Central Intelligence Agency (CIA), Office of Public Affairs, Washington, DC, 20505, USA, (703) 482-0623, https://www.cia.gov; The World Factbook.

Inter-American Development Bank (IDB), 1300 New York Ave. NW, Washington, DC, 20577, USA, (202) 623-1000, (202) 623-3096, https://www.iadb.org/en; Latin Macro Watch (LMW).

Palgrave Macmillan, 1 New York Plaza, Ste. 4500, New York, NY, 10004-1562, USA, (800) 777-4643, orders@palgrave.com, https://www.palgrave.com/us; The Statesman's Yearbook, 2023.

Routledge - Taylor & Francis Group, 6000 Broken Sound Pkwy. NW, Ste. 300, Boca Raton, FL, 33487, USA, (800) 634-1420, (800) 634-7064, orders@taylorandfrancis.com, https://www.routledge.com/; The Europa World Year Book 2022.

UNESCO Institute for Statistics, C.P 250 Succursale H, Montreal, QC, H3G 2K8, CAN, (514) 343-6880 (Dial from U.S.), (514) 343-5740 (Fax from U.S.), uis.publications@unesco.org, http://uis.unesco.org/; UIS.Stat.

The World Bank, 1818 H St. NW, Washington, DC, 20433, USA, (202) 473-1000, (202) 477-6391, eds03@worldbank.org, https://www.worldbank.org/; Costa Rica (report) and World Development Report 2022: Finance for an Equitable Recovery.

COSTA RICA-POWER RESOURCES

Euromonitor International, Inc., 1 N Dearborn St., Ste. 1700, Chicago, IL, 60602, USA, (312) 922-1115, (312) 922-1157, info-usa@euromonitor.com, https://www.euromonitor.com/; Geographies.

Palgrave Macmillan, 1 New York Plaza, Ste. 4500, New York, NY, 10004-1562, USA, (800) 777-4643, orders@palgrave.com, https://www.palgrave.com/us; The Statesman's Yearbook, 2023.

U.S. Energy Information Administration (EIA), 1000 Independence Ave. SW, Washington, DC, 20585, USA, (202) 586-8800, infoctr@eia.gov, https://www.eia.gov; International Energy Outlook 2021.

United Nations Food and Agricultural Organization (FAO), 2121 K St., Ste. 800B, Washington, DC, 20037, USA, (202) 653-2400 (Dial from U.S.), (202) 653-5760 (Fax from U.S.), fao-hq@fao.org, https://www.fao.org; The State of Food and Agriculture (SOFA) 2022.

United Nations Statistics Division (UNSD), United Nations Plz., New York, NY, 10017, USA, (800) 253-9646, (212) 963-9851, statistics@un.org, https://unstats.un.org; Energy Statistics Yearbook 2019; Statistical Yearbook of the United Nations 2021; and World Statistics Pocketbook 2021.

The World Bank, 1818 H St. NW, Washington, DC, 20433, USA, (202) 473-1000, (202) 477-6391, eds03@worldbank.org, https://www.worldbank.org/; World Development Report 2022: Finance for an Equitable Recovery.

COSTA RICA-PRICES

Euromonitor International, Inc., 1 N Dearborn St., Ste. 1700, Chicago, IL, 60602, USA, (312) 922-1115, (312) 922-1157, info-usa@euromonitor.com, https://www.euromonitor.com/; Geographies.

International Monetary Fund (IMF), 700 19th St. NW, Washington, DC, 20431, USA, (202) 623-7000, (202) 623-4661, publications@imf.org, https://www.imf.org; International Financial Statistics (IFS).

United Nations Economic Commission for Latin America and the Caribbean (ECLAC), Casilla 179-D, Santiago, 7630412, CHL, (202) 596-3713, prensa@cepal.org, https://www.cepal.org/en; Economic Survey of Latin America and the Caribbean 2021: Labour Dynamics and Employment Policies for Sustainable and Inclusive Recovery Beyond the COVID-19 Crisis.

The World Bank, 1818 H St. NW, Washington, DC, 20433, USA, (202) 473-1000, (202) 477-6391, eds03@worldbank.org, https://www.worldbank.org/; Costa Rica (report).

COSTA RICA-PUBLIC HEALTH

Euromonitor International, Inc., 1 N Dearborn St., Ste. 1700, Chicago, IL, 60602, USA, (312) 922-1115, (312) 922-1157, info-usa@euromonitor.com, https://www.euromonitor.com/; Geographies.

Palgrave Macmillan, 1 New York Plaza, Ste. 4500, New York, NY, 10004-1562, USA, (800) 777-4643, orders@palgrave.com, https://www.palgrave.com/us; The Statesman's Yearbook, 2023.

U.S. Census Bureau, 4600 Silver Hill Rd., Washington, DC, 20233, USA, (301) 763-4636, (800) 923-8282, https://www.census.gov; HIV/AIDS Surveillance Data Base.

UNICEF, 3 United Nations Plz., New York, NY, 10017, USA, (212) 303-7984, (917) 244-2215, https://www.unicef.org; The State of the World's Children 2023.

United Nations Department of Economic and Social Affairs (DESA), Population Division, 2 United Nations Plz., Rm. DC2-1950, New York, NY, 10017, USA, (212) 963-3209, (212) 963-2147, population@un.org, https://www.un.org/development/desa/pd/; World Fertility Data 2019.

United Nations Development Programme (UNDP), One United Nations Plz., New York, NY, 10017, USA, (212) 906-5000, (212) 906-5001, https://www.undp.org; Human Development Report 2021-2022.

United Nations Statistics Division (UNSD), United Nations Plz., New York, NY, 10017, USA, (800) 253-9646, (212) 963-9851, statistics@un.org, https://unstats.un.org; Millennium Development Goal Indicators and Statistical Yearbook of the United Nations 2021.

The World Bank, 1818 H St. NW, Washington, DC, 20433, USA, (202) 473-1000, (202) 477-6391, eds03@worldbank.org, https://www.worldbank.org/; Costa Rica (report).

World Health Organization (WHO), Ave. Appia 20, Geneva, CH-1211, SWI, (202) 974-3000 (Telephone in U.S.), publications@who.int, https://www.who.int/; Global Health Observatory (GHO) and Health Statistics and Information Systems.

COSTA RICA-PUBLISHERS AND PUBLISHING

UNESCO Institute for Statistics, C.P 250 Succursale H, Montreal, QC, H3G 2K8, CAN, (514) 343-6880 (Dial from U.S.), (514) 343-5740 (Fax from U.S.), uis.publications@unesco.org, http://uis.unesco.org/; UIS.Stat.

COSTA RICA-RAILROADS

Janes, USA, (703) 574-7580, (888) 977-1519, customer.care@janes.com, https://www.janes.com; Janes World Railways 2021-2022.

Palgrave Macmillan, 1 New York Plaza, Ste. 4500, New York, NY, 10004-1562, USA, (800) 777-4643, orders@palgrave.com, https://www.palgrave.com/us; The Statesman's Yearbook, 2023.

Routledge - Taylor & Francis Group, 6000 Broken Sound Pkwy. NW, Ste. 300, Boca Raton, FL, 33487, USA, (800) 634-1420, (800) 634-7064, orders@taylorandfrancis.com, https://www.routledge.com/; The Europa World Year Book 2022.

United Nations Statistics Division (UNSD), United Nations Plz., New York, NY, 10017, USA, (800) 253-9646, (212) 963-9851, statistics@un.org, https://unstats.un.org; Statistical Yearbook of the United Nations 2021.

COSTA RICA-RELIGION

Central Intelligence Agency (CIA), Office of Public Affairs, Washington, DC, 20505, USA, (703) 482-0623, https://www.cia.gov; The World Factbook.

Palgrave Macmillan, 1 New York Plaza, Ste. 4500, New York, NY, 10004-1562, USA, (800) 777-4643, orders@palgrave.com, https://www.palgrave.com/us; The Statesman's Yearbook, 2023.

COSTA RICA-RETAIL TRADE

Banque de France, 31 rue Croix des Petits-Champs, Paris, 75049, FRA, infos@banque-france.fr, https://www.banque-france.fr/en; Key Figures France and Abroad.

Euromonitor International, Inc., 1 N Dearborn St., Ste. 1700, Chicago, IL, 60602, USA, (312) 922-1115, (312) 922-1157, info-usa@euromonitor.com, https://www.euromonitor.com/; Geographies.

Inter-American Development Bank (IDB), 1300 New York Ave. NW, Washington, DC, 20577, USA, (202) 623-1000, (202) 623-3096, https://www.iadb.org/en; Latin Macro Watch (LMW).

COSTA RICA-RICE TRADE

United Nations Statistics Division (UNSD), United Nations Plz., New York, NY, 10017, USA, (800) 253-9646, (212) 963-9851, statistics@un.org, https://unstats.un.org; Statistical Yearbook of the United Nations 2021.

COSTA RICA-ROADS

International Road Federation (IRF), Madison Place, 500 Montgomery St., 5th Fl., Alexandria, VA, 22314, USA, (703) 535-1001, (703) 535-1007, info@irf.global, https://www.irf.global/; World Road Statistics (WRS).

COSTA RICA-RUBBER INDUSTRY AND TRADE

International Rubber Study Group (IRSG), 51 Changi Business Park Central 2, Unit No. 6, 486066, SGP, https://www.rubberstudy.org; Monthly Rubber Bulletin (MRB); Rubber Statistical Bulletin; and World Rubber Industry Report (WRIO).

COSTA RICA-SHIPPING

Routledge - Taylor & Francis Group, 6000 Broken Sound Pkwy. NW, Ste. 300, Boca Raton, FL, 33487, USA, (800) 634-1420, (800) 634-7064, orders@taylorandfrancis.com, https://www.routledge.com/; The Europa World Year Book 2022.

United Nations Statistics Division (UNSD), United Nations Plz., New York, NY, 10017, USA, (800) 253-9646, (212) 963-9851, statistics@un.org, https://unstats.un.org; Statistical Yearbook of the United Nations 2021.

COSTA RICA-SOYBEAN PRODUCTION

See COSTA RICA-CROPS

COSTA RICA-STEEL PRODUCTION

See COSTA RICA-MINERAL INDUSTRIES

COSTA RICA-SUGAR PRODUCTION

See COSTA RICA-CROPS

COSTA RICA-TAXATION

Inter-American Development Bank (IDB), 1300 New York Ave. NW, Washington, DC, 20577, USA, (202) 623-1000, (202) 623-3096, https://www.iadb.org/en; Latin Macro Watch (LMW).

International Road Federation (IRF), Madison Place, 500 Montgomery St., 5th Fl., Alexandria, VA, 22314, USA, (703) 535-1001, (703) 535-1007, info@irf.global, https://www.irf.global/; World Road Statistics (WRS).

Palgrave Macmillan, 1 New York Plaza, Ste. 4500, New York, NY, 10004-1562, USA, (800) 777-4643, orders@palgrave.com, https://www.palgrave.com/us; The Statesman's Yearbook, 2023.

The World Bank, 1818 H St. NW, Washington, DC, 20433, USA, (202) 473-1000, (202) 477-6391, eds03@worldbank.org, https://www.worldbank.org/; World Development Indicators (WDI) 2022.

COSTA RICA-TELEPHONE

Palgrave Macmillan, 1 New York Plaza, Ste. 4500, New York, NY, 10004-1562, USA, (800) 777-4643, orders@palgrave.com, https://www.palgrave.com/us; The Statesman's Yearbook, 2023.

Routledge - Taylor & Francis Group, 6000 Broken Sound Pkwy. NW, Ste. 300, Boca Raton, FL, 33487, USA, (800) 634-1420, (800) 634-7064, orders@taylorandfrancis.com, https://www.routledge.com/; The Europa World Year Book 2022.

United Nations Statistics Division (UNSD), United Nations Plz., New York, NY, 10017, USA, (800) 253-9646, (212) 963-9851, statistics@un.org, https://unstats.un.org; World Statistics Pocketbook 2021.

COSTA RICA-TEXTILE INDUSTRY

Palgrave Macmillan, 1 New York Plaza, Ste. 4500, New York, NY, 10004-1562, USA, (800) 777-4643, orders@palgrave.com, https://www.palgrave.com/us; The Statesman's Yearbook, 2023.

COSTA RICA-THEATER

UNESCO Institute for Statistics, C.P 250 Succursale H, Montreal, QC, H3G 2K8, CAN, (514) 343-6880 (Dial from U.S.), (514) 343-5740 (Fax from U.S.), uis.publications@unesco.org, http://uis.unesco.org/; UIS.Stat.

COSTA RICA-TOBACCO INDUSTRY

United Nations Statistics Division (UNSD), United Nations Plz., New York, NY, 10017, USA, (800) 253-9646, (212) 963-9851, statistics@un.org, https://unstats.un.org; Statistical Yearbook of the United Nations 2021.

COSTA RICA-TOURISM

Euromonitor International, Inc., 1 N Dearborn St., Ste. 1700, Chicago, IL, 60602, USA, (312) 922-1115, (312) 922-1157, info-usa@euromonitor.com, https://www.euromonitor.com/; Geographies.

Palgrave Macmillan, 1 New York Plaza, Ste. 4500, New York, NY, 10004-1562, USA, (800) 777-4643, orders@palgrave.com, https://www.palgrave.com/us; The Statesman's Yearbook, 2023.

Routledge - Taylor & Francis Group, 6000 Broken Sound Pkwy. NW, Ste. 300, Boca Raton, FL, 33487, USA, (800) 634-1420, (800) 634-7064, orders@taylorandfrancis.com, https://www.routledge.com/; The Europa World Year Book 2022.

United Nations Statistics Division (UNSD), United Nations Plz., New York, NY, 10017, USA, (800) 253-9646, (212) 963-9851, statistics@un.org, https://unstats.un.org; Statistical Yearbook of the United Nations 2021.

United Nations World Tourism Organization (UNWTO), Calle Poeta Joan Maragall 42, Madrid, 28020, SPA, info@unwto.org, https://www.unwto.org/; Yearbook of Tourism Statistics, 2021 Edition.

The World Bank, 1818 H St. NW, Washington, DC, 20433, USA, (202) 473-1000, (202) 477-6391, eds03@worldbank.org, https://www.worldbank.org/; Costa Rica (report).

COSTA RICA-TRADE

See COSTA RICA-INTERNATIONAL TRADE

COSTA RICA-TRANSPORTATION

Central Intelligence Agency (CIA), Office of Public Affairs, Washington, DC, 20505, USA, (703) 482-0623, https://www.cia.gov; The World Factbook.

Euromonitor International, Inc., 1 N Dearborn St., Ste. 1700, Chicago, IL, 60602, USA, (312) 922-1115, (312) 922-1157, info-usa@euromonitor.com, https://www.euromonitor.com/; Geographies.

Inter-American Development Bank (IDB), 1300 New York Ave. NW, Washington, DC, 20577, USA, (202) 623-1000, (202) 623-3096, https://www.iadb.org/en; Latin Macro Watch (LMW).

Palgrave Macmillan, 1 New York Plaza, Ste. 4500, New York, NY, 10004-1562, USA, (800) 777-4643, orders@palgrave.com, https://www.palgrave.com/us; The Statesman's Yearbook, 2023.

Routledge - Taylor & Francis Group, 6000 Broken Sound Pkwy. NW, Ste. 300, Boca Raton, FL, 33487, USA, (800) 634-1420, (800) 634-7064, orders@taylorandfrancis.com, https://www.routledge.com/; The Europa World Year Book 2022.

The World Bank, 1818 H St. NW, Washington, DC, 20433, USA, (202) 473-1000, (202) 477-6391, eds03@worldbank.org, https://www.worldbank.org/; Costa Rica (report).

COSTA RICA-UNEMPLOYMENT

International Labour Organization (ILO), 4 Rte. des Morillons, Geneva, CH-1211, SWI, ilo@ilo.org,

https://www.ilo.org; NORMLEX Information System on International Labour Standards.

United Nations Statistics Division (UNSD), United Nations Plz., New York, NY, 10017, USA, (800) 253-9646, (212) 963-9851, statistics@un.org, https://unstats.un.org; Statistical Yearbook of the United Nations 2021.

COSTA RICA-VITAL STATISTICS

U.S. Census Bureau, 4600 Silver Hill Rd., Washington, DC, 20233, USA, (301) 763-4636, (800) 923-8282, https://www.census.gov; HIV/AIDS Surveillance Data Base.

United Nations Department of Economic and Social Affairs (DESA), Population Division, 2 United Nations Plz., Rm. DC2-1950, New York, NY, 10017, USA, (212) 963-3209, (212) 963-2147, population@un.org, https://www.un.org/development/desa/pd/; World Contraceptive Use 2021: Estimates and Projections of Family Planning Indicators and World Marriage Data 2019.

United Nations Statistics Division (UNSD), United Nations Plz., New York, NY, 10017, USA, (800) 253-9646, (212) 963-9851, statistics@un.org, https://unstats.un.org; Statistical Yearbook of the United Nations 2021.

COSTA RICA-WAGES

International Labour Organization (ILO), 4 Rte. des Morillons, Geneva, CH-1211, SWI, ilo@ilo.org, https://www.ilo.org; NORMLEX Information System on International Labour Standards.

The World Bank, 1818 H St. NW, Washington, DC, 20433, USA, (202) 473-1000, (202) 477-6391, eds03@worldbank.org, https://www.worldbank.org/; Costa Rica (report).

COSTA RICA-WEATHER

See COSTA RICA-CLIMATE

COSTA RICA-WHEAT PRODUCTION

See COSTA RICA-CROPS

COSTA RICA-WHOLESALE PRICE INDEXES

Inter-American Development Bank (IDB), 1300 New York Ave. NW, Washington, DC, 20577, USA, (202) 623-1000, (202) 623-3096, https://www.iadb.org/en; Latin Macro Watch (LMW).

International Monetary Fund (IMF), 700 19th St. NW, Washington, DC, 20431, USA, (202) 623-7000, (202) 623-4661, publications@imf.org, https://www.imf.org; International Financial Statistics (IFS).

COSTA RICA-WHOLESALE TRADE

Inter-American Development Bank (IDB), 1300 New York Ave. NW, Washington, DC, 20577, USA, (202) 623-1000, (202) 623-3096, https://www.iadb.org/en; Latin Macro Watch (LMW).

COSTA RICA-WOOL PRODUCTION

See COSTA RICA-TEXTILE INDUSTRY

COSTUME JEWELRY AND NOTIONS-MANUFACTURING-EARNINGS

U.S. Census Bureau, 4600 Silver Hill Rd., Washington, DC, 20233, USA, (301) 763-4636, (800) 923-8282, https://www.census.gov; Annual Survey of Manufactures (ASM) 2021.

COSTUME JEWELRY AND NOTIONS-MANUFACTURING-EMPLOYEES

U.S. Census Bureau, 4600 Silver Hill Rd., Washington, DC, 20233, USA, (301) 763-4636, (800) 923-8282, https://www.census.gov; Annual Survey of Manufactures (ASM) 2021.

COTE d'IVOIRE-NATIONAL STATISTICAL OFFICE

Institut National de la Statistique, COTE d'IVOIRE, BP V 55, Abidjan, 01, COT, ins.rci.diffusion@gmail.com, https://www.ins.ci/n/; National Data Reports (COTE d'IVOIRE).

COTE d'IVOIRE-AGRICULTURE

African Development Bank Group (AfDB), Avenue Joseph Anoma, 01 BP 1387, Abidjan, 01, COT, https://www.afdb.org; African Economic Outlook 2021 and Compendium of Statistics on Bank Group Operations 2019.

The Economist Group: Economist Intelligence Unit (EIU), 900 3rd Ave., 16th Fl., New York, NY, 10022, USA, (212) 541-0500, americas@eiu.com, https://www.eiu.com; COTE d'IVOIRE Country Report.

Euromonitor International, Inc., 1 N Dearborn St., Ste. 1700, Chicago, IL, 60602, USA, (312) 922-1115, (312) 922-1157, info-usa@euromonitor.com, https://www.euromonitor.com/; Geographies.

Organisation of Islamic Cooperation (OIC), Statistical, Economic and Social Research and Training Centre for Islamic Countries (SESRIC), Kudus Cad. No. 9, Diplomatik Site, Ankara, 06450, TUR, statistics@sesric.org, https://www.sesric.org/; OIC Statistics (OICStat) Database and OIC-Countries in Figures (OIC-CIF).

Palgrave Macmillan, 1 New York Plaza, Ste. 4500, New York, NY, 10004-1562, USA, (800) 777-4643, orders@palgrave.com, https://www.palgrave.com/us; The Statesman's Yearbook, 2023.

Routledge - Taylor & Francis Group, 6000 Broken Sound Pkwy. NW, Ste. 300, Boca Raton, FL, 33487, USA, (800) 634-1420, (800) 634-7064, orders@taylorandfrancis.com, https://www.routledge.com/; The Europa World Year Book 2022.

United Nations Economic Commission for Africa (UNECA), PO Box 3001, Addis Ababa, ETH, ecainfo@uneca.org, https://www.uneca.org/; African Statistical Yearbook 2020 and Economic Report on Africa 2021.

United Nations Food and Agricultural Organization (FAO), 2121 K St., Ste. 800B, Washington, DC, 20037, USA, (202) 653-2400 (Dial from U.S.), (202) 653-5760 (Fax from U.S.), fao-hq@fao.org, https://www.fao.org; AQUASTAT and The State of Food and Agriculture (SOFA) 2022.

United Nations Statistics Division (UNSD), United Nations Plz., New York, NY, 10017, USA, (800) 253-9646, (212) 963-9851, statistics@un.org, https://unstats.un.org; Statistical Yearbook of the United Nations 2021.

The World Bank, 1818 H St. NW, Washington, DC, 20433, USA, (202) 473-1000, (202) 477-6391, eds03@worldbank.org, https://www.worldbank.org/; COTE d'IVOIRE (report) and World Development Indicators (WDI) 2022.

COTE d'IVOIRE-AIRLINES

Palgrave Macmillan, 1 New York Plaza, Ste. 4500, New York, NY, 10004-1562, USA, (800) 777-4643, orders@palgrave.com, https://www.palgrave.com/us; The Statesman's Yearbook, 2023.

Routledge - Taylor & Francis Group, 6000 Broken Sound Pkwy. NW, Ste. 300, Boca Raton, FL, 33487, USA, (800) 634-1420, (800) 634-7064, orders@taylorandfrancis.com, https://www.routledge.com/; The Europa World Year Book 2022.

United Nations Economic Commission for Africa (UNECA), PO Box 3001, Addis Ababa, ETH, ecainfo@uneca.org, https://www.uneca.org/; African Statistical Yearbook 2020.

COTE d'IVOIRE-ALUMINUM PRODUCTION

See COTE d'IVOIRE-MINERAL INDUSTRIES

COTE d'IVOIRE-ARMED FORCES

Central Intelligence Agency (CIA), Office of Public Affairs, Washington, DC, 20505, USA, (703) 482-0623, https://www.cia.gov; The World Factbook.

International Institute for Strategic Studies (IISS) - Americas, 2121 K St. NW, Ste. 600, Washington, DC, 20037, USA, (202) 659-1490, (202) 659-1499, https://www.iiss.org/; Armed Conflict Survey 2021 and The Military Balance 2022.

Palgrave Macmillan, 1 New York Plaza, Ste. 4500, New York, NY, 10004-1562, USA, (800) 777-4643, orders@palgrave.com, https://www.palgrave.com/us; The Statesman's Yearbook, 2023.

Stockholm International Peace Research Institute (SIPRI), Signalistgatan 9, Stockholm, SE 169 72, SWE, https://www.sipri.org/; SIPRI Arms Transfers Database and SIPRI Military Expenditure Database.

COTE d'IVOIRE-BALANCE OF PAYMENTS

African Development Bank Group (AfDB), Avenue Joseph Anoma, 01 BP 1387, Abidjan, 01, COT, https://www.afdb.org; The AfDB Statistics Pocketbook 2019.

International Monetary Fund (IMF), 700 19th St. NW, Washington, DC, 20431, USA, (202) 623-7000, (202) 623-4661, publications@imf.org, https://www.imf.org; Balance of Payments Statistics: Annual Report 2021.

Routledge - Taylor & Francis Group, 6000 Broken Sound Pkwy. NW, Ste. 300, Boca Raton, FL, 33487, USA, (800) 634-1420, (800) 634-7064, orders@taylorandfrancis.com, https://www.routledge.com/; The Europa World Year Book 2022.

United Nations Conference on Trade and Development (UNCTAD), Palais des Nations, Geneva, 1211, SWI, (212) 963-6896, unctadinfo@unctad.org, https://unctad.org; Handbook of Statistics 2021.

United Nations Economic Commission for Africa (UNECA), PO Box 3001, Addis Ababa, ETH, ecainfo@uneca.org, https://www.uneca.org/; African Statistical Yearbook 2020.

The World Bank, 1818 H St. NW, Washington, DC, 20433, USA, (202) 473-1000, (202) 477-6391, eds03@worldbank.org, https://www.worldbank.org/; COTE d'IVOIRE (report); World Development Indicators (WDI) 2022; and World Development Report 2022: Finance for an Equitable Recovery.

COTE d'IVOIRE-BANKS AND BANKING

Euromonitor International, Inc., 1 N Dearborn St., Ste. 1700, Chicago, IL, 60602, USA, (312) 922-1115, (312) 922-1157, info-usa@euromonitor.com, https://www.euromonitor.com/; Geographies.

Routledge - Taylor & Francis Group, 6000 Broken Sound Pkwy. NW, Ste. 300, Boca Raton, FL, 33487, USA, (800) 634-1420, (800) 634-7064, orders@taylorandfrancis.com, https://www.routledge.com/; The Europa World Year Book 2022.

United Nations Economic Commission for Africa (UNECA), PO Box 3001, Addis Ababa, ETH, ecainfo@uneca.org, https://www.uneca.org/; African Statistical Yearbook 2020.

United Nations Statistics Division (UNSD), United Nations Plz., New York, NY, 10017, USA, (800) 253-9646, (212) 963-9851, statistics@un.org, https://unstats.un.org; Statistical Yearbook of the United Nations 2021.

COTE d'IVOIRE-BARLEY PRODUCTION

See COTE d'IVOIRE-CROPS

COTE d'IVOIRE-BROADCASTING

Central Intelligence Agency (CIA), Office of Public Affairs, Washington, DC, 20505, USA, (703) 482-0623, https://www.cia.gov; The World Factbook.

Euromonitor International, Inc., 1 N Dearborn St., Ste. 1700, Chicago, IL, 60602, USA, (312) 922-1115, (312) 922-1157, info-usa@euromonitor.com, https://www.euromonitor.com/; Geographies.

Palgrave Macmillan, 1 New York Plaza, Ste. 4500, New York, NY, 10004-1562, USA, (800) 777-4643, orders@palgrave.com, https://www.palgrave.com/us; The Statesman's Yearbook, 2023.

UNESCO Institute for Statistics, C.P 250 Succursale H, Montreal, QC, H3G 2K8, CAN, (514) 343-6880 (Dial from U.S.), (514) 343-5740 (Fax from U.S.), uis.publications@unesco.org, http://uis.unesco.org/; UIS.Stat.

WRTH Publications Limited, PO Box 290, Oxford, OX2 7FT, GBR, sales@wrth.com, https://www.wrth.com; World Radio TV Handbook 2023.

COTE d'IVOIRE-BUDGET

Central Intelligence Agency (CIA), Office of Public Affairs, Washington, DC, 20505, USA, (703) 482-0623, https://www.cia.gov; The World Factbook.

COTE d'IVOIRE-CHILDBIRTH-STATISTICS

The World Bank, 1818 H St. NW, Washington, DC, 20433, USA, (202) 473-1000, (202) 477-6391, eds03@worldbank.org, https://www.worldbank.org/; World Development Indicators (WDI) 2022.

COTE d'IVOIRE-CLIMATE

International Institute for Environment and Development (IIED), 235 High Holborn, London, WC1V 7DN, GBR, inforequest@iied.org, https://www.iied.org; Environment & Urbanization.

Palgrave Macmillan, 1 New York Plaza, Ste. 4500, New York, NY, 10004-1562, USA, (800) 777-4643, orders@palgrave.com, https://www.palgrave.com/us; The Statesman's Yearbook, 2023.

COTE d'IVOIRE-COAL PRODUCTION

See COTE d'IVOIRE-MINERAL INDUSTRIES

COTE d'IVOIRE-COCOA PRODUCTION

See COTE d'IVOIRE-CROPS

COTE d'IVOIRE-COFFEE

See COTE d'IVOIRE-CROPS

COTE d'IVOIRE-COMMERCE

Palgrave Macmillan, 1 New York Plaza, Ste. 4500, New York, NY, 10004-1562, USA, (800) 777-4643, orders@palgrave.com, https://www.palgrave.com/us; The Statesman's Yearbook, 2023.

UK Data Service, University of Essex, Wivenhoe Park, Colchester, Essex, CO4 3SQ, GBR, https://ukdataservice.ac.uk/; International Aggregate Data.

COTE d'IVOIRE-CONSTRUCTION INDUSTRY

United Nations Economic Commission for Africa (UNECA), PO Box 3001, Addis Ababa, ETH, ecainfo@uneca.org, https://www.uneca.org/; African Statistical Yearbook 2020.

United Nations Statistics Division (UNSD), United Nations Plz., New York, NY, 10017, USA, (800) 253-9646, (212) 963-9851, statistics@un.org, https://unstats.un.org; Statistical Yearbook of the United Nations 2021.

COTE d'IVOIRE-CONSUMER PRICE INDEXES

Routledge - Taylor & Francis Group, 6000 Broken Sound Pkwy. NW, Ste. 300, Boca Raton, FL, 33487, USA, (800) 634-1420, (800) 634-7064, orders@taylorandfrancis.com, https://www.routledge.com/; The Europa World Year Book 2022.

United Nations Economic Commission for Africa (UNECA), PO Box 3001, Addis Ababa, ETH, ecainfo@uneca.org, https://www.uneca.org/; African Statistical Yearbook 2020.

COTE d'IVOIRE-CONSUMPTION (ECONOMICS)

African Development Bank Group (AfDB), Avenue Joseph Anoma, 01 BP 1387, Abidjan, 01, COT, https://www.afdb.org; The AfDB Statistics Pocketbook 2019.

COTE d'IVOIRE-COPPER INDUSTRY AND TRADE

See COTE d'IVOIRE-MINERAL INDUSTRIES

COTE d'IVOIRE-CORN INDUSTRY

See COTE d'IVOIRE-CROPS

COTE d'IVOIRE-COTTON

See COTE d'IVOIRE-CROPS

COTE d'IVOIRE-CROPS

Palgrave Macmillan, 1 New York Plaza, Ste. 4500, New York, NY, 10004-1562, USA, (800) 777-4643, orders@palgrave.com, https://www.palgrave.com/us; The Statesman's Yearbook, 2023.

United Nations Economic Commission for Africa (UNECA), PO Box 3001, Addis Ababa, ETH, ecainfo@uneca.org, https://www.uneca.org/; African Statistical Yearbook 2020.

United Nations Food and Agricultural Organization (FAO), 2121 K St., Ste. 800B, Washington, DC, 20037, USA, (202) 653-2400 (Dial from U.S.), (202) 653-5760 (Fax from U.S.), fao-hq@fao.org, https://www.fao.org; The State of Food and Agriculture (SOFA) 2022.

United Nations Statistics Division (UNSD), United Nations Plz., New York, NY, 10017, USA, (800) 253-9646, (212) 963-9851, statistics@un.org, https://unstats.un.org; Statistical Yearbook of the United Nations 2021.

COTE d'IVOIRE-DAIRY PROCESSING

Palgrave Macmillan, 1 New York Plaza, Ste. 4500, New York, NY, 10004-1562, USA, (800) 777-4643, orders@palgrave.com, https://www.palgrave.com/us; The Statesman's Yearbook, 2023.

United Nations Food and Agricultural Organization (FAO), 2121 K St., Ste. 800B, Washington, DC, 20037, USA, (202) 653-2400 (Dial from U.S.), (202) 653-5760 (Fax from U.S.), fao-hq@fao.org, https://www.fao.org; The State of Food and Agriculture (SOFA) 2022.

COTE d'IVOIRE-DEBTS, EXTERNAL

African Development Bank Group (AfDB), Avenue Joseph Anoma, 01 BP 1387, Abidjan, 01, COT, https://www.afdb.org; The AfDB Statistics Pocketbook 2019; African Economic Outlook 2021; and Compendium of Statistics on Bank Group Operations 2019.

Palgrave Macmillan, 1 New York Plaza, Ste. 4500, New York, NY, 10004-1562, USA, (800) 777-4643, orders@palgrave.com, https://www.palgrave.com/us; The Statesman's Yearbook, 2023.

United Nations Economic Commission for Africa (UNECA), PO Box 3001, Addis Ababa, ETH, ecainfo@uneca.org, https://www.uneca.org/; Economic Report on Africa 2021.

The World Bank, 1818 H St. NW, Washington, DC, 20433, USA, (202) 473-1000, (202) 477-6391, eds03@worldbank.org, https://www.worldbank.org/; World Development Indicators (WDI) 2022 and World Development Report 2022: Finance for an Equitable Recovery.

COTE d'IVOIRE-DEFENSE EXPENDITURES

See COTE d'IVOIRE-ARMED FORCES

COTE d'IVOIRE-DIAMONDS

See COTE d'IVOIRE-MINERAL INDUSTRIES

COTE d'IVOIRE-ECONOMIC ASSISTANCE

United Nations Statistics Division (UNSD), United Nations Plz., New York, NY, 10017, USA, (800) 253-9646, (212) 963-9851, statistics@un.org, https://unstats.un.org; Statistical Yearbook of the United Nations 2021.

COTE d'IVOIRE-ECONOMIC CONDITIONS

African Development Bank Group (AfDB), Avenue Joseph Anoma, 01 BP 1387, Abidjan, 01, COT, https://www.afdb.org; The AfDB Statistics Pocketbook 2019; Africa Economic Brief - COVID-19 Pandemic Potential Risks for Trade and Trade Finance in Africa; African Economic Outlook 2021; The African Statistical Journal; Compendium of Statistics on Bank Group Operations 2019; and Gender, Poverty and Environmental Indicators on African Countries 2019.

Bernan Press, 15250 NBN Way, Bldg. C, Blue Ridge Summit, PA, 17214, USA, (301) 459-2255, (800) 865-3457, (800) 865-3450, customercare@bernan.com, https://rowman.com/Page/Bernan; World Economic Outlook, April 2022.

Central Intelligence Agency (CIA), Office of Public Affairs, Washington, DC, 20505, USA, (703) 482-0623, https://www.cia.gov; The World Factbook.

The Economist Group: Economist Intelligence Unit (EIU), 900 3rd Ave., 16th Fl., New York, NY, 10022, USA, (212) 541-0500, americas@eiu.com, https://www.eiu.com; COTE d'IVOIRE Country Report.

Euromonitor International, Inc., 1 N Dearborn St., Ste. 1700, Chicago, IL, 60602, USA, (312) 922-1115, (312) 922-1157, info-usa@euromonitor.com, https://www.euromonitor.com/; Geographies.

Organisation of Islamic Cooperation (OIC), Statistical, Economic and Social Research and Training Centre for Islamic Countries (SESRIC), Kudus Cad. No. 9, Diplomatik Site, Ankara, 06450, TUR, statistics@sesric.org, https://www.sesric.org/; OIC Economic Outlook 2021; OIC Statistics (OICStat) Database; and OIC-Countries in Figures (OIC-CIF).

Palgrave Macmillan, 1 New York Plaza, Ste. 4500, New York, NY, 10004-1562, USA, (800) 777-4643, orders@palgrave.com, https://www.palgrave.com/us; The Statesman's Yearbook, 2023.

Routledge - Taylor & Francis Group, 6000 Broken Sound Pkwy. NW, Ste. 300, Boca Raton, FL, 33487, USA, (800) 634-1420, (800) 634-7064, orders@taylorandfrancis.com, https://www.routledge.com/; The Europa World Year Book 2022.

United Nations Economic Commission for Africa (UNECA), PO Box 3001, Addis Ababa, ETH, ecainfo@uneca.org, https://www.uneca.org/; Economic Report on Africa 2021.

United Nations Statistics Division (UNSD), United Nations Plz., New York, NY, 10017, USA, (800) 253-9646, (212) 963-9851, statistics@un.org, https://unstats.un.org; World Statistics Pocketbook 2021.

The World Bank, 1818 H St. NW, Washington, DC, 20433, USA, (202) 473-1000, (202) 477-6391, eds03@worldbank.org, https://www.worldbank.org/; COTE d'IVOIRE (report); The Global Findex Database 2021; and World Development Report 2022: Finance for an Equitable Recovery.

COTE d'IVOIRE-EDUCATION

African Development Bank Group (AfDB), Avenue Joseph Anoma, 01 BP 1387, Abidjan, 01, COT, https://www.afdb.org; The AfDB Statistics Pocketbook 2019.

Euromonitor International, Inc., 1 N Dearborn St., Ste. 1700, Chicago, IL, 60602, USA, (312) 922-1115, (312) 922-1157, info-usa@euromonitor.com, https://www.euromonitor.com/; Geographies.

Organisation of Islamic Cooperation (OIC), Statistical, Economic and Social Research and Training Centre for Islamic Countries (SESRIC), Kudus Cad. No. 9, Diplomatik Site, Ankara, 06450, TUR, statistics@sesric.org, https://www.sesric.org/; OIC Statistics (OICStat) Database.

Palgrave Macmillan, 1 New York Plaza, Ste. 4500, New York, NY, 10004-1562, USA, (800) 777-4643, orders@palgrave.com, https://www.palgrave.com/us; The Statesman's Yearbook, 2023.

Routledge - Taylor & Francis Group, 6000 Broken Sound Pkwy. NW, Ste. 300, Boca Raton, FL, 33487, USA, (800) 634-1420, (800) 634-7064, orders@taylorandfrancis.com, https://www.routledge.com/; The Europa World Year Book 2022.

UNESCO Institute for Statistics, C.P 250 Succursale H, Montreal, QC, H3G 2K8, CAN, (514) 343-6880 (Dial from U.S.), (514) 343-5740 (Fax from U.S.), uis.publications@unesco.org, http://uis.unesco.org/; UIS.Stat.

United Nations Economic Commission for Africa (UNECA), PO Box 3001, Addis Ababa, ETH, ecainfo@uneca.org, https://www.uneca.org/; African Statistical Yearbook 2020.

The World Bank, 1818 H St. NW, Washington, DC, 20433, USA, (202) 473-1000, (202) 477-6391, eds03@worldbank.org, https://www.worldbank.org/;

COTE d'IVOIRE (report); World Development Indicators (WDI) 2022; and World Development Report 2022: Finance for an Equitable Recovery.

COTE d'IVOIRE-ELECTRICITY

International Energy Agency (IEA), 9 Rue de la Federation, Paris, 75739, FRA, info@iea.org, https://www.iea.org/; World Energy Outlook 2021.

U.S. Energy Information Administration (EIA), 1000 Independence Ave. SW, Washington, DC, 20585, USA, (202) 586-8800, infoctr@eia.gov, https://www.eia.gov; International Energy Outlook 2021.

United Nations Statistics Division (UNSD), United Nations Plz., New York, NY, 10017, USA, (800) 253-9646, (212) 963-9851, statistics@un.org, https://unstats.un.org; Statistical Yearbook of the United Nations 2021.

COTE d'IVOIRE-EMPLOYMENT

UK Data Service, University of Essex, Wivenhoe Park, Colchester, Essex, CO4 3SQ, GBR, https://ukdataservice.ac.uk/; International Aggregate Data.

United Nations Economic Commission for Africa (UNECA), PO Box 3001, Addis Ababa, ETH, ecainfo@uneca.org, https://www.uneca.org/; African Statistical Yearbook 2020.

United Nations Statistics Division (UNSD), United Nations Plz., New York, NY, 10017, USA, (800) 253-9646, (212) 963-9851, statistics@un.org, https://unstats.un.org; Statistical Yearbook of the United Nations 2021.

The World Bank, 1818 H St. NW, Washington, DC, 20433, USA, (202) 473-1000, (202) 477-6391, eds03@worldbank.org, https://www.worldbank.org/; COTE d'IVOIRE (report).

COTE d'IVOIRE-ENVIRONMENTAL CONDITIONS

The Economist Group: Economist Intelligence Unit (EIU), 900 3rd Ave., 16th Fl., New York, NY, 10022, USA, (212) 541-0500, americas@eiu.com, https://www.eiu.com; COTE d'IVOIRE Country Report.

International Institute for Environment and Development (IIED), 235 High Holborn, London, WC1V 7DN, GBR, inforequest@iied.org, https://www.iied.org; Environment & Urbanization.

Organisation of Islamic Cooperation (OIC), Statistical, Economic and Social Research and Training Centre for Islamic Countries (SESRIC), Kudus Cad. No. 9, Diplomatik Site, Ankara, 06450, TUR, statistics@sesric.org, https://www.sesric.org/; OIC Statistics (OICStat) Database and OIC-Countries in Figures (OIC-CIF).

United Nations Statistics Division (UNSD), United Nations Plz., New York, NY, 10017, USA, (800) 253-9646, (212) 963-9851, statistics@un.org, https://unstats.un.org; World Statistics Pocketbook 2021.

COTE d'IVOIRE-EXPORTS

African Development Bank Group (AfDB), Avenue Joseph Anoma, 01 BP 1387, Abidjan, 01, COT, https://www.afdb.org; African Economic Outlook 2021.

Central Intelligence Agency (CIA), Office of Public Affairs, Washington, DC, 20505, USA, (703) 482-0623, https://www.cia.gov; The World Factbook.

The Economist Group: Economist Intelligence Unit (EIU), 900 3rd Ave., 16th Fl., New York, NY, 10022, USA, (212) 541-0500, americas@eiu.com, https://www.eiu.com; COTE d'IVOIRE Country Report.

International Monetary Fund (IMF), 700 19th St. NW, Washington, DC, 20431, USA, (202) 623-7000, (202) 623-4661, publications@imf.org, https://www.imf.org; Direction of Trade Statistics (DOTS).

Organisation of Islamic Cooperation (OIC), Statistical, Economic and Social Research and Training Centre for Islamic Countries (SESRIC), Kudus Cad. No. 9, Diplomatik Site, Ankara, 06450, TUR, statistics@sesric.org, https://www.sesric.org/; OIC Statistics (OICStat) Database.

S&P Global, IHS Markit, 15 Inverness Way E, Englewood, CO, 80112, USA, (800) 447-2273, (800) 854-7179, https://ihsmarkit.com; Global Trade Atlas (GTA).

United Nations Conference on Trade and Development (UNCTAD), Palais des Nations, Geneva, 1211, SWI, (212) 963-6896, unctadinfo@unctad.org, https://unctad.org; Handbook of Statistics 2021.

The World Bank, 1818 H St. NW, Washington, DC, 20433, USA, (202) 473-1000, (202) 477-6391, eds03@worldbank.org, https://www.worldbank.org/; World Development Report 2022: Finance for an Equitable Recovery.

COTE d'IVOIRE-FEMALE WORKING POPULATION

See COTE d'IVOIRE-EMPLOYMENT

COTE d'IVOIRE-FERTILITY, HUMAN

Central Intelligence Agency (CIA), Office of Public Affairs, Washington, DC, 20505, USA, (703) 482-0623, https://www.cia.gov; The World Factbook.

COTE d'IVOIRE-FERTILIZER INDUSTRY

United Nations Food and Agricultural Organization (FAO), 2121 K St., Ste. 800B, Washington, DC, 20037, USA, (202) 653-2400 (Dial from U.S.), (202) 653-5760 (Fax from U.S.), fao-hq@fao.org, https://www.fao.org; The State of Food and Agriculture (SOFA) 2022.

COTE d'IVOIRE-FETAL MORTALITY

See COTE d'IVOIRE-MORTALITY

COTE d'IVOIRE-FINANCE

Stockholm International Peace Research Institute (SIPRI), Signalistgatan 9, Stockholm, SE 169 72, SWE, https://www.sipri.org/; SIPRI Arms Transfers Database and SIPRI Military Expenditure Database.

United Nations Economic Commission for Africa (UNECA), PO Box 3001, Addis Ababa, ETH, ecainfo@uneca.org, https://www.uneca.org/; African Statistical Yearbook 2020.

United Nations Statistics Division (UNSD), United Nations Plz., New York, NY, 10017, USA, (800) 253-9646, (212) 963-9851, statistics@un.org, https://unstats.un.org; Statistical Yearbook of the United Nations 2021.

The World Bank, 1818 H St. NW, Washington, DC, 20433, USA, (202) 473-1000, (202) 477-6391, eds03@worldbank.org, https://www.worldbank.org/; COTE d'IVOIRE (report).

COTE d'IVOIRE-FINANCE, PUBLIC

African Development Bank Group (AfDB), Avenue Joseph Anoma, 01 BP 1387, Abidjan, 01, COT, https://www.afdb.org; The AfDB Statistics Pocketbook 2019.

The Economist Group: Economist Intelligence Unit (EIU), 900 3rd Ave., 16th Fl., New York, NY, 10022, USA, (212) 541-0500, americas@eiu.com, https://www.eiu.com; COTE d'IVOIRE Country Report.

International Monetary Fund (IMF), 700 19th St. NW, Washington, DC, 20431, USA, (202) 623-7000, (202) 623-4661, publications@imf.org, https://www.imf.org; International Financial Statistics (IFS).

Palgrave Macmillan, 1 New York Plaza, Ste. 4500, New York, NY, 10004-1562, USA, (800) 777-4643, orders@palgrave.com, https://www.palgrave.com/us; The Statesman's Yearbook, 2023.

Routledge - Taylor & Francis Group, 6000 Broken Sound Pkwy. NW, Ste. 300, Boca Raton, FL, 33487, USA, (800) 634-1420, (800) 634-7064, orders@taylorandfrancis.com, https://www.routledge.com/; The Europa World Year Book 2022.

United Nations Economic Commission for Africa (UNECA), PO Box 3001, Addis Ababa, ETH, ecainfo@uneca.org, https://www.uneca.org/; African Statistical Yearbook 2020.

United Nations Statistics Division (UNSD), United Nations Plz., New York, NY, 10017, USA, (800) 253-9646, (212) 963-9851, statistics@un.org, https://unstats.un.org; National Accounts Main Aggregates Database and National Accounts Statistics: Main Aggregates and Detailed Tables.

The World Bank, 1818 H St. NW, Washington, DC, 20433, USA, (202) 473-1000, (202) 477-6391, eds03@worldbank.org, https://www.worldbank.org/; COTE d'IVOIRE (report).

COTE d'IVOIRE-FISHERIES

Palgrave Macmillan, 1 New York Plaza, Ste. 4500, New York, NY, 10004-1562, USA, (800) 777-4643, orders@palgrave.com, https://www.palgrave.com/us; The Statesman's Yearbook, 2023.

Routledge - Taylor & Francis Group, 6000 Broken Sound Pkwy. NW, Ste. 300, Boca Raton, FL, 33487, USA, (800) 634-1420, (800) 634-7064, orders@taylorandfrancis.com, https://www.routledge.com/; The Europa World Year Book 2022.

United Nations Economic Commission for Africa (UNECA), PO Box 3001, Addis Ababa, ETH, ecainfo@uneca.org, https://www.uneca.org/; African Statistical Yearbook 2020.

United Nations Food and Agricultural Organization (FAO), 2121 K St., Ste. 800B, Washington, DC, 20037, USA, (202) 653-2400 (Dial from U.S.), (202) 653-5760 (Fax from U.S.), fao-hq@fao.org, https://www.fao.org; FAO Yearbook of Fishery and Aquaculture Statistics 2019; Fishery Statistical Collections Global Capture Production; FishStatJ; and The State of Food and Agriculture (SOFA) 2022.

United Nations Statistics Division (UNSD), United Nations Plz., New York, NY, 10017, USA, (800) 253-9646, (212) 963-9851, statistics@un.org, https://unstats.un.org; Statistical Yearbook of the United Nations 2021.

The World Bank, 1818 H St. NW, Washington, DC, 20433, USA, (202) 473-1000, (202) 477-6391, eds03@worldbank.org, https://www.worldbank.org/; COTE d'IVOIRE (report).

COTE d'IVOIRE-FOOD

African Development Bank Group (AfDB), Avenue Joseph Anoma, 01 BP 1387, Abidjan, 01, COT, https://www.afdb.org; The AfDB Statistics Pocketbook 2019.

United Nations Food and Agricultural Organization (FAO), 2121 K St., Ste. 800B, Washington, DC, 20037, USA, (202) 653-2400 (Dial from U.S.), (202) 653-5760 (Fax from U.S.), fao-hq@fao.org, https://www.fao.org; The State of Food and Agriculture (SOFA) 2022.

COTE d'IVOIRE-FOREIGN EXCHANGE RATES

African Development Bank Group (AfDB), Avenue Joseph Anoma, 01 BP 1387, Abidjan, 01, COT, https://www.afdb.org; The AfDB Statistics Pocketbook 2019 and African Economic Outlook 2021.

COTE d'IVOIRE-FORESTS AND FORESTRY

Palgrave Macmillan, 1 New York Plaza, Ste. 4500, New York, NY, 10004-1562, USA, (800) 777-4643, orders@palgrave.com, https://www.palgrave.com/us; The Statesman's Yearbook, 2023.

Routledge - Taylor & Francis Group, 6000 Broken Sound Pkwy. NW, Ste. 300, Boca Raton, FL, 33487, USA, (800) 634-1420, (800) 634-7064, orders@taylorandfrancis.com, https://www.routledge.com/; The Europa World Year Book 2022.

UNESCO Institute for Statistics, C.P 250 Succursale H, Montreal, QC, H3G 2K8, CAN, (514) 343-6880 (Dial from U.S.), (514) 343-5740 (Fax from U.S.), uis.publications@unesco.org, http://uis.unesco.org/; UIS.Stat.

United Nations Economic Commission for Africa (UNECA), PO Box 3001, Addis Ababa, ETH, ecainfo@uneca.org, https://www.uneca.org/; African Statistical Yearbook 2020.

United Nations Food and Agricultural Organization (FAO), 2121 K St., Ste. 800B, Washington, DC,

20037, USA, (202) 653-2400 (Dial from U.S.), (202) 653-5760 (Fax from U.S.), fao-hq@fao.org, https://www.fao.org; FAO Yearbook of Forest Products 2019 and The State of Food and Agriculture (SOFA) 2022.

United Nations Statistics Division (UNSD), United Nations Plz., New York, NY, 10017, USA, (800) 253-9646, (212) 963-9851, statistics@un.org, https://unstats.un.org; Statistical Yearbook of the United Nations 2021.

The World Bank, 1818 H St. NW, Washington, DC, 20433, USA, (202) 473-1000, (202) 477-6391, eds03@worldbank.org, https://www.worldbank.org/; COTE d'IVOIRE (report) and World Development Report 2022: Finance for an Equitable Recovery.

COTE d'IVOIRE-GAS PRODUCTION

See COTE d'IVOIRE-MINERAL INDUSTRIES

COTE d'IVOIRE-GOLD INDUSTRY

The World Bank, 1818 H St. NW, Washington, DC, 20433, USA, (202) 473-1000, (202) 477-6391, eds03@worldbank.org, https://www.worldbank.org/; World Development Indicators (WDI) 2022.

COTE d'IVOIRE-GOLD PRODUCTION

See COTE d'IVOIRE-MINERAL INDUSTRIES

COTE d'IVOIRE-GROSS DOMESTIC PRODUCT

African Development Bank Group (AfDB), Avenue Joseph Anoma, 01 BP 1387, Abidjan, 01, COT, https://www.afdb.org; The AfDB Statistics Pocketbook 2019.

The Economist Group: Economist Intelligence Unit (EIU), 900 3rd Ave., 16th Fl., New York, NY, 10022, USA, (212) 541-0500, americas@eiu.com, https://www.eiu.com; COTE d'IVOIRE Country Report.

Routledge - Taylor & Francis Group, 6000 Broken Sound Pkwy. NW, Ste. 300, Boca Raton, FL, 33487, USA, (800) 634-1420, (800) 634-7064, orders@taylorandfrancis.com, https://www.routledge.com/; The Europa World Year Book 2022.

United Nations Economic Commission for Africa (UNECA), PO Box 3001, Addis Ababa, ETH, ecainfo@uneca.org, https://www.uneca.org/; African Statistical Yearbook 2020.

United Nations Statistics Division (UNSD), United Nations Plz., New York, NY, 10017, USA, (800) 253-9646, (212) 963-9851, statistics@un.org, https://unstats.un.org; Statistical Yearbook of the United Nations 2021.

The World Bank, 1818 H St. NW, Washington, DC, 20433, USA, (202) 473-1000, (202) 477-6391, eds03@worldbank.org, https://www.worldbank.org/; World Development Indicators (WDI) 2022 and World Development Report 2022: Finance for an Equitable Recovery.

COTE d'IVOIRE-GROSS NATIONAL PRODUCT

Routledge - Taylor & Francis Group, 6000 Broken Sound Pkwy. NW, Ste. 300, Boca Raton, FL, 33487, USA, (800) 634-1420, (800) 634-7064, orders@taylorandfrancis.com, https://www.routledge.com/; The Europa World Year Book 2022.

United Nations Statistics Division (UNSD), United Nations Plz., New York, NY, 10017, USA, (800) 253-9646, (212) 963-9851, statistics@un.org, https://unstats.un.org; Statistical Yearbook of the United Nations 2021.

The World Bank, 1818 H St. NW, Washington, DC, 20433, USA, (202) 473-1000, (202) 477-6391, eds03@worldbank.org, https://www.worldbank.org/; World Development Indicators (WDI) 2022 and World Development Report 2022: Finance for an Equitable Recovery.

COTE d'IVOIRE-HOUSING

Euromonitor International, Inc., 1 N Dearborn St., Ste. 1700, Chicago, IL, 60602, USA, (312) 922-1115, (312) 922-1157, info-usa@euromonitor.com, https://www.euromonitor.com/; Geographies.

COTE d'IVOIRE-ILLITERATE PERSONS

UNESCO Institute for Statistics, C.P 250 Succursale H, Montreal, QC, H3G 2K8, CAN, (514) 343-6880 (Dial from U.S.), (514) 343-5740 (Fax from U.S.), uis.publications@unesco.org, http://uis.unesco.org/; UIS.Stat.

COTE d'IVOIRE-IMPORTS

African Development Bank Group (AfDB), Avenue Joseph Anoma, 01 BP 1387, Abidjan, 01, COT, https://www.afdb.org; African Economic Outlook 2021.

Central Intelligence Agency (CIA), Office of Public Affairs, Washington, DC, 20505, USA, (703) 482-0623, https://www.cia.gov; The World Factbook.

The Economist Group: Economist Intelligence Unit (EIU), 900 3rd Ave., 16th Fl., New York, NY, 10022, USA, (212) 541-0500, americas@eiu.com, https://www.eiu.com; COTE d'IVOIRE Country Report.

International Monetary Fund (IMF), 700 19th St. NW, Washington, DC, 20431, USA, (202) 623-7000, (202) 623-4661, publications@imf.org, https://www.imf.org; Direction of Trade Statistics (DOTS).

S&P Global, IHS Markit, 15 Inverness Way E, Englewood, CO, 80112, USA, (800) 447-2273, (800) 854-7179, https://ihsmarkit.com; Global Trade Atlas (GTA).

United Nations Conference on Trade and Development (UNCTAD), Palais des Nations, Geneva, 1211, SWI, (212) 963-6896, unctadinfo@unctad.org, https://unctad.org; Handbook of Statistics 2021.

The World Bank, 1818 H St. NW, Washington, DC, 20433, USA, (202) 473-1000, (202) 477-6391, eds03@worldbank.org, https://www.worldbank.org/; World Development Report 2022: Finance for an Equitable Recovery.

COTE d'IVOIRE-INDUSTRIES

Central Intelligence Agency (CIA), Office of Public Affairs, Washington, DC, 20505, USA, (703) 482-0623, https://www.cia.gov; The World Factbook.

The Economist Group: Economist Intelligence Unit (EIU), 900 3rd Ave., 16th Fl., New York, NY, 10022, USA, (212) 541-0500, americas@eiu.com, https://www.eiu.com; COTE d'IVOIRE Country Report.

Euromonitor International, Inc., 1 N Dearborn St., Ste. 1700, Chicago, IL, 60602, USA, (312) 922-1115, (312) 922-1157, info-usa@euromonitor.com, https://www.euromonitor.com/; Geographies.

Palgrave Macmillan, 1 New York Plaza, Ste. 4500, New York, NY, 10004-1562, USA, (800) 777-4643, orders@palgrave.com, https://www.palgrave.com/us; The Statesman's Yearbook, 2023.

Routledge - Taylor & Francis Group, 6000 Broken Sound Pkwy. NW, Ste. 300, Boca Raton, FL, 33487, USA, (800) 634-1420, (800) 634-7064, orders@taylorandfrancis.com, https://www.routledge.com/; The Europa World Year Book 2022.

United Nations Economic Commission for Africa (UNECA), PO Box 3001, Addis Ababa, ETH, ecainfo@uneca.org, https://www.uneca.org/; African Statistical Yearbook 2020.

The World Bank, 1818 H St. NW, Washington, DC, 20433, USA, (202) 473-1000, (202) 477-6391, eds03@worldbank.org, https://www.worldbank.org/; COTE d'IVOIRE (report) and World Development Indicators (WDI) 2022.

COTE d'IVOIRE-INFANT AND MATERNAL MORTALITY

See COTE d'IVOIRE-MORTALITY

COTE d'IVOIRE-INTERNATIONAL TRADE

African Development Bank Group (AfDB), Avenue Joseph Anoma, 01 BP 1387, Abidjan, 01, COT, https://www.afdb.org; The AfDB Statistics Pocketbook 2019 and African Economic Outlook 2021.

The Economist Group: Economist Intelligence Unit (EIU), 900 3rd Ave., 16th Fl., New York, NY, 10022, USA, (212) 541-0500, americas@eiu.com, https://www.eiu.com; COTE d'IVOIRE Country Report.

Euromonitor International, Inc., 1 N Dearborn St., Ste. 1700, Chicago, IL, 60602, USA, (312) 922-1115, (312) 922-1157, info-usa@euromonitor.com, https://www.euromonitor.com/; Geographies.

Palgrave Macmillan, 1 New York Plaza, Ste. 4500, New York, NY, 10004-1562, USA, (800) 777-4643, orders@palgrave.com, https://www.palgrave.com/us; The Statesman's Yearbook, 2023.

Routledge - Taylor & Francis Group, 6000 Broken Sound Pkwy. NW, Ste. 300, Boca Raton, FL, 33487, USA, (800) 634-1420, (800) 634-7064, orders@taylorandfrancis.com, https://www.routledge.com/; The Europa World Year Book 2022.

United Nations Conference on Trade and Development (UNCTAD), Palais des Nations, Geneva, 1211, SWI, (212) 963-6896, unctadinfo@unctad.org, https://unctad.org; Trade and Development Report 2021.

United Nations Economic Commission for Africa (UNECA), PO Box 3001, Addis Ababa, ETH, ecainfo@uneca.org, https://www.uneca.org/; African Statistical Yearbook 2020.

United Nations Food and Agricultural Organization (FAO), 2121 K St., Ste. 800B, Washington, DC, 20037, USA, (202) 653-2400 (Dial from U.S.), (202) 653-5760 (Fax from U.S.), fao-hq@fao.org, https://www.fao.org; The State of Food and Agriculture (SOFA) 2022.

United Nations Statistics Division (UNSD), United Nations Plz., New York, NY, 10017, USA, (800) 253-9646, (212) 963-9851, statistics@un.org, https://unstats.un.org; International Trade Statistics Yearbook 2020 and Statistical Yearbook of the United Nations 2021.

The World Bank, 1818 H St. NW, Washington, DC, 20433, USA, (202) 473-1000, (202) 477-6391, eds03@worldbank.org, https://www.worldbank.org/; COTE d'IVOIRE (report); World Development Indicators (WDI) 2022; and World Development Report 2022: Finance for an Equitable Recovery.

World Trade Organization (WTO), Ctre. William Rappard, Rue de Lausanne 154, Case postale, Geneva, CH-1211, SWI, enquiries@wto.org, https://www.wto.org; World Trade Statistical Review 2022.

COTE d'IVOIRE-LABOR

African Development Bank Group (AfDB), Avenue Joseph Anoma, 01 BP 1387, Abidjan, 01, COT, https://www.afdb.org; The AfDB Statistics Pocketbook 2019.

Central Intelligence Agency (CIA), Office of Public Affairs, Washington, DC, 20505, USA, (703) 482-0623, https://www.cia.gov; The World Factbook.

Euromonitor International, Inc., 1 N Dearborn St., Ste. 1700, Chicago, IL, 60602, USA, (312) 922-1115, (312) 922-1157, info-usa@euromonitor.com, https://www.euromonitor.com/; Geographies.

Organisation of Islamic Cooperation (OIC), Statistical, Economic and Social Research and Training Centre for Islamic Countries (SESRIC), Kudus Cad. No. 9, Diplomatik Site, Ankara, 06450, TUR, statistics@sesric.org, https://www.sesric.org/; OIC Statistics (OICStat) Database.

Palgrave Macmillan, 1 New York Plaza, Ste. 4500, New York, NY, 10004-1562, USA, (800) 777-4643, orders@palgrave.com, https://www.palgrave.com/us; The Statesman's Yearbook, 2023.

U.S. Energy Information Administration (EIA), 1000 Independence Ave. SW, Washington, DC, 20585, USA, (202) 586-8800, infoctr@eia.gov, https://www.eia.gov; International Energy Outlook 2021.

United Nations Food and Agricultural Organization (FAO), 2121 K St., Ste. 800B, Washington, DC, 20037, USA, (202) 653-2400 (Dial from U.S.), (202) 653-5760 (Fax from U.S.), fao-hq@fao.org, https://www.fao.org; The State of Food and Agriculture (SOFA) 2022.

The World Bank, 1818 H St. NW, Washington, DC, 20433, USA, (202) 473-1000, (202) 477-6391, eds03@worldbank.org, https://www.worldbank.org/; World Development Indicators (WDI) 2022 and World Development Report 2022: Finance for an Equitable Recovery.

COTE d'IVOIRE-LAND USE

The World Bank, 1818 H St. NW, Washington, DC, 20433, USA, (202) 473-1000, (202) 477-6391, eds03@worldbank.org, https://www.worldbank.org/; World Development Report 2022: Finance for an Equitable Recovery.

COTE d'IVOIRE-LIBRARIES

UNESCO Institute for Statistics, C.P 250 Succursale H, Montreal, QC, H3G 2K8, CAN, (514) 343-6880 (Dial from U.S.), (514) 343-5740 (Fax from U.S.), uis.publications@unesco.org, http://uis.unesco.org/; UIS.Stat.

COTE d'IVOIRE-LIFE EXPECTANCY

African Development Bank Group (AfDB), Avenue Joseph Anoma, 01 BP 1387, Abidjan, 01, COT, https://www.afdb.org; The AfDB Statistics Pocketbook 2019.

Central Intelligence Agency (CIA), Office of Public Affairs, Washington, DC, 20505, USA, (703) 482-0623, https://www.cia.gov; The World Factbook.

United Nations Department of Economic and Social Affairs (DESA), Population Division, 2 United Nations Plz., Rm. DC2-1950, New York, NY, 10017, USA, (212) 963-3209, (212) 963-2147, population@un.org, https://www.un.org/development/desa/pd/; World Population Ageing 2020 Highlights.

COTE d'IVOIRE-LITERACY

Euromonitor International, Inc., 1 N Dearborn St., Ste. 1700, Chicago, IL, 60602, USA, (312) 922-1115, (312) 922-1157, info-usa@euromonitor.com, https://www.euromonitor.com/; Geographies.

COTE d'IVOIRE-LIVESTOCK

Palgrave Macmillan, 1 New York Plaza, Ste. 4500, New York, NY, 10004-1562, USA, (800) 777-4643, orders@palgrave.com, https://www.palgrave.com/us; The Statesman's Yearbook, 2023.

Routledge - Taylor & Francis Group, 6000 Broken Sound Pkwy. NW, Ste. 300, Boca Raton, FL, 33487, USA, (800) 634-1420, (800) 634-7064, orders@taylorandfrancis.com, https://www.routledge.com/; The Europa World Year Book 2022.

United Nations Economic Commission for Africa (UNECA), PO Box 3001, Addis Ababa, ETH, ecainfo@uneca.org, https://www.uneca.org/; African Statistical Yearbook 2020.

United Nations Food and Agricultural Organization (FAO), 2121 K St., Ste. 800B, Washington, DC, 20037, USA, (202) 653-2400 (Dial from U.S.), (202) 653-5760 (Fax from U.S.), fao-hq@fao.org, https://www.fao.org; The State of Food and Agriculture (SOFA) 2022.

United Nations Statistics Division (UNSD), United Nations Plz., New York, NY, 10017, USA, (800) 253-9646, (212) 963-9851, statistics@un.org, https://unstats.un.org; Statistical Yearbook of the United Nations 2021.

COTE d'IVOIRE-MINERAL INDUSTRIES

International Energy Agency (IEA), 9 Rue de la Federation, Paris, 75739, FRA, info@iea.org, https://www.iea.org/; World Energy Outlook 2021.

Palgrave Macmillan, 1 New York Plaza, Ste. 4500, New York, NY, 10004-1562, USA, (800) 777-4643, orders@palgrave.com, https://www.palgrave.com/us; The Statesman's Yearbook, 2023.

Routledge - Taylor & Francis Group, 6000 Broken Sound Pkwy. NW, Ste. 300, Boca Raton, FL, 33487, USA, (800) 634-1420, (800) 634-7064, orders@taylorandfrancis.com, https://www.routledge.com/; The Europa World Year Book 2022.

United Nations Conference on Trade and Development (UNCTAD), Palais des Nations, Geneva, 1211, SWI, (212) 963-6896, unctadinfo@unctad.org, https://unctad.org; Trade and Development Report 2021.

United Nations Economic Commission for Africa (UNECA), PO Box 3001, Addis Ababa, ETH, ecainfo@uneca.org, https://www.uneca.org/; African Statistical Yearbook 2020.

United Nations Statistics Division (UNSD), United Nations Plz., New York, NY, 10017, USA, (800) 253-9646, (212) 963-9851, statistics@un.org, https://unstats.un.org; Statistical Yearbook of the United Nations 2021.

COTE d'IVOIRE-MONEY SUPPLY

The Economist Group: Economist Intelligence Unit (EIU), 900 3rd Ave., 16th Fl., New York, NY, 10022, USA, (212) 541-0500, americas@eiu.com, https://www.eiu.com; COTE d'IVOIRE Country Report.

Routledge - Taylor & Francis Group, 6000 Broken Sound Pkwy. NW, Ste. 300, Boca Raton, FL, 33487, USA, (800) 634-1420, (800) 634-7064, orders@taylorandfrancis.com, https://www.routledge.com/; The Europa World Year Book 2022.

United Nations Statistics Division (UNSD), United Nations Plz., New York, NY, 10017, USA, (800) 253-9646, (212) 963-9851, statistics@un.org, https://unstats.un.org; Statistical Yearbook of the United Nations 2021.

The World Bank, 1818 H St. NW, Washington, DC, 20433, USA, (202) 473-1000, (202) 477-6391, eds03@worldbank.org, https://www.worldbank.org/; COTE d'IVOIRE (report).

COTE d'IVOIRE-MORTALITY

UNICEF, 3 United Nations Plz., New York, NY, 10017, USA, (212) 303-7984, (917) 244-2215, https://www.unicef.org; The State of the World's Children 2023.

United Nations Statistics Division (UNSD), United Nations Plz., New York, NY, 10017, USA, (800) 253-9646, (212) 963-9851, statistics@un.org, https://unstats.un.org; Statistical Yearbook of the United Nations 2021 and World Statistics Pocketbook 2021.

The World Bank, 1818 H St. NW, Washington, DC, 20433, USA, (202) 473-1000, (202) 477-6391, eds03@worldbank.org, https://www.worldbank.org/; World Development Indicators (WDI) 2022.

COTE d'IVOIRE-MOTOR VEHICLES

International Road Federation (IRF), Madison Place, 500 Montgomery St., 5th Fl., Alexandria, VA, 22314, USA, (703) 535-1001, (703) 535-1007, info@irf.global, https://www.irf.global/; World Road Statistics (WRS).

COTE d'IVOIRE-NATURAL GAS PRODUCTION

See COTE d'IVOIRE-MINERAL INDUSTRIES

COTE d'IVOIRE-NUTRITION

United Nations Food and Agricultural Organization (FAO), 2121 K St., Ste. 800B, Washington, DC, 20037, USA, (202) 653-2400 (Dial from U.S.), (202) 653-5760 (Fax from U.S.), fao-hq@fao.org, https://www.fao.org; The State of Food and Agriculture (SOFA) 2022.

COTE d'IVOIRE-PAPER

See COTE d'IVOIRE-FORESTS AND FORESTRY

COTE d'IVOIRE-PEANUT PRODUCTION

See COTE d'IVOIRE-CROPS

COTE d'IVOIRE-PESTICIDES

United Nations Food and Agricultural Organization (FAO), 2121 K St., Ste. 800B, Washington, DC, 20037, USA, (202) 653-2400 (Dial from U.S.), (202) 653-5760 (Fax from U.S.), fao-hq@fao.org, https://www.fao.org; The State of Food and Agriculture (SOFA) 2022.

COTE d'IVOIRE-PETROLEUM INDUSTRY AND TRADE

International Energy Agency (IEA), 9 Rue de la Federation, Paris, 75739, FRA, info@iea.org, https://www.iea.org/; World Energy Outlook 2021.

U.S. Energy Information Administration (EIA), 1000 Independence Ave. SW, Washington, DC, 20585, USA, (202) 586-8800, infoctr@eia.gov, https://www.eia.gov; International Energy Outlook 2021.

United Nations Food and Agricultural Organization (FAO), 2121 K St., Ste. 800B, Washington, DC, 20037, USA, (202) 653-2400 (Dial from U.S.), (202) 653-5760 (Fax from U.S.), fao-hq@fao.org, https://www.fao.org; The State of Food and Agriculture (SOFA) 2022.

United Nations Statistics Division (UNSD), United Nations Plz., New York, NY, 10017, USA, (800) 253-9646, (212) 963-9851, statistics@un.org, https://unstats.un.org; Statistical Yearbook of the United Nations 2021.

COTE d'IVOIRE-POPULATION

African Development Bank Group (AfDB), Avenue Joseph Anoma, 01 BP 1387, Abidjan, 01, COT, https://www.afdb.org; The AfDB Statistics Pocketbook 2019; Africa Economic Brief - COVID-19 Pandemic Potential Risks for Trade and Trade Finance in Africa; The African Statistical Journal; and Gender, Poverty and Environmental Indicators on African Countries 2019.

Central Intelligence Agency (CIA), Office of Public Affairs, Washington, DC, 20505, USA, (703) 482-0623, https://www.cia.gov; The World Factbook.

The Economist Group: Economist Intelligence Unit (EIU), 900 3rd Ave., 16th Fl., New York, NY, 10022, USA, (212) 541-0500, americas@eiu.com, https://www.eiu.com; COTE d'IVOIRE Country Report.

European Commission, Eurostat, Luxembourg, 2920, LUX, https://ec.europa.eu/eurostat/; EU in the World 2020.

International Labour Organization (ILO), 4 Rte. des Morillons, Geneva, CH-1211, SWI, ilo@ilo.org, https://www.ilo.org; NORMLEX Information System on International Labour Standards.

Palgrave Macmillan, 1 New York Plaza, Ste. 4500, New York, NY, 10004-1562, USA, (800) 777-4643, orders@palgrave.com, https://www.palgrave.com/us; The Statesman's Yearbook, 2023.

Routledge - Taylor & Francis Group, 6000 Broken Sound Pkwy. NW, Ste. 300, Boca Raton, FL, 33487, USA, (800) 634-1420, (800) 634-7064, orders@taylorandfrancis.com, https://www.routledge.com/; The Europa World Year Book 2022.

UK Data Service, University of Essex, Wivenhoe Park, Colchester, Essex, CO4 3SQ, GBR, https://ukdataservice.ac.uk/; International Aggregate Data.

UNESCO Institute for Statistics, C.P 250 Succursale H, Montreal, QC, H3G 2K8, CAN, (514) 343-6880 (Dial from U.S.), (514) 343-5740 (Fax from U.S.), uis.publications@unesco.org, http://uis.unesco.org/; UIS.Stat.

United Nations Department of Economic and Social Affairs (DESA), Population Division, 2 United Nations Plz., Rm. DC2-1950, New York, NY, 10017, USA, (212) 963-3209, (212) 963-2147, population@un.org, https://www.un.org/development/desa/pd/; Revision of World Urbanization Prospects and World Population Ageing 2020 Highlights.

United Nations Development Programme (UNDP), One United Nations Plz., New York, NY, 10017, USA, (212) 906-5000, (212) 906-5001, https://www.undp.org; Human Development Report 2021-2022.

United Nations Statistics Division (UNSD), United Nations Plz., New York, NY, 10017, USA, (800) 253-9646, (212) 963-9851, statistics@un.org, https://unstats.un.org; Statistical Yearbook of the United Nations 2021 and World Statistics Pocketbook 2021.

The World Bank, 1818 H St. NW, Washington, DC, 20433, USA, (202) 473-1000, (202) 477-6391, eds03@worldbank.org, https://www.worldbank.org/;

COTE d'IVOIRE (report); The Global Findex Database 2021; and World Development Report 2022: Finance for an Equitable Recovery.

COTE d'IVOIRE-POPULATION DENSITY

African Development Bank Group (AfDB), Avenue Joseph Anoma, 01 BP 1387, Abidjan, 01, COT, https://www.afdb.org; The AfDB Statistics Pocketbook 2019.

Central Intelligence Agency (CIA), Office of Public Affairs, Washington, DC, 20505, USA, (703) 482-0623, https://www.cia.gov; The World Factbook.

Palgrave Macmillan, 1 New York Plaza, Ste. 4500, New York, NY, 10004-1562, USA, (800) 777-4643, orders@palgrave.com, https://www.palgrave.com/us; The Statesman's Yearbook, 2023.

Routledge - Taylor & Francis Group, 6000 Broken Sound Pkwy. NW, Ste. 300, Boca Raton, FL, 33487, USA, (800) 634-1420, (800) 634-7064, orders@taylorandfrancis.com, https://www.routledge.com/; The Europa World Year Book 2022.

UNESCO Institute for Statistics, C.P 250 Succursale H, Montreal, QC, H3G 2K8, CAN, (514) 343-6880 (Dial from U.S.), (514) 343-5740 (Fax from U.S.), uis.publications@unesco.org, http://uis.unesco.org/; UIS.Stat.

The World Bank, 1818 H St. NW, Washington, DC, 20433, USA, (202) 473-1000, (202) 477-6391, eds03@worldbank.org, https://www.worldbank.org/; COTE d'IVOIRE (report) and World Development Report 2022: Finance for an Equitable Recovery.

COTE d'IVOIRE-POWER RESOURCES

Euromonitor International, Inc., 1 N Dearborn St., Ste. 1700, Chicago, IL, 60602, USA, (312) 922-1115, (312) 922-1157, info-usa@euromonitor.com, https://www.euromonitor.com/; Geographies.

International Energy Agency (IEA), 9 Rue de la Federation, Paris, 75739, FRA, info@iea.org, https://www.iea.org/; World Energy Outlook 2021.

Palgrave Macmillan, 1 New York Plaza, Ste. 4500, New York, NY, 10004-1562, USA, (800) 777-4643, orders@palgrave.com, https://www.palgrave.com/us; The Statesman's Yearbook, 2023.

U.S. Energy Information Administration (EIA), 1000 Independence Ave. SW, Washington, DC, 20585, USA, (202) 586-8800, infoctr@eia.gov, https://www.eia.gov; International Energy Outlook 2021.

United Nations Economic Commission for Africa (UNECA), PO Box 3001, Addis Ababa, ETH, ecainfo@uneca.org, https://www.uneca.org/; African Statistical Yearbook 2020.

United Nations Food and Agricultural Organization (FAO), 2121 K St., Ste. 800B, Washington, DC, 20037, USA, (202) 653-2400 (Dial from U.S.), (202) 653-5760 (Fax from U.S.), fao-hq@fao.org, https://www.fao.org; The State of Food and Agriculture (SOFA) 2022.

United Nations Statistics Division (UNSD), United Nations Plz., New York, NY, 10017, USA, (800) 253-9646, (212) 963-9851, statistics@un.org, https://unstats.un.org; Energy Statistics Yearbook 2019; Statistical Yearbook of the United Nations 2021; and World Statistics Pocketbook 2021.

The World Bank, 1818 H St. NW, Washington, DC, 20433, USA, (202) 473-1000, (202) 477-6391, eds03@worldbank.org, https://www.worldbank.org/; World Development Report 2022: Finance for an Equitable Recovery.

COTE d'IVOIRE-PRICES

Euromonitor International, Inc., 1 N Dearborn St., Ste. 1700, Chicago, IL, 60602, USA, (312) 922-1115, (312) 922-1157, info-usa@euromonitor.com, https://www.euromonitor.com/; Geographies.

United Nations Economic Commission for Africa (UNECA), PO Box 3001, Addis Ababa, ETH, ecainfo@uneca.org, https://www.uneca.org/; African Statistical Yearbook 2020.

The World Bank, 1818 H St. NW, Washington, DC, 20433, USA, (202) 473-1000, (202) 477-6391, eds03@worldbank.org, https://www.worldbank.org/; COTE d'IVOIRE (report).

COTE d'IVOIRE-PUBLIC HEALTH

African Development Bank Group (AfDB), Avenue Joseph Anoma, 01 BP 1387, Abidjan, 01, COT, https://www.afdb.org; The AfDB Statistics Pocketbook 2019.

Euromonitor International, Inc., 1 N Dearborn St., Ste. 1700, Chicago, IL, 60602, USA, (312) 922-1115, (312) 922-1157, info-usa@euromonitor.com, https://www.euromonitor.com/; Geographies.

Organisation of Islamic Cooperation (OIC), Statistical, Economic and Social Research and Training Centre for Islamic Countries (SESRIC), Kudus Cad. No. 9, Diplomatik Site, Ankara, 06450, TUR, statistics@sesric.org, https://www.sesric.org/; OIC Statistics (OICStat) Database.

Palgrave Macmillan, 1 New York Plaza, Ste. 4500, New York, NY, 10004-1562, USA, (800) 777-4643, orders@palgrave.com, https://www.palgrave.com/us; The Statesman's Yearbook, 2023.

U.S. Census Bureau, 4600 Silver Hill Rd., Washington, DC, 20233, USA, (301) 763-4636, (800) 923-8282, https://www.census.gov; HIV/AIDS Surveillance Data Base.

UNICEF, 3 United Nations Plz., New York, NY, 10017, USA, (212) 303-7984, (917) 244-2215, https://www.unicef.org; The State of the World's Children 2023.

United Nations Department of Economic and Social Affairs (DESA), Population Division, 2 United Nations Plz., Rm. DC2-1950, New York, NY, 10017, USA, (212) 963-3209, (212) 963-2147, population@un.org, https://www.un.org/development/desa/pd/; World Fertility Data 2019.

United Nations Development Programme (UNDP), One United Nations Plz., New York, NY, 10017, USA, (212) 906-5000, (212) 906-5001, https://www.undp.org; Human Development Report 2021-2022.

United Nations Economic Commission for Africa (UNECA), PO Box 3001, Addis Ababa, ETH, ecainfo@uneca.org, https://www.uneca.org/; African Statistical Yearbook 2020.

United Nations Statistics Division (UNSD), United Nations Plz., New York, NY, 10017, USA, (800) 253-9646, (212) 963-9851, statistics@un.org, https://unstats.un.org; Statistical Yearbook of the United Nations 2021.

The World Bank, 1818 H St. NW, Washington, DC, 20433, USA, (202) 473-1000, (202) 477-6391, eds03@worldbank.org, https://www.worldbank.org/; COTE d'IVOIRE (report).

COTE d'IVOIRE-PUBLISHERS AND PUBLISHING

Routledge - Taylor & Francis Group, 6000 Broken Sound Pkwy. NW, Ste. 300, Boca Raton, FL, 33487, USA, (800) 634-1420, (800) 634-7064, orders@taylorandfrancis.com, https://www.routledge.com/; The Europa World Year Book 2022.

UNESCO Institute for Statistics, C.P 250 Succursale H, Montreal, QC, H3G 2K8, CAN, (514) 343-6880 (Dial from U.S.), (514) 343-5740 (Fax from U.S.), uis.publications@unesco.org, http://uis.unesco.org/; UIS.Stat.

COTE d'IVOIRE-RAILROADS

Janes, USA, (703) 574-7580, (888) 977-1519, customer.care@janes.com, https://www.janes.com; Janes World Railways 2021-2022.

Palgrave Macmillan, 1 New York Plaza, Ste. 4500, New York, NY, 10004-1562, USA, (800) 777-4643, orders@palgrave.com, https://www.palgrave.com/us; The Statesman's Yearbook, 2023.

Routledge - Taylor & Francis Group, 6000 Broken Sound Pkwy. NW, Ste. 300, Boca Raton, FL, 33487, USA, (800) 634-1420, (800) 634-7064, orders@taylorandfrancis.com, https://www.routledge.com/; The Europa World Year Book 2022.

United Nations Economic Commission for Africa (UNECA), PO Box 3001, Addis Ababa, ETH, ecainfo@uneca.org, https://www.uneca.org/; African Statistical Yearbook 2020.

United Nations Statistics Division (UNSD), United Nations Plz., New York, NY, 10017, USA, (800) 253-9646, (212) 963-9851, statistics@un.org, https://unstats.un.org; Statistical Yearbook of the United Nations 2021.

COTE d'IVOIRE-RELIGION

Central Intelligence Agency (CIA), Office of Public Affairs, Washington, DC, 20505, USA, (703) 482-0623, https://www.cia.gov; The World Factbook.

Palgrave Macmillan, 1 New York Plaza, Ste. 4500, New York, NY, 10004-1562, USA, (800) 777-4643, orders@palgrave.com, https://www.palgrave.com/us; The Statesman's Yearbook, 2023.

COTE d'IVOIRE-RETAIL TRADE

Euromonitor International, Inc., 1 N Dearborn St., Ste. 1700, Chicago, IL, 60602, USA, (312) 922-1115, (312) 922-1157, info-usa@euromonitor.com, https://www.euromonitor.com/; Geographies.

COTE d'IVOIRE-RICE PRODUCTION

See COTE d'IVOIRE-CROPS

COTE d'IVOIRE-ROADS

International Road Federation (IRF), Madison Place, 500 Montgomery St., 5th Fl., Alexandria, VA, 22314, USA, (703) 535-1001, (703) 535-1007, info@irf.global, https://www.irf.global/; World Road Statistics (WRS).

United Nations Economic Commission for Africa (UNECA), PO Box 3001, Addis Ababa, ETH, ecainfo@uneca.org, https://www.uneca.org/; African Statistical Yearbook 2020.

COTE d'IVOIRE-RUBBER INDUSTRY AND TRADE

International Rubber Study Group (IRSG), 51 Changi Business Park Central 2, Unit No. 6, 486066, SGP, https://www.rubberstudy.org; Monthly Rubber Bulletin (MRB); Rubber Statistical Bulletin; and World Rubber Industry Report (WRIO).

United Nations Statistics Division (UNSD), United Nations Plz., New York, NY, 10017, USA, (800) 253-9646, (212) 963-9851, statistics@un.org, https://unstats.un.org; Statistical Yearbook of the United Nations 2021.

COTE d'IVOIRE-SHIPPING

Routledge - Taylor & Francis Group, 6000 Broken Sound Pkwy. NW, Ste. 300, Boca Raton, FL, 33487, USA, (800) 634-1420, (800) 634-7064, orders@taylorandfrancis.com, https://www.routledge.com/; The Europa World Year Book 2022.

United Nations Economic Commission for Africa (UNECA), PO Box 3001, Addis Ababa, ETH, ecainfo@uneca.org, https://www.uneca.org/; African Statistical Yearbook 2020.

United Nations Statistics Division (UNSD), United Nations Plz., New York, NY, 10017, USA, (800) 253-9646, (212) 963-9851, statistics@un.org, https://unstats.un.org; Statistical Yearbook of the United Nations 2021.

COTE d'IVOIRE-STEEL PRODUCTION

See COTE d'IVOIRE-MINERAL INDUSTRIES

COTE d'IVOIRE-SUGAR PRODUCTION

See COTE d'IVOIRE-CROPS

COTE d'IVOIRE-TAXATION

International Road Federation (IRF), Madison Place, 500 Montgomery St., 5th Fl., Alexandria, VA, 22314, USA, (703) 535-1001, (703) 535-1007, info@irf.global, https://www.irf.global/; World Road Statistics (WRS).

The World Bank, 1818 H St. NW, Washington, DC, 20433, USA, (202) 473-1000, (202) 477-6391, eds03@worldbank.org, https://www.worldbank.org/; World Development Indicators (WDI) 2022.

COTE d'IVOIRE-TELEPHONE

Palgrave Macmillan, 1 New York Plaza, Ste. 4500, New York, NY, 10004-1562, USA, (800) 777-4643, orders@palgrave.com, https://www.palgrave.com/us; The Statesman's Yearbook, 2023.

Routledge - Taylor & Francis Group, 6000 Broken Sound Pkwy. NW, Ste. 300, Boca Raton, FL, 33487, USA, (800) 634-1420, (800) 634-7064, orders@taylorandfrancis.com, https://www.routledge.com/; The Europa World Year Book 2022.

United Nations Statistics Division (UNSD), United Nations Plz., New York, NY, 10017, USA, (800) 253-9646, (212) 963-9851, statistics@un.org, https://unstats.un.org; World Statistics Pocketbook 2021.

COTE d'IVOIRE-TEXTILE INDUSTRY

Palgrave Macmillan, 1 New York Plaza, Ste. 4500, New York, NY, 10004-1562, USA, (800) 777-4643, orders@palgrave.com, https://www.palgrave.com/us; The Statesman's Yearbook, 2023.

United Nations Statistics Division (UNSD), United Nations Plz., New York, NY, 10017, USA, (800) 253-9646, (212) 963-9851, statistics@un.org, https://unstats.un.org; Statistical Yearbook of the United Nations 2021.

COTE d'IVOIRE-TOBACCO INDUSTRY

United Nations Statistics Division (UNSD), United Nations Plz., New York, NY, 10017, USA, (800) 253-9646, (212) 963-9851, statistics@un.org, https://unstats.un.org; Statistical Yearbook of the United Nations 2021.

COTE d'IVOIRE-TOURISM

Euromonitor International, Inc., 1 N Dearborn St., Ste. 1700, Chicago, IL, 60602, USA, (312) 922-1115, (312) 922-1157, info-usa@euromonitor.com, https://www.euromonitor.com/; Geographies.

Organisation of Islamic Cooperation (OIC), Statistical, Economic and Social Research and Training Centre for Islamic Countries (SESRIC), Kudus Cad. No. 9, Diplomatik Site, Ankara, 06450, TUR, statistics@sesric.org, https://www.sesric.org/; International Tourism in the OIC Countries: Prospects and Challenges, 2020 and OIC Statistics (OICStat) Database.

Routledge - Taylor & Francis Group, 6000 Broken Sound Pkwy. NW, Ste. 300, Boca Raton, FL, 33487, USA, (800) 634-1420, (800) 634-7064, orders@taylorandfrancis.com, https://www.routledge.com/; The Europa World Year Book 2022.

United Nations Economic Commission for Africa (UNECA), PO Box 3001, Addis Ababa, ETH, ecainfo@uneca.org, https://www.uneca.org/; African Statistical Yearbook 2020.

United Nations Statistics Division (UNSD), United Nations Plz., New York, NY, 10017, USA, (800) 253-9646, (212) 963-9851, statistics@un.org, https://unstats.un.org; Statistical Yearbook of the United Nations 2021.

United Nations World Tourism Organization (UNWTO), Calle Poeta Joan Maragall 42, Madrid, 28020, SPA, info@unwto.org, https://www.unwto.org/; Yearbook of Tourism Statistics, 2021 Edition.

The World Bank, 1818 H St. NW, Washington, DC, 20433, USA, (202) 473-1000, (202) 477-6391, eds03@worldbank.org, https://www.worldbank.org/; COTE d'IVOIRE (report).

COTE d'IVOIRE-TRADE

See COTE d'IVOIRE-INTERNATIONAL TRADE

COTE d'IVOIRE-TRANSPORTATION

Central Intelligence Agency (CIA), Office of Public Affairs, Washington, DC, 20505, USA, (703) 482-0623, https://www.cia.gov; The World Factbook.

Euromonitor International, Inc., 1 N Dearborn St., Ste. 1700, Chicago, IL, 60602, USA, (312) 922-1115, (312) 922-1157, info-usa@euromonitor.com, https://www.euromonitor.com/; Geographies.

Organisation of Islamic Cooperation (OIC), Statistical, Economic and Social Research and Training Centre for Islamic Countries (SESRIC), Kudus Cad. No. 9, Diplomatik Site, Ankara, 06450, TUR, statistics@sesric.org, https://www.sesric.org/; OIC Statistics (OICStat) Database.

Palgrave Macmillan, 1 New York Plaza, Ste. 4500, New York, NY, 10004-1562, USA, (800) 777-4643, orders@palgrave.com, https://www.palgrave.com/us; The Statesman's Yearbook, 2023.

Routledge - Taylor & Francis Group, 6000 Broken Sound Pkwy. NW, Ste. 300, Boca Raton, FL, 33487, USA, (800) 634-1420, (800) 634-7064, orders@taylorandfrancis.com, https://www.routledge.com/; The Europa World Year Book 2022.

United Nations Economic Commission for Africa (UNECA), PO Box 3001, Addis Ababa, ETH, ecainfo@uneca.org, https://www.uneca.org/; African Statistical Yearbook 2020.

The World Bank, 1818 H St. NW, Washington, DC, 20433, USA, (202) 473-1000, (202) 477-6391, eds03@worldbank.org, https://www.worldbank.org/; COTE d'IVOIRE (report).

COTE d'IVOIRE-VITAL STATISTICS

U.S. Census Bureau, 4600 Silver Hill Rd., Washington, DC, 20233, USA, (301) 763-4636, (800) 923-8282, https://www.census.gov; HIV/AIDS Surveillance Data Base.

United Nations Department of Economic and Social Affairs (DESA), Population Division, 2 United Nations Plz., Rm. DC2-1950, New York, NY, 10017, USA, (212) 963-3209, (212) 963-2147, population@un.org, https://www.un.org/development/desa/pd/; World Contraceptive Use 2021: Estimates and Projections of Family Planning Indicators and World Marriage Data 2019.

United Nations Statistics Division (UNSD), United Nations Plz., New York, NY, 10017, USA, (800) 253-9646, (212) 963-9851, statistics@un.org, https://unstats.un.org; Statistical Yearbook of the United Nations 2021.

COTE d'IVOIRE-WAGES

The World Bank, 1818 H St. NW, Washington, DC, 20433, USA, (202) 473-1000, (202) 477-6391, eds03@worldbank.org, https://www.worldbank.org/; COTE d'IVOIRE (report).

COTE d'IVOIRE-WHEAT PRODUCTION

See COTE d'IVOIRE-CROPS

COTE d'IVOIRE-WOOL PRODUCTION

See COTE d'IVOIRE-TEXTILE INDUSTRY

COTTON-ACREAGE

U.S. Department of Agriculture (USDA), National Agricultural Statistics Service (USDA-NASS), 1400 Independence Ave. SW, Washington, DC, 20250, USA, (800) 727-9540, nass@nass.usda.gov, https://www.nass.usda.gov; Crop Production and Crop Values Annual Summary.

COTTON-GENETICS

U.S. Department of Agriculture (USDA), National Agricultural Statistics Service (USDA-NASS), 1400 Independence Ave. SW, Washington, DC, 20250, USA, (800) 727-9540, nass@nass.usda.gov, https://www.nass.usda.gov; Acreage.

COTTON-INTERNATIONAL TRADE

U.S. Census Bureau, International Trade Program, 4600 Silver Hill Rd., Washington, DC, 20233, USA, (800) 549-0595, eid.international.trade.data@census.gov, https://www.census.gov/foreign-trade; International Trade Data.

U.S. Department of Agriculture (USDA), Economic Research Service (ERS), 1400 Independence Ave. SW, Mail Stop 1800, Washington, DC, 20250-0002, USA, (202) 720-2791, https://www.ers.usda.gov/; Cotton and Wool Outlook; Foreign Agricultural Trade of the United States (FATUS); and Outlook for U.S. Agricultural Trade: May 2022.

U.S. Department of Agriculture (USDA), Foreign Agricultural Service (FAS), 1400 Independence Ave. SW, Mail Stop 1001, Washington, DC, 20250, USA, (202) 720-3935, https://www.fas.usda.gov/; Cotton: World Markets and Trade.

U.S. Department of Agriculture (USDA), National Agricultural Statistics Service (USDA-NASS), 1400 Independence Ave. SW, Washington, DC, 20250, USA, (800) 727-9540, nass@nass.usda.gov, https://www.nass.usda.gov; Crop Production and Crop Values Annual Summary.

U.S. Department of Agriculture (USDA), World Agricultural Outlook Board, (WAOB), 1400 Independence Ave. SW, Mail Stop 3812, Washington, DC, 20250, USA, (202) 720-9805, mark.jekanowski@usda.gov, https://www.usda.gov/oce/commodity-markets/waob; World Agricultural Supply and Demand Estimates (WASDE) Report.

COTTON-PESTICIDES

U.S. Department of Agriculture (USDA), Foreign Agricultural Service (FAS), 1400 Independence Ave. SW, Mail Stop 1001, Washington, DC, 20250, USA, (202) 720-3935, https://www.fas.usda.gov/; Production, Supply and Distribution Online (PSD) Online.

COTTON-PRICES

U.S. Department of Agriculture (USDA), Economic Research Service (ERS), 1400 Independence Ave. SW, Mail Stop 1800, Washington, DC, 20250-0002, USA, (202) 720-2791, https://www.ers.usda.gov/; Cotton and Wool Outlook.

U.S. Department of Agriculture (USDA), National Agricultural Statistics Service (USDA-NASS), 1400 Independence Ave. SW, Washington, DC, 20250, USA, (800) 727-9540, nass@nass.usda.gov, https://www.nass.usda.gov; Agricultural Prices; Crop Production; and Crop Values Annual Summary.

U.S. Department of Agriculture (USDA), World Agricultural Outlook Board, (WAOB), 1400 Independence Ave. SW, Mail Stop 3812, Washington, DC, 20250, USA, (202) 720-9805, mark.jekanowski@usda.gov, https://www.usda.gov/oce/commodity-markets/waob; World Agricultural Supply and Demand Estimates (WASDE) Report.

COTTON-PRODUCTION

U.S. Department of Agriculture (USDA), Economic Research Service (ERS), 1400 Independence Ave. SW, Mail Stop 1800, Washington, DC, 20250-0002, USA, (202) 720-2791, https://www.ers.usda.gov/; Cotton and Wool Outlook.

U.S. Department of Agriculture (USDA), National Agricultural Statistics Service (USDA-NASS), 1400 Independence Ave. SW, Washington, DC, 20250, USA, (800) 727-9540, nass@nass.usda.gov, https://www.nass.usda.gov; Crop Production; Crop Progress; Crop Values Annual Summary; and Quick Stats.

U.S. Department of Agriculture (USDA), World Agricultural Outlook Board, (WAOB), 1400 Independence Ave. SW, Mail Stop 3812, Washington, DC, 20250, USA, (202) 720-9805, mark.jekanowski@usda.gov, https://www.usda.gov/oce/commodity-markets/waob; World Agricultural Supply and Demand Estimates (WASDE) Report.

COTTON-PRODUCTION-WORLD

United Nations Statistics Division (UNSD), United Nations Plz., New York, NY, 10017, USA, (800) 253-9646, (212) 963-9851, statistics@un.org, https://unstats.un.org; Monthly Bulletin of Statistics Online.

COTTON-SUPPLY AND DISAPPEARANCE

U.S. Department of Agriculture (USDA), Economic Research Service (ERS), 1400 Independence Ave.

SW, Mail Stop 1800, Washington, DC, 20250-0002, USA, (202) 720-2791, https://www.ers.usda.gov/; Cotton and Wool Outlook.

U.S. Department of Agriculture (USDA), World Agricultural Outlook Board, (WAOB), 1400 Independence Ave. SW, Mail Stop 3812, Washington, DC, 20250, USA, (202) 720-9805, mark.jekanowski@usda.gov, https://www.usda.gov/oce/commodity-markets/waob; World Agricultural Supply and Demand Estimates (WASDE) Report.

COUNTY GOVERNMENTS-DEBT

U.S. Census Bureau, Public Sector, 4600 Silver Hill Rd., Washington, DC, 20233, USA, (800) 923-8282, (301) 763-4636, ewd.outreach@census.gov, https://www.census.gov/topics/public-sector.html; Annual Survey of State and Local Government Finances.

COUNTY GOVERNMENTS-ELECTED OFFICIALS

National Association of Latino Elected and Appointed Officials (NALEO) Educational Fund, 1000 Corporate Center Dr., Ste. 310, Los Angeles, CA, 90015, USA, (213) 747-7606, (213) 747-7664, avargas@naleo.org, https://naleo.org/; National Directory of Latino Elected Officials 2021.

COUNTY GOVERNMENTS-EMPLOYEES, EARNINGS, PAYROLL

U.S. Census Bureau, Public Sector, 4600 Silver Hill Rd., Washington, DC, 20233, USA, (800) 923-8282, (301) 763-4636, ewd.outreach@census.gov, https://www.census.gov/topics/public-sector.html; Annual Survey of Public Employment & Payroll (ASPEP).

COUNTY GOVERNMENTS-FINANCES OF COUNTY GOVERNMENTS

U.S. Census Bureau, Public Sector, 4600 Silver Hill Rd., Washington, DC, 20233, USA, (800) 923-8282, (301) 763-4636, ewd.outreach@census.gov, https://www.census.gov/topics/public-sector.html; Annual Survey of State and Local Government Finances.

COURIERS AND MESSENGERS-EARNINGS

U.S. Census Bureau, 4600 Silver Hill Rd., Washington, DC, 20233, USA, (301) 763-4636, (800) 923-8282, https://www.census.gov; County Business Patterns (CBP) 2020.

U.S. Census Bureau, Center for Economic Studies (CES), 4600 Silver Hill Rd., Washington, DC, 20233, USA, (301) 763-6460, (301) 763-5935, ces.contacts@census.gov, https://www.census.gov/programs-surveys/ces.html; Transportation and Warehousing, 2017 Economic Census.

COURIERS AND MESSENGERS-EMPLOYEES

U.S. Census Bureau, 4600 Silver Hill Rd., Washington, DC, 20233, USA, (301) 763-4636, (800) 923-8282, https://www.census.gov; County Business Patterns (CBP) 2020.

U.S. Census Bureau, Center for Economic Studies (CES), 4600 Silver Hill Rd., Washington, DC, 20233, USA, (301) 763-6460, (301) 763-5935, ces.contacts@census.gov, https://www.census.gov/programs-surveys/ces.html; Transportation and Warehousing, 2017 Economic Census.

COURIERS AND MESSENGERS-ESTABLISHMENTS

U.S. Census Bureau, 4600 Silver Hill Rd., Washington, DC, 20233, USA, (301) 763-4636, (800) 923-8282, https://www.census.gov; County Business Patterns (CBP) 2020.

U.S. Census Bureau, Center for Economic Studies (CES), 4600 Silver Hill Rd., Washington, DC, 20233, USA, (301) 763-6460, (301) 763-5935, ces.contacts@census.gov, https://www.census.gov/programs-surveys/ces.html; Transportation and Warehousing, 2017 Economic Census.

COURIERS AND MESSENGERS-REVENUE

U.S. Census Bureau, 4600 Silver Hill Rd., Washington, DC, 20233, USA, (301) 763-4636, (800) 923-8282, https://www.census.gov; County Business Patterns (CBP) 2020.

U.S. Census Bureau, Center for Economic Studies (CES), 4600 Silver Hill Rd., Washington, DC, 20233, USA, (301) 763-6460, (301) 763-5935, ces.contacts@census.gov, https://www.census.gov/programs-surveys/ces.html; Transportation and Warehousing, 2017 Economic Census.

COURTS

Administrative Office of the United States Courts, One Columbus Cir. NE, Washington, DC, 20544, USA, (202) 502-2600, https://www.uscourts.gov; Federal Court Management Statistics 2022; Judicial Business of the U.S. Courts, 2022; Judicial Facts and Figures 2022; and Statistical Tables for the Federal Judiciary 2022.

Justice Research and Statistics Association (JRSA), 1000 Vermont Ave. NW, Ste. 450, Washington, DC, 20005, USA, (202) 842-9330, (202) 304-1417, cjinfo@jrsa.org, https://www.jrsa.org; SAC Publication Digest 2022.

National Center for Juvenile Justice (NCJJ), 3700 S Water St., Ste. 200, Pittsburgh, PA, 15203, USA, (412) 227-6950, (412) 227-6955, ncjj@ncjfcj.org, https://www.ncjj.org/; Criminological Highlights: Children and Youth.

National Center for State Courts (NCSC), 300 Newport Ave., Williamsburg, VA, 23185, USA, (800) 616-6164, (757) 220-0449, https://www.ncsc.org/; Court Statistics Project (CSP).

U.S. Department of Justice (DOJ), Office of the Attorney General, 950 Pennsylvania Ave. NW, Washington, DC, 20530-0001, USA, (202) 514-2000, (800) 877-8339 (TTY), askdoj@usdoj.gov, https://www.justice.gov/ag; Attorney General's Annual Report to Congress and Assessment of U.S. Government Activities to Combat Trafficking in Persons.

U.S. Supreme Court, 1 First St. NE, Washington, DC, 20543, USA, (202) 479-3000, (202) 479-3472 (TTY), https://www.supremecourt.gov/; unpublished data.

COURTS-DISTRICT COURTS, UNITED STATES

Administrative Office of the United States Courts, One Columbus Cir. NE, Washington, DC, 20544, USA, (202) 502-2600, https://www.uscourts.gov; Civil Justice Reform Act Report 2022; Federal Judicial Caseload Statistics 2022; Judicial Business of the U.S. Courts, 2022; and Statistical Tables for the Federal Judiciary 2022.

COURTS-JUVENILE COURT CASES HANDLED

National Center for Juvenile Justice (NCJJ), 3700 S Water St., Ste. 200, Pittsburgh, PA, 15203, USA, (412) 227-6950, (412) 227-6955, ncjj@ncjfcj.org, https://www.ncjj.org/; Criminological Highlights: Children and Youth; Trends and Characteristics of Delinquency Cases Handled in Juvenile Court, 2019; and Youth Younger than 18 Prosecuted in Criminal Court: National Estimate, 2019 Cases.

U.S. Department of Justice (DOJ), Office of Juvenile Justice and Delinquency Prevention (OJJDP), 810 7th St. NW, Washington, DC, 20531, USA, (202) 307-5911, https://www.ojjdp.gov/; Statistical Briefing Book (SBB).

COURTS-PUBLIC OFFICERS-PROSECUTIONS

U.S. Department of Justice (DOJ), Criminal Division, 950 Pennsylvania Ave. NW, Washington, DC, 20530-0001, USA, (202) 514-2000, criminal.division@usdoj.gov, https://www.justice.gov/criminal; Report to Congress on the Activities and Operations of the Public Integrity Section for 2020.

COURTS-SENTENCING

The Gallup Organization, 901 F St. NW, Washington, DC, 20004, USA, (202) 715-3030, (800) 204-1192, (202) 715-3045, https://www.gallup.com; Record-Low 54% in U.S. Say Death Penalty Morally Acceptable.

COURTS-SUPREME COURT, UNITED STATES

The Minority Corporate Counsel Association (MCCA), 1111 Pennsylvania Ave. NW, Washington, DC, 20004, USA, (202) 739-5901, https://www.mcca.com/; Tracking the Integration of the Federal Judiciary.

Pew Research Center, Politics & Policy, 1615 L St. NW, Ste. 800, Washington, DC, 20036, USA, (202) 419-4300, (202) 857-8562, https://www.pewresearch.org/topic/politics-policy/; Americans Divided on Kavanaugh's Nomination to the Supreme Court: Democrats Are Worried He Will Make Court Too Conservative.

PollingReport.com, USA, https://www.pollingreport.com/; State of the Union.

SAE International, 400 Commonwealth Dr., Warrendale, PA, 15096, USA, (724) 776-4790, (724) 776-4841, (724) 776-0790, customerservice@sae.org, https://www.sae.org/; SAE International Journal of Aerospace.

COVID-19 (DISEASE)

Act Now Coalition, USA, https://www.actnowcoalition.org/; unpublished data.

Act Now Coalition: COVID Act Now, USA, info@covidactnow.org, https://covidactnow.org; U.S. COVID Tracker.

American Academy of Pediatrics (AAP), 345 Park Blvd., Itasca, IL, 60143, USA, (800) 433-9016, (847) 434-8000, mcc@aap.org, https://www.aap.org; Children and COVID-19: State-Level Data Report.

American Chemical Society (ACS), 1155 16th St. NW, Washington, DC, 20036, USA, (800) 227-5558, (202) 872-4600, help@services.acs.org, https://www.acs.org; Aerosol Filtration Efficiency of Common Fabrics Used in Respiratory Cloth Masks; Filtration Efficiencies of Nanoscale Aerosol by Cloth Mask Materials Used to Slow the Spread of SARS-CoV-2; and Household Materials Selection for Homemade Cloth Face Coverings and Their Filtration Efficiency Enhancement with Triboelectric Charging.

American Immigration Council, 1331 G St. NW , Ste. 200, Washington, DC, 20005, USA, (202) 507-7500, info@immcouncil.org, https://www.americanimmigrationcouncil.org/; Immigration and Covid-19 and Undocumented Immigrants and the Covid-19 Crisis.

American Psychological Association (APA), 750 First St. NE, Washington, DC, 20002-4242, USA, (800) 374-2721, (202) 336-5500, https://www.apa.org/; One Year On: Unhealthy Weight Gains, Increased Drinking Reported by Americans Coping with Pandemic Stress.

Biotechnology Innovation Organization (BIO), 1201 New York NW, Ste. 1300, Washington, DC, 20005, USA, (202) 962-9200, info@bio.org, https://www.bio.org/; BIO COVID-19 Therapeutic Development Tracker.

Board of Governors of the Federal Reserve System, Constitution Ave. NW, Washington, DC, 20551, USA, (202) 452-3000, (202) 263-4869 (TDD), https://www.federalreserve.gov; Reconciling Unemployment Claims with Job Losses in the First Months of the COVID-19 Crisis.

Boston Consulting Group (BCG), 200 Pier 4 Blvd., Boston, MA, 02210, USA, (617) 973-1200, https://www.bcg.com/; The Business Impact of COVID-19.

The Brookings Institution, 1775 Massachusetts Ave. NW, Washington, DC, 20036, USA, (202) 797-6000, communications@brookings.edu, https://www.brookings.edu/; Metro Recovery Index.

California Department of Public Health (CDPH), PO Box 997377, MS 0500, Sacramento, CA, 95899-7377, USA, (916) 558-1784, https://www.cdph.ca.gov; COVID-19 by the Numbers.

Center on Budget and Policy Priorities, 1275 First St. NE, Ste. 1200, Washington, DC, 20002, USA, (202) 408-1080, (202) 408-1056, center@cbpp.org, https://www.cbpp.org/; Tracking the COVID-19 Recession's Effects on Food, Housing, and Employment Hardships.

Civis Analytics, 200 W Monroe St., 22nd Fl., Chicago, IL, 60606, USA, https://www.civisanalytics.com/; COVID-19 Impact Research.

Climate Analytics, 135 Madison Ave., 5th Fl., Ste. 05-115, New York, NY, 10016, USA, info.ny@climateanalytics.org, https://climateanalytics.org/; 2 Steps Down the Debt Spiral: COVID-19 and Tropical Cyclones Severely Limit the Fiscal Space of Many Small Island Developing States.

Council on Criminal Justice (CCJ), National Commission on COVID-19 and Criminal Justice, 700 Pennsylvania Ave. SE, Washington, DC, 20020, USA, info@counciloncj.org, https://counciloncj.org/covid-19/; COVID-19 in U.S. State and Federal Prisons; Impact Report: COVID-19 and Prisons; and Impact Report: COVID-19 Testing in State Prisons.

The COVID Tracking Project at The Atlantic, support@covidtracking.com, https://covidtracking.com; The COVID Racial Data Tracker and COVID Tracking Project Data.

COVID-19 Forecast Hub, University of Massachusetts Amherst, Reich Lab, Amherst, MA, 10022, USA, https://covid19forecasthub.org; COVID-19 US Weekly Forecast Summary.

Democracy Fund Voter Study Group, 1200 17th St. NW, Ste. 300, Washington, DC, 20036, USA, (202) 420-7900, https://www.voterstudygroup.org/; COVID-19: Tracking American Perspectives.

District of Columbia Corrections Information Council (CIC), 1400 I St. NW, Ste. 400, Washington, DC, 20005, USA, (202) 478-9211, dccic@dc.gov, https://cic.dc.gov/page/about-cic; COVID-19 Survey Final Report.

Duke Global Health Institute, Center for Policy Impact in Global Health, 310 Trent Dr., Durham, NC, 27710, USA, (919) 613-6249, cpigh@duke.edu, https://centerforpolicyimpact.org; Achieving Global Mortality Reduction Targets and Universal Health Coverage: The Impact of COVID-19.

The Economist Group, 900 3rd Ave., 16th Fl., New York, NY, 10022, USA, (212) 541-0500, (202) 429-0890, customerhelp@economist.com, https://www.economistgroup.com; Covid-19 Data: The Global Normalcy Index.

Elsevier, Radarweg 29, Amsterdam, 1043 NX, NLD, https://www.elsevier.com; Novel Coronavirus Information Center.

Euromonitor International, Inc., 1 N Dearborn St., Ste. 1700, Chicago, IL, 60602, USA, (312) 922-1115, (312) 922-1157, info-usa@euromonitor.com, https://www.euromonitor.com/; The Impact of Coronavirus on Consumer Finance; The Impact of Coronavirus on Consumer Goods and Services in the Middle East; and The Impact of Coronavirus on Top 10 Global Consumer Trends 2020.

Federal Bureau of Prisons (BOP), 320 First St. NW, Washington, DC, 20534 , USA, (202) 307-3198, https://www.bop.gov/; Inmate COVID-19 Data: A Look at the Impact of COVID-19 on Individuals in Federal Custody.

FiveThirtyEight, 47 W 66th St., 2nd Fl., New York, NY, 10023, USA, contact@fivethirtyeight.com, https://fivethirtyeight.com/; Where the Latest COVID-19 Models Think We're Headed - And Why They Disagree.

Frontier Group, 1129 State St., No. 10, Santa Barbara, CA, 93101, USA, (805) 730-1391, https://frontiergroup.org/; Healthy Parks, Healthy People: The COVID-19 Pandemic Spotlights the Importance of Public Lands.

GISAID Initiative, Munich, GER, https://www.gisaid.org; Tracking of hCoV-19 Variants.

Global Change Data Lab, Our World in Data, GBR, info@ourworldindata.org, https://ourworldindata.org; Coronavirus Pandemic (COVID-19) and COVID-19 Database.

Harvard Global Health Institute (HGHI), 42 Church St., Cambridge, MA, 02138, USA, (617) 384-5431, globalhealth@harvard.edu, https://globalhealth.harvard.edu/; COVID Risk Levels Dashboard and COVID-19 Hospital Capacity Estimates 2020.

Harvard T.H. Chan School of Public Health, 677 Huntington Ave., Boston, MA, 02115, USA, (617) 495-1000, https://www.hsph.harvard.edu/; Air Pollution and COVID-19 Mortality in the United States: Strengths and Limitations of an Ecological Regression Analysis.

hc1, 6100 Technology Center Dr., Indianapolis, IN, 46278, USA, (317) 219-4646, info@hc1.com, https://www.hc1.com; CV19 Lab Testing Dashboard.

The Henry J. Kaiser Family Foundation (KFF), 185 Berry St., Ste. 2000, San Francisco, CA, 94107, USA, (650) 854-9400, (650) 854-4800, https://www.kff.org; About 1.5 Million Teachers Are at Higher Risk of Serious Illness From COVID-19; Almost One in Four Adult Workers Is Vulnerable to Severe Illness from COVID-19; The Implications of COVID-19 for Mental Health and Substance Use; KFF COVID-19 Vaccine Monitor: January 2022 Parents and Kids Update; KFF COVID-19 Vaccine Monitor: Views on the Pandemic at Two Years; KFF Health Tracking Poll: Coronavirus, Delayed Care and 2020 Election; KFF Health Tracking Poll: Coronavirus: Reopening, Schools, and the Government Response; More Than 3 Million People Age 65 or Older Live with School-Age Children, and Could Be at Heightened Risk of COVID-19 Infection if Children Bring the Virus Home from School; Rising Cases in Long-term Care Facilities Are Cause for Concern; State COVID-19 Data and Policy Actions; Temporary Enhanced Federal Medicaid Funding Can Soften the Economic Blow of the COVID-19 Pandemic on States, But Is Unlikely to Fully Offset State Revenue Declines or Forestall Budget Shortfalls; and Where are the COVID-19 Hotspots? Tracking State Outbreaks.

Human Cell Atlas (HCA), hca@humancellatlas.org, https://www.humancellatlas.org/; The Local and Systemic Response to SARS-CoV-2 Infection in Children and Adults and Pre-Activated Anti-Viral Innate Immunity in the Upper Airways Controls Early SARS-CoV-2 Infection in Children.

IDTechEx, One Boston Place, Ste. 2600, Boston, MA, 02108, USA, (617) 577-7890, (617) 577-7810, research@idtechex.com, https://www.idtechex.com/; 3D Printing and Additive Manufacturing 2022-2032: Technology and Market Outlook.

The Immigrant Learning Center (ILC), 442 Main St., Malden, MA, 02148-5177, USA, (781) 322-9777, (800) 439-2370 (TTY), (781) 321-1963, info@ilctr.org, https://www.ilctr.org/; Health and Financial Risks for Noncitizen Immigrants due to the COVID-19 Pandemic; Immigrant Detention and COVID-19: How a Pandemic Exploited and Spread through the US Immigrant Detention System; and Latinx Workers - Particularly Women - Face Devastating Job Losses in the COVID-19 Recession.

Imperial College London, South Kensington Campus, London, SW7 2AZ, GBR, https://www.imperial.ac.uk/; Estimating the Effects of Non-Pharmaceutical Interventions on COVID-19 in Europe.

Institute for Strategic Dialogue (ISD), PO Box 75769, London, SW1P 9ER, GBR, info@isdglobal.org, https://www.isdglobal.org/; The Conspiracy Consortium: Examining Discussions of COVID-19 Among Right-Wing Extremist Telegram Channels and Ill Advice: A Case Study in Facebook's Failure to Tackle COVID-19 Disinformation.

International Consortium of Investigative Journalists (ICIJ), 1730 Rhode Island Ave. NW, Ste. 317, Washington, DC, 20036, USA, (202) 808-3310, contact@icij.org, https://www.icij.org/; Indian Reporters Find New Ways to Expose 'Vaccine Inequity' and COVID-19 Data.

Ipsos, 360 Park Ave. S, 17th Fl., New York, NY, 10010, USA, (212) 265-3200, https://www.ipsos.com/en-us; Most Americans Not Worrying About COVID Going into 2022 Holidays.

Italian National Agency for New Technologies, Energy and Sustainable Economic Development (ENEA), Lungotevere Thaon di Revel, 76, Rome, 00196, ITA, https://www.enea.it/en; ENEA CRESCO in the Fight Against COVID-19.

Johns Hopkins Center for Health Security, 621 E Pratt St., Ste. 210, Baltimore, MD, 21202, USA, (443) 573-3304, (443) 573-3305, centerhealthsecurity@jhu.edu, https://www.centerforhealthsecurity.org/; COVID-19 Situation Reports.

Johns Hopkins Coronavirus Resource Center, 3400 N Charles St., Baltimore, MD, 21218, USA, https://coronavirus.jhu.edu/; COVID-19 Testing Insights Initiative and Testing Trends Tool: Track Trends in COVID-19 Cases and Tests.

La Jolla Institute for Immunology, 9420 Athena Circle, La Jolla, CA, 92037, USA, (858) 752-6500, https://www.lji.org; Database of Immune Cell Epigenomes (DICE).

The Lancet, 230 Park Ave., New York, NY, 10169, USA, (212) 633-3800, editorial@lancet.com, https://www.thelancet.com/; COVID-19 Resource Centre.

The Marshall Project, 156 W 56th St., 3rd Fl., New York, NY, 10019, USA, (212) 803-5200, info@themarshallproject.org, https://www.themarshallproject.org/; COVID Cases in Prisons and A State-By-State Look at 15 Months of Coronavirus in Prisons.

Massachusetts Institute of Technology (MIT), Living Wage Calculator, 77 Massachusetts Ave., Cambridge, MA, 02139, USA, (617) 324-6565, (617) 253-1000, amyglas@mit.edu, https://livingwage.mit.edu; Double Whammy: Essential Workers Threatened by Job Loss While Facing the Highest Risk of COVID Infection.

McKinsey & Company, 725 Ponce de Leon Ave., Ste. 700, Atlanta, GA, 30306, USA, (404) 335-3000, (404) 521-1743, https://www.mckinsey.com; Tracking the Impact of COVID-19.

National Academies of Sciences, Engineering, and Medicine (The National Academies), 500 5th St. NW, Washington, DC, 20001, USA, (202) 334-2000, contact@nas.edu, https://www.nationalacademies.org/; Rapid Expert Consultation on SARS-CoV-2 Viral Shedding and Antibody Response for the COVID-19 Pandemic; Rapid Expert Consultation on the Effectiveness of Fabric Masks for the COVID-19 Pandemic; and Rapid Expert Consultation on the Possibility of Bioaerosol Spread of SARS-CoV-2 for the COVID-19 Pandemic.

National Academy of Social Insurance (NASI), 1441 L St. NW, Ste. 530, Washington, DC, 20005, USA, (202) 452-8097, (202) 452-8111, nasi@nasi.org, https://www.nasi.org; The Impact of the COVID-19 Pandemic on Access to Health Care.

National Bureau of Economic Research (NBER), 1050 Massachusetts Ave., Cambridge, MA, 02138, USA, (617) 868-3900, info@nber.org, https://www.nber.org/; Misinformation During a Pandemic.

National Highway Traffic Safety Administration (NHTSA), National Center for Statistics and Analysis (NCSA), 1200 New Jersey Ave. SE, West Bldg., Washington, DC, 20590, USA, (800) 934-8517, (202) 366-2746, ncsarequests@dot.gov, https://www.nhtsa.gov/research-data/national-center-statistics-and-analysis-ncsa; Update to Special Reports on Traffic Safety During the COVID-19 Public Health Emergency.

National Women's Law Center (NWLC), 1350 I St. NW, Ste. 700, Washington, DC, 20005, USA, (202) 588-5180, https://nwlc.org; A Year of Strength & Loss: The Pandemic, the Economy, & the Value of Women's Work.

New York University School of Law, Institute for Policy Integrity, 139 MacDougal St., Wilf Hall, 3rd Fl., New York, NY, 10012, USA, (212) 992-8932, (212) 995-4592, https://policyintegrity.org/; Weakening Our Defenses: How the Trump Administration's Deregulatory Push Has Exacerbated the Covid-19 Pandemic.

NewClimate Institute, Waidmarkt 11a, Cologne, D-50676, GER, info@newclimate.org, https://newclimate.org/; Exploring the Impact of the COVID-19 Pandemic on Global Emission Projections.

Oxford University Centre for the Environment, Centre for Research into Energy Demand Solutions (CREDS), South Parks Rd., Oxford, OX1 3QY, GBR, credsadmin@ouce.ox.ac.uk, https://www.creds.ac.uk; House of Lords Covid Committee: Inquiry into the Long-Term Impact of the Pandemic on the UK's Towns and Cities.

Pew Research Center, 1615 L St. NW, Ste. 800, Washington, DC, 20036, USA, (202) 419-4300, (202) 857-8562, info@pewresearch.org, https://www.pewresearch.org/; American News Pathways Data Tool and U.S. Labor Market Inches Back From the COVID-19 Shock, But Recovery Is Far From Complete.

Pew Research Center, Internet & Technology, 1615 L St. NW, Ste. 800, Washington, DC, 20036, USA, (202) 419-4300, (202) 857-8562, https://www.pewresearch.org/topic/internet-technology/; The Internet and the Pandemic.

Prison Policy Initiative, PO Box 127, Northampton, MA, 01061, USA, https://www.prisonpolicy.org/; Mass Incarceration, COVID-19, and Community Spread.

ProPublica, 155 Avenue of the Americas, 13th Fl., New York, NY, 10013, USA, (212) 514-5250, (212) 785-2634, hello@propublica.org, https://www.propublica.org/; Hazardous Air Pollutant Exposure as a Contributing Factor to COVID-19 Mortality in the United States.

Robert Wood Johnson Foundation (RWJF), 50 College Rd. E, Princeton, NJ, 08540-6614, USA, (877) 843-7953, (609) 627-6000, https://www.rwjf.org/; Marketplace Pulse: COVID-19 and the Coverage Gap.

SAGE Publications, 2455 Teller Rd., Thousand Oaks, CA, 91320, USA, (800) 818-7243, (800) 583-2665, journals@sagepub.com, https://www.sagepub.com; Experimental Biology and Medicine - The Role of Chest Computed Tomography in the Management of COVID-19: A Review of Results and Recommendations and Palliative Medicine - End-of-Life Care in COVID-19: An Audit of Pharmacological Management in Hospital Inpatients.

Save the Children, 501 Kings Hwy. E, Ste. 400, Fairfield, CT, 06825, USA, (203) 221-4000, (800) 728-3843, https://www.savethechildren.org/; Childhood in the Time of COVID: U.S. Complement to the Global Childhood Report 2021.

State Health Access Data Assistance Center (SHADAC), 2221 University Ave. SE, Ste. 345, Minneapolis, MN, 55414, USA, (612) 624-4802, (612) 624-1493, shadac@umn.edu, https://www.shadac.org/; 90 Percent of U.S. Adults Report Increased Stress Due to Coronavirus Pandemic; Coronavirus Pandemic Caused More than 10 million U.S. Adults to Lose Health Insurance; and Emergency Flexibility for States to Increase and Maintain Medicaid Eligibility for LTSS under COVID-19.

U.S. Census Bureau, 4600 Silver Hill Rd., Washington, DC, 20233, USA, (301) 763-4636, (800) 923-8282, https://www.census.gov; Measuring Household Experiences During the Coronavirus Pandemic: Household Pulse Survey.

U.S. Department of Health and Human Services (HHS), National Institutes of Health (NIH), National Center for Advancing Translational Sciences (NCATS), 31 Center Dr., Ste. 3B11, Bethesda, MD, 20892-2128, USA, (301) 594-8966, info@ncats.nih.gov, https://ncats.nih.gov/; OpenData COVID-19 Portal.

U.S. Department of Health and Human Services (HHS), National Institutes of Health (NIH), Office of Data Science Strategy (ODSS), 9000 Rockville Pike, Bethesda, MD, 20892, USA, (301) 827-7212, datascience@nih.gov, https://datascience.nih.gov/; Open-Access Data and Computational Resources to Address COVID-19.

U.S. Department of Health and Human Services (HHS), U.S. National Library of Medicine (NLM), National Center for Biotechnology Information (NCBI), 8600 Rockville Pike, Bethesda, MD, 20894, USA, info@ncbi.nlm.nih.gov, https://www.ncbi.nlm.nih.gov; NCBI SARS-CoV-2 Resources.

U.S. Department of Health and Human Services, Centers for Disease Control and Prevention (CDC), 1600 Clifton Rd., Atlanta, GA, 30329-4027, USA, (800) 232-4636, (888) 232-6348 (TTY), cdcinfo@cdc.gov, https://www.cdc.gov; COVID Data Tracker; COVID Data Tracker Weekly Review; COVID-19 Case Surveillance Public Use Data Profile; COVID-19 Forecasts: Deaths; COVID-19 Vaccine Breakthrough Infections Reported to CDC - United States, January 1-April 30, 2021; COVID-19: U.S. Impact on Antimicrobial Resistance; Detection of Severe Acute Respiratory Syndrome Coronavirus 2 RNA on Surfaces in Quarantine Rooms; Effectiveness of a COVID-19 Additional Primary or Booster Vaccine Dose in Preventing SARS-CoV-2 Infection Among Nursing Home Residents During Widespread Circulation of the Omicron Variant - United States, February 14 - March 27, 2022; Efficacy of Portable Air Cleaners and Masking for Reducing Indoor Exposure to Simulated Exhaled SARS-CoV-2 Aerosols - United States, 2021; Emergency Department Visits for COVID-19 by Race and Ethnicity - 13 States, October - December 2020; Emergency Department Visits for Suspected Suicide Attempts Among Persons Aged 12-25 Years Before and During the COVID-19 Pandemic - United States, January 2019 - May 2021; Mask Use and Ventilation Improvements to Reduce COVID-19 Incidence in Elementary Schools - Georgia, November 16 - December 11, 2020; Mass Testing for SARS-CoV-2 in 16 Prisons and Jails - Six Jurisdictions, United States, April-May 2020; Provisional COVID-19 Deaths: Distribution of Deaths by Race and Hispanic Origin; Sexual Orientation Disparities in Risk Factors for Adverse COVID-19-Related Outcomes, by Race/Ethnicity - Behavioral Risk Factor Surveillance System, United States, 2017-2019; Symptoms of Anxiety or Depressive Disorder and Use of Mental Health Care Among Adults During the COVID-19 Pandemic - United States, August 2020 - February 2021; and Trends in Racial and Ethnic Disparities in COVID-19 Hospitalizations, by Region - United States, March - December 2020.

U.S. Department of Health and Human Services, Centers for Disease Control and Prevention (CDC), Coronavirus Disease 2019 (COVID-19)-Associated Hospitalization Surveillance Network (COVID-NET), 1600 Clifton Rd., Atlanta, GA, 30329-4027, USA, (800) 232-4636, cdcinfo@cdc.gov, https://www.cdc.gov/coronavirus/2019-ncov/covid-data/covid-net/purpose-methods.html; Hospitalizations of Children and Adolescents with Laboratory-Confirmed COVID-19 - COVID-NET, 14 States, July 2021-January 2022 and Laboratory-Confirmed COVID-19-Associated Hospitalizations.

U.S. Department of Health and Human Services, Centers for Disease Control and Prevention (CDC), National Center for Health Statistics (NCHS), 3311 Toledo Rd., Hyattsville, MD, 20782-2064, USA, (800) 232-4636, (301) 458-4000, https://www.cdc.gov/nchs; COVID-19 Death Data and Resources; Household Pulse Survey: Anxiety and Depression; Household Pulse Survey: Health Insurance Coverage; Household Pulse Survey: Mental Health Care; Household Pulse Survey: Reduced Access to Care; and Household Pulse Survey: Telemedicine Use.

U.S. Department of Homeland Security (DHS), Federal Emergency Management Agency (FEMA), PO Box 10055, Hyattsville, MD, 20782-8055, USA, (202) 646-2500, https://www.fema.gov/; Coronavirus Disease (COVID-19) Initial Assessment Report.

U.S. Department of State (DOS), 2201 C St. NW, Washington, DC, 20520, USA, (202) 647-4000, ofm-info@state.gov, https://www.state.gov; Update: The United States Continues to Lead the Global Response to COVID-19.

U.S. Department of Transportation (DOT), Federal Railroad Administration (FRA), 1200 New Jersey Ave. SE, Washington, DC, 20590, USA, (202) 366-4000, (202) 493-6014, (202) 493-6481, frapa@dot.gov, https://railroads.dot.gov/; Coronavirus (COVID-19) Information from the FRA.

UK Health Security Agency (UKHSA), Nobel House, 17 Smith Sq., London, SW1P 3JR, GBR, enquiries@ukhsa.gov.uk, https://www.gov.uk/government/organisations/uk-health-security-agency; COVID-19 Vaccine Surveillance Reports and COVID-19 Variants: Genomically Confirmed Case Numbers.

UNICEF, 3 United Nations Plz., New York, NY, 10017, USA, (212) 303-7984, (917) 244-2215, https://www.unicef.org; COVID-19 and Children: UNICEF Data Hub.

Uniformed Services University, Department of Psychiatry, Center for the Study of Traumatic Stress (CSTS), 4301 Jones Bridge Rd., Bethesda, MD, 20814-4799, USA, cstsinfo@usuhs.edu, https://www.cstsonline.org/; Annals for Hospitalists Inpatient Notes - Preparing for Battle: How Hospitalists Can Manage the Stress of COVID-19.

United Kingdom Office for National Statistics (ONS), Cardiff Rd., Government Bldgs., Rm. D265 , Newport, NP10 8XG, GBR, info@ons.gsi.gov.uk, https://www.ons.gov.uk/; COVID-19 Infection Survey.

United Nations Human Settlements Programme (UN-HABITAT), PO Box 30030, Nairobi, 00100, KEN, unhabitat-info@un.org, https://unhabitat.org/; Cities and Pandemics: Towards a More Just, Green and Healthy Future.

United Nations UN Women, 405 E 42nd St., New York, NY, 10017-3599, USA, (646) 781-4400, (646) 781-4444, https://www.unwomen.org; COVID-19: Emerging Gender Data and Why it Matters and From Insights to Action: Gender Equality in the Wake of COVID-19.

University of California Los Angeles (UCLA) School of Law, Covid-19 Behind Bars Data Project, 385 Charles E. Young Dr. E, Los Angeles, CA, 90095, USA, (310) 206-5568, covidbehindbars@law.ucla.edu, https://uclacovidbehindbars.org; Covid Behind Bars Data Project; Georgia Custodial Death Records Summary Report; In California Jails, Sherrifs Have Been Left in Charge of Covid Mitigation. The Results Have Been Disastrous.; Racial And Ethnic Inequalities in COVID-19 Mortality Within Carceral Settings: An Analysis of Texas Prisons; and What We Won't Know When the Next Surge Arrives.

University of California Los Angeles (UCLA), Luskin Center for Innovation, 3323 Public Affairs Bldg., PO Box 951656, Los Angeles, CA, 90095-1656, USA, (310) 267-5435, (310) 267-5443, https://innovation.luskin.ucla.edu/; Keeping the Lights and Heat On: COVID-19 Utility Debt in Communities Served by Pacific Gas and Electric Company.

University of California, Berkeley, Global Policy Lab, California Memorial Stadium, 2227 Piedmont Ave., Berkeley, CA, 94720, USA, (510) 643-5751, https://www.globalpolicy.science/; Public Mobility Data Enables COVID-19 Forecasting and Management at Local and Global Scales.

University of Minnesota, Center for Infectious Disease Research and Policy (CIDRAP), Office of the Vice President for Research, 420 Delaware St. SE, MMC 263, C315 Mayo, Minneapolis, MN, 55455, USA, (612) 626-6770, (612) 626-6783, https://www.cidrap.umn.edu/; Novel Coronavirus (COVID-19) Resource Center.

University of Washington, Institute for Health Metrics and Evaluation (IHME), Population Health Building/Hans Rosling Center, UW Campus Box 351615, 3980 15th Ave. NE, Seattle, WA, 98195, USA, (206) 897-2800, (206) 897-2899, engage@healthdata.org, https://www.healthdata.org; Estimation of Excess Mortality Due to COVID-19; Global Access to Handwashing: Implications for COVID-19 Control in Low-Income Countries; and Vaccine Hesitancy by County.

The Urban Institute, 500 L'Enfant Plaza SW, Washington, DC, 20024, USA, (202) 833-7200, https://

www.urban.org/; Local Government Efforts to Mitigate the Novel Coronavirus Pandemic Among Older Adults.

Western Washington University, Border Policy Research Institute (BPRI), 516 High St., Bellingham, WA, 98225, USA, (360) 650-3000, laurie.trautman@wwu.edu, https://bpri.wwu.edu/; COVID-19 and the US-Canada Border.

World Health Organization (WHO), Ave. Appia 20, Geneva, CH-1211, SWI, (202) 974-3000 (Telephone in U.S.), publications@who.int, https://www.who.int/; Advice on the Use of Masks in the Context of COVID-19; Coronavirus Disease (COVID-19) Situation Report; Global Health Observatory (GHO) Data; and Global Research on Coronavirus Disease (COVID-19).

World Health Organization (WHO), Pan American Health Organization (PAHO), 525 23rd St. NW, Washington, DC, 20037, USA, (202) 974-3000, (202) 974-3663, pubrights@paho.org, https://www.paho.org; A New Agenda for Mental Health in the Americas: Report of the Pan American Health Organization High-Level Commission on Mental Health and COVID-19.

Worldometer, https://www.worldometers.info/; COVID-19 Coronavirus Pandemic.

Yale University, Tobin Center for Economic Policy, 37 Hillhouse Ave., New Haven, CT, 06520, USA, tobincenter@yale.edu, https://tobin.yale.edu/; Employment Effects of Unemployment Insurance Generosity During the Pandemic.

COVID-19 (DISEASE)-PATIENTS

African Women's Development and Communication Network (FEMNET), 12 Masaba Rd., Lowerhill, PO Box 54562, Nairobi, 00200, KEN, admin@femnet.or.ke, https://femnet.org; Qualitative Study on the Impact of COVID-19 on Sexual and Reproductive Health and Rights (SRHR) of Women & Girls in Africa.

American Association of Retired Persons (AARP) Public Policy Institute (PPI), 601 E St. NW, Washington, DC, 20049, USA, (202) 434-3840, ppi@aarp.org, https://www.aarp.org/ppi; Estimating Impacts of Pandemic-Related Job Loss on Health Insurance Coverage Among Adults Ages 50 to 64 During the First Year of COVID-19.

American Civil Liberties Union (ACLU), 125 Broad St. , 18th Fl., New York, NY, 10004, USA, (212) 549-2500, https://www.aclu.org/; COVID-19 Model Finds Nearly 100,000 More Deaths Than Current Estimates, Due to Failures to Reduce Jails.

Council on Criminal Justice (CCJ), National Commission on COVID-19 and Criminal Justice, 700 Pennsylvania Ave. SE, Washington, DC, 20020, USA, info@counciloncj.org, https://counciloncj.org/covid-19/; COVID-19 in U.S. State and Federal Prisons; Impact Report: COVID-19 and Prisons; Impact Report: COVID-19 and SUD Treatment; and Impact Report: COVID-19 Testing in State Prisons.

The Henry J. Kaiser Family Foundation (KFF), 185 Berry St., Ste. 2000, San Francisco, CA, 94107, USA, (650) 854-9400, (650) 854-4800, https://www.kff.org; KFF COVID-19 Vaccine Monitor: The Pandemic's Toll on Workers and Family Finances During the Omicron Surge and Long COVID: What Do the Latest Data Show?.

The Marshall Project, 156 W 56th St., 3rd Fl., New York, NY, 10019, USA, (212) 803-5200, info@themarshallproject.org, https://www.themarshallproject.org/; A State-By-State Look at 15 Months of Coronavirus in Prisons.

McKinsey & Company, 725 Ponce de Leon Ave., Ste. 700, Atlanta, GA, 30306, USA, (404) 335-3000, (404) 521-1743, https://www.mckinsey.com; Tracking the Impact of COVID-19.

NielsenIQ (NIQ), 200 W Jackson Blvd., Chicago, IL, 60606, USA, https://nielseniq.com; Covid-Positive Households Are Altering Their Eating Habits.

U.S. Department of Health and Human Services (HHS), National Institutes of Health (NIH), Researching COVID to Enhance Recovery (RECOVER), 9000 Rockville Pike, Bethesda, MD, 20892, USA, (301) 496-4000, (301) 402-9612 (TTY), https://recovercovid.org; Can Multisystem Inflammatory Syndrome in Children Be Managed in the Outpatient Setting? An EHR-Based Cohort Study From the RECOVER Program; Development of a Definition of Postacute Sequelae of SARS-CoV-2 Infection; Racial/Ethnic Disparities in Post-Acute Sequelae of SARS-CoV-2 Infection in New York: An EHR-Based Cohort Study from the RECOVER Program; and Risk of Post-Acute Sequelae of SARS-CoV-2 Infection Associated with Pre-Coronavirus Disease Obstructive Sleep Apnea Diagnoses: An Electronic Health Record-Based Analysis from the RECOVER Initiative.

U.S. Department of Health and Human Services (HHS), Office of Inspector General (OIG), 330 Independence Ave. SW, Washington, DC, 20201, USA, (877) 696-6775, public.affairs@oig.hhs.gov, https://oig.hhs.gov/; COVID-19 Had a Devastating Impact on Medicare Beneficiaries in Nursing Homes During 2020.

U.S. Department of Health and Human Services, Centers for Disease Control and Prevention (CDC), 1600 Clifton Rd., Atlanta, GA, 30329-4027, USA, (800) 232-4636, (888) 232-6348 (TTY), cdcinfo@cdc.gov, https://www.cdc.gov; COVID Data Tracker; COVID Data Tracker: Rates of COVID-19 Cases and Deaths by Vaccination Status; COVID-19 Forecasts: Deaths; Emergency Department Visits for COVID-19 by Race and Ethnicity - 13 States, October - December 2020; Nearly One in Five American Adults Who Have Had COVID-19 Still Have Long COVID; Provisional COVID-19 Deaths: Distribution of Deaths by Race and Hispanic Origin; Rates of COVID-19 Cases or Deaths by Age Group and Vaccination Status and Booster Dose; and Trends in Racial and Ethnic Disparities in COVID-19 Hospitalizations, by Region - United States, March - December 2020.

U.S. Department of Health and Human Services, Centers for Disease Control and Prevention (CDC), Coronavirus Disease 2019 (COVID-19)-Associated Hospitalization Surveillance Network (COVID-NET), 1600 Clifton Rd., Atlanta, GA, 30329-4027, USA, (800) 232-4636, cdcinfo@cdc.gov, https://www.cdc.gov/coronavirus/2019-ncov/covid-data/covid-net/purpose-methods.html; Hospitalization Rates and Characteristics of Children Aged Less than 18 Years Hospitalized with Laboratory-Confirmed COVID-19 - COVID-NET, 14 States, March 1-July 25, 2020; Hospitalizations of Children and Adolescents with Laboratory-Confirmed COVID-19 - COVID-NET, 14 States, July 2021-January 2022; and Laboratory-Confirmed COVID-19-Associated Hospitalizations.

U.S. Department of Health and Human Services, Centers for Disease Control and Prevention (CDC), National Center for Health Statistics (NCHS), 3311 Toledo Rd., Hyattsville, MD, 20782-2064, USA, (800) 232-4636, (301) 458-4000, https://www.cdc.gov/nchs; Excess Deaths Associated with COVID-19 and Household Pulse Survey: Telemedicine Use.

UK Health Security Agency (UKHSA), Nobel House, 17 Smith Sq., London, SW1P 3JR, GBR, enquiries@ukhsa.gov.uk, https://www.gov.uk/government/organisations/uk-health-security-agency; COVID-19 Variants: Genomically Confirmed Case Numbers.

University of Washington, Institute for Health Metrics and Evaluation (IHME), Population Health Building/Hans Rosling Center, UW Campus Box 351615, 3980 15th Ave. NE, Seattle, WA, 98195, USA, (206) 897-2800, (206) 897-2899, engage@healthdata.org, https://www.healthdata.org; Estimated Global Proportions of Individuals With Persistent Fatigue, Cognitive, and Respiratory Symptom Clusters Following Symptomatic COVID-19 in 2020 and 2021 and Estimation of Excess Mortality Due to COVID-19.

World Health Organization (WHO), Ave. Appia 20, Geneva, CH-1211, SWI, (202) 974-3000 (Telephone in U.S.), publications@who.int, https://www.who.int/; Global Excess Deaths Associated with COVID-19, January 2020 - December 2021.

COVID-19 (DISEASE)-PREVENTION

Brown School of Public Health, Global Epidemics, 121 South Main St., Providence, RI, 02903, USA, (401) 863-3375, https://globalepidemics.org/; Vaccine Preventable Deaths Analysis.

Commonwealth Fund, 1 E 75th St., New York, NY, 10021, USA, (212) 606-3800 , info@cmwf.org, https://www.commonwealthfund.org/; Two Years of U.S. COVID-19 Vaccines Have Prevented Millions of Hospitalizations and Deaths.

Council on Criminal Justice (CCJ), National Commission on COVID-19 and Criminal Justice, 700 Pennsylvania Ave. SE, Washington, DC, 20020, USA, info@counciloncj.org, https://counciloncj.org/covid-19/; Impact Report: COVID-19 Testing in State Prisons.

Global Change Data Lab, Our World in Data, GBR, info@ourworldindata.org, https://ourworldindata.org; Which Countries Have Protected Both Health and the Economy in the Pandemic?.

The Henry J. Kaiser Family Foundation (KFF), 185 Berry St., Ste. 2000, San Francisco, CA, 94107, USA, (650) 854-9400, (650) 854-4800, https://www.kff.org; KFF COVID-19 Vaccine Monitor and KFF COVID-19 Vaccine Monitor: The Increasing Importance of Partisanship in Predicting COVID-19 Vaccination Status.

Imperial College London, School of Public Health, MRC Centre for Global Infectious Disease Analysis, Medical School Bldg., Norfolk Place, London, W2 1PG, GBR, mrc.gida@imperial.ac.uk, https://www.imperial.ac.uk/mrc-global-infectious-disease-analysis/; Evaluation of Individual and Ensemble Probabilistic Forecasts of COVID-19 Mortality in the United States and Genetic Evidence for the Association Between COVID-19 Epidemic Severity and Timing of Non-Pharmaceutical Interventions.

KFF Health News, 1330 G St. NW, Washington, DC, 20005, USA, (202) 347-5270, https://khn.org/; Medicaid Vaccination Rates Founder as States Struggle to Immunize Their Poorest Residents.

McKinsey & Company, 725 Ponce de Leon Ave., Ste. 700, Atlanta, GA, 30306, USA, (404) 335-3000, (404) 521-1743, https://www.mckinsey.com; Fast-Forward: Will the Speed of COVID-19 Vaccine Development Reset Industry Norms?.

Media Matters for America, PO Box 44811, Washington, DC, 20026, USA, (202) 756-4100, action@mediamatters.org, https://www.mediamatters.org; Fox Has Undermined Vaccination Efforts in Nearly 60% of All Vaccination Segments in a 2-Week Period.

National Nurses United (NNU), 8455 Colesville Rd., Ste. 1100, Silver Spring, MD, 20910, USA, (240) 235-2000, (240) 235-2019, info@nationalnursesunited.org, https://www.nationalnursesunited.org; Deadly Shame: Redressing the Devaluation of Registered Nurse Labor Through Pandemic Equity and Sins of Omission: How Government Failures to Track Covid-19 Data Have Led to More Than 3,200 Health Care Worker Deaths and Jeopardize Public Health.

Pew Research Center, Religion & Public Life, 1615 L St. NW, Ste. 800, Washington, DC, 20036, USA, (202) 419-4300, (202) 857-8562, https://www.pewforum.org/; How COVID-19 Restrictions Affected Religious Groups Around the World in 2020.

Public Religion Research Institute (PRRI), 1023 15th St. NW, 9th Fl., Washington, DC, 20005, USA, (202) 238-9424, info@prri.org, https://www.prri.org/; Religious Identities and the Race Against the Virus: Engaging Faith Communities on COVID-19 Vaccination.

Rockefeller Foundation, 420 5th Ave., New York, NY, 10018, USA, (212) 869-8500, https://www.rockefellerfoundation.org; Implementing Covid-19 Routine Testing in K-12 Schools: Lessons and Recommendations from Pilot Sites.

Statistics Poland, Aleja Niepodleglosci 208, Warsaw, 00-925, POL, kancelariaogolnagus@stat.gov.pl, https://stat.gov.pl/en/; Production of Industrial

Products Related to the Prevention of Spreading/ Combating COVID-19 in March 2022.

U.S. Department of Health and Human Services, Centers for Disease Control and Prevention (CDC), 1600 Clifton Rd., Atlanta, GA, 30329-4027, USA, (800) 232-4636, (888) 232-6348 (TTY), cdcinfo@cdc.gov, https://www.cdc.gov; COVID Data Tracker; COVID Data Tracker: Rates of COVID-19 Cases and Deaths by Vaccination Status; Early Estimates of Bivalent mRNA Vaccine Effectiveness in Preventing COVID-19-Associated Emergency Department or Urgent Care Encounters and Hospitalizations Among Immunocompetent Adults - VISION Network, Nine States, September-November 2022; Efficacy of Portable Air Cleaners and Masking for Reducing Indoor Exposure to Simulated Exhaled SARS-CoV-2 Aerosols - United States, 2021; Mask Use and Ventilation Improvements to Reduce COVID-19 Incidence in Elementary Schools - Georgia, November 16 - December 11, 2020; and SARS-CoV-2 Incidence in K-12 School Districts with Mask-Required Versus Mask-Optional Policies: Arkansas, August-October 2021.

U.S. Department of State (DOS), 2201 C St. NW, Washington, DC, 20520, USA, (202) 647-4000, ofminfo@state.gov, https://www.state.gov; Update: The United States Continues to Lead the Global Response to COVID-19.

UK Health Security Agency (UKHSA), Nobel House, 17 Smith Sq., London, SW1P 3JR, GBR, enquiries@ukhsa.gov.uk, https://www.gov.uk/government/organisations/uk-health-security-agency; COVID-19 Vaccine Surveillance Reports and Effectiveness of COVID-19 Vaccines Against the B.1.617.2 Variant.

University of California Los Angeles (UCLA), Center for Health Policy Research (CHPR), 10960 Wilshire Blvd., Ste. 1550, Campus Mail Code 714346, Los Angeles, CA, 90024, USA, (310) 794-0909, (310) 794-2686, healthpolicy@ucla.edu, https://healthpolicy.ucla.edu; Coronavirus Disease 2019 and the Case to Cover Undocumented Immigrants in California (Health Equity).

University of Washington, Institute for Health Metrics and Evaluation (IHME), Population Health Building/ Hans Rosling Center, UW Campus Box 351615, 3980 15th Ave. NE, Seattle, WA, 98195, USA, (206) 897-2800, (206) 897-2899, engage@healthdata.org, https://www.healthdata.org; Vaccine Hesitancy by County.

COVID-19 (DISEASE)-TREATMENT

Consumer Technology Association (CTA), 1919 S Eads St., Arlington, VA, 22202, USA, (703) 907-7600, (866) 858-1555, (703) 907-7675, cta@cta.tech, https://www.cta.tech; The Future of Telehealth and Remote Patient Monitoring in the Age of COVID-19.

Council on Criminal Justice (CCJ), National Commission on COVID-19 and Criminal Justice, 700 Pennsylvania Ave. SE, Washington, DC, 20020, USA, info@counciloncj.org, https://counciloncj.org/covid-19/; COVID-19 in U.S. State and Federal Prisons and Impact Report: COVID-19 and Prisons.

Physicians for Human Rights (PHR), 256 W 38th St., 9th Fl., New York, NY, 10018, USA, (646) 564-3720, (646) 564-3750, https://phr.org/; Silenced and Endangered: Clinicians' Human Rights and Health Concerns about Their Facilities' Response to COVID-19.

U.S. Department of Health and Human Services (HHS), National Institutes of Health (NIH), Researching COVID to Enhance Recovery (RECOVER), 9000 Rockville Pike, Bethesda, MD, 20892, USA, (301) 496-4000, (301) 402-9612 (TTY), https://recovercovid.org; Can Multisystem Inflammatory Syndrome in Children Be Managed in the Outpatient Setting? An EHR-Based Cohort Study From the RECOVER Program; Development of a Definition of Postacute Sequelae of SARS-CoV-2 Infection; Racial/Ethnic Disparities in Post-Acute Sequelae of SARS-CoV-2 Infection in New York: An EHR-Based Cohort Study from the RECOVER Program; and Risk of Post-Acute Sequelae of SARS-CoV-2 Infection Associated with Pre-Coronavirus Disease Obstructive Sleep Apnea Diagnoses: An Electronic Health Record-Based Analysis from the RECOVER Initiative.

U.S. Department of Health and Human Services, Centers for Disease Control and Prevention (CDC), 1600 Clifton Rd., Atlanta, GA, 30329-4027, USA, (800) 232-4636, (888) 232-6348 (TTY), cdcinfo@cdc.gov, https://www.cdc.gov; Trends in Racial and Ethnic Disparities in COVID-19 Hospitalizations, by Region - United States, March - December 2020.

U.S. Department of Health and Human Services, Centers for Disease Control and Prevention (CDC), Coronavirus Disease 2019 (COVID-19)-Associated Hospitalization Surveillance Network (COVID-NET), 1600 Clifton Rd., Atlanta, GA, 30329-4027, USA, (800) 232-4636, cdcinfo@cdc.gov, https://www.cdc.gov/coronavirus/2019-ncov/covid-data/covid-net/purpose-methods.html; Hospitalization Rates and Characteristics of Children Aged Less than 18 Years Hospitalized with Laboratory-Confirmed COVID-19 - COVID-NET, 14 States, March 1-July 25, 2020; Hospitalizations of Children and Adolescents with Laboratory-Confirmed COVID-19 - COVID-NET, 14 States, July 2021-January 2022; and Laboratory-Confirmed COVID-19-Associated Hospitalizations.

U.S. Department of Health and Human Services, Centers for Disease Control and Prevention (CDC), National Center for Health Statistics (NCHS), 3311 Toledo Rd., Hyattsville, MD, 20782-2064, USA, (800) 232-4636, (301) 458-4000, https://www.cdc.gov/nchs; Household Pulse Survey: Telemedicine Use.

COVID-19 (DISEASE)-VACCINES

American Association for the Advancement of Science (AAAS), 1200 New York Ave. NW, Washington, DC, 20005, USA, (202) 326-6400, https://www.aaas.org; Science Immunology.

Center for Countering Digital Hate (CCDH), Langley House, Park Rd. , East Finchley, London, N2 8EY, GBR, info@counterhate.com, https://www.counterhate.com; The Disinformation Dozen: Why Platforms Must Act on Twelve Leading Online Anti-Vaxxers and Malgorithm: How Instagram's Algorithm Publishes Misinformation and Hate to Millions During a Pandemic.

Commonwealth Fund, 1 E 75th St., New York, NY, 10021, USA, (212) 606-3800 , info@cmwf.org, https://www.commonwealthfund.org/; Two Years of U.S. COVID-19 Vaccines Have Prevented Millions of Hospitalizations and Deaths.

Global Change Data Lab, Our World in Data, GBR, info@ourworldindata.org, https://ourworldindata.org; Coronavirus (COVID-19) Vaccinations.

The Henry J. Kaiser Family Foundation (KFF), 185 Berry St., Ste. 2000, San Francisco, CA, 94107, USA, (650) 854-9400, (650) 854-4800, https://www.kff.org; KFF COVID-19 Vaccine Monitor; KFF COVID-19 Vaccine Monitor: January 2022 Parents and Kids Update; KFF COVID-19 Vaccine Monitor: The Increasing Importance of Partisanship in Predicting COVID-19 Vaccination Status; and KFF COVID-19 Vaccine Monitor: Views on the Pandemic at Two Years.

KFF Health News, 1330 G St. NW, Washington, DC, 20005, USA, (202) 347-5270, https://khn.org/; Medicaid Vaccination Rates Founder as States Struggle to Immunize Their Poorest Residents.

McKinsey & Company, 725 Ponce de Leon Ave., Ste. 700, Atlanta, GA, 30306, USA, (404) 335-3000, (404) 521-1743, https://www.mckinsey.com; Fast-Forward: Will the Speed of COVID-19 Vaccine Development Reset Industry Norms?.

Media Matters for America, PO Box 44811, Washington, DC, 20026, USA, (202) 756-4100, action@mediamatters.org, https://www.mediamatters.org; Fox Has Undermined Vaccination Efforts in Nearly 60% of All Vaccination Segments in a 2-Week Period.

NewsGuard, 25 W 52nd St., 15th Fl., New York, NY, 10019, USA, https://www.newsguardtech.com/; COVID-19 Vaccine Misinformation Targeting Children, Teenagers and Parents on Social Media: A Report for Governments and the WHO.

Public Religion Research Institute (PRRI), 1023 15th St. NW, 9th Fl., Washington, DC, 20005, USA, (202) 238-9424, info@prri.org, https://www.prri.org/; Religious Identities and the Race Against the Virus: Engaging Faith Communities on COVID-19 Vaccination.

U.S. Department of Health and Human Services, Centers for Disease Control and Prevention (CDC), 1600 Clifton Rd., Atlanta, GA, 30329-4027, USA, (800) 232-4636, (888) 232-6348 (TTY), cdcinfo@cdc.gov, https://www.cdc.gov; COVID Data Tracker: Rates of COVID-19 Cases and Deaths by Vaccination Status; COVID-19 Bivalent Booster Vaccination Coverage and Intent to Receive Booster Vaccination Among Adolescents and Adults - United States, November-December 2022; COVID-19 Primary Series and Booster Dose Vaccination Coverage Among Pregnant Individuals by Key Demographics, High-Risk Conditions for Severe Illness from COVID-19, Pregnancy Comorbidities, and Timing of Vaccination - United States, January 2022-April 202; Early Estimates of Bivalent mRNA Vaccine Effectiveness in Preventing COVID-19-Associated Emergency Department or Urgent Care Encounters and Hospitalizations Among Immunocompetent Adults - VISION Network, Nine States, September-November 2022; Rates of COVID-19 Cases or Deaths by Age Group and Vaccination Status and Booster Dose; Vaccine Adverse Event Reporting System (VAERS) Publications; and VaxView: Vaccination Coverage in the U.S..

UK Health Security Agency (UKHSA), Nobel House, 17 Smith Sq., London, SW1P 3JR, GBR, enquiries@ukhsa.gov.uk, https://www.gov.uk/government/organisations/uk-health-security-agency; COVID-19 Vaccine Surveillance Reports and Effectiveness of COVID-19 Vaccines Against the B.1.617.2 Variant.

University of Washington, Institute for Health Metrics and Evaluation (IHME), Population Health Building/ Hans Rosling Center, UW Campus Box 351615, 3980 15th Ave. NE, Seattle, WA, 98195, USA, (206) 897-2800, (206) 897-2899, engage@healthdata.org, https://www.healthdata.org; Vaccine Hesitancy by County.

COVID-19 PANDEMIC, 2020-

ACT, PO Box 168, Iowa City, IA, 52243-0168, USA, (319) 337-1270, https://www.act.org; College Preparation Opportunities, the Pandemic, and Student Preparedness: Perspectives From Class of 2021 College-Bound ACT Test-Takers.

Act Now Coalition, USA, https://www.actnowcoalition.org/; unpublished data.

Act Now Coalition: COVID Act Now, USA, info@covidactnow.org, https://covidactnow.org; U.S. COVID Tracker.

America's Health Insurance Plans (AHIP), 601 Pennsylvania Ave. NW, South Bldg., Ste. 500, Washington, DC, 20004, USA, (202) 778-3200, (202) 331-7487, info@ahip.org, https://www.ahip.org; Telehealth Coverage During the COVID-19 Pandemic.

American Academy of Pediatrics (AAP), 345 Park Blvd., Itasca, IL, 60143, USA, (800) 433-9016, (847) 434-8000, mcc@aap.org, https://www.aap.org; Children and COVID-19: State-Level Data Report.

American Civil Liberties Union (ACLU), 125 Broad St. , 18th Fl., New York, NY, 10004, USA, (212) 549-2500, https://www.aclu.org/; COVID-19 Model Finds Nearly 100,000 More Deaths Than Current Estimates, Due to Failures to Reduce Jails and The Other Epidemic: Fatal Police Shootings in the Time of COVID-19.

The Annie E. Casey Foundation, 701 Saint Paul St., Baltimore, MD, 21202, USA, (410) 547-6600, (410) 547-6624, https://www.aecf.org/; Kids, Families and COVID-19: Pandemic Pain Points and the Urgent Need to Respond.

Australian Institute of Family Studies, Child Family Community Australia (CFCA), 40 City Rd., Level 4,

Southbank, VIC, 3006, AUS, enquiries@aifs.gov.au, https://aifs.gov.au/research_programs/child-family-community-australia; Child Wellbeing During the COVID Pandemic: Parental Concerns.

Biotechnology Innovation Organization (BIO), 1201 New York NW, Ste. 1300, Washington, DC, 20005, USA, (202) 962-9200, info@bio.org, https://www.bio.org/; BIO COVID-19 Therapeutic Development Tracker.

The Brookings Institution, 1775 Massachusetts Ave. NW, Washington, DC, 20036, USA, (202) 797-6000, communications@brookings.edu, https://www.brookings.edu/; Metro Recovery Index.

Brown School of Public Health, Global Epidemics, 121 South Main St., Providence, RI, 02903, USA, (401) 863-3375, https://globalepidemics.org/; Vaccine Preventable Deaths Analysis.

Bulletin of the Atomic Scientists, PO Box 15461, Chicago, IL, 60615-5146, USA, (773) 834-3779, admin@thebulletin.org, https://thebulletin.org/; An Illustrated History of the World's Deadliest Epidemics, from Ancient Rome to Covid-19.

California Department of Public Health (CDPH), PO Box 997377, MS 0500, Sacramento, CA, 95899-7377, USA, (916) 558-1784, https://www.cdph.ca.gov; COVID-19 by the Numbers.

Center for Countering Digital Hate (CCDH), Langley House, Park Rd. , East Finchley, London, N2 8EY, GBR, info@counterhate.com, https://www.counterhate.com; The Disinformation Dozen: Why Platforms Must Act on Twelve Leading Online Anti-Vaxxers and Malgorithm: How Instagram's Algorithm Publishes Misinformation and Hate to Millions During a Pandemic.

Center for Economic and Policy Research (CEPR), 1611 Connecticut Ave. NW, Ste. 400, Washington, DC, 20009, USA, (202) 293-5380, (202) 588-1356, info@cepr.net, https://cepr.net/; A Basic Demographic Profile of Workers in Frontline Industries.

Charities Aid Foundation (CAF), 25 Kings Hill Ave., Kings Hill, West Malling, Kent, ME19 4TA, GBR, cafbank@cafonline.org, https://www.cafonline.org/; The Global Response to the COVID-19 Pandemic: Lessons in Compassion, Innovation and Resilience.

Civis Analytics, 200 W Monroe St., 22nd Fl., Chicago, IL, 60606, USA, https://www.civisanalytics.com/; Coronavirus Pulse Survey Research and COVID-19 Impact Research.

Climate Analytics, 135 Madison Ave., 5th Fl., Ste. 05-115, New York, NY, 10016, USA, info.ny@climateanalytics.org, https://climateanalytics.org/; 2 Steps Down the Debt Spiral: COVID-19 and Tropical Cyclones Severely Limit the Fiscal Space of Many Small Island Developing States.

Commonwealth Fund, 1 E 75th St., New York, NY, 10021, USA, (212) 606-3800 , info@cmwf.org, https://www.commonwealthfund.org/; Two Years of U.S. COVID-19 Vaccines Have Prevented Millions of Hospitalizations and Deaths.

Consumer Technology Association (CTA), 1919 S Eads St., Arlington, VA, 22202, USA, (703) 907-7600, (866) 858-1555, (703) 907-7675, cta@cta.tech, https://www.cta.tech; The Future of Telehealth and Remote Patient Monitoring in the Age of COVID-19.

Council on Criminal Justice (CCJ), National Commission on COVID-19 and Criminal Justice, 700 Pennsylvania Ave. SE, Washington, DC, 20020, USA, info@counciloncj.org, https://counciloncj.org/covid-19/; COVID-19 in U.S. State and Federal Prisons; Impact Report: COVID-19 and Crime; Impact Report: COVID-19 and Domestic Violence Trends; Impact Report: COVID-19 and Prisons; and Impact Report: COVID-19 Testing in State Prisons.

The COVID Tracking Project at The Atlantic, support@covidtracking.com, https://covidtracking.com; COVID Tracking Project Data.

COVID-19 Forecast Hub, University of Massachusetts Amherst, Reich Lab, Amherst, MA, 10022, USA, https://covid19forecasthub.org; COVID-19 US Weekly Forecast Summary.

COVID-19 Transport, Travel and Social Adaptation Study (COVID-19 TRANSAS), GBR, decarbon8@leeds.ac.uk, https://covid19transas.org; At a Crossroads: Travel Adaptations During Covid-19 Restrictions and Where Next?.

Democracy Fund Voter Study Group, 1200 17th St. NW, Ste. 300, Washington, DC, 20036, USA, (202) 420-7900, https://www.voterstudygroup.org/; COVID-19: Tracking American Perspectives.

District of Columbia Corrections Information Council (CIC), 1400 I St. NW, Ste. 400, Washington, DC, 20005, USA, (202) 478-9211, dccic@dc.gov, https://cic.dc.gov/page/about-cic; COVID-19 Survey Final Report.

Duke Global Health Institute, Center for Policy Impact in Global Health, 310 Trent Dr., Durham, NC, 27710, USA, (919) 613-6249, cpigh@duke.edu, https://centerforpolicyimpact.org; Achieving Global Mortality Reduction Targets and Universal Health Coverage: The Impact of COVID-19.

Elsevier, Radarweg 29, Amsterdam, 1043 NX, NLD, https://www.elsevier.com; Novel Coronavirus Information Center.

European Centre for Disease Prevention and Control (ECDC), Stockholm, SE 171 83, SWE, ecdc.info@ecdc.europa.eu, https://ecdc.europa.eu; COVID-19: Country Overview Report.

European Cockpit Association (ECA), Rue du Commerce 20-22, Brussels, B-1000, BEL, eca@eurocockpit.be, https://www.eurocockpit.be/; COVID-19: Thousands of Aircrew Redundant.

Federal Bureau of Prisons (BOP), 320 First St. NW, Washington, DC, 20534 , USA, (202) 307-3198, https://www.bop.gov/; Inmate COVID-19 Data: A Look at the Impact of COVID-19 on Individuals in Federal Custody.

FiveThirtyEight, 47 W 66th St., 2nd Fl., New York, NY, 10023, USA, contact@fivethirtyeight.com, https://fivethirtyeight.com/; All the Science You Need to Make Your COVID-19 Decisions.

The Gallup Organization, 901 F St. NW, Washington, DC, 20004, USA, (202) 715-3030, (800) 204-1192, (202) 715-3045, https://www.gallup.com; State of the Global Workplace 2023.

GISAID Initiative, Munich, GER, https://www.gisaid.org; Tracking of hCoV-19 Variants.

Global Change Data Lab, Our World in Data, GBR, info@ourworldindata.org, https://ourworldindata.org; Coronavirus (COVID-19) Vaccinations; Coronavirus Pandemic (COVID-19); and COVID-19 Database.

Global Wellness Institute (GWI), 333 SE 2nd Ave., Ste. 2048, Miami, FL, 33131, USA, info@globalwellnessinstitute.org, https://www.globalwellnessinstitute.org/; Resetting the World with Wellness: A New Vision for a Post COVID Future.

Harvard Global Health Institute (HGHI), 42 Church St., Cambridge, MA, 02138, USA, (617) 384-5431, globalhealth@harvard.edu, https://globalhealth.harvard.edu/; COVID Risk Levels Dashboard and COVID-19 Hospital Capacity Estimates 2020.

Harvard T.H. Chan School of Public Health, 677 Huntington Ave., Boston, MA, 02115, USA, (617) 495-1000, https://www.hsph.harvard.edu/; Air Pollution and COVID-19 Mortality in the United States: Strengths and Limitations of an Ecological Regression Analysis.

hc1, 6100 Technology Center Dr., Indianapolis, IN, 46278, USA, (317) 219-4646, info@hc1.com, https://www.hc1.com; CV19 Lab Testing Dashboard.

The Hechinger Report, 525 W 120th St., Ste. 127, New York, NY, 10027, USA, (212) 678-7556, (212) 678-7556, hechinger@hechingerreport.org, https://hechingerreport.org; What Has Happened When Campuses Shut Down for Other Disasters? A Coronavirus Case Study.

The Henry J. Kaiser Family Foundation (KFF), 185 Berry St., Ste. 2000, San Francisco, CA, 94107, USA, (650) 854-9400, (650) 854-4800, https://www.kff.org; KFF COVID-19 Vaccine Monitor; KFF COVID-19 Vaccine Monitor: January 2022 Parents and Kids Update; KFF COVID-19 Vaccine Monitor: Views on the Pandemic at Two Years; Long COVID: What Do the Latest Data Show?; State COVID-19 Data and Policy Actions; and Where are the COVID-19 Hotspots? Tracking State Outbreaks.

Horatio Alger Association of Distinguished Americans, 99 Canal Center Plaza, Ste. 320, Alexandria, VA, 22314, USA, (703) 684-9444, (703) 684-9445, https://horatioalger.org/; The Pandemic's Financial and Emotional Impact on Student Futures.

Human Rights Watch, 350 5th Ave., 34th Fl., New York, NY, 10118-3299, USA, (212) 290-4700, (212) 736-1300, https://www.hrw.org; I Must Work to Eat: Covid-19, Poverty, and Child Labor in Ghana, Nepal, and Uganda and World Report 2023: Our Annual Review of Human Rights Around the Globe.

Imperial College London, South Kensington Campus, London, SW7 2AZ, GBR, https://www.imperial.ac.uk/; Estimating the Effects of Non-Pharmaceutical Interventions on COVID-19 in Europe.

Imperial College London, School of Public Health, MRC Centre for Global Infectious Disease Analysis, Medical School Bldg., Norfolk Place, London, W2 1PG, GBR, mrc.gida@imperial.ac.uk, https://www.imperial.ac.uk/mrc-global-infectious-disease-analysis/; Evaluation of Individual and Ensemble Probabilistic Forecasts of COVID-19 Mortality in the United States and Genetic Evidence for the Association Between COVID-19 Epidemic Severity and Timing of Non-Pharmaceutical Interventions.

International Consortium of Investigative Journalists (ICIJ), 1730 Rhode Island Ave. NW, Ste. 317, Washington, DC, 20036, USA, (202) 808-3310, contact@icij.org, https://www.icij.org/; Indian Reporters Find New Ways to Expose 'Vaccine Inequity' and COVID-19 Data.

International Energy Agency (IEA), 9 Rue de la Federation, Paris, 75739, FRA, info@iea.org, https://www.iea.org/; Global Energy Review: CO2 Emissions in 2020.

International Food Policy Research Institute (IFPRI), 1201 Eye St. NW, Washington, DC, 20005-3915, USA, (202) 862-5600, (202) 862-5606, ifpri@cgiar.org, https://www.ifpri.org/; The COVID-19 Crisis Will Exacerbate Maternal and Child Undernutrition and Child Mortality in Low- and Middle-Income Countries and 2021 Global Food Policy Report: Transforming Food Systems After COVID-19.

Ipsos, 360 Park Ave. S, 17th Fl., New York, NY, 10010, USA, (212) 265-3200, https://www.ipsos.com/en-us; Most Americans Not Worrying About COVID Going into 2022 Holidays.

Italian National Agency for New Technologies, Energy and Sustainable Economic Development (ENEA), Lungotevere Thaon di Revel, 76, Rome, 00196, ITA, https://www.enea.it/en; ENEA CRESCO in the Fight Against COVID-19.

Johns Hopkins Center for a Livable Future, 111 Market Pl., Ste. 840, Baltimore, MD, 21202, USA, (410) 223-1811, (410) 223-1829, clf@jhsph.edu, https://clf.jhsph.edu; Emerging COVID-19 Impacts, Responses, and Lessons for Building Resilience in the Seafood System; Essential and in Crisis: A Review of the Public Health Threats Facing Farmworkers in the US; Exploring U.S. Food System Workers' Intentions to Work While Ill during the Early COVID-19 Pandemic: A National Survey; and Frequency of Workplace Controls and Associations with Safety Perceptions among a National Sample of U.S. Food Retail Workers during the COVID-19 Pandemic.

Johns Hopkins Center for Health Security, 621 E Pratt St., Ste. 210, Baltimore, MD, 21202, USA, (443) 573-3304, (443) 573-3305, centerhealthsecurity@jhu.edu, https://www.centerforhealthsecurity.org/; COVID-19 Situation Reports.

Johns Hopkins Coronavirus Resource Center, 3400 N Charles St., Baltimore, MD, 21218, USA, https://coronavirus.jhu.edu/; COVID-19 Testing Insights Initiative and Testing Trends Tool: Track Trends in COVID-19 Cases and Tests.

The Marshall Project, 156 W 56th St., 3rd Fl., New York, NY, 10019, USA, (212) 803-5200, info@themarshallproject.org, https://www.themarshallproject.org/; COVID Cases in Prisons.

McKinsey & Company, 725 Ponce de Leon Ave., Ste. 700, Atlanta, GA, 30306, USA, (404) 335-3000, (404) 521-1743, https://www.mckinsey.com; Tracking the Impact of COVID-19.

Media Matters for America, PO Box 44811, Washington, DC, 20026, USA, (202) 756-4100, action@mediamatters.org, https://www.mediamatters.org; Fox Has Undermined Vaccination Efforts in Nearly 60% of All Vaccination Segments in a 2-Week Period.

Migration Policy Institute (MPI), 1275 K St. NW, Ste. 800, Washington, DC, 20005, USA, (202) 266-1940, (202) 266-1900, info@migrationpolicy.org, https://www.migrationpolicy.org/; COVID-19's Effects on U.S. Immigration and Immigrant Communities, Two Years On.

National Academies of Sciences, Engineering, and Medicine (The National Academies), 500 5th St. NW, Washington, DC, 20001, USA, (202) 334-2000, contact@nas.edu, https://www.nationalacademies.org/; Rapid Expert Consultation on SARS-CoV-2 Viral Shedding and Antibody Response for the COVID-19 Pandemic.

National Highway Traffic Safety Administration (NHTSA), National Center for Statistics and Analysis (NCSA), 1200 New Jersey Ave. SE, West Bldg., Washington, DC, 20590, USA, (800) 934-8517, (202) 366-2746, ncsarequests@dot.gov, https://www.nhtsa.gov/research-data/national-center-statistics-and-analysis-ncsa; Update to Special Reports on Traffic Safety During the COVID-19 Public Health Emergency.

National Nurses United (NNU), 8455 Colesville Rd., Ste. 1100, Silver Spring, MD, 20910, USA, (240) 235-2000, (240) 235-2019, info@nationalnursesunited.org, https://www.nationalnursesunited.org; Deadly Shame: Redressing the Devaluation of Registered Nurse Labor Through Pandemic Equity and Sins of Omission: How Government Failures to Track Covid-19 Data Have Led to More Than 3,200 Health Care Worker Deaths and Jeopardize Public Health.

NewClimate Institute, Waidmarkt 11a, Cologne, D-50676, GER, info@newclimate.org, https://newclimate.org/; Exploring the Impact of the COVID-19 Pandemic on Global Emission Projections.

Oxford University Centre for the Environment, Centre for Research into Energy Demand Solutions (CREDS), South Parks Rd., Oxford, OX1 3QY, GBR, credsadmin@ouce.ox.ac.uk, https://www.creds.ac.uk; House of Lords Covid Committee: Inquiry into the Long-Term Impact of the Pandemic on the UK's Towns and Cities.

PeopleForBikes, PO Box 2359, Boulder, CO, 80306, USA, (303) 449-4893, info@peopleforbikes.org, https://www.peopleforbikes.org; COVID Participation Study.

Pew Research Center, 1615 L St. NW, Ste. 800, Washington, DC, 20036, USA, (202) 419-4300, (202) 857-8562, info@pewresearch.org, https://www.pewresearch.org/; American News Pathways Data Tool.

Physicians for Human Rights (PHR), 256 W 38th St., 9th Fl., New York, NY, 10018, USA, (646) 564-3720, (646) 564-3750, https://phr.org/; Silenced and Endangered: Clinicians' Human Rights and Health Concerns about Their Facilities' Response to COVID-19.

PLOS, 1265 Battery St., Ste. 200, San Francisco, CA, 94111, USA, (415) 624-1200, (415) 795-1584, plos@plos.org, https://www.plos.org/; Outbreak Analysis with a Logistic Growth Model Shows COVID-19 Suppression Dynamics in China.

Prison Policy Initiative, PO Box 127, Northampton, MA, 01061, USA, https://www.prisonpolicy.org/; Mass Incarceration, COVID-19, and Community Spread.

ProPublica, 155 Avenue of the Americas, 13th Fl., New York, NY, 10013, USA, (212) 514-5250, (212) 785-2634, hello@propublica.org, https://www.propublica.org/; Hazardous Air Pollutant Exposure as a Contributing Factor to COVID-19 Mortality in the United States.

Robert Wood Johnson Foundation (RWJF), 50 College Rd. E, Princeton, NJ, 08540-6614, USA, (877) 843-7953, (609) 627-6000, https://www.rwjf.org/; Marketplace Pulse: COVID-19 and the Coverage Gap.

Rockefeller Foundation, 420 5th Ave., New York, NY, 10018, USA, (212) 869-8500, https://www.rockefellerfoundation.org; Implementing Covid-19 Routine Testing in K-12 Schools: Lessons and Recommendations from Pilot Sites.

Save the Children, 501 Kings Hwy. E, Ste. 400, Fairfield, CT, 06825, USA, (203) 221-4000, (800) 728-3843, https://www.savethechildren.org/; Childhood in the Time of COVID: U.S. Complement to the Global Childhood Report 2021.

Statistics Poland, Aleja Niepodleglosci 208, Warsaw, 00-925, POL, kancelariaogolnagus@stat.gov.pl, https://stat.gov.pl/en/; Production of Industrial Products Related to the Prevention of Spreading/Combating COVID-19 in March 2022.

U.S. Department of Health and Human Services (HHS), National Institutes of Health (NIH), National Center for Advancing Translational Sciences (NCATS), 31 Center Dr., Ste. 3B11, Bethesda, MD, 20892-2128, USA, (301) 594-8966, info@ncats.nih.gov, https://ncats.nih.gov/; OpenData COVID-19 Portal.

U.S. Department of Health and Human Services (HHS), National Institutes of Health (NIH), Office of Data Science Strategy (ODSS), 9000 Rockville Pike, Bethesda, MD, 20892, USA, (301) 827-7212, datascience@nih.gov, https://datascience.nih.gov/; Open-Access Data and Computational Resources to Address COVID-19.

U.S. Department of Health and Human Services (HHS), U.S. National Library of Medicine (NLM), National Center for Biotechnology Information (NCBI), 8600 Rockville Pike, Bethesda, MD, 20894, USA, info@ncbi.nlm.nih.gov, https://www.ncbi.nlm.nih.gov; NCBI SARS-CoV-2 Resources.

U.S. Department of Health and Human Services, Centers for Disease Control and Prevention (CDC), 1600 Clifton Rd., Atlanta, GA, 30329-4027, USA, (800) 232-4636, (888) 232-6348 (TTY), cdcinfo@cdc.gov, https://www.cdc.gov; COVID Data Tracker; COVID Data Tracker Weekly Review; COVID Data Tracker: Rates of COVID-19 Cases and Deaths by Vaccination Status; COVID-19 Case Surveillance Public Use Data Profile; COVID-19 Forecasts: Deaths; COVID-19 Vaccine Breakthrough Infections Reported to CDC - United States, January 1-April 30, 2021; COVID-19: U.S. Impact on Antimicrobial Resistance; Early Estimates of Bivalent mRNA Vaccine Effectiveness in Preventing COVID-19-Associated Emergency Department or Urgent Care Encounters and Hospitalizations Among Immunocompetent Adults - VISION Network, Nine States, September-November 2022; Effectiveness of a COVID-19 Additional Primary or Booster Vaccine Dose in Preventing SARS-CoV-2 Infection Among Nursing Home Residents During Widespread Circulation of the Omicron Variant - United States, February 14 - March 27, 2022; Efficacy of Portable Air Cleaners and Masking for Reducing Indoor Exposure to Simulated Exhaled SARS-CoV-2 Aerosols - United States, 2021; Mass Testing for SARS-CoV-2 in 16 Prisons and Jails - Six Jurisdictions, United States, April-May 2020; and Nearly One in Five American Adults Who Have Had COVID-19 Still Have Long COVID.

U.S. Department of Health and Human Services, Centers for Disease Control and Prevention (CDC), National Center for Health Statistics (NCHS), 3311 Toledo Rd., Hyattsville, MD, 20782-2064, USA, (800) 232-4636, (301) 458-4000, https://www.cdc.gov/nchs; COVID-19 Death Data and Resources and Excess Deaths Associated with COVID-19.

U.S. Department of Justice (DOJ), Office of Community Oriented Policing Services (COPS), 145 N St. NE, Washington, DC, 20530, USA, (800) 421-6770, askcopsrc@usdoj.gov, https://cops.usdoj.gov/; Officer Safety and Wellness Group Meeting Summary: Pandemic Policing.

U.S. Department of Transportation (DOT), Federal Railroad Administration (FRA), 1200 New Jersey Ave. SE, Washington, DC, 20590, USA, (202) 366-4000, (202) 493-6014, (202) 493-6481, frapa@dot.gov, https://railroads.dot.gov/; Coronavirus (COVID-19) Information from the FRA.

UK Health Security Agency (UKHSA), Nobel House, 17 Smith Sq., London, SW1P 3JR, GBR, enquiries@ukhsa.gov.uk, https://www.gov.uk/government/organisations/uk-health-security-agency; COVID-19 Vaccine Surveillance Reports; COVID-19 Variants: Genomically Confirmed Case Numbers; and Effectiveness of COVID-19 Vaccines Against the B.1.617.2 Variant.

UNICEF, 3 United Nations Plz., New York, NY, 10017, USA, (212) 303-7984, (917) 244-2215, https://www.unicef.org; COVID-19 and Children: UNICEF Data Hub.

United Nations Human Settlements Programme (UN-HABITAT), PO Box 30030, Nairobi, 00100, KEN, unhabitat-info@un.org, https://unhabitat.org/; Cities and Pandemics: Towards a More Just, Green and Healthy Future.

University of California Davis, Violence Prevention Research Program (VPRP), 2315 Stockton Blvd., Sacramento, CA, 95817, USA, (916) 734-3539 , hs-vprp@ucdavis.edu, https://health.ucdavis.edu/vprp/; Physical Distancing, Violence, and Crime in US Cities during the Coronavirus Pandemic.

University of California Los Angeles (UCLA) School of Law, Covid-19 Behind Bars Data Project, 385 Charles E. Young Dr. E, Los Angeles, CA, 90095, USA, (310) 206-5568, covidbehindbars@law.ucla.edu, https://uclacovidbehindbars.org; Covid Behind Bars Data Project; Georgia Custodial Death Records Summary Report; In California Jails, Sherrifs Have Been Left in Charge of Covid Mitigation. The Results Have Been Disastrous.; Racial And Ethnic Inequalities in COVID-19 Mortality Within Carceral Settings: An Analysis of Texas Prisons; and What We Won't Know When the Next Surge Arrives.

University of California Los Angeles (UCLA), Center for Health Policy Research (CHPR), 10960 Wilshire Blvd., Ste. 1550, Campus Mail Code 714346, Los Angeles, CA, 90024, USA, (310) 794-0909, (310) 794-2686, healthpolicy@ucla.edu, https://healthpolicy.ucla.edu; Coronavirus Disease 2019 and the Case to Cover Undocumented Immigrants in California (Health Equity).

University of California, Berkeley, Global Policy Lab, California Memorial Stadium, 2227 Piedmont Ave., Berkeley, CA, 94720, USA, (510) 643-5751, https://www.globalpolicy.science/; Public Mobility Data Enables COVID-19 Forecasting and Management at Local and Global Scales.

University of Minnesota, Center for Infectious Disease Research and Policy (CIDRAP), Office of the Vice President for Research, 420 Delaware St. SE, MMC 263, C315 Mayo, Minneapolis, MN, 55455, USA, (612) 626-6770, (612) 626-6783, https://www.cidrap.umn.edu/; Novel Coronavirus (COVID-19) Resource Center.

University of Texas at Austin, COVID-19 Modeling Consortium, 1 University Station C0930, Austin, TX, 78712, USA, utpandemics@austin.utexas.edu, https://covid-19.tacc.utexas.edu/; Estimated COVID-19 Mortality in China, December 16, 2022 - January 19, 2023 and Scenario Projections for the Spread of SARS-CoV-2 Omicron BA.4 and BA.5 Subvariants in the US and Texas.

University of Washington, Institute for Health Metrics and Evaluation (IHME), Population Health Building/Hans Rosling Center, UW Campus Box 351615, 3980 15th Ave. NE, Seattle, WA, 98195, USA, (206) 897-2800, (206) 897-2899, engage@healthdata.org, https://www.healthdata.org; Estimated Global Proportions of Individuals With Persistent Fatigue,

Cognitive, and Respiratory Symptom Clusters Following Symptomatic COVID-19 in 2020 and 2021; Estimation of Excess Mortality Due to COVID-19; and Global Access to Handwashing: Implications for COVID-19 Control in Low-Income Countries.

Western Washington University, Border Policy Research Institute (BPRI), 516 High St., Bellingham, WA, 98225, USA, (360) 650-3000, laurie.trautman@wwu.edu, https://bpri.wwu.edu/; COVID-19 and the US-Canada Border.

World Health Organization (WHO), Ave. Appia 20, Geneva, CH-1211, SWI, (202) 974-3000 (Telephone in U.S.), publications@who.int, https://www.who.int/; Coronavirus Disease (COVID-19) Situation Report; European Health Report 2021: Taking stock of the health-related Sustainable Development Goals in the COVID-19 era with a focus on leaving no one behind; Global Excess Deaths Associated with COVID-19, January 2020 - December 2021; Global Health Observatory (GHO) Data; Global Research on Coronavirus Disease (COVID-19); and The Impact of the COVID-19 Pandemic on Noncommunicable Disease Resources and Services: Results of a Rapid Assessment.

World Health Organization (WHO), Pan American Health Organization (PAHO), 525 23rd St. NW, Washington, DC, 20037, USA, (202) 974-3000, (202) 974-3663, pubrights@paho.org, https://www.paho.org; Health in the Americas+.

Worldometer, https://www.worldometers.info/; COVID-19 Coronavirus Pandemic.

COVID-19 PANDEMIC, 2020—ECONOMIC ASPECTS

American Association of Retired Persons (AARP) Public Policy Institute (PPI), 601 E St. NW, Washington, DC, 20049, USA, (202) 434-3840, ppi@aarp.org, https://www.aarp.org/ppi; Estimating Impacts of Pandemic-Related Job Loss on Health Insurance Coverage Among Adults Ages 50 to 64 During the First Year of COVID-19.

American Water Works Association (AWWA), 6666 W Quincy Ave., Denver, CO, 80235, USA, (303) 794-7711, (800) 926-7337, (303) 347-0804, https://www.awwa.org/; COVID-19 Utility and Water Sector Organization Impact Survey.

Australian Government Department of Agriculture, Water and the Environment, GPO Box 858, Canberra, ACT, 2601, AUS, https://www.agriculture.gov.au/; Australian Agricultural Trade and the COVID-19 Pandemic.

Board of Governors of the Federal Reserve System, Constitution Ave. NW, Washington, DC, 20551, USA, (202) 452-3000, (202) 263-4869 (TDD), https://www.federalreserve.gov; Reconciling Unemployment Claims with Job Losses in the First Months of the COVID-19 Crisis.

Boston Consulting Group (BCG), 200 Pier 4 Blvd., Boston, MA, 02210, USA, (617) 973-1200, https://www.bcg.com/; The Business Impact of COVID-19.

Center on Budget and Policy Priorities, 1275 First St. NE, Ste. 1200, Washington, DC, 20002, USA, (202) 408-1080, (202) 408-1056, center@cbpp.org, https://www.cbpp.org/; Tracking the COVID-19 Recession's Effects on Food, Housing, and Employment Hardships.

Cirium, 230 Park Ave., 7th Fl., New York, NY, 10169, USA, (646) 746-6851, https://www.cirium.com/; The Impact of COVID-19 on Aviation.

Civis Analytics, 200 W Monroe St., 22nd Fl., Chicago, IL, 60606, USA, https://www.civisanalytics.com/; COVID-19 in the U.S.: Consumer Insights for Business.

Climate Analytics, 135 Madison Ave., 5th Fl., Ste. 05-115, New York, NY, 10016, USA, info.ny@climateanalytics.org, https://climateanalytics.org/; Climate Action Tracker: How a Renewable Energy COVID-19 Recovery Creates Opportunities for India; Exploring New Electric Vehicle Roadmaps for China in a Post-COVID-19 Era; and 2 Steps Down the Debt Spiral: COVID-19 and Tropical Cyclones Severely Limit the Fiscal Space of Many Small Island Developing States.

Consumer Technology Association (CTA), 1919 S Eads St., Arlington, VA, 22202, USA, (703) 907-7600, (866) 858-1555, (703) 907-7675, cta@cta.tech, https://www.cta.tech; Mobility and Auto Technology in the COVID-19 Era.

The Economist Group, 900 3rd Ave., 16th Fl., New York, NY, 10022, USA, (212) 541-0500, (202) 429-0890, customerhelp@economist.com, https://www.economistgroup.com; Covid-19 Data: The Global Normalcy Index.

Euromonitor International, Inc., 1 N Dearborn St., Ste. 1700, Chicago, IL, 60602, USA, (312) 922-1115, (312) 922-1157, info-usa@euromonitor.com, https://www.euromonitor.com/; The Impact of Coronavirus on Consumer Finance; The Impact of Coronavirus on Consumer Goods and Services in the Middle East; and The Impact of Coronavirus on Top 10 Global Consumer Trends 2020.

Ewing Marion Kauffman Foundation, 4801 Rockhill Rd., Kansas City, MO, 64110, USA, (816) 932-1000, https://www.kauffman.org/; COVID-19 and Entrepreneurial Firms: Seeding an Inclusive and Equitable Recovery.

Feeding America, 161 N Clark St., Ste. 700, Chicago, IL, 60601, USA, (800) 771-2303, (312) 263-5626, https://www.feedingamerica.org/; The Impact of the Coronavirus on Local Food Insecurity in 2020 and 2021.

FiveThirtyEight, 47 W 66th St., 2nd Fl., New York, NY, 10023, USA, contact@fivethirtyeight.com, https://fivethirtyeight.com/; Where the Latest COVID-19 Models Think We're Headed - And Why They Disagree.

Global Change Data Lab, Our World in Data, GBR, info@ourworldindata.org, https://ourworldindata.org; Which Countries Have Protected Both Health and the Economy in the Pandemic?.

The Hechinger Report, 525 W 120th St., Ste. 127, New York, NY, 10027, USA, (212) 678-7556, (212) 678-7556, hechinger@hechingerreport.org, https://hechingerreport.org; Analysis: Hundreds of Colleges and Universities Show Financial Warning Signs and How Higher Education's Own Choices Left it Vulnerable to the Pandemic Crisis.

The Henry J. Kaiser Family Foundation (KFF), 185 Berry St., Ste. 2000, San Francisco, CA, 94107, USA, (650) 854-9400, (650) 854-4800, https://www.kff.org; About 1.5 Million Teachers Are at Higher Risk of Serious Illness From COVID-19; Almost One in Four Adult Workers Is Vulnerable to Severe Illness from COVID-19; KFF COVID-19 Vaccine Monitor: The Pandemic's Toll on Workers and Family Finances During the Omicron Surge; and Temporary Enhanced Federal Medicaid Funding Can Soften the Economic Blow of the COVID-19 Pandemic on States, But Is Unlikely to Fully Offset State Revenue Declines or Forestall Budget Shortfalls.

IDTechEx, One Boston Place, Ste. 2600, Boston, MA, 02108, USA, (617) 577-7890, (617) 577-7810, research@idtechex.com, https://www.idtechex.com/; 3D Printing and Additive Manufacturing 2022-2032: Technology and Market Outlook.

The Immigrant Learning Center (ILC), 442 Main St., Malden, MA, 02148-5177, USA, (781) 322-9777, (800) 439-2370 (TTY), (781) 321-1963, info@ilctr.org, https://www.ilctr.org/; Health and Financial Risks for Noncitizen Immigrants due to the COVID-19 Pandemic; Immigrant Detention and COVID-19: How a Pandemic Exploited and Spread through the US Immigrant Detention System; and Latinx Workers - Particularly Women - Face Devastating Job Losses in the COVID-19 Recession.

INRIX, 10210 NE Points Dr., No. 400, Kirkland, WA, 98033, USA, (425) 284-3800, https://inrix.com; Holiday Shopping Update.

International Institute for Environment and Development (IIED), 235 High Holborn, London, WC1V 7DN, GBR, inforequest@iied.org, https://www.iied.org; Redesigning Debt: Lessons from HIPC for COVID, Climate and Nature.

Ipsos, 360 Park Ave. S, 17th Fl., New York, NY, 10010, USA, (212) 265-3200, https://www.ipsos.com/en-us; U.S. Consumer Confidence Takes a Small Step Back: Expectations Dampen with Surge of New Coronavirus Cases.

Japan Center for Economic Research (JCER), Nikkei Inc. Bldg. 11F, 1-3-7 Otemachi, Chiyoda-ku, Tokyo, 100-8066, JPN, https://www.jcer.or.jp/en; New Threat to the Financial System in the Post-COVID-19 Era.

KFF Health News, 1330 G St. NW, Washington, DC, 20005, USA, (202) 347-5270, https://khn.org/; Medicaid Vaccination Rates Founder as States Struggle to Immunize Their Poorest Residents.

League of American Orchestras, 520 8th Ave., Ste. 2005, New York, NY, 10018, USA, (212) 262-5161, (212) 262-5198, knowledge@americanorchestras.org, https://americanorchestras.org/; The League's COVID-19 Impact Survey.

Massachusetts Institute of Technology (MIT), Living Wage Calculator, 77 Massachusetts Ave., Cambridge, MA, 02139, USA, (617) 324-6565, (617) 253-1000, amyglas@mit.edu, https://livingwage.mit.edu; Double Whammy: Essential Workers Threatened by Job Loss While Facing the Highest Risk of COVID Infection.

Mathematica, PO Box 2393, Princeton, NJ, 08543-2393, USA, (609) 275-2350, (609) 799-3535, (609) 799-0005, info@mathematica-mpr.com, https://www.mathematica.org; Tracking Youth Unemployment During the COVID-19 Pandemic.

Morning Consult, 729 15th St. NW, Washington, DC, 20005, USA, (202) 506-1957, contact@morningconsult.com, https://morningconsult.com; The U.S. Consumer Confidence Dashboard and When Will Consumers Feel Safe? Weekly Updates on Consumers' Comfort Level with Various Pastimes.

National Women's Law Center (NWLC), 1350 I St. NW, Ste. 700, Washington, DC, 20005, USA, (202) 588-5180, https://nwlc.org; A Year of Strength & Loss: The Pandemic, the Economy, & the Value of Women's Work.

NielsenIQ (NIQ), 200 W Jackson Blvd., Chicago, IL, 60606, USA, https://nielseniq.com; Covid-Positive Households Are Altering Their Eating Habits.

Organization for Economic Cooperation and Development (OECD), 2001 L St. NW, Ste. 650, Washington, DC, 20036-4922, USA, (202) 785-6323, (800) 456-6323, (202) 785-0350, washington.contact@oecd.org, https://www.oecd.org/; The Future of Corporate Governance in Capital Markets Following the COVID-19 Crisis.

Pew Research Center, 1615 L St. NW, Ste. 800, Washington, DC, 20036, USA, (202) 419-4300, (202) 857-8562, info@pewresearch.org, https://www.pewresearch.org/; U.S. Labor Market Inches Back From the COVID-19 Shock, But Recovery Is Far From Complete.

Plant Based Foods Association (PBFA), 4 Embarcadero Center, Ste. 1400, San Francisco, CA, 94111, USA, (415) 236-5048, info@plantbasedfoods.org, https://plantbasedfoods.org/; New Data Shows Plant-Based Food Outpacing Total Food Sales During COVID-19.

Poor People's Campaign, USA, https://www.poorpeoplescampaign.org/; A Poor People's Pandemic Report: Mapping the Intersections of Poverty, Race and COVID-19.

Realtime Inequality, Berkeley, CA, USA, realtimeinequality@gmail.com, https://realtimeinequality.org/; COVID-19: Factor Income During the Pandemic.

Restaurant Opportunities Centers United (ROC United), 275 7th. Ave., New York, NY, 10001, USA, (212) 343-1771, info@rocunited.org, https://rocunited.org/; COVID Impact Report: The Impact of COVID-19 on Restaurant Workers Across America.

S&P Global, 55 Water St., New York, NY, 10041, USA, (212) 438-2000, market.intelligence@spglobal.com, https://www.spglobal.com/; Update: Aerospace and Defense North America.

State Health Access Data Assistance Center (SHADAC), 2221 University Ave. SE, Ste. 345, Minneapolis, MN, 55414, USA, (612) 624-4802, (612) 624-1493, shadac@umn.edu, https://www.shadac.org/; Coronavirus Pandemic Caused More than 10 million U.S. Adults to Lose Health Insurance.

Temple University, Hope Center for College, Community, and Justice, Medical Education & Research Bldg., 3500N Broad St., Philadelphia, PA, 19140, USA, (215) 204-7000, hopectr@temple.edu, https://hope4college.com/; The Hope Center Survey 2021: Basic Needs Insecurity During the Ongoing Pandemic.

UNESCO Institute for Statistics, C.P 250 Succursale H, Montreal, QC, H3G 2K8, CAN, (514) 343-6880 (Dial from U.S.), (514) 343-5740 (Fax from U.S.), uis.publications@unesco.org, http://uis.unesco.org/; COVID-19 Is a Serious Threat to Aid to Education Recovery.

United Nations UN Women, 405 E 42nd St., New York, NY, 10017-3599, USA, (646) 781-4400, (646) 781-4444, https://www.unwomen.org; COVID-19: Emerging Gender Data and Why it Matters and From Insights to Action: Gender Equality in the Wake of COVID-19.

University of California Los Angeles (UCLA), Luskin Center for Innovation, 3323 Public Affairs Bldg., PO Box 951656, Los Angeles, CA, 90095-1656, USA, (310) 267-5435, (310) 267-5443, https://innovation.luskin.ucla.edu/; Keeping the Lights and Heat On: COVID-19 Utility Debt in Communities Served by Pacific Gas and Electric Company.

University of Michigan, Poverty Solutions, 735 S State St., Ste. 5100, Ann Arbor, MI, 48109-3091, USA, povertysolutions@umich.edu, https://poverty.umich.edu/; Housing and Health Inequities During COVID-19: Findings from the National Household Pulse Survey.

USAFacts, USA, info@usafacts.org, https://usafacts.org/; COVID-19 Recovery Indicators.

Yale University, Tobin Center for Economic Policy, 37 Hillhouse Ave., New Haven, CT, 06520, USA, tobincenter@yale.edu, https://tobin.yale.edu/; Employment Effects of Unemployment Insurance Generosity During the Pandemic.

COVID-19 PANDEMIC, 2020--GOVERNMENT POLICY

American Immigration Council, 1331 G St. NW , Ste. 200, Washington, DC, 20005, USA, (202) 507-7500, info@immcouncil.org, https://www.americanimmigrationcouncil.org/; Immigration and Covid-19 and Undocumented Immigrants and the Covid-19 Crisis.

Civiqs, PO Box 70008, Oakland, CA, 94612, USA, (510) 394-5664, inquiries@civiqs.com, https://civiqs.com/; How Satisfied Are You With the U.S. Government's Current Response to the Coronavirus Outbreak?.

Council on Criminal Justice (CCJ), National Commission on COVID-19 and Criminal Justice, 700 Pennsylvania Ave. SE, Washington, DC, 20020, USA, info@counciloncj.org, https://counciloncj.org/covid-19/; Experience to Action: Reshaping Criminal Justice After COVID-19.

Guttmacher Institute, 125 Maiden Ln., 7th Fl., New York, NY, 10038, USA, (212) 248-1111, (800) 355-0244, (212) 248-1951, info@guttmacher.org, https://www.guttmacher.org/; State Policy Trends at Midyear 2022: With Roe About to Be Overturned, Some States Double Down on Abortion Restrictions.

The Henry J. Kaiser Family Foundation (KFF), 185 Berry St., Ste. 2000, San Francisco, CA, 94107, USA, (650) 854-9400, (650) 854-4800, https://www.kff.org; KFF Health Tracking Poll: Coronavirus: Reopening, Schools, and the Government Response and Temporary Enhanced Federal Medicaid Funding Can Soften the Economic Blow of the COVID-19 Pandemic on States, But Is Unlikely to Fully Offset State Revenue Declines or Forestall Budget Shortfalls.

Institute for Strategic Dialogue (ISD), PO Box 75769, London, SW1P 9ER, GBR, info@isdglobal.org, https://www.isdglobal.org/; 'Climate Lockdown' and the Culture Wars: How COVID-19 Sparked a New Narrative Against Climate Action.

New York University School of Law, Institute for Policy Integrity, 139 MacDougal St., Wilf Hall, 3rd Fl., New York, NY, 10012, USA, (212) 992-8932, (212) 995-4592, https://policyintegrity.org/; Weakening Our Defenses: How the Trump Administration's Deregulatory Push Has Exacerbated the Covid-19 Pandemic.

Pew Research Center, 1615 L St. NW, Ste. 800, Washington, DC, 20036, USA, (202) 419-4300, (202) 857-8562, info@pewresearch.org, https://www.pewresearch.org/; U.S. Labor Market Inches Back From the COVID-19 Shock, But Recovery Is Far From Complete.

Physicians for Human Rights (PHR), 256 W 38th St., 9th Fl., New York, NY, 10018, USA, (646) 564-3720, (646) 564-3750, https://phr.org/; Neither Safety nor Health: How Title 42 Expulsions Harm Health and Violate Rights.

PLOS, 1265 Battery St., Ste. 200, San Francisco, CA, 94111, USA, (415) 624-1200, (415) 795-1584, plos@plos.org, https://www.plos.org/; Outbreak Analysis with a Logistic Growth Model Shows COVID-19 Suppression Dynamics in China.

State Health Access Data Assistance Center (SHADAC), 2221 University Ave. SE, Ste. 345, Minneapolis, MN, 55414, USA, (612) 624-4802, (612) 624-1493, shadac@umn.edu, https://www.shadac.org/; Emergency Flexibility for States to Increase and Maintain Medicaid Eligibility for LTSS under COVID-19.

U.S. Department of Health and Human Services, Centers for Disease Control and Prevention (CDC), 1600 Clifton Rd., Atlanta, GA, 30329-4027, USA, (800) 232-4636, (888) 232-6348 (TTY), cdcinfo@cdc.gov, https://www.cdc.gov; SARS-CoV-2 Incidence in K-12 School Districts with Mask-Required Versus Mask-Optional Policies: Arkansas, August-October 2021.

U.S. Department of Homeland Security (DHS), Federal Emergency Management Agency (FEMA), PO Box 10055, Hyattsville, MD, 20782-8055, USA, (202) 646-2500, https://www.fema.gov/; Coronavirus Disease (COVID-19) Initial Assessment Report.

U.S. Department of State (DOS), 2201 C St. NW, Washington, DC, 20520, USA, (202) 647-4000, ofm-info@state.gov, https://www.state.gov; Update: The United States Continues to Lead the Global Response to COVID-19.

U.S. Government Accountablity Office (GAO), 441 G St. NW, Washington, DC, 20548, USA, (202) 512-3000, contact@gao.gov, https://www.gao.gov/; COVID-19: Opportunities to Improve Federal Response and Recovery Efforts.

University of California, Berkeley, Global Policy Lab, California Memorial Stadium, 2227 Piedmont Ave., Berkeley, CA, 94720, USA, (510) 643-5751, https://www.globalpolicy.science/; The Effect of Large-Scale Anti-Contagion Policies on the COVID-19 Pandemic.

The Urban Institute, 500 L'Enfant Plaza SW, Washington, DC, 20024, USA, (202) 833-7200, https://www.urban.org/; Local Government Efforts to Mitigate the Novel Coronavirus Pandemic Among Older Adults.

COVID-19 PANDEMIC, 2020--POLITICAL ASPECTS

American Immigration Council, 1331 G St. NW , Ste. 200, Washington, DC, 20005, USA, (202) 507-7500, info@immcouncil.org, https://www.americanimmigrationcouncil.org/; Immigration and Covid-19 and Undocumented Immigrants and the Covid-19 Crisis.

The Henry J. Kaiser Family Foundation (KFF), 185 Berry St., Ste. 2000, San Francisco, CA, 94107, USA, (650) 854-9400, (650) 854-4800, https://www.kff.org; KFF COVID-19 Vaccine Monitor: The Increasing Importance of Partisanship in Predicting COVID-19 Vaccination Status and KFF Health Tracking Poll: Coronavirus, Delayed Care and 2020 Election.

The Immigrant Learning Center (ILC), 442 Main St., Malden, MA, 02148-5177, USA, (781) 322-9777, (800) 439-2370 (TTY), (781) 321-1963, info@ilctr.org, https://www.ilctr.org/; Immigrant Detention and COVID-19: How a Pandemic Exploited and Spread through the US Immigrant Detention System.

Institute for Strategic Dialogue (ISD), PO Box 75769, London, SW1P 9ER, GBR, info@isdglobal.org, https://www.isdglobal.org/; 'Climate Lockdown' and the Culture Wars: How COVID-19 Sparked a New Narrative Against Climate Action.

Ipsos, 360 Park Ave. S, 17th Fl., New York, NY, 10010, USA, (212) 265-3200, https://www.ipsos.com/en-us; COVID-19, Racial Inequality Among Top Political Issues for Americans.

National Bureau of Economic Research (NBER), 1050 Massachusetts Ave., Cambridge, MA, 02138, USA, (617) 868-3900, info@nber.org, https://www.nber.org/; Misinformation During a Pandemic.

New York University School of Law, Institute for Policy Integrity, 139 MacDougal St., Wilf Hall, 3rd Fl., New York, NY, 10012, USA, (212) 992-8932, (212) 995-4592, https://policyintegrity.org/; Weakening Our Defenses: How the Trump Administration's Deregulatory Push Has Exacerbated the Covid-19 Pandemic.

Pew Research Center, Politics & Policy, 1615 L St. NW, Ste. 800, Washington, DC, 20036, USA, (202) 419-4300, (202) 857-8562, https://www.pewresearch.org/topic/politics-policy/; Republicans, Democrats Move Even Further Apart in Coronavirus Concerns: Growing Share of Republicans Say 'The Worst Is Behind Us'.

Southern Poverty Law Center (SPLC), 400 Washington Ave., Montgomery, AL, 36104, USA, (334) 956-8200, (888) 414-7752, https://www.splcenter.org/; Overcoming the Unprecedented: Southern Voters' Battle Against Voter Suppression, Intimidation, and a Virus.

U.S. Department of State (DOS), 2201 C St. NW, Washington, DC, 20520, USA, (202) 647-4000, ofm-info@state.gov, https://www.state.gov; Update: The United States Continues to Lead the Global Response to COVID-19.

United Kingdom Office for National Statistics (ONS), Cardiff Rd., Government Bldgs., Rm. D265 , Newport, NP10 8XG, GBR, info@ons.gsi.gov.uk, https://www.ons.gov.uk/; COVID-19 Infection Survey.

COVID-19 PANDEMIC, 2020--PSYCHOLOGICAL ASPECTS

American Psychological Association (APA), 750 First St. NE, Washington, DC, 20002-4242, USA, (800) 374-2721, (202) 336-5500, https://www.apa.org/; One Year On: Unhealthy Weight Gains, Increased Drinking Reported by Americans Coping with Pandemic Stress.

Center on Budget and Policy Priorities, 1275 First St. NE, Ste. 1200, Washington, DC, 20002, USA, (202) 408-1080, (202) 408-1056, center@cbpp.org, https://www.cbpp.org/; Tracking the COVID-19 Recession's Effects on Food, Housing, and Employment Hardships.

Council on Criminal Justice (CCJ), National Commission on COVID-19 and Criminal Justice, 700 Pennsylvania Ave. SE, Washington, DC, 20020, USA, info@counciloncj.org, https://counciloncj.org/covid-19/; Impact Report: COVID-19 and SUD Treatment and Research in Brief: Domestic Violence Calls for Service.

Frontier Group, 1129 State St., No. 10, Santa Barbara, CA, 93101, USA, (805) 730-1391, https://frontiergroup.org/; Healthy Parks, Healthy People: The COVID-19 Pandemic Spotlights the Importance of Public Lands.

The Gallup Organization, 901 F St. NW, Washington, DC, 20004, USA, (202) 715-3030, (800) 204-1192, (202) 715-3045, https://www.gallup.com; 2020 Sets Records for Negative Emotions.

The Henry J. Kaiser Family Foundation (KFF), 185 Berry St., Ste. 2000, San Francisco, CA, 94107, USA, (650) 854-9400, (650) 854-4800, https://www.kff.org; The Implications of COVID-19 for Mental Health and Substance Use and KFF Health Tracking Poll: Coronavirus, Delayed Care and 2020 Election.

Indiana University, Kinsey Institute, 150 S Woodlawn Ave., Lindley Hall 428, Bloomington, IN, 47405, USA, (812) 855-7686, (812) 855-3058, kinsey@indiana.edu, https://kinseyinstitute.org; Sexual Desire in the Time of COVID-19: How COVID-Related Stressors Are Associated with Sexual Desire in Romantic Relationships.

Mediterranean Institute of Gender Studies (MIGS), 46 Makedonitissas Ave., PO Box 24005, Nicosia, 1703, CYP, info@medinstgenderstudies.org, https://medinstgenderstudies.org/; Workers' Individual and Dyadic Coping with the COVID-19 Health Emergency: A Cross Cultural Study.

National Bureau of Economic Research (NBER), 1050 Massachusetts Ave., Cambridge, MA, 02138, USA, (617) 868-3900, info@nber.org, https://www.nber.org/; Misinformation During a Pandemic.

Public Religion Research Institute (PRRI), 1023 15th St. NW, 9th Fl., Washington, DC, 20005, USA, (202) 238-9424, info@prri.org, https://www.prri.org/; Religious Identities and the Race Against the Virus: Engaging Faith Communities on COVID-19 Vaccination.

SAGE Publications, 2455 Teller Rd., Thousand Oaks, CA, 91320, USA, (800) 818-7243, (800) 583-2665, journals@sagepub.com, https://www.sagepub.com; Palliative Medicine - End-of-Life Care in COVID-19: An Audit of Pharmacological Management in Hospital Inpatients.

State Health Access Data Assistance Center (SHADAC), 2221 University Ave. SE, Ste. 345, Minneapolis, MN, 55414, USA, (612) 624-4802, (612) 624-1493, shadac@umn.edu, https://www.shadac.org/; 90 Percent of U.S. Adults Report Increased Stress Due to Coronavirus Pandemic.

Temple University, Hope Center for College, Community, and Justice, Medical Education & Research Bldg., 3500N Broad St., Philadelphia, PA, 19140, USA, (215) 204-7000, hopectr@temple.edu, https://hope4college.com/; The Hope Center Survey 2021: Basic Needs Insecurity During the Ongoing Pandemic.

U.S. Department of Health and Human Services, Centers for Disease Control and Prevention (CDC), 1600 Clifton Rd., Atlanta, GA, 30329-4027, USA, (800) 232-4636, (888) 232-6348 (TTY), cdcinfo@cdc.gov, https://www.cdc.gov; Emergency Department Visits for Suspected Suicide Attempts Among Persons Aged 12-25 Years Before and During the COVID-19 Pandemic - United States, January 2019 - May 2021 and Symptoms of Anxiety or Depressive Disorder and Use of Mental Health Care Among Adults During the COVID-19 Pandemic - United States, August 2020 - February 2021.

U.S. Department of Health and Human Services, Centers for Disease Control and Prevention (CDC), National Center for Health Statistics (NCHS), 3311 Toledo Rd., Hyattsville, MD, 20782-2064, USA, (800) 232-4636, (301) 458-4000, https://www.cdc.gov/nchs; Household Pulse Survey: Anxiety and Depression and Household Pulse Survey: Mental Health Care.

United Nations UN Women, 405 E 42nd St., New York, NY, 10017-3599, USA, (646) 781-4400, (646) 781-4444, https://www.unwomen.org; COVID-19: Emerging Gender Data and Why it Matters.

University of Washington, Institute for Health Metrics and Evaluation (IHME), Population Health Building/Hans Rosling Center, UW Campus Box 351615, 3980 15th Ave. NE, Seattle, WA, 98195, USA, (206) 897-2800, (206) 897-2899, engage@healthdata.org, https://www.healthdata.org; Vaccine Hesitancy by County.

World Health Organization (WHO), Pan American Health Organization (PAHO), 525 23rd St. NW, Washington, DC, 20037, USA, (202) 974-3000, (202) 974-3663, pubrights@paho.org, https://www.paho.org; A New Agenda for Mental Health in the Americas: Report of the Pan American Health Organization High-Level Commission on Mental Health and COVID-19.

COVID-19 PANDEMIC, 2020--SOCIAL ASPECTS

African Women's Development and Communication Network (FEMNET), 12 Masaba Rd., Lowerhill, PO Box 54562, Nairobi, 00200, KEN, admin@femnet.or.ke, https://femnet.org; Qualitative Study on the Impact of COVID-19 on Sexual and Reproductive Health and Rights (SRHR) of Women & Girls in Africa.

American Association of Retired Persons (AARP) Public Policy Institute (PPI), 601 E St. NW, Washington, DC, 20049, USA, (202) 434-3840, ppi@aarp.org, https://www.aarp.org/ppi; Estimating Impacts of Pandemic-Related Job Loss on Health Insurance Coverage Among Adults Ages 50 to 64 During the First Year of COVID-19.

American Immigration Council, 1331 G St. NW , Ste. 200, Washington, DC, 20005, USA, (202) 507-7500, info@immcouncil.org, https://www.americanimmigrationcouncil.org/; Immigration and Covid-19 and Undocumented Immigrants and the Covid-19 Crisis.

American Psychological Association (APA), 750 First St. NE, Washington, DC, 20002-4242, USA, (800) 374-2721, (202) 336-5500, https://www.apa.org/; One Year On: Unhealthy Weight Gains, Increased Drinking Reported by Americans Coping with Pandemic Stress.

American Sociological Association (ASA), 1430 K St. NW, Ste. 600, Washington, DC, 20005, USA, (202) 383-9005, (202) 638-0882, publications@asanet.org, https://www.asanet.org/; Footnotes: Sociologists and Sociology During COVID-19.

Australian Institute of Family Studies, Child Family Community Australia (CFCA), 40 City Rd., Level 4, Southbank, VIC, 3006, AUS, enquiries@aifs.gov.au, https://aifs.gov.au/research_programs/child-family-community-australia; Alcohol-Related Harm in Families and Alcohol Consumption During COVID-19.

The Brookings Institution, 1775 Massachusetts Ave. NW, Washington, DC, 20036, USA, (202) 797-6000, communications@brookings.edu, https://www.brookings.edu/; Three Million More Guns: The Spring 2020 Spike in Firearm Sales.

Charities Aid Foundation (CAF), 25 Kings Hill Ave., Kings Hill, West Malling, Kent, ME19 4TA, GBR, cafbank@cafonline.org, https://www.cafonline.org/; UK Giving Report 2020: COVID-19 Special Report.

Charities Aid Foundation of America (CAF America), 225 Reinekers Ln., Ste. 375, Alexandria, VA, 22314, USA, (202) 793-2232, (703) 549-8934, info@cafamerica.org, https://www.cafamerica.org/; COVID-19 Reports Series.

Clayton Christensen Institute, 92 Hayden Ave., Lexington, MA, 02421, USA, (781) 325-9558, info@christenseninstitute.org, https://www.christenseninstitute.org/; Not a Lost Year: K-12 Innovation During 2020-21 and How to Nurture it Post-Pandemic and Potential Unfulfilled: COVID-19, the Rapid Adoption of Online Learning, and What Could be Unlocked this Year.

Consumer Technology Association (CTA), 1919 S Eads St., Arlington, VA, 22202, USA, (703) 907-7600, (866) 858-1555, (703) 907-7675, cta@cta.tech, https://www.cta.tech; Mobility and Auto Technology in the COVID-19 Era.

Council on Criminal Justice (CCJ), National Commission on COVID-19 and Criminal Justice, 700 Pennsylvania Ave. SE, Washington, DC, 20020, USA, info@counciloncj.org, https://counciloncj.org/covid-19/; Impact Report: COVID-19 and SUD Treatment and Research in Brief: Domestic Violence Calls for Service.

The COVID Tracking Project at The Atlantic, support@covidtracking.com, https://covidtracking.com; The COVID Racial Data Tracker.

Death Penalty Information Center (DPIC), 1701 K St. NW, Ste. 205, Washington, DC, 20006, USA, (202) 289-2275, dpic@deathpenaltyinfo.org, https://deathpenaltyinfo.org/; DPIC Mid-Year Review: Pandemic and Continuing Historic Decline Produce Record-Low Death Penalty Use in First Half of 2020.

The Economist Group, 900 3rd Ave., 16th Fl., New York, NY, 10022, USA, (212) 541-0500, (202) 429-0890, customerhelp@economist.com, https://www.economistgroup.com; Covid-19 Data: The Global Normalcy Index.

Feeding America, 161 N Clark St., Ste. 700, Chicago, IL, 60601, USA, (800) 771-2303, (312) 263-5626, https://www.feedingamerica.org/; The Impact of the Coronavirus on Local Food Insecurity in 2020 and 2021.

Frontier Group, 1129 State St., No. 10, Santa Barbara, CA, 93101, USA, (805) 730-1391, https://frontiergroup.org/; Healthy Parks, Healthy People: The COVID-19 Pandemic Spotlights the Importance of Public Lands.

The Gallup Organization, 901 F St. NW, Washington, DC, 20004, USA, (202) 715-3030, (800) 204-1192, (202) 715-3045, https://www.gallup.com; 2020 Sets Records for Negative Emotions.

Global Change Data Lab, Our World in Data, GBR, info@ourworldindata.org, https://ourworldindata.org; Which Countries Have Protected Both Health and the Economy in the Pandemic?.

Guttmacher Institute, 125 Maiden Ln., 7th Fl., New York, NY, 10038, USA, (212) 248-1111, (800) 355-0244, (212) 248-1951, info@guttmacher.org, https://www.guttmacher.org/; Early Impacts of the COVID-19 Pandemic: Findings from the 2020 Guttmacher Survey of Reproductive Health Experiences.

Harvard John F. Kennedy School of Government, 79 John F. Kennedy St., Cambridge, MA, 02138, USA, (617) 495-1100, https://www.hks.harvard.edu/; Harvard Kennedy School Misinformation Review - The Causes and Consequences of COVID-19 Misperceptions: Understanding the Role of News and Social Media and Harvard Kennedy School Misinformation Review - The Relation between Media Consumption and Misinformation at the Outset of the SARS-CoV-2 Pandemic in the US.

The Henry J. Kaiser Family Foundation (KFF), 185 Berry St., Ste. 2000, San Francisco, CA, 94107, USA, (650) 854-9400, (650) 854-4800, https://www.kff.org; About 1.5 Million Teachers Are at Higher Risk of Serious Illness From COVID-19; Almost One in Four Adult Workers Is Vulnerable to Severe Illness from COVID-19; KFF COVID-19 Vaccine Monitor: The Increasing Importance of Partisanship in Predicting COVID-19 Vaccination Status; KFF COVID-19 Vaccine Monitor: The Pandemic's Toll on Workers and Family Finances During the Omicron Surge; KFF Health Tracking Poll: Coronavirus, Delayed Care and 2020 Election; KFF Health Tracking Poll: Coronavirus: Reopening, Schools, and the Government Response; More Than 3 Million People Age 65 or Older Live with School-Age Children, and Could Be at Heightened Risk of COVID-19 Infection if Children Bring the Virus Home from School; and Rising Cases in Long-term Care Facilities Are Cause for Concern.

The Immigrant Learning Center (ILC), 442 Main St., Malden, MA, 02148-5177, USA, (781) 322-9777, (800) 439-2370 (TTY), (781) 321-1963, info@ilctr.org, https://www.ilctr.org/; Health and Financial Risks for Noncitizen Immigrants due to the COVID-19 Pandemic.

Indiana University, Kinsey Institute, 150 S Woodlawn Ave., Lindley Hall 428, Bloomington, IN, 47405, USA, (812) 855-7686, (812) 855-3058, kinsey@indiana.edu, https://kinseyinstitute.org; Sexual Desire in the Time of COVID-19: How COVID-Related Stressors Are Associated with Sexual Desire in Romantic Relationships.

INRIX, 10210 NE Points Dr., No. 400, Kirkland, WA, 98033, USA, (425) 284-3800, https://inrix.com; COVID-19 Effect on Collisions on Interstates and Highways.

Institute for Strategic Dialogue (ISD), PO Box 75769, London, SW1P 9ER, GBR, info@isdglobal.org, https://www.isdglobal.org/; 'Climate Lockdown' and the Culture Wars: How COVID-19 Sparked a New Narrative Against Climate Action; The Conspiracy Consortium: Examining Discussions of COVID-19 Among Right-Wing Extremist Telegram Channels; and Ill Advice: A Case Study in Facebook's Failure to Tackle COVID-19 Disinformation.

International Institute for Applied Systems Analysis (IIASA), Schlossplatz 1, Laxenburg, A-2361, AUT, info@iiasa.ac.at, https://iiasa.ac.at/; Understanding Patterns of Internal Migration During the COVID-19 Pandemic in Spain.

International Women's Media Foundation (IWMF), 1625 K St. NW, Ste. 1275, Washington, DC, 20006, USA, (202) 496-1992, info@iwmf.org, https://www.iwmf.org/; The Missing Perspectives of Women in COVID-19 News.

KFF Health News, 1330 G St. NW, Washington, DC, 20005, USA, (202) 347-5270, https://khn.org/; Medicaid Vaccination Rates Founder as States Struggle to Immunize Their Poorest Residents.

The Lancet, 230 Park Ave., New York, NY, 10169, USA, (212) 633-3800, editorial@lancet.com, https://www.thelancet.com/; Global, Regional, and National Minimum Estimates of Children Affected by COVID-19-Associated Orphanhood and Caregiver Death, by Age and Family Circumstance up to Oct 31, 2021: An Updated Modelling Study.

League of American Orchestras, 520 8th Ave., Ste. 2005, New York, NY, 10018, USA, (212) 262-5161, (212) 262-5198, knowledge@americanorchestras.org, https://americanorchestras.org/; The League's COVID-19 Impact Survey.

The Marshall Project, 156 W 56th St., 3rd Fl., New York, NY, 10019, USA, (212) 803-5200, info@themarshallproject.org, https://www.themarshallproject.org/; A State-By-State Look at 15 Months of Coronavirus in Prisons.

Massachusetts Institute of Technology (MIT), Living Wage Calculator, 77 Massachusetts Ave., Cambridge, MA, 02139, USA, (617) 324-6565, (617) 253-1000, amyglas@mit.edu, https://livingwage.mit.edu; Nothing New Under the Sun: Covid-19 Brings to Light Persistent Issues in the Navajo Nation.

Mathematica, PO Box 2393, Princeton, NJ, 08543-2393, USA, (609) 275-2350, (609) 799-3535, (609) 799-0005, info@mathematica-mpr.com, https://www.mathematica.org; Tracking Youth Unemployment During the COVID-19 Pandemic.

Mediterranean Institute of Gender Studies (MIGS), 46 Makedonitissas Ave., PO Box 24005, Nicosia, 1703, CYP, info@medinstgenderstudies.org, https://medinstgenderstudies.org/; Workers' Individual and Dyadic Coping with the COVID-19 Health Emergency: A Cross Cultural Study.

Morning Consult, 729 15th St. NW, Washington, DC, 20005, USA, (202) 506-1957, contact@morningconsult.com, https://morningconsult.com; How 2020 Is Impacting Gen Z's Worldview: A Tracking Report Dedicated to Understanding How a Tumultuous Year Is Altering the Young Generation's Habits, Values, and Outlook.

National Academy of Social Insurance (NASI), 1441 L St. NW, Ste. 530, Washington, DC, 20005, USA, (202) 452-8097, (202) 452-8111, nasi@nasi.org, https://www.nasi.org; The Impact of the COVID-19 Pandemic on Access to Health Care.

National Alliance for Public Charter Schools, 800 Connecticut Ave. NW, Ste. 300, Washington, DC, 20006, USA, (202) 289-2700, (202) 289-4009, datarequest@publiccharters.org, https://www.publiccharters.org/; Learning in Real Time: How Charter Schools Served Students During COVID-19 Closures.

National Bureau of Economic Research (NBER), 1050 Massachusetts Ave., Cambridge, MA, 02138, USA, (617) 868-3900, info@nber.org, https://www.nber.org/; Misinformation During a Pandemic; Pandemic Schooling Mode and Student Test Scores: Evidence from US States; and The Persuasive Effect of Fox News: Non-Compliance with Social Distancing During the Covid-19 Pandemic.

National Coalition of Anti-Violence Programs (NCAVP), 116 Nassau St., 3rd Fl., New York, NY, 10038, USA, (212) 714-1184, ecruz@avp.org, https://avp.org/ncavp/; Supporting LGBTQ Survivors of Violence During the COVID-19 Pandemic.

National Law Enforcement Officers Memorial Fund (NLEOMF), 444 E St. NW, Washington, DC, 20001, USA, (202) 737-3400, (202) 737-3405, info@nleomf.org, https://nleomf.org/; The Takeaway: Covid-19 Fatalities.

National Student Clearinghouse Research Center, 2300 Dulles Station Blvd., Ste. 220, Herndon, VA, 21071, USA, https://nscresearchcenter.org; Spring 2022 Current Term Enrollment Estimates.

National Women's Law Center (NWLC), 1350 I St. NW, Ste. 700, Washington, DC, 20005, USA, (202) 588-5180, https://nwlc.org; A Year of Strength & Loss: The Pandemic, the Economy, & the Value of Women's Work.

Network Contagion Research Institute (NCRI), https://networkcontagion.us/; Mapping Mistrust: The NCRI's Geospatial Analysis of Civil-Unrest Activity, Relating to the COVID-19 Pandemic, in the United States (2020).

NewsGuard, 25 W 52nd St., 15th Fl., New York, NY, 10019, USA, https://www.newsguardtech.com/; COVID-19 Vaccine Misinformation Targeting Children, Teenagers and Parents on Social Media: A Report for Governments and the WHO.

Nielsen, 675 6th Ave., New York, NY, 10011, USA, (800) 864-1224, https://www.nielsen.com; Nielsen Total Audience Report: August 2020 Special Edition on Work-From-Home.

Pew Research Center, 1615 L St. NW, Ste. 800, Washington, DC, 20036, USA, (202) 419-4300, (202) 857-8562, info@pewresearch.org, https://www.pewresearch.org/; Americans Are Following News about Presidential Candidates Much Less Closely than COVID-19 News; Local News Is Playing an Important Role for Americans During COVID-19 Outbreak; Many Black and Asian Americans Say They Have Experienced Discrimination Amid the COVID-19 Outbreak; Three Months In, Many Americans See Exaggeration, Conspiracy Theories and Partisanship in COVID-19 News; and Younger Adults Differ from Older Ones in Perceptions of News about COVID-19, George Floyd Protests.

Pew Research Center, Internet & Technology, 1615 L St. NW, Ste. 800, Washington, DC, 20036, USA, (202) 419-4300, (202) 857-8562, https://www.pewresearch.org/topic/internet-technology/; The Internet and the Pandemic.

Pew Research Center, Religion & Public Life, 1615 L St. NW, Ste. 800, Washington, DC, 20036, USA, (202) 419-4300, (202) 857-8562, https://www.pewforum.org/; How COVID-19 Restrictions Affected Religious Groups Around the World in 2020.

Police Executive Research Forum (PERF), 1120 Connecticut Ave. NW, Ste. 930, Washington, DC, 20036, USA, (202) 466-7820, https://www.policeforum.org; Lessons from the COVID-19 Pandemic: What Police Learned from One of the Most Challenging Periods of Our Lives.

Poor People's Campaign, USA, https://www.poorpeoplescampaign.org/; A Poor People's Pandemic Report: Mapping the Intersections of Poverty, Race and COVID-19.

Princeton University Eviction Lab, Princeton, NY, 08544, research@evictionlab.org, https://evictionlab.org; Preliminary Analysis: Eviction Filing Trends After the CDC Moratorium Expiration.

Public Agenda, 1 Dock 72 Way, No. 6101, Brooklyn, NY, 11205-1242, USA, (212) 686-6610, info@publicagenda.org, https://www.publicagenda.org/; America's Hidden Common Ground on the Coronavirus Crisis: Results from a Public Agenda/USA Today/Ipsos Snapshot Survey on How Communities Are Responding and the Policies People Support and America's Hidden Common Ground on the Coronavirus Crisis: Results from a Public Agenda/USA Today/Ipsos Survey of Americans' Views on Reopening Their Communities.

Public Religion Research Institute (PRRI), 1023 15th St. NW, 9th Fl., Washington, DC, 20005, USA, (202) 238-9424, info@prri.org, https://www.prri.org/; Religious Identities and the Race Against the Virus: Engaging Faith Communities on COVID-19 Vaccination.

Resolve to Save Lives, 100 Broadway, 4th Fl., New York, NY, 10005, USA, info@resolvetosavelives.org, https://resolvetosavelives.org/; Tracking COVID-19 in the United States: From Information Catastrophe to Empowered Communities.

Restaurant Opportunities Centers United (ROC United), 275 7th. Ave., New York, NY, 10001, USA, (212) 343-1771, info@rocunited.org, https://rocunited.org/; COVID Impact Report: The Impact of COVID-19 on Restaurant Workers Across America.

SAGE Publications, 2455 Teller Rd., Thousand Oaks, CA, 91320, USA, (800) 818-7243, (800) 583-2665, journals@sagepub.com, https://www.sagepub.com; Dialogues in Human Geography - Geographies of the COVID-19 Pandemic and Palliative Medicine - End-of-Life Care in COVID-19: An Audit of Pharmacological Management in Hospital Inpatients.

State Health Access Data Assistance Center (SHADAC), 2221 University Ave. SE, Ste. 345, Minneapolis, MN, 55414, USA, (612) 624-4802, (612) 624-1493, shadac@umn.edu, https://www.shadac.org/; Coronavirus Pandemic Caused More than 10 million U.S. Adults to Lose Health Insurance.

Temple University, Hope Center for College, Community, and Justice, Medical Education & Research Bldg., 3500N Broad St., Philadelphia, PA, 19140, USA, (215) 204-7000, hopectr@temple.edu, https://hope4college.com/; The Hope Center Survey 2021: Basic Needs Insecurity During the Ongoing Pandemic.

U.S. Census Bureau, 4600 Silver Hill Rd., Washington, DC, 20233, USA, (301) 763-4636, (800) 923-8282, https://www.census.gov; Domestic Migration Plays Larger Role in Population Growth of Many Counties in Recent Years; New Census Bureau Population Estimates Show COVID-19 Impact on Fertility and Mortality Across the Nation; and Pandemic Disrupted Historical Mortality Patterns, Caused Largest Jump in Deaths in 100 Years.

U.S. Department of Education (ED), Institute of Education Sciences (IES), 550 12th St. SW, Washington, DC, 20024, USA, (202) 245-6940, contact.ies@ed.gov, https://ies.ed.gov/; School Pulse Panel.

U.S. Department of Health and Human Services (HHS), Office of Inspector General (OIG), 330 Independence Ave. SW, Washington, DC, 20201, USA, (877) 696-6775, public.affairs@oig.hhs.gov, https://oig.hhs.gov/; COVID-19 Had a Devastating Impact on Medicare Beneficiaries in Nursing Homes During 2020.

U.S. Department of Health and Human Services, Centers for Disease Control and Prevention (CDC), 1600 Clifton Rd., Atlanta, GA, 30329-4027, USA, (800) 232-4636, (888) 232-6348 (TTY), cdcinfo@cdc.gov, https://www.cdc.gov; Emergency Department Visits for COVID-19 by Race and Ethnicity - 13 States, October - December 2020; Emergency Department Visits for Suspected Suicide Attempts Among Persons Aged 12-25 Years Before and During the COVID-19 Pandemic - United States, January 2019 - May 2021; Mask Use and Ventilation Improvements to Reduce COVID-19 Incidence in Elementary Schools - Georgia, November 16 - December 11, 2020; Provisional COVID-19 Deaths: Distribution of Deaths by Race and Hispanic Origin; SARS-CoV-2 Incidence in K-12 School Districts with Mask-Required Versus Mask-Optional Policies: Arkansas, August-October 2021; and

Trends in Racial and Ethnic Disparities in COVID-19 Hospitalizations, by Region - United States, March - December 2020.

U.S. Department of Health and Human Services, Centers for Disease Control and Prevention (CDC), National Center for Health Statistics (NCHS), 3311 Toledo Rd., Hyattsville, MD, 20782-2064, USA, (800) 232-4636, (301) 458-4000, https://www.cdc.gov/nchs; Household Pulse Survey: Anxiety and Depression; Household Pulse Survey: Health Insurance Coverage; Household Pulse Survey: Mental Health Care; Household Pulse Survey: Reduced Access to Care; and Household Pulse Survey: Telemedicine Use.

UNESCO Global Education Coalition, C. P. 6128 Succursale Centre-Ville, Montreal, QC, H3C 3J7, CAN, (514) 343-6880 (Dial from U.S.), (514) 343-5740 (Fax from U.S.), https://en.unesco.org/covid19/educationresponse/globalcoalition ; Education: From Disruption to Recovery.

UNESCO Institute for Statistics, C.P 250 Succursale H, Montreal, QC, H3G 2K8, CAN, (514) 343-6880 (Dial from U.S.), (514) 343-5740 (Fax from U.S.), uis.publications@unesco.org, http://uis.unesco.org/; COVID-19 Recovery: Education.

United Nations UN Women, 405 E 42nd St., New York, NY, 10017-3599, USA, (646) 781-4400, (646) 781-4444, https://www.unwomen.org; COVID-19: Emerging Gender Data and Why it Matters and From Insights to Action: Gender Equality in the Wake of COVID-19.

University of Michigan, Poverty Solutions, 735 S State St., Ste. 5100, Ann Arbor, MI, 48109-3091, USA, povertysolutions@umich.edu, https://poverty.umich.edu/; Housing and Health Inequities During COVID-19: Findings from the National Household Pulse Survey.

University of Washington, Institute for Health Metrics and Evaluation (IHME), Population Health Building/Hans Rosling Center, UW Campus Box 351615, 3980 15th Ave. NE, Seattle, WA, 98195, USA, (206) 897-2800, (206) 897-2899, engage@healthdata.org, https://www.healthdata.org; Vaccine Hesitancy by County.

World Health Organization (WHO), Ave. Appia 20, Geneva, CH-1211, SWI, (202) 974-3000 (Telephone in U.S.), publications@who.int, https://www.who.int/; Whose Life Matters? Challenges, Barriers and Impact of COVID-19 Pandemic on Persons with Disability and Their Caregivers.

World Health Organization (WHO), Pan American Health Organization (PAHO), 525 23rd St. NW, Washington, DC, 20037, USA, (202) 974-3000, (202) 974-3663, pubrights@paho.org, https://www.paho.org; A New Agenda for Mental Health in the Americas: Report of the Pan American Health Organization High-Level Commission on Mental Health and COVID-19.

COWS

See CATTLE

CPR (FIRST AID)

Cardiac Arrest Registry to Enhance Survival (CARES), 1599 Clifton Rd. NE, Woodruff Health Sciences Center, Mailstop 1599/001/1BQ, Atlanta, GA, 30322, USA, cares@emory.edu, https://mycares.net; Race/Ethnicity and Neighborhood Characteristics Are Associated With Bystander Cardiopulmonary Resuscitation in Pediatric Out-of-Hospital Cardiac Arrest in the United States.

CRABS

National Oceanic and Atmospheric Administration (NOAA), National Marine Fisheries Service (NOAA Fisheries), 1315 East-West Hwy., 14th Fl., Silver Spring, MD, 20910, USA, (301) 427-8000, https://www.fisheries.noaa.gov/; Fisheries of the United States, 2020.

CRACK COCAINE

Drug Policy Alliance (DPA), 131 W 33rd St., 15th Fl., New York, NY, 10001, USA, (212) 613-8020, (212) 613-8021, contact@drugpolicy.org, https://drugpolicy.org/; Drug Facts.

Substance Abuse and Mental Health Services Administration (SAMHSA), 5600 Fishers Ln., Rockville, MD, 20857, USA, (877) 726-4727, (800) 487-4889 (TTY), samhsainfo@samhsa.hhs.gov, https://www.samhsa.gov/; 2019-2020 National Survey on Drug Use and Health (NSDUH).

CRANBERRIES

U.S. Department of Agriculture (USDA), National Agricultural Statistics Service (USDA-NASS), 1400 Independence Ave. SW, Washington, DC, 20250, USA, (800) 727-9540, nass@nass.usda.gov, https://www.nass.usda.gov; Quick Stats.

CREDIT CARDS

Board of Governors of the Federal Reserve System, Constitution Ave. NW, Washington, DC, 20551, USA, (202) 452-3000, (202) 263-4869 (TDD), https://www.federalreserve.gov; Federal Reserve Bulletin.

Federal Financial Institutions Examination Council (FFIEC), 3501 Fairfax Dr., L. William Seidman Center, Mail Stop: B-7081a, Arlington, VA, 22226-3550 , USA, (703) 516-5590, https://www.ffiec.gov/; Uniform Bank Performance Report (UBPR).

The Nilson Report, PO Box 50539, Santa Barbara, CA, 93150, USA, (805) 684-8800, (805) 684-8825, info@nilsonreport.com, https://www.nilsonreport.com; The Nilson Report and The World's Top Card Issuers and Merchant Acquirers.

CREDIT MARKETS

Board of Governors of the Federal Reserve System, Constitution Ave. NW, Washington, DC, 20551, USA, (202) 452-3000, (202) 263-4869 (TDD), https://www.federalreserve.gov; Federal Reserve Bulletin and Financial Accounts of the United States 2023.

CREDIT MARKETS-FEDERAL PARTICIPATION

U.S. Office of Management and Budget (OMB), 725 17th St. NW, Washington, DC, 20503, USA, (202) 395-3080, https://www.whitehouse.gov/omb/; Analytical Perspectives: Budget of the United States Government and Budget of the United States Government, Fiscal Year 2023.

CREDIT SCORING SYSTEMS

Experian, 475 Anton Blvd., Costa Mesa, CA, 92626, USA, (714) 830-7000, https://www.experian.com/; Credit Scores Steady as Consumer Debt Balances Rise in 2022.

CREDIT UNIONS-EARNINGS

U.S. Census Bureau, 4600 Silver Hill Rd., Washington, DC, 20233, USA, (301) 763-4636, (800) 923-8282, https://www.census.gov; County Business Patterns (CBP) 2020.

CREDIT UNIONS-EMPLOYEES

U.S. Census Bureau, 4600 Silver Hill Rd., Washington, DC, 20233, USA, (301) 763-4636, (800) 923-8282, https://www.census.gov; County Business Patterns (CBP) 2020.

CREDIT UNIONS-ESTABLISHMENTS

Federal Deposit Insurance Corporation (FDIC), 550 17th St. NW, Washington, DC, 20429-9990, USA, (877) 275-3342, (800) 925-4618 (TTY), publicinfo@fdic.gov, https://www.fdic.gov; FDIC State Profiles.

National Credit Union Administration (NCUA), 1775 Duke St., Alexandria, VA, 22314, USA, (703) 518-6300, easternmail@ncua.gov, https://www.ncua.gov; Annual Report of NCUA, 2021; Credit Union and Corporate Call Report Data; and Industry at a Glance.

CREDIT UNIONS-FINANCES

Board of Governors of the Federal Reserve System, Constitution Ave. NW, Washington, DC, 20551, USA, (202) 452-3000, (202) 263-4869 (TDD), https://www.federalreserve.gov; Federal Reserve Bulletin and Financial Accounts of the United States 2023.

Federal Deposit Insurance Corporation (FDIC), 550 17th St. NW, Washington, DC, 20429-9990, USA, (877) 275-3342, (800) 925-4618 (TTY), publicinfo@fdic.gov, https://www.fdic.gov; FDIC State Profiles.

National Credit Union Administration (NCUA), 1775 Duke St., Alexandria, VA, 22314, USA, (703) 518-6300, easternmail@ncua.gov, https://www.ncua.gov; Annual Report of NCUA, 2021; Credit Union and Corporate Call Report Data; and Industry at a Glance.

CREDIT UNIONS-INDIVIDUAL RETIREMENT ACCOUNTS

Investment Company Institute (ICI), 1401 H St. NW, Ste. 1200, Washington, DC, 20005, USA, (202) 326-5800, doug.richardson@ici.org, https://www.ici.org/; 2022 Investment Company Fact Book.

CREMATION

Green Burial Council (GBC), 2720 Cold Springs Rd., Placerville, CA, 95667, USA, (888) 966-3330, info@greenburialcouncil.org, https://www.greenburialcouncil.org; Disposition Statistics.

CREW

National Collegiate Athletic Association (NCAA), PO Box 6222, Indianapolis, IN, 46206-6222, USA, (317) 917-6222, (317) 917-6888, https://www.ncaa.org/; NCAA Sports Sponsorship and Participation Rates Report: 1956-1957 through 2020-2021.

CRIME

See also CRIMINAL VICTIMIZATION

Anti-Defamation League (ADL), 605 3rd Ave., New York, NY, 10158-3650, USA, (212) 885-7700, adlmedia@adl.org, https://www.adl.org; Murder and Extremism in the United States in 2021.

Australian Institute of Criminology (AIC), GPO Box 1936, Canberra, ACT, 2601, AUS, front.desk@aic.gov.au, https://www.aic.gov.au/; Estimating the Costs of Serious and Organised Crime in Australia, 2020-2021.

Bernan Press, 15250 NBN Way, Bldg. C, Blue Ridge Summit, PA, 17214, USA, (301) 459-2255, (800) 865-3457, (800) 865-3450, customercare@bernan.com, https://rowman.com/Page/Bernan; Crime in the United States 2022 and Justice Statistics: An Extended Look at Crime in the United States 2021.

Bureau of Alcohol, Tobacco, Firearms and Explosives (ATF), Office of Public Affairs, 99 New York Ave. NE, Washington, DC, 20226, USA, (202) 648-8520, https://www.atf.gov; Firearms Commerce in the United States, Annual Statistical Update 2021.

Cato Institute, 1000 Massachusetts Ave. NW, Washington, DC, 20001-5403, USA, (202) 842-0200, https://www.cato.org/; Immigrants' Deportations, Local Crime, and Police Effectiveness.

Council on American-Islamic Relations (CAIR), 453 New Jersey Ave. SE, Washington, DC, 20003, USA, (202) 488-8787, (202) 488-0833, info@cair.com, https://www.islamophobia.org/; 2023 Civil Rights Report: Progress in the Shadow of Prejudice.

Council on Criminal Justice (CCJ), National Commission on COVID-19 and Criminal Justice, 700 Pennsylvania Ave. SE, Washington, DC, 20020, USA, info@counciloncj.org, https://counciloncj.org/covid-19/; Experience to Action: Reshaping Criminal Justice After COVID-19.

District of Columbia, Metropolitan Police Department, 441 4th St. NW, 7th Fl., Washington, DC, 20001, USA, (202) 727-9099, (202) 727-4106, mpd@dc.gov, https://mpdc.dc.gov/; Crime Cards and District Crime Data at a Glance.

District of Columbia, Office of Planning, 1100 4th St. SW, Ste. 650 E, Washington, DC, 20024, USA, (202) 442-7600, (202) 442-7638, planning@dc.gov, https://planning.dc.gov/; DC Data Reports 2023.

European Commission, Eurostat, Luxembourg, 2920, LUX, https://ec.europa.eu/eurostat/; Crime and Criminal Justice Database and Crime Statistics.

The European Institute for Crime Prevention and Control, Affiliated with the United Nations (HEUNI), Vilhonkatu 4 B 19, Helsinki, FI-00101, FIN, heuni@om.fi, https://heuni.fi/; Trafficking of Children and Young Persons in Finland.

European Society of Criminology (ESC), University of Lausanne , ESC - ICDP, Sorge - BCH, Lausanne, CH-1015, SWI, secretariat@esc-eurocrim.org, https://www.esc-eurocrim.org/; European Journal of Criminology.

Google Public Data Directory, USA, https://www.google.com/publicdata/directory; Google Public Data Directory.

Home Office of the Government of the United Kingdom, Direct Communications Unit, 2 Marsham St., London, SW1P 4DF, GBR, public.enquiries@homeoffice.gov.uk, https://www.gov.uk/government/organisations/home-office; Crime Outcomes in England and Wales, 2021 to 2022; Criminal Justice Statistics Quarterly; and Police Use of Firearms Statistics.

Institute of Criminology and Legal Policy, University of Helsinki Department of Social Research, PO Box 16, Helsinki, FI-00014, FIN, https://www.helsinki.fi/en/institute-criminology-and-legal-policy; The Historical Criminal Statistics of Finland 1842-2015 - A Systematic Comparison to Sweden.

International Criminal Police Organization (INTERPOL), General Secretariat, 200 quai Charles de Gaulle, Lyon, 69006, FRA, https://www.interpol.int; Automatic Fingerprint Identification System (AFIS) Database; Ballistic Information Network (IBIN); DNA Database; Firearms Reference Table (IFRT); Illicit Arms Records and tracing Management System (iARMS); International Child Sexual Exploitation ((ICSE)) Database; Nominal Data; Stolen Administrative Documents (SAD) Database; Stolen Motor Vehicle Database; and Stolen Works of Art Database.

Justice Policy Institute (JPI), 1012 14th St. NW, Ste. 600, Washington, DC, 20005, USA, (202) 558-7974, (202) 558-7978, info@justicepolicy.org, https://www.justicepolicy.org; Sticker Shock: The Cost of New York's Youth Prisons Approaches $1 Million Per Kid.

Justice Research and Statistics Association (JRSA), 1000 Vermont Ave. NW, Ste. 450, Washington, DC, 20005, USA, (202) 842-9330, (202) 304-1417, cjinfo@jrsa.org, https://www.jrsa.org; SAC Publication Digest 2022.

National Academies of Sciences, Engineering, and Medicine (The National Academies), 500 5th St. NW, Washington, DC, 20001, USA, (202) 334-2000, contact@nas.edu, https://www.nationalacademies.org/; Proactive Policing: Effects on Crime and Communities.

National Bureau of Economic Research (NBER), 1050 Massachusetts Ave., Cambridge, MA, 02138, USA, (617) 868-3900, info@nber.org, https://www.nber.org/; The Urban Crime and Heat Gradient in High and Low Poverty Areas.

National Center for Juvenile Justice (NCJJ), 3700 S Water St., Ste. 200, Pittsburgh, PA, 15203, USA, (412) 227-6950, (412) 227-6955, ncjj@ncjfcj.org, https://www.ncjj.org/; Criminological Highlights: Children and Youth and Trends and Characteristics of Delinquency Cases Handled in Juvenile Court, 2019.

New York University School of Law, Brennan Center for Justice, 120 Broadway, Ste. 1750, New York, NY, 10271, USA, (646) 292-8310, (202) 249-7190, (212) 463-7308, brennancenter@nyu.edu, https://www.brennancenter.org; Myths and Realities: Understanding Recent Trends in Violent Crime.

Pew Research Center, 1615 L St. NW, Ste. 800, Washington, DC, 20036, USA, (202) 419-4300, (202) 857-8562, info@pewresearch.org, https://www.pewresearch.org/; What the Data Says (and Doesn't Say) about Crime in the United States.

PollingReport.com, USA, https://www.pollingreport.com/; Issues Facing the Nation.

RAND Corporation, PO Box 2138, 1776 Main St., Santa Monica, CA, 90407-2138, USA, (310) 451-7002, (412) 802-4981, order@rand.org, https://www.rand.org/; RAND Database of Worldwide Terrorism Incidents (RDWTI).

Rapid Intelligence, Sydney, NSW, 2001, AUS, https://www.rapint.com/; NationMaster.com.

The Sentencing Project, 1705 DeSales St. NW, 8th Fl., Washington, DC, 20036, USA, (202) 628-0871, staff@sentencingproject.org, https://www.sentencingproject.org; Growth in Mass Incarceration; Mass Incarceration Trends; and U.S. Criminal Justice Data.

Trustwave, 70 W Madison St., Ste. 600, Chicago, IL, 60602, USA, (312) 873-7500, https://www.trustwave.com; 2020 Trustwave Global Security Report.

U.S. Department of Education (ED), Office of Postsecondary Education (OPE), Lyndon Baines Johnson Bldg., 400 Maryland Ave. SW, Washington, DC, 20202, USA, (202) 453-6914, https://www2.ed.gov/about/offices/list/ope; The Campus Safety and Security Data Analysis Cutting Tool.

U.S. Department of Justice (DOJ), Bureau of Justice Statistics (BJS), 810 7th St. NW, Washington, DC, 20531, USA, (202) 307-0765, askbjs@usdoj.gov, https://www.bjs.gov/; Annual Survey of Jails, 2019.

U.S. Department of Justice (DOJ), Federal Bureau of Investigation (FBI), 935 Pennsylvania Ave. NW, Washington, DC, 20535-0001, USA, (202) 324-3000, https://www.fbi.gov/; Hate Crime in the United States Incident Analysis.

U.S. Department of Justice (DOJ), National Institute of Justice (NIJ), 810 7th St. NW, Washington, DC, 20531, USA, (202) 307-2942, (800) 851-3420, https://www.nij.gov/; Forensic Evidence and Criminal Justice Outcomes in Sexual Assault Cases; NIJ Journal; and Risk Factors and Indicators Associated with Radicalization to Terrorism in the United States: What Research Sponsored by the National Institute of Justice Tells Us.

U.S. Department of Justice (DOJ), Office of Justice Programs (OJP), 810 7th St. NW, Washington, DC, 20531, USA, (202) 514-2000, askojp@ncjrs.gov, https://ojp.gov/; unpublished data.

U.S. Department of Justice (DOJ), Office of Justice Programs (OJP), National Criminal Justice Reference Service (NCJRS), PO Box 6000, Rockville, MD, 20849-6000, USA, (800) 851-3420, (301) 240-6310 (TTY), responsecenter@ncjrs.gov, https://www.ojp.gov/ncjrs; National Criminal Justice Reference Service (NCJRS) Virtual Library.

U.S. Department of Justice (DOJ), Office of the Attorney General, 950 Pennsylvania Ave. NW, Washington, DC, 20530-0001, USA, (202) 514-2000, (800) 877-8339 (TTY), askdoj@usdoj.gov, https://www.justice.gov/ag; Attorney General's Annual Report to Congress and Assessment of U.S. Government Activities to Combat Trafficking in Persons.

U.S. Department of Justice (DOJ), Office on Violence Against Women (OVW), 145 N St. NE, Ste. 10W.121, Washington, DC, 20530, USA, (202) 307-6026, (202) 307-2277 (TTY), (202) 305-2589, ovw.info@usdoj.gov, https://www.justice.gov/ovw; 2020 Biennial Report to Congress on the Effectiveness of Grant Programs Under the Violence Against Women Act and Office on Violence Against Women 2021 Tribal Consultation Report.

U.S. Department of State (DOS), Bureau of Counterterrorism, Office of Public Affairs, 2201 C St. NW, Rm. 2509, Washington, DC, 20520, USA, (202) 647-4000, https://www.state.gov/bureaus-offices/under-secretary-for-civilian-security-democracy-and-human-rights/bureau-of-counterterrorism/; Country Reports on Terrorism 2020.

United Kingdom National Wildlife Crime Unit (NWCU), GBR, https://www.nwcu.police.uk/; U.K. Wildlife Crime 2020 and Wildlife Crime in Scotland: 2021 Annual Report.

United Nations Office on Drugs and Crime (UNODC), Vienna International Ctre., PO Box 500, Vienna, A-1400, AUT, unodc@unodc.org, https://www.unodc.org/; Global Report on Trafficking in Persons 2022 and Myanmar Opium Survey 2022 - Cultivation, Production and Implications.

University of California Davis, Violence Prevention Research Program (VPRP), 2315 Stockton Blvd., Sacramento, CA, 95817, USA, (916) 734-3539 , hs-vprp@ucdavis.edu, https://health.ucdavis.edu/vprp/; Physical Distancing, Violence, and Crime in US Cities during the Coronavirus Pandemic.

University of Michigan Institute for Social Research, Inter-University Consortium for Political and Social Science Research (ICPSR), PO Box 1248, Ann Arbor, MI, 48106-1248, USA, (734) 615-8400, icpsr-help@umich.edu, https://www.icpsr.umich.edu; ICPSR Bibliography of Data-Related Literature.

University of Michigan Institute for Social Research, Inter-University Consortium for Political and Social Science Research (ICPSR), National Archive of Criminal Justice Data (NACJD), PO Box 1248, Ann Arbor, MI, 48106-1248, USA, (734) 615-8400, nacjd@icpsr.umich.edu, https://www.icpsr.umich.edu/web/pages/NACJD/; Capital Punishment in the United States, 1973-2020 and Violence Against Women (VAW) Resource Guide.

Verizon, 1095 Avenue of the Americas, New York, NY, 10036, USA, (212) 395-1000, https://enterprise.verizon.com/resources/reports; Data Breach Investigations Report (DBIR) 2023.

Washington Coalition of Sexual Assault Programs (WCSAP), 5426 N Rd. 68, Ste. D 311, Pasco, WA, 99301, USA, (360) 754-7356, https://www.wcsap.org/; unpublished data.

CRIME-AGGRAVATING CIRCUMSTANCES

Media Matters for America, PO Box 44811, Washington, DC, 20026, USA, (202) 756-4100, action@mediamatters.org, https://www.mediamatters.org; Fact-Checking Fox News' Narrative on America's 'Crime Crisis'.

U.S. Department of Justice (DOJ), Federal Bureau of Investigation (FBI), 935 Pennsylvania Ave. NW, Washington, DC, 20535-0001, USA, (202) 324-3000, https://www.fbi.gov/; Crime in the United States 2019 and A Study of Pre-Attack Behaviors of Active Shooters in the United States Between 2000 and 2013.

CRIME-ARSON

Bureau of Alcohol, Tobacco, Firearms and Explosives (ATF), Office of Public Affairs, 99 New York Ave. NE, Washington, DC, 20226, USA, (202) 648-8520, https://www.atf.gov; Bomb Arson Tracking System (BATS).

Bureau of Alcohol, Tobacco, Firearms and Explosives (ATF), United States Bomb Data Center (USBDC), 3750 Corporal Rd., Huntsville, AL, 35898 , USA, (800) 461-8841, usbdc@atf.gov, https://www.atf.gov/explosives/us-bomb-data-center; 2020 Arson Incident Report; 2019 House of Worship Incidents in the United States; and 2019 Juvenile Offender (Fire) Incident Report.

National Fire Protection Association (NFPA), 1 Batterymarch Park, Quincy, MA, 02169-7471, USA, (617) 770-3000, (800) 344-3555, (508) 895-8301, https://www.nfpa.org/; NFPA Journal.

U.S. Department of Justice (DOJ), Federal Bureau of Investigation (FBI), 935 Pennsylvania Ave. NW, Washington, DC, 20535-0001, USA, (202) 324-3000, https://www.fbi.gov/; Crime in the United States 2019 and Uniform Crime Reporting (UCR) Program Data.

CRIME-ASSAULT

Delegation of the European Union to the United States, 2175 K St. NW, Washington, DC, 20037, USA, (202) 862-9500, (202) 429-1766, delegation-usa-info@eeas.europa.eu, https://www.eeas.europa.eu/delegations/united-states-america_en ; End Violence against Women & Girls.

Gun Violence Archive (GVA), 1133 Connecticut Ave. NW, Washington, DC, 20036, USA, inquiry@gva.us.

com, https://www.gunviolencearchive.org/; Gun Violence Archive 2023 and Mass Shootings in 2023.

New York University School of Law, Brennan Center for Justice, 120 Broadway, Ste. 1750, New York, NY, 10271, USA, (646) 292-8310, (202) 249-7190, (212) 463-7308, brennancenter@nyu.edu, https://www.brennancenter.org; Myths and Realities: Understanding Recent Trends in Violent Crime.

U.S. Department of Justice (DOJ), Bureau of Justice Statistics (BJS), 810 7th St. NW, Washington, DC, 20531, USA, (202) 307-0765, askbjs@usdoj.gov, https://www.bjs.gov/; Criminal Victimization, 2020.

U.S. Department of Justice (DOJ), Federal Bureau of Investigation (FBI), 935 Pennsylvania Ave. NW, Washington, DC, 20535-0001, USA, (202) 324-3000, https://www.fbi.gov/; Crime in the United States 2019; Hate Crime in the United States Incident Analysis; and Uniform Crime Reporting (UCR) Program Data.

U.S. Department of Justice (DOJ), Office on Violence Against Women (OVW), 145 N St. NE, Ste. 10W.121, Washington, DC, 20530, USA, (202) 307-6026, (202) 307-2277 (TTY), (202) 305-2589, ovw.info@usdoj.gov, https://www.justice.gov/ovw; 2020 Biennial Report to Congress on the Effectiveness of Grant Programs Under the Violence Against Women Act and Office on Violence Against Women 2021 Tribal Consultation Report.

V-Day, 4104 24th St., No. 4515, San Francisco, CA, 94114, USA, (212) 645-8329, info@vday.org, https://www.vday.org/; unpublished data.

The Violence Project, USA, admin@theviolenceproject.org, https://www.theviolenceproject.org/; Mass Shooter Database.

CRIME-AVERAGE VALUE LOST

U.S. Department of Justice (DOJ), Federal Bureau of Investigation (FBI), 935 Pennsylvania Ave. NW, Washington, DC, 20535-0001, USA, (202) 324-3000, https://www.fbi.gov/; Crime in the United States 2019.

CRIME-BURGLARY

U.S. Department of Justice (DOJ), Bureau of Justice Statistics (BJS), 810 7th St. NW, Washington, DC, 20531, USA, (202) 307-0765, askbjs@usdoj.gov, https://www.bjs.gov/; Criminal Victimization, 2020.

U.S. Department of Justice (DOJ), Federal Bureau of Investigation (FBI), 935 Pennsylvania Ave. NW, Washington, DC, 20535-0001, USA, (202) 324-3000, https://www.fbi.gov/; Crime in the United States 2019.

CRIME-CHILD ABUSE AND NEGLECT

Children's Defense Fund (CDF), 840 1st St. NE, Ste. 300, Washington, DC, 20002, USA, (202) 628-8787, cdfinfo@childrensdefense.org, https://www.childrensdefense.org/; The State of America's Children 2021.

Human Rights Watch, 350 5th Ave., 34th Fl., New York, NY, 10118-3299, USA, (212) 290-4700, (212) 736-1300, https://www.hrw.org; Like I'm Drowning: Children and Families Sent to Harm by the US 'Remain in Mexico' Program.

Institute on Violence, Abuse and Trauma (IVAT), 10065 Old Grove Rd. , Ste. 101, San Diego, CA, 92131, USA, (858) 527-1860, (858) 527-1743, https://www.ivatcenters.org/; Journal of Child Sexual Abuse (JCSA) and Journal of Family Trauma, Child Custody, and Child Development (JFT).

International Criminal Police Organization (INTERPOL), General Secretariat, 200 quai Charles de Gaulle, Lyon, 69006, FRA, https://www.interpol.int; International Child Sexual Exploitation ((ICSE)) Database.

National Indian Child Welfare Association (NICWA), 5100 SW Macadam Ave., Ste. 300, Portland, OR, 97239, USA, (503) 222-4044, info@nicwa.org, https://www.nicwa.org/; unpublished data.

U.S. Department of Health and Human Services (HHS), Administration for Children and Families (ACF), Children's Bureau, 330 C St. SW, Washington, DC, 20201, USA, https://www.acf.hhs.gov/cb; Child Maltreatment 2020.

U.S. Department of Health and Human Services (HHS), Administration for Children and Families (ACF), Children's Bureau, Child Welfare Information Gateway, 330 C St. SW, Washington, DC, 20201, USA, (800) 394-3366, info@childwelfare.gov, https://www.childwelfare.gov/; Adoption Statistics; Child Abuse & Neglect Fatalities; Child Abuse & Neglect Statistics; and Foster Care Statistics.

University of New Hampshire, Crimes Against Children Research Center (CCRC), 125 McConnell Hall, 15 Academic Way, Durham, NH, 03824, USA, (603) 862-3541, (603) 862-1122, david.finkelhor@unh.edu, https://www.unh.edu/ccrc/; unpublished data.

CRIME-CONTACT WITH POLICE

American Civil Liberties Union (ACLU), 125 Broad St. , 18th Fl., New York, NY, 10004, USA, (212) 549-2500, https://www.aclu.org/; License to Abuse: How ICE's 287(g) Program Empowers Racist Sheriffs and Civil Rights Violations and The Other Epidemic: Fatal Police Shootings in the Time of COVID-19.

Campaign Zero, USA, info@campaignzero.org, https://campaignzero.org; Mapping Police Violence.

Cato Institute, 1000 Massachusetts Ave. NW, Washington, DC, 20001-5403, USA, (202) 842-0200, https://www.cato.org/; Does Greater Police Funding Help Catch More Murderers? and Immigrants' Deportations, Local Crime, and Police Effectiveness.

Center for Policing Equity (CPE), 8605 Santa Monica Blvd., PMB 54596, West Hollywood, CA, 90069-4109, USA, (347) 948-9953, https://policingequity.org/; National Justice Database (NJD).

Civis Analytics, 200 W Monroe St., 22nd Fl., Chicago, IL, 60606, USA, https://www.civisanalytics.com/; BLM and Policing Survey Identifies Broad Support for Common-Sense Reform.

Council on Criminal Justice (CCJ), Task Force on Policing, 700 Pennsylvania Ave. SE, Washington, DC, 20020, USA, info@counciloncj.org, https://counciloncj.org/tfp/; Policing by the Numbers; Policy Assessment: Chokeholds and Other Neck Restraints; Policy Assessment: Civilian Oversight; Policy Assessment: No-Knock Warrants and Police Raids; Policy Assessment: Qualified Immunity; and Policy Assessment: Shifting Police Functions.

The Guardian, 61 Broadway, New York, NY, 10006, USA, (844) 632-2010, (917) 900-4663, usinfo@theguardian.com, https://www.theguardian.com; 'No Progress' Since George Floyd: US Police Killing Three People a Day.

Home Office of the Government of the United Kingdom, Direct Communications Unit, 2 Marsham St., London, SW1P 4DF, GBR, public.enquiries@homeoffice.gov.uk, https://www.gov.uk/government/organisations/home-office; Criminal Justice Statistics Quarterly and Police Use of Firearms Statistics.

International Association of Chiefs of Police (IACP), 44 Canal Center Plz., Ste. 200, Alexandria, VA, 22314, USA, (703) 836-6767, (800) 843-4227, socialmedia@theiacp.org, https://www.theiacp.org/; unpublished data.

The Leadership Conference Education Fund (The Education Fund), 1620 L St. NW, Ste. 1100, Washington, DC, 20036, USA, (202) 466-3311, https://civilrights.org/edfund/#; A Matter of Life and Death: The Importance of the Death in Custody Reporting Act.

National Academies of Sciences, Engineering, and Medicine (The National Academies), 500 5th St. NW, Washington, DC, 20001, USA, (202) 334-2000, contact@nas.edu, https://www.nationalacademies.org/; Proactive Policing: Effects on Crime and Communities.

National Policing Institute, 2550 S Clark St., Ste. 1130, Arlington, VA, 22202, USA, (202) 833-1460, (202) 659-9149, info@policinginstitute.org, https://www.policefoundation.org; National Survey on Officer Safety Training: Findings and Implications.

Pew Research Center, 1615 L St. NW, Ste. 800, Washington, DC, 20036, USA, (202) 419-4300, (202) 857-8562, info@pewresearch.org, https://www.pewresearch.org/; What the Data Says (and Doesn't Say) about Crime in the United States.

Physicians for Human Rights (PHR), 256 W 38th St., 9th Fl., New York, NY, 10018, USA, (646) 564-3720, (646) 564-3750, https://phr.org/; 'Excited Delirium' and Deaths in Police Custody: The Deadly Impact of a Baseless Diagnosis.

Police Executive Research Forum (PERF), 1120 Connecticut Ave. NW, Ste. 930, Washington, DC, 20036, USA, (202) 466-7820, https://www.policeforum.org; Municipal and Campus Police: Strategies for Working Together During Turbulent Times.

Public Agenda, 1 Dock 72 Way, No. 6101, Brooklyn, NY, 11205-1242, USA, (212) 686-6610, info@publicagenda.org, https://www.publicagenda.org/; America's Hidden Common Ground on Race and Police Reform.

U.S. Department of Justice (DOJ), Office of Community Oriented Policing Services (COPS), 145 N St. NE, Washington, DC, 20530, USA, (800) 421-6770, askcopsrc@usdoj.gov, https://cops.usdoj.gov/; Officer Safety and Wellness Group Meeting Summary: Pandemic Policing.

University of California Los Angeles (UCLA) School of Law, The Williams Institute, 1060 Veteran Ave., Ste. 134, PO Box 957092, Los Angeles, CA, 90095-7092, USA, (310) 267-4382, (310) 825-7270, williamsinstitute@law.ucla.edu, https://williamsinstitute.law.ucla.edu/; Police and the Criminalization of LGBT People.

Vera Institute of Justice, 34 35th St., Ste. 4-2A, Brooklyn, NY, 11232, USA, (212) 334-1300, (212) 941-9407, contactvera@vera.org, https://www.vera.org/; What Policing Costs: A Look at Spending in America's Biggest Cities.

The Washington Post, 1301 K St. NW, Washington, DC, 20071, USA, (800) 477-4679, https://www.washingtonpost.com/; Fatal Force: Database of People Shot and Killed by Police.

CRIME-DRUG ABUSE VIOLATIONS

U.S. Department of Justice (DOJ), Federal Bureau of Investigation (FBI), 935 Pennsylvania Ave. NW, Washington, DC, 20535-0001, USA, (202) 324-3000, https://www.fbi.gov/; Crime in the United States 2019.

United Nations Office on Drugs and Crime (UNODC), Vienna International Ctre., PO Box 500, Vienna, A-1400, AUT, unodc@unodc.org, https://www.unodc.org/; Afghanistan Opium Survey 2020: Cultivation and Production; Myanmar Opium Survey 2022 - Cultivation, Production and Implications; and World Drug Report 2022.

University of Alaska Anchorage Justice Center, 3211 Providence Dr., PSB Ste. 234, Anchorage, AK, 99508, USA, (907) 786-1810, (907) 786-7777, uaa_justicecenter@alaska.edu, https://www.uaa.alaska.edu/academics/college-of-health/departments/justice-center/; Adverse Childhood Experiences, Intimate Partner Violence, and Sexual Violence Among Persons Who May Be Alaska Mental Health Trust Beneficiaries: Findings from the Alaska Victimization Survey.

CRIME-FRAUD

Center for Fraud Prevention, USA, info@thefraudcenter.org, http://thefraudcenter.org; unpublished data.

International Consortium of Investigative Journalists (ICIJ), 1730 Rhode Island Ave. NW, Ste. 317, Washington, DC, 20036, USA, (202) 808-3310, contact@icij.org, https://www.icij.org/; Offshore Leaks Database.

Oceana, 1025 Connecticut Ave. NW, Washington, DC, 20036, USA, (202) 833-3900, (877) 762-3262,

(202) 833-2070, info@oceana.org, https://oceana.org/; Transparency and Traceability: Tools to Stop Illegal Fishing.

U.S. Government Accountablity Office (GAO), 441 G St. NW, Washington, DC, 20548, USA, (202) 512-3000, contact@gao.gov, https://www.gao.gov/; School Meals Program: USDA Has Reported Taking Some Steps to Reduce Improper Payments but Should Comprehensively Assess Fraud Risks.

CRIME-HATE CRIMES

Anti-Defamation League (ADL), 605 3rd Ave., New York, NY, 10158-3650, USA, (212) 885-7700, adlmedia@adl.org, https://www.adl.org; ADL H.E.A.T. Map: Hate, Extremism, Antisemitism and Terrorism; ADL Hate Crime Map; Audit of Antisemitic Incidents 2022; and Murder and Extremism in the United States in 2021.

Bureau of Alcohol, Tobacco, Firearms and Explosives (ATF), United States Bomb Data Center (USBDC), 3750 Corporal Rd., Huntsville, AL, 35898 , USA, (800) 461-8841, usbdc@atf.gov, https://www.atf.gov/explosives/us-bomb-data-center; 2019 House of Worship Incidents in the United States.

California State University San Bernardino, Center for the Study of Hate and Extremism, 5500 University Pkwy., San Bernardino, CA, 92407, USA, (909) 537-7503, (909) 537-7711, blevin8@aol.com, https://csbs.csusb.edu/hate-and-extremism-center; Report to the Nation: Anti-Asian Prejudice & Hate Crime; Report to the Nation: Factbook on Hate and Extremism in the U.S. and Internationally; Report to the Nation: Illustrated Almanac; Report to the Nation: Visual Almanac 2020 Preview, with the Latest FBI/DHS Data; and Special Status Report: Hate Crime in the U.S. 1992-2016.

Center for Strategic & International Studies (CSIS), 1616 Rhode Island Ave. NW, Washington, DC, 20036, USA, (202) 887-0200, (202) 775-3199, https://www.csis.org; The Military, Police, and the Rise of Terrorism in the United States and The War Comes Home: The Evolution of Domestic Terrorism in the United States.

Council on American-Islamic Relations (CAIR), 453 New Jersey Ave. SE, Washington, DC, 20003, USA, (202) 488-8787, (202) 488-0833, info@cair.com, https://www.islamophobia.org/; 2023 Civil Rights Report: Progress in the Shadow of Prejudice.

District of Columbia, Metropolitan Police Department, 441 4th St. NW, 7th Fl., Washington, DC, 20001, USA, (202) 727-9099, (202) 727-4106, mpd@dc.gov, https://mpdc.dc.gov/; Bias-Related Crimes (Hate Crimes) Data.

District of Columbia, Office of Planning, 1100 4th St. SW, Ste. 650 E, Washington, DC, 20024, USA, (202) 442-7600, (202) 442-7638, planning@dc.gov, https://planning.dc.gov/; DC Data Reports 2023.

Everytown for Gun Safety Support Fund, Washington, DC, 20001, USA, (646) 324-8250, info@everytown.org, https://everytownresearch.org; Disarm Hate: The Deadly Intersection of Guns and Hate Crimes.

Human Rights Campaign (HRC), 1640 Rhode Island Ave. NW, Washington, DC, 20036-3278, USA, (202) 628-4160, (202) 216-1572 (TTY), (202) 347-5323, feedback@hrc.org, https://www.hrc.org/; Dismantling a Culture of Violence: Understanding Violence Against Transgender and Non-Binary People and Ending the Crisis and A National Epidemic: Fatal Anti-Transgender Violence in the United States in 2019.

National Coalition of Anti-Violence Programs (NCAVP), 116 Nassau St., 3rd Fl., New York, NY, 10038, USA, (212) 714-1184, ecruz@avp.org, https://avp.org/ncavp/; Pride and Pain: A Snapshot of Anti-LGBTQ Hate and Violence During Pride Season 2019 and Supporting LGBTQ Survivors of Violence During the COVID-19 Pandemic.

Southern Poverty Law Center (SPLC), 400 Washington Ave., Montgomery, AL, 36104, USA, (334) 956-8200, (888) 414-7752, https://www.splcenter.org/; Hate Map and The Year in Hate and Extremism 2021.

Stop AAPI Hate, C/O Chinese for Affirmative Action, 17 Walter U. Lum Place, San Francisco, CA, 94108, USA, (415) 274-6750, (415) 397-8770, community@stopaapihate.org, https://stopaapihate.org; The Rising Tide of Violence and Discrimination Against Asian American and Pacific Islander Women and Girls; Stop AAPI Hate Mental Health Report; Stop AAPI Hate National Report; and Two Years and Thousands of Voices: What Community-Generated Data Tells Us About Anti-AAPI Hate.

U.S. Department of Homeland Security (DHS), 2707 Martin Luther King Jr. Ave. SE, Washington, DC, 20528-0525, USA, (202) 282-8000, https://www.dhs.gov; 2020 Homeland Threat Assessment.

U.S. Department of Justice (DOJ), Bureau of Justice Statistics (BJS), 810 7th St. NW, Washington, DC, 20531, USA, (202) 307-0765, askbjs@usdoj.gov, https://www.bjs.gov/; Hate Crime Victimization, 2005-2019.

U.S. Department of Justice (DOJ), Federal Bureau of Investigation (FBI), 935 Pennsylvania Ave. NW, Washington, DC, 20535-0001, USA, (202) 324-3000, https://www.fbi.gov/; Hate Crime in the United States Incident Analysis; Hate Crime Statistics 2019; and A Study of Pre-Attack Behaviors of Active Shooters in the United States Between 2000 and 2013.

University of Maryland, National Consortium for the Study of Terrorism and Responses to Terrorism (START), PO Box 266, 5245 Greenbelt Rd., College Park, MD, 20740, USA, (301) 405-6600, (301) 314-1980, infostart@start.umd.edu, https://www.start.umd.edu; Characteristics and Targets of Mass Casualty Hate Crime Offenders.

The Violence Project, USA, admin@theviolenceproject.org, https://www.theviolenceproject.org/; Mass Shooter Database.

The Washington Post, 1301 K St. NW, Washington, DC, 20071, USA, (800) 477-4679, https://www.washingtonpost.com/; The Rise of Domestic Extremism in America.

CRIME-HOMICIDES

Amnesty International USA, 311 W 43rd St., 7th Fl., New York, NY, 10036, USA, (212) 807-8400, (800) 266-3789, (212) 627-1451, aimember@aiusa.org, https://www.amnestyusa.org/; Scars of Survival: Gun Violence and Barriers to Reparation in the USA.

Cato Institute, 1000 Massachusetts Ave. NW, Washington, DC, 20001-5403, USA, (202) 842-0200, https://www.cato.org/; Does Greater Police Funding Help Catch More Murderers?.

Committee to Protect Journalists (CPJ), PO Box 2675, New York, NY, 10108, USA, (212) 465-1004, (212) 214-0640, info@cpj.org, https://cpj.org; Deadly Year for Journalists as Killings Rose Sharply in 2022 and Killing with Impunity: Vast Majority of Journalists' Murderers Go Free.

Council on Criminal Justice (CCJ), National Commission on COVID-19 and Criminal Justice, 700 Pennsylvania Ave. SE, Washington, DC, 20020, USA, info@counciloncj.org, https://counciloncj.org/covid-19/; Impact Report: COVID-19 and Crime.

District of Columbia, Office of Planning, 1100 4th St. SW, Ste. 650 E, Washington, DC, 20024, USA, (202) 442-7600, (202) 442-7638, planning@dc.gov, https://planning.dc.gov/; DC Data Reports 2023.

Gun Violence Archive (GVA), 1133 Connecticut Ave. NW, Washington, DC, 20036, USA, inquiry@gva.us.com, https://www.gunviolencearchive.org/; Gun Violence Archive 2023 and Mass Shootings in 2023.

Igarape Institute, Rio de Janeiro, 20271-205, BRZ, contato@igarape.org.br, https://igarape.org.br/en/; Homicide Monitor.

New York University School of Law, Brennan Center for Justice, 120 Broadway, Ste. 1750, New York, NY, 10271, USA, (646) 292-8310, (202) 249-7190, (212) 463-7308, brennancenter@nyu.edu, https://www.brennancenter.org; Myths and Realities: Understanding Recent Trends in Violent Crime.

U.S. Department of Justice (DOJ), Federal Bureau of Investigation (FBI), 935 Pennsylvania Ave. NW, Washington, DC, 20535-0001, USA, (202) 324-3000, https://www.fbi.gov/; A Study of Pre-Attack Behaviors of Active Shooters in the United States Between 2000 and 2013.

U.S. Department of Justice (DOJ), National Institute of Justice (NIJ), 810 7th St. NW, Washington, DC, 20531, USA, (202) 307-2942, (800) 851-3420, https://www.nij.gov/; Compendium of Research on Violence Against Women 1993-2020.

United Nations Office on Drugs and Crime (UNODC), Vienna International Ctre., PO Box 500, Vienna, A-1400, AUT, unodc@unodc.org, https://www.unodc.org/; Global Study on Homicide 2019.

University of Sydney, Sydney School of Public Health, GunPolicy.org, Edward Ford Bldg. , Sydney, NSW, 2006, AUS, ssph.education-support@sydney.edu.au, https://www.gunpolicy.org/; Armed Violence and Gun Laws, Country by Country.

The Urban Institute, Greater D.C. (Urban-Greater D.C), 500 L'Enfant Plaza SW, Washington, DC, 20024, USA, (202) 833-7200, https://greaterdc.urban.org/; Strengthening Nonpolice Safety Infrastructure in DC.

Violence Policy Center (VPC), 1025 Connecticut Ave. NW, Ste. 1210, Washington, DC, 20036, USA, (202) 822-8200, https://vpc.org/; American Roulette: The Untold Story of Murder-Suicide in the United States and States with Weak Gun Laws and Higher Gun Ownership Lead Nation in Gun Deaths, New Data for 2020 Confirms.

CRIME-HOMICIDES-RACE AND SEX

U.S. Department of Health and Human Services, Centers for Disease Control and Prevention (CDC), 1600 Clifton Rd., Atlanta, GA, 30329-4027, USA, (800) 232-4636, (888) 232-6348 (TTY), cdcinfo@cdc.gov, https://www.cdc.gov; Racial and Ethnic Differences in Homicides of Adult Women and the Role of Intimate Partner Violence.

U.S. Department of Health and Human Services, Centers for Disease Control and Prevention (CDC), National Center for Health Statistics (NCHS), 3311 Toledo Rd., Hyattsville, MD, 20782-2064, USA, (800) 232-4636, (301) 458-4000, https://www.cdc.gov/nchs; Vital Statistics Online Data Portal.

U.S. Department of Justice (DOJ), Bureau of Justice Statistics (BJS), 810 7th St. NW, Washington, DC, 20531, USA, (202) 307-0765, askbjs@usdoj.gov, https://www.bjs.gov/; Mortality in State and Federal Prisons, 2001-2019 - Statistical Tables.

CRIME-HUMAN TRAFFICKING

American Hotel & Lodging Association (AHLA), 1250 Eye St. NW, Ste. 1100, Washington, DC, 20005, USA, (202) 289-3100, informationcenter@ahla.com, https://www.ahla.com; Unpacking Human Trafficking: A Survey of State Laws Targeting Human Trafficking in the Hospitality Industry.

The European Institute for Crime Prevention and Control, Affiliated with the United Nations (HEUNI), Vilhonkatu 4 B 19, Helsinki, FI-00101, FIN, heuni@om.fi, https://heuni.fi/; Trafficking of Children and Young Persons in Finland.

Global Alliance Against Traffic in Women (GAATW), Soi 33 Itsaraphap Rd., Sivalai Condominium, 6th Fl., Bangkok, 10600, THA, gaatw@gaatw.org, https://www.gaatw.org/; Anti-Trafficking Review.

Mediterranean Institute of Gender Studies (MIGS), 46 Makedonitissas Ave., PO Box 24005, Nicosia, 1703, CYP, info@medinstgenderstudies.org, https://medinstgenderstudies.org/; Mind the Gap Report: COALESCE for Support in Cyprus.

U.S. Department of Justice (DOJ), National Institute of Justice (NIJ), 810 7th St. NW, Washington, DC, 20531, USA, (202) 307-2942, (800) 851-3420, https://www.nij.gov/; Gaps in Reporting Human Trafficking Incidents Result in Significant Undercounting.

U.S. Department of Justice (DOJ), Office of the Attorney General, 950 Pennsylvania Ave. NW, Washington, DC, 20530-0001, USA, (202) 514-2000, (800) 877-8339 (TTY), askdoj@usdoj.gov, https://

www.justice.gov/ag; Attorney General's Annual Report to Congress and Assessment of U.S. Government Activities to Combat Trafficking in Persons.

U.S. Department of State (DOS), 2201 C St. NW, Washington, DC, 20520, USA, (202) 647-4000, ofminfo@state.gov, https://www.state.gov; 2021 Trafficking in Persons Repor.

U.S. Government Accountablity Office (GAO), 441 G St. NW, Washington, DC, 20548, USA, (202) 512-3000, contact@gao.gov, https://www.gao.gov/; Human Trafficking: Department of State Collaborates with Partner Governments on Child Protection Compacts but Should Strengthen Oversight.

United Nations Office on Drugs and Crime (UNODC), Vienna International Ctre., PO Box 500, Vienna, A-1400, AUT, unodc@unodc.org, https://www.unodc.org/; Global Report on Trafficking in Persons 2022.

CRIME-IDENTITY THEFT

Identity Theft Resource Center (ITRC), 2514 Jamacha Rd., Ste. 502-525, El Cajon, CA, 92019-4492, USA, (888) 400-5530, itrc@idtheftcenter.org, https://www.idtheftcenter.org/; notified: Data Breach Information.

Trustwave, 70 W Madison St., Ste. 600, Chicago, IL, 60602, USA, (312) 873-7500, https://www.trustwave.com; 2020 Trustwave Global Security Report.

Verizon, 1095 Avenue of the Americas, New York, NY, 10036, USA, (212) 395-1000, https://enterprise.verizon.com/resources/reports; Data Breach Investigations Report (DBIR) 2023.

CRIME-IMMIGRATION VIOLATIONS

U.S. Department of Homeland Security (DHS), Office of Immigration Statistics (OIS), 2707 Martin Luther King Jr. Ave. SE, Washington, DC, 20528-0525, USA, (202) 282-8000, immigrationstatistics@hq.dhs.gov, https://www.dhs.gov/office-immigration-statistics; Yearbook of Immigration Statistics 2020.

United Nations Office on Drugs and Crime (UNODC), Vienna International Ctre., PO Box 500, Vienna, A-1400, AUT, unodc@unodc.org, https://www.unodc.org/; Global Report on Trafficking in Persons 2022.

Vera Institute of Justice, 34 35th St., Ste. 4-2A, Brooklyn, NY, 11232, USA, (212) 334-1300, (212) 941-9407, contactvera@vera.org, https://www.vera.org/; Operation Streamline: No Evidence that Criminal Prosecution Deters Migration.

CRIME-LARCENY-THEFT

U.S. Department of Justice (DOJ), Federal Bureau of Investigation (FBI), 935 Pennsylvania Ave. NW, Washington, DC, 20535-0001, USA, (202) 324-3000, https://www.fbi.gov/; Crime in the United States 2019.

CRIME-MOTOR VEHICLE THEFT

National Insurance Crime Bureau (NICB), 1111 E Touhy Ave., Ste. 400, Des Plaines, IL, 60018, USA, (800) 447-6282, (847) 544-7000, (847) 544-7100, https://www.nicb.org/; 2019 Hot Spots National Interactive Map and NICB's Hot Wheels: America's 10 Most Stolen Vehicles.

U.S. Department of Justice (DOJ), Bureau of Justice Statistics (BJS), 810 7th St. NW, Washington, DC, 20531, USA, (202) 307-0765, askbjs@usdoj.gov, https://www.bjs.gov/; Criminal Victimization, 2020.

CRIME-MURDER

Amnesty International USA, 311 W 43rd St., 7th Fl., New York, NY, 10036, USA, (212) 807-8400, (800) 266-3789, (212) 627-1451, aimember@aiusa.org, https://www.amnestyusa.org/; Scars of Survival: Gun Violence and Barriers to Reparation in the USA.

Anti-Defamation League (ADL), 605 3rd Ave., New York, NY, 10158-3650, USA, (212) 885-7700, adlmedia@adl.org, https://www.adl.org; Murder and Extremism in the United States in 2021.

Cato Institute, 1000 Massachusetts Ave. NW, Washington, DC, 20001-5403, USA, (202) 842-0200, https://www.cato.org/; Does Greater Police Funding Help Catch More Murderers?.

District of Columbia, Office of Planning, 1100 4th St. SW, Ste. 650 E, Washington, DC, 20024, USA, (202) 442-7600, (202) 442-7638, planning@dc.gov, https://planning.dc.gov/; DC Data Reports 2023.

Gun Violence Archive (GVA), 1133 Connecticut Ave. NW, Washington, DC, 20036, USA, inquiry@gva.us.com, https://www.gunviolencearchive.org/; Gun Violence Archive 2023 and Mass Shootings in 2023.

Human Rights Campaign (HRC), 1640 Rhode Island Ave. NW, Washington, DC, 20036-3278, USA, (202) 628-4160, (202) 216-1572 (TTY), (202) 347-5323, feedback@hrc.org, https://www.hrc.org/; A National Epidemic: Fatal Anti-Transgender Violence in the United States in 2019.

Igarape Institute, Rio de Janeiro, 20271-205, BRZ, contato@igarape.org.br, https://igarape.org.br/en/; Homicide Monitor.

New York University School of Law, Brennan Center for Justice, 120 Broadway, Ste. 1750, New York, NY, 10271, USA, (646) 292-8310, (202) 249-7190, (212) 463-7308, brennancenter@nyu.edu, https://www.brennancenter.org; Myths and Realities: Understanding Recent Trends in Violent Crime.

U.S. Department of Justice (DOJ), Federal Bureau of Investigation (FBI), 935 Pennsylvania Ave. NW, Washington, DC, 20535-0001, USA, (202) 324-3000, https://www.fbi.gov/; Active Shooter Incidents in the United States in 2021; A Study of Pre-Attack Behaviors of Active Shooters in the United States Between 2000 and 2013; and Uniform Crime Reporting (UCR) Program Data.

U.S. Department of Justice (DOJ), National Institute of Justice (NIJ), 810 7th St. NW, Washington, DC, 20531, USA, (202) 307-2942, (800) 851-3420, https://www.nij.gov/; Compendium of Research on Violence Against Women 1993-2020.

United Nations Office on Drugs and Crime (UNODC), Vienna International Ctre., PO Box 500, Vienna, A-1400, AUT, unodc@unodc.org, https://www.unodc.org/; Global Study on Homicide 2019.

University of Maryland, National Consortium for the Study of Terrorism and Responses to Terrorism (START), PO Box 266, 5245 Greenbelt Rd., College Park, MD, 20740, USA, (301) 405-6600, (301) 314-1980, infostart@start.umd.edu, https://www.start.umd.edu; Characteristics and Targets of Mass Casualty Hate Crime Offenders.

University of Sydney, Sydney School of Public Health, GunPolicy.org, Edward Ford Bldg. , Sydney, NSW, 2006, AUS, ssph.education-support@sydney.edu.au, https://www.gunpolicy.org/; Armed Violence and Gun Laws, Country by Country.

The Urban Institute, Greater D.C. (Urban-Greater D.C), 500 L'Enfant Plaza SW, Washington, DC, 20024, USA, (202) 833-7200, https://greaterdc.urban.org/; Strengthening Nonpolice Safety Infrastructure in DC.

The Violence Project, USA, admin@theviolenceproject.org, https://www.theviolenceproject.org/; Mass Shooter Database.

CRIME-MURDER-MURDER CIRCUMSTANCES

U.S. Department of Justice (DOJ), Federal Bureau of Investigation (FBI), 935 Pennsylvania Ave. NW, Washington, DC, 20535-0001, USA, (202) 324-3000, https://www.fbi.gov/; Crime in the United States 2019 and A Study of Pre-Attack Behaviors of Active Shooters in the United States Between 2000 and 2013.

Violence Policy Center (VPC), 1025 Connecticut Ave. NW, Ste. 1210, Washington, DC, 20036, USA, (202) 822-8200, https://vpc.org/; American Roulette: The Untold Story of Murder-Suicide in the United States and States with Weak Gun Laws and Higher Gun Ownership Lead Nation in Gun Deaths, New Data for 2020 Confirms.

CRIME-PLACE AND TIME OF OCCURRENCE

Bureau of Alcohol, Tobacco, Firearms and Explosives (ATF), United States Bomb Data Center (USBDC), 3750 Corporal Rd., Huntsville, AL, 35898 , USA, (800) 461-8841, usbdc@atf.gov, https://www.atf.gov/explosives/us-bomb-data-center; 2020 Arson Incident Report; 2021 Explosives Incident Report; 2019 House of Worship Incidents in the United States; and 2019 Juvenile Offender (Fire) Incident Report.

U.S. Department of Justice (DOJ), Bureau of Justice Statistics (BJS), 810 7th St. NW, Washington, DC, 20531, USA, (202) 307-0765, askbjs@usdoj.gov, https://www.bjs.gov/; Criminal Victimization, 2020.

U.S. Department of Justice (DOJ), Federal Bureau of Investigation (FBI), 935 Pennsylvania Ave. NW, Washington, DC, 20535-0001, USA, (202) 324-3000, https://www.fbi.gov/; Active Shooter Incidents in the United States in 2021.

CRIME-POLICE OFFICERS ASSAULTED, KILLED

National Law Enforcement Officers Memorial Fund (NLEOMF), 444 E St. NW, Washington, DC, 20001, USA, (202) 737-3400, (202) 737-3405, info@nleomf.org, https://nleomf.org/; 2021 End-of-Year Preliminary Law Enforcement Officers Fatalities Report and Officer Fatalities by State.

National Policing Institute, 2550 S Clark St., Ste. 1130, Arlington, VA, 22202, USA, (202) 833-1460, (202) 659-9149, info@policinginstitute.org, https://www.policefoundation.org; National Survey on Officer Safety Training: Findings and Implications.

U.S. Department of Justice (DOJ), Federal Bureau of Investigation (FBI), 935 Pennsylvania Ave. NW, Washington, DC, 20535-0001, USA, (202) 324-3000, https://www.fbi.gov/; Law Enforcement Officers Killed and Assaulted (LEOKA) 2020.

CRIME-PROPERTY CRIME

Bureau of Alcohol, Tobacco, Firearms and Explosives (ATF), United States Bomb Data Center (USBDC), 3750 Corporal Rd., Huntsville, AL, 35898 , USA, (800) 461-8841, usbdc@atf.gov, https://www.atf.gov/explosives/us-bomb-data-center; 2020 Arson Incident Report; 2021 Explosives Incident Report; 2019 House of Worship Incidents in the United States; and 2019 Juvenile Offender (Fire) Incident Report.

Council on Criminal Justice (CCJ), National Commission on COVID-19 and Criminal Justice, 700 Pennsylvania Ave. SE, Washington, DC, 20020, USA, info@counciloncj.org, https://counciloncj.org/covid-19/; Impact Report: COVID-19 and Crime.

U.S. Department of Justice (DOJ), Bureau of Justice Statistics (BJS), 810 7th St. NW, Washington, DC, 20531, USA, (202) 307-0765, askbjs@usdoj.gov, https://www.bjs.gov/; Crime Against Persons with Disabilities 2009-2019.

U.S. Department of Justice (DOJ), Federal Bureau of Investigation (FBI), 935 Pennsylvania Ave. NW, Washington, DC, 20535-0001, USA, (202) 324-3000, https://www.fbi.gov/; Crime in the United States 2019.

University of California Davis, Violence Prevention Research Program (VPRP), 2315 Stockton Blvd., Sacramento, CA, 95817, USA, (916) 734-3539 , hs-vprp@ucdavis.edu, https://health.ucdavis.edu/vprp/; Physical Distancing, Violence, and Crime in US Cities during the Coronavirus Pandemic.

CRIME-RAPE

District of Columbia, Office of Planning, 1100 4th St. SW, Ste. 650 E, Washington, DC, 20024, USA, (202) 442-7600, (202) 442-7638, planning@dc.gov, https://planning.dc.gov/; DC Data Reports 2023.

Mediterranean Institute of Gender Studies (MIGS), 46 Makedonitissas Ave., PO Box 24005, Nicosia, 1703, CYP, info@medinstgenderstudies.org, https://medinstgenderstudies.org/; Mind the Gap Report: COALESCE for Support in Cyprus.

National Sexual Violence Resource Center (NSVRC), Governor's Plaza N, Bldg. 2, 2101 N Front St., Harrisburg, PA, 17110, USA, (877) 739-3895, (717) 909-0715 (TTY), (717) 909-0714, https://www.nsvrc.org/resources@nsvrc.org, https://www.nsvrc.org/; National Sexual Violence Resource Center Library Catalog; Serving Teen Survivors: A Manual for Advocates; and Statistics.

Rape, Abuse & Incest National Network (RAINN), 635 Pennsylvania Ave. SE, Ste. B, Washington, DC, 20003, USA, (202) 544-1034, (800) 656-4673 , info@rainn.org, https://www.rainn.org/; Statistics.

U.S. Department of Defense (DOD), Sexual Assault Prevention and Response Office (SAPRO), 1400 Defense Pentagon, Washington, DC, 20301, USA, (571) 372-2657, whs.mc-alex.wso.mbx.sapro@mail.mil, https://www.sapr.mil/; Annual Report on Sexual Assault in the Military, Fiscal Year 2022.

U.S. Department of Justice (DOJ), Bureau of Justice Statistics (BJS), 810 7th St. NW, Washington, DC, 20531, USA, (202) 307-0765, askbjs@usdoj.gov, https://www.bjs.gov/; PREA (Prison Rape Elimination Act) Data Collection Activities, 2021 and Rape and Sexual Assault Among College-Age Females, 1995-2013.

U.S. Department of Justice (DOJ), Federal Bureau of Investigation (FBI), 935 Pennsylvania Ave. NW, Washington, DC, 20535-0001, USA, (202) 324-3000, https://www.fbi.gov/; Crime in the United States 2019 and Uniform Crime Reporting (UCR) Program Data.

U.S. Department of Justice (DOJ), National Institute of Justice (NIJ), 810 7th St. NW, Washington, DC, 20531, USA, (202) 307-2942, (800) 851-3420, https://www.nij.gov/; Compendium of Research on Violence Against Women 1993-2020 and Forensic Evidence and Criminal Justice Outcomes in Sexual Assault Cases.

U.S. Department of Justice (DOJ), Office on Violence Against Women (OVW), 145 N St. NE, Ste. 10W.121, Washington, DC, 20530, USA, (202) 307-6026, (202) 307-2277 (TTY), (202) 305-2589, ovw.info@usdoj.gov, https://www.justice.gov/ovw; 2020 Biennial Report to Congress on the Effectiveness of Grant Programs Under the Violence Against Women Act and Office on Violence Against Women 2021 Tribal Consultation Report.

United Nations Office on Drugs and Crime (UNODC), Vienna International Ctre., PO Box 500, Vienna, A-1400, AUT, unodc@unodc.org, https://www.unodc.org/; Global Report on Trafficking in Persons 2022.

United Nations UN Women, 405 E 42nd St., New York, NY, 10017-3599, USA, (646) 781-4400, (646) 781-4444, https://www.unwomen.org; Progress on the Sustainable Development Goals: The Gender Snapshot 2021.

United States Merchant Marine Academy (USMMA), 300 Steamboat Rd., Kings Point, NY, 11024, USA, (516) 726-5800, (516) 726-6048, https://www.usmma.edu/; Final Signed 2018-2019 Sexual Harassment Report.

Washington Coalition of Sexual Assault Programs (WCSAP), 5426 N Rd. 68, Ste. D 311, Pasco, WA, 99301, USA, (360) 754-7356, https://www.wcsap.org/; unpublished data.

CRIME-ROBBERY

Council on Criminal Justice (CCJ), National Commission on COVID-19 and Criminal Justice, 700 Pennsylvania Ave. SE, Washington, DC, 20020, USA, info@counciloncj.org, https://counciloncj.org/covid-19/; Impact Report: COVID-19 and Crime.

District of Columbia, Office of Planning, 1100 4th St. SW, Ste. 650 E, Washington, DC, 20024, USA, (202) 442-7600, (202) 442-7638, planning@dc.gov, https://planning.dc.gov/; DC Data Reports 2023.

U.S. Department of Justice (DOJ), Federal Bureau of Investigation (FBI), 935 Pennsylvania Ave. NW, Washington, DC, 20535-0001, USA, (202) 324-3000, https://www.fbi.gov/; Crime in the United States 2019.

CRIME-SHOPLIFTING

National Association for Shoplifting Prevention (NASP), 33 Walt Whitman Rd., Ste. 233W, Huntington Station, NY, 11746, USA, (800) 848-9595, (631) 923-2737, (631) 923-2743, nasp@shopliftingprevention.org, https://www.shopliftingprevention.org/; The Cost of Repeat Offenses by Consumer Shoplifters.

U.S. Department of Justice (DOJ), Federal Bureau of Investigation (FBI), 935 Pennsylvania Ave. NW, Washington, DC, 20535-0001, USA, (202) 324-3000, https://www.fbi.gov/; Crime in the United States 2019.

CRIME-VIOLENT CRIME

Amnesty International USA, 311 W 43rd St., 7th Fl., New York, NY, 10036, USA, (212) 807-8400, (800) 266-3789, (212) 627-1451, aimember@aiusa.org, https://www.amnestyusa.org/; Scars of Survival: Gun Violence and Barriers to Reparation in the USA.

Bureau of Alcohol, Tobacco, Firearms and Explosives (ATF), United States Bomb Data Center (USBDC), 3750 Corporal Rd., Huntsville, AL, 35898 , USA, (800) 461-8841, usbdc@atf.gov, https://www.atf.gov/explosives/us-bomb-data-center; 2019 House of Worship Incidents in the United States.

Cato Institute, 1000 Massachusetts Ave. NW, Washington, DC, 20001-5403, USA, (202) 842-0200, https://www.cato.org/; Does Greater Police Funding Help Catch More Murderers?.

Center for Strategic & International Studies (CSIS), 1616 Rhode Island Ave. NW, Washington, DC, 20036, USA, (202) 887-0200, (202) 775-3199, https://www.csis.org; The Military, Police, and the Rise of Terrorism in the United States and The War Comes Home: The Evolution of Domestic Terrorism in the United States.

Council on Criminal Justice (CCJ), National Commission on COVID-19 and Criminal Justice, 700 Pennsylvania Ave. SE, Washington, DC, 20020, USA, info@counciloncj.org, https://counciloncj.org/covid-19/; Impact Report: COVID-19 and Crime; Impact Report: COVID-19 and Domestic Violence Trends; and Research in Brief: Domestic Violence Calls for Service.

District of Columbia, Office of Planning, 1100 4th St. SW, Ste. 650 E, Washington, DC, 20024, USA, (202) 442-7600, (202) 442-7638, planning@dc.gov, https://planning.dc.gov/; DC Data Reports 2023.

The European Institute for Crime Prevention and Control, Affiliated with the United Nations (HEUNI), Vilhonkatu 4 B 19, Helsinki, FI-00101, FIN, heuni@om.fi, https://heuni.fi/; Unseen Victims: Why Refugee Women Victims of Gender-Based Violence Do Not Receive Assistance in the EU.

Everytown for Gun Safety Support Fund, Washington, DC, 20001, USA, (646) 324-8250, info@everytown.org, https://everytownresearch.org; Disarm Hate: The Deadly Intersection of Guns and Hate Crimes; EveryStat Database; 2023 Gun Law Rankings; and Mass Shootings in America.

Gun Violence Archive (GVA), 1133 Connecticut Ave. NW, Washington, DC, 20036, USA, inquiry@gva.us.com, https://www.gunviolencearchive.org/; Gun Violence Archive 2023 and Mass Shootings in 2023.

Human Rights Campaign (HRC), 1640 Rhode Island Ave. NW, Washington, DC, 20036-3278, USA, (202) 628-4160, (202) 216-1572 (TTY), (202) 347-5323, feedback@hrc.org, https://www.hrc.org/; Dismantling a Culture of Violence: Understanding Violence Against Transgender and Non-Binary People and Ending the Crisis.

Institute for Economics & Peace (IEP), 3 E 54th St., New York, NY, 10022, USA, (332) 213-1666, info@economicsandpeace.org, https://www.economicsandpeace.org/; Global Peace Index 2022; Global Terrorism Index 2022; Mexico Peace Index 2022; and Ukraine Russia Crisis: Terrorism Briefing.

Institute on Violence, Abuse and Trauma (IVAT), 10065 Old Grove Rd. , Ste. 101, San Diego, CA, 92131, USA, (858) 527-1860, (858) 527-1743, https://www.ivatcenters.org/; Journal of Family Trauma, Child Custody, and Child Development (JFT).

Issue Lab by Candid, 32 Old Slip, 24th Fl., New York, NY, 10003, USA, (800) 424-9836, https://www.issuelab.org/; Issue Lab Special Collection: Gun Violence.

Major Cities Chiefs Association (MCCA), PO Box 71690, Salt Lake City, UT, 84171, USA, (801) 209-1815, patricia@majorcitieschiefs.com, https://majorcitieschiefs.com/; MCCA Report on the 2020 Protest and Civil Unrest.

Media Matters for America, PO Box 44811, Washington, DC, 20026, USA, (202) 756-4100, action@mediamatters.org, https://www.mediamatters.org; Fact-Checking Fox News' Narrative on America's 'Crime Crisis'.

National Bureau of Economic Research (NBER), 1050 Massachusetts Ave., Cambridge, MA, 02138, USA, (617) 868-3900, info@nber.org, https://www.nber.org/; The Urban Crime and Heat Gradient in High and Low Poverty Areas.

National Policing Institute, 2550 S Clark St., Ste. 1130, Arlington, VA, 22202, USA, (202) 833-1460, (202) 659-9149, info@policinginstitute.org, https://www.policefoundation.org; Averted School Violence (ASV) Database: 2021 Analysis Update.

New York University School of Law, Brennan Center for Justice, 120 Broadway, Ste. 1750, New York, NY, 10271, USA, (646) 292-8310, (202) 249-7190, (212) 463-7308, brennancenter@nyu.edu, https://www.brennancenter.org; Myths and Realities: Understanding Recent Trends in Violent Crime.

Office of the Director of National Intelligence (ODNI), National Counterterrorism Center (NCTC), Washington, DC, 20511, USA, nctcpao@nctc.gov, https://www.dni.gov/index.php/nctc-home; unpublished data.

Police Executive Research Forum (PERF), 1120 Connecticut Ave. NW, Ste. 930, Washington, DC, 20036, USA, (202) 466-7820, https://www.policeforum.org; Reducing Gun Violence: What Works, and What Can Be Done Now.

Public Health Agency of Canada, 130 Colonnade Rd., Ottawa, ON, K1A 0K9, CAN, (844) 280-5020 (Dial from U.S.), https://www.phac-aspc.gc.ca/; Victims of Police-Reported Family and Intimate Partner Violence in Canada, 2021.

RAND Corporation, PO Box 2138, 1776 Main St., Santa Monica, CA, 90407-2138, USA, (310) 451-7002, (412) 802-4981, order@rand.org, https://www.rand.org/; RAND Database of Worldwide Terrorism Incidents (RDWTI).

Small Arms Survey, Maison de la Paix, Chemin Eugene-Rigot 2E, Geneva, CH-1202, SWI, sas@smallarmssurvey.org, https://www.smallarmssurvey.org/; Global Firearms Holdings; Global Violent Deaths (GVD) Database; 2021 Small Arms Trade Transparency Barometer; and Unplanned Explosions at Munitions Sites (UEMS).

U.S. Department of Homeland Security (DHS), 2707 Martin Luther King Jr. Ave. SE, Washington, DC, 20528-0525, USA, (202) 282-8000, https://www.dhs.gov; 2020 Homeland Threat Assessment.

U.S. Department of Justice (DOJ), Bureau of Justice Statistics (BJS), 810 7th St. NW, Washington, DC, 20531, USA, (202) 307-0765, askbjs@usdoj.gov, https://www.bjs.gov/; Crime Against Persons with Disabilities 2009-2019; Criminal Victimization, 2020; and Rape and Sexual Assault Among College-Age Females, 1995-2013.

U.S. Department of Justice (DOJ), Federal Bureau of Investigation (FBI), 935 Pennsylvania Ave. NW, Washington, DC, 20535-0001, USA, (202) 324-3000, https://www.fbi.gov/; Active Shooter Incidents in the United States in 2021; Crime in the United States 2019; A Study of Pre-Attack Behaviors of Active Shooters in the United States Between 2000 and 2013; and Uniform Crime Reporting (UCR) Program Data.

U.S. Department of Justice (DOJ), National Institute of Justice (NIJ), 810 7th St. NW, Washington, DC, 20531, USA, (202) 307-2942, (800) 851-3420, https://www.nij.gov/; Compendium of Research on Violence Against Women 1993-2020.

U.S. Department of State (DOS), Bureau of Counterterrorism, Office of Public Affairs, 2201 C St. NW, Rm. 2509, Washington, DC, 20520, USA, (202) 647-4000, https://www.state.gov/bureaus-offices/under-secretary-for-civilian-security-democracy-and-human-rights/bureau-of-counterterrorism/; Country Reports on Terrorism 2020.

University of Alaska Anchorage Justice Center, 3211 Providence Dr., PSB Ste. 234, Anchorage, AK, 99508, USA, (907) 786-1810, (907) 786-7777, uaa_justicecenter@alaska.edu, https://www.uaa.alaska.edu/academics/college-of-health/departments/justice-center/; Alaska Victimization Survey.

University of California Davis, Violence Prevention Research Program (VPRP), 2315 Stockton Blvd., Sacramento, CA, 95817, USA, (916) 734-3539 , hs-vprp@ucdavis.edu, https://health.ucdavis.edu/vprp/; Ghost Guns: Spookier Than You Think They Are and Physical Distancing, Violence, and Crime in US Cities during the Coronavirus Pandemic.

University of Maryland, National Consortium for the Study of Terrorism and Responses to Terrorism (START), PO Box 266, 5245 Greenbelt Rd., College Park, MD, 20740, USA, (301) 405-6600, (301) 314-1980, infostart@start.umd.edu, https://www.start.umd.edu; Characteristics and Targets of Mass Casualty Hate Crime Offenders.

University of Michigan Institute for Social Research, Inter-University Consortium for Political and Social Science Research (ICPSR), National Archive of Criminal Justice Data (NACJD), PO Box 1248, Ann Arbor, MI, 48106-1248, USA, (734) 615-8400, nacjd@icpsr.umich.edu, https://www.icpsr.umich.edu/web/pages/NACJD/; Capital Punishment in the United States, 1973-2020.

University of Sydney, Sydney School of Public Health, GunPolicy.org, Edward Ford Bldg. , Sydney, NSW, 2006, AUS, ssph.education-support@sydney.edu.au, https://www.gunpolicy.org/; Armed Violence and Gun Laws, Country by Country.

The Urban Institute, Greater D.C. (Urban-Greater D.C), 500 L'Enfant Plaza SW, Washington, DC, 20024, USA, (202) 833-7200, https://greaterdc.urban.org/; Strengthening Nonpolice Safety Infrastructure in DC.

The Violence Project, USA, admin@theviolenceproject.org, https://www.theviolenceproject.org/; Mass Shooter Database.

The Washington Post, 1301 K St. NW, Washington, DC, 20071, USA, (800) 477-4679, https://www.washingtonpost.com/; The Rise of Domestic Extremism in America.

CRIME-WORKPLACE

U.S. Department of Labor (DOL), Bureau of Labor Statistics (BLS), Postal Square Bldg., 2 Massachusetts Ave. NE, Washington, DC, 20212-0001, USA, (202) 691-5200, (202) 691-7890, blsdata_staff@bls.gov, https://www.bls.gov; Monthly Labor Review.

CRIME LABORATORIES

U.S. Department of Justice (DOJ), National Institute of Justice (NIJ), 810 7th St. NW, Washington, DC, 20531, USA, (202) 307-2942, (800) 851-3420, https://www.nij.gov/; Forensic Evidence and Criminal Justice Outcomes in Sexual Assault Cases.

CRIME PREVENTION

Media Matters for America, PO Box 44811, Washington, DC, 20026, USA, (202) 756-4100, action@mediamatters.org, https://www.mediamatters.org; Fact-Checking Fox News' Narrative on America's 'Crime Crisis'.

National Academies of Sciences, Engineering, and Medicine (The National Academies), 500 5th St. NW, Washington, DC, 20001, USA, (202) 334-2000, contact@nas.edu, https://www.nationalacademies.org/; Proactive Policing: Effects on Crime and Communities.

CRIME SCENES

Media Matters for America, PO Box 44811, Washington, DC, 20026, USA, (202) 756-4100, action@mediamatters.org, https://www.mediamatters.org; Fact-Checking Fox News' Narrative on America's 'Crime Crisis'.

U.S. Department of Justice (DOJ), Federal Bureau of Investigation (FBI), 935 Pennsylvania Ave. NW, Washington, DC, 20535-0001, USA, (202) 324-3000, https://www.fbi.gov/; Active Shooter Incidents in the United States in 2021.

CRIME VICTIMS' FAMILIES

Amnesty International USA, 311 W 43rd St., 7th Fl., New York, NY, 10036, USA, (212) 807-8400, (800) 266-3789, (212) 627-1451, aimember@aiusa.org, https://www.amnestyusa.org/; Scars of Survival: Gun Violence and Barriers to Reparation in the USA.

CRIMES AGAINST HUMANITY

Amnesty International USA, 311 W 43rd St., 7th Fl., New York, NY, 10036, USA, (212) 807-8400, (800) 266-3789, (212) 627-1451, aimember@aiusa.org, https://www.amnestyusa.org/; Hunger for Justice: Crimes Against Humanity in Venezuela.

Human Rights Watch, 350 5th Ave., 34th Fl., New York, NY, 10118-3299, USA, (212) 290-4700, (212) 736-1300, https://www.hrw.org; Break Their Lineage, Break Their Roots: China's Crimes against Humanity Targeting Uyghurs and Other Turkic Muslims and A Threshold Crossed: Israeli Authorities and the Crimes of Apartheid and Persecution.

CRIMINAL BEHAVIOR

Pew Research Center, 1615 L St. NW, Ste. 800, Washington, DC, 20036, USA, (202) 419-4300, (202) 857-8562, info@pewresearch.org, https://www.pewresearch.org/; What the Data Says (and Doesn't Say) about Crime in the United States.

U.S. Department of Justice (DOJ), Federal Bureau of Investigation (FBI), 935 Pennsylvania Ave. NW, Washington, DC, 20535-0001, USA, (202) 324-3000, https://www.fbi.gov/; A Study of Pre-Attack Behaviors of Active Shooters in the United States Between 2000 and 2013.

University of Maryland, National Consortium for the Study of Terrorism and Responses to Terrorism (START), PO Box 266, 5245 Greenbelt Rd., College Park, MD, 20740, USA, (301) 405-6600, (301) 314-1980, infostart@start.umd.edu, https://www.start.umd.edu; Characteristics and Targets of Mass Casualty Hate Crime Offenders; Proud Boys Crimes and Characteristics; QAnon Offenders in the United States; and Radicalization in the Ranks.

CRIMINAL INVESTIGATION

Bernan Press, 15250 NBN Way, Bldg. C, Blue Ridge Summit, PA, 17214, USA, (301) 459-2255, (800) 865-3457, (800) 865-3450, customercare@bernan.com, https://rowman.com/Page/Bernan; Crime in the United States 2022 and Justice Statistics: An Extended Look at Crime in the United States 2021.

Bureau of Alcohol, Tobacco, Firearms and Explosives (ATF), Office of Public Affairs, 99 New York Ave. NE, Washington, DC, 20226, USA, (202) 648-8520, https://www.atf.gov; Firearms Trace Data 2020.

District of Columbia, Metropolitan Police Department, 441 4th St. NW, 7th Fl., Washington, DC, 20001, USA, (202) 727-9099, (202) 727-4106, mpd@dc.gov, https://mpdc.dc.gov/; Crime Cards and District Crime Data at a Glance.

Justice Research and Statistics Association (JRSA), 1000 Vermont Ave. NW, Ste. 450, Washington, DC, 20005, USA, (202) 842-9330, (202) 304-1417, cjinfo@jrsa.org, https://www.jrsa.org; SAC Publication Digest 2022.

Pew Research Center, 1615 L St. NW, Ste. 800, Washington, DC, 20036, USA, (202) 419-4300, (202) 857-8562, info@pewresearch.org, https://www.pewresearch.org/; What the Data Says (and Doesn't Say) about Crime in the United States.

U.S. Department of Justice (DOJ), National Institute of Justice (NIJ), 810 7th St. NW, Washington, DC, 20531, USA, (202) 307-2942, (800) 851-3420, https://www.nij.gov/; Forensic Evidence and Criminal Justice Outcomes in Sexual Assault Cases.

U.S. Department of Justice (DOJ), Office of the Attorney General, 950 Pennsylvania Ave. NW, Washington, DC, 20530-0001, USA, (202) 514-2000, (800) 877-8339 (TTY), askdoj@usdoj.gov, https://www.justice.gov/ag; Attorney General's Annual Report to Congress and Assessment of U.S. Government Activities to Combat Trafficking in Persons.

CRIMINAL JUSTICE, ADMINISTRATION OF

Academy of Criminal Justice Sciences (ACJS), PO Box 960, Greenbelt, MD, 20768-0960, USA, (301) 446-6300, (800) 757-2257, info@acjs.org, https://www.acjs.org/; Justice Quarterly (JQ).

Administrative Office of the United States Courts, One Columbus Cir. NE, Washington, DC, 20544, USA, (202) 502-2600, https://www.uscourts.gov; Judicial Business of the U.S. Courts, 2022.

Bernan Press, 15250 NBN Way, Bldg. C, Blue Ridge Summit, PA, 17214, USA, (301) 459-2255, (800) 865-3457, (800) 865-3450, customercare@bernan.com, https://rowman.com/Page/Bernan; Crime in the United States 2022 and Justice Statistics: An Extended Look at Crime in the United States 2021.

Chicago Police Accountability Task Force, PO Box 6289, Chicago, IL, 60606-6289, USA, comments@chicagopatf.org, https://chicagopatf.org; unpublished data.

Committee to Protect Journalists (CPJ), PO Box 2675, New York, NY, 10108, USA, (212) 465-1004, (212) 214-0640, info@cpj.org, https://cpj.org; Deadly Year for Journalists as Killings Rose Sharply in 2022 and Killing with Impunity: Vast Majority of Journalists' Murderers Go Free.

Council on Criminal Justice (CCJ), 700 Pennsylvania Ave. SE, Washington, DC, 20003, USA, info@counciloncj.org, https://counciloncj.org; Justice System Disparities: Black-White National Imprisonment Trends, 2000 to 2020 and The 1994 Crime Bill: Legacy and Lessons.

Council on Criminal Justice (CCJ), National Commission on COVID-19 and Criminal Justice, 700 Pennsylvania Ave. SE, Washington, DC, 20020, USA, info@counciloncj.org, https://counciloncj.org/covid-19/; Experience to Action: Reshaping Criminal Justice After COVID-19.

Council on Criminal Justice (CCJ), Task Force on Policing, 700 Pennsylvania Ave. SE, Washington, DC, 20020, USA, info@counciloncj.org, https://counciloncj.org/tfp/; Policy Assessment: No-Knock Warrants and Police Raids and Policy Assessment: Shifting Police Functions.

Death Penalty Information Center (DPIC), 1701 K St. NW, Ste. 205, Washington, DC, 20006, USA, (202) 289-2275, dpic@deathpenaltyinfo.org, https://deathpenaltyinfo.org/; The Death Penalty in 2022: Year End Report; DPIC Analysis: At Least 1,300 Prisoners Are on U.S. Death Rows in Violation of U.S. Human Rights Obligations; DPIC Mid-Year Review: Pandemic and Continuing Historic Decline Produce Record-Low Death Penalty Use in First Half of 2020; Execution Database; and Study: Dehumanizing Belief Systems Linked to Support for Guns Rights, the Death Penalty, and Anti-Immigration Practices.

District of Columbia, Metropolitan Police Department, 441 4th St. NW, 7th Fl., Washington, DC, 20001, USA, (202) 727-9099, (202) 727-4106, mpd@dc.gov, https://mpdc.dc.gov/; Crime Cards and District Crime Data at a Glance.

The Gallup Organization, 901 F St. NW, Washington, DC, 20004, USA, (202) 715-3030, (800) 204-1192,

(202) 715-3045, https://www.gallup.com; Record-Low 54% in U.S. Say Death Penalty Morally Acceptable.

Institute of Criminology and Legal Policy, University of Helsinki Department of Social Research, PO Box 16, Helsinki, FI-00014, FIN, https://www.helsinki.fi/en/institute-criminology-and-legal-policy; The Historical Criminal Statistics of Finland 1842-2015 - A Systematic Comparison to Sweden.

Justice Research and Statistics Association (JRSA), 1000 Vermont Ave. NW, Ste. 450, Washington, DC, 20005, USA, (202) 842-9330, (202) 304-1417, cjinfo@jrsa.org, https://www.jrsa.org; SAC Publication Digest 2022.

The Marshall Project, 156 W 56th St., 3rd Fl., New York, NY, 10019, USA, (212) 803-5200, info@themarshallproject.org, https://www.themarshallproject.org/; Diversity and Inclusion, 2022.

National Academies of Sciences, Engineering, and Medicine (The National Academies), Committee on Law and Justice (CLAJ), 500 5th St. NW, Washington, DC, 20001, USA, (202) 334-1993, (202) 334-2000, claj@nas.edu, https://www.nationalacademies.org/claj/committee-on-law-and-justice; unpublished data.

National Center for State Courts (NCSC), 300 Newport Ave., Williamsburg, VA, 23185, USA, (800) 616-6164, (757) 220-0449, https://www.ncsc.org/; Court Statistics Project (CSP).

National Registry of Exonerations, USA, https://www.law.umich.edu/special/exoneration/; The National Registry of Exonerations Annual Report, March 30, 2021 and Race and Wrongful Convictions in the United States 2022.

New York University School of Law, Brennan Center for Justice, 120 Broadway, Ste. 1750, New York, NY, 10271, USA, (646) 292-8310, (202) 249-7190, (212) 463-7308, brennancenter@nyu.edu, https://www.brennancenter.org; Revenue Over Public Safety.

Physicians for Human Rights (PHR), 256 W 38th St., 9th Fl., New York, NY, 10018, USA, (646) 564-3720, (646) 564-3750, https://phr.org/; 'Excited Delirium' and Deaths in Police Custody: The Deadly Impact of a Baseless Diagnosis.

Prison Policy Initiative, PO Box 127, Northampton, MA, 01061, USA, https://www.prisonpolicy.org/; Grading the Parole Release Systems of All 50 States; Mass Incarceration: The Whole Pie 2023; State of Phone Justice 2022: The Problem, the Progress, and What's Next; States of Incarceration: The Global Context 2021; Where People in Prison Come From: The Geography of Mass Incarceration; and Women's Mass Incarceration: The Whole Pie 2023.

Routledge - Taylor & Francis Group, 6000 Broken Sound Pkwy. NW, Ste. 300, Boca Raton, FL, 33487, USA, (800) 634-1420, (800) 634-7064, orders@taylorandfrancis.com, https://www.routledge.com/; Journal of Ethnicity in Criminal Justice.

The Sentencing Project, 1705 DeSales St. NW, 8th Fl., Washington, DC, 20036, USA, (202) 628-0871, staff@sentencingproject.org, https://www.sentencingproject.org; Growth in Mass Incarceration; Mass Incarceration Trends; and U.S. Criminal Justice Data.

U.S. Commission on Civil Rights (USCCR), 1331 Pennsylvania Ave. NW, Ste. 1150, Washington, DC, 20425, USA, (202) 376-7700, (202) 376-8116 (TTY), publications@usccr.gov, https://www.usccr.gov/; 2019 Statutory Enforcement Report: Are Rights A Reality? Evaluating Federal Civil Rights Enforcement.

U.S. Department of Justice (DOJ), Bureau of Justice Statistics (BJS), 810 7th St. NW, Washington, DC, 20531, USA, (202) 307-0765, askbjs@usdoj.gov, https://www.bjs.gov/; Data Collection: National Corrections Reporting Program (NCRP).

U.S. Department of Justice (DOJ), Criminal Division, 950 Pennsylvania Ave. NW, Washington, DC, 20530-0001, USA, (202) 514-2000, criminal.division@usdoj.gov, https://www.justice.gov/criminal; Report to Congress on the Activities and Operations of the Public Integrity Section for 2020.

U.S. Department of Justice (DOJ), National Institute of Justice (NIJ), 810 7th St. NW, Washington, DC, 20531, USA, (202) 307-2942, (800) 851-3420, https://www.nij.gov/; NIJ Journal.

U.S. Department of Justice (DOJ), Office of Justice Programs (OJP), 810 7th St. NW, Washington, DC, 20531, USA, (202) 514-2000, askojp@ncjrs.gov, https://ojp.gov/; unpublished data.

U.S. Department of Justice (DOJ), Office of Justice Programs (OJP), National Criminal Justice Reference Service (NCJRS), PO Box 6000, Rockville, MD, 20849-6000, USA, (800) 851-3420, (301) 240-6310 (TTY), responsecenter@ncjrs.gov, https://www.ojp.gov/ncjrs; National Criminal Justice Reference Service (NCJRS) Virtual Library.

U.S. Department of Justice (DOJ), Office of the Attorney General, 950 Pennsylvania Ave. NW, Washington, DC, 20530-0001, USA, (202) 514-2000, (800) 877-8339 (TTY), askdoj@usdoj.gov, https://www.justice.gov/ag; Attorney General's Annual Report to Congress and Assessment of U.S. Government Activities to Combat Trafficking in Persons.

University of California Los Angeles (UCLA) School of Law, The Williams Institute, 1060 Veteran Ave., Ste. 134, PO Box 957092, Los Angeles, CA, 90095-7092, USA, (310) 267-4382, (310) 825-7270, williamsinstitute@law.ucla.edu, https://williamsinstitute.law.ucla.edu/; Police and the Criminalization of LGBT People.

University of Michigan Institute for Social Research, Inter-University Consortium for Political and Social Science Research (ICPSR), National Archive of Criminal Justice Data (NACJD), PO Box 1248, Ann Arbor, MI, 48106-1248, USA, (734) 615-8400, nacjd@icpsr.umich.edu, https://www.icpsr.umich.edu/web/pages/NACJD/; Capital Punishment in the United States, 1973-2020.

Vera Institute of Justice, 34 35th St., Ste. 4-2A, Brooklyn, NY, 11232, USA, (212) 334-1300, (212) 941-9407, contactvera@vera.org, https://www.vera.org/; The New Dynamics of Mass Incarceration; Operation Streamline: No Evidence that Criminal Prosecution Deters Migration; and An Unjust Burden: The Disparate Treatment of Black Americans in the Criminal Justice System.

CRIMINAL VICTIMIZATION

Amnesty International USA, 311 W 43rd St., 7th Fl., New York, NY, 10036, USA, (212) 807-8400, (800) 266-3789, (212) 627-1451, aimember@aiusa.org, https://www.amnestyusa.org/; Scars of Survival: Gun Violence and Barriers to Reparation in the USA.

Childhelp, 6730 N Scottsdale Rd., Ste. 150, Scottsdale, AZ, 85253, USA, (480) 922-8212, https://www.childhelp.org/; Child Abuse Statistics.

Children's Defense Fund (CDF), 840 1st St. NE, Ste. 300, Washington, DC, 20002, USA, (202) 628-8787, cdfinfo@childrensdefense.org, https://www.childrensdefense.org/; Protect Children, Not Guns 2019.

Council on American-Islamic Relations (CAIR), 453 New Jersey Ave. SE, Washington, DC, 20003, USA, (202) 488-8787, (202) 488-0833, info@cair.com, https://www.islamophobia.org/; 2023 Civil Rights Report: Progress in the Shadow of Prejudice.

District of Columbia, Metropolitan Police Department, 441 4th St. NW, 7th Fl., Washington, DC, 20001, USA, (202) 727-9099, (202) 727-4106, mpd@dc.gov, https://mpdc.dc.gov/; Crime Cards and District Crime Data at a Glance.

European Commission, Eurostat, Luxembourg, 2920, LUX, https://ec.europa.eu/eurostat/; Crime and Criminal Justice Database and Crime Statistics.

Home Office of the Government of the United Kingdom, Direct Communications Unit, 2 Marsham St., London, SW1P 4DF, GBR, public.enquiries@homeoffice.gov.uk, https://www.gov.uk/government/organisations/home-office; Crime Outcomes in England and Wales, 2021 to 2022.

Human Rights Watch, 350 5th Ave., 34th Fl., New York, NY, 10118-3299, USA, (212) 290-4700, (212) 736-1300, https://www.hrw.org; Like I'm Drowning: Children and Families Sent to Harm by the US 'Remain in Mexico' Program and World Report 2023: Our Annual Review of Human Rights Around the Globe.

Pew Research Center, 1615 L St. NW, Ste. 800, Washington, DC, 20036, USA, (202) 419-4300, (202) 857-8562, info@pewresearch.org, https://www.pewresearch.org/; What the Data Says (and Doesn't Say) about Crime in the United States.

Statistic Brain Research Institute, 1100 Glendon Ave., Los Angeles, CA, 90024, USA, https://www.statisticbrain.com/; AMBER Alert Statistics.

U.S. Department of Education (ED), Institute of Education Sciences (IES), National Center for Education Statistics (NCES), Potomac Center Plaza, 550 12th St. SW, Washington, DC, 20202, USA, (202) 403-5551, https://nces.ed.gov/; Students' Perceptions of Bullying.

U.S. Department of Education (ED), Office of Postsecondary Education (OPE), Lyndon Baines Johnson Bldg., 400 Maryland Ave. SW, Washington, DC, 20202, USA, (202) 453-6914, https://www2.ed.gov/about/offices/list/ope; The Campus Safety and Security Data Analysis Cutting Tool.

U.S. Department of Justice (DOJ), Bureau of Justice Statistics (BJS), 810 7th St. NW, Washington, DC, 20531, USA, (202) 307-0765, askbjs@usdoj.gov, https://www.bjs.gov/; Crime Against Persons with Disabilities 2009-2019; Criminal Victimization, 2020; Hate Crime Victimization, 2005-2019; Rape and Sexual Assault Among College-Age Females, 1995-2013; and Report on Indicators of School Crime and Safety: 2020.

U.S. Department of Justice (DOJ), Federal Bureau of Investigation (FBI), 935 Pennsylvania Ave. NW, Washington, DC, 20535-0001, USA, (202) 324-3000, https://www.fbi.gov/; Hate Crime in the United States Incident Analysis and 2021 NCIC Missing Person and Unidentified Person Statistics.

U.S. Department of Justice (DOJ), Office of Justice Programs (OJP), National Criminal Justice Reference Service (NCJRS), PO Box 6000, Rockville, MD, 20849-6000, USA, (800) 851-3420, (301) 240-6310 (TTY), responsecenter@ncjrs.gov, https://www.ojp.gov/ncjrs; National Criminal Justice Reference Service (NCJRS) Virtual Library.

U.S. Department of Justice (DOJ), Office of the Attorney General, 950 Pennsylvania Ave. NW, Washington, DC, 20530-0001, USA, (202) 514-2000, (800) 877-8339 (TTY), askdoj@usdoj.gov, https://www.justice.gov/ag; Attorney General's Annual Report to Congress and Assessment of U.S. Government Activities to Combat Trafficking in Persons.

U.S. Department of Justice (DOJ), Office on Violence Against Women (OVW), 145 N St. NE, Ste. 10W.121, Washington, DC, 20530, USA, (202) 307-6026, (202) 307-2277 (TTY), (202) 305-2589, ovw.info@usdoj.gov, https://www.justice.gov/ovw; 2020 Biennial Report to Congress on the Effectiveness of Grant Programs Under the Violence Against Women Act and Office on Violence Against Women 2021 Tribal Consultation Report.

U.S. Department of State (DOS), 2201 C St. NW, Washington, DC, 20520, USA, (202) 647-4000, ofm-info@state.gov, https://www.state.gov; 2022 Country Reports on Human Rights Practices and 2021 Trafficking in Persons Repor.

University of Alaska Anchorage Justice Center, 3211 Providence Dr., PSB Ste. 234, Anchorage, AK, 99508, USA, (907) 786-1810, (907) 786-7777, uaa_justicecenter@alaska.edu, https://www.uaa.alaska.edu/academics/college-of-health/departments/justice-center/; Alaska Victimization Survey.

University of Michigan Institute for Social Research, Inter-University Consortium for Political and Social Science Research (ICPSR), National Archive of

Criminal Justice Data (NACJD), PO Box 1248, Ann Arbor, MI, 48106-1248, USA, (734) 615-8400, nacjd@icpsr.umich.edu, https://www.icpsr.umich.edu/web/pages/NACJD/; Violence Against Women (VAW) Resource Guide.

Youth Pride, Inc. (YPI), 743 Westminster St., Providence, RI, 02903, USA, (401) 421-5626, (401) 274-1990, info@youthprideri.org, https://www.youthprideri.org/; unpublished data.

CRIMINAL VICTIMIZATION-HOUSEHOLDS

University of New Hampshire, Crimes Against Children Research Center (CCRC), 125 McConnell Hall, 15 Academic Way, Durham, NH, 03824, USA, (603) 862-3541, (603) 862-1122, david.finkelhor@unh.edu, https://www.unh.edu/ccrc/; unpublished data.

CRIMINAL VICTIMIZATION-PLACE OF OCCURRENCE

U.S. Department of Justice (DOJ), Bureau of Justice Statistics (BJS), 810 7th St. NW, Washington, DC, 20531, USA, (202) 307-0765, askbjs@usdoj.gov, https://www.bjs.gov/; Criminal Victimization, 2020 and PREA (Prison Rape Elimination Act) Data Collection Activities, 2021.

CRIMINAL VICTIMIZATION-WEAPONS INVOLVED

Amnesty International USA, 311 W 43rd St., 7th Fl., New York, NY, 10036, USA, (212) 807-8400, (800) 266-3789, (212) 627-1451, aimember@aiusa.org, https://www.amnestyusa.org/; Scars of Survival: Gun Violence and Barriers to Reparation in the USA.

International Criminal Police Organization (INTERPOL), General Secretariat, 200 quai Charles de Gaulle, Lyon, 69006, FRA, https://www.interpol.int; Ballistic Information Network (IBIN).

National Rifle Association of America (NRA), Institute for Legislative Action (ILA), 11250 Waples Mill Rd., Fairfax, VA, 22030, USA, (800) 392-8683, https://www.nraila.org/; unpublished data.

Police Executive Research Forum (PERF), 1120 Connecticut Ave. NW, Ste. 930, Washington, DC, 20036, USA, (202) 466-7820, https://www.policeforum.org; Reducing Gun Violence: What Works, and What Can Be Done Now.

U.S. Department of Justice (DOJ), Bureau of Justice Statistics (BJS), 810 7th St. NW, Washington, DC, 20531, USA, (202) 307-0765, askbjs@usdoj.gov, https://www.bjs.gov/; Criminal Victimization, 2020.

Violence Policy Center (VPC), 1025 Connecticut Ave. NW, Ste. 1210, Washington, DC, 20036, USA, (202) 822-8200, https://vpc.org/; American Roulette: The Untold Story of Murder-Suicide in the United States; Concealed Carry Killers; States with Lower Gun Ownership and Strong Gun Laws Have Lowest Suicide Rates; and States with Weak Gun Laws and Higher Gun Ownership Lead Nation in Gun Deaths, New Data for 2020 Confirms.

CRIMINAL VICTIMIZATION-WORKPLACE

U.S. Department of Labor (DOL), Bureau of Labor Statistics (BLS), Postal Square Bldg., 2 Massachusetts Ave. NE, Washington, DC, 20212-0001, USA, (202) 691-5200, (202) 691-7890, blsdata_staff@bls.gov, https://www.bls.gov; Monthly Labor Review.

CRIMINALS

Cato Institute, 1000 Massachusetts Ave. NW, Washington, DC, 20001-5403, USA, (202) 842-0200, https://www.cato.org/; Immigrants' Deportations, Local Crime, and Police Effectiveness.

U.S. Department of Justice (DOJ), Federal Bureau of Investigation (FBI), 935 Pennsylvania Ave. NW, Washington, DC, 20535-0001, USA, (202) 324-3000, https://www.fbi.gov/; Active Shooter Incidents in the United States in 2021.

University of Maryland, National Consortium for the Study of Terrorism and Responses to Terrorism (START), PO Box 266, 5245 Greenbelt Rd., College Park, MD, 20740, USA, (301) 405-6600, (301) 314-1980, infostart@start.umd.edu, https://www.start.umd.edu; Characteristics and Targets of Mass Casualty Hate Crime Offenders; Proud Boys Crimes and Characteristics; QAnon Offenders in the United States; and Radicalization in the Ranks.

CRIMINOLOGY

European Society of Criminology (ESC), University of Lausanne , ESC - ICDP, Sorge - BCH, Lausanne, CH-1015, SWI, secretariat@esc-eurocrim.org, https://www.esc-eurocrim.org/; European Journal of Criminology.

CRISIS MANAGEMENT

National Bureau of Economic Research (NBER), 1050 Massachusetts Ave., Cambridge, MA, 02138, USA, (617) 868-3900, info@nber.org, https://www.nber.org/; Destructive Behavior, Judgment, and Economic Decision-Making Under Thermal Stress.

CRISIS MANAGEMENT IN GOVERNMENT

American Society of Civil Engineers (AMCE), 1801 Alexander Bell Dr., Reston, VA, 20191, USA, (800) 548-2723, (703) 295-6300, customercare@asce.org, https://www.asce.org/; Report Card for America's Infrastructure.

Amnesty International USA, 311 W 43rd St., 7th Fl., New York, NY, 10036, USA, (212) 807-8400, (800) 266-3789, (212) 627-1451, aimember@aiusa.org, https://www.amnestyusa.org/; Hunger for Justice: Crimes Against Humanity in Venezuela.

CRITICAL RACE THEORY

FiveThirtyEight, 47 W 66th St., 2nd Fl., New York, NY, 10023, USA, contact@fivethirtyeight.com, https://fivethirtyeight.com/; How the Rise of White Identity Politics Explains the Fight over Critical Race Theory.

CROAKER

National Oceanic and Atmospheric Administration (NOAA), National Marine Fisheries Service (NOAA Fisheries), 1315 East-West Hwy., 14th Fl., Silver Spring, MD, 20910, USA, (301) 427-8000, https://www.fisheries.noaa.gov/; Fisheries of the United States, 2020.

CROATIA-NATIONAL STATISTICAL OFFICE

Croatian Bureau of Statistics, Ilica 3, Zagreb, 10000, CTA, stat.info@dzs.hr, https://www.dzs.hr/; National Data Reports (Croatia).

CROATIA-PRIMARY STATISTICS SOURCES

Croatian Bureau of Statistics, Ilica 3, Zagreb, 10000, CTA, stat.info@dzs.hr, https://www.dzs.hr/; Croatia in Figures 2022.

European Commission, Eurostat, Luxembourg, 2920, LUX, https://ec.europa.eu/eurostat/; Key Figures on Enlargement Countries, 2019.

CROATIA-AGRICULTURE

The Economist Group: Economist Intelligence Unit (EIU), 900 3rd Ave., 16th Fl., New York, NY, 10022, USA, (212) 541-0500, americas@eiu.com, https://www.eiu.com; Croatia Country Report.

Euromonitor International, Inc., 1 N Dearborn St., Ste. 1700, Chicago, IL, 60602, USA, (312) 922-1115, (312) 922-1157, info-usa@euromonitor.com, https://www.euromonitor.com/; Geographies.

Palgrave Macmillan, 1 New York Plaza, Ste. 4500, New York, NY, 10004-1562, USA, (800) 777-4643, orders@palgrave.com, https://www.palgrave.com/us; The Statesman's Yearbook, 2023.

Routledge - Taylor & Francis Group, 6000 Broken Sound Pkwy. NW, Ste. 300, Boca Raton, FL, 33487, USA, (800) 634-1420, (800) 634-7064, orders@taylorandfrancis.com, https://www.routledge.com/; The Europa World Year Book 2022.

United Nations Food and Agricultural Organization (FAO), 2121 K St., Ste. 800B, Washington, DC, 20037, USA, (202) 653-2400 (Dial from U.S.), (202) 653-5760 (Fax from U.S.), fao-hq@fao.org, https://www.fao.org; AQUASTAT and The State of Food and Agriculture (SOFA) 2022.

United Nations Statistics Division (UNSD), United Nations Plz., New York, NY, 10017, USA, (800) 253-9646, (212) 963-9851, statistics@un.org, https://unstats.un.org; Statistical Yearbook of the United Nations 2021.

The World Bank, 1818 H St. NW, Washington, DC, 20433, USA, (202) 473-1000, (202) 477-6391, eds03@worldbank.org, https://www.worldbank.org/; Croatia (report).

CROATIA-AIRLINES

International Civil Aviation Organization (ICAO), 999 Robert-Bourassa Blvd., Montreal, QC, H3C 5H7, CAN, (514) 954-8219 (Dial from U.S.), (514) 954-6077 (Fax from U.S.), icaohq@icao.int, https://www.icao.int; ICAO Regional Reports.

Palgrave Macmillan, 1 New York Plaza, Ste. 4500, New York, NY, 10004-1562, USA, (800) 777-4643, orders@palgrave.com, https://www.palgrave.com/us; The Statesman's Yearbook, 2023.

CROATIA-ARMED FORCES

Central Intelligence Agency (CIA), Office of Public Affairs, Washington, DC, 20505, USA, (703) 482-0623, https://www.cia.gov; The World Factbook.

International Institute for Strategic Studies (IISS) - Americas, 2121 K St. NW, Ste. 600, Washington, DC, 20037, USA, (202) 659-1490, (202) 659-1499, https://www.iiss.org/; The Military Balance 2022.

Palgrave Macmillan, 1 New York Plaza, Ste. 4500, New York, NY, 10004-1562, USA, (800) 777-4643, orders@palgrave.com, https://www.palgrave.com/us; The Statesman's Yearbook, 2023.

Stockholm International Peace Research Institute (SIPRI), Signalistgatan 9, Stockholm, SE 169 72, SWE, https://www.sipri.org/; SIPRI Arms Transfers Database and SIPRI Military Expenditure Database.

CROATIA-BALANCE OF PAYMENTS

Routledge - Taylor & Francis Group, 6000 Broken Sound Pkwy. NW, Ste. 300, Boca Raton, FL, 33487, USA, (800) 634-1420, (800) 634-7064, orders@taylorandfrancis.com, https://www.routledge.com/; The Europa World Year Book 2022.

United Nations Conference on Trade and Development (UNCTAD), Palais des Nations, Geneva, 1211, SWI, (212) 963-6896, unctadinfo@unctad.org, https://unctad.org; Handbook of Statistics 2021.

The World Bank, 1818 H St. NW, Washington, DC, 20433, USA, (202) 473-1000, (202) 477-6391, eds03@worldbank.org, https://www.worldbank.org/; Croatia (report) and World Development Report 2022: Finance for an Equitable Recovery.

CROATIA-BANKS AND BANKING

Euromonitor International, Inc., 1 N Dearborn St., Ste. 1700, Chicago, IL, 60602, USA, (312) 922-1115, (312) 922-1157, info-usa@euromonitor.com, https://www.euromonitor.com/; Geographies.

CROATIA-BROADCASTING

Central Intelligence Agency (CIA), Office of Public Affairs, Washington, DC, 20505, USA, (703) 482-0623, https://www.cia.gov; The World Factbook.

Euromonitor International, Inc., 1 N Dearborn St., Ste. 1700, Chicago, IL, 60602, USA, (312) 922-1115, (312) 922-1157, info-usa@euromonitor.com, https://www.euromonitor.com/; Geographies.

Palgrave Macmillan, 1 New York Plaza, Ste. 4500, New York, NY, 10004-1562, USA, (800) 777-4643, orders@palgrave.com, https://www.palgrave.com/us; The Statesman's Yearbook, 2023.

UNESCO Institute for Statistics, C.P 250 Succursale H, Montreal, QC, H3G 2K8, CAN, (514) 343-6880 (Dial from U.S.), (514) 343-5740 (Fax from U.S.), uis.publications@unesco.org, http://uis.unesco.org/; UIS.Stat.

CROATIA-BUDGET

Central Intelligence Agency (CIA), Office of Public Affairs, Washington, DC, 20505, USA, (703) 482-0623, https://www.cia.gov; The World Factbook.

CROATIA-BUSINESS

Global Entrepreneurship Monitor (GEM), Babson College, 231 Forest St., Babson Park, MA, 02457, USA, (781) 235-1200, info@gemconsortium.org, https://www.gemconsortium.org/; GEM 2022-2023 Global Report.

United Nations Statistics Division (UNSD), United Nations Plz., New York, NY, 10017, USA, (800) 253-9646, (212) 963-9851, statistics@un.org, https://unstats.un.org; Statistical Yearbook of the United Nations 2021.

CROATIA-CLIMATE

Palgrave Macmillan, 1 New York Plaza, Ste. 4500, New York, NY, 10004-1562, USA, (800) 777-4643, orders@palgrave.com, https://www.palgrave.com/us; The Statesman's Yearbook, 2023.

CROATIA-COMMERCE

Palgrave Macmillan, 1 New York Plaza, Ste. 4500, New York, NY, 10004-1562, USA, (800) 777-4643, orders@palgrave.com, https://www.palgrave.com/us; The Statesman's Yearbook, 2023.

UK Data Service, University of Essex, Wivenhoe Park, Colchester, Essex, CO4 3SQ, GBR, https://ukdataservice.ac.uk/; International Aggregate Data.

CROATIA-CONSTRUCTION INDUSTRY

United Nations Statistics Division (UNSD), United Nations Plz., New York, NY, 10017, USA, (800) 253-9646, (212) 963-9851, statistics@un.org, https://unstats.un.org; Statistical Yearbook of the United Nations 2021.

CROATIA-CONSUMER PRICE INDEXES

Routledge - Taylor & Francis Group, 6000 Broken Sound Pkwy. NW, Ste. 300, Boca Raton, FL, 33487, USA, (800) 634-1420, (800) 634-7064, orders@taylorandfrancis.com, https://www.routledge.com/; The Europa World Year Book 2022.

The World Bank, 1818 H St. NW, Washington, DC, 20433, USA, (202) 473-1000, (202) 477-6391, eds03@worldbank.org, https://www.worldbank.org/; Croatia (report).

CROATIA-CROPS

Palgrave Macmillan, 1 New York Plaza, Ste. 4500, New York, NY, 10004-1562, USA, (800) 777-4643, orders@palgrave.com, https://www.palgrave.com/us; The Statesman's Yearbook, 2023.

United Nations Food and Agricultural Organization (FAO), 2121 K St., Ste. 800B, Washington, DC, 20037, USA, (202) 653-2400 (Dial from U.S.), (202) 653-5760 (Fax from U.S.), fao-hq@fao.org, https://www.fao.org; The State of Food and Agriculture (SOFA) 2022.

United Nations Statistics Division (UNSD), United Nations Plz., New York, NY, 10017, USA, (800) 253-9646, (212) 963-9851, statistics@un.org, https://unstats.un.org; Statistical Yearbook of the United Nations 2021.

CROATIA-DAIRY PROCESSING

Palgrave Macmillan, 1 New York Plaza, Ste. 4500, New York, NY, 10004-1562, USA, (800) 777-4643, orders@palgrave.com, https://www.palgrave.com/us; The Statesman's Yearbook, 2023.

United Nations Food and Agricultural Organization (FAO), 2121 K St., Ste. 800B, Washington, DC, 20037, USA, (202) 653-2400 (Dial from U.S.), (202) 653-5760 (Fax from U.S.), fao-hq@fao.org, https://www.fao.org; The State of Food and Agriculture (SOFA) 2022.

CROATIA-DEBTS, EXTERNAL

The World Bank, 1818 H St. NW, Washington, DC, 20433, USA, (202) 473-1000, (202) 477-6391, eds03@worldbank.org, https://www.worldbank.org/; Global Financial Development Report 2019-2020: Bank Regulation and Supervision a Decade after the Global Financial Crisis and World Development Report 2022: Finance for an Equitable Recovery.

CROATIA-ECONOMIC CONDITIONS

Bernan Press, 15250 NBN Way, Bldg. C, Blue Ridge Summit, PA, 17214, USA, (301) 459-2255, (800) 865-3457, (800) 865-3450, customercare@bernan.com, https://rowman.com/Page/Bernan; World Economic Outlook, April 2022.

Central Intelligence Agency (CIA), Office of Public Affairs, Washington, DC, 20505, USA, (703) 482-0623, https://www.cia.gov; The World Factbook.

The Economist Group: Economist Intelligence Unit (EIU), 900 3rd Ave., 16th Fl., New York, NY, 10022, USA, (212) 541-0500, americas@eiu.com, https://www.eiu.com; Croatia Country Report.

Euromonitor International, Inc., 1 N Dearborn St., Ste. 1700, Chicago, IL, 60602, USA, (312) 922-1115, (312) 922-1157, info-usa@euromonitor.com, https://www.euromonitor.com/; Geographies and Market Research on the Consumer Finance Industry.

Global Entrepreneurship Monitor (GEM), Babson College, 231 Forest St., Babson Park, MA, 02457, USA, (781) 235-1200, info@gemconsortium.org, https://www.gemconsortium.org/; GEM 2022-2023 Global Report.

International Monetary Fund (IMF), 700 19th St. NW, Washington, DC, 20431, USA, (202) 623-7000, (202) 623-4661, publications@imf.org, https://www.imf.org; IMF Data and World Economic Outlook.

Palgrave Macmillan, 1 New York Plaza, Ste. 4500, New York, NY, 10004-1562, USA, (800) 777-4643, orders@palgrave.com, https://www.palgrave.com/us; The Statesman's Yearbook, 2023.

Routledge - Taylor & Francis Group, 6000 Broken Sound Pkwy. NW, Ste. 300, Boca Raton, FL, 33487, USA, (800) 634-1420, (800) 634-7064, orders@taylorandfrancis.com, https://www.routledge.com/; The Europa World Year Book 2022.

United Nations Statistics Division (UNSD), United Nations Plz., New York, NY, 10017, USA, (800) 253-9646, (212) 963-9851, statistics@un.org, https://unstats.un.org; World Statistics Pocketbook 2021.

The World Bank, 1818 H St. NW, Washington, DC, 20433, USA, (202) 473-1000, (202) 477-6391, eds03@worldbank.org, https://www.worldbank.org/; Croatia (report); Global Economic Monitor (GEM); Global Economic Prospects, June 2022; The Global Findex Database 2021; and World Development Report 2022: Finance for an Equitable Recovery.

CROATIA-EDUCATION

Euromonitor International, Inc., 1 N Dearborn St., Ste. 1700, Chicago, IL, 60602, USA, (312) 922-1115, (312) 922-1157, info-usa@euromonitor.com, https://www.euromonitor.com/; Geographies.

Infoplease, c/o Sandbox Networks, Inc., 1 Lincoln St., 24th Fl., Boston, MA, 02111, USA, https://www.infoplease.com; Countries of the World.

Palgrave Macmillan, 1 New York Plaza, Ste. 4500, New York, NY, 10004-1562, USA, (800) 777-4643, orders@palgrave.com, https://www.palgrave.com/us; The Statesman's Yearbook, 2023.

Routledge - Taylor & Francis Group, 6000 Broken Sound Pkwy. NW, Ste. 300, Boca Raton, FL, 33487, USA, (800) 634-1420, (800) 634-7064, orders@taylorandfrancis.com, https://www.routledge.com/; The Europa World Year Book 2022.

UNESCO Institute for Statistics, C.P 250 Succursale H, Montreal, QC, H3G 2K8, CAN, (514) 343-6880 (Dial from U.S.), (514) 343-5740 (Fax from U.S.), uis.publications@unesco.org, http://uis.unesco.org/; Literacy and UIS.Stat.

United Nations Statistics Division (UNSD), United Nations Plz., New York, NY, 10017, USA, (800) 253-9646, (212) 963-9851, statistics@un.org, https://unstats.un.org; Millennium Development Goal Indicators.

The World Bank, 1818 H St. NW, Washington, DC, 20433, USA, (202) 473-1000, (202) 477-6391, eds03@worldbank.org, https://www.worldbank.org/; Croatia (report) and World Development Report 2022: Finance for an Equitable Recovery.

CROATIA-ELECTRICITY

Central Intelligence Agency (CIA), Office of Public Affairs, Washington, DC, 20505, USA, (703) 482-0623, https://www.cia.gov; The World Factbook.

S&P Global Commodity Insights, One World Trade Center, New York, NY, 10007, USA, (800) 752-8878, support@platts.com, https://www.spglobal.com/commodityinsights/en; Platts European Power Alert.

U.S. Energy Information Administration (EIA), 1000 Independence Ave. SW, Washington, DC, 20585, USA, (202) 586-8800, infoctr@eia.gov, https://www.eia.gov; International Energy Outlook 2021.

United Nations Statistics Division (UNSD), United Nations Plz., New York, NY, 10017, USA, (800) 253-9646, (212) 963-9851, statistics@un.org, https://unstats.un.org; Energy Statistics Yearbook 2019 and Statistical Yearbook of the United Nations 2021.

CROATIA-EMPLOYMENT

UK Data Service, University of Essex, Wivenhoe Park, Colchester, Essex, CO4 3SQ, GBR, https://ukdataservice.ac.uk/; International Aggregate Data.

United Nations Statistics Division (UNSD), United Nations Plz., New York, NY, 10017, USA, (800) 253-9646, (212) 963-9851, statistics@un.org, https://unstats.un.org; Statistical Yearbook of the United Nations 2021.

The World Bank, 1818 H St. NW, Washington, DC, 20433, USA, (202) 473-1000, (202) 477-6391, eds03@worldbank.org, https://www.worldbank.org/; Croatia (report).

CROATIA-ENERGY INDUSTRIES

European Institute for Energy Research (EIFER), Emmy-Noether-Strasse 11, Ground Fl., Karlsruhe, D-76131, GER, contact@eifer.org, https://www.eifer.kit.edu/; unpublished data.

University of Georgia, Terry College of Business, Selig Center for Economic Growth, E201 Ivester Hall, 650 S Lumpkin St., Athens, GA, 30602, USA, (706) 425-9782, jhumphre@uga.edu, https://www.terry.uga.edu/about/selig//; Georgia Economic Outlook 2022.

CROATIA-ENVIRONMENTAL CONDITIONS

DSI Data Service & Information, Xantener Strasse 51a, Rheinberg, D-47495, GER, dsi@dsidata.com, https://www.dsidata.com/; Global Environmental Database.

The Economist Group: Economist Intelligence Unit (EIU), 900 3rd Ave., 16th Fl., New York, NY, 10022, USA, (212) 541-0500, americas@eiu.com, https://www.eiu.com; Croatia Country Report.

United Nations Statistics Division (UNSD), United Nations Plz., New York, NY, 10017, USA, (800) 253-9646, (212) 963-9851, statistics@un.org, https://unstats.un.org; Statistical Yearbook of the United Nations 2021 and World Statistics Pocketbook 2021.

CROATIA-EXPORTS

Central Intelligence Agency (CIA), Office of Public Affairs, Washington, DC, 20505, USA, (703) 482-0623, https://www.cia.gov; The World Factbook.

The Economist Group: Economist Intelligence Unit (EIU), 900 3rd Ave., 16th Fl., New York, NY, 10022, USA, (212) 541-0500, americas@eiu.com, https://www.eiu.com; Croatia Country Report.

United Nations Conference on Trade and Development (UNCTAD), Palais des Nations, Geneva, 1211, SWI, (212) 963-6896, unctadinfo@unctad.org, https://unctad.org; Handbook of Statistics 2021.

United Nations Statistics Division (UNSD), United Nations Plz., New York, NY, 10017, USA, (800) 253-9646, (212) 963-9851, statistics@un.org, https://unstats.un.org; International Trade Statistics Yearbook 2020.

The World Bank, 1818 H St. NW, Washington, DC, 20433, USA, (202) 473-1000, (202) 477-6391, eds03@worldbank.org, https://www.worldbank.org/; World Development Report 2022: Finance for an Equitable Recovery.

CROATIA-FINANCE

Stockholm International Peace Research Institute (SIPRI), Signalistgatan 9, Stockholm, SE 169 72, SWE, https://www.sipri.org/; SIPRI Arms Transfers Database and SIPRI Military Expenditure Database.

United Nations Statistics Division (UNSD), United Nations Plz., New York, NY, 10017, USA, (800) 253-9646, (212) 963-9851, statistics@un.org, https://unstats.un.org; Statistical Yearbook of the United Nations 2021.

The World Bank, 1818 H St. NW, Washington, DC, 20433, USA, (202) 473-1000, (202) 477-6391, eds03@worldbank.org, https://www.worldbank.org/; Croatia (report).

CROATIA-FINANCE, PUBLIC

Bernan Press, 15250 NBN Way, Bldg. C, Blue Ridge Summit, PA, 17214, USA, (301) 459-2255, (800) 865-3457, (800) 865-3450, customercare@bernan.com, https://rowman.com/Page/Bernan; National Accounts Statistics: Analysis of Main Aggregates 2020.

The Economist Group: Economist Intelligence Unit (EIU), 900 3rd Ave., 16th Fl., New York, NY, 10022, USA, (212) 541-0500, americas@eiu.com, https://www.eiu.com; Croatia Country Report.

International Monetary Fund (IMF), 700 19th St. NW, Washington, DC, 20431, USA, (202) 623-7000, (202) 623-4661, publications@imf.org, https://www.imf.org; Regional Economic Outlook.

Palgrave Macmillan, 1 New York Plaza, Ste. 4500, New York, NY, 10004-1562, USA, (800) 777-4643, orders@palgrave.com, https://www.palgrave.com/us; The Statesman's Yearbook, 2023.

Routledge - Taylor & Francis Group, 6000 Broken Sound Pkwy. NW, Ste. 300, Boca Raton, FL, 33487, USA, (800) 634-1420, (800) 634-7064, orders@taylorandfrancis.com, https://www.routledge.com/; The Europa World Year Book 2022.

United Nations Statistics Division (UNSD), United Nations Plz., New York, NY, 10017, USA, (800) 253-9646, (212) 963-9851, statistics@un.org, https://unstats.un.org; National Accounts Main Aggregates Database and National Accounts Statistics: Main Aggregates and Detailed Tables.

The World Bank, 1818 H St. NW, Washington, DC, 20433, USA, (202) 473-1000, (202) 477-6391, eds03@worldbank.org, https://www.worldbank.org/; Croatia (report).

CROATIA-FISHERIES

Palgrave Macmillan, 1 New York Plaza, Ste. 4500, New York, NY, 10004-1562, USA, (800) 777-4643, orders@palgrave.com, https://www.palgrave.com/us; The Statesman's Yearbook, 2023.

Routledge - Taylor & Francis Group, 6000 Broken Sound Pkwy. NW, Ste. 300, Boca Raton, FL, 33487, USA, (800) 634-1420, (800) 634-7064, orders@taylorandfrancis.com, https://www.routledge.com/; The Europa World Year Book 2022.

United Nations Food and Agricultural Organization (FAO), 2121 K St., Ste. 800B, Washington, DC, 20037, USA, (202) 653-2400 (Dial from U.S.), (202) 653-5760 (Fax from U.S.), fao-hq@fao.org, https://www.fao.org; FAO Yearbook of Fishery and Aquaculture Statistics 2019; Fishery Statistical Collections Global Capture Production; FishStatJ; and The State of Food and Agriculture (SOFA) 2022.

United Nations Statistics Division (UNSD), United Nations Plz., New York, NY, 10017, USA, (800) 253-9646, (212) 963-9851, statistics@un.org, https://unstats.un.org; Statistical Yearbook of the United Nations 2021.

The World Bank, 1818 H St. NW, Washington, DC, 20433, USA, (202) 473-1000, (202) 477-6391, eds03@worldbank.org, https://www.worldbank.org/; Croatia (report).

CROATIA-FOOD

United Nations Food and Agricultural Organization (FAO), 2121 K St., Ste. 800B, Washington, DC, 20037, USA, (202) 653-2400 (Dial from U.S.), (202) 653-5760 (Fax from U.S.), fao-hq@fao.org, https://www.fao.org; The State of Food and Agriculture (SOFA) 2022.

CROATIA-FORESTS AND FORESTRY

Palgrave Macmillan, 1 New York Plaza, Ste. 4500, New York, NY, 10004-1562, USA, (800) 777-4643, orders@palgrave.com, https://www.palgrave.com/us; The Statesman's Yearbook, 2023.

Routledge - Taylor & Francis Group, 6000 Broken Sound Pkwy. NW, Ste. 300, Boca Raton, FL, 33487, USA, (800) 634-1420, (800) 634-7064, orders@taylorandfrancis.com, https://www.routledge.com/; The Europa World Year Book 2022.

UNESCO Institute for Statistics, C.P 250 Succursale H, Montreal, QC, H3G 2K8, CAN, (514) 343-6880 (Dial from U.S.), (514) 343-5740 (Fax from U.S.), uis.publications@unesco.org, http://uis.unesco.org/; UIS.Stat.

United Nations Food and Agricultural Organization (FAO), 2121 K St., Ste. 800B, Washington, DC, 20037, USA, (202) 653-2400 (Dial from U.S.), (202) 653-5760 (Fax from U.S.), fao-hq@fao.org, https://www.fao.org; FAO Yearbook of Forest Products 2019 and The State of Food and Agriculture (SOFA) 2022.

United Nations Statistics Division (UNSD), United Nations Plz., New York, NY, 10017, USA, (800) 253-9646, (212) 963-9851, statistics@un.org, https://unstats.un.org; Statistical Yearbook of the United Nations 2021.

The World Bank, 1818 H St. NW, Washington, DC, 20433, USA, (202) 473-1000, (202) 477-6391, eds03@worldbank.org, https://www.worldbank.org/; Croatia (report) and World Development Report 2022: Finance for an Equitable Recovery.

CROATIA-GROSS DOMESTIC PRODUCT

The Economist Group: Economist Intelligence Unit (EIU), 900 3rd Ave., 16th Fl., New York, NY, 10022, USA, (212) 541-0500, americas@eiu.com, https://www.eiu.com; Croatia Country Report.

United Nations Statistics Division (UNSD), United Nations Plz., New York, NY, 10017, USA, (800) 253-9646, (212) 963-9851, statistics@un.org, https://unstats.un.org; Statistical Yearbook of the United Nations 2021.

The World Bank, 1818 H St. NW, Washington, DC, 20433, USA, (202) 473-1000, (202) 477-6391, eds03@worldbank.org, https://www.worldbank.org/; World Development Report 2022: Finance for an Equitable Recovery.

CROATIA-GROSS NATIONAL PRODUCT

Palgrave Macmillan, 1 New York Plaza, Ste. 4500, New York, NY, 10004-1562, USA, (800) 777-4643, orders@palgrave.com, https://www.palgrave.com/us; The Statesman's Yearbook, 2023.

United Nations Statistics Division (UNSD), United Nations Plz., New York, NY, 10017, USA, (800) 253-9646, (212) 963-9851, statistics@un.org, https://unstats.un.org; Statistical Yearbook of the United Nations 2021.

The World Bank, 1818 H St. NW, Washington, DC, 20433, USA, (202) 473-1000, (202) 477-6391, eds03@worldbank.org, https://www.worldbank.org/; World Development Report 2022: Finance for an Equitable Recovery.

CROATIA-HOUSING

Euromonitor International, Inc., 1 N Dearborn St., Ste. 1700, Chicago, IL, 60602, USA, (312) 922-1115, (312) 922-1157, info-usa@euromonitor.com, https://www.euromonitor.com/; Geographies.

CROATIA-ILLITERATE PERSONS

UNESCO Institute for Statistics, C.P 250 Succursale H, Montreal, QC, H3G 2K8, CAN, (514) 343-6880 (Dial from U.S.), (514) 343-5740 (Fax from U.S.), uis.publications@unesco.org, http://uis.unesco.org/; UIS.Stat.

CROATIA-IMPORTS

Central Intelligence Agency (CIA), Office of Public Affairs, Washington, DC, 20505, USA, (703) 482-0623, https://www.cia.gov; The World Factbook.

The Economist Group: Economist Intelligence Unit (EIU), 900 3rd Ave., 16th Fl., New York, NY, 10022, USA, (212) 541-0500, americas@eiu.com, https://www.eiu.com; Croatia Country Report.

United Nations Conference on Trade and Development (UNCTAD), Palais des Nations, Geneva, 1211, SWI, (212) 963-6896, unctadinfo@unctad.org, https://unctad.org; Handbook of Statistics 2021.

United Nations Statistics Division (UNSD), United Nations Plz., New York, NY, 10017, USA, (800) 253-9646, (212) 963-9851, statistics@un.org, https://unstats.un.org; International Trade Statistics Yearbook 2020.

The World Bank, 1818 H St. NW, Washington, DC, 20433, USA, (202) 473-1000, (202) 477-6391, eds03@worldbank.org, https://www.worldbank.org/; World Development Report 2022: Finance for an Equitable Recovery.

CROATIA-INDUSTRIES

Central Intelligence Agency (CIA), Office of Public Affairs, Washington, DC, 20505, USA, (703) 482-0623, https://www.cia.gov; The World Factbook.

The Economist Group: Economist Intelligence Unit (EIU), 900 3rd Ave., 16th Fl., New York, NY, 10022, USA, (212) 541-0500, americas@eiu.com, https://www.eiu.com; Croatia Country Report.

Euromonitor International, Inc., 1 N Dearborn St., Ste. 1700, Chicago, IL, 60602, USA, (312) 922-1115, (312) 922-1157, info-usa@euromonitor.com, https://www.euromonitor.com/; Geographies.

Palgrave Macmillan, 1 New York Plaza, Ste. 4500, New York, NY, 10004-1562, USA, (800) 777-4643, orders@palgrave.com, https://www.palgrave.com/us; The Statesman's Yearbook, 2023.

Routledge - Taylor & Francis Group, 6000 Broken Sound Pkwy. NW, Ste. 300, Boca Raton, FL, 33487, USA, (800) 634-1420, (800) 634-7064, orders@taylorandfrancis.com, https://www.routledge.com/; The Europa World Year Book 2022.

United Nations Industrial Development Organization (UNIDO), 1 United Nations Plz., Rm. DC1-1118, New York, NY, 10017, USA, (212) 963-6890, (212) 963 6885, (212) 963-7904, office.newyork@unido.org, https://www.unido.org/; Industrial Statistics Databases and International Yearbook of Industrial Statistics 2021.

The World Bank, 1818 H St. NW, Washington, DC, 20433, USA, (202) 473-1000, (202) 477-6391, eds03@worldbank.org, https://www.worldbank.org/; Croatia (report).

CROATIA-INTERNATIONAL TRADE

The Economist Group: Economist Intelligence Unit (EIU), 900 3rd Ave., 16th Fl., New York, NY, 10022, USA, (212) 541-0500, americas@eiu.com, https://www.eiu.com; Croatia Country Report.

Euromonitor International, Inc., 1 N Dearborn St., Ste. 1700, Chicago, IL, 60602, USA, (312) 922-1115, (312) 922-1157, info-usa@euromonitor.com, https://www.euromonitor.com/; Geographies.

Palgrave Macmillan, 1 New York Plaza, Ste. 4500, New York, NY, 10004-1562, USA, (800) 777-4643,

orders@palgrave.com, https://www.palgrave.com/us; The Statesman's Yearbook, 2023.

Routledge - Taylor & Francis Group, 6000 Broken Sound Pkwy. NW, Ste. 300, Boca Raton, FL, 33487, USA, (800) 634-1420, (800) 634-7064, orders@taylorandfrancis.com, https://www.routledge.com/; The Europa World Year Book 2022.

United Nations Statistics Division (UNSD), United Nations Plz., New York, NY, 10017, USA, (800) 253-9646, (212) 963-9851, statistics@un.org, https://unstats.un.org; International Trade Statistics Yearbook 2020 and Statistical Yearbook of the United Nations 2021.

The World Bank, 1818 H St. NW, Washington, DC, 20433, USA, (202) 473-1000, (202) 477-6391, eds03@worldbank.org, https://www.worldbank.org/; Croatia (report) and World Development Report 2022: Finance for an Equitable Recovery.

World Trade Organization (WTO), Ctre. William Rappard, Rue de Lausanne 154, Case postale, Geneva, CH-1211, SWI, enquiries@wto.org, https://www.wto.org; World Trade Statistical Review 2022.

CROATIA-INTERNET USERS

International Telecommunication Union (ITU), Place des Nations, Geneva, CH-1211, SWI, itumail@itu.int, https://www.itu.int; Global Connectivity Report 2022; World Telecommunication/ICT Indicators Database 2021; and Yearbook of Statistics 2019.

The World Bank, 1818 H St. NW, Washington, DC, 20433, USA, (202) 473-1000, (202) 477-6391, eds03@worldbank.org, https://www.worldbank.org/; Croatia (report).

CROATIA-LABOR

Central Intelligence Agency (CIA), Office of Public Affairs, Washington, DC, 20505, USA, (703) 482-0623, https://www.cia.gov; The World Factbook.

Euromonitor International, Inc., 1 N Dearborn St., Ste. 1700, Chicago, IL, 60602, USA, (312) 922-1115, (312) 922-1157, info-usa@euromonitor.com, https://www.euromonitor.com/; Geographies.

Palgrave Macmillan, 1 New York Plaza, Ste. 4500, New York, NY, 10004-1562, USA, (800) 777-4643, orders@palgrave.com, https://www.palgrave.com/us; The Statesman's Yearbook, 2023.

United Nations Statistics Division (UNSD), United Nations Plz., New York, NY, 10017, USA, (800) 253-9646, (212) 963-9851, statistics@un.org, https://unstats.un.org; Statistical Yearbook of the United Nations 2021.

The World Bank, 1818 H St. NW, Washington, DC, 20433, USA, (202) 473-1000, (202) 477-6391, eds03@worldbank.org, https://www.worldbank.org/; World Development Report 2022: Finance for an Equitable Recovery.

CROATIA-LAND USE

United Nations Statistics Division (UNSD), United Nations Plz., New York, NY, 10017, USA, (800) 253-9646, (212) 963-9851, statistics@un.org, https://unstats.un.org; Millennium Development Goal Indicators.

The World Bank, 1818 H St. NW, Washington, DC, 20433, USA, (202) 473-1000, (202) 477-6391, eds03@worldbank.org, https://www.worldbank.org/; World Development Report 2022: Finance for an Equitable Recovery.

CROATIA-LIBRARIES

UNESCO Institute for Statistics, C.P 250 Succursale H, Montreal, QC, H3G 2K8, CAN, (514) 343-6880 (Dial from U.S.), (514) 343-5740 (Fax from U.S.), uis.publications@unesco.org, http://uis.unesco.org/; UIS.Stat.

CROATIA-LIFE EXPECTANCY

Central Intelligence Agency (CIA), Office of Public Affairs, Washington, DC, 20505, USA, (703) 482-0623, https://www.cia.gov; The World Factbook.

United Nations Department of Economic and Social Affairs (DESA), Population Division, 2 United Nations Plz., Rm. DC2-1950, New York, NY, 10017, USA, (212) 963-3209, (212) 963-2147, population@un.org, https://www.un.org/development/desa/pd/; World Population Ageing 2020 Highlights.

United Nations Statistics Division (UNSD), United Nations Plz., New York, NY, 10017, USA, (800) 253-9646, (212) 963-9851, statistics@un.org, https://unstats.un.org; Millennium Development Goal Indicators.

CROATIA-LITERACY

Euromonitor International, Inc., 1 N Dearborn St., Ste. 1700, Chicago, IL, 60602, USA, (312) 922-1115, (312) 922-1157, info-usa@euromonitor.com, https://www.euromonitor.com/; Geographies.

UNESCO Institute for Statistics, C.P 250 Succursale H, Montreal, QC, H3G 2K8, CAN, (514) 343-6880 (Dial from U.S.), (514) 343-5740 (Fax from U.S.), uis.publications@unesco.org, http://uis.unesco.org/; Literacy.

CROATIA-LIVESTOCK

Palgrave Macmillan, 1 New York Plaza, Ste. 4500, New York, NY, 10004-1562, USA, (800) 777-4643, orders@palgrave.com, https://www.palgrave.com/us; The Statesman's Yearbook, 2023.

Routledge - Taylor & Francis Group, 6000 Broken Sound Pkwy. NW, Ste. 300, Boca Raton, FL, 33487, USA, (800) 634-1420, (800) 634-7064, orders@taylorandfrancis.com, https://www.routledge.com/; The Europa World Year Book 2022.

United Nations Food and Agricultural Organization (FAO), 2121 K St., Ste. 800B, Washington, DC, 20037, USA, (202) 653-2400 (Dial from U.S.), (202) 653-5760 (Fax from U.S.), fao-hq@fao.org, https://www.fao.org; The State of Food and Agriculture (SOFA) 2022.

United Nations Statistics Division (UNSD), United Nations Plz., New York, NY, 10017, USA, (800) 253-9646, (212) 963-9851, statistics@un.org, https://unstats.un.org; Statistical Yearbook of the United Nations 2021.

CROATIA-MARRIAGE

Routledge - Taylor & Francis Group, 6000 Broken Sound Pkwy. NW, Ste. 300, Boca Raton, FL, 33487, USA, (800) 634-1420, (800) 634-7064, orders@taylorandfrancis.com, https://www.routledge.com/; The Europa World Year Book 2022.

United Nations Statistics Division (UNSD), United Nations Plz., New York, NY, 10017, USA, (800) 253-9646, (212) 963-9851, statistics@un.org, https://unstats.un.org; Statistical Yearbook of the United Nations 2021.

CROATIA-MINERAL INDUSTRIES

Routledge - Taylor & Francis Group, 6000 Broken Sound Pkwy. NW, Ste. 300, Boca Raton, FL, 33487, USA, (800) 634-1420, (800) 634-7064, orders@taylorandfrancis.com, https://www.routledge.com/; The Europa World Year Book 2022.

United Nations Statistics Division (UNSD), United Nations Plz., New York, NY, 10017, USA, (800) 253-9646, (212) 963-9851, statistics@un.org, https://unstats.un.org; Energy Statistics Yearbook 2019 and Statistical Yearbook of the United Nations 2021.

The World Bank, 1818 H St. NW, Washington, DC, 20433, USA, (202) 473-1000, (202) 477-6391, eds03@worldbank.org, https://www.worldbank.org/; Croatia (report).

CROATIA-MONEY SUPPLY

The Economist Group: Economist Intelligence Unit (EIU), 900 3rd Ave., 16th Fl., New York, NY, 10022, USA, (212) 541-0500, americas@eiu.com, https://www.eiu.com; Croatia Country Report.

The World Bank, 1818 H St. NW, Washington, DC, 20433, USA, (202) 473-1000, (202) 477-6391, eds03@worldbank.org, https://www.worldbank.org/; Croatia (report).

CROATIA-MONUMENTS AND HISTORIC SITES

Palgrave Macmillan, 1 New York Plaza, Ste. 4500, New York, NY, 10004-1562, USA, (800) 777-4643, orders@palgrave.com, https://www.palgrave.com/us; The Statesman's Yearbook, 2023.

UNESCO Institute for Statistics, C.P 250 Succursale H, Montreal, QC, H3G 2K8, CAN, (514) 343-6880 (Dial from U.S.), (514) 343-5740 (Fax from U.S.), uis.publications@unesco.org, http://uis.unesco.org/; UIS.Stat.

CROATIA-MORTALITY

UNICEF, 3 United Nations Plz., New York, NY, 10017, USA, (212) 303-7984, (917) 244-2215, https://www.unicef.org; The State of the World's Children 2023.

United Nations Statistics Division (UNSD), United Nations Plz., New York, NY, 10017, USA, (800) 253-9646, (212) 963-9851, statistics@un.org, https://unstats.un.org; Millennium Development Goal Indicators; Statistical Yearbook of the United Nations 2021; and World Statistics Pocketbook 2021.

World Health Organization (WHO), Ave. Appia 20, Geneva, CH-1211, SWI, (202) 974-3000 (Telephone in U.S.), publications@who.int, https://www.who.int/; Global Health Observatory (GHO).

CROATIA-MOTION PICTURES

Palgrave Macmillan, 1 New York Plaza, Ste. 4500, New York, NY, 10004-1562, USA, (800) 777-4643, orders@palgrave.com, https://www.palgrave.com/us; The Statesman's Yearbook, 2023.

CROATIA-PETROLEUM INDUSTRY AND TRADE

Palgrave Macmillan, 1 New York Plaza, Ste. 4500, New York, NY, 10004-1562, USA, (800) 777-4643, orders@palgrave.com, https://www.palgrave.com/us; The Statesman's Yearbook, 2023.

U.S. Energy Information Administration (EIA), 1000 Independence Ave. SW, Washington, DC, 20585, USA, (202) 586-8800, infoctr@eia.gov, https://www.eia.gov; International Energy Outlook 2021.

United Nations Food and Agricultural Organization (FAO), 2121 K St., Ste. 800B, Washington, DC, 20037, USA, (202) 653-2400 (Dial from U.S.), (202) 653-5760 (Fax from U.S.), fao-hq@fao.org, https://www.fao.org; The State of Food and Agriculture (SOFA) 2022.

United Nations Statistics Division (UNSD), United Nations Plz., New York, NY, 10017, USA, (800) 253-9646, (212) 963-9851, statistics@un.org, https://unstats.un.org; Energy Statistics Yearbook 2019 and Statistical Yearbook of the United Nations 2021.

CROATIA-POPULATION

Central Intelligence Agency (CIA), Office of Public Affairs, Washington, DC, 20505, USA, (703) 482-0623, https://www.cia.gov; The World Factbook.

The Economist Group: Economist Intelligence Unit (EIU), 900 3rd Ave., 16th Fl., New York, NY, 10022, USA, (212) 541-0500, americas@eiu.com, https://www.eiu.com; Croatia Country Report.

Infoplease, c/o Sandbox Networks, Inc., 1 Lincoln St., 24th Fl., Boston, MA, 02111, USA, https://www.infoplease.com; Countries of the World.

Palgrave Macmillan, 1 New York Plaza, Ste. 4500, New York, NY, 10004-1562, USA, (800) 777-4643, orders@palgrave.com, https://www.palgrave.com/us; The Statesman's Yearbook, 2023.

Routledge - Taylor & Francis Group, 6000 Broken Sound Pkwy. NW, Ste. 300, Boca Raton, FL, 33487, USA, (800) 634-1420, (800) 634-7064, orders@taylorandfrancis.com, https://www.routledge.com/; The Europa World Year Book 2022.

UK Data Service, University of Essex, Wivenhoe Park, Colchester, Essex, CO4 3SQ, GBR, https://ukdataservice.ac.uk/; International Aggregate Data.

UNESCO Institute for Statistics, C.P 250 Succursale H, Montreal, QC, H3G 2K8, CAN, (514) 343-

6880 (Dial from U.S.), (514) 343-5740 (Fax from U.S.), uis.publications@unesco.org, http://uis.unesco.org/; UIS.Stat.

United Nations Department of Economic and Social Affairs (DESA), Population Division, 2 United Nations Plz., Rm. DC2-1950, New York, NY, 10017, USA, (212) 963-3209, (212) 963-2147, population@un.org, https://www.un.org/development/desa/pd/; Revision of World Urbanization Prospects and World Population Ageing 2020 Highlights.

United Nations Development Programme (UNDP), One United Nations Plz., New York, NY, 10017, USA, (212) 906-5000, (212) 906-5001, https://www.undp.org; Human Development Report 2021-2022.

United Nations Statistics Division (UNSD), United Nations Plz., New York, NY, 10017, USA, (800) 253-9646, (212) 963-9851, statistics@un.org, https://unstats.un.org; Statistical Yearbook of the United Nations 2021 and World Statistics Pocketbook 2021.

The World Bank, 1818 H St. NW, Washington, DC, 20433, USA, (202) 473-1000, (202) 477-6391, eds03@worldbank.org, https://www.worldbank.org/; Croatia (report); The Global Findex Database 2021; and World Development Report 2022: Finance for an Equitable Recovery.

CROATIA-POPULATION DENSITY

Central Intelligence Agency (CIA), Office of Public Affairs, Washington, DC, 20505, USA, (703) 482-0623, https://www.cia.gov; The World Factbook.

Palgrave Macmillan, 1 New York Plaza, Ste. 4500, New York, NY, 10004-1562, USA, (800) 777-4643, orders@palgrave.com, https://www.palgrave.com/us; The Statesman's Yearbook, 2023.

Routledge - Taylor & Francis Group, 6000 Broken Sound Pkwy. NW, Ste. 300, Boca Raton, FL, 33487, USA, (800) 634-1420, (800) 634-7064, orders@taylorandfrancis.com, https://www.routledge.com/; The Europa World Year Book 2022.

UNESCO Institute for Statistics, C.P 250 Succursale H, Montreal, QC, H3G 2K8, CAN, (514) 343-6880 (Dial from U.S.), (514) 343-5740 (Fax from U.S.), uis.publications@unesco.org, http://uis.unesco.org/; UIS.Stat.

The World Bank, 1818 H St. NW, Washington, DC, 20433, USA, (202) 473-1000, (202) 477-6391, eds03@worldbank.org, https://www.worldbank.org/; Croatia (report) and World Development Report 2022: Finance for an Equitable Recovery.

CROATIA-POWER RESOURCES

Euromonitor International, Inc., 1 N Dearborn St., Ste. 1700, Chicago, IL, 60602, USA, (312) 922-1115, (312) 922-1157, info-usa@euromonitor.com, https://www.euromonitor.com/; Geographies.

Palgrave Macmillan, 1 New York Plaza, Ste. 4500, New York, NY, 10004-1562, USA, (800) 777-4643, orders@palgrave.com, https://www.palgrave.com/us; The Statesman's Yearbook, 2023.

U.S. Energy Information Administration (EIA), 1000 Independence Ave. SW, Washington, DC, 20585, USA, (202) 586-8800, infoctr@eia.gov, https://www.eia.gov; International Energy Outlook 2021.

United Nations Statistics Division (UNSD), United Nations Plz., New York, NY, 10017, USA, (800) 253-9646, (212) 963-9851, statistics@un.org, https://unstats.un.org; Energy Statistics Yearbook 2019; Statistical Yearbook of the United Nations 2021; and World Statistics Pocketbook 2021.

The World Bank, 1818 H St. NW, Washington, DC, 20433, USA, (202) 473-1000, (202) 477-6391, eds03@worldbank.org, https://www.worldbank.org/; World Development Report 2022: Finance for an Equitable Recovery.

CROATIA-PRICES

Euromonitor International, Inc., 1 N Dearborn St., Ste. 1700, Chicago, IL, 60602, USA, (312) 922-1115, (312) 922-1157, info-usa@euromonitor.com, https://www.euromonitor.com/; Geographies.

The World Bank, 1818 H St. NW, Washington, DC, 20433, USA, (202) 473-1000, (202) 477-6391, eds03@worldbank.org, https://www.worldbank.org/; Croatia (report).

CROATIA-PUBLIC HEALTH

Euromonitor International, Inc., 1 N Dearborn St., Ste. 1700, Chicago, IL, 60602, USA, (312) 922-1115, (312) 922-1157, info-usa@euromonitor.com, https://www.euromonitor.com/; Geographies and Market Research on the Health and Wellness Industry.

Palgrave Macmillan, 1 New York Plaza, Ste. 4500, New York, NY, 10004-1562, USA, (800) 777-4643, orders@palgrave.com, https://www.palgrave.com/us; The Statesman's Yearbook, 2023.

U.S. Census Bureau, 4600 Silver Hill Rd., Washington, DC, 20233, USA, (301) 763-4636, (800) 923-8282, https://www.census.gov; HIV/AIDS Surveillance Data Base.

UNICEF, 3 United Nations Plz., New York, NY, 10017, USA, (212) 303-7984, (917) 244-2215, https://www.unicef.org; The State of the World's Children 2023.

United Nations Department of Economic and Social Affairs (DESA), Population Division, 2 United Nations Plz., Rm. DC2-1950, New York, NY, 10017, USA, (212) 963-3209, (212) 963-2147, population@un.org, https://www.un.org/development/desa/pd/; World Fertility Data 2019.

United Nations Development Programme (UNDP), One United Nations Plz., New York, NY, 10017, USA, (212) 906-5000, (212) 906-5001, https://www.undp.org; Human Development Report 2021-2022.

United Nations Statistics Division (UNSD), United Nations Plz., New York, NY, 10017, USA, (800) 253-9646, (212) 963-9851, statistics@un.org, https://unstats.un.org; Millennium Development Goal Indicators and Statistical Yearbook of the United Nations 2021.

The World Bank, 1818 H St. NW, Washington, DC, 20433, USA, (202) 473-1000, (202) 477-6391, eds03@worldbank.org, https://www.worldbank.org/; Croatia (report).

World Health Organization (WHO), Ave. Appia 20, Geneva, CH-1211, SWI, (202) 974-3000 (Telephone in U.S.), publications@who.int, https://www.who.int/; Global Health Observatory (GHO).

CROATIA-PUBLISHERS AND PUBLISHING

Routledge - Taylor & Francis Group, 6000 Broken Sound Pkwy. NW, Ste. 300, Boca Raton, FL, 33487, USA, (800) 634-1420, (800) 634-7064, orders@taylorandfrancis.com, https://www.routledge.com/; The Europa World Year Book 2022.

UNESCO Institute for Statistics, C.P 250 Succursale H, Montreal, QC, H3G 2K8, CAN, (514) 343-6880 (Dial from U.S.), (514) 343-5740 (Fax from U.S.), uis.publications@unesco.org, http://uis.unesco.org/; UIS.Stat.

CROATIA-RAILROADS

Palgrave Macmillan, 1 New York Plaza, Ste. 4500, New York, NY, 10004-1562, USA, (800) 777-4643, orders@palgrave.com, https://www.palgrave.com/us; The Statesman's Yearbook, 2023.

Routledge - Taylor & Francis Group, 6000 Broken Sound Pkwy. NW, Ste. 300, Boca Raton, FL, 33487, USA, (800) 634-1420, (800) 634-7064, orders@taylorandfrancis.com, https://www.routledge.com/; The Europa World Year Book 2022.

United Nations Statistics Division (UNSD), United Nations Plz., New York, NY, 10017, USA, (800) 253-9646, (212) 963-9851, statistics@un.org, https://unstats.un.org; Statistical Yearbook of the United Nations 2021.

CROATIA-RELIGION

Central Intelligence Agency (CIA), Office of Public Affairs, Washington, DC, 20505, USA, (703) 482-0623, https://www.cia.gov; The World Factbook.

Palgrave Macmillan, 1 New York Plaza, Ste. 4500, New York, NY, 10004-1562, USA, (800) 777-4643, orders@palgrave.com, https://www.palgrave.com/us; The Statesman's Yearbook, 2023.

CROATIA-RETAIL TRADE

Euromonitor International, Inc., 1 N Dearborn St., Ste. 1700, Chicago, IL, 60602, USA, (312) 922-1115, (312) 922-1157, info-usa@euromonitor.com, https://www.euromonitor.com/; Geographies.

United Nations Statistics Division (UNSD), United Nations Plz., New York, NY, 10017, USA, (800) 253-9646, (212) 963-9851, statistics@un.org, https://unstats.un.org; Statistical Yearbook of the United Nations 2021.

CROATIA-RUBBER INDUSTRY AND TRADE

International Rubber Study Group (IRSG), 51 Changi Business Park Central 2, Unit No. 6, 486066, SGP, https://www.rubberstudy.org; Monthly Rubber Bulletin (MRB); Rubber Industry Report; Rubber Statistical Bulletin; and World Rubber Industry Report (WRIO).

United Nations Statistics Division (UNSD), United Nations Plz., New York, NY, 10017, USA, (800) 253-9646, (212) 963-9851, statistics@un.org, https://unstats.un.org; Statistical Yearbook of the United Nations 2021.

CROATIA-SHIPPING

Routledge - Taylor & Francis Group, 6000 Broken Sound Pkwy. NW, Ste. 300, Boca Raton, FL, 33487, USA, (800) 634-1420, (800) 634-7064, orders@taylorandfrancis.com, https://www.routledge.com/; The Europa World Year Book 2022.

United Nations Statistics Division (UNSD), United Nations Plz., New York, NY, 10017, USA, (800) 253-9646, (212) 963-9851, statistics@un.org, https://unstats.un.org; Statistical Yearbook of the United Nations 2021.

CROATIA-TELEPHONE

Palgrave Macmillan, 1 New York Plaza, Ste. 4500, New York, NY, 10004-1562, USA, (800) 777-4643, orders@palgrave.com, https://www.palgrave.com/us; The Statesman's Yearbook, 2023.

Routledge - Taylor & Francis Group, 6000 Broken Sound Pkwy. NW, Ste. 300, Boca Raton, FL, 33487, USA, (800) 634-1420, (800) 634-7064, orders@taylorandfrancis.com, https://www.routledge.com/; The Europa World Year Book 2022.

United Nations Statistics Division (UNSD), United Nations Plz., New York, NY, 10017, USA, (800) 253-9646, (212) 963-9851, statistics@un.org, https://unstats.un.org; World Statistics Pocketbook 2021.

CROATIA-TEXTILE INDUSTRY

United Nations Statistics Division (UNSD), United Nations Plz., New York, NY, 10017, USA, (800) 253-9646, (212) 963-9851, statistics@un.org, https://unstats.un.org; Statistical Yearbook of the United Nations 2021.

CROATIA-THEATER

UNESCO Institute for Statistics, C.P 250 Succursale H, Montreal, QC, H3G 2K8, CAN, (514) 343-6880 (Dial from U.S.), (514) 343-5740 (Fax from U.S.), uis.publications@unesco.org, http://uis.unesco.org/; UIS.Stat.

CROATIA-TOBACCO INDUSTRY

United Nations Statistics Division (UNSD), United Nations Plz., New York, NY, 10017, USA, (800) 253-9646, (212) 963-9851, statistics@un.org, https://unstats.un.org; Statistical Yearbook of the United Nations 2021.

CROATIA-TOURISM

Euromonitor International, Inc., 1 N Dearborn St., Ste. 1700, Chicago, IL, 60602, USA, (312) 922-

1115, (312) 922-1157, info-usa@euromonitor.com, https://www.euromonitor.com/; Geographies.

Palgrave Macmillan, 1 New York Plaza, Ste. 4500, New York, NY, 10004-1562, USA, (800) 777-4643, orders@palgrave.com, https://www.palgrave.com/us; The Statesman's Yearbook, 2023.

Routledge - Taylor & Francis Group, 6000 Broken Sound Pkwy. NW, Ste. 300, Boca Raton, FL, 33487, USA, (800) 634-1420, (800) 634-7064, orders@taylorandfrancis.com, https://www.routledge.com/; The Europa World Year Book 2022.

United Nations Statistics Division (UNSD), United Nations Plz., New York, NY, 10017, USA, (800) 253-9646, (212) 963-9851, statistics@un.org, https://unstats.un.org; Statistical Yearbook of the United Nations 2021.

The World Bank, 1818 H St. NW, Washington, DC, 20433, USA, (202) 473-1000, (202) 477-6391, eds03@worldbank.org, https://www.worldbank.org/; Croatia (report).

CROATIA-TRANSPORTATION

Central Intelligence Agency (CIA), Office of Public Affairs, Washington, DC, 20505, USA, (703) 482-0623, https://www.cia.gov; The World Factbook.

Euromonitor International, Inc., 1 N Dearborn St., Ste. 1700, Chicago, IL, 60602, USA, (312) 922-1115, (312) 922-1157, info-usa@euromonitor.com, https://www.euromonitor.com/; Geographies.

European Commission, Eurostat, Luxembourg, 2920, LUX, https://ec.europa.eu/eurostat/; Air Transport Statistics.

Palgrave Macmillan, 1 New York Plaza, Ste. 4500, New York, NY, 10004-1562, USA, (800) 777-4643, orders@palgrave.com, https://www.palgrave.com/us; The Statesman's Yearbook, 2023.

Routledge - Taylor & Francis Group, 6000 Broken Sound Pkwy. NW, Ste. 300, Boca Raton, FL, 33487, USA, (800) 634-1420, (800) 634-7064, orders@taylorandfrancis.com, https://www.routledge.com/; The Europa World Year Book 2022.

The World Bank, 1818 H St. NW, Washington, DC, 20433, USA, (202) 473-1000, (202) 477-6391, eds03@worldbank.org, https://www.worldbank.org/; Croatia (report).

CROATIA-UNEMPLOYMENT

Palgrave Macmillan, 1 New York Plaza, Ste. 4500, New York, NY, 10004-1562, USA, (800) 777-4643, orders@palgrave.com, https://www.palgrave.com/us; The Statesman's Yearbook, 2023.

United Nations Statistics Division (UNSD), United Nations Plz., New York, NY, 10017, USA, (800) 253-9646, (212) 963-9851, statistics@un.org, https://unstats.un.org; Statistical Yearbook of the United Nations 2021.

The World Bank, 1818 H St. NW, Washington, DC, 20433, USA, (202) 473-1000, (202) 477-6391, eds03@worldbank.org, https://www.worldbank.org/; Croatia (report).

CROATIA-VITAL STATISTICS

Palgrave Macmillan, 1 New York Plaza, Ste. 4500, New York, NY, 10004-1562, USA, (800) 777-4643, orders@palgrave.com, https://www.palgrave.com/us; The Statesman's Yearbook, 2023.

U.S. Census Bureau, 4600 Silver Hill Rd., Washington, DC, 20233, USA, (301) 763-4636, (800) 923-8282, https://www.census.gov; HIV/AIDS Surveillance Data Base.

United Nations Department of Economic and Social Affairs (DESA), Population Division, 2 United Nations Plz., Rm. DC2-1950, New York, NY, 10017, USA, (212) 963-3209, (212) 963-2147, population@un.org, https://www.un.org/development/desa/pd/; World Contraceptive Use 2021: Estimates and Projections of Family Planning Indicators and World Marriage Data 2019.

United Nations Statistics Division (UNSD), United Nations Plz., New York, NY, 10017, USA, (800) 253-9646, (212) 963-9851, statistics@un.org, https://unstats.un.org; Statistical Yearbook of the United Nations 2021.

CROATIA-WAGES

United Nations Statistics Division (UNSD), United Nations Plz., New York, NY, 10017, USA, (800) 253-9646, (212) 963-9851, statistics@un.org, https://unstats.un.org; Statistical Yearbook of the United Nations 2021.

The World Bank, 1818 H St. NW, Washington, DC, 20433, USA, (202) 473-1000, (202) 477-6391, eds03@worldbank.org, https://www.worldbank.org/; Croatia (report).

CROATIA-WHOLESALE TRADE

United Nations Statistics Division (UNSD), United Nations Plz., New York, NY, 10017, USA, (800) 253-9646, (212) 963-9851, statistics@un.org, https://unstats.un.org; Statistical Yearbook of the United Nations 2021.

CROPS

See also FARMS and Individual crops

CROPS-ACREAGE

U.S. Department of Agriculture (USDA), Economic Research Service (ERS), 1400 Independence Ave. SW, Mail Stop 1800, Washington, DC, 20250-0002, USA, (202) 720-2791, https://www.ers.usda.gov/; Agricultural Resource Management Survey (ARMS) Tailored Reports.

U.S. Department of Agriculture (USDA), National Agricultural Statistics Service (USDA-NASS), 1400 Independence Ave. SW, Washington, DC, 20250, USA, (800) 727-9540, nass@nass.usda.gov, https://www.nass.usda.gov; Agricultural Statistics; Crop Production; and Crop Values Annual Summary.

CROPS-FARM MARKETINGS, SALES

U.S. Department of Agriculture (USDA), Economic Research Service (ERS), 1400 Independence Ave. SW, Mail Stop 1800, Washington, DC, 20250-0002, USA, (202) 720-2791, https://www.ers.usda.gov/; Agricultural Baseline Database and 2022 Farm Sector Income Forecast.

CROPS-INTERNATIONAL TRADE

U.S. Department of Agriculture (USDA), Economic Research Service (ERS), 1400 Independence Ave. SW, Mail Stop 1800, Washington, DC, 20250-0002, USA, (202) 720-2791, https://www.ers.usda.gov/; Foreign Agricultural Trade of the United States (FATUS).

U.S. Department of Agriculture (USDA), National Agricultural Statistics Service (USDA-NASS), 1400 Independence Ave. SW, Washington, DC, 20250, USA, (800) 727-9540, nass@nass.usda.gov, https://www.nass.usda.gov; Agricultural Statistics.

U.S. Department of Agriculture (USDA), World Agricultural Outlook Board, (WAOB), 1400 Independence Ave. SW, Mail Stop 3812, Washington, DC, 20250, USA, (202) 720-9805, mark.jekanowski@usda.gov, https://www.usda.gov/oce/commodity-markets/waob; World Agricultural Supply and Demand Estimates (WASDE) Report.

CROPS-PRICES

U.S. Department of Agriculture (USDA), Economic Research Service (ERS), 1400 Independence Ave. SW, Mail Stop 1800, Washington, DC, 20250-0002, USA, (202) 720-2791, https://www.ers.usda.gov/; Agricultural Baseline Database.

U.S. Department of Agriculture (USDA), National Agricultural Statistics Service (USDA-NASS), 1400 Independence Ave. SW, Washington, DC, 20250, USA, (800) 727-9540, nass@nass.usda.gov, https://www.nass.usda.gov; Agricultural Prices; Agricultural Statistics; Crop Production; and Crop Values Annual Summary.

CROPS-PRODUCTION

U.S. Department of Agriculture (USDA), Economic Research Service (ERS), 1400 Independence Ave. SW, Mail Stop 1800, Washington, DC, 20250-0002, USA, (202) 720-2791, https://www.ers.usda.gov/; Agricultural Baseline Database.

U.S. Department of Agriculture (USDA), National Agricultural Statistics Service (USDA-NASS), 1400 Independence Ave. SW, Washington, DC, 20250, USA, (800) 727-9540, nass@nass.usda.gov, https://www.nass.usda.gov; Agricultural Statistics; Crop Production; Crop Progress; Crop Values Annual Summary; and Quick Stats.

CROPS-PRODUCTIVITY

U.S. Department of Agriculture (USDA), Economic Research Service (ERS), 1400 Independence Ave. SW, Mail Stop 1800, Washington, DC, 20250-0002, USA, (202) 720-2791, https://www.ers.usda.gov/; Agricultural Resource Management Survey (ARMS) Tailored Reports.

CROPS-SUPPLY AND DISAPPEARANCE

U.S. Department of Agriculture (USDA), Economic Research Service (ERS), 1400 Independence Ave. SW, Mail Stop 1800, Washington, DC, 20250-0002, USA, (202) 720-2791, https://www.ers.usda.gov/; Cotton and Wool Outlook; Feed Yearbook: Report; and Wheat Data.

U.S. Department of Agriculture (USDA), World Agricultural Outlook Board, (WAOB), 1400 Independence Ave. SW, Mail Stop 3812, Washington, DC, 20250, USA, (202) 720-9805, mark.jekanowski@usda.gov, https://www.usda.gov/oce/commodity-markets/waob; World Agricultural Supply and Demand Estimates (WASDE) Report.

CROSS COUNTRY (RUNNING)

National Collegiate Athletic Association (NCAA), PO Box 6222, Indianapolis, IN, 46206-6222, USA, (317) 917-6222, (317) 917-6888, https://www.ncaa.org/; NCAA Sports Sponsorship and Participation Rates Report: 1956-1957 through 2020-2021.

National Federation of State High School Associations (NFHS), PO Box 690, Indianapolis, IN, 46206, USA, (317) 972-6900, https://www.nfhs.org/; High School Athletics Participation Survey, 2021-2022.

The NPD Group, 900 W Shore Rd., Port Washington, NY, 11050, USA, (516) 625-0700, contactnpd@npd.com, https://www.npd.com; Sports.

CROSSWORD PUZZLES

MRI Simmons, 200 Liberty St., 4th Fl., New York, NY, 10281, USA, (866) 256-4468, info.ms@mrisimmons.com, https://www.mrisimmons.com/; MRI-Simmons USA.

CRUDE MATERIALS

U.S. Energy Information Administration (EIA), 1000 Independence Ave. SW, Washington, DC, 20585, USA, (202) 586-8800, infoctr@eia.gov, https://www.eia.gov; International Energy Outlook 2021 and Monthly Energy Review (MER).

CRUDE MATERIALS-PRODUCER PRICE INDEXES

U.S. Department of Labor (DOL), Bureau of Labor Statistics (BLS), Postal Square Bldg., 2 Massachusetts Ave. NE, Washington, DC, 20212-0001, USA, (202) 691-5200, (202) 691-7890, blsdata_staff@bls.gov, https://www.bls.gov; Producer Price Indexes (PPI).

CRUDE OIL

See also PETROLEUM INDUSTRY AND TRADE

American Petroleum Institute (API), 200 Massachusetts Ave. NW, Ste. 1100, Washington, DC, 20001-5571, USA, (202) 682-8000, https://www.api.org/; Monthly Statistical Report and Weekly Statistical Bulletin.

Lundberg Survey, Inc. (LSI), 911 Via Alondra, Camarillo, CA, 93012, USA, (805) 383-2400, (805) 383-2424, lsi@lundbergsurvey.com, https://www.lundbergsurvey.com; Energy Detente; Lundberg Letter; and Market Share Reports.

OilPrice.com, USA, https://oilprice.com/; OilPrice.com.

CRUDE OIL-INTERNATIONAL TRADE

U.S. Census Bureau, International Trade Program, 4600 Silver Hill Rd., Washington, DC, 20233, USA, (800) 549-0595, eid.international.trade.data@census.gov, https://www.census.gov/foreign-trade; International Trade Data.

U.S. Energy Information Administration (EIA), 1000 Independence Ave. SW, Washington, DC, 20585, USA, (202) 586-8800, infoctr@eia.gov, https://www.eia.gov; Annual Energy Outlook 2022; International Energy Outlook 2021; Monthly Energy Review (MER); Petroleum Supply Annual 2021; and U.S. Crude Oil and Natural Gas Proved Reserves, Year-End 2020.

CRUDE OIL-PRICES

OilPrice.com, USA, https://oilprice.com/; OilPrice.com.

CRUDE OIL-PRODUCTION

U.S. Energy Information Administration (EIA), 1000 Independence Ave. SW, Washington, DC, 20585, USA, (202) 586-8800, infoctr@eia.gov, https://www.eia.gov; Monthly Energy Review (MER); Petroleum Supply Annual 2021; and U.S. Crude Oil and Natural Gas Proved Reserves, Year-End 2020.

CRUDE OIL-WORLD PRODUCTION

Endeavor Business Media, 30 Burton Hills Blvd., Ste. 185, Nashville, TN, 37215, USA, (800) 547-7377, https://www.endeavorbusinessmedia.com/; Oil & Gas Journal.

U.S. Energy Information Administration (EIA), 1000 Independence Ave. SW, Washington, DC, 20585, USA, (202) 586-8800, infoctr@eia.gov, https://www.eia.gov; International Energy Outlook 2021.

CRYOSPHERE

Intergovernmental Panel on Climate Change (IPCC), C/O World Meteorological Organization, 7 bis Avenue de la Paix, C.P. 2300, Geneva, CH-1211, SWI, ipcc-sec@wmo.int, https://www.ipcc.ch/; The Ocean and Cryosphere in a Changing Climate.

CRYPTOCURRENCIES

Greenpeace, 1300 I St. NW, Ste. 1100 E, Washington, DC, 20001, USA, (800) 722-6995, (202) 462-1177, (202) 462-4507, connect@greenpeace.us, https://www.greenpeace.org; Financial Institutions Need to Support a Code Change to Cleanup Bitcoin.

Thomson Reuters, 3 Times Square, New York, NY, 10036, USA, (646) 540-3000, general.info@thomsonreuters.com, https://thomsonreuters.com/; Cryptos on the Rise 2022.

CRYPTOSPORIDIOSIS

U.S. Department of Health and Human Services, Centers for Disease Control and Prevention (CDC), 1600 Clifton Rd., Atlanta, GA, 30329-4027, USA, (800) 232-4636, (888) 232-6348 (TTY), cdcinfo@cdc.gov, https://www.cdc.gov; Morbidity and Mortality Weekly Report (MMWR) and National Notifiable Diseases Surveillance System (NNDSS).

CUBA-NATIONAL STATISTICAL OFFICE

Oficina Nacional de Estadisticas e Informacion, Cuba, Vedado, Plz. de la Revolucion, Paseo No. 60 e/ 3ra y 5ta, Havana, CP 10400, CUB, difusion@onei.gob.cu, http://www.onei.gob.cu/; National Data Reports of Cuba.

CUBA-PRIMARY STATISTICS SOURCES

Oficina Nacional de Estadisticas e Informacion, Cuba, Vedado, Plz. de la Revolucion, Paseo No. 60 e/ 3ra y 5ta, Havana, CP 10400, CUB, difusion@onei.gob.cu, http://www.onei.gob.cu/; Anuario Estadistico de Cuba 2020.

CUBA-AGRICULTURE

The Economist Group: Economist Intelligence Unit (EIU), 900 3rd Ave., 16th Fl., New York, NY, 10022, USA, (212) 541-0500, americas@eiu.com, https://www.eiu.com; Cuba Country Report.

Euromonitor International, Inc., 1 N Dearborn St., Ste. 1700, Chicago, IL, 60602, USA, (312) 922-1115, (312) 922-1157, info-usa@euromonitor.com, https://www.euromonitor.com/; Geographies.

Palgrave Macmillan, 1 New York Plaza, Ste. 4500, New York, NY, 10004-1562, USA, (800) 777-4643, orders@palgrave.com, https://www.palgrave.com/us; The Statesman's Yearbook, 2023.

Routledge - Taylor & Francis Group, 6000 Broken Sound Pkwy. NW, Ste. 300, Boca Raton, FL, 33487, USA, (800) 634-1420, (800) 634-7064, orders@taylorandfrancis.com, https://www.routledge.com/; The Europa World Year Book 2022.

United Nations Food and Agricultural Organization (FAO), 2121 K St., Ste. 800B, Washington, DC, 20037, USA, (202) 653-2400 (Dial from U.S.), (202) 653-5760 (Fax from U.S.), fao-hq@fao.org, https://www.fao.org; AQUASTAT and The State of Food and Agriculture (SOFA) 2022.

United Nations Statistics Division (UNSD), United Nations Plz., New York, NY, 10017, USA, (800) 253-9646, (212) 963-9851, statistics@un.org, https://unstats.un.org; Statistical Yearbook of the United Nations 2021.

CUBA-AIRLINES

Palgrave Macmillan, 1 New York Plaza, Ste. 4500, New York, NY, 10004-1562, USA, (800) 777-4643, orders@palgrave.com, https://www.palgrave.com/us; The Statesman's Yearbook, 2023.

Routledge - Taylor & Francis Group, 6000 Broken Sound Pkwy. NW, Ste. 300, Boca Raton, FL, 33487, USA, (800) 634-1420, (800) 634-7064, orders@taylorandfrancis.com, https://www.routledge.com/; The Europa World Year Book 2022.

CUBA-ALUMINUM PRODUCTION

See CUBA-MINERAL INDUSTRIES

CUBA-ARMED FORCES

Central Intelligence Agency (CIA), Office of Public Affairs, Washington, DC, 20505, USA, (703) 482-0623, https://www.cia.gov; The World Factbook.

International Institute for Strategic Studies (IISS) - Americas, 2121 K St. NW, Ste. 600, Washington, DC, 20037, USA, (202) 659-1490, (202) 659-1499, https://www.iiss.org/; The Military Balance 2022.

Palgrave Macmillan, 1 New York Plaza, Ste. 4500, New York, NY, 10004-1562, USA, (800) 777-4643, orders@palgrave.com, https://www.palgrave.com/us; The Statesman's Yearbook, 2023.

Stockholm International Peace Research Institute (SIPRI), Signalistgatan 9, Stockholm, SE 169 72, SWE, https://www.sipri.org/; SIPRI Arms Transfers Database and SIPRI Military Expenditure Database.

CUBA-BALANCE OF PAYMENTS

United Nations Economic Commission for Latin America and the Caribbean (ECLAC), Casilla 179-D, Santiago, 7630412, CHL, (202) 596-3713, prensa@cepal.org, https://www.cepal.org/en; Economic Survey of Latin America and the Caribbean 2021: Labour Dynamics and Employment Policies for Sustainable and Inclusive Recovery Beyond the COVID-19 Crisis.

CUBA-BANKS AND BANKING

Euromonitor International, Inc., 1 N Dearborn St., Ste. 1700, Chicago, IL, 60602, USA, (312) 922-1115, (312) 922-1157, info-usa@euromonitor.com, https://www.euromonitor.com/; Geographies.

Routledge - Taylor & Francis Group, 6000 Broken Sound Pkwy. NW, Ste. 300, Boca Raton, FL, 33487, USA, (800) 634-1420, (800) 634-7064, orders@taylorandfrancis.com, https://www.routledge.com/; The Europa World Year Book 2022.

CUBA-BARLEY PRODUCTION

See CUBA-CROPS

CUBA-BROADCASTING

Central Intelligence Agency (CIA), Office of Public Affairs, Washington, DC, 20505, USA, (703) 482-0623, https://www.cia.gov; The World Factbook.

Euromonitor International, Inc., 1 N Dearborn St., Ste. 1700, Chicago, IL, 60602, USA, (312) 922-1115, (312) 922-1157, info-usa@euromonitor.com, https://www.euromonitor.com/; Geographies.

Palgrave Macmillan, 1 New York Plaza, Ste. 4500, New York, NY, 10004-1562, USA, (800) 777-4643, orders@palgrave.com, https://www.palgrave.com/us; The Statesman's Yearbook, 2023.

UNESCO Institute for Statistics, C.P 250 Succursale H, Montreal, QC, H3G 2K8, CAN, (514) 343-6880 (Dial from U.S.), (514) 343-5740 (Fax from U.S.), uis.publications@unesco.org, http://uis.unesco.org/; UIS.Stat.

WRTH Publications Limited, PO Box 290, Oxford, OX2 7FT, GBR, sales@wrth.com, https://www.wrth.com; World Radio TV Handbook 2023.

CUBA-BUDGET

Central Intelligence Agency (CIA), Office of Public Affairs, Washington, DC, 20505, USA, (703) 482-0623, https://www.cia.gov; The World Factbook.

CUBA-CLIMATE

Palgrave Macmillan, 1 New York Plaza, Ste. 4500, New York, NY, 10004-1562, USA, (800) 777-4643, orders@palgrave.com, https://www.palgrave.com/us; The Statesman's Yearbook, 2023.

CUBA-COAL PRODUCTION

See CUBA-MINERAL INDUSTRIES

CUBA-COCOA PRODUCTION

See CUBA-CROPS

CUBA-COFFEE

See CUBA-CROPS

CUBA-COMMERCE

Palgrave Macmillan, 1 New York Plaza, Ste. 4500, New York, NY, 10004-1562, USA, (800) 777-4643, orders@palgrave.com, https://www.palgrave.com/us; The Statesman's Yearbook, 2023.

UK Data Service, University of Essex, Wivenhoe Park, Colchester, Essex, CO4 3SQ, GBR, https://ukdataservice.ac.uk/; International Aggregate Data.

CUBA-COMMODITY EXCHANGES

Barchart, 209 W Jackson Blvd., 2nd Fl., Chicago, IL, 60606, USA, (877) 247-4394, commodities@barchart.com, https://www.barchart.com/cmdty; The cmdty Yearbook 2023; cmdtyStats: Commodity Statistics and Fundamental Data; cmdtyView: Commodity Index; and Commodity Data and Prices.

International Monetary Fund (IMF), 700 19th St. NW, Washington, DC, 20431, USA, (202) 623-7000, (202) 623-4661, publications@imf.org, https://www.imf.org; IMF Primary Commodity Prices.

CUBA-CONSTRUCTION INDUSTRY

United Nations Statistics Division (UNSD), United Nations Plz., New York, NY, 10017, USA, (800) 253-9646, (212) 963-9851, statistics@un.org, https://unstats.un.org; Statistical Yearbook of the United Nations 2021.

CUBA-COPPER INDUSTRY AND TRADE

See CUBA-MINERAL INDUSTRIES

CUBA-CORN INDUSTRY

See CUBA-CROPS

CUBA-COTTON

See CUBA-CROPS

CUBA-CROPS

Palgrave Macmillan, 1 New York Plaza, Ste. 4500, New York, NY, 10004-1562, USA, (800) 777-4643, orders@palgrave.com, https://www.palgrave.com/us; The Statesman's Yearbook, 2023.

United Nations Food and Agricultural Organization (FAO), 2121 K St., Ste. 800B, Washington, DC, 20037, USA, (202) 653-2400 (Dial from U.S.), (202) 653-5760 (Fax from U.S.), fao-hq@fao.org, https://www.fao.org; The State of Food and Agriculture (SOFA) 2022.

United Nations Statistics Division (UNSD), United Nations Plz., New York, NY, 10017, USA, (800) 253-9646, (212) 963-9851, statistics@un.org, https://unstats.un.org; Statistical Yearbook of the United Nations 2021.

CUBA-DAIRY PROCESSING

Palgrave Macmillan, 1 New York Plaza, Ste. 4500, New York, NY, 10004-1562, USA, (800) 777-4643, orders@palgrave.com, https://www.palgrave.com/us; The Statesman's Yearbook, 2023.

United Nations Food and Agricultural Organization (FAO), 2121 K St., Ste. 800B, Washington, DC, 20037, USA, (202) 653-2400 (Dial from U.S.), (202) 653-5760 (Fax from U.S.), fao-hq@fao.org, https://www.fao.org; The State of Food and Agriculture (SOFA) 2022.

CUBA-DEBTS, EXTERNAL

Palgrave Macmillan, 1 New York Plaza, Ste. 4500, New York, NY, 10004-1562, USA, (800) 777-4643, orders@palgrave.com, https://www.palgrave.com/us; The Statesman's Yearbook, 2023.

United Nations Economic Commission for Latin America and the Caribbean (ECLAC), Casilla 179-D, Santiago, 7630412, CHL, (202) 596-3713, prensa@cepal.org, https://www.cepal.org/en; Economic Survey of Latin America and the Caribbean 2021: Labour Dynamics and Employment Policies for Sustainable and Inclusive Recovery Beyond the COVID-19 Crisis.

The World Bank, 1818 H St. NW, Washington, DC, 20433, USA, (202) 473-1000, (202) 477-6391, eds03@worldbank.org, https://www.worldbank.org/; Global Financial Development Report 2019-2020: Bank Regulation and Supervision a Decade after the Global Financial Crisis.

CUBA-DEFENSE EXPENDITURES

See CUBA-ARMED FORCES

CUBA-DIAMONDS

See CUBA-MINERAL INDUSTRIES

CUBA-ECONOMIC ASSISTANCE

United Nations Statistics Division (UNSD), United Nations Plz., New York, NY, 10017, USA, (800) 253-9646, (212) 963-9851, statistics@un.org, https://unstats.un.org; Statistical Yearbook of the United Nations 2021.

CUBA-ECONOMIC CONDITIONS

Bernan Press, 15250 NBN Way, Bldg. C, Blue Ridge Summit, PA, 17214, USA, (301) 459-2255, (800) 865-3457, (800) 865-3450, customercare@bernan.com, https://rowman.com/Page/Bernan; World Economic Outlook, April 2022.

Central Intelligence Agency (CIA), Office of Public Affairs, Washington, DC, 20505, USA, (703) 482-0623, https://www.cia.gov; The World Factbook.

The Economist Group: Economist Intelligence Unit (EIU), 900 3rd Ave., 16th Fl., New York, NY, 10022, USA, (212) 541-0500, americas@eiu.com, https://www.eiu.com; Cuba Country Report.

Euromonitor International, Inc., 1 N Dearborn St., Ste. 1700, Chicago, IL, 60602, USA, (312) 922-1115, (312) 922-1157, info-usa@euromonitor.com, https://www.euromonitor.com/; Geographies.

International Monetary Fund (IMF), 700 19th St. NW, Washington, DC, 20431, USA, (202) 623-7000, (202) 623-4661, publications@imf.org, https://www.imf.org; IMF Data and World Economic Outlook.

Palgrave Macmillan, 1 New York Plaza, Ste. 4500, New York, NY, 10004-1562, USA, (800) 777-4643, orders@palgrave.com, https://www.palgrave.com/us; The Statesman's Yearbook, 2023.

Routledge - Taylor & Francis Group, 6000 Broken Sound Pkwy. NW, Ste. 300, Boca Raton, FL, 33487, USA, (800) 634-1420, (800) 634-7064, orders@taylorandfrancis.com, https://www.routledge.com/; The Europa World Year Book 2022.

United Nations Economic Commission for Latin America and the Caribbean (ECLAC), Casilla 179-D, Santiago, 7630412, CHL, (202) 596-3713, prensa@cepal.org, https://www.cepal.org/en; CEPALSTAT; Economic Survey of Latin America and the Caribbean 2021: Labour Dynamics and Employment Policies for Sustainable and Inclusive Recovery Beyond the COVID-19 Crisis; Foreign Direct Investment in Latin America and the Caribbean 2022; and Social Panorama of Latin America and the Caribbean 2022: Transforming Education as a Basis for Sustainable Development.

United Nations Statistics Division (UNSD), United Nations Plz., New York, NY, 10017, USA, (800) 253-9646, (212) 963-9851, statistics@un.org, https://unstats.un.org; World Statistics Pocketbook 2021.

The World Bank, 1818 H St. NW, Washington, DC, 20433, USA, (202) 473-1000, (202) 477-6391, eds03@worldbank.org, https://www.worldbank.org/; Global Economic Monitor (GEM); Global Economic Prospects, June 2022; and The Global Findex Database 2021.

CUBA-EDUCATION

Euromonitor International, Inc., 1 N Dearborn St., Ste. 1700, Chicago, IL, 60602, USA, (312) 922-1115, (312) 922-1157, info-usa@euromonitor.com, https://www.euromonitor.com/; Geographies.

Infoplease, c/o Sandbox Networks, Inc., 1 Lincoln St., 24th Fl., Boston, MA, 02111, USA, https://www.infoplease.com; Countries of the World.

Oficina Nacional de Estadisticas e Informacion, Cuba, Vedado, Plz. de la Revolucion, Paseo No. 60 e/ 3ra y 5ta, Havana, CP 10400, CUB, difusion@onei.gob.cu, http://www.onei.gob.cu/; Series Estadisticas Educacion 1985-2019.

Palgrave Macmillan, 1 New York Plaza, Ste. 4500, New York, NY, 10004-1562, USA, (800) 777-4643, orders@palgrave.com, https://www.palgrave.com/us; The Statesman's Yearbook, 2023.

Routledge - Taylor & Francis Group, 6000 Broken Sound Pkwy. NW, Ste. 300, Boca Raton, FL, 33487, USA, (800) 634-1420, (800) 634-7064, orders@taylorandfrancis.com, https://www.routledge.com/; The Europa World Year Book 2022.

UNESCO Institute for Statistics, C.P 250 Succursale H, Montreal, QC, H3G 2K8, CAN, (514) 343-6880 (Dial from U.S.), (514) 343-5740 (Fax from U.S.), uis.publications@unesco.org, http://uis.unesco.org/; Literacy and UIS.Stat.

United Nations Statistics Division (UNSD), United Nations Plz., New York, NY, 10017, USA, (800) 253-9646, (212) 963-9851, statistics@un.org, https://unstats.un.org; Millennium Development Goal Indicators.

CUBA-ELECTRICITY

International Energy Agency (IEA), 9 Rue de la Federation, Paris, 75739, FRA, info@iea.org, https://www.iea.org/; World Energy Outlook 2021.

U.S. Energy Information Administration (EIA), 1000 Independence Ave. SW, Washington, DC, 20585, USA, (202) 586-8800, infoctr@eia.gov, https://www.eia.gov; International Energy Outlook 2021.

United Nations Statistics Division (UNSD), United Nations Plz., New York, NY, 10017, USA, (800) 253-9646, (212) 963-9851, statistics@un.org, https://unstats.un.org; Statistical Yearbook of the United Nations 2021.

CUBA-EMPLOYMENT

International Labour Organization (ILO), 4 Rte. des Morillons, Geneva, CH-1211, SWI, ilo@ilo.org, https://www.ilo.org; NORMLEX Information System on International Labour Standards.

UK Data Service, University of Essex, Wivenhoe Park, Colchester, Essex, CO4 3SQ, GBR, https://ukdataservice.ac.uk/; International Aggregate Data.

United Nations Statistics Division (UNSD), United Nations Plz., New York, NY, 10017, USA, (800) 253-9646, (212) 963-9851, statistics@un.org, https://unstats.un.org; Statistical Yearbook of the United Nations 2021.

CUBA-ENVIRONMENTAL CONDITIONS

DSI Data Service & Information, Xantener Strasse 51a, Rheinberg, D-47495, GER, dsi@dsidata.com, https://www.dsidata.com/; Global Environmental Database.

The Economist Group: Economist Intelligence Unit (EIU), 900 3rd Ave., 16th Fl., New York, NY, 10022, USA, (212) 541-0500, americas@eiu.com, https://www.eiu.com; Cuba Country Report.

United Nations Economic Commission for Latin America and the Caribbean (ECLAC), Casilla 179-D, Santiago, 7630412, CHL, (202) 596-3713, prensa@cepal.org, https://www.cepal.org/en; CEPALSTAT.

United Nations Statistics Division (UNSD), United Nations Plz., New York, NY, 10017, USA, (800) 253-9646, (212) 963-9851, statistics@un.org, https://unstats.un.org; World Statistics Pocketbook 2021.

CUBA-EXPORTS

Central Intelligence Agency (CIA), Office of Public Affairs, Washington, DC, 20505, USA, (703) 482-0623, https://www.cia.gov; The World Factbook.

The Economist Group: Economist Intelligence Unit (EIU), 900 3rd Ave., 16th Fl., New York, NY, 10022, USA, (212) 541-0500, americas@eiu.com, https://www.eiu.com; Cuba Country Report.

International Monetary Fund (IMF), 700 19th St. NW, Washington, DC, 20431, USA, (202) 623-7000, (202) 623-4661, publications@imf.org, https://www.imf.org; Direction of Trade Statistics (DOTS).

S&P Global, IHS Markit, 15 Inverness Way E, Englewood, CO, 80112, USA, (800) 447-2273, (800) 854-7179, https://ihsmarkit.com; Global Trade Atlas (GTA).

CUBA-FEMALE WORKING POPULATION

See CUBA-EMPLOYMENT

CUBA-FERTILITY, HUMAN

Central Intelligence Agency (CIA), Office of Public Affairs, Washington, DC, 20505, USA, (703) 482-0623, https://www.cia.gov; The World Factbook.

CUBA-FERTILIZER INDUSTRY

United Nations Food and Agricultural Organization (FAO), 2121 K St., Ste. 800B, Washington, DC, 20037, USA, (202) 653-2400 (Dial from U.S.), (202) 653-5760 (Fax from U.S.), fao-hq@fao.org, https://www.fao.org; The State of Food and Agriculture (SOFA) 2022.

CUBA-FETAL MORTALITY

See CUBA-MORTALITY

CUBA-FINANCE

Stockholm International Peace Research Institute (SIPRI), Signalistgatan 9, Stockholm, SE 169 72,

SWE, https://www.sipri.org/; SIPRI Arms Transfers Database and SIPRI Military Expenditure Database.

United Nations Statistics Division (UNSD), United Nations Plz., New York, NY, 10017, USA, (800) 253-9646, (212) 963-9851, statistics@un.org, https://unstats.un.org; Statistical Yearbook of the United Nations 2021.

CUBA-FINANCE, PUBLIC

Bernan Press, 15250 NBN Way, Bldg. C, Blue Ridge Summit, PA, 17214, USA, (301) 459-2255, (800) 865-3457, (800) 865-3450, customercare@bernan.com, https://rowman.com/Page/Bernan; National Accounts Statistics: Analysis of Main Aggregates 2020.

The Economist Group: Economist Intelligence Unit (EIU), 900 3rd Ave., 16th Fl., New York, NY, 10022, USA, (212) 541-0500, americas@eiu.com, https://www.eiu.com; Cuba Country Report.

International Monetary Fund (IMF), 700 19th St. NW, Washington, DC, 20431, USA, (202) 623-7000, (202) 623-4661, publications@imf.org, https://www.imf.org; Regional Economic Outlook.

Palgrave Macmillan, 1 New York Plaza, Ste. 4500, New York, NY, 10004-1562, USA, (800) 777-4643, orders@palgrave.com, https://www.palgrave.com/us; The Statesman's Yearbook, 2023.

Routledge - Taylor & Francis Group, 6000 Broken Sound Pkwy. NW, Ste. 300, Boca Raton, FL, 33487, USA, (800) 634-1420, (800) 634-7064, orders@taylorandfrancis.com, https://www.routledge.com/; The Europa World Year Book 2022.

United Nations Statistics Division (UNSD), United Nations Plz., New York, NY, 10017, USA, (800) 253-9646, (212) 963-9851, statistics@un.org, https://unstats.un.org; National Accounts Main Aggregates Database and National Accounts Statistics: Main Aggregates and Detailed Tables.

CUBA-FISHERIES

Palgrave Macmillan, 1 New York Plaza, Ste. 4500, New York, NY, 10004-1562, USA, (800) 777-4643, orders@palgrave.com, https://www.palgrave.com/us; The Statesman's Yearbook, 2023.

Routledge - Taylor & Francis Group, 6000 Broken Sound Pkwy. NW, Ste. 300, Boca Raton, FL, 33487, USA, (800) 634-1420, (800) 634-7064, orders@taylorandfrancis.com, https://www.routledge.com/; The Europa World Year Book 2022.

United Nations Food and Agricultural Organization (FAO), 2121 K St., Ste. 800B, Washington, DC, 20037, USA, (202) 653-2400 (Dial from U.S.), (202) 653-5760 (Fax from U.S.), fao-hq@fao.org, https://www.fao.org; FAO Yearbook of Fishery and Aquaculture Statistics 2019; Fishery Statistical Collections Global Capture Production; FishStatJ; and The State of Food and Agriculture (SOFA) 2022.

United Nations Statistics Division (UNSD), United Nations Plz., New York, NY, 10017, USA, (800) 253-9646, (212) 963-9851, statistics@un.org, https://unstats.un.org; Statistical Yearbook of the United Nations 2021.

CUBA-FOOD

United Nations Food and Agricultural Organization (FAO), 2121 K St., Ste. 800B, Washington, DC, 20037, USA, (202) 653-2400 (Dial from U.S.), (202) 653-5760 (Fax from U.S.), fao-hq@fao.org, https://www.fao.org; The State of Food and Agriculture (SOFA) 2022.

CUBA-FORESTS AND FORESTRY

Palgrave Macmillan, 1 New York Plaza, Ste. 4500, New York, NY, 10004-1562, USA, (800) 777-4643, orders@palgrave.com, https://www.palgrave.com/us; The Statesman's Yearbook, 2023.

Routledge - Taylor & Francis Group, 6000 Broken Sound Pkwy. NW, Ste. 300, Boca Raton, FL, 33487, USA, (800) 634-1420, (800) 634-7064, orders@taylorandfrancis.com, https://www.routledge.com/; The Europa World Year Book 2022.

UNESCO Institute for Statistics, C.P 250 Succursale H, Montreal, QC, H3G 2K8, CAN, (514) 343-6880 (Dial from U.S.), (514) 343-5740 (Fax from U.S.), uis.publications@unesco.org, http://uis.unesco.org/; UIS.Stat.

United Nations Food and Agricultural Organization (FAO), 2121 K St., Ste. 800B, Washington, DC, 20037, USA, (202) 653-2400 (Dial from U.S.), (202) 653-5760 (Fax from U.S.), fao-hq@fao.org, https://www.fao.org; FAO Yearbook of Forest Products 2019 and The State of Food and Agriculture (SOFA) 2022.

United Nations Statistics Division (UNSD), United Nations Plz., New York, NY, 10017, USA, (800) 253-9646, (212) 963-9851, statistics@un.org, https://unstats.un.org; Statistical Yearbook of the United Nations 2021.

CUBA-GAS PRODUCTION

See CUBA-MINERAL INDUSTRIES

CUBA-GOLD PRODUCTION

See CUBA-MINERAL INDUSTRIES

CUBA-GROSS DOMESTIC PRODUCT

The Economist Group: Economist Intelligence Unit (EIU), 900 3rd Ave., 16th Fl., New York, NY, 10022, USA, (212) 541-0500, americas@eiu.com, https://www.eiu.com; Cuba Country Report.

United Nations Statistics Division (UNSD), United Nations Plz., New York, NY, 10017, USA, (800) 253-9646, (212) 963-9851, statistics@un.org, https://unstats.un.org; Statistical Yearbook of the United Nations 2021.

CUBA-GROSS NATIONAL PRODUCT

United Nations Statistics Division (UNSD), United Nations Plz., New York, NY, 10017, USA, (800) 253-9646, (212) 963-9851, statistics@un.org, https://unstats.un.org; Statistical Yearbook of the United Nations 2021.

CUBA-HOUSING

Euromonitor International, Inc., 1 N Dearborn St., Ste. 1700, Chicago, IL, 60602, USA, (312) 922-1115, (312) 922-1157, info-usa@euromonitor.com, https://www.euromonitor.com/; Geographies.

CUBA-ILLITERATE PERSONS

UNESCO Institute for Statistics, C.P 250 Succursale H, Montreal, QC, H3G 2K8, CAN, (514) 343-6880 (Dial from U.S.), (514) 343-5740 (Fax from U.S.), uis.publications@unesco.org, http://uis.unesco.org/; UIS.Stat.

CUBA-IMPORTS

Central Intelligence Agency (CIA), Office of Public Affairs, Washington, DC, 20505, USA, (703) 482-0623, https://www.cia.gov; The World Factbook.

The Economist Group: Economist Intelligence Unit (EIU), 900 3rd Ave., 16th Fl., New York, NY, 10022, USA, (212) 541-0500, americas@eiu.com, https://www.eiu.com; Cuba Country Report.

International Monetary Fund (IMF), 700 19th St. NW, Washington, DC, 20431, USA, (202) 623-7000, (202) 623-4661, publications@imf.org, https://www.imf.org; Direction of Trade Statistics (DOTS).

S&P Global, IHS Markit, 15 Inverness Way E, Englewood, CO, 80112, USA, (800) 447-2273, (800) 854-7179, https://ihsmarkit.com; Global Trade Atlas (GTA).

CUBA-INDUSTRIAL METALS PRODUCTION

See CUBA-MINERAL INDUSTRIES

CUBA-INDUSTRIAL PROPERTY

World Intellectual Property Organization (WIPO), 34, chemin des Colombettes, Geneva, CH-1211, SWI, https://www.wipo.int; Madrid Yearly Review 2022: International Registrations of Marks.

CUBA-INDUSTRIES

Central Intelligence Agency (CIA), Office of Public Affairs, Washington, DC, 20505, USA, (703) 482-0623, https://www.cia.gov; The World Factbook.

The Economist Group: Economist Intelligence Unit (EIU), 900 3rd Ave., 16th Fl., New York, NY, 10022, USA, (212) 541-0500, americas@eiu.com, https://www.eiu.com; Cuba Country Report.

Euromonitor International, Inc., 1 N Dearborn St., Ste. 1700, Chicago, IL, 60602, USA, (312) 922-1115, (312) 922-1157, info-usa@euromonitor.com, https://www.euromonitor.com/; Geographies.

International Labour Organization (ILO), 4 Rte. des Morillons, Geneva, CH-1211, SWI, ilo@ilo.org, https://www.ilo.org; NORMLEX Information System on International Labour Standards.

Palgrave Macmillan, 1 New York Plaza, Ste. 4500, New York, NY, 10004-1562, USA, (800) 777-4643, orders@palgrave.com, https://www.palgrave.com/us; The Statesman's Yearbook, 2023.

Routledge - Taylor & Francis Group, 6000 Broken Sound Pkwy. NW, Ste. 300, Boca Raton, FL, 33487, USA, (800) 634-1420, (800) 634-7064, orders@taylorandfrancis.com, https://www.routledge.com/; The Europa World Year Book 2022.

United Nations Economic Commission for Latin America and the Caribbean (ECLAC), Casilla 179-D, Santiago, 7630412, CHL, (202) 596-3713, prensa@cepal.org, https://www.cepal.org/en; Economic Survey of Latin America and the Caribbean 2021: Labour Dynamics and Employment Policies for Sustainable and Inclusive Recovery Beyond the COVID-19 Crisis.

United Nations Industrial Development Organization (UNIDO), 1 United Nations Plz., Rm. DC1-1118, New York, NY, 10017, USA, (212) 963-6890, (212) 963 6885, (212) 963-7904, office.newyork@unido.org, https://www.unido.org/; Industrial Statistics Databases and International Yearbook of Industrial Statistics 2021.

CUBA-INFANT AND MATERNAL MORTALITY

See CUBA-MORTALITY

CUBA-INFLATION (FINANCE)

United Nations Economic Commission for Latin America and the Caribbean (ECLAC), Casilla 179-D, Santiago, 7630412, CHL, (202) 596-3713, prensa@cepal.org, https://www.cepal.org/en; Economic Survey of Latin America and the Caribbean 2021: Labour Dynamics and Employment Policies for Sustainable and Inclusive Recovery Beyond the COVID-19 Crisis.

CUBA-INTERNATIONAL TRADE

The Economist Group: Economist Intelligence Unit (EIU), 900 3rd Ave., 16th Fl., New York, NY, 10022, USA, (212) 541-0500, americas@eiu.com, https://www.eiu.com; Cuba Country Report.

Euromonitor International, Inc., 1 N Dearborn St., Ste. 1700, Chicago, IL, 60602, USA, (312) 922-1115, (312) 922-1157, info-usa@euromonitor.com, https://www.euromonitor.com/; Geographies.

Palgrave Macmillan, 1 New York Plaza, Ste. 4500, New York, NY, 10004-1562, USA, (800) 777-4643, orders@palgrave.com, https://www.palgrave.com/us; The Statesman's Yearbook, 2023.

Routledge - Taylor & Francis Group, 6000 Broken Sound Pkwy. NW, Ste. 300, Boca Raton, FL, 33487, USA, (800) 634-1420, (800) 634-7064, orders@taylorandfrancis.com, https://www.routledge.com/; The Europa World Year Book 2022.

United Nations Conference on Trade and Development (UNCTAD), Palais des Nations, Geneva, 1211, SWI, (212) 963-6896, unctadinfo@unctad.org, https://unctad.org; Trade and Development Report 2021.

United Nations Economic Commission for Latin America and the Caribbean (ECLAC), Casilla 179-D, Santiago, 7630412, CHL, (202) 596-3713, prensa@cepal.org, https://www.cepal.org/en; Economic Survey of Latin America and the Caribbean 2021: Labour Dynamics and Employment Policies for Sustainable and Inclusive Recovery Beyond the COVID-19 Crisis.

United Nations Food and Agricultural Organization (FAO), 2121 K St., Ste. 800B, Washington, DC, 20037, USA, (202) 653-2400 (Dial from U.S.), (202) 653-5760 (Fax from U.S.), fao-hq@fao.org, https://www.fao.org; The State of Food and Agriculture (SOFA) 2022.

United Nations Statistics Division (UNSD), United Nations Plz., New York, NY, 10017, USA, (800) 253-9646, (212) 963-9851, statistics@un.org, https://unstats.un.org; International Trade Statistics Yearbook 2020 and Statistical Yearbook of the United Nations 2021.

World Trade Organization (WTO), Ctre. William Rappard, Rue de Lausanne 154, Case postale, Geneva, CH-1211, SWI, enquiries@wto.org, https://www.wto.org; World Trade Statistical Review 2022.

CUBA-INTERNET USERS

International Telecommunication Union (ITU), Place des Nations, Geneva, CH-1211, SWI, itumail@itu.int, https://www.itu.int; Global Connectivity Report 2022; World Telecommunication/ICT Indicators Database 2021; and Yearbook of Statistics 2019.

CUBA-LABOR

Central Intelligence Agency (CIA), Office of Public Affairs, Washington, DC, 20505, USA, (703) 482-0623, https://www.cia.gov; The World Factbook.

Euromonitor International, Inc., 1 N Dearborn St., Ste. 1700, Chicago, IL, 60602, USA, (312) 922-1115, (312) 922-1157, info-usa@euromonitor.com, https://www.euromonitor.com/; Geographies.

International Labour Organization (ILO), 4 Rte. des Morillons, Geneva, CH-1211, SWI, ilo@ilo.org, https://www.ilo.org; NORMLEX Information System on International Labour Standards.

Palgrave Macmillan, 1 New York Plaza, Ste. 4500, New York, NY, 10004-1562, USA, (800) 777-4643, orders@palgrave.com, https://www.palgrave.com/us; The Statesman's Yearbook, 2023.

United Nations Food and Agricultural Organization (FAO), 2121 K St., Ste. 800B, Washington, DC, 20037, USA, (202) 653-2400 (Dial from U.S.), (202) 653-5760 (Fax from U.S.), fao-hq@fao.org, https://www.fao.org; The State of Food and Agriculture (SOFA) 2022.

CUBA-LAND USE

United Nations Statistics Division (UNSD), United Nations Plz., New York, NY, 10017, USA, (800) 253-9646, (212) 963-9851, statistics@un.org, https://unstats.un.org; Millennium Development Goal Indicators.

CUBA-LIFE EXPECTANCY

Central Intelligence Agency (CIA), Office of Public Affairs, Washington, DC, 20505, USA, (703) 482-0623, https://www.cia.gov; The World Factbook.

United Nations Department of Economic and Social Affairs (DESA), Population Division, 2 United Nations Plz., Rm. DC2-1950, New York, NY, 10017, USA, (212) 963-3209, (212) 963-2147, population@un.org, https://www.un.org/development/desa/pd/; World Population Ageing 2020 Highlights.

United Nations Statistics Division (UNSD), United Nations Plz., New York, NY, 10017, USA, (800) 253-9646, (212) 963-9851, statistics@un.org, https://unstats.un.org; Millennium Development Goal Indicators.

CUBA-LITERACY

Euromonitor International, Inc., 1 N Dearborn St., Ste. 1700, Chicago, IL, 60602, USA, (312) 922-1115, (312) 922-1157, info-usa@euromonitor.com, https://www.euromonitor.com/; Geographies.

UNESCO Institute for Statistics, C.P 250 Succursale H, Montreal, QC, H3G 2K8, CAN, (514) 343-6880 (Dial from U.S.), (514) 343-5740 (Fax from U.S.), uis.publications@unesco.org, http://uis.unesco.org/; Literacy.

CUBA-LIVESTOCK

Palgrave Macmillan, 1 New York Plaza, Ste. 4500, New York, NY, 10004-1562, USA, (800) 777-4643, orders@palgrave.com, https://www.palgrave.com/us; The Statesman's Yearbook, 2023.

Routledge - Taylor & Francis Group, 6000 Broken Sound Pkwy. NW, Ste. 300, Boca Raton, FL, 33487, USA, (800) 634-1420, (800) 634-7064, orders@taylorandfrancis.com, https://www.routledge.com/; The Europa World Year Book 2022.

United Nations Food and Agricultural Organization (FAO), 2121 K St., Ste. 800B, Washington, DC, 20037, USA, (202) 653-2400 (Dial from U.S.), (202) 653-5760 (Fax from U.S.), fao-hq@fao.org, https://www.fao.org; The State of Food and Agriculture (SOFA) 2022.

United Nations Statistics Division (UNSD), United Nations Plz., New York, NY, 10017, USA, (800) 253-9646, (212) 963-9851, statistics@un.org, https://unstats.un.org; Statistical Yearbook of the United Nations 2021.

CUBA-MARRIAGE

Routledge - Taylor & Francis Group, 6000 Broken Sound Pkwy. NW, Ste. 300, Boca Raton, FL, 33487, USA, (800) 634-1420, (800) 634-7064, orders@taylorandfrancis.com, https://www.routledge.com/; The Europa World Year Book 2022.

United Nations Statistics Division (UNSD), United Nations Plz., New York, NY, 10017, USA, (800) 253-9646, (212) 963-9851, statistics@un.org, https://unstats.un.org; Statistical Yearbook of the United Nations 2021.

CUBA-MINERAL INDUSTRIES

Barchart, 209 W Jackson Blvd., 2nd Fl., Chicago, IL, 60606, USA, (877) 247-4394, commodities@barchart.com, https://www.barchart.com/cmdty; The cmdty Yearbook 2023; cmdtyStats: Commodity Statistics and Fundamental Data; cmdtyView: Commodity Index; and Commodity Data and Prices.

International Energy Agency (IEA), 9 Rue de la Federation, Paris, 75739, FRA, info@iea.org, https://www.iea.org/; World Energy Outlook 2021.

Palgrave Macmillan, 1 New York Plaza, Ste. 4500, New York, NY, 10004-1562, USA, (800) 777-4643, orders@palgrave.com, https://www.palgrave.com/us; The Statesman's Yearbook, 2023.

Routledge - Taylor & Francis Group, 6000 Broken Sound Pkwy. NW, Ste. 300, Boca Raton, FL, 33487, USA, (800) 634-1420, (800) 634-7064, orders@taylorandfrancis.com, https://www.routledge.com/; The Europa World Year Book 2022.

United Nations Conference on Trade and Development (UNCTAD), Palais des Nations, Geneva, 1211, SWI, (212) 963-6896, unctadinfo@unctad.org, https://unctad.org; Trade and Development Report 2021.

United Nations Statistics Division (UNSD), United Nations Plz., New York, NY, 10017, USA, (800) 253-9646, (212) 963-9851, statistics@un.org, https://unstats.un.org; Statistical Yearbook of the United Nations 2021.

CUBA-MOLASSES PRODUCTION

See CUBA-CROPS

CUBA-MONEY SUPPLY

The Economist Group: Economist Intelligence Unit (EIU), 900 3rd Ave., 16th Fl., New York, NY, 10022, USA, (212) 541-0500, americas@eiu.com, https://www.eiu.com; Cuba Country Report.

CUBA-MORTALITY

UNICEF, 3 United Nations Plz., New York, NY, 10017, USA, (212) 303-7984, (917) 244-2215, https://www.unicef.org; The State of the World's Children 2023.

United Nations Statistics Division (UNSD), United Nations Plz., New York, NY, 10017, USA, (800) 253-9646, (212) 963-9851, statistics@un.org, https://unstats.un.org; Millennium Development Goal Indicators; Statistical Yearbook of the United Nations 2021; and World Statistics Pocketbook 2021.

World Health Organization (WHO), Ave. Appia 20, Geneva, CH-1211, SWI, (202) 974-3000 (Telephone in U.S.), publications@who.int, https://www.who.int/; Global Health Observatory (GHO).

CUBA-MOTION PICTURES

Palgrave Macmillan, 1 New York Plaza, Ste. 4500, New York, NY, 10004-1562, USA, (800) 777-4643, orders@palgrave.com, https://www.palgrave.com/us; The Statesman's Yearbook, 2023.

CUBA-NATURAL GAS PRODUCTION

See CUBA-MINERAL INDUSTRIES

CUBA-NICKEL AND NICKEL ORE

See CUBA-MINERAL INDUSTRIES

CUBA-NUTRITION

United Nations Food and Agricultural Organization (FAO), 2121 K St., Ste. 800B, Washington, DC, 20037, USA, (202) 653-2400 (Dial from U.S.), (202) 653-5760 (Fax from U.S.), fao-hq@fao.org, https://www.fao.org; The State of Food and Agriculture (SOFA) 2022.

United Nations Statistics Division (UNSD), United Nations Plz., New York, NY, 10017, USA, (800) 253-9646, (212) 963-9851, statistics@un.org, https://unstats.un.org; Millennium Development Goal Indicators.

CUBA-PAPER

See CUBA-FORESTS AND FORESTRY

CUBA-PEANUT PRODUCTION

See CUBA-CROPS

CUBA-PESTICIDES

United Nations Food and Agricultural Organization (FAO), 2121 K St., Ste. 800B, Washington, DC, 20037, USA, (202) 653-2400 (Dial from U.S.), (202) 653-5760 (Fax from U.S.), fao-hq@fao.org, https://www.fao.org; The State of Food and Agriculture (SOFA) 2022.

CUBA-PETROLEUM INDUSTRY AND TRADE

International Energy Agency (IEA), 9 Rue de la Federation, Paris, 75739, FRA, info@iea.org, https://www.iea.org/; World Energy Outlook 2021.

Palgrave Macmillan, 1 New York Plaza, Ste. 4500, New York, NY, 10004-1562, USA, (800) 777-4643, orders@palgrave.com, https://www.palgrave.com/us; The Statesman's Yearbook, 2023.

U.S. Energy Information Administration (EIA), 1000 Independence Ave. SW, Washington, DC, 20585, USA, (202) 586-8800, infoctr@eia.gov, https://www.eia.gov; International Energy Outlook 2021.

United Nations Food and Agricultural Organization (FAO), 2121 K St., Ste. 800B, Washington, DC, 20037, USA, (202) 653-2400 (Dial from U.S.), (202) 653-5760 (Fax from U.S.), fao-hq@fao.org, https://www.fao.org; The State of Food and Agriculture (SOFA) 2022.

United Nations Statistics Division (UNSD), United Nations Plz., New York, NY, 10017, USA, (800) 253-9646, (212) 963-9851, statistics@un.org, https://unstats.un.org; Statistical Yearbook of the United Nations 2021.

CUBA-POPULATION

Central Intelligence Agency (CIA), Office of Public Affairs, Washington, DC, 20505, USA, (703) 482-0623, https://www.cia.gov; The World Factbook.

The Economist Group: Economist Intelligence Unit (EIU), 900 3rd Ave., 16th Fl., New York, NY, 10022, USA, (212) 541-0500, americas@eiu.com, https://www.eiu.com; Cuba Country Report.

European Commission, Eurostat, Luxembourg, 2920, LUX, https://ec.europa.eu/eurostat/; EU in the World 2020.

Infoplease, c/o Sandbox Networks, Inc., 1 Lincoln St., 24th Fl., Boston, MA, 02111, USA, https://www.infoplease.com; Countries of the World.

International Labour Organization (ILO), 4 Rte. des Morillons, Geneva, CH-1211, SWI, ilo@ilo.org, https://www.ilo.org; NORMLEX Information System on International Labour Standards.

Palgrave Macmillan, 1 New York Plaza, Ste. 4500, New York, NY, 10004-1562, USA, (800) 777-4643, orders@palgrave.com, https://www.palgrave.com/us; The Statesman's Yearbook, 2023.

Routledge - Taylor & Francis Group, 6000 Broken Sound Pkwy. NW, Ste. 300, Boca Raton, FL, 33487, USA, (800) 634-1420, (800) 634-7064, orders@taylorandfrancis.com, https://www.routledge.com/; The Europa World Year Book 2022.

UK Data Service, University of Essex, Wivenhoe Park, Colchester, Essex, CO4 3SQ, GBR, https://ukdataservice.ac.uk/; International Aggregate Data.

UNESCO Institute for Statistics, C.P 250 Succursale H, Montreal, QC, H3G 2K8, CAN, (514) 343-6880 (Dial from U.S.), (514) 343-5740 (Fax from U.S.), uis.publications@unesco.org, http://uis.unesco.org/; UIS.Stat.

United Nations Department of Economic and Social Affairs (DESA), Population Division, 2 United Nations Plz., Rm. DC2-1950, New York, NY, 10017, USA, (212) 963-3209, (212) 963-2147, population@un.org, https://www.un.org/development/desa/pd/; Revision of World Urbanization Prospects and World Population Ageing 2020 Highlights.

United Nations Development Programme (UNDP), One United Nations Plz., New York, NY, 10017, USA, (212) 906-5000, (212) 906-5001, https://www.undp.org; Human Development Report 2021-2022.

United Nations Economic Commission for Latin America and the Caribbean (ECLAC), Casilla 179-D, Santiago, 7630412, CHL, (202) 596-3713, prensa@cepal.org, https://www.cepal.org/en; CEPALSTAT and Social Panorama of Latin America and the Caribbean 2022: Transforming Education as a Basis for Sustainable Development.

United Nations Statistics Division (UNSD), United Nations Plz., New York, NY, 10017, USA, (800) 253-9646, (212) 963-9851, statistics@un.org, https://unstats.un.org; Statistical Yearbook of the United Nations 2021 and World Statistics Pocketbook 2021.

The World Bank, 1818 H St. NW, Washington, DC, 20433, USA, (202) 473-1000, (202) 477-6391, eds03@worldbank.org, https://www.worldbank.org/; The Global Findex Database 2021.

CUBA-POPULATION DENSITY

Central Intelligence Agency (CIA), Office of Public Affairs, Washington, DC, 20505, USA, (703) 482-0623, https://www.cia.gov; The World Factbook.

Palgrave Macmillan, 1 New York Plaza, Ste. 4500, New York, NY, 10004-1562, USA, (800) 777-4643, orders@palgrave.com, https://www.palgrave.com/us; The Statesman's Yearbook, 2023.

Routledge - Taylor & Francis Group, 6000 Broken Sound Pkwy. NW, Ste. 300, Boca Raton, FL, 33487, USA, (800) 634-1420, (800) 634-7064, orders@taylorandfrancis.com, https://www.routledge.com/; The Europa World Year Book 2022.

UNESCO Institute for Statistics, C.P 250 Succursale H, Montreal, QC, H3G 2K8, CAN, (514) 343-6880 (Dial from U.S.), (514) 343-5740 (Fax from U.S.), uis.publications@unesco.org, http://uis.unesco.org/; UIS.Stat.

CUBA-POWER RESOURCES

Euromonitor International, Inc., 1 N Dearborn St., Ste. 1700, Chicago, IL, 60602, USA, (312) 922-1115, (312) 922-1157, info-usa@euromonitor.com, https://www.euromonitor.com/; Geographies.

International Energy Agency (IEA), 9 Rue de la Federation, Paris, 75739, FRA, info@iea.org, https://www.iea.org/; World Energy Outlook 2021.

Palgrave Macmillan, 1 New York Plaza, Ste. 4500, New York, NY, 10004-1562, USA, (800) 777-4643, orders@palgrave.com, https://www.palgrave.com/us; The Statesman's Yearbook, 2023.

U.S. Energy Information Administration (EIA), 1000 Independence Ave. SW, Washington, DC, 20585, USA, (202) 586-8800, infoctr@eia.gov, https://www.eia.gov; International Energy Outlook 2021.

United Nations Food and Agricultural Organization (FAO), 2121 K St., Ste. 800B, Washington, DC, 20037, USA, (202) 653-2400 (Dial from U.S.), (202) 653-5760 (Fax from U.S.), fao-hq@fao.org, https://www.fao.org; The State of Food and Agriculture (SOFA) 2022.

United Nations Statistics Division (UNSD), United Nations Plz., New York, NY, 10017, USA, (800) 253-9646, (212) 963-9851, statistics@un.org, https://unstats.un.org; Energy Statistics Yearbook 2019; Statistical Yearbook of the United Nations 2021; and World Statistics Pocketbook 2021.

CUBA-PRICES

Euromonitor International, Inc., 1 N Dearborn St., Ste. 1700, Chicago, IL, 60602, USA, (312) 922-1115, (312) 922-1157, info-usa@euromonitor.com, https://www.euromonitor.com/; Geographies.

United Nations Economic Commission for Latin America and the Caribbean (ECLAC), Casilla 179-D, Santiago, 7630412, CHL, (202) 596-3713, prensa@cepal.org, https://www.cepal.org/en; Economic Survey of Latin America and the Caribbean 2021: Labour Dynamics and Employment Policies for Sustainable and Inclusive Recovery Beyond the COVID-19 Crisis.

CUBA-PUBLIC HEALTH

Euromonitor International, Inc., 1 N Dearborn St., Ste. 1700, Chicago, IL, 60602, USA, (312) 922-1115, (312) 922-1157, info-usa@euromonitor.com, https://www.euromonitor.com/; Geographies.

Palgrave Macmillan, 1 New York Plaza, Ste. 4500, New York, NY, 10004-1562, USA, (800) 777-4643, orders@palgrave.com, https://www.palgrave.com/us; The Statesman's Yearbook, 2023.

U.S. Census Bureau, 4600 Silver Hill Rd., Washington, DC, 20233, USA, (301) 763-4636, (800) 923-8282, https://www.census.gov; HIV/AIDS Surveillance Data Base.

UNICEF, 3 United Nations Plz., New York, NY, 10017, USA, (212) 303-7984, (917) 244-2215, https://www.unicef.org; The State of the World's Children 2023.

United Nations Department of Economic and Social Affairs (DESA), Population Division, 2 United Nations Plz., Rm. DC2-1950, New York, NY, 10017, USA, (212) 963-3209, (212) 963-2147, population@un.org, https://www.un.org/development/desa/pd/; World Fertility Data 2019.

United Nations Development Programme (UNDP), One United Nations Plz., New York, NY, 10017, USA, (212) 906-5000, (212) 906-5001, https://www.undp.org; Human Development Report 2021-2022.

United Nations Statistics Division (UNSD), United Nations Plz., New York, NY, 10017, USA, (800) 253-9646, (212) 963-9851, statistics@un.org, https://unstats.un.org; Millennium Development Goal Indicators and Statistical Yearbook of the United Nations 2021.

World Health Organization (WHO), Ave. Appia 20, Geneva, CH-1211, SWI, (202) 974-3000 (Telephone in U.S.), publications@who.int, https://www.who.int/; Global Health Observatory (GHO) and Health Statistics and Information Systems.

CUBA-PUBLISHERS AND PUBLISHING

UNESCO Institute for Statistics, C.P 250 Succursale H, Montreal, QC, H3G 2K8, CAN, (514) 343-6880 (Dial from U.S.), (514) 343-5740 (Fax from U.S.), uis.publications@unesco.org, http://uis.unesco.org/; UIS.Stat.

CUBA-RAILROADS

Janes, USA, (703) 574-7580, (888) 977-1519, customer.care@janes.com, https://www.janes.com; Janes World Railways 2021-2022.

Palgrave Macmillan, 1 New York Plaza, Ste. 4500, New York, NY, 10004-1562, USA, (800) 777-4643, orders@palgrave.com, https://www.palgrave.com/us; The Statesman's Yearbook, 2023.

Routledge - Taylor & Francis Group, 6000 Broken Sound Pkwy. NW, Ste. 300, Boca Raton, FL, 33487, USA, (800) 634-1420, (800) 634-7064, orders@taylorandfrancis.com, https://www.routledge.com/; The Europa World Year Book 2022.

United Nations Statistics Division (UNSD), United Nations Plz., New York, NY, 10017, USA, (800) 253-9646, (212) 963-9851, statistics@un.org, https://unstats.un.org; Statistical Yearbook of the United Nations 2021.

CUBA-RELIGION

Central Intelligence Agency (CIA), Office of Public Affairs, Washington, DC, 20505, USA, (703) 482-0623, https://www.cia.gov; The World Factbook.

Palgrave Macmillan, 1 New York Plaza, Ste. 4500, New York, NY, 10004-1562, USA, (800) 777-4643, orders@palgrave.com, https://www.palgrave.com/us; The Statesman's Yearbook, 2023.

CUBA-RETAIL TRADE

Euromonitor International, Inc., 1 N Dearborn St., Ste. 1700, Chicago, IL, 60602, USA, (312) 922-1115, (312) 922-1157, info-usa@euromonitor.com, https://www.euromonitor.com/; Geographies.

United Nations Statistics Division (UNSD), United Nations Plz., New York, NY, 10017, USA, (800) 253-9646, (212) 963-9851, statistics@un.org, https://unstats.un.org; Statistical Yearbook of the United Nations 2021.

CUBA-RICE PRODUCTION

See CUBA-CROPS

CUBA-RUBBER INDUSTRY AND TRADE

International Rubber Study Group (IRSG), 51 Changi Business Park Central 2, Unit No. 6, 486066, SGP, https://www.rubberstudy.org; Monthly Rubber Bulletin (MRB); Rubber Industry Report; Rubber Statistical Bulletin; and World Rubber Industry Report (WRIO).

CUBA-SHIPPING

Routledge - Taylor & Francis Group, 6000 Broken Sound Pkwy. NW, Ste. 300, Boca Raton, FL, 33487, USA, (800) 634-1420, (800) 634-7064, orders@taylorandfrancis.com, https://www.routledge.com/; The Europa World Year Book 2022.

United Nations Statistics Division (UNSD), United Nations Plz., New York, NY, 10017, USA, (800) 253-9646, (212) 963-9851, statistics@un.org, https://unstats.un.org; Statistical Yearbook of the United Nations 2021.

CUBA-STEEL PRODUCTION

See CUBA-MINERAL INDUSTRIES

CUBA-SUGAR PRODUCTION

See CUBA-CROPS

CUBA-TELEPHONE

Palgrave Macmillan, 1 New York Plaza, Ste. 4500, New York, NY, 10004-1562, USA, (800) 777-4643,

orders@palgrave.com, https://www.palgrave.com/us; The Statesman's Yearbook, 2023.

Routledge - Taylor & Francis Group, 6000 Broken Sound Pkwy. NW, Ste. 300, Boca Raton, FL, 33487, USA, (800) 634-1420, (800) 634-7064, orders@taylorandfrancis.com, https://www.routledge.com/; The Europa World Year Book 2022.

United Nations Statistics Division (UNSD), United Nations Plz., New York, NY, 10017, USA, (800) 253-9646, (212) 963-9851, statistics@un.org, https://unstats.un.org; World Statistics Pocketbook 2021.

CUBA-TEXTILE INDUSTRY

Palgrave Macmillan, 1 New York Plaza, Ste. 4500, New York, NY, 10004-1562, USA, (800) 777-4643, orders@palgrave.com, https://www.palgrave.com/us; The Statesman's Yearbook, 2023.

United Nations Statistics Division (UNSD), United Nations Plz., New York, NY, 10017, USA, (800) 253-9646, (212) 963-9851, statistics@un.org, https://unstats.un.org; Statistical Yearbook of the United Nations 2021.

CUBA-TOBACCO INDUSTRY

United Nations Statistics Division (UNSD), United Nations Plz., New York, NY, 10017, USA, (800) 253-9646, (212) 963-9851, statistics@un.org, https://unstats.un.org; Statistical Yearbook of the United Nations 2021.

CUBA-TOURISM

Euromonitor International, Inc., 1 N Dearborn St., Ste. 1700, Chicago, IL, 60602, USA, (312) 922-1115, (312) 922-1157, info-usa@euromonitor.com, https://www.euromonitor.com/; Geographies.

Oficina Nacional de Estadisticas e Informacion, Cuba, Vedado, Plz. de la Revolucion, Paseo No. 60 e/ 3ra y 5ta, Havana, CP 10400, CUB, difusion@onei.gob.cu, http://www.onei.gob.cu/; Turismo Nacional.

Palgrave Macmillan, 1 New York Plaza, Ste. 4500, New York, NY, 10004-1562, USA, (800) 777-4643, orders@palgrave.com, https://www.palgrave.com/us; The Statesman's Yearbook, 2023.

Routledge - Taylor & Francis Group, 6000 Broken Sound Pkwy. NW, Ste. 300, Boca Raton, FL, 33487, USA, (800) 634-1420, (800) 634-7064, orders@taylorandfrancis.com, https://www.routledge.com/; The Europa World Year Book 2022.

United Nations World Tourism Organization (UNWTO), Calle Poeta Joan Maragall 42, Madrid, 28020, SPA, info@unwto.org, https://www.unwto.org/; Yearbook of Tourism Statistics, 2021 Edition.

CUBA-TRADE

See CUBA-INTERNATIONAL TRADE

CUBA-TRANSPORTATION

Central Intelligence Agency (CIA), Office of Public Affairs, Washington, DC, 20505, USA, (703) 482-0623, https://www.cia.gov; The World Factbook.

CUBA-UNEMPLOYMENT

International Labour Organization (ILO), 4 Rte. des Morillons, Geneva, CH-1211, SWI, ilo@ilo.org, https://www.ilo.org; NORMLEX Information System on International Labour Standards.

United Nations Statistics Division (UNSD), United Nations Plz., New York, NY, 10017, USA, (800) 253-9646, (212) 963-9851, statistics@un.org, https://unstats.un.org; Statistical Yearbook of the United Nations 2021.

CUBA-VITAL STATISTICS

Oficina Nacional de Estadisticas e Informacion, Cuba, Vedado, Plz. de la Revolucion, Paseo No. 60 e/ 3ra y 5ta, Havana, CP 10400, CUB, difusion@onei.gob.cu, http://www.onei.gob.cu/; Anuario Estadistico de Cuba 2020.

U.S. Census Bureau, 4600 Silver Hill Rd., Washington, DC, 20233, USA, (301) 763-4636, (800) 923-8282, https://www.census.gov; HIV/AIDS Surveillance Data Base.

United Nations Department of Economic and Social Affairs (DESA), Population Division, 2 United Nations Plz., Rm. DC2-1950, New York, NY, 10017, USA, (212) 963-3209, (212) 963-2147, population@un.org, https://www.un.org/development/desa/pd/; World Contraceptive Use 2021: Estimates and Projections of Family Planning Indicators and World Marriage Data 2019.

CUBA-WAGES

International Labour Organization (ILO), 4 Rte. des Morillons, Geneva, CH-1211, SWI, ilo@ilo.org, https://www.ilo.org; NORMLEX Information System on International Labour Standards.

United Nations Statistics Division (UNSD), United Nations Plz., New York, NY, 10017, USA, (800) 253-9646, (212) 963-9851, statistics@un.org, https://unstats.un.org; Statistical Yearbook of the United Nations 2021.

CUBA-WHEAT PRODUCTION

See CUBA-CROPS

CUBA-WHOLESALE TRADE

United Nations Statistics Division (UNSD), United Nations Plz., New York, NY, 10017, USA, (800) 253-9646, (212) 963-9851, statistics@un.org, https://unstats.un.org; Statistical Yearbook of the United Nations 2021.

CUBA-WOOL PRODUCTION

See CUBA-TEXTILE INDUSTRY

CUBAN POPULATION-EDUCATIONAL ATTAINMENT

U.S. Census Bureau, 4600 Silver Hill Rd., Washington, DC, 20233, USA, (301) 763-4636, (800) 923-8282, https://www.census.gov; Decennial Census of Population and Housing Data.

CUCUMBERS

U.S. Department of Agriculture (USDA), Economic Research Service (ERS), 1400 Independence Ave. SW, Mail Stop 1800, Washington, DC, 20250-0002, USA, (202) 720-2791, https://www.ers.usda.gov/; Food Price Outlook.

U.S. Department of Agriculture (USDA), National Agricultural Statistics Service (USDA-NASS), 1400 Independence Ave. SW, Washington, DC, 20250, USA, (800) 727-9540, nass@nass.usda.gov, https://www.nass.usda.gov; Quick Stats and Vegetables Annual Summary.

CULTS

Cult Education Institute (CEI), 1977 N Olden Ave., Ext. 272, Trenton, NJ, 08618, USA, (609) 396-6684, info@culteducation.com, https://www.culteducation.com; unpublished data.

CULTURE

Pew Research Center, 1615 L St. NW, Ste. 800, Washington, DC, 20036, USA, (202) 419-4300, (202) 857-8562, info@pewresearch.org, https://www.pewresearch.org/; Generation Z Looks a Lot Like Millennials on Key Social and Political Issues.

SMU DataArts, 461 N 3rd St., 4th Fl., Philadelphia, PA, 19123, USA, (215) 383-0700, (215) 383-0750, info@culturaldata.org, https://culturaldata.org/; Cultural Data Profile (CDP).

University of Chicago, Center for the Study of Race, Politics and Culture, Black Youth Project, 5733 S University Ave., Chicago, IL, 60637, USA, info@blackyouthproject.com, https://www.blackyouthproject.com/; GenForward Survey 2022.

CULTURE AND GLOBALIZATION

Institute for Strategic Dialogue (ISD), PO Box 75769, London, SW1P 9ER, GBR, info@isdglobal.org, https://www.isdglobal.org/; 'Climate Lockdown' and the Culture Wars: How COVID-19 Sparked a New Narrative Against Climate Action.

Public Religion Research Institute (PRRI), 1023 15th St. NW, 9th Fl., Washington, DC, 20005, USA, (202) 238-9424, info@prri.org, https://www.prri.org/; Dueling Realities: Amid Multiple Crises, Trump and Biden Supporters See Different Priorities and Futures for the Nation and White Too Long: The Legacy of White Supremacy in American Christianity.

CULTURE CONFLICT

Mercy Corps, 45 SW Ankeny St., Portland, OR, 97204, USA, (800) 292-3355, (503) 896-5000, https://www.mercycorps.org/; Time to Turn Around: The Decline of UK Peacebuilding.

Public Religion Research Institute (PRRI), 1023 15th St. NW, 9th Fl., Washington, DC, 20005, USA, (202) 238-9424, info@prri.org, https://www.prri.org/; Dueling Realities: Amid Multiple Crises, Trump and Biden Supporters See Different Priorities and Futures for the Nation.

University of Chicago, Center for the Study of Race, Politics and Culture, Black Youth Project, 5733 S University Ave., Chicago, IL, 60637, USA, info@blackyouthproject.com, https://www.blackyouthproject.com/; GenForward Survey 2022.

CULTURE CONFLICT-RELIGIOUS ASPECTS

Public Religion Research Institute (PRRI), 1023 15th St. NW, 9th Fl., Washington, DC, 20005, USA, (202) 238-9424, info@prri.org, https://www.prri.org/; Dueling Realities: Amid Multiple Crises, Trump and Biden Supporters See Different Priorities and Futures for the Nation and White Too Long: The Legacy of White Supremacy in American Christianity.

CURACAO-AGRICULTURE

The Economist Group: Economist Intelligence Unit (EIU), 900 3rd Ave., 16th Fl., New York, NY, 10022, USA, (212) 541-0500, americas@eiu.com, https://www.eiu.com; Netherlands Antilles Country Report.

Euromonitor International, Inc., 1 N Dearborn St., Ste. 1700, Chicago, IL, 60602, USA, (312) 922-1115, (312) 922-1157, info-usa@euromonitor.com, https://www.euromonitor.com/; Geographies.

Palgrave Macmillan, 1 New York Plaza, Ste. 4500, New York, NY, 10004-1562, USA, (800) 777-4643, orders@palgrave.com, https://www.palgrave.com/us; The Statesman's Yearbook, 2023.

Routledge - Taylor & Francis Group, 6000 Broken Sound Pkwy. NW, Ste. 300, Boca Raton, FL, 33487, USA, (800) 634-1420, (800) 634-7064, orders@taylorandfrancis.com, https://www.routledge.com/; The Europa World Year Book 2022.

United Nations Food and Agricultural Organization (FAO), 2121 K St., Ste. 800B, Washington, DC, 20037, USA, (202) 653-2400 (Dial from U.S.), (202) 653-5760 (Fax from U.S.), fao-hq@fao.org, https://www.fao.org; AQUASTAT and The State of Food and Agriculture (SOFA) 2022.

United Nations Statistics Division (UNSD), United Nations Plz., New York, NY, 10017, USA, (800) 253-9646, (212) 963-9851, statistics@un.org, https://unstats.un.org; Statistical Yearbook of the United Nations 2021.

CURACAO-AIRLINES

Palgrave Macmillan, 1 New York Plaza, Ste. 4500, New York, NY, 10004-1562, USA, (800) 777-4643, orders@palgrave.com, https://www.palgrave.com/us; The Statesman's Yearbook, 2023.

CURACAO-ARMED FORCES

Central Intelligence Agency (CIA), Office of Public Affairs, Washington, DC, 20505, USA, (703) 482-0623, https://www.cia.gov; The World Factbook.

Stockholm International Peace Research Institute (SIPRI), Signalistgatan 9, Stockholm, SE 169 72, SWE, https://www.sipri.org/; SIPRI Arms Transfers Database and SIPRI Military Expenditure Database.

CURACAO-BALANCE OF PAYMENTS

International Monetary Fund (IMF), 700 19th St. NW, Washington, DC, 20431, USA, (202) 623-7000,

(202) 623-4661, publications@imf.org, https://www.imf.org; Balance of Payments Statistics: Annual Report 2021.

Routledge - Taylor & Francis Group, 6000 Broken Sound Pkwy. NW, Ste. 300, Boca Raton, FL, 33487, USA, (800) 634-1420, (800) 634-7064, orders@taylorandfrancis.com, https://www.routledge.com/; The Europa World Year Book 2022.

CURACAO-BANKS AND BANKING

Euromonitor International, Inc., 1 N Dearborn St., Ste. 1700, Chicago, IL, 60602, USA, (312) 922-1115, (312) 922-1157, info-usa@euromonitor.com, https://www.euromonitor.com/; Geographies.

International Monetary Fund (IMF), 700 19th St. NW, Washington, DC, 20431, USA, (202) 623-7000, (202) 623-4661, publications@imf.org, https://www.imf.org; International Financial Statistics (IFS).

Routledge - Taylor & Francis Group, 6000 Broken Sound Pkwy. NW, Ste. 300, Boca Raton, FL, 33487, USA, (800) 634-1420, (800) 634-7064, orders@taylorandfrancis.com, https://www.routledge.com/; The Europa World Year Book 2022.

CURACAO-BROADCASTING

Central Intelligence Agency (CIA), Office of Public Affairs, Washington, DC, 20505, USA, (703) 482-0623, https://www.cia.gov; The World Factbook.

Euromonitor International, Inc., 1 N Dearborn St., Ste. 1700, Chicago, IL, 60602, USA, (312) 922-1115, (312) 922-1157, info-usa@euromonitor.com, https://www.euromonitor.com/; Geographies.

Palgrave Macmillan, 1 New York Plaza, Ste. 4500, New York, NY, 10004-1562, USA, (800) 777-4643, orders@palgrave.com, https://www.palgrave.com/us; The Statesman's Yearbook, 2023.

Routledge - Taylor & Francis Group, 6000 Broken Sound Pkwy. NW, Ste. 300, Boca Raton, FL, 33487, USA, (800) 634-1420, (800) 634-7064, orders@taylorandfrancis.com, https://www.routledge.com/; The Europa World Year Book 2022.

WRTH Publications Limited, PO Box 290, Oxford, OX2 7FT, GBR, sales@wrth.com, https://www.wrth.com; World Radio TV Handbook 2023.

CURACAO-BUDGET

Central Intelligence Agency (CIA), Office of Public Affairs, Washington, DC, 20505, USA, (703) 482-0623, https://www.cia.gov; The World Factbook.

CURACAO-CLIMATE

Palgrave Macmillan, 1 New York Plaza, Ste. 4500, New York, NY, 10004-1562, USA, (800) 777-4643, orders@palgrave.com, https://www.palgrave.com/us; The Statesman's Yearbook, 2023.

CURACAO-COMMERCE

Palgrave Macmillan, 1 New York Plaza, Ste. 4500, New York, NY, 10004-1562, USA, (800) 777-4643, orders@palgrave.com, https://www.palgrave.com/us; The Statesman's Yearbook, 2023.

UK Data Service, University of Essex, Wivenhoe Park, Colchester, Essex, CO4 3SQ, GBR, https://ukdataservice.ac.uk/; International Aggregate Data.

CURACAO-CONSTRUCTION INDUSTRY

United Nations Statistics Division (UNSD), United Nations Plz., New York, NY, 10017, USA, (800) 253-9646, (212) 963-9851, statistics@un.org, https://unstats.un.org; Statistical Yearbook of the United Nations 2021.

CURACAO-CONSUMER PRICE INDEXES

Routledge - Taylor & Francis Group, 6000 Broken Sound Pkwy. NW, Ste. 300, Boca Raton, FL, 33487, USA, (800) 634-1420, (800) 634-7064, orders@taylorandfrancis.com, https://www.routledge.com/; The Europa World Year Book 2022.

CURACAO-CROPS

United Nations Food and Agricultural Organization (FAO), 2121 K St., Ste. 800B, Washington, DC, 20037, USA, (202) 653-2400 (Dial from U.S.), (202) 653-5760 (Fax from U.S.), fao-hq@fao.org, https://www.fao.org; The State of Food and Agriculture (SOFA) 2022.

CURACAO-DAIRY PROCESSING

United Nations Food and Agricultural Organization (FAO), 2121 K St., Ste. 800B, Washington, DC, 20037, USA, (202) 653-2400 (Dial from U.S.), (202) 653-5760 (Fax from U.S.), fao-hq@fao.org, https://www.fao.org; The State of Food and Agriculture (SOFA) 2022.

CURACAO-ECONOMIC CONDITIONS

Bernan Press, 15250 NBN Way, Bldg. C, Blue Ridge Summit, PA, 17214, USA, (301) 459-2255, (800) 865-3457, (800) 865-3450, customercare@bernan.com, https://rowman.com/Page/Bernan; World Economic Outlook, April 2022.

Central Intelligence Agency (CIA), Office of Public Affairs, Washington, DC, 20505, USA, (703) 482-0623, https://www.cia.gov; The World Factbook.

The Economist Group: Economist Intelligence Unit (EIU), 900 3rd Ave., 16th Fl., New York, NY, 10022, USA, (212) 541-0500, americas@eiu.com, https://www.eiu.com; Netherlands Antilles Country Report.

Euromonitor International, Inc., 1 N Dearborn St., Ste. 1700, Chicago, IL, 60602, USA, (312) 922-1115, (312) 922-1157, info-usa@euromonitor.com, https://www.euromonitor.com/; Geographies.

Palgrave Macmillan, 1 New York Plaza, Ste. 4500, New York, NY, 10004-1562, USA, (800) 777-4643, orders@palgrave.com, https://www.palgrave.com/us; The Statesman's Yearbook, 2023.

Routledge - Taylor & Francis Group, 6000 Broken Sound Pkwy. NW, Ste. 300, Boca Raton, FL, 33487, USA, (800) 634-1420, (800) 634-7064, orders@taylorandfrancis.com, https://www.routledge.com/; The Europa World Year Book 2022.

United Nations Economic Commission for Latin America and the Caribbean (ECLAC), Casilla 179-D, Santiago, 7630412, CHL, (202) 596-3713, prensa@cepal.org, https://www.cepal.org/en; CEPALSTAT.

United Nations Statistics Division (UNSD), United Nations Plz., New York, NY, 10017, USA, (800) 253-9646, (212) 963-9851, statistics@un.org, https://unstats.un.org; World Statistics Pocketbook 2021.

CURACAO-EDUCATION

Euromonitor International, Inc., 1 N Dearborn St., Ste. 1700, Chicago, IL, 60602, USA, (312) 922-1115, (312) 922-1157, info-usa@euromonitor.com, https://www.euromonitor.com/; Geographies.

UNESCO Institute for Statistics, C.P 250 Succursale H, Montreal, QC, H3G 2K8, CAN, (514) 343-6880 (Dial from U.S.), (514) 343-5740 (Fax from U.S.), uis.publications@unesco.org, http://uis.unesco.org/; UIS.Stat.

CURACAO-ELECTRICITY

U.S. Energy Information Administration (EIA), 1000 Independence Ave. SW, Washington, DC, 20585, USA, (202) 586-8800, infoctr@eia.gov, https://www.eia.gov; International Energy Outlook 2021.

United Nations Statistics Division (UNSD), United Nations Plz., New York, NY, 10017, USA, (800) 253-9646, (212) 963-9851, statistics@un.org, https://unstats.un.org; Statistical Yearbook of the United Nations 2021.

CURACAO-EMPLOYMENT

International Labour Organization (ILO), 4 Rte. des Morillons, Geneva, CH-1211, SWI, ilo@ilo.org, https://www.ilo.org; NORMLEX Information System on International Labour Standards.

UK Data Service, University of Essex, Wivenhoe Park, Colchester, Essex, CO4 3SQ, GBR, https://ukdataservice.ac.uk/; International Aggregate Data.

CURACAO-ENVIRONMENTAL CONDITIONS

The Economist Group: Economist Intelligence Unit (EIU), 900 3rd Ave., 16th Fl., New York, NY, 10022, USA, (212) 541-0500, americas@eiu.com, https://www.eiu.com; Netherlands Antilles Country Report.

United Nations Economic Commission for Latin America and the Caribbean (ECLAC), Casilla 179-D, Santiago, 7630412, CHL, (202) 596-3713, prensa@cepal.org, https://www.cepal.org/en; CEPALSTAT.

United Nations Statistics Division (UNSD), United Nations Plz., New York, NY, 10017, USA, (800) 253-9646, (212) 963-9851, statistics@un.org, https://unstats.un.org; World Statistics Pocketbook 2021.

CURACAO-EXPORTS

Central Intelligence Agency (CIA), Office of Public Affairs, Washington, DC, 20505, USA, (703) 482-0623, https://www.cia.gov; The World Factbook.

The Economist Group: Economist Intelligence Unit (EIU), 900 3rd Ave., 16th Fl., New York, NY, 10022, USA, (212) 541-0500, americas@eiu.com, https://www.eiu.com; Netherlands Antilles Country Report.

International Monetary Fund (IMF), 700 19th St. NW, Washington, DC, 20431, USA, (202) 623-7000, (202) 623-4661, publications@imf.org, https://www.imf.org; Direction of Trade Statistics (DOTS).

S&P Global, IHS Markit, 15 Inverness Way E, Englewood, CO, 80112, USA, (800) 447-2273, (800) 854-7179, https://ihsmarkit.com; Global Trade Atlas (GTA).

CURACAO-FERTILITY, HUMAN

Central Intelligence Agency (CIA), Office of Public Affairs, Washington, DC, 20505, USA, (703) 482-0623, https://www.cia.gov; The World Factbook.

CURACAO-FINANCE

Stockholm International Peace Research Institute (SIPRI), Signalistgatan 9, Stockholm, SE 169 72, SWE, https://www.sipri.org/; SIPRI Arms Transfers Database and SIPRI Military Expenditure Database.

United Nations Statistics Division (UNSD), United Nations Plz., New York, NY, 10017, USA, (800) 253-9646, (212) 963-9851, statistics@un.org, https://unstats.un.org; Statistical Yearbook of the United Nations 2021.

CURACAO-FINANCE, PUBLIC

The Economist Group: Economist Intelligence Unit (EIU), 900 3rd Ave., 16th Fl., New York, NY, 10022, USA, (212) 541-0500, americas@eiu.com, https://www.eiu.com; Netherlands Antilles Country Report.

Palgrave Macmillan, 1 New York Plaza, Ste. 4500, New York, NY, 10004-1562, USA, (800) 777-4643, orders@palgrave.com, https://www.palgrave.com/us; The Statesman's Yearbook, 2023.

Routledge - Taylor & Francis Group, 6000 Broken Sound Pkwy. NW, Ste. 300, Boca Raton, FL, 33487, USA, (800) 634-1420, (800) 634-7064, orders@taylorandfrancis.com, https://www.routledge.com/; The Europa World Year Book 2022.

United Nations Statistics Division (UNSD), United Nations Plz., New York, NY, 10017, USA, (800) 253-9646, (212) 963-9851, statistics@un.org, https://unstats.un.org; National Accounts Main Aggregates Database and National Accounts Statistics: Main Aggregates and Detailed Tables.

CURACAO-FISHERIES

Palgrave Macmillan, 1 New York Plaza, Ste. 4500, New York, NY, 10004-1562, USA, (800) 777-4643, orders@palgrave.com, https://www.palgrave.com/us; The Statesman's Yearbook, 2023.

Routledge - Taylor & Francis Group, 6000 Broken Sound Pkwy. NW, Ste. 300, Boca Raton, FL, 33487, USA, (800) 634-1420, (800) 634-7064, orders@taylorandfrancis.com, https://www.routledge.com/; The Europa World Year Book 2022.

United Nations Food and Agricultural Organization (FAO), 2121 K St., Ste. 800B, Washington, DC, 20037, USA, (202) 653-2400 (Dial from U.S.), (202) 653-5760 (Fax from U.S.), fao-hq@fao.org, https://

www.fao.org; FAO Yearbook of Fishery and Aquaculture Statistics 2019; Fishery Statistical Collections Global Capture Production; FishStatJ; and The State of Food and Agriculture (SOFA) 2022.

United Nations Statistics Division (UNSD), United Nations Plz., New York, NY, 10017, USA, (800) 253-9646, (212) 963-9851, statistics@un.org, https://unstats.un.org; Statistical Yearbook of the United Nations 2021.

CURACAO-FOOD

United Nations Food and Agricultural Organization (FAO), 2121 K St., Ste. 800B, Washington, DC, 20037, USA, (202) 653-2400 (Dial from U.S.), (202) 653-5760 (Fax from U.S.), fao-hq@fao.org, https://www.fao.org; The State of Food and Agriculture (SOFA) 2022.

CURACAO-FOREIGN EXCHANGE RATES

International Monetary Fund (IMF), 700 19th St. NW, Washington, DC, 20431, USA, (202) 623-7000, (202) 623-4661, publications@imf.org, https://www.imf.org; International Financial Statistics (IFS).

CURACAO-FORESTS AND FORESTRY

UNESCO Institute for Statistics, C.P 250 Succursale H, Montreal, QC, H3G 2K8, CAN, (514) 343-6880 (Dial from U.S.), (514) 343-5740 (Fax from U.S.), uis.publications@unesco.org, http://uis.unesco.org/; UIS.Stat.

United Nations Food and Agricultural Organization (FAO), 2121 K St., Ste. 800B, Washington, DC, 20037, USA, (202) 653-2400 (Dial from U.S.), (202) 653-5760 (Fax from U.S.), fao-hq@fao.org, https://www.fao.org; FAO Yearbook of Forest Products 2019 and The State of Food and Agriculture (SOFA) 2022.

United Nations Statistics Division (UNSD), United Nations Plz., New York, NY, 10017, USA, (800) 253-9646, (212) 963-9851, statistics@un.org, https://unstats.un.org; Statistical Yearbook of the United Nations 2021.

CURACAO-GROSS DOMESTIC PRODUCT

The Economist Group: Economist Intelligence Unit (EIU), 900 3rd Ave., 16th Fl., New York, NY, 10022, USA, (212) 541-0500, americas@eiu.com, https://www.eiu.com; Netherlands Antilles Country Report.

Routledge - Taylor & Francis Group, 6000 Broken Sound Pkwy. NW, Ste. 300, Boca Raton, FL, 33487, USA, (800) 634-1420, (800) 634-7064, orders@taylorandfrancis.com, https://www.routledge.com/; The Europa World Year Book 2022.

United Nations Statistics Division (UNSD), United Nations Plz., New York, NY, 10017, USA, (800) 253-9646, (212) 963-9851, statistics@un.org, https://unstats.un.org; Statistical Yearbook of the United Nations 2021.

CURACAO-HOUSING

Euromonitor International, Inc., 1 N Dearborn St., Ste. 1700, Chicago, IL, 60602, USA, (312) 922-1115, (312) 922-1157, info-usa@euromonitor.com, https://www.euromonitor.com/; Geographies.

CURACAO-ILLITERATE PERSONS

UNESCO Institute for Statistics, C.P 250 Succursale H, Montreal, QC, H3G 2K8, CAN, (514) 343-6880 (Dial from U.S.), (514) 343-5740 (Fax from U.S.), uis.publications@unesco.org, http://uis.unesco.org/; UIS.Stat.

CURACAO-IMPORTS

Central Intelligence Agency (CIA), Office of Public Affairs, Washington, DC, 20505, USA, (703) 482-0623, https://www.cia.gov; The World Factbook.

The Economist Group: Economist Intelligence Unit (EIU), 900 3rd Ave., 16th Fl., New York, NY, 10022, USA, (212) 541-0500, americas@eiu.com, https://www.eiu.com; Netherlands Antilles Country Report.

International Monetary Fund (IMF), 700 19th St. NW, Washington, DC, 20431, USA, (202) 623-7000, (202) 623-4661, publications@imf.org, https://www.imf.org; Direction of Trade Statistics (DOTS).

S&P Global, IHS Markit, 15 Inverness Way E, Englewood, CO, 80112, USA, (800) 447-2273, (800) 854-7179, https://ihsmarkit.com; Global Trade Atlas (GTA).

CURACAO-INDUSTRIES

Central Intelligence Agency (CIA), Office of Public Affairs, Washington, DC, 20505, USA, (703) 482-0623, https://www.cia.gov; The World Factbook.

The Economist Group: Economist Intelligence Unit (EIU), 900 3rd Ave., 16th Fl., New York, NY, 10022, USA, (212) 541-0500, americas@eiu.com, https://www.eiu.com; Netherlands Antilles Country Report.

Euromonitor International, Inc., 1 N Dearborn St., Ste. 1700, Chicago, IL, 60602, USA, (312) 922-1115, (312) 922-1157, info-usa@euromonitor.com, https://www.euromonitor.com/; Geographies.

International Labour Organization (ILO), 4 Rte. des Morillons, Geneva, CH-1211, SWI, ilo@ilo.org, https://www.ilo.org; NORMLEX Information System on International Labour Standards.

Palgrave Macmillan, 1 New York Plaza, Ste. 4500, New York, NY, 10004-1562, USA, (800) 777-4643, orders@palgrave.com, https://www.palgrave.com/us; The Statesman's Yearbook, 2023.

Routledge - Taylor & Francis Group, 6000 Broken Sound Pkwy. NW, Ste. 300, Boca Raton, FL, 33487, USA, (800) 634-1420, (800) 634-7064, orders@taylorandfrancis.com, https://www.routledge.com/; The Europa World Year Book 2022.

CURACAO-INTERNATIONAL TRADE

The Economist Group: Economist Intelligence Unit (EIU), 900 3rd Ave., 16th Fl., New York, NY, 10022, USA, (212) 541-0500, americas@eiu.com, https://www.eiu.com; Netherlands Antilles Country Report.

Euromonitor International, Inc., 1 N Dearborn St., Ste. 1700, Chicago, IL, 60602, USA, (312) 922-1115, (312) 922-1157, info-usa@euromonitor.com, https://www.euromonitor.com/; Geographies.

Palgrave Macmillan, 1 New York Plaza, Ste. 4500, New York, NY, 10004-1562, USA, (800) 777-4643, orders@palgrave.com, https://www.palgrave.com/us; The Statesman's Yearbook, 2023.

Routledge - Taylor & Francis Group, 6000 Broken Sound Pkwy. NW, Ste. 300, Boca Raton, FL, 33487, USA, (800) 634-1420, (800) 634-7064, orders@taylorandfrancis.com, https://www.routledge.com/; The Europa World Year Book 2022.

United Nations Conference on Trade and Development (UNCTAD), Palais des Nations, Geneva, 1211, SWI, (212) 963-6896, unctadinfo@unctad.org, https://unctad.org; Trade and Development Report 2021.

United Nations Food and Agricultural Organization (FAO), 2121 K St., Ste. 800B, Washington, DC, 20037, USA, (202) 653-2400 (Dial from U.S.), (202) 653-5760 (Fax from U.S.), fao-hq@fao.org, https://www.fao.org; The State of Food and Agriculture (SOFA) 2022.

United Nations Statistics Division (UNSD), United Nations Plz., New York, NY, 10017, USA, (800) 253-9646, (212) 963-9851, statistics@un.org, https://unstats.un.org; International Trade Statistics Yearbook 2020 and Statistical Yearbook of the United Nations 2021.

World Trade Organization (WTO), Ctre. William Rappard, Rue de Lausanne 154, Case postale, Geneva, CH-1211, SWI, enquiries@wto.org, https://www.wto.org; World Trade Statistical Review 2022.

CURACAO-LABOR

Central Intelligence Agency (CIA), Office of Public Affairs, Washington, DC, 20505, USA, (703) 482-0623, https://www.cia.gov; The World Factbook.

Euromonitor International, Inc., 1 N Dearborn St., Ste. 1700, Chicago, IL, 60602, USA, (312) 922-1115, (312) 922-1157, info-usa@euromonitor.com, https://www.euromonitor.com/; Geographies.

International Labour Organization (ILO), 4 Rte. des Morillons, Geneva, CH-1211, SWI, ilo@ilo.org, https://www.ilo.org; NORMLEX Information System on International Labour Standards.

Palgrave Macmillan, 1 New York Plaza, Ste. 4500, New York, NY, 10004-1562, USA, (800) 777-4643, orders@palgrave.com, https://www.palgrave.com/us; The Statesman's Yearbook, 2023.

United Nations Food and Agricultural Organization (FAO), 2121 K St., Ste. 800B, Washington, DC, 20037, USA, (202) 653-2400 (Dial from U.S.), (202) 653-5760 (Fax from U.S.), fao-hq@fao.org, https://www.fao.org; The State of Food and Agriculture (SOFA) 2022.

CURACAO-LIBRARIES

UNESCO Institute for Statistics, C.P 250 Succursale H, Montreal, QC, H3G 2K8, CAN, (514) 343-6880 (Dial from U.S.), (514) 343-5740 (Fax from U.S.), uis.publications@unesco.org, http://uis.unesco.org/; UIS.Stat.

CURACAO-LIFE EXPECTANCY

Central Intelligence Agency (CIA), Office of Public Affairs, Washington, DC, 20505, USA, (703) 482-0623, https://www.cia.gov; The World Factbook.

United Nations Department of Economic and Social Affairs (DESA), Population Division, 2 United Nations Plz., Rm. DC2-1950, New York, NY, 10017, USA, (212) 963-3209, (212) 963-2147, population@un.org, https://www.un.org/development/desa/pd/; World Population Ageing 2020 Highlights.

CURACAO-LITERACY

Euromonitor International, Inc., 1 N Dearborn St., Ste. 1700, Chicago, IL, 60602, USA, (312) 922-1115, (312) 922-1157, info-usa@euromonitor.com, https://www.euromonitor.com/; Geographies.

CURACAO-LIVESTOCK

Palgrave Macmillan, 1 New York Plaza, Ste. 4500, New York, NY, 10004-1562, USA, (800) 777-4643, orders@palgrave.com, https://www.palgrave.com/us; The Statesman's Yearbook, 2023.

Routledge - Taylor & Francis Group, 6000 Broken Sound Pkwy. NW, Ste. 300, Boca Raton, FL, 33487, USA, (800) 634-1420, (800) 634-7064, orders@taylorandfrancis.com, https://www.routledge.com/; The Europa World Year Book 2022.

United Nations Food and Agricultural Organization (FAO), 2121 K St., Ste. 800B, Washington, DC, 20037, USA, (202) 653-2400 (Dial from U.S.), (202) 653-5760 (Fax from U.S.), fao-hq@fao.org, https://www.fao.org; The State of Food and Agriculture (SOFA) 2022.

United Nations Statistics Division (UNSD), United Nations Plz., New York, NY, 10017, USA, (800) 253-9646, (212) 963-9851, statistics@un.org, https://unstats.un.org; Statistical Yearbook of the United Nations 2021.

CURACAO-MARRIAGE

Routledge - Taylor & Francis Group, 6000 Broken Sound Pkwy. NW, Ste. 300, Boca Raton, FL, 33487, USA, (800) 634-1420, (800) 634-7064, orders@taylorandfrancis.com, https://www.routledge.com/; The Europa World Year Book 2022.

United Nations Statistics Division (UNSD), United Nations Plz., New York, NY, 10017, USA, (800) 253-9646, (212) 963-9851, statistics@un.org, https://unstats.un.org; Statistical Yearbook of the United Nations 2021.

CURACAO-MINERAL INDUSTRIES

Palgrave Macmillan, 1 New York Plaza, Ste. 4500, New York, NY, 10004-1562, USA, (800) 777-4643, orders@palgrave.com, https://www.palgrave.com/us; The Statesman's Yearbook, 2023.

Routledge - Taylor & Francis Group, 6000 Broken Sound Pkwy. NW, Ste. 300, Boca Raton, FL, 33487,

USA, (800) 634-1420, (800) 634-7064, orders@taylorandfrancis.com, https://www.routledge.com/; The Europa World Year Book 2022.

United Nations Conference on Trade and Development (UNCTAD), Palais des Nations, Geneva, 1211, SWI, (212) 963-6896, unctadinfo@unctad.org, https://unctad.org; Trade and Development Report 2021.

United Nations Statistics Division (UNSD), United Nations Plz., New York, NY, 10017, USA, (800) 253-9646, (212) 963-9851, statistics@un.org, https://unstats.un.org; Statistical Yearbook of the United Nations 2021.

CURACAO-MONEY SUPPLY

The Economist Group: Economist Intelligence Unit (EIU), 900 3rd Ave., 16th Fl., New York, NY, 10022, USA, (212) 541-0500, americas@eiu.com, https://www.eiu.com; Netherlands Antilles Country Report.

International Monetary Fund (IMF), 700 19th St. NW, Washington, DC, 20431, USA, (202) 623-7000, (202) 623-4661, publications@imf.org, https://www.imf.org; International Financial Statistics (IFS).

Routledge - Taylor & Francis Group, 6000 Broken Sound Pkwy. NW, Ste. 300, Boca Raton, FL, 33487, USA, (800) 634-1420, (800) 634-7064, orders@taylorandfrancis.com, https://www.routledge.com/; The Europa World Year Book 2022.

CURACAO-MORTALITY

United Nations Statistics Division (UNSD), United Nations Plz., New York, NY, 10017, USA, (800) 253-9646, (212) 963-9851, statistics@un.org, https://unstats.un.org; Statistical Yearbook of the United Nations 2021 and World Statistics Pocketbook 2021.

CURACAO-NUTRITION

United Nations Food and Agricultural Organization (FAO), 2121 K St., Ste. 800B, Washington, DC, 20037, USA, (202) 653-2400 (Dial from U.S.), (202) 653-5760 (Fax from U.S.), fao-hq@fao.org, https://www.fao.org; The State of Food and Agriculture (SOFA) 2022.

CURACAO-PESTICIDES

United Nations Food and Agricultural Organization (FAO), 2121 K St., Ste. 800B, Washington, DC, 20037, USA, (202) 653-2400 (Dial from U.S.), (202) 653-5760 (Fax from U.S.), fao-hq@fao.org, https://www.fao.org; The State of Food and Agriculture (SOFA) 2022.

CURACAO-PETROLEUM INDUSTRY AND TRADE

Palgrave Macmillan, 1 New York Plaza, Ste. 4500, New York, NY, 10004-1562, USA, (800) 777-4643, orders@palgrave.com, https://www.palgrave.com/us; The Statesman's Yearbook, 2023.

U.S. Energy Information Administration (EIA), 1000 Independence Ave. SW, Washington, DC, 20585, USA, (202) 586-8800, infoctr@eia.gov, https://www.eia.gov; International Energy Outlook 2021.

United Nations Food and Agricultural Organization (FAO), 2121 K St., Ste. 800B, Washington, DC, 20037, USA, (202) 653-2400 (Dial from U.S.), (202) 653-5760 (Fax from U.S.), fao-hq@fao.org, https://www.fao.org; The State of Food and Agriculture (SOFA) 2022.

United Nations Statistics Division (UNSD), United Nations Plz., New York, NY, 10017, USA, (800) 253-9646, (212) 963-9851, statistics@un.org, https://unstats.un.org; Statistical Yearbook of the United Nations 2021.

CURACAO-POPULATION

Caribbean Public Health Agency (CARPHA), Federation Park, 16-18 Jamaica Blvd., Port of Spain, TTO, (868) 622-4261 (Dial from U.S.), (868) 299-0820 (Dial from U.S.), postmaster@carpha.org, https://carpha.org/; unpublished data.

Central Intelligence Agency (CIA), Office of Public Affairs, Washington, DC, 20505, USA, (703) 482-0623, https://www.cia.gov; The World Factbook.

The Economist Group: Economist Intelligence Unit (EIU), 900 3rd Ave., 16th Fl., New York, NY, 10022, USA, (212) 541-0500, americas@eiu.com, https://www.eiu.com; Netherlands Antilles Country Report.

International Labour Organization (ILO), 4 Rte. des Morillons, Geneva, CH-1211, SWI, ilo@ilo.org, https://www.ilo.org; NORMLEX Information System on International Labour Standards.

Palgrave Macmillan, 1 New York Plaza, Ste. 4500, New York, NY, 10004-1562, USA, (800) 777-4643, orders@palgrave.com, https://www.palgrave.com/us; The Statesman's Yearbook, 2023.

Routledge - Taylor & Francis Group, 6000 Broken Sound Pkwy. NW, Ste. 300, Boca Raton, FL, 33487, USA, (800) 634-1420, (800) 634-7064, orders@taylorandfrancis.com, https://www.routledge.com/; The Europa World Year Book 2022.

UK Data Service, University of Essex, Wivenhoe Park, Colchester, Essex, CO4 3SQ, GBR, https://ukdataservice.ac.uk/; International Aggregate Data.

UNESCO Institute for Statistics, C.P 250 Succursale H, Montreal, QC, H3G 2K8, CAN, (514) 343-6880 (Dial from U.S.), (514) 343-5740 (Fax from U.S.), uis.publications@unesco.org, http://uis.unesco.org/; UIS.Stat.

United Nations Department of Economic and Social Affairs (DESA), Population Division, 2 United Nations Plz., Rm. DC2-1950, New York, NY, 10017, USA, (212) 963-3209, (212) 963-2147, population@un.org, https://www.un.org/development/desa/pd/; Revision of World Urbanization Prospects and World Population Ageing 2020 Highlights.

United Nations Economic Commission for Latin America and the Caribbean (ECLAC), Casilla 179-D, Santiago, 7630412, CHL, (202) 596-3713, prensa@cepal.org, https://www.cepal.org/en; CEPALSTAT.

United Nations Statistics Division (UNSD), United Nations Plz., New York, NY, 10017, USA, (800) 253-9646, (212) 963-9851, statistics@un.org, https://unstats.un.org; Statistical Yearbook of the United Nations 2021 and World Statistics Pocketbook 2021.

The World Bank, 1818 H St. NW, Washington, DC, 20433, USA, (202) 473-1000, (202) 477-6391, eds03@worldbank.org, https://www.worldbank.org/; The Global Findex Database 2021.

CURACAO-POPULATION DENSITY

Central Intelligence Agency (CIA), Office of Public Affairs, Washington, DC, 20505, USA, (703) 482-0623, https://www.cia.gov; The World Factbook.

Palgrave Macmillan, 1 New York Plaza, Ste. 4500, New York, NY, 10004-1562, USA, (800) 777-4643, orders@palgrave.com, https://www.palgrave.com/us; The Statesman's Yearbook, 2023.

Routledge - Taylor & Francis Group, 6000 Broken Sound Pkwy. NW, Ste. 300, Boca Raton, FL, 33487, USA, (800) 634-1420, (800) 634-7064, orders@taylorandfrancis.com, https://www.routledge.com/; The Europa World Year Book 2022.

UNESCO Institute for Statistics, C.P 250 Succursale H, Montreal, QC, H3G 2K8, CAN, (514) 343-6880 (Dial from U.S.), (514) 343-5740 (Fax from U.S.), uis.publications@unesco.org, http://uis.unesco.org/; UIS.Stat.

CURACAO-POWER RESOURCES

Euromonitor International, Inc., 1 N Dearborn St., Ste. 1700, Chicago, IL, 60602, USA, (312) 922-1115, (312) 922-1157, info-usa@euromonitor.com, https://www.euromonitor.com/; Geographies.

Palgrave Macmillan, 1 New York Plaza, Ste. 4500, New York, NY, 10004-1562, USA, (800) 777-4643, orders@palgrave.com, https://www.palgrave.com/us; The Statesman's Yearbook, 2023.

U.S. Energy Information Administration (EIA), 1000 Independence Ave. SW, Washington, DC, 20585, USA, (202) 586-8800, infoctr@eia.gov, https://www.eia.gov; International Energy Outlook 2021.

United Nations Food and Agricultural Organization (FAO), 2121 K St., Ste. 800B, Washington, DC, 20037, USA, (202) 653-2400 (Dial from U.S.), (202) 653-5760 (Fax from U.S.), fao-hq@fao.org, https://www.fao.org; The State of Food and Agriculture (SOFA) 2022.

United Nations Statistics Division (UNSD), United Nations Plz., New York, NY, 10017, USA, (800) 253-9646, (212) 963-9851, statistics@un.org, https://unstats.un.org; Energy Statistics Yearbook 2019; Statistical Yearbook of the United Nations 2021; and World Statistics Pocketbook 2021.

CURACAO-PRICES

Euromonitor International, Inc., 1 N Dearborn St., Ste. 1700, Chicago, IL, 60602, USA, (312) 922-1115, (312) 922-1157, info-usa@euromonitor.com, https://www.euromonitor.com/; Geographies.

International Monetary Fund (IMF), 700 19th St. NW, Washington, DC, 20431, USA, (202) 623-7000, (202) 623-4661, publications@imf.org, https://www.imf.org; International Financial Statistics (IFS).

CURACAO-PRIMARY STATISTICS SOURCES

Curacao Central Bureau of Statistics, WTC Unit-IBC.II.2, Willemstad, NAT, info@cbs.cw, https://www.cbs.cw/; Statistical Orientation Curacao 2020.

CURACAO-PUBLIC HEALTH

Euromonitor International, Inc., 1 N Dearborn St., Ste. 1700, Chicago, IL, 60602, USA, (312) 922-1115, (312) 922-1157, info-usa@euromonitor.com, https://www.euromonitor.com/; Geographies.

Palgrave Macmillan, 1 New York Plaza, Ste. 4500, New York, NY, 10004-1562, USA, (800) 777-4643, orders@palgrave.com, https://www.palgrave.com/us; The Statesman's Yearbook, 2023.

U.S. Census Bureau, 4600 Silver Hill Rd., Washington, DC, 20233, USA, (301) 763-4636, (800) 923-8282, https://www.census.gov; HIV/AIDS Surveillance Data Base.

United Nations Department of Economic and Social Affairs (DESA), Population Division, 2 United Nations Plz., Rm. DC2-1950, New York, NY, 10017, USA, (212) 963-3209, (212) 963-2147, population@un.org, https://www.un.org/development/desa/pd/; World Fertility Data 2019.

United Nations Statistics Division (UNSD), United Nations Plz., New York, NY, 10017, USA, (800) 253-9646, (212) 963-9851, statistics@un.org, https://unstats.un.org; Statistical Yearbook of the United Nations 2021.

CURACAO-PUBLISHERS AND PUBLISHING

Routledge - Taylor & Francis Group, 6000 Broken Sound Pkwy. NW, Ste. 300, Boca Raton, FL, 33487, USA, (800) 634-1420, (800) 634-7064, orders@taylorandfrancis.com, https://www.routledge.com/; The Europa World Year Book 2022.

UNESCO Institute for Statistics, C.P 250 Succursale H, Montreal, QC, H3G 2K8, CAN, (514) 343-6880 (Dial from U.S.), (514) 343-5740 (Fax from U.S.), uis.publications@unesco.org, http://uis.unesco.org/; UIS.Stat.

CURACAO-RELIGION

Central Intelligence Agency (CIA), Office of Public Affairs, Washington, DC, 20505, USA, (703) 482-0623, https://www.cia.gov; The World Factbook.

Palgrave Macmillan, 1 New York Plaza, Ste. 4500, New York, NY, 10004-1562, USA, (800) 777-4643, orders@palgrave.com, https://www.palgrave.com/us; The Statesman's Yearbook, 2023.

CURACAO-RETAIL TRADE

Euromonitor International, Inc., 1 N Dearborn St., Ste. 1700, Chicago, IL, 60602, USA, (312) 922-

1115, (312) 922-1157, info-usa@euromonitor.com, https://www.euromonitor.com/; Geographies.

CURACAO-SHIPPING

Routledge - Taylor & Francis Group, 6000 Broken Sound Pkwy. NW, Ste. 300, Boca Raton, FL, 33487, USA, (800) 634-1420, (800) 634-7064, orders@taylorandfrancis.com, https://www.routledge.com/; The Europa World Year Book 2022.

United Nations Statistics Division (UNSD), United Nations Plz., New York, NY, 10017, USA, (800) 253-9646, (212) 963-9851, statistics@un.org, https://unstats.un.org; Statistical Yearbook of the United Nations 2021.

CURACAO-TELEPHONE

Palgrave Macmillan, 1 New York Plaza, Ste. 4500, New York, NY, 10004-1562, USA, (800) 777-4643, orders@palgrave.com, https://www.palgrave.com/us; The Statesman's Yearbook, 2023.

Routledge - Taylor & Francis Group, 6000 Broken Sound Pkwy. NW, Ste. 300, Boca Raton, FL, 33487, USA, (800) 634-1420, (800) 634-7064, orders@taylorandfrancis.com, https://www.routledge.com/; The Europa World Year Book 2022.

United Nations Statistics Division (UNSD), United Nations Plz., New York, NY, 10017, USA, (800) 253-9646, (212) 963-9851, statistics@un.org, https://unstats.un.org; World Statistics Pocketbook 2021.

CURACAO-TOURISM

Euromonitor International, Inc., 1 N Dearborn St., Ste. 1700, Chicago, IL, 60602, USA, (312) 922-1115, (312) 922-1157, info-usa@euromonitor.com, https://www.euromonitor.com/; Geographies.

Palgrave Macmillan, 1 New York Plaza, Ste. 4500, New York, NY, 10004-1562, USA, (800) 777-4643, orders@palgrave.com, https://www.palgrave.com/us; The Statesman's Yearbook, 2023.

Routledge - Taylor & Francis Group, 6000 Broken Sound Pkwy. NW, Ste. 300, Boca Raton, FL, 33487, USA, (800) 634-1420, (800) 634-7064, orders@taylorandfrancis.com, https://www.routledge.com/; The Europa World Year Book 2022.

United Nations Statistics Division (UNSD), United Nations Plz., New York, NY, 10017, USA, (800) 253-9646, (212) 963-9851, statistics@un.org, https://unstats.un.org; Statistical Yearbook of the United Nations 2021.

CURACAO-TRANSPORTATION

Central Intelligence Agency (CIA), Office of Public Affairs, Washington, DC, 20505, USA, (703) 482-0623, https://www.cia.gov; The World Factbook.

Euromonitor International, Inc., 1 N Dearborn St., Ste. 1700, Chicago, IL, 60602, USA, (312) 922-1115, (312) 922-1157, info-usa@euromonitor.com, https://www.euromonitor.com/; Geographies.

Palgrave Macmillan, 1 New York Plaza, Ste. 4500, New York, NY, 10004-1562, USA, (800) 777-4643, orders@palgrave.com, https://www.palgrave.com/us; The Statesman's Yearbook, 2023.

Routledge - Taylor & Francis Group, 6000 Broken Sound Pkwy. NW, Ste. 300, Boca Raton, FL, 33487, USA, (800) 634-1420, (800) 634-7064, orders@taylorandfrancis.com, https://www.routledge.com/; The Europa World Year Book 2022.

CURACAO-UNEMPLOYMENT

International Labour Organization (ILO), 4 Rte. des Morillons, Geneva, CH-1211, SWI, ilo@ilo.org, https://www.ilo.org; NORMLEX Information System on International Labour Standards.

CURACAO-VITAL STATISTICS

Palgrave Macmillan, 1 New York Plaza, Ste. 4500, New York, NY, 10004-1562, USA, (800) 777-4643, orders@palgrave.com, https://www.palgrave.com/us; The Statesman's Yearbook, 2023.

U.S. Census Bureau, 4600 Silver Hill Rd., Washington, DC, 20233, USA, (301) 763-4636, (800) 923-8282, https://www.census.gov; HIV/AIDS Surveillance Data Base.

United Nations Department of Economic and Social Affairs (DESA), Population Division, 2 United Nations Plz., Rm. DC2-1950, New York, NY, 10017, USA, (212) 963-3209, (212) 963-2147, population@un.org, https://www.un.org/development/desa/pd/; World Contraceptive Use 2021: Estimates and Projections of Family Planning Indicators and World Marriage Data 2019.

United Nations Statistics Division (UNSD), United Nations Plz., New York, NY, 10017, USA, (800) 253-9646, (212) 963-9851, statistics@un.org, https://unstats.un.org; Statistical Yearbook of the United Nations 2021.

CURACAO-WAGES

International Labour Organization (ILO), 4 Rte. des Morillons, Geneva, CH-1211, SWI, ilo@ilo.org, https://www.ilo.org; NORMLEX Information System on International Labour Standards.

United Nations Statistics Division (UNSD), United Nations Plz., New York, NY, 10017, USA, (800) 253-9646, (212) 963-9851, statistics@un.org, https://unstats.un.org; Statistical Yearbook of the United Nations 2021.

CURACAO ANTILLES-NATIONAL STATISTICAL OFFICE

Curacao Central Bureau of Statistics, WTC Unit-IBC.II.2, Willemstad, NAT, info@cbs.cw, https://www.cbs.cw/; National Data Reports (Curacao).

CURCUMIN

ConsumerLab, 333 Mamaroneck Ave., White Plains, NY, 10605, USA, (914) 722-9149, info@consumerlab.com, https://www.consumerlab.com; Product Review: Turmeric and Curcumin Supplements and Spices.

CURRENCY

Rapid Intelligence, Sydney, NSW, 2001, AUS, https://www.rapint.com/; NationMaster.com.

CURRENCY-FOREIGN EXCHANGE RATE

International Monetary Fund (IMF), 700 19th St. NW, Washington, DC, 20431, USA, (202) 623-7000, (202) 623-4661, publications@imf.org, https://www.imf.org; International Financial Statistics (IFS).

CURRENCY-PERSONAL SAVING COMPONENT

U.S. Department of Commerce (DOC), Bureau of Economic Analysis (BEA), 4600 Silver Hill Rd., Washington, DC, 20233, USA, (301) 278-9004, customerservice@bea.gov, https://www.bea.gov; National Income and Product Accounts (NIPA): 2022 Update and Survey of Current Business (SCB).

CURRENCY-SUPPLY

Board of Governors of the Federal Reserve System, Constitution Ave. NW, Washington, DC, 20551, USA, (202) 452-3000, (202) 263-4869 (TDD), https://www.federalreserve.gov; Federal Reserve Bulletin and Money Stock Measures 2023.

CUSTODY OF CHILDREN

Institute on Violence, Abuse and Trauma (IVAT), 10065 Old Grove Rd. , Ste. 101, San Diego, CA, 92131, USA, (858) 527-1860, (858) 527-1743, https://www.ivatcenters.org/; Journal of Family Trauma, Child Custody, and Child Development (JFT).

The Lancet, 230 Park Ave., New York, NY, 10169, USA, (212) 633-3800, editorial@lancet.com, https://www.thelancet.com/; Global, Regional, and National Minimum Estimates of Children Affected by COVID-19-Associated Orphanhood and Caregiver Death, by Age and Family Circumstance up to Oct 31, 2021: An Updated Modelling Study.

CUSTOMS ADMINISTRATION

U.S. Department of Homeland Security (DHS), U.S. Customs and Border Protection (CBP), 1300 Pennsylvania Ave. NW, Washington, DC, 20229, USA, (877) 227-5511, (202) 325-8000, https://www.cbp.gov; Intellectual Property Rights (IPR) Seizure Statistics - Fiscal Year 2020.

U.S. Office of Management and Budget (OMB), 725 17th St. NW, Washington, DC, 20503, USA, (202) 395-3080, https://www.whitehouse.gov/omb/; Historical Tables.

United States International Trade Commission (USITC), 500 E St. SW, Washington, DC, 20436, USA, (202) 205-2000, (202) 205-1810 (TDD), https://www.usitc.gov/; Recent Trends in U.S. Services Trade: 2020 Annual Report.

CYBERBULLYING

Cyberbullying Research Center, USA, hinduja@cyberbullying.org, https://cyberbullying.org; Bullying, Cyberbullying, and Sexting by State; 2021 Cyberbullying Data; Summary of Our Cyberbullying Research (2007-2021); and Tween Cyberbullying in 2020.

Plan International Canada, 245 Eglinton Ave. E, Ste. 300, Toronto, ON, M4P 0B3, CAN, (800) 387-1418 (Dial from U.S.), info@plancanada.ca, https://plancanada.ca/; State of the World's Girls Report: Free to Be Online?.

U.S. Department of Education (ED), Institute of Education Sciences (IES), National Center for Education Statistics (NCES), Potomac Center Plaza, 550 12th St. SW, Washington, DC, 20202, USA, (202) 403-5551, https://nces.ed.gov/; Students' Perceptions of Bullying.

CYBERSTALKING

Plan International Canada, 245 Eglinton Ave. E, Ste. 300, Toronto, ON, M4P 0B3, CAN, (800) 387-1418 (Dial from U.S.), info@plancanada.ca, https://plancanada.ca/; State of the World's Girls Report: Free to Be Online?.

CYBERTERRORISM

The German Marshall Fund of the United States (GMF), 1744 R St. NW, Washington, DC, 20009, USA, (202) 683-2650, (202) 265-1662, info@gmfus.org, https://www.gmfus.org/; Russian Information Warfare in Central and Eastern Europe: Strategies, Impact, and Counter-Measures.

University of Maryland, National Consortium for the Study of Terrorism and Responses to Terrorism (START), PO Box 266, 5245 Greenbelt Rd., College Park, MD, 20740, USA, (301) 405-6600, (301) 314-1980, infostart@start.umd.edu, https://www.start.umd.edu; Global Terrorism Overview: Terrorism in 2019.

CYCLONES

National Oceanic and Atmospheric Administration (NOAA), National Centers for Environmental Information (NCEI), Federal Bldg., 151 Patton Ave., Asheville, NC, 28801-5001, USA, (828) 271-4800, (828) 271-4010 (TTY), (828) 271-4876, ncei.info@noaa.gov, https://www.ncei.noaa.gov/; Storm Events Database.

Proceedings of the National Academy of Sciences (PNAS), 500 Fifth St. NW, NAS 338, Washington, DC, 20001, USA, (202) 334-2679, pnas@nas.edu, https://www.pnas.org; Global Increase in Major Tropical Cyclone Exceedance Probability Over the Past Four Decades.

CYPRUS-NATIONAL STATISTICAL OFFICE

Republic of Cyprus Statistical Service (CYSTAT), Michael Karaolis St., Lefkosia, 1444, CYP, enquiries@cystat.mof.gov.cy, https://www.cystat.gov.cy/en/; National Data Reports (Cyprus).

CYPRUS-PRIMARY STATISTICS SOURCES

European Commission, Eurostat, Luxembourg, 2920, LUX, https://ec.europa.eu/eurostat/; Key Figures on Enlargement Countries, 2019.

CYPRUS-AGRICULTURE

The Economist Group: Economist Intelligence Unit (EIU), 900 3rd Ave., 16th Fl., New York, NY, 10022, USA, (212) 541-0500, americas@eiu.com, https://www.eiu.com; Cyprus Country Report.

Euromonitor International, Inc., 1 N Dearborn St., Ste. 1700, Chicago, IL, 60602, USA, (312) 922-1115, (312) 922-1157, info-usa@euromonitor.com, https://www.euromonitor.com/; Geographies.

European Commission, Rue de la Loi, 170, Brussels, B-1040, BEL, https://ec.europa.eu; Common Agricultural Policy (CAPF) Context Indicators, 2019 Update.

European Commission, Eurostat, Luxembourg, 2920, LUX, https://ec.europa.eu/eurostat/; Farmers and the Agricultural Labour Force - Statistics.

Palgrave Macmillan, 1 New York Plaza, Ste. 4500, New York, NY, 10004-1562, USA, (800) 777-4643, orders@palgrave.com, https://www.palgrave.com/us; The Statesman's Yearbook, 2023.

Routledge - Taylor & Francis Group, 6000 Broken Sound Pkwy. NW, Ste. 300, Boca Raton, FL, 33487, USA, (800) 634-1420, (800) 634-7064, orders@taylorandfrancis.com, https://www.routledge.com/; The Europa World Year Book 2022.

United Nations Food and Agricultural Organization (FAO), 2121 K St., Ste. 800B, Washington, DC, 20037, USA, (202) 653-2400 (Dial from U.S.), (202) 653-5760 (Fax from U.S.), fao-hq@fao.org, https://www.fao.org; AQUASTAT and The State of Food and Agriculture (SOFA) 2022.

United Nations Statistics Division (UNSD), United Nations Plz., New York, NY, 10017, USA, (800) 253-9646, (212) 963-9851, statistics@un.org, https://unstats.un.org; Statistical Yearbook of the United Nations 2021.

The World Bank, 1818 H St. NW, Washington, DC, 20433, USA, (202) 473-1000, (202) 477-6391, eds03@worldbank.org, https://www.worldbank.org/; World Development Indicators (WDI) 2022.

CYPRUS-AIRLINES

European Commission, Eurostat, Luxembourg, 2920, LUX, https://ec.europa.eu/eurostat/; Air Transport Statistics.

International Civil Aviation Organization (ICAO), 999 Robert-Bourassa Blvd., Montreal, QC, H3C 5H7, CAN, (514) 954-8219 (Dial from U.S.), (514) 954-6077 (Fax from U.S.), icaohq@icao.int, https://www.icao.int; ICAO Regional Reports.

Palgrave Macmillan, 1 New York Plaza, Ste. 4500, New York, NY, 10004-1562, USA, (800) 777-4643, orders@palgrave.com, https://www.palgrave.com/us; The Statesman's Yearbook, 2023.

Routledge - Taylor & Francis Group, 6000 Broken Sound Pkwy. NW, Ste. 300, Boca Raton, FL, 33487, USA, (800) 634-1420, (800) 634-7064, orders@taylorandfrancis.com, https://www.routledge.com/; The Europa World Year Book 2022.

CYPRUS-ALUMINUM PRODUCTION

See CYPRUS-MINERAL INDUSTRIES

CYPRUS-ARMED FORCES

Central Intelligence Agency (CIA), Office of Public Affairs, Washington, DC, 20505, USA, (703) 482-0623, https://www.cia.gov; The World Factbook.

International Institute for Strategic Studies (IISS) - Americas, 2121 K St. NW, Ste. 600, Washington, DC, 20037, USA, (202) 659-1490, (202) 659-1499, https://www.iiss.org/; Armed Conflict Survey 2021 and The Military Balance 2022.

Palgrave Macmillan, 1 New York Plaza, Ste. 4500, New York, NY, 10004-1562, USA, (800) 777-4643, orders@palgrave.com, https://www.palgrave.com/us; The Statesman's Yearbook, 2023.

Stockholm International Peace Research Institute (SIPRI), Signalistgatan 9, Stockholm, SE 169 72, SWE, https://www.sipri.org/; SIPRI Arms Transfers Database and SIPRI Military Expenditure Database.

CYPRUS-ARTICHOKE PRODUCTION

See CYPRUS-CROPS

CYPRUS-BALANCE OF PAYMENTS

International Monetary Fund (IMF), 700 19th St. NW, Washington, DC, 20431, USA, (202) 623-7000, (202) 623-4661, publications@imf.org, https://www.imf.org; Balance of Payments Statistics: Annual Report 2021.

Routledge - Taylor & Francis Group, 6000 Broken Sound Pkwy. NW, Ste. 300, Boca Raton, FL, 33487, USA, (800) 634-1420, (800) 634-7064, orders@taylorandfrancis.com, https://www.routledge.com/; The Europa World Year Book 2022.

United Nations Conference on Trade and Development (UNCTAD), Palais des Nations, Geneva, 1211, SWI, (212) 963-6896, unctadinfo@unctad.org, https://unctad.org; Handbook of Statistics 2021.

The World Bank, 1818 H St. NW, Washington, DC, 20433, USA, (202) 473-1000, (202) 477-6391, eds03@worldbank.org, https://www.worldbank.org/; World Development Indicators (WDI) 2022.

CYPRUS-BANKS AND BANKING

Euromonitor International, Inc., 1 N Dearborn St., Ste. 1700, Chicago, IL, 60602, USA, (312) 922-1115, (312) 922-1157, info-usa@euromonitor.com, https://www.euromonitor.com/; Geographies.

International Monetary Fund (IMF), 700 19th St. NW, Washington, DC, 20431, USA, (202) 623-7000, (202) 623-4661, publications@imf.org, https://www.imf.org; International Financial Statistics (IFS).

Routledge - Taylor & Francis Group, 6000 Broken Sound Pkwy. NW, Ste. 300, Boca Raton, FL, 33487, USA, (800) 634-1420, (800) 634-7064, orders@taylorandfrancis.com, https://www.routledge.com/; The Europa World Year Book 2022.

CYPRUS-BARLEY PRODUCTION

See CYPRUS-CROPS

CYPRUS-BEVERAGE INDUSTRY

International Monetary Fund (IMF), 700 19th St. NW, Washington, DC, 20431, USA, (202) 623-7000, (202) 623-4661, publications@imf.org, https://www.imf.org; International Financial Statistics (IFS).

CYPRUS-BROADCASTING

Central Intelligence Agency (CIA), Office of Public Affairs, Washington, DC, 20505, USA, (703) 482-0623, https://www.cia.gov; The World Factbook.

Euromonitor International, Inc., 1 N Dearborn St., Ste. 1700, Chicago, IL, 60602, USA, (312) 922-1115, (312) 922-1157, info-usa@euromonitor.com, https://www.euromonitor.com/; Geographies.

Palgrave Macmillan, 1 New York Plaza, Ste. 4500, New York, NY, 10004-1562, USA, (800) 777-4643, orders@palgrave.com, https://www.palgrave.com/us; The Statesman's Yearbook, 2023.

UNESCO Institute for Statistics, C.P 250 Succursale H, Montreal, QC, H3G 2K8, CAN, (514) 343-6880 (Dial from U.S.), (514) 343-5740 (Fax from U.S.), uis.publications@unesco.org, http://uis.unesco.org/; UIS.Stat.

WRTH Publications Limited, PO Box 290, Oxford, OX2 7FT, GBR, sales@wrth.com, https://www.wrth.com; World Radio TV Handbook 2023.

CYPRUS-BUDGET

Central Intelligence Agency (CIA), Office of Public Affairs, Washington, DC, 20505, USA, (703) 482-0623, https://www.cia.gov; The World Factbook.

European Commission, Eurostat, Luxembourg, 2920, LUX, https://ec.europa.eu/eurostat/; Share of Government Budget Appropriations or Outlays on Research and Development.

CYPRUS-CHILDBIRTH-STATISTICS

The World Bank, 1818 H St. NW, Washington, DC, 20433, USA, (202) 473-1000, (202) 477-6391, eds03@worldbank.org, https://www.worldbank.org/; World Development Indicators (WDI) 2022.

CYPRUS-CLIMATE

Palgrave Macmillan, 1 New York Plaza, Ste. 4500, New York, NY, 10004-1562, USA, (800) 777-4643, orders@palgrave.com, https://www.palgrave.com/us; The Statesman's Yearbook, 2023.

CYPRUS-COAL PRODUCTION

See CYPRUS-MINERAL INDUSTRIES

CYPRUS-COFFEE

See CYPRUS-CROPS

CYPRUS-COMMERCE

Palgrave Macmillan, 1 New York Plaza, Ste. 4500, New York, NY, 10004-1562, USA, (800) 777-4643, orders@palgrave.com, https://www.palgrave.com/us; The Statesman's Yearbook, 2023.

UK Data Service, University of Essex, Wivenhoe Park, Colchester, Essex, CO4 3SQ, GBR, https://ukdataservice.ac.uk/; International Aggregate Data.

CYPRUS-COMMODITY EXCHANGES

Barchart, 209 W Jackson Blvd., 2nd Fl., Chicago, IL, 60606, USA, (877) 247-4394, commodities@barchart.com, https://www.barchart.com/cmdty; The cmdty Yearbook 2023; cmdtyStats: Commodity Statistics and Fundamental Data; cmdtyView: Commodity Index; and Commodity Data and Prices.

International Monetary Fund (IMF), 700 19th St. NW, Washington, DC, 20431, USA, (202) 623-7000, (202) 623-4661, publications@imf.org, https://www.imf.org; IMF Primary Commodity Prices.

CYPRUS-CONSTRUCTION INDUSTRY

United Nations Statistics Division (UNSD), United Nations Plz., New York, NY, 10017, USA, (800) 253-9646, (212) 963-9851, statistics@un.org, https://unstats.un.org; Statistical Yearbook of the United Nations 2021.

CYPRUS-CONSUMER PRICE INDEXES

Routledge - Taylor & Francis Group, 6000 Broken Sound Pkwy. NW, Ste. 300, Boca Raton, FL, 33487, USA, (800) 634-1420, (800) 634-7064, orders@taylorandfrancis.com, https://www.routledge.com/; The Europa World Year Book 2022.

CYPRUS-COPPER INDUSTRY AND TRADE

See CYPRUS-MINERAL INDUSTRIES

CYPRUS-CORN INDUSTRY

See CYPRUS-CROPS

CYPRUS-COTTON

See CYPRUS-CROPS

CYPRUS-CRIME

European Commission, Eurostat, Luxembourg, 2920, LUX, https://ec.europa.eu/eurostat/; Crime and Criminal Justice Database and Crime Statistics.

Mediterranean Institute of Gender Studies (MIGS), 46 Makedonitissas Ave., PO Box 24005, Nicosia, 1703, CYP, info@medinstgenderstudies.org, https://medinstgenderstudies.org/; Mind the Gap Report: COALESCE for Support in Cyprus.

CYPRUS-CROPS

International Monetary Fund (IMF), 700 19th St. NW, Washington, DC, 20431, USA, (202) 623-7000, (202) 623-4661, publications@imf.org, https://www.imf.org; International Financial Statistics (IFS).

Palgrave Macmillan, 1 New York Plaza, Ste. 4500, New York, NY, 10004-1562, USA, (800) 777-4643, orders@palgrave.com, https://www.palgrave.com/us; The Statesman's Yearbook, 2023.

United Nations Food and Agricultural Organization (FAO), 2121 K St., Ste. 800B, Washington, DC, 20037, USA, (202) 653-2400 (Dial from U.S.), (202) 653-5760 (Fax from U.S.), fao-hq@fao.org, https://www.fao.org; The State of Food and Agriculture (SOFA) 2022.

United Nations Statistics Division (UNSD), United Nations Plz., New York, NY, 10017, USA, (800) 253-9646, (212) 963-9851, statistics@un.org, https://unstats.un.org; Statistical Yearbook of the United Nations 2021.

CYPRUS-DAIRY PROCESSING

Palgrave Macmillan, 1 New York Plaza, Ste. 4500, New York, NY, 10004-1562, USA, (800) 777-4643, orders@palgrave.com, https://www.palgrave.com/us; The Statesman's Yearbook, 2023.

United Nations Food and Agricultural Organization (FAO), 2121 K St., Ste. 800B, Washington, DC, 20037, USA, (202) 653-2400 (Dial from U.S.), (202) 653-5760 (Fax from U.S.), fao-hq@fao.org, https://www.fao.org; The State of Food and Agriculture (SOFA) 2022.

CYPRUS-DEBTS, EXTERNAL

Palgrave Macmillan, 1 New York Plaza, Ste. 4500, New York, NY, 10004-1562, USA, (800) 777-4643, orders@palgrave.com, https://www.palgrave.com/us; The Statesman's Yearbook, 2023.

The World Bank, 1818 H St. NW, Washington, DC, 20433, USA, (202) 473-1000, (202) 477-6391, eds03@worldbank.org, https://www.worldbank.org/; Global Financial Development Report 2019-2020: Bank Regulation and Supervision a Decade after the Global Financial Crisis and World Development Indicators (WDI) 2022.

CYPRUS-DEFENSE EXPENDITURES

See CYPRUS-ARMED FORCES

CYPRUS-DIAMONDS

See CYPRUS-MINERAL INDUSTRIES

CYPRUS-ECONOMIC ASSISTANCE

United Nations Statistics Division (UNSD), United Nations Plz., New York, NY, 10017, USA, (800) 253-9646, (212) 963-9851, statistics@un.org, https://unstats.un.org; Statistical Yearbook of the United Nations 2021.

CYPRUS-ECONOMIC CONDITIONS

Bernan Press, 15250 NBN Way, Bldg. C, Blue Ridge Summit, PA, 17214, USA, (301) 459-2255, (800) 865-3457, (800) 865-3450, customercare@bernan.com, https://rowman.com/Page/Bernan; World Economic Outlook, April 2022.

Central Intelligence Agency (CIA), Office of Public Affairs, Washington, DC, 20505, USA, (703) 482-0623, https://www.cia.gov; The World Factbook.

The Economist Group: Economist Intelligence Unit (EIU), 900 3rd Ave., 16th Fl., New York, NY, 10022, USA, (212) 541-0500, americas@eiu.com, https://www.eiu.com; Cyprus Country Report.

Euromonitor International, Inc., 1 N Dearborn St., Ste. 1700, Chicago, IL, 60602, USA, (312) 922-1115, (312) 922-1157, info-usa@euromonitor.com, https://www.euromonitor.com/; Geographies.

European Commission, Rue de la Loi, 170, Brussels, B-1040, BEL, https://ec.europa.eu; Common Agricultural Policy (CAPF) Context Indicators, 2019 Update.

International Monetary Fund (IMF), 700 19th St. NW, Washington, DC, 20431, USA, (202) 623-7000, (202) 623-4661, publications@imf.org, https://www.imf.org; IMF Data and World Economic Outlook.

Palgrave Macmillan, 1 New York Plaza, Ste. 4500, New York, NY, 10004-1562, USA, (800) 777-4643, orders@palgrave.com, https://www.palgrave.com/us; The Statesman's Yearbook, 2023.

Routledge - Taylor & Francis Group, 6000 Broken Sound Pkwy. NW, Ste. 300, Boca Raton, FL, 33487, USA, (800) 634-1420, (800) 634-7064, orders@taylorandfrancis.com, https://www.routledge.com/; The Europa World Year Book 2022.

United Nations Economic and Social Commission for Western Asia (ESCWA), Riad el-Solh Sq., PO Box 11-8575, Beirut, LBN, escwa-ciu@un.org, https://www.unescwa.org; ESCWA Annual Report 2019; ESCWA Data Portal for the Arab Region; and Survey of Economic and Social Developments in the Arab Region 2020-2021.

United Nations Statistics Division (UNSD), United Nations Plz., New York, NY, 10017, USA, (800) 253-9646, (212) 963-9851, statistics@un.org, https://unstats.un.org; World Statistics Pocketbook 2021.

The World Bank, 1818 H St. NW, Washington, DC, 20433, USA, (202) 473-1000, (202) 477-6391, eds03@worldbank.org, https://www.worldbank.org/; Global Economic Monitor (GEM); Global Economic Prospects, June 2022; and The Global Findex Database 2021.

CYPRUS-EDUCATION

Euromonitor International, Inc., 1 N Dearborn St., Ste. 1700, Chicago, IL, 60602, USA, (312) 922-1115, (312) 922-1157, info-usa@euromonitor.com, https://www.euromonitor.com/; Geographies.

European Commission, Rue de la Loi, 170, Brussels, B-1040, BEL, https://ec.europa.eu; Common Agricultural Policy (CAPF) Context Indicators, 2019 Update.

Infoplease, c/o Sandbox Networks, Inc., 1 Lincoln St., 24th Fl., Boston, MA, 02111, USA, https://www.infoplease.com; Countries of the World.

Palgrave Macmillan, 1 New York Plaza, Ste. 4500, New York, NY, 10004-1562, USA, (800) 777-4643, orders@palgrave.com, https://www.palgrave.com/us; The Statesman's Yearbook, 2023.

UNESCO Institute for Statistics, C.P 250 Succursale H, Montreal, QC, H3G 2K8, CAN, (514) 343-6880 (Dial from U.S.), (514) 343-5740 (Fax from U.S.), uis.publications@unesco.org, http://uis.unesco.org/; Literacy and UIS.Stat.

United Nations Statistics Division (UNSD), United Nations Plz., New York, NY, 10017, USA, (800) 253-9646, (212) 963-9851, statistics@un.org, https://unstats.un.org; Millennium Development Goal Indicators.

The World Bank, 1818 H St. NW, Washington, DC, 20433, USA, (202) 473-1000, (202) 477-6391, eds03@worldbank.org, https://www.worldbank.org/; World Development Indicators (WDI) 2022.

CYPRUS-ELECTRICITY

European Commission, Eurostat, Luxembourg, 2920, LUX, https://ec.europa.eu/eurostat/; Final Energy Consumption in Transport by Type of Fuel.

S&P Global Commodity Insights, One World Trade Center, New York, NY, 10007, USA, (800) 752-8878, support@platts.com, https://www.spglobal.com/commodityinsights/en; Platts European Power Alert and Platts Power in Europe.

U.S. Energy Information Administration (EIA), 1000 Independence Ave. SW, Washington, DC, 20585, USA, (202) 586-8800, infoctr@eia.gov, https://www.eia.gov; International Energy Outlook 2021.

United Nations Statistics Division (UNSD), United Nations Plz., New York, NY, 10017, USA, (800) 253-9646, (212) 963-9851, statistics@un.org, https://unstats.un.org; Statistical Yearbook of the United Nations 2021.

CYPRUS-EMPLOYMENT

International Labour Organization (ILO), 4 Rte. des Morillons, Geneva, CH-1211, SWI, ilo@ilo.org, https://www.ilo.org; NORMLEX Information System on International Labour Standards.

UK Data Service, University of Essex, Wivenhoe Park, Colchester, Essex, CO4 3SQ, GBR, https://ukdataservice.ac.uk/; International Aggregate Data.

United Nations Statistics Division (UNSD), United Nations Plz., New York, NY, 10017, USA, (800) 253-9646, (212) 963-9851, statistics@un.org, https://unstats.un.org; Statistical Yearbook of the United Nations 2021.

CYPRUS-ENERGY INDUSTRIES

European Commission, Eurostat, Luxembourg, 2920, LUX, https://ec.europa.eu/eurostat/; Final Energy Consumption in Transport by Type of Fuel.

S&P Global Commodity Insights, One World Trade Center, New York, NY, 10007, USA, (800) 752-8878, support@platts.com, https://www.spglobal.com/commodityinsights/en; Platts Power in Europe.

CYPRUS-ENVIRONMENTAL CONDITIONS

DSI Data Service & Information, Xantener Strasse 51a, Rheinberg, D-47495, GER, dsi@dsidata.com, https://www.dsidata.com/; Global Environmental Database.

The Economist Group: Economist Intelligence Unit (EIU), 900 3rd Ave., 16th Fl., New York, NY, 10022, USA, (212) 541-0500, americas@eiu.com, https://www.eiu.com; Cyprus Country Report.

European Commission, Rue de la Loi, 170, Brussels, B-1040, BEL, https://ec.europa.eu; Common Agricultural Policy (CAPF) Context Indicators, 2019 Update.

United Nations Statistics Division (UNSD), United Nations Plz., New York, NY, 10017, USA, (800) 253-9646, (212) 963-9851, statistics@un.org, https://unstats.un.org; World Statistics Pocketbook 2021.

CYPRUS-EXPORTS

Central Intelligence Agency (CIA), Office of Public Affairs, Washington, DC, 20505, USA, (703) 482-0623, https://www.cia.gov; The World Factbook.

The Economist Group: Economist Intelligence Unit (EIU), 900 3rd Ave., 16th Fl., New York, NY, 10022, USA, (212) 541-0500, americas@eiu.com, https://www.eiu.com; Cyprus Country Report.

International Monetary Fund (IMF), 700 19th St. NW, Washington, DC, 20431, USA, (202) 623-7000, (202) 623-4661, publications@imf.org, https://www.imf.org; Direction of Trade Statistics (DOTS) and International Financial Statistics (IFS).

S&P Global, IHS Markit, 15 Inverness Way E, Englewood, CO, 80112, USA, (800) 447-2273, (800) 854-7179, https://ihsmarkit.com; Global Trade Atlas (GTA).

United Nations Conference on Trade and Development (UNCTAD), Palais des Nations, Geneva, 1211, SWI, (212) 963-6896, unctadinfo@unctad.org, https://unctad.org; Handbook of Statistics 2021.

CYPRUS-FERTILITY, HUMAN

Central Intelligence Agency (CIA), Office of Public Affairs, Washington, DC, 20505, USA, (703) 482-0623, https://www.cia.gov; The World Factbook.

CYPRUS-FERTILIZER INDUSTRY

United Nations Food and Agricultural Organization (FAO), 2121 K St., Ste. 800B, Washington, DC, 20037, USA, (202) 653-2400 (Dial from U.S.), (202) 653-5760 (Fax from U.S.), fao-hq@fao.org, https://www.fao.org; The State of Food and Agriculture (SOFA) 2022.

CYPRUS-FETAL MORTALITY

See CYPRUS-MORTALITY

CYPRUS-FINANCE

Stockholm International Peace Research Institute (SIPRI), Signalistgatan 9, Stockholm, SE 169 72,

SWE, https://www.sipri.org/; SIPRI Arms Transfers Database and SIPRI Military Expenditure Database.

United Nations Statistics Division (UNSD), United Nations Plz., New York, NY, 10017, USA, (800) 253-9646, (212) 963-9851, statistics@un.org, https://unstats.un.org; Statistical Yearbook of the United Nations 2021.

CYPRUS-FINANCE, PUBLIC

Bernan Press, 15250 NBN Way, Bldg. C, Blue Ridge Summit, PA, 17214, USA, (301) 459-2255, (800) 865-3457, (800) 865-3450, customercare@bernan.com, https://rowman.com/Page/Bernan; National Accounts Statistics: Analysis of Main Aggregates 2020.

The Economist Group: Economist Intelligence Unit (EIU), 900 3rd Ave., 16th Fl., New York, NY, 10022, USA, (212) 541-0500, americas@eiu.com, https://www.eiu.com; Cyprus Country Report.

International Monetary Fund (IMF), 700 19th St. NW, Washington, DC, 20431, USA, (202) 623-7000, (202) 623-4661, publications@imf.org, https://www.imf.org; International Financial Statistics (IFS) and Regional Economic Outlook.

Palgrave Macmillan, 1 New York Plaza, Ste. 4500, New York, NY, 10004-1562, USA, (800) 777-4643, orders@palgrave.com, https://www.palgrave.com/us; The Statesman's Yearbook, 2023.

Routledge - Taylor & Francis Group, 6000 Broken Sound Pkwy. NW, Ste. 300, Boca Raton, FL, 33487, USA, (800) 634-1420, (800) 634-7064, orders@taylorandfrancis.com, https://www.routledge.com/; The Europa World Year Book 2022.

United Nations Statistics Division (UNSD), United Nations Plz., New York, NY, 10017, USA, (800) 253-9646, (212) 963-9851, statistics@un.org, https://unstats.un.org; National Accounts Main Aggregates Database and National Accounts Statistics: Main Aggregates and Detailed Tables.

CYPRUS-FISHERIES

Palgrave Macmillan, 1 New York Plaza, Ste. 4500, New York, NY, 10004-1562, USA, (800) 777-4643, orders@palgrave.com, https://www.palgrave.com/us; The Statesman's Yearbook, 2023.

Routledge - Taylor & Francis Group, 6000 Broken Sound Pkwy. NW, Ste. 300, Boca Raton, FL, 33487, USA, (800) 634-1420, (800) 634-7064, orders@taylorandfrancis.com, https://www.routledge.com/; The Europa World Year Book 2022.

United Nations Food and Agricultural Organization (FAO), 2121 K St., Ste. 800B, Washington, DC, 20037, USA, (202) 653-2400 (Dial from U.S.), (202) 653-5760 (Fax from U.S.), fao-hq@fao.org, https://www.fao.org; FAO Yearbook of Fishery and Aquaculture Statistics 2019; Fishery Statistical Collections Global Capture Production; FishStatJ; and The State of Food and Agriculture (SOFA) 2022.

United Nations Statistics Division (UNSD), United Nations Plz., New York, NY, 10017, USA, (800) 253-9646, (212) 963-9851, statistics@un.org, https://unstats.un.org; Statistical Yearbook of the United Nations 2021.

CYPRUS-FOOD

United Nations Food and Agricultural Organization (FAO), 2121 K St., Ste. 800B, Washington, DC, 20037, USA, (202) 653-2400 (Dial from U.S.), (202) 653-5760 (Fax from U.S.), fao-hq@fao.org, https://www.fao.org; The State of Food and Agriculture (SOFA) 2022.

CYPRUS-FOREIGN EXCHANGE RATES

International Monetary Fund (IMF), 700 19th St. NW, Washington, DC, 20431, USA, (202) 623-7000, (202) 623-4661, publications@imf.org, https://www.imf.org; International Financial Statistics (IFS).

CYPRUS-FORESTS AND FORESTRY

Palgrave Macmillan, 1 New York Plaza, Ste. 4500, New York, NY, 10004-1562, USA, (800) 777-4643, orders@palgrave.com, https://www.palgrave.com/us; The Statesman's Yearbook, 2023.

UNESCO Institute for Statistics, C.P 250 Succursale H, Montreal, QC, H3G 2K8, CAN, (514) 343-6880 (Dial from U.S.), (514) 343-5740 (Fax from U.S.), uis.publications@unesco.org, http://uis.unesco.org/; UIS.Stat.

United Nations Food and Agricultural Organization (FAO), 2121 K St., Ste. 800B, Washington, DC, 20037, USA, (202) 653-2400 (Dial from U.S.), (202) 653-5760 (Fax from U.S.), fao-hq@fao.org, https://www.fao.org; FAO Yearbook of Forest Products 2019 and The State of Food and Agriculture (SOFA) 2022.

United Nations Statistics Division (UNSD), United Nations Plz., New York, NY, 10017, USA, (800) 253-9646, (212) 963-9851, statistics@un.org, https://unstats.un.org; Statistical Yearbook of the United Nations 2021.

CYPRUS-FRUIT TRADE

International Monetary Fund (IMF), 700 19th St. NW, Washington, DC, 20431, USA, (202) 623-7000, (202) 623-4661, publications@imf.org, https://www.imf.org; International Financial Statistics (IFS).

CYPRUS-GAS PRODUCTION

See CYPRUS-MINERAL INDUSTRIES

CYPRUS-GOLD INDUSTRY

The World Bank, 1818 H St. NW, Washington, DC, 20433, USA, (202) 473-1000, (202) 477-6391, eds03@worldbank.org, https://www.worldbank.org/; World Development Indicators (WDI) 2022.

CYPRUS-GOLD PRODUCTION

See CYPRUS-MINERAL INDUSTRIES

CYPRUS-GROSS DOMESTIC PRODUCT

The Economist Group: Economist Intelligence Unit (EIU), 900 3rd Ave., 16th Fl., New York, NY, 10022, USA, (212) 541-0500, americas@eiu.com, https://www.eiu.com; Cyprus Country Report.

Routledge - Taylor & Francis Group, 6000 Broken Sound Pkwy. NW, Ste. 300, Boca Raton, FL, 33487, USA, (800) 634-1420, (800) 634-7064, orders@taylorandfrancis.com, https://www.routledge.com/; The Europa World Year Book 2022.

United Nations Statistics Division (UNSD), United Nations Plz., New York, NY, 10017, USA, (800) 253-9646, (212) 963-9851, statistics@un.org, https://unstats.un.org; Statistical Yearbook of the United Nations 2021.

The World Bank, 1818 H St. NW, Washington, DC, 20433, USA, (202) 473-1000, (202) 477-6391, eds03@worldbank.org, https://www.worldbank.org/; World Development Indicators (WDI) 2022.

CYPRUS-GROSS NATIONAL PRODUCT

Palgrave Macmillan, 1 New York Plaza, Ste. 4500, New York, NY, 10004-1562, USA, (800) 777-4643, orders@palgrave.com, https://www.palgrave.com/us; The Statesman's Yearbook, 2023.

United Nations Statistics Division (UNSD), United Nations Plz., New York, NY, 10017, USA, (800) 253-9646, (212) 963-9851, statistics@un.org, https://unstats.un.org; Statistical Yearbook of the United Nations 2021.

The World Bank, 1818 H St. NW, Washington, DC, 20433, USA, (202) 473-1000, (202) 477-6391, eds03@worldbank.org, https://www.worldbank.org/; World Development Indicators (WDI) 2022.

CYPRUS-HAZELNUT PRODUCTION

See CYPRUS-CROPS

CYPRUS-HOUSING

Euromonitor International, Inc., 1 N Dearborn St., Ste. 1700, Chicago, IL, 60602, USA, (312) 922-1115, (312) 922-1157, info-usa@euromonitor.com, https://www.euromonitor.com/; Geographies.

CYPRUS-ILLITERATE PERSONS

UNESCO Institute for Statistics, C.P 250 Succursale H, Montreal, QC, H3G 2K8, CAN, (514) 343-6880 (Dial from U.S.), (514) 343-5740 (Fax from U.S.), uis.publications@unesco.org, http://uis.unesco.org/; UIS.Stat.

CYPRUS-IMPORTS

Central Intelligence Agency (CIA), Office of Public Affairs, Washington, DC, 20505, USA, (703) 482-0623, https://www.cia.gov; The World Factbook.

The Economist Group: Economist Intelligence Unit (EIU), 900 3rd Ave., 16th Fl., New York, NY, 10022, USA, (212) 541-0500, americas@eiu.com, https://www.eiu.com; Cyprus Country Report.

International Monetary Fund (IMF), 700 19th St. NW, Washington, DC, 20431, USA, (202) 623-7000, (202) 623-4661, publications@imf.org, https://www.imf.org; Direction of Trade Statistics (DOTS) and International Financial Statistics (IFS).

S&P Global, IHS Markit, 15 Inverness Way E, Englewood, CO, 80112, USA, (800) 447-2273, (800) 854-7179, https://ihsmarkit.com; Global Trade Atlas (GTA).

United Nations Conference on Trade and Development (UNCTAD), Palais des Nations, Geneva, 1211, SWI, (212) 963-6896, unctadinfo@unctad.org, https://unctad.org; Handbook of Statistics 2021.

CYPRUS-INDUSTRIAL PROPERTY

World Intellectual Property Organization (WIPO), 34, chemin des Colombettes, Geneva, CH-1211, SWI, https://www.wipo.int; Madrid Yearly Review 2022: International Registrations of Marks.

CYPRUS-INDUSTRIES

Central Intelligence Agency (CIA), Office of Public Affairs, Washington, DC, 20505, USA, (703) 482-0623, https://www.cia.gov; The World Factbook.

The Economist Group: Economist Intelligence Unit (EIU), 900 3rd Ave., 16th Fl., New York, NY, 10022, USA, (212) 541-0500, americas@eiu.com, https://www.eiu.com; Cyprus Country Report.

Euromonitor International, Inc., 1 N Dearborn St., Ste. 1700, Chicago, IL, 60602, USA, (312) 922-1115, (312) 922-1157, info-usa@euromonitor.com, https://www.euromonitor.com/; Geographies.

International Labour Organization (ILO), 4 Rte. des Morillons, Geneva, CH-1211, SWI, ilo@ilo.org, https://www.ilo.org; NORMLEX Information System on International Labour Standards.

International Monetary Fund (IMF), 700 19th St. NW, Washington, DC, 20431, USA, (202) 623-7000, (202) 623-4661, publications@imf.org, https://www.imf.org; International Financial Statistics (IFS).

Palgrave Macmillan, 1 New York Plaza, Ste. 4500, New York, NY, 10004-1562, USA, (800) 777-4643, orders@palgrave.com, https://www.palgrave.com/us; The Statesman's Yearbook, 2023.

Routledge - Taylor & Francis Group, 6000 Broken Sound Pkwy. NW, Ste. 300, Boca Raton, FL, 33487, USA, (800) 634-1420, (800) 634-7064, orders@taylorandfrancis.com, https://www.routledge.com/; The Europa World Year Book 2022.

United Nations Industrial Development Organization (UNIDO), 1 United Nations Plz., Rm. DC1-1118, New York, NY, 10017, USA, (212) 963-6890, (212) 963 6885, (212) 963-7904, office.newyork@unido.org, https://www.unido.org/; Industrial Statistics Databases and International Yearbook of Industrial Statistics 2021.

The World Bank, 1818 H St. NW, Washington, DC, 20433, USA, (202) 473-1000, (202) 477-6391, eds03@worldbank.org, https://www.worldbank.org/; World Development Indicators (WDI) 2022.

CYPRUS-INFANT AND MATERNAL MORTALITY

See CYPRUS-MORTALITY

CYPRUS-INTERNATIONAL TRADE

The Economist Group: Economist Intelligence Unit (EIU), 900 3rd Ave., 16th Fl., New York, NY, 10022,

USA, (212) 541-0500, americas@eiu.com, https://www.eiu.com; Cyprus Country Report.

Euromonitor International, Inc., 1 N Dearborn St., Ste. 1700, Chicago, IL, 60602, USA, (312) 922-1115, (312) 922-1157, info-usa@euromonitor.com, https://www.euromonitor.com/; Geographies.

European Commission, Eurostat, Luxembourg, 2920, LUX, https://ec.europa.eu/eurostat/; Extra-EU Trade in Goods.

International Monetary Fund (IMF), 700 19th St. NW, Washington, DC, 20431, USA, (202) 623-7000, (202) 623-4661, publications@imf.org, https://www.imf.org; International Financial Statistics (IFS).

Palgrave Macmillan, 1 New York Plaza, Ste. 4500, New York, NY, 10004-1562, USA, (800) 777-4643, orders@palgrave.com, https://www.palgrave.com/us; The Statesman's Yearbook, 2023.

Routledge - Taylor & Francis Group, 6000 Broken Sound Pkwy. NW, Ste. 300, Boca Raton, FL, 33487, USA, (800) 634-1420, (800) 634-7064, orders@taylorandfrancis.com, https://www.routledge.com/; The Europa World Year Book 2022.

United Nations Conference on Trade and Development (UNCTAD), Palais des Nations, Geneva, 1211, SWI, (212) 963-6896, unctadinfo@unctad.org, https://unctad.org; Trade and Development Report 2021.

United Nations Food and Agricultural Organization (FAO), 2121 K St., Ste. 800B, Washington, DC, 20037, USA, (202) 653-2400 (Dial from U.S.), (202) 653-5760 (Fax from U.S.), fao-hq@fao.org, https://www.fao.org; The State of Food and Agriculture (SOFA) 2022.

United Nations Statistics Division (UNSD), United Nations Plz., New York, NY, 10017, USA, (800) 253-9646, (212) 963-9851, statistics@un.org, https://unstats.un.org; International Trade Statistics Yearbook 2020 and Statistical Yearbook of the United Nations 2021.

The World Bank, 1818 H St. NW, Washington, DC, 20433, USA, (202) 473-1000, (202) 477-6391, eds03@worldbank.org, https://www.worldbank.org/; World Development Indicators (WDI) 2022.

World Trade Organization (WTO), Ctre. William Rappard, Rue de Lausanne 154, Case postale, Geneva, CH-1211, SWI, enquiries@wto.org, https://www.wto.org; World Trade Statistical Review 2022.

CYPRUS-INTERNET USERS

International Telecommunication Union (ITU), Place des Nations, Geneva, CH-1211, SWI, itumail@itu.int, https://www.itu.int; Global Connectivity Report 2022; World Telecommunication/ICT Indicators Database 2021; and Yearbook of Statistics 2019.

CYPRUS-LABOR

Central Intelligence Agency (CIA), Office of Public Affairs, Washington, DC, 20505, USA, (703) 482-0623, https://www.cia.gov; The World Factbook.

Euromonitor International, Inc., 1 N Dearborn St., Ste. 1700, Chicago, IL, 60602, USA, (312) 922-1115, (312) 922-1157, info-usa@euromonitor.com, https://www.euromonitor.com/; Geographies.

International Labour Organization (ILO), 4 Rte. des Morillons, Geneva, CH-1211, SWI, ilo@ilo.org, https://www.ilo.org; NORMLEX Information System on International Labour Standards.

Palgrave Macmillan, 1 New York Plaza, Ste. 4500, New York, NY, 10004-1562, USA, (800) 777-4643, orders@palgrave.com, https://www.palgrave.com/us; The Statesman's Yearbook, 2023.

United Nations Food and Agricultural Organization (FAO), 2121 K St., Ste. 800B, Washington, DC, 20037, USA, (202) 653-2400 (Dial from U.S.), (202) 653-5760 (Fax from U.S.), fao-hq@fao.org, https://www.fao.org; The State of Food and Agriculture (SOFA) 2022.

The World Bank, 1818 H St. NW, Washington, DC, 20433, USA, (202) 473-1000, (202) 477-6391, eds03@worldbank.org, https://www.worldbank.org/; World Development Indicators (WDI) 2022.

CYPRUS-LAND USE

United Nations Statistics Division (UNSD), United Nations Plz., New York, NY, 10017, USA, (800) 253-9646, (212) 963-9851, statistics@un.org, https://unstats.un.org; Millennium Development Goal Indicators.

CYPRUS-LIBRARIES

UNESCO Institute for Statistics, C.P 250 Succursale H, Montreal, QC, H3G 2K8, CAN, (514) 343-6880 (Dial from U.S.), (514) 343-5740 (Fax from U.S.), uis.publications@unesco.org, http://uis.unesco.org/; UIS.Stat.

CYPRUS-LIFE EXPECTANCY

Central Intelligence Agency (CIA), Office of Public Affairs, Washington, DC, 20505, USA, (703) 482-0623, https://www.cia.gov; The World Factbook.

United Nations Department of Economic and Social Affairs (DESA), Population Division, 2 United Nations Plz., Rm. DC2-1950, New York, NY, 10017, USA, (212) 963-3209, (212) 963-2147, population@un.org, https://www.un.org/development/desa/pd/; World Population Ageing 2020 Highlights.

United Nations Statistics Division (UNSD), United Nations Plz., New York, NY, 10017, USA, (800) 253-9646, (212) 963-9851, statistics@un.org, https://unstats.un.org; Millennium Development Goal Indicators.

CYPRUS-LIVESTOCK

Palgrave Macmillan, 1 New York Plaza, Ste. 4500, New York, NY, 10004-1562, USA, (800) 777-4643, orders@palgrave.com, https://www.palgrave.com/us; The Statesman's Yearbook, 2023.

Routledge - Taylor & Francis Group, 6000 Broken Sound Pkwy. NW, Ste. 300, Boca Raton, FL, 33487, USA, (800) 634-1420, (800) 634-7064, orders@taylorandfrancis.com, https://www.routledge.com/; The Europa World Year Book 2022.

United Nations Food and Agricultural Organization (FAO), 2121 K St., Ste. 800B, Washington, DC, 20037, USA, (202) 653-2400 (Dial from U.S.), (202) 653-5760 (Fax from U.S.), fao-hq@fao.org, https://www.fao.org; The State of Food and Agriculture (SOFA) 2022.

United Nations Statistics Division (UNSD), United Nations Plz., New York, NY, 10017, USA, (800) 253-9646, (212) 963-9851, statistics@un.org, https://unstats.un.org; Statistical Yearbook of the United Nations 2021.

CYPRUS-MARRIAGE

United Nations Statistics Division (UNSD), United Nations Plz., New York, NY, 10017, USA, (800) 253-9646, (212) 963-9851, statistics@un.org, https://unstats.un.org; Statistical Yearbook of the United Nations 2021.

CYPRUS-MINERAL INDUSTRIES

European Commission, Eurostat, Luxembourg, 2920, LUX, https://ec.europa.eu/eurostat/; Final Energy Consumption in Transport by Type of Fuel.

International Monetary Fund (IMF), 700 19th St. NW, Washington, DC, 20431, USA, (202) 623-7000, (202) 623-4661, publications@imf.org, https://www.imf.org; International Financial Statistics (IFS).

Palgrave Macmillan, 1 New York Plaza, Ste. 4500, New York, NY, 10004-1562, USA, (800) 777-4643, orders@palgrave.com, https://www.palgrave.com/us; The Statesman's Yearbook, 2023.

Routledge - Taylor & Francis Group, 6000 Broken Sound Pkwy. NW, Ste. 300, Boca Raton, FL, 33487, USA, (800) 634-1420, (800) 634-7064, orders@taylorandfrancis.com, https://www.routledge.com/; The Europa World Year Book 2022.

S&P Global Commodity Insights, One World Trade Center, New York, NY, 10007, USA, (800) 752-8878, support@platts.com, https://www.spglobal.com/commodityinsights/en; Platts Power in Europe.

United Nations Conference on Trade and Development (UNCTAD), Palais des Nations, Geneva, 1211, SWI, (212) 963-6896, unctadinfo@unctad.org, https://unctad.org; Trade and Development Report 2021.

United Nations Statistics Division (UNSD), United Nations Plz., New York, NY, 10017, USA, (800) 253-9646, (212) 963-9851, statistics@un.org, https://unstats.un.org; Statistical Yearbook of the United Nations 2021.

CYPRUS-MONEY SUPPLY

The Economist Group: Economist Intelligence Unit (EIU), 900 3rd Ave., 16th Fl., New York, NY, 10022, USA, (212) 541-0500, americas@eiu.com, https://www.eiu.com; Cyprus Country Report.

International Monetary Fund (IMF), 700 19th St. NW, Washington, DC, 20431, USA, (202) 623-7000, (202) 623-4661, publications@imf.org, https://www.imf.org; International Financial Statistics (IFS).

Routledge - Taylor & Francis Group, 6000 Broken Sound Pkwy. NW, Ste. 300, Boca Raton, FL, 33487, USA, (800) 634-1420, (800) 634-7064, orders@taylorandfrancis.com, https://www.routledge.com/; The Europa World Year Book 2022.

United Nations Statistics Division (UNSD), United Nations Plz., New York, NY, 10017, USA, (800) 253-9646, (212) 963-9851, statistics@un.org, https://unstats.un.org; Statistical Yearbook of the United Nations 2021.

CYPRUS-MONUMENTS AND HISTORIC SITES

UNESCO Institute for Statistics, C.P 250 Succursale H, Montreal, QC, H3G 2K8, CAN, (514) 343-6880 (Dial from U.S.), (514) 343-5740 (Fax from U.S.), uis.publications@unesco.org, http://uis.unesco.org/; UIS.Stat.

CYPRUS-MORTALITY

United Nations Statistics Division (UNSD), United Nations Plz., New York, NY, 10017, USA, (800) 253-9646, (212) 963-9851, statistics@un.org, https://unstats.un.org; Millennium Development Goal Indicators; Statistical Yearbook of the United Nations 2021; and World Statistics Pocketbook 2021.

The World Bank, 1818 H St. NW, Washington, DC, 20433, USA, (202) 473-1000, (202) 477-6391, eds03@worldbank.org, https://www.worldbank.org/; World Development Indicators (WDI) 2022.

World Health Organization (WHO), Ave. Appia 20, Geneva, CH-1211, SWI, (202) 974-3000 (Telephone in U.S.), publications@who.int, https://www.who.int/; Global Health Observatory (GHO).

CYPRUS-MOTION PICTURES

Palgrave Macmillan, 1 New York Plaza, Ste. 4500, New York, NY, 10004-1562, USA, (800) 777-4643, orders@palgrave.com, https://www.palgrave.com/us; The Statesman's Yearbook, 2023.

CYPRUS-MOTOR VEHICLES

International Road Federation (IRF), Madison Place, 500 Montgomery St., 5th Fl., Alexandria, VA, 22314, USA, (703) 535-1001, (703) 535-1007, info@irf.global, https://www.irf.global/; World Road Statistics (WRS).

CYPRUS-NATURAL GAS PRODUCTION

See CYPRUS-MINERAL INDUSTRIES

CYPRUS-NUTRITION

United Nations Food and Agricultural Organization (FAO), 2121 K St., Ste. 800B, Washington, DC, 20037, USA, (202) 653-2400 (Dial from U.S.), (202) 653-5760 (Fax from U.S.), fao-hq@fao.org, https://www.fao.org; The State of Food and Agriculture (SOFA) 2022.

United Nations Statistics Division (UNSD), United Nations Plz., New York, NY, 10017, USA, (800) 253-

9646, (212) 963-9851, statistics@un.org, https://unstats.un.org; Millennium Development Goal Indicators.

CYPRUS-PAPER

See CYPRUS-FORESTS AND FORESTRY

CYPRUS-PEANUT PRODUCTION

See CYPRUS-CROPS

CYPRUS-PESTICIDES

United Nations Food and Agricultural Organization (FAO), 2121 K St., Ste. 800B, Washington, DC, 20037, USA, (202) 653-2400 (Dial from U.S.), (202) 653-5760 (Fax from U.S.), fao-hq@fao.org, https://www.fao.org; The State of Food and Agriculture (SOFA) 2022.

CYPRUS-PETROLEUM INDUSTRY AND TRADE

U.S. Energy Information Administration (EIA), 1000 Independence Ave. SW, Washington, DC, 20585, USA, (202) 586-8800, infoctr@eia.gov, https://www.eia.gov; International Energy Outlook 2021.

United Nations Food and Agricultural Organization (FAO), 2121 K St., Ste. 800B, Washington, DC, 20037, USA, (202) 653-2400 (Dial from U.S.), (202) 653-5760 (Fax from U.S.), fao-hq@fao.org, https://www.fao.org; The State of Food and Agriculture (SOFA) 2022.

United Nations Statistics Division (UNSD), United Nations Plz., New York, NY, 10017, USA, (800) 253-9646, (212) 963-9851, statistics@un.org, https://unstats.un.org; Statistical Yearbook of the United Nations 2021.

CYPRUS-POPULATION

Central Intelligence Agency (CIA), Office of Public Affairs, Washington, DC, 20505, USA, (703) 482-0623, https://www.cia.gov; The World Factbook.

The Economist Group: Economist Intelligence Unit (EIU), 900 3rd Ave., 16th Fl., New York, NY, 10022, USA, (212) 541-0500, americas@eiu.com, https://www.eiu.com; Cyprus Country Report.

Infoplease, c/o Sandbox Networks, Inc., 1 Lincoln St., 24th Fl., Boston, MA, 02111, USA, https://www.infoplease.com; Countries of the World.

International Labour Organization (ILO), 4 Rte. des Morillons, Geneva, CH-1211, SWI, ilo@ilo.org, https://www.ilo.org; NORMLEX Information System on International Labour Standards.

Mediterranean Institute of Gender Studies (MIGS), 46 Makedonitissas Ave., PO Box 24005, Nicosia, 1703, CYP, info@medinstgenderstudies.org, https://medinstgenderstudies.org/; Mind the Gap Report: COALESCE for Support in Cyprus.

Palgrave Macmillan, 1 New York Plaza, Ste. 4500, New York, NY, 10004-1562, USA, (800) 777-4643, orders@palgrave.com, https://www.palgrave.com/us; The Statesman's Yearbook, 2023.

Routledge - Taylor & Francis Group, 6000 Broken Sound Pkwy. NW, Ste. 300, Boca Raton, FL, 33487, USA, (800) 634-1420, (800) 634-7064, orders@taylorandfrancis.com, https://www.routledge.com/; The Europa World Year Book 2022.

UK Data Service, University of Essex, Wivenhoe Park, Colchester, Essex, CO4 3SQ, GBR, https://ukdataservice.ac.uk/; International Aggregate Data.

UNESCO Institute for Statistics, C.P 250 Succursale H, Montreal, QC, H3G 2K8, CAN, (514) 343-6880 (Dial from U.S.), (514) 343-5740 (Fax from U.S.), uis.publications@unesco.org, http://uis.unesco.org/; UIS.Stat.

United Nations Department of Economic and Social Affairs (DESA), Population Division, 2 United Nations Plz., Rm. DC2-1950, New York, NY, 10017, USA, (212) 963-3209, (212) 963-2147, population@un.org, https://www.un.org/development/desa/pd/; Revision of World Urbanization Prospects and World Population Ageing 2020 Highlights.

United Nations Development Programme (UNDP), One United Nations Plz., New York, NY, 10017, USA, (212) 906-5000, (212) 906-5001, https://www.undp.org; Human Development Report 2021-2022.

United Nations Statistics Division (UNSD), United Nations Plz., New York, NY, 10017, USA, (800) 253-9646, (212) 963-9851, statistics@un.org, https://unstats.un.org; Statistical Yearbook of the United Nations 2021 and World Statistics Pocketbook 2021.

The World Bank, 1818 H St. NW, Washington, DC, 20433, USA, (202) 473-1000, (202) 477-6391, eds03@worldbank.org, https://www.worldbank.org/; The Global Findex Database 2021.

World Health Organization (WHO), Ave. Appia 20, Geneva, CH-1211, SWI, (202) 974-3000 (Telephone in U.S.), publications@who.int, https://www.who.int/; Eastern Mediterranean Health Journal.

CYPRUS-POPULATION DENSITY

Central Intelligence Agency (CIA), Office of Public Affairs, Washington, DC, 20505, USA, (703) 482-0623, https://www.cia.gov; The World Factbook.

Palgrave Macmillan, 1 New York Plaza, Ste. 4500, New York, NY, 10004-1562, USA, (800) 777-4643, orders@palgrave.com, https://www.palgrave.com/us; The Statesman's Yearbook, 2023.

Routledge - Taylor & Francis Group, 6000 Broken Sound Pkwy. NW, Ste. 300, Boca Raton, FL, 33487, USA, (800) 634-1420, (800) 634-7064, orders@taylorandfrancis.com, https://www.routledge.com/; The Europa World Year Book 2022.

UNESCO Institute for Statistics, C.P 250 Succursale H, Montreal, QC, H3G 2K8, CAN, (514) 343-6880 (Dial from U.S.), (514) 343-5740 (Fax from U.S.), uis.publications@unesco.org, http://uis.unesco.org/; UIS.Stat.

CYPRUS-POSTAL SERVICE

Palgrave Macmillan, 1 New York Plaza, Ste. 4500, New York, NY, 10004-1562, USA, (800) 777-4643, orders@palgrave.com, https://www.palgrave.com/us; The Statesman's Yearbook, 2023.

CYPRUS-POWER RESOURCES

Euromonitor International, Inc., 1 N Dearborn St., Ste. 1700, Chicago, IL, 60602, USA, (312) 922-1115, (312) 922-1157, info-usa@euromonitor.com, https://www.euromonitor.com/; Geographies.

Palgrave Macmillan, 1 New York Plaza, Ste. 4500, New York, NY, 10004-1562, USA, (800) 777-4643, orders@palgrave.com, https://www.palgrave.com/us; The Statesman's Yearbook, 2023.

S&P Global Commodity Insights, One World Trade Center, New York, NY, 10007, USA, (800) 752-8878, support@platts.com, https://www.spglobal.com/commodityinsights/en; Platts European Power Daily.

U.S. Energy Information Administration (EIA), 1000 Independence Ave. SW, Washington, DC, 20585, USA, (202) 586-8800, infoctr@eia.gov, https://www.eia.gov; International Energy Outlook 2021.

United Nations Food and Agricultural Organization (FAO), 2121 K St., Ste. 800B, Washington, DC, 20037, USA, (202) 653-2400 (Dial from U.S.), (202) 653-5760 (Fax from U.S.), fao-hq@fao.org, https://www.fao.org; The State of Food and Agriculture (SOFA) 2022.

United Nations Statistics Division (UNSD), United Nations Plz., New York, NY, 10017, USA, (800) 253-9646, (212) 963-9851, statistics@un.org, https://unstats.un.org; Energy Statistics Yearbook 2019; Statistical Yearbook of the United Nations 2021; and World Statistics Pocketbook 2021.

CYPRUS-PRICES

Euromonitor International, Inc., 1 N Dearborn St., Ste. 1700, Chicago, IL, 60602, USA, (312) 922-1115, (312) 922-1157, info-usa@euromonitor.com, https://www.euromonitor.com/; Geographies.

International Monetary Fund (IMF), 700 19th St. NW, Washington, DC, 20431, USA, (202) 623-7000, (202) 623-4661, publications@imf.org, https://www.imf.org; International Financial Statistics (IFS).

CYPRUS-PUBLIC HEALTH

Euromonitor International, Inc., 1 N Dearborn St., Ste. 1700, Chicago, IL, 60602, USA, (312) 922-1115, (312) 922-1157, info-usa@euromonitor.com, https://www.euromonitor.com/; Geographies.

European Commission, Directorate-General for Health and Food Safety, Brussels, B-1049, BEL, https://ec.europa.eu/info/departments/health-and-food-safety_en ; zzunpublished data.

U.S. Census Bureau, 4600 Silver Hill Rd., Washington, DC, 20233, USA, (301) 763-4636, (800) 923-8282, https://www.census.gov; HIV/AIDS Surveillance Data Base.

United Nations Department of Economic and Social Affairs (DESA), Population Division, 2 United Nations Plz., Rm. DC2-1950, New York, NY, 10017, USA, (212) 963-3209, (212) 963-2147, population@un.org, https://www.un.org/development/desa/pd/; World Fertility Data 2019.

United Nations Development Programme (UNDP), One United Nations Plz., New York, NY, 10017, USA, (212) 906-5000, (212) 906-5001, https://www.undp.org; Human Development Report 2021-2022.

United Nations Statistics Division (UNSD), United Nations Plz., New York, NY, 10017, USA, (800) 253-9646, (212) 963-9851, statistics@un.org, https://unstats.un.org; Millennium Development Goal Indicators and Statistical Yearbook of the United Nations 2021.

World Health Organization (WHO), Ave. Appia 20, Geneva, CH-1211, SWI, (202) 974-3000 (Telephone in U.S.), publications@who.int, https://www.who.int/; Eastern Mediterranean Health Journal; Global Health Observatory (GHO); and Health Statistics and Information Systems.

CYPRUS-PUBLISHERS AND PUBLISHING

UNESCO Institute for Statistics, C.P 250 Succursale H, Montreal, QC, H3G 2K8, CAN, (514) 343-6880 (Dial from U.S.), (514) 343-5740 (Fax from U.S.), uis.publications@unesco.org, http://uis.unesco.org/; UIS.Stat.

CYPRUS-RELIGION

Central Intelligence Agency (CIA), Office of Public Affairs, Washington, DC, 20505, USA, (703) 482-0623, https://www.cia.gov; The World Factbook.

Palgrave Macmillan, 1 New York Plaza, Ste. 4500, New York, NY, 10004-1562, USA, (800) 777-4643, orders@palgrave.com, https://www.palgrave.com/us; The Statesman's Yearbook, 2023.

CYPRUS-RETAIL TRADE

Euromonitor International, Inc., 1 N Dearborn St., Ste. 1700, Chicago, IL, 60602, USA, (312) 922-1115, (312) 922-1157, info-usa@euromonitor.com, https://www.euromonitor.com/; Geographies.

United Nations Statistics Division (UNSD), United Nations Plz., New York, NY, 10017, USA, (800) 253-9646, (212) 963-9851, statistics@un.org, https://unstats.un.org; Statistical Yearbook of the United Nations 2021.

CYPRUS-RICE PRODUCTION

See CYPRUS-CROPS

CYPRUS-ROADS

International Road Federation (IRF), Madison Place, 500 Montgomery St., 5th Fl., Alexandria, VA, 22314, USA, (703) 535-1001, (703) 535-1007, info@irf.global, https://www.irf.global/; World Road Statistics (WRS).

CYPRUS-RUBBER INDUSTRY AND TRADE

International Rubber Study Group (IRSG), 51 Changi Business Park Central 2, Unit No. 6, 486066, SGP, https://www.rubberstudy.org; Monthly Rubber

Bulletin (MRB); Rubber Industry Report; Rubber Statistical Bulletin; and World Rubber Industry Report (WRIO).

CYPRUS-SHIPPING

Routledge - Taylor & Francis Group, 6000 Broken Sound Pkwy. NW, Ste. 300, Boca Raton, FL, 33487, USA, (800) 634-1420, (800) 634-7064, orders@taylorandfrancis.com, https://www.routledge.com/; The Europa World Year Book 2022.

S&P Global, IHS Markit, 15 Inverness Way E, Englewood, CO, 80112, USA, (800) 447-2273, (800) 854-7179, https://ihsmarkit.com; IHS Maritime World Shipbuilding Statistics; Journal of Commerce; Lloyd's Register of Ships 2021-2022; and Maritime Portal Desktop.

United Nations Statistics Division (UNSD), United Nations Plz., New York, NY, 10017, USA, (800) 253-9646, (212) 963-9851, statistics@un.org, https://unstats.un.org; Statistical Yearbook of the United Nations 2021.

CYPRUS-STEEL PRODUCTION

See CYPRUS-MINERAL INDUSTRIES

CYPRUS-SUGAR PRODUCTION

See CYPRUS-CROPS

CYPRUS-TAXATION

European Commission, Eurostat, Luxembourg, 2920, LUX, https://ec.europa.eu/eurostat/; Taxation Trends in the European Union.

The World Bank, 1818 H St. NW, Washington, DC, 20433, USA, (202) 473-1000, (202) 477-6391, eds03@worldbank.org, https://www.worldbank.org/; World Development Indicators (WDI) 2022.

CYPRUS-TELEPHONE

Palgrave Macmillan, 1 New York Plaza, Ste. 4500, New York, NY, 10004-1562, USA, (800) 777-4643, orders@palgrave.com, https://www.palgrave.com/us; The Statesman's Yearbook, 2023.

United Nations Statistics Division (UNSD), United Nations Plz., New York, NY, 10017, USA, (800) 253-9646, (212) 963-9851, statistics@un.org, https://unstats.un.org; World Statistics Pocketbook 2021.

CYPRUS-TEXTILE INDUSTRY

Palgrave Macmillan, 1 New York Plaza, Ste. 4500, New York, NY, 10004-1562, USA, (800) 777-4643, orders@palgrave.com, https://www.palgrave.com/us; The Statesman's Yearbook, 2023.

CYPRUS-THEATER

UNESCO Institute for Statistics, C.P 250 Succursale H, Montreal, QC, H3G 2K8, CAN, (514) 343-6880 (Dial from U.S.), (514) 343-5740 (Fax from U.S.), uis.publications@unesco.org, http://uis.unesco.org/; UIS.Stat.

CYPRUS-TOBACCO INDUSTRY

United Nations Statistics Division (UNSD), United Nations Plz., New York, NY, 10017, USA, (800) 253-9646, (212) 963-9851, statistics@un.org, https://unstats.un.org; Statistical Yearbook of the United Nations 2021.

CYPRUS-TOURISM

Euromonitor International, Inc., 1 N Dearborn St., Ste. 1700, Chicago, IL, 60602, USA, (312) 922-1115, (312) 922-1157, info-usa@euromonitor.com, https://www.euromonitor.com/; Geographies.

European Commission, Rue de la Loi, 170, Brussels, B-1040, BEL, https://ec.europa.eu; Common Agricultural Policy (CAPF) Context Indicators, 2019 Update.

International Road Federation (IRF), Madison Place, 500 Montgomery St., 5th Fl., Alexandria, VA, 22314, USA, (703) 535-1001, (703) 535-1007, info@irf.global, https://www.irf.global/; World Road Statistics (WRS).

Palgrave Macmillan, 1 New York Plaza, Ste. 4500, New York, NY, 10004-1562, USA, (800) 777-4643, orders@palgrave.com, https://www.palgrave.com/us; The Statesman's Yearbook, 2023.

Routledge - Taylor & Francis Group, 6000 Broken Sound Pkwy. NW, Ste. 300, Boca Raton, FL, 33487, USA, (800) 634-1420, (800) 634-7064, orders@taylorandfrancis.com, https://www.routledge.com/; The Europa World Year Book 2022.

United Nations Statistics Division (UNSD), United Nations Plz., New York, NY, 10017, USA, (800) 253-9646, (212) 963-9851, statistics@un.org, https://unstats.un.org; Statistical Yearbook of the United Nations 2021.

United Nations World Tourism Organization (UNWTO), Calle Poeta Joan Maragall 42, Madrid, 28020, SPA, info@unwto.org, https://www.unwto.org/; Yearbook of Tourism Statistics, 2021 Edition.

CYPRUS-TRADE

See CYPRUS-INTERNATIONAL TRADE

CYPRUS-TRANSPORTATION

Central Intelligence Agency (CIA), Office of Public Affairs, Washington, DC, 20505, USA, (703) 482-0623, https://www.cia.gov; The World Factbook.

Euromonitor International, Inc., 1 N Dearborn St., Ste. 1700, Chicago, IL, 60602, USA, (312) 922-1115, (312) 922-1157, info-usa@euromonitor.com, https://www.euromonitor.com/; Geographies.

European Commission, Eurostat, Luxembourg, 2920, LUX, https://ec.europa.eu/eurostat/; Air Transport Statistics.

Palgrave Macmillan, 1 New York Plaza, Ste. 4500, New York, NY, 10004-1562, USA, (800) 777-4643, orders@palgrave.com, https://www.palgrave.com/us; The Statesman's Yearbook, 2023.

Routledge - Taylor & Francis Group, 6000 Broken Sound Pkwy. NW, Ste. 300, Boca Raton, FL, 33487, USA, (800) 634-1420, (800) 634-7064, orders@taylorandfrancis.com, https://www.routledge.com/; The Europa World Year Book 2022.

CYPRUS-UNEMPLOYMENT

International Labour Organization (ILO), 4 Rte. des Morillons, Geneva, CH-1211, SWI, ilo@ilo.org, https://www.ilo.org; NORMLEX Information System on International Labour Standards.

Palgrave Macmillan, 1 New York Plaza, Ste. 4500, New York, NY, 10004-1562, USA, (800) 777-4643, orders@palgrave.com, https://www.palgrave.com/us; The Statesman's Yearbook, 2023.

United Nations Statistics Division (UNSD), United Nations Plz., New York, NY, 10017, USA, (800) 253-9646, (212) 963-9851, statistics@un.org, https://unstats.un.org; Statistical Yearbook of the United Nations 2021.

CYPRUS-VITAL STATISTICS

Palgrave Macmillan, 1 New York Plaza, Ste. 4500, New York, NY, 10004-1562, USA, (800) 777-4643, orders@palgrave.com, https://www.palgrave.com/us; The Statesman's Yearbook, 2023.

U.S. Census Bureau, 4600 Silver Hill Rd., Washington, DC, 20233, USA, (301) 763-4636, (800) 923-8282, https://www.census.gov; HIV/AIDS Surveillance Data Base.

United Nations Department of Economic and Social Affairs (DESA), Population Division, 2 United Nations Plz., Rm. DC2-1950, New York, NY, 10017, USA, (212) 963-3209, (212) 963-2147, population@un.org, https://www.un.org/development/desa/pd/; World Contraceptive Use 2021: Estimates and Projections of Family Planning Indicators and World Marriage Data 2019.

United Nations Economic and Social Commission for Western Asia (ESCWA), Riad el-Solh Sq., PO Box 11-8575, Beirut, LBN, escwa-ciu@un.org, https://www.unescwa.org; ESCWA Annual Report 2019; ESCWA Data Portal for the Arab Region; and Survey of Economic and Social Developments in the Arab Region 2020-2021.

United Nations Statistics Division (UNSD), United Nations Plz., New York, NY, 10017, USA, (800) 253-9646, (212) 963-9851, statistics@un.org, https://unstats.un.org; Statistical Yearbook of the United Nations 2021.

CYPRUS-WAGES

International Labour Organization (ILO), 4 Rte. des Morillons, Geneva, CH-1211, SWI, ilo@ilo.org, https://www.ilo.org; NORMLEX Information System on International Labour Standards.

United Nations Statistics Division (UNSD), United Nations Plz., New York, NY, 10017, USA, (800) 253-9646, (212) 963-9851, statistics@un.org, https://unstats.un.org; Statistical Yearbook of the United Nations 2021.

CYPRUS-WHEAT PRODUCTION

See CYPRUS-CROPS

CYPRUS-WHOLESALE PRICE INDEXES

International Monetary Fund (IMF), 700 19th St. NW, Washington, DC, 20431, USA, (202) 623-7000, (202) 623-4661, publications@imf.org, https://www.imf.org; International Financial Statistics (IFS).

CYPRUS-WHOLESALE TRADE

United Nations Statistics Division (UNSD), United Nations Plz., New York, NY, 10017, USA, (800) 253-9646, (212) 963-9851, statistics@un.org, https://unstats.un.org; Statistical Yearbook of the United Nations 2021.

CYPRUS-WOOL PRODUCTION

See CYPRUS-TEXTILE INDUSTRY

CZECH REPUBLIC-NATIONAL STATISTICAL OFFICE

Czech Statistical Office, Na padesatem 3268/81, Praha 10, Strasnice, 100 82, CZE, infoservis@czso.cz, https://www.czso.cz; National Data Reports (Czech Republic).

CZECH REPUBLIC-PRIMARY STATISTICS SOURCES

Czech Statistical Office, Na padesatem 3268/81, Praha 10, Strasnice, 100 82, CZE, infoservis@czso.cz, https://www.czso.cz; Statistical Yearbook of the Czech Republic, 2021 and Statistika: Statistics and Economy Journal.

European Commission, Eurostat, Luxembourg, 2920, LUX, https://ec.europa.eu/eurostat/; Key Figures on Enlargement Countries, 2019.

CZECH REPUBLIC-AGRICULTURE

Czech Statistical Office, Na padesatem 3268/81, Praha 10, Strasnice, 100 82, CZE, infoservis@czso.cz, https://www.czso.cz; Agricultural Producer Price Indices.

The Economist Group: Economist Intelligence Unit (EIU), 900 3rd Ave., 16th Fl., New York, NY, 10022, USA, (212) 541-0500, americas@eiu.com, https://www.eiu.com; Czech Republic Country Report.

Euromonitor International, Inc., 1 N Dearborn St., Ste. 1700, Chicago, IL, 60602, USA, (312) 922-1115, (312) 922-1157, info-usa@euromonitor.com, https://www.euromonitor.com/; Geographies.

European Commission, Rue de la Loi, 170, Brussels, B-1040, BEL, https://ec.europa.eu; Common Agricultural Policy (CAPF) Context Indicators, 2019 Update.

European Commission, Eurostat, Luxembourg, 2920, LUX, https://ec.europa.eu/eurostat/; Farmers and the Agricultural Labour Force - Statistics.

Organization for Economic Cooperation and Development (OECD), 2001 L St. NW, Ste. 650, Washington, DC, 20036-4922, USA, (202) 785-6323, (800) 456-6323, (202) 785-0350, washington.contact@oecd.org, https://www.oecd.org/; Economic Survey of Czech Republic 2023.

Palgrave Macmillan, 1 New York Plaza, Ste. 4500, New York, NY, 10004-1562, USA, (800) 777-4643, orders@palgrave.com, https://www.palgrave.com/us; The Statesman's Yearbook, 2023.

Routledge - Taylor & Francis Group, 6000 Broken Sound Pkwy. NW, Ste. 300, Boca Raton, FL, 33487, USA, (800) 634-1420, (800) 634-7064, orders@taylorandfrancis.com, https://www.routledge.com/; The Europa World Year Book 2022.

United Nations Food and Agricultural Organization (FAO), 2121 K St., Ste. 800B, Washington, DC, 20037, USA, (202) 653-2400 (Dial from U.S.), (202) 653-5760 (Fax from U.S.), fao-hq@fao.org, https://www.fao.org; AQUASTAT and The State of Food and Agriculture (SOFA) 2022.

United Nations Statistics Division (UNSD), United Nations Plz., New York, NY, 10017, USA, (800) 253-9646, (212) 963-9851, statistics@un.org, https://unstats.un.org; Statistical Yearbook of the United Nations 2021.

CZECH REPUBLIC-AIRLINES

European Commission, Eurostat, Luxembourg, 2920, LUX, https://ec.europa.eu/eurostat/; Air Transport Statistics.

International Civil Aviation Organization (ICAO), 999 Robert-Bourassa Blvd., Montreal, QC, H3C 5H7, CAN, (514) 954-8219 (Dial from U.S.), (514) 954-6077 (Fax from U.S.), icaohq@icao.int, https://www.icao.int; ICAO Regional Reports.

Palgrave Macmillan, 1 New York Plaza, Ste. 4500, New York, NY, 10004-1562, USA, (800) 777-4643, orders@palgrave.com, https://www.palgrave.com/us; The Statesman's Yearbook, 2023.

Routledge - Taylor & Francis Group, 6000 Broken Sound Pkwy. NW, Ste. 300, Boca Raton, FL, 33487, USA, (800) 634-1420, (800) 634-7064, orders@taylorandfrancis.com, https://www.routledge.com/; The Europa World Year Book 2022.

CZECH REPUBLIC-ALUMINUM PRODUCTION

See CZECH REPUBLIC-MINERAL INDUSTRIES

CZECH REPUBLIC-ARMED FORCES

Central Intelligence Agency (CIA), Office of Public Affairs, Washington, DC, 20505, USA, (703) 482-0623, https://www.cia.gov; The World Factbook.

International Institute for Strategic Studies (IISS) - Americas, 2121 K St. NW, Ste. 600, Washington, DC, 20037, USA, (202) 659-1490, (202) 659-1499, https://www.iiss.org/; The Military Balance 2022.

Palgrave Macmillan, 1 New York Plaza, Ste. 4500, New York, NY, 10004-1562, USA, (800) 777-4643, orders@palgrave.com, https://www.palgrave.com/us; The Statesman's Yearbook, 2023.

Stockholm International Peace Research Institute (SIPRI), Signalistgatan 9, Stockholm, SE 169 72, SWE, https://www.sipri.org/; SIPRI Arms Transfers Database and SIPRI Military Expenditure Database.

CZECH REPUBLIC-BALANCE OF PAYMENTS

Organization for Economic Cooperation and Development (OECD), 2001 L St. NW, Ste. 650, Washington, DC, 20036-4922, USA, (202) 785-6323, (800) 456-6323, (202) 785-0350, washington.contact@oecd.org, https://www.oecd.org/; Economic Survey of Czech Republic 2023.

Routledge - Taylor & Francis Group, 6000 Broken Sound Pkwy. NW, Ste. 300, Boca Raton, FL, 33487, USA, (800) 634-1420, (800) 634-7064, orders@taylorandfrancis.com, https://www.routledge.com/; The Europa World Year Book 2022.

United Nations Conference on Trade and Development (UNCTAD), Palais des Nations, Geneva, 1211, SWI, (212) 963-6896, unctadinfo@unctad.org, https://unctad.org; Handbook of Statistics 2021.

The World Bank, 1818 H St. NW, Washington, DC, 20433, USA, (202) 473-1000, (202) 477-6391, eds03@worldbank.org, https://www.worldbank.org/; World Development Report 2022: Finance for an Equitable Recovery.

CZECH REPUBLIC-BANKS AND BANKING

Euromonitor International, Inc., 1 N Dearborn St., Ste. 1700, Chicago, IL, 60602, USA, (312) 922-1115, (312) 922-1157, info-usa@euromonitor.com, https://www.euromonitor.com/; Geographies.

Organization for Economic Cooperation and Development (OECD), 2001 L St. NW, Ste. 650, Washington, DC, 20036-4922, USA, (202) 785-6323, (800) 456-6323, (202) 785-0350, washington.contact@oecd.org, https://www.oecd.org/; Economic Survey of Czech Republic 2023.

Routledge - Taylor & Francis Group, 6000 Broken Sound Pkwy. NW, Ste. 300, Boca Raton, FL, 33487, USA, (800) 634-1420, (800) 634-7064, orders@taylorandfrancis.com, https://www.routledge.com/; The Europa World Year Book 2022.

CZECH REPUBLIC-BARLEY PRODUCTION

See CZECH REPUBLIC-CROPS

CZECH REPUBLIC-BROADCASTING

Central Intelligence Agency (CIA), Office of Public Affairs, Washington, DC, 20505, USA, (703) 482-0623, https://www.cia.gov; The World Factbook.

Euromonitor International, Inc., 1 N Dearborn St., Ste. 1700, Chicago, IL, 60602, USA, (312) 922-1115, (312) 922-1157, info-usa@euromonitor.com, https://www.euromonitor.com/; Geographies.

Palgrave Macmillan, 1 New York Plaza, Ste. 4500, New York, NY, 10004-1562, USA, (800) 777-4643, orders@palgrave.com, https://www.palgrave.com/us; The Statesman's Yearbook, 2023.

WRTH Publications Limited, PO Box 290, Oxford, OX2 7FT, GBR, sales@wrth.com, https://www.wrth.com; World Radio TV Handbook 2023.

CZECH REPUBLIC-BUDGET

Central Intelligence Agency (CIA), Office of Public Affairs, Washington, DC, 20505, USA, (703) 482-0623, https://www.cia.gov; The World Factbook.

European Commission, Eurostat, Luxembourg, 2920, LUX, https://ec.europa.eu/eurostat/; Share of Government Budget Appropriations or Outlays on Research and Development.

CZECH REPUBLIC-BUSINESS

Czech Statistical Office, Na padesatem 3268/81, Praha 10, Strasnice, 100 82, CZE, infoservis@czso.cz, https://www.czso.cz; Labour Costs in Czech Republic, 2020.

United Nations Statistics Division (UNSD), United Nations Plz., New York, NY, 10017, USA, (800) 253-9646, (212) 963-9851, statistics@un.org, https://unstats.un.org; Statistical Yearbook of the United Nations 2021.

CZECH REPUBLIC-CHILDBIRTH-STATISTICS

World Health Organization (WHO), Ave. Appia 20, Geneva, CH-1211, SWI, (202) 974-3000 (Telephone in U.S.), publications@who.int, https://www.who.int/; Health Statistics and Information Systems.

CZECH REPUBLIC-CLIMATE

Palgrave Macmillan, 1 New York Plaza, Ste. 4500, New York, NY, 10004-1562, USA, (800) 777-4643, orders@palgrave.com, https://www.palgrave.com/us; The Statesman's Yearbook, 2023.

CZECH REPUBLIC-COAL PRODUCTION

See CZECH REPUBLIC-MINERAL INDUSTRIES

CZECH REPUBLIC-COFFEE

See CZECH REPUBLIC-CROPS

CZECH REPUBLIC-COMMERCE

Palgrave Macmillan, 1 New York Plaza, Ste. 4500, New York, NY, 10004-1562, USA, (800) 777-4643, orders@palgrave.com, https://www.palgrave.com/us; The Statesman's Yearbook, 2023.

UK Data Service, University of Essex, Wivenhoe Park, Colchester, Essex, CO4 3SQ, GBR, https://ukdataservice.ac.uk/; International Aggregate Data.

CZECH REPUBLIC-COMMODITY EXCHANGES

Barchart, 209 W Jackson Blvd., 2nd Fl., Chicago, IL, 60606, USA, (877) 247-4394, commodities@barchart.com, https://www.barchart.com/cmdty; The cmdty Yearbook 2023; cmdtyStats: Commodity Statistics and Fundamental Data; cmdtyView: Commodity Index; and Commodity Data and Prices.

International Monetary Fund (IMF), 700 19th St. NW, Washington, DC, 20431, USA, (202) 623-7000, (202) 623-4661, publications@imf.org, https://www.imf.org; IMF Primary Commodity Prices.

CZECH REPUBLIC-CONSTRUCTION INDUSTRY

Organization for Economic Cooperation and Development (OECD), 2001 L St. NW, Ste. 650, Washington, DC, 20036-4922, USA, (202) 785-6323, (800) 456-6323, (202) 785-0350, washington.contact@oecd.org, https://www.oecd.org/; Economic Survey of Czech Republic 2023.

United Nations Statistics Division (UNSD), United Nations Plz., New York, NY, 10017, USA, (800) 253-9646, (212) 963-9851, statistics@un.org, https://unstats.un.org; Statistical Yearbook of the United Nations 2021.

CZECH REPUBLIC-CONSUMER PRICE INDEXES

Routledge - Taylor & Francis Group, 6000 Broken Sound Pkwy. NW, Ste. 300, Boca Raton, FL, 33487, USA, (800) 634-1420, (800) 634-7064, orders@taylorandfrancis.com, https://www.routledge.com/; The Europa World Year Book 2022.

CZECH REPUBLIC-COPPER INDUSTRY AND TRADE

See CZECH REPUBLIC-MINERAL INDUSTRIES

CZECH REPUBLIC-CORN INDUSTRY

See CZECH REPUBLIC-CROPS

CZECH REPUBLIC-COTTON

See CZECH REPUBLIC-CROPS

CZECH REPUBLIC-CRIME

European Commission, Eurostat, Luxembourg, 2920, LUX, https://ec.europa.eu/eurostat/; Crime and Criminal Justice Database and Crime Statistics.

CZECH REPUBLIC-CROPS

Palgrave Macmillan, 1 New York Plaza, Ste. 4500, New York, NY, 10004-1562, USA, (800) 777-4643, orders@palgrave.com, https://www.palgrave.com/us; The Statesman's Yearbook, 2023.

United Nations Food and Agricultural Organization (FAO), 2121 K St., Ste. 800B, Washington, DC, 20037, USA, (202) 653-2400 (Dial from U.S.), (202) 653-5760 (Fax from U.S.), fao-hq@fao.org, https://www.fao.org; The State of Food and Agriculture (SOFA) 2022.

United Nations Statistics Division (UNSD), United Nations Plz., New York, NY, 10017, USA, (800) 253-9646, (212) 963-9851, statistics@un.org, https://unstats.un.org; Statistical Yearbook of the United Nations 2021.

CZECH REPUBLIC-DAIRY PROCESSING

Palgrave Macmillan, 1 New York Plaza, Ste. 4500, New York, NY, 10004-1562, USA, (800) 777-4643, orders@palgrave.com, https://www.palgrave.com/us; The Statesman's Yearbook, 2023.

United Nations Food and Agricultural Organization (FAO), 2121 K St., Ste. 800B, Washington, DC, 20037, USA, (202) 653-2400 (Dial from U.S.), (202) 653-5760 (Fax from U.S.), fao-hq@fao.org, https://www.fao.org; The State of Food and Agriculture (SOFA) 2022.

CZECH REPUBLIC-DEBTS, EXTERNAL

The World Bank, 1818 H St. NW, Washington, DC, 20433, USA, (202) 473-1000, (202) 477-6391, eds03@worldbank.org, https://www.worldbank.org/; Global Financial Development Report 2019-2020: Bank Regulation and Supervision a Decade after the Global Financial Crisis and World Development Report 2022: Finance for an Equitable Recovery.

CZECH REPUBLIC-DEFENSE EXPENDITURES

See CZECH REPUBLIC-ARMED FORCES

CZECH REPUBLIC-DIAMONDS

See CZECH REPUBLIC-MINERAL INDUSTRIES

CZECH REPUBLIC-DISPOSABLE INCOME

Czech Statistical Office, Na padesatem 3268/81, Praha 10, Strasnice, 100 82, CZE, infoservis@czso.cz, https://www.czso.cz; Household Income and Living Conditions in the Czech Republic, 2021.

CZECH REPUBLIC-ECONOMIC ASSISTANCE

United Nations Statistics Division (UNSD), United Nations Plz., New York, NY, 10017, USA, (800) 253-9646, (212) 963-9851, statistics@un.org, https://unstats.un.org; Statistical Yearbook of the United Nations 2021.

CZECH REPUBLIC-ECONOMIC CONDITIONS

Banque de France, 31 rue Croix des Petits-Champs, Paris, 75049, FRA, infos@banque-france.fr, https://www.banque-france.fr/en; Webstat: Access to Statistical Series of Banque de France.

Bernan Press, 15250 NBN Way, Bldg. C, Blue Ridge Summit, PA, 17214, USA, (301) 459-2255, (800) 865-3457, (800) 865-3450, customercare@bernan.com, https://rowman.com/Page/Bernan; World Economic Outlook, April 2022.

Central Intelligence Agency (CIA), Office of Public Affairs, Washington, DC, 20505, USA, (703) 482-0623, https://www.cia.gov; The World Factbook.

Czech Statistical Office, Na padesatem 3268/81, Praha 10, Strasnice, 100 82, CZE, infoservis@czso.cz, https://www.czso.cz; Czechia in Figures, 2021.

The Economist Group: Economist Intelligence Unit (EIU), 900 3rd Ave., 16th Fl., New York, NY, 10022, USA, (212) 541-0500, americas@eiu.com, https://www.eiu.com; Czech Republic Country Report.

Euromonitor International, Inc., 1 N Dearborn St., Ste. 1700, Chicago, IL, 60602, USA, (312) 922-1115, (312) 922-1157, info-usa@euromonitor.com, https://www.euromonitor.com/; Geographies and Market Research on the Consumer Finance Industry.

European Commission, Rue de la Loi, 170, Brussels, B-1040, BEL, https://ec.europa.eu; Common Agricultural Policy (CAPF) Context Indicators, 2019 Update.

International Monetary Fund (IMF), 700 19th St. NW, Washington, DC, 20431, USA, (202) 623-7000, (202) 623-4661, publications@imf.org, https://www.imf.org; IMF Data and World Economic Outlook.

Organization for Economic Cooperation and Development (OECD), 2001 L St. NW, Ste. 650, Washington, DC, 20036-4922, USA, (202) 785-6323, (800) 456-6323, (202) 785-0350, washington.contact@oecd.org, https://www.oecd.org/; Economic Survey of Czech Republic 2023; OECD Composite Leading Indicator (CLI); and OECD Labour Force Statistics 2022.

Palgrave Macmillan, 1 New York Plaza, Ste. 4500, New York, NY, 10004-1562, USA, (800) 777-4643, orders@palgrave.com, https://www.palgrave.com/us; The Statesman's Yearbook, 2023.

Routledge - Taylor & Francis Group, 6000 Broken Sound Pkwy. NW, Ste. 300, Boca Raton, FL, 33487, USA, (800) 634-1420, (800) 634-7064, orders@taylorandfrancis.com, https://www.routledge.com/; The Europa World Year Book 2022.

United Nations Economic Commission for Europe (UNECE), Palais des Nations, Geneva, CH-1211, SWI, unece_info@un.org, https://unece.org/; UNECE Countries in Figures 2019.

United Nations Statistics Division (UNSD), United Nations Plz., New York, NY, 10017, USA, (800) 253-9646, (212) 963-9851, statistics@un.org, https://unstats.un.org; World Statistics Pocketbook 2021.

The World Bank, 1818 H St. NW, Washington, DC, 20433, USA, (202) 473-1000, (202) 477-6391, eds03@worldbank.org, https://www.worldbank.org/; Global Economic Monitor (GEM); Global Economic Prospects, June 2022; The Global Findex Database 2021; and World Development Report 2022: Finance for an Equitable Recovery.

CZECH REPUBLIC-EDUCATION

Euromonitor International, Inc., 1 N Dearborn St., Ste. 1700, Chicago, IL, 60602, USA, (312) 922-1115, (312) 922-1157, info-usa@euromonitor.com, https://www.euromonitor.com/; Geographies.

European Commission, Rue de la Loi, 170, Brussels, B-1040, BEL, https://ec.europa.eu; Common Agricultural Policy (CAPF) Context Indicators, 2019 Update.

Infoplease, c/o Sandbox Networks, Inc., 1 Lincoln St., 24th Fl., Boston, MA, 02111, USA, https://www.infoplease.com; Countries of the World.

Routledge - Taylor & Francis Group, 6000 Broken Sound Pkwy. NW, Ste. 300, Boca Raton, FL, 33487, USA, (800) 634-1420, (800) 634-7064, orders@taylorandfrancis.com, https://www.routledge.com/; The Europa World Year Book 2022.

UNESCO Institute for Statistics, C.P 250 Succursale H, Montreal, QC, H3G 2K8, CAN, (514) 343-6880 (Dial from U.S.), (514) 343-5740 (Fax from U.S.), uis.publications@unesco.org, http://uis.unesco.org/; Literacy and UIS.Stat.

United Nations Statistics Division (UNSD), United Nations Plz., New York, NY, 10017, USA, (800) 253-9646, (212) 963-9851, statistics@un.org, https://unstats.un.org; Millennium Development Goal Indicators.

The World Bank, 1818 H St. NW, Washington, DC, 20433, USA, (202) 473-1000, (202) 477-6391, eds03@worldbank.org, https://www.worldbank.org/; World Development Report 2022: Finance for an Equitable Recovery.

CZECH REPUBLIC-ELECTRICITY

European Commission, Eurostat, Luxembourg, 2920, LUX, https://ec.europa.eu/eurostat/; Final Energy Consumption in Transport by Type of Fuel.

International Energy Agency (IEA), 9 Rue de la Federation, Paris, 75739, FRA, info@iea.org, https://www.iea.org/; World Energy Outlook 2021.

S&P Global Commodity Insights, One World Trade Center, New York, NY, 10007, USA, (800) 752-8878, support@platts.com, https://www.spglobal.com/commodityinsights/en; Platts European Power Alert and Platts Power in Europe.

U.S. Energy Information Administration (EIA), 1000 Independence Ave. SW, Washington, DC, 20585, USA, (202) 586-8800, infoctr@eia.gov, https://www.eia.gov; International Energy Outlook 2021.

United Nations Statistics Division (UNSD), United Nations Plz., New York, NY, 10017, USA, (800) 253-9646, (212) 963-9851, statistics@un.org, https://unstats.un.org; Energy Statistics Yearbook 2019 and Statistical Yearbook of the United Nations 2021.

CZECH REPUBLIC-EMIGRATION AND IMMIGRATION

Czech Statistical Office, Na padesatem 3268/81, Praha 10, Strasnice, 100 82, CZE, infoservis@czso.cz, https://www.czso.cz; Foreigners in the Czech Republic, 2020.

CZECH REPUBLIC-EMPLOYMENT

International Labour Organization (ILO), 4 Rte. des Morillons, Geneva, CH-1211, SWI, ilo@ilo.org, https://www.ilo.org; NORMLEX Information System on International Labour Standards.

Organization for Economic Cooperation and Development (OECD), 2001 L St. NW, Ste. 650, Washington, DC, 20036-4922, USA, (202) 785-6323, (800) 456-6323, (202) 785-0350, washington.contact@oecd.org, https://www.oecd.org/; Economic Survey of Czech Republic 2023; OECD Composite Leading Indicator (CLI); and OECD Labour Force Statistics 2022.

UK Data Service, University of Essex, Wivenhoe Park, Colchester, Essex, CO4 3SQ, GBR, https://ukdataservice.ac.uk/; International Aggregate Data.

United Nations Statistics Division (UNSD), United Nations Plz., New York, NY, 10017, USA, (800) 253-9646, (212) 963-9851, statistics@un.org, https://unstats.un.org; Statistical Yearbook of the United Nations 2021.

CZECH REPUBLIC-ENERGY INDUSTRIES

Enerdata, 47 avenue Alsace Lorraine, Grenoble, 38027, FRA, (332) 216-4534, research@enerdata.net, https://www.enerdata.net; World Refinery Database.

European Commission, Eurostat, Luxembourg, 2920, LUX, https://ec.europa.eu/eurostat/; Final Energy Consumption in Transport by Type of Fuel.

European Institute for Energy Research (EIFER), Emmy-Noether-Strasse 11, Ground Fl., Karlsruhe, D-76131, GER, contact@eifer.org, https://www.eifer.kit.edu/; unpublished data.

International Energy Agency (IEA), 9 Rue de la Federation, Paris, 75739, FRA, info@iea.org, https://www.iea.org/; Renewables Information and World Energy Statistics and Balances.

S&P Global Commodity Insights, One World Trade Center, New York, NY, 10007, USA, (800) 752-8878, support@platts.com, https://www.spglobal.com/commodityinsights/en; Platts European Power Daily and Platts Power in Europe.

United Nations Statistics Division (UNSD), United Nations Plz., New York, NY, 10017, USA, (800) 253-9646, (212) 963-9851, statistics@un.org, https://unstats.un.org; Statistical Yearbook of the United Nations 2021.

CZECH REPUBLIC-ENVIRONMENTAL CONDITIONS

Czech Statistical Office, Na padesatem 3268/81, Praha 10, Strasnice, 100 82, CZE, infoservis@czso.cz, https://www.czso.cz; Environmental Protection Expenditure in the Czech Republic, 2020.

DSI Data Service & Information, Xantener Strasse 51a, Rheinberg, D-47495, GER, dsi@dsidata.com, https://www.dsidata.com/; Global Environmental Database.

The Economist Group: Economist Intelligence Unit (EIU), 900 3rd Ave., 16th Fl., New York, NY, 10022, USA, (212) 541-0500, americas@eiu.com, https://www.eiu.com; Czech Republic Country Report.

European Commission, Rue de la Loi, 170, Brussels, B-1040, BEL, https://ec.europa.eu; Common Agricultural Policy (CAPF) Context Indicators, 2019 Update.

European Commission, Eurostat, Luxembourg, 2920, LUX, https://ec.europa.eu/eurostat/; Environment Statistics Introduced.

United Nations Statistics Division (UNSD), United Nations Plz., New York, NY, 10017, USA, (800) 253-9646, (212) 963-9851, statistics@un.org, https://unstats.un.org; Statistical Yearbook of the United Nations 2021 and World Statistics Pocketbook 2021.

CZECH REPUBLIC-EXPENDITURES, PUBLIC

Czech Statistical Office, Na padesatem 3268/81, Praha 10, Strasnice, 100 82, CZE, infoservis@czso.cz, https://www.czso.cz; Environmental Protection Expenditure in the Czech Republic, 2020.

CZECH REPUBLIC-EXPORTS

Central Intelligence Agency (CIA), Office of Public Affairs, Washington, DC, 20505, USA, (703) 482-0623, https://www.cia.gov; The World Factbook.

Czech Statistical Office, Na padesatem 3268/81, Praha 10, Strasnice, 100 82, CZE, infoservis@czso.cz, https://www.czso.cz; External Trade of the Czech Republic.

The Economist Group: Economist Intelligence Unit (EIU), 900 3rd Ave., 16th Fl., New York, NY, 10022, USA, (212) 541-0500, americas@eiu.com, https://www.eiu.com; Czech Republic Country Report.

International Monetary Fund (IMF), 700 19th St. NW, Washington, DC, 20431, USA, (202) 623-7000, (202) 623-4661, publications@imf.org, https://www.imf.org; Direction of Trade Statistics (DOTS).

Organization for Economic Cooperation and Development (OECD), 2001 L St. NW, Ste. 650, Washington, DC, 20036-4922, USA, (202) 785-6323, (800) 456-6323, (202) 785-0350, washington.contact@oecd.org, https://www.oecd.org/; Economic Survey of Czech Republic 2023.

S&P Global, IHS Markit, 15 Inverness Way E, Englewood, CO, 80112, USA, (800) 447-2273, (800) 854-7179, https://ihsmarkit.com; Global Trade Atlas (GTA).

United Nations Conference on Trade and Development (UNCTAD), Palais des Nations, Geneva, 1211, SWI, (212) 963-6896, unctadinfo@unctad.org, https://unctad.org; Handbook of Statistics 2021.

United Nations Statistics Division (UNSD), United Nations Plz., New York, NY, 10017, USA, (800) 253-9646, (212) 963-9851, statistics@un.org, https://unstats.un.org; International Trade Statistics Yearbook 2020.

The World Bank, 1818 H St. NW, Washington, DC, 20433, USA, (202) 473-1000, (202) 477-6391, eds03@worldbank.org, https://www.worldbank.org/; World Development Report 2022: Finance for an Equitable Recovery.

CZECH REPUBLIC-FERTILITY, HUMAN

Central Intelligence Agency (CIA), Office of Public Affairs, Washington, DC, 20505, USA, (703) 482-0623, https://www.cia.gov; The World Factbook.

Czech Statistical Office, Na padesatem 3268/81, Praha 10, Strasnice, 100 82, CZE, infoservis@czso.cz, https://www.czso.cz; Demographic Yearbook of the Czech Republic, 2020.

CZECH REPUBLIC-FERTILIZER INDUSTRY

United Nations Food and Agricultural Organization (FAO), 2121 K St., Ste. 800B, Washington, DC, 20037, USA, (202) 653-2400 (Dial from U.S.), (202) 653-5760 (Fax from U.S.), fao-hq@fao.org, https://www.fao.org; The State of Food and Agriculture (SOFA) 2022.

CZECH REPUBLIC-FETAL MORTALITY

See CZECH REPUBLIC-MORTALITY

CZECH REPUBLIC-FINANCE

Stockholm International Peace Research Institute (SIPRI), Signalistgatan 9, Stockholm, SE 169 72, SWE, https://www.sipri.org/; SIPRI Arms Transfers Database and SIPRI Military Expenditure Database.

United Nations Statistics Division (UNSD), United Nations Plz., New York, NY, 10017, USA, (800) 253-9646, (212) 963-9851, statistics@un.org, https://unstats.un.org; Statistical Yearbook of the United Nations 2021.

CZECH REPUBLIC-FINANCE, PUBLIC

Banque de France, 31 rue Croix des Petits-Champs, Paris, 75049, FRA, infos@banque-france.fr, https://www.banque-france.fr/en; Webstat: Access to Statistical Series of Banque de France.

Bernan Press, 15250 NBN Way, Bldg. C, Blue Ridge Summit, PA, 17214, USA, (301) 459-2255, (800) 865-3457, (800) 865-3450, customercare@bernan.com, https://rowman.com/Page/Bernan; National Accounts Statistics: Analysis of Main Aggregates 2020.

The Economist Group: Economist Intelligence Unit (EIU), 900 3rd Ave., 16th Fl., New York, NY, 10022, USA, (212) 541-0500, americas@eiu.com, https://www.eiu.com; Czech Republic Country Report.

International Monetary Fund (IMF), 700 19th St. NW, Washington, DC, 20431, USA, (202) 623-7000, (202) 623-4661, publications@imf.org, https://www.imf.org; Regional Economic Outlook.

Palgrave Macmillan, 1 New York Plaza, Ste. 4500, New York, NY, 10004-1562, USA, (800) 777-4643, orders@palgrave.com, https://www.palgrave.com/us; The Statesman's Yearbook, 2023.

Routledge - Taylor & Francis Group, 6000 Broken Sound Pkwy. NW, Ste. 300, Boca Raton, FL, 33487, USA, (800) 634-1420, (800) 634-7064, orders@taylorandfrancis.com, https://www.routledge.com/; The Europa World Year Book 2022.

United Nations Statistics Division (UNSD), United Nations Plz., New York, NY, 10017, USA, (800) 253-9646, (212) 963-9851, statistics@un.org, https://unstats.un.org; National Accounts Main Aggregates Database and National Accounts Statistics: Main Aggregates and Detailed Tables.

CZECH REPUBLIC-FISHERIES

Routledge - Taylor & Francis Group, 6000 Broken Sound Pkwy. NW, Ste. 300, Boca Raton, FL, 33487, USA, (800) 634-1420, (800) 634-7064, orders@taylorandfrancis.com, https://www.routledge.com/; The Europa World Year Book 2022.

United Nations Food and Agricultural Organization (FAO), 2121 K St., Ste. 800B, Washington, DC, 20037, USA, (202) 653-2400 (Dial from U.S.), (202) 653-5760 (Fax from U.S.), fao-hq@fao.org, https://www.fao.org; FAO Yearbook of Fishery and Aquaculture Statistics 2019; Fishery Statistical Collections Global Capture Production; FishStatJ; and The State of Food and Agriculture (SOFA) 2022.

United Nations Statistics Division (UNSD), United Nations Plz., New York, NY, 10017, USA, (800) 253-9646, (212) 963-9851, statistics@un.org, https://unstats.un.org; Statistical Yearbook of the United Nations 2021.

CZECH REPUBLIC-FOOD

Czech Statistical Office, Na padesatem 3268/81, Praha 10, Strasnice, 100 82, CZE, infoservis@czso.cz, https://www.czso.cz; Food Consumption in Czech Republic, 2020.

Euromonitor International, Inc., 1 N Dearborn St., Ste. 1700, Chicago, IL, 60602, USA, (312) 922-1115, (312) 922-1157, info-usa@euromonitor.com, https://www.euromonitor.com/; Market Research on the Retailing Industry.

United Nations Food and Agricultural Organization (FAO), 2121 K St., Ste. 800B, Washington, DC, 20037, USA, (202) 653-2400 (Dial from U.S.), (202) 653-5760 (Fax from U.S.), fao-hq@fao.org, https://www.fao.org; The State of Food and Agriculture (SOFA) 2022.

CZECH REPUBLIC-FORESTS AND FORESTRY

Palgrave Macmillan, 1 New York Plaza, Ste. 4500, New York, NY, 10004-1562, USA, (800) 777-4643, orders@palgrave.com, https://www.palgrave.com/us; The Statesman's Yearbook, 2023.

Routledge - Taylor & Francis Group, 6000 Broken Sound Pkwy. NW, Ste. 300, Boca Raton, FL, 33487, USA, (800) 634-1420, (800) 634-7064, orders@taylorandfrancis.com, https://www.routledge.com/; The Europa World Year Book 2022.

UNESCO Institute for Statistics, C.P 250 Succursale H, Montreal, QC, H3G 2K8, CAN, (514) 343-6880 (Dial from U.S.), (514) 343-5740 (Fax from U.S.), uis.publications@unesco.org, http://uis.unesco.org/; UIS.Stat.

United Nations Food and Agricultural Organization (FAO), 2121 K St., Ste. 800B, Washington, DC, 20037, USA, (202) 653-2400 (Dial from U.S.), (202) 653-5760 (Fax from U.S.), fao-hq@fao.org, https://www.fao.org; FAO Yearbook of Forest Products 2019 and The State of Food and Agriculture (SOFA) 2022.

United Nations Statistics Division (UNSD), United Nations Plz., New York, NY, 10017, USA, (800) 253-9646, (212) 963-9851, statistics@un.org, https://unstats.un.org; Statistical Yearbook of the United Nations 2021.

The World Bank, 1818 H St. NW, Washington, DC, 20433, USA, (202) 473-1000, (202) 477-6391, eds03@worldbank.org, https://www.worldbank.org/; World Development Report 2022: Finance for an Equitable Recovery.

CZECH REPUBLIC-GAS PRODUCTION

See CZECH REPUBLIC-MINERAL INDUSTRIES

CZECH REPUBLIC-GOLD PRODUCTION

See CZECH REPUBLIC-MINERAL INDUSTRIES

CZECH REPUBLIC-GROSS DOMESTIC PRODUCT

The Economist Group: Economist Intelligence Unit (EIU), 900 3rd Ave., 16th Fl., New York, NY, 10022, USA, (212) 541-0500, americas@eiu.com, https://www.eiu.com; Czech Republic Country Report.

United Nations Statistics Division (UNSD), United Nations Plz., New York, NY, 10017, USA, (800) 253-9646, (212) 963-9851, statistics@un.org, https://unstats.un.org; Statistical Yearbook of the United Nations 2021.

The World Bank, 1818 H St. NW, Washington, DC, 20433, USA, (202) 473-1000, (202) 477-6391, eds03@worldbank.org, https://www.worldbank.org/; World Development Report 2022: Finance for an Equitable Recovery.

CZECH REPUBLIC-GROSS NATIONAL PRODUCT

Organization for Economic Cooperation and Development (OECD), 2001 L St. NW, Ste. 650, Washington, DC, 20036-4922, USA, (202) 785-6323, (800) 456-6323, (202) 785-0350, washington.contact@oecd.org, https://www.oecd.org/; OECD Composite Leading Indicator (CLI).

United Nations Statistics Division (UNSD), United Nations Plz., New York, NY, 10017, USA, (800) 253-9646, (212) 963-9851, statistics@un.org, https://unstats.un.org; Statistical Yearbook of the United Nations 2021.

The World Bank, 1818 H St. NW, Washington, DC, 20433, USA, (202) 473-1000, (202) 477-6391, eds03@worldbank.org, https://www.worldbank.org/; World Development Report 2022: Finance for an Equitable Recovery.

CZECH REPUBLIC-HEMP FIBRE PRODUCTION

See CZECH REPUBLIC-TEXTILE INDUSTRY

CZECH REPUBLIC-HOUSING

Czech Statistical Office, Na padesatem 3268/81, Praha 10, Strasnice, 100 82, CZE, infoservis@czso.cz, https://www.czso.cz; Household Income and Living Conditions in the Czech Republic, 2021.

Euromonitor International, Inc., 1 N Dearborn St., Ste. 1700, Chicago, IL, 60602, USA, (312) 922-1115, (312) 922-1157, info-usa@euromonitor.com, https://www.euromonitor.com/; Geographies.

CZECH REPUBLIC-ILLITERATE PERSONS

UNESCO Institute for Statistics, C.P 250 Succursale H, Montreal, QC, H3G 2K8, CAN, (514) 343-6880 (Dial from U.S.), (514) 343-5740 (Fax from U.S.), uis.publications@unesco.org, http://uis.unesco.org/; UIS.Stat.

CZECH REPUBLIC-IMPORTS

Central Intelligence Agency (CIA), Office of Public Affairs, Washington, DC, 20505, USA, (703) 482-0623, https://www.cia.gov; The World Factbook.

The Economist Group: Economist Intelligence Unit (EIU), 900 3rd Ave., 16th Fl., New York, NY, 10022, USA, (212) 541-0500, americas@eiu.com, https://www.eiu.com; Czech Republic Country Report.

International Monetary Fund (IMF), 700 19th St. NW, Washington, DC, 20431, USA, (202) 623-7000, (202) 623-4661, publications@imf.org, https://www.imf.org; Direction of Trade Statistics (DOTS).

Organization for Economic Cooperation and Development (OECD), 2001 L St. NW, Ste. 650, Washington, DC, 20036-4922, USA, (202) 785-6323, (800) 456-6323, (202) 785-0350, washington.contact@oecd.org, https://www.oecd.org/; Economic Survey of Czech Republic 2023.

S&P Global, IHS Markit, 15 Inverness Way E, Englewood, CO, 80112, USA, (800) 447-2273, (800) 854-7179, https://ihsmarkit.com; Global Trade Atlas (GTA).

United Nations Conference on Trade and Development (UNCTAD), Palais des Nations, Geneva, 1211, SWI, (212) 963-6896, unctadinfo@unctad.org, https://unctad.org; Handbook of Statistics 2021.

United Nations Statistics Division (UNSD), United Nations Plz., New York, NY, 10017, USA, (800) 253-9646, (212) 963-9851, statistics@un.org, https://unstats.un.org; International Trade Statistics Yearbook 2020.

The World Bank, 1818 H St. NW, Washington, DC, 20433, USA, (202) 473-1000, (202) 477-6391, eds03@worldbank.org, https://www.worldbank.org/; World Development Report 2022: Finance for an Equitable Recovery.

CZECH REPUBLIC-INDUSTRIAL METALS PRODUCTION

See CZECH REPUBLIC-MINERAL INDUSTRIES

CZECH REPUBLIC-INDUSTRIAL PRODUCTIVITY

International Lead and Zinc Study Group (ILZSG), Rua Almirante Barroso 38, 5th Fl., Lisbon, 1000-013, PRT, sales@ilzsg.org, https://www.ilzsg.org; Interactive Statistical Database.

CZECH REPUBLIC-INDUSTRIAL PROPERTY

World Intellectual Property Organization (WIPO), 34, chemin des Colombettes, Geneva, CH-1211, SWI, https://www.wipo.int; Madrid Yearly Review 2022: International Registrations of Marks.

CZECH REPUBLIC-INDUSTRIES

Central Intelligence Agency (CIA), Office of Public Affairs, Washington, DC, 20505, USA, (703) 482-0623, https://www.cia.gov; The World Factbook.

The Economist Group: Economist Intelligence Unit (EIU), 900 3rd Ave., 16th Fl., New York, NY, 10022, USA, (212) 541-0500, americas@eiu.com, https://www.eiu.com; Czech Republic Country Report.

Euromonitor International, Inc., 1 N Dearborn St., Ste. 1700, Chicago, IL, 60602, USA, (312) 922-1115, (312) 922-1157, info-usa@euromonitor.com, https://www.euromonitor.com/; Geographies.

International Labour Organization (ILO), 4 Rte. des Morillons, Geneva, CH-1211, SWI, ilo@ilo.org, https://www.ilo.org; NORMLEX Information System on International Labour Standards.

Palgrave Macmillan, 1 New York Plaza, Ste. 4500, New York, NY, 10004-1562, USA, (800) 777-4643, orders@palgrave.com, https://www.palgrave.com/us; The Statesman's Yearbook, 2023.

Routledge - Taylor & Francis Group, 6000 Broken Sound Pkwy. NW, Ste. 300, Boca Raton, FL, 33487, USA, (800) 634-1420, (800) 634-7064, orders@taylorandfrancis.com, https://www.routledge.com/; The Europa World Year Book 2022.

United Nations Industrial Development Organization (UNIDO), 1 United Nations Plz., Rm. DC1-1118, New York, NY, 10017, USA, (212) 963-6890, (212) 963 6885, (212) 963-7904, office.newyork@unido.org, https://www.unido.org/; Industrial Statistics Databases and International Yearbook of Industrial Statistics 2021.

CZECH REPUBLIC-INFANT AND MATERNAL MORTALITY

See CZECH REPUBLIC-MORTALITY

CZECH REPUBLIC-INTERNATIONAL TRADE

Banque de France, 31 rue Croix des Petits-Champs, Paris, 75049, FRA, infos@banque-france.fr, https://www.banque-france.fr/en; Key Figures France and Abroad.

Czech Statistical Office, Na padesatem 3268/81, Praha 10, Strasnice, 100 82, CZE, infoservis@czso.cz, https://www.czso.cz; External Trade of the Czech Republic.

The Economist Group: Economist Intelligence Unit (EIU), 900 3rd Ave., 16th Fl., New York, NY, 10022, USA, (212) 541-0500, americas@eiu.com, https://www.eiu.com; Czech Republic Country Report.

Euromonitor International, Inc., 1 N Dearborn St., Ste. 1700, Chicago, IL, 60602, USA, (312) 922-1115, (312) 922-1157, info-usa@euromonitor.com, https://www.euromonitor.com/; Geographies.

European Commission, Eurostat, Luxembourg, 2920, LUX, https://ec.europa.eu/eurostat/; Extra-EU Trade in Goods.

Organization for Economic Cooperation and Development (OECD), 2001 L St. NW, Ste. 650, Washington, DC, 20036-4922, USA, (202) 785-6323, (800) 456-6323, (202) 785-0350, washington.contact@oecd.org, https://www.oecd.org/; Economic Survey of Czech Republic 2023.

Palgrave Macmillan, 1 New York Plaza, Ste. 4500, New York, NY, 10004-1562, USA, (800) 777-4643, orders@palgrave.com, https://www.palgrave.com/us; The Statesman's Yearbook, 2023.

Routledge - Taylor & Francis Group, 6000 Broken Sound Pkwy. NW, Ste. 300, Boca Raton, FL, 33487, USA, (800) 634-1420, (800) 634-7064, orders@taylorandfrancis.com, https://www.routledge.com/; The Europa World Year Book 2022.

United Nations Conference on Trade and Development (UNCTAD), Palais des Nations, Geneva, 1211, SWI, (212) 963-6896, unctadinfo@unctad.org, https://unctad.org; Trade and Development Report 2021.

United Nations Food and Agricultural Organization (FAO), 2121 K St., Ste. 800B, Washington, DC, 20037, USA, (202) 653-2400 (Dial from U.S.), (202) 653-5760 (Fax from U.S.), fao-hq@fao.org, https://www.fao.org; The State of Food and Agriculture (SOFA) 2022.

United Nations Statistics Division (UNSD), United Nations Plz., New York, NY, 10017, USA, (800) 253-9646, (212) 963-9851, statistics@un.org, https://unstats.un.org; International Trade Statistics Yearbook 2020 and Statistical Yearbook of the United Nations 2021.

The World Bank, 1818 H St. NW, Washington, DC, 20433, USA, (202) 473-1000, (202) 477-6391, eds03@worldbank.org, https://www.worldbank.org/; World Development Report 2022: Finance for an Equitable Recovery.

World Trade Organization (WTO), Ctre. William Rappard, Rue de Lausanne 154, Case postale, Geneva, CH-1211, SWI, enquiries@wto.org, https://www.wto.org; World Trade Statistical Review 2022.

CZECH REPUBLIC-INTERNET USERS

International Telecommunication Union (ITU), Place des Nations, Geneva, CH-1211, SWI, itumail@itu.int, https://www.itu.int; Global Connectivity Report 2022; World Telecommunication/ICT Indicators Database 2021; and Yearbook of Statistics 2019.

CZECH REPUBLIC-LABOR

Central Intelligence Agency (CIA), Office of Public Affairs, Washington, DC, 20505, USA, (703) 482-0623, https://www.cia.gov; The World Factbook.

Czech Statistical Office, Na padesatem 3268/81, Praha 10, Strasnice, 100 82, CZE, infoservis@czso.cz, https://www.czso.cz; Labour Costs in Czech Republic, 2020.

Euromonitor International, Inc., 1 N Dearborn St., Ste. 1700, Chicago, IL, 60602, USA, (312) 922-1115, (312) 922-1157, info-usa@euromonitor.com, https://www.euromonitor.com/; Geographies.

International Labour Organization (ILO), 4 Rte. des Morillons, Geneva, CH-1211, SWI, ilo@ilo.org, https://www.ilo.org; NORMLEX Information System on International Labour Standards.

Organization for Economic Cooperation and Development (OECD), 2001 L St. NW, Ste. 650, Washington, DC, 20036-4922, USA, (202) 785-6323, (800) 456-6323, (202) 785-0350, washington.contact@oecd.org, https://www.oecd.org/; Economic Survey of Czech Republic 2023.

Palgrave Macmillan, 1 New York Plaza, Ste. 4500, New York, NY, 10004-1562, USA, (800) 777-4643, orders@palgrave.com, https://www.palgrave.com/us; The Statesman's Yearbook, 2023.

United Nations Economic Commission for Europe (UNECE), Palais des Nations, Geneva, CH-1211, SWI, unece_info@un.org, https://unece.org/; UNECE Countries in Figures 2019.

United Nations Food and Agricultural Organization (FAO), 2121 K St., Ste. 800B, Washington, DC, 20037, USA, (202) 653-2400 (Dial from U.S.), (202) 653-5760 (Fax from U.S.), fao-hq@fao.org, https://www.fao.org; The State of Food and Agriculture (SOFA) 2022.

United Nations Statistics Division (UNSD), United Nations Plz., New York, NY, 10017, USA, (800) 253-9646, (212) 963-9851, statistics@un.org, https://unstats.un.org; Statistical Yearbook of the United Nations 2021.

The World Bank, 1818 H St. NW, Washington, DC, 20433, USA, (202) 473-1000, (202) 477-6391, eds03@worldbank.org, https://www.worldbank.org/; World Development Report 2022: Finance for an Equitable Recovery.

CZECH REPUBLIC-LAND USE

United Nations Statistics Division (UNSD), United Nations Plz., New York, NY, 10017, USA, (800) 253-9646, (212) 963-9851, statistics@un.org, https://unstats.un.org; Millennium Development Goal Indicators.

CZECH REPUBLIC-LIBRARIES

UNESCO Institute for Statistics, C.P 250 Succursale H, Montreal, QC, H3G 2K8, CAN, (514) 343-6880 (Dial from U.S.), (514) 343-5740 (Fax from U.S.), uis.publications@unesco.org, http://uis.unesco.org/; UIS.Stat.

CZECH REPUBLIC-LIFE EXPECTANCY

Central Intelligence Agency (CIA), Office of Public Affairs, Washington, DC, 20505, USA, (703) 482-0623, https://www.cia.gov; The World Factbook.

United Nations Department of Economic and Social Affairs (DESA), Population Division, 2 United Nations Plz., Rm. DC2-1950, New York, NY, 10017, USA, (212) 963-3209, (212) 963-2147, population@un.org, https://www.un.org/development/desa/pd/; World Population Ageing 2020 Highlights.

United Nations Economic Commission for Europe (UNECE), Palais des Nations, Geneva, CH-1211, SWI, unece_info@un.org, https://unece.org/; UN-ECE Countries in Figures 2019.

United Nations Statistics Division (UNSD), United Nations Plz., New York, NY, 10017, USA, (800) 253-9646, (212) 963-9851, statistics@un.org, https://unstats.un.org; Millennium Development Goal Indicators.

CZECH REPUBLIC-LITERACY

Euromonitor International, Inc., 1 N Dearborn St., Ste. 1700, Chicago, IL, 60602, USA, (312) 922-1115, (312) 922-1157, info-usa@euromonitor.com, https://www.euromonitor.com/; Geographies.

UNESCO Institute for Statistics, C.P 250 Succursale H, Montreal, QC, H3G 2K8, CAN, (514) 343-6880 (Dial from U.S.), (514) 343-5740 (Fax from U.S.), uis.publications@unesco.org, http://uis.unesco.org/; Literacy.

CZECH REPUBLIC-LIVESTOCK

Palgrave Macmillan, 1 New York Plaza, Ste. 4500, New York, NY, 10004-1562, USA, (800) 777-4643, orders@palgrave.com, https://www.palgrave.com/us; The Statesman's Yearbook, 2023.

Routledge - Taylor & Francis Group, 6000 Broken Sound Pkwy. NW, Ste. 300, Boca Raton, FL, 33487, USA, (800) 634-1420, (800) 634-7064, orders@taylorandfrancis.com, https://www.routledge.com/; The Europa World Year Book 2022.

United Nations Food and Agricultural Organization (FAO), 2121 K St., Ste. 800B, Washington, DC, 20037, USA, (202) 653-2400 (Dial from U.S.), (202) 653-5760 (Fax from U.S.), fao-hq@fao.org, https://www.fao.org; The State of Food and Agriculture (SOFA) 2022.

United Nations Statistics Division (UNSD), United Nations Plz., New York, NY, 10017, USA, (800) 253-9646, (212) 963-9851, statistics@un.org, https://unstats.un.org; Statistical Yearbook of the United Nations 2021.

CZECH REPUBLIC-MANUFACTURES

Organization for Economic Cooperation and Development (OECD), 2001 L St. NW, Ste. 650, Washington, DC, 20036-4922, USA, (202) 785-6323, (800) 456-6323, (202) 785-0350, washington.contact@oecd.org, https://www.oecd.org/; Economic Survey of Czech Republic 2023.

CZECH REPUBLIC-MARRIAGE

Routledge - Taylor & Francis Group, 6000 Broken Sound Pkwy. NW, Ste. 300, Boca Raton, FL, 33487, USA, (800) 634-1420, (800) 634-7064, orders@taylorandfrancis.com, https://www.routledge.com/; The Europa World Year Book 2022.

UNESCO Institute for Statistics, C.P 250 Succursale H, Montreal, QC, H3G 2K8, CAN, (514) 343-6880 (Dial from U.S.), (514) 343-5740 (Fax from U.S.), uis.publications@unesco.org, http://uis.unesco.org/; UIS.Stat.

United Nations Statistics Division (UNSD), United Nations Plz., New York, NY, 10017, USA, (800) 253-9646, (212) 963-9851, statistics@un.org, https://unstats.un.org; Statistical Yearbook of the United Nations 2021.

CZECH REPUBLIC-MERCURY PRODUCTION

See CZECH REPUBLIC-MINERAL INDUSTRIES

CZECH REPUBLIC-MINERAL INDUSTRIES

Barchart, 209 W Jackson Blvd., 2nd Fl., Chicago, IL, 60606, USA, (877) 247-4394, commodities@barchart.com, https://www.barchart.com/cmdty; The cmdty Yearbook 2023; cmdtyStats: Commodity Statistics and Fundamental Data; cmdtyView: Commodity Index; and Commodity Data and Prices.

European Commission, Eurostat, Luxembourg, 2920, LUX, https://ec.europa.eu/eurostat/; Final Energy Consumption in Transport by Type of Fuel.

International Energy Agency (IEA), 9 Rue de la Federation, Paris, 75739, FRA, info@iea.org, https://www.iea.org/; World Energy Outlook 2021 and World Energy Statistics and Balances.

International Lead and Zinc Study Group (ILZSG), Rua Almirante Barroso 38, 5th Fl., Lisbon, 1000-013, PRT, sales@ilzsg.org, https://www.ilzsg.org; Interactive Statistical Database.

Palgrave Macmillan, 1 New York Plaza, Ste. 4500, New York, NY, 10004-1562, USA, (800) 777-4643, orders@palgrave.com, https://www.palgrave.com/us; The Statesman's Yearbook, 2023.

Routledge - Taylor & Francis Group, 6000 Broken Sound Pkwy. NW, Ste. 300, Boca Raton, FL, 33487, USA, (800) 634-1420, (800) 634-7064, orders@taylorandfrancis.com, https://www.routledge.com/; The Europa World Year Book 2022.

S&P Global Commodity Insights, One World Trade Center, New York, NY, 10007, USA, (800) 752-8878, support@platts.com, https://www.spglobal.com/commodityinsights/en; Platts Power in Europe.

United Nations Conference on Trade and Development (UNCTAD), Palais des Nations, Geneva, 1211, SWI, (212) 963-6896, unctadinfo@unctad.org, https://unctad.org; Trade and Development Report 2021.

United Nations Statistics Division (UNSD), United Nations Plz., New York, NY, 10017, USA, (800) 253-9646, (212) 963-9851, statistics@un.org, https://unstats.un.org; Energy Statistics Yearbook 2019 and Statistical Yearbook of the United Nations 2021.

CZECH REPUBLIC-MONEY SUPPLY

The Economist Group: Economist Intelligence Unit (EIU), 900 3rd Ave., 16th Fl., New York, NY, 10022, USA, (212) 541-0500, americas@eiu.com, https://www.eiu.com; Czech Republic Country Report.

Organization for Economic Cooperation and Development (OECD), 2001 L St. NW, Ste. 650, Washington, DC, 20036-4922, USA, (202) 785-6323, (800) 456-6323, (202) 785-0350, washington.contact@oecd.org, https://www.oecd.org/; Economic Survey of Czech Republic 2023.

Routledge - Taylor & Francis Group, 6000 Broken Sound Pkwy. NW, Ste. 300, Boca Raton, FL, 33487, USA, (800) 634-1420, (800) 634-7064, orders@taylorandfrancis.com, https://www.routledge.com/; The Europa World Year Book 2022.

CZECH REPUBLIC-MONUMENTS AND HISTORIC SITES

UNESCO Institute for Statistics, C.P 250 Succursale H, Montreal, QC, H3G 2K8, CAN, (514) 343-6880 (Dial from U.S.), (514) 343-5740 (Fax from U.S.), uis.publications@unesco.org, http://uis.unesco.org/; UIS.Stat.

CZECH REPUBLIC-MORTALITY

UNICEF, 3 United Nations Plz., New York, NY, 10017, USA, (212) 303-7984, (917) 244-2215, https://www.unicef.org; The State of the World's Children 2023.

United Nations Statistics Division (UNSD), United Nations Plz., New York, NY, 10017, USA, (800) 253-9646, (212) 963-9851, statistics@un.org, https://unstats.un.org; Millennium Development Goal Indicators; Statistical Yearbook of the United Nations 2021; and World Statistics Pocketbook 2021.

World Health Organization (WHO), Ave. Appia 20, Geneva, CH-1211, SWI, (202) 974-3000 (Telephone in U.S.), publications@who.int, https://www.who.int/; Global Health Observatory (GHO) and Health Statistics and Information Systems.

CZECH REPUBLIC-MOTOR VEHICLES

International Road Federation (IRF), Madison Place, 500 Montgomery St., 5th Fl., Alexandria, VA, 22314, USA, (703) 535-1001, (703) 535-1007, info@irf.global, https://www.irf.global/; World Road Statistics (WRS).

CZECH REPUBLIC-NATURAL GAS PRODUCTION

See CZECH REPUBLIC-MINERAL INDUSTRIES

CZECH REPUBLIC-NICKEL AND NICKEL ORE

See CZECH REPUBLIC-MINERAL INDUSTRIES

CZECH REPUBLIC-NUTRITION

United Nations Food and Agricultural Organization (FAO), 2121 K St., Ste. 800B, Washington, DC, 20037, USA, (202) 653-2400 (Dial from U.S.), (202) 653-5760 (Fax from U.S.), fao-hq@fao.org, https://www.fao.org; The State of Food and Agriculture (SOFA) 2022.

United Nations Statistics Division (UNSD), United Nations Plz., New York, NY, 10017, USA, (800) 253-9646, (212) 963-9851, statistics@un.org, https://unstats.un.org; Millennium Development Goal Indicators.

CZECH REPUBLIC-PAPER

See CZECH REPUBLIC-FORESTS AND FORESTRY

CZECH REPUBLIC-PEANUT PRODUCTION

See CZECH REPUBLIC-CROPS

CZECH REPUBLIC-PESTICIDES

United Nations Food and Agricultural Organization (FAO), 2121 K St., Ste. 800B, Washington, DC, 20037, USA, (202) 653-2400 (Dial from U.S.), (202) 653-5760 (Fax from U.S.), fao-hq@fao.org, https://www.fao.org; The State of Food and Agriculture (SOFA) 2022.

CZECH REPUBLIC-PETROLEUM INDUSTRY AND TRADE

International Energy Agency (IEA), 9 Rue de la Federation, Paris, 75739, FRA, info@iea.org, https://www.iea.org/; World Energy Outlook 2021 and World Energy Statistics and Balances.

U.S. Energy Information Administration (EIA), 1000 Independence Ave. SW, Washington, DC, 20585, USA, (202) 586-8800, infoctr@eia.gov, https://www.eia.gov; International Energy Outlook 2021.

United Nations Food and Agricultural Organization (FAO), 2121 K St., Ste. 800B, Washington, DC, 20037, USA, (202) 653-2400 (Dial from U.S.), (202) 653-5760 (Fax from U.S.), fao-hq@fao.org, https://www.fao.org; The State of Food and Agriculture (SOFA) 2022.

United Nations Statistics Division (UNSD), United Nations Plz., New York, NY, 10017, USA, (800) 253-9646, (212) 963-9851, statistics@un.org, https://unstats.un.org; Energy Statistics Yearbook 2019 and Statistical Yearbook of the United Nations 2021.

CZECH REPUBLIC-PLASTICS INDUSTRY AND TRADE

United Nations Statistics Division (UNSD), United Nations Plz., New York, NY, 10017, USA, (800) 253-9646, (212) 963-9851, statistics@un.org, https://unstats.un.org; Statistical Yearbook of the United Nations 2021.

CZECH REPUBLIC-POPULATION

Banque de France, 31 rue Croix des Petits-Champs, Paris, 75049, FRA, infos@banque-france.fr, https://www.banque-france.fr/en; Webstat: Access to Statistical Series of Banque de France.

Central Intelligence Agency (CIA), Office of Public Affairs, Washington, DC, 20505, USA, (703) 482-0623, https://www.cia.gov; The World Factbook.

Czech Statistical Office, Na padesatem 3268/81, Praha 10, Strasnice, 100 82, CZE, infoservis@czso.cz, https://www.czso.cz; Czechia in Figures, 2021; Demographic Yearbook of the Czech Republic, 2020; Household Income and Living Conditions in the Czech Republic, 2021; and Population of the Czech Republic, 2021.

The Economist Group: Economist Intelligence Unit (EIU), 900 3rd Ave., 16th Fl., New York, NY, 10022, USA, (212) 541-0500, americas@eiu.com, https://www.eiu.com; Czech Republic Country Report.

Infoplease, c/o Sandbox Networks, Inc., 1 Lincoln St., 24th Fl., Boston, MA, 02111, USA, https://www.infoplease.com; Countries of the World.

International Labour Organization (ILO), 4 Rte. des Morillons, Geneva, CH-1211, SWI, ilo@ilo.org, https://www.ilo.org; NORMLEX Information System on International Labour Standards.

Organization for Economic Cooperation and Development (OECD), 2001 L St. NW, Ste. 650, Washington, DC, 20036-4922, USA, (202) 785-6323, (800) 456-6323, (202) 785-0350, washington.contact@oecd.org, https://www.oecd.org/; OECD Labour Force Statistics 2022.

Palgrave Macmillan, 1 New York Plaza, Ste. 4500, New York, NY, 10004-1562, USA, (800) 777-4643, orders@palgrave.com, https://www.palgrave.com/us; The Statesman's Yearbook, 2023.

Routledge - Taylor & Francis Group, 6000 Broken Sound Pkwy. NW, Ste. 300, Boca Raton, FL, 33487, USA, (800) 634-1420, (800) 634-7064, orders@taylorandfrancis.com, https://www.routledge.com/; The Europa World Year Book 2022.

UK Data Service, University of Essex, Wivenhoe Park, Colchester, Essex, CO4 3SQ, GBR, https://ukdataservice.ac.uk/; International Aggregate Data.

UNESCO Institute for Statistics, C.P 250 Succursale H, Montreal, QC, H3G 2K8, CAN, (514) 343-6880 (Dial from U.S.), (514) 343-5740 (Fax from U.S.), uis.publications@unesco.org, http://uis.unesco.org/; UIS.Stat.

United Nations Department of Economic and Social Affairs (DESA), Population Division, 2 United Nations Plz., Rm. DC2-1950, New York, NY, 10017, USA, (212) 963-3209, (212) 963-2147, population@un.org, https://www.un.org/development/desa/pd/; Revision of World Urbanization Prospects and World Population Ageing 2020 Highlights.

United Nations Development Programme (UNDP), One United Nations Plz., New York, NY, 10017, USA, (212) 906-5000, (212) 906-5001, https://www.undp.org; Human Development Report 2021-2022.

United Nations Statistics Division (UNSD), United Nations Plz., New York, NY, 10017, USA, (800) 253-9646, (212) 963-9851, statistics@un.org, https://unstats.un.org; Statistical Yearbook of the United Nations 2021 and World Statistics Pocketbook 2021.

The World Bank, 1818 H St. NW, Washington, DC, 20433, USA, (202) 473-1000, (202) 477-6391, eds03@worldbank.org, https://www.worldbank.org/; The Global Findex Database 2021 and World Development Report 2022: Finance for an Equitable Recovery.

World Health Organization (WHO), Ave. Appia 20, Geneva, CH-1211, SWI, (202) 974-3000 (Telephone in U.S.), publications@who.int, https://www.who.int/; Health Statistics and Information Systems.

CZECH REPUBLIC-POPULATION DENSITY

Central Intelligence Agency (CIA), Office of Public Affairs, Washington, DC, 20505, USA, (703) 482-0623, https://www.cia.gov; The World Factbook.

Palgrave Macmillan, 1 New York Plaza, Ste. 4500, New York, NY, 10004-1562, USA, (800) 777-4643, orders@palgrave.com, https://www.palgrave.com/us; The Statesman's Yearbook, 2023.

Routledge - Taylor & Francis Group, 6000 Broken Sound Pkwy. NW, Ste. 300, Boca Raton, FL, 33487, USA, (800) 634-1420, (800) 634-7064, orders@taylorandfrancis.com, https://www.routledge.com/; The Europa World Year Book 2022.

UNESCO Institute for Statistics, C.P 250 Succursale H, Montreal, QC, H3G 2K8, CAN, (514) 343-6880 (Dial from U.S.), (514) 343-5740 (Fax from U.S.), uis.publications@unesco.org, http://uis.unesco.org/; UIS.Stat.

The World Bank, 1818 H St. NW, Washington, DC, 20433, USA, (202) 473-1000, (202) 477-6391, eds03@worldbank.org, https://www.worldbank.org/; World Development Report 2022: Finance for an Equitable Recovery.

CZECH REPUBLIC-POWER RESOURCES

Euromonitor International, Inc., 1 N Dearborn St., Ste. 1700, Chicago, IL, 60602, USA, (312) 922-1115, (312) 922-1157, info-usa@euromonitor.com, https://www.euromonitor.com/; Geographies.

International Energy Agency (IEA), 9 Rue de la Federation, Paris, 75739, FRA, info@iea.org, https://www.iea.org/; World Energy Outlook 2021.

Palgrave Macmillan, 1 New York Plaza, Ste. 4500, New York, NY, 10004-1562, USA, (800) 777-4643, orders@palgrave.com, https://www.palgrave.com/us; The Statesman's Yearbook, 2023.

S&P Global Commodity Insights, One World Trade Center, New York, NY, 10007, USA, (800) 752-8878, support@platts.com, https://www.spglobal.com/commodityinsights/en; Platts European Power Daily.

U.S. Energy Information Administration (EIA), 1000 Independence Ave. SW, Washington, DC, 20585, USA, (202) 586-8800, infoctr@eia.gov, https://www.eia.gov; International Energy Outlook 2021.

United Nations Food and Agricultural Organization (FAO), 2121 K St., Ste. 800B, Washington, DC, 20037, USA, (202) 653-2400 (Dial from U.S.), (202) 653-5760 (Fax from U.S.), fao-hq@fao.org, https://www.fao.org; The State of Food and Agriculture (SOFA) 2022.

United Nations Statistics Division (UNSD), United Nations Plz., New York, NY, 10017, USA, (800) 253-9646, (212) 963-9851, statistics@un.org, https://unstats.un.org; Energy Statistics Yearbook 2019; Statistical Yearbook of the United Nations 2021; and World Statistics Pocketbook 2021.

The World Bank, 1818 H St. NW, Washington, DC, 20433, USA, (202) 473-1000, (202) 477-6391, eds03@worldbank.org, https://www.worldbank.org/; World Development Report 2022: Finance for an Equitable Recovery.

CZECH REPUBLIC-PRICES

Euromonitor International, Inc., 1 N Dearborn St., Ste. 1700, Chicago, IL, 60602, USA, (312) 922-1115, (312) 922-1157, info-usa@euromonitor.com, https://www.euromonitor.com/; Geographies.

CZECH REPUBLIC-PUBLIC HEALTH

Euromonitor International, Inc., 1 N Dearborn St., Ste. 1700, Chicago, IL, 60602, USA, (312) 922-1115, (312) 922-1157, info-usa@euromonitor.com, https://www.euromonitor.com/; Geographies and Market Research on the Health and Wellness Industry.

European Centre for Disease Prevention and Control (ECDC), Stockholm, SE 171 83, SWE, ecdc.info@ecdc.europa.eu, https://ecdc.europa.eu; Eurosurveillance.

European Commission, Directorate-General for Health and Food Safety, Brussels, B-1049, BEL, https://ec.europa.eu/info/departments/health-and-food-safety_en ; zzunpublished data.

U.S. Census Bureau, 4600 Silver Hill Rd., Washington, DC, 20233, USA, (301) 763-4636, (800) 923-8282, https://www.census.gov; HIV/AIDS Surveillance Data Base.

UNICEF, 3 United Nations Plz., New York, NY, 10017, USA, (212) 303-7984, (917) 244-2215, https://www.unicef.org; The State of the World's Children 2023.

United Nations Department of Economic and Social Affairs (DESA), Population Division, 2 United Nations Plz., Rm. DC2-1950, New York, NY, 10017, USA, (212) 963-3209, (212) 963-2147, population@un.org, https://www.un.org/development/desa/pd/; World Fertility Data 2019.

United Nations Development Programme (UNDP), One United Nations Plz., New York, NY, 10017, USA, (212) 906-5000, (212) 906-5001, https://www.undp.org; Human Development Report 2021-2022.

United Nations Statistics Division (UNSD), United Nations Plz., New York, NY, 10017, USA, (800) 253-9646, (212) 963-9851, statistics@un.org, https://unstats.un.org; Millennium Development Goal Indicators and Statistical Yearbook of the United Nations 2021.

World Health Organization (WHO), Ave. Appia 20, Geneva, CH-1211, SWI, (202) 974-3000 (Telephone in U.S.), publications@who.int, https://www.who.int/; Global Health Observatory (GHO).

CZECH REPUBLIC-PUBLISHERS AND PUBLISHING

Routledge - Taylor & Francis Group, 6000 Broken Sound Pkwy. NW, Ste. 300, Boca Raton, FL, 33487, USA, (800) 634-1420, (800) 634-7064, orders@taylorandfrancis.com, https://www.routledge.com/; The Europa World Year Book 2022.

UNESCO Institute for Statistics, C.P 250 Succursale H, Montreal, QC, H3G 2K8, CAN, (514) 343-6880 (Dial from U.S.), (514) 343-5740 (Fax from U.S.), uis.publications@unesco.org, http://uis.unesco.org/; UIS.Stat.

CZECH REPUBLIC-RAILROADS

Janes, USA, (703) 574-7580, (888) 977-1519, customer.care@janes.com, https://www.janes.com; Janes World Railways 2021-2022.

Palgrave Macmillan, 1 New York Plaza, Ste. 4500, New York, NY, 10004-1562, USA, (800) 777-4643, orders@palgrave.com, https://www.palgrave.com/us; The Statesman's Yearbook, 2023.

Routledge - Taylor & Francis Group, 6000 Broken Sound Pkwy. NW, Ste. 300, Boca Raton, FL, 33487, USA, (800) 634-1420, (800) 634-7064, orders@taylorandfrancis.com, https://www.routledge.com/; The Europa World Year Book 2022.

United Nations Statistics Division (UNSD), United Nations Plz., New York, NY, 10017, USA, (800) 253-9646, (212) 963-9851, statistics@un.org, https://unstats.un.org; Statistical Yearbook of the United Nations 2021.

CZECH REPUBLIC-RELIGION

Central Intelligence Agency (CIA), Office of Public Affairs, Washington, DC, 20505, USA, (703) 482-0623, https://www.cia.gov; The World Factbook.

Palgrave Macmillan, 1 New York Plaza, Ste. 4500, New York, NY, 10004-1562, USA, (800) 777-4643, orders@palgrave.com, https://www.palgrave.com/us; The Statesman's Yearbook, 2023.

CZECH REPUBLIC-RETAIL TRADE

Banque de France, 31 rue Croix des Petits-Champs, Paris, 75049, FRA, infos@banque-france.fr, https://www.banque-france.fr/en; Key Figures France and Abroad.

Euromonitor International, Inc., 1 N Dearborn St., Ste. 1700, Chicago, IL, 60602, USA, (312) 922-1115, (312) 922-1157, info-usa@euromonitor.com, https://www.euromonitor.com/; Geographies and Market Research on the Retailing Industry.

United Nations Statistics Division (UNSD), United Nations Plz., New York, NY, 10017, USA, (800) 253-9646, (212) 963-9851, statistics@un.org, https://unstats.un.org; Statistical Yearbook of the United Nations 2021.

CZECH REPUBLIC-RICE PRODUCTION

See CZECH REPUBLIC-CROPS

CZECH REPUBLIC-ROADS

International Road Federation (IRF), Madison Place, 500 Montgomery St., 5th Fl., Alexandria, VA, 22314,

USA, (703) 535-1001, (703) 535-1007, info@irf.global, https://www.irf.global/; World Road Statistics (WRS).

CZECH REPUBLIC-RUBBER INDUSTRY AND TRADE

International Rubber Study Group (IRSG), 51 Changi Business Park Central 2, Unit No. 6, 486066, SGP, https://www.rubberstudy.org; Monthly Rubber Bulletin (MRB); Rubber Industry Report; Rubber Statistical Bulletin; and World Rubber Industry Report (WRIO).

United Nations Statistics Division (UNSD), United Nations Plz., New York, NY, 10017, USA, (800) 253-9646, (212) 963-9851, statistics@un.org, https://unstats.un.org; Statistical Yearbook of the United Nations 2021.

CZECH REPUBLIC-RYE PRODUCTION

See CZECH REPUBLIC-CROPS

CZECH REPUBLIC-SHIPPING

Routledge - Taylor & Francis Group, 6000 Broken Sound Pkwy. NW, Ste. 300, Boca Raton, FL, 33487, USA, (800) 634-1420, (800) 634-7064, orders@taylorandfrancis.com, https://www.routledge.com/; The Europa World Year Book 2022.

United Nations Statistics Division (UNSD), United Nations Plz., New York, NY, 10017, USA, (800) 253-9646, (212) 963-9851, statistics@un.org, https://unstats.un.org; Statistical Yearbook of the United Nations 2021.

CZECH REPUBLIC-STEEL PRODUCTION

See CZECH REPUBLIC-MINERAL INDUSTRIES

CZECH REPUBLIC-SUGAR PRODUCTION

See CZECH REPUBLIC-CROPS

CZECH REPUBLIC-TAXATION

European Commission, Eurostat, Luxembourg, 2920, LUX, https://ec.europa.eu/eurostat/; Taxation Trends in the European Union.

International Road Federation (IRF), Madison Place, 500 Montgomery St., 5th Fl., Alexandria, VA, 22314, USA, (703) 535-1001, (703) 535-1007, info@irf.global, https://www.irf.global/; World Road Statistics (WRS).

CZECH REPUBLIC-TEA PRODUCTION

See CZECH REPUBLIC-CROPS

CZECH REPUBLIC-TELEPHONE

Palgrave Macmillan, 1 New York Plaza, Ste. 4500, New York, NY, 10004-1562, USA, (800) 777-4643, orders@palgrave.com, https://www.palgrave.com/us; The Statesman's Yearbook, 2023.

Routledge - Taylor & Francis Group, 6000 Broken Sound Pkwy. NW, Ste. 300, Boca Raton, FL, 33487, USA, (800) 634-1420, (800) 634-7064, orders@taylorandfrancis.com, https://www.routledge.com/; The Europa World Year Book 2022.

United Nations Statistics Division (UNSD), United Nations Plz., New York, NY, 10017, USA, (800) 253-9646, (212) 963-9851, statistics@un.org, https://unstats.un.org; World Statistics Pocketbook 2021.

CZECH REPUBLIC-TEXTILE INDUSTRY

Euromonitor International, Inc., 1 N Dearborn St., Ste. 1700, Chicago, IL, 60602, USA, (312) 922-1115, (312) 922-1157, info-usa@euromonitor.com, https://www.euromonitor.com/; Market Research on the Retailing Industry.

Palgrave Macmillan, 1 New York Plaza, Ste. 4500, New York, NY, 10004-1562, USA, (800) 777-4643, orders@palgrave.com, https://www.palgrave.com/us; The Statesman's Yearbook, 2023.

United Nations Statistics Division (UNSD), United Nations Plz., New York, NY, 10017, USA, (800) 253-9646, (212) 963-9851, statistics@un.org, https://unstats.un.org; Statistical Yearbook of the United Nations 2021.

CZECH REPUBLIC-THEATER

UNESCO Institute for Statistics, C.P 250 Succursale H, Montreal, QC, H3G 2K8, CAN, (514) 343-6880 (Dial from U.S.), (514) 343-5740 (Fax from U.S.), uis.publications@unesco.org, http://uis.unesco.org/; UIS.Stat.

CZECH REPUBLIC-TOBACCO INDUSTRY

United Nations Statistics Division (UNSD), United Nations Plz., New York, NY, 10017, USA, (800) 253-9646, (212) 963-9851, statistics@un.org, https://unstats.un.org; Statistical Yearbook of the United Nations 2021.

CZECH REPUBLIC-TOURISM

Euromonitor International, Inc., 1 N Dearborn St., Ste. 1700, Chicago, IL, 60602, USA, (312) 922-1115, (312) 922-1157, info-usa@euromonitor.com, https://www.euromonitor.com/; Geographies.

European Commission, Rue de la Loi, 170, Brussels, B-1040, BEL, https://ec.europa.eu; Common Agricultural Policy (CAPF) Context Indicators, 2019 Update.

European Commission, Eurostat, Luxembourg, 2920, LUX, https://ec.europa.eu/eurostat/; European Union Tourism Database.

International Road Federation (IRF), Madison Place, 500 Montgomery St., 5th Fl., Alexandria, VA, 22314, USA, (703) 535-1001, (703) 535-1007, info@irf.global, https://www.irf.global/; World Road Statistics (WRS).

Routledge - Taylor & Francis Group, 6000 Broken Sound Pkwy. NW, Ste. 300, Boca Raton, FL, 33487, USA, (800) 634-1420, (800) 634-7064, orders@taylorandfrancis.com, https://www.routledge.com/; The Europa World Year Book 2022.

United Nations Statistics Division (UNSD), United Nations Plz., New York, NY, 10017, USA, (800) 253-9646, (212) 963-9851, statistics@un.org, https://unstats.un.org; Statistical Yearbook of the United Nations 2021.

United Nations World Tourism Organization (UNWTO), Calle Poeta Joan Maragall 42, Madrid, 28020, SPA, info@unwto.org, https://www.unwto.org/; Yearbook of Tourism Statistics, 2021 Edition.

CZECH REPUBLIC-TRADE

See CZECH REPUBLIC-INTERNATIONAL TRADE

CZECH REPUBLIC-TRANSPORTATION

Central Intelligence Agency (CIA), Office of Public Affairs, Washington, DC, 20505, USA, (703) 482-0623, https://www.cia.gov; The World Factbook.

Euromonitor International, Inc., 1 N Dearborn St., Ste. 1700, Chicago, IL, 60602, USA, (312) 922-1115, (312) 922-1157, info-usa@euromonitor.com, https://www.euromonitor.com/; Geographies.

European Commission, Eurostat, Luxembourg, 2920, LUX, https://ec.europa.eu/eurostat/; Air Transport Statistics.

Palgrave Macmillan, 1 New York Plaza, Ste. 4500, New York, NY, 10004-1562, USA, (800) 777-4643, orders@palgrave.com, https://www.palgrave.com/us; The Statesman's Yearbook, 2023.

Routledge - Taylor & Francis Group, 6000 Broken Sound Pkwy. NW, Ste. 300, Boca Raton, FL, 33487, USA, (800) 634-1420, (800) 634-7064, orders@taylorandfrancis.com, https://www.routledge.com/; The Europa World Year Book 2022.

United Nations Economic Commission for Europe (UNECE), Palais des Nations, Geneva, CH-1211, SWI, unece_info@un.org, https://unece.org/; UN-ECE Countries in Figures 2019.

CZECH REPUBLIC-UNEMPLOYMENT

International Labour Organization (ILO), 4 Rte. des Morillons, Geneva, CH-1211, SWI, ilo@ilo.org, https://www.ilo.org; NORMLEX Information System on International Labour Standards.

Organization for Economic Cooperation and Development (OECD), 2001 L St. NW, Ste. 650, Washington, DC, 20036-4922, USA, (202) 785-6323, (800) 456-6323, (202) 785-0350, washington.contact@oecd.org, https://www.oecd.org/; Economic Survey of Czech Republic 2023; OECD Composite Leading Indicator (CLI); and OECD Labour Force Statistics 2022.

Palgrave Macmillan, 1 New York Plaza, Ste. 4500, New York, NY, 10004-1562, USA, (800) 777-4643, orders@palgrave.com, https://www.palgrave.com/us; The Statesman's Yearbook, 2023.

United Nations Statistics Division (UNSD), United Nations Plz., New York, NY, 10017, USA, (800) 253-9646, (212) 963-9851, statistics@un.org, https://unstats.un.org; Statistical Yearbook of the United Nations 2021.

CZECH REPUBLIC-VITAL STATISTICS

Czech Statistical Office, Na padesatem 3268/81, Praha 10, Strasnice, 100 82, CZE, infoservis@czso.cz, https://www.czso.cz; Demographic Yearbook of the Czech Republic, 2020 and Population of the Czech Republic, 2021.

Palgrave Macmillan, 1 New York Plaza, Ste. 4500, New York, NY, 10004-1562, USA, (800) 777-4643, orders@palgrave.com, https://www.palgrave.com/us; The Statesman's Yearbook, 2023.

U.S. Census Bureau, 4600 Silver Hill Rd., Washington, DC, 20233, USA, (301) 763-4636, (800) 923-8282, https://www.census.gov; HIV/AIDS Surveillance Data Base.

United Nations Department of Economic and Social Affairs (DESA), Population Division, 2 United Nations Plz., Rm. DC2-1950, New York, NY, 10017, USA, (212) 963-3209, (212) 963-2147, population@un.org, https://www.un.org/development/desa/pd/; World Contraceptive Use 2021: Estimates and Projections of Family Planning Indicators and World Marriage Data 2019.

United Nations Statistics Division (UNSD), United Nations Plz., New York, NY, 10017, USA, (800) 253-9646, (212) 963-9851, statistics@un.org, https://unstats.un.org; Statistical Yearbook of the United Nations 2021.

World Health Organization (WHO), Ave. Appia 20, Geneva, CH-1211, SWI, (202) 974-3000 (Telephone in U.S.), publications@who.int, https://www.who.int/; Health Statistics and Information Systems.

CZECH REPUBLIC-WAGES

International Labour Organization (ILO), 4 Rte. des Morillons, Geneva, CH-1211, SWI, ilo@ilo.org, https://www.ilo.org; NORMLEX Information System on International Labour Standards.

United Nations Statistics Division (UNSD), United Nations Plz., New York, NY, 10017, USA, (800) 253-9646, (212) 963-9851, statistics@un.org, https://unstats.un.org; Statistical Yearbook of the United Nations 2021.

CZECH REPUBLIC-WHEAT PRODUCTION

See CZECH REPUBLIC-CROPS

CZECH REPUBLIC-WHOLESALE TRADE

United Nations Statistics Division (UNSD), United Nations Plz., New York, NY, 10017, USA, (800) 253-9646, (212) 963-9851, statistics@un.org, https://unstats.un.org; Statistical Yearbook of the United Nations 2021.

DAIRY PRODUCTS-CONSUMER EXPENDITURES

EnsembleIQ, 8550 W Bryn Mawr Ave., Ste. 200, Chicago, IL, 60631, USA, (877) 687-7321, https://ensembleiq.com/; 2021 Consumer Expenditures Report.

U.S. Department of Labor (DOL), Bureau of Labor Statistics (BLS), Postal Square Bldg., 2 Massachusetts Ave. NE, Washington, DC, 20212-0001, USA, (202) 691-5200, (202) 691-7890, blsdata_staff@bls.gov, https://www.bls.gov; Consumer Expenditure Survey (CE).

DAIRY PRODUCTS-CONSUMPTION

Department for Environment, Food and Rural Affairs (Defra), Seacole Bldg., 2 Marsham St., London, SW1P 4DF, GBR, defra.helpline@defra.gov.uk, https://www.gov.uk/defra; United Kingdom Milk Prices and Composition of Milk 2023.

U.S. Department of Agriculture (USDA), Economic Research Service (ERS), 1400 Independence Ave. SW, Mail Stop 1800, Washington, DC, 20250-0002, USA, (202) 720-2791, https://www.ers.usda.gov/; Food Price Outlook.

U.S. Department of Agriculture (USDA), Foreign Agricultural Service (FAS), 1400 Independence Ave. SW, Mail Stop 1001, Washington, DC, 20250, USA, (202) 720-3935, https://www.fas.usda.gov/; Dairy Monthly Imports.

DAIRY PRODUCTS-FARM MARKETINGS-SALES

U.S. Department of Agriculture (USDA), Economic Research Service (ERS), 1400 Independence Ave. SW, Mail Stop 1800, Washington, DC, 20250-0002, USA, (202) 720-2791, https://www.ers.usda.gov/; U.S. and State Farm Income and Wealth Statistics.

U.S. Department of Agriculture (USDA), National Agricultural Statistics Service (USDA-NASS), 1400 Independence Ave. SW, Washington, DC, 20250, USA, (800) 727-9540, nass@nass.usda.gov, https://www.nass.usda.gov; Dairy Products and Milk Production.

DAIRY PRODUCTS-INTERNATIONAL TRADE

U.S. Census Bureau, International Trade Program, 4600 Silver Hill Rd., Washington, DC, 20233, USA, (800) 549-0595, eid.international.trade.data@census.gov, https://www.census.gov/foreign-trade; International Trade Data.

U.S. Department of Agriculture (USDA), Economic Research Service (ERS), 1400 Independence Ave. SW, Mail Stop 1800, Washington, DC, 20250-0002, USA, (202) 720-2791, https://www.ers.usda.gov/; Food Price Outlook; Foreign Agricultural Trade of the United States (FATUS); and Outlook for U.S. Agricultural Trade: May 2022.

U.S. Department of Agriculture (USDA), Foreign Agricultural Service (FAS), 1400 Independence Ave. SW, Mail Stop 1001, Washington, DC, 20250, USA, (202) 720-3935, https://www.fas.usda.gov/; Dairy Monthly Imports and Dairy: World Markets and Trade.

DAIRY PRODUCTS-MANUFACTURING

U.S. Department of Agriculture (USDA), National Agricultural Statistics Service (USDA-NASS), 1400 Independence Ave. SW, Washington, DC, 20250, USA, (800) 727-9540, nass@nass.usda.gov, https://www.nass.usda.gov; Dairy Products and Milk Production.

DAIRY PRODUCTS-PRICES

U.S. Department of Agriculture (USDA), National Agricultural Statistics Service (USDA-NASS), 1400 Independence Ave. SW, Washington, DC, 20250, USA, (800) 727-9540, nass@nass.usda.gov, https://www.nass.usda.gov; Agricultural Prices.

DAIRY PRODUCTS-PRODUCTION

Cornucopia Institute, PO Box 826, Viroqua, WI, 54665, USA, (608) 636-8278, cultivate@cornucopia.org, https://www.cornucopia.org/; USDA-Backed 'Factory Farm' Takeover of Organic Milk Production Crushing Family-Scale Farmers and Forcing Them Out of Business.

U.S. Department of Agriculture (USDA), National Agricultural Statistics Service (USDA-NASS), 1400 Independence Ave. SW, Washington, DC, 20250, USA, (800) 727-9540, nass@nass.usda.gov, https://www.nass.usda.gov; Dairy Products; Milk Production; and Quick Stats.

DAMS

U.S. Army Corps of Engineers (USACE), 441 G St. NW, Washington, DC, 20314-1000, USA, (202) 761-0011, (202) 761-0001, hq-publicaffairs@usace.army.mil, https://www.usace.army.mil/; National Inventory of Dams (NID).

DANCE

National Assembly of State Arts Agencies (NASAA), 1200 18th St. NW, Ste. 1100, Washington, DC, 20036, USA, (202) 347-6352, (202) 296-0567 (TDD), (202) 737-0526, nasaa@nasaa-arts.org, https://nasaa-arts.org/; State Arts Agency Revenues Report, Fiscal Year 2022.

DARK TOURISM

University of Central Lancashire, Institute for Dark Tourism Research (iDTR), Preston, Lancashire, PR1 2HE, GBR, https://www.uclan.ac.uk/research/activity/dark-tourism; unpublished data.

DART THROWING

National Sporting Goods Association (NSGA), 3041 Woodcreek Dr., Ste. 210, Downers Grove, IL, 60515, USA, (847) 296-6742, (847) 391-9827, info@nsga.org, https://www.nsga.org; Sports Participation in the United States 2022.

DATA PROTECTION

Common Sense, 699 8th St., Ste. C150, San Francisco, CA, 94103, USA, (415) 863-0600, (415) 863-0601, https://www.commonsensemedia.org/; 2023 State of Kids' Privacy.

Federation of American Scientists (FAS), 1112 16th St. NW, Ste. 600, Washington, DC, 20036, USA, (202) 546-3300, (202) 675-1010, fas@fas.org, https://fas.org/; A More Responsible Digital Surveillance Future.

Network for Public Education (NPE), PO Box 227, New York, NY, 10156, USA, (646) 678-4477, info@networkforpubliceducation.org, https://networkforpubliceducation.org/; The State Student Privacy Report Cards: Grading the States on Protecting Student Data Privacy.

Princeton University Center for Information Technology Policy (CITP), Princeton Web Transparency & Accountability Project (WebTAP), 308 Sherrerd Hall, Princeton, NJ, 08544, USA, (609) 258-9302, arvindn@cs.princeton.edu, https://webtap.princeton.edu/; Dark Patterns at Scale: Findings from a Crawl of 11K Shopping Websites and The Impact of User Location on Cookie Notices (Inside and Outside of the European Union).

SAE International, 400 Commonwealth Dr., Warrendale, PA, 15096, USA, (724) 776-4790, (724) 776-4841, (724) 776-0790, customerservice@sae.org, https://www.sae.org/; SAE International Journal of Transportation Cybersecurity and Privacy.

U.S. Department of Commerce (DOC), National Telecommunications and Information Administration (NTIA), Herbert C. Hoover Bldg., 1401 Constitution Ave. NW, Washington, DC, 20230, USA, (202) 482-2000, https://www.ntia.doc.gov; Data Central.

Verizon, 1095 Avenue of the Americas, New York, NY, 10036, USA, (212) 395-1000, https://enterprise.verizon.com/resources/reports; Data Breach Investigations Report (DBIR) 2023.

DATES

U.S. Department of Agriculture (USDA), National Agricultural Statistics Service (USDA-NASS), 1400 Independence Ave. SW, Washington, DC, 20250, USA, (800) 727-9540, nass@nass.usda.gov, https://www.nass.usda.gov; Quick Stats.

DATING

OkCupid Blog, USA, https://theblog.okcupid.com/; OkCupid Data.

DATING VIOLENCE

National Coalition of Anti-Violence Programs (NCAVP), 116 Nassau St., 3rd Fl., New York, NY, 10038, USA, (212) 714-1184, ecruz@avp.org, https://avp.org/ncavp/; Pride and Pain: A Snapshot of Anti-LGBTQ Hate and Violence During Pride Season 2019 and Supporting LGBTQ Survivors of Violence During the COVID-19 Pandemic.

DAY CARE

See CHILD DAY CARE SERVICES

DEAD

Green Burial Council (GBC), 2720 Cold Springs Rd., Placerville, CA, 95667, USA, (888) 966-3330, info@greenburialcouncil.org, https://www.greenburialcouncil.org; Disposition Statistics.

DEATH

See also MORTALITY

The Lancet, 230 Park Ave., New York, NY, 10169, USA, (212) 633-3800, editorial@lancet.com, https://www.thelancet.com/; Global, Regional, and National Minimum Estimates of Children Affected by COVID-19-Associated Orphanhood and Caregiver Death, by Age and Family Circumstance up to Oct 31, 2021: An Updated Modelling Study.

National Bureau of Economic Research (NBER), 1050 Massachusetts Ave., Cambridge, MA, 02138, USA, (617) 868-3900, info@nber.org, https://www.nber.org/; Medicaid and Mortality: New Evidence from Linked Survey and Administrative Data.

DEATH CARE INDUSTRY

National Funeral Directors Association (NFDA), 13625 Bishop's Dr., Brookfield, WI, 53005, USA, (800) 228-6332, (262) 789-1880, (262) 789-6977, nfda@nfda.org, https://nfda.org/; Memorial Business Journal.

SAGE Publications, 2455 Teller Rd., Thousand Oaks, CA, 91320, USA, (800) 818-7243, (800) 583-2665, journals@sagepub.com, https://www.sagepub.com; Palliative Medicine and Palliative Medicine - End-of-Life Care in COVID-19: An Audit of Pharmacological Management in Hospital Inpatients.

DEATH PENALTY

See CAPITAL PUNISHMENT

DEATH RATES

See MORTALITY

DEATH ROW

Death Penalty Information Center (DPIC), 1701 K St. NW, Ste. 205, Washington, DC, 20006, USA, (202) 289-2275, dpic@deathpenaltyinfo.org, https://deathpenaltyinfo.org/; Study: Dehumanizing Belief Systems Linked to Support for Guns Rights, the Death Penalty, and Anti-Immigration Practices.

DEATH ROW INMATES

Death Penalty Information Center (DPIC), 1701 K St. NW, Ste. 205, Washington, DC, 20006, USA, (202) 289-2275, dpic@deathpenaltyinfo.org, https://deathpenaltyinfo.org/; The Death Penalty in 2022: Year End Report; DPIC Analysis: At Least 1,300 Prisoners Are on U.S. Death Rows in Violation of U.S. Human Rights Obligations; DPIC Mid-Year Review: Pandemic and Continuing Historic Decline Produce Record-Low Death Penalty Use in First Half of 2020; and Execution Database.

DEBIT CARDS

The Nilson Report, PO Box 50539, Santa Barbara, CA, 93150, USA, (805) 684-8800, (805) 684-8825, info@nilsonreport.com, https://www.nilsonreport.com; The Nilson Report and The World's Top Card Issuers and Merchant Acquirers.

DEBT-CONSUMER

Board of Governors of the Federal Reserve System, Constitution Ave. NW, Washington, DC, 20551, USA, (202) 452-3000, (202) 263-4869 (TDD), https://www.federalreserve.gov; Federal Reserve Bulletin and Household Debt Service and Financial Obligations Ratios 2022.

University of California Los Angeles (UCLA), Luskin Center for Innovation, 3323 Public Affairs Bldg., PO Box 951656, Los Angeles, CA, 90095-1656, USA, (310) 267-5435, (310) 267-5443, https://innovation.luskin.ucla.edu/; Keeping the Lights and Heat On: COVID-19 Utility Debt in Communities Served by Pacific Gas and Electric Company.

DEBT-FARM

U.S. Department of Agriculture (USDA), Economic Research Service (ERS), 1400 Independence Ave. SW, Mail Stop 1800, Washington, DC, 20250-0002, USA, (202) 720-2791, https://www.ers.usda.gov/; Amber Waves: The Economics of Food, Farming, Natural Resources, and Rural America and U.S. and State Farm Income and Wealth Statistics.

DEBT-FEDERAL GOVERNMENT

Internal Revenue Service (IRS), Statistics of Income Division (SOI), 1111 Constitution Ave. NW, K-Room 4100-123, Washington, DC, 20224-0002, USA, (202) 874-0410, (202) 874-0964, sis@irs.gov, https://www.irs.gov/uac/soi-tax-stats-statistics-of-income; Tax Stats - Individual Tax Statistics.

U.S. Census Bureau, Public Sector, 4600 Silver Hill Rd., Washington, DC, 20233, USA, (800) 923-8282, (301) 763-4636, ewd.outreach@census.gov, https://www.census.gov/topics/public-sector.html; Annual Survey of State and Local Government Finances and Census of Governments.

U.S. Department of the Treasury (DOT), 1500 Pennsylvania Ave. NW, Washington, DC, 20220, USA, (202) 622-2000, (202) 622-6415, https://home.treasury.gov; Treasury Bulletin.

U.S. Office of Management and Budget (OMB), 725 17th St. NW, Washington, DC, 20503, USA, (202) 395-3080, https://www.whitehouse.gov/omb/; Historical Tables.

usdebtclock.org, USA, feedback@usdebtclock.org, https://www.usdebtclock.org/; usdebtclock.org.

DEBT-FOREIGN COUNTRIES

Climate Analytics, 135 Madison Ave., 5th Fl., Ste. 05-115, New York, NY, 10016, USA, info.ny@climateanalytics.org, https://climateanalytics.org/; 2 Steps Down the Debt Spiral: COVID-19 and Tropical Cyclones Severely Limit the Fiscal Space of Many Small Island Developing States.

International Institute for Environment and Development (IIED), 235 High Holborn, London, WC1V 7DN, GBR, inforequest@iied.org, https://www.iied.org; Redesigning Debt: Lessons from HIPC for COVID, Climate and Nature.

International Monetary Fund (IMF), 700 19th St. NW, Washington, DC, 20431, USA, (202) 623-7000, (202) 623-4661, publications@imf.org, https://www.imf.org; Joint External Debt Hub (JEDH).

The World Bank, 1818 H St. NW, Washington, DC, 20433, USA, (202) 473-1000, (202) 477-6391, eds03@worldbank.org, https://www.worldbank.org/; World Bank Quarterly External Debt Statistics (QEDS) SDDS and World Development Indicators (WDI) 2022.

DEBT-HOUSEHOLDS

Board of Governors of the Federal Reserve System, Constitution Ave. NW, Washington, DC, 20551, USA, (202) 452-3000, (202) 263-4869 (TDD), https://www.federalreserve.gov; Federal Reserve Bulletin and Financial Accounts of the United States 2023.

DEBT-LOCAL GOVERNMENTS

U.S. Census Bureau, Public Sector, 4600 Silver Hill Rd., Washington, DC, 20233, USA, (800) 923-8282, (301) 763-4636, ewd.outreach@census.gov, https://www.census.gov/topics/public-sector.html; Annual Survey of State and Local Government Finances and Census of Governments.

DEBT-PUBLIC-STATE AND LOCAL GOVERNMENT-HIGHWAYS

U.S. Department of Transportation (DOT), Federal Highway Administration (FHA), 1200 New Jersey Ave. SE, Washington, DC, 20590, USA, (202) 366-4000, https://highways.dot.gov/; Highway Statistics 2020.

DEBT-PUBLIC-STATE GOVERNMENT

U.S. Census Bureau, Public Sector, 4600 Silver Hill Rd., Washington, DC, 20233, USA, (800) 923-8282, (301) 763-4636, ewd.outreach@census.gov, https://www.census.gov/topics/public-sector.html; Annual Survey of State and Local Government Finances.

DEBT-STATE AND LOCAL GOVERNMENTS

U.S. Census Bureau, Public Sector, 4600 Silver Hill Rd., Washington, DC, 20233, USA, (800) 923-8282, (301) 763-4636, ewd.outreach@census.gov, https://www.census.gov/topics/public-sector.html; Annual Survey of State and Local Government Finances.

DECISION MAKING

Brown University, Population Studies and Training Center (PSTC), 68 Waterman St., PO Box 1836, Providence, RI, 02912, USA, (401) 863-2668, (401) 863-3351, population_studies@brown.edu, https://www.brown.edu/academics/population-studies/; The Determinants of Efficient Behavior in Coordination Games.

Civis Analytics, 200 W Monroe St., 22nd Fl., Chicago, IL, 60606, USA, https://www.civisanalytics.com/; How Do You Persuade People to Get a Flu Shot?.

National Bureau of Economic Research (NBER), 1050 Massachusetts Ave., Cambridge, MA, 02138, USA, (617) 868-3900, info@nber.org, https://www.nber.org/; Destructive Behavior, Judgment, and Economic Decision-Making Under Thermal Stress.

DEDUCTIONS (TAXES)

Internal Revenue Service (IRS), Statistics of Income Division (SOI), 1111 Constitution Ave. NW, K-Room 4100-123, Washington, DC, 20224-0002, USA, (202) 874-0410, (202) 874-0964, sis@irs.gov, https://www.irs.gov/uac/soi-tax-stats-statistics-of-income; Tax Stats - Individual Tax Statistics.

DEFENSE INDUSTRIES

S&P Global, 55 Water St., New York, NY, 10041, USA, (212) 438-2000, market.intelligence@spglobal.com, https://www.spglobal.com/; Update: Aerospace and Defense North America.

Small Arms Survey, Maison de la Paix, Chemin Eugene-Rigot 2E, Geneva, CH-1202, SWI, sas@smallarmssurvey.org, https://www.smallarmssurvey.org/; Global Firearms Holdings; Global Violent Deaths (GVD) Database; 2021 Small Arms Trade Transparency Barometer; and Unplanned Explosions at Munitions Sites (UEMS).

DEFENSE, DEPARTMENT OF-BUDGET AUTHORITY, OUTLAYS

U.S. Department of Defense (DOD), 1400 Defense Pentagon, Washington, DC, 20301-1400, USA, (703) 571-3343, https://www.defense.gov; Agency Financial Report: Fiscal Year 2021.

U.S. Office of Management and Budget (OMB), 725 17th St. NW, Washington, DC, 20503, USA, (202) 395-3080, https://www.whitehouse.gov/omb/; Historical Tables.

DEFENSE, DEPARTMENT OF-EXPENDITURES

S&P Global, 55 Water St., New York, NY, 10041, USA, (212) 438-2000, market.intelligence@spglobal.com, https://www.spglobal.com/; Update: Aerospace and Defense North America.

U.S. Department of Defense (DOD), 1400 Defense Pentagon, Washington, DC, 20301-1400, USA, (703) 571-3343, https://www.defense.gov; Agency Financial Report: Fiscal Year 2021.

U.S. Office of Management and Budget (OMB), 725 17th St. NW, Washington, DC, 20503, USA, (202) 395-3080, https://www.whitehouse.gov/omb/; Historical Tables.

DEFENSE, DEPARTMENT OF-FUNDS AVAILABLE AND OUTLAYS

U.S. Office of Management and Budget (OMB), 725 17th St. NW, Washington, DC, 20503, USA, (202) 395-3080, https://www.whitehouse.gov/omb/; Historical Tables.

DEFENSE, DEPARTMENT OF-PROPERTY-REAL AND PERSONAL

U.S. General Services Administration (GSA), 1800 F St. NW, Washington, DC, 20405, USA, (844) 472-4111, https://www.gsa.gov/; Federal Real Property Profile (FRPP) Summary Reports.

DEFORESTATION-CONTROL

Environmental Defense Fund (EDF), 1875 Connecticut Ave. NW, Ste. 600, Washington, DC, 20009, USA, (202) 572-3298, (202) 387-3500, (202) 234-6049, https://www.edf.org; Justification for High Forest, Low Deforestation Crediting: How Jurisdictional HFLD Credits Meet Integrity and Additionality Thresholds for Fungibility.

DEGREES CONFERRED

See also Individual Fields

National Science Foundation, National Center for Science and Engineering Statistics (NCSES), 2415 Eisenhower Ave., Ste. W14200, Arlington, VA, 22314, USA, (703) 292-8780, (703) 292-9092, info@nsf.gov, https://www.nsf.gov/statistics/; Survey of Doctorate Recipients and Survey of Earned Doctorates.

U.S. Department of Education (ED), Institute of Education Sciences (IES), National Center for Education Statistics (NCES), Potomac Center Plaza, 550 12th St. SW, Washington, DC, 20202, USA, (202) 403-5551, https://nces.ed.gov/; Digest of Education Statistics, 2020.

DEGREES CONFERRED-SALARY OFFERS

National Association of Colleges and Employers (NACE), 1 E Broad St., Ste 130-1005, Bethlehem, PA, 18018, USA, (610) 868-1421, customerservice@naceweb.org, https://www.naceweb.org/; Recruiting Benchmarks Survey Report 2022 and Salary Survey.

DELAWARE

See also-STATE DATA (FOR INDIVIDUAL STATES)

DELAWARE-STATE DATA CENTERS

Delaware Office of Management and Budget, Haslet Armory, 122 Martin Luther King Jr. Blvd. S, Dover, DE, 19901, USA, (302) 739-4206, (302) 739-5661, https://omb.delaware.gov/; State Data Reports (DE).

University of Delaware, Center for Applied Demography and Survey Research (CADSR), 111 Academy St., Newark, DE, 19716, USA, (302) 831-8406, udelcadsr@udel.edu, https://www.bidenschool.udel.edu/cadsr; State Data Reports (DE).

DELAWARE-PRIMARY STATISTICS SOURCES

Delaware Department of Education, The Townsend Bldg., 401 Federal St., Ste. 2, Dover, DE, 19901-3639, USA, (302) 735-4000, (302) 739-4654, dedoe@doe.k12.de.us, https://education.delaware.gov/; Delaware Educator Data System (DEEDS) and Delaware Report Card.

Delaware Division of Small Business, 99 Kings Hwy., Dover, DE, 19901, USA, (302) 739-4271, https://business.delaware.gov/; SizeUpDelaware.

SAGE Publications, 2455 Teller Rd., Thousand Oaks, CA, 91320, USA, (800) 818-7243, (800) 583-2665, journals@sagepub.com, https://www.sagepub.com; Data Planet.

DELINQUENCY

See JUVENILE DELINQUENCY

DEMENTIA

AlzForum Foundation Inc., 7 Water St., Boston, MA, 02109, USA, contact@alzforum.org, https://www.alzforum.org; AlzForum.

Alzheimer's Association, 225 N Michigan Ave., 17th Fl., Chicago, IL, 60601, USA, (312) 335-8700, (800) 272-3900, (866) 699-1246, info@alz.org, https://www.alz.org/; Alzheimer's & Dementia: The Journal of the Alzheimer's Association and 2022 Alzheimer's Disease Facts and Figures.

Alzheimer's Disease International (ADI), 15 Blue Lion Pl., London, SE1 4PU, GBR, info@alzint.org, https://www.alzint.org; Global Perspective Newsletter; World Alzheimer Report 2020: Design, Dignity, Dementia: Dementia-Related Design and the Built Environment; World Alzheimer Report 2021: Journey to a Diagnosis of Dementia; and World Alzheimer Report 2022: Life After Diagnosis: Navigating Treatment, Care and Support.

Alzheimer's Foundation of America (AFA), 322 8th Ave., 16th Fl., New York, NY, 10001, USA, (866) 232-8484, (646) 638-1542, (646) 638-1546, info@alzfdn.org, https://alzfdn.org; unpublished data.

Dementia Singapore, 20 Bendemeer Rd. , No. 01-02, BS Bendemeer Centre, 339914, SGP, https://dementia.org.sg/; Voice of Dementia 2023.

Rush Alzheimer's Disease Center (RADC), 1620 W Harrison St., Chicago, IL, 60612, USA, (312) 942-0050, (312) 942-7100, https://www.rushu.rush.edu/research/departmental-research/rush-alzheimers-disease-center; RADC Research Resource Sharing Hub and Rush Memory Clinic Data Repository.

Springer Nature, BMC, 1 New York Plaza, Ste. 4600, New York, NY, 10004-1562, USA, info@biomedcentral.com, https://www.biomedcentral.com/; Alzheimer's Research & Therapy.

U.S. Department of Health and Human Services (HHS), National Institutes of Health (NIH), National Institute on Aging (NIA), Alzheimer's Disease Education and Referral (ADEAR) Center, PO Box 8057, Gaithersburg, MD, 20898, USA, (800) 438-4380, adear@nia.nih.gov, https://www.nia.nih.gov/health/alzheimers; alzheimers.gov.

DEMOCRACY

Democracy Fund Voter Study Group, 1200 17th St. NW, Ste. 300, Washington, DC, 20036, USA, (202) 420-7900, https://www.voterstudygroup.org/; Democracy Maybe: Attitudes on Authoritarianism in America and Nationscape: A Comprehensive View of the American Electorate.

The Economist Group: Economist Intelligence Unit (EIU), 900 3rd Ave., 16th Fl., New York, NY, 10022, USA, (212) 541-0500, americas@eiu.com, https://www.eiu.com; Democracy Index 2022.

Freedom House, 1850 M St. NW, 11th Fl., Washington, DC, 20036, USA, (202) 296-5101, info@freedomhouse.org, https://freedomhouse.org; The Democracy Project and Freedom in the World 2022: The Global Expansion of Authoritarian Rule.

International Institute for Democracy and Electoral Assistance (International IDEA), Stromsborg, Stockholm, SE 103 34, SWE, https://www.idea.int/; Gender Quotas Database; The Integrity of Political Finance Systems in Africa: Tackling Political Corruption; and The Integrity of Political Finance Systems in Asia: Tackling Political Corruption.

Pew Research Center, International Affairs, 1615 L St. NW, Ste. 800, Washington, DC, 20036, USA, (202) 419-4300, (202) 857-8562, https://www.pewresearch.org/topic/international-affairs/; Social Media Seen as Mostly Good for Democracy Across Many Nations, But U.S. Is a Major Outlier.

Public Religion Research Institute (PRRI), 1023 15th St. NW, 9th Fl., Washington, DC, 20005, USA, (202) 238-9424, info@prri.org, https://www.prri.org/; American Democracy in Crisis: The Fate of Pluralism in a Divided Nation.

U.S. Commission on Civil Rights (USCCR), 1331 Pennsylvania Ave. NW, Ste. 1150, Washington, DC, 20425, USA, (202) 376-7700, (202) 376-8116 (TTY), publications@usccr.gov, https://www.usccr.gov/; 2019 Statutory Enforcement Report: Are Rights A Reality? Evaluating Federal Civil Rights Enforcement.

DEMOCRATIC KAMPUCHEA

See CAMBODIA

DEMOCRATIC PARTY (U.S.)

Associated Press-NORC Center for Public Affairs Research (AP-NORC), 55 E Monroe St., 30th Fl., Chicago, IL, 60603, USA, (312) 759-4000, info@apnorc.org, https://apnorc.org/; Feeling the Sting of Rising Prices, Most Are Critical of the National Economy and Biden's Management of It.

FiveThirtyEight, 47 W 66th St., 2nd Fl., New York, NY, 10023, USA, contact@fivethirtyeight.com, https://fivethirtyeight.com/; Do Voters Want Democrats or Republicans In Congress?.

The Gallup Organization, 901 F St. NW, Washington, DC, 20004, USA, (202) 715-3030, (800) 204-1192, (202) 715-3045, https://www.gallup.com; Mixed Views Among Americans on Transgender Issues and Social Conservatism in U.S. Highest in About a Decade.

The Henry J. Kaiser Family Foundation (KFF), 185 Berry St., Ste. 2000, San Francisco, CA, 94107, USA, (650) 854-9400, (650) 854-4800, https://www.kff.org; KFF COVID-19 Vaccine Monitor: The Increasing Importance of Partisanship in Predicting COVID-19 Vaccination Status.

Marist College Institute for Public Opinion, 3399 North Rd., Poughkeepsie, NY, 12601, USA, (845) 575-5050, https://maristpoll.marist.edu; The 2022 Midterms & Biden's Job Performance, April 2022.

Pew Research Center, 1615 L St. NW, Ste. 800, Washington, DC, 20036, USA, (202) 419-4300, (202) 857-8562, info@pewresearch.org, https://www.pewresearch.org/; Deep Partisan Divide on Whether Greater Acceptance of Transgender People Is Good for Society.

Quinnipiac University Poll, Mount Carmel Campus, 275 Mount Carmel Ave., Hamden, CT, 06518, USA, (203) 582-5201, (800) 462-1944, poll@qu.edu, https://poll.qu.edu; 78% of Republicans Want to See Trump Run for President in 2024, Quinnipiac University National Poll Finds; Americans Now Split on Border Wall as Opposition Softens.

Yale Project on Climate Change Communication (YPCCC), Yale School of the Environment, 195 Prospect St., New Haven, CT, 06511, USA, (203) 432-5055, climatechange@yale.edu, https://climatecommunication.yale.edu/; Politics & Global Warming, April 2022.

YouGov, 38 W 21st St., New York, NY, 10010, USA, (646) 213-7414, help.us@yougov.com, https://today.yougov.com/; On Issues Relating to Transgender Youth, Democrats and Republicans Are Far Apart.

DENMARK-NATIONAL STATISTICAL OFFICE

Statistics Denmark (Danmarks Statistik), Sejroegade 11, Copenhagen, DK-2100, DEN, dst@dst.dk, https://www.dst.dk/en; National Data Reports (Denmark).

DENMARK-PRIMARY STATISTICS SOURCES

European Commission, Eurostat, Luxembourg, 2920, LUX, https://ec.europa.eu/eurostat/; Key Figures on Enlargement Countries, 2019.

Statistics Denmark (Danmarks Statistik), Sejroegade 11, Copenhagen, DK-2100, DEN, dst@dst.dk, https://www.dst.dk/en; Denmark in Figures 2019.

DENMARK-DATABASES

Statistics Denmark (Danmarks Statistik), Sejroegade 11, Copenhagen, DK-2100, DEN, dst@dst.dk, https://www.dst.dk/en; StatBank Denmark.

DENMARK-ABORTION

Nordic Council of Ministers, Ved Stranden 18, Copenhagen, DK-1061, DEN, nmr@norden.org, https://www.norden.org/en; Nordic Children and Young People in Figures 2021 and Nordic Statistics Database.

DENMARK-AGRICULTURAL MACHINERY

European Commission, Rue de la Loi, 170, Brussels, B-1040, BEL, https://ec.europa.eu; EU Energy in Figures: Statistical Pocketbook 2021.

DENMARK-AGRICULTURE

The Economist Group: Economist Intelligence Unit (EIU), 900 3rd Ave., 16th Fl., New York, NY, 10022, USA, (212) 541-0500, americas@eiu.com, https://www.eiu.com; Denmark Country Report.

Euromonitor International, Inc., 1 N Dearborn St., Ste. 1700, Chicago, IL, 60602, USA, (312) 922-1115, (312) 922-1157, info-usa@euromonitor.com, https://www.euromonitor.com/; Geographies.

European Commission, Rue de la Loi, 170, Brussels, B-1040, BEL, https://ec.europa.eu; Common Agricultural Policy (CAPF) Context Indicators, 2019 Update.

European Commission, Eurostat, Luxembourg, 2920, LUX, https://ec.europa.eu/eurostat/; Eurostat Regional Yearbook 2021 and Farmers and the Agricultural Labour Force - Statistics.

International Monetary Fund (IMF), 700 19th St. NW, Washington, DC, 20431, USA, (202) 623-7000, (202) 623-4661, publications@imf.org, https://www.imf.org; International Financial Statistics (IFS).

Nordic Council of Ministers, Ved Stranden 18, Copenhagen, DK-1061, DEN, nmr@norden.org, https://www.norden.org/en; Nordic Children and Young People in Figures 2021 and Nordic Statistics Database.

Organization for Economic Cooperation and Development (OECD), 2001 L St. NW, Ste. 650, Washington, DC, 20036-4922, USA, (202) 785-6323, (800) 456-6323, (202) 785-0350, washington.contact@oecd.org, https://www.oecd.org/; Economic Survey of Denmark 2021; OECD-FAO Agricultural Outlook 2022-2031; and STAN (STructural ANalysis) Database.

Palgrave Macmillan, 1 New York Plaza, Ste. 4500, New York, NY, 10004-1562, USA, (800) 777-4643, orders@palgrave.com, https://www.palgrave.com/us; The Statesman's Yearbook, 2023.

Routledge - Taylor & Francis Group, 6000 Broken Sound Pkwy. NW, Ste. 300, Boca Raton, FL, 33487, USA, (800) 634-1420, (800) 634-7064, orders@taylorandfrancis.com, https://www.routledge.com/; The Europa World Year Book 2022.

United Nations Food and Agricultural Organization (FAO), 2121 K St., Ste. 800B, Washington, DC, 20037, USA, (202) 653-2400 (Dial from U.S.), (202) 653-5760 (Fax from U.S.), fao-hq@fao.org, https://www.fao.org; AQUASTAT and The State of Food and Agriculture (SOFA) 2022.

United Nations Statistics Division (UNSD), United Nations Plz., New York, NY, 10017, USA, (800) 253-9646, (212) 963-9851, statistics@un.org, https://unstats.un.org; Statistical Yearbook of the United Nations 2021.

The World Bank, 1818 H St. NW, Washington, DC, 20433, USA, (202) 473-1000, (202) 477-6391, eds03@worldbank.org, https://www.worldbank.org/; Denmark (report) and World Development Indicators (WDI) 2022.

DENMARK-AIRLINES

European Commission, Rue de la Loi, 170, Brussels, B-1040, BEL, https://ec.europa.eu; EU Energy in Figures: Statistical Pocketbook 2021.

European Commission, Eurostat, Luxembourg, 2920, LUX, https://ec.europa.eu/eurostat/; Air Transport Statistics.

International Civil Aviation Organization (ICAO), 999 Robert-Bourassa Blvd., Montreal, QC, H3C 5H7, CAN, (514) 954-8219 (Dial from U.S.), (514) 954-6077 (Fax from U.S.), icaohq@icao.int, https://www.icao.int; ICAO Regional Reports.

Nordic Council of Ministers, Ved Stranden 18, Copenhagen, DK-1061, DEN, nmr@norden.org, https://www.norden.org/en; Nordic Children and Young People in Figures 2021 and Nordic Statistics Database.

Organization for Economic Cooperation and Development (OECD), 2001 L St. NW, Ste. 650, Washington, DC, 20036-4922, USA, (202) 785-6323, (800) 456-6323, (202) 785-0350, washington.contact@oecd.org, https://www.oecd.org/; OECD Tourism Trends and Policies 2022.

Palgrave Macmillan, 1 New York Plaza, Ste. 4500, New York, NY, 10004-1562, USA, (800) 777-4643, orders@palgrave.com, https://www.palgrave.com/us; The Statesman's Yearbook, 2023.

Routledge - Taylor & Francis Group, 6000 Broken Sound Pkwy. NW, Ste. 300, Boca Raton, FL, 33487, USA, (800) 634-1420, (800) 634-7064, orders@taylorandfrancis.com, https://www.routledge.com/; The Europa World Year Book 2022.

DENMARK-ALUMINUM PRODUCTION

See DENMARK-MINERAL INDUSTRIES

DENMARK-ANIMAL FEEDING

United Nations Statistics Division (UNSD), United Nations Plz., New York, NY, 10017, USA, (800) 253-9646, (212) 963-9851, statistics@un.org, https://unstats.un.org; Statistical Yearbook of the United Nations 2021.

DENMARK-ARMED FORCES

Central Intelligence Agency (CIA), Office of Public Affairs, Washington, DC, 20505, USA, (703) 482-0623, https://www.cia.gov; The World Factbook.

International Institute for Strategic Studies (IISS) - Americas, 2121 K St. NW, Ste. 600, Washington, DC, 20037, USA, (202) 659-1490, (202) 659-1499, https://www.iiss.org/; The Military Balance 2022.

Nordic Council of Ministers, Ved Stranden 18, Copenhagen, DK-1061, DEN, nmr@norden.org, https://www.norden.org/en; Nordic Children and Young People in Figures 2021 and Nordic Statistics Database.

Palgrave Macmillan, 1 New York Plaza, Ste. 4500, New York, NY, 10004-1562, USA, (800) 777-4643, orders@palgrave.com, https://www.palgrave.com/us; The Statesman's Yearbook, 2023.

Stockholm International Peace Research Institute (SIPRI), Signalistgatan 9, Stockholm, SE 169 72, SWE, https://www.sipri.org/; SIPRI Arms Transfers Database and SIPRI Military Expenditure Database.

DENMARK-BALANCE OF PAYMENTS

European Commission, Eurostat, Luxembourg, 2920, LUX, https://ec.europa.eu/eurostat/; Eurostat Regional Yearbook 2021.

International Monetary Fund (IMF), 700 19th St. NW, Washington, DC, 20431, USA, (202) 623-7000, (202) 623-4661, publications@imf.org, https://www.imf.org; Balance of Payments Statistics: Annual Report 2021 and International Financial Statistics (IFS).

Nordic Council of Ministers, Ved Stranden 18, Copenhagen, DK-1061, DEN, nmr@norden.org, https://www.norden.org/en; Nordic Children and Young People in Figures 2021 and Nordic Statistics Database.

Organization for Economic Cooperation and Development (OECD), 2001 L St. NW, Ste. 650, Washington, DC, 20036-4922, USA, (202) 785-6323, (800) 456-6323, (202) 785-0350, washington.contact@oecd.org, https://www.oecd.org/; Economic Survey of Denmark 2021; Geographical Distribution of Financial Flows to Developing Countries 2023; and OECD Digital Economy Outlook 2020.

Routledge - Taylor & Francis Group, 6000 Broken Sound Pkwy. NW, Ste. 300, Boca Raton, FL, 33487, USA, (800) 634-1420, (800) 634-7064, orders@taylorandfrancis.com, https://www.routledge.com/; The Europa World Year Book 2022.

United Nations Conference on Trade and Development (UNCTAD), Palais des Nations, Geneva, 1211, SWI, (212) 963-6896, unctadinfo@unctad.org, https://unctad.org; Handbook of Statistics 2021.

United Nations Statistics Division (UNSD), United Nations Plz., New York, NY, 10017, USA, (800) 253-9646, (212) 963-9851, statistics@un.org, https://unstats.un.org; Energy Statistics Yearbook 2019.

The World Bank, 1818 H St. NW, Washington, DC, 20433, USA, (202) 473-1000, (202) 477-6391, eds03@worldbank.org, https://www.worldbank.org/; Denmark (report); World Development Indicators (WDI) 2022; and World Development Report 2022: Finance for an Equitable Recovery.

DENMARK-BANANAS

See DENMARK-CROPS

DENMARK-BANKS AND BANKING

Euromonitor International, Inc., 1 N Dearborn St., Ste. 1700, Chicago, IL, 60602, USA, (312) 922-1115, (312) 922-1157, info-usa@euromonitor.com, https://www.euromonitor.com/; Geographies.

European Commission, Eurostat, Luxembourg, 2920, LUX, https://ec.europa.eu/eurostat/; Eurostat Regional Yearbook 2021.

International Monetary Fund (IMF), 700 19th St. NW, Washington, DC, 20431, USA, (202) 623-7000, (202) 623-4661, publications@imf.org, https://www.imf.org; International Financial Statistics (IFS).

Nordic Council of Ministers, Ved Stranden 18, Copenhagen, DK-1061, DEN, nmr@norden.org, https://www.norden.org/en; Nordic Children and Young People in Figures 2021 and Nordic Statistics Database.

Organization for Economic Cooperation and Development (OECD), 2001 L St. NW, Ste. 650, Washington, DC, 20036-4922, USA, (202) 785-6323, (800) 456-6323, (202) 785-0350, washington.contact@oecd.org, https://www.oecd.org/; Economic Survey of Denmark 2021; OECD Business and Finance Outlook 2021; and OECD Digital Economy Outlook 2020.

Routledge - Taylor & Francis Group, 6000 Broken Sound Pkwy. NW, Ste. 300, Boca Raton, FL, 33487, USA, (800) 634-1420, (800) 634-7064, orders@taylorandfrancis.com, https://www.routledge.com/; The Europa World Year Book 2022.

United Nations Statistics Division (UNSD), United Nations Plz., New York, NY, 10017, USA, (800) 253-9646, (212) 963-9851, statistics@un.org, https://unstats.un.org; Statistical Yearbook of the United Nations 2021.

DENMARK-BARLEY PRODUCTION

See DENMARK-CROPS

DENMARK-BONDS

Organization for Economic Cooperation and Development (OECD), 2001 L St. NW, Ste. 650, Washington, DC, 20036-4922, USA, (202) 785-6323, (800) 456-6323, (202) 785-0350, washington.contact@oecd.org, https://www.oecd.org/; OECD Business and Finance Outlook 2021.

United Nations Statistics Division (UNSD), United Nations Plz., New York, NY, 10017, USA, (800) 253-9646, (212) 963-9851, statistics@un.org, https://unstats.un.org; Statistical Yearbook of the United Nations 2021.

DENMARK-BROADCASTING

Central Intelligence Agency (CIA), Office of Public Affairs, Washington, DC, 20505, USA, (703) 482-0623, https://www.cia.gov; The World Factbook.

Euromonitor International, Inc., 1 N Dearborn St., Ste. 1700, Chicago, IL, 60602, USA, (312) 922-1115, (312) 922-1157, info-usa@euromonitor.com, https://www.euromonitor.com/; Geographies.

Palgrave Macmillan, 1 New York Plaza, Ste. 4500, New York, NY, 10004-1562, USA, (800) 777-4643,

orders@palgrave.com, https://www.palgrave.com/us; The Statesman's Yearbook, 2023.

UNESCO Institute for Statistics, C.P 250 Succursale H, Montreal, QC, H3G 2K8, CAN, (514) 343-6880 (Dial from U.S.), (514) 343-5740 (Fax from U.S.), uis.publications@unesco.org, http://uis.unesco.org/; UIS.Stat.

WRTH Publications Limited, PO Box 290, Oxford, OX2 7FT, GBR, sales@wrth.com, https://www.wrth.com; World Radio TV Handbook 2023.

DENMARK-BUDGET

Central Intelligence Agency (CIA), Office of Public Affairs, Washington, DC, 20505, USA, (703) 482-0623, https://www.cia.gov; The World Factbook.

European Commission, Eurostat, Luxembourg, 2920, LUX, https://ec.europa.eu/eurostat/; Share of Government Budget Appropriations or Outlays on Research and Development.

DENMARK-BUSINESS

European Commission, Eurostat, Luxembourg, 2920, LUX, https://ec.europa.eu/eurostat/; Eurostat Regional Yearbook 2021.

Global Entrepreneurship Monitor (GEM), Babson College, 231 Forest St., Babson Park, MA, 02457, USA, (781) 235-1200, info@gemconsortium.org, https://www.gemconsortium.org/; GEM 2022-2023 Global Report.

Nordic Council of Ministers, Ved Stranden 18, Copenhagen, DK-1061, DEN, nmr@norden.org, https://www.norden.org/en; Nordic Children and Young People in Figures 2021 and Nordic Statistics Database.

DENMARK-CAPITAL INVESTMENTS

Organization for Economic Cooperation and Development (OECD), 2001 L St. NW, Ste. 650, Washington, DC, 20036-4922, USA, (202) 785-6323, (800) 456-6323, (202) 785-0350, washington.contact@oecd.org, https://www.oecd.org/; OECD Business and Finance Outlook 2021.

DENMARK-CHESTNUT PRODUCTION

See DENMARK-CROPS

DENMARK-CHILDBIRTH-STATISTICS

European Commission, Eurostat, Luxembourg, 2920, LUX, https://ec.europa.eu/eurostat/; Eurostat Regional Yearbook 2021.

The World Bank, 1818 H St. NW, Washington, DC, 20433, USA, (202) 473-1000, (202) 477-6391, eds03@worldbank.org, https://www.worldbank.org/; World Development Indicators (WDI) 2022.

DENMARK-CLIMATE

Danish Energy Agency, Carsten Niebuhrs Gade 43, Copenhagen, DK-1577, DEN, ens@ens.dk, https://www.ens.dk/en; Denmark's Climate Status and Outlook 2022 (CSO22) and Energy Statistics 2021.

Nordic Council of Ministers, Ved Stranden 18, Copenhagen, DK-1061, DEN, nmr@norden.org, https://www.norden.org/en; Nordic Children and Young People in Figures 2021 and Nordic Statistics Database.

Palgrave Macmillan, 1 New York Plaza, Ste. 4500, New York, NY, 10004-1562, USA, (800) 777-4643, orders@palgrave.com, https://www.palgrave.com/us; The Statesman's Yearbook, 2023.

DENMARK-COAL PRODUCTION

See DENMARK-MINERAL INDUSTRIES

DENMARK-COCOA PRODUCTION

See DENMARK-CROPS

DENMARK-COFFEE

See DENMARK-CROPS

DENMARK-COMMERCE

Palgrave Macmillan, 1 New York Plaza, Ste. 4500, New York, NY, 10004-1562, USA, (800) 777-4643, orders@palgrave.com, https://www.palgrave.com/us; The Statesman's Yearbook, 2023.

UK Data Service, University of Essex, Wivenhoe Park, Colchester, Essex, CO4 3SQ, GBR, https://ukdataservice.ac.uk/; International Aggregate Data.

DENMARK-COMMODITY EXCHANGES

Barchart, 209 W Jackson Blvd., 2nd Fl., Chicago, IL, 60606, USA, (877) 247-4394, commodities@barchart.com, https://www.barchart.com/cmdty; The cmdty Yearbook 2023; cmdtyStats: Commodity Statistics and Fundamental Data; cmdtyView: Commodity Index; and Commodity Data and Prices.

International Lead and Zinc Study Group (ILZSG), Rua Almirante Barroso 38, 5th Fl., Lisbon, 1000-013, PRT, sales@ilzsg.org, https://www.ilzsg.org; Interactive Statistical Database.

International Monetary Fund (IMF), 700 19th St. NW, Washington, DC, 20431, USA, (202) 623-7000, (202) 623-4661, publications@imf.org, https://www.imf.org; IMF Primary Commodity Prices.

World Bureau of Metal Statistics (WBMS), 31 Star St., Ware, Hertfordshire, SG12 9BA, GBR, https://www.refinitiv.com/en/trading-solutions/world-bureau-metal-statistics; Annual Stainless Steel Statistics; Long Term Production/Consumption Series - All Metals; World Flow Charts; and World Metal Statistics.

DENMARK-CONSTRUCTION INDUSTRY

Nordic Council of Ministers, Ved Stranden 18, Copenhagen, DK-1061, DEN, nmr@norden.org, https://www.norden.org/en; Nordic Children and Young People in Figures 2021 and Nordic Statistics Database.

Organization for Economic Cooperation and Development (OECD), 2001 L St. NW, Ste. 650, Washington, DC, 20036-4922, USA, (202) 785-6323, (800) 456-6323, (202) 785-0350, washington.contact@oecd.org, https://www.oecd.org/; Economic Survey of Denmark 2021 and STAN (STructural ANalysis) Database.

Palgrave Macmillan, 1 New York Plaza, Ste. 4500, New York, NY, 10004-1562, USA, (800) 777-4643, orders@palgrave.com, https://www.palgrave.com/us; The Statesman's Yearbook, 2023.

United Nations Statistics Division (UNSD), United Nations Plz., New York, NY, 10017, USA, (800) 253-9646, (212) 963-9851, statistics@un.org, https://unstats.un.org; Statistical Yearbook of the United Nations 2021.

DENMARK-CONSUMER PRICE INDEXES

European Commission, Eurostat, Luxembourg, 2920, LUX, https://ec.europa.eu/eurostat/; Eurostat Regional Yearbook 2021.

Organization for Economic Cooperation and Development (OECD), 2001 L St. NW, Ste. 650, Washington, DC, 20036-4922, USA, (202) 785-6323, (800) 456-6323, (202) 785-0350, washington.contact@oecd.org, https://www.oecd.org/; OECD Digital Economy Outlook 2020.

Routledge - Taylor & Francis Group, 6000 Broken Sound Pkwy. NW, Ste. 300, Boca Raton, FL, 33487, USA, (800) 634-1420, (800) 634-7064, orders@taylorandfrancis.com, https://www.routledge.com/; The Europa World Year Book 2022.

The World Bank, 1818 H St. NW, Washington, DC, 20433, USA, (202) 473-1000, (202) 477-6391, eds03@worldbank.org, https://www.worldbank.org/; Denmark (report).

DENMARK-CONSUMPTION (ECONOMICS)

European Commission, Eurostat, Luxembourg, 2920, LUX, https://ec.europa.eu/eurostat/; Eurostat Regional Yearbook 2021.

Nordic Council of Ministers, Ved Stranden 18, Copenhagen, DK-1061, DEN, nmr@norden.org, https://www.norden.org/en; Nordic Children and Young People in Figures 2021 and Nordic Statistics Database.

Organization for Economic Cooperation and Development (OECD), 2001 L St. NW, Ste. 650, Washington, DC, 20036-4922, USA, (202) 785-6323, (800) 456-6323, (202) 785-0350, washington.contact@oecd.org, https://www.oecd.org/; OECD-FAO Agricultural Outlook 2022-2031 and Revenue Statistics 2022.

TAPPI - Technical Association of the Pulp and Paper Industry, 15 Technology Pkwy. S, Ste. 115, Peachtree Corners, GA, 30092, USA, (770) 446-1400, (800) 332-8686, (770) 446-6947, memberconnection@tappi.org, https://www.tappi.org/; TAPPI Journal.

DENMARK-COPPER INDUSTRY AND TRADE

See DENMARK-MINERAL INDUSTRIES

DENMARK-CORN INDUSTRY

See DENMARK-CROPS

DENMARK-COST AND STANDARD OF LIVING

European Commission, Eurostat, Luxembourg, 2920, LUX, https://ec.europa.eu/eurostat/; Eurostat Regional Yearbook 2021.

DENMARK-COTTON

See DENMARK-CROPS

DENMARK-CRIME

European Commission, Eurostat, Luxembourg, 2920, LUX, https://ec.europa.eu/eurostat/; Crime and Criminal Justice Database and Crime Statistics.

Nordic Council of Ministers, Ved Stranden 18, Copenhagen, DK-1061, DEN, nmr@norden.org, https://www.norden.org/en; Nordic Children and Young People in Figures 2021 and Nordic Statistics Database.

DENMARK-CROPS

European Commission, Eurostat, Luxembourg, 2920, LUX, https://ec.europa.eu/eurostat/; Eurostat Regional Yearbook 2021.

International Grains Council (IGC), 1 Canada Sq., Canary Wharf, London, E14 5AE, GBR, igc@igc.int, https://www.igc.int/en/; Grain Market Report.

Organization for Economic Cooperation and Development (OECD), 2001 L St. NW, Ste. 650, Washington, DC, 20036-4922, USA, (202) 785-6323, (800) 456-6323, (202) 785-0350, washington.contact@oecd.org, https://www.oecd.org/; OECD-FAO Agricultural Outlook 2022-2031.

Palgrave Macmillan, 1 New York Plaza, Ste. 4500, New York, NY, 10004-1562, USA, (800) 777-4643, orders@palgrave.com, https://www.palgrave.com/us; The Statesman's Yearbook, 2023.

United Nations Food and Agricultural Organization (FAO), 2121 K St., Ste. 800B, Washington, DC, 20037, USA, (202) 653-2400 (Dial from U.S.), (202) 653-5760 (Fax from U.S.), fao-hq@fao.org, https://www.fao.org; The State of Food and Agriculture (SOFA) 2022.

United Nations Statistics Division (UNSD), United Nations Plz., New York, NY, 10017, USA, (800) 253-9646, (212) 963-9851, statistics@un.org, https://unstats.un.org; Statistical Yearbook of the United Nations 2021.

DENMARK-CUSTOMS ADMINISTRATION

European Commission, Eurostat, Luxembourg, 2920, LUX, https://ec.europa.eu/eurostat/; Eurostat Regional Yearbook 2021.

DENMARK-DAIRY PROCESSING

Organization for Economic Cooperation and Development (OECD), 2001 L St. NW, Ste. 650, Washington, DC, 20036-4922, USA, (202) 785-6323, (800) 456-6323, (202) 785-0350, washington.contact@oecd.org, https://www.oecd.org/; OECD-FAO Agricultural Outlook 2022-2031.

Palgrave Macmillan, 1 New York Plaza, Ste. 4500, New York, NY, 10004-1562, USA, (800) 777-4643, orders@palgrave.com, https://www.palgrave.com/us; The Statesman's Yearbook, 2023.

United Nations Food and Agricultural Organization (FAO), 2121 K St., Ste. 800B, Washington, DC, 20037, USA, (202) 653-2400 (Dial from U.S.), (202) 653-5760 (Fax from U.S.), fao-hq@fao.org, https://www.fao.org; The State of Food and Agriculture (SOFA) 2022.

DENMARK-DEBTS, EXTERNAL

Organization for Economic Cooperation and Development (OECD), 2001 L St. NW, Ste. 650, Washington, DC, 20036-4922, USA, (202) 785-6323, (800) 456-6323, (202) 785-0350, washington.contact@oecd.org, https://www.oecd.org/; Geographical Distribution of Financial Flows to Developing Countries 2023; OECD Business and Finance Outlook 2021; and OECD Digital Economy Outlook 2020.

Palgrave Macmillan, 1 New York Plaza, Ste. 4500, New York, NY, 10004-1562, USA, (800) 777-4643, orders@palgrave.com, https://www.palgrave.com/us; The Statesman's Yearbook, 2023.

The World Bank, 1818 H St. NW, Washington, DC, 20433, USA, (202) 473-1000, (202) 477-6391, eds03@worldbank.org, https://www.worldbank.org/; Global Financial Development Report 2019-2020: Bank Regulation and Supervision a Decade after the Global Financial Crisis; World Development Indicators (WDI) 2022; and World Development Report 2022: Finance for an Equitable Recovery.

DENMARK-DEFENSE EXPENDITURES

See DENMARK-ARMED FORCES

DENMARK-DIAMONDS

See DENMARK-MINERAL INDUSTRIES

DENMARK-DISPOSABLE INCOME

Nordic Council of Ministers, Ved Stranden 18, Copenhagen, DK-1061, DEN, nmr@norden.org, https://www.norden.org/en; Nordic Children and Young People in Figures 2021 and Nordic Statistics Database.

DENMARK-DIVORCE

Nordic Council of Ministers, Ved Stranden 18, Copenhagen, DK-1061, DEN, nmr@norden.org, https://www.norden.org/en; Nordic Children and Young People in Figures 2021 and Nordic Statistics Database.

DENMARK-ECONOMIC ASSISTANCE

Organization for Economic Cooperation and Development (OECD), 2001 L St. NW, Ste. 650, Washington, DC, 20036-4922, USA, (202) 785-6323, (800) 456-6323, (202) 785-0350, washington.contact@oecd.org, https://www.oecd.org/; Geographical Distribution of Financial Flows to Developing Countries 2023.

United Nations Statistics Division (UNSD), United Nations Plz., New York, NY, 10017, USA, (800) 253-9646, (212) 963-9851, statistics@un.org, https://unstats.un.org; Statistical Yearbook of the United Nations 2021.

DENMARK-ECONOMIC CONDITIONS

Banque de France, 31 rue Croix des Petits-Champs, Paris, 75049, FRA, infos@banque-france.fr, https://www.banque-france.fr/en; Webstat: Access to Statistical Series of Banque de France.

Bernan Press, 15250 NBN Way, Bldg. C, Blue Ridge Summit, PA, 17214, USA, (301) 459-2255, (800) 865-3457, (800) 865-3450, customercare@bernan.com, https://rowman.com/Page/Bernan; World Economic Outlook, April 2022.

Central Intelligence Agency (CIA), Office of Public Affairs, Washington, DC, 20505, USA, (703) 482-0623, https://www.cia.gov; The World Factbook.

The Economist Group: Economist Intelligence Unit (EIU), 900 3rd Ave., 16th Fl., New York, NY, 10022, USA, (212) 541-0500, americas@eiu.com, https://www.eiu.com; Denmark Country Report.

Euromonitor International, Inc., 1 N Dearborn St., Ste. 1700, Chicago, IL, 60602, USA, (312) 922-1115, (312) 922-1157, info-usa@euromonitor.com, https://www.euromonitor.com/; Geographies and Market Research on the Consumer Finance Industry.

European Commission, Rue de la Loi, 170, Brussels, B-1040, BEL, https://ec.europa.eu; Common Agricultural Policy (CAPF) Context Indicators, 2019 Update.

European Commission, Eurostat, Luxembourg, 2920, LUX, https://ec.europa.eu/eurostat/; Eurostat Regional Yearbook 2021.

Global Entrepreneurship Monitor (GEM), Babson College, 231 Forest St., Babson Park, MA, 02457, USA, (781) 235-1200, info@gemconsortium.org, https://www.gemconsortium.org/; GEM 2022-2023 Global Report.

International Monetary Fund (IMF), 700 19th St. NW, Washington, DC, 20431, USA, (202) 623-7000, (202) 623-4661, publications@imf.org, https://www.imf.org; IMF Data and World Economic Outlook.

Organization for Economic Cooperation and Development (OECD), 2001 L St. NW, Ste. 650, Washington, DC, 20036-4922, USA, (202) 785-6323, (800) 456-6323, (202) 785-0350, washington.contact@oecd.org, https://www.oecd.org/; Economic Survey of Denmark 2021; Geographical Distribution of Financial Flows to Developing Countries 2023; OECD Composite Leading Indicator (CLI); OECD Digital Economy Outlook 2020; OECD Employment Outlook 2022: Building Back More Inclusive Labour Markets; OECD Labour Force Statistics 2022; and OECD Main Economic Indicators (MEI).

Palgrave Macmillan, 1 New York Plaza, Ste. 4500, New York, NY, 10004-1562, USA, (800) 777-4643, orders@palgrave.com, https://www.palgrave.com/us; The Statesman's Yearbook, 2023.

Routledge - Taylor & Francis Group, 6000 Broken Sound Pkwy. NW, Ste. 300, Boca Raton, FL, 33487, USA, (800) 634-1420, (800) 634-7064, orders@taylorandfrancis.com, https://www.routledge.com/; The Europa World Year Book 2022.

United Nations Economic Commission for Europe (UNECE), Palais des Nations, Geneva, CH-1211, SWI, unece_info@un.org, https://unece.org/; UNECE Countries in Figures 2019.

United Nations Statistics Division (UNSD), United Nations Plz., New York, NY, 10017, USA, (800) 253-9646, (212) 963-9851, statistics@un.org, https://unstats.un.org; Energy Statistics Yearbook 2019; Statistical Yearbook of the United Nations 2021; and World Statistics Pocketbook 2021.

The World Bank, 1818 H St. NW, Washington, DC, 20433, USA, (202) 473-1000, (202) 477-6391, eds03@worldbank.org, https://www.worldbank.org/; Denmark (report); Global Economic Monitor (GEM); Global Economic Prospects, June 2022; The Global Findex Database 2021; and World Development Report 2022: Finance for an Equitable Recovery.

DENMARK-EDUCATION

Euromonitor International, Inc., 1 N Dearborn St., Ste. 1700, Chicago, IL, 60602, USA, (312) 922-1115, (312) 922-1157, info-usa@euromonitor.com, https://www.euromonitor.com/; Geographies.

European Commission, Rue de la Loi, 170, Brussels, B-1040, BEL, https://ec.europa.eu; Common Agricultural Policy (CAPF) Context Indicators, 2019 Update.

European Commission, Eurostat, Luxembourg, 2920, LUX, https://ec.europa.eu/eurostat/; Eurostat Regional Yearbook 2021.

Infoplease, c/o Sandbox Networks, Inc., 1 Lincoln St., 24th Fl., Boston, MA, 02111, USA, https://www.infoplease.com; Countries of the World.

Nordic Council of Ministers, Ved Stranden 18, Copenhagen, DK-1061, DEN, nmr@norden.org, https://www.norden.org/en; Nordic Children and Young People in Figures 2021 and Nordic Statistics Database.

Organization for Economic Cooperation and Development (OECD), 2001 L St. NW, Ste. 650, Washington, DC, 20036-4922, USA, (202) 785-6323, (800) 456-6323, (202) 785-0350, washington.contact@oecd.org, https://www.oecd.org/; Education at a Glance 2022: OECD Indicators.

Palgrave Macmillan, 1 New York Plaza, Ste. 4500, New York, NY, 10004-1562, USA, (800) 777-4643, orders@palgrave.com, https://www.palgrave.com/us; The Statesman's Yearbook, 2023.

Routledge - Taylor & Francis Group, 6000 Broken Sound Pkwy. NW, Ste. 300, Boca Raton, FL, 33487, USA, (800) 634-1420, (800) 634-7064, orders@taylorandfrancis.com, https://www.routledge.com/; The Europa World Year Book 2022.

UNESCO Institute for Statistics, C.P 250 Succursale H, Montreal, QC, H3G 2K8, CAN, (514) 343-6880 (Dial from U.S.), (514) 343-5740 (Fax from U.S.), uis.publications@unesco.org, http://uis.unesco.org/; Literacy and UIS.Stat.

United Nations Statistics Division (UNSD), United Nations Plz., New York, NY, 10017, USA, (800) 253-9646, (212) 963-9851, statistics@un.org, https://unstats.un.org; Millennium Development Goal Indicators.

The World Bank, 1818 H St. NW, Washington, DC, 20433, USA, (202) 473-1000, (202) 477-6391, eds03@worldbank.org, https://www.worldbank.org/; Denmark (report); World Development Indicators (WDI) 2022; and World Development Report 2022: Finance for an Equitable Recovery.

DENMARK-ELECTRICITY

Danish Energy Agency, Carsten Niebuhrs Gade 43, Copenhagen, DK-1577, DEN, ens@ens.dk, https://www.ens.dk/en; Denmark's Climate Status and Outlook 2022 (CSO22) and Energy Statistics 2021.

European Commission, Eurostat, Luxembourg, 2920, LUX, https://ec.europa.eu/eurostat/; Eurostat Regional Yearbook 2021 and Final Energy Consumption in Transport by Type of Fuel.

International Energy Agency (IEA), 9 Rue de la Federation, Paris, 75739, FRA, info@iea.org, https://www.iea.org/; Coal 2021: Analysis and Forecast to 2024 and World Energy Outlook 2021.

Organization for Economic Cooperation and Development (OECD), 2001 L St. NW, Ste. 650, Washington, DC, 20036-4922, USA, (202) 785-6323, (800) 456-6323, (202) 785-0350, washington.contact@oecd.org, https://www.oecd.org/; Energy Prices and Taxes for OECD Countries 2020 and STAN (STructural ANalysis) Database.

S&P Global Commodity Insights, One World Trade Center, New York, NY, 10007, USA, (800) 752-8878, support@platts.com, https://www.spglobal.com/commodityinsights/en; Platts European Power Alert and Platts Power in Europe.

U.S. Energy Information Administration (EIA), 1000 Independence Ave. SW, Washington, DC, 20585, USA, (202) 586-8800, infoctr@eia.gov, https://www.eia.gov; International Energy Outlook 2021.

United Nations Statistics Division (UNSD), United Nations Plz., New York, NY, 10017, USA, (800) 253-9646, (212) 963-9851, statistics@un.org, https://unstats.un.org; Energy Statistics Yearbook 2019 and Statistical Yearbook of the United Nations 2021.

DENMARK-EMPLOYMENT

European Commission, Eurostat, Luxembourg, 2920, LUX, https://ec.europa.eu/eurostat/; Eurostat Regional Yearbook 2021.

International Labour Organization (ILO), 4 Rte. des Morillons, Geneva, CH-1211, SWI, ilo@ilo.org,

https://www.ilo.org; NORMLEX Information System on International Labour Standards.

Nordic Council of Ministers, Ved Stranden 18, Copenhagen, DK-1061, DEN, nmr@norden.org, https://www.norden.org/en; Nordic Children and Young People in Figures 2021 and Nordic Statistics Database.

Organization for Economic Cooperation and Development (OECD), 2001 L St. NW, Ste. 650, Washington, DC, 20036-4922, USA, (202) 785-6323, (800) 456-6323, (202) 785-0350, washington.contact@oecd.org, https://www.oecd.org/; Economic Survey of Denmark 2021; OECD Composite Leading Indicator (CLI); OECD Digital Economy Outlook 2020; OECD Employment Outlook 2022: Building Back More Inclusive Labour Markets; and OECD Labour Force Statistics 2022.

UK Data Service, University of Essex, Wivenhoe Park, Colchester, Essex, CO4 3SQ, GBR, https://ukdataservice.ac.uk/; International Aggregate Data.

United Nations Statistics Division (UNSD), United Nations Plz., New York, NY, 10017, USA, (800) 253-9646, (212) 963-9851, statistics@un.org, https://unstats.un.org; Statistical Yearbook of the United Nations 2021.

The World Bank, 1818 H St. NW, Washington, DC, 20433, USA, (202) 473-1000, (202) 477-6391, eds03@worldbank.org, https://www.worldbank.org/; Denmark (report).

DENMARK-ENERGY INDUSTRIES

Danish Energy Agency, Carsten Niebuhrs Gade 43, Copenhagen, DK-1577, DEN, ens@ens.dk, https://www.ens.dk/en; Denmark's Climate Status and Outlook 2022 (CSO22) and Energy Statistics 2021.

EMD International A/S, Niels Jernes Vej 10, Aalborg, DK-9220, DEN, emd@emd.dk, https://www.emd-international.com/; windPRO Newsletter.

Enerdata, 47 avenue Alsace Lorraine, Grenoble, 38027, FRA, (332) 216-4534, research@enerdata.net, https://www.enerdata.net; World Refinery Database.

European Commission, Rue de la Loi, 170, Brussels, B-1040, BEL, https://ec.europa.eu; EU Energy in Figures: Statistical Pocketbook 2021.

European Commission, Eurostat, Luxembourg, 2920, LUX, https://ec.europa.eu/eurostat/; Eurostat Regional Yearbook 2021 and Final Energy Consumption in Transport by Type of Fuel.

European Institute for Energy Research (EIFER), Emmy-Noether-Strasse 11, Ground Fl., Karlsruhe, D-76131, GER, contact@eifer.org, https://www.eifer.kit.edu/; unpublished data.

International Energy Agency (IEA), 9 Rue de la Federation, Paris, 75739, FRA, info@iea.org, https://www.iea.org/; Renewables Information and World Energy Statistics and Balances.

S&P Global Commodity Insights, One World Trade Center, New York, NY, 10007, USA, (800) 752-8878, support@platts.com, https://www.spglobal.com/commodityinsights/en; Platts European Power Daily and Platts Power in Europe.

DENMARK-ENVIRONMENTAL CONDITIONS

Danish Energy Agency, Carsten Niebuhrs Gade 43, Copenhagen, DK-1577, DEN, ens@ens.dk, https://www.ens.dk/en; Denmark's Climate Status and Outlook 2022 (CSO22) and Energy Statistics 2021.

DSI Data Service & Information, Xantener Strasse 51a, Rheinberg, D-47495, GER, dsi@dsidata.com, https://www.dsidata.com/; Global Environmental Database.

The Economist Group: Economist Intelligence Unit (EIU), 900 3rd Ave., 16th Fl., New York, NY, 10022, USA, (212) 541-0500, americas@eiu.com, https://www.eiu.com; Denmark Country Report.

European Commission, Rue de la Loi, 170, Brussels, B-1040, BEL, https://ec.europa.eu; Common Agricultural Policy (CAPF) Context Indicators, 2019 Update.

European Commission, Eurostat, Luxembourg, 2920, LUX, https://ec.europa.eu/eurostat/; Environment Statistics Introduced.

Organization for Economic Cooperation and Development (OECD), 2001 L St. NW, Ste. 650, Washington, DC, 20036-4922, USA, (202) 785-6323, (800) 456-6323, (202) 785-0350, washington.contact@oecd.org, https://www.oecd.org/; Environment Statistics.

United Nations Statistics Division (UNSD), United Nations Plz., New York, NY, 10017, USA, (800) 253-9646, (212) 963-9851, statistics@un.org, https://unstats.un.org; World Statistics Pocketbook 2021.

DENMARK-EXPENDITURES, PUBLIC

European Commission, Eurostat, Luxembourg, 2920, LUX, https://ec.europa.eu/eurostat/; Eurostat Regional Yearbook 2021.

Organization for Economic Cooperation and Development (OECD), 2001 L St. NW, Ste. 650, Washington, DC, 20036-4922, USA, (202) 785-6323, (800) 456-6323, (202) 785-0350, washington.contact@oecd.org, https://www.oecd.org/; Revenue Statistics 2022.

DENMARK-EXPORTS

BC Stats, Stn Prov Govt, PO Box 9410, Victoria, BC, V8W 9V1, CAN, (250) 387-6121 (Dial from U.S.), bc.stats@gov.bc.ca, https://www2.gov.bc.ca/gov/content/data/about-data-management/bc-stats; Country Trade Profile - Denmark.

Central Intelligence Agency (CIA), Office of Public Affairs, Washington, DC, 20505, USA, (703) 482-0623, https://www.cia.gov; The World Factbook.

The Economist Group: Economist Intelligence Unit (EIU), 900 3rd Ave., 16th Fl., New York, NY, 10022, USA, (212) 541-0500, americas@eiu.com, https://www.eiu.com; Denmark Country Report.

European Commission, Eurostat, Luxembourg, 2920, LUX, https://ec.europa.eu/eurostat/; Eurostat Regional Yearbook 2021.

International Monetary Fund (IMF), 700 19th St. NW, Washington, DC, 20431, USA, (202) 623-7000, (202) 623-4661, publications@imf.org, https://www.imf.org; Direction of Trade Statistics (DOTS) and International Financial Statistics (IFS).

Nordic Council of Ministers, Ved Stranden 18, Copenhagen, DK-1061, DEN, nmr@norden.org, https://www.norden.org/en; Nordic Children and Young People in Figures 2021 and Nordic Statistics Database.

Organization for Economic Cooperation and Development (OECD), 2001 L St. NW, Ste. 650, Washington, DC, 20036-4922, USA, (202) 785-6323, (800) 456-6323, (202) 785-0350, washington.contact@oecd.org, https://www.oecd.org/; Economic Survey of Denmark 2021; Geographical Distribution of Financial Flows to Developing Countries 2023; OECD Digital Economy Outlook 2020; OECD Review of Fisheries 2022; OECD-FAO Agricultural Outlook 2022-2031; and STAN (STructural ANalysis) Database.

S&P Global, IHS Markit, 15 Inverness Way E, Englewood, CO, 80112, USA, (800) 447-2273, (800) 854-7179, https://ihsmarkit.com; Global Trade Atlas (GTA).

TAPPI - Technical Association of the Pulp and Paper Industry, 15 Technology Pkwy. S, Ste. 115, Peachtree Corners, GA, 30092, USA, (770) 446-1400, (800) 332-8686, (770) 446-6947, memberconnection@tappi.org, https://www.tappi.org/; TAPPI Journal.

United Nations Conference on Trade and Development (UNCTAD), Palais des Nations, Geneva, 1211, SWI, (212) 963-6896, unctadinfo@unctad.org, https://unctad.org; Handbook of Statistics 2021.

United Nations Statistics Division (UNSD), United Nations Plz., New York, NY, 10017, USA, (800) 253-9646, (212) 963-9851, statistics@un.org, https://unstats.un.org; Energy Statistics Yearbook 2019.

The World Bank, 1818 H St. NW, Washington, DC, 20433, USA, (202) 473-1000, (202) 477-6391, eds03@worldbank.org, https://www.worldbank.org/; World Development Report 2022: Finance for an Equitable Recovery.

DENMARK-FEMALE WORKING POPULATION

See DENMARK-EMPLOYMENT

DENMARK-FERTILITY, HUMAN

Central Intelligence Agency (CIA), Office of Public Affairs, Washington, DC, 20505, USA, (703) 482-0623, https://www.cia.gov; The World Factbook.

DENMARK-FERTILIZER INDUSTRY

Organization for Economic Cooperation and Development (OECD), 2001 L St. NW, Ste. 650, Washington, DC, 20036-4922, USA, (202) 785-6323, (800) 456-6323, (202) 785-0350, washington.contact@oecd.org, https://www.oecd.org/; OECD-FAO Agricultural Outlook 2022-2031.

United Nations Food and Agricultural Organization (FAO), 2121 K St., Ste. 800B, Washington, DC, 20037, USA, (202) 653-2400 (Dial from U.S.), (202) 653-5760 (Fax from U.S.), fao-hq@fao.org, https://www.fao.org; The State of Food and Agriculture (SOFA) 2022.

DENMARK-FETAL MORTALITY

See DENMARK-MORTALITY

DENMARK-FINANCE

European Commission, Eurostat, Luxembourg, 2920, LUX, https://ec.europa.eu/eurostat/; Eurostat Regional Yearbook 2021.

International Monetary Fund (IMF), 700 19th St. NW, Washington, DC, 20431, USA, (202) 623-7000, (202) 623-4661, publications@imf.org, https://www.imf.org; International Financial Statistics (IFS).

Nordic Council of Ministers, Ved Stranden 18, Copenhagen, DK-1061, DEN, nmr@norden.org, https://www.norden.org/en; Nordic Children and Young People in Figures 2021 and Nordic Statistics Database.

Organization for Economic Cooperation and Development (OECD), 2001 L St. NW, Ste. 650, Washington, DC, 20036-4922, USA, (202) 785-6323, (800) 456-6323, (202) 785-0350, washington.contact@oecd.org, https://www.oecd.org/; OECD Digital Economy Outlook 2020.

Stockholm International Peace Research Institute (SIPRI), Signalistgatan 9, Stockholm, SE 169 72, SWE, https://www.sipri.org/; SIPRI Arms Transfers Database and SIPRI Military Expenditure Database.

United Nations Statistics Division (UNSD), United Nations Plz., New York, NY, 10017, USA, (800) 253-9646, (212) 963-9851, statistics@un.org, https://unstats.un.org; Statistical Yearbook of the United Nations 2021.

The World Bank, 1818 H St. NW, Washington, DC, 20433, USA, (202) 473-1000, (202) 477-6391, eds03@worldbank.org, https://www.worldbank.org/; Denmark (report).

DENMARK-FINANCE, PUBLIC

Banque de France, 31 rue Croix des Petits-Champs, Paris, 75049, FRA, infos@banque-france.fr, https://www.banque-france.fr/en; Webstat: Access to Statistical Series of Banque de France.

Bernan Press, 15250 NBN Way, Bldg. C, Blue Ridge Summit, PA, 17214, USA, (301) 459-2255, (800) 865-3457, (800) 865-3450, customercare@bernan.com, https://rowman.com/Page/Bernan; National Accounts Statistics: Analysis of Main Aggregates 2020.

The Economist Group: Economist Intelligence Unit (EIU), 900 3rd Ave., 16th Fl., New York, NY, 10022, USA, (212) 541-0500, americas@eiu.com, https://www.eiu.com; Denmark Country Report.

European Commission, Eurostat, Luxembourg, 2920, LUX, https://ec.europa.eu/eurostat/; Eurostat Regional Yearbook 2021.

International Monetary Fund (IMF), 700 19th St. NW, Washington, DC, 20431, USA, (202) 623-7000, (202) 623-4661, publications@imf.org, https://www.imf.org; International Financial Statistics (IFS) and Regional Economic Outlook.

Organization for Economic Cooperation and Development (OECD), 2001 L St. NW, Ste. 650, Washington, DC, 20036-4922, USA, (202) 785-6323, (800) 456-6323, (202) 785-0350, washington.contact@oecd.org, https://www.oecd.org/; Geographical Distribution of Financial Flows to Developing Countries 2023; OECD Business and Finance Outlook 2021; OECD Digital Economy Outlook 2020; and Revenue Statistics 2022.

Palgrave Macmillan, 1 New York Plaza, Ste. 4500, New York, NY, 10004-1562, USA, (800) 777-4643, orders@palgrave.com, https://www.palgrave.com/us; The Statesman's Yearbook, 2023.

Routledge - Taylor & Francis Group, 6000 Broken Sound Pkwy. NW, Ste. 300, Boca Raton, FL, 33487, USA, (800) 634-1420, (800) 634-7064, orders@taylorandfrancis.com, https://www.routledge.com/; The Europa World Year Book 2022.

United Nations Statistics Division (UNSD), United Nations Plz., New York, NY, 10017, USA, (800) 253-9646, (212) 963-9851, statistics@un.org, https://unstats.un.org; National Accounts Main Aggregates Database and National Accounts Statistics: Main Aggregates and Detailed Tables.

The World Bank, 1818 H St. NW, Washington, DC, 20433, USA, (202) 473-1000, (202) 477-6391, eds03@worldbank.org, https://www.worldbank.org/; Denmark (report).

DENMARK-FISHERIES

European Commission, Eurostat, Luxembourg, 2920, LUX, https://ec.europa.eu/eurostat/; Eurostat Regional Yearbook 2021.

Nordic Council of Ministers, Ved Stranden 18, Copenhagen, DK-1061, DEN, nmr@norden.org, https://www.norden.org/en; Nordic Children and Young People in Figures 2021 and Nordic Statistics Database.

Organization for Economic Cooperation and Development (OECD), 2001 L St. NW, Ste. 650, Washington, DC, 20036-4922, USA, (202) 785-6323, (800) 456-6323, (202) 785-0350, washington.contact@oecd.org, https://www.oecd.org/; OECD Review of Fisheries 2022 and STAN (STructural ANalysis) Database.

Palgrave Macmillan, 1 New York Plaza, Ste. 4500, New York, NY, 10004-1562, USA, (800) 777-4643, orders@palgrave.com, https://www.palgrave.com/us; The Statesman's Yearbook, 2023.

Routledge - Taylor & Francis Group, 6000 Broken Sound Pkwy. NW, Ste. 300, Boca Raton, FL, 33487, USA, (800) 634-1420, (800) 634-7064, orders@taylorandfrancis.com, https://www.routledge.com/; The Europa World Year Book 2022.

United Nations Food and Agricultural Organization (FAO), 2121 K St., Ste. 800B, Washington, DC, 20037, USA, (202) 653-2400 (Dial from U.S.), (202) 653-5760 (Fax from U.S.), fao-hq@fao.org, https://www.fao.org; FAO Yearbook of Fishery and Aquaculture Statistics 2019; Fishery Statistical Collections Global Capture Production; FishStatJ; and The State of Food and Agriculture (SOFA) 2022.

United Nations Statistics Division (UNSD), United Nations Plz., New York, NY, 10017, USA, (800) 253-9646, (212) 963-9851, statistics@un.org, https://unstats.un.org; Statistical Yearbook of the United Nations 2021.

The World Bank, 1818 H St. NW, Washington, DC, 20433, USA, (202) 473-1000, (202) 477-6391, eds03@worldbank.org, https://www.worldbank.org/; Denmark (report).

DENMARK-FOOD

Euromonitor International, Inc., 1 N Dearborn St., Ste. 1700, Chicago, IL, 60602, USA, (312) 922-1115, (312) 922-1157, info-usa@euromonitor.com, https://www.euromonitor.com/; Market Research on the Retailing Industry.

European Commission, Eurostat, Luxembourg, 2920, LUX, https://ec.europa.eu/eurostat/; Eurostat Regional Yearbook 2021.

United Nations Food and Agricultural Organization (FAO), 2121 K St., Ste. 800B, Washington, DC, 20037, USA, (202) 653-2400 (Dial from U.S.), (202) 653-5760 (Fax from U.S.), fao-hq@fao.org, https://www.fao.org; The State of Food and Agriculture (SOFA) 2022.

DENMARK-FOREIGN EXCHANGE RATES

European Commission, Eurostat, Luxembourg, 2920, LUX, https://ec.europa.eu/eurostat/; Eurostat Regional Yearbook 2021.

International Monetary Fund (IMF), 700 19th St. NW, Washington, DC, 20431, USA, (202) 623-7000, (202) 623-4661, publications@imf.org, https://www.imf.org; International Financial Statistics (IFS).

Nordic Council of Ministers, Ved Stranden 18, Copenhagen, DK-1061, DEN, nmr@norden.org, https://www.norden.org/en; Nordic Children and Young People in Figures 2021 and Nordic Statistics Database.

Organization for Economic Cooperation and Development (OECD), 2001 L St. NW, Ste. 650, Washington, DC, 20036-4922, USA, (202) 785-6323, (800) 456-6323, (202) 785-0350, washington.contact@oecd.org, https://www.oecd.org/; OECD Business and Finance Outlook 2021; OECD Digital Economy Outlook 2020; OECD Tourism Trends and Policies 2022; and Revenue Statistics 2022.

DENMARK-FORESTS AND FORESTRY

European Commission, Eurostat, Luxembourg, 2920, LUX, https://ec.europa.eu/eurostat/; Eurostat Regional Yearbook 2021.

Nordic Council of Ministers, Ved Stranden 18, Copenhagen, DK-1061, DEN, nmr@norden.org, https://www.norden.org/en; Nordic Children and Young People in Figures 2021 and Nordic Statistics Database.

Organization for Economic Cooperation and Development (OECD), 2001 L St. NW, Ste. 650, Washington, DC, 20036-4922, USA, (202) 785-6323, (800) 456-6323, (202) 785-0350, washington.contact@oecd.org, https://www.oecd.org/; STAN (STructural ANalysis) Database.

Palgrave Macmillan, 1 New York Plaza, Ste. 4500, New York, NY, 10004-1562, USA, (800) 777-4643, orders@palgrave.com, https://www.palgrave.com/us; The Statesman's Yearbook, 2023.

Routledge - Taylor & Francis Group, 6000 Broken Sound Pkwy. NW, Ste. 300, Boca Raton, FL, 33487, USA, (800) 634-1420, (800) 634-7064, orders@taylorandfrancis.com, https://www.routledge.com/; The Europa World Year Book 2022.

TAPPI - Technical Association of the Pulp and Paper Industry, 15 Technology Pkwy. S, Ste. 115, Peachtree Corners, GA, 30092, USA, (770) 446-1400, (800) 332-8686, (770) 446-6947, memberconnection@tappi.org, https://www.tappi.org/; TAPPI Journal.

UNESCO Institute for Statistics, C.P 250 Succursale H, Montreal, QC, H3G 2K8, CAN, (514) 343-6880 (Dial from U.S.), (514) 343-5740 (Fax from U.S.), uis.publications@unesco.org, http://uis.unesco.org/; UIS.Stat.

United Nations Food and Agricultural Organization (FAO), 2121 K St., Ste. 800B, Washington, DC, 20037, USA, (202) 653-2400 (Dial from U.S.), (202) 653-5760 (Fax from U.S.), fao-hq@fao.org, https://www.fao.org; FAO Yearbook of Forest Products 2019 and The State of Food and Agriculture (SOFA) 2022.

United Nations Statistics Division (UNSD), United Nations Plz., New York, NY, 10017, USA, (800) 253-9646, (212) 963-9851, statistics@un.org, https://unstats.un.org; Statistical Yearbook of the United Nations 2021.

The World Bank, 1818 H St. NW, Washington, DC, 20433, USA, (202) 473-1000, (202) 477-6391, eds03@worldbank.org, https://www.worldbank.org/; Denmark (report) and World Development Report 2022: Finance for an Equitable Recovery.

DENMARK-FRUIT PRODUCTION

See DENMARK-CROPS

DENMARK-GAS PRODUCTION

See DENMARK-MINERAL INDUSTRIES

DENMARK-GEOGRAPHIC INFORMATION SYSTEMS

The World Bank, 1818 H St. NW, Washington, DC, 20433, USA, (202) 473-1000, (202) 477-6391, eds03@worldbank.org, https://www.worldbank.org/; Denmark (report).

DENMARK-GOLD INDUSTRY

The World Bank, 1818 H St. NW, Washington, DC, 20433, USA, (202) 473-1000, (202) 477-6391, eds03@worldbank.org, https://www.worldbank.org/; World Development Indicators (WDI) 2022.

DENMARK-GOLD PRODUCTION

See DENMARK-MINERAL INDUSTRIES

DENMARK-GRANTS-IN-AID

Organization for Economic Cooperation and Development (OECD), 2001 L St. NW, Ste. 650, Washington, DC, 20036-4922, USA, (202) 785-6323, (800) 456-6323, (202) 785-0350, washington.contact@oecd.org, https://www.oecd.org/; Geographical Distribution of Financial Flows to Developing Countries 2023.

DENMARK-GROSS DOMESTIC PRODUCT

The Economist Group: Economist Intelligence Unit (EIU), 900 3rd Ave., 16th Fl., New York, NY, 10022, USA, (212) 541-0500, americas@eiu.com, https://www.eiu.com; Denmark Country Report.

European Commission, Eurostat, Luxembourg, 2920, LUX, https://ec.europa.eu/eurostat/; Eurostat Regional Yearbook 2021.

Nordic Council of Ministers, Ved Stranden 18, Copenhagen, DK-1061, DEN, nmr@norden.org, https://www.norden.org/en; Nordic Children and Young People in Figures 2021 and Nordic Statistics Database.

Organization for Economic Cooperation and Development (OECD), 2001 L St. NW, Ste. 650, Washington, DC, 20036-4922, USA, (202) 785-6323, (800) 456-6323, (202) 785-0350, washington.contact@oecd.org, https://www.oecd.org/; Geographical Distribution of Financial Flows to Developing Countries 2023; OECD Digital Economy Outlook 2020; and Revenue Statistics 2022.

United Nations Statistics Division (UNSD), United Nations Plz., New York, NY, 10017, USA, (800) 253-9646, (212) 963-9851, statistics@un.org, https://unstats.un.org; Statistical Yearbook of the United Nations 2021.

The World Bank, 1818 H St. NW, Washington, DC, 20433, USA, (202) 473-1000, (202) 477-6391, eds03@worldbank.org, https://www.worldbank.org/; World Development Indicators (WDI) 2022 and World Development Report 2022: Finance for an Equitable Recovery.

DENMARK-GROSS NATIONAL PRODUCT

European Commission, Eurostat, Luxembourg, 2920, LUX, https://ec.europa.eu/eurostat/; Eurostat Regional Yearbook 2021.

Organization for Economic Cooperation and Development (OECD), 2001 L St. NW, Ste. 650, Washington, DC, 20036-4922, USA, (202) 785-6323, (800) 456-6323, (202) 785-0350, washington.contact@oecd.org, https://www.oecd.org/; Geographical Distribution of Financial Flows to Developing Countries 2023; OECD Composite Leading Indicator (CLI); and OECD Digital Economy Outlook 2020.

Palgrave Macmillan, 1 New York Plaza, Ste. 4500, New York, NY, 10004-1562, USA, (800) 777-4643, orders@palgrave.com, https://www.palgrave.com/us; The Statesman's Yearbook, 2023.

United Nations Statistics Division (UNSD), United Nations Plz., New York, NY, 10017, USA, (800) 253-9646, (212) 963-9851, statistics@un.org, https://unstats.un.org; Statistical Yearbook of the United Nations 2021.

The World Bank, 1818 H St. NW, Washington, DC, 20433, USA, (202) 473-1000, (202) 477-6391, eds03@worldbank.org, https://www.worldbank.org/; World Development Indicators (WDI) 2022 and World Development Report 2022: Finance for an Equitable Recovery.

DENMARK-HAY PRODUCTION

See DENMARK-CROPS

DENMARK-HAZELNUT PRODUCTION

See DENMARK-CROPS

DENMARK-HEALTH

See DENMARK-PUBLIC HEALTH

DENMARK-HEMP FIBRE PRODUCTION

See DENMARK-TEXTILE INDUSTRY

DENMARK-HOUSING

Euromonitor International, Inc., 1 N Dearborn St., Ste. 1700, Chicago, IL, 60602, USA, (312) 922-1115, (312) 922-1157, info-usa@euromonitor.com, https://www.euromonitor.com/; Geographies.

European Commission, Eurostat, Luxembourg, 2920, LUX, https://ec.europa.eu/eurostat/; Eurostat Regional Yearbook 2021.

Nordic Council of Ministers, Ved Stranden 18, Copenhagen, DK-1061, DEN, nmr@norden.org, https://www.norden.org/en; Nordic Children and Young People in Figures 2021 and Nordic Statistics Database.

DENMARK-HOUSING CONSTRUCTION

See DENMARK-CONSTRUCTION INDUSTRY

DENMARK-IMPORTS

BC Stats, Stn Prov Govt, PO Box 9410, Victoria, BC, V8W 9V1, CAN, (250) 387-6121 (Dial from U.S.), bc.stats@gov.bc.ca, https://www2.gov.bc.ca/gov/content/data/about-data-management/bc-stats; Country Trade Profile - Denmark.

Central Intelligence Agency (CIA), Office of Public Affairs, Washington, DC, 20505, USA, (703) 482-0623, https://www.cia.gov; The World Factbook.

The Economist Group: Economist Intelligence Unit (EIU), 900 3rd Ave., 16th Fl., New York, NY, 10022, USA, (212) 541-0500, americas@eiu.com, https://www.eiu.com; Denmark Country Report.

European Commission, Eurostat, Luxembourg, 2920, LUX, https://ec.europa.eu/eurostat/; Eurostat Regional Yearbook 2021.

International Monetary Fund (IMF), 700 19th St. NW, Washington, DC, 20431, USA, (202) 623-7000, (202) 623-4661, publications@imf.org, https://www.imf.org; Direction of Trade Statistics (DOTS) and International Financial Statistics (IFS).

Organization for Economic Cooperation and Development (OECD), 2001 L St. NW, Ste. 650, Washington, DC, 20036-4922, USA, (202) 785-6323, (800) 456-6323, (202) 785-0350, washington.contact@oecd.org, https://www.oecd.org/; Economic Survey of Denmark 2021; OECD Digital Economy Outlook 2020; OECD Review of Fisheries 2022; OECD-FAO Agricultural Outlook 2022-2031; and STAN (STructural ANalysis) Database.

S&P Global, IHS Markit, 15 Inverness Way E, Englewood, CO, 80112, USA, (800) 447-2273, (800) 854-7179, https://ihsmarkit.com; Global Trade Atlas (GTA).

TAPPI - Technical Association of the Pulp and Paper Industry, 15 Technology Pkwy. S, Ste. 115, Peachtree Corners, GA, 30092, USA, (770) 446-1400, (800) 332-8686, (770) 446-6947, memberconnection@tappi.org, https://www.tappi.org/; TAPPI Journal.

United Nations Conference on Trade and Development (UNCTAD), Palais des Nations, Geneva, 1211, SWI, (212) 963-6896, unctadinfo@unctad.org, https://unctad.org; Handbook of Statistics 2021.

United Nations Statistics Division (UNSD), United Nations Plz., New York, NY, 10017, USA, (800) 253-9646, (212) 963-9851, statistics@un.org, https://unstats.un.org; Energy Statistics Yearbook 2019.

The World Bank, 1818 H St. NW, Washington, DC, 20433, USA, (202) 473-1000, (202) 477-6391, eds03@worldbank.org, https://www.worldbank.org/; World Development Report 2022: Finance for an Equitable Recovery.

DENMARK-INDUSTRIAL METALS PRODUCTION

See DENMARK-MINERAL INDUSTRIES

DENMARK-INDUSTRIAL PRODUCTIVITY

European Commission, Eurostat, Luxembourg, 2920, LUX, https://ec.europa.eu/eurostat/; Eurostat Regional Yearbook 2021.

International Lead and Zinc Study Group (ILZSG), Rua Almirante Barroso 38, 5th Fl., Lisbon, 1000-013, PRT, sales@ilzsg.org, https://www.ilzsg.org; Interactive Statistical Database.

Organization for Economic Cooperation and Development (OECD), 2001 L St. NW, Ste. 650, Washington, DC, 20036-4922, USA, (202) 785-6323, (800) 456-6323, (202) 785-0350, washington.contact@oecd.org, https://www.oecd.org/; OECD Digital Economy Outlook 2020; OECD-FAO Agricultural Outlook 2022-2031; and STAN (STructural ANalysis) Database.

TAPPI - Technical Association of the Pulp and Paper Industry, 15 Technology Pkwy. S, Ste. 115, Peachtree Corners, GA, 30092, USA, (770) 446-1400, (800) 332-8686, (770) 446-6947, memberconnection@tappi.org, https://www.tappi.org/; TAPPI Journal.

DENMARK-INDUSTRIAL PROPERTY

World Intellectual Property Organization (WIPO), 34, chemin des Colombettes, Geneva, CH-1211, SWI, https://www.wipo.int; Madrid Yearly Review 2022: International Registrations of Marks.

DENMARK-INDUSTRIES

Central Intelligence Agency (CIA), Office of Public Affairs, Washington, DC, 20505, USA, (703) 482-0623, https://www.cia.gov; The World Factbook.

Danish Energy Agency, Carsten Niebuhrs Gade 43, Copenhagen, DK-1577, DEN, ens@ens.dk, https://www.ens.dk/en; Denmark's Climate Status and Outlook 2022 (CSO22) and Energy Statistics 2021.

The Economist Group: Economist Intelligence Unit (EIU), 900 3rd Ave., 16th Fl., New York, NY, 10022, USA, (212) 541-0500, americas@eiu.com, https://www.eiu.com; Denmark Country Report.

Euromonitor International, Inc., 1 N Dearborn St., Ste. 1700, Chicago, IL, 60602, USA, (312) 922-1115, (312) 922-1157, info-usa@euromonitor.com, https://www.euromonitor.com/; Geographies.

European Commission, Eurostat, Luxembourg, 2920, LUX, https://ec.europa.eu/eurostat/; Eurostat Regional Yearbook 2021.

International Labour Organization (ILO), 4 Rte. des Morillons, Geneva, CH-1211, SWI, ilo@ilo.org, https://www.ilo.org; NORMLEX Information System on International Labour Standards.

Nordic Council of Ministers, Ved Stranden 18, Copenhagen, DK-1061, DEN, nmr@norden.org, https://www.norden.org/en; Nordic Children and Young People in Figures 2021 and Nordic Statistics Database.

Organization for Economic Cooperation and Development (OECD), 2001 L St. NW, Ste. 650, Washington, DC, 20036-4922, USA, (202) 785-6323, (800) 456-6323, (202) 785-0350, washington.contact@oecd.org, https://www.oecd.org/; Environment Statistics; OECD Digital Economy Outlook 2020; and STAN (STructural ANalysis) Database.

Palgrave Macmillan, 1 New York Plaza, Ste. 4500, New York, NY, 10004-1562, USA, (800) 777-4643, orders@palgrave.com, https://www.palgrave.com/us; The Statesman's Yearbook, 2023.

Routledge - Taylor & Francis Group, 6000 Broken Sound Pkwy. NW, Ste. 300, Boca Raton, FL, 33487, USA, (800) 634-1420, (800) 634-7064, orders@taylorandfrancis.com, https://www.routledge.com/; The Europa World Year Book 2022.

United Nations Industrial Development Organization (UNIDO), 1 United Nations Plz., Rm. DC1-1118, New York, NY, 10017, USA, (212) 963-6890, (212) 963 6885, (212) 963-7904, office.newyork@unido.org, https://www.unido.org/; Industrial Statistics Databases and International Yearbook of Industrial Statistics 2021.

The World Bank, 1818 H St. NW, Washington, DC, 20433, USA, (202) 473-1000, (202) 477-6391, eds03@worldbank.org, https://www.worldbank.org/; Denmark (report) and World Development Indicators (WDI) 2022.

DENMARK-INFANT AND MATERNAL MORTALITY

See DENMARK-MORTALITY

DENMARK-INTEREST RATES

Organization for Economic Cooperation and Development (OECD), 2001 L St. NW, Ste. 650, Washington, DC, 20036-4922, USA, (202) 785-6323, (800) 456-6323, (202) 785-0350, washington.contact@oecd.org, https://www.oecd.org/; OECD Business and Finance Outlook 2021 and OECD Digital Economy Outlook 2020.

DENMARK-INTERNAL REVENUE

Organization for Economic Cooperation and Development (OECD), 2001 L St. NW, Ste. 650, Washington, DC, 20036-4922, USA, (202) 785-6323, (800) 456-6323, (202) 785-0350, washington.contact@oecd.org, https://www.oecd.org/; Revenue Statistics 2022.

DENMARK-INTERNATIONAL FINANCE

European Commission, Eurostat, Luxembourg, 2920, LUX, https://ec.europa.eu/eurostat/; Eurostat Regional Yearbook 2021.

Organization for Economic Cooperation and Development (OECD), 2001 L St. NW, Ste. 650, Washington, DC, 20036-4922, USA, (202) 785-6323, (800) 456-6323, (202) 785-0350, washington.contact@oecd.org, https://www.oecd.org/; OECD Business and Finance Outlook 2021 and OECD Digital Economy Outlook 2020.

DENMARK-INTERNATIONAL LIQUIDITY

Organization for Economic Cooperation and Development (OECD), 2001 L St. NW, Ste. 650, Washington, DC, 20036-4922, USA, (202) 785-6323, (800) 456-6323, (202) 785-0350, washington.contact@oecd.org, https://www.oecd.org/; OECD Business and Finance Outlook 2021.

DENMARK-INTERNATIONAL TRADE

Banque de France, 31 rue Croix des Petits-Champs, Paris, 75049, FRA, infos@banque-france.fr, https://www.banque-france.fr/en; Key Figures France and Abroad.

The Economist Group: Economist Intelligence Unit (EIU), 900 3rd Ave., 16th Fl., New York, NY, 10022, USA, (212) 541-0500, americas@eiu.com, https://www.eiu.com; Denmark Country Report.

Euromonitor International, Inc., 1 N Dearborn St., Ste. 1700, Chicago, IL, 60602, USA, (312) 922-

1115, (312) 922-1157, info-usa@euromonitor.com, https://www.euromonitor.com/; Geographies.

European Commission, Eurostat, Luxembourg, 2920, LUX, https://ec.europa.eu/eurostat/; Eurostat Regional Yearbook 2021 and Extra-EU Trade in Goods.

International Monetary Fund (IMF), 700 19th St. NW, Washington, DC, 20431, USA, (202) 623-7000, (202) 623-4661, publications@imf.org, https://www.imf.org; International Financial Statistics (IFS).

Nordic Council of Ministers, Ved Stranden 18, Copenhagen, DK-1061, DEN, nmr@norden.org, https://www.norden.org/en; Nordic Children and Young People in Figures 2021 and Nordic Statistics Database.

Organization for Economic Cooperation and Development (OECD), 2001 L St. NW, Ste. 650, Washington, DC, 20036-4922, USA, (202) 785-6323, (800) 456-6323, (202) 785-0350, washington.contact@oecd.org, https://www.oecd.org/; Economic Survey of Denmark 2021; OECD Digital Economy Outlook 2020; and OECD-FAO Agricultural Outlook 2022-2031.

Palgrave Macmillan, 1 New York Plaza, Ste. 4500, New York, NY, 10004-1562, USA, (800) 777-4643, orders@palgrave.com, https://www.palgrave.com/us; The Statesman's Yearbook, 2023.

Routledge - Taylor & Francis Group, 6000 Broken Sound Pkwy. NW, Ste. 300, Boca Raton, FL, 33487, USA, (800) 634-1420, (800) 634-7064, orders@taylorandfrancis.com, https://www.routledge.com/; The Europa World Year Book 2022.

United Nations Conference on Trade and Development (UNCTAD), Palais des Nations, Geneva, 1211, SWI, (212) 963-6896, unctadinfo@unctad.org, https://unctad.org; Trade and Development Report 2021.

United Nations Food and Agricultural Organization (FAO), 2121 K St., Ste. 800B, Washington, DC, 20037, USA, (202) 653-2400 (Dial from U.S.), (202) 653-5760 (Fax from U.S.), fao-hq@fao.org, https://www.fao.org; The State of Food and Agriculture (SOFA) 2022.

United Nations Statistics Division (UNSD), United Nations Plz., New York, NY, 10017, USA, (800) 253-9646, (212) 963-9851, statistics@un.org, https://unstats.un.org; International Trade Statistics Yearbook 2020 and Statistical Yearbook of the United Nations 2021.

The World Bank, 1818 H St. NW, Washington, DC, 20433, USA, (202) 473-1000, (202) 477-6391, eds03@worldbank.org, https://www.worldbank.org/; Denmark (report); World Development Indicators (WDI) 2022; and World Development Report 2022: Finance for an Equitable Recovery.

World Bureau of Metal Statistics (WBMS), 31 Star St., Ware, Hertfordshire, SG12 9BA, GBR, https://www.refinitiv.com/en/trading-solutions/world-bureau-metal-statistics; Long Term Production/Consumption Series - All Metals; World Flow Charts; and World Metal Statistics.

World Trade Organization (WTO), Ctre. William Rappard, Rue de Lausanne 154, Case postale, Geneva, CH-1211, SWI, enquiries@wto.org, https://www.wto.org; World Trade Statistical Review 2022.

DENMARK-INTERNET USERS

International Telecommunication Union (ITU), Place des Nations, Geneva, CH-1211, SWI, itumail@itu.int, https://www.itu.int; Global Connectivity Report 2022; World Telecommunication/ICT Indicators Database 2021; and Yearbook of Statistics 2019.

The World Bank, 1818 H St. NW, Washington, DC, 20433, USA, (202) 473-1000, (202) 477-6391, eds03@worldbank.org, https://www.worldbank.org/; Denmark (report).

DENMARK-INVESTMENTS

International Monetary Fund (IMF), 700 19th St. NW, Washington, DC, 20431, USA, (202) 623-7000, (202) 623-4661, publications@imf.org, https://www.imf.org; International Financial Statistics (IFS).

Organization for Economic Cooperation and Development (OECD), 2001 L St. NW, Ste. 650, Washington, DC, 20036-4922, USA, (202) 785-6323, (800) 456-6323, (202) 785-0350, washington.contact@oecd.org, https://www.oecd.org/; OECD Business and Finance Outlook 2021; OECD Digital Economy Outlook 2020; and STAN (STructural ANalysis) Database.

DENMARK-LABOR

Central Intelligence Agency (CIA), Office of Public Affairs, Washington, DC, 20505, USA, (703) 482-0623, https://www.cia.gov; The World Factbook.

Euromonitor International, Inc., 1 N Dearborn St., Ste. 1700, Chicago, IL, 60602, USA, (312) 922-1115, (312) 922-1157, info-usa@euromonitor.com, https://www.euromonitor.com/; Geographies.

European Commission, Eurostat, Luxembourg, 2920, LUX, https://ec.europa.eu/eurostat/; Eurostat Regional Yearbook 2021.

International Labour Organization (ILO), 4 Rte. des Morillons, Geneva, CH-1211, SWI, ilo@ilo.org, https://www.ilo.org; NORMLEX Information System on International Labour Standards.

Nordic Council of Ministers, Ved Stranden 18, Copenhagen, DK-1061, DEN, nmr@norden.org, https://www.norden.org/en; Nordic Children and Young People in Figures 2021 and Nordic Statistics Database.

Organization for Economic Cooperation and Development (OECD), 2001 L St. NW, Ste. 650, Washington, DC, 20036-4922, USA, (202) 785-6323, (800) 456-6323, (202) 785-0350, washington.contact@oecd.org, https://www.oecd.org/; Economic Survey of Denmark 2021; OECD Digital Economy Outlook 2020; and OECD Employment Outlook 2022: Building Back More Inclusive Labour Markets.

Palgrave Macmillan, 1 New York Plaza, Ste. 4500, New York, NY, 10004-1562, USA, (800) 777-4643, orders@palgrave.com, https://www.palgrave.com/us; The Statesman's Yearbook, 2023.

United Nations Economic Commission for Europe (UNECE), Palais des Nations, Geneva, CH-1211, SWI, unece_info@un.org, https://unece.org/; UNECE Countries in Figures 2019.

United Nations Food and Agricultural Organization (FAO), 2121 K St., Ste. 800B, Washington, DC, 20037, USA, (202) 653-2400 (Dial from U.S.), (202) 653-5760 (Fax from U.S.), fao-hq@fao.org, https://www.fao.org; The State of Food and Agriculture (SOFA) 2022.

The World Bank, 1818 H St. NW, Washington, DC, 20433, USA, (202) 473-1000, (202) 477-6391, eds03@worldbank.org, https://www.worldbank.org/; World Development Indicators (WDI) 2022 and World Development Report 2022: Finance for an Equitable Recovery.

DENMARK-LAND USE

European Commission, Eurostat, Luxembourg, 2920, LUX, https://ec.europa.eu/eurostat/; Eurostat Regional Yearbook 2021.

United Nations Statistics Division (UNSD), United Nations Plz., New York, NY, 10017, USA, (800) 253-9646, (212) 963-9851, statistics@un.org, https://unstats.un.org; Millennium Development Goal Indicators.

The World Bank, 1818 H St. NW, Washington, DC, 20433, USA, (202) 473-1000, (202) 477-6391, eds03@worldbank.org, https://www.worldbank.org/; World Development Report 2022: Finance for an Equitable Recovery.

DENMARK-LIBRARIES

Nordic Council of Ministers, Ved Stranden 18, Copenhagen, DK-1061, DEN, nmr@norden.org, https://www.norden.org/en; Nordic Children and Young People in Figures 2021 and Nordic Statistics Database.

UNESCO Institute for Statistics, C.P 250 Succursale H, Montreal, QC, H3G 2K8, CAN, (514) 343-6880 (Dial from U.S.), (514) 343-5740 (Fax from U.S.), uis.publications@unesco.org, http://uis.unesco.org/; UIS.Stat.

DENMARK-LIFE EXPECTANCY

Central Intelligence Agency (CIA), Office of Public Affairs, Washington, DC, 20505, USA, (703) 482-0623, https://www.cia.gov; The World Factbook.

United Nations Department of Economic and Social Affairs (DESA), Population Division, 2 United Nations Plz., Rm. DC2-1950, New York, NY, 10017, USA, (212) 963-3209, (212) 963-2147, population@un.org, https://www.un.org/development/desa/pd/; World Population Ageing 2020 Highlights.

United Nations Economic Commission for Europe (UNECE), Palais des Nations, Geneva, CH-1211, SWI, unece_info@un.org, https://unece.org/; UNECE Countries in Figures 2019.

United Nations Statistics Division (UNSD), United Nations Plz., New York, NY, 10017, USA, (800) 253-9646, (212) 963-9851, statistics@un.org, https://unstats.un.org; Millennium Development Goal Indicators.

DENMARK-LITERACY

Euromonitor International, Inc., 1 N Dearborn St., Ste. 1700, Chicago, IL, 60602, USA, (312) 922-1115, (312) 922-1157, info-usa@euromonitor.com, https://www.euromonitor.com/; Geographies.

UNESCO Institute for Statistics, C.P 250 Succursale H, Montreal, QC, H3G 2K8, CAN, (514) 343-6880 (Dial from U.S.), (514) 343-5740 (Fax from U.S.), uis.publications@unesco.org, http://uis.unesco.org/; Literacy.

DENMARK-LIVESTOCK

European Commission, Eurostat, Luxembourg, 2920, LUX, https://ec.europa.eu/eurostat/; Eurostat Regional Yearbook 2021.

Nordic Council of Ministers, Ved Stranden 18, Copenhagen, DK-1061, DEN, nmr@norden.org, https://www.norden.org/en; Nordic Children and Young People in Figures 2021 and Nordic Statistics Database.

Organization for Economic Cooperation and Development (OECD), 2001 L St. NW, Ste. 650, Washington, DC, 20036-4922, USA, (202) 785-6323, (800) 456-6323, (202) 785-0350, washington.contact@oecd.org, https://www.oecd.org/; OECD-FAO Agricultural Outlook 2022-2031.

Palgrave Macmillan, 1 New York Plaza, Ste. 4500, New York, NY, 10004-1562, USA, (800) 777-4643, orders@palgrave.com, https://www.palgrave.com/us; The Statesman's Yearbook, 2023.

Routledge - Taylor & Francis Group, 6000 Broken Sound Pkwy. NW, Ste. 300, Boca Raton, FL, 33487, USA, (800) 634-1420, (800) 634-7064, orders@taylorandfrancis.com, https://www.routledge.com/; The Europa World Year Book 2022.

United Nations Food and Agricultural Organization (FAO), 2121 K St., Ste. 800B, Washington, DC, 20037, USA, (202) 653-2400 (Dial from U.S.), (202) 653-5760 (Fax from U.S.), fao-hq@fao.org, https://www.fao.org; The State of Food and Agriculture (SOFA) 2022.

United Nations Statistics Division (UNSD), United Nations Plz., New York, NY, 10017, USA, (800) 253-9646, (212) 963-9851, statistics@un.org, https://unstats.un.org; Statistical Yearbook of the United Nations 2021.

DENMARK-MAGNESIUM PRODUCTION AND CONSUMPTION

See DENMARK-MINERAL INDUSTRIES

DENMARK-MANUFACTURES

European Commission, Eurostat, Luxembourg, 2920, LUX, https://ec.europa.eu/eurostat/; Eurostat Regional Yearbook 2021.

International Monetary Fund (IMF), 700 19th St. NW, Washington, DC, 20431, USA, (202) 623-7000,

(202) 623-4661, publications@imf.org, https://www.imf.org; International Financial Statistics (IFS).

Nordic Council of Ministers, Ved Stranden 18, Copenhagen, DK-1061, DEN, nmr@norden.org, https://www.norden.org/en; Nordic Children and Young People in Figures 2021 and Nordic Statistics Database.

Organization for Economic Cooperation and Development (OECD), 2001 L St. NW, Ste. 650, Washington, DC, 20036-4922, USA, (202) 785-6323, (800) 456-6323, (202) 785-0350, washington.contact@oecd.org, https://www.oecd.org/; Economic Survey of Denmark 2021 and STAN (STructural ANalysis) Database.

DENMARK-MARRIAGE

European Commission, Eurostat, Luxembourg, 2920, LUX, https://ec.europa.eu/eurostat/; Eurostat Regional Yearbook 2021.

Nordic Council of Ministers, Ved Stranden 18, Copenhagen, DK-1061, DEN, nmr@norden.org, https://www.norden.org/en; Nordic Children and Young People in Figures 2021 and Nordic Statistics Database.

Routledge - Taylor & Francis Group, 6000 Broken Sound Pkwy. NW, Ste. 300, Boca Raton, FL, 33487, USA, (800) 634-1420, (800) 634-7064, orders@taylorandfrancis.com, https://www.routledge.com/; The Europa World Year Book 2022.

United Nations Statistics Division (UNSD), United Nations Plz., New York, NY, 10017, USA, (800) 253-9646, (212) 963-9851, statistics@un.org, https://unstats.un.org; Statistical Yearbook of the United Nations 2021.

DENMARK-MERCURY PRODUCTION

See DENMARK-MINERAL INDUSTRIES

DENMARK-METAL PRODUCTS

European Commission, Eurostat, Luxembourg, 2920, LUX, https://ec.europa.eu/eurostat/; Eurostat Regional Yearbook 2021.

DENMARK-MINERAL INDUSTRIES

Danish Energy Agency, Carsten Niebuhrs Gade 43, Copenhagen, DK-1577, DEN, ens@ens.dk, https://www.ens.dk/en; Denmark's Climate Status and Outlook 2022 (CSO22) and Energy Statistics 2021.

European Commission, Eurostat, Luxembourg, 2920, LUX, https://ec.europa.eu/eurostat/; Eurostat Regional Yearbook 2021 and Final Energy Consumption in Transport by Type of Fuel.

International Energy Agency (IEA), 9 Rue de la Federation, Paris, 75739, FRA, info@iea.org, https://www.iea.org/; Coal 2021: Analysis and Forecast to 2024; World Energy Outlook 2021; and World Energy Statistics and Balances.

International Lead and Zinc Study Group (ILZSG), Rua Almirante Barroso 38, 5th Fl., Lisbon, 1000-013, PRT, sales@ilzsg.org, https://www.ilzsg.org; Interactive Statistical Database.

Nordic Council of Ministers, Ved Stranden 18, Copenhagen, DK-1061, DEN, nmr@norden.org, https://www.norden.org/en; Nordic Children and Young People in Figures 2021 and Nordic Statistics Database.

Organization for Economic Cooperation and Development (OECD), 2001 L St. NW, Ste. 650, Washington, DC, 20036-4922, USA, (202) 785-6323, (800) 456-6323, (202) 785-0350, washington.contact@oecd.org, https://www.oecd.org/; Economic Survey of Denmark 2021; Energy Prices and Taxes for OECD Countries 2020; and STAN (STructural ANalysis) Database.

Palgrave Macmillan, 1 New York Plaza, Ste. 4500, New York, NY, 10004-1562, USA, (800) 777-4643, orders@palgrave.com, https://www.palgrave.com/us; The Statesman's Yearbook, 2023.

Routledge - Taylor & Francis Group, 6000 Broken Sound Pkwy. NW, Ste. 300, Boca Raton, FL, 33487, USA, (800) 634-1420, (800) 634-7064, orders@taylorandfrancis.com, https://www.routledge.com/; The Europa World Year Book 2022.

S&P Global Commodity Insights, One World Trade Center, New York, NY, 10007, USA, (800) 752-8878, support@platts.com, https://www.spglobal.com/commodityinsights/en; Platts Power in Europe.

United Nations Conference on Trade and Development (UNCTAD), Palais des Nations, Geneva, 1211, SWI, (212) 963-6896, unctadinfo@unctad.org, https://unctad.org; Trade and Development Report 2021.

United Nations Statistics Division (UNSD), United Nations Plz., New York, NY, 10017, USA, (800) 253-9646, (212) 963-9851, statistics@un.org, https://unstats.un.org; Energy Statistics Yearbook 2019 and Statistical Yearbook of the United Nations 2021.

World Bureau of Metal Statistics (WBMS), 31 Star St., Ware, Hertfordshire, SG12 9BA, GBR, https://www.refinitiv.com/en/trading-solutions/world-bureau-metal-statistics; Annual Stainless Steel Statistics; Long Term Production/Consumption Series - All Metals; World Flow Charts; and World Metal Statistics.

DENMARK-MONEY

European Central Bank (ECB), Frankfurt am Main, D-60640, GER, info@ecb.europa.eu, https://www.ecb.europa.eu; Economic Bulletin; Monetary Developments in the Euro Area; and Research Bulletin.

Organization for Economic Cooperation and Development (OECD), 2001 L St. NW, Ste. 650, Washington, DC, 20036-4922, USA, (202) 785-6323, (800) 456-6323, (202) 785-0350, washington.contact@oecd.org, https://www.oecd.org/; Economic Survey of Denmark 2021.

DENMARK-MONEY SUPPLY

The Economist Group: Economist Intelligence Unit (EIU), 900 3rd Ave., 16th Fl., New York, NY, 10022, USA, (212) 541-0500, americas@eiu.com, https://www.eiu.com; Denmark Country Report.

International Monetary Fund (IMF), 700 19th St. NW, Washington, DC, 20431, USA, (202) 623-7000, (202) 623-4661, publications@imf.org, https://www.imf.org; International Financial Statistics (IFS).

Nordic Council of Ministers, Ved Stranden 18, Copenhagen, DK-1061, DEN, nmr@norden.org, https://www.norden.org/en; Nordic Children and Young People in Figures 2021 and Nordic Statistics Database.

Routledge - Taylor & Francis Group, 6000 Broken Sound Pkwy. NW, Ste. 300, Boca Raton, FL, 33487, USA, (800) 634-1420, (800) 634-7064, orders@taylorandfrancis.com, https://www.routledge.com/; The Europa World Year Book 2022.

United Nations Statistics Division (UNSD), United Nations Plz., New York, NY, 10017, USA, (800) 253-9646, (212) 963-9851, statistics@un.org, https://unstats.un.org; Statistical Yearbook of the United Nations 2021.

The World Bank, 1818 H St. NW, Washington, DC, 20433, USA, (202) 473-1000, (202) 477-6391, eds03@worldbank.org, https://www.worldbank.org/; Denmark (report).

DENMARK-MONUMENTS AND HISTORIC SITES

UNESCO Institute for Statistics, C.P 250 Succursale H, Montreal, QC, H3G 2K8, CAN, (514) 343-6880 (Dial from U.S.), (514) 343-5740 (Fax from U.S.), uis.publications@unesco.org, http://uis.unesco.org/; UIS.Stat.

DENMARK-MORTALITY

European Commission, Eurostat, Luxembourg, 2920, LUX, https://ec.europa.eu/eurostat/; Eurostat Regional Yearbook 2021.

Nordic Council of Ministers, Ved Stranden 18, Copenhagen, DK-1061, DEN, nmr@norden.org, https://www.norden.org/en; Nordic Children and Young People in Figures 2021 and Nordic Statistics Database.

United Nations Conference on Trade and Development (UNCTAD), Palais des Nations, Geneva, 1211, SWI, (212) 963-6896, unctadinfo@unctad.org, https://unctad.org; Handbook of Statistics 2021.

United Nations Statistics Division (UNSD), United Nations Plz., New York, NY, 10017, USA, (800) 253-9646, (212) 963-9851, statistics@un.org, https://unstats.un.org; Millennium Development Goal Indicators; Statistical Yearbook of the United Nations 2021; and World Statistics Pocketbook 2021.

The World Bank, 1818 H St. NW, Washington, DC, 20433, USA, (202) 473-1000, (202) 477-6391, eds03@worldbank.org, https://www.worldbank.org/; World Development Indicators (WDI) 2022.

World Health Organization (WHO), Ave. Appia 20, Geneva, CH-1211, SWI, (202) 974-3000 (Telephone in U.S.), publications@who.int, https://www.who.int/; Global Health Observatory (GHO).

DENMARK-MOTION PICTURES

Palgrave Macmillan, 1 New York Plaza, Ste. 4500, New York, NY, 10004-1562, USA, (800) 777-4643, orders@palgrave.com, https://www.palgrave.com/us; The Statesman's Yearbook, 2023.

DENMARK-MOTOR VEHICLES

European Commission, Rue de la Loi, 170, Brussels, B-1040, BEL, https://ec.europa.eu; EU Energy in Figures: Statistical Pocketbook 2021.

European Commission, Eurostat, Luxembourg, 2920, LUX, https://ec.europa.eu/eurostat/; Eurostat Regional Yearbook 2021.

International Road Federation (IRF), Madison Place, 500 Montgomery St., 5th Fl., Alexandria, VA, 22314, USA, (703) 535-1001, (703) 535-1007, info@irf.global, https://www.irf.global/; World Road Statistics (WRS).

Nordic Council of Ministers, Ved Stranden 18, Copenhagen, DK-1061, DEN, nmr@norden.org, https://www.norden.org/en; Nordic Children and Young People in Figures 2021 and Nordic Statistics Database.

DENMARK-NATURAL GAS PRODUCTION

See DENMARK-MINERAL INDUSTRIES

DENMARK-NICKEL AND NICKEL ORE

See DENMARK-MINERAL INDUSTRIES

DENMARK-NUTRITION

United Nations Food and Agricultural Organization (FAO), 2121 K St., Ste. 800B, Washington, DC, 20037, USA, (202) 653-2400 (Dial from U.S.), (202) 653-5760 (Fax from U.S.), fao-hq@fao.org, https://www.fao.org; The State of Food and Agriculture (SOFA) 2022.

United Nations Statistics Division (UNSD), United Nations Plz., New York, NY, 10017, USA, (800) 253-9646, (212) 963-9851, statistics@un.org, https://unstats.un.org; Millennium Development Goal Indicators.

DENMARK-PAPER

See DENMARK-FORESTS AND FORESTRY

DENMARK-PEANUT PRODUCTION

See DENMARK-CROPS

DENMARK-PEPPER PRODUCTION

See DENMARK-CROPS

DENMARK-PESTICIDES

United Nations Food and Agricultural Organization (FAO), 2121 K St., Ste. 800B, Washington, DC, 20037, USA, (202) 653-2400 (Dial from U.S.), (202) 653-5760 (Fax from U.S.), fao-hq@fao.org, https://www.fao.org; The State of Food and Agriculture (SOFA) 2022.

DENMARK-PETROLEUM INDUSTRY AND TRADE

Danish Energy Agency, Carsten Niebuhrs Gade 43, Copenhagen, DK-1577, DEN, ens@ens.dk, https://

www.ens.dk/en; Denmark's Climate Status and Outlook 2022 (CSO22) and Energy Statistics 2021.

International Energy Agency (IEA), 9 Rue de la Federation, Paris, 75739, FRA, info@iea.org, https://www.iea.org/; World Energy Outlook 2021 and World Energy Statistics and Balances.

Organization for Economic Cooperation and Development (OECD), 2001 L St. NW, Ste. 650, Washington, DC, 20036-4922, USA, (202) 785-6323, (800) 456-6323, (202) 785-0350, washington.contact@oecd.org, https://www.oecd.org/; Energy Prices and Taxes for OECD Countries 2020.

Palgrave Macmillan, 1 New York Plaza, Ste. 4500, New York, NY, 10004-1562, USA, (800) 777-4643, orders@palgrave.com, https://www.palgrave.com/us; The Statesman's Yearbook, 2023.

U.S. Energy Information Administration (EIA), 1000 Independence Ave. SW, Washington, DC, 20585, USA, (202) 586-8800, infoctr@eia.gov, https://www.eia.gov; International Energy Outlook 2021.

United Nations Food and Agricultural Organization (FAO), 2121 K St., Ste. 800B, Washington, DC, 20037, USA, (202) 653-2400 (Dial from U.S.), (202) 653-5760 (Fax from U.S.), fao-hq@fao.org, https://www.fao.org; The State of Food and Agriculture (SOFA) 2022.

United Nations Statistics Division (UNSD), United Nations Plz., New York, NY, 10017, USA, (800) 253-9646, (212) 963-9851, statistics@un.org, https://unstats.un.org; Energy Statistics Yearbook 2019 and Statistical Yearbook of the United Nations 2021.

DENMARK-PHOSPHATES PRODUCTION

See DENMARK-MINERAL INDUSTRIES

DENMARK-PIPELINES

European Commission, Rue de la Loi, 170, Brussels, B-1040, BEL, https://ec.europa.eu; EU Energy in Figures: Statistical Pocketbook 2021.

DENMARK-PLASTICS INDUSTRY AND TRADE

European Commission, Eurostat, Luxembourg, 2920, LUX, https://ec.europa.eu/eurostat/; Eurostat Regional Yearbook 2021.

United Nations Statistics Division (UNSD), United Nations Plz., New York, NY, 10017, USA, (800) 253-9646, (212) 963-9851, statistics@un.org, https://unstats.un.org; Statistical Yearbook of the United Nations 2021.

DENMARK-PLATINUM PRODUCTION

See DENMARK-MINERAL INDUSTRIES

DENMARK-POPULATION

Banque de France, 31 rue Croix des Petits-Champs, Paris, 75049, FRA, infos@banque-france.fr, https://www.banque-france.fr/en; Webstat: Access to Statistical Series of Banque de France.

Central Intelligence Agency (CIA), Office of Public Affairs, Washington, DC, 20505, USA, (703) 482-0623, https://www.cia.gov; The World Factbook.

The Economist Group: Economist Intelligence Unit (EIU), 900 3rd Ave., 16th Fl., New York, NY, 10022, USA, (212) 541-0500, americas@eiu.com, https://www.eiu.com; Denmark Country Report.

European Commission, Eurostat, Luxembourg, 2920, LUX, https://ec.europa.eu/eurostat/; Eurostat Regional Yearbook 2021.

Infoplease, c/o Sandbox Networks, Inc., 1 Lincoln St., 24th Fl., Boston, MA, 02111, USA, https://www.infoplease.com; Countries of the World.

International Labour Organization (ILO), 4 Rte. des Morillons, Geneva, CH-1211, SWI, ilo@ilo.org, https://www.ilo.org; NORMLEX Information System on International Labour Standards.

Nordic Council of Ministers, Ved Stranden 18, Copenhagen, DK-1061, DEN, nmr@norden.org, https://www.norden.org/en; Nordic Children and Young People in Figures 2021 and Nordic Statistics Database.

Organization for Economic Cooperation and Development (OECD), 2001 L St. NW, Ste. 650, Washington, DC, 20036-4922, USA, (202) 785-6323, (800) 456-6323, (202) 785-0350, washington.contact@oecd.org, https://www.oecd.org/; OECD Labour Force Statistics 2022.

Palgrave Macmillan, 1 New York Plaza, Ste. 4500, New York, NY, 10004-1562, USA, (800) 777-4643, orders@palgrave.com, https://www.palgrave.com/us; The Statesman's Yearbook, 2023.

Routledge - Taylor & Francis Group, 6000 Broken Sound Pkwy. NW, Ste. 300, Boca Raton, FL, 33487, USA, (800) 634-1420, (800) 634-7064, orders@taylorandfrancis.com, https://www.routledge.com/; The Europa World Year Book 2022.

UK Data Service, University of Essex, Wivenhoe Park, Colchester, Essex, CO4 3SQ, GBR, https://ukdataservice.ac.uk/; International Aggregate Data.

UNESCO Institute for Statistics, C.P 250 Succursale H, Montreal, QC, H3G 2K8, CAN, (514) 343-6880 (Dial from U.S.), (514) 343-5740 (Fax from U.S.), uis.publications@unesco.org, http://uis.unesco.org/; UIS.Stat.

United Nations Department of Economic and Social Affairs (DESA), Population Division, 2 United Nations Plz., Rm. DC2-1950, New York, NY, 10017, USA, (212) 963-3209, (212) 963-2147, population@un.org, https://www.un.org/development/desa/pd/; Revision of World Urbanization Prospects and World Population Ageing 2020 Highlights.

United Nations Development Programme (UNDP), One United Nations Plz., New York, NY, 10017, USA, (212) 906-5000, (212) 906-5001, https://www.undp.org; Human Development Report 2021-2022.

United Nations Statistics Division (UNSD), United Nations Plz., New York, NY, 10017, USA, (800) 253-9646, (212) 963-9851, statistics@un.org, https://unstats.un.org; Statistical Yearbook of the United Nations 2021 and World Statistics Pocketbook 2021.

VisitDenmark, Islands Brygge 43, 3, Copenhagen, DK-2300, DEN, contact@visitdenmark.com, https://www.visitdenmark.com; VisitDenmark.com.

The World Bank, 1818 H St. NW, Washington, DC, 20433, USA, (202) 473-1000, (202) 477-6391, eds03@worldbank.org, https://www.worldbank.org/; Denmark (report); The Global Findex Database 2021; and World Development Report 2022: Finance for an Equitable Recovery.

DENMARK-POPULATION DENSITY

Central Intelligence Agency (CIA), Office of Public Affairs, Washington, DC, 20505, USA, (703) 482-0623, https://www.cia.gov; The World Factbook.

European Commission, Eurostat, Luxembourg, 2920, LUX, https://ec.europa.eu/eurostat/; Eurostat Regional Yearbook 2021.

Palgrave Macmillan, 1 New York Plaza, Ste. 4500, New York, NY, 10004-1562, USA, (800) 777-4643, orders@palgrave.com, https://www.palgrave.com/us; The Statesman's Yearbook, 2023.

Routledge - Taylor & Francis Group, 6000 Broken Sound Pkwy. NW, Ste. 300, Boca Raton, FL, 33487, USA, (800) 634-1420, (800) 634-7064, orders@taylorandfrancis.com, https://www.routledge.com/; The Europa World Year Book 2022.

UNESCO Institute for Statistics, C.P 250 Succursale H, Montreal, QC, H3G 2K8, CAN, (514) 343-6880 (Dial from U.S.), (514) 343-5740 (Fax from U.S.), uis.publications@unesco.org, http://uis.unesco.org/; UIS.Stat.

The World Bank, 1818 H St. NW, Washington, DC, 20433, USA, (202) 473-1000, (202) 477-6391, eds03@worldbank.org, https://www.worldbank.org/; Denmark (report) and World Development Report 2022: Finance for an Equitable Recovery.

DENMARK-POSTAL SERVICE

European Commission, Rue de la Loi, 170, Brussels, B-1040, BEL, https://ec.europa.eu; EU Energy in Figures: Statistical Pocketbook 2021.

Palgrave Macmillan, 1 New York Plaza, Ste. 4500, New York, NY, 10004-1562, USA, (800) 777-4643, orders@palgrave.com, https://www.palgrave.com/us; The Statesman's Yearbook, 2023.

DENMARK-POULTRY

See DENMARK-LIVESTOCK

DENMARK-POWER RESOURCES

Danish Energy Agency, Carsten Niebuhrs Gade 43, Copenhagen, DK-1577, DEN, ens@ens.dk, https://www.ens.dk/en; Denmark's Climate Status and Outlook 2022 (CSO22) and Energy Statistics 2021.

Euromonitor International, Inc., 1 N Dearborn St., Ste. 1700, Chicago, IL, 60602, USA, (312) 922-1115, (312) 922-1157, info-usa@euromonitor.com, https://www.euromonitor.com/; Geographies.

European Commission, Rue de la Loi, 170, Brussels, B-1040, BEL, https://ec.europa.eu; EU Energy in Figures: Statistical Pocketbook 2021.

European Commission, Eurostat, Luxembourg, 2920, LUX, https://ec.europa.eu/eurostat/; Eurostat Regional Yearbook 2021.

International Energy Agency (IEA), 9 Rue de la Federation, Paris, 75739, FRA, info@iea.org, https://www.iea.org/; Coal 2021: Analysis and Forecast to 2024 and World Energy Outlook 2021.

Organization for Economic Cooperation and Development (OECD), 2001 L St. NW, Ste. 650, Washington, DC, 20036-4922, USA, (202) 785-6323, (800) 456-6323, (202) 785-0350, washington.contact@oecd.org, https://www.oecd.org/; Energy Prices and Taxes for OECD Countries 2020 and Environment Statistics.

Palgrave Macmillan, 1 New York Plaza, Ste. 4500, New York, NY, 10004-1562, USA, (800) 777-4643, orders@palgrave.com, https://www.palgrave.com/us; The Statesman's Yearbook, 2023.

S&P Global Commodity Insights, One World Trade Center, New York, NY, 10007, USA, (800) 752-8878, support@platts.com, https://www.spglobal.com/commodityinsights/en; Platts European Power Daily.

U.S. Energy Information Administration (EIA), 1000 Independence Ave. SW, Washington, DC, 20585, USA, (202) 586-8800, infoctr@eia.gov, https://www.eia.gov; International Energy Outlook 2021.

United Nations Food and Agricultural Organization (FAO), 2121 K St., Ste. 800B, Washington, DC, 20037, USA, (202) 653-2400 (Dial from U.S.), (202) 653-5760 (Fax from U.S.), fao-hq@fao.org, https://www.fao.org; The State of Food and Agriculture (SOFA) 2022.

United Nations Statistics Division (UNSD), United Nations Plz., New York, NY, 10017, USA, (800) 253-9646, (212) 963-9851, statistics@un.org, https://unstats.un.org; Energy Statistics Yearbook 2019; Statistical Yearbook of the United Nations 2021; and World Statistics Pocketbook 2021.

The World Bank, 1818 H St. NW, Washington, DC, 20433, USA, (202) 473-1000, (202) 477-6391, eds03@worldbank.org, https://www.worldbank.org/; World Development Report 2022: Finance for an Equitable Recovery.

DENMARK-PRICES

Euromonitor International, Inc., 1 N Dearborn St., Ste. 1700, Chicago, IL, 60602, USA, (312) 922-1115, (312) 922-1157, info-usa@euromonitor.com, https://www.euromonitor.com/; Geographies.

European Commission, Eurostat, Luxembourg, 2920, LUX, https://ec.europa.eu/eurostat/; Eurostat Regional Yearbook 2021.

International Monetary Fund (IMF), 700 19th St. NW, Washington, DC, 20431, USA, (202) 623-7000, (202) 623-4661, publications@imf.org, https://www.imf.org; International Financial Statistics (IFS).

Nordic Council of Ministers, Ved Stranden 18, Copenhagen, DK-1061, DEN, nmr@norden.org, https://www.norden.org/en; Nordic Children and Young People in Figures 2021 and Nordic Statistics Database.

Organization for Economic Cooperation and Development (OECD), 2001 L St. NW, Ste. 650, Washington, DC, 20036-4922, USA, (202) 785-6323, (800) 456-6323, (202) 785-0350, washington.contact@oecd.org, https://www.oecd.org/; OECD Digital Economy Outlook 2020.

TAPPI - Technical Association of the Pulp and Paper Industry, 15 Technology Pkwy. S, Ste. 115, Peachtree Corners, GA, 30092, USA, (770) 446-1400, (800) 332-8686, (770) 446-6947, memberconnection@tappi.org, https://www.tappi.org/; TAPPI Journal.

The World Bank, 1818 H St. NW, Washington, DC, 20433, USA, (202) 473-1000, (202) 477-6391, eds03@worldbank.org, https://www.worldbank.org/; Denmark (report).

World Bureau of Metal Statistics (WBMS), 31 Star St., Ware, Hertfordshire, SG12 9BA, GBR, https://www.refinitiv.com/en/trading-solutions/world-bureau-metal-statistics; Long Term Production/Consumption Series - All Metals; World Flow Charts; and World Metal Statistics.

DENMARK-PUBLIC HEALTH

Euromonitor International, Inc., 1 N Dearborn St., Ste. 1700, Chicago, IL, 60602, USA, (312) 922-1115, (312) 922-1157, info-usa@euromonitor.com, https://www.euromonitor.com/; Geographies and Market Research on the Health and Wellness Industry.

European Commission, Directorate-General for Health and Food Safety, Brussels, B-1049, BEL, https://ec.europa.eu/info/departments/health-and-food-safety_en; unpublished data.

European Commission, Eurostat, Luxembourg, 2920, LUX, https://ec.europa.eu/eurostat/; Eurostat Regional Yearbook 2021.

Nordic Council of Ministers, Ved Stranden 18, Copenhagen, DK-1061, DEN, nmr@norden.org, https://www.norden.org/en; Nordic Children and Young People in Figures 2021 and Nordic Statistics Database.

Organization for Economic Cooperation and Development (OECD), 2001 L St. NW, Ste. 650, Washington, DC, 20036-4922, USA, (202) 785-6323, (800) 456-6323, (202) 785-0350, washington.contact@oecd.org, https://www.oecd.org/; Health at a Glance 2021.

U.S. Census Bureau, 4600 Silver Hill Rd., Washington, DC, 20233, USA, (301) 763-4636, (800) 923-8282, https://www.census.gov; HIV/AIDS Surveillance Data Base.

United Nations Conference on Trade and Development (UNCTAD), Palais des Nations, Geneva, 1211, SWI, (212) 963-6896, unctadinfo@unctad.org, https://unctad.org; Handbook of Statistics 2021.

United Nations Department of Economic and Social Affairs (DESA), Population Division, 2 United Nations Plz., Rm. DC2-1950, New York, NY, 10017, USA, (212) 963-3209, (212) 963-2147, population@un.org, https://www.un.org/development/desa/pd/; World Fertility Data 2019.

United Nations Development Programme (UNDP), One United Nations Plz., New York, NY, 10017, USA, (212) 906-5000, (212) 906-5001, https://www.undp.org; Human Development Report 2021-2022.

United Nations Statistics Division (UNSD), United Nations Plz., New York, NY, 10017, USA, (800) 253-9646, (212) 963-9851, statistics@un.org, https://unstats.un.org; Millennium Development Goal Indicators and Statistical Yearbook of the United Nations 2021.

The World Bank, 1818 H St. NW, Washington, DC, 20433, USA, (202) 473-1000, (202) 477-6391, eds03@worldbank.org, https://www.worldbank.org/; Denmark (report).

World Health Organization (WHO), Ave. Appia 20, Geneva, CH-1211, SWI, (202) 974-3000 (Telephone in U.S.), publications@who.int, https://www.who.int/; Global Health Observatory (GHO) and Health Statistics and Information Systems.

DENMARK-PUBLIC UTILITIES

Danish Energy Agency, Carsten Niebuhrs Gade 43, Copenhagen, DK-1577, DEN, ens@ens.dk, https://www.ens.dk/en; Denmark's Climate Status and Outlook 2022 (CSO22) and Energy Statistics 2021.

DENMARK-PUBLISHERS AND PUBLISHING

Nordic Council of Ministers, Ved Stranden 18, Copenhagen, DK-1061, DEN, nmr@norden.org, https://www.norden.org/en; Nordic Children and Young People in Figures 2021 and Nordic Statistics Database.

Palgrave Macmillan, 1 New York Plaza, Ste. 4500, New York, NY, 10004-1562, USA, (800) 777-4643, orders@palgrave.com, https://www.palgrave.com/us; The Statesman's Yearbook, 2023.

Routledge - Taylor & Francis Group, 6000 Broken Sound Pkwy. NW, Ste. 300, Boca Raton, FL, 33487, USA, (800) 634-1420, (800) 634-7064, orders@taylorandfrancis.com, https://www.routledge.com/; The Europa World Year Book 2022.

UNESCO Institute for Statistics, C.P 250 Succursale H, Montreal, QC, H3G 2K8, CAN, (514) 343-6880 (Dial from U.S.), (514) 343-5740 (Fax from U.S.), uis.publications@unesco.org, http://uis.unesco.org/; UIS.Stat.

DENMARK-RAILROADS

European Commission, Rue de la Loi, 170, Brussels, B-1040, BEL, https://ec.europa.eu; EU Energy in Figures: Statistical Pocketbook 2021.

Janes, USA, (703) 574-7580, (888) 977-1519, customer.care@janes.com, https://www.janes.com; Janes World Railways 2021-2022.

Nordic Council of Ministers, Ved Stranden 18, Copenhagen, DK-1061, DEN, nmr@norden.org, https://www.norden.org/en; Nordic Children and Young People in Figures 2021 and Nordic Statistics Database.

Palgrave Macmillan, 1 New York Plaza, Ste. 4500, New York, NY, 10004-1562, USA, (800) 777-4643, orders@palgrave.com, https://www.palgrave.com/us; The Statesman's Yearbook, 2023.

Routledge - Taylor & Francis Group, 6000 Broken Sound Pkwy. NW, Ste. 300, Boca Raton, FL, 33487, USA, (800) 634-1420, (800) 634-7064, orders@taylorandfrancis.com, https://www.routledge.com/; The Europa World Year Book 2022.

United Nations Statistics Division (UNSD), United Nations Plz., New York, NY, 10017, USA, (800) 253-9646, (212) 963-9851, statistics@un.org, https://unstats.un.org; Statistical Yearbook of the United Nations 2021.

DENMARK-RELIGION

Central Intelligence Agency (CIA), Office of Public Affairs, Washington, DC, 20505, USA, (703) 482-0623, https://www.cia.gov; The World Factbook.

Palgrave Macmillan, 1 New York Plaza, Ste. 4500, New York, NY, 10004-1562, USA, (800) 777-4643, orders@palgrave.com, https://www.palgrave.com/us; The Statesman's Yearbook, 2023.

DENMARK-RETAIL TRADE

Banque de France, 31 rue Croix des Petits-Champs, Paris, 75049, FRA, infos@banque-france.fr, https://www.banque-france.fr/en; Key Figures France and Abroad.

Euromonitor International, Inc., 1 N Dearborn St., Ste. 1700, Chicago, IL, 60602, USA, (312) 922-1115, (312) 922-1157, info-usa@euromonitor.com, https://www.euromonitor.com/; Geographies and Market Research on the Retailing Industry.

United Nations Statistics Division (UNSD), United Nations Plz., New York, NY, 10017, USA, (800) 253-9646, (212) 963-9851, statistics@un.org, https://unstats.un.org; Statistical Yearbook of the United Nations 2021.

DENMARK-RICE PRODUCTION

See DENMARK-CROPS

DENMARK-ROADS

European Commission, Rue de la Loi, 170, Brussels, B-1040, BEL, https://ec.europa.eu; EU Energy in Figures: Statistical Pocketbook 2021.

International Road Federation (IRF), Madison Place, 500 Montgomery St., 5th Fl., Alexandria, VA, 22314, USA, (703) 535-1001, (703) 535-1007, info@irf.global, https://www.irf.global/; World Road Statistics (WRS).

Nordic Council of Ministers, Ved Stranden 18, Copenhagen, DK-1061, DEN, nmr@norden.org, https://www.norden.org/en; Nordic Children and Young People in Figures 2021 and Nordic Statistics Database.

DENMARK-RUBBER INDUSTRY AND TRADE

International Rubber Study Group (IRSG), 51 Changi Business Park Central 2, Unit No. 6, 486066, SGP, https://www.rubberstudy.org; Monthly Rubber Bulletin (MRB); Rubber Industry Report; Rubber Statistical Bulletin; and World Rubber Industry Report (WRIO).

DENMARK-RYE PRODUCTION

See DENMARK-CROPS

DENMARK-SAVINGS ACCOUNT DEPOSITS

See DENMARK-BANKS AND BANKING

DENMARK-SHIPPING

European Commission, Rue de la Loi, 170, Brussels, B-1040, BEL, https://ec.europa.eu; EU Energy in Figures: Statistical Pocketbook 2021.

Nordic Council of Ministers, Ved Stranden 18, Copenhagen, DK-1061, DEN, nmr@norden.org, https://www.norden.org/en; Nordic Children and Young People in Figures 2021 and Nordic Statistics Database.

Routledge - Taylor & Francis Group, 6000 Broken Sound Pkwy. NW, Ste. 300, Boca Raton, FL, 33487, USA, (800) 634-1420, (800) 634-7064, orders@taylorandfrancis.com, https://www.routledge.com/; The Europa World Year Book 2022.

S&P Global, IHS Markit, 15 Inverness Way E, Englewood, CO, 80112, USA, (800) 447-2273, (800) 854-7179, https://ihsmarkit.com; IHS Maritime World Shipbuilding Statistics; Journal of Commerce; Lloyd's Register of Ships 2021-2022; and Maritime Portal Desktop.

United Nations Statistics Division (UNSD), United Nations Plz., New York, NY, 10017, USA, (800) 253-9646, (212) 963-9851, statistics@un.org, https://unstats.un.org; Statistical Yearbook of the United Nations 2021.

DENMARK-SOYBEAN PRODUCTION

See DENMARK-CROPS

DENMARK-STEEL PRODUCTION

See DENMARK-MINERAL INDUSTRIES

DENMARK-STRAW PRODUCTION

See DENMARK-CROPS

DENMARK-SUGAR PRODUCTION

See DENMARK-CROPS

DENMARK-SULPHUR PRODUCTION

See DENMARK-MINERAL INDUSTRIES

DENMARK-SUNFLOWER PRODUCTION

See DENMARK-CROPS

DENMARK-TAXATION

European Commission, Eurostat, Luxembourg, 2920, LUX, https://ec.europa.eu/eurostat/; Eurostat Regional Yearbook 2021 and Taxation Trends in the European Union.

International Road Federation (IRF), Madison Place, 500 Montgomery St., 5th Fl., Alexandria, VA, 22314, USA, (703) 535-1001, (703) 535-1007, info@irf.global, https://www.irf.global/; World Road Statistics (WRS).

Nordic Council of Ministers, Ved Stranden 18, Copenhagen, DK-1061, DEN, nmr@norden.org, https://www.norden.org/en; Nordic Children and Young People in Figures 2021 and Nordic Statistics Database.

Organization for Economic Cooperation and Development (OECD), 2001 L St. NW, Ste. 650, Washington, DC, 20036-4922, USA, (202) 785-6323, (800) 456-6323, (202) 785-0350, washington.contact@oecd.org, https://www.oecd.org/; Revenue Statistics 2022.

Palgrave Macmillan, 1 New York Plaza, Ste. 4500, New York, NY, 10004-1562, USA, (800) 777-4643, orders@palgrave.com, https://www.palgrave.com/us; The Statesman's Yearbook, 2023.

The World Bank, 1818 H St. NW, Washington, DC, 20433, USA, (202) 473-1000, (202) 477-6391, eds03@worldbank.org, https://www.worldbank.org/; World Development Indicators (WDI) 2022.

DENMARK-TEA PRODUCTION

See DENMARK-CROPS

DENMARK-TELEPHONE

European Commission, Rue de la Loi, 170, Brussels, B-1040, BEL, https://ec.europa.eu; EU Energy in Figures: Statistical Pocketbook 2021.

Palgrave Macmillan, 1 New York Plaza, Ste. 4500, New York, NY, 10004-1562, USA, (800) 777-4643, orders@palgrave.com, https://www.palgrave.com/us; The Statesman's Yearbook, 2023.

Routledge - Taylor & Francis Group, 6000 Broken Sound Pkwy. NW, Ste. 300, Boca Raton, FL, 33487, USA, (800) 634-1420, (800) 634-7064, orders@taylorandfrancis.com, https://www.routledge.com/; The Europa World Year Book 2022.

United Nations Statistics Division (UNSD), United Nations Plz., New York, NY, 10017, USA, (800) 253-9646, (212) 963-9851, statistics@un.org, https://unstats.un.org; World Statistics Pocketbook 2021.

DENMARK-TEXTILE INDUSTRY

Euromonitor International, Inc., 1 N Dearborn St., Ste. 1700, Chicago, IL, 60602, USA, (312) 922-1115, (312) 922-1157, info-usa@euromonitor.com, https://www.euromonitor.com/; Market Research on the Retailing Industry.

European Commission, Eurostat, Luxembourg, 2920, LUX, https://ec.europa.eu/eurostat/; Eurostat Regional Yearbook 2021.

Organization for Economic Cooperation and Development (OECD), 2001 L St. NW, Ste. 650, Washington, DC, 20036-4922, USA, (202) 785-6323, (800) 456-6323, (202) 785-0350, washington.contact@oecd.org, https://www.oecd.org/; OECD-FAO Agricultural Outlook 2022-2031 and STAN (STructural ANalysis) Database.

Palgrave Macmillan, 1 New York Plaza, Ste. 4500, New York, NY, 10004-1562, USA, (800) 777-4643, orders@palgrave.com, https://www.palgrave.com/us; The Statesman's Yearbook, 2023.

United Nations Statistics Division (UNSD), United Nations Plz., New York, NY, 10017, USA, (800) 253-9646, (212) 963-9851, statistics@un.org, https://unstats.un.org; Statistical Yearbook of the United Nations 2021 and United Nations Commodity Trade Statistics Database (UN Comtrade).

DENMARK-TOBACCO INDUSTRY

European Commission, Eurostat, Luxembourg, 2920, LUX, https://ec.europa.eu/eurostat/; Eurostat Regional Yearbook 2021.

Organization for Economic Cooperation and Development (OECD), 2001 L St. NW, Ste. 650, Washington, DC, 20036-4922, USA, (202) 785-6323, (800) 456-6323, (202) 785-0350, washington.contact@oecd.org, https://www.oecd.org/; STAN (STructural ANalysis) Database.

United Nations Statistics Division (UNSD), United Nations Plz., New York, NY, 10017, USA, (800) 253-9646, (212) 963-9851, statistics@un.org, https://unstats.un.org; Statistical Yearbook of the United Nations 2021.

DENMARK-TOURISM

Euromonitor International, Inc., 1 N Dearborn St., Ste. 1700, Chicago, IL, 60602, USA, (312) 922-1115, (312) 922-1157, info-usa@euromonitor.com, https://www.euromonitor.com/; Geographies.

European Commission, Rue de la Loi, 170, Brussels, B-1040, BEL, https://ec.europa.eu; Common Agricultural Policy (CAPF) Context Indicators, 2019 Update and EU Energy in Figures: Statistical Pocketbook 2021.

European Commission, Eurostat, Luxembourg, 2920, LUX, https://ec.europa.eu/eurostat/; European Union Tourism Database.

Organization for Economic Cooperation and Development (OECD), 2001 L St. NW, Ste. 650, Washington, DC, 20036-4922, USA, (202) 785-6323, (800) 456-6323, (202) 785-0350, washington.contact@oecd.org, https://www.oecd.org/; OECD Tourism Trends and Policies 2022.

Palgrave Macmillan, 1 New York Plaza, Ste. 4500, New York, NY, 10004-1562, USA, (800) 777-4643, orders@palgrave.com, https://www.palgrave.com/us; The Statesman's Yearbook, 2023.

Routledge - Taylor & Francis Group, 6000 Broken Sound Pkwy. NW, Ste. 300, Boca Raton, FL, 33487, USA, (800) 634-1420, (800) 634-7064, orders@taylorandfrancis.com, https://www.routledge.com/; The Europa World Year Book 2022.

United Nations Statistics Division (UNSD), United Nations Plz., New York, NY, 10017, USA, (800) 253-9646, (212) 963-9851, statistics@un.org, https://unstats.un.org; Statistical Yearbook of the United Nations 2021.

United Nations World Tourism Organization (UNWTO), Calle Poeta Joan Maragall 42, Madrid, 28020, SPA, info@unwto.org, https://www.unwto.org/; Yearbook of Tourism Statistics, 2021 Edition.

VisitDenmark, Islands Brygge 43, 3, Copenhagen, DK-2300, DEN, contact@visitdenmark.com, https://www.visitdenmark.com; VisitDenmark.com.

The World Bank, 1818 H St. NW, Washington, DC, 20433, USA, (202) 473-1000, (202) 477-6391, eds03@worldbank.org, https://www.worldbank.org/; Denmark (report).

DENMARK-TRADE

See DENMARK-INTERNATIONAL TRADE

DENMARK-TRANSPORTATION

Central Intelligence Agency (CIA), Office of Public Affairs, Washington, DC, 20505, USA, (703) 482-0623, https://www.cia.gov; The World Factbook.

Euromonitor International, Inc., 1 N Dearborn St., Ste. 1700, Chicago, IL, 60602, USA, (312) 922-1115, (312) 922-1157, info-usa@euromonitor.com, https://www.euromonitor.com/; Geographies.

European Commission, Rue de la Loi, 170, Brussels, B-1040, BEL, https://ec.europa.eu; EU Energy in Figures: Statistical Pocketbook 2021.

European Commission, Eurostat, Luxembourg, 2920, LUX, https://ec.europa.eu/eurostat/; Air Transport Statistics and Eurostat Regional Yearbook 2021.

Nordic Council of Ministers, Ved Stranden 18, Copenhagen, DK-1061, DEN, nmr@norden.org, https://www.norden.org/en; Nordic Children and Young People in Figures 2021 and Nordic Statistics Database.

Palgrave Macmillan, 1 New York Plaza, Ste. 4500, New York, NY, 10004-1562, USA, (800) 777-4643, orders@palgrave.com, https://www.palgrave.com/us; The Statesman's Yearbook, 2023.

Routledge - Taylor & Francis Group, 6000 Broken Sound Pkwy. NW, Ste. 300, Boca Raton, FL, 33487, USA, (800) 634-1420, (800) 634-7064, orders@taylorandfrancis.com, https://www.routledge.com/; The Europa World Year Book 2022.

United Nations Economic Commission for Europe (UNECE), Palais des Nations, Geneva, CH-1211, SWI, unece_info@un.org, https://unece.org/; UNECE Countries in Figures 2019.

United Nations Statistics Division (UNSD), United Nations Plz., New York, NY, 10017, USA, (800) 253-9646, (212) 963-9851, statistics@un.org, https://unstats.un.org; Energy Statistics Yearbook 2019.

The World Bank, 1818 H St. NW, Washington, DC, 20433, USA, (202) 473-1000, (202) 477-6391, eds03@worldbank.org, https://www.worldbank.org/; Denmark (report).

DENMARK-UNEMPLOYMENT

European Commission, Eurostat, Luxembourg, 2920, LUX, https://ec.europa.eu/eurostat/; Eurostat Regional Yearbook 2021.

International Labour Organization (ILO), 4 Rte. des Morillons, Geneva, CH-1211, SWI, ilo@ilo.org, https://www.ilo.org; NORMLEX Information System on International Labour Standards.

Nordic Council of Ministers, Ved Stranden 18, Copenhagen, DK-1061, DEN, nmr@norden.org, https://www.norden.org/en; Nordic Children and Young People in Figures 2021 and Nordic Statistics Database.

Organization for Economic Cooperation and Development (OECD), 2001 L St. NW, Ste. 650, Washington, DC, 20036-4922, USA, (202) 785-6323, (800) 456-6323, (202) 785-0350, washington.contact@oecd.org, https://www.oecd.org/; Economic Survey of Denmark 2021; OECD Composite Leading Indicator (CLI); OECD Employment Outlook 2022: Building Back More Inclusive Labour Markets; and OECD Labour Force Statistics 2022.

Palgrave Macmillan, 1 New York Plaza, Ste. 4500, New York, NY, 10004-1562, USA, (800) 777-4643, orders@palgrave.com, https://www.palgrave.com/us; The Statesman's Yearbook, 2023.

United Nations Statistics Division (UNSD), United Nations Plz., New York, NY, 10017, USA, (800) 253-9646, (212) 963-9851, statistics@un.org, https://unstats.un.org; Statistical Yearbook of the United Nations 2021.

DENMARK-URANIUM PRODUCTION AND CONSUMPTION

See DENMARK-MINERAL INDUSTRIES

DENMARK-VITAL STATISTICS

Danish Energy Agency, Carsten Niebuhrs Gade 43, Copenhagen, DK-1577, DEN, ens@ens.dk, https://www.ens.dk/en; Denmark's Climate Status and Outlook 2022 (CSO22) and Energy Statistics 2021.

European Commission, Eurostat, Luxembourg, 2920, LUX, https://ec.europa.eu/eurostat/; Eurostat Regional Yearbook 2021.

Nordic Council of Ministers, Ved Stranden 18, Copenhagen, DK-1061, DEN, nmr@norden.org, https://www.norden.org/en; Nordic Children and Young People in Figures 2021 and Nordic Statistics Database.

Palgrave Macmillan, 1 New York Plaza, Ste. 4500, New York, NY, 10004-1562, USA, (800) 777-4643, orders@palgrave.com, https://www.palgrave.com/us; The Statesman's Yearbook, 2023.

U.S. Census Bureau, 4600 Silver Hill Rd., Washington, DC, 20233, USA, (301) 763-4636, (800) 923-8282, https://www.census.gov; HIV/AIDS Surveillance Data Base.

United Nations Department of Economic and Social Affairs (DESA), Population Division, 2 United Nations Plz., Rm. DC2-1950, New York, NY, 10017, USA, (212) 963-3209, (212) 963-2147, population@un.org, https://www.un.org/development/desa/pd/; World Contraceptive Use

2021: Estimates and Projections of Family Planning Indicators and World Marriage Data 2019.

United Nations Statistics Division (UNSD), United Nations Plz., New York, NY, 10017, USA, (800) 253-9646, (212) 963-9851, statistics@un.org, https://unstats.un.org; Statistical Yearbook of the United Nations 2021.

DENMARK-WAGES

European Commission, Eurostat, Luxembourg, 2920, LUX, https://ec.europa.eu/eurostat/; Eurostat Regional Yearbook 2021.

International Labour Organization (ILO), 4 Rte. des Morillons, Geneva, CH-1211, SWI, ilo@ilo.org, https://www.ilo.org; NORMLEX Information System on International Labour Standards.

Nordic Council of Ministers, Ved Stranden 18, Copenhagen, DK-1061, DEN, nmr@norden.org, https://www.norden.org/en; Nordic Children and Young People in Figures 2021 and Nordic Statistics Database.

Organization for Economic Cooperation and Development (OECD), 2001 L St. NW, Ste. 650, Washington, DC, 20036-4922, USA, (202) 785-6323, (800) 456-6323, (202) 785-0350, washington.contact@oecd.org, https://www.oecd.org/; OECD Digital Economy Outlook 2020 and STAN (STructural ANalysis) Database.

United Nations Statistics Division (UNSD), United Nations Plz., New York, NY, 10017, USA, (800) 253-9646, (212) 963-9851, statistics@un.org, https://unstats.un.org; Statistical Yearbook of the United Nations 2021.

The World Bank, 1818 H St. NW, Washington, DC, 20433, USA, (202) 473-1000, (202) 477-6391, eds03@worldbank.org, https://www.worldbank.org/; Denmark (report).

DENMARK-WEATHER

See DENMARK-CLIMATE

DENMARK-WHALES

See DENMARK-FISHERIES

DENMARK-WHEAT PRODUCTION

See DENMARK-CROPS

DENMARK-WHOLESALE TRADE

European Commission, Eurostat, Luxembourg, 2920, LUX, https://ec.europa.eu/eurostat/; Eurostat Regional Yearbook 2021.

United Nations Statistics Division (UNSD), United Nations Plz., New York, NY, 10017, USA, (800) 253-9646, (212) 963-9851, statistics@un.org, https://unstats.un.org; Statistical Yearbook of the United Nations 2021.

DENMARK-WOOD AND WOOD PULP

See DENMARK-FORESTS AND FORESTRY

DENMARK-WOOD PRODUCTS

Organization for Economic Cooperation and Development (OECD), 2001 L St. NW, Ste. 650, Washington, DC, 20036-4922, USA, (202) 785-6323, (800) 456-6323, (202) 785-0350, washington.contact@oecd.org, https://www.oecd.org/; STAN (STructural ANalysis) Database.

DENMARK-WOOL PRODUCTION

See DENMARK-TEXTILE INDUSTRY

DENMARK-ZINC AND ZINC ORE

See DENMARK-MINERAL INDUSTRIES

DENMARK-ZOOS

UNESCO Institute for Statistics, C.P 250 Succursale H, Montreal, QC, H3G 2K8, CAN, (514) 343-6880 (Dial from U.S.), (514) 343-5740 (Fax from U.S.), uis.publications@unesco.org, http://uis.unesco.org/; UIS.Stat.

DENTAL CARE

Bank Street Graduate School of Education, National Center for Children in Poverty (NCCP), 475 Riverside Dr., Ste. 1400, New York, NY, 10115, USA, info@nccp.org, https://www.nccp.org/; Medicaid Oral Health Coverage for Adults with Intellectual & Developmental Disabilities - A Fiscal Analysis.

DENTISTS-CHARGES AND EXPENDITURES FOR

U.S. Department of Labor (DOL), Bureau of Labor Statistics (BLS), Postal Square Bldg., 2 Massachusetts Ave. NE, Washington, DC, 20212-0001, USA, (202) 691-5200, (202) 691-7890, blsdata_staff@bls.gov, https://www.bls.gov; Consumer Price Index (CPI) Databases.

DENTISTS-DENTAL SCHOOLS-STUDENTS, AND GRADUATES

U.S. Department of Education (ED), Institute of Education Sciences (IES), National Center for Education Statistics (NCES), Potomac Center Plaza, 550 12th St. SW, Washington, DC, 20202, USA, (202) 403-5551, https://nces.ed.gov/; Digest of Education Statistics, 2020.

U.S. Department of Health and Human Services, Centers for Disease Control and Prevention (CDC), National Center for Health Statistics (NCHS), 3311 Toledo Rd., Hyattsville, MD, 20782-2064, USA, (800) 232-4636, (301) 458-4000, https://www.cdc.gov/nchs; Health, United States, 2020-2021.

DENTISTS-MEDICAID PAYMENTS AND RECIPIENTS

Bank Street Graduate School of Education, National Center for Children in Poverty (NCCP), 475 Riverside Dr., Ste. 1400, New York, NY, 10115, USA, info@nccp.org, https://www.nccp.org/; Medicaid Oral Health Coverage for Adults with Intellectual & Developmental Disabilities - A Fiscal Analysis.

U.S. Department of Health and Human Services (HHS), Centers for Medicare and Medicaid Services (CMS), 7500 Security Blvd., Baltimore, MD, 21244, USA, (410) 786-3000, (877) 267-2323, https://www.cms.gov; Medicare Current Beneficiary Survey (MCBS).

DENTISTS-OFFICES

U.S. Census Bureau, 4600 Silver Hill Rd., Washington, DC, 20233, USA, (301) 763-4636, (800) 923-8282, https://www.census.gov; County Business Patterns (CBP) 2020.

U.S. Census Bureau, Center for Economic Studies (CES), 4600 Silver Hill Rd., Washington, DC, 20233, USA, (301) 763-6460, (301) 763-5935, ces.contacts@census.gov, https://www.census.gov/programs-surveys/ces.html; Professional, Scientific and Technical Services, 2017 Economic Census.

DEPARTMENT STORES-EARNINGS

U.S. Census Bureau, 4600 Silver Hill Rd., Washington, DC, 20233, USA, (301) 763-4636, (800) 923-8282, https://www.census.gov; County Business Patterns (CBP) 2020.

U.S. Census Bureau, Center for Economic Studies (CES), 4600 Silver Hill Rd., Washington, DC, 20233, USA, (301) 763-6460, (301) 763-5935, ces.contacts@census.gov, https://www.census.gov/programs-surveys/ces.html; Retail Trade, 2017 Economic Census and Wholesale Trade, 2017 Economic Census.

U.S. Department of Commerce (DOC), International Trade Administration (ITA), 1401 Constitution Ave. NW, Washington, DC, 20230, USA, (800) 872-8723, https://www.trade.gov/; TradeStats Express (TSE).

DEPARTMENT STORES-EMPLOYEES

U.S. Census Bureau, 4600 Silver Hill Rd., Washington, DC, 20233, USA, (301) 763-4636, (800) 923-8282, https://www.census.gov; County Business Patterns (CBP) 2020.

U.S. Census Bureau, Center for Economic Studies (CES), 4600 Silver Hill Rd., Washington, DC, 20233, USA, (301) 763-6460, (301) 763-5935, ces.contacts@census.gov, https://www.census.gov/programs-surveys/ces.html; Retail Trade, 2017 Economic Census.

DEPARTMENT STORES-ESTABLISHMENTS

U.S. Census Bureau, 4600 Silver Hill Rd., Washington, DC, 20233, USA, (301) 763-4636, (800) 923-8282, https://www.census.gov; County Business Patterns (CBP) 2020.

U.S. Census Bureau, Center for Economic Studies (CES), 4600 Silver Hill Rd., Washington, DC, 20233, USA, (301) 763-6460, (301) 763-5935, ces.contacts@census.gov, https://www.census.gov/programs-surveys/ces.html; Retail Trade, 2017 Economic Census.

U.S. Department of Commerce (DOC), International Trade Administration (ITA), 1401 Constitution Ave. NW, Washington, DC, 20230, USA, (800) 872-8723, https://www.trade.gov/; TradeStats Express (TSE).

DEPARTMENT STORES-INVENTORIES

U.S. Census Bureau, Center for Economic Studies (CES), 4600 Silver Hill Rd., Washington, DC, 20233, USA, (301) 763-6460, (301) 763-5935, ces.contacts@census.gov, https://www.census.gov/programs-surveys/ces.html; Retail Trade, 2017 Economic Census.

U.S. Department of Commerce (DOC), International Trade Administration (ITA), 1401 Constitution Ave. NW, Washington, DC, 20230, USA, (800) 872-8723, https://www.trade.gov/; TradeStats Express (TSE).

DEPARTMENT STORES-PRODUCTIVITY

U.S. Department of Labor (DOL), Bureau of Labor Statistics (BLS), Postal Square Bldg., 2 Massachusetts Ave. NE, Washington, DC, 20212-0001, USA, (202) 691-5200, (202) 691-7890, blsdata_staff@bls.gov, https://www.bls.gov; Current Employment Statistics (CES).

DEPARTMENT STORES-SALES

U.S. Census Bureau, Center for Economic Studies (CES), 4600 Silver Hill Rd., Washington, DC, 20233, USA, (301) 763-6460, (301) 763-5935, ces.contacts@census.gov, https://www.census.gov/programs-surveys/ces.html; Retail Trade, 2017 Economic Census.

U.S. Department of Commerce (DOC), International Trade Administration (ITA), 1401 Constitution Ave. NW, Washington, DC, 20230, USA, (800) 872-8723, https://www.trade.gov/; TradeStats Express (TSE).

DEPORTATION

Cato Institute, 1000 Massachusetts Ave. NW, Washington, DC, 20001-5403, USA, (202) 842-0200, https://www.cato.org/; Immigrants' Deportations, Local Crime, and Police Effectiveness.

Civiqs, PO Box 70008, Oakland, CA, 94612, USA, (510) 394-5664, inquiries@civiqs.com, https://civiqs.com/; Should the United States Deport Immigrants Living Here Illegally, or Offer Them a Path to Citizenship?.

DEPOSITS

See BANKS, COMMERCIAL-DEPOSITS

DEPRESSION, MENTAL

The Henry J. Kaiser Family Foundation (KFF), 185 Berry St., Ste. 2000, San Francisco, CA, 94107, USA, (650) 854-9400, (650) 854-4800, https://www.kff.org; The Implications of COVID-19 for Mental Health and Substance Use.

U.S. Department of Health and Human Services (HHS), National Institutes of Health (NIH), National Institute of Mental Health (NIMH), 6001 Executive Blvd., Room 6200, MSC 9663, Bethesda, MD, 20892-9663, USA, (866) 615-6464, (301) 443-8431 (TTY), (301) 443-4279, nimhinfo@nih.gov, https://www.nimh.nih.gov/; Mental Health Statistics.

U.S. Department of Health and Human Services, Centers for Disease Control and Prevention (CDC), 1600 Clifton Rd., Atlanta, GA, 30329-4027, USA, (800) 232-4636, (888) 232-6348 (TTY), cdcinfo@cdc.gov, https://www.cdc.gov; Symptoms of Anxiety or Depressive Disorder and Use of Mental Health Care Among Adults During the COVID-19 Pandemic - United States, August 2020 - February 2021.

U.S. Department of Health and Human Services, Centers for Disease Control and Prevention (CDC), National Center for Health Statistics (NCHS), 3311 Toledo Rd., Hyattsville, MD, 20782-2064, USA, (800) 232-4636, (301) 458-4000, https://www.cdc.gov/nchs; Household Pulse Survey: Anxiety and Depression.

World Health Organization (WHO), Ave. Appia 20, Geneva, CH-1211, SWI, (202) 974-3000 (Telephone in U.S.), publications@who.int, https://www.who.int/; Mental Health Atlas 2020.

Yale School of Medicine, Yale Child Study Center, 230 S Frontage Rd., New Haven, CT, 06520, USA, (844) 362-9272, https://medicine.yale.edu/childstudy; unpublished data.

DERMATOLOGY

American Medical Association (AMA), AMA Plaza, 330 N Wabash Ave., Ste. 39300, Chicago, IL, 60611-5885, USA, (312) 464-4782, amacatalog@ama-assn.org, https://www.ama-assn.org; JAMA Dermatology.

DESERT

International Institute for Environment and Development (IIED), 235 High Holborn, London, WC1V 7DN, GBR, inforequest@iied.org, https://www.iied.org; Environment & Urbanization.

United Nations Food and Agricultural Organization (FAO), 2121 K St., Ste. 800B, Washington, DC, 20037, USA, (202) 653-2400 (Dial from U.S.), (202) 653-5760 (Fax from U.S.), fao-hq@fao.org, https://www.fao.org; FAO Soils Portal: Legacy Soil Maps and Soils Databases.

DESIGN

Alzheimer's Disease International (ADI), 15 Blue Lion Pl., London, SE1 4PU, GBR, info@alzint.org, https://www.alzint.org; World Alzheimer Report 2020: Design, Dignity, Dementia: Dementia-Related Design and the Built Environment.

DETENTION OF PERSONS-UNITED STATES

Amnesty International USA, 311 W 43rd St., 7th Fl., New York, NY, 10036, USA, (212) 807-8400, (800) 266-3789, (212) 627-1451, aimember@aiusa.org, https://www.amnestyusa.org/; No Home for Children: The Homestead 'Temporary Emergency' Facility.

The Immigrant Learning Center (ILC), 442 Main St., Malden, MA, 02148-5177, USA, (781) 322-9777, (800) 439-2370 (TTY), (781) 321-1963, info@ilctr.org, https://www.ilctr.org/; Immigrant Detention and COVID-19: How a Pandemic Exploited and Spread through the US Immigrant Detention System.

Pennsylvania State University, Penn State Law Center for Immigrants' Rights Clinic, Lewis Katz Bldg., University Park, PA, 16802, USA, (814) 865-8900, (814) 863-7274, centerforimmigrantsr@pennstatelaw.psu.edu, https://pennstatelaw.psu.edu/practice-skills/clinics/center-immigrants-rights; Inside Berks Family Detention: Observations by Penn State Law Center for Immigrants' Rights Clinic.

U.S. Department of Health and Human Services (HHS), Office of Inspector General (OIG), 330 Independence Ave. SW, Washington, DC, 20201, USA, (877) 696-6775, public.affairs@oig.hhs.gov, https://oig.hhs.gov/; Care Provider Facilities Described Challenges Addressing Mental Health Needs of Children in HHS Custody.

University of California Los Angeles (UCLA) School of Law, Covid-19 Behind Bars Data Project, 385 Charles E. Young Dr. E, Los Angeles, CA, 90095, USA, (310) 206-5568, covidbehindbars@law.ucla.edu, https://uclacovidbehindbars.org; Covid Behind Bars Data Project.

DEVELOPING COUNTRIES-ECONOMIC CONDITIONS

Climate Analytics, 135 Madison Ave., 5th Fl., Ste. 05-115, New York, NY, 10016, USA, info.ny@climateanalytics.org, https://climateanalytics.org/; 2 Steps Down the Debt Spiral: COVID-19 and Tropical Cyclones Severely Limit the Fiscal Space of Many Small Island Developing States.

Global Change Data Lab, Our World in Data, GBR, info@ourworldindata.org, https://ourworldindata.org; Measuring Progress Towards the Sustainable Development Goals.

International Food Policy Research Institute (IFPRI), 1201 Eye St. NW, Washington, DC, 20005-3915, USA, (202) 862-5600, (202) 862-5606, ifpri@cgiar.org, https://www.ifpri.org/; The COVID-19 Crisis Will Exacerbate Maternal and Child Undernutrition and Child Mortality in Low- and Middle-Income Countries.

International Fund for Agricultural Development (IFAD), Via Paolo di Dono, 44, Rome, 00142, ITA, ifad@ifad.org, https://www.ifad.org/; The State of Food Security and Nutrition in the World 2021.

International Institute for Environment and Development (IIED), 235 High Holborn, London, WC1V 7DN, GBR, inforequest@iied.org, https://www.iied.org; Redesigning Debt: Lessons from HIPC for COVID, Climate and Nature.

Pew Research Center, Internet & Technology, 1615 L St. NW, Ste. 800, Washington, DC, 20036, USA, (202) 419-4300, (202) 857-8562, https://www.pewresearch.org/topic/internet-technology/; Mobile Divides in Emerging Economies.

Swedish International Development Cooperation Agency (SIDA), Box 2025, Sundbyberg, SE-174 02, SWE, sida@sida.se, https://www.sida.se/en; Environment and Climate Change 2020: Towards Environmental Sustainability and Resilience and Migration and Displacement 2020: Inclusion of Migrants and Displaced in Global Development.

The World Bank, 1818 H St. NW, Washington, DC, 20433, USA, (202) 473-1000, (202) 477-6391, eds03@worldbank.org, https://www.worldbank.org/; The Global Findex Database 2021 and World Bank Open Data.

DEVELOPING COUNTRIES-FOREIGN ECONOMIC RELATIONS

AidData, William & Mary Global Research Institute, 427 Scotland St., Williamsburg, VA, 23185, USA, (757) 221-1468, info@aiddata.org, https://www.aiddata.org/; Datasets Database and Ties That Bind: Quantifying China's Public Diplomacy and Its 'Good Neighbor' Effect.

The World Bank, 1818 H St. NW, Washington, DC, 20433, USA, (202) 473-1000, (202) 477-6391, eds03@worldbank.org, https://www.worldbank.org/; World Bank Open Data.

DEVELOPING COUNTRIES-POPULATION

African Gender Institute (AGI), University of Cape Town, Private Bag, Rondebosch, 7701, SAF, afs@uct.ac.za, http://www.agi.uct.ac.za/; Feminist Africa Journal.

Climate Analytics, 135 Madison Ave., 5th Fl., Ste. 05-115, New York, NY, 10016, USA, info.ny@climateanalytics.org, https://climateanalytics.org/; 2 Steps Down the Debt Spiral: COVID-19 and Tropical Cyclones Severely Limit the Fiscal Space of Many Small Island Developing States.

Global Change Data Lab, Our World in Data, GBR, info@ourworldindata.org, https://ourworldindata.org; Measuring Progress Towards the Sustainable Development Goals.

International Food Policy Research Institute (IFPRI), 1201 Eye St. NW, Washington, DC, 20005-3915, USA, (202) 862-5600, (202) 862-5606, ifpri@cgiar.org, https://www.ifpri.org/; The COVID-19 Crisis Will Exacerbate Maternal and Child Undernutrition and Child Mortality in Low- and Middle-Income Countries.

International Fund for Agricultural Development (IFAD), Via Paolo di Dono, 44, Rome, 00142, ITA, ifad@ifad.org, https://www.ifad.org/; The State of Food Security and Nutrition in the World 2021.

Pew Research Center, Internet & Technology, 1615 L St. NW, Ste. 800, Washington, DC, 20036, USA, (202) 419-4300, (202) 857-8562, https://www.pewresearch.org/topic/internet-technology/; Mobile Divides in Emerging Economies.

Swedish International Development Cooperation Agency (SIDA), Box 2025, Sundbyberg, SE-174 02, SWE, sida@sida.se, https://www.sida.se/en; Environment and Climate Change 2020: Towards Environmental Sustainability and Resilience and Migration and Displacement 2020: Inclusion of Migrants and Displaced in Global Development.

United Nations Educational, Scientific and Cultural Organization (UNESCO), 7, place de Fontenoy, Paris, 75007, FRA, https://www.unesco.org; World Water Development Report (WWDR) 2023: Partnerships and Cooperation for Water.

University of Washington, Institute for Health Metrics and Evaluation (IHME), Population Health Building/Hans Rosling Center, UW Campus Box 351615, 3980 15th Ave. NE, Seattle, WA, 98195, USA, (206) 897-2800, (206) 897-2899, engage@healthdata.org, https://www.healthdata.org; Global Access to Handwashing: Implications for COVID-19 Control in Low-Income Countries.

The World Bank, 1818 H St. NW, Washington, DC, 20433, USA, (202) 473-1000, (202) 477-6391, eds03@worldbank.org, https://www.worldbank.org/; The Global Findex Database 2021.

DEVELOPING COUNTRIES AND GLOBAL CLIMATE CHANGE

Global Change Data Lab, Our World in Data, GBR, info@ourworldindata.org, https://ourworldindata.org; Measuring Progress Towards the Sustainable Development Goals.

Global Facility for Disaster Reduction and Recovery (GFDRR), 1818 H St. NW, Washington, DC, 20433, USA, (202) 473-1000, gfdrr@worldbank.org, https://www.gfdrr.org/; Overlooked : Examining the Impact of Disasters and Climate Shocks on Poverty in the Europe and Central Asia Region.

International Fund for Agricultural Development (IFAD), Via Paolo di Dono, 44, Rome, 00142, ITA, ifad@ifad.org, https://www.ifad.org/; Climate Change and Food System Activities - A Review of Emission Trends, Climate Impacts and the Effects of Dietary Change.

International Institute for Environment and Development (IIED), 235 High Holborn, London, WC1V 7DN, GBR, inforequest@iied.org, https://www.iied.org; Redesigning Debt: Lessons from HIPC for COVID, Climate and Nature.

Swedish International Development Cooperation Agency (SIDA), Box 2025, Sundbyberg, SE-174 02, SWE, sida@sida.se, https://www.sida.se/en; Environment and Climate Change 2020: Towards Environmental Sustainability and Resilience.

UNICEF, 3 United Nations Plz., New York, NY, 10017, USA, (212) 303-7984, (917) 244-2215, https://www.unicef.org; Children's Climate Risk Index (CCRI).

United Nations Educational, Scientific and Cultural Organization (UNESCO), 7, place de Fontenoy, Paris, 75007, FRA, https://www.unesco.org; World Water Development Report (WWDR) 2023: Partnerships and Cooperation for Water.

The World Bank, 1818 H St. NW, Washington, DC, 20433, USA, (202) 473-1000, (202) 477-6391, eds03@worldbank.org, https://www.worldbank.org/; Atlas of Sustainable Development Goals 2020: From World Development Indicators.

World Economic Forum (WEF), 350 Madison Ave., 11th Fl., New York, NY, 10017, USA, (212) 703-2300, forumusa@weforum.org, https://www.weforum.org/; The Global Risks Report 2022.

World Meteorological Organization (WMO), 7bis, ave. de la Paix, PO Box 2300, Geneva, CH-1211, SWI, wmo@wmo.int, https://public.wmo.int/en; Atlas of Mortality and Economic Losses from Weather, Climate and Water Extremes (1970-2019).

DIABETES

Australian Institute of Health and Welfare (AIHW), GPO Box 570, Canberra, ACT, 2601, AUS, info@aihw.gov.au, https://www.aihw.gov.au/; Incidence of Insulin-Treated Diabetes in Australia.

Bernan Press, 15250 NBN Way, Bldg. C, Blue Ridge Summit, PA, 17214, USA, (301) 459-2255, (800) 865-3457, (800) 865-3450, customercare@bernan.com, https://rowman.com/Page/Bernan; Vital Statistics of the United States 2022: Births, Life Expectancy, Deaths, and Selected Health Data.

Novo Nordisk Inc., 800 Scudders Mill Rd., Plainsboro, NJ, 08536, USA, (609) 987-5800, (800) 727-6500, https://www.novonordisk-us.com/; unpublished data.

U.S. Department of Health and Human Services, Centers for Disease Control and Prevention (CDC), 1600 Clifton Rd., Atlanta, GA, 30329-4027, USA, (800) 232-4636, (888) 232-6348 (TTY), cdcinfo@cdc.gov, https://www.cdc.gov; Behavioral Risk Factor Surveillance System (BRFSS) Data; Diabetes Data and Statistics; and National Diabetes Statistics Report.

U.S. Department of Health and Human Services, Centers for Disease Control and Prevention (CDC), National Center for Chronic Disease Prevention and Health Promotion (NCCDPHP), 1600 Clifton Rd., Atlanta, GA, 30329, USA, (800) 232-4636, (888) 232-6348 (TTY), https://www.cdc.gov/chronicdisease/; Leading Indicators for Chronic Diseases and Risk Factors Open Data Portal.

U.S. Department of Health and Human Services, Centers for Disease Control and Prevention (CDC), National Center for Health Statistics (NCHS), 3311 Toledo Rd., Hyattsville, MD, 20782-2064, USA, (800) 232-4636, (301) 458-4000, https://www.cdc.gov/nchs; FastStats - Statistics by Topic; National Vital Statistics Reports (NVSR); and Vital Statistics Online Data Portal.

DIAGNOSIS

Alzheimer's Disease International (ADI), 15 Blue Lion Pl., London, SE1 4PU, GBR, info@alzint.org, https://www.alzint.org; World Alzheimer Report 2021: Journey to a Diagnosis of Dementia.

SAGE Publications, 2455 Teller Rd., Thousand Oaks, CA, 91320, USA, (800) 818-7243, (800) 583-2665, journals@sagepub.com, https://www.sagepub.com; Experimental Biology and Medicine - The Role of Chest Computed Tomography in the Management of COVID-19: A Review of Results and Recommendations.

DIAGNOSTIC HEALTH PROCEDURES

Alzheimer's Disease International (ADI), 15 Blue Lion Pl., London, SE1 4PU, GBR, info@alzint.org, https://www.alzint.org; World Alzheimer Report 2021: Journey to a Diagnosis of Dementia.

DIAMONDS

U.S. Department of the Interior (DOI), U.S. Geological Survey (USGS), National Minerals Information Center (NMIC), 12201 Sunrise Valley Dr., Reston, VA, 20192, USA, (703) 648-4920, (703) 648-7971, (703) 648-4995, sfortier@usgs.gov, https://www.usgs.gov/centers/nmic; Mineral Commodity Summaries 2022 and Minerals Yearbook.

DIAMONDS-INTERNATIONAL TRADE

U.S. Census Bureau, International Trade Program, 4600 Silver Hill Rd., Washington, DC, 20233, USA, (800) 549-0595, eid.international.trade.data@census.gov, https://www.census.gov/foreign-trade; International Trade Data.

DIAMONDS-WORLD PRODUCTION

U.S. Department of the Interior (DOI), U.S. Geological Survey (USGS), National Minerals Information Center (NMIC), 12201 Sunrise Valley Dr., Reston, VA, 20192, USA, (703) 648-4920, (703) 648-7971, (703) 648-4995, sfortier@usgs.gov, https://www.usgs.gov/centers/nmic; Mineral Commodity Summaries 2022 and Minerals Yearbook.

DIATOMITE

U.S. Department of the Interior (DOI), U.S. Geological Survey (USGS), National Minerals Information Center (NMIC), 12201 Sunrise Valley Dr., Reston, VA, 20192, USA, (703) 648-4920, (703) 648-7971, (703) 648-4995, sfortier@usgs.gov, https://www.usgs.gov/centers/nmic; Mineral Commodity Summaries 2022 and Minerals Yearbook.

DIESEL AUTOMOBILES

International Council on Clean Transportation (ICCT), 1500 K St. NW, Ste. 650, Washington, DC, 20005, USA, (202) 798-3986, https://theicct.org; Reassessment of Excess NOx from Diesel Cars in Europe Following the Court Justice of the European Union Rulings.

DIESEL TRUCKS

The Real Urban Emissions Initiative (TRUE), 60 Trafalgar Square, London, WC2N 5DS, GBR, info@trueinitiative.org, https://www.trueinitiative.org/; Air Quality and Health Impacts of Diesel Truck Emissions in New York City and Policy Implications.

DIET

International Fund for Agricultural Development (IFAD), Via Paolo di Dono, 44, Rome, 00142, ITA, ifad@ifad.org, https://www.ifad.org/; Climate Change and Food System Activities - A Review of Emission Trends, Climate Impacts and the Effects of Dietary Change.

NielsenIQ (NIQ), 200 W Jackson Blvd., Chicago, IL, 60606, USA, https://nielseniq.com; Covid-Positive Households Are Altering Their Eating Habits and The F Word: Flexitarian Is Not a Curse to the Meat Industry.

Numerator, 24 E Washington St., Ste. 1200, Chicago, IL, 60602, USA, (312) 585-3927, https://www.numerator.com; The Real Deal with Fake Meat: Understanding the Plant-Based Meat Alternative Buyer.

Produce for Better Health (PBH) Foundation, USA, https://fruitsandveggies.org/; 2020 State of the Plate.

DIETARY SUPPLEMENTS

ConsumerLab, 333 Mamaroneck Ave., White Plains, NY, 10605, USA, (914) 722-9149, info@consumerlab.com, https://www.consumerlab.com; Product Review: Turmeric and Curcumin Supplements and Spices and Product Reviews: CBD and Hemp Extract Supplements, Lotions, and Balms Review.

DIETICIANS AND THERAPISTS

U.S. Department of Labor (DOL), Bureau of Labor Statistics (BLS), Postal Square Bldg., 2 Massachusetts Ave. NE, Washington, DC, 20212-0001, USA, (202) 691-5200, (202) 691-7890, blsdata_staff@bls.gov, https://www.bls.gov; Monthly Labor Review.

DIGITAL COMMUNICATION

Girl Scouts of the USA, 420 Fifth Ave., New York, NY, 10018, USA, (212) 852-8000, (800) 478-7248, https://www.girlscouts.org/; Decoding the Digital Girl: Defining and Supporting Girls' Digital Leadership.

Microsoft Research, 14820 NE 36th St., Bldg. 99, Redmond, WA, 98052, USA, https://research.microsoft.com; Design of Digital Workplace Stress-Reduction Intervention Systems: Effects of Intervention Type and Timing.

PricewaterhouseCoopers (PwC) Strategy&, 90 Park Ave., Ste. 400, New York, NY, 10016, USA, (212) 697-1900, (212) 551-6732, https://www.strategyand.pwc.com/gx/en/; 2019 Chief Digital Officer Study.

DIGITAL CURRENCY

Thomson Reuters, 3 Times Square, New York, NY, 10036, USA, (646) 540-3000, general.info@thomsonreuters.com, https://thomsonreuters.com/; Cryptos on the Rise 2022.

DIGITAL MEDIA

Data & Society Research Institute, 36 W 20th St., 11th Fl., New York, NY, 10011, USA, (646) 832-2038, info@datasociety.net, https://datasociety.net/; unpublished data.

DoubleVerify, 28 Crosby St., 6th Fl., New York, NY, 10003, USA, info@doubleverify.com, https://doubleverify.com; 2023 Global Insights Report.

Girl Scouts of the USA, 420 Fifth Ave., New York, NY, 10018, USA, (212) 852-8000, (800) 478-7248, https://www.girlscouts.org/; Decoding the Digital Girl: Defining and Supporting Girls' Digital Leadership.

Pew Research Center, 1615 L St. NW, Ste. 800, Washington, DC, 20036, USA, (202) 419-4300, (202) 857-8562, info@pewresearch.org, https://www.pewresearch.org/; For Local News, Americans Embrace Digital but Still Want Strong Community Connection.

Pew Research Center, News Habits & Media, 1615 L St. NW, Ste. 800, Washington, DC, 20036, USA, (202) 419-4300, (202) 857-8562, https://www.pewresearch.org/topic/news-habits-media/; Digital News Fact Sheet.

University of Michigan, Institute for Social Research, Population Studies Center, 426 Thompson St., 2nd Fl., Ann Arbor, MI, 48106-1248, USA, (734) 764-8354, (734) 615-9538, psc-director@umich.edu, https://www.psc.isr.umich.edu; How Do I Learn More About this?: Utilization and Trust of Psychedelic Information Sources Among People Naturalistically Using Psychedelics.

DIGITAL VIDEO AND AUDIO

Interactive Advertising Bureau (IAB), 116 E 27th St., 6th Fl., New York, NY, 10016, USA, (212) 380-4700, https://www.iab.com/; 2022 Video Ad Spend & 2023 Outlook: Defining the Next Generation.

DIPHTHERIA

U.S. Department of Health and Human Services, Centers for Disease Control and Prevention (CDC), 1600 Clifton Rd., Atlanta, GA, 30329-4027, USA, (800) 232-4636, (888) 232-6348 (TTY), cdcinfo@cdc.gov, https://www.cdc.gov; Morbidity and Mortality Weekly Report (MMWR) and VaxView: Vaccination Coverage in the U.S..

U.S. Department of Health and Human Services, Centers for Disease Control and Prevention (CDC), National Center for Health Statistics (NCHS), 3311 Toledo Rd., Hyattsville, MD, 20782-2064, USA, (800) 232-4636, (301) 458-4000, https://www.cdc.gov/nchs; National Immunization Surveys (NIS).

DIPLOMACY

Institute for the Study of War (ISW), 1400 16th St. NW, Ste. 515, Washington, DC, 20036, USA, (202) 293-5550, https://www.understandingwar.org/; ISIS's Opportunity in Northern Syria.

DISABILITY INSURANCE

Cornell University ILR School, Yang-Tan Institute on Employment and Disability, 201 Dolgen Hall, Ithaca, NY, 14853, USA, (607) 255-7727, ilr_yti@cornell.edu, https://www.yti.cornell.edu/; Disability Statistics: Online Resource for U.S. Disability Statistics.

National Rehabilitation Information Center (NARIC), 8400 Corporate Dr., Ste. 500, Landover, MD, 20785, USA, (800) 346-2742, (301) 459-5984 (TTY), (301) 459-4263, https://www.naric.com/; NARIC Knowledgebase.

National Safety Council (NSC), 1121 Spring Lake Dr., Itasca, IL, 60143-3201, USA, (630) 285-1121, (800) 621-7615, customerservice@nsc.org, https://www.nsc.org/; National Safety Council Injury Facts.

U.S. Department of Education (ED), Office of Special Education and Rehabilitative Services (OSERS), 400 Maryland Ave. SW, Washington, DC, 20202-7100, USA, (202) 245-7468, https://www2.ed.gov/about/offices/list/osers; Annual Reports to Congress on the Implementation of the Individuals with Disabilities Education Act (IDEA).

U.S. Department of Health and Human Services (HHS), National Institutes of Health (NIH), National Institute of Mental Health (NIMH), 6001 Executive Blvd., Room 6200, MSC 9663, Bethesda, MD, 20892-9663, USA, (866) 615-6464, (301) 443-8431 (TTY), (301) 443-4279, nimhinfo@nih.gov, https://www.nimh.nih.gov/; Mental Health Statistics.

U.S. Department of Health and Human Services, Centers for Disease Control and Prevention (CDC), 1600 Clifton Rd., Atlanta, GA, 30329-4027, USA, (800) 232-4636, (888) 232-6348 (TTY), cdcinfo@cdc.gov, https://www.cdc.gov; Behavioral Risk Factor Surveillance System (BRFSS) Data and Health-Related Quality of Life (HRQOL).

U.S. Department of Health and Human Services, Centers for Disease Control and Prevention (CDC), National Center for Health Statistics (NCHS), 3311 Toledo Rd., Hyattsville, MD, 20782-2064, USA, (800) 232-4636, (301) 458-4000, https://www.cdc.gov/nchs; FastStats - Statistics by Topic.

U.S. Department of Justice (DOJ), Civil Rights Division, 950 Pennsylvania Ave. NW, Washington, DC, 20530, USA, (202) 514-3847, (202) 514-0716 (TTY), https://www.justice.gov/crt; unpublished data.

World Health Organization (WHO), Ave. Appia 20, Geneva, CH-1211, SWI, (202) 974-3000 (Telephone in U.S.), publications@who.int, https://www.who.int/; Mental Health Atlas 2020.

DISABILITY INSURANCE CLAIMS

Cornell University ILR School, Yang-Tan Institute on Employment and Disability, 201 Dolgen Hall, Ithaca, NY, 14853, USA, (607) 255-7727, ilr_yti@cornell.edu, https://www.yti.cornell.edu/; Disability Statistics: Online Resource for U.S. Disability Statistics.

IDEA Data Center (IDC) at Westat, RA 1200, 1600 Research Blvd., Rockville, MD, 20850-3129, USA, (888) 819-7024, ideadata@westat.com, https://ideadata.org/; unpublished data.

National Bureau of Economic Research (NBER), 1050 Massachusetts Ave., Cambridge, MA, 02138, USA, (617) 868-3900, info@nber.org, https://www.nber.org/; The Bulletin on Retirement and Disability and Medicaid and Mortality: New Evidence from Linked Survey and Administrative Data.

Social Security Administration (SSA), Office of Public Inquiries and Communications Support, 1100 W High Rise, 6401 Security Blvd., Baltimore, MD, 21235, USA, (800) 772-1213, (800) 325-0778 (TTY), https://www.ssa.gov; Annual Statistical Supplement, 2021; Detailed Reports on the Financial Outlook for Social Security's 'Old-Age, Survivors, and Disability Insurance' (OASDI) Trust Funds, 2020; Social Security Bulletin; and SSI Monthly Statistics.

U.S. Department of Commerce (DOC), Bureau of Economic Analysis (BEA), 4600 Silver Hill Rd., Washington, DC, 20233, USA, (301) 278-9004, customerservice@bea.gov, https://www.bea.gov; Personal Income by State, 1st Quarter 2022.

U.S. Department of Health and Human Services (HHS), Centers for Medicare and Medicaid Services (CMS), 7500 Security Blvd., Baltimore, MD, 21244, USA, (410) 786-3000, (877) 267-2323, https://www.cms.gov; Medicare Current Beneficiary Survey (MCBS).

U.S. Department of Health and Human Services, Centers for Disease Control and Prevention (CDC), 1600 Clifton Rd., Atlanta, GA, 30329-4027, USA, (800) 232-4636, (888) 232-6348 (TTY), cdcinfo@cdc.gov, https://www.cdc.gov; State Medicaid Coverage for Tobacco Cessation Treatments and Barriers to Accessing Treatments - United States, 2008-2018.

U.S. Department of Veterans Affairs (VA), National Center for Veterans Analysis and Statistics (NCVAS), 810 Vermont Ave. NW, Washington, DC, 20420, USA, (800) 698-2411, vancvas@va.gov, https://www.va.gov/vetdata/; Veterans' Utiliization of Benefits.

DISABILITY INSURANCE TRUST FUND (SOCIAL SECURITY)

Social Security Administration (SSA), Office of Public Inquiries and Communications Support, 1100 W High Rise, 6401 Security Blvd., Baltimore, MD, 21235, USA, (800) 772-1213, (800) 325-0778 (TTY), https://www.ssa.gov; Detailed Reports on the Financial Outlook for Social Security's 'Old-Age, Survivors, and Disability Insurance' (OASDI) Trust Funds, 2020 and Social Security Bulletin.

U.S. Office of Management and Budget (OMB), 725 17th St. NW, Washington, DC, 20503, USA, (202) 395-3080, https://www.whitehouse.gov/omb/; Analytical Perspectives: Budget of the United States Government.

DISAPPEARED PERSONS

U.S. Department of Justice (DOJ), Federal Bureau of Investigation (FBI), 935 Pennsylvania Ave. NW, Washington, DC, 20535-0001, USA, (202) 324-3000, https://www.fbi.gov/; 2021 NCIC Missing Person and Unidentified Person Statistics.

DISASTER RELIEF

Network for Public Education (NPE), PO Box 227, New York, NY, 10156, USA, (646) 678-4477, info@networkforpubliceducation.org, https://networkforpubliceducation.org/; What Should We Really Learn from New Orleans After the Storm?.

United Nations Population Fund (UNFPA), 605 3rd Ave., New York, NY, 10158, USA, https://www.unfpa.org/; Humanitarian Action Overview Report 2023.

DISASTERS

American Meteorological Society (AMS), 45 Beacon St., Boston, MA, 02108-3693, USA, (617) 227-2425, (617) 742-8718, amsinfo@ametsoc.org, https://www.ametsoc.org/ams/; Explaining Extreme Events in 2021 and 2022 from a Climate Perspective and State of the Climate in 2020.

Centre for Research on the Epidemiology of Disasters (CRED), Universite Catholique de Louvain School of Public Health, Clos Chapelle-aux-Champs, Bte B1.30.15, Brussels, B-1200, BEL, contact@cred.be, https://www.cred.be/; Cred Crunch Newsletter; 2021 Disasters in Numbers; EM-DAT: The International Disaster Database; and Natural Disasters 2019: Now Is the Time to Not Give Up.

Climate Analytics, 135 Madison Ave., 5th Fl., Ste. 05-115, New York, NY, 10016, USA, info.ny@climateanalytics.org, https://climateanalytics.org/; Extreme Atlantic Hurricane Seasons Made Twice as Likely by Ocean Warming.

Climate Central, One Palmer Square, Ste. 402, Princeton, NJ, 08542, USA, (609) 924-3800, (877) 425-4724, https://www.climatecentral.org/; Flooded Future: Global Vulnerability to Sea Level Rise Worse than Previously Understood.

Colorado Avalanche Information Center (CAIC), 1313 Sherman St., Rm. 423, Denver, CO, 80203, USA, (303) 499-9650, help@caic.com, https://www.avalanche.state.co.us; US Avalanche Accidents 2022.

CoreLogic, 40 Pacifica, Ste. 900, Irvine, CA, 92618, USA, (800) 426-1466, (949) 214-1000, https://www.corelogic.com/; 2021 Climate Change Catastrophe Report.

European Commission, Eurostat, Luxembourg, 2920, LUX, https://ec.europa.eu/eurostat/; Environment Statistics Introduced.

European Severe Storms Laboratory (ESSL), c/o DLR, Muenchener Str. 20, Wessling, D-82234, GER, https://www.essl.org/, https://www.essl.org/cms/; European Severe Weather Database (ESWD).

Germanwatch, Kaiserstrasse 201, Bonn, D-53113, GER, info@germanwatch.org, https://germanwatch.org; Global Climate Risk Index 2021.

Global Facility for Disaster Reduction and Recovery (GFDRR), 1818 H St. NW, Washington, DC, 20433, USA, (202) 473-1000, gfdrr@worldbank.org, https://www.gfdrr.org/; Overlooked : Examining the Impact of Disasters and Climate Shocks on Poverty in the Europe and Central Asia Region and Turning Flood Risk Into Economic Opportunity in Dar es Salaam, Tanzania.

Google Public Data Directory, USA, https://www.google.com/publicdata/directory; Google Public Data Directory.

Gulf Coast Ecosystem Restoration Council, 500 Poydras St., Ste. 1117, New Orleans, LA, 70130, USA, (504) 717-7235, restorecouncil@restorethegulf.gov, https://www.restorethegulf.gov/; RESTORE Council - 10 Year Commemoration Report.

Harvard T.H. Chan School of Public Health, Center for Climate, Health, and the Global Environment (Harvard C-CHANGE), 401 Park Dr., 4th Fl. W, Ste. 415, Boston, MA, 02215, USA, (617) 384-8350, cchange@hsph.harvard.edu, https://www.hsph.harvard.edu/c-change/; Flood Risk to Hospitals on the United States Atlantic and Gulf Coasts From Hurricanes and Sea Level Rise.

The Hechinger Report, 525 W 120th St., Ste. 127, New York, NY, 10027, USA, (212) 678-7556, (212) 678-7556, hechinger@hechingerreport.org, https://hechingerreport.org; What Has Happened When Campuses Shut Down for Other Disasters? A Coronavirus Case Study.

Intergovernmental Panel on Climate Change (IPCC), C/O World Meteorological Organization, 7 bis Avenue de la Paix, C.P. 2300, Geneva, CH-1211, SWI, ipcc-sec@wmo.int, https://www.ipcc.ch/; AR6 Synthesis Report: Climate Change 2023.

National Oceanic and Atmospheric Administration (NOAA), National Centers for Environmental Information (NCEI), Federal Bldg., 151 Patton Ave., Asheville, NC, 28801-5001, USA, (828) 271-4800, (828) 271-4010 (TTY), (828) 271-4876, ncei.info@noaa.gov, https://www.ncei.noaa.gov/; Billion-Dollar Weather and Climate Disasters: Overview; Climate Monitoring; Global Historical Tsunami Database; Significant Earthquake Database; Significant Volcanic Eruption Database; Storm Events Database; and U.S. Earthquake Intensity Database (1638-1985).

National Oceanic and Atmospheric Administration (NOAA), National Centers for Environmental Information (NCEI), National Integrated Drought Information System (NIDIS), 151 Patton Ave., Asheville, ND, 28801-5001, USA, drought.portal@noaa.gov, https://www.drought.gov; Drought Status Update for California-Nevada; Drought Status Update for the Pacific Northwest; and Drought.gov.

National Oceanic and Atmospheric Administration (NOAA), National Hurricane Center (NHC), 11691 SW 17th St., Miami, FL, 33165, USA, (305) 229-4400, nhc.public.affairs@noaa.gov, https://www.nhc.noaa.gov/; unpublished data.

Network for Public Education (NPE), PO Box 227, New York, NY, 10156, USA, (646) 678-4477, info@networkforpubliceducation.org, https://networkforpubliceducation.org/; What Should We Really Learn from New Orleans After the Storm?.

PollingReport.com, USA, https://www.pollingreport.com/; Issues Facing the Nation.

Proceedings of the National Academy of Sciences (PNAS), 500 Fifth St. NW, NAS 338, Washington, DC, 20001, USA, (202) 334-2679, pnas@nas.edu, https://www.pnas.org; Global Increase in Major Tropical Cyclone Exceedance Probability Over the Past Four Decades.

Rapid Intelligence, Sydney, NSW, 2001, AUS, https://www.rapint.com/; NationMaster.com.

U.S. Commission on Civil Rights (USCCR), 1331 Pennsylvania Ave. NW, Ste. 1150, Washington, DC, 20425, USA, (202) 376-7700, (202) 376-8116 (TTY), publications@usccr.gov, https://www.usccr.gov/; 2022 Statutory Enforcement Report: Civil Rights and Protections During the Federal Response to Hurricanes Harvey and Maria.

U.S. Department of Commerce (DOC), National Institute of Standards and Technology (NIST), 100 Bureau Dr., Gaithersburg, MD, 20899, USA, (301) 975-2000, https://www.nist.gov; Data-Based Models for Hurricane Evolution Prediction: A Deep Learning Approach.

U.S. Department of the Interior (DOI), Fish & Wildlife Service (FWS), 1849 C St. NW, Washington, DC, 20240, USA, (800) 344-9453, https://www.fws.gov; Fire Management.

U.S. Department of the Interior (DOI), U.S. Geological Survey (USGS), 12201 Sunrise Valley Dr., Reston, VA, 20192, USA, (888) 392-8545, https://www.usgs.gov/; Earthquake Catalog; Earthquake Hazards Program Lists, Maps, and Statistics; Significant Earthquakes - 2023; and USGS Magnitude 2.5+ Earthquakes, Past Day.

United Nations Department of Economic and Social Affairs (DESA), United Nations Plz., New York, NY, 10017, USA, (212) 963-4849, statistics@un.org, https://www.un.org/en/desa; The Sustainable Development Goals Report 2022.

United Nations Economic Commission for Europe (UNECE), Palais des Nations, Geneva, CH-1211, SWI, unece_info@un.org, https://unece.org/; Resilience to Disasters for Sustainable Development.

United Nations Office for Disaster Risk Reduction (UNDRR), 2 United Nations Plaza, 11th Fl., New York, NY, 10017, SWI, (212) 963-5385, (917) 367-1578, isdr@un.org, https://www.unisdr.org/; Global Assessment Report on Disaster Risk Reduction (GAR) 2019.

University of Central Lancashire, Institute for Dark Tourism Research (iDTR), Preston, Lancashire, PR1 2HE, GBR, https://www.uclan.ac.uk/research/activity/dark-tourism; unpublished data.

University of Colorado Boulder, Natural Hazards Center, 483 UCB, Boulder, CO, 80309-0483, USA, (303) 735-5844, hazctr@colorado.edu, https://hazards.colorado.edu/; Disaster Research and Natural Hazards Review.

The Washington Post, 1301 K St. NW, Washington, DC, 20071, USA, (800) 477-4679, https://www.washingtonpost.com/; Mapping America's Wicked Weather and Deadly Disasters and 2020 Rivals Hottest Year on Record, Pushing Earth Closer to a Critical Climate Threshold.

Yale Project on Climate Change Communication (YPCCC), Yale School of the Environment, 195 Prospect St., New Haven, CT, 06511, USA, (203) 432-5055, climatechange@yale.edu, https://climatecommunication.yale.edu/; Are Hurricane-prone States More Concerned about Climate Change?.

DISCIPLINE

Thomas B. Fordham Institute, 1015 18th St. NW, Ste. 902, Washington, DC, 20036, USA, (202) 223-5452, thegadfly@fordhaminstitute.org, https://fordhaminstitute.org/; Discipline Reform Through the Eyes of Teachers.

DISCOUNT RATES-FEDERAL RESERVE BANK OF NEW YORK

Board of Governors of the Federal Reserve System, Constitution Ave. NW, Washington, DC, 20551, USA, (202) 452-3000, (202) 263-4869 (TDD), https://www.federalreserve.gov; Federal Reserve Bulletin.

DISCRIMINATION

California State University San Bernardino, Center for the Study of Hate and Extremism, 5500 University Pkwy., San Bernardino, CA, 92407, USA, (909) 537-7503, (909) 537-7711, blevin8@aol.com, https://csbs.csusb.edu/hate-and-extremism-center; Report to the Nation: Anti-Asian Prejudice & Hate Crime.

Center for American Progress (CAP), 1333 H St. NW, 10th Fl., Washington, DC, 20005, USA, (202) 682-1611, https://www.americanprogress.org/; Systemic Inequality: Displacement, Exclusion, and Segregation - How America's Housing System Undermines Wealth Building in Communities of Color.

The Gallup Organization, 901 F St. NW, Washington, DC, 20004, USA, (202) 715-3030, (800) 204-1192, (202) 715-3045, https://www.gallup.com; New Low: 35% in U.S. Satisfied With Treatment of Black People.

GLAAD, USA, rferraro@glaad.org, https://www.glaad.org/; Accelerating Acceptance 2021; Social Media Safety Index (SMSI); and Where We Are on TV Report 2021-2022.

Institute for Strategic Dialogue (ISD), Strong Cities Network (SCN), PO Box 75769, London, SW1P 9ER, GBR, https://strongcitiesnetwork.org; Online Russian-Language Hate and Discrimination Against Central Asian Migrants: Challenges and Ways Forward.

LGBT Freedom and Asylum Network (LGBT-FAN), USA, info@lgbt-fan.org, https://www.lgbt-fan.org; unpublished data.

National Asian Pacific American Women's Forum (NAPAWF), PO Box 13255, Chicago, IL, 60613, USA, info@napawf.org, https://www.napawf.org/; The State of Safety for Asian American, Native Hawaiian, and Pacific Islander Women.

National Center for Transgender Equality (NCTE), 1032 15th St. NW, Ste. 199, Washington, DC, 20005, USA, (202) 642-4542, ncte@transequality.org, https://transequality.org/; unpublished data.

National LGBTQ Task Force, 1050 Connecticut Ave. NW, Ste. 65500, Washington, DC, 20035, USA, (202) 393-5177, (202) 393-2241, https://www.thetaskforce.org/; unpublished data.

National Organization for Women (NOW), 1100 H St. NW, Ste. 300, Washington, DC, 20005, USA, (202) 628-8669, (202) 331-9002 (TTY), https://now.org/; unpublished data.

Pew Research Center, 1615 L St. NW, Ste. 800, Washington, DC, 20036, USA, (202) 419-4300, (202) 857-8562, info@pewresearch.org, https://www.pewresearch.org/; Many Black and Asian Americans Say They Have Experienced Discrimination Amid the COVID-19 Outbreak.

Pew Research Center, Internet & Technology, 1615 L St. NW, Ste. 800, Washington, DC, 20036, USA, (202) 419-4300, (202) 857-8562, https://www.pewresearch.org/topic/internet-technology/; Most Americans Think Social Media Sites Censor Political Viewpoints.

Public Religion Research Institute (PRRI), 1023 15th St. NW, 9th Fl., Washington, DC, 20005, USA, (202) 238-9424, info@prri.org, https://www.prri.org/; Increasing Support for Religiously Based Service Refusals.

Transgender American Veterans Association (TAVA), 2020 Pennsylvania Ave., Ste. 465, Akron, OH, 44310, USA, (516) 828-2911, office@transveteran.org, https://transveteran.org/; unpublished data.

U.S. Commission on Civil Rights (USCCR), 1331 Pennsylvania Ave. NW, Ste. 1150, Washington, DC, 20425, USA, (202) 376-7700, (202) 376-8116 (TTY), publications@usccr.gov, https://www.usccr.gov/; 2019 Statutory Enforcement Report: Are Rights A Reality? Evaluating Federal Civil Rights Enforcement and 2022 Statutory Enforcement Report: Civil Rights and Protections During the Federal Response to Hurricanes Harvey and Maria.

U.S. Equal Employment Opportunity Commission (EEOC), 131 M St. NE, Washington, DC, 20507, USA, (202) 921-3191, (202) 663-4900, info@eeoc.gov, https://www.eeoc.gov; Annual Report on the Federal Work Force, Fiscal Year 2019; EEOC Litigation Statistics, FY 1997 through FY 2021; and Equal Employment Opportunity Data Posted Pursuant to the No Fear Act.

University of Chicago, Center for the Study of Race, Politics and Culture, Black Youth Project, 5733 S University Ave., Chicago, IL, 60637, USA, info@blackyouthproject.com, https://www.blackyouthproject.com/; GenForward Survey 2022.

University of Washington, Center for an Informed Public (CIP), Seattle, WA, USA, uwcip@uw.edu, https://www.cip.uw.edu/; Recognize the Bias? News Media Partisanship Shapes the Coverage of Facial Recognition Technology in the United States.

DISCRIMINATION-LAW AND LEGISLATION

The Henry J. Kaiser Family Foundation (KFF), 185 Berry St., Ste. 2000, San Francisco, CA, 94107, USA, (650) 854-9400, (650) 854-4800, https://www.kff.org; Majorities Support Policies Banning Discrimination Against LGBTQ Individuals' Health Care Access.

Public Religion Research Institute (PRRI), 1023 15th St. NW, 9th Fl., Washington, DC, 20005, USA, (202) 238-9424, info@prri.org, https://www.prri.org/; Wedding Cakes, Same-Sex Marriage, and the Future of LGBT Rights in America.

University of California Los Angeles (UCLA) School of Law, The Williams Institute, 1060 Veteran Ave., Ste. 134, PO Box 957092, Los Angeles, CA, 90095-7092, USA, (310) 267-4382, (310) 825-7270, williamsinstitute@law.ucla.edu, https://williamsinstitute.law.ucla.edu/; Public Attitudes Toward the Use of Religious Beliefs to Discriminate Against LGBTQ People.

DISCRIMINATION-RELIGIOUS ASPECTS

Federal Housing Finance Agency (FHFA), 400 7th St. SW, Washington, DC, 20019, USA, (202) 649-3800, (202) 649-1071, https://www.fhfa.gov/; No Fear Act Data.

Pew Research Center, 1615 L St. NW, Ste. 800, Washington, DC, 20036, USA, (202) 419-4300, (202) 857-8562, info@pewresearch.org, https://www.pewresearch.org/; Many Americans See Religious Discrimination in U.S. - Especially Against Muslims.

Public Religion Research Institute (PRRI), 1023 15th St. NW, 9th Fl., Washington, DC, 20005, USA, (202) 238-9424, info@prri.org, https://www.prri.org/; Wedding Cakes, Same-Sex Marriage, and the Future of LGBT Rights in America.

University of California Los Angeles (UCLA) School of Law, The Williams Institute, 1060 Veteran Ave., Ste. 134, PO Box 957092, Los Angeles, CA, 90095-7092, USA, (310) 267-4382, (310) 825-7270, williamsinstitute@law.ucla.edu, https://williamsinstitute.law.ucla.edu/; Public Attitudes Toward the Use of Religious Beliefs to Discriminate Against LGBTQ People.

DISCRIMINATION AGAINST INTERSEX PEOPLE

GLAAD, USA, rferraro@glaad.org, https://www.glaad.org/; Accelerating Acceptance 2021; Social Media Safety Index (SMSI); and Where We Are on TV Report 2021-2022.

The Henry J. Kaiser Family Foundation (KFF), 185 Berry St., Ste. 2000, San Francisco, CA, 94107, USA, (650) 854-9400, (650) 854-4800, https://www.kff.org; Majorities Support Policies Banning Discrimination Against LGBTQ Individuals' Health Care Access.

Human Rights Campaign (HRC), 1640 Rhode Island Ave. NW, Washington, DC, 20036-3278, USA, (202) 628-4160, (202) 216-1572 (TTY), (202) 347-5323, feedback@hrc.org, https://www.hrc.org/; Dismantling a Culture of Violence: Understanding Violence Against Transgender and Non-Binary People and Ending the Crisis.

DISCRIMINATION AGAINST PEOPLE WITH DISABILITIES

Federal Housing Finance Agency (FHFA), 400 7th St. SW, Washington, DC, 20019, USA, (202) 649-3800, (202) 649-1071, https://www.fhfa.gov/; No Fear Act Data.

U.S. Commission on Civil Rights (USCCR), 1331 Pennsylvania Ave. NW, Ste. 1150, Washington, DC, 20425, USA, (202) 376-7700, (202) 376-8116 (TTY), publications@usccr.gov, https://www.usccr.gov/; 2020 Statutory Enforcement Report: Subminimum Wages: Impacts on the Civil Rights of People with Disabilities.

DISCRIMINATION IN CRIMINAL JUSTICE ADMINISTRATION

Chicago Police Accountability Task Force, PO Box 6289, Chicago, IL, 60606-6289, USA, comments@chicagopatf.org, https://chicagopatf.org; unpublished data.

Council on Criminal Justice (CCJ), 700 Pennsylvania Ave. SE, Washington, DC, 20003, USA, info@counciloncj.org, https://counciloncj.org; Justice System Disparities: Black-White National Imprisonment Trends, 2000 to 2020 and The 1994 Crime Bill: Legacy and Lessons.

Council on Criminal Justice (CCJ), National Commission on COVID-19 and Criminal Justice, 700 Pennsylvania Ave. SE, Washington, DC, 20020, USA, info@counciloncj.org, https://counciloncj.org/covid-19/; Experience to Action: Reshaping Criminal Justice After COVID-19.

National Registry of Exonerations, USA, https://www.law.umich.edu/special/exoneration/; The National Registry of Exonerations Annual Report, March 30, 2021 and Race and Wrongful Convictions in the United States 2022.

New York University School of Law, Brennan Center for Justice, 120 Broadway, Ste. 1750, New York, NY, 10271, USA, (646) 292-8310, (202) 249-7190, (212) 463-7308, brennancenter@nyu.edu, https://www.brennancenter.org; Revenue Over Public Safety.

Physicians for Human Rights (PHR), 256 W 38th St., 9th Fl., New York, NY, 10018, USA, (646) 564-3720, (646) 564-3750, https://phr.org/; 'Excited Delirium' and Deaths in Police Custody: The Deadly Impact of a Baseless Diagnosis.

Prison Policy Initiative, PO Box 127, Northampton, MA, 01061, USA, https://www.prisonpolicy.org/; Grading the Parole Release Systems of All 50 States and State of Phone Justice 2022: The Problem, the Progress, and What's Next.

Public Religion Research Institute (PRRI), 1023 15th St. NW, 9th Fl., Washington, DC, 20005, USA, (202) 238-9424, info@prri.org, https://www.prri.org/; Summer Unrest over Racial Injustice Moves the Country, But Not Republicans or White Evangelicals.

The Sentencing Project, 1705 DeSales St. NW, 8th Fl., Washington, DC, 20036, USA, (202) 628-0871, staff@sentencingproject.org, https://www.sentencingproject.org; Mass Incarceration Trends.

U.S. Commission on Civil Rights (USCCR), 1331 Pennsylvania Ave. NW, Ste. 1150, Washington, DC, 20425, USA, (202) 376-7700, (202) 376-8116 (TTY), publications@usccr.gov, https://www.usccr.gov/; 2019 Statutory Enforcement Report: Are Rights A Reality? Evaluating Federal Civil Rights Enforcement.

University of California Los Angeles (UCLA) School of Law, The Williams Institute, 1060 Veteran Ave., Ste. 134, PO Box 957092, Los Angeles, CA, 90095-7092, USA, (310) 267-4382, (310) 825-7270, williamsinstitute@law.ucla.edu, https://williamsinstitute.law.ucla.edu/; Police and the Criminalization of LGBT People.

DISCRIMINATION IN EMPLOYMENT

Federal Housing Finance Agency (FHFA), 400 7th St. SW, Washington, DC, 20019, USA, (202) 649-3800, (202) 649-1071, https://www.fhfa.gov/; No Fear Act Data.

Pew Research Center, 1615 L St. NW, Ste. 800, Washington, DC, 20036, USA, (202) 419-4300, (202) 857-8562, info@pewresearch.org, https://www.pewresearch.org/; A Century After Women Gained the Right to Vote, Majority of Americans See Work to Do on Gender Equality.

U.S. Commission on Civil Rights (USCCR), 1331 Pennsylvania Ave. NW, Ste. 1150, Washington, DC, 20425, USA, (202) 376-7700, (202) 376-8116 (TTY), publications@usccr.gov, https://www.usccr.gov/; 2020 Statutory Enforcement Report: Subminimum Wages: Impacts on the Civil Rights of People with Disabilities.

University of California Hastings College of the Law, Center for WorkLife Law, Project for Attorney Retention (PAR-Davis) Research Institute, 200 McAllister St., San Francisco, CA, 94102, USA, (415) 565-4640, https://worklifelaw.org/projects/women-in-the-legal-profession/ ; Exposed: Discrimination Against Breastfeeding Workers.

DISCRIMINATION IN LAW ENFORCEMENT

American Civil Liberties Union (ACLU), 125 Broad St. , 18th Fl., New York, NY, 10004, USA, (212) 549-2500, https://www.aclu.org/; License to Abuse: How ICE's 287(g) Program Empowers Racist Sheriffs and Civil Rights Violations.

Center for Policing Equity (CPE), 8605 Santa Monica Blvd., PMB 54596, West Hollywood, CA, 90069-4109, USA, (347) 948-9953, https://policingequity.org/; National Justice Database (NJD).

DISCRIMINATION IN MEDICAL CARE

The Henry J. Kaiser Family Foundation (KFF), 185 Berry St., Ste. 2000, San Francisco, CA, 94107, USA, (650) 854-9400, (650) 854-4800, https://www.kff.org; Majorities Support Policies Banning Discrimination Against LGBTQ Individuals' Health Care Access and Racial Disparities in Maternal and Infant Health: Current Status and Efforts to Address Them.

National Bureau of Economic Research (NBER), 1050 Massachusetts Ave., Cambridge, MA, 02138, USA, (617) 868-3900, info@nber.org, https://www.nber.org/; Maternal and Infant Health Inequality: New Evidence from Linked Administrative Data.

DISCRIMINATION IN SPORTS

The Gallup Organization, 901 F St. NW, Washington, DC, 20004, USA, (202) 715-3030, (800) 204-1192, (202) 715-3045, https://www.gallup.com; Mixed Views Among Americans on Transgender Issues.

DISEASE MANAGEMENT

National Foundation for Infectious Diseases (NFID), 1629 K St. NW, Ste. 300, Washington, DC, 20006, USA, (301) 656-0003, https://www.nfid.org/; 2021 Chronic Health Conditions Surveys: Gaps between Healthcare Professionals and Adult Patients.

Pew Research Center, Religion & Public Life, 1615 L St. NW, Ste. 800, Washington, DC, 20036, USA, (202) 419-4300, (202) 857-8562, https://www.pewforum.org/; How COVID-19 Restrictions Affected Religious Groups Around the World in 2020.

U.S. Department of Health and Human Services (HHS), National Institutes of Health (NIH), Researching COVID to Enhance Recovery (RECOVER), 9000 Rockville Pike, Bethesda, MD, 20892, USA, (301) 496-4000, (301) 402-9612 (TTY), https://recovercovid.org; Can Multisystem Inflammatory Syndrome in Children Be Managed in the Outpatient Setting? An EHR-Based Cohort Study From the RECOVER Program; Development of a Definition of Postacute Sequelae of SARS-CoV-2 Infection; Racial/Ethnic Disparities in Post-Acute Sequelae of SARS-CoV-2 Infection in New York: An EHR-Based Cohort Study from the RECOVER Program; and Risk of Post-Acute Sequelae of SARS-CoV-2 Infection Associated with Pre-Coronavirus Disease Obstructive Sleep Apnea Diagnoses: An Electronic Health Record-Based Analysis from the RECOVER Initiative.

World Health Organization (WHO), Ave. Appia 20, Geneva, CH-1211, SWI, (202) 974-3000 (Telephone in U.S.), publications@who.int, https://www.who.int/; The Impact of the COVID-19 Pandemic on Noncommunicable Disease Resources and Services: Results of a Rapid Assessment.

DISEASE SUSCEPTIBILITY

World Health Organization (WHO), International Agency for Research on Cancer (IARC), 25 Avenue Tony Garnier, CS 90627, Lyon, 69366, FRA, https://www.iarc.who.int; World Cancer Report: Cancer Research for Cancer Prevention.

DISEASES

AlzForum Foundation Inc., 7 Water St., Boston, MA, 02109, USA, contact@alzforum.org, https://www.alzforum.org; AlzForum.

Alzheimer's Association, 225 N Michigan Ave., 17th Fl., Chicago, IL, 60601, USA, (312) 335-8700, (800) 272-3900, (866) 699-1246, info@alz.org, https://www.alz.org/; Alzheimer's & Dementia: The Journal of the Alzheimer's Association and 2022 Alzheimer's Disease Facts and Figures.

Alzheimer's Foundation of America (AFA), 322 8th Ave., 16th Fl., New York, NY, 10001, USA, (866) 232-8484, (646) 638-1542, (646) 638-1546, info@alzfdn.org, https://alzfdn.org; unpublished data.

American Cancer Society (ACS), 3380 Chastain Meadows Pkwy NW, Ste. 200, Kennesaw, GA, 30144, USA, (800) 227-2345, https://www.cancer.org; Cancer Treatment & Survivorship Facts & Figures 2022-2024.

American Heart Association (AHA), 7272 Greenville Ave., Dallas, TX, 75231, USA, (800) 242-8721, (214) 570-5943, https://www.heart.org; Heart Disease and Stroke Statistics.

Australian Institute of Health and Welfare (AIHW), GPO Box 570, Canberra, ACT, 2601, AUS, info@aihw.gov.au, https://www.aihw.gov.au/; Heart, Stroke and Vascular Disease: Australian Facts and Incidence of Insulin-Treated Diabetes in Australia.

Boston University Alzheimer's Disease Center (ADC), 72 East Concord St., B-7800, Boston, MA, 02118, USA, (857) 364-2140, (888) 458-2823, (617) 358-6544, https://www.bu.edu/alzresearch/; unpublished data.

California Department of Public Health (CDPH), PO Box 997377, MS 0500, Sacramento, CA, 95899-7377, USA, (916) 558-1784, https://www.cdph.ca.gov; Vital Records.

Commonwealth Fund, 1 E 75th St., New York, NY, 10021, USA, (212) 606-3800 , info@cmwf.org, https://www.commonwealthfund.org/; State Health Data Center.

The COVID Tracking Project at The Atlantic, support@covidtracking.com, https://covidtracking.com; COVID Tracking Project Data.

COVID-19 Forecast Hub, University of Massachusetts Amherst, Reich Lab, Amherst, MA, 10022, USA, https://covid19forecasthub.org; COVID-19 US Weekly Forecast Summary.

Elsevier, Radarweg 29, Amsterdam, 1043 NX, NLD, https://www.elsevier.com; Novel Coronavirus Information Center and ScienceDirect.

European Centre for Disease Prevention and Control (ECDC), Stockholm, SE 171 83, SWE, ecdc.info@ecdc.europa.eu, https://ecdc.europa.eu; Annual Epidemiological Reports (AERs); Disease Surveillance Reports; The European Union One Health 2021 Zoonoses Report; and Eurosurveillance.

Global Lyme Alliance (GLA), 1290 E Main St., 3rd Fl., Stamford, CT, 06902, USA, (203) 969-1333, info@gla.org, https://globallymealliance.org/; Botanical Medicines Cryptolepsis Sanguinolenta, Artemisia Annua, Scutellaria Baicalensis, Polygonum Cuspidatum, and Alchornea Cordifolia Demonstrate Inhibitory Activity against Babesia Duncani and Interactions Between Ticks and Lyme Disease Spirochetes.

Google Public Data Directory, USA, https://www.google.com/publicdata/directory; Google Public Data Directory.

Health Protection Surveillance Centre (HPSC), 25-27 Middle Gardiner St., Dublin, D01 A4A3, IRL, hpsc@hse.ie, https://www.hpsc.ie/; Tuberculosis in Ireland: Trends in Surveillance Data.

The Henry J. Kaiser Family Foundation (KFF), 185 Berry St., Ste. 2000, San Francisco, CA, 94107, USA, (650) 854-9400, (650) 854-4800, https://www.kff.org; Long COVID: What Do the Latest Data Show?.

Imperial College London, South Kensington Campus, London, SW7 2AZ, GBR, https://www.imperial.ac.uk/; The Effect of Climate Change on Yellow Fever Disease Burden in Africa.

Indiana University School of Public Health-Bloomington, 1025 E 7th St., Ste. 111, Bloomington, IN, 47405, USA, (812) 855-1561, (812) 855-4983, iusph@indiana.edu, https://publichealth.indiana.edu/; unpublished data.

Johns Hopkins Coronavirus Resource Center, 3400 N Charles St., Baltimore, MD, 21218, USA, https://coronavirus.jhu.edu/; COVID-19 Testing Insights Initiative and Testing Trends Tool: Track Trends in COVID-19 Cases and Tests.

The Lancet, 230 Park Ave., New York, NY, 10169, USA, (212) 633-3800, editorial@lancet.com, https://www.thelancet.com/; Alcohol Use and Burden for 195 Countries and Territories, 1990-2016: A Systematic Analysis for the Global Burden of Disease Study 2016; The Lancet; The Lancet Infectious Diseases; The Lancet Neurology; and The Lancet Oncology.

National Alliance for Caregiving (NAC), 1730 Rhode Island Ave. NW, Ste. 812, Washington, DC, 20036, USA, (202) 918-1013, (202) 918-1014, info@caregiving.org, https://www.caregiving.org/; Caregiving in the U.S. 2020.

National Institute for Public Health and the Environment (RIVM), PO Box 1, Bilthoven, 3720 BA, NLD, info@rivm.nl, https://www.rivm.nl/en; Informative Inventory Report 2021: Emissions of Transboundary Air Pollutants in the Netherlands 1990-2019.

Novo Nordisk Inc., 800 Scudders Mill Rd., Plainsboro, NJ, 08536, USA, (609) 987-5800, (800) 727-6500, https://www.novonordisk-us.com/; unpublished data.

Public Health Agency of Canada, 130 Colonnade Rd., Ottawa, ON, K1A 0K9, CAN, (844) 280-5020 (Dial from U.S.), https://www.phac-aspc.gc.ca/; Canada Communicable Disease Report (CCDR), 2023; Mpox (Monkeypox); Surveillance of Hepatitis C in Canada; and Tuberculosis in Canada, 2020.

Robert Koch Institute, Nordufer 20, Berlin, D-13353, GER, https://www.rki.de; Journal of Health Monitoring.

SAGE Publications, 2455 Teller Rd., Thousand Oaks, CA, 91320, USA, (800) 818-7243, (800) 583-2665, journals@sagepub.com, https://www.sagepub.com; American Journal of Alzheimer's Disease and Other Dementias.

Springer Nature, BMC, 1 New York Plaza, Ste. 4600, New York, NY, 10004-1562, USA, info@biomedcentral.com, https://www.biomedcentral.com/; Alzheimer's Research & Therapy.

U.S. Department of Health and Human Services (HHS), National Institutes of Health (NIH), National Cancer Institute (NCI), 9609 Medical Center Dr., Bethesda, MD, 20850, USA, (800) 422-6237, nciinfo@nih.gov, https://www.cancer.gov; Annual Report to the Nation on the Status of Cancer; Surveillance, Epidemiology, and End Results (SEER) Incidence Data, 1975-2020; and U.S. Atlas of Cancer Mortality 1950-1994.

U.S. Department of Health and Human Services (HHS), National Institutes of Health (NIH), National Center for Advancing Translational Sciences (NCATS), Genetic and Rare Diseases Information Center (GARD), PO Box 8126, Gaithersburg, MD, 20898-8126, USA, (888) 205-2311, info@ncats.nih.gov, https://rarediseases.info.nih.gov/; Genetic and Rare Diseases Information Center (GARD).

U.S. Department of Health and Human Services (HHS), National Institutes of Health (NIH), National Institute of Allergy and Infectious Diseases (NIAID), Office of Communications and Government Relations, 5601 Fishers Ln., MSC 9806, Bethesda, MD, 20892-9806, USA, (866) 284-4107, (301) 496-5717, (301) 402-3573, ocpostoffice@niaid.nih.gov, https://www.niaid.nih.gov; Diseases & Conditions.

U.S. Department of Health and Human Services (HHS), National Institutes of Health (NIH), Researching COVID to Enhance Recovery (RECOVER), 9000 Rockville Pike, Bethesda, MD, 20892, USA, (301) 496-4000, (301) 402-9612 (TTY), https://recovercovid.org; Can Multisystem Inflammatory Syndrome in Children Be Managed in the Outpatient Setting? An EHR-Based Cohort Study From the RECOVER Program; Development of a Definition of Postacute Sequelae of SARS-CoV-2 Infection; Racial/Ethnic Disparities in Post-Acute Sequelae of SARS-CoV-2 Infection in New York: An EHR-Based Cohort Study from the RECOVER Program; and Risk of Post-Acute Sequelae of SARS-CoV-2 Infection Associated with Pre-Coronavirus Disease Obstructive Sleep Apnea Diagnoses: An Electronic Health Record-Based Analysis from the RECOVER Initiative.

U.S. Department of Health and Human Services, Centers for Disease Control and Prevention (CDC), 1600 Clifton Rd., Atlanta, GA, 30329-4027, USA, (800) 232-4636, (888) 232-6348 (TTY), cdcinfo@cdc.gov, https://www.cdc.gov; CDC Wonder Databases; Chronic Disease Indicators; COVID Data Tracker Weekly Review; Diabetes Data and Statistics; Emerging Infectious Diseases; Heart Disease Facts; Mask Use and Ventilation Improvements to Reduce COVID-19 Incidence in Elementary Schools - Georgia, November 16 - December 11, 2020; Morbidity and Mortality Weekly Report (MMWR); National Diabetes Statistics Report; National Health and Nutrition Examination Survey (NHANES); National Notifiable Diseases Surveillance System (NNDSS); Nearly One in Five American Adults Who Have Had COVID-19 Still Have Long COVID; Preventing Chronic Disease: Public Health Research, Practice, and Policy; and United States Cancer Statistics (USCS): Data Visualizations.

U.S. Department of Health and Human Services, Centers for Disease Control and Prevention (CDC), National Center for Chronic Disease Prevention and Health Promotion (NCCDPHP), 1600 Clifton Rd., Atlanta, GA, 30329, USA, (800) 232-4636, (888) 232-6348 (TTY), https://www.cdc.gov/chronicdisease/; Leading Indicators for Chronic Diseases and Risk Factors Open Data Portal.

U.S. Department of Health and Human Services, Centers for Disease Control and Prevention (CDC), National Center for Health Statistics (NCHS), 3311 Toledo Rd., Hyattsville, MD, 20782-2064, USA, (800) 232-4636, (301) 458-4000, https://www.cdc.gov/nchs; FastStats - Statistics by Topic; Health, United States, 2020-2021; HPV-Associated Cancer Statistics; and National Health Interview Survey (NHIS).

U.S. Department of Health and Human Services, Centers for Disease Control and Prevention (CDC), National Center for HIV, Viral Hepatitis, STD, and TB Prevention (NCHHSTP), 1600 Clifton Rd., Atlanta, GA, 30329-4027, USA, (800) 232-4636, (888) 232-6348 (TTY), https://www.cdc.gov/nchhstp/; NCHHSTP AtlasPlus.

UK Health Security Agency (UKHSA), Nobel House, 17 Smith Sq., London, SW1P 3JR, GBR, enquiries@ukhsa.gov.uk, https://www.gov.uk/government/organisations/uk-health-security-agency; Hepatitis C in the UK 2022; Monkeypox Outbreak: Epidemiological Overview; and Trends in HIV Testing, New Diagnoses and People Receiving HIV-Related Care in the United Kingdom: Data to the End of December 2019.

UNAIDS, 20, Avenue Appia, Geneva, CH-1211, SWI, unaids@unaids.org, https://www.unaids.org; 2020 AIDS Progress Reports Submitted by Countries; AIDSinfo Database; Key Populations Atlas; and UNAIDS Global AIDS Update 2022 - In Danger.

United Nations UN Women, 405 E 42nd St., New York, NY, 10017-3599, USA, (646) 781-4400, (646) 781-4444, https://www.unwomen.org; COVID-19: Emerging Gender Data and Why it Matters.

University of California San Diego, U.S. Immigration Policy Center (USIPC), 9500 Gilman Dr., La Jolla, CA, 92093, USA, (858) 534-2230, usipc@ucsd.edu, https://usipc.ucsd.edu/; COVID-19 and the Remaking of U.S. Immigration Policy? Empirically Evaluating the Myth of Immigration and Disease.

University of Texas at Austin, COVID-19 Modeling Consortium, 1 University Station C0930, Austin, TX, 78712, USA, utpandemics@austin.utexas.edu, https://covid-19.tacc.utexas.edu/; Scenario Projections for the Spread of SARS-CoV-2 Omicron BA.4 and BA.5 Subvariants in the US and Texas.

University of Washington, Institute for Health Metrics and Evaluation (IHME), Population Health Building/Hans Rosling Center, UW Campus Box 351615, 3980 15th Ave. NE, Seattle, WA, 98195, USA, (206) 897-2800, (206) 897-2899, engage@healthdata.org, https://www.healthdata.org; Estimated Global Proportions of Individuals With Persistent Fatigue, Cognitive, and Respiratory Symptom Clusters Following Symptomatic COVID-19 in 2020 and 2021; Global Access to Handwashing: Implications for COVID-19 Control in Low-Income Countries; and Global Burden of Disease (GBD).

World Health Organization (WHO), Ave. Appia 20, Geneva, CH-1211, SWI, (202) 974-3000 (Telephone in U.S.), publications@who.int, https://www.who.int/; Eastern Mediterranean Health Journal; Global Health Observatory (GHO); Global Health Observatory (GHO) Data; Global Tuberculosis Report 2022; The Impact of the COVID-19 Pandemic on Noncommunicable Disease Resources and Services: Results of a Rapid Assessment; Noncommunicable Diseases Progress Monitor 2022; Weekly Epidemiological Record (WER); Western Pacific Surveillance and Response Journal; WHO Drug Information 2023; WHO Report on the Global Tobacco Epidemic 2021; and World Malaria Report 2022.

DISEASES-DEATHS FROM

Bernan Press, 15250 NBN Way, Bldg. C, Blue Ridge Summit, PA, 17214, USA, (301) 459-2255, (800) 865-3457, (800) 865-3450, customercare@bernan.com, https://rowman.com/Page/Bernan; Vital Statistics of the United States 2022: Births, Life Expectancy, Deaths, and Selected Health Data.

The Lancet, 230 Park Ave., New York, NY, 10169, USA, (212) 633-3800, editorial@lancet.com, https://www.thelancet.com/; Alcohol Use and Burden for 195 Countries and Territories, 1990-2016: A Systematic Analysis for the Global Burden of Disease Study 2016 and Global, Regional, and National Minimum Estimates of Children Affected by COVID-19-Associated Orphanhood and Caregiver Death, by Age and Family Circumstance up to Oct 31, 2021: An Updated Modelling Study.

SAGE Publications, 2455 Teller Rd., Thousand Oaks, CA, 91320, USA, (800) 818-7243, (800) 583-2665, journals@sagepub.com, https://www.sagepub.com; American Journal of Alzheimer's Disease and Other Dementias.

U.S. Census Bureau, 4600 Silver Hill Rd., Washington, DC, 20233, USA, (301) 763-4636, (800) 923-8282, https://www.census.gov; New Census Bureau Population Estimates Show COVID-19 Impact on Fertility and Mortality Across the Nation and Pandemic Disrupted Historical Mortality Patterns, Caused Largest Jump in Deaths in 100 Years.

U.S. Department of Health and Human Services (HHS), National Institutes of Health (NIH), National Cancer Institute (NCI), 9609 Medical Center Dr., Bethesda, MD, 20850, USA, (800) 422-6237, nciinfo@nih.gov, https://www.cancer.gov; NCI Cancer Atlas.

U.S. Department of Health and Human Services (HHS), Office of Inspector General (OIG), 330 Independence Ave. SW, Washington, DC, 20201, USA, (877) 696-6775, public.affairs@oig.hhs.gov, https://oig.hhs.gov/; COVID-19 Had a Devastating Impact on Medicare Beneficiaries in Nursing Homes During 2020.

U.S. Department of Health and Human Services, Centers for Disease Control and Prevention (CDC), 1600 Clifton Rd., Atlanta, GA, 30329-4027, USA, (800) 232-4636, (888) 232-6348 (TTY), cdcinfo@cdc.gov, https://www.cdc.gov; CDC Wonder Databases; COVID Data Tracker Weekly Review; COVID-19 Case Surveillance Public Use Data Profile; HIV Surveillance Reports; and Rates of COVID-19 Cases or Deaths by Age Group and Vaccination Status and Booster Dose.

U.S. Department of Health and Human Services, Centers for Disease Control and Prevention (CDC), National Center for Health Statistics (NCHS), 3311 Toledo Rd., Hyattsville, MD, 20782-2064, USA, (800) 232-4636, (301) 458-4000, https://www.cdc.gov/nchs; Excess Deaths Associated with COVID-19; FastStats - Statistics by Topic; National Vital Statistics Reports (NVSR); and Vital Statistics Online Data Portal.

UK Health Security Agency (UKHSA), Nobel House, 17 Smith Sq., London, SW1P 3JR, GBR, enquiries@ukhsa.gov.uk, https://www.gov.uk/government/organisations/uk-health-security-agency; Quarterly Epidemiological Commentary: Mandatory MRSA, MSSA and Gram-Negative Bacteraemia, and C. Difficile Infections Data (up to October to December 2021).

University of Texas at Austin, COVID-19 Modeling Consortium, 1 University Station C0930, Austin, TX, 78712, USA, utpandemics@austin.utexas.edu, https://covid-19.tacc.utexas.edu/; Estimated COVID-19 Mortality in China, December 16, 2022 - January 19, 2023.

University of Washington, Institute for Health Metrics and Evaluation (IHME), Population Health Building/ Hans Rosling Center, UW Campus Box 351615, 3980 15th Ave. NE, Seattle, WA, 98195, USA, (206) 897-2800, (206) 897-2899, engage@healthdata.org, https://www.healthdata.org; Global Burden of Disease (GBD).

World Health Organization (WHO), Ave. Appia 20, Geneva, CH-1211, SWI, (202) 974-3000 (Telephone in U.S.), publications@who.int, https://www.who.int/; Global Excess Deaths Associated with COVID-19, January 2020 - December 2021; HIV/AIDS Surveillance in Europe 2022; and WHO Report on the Global Tobacco Epidemic 2021.

DISEASES-GENETIC ASPECTS

Global Lyme Alliance (GLA), 1290 E Main St., 3rd Fl., Stamford, CT, 06902, USA, (203) 969-1333, info@gla.org, https://globallymealliance.org/; Botanical Medicines Cryptolepsis Sanguinolenta, Artemisia Annua, Scutellaria Baicalensis, Polygonum Cuspidatum, and Alchornea Cordifolia Demonstrate Inhibitory Activity against Babesia Duncani.

Scripps Research, 10550 N Torrey Pines Rd., La Jolla, CA, 92037, USA, (858) 784-1000, https://www.scripps.edu; OMNI Browser.

U.S. Department of Health and Human Services (HHS), National Institutes of Health (NIH), National Center for Advancing Translational Sciences (NCATS), Genetic and Rare Diseases Information Center (GARD), PO Box 8126, Gaithersburg, MD, 20898-8126, USA, (888) 205-2311, info@ncats.nih.gov, https://rarediseases.info.nih.gov/; Genetic and Rare Diseases Information Center (GARD).

UK Health Security Agency (UKHSA), Nobel House, 17 Smith Sq., London, SW1P 3JR, GBR, enquiries@ukhsa.gov.uk, https://www.gov.uk/government/organisations/uk-health-security-agency; COVID-19 Variants: Genomically Confirmed Case Numbers and Effectiveness of COVID-19 Vaccines Against the B.1.617.2 Variant.

DISEASES-RISK FACTORS

World Health Organization (WHO), International Agency for Research on Cancer (IARC), 25 Avenue Tony Garnier, CS 90627, Lyon, 69366, FRA, https://www.iarc.who.int; World Cancer Report: Cancer Research for Cancer Prevention.

DISEASES-SOCIAL ASPECTS

Pew Research Center, Religion & Public Life, 1615 L St. NW, Ste. 800, Washington, DC, 20036, USA, (202) 419-4300, (202) 857-8562, https://www.pewforum.org/; How COVID-19 Restrictions Affected Religious Groups Around the World in 2020.

U.S. Department of Health and Human Services (HHS), Office of Inspector General (OIG), 330 Independence Ave. SW, Washington, DC, 20201, USA, (877) 696-6775, public.affairs@oig.hhs.gov, https://oig.hhs.gov/; COVID-19 Had a Devastating Impact on Medicare Beneficiaries in Nursing Homes During 2020.

University of California, Berkeley, Global Policy Lab, California Memorial Stadium, 2227 Piedmont Ave., Berkeley, CA, 94720, USA, (510) 643-5751, https://www.globalpolicy.science/; Public Mobility Data Enables COVID-19 Forecasting and Management at Local and Global Scales.

DISINFORMATION

Center for Countering Digital Hate (CCDH), Langley House, Park Rd. , East Finchley, London, N2 8EY, GBR, info@counterhate.com, https://www.counterhate.com; The Disinformation Dozen: Why Platforms Must Act on Twelve Leading Online Anti-Vaxxers and Malgorithm: How Instagram's Algorithm Publishes Misinformation and Hate to Millions During a Pandemic.

Democracy Fund Voter Study Group, 1200 17th St. NW, Ste. 300, Washington, DC, 20036, USA, (202) 420-7900, https://www.voterstudygroup.org/; Theft Perception: Examining the Views of Americans Who Believe the 2020 Election was Stolen.

Greenpeace, 1300 I St. NW, Ste. 1100 E, Washington, DC, 20001, USA, (800) 722-6995, (202) 462-1177, (202) 462-4507, connect@greenpeace.us, https://www.greenpeace.org; In the Dark: How Social Media Companies' Climate Disinformation Problem is Hidden from the Public.

Institute for Strategic Dialogue (ISD), PO Box 75769, London, SW1P 9ER, GBR, info@isdglobal.org, https://www.isdglobal.org/; What's New (and What's Not) With News Front.

Network Contagion Research Institute (NCRI), https://networkcontagion.us/; Exploiting Tragedy: The Rise of Computer-Generative Enabled Hoaxes and Malicious Information in the Wake of Mass Shootings.

NewsGuard, 25 W 52nd St., 15th Fl., New York, NY, 10019, USA, https://www.newsguardtech.com/; COVID-19 Vaccine Misinformation Targeting Children, Teenagers and Parents on Social Media: A Report for Governments and the WHO.

Pew Research Center, International Affairs, 1615 L St. NW, Ste. 800, Washington, DC, 20036, USA, (202) 419-4300, (202) 857-8562, https://www.pewresearch.org/topic/international-affairs/; A Look Back at How Fear and False Beliefs Bolstered U.S. Public Support for War in Iraq.

DISPOSABLE PERSONAL INCOME

See also INCOME

Board of Governors of the Federal Reserve System, Constitution Ave. NW, Washington, DC, 20551, USA, (202) 452-3000, (202) 263-4869 (TDD), https://www.federalreserve.gov; Household Debt Service and Financial Obligations Ratios 2022.

U.S. Department of Commerce (DOC), Bureau of Economic Analysis (BEA), 4600 Silver Hill Rd., Washington, DC, 20233, USA, (301) 278-9004, customerservice@bea.gov, https://www.bea.gov; National Income and Product Accounts (NIPA): 2022 Update and Survey of Current Business (SCB).

DISTANCE EDUCATION

Inside Higher Ed, 1150 Connecticut Ave. NW, Ste. 400, Washington, DC, 20036, USA, (202) 659-9208, (202) 659-9381, info@insidehighered.com, https://www.insidehighered.com/; Survey of College and University Chief Academic Officers, 2023 and Survey of Faculty Attitudes on Technology, 2020.

Market Data Retrieval (MDR), A Dun & Bradstreet Division, 5335 Gate Pkwy., Jacksonville, FL, 32256, USA, (973) 921-5500, (800) 333-8802, mdrinfo@dnb.com, https://mdreducation.com/; How 2020 Shifted Perceptions of Technology in the Classroom.

DISTRACTED DRIVING

AAA Foundation for Traffic Safety (FTS), 607 14th St. NW, Ste. 201, Washington, DC, 20005, USA, (202) 638-5944, (202) 638-5943, info@aaafoundation.org, https://www.aaafoundation.org/; 2021 Traffic Safety Culture Index and Use of Potentially Impairing Medications in Relation to Driving, United States, 2021.

Association for the Advancement of Automotive Medicine (AAAM), 35 E Wacker Dr., Ste. 850, Chicago, IL, 60601, USA, (847) 844-3880, info@aaam.org, https://www.aaam.org; unpublished data.

IDTechEx, One Boston Place, Ste. 2600, Boston, MA, 02108, USA, (617) 577-7890, (617) 577-7810, research@idtechex.com, https://www.idtechex.com/; Electric Vehicles: Land, Sea & Air 2022-2042.

Insurance Institute for Highway Safety/Highway Loss Data Institute (IIHS/HLDI), 4121 Wilson Blvd., 6th Fl., Arlington, VA, 22203, USA, (703) 247-1500, (434) 985 4600, cmatthew@iihs.org, https://www.iihs.org/; Fatality Facts 2021: Yearly Snapshot and Highway Safety Topics.

DISTRESS (PSYCHOLOGY)

The Gallup Organization, 901 F St. NW, Washington, DC, 20004, USA, (202) 715-3030, (800) 204-1192, (202) 715-3045, https://www.gallup.com; Gallup Global Emotions 2022; 2020 Sets Records for Negative Emotions; and State of the Global Workplace 2023.

Indiana University, Kinsey Institute, 150 S Woodlawn Ave., Lindley Hall 428, Bloomington, IN, 47405, USA, (812) 855-7686, (812) 855-3058, kinsey@indiana.edu, https://kinseyinstitute.org; Sexual Desire in the Time of COVID-19: How COVID-Related Stressors Are Associated with Sexual Desire in Romantic Relationships.

Microsoft Research, 14820 NE 36th St., Bldg. 99, Redmond, WA, 98052, USA, https://research.microsoft.com; Design of Digital Workplace Stress-Reduction Intervention Systems: Effects of Intervention Type and Timing.

Physicians for Human Rights (PHR), 256 W 38th St., 9th Fl., New York, NY, 10018, USA, (646) 564-3720, (646) 564-3750, https://phr.org/; 'Excited Delirium' and Deaths in Police Custody: The Deadly Impact of a Baseless Diagnosis.

DISTRICT COURTS, UNITED STATES

Administrative Office of the United States Courts, One Columbus Cir. NE, Washington, DC, 20544, USA, (202) 502-2600, https://www.uscourts.gov; Civil Justice Reform Act Report 2022; Federal Court Management Statistics 2022; Federal Judicial Caseload Statistics 2022; Judicial Facts and Figures 2022; and Statistical Tables for the Federal Judiciary 2022.

Justice Research and Statistics Association (JRSA), 1000 Vermont Ave. NW, Ste. 450, Washington, DC, 20005, USA, (202) 842-9330, (202) 304-1417, cjinfo@jrsa.org, https://www.jrsa.org; SAC Publication Digest 2022.

DISTRICT OF COLUMBIA-STATE DATA CENTERS

DC Public Libraries, Washingtoniana Collection in the People's Archive, 901 G St. NW, Rm. 307, Washington, DC, 20001-4531, USA, (202) 727-1213, peoples.archive@dc.gov, https://www.dclibrary.org/washingtoniana; State Data Reports (DC).

District of Columbia, Department of Health, Research and Analysis Division, 899 N Capitol St. NE, Washington, DC, 20002, USA, (202) 442-5955, (202) 442-4795, doh@dc.gov, https://dchealth.dc.gov/; State Data Reports (DC).

District of Columbia, Office of Planning, 1100 4th St. SW, Ste. 650 E, Washington, DC, 20024, USA, (202) 442-7600, (202) 442-7638, planning@dc.gov, https://planning.dc.gov/; State Data Reports (DC).

Metropolitan Washington Council of Governments (COG), 777 N Capitol St. NE, Ste. 300, Washington, DC, 20002, USA, (202) 962-3200, (202) 962-3213 (TDD), (202) 962-3201, pdesjardin@mwcog.org, https://www.mwcog.org; State Data Reports (DC).

DISTRICT OF COLUMBIA-PRIMARY STATISTICS SOURCES

District of Columbia, Public Schools, 1200 First St. NE, Washington, DC, 20002, USA, (202) 442-5885, (202) 442-5026, https://dcps.dc.gov/; District of Columbia Public Schools.

DISTRICT OF COLUMBIA

See also-STATE DATA (FOR INDIVIDUAL STATES)

Casey Trees, 3030 12th St. NE, Washington, DC, 20017, USA, (202) 833-4010, (202) 833-4092, friends@caseytrees.org, https://www.caseytrees.org; Tree Report Card 2020.

District of Columbia Corrections Information Council (CIC), 1400 I St. NW, Ste. 400, Washington, DC, 20005, USA, (202) 478-9211, dccic@dc.gov, https://cic.dc.gov/page/about-cic; COVID-19 Survey Final Report.

District of Columbia, Department of Employment Services (DOES), 4058 Minnesota Ave. NE, Washington, DC, 20019, USA, (202) 724-7000, (202) 698-4817 (TTY), (202) 673-6993, does@dc.gov, https://does.dc.gov/; DC Monthly Labor Market Indicators; Department of Employment Services Talent Forward DC: Annual Economic and Workforce Report, Fiscal Year 2020; and District of Columbia Labor Force Statistics Seasonally Adjusted 1976-2020.

District of Columbia, Metropolitan Police Department, 441 4th St. NW, 7th Fl., Washington, DC, 20001, USA, (202) 727-9099, (202) 727-4106, mpd@dc.gov, https://mpdc.dc.gov/; Bias-Related Crimes (Hate Crimes) Data; Crime Cards; and District Crime Data at a Glance.

District of Columbia, Office of Planning, 1100 4th St. SW, Ste. 650 E, Washington, DC, 20024, USA, (202) 442-7600, (202) 442-7638, planning@dc.gov, https://planning.dc.gov/; Census and Demographic Data by Ward.

District of Columbia, Office of the Chief Financial Officer, 1350 Pennsylvania Ave. NW, Ste. 203, Washington, DC, 20004, USA, (202) 727-2476, (202) 727-1643, ocfo@dc.gov, https://cfo.dc.gov/; Tax Rates and Tax Burdens 2020: A Nationwide Comparison.

The Federal Reserve Bank of Richmond, PO Box 27622, Richmond, VA, 23261, USA, (804) 697-8000, (410) 576-3300, https://www.richmondfed.org/; Fifth District Survey of Manufacturing Activity and Fifth District Survey of Service Sector Activity.

Greater Washington Board of Trade (BOT), 800 Connecticut Ave. NW, Ste. 1001, Washington, DC, 20006, USA, (202) 857-5900, info@bot.org, https://www.bot.org/; unpublished data.

The Urban Institute, Greater D.C. (Urban-Greater D.C), 500 L'Enfant Plaza SW, Washington, DC, 20024, USA, (202) 833-7200, https://greaterdc.urban.org/; DC Flexible Rent Subsidy Program: Findings from the Program's First Year.

Washington Area Women's Foundation, 712 H St. NE, Ste. 1099, Washington, DC, 20002, USA, (202) 347-7737, (202) 347-7739, info@wawf.org, https://thewomensfoundation.org; unpublished data.

DIVERSITY IN THE WORKPLACE

Directors UK, 22 Stukeley St., 3rd & 4th Fl., London, WC2B 5LR, GBR, info@directors.uk.com, https://www.directors.uk.com; zzunpublished data.

Geena Davis Institute on Gender in Media, 4712 Admiralty Way, Ste. 455, Marina del Rey, CA, 90292, USA, https://seejane.org/; From Real to Reel: Representation and Inclusion in Film and Television Produced in British Columbia.

The Marshall Project, 156 W 56th St., 3rd Fl., New York, NY, 10019, USA, (212) 803-5200, info@themarshallproject.org, https://www.themarshallproject.org/; Diversity and Inclusion, 2022.

The Minority Corporate Counsel Association (MCCA), 1111 Pennsylvania Ave. NW, Washington, DC, 20004, USA, (202) 739-5901, https://www.mcca.com/; 2022 Global Law Firm Diversity Database; 2020 Inclusion Index Survey Report; and Tracking the Integration of the Federal Judiciary.

Pew Research Center, 1615 L St. NW, Ste. 800, Washington, DC, 20036, USA, (202) 419-4300, (202) 857-8562, info@pewresearch.org, https://www.pewresearch.org/; Americans See Advantages and Challenges in Country's Growing Racial and Ethnic Diversity.

Statistics Canada (StatCan), 150 Tunney's Pasture Driveway, Ottawa, ON, K1A 0T6, CAN, (800) 263-1136 (Dial from U.S.), (514) 283-8300 (Dial from U.S.), (514) 283-9350 (Fax from U.S.), infostats@statcan.gc.ca, https://www.statcan.gc.ca; Gender, Diversity and Inclusion Statistics (GDIS) Hub.

University of Southern California (USC), Annenberg School for Communication and Journalism, Annenberg Inclusion Initiative, 3630 Watt Way, Ste. 402, Los Angeles, CA, 90089, USA, (213) 740-6180, (213) 740-3772, aii@usc.edu, https://annenberg.usc.edu/research/aii; Inclusion at Film Festivals: Examining the Gender and Race/Ethnicity of Narrative Directors from 2017-2019; Inclusion in the Director's Chair: Analysis of Director Gender & Race/Ethnicity Across 1,500 Top Films from 2007 to 2021; Inclusion in the Recording Studio? Gender and Race/Ethnicity of Artists, Songwriters & Producers Across 900 Popular Songs from 2012-2020; Inequality Across 1,600 Popular Films: Examining Gender, Race/Ethnicity & Age of Leads/Co Leads From 2007 to 2022; and Mental Health Conditions in Film & TV: Portrayals that Dehumanize and Trivialize Characters.

DIVIDENDS-CORPORATION

U.S. Department of Commerce (DOC), Bureau of Economic Analysis (BEA), 4600 Silver Hill Rd., Washington, DC, 20233, USA, (301) 278-9004, customerservice@bea.gov, https://www.bea.gov; National Income and Product Accounts (NIPA): 2022 Update and Survey of Current Business (SCB).

DIVIDENDS-INDIVIDUAL INCOME TAX RETURNS

Internal Revenue Service (IRS), Statistics of Income Division (SOI), 1111 Constitution Ave. NW, K-Room 4100-123, Washington, DC, 20224-0002, USA, (202) 874-0410, (202) 874-0964, sis@irs.gov, https://www.irs.gov/uac/soi-tax-stats-statistics-of-income; Statistics of Income Bulletin.

DIVIDENDS-NATIONAL AND/OR PERSONAL INCOME COMPONENTS

U.S. Department of Commerce (DOC), Bureau of Economic Analysis (BEA), 4600 Silver Hill Rd., Washington, DC, 20233, USA, (301) 278-9004, customerservice@bea.gov, https://www.bea.gov; National Income and Product Accounts (NIPA): 2022 Update and Survey of Current Business (SCB).

DIVIDENDS-RAILROAD STOCK

Association of American Railroads (AAR), 425 3rd St. SW, Washington, DC, 20024, USA, (202) 639-2100, https://www.aar.org; Analysis of Class I Railroads 2021 and Railroad Facts 2022.

DIVORCE

See MARITAL STATUS

DJIBOUTI-NATIONAL STATISTICAL OFFICE

Djibouti Ministere de l'Economie, des Finances, Charge de l'Industrie, BP 13, Djibouti, DJI, http://www.ministere-finances.dj/; National Data Reports (Djibouti).

DJIBOUTI-AGRICULTURE

African Development Bank Group (AfDB), Avenue Joseph Anoma, 01 BP 1387, Abidjan, 01, COT, https://www.afdb.org; African Economic Outlook 2021 and Compendium of Statistics on Bank Group Operations 2019.

The Economist Group: Economist Intelligence Unit (EIU), 900 3rd Ave., 16th Fl., New York, NY, 10022, USA, (212) 541-0500, americas@eiu.com, https://www.eiu.com; Djibouti Country Report.

Euromonitor International, Inc., 1 N Dearborn St., Ste. 1700, Chicago, IL, 60602, USA, (312) 922-1115, (312) 922-1157, info-usa@euromonitor.com, https://www.euromonitor.com/; Geographies.

Organisation of Islamic Cooperation (OIC), Statistical, Economic and Social Research and Training Centre for Islamic Countries (SESRIC), Kudus Cad. No. 9, Diplomatik Site, Ankara, 06450, TUR, statistics@sesric.org, https://www.sesric.org/; OIC Statistics (OICStat) Database and OIC-Countries in Figures (OIC-CIF).

Palgrave Macmillan, 1 New York Plaza, Ste. 4500, New York, NY, 10004-1562, USA, (800) 777-4643, orders@palgrave.com, https://www.palgrave.com/us; The Statesman's Yearbook, 2023.

Routledge - Taylor & Francis Group, 6000 Broken Sound Pkwy. NW, Ste. 300, Boca Raton, FL, 33487, USA, (800) 634-1420, (800) 634-7064, orders@taylorandfrancis.com, https://www.routledge.com/; The Europa World Year Book 2022.

United Nations Economic Commission for Africa (UNECA), PO Box 3001, Addis Ababa, ETH, ecainfo@uneca.org, https://www.uneca.org/; African Statistical Yearbook 2020 and Economic Report on Africa 2021.

United Nations Food and Agricultural Organization (FAO), 2121 K St., Ste. 800B, Washington, DC, 20037, USA, (202) 653-2400 (Dial from U.S.), (202) 653-5760 (Fax from U.S.), fao-hq@fao.org, https://www.fao.org; AQUASTAT and The State of Food and Agriculture (SOFA) 2022.

United Nations Statistics Division (UNSD), United Nations Plz., New York, NY, 10017, USA, (800) 253-9646, (212) 963-9851, statistics@un.org, https://unstats.un.org; Statistical Yearbook of the United Nations 2021.

The World Bank, 1818 H St. NW, Washington, DC, 20433, USA, (202) 473-1000, (202) 477-6391, eds03@worldbank.org, https://www.worldbank.org/; Djibouti (report).

DJIBOUTI-AIRLINES

Palgrave Macmillan, 1 New York Plaza, Ste. 4500, New York, NY, 10004-1562, USA, (800) 777-4643, orders@palgrave.com, https://www.palgrave.com/us; The Statesman's Yearbook, 2023.

Routledge - Taylor & Francis Group, 6000 Broken Sound Pkwy. NW, Ste. 300, Boca Raton, FL, 33487, USA, (800) 634-1420, (800) 634-7064, orders@taylorandfrancis.com, https://www.routledge.com/; The Europa World Year Book 2022.

United Nations Economic Commission for Africa (UNECA), PO Box 3001, Addis Ababa, ETH, ecainfo@uneca.org, https://www.uneca.org/; African Statistical Yearbook 2020.

DJIBOUTI-ARMED FORCES

Central Intelligence Agency (CIA), Office of Public Affairs, Washington, DC, 20505, USA, (703) 482-0623, https://www.cia.gov; The World Factbook.

International Institute for Strategic Studies (IISS) - Americas, 2121 K St. NW, Ste. 600, Washington, DC, 20037, USA, (202) 659-1490, (202) 659-1499, https://www.iiss.org/; The Military Balance 2022.

Palgrave Macmillan, 1 New York Plaza, Ste. 4500, New York, NY, 10004-1562, USA, (800) 777-4643, orders@palgrave.com, https://www.palgrave.com/us; The Statesman's Yearbook, 2023.

Stockholm International Peace Research Institute (SIPRI), Signalistgatan 9, Stockholm, SE 169 72, SWE, https://www.sipri.org/; SIPRI Arms Transfers Database and SIPRI Military Expenditure Database.

DJIBOUTI-BALANCE OF PAYMENTS

African Development Bank Group (AfDB), Avenue Joseph Anoma, 01 BP 1387, Abidjan, 01, COT, https://www.afdb.org; The AfDB Statistics Pocketbook 2019.

Routledge - Taylor & Francis Group, 6000 Broken Sound Pkwy. NW, Ste. 300, Boca Raton, FL, 33487, USA, (800) 634-1420, (800) 634-7064, orders@taylorandfrancis.com, https://www.routledge.com/; The Europa World Year Book 2022.

United Nations Conference on Trade and Development (UNCTAD), Palais des Nations, Geneva, 1211, SWI, (212) 963-6896, unctadinfo@unctad.org, https://unctad.org; Handbook of Statistics 2021.

United Nations Economic Commission for Africa (UNECA), PO Box 3001, Addis Ababa, ETH, ecainfo@uneca.org, https://www.uneca.org/; African Statistical Yearbook 2020.

The World Bank, 1818 H St. NW, Washington, DC, 20433, USA, (202) 473-1000, (202) 477-6391, eds03@worldbank.org, https://www.worldbank.org/; Djibouti (report).

DJIBOUTI-BANKS AND BANKING

Euromonitor International, Inc., 1 N Dearborn St., Ste. 1700, Chicago, IL, 60602, USA, (312) 922-1115, (312) 922-1157, info-usa@euromonitor.com, https://www.euromonitor.com/; Geographies.

Routledge - Taylor & Francis Group, 6000 Broken Sound Pkwy. NW, Ste. 300, Boca Raton, FL, 33487, USA, (800) 634-1420, (800) 634-7064, orders@taylorandfrancis.com, https://www.routledge.com/; The Europa World Year Book 2022.

United Nations Economic Commission for Africa (UNECA), PO Box 3001, Addis Ababa, ETH, ecainfo@uneca.org, https://www.uneca.org/; African Statistical Yearbook 2020.

DJIBOUTI-BROADCASTING

Central Intelligence Agency (CIA), Office of Public Affairs, Washington, DC, 20505, USA, (703) 482-0623, https://www.cia.gov; The World Factbook.

Euromonitor International, Inc., 1 N Dearborn St., Ste. 1700, Chicago, IL, 60602, USA, (312) 922-1115, (312) 922-1157, info-usa@euromonitor.com, https://www.euromonitor.com/; Geographies.

Palgrave Macmillan, 1 New York Plaza, Ste. 4500, New York, NY, 10004-1562, USA, (800) 777-4643, orders@palgrave.com, https://www.palgrave.com/us; The Statesman's Yearbook, 2023.

WRTH Publications Limited, PO Box 290, Oxford, OX2 7FT, GBR, sales@wrth.com, https://www.wrth.com; World Radio TV Handbook 2023.

DJIBOUTI-BUDGET

Central Intelligence Agency (CIA), Office of Public Affairs, Washington, DC, 20505, USA, (703) 482-0623, https://www.cia.gov; The World Factbook.

DJIBOUTI-CLIMATE

International Institute for Environment and Development (IIED), 235 High Holborn, London, WC1V 7DN, GBR, inforequest@iied.org, https://www.iied.org; Environment & Urbanization.

Palgrave Macmillan, 1 New York Plaza, Ste. 4500, New York, NY, 10004-1562, USA, (800) 777-4643, orders@palgrave.com, https://www.palgrave.com/us; The Statesman's Yearbook, 2023.

DJIBOUTI-COAL PRODUCTION

See DJIBOUTI-MINERAL INDUSTRIES

DJIBOUTI-COMMERCE

Palgrave Macmillan, 1 New York Plaza, Ste. 4500, New York, NY, 10004-1562, USA, (800) 777-4643, orders@palgrave.com, https://www.palgrave.com/us; The Statesman's Yearbook, 2023.

UK Data Service, University of Essex, Wivenhoe Park, Colchester, Essex, CO4 3SQ, GBR, https://ukdataservice.ac.uk/; International Aggregate Data.

DJIBOUTI-COMMODITY EXCHANGES

Barchart, 209 W Jackson Blvd., 2nd Fl., Chicago, IL, 60606, USA, (877) 247-4394, commodities@barchart.com, https://www.barchart.com/cmdty; The cmdty Yearbook 2023; cmdtyStats: Commodity Statistics and Fundamental Data; cmdtyView: Commodity Index; and Commodity Data and Prices.

International Monetary Fund (IMF), 700 19th St. NW, Washington, DC, 20431, USA, (202) 623-7000, (202) 623-4661, publications@imf.org, https://www.imf.org; IMF Primary Commodity Prices.

DJIBOUTI-CONSTRUCTION INDUSTRY

Palgrave Macmillan, 1 New York Plaza, Ste. 4500, New York, NY, 10004-1562, USA, (800) 777-4643, orders@palgrave.com, https://www.palgrave.com/us; The Statesman's Yearbook, 2023.

United Nations Economic Commission for Africa (UNECA), PO Box 3001, Addis Ababa, ETH, ecainfo@uneca.org, https://www.uneca.org/; African Statistical Yearbook 2020.

United Nations Statistics Division (UNSD), United Nations Plz., New York, NY, 10017, USA, (800) 253-9646, (212) 963-9851, statistics@un.org, https://unstats.un.org; Statistical Yearbook of the United Nations 2021.

DJIBOUTI-CONSUMER PRICE INDEXES

United Nations Economic Commission for Africa (UNECA), PO Box 3001, Addis Ababa, ETH, ecainfo@uneca.org, https://www.uneca.org/; African Statistical Yearbook 2020.

The World Bank, 1818 H St. NW, Washington, DC, 20433, USA, (202) 473-1000, (202) 477-6391, eds03@worldbank.org, https://www.worldbank.org/; Djibouti (report).

DJIBOUTI-CONSUMPTION (ECONOMICS)

African Development Bank Group (AfDB), Avenue Joseph Anoma, 01 BP 1387, Abidjan, 01, COT, https://www.afdb.org; The AfDB Statistics Pocketbook 2019.

DJIBOUTI-CORN INDUSTRY

See DJIBOUTI-CROPS

DJIBOUTI-CROPS

Palgrave Macmillan, 1 New York Plaza, Ste. 4500, New York, NY, 10004-1562, USA, (800) 777-4643, orders@palgrave.com, https://www.palgrave.com/us; The Statesman's Yearbook, 2023.

United Nations Economic Commission for Africa (UNECA), PO Box 3001, Addis Ababa, ETH, ecainfo@uneca.org, https://www.uneca.org/; African Statistical Yearbook 2020.

United Nations Food and Agricultural Organization (FAO), 2121 K St., Ste. 800B, Washington, DC, 20037, USA, (202) 653-2400 (Dial from U.S.), (202) 653-5760 (Fax from U.S.), fao-hq@fao.org, https://www.fao.org; The State of Food and Agriculture (SOFA) 2022.

DJIBOUTI-DAIRY PROCESSING

United Nations Food and Agricultural Organization (FAO), 2121 K St., Ste. 800B, Washington, DC, 20037, USA, (202) 653-2400 (Dial from U.S.), (202) 653-5760 (Fax from U.S.), fao-hq@fao.org, https://www.fao.org; The State of Food and Agriculture (SOFA) 2022.

DJIBOUTI-DEBTS, EXTERNAL

African Development Bank Group (AfDB), Avenue Joseph Anoma, 01 BP 1387, Abidjan, 01, COT, https://www.afdb.org; The AfDB Statistics Pocketbook 2019; African Economic Outlook 2021; and Compendium of Statistics on Bank Group Operations 2019.

Palgrave Macmillan, 1 New York Plaza, Ste. 4500, New York, NY, 10004-1562, USA, (800) 777-4643, orders@palgrave.com, https://www.palgrave.com/us; The Statesman's Yearbook, 2023.

United Nations Economic Commission for Africa (UNECA), PO Box 3001, Addis Ababa, ETH, ecainfo@uneca.org, https://www.uneca.org/; Economic Report on Africa 2021.

The World Bank, 1818 H St. NW, Washington, DC, 20433, USA, (202) 473-1000, (202) 477-6391, eds03@worldbank.org, https://www.worldbank.org/; Global Financial Development Report 2019-2020: Bank Regulation and Supervision a Decade after the Global Financial Crisis.

DJIBOUTI-DEFENSE EXPENDITURES

See DJIBOUTI-ARMED FORCES

DJIBOUTI-ECONOMIC ASSISTANCE

United Nations Statistics Division (UNSD), United Nations Plz., New York, NY, 10017, USA, (800) 253-9646, (212) 963-9851, statistics@un.org, https://unstats.un.org; Statistical Yearbook of the United Nations 2021.

DJIBOUTI-ECONOMIC CONDITIONS

African Development Bank Group (AfDB), Avenue Joseph Anoma, 01 BP 1387, Abidjan, 01, COT, https://www.afdb.org; The AfDB Statistics Pocketbook 2019; Africa Economic Brief - COVID-19 Pandemic Potential Risks for Trade and Trade Finance in Africa; African Economic Outlook 2021; The African Statistical Journal; Compendium of Statistics on Bank Group Operations 2019; and Gender, Poverty and Environmental Indicators on African Countries 2019.

Bernan Press, 15250 NBN Way, Bldg. C, Blue Ridge Summit, PA, 17214, USA, (301) 459-2255, (800) 865-3457, (800) 865-3450, customercare@bernan.com, https://rowman.com/Page/Bernan; World Economic Outlook, April 2022.

Central Intelligence Agency (CIA), Office of Public Affairs, Washington, DC, 20505, USA, (703) 482-0623, https://www.cia.gov; The World Factbook.

The Economist Group: Economist Intelligence Unit (EIU), 900 3rd Ave., 16th Fl., New York, NY, 10022, USA, (212) 541-0500, americas@eiu.com, https://www.eiu.com; Djibouti Country Report.

Euromonitor International, Inc., 1 N Dearborn St., Ste. 1700, Chicago, IL, 60602, USA, (312) 922-1115, (312) 922-1157, info-usa@euromonitor.com, https://www.euromonitor.com/; Geographies.

International Monetary Fund (IMF), 700 19th St. NW, Washington, DC, 20431, USA, (202) 623-7000, (202) 623-4661, publications@imf.org, https://www.imf.org; IMF Data and World Economic Outlook.

Organisation of Islamic Cooperation (OIC), Statistical, Economic and Social Research and Training Centre for Islamic Countries (SESRIC), Kudus Cad. No. 9, Diplomatik Site, Ankara, 06450, TUR, statistics@sesric.org, https://www.sesric.org/; OIC Economic Outlook 2021; OIC Statistics (OICStat) Database; and OIC-Countries in Figures (OIC-CIF).

Palgrave Macmillan, 1 New York Plaza, Ste. 4500, New York, NY, 10004-1562, USA, (800) 777-4643, orders@palgrave.com, https://www.palgrave.com/us; The Statesman's Yearbook, 2023.

United Nations Economic Commission for Africa (UNECA), PO Box 3001, Addis Ababa, ETH,

ecainfo@uneca.org, https://www.uneca.org/; Economic Report on Africa 2021.

United Nations Statistics Division (UNSD), United Nations Plz., New York, NY, 10017, USA, (800) 253-9646, (212) 963-9851, statistics@un.org, https://unstats.un.org; World Statistics Pocketbook 2021.

The World Bank, 1818 H St. NW, Washington, DC, 20433, USA, (202) 473-1000, (202) 477-6391, eds03@worldbank.org, https://www.worldbank.org/; Djibouti (report); Global Economic Monitor (GEM); Global Economic Prospects, June 2022; and The Global Findex Database 2021.

DJIBOUTI-EDUCATION

African Development Bank Group (AfDB), Avenue Joseph Anoma, 01 BP 1387, Abidjan, 01, COT, https://www.afdb.org; The AfDB Statistics Pocketbook 2019.

Euromonitor International, Inc., 1 N Dearborn St., Ste. 1700, Chicago, IL, 60602, USA, (312) 922-1115, (312) 922-1157, info-usa@euromonitor.com, https://www.euromonitor.com/; Geographies.

Infoplease, c/o Sandbox Networks, Inc., 1 Lincoln St., 24th Fl., Boston, MA, 02111, USA, https://www.infoplease.com; Countries of the World.

Organisation of Islamic Cooperation (OIC), Statistical, Economic and Social Research and Training Centre for Islamic Countries (SESRIC), Kudus Cad. No. 9, Diplomatik Site, Ankara, 06450, TUR, statistics@sesric.org, https://www.sesric.org/; OIC Statistics (OICStat) Database.

Palgrave Macmillan, 1 New York Plaza, Ste. 4500, New York, NY, 10004-1562, USA, (800) 777-4643, orders@palgrave.com, https://www.palgrave.com/us; The Statesman's Yearbook, 2023.

Routledge - Taylor & Francis Group, 6000 Broken Sound Pkwy. NW, Ste. 300, Boca Raton, FL, 33487, USA, (800) 634-1420, (800) 634-7064, orders@taylorandfrancis.com, https://www.routledge.com/; The Europa World Year Book 2022.

UNESCO Institute for Statistics, C.P 250 Succursale H, Montreal, QC, H3G 2K8, CAN, (514) 343-6880 (Dial from U.S.), (514) 343-5740 (Fax from U.S.), uis.publications@unesco.org, http://uis.unesco.org/; Literacy and UIS.Stat.

United Nations Economic Commission for Africa (UNECA), PO Box 3001, Addis Ababa, ETH, ecainfo@uneca.org, https://www.uneca.org/; African Statistical Yearbook 2020.

United Nations Statistics Division (UNSD), United Nations Plz., New York, NY, 10017, USA, (800) 253-9646, (212) 963-9851, statistics@un.org, https://unstats.un.org; Millennium Development Goal Indicators.

The World Bank, 1818 H St. NW, Washington, DC, 20433, USA, (202) 473-1000, (202) 477-6391, eds03@worldbank.org, https://www.worldbank.org/; Djibouti (report).

DJIBOUTI-ELECTRICITY

United Nations Statistics Division (UNSD), United Nations Plz., New York, NY, 10017, USA, (800) 253-9646, (212) 963-9851, statistics@un.org, https://unstats.un.org; Statistical Yearbook of the United Nations 2021.

DJIBOUTI-EMPLOYMENT

International Labour Organization (ILO), 4 Rte. des Morillons, Geneva, CH-1211, SWI, ilo@ilo.org, https://www.ilo.org; NORMLEX Information System on International Labour Standards.

UK Data Service, University of Essex, Wivenhoe Park, Colchester, Essex, CO4 3SQ, GBR, https://ukdataservice.ac.uk/; International Aggregate Data.

United Nations Economic Commission for Africa (UNECA), PO Box 3001, Addis Ababa, ETH, ecainfo@uneca.org, https://www.uneca.org/; African Statistical Yearbook 2020.

The World Bank, 1818 H St. NW, Washington, DC, 20433, USA, (202) 473-1000, (202) 477-6391, eds03@worldbank.org, https://www.worldbank.org/; Djibouti (report).

DJIBOUTI-ENVIRONMENTAL CONDITIONS

DSI Data Service & Information, Xantener Strasse 51a, Rheinberg, D-47495, GER, dsi@dsidata.com, https://www.dsidata.com/; Global Environmental Database.

The Economist Group: Economist Intelligence Unit (EIU), 900 3rd Ave., 16th Fl., New York, NY, 10022, USA, (212) 541-0500, americas@eiu.com, https://www.eiu.com; Djibouti Country Report.

International Institute for Environment and Development (IIED), 235 High Holborn, London, WC1V 7DN, GBR, inforequest@iied.org, https://www.iied.org; Environment & Urbanization.

Organisation of Islamic Cooperation (OIC), Statistical, Economic and Social Research and Training Centre for Islamic Countries (SESRIC), Kudus Cad. No. 9, Diplomatik Site, Ankara, 06450, TUR, statistics@sesric.org, https://www.sesric.org/; OIC Statistics (OICStat) Database and OIC-Countries in Figures (OIC-CIF).

United Nations Statistics Division (UNSD), United Nations Plz., New York, NY, 10017, USA, (800) 253-9646, (212) 963-9851, statistics@un.org, https://unstats.un.org; World Statistics Pocketbook 2021.

DJIBOUTI-EXPORTS

African Development Bank Group (AfDB), Avenue Joseph Anoma, 01 BP 1387, Abidjan, 01, COT, https://www.afdb.org; African Economic Outlook 2021.

Central Intelligence Agency (CIA), Office of Public Affairs, Washington, DC, 20505, USA, (703) 482-0623, https://www.cia.gov; The World Factbook.

The Economist Group: Economist Intelligence Unit (EIU), 900 3rd Ave., 16th Fl., New York, NY, 10022, USA, (212) 541-0500, americas@eiu.com, https://www.eiu.com; Djibouti Country Report.

Inter-American Development Bank (IDB), 1300 New York Ave. NW, Washington, DC, 20577, USA, (202) 623-1000, (202) 623-3096, https://www.iadb.org/en; Latin Macro Watch (LMW).

Organisation of Islamic Cooperation (OIC), Statistical, Economic and Social Research and Training Centre for Islamic Countries (SESRIC), Kudus Cad. No. 9, Diplomatik Site, Ankara, 06450, TUR, statistics@sesric.org, https://www.sesric.org/; OIC Statistics (OICStat) Database.

United Nations Conference on Trade and Development (UNCTAD), Palais des Nations, Geneva, 1211, SWI, (212) 963-6896, unctadinfo@unctad.org, https://unctad.org; Handbook of Statistics 2021.

DJIBOUTI-FERTILITY, HUMAN

Central Intelligence Agency (CIA), Office of Public Affairs, Washington, DC, 20505, USA, (703) 482-0623, https://www.cia.gov; The World Factbook.

DJIBOUTI-FERTILIZER INDUSTRY

United Nations Food and Agricultural Organization (FAO), 2121 K St., Ste. 800B, Washington, DC, 20037, USA, (202) 653-2400 (Dial from U.S.), (202) 653-5760 (Fax from U.S.), fao-hq@fao.org, https://www.fao.org; The State of Food and Agriculture (SOFA) 2022.

DJIBOUTI-FETAL MORTALITY

See DJIBOUTI-MORTALITY

DJIBOUTI-FINANCE

Stockholm International Peace Research Institute (SIPRI), Signalistgatan 9, Stockholm, SE 169 72, SWE, https://www.sipri.org/; SIPRI Arms Transfers Database and SIPRI Military Expenditure Database.

United Nations Economic Commission for Africa (UNECA), PO Box 3001, Addis Ababa, ETH, ecainfo@uneca.org, https://www.uneca.org/; African Statistical Yearbook 2020.

The World Bank, 1818 H St. NW, Washington, DC, 20433, USA, (202) 473-1000, (202) 477-6391, eds03@worldbank.org, https://www.worldbank.org/; Djibouti (report).

DJIBOUTI-FINANCE, PUBLIC

African Development Bank Group (AfDB), Avenue Joseph Anoma, 01 BP 1387, Abidjan, 01, COT, https://www.afdb.org; The AfDB Statistics Pocketbook 2019.

Bernan Press, 15250 NBN Way, Bldg. C, Blue Ridge Summit, PA, 17214, USA, (301) 459-2255, (800) 865-3457, (800) 865-3450, customercare@bernan.com, https://rowman.com/Page/Bernan; National Accounts Statistics: Analysis of Main Aggregates 2020.

The Economist Group: Economist Intelligence Unit (EIU), 900 3rd Ave., 16th Fl., New York, NY, 10022, USA, (212) 541-0500, americas@eiu.com, https://www.eiu.com; Djibouti Country Report.

International Monetary Fund (IMF), 700 19th St. NW, Washington, DC, 20431, USA, (202) 623-7000, (202) 623-4661, publications@imf.org, https://www.imf.org; Regional Economic Outlook.

Palgrave Macmillan, 1 New York Plaza, Ste. 4500, New York, NY, 10004-1562, USA, (800) 777-4643, orders@palgrave.com, https://www.palgrave.com/us; The Statesman's Yearbook, 2023.

Routledge - Taylor & Francis Group, 6000 Broken Sound Pkwy. NW, Ste. 300, Boca Raton, FL, 33487, USA, (800) 634-1420, (800) 634-7064, orders@taylorandfrancis.com, https://www.routledge.com/; The Europa World Year Book 2022.

United Nations Economic Commission for Africa (UNECA), PO Box 3001, Addis Ababa, ETH, ecainfo@uneca.org, https://www.uneca.org/; African Statistical Yearbook 2020.

United Nations Statistics Division (UNSD), United Nations Plz., New York, NY, 10017, USA, (800) 253-9646, (212) 963-9851, statistics@un.org, https://unstats.un.org; National Accounts Main Aggregates Database and National Accounts Statistics: Main Aggregates and Detailed Tables.

The World Bank, 1818 H St. NW, Washington, DC, 20433, USA, (202) 473-1000, (202) 477-6391, eds03@worldbank.org, https://www.worldbank.org/; Djibouti (report).

DJIBOUTI-FISHERIES

Palgrave Macmillan, 1 New York Plaza, Ste. 4500, New York, NY, 10004-1562, USA, (800) 777-4643, orders@palgrave.com, https://www.palgrave.com/us; The Statesman's Yearbook, 2023.

Routledge - Taylor & Francis Group, 6000 Broken Sound Pkwy. NW, Ste. 300, Boca Raton, FL, 33487, USA, (800) 634-1420, (800) 634-7064, orders@taylorandfrancis.com, https://www.routledge.com/; The Europa World Year Book 2022.

United Nations Economic Commission for Africa (UNECA), PO Box 3001, Addis Ababa, ETH, ecainfo@uneca.org, https://www.uneca.org/; African Statistical Yearbook 2020.

United Nations Food and Agricultural Organization (FAO), 2121 K St., Ste. 800B, Washington, DC, 20037, USA, (202) 653-2400 (Dial from U.S.), (202) 653-5760 (Fax from U.S.), fao-hq@fao.org, https://www.fao.org; FAO Yearbook of Fishery and Aquaculture Statistics 2019; Fishery Statistical Collections Global Capture Production; FishStatJ; and The State of Food and Agriculture (SOFA) 2022.

The World Bank, 1818 H St. NW, Washington, DC, 20433, USA, (202) 473-1000, (202) 477-6391, eds03@worldbank.org, https://www.worldbank.org/; Djibouti (report).

DJIBOUTI-FOOD

African Development Bank Group (AfDB), Avenue Joseph Anoma, 01 BP 1387, Abidjan, 01, COT, https://www.afdb.org; The AfDB Statistics Pocketbook 2019.

United Nations Food and Agricultural Organization (FAO), 2121 K St., Ste. 800B, Washington, DC, 20037, USA, (202) 653-2400 (Dial from U.S.), (202) 653-5760 (Fax from U.S.), fao-hq@fao.org, https://www.fao.org; The State of Food and Agriculture (SOFA) 2022.

DJIBOUTI-FOREIGN EXCHANGE RATES

African Development Bank Group (AfDB), Avenue Joseph Anoma, 01 BP 1387, Abidjan, 01, COT, https://www.afdb.org; The AfDB Statistics Pocketbook 2019 and African Economic Outlook 2021.

Inter-American Development Bank (IDB), 1300 New York Ave. NW, Washington, DC, 20577, USA, (202) 623-1000, (202) 623-3096, https://www.iadb.org/en; Latin Macro Watch (LMW).

DJIBOUTI-FORESTS AND FORESTRY

UNESCO Institute for Statistics, C.P 250 Succursale H, Montreal, QC, H3G 2K8, CAN, (514) 343-6880 (Dial from U.S.), (514) 343-5740 (Fax from U.S.), uis.publications@unesco.org, http://uis.unesco.org/; UIS.Stat.

United Nations Economic Commission for Africa (UNECA), PO Box 3001, Addis Ababa, ETH, ecainfo@uneca.org, https://www.uneca.org/; African Statistical Yearbook 2020.

United Nations Food and Agricultural Organization (FAO), 2121 K St., Ste. 800B, Washington, DC, 20037, USA, (202) 653-2400 (Dial from U.S.), (202) 653-5760 (Fax from U.S.), fao-hq@fao.org, https://www.fao.org; FAO Yearbook of Forest Products 2019 and The State of Food and Agriculture (SOFA) 2022.

United Nations Statistics Division (UNSD), United Nations Plz., New York, NY, 10017, USA, (800) 253-9646, (212) 963-9851, statistics@un.org, https://unstats.un.org; Statistical Yearbook of the United Nations 2021.

The World Bank, 1818 H St. NW, Washington, DC, 20433, USA, (202) 473-1000, (202) 477-6391, eds03@worldbank.org, https://www.worldbank.org/; Djibouti (report).

DJIBOUTI-GEOGRAPHIC INFORMATION SYSTEMS

The World Bank, 1818 H St. NW, Washington, DC, 20433, USA, (202) 473-1000, (202) 477-6391, eds03@worldbank.org, https://www.worldbank.org/; Djibouti (report).

DJIBOUTI-GROSS DOMESTIC PRODUCT

African Development Bank Group (AfDB), Avenue Joseph Anoma, 01 BP 1387, Abidjan, 01, COT, https://www.afdb.org; The AfDB Statistics Pocketbook 2019.

The Economist Group: Economist Intelligence Unit (EIU), 900 3rd Ave., 16th Fl., New York, NY, 10022, USA, (212) 541-0500, americas@eiu.com, https://www.eiu.com; Djibouti Country Report.

Routledge - Taylor & Francis Group, 6000 Broken Sound Pkwy. NW, Ste. 300, Boca Raton, FL, 33487, USA, (800) 634-1420, (800) 634-7064, orders@taylorandfrancis.com, https://www.routledge.com/; The Europa World Year Book 2022.

United Nations Economic Commission for Africa (UNECA), PO Box 3001, Addis Ababa, ETH, ecainfo@uneca.org, https://www.uneca.org/; African Statistical Yearbook 2020.

United Nations Statistics Division (UNSD), United Nations Plz., New York, NY, 10017, USA, (800) 253-9646, (212) 963-9851, statistics@un.org, https://unstats.un.org; Statistical Yearbook of the United Nations 2021.

DJIBOUTI-GROSS NATIONAL PRODUCT

Palgrave Macmillan, 1 New York Plaza, Ste. 4500, New York, NY, 10004-1562, USA, (800) 777-4643, orders@palgrave.com, https://www.palgrave.com/us; The Statesman's Yearbook, 2023.

United Nations Statistics Division (UNSD), United Nations Plz., New York, NY, 10017, USA, (800) 253-9646, (212) 963-9851, statistics@un.org, https://unstats.un.org; Statistical Yearbook of the United Nations 2021.

DJIBOUTI-HOUSING

Euromonitor International, Inc., 1 N Dearborn St., Ste. 1700, Chicago, IL, 60602, USA, (312) 922-1115, (312) 922-1157, info-usa@euromonitor.com, https://www.euromonitor.com/; Geographies.

DJIBOUTI-IMPORTS

African Development Bank Group (AfDB), Avenue Joseph Anoma, 01 BP 1387, Abidjan, 01, COT, https://www.afdb.org; African Economic Outlook 2021.

Central Intelligence Agency (CIA), Office of Public Affairs, Washington, DC, 20505, USA, (703) 482-0623, https://www.cia.gov; The World Factbook.

The Economist Group: Economist Intelligence Unit (EIU), 900 3rd Ave., 16th Fl., New York, NY, 10022, USA, (212) 541-0500, americas@eiu.com, https://www.eiu.com; Djibouti Country Report.

Inter-American Development Bank (IDB), 1300 New York Ave. NW, Washington, DC, 20577, USA, (202) 623-1000, (202) 623-3096, https://www.iadb.org/en; Latin Macro Watch (LMW).

International Monetary Fund (IMF), 700 19th St. NW, Washington, DC, 20431, USA, (202) 623-7000, (202) 623-4661, publications@imf.org, https://www.imf.org; Direction of Trade Statistics (DOTS).

S&P Global, IHS Markit, 15 Inverness Way E, Englewood, CO, 80112, USA, (800) 447-2273, (800) 854-7179, https://ihsmarkit.com; Global Trade Atlas (GTA).

United Nations Conference on Trade and Development (UNCTAD), Palais des Nations, Geneva, 1211, SWI, (212) 963-6896, unctadinfo@unctad.org, https://unctad.org; Handbook of Statistics 2021.

DJIBOUTI-INDUSTRIES

Central Intelligence Agency (CIA), Office of Public Affairs, Washington, DC, 20505, USA, (703) 482-0623, https://www.cia.gov; The World Factbook.

The Economist Group: Economist Intelligence Unit (EIU), 900 3rd Ave., 16th Fl., New York, NY, 10022, USA, (212) 541-0500, americas@eiu.com, https://www.eiu.com; Djibouti Country Report.

Euromonitor International, Inc., 1 N Dearborn St., Ste. 1700, Chicago, IL, 60602, USA, (312) 922-1115, (312) 922-1157, info-usa@euromonitor.com, https://www.euromonitor.com/; Geographies.

International Labour Organization (ILO), 4 Rte. des Morillons, Geneva, CH-1211, SWI, ilo@ilo.org, https://www.ilo.org; NORMLEX Information System on International Labour Standards.

Palgrave Macmillan, 1 New York Plaza, Ste. 4500, New York, NY, 10004-1562, USA, (800) 777-4643, orders@palgrave.com, https://www.palgrave.com/us; The Statesman's Yearbook, 2023.

Routledge - Taylor & Francis Group, 6000 Broken Sound Pkwy. NW, Ste. 300, Boca Raton, FL, 33487, USA, (800) 634-1420, (800) 634-7064, orders@taylorandfrancis.com, https://www.routledge.com/; The Europa World Year Book 2022.

United Nations Economic Commission for Africa (UNECA), PO Box 3001, Addis Ababa, ETH, ecainfo@uneca.org, https://www.uneca.org/; African Statistical Yearbook 2020.

United Nations Industrial Development Organization (UNIDO), 1 United Nations Plz., Rm. DC1-1118, New York, NY, 10017, USA, (212) 963-6890, (212) 963 6885, (212) 963-7904, office.newyork@unido.org, https://www.unido.org/; Industrial Statistics Databases and International Yearbook of Industrial Statistics 2021.

The World Bank, 1818 H St. NW, Washington, DC, 20433, USA, (202) 473-1000, (202) 477-6391, eds03@worldbank.org, https://www.worldbank.org/; Djibouti (report).

DJIBOUTI-INFANT AND MATERNAL MORTALITY

See DJIBOUTI-MORTALITY

DJIBOUTI-INTERNATIONAL TRADE

African Development Bank Group (AfDB), Avenue Joseph Anoma, 01 BP 1387, Abidjan, 01, COT, https://www.afdb.org; The AfDB Statistics Pocketbook 2019 and African Economic Outlook 2021.

The Economist Group: Economist Intelligence Unit (EIU), 900 3rd Ave., 16th Fl., New York, NY, 10022, USA, (212) 541-0500, americas@eiu.com, https://www.eiu.com; Djibouti Country Report.

Euromonitor International, Inc., 1 N Dearborn St., Ste. 1700, Chicago, IL, 60602, USA, (312) 922-1115, (312) 922-1157, info-usa@euromonitor.com, https://www.euromonitor.com/; Geographies.

Inter-American Development Bank (IDB), 1300 New York Ave. NW, Washington, DC, 20577, USA, (202) 623-1000, (202) 623-3096, https://www.iadb.org/en; Latin Macro Watch (LMW).

Palgrave Macmillan, 1 New York Plaza, Ste. 4500, New York, NY, 10004-1562, USA, (800) 777-4643, orders@palgrave.com, https://www.palgrave.com/us; The Statesman's Yearbook, 2023.

Routledge - Taylor & Francis Group, 6000 Broken Sound Pkwy. NW, Ste. 300, Boca Raton, FL, 33487, USA, (800) 634-1420, (800) 634-7064, orders@taylorandfrancis.com, https://www.routledge.com/; The Europa World Year Book 2022.

United Nations Conference on Trade and Development (UNCTAD), Palais des Nations, Geneva, 1211, SWI, (212) 963-6896, unctadinfo@unctad.org, https://unctad.org; Trade and Development Report 2021.

United Nations Economic Commission for Africa (UNECA), PO Box 3001, Addis Ababa, ETH, ecainfo@uneca.org, https://www.uneca.org/; African Statistical Yearbook 2020.

United Nations Food and Agricultural Organization (FAO), 2121 K St., Ste. 800B, Washington, DC, 20037, USA, (202) 653-2400 (Dial from U.S.), (202) 653-5760 (Fax from U.S.), fao-hq@fao.org, https://www.fao.org; The State of Food and Agriculture (SOFA) 2022.

United Nations Statistics Division (UNSD), United Nations Plz., New York, NY, 10017, USA, (800) 253-9646, (212) 963-9851, statistics@un.org, https://unstats.un.org; Statistical Yearbook of the United Nations 2021.

The World Bank, 1818 H St. NW, Washington, DC, 20433, USA, (202) 473-1000, (202) 477-6391, eds03@worldbank.org, https://www.worldbank.org/; Djibouti (report).

World Trade Organization (WTO), Ctre. William Rappard, Rue de Lausanne 154, Case postale, Geneva, CH-1211, SWI, enquiries@wto.org, https://www.wto.org; World Trade Statistical Review 2022.

DJIBOUTI-INTERNET USERS

International Telecommunication Union (ITU), Place des Nations, Geneva, CH-1211, SWI, itumail@itu.int, https://www.itu.int; Global Connectivity Report 2022; World Telecommunication/ICT Indicators Database 2021; and Yearbook of Statistics 2019.

The World Bank, 1818 H St. NW, Washington, DC, 20433, USA, (202) 473-1000, (202) 477-6391, eds03@worldbank.org, https://www.worldbank.org/; Djibouti (report).

DJIBOUTI-LABOR

African Development Bank Group (AfDB), Avenue Joseph Anoma, 01 BP 1387, Abidjan, 01, COT, https://www.afdb.org; The AfDB Statistics Pocketbook 2019.

Central Intelligence Agency (CIA), Office of Public Affairs, Washington, DC, 20505, USA, (703) 482-0623, https://www.cia.gov; The World Factbook.

Euromonitor International, Inc., 1 N Dearborn St., Ste. 1700, Chicago, IL, 60602, USA, (312) 922-1115, (312) 922-1157, info-usa@euromonitor.com, https://www.euromonitor.com/; Geographies.

International Labour Organization (ILO), 4 Rte. des Morillons, Geneva, CH-1211, SWI, ilo@ilo.org, https://www.ilo.org; NORMLEX Information System on International Labour Standards.

Organisation of Islamic Cooperation (OIC), Statistical, Economic and Social Research and Training

Centre for Islamic Countries (SESRIC), Kudus Cad. No. 9, Diplomatik Site, Ankara, 06450, TUR, statistics@sesric.org, https://www.sesric.org/; OIC Statistics (OICStat) Database.

Palgrave Macmillan, 1 New York Plaza, Ste. 4500, New York, NY, 10004-1562, USA, (800) 777-4643, orders@palgrave.com, https://www.palgrave.com/us; The Statesman's Yearbook, 2023.

United Nations Food and Agricultural Organization (FAO), 2121 K St., Ste. 800B, Washington, DC, 20037, USA, (202) 653-2400 (Dial from U.S.), (202) 653-5760 (Fax from U.S.), fao-hq@fao.org, https://www.fao.org; The State of Food and Agriculture (SOFA) 2022.

DJIBOUTI-LAND USE

United Nations Statistics Division (UNSD), United Nations Plz., New York, NY, 10017, USA, (800) 253-9646, (212) 963-9851, statistics@un.org, https://unstats.un.org; Millennium Development Goal Indicators.

DJIBOUTI-LIBRARIES

UNESCO Institute for Statistics, C.P 250 Succursale H, Montreal, QC, H3G 2K8, CAN, (514) 343-6880 (Dial from U.S.), (514) 343-5740 (Fax from U.S.), uis.publications@unesco.org, http://uis.unesco.org/; UIS.Stat.

DJIBOUTI-LIFE EXPECTANCY

African Development Bank Group (AfDB), Avenue Joseph Anoma, 01 BP 1387, Abidjan, 01, COT, https://www.afdb.org; The AfDB Statistics Pocketbook 2019.

Central Intelligence Agency (CIA), Office of Public Affairs, Washington, DC, 20505, USA, (703) 482-0623, https://www.cia.gov; The World Factbook.

United Nations Department of Economic and Social Affairs (DESA), Population Division, 2 United Nations Plz., Rm. DC2-1950, New York, NY, 10017, USA, (212) 963-3209, (212) 963-2147, population@un.org, https://www.un.org/development/desa/pd/; World Population Ageing 2020 Highlights.

United Nations Statistics Division (UNSD), United Nations Plz., New York, NY, 10017, USA, (800) 253-9646, (212) 963-9851, statistics@un.org, https://unstats.un.org; Millennium Development Goal Indicators.

DJIBOUTI-LITERACY

Euromonitor International, Inc., 1 N Dearborn St., Ste. 1700, Chicago, IL, 60602, USA, (312) 922-1115, (312) 922-1157, info-usa@euromonitor.com, https://www.euromonitor.com/; Geographies.

UNESCO Institute for Statistics, C.P 250 Succursale H, Montreal, QC, H3G 2K8, CAN, (514) 343-6880 (Dial from U.S.), (514) 343-5740 (Fax from U.S.), uis.publications@unesco.org, http://uis.unesco.org/; Literacy.

DJIBOUTI-LIVESTOCK

Palgrave Macmillan, 1 New York Plaza, Ste. 4500, New York, NY, 10004-1562, USA, (800) 777-4643, orders@palgrave.com, https://www.palgrave.com/us; The Statesman's Yearbook, 2023.

Routledge - Taylor & Francis Group, 6000 Broken Sound Pkwy. NW, Ste. 300, Boca Raton, FL, 33487, USA, (800) 634-1420, (800) 634-7064, orders@taylorandfrancis.com, https://www.routledge.com/; The Europa World Year Book 2022.

United Nations Economic Commission for Africa (UNECA), PO Box 3001, Addis Ababa, ETH, ecainfo@uneca.org, https://www.uneca.org/; African Statistical Yearbook 2020.

United Nations Food and Agricultural Organization (FAO), 2121 K St., Ste. 800B, Washington, DC, 20037, USA, (202) 653-2400 (Dial from U.S.), (202) 653-5760 (Fax from U.S.), fao-hq@fao.org, https://www.fao.org; The State of Food and Agriculture (SOFA) 2022.

United Nations Statistics Division (UNSD), United Nations Plz., New York, NY, 10017, USA, (800) 253-9646, (212) 963-9851, statistics@un.org, https://unstats.un.org; Statistical Yearbook of the United Nations 2021.

DJIBOUTI-MINERAL INDUSTRIES

Palgrave Macmillan, 1 New York Plaza, Ste. 4500, New York, NY, 10004-1562, USA, (800) 777-4643, orders@palgrave.com, https://www.palgrave.com/us; The Statesman's Yearbook, 2023.

United Nations Conference on Trade and Development (UNCTAD), Palais des Nations, Geneva, 1211, SWI, (212) 963-6896, unctadinfo@unctad.org, https://unctad.org; Trade and Development Report 2021.

United Nations Economic Commission for Africa (UNECA), PO Box 3001, Addis Ababa, ETH, ecainfo@uneca.org, https://www.uneca.org/; African Statistical Yearbook 2020.

DJIBOUTI-MONEY SUPPLY

The Economist Group: Economist Intelligence Unit (EIU), 900 3rd Ave., 16th Fl., New York, NY, 10022, USA, (212) 541-0500, americas@eiu.com, https://www.eiu.com; Djibouti Country Report.

Routledge - Taylor & Francis Group, 6000 Broken Sound Pkwy. NW, Ste. 300, Boca Raton, FL, 33487, USA, (800) 634-1420, (800) 634-7064, orders@taylorandfrancis.com, https://www.routledge.com/; The Europa World Year Book 2022.

The World Bank, 1818 H St. NW, Washington, DC, 20433, USA, (202) 473-1000, (202) 477-6391, eds03@worldbank.org, https://www.worldbank.org/; Djibouti (report).

DJIBOUTI-MORTALITY

United Nations Statistics Division (UNSD), United Nations Plz., New York, NY, 10017, USA, (800) 253-9646, (212) 963-9851, statistics@un.org, https://unstats.un.org; Millennium Development Goal Indicators; Statistical Yearbook of the United Nations 2021; and World Statistics Pocketbook 2021.

World Health Organization (WHO), Ave. Appia 20, Geneva, CH-1211, SWI, (202) 974-3000 (Telephone in U.S.), publications@who.int, https://www.who.int/; Global Health Observatory (GHO).

DJIBOUTI-NUTRITION

United Nations Food and Agricultural Organization (FAO), 2121 K St., Ste. 800B, Washington, DC, 20037, USA, (202) 653-2400 (Dial from U.S.), (202) 653-5760 (Fax from U.S.), fao-hq@fao.org, https://www.fao.org; The State of Food and Agriculture (SOFA) 2022.

United Nations Statistics Division (UNSD), United Nations Plz., New York, NY, 10017, USA, (800) 253-9646, (212) 963-9851, statistics@un.org, https://unstats.un.org; Millennium Development Goal Indicators.

DJIBOUTI-PAPER

See DJIBOUTI-FORESTS AND FORESTRY

DJIBOUTI-PESTICIDES

United Nations Food and Agricultural Organization (FAO), 2121 K St., Ste. 800B, Washington, DC, 20037, USA, (202) 653-2400 (Dial from U.S.), (202) 653-5760 (Fax from U.S.), fao-hq@fao.org, https://www.fao.org; The State of Food and Agriculture (SOFA) 2022.

DJIBOUTI-PETROLEUM INDUSTRY AND TRADE

United Nations Food and Agricultural Organization (FAO), 2121 K St., Ste. 800B, Washington, DC, 20037, USA, (202) 653-2400 (Dial from U.S.), (202) 653-5760 (Fax from U.S.), fao-hq@fao.org, https://www.fao.org; The State of Food and Agriculture (SOFA) 2022.

DJIBOUTI-POPULATION

African Development Bank Group (AfDB), Avenue Joseph Anoma, 01 BP 1387, Abidjan, 01, COT, https://www.afdb.org; The AfDB Statistics Pocketbook 2019; Africa Economic Brief - COVID-19 Pandemic Potential Risks for Trade and Trade Finance in Africa; The African Statistical Journal; and Gender, Poverty and Environmental Indicators on African Countries 2019.

Central Intelligence Agency (CIA), Office of Public Affairs, Washington, DC, 20505, USA, (703) 482-0623, https://www.cia.gov; The World Factbook.

The Economist Group: Economist Intelligence Unit (EIU), 900 3rd Ave., 16th Fl., New York, NY, 10022, USA, (212) 541-0500, americas@eiu.com, https://www.eiu.com; Djibouti Country Report.

European Commission, Eurostat, Luxembourg, 2920, LUX, https://ec.europa.eu/eurostat/; EU in the World 2020.

Infoplease, c/o Sandbox Networks, Inc., 1 Lincoln St., 24th Fl., Boston, MA, 02111, USA, https://www.infoplease.com; Countries of the World.

International Labour Organization (ILO), 4 Rte. des Morillons, Geneva, CH-1211, SWI, ilo@ilo.org, https://www.ilo.org; NORMLEX Information System on International Labour Standards.

Palgrave Macmillan, 1 New York Plaza, Ste. 4500, New York, NY, 10004-1562, USA, (800) 777-4643, orders@palgrave.com, https://www.palgrave.com/us; The Statesman's Yearbook, 2023.

Routledge - Taylor & Francis Group, 6000 Broken Sound Pkwy. NW, Ste. 300, Boca Raton, FL, 33487, USA, (800) 634-1420, (800) 634-7064, orders@taylorandfrancis.com, https://www.routledge.com/; The Europa World Year Book 2022.

UK Data Service, University of Essex, Wivenhoe Park, Colchester, Essex, CO4 3SQ, GBR, https://ukdataservice.ac.uk/; International Aggregate Data.

United Nations Department of Economic and Social Affairs (DESA), Population Division, 2 United Nations Plz., Rm. DC2-1950, New York, NY, 10017, USA, (212) 963-3209, (212) 963-2147, population@un.org, https://www.un.org/development/desa/pd/; Revision of World Urbanization Prospects and World Population Ageing 2020 Highlights.

United Nations Development Programme (UNDP), One United Nations Plz., New York, NY, 10017, USA, (212) 906-5000, (212) 906-5001, https://www.undp.org; Human Development Report 2021-2022.

United Nations Statistics Division (UNSD), United Nations Plz., New York, NY, 10017, USA, (800) 253-9646, (212) 963-9851, statistics@un.org, https://unstats.un.org; Statistical Yearbook of the United Nations 2021 and World Statistics Pocketbook 2021.

The World Bank, 1818 H St. NW, Washington, DC, 20433, USA, (202) 473-1000, (202) 477-6391, eds03@worldbank.org, https://www.worldbank.org/; Djibouti (report) and The Global Findex Database 2021.

DJIBOUTI-POPULATION DENSITY

African Development Bank Group (AfDB), Avenue Joseph Anoma, 01 BP 1387, Abidjan, 01, COT, https://www.afdb.org; The AfDB Statistics Pocketbook 2019.

Central Intelligence Agency (CIA), Office of Public Affairs, Washington, DC, 20505, USA, (703) 482-0623, https://www.cia.gov; The World Factbook.

Palgrave Macmillan, 1 New York Plaza, Ste. 4500, New York, NY, 10004-1562, USA, (800) 777-4643, orders@palgrave.com, https://www.palgrave.com/us; The Statesman's Yearbook, 2023.

Routledge - Taylor & Francis Group, 6000 Broken Sound Pkwy. NW, Ste. 300, Boca Raton, FL, 33487, USA, (800) 634-1420, (800) 634-7064, orders@taylorandfrancis.com, https://www.routledge.com/; The Europa World Year Book 2022.

The World Bank, 1818 H St. NW, Washington, DC, 20433, USA, (202) 473-1000, (202) 477-6391, eds03@worldbank.org, https://www.worldbank.org/; Djibouti (report).

DJIBOUTI-POWER RESOURCES

Euromonitor International, Inc., 1 N Dearborn St., Ste. 1700, Chicago, IL, 60602, USA, (312) 922-1115, (312) 922-1157, info-usa@euromonitor.com, https://www.euromonitor.com/; Geographies.

Palgrave Macmillan, 1 New York Plaza, Ste. 4500, New York, NY, 10004-1562, USA, (800) 777-4643, orders@palgrave.com, https://www.palgrave.com/us; The Statesman's Yearbook, 2023.

United Nations Economic Commission for Africa (UNECA), PO Box 3001, Addis Ababa, ETH, ecainfo@uneca.org, https://www.uneca.org/; African Statistical Yearbook 2020.

United Nations Food and Agricultural Organization (FAO), 2121 K St., Ste. 800B, Washington, DC, 20037, USA, (202) 653-2400 (Dial from U.S.), (202) 653-5760 (Fax from U.S.), fao-hq@fao.org, https://www.fao.org; The State of Food and Agriculture (SOFA) 2022.

United Nations Statistics Division (UNSD), United Nations Plz., New York, NY, 10017, USA, (800) 253-9646, (212) 963-9851, statistics@un.org, https://unstats.un.org; Statistical Yearbook of the United Nations 2021 and World Statistics Pocketbook 2021.

DJIBOUTI-PRICES

Euromonitor International, Inc., 1 N Dearborn St., Ste. 1700, Chicago, IL, 60602, USA, (312) 922-1115, (312) 922-1157, info-usa@euromonitor.com, https://www.euromonitor.com/; Geographies.

United Nations Economic Commission for Africa (UNECA), PO Box 3001, Addis Ababa, ETH, ecainfo@uneca.org, https://www.uneca.org/; African Statistical Yearbook 2020.

The World Bank, 1818 H St. NW, Washington, DC, 20433, USA, (202) 473-1000, (202) 477-6391, eds03@worldbank.org, https://www.worldbank.org/; Djibouti (report).

DJIBOUTI-PUBLIC HEALTH

African Development Bank Group (AfDB), Avenue Joseph Anoma, 01 BP 1387, Abidjan, 01, COT, https://www.afdb.org; The AfDB Statistics Pocketbook 2019.

Euromonitor International, Inc., 1 N Dearborn St., Ste. 1700, Chicago, IL, 60602, USA, (312) 922-1115, (312) 922-1157, info-usa@euromonitor.com, https://www.euromonitor.com/; Geographies.

Organisation of Islamic Cooperation (OIC), Statistical, Economic and Social Research and Training Centre for Islamic Countries (SESRIC), Kudus Cad. No. 9, Diplomatik Site, Ankara, 06450, TUR, statistics@sesric.org, https://www.sesric.org/; OIC Statistics (OICStat) Database.

Palgrave Macmillan, 1 New York Plaza, Ste. 4500, New York, NY, 10004-1562, USA, (800) 777-4643, orders@palgrave.com, https://www.palgrave.com/us; The Statesman's Yearbook, 2023.

U.S. Census Bureau, 4600 Silver Hill Rd., Washington, DC, 20233, USA, (301) 763-4636, (800) 923-8282, https://www.census.gov; HIV/AIDS Surveillance Data Base.

United Nations Department of Economic and Social Affairs (DESA), Population Division, 2 United Nations Plz., Rm. DC2-1950, New York, NY, 10017, USA, (212) 963-3209, (212) 963-2147, population@un.org, https://www.un.org/development/desa/pd/; World Fertility Data 2019.

United Nations Development Programme (UNDP), One United Nations Plz., New York, NY, 10017, USA, (212) 906-5000, (212) 906-5001, https://www.undp.org; Human Development Report 2021-2022.

United Nations Economic Commission for Africa (UNECA), PO Box 3001, Addis Ababa, ETH, ecainfo@uneca.org, https://www.uneca.org/; African Statistical Yearbook 2020.

United Nations Statistics Division (UNSD), United Nations Plz., New York, NY, 10017, USA, (800) 253-9646, (212) 963-9851, statistics@un.org, https://unstats.un.org; Millennium Development Goal Indicators and Statistical Yearbook of the United Nations 2021.

The World Bank, 1818 H St. NW, Washington, DC, 20433, USA, (202) 473-1000, (202) 477-6391, eds03@worldbank.org, https://www.worldbank.org/; Djibouti (report).

World Health Organization (WHO), Ave. Appia 20, Geneva, CH-1211, SWI, (202) 974-3000 (Telephone in U.S.), publications@who.int, https://www.who.int/; Global Health Observatory (GHO).

DJIBOUTI-RAILROADS

Palgrave Macmillan, 1 New York Plaza, Ste. 4500, New York, NY, 10004-1562, USA, (800) 777-4643, orders@palgrave.com, https://www.palgrave.com/us; The Statesman's Yearbook, 2023.

Routledge - Taylor & Francis Group, 6000 Broken Sound Pkwy. NW, Ste. 300, Boca Raton, FL, 33487, USA, (800) 634-1420, (800) 634-7064, orders@taylorandfrancis.com, https://www.routledge.com/; The Europa World Year Book 2022.

United Nations Economic Commission for Africa (UNECA), PO Box 3001, Addis Ababa, ETH, ecainfo@uneca.org, https://www.uneca.org/; African Statistical Yearbook 2020.

DJIBOUTI-RELIGION

Central Intelligence Agency (CIA), Office of Public Affairs, Washington, DC, 20505, USA, (703) 482-0623, https://www.cia.gov; The World Factbook.

Palgrave Macmillan, 1 New York Plaza, Ste. 4500, New York, NY, 10004-1562, USA, (800) 777-4643, orders@palgrave.com, https://www.palgrave.com/us; The Statesman's Yearbook, 2023.

DJIBOUTI-RETAIL TRADE

Euromonitor International, Inc., 1 N Dearborn St., Ste. 1700, Chicago, IL, 60602, USA, (312) 922-1115, (312) 922-1157, info-usa@euromonitor.com, https://www.euromonitor.com/; Geographies.

DJIBOUTI-ROADS

United Nations Economic Commission for Africa (UNECA), PO Box 3001, Addis Ababa, ETH, ecainfo@uneca.org, https://www.uneca.org/; African Statistical Yearbook 2020.

DJIBOUTI-SHIPPING

Routledge - Taylor & Francis Group, 6000 Broken Sound Pkwy. NW, Ste. 300, Boca Raton, FL, 33487, USA, (800) 634-1420, (800) 634-7064, orders@taylorandfrancis.com, https://www.routledge.com/; The Europa World Year Book 2022.

United Nations Economic Commission for Africa (UNECA), PO Box 3001, Addis Ababa, ETH, ecainfo@uneca.org, https://www.uneca.org/; African Statistical Yearbook 2020.

United Nations Statistics Division (UNSD), United Nations Plz., New York, NY, 10017, USA, (800) 253-9646, (212) 963-9851, statistics@un.org, https://unstats.un.org; Statistical Yearbook of the United Nations 2021.

DJIBOUTI-TELEPHONE

Palgrave Macmillan, 1 New York Plaza, Ste. 4500, New York, NY, 10004-1562, USA, (800) 777-4643, orders@palgrave.com, https://www.palgrave.com/us; The Statesman's Yearbook, 2023.

Routledge - Taylor & Francis Group, 6000 Broken Sound Pkwy. NW, Ste. 300, Boca Raton, FL, 33487, USA, (800) 634-1420, (800) 634-7064, orders@taylorandfrancis.com, https://www.routledge.com/; The Europa World Year Book 2022.

United Nations Statistics Division (UNSD), United Nations Plz., New York, NY, 10017, USA, (800) 253-9646, (212) 963-9851, statistics@un.org, https://unstats.un.org; World Statistics Pocketbook 2021.

DJIBOUTI-TOURISM

Euromonitor International, Inc., 1 N Dearborn St., Ste. 1700, Chicago, IL, 60602, USA, (312) 922-1115, (312) 922-1157, info-usa@euromonitor.com, https://www.euromonitor.com/; Geographies.

Organisation of Islamic Cooperation (OIC), Statistical, Economic and Social Research and Training Centre for Islamic Countries (SESRIC), Kudus Cad. No. 9, Diplomatik Site, Ankara, 06450, TUR, statistics@sesric.org, https://www.sesric.org/; International Tourism in the OIC Countries: Prospects and Challenges, 2020 and OIC Statistics (OICStat) Database.

Palgrave Macmillan, 1 New York Plaza, Ste. 4500, New York, NY, 10004-1562, USA, (800) 777-4643, orders@palgrave.com, https://www.palgrave.com/us; The Statesman's Yearbook, 2023.

Routledge - Taylor & Francis Group, 6000 Broken Sound Pkwy. NW, Ste. 300, Boca Raton, FL, 33487, USA, (800) 634-1420, (800) 634-7064, orders@taylorandfrancis.com, https://www.routledge.com/; The Europa World Year Book 2022.

United Nations Economic Commission for Africa (UNECA), PO Box 3001, Addis Ababa, ETH, ecainfo@uneca.org, https://www.uneca.org/; African Statistical Yearbook 2020.

The World Bank, 1818 H St. NW, Washington, DC, 20433, USA, (202) 473-1000, (202) 477-6391, eds03@worldbank.org, https://www.worldbank.org/; Djibouti (report).

DJIBOUTI-TRADE

See DJIBOUTI-INTERNATIONAL TRADE

DJIBOUTI-TRANSPORTATION

Central Intelligence Agency (CIA), Office of Public Affairs, Washington, DC, 20505, USA, (703) 482-0623, https://www.cia.gov; The World Factbook.

Euromonitor International, Inc., 1 N Dearborn St., Ste. 1700, Chicago, IL, 60602, USA, (312) 922-1115, (312) 922-1157, info-usa@euromonitor.com, https://www.euromonitor.com/; Geographies.

Organisation of Islamic Cooperation (OIC), Statistical, Economic and Social Research and Training Centre for Islamic Countries (SESRIC), Kudus Cad. No. 9, Diplomatik Site, Ankara, 06450, TUR, statistics@sesric.org, https://www.sesric.org/; OIC Statistics (OICStat) Database.

Palgrave Macmillan, 1 New York Plaza, Ste. 4500, New York, NY, 10004-1562, USA, (800) 777-4643, orders@palgrave.com, https://www.palgrave.com/us; The Statesman's Yearbook, 2023.

Routledge - Taylor & Francis Group, 6000 Broken Sound Pkwy. NW, Ste. 300, Boca Raton, FL, 33487, USA, (800) 634-1420, (800) 634-7064, orders@taylorandfrancis.com, https://www.routledge.com/; The Europa World Year Book 2022.

United Nations Economic Commission for Africa (UNECA), PO Box 3001, Addis Ababa, ETH, ecainfo@uneca.org, https://www.uneca.org/; African Statistical Yearbook 2020.

The World Bank, 1818 H St. NW, Washington, DC, 20433, USA, (202) 473-1000, (202) 477-6391, eds03@worldbank.org, https://www.worldbank.org/; Djibouti (report).

DJIBOUTI-UNEMPLOYMENT

International Labour Organization (ILO), 4 Rte. des Morillons, Geneva, CH-1211, SWI, ilo@ilo.org, https://www.ilo.org; NORMLEX Information System on International Labour Standards.

DJIBOUTI-VITAL STATISTICS

Palgrave Macmillan, 1 New York Plaza, Ste. 4500, New York, NY, 10004-1562, USA, (800) 777-4643, orders@palgrave.com, https://www.palgrave.com/us; The Statesman's Yearbook, 2023.

U.S. Census Bureau, 4600 Silver Hill Rd., Washington, DC, 20233, USA, (301) 763-4636, (800) 923-8282, https://www.census.gov; HIV/AIDS Surveillance Data Base.

United Nations Department of Economic and Social Affairs (DESA), Population Division, 2 United Nations Plz., Rm. DC2-1950, New York, NY, 10017, USA, (212) 963-3209, (212) 963-2147, population@un.org, https://www.un.org/development/desa/pd/; World Contraceptive Use 2021: Estimates and Projections of Family Planning Indicators and World Marriage Data 2019.

United Nations Statistics Division (UNSD), United Nations Plz., New York, NY, 10017, USA, (800) 253-9646, (212) 963-9851, statistics@un.org, https://unstats.un.org; Statistical Yearbook of the United Nations 2021.

DJIBOUTI-WAGES

International Labour Organization (ILO), 4 Rte. des Morillons, Geneva, CH-1211, SWI, ilo@ilo.org, https://www.ilo.org; NORMLEX Information System on International Labour Standards.

The World Bank, 1818 H St. NW, Washington, DC, 20433, USA, (202) 473-1000, (202) 477-6391, eds03@worldbank.org, https://www.worldbank.org/; Djibouti (report).

DOCTORS, M.D.s

See PHYSICIANS

DOGS-OWNERSHIP

American Humane, 1400 16th St. NW, Ste. 360, Washington, DC, 20036, USA, (800) 227-4645, info@americanhumane.org, https://www.americanhumane.org/; unpublished data.

DOGS-RACING

Association of Racing Commissioners International (ARCI), 2365 Harrodsburg Rd., Ste. B-450, Lexington, KY, 40504, USA, (859) 224-7070, info@arci.com, https://www.arci.com/; ARCI Online Database.

DOLPHINS

The Whale Sanctuary Project, 4100 Kanab Canyon Rd., Kanab, UT, 84741, USA, info@whalesanctuaryproject.org, https://whalesanctuaryproject.org; unpublished data.

DOMESTIC INTELLIGENCE

Syria Justice and Accountability Centre (SJAC), 1612 K St. NW, Ste. 400, Washington, DC, 20006, USA, (202) 791-0426, info@syriaaccountability.org, https://syriaaccountability.org/; Walls Have Ears: An Analysis of Classified Syrian Security Sector Documents.

DOMESTIC SERVICE

See HOUSEHOLD WORKERS

DOMESTIC TERRORISM

Center for Strategic & International Studies (CSIS), 1616 Rhode Island Ave. NW, Washington, DC, 20036, USA, (202) 887-0200, (202) 775-3199, https://www.csis.org; The Military, Police, and the Rise of Terrorism in the United States and The War Comes Home: The Evolution of Domestic Terrorism in the United States.

Institute for Strategic Dialogue (ISD), PO Box 75769, London, SW1P 9ER, GBR, info@isdglobal.org, https://www.isdglobal.org/; Inspiration and Influence: Discussions of the US Military in Extreme Right-Wing Telegram Channels.

U.S. Department of Homeland Security (DHS), 2707 Martin Luther King Jr. Ave. SE, Washington, DC, 20528-0525, USA, (202) 282-8000, https://www.dhs.gov; 2020 Homeland Threat Assessment.

U.S. Department of Justice (DOJ), Federal Bureau of Investigation (FBI), 935 Pennsylvania Ave. NW, Washington, DC, 20535-0001, USA, (202) 324-3000, https://www.fbi.gov/; A Study of Pre-Attack Behaviors of Active Shooters in the United States Between 2000 and 2013.

U.S. Library of Congress (LOC), Congressional Research Service (CRS), 101 Independence Ave. SE, Washington, DC, 20540, USA, (202) 707-5000, https://www.loc.gov/crsinfo/; Terrorism Risk Insurance: Overview and Issue Analysis.

University of Maryland, National Consortium for the Study of Terrorism and Responses to Terrorism (START), PO Box 266, 5245 Greenbelt Rd., College Park, MD, 20740, USA, (301) 405-6600, (301) 314-1980, infostart@start.umd.edu, https://www.start.umd.edu; American Deaths in Terrorist Attacks, 1995-2019; Anti-Muslim Terrorism in the United States; Global Terrorism Overview: Terrorism in 2019; and Profiles of Individual Radicalization in the United States - PIRUS (Keshif).

The Washington Post, 1301 K St. NW, Washington, DC, 20071, USA, (800) 477-4679, https://www.washingtonpost.com/; The Rise of Domestic Extremism in America.

DOMESTIC VIOLENCE

See FAMILY VIOLENCE and INTIMATE PARTNER VIOLENCE

DOMINICA-NATIONAL STATISTICAL OFFICE

Central Statistical Office of Dominica, Ministry of Finance, Financial Centre, Kennedy Ave., Roseau, DMA, (767) 266-3400 (Dial from U.S.), (767) 266-3407 (Dial from U.S.), cso@dominica.gov.dm, https://stats.gov.dm/; National Data Reports (Dominica).

DOMINICA-AGRICULTURE

Euromonitor International, Inc., 1 N Dearborn St., Ste. 1700, Chicago, IL, 60602, USA, (312) 922-1115, (312) 922-1157, info-usa@euromonitor.com, https://www.euromonitor.com/; Geographies.

Palgrave Macmillan, 1 New York Plaza, Ste. 4500, New York, NY, 10004-1562, USA, (800) 777-4643, orders@palgrave.com, https://www.palgrave.com/us; The Statesman's Yearbook, 2023.

Routledge - Taylor & Francis Group, 6000 Broken Sound Pkwy. NW, Ste. 300, Boca Raton, FL, 33487, USA, (800) 634-1420, (800) 634-7064, orders@taylorandfrancis.com, https://www.routledge.com/; The Europa World Year Book 2022.

United Nations Food and Agricultural Organization (FAO), 2121 K St., Ste. 800B, Washington, DC, 20037, USA, (202) 653-2400 (Dial from U.S.), (202) 653-5760 (Fax from U.S.), fao-hq@fao.org, https://www.fao.org; AQUASTAT and The State of Food and Agriculture (SOFA) 2022.

United Nations Statistics Division (UNSD), United Nations Plz., New York, NY, 10017, USA, (800) 253-9646, (212) 963-9851, statistics@un.org, https://unstats.un.org; Statistical Yearbook of the United Nations 2021.

The World Bank, 1818 H St. NW, Washington, DC, 20433, USA, (202) 473-1000, (202) 477-6391, eds03@worldbank.org, https://www.worldbank.org/; World Development Indicators (WDI) 2022.

DOMINICA-AIRLINES

Routledge - Taylor & Francis Group, 6000 Broken Sound Pkwy. NW, Ste. 300, Boca Raton, FL, 33487, USA, (800) 634-1420, (800) 634-7064, orders@taylorandfrancis.com, https://www.routledge.com/; The Europa World Year Book 2022.

DOMINICA-ARMED FORCES

Central Intelligence Agency (CIA), Office of Public Affairs, Washington, DC, 20505, USA, (703) 482-0623, https://www.cia.gov; The World Factbook.

Stockholm International Peace Research Institute (SIPRI), Signalistgatan 9, Stockholm, SE 169 72, SWE, https://www.sipri.org/; SIPRI Arms Transfers Database and SIPRI Military Expenditure Database.

DOMINICA-BALANCE OF PAYMENTS

Routledge - Taylor & Francis Group, 6000 Broken Sound Pkwy. NW, Ste. 300, Boca Raton, FL, 33487, USA, (800) 634-1420, (800) 634-7064, orders@taylorandfrancis.com, https://www.routledge.com/; The Europa World Year Book 2022.

United Nations Conference on Trade and Development (UNCTAD), Palais des Nations, Geneva, 1211, SWI, (212) 963-6896, unctadinfo@unctad.org, https://unctad.org; Handbook of Statistics 2021.

United Nations Economic Commission for Latin America and the Caribbean (ECLAC), Casilla 179-D, Santiago, 7630412, CHL, (202) 596-3713, prensa@cepal.org, https://www.cepal.org/en; Economic Survey of Latin America and the Caribbean 2021: Labour Dynamics and Employment Policies for Sustainable and Inclusive Recovery Beyond the COVID-19 Crisis.

The World Bank, 1818 H St. NW, Washington, DC, 20433, USA, (202) 473-1000, (202) 477-6391, eds03@worldbank.org, https://www.worldbank.org/; World Development Indicators (WDI) 2022.

DOMINICA-BANKS AND BANKING

Euromonitor International, Inc., 1 N Dearborn St., Ste. 1700, Chicago, IL, 60602, USA, (312) 922-1115, (312) 922-1157, info-usa@euromonitor.com, https://www.euromonitor.com/; Geographies.

Routledge - Taylor & Francis Group, 6000 Broken Sound Pkwy. NW, Ste. 300, Boca Raton, FL, 33487, USA, (800) 634-1420, (800) 634-7064, orders@taylorandfrancis.com, https://www.routledge.com/; The Europa World Year Book 2022.

DOMINICA-BROADCASTING

Central Intelligence Agency (CIA), Office of Public Affairs, Washington, DC, 20505, USA, (703) 482-0623, https://www.cia.gov; The World Factbook.

Euromonitor International, Inc., 1 N Dearborn St., Ste. 1700, Chicago, IL, 60602, USA, (312) 922-1115, (312) 922-1157, info-usa@euromonitor.com, https://www.euromonitor.com/; Geographies.

Palgrave Macmillan, 1 New York Plaza, Ste. 4500, New York, NY, 10004-1562, USA, (800) 777-4643, orders@palgrave.com, https://www.palgrave.com/us; The Statesman's Yearbook, 2023.

WRTH Publications Limited, PO Box 290, Oxford, OX2 7FT, GBR, sales@wrth.com, https://www.wrth.com; World Radio TV Handbook 2023.

DOMINICA-BUDGET

Central Intelligence Agency (CIA), Office of Public Affairs, Washington, DC, 20505, USA, (703) 482-0623, https://www.cia.gov; The World Factbook.

DOMINICA-CHILDBIRTH-STATISTICS

The World Bank, 1818 H St. NW, Washington, DC, 20433, USA, (202) 473-1000, (202) 477-6391, eds03@worldbank.org, https://www.worldbank.org/; World Development Indicators (WDI) 2022.

DOMINICA-CLIMATE

Palgrave Macmillan, 1 New York Plaza, Ste. 4500, New York, NY, 10004-1562, USA, (800) 777-4643, orders@palgrave.com, https://www.palgrave.com/us; The Statesman's Yearbook, 2023.

DOMINICA-COCOA PRODUCTION

See DOMINICA-CROPS

DOMINICA-COMMERCE

Palgrave Macmillan, 1 New York Plaza, Ste. 4500, New York, NY, 10004-1562, USA, (800) 777-4643, orders@palgrave.com, https://www.palgrave.com/us; The Statesman's Yearbook, 2023.

UK Data Service, University of Essex, Wivenhoe Park, Colchester, Essex, CO4 3SQ, GBR, https://ukdataservice.ac.uk/; International Aggregate Data.

DOMINICA-COMMODITY EXCHANGES

Barchart, 209 W Jackson Blvd., 2nd Fl., Chicago, IL, 60606, USA, (877) 247-4394, commodities@barchart.com, https://www.barchart.

com/cmdty; The cmdty Yearbook 2023; cmdtyStats: Commodity Statistics and Fundamental Data; cmdtyView: Commodity Index; and Commodity Data and Prices.

International Monetary Fund (IMF), 700 19th St. NW, Washington, DC, 20431, USA, (202) 623-7000, (202) 623-4661, publications@imf.org, https://www.imf.org; IMF Primary Commodity Prices.

DOMINICA-CONSUMER PRICE INDEXES

Routledge - Taylor & Francis Group, 6000 Broken Sound Pkwy. NW, Ste. 300, Boca Raton, FL, 33487, USA, (800) 634-1420, (800) 634-7064, orders@taylorandfrancis.com, https://www.routledge.com/; The Europa World Year Book 2022.

DOMINICA-CORN INDUSTRY

See DOMINICA-CROPS

DOMINICA-CROPS

Palgrave Macmillan, 1 New York Plaza, Ste. 4500, New York, NY, 10004-1562, USA, (800) 777-4643, orders@palgrave.com, https://www.palgrave.com/us; The Statesman's Yearbook, 2023.

United Nations Food and Agricultural Organization (FAO), 2121 K St., Ste. 800B, Washington, DC, 20037, USA, (202) 653-2400 (Dial from U.S.), (202) 653-5760 (Fax from U.S.), fao-hq@fao.org, https://www.fao.org; The State of Food and Agriculture (SOFA) 2022.

United Nations Statistics Division (UNSD), United Nations Plz., New York, NY, 10017, USA, (800) 253-9646, (212) 963-9851, statistics@un.org, https://unstats.un.org; Statistical Yearbook of the United Nations 2021.

DOMINICA-DAIRY PROCESSING

United Nations Food and Agricultural Organization (FAO), 2121 K St., Ste. 800B, Washington, DC, 20037, USA, (202) 653-2400 (Dial from U.S.), (202) 653-5760 (Fax from U.S.), fao-hq@fao.org, https://www.fao.org; The State of Food and Agriculture (SOFA) 2022.

DOMINICA-DEBTS, EXTERNAL

United Nations Economic Commission for Latin America and the Caribbean (ECLAC), Casilla 179-D, Santiago, 7630412, CHL, (202) 596-3713, prensa@cepal.org, https://www.cepal.org/en; Economic Survey of Latin America and the Caribbean 2021: Labour Dynamics and Employment Policies for Sustainable and Inclusive Recovery Beyond the COVID-19 Crisis.

The World Bank, 1818 H St. NW, Washington, DC, 20433, USA, (202) 473-1000, (202) 477-6391, eds03@worldbank.org, https://www.worldbank.org/; Global Financial Development Report 2019-2020: Bank Regulation and Supervision a Decade after the Global Financial Crisis and World Development Indicators (WDI) 2022.

DOMINICA-DEFENSE EXPENDITURES

See DOMINICA-ARMED FORCES

DOMINICA-ECONOMIC CONDITIONS

Bernan Press, 15250 NBN Way, Bldg. C, Blue Ridge Summit, PA, 17214, USA, (301) 459-2255, (800) 865-3457, (800) 865-3450, customercare@bernan.com, https://rowman.com/Page/Bernan; World Economic Outlook, April 2022.

Central Intelligence Agency (CIA), Office of Public Affairs, Washington, DC, 20505, USA, (703) 482-0623, https://www.cia.gov; The World Factbook.

Euromonitor International, Inc., 1 N Dearborn St., Ste. 1700, Chicago, IL, 60602, USA, (312) 922-1115, (312) 922-1157, info-usa@euromonitor.com, https://www.euromonitor.com/; Geographies.

International Monetary Fund (IMF), 700 19th St. NW, Washington, DC, 20431, USA, (202) 623-7000, (202) 623-4661, publications@imf.org, https://www.imf.org; IMF Data and World Economic Outlook.

Palgrave Macmillan, 1 New York Plaza, Ste. 4500, New York, NY, 10004-1562, USA, (800) 777-4643, orders@palgrave.com, https://www.palgrave.com/us; The Statesman's Yearbook, 2023.

Routledge - Taylor & Francis Group, 6000 Broken Sound Pkwy. NW, Ste. 300, Boca Raton, FL, 33487, USA, (800) 634-1420, (800) 634-7064, orders@taylorandfrancis.com, https://www.routledge.com/; The Europa World Year Book 2022.

United Nations Economic Commission for Latin America and the Caribbean (ECLAC), Casilla 179-D, Santiago, 7630412, CHL, (202) 596-3713, prensa@cepal.org, https://www.cepal.org/en; CEPALSTAT; Economic Survey of Latin America and the Caribbean 2021: Labour Dynamics and Employment Policies for Sustainable and Inclusive Recovery Beyond the COVID-19 Crisis; Foreign Direct Investment in Latin America and the Caribbean 2022; and Social Panorama of Latin America and the Caribbean 2022: Transforming Education as a Basis for Sustainable Development.

United Nations Statistics Division (UNSD), United Nations Plz., New York, NY, 10017, USA, (800) 253-9646, (212) 963-9851, statistics@un.org, https://unstats.un.org; World Statistics Pocketbook 2021.

The World Bank, 1818 H St. NW, Washington, DC, 20433, USA, (202) 473-1000, (202) 477-6391, eds03@worldbank.org, https://www.worldbank.org/; Caribbean (report); Global Economic Monitor (GEM); Global Economic Prospects, June 2022; and The Global Findex Database 2021.

DOMINICA-EDUCATION

Infoplease, c/o Sandbox Networks, Inc., 1 Lincoln St., 24th Fl., Boston, MA, 02111, USA, https://www.infoplease.com; Countries of the World.

Palgrave Macmillan, 1 New York Plaza, Ste. 4500, New York, NY, 10004-1562, USA, (800) 777-4643, orders@palgrave.com, https://www.palgrave.com/us; The Statesman's Yearbook, 2023.

Routledge - Taylor & Francis Group, 6000 Broken Sound Pkwy. NW, Ste. 300, Boca Raton, FL, 33487, USA, (800) 634-1420, (800) 634-7064, orders@taylorandfrancis.com, https://www.routledge.com/; The Europa World Year Book 2022.

UNESCO Institute for Statistics, C.P 250 Succursale H, Montreal, QC, H3G 2K8, CAN, (514) 343-6880 (Dial from U.S.), (514) 343-5740 (Fax from U.S.), uis.publications@unesco.org, http://uis.unesco.org/; Literacy and UIS.Stat.

United Nations Statistics Division (UNSD), United Nations Plz., New York, NY, 10017, USA, (800) 253-9646, (212) 963-9851, statistics@un.org, https://unstats.un.org; Millennium Development Goal Indicators.

The World Bank, 1818 H St. NW, Washington, DC, 20433, USA, (202) 473-1000, (202) 477-6391, eds03@worldbank.org, https://www.worldbank.org/; Caribbean (report) and World Development Indicators (WDI) 2022.

DOMINICA-EMPLOYMENT

International Labour Organization (ILO), 4 Rte. des Morillons, Geneva, CH-1211, SWI, ilo@ilo.org, https://www.ilo.org; NORMLEX Information System on International Labour Standards.

UK Data Service, University of Essex, Wivenhoe Park, Colchester, Essex, CO4 3SQ, GBR, https://ukdataservice.ac.uk/; International Aggregate Data.

DOMINICA-ENVIRONMENTAL CONDITIONS

DSI Data Service & Information, Xantener Strasse 51a, Rheinberg, D-47495, GER, dsi@dsidata.com, https://www.dsidata.com/; Global Environmental Database.

United Nations Economic Commission for Latin America and the Caribbean (ECLAC), Casilla 179-D, Santiago, 7630412, CHL, (202) 596-3713, prensa@cepal.org, https://www.cepal.org/en; CEPALSTAT.

United Nations Statistics Division (UNSD), United Nations Plz., New York, NY, 10017, USA, (800) 253-9646, (212) 963-9851, statistics@un.org, https://unstats.un.org; World Statistics Pocketbook 2021.

The World Bank, 1818 H St. NW, Washington, DC, 20433, USA, (202) 473-1000, (202) 477-6391, eds03@worldbank.org, https://www.worldbank.org/; Caribbean (report).

DOMINICA-EXCISE TAX

Routledge - Taylor & Francis Group, 6000 Broken Sound Pkwy. NW, Ste. 300, Boca Raton, FL, 33487, USA, (800) 634-1420, (800) 634-7064, orders@taylorandfrancis.com, https://www.routledge.com/; The Europa World Year Book 2022.

United Nations Statistics Division (UNSD), United Nations Plz., New York, NY, 10017, USA, (800) 253-9646, (212) 963-9851, statistics@un.org, https://unstats.un.org; World Statistics Pocketbook 2021.

DOMINICA-EXPORTS

Central Intelligence Agency (CIA), Office of Public Affairs, Washington, DC, 20505, USA, (703) 482-0623, https://www.cia.gov; The World Factbook.

United Nations Conference on Trade and Development (UNCTAD), Palais des Nations, Geneva, 1211, SWI, (212) 963-6896, unctadinfo@unctad.org, https://unctad.org; Handbook of Statistics 2021.

DOMINICA-FERTILITY, HUMAN

Central Intelligence Agency (CIA), Office of Public Affairs, Washington, DC, 20505, USA, (703) 482-0623, https://www.cia.gov; The World Factbook.

DOMINICA-FERTILIZER INDUSTRY

United Nations Food and Agricultural Organization (FAO), 2121 K St., Ste. 800B, Washington, DC, 20037, USA, (202) 653-2400 (Dial from U.S.), (202) 653-5760 (Fax from U.S.), fao-hq@fao.org, https://www.fao.org; The State of Food and Agriculture (SOFA) 2022.

DOMINICA-FETAL MORTALITY

See DOMINICA-MORTALITY

DOMINICA-FINANCE

Stockholm International Peace Research Institute (SIPRI), Signalistgatan 9, Stockholm, SE 169 72, SWE, https://www.sipri.org/; SIPRI Arms Transfers Database and SIPRI Military Expenditure Database.

United Nations Statistics Division (UNSD), United Nations Plz., New York, NY, 10017, USA, (800) 253-9646, (212) 963-9851, statistics@un.org, https://unstats.un.org; Statistical Yearbook of the United Nations 2021.

The World Bank, 1818 H St. NW, Washington, DC, 20433, USA, (202) 473-1000, (202) 477-6391, eds03@worldbank.org, https://www.worldbank.org/; Caribbean (report).

DOMINICA-FINANCE, PUBLIC

Bernan Press, 15250 NBN Way, Bldg. C, Blue Ridge Summit, PA, 17214, USA, (301) 459-2255, (800) 865-3457, (800) 865-3450, customercare@bernan.com, https://rowman.com/Page/Bernan; National Accounts Statistics: Analysis of Main Aggregates 2020.

International Monetary Fund (IMF), 700 19th St. NW, Washington, DC, 20431, USA, (202) 623-7000, (202) 623-4661, publications@imf.org, https://www.imf.org; Regional Economic Outlook.

Palgrave Macmillan, 1 New York Plaza, Ste. 4500, New York, NY, 10004-1562, USA, (800) 777-4643, orders@palgrave.com, https://www.palgrave.com/us; The Statesman's Yearbook, 2023.

Routledge - Taylor & Francis Group, 6000 Broken Sound Pkwy. NW, Ste. 300, Boca Raton, FL, 33487, USA, (800) 634-1420, (800) 634-7064, orders@taylorandfrancis.com, https://www.routledge.com/; The Europa World Year Book 2022.

United Nations Statistics Division (UNSD), United Nations Plz., New York, NY, 10017, USA, (800) 253-9646, (212) 963-9851, statistics@un.org, https://

unstats.un.org; National Accounts Main Aggregates Database and National Accounts Statistics: Main Aggregates and Detailed Tables.

DOMINICA-FISHERIES

Routledge - Taylor & Francis Group, 6000 Broken Sound Pkwy. NW, Ste. 300, Boca Raton, FL, 33487, USA, (800) 634-1420, (800) 634-7064, orders@taylorandfrancis.com, https://www.routledge.com/; The Europa World Year Book 2022.

United Nations Food and Agricultural Organization (FAO), 2121 K St., Ste. 800B, Washington, DC, 20037, USA, (202) 653-2400 (Dial from U.S.), (202) 653-5760 (Fax from U.S.), fao-hq@fao.org, https://www.fao.org; FAO Yearbook of Fishery and Aquaculture Statistics 2019; Fishery Statistical Collections Global Capture Production; FishStatJ; and The State of Food and Agriculture (SOFA) 2022.

DOMINICA-FOOD

United Nations Food and Agricultural Organization (FAO), 2121 K St., Ste. 800B, Washington, DC, 20037, USA, (202) 653-2400 (Dial from U.S.), (202) 653-5760 (Fax from U.S.), fao-hq@fao.org, https://www.fao.org; The State of Food and Agriculture (SOFA) 2022.

DOMINICA-FORESTS AND FORESTRY

Routledge - Taylor & Francis Group, 6000 Broken Sound Pkwy. NW, Ste. 300, Boca Raton, FL, 33487, USA, (800) 634-1420, (800) 634-7064, orders@taylorandfrancis.com, https://www.routledge.com/; The Europa World Year Book 2022.

United Nations Food and Agricultural Organization (FAO), 2121 K St., Ste. 800B, Washington, DC, 20037, USA, (202) 653-2400 (Dial from U.S.), (202) 653-5760 (Fax from U.S.), fao-hq@fao.org, https://www.fao.org; FAO Yearbook of Forest Products 2019 and The State of Food and Agriculture (SOFA) 2022.

DOMINICA-GOLD INDUSTRY

The World Bank, 1818 H St. NW, Washington, DC, 20433, USA, (202) 473-1000, (202) 477-6391, eds03@worldbank.org, https://www.worldbank.org/; World Development Indicators (WDI) 2022.

DOMINICA-GROSS DOMESTIC PRODUCT

Routledge - Taylor & Francis Group, 6000 Broken Sound Pkwy. NW, Ste. 300, Boca Raton, FL, 33487, USA, (800) 634-1420, (800) 634-7064, orders@taylorandfrancis.com, https://www.routledge.com/; The Europa World Year Book 2022.

United Nations Statistics Division (UNSD), United Nations Plz., New York, NY, 10017, USA, (800) 253-9646, (212) 963-9851, statistics@un.org, https://unstats.un.org; Statistical Yearbook of the United Nations 2021.

The World Bank, 1818 H St. NW, Washington, DC, 20433, USA, (202) 473-1000, (202) 477-6391, eds03@worldbank.org, https://www.worldbank.org/; World Development Indicators (WDI) 2022.

DOMINICA-GROSS NATIONAL PRODUCT

Palgrave Macmillan, 1 New York Plaza, Ste. 4500, New York, NY, 10004-1562, USA, (800) 777-4643, orders@palgrave.com, https://www.palgrave.com/us; The Statesman's Yearbook, 2023.

The World Bank, 1818 H St. NW, Washington, DC, 20433, USA, (202) 473-1000, (202) 477-6391, eds03@worldbank.org, https://www.worldbank.org/; World Development Indicators (WDI) 2022.

DOMINICA-HOUSING

Euromonitor International, Inc., 1 N Dearborn St., Ste. 1700, Chicago, IL, 60602, USA, (312) 922-1115, (312) 922-1157, info-usa@euromonitor.com, https://www.euromonitor.com/; Geographies.

United Nations Statistics Division (UNSD), United Nations Plz., New York, NY, 10017, USA, (800) 253-9646, (212) 963-9851, statistics@un.org, https://unstats.un.org; Statistical Yearbook of the United Nations 2021.

DOMINICA-ILLITERATE PERSONS

UNESCO Institute for Statistics, C.P 250 Succursale H, Montreal, QC, H3G 2K8, CAN, (514) 343-6880 (Dial from U.S.), (514) 343-5740 (Fax from U.S.), uis.publications@unesco.org, http://uis.unesco.org/; UIS.Stat.

DOMINICA-IMPORTS

Central Intelligence Agency (CIA), Office of Public Affairs, Washington, DC, 20505, USA, (703) 482-0623, https://www.cia.gov; The World Factbook.

United Nations Conference on Trade and Development (UNCTAD), Palais des Nations, Geneva, 1211, SWI, (212) 963-6896, unctadinfo@unctad.org, https://unctad.org; Handbook of Statistics 2021.

DOMINICA-INDUSTRIES

Central Intelligence Agency (CIA), Office of Public Affairs, Washington, DC, 20505, USA, (703) 482-0623, https://www.cia.gov; The World Factbook.

Euromonitor International, Inc., 1 N Dearborn St., Ste. 1700, Chicago, IL, 60602, USA, (312) 922-1115, (312) 922-1157, info-usa@euromonitor.com, https://www.euromonitor.com/; Geographies.

International Labour Organization (ILO), 4 Rte. des Morillons, Geneva, CH-1211, SWI, ilo@ilo.org, https://www.ilo.org; NORMLEX Information System on International Labour Standards.

Routledge - Taylor & Francis Group, 6000 Broken Sound Pkwy. NW, Ste. 300, Boca Raton, FL, 33487, USA, (800) 634-1420, (800) 634-7064, orders@taylorandfrancis.com, https://www.routledge.com/; The Europa World Year Book 2022.

United Nations Economic Commission for Latin America and the Caribbean (ECLAC), Casilla 179-D, Santiago, 7630412, CHL, (202) 596-3713, prensa@cepal.org, https://www.cepal.org/en; Economic Survey of Latin America and the Caribbean 2021: Labour Dynamics and Employment Policies for Sustainable and Inclusive Recovery Beyond the COVID-19 Crisis.

United Nations Industrial Development Organization (UNIDO), 1 United Nations Plz., Rm. DC1-1118, New York, NY, 10017, USA, (212) 963-6890, (212) 963 6885, (212) 963-7904, office.newyork@unido.org, https://www.unido.org/; Industrial Statistics Databases and International Yearbook of Industrial Statistics 2021.

The World Bank, 1818 H St. NW, Washington, DC, 20433, USA, (202) 473-1000, (202) 477-6391, eds03@worldbank.org, https://www.worldbank.org/; World Development Indicators (WDI) 2022.

DOMINICA-INFANT AND MATERNAL MORTALITY

See DOMINICA-MORTALITY

DOMINICA-INFLATION (FINANCE)

United Nations Economic Commission for Latin America and the Caribbean (ECLAC), Casilla 179-D, Santiago, 7630412, CHL, (202) 596-3713, prensa@cepal.org, https://www.cepal.org/en; Economic Survey of Latin America and the Caribbean 2021: Labour Dynamics and Employment Policies for Sustainable and Inclusive Recovery Beyond the COVID-19 Crisis.

DOMINICA-INTERNATIONAL TRADE

Euromonitor International, Inc., 1 N Dearborn St., Ste. 1700, Chicago, IL, 60602, USA, (312) 922-1115, (312) 922-1157, info-usa@euromonitor.com, https://www.euromonitor.com/; Geographies.

Palgrave Macmillan, 1 New York Plaza, Ste. 4500, New York, NY, 10004-1562, USA, (800) 777-4643, orders@palgrave.com, https://www.palgrave.com/us; The Statesman's Yearbook, 2023.

Routledge - Taylor & Francis Group, 6000 Broken Sound Pkwy. NW, Ste. 300, Boca Raton, FL, 33487, USA, (800) 634-1420, (800) 634-7064, orders@taylorandfrancis.com, https://www.routledge.com/; The Europa World Year Book 2022.

United Nations Conference on Trade and Development (UNCTAD), Palais des Nations, Geneva, 1211, SWI, (212) 963-6896, unctadinfo@unctad.org, https://unctad.org; Trade and Development Report 2021.

United Nations Economic Commission for Latin America and the Caribbean (ECLAC), Casilla 179-D, Santiago, 7630412, CHL, (202) 596-3713, prensa@cepal.org, https://www.cepal.org/en; Economic Survey of Latin America and the Caribbean 2021: Labour Dynamics and Employment Policies for Sustainable and Inclusive Recovery Beyond the COVID-19 Crisis.

United Nations Food and Agricultural Organization (FAO), 2121 K St., Ste. 800B, Washington, DC, 20037, USA, (202) 653-2400 (Dial from U.S.), (202) 653-5760 (Fax from U.S.), fao-hq@fao.org, https://www.fao.org; The State of Food and Agriculture (SOFA) 2022.

United Nations Statistics Division (UNSD), United Nations Plz., New York, NY, 10017, USA, (800) 253-9646, (212) 963-9851, statistics@un.org, https://unstats.un.org; International Trade Statistics Yearbook 2020.

The World Bank, 1818 H St. NW, Washington, DC, 20433, USA, (202) 473-1000, (202) 477-6391, eds03@worldbank.org, https://www.worldbank.org/; World Development Indicators (WDI) 2022.

World Trade Organization (WTO), Ctre. William Rappard, Rue de Lausanne 154, Case postale, Geneva, CH-1211, SWI, enquiries@wto.org, https://www.wto.org; World Trade Statistical Review 2022.

DOMINICA-INTERNET USERS

International Telecommunication Union (ITU), Place des Nations, Geneva, CH-1211, SWI, itumail@itu.int, https://www.itu.int; Global Connectivity Report 2022; World Telecommunication/ICT Indicators Database 2021; and Yearbook of Statistics 2019.

DOMINICA-LABOR

Central Intelligence Agency (CIA), Office of Public Affairs, Washington, DC, 20505, USA, (703) 482-0623, https://www.cia.gov; The World Factbook.

Euromonitor International, Inc., 1 N Dearborn St., Ste. 1700, Chicago, IL, 60602, USA, (312) 922-1115, (312) 922-1157, info-usa@euromonitor.com, https://www.euromonitor.com/; Geographies.

International Labour Organization (ILO), 4 Rte. des Morillons, Geneva, CH-1211, SWI, ilo@ilo.org, https://www.ilo.org; NORMLEX Information System on International Labour Standards.

United Nations Food and Agricultural Organization (FAO), 2121 K St., Ste. 800B, Washington, DC, 20037, USA, (202) 653-2400 (Dial from U.S.), (202) 653-5760 (Fax from U.S.), fao-hq@fao.org, https://www.fao.org; The State of Food and Agriculture (SOFA) 2022.

The World Bank, 1818 H St. NW, Washington, DC, 20433, USA, (202) 473-1000, (202) 477-6391, eds03@worldbank.org, https://www.worldbank.org/; World Development Indicators (WDI) 2022.

DOMINICA-LAND USE

United Nations Statistics Division (UNSD), United Nations Plz., New York, NY, 10017, USA, (800) 253-9646, (212) 963-9851, statistics@un.org, https://unstats.un.org; Millennium Development Goal Indicators.

DOMINICA-LIFE EXPECTANCY

Central Intelligence Agency (CIA), Office of Public Affairs, Washington, DC, 20505, USA, (703) 482-0623, https://www.cia.gov; The World Factbook.

United Nations Department of Economic and Social Affairs (DESA), Population Division, 2 United Nations Plz., Rm. DC2-1950, New York, NY, 10017, USA, (212) 963-3209, (212) 963-2147, population@un.org, https://www.un.org/development/desa/pd/; World Population Ageing 2020 Highlights.

United Nations Statistics Division (UNSD), United Nations Plz., New York, NY, 10017, USA, (800) 253-9646, (212) 963-9851, statistics@un.org, https://unstats.un.org; Millennium Development Goal Indicators.

The World Bank, 1818 H St. NW, Washington, DC, 20433, USA, (202) 473-1000, (202) 477-6391, eds03@worldbank.org, https://www.worldbank.org/; Caribbean (report).

DOMINICA-LITERACY

Euromonitor International, Inc., 1 N Dearborn St., Ste. 1700, Chicago, IL, 60602, USA, (312) 922-1115, (312) 922-1157, info-usa@euromonitor.com, https://www.euromonitor.com/; Geographies.

UNESCO Institute for Statistics, C.P 250 Succursale H, Montreal, QC, H3G 2K8, CAN, (514) 343-6880 (Dial from U.S.), (514) 343-5740 (Fax from U.S.), uis.publications@unesco.org, http://uis.unesco.org/; Literacy.

DOMINICA-LIVESTOCK

Palgrave Macmillan, 1 New York Plaza, Ste. 4500, New York, NY, 10004-1562, USA, (800) 777-4643, orders@palgrave.com, https://www.palgrave.com/us; The Statesman's Yearbook, 2023.

Routledge - Taylor & Francis Group, 6000 Broken Sound Pkwy. NW, Ste. 300, Boca Raton, FL, 33487, USA, (800) 634-1420, (800) 634-7064, orders@taylorandfrancis.com, https://www.routledge.com/; The Europa World Year Book 2022.

United Nations Food and Agricultural Organization (FAO), 2121 K St., Ste. 800B, Washington, DC, 20037, USA, (202) 653-2400 (Dial from U.S.), (202) 653-5760 (Fax from U.S.), fao-hq@fao.org, https://www.fao.org; The State of Food and Agriculture (SOFA) 2022.

United Nations Statistics Division (UNSD), United Nations Plz., New York, NY, 10017, USA, (800) 253-9646, (212) 963-9851, statistics@un.org, https://unstats.un.org; Statistical Yearbook of the United Nations 2021.

DOMINICA-MARRIAGE

Routledge - Taylor & Francis Group, 6000 Broken Sound Pkwy. NW, Ste. 300, Boca Raton, FL, 33487, USA, (800) 634-1420, (800) 634-7064, orders@taylorandfrancis.com, https://www.routledge.com/; The Europa World Year Book 2022.

United Nations Statistics Division (UNSD), United Nations Plz., New York, NY, 10017, USA, (800) 253-9646, (212) 963-9851, statistics@un.org, https://unstats.un.org; Statistical Yearbook of the United Nations 2021.

DOMINICA-MINERAL INDUSTRIES

Routledge - Taylor & Francis Group, 6000 Broken Sound Pkwy. NW, Ste. 300, Boca Raton, FL, 33487, USA, (800) 634-1420, (800) 634-7064, orders@taylorandfrancis.com, https://www.routledge.com/; The Europa World Year Book 2022.

United Nations Conference on Trade and Development (UNCTAD), Palais des Nations, Geneva, 1211, SWI, (212) 963-6896, unctadinfo@unctad.org, https://unctad.org; Trade and Development Report 2021.

DOMINICA-MONEY SUPPLY

Routledge - Taylor & Francis Group, 6000 Broken Sound Pkwy. NW, Ste. 300, Boca Raton, FL, 33487, USA, (800) 634-1420, (800) 634-7064, orders@taylorandfrancis.com, https://www.routledge.com/; The Europa World Year Book 2022.

DOMINICA-MORTALITY

UNICEF, 3 United Nations Plz., New York, NY, 10017, USA, (212) 303-7984, (917) 244-2215, https://www.unicef.org; The State of the World's Children 2023.

United Nations Statistics Division (UNSD), United Nations Plz., New York, NY, 10017, USA, (800) 253-9646, (212) 963-9851, statistics@un.org, https://unstats.un.org; Millennium Development Goal Indicators; Statistical Yearbook of the United Nations 2021; and World Statistics Pocketbook 2021.

The World Bank, 1818 H St. NW, Washington, DC, 20433, USA, (202) 473-1000, (202) 477-6391, eds03@worldbank.org, https://www.worldbank.org/; World Development Indicators (WDI) 2022.

World Health Organization (WHO), Ave. Appia 20, Geneva, CH-1211, SWI, (202) 974-3000 (Telephone in U.S.), publications@who.int, https://www.who.int/; Global Health Observatory (GHO).

DOMINICA-MOTION PICTURES

Palgrave Macmillan, 1 New York Plaza, Ste. 4500, New York, NY, 10004-1562, USA, (800) 777-4643, orders@palgrave.com, https://www.palgrave.com/us; The Statesman's Yearbook, 2023.

DOMINICA-NUTRITION

United Nations Food and Agricultural Organization (FAO), 2121 K St., Ste. 800B, Washington, DC, 20037, USA, (202) 653-2400 (Dial from U.S.), (202) 653-5760 (Fax from U.S.), fao-hq@fao.org, https://www.fao.org; The State of Food and Agriculture (SOFA) 2022.

United Nations Statistics Division (UNSD), United Nations Plz., New York, NY, 10017, USA, (800) 253-9646, (212) 963-9851, statistics@un.org, https://unstats.un.org; Millennium Development Goal Indicators.

DOMINICA-PESTICIDES

United Nations Food and Agricultural Organization (FAO), 2121 K St., Ste. 800B, Washington, DC, 20037, USA, (202) 653-2400 (Dial from U.S.), (202) 653-5760 (Fax from U.S.), fao-hq@fao.org, https://www.fao.org; The State of Food and Agriculture (SOFA) 2022.

DOMINICA-PETROLEUM INDUSTRY AND TRADE

United Nations Food and Agricultural Organization (FAO), 2121 K St., Ste. 800B, Washington, DC, 20037, USA, (202) 653-2400 (Dial from U.S.), (202) 653-5760 (Fax from U.S.), fao-hq@fao.org, https://www.fao.org; The State of Food and Agriculture (SOFA) 2022.

DOMINICA-POPULATION

Caribbean Public Health Agency (CARPHA), Federation Park, 16-18 Jamaica Blvd., Port of Spain, TTO, (868) 622-4261 (Dial from U.S.), (868) 299-0820 (Dial from U.S.), postmaster@carpha.org, https://carpha.org/; unpublished data.

Central Intelligence Agency (CIA), Office of Public Affairs, Washington, DC, 20505, USA, (703) 482-0623, https://www.cia.gov; The World Factbook.

European Commission, Eurostat, Luxembourg, 2920, LUX, https://ec.europa.eu/eurostat/; EU in the World 2020.

Infoplease, c/o Sandbox Networks, Inc., 1 Lincoln St., 24th Fl., Boston, MA, 02111, USA, https://www.infoplease.com; Countries of the World.

International Labour Organization (ILO), 4 Rte. des Morillons, Geneva, CH-1211, SWI, ilo@ilo.org, https://www.ilo.org; NORMLEX Information System on International Labour Standards.

Palgrave Macmillan, 1 New York Plaza, Ste. 4500, New York, NY, 10004-1562, USA, (800) 777-4643, orders@palgrave.com, https://www.palgrave.com/us; The Statesman's Yearbook, 2023.

Routledge - Taylor & Francis Group, 6000 Broken Sound Pkwy. NW, Ste. 300, Boca Raton, FL, 33487, USA, (800) 634-1420, (800) 634-7064, orders@taylorandfrancis.com, https://www.routledge.com/; The Europa World Year Book 2022.

UK Data Service, University of Essex, Wivenhoe Park, Colchester, Essex, CO4 3SQ, GBR, https://ukdataservice.ac.uk/; International Aggregate Data.

UNESCO Institute for Statistics, C.P 250 Succursale H, Montreal, QC, H3G 2K8, CAN, (514) 343-6880 (Dial from U.S.), (514) 343-5740 (Fax from U.S.), uis.publications@unesco.org, http://uis.unesco.org/; UIS.Stat.

United Nations Department of Economic and Social Affairs (DESA), Population Division, 2 United Nations Plz., Rm. DC2-1950, New York, NY, 10017, USA, (212) 963-3209, (212) 963-2147, population@un.org, https://www.un.org/development/desa/pd/; Revision of World Urbanization Prospects and World Population Ageing 2020 Highlights.

United Nations Development Programme (UNDP), One United Nations Plz., New York, NY, 10017, USA, (212) 906-5000, (212) 906-5001, https://www.undp.org; Human Development Report 2021-2022.

United Nations Economic Commission for Latin America and the Caribbean (ECLAC), Casilla 179-D, Santiago, 7630412, CHL, (202) 596-3713, prensa@cepal.org, https://www.cepal.org/en; CEPALSTAT and Social Panorama of Latin America and the Caribbean 2022: Transforming Education as a Basis for Sustainable Development.

United Nations Statistics Division (UNSD), United Nations Plz., New York, NY, 10017, USA, (800) 253-9646, (212) 963-9851, statistics@un.org, https://unstats.un.org; Statistical Yearbook of the United Nations 2021 and World Statistics Pocketbook 2021.

The World Bank, 1818 H St. NW, Washington, DC, 20433, USA, (202) 473-1000, (202) 477-6391, eds03@worldbank.org, https://www.worldbank.org/; Caribbean (report) and The Global Findex Database 2021.

DOMINICA-POPULATION DENSITY

Central Intelligence Agency (CIA), Office of Public Affairs, Washington, DC, 20505, USA, (703) 482-0623, https://www.cia.gov; The World Factbook.

Palgrave Macmillan, 1 New York Plaza, Ste. 4500, New York, NY, 10004-1562, USA, (800) 777-4643, orders@palgrave.com, https://www.palgrave.com/us; The Statesman's Yearbook, 2023.

Routledge - Taylor & Francis Group, 6000 Broken Sound Pkwy. NW, Ste. 300, Boca Raton, FL, 33487, USA, (800) 634-1420, (800) 634-7064, orders@taylorandfrancis.com, https://www.routledge.com/; The Europa World Year Book 2022.

UNESCO Institute for Statistics, C.P 250 Succursale H, Montreal, QC, H3G 2K8, CAN, (514) 343-6880 (Dial from U.S.), (514) 343-5740 (Fax from U.S.), uis.publications@unesco.org, http://uis.unesco.org/; UIS.Stat.

DOMINICA-POWER RESOURCES

Palgrave Macmillan, 1 New York Plaza, Ste. 4500, New York, NY, 10004-1562, USA, (800) 777-4643, orders@palgrave.com, https://www.palgrave.com/us; The Statesman's Yearbook, 2023.

United Nations Food and Agricultural Organization (FAO), 2121 K St., Ste. 800B, Washington, DC, 20037, USA, (202) 653-2400 (Dial from U.S.), (202) 653-5760 (Fax from U.S.), fao-hq@fao.org, https://www.fao.org; The State of Food and Agriculture (SOFA) 2022.

United Nations Statistics Division (UNSD), United Nations Plz., New York, NY, 10017, USA, (800) 253-9646, (212) 963-9851, statistics@un.org, https://unstats.un.org; Energy Statistics Yearbook 2019 and World Statistics Pocketbook 2021.

DOMINICA-PRICES

Euromonitor International, Inc., 1 N Dearborn St., Ste. 1700, Chicago, IL, 60602, USA, (312) 922-1115, (312) 922-1157, info-usa@euromonitor.com, https://www.euromonitor.com/; Geographies.

United Nations Economic Commission for Latin America and the Caribbean (ECLAC), Casilla 179-D, Santiago, 7630412, CHL, (202) 596-3713, prensa@cepal.org, https://www.cepal.org/en; Economic Survey of Latin America and the Caribbean 2021: Labour Dynamics and Employment Policies for Sustainable and Inclusive Recovery Beyond the COVID-19 Crisis.

DOMINICA-PUBLIC HEALTH

Euromonitor International, Inc., 1 N Dearborn St., Ste. 1700, Chicago, IL, 60602, USA, (312) 922-1115, (312) 922-1157, info-usa@euromonitor.com, https://www.euromonitor.com/; Geographies.

Palgrave Macmillan, 1 New York Plaza, Ste. 4500, New York, NY, 10004-1562, USA, (800) 777-4643, orders@palgrave.com, https://www.palgrave.com/us; The Statesman's Yearbook, 2023.

U.S. Census Bureau, 4600 Silver Hill Rd., Washington, DC, 20233, USA, (301) 763-4636, (800) 923-8282, https://www.census.gov; HIV/AIDS Surveillance Data Base.

UNICEF, 3 United Nations Plz., New York, NY, 10017, USA, (212) 303-7984, (917) 244-2215, https://www.unicef.org; The State of the World's Children 2023.

United Nations Department of Economic and Social Affairs (DESA), Population Division, 2 United Nations Plz., Rm. DC2-1950, New York, NY, 10017, USA, (212) 963-3209, (212) 963-2147, population@un.org, https://www.un.org/development/desa/pd/; World Fertility Data 2019.

United Nations Development Programme (UNDP), One United Nations Plz., New York, NY, 10017, USA, (212) 906-5000, (212) 906-5001, https://www.undp.org; Human Development Report 2021-2022.

United Nations Statistics Division (UNSD), United Nations Plz., New York, NY, 10017, USA, (800) 253-9646, (212) 963-9851, statistics@un.org, https://unstats.un.org; Millennium Development Goal Indicators and Statistical Yearbook of the United Nations 2021.

The World Bank, 1818 H St. NW, Washington, DC, 20433, USA, (202) 473-1000, (202) 477-6391, eds03@worldbank.org, https://www.worldbank.org/; Caribbean (report).

World Health Organization (WHO), Ave. Appia 20, Geneva, CH-1211, SWI, (202) 974-3000 (Telephone in U.S.), publications@who.int, https://www.who.int/; Global Health Observatory (GHO) and Health Statistics and Information Systems.

DOMINICA-RELIGION

Central Intelligence Agency (CIA), Office of Public Affairs, Washington, DC, 20505, USA, (703) 482-0623, https://www.cia.gov; The World Factbook.

Palgrave Macmillan, 1 New York Plaza, Ste. 4500, New York, NY, 10004-1562, USA, (800) 777-4643, orders@palgrave.com, https://www.palgrave.com/us; The Statesman's Yearbook, 2023.

DOMINICA-RETAIL TRADE

Euromonitor International, Inc., 1 N Dearborn St., Ste. 1700, Chicago, IL, 60602, USA, (312) 922-1115, (312) 922-1157, info-usa@euromonitor.com, https://www.euromonitor.com/; Geographies.

DOMINICA-SHIPPING

Routledge - Taylor & Francis Group, 6000 Broken Sound Pkwy. NW, Ste. 300, Boca Raton, FL, 33487, USA, (800) 634-1420, (800) 634-7064, orders@taylorandfrancis.com, https://www.routledge.com/; The Europa World Year Book 2022.

United Nations Statistics Division (UNSD), United Nations Plz., New York, NY, 10017, USA, (800) 253-9646, (212) 963-9851, statistics@un.org, https://unstats.un.org; Statistical Yearbook of the United Nations 2021.

DOMINICA-TAXATION

The World Bank, 1818 H St. NW, Washington, DC, 20433, USA, (202) 473-1000, (202) 477-6391, eds03@worldbank.org, https://www.worldbank.org/; World Development Indicators (WDI) 2022.

DOMINICA-TELEPHONE

Palgrave Macmillan, 1 New York Plaza, Ste. 4500, New York, NY, 10004-1562, USA, (800) 777-4643, orders@palgrave.com, https://www.palgrave.com/us; The Statesman's Yearbook, 2023.

Routledge - Taylor & Francis Group, 6000 Broken Sound Pkwy. NW, Ste. 300, Boca Raton, FL, 33487, USA, (800) 634-1420, (800) 634-7064, orders@taylorandfrancis.com, https://www.routledge.com/; The Europa World Year Book 2022.

United Nations Statistics Division (UNSD), United Nations Plz., New York, NY, 10017, USA, (800) 253-9646, (212) 963-9851, statistics@un.org, https://unstats.un.org; World Statistics Pocketbook 2021.

DOMINICA-TOURISM

Euromonitor International, Inc., 1 N Dearborn St., Ste. 1700, Chicago, IL, 60602, USA, (312) 922-1115, (312) 922-1157, info-usa@euromonitor.com, https://www.euromonitor.com/; Geographies.

Palgrave Macmillan, 1 New York Plaza, Ste. 4500, New York, NY, 10004-1562, USA, (800) 777-4643, orders@palgrave.com, https://www.palgrave.com/us; The Statesman's Yearbook, 2023.

Routledge - Taylor & Francis Group, 6000 Broken Sound Pkwy. NW, Ste. 300, Boca Raton, FL, 33487, USA, (800) 634-1420, (800) 634-7064, orders@taylorandfrancis.com, https://www.routledge.com/; The Europa World Year Book 2022.

United Nations World Tourism Organization (UNWTO), Calle Poeta Joan Maragall 42, Madrid, 28020, SPA, info@unwto.org, https://www.unwto.org/; Yearbook of Tourism Statistics, 2021 Edition.

DOMINICA-TRADE

See DOMINICA-INTERNATIONAL TRADE

DOMINICA-TRANSPORTATION

Central Intelligence Agency (CIA), Office of Public Affairs, Washington, DC, 20505, USA, (703) 482-0623, https://www.cia.gov; The World Factbook.

Euromonitor International, Inc., 1 N Dearborn St., Ste. 1700, Chicago, IL, 60602, USA, (312) 922-1115, (312) 922-1157, info-usa@euromonitor.com, https://www.euromonitor.com/; Geographies.

Palgrave Macmillan, 1 New York Plaza, Ste. 4500, New York, NY, 10004-1562, USA, (800) 777-4643, orders@palgrave.com, https://www.palgrave.com/us; The Statesman's Yearbook, 2023.

Routledge - Taylor & Francis Group, 6000 Broken Sound Pkwy. NW, Ste. 300, Boca Raton, FL, 33487, USA, (800) 634-1420, (800) 634-7064, orders@taylorandfrancis.com, https://www.routledge.com/; The Europa World Year Book 2022.

DOMINICA-UNEMPLOYMENT

International Labour Organization (ILO), 4 Rte. des Morillons, Geneva, CH-1211, SWI, ilo@ilo.org, https://www.ilo.org; NORMLEX Information System on International Labour Standards.

DOMINICA-VITAL STATISTICS

U.S. Census Bureau, 4600 Silver Hill Rd., Washington, DC, 20233, USA, (301) 763-4636, (800) 923-8282, https://www.census.gov; HIV/AIDS Surveillance Data Base.

United Nations Department of Economic and Social Affairs (DESA), Population Division, 2 United Nations Plz., Rm. DC2-1950, New York, NY, 10017, USA, (212) 963-3209, (212) 963-2147, population@un.org, https://www.un.org/development/desa/pd/; World Contraceptive Use 2021: Estimates and Projections of Family Planning Indicators and World Marriage Data 2019.

DOMINICA-WAGES

International Labour Organization (ILO), 4 Rte. des Morillons, Geneva, CH-1211, SWI, ilo@ilo.org, https://www.ilo.org; NORMLEX Information System on International Labour Standards.

DOMINICAN REPUBLIC-NATIONAL STATISTICAL OFFICE

Oficina Nacional de Estadistica, Av. Mexico Esq. Leopoldo Navarro, Edif. Oficinas Gubernamentales Juan Pablo Duarte, Piso 9, Santo Domingo, DOM, (809) 682-7777 (Dial from U.S.), info@one.gob.do, https://www.one.gob.do/; National Data Reports (Dominican Republic).

DOMINICAN REPUBLIC-AGRICULTURE

The Economist Group: Economist Intelligence Unit (EIU), 900 3rd Ave., 16th Fl., New York, NY, 10022, USA, (212) 541-0500, americas@eiu.com, https://www.eiu.com; Dominican Republic Country Report.

Euromonitor International, Inc., 1 N Dearborn St., Ste. 1700, Chicago, IL, 60602, USA, (312) 922-1115, (312) 922-1157, info-usa@euromonitor.com, https://www.euromonitor.com/; Geographies.

Inter-American Development Bank (IDB), 1300 New York Ave. NW, Washington, DC, 20577, USA, (202) 623-1000, (202) 623-3096, https://www.iadb.org/en; Latin Macro Watch (LMW).

Palgrave Macmillan, 1 New York Plaza, Ste. 4500, New York, NY, 10004-1562, USA, (800) 777-4643, orders@palgrave.com, https://www.palgrave.com/us; The Statesman's Yearbook, 2023.

Routledge - Taylor & Francis Group, 6000 Broken Sound Pkwy. NW, Ste. 300, Boca Raton, FL, 33487, USA, (800) 634-1420, (800) 634-7064, orders@taylorandfrancis.com, https://www.routledge.com/; The Europa World Year Book 2022.

United Nations Food and Agricultural Organization (FAO), 2121 K St., Ste. 800B, Washington, DC, 20037, USA, (202) 653-2400 (Dial from U.S.), (202) 653-5760 (Fax from U.S.), fao-hq@fao.org, https://www.fao.org; AQUASTAT and The State of Food and Agriculture (SOFA) 2022.

United Nations Statistics Division (UNSD), United Nations Plz., New York, NY, 10017, USA, (800) 253-9646, (212) 963-9851, statistics@un.org, https://unstats.un.org; Statistical Yearbook of the United Nations 2021.

The World Bank, 1818 H St. NW, Washington, DC, 20433, USA, (202) 473-1000, (202) 477-6391, eds03@worldbank.org, https://www.worldbank.org/; Dominican Republic (report) and World Development Indicators (WDI) 2022.

DOMINICAN REPUBLIC-AIRLINES

International Civil Aviation Organization (ICAO), 999 Robert-Bourassa Blvd., Montreal, QC, H3C 5H7, CAN, (514) 954-8219 (Dial from U.S.), (514) 954-6077 (Fax from U.S.), icaohq@icao.int, https://www.icao.int; ICAO Regional Reports.

Palgrave Macmillan, 1 New York Plaza, Ste. 4500, New York, NY, 10004-1562, USA, (800) 777-4643, orders@palgrave.com, https://www.palgrave.com/us; The Statesman's Yearbook, 2023.

Routledge - Taylor & Francis Group, 6000 Broken Sound Pkwy. NW, Ste. 300, Boca Raton, FL, 33487, USA, (800) 634-1420, (800) 634-7064, orders@taylorandfrancis.com, https://www.routledge.com/; The Europa World Year Book 2022.

DOMINICAN REPUBLIC-ALUMINUM PRODUCTION

See DOMINICAN REPUBLIC-MINERAL INDUSTRIES

DOMINICAN REPUBLIC-ARMED FORCES

Central Intelligence Agency (CIA), Office of Public Affairs, Washington, DC, 20505, USA, (703) 482-0623, https://www.cia.gov; The World Factbook.

International Institute for Strategic Studies (IISS) - Americas, 2121 K St. NW, Ste. 600, Washington, DC, 20037, USA, (202) 659-1490, (202) 659-1499, https://www.iiss.org/; The Military Balance 2022.

Palgrave Macmillan, 1 New York Plaza, Ste. 4500, New York, NY, 10004-1562, USA, (800) 777-4643, orders@palgrave.com, https://www.palgrave.com/us; The Statesman's Yearbook, 2023.

Stockholm International Peace Research Institute (SIPRI), Signalistgatan 9, Stockholm, SE 169 72, SWE, https://www.sipri.org/; SIPRI Arms Transfers Database and SIPRI Military Expenditure Database.

DOMINICAN REPUBLIC-BALANCE OF PAYMENTS

Inter-American Development Bank (IDB), 1300 New York Ave. NW, Washington, DC, 20577, USA, (202) 623-1000, (202) 623-3096, https://www.iadb.org/en; Latin Macro Watch (LMW).

International Monetary Fund (IMF), 700 19th St. NW, Washington, DC, 20431, USA, (202) 623-7000, (202) 623-4661, publications@imf.org, https://www.imf.org; Balance of Payments Statistics: Annual Report 2021.

Routledge - Taylor & Francis Group, 6000 Broken Sound Pkwy. NW, Ste. 300, Boca Raton, FL, 33487, USA, (800) 634-1420, (800) 634-7064, orders@taylorandfrancis.com, https://www.routledge.com/; The Europa World Year Book 2022.

United Nations Conference on Trade and Development (UNCTAD), Palais des Nations, Geneva, 1211, SWI, (212) 963-6896, unctadinfo@unctad.org, https://unctad.org; Handbook of Statistics 2021.

The World Bank, 1818 H St. NW, Washington, DC, 20433, USA, (202) 473-1000, (202) 477-6391, eds03@worldbank.org, https://www.worldbank.org/; Dominican Republic (report); World Development Indicators (WDI) 2022; and World Development Report 2022: Finance for an Equitable Recovery.

DOMINICAN REPUBLIC-BANKS AND BANKING

Euromonitor International, Inc., 1 N Dearborn St., Ste. 1700, Chicago, IL, 60602, USA, (312) 922-1115, (312) 922-1157, info-usa@euromonitor.com, https://www.euromonitor.com/; Geographies.

Inter-American Development Bank (IDB), 1300 New York Ave. NW, Washington, DC, 20577, USA, (202) 623-1000, (202) 623-3096, https://www.iadb.org/en; Latin Macro Watch (LMW).

International Monetary Fund (IMF), 700 19th St. NW, Washington, DC, 20431, USA, (202) 623-7000, (202) 623-4661, publications@imf.org, https://www.imf.org; International Financial Statistics (IFS).

Routledge - Taylor & Francis Group, 6000 Broken Sound Pkwy. NW, Ste. 300, Boca Raton, FL, 33487, USA, (800) 634-1420, (800) 634-7064, orders@taylorandfrancis.com, https://www.routledge.com/; The Europa World Year Book 2022.

DOMINICAN REPUBLIC-BARLEY PRODUCTION

See DOMINICAN REPUBLIC-CROPS

DOMINICAN REPUBLIC-BONDS

Inter-American Development Bank (IDB), 1300 New York Ave. NW, Washington, DC, 20577, USA, (202) 623-1000, (202) 623-3096, https://www.iadb.org/en; Latin Macro Watch (LMW).

DOMINICAN REPUBLIC-BROADCASTING

Central Intelligence Agency (CIA), Office of Public Affairs, Washington, DC, 20505, USA, (703) 482-0623, https://www.cia.gov; The World Factbook.

Euromonitor International, Inc., 1 N Dearborn St., Ste. 1700, Chicago, IL, 60602, USA, (312) 922-1115, (312) 922-1157, info-usa@euromonitor.com, https://www.euromonitor.com/; Geographies.

Palgrave Macmillan, 1 New York Plaza, Ste. 4500, New York, NY, 10004-1562, USA, (800) 777-4643, orders@palgrave.com, https://www.palgrave.com/us; The Statesman's Yearbook, 2023.

WRTH Publications Limited, PO Box 290, Oxford, OX2 7FT, GBR, sales@wrth.com, https://www.wrth.com; World Radio TV Handbook 2023.

DOMINICAN REPUBLIC-BUDGET

Central Intelligence Agency (CIA), Office of Public Affairs, Washington, DC, 20505, USA, (703) 482-0623, https://www.cia.gov; The World Factbook.

DOMINICAN REPUBLIC-BUSINESS

Global Entrepreneurship Monitor (GEM), Babson College, 231 Forest St., Babson Park, MA, 02457, USA, (781) 235-1200, info@gemconsortium.org, https://www.gemconsortium.org/; GEM 2022-2023 Global Report.

Inter-American Development Bank (IDB), 1300 New York Ave. NW, Washington, DC, 20577, USA, (202) 623-1000, (202) 623-3096, https://www.iadb.org/en; Latin Macro Watch (LMW).

United Nations Statistics Division (UNSD), United Nations Plz., New York, NY, 10017, USA, (800) 253-9646, (212) 963-9851, statistics@un.org, https://unstats.un.org; Statistical Yearbook of the United Nations 2021.

DOMINICAN REPUBLIC-CACAO

See DOMINICAN REPUBLIC-CROPS

DOMINICAN REPUBLIC-CAPITAL INVESTMENTS

Inter-American Development Bank (IDB), 1300 New York Ave. NW, Washington, DC, 20577, USA, (202) 623-1000, (202) 623-3096, https://www.iadb.org/en; Latin Macro Watch (LMW).

DOMINICAN REPUBLIC-CHILDBIRTH-STATISTICS

The World Bank, 1818 H St. NW, Washington, DC, 20433, USA, (202) 473-1000, (202) 477-6391, eds03@worldbank.org, https://www.worldbank.org/; World Development Indicators (WDI) 2022.

World Health Organization (WHO), Ave. Appia 20, Geneva, CH-1211, SWI, (202) 974-3000 (Telephone in U.S.), publications@who.int, https://www.who.int/; Health Statistics and Information Systems.

DOMINICAN REPUBLIC-CLIMATE

Palgrave Macmillan, 1 New York Plaza, Ste. 4500, New York, NY, 10004-1562, USA, (800) 777-4643, orders@palgrave.com, https://www.palgrave.com/us; The Statesman's Yearbook, 2023.

DOMINICAN REPUBLIC-COAL PRODUCTION

See DOMINICAN REPUBLIC-MINERAL INDUSTRIES

DOMINICAN REPUBLIC-COCOA PRODUCTION

See DOMINICAN REPUBLIC-CROPS

DOMINICAN REPUBLIC-COFFEE

See DOMINICAN REPUBLIC-CROPS

DOMINICAN REPUBLIC-COMMERCE

Palgrave Macmillan, 1 New York Plaza, Ste. 4500, New York, NY, 10004-1562, USA, (800) 777-4643, orders@palgrave.com, https://www.palgrave.com/us; The Statesman's Yearbook, 2023.

UK Data Service, University of Essex, Wivenhoe Park, Colchester, Essex, CO4 3SQ, GBR, https://ukdataservice.ac.uk/; International Aggregate Data.

DOMINICAN REPUBLIC-COMMODITY EXCHANGES

Barchart, 209 W Jackson Blvd., 2nd Fl., Chicago, IL, 60606, USA, (877) 247-4394, commodities@barchart.com, https://www.barchart.com/cmdty; The cmdty Yearbook 2023; cmdtyStats: Commodity Statistics and Fundamental Data; cmdtyView: Commodity Index; and Commodity Data and Prices.

International Monetary Fund (IMF), 700 19th St. NW, Washington, DC, 20431, USA, (202) 623-7000, (202) 623-4661, publications@imf.org, https://www.imf.org; IMF Primary Commodity Prices.

DOMINICAN REPUBLIC-CONSTRUCTION INDUSTRY

Inter-American Development Bank (IDB), 1300 New York Ave. NW, Washington, DC, 20577, USA, (202) 623-1000, (202) 623-3096, https://www.iadb.org/en; Latin Macro Watch (LMW).

United Nations Statistics Division (UNSD), United Nations Plz., New York, NY, 10017, USA, (800) 253-9646, (212) 963-9851, statistics@un.org, https://unstats.un.org; Statistical Yearbook of the United Nations 2021.

DOMINICAN REPUBLIC-CONSUMER PRICE INDEXES

International Labour Organization (ILO), 4 Rte. des Morillons, Geneva, CH-1211, SWI, ilo@ilo.org, https://www.ilo.org; NORMLEX Information System on International Labour Standards.

Routledge - Taylor & Francis Group, 6000 Broken Sound Pkwy. NW, Ste. 300, Boca Raton, FL, 33487, USA, (800) 634-1420, (800) 634-7064, orders@taylorandfrancis.com, https://www.routledge.com/; The Europa World Year Book 2022.

The World Bank, 1818 H St. NW, Washington, DC, 20433, USA, (202) 473-1000, (202) 477-6391, eds03@worldbank.org, https://www.worldbank.org/; Dominican Republic (report).

DOMINICAN REPUBLIC-CONSUMPTION (ECONOMICS)

Inter-American Development Bank (IDB), 1300 New York Ave. NW, Washington, DC, 20577, USA, (202) 623-1000, (202) 623-3096, https://www.iadb.org/en; Latin Macro Watch (LMW).

DOMINICAN REPUBLIC-COPPER INDUSTRY AND TRADE

See DOMINICAN REPUBLIC-MINERAL INDUSTRIES

DOMINICAN REPUBLIC-CORN INDUSTRY

See DOMINICAN REPUBLIC-CROPS

DOMINICAN REPUBLIC-COTTON

See DOMINICAN REPUBLIC-CROPS

DOMINICAN REPUBLIC-CROPS

International Monetary Fund (IMF), 700 19th St. NW, Washington, DC, 20431, USA, (202) 623-7000, (202) 623-4661, publications@imf.org, https://www.imf.org; International Financial Statistics (IFS).

Palgrave Macmillan, 1 New York Plaza, Ste. 4500, New York, NY, 10004-1562, USA, (800) 777-4643, orders@palgrave.com, https://www.palgrave.com/us; The Statesman's Yearbook, 2023.

United Nations Food and Agricultural Organization (FAO), 2121 K St., Ste. 800B, Washington, DC, 20037, USA, (202) 653-2400 (Dial from U.S.), (202) 653-5760 (Fax from U.S.), fao-hq@fao.org, https://www.fao.org; The State of Food and Agriculture (SOFA) 2022.

United Nations Statistics Division (UNSD), United Nations Plz., New York, NY, 10017, USA, (800) 253-9646, (212) 963-9851, statistics@un.org, https://unstats.un.org; Statistical Yearbook of the United Nations 2021.

DOMINICAN REPUBLIC-CUSTOMS ADMINISTRATION

Inter-American Development Bank (IDB), 1300 New York Ave. NW, Washington, DC, 20577, USA, (202) 623-1000, (202) 623-3096, https://www.iadb.org/en; Latin Macro Watch (LMW).

DOMINICAN REPUBLIC-DAIRY PROCESSING

Palgrave Macmillan, 1 New York Plaza, Ste. 4500, New York, NY, 10004-1562, USA, (800) 777-4643, orders@palgrave.com, https://www.palgrave.com/us; The Statesman's Yearbook, 2023.

United Nations Food and Agricultural Organization (FAO), 2121 K St., Ste. 800B, Washington, DC, 20037, USA, (202) 653-2400 (Dial from U.S.), (202) 653-5760 (Fax from U.S.), fao-hq@fao.org, https://www.fao.org; The State of Food and Agriculture (SOFA) 2022.

DOMINICAN REPUBLIC-DEBT

The World Bank, 1818 H St. NW, Washington, DC, 20433, USA, (202) 473-1000, (202) 477-6391, eds03@worldbank.org, https://www.worldbank.org/; Global Financial Development Report 2019-2020: Bank Regulation and Supervision a Decade after the Global Financial Crisis.

DOMINICAN REPUBLIC-DEBTS, EXTERNAL

Inter-American Development Bank (IDB), 1300 New York Ave. NW, Washington, DC, 20577, USA, (202) 623-1000, (202) 623-3096, https://www.iadb.org/en; Latin Macro Watch (LMW).

Palgrave Macmillan, 1 New York Plaza, Ste. 4500, New York, NY, 10004-1562, USA, (800) 777-4643, orders@palgrave.com, https://www.palgrave.com/us; The Statesman's Yearbook, 2023.

The World Bank, 1818 H St. NW, Washington, DC, 20433, USA, (202) 473-1000, (202) 477-6391, eds03@worldbank.org, https://www.worldbank.org/; Global Financial Development Report 2019-2020: Bank Regulation and Supervision a Decade after the Global Financial Crisis; World Development Indicators (WDI) 2022; and World Development Report 2022: Finance for an Equitable Recovery.

DOMINICAN REPUBLIC-DEFENSE EXPENDITURES

See DOMINICAN REPUBLIC-ARMED FORCES

DOMINICAN REPUBLIC-DIAMONDS

See DOMINICAN REPUBLIC-MINERAL INDUSTRIES

DOMINICAN REPUBLIC-DISPOSABLE INCOME

Inter-American Development Bank (IDB), 1300 New York Ave. NW, Washington, DC, 20577, USA, (202) 623-1000, (202) 623-3096, https://www.iadb.org/en; Latin Macro Watch (LMW).

DOMINICAN REPUBLIC-ECONOMIC ASSISTANCE

Inter-American Development Bank (IDB), 1300 New York Ave. NW, Washington, DC, 20577, USA, (202) 623-1000, (202) 623-3096, https://www.iadb.org/en; Latin Macro Watch (LMW).

United Nations Statistics Division (UNSD), United Nations Plz., New York, NY, 10017, USA, (800) 253-9646, (212) 963-9851, statistics@un.org, https://unstats.un.org; Statistical Yearbook of the United Nations 2021.

DOMINICAN REPUBLIC-ECONOMIC CONDITIONS

Bernan Press, 15250 NBN Way, Bldg. C, Blue Ridge Summit, PA, 17214, USA, (301) 459-2255, (800) 865-3457, (800) 865-3450, customercare@bernan.com, https://rowman.com/Page/Bernan; World Economic Outlook, April 2022.

Central Intelligence Agency (CIA), Office of Public Affairs, Washington, DC, 20505, USA, (703) 482-0623, https://www.cia.gov; The World Factbook.

The Economist Group: Economist Intelligence Unit (EIU), 900 3rd Ave., 16th Fl., New York, NY, 10022, USA, (212) 541-0500, americas@eiu.com, https://www.eiu.com; Dominican Republic Country Report.

Euromonitor International, Inc., 1 N Dearborn St., Ste. 1700, Chicago, IL, 60602, USA, (312) 922-1115, (312) 922-1157, info-usa@euromonitor.com, https://www.euromonitor.com/; Geographies.

Global Entrepreneurship Monitor (GEM), Babson College, 231 Forest St., Babson Park, MA, 02457, USA, (781) 235-1200, info@gemconsortium.org, https://www.gemconsortium.org/; GEM 2022-2023 Global Report.

Inter-American Development Bank (IDB), 1300 New York Ave. NW, Washington, DC, 20577, USA, (202) 623-1000, (202) 623-3096, https://www.iadb.org/en; Latin Macro Watch (LMW).

International Monetary Fund (IMF), 700 19th St. NW, Washington, DC, 20431, USA, (202) 623-7000, (202) 623-4661, publications@imf.org, https://www.imf.org; IMF Data and World Economic Outlook.

Palgrave Macmillan, 1 New York Plaza, Ste. 4500, New York, NY, 10004-1562, USA, (800) 777-4643, orders@palgrave.com, https://www.palgrave.com/us; The Statesman's Yearbook, 2023.

Routledge - Taylor & Francis Group, 6000 Broken Sound Pkwy. NW, Ste. 300, Boca Raton, FL, 33487, USA, (800) 634-1420, (800) 634-7064, orders@taylorandfrancis.com, https://www.routledge.com/; The Europa World Year Book 2022.

United Nations Economic Commission for Latin America and the Caribbean (ECLAC), Casilla 179-D, Santiago, 7630412, CHL, (202) 596-3713, prensa@cepal.org, https://www.cepal.org/en; CEPALSTAT.

United Nations Statistics Division (UNSD), United Nations Plz., New York, NY, 10017, USA, (800) 253-9646, (212) 963-9851, statistics@un.org, https://unstats.un.org; World Statistics Pocketbook 2021.

The World Bank, 1818 H St. NW, Washington, DC, 20433, USA, (202) 473-1000, (202) 477-6391, eds03@worldbank.org, https://www.worldbank.org/; Caribbean (report); Dominican Republic (report); Global Economic Monitor (GEM); Global Economic Prospects, June 2022; The Global Findex Database 2021; and World Development Report 2022: Finance for an Equitable Recovery.

DOMINICAN REPUBLIC-EDUCATION

Euromonitor International, Inc., 1 N Dearborn St., Ste. 1700, Chicago, IL, 60602, USA, (312) 922-1115, (312) 922-1157, info-usa@euromonitor.com, https://www.euromonitor.com/; Geographies.

Infoplease, c/o Sandbox Networks, Inc., 1 Lincoln St., 24th Fl., Boston, MA, 02111, USA, https://www.infoplease.com; Countries of the World.

Palgrave Macmillan, 1 New York Plaza, Ste. 4500, New York, NY, 10004-1562, USA, (800) 777-4643, orders@palgrave.com, https://www.palgrave.com/us; The Statesman's Yearbook, 2023.

Routledge - Taylor & Francis Group, 6000 Broken Sound Pkwy. NW, Ste. 300, Boca Raton, FL, 33487, USA, (800) 634-1420, (800) 634-7064, orders@taylorandfrancis.com, https://www.routledge.com/; The Europa World Year Book 2022.

UNESCO Institute for Statistics, C.P 250 Succursale H, Montreal, QC, H3G 2K8, CAN, (514) 343-6880 (Dial from U.S.), (514) 343-5740 (Fax from U.S.), uis.publications@unesco.org, http://uis.unesco.org/; Literacy and UIS.Stat.

United Nations Statistics Division (UNSD), United Nations Plz., New York, NY, 10017, USA, (800) 253-9646, (212) 963-9851, statistics@un.org, https://unstats.un.org; Millennium Development Goal Indicators.

The World Bank, 1818 H St. NW, Washington, DC, 20433, USA, (202) 473-1000, (202) 477-6391, eds03@worldbank.org, https://www.worldbank.org/; Dominican Republic (report); World Development Indicators (WDI) 2022; and World Development Report 2022: Finance for an Equitable Recovery.

DOMINICAN REPUBLIC-ELECTRICITY

Inter-American Development Bank (IDB), 1300 New York Ave. NW, Washington, DC, 20577, USA, (202) 623-1000, (202) 623-3096, https://www.iadb.org/en; Latin Macro Watch (LMW).

U.S. Energy Information Administration (EIA), 1000 Independence Ave. SW, Washington, DC, 20585, USA, (202) 586-8800, infoctr@eia.gov, https://www.eia.gov; International Energy Outlook 2021.

United Nations Statistics Division (UNSD), United Nations Plz., New York, NY, 10017, USA, (800) 253-9646, (212) 963-9851, statistics@un.org, https://unstats.un.org; Statistical Yearbook of the United Nations 2021.

DOMINICAN REPUBLIC-EMPLOYMENT

International Labour Organization (ILO), 4 Rte. des Morillons, Geneva, CH-1211, SWI, ilo@ilo.org, https://www.ilo.org; NORMLEX Information System on International Labour Standards.

UK Data Service, University of Essex, Wivenhoe Park, Colchester, Essex, CO4 3SQ, GBR, https://ukdataservice.ac.uk/; International Aggregate Data.

United Nations Statistics Division (UNSD), United Nations Plz., New York, NY, 10017, USA, (800) 253-9646, (212) 963-9851, statistics@un.org, https://unstats.un.org; Statistical Yearbook of the United Nations 2021.

The World Bank, 1818 H St. NW, Washington, DC, 20433, USA, (202) 473-1000, (202) 477-6391, eds03@worldbank.org, https://www.worldbank.org/; Dominican Republic (report).

DOMINICAN REPUBLIC-ENERGY INDUSTRIES

Enerdata, 47 avenue Alsace Lorraine, Grenoble, 38027, FRA, (332) 216-4534, research@enerdata.net, https://www.enerdata.net; World Refinery Database.

United Nations Statistics Division (UNSD), United Nations Plz., New York, NY, 10017, USA, (800) 253-9646, (212) 963-9851, statistics@un.org, https://unstats.un.org; Statistical Yearbook of the United Nations 2021.

DOMINICAN REPUBLIC-ENVIRONMENTAL CONDITIONS

DSI Data Service & Information, Xantener Strasse 51a, Rheinberg, D-47495, GER, dsi@dsidata.com, https://www.dsidata.com/; Global Environmental Database.

The Economist Group: Economist Intelligence Unit (EIU), 900 3rd Ave., 16th Fl., New York, NY, 10022, USA, (212) 541-0500, americas@eiu.com, https://www.eiu.com; Dominican Republic Country Report.

United Nations Economic Commission for Latin America and the Caribbean (ECLAC), Casilla 179-D, Santiago, 7630412, CHL, (202) 596-3713, prensa@cepal.org, https://www.cepal.org/en; CEPALSTAT.

United Nations Statistics Division (UNSD), United Nations Plz., New York, NY, 10017, USA, (800) 253-9646, (212) 963-9851, statistics@un.org, https://unstats.un.org; World Statistics Pocketbook 2021.

DOMINICAN REPUBLIC-EXPENDITURES, PUBLIC

Inter-American Development Bank (IDB), 1300 New York Ave. NW, Washington, DC, 20577, USA, (202) 623-1000, (202) 623-3096, https://www.iadb.org/en; Latin Macro Watch (LMW).

DOMINICAN REPUBLIC-EXPORTS

Central Intelligence Agency (CIA), Office of Public Affairs, Washington, DC, 20505, USA, (703) 482-0623, https://www.cia.gov; The World Factbook.

The Economist Group: Economist Intelligence Unit (EIU), 900 3rd Ave., 16th Fl., New York, NY, 10022, USA, (212) 541-0500, americas@eiu.com, https://www.eiu.com; Dominican Republic Country Report.

Inter-American Development Bank (IDB), 1300 New York Ave. NW, Washington, DC, 20577, USA, (202) 623-1000, (202) 623-3096, https://www.iadb.org/en; Latin Macro Watch (LMW).

International Monetary Fund (IMF), 700 19th St. NW, Washington, DC, 20431, USA, (202) 623-7000, (202) 623-4661, publications@imf.org, https://www.imf.org; Direction of Trade Statistics (DOTS) and International Financial Statistics (IFS).

S&P Global, IHS Markit, 15 Inverness Way E, Englewood, CO, 80112, USA, (800) 447-2273, (800) 854-7179, https://ihsmarkit.com; Global Trade Atlas (GTA).

United Nations Conference on Trade and Development (UNCTAD), Palais des Nations, Geneva, 1211,

SWI, (212) 963-6896, unctadinfo@unctad.org, https://unctad.org; Handbook of Statistics 2021.

The World Bank, 1818 H St. NW, Washington, DC, 20433, USA, (202) 473-1000, (202) 477-6391, eds03@worldbank.org, https://www.worldbank.org/; World Development Report 2022: Finance for an Equitable Recovery.

DOMINICAN REPUBLIC-FEMALE WORKING POPULATION

See DOMINICAN REPUBLIC-EMPLOYMENT

DOMINICAN REPUBLIC-FERTILITY, HUMAN

Central Intelligence Agency (CIA), Office of Public Affairs, Washington, DC, 20505, USA, (703) 482-0623, https://www.cia.gov; The World Factbook.

DOMINICAN REPUBLIC-FERTILIZER INDUSTRY

United Nations Food and Agricultural Organization (FAO), 2121 K St., Ste. 800B, Washington, DC, 20037, USA, (202) 653-2400 (Dial from U.S.), (202) 653-5760 (Fax from U.S.), fao-hq@fao.org, https://www.fao.org; The State of Food and Agriculture (SOFA) 2022.

DOMINICAN REPUBLIC-FETAL MORTALITY

See DOMINICAN REPUBLIC-MORTALITY

DOMINICAN REPUBLIC-FINANCE

Inter-American Development Bank (IDB), 1300 New York Ave. NW, Washington, DC, 20577, USA, (202) 623-1000, (202) 623-3096, https://www.iadb.org/en; Latin Macro Watch (LMW).

International Monetary Fund (IMF), 700 19th St. NW, Washington, DC, 20431, USA, (202) 623-7000, (202) 623-4661, publications@imf.org, https://www.imf.org; International Financial Statistics (IFS).

Stockholm International Peace Research Institute (SIPRI), Signalistgatan 9, Stockholm, SE 169 72, SWE, https://www.sipri.org/; SIPRI Arms Transfers Database and SIPRI Military Expenditure Database.

United Nations Statistics Division (UNSD), United Nations Plz., New York, NY, 10017, USA, (800) 253-9646, (212) 963-9851, statistics@un.org, https://unstats.un.org; Statistical Yearbook of the United Nations 2021.

The World Bank, 1818 H St. NW, Washington, DC, 20433, USA, (202) 473-1000, (202) 477-6391, eds03@worldbank.org, https://www.worldbank.org/; Dominican Republic (report).

DOMINICAN REPUBLIC-FINANCE, PUBLIC

Bernan Press, 15250 NBN Way, Bldg. C, Blue Ridge Summit, PA, 17214, USA, (301) 459-2255, (800) 865-3457, (800) 865-3450, customercare@bernan.com, https://rowman.com/Page/Bernan; National Accounts Statistics: Analysis of Main Aggregates 2020.

The Economist Group: Economist Intelligence Unit (EIU), 900 3rd Ave., 16th Fl., New York, NY, 10022, USA, (212) 541-0500, americas@eiu.com, https://www.eiu.com; Dominican Republic Country Report.

Inter-American Development Bank (IDB), 1300 New York Ave. NW, Washington, DC, 20577, USA, (202) 623-1000, (202) 623-3096, https://www.iadb.org/en; Latin Macro Watch (LMW).

International Monetary Fund (IMF), 700 19th St. NW, Washington, DC, 20431, USA, (202) 623-7000, (202) 623-4661, publications@imf.org, https://www.imf.org; International Financial Statistics (IFS) and Regional Economic Outlook.

Palgrave Macmillan, 1 New York Plaza, Ste. 4500, New York, NY, 10004-1562, USA, (800) 777-4643, orders@palgrave.com, https://www.palgrave.com/us; The Statesman's Yearbook, 2023.

Routledge - Taylor & Francis Group, 6000 Broken Sound Pkwy. NW, Ste. 300, Boca Raton, FL, 33487, USA, (800) 634-1420, (800) 634-7064, orders@taylorandfrancis.com, https://www.routledge.com/; The Europa World Year Book 2022.

United Nations Statistics Division (UNSD), United Nations Plz., New York, NY, 10017, USA, (800) 253-9646, (212) 963-9851, statistics@un.org, https://unstats.un.org; National Accounts Main Aggregates Database and National Accounts Statistics: Main Aggregates and Detailed Tables.

The World Bank, 1818 H St. NW, Washington, DC, 20433, USA, (202) 473-1000, (202) 477-6391, eds03@worldbank.org, https://www.worldbank.org/; Dominican Republic (report).

DOMINICAN REPUBLIC-FISHERIES

Inter-American Development Bank (IDB), 1300 New York Ave. NW, Washington, DC, 20577, USA, (202) 623-1000, (202) 623-3096, https://www.iadb.org/en; Latin Macro Watch (LMW).

Palgrave Macmillan, 1 New York Plaza, Ste. 4500, New York, NY, 10004-1562, USA, (800) 777-4643, orders@palgrave.com, https://www.palgrave.com/us; The Statesman's Yearbook, 2023.

Routledge - Taylor & Francis Group, 6000 Broken Sound Pkwy. NW, Ste. 300, Boca Raton, FL, 33487, USA, (800) 634-1420, (800) 634-7064, orders@taylorandfrancis.com, https://www.routledge.com/; The Europa World Year Book 2022.

United Nations Food and Agricultural Organization (FAO), 2121 K St., Ste. 800B, Washington, DC, 20037, USA, (202) 653-2400 (Dial from U.S.), (202) 653-5760 (Fax from U.S.), fao-hq@fao.org, https://www.fao.org; FAO Yearbook of Fishery and Aquaculture Statistics 2019; Fishery Statistical Collections Global Capture Production; FishStatJ; and The State of Food and Agriculture (SOFA) 2022.

United Nations Statistics Division (UNSD), United Nations Plz., New York, NY, 10017, USA, (800) 253-9646, (212) 963-9851, statistics@un.org, https://unstats.un.org; Statistical Yearbook of the United Nations 2021.

The World Bank, 1818 H St. NW, Washington, DC, 20433, USA, (202) 473-1000, (202) 477-6391, eds03@worldbank.org, https://www.worldbank.org/; Dominican Republic (report).

DOMINICAN REPUBLIC-FOOD

United Nations Food and Agricultural Organization (FAO), 2121 K St., Ste. 800B, Washington, DC, 20037, USA, (202) 653-2400 (Dial from U.S.), (202) 653-5760 (Fax from U.S.), fao-hq@fao.org, https://www.fao.org; The State of Food and Agriculture (SOFA) 2022.

DOMINICAN REPUBLIC-FOREIGN EXCHANGE RATES

Inter-American Development Bank (IDB), 1300 New York Ave. NW, Washington, DC, 20577, USA, (202) 623-1000, (202) 623-3096, https://www.iadb.org/en; Latin Macro Watch (LMW).

International Monetary Fund (IMF), 700 19th St. NW, Washington, DC, 20431, USA, (202) 623-7000, (202) 623-4661, publications@imf.org, https://www.imf.org; International Financial Statistics (IFS).

DOMINICAN REPUBLIC-FORESTS AND FORESTRY

Inter-American Development Bank (IDB), 1300 New York Ave. NW, Washington, DC, 20577, USA, (202) 623-1000, (202) 623-3096, https://www.iadb.org/en; Latin Macro Watch (LMW).

Palgrave Macmillan, 1 New York Plaza, Ste. 4500, New York, NY, 10004-1562, USA, (800) 777-4643, orders@palgrave.com, https://www.palgrave.com/us; The Statesman's Yearbook, 2023.

Routledge - Taylor & Francis Group, 6000 Broken Sound Pkwy. NW, Ste. 300, Boca Raton, FL, 33487, USA, (800) 634-1420, (800) 634-7064, orders@taylorandfrancis.com, https://www.routledge.com/; The Europa World Year Book 2022.

UNESCO Institute for Statistics, C.P 250 Succursale H, Montreal, QC, H3G 2K8, CAN, (514) 343-6880 (Dial from U.S.), (514) 343-5740 (Fax from U.S.), uis.publications@unesco.org, http://uis.unesco.org/; UIS.Stat.

United Nations Food and Agricultural Organization (FAO), 2121 K St., Ste. 800B, Washington, DC, 20037, USA, (202) 653-2400 (Dial from U.S.), (202) 653-5760 (Fax from U.S.), fao-hq@fao.org, https://www.fao.org; FAO Yearbook of Forest Products 2019 and The State of Food and Agriculture (SOFA) 2022.

United Nations Statistics Division (UNSD), United Nations Plz., New York, NY, 10017, USA, (800) 253-9646, (212) 963-9851, statistics@un.org, https://unstats.un.org; Statistical Yearbook of the United Nations 2021.

The World Bank, 1818 H St. NW, Washington, DC, 20433, USA, (202) 473-1000, (202) 477-6391, eds03@worldbank.org, https://www.worldbank.org/; Dominican Republic (report) and World Development Report 2022: Finance for an Equitable Recovery.

DOMINICAN REPUBLIC-GAS PRODUCTION

See DOMINICAN REPUBLIC-MINERAL INDUSTRIES

DOMINICAN REPUBLIC-GEOGRAPHIC INFORMATION SYSTEMS

The World Bank, 1818 H St. NW, Washington, DC, 20433, USA, (202) 473-1000, (202) 477-6391, eds03@worldbank.org, https://www.worldbank.org/; Dominican Republic (report).

DOMINICAN REPUBLIC-GOLD INDUSTRY

The World Bank, 1818 H St. NW, Washington, DC, 20433, USA, (202) 473-1000, (202) 477-6391, eds03@worldbank.org, https://www.worldbank.org/; World Development Indicators (WDI) 2022.

DOMINICAN REPUBLIC-GOLD PRODUCTION

See DOMINICAN REPUBLIC-MINERAL INDUSTRIES

DOMINICAN REPUBLIC-GROSS DOMESTIC PRODUCT

The Economist Group: Economist Intelligence Unit (EIU), 900 3rd Ave., 16th Fl., New York, NY, 10022, USA, (212) 541-0500, americas@eiu.com, https://www.eiu.com; Dominican Republic Country Report.

Inter-American Development Bank (IDB), 1300 New York Ave. NW, Washington, DC, 20577, USA, (202) 623-1000, (202) 623-3096, https://www.iadb.org/en; Latin Macro Watch (LMW).

Routledge - Taylor & Francis Group, 6000 Broken Sound Pkwy. NW, Ste. 300, Boca Raton, FL, 33487, USA, (800) 634-1420, (800) 634-7064, orders@taylorandfrancis.com, https://www.routledge.com/; The Europa World Year Book 2022.

United Nations Statistics Division (UNSD), United Nations Plz., New York, NY, 10017, USA, (800) 253-9646, (212) 963-9851, statistics@un.org, https://unstats.un.org; Statistical Yearbook of the United Nations 2021.

The World Bank, 1818 H St. NW, Washington, DC, 20433, USA, (202) 473-1000, (202) 477-6391, eds03@worldbank.org, https://www.worldbank.org/; World Development Indicators (WDI) 2022 and World Development Report 2022: Finance for an Equitable Recovery.

DOMINICAN REPUBLIC-GROSS NATIONAL PRODUCT

Inter-American Development Bank (IDB), 1300 New York Ave. NW, Washington, DC, 20577, USA, (202) 623-1000, (202) 623-3096, https://www.iadb.org/en; Latin Macro Watch (LMW).

Palgrave Macmillan, 1 New York Plaza, Ste. 4500, New York, NY, 10004-1562, USA, (800) 777-4643, orders@palgrave.com, https://www.palgrave.com/us; The Statesman's Yearbook, 2023.

Routledge - Taylor & Francis Group, 6000 Broken Sound Pkwy. NW, Ste. 300, Boca Raton, FL, 33487, USA, (800) 634-1420, (800) 634-7064, orders@taylorandfrancis.com, https://www.routledge.com/; The Europa World Year Book 2022.

United Nations Statistics Division (UNSD), United Nations Plz., New York, NY, 10017, USA, (800) 253-9646, (212) 963-9851, statistics@un.org, https://unstats.un.org; Statistical Yearbook of the United Nations 2021.

The World Bank, 1818 H St. NW, Washington, DC, 20433, USA, (202) 473-1000, (202) 477-6391, eds03@worldbank.org, https://www.worldbank.org/; World Development Indicators (WDI) 2022 and World Development Report 2022: Finance for an Equitable Recovery.

DOMINICAN REPUBLIC-HARDWOOD INDUSTRY

Inter-American Development Bank (IDB), 1300 New York Ave. NW, Washington, DC, 20577, USA, (202) 623-1000, (202) 623-3096, https://www.iadb.org/en; Latin Macro Watch (LMW).

United Nations Food and Agricultural Organization (FAO), 2121 K St., Ste. 800B, Washington, DC, 20037, USA, (202) 653-2400 (Dial from U.S.), (202) 653-5760 (Fax from U.S.), fao-hq@fao.org, https://www.fao.org; FAO Yearbook of Forest Products 2019.

United Nations Statistics Division (UNSD), United Nations Plz., New York, NY, 10017, USA, (800) 253-9646, (212) 963-9851, statistics@un.org, https://unstats.un.org; Statistical Yearbook of the United Nations 2021.

DOMINICAN REPUBLIC-HOUSING

Euromonitor International, Inc., 1 N Dearborn St., Ste. 1700, Chicago, IL, 60602, USA, (312) 922-1115, (312) 922-1157, info-usa@euromonitor.com, https://www.euromonitor.com/; Geographies.

DOMINICAN REPUBLIC-ILLITERATE PERSONS

UNESCO Institute for Statistics, C.P 250 Succursale H, Montreal, QC, H3G 2K8, CAN, (514) 343-6880 (Dial from U.S.), (514) 343-5740 (Fax from U.S.), uis.publications@unesco.org, http://uis.unesco.org/; UIS.Stat.

DOMINICAN REPUBLIC-IMPORTS

Central Intelligence Agency (CIA), Office of Public Affairs, Washington, DC, 20505, USA, (703) 482-0623, https://www.cia.gov; The World Factbook.

The Economist Group: Economist Intelligence Unit (EIU), 900 3rd Ave., 16th Fl., New York, NY, 10022, USA, (212) 541-0500, americas@eiu.com, https://www.eiu.com; Dominican Republic Country Report.

Inter-American Development Bank (IDB), 1300 New York Ave. NW, Washington, DC, 20577, USA, (202) 623-1000, (202) 623-3096, https://www.iadb.org/en; Latin Macro Watch (LMW).

International Monetary Fund (IMF), 700 19th St. NW, Washington, DC, 20431, USA, (202) 623-7000, (202) 623-4661, publications@imf.org, https://www.imf.org; Direction of Trade Statistics (DOTS) and International Financial Statistics (IFS).

S&P Global, IHS Markit, 15 Inverness Way E, Englewood, CO, 80112, USA, (800) 447-2273, (800) 854-7179, https://ihsmarkit.com; Global Trade Atlas (GTA).

United Nations Conference on Trade and Development (UNCTAD), Palais des Nations, Geneva, 1211, SWI, (212) 963-6896, unctadinfo@unctad.org, https://unctad.org; Handbook of Statistics 2021.

The World Bank, 1818 H St. NW, Washington, DC, 20433, USA, (202) 473-1000, (202) 477-6391, eds03@worldbank.org, https://www.worldbank.org/; World Development Report 2022: Finance for an Equitable Recovery.

DOMINICAN REPUBLIC-INDUSTRIES

Central Intelligence Agency (CIA), Office of Public Affairs, Washington, DC, 20505, USA, (703) 482-0623, https://www.cia.gov; The World Factbook.

The Economist Group: Economist Intelligence Unit (EIU), 900 3rd Ave., 16th Fl., New York, NY, 10022, USA, (212) 541-0500, americas@eiu.com, https://www.eiu.com; Dominican Republic Country Report.

Euromonitor International, Inc., 1 N Dearborn St., Ste. 1700, Chicago, IL, 60602, USA, (312) 922-1115, (312) 922-1157, info-usa@euromonitor.com, https://www.euromonitor.com/; Geographies.

International Labour Organization (ILO), 4 Rte. des Morillons, Geneva, CH-1211, SWI, ilo@ilo.org, https://www.ilo.org; NORMLEX Information System on International Labour Standards.

Palgrave Macmillan, 1 New York Plaza, Ste. 4500, New York, NY, 10004-1562, USA, (800) 777-4643, orders@palgrave.com, https://www.palgrave.com/us; The Statesman's Yearbook, 2023.

Routledge - Taylor & Francis Group, 6000 Broken Sound Pkwy. NW, Ste. 300, Boca Raton, FL, 33487, USA, (800) 634-1420, (800) 634-7064, orders@taylorandfrancis.com, https://www.routledge.com/; The Europa World Year Book 2022.

United Nations Industrial Development Organization (UNIDO), 1 United Nations Plz., Rm. DC1-1118, New York, NY, 10017, USA, (212) 963-6890, (212) 963 6885, (212) 963-7904, office.newyork@unido.org, https://www.unido.org/; Industrial Statistics Databases and International Yearbook of Industrial Statistics 2021.

The World Bank, 1818 H St. NW, Washington, DC, 20433, USA, (202) 473-1000, (202) 477-6391, eds03@worldbank.org, https://www.worldbank.org/; Dominican Republic (report) and World Development Indicators (WDI) 2022.

DOMINICAN REPUBLIC-INFANT AND MATERNAL MORTALITY

See DOMINICAN REPUBLIC-MORTALITY

DOMINICAN REPUBLIC-INTEREST RATES

Inter-American Development Bank (IDB), 1300 New York Ave. NW, Washington, DC, 20577, USA, (202) 623-1000, (202) 623-3096, https://www.iadb.org/en; Latin Macro Watch (LMW).

DOMINICAN REPUBLIC-INTERNAL REVENUE

Inter-American Development Bank (IDB), 1300 New York Ave. NW, Washington, DC, 20577, USA, (202) 623-1000, (202) 623-3096, https://www.iadb.org/en; Latin Macro Watch (LMW).

DOMINICAN REPUBLIC-INTERNATIONAL FINANCE

Inter-American Development Bank (IDB), 1300 New York Ave. NW, Washington, DC, 20577, USA, (202) 623-1000, (202) 623-3096, https://www.iadb.org/en; Latin Macro Watch (LMW).

DOMINICAN REPUBLIC-INTERNATIONAL LIQUIDITY

Inter-American Development Bank (IDB), 1300 New York Ave. NW, Washington, DC, 20577, USA, (202) 623-1000, (202) 623-3096, https://www.iadb.org/en; Latin Macro Watch (LMW).

DOMINICAN REPUBLIC-INTERNATIONAL TRADE

The Economist Group: Economist Intelligence Unit (EIU), 900 3rd Ave., 16th Fl., New York, NY, 10022, USA, (212) 541-0500, americas@eiu.com, https://www.eiu.com; Dominican Republic Country Report.

Euromonitor International, Inc., 1 N Dearborn St., Ste. 1700, Chicago, IL, 60602, USA, (312) 922-1115, (312) 922-1157, info-usa@euromonitor.com, https://www.euromonitor.com/; Geographies.

Inter-American Development Bank (IDB), 1300 New York Ave. NW, Washington, DC, 20577, USA, (202) 623-1000, (202) 623-3096, https://www.iadb.org/en; Latin Macro Watch (LMW).

International Monetary Fund (IMF), 700 19th St. NW, Washington, DC, 20431, USA, (202) 623-7000, (202) 623-4661, publications@imf.org, https://www.imf.org; International Financial Statistics (IFS).

Palgrave Macmillan, 1 New York Plaza, Ste. 4500, New York, NY, 10004-1562, USA, (800) 777-4643, orders@palgrave.com, https://www.palgrave.com/us; The Statesman's Yearbook, 2023.

Routledge - Taylor & Francis Group, 6000 Broken Sound Pkwy. NW, Ste. 300, Boca Raton, FL, 33487, USA, (800) 634-1420, (800) 634-7064, orders@taylorandfrancis.com, https://www.routledge.com/; The Europa World Year Book 2022.

United Nations Conference on Trade and Development (UNCTAD), Palais des Nations, Geneva, 1211, SWI, (212) 963-6896, unctadinfo@unctad.org, https://unctad.org; Trade and Development Report 2021.

United Nations Food and Agricultural Organization (FAO), 2121 K St., Ste. 800B, Washington, DC, 20037, USA, (202) 653-2400 (Dial from U.S.), (202) 653-5760 (Fax from U.S.), fao-hq@fao.org, https://www.fao.org; The State of Food and Agriculture (SOFA) 2022.

United Nations Statistics Division (UNSD), United Nations Plz., New York, NY, 10017, USA, (800) 253-9646, (212) 963-9851, statistics@un.org, https://unstats.un.org; International Trade Statistics Yearbook 2020 and Statistical Yearbook of the United Nations 2021.

The World Bank, 1818 H St. NW, Washington, DC, 20433, USA, (202) 473-1000, (202) 477-6391, eds03@worldbank.org, https://www.worldbank.org/; Dominican Republic (report); World Development Indicators (WDI) 2022; and World Development Report 2022: Finance for an Equitable Recovery.

World Trade Organization (WTO), Ctre. William Rappard, Rue de Lausanne 154, Case postale, Geneva, CH-1211, SWI, enquiries@wto.org, https://www.wto.org; World Trade Statistical Review 2022.

DOMINICAN REPUBLIC-INTERNET USERS

International Telecommunication Union (ITU), Place des Nations, Geneva, CH-1211, SWI, itumail@itu.int, https://www.itu.int; Global Connectivity Report 2022; World Telecommunication/ICT Indicators Database 2021; and Yearbook of Statistics 2019.

The World Bank, 1818 H St. NW, Washington, DC, 20433, USA, (202) 473-1000, (202) 477-6391, eds03@worldbank.org, https://www.worldbank.org/; Dominican Republic (report).

DOMINICAN REPUBLIC-INVESTMENTS

Inter-American Development Bank (IDB), 1300 New York Ave. NW, Washington, DC, 20577, USA, (202) 623-1000, (202) 623-3096, https://www.iadb.org/en; Latin Macro Watch (LMW).

DOMINICAN REPUBLIC-IRRIGATION

Inter-American Development Bank (IDB), 1300 New York Ave. NW, Washington, DC, 20577, USA, (202) 623-1000, (202) 623-3096, https://www.iadb.org/en; Latin Macro Watch (LMW).

DOMINICAN REPUBLIC-LABOR

Central Intelligence Agency (CIA), Office of Public Affairs, Washington, DC, 20505, USA, (703) 482-0623, https://www.cia.gov; The World Factbook.

Euromonitor International, Inc., 1 N Dearborn St., Ste. 1700, Chicago, IL, 60602, USA, (312) 922-1115, (312) 922-1157, info-usa@euromonitor.com, https://www.euromonitor.com/; Geographies.

International Labour Organization (ILO), 4 Rte. des Morillons, Geneva, CH-1211, SWI, ilo@ilo.org, https://www.ilo.org; NORMLEX Information System on International Labour Standards.

Palgrave Macmillan, 1 New York Plaza, Ste. 4500, New York, NY, 10004-1562, USA, (800) 777-4643, orders@palgrave.com, https://www.palgrave.com/us; The Statesman's Yearbook, 2023.

U.S. Energy Information Administration (EIA), 1000 Independence Ave. SW, Washington, DC, 20585,

USA, (202) 586-8800, infoctr@eia.gov, https://www.eia.gov; International Energy Outlook 2021.

United Nations Food and Agricultural Organization (FAO), 2121 K St., Ste. 800B, Washington, DC, 20037, USA, (202) 653-2400 (Dial from U.S.), (202) 653-5760 (Fax from U.S.), fao-hq@fao.org, https://www.fao.org; The State of Food and Agriculture (SOFA) 2022.

The World Bank, 1818 H St. NW, Washington, DC, 20433, USA, (202) 473-1000, (202) 477-6391, eds03@worldbank.org, https://www.worldbank.org/; World Development Indicators (WDI) 2022 and World Development Report 2022: Finance for an Equitable Recovery.

DOMINICAN REPUBLIC-LAND USE

Inter-American Development Bank (IDB), 1300 New York Ave. NW, Washington, DC, 20577, USA, (202) 623-1000, (202) 623-3096, https://www.iadb.org/en; Latin Macro Watch (LMW).

United Nations Statistics Division (UNSD), United Nations Plz., New York, NY, 10017, USA, (800) 253-9646, (212) 963-9851, statistics@un.org, https://unstats.un.org; Millennium Development Goal Indicators.

The World Bank, 1818 H St. NW, Washington, DC, 20433, USA, (202) 473-1000, (202) 477-6391, eds03@worldbank.org, https://www.worldbank.org/; World Development Report 2022: Finance for an Equitable Recovery.

DOMINICAN REPUBLIC-LIFE EXPECTANCY

Central Intelligence Agency (CIA), Office of Public Affairs, Washington, DC, 20505, USA, (703) 482-0623, https://www.cia.gov; The World Factbook.

United Nations Department of Economic and Social Affairs (DESA), Population Division, 2 United Nations Plz., Rm. DC2-1950, New York, NY, 10017, USA, (212) 963-3209, (212) 963-2147, population@un.org, https://www.un.org/development/desa/pd/; World Population Ageing 2020 Highlights.

United Nations Statistics Division (UNSD), United Nations Plz., New York, NY, 10017, USA, (800) 253-9646, (212) 963-9851, statistics@un.org, https://unstats.un.org; Millennium Development Goal Indicators.

DOMINICAN REPUBLIC-LITERACY

Euromonitor International, Inc., 1 N Dearborn St., Ste. 1700, Chicago, IL, 60602, USA, (312) 922-1115, (312) 922-1157, info-usa@euromonitor.com, https://www.euromonitor.com/; Geographies.

UNESCO Institute for Statistics, C.P 250 Succursale H, Montreal, QC, H3G 2K8, CAN, (514) 343-6880 (Dial from U.S.), (514) 343-5740 (Fax from U.S.), uis.publications@unesco.org, http://uis.unesco.org/; Literacy.

DOMINICAN REPUBLIC-LIVESTOCK

Palgrave Macmillan, 1 New York Plaza, Ste. 4500, New York, NY, 10004-1562, USA, (800) 777-4643, orders@palgrave.com, https://www.palgrave.com/us; The Statesman's Yearbook, 2023.

Routledge - Taylor & Francis Group, 6000 Broken Sound Pkwy. NW, Ste. 300, Boca Raton, FL, 33487, USA, (800) 634-1420, (800) 634-7064, orders@taylorandfrancis.com, https://www.routledge.com/; The Europa World Year Book 2022.

United Nations Food and Agricultural Organization (FAO), 2121 K St., Ste. 800B, Washington, DC, 20037, USA, (202) 653-2400 (Dial from U.S.), (202) 653-5760 (Fax from U.S.), fao-hq@fao.org, https://www.fao.org; The State of Food and Agriculture (SOFA) 2022.

United Nations Statistics Division (UNSD), United Nations Plz., New York, NY, 10017, USA, (800) 253-9646, (212) 963-9851, statistics@un.org, https://unstats.un.org; Statistical Yearbook of the United Nations 2021.

DOMINICAN REPUBLIC-MANUFACTURES

Inter-American Development Bank (IDB), 1300 New York Ave. NW, Washington, DC, 20577, USA, (202) 623-1000, (202) 623-3096, https://www.iadb.org/en; Latin Macro Watch (LMW).

DOMINICAN REPUBLIC-MARRIAGE

United Nations Statistics Division (UNSD), United Nations Plz., New York, NY, 10017, USA, (800) 253-9646, (212) 963-9851, statistics@un.org, https://unstats.un.org; Statistical Yearbook of the United Nations 2021.

DOMINICAN REPUBLIC-MINERAL INDUSTRIES

Inter-American Development Bank (IDB), 1300 New York Ave. NW, Washington, DC, 20577, USA, (202) 623-1000, (202) 623-3096, https://www.iadb.org/en; Latin Macro Watch (LMW).

International Monetary Fund (IMF), 700 19th St. NW, Washington, DC, 20431, USA, (202) 623-7000, (202) 623-4661, publications@imf.org, https://www.imf.org; International Financial Statistics (IFS).

Palgrave Macmillan, 1 New York Plaza, Ste. 4500, New York, NY, 10004-1562, USA, (800) 777-4643, orders@palgrave.com, https://www.palgrave.com/us; The Statesman's Yearbook, 2023.

Routledge - Taylor & Francis Group, 6000 Broken Sound Pkwy. NW, Ste. 300, Boca Raton, FL, 33487, USA, (800) 634-1420, (800) 634-7064, orders@taylorandfrancis.com, https://www.routledge.com/; The Europa World Year Book 2022.

United Nations Conference on Trade and Development (UNCTAD), Palais des Nations, Geneva, 1211, SWI, (212) 963-6896, unctadinfo@unctad.org, https://unctad.org; Trade and Development Report 2021.

United Nations Statistics Division (UNSD), United Nations Plz., New York, NY, 10017, USA, (800) 253-9646, (212) 963-9851, statistics@un.org, https://unstats.un.org; Statistical Yearbook of the United Nations 2021.

DOMINICAN REPUBLIC-MONEY SUPPLY

The Economist Group: Economist Intelligence Unit (EIU), 900 3rd Ave., 16th Fl., New York, NY, 10022, USA, (212) 541-0500, americas@eiu.com, https://www.eiu.com; Dominican Republic Country Report.

Inter-American Development Bank (IDB), 1300 New York Ave. NW, Washington, DC, 20577, USA, (202) 623-1000, (202) 623-3096, https://www.iadb.org/en; Latin Macro Watch (LMW).

International Monetary Fund (IMF), 700 19th St. NW, Washington, DC, 20431, USA, (202) 623-7000, (202) 623-4661, publications@imf.org, https://www.imf.org; International Financial Statistics (IFS).

Routledge - Taylor & Francis Group, 6000 Broken Sound Pkwy. NW, Ste. 300, Boca Raton, FL, 33487, USA, (800) 634-1420, (800) 634-7064, orders@taylorandfrancis.com, https://www.routledge.com/; The Europa World Year Book 2022.

United Nations Statistics Division (UNSD), United Nations Plz., New York, NY, 10017, USA, (800) 253-9646, (212) 963-9851, statistics@un.org, https://unstats.un.org; Statistical Yearbook of the United Nations 2021.

The World Bank, 1818 H St. NW, Washington, DC, 20433, USA, (202) 473-1000, (202) 477-6391, eds03@worldbank.org, https://www.worldbank.org/; Dominican Republic (report).

DOMINICAN REPUBLIC-MORTALITY

United Nations Statistics Division (UNSD), United Nations Plz., New York, NY, 10017, USA, (800) 253-9646, (212) 963-9851, statistics@un.org, https://unstats.un.org; Millennium Development Goal Indicators; Statistical Yearbook of the United Nations 2021; and World Statistics Pocketbook 2021.

The World Bank, 1818 H St. NW, Washington, DC, 20433, USA, (202) 473-1000, (202) 477-6391, eds03@worldbank.org, https://www.worldbank.org/; World Development Indicators (WDI) 2022.

World Health Organization (WHO), Ave. Appia 20, Geneva, CH-1211, SWI, (202) 974-3000 (Telephone in U.S.), publications@who.int, https://www.who.int/; Global Health Observatory (GHO) and Health Statistics and Information Systems.

DOMINICAN REPUBLIC-MOTOR VEHICLES

International Road Federation (IRF), Madison Place, 500 Montgomery St., 5th Fl., Alexandria, VA, 22314, USA, (703) 535-1001, (703) 535-1007, info@irf.global, https://www.irf.global/; World Road Statistics (WRS).

DOMINICAN REPUBLIC-NATURAL GAS PRODUCTION

See DOMINICAN REPUBLIC-MINERAL INDUSTRIES

DOMINICAN REPUBLIC-NICKEL AND NICKEL ORE

See DOMINICAN REPUBLIC-MINERAL INDUSTRIES

DOMINICAN REPUBLIC-NUTRITION

United Nations Food and Agricultural Organization (FAO), 2121 K St., Ste. 800B, Washington, DC, 20037, USA, (202) 653-2400 (Dial from U.S.), (202) 653-5760 (Fax from U.S.), fao-hq@fao.org, https://www.fao.org; The State of Food and Agriculture (SOFA) 2022.

United Nations Statistics Division (UNSD), United Nations Plz., New York, NY, 10017, USA, (800) 253-9646, (212) 963-9851, statistics@un.org, https://unstats.un.org; Millennium Development Goal Indicators.

DOMINICAN REPUBLIC-PAPER

See DOMINICAN REPUBLIC-FORESTS AND FORESTRY

DOMINICAN REPUBLIC-PEANUT PRODUCTION

See DOMINICAN REPUBLIC-CROPS

DOMINICAN REPUBLIC-PESTICIDES

United Nations Food and Agricultural Organization (FAO), 2121 K St., Ste. 800B, Washington, DC, 20037, USA, (202) 653-2400 (Dial from U.S.), (202) 653-5760 (Fax from U.S.), fao-hq@fao.org, https://www.fao.org; The State of Food and Agriculture (SOFA) 2022.

DOMINICAN REPUBLIC-PETROLEUM INDUSTRY AND TRADE

Inter-American Development Bank (IDB), 1300 New York Ave. NW, Washington, DC, 20577, USA, (202) 623-1000, (202) 623-3096, https://www.iadb.org/en; Latin Macro Watch (LMW).

U.S. Energy Information Administration (EIA), 1000 Independence Ave. SW, Washington, DC, 20585, USA, (202) 586-8800, infoctr@eia.gov, https://www.eia.gov; International Energy Outlook 2021.

United Nations Food and Agricultural Organization (FAO), 2121 K St., Ste. 800B, Washington, DC, 20037, USA, (202) 653-2400 (Dial from U.S.), (202) 653-5760 (Fax from U.S.), fao-hq@fao.org, https://www.fao.org; The State of Food and Agriculture (SOFA) 2022.

United Nations Statistics Division (UNSD), United Nations Plz., New York, NY, 10017, USA, (800) 253-9646, (212) 963-9851, statistics@un.org, https://unstats.un.org; Statistical Yearbook of the United Nations 2021.

DOMINICAN REPUBLIC-POPULATION

Central Intelligence Agency (CIA), Office of Public Affairs, Washington, DC, 20505, USA, (703) 482-0623, https://www.cia.gov; The World Factbook.

The Economist Group: Economist Intelligence Unit (EIU), 900 3rd Ave., 16th Fl., New York, NY, 10022, USA, (212) 541-0500, americas@eiu.com, https://www.eiu.com; Dominican Republic Country Report.

European Commission, Eurostat, Luxembourg, 2920, LUX, https://ec.europa.eu/eurostat/; EU in the World 2020.

Infoplease, c/o Sandbox Networks, Inc., 1 Lincoln St., 24th Fl., Boston, MA, 02111, USA, https://www.infoplease.com; Countries of the World.

Inter-American Development Bank (IDB), 1300 New York Ave. NW, Washington, DC, 20577, USA, (202) 623-1000, (202) 623-3096, https://www.iadb.org/en; Latin Macro Watch (LMW).

International Labour Organization (ILO), 4 Rte. des Morillons, Geneva, CH-1211, SWI, ilo@ilo.org, https://www.ilo.org; NORMLEX Information System on International Labour Standards.

Palgrave Macmillan, 1 New York Plaza, Ste. 4500, New York, NY, 10004-1562, USA, (800) 777-4643, orders@palgrave.com, https://www.palgrave.com/us; The Statesman's Yearbook, 2023.

Routledge - Taylor & Francis Group, 6000 Broken Sound Pkwy. NW, Ste. 300, Boca Raton, FL, 33487, USA, (800) 634-1420, (800) 634-7064, orders@taylorandfrancis.com, https://www.routledge.com/; The Europa World Year Book 2022.

UK Data Service, University of Essex, Wivenhoe Park, Colchester, Essex, CO4 3SQ, GBR, https://ukdataservice.ac.uk/; International Aggregate Data.

UNESCO Institute for Statistics, C.P 250 Succursale H, Montreal, QC, H3G 2K8, CAN, (514) 343-6880 (Dial from U.S.), (514) 343-5740 (Fax from U.S.), uis.publications@unesco.org, http://uis.unesco.org/; UIS.Stat.

United Nations Department of Economic and Social Affairs (DESA), Population Division, 2 United Nations Plz., Rm. DC2-1950, New York, NY, 10017, USA, (212) 963-3209, (212) 963-2147, population@un.org, https://www.un.org/development/desa/pd/; Revision of World Urbanization Prospects and World Population Ageing 2020 Highlights.

United Nations Development Programme (UNDP), One United Nations Plz., New York, NY, 10017, USA, (212) 906-5000, (212) 906-5001, https://www.undp.org; Human Development Report 2021-2022.

United Nations Economic Commission for Latin America and the Caribbean (ECLAC), Casilla 179-D, Santiago, 7630412, CHL, (202) 596-3713, prensa@cepal.org, https://www.cepal.org/en; CEPALSTAT.

United Nations Statistics Division (UNSD), United Nations Plz., New York, NY, 10017, USA, (800) 253-9646, (212) 963-9851, statistics@un.org, https://unstats.un.org; Statistical Yearbook of the United Nations 2021 and World Statistics Pocketbook 2021.

The World Bank, 1818 H St. NW, Washington, DC, 20433, USA, (202) 473-1000, (202) 477-6391, eds03@worldbank.org, https://www.worldbank.org/; Caribbean (report); Dominican Republic (report); The Global Findex Database 2021; and World Development Report 2022: Finance for an Equitable Recovery.

World Health Organization (WHO), Ave. Appia 20, Geneva, CH-1211, SWI, (202) 974-3000 (Telephone in U.S.), publications@who.int, https://www.who.int/; Health Statistics and Information Systems.

DOMINICAN REPUBLIC-POPULATION DENSITY

Central Intelligence Agency (CIA), Office of Public Affairs, Washington, DC, 20505, USA, (703) 482-0623, https://www.cia.gov; The World Factbook.

Inter-American Development Bank (IDB), 1300 New York Ave. NW, Washington, DC, 20577, USA, (202) 623-1000, (202) 623-3096, https://www.iadb.org/en; Latin Macro Watch (LMW).

Palgrave Macmillan, 1 New York Plaza, Ste. 4500, New York, NY, 10004-1562, USA, (800) 777-4643, orders@palgrave.com, https://www.palgrave.com/us; The Statesman's Yearbook, 2023.

Routledge - Taylor & Francis Group, 6000 Broken Sound Pkwy. NW, Ste. 300, Boca Raton, FL, 33487, USA, (800) 634-1420, (800) 634-7064, orders@taylorandfrancis.com, https://www.routledge.com/; The Europa World Year Book 2022.

The World Bank, 1818 H St. NW, Washington, DC, 20433, USA, (202) 473-1000, (202) 477-6391, eds03@worldbank.org, https://www.worldbank.org/; Dominican Republic (report) and World Development Report 2022: Finance for an Equitable Recovery.

DOMINICAN REPUBLIC-POWER RESOURCES

Euromonitor International, Inc., 1 N Dearborn St., Ste. 1700, Chicago, IL, 60602, USA, (312) 922-1115, (312) 922-1157, info-usa@euromonitor.com, https://www.euromonitor.com/; Geographies.

Palgrave Macmillan, 1 New York Plaza, Ste. 4500, New York, NY, 10004-1562, USA, (800) 777-4643, orders@palgrave.com, https://www.palgrave.com/us; The Statesman's Yearbook, 2023.

U.S. Energy Information Administration (EIA), 1000 Independence Ave. SW, Washington, DC, 20585, USA, (202) 586-8800, infoctr@eia.gov, https://www.eia.gov; International Energy Outlook 2021.

United Nations Food and Agricultural Organization (FAO), 2121 K St., Ste. 800B, Washington, DC, 20037, USA, (202) 653-2400 (Dial from U.S.), (202) 653-5760 (Fax from U.S.), fao-hq@fao.org, https://www.fao.org; The State of Food and Agriculture (SOFA) 2022.

United Nations Statistics Division (UNSD), United Nations Plz., New York, NY, 10017, USA, (800) 253-9646, (212) 963-9851, statistics@un.org, https://unstats.un.org; Energy Statistics Yearbook 2019; Statistical Yearbook of the United Nations 2021; and World Statistics Pocketbook 2021.

The World Bank, 1818 H St. NW, Washington, DC, 20433, USA, (202) 473-1000, (202) 477-6391, eds03@worldbank.org, https://www.worldbank.org/; World Development Report 2022: Finance for an Equitable Recovery.

DOMINICAN REPUBLIC-PRICES

Euromonitor International, Inc., 1 N Dearborn St., Ste. 1700, Chicago, IL, 60602, USA, (312) 922-1115, (312) 922-1157, info-usa@euromonitor.com, https://www.euromonitor.com/; Geographies.

International Monetary Fund (IMF), 700 19th St. NW, Washington, DC, 20431, USA, (202) 623-7000, (202) 623-4661, publications@imf.org, https://www.imf.org; International Financial Statistics (IFS).

The World Bank, 1818 H St. NW, Washington, DC, 20433, USA, (202) 473-1000, (202) 477-6391, eds03@worldbank.org, https://www.worldbank.org/; Dominican Republic (report).

DOMINICAN REPUBLIC-PUBLIC HEALTH

Euromonitor International, Inc., 1 N Dearborn St., Ste. 1700, Chicago, IL, 60602, USA, (312) 922-1115, (312) 922-1157, info-usa@euromonitor.com, https://www.euromonitor.com/; Geographies.

Palgrave Macmillan, 1 New York Plaza, Ste. 4500, New York, NY, 10004-1562, USA, (800) 777-4643, orders@palgrave.com, https://www.palgrave.com/us; The Statesman's Yearbook, 2023.

U.S. Census Bureau, 4600 Silver Hill Rd., Washington, DC, 20233, USA, (301) 763-4636, (800) 923-8282, https://www.census.gov; HIV/AIDS Surveillance Data Base.

United Nations Department of Economic and Social Affairs (DESA), Population Division, 2 United Nations Plz., Rm. DC2-1950, New York, NY, 10017, USA, (212) 963-3209, (212) 963-2147, population@un.org, https://www.un.org/development/desa/pd/; World Fertility Data 2019.

United Nations Development Programme (UNDP), One United Nations Plz., New York, NY, 10017, USA, (212) 906-5000, (212) 906-5001, https://www.undp.org; Human Development Report 2021-2022.

United Nations Statistics Division (UNSD), United Nations Plz., New York, NY, 10017, USA, (800) 253-9646, (212) 963-9851, statistics@un.org, https://unstats.un.org; Millennium Development Goal Indicators and Statistical Yearbook of the United Nations 2021.

The World Bank, 1818 H St. NW, Washington, DC, 20433, USA, (202) 473-1000, (202) 477-6391, eds03@worldbank.org, https://www.worldbank.org/; Dominican Republic (report).

World Health Organization (WHO), Ave. Appia 20, Geneva, CH-1211, SWI, (202) 974-3000 (Telephone in U.S.), publications@who.int, https://www.who.int/; Global Health Observatory (GHO) and Health Statistics and Information Systems.

DOMINICAN REPUBLIC-RAILROADS

Janes, USA, (703) 574-7580, (888) 977-1519, customer.care@janes.com, https://www.janes.com; Janes World Railways 2021-2022.

Palgrave Macmillan, 1 New York Plaza, Ste. 4500, New York, NY, 10004-1562, USA, (800) 777-4643, orders@palgrave.com, https://www.palgrave.com/us; The Statesman's Yearbook, 2023.

DOMINICAN REPUBLIC-RELIGION

Central Intelligence Agency (CIA), Office of Public Affairs, Washington, DC, 20505, USA, (703) 482-0623, https://www.cia.gov; The World Factbook.

Palgrave Macmillan, 1 New York Plaza, Ste. 4500, New York, NY, 10004-1562, USA, (800) 777-4643, orders@palgrave.com, https://www.palgrave.com/us; The Statesman's Yearbook, 2023.

DOMINICAN REPUBLIC-RETAIL TRADE

Euromonitor International, Inc., 1 N Dearborn St., Ste. 1700, Chicago, IL, 60602, USA, (312) 922-1115, (312) 922-1157, info-usa@euromonitor.com, https://www.euromonitor.com/; Geographies.

Inter-American Development Bank (IDB), 1300 New York Ave. NW, Washington, DC, 20577, USA, (202) 623-1000, (202) 623-3096, https://www.iadb.org/en; Latin Macro Watch (LMW).

DOMINICAN REPUBLIC-RICE PRODUCTION

See DOMINICAN REPUBLIC-CROPS

DOMINICAN REPUBLIC-ROADS

International Road Federation (IRF), Madison Place, 500 Montgomery St., 5th Fl., Alexandria, VA, 22314, USA, (703) 535-1001, (703) 535-1007, info@irf.global, https://www.irf.global/; World Road Statistics (WRS).

DOMINICAN REPUBLIC-RUBBER INDUSTRY AND TRADE

International Rubber Study Group (IRSG), 51 Changi Business Park Central 2, Unit No. 6, 486066, SGP, https://www.rubberstudy.org; Monthly Rubber Bulletin (MRB); Rubber Industry Report; Rubber Statistical Bulletin; and World Rubber Industry Report (WRIO).

DOMINICAN REPUBLIC-SHIPPING

Routledge - Taylor & Francis Group, 6000 Broken Sound Pkwy. NW, Ste. 300, Boca Raton, FL, 33487, USA, (800) 634-1420, (800) 634-7064, orders@taylorandfrancis.com, https://www.routledge.com/; The Europa World Year Book 2022.

United Nations Statistics Division (UNSD), United Nations Plz., New York, NY, 10017, USA, (800) 253-9646, (212) 963-9851, statistics@un.org, https://unstats.un.org; Statistical Yearbook of the United Nations 2021.

DOMINICAN REPUBLIC-SOYBEAN PRODUCTION

See DOMINICAN REPUBLIC-CROPS

DOMINICAN REPUBLIC-STEEL PRODUCTION

See DOMINICAN REPUBLIC-MINERAL INDUSTRIES

DOMINICAN REPUBLIC-SUGAR PRODUCTION

See DOMINICAN REPUBLIC-CROPS

DOMINICAN REPUBLIC-TAXATION

Inter-American Development Bank (IDB), 1300 New York Ave. NW, Washington, DC, 20577, USA, (202) 623-1000, (202) 623-3096, https://www.iadb.org/en; Latin Macro Watch (LMW).

International Road Federation (IRF), Madison Place, 500 Montgomery St., 5th Fl., Alexandria, VA, 22314, USA, (703) 535-1001, (703) 535-1007, info@irf.global, https://www.irf.global/; World Road Statistics (WRS).

The World Bank, 1818 H St. NW, Washington, DC, 20433, USA, (202) 473-1000, (202) 477-6391, eds03@worldbank.org, https://www.worldbank.org/; World Development Indicators (WDI) 2022.

DOMINICAN REPUBLIC-TELEPHONE

Palgrave Macmillan, 1 New York Plaza, Ste. 4500, New York, NY, 10004-1562, USA, (800) 777-4643, orders@palgrave.com, https://www.palgrave.com/us; The Statesman's Yearbook, 2023.

United Nations Statistics Division (UNSD), United Nations Plz., New York, NY, 10017, USA, (800) 253-9646, (212) 963-9851, statistics@un.org, https://unstats.un.org; World Statistics Pocketbook 2021.

DOMINICAN REPUBLIC-TEXTILE INDUSTRY

United Nations Statistics Division (UNSD), United Nations Plz., New York, NY, 10017, USA, (800) 253-9646, (212) 963-9851, statistics@un.org, https://unstats.un.org; Statistical Yearbook of the United Nations 2021.

DOMINICAN REPUBLIC-TOBACCO INDUSTRY

International Monetary Fund (IMF), 700 19th St. NW, Washington, DC, 20431, USA, (202) 623-7000, (202) 623-4661, publications@imf.org, https://www.imf.org; International Financial Statistics (IFS).

United Nations Statistics Division (UNSD), United Nations Plz., New York, NY, 10017, USA, (800) 253-9646, (212) 963-9851, statistics@un.org, https://unstats.un.org; Statistical Yearbook of the United Nations 2021.

DOMINICAN REPUBLIC-TOURISM

Euromonitor International, Inc., 1 N Dearborn St., Ste. 1700, Chicago, IL, 60602, USA, (312) 922-1115, (312) 922-1157, info-usa@euromonitor.com, https://www.euromonitor.com/; Geographies.

Palgrave Macmillan, 1 New York Plaza, Ste. 4500, New York, NY, 10004-1562, USA, (800) 777-4643, orders@palgrave.com, https://www.palgrave.com/us; The Statesman's Yearbook, 2023.

Routledge - Taylor & Francis Group, 6000 Broken Sound Pkwy. NW, Ste. 300, Boca Raton, FL, 33487, USA, (800) 634-1420, (800) 634-7064, orders@taylorandfrancis.com, https://www.routledge.com/; The Europa World Year Book 2022.

United Nations Statistics Division (UNSD), United Nations Plz., New York, NY, 10017, USA, (800) 253-9646, (212) 963-9851, statistics@un.org, https://unstats.un.org; Statistical Yearbook of the United Nations 2021.

United Nations World Tourism Organization (UNWTO), Calle Poeta Joan Maragall 42, Madrid, 28020, SPA, info@unwto.org, https://www.unwto.org/; Yearbook of Tourism Statistics, 2021 Edition.

The World Bank, 1818 H St. NW, Washington, DC, 20433, USA, (202) 473-1000, (202) 477-6391, eds03@worldbank.org, https://www.worldbank.org/; Dominican Republic (report).

DOMINICAN REPUBLIC-TRADE

See DOMINICAN REPUBLIC-INTERNATIONAL TRADE

DOMINICAN REPUBLIC-TRANSPORTATION

Central Intelligence Agency (CIA), Office of Public Affairs, Washington, DC, 20505, USA, (703) 482-0623, https://www.cia.gov; The World Factbook.

Euromonitor International, Inc., 1 N Dearborn St., Ste. 1700, Chicago, IL, 60602, USA, (312) 922-1115, (312) 922-1157, info-usa@euromonitor.com, https://www.euromonitor.com/; Geographies.

Inter-American Development Bank (IDB), 1300 New York Ave. NW, Washington, DC, 20577, USA, (202) 623-1000, (202) 623-3096, https://www.iadb.org/en; Latin Macro Watch (LMW).

Palgrave Macmillan, 1 New York Plaza, Ste. 4500, New York, NY, 10004-1562, USA, (800) 777-4643, orders@palgrave.com, https://www.palgrave.com/us; The Statesman's Yearbook, 2023.

Routledge - Taylor & Francis Group, 6000 Broken Sound Pkwy. NW, Ste. 300, Boca Raton, FL, 33487, USA, (800) 634-1420, (800) 634-7064, orders@taylorandfrancis.com, https://www.routledge.com/; The Europa World Year Book 2022.

The World Bank, 1818 H St. NW, Washington, DC, 20433, USA, (202) 473-1000, (202) 477-6391, eds03@worldbank.org, https://www.worldbank.org/; Dominican Republic (report).

DOMINICAN REPUBLIC-UNEMPLOYMENT

International Labour Organization (ILO), 4 Rte. des Morillons, Geneva, CH-1211, SWI, ilo@ilo.org, https://www.ilo.org; NORMLEX Information System on International Labour Standards.

DOMINICAN REPUBLIC-VITAL STATISTICS

U.S. Census Bureau, 4600 Silver Hill Rd., Washington, DC, 20233, USA, (301) 763-4636, (800) 923-8282, https://www.census.gov; HIV/AIDS Surveillance Data Base.

United Nations Department of Economic and Social Affairs (DESA), Population Division, 2 United Nations Plz., Rm. DC2-1950, New York, NY, 10017, USA, (212) 963-3209, (212) 963-2147, population@un.org, https://www.un.org/development/desa/pd/; World Contraceptive Use 2021: Estimates and Projections of Family Planning Indicators and World Marriage Data 2019.

United Nations Statistics Division (UNSD), United Nations Plz., New York, NY, 10017, USA, (800) 253-9646, (212) 963-9851, statistics@un.org, https://unstats.un.org; Statistical Yearbook of the United Nations 2021.

World Health Organization (WHO), Ave. Appia 20, Geneva, CH-1211, SWI, (202) 974-3000 (Telephone in U.S.), publications@who.int, https://www.who.int/; Health Statistics and Information Systems.

DOMINICAN REPUBLIC-WAGES

International Labour Organization (ILO), 4 Rte. des Morillons, Geneva, CH-1211, SWI, ilo@ilo.org, https://www.ilo.org; NORMLEX Information System on International Labour Standards.

United Nations Statistics Division (UNSD), United Nations Plz., New York, NY, 10017, USA, (800) 253-9646, (212) 963-9851, statistics@un.org, https://unstats.un.org; Statistical Yearbook of the United Nations 2021.

The World Bank, 1818 H St. NW, Washington, DC, 20433, USA, (202) 473-1000, (202) 477-6391, eds03@worldbank.org, https://www.worldbank.org/; Dominican Republic (report).

DOMINICAN REPUBLIC-WHEAT PRODUCTION

See DOMINICAN REPUBLIC-CROPS

DOMINICAN REPUBLIC-WHOLESALE PRICE INDEXES

Inter-American Development Bank (IDB), 1300 New York Ave. NW, Washington, DC, 20577, USA, (202) 623-1000, (202) 623-3096, https://www.iadb.org/en; Latin Macro Watch (LMW).

DOMINICAN REPUBLIC-WHOLESALE TRADE

Inter-American Development Bank (IDB), 1300 New York Ave. NW, Washington, DC, 20577, USA, (202) 623-1000, (202) 623-3096, https://www.iadb.org/en; Latin Macro Watch (LMW).

DOMINICAN REPUBLIC-WOOL PRODUCTION

See DOMINICAN REPUBLIC-TEXTILE INDUSTRY

DOW JONES STOCK INDICES

Global Financial Data, Inc., 29122 Rancho Viejo Rd., Ste. 215, San Juan Capistrano, CA, 92675, USA, (949) 542-4200, sales@globalfinancialdata.com, https://globalfinancialdata.com/; GFD Finaeon: U.S. Equities Database.

DRINKING AND TRAFFIC ACCIDENTS

National Highway Traffic Safety Administration (NHTSA), National Center for Statistics and Analysis (NCSA), 1200 New Jersey Ave. SE, West Bldg., Washington, DC, 20590, USA, (800) 934-8517, (202) 366-2746, ncsarequests@dot.gov, https://www.nhtsa.gov/research-data/national-center-statistics-and-analysis-ncsa; Traffic Safety Facts and Traffic Safety Facts, 2020 Data - Alcohol-Impaired Driving.

DRINKING PLACES

See RESTAURANTS

DRINKING WATER

American Chemical Society (ACS), 1155 16th St. NW, Washington, DC, 20036, USA, (800) 227-5558, (202) 872-4600, help@services.acs.org, https://www.acs.org; Population-Wide Exposure to Per- and Polyfluoroalkyl Substances from Drinking Water in the United States.

Environmental Working Group (EWG), 1250 U St. NW, Ste. 1000, Washington, DC, 20005, USA, (202) 667-6982, https://www.ewg.org/; EWG's Tap Water Database and PFAS Contamination in the U.S..

Silent Spring Institute, 320 Nevada St., Ste. 302, Newton, MA, 02460, USA, (617) 332-4288, (617) 332-4284, info@silentspring.org, https://silentspring.org/; Sociodemographic Factors Are Associated with the Abundance of PFAS Sources and Detection in U.S. Community Water Systems.

U.S. Department of the Interior (DOI), U.S. Geological Survey (USGS), 12201 Sunrise Valley Dr., Reston, VA, 20192, USA, (888) 392-8545, https://www.usgs.gov/; Per- and Polyfluoroalkyl Substances (PFAS) in United States Tapwater: Comparison of Underserved Private-Well and Public-Supply Exposures and Associated Health Implications.

DRIVERLESS CARS

See AUTONOMOUS VEHICLES

DRIVING

See also MOTOR VEHICLES

Governors Highway Safety Association (GHSA), 660 N Capitol St. NW, Ste. 220, Washington, DC, 20001-1642, USA, (202) 789-0942, headquarters@ghsa.org, https://www.ghsa.org/; High-Risk Impaired Drivers: Combating a Critical Threat; Motorcyclists' Attitudes on Using High-Visibility Gear to Improve Conspicuity; and Pedestrian Traffic Fatalities by State: 2022 Preliminary Data.

INRIX, 10210 NE Points Dr., No. 400, Kirkland, WA, 98033, USA, (425) 284-3800, https://inrix.com; COVID-19 Effect on Collisions on Interstates and

Highways; 2021 Global Traffic Scorecard; Signal Optimization and Climate Outcomes; and U.S. Signals Scorecard.

Insurance Institute for Highway Safety/Highway Loss Data Institute (IIHS/HLDI), 4121 Wilson Blvd., 6th Fl., Arlington, VA, 22203, USA, (703) 247-1500, (434) 985 4600, cmatthew@iihs.org, https://www.iihs.org/; Highway Safety Topics.

National Highway Traffic Safety Administration (NHTSA), National Center for Statistics and Analysis (NCSA), 1200 New Jersey Ave. SE, West Bldg., Washington, DC, 20590, USA, (800) 934-8517, (202) 366-2746, ncsarequests@dot.gov, https://www.nhtsa.gov/research-data/national-center-statistics-and-analysis-ncsa; Analysis of Real-World Crashes Where Involved Vehicles Were Equipped With Adaptive Equipment; Traffic Safety Facts; Traffic Safety Facts, 2020 Data - Children; Traffic Safety Facts, 2020 Data - Pedestrians; Traffic Safety Facts, 2020 Data - Speeding; and Traffic Safety Facts, 2020 Data - Young Drivers.

U.S. Department of Transportation (DOT), Federal Highway Administration (FHA), 1200 New Jersey Ave. SE, Washington, DC, 20590, USA, (202) 366-4000, https://highways.dot.gov/; Monthly Motor Fuel Reported by States.

DRIVING-FATAL ACCIDENTS

AAA Foundation for Traffic Safety (FTS), 607 14th St. NW, Ste. 201, Washington, DC, 20005, USA, (202) 638-5944, (202) 638-5943, info@aaafoundation.org, https://www.aaafoundation.org/; Cannabis Use Among Drivers in Fatal Crashes in Washington State Before and After Legalization.

Advocates for Highway and Auto Safety, 750 1st St. NE, Ste. 1130, Washington, DC, 20002, USA, (202) 408-1711, (202) 408-1699, advocates@saferoads.org, https://saferoads.org/; 2022 Roadmap of State Highway Safety Laws and 2023 Roadmap to Safety.

Centre for Research on the Epidemiology of Disasters (CRED), Universite Catholique de Louvain School of Public Health, Clos Chapelle-aux-Champs, Bte B1.30.15, Brussels, B-1200, BEL, contact@cred.be, https://www.cred.be/; Technological Disasters: Trends & Transport Accidents.

Governors Highway Safety Association (GHSA), 660 N Capitol St. NW, Ste. 220, Washington, DC, 20001-1642, USA, (202) 789-0942, headquarters@ghsa.org, https://www.ghsa.org/; An Analysis of Traffic Fatalities by Race and Ethnicity; Motorcyclists' Attitudes on Using High-Visibility Gear to Improve Conspicuity; and Pedestrian Traffic Fatalities by State: 2022 Preliminary Data.

Insurance Institute for Highway Safety/Highway Loss Data Institute (IIHS/HLDI), 4121 Wilson Blvd., 6th Fl., Arlington, VA, 22203, USA, (703) 247-1500, (434) 985 4600, cmatthew@iihs.org, https://www.iihs.org/; Fatality Facts 2021: Yearly Snapshot and Highway Safety Topics.

National Safety Council (NSC), 1121 Spring Lake Dr., Itasca, IL, 60143-3201, USA, (630) 285-1121, (800) 621-7615, customerservice@nsc.org, https://www.nsc.org/; Motor Vehicles.

U.S. Department of Transportation (DOT), Office of the Assistant Secretary for Research and Technology (OST-R), Bureau of Transportation Statistics (BTS), 1200 New Jersey Ave. SE, Washington, DC, 20590, USA, (800) 853-1351, (202) 366-3282, https://www.bts.gov; TranStats.

U.S. Department of Transportation (DOT), Office of the Secretary of Transportation, 1200 New Jersey Ave. SE, Washington, DC, 20590, USA, (202) 366-4200, https://www.transportation.gov/tags/office-secretary; Our Nation's Roadway Safety Crisis.

World Health Organization (WHO), Ave. Appia 20, Geneva, CH-1211, SWI, (202) 974-3000 (Telephone in U.S.), publications@who.int, https://www.who.int/; Road Traffic Injuries.

DRIVING-INTOXICATED

Insurance Institute for Highway Safety/Highway Loss Data Institute (IIHS/HLDI), 4121 Wilson Blvd., 6th Fl., Arlington, VA, 22203, USA, (703) 247-1500, (434) 985 4600, cmatthew@iihs.org, https://www.iihs.org/; Highway Safety Topics.

National Highway Traffic Safety Administration (NHTSA), National Center for Statistics and Analysis (NCSA), 1200 New Jersey Ave. SE, West Bldg., Washington, DC, 20590, USA, (800) 934-8517, (202) 366-2746, ncsarequests@dot.gov, https://www.nhtsa.gov/research-data/national-center-statistics-and-analysis-ncsa; Traffic Safety Facts and Traffic Safety Facts, 2020 Data - Alcohol-Impaired Driving.

DRIVING-LICENSED DRIVERS

U.S. Department of Transportation (DOT), Federal Highway Administration (FHA), 1200 New Jersey Ave. SE, Washington, DC, 20590, USA, (202) 366-4000, https://highways.dot.gov/; Core Highway Topics and Highway Statistics 2020.

DRIVING-TRAFFIC OFFENSE

National Highway Traffic Safety Administration (NHTSA), National Center for Statistics and Analysis (NCSA), 1200 New Jersey Ave. SE, West Bldg., Washington, DC, 20590, USA, (800) 934-8517, (202) 366-2746, ncsarequests@dot.gov, https://www.nhtsa.gov/research-data/national-center-statistics-and-analysis-ncsa; Traffic Safety Facts and Traffic Safety Facts, 2020 Data - Speeding.

U.S. Department of Justice (DOJ), Federal Bureau of Investigation (FBI), 935 Pennsylvania Ave. NW, Washington, DC, 20535-0001, USA, (202) 324-3000, https://www.fbi.gov/; Crime in the United States 2019.

DRONE AIRCRAFT

New America, 740 15th St. NW, Ste. 900, Washington, DC, 20005, USA, (202) 986-2700, https://www.newamerica.org/; America's Counterterrorism Wars: Tracking the United States' Drone Strikes and Other Operations in Pakistan, Yemen, Somalia, and Libya.

DROUGHTS

Media Matters for America, PO Box 44811, Washington, DC, 20026, USA, (202) 756-4100, action@mediamatters.org, https://www.mediamatters.org; Broadcast TV News Shows Link Western Heat Wave and Drought to Climate Change in 27% of Segments.

National Oceanic and Atmospheric Administration (NOAA), National Centers for Environmental Information (NCEI), National Integrated Drought Information System (NIDIS), 151 Patton Ave., Asheville, ND, 28801-5001, USA, drought.portal@noaa.gov, https://www.drought.gov; Drought Status Update for California-Nevada; Drought Status Update for the Pacific Northwest; Drought.gov; and National Current Conditions.

Public Policy Institute of California (PPIC), 500 Washington St., Ste. 600, San Francisco, CA, 94111, USA, (415) 291-4400, (916) 440-1120, (415) 291-4401, https://www.ppic.org/; Droughts in California.

Public Policy Institute of California (PPIC) Water Policy Center, 500 Washington St., Ste. 600, San Francisco, CA, 94111, USA, (415) 291-4433, (415) 291-4400, (415) 291-4401, https://www.ppic.org/water/; Policy Brief: Drought and California's Agriculture.

University of Nebraska-Lincoln, National Drought Mitigation Center, 3310 Holdrege St., PO Box 830988, Lincoln, NE, 68583-0988, USA, (402) 472-6707, (402) 472-2946, https://droughtmonitor.unl.edu/; U.S. Drought Monitor.

World Meteorological Organization (WMO), 7bis, ave. de la Paix, PO Box 2300, Geneva, CH-1211, SWI, wmo@wmo.int, https://public.wmo.int/en; Atlas of Mortality and Economic Losses from Weather, Climate and Water Extremes (1970-2019).

DROWSINESS

National Sleep Foundation (NSF), 1414 NE 42nd St., Ste. 400, Seattle, WA, 98105, USA, (703) 243-1697, contact@sleepfoundation.org, https://sleepfoundation.org/; Sleep In America Poll 2022.

DROWSY DRIVING

Insurance Institute for Highway Safety/Highway Loss Data Institute (IIHS/HLDI), 4121 Wilson Blvd., 6th Fl., Arlington, VA, 22203, USA, (703) 247-1500, (434) 985 4600, cmatthew@iihs.org, https://www.iihs.org/; Highway Safety Topics.

DRUG ADDICTION

Health Canada, Address Locator 1801B, Ottawa, ON, K1A 0K9, CAN, (613) 957-2991 (Dial from U.S.), (613) 941-5366 (Fax from U.S.), hcinfo.infosc@canada.ca, https://www.hc-sc.gc.ca/; Canadian Alcohol and Drugs Survey (CADS): Summary of Results for 2019.

KFF Health News, 1330 G St. NW, Washington, DC, 20005, USA, (202) 347-5270, https://khn.org/; $50 Billion in Opioid Settlement Cash Is on the Way. We're Tracking How It's Spent..

Partnership to End Addiction, 711 3rd Ave., 5th Fl., Ste. 500, New York, NY, 10017, USA, (212) 841-5200, contact@toendaddiction.org, https://drugfree.org/; unpublished data.

Recovery Research Institute (RRI), 151 Merrimac St., 6th Fl., Boston, MA, 02114, USA, https://www.recoveryanswers.org/; Can Buprenorphine-Equipped Ambulances Help Link Overdose Survivors to Addiction Treatment?.

DRUG RESISTANCE IN MICROORGANISMS

Biotechnology Innovation Organization (BIO), 1201 New York NW, Ste. 1300, Washington, DC, 20005, USA, (202) 962-9200, info@bio.org, https://www.bio.org/; The State of Innovation in Antibacterial Therapeutics.

Johns Hopkins Center for a Livable Future, 111 Market Pl., Ste. 840, Baltimore, MD, 21202, USA, (410) 223-1811, (410) 223-1829, clf@jhsph.edu, https://clf.jhsph.edu; Contamination of Retail Meat Samples with Multidrug-Resistant Organisms in Relation to Organic and Conventional Production and Processing: A Cross-Sectional Analysis of Data from the United States National Antimicrobial Resistance Monitoring System.

Review on Antimicrobial Resistance, Gibbs Bldg., 215 Euston Rd., London, NW1 2BE, GBR, info@amr-review.org, https://amr-review.org/; unpublished data.

U.S. Department of Health and Human Services, Centers for Disease Control and Prevention (CDC), 1600 Clifton Rd., Atlanta, GA, 30329-4027, USA, (800) 232-4636, (888) 232-6348 (TTY), cdcinfo@cdc.gov, https://www.cdc.gov; COVID-19: U.S. Impact on Antimicrobial Resistance.

DRUG STORES AND PROPRIETARY STORES

See PHARMACIES AND DRUG STORES

DRUG TRAFFIC

Australian Institute of Criminology (AIC), GPO Box 1936, Canberra, ACT, 2601, AUS, front.desk@aic.gov.au, https://www.aic.gov.au/; Drug Use Monitoring in Australia: Drug Use Among Police Detainees, 2021.

Drug Policy Alliance (DPA), 131 W 33rd St., 15th Fl., New York, NY, 10001, USA, (212) 613-8020, (212) 613-8021, contact@drugpolicy.org, https://drugpolicy.org/; Drug Facts.

Marijuana Policy Project (MPP), PO Box 21824, Washington, DC, 20009, USA, (202) 462-5747, info@mpp.org, https://www.mpp.org/; State Polling: Support for Marijuana Policy Reform.

Mathematica, PO Box 2393, Princeton, NJ, 08543-2393, USA, (609) 275-2350, (609) 799-3535, (609) 799-0005, info@mathematica-mpr.com, https://www.mathematica.org; Marijuana Legalization: Public Health, Safety, and Economic Factors for States to Consider.

National Cannabis Industry Association (NCIA), 126 C St. NW, Washington, DC, 20001, USA, (888) 683-5650, (888) 683-5670, info@thecannabisindustry.org, https://thecannabisindustry.org/; The Key to Consumer Safety: Displacing the Illicit Cannabis Market - Recommendations for Safe Vaping.

National Organization for the Reform of Marijuana Laws (NORML), 1420 K St. NW, Ste. 350, Washington, DC, 20005, USA, (202) 483-5500, norml@norml.org, https://norml.org/; Marijuana Regulation: Impact on Health, Safety, Economy.

Police Executive Research Forum (PERF), 1120 Connecticut Ave. NW, Ste. 930, Washington, DC, 20036, USA, (202) 466-7820, https://www.policeforum.org; Policing on the Front Lines of the Opioid Crisis.

PollingReport.com, USA, https://www.pollingreport.com/; Issues Facing the Nation.

U.S. Department of Justice (DOJ), Drug Enforcement Administration (DEA), 8701 Morrissette Dr., Springfield, VA, 22152, USA, (202) 307-1000, info@dea.gov, https://www.dea.gov; Drugs of Abuse: A DEA Resource Guide 2020 and Responding to Nationwide Increases in Fentanyl-Related Mass-Overdose Events.

U.S. Department of State (DOS), 2201 C St. NW, Washington, DC, 20520, USA, (202) 647-4000, ofm-info@state.gov, https://www.state.gov; International Narcotics Control Strategy Report (INCSR) 2021.

UK Health Security Agency (UKHSA), Nobel House, 17 Smith Sq., London, SW1P 3JR, GBR, enquiries@ukhsa.gov.uk, https://www.gov.uk/government/organisations/uk-health-security-agency; Shooting Up: Infections and Injecting-Related Harms Among People Who Inject Drugs in the UK: Update, December 2021.

United Nations Office on Drugs and Crime (UNODC), Vienna International Ctre., PO Box 500, Vienna, A-1400, AUT, unodc@unodc.org, https://www.unodc.org/; World Drug Report 2022.

DRUG TRAFFIC-ARRESTS

Council on Criminal Justice (CCJ), National Commission on COVID-19 and Criminal Justice, 700 Pennsylvania Ave. SE, Washington, DC, 20020, USA, info@counciloncj.org, https://counciloncj.org/covid-19/; Impact Report: COVID-19 and Crime.

Drug Policy Alliance (DPA), 131 W 33rd St., 15th Fl., New York, NY, 10001, USA, (212) 613-8020, (212) 613-8021, contact@drugpolicy.org, https://drugpolicy.org/; Drug War Statistics and From Prohibition to Progress: A Status Report on Marijuana Legalization.

U.S. Department of Homeland Security (DHS), Office of Immigration Statistics (OIS), 2707 Martin Luther King Jr. Ave. SE, Washington, DC, 20528-0525, USA, (202) 282-8000, immigrationstatistics@hq.dhs.gov, https://www.dhs.gov/office-immigration-statistics; Yearbook of Immigration Statistics 2020.

U.S. Department of Homeland Security (DHS), U.S. Customs and Border Protection (CBP), 1300 Pennsylvania Ave. NW, Washington, DC, 20229, USA, (877) 227-5511, (202) 325-8000, https://www.cbp.gov; Snapshot: A Summary of CBP Facts and Figures.

U.S. Department of Justice (DOJ), Drug Enforcement Administration (DEA), 8701 Morrissette Dr., Springfield, VA, 22152, USA, (202) 307-1000, info@dea.gov, https://www.dea.gov; Illicit Opioid Availability in Pennsylvania 2020 and 2020 National Drug Threat Assessment.

U.S. Department of Justice (DOJ), Federal Bureau of Investigation (FBI), 935 Pennsylvania Ave. NW, Washington, DC, 20535-0001, USA, (202) 324-3000, https://www.fbi.gov/; Crime in the United States 2019.

United Nations Office on Drugs and Crime (UNODC), Vienna International Ctre., PO Box 500, Vienna, A-1400, AUT, unodc@unodc.org, https://www.unodc.org/; Afghanistan Opium Survey 2020: Cultivation and Production.

University of Alaska Anchorage Justice Center, 3211 Providence Dr., PSB Ste. 234, Anchorage, AK, 99508, USA, (907) 786-1810, (907) 786-7777, uaa_justicecenter@alaska.edu, https://www.uaa.alaska.edu/academics/college-of-health/departments/justice-center/; Adverse Childhood Experiences, Intimate Partner Violence, and Sexual Violence Among Persons Who May Be Alaska Mental Health Trust Beneficiaries: Findings from the Alaska Victimization Survey.

White House Office of National Drug Control Policy (ONDCP), 1600 Pennsylvania Ave. NW, Washington, DC, 20500, USA, https://www.whitehouse.gov/ondcp; unpublished data.

DRUG TRAFFIC-COURT CASES

Justice Research and Statistics Association (JRSA), 1000 Vermont Ave. NW, Ste. 450, Washington, DC, 20005, USA, (202) 842-9330, (202) 304-1417, cjinfo@jrsa.org, https://www.jrsa.org; SAC Publication Digest 2022.

United Nations Office on Drugs and Crime (UNODC), Vienna International Ctre., PO Box 500, Vienna, A-1400, AUT, unodc@unodc.org, https://www.unodc.org/; World Drug Report 2022.

DRUG TRAFFIC-DRUG ABUSE TREATMENT

Council on Criminal Justice (CCJ), National Commission on COVID-19 and Criminal Justice, 700 Pennsylvania Ave. SE, Washington, DC, 20020, USA, info@counciloncj.org, https://counciloncj.org/covid-19/; Impact Report: COVID-19 and SUD Treatment.

Substance Abuse and Mental Health Services Administration (SAMHSA), 5600 Fishers Ln., Rockville, MD, 20857, USA, (877) 726-4727, (800) 487-4889 (TTY), samhsainfo@samhsa.hhs.gov, https://www.samhsa.gov/; 2020 National Survey of Substance Abuse Treatment Services (N-SSATS) and Treatment Episode Data Set (TEDS).

U.S. Department of Justice (DOJ), Drug Enforcement Administration (DEA), 8701 Morrissette Dr., Springfield, VA, 22152, USA, (202) 307-1000, info@dea.gov, https://www.dea.gov; Illicit Opioid Availability in Pennsylvania 2020.

University of Maryland Center for Substance Use, Addiction & Health Research (CESAR), 7401 Preinkert Dr., 1114 Chincoteague Hall, College Park, MD, 20742, USA, (301) 405-9770, cesar@umd.edu, https://cesar.umd.edu/; Characterizing Knowledge, Attitudes, Behaviors, and Practices Related to Bystander Naloxone in Methadone-Maintained Individuals with Opioid Use Disorder and Highlights from the Naloxone Phase II Studies.

DRUG TRAFFIC-ENFORCEMENT ACTIVITIES

Drug Policy Alliance (DPA), 131 W 33rd St., 15th Fl., New York, NY, 10001, USA, (212) 613-8020, (212) 613-8021, contact@drugpolicy.org, https://drugpolicy.org/; Drug War Statistics and From Prohibition to Progress: A Status Report on Marijuana Legalization.

U.S. Department of Homeland Security (DHS), Office of Immigration Statistics (OIS), 2707 Martin Luther King Jr. Ave. SE, Washington, DC, 20528-0525, USA, (202) 282-8000, immigrationstatistics@hq.dhs.gov, https://www.dhs.gov/office-immigration-statistics; Yearbook of Immigration Statistics 2020.

U.S. Department of Justice (DOJ), Drug Enforcement Administration (DEA), 8701 Morrissette Dr., Springfield, VA, 22152, USA, (202) 307-1000, info@dea.gov, https://www.dea.gov; Illicit Opioid Availability in Pennsylvania 2020 and 2020 National Drug Threat Assessment.

United Nations Office on Drugs and Crime (UNODC), Vienna International Ctre., PO Box 500, Vienna, A-1400, AUT, unodc@unodc.org, https://www.unodc.org/; Afghanistan Opium Survey 2020: Cultivation and Production; Myanmar Opium Survey 2022 - Cultivation, Production and Implications; and World Drug Report 2022.

White House Office of National Drug Control Policy (ONDCP), 1600 Pennsylvania Ave. NW, Washington, DC, 20500, USA, https://www.whitehouse.gov/ondcp; unpublished data.

DRUG TRAFFIC-JUVENILES

Health Canada, Address Locator 1801B, Ottawa, ON, K1A 0K9, CAN, (613) 957-2991 (Dial from U.S.), (613) 941-5366 (Fax from U.S.), hcinfo.infosc@canada.ca, https://www.hc-sc.gc.ca/; Canadian Alcohol and Drugs Survey (CADS): Summary of Results for 2019.

National Center for Juvenile Justice (NCJJ), 3700 S Water St., Ste. 200, Pittsburgh, PA, 15203, USA, (412) 227-6950, (412) 227-6955, ncjj@ncjfcj.org, https://www.ncjj.org/; Criminological Highlights: Children and Youth; Trends and Characteristics of Delinquency Cases Handled in Juvenile Court, 2019; and Youth Younger than 18 Prosecuted in Criminal Court: National Estimate, 2019 Cases.

Trust for America's Health (TFAH), 1730 M St. NW, Ste. 900, Washington, DC, 20036, USA, (202) 223-9870, (202) 223-9871, info@tfah.org, https://www.tfah.org/; Alcohol and Drug Misuse and Suicide and the Millennial Generation - A Devastating Impact and Pain in the Nation Series Update: Alcohol, Drug and Suicide Deaths at Record Highs.

U.S. Department of Health and Human Services (HHS), National Institutes of Health (NIH), National Institute on Drug Abuse (NIDA), Office of Science Policy and Communications, 3WFN MSC 6024, 16071 Industrial Dr - Dock 11, Bethesda, MD, 20892, USA, (301) 443-6441, https://www.drugabuse.gov/; Vaping Devices (Electronic Cigarettes) DrugFacts.

U.S. Department of Justice (DOJ), Office of Juvenile Justice and Delinquency Prevention (OJJDP), 810 7th St. NW, Washington, DC, 20531, USA, (202) 307-5911, https://www.ojjdp.gov/; Statistical Briefing Book (SBB).

United Nations Office on Drugs and Crime (UNODC), Vienna International Ctre., PO Box 500, Vienna, A-1400, AUT, unodc@unodc.org, https://www.unodc.org/; World Drug Report 2022.

DRUG TRAFFIC-OVERDOSE

American Academy of Pediatrics (AAP), 345 Park Blvd., Itasca, IL, 60143, USA, (800) 433-9016, (847) 434-8000, mcc@aap.org, https://www.aap.org; Pediatric Edible Cannabis Exposures and Acute Toxicity: 2017-2021.

Council on Criminal Justice (CCJ), National Commission on COVID-19 and Criminal Justice, 700 Pennsylvania Ave. SE, Washington, DC, 20020, USA, info@counciloncj.org, https://counciloncj.org/covid-19/; Impact Report: COVID-19 and SUD Treatment.

Partnership to End Addiction, 711 3rd Ave., 5th Fl., Ste. 500, New York, NY, 10017, USA, (212) 841-5200, contact@toendaddiction.org, https://drugfree.org/; unpublished data.

Recovery Research Institute (RRI), 151 Merrimac St., 6th Fl., Boston, MA, 02114, USA, https://www.recoveryanswers.org/; Can Buprenorphine-Equipped Ambulances Help Link Overdose Survivors to Addiction Treatment?.

Trust for America's Health (TFAH), 1730 M St. NW, Ste. 900, Washington, DC, 20036, USA, (202) 223-9870, (202) 223-9871, info@tfah.org, https://www.tfah.org/; Alcohol and Drug Misuse and Suicide and the Millennial Generation - A Devastating Impact and Pain in the Nation Series Update: Alcohol, Drug and Suicide Deaths at Record Highs.

U.S. Department of Health and Human Services, Centers for Disease Control and Prevention (CDC), National Center for Health Statistics (NCHS), 3311 Toledo Rd., Hyattsville, MD, 20782-2064, USA, (800) 232-4636, (301) 458-4000, https://www.cdc.gov/nchs; Drug Overdose Deaths.

U.S. Department of Justice (DOJ), Drug Enforcement Administration (DEA), 8701 Morrissette Dr., Springfield, VA, 22152, USA, (202) 307-1000, info@dea.gov, https://www.dea.gov; Responding to Nationwide Increases in Fentanyl-Related Mass-Overdose Events.

University of Maryland Center for Substance Use, Addiction & Health Research (CESAR), 7401 Preinkert Dr., 1114 Chincoteague Hall, College Park, MD, 20742, USA, (301) 405-9770, cesar@umd.edu, https://cesar.umd.edu/; Characterizing Knowledge, Attitudes, Behaviors, and Practices Related to Bystander Naloxone in Methadone-Maintained Individuals with Opioid Use Disorder and Highlights from the Naloxone Phase II Studies.

DRUG TRAFFIC-USAGE

Council on Criminal Justice (CCJ), National Commission on COVID-19 and Criminal Justice, 700 Pennsylvania Ave. SE, Washington, DC, 20020, USA, info@counciloncj.org, https://counciloncj.org/covid-19/; Impact Report: COVID-19 and SUD Treatment.

Health Canada, Address Locator 1801B, Ottawa, ON, K1A 0K9, CAN, (613) 957-2991 (Dial from U.S.), (613) 941-5366 (Fax from U.S.), hcinfo.infosc@canada.ca, https://www.hc-sc.gc.ca/; Canadian Alcohol and Drugs Survey (CADS): Summary of Results for 2019.

Partnership to End Addiction, 711 3rd Ave., 5th Fl., Ste. 500, New York, NY, 10017, USA, (212) 841-5200, contact@toendaddiction.org, https://drugfree.org/; unpublished data.

PLOS, 1265 Battery St., Ste. 200, San Francisco, CA, 94111, USA, (415) 624-1200, (415) 795-1584, plos@plos.org, https://www.plos.org/; A Systematic Study of Microdosing Psychedelics.

Substance Abuse and Mental Health Services Administration (SAMHSA), 5600 Fishers Ln., Rockville, MD, 20857, USA, (877) 726-4727, (800) 487-4889 (TTY), samhsainfo@samhsa.hhs.gov, https://www.samhsa.gov/; 2019-2020 National Survey on Drug Use and Health (NSDUH).

Trust for America's Health (TFAH), 1730 M St. NW, Ste. 900, Washington, DC, 20036, USA, (202) 223-9870, (202) 223-9871, info@tfah.org, https://www.tfah.org/; Alcohol and Drug Misuse and Suicide and the Millennial Generation - A Devastating Impact and Pain in the Nation Series Update: Alcohol, Drug and Suicide Deaths at Record Highs.

U.S. Department of Justice (DOJ), Drug Enforcement Administration (DEA), 8701 Morrissette Dr., Springfield, VA, 22152, USA, (202) 307-1000, info@dea.gov, https://www.dea.gov; Illicit Opioid Availability in Pennsylvania 2020.

U.S. Department of Justice (DOJ), Federal Bureau of Investigation (FBI), 935 Pennsylvania Ave. NW, Washington, DC, 20535-0001, USA, (202) 324-3000, https://www.fbi.gov/; Crime in the United States 2019.

U.S. Department of Justice (DOJ), National Institute of Justice (NIJ), 810 7th St. NW, Washington, DC, 20531, USA, (202) 307-2942, (800) 851-3420, https://www.nij.gov/; 2021 Annual Report to Congress.

United Nations Office on Drugs and Crime (UNODC), Vienna International Ctre., PO Box 500, Vienna, A-1400, AUT, unodc@unodc.org, https://www.unodc.org/; Afghanistan Opium Survey 2020: Cultivation and Production; Myanmar Opium Survey 2022 - Cultivation, Production and Implications; and World Drug Report 2022.

White House Office of National Drug Control Policy (ONDCP), 1600 Pennsylvania Ave. NW, Washington, DC, 20500, USA, https://www.whitehouse.gov/ondcp; unpublished data.

DRUGGED DRIVING

AAA Foundation for Traffic Safety (FTS), 607 14th St. NW, Ste. 201, Washington, DC, 20005, USA, (202) 638-5944, (202) 638-5943, info@aaafoundation.org, https://www.aaafoundation.org/; Use of Potentially Impairing Medications in Relation to Driving, United States, 2021.

Governors Highway Safety Association (GHSA), 660 N Capitol St. NW, Ste. 220, Washington, DC, 20001-1642, USA, (202) 789-0942, headquarters@ghsa.org, https://www.ghsa.org/; High-Risk Impaired Drivers: Combating a Critical Threat.

DRUGS

AAA Foundation for Traffic Safety (FTS), 607 14th St. NW, Ste. 201, Washington, DC, 20005, USA, (202) 638-5944, (202) 638-5943, info@aaafoundation.org, https://www.aaafoundation.org/; Use of Potentially Impairing Medications in Relation to Driving, United States, 2021.

Access to Medicine Foundation, Naritaweg 227-A, Amsterdam, 1043 CB, NLD, info@accesstomedicinefoundation.org, https://accesstomedicinefoundation.org/; Access to Medicine Index, 2021 and Access to Vaccines Index.

American Association for the Advancement of Science (AAAS), 1200 New York Ave. NW, Washington, DC, 20005, USA, (202) 326-6400, https://www.aaas.org; Science Translational Medicine.

American Association of Retired Persons (AARP), 601 E St. NW, Washington, DC, 20049, USA, (202) 434-3525, (888) 687-2277, member@aarp.org, https://www.aarp.org/; 2019 Survey on Prescription Drugs.

Biotechnology Innovation Organization (BIO), 1201 New York NW, Ste. 1300, Washington, DC, 20005, USA, (202) 962-9200, info@bio.org, https://www.bio.org/; BIO COVID-19 Therapeutic Development Tracker and The State of Innovation in Antibacterial Therapeutics.

Broad Institute of MIT and Harvard, 415 Main St., Cambridge, MA, 02142, USA, (617) 714-7000, https://www.broadinstitute.org/; Drug Repurposing Hub.

Elsevier, Radarweg 29, Amsterdam, 1043 NX, NLD, https://www.elsevier.com; ScienceDirect.

Global Lyme Alliance (GLA), 1290 E Main St., 3rd Fl., Stamford, CT, 06902, USA, (203) 969-1333, info@gla.org, https://globallymealliance.org/; Botanical Medicines Cryptolepsis Sanguinolenta, Artemisia Annua, Scutellaria Baicalensis, Polygonum Cuspidatum, and Alchornea Cordifolia Demonstrate Inhibitory Activity against Babesia Duncani.

Johns Hopkins Center for a Livable Future, 111 Market Pl., Ste. 840, Baltimore, MD, 21202, USA, (410) 223-1811, (410) 223-1829, clf@jhsph.edu, https://clf.jhsph.edu; Contamination of Retail Meat Samples with Multidrug-Resistant Organisms in Relation to Organic and Conventional Production and Processing: A Cross-Sectional Analysis of Data from the United States National Antimicrobial Resistance Monitoring System.

KFF Health News, 1330 G St. NW, Washington, DC, 20005, USA, (202) 347-5270, https://khn.org/; $50 Billion in Opioid Settlement Cash Is on the Way. We're Tracking How It's Spent..

The Lancet, 230 Park Ave., New York, NY, 10169, USA, (212) 633-3800, editorial@lancet.com, https://www.thelancet.com/; The Lancet; The Lancet Infectious Diseases; The Lancet Neurology; and The Lancet Oncology.

Merative, 100 Phoenix Dr., Ann Arbor, MI, 48108, USA, (844) 6372848, https://www.merative.com/; Health Insights.

National Academies of Sciences, Engineering, and Medicine (The National Academies), 500 5th St. NW, Washington, DC, 20001, USA, (202) 334-2000, contact@nas.edu, https://www.nationalacademies.org/; Proceedings of the National Academy of Sciences (PNAS).

Novo Nordisk Inc., 800 Scudders Mill Rd., Plainsboro, NJ, 08536, USA, (609) 987-5800, (800) 727-6500, https://www.novonordisk-us.com/; unpublished data.

SAGE Publications, 2455 Teller Rd., Thousand Oaks, CA, 91320, USA, (800) 818-7243, (800) 583-2665, journals@sagepub.com, https://www.sagepub.com; Palliative Medicine - End-of-Life Care in COVID-19: An Audit of Pharmacological Management in Hospital Inpatients.

U.S. Census Bureau, 4600 Silver Hill Rd., Washington, DC, 20233, USA, (301) 763-4636, (800) 923-8282, https://www.census.gov; 2019 E-Stats Report: Measuring the Electronic Economy.

U.S. Census Bureau, Center for Economic Studies (CES), 4600 Silver Hill Rd., Washington, DC, 20233, USA, (301) 763-6460, (301) 763-5935, ces.contacts@census.gov, https://www.census.gov/programs-surveys/ces.html; Retail Trade, 2017 Economic Census and Wholesale Trade, 2017 Economic Census.

U.S. Department of Commerce (DOC), International Trade Administration (ITA), 1401 Constitution Ave. NW, Washington, DC, 20230, USA, (800) 872-8723, https://www.trade.gov/; TradeStats Express (TSE).

World Anti-Doping Agency (WADA), 800 Place Victoria, Ste. 1700, Montreal, QC, H4Z 1B7, CAN, (514) 904-9232 (Dial from U.S.), https://www.wada-ama.org; 2020 Anti-Doping Testing Figures.

World Health Organization (WHO), Ave. Appia 20, Geneva, CH-1211, SWI, (202) 974-3000 (Telephone in U.S.), publications@who.int, https://www.who.int/; WHO Drug Information 2023.

DRUGS-ADVERTISING EXPENDITURES

Magazine Publishers of America (MPA) - The Association of Magazine Media, 1211 Connecticut Ave. NW, Ste. 610, Washington, DC, 20036, USA, (202) 296-7277, mpa@magazine.org, https://www.magazine.org/; Magazine Media Factbook 2021.

DRUGS-CONSUMER PRICE INDEXES

U.S. Department of Labor (DOL), Bureau of Labor Statistics (BLS), Postal Square Bldg., 2 Massachusetts Ave. NE, Washington, DC, 20212-0001, USA, (202) 691-5200, (202) 691-7890, blsdata_staff@bls.gov, https://www.bls.gov; Consumer Price Index (CPI) Databases.

DRUGS-DRUG ABUSE TREATMENT

Substance Abuse and Mental Health Services Administration (SAMHSA), 5600 Fishers Ln., Rockville, MD, 20857, USA, (877) 726-4727, (800) 487-4889 (TTY), samhsainfo@samhsa.hhs.gov, https://www.samhsa.gov/; 2020 National Survey of Substance Abuse Treatment Services (N-SSATS).

University of Maryland Center for Substance Use, Addiction & Health Research (CESAR), 7401 Preinkert Dr., 1114 Chincoteague Hall, College Park, MD, 20742, USA, (301) 405-9770, cesar@umd.edu, https://cesar.umd.edu/; Characterizing Knowledge, Attitudes, Behaviors, and Practices Related to Bystander Naloxone in Methadone-Maintained Individuals with Opioid Use Disorder and Highlights from the Naloxone Phase II Studies.

DRUGS-EXPENDITURES FOR

U.S. Department of Labor (DOL), Bureau of Labor Statistics (BLS), Postal Square Bldg., 2 Massachusetts Ave. NE, Washington, DC, 20212-0001, USA, (202) 691-5200, (202) 691-7890, blsdata_staff@bls.gov, https://www.bls.gov; Consumer Expenditure Survey (CE).

World Health Organization (WHO), Ave. Appia 20, Geneva, CH-1211, SWI, (202) 974-3000 (Telephone in U.S.), publications@who.int, https://www.who.int/; WHO Drug Information 2023.

DRUGS-INTERNATIONAL TRADE

U.S. Census Bureau, International Trade Program, 4600 Silver Hill Rd., Washington, DC, 20233, USA, (800) 549-0595, eid.international.trade.data@census.gov, https://www.census.gov/foreign-trade; International Trade Data.

DRUGS-MEDICAID PAYMENTS AND RECIPIENTS

U.S. Department of Health and Human Services (HHS), Centers for Medicare and Medicaid Services (CMS), 7500 Security Blvd., Baltimore, MD, 21244, USA, (410) 786-3000, (877) 267-2323, https://www.cms.gov; Medicare Current Beneficiary Survey (MCBS).

U.S. Department of Health and Human Services, Centers for Disease Control and Prevention (CDC), 1600 Clifton Rd., Atlanta, GA, 30329-4027, USA, (800) 232-4636, (888) 232-6348 (TTY), cdcinfo@cdc.gov, https://www.cdc.gov; State Medicaid Coverage for Tobacco Cessation Treatments and Barriers to Accessing Treatments - United States, 2008-2018.

DRUGS-NONMEDICAL USE

KFF Health News, 1330 G St. NW, Washington, DC, 20005, USA, (202) 347-5270, https://khn.org/; $50 Billion in Opioid Settlement Cash Is on the Way. We're Tracking How It's Spent..

Partnership to End Addiction, 711 3rd Ave., 5th Fl., Ste. 500, New York, NY, 10017, USA, (212) 841-5200, contact@toendaddiction.org, https://drugfree.org/; unpublished data.

DRUGS-PRICE INDEXES

U.S. Department of Labor (DOL), Bureau of Labor Statistics (BLS), Postal Square Bldg., 2 Massachusetts Ave. NE, Washington, DC, 20212-0001, USA, (202) 691-5200, (202) 691-7890, blsdata_staff@bls.gov, https://www.bls.gov; Consumer Price Index (CPI) Databases.

DRUNK DRIVING

Insurance Institute for Highway Safety/Highway Loss Data Institute (IIHS/HLDI), 4121 Wilson Blvd., 6th Fl., Arlington, VA, 22203, USA, (703) 247-1500, (434) 985 4600, cmatthew@iihs.org, https://www.iihs.org/; Highway Safety Topics.

U.S. Department of Health and Human Services (HHS), National Institutes of Health (NIH), National Institute on Alcohol Abuse and Alcoholism (NIAAA), 9000 Rockville Pike, Bethesda, MD, 20892, USA, (888) 696-4222, (301) 443-3860, askniaaa@nih.gov, https://www.niaaa.nih.gov/; Alcohol Facts and Statistics; Alcohol Policy Information System (APIS); and Surveillance Reports.

DRUNK DRIVING-ARRESTS

U.S. Department of Justice (DOJ), Federal Bureau of Investigation (FBI), 935 Pennsylvania Ave. NW, Washington, DC, 20535-0001, USA, (202) 324-3000, https://www.fbi.gov/; Crime in the United States 2019.

DRYCLEANING AND LAUNDRY SERVICES-EARNINGS

U.S. Census Bureau, 4600 Silver Hill Rd., Washington, DC, 20233, USA, (301) 763-4636, (800) 923-8282, https://www.census.gov; County Business Patterns (CBP) 2020.

U.S. Department of Labor (DOL), Bureau of Labor Statistics (BLS), Postal Square Bldg., 2 Massachusetts Ave. NE, Washington, DC, 20212-0001, USA, (202) 691-5200, (202) 691-7890, blsdata_staff@bls.gov, https://www.bls.gov; Current Employment Statistics (CES).

DRYCLEANING AND LAUNDRY SERVICES-EMPLOYEES

U.S. Census Bureau, 4600 Silver Hill Rd., Washington, DC, 20233, USA, (301) 763-4636, (800) 923-8282, https://www.census.gov; County Business Patterns (CBP) 2020.

U.S. Census Bureau, Center for Economic Studies (CES), 4600 Silver Hill Rd., Washington, DC, 20233, USA, (301) 763-6460, (301) 763-5935, ces.contacts@census.gov, https://www.census.gov/programs-surveys/ces.html; Other Services (except Public Administration), 2017 Economic Census.

U.S. Department of Labor (DOL), Bureau of Labor Statistics (BLS), Postal Square Bldg., 2 Massachusetts Ave. NE, Washington, DC, 20212-0001, USA, (202) 691-5200, (202) 691-7890, blsdata_staff@bls.gov, https://www.bls.gov; Current Employment Statistics (CES).

DRYCLEANING AND LAUNDRY SERVICES-ESTABLISHMENTS

U.S. Census Bureau, 4600 Silver Hill Rd., Washington, DC, 20233, USA, (301) 763-4636, (800) 923-8282, https://www.census.gov; County Business Patterns (CBP) 2020.

U.S. Census Bureau, Center for Economic Studies (CES), 4600 Silver Hill Rd., Washington, DC, 20233, USA, (301) 763-6460, (301) 763-5935, ces.contacts@census.gov, https://www.census.gov/programs-surveys/ces.html; Other Services (except Public Administration), 2017 Economic Census.

DRYCLEANING AND LAUNDRY SERVICES-PRODUCTIVITY

U.S. Department of Labor (DOL), Bureau of Labor Statistics (BLS), Postal Square Bldg., 2 Massachusetts Ave. NE, Washington, DC, 20212-0001, USA, (202) 691-5200, (202) 691-7890, blsdata_staff@bls.gov, https://www.bls.gov; Productivity.

DRYCLEANING AND LAUNDRY SERVICES-RECEIPTS

U.S. Census Bureau, Center for Economic Studies (CES), 4600 Silver Hill Rd., Washington, DC, 20233, USA, (301) 763-6460, (301) 763-5935, ces.contacts@census.gov, https://www.census.gov/programs-surveys/ces.html; Other Services (except Public Administration), 2017 Economic Census.

Printed in the USA
CPSIA information can be obtained
at www.ICGtesting.com
JSHW061542101223
53367JS00007B/34